FINANCIAL TIMES

WORLD DESK REFERENCE

DORLING KINDERSLEY PUBLISHING, INC.
LONDON • NEW YORK • MUNICH • MELBOURNE • DELHI

For the very latest information, visit:
www.dk.com and click on the Maps & Atlases icon

A DORLING KINDERSLEY BOOK
www.dk.com

FOR THE SEVENTH EDITION

EDITOR-IN-CHIEF
Andrew Heritage

SENIOR CARTOGRAPHIC MANAGER
David Roberts

SENIOR CARTOGRAPHIC EDITOR
Simon Mumford

SYSTEMS COORDINATOR
Phil Rowles

SEVENTH EDITION UPDATED AND EDITED BY
Cambridge International Reference on Current Affairs (CIRCA)

PROJECT MANAGER
Catherine Jagger

EDITORIAL SUPERVISION
Roger East

EDITORS
Richard J. Thomas, Philippa Youngman, Carina O'Reilly

DATABASE & GRAPHICS
Carolyn Postgate, Jenny Durham

EDITORIAL AND RESEARCH
Patrick Chabal, John Coggins, Alan Day, Ian Gorvin, Amra Hewitt, Lawrence Joffe, Kylie Jerome, Wim Mellaerts, Rory Miller, Frances Nicholson, Gabriella Ramos, Sanna Rimpilainen, Darren Sugar, Farzana Shaikh, Jo Skelt, Paul Sutton, Tim Shaw, Edmund Waite

DIGITAL CONTENT MANAGEMENT
Nina Blackett, Nishi Bhasin, Pooja Huria

PICTURE RESEARCH
Louise Thomas

DORLING KINDERSLEY CARTOGRAPHY

EDITORIAL DIRECTION
Andrew Heritage

MANAGING EDITORS
Ian Castello-Cortes, Wim Jenkins

PROJECT EDITORS
Debra Clapson, Catherine Day, Jo Edwards, Jane Oliver

EDITORS
Alastair Dougall, Ailsa Heritage, Nicholas Kynaston, Lisa Thomas, Susan Turner, Chris Whitwell, Elizabeth Wyse

ADDITIONAL EDITORIAL ASSISTANCE
Sam Atkinson, Louise Keane, Zoë Ellinson, Caroline Lucas, Sophie Park, Laura Porter, Jo Russ, Crispian Martin St. Valery, Sally Wood, Ulrike Fritz-Weltz

READERS
Jane Bruton, Reg Grant, Ann Kramer, Lesley Riley

ART DIRECTION
Chez Picthall, Philip Lord

PROJECT DESIGNERS
Martin Biddulph, Scott David, Carol Ann Davis, David Douglas, Yahya El-Droubie, Karen Gregory

DESIGNERS
Tony Cutting, Rhonda Fisher, Nicola Liddiard, Katy Wall

ADDITIONAL DESIGN ASSISTANCE
Paul Bayliss, Carol Ann Davis, Adam Dobney, Kenny Laurenson, Paul Williams

DIGITAL CONTENT MANAGER
Nina Blackett

PRODUCTION
Wendy Penn

PROJECT CARTOGRAPHERS
Caroline Bowie, Ruth Duxbury, James Mills-Hicks, John Plumer, Julie Turner

CARTOGRAPHERS
James Anderson, Dale Buckton, Roger Bullen, Tony Chambers, Jan Clark, Tom Coulson, Martin Darlison, Claire Ellam, Julia Lunn, Michael Martin, Alka Ranger, Peter Winfield, Claudine Zante

PICTURE RESEARCH
Alison McKittrick, Sarah Moule, Christine Rista, Louise Thomas

DATABASE MANAGER
Simon Lewis

INDEX GAZETTEER
Margaret Hynes, Julia Lynch, Barbara Nash, Jayne Parsons, Janet Smy

Printed and bound in Portugal by Printer Portuguesa

Published in the United States
by Dorling Kindersley Publishing Inc.
375 Hudson Street, New York, New York 10014
A Penguin Company

Previously published as the DK World Reference Atlas

First American Edition 1994
10 9 8 7
Second Edition 1996. Revised 1998. Third Edition (revised) 2000. Fourth Edition (revised) 2002.
Fifth Edition (revised) 2003. Sixth Edition (revised) 2004. Seventh Edition (revised) 2004.

A catalog record for this book is available from the Library of Congress.

ISBN: 0-7566-1099-0

FOREWORD

THIS DESK REFERENCE is presented to the public in the full knowledge that the world is in a state of continual flux. Political fashions and personalities come and go, while the ebb and flow of peoples and ideas across the face of the planet creates constant shifts in the cultural landscape. All the material assembled for this book has been researched from the most up-to-date and authoritative sources; our team of consultants and contributors, designers, editors, and cartographers have endeavored not only to explain the meaning of this material, to place it in a useful and clear context, but also to present it in a way that has a lasting value and relevance, regardless of the turmoil of daily events. This new edition, bearing the imprimatur of the *Financial Times*, has been completely revised and updated, to reflect the global changes of the past few years. It includes the latest statistical data, and over 60 new photographs.

The publishers would like to thank the many consultants and contributors whose diligence, perseverance, and attention to detail made this book possible.

GENERAL CONSULTANTS

Anthony Goldstone, Senior Editor Asia-Pacific, *The Economist* Intelligence Unit, London
Professor Jack Spence, Director of Studies, The Royal Institute of International Affairs, London

REGIONAL CONSULTANTS

ASIA
Anthony Goldstone, London

AFRICA
James Hammill, Lecturer in African Politics, University of Leicester
Kaye Whiteman, Editor-in-Chief, *West Africa Magazine*, London

RUSSIA AND CIS
Martin McCauley, Senior Lecturer, School of Slavonic and East European Studies, University of London

CENTRAL AND SOUTH AMERICA
Nick Caistor, Producer, Latin American Section, BBC World Service

USA
Michael Elliot, Diplomatic Editor, *Newsweek*, Washington DC

EUROPE
John Ardagh, London
Rory Clarke, Senior Editor Europe, *The Economist* Intelligence Unit, London
Charles Powell, Centre for European Studies, St Antony's College, Oxford

MIDDLE EAST
John Whelan, Ex Editor-in-Chief, *Middle East Economic Digest*

PACIFIC
Jim Boutilier, Professor in History, Royal Roads Military College, Victoria, Canada

CARIBBEAN
Canute James, *Financial Times*, Kingston, Jamaica

CONTRIBUTORS

Janice Bell, School of Slavonic and East European Studies, University of London
Gerry Bourke, Asia Correspondent, *The Guardian*, Islamabad
Vincent Cable, Director, International Economics Programme
P K Clark, MA, Former Chief Map Research Officer, Ministry of Defence
Ken Davies, Senior Editor, *The Economist* Intelligence Unit, London
Roger Dunn, Analyst, Control Risks Group, London
Aidan Foster-Carter, Senior Lecturer in Sociology, University of Leeds
Professor Murray Forsyth, Centre for Federal Studies, University of Leicester
Natasha Franklin, School of Slavonic and East European Studies, London
Adam Hannestad, *Blomberg Business News*, Copenhagen
Peter Holden, *The Economist* Research Department, London
Tim Jones, Knight Ritter, Brussels
Angella Johnstone, Home Affairs Correspondent, *The Guardian*, London
Oliver Keserü, International Chamber of Commerce, Paris
Robert Macdonald, *The Economist* Intelligence Unit
William Mader, Former Europe Bureau Chief, *Time Magazine*, Washington DC
Professor Brian Matthews, Institute of Commonwealth Studies, London
Nick Middleton, Oriel College, Oxford
Professor Mya Maung, Department of Finance, Boston College, Massachusetts
Judith Nordby, Leeds University
Simon Orme, London
Professor Richard Overy, Department of History, King's College, London
Steve Percy, East Asia Service, BBC World Service
Douglas Rimmer, Honorary Senior Research Fellow, Centre for West African Studies, University of Birmingham
Donna Rispoli, Linacre College, Oxford
Ian Rodger, *The Financial Times*, Zürich
The Royal Institute of International Affairs, London
Struan Simpson, St. James Research, London
Julie Smith, Brasenose College, Oxford
Elizabeth Spencer, London
Michiel Van Kuyen, Erasmus University, Rotterdam
Steven Whitefield, Pembroke College, Oxford
Georgina Wilde, Regional Director, Asia-Pacific, *The Economist* Intelligence Unit, London
H P Willmott, Visiting Professor, Dept. of Military Strategy & Operations, The National War College, Washington DC
Andrew Wilson, Sydney Sussex College, Cambridge
Tom Wingfield, *Reuters*, Bangkok
The World Conservation Monitoring Centre, Cambridge
Cambridge International Reference on Current Affairs (CIRCA)

CONTENTS

FOREWORD 3
THE CONTRIBUTORS 3
CONTENTS 4–5
ICON & CHART KEY 6–7
(see also flaps on front and back cover)
DATA SOURCES 8

1 WORLD FACTFILE

THE PHYSICAL WORLD 10–11
THE POLITICAL WORLD 12–13
THE SOLAR SYSTEM 14–15
CLIMATE 16–17
ENVIRONMENT 18–19
NORTH AMERICA 20–21
SOUTH AMERICA 22–23
EUROPE 24–25
AFRICA 26–27
WEST ASIA 28–29
NORTH ASIA 30–31
SOUTH ASIA 32–33
AUSTRALASIA AND OCEANIA 34–35
TIMELINE OF GLOBAL HISTORY 36–39
THE FORMATION OF THE MODERN WORLD 40–41
THE WORLD IN 1492 42–43
THE AGE OF DISCOVERY 1492–1648 44–45
THE AGE OF EXPANSION 1648–1789 46–47
THE AGE OF REVOLUTION 1789–1830 48–49
THE AGE OF EMPIRE 1830–1914 50–51
THE AGE OF GLOBAL WAR 1914–1945 52–53
THE MODERN AGE From 1945 54–55
POPULATION 56–57
THE WORLD ECONOMY 58–61
GLOBAL TOURISM 62–63
GLOBAL SECURITY 64–65
TIME ZONES 66–67
WORLD CHRONOLOGY OF 2002–2003 68–69
INTERNATIONAL ORGANIZATIONS 70–73

2 THE NATIONS OF THE WORLD

AFGHANISTAN 76–79
ALBANIA 80–81
ALGERIA 82–85
ANDORRA 86–87
ANGOLA 88–89
ANTARCTICA 90–91
ANTIGUA & BARBUDA 92–93
ARGENTINA 94–97
ARMENIA 98–99
AUSTRALIA 100–105
AUSTRIA 106–109
AZERBAIJAN 110–111

BAHAMAS 112–113
BAHRAIN 114–115
BANGLADESH 116–119
BARBADOS 120–121
BELARUS 122–125
BELGIUM 126–129
BELIZE 130–131
BENIN 132–133
BHUTAN 134–135
BOLIVIA 136–139
BOSNIA & HERZEGOVINA 140–141
BOTSWANA 142–143
BRAZIL 144–149
BRUNEI 150–151
BULGARIA 152–155
BURKINA 156–157
BURMA (MYANMAR) 158–161
BURUNDI 162–163

CAMBODIA 164–167
CAMEROON 168–169
CANADA 170–175
CAPE VERDE 176–177
CENTRAL AFRICAN REPUBLIC 178–179
CHAD 180–181
CHILE 182–185
CHINA 186–193
COLOMBIA 194–197
COMOROS 198–199
CONGO 200–201
CONGO, DEM. REP. 202–205
COSTA RICA 206–207
CÔTE D'IVOIRE ....see IVORY COAST
CROATIA 208–209
CUBA 210–213
CYPRUS 214–215
CZECH REPUBLIC 216–217

DENMARK 218–221
DJIBOUTI 222–223
DOMINICA 224–225
DOMINICAN REPUBLIC 226–227

EAST TIMOR 228–229
ECUADOR 230–231
EGYPT 232–235
EL SALVADOR 236–237
EQUATORIAL GUINEA 238–239
ERITREA 240–241
ESTONIA 242–243
ETHIOPIA 244–247

FIJI 248–249
FINLAND 250–253
FRANCE 254–259

GABON 260–261
GAMBIA 262–263
GEORGIA 264–265
GERMANY 266–271
GHANA 272–273
GREECE 274–277
GRENADA 278–279
GUATEMALA 280–281
GUINEA 282–283
GUINEA-BISSAU 284–285
GUYANA 286–287

HAITI 288–289
HONDURAS 290–291
HUNGARY 292–295

ICELAND 296–297
INDIA 298–303
INDONESIA 304–307
IRAN 308–311
IRAQ 312–315
IRELAND 316–317
ISRAEL 318–321
ITALY 322–327
IVORY COAST (CÔTE D'IVOIRE).................... 328–329

JAMAICA 330–331
JAPAN 332–337
JORDAN 338–339

KAZAKHSTAN 340–343
KENYA 344–347
KIRIBATI 348–349
KOREA, NORTH 350–351
KOREA, SOUTH 352–355
KUWAIT 356–357
KYRGYZSTAN 358–359

LAOS 360–361
LATVIA 362–363

LEBANON 364–365
LESOTHO 366–367
LIBERIA 368–369
LIBYA 370–373
LIECHTENSTEIN 374–375
LITHUANIA 376–377
LUXEMBOURG 378–379

MACEDONIA 380–381
MADAGASCAR 382–383
MALAWI 384–385
MALAYSIA 386–389
MALDIVES 390–391
MALI 392–393
MALTA 394–395
MARSHALL ISLANDS 396–397
MAURITANIA 398–399
MAURITIUS 400–401
MEXICO 402–405
MICRONESIA 406–407
MOLDOVA 408–409
MONACO 410–411
MONGOLIA 412–413
MOROCCO 414–417
MOZAMBIQUE 418–421
MYANMAR .... see BURMA

NAMIBIA 422–423
NAURU 424–425
NEPAL 426–427
NETHERLANDS 428–431
NEW ZEALAND 432–435
NICARAGUA 436–437
NIGER 438–439
NIGERIA 440–443
NORWAY 444–447

OMAN 448–449

PAKISTAN 450–453
PALAU 454–455
PANAMA 456–457
PAPUA NEW GUINEA 458–459
PARAGUAY 460–461
PERU 462–465
PHILIPPINES 466–469
POLAND 470–473
PORTUGAL 474–477

QATAR 478–479

ROMANIA 480–483
RUSSIAN FEDERATION 484–491
RWANDA 492–493

ST. KITTS & NEVIS 494–495
ST. LUCIA 496–497
ST. VINCENT & THE GRENADINES 498–499
SAMOA 500–501
SAN MARINO 502–503
SÃO TOMÉ & PRÍNCIPE 504–505
SAUDI ARABIA 506–509
SENEGAL 510–511
SERBIA & MONTENEGRO (YUGOSLAVIA) 512–515
SEYCHELLES 516–517
SIERRA LEONE 518–519
SINGAPORE 520–521
SLOVAKIA 522–523
SLOVENIA 524–525
SOLOMON ISLANDS 526–527
SOMALIA 528–529
SOUTH AFRICA 530–533
SPAIN 534–537
SRI LANKA 538–539
SUDAN 540–541
SURINAME 542–543
SWAZILAND 544–545
SWEDEN 546–549
SWITZERLAND 550–553
SYRIA 554–557

TAIWAN 558–561
TAJIKISTAN 562–563
TANZANIA 564–565
THAILAND 566–569
TOGO 570–571
TONGA 572–573
TRINIDAD & TOBAGO 574–575
TUNISIA 576–579
TURKEY 580–583
TURKMENISTAN 584–585
TUVALU 586–587

UGANDA 588–589
UKRAINE 590–593
UNITED ARAB EMIRATES 594–595
UNITED KINGDOM 596–601
UNITED STATES 602–609
URUGUAY 610–613
UZBEKISTAN 614–617

VANUATU 618–619
VATICAN CITY 620–621
VENEZUELA 622–625
VIETNAM 626–629

YEMEN 630–633
YUGOSLAVIA .... see SERBIA & MONTENEGRO

ZAMBIA 634–635
ZIMBABWE 636–639

OVERSEAS TERRITORIES & DEPENDENCIES

WORLD MAP 640–641

AMERICAN SAMOA, ANGUILLA, ARUBA, BERMUDA, BRITISH INDIAN OCEAN TERRITORY, BRITISH VIRGIN ISLANDS 642–643

CAYMAN ISLANDS, CHRISTMAS ISLAND, COCOS (KEELING) ISLANDS, COOK ISLANDS, FAEROE ISLANDS, FALKLAND ISLANDS, FRENCH GUIANA 644–645

FRENCH POLYNESIA, GIBRALTAR, GREENLAND, GUADELOUPE, GUAM, GUERNSEY, ISLE OF MAN 646–647

JERSEY, JOHNSTON ATOLL, MARTINIQUE, MAYOTTE, MIDWAY ISLANDS, MONTSERRAT, NETHERLANDS ANTILLES .. 648–649

NEW CALEDONIA, NIUE, NORFOLK ISLAND, NORTHERN MARIANA ISLANDS, PARACEL ISLANDS, PITCAIRN ISLANDS, PUERTO RICO 650–651

RÉUNION, ST. HELENA & DEPENDENCIES, ST. PIERRE & MIQUELON, SPRATLY ISLANDS, SVALBARD, TOKELAU, TURKS & CAICOS ISLANDS, VIRGIN ISLANDS (US), WAKE ISLAND, WALLIS & FUTUNA 652–653

3
GLOSSARIES

GLOSSARY OF GEOGRAPHIC TERMS 654–655
GLOSSARY OF ABBREVIATIONS 655
ACKNOWLEDGEMENTS AND PICTURE CREDITS 656

COVER FLAPS

KEY TO SYMBOLS, ICONS, AND ABBREVIATIONS USED IN THE ATLAS

KEY TO CHARTS AND ICONS

ICONS AND TREND INDICATORS vary. Not all variations are shown in the key below, but where they do occur the symbols have been "stacked."

COUNTRY PROFILES

1952
Date of country's independence, or formation.

1847
Date when the country's current borders were established.

Aug 2
National Day

GB
Vehicle country identifying code

+3
Time zone(s) of country (hours plus or minus from GMT)

+44
International telephone dialling code

.de
Internet country identifying code

CLIMATE

Indication of the climatic types and zones found in each country.

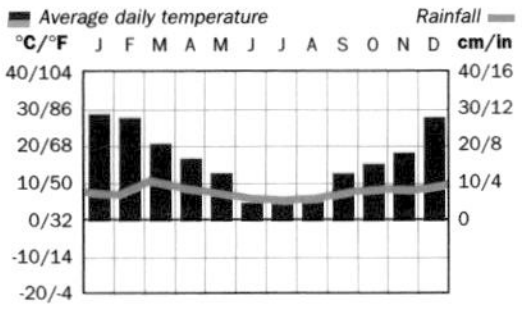
Average daily temperature
Rainfall
°C/°F
J F M A M J J A S O N D
cm/in
40/104
30/86
20/68
10/50
0/32
-10/14
-20/4
40/16
30/12
20/8
10/4
0

Statistics are given for the national capital. They represent maximum summer and minimum winter averages.

TRANSPORTATION

Indicates on which side of the road vehicles are driven in each country.

The country's principal international airport with annual passenger numbers.

Total size of national merchant or cargo fleet.

THE TRANSPORTATION NETWORK

National communications infrastructure given in kilometers and miles.

Extent of national paved road network

Extent of expressways, freeways, or major highways

Extent of commercial rail network

Extent of inland waterways navigable by commercial craft

TOURISM

The ratio of foreign visitors to population.

Number of visitors per year, including business travelers.

Indicators showing trend in recent visitor numbers (up/level/down).

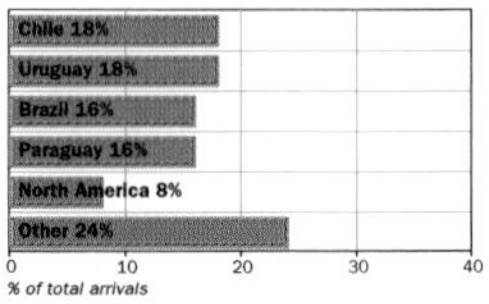
Chile 18%
Uruguay 18%
Brazil 16%
Paraguay 16%
North America 8%
Other 24%
0
10
20
30
40
% of total arrivals

The state of each nation's tourism is explained, with reasons given when there is no significant tourist industry. The chart shows the percentage of total visitors by country of origin.

PEOPLE

An easy indication of the population density in each country (high/medium/low).

Main languages spoken, including official languages.

Population density. This is an average over the whole country.

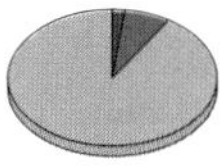

The pie chart proportions show the religious affiliations of those who profess a belief.

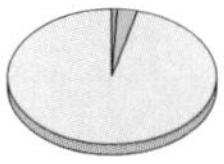

This pie chart illustrates the ethnic origin of the country's population.

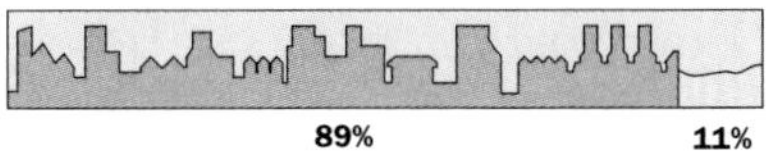
89%
11%

This graph represents the proportion of the population living in urban areas (gray) and rural areas (green).

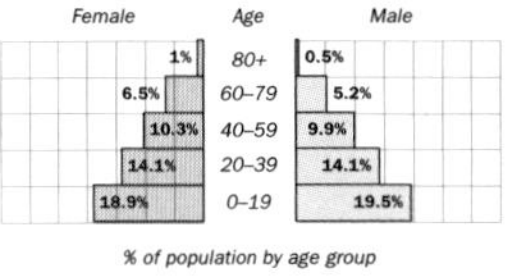
Female
Age
Male
1%
80+
0.5%
6.5%
60–79
5.2%
10.3%
40–59
9.9%
14.1%
20–39
14.1%
18.9%
0–19
19.5%
% of population by age group

This chart shows the breakdown of the population by age groupings, providing an interesting insight into the country's demography.

POLITICS

Indicates the type of elections held within each country.

Dates of last and next legislative elections for Lower (L.) and Upper (U.) Houses.

Name of head of state. In many cases this is a nominal position and does not indicate that this is the country's most powerful person.

A graphic representation of the political makeup of the country's government, based on each party's showing at the last election. Where there are two houses, the more important elected body is shown first.

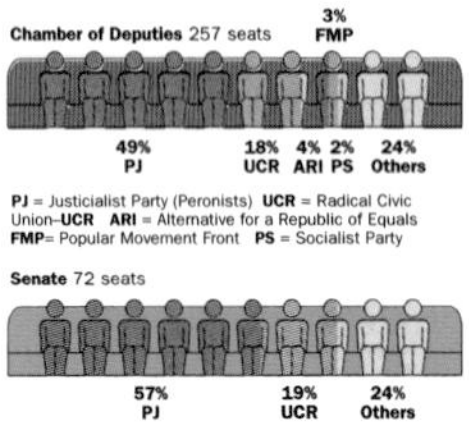
Chamber of Deputies 257 seats
3%
FMP
49%
PJ
18%
UCR
4%
ARI
2%
PS
24%
Others
PJ = Justicialist Party (Peronists) UCR = Radical Civic Union-UCR ARI = Alternative for a Republic of Equals FMP= Popular Movement Front PS = Socialist Party
Senate 72 seats
57%
PJ
19%
UCR
24%
Others

WORLD AFFAIRS

Indication of membership of the UN (United Nations), and date of entry.

Comm
Abbreviations indicate membership of international organizations.

Nonmembership of additional international organizations.

AID

Indication as to which countries are aid givers (donors) or aid recipients.

The amount of net international aid given or received is shown in US$. Undisclosed military aid is not included.

Symbols indicate whether aid payments or receipts are rising, level, or declining.

DEFENSE

An indication of the status of conscription and mandatory military service.

The defense budget, the country's annual expenditure (in US$) on arms and military personnel.

Symbols indicate if the trend in defense spending is rising, level, or declining.

THE ARMED FORCES

Icons represent the main branches of the national armed forces.

Army: equipment and personnel

Navy: equipment and personnel

Air force: equipment and personnel

Nuclear capability: armaments

ECONOMICS

An indication of the average rate of inflation per annum, over the period indicated.

Gross National Product (GNP) – the total value (in US$) of goods and services produced by a country.

Latest midyear exchange rate against the US$, with previous year's rate for comparison.

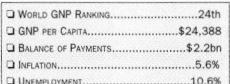

World GNP Ranking	24th
GNP per Capita	$24,388
Balance of Payments	$2.2bn
Inflation	5.6%
Unemployment	10.6%

The score cards are intended to give a broad picture of the country's economy. Gross National Product (GNP), unlike GDP, includes income from investments and businesses held abroad. Balance of payments is the difference between a country's payments to and receipts from abroad.

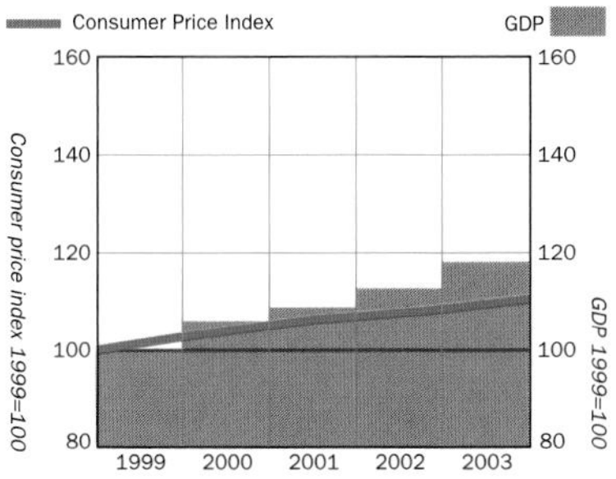

Consumer Price Index
GDP
160
140
120
100
80
1999
2000
2001
2002
2003
Consumer price index 1999=100
GDP 1999=100

This graph shows year-on-year variations in GDP and consumer prices.

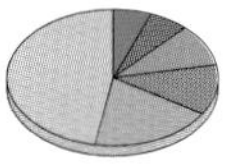

This pie chart gives a broad picture of the country's principal export trading partners.

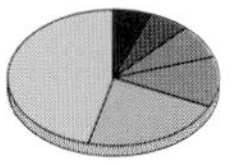

This pie chart gives a broad picture of the country's principal import trading partners.

RESOURCES

Indicates the capacity of the combined national electricity generating sources (in kilowatts).

Fish catch per year.

Oil produced in barrels per day (b/d). Refining output and oil reserves are given where applicable.

Estimated livestock resources.

Main mineral reserves are listed in descending order of economic importance.

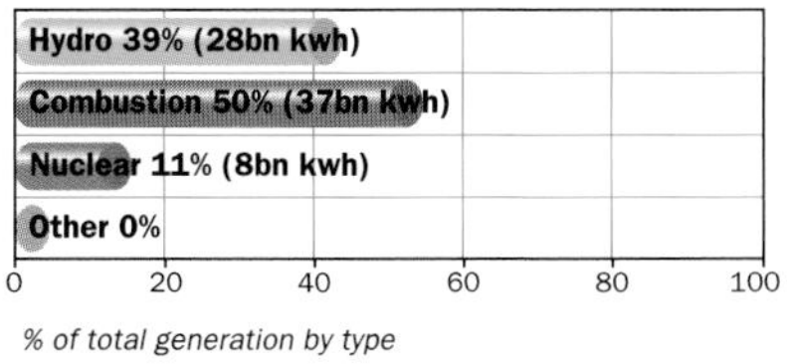

Hydro 39% (28bn kwh)
Combustion 50% (37bn kwh)
Nuclear 11% (8bn kwh)
Other 0%
0
20
40
60
80
100
% of total generation by type

Percentages of the different energy sources used for the generation of electricity are represented graphically ("Combustion" indicates the burning of fossil fuels, wood etc.). An account of the country's resource base is given in the text.

ENVIRONMENT

The 2002 Index of progress toward environmental sustainability, based on 22 core indicators. Compiled by the World Economic Forum taskforce.

Protected area (including marine areas) as a percentage of total land area. Protection is often theoretical.

Trend in total CO_2 emissions since 1990 (up/level/down) and current emissions per capita.

ENVIRONMENTAL TREATIES

National parties to international environmental treaties.

Ramsar: (wetlands)

Basel: (hazardous wastes)

CITES: (endangered species)

Montreal Protocol: (CFC emissions)

CBD: (biological diversity)

Kyoto: (greenhouse gases)

MEDIA

Indicates the average rates of television ownership across the country.

Media free to express critical views.

Partial controls or constraints on media freedom.

Severe restrictions on media freedom.

PUBLISHING AND BROADCAST MEDIA

National broadcast and print media, by size and ownership.

Main national newspapers

Television services: state-owned/independent

Radio services: state-owned/independent

CRIME

An indication of the status of capital punishment and the death penalty.

Prison population statistics

Symbols show general trend in crime figures.

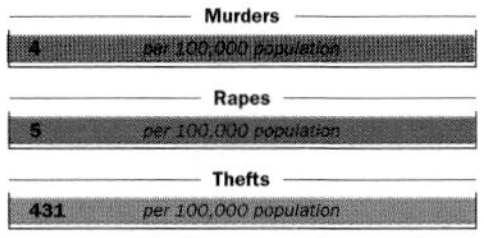

Murders
4
per 100,000 population
Rapes
5
per 100,000 population
Thefts
431
per 100,000 population

This section records official crime figures only. Reported statistics are normally lower than the actual figures.

CHRONOLOGY

Beginning at a significant date in the recent history of the country, the outline chronology continues through to the present day, and highlights key dates and turning points.

EDUCATION

Displays the age until which children are legally required to attend school.

Literacy rate. UNESCO defines as literate anyone who can read and write a short statement.

The number of students in all forms of tertiary education within that country.

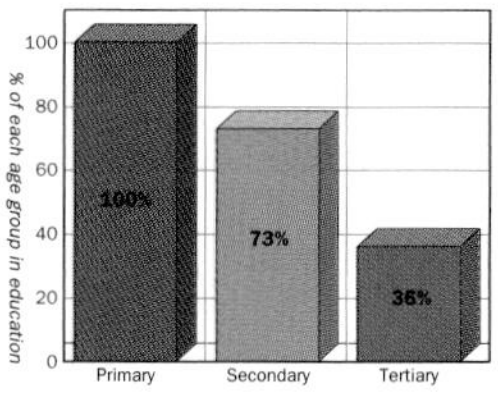

100
80
60
40
20
0
100%
73%
36%
Primary
Secondary
Tertiary
% of each age group in education

This graph shows, for each level of education, the total enrollment, regardless of age, as a percentage of the population of the age group that officially corresponds to that level.

HEALTH

An indication of the existence of health benefits provided by the state.

Ratio of the number of people per doctor is given as a national average.

Major causes of death are listed.

SPENDING

Indicates the trend in GDP per capita since 1990.

Levels of car ownership (per 1000 head of population)

Rates of telephone landline connectivity (per 1000 head of population)

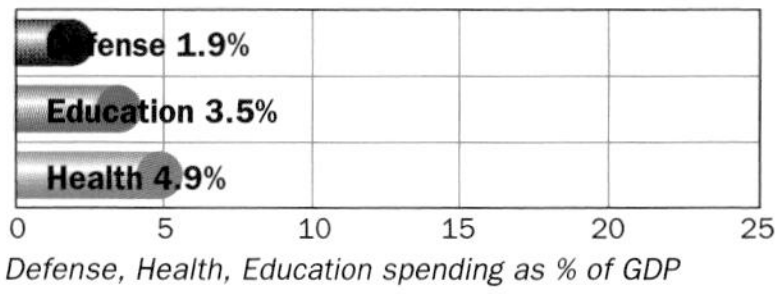

Defense 1.9%
Education 3.5%
Health 4.9%
0
5
10
15
20
25
Defense, Health, Education spending as % of GDP

Percentage of the country's GDP that is spent by the government on defense, education, and health.

WORLD RANKING

Each country is ranked in the world by four key indicators and by the UN Human Development Index, which reflects all-around attainment in health, education, and wealth (covering 176 countries and Hong Kong).

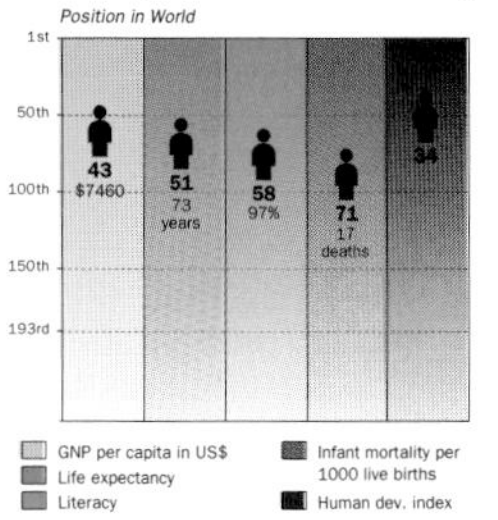

Position in World
1st
50th
100th
150th
193rd
43
$7460
51
73 years
58
97%
71
17 deaths
34
GNP per capita in US$
Life expectancy
Literacy
Infant mortality per 1000 live births
Human dev. index

SOURCES OF STATISTICAL DATA USED IN THIS BOOK

Airports Council International

Amnesty International

Automobile Association (AA)

British Petroleum (BP):
World Energy Data

Cambridge International Reference on Current Affairs (CIRCA)

Canadian International Development Agency

Commonwealth Secretariat:
Small States Economic Review and Basic Statistics

Dorling Kindersley

Europa World Yearbook

European Bank for Reconstruction and Development (EBRD)

Financial Times

Fischer Weltalmanach

Food and Agriculture Organization (FAO)

International Atomic Energy Agency (IAEA)

International Institute for Strategic Studies (IISS):
The Military Balance

International Labor Organization (ILO):
World Labor Report

International Monetary Fund (IMF):
Balance of Payments Statistics Yearbook,
Direction of Trade Statistics Yearbook,
Government Financial Statistics Yearbook,
International Financial Statistics,
World Economic Outlook

International Road Federation

International Union for Conservation of Nature (IUCN)

International Union of Railways

INTERPOL International Crime Statistics

Lloyd's Register of Shipping

Organization for Economic Cooperation Development (OECD):
Economic surveys

OECD Development Assistance Committee (DAC):
Development Cooperation Report

Organization of Petroleum Exporting Countries (OPEC)

People in Power

Ramsar Convention Bureau

Reporters without Borders

Royal Automobile Club (RAC)

UK Home Office:
World Prison Population List (Research, Development, and Statistics Directorate)

United Nations (UN)
Department of Economic and Social Affairs Statistics Division:
United Nations Demographic Yearbook,
United Nations Energy Statistics Yearbook,
United Nations Industrial Commodity Statistics Yearbook,
United Nations International Trade Statistics Yearbook,
United Nations Statistical Yearbook

United Nations Children's Fund (UNICEF)

United Nations Development Program (UNDP):
Human Development Report

United Nations Economic and Social Commission for Asia and the Pacific (UNESCAP):
United Nations Statistical Yearbook of Asia and the Pacific

United Nations Educational, Scientific, and Cultural Organization (UNESCO):
Statistical Yearbook

United Nations Environment Program (UNEP):
Ozone Secretariat
Secretariat of the Basel Convention
Secretariat of the Convention on Biological Diversity (CBD)
Secretariat of the Convention on International Trade in Endangered Species (CITES)

United Nations Framework Convention on Climate Change

United Nations Office on Drugs and Crime (UNODC):
Surveys on Crime Trends and the Operations of Criminal Justice Systems

United Nations Population Fund (UNFPA):
The State of World Population

United States Central Intelligence Agency (CIA)

World Bank (IBRD):
World Development Indicators,
World Development Report,
World Bank Atlas

World Conservation Monitoring Center (WCMC):
Biodiversity Data Sourcebook

World Economic Forum

World Health Organization (WHO)

World Tourist Organization (WTO)

Worldwide Fund for Nature (WWF)

1

WORLD FACTFILE

The Physical World

THE EARTH'S SURFACE IS constantly being transformed: it is uplifted, folded, and faulted by tectonic forces; weathered and eroded by wind, water, and ice. Sometimes change is dramatic, the spectacular results of earthquakes or floods. More often it is a slow process lasting millions of years. A physical map of the world represents a snapshot of the ever-evolving architecture of the Earth. This terrain map shows the whole surface of the Earth, both above and below the sea. The size of the Earth can be measured in different ways. When taken from the Equator, the diameter of the Earth measures 12,756 km (7927 miles); when taken from pole to pole, the diameter measures 12,714 km (7900 miles). Two-thirds of the Earth's surface is covered by oceans. The landscape of the ocean floor, like the surface of the land, has been shaped by movements of the Earth's crust over millions of years to form volcanic mountain ranges, deep trenches, basins, and plateaus. Ocean currents constantly redistribute warm and cold water around the world. The largest ocean in the world is the Pacific, which covers an area of over 181 million sq. km (70 million sq. miles).

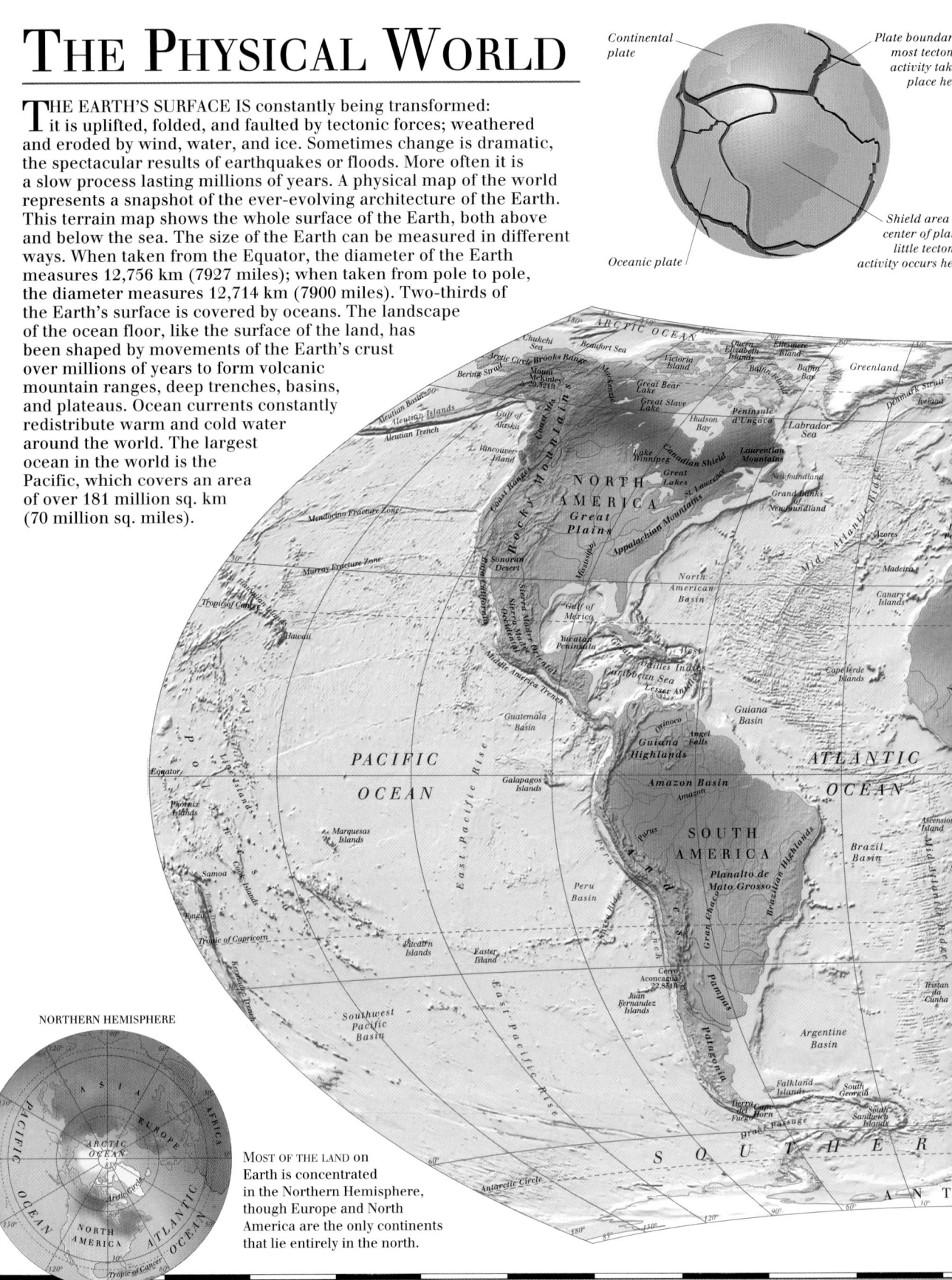

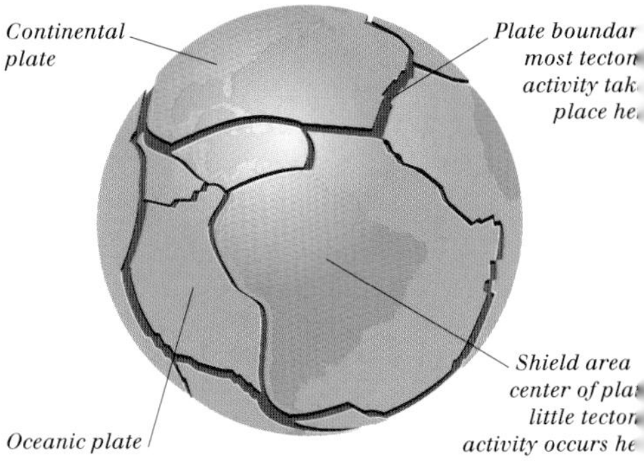
Continental plate
Plate boundar
most tecton
activity tak
place he
Shield area
center of pla
little tecton
activity occurs he
Oceanic plate

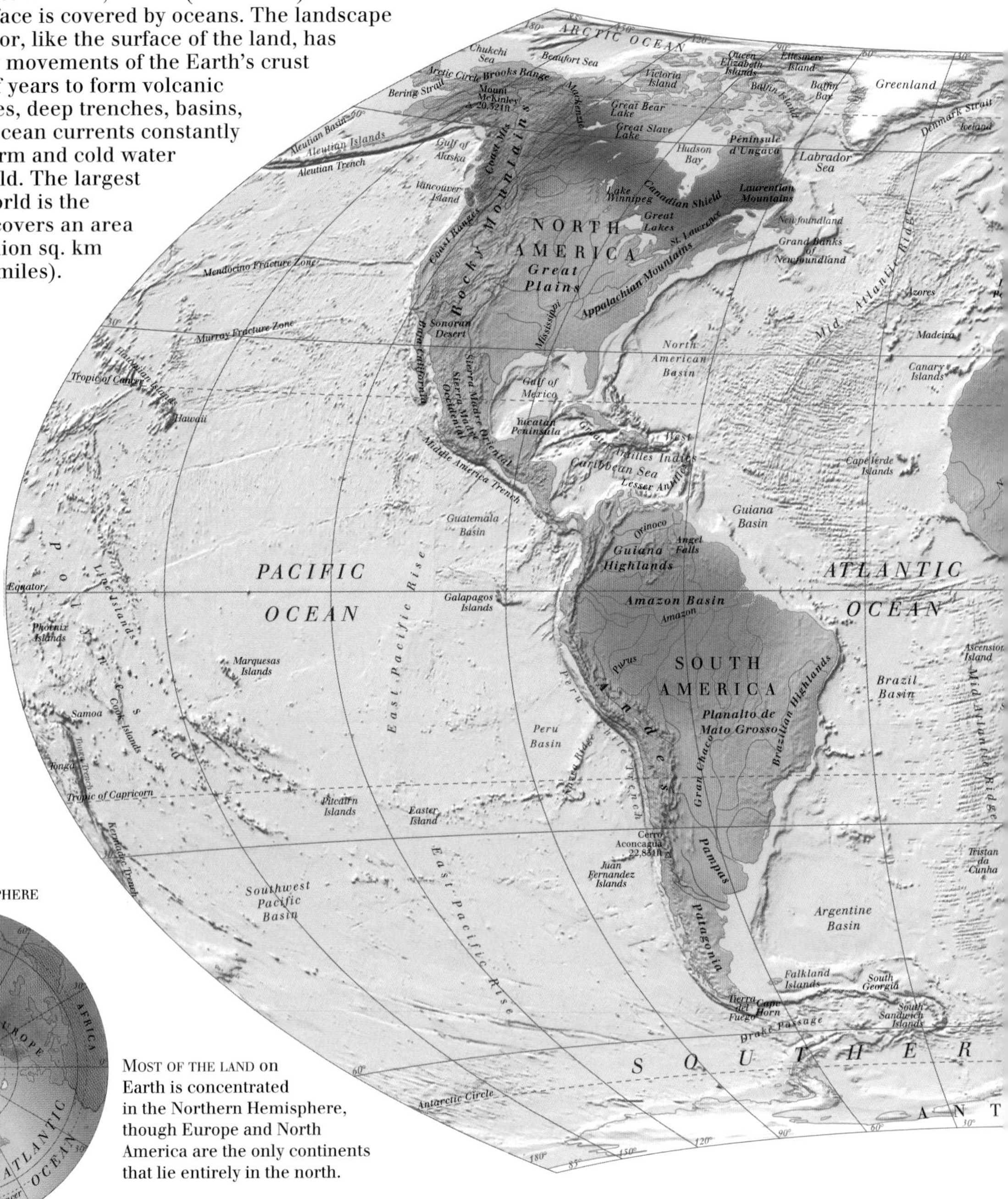
ARCTIC OCEAN
Chukchi Sea
Beaufort Sea
Arctic Circle
Brooks Range
Bering Strait
Mount McKinley
Victoria Island
Queen Elizabeth Islands
Ellesmere Island
Baffin Island
Baffin Bay
Greenland
Denmark Strait
Iceland
Great Bear Lake
Great Slave Lake
Hudson Bay
Péninsule d'Ungava
Labrador Sea
Aleutian Basin
Aleutian Islands
Aleutian Trench
Gulf of Alaska
Coast Mountains
Vancouver Island
Lake Winnipeg
Canadian Shield
Laurentian Mountains
Great Lakes
St. Lawrence
Newfoundland
Grand Banks of Newfoundland
NORTH AMERICA
Great Plains
Rocky Mountains
Coast Ranges
Mendocino Fracture Zone
Appalachian Mountains
Mississippi
Mid-Atlantic Ridge
Azores
Sonoran Desert
Murray Fracture Zone
Baja California
North American Basin
Madeira
Canary Islands
Tropic of Cancer
Hawaiian Islands
Hawaii
Sierra Madre Occidental
Sierra Madre Oriental
Gulf of Mexico
Yucatan Peninsula
Greater Antilles
West Indies
Caribbean Sea
Lesser Antilles
Middle America Trench
Cape Verde Islands
Guatemala Basin
Guiana Basin
Orinoco
Angel Falls
Guiana Highlands
PACIFIC OCEAN
ATLANTIC OCEAN
Equator
Galapagos Islands
Amazon Basin
Amazon
Phoenix Islands
Line Islands
Polynesia
Marquesas Islands
East Pacific Rise
Peru Basin
Purus
SOUTH AMERICA
Andes
Planalto de Mato Grosso
Brazilian Highlands
Ascension Island
Brazil Basin
Samoa
Cook Islands
Tonga
Tonga Trench
Tropic of Capricorn
Peru-Chile Trench
Gran Chaco
Pitcairn Islands
Easter Island
Kermadec Trench
Cerro Aconcagua 22,831ft
Juan Fernandez Islands
Pampas
Tristan da Cunha
Southwest Pacific Basin
Patagonia
Argentine Basin
Falkland Islands
South Georgia
Tierra del Fuego
Cape Horn
Drake Passage
South Sandwich Islands
SOUTHERN
Antarctic Circle
ANT

NORTHERN HEMISPHERE

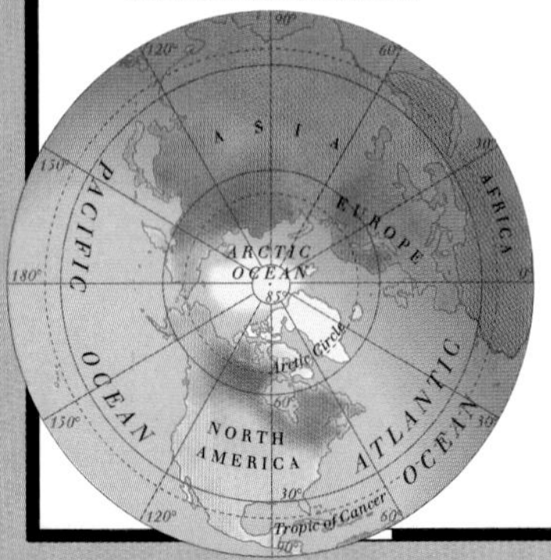
ASIA
EUROPE
AFRICA
PACIFIC OCEAN
ARCTIC OCEAN
Arctic Circle
NORTH AMERICA
ATLANTIC OCEAN
Tropic of Cancer

MOST OF THE LAND on Earth is concentrated in the Northern Hemisphere, though Europe and North America are the only continents that lie entirely in the north.

THE DYNAMIC EARTH

THE EARTH'S CRUST is made up of eight major (and several minor) rigid continental and oceanic tectonic plates, which constantly move relative to one another. It is this movement which causes volcanic eruptions, earthquakes, and sometimes tsunamis along the plate boundaries. The largest volcanoes formed by this process are Aconcagua in Argentina at 6959 m (22,831 ft) and Kilimanjaro in Tanzania at 5895 m (19,340 ft), both of which are now extinct. Plate tectonics are responsible for the formation of the Himalayas – which were created by two colliding plates – and the Hawaiian Islands, created by the Pacific plate's movement over a "hot spot" of magma.

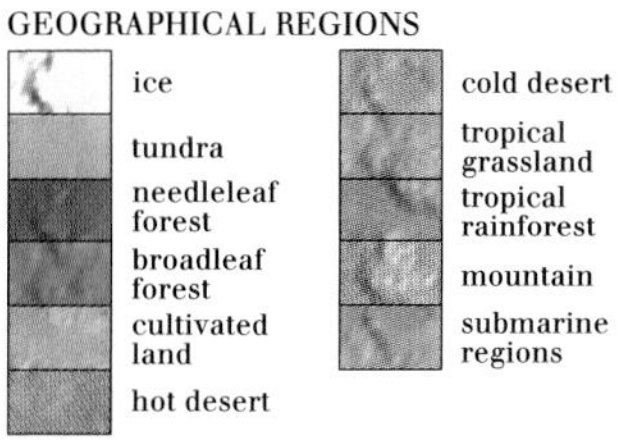
GEOGRAPHICAL REGIONS
ice
tundra
needleleaf forest
broadleaf forest
cultivated land
hot desert
cold desert
tropical grassland
tropical rainforest
mountain
submarine regions

PHYSICAL WORLD FACTFILE

HIGHEST MOUNTAINS

1 **Everest**	8850 m	(29,035 ft)
2 **K2**	8611 m	(28,253 ft)
3 **Kangchenjunga I**	8590 m	(28,169 ft)
4 **Makalu I**	8463 m	(27,766 ft)
5 **Cho Oyu**	8201 m	(26,906 ft)

LONGEST RIVERS

1 **Nile**	6695 km	(4160 mi.)
2 **Amazon**	6516 km	(4049 mi.)
3 **Chang Jiang**	6299 km	(3915 mi.)
4 **Mississippi /Missouri**	5969 km	(3710 mi.)
5 **Ob'-Irtysh**	5570 km	(3461 mi.)

LARGEST DESERTS

1 **Sahara**	9,065,000 km²	(3,263,400 mi²)
2 **Australian**	3,750,000 km²	(1,350,000 mi²)
3 **Gobi**	1,295,000 km²	(466,200 mi²)
4 **Arabian**	750,000 km²	(270,000 mi²)
5 **Sonoran**	311,000 km²	(111,960 mi²)

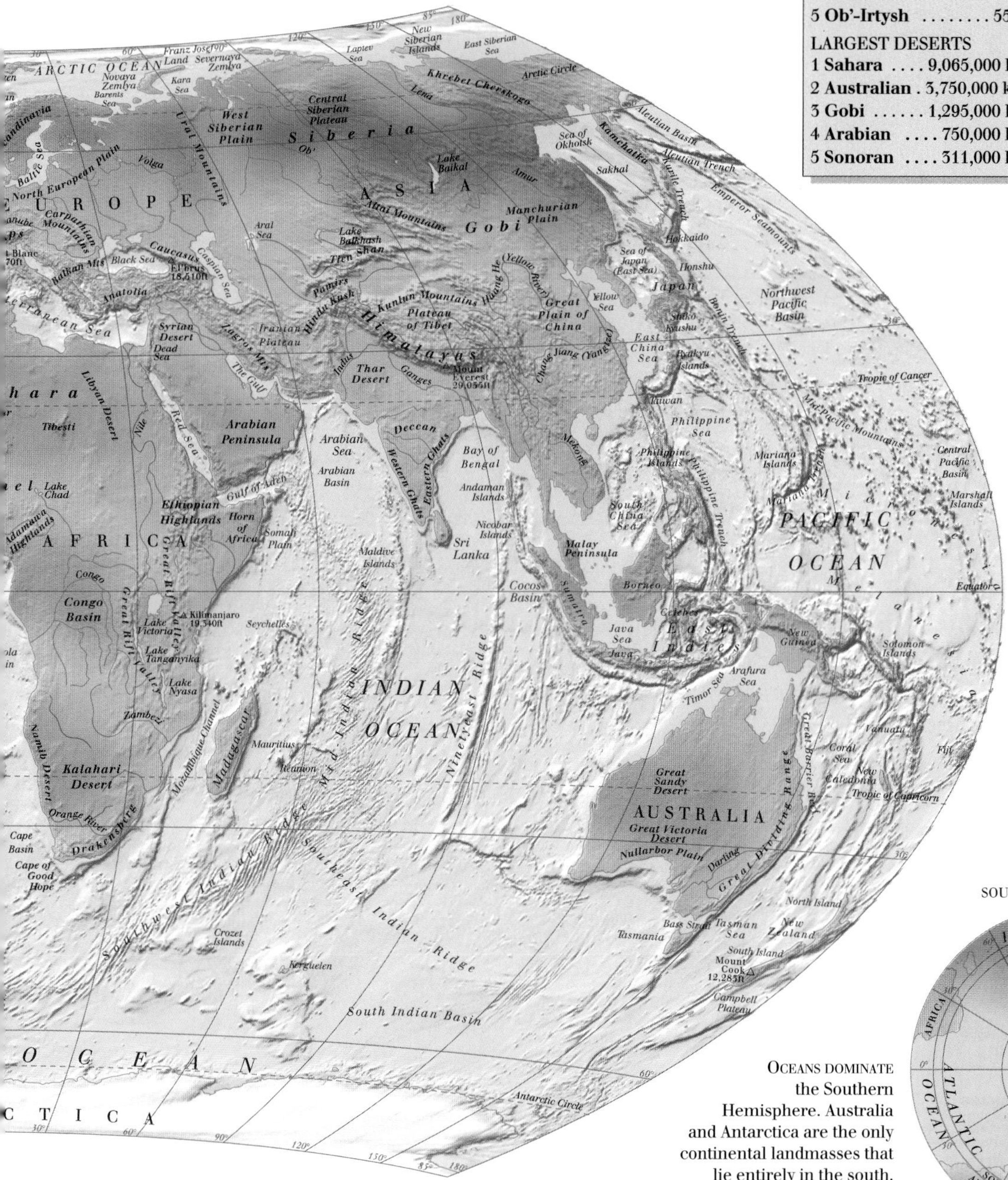
ARCTIC OCEAN
Siberia
ASIA
EUROPE
Gobi
Himalayas
Mount Everest 29,035ft
Plateau of Tibet
Arabian Peninsula
AFRICA
Congo Basin
Kalahari Desert
INDIAN OCEAN
PACIFIC OCEAN
AUSTRALIA
Great Sandy Desert
Great Victoria Desert
Nullarbor Plain
Malay Peninsula
Borneo
Java Sea
Philippine Sea
Philippine Trench
Japan
Kamchatka
Sea of Okhotsk
Lake Baikal
Ural Mountains
Caspian Sea
Black Sea
Aral Sea
Bay of Bengal
Arabian Sea
Red Sea
Madagascar
Kilimanjaro 19,340ft
Lake Victoria
Tropic of Cancer
Equator
Tropic of Capricorn
Antarctic Circle
Tasmania
New Zealand
Mount Cook 12,283ft
Kerguelen
South Indian Basin
Southeast Indian Ridge
Southwest Indian Ridge
Ninetyeast Ridge
Mid-Indian Ridge

SOUTHERN HEMISPHERE

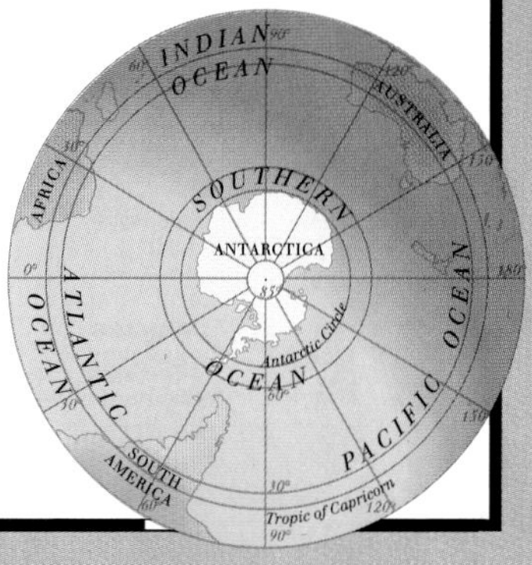
INDIAN OCEAN
SOUTHERN OCEAN
ANTARCTICA
ATLANTIC OCEAN
PACIFIC OCEAN
AFRICA
AUSTRALIA
SOUTH AMERICA
Antarctic Circle
Tropic of Capricorn

OCEANS DOMINATE the Southern Hemisphere. Australia and Antarctica are the only continental landmasses that lie entirely in the south.

THE POLITICAL WORLD

IN 2002, EAST TIMOR joined the international community, becoming the world's 193rd recognized independent state. In 1950 there were only 82. With the exception of Antarctica, where territorial claims have been deferred by international treaty, every land area of the Earth's surface either belongs to, or is claimed by, one country or another. Some 60 overseas dependent territories remain, administered variously by Australia, Denmark, France, the Netherlands, New Zealand, Norway, the UK, and the US. Over the last half-century, national self-determination has been a driving force for many states with a history of colonialism or oppression. While some new states on gaining independence moved peacefully to establish a democracy, many others have been torn by religious or ethnic conflicts or became submerged in power struggles resulting in dictatorship by a military regime or an individual despot.

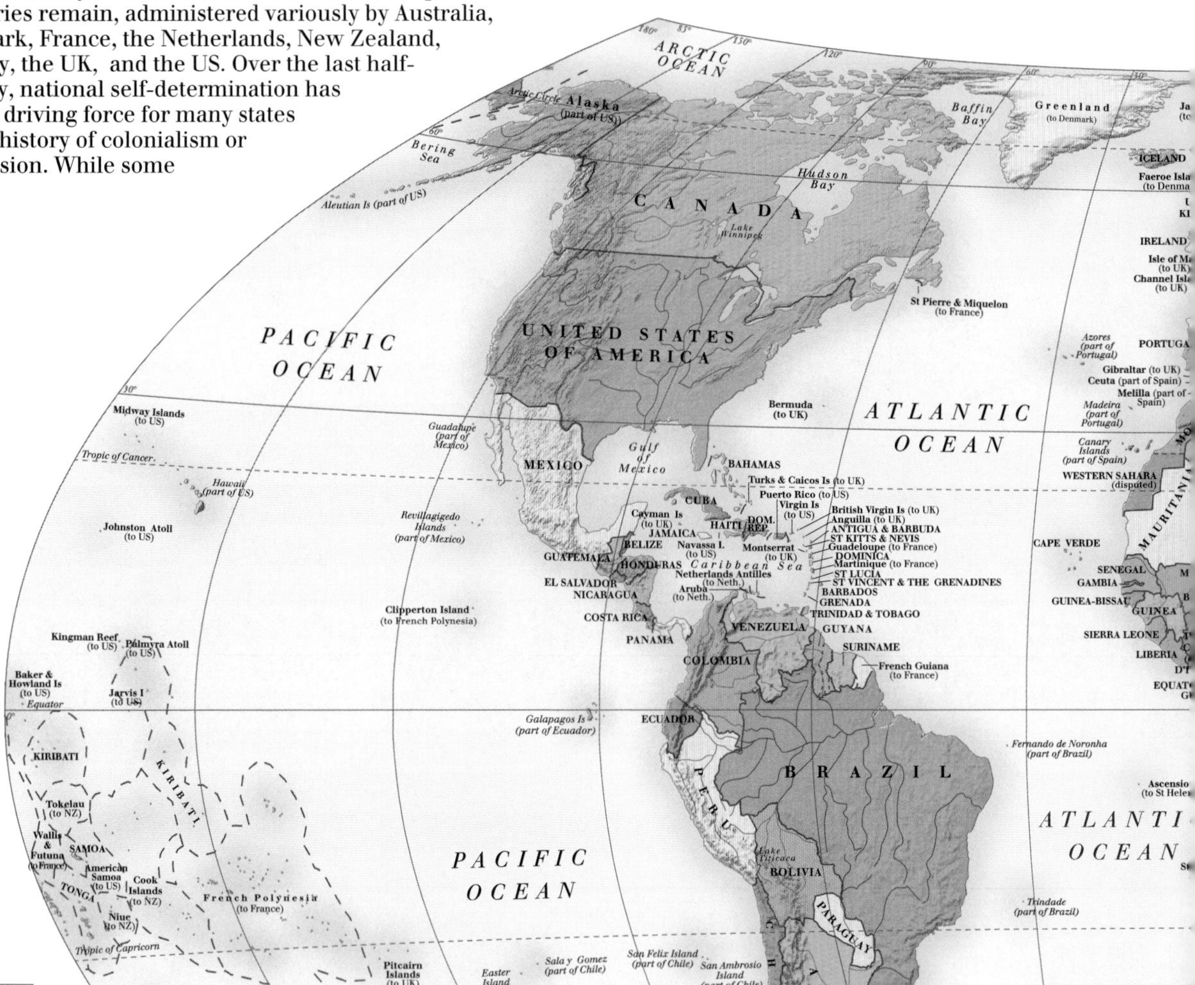
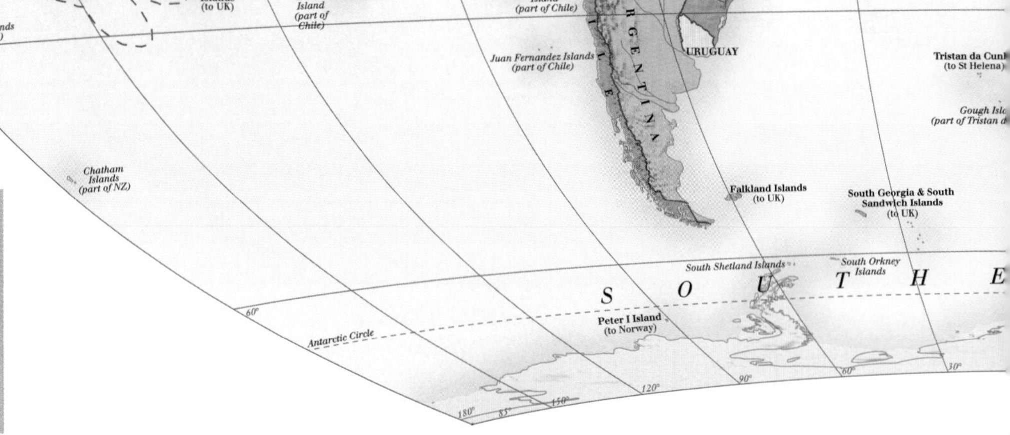
ARCTIC OCEAN
Arctic Circle
Alaska (part of US)
Bering Sea
Aleutian Is (part of US)
Baffin Bay
Greenland (to Denmark)
Hudson Bay
CANADA
Lake Winnipeg
ICELAND
Faeroe Isla (to Denma
IRELAND
Isle of M (to UK)
Channel Isl (to UK)
St Pierre & Miquelon (to France)
UNITED STATES OF AMERICA
PACIFIC OCEAN
Azores (part of Portugal)
PORTUGA
Gibraltar (to UK)
Ceuta (part of Spain)
Melilla (part of Spain)
Madeira (part of Portugal)
Bermuda (to UK)
ATLANTIC OCEAN
Midway Islands (to US)
Guadalupe (part of Mexico)
Gulf of Mexico
Canary Islands (part of Spain)
WESTERN SAHARA (disputed)
Tropic of Cancer
MEXICO
BAHAMAS
Turks & Caicos Is (to UK)
Puerto Rico (to US)
Hawaii (part of US)
CUBA
Virgin Is (to US)
British Virgin Is (to UK)
Anguilla (to UK)
ANTIGUA & BARBUDA
ST KITTS & NEVIS
Guadeloupe (to France)
DOMINICA
Martinique (to France)
ST LUCIA
ST VINCENT & THE GRENADINES
BARBADOS
GRENADA
TRINIDAD & TOBAGO
Johnston Atoll (to US)
Revillagigedo Islands (part of Mexico)
Cayman Is (to UK)
JAMAICA
HAITI
DOM. REP.
BELIZE
Navassa I. (to US)
Montserrat (to UK)
Caribbean Sea
Netherlands Antilles (to Neth.)
Aruba (to Neth.)
GUATEMALA
HONDURAS
EL SALVADOR
NICARAGUA
COSTA RICA
PANAMA
CAPE VERDE
SENEGAL
GAMBIA
GUINEA-BISSAU
GUINEA
SIERRA LEONE
LIBERIA
Clipperton Island (to French Polynesia)
VENEZUELA
GUYANA
SURINAME
French Guiana (to France)
COLOMBIA
Kingman Reef (to US)
Palmyra Atoll (to US)
Baker & Howland Is (to US)
Jarvis I (to US)
Equator
Galapagos Is (part of Ecuador)
ECUADOR
Fernando de Noronha (part of Brazil)
KIRIBATI
BRAZIL
PERU
Ascension (to St Helen
Tokelau (to NZ)
Wallis & Futuna (to France)
SAMOA
American Samoa (to US)
Cook Islands (to NZ)
TONGA
Niue (to NZ)
French Polynesia (to France)
PACIFIC OCEAN
Lake Titicaca
BOLIVIA
ATLANTIC OCEAN
Trindade (part of Brazil)
PARAGUAY
Tropic of Capricorn
Pitcairn Islands (to UK)
Easter Island (part of Chile)
Sala y Gomez (part of Chile)
San Felix Island (part of Chile)
San Ambrosio Island (part of Chile)
CHILE
ARGENTINA
Kermadec Islands (part of NZ)
URUGUAY
Juan Fernandez Islands (part of Chile)
Tristan da Cun (to St Helena)
Gough Isl (part of Tristan d
Chatham Islands (part of NZ)
Falkland Islands (to UK)
South Georgia & South Sandwich Islands (to UK)
South Shetland Islands
South Orkney Islands
SOUTHE
Peter I Island (to Norway)
Antarctic Circle

OLDEST COUNTRIES

Denmark
950 CE

China
960 CE

Portugal
1139 CE

France
987 CE

Thailand
1238 CE

KEY

- Full borders
- Disputed borders
- Undefined borders
- Extent of dependent island territories
- Extent of country boundaries for island territories
- Tristan da Cunha (to St Helena) — Dependent territory with self-government
- *Gough Island (part of Tristan da Cunha)* — Territory without self-government (the state it belongs to is given in brackets)

INTERNATIONAL BORDERS

BOUNDARIES BETWEEN states fall into three categories. Full borders are internationally recognized territorial boundaries. Undefined borders exist where no fixed boundary has been demarcated. A disputed border is where a de facto boundary exists which is not agreed upon or is subject to arbitration. Disputed borders exist throughout the world, such as the land borders between India and China and between Ethiopia and Eritrea, and the maritime border between Samoa and American Samoa.

COUNTRIES WITH THE MOST LAND BORDERS

1 **China:** *14* (Afghanistan, Bhutan, Burma, India, Kazakhstan, North Korea, Kyrgyzstan, Laos, Mongolia, Nepal, Pakistan, Russian Federation, Tajikistan, Vietnam)

Russian Federation: *14* (Azerbaijan, Belarus, China, Estonia, Finland, Georgia, Kazakhstan, North Korea, Latvia, Lithuania, Mongolia, Norway, Poland, Ukraine)

2 **Brazil:** *10* (Argentina, Bolivia, Colombia, French Guiana, Guyana, Paraguay, Peru, Suriname, Uruguay, Venezuela)

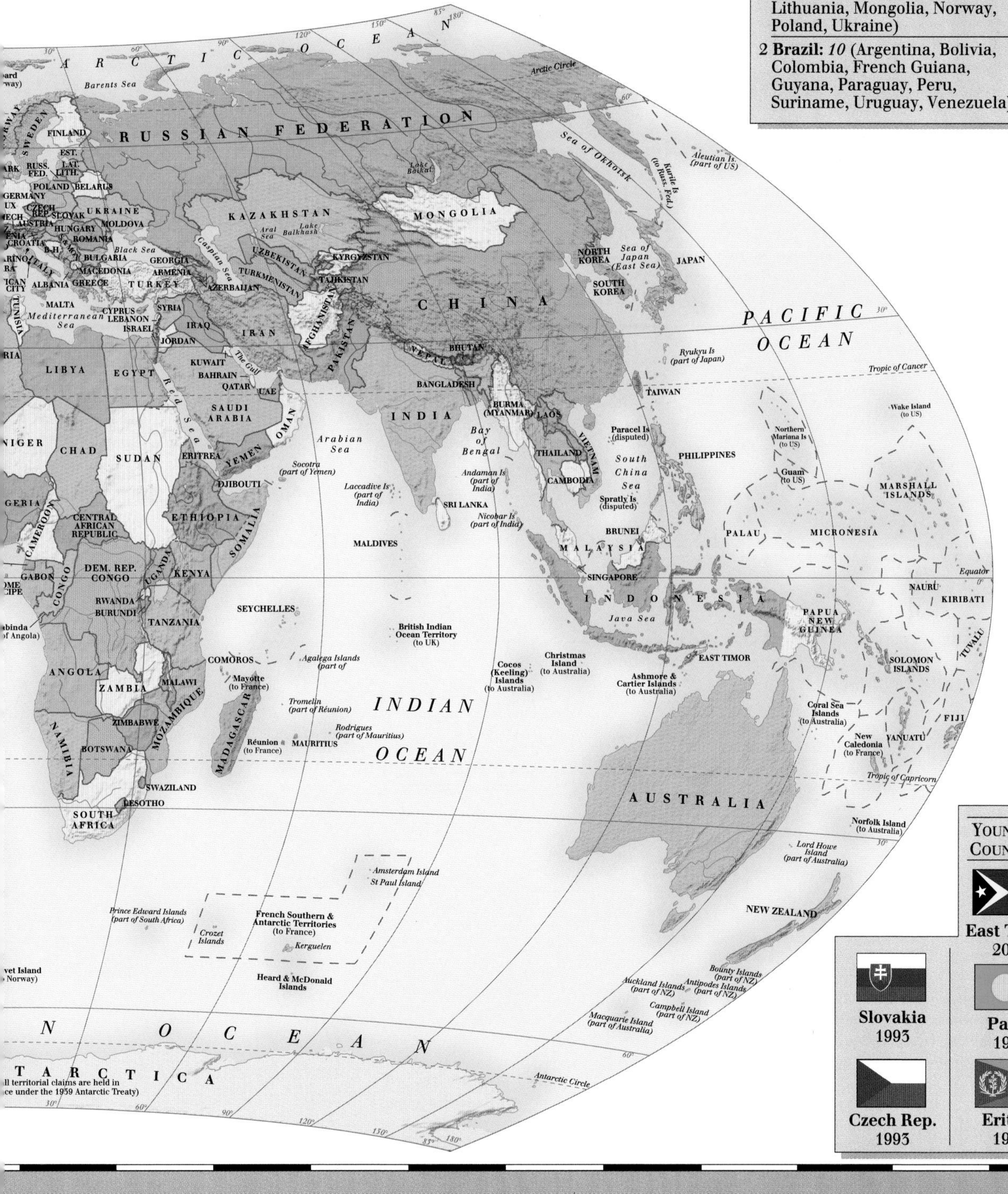
ARCTIC OCEAN
Barents Sea
Arctic Circle
RUSSIAN FEDERATION
FINLAND
EST.
LAT.
LITH.
RUSS. FED.
POLAND
BELARUS
GERMANY
UKRAINE
MOLDOVA
HUNGARY
ROMANIA
BULGARIA
MACEDONIA
GREECE
ALBANIA
MALTA
Mediterranean Sea
Black Sea
GEORGIA
ARMENIA
AZERBAIJAN
TURKEY
CYPRUS
LEBANON
ISRAEL
SYRIA
JORDAN
IRAQ
IRAN
KUWAIT
BAHRAIN
QATAR
UAE
The Gulf
SAUDI ARABIA
OMAN
YEMEN
Red Sea
LIBYA
EGYPT
SUDAN
CHAD
ERITREA
DJIBOUTI
ETHIOPIA
SOMALIA
CENTRAL AFRICAN REPUBLIC
CAMEROON
GABON
CONGO
DEM. REP. CONGO
UGANDA
KENYA
RWANDA
BURUNDI
TANZANIA
ANGOLA
ZAMBIA
MALAWI
MOZAMBIQUE
ZIMBABWE
NAMIBIA
BOTSWANA
SWAZILAND
LESOTHO
SOUTH AFRICA
MADAGASCAR
COMOROS
Mayotte (to France)
Réunion (to France)
MAURITIUS
Tromelin (part of Réunion)
Rodrigues (part of Mauritius)
Agalega Islands (part of
SEYCHELLES
Caspian Sea
KAZAKHSTAN
Aral Sea
Lake Balkhash
UZBEKISTAN
TURKMENISTAN
KYRGYZSTAN
TAJIKISTAN
AFGHANISTAN
PAKISTAN
MONGOLIA
Lake Baikal
CHINA
NEPAL
BHUTAN
BANGLADESH
INDIA
BURMA (MYANMAR)
LAOS
THAILAND
CAMBODIA
VIETNAM
Arabian Sea
Bay of Bengal
Socotra (part of Yemen)
Laccadive Is (part of India)
Andaman Is (part of India)
Nicobar Is (part of India)
SRI LANKA
MALDIVES
British Indian Ocean Territory (to UK)
Sea of Okhotsk
Kurile Is (to Russ. Fed.)
Aleutian Is. (part of US)
NORTH KOREA
SOUTH KOREA
Sea of Japan (East Sea)
JAPAN
PACIFIC OCEAN
Ryukyu Is (part of Japan)
Tropic of Cancer
TAIWAN
Paracel Is (disputed)
South China Sea
Spratly Is (disputed)
PHILIPPINES
BRUNEI
MALAYSIA
SINGAPORE
INDONESIA
Java Sea
EAST TIMOR
PALAU
MICRONESIA
Northern Mariana Is (to US)
Guam (to US)
Wake Island (to US)
MARSHALL ISLANDS
NAURU
KIRIBATI
Equator
PAPUA NEW GUINEA
SOLOMON ISLANDS
TUVALU
FIJI
VANUATU
New Caledonia (to France)
Coral Sea Islands (to Australia)
Tropic of Capricorn
Cocos (Keeling) Islands (to Australia)
Christmas Island (to Australia)
Ashmore & Cartier Islands (to Australia)
INDIAN OCEAN
AUSTRALIA
Norfolk Island (to Australia)
Lord Howe Island (part of Australia)
NEW ZEALAND
Bounty Islands (part of NZ)
Antipodes Islands (part of NZ)
Auckland Islands (part of NZ)
Campbell Island (part of NZ)
Macquarie Island (part of Australia)
Amsterdam Island
St Paul Island
French Southern & Antarctic Territories (to France)
Crozet Islands
Kerguelen
Heard & McDonald Islands
Prince Edward Islands (part of South Africa)
vet Island
Norway)
OCEAN
ANTARCTICA
ll territorial claims are held in
ce under the 1959 Antarctic Treaty)
Antarctic Circle

YOUNGEST COUNTRIES

East Timor 2002

Slovakia 1993

Palau 1994

Czech Rep. 1993

Eritrea 1993

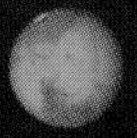

MARS

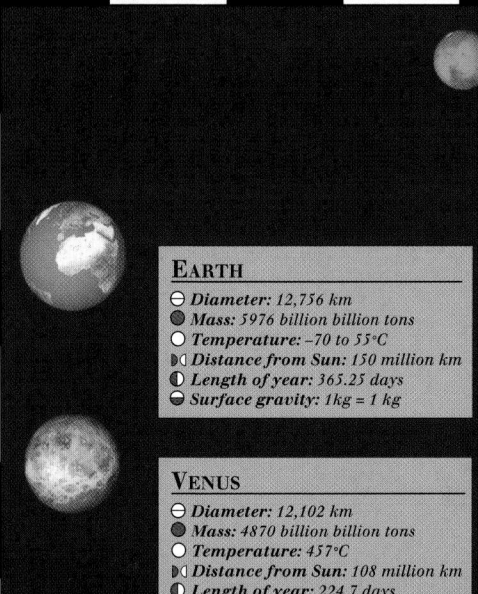

- *Diameter: 6786 km*
- *Mass: 642 billion billion tons*
- *Temperature: –137 to 37°C*
- *Distance from Sun: 228 million km*
- *Length of year: 1.88 years*
- *Surface gravity: 1 kg = 0.38 kg*

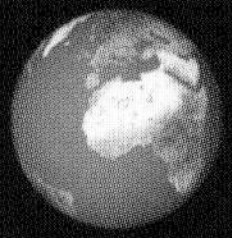

EARTH

- *Diameter: 12,756 km*
- *Mass: 5976 billion billion tons*
- *Temperature: –70 to 55°C*
- *Distance from Sun: 150 million km*
- *Length of year: 365.25 days*
- *Surface gravity: 1kg = 1 kg*

THE EARTH

GASES SUCH AS CARBON dioxide are known as "greenhouse gases" because they prevent shortwave solar radiation from entering the Earth's atmosphere, but help to stop longwave radiation from escaping. This traps heat, raising the Earth's temperature. An excess of these gases traps more heat and can lead to global warming.

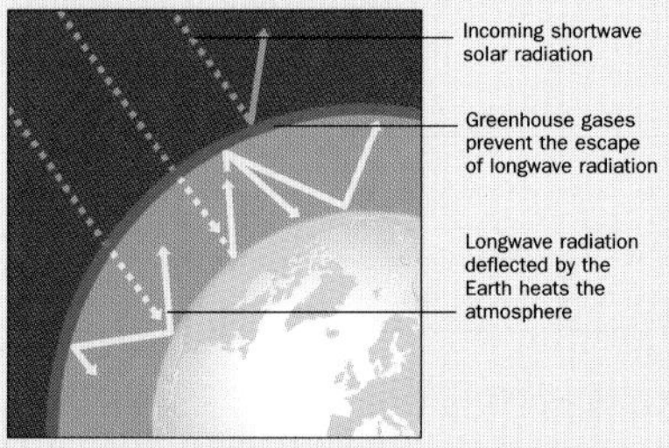
Incoming shortwave solar radiation
Greenhouse gases prevent the escape of longwave radiation
Longwave radiation deflected by the Earth heats the atmosphere

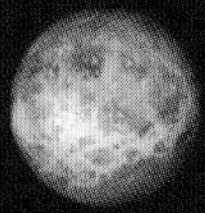

VENUS

- *Diameter: 12,102 km*
- *Mass: 4870 billion billion tons*
- *Temperature: 457°C*
- *Distance from Sun: 108 million km*
- *Length of year: 224.7 days*
- *Surface gravity: 1 kg = 0.88 kg*

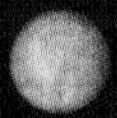

MERCURY

- *Diameter: 4878 km*
- *Mass: 330 billion billion tons*
- *Temperature: –173 to 427°C*
- *Distance from Sun: 58 million km*
- *Length of year: 87.97 days*
- *Surface gravity: 1 kg = 0.38 kg*

THE SOLAR SYSTEM

THE SOLAR SYSTEM CONSISTS of the nine major planets, their moons, the asteroids, and the comets that orbit around the Sun. The Sun itself is composed of 70% hydrogen and 30% helium, and at its core nuclear fusion reactions turning hydrogen into helium produce the heat and light which make life possible on Earth. Of the planets, the inner four (Mercury, Venus, Earth, and Mars) are termed terrestrial, while the next four (Jupiter, Saturn, Uranus, and Neptune) are termed gas giants. Pluto, at the edge of the solar system, is much smaller, and made of rock. The largest natural satellite in the Solar System is Ganymede (5262 km – 3270 miles – in diameter), which orbits around Jupiter, the largest planet. Halley's comet is the brightest comet when seen from Earth, and orbits the Sun once every 76 years. The largest asteroid is named Ceres (940 km – 584 miles – in diameter), which is found in the asteroid belt between Mars and Jupiter. The planet Earth is unique within the solar system (and possibly the universe), being the only planet capable of sustaining life.

JUPITER

- *Diameter: 142,984 km*
- *Mass: 1,900,000,000 billion billion tons*
- *Temperature: –153°C*
- *Distance from Sun: 77*
- *Length of year: 11.86 y*
- *Surface gravity: 1 kg =*

SATURN

- Diameter: 120,660 km
- Mass: 570,000 billion billion tons
- Temperature: –185°C
- Distance from Sun: 1427 million km
- Length of year: 29.46 years
- Surface gravity: 1 kg = 1.07 kg

URANUS

- Diameter: 51,118 km
- Mass: 102,000 billion billion tons
- Temperature: –214°C
- Distance from Sun: 2870 million km
- Length of year: 84.01 years
- Surface gravity: 1 kg = 0.92 kg

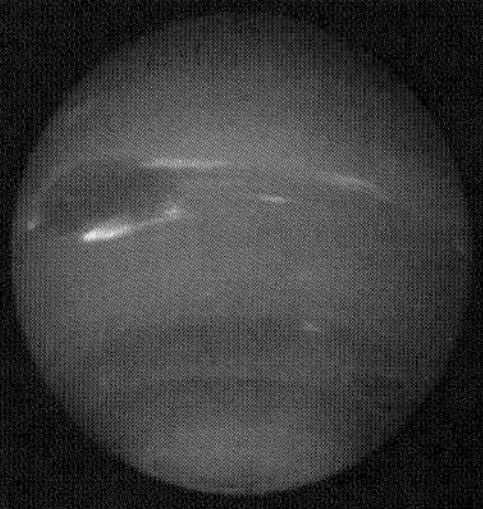

NEPTUNE

- Diameter: 49,528 km
- Mass: 13 billion billion tons
- Temperature: –225°C
- Distance from Sun: 4497 million km
- Length of year: 164.79 years
- Surface gravity: 1 kg = 1.18 kg

PLUTO

- Diameter: 2300 km
- Mass: 13 billion billion tons
- Temperature: –236°C
- Distance from Sun: 5900 million km
- Length of year: 248.54 years
- Surface gravity: 1 kg = 0.30 kg

MOON AND TIDES

TIDES ARE CREATED by the pull of the Sun's and the Moon's gravity on the surface of the oceans. Waves are formed by wind blowing over the surface of the oceans. The highest tides occur when the Earth, the Moon, and the Sun are aligned (*below left*). The lowest tides are experienced when the Sun and Moon align at right angles to one another (*below right*).

NEAR SIDE OF THE MOON

FAR SIDE OF THE MOON

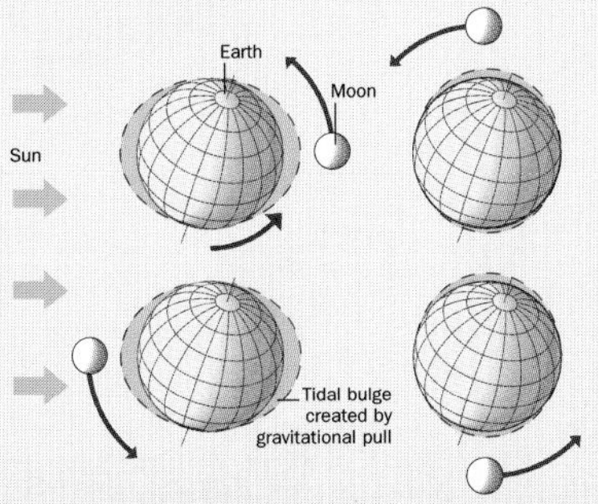
HIGHEST HIGH TIDES
LOWEST HIGH TIDES
Earth
Moon
Sun
Tidal bulge created by gravitational pull

Timeline of Space Exploration

- **1957:** USSR launches *Sputnik 1* - first artificial satellite
- **Oct 10, 1959:** *Luna 3* sends back first pictures of dark side of the Moon
- **Apr 12, 1961:** Yuri Gagarin (USSR) first person in space
- **Jul 10, 1962:** Launch of *Telstar 1*, first commercial communications satellite
- **Feb 13, 1966:** *Luna 9* first probe to land on Moon
- **Jul 21, 1969:** Neil Armstrong and Buzz Aldrin first people to land on Moon
- **1976:** Missions of *Viking 1* and *2* analyze surface of Mars
- **Jan 28, 1986:** *Challenger* shuttle explodes; all seven crew members killed
- **Feb 20, 1986:** Launch of space station *Mir*
- **Aug 25, 1989:** *Voyager 2* probe passes Neptune on way out of Solar System
- **Apr 24, 1990:** Launch of Hubble Space Telescope
- **1998:** Launch of first part of International Space Station
- **2001:** *Near* probe lands on Eros asteroid. *Mir* brought to earth. Dennis Tito is first space tourist. 100th shuttle mission completed
- **2003:** *Columbia* space shuttle explodes. Three separate missions launched to Mars: ESA's *Mars Express*, NASA's Rovers, and Japan's *Nozomi*. First Chinese manned space flight
- **2005:** *Cassini* probe to land on Titan (Saturn's largest moon)

1955 1960 1970 1980 1990 2000 2010

The Climate

THE EARTH'S CLIMATIC REGIONS consist of stable patterns of weather conditions averaged out over a long period of time. Different climates are categorized according to particular combinations of temperature and humidity. By contrast, weather consists of short-term fluctuations in wind, temperature, and humidity conditions. Different climates are determined by latitude, altitude, the prevailing wind, and circulation of ocean currents. Longer-term changes in climate, such as global warming or the onset of ice ages, are punctuated by shorter-term events which comprise the day-to-day weather of a region, such as frontal depressions, hurricanes, and blizzards.

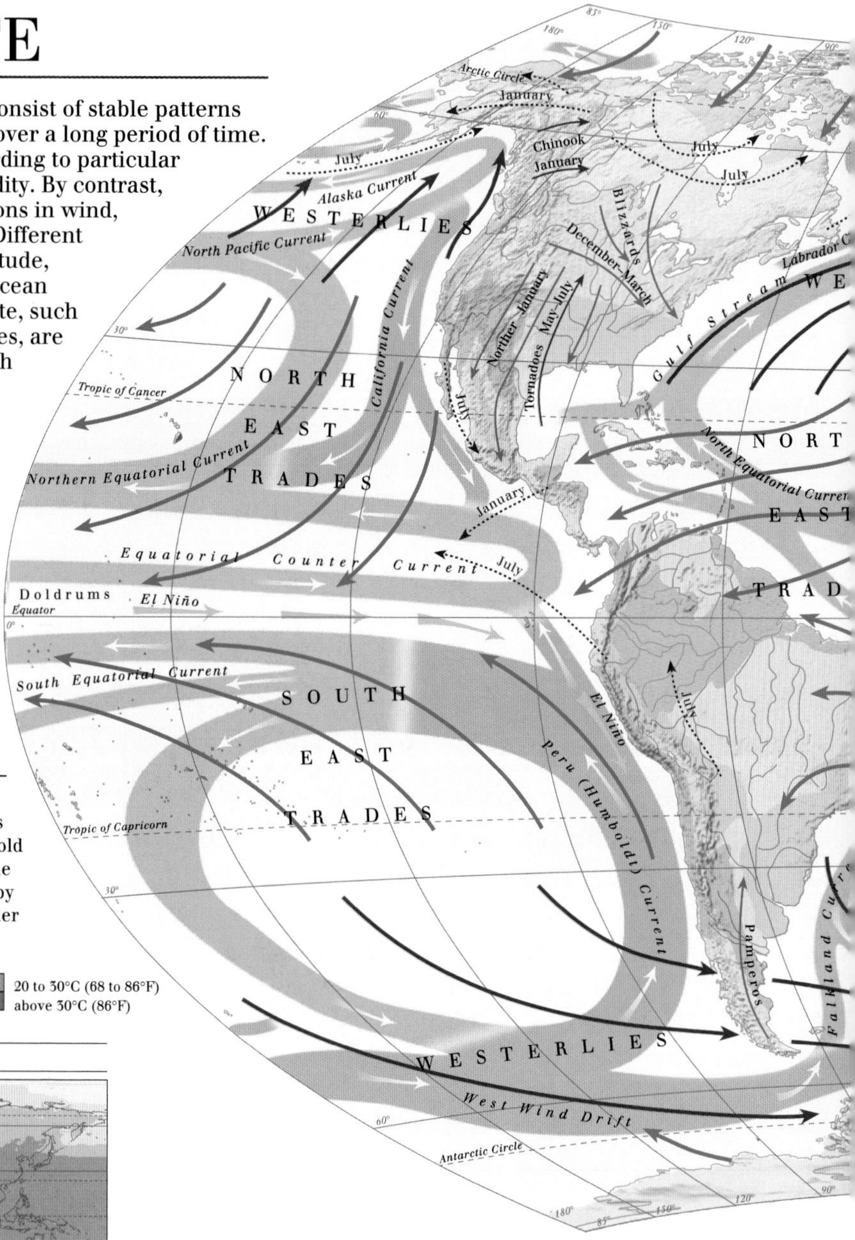
Arctic Circle
January
Chinook
January
July
July
July
Alaska Current
WESTERLIES
North Pacific Current
Blizzards
December-March
Labrador C
Gulf Stream
Norther January
Tornadoes May-July
California Current
Tropic of Cancer
NORTH
EAST
TRADES
July
Northern Equatorial Current
North Equatorial Current
NORT
EAST
TRAD
January
Equatorial Counter Current
July
Doldrums
El Niño
Equator
South Equatorial Current
SOUTH
EAST
TRADES
El Niño
July
Peru (Humboldt) Current
Tropic of Capricorn
Pamperos
Falkland Current
WESTERLIES
West Wind Drift
Antarctic Circle

CLIMATE ZONES

- Ice cap
- Tundra
- Subarctic
- Cool continental
- Warm humid
- Mediterranean
- Semi-arid
- Arid
- Tropical
- Humid equatorial

OCEAN CURRENTS
- Warm
- Cold

PREVAILING WINDS
- Warm
- Cold

LOCAL WINDS
- Warm
- Cold
- June Seasonal*

* (seasonal winds which can either be warm or cold)

TEMPERATURE

THE WORLD CAN BE DIVIDED into three major climatic zones, stretching like large belts across the latitudes: the tropics which are warm, the cold polar regions, and the temperate zones which lie between them. Temperature is also controlled by altitude: mountainous regions are typically colder than those at sea level.

- below - 30°C (-22°F)
- -30 to - 20°C (-22 to -4°F)
- -20 to - 10°C (-4 to 14°F)
- -10 to 0°C (14 to 32°F)
- 0 to 10°C (32 to 50°F)
- 10 to 20°C (50 to 68°F)
- 20 to 30°C (68 to 86°F)
- above 30°C (86°F)

AVERAGE JULY TEMPERATURE

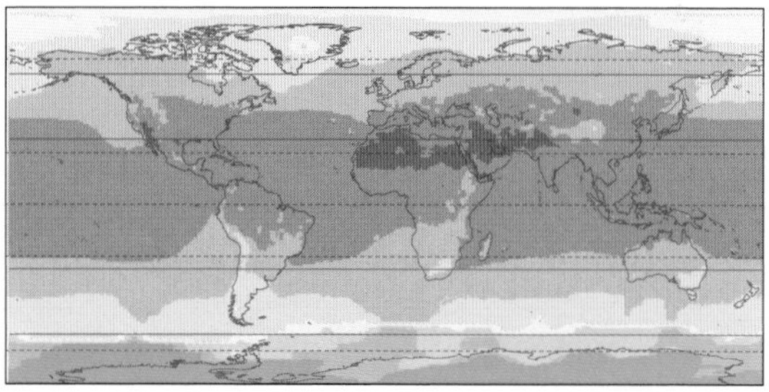

AVERAGE JANUARY TEMPERATURE

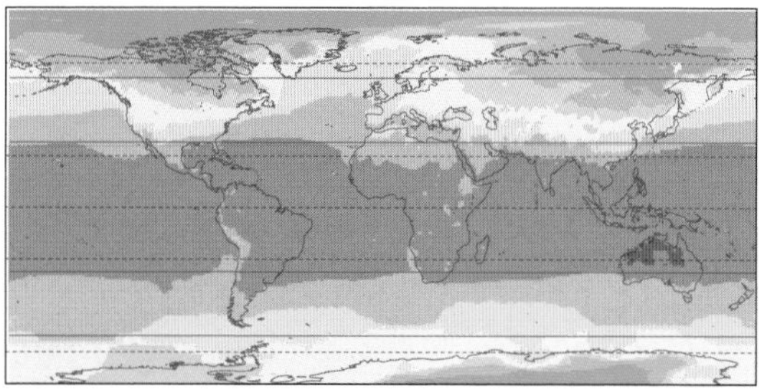

AVERAGE JULY RAINFALL

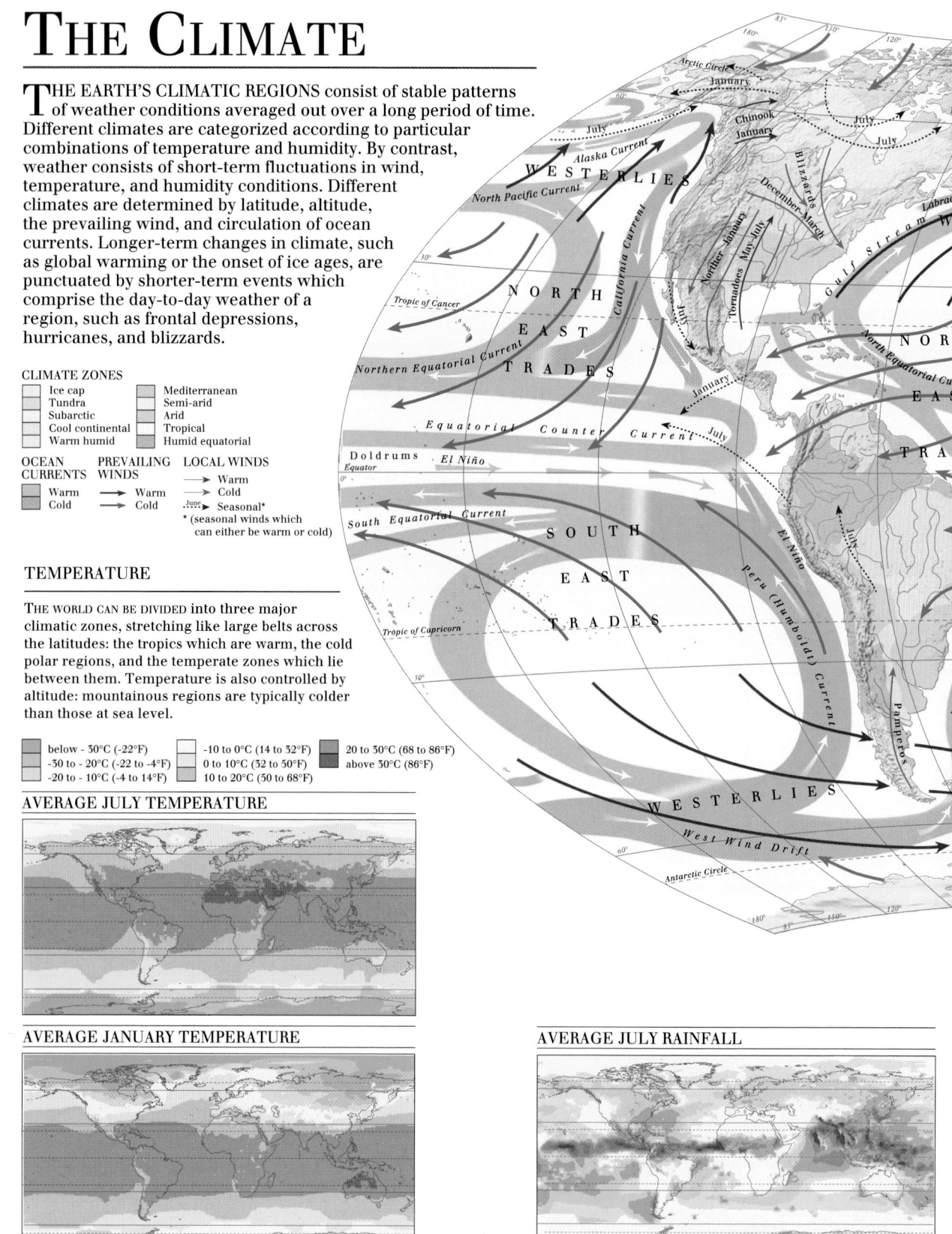

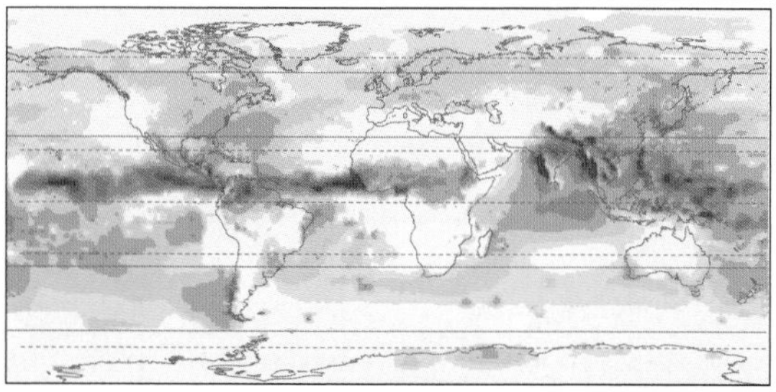

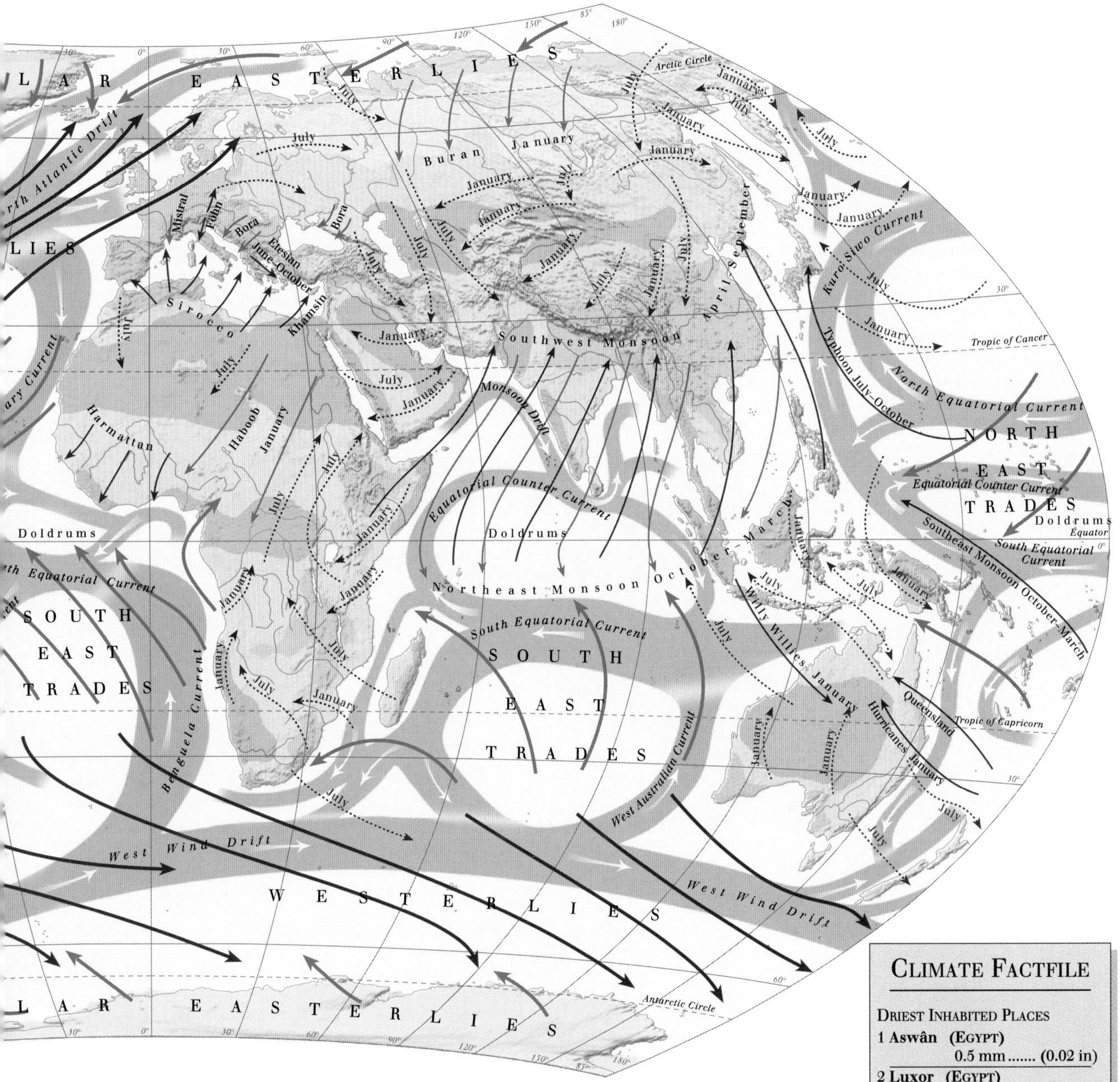

EASTERLIES
North Atlantic Drift
LIES
July
January
Buran
Mistral
Föhn
Bora
Etesian June–October
Sirocco
Khamsin
Harmattan
Haboob
Southwest Monsoon
Monsoon Drift
April–September
Kuro Siwo Current
Typhoon July–October
Tropic of Cancer
North Equatorial Current
NORTH EAST TRADES
Equatorial Counter Current
Doldrums
Equator
South Equatorial Current
Southeast Monsoon October–March
Northeast Monsoon
October–March
Willy Willies January
SOUTH EAST TRADES
Benguela Current
West Australian Current
Queensland
Hurricanes January
Tropic of Capricorn
West Wind Drift
WESTERLIES
Arctic Circle
Antarctic Circle

0–25 mm (0–1 in)
25–50 mm (1–2 in)
50–100 mm (2–4 in)
100–200 mm (4–8 in)
200–300 mm (8–12 in)
300–400 mm (12–16 in)
400–500 mm (16–20 in)
above 500 mm (20 in)

AVERAGE JANUARY RAINFALL

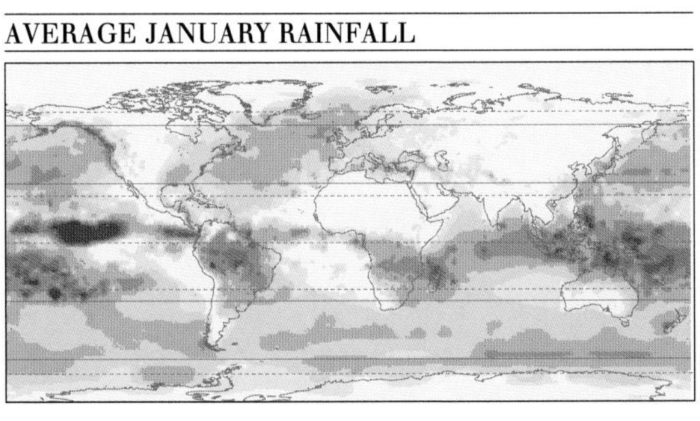

RAINFALL

WHEN AIR IS HEATED, it expands, rises, and cools, and the water vapor it carries condenses to form clouds. Heavy, regular rainfall is characteristic of the equatorial region, while the poles, being cold, receive only slight snowfall. Tropical regions have marked dry and rainy seasons, while in temperate regions rainfall is unpredictable.

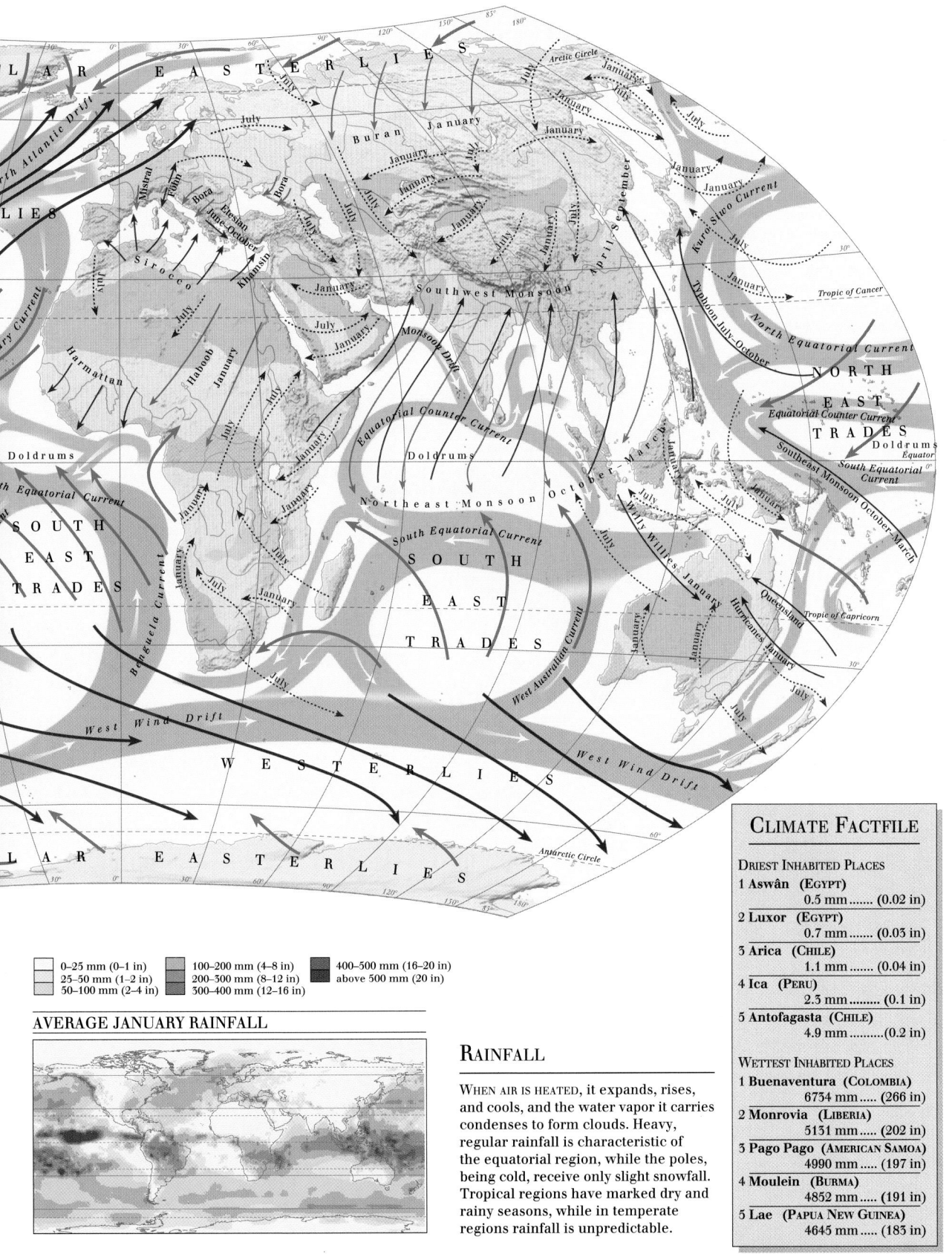

CLIMATE FACTFILE

DRIEST INHABITED PLACES

1 **Aswân** (**EGYPT**) 0.5 mm .... (0.02 in)
2 **Luxor** (**EGYPT**) 0.7 mm .... (0.03 in)
3 **Arica** (**CHILE**) 1.1 mm .... (0.04 in)
4 **Ica** (**PERU**) 2.3 mm .... (0.1 in)
5 **Antofagasta** (**CHILE**) 4.9 mm ....(0.2 in)

WETTEST INHABITED PLACES

1 **Buenaventura** (**COLOMBIA**) 6734 mm ..... (266 in)
2 **Monrovia** (**LIBERIA**) 5131 mm ..... (202 in)
3 **Pago Pago** (**AMERICAN SAMOA**) 4990 mm ..... (197 in)
4 **Moulein** (**BURMA**) 4852 mm ..... (191 in)
5 **Lae** (**PAPUA NEW GUINEA**) 4645 mm ..... (183 in)

THE ENVIRONMENT

THE EARTH CAN BE DIVIDED into a series of biogeographic regions, or biomes – ecological communities where certain species of plant and animal coexist within particular climatic conditions. Within these broad classifications, other factors affect the local distribution of species in each biome, including soil richness, altitude, and human activities such as urbanization, intensive agriculture, and deforestation. Apart from the polar ice caps, there are few areas which have not been colonized by animals or plants over the course of the Earth's history. Because of all animals' reliance on plants for survival, plants are known as primary producers. The availability of nutrients and the temperature of an area define its primary productivity, which affects the number and type of animals which are able to live there; the level of humidity or aridity is also a determining factor.

BIODIVERSITY

THE NUMBER OF PLANT AND ANIMAL SPECIES, and the range of genetic diversity within the populations of each species, make up the Earth's biodiversity. The plants and animals which are endemic to a region – that is, those which are found nowhere else in the world – are also important in determining levels of biodiversity. Human settlement and intervention have encroached on many areas of the world once rich in endemic plant and animal species. Increasing international efforts are being made to monitor and conserve the biodiversity of the Earth's remaining wild places.

Arctic Circle
Rocky Mountains
Great Plains
Canadian Shield
North European Plain
Mediterranean Sea
ATLANTIC OCEAN
Tropic of Cancer
Sahara
Caribbean Sea
Sahel
PACIFIC OCEAN
Equator
Amazon Basin
Congo Basin
ATLANTIC OCEAN
Gran Chaco
Kalahari Desert
Tropic of Capricorn
Pampas
SOUTHERN OCE
Antarctic Circle
ANTARCT

ANIMALS

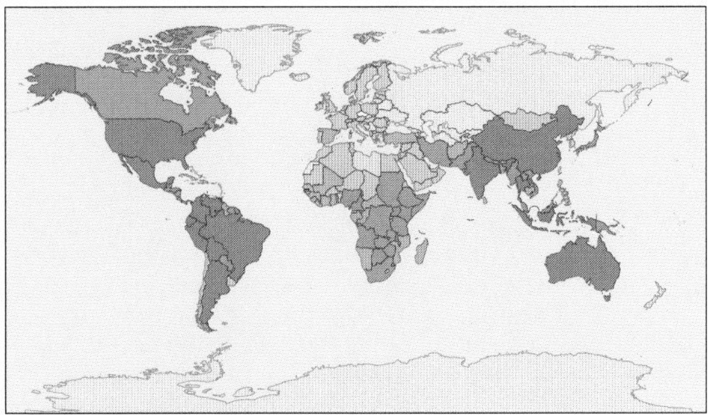

Number of animal species per country

- More than 2000
- 1000–1999
- 700–999
- 400–699
- 200–399
- 100–199
- 0–99
- Data not available

ANIMAL ADAPTATION

THE DEGREE OF AN ANIMAL'S ADAPTABILITY to different climates and conditions is extremely important in ensuring its success as a species. Many animals, particularly the largest mammals, are becoming restricted to ever-smaller regions as human development and agricultural practices reduce their natural habitats. In contrast, humans have been responsible – deliberately and accidentally – for the spread of some of the world's most successful species, many of which now outnumber the indigenous animal populations.

PLANTS

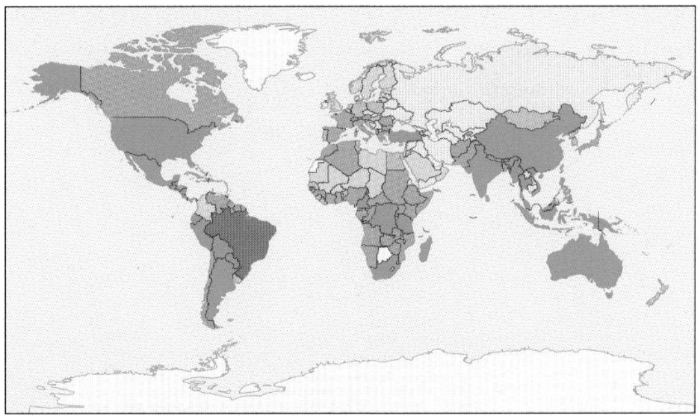

Number of plant species per country

- More than 50,000
- 7000–49,999
- 3000–6999
- 2000–2999
- 1000–1999
- 600–999
- 0–599
- Data not available

PLANT ADAPTATION

ENVIRONMENTAL CONDITIONS, such as climate, soil type, and competition with other organisms, influence the development of plants into distinctive forms. Similar conditions in different parts of the world create similar adaptations in the plants, which may then be modified by other, local, factors specific to the region.

OCEAN
Arctic Circle
Siberia
Gobi
Himalayas
Thar Desert
Deccan
Tropic of Cancer
PACIFIC OCEAN
Equator
INDIAN OCEAN
Tropic of Capricorn
Great Victoria Desert
Antarctic Circle
A

BIOME TYPES

- Mountains
- Polar regions
- Tundra
- Tropical rainforests
- Dry woodlands
- Savanna
- Temperate grasslands
- Mediterranean
- Coniferous forests
- Temperate rainforests
- Broadleaf forests
- Cold deserts
- Hot deserts
- Wetlands

ENVIRONMENT FACTFILE

LARGEST PROTECTED AREAS
(Land and marine, as percentage of land area)

Dominican Republic	174%
Tuvalu	132%
Seychelles	111%
Cuba	69%
Venezuela	64%

HIGHEST ANNUAL DEFORESTATION

Brazil	24,130 km²	(9317 mi²)
Indonesia	11,000 km²	(4247 mi²)
Sudan	9590 km²	(3711 mi²)
Zambia	8510 km²	(3293 mi²)
Mexico	6310 km²	(2436 mi²)

DESCRIBED SPECIES

Invertebrates	1,190,200
Plants	322,500
Fish	28,100
Reptiles & amphibians	13,712
Birds	9932
Mammals	4842

THREATENED SPECIES

Plants	6774
Invertebrates	1959
Birds	1194
Mammals	1130
Fish	750
Reptiles & amphibians	450

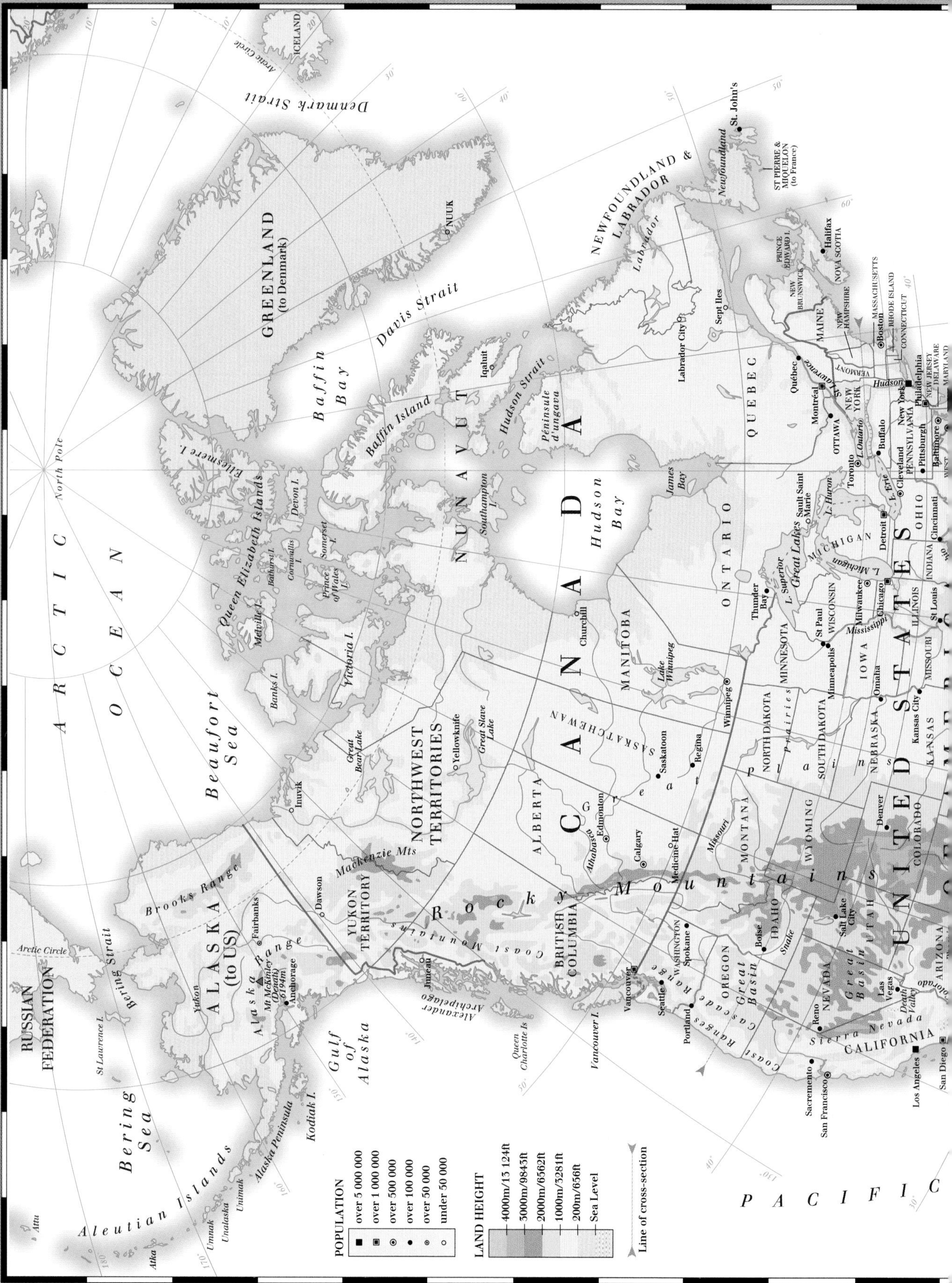

ARCTIC OCEAN
North Pole
Arctic Circle
Denmark Strait
ICELAND
GREENLAND (to Denmark)
NUUK
Davis Strait
Baffin Bay
Baffin Island
Ellesmere I.
Queen Elizabeth Islands
Devon I.
Bathurst I.
Cornwallis I.
Somerset I.
Prince of Wales I.
Melville I.
Banks I.
Victoria I.
Beaufort Sea
NUNAVUT
Iqaluit
Hudson Strait
Péninsule d'ungava
Southampton I.
Hudson Bay
James Bay
CANADA
NORTHWEST TERRITORIES
Great Bear Lake
Great Slave Lake
Yellowknife
Inuvik
Mackenzie Mts
YUKON TERRITORY
Dawson
Rocky Mountains
Coast Mountains
BRITISH COLUMBIA
ALBERTA
SASKATCHEWAN
MANITOBA
ONTARIO
QUEBEC
NEWFOUNDLAND & LABRADOR
Labrador
Newfoundland
St. John's
ST PIERRE & MIQUELON (to France)
Labrador City
Sept Iles
Churchill
Lake Winnipeg
Winnipeg
Edmonton
Athabasca
Calgary
Medicine Hat
Saskatoon
Regina
Great Plains
Thunder Bay
Sault Saint Marie
Great Lakes
L. Superior
L. Michigan
L. Huron
L. Erie
L. Ontario
Toronto
OTTAWA
Montréal
Québec
St Lawrence
PRINCE EDWARD I.
NEW BRUNSWICK
NOVA SCOTIA
Halifax
MAINE
NEW HAMPSHIRE
VERMONT
MASSACHUSETTS
RHODE ISLAND
CONNECTICUT
Boston
NEW YORK
New York
Hudson
NEW JERSEY
DELAWARE
MARYLAND
PENNSYLVANIA
Philadelphia
Pittsburgh
Baltimore
Buffalo
Cleveland
Detroit
OHIO
Cincinnati
INDIANA
MICHIGAN
Chicago
Milwaukee
ILLINOIS
St Louis
WISCONSIN
MINNESOTA
St Paul
Minneapolis
IOWA
Mississippi
MISSOURI
Kansas City
KANSAS
NEBRASKA
Omaha
NORTH DAKOTA
SOUTH DAKOTA
Prairies
MONTANA
Missouri
WYOMING
COLORADO
Denver
UTAH
Salt Lake City
IDAHO
Boise
Snake
WASHINGTON
Spokane
Seattle
OREGON
Portland
Cascade Range
Great Basin
NEVADA
Reno
Las Vegas
Death Valley
Sierra Nevada
CALIFORNIA
Sacremento
San Francisco
Los Angeles
San Diego
Coast Ranges
ARIZONA
Colorado
UNITED STATES
Vancouver
Vancouver I.
Queen Charlotte Is
Alexander Archipelago
Juneau
Gulf of Alaska
ALASKA (to US)
Brooks Range
Alaska Range
Fairbanks
Mt McKinley (Denali) 6194m
Anchorage
Yukon
Kodiak I.
Alaska Peninsula
Aleutian Islands
Unimak
Unalaska
Umnak
Atka
Attu
Bering Strait
Bering Sea
St Lawrence I.
RUSSIAN FEDERATION
PACIFIC
POPULATION
over 5 000 000
over 1 000 000
over 500 000
over 100 000
over 50 000
under 50 000
LAND HEIGHT
4000m/13 124ft
3000m/9843ft
2000m/6562ft
1000m/3281ft
200m/656ft
Sea Level
Line of cross-section

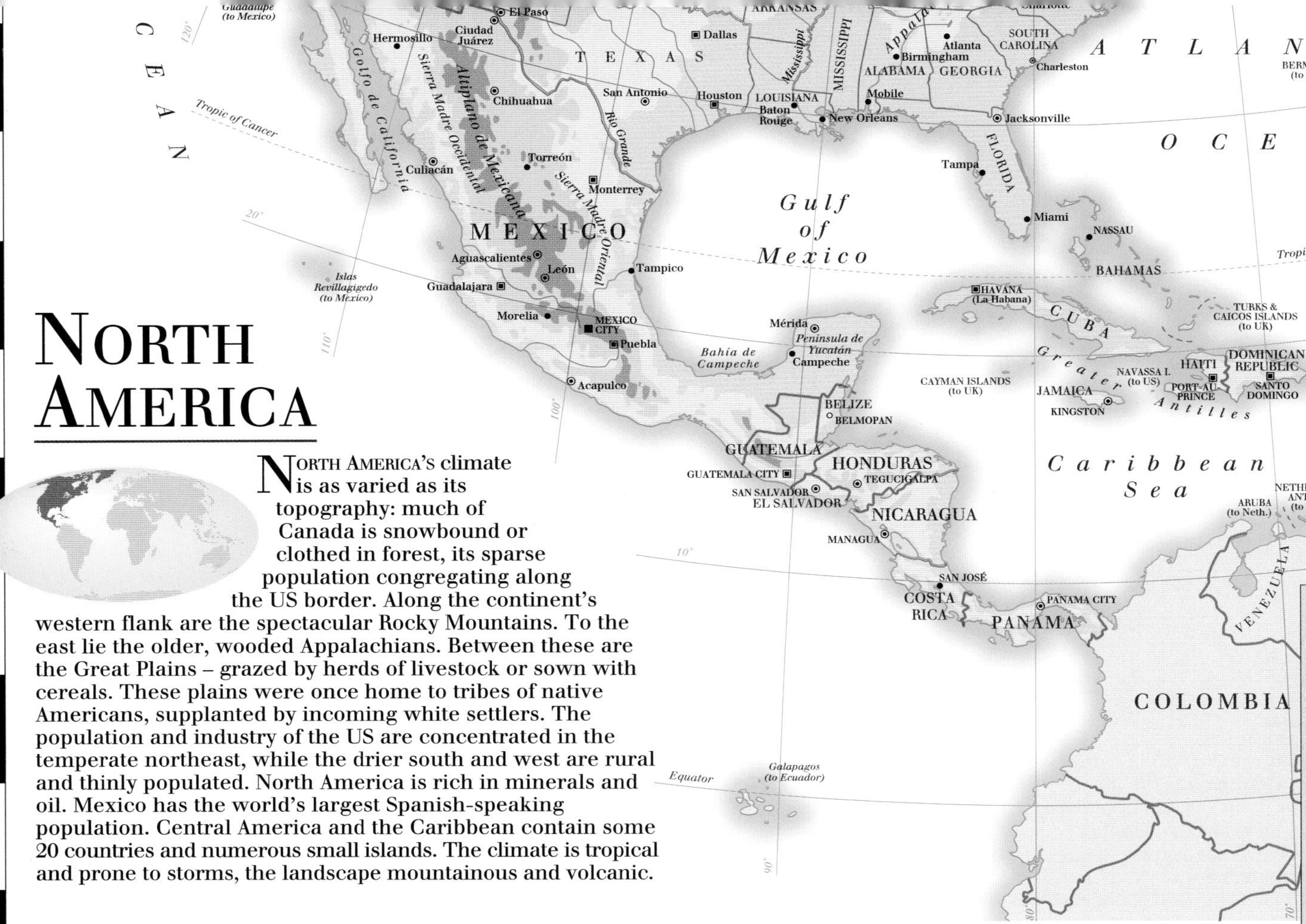
ATLANTIC OCEAN
BERMUDA (to UK)
Scale : 1:32 500 000
0 250 500 km
0 250 500 miles
Tropic of Cancer
Gulf of Mexico
Caribbean Sea
Greater Antilles
Lesser Antilles
MEXICO
TEXAS
LOUISIANA
MISSISSIPPI
ALABAMA
GEORGIA
SOUTH CAROLINA
FLORIDA
ARKANSAS
El Paso
Ciudad Juárez
Hermosillo
Chihuahua
Culiacán
Torreón
Monterrey
San Antonio
Houston
Dallas
Baton Rouge
New Orleans
Mobile
Birmingham
Atlanta
Charleston
Jacksonville
Tampa
Miami
Golfo de California
Sierra Madre Occidental
Altiplano de Mexicana
Sierra Madre Oriental
Rio Grande
Mississippi
Aguascalientes
León
Guadalajara
Morelia
MEXICO CITY
Puebla
Tampico
Acapulco
Islas Revillagigedo (to Mexico)
Bahía de Campeche
Mérida
Península de Yucatán
Campeche
BELIZE
BELMOPAN
GUATEMALA
GUATEMALA CITY
HONDURAS
TEGUCIGALPA
SAN SALVADOR
EL SALVADOR
NICARAGUA
MANAGUA
SAN JOSÉ
COSTA RICA
PANAMA CITY
PANAMA
COLOMBIA
VENEZUELA
Equator
Galapagos (to Ecuador)
NASSAU
BAHAMAS
HAVANA (La Habana)
CUBA
CAYMAN ISLANDS (to UK)
JAMAICA
KINGSTON
NAVASSA I. (to US)
HAITI
PORT-AU-PRINCE
DOMINICAN REPUBLIC
SANTO DOMINGO
TURKS & CAICOS ISLANDS (to UK)
PUERTO RICO (to US)
SAN JUAN
VIRGIN IS (to US)
BRITISH VIRGIN IS (to UK)
ANGUILLA (to UK)
ANTIGUA & BARBUDA
ST KITTS & NEVIS
MONTSERRAT (to UK)
GUADELOUPE (to France)
DOMINICA
MARTINIQUE (to France)
ST LUCIA
BARBADOS
ST VINCENT & THE GRENADINES
GRENADA
TRINIDAD & TOBAGO
ARUBA (to Neth.)
NETHERLANDS ANTILLES (to Neth.)

NORTH AMERICA

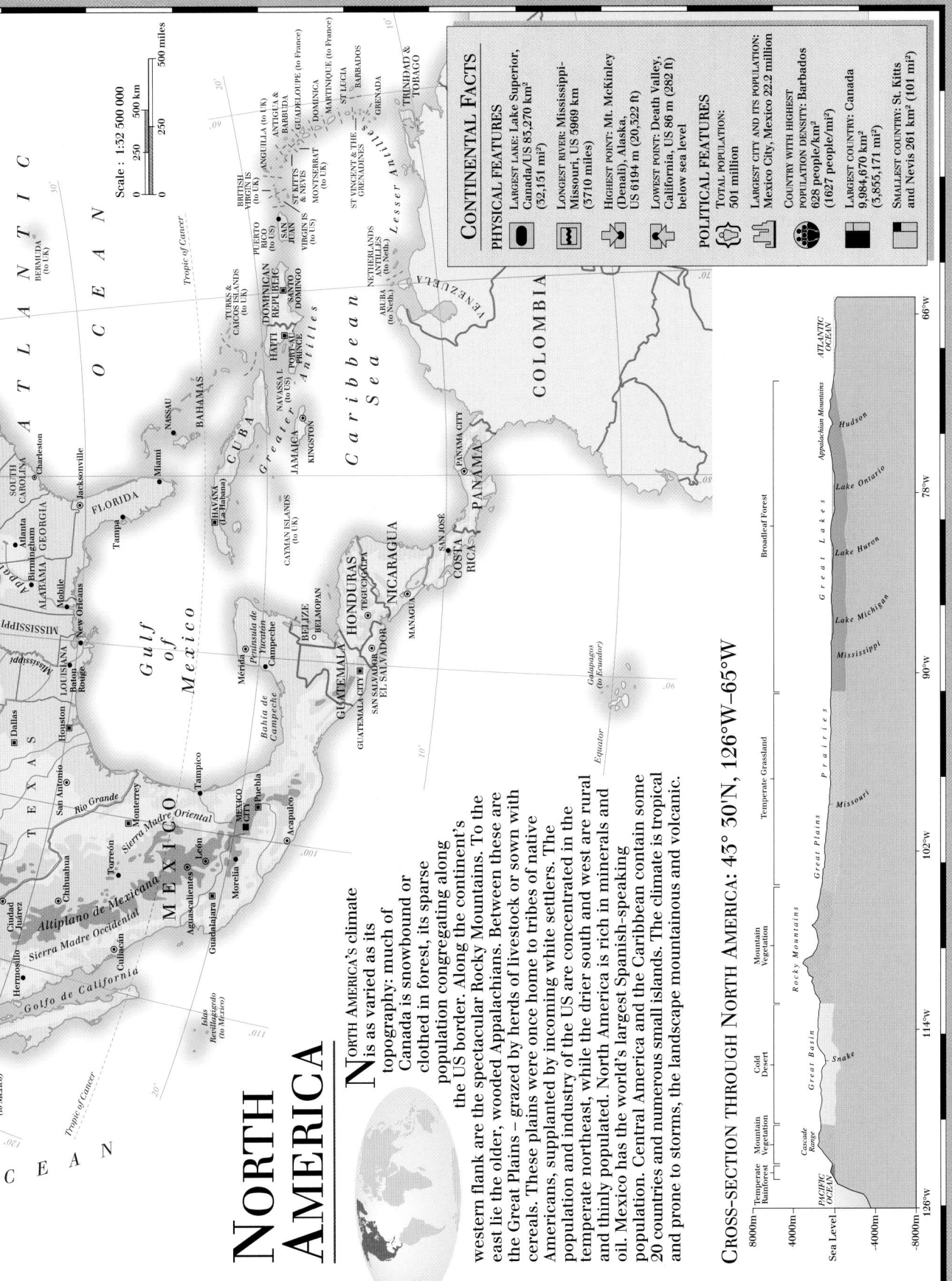

NORTH AMERICA'S climate is as varied as its topography: much of Canada is snowbound or clothed in forest, its sparse population congregating along the US border. Along the continent's western flank are the spectacular Rocky Mountains. To the east lie the older, wooded Appalachians. Between these are the Great Plains – grazed by herds of livestock or sown with cereals. These plains were once home to tribes of native Americans, supplanted by incoming white settlers. The population and industry of the US are concentrated in the temperate northeast, while the drier south and west are rural and thinly populated. North America is rich in minerals and oil. Mexico has the world's largest Spanish-speaking population. Central America and the Caribbean contain some 20 countries and numerous small islands. The climate is tropical and prone to storms, the landscape mountainous and volcanic.

CONTINENTAL FACTS

PHYSICAL FEATURES

- LARGEST LAKE: Lake Superior, Canada/US 83,270 km² (32,151 mi²)
- LONGEST RIVER: Mississippi-Missouri, US 5969 km (3710 miles)
- HIGHEST POINT: Mt. McKinley (Denali), Alaska, US 6194 m (20,322 ft)
- LOWEST POINT: Death Valley, California, US 86 m (282 ft) below sea level

POLITICAL FEATURES

- TOTAL POPULATION: 501 million
- LARGEST CITY AND ITS POPULATION: Mexico City, Mexico 22.2 million
- COUNTRY WITH HIGHEST POPULATION DENSITY: Barbados 628 people/km² (1627 people/mi²)
- LARGEST COUNTRY: Canada 9,984,670 km² (3,855,171 mi²)
- SMALLEST COUNTRY: St. Kitts and Nevis 261 km² (101 mi²)

CROSS-SECTION THROUGH NORTH AMERICA: 43° 30'N, 126°W–65°W

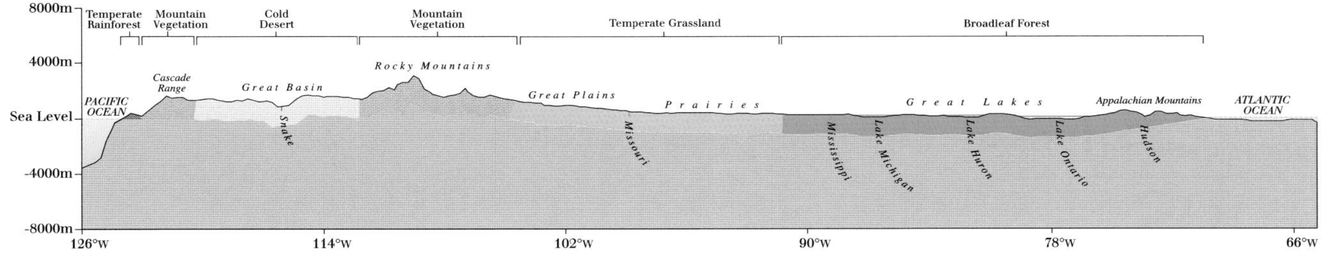
8000m
4000m
Sea Level
-4000m
-8000m
126°W
114°W
102°W
90°W
78°W
66°W
Temperate Rainforest
Mountain Vegetation
Cold Desert
Mountain Vegetation
Temperate Grassland
Broadleaf Forest
PACIFIC OCEAN
Cascade Range
Great Basin
Snake
Rocky Mountains
Great Plains
Missouri
Prairies
Mississippi
Lake Michigan
Great Lakes
Lake Huron
Lake Ontario
Appalachian Mountains
Hudson
ATLANTIC OCEAN

South America

The world's fourth-largest continent includes one of its most important resources – the Amazonian rainforest. It is a major source of oxygen and includes a third of all known living species, while the Amazon – the world's second-longest river – contains one-fifth of the world's fresh water. The Andes mountain chain reaches down South America's western flank, sheltering the prairies of the Gran Chaco, the Pampas, and the wastes of the far south. Most South Americans are *mestizo* – of mixed European and Amerindian descent – and live in the coastal regions. Spanish is the most widely spoken language, and over 90% of South Americans are Roman Catholic. South America has massive mineral resources, many exploited by US and European multinationals.

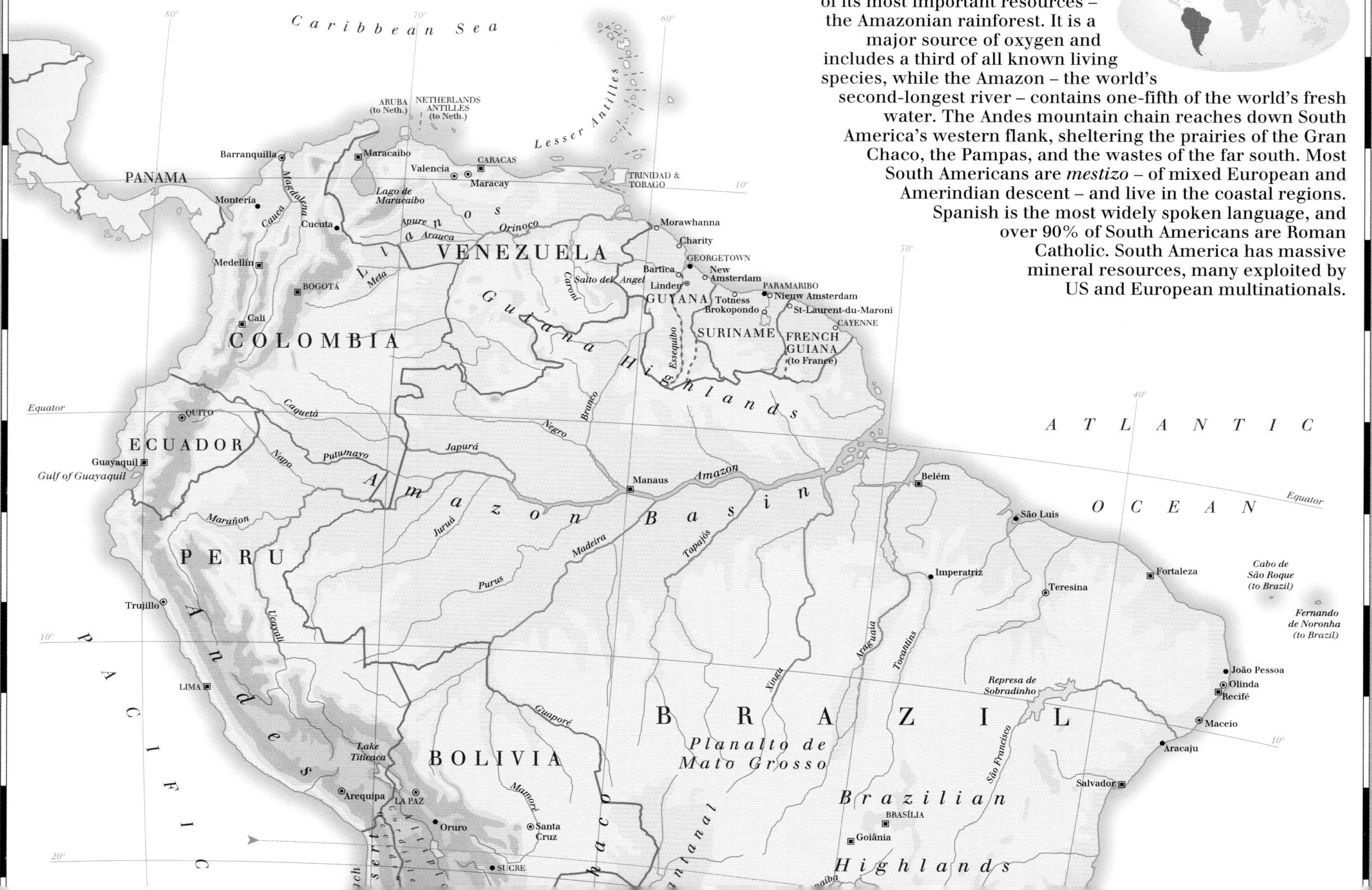

Caribbean Sea
Lesser Antilles
ARUBA (to Neth.)
NETHERLANDS ANTILLES (to Neth.)
TRINIDAD & TOBAGO
PANAMA
Barranquilla
Montería
Medellín
Cali
BOGOTÁ
Cucuta
Maracaibo
Lago de Maracaibo
Valencia
CARACAS
Maracay
Magdalena
Cauca
Meta
Apure
Arauca
Orinoco
Llanos
VENEZUELA
COLOMBIA
Caroní
Salto del Angel
Guiana Highlands
Morawhanna
Charity
GEORGETOWN
Bartica
New Amsterdam
Linden
GUYANA
Totness
Brokopondo
PARAMARIBO
Nieuw Amsterdam
St-Laurent-du-Maroni
CAYENNE
SURINAME
FRENCH GUIANA (to France)
Essequibo
Equator
QUITO
ECUADOR
Guayaquil
Gulf of Guayaquil
Caquetá
Putumayo
Napo
Japurá
Negro
Branco
Manaus
Amazon
Amazon Basin
Juruá
Purus
Madeira
Tapajós
Marañon
PERU
Ucayali
Trujillo
LIMA
Andes
PACIFIC
Lake Titicaca
Arequipa
LA PAZ
Oruro
SUCRE
Santa Cruz
Mamoré
Guaporé
BOLIVIA
BRAZIL
Planalto de Mato Grosso
Brazilian Highlands
BRASÍLIA
Goiânia
Xingu
Araguaia
Tocantins
São Francisco
Represa de Sobradinho
Belém
Imperatriz
São Luis
Teresina
Fortaleza
ATLANTIC OCEAN
Cabo de São Roque (to Brazil)
Fernando de Noronha (to Brazil)
João Pessoa
Olinda
Recifé
Maceio
Aracaju
Salvador
80°
70°
60°
50°
40°
10°
20°

Islas de los Desventurados (to Chile)
OCEAN
Peru - Ataca
PARAGUAY
Fernando de la Mora
ASUNCIÓN
Lambaré
Campinas
São Paulo
Sorocaba
Santos
Juiz de Fora
Nova Iguaçu
Rio de Janeiro
Tropic of Capricorn
Curitiba
Uruguay
Salado
L. Mar Chiquita
Córdoba
Paraná
Porto Alegre
Salto
Paysandú
Cerro Aconcagua 6959m
Valparaiso
SANTIAGO
Rosario
URUGUAY
Islas Juan Fernández (to Chile)
BUENOS AIRES
La Plata
Las Piedras
MONTEVIDEO
Río de la Plata
Concepción
Colorado
Negro
Bahía Blanca
Puerto Montt
Golfo San Matías
Península Valdés
Isla de Chiloé
Chubut
Deseado
Golfo San Jorge
Isla Wellington
Bahía Grande
FALKLAND ISLANDS (to UK)
Strait of Magellan
Tierra del Fuego
Beagle Channel
Cape Horn
ATLANTIC OCEAN
CHILE
ARGENTINA
Andes
Pampas
Patagonia

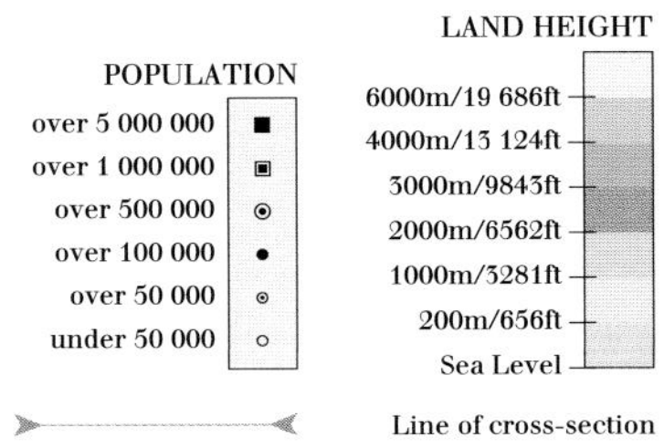
POPULATION
over 5 000 000
over 1 000 000
over 500 000
over 100 000
over 50 000
under 50 000
LAND HEIGHT
6000m/19 686ft
4000m/13 124ft
3000m/9843ft
2000m/6562ft
1000m/3281ft
200m/656ft
Sea Level
Line of cross-section

CONTINENTAL FACTS

PHYSICAL FEATURES

LARGEST LAKE: Lake Titicaca, Bolivia/Peru 8340 km² (3220 mi²)

LONGEST RIVER: Amazon, Brazil 6516 km (4049 miles)

HIGHEST POINT: Cerro Aconcagua, Argentina 6959 m (22,831 ft)

LOWEST POINT: Península Valdés, Argentina 40 m (131 ft) below sea level

POLITICAL FEATURES

TOTAL POPULATION: 362 million

LARGEST CITY AND ITS POPULATION: São Paulo, Brazil 19.9 million

COUNTRY WITH HIGHEST POPULATION DENSITY: Ecuador 47 people/km² (122 people/mi²)

LARGEST COUNTRY: Brazil 8,511,965 km² (3,286,470 mi²)

SMALLEST COUNTRY: Suriname 163,270 km² (63,039 mi²)

Scale : 1:26 500 000
0 250 500 km
0 250 500 miles

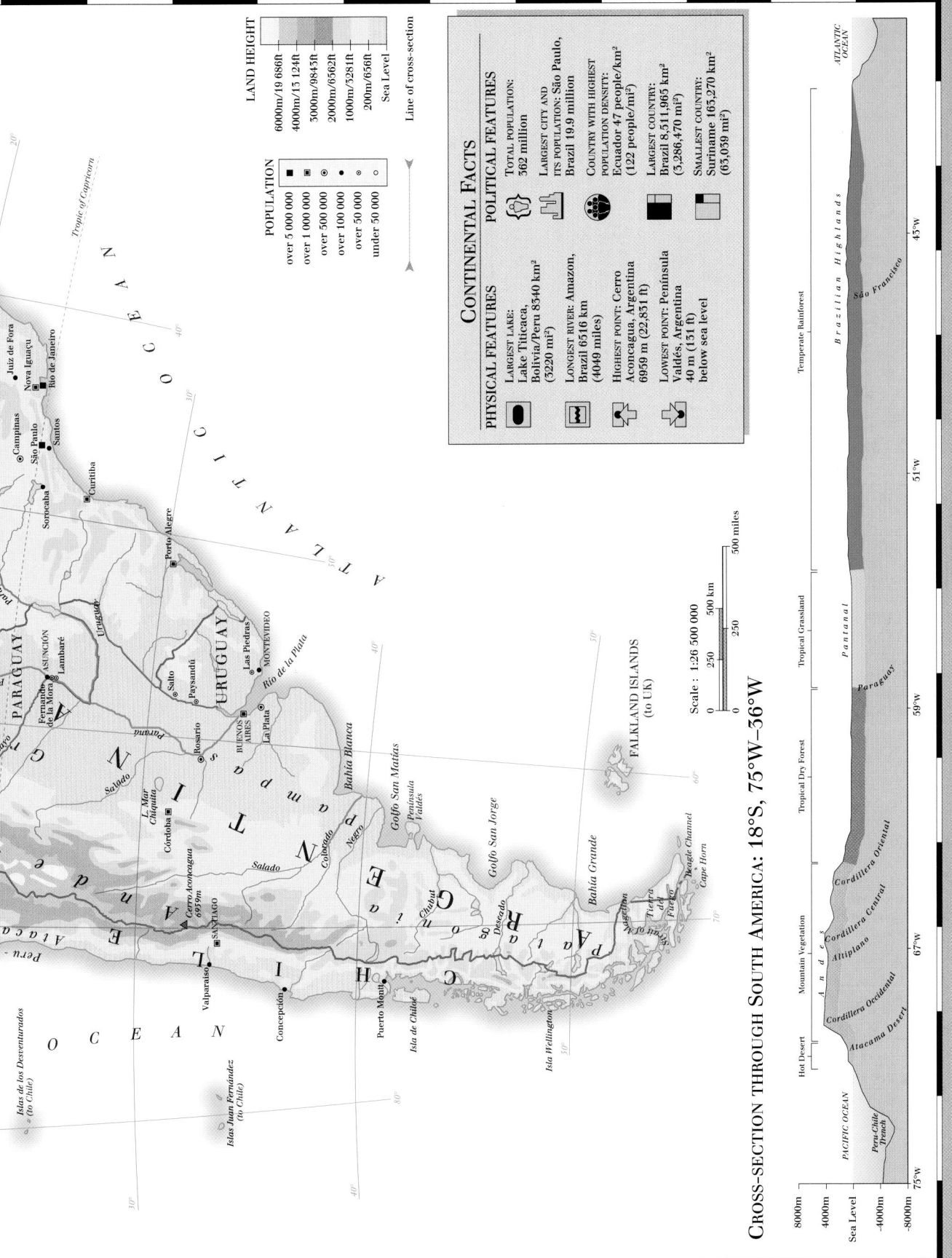

CROSS-SECTION THROUGH SOUTH AMERICA: 18°S, 75°W–36°W

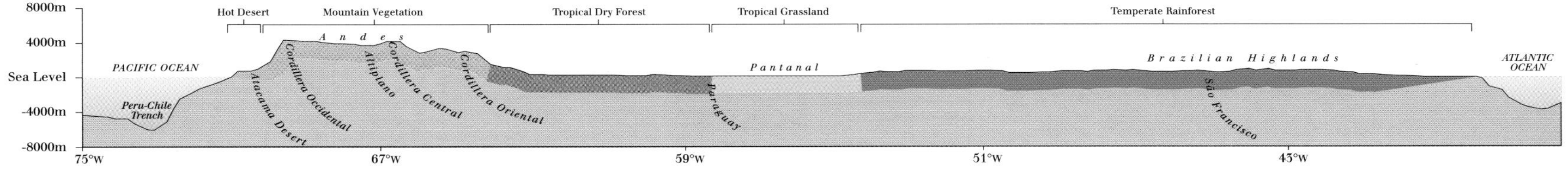
8000m
4000m
Sea Level
-4000m
-8000m
Hot Desert
Mountain Vegetation
Tropical Dry Forest
Tropical Grassland
Temperate Rainforest
PACIFIC OCEAN
Peru-Chile Trench
Atacama Desert
Andes
Cordillera Occidental
Altiplano
Cordillera Central
Cordillera Oriental
Pantanal
Paraguay
Brazilian Highlands
São Francisco
ATLANTIC OCEAN
75°W
67°W
59°W
51°W
43°W

EUROPE

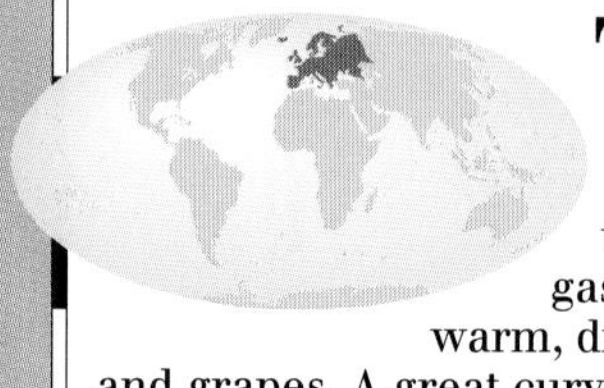

THE SMALLEST CONTINENT AFTER AUSTRALIA, Europe has a wide variety of climates and landscapes. The tundra of the far north gives way to a cool, wet, heavily forested region. The North European Plain is well-drained, fertile, and rich in oil, coal, and natural gas. The shores of the Mediterranean are generally warm, dry, and hilly, ideal for cultivating olives, citrus fruit, and grapes. A great curve of mountain ranges, including the Pyrenees, Alps, and Carpathians, divides north from south. To the east, the rolling plains of European Russia and Ukraine, clad in coniferous forests or cultivated for wheat, run up to the Ural Mountains. Europeans are mainly Christian – Catholic, Orthodox, or Protestant – and speak a variety of languages, most of which spring from Latin (Romance), Germanic, or Slavic roots.

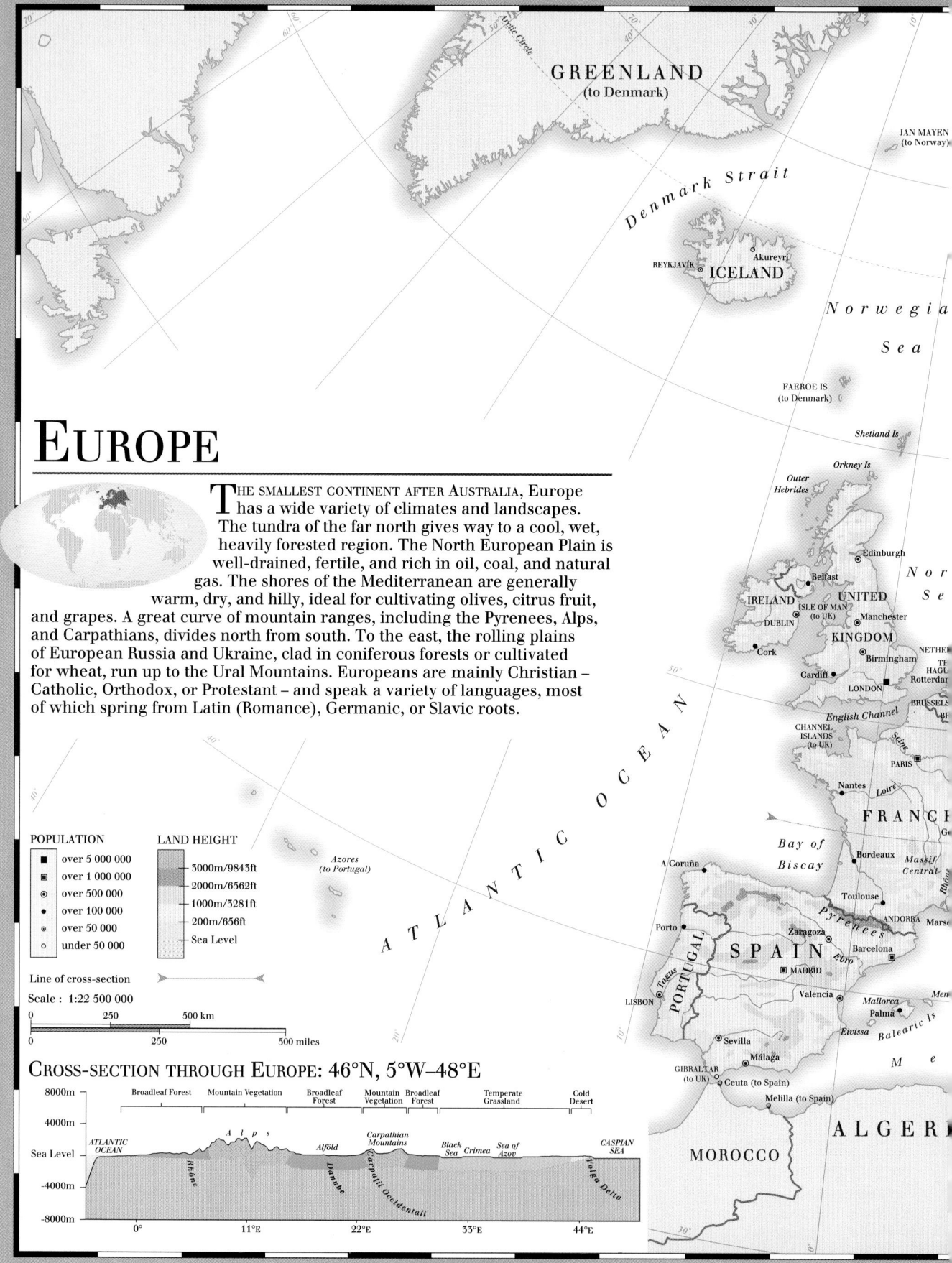

GREENLAND
(to Denmark)
Arctic Circle
JAN MAYEN
(to Norway)
Denmark Strait
Akureyri
REYKJAVÍK
ICELAND
Norwegian
Sea
FAEROE IS
(to Denmark)
Shetland Is
Orkney Is
Outer
Hebrides
Edinburgh
Belfast
IRELAND
ISLE OF MAN
(to UK)
DUBLIN
UNITED
KINGDOM
Manchester
Birmingham
Cork
Cardiff
LONDON
English Channel
CHANNEL
ISLANDS
(to UK)
Seine
PARIS
Nantes
Loire
FRANC
Bay of
Biscay
Bordeaux
Massif
Central
Toulouse
ANDORRA
Pyrenees
A Coruña
Porto
Zaragoza
SPAIN
Ebro
Barcelona
MADRID
Tagus
PORTUGAL
LISBON
Valencia
Mallorca
Palma
Eivissa
Balearic Is
Sevilla
Málaga
GIBRALTAR
(to UK)
Ceuta (to Spain)
Melilla (to Spain)
MOROCCO
ALGER
ATLANTIC OCEAN
Azores
(to Portugal)
Rotterdam
BRUSSELS

POPULATION

- ■ over 5 000 000
- ▣ over 1 000 000
- ◉ over 500 000
- ● over 100 000
- ⊙ over 50 000
- ○ under 50 000

LAND HEIGHT

- 3000m/9843ft
- 2000m/6562ft
- 1000m/3281ft
- 200m/656ft
- Sea Level

Line of cross-section

Scale : 1:22 500 000

0 250 500 km

0 250 500 miles

CROSS-SECTION THROUGH EUROPE: 46°N, 5°W–48°E

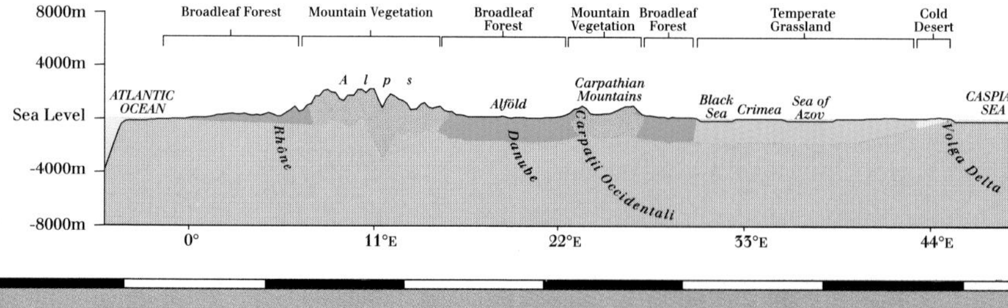
8000m
4000m
Sea Level
-4000m
-8000m
Broadleaf Forest
Mountain Vegetation
Broadleaf Forest
Mountain Vegetation
Broadleaf Forest
Temperate Grassland
Cold Desert
ATLANTIC OCEAN
Alps
Rhône
Alföld
Danube
Carpathian Mountains
Carpatii Occidentali
Black Sea
Crimea
Sea of Azov
CASPIAN SEA
Volga Delta
0°
11°E
22°E
33°E
44°E

CONTINENTAL FACTS

PHYSICAL FEATURES

LARGEST LAKE: Ladoga, European Russia 18,390 km² (7100 mi²)

LONGEST RIVER: Volga, European Russia 3688 km (2290 miles)

HIGHEST POINT: El' brus, Caucasus, European Russia 5642 m (18,510 ft)

LOWEST POINT: Volga Delta, Caspian Sea, European Russia 28 m (92 ft) below sea level

POLITICAL FEATURES

TOTAL POPULATION: 774 million

COUNTRY WITH HIGHEST POPULATION DENSITY: Monaco 16,477 people/km² (42,840 people/mi²)

LARGEST CITY AND ITS POPULATION: Moscow, European Russia 15.5 million

LARGEST COUNTRY: European Russia 3,955,818 km² (1,527,341 mi²)

SMALLEST COUNTRY: Vatican City, Italy 0.44 km² (0.17 mi²)

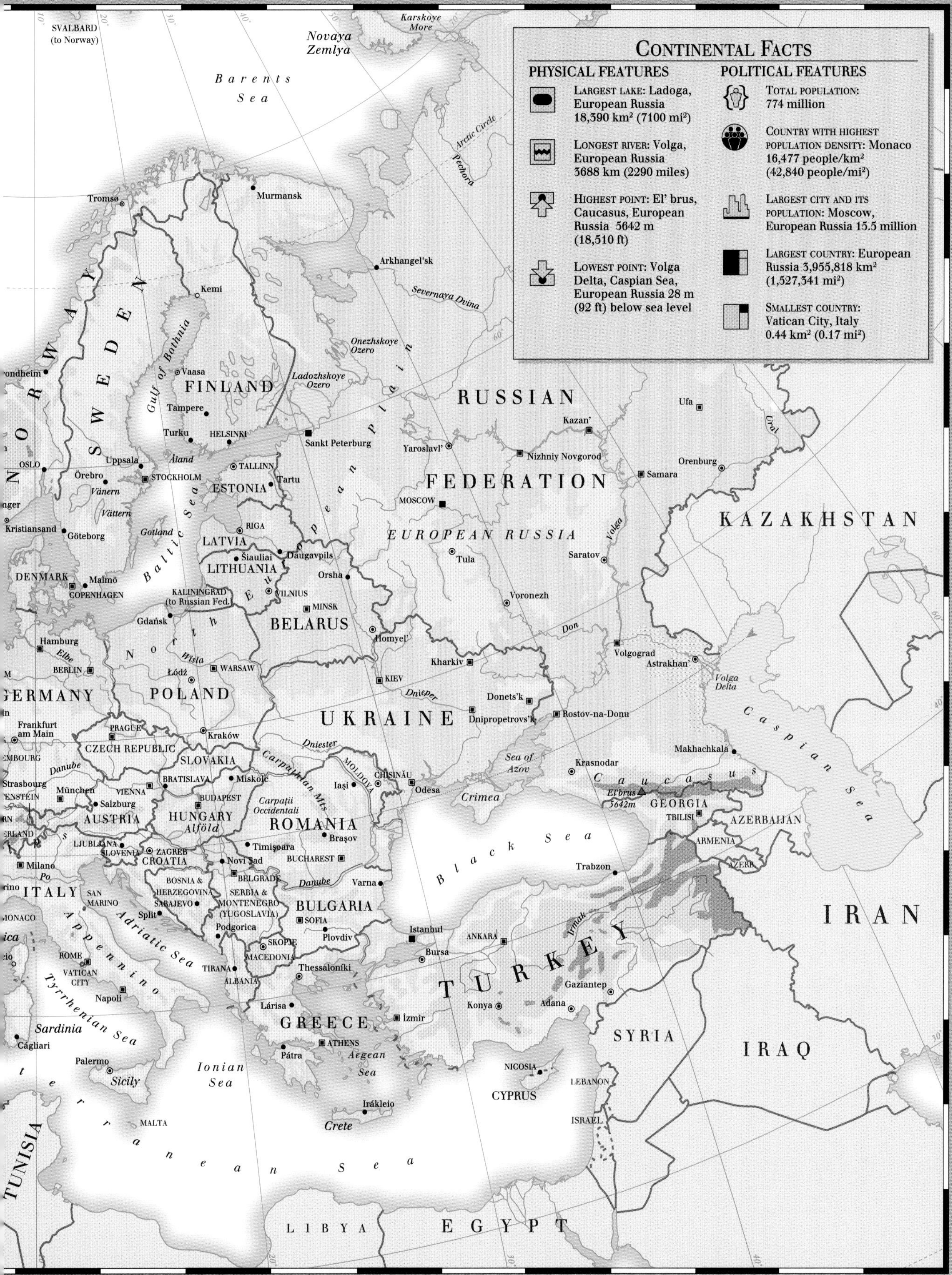
SVALBARD (to Norway)
Novaya Zemlya
Karskoye More
Barents Sea
Arctic Circle
Pechora
Murmansk
Tromsø
Arkhangel'sk
Severnaya Dvina
Kemi
Gulf of Bothnia
Vaasa
FINLAND
Tampere
Turku
HELSINKI
Åland
Onezhskoye Ozero
Ladozhskoye Ozero
RUSSIAN FEDERATION
Sankt Peterburg
Yaroslavl'
Kazan'
Ufa
Ural
Nizhniy Novgorod
Orenburg
Samara
MOSCOW
EUROPEAN RUSSIA
Volga
Tula
Saratov
KAZAKHSTAN
NORWAY
SWEDEN
Trondheim
OSLO
Uppsala
Örebro
STOCKHOLM
Vänern
Vättern
Kristiansand
Göteborg
Gotland
Baltic Sea
TALLINN
ESTONIA
Tartu
RIGA
LATVIA
Šiauliai
Daugavpils
LITHUANIA
VILNIUS
Orsha
DENMARK
Malmö
COPENHAGEN
KALININGRAD (to Russian Fed.)
MINSK
BELARUS
Voronezh
Gdańsk
North European Plain
Homyel'
Don
Hamburg
Elbe
BERLIN
Wisla
WARSAW
Łódź
GERMANY
POLAND
Kharkiv
Volgograd
Astrakhan'
Volga Delta
KIEV
Dnieper
Donets'k
UKRAINE
Dnipropetrovs'k
Rostov-na-Donu
Caspian Sea
Frankfurt am Main
PRAGUE
Kraków
CZECH REPUBLIC
Dniester
Danube
SLOVAKIA
Carpathian Mts
MOLDOVA
CHIŞINĂU
Sea of Azov
Krasnodar
Makhachkala
Caucasus
Strasbourg
München
VIENNA
BRATISLAVA
Miskolc
Iaşi
Odesa
Crimea
El'brus 5642m
GEORGIA
TBILISI
AZERBAIJAN
Salzburg
BUDAPEST
Carpaţii Occidentali
AUSTRIA
HUNGARY
Alföld
ROMANIA
Braşov
ARMENIA
LJUBLJANA
SLOVENIA
ZAGREB
CROATIA
Timişoara
Novi Sad
BUCHAREST
Black Sea
Trabzon
AZERB.
Milano
Po
BELGRADE
ITALY
SAN MARINO
BOSNIA & HERZEGOVINA
SARAJEVO
SERBIA & MONTENEGRO (YUGOSLAVIA)
Danube
Varna
BULGARIA
SOFIA
IRAN
MONACO
Appennino
Adriatic Sea
Split
Podgorica
SKOPJE
MACEDONIA
Plovdiv
Istanbul
ANKARA
Irmak
TURKEY
Bursa
ROME
VATICAN CITY
TIRANA
ALBANIA
Thessaloníki
Napoli
Tyrrhenian Sea
Gaziantep
Lárisa
Konya
Adana
Sardinia
GREECE
İzmir
Cágliari
ATHENS
Pátra
Aegean Sea
SYRIA
IRAQ
Palermo
Sicily
Ionian Sea
NICOSIA
CYPRUS
LEBANON
Mediterranean Sea
Iráklеio
Crete
MALTA
ISRAEL
TUNISIA
LIBYA
EGYPT

ATLANTIC OCEAN
INDIAN OCEAN
ATLANTI
Mediterranean Sea
Black Sea
Red Sea
Gulf of Aden
Gulf of Guinea
Tropic of Cancer
Equator
PORTUGAL
SPAIN
FRANCE
ITALY
GREECE
TURKEY
SYRIA
LEBANON
ISRAEL
JORDAN
CYPRUS
MALTA
SAUDI ARABIA
YEMEN
MOROCCO
ALGERIA
TUNISIA
LIBYA
EGYPT
SUDAN
ERITREA
DJIBOUTI
ETHIOPIA
SOMALIA
KENYA
UGANDA
RWANDA
BURUNDI
TANZANIA
WESTERN SAHARA (Occupied by Morocco)
MAURITANIA
MALI
NIGER
CHAD
SENEGAL
GAMBIA
GUINEA-BISSAU
GUINEA
SIERRA LEONE
LIBERIA
IVORY COAST (CÔTE D'IVOIRE)
BURKINA
GHANA
TOGO
BENIN
NIGERIA
CAMEROON
CENTRAL AFRICAN REPUBLIC
EQUATORIAL GUINEA
SAO TOME & PRINCIPE
GABON
CONGO
DEM. REP. CONGO
ANGOLA
CABINDA (to Angola)
SEYCHELLES
VICTORIA
ASCENSION (to St Helena)
Madeira (to Portugal)
Islas Canarias (to Spain)
GIBRALTAR (to UK)
Ceuta (to Spain)
Melilla (to Spain)
Atlas Mts
Ahaggar
Sahara
Sahel
Nubian Desert
Ethiopian Highlands
Horn of Africa
Adamawa Highlands
Great Rift Valley
Kilimanjaro 5895m
Nile
Blue Nile
White Nile
Niger
Congo
Sudd
L. Chad
L. Victoria
L. Tanganyika
Lake Volta
Lac Assal
Buheiret Nâsir
Suez Canal
RABAT
Tanger
Fez
Oran
Casablanca
Marrakech
ALGIERS
Constantine
TUNIS
Sfax
TRIPOLI
Banghāzī
Sabhā
Alexandria
CAIRO
Aswân
Port Sudan
KHARTOUM
El Obeid
ASMARA
DJIBOUTI
Hargeysa
Dirē Dawa
ADDIS ABABA
MOGADISHU
Kismaayo
Laâyoune
NOUAKCHOTT
Nouâdhibou
DAKAR
BANJUL
BISSAU
CONAKRY
FREETOWN
MONROVIA
BAMAKO
YAMOUSSOUKRO
Abidjan
OUAGADOUGOU
ACCRA
LOMÉ
PORTO-NOVO
Lagos
Ibadan
NIAMEY
Agadez
Kano
ABUJA
Port Harcourt
N'DJAMENA
Abéché
BANGUI
YAOUNDÉ
Douala
MALABO
Bata
SÃO TOMÉ
Príncipe
LIBREVILLE
Pointe-Noire
BRAZZAVILLE
KINSHASA
LUANDA
Kisangani
Kananga
Mbuji-Mayi
Juba
KAMPALA
KIGALI
BUJUMBURA
Kisumu
Mbale
NAIROBI
Mwanza
DODOMA
Mombasa
Zanzibar
Dar es Salaam

ST HELENA (to UK)
OCEAN
Namibe
Walvis Bay
Tropic of Capricorn
NAMIBIA
WINDHOEK
Kalahari Desert
BOTSWANA
GABORONE
Francistown
LUSAKA
HARARE
ZIMBABWE
Bulawayo
Zambezi
Limpopo
PRETORIA
Johannesburg
MAPUTO
MBABANE
SWAZILAND
BLOEMFONTEIN
MASERU
LESOTHO
Orange
SOUTH AFRICA
Durban
Drakensberg
East London
Port Elizabeth
CAPE TOWN
Cape of Good Hope
Blantyre
Quelimane
Beira
MOZAMBIQUE
Mozambique Channel
Mahajanga
MADAGASCAR
ANTANANARIVO
Fianarantsoa
Farafangana
MAURITIUS
PORT LOUIS
RÉUNION (to France)
Scale : 1:36 000 000
0 500 1000 km
0 500 1000 miles
POPULATION
over 5 000 000
over 1 000 000
over 500 000
over 100 000
over 50 000
under 50 000
LAND HEIGHT
4000m/13 124ft
3000m/9843ft
2000m/6562ft
1000m/3281ft
200m/656ft
Sea Level
Line of cross-section

AFRICA

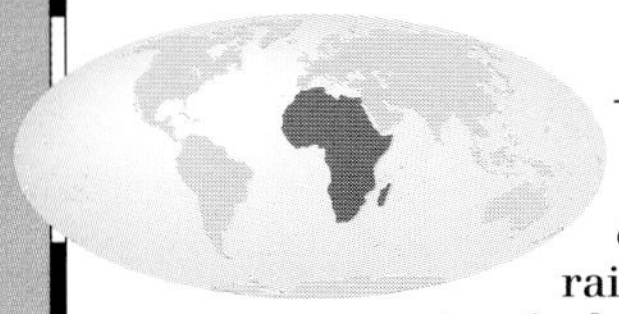

AFRICA IS THE SECOND-LARGEST CONTINENT after Asia. It is dominated by the Sahara in the north and the Great Rift Valley in the east. The Mediterranean climate of the extreme north and south enables cultivation of grapes and other fruit. A belt of tropical rainforest lies along the Equator, while Africa's great tropical grasslands provide grazing for herds of wild animals and domestic livestock. A narrow strip of Egypt is watered by the world's longest river, the Nile, which has sustained communities from prehistoric times. The center and south of the continent are rich in minerals. Just over one-eighth of the world's population lives in Africa – a wide variety of peoples with their own distinctive languages and cultures. Though Islam and Christianity are widespread, many Africans adhere to their own local customs and religious beliefs.

CONTINENTAL FACTS

PHYSICAL FEATURES

- LARGEST LAKE: Lake Victoria, Kenya/Tanzania/Uganda 68,880 km² (26,560 mi²)
- LONGEST RIVER: Nile, Uganda/Sudan/Egypt 6695 km (4160 miles)
- HIGHEST POINT: Kilimanjaro, Tanzania 5895 m (19,340 ft)
- LOWEST POINT: Lac' Assal, Djibouti 156 m (512 ft) below sea level

POLITICAL FEATURES

- TOTAL POPULATION: 849 million
- LARGEST CITY AND ITS POPULATION: Cairo, Egypt 15.1 million
- COUNTRY WITH HIGHEST POPULATION DENSITY: Mauritius 645 people/km² (1671 people/mi²)
- LARGEST COUNTRY: Sudan 2,505,810 km² (967,493 mi²)
- SMALLEST COUNTRY: Seychelles 455 km² (176 mi²)

CROSS-SECTION THROUGH AFRICA 7°N, 15°W–55°E

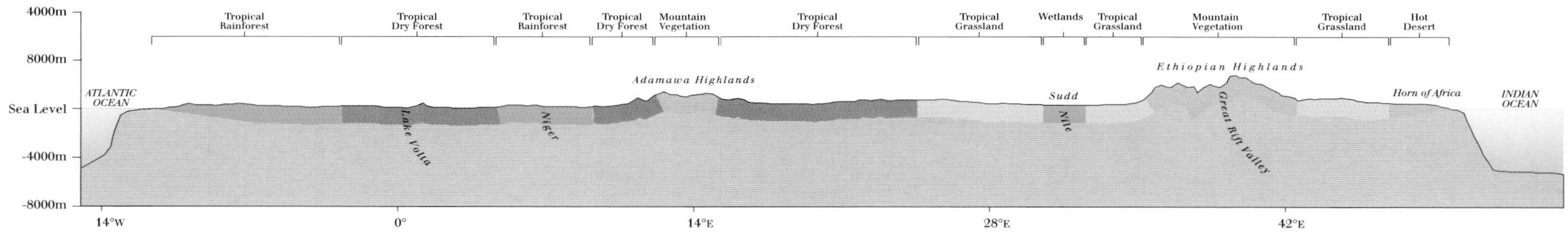
4000m
8000m
Sea Level
-4000m
-8000m
Tropical Rainforest
Tropical Dry Forest
Tropical Rainforest
Tropical Dry Forest
Mountain Vegetation
Tropical Dry Forest
Tropical Grassland
Wetlands
Tropical Grassland
Mountain Vegetation
Tropical Grassland
Hot Desert
ATLANTIC OCEAN
Lake Volta
Niger
Adamawa Highlands
Sudd
Nile
Ethiopian Highlands
Great Rift Valley
Horn of Africa
INDIAN OCEAN
14°W
0°
14°E
28°E
42°E

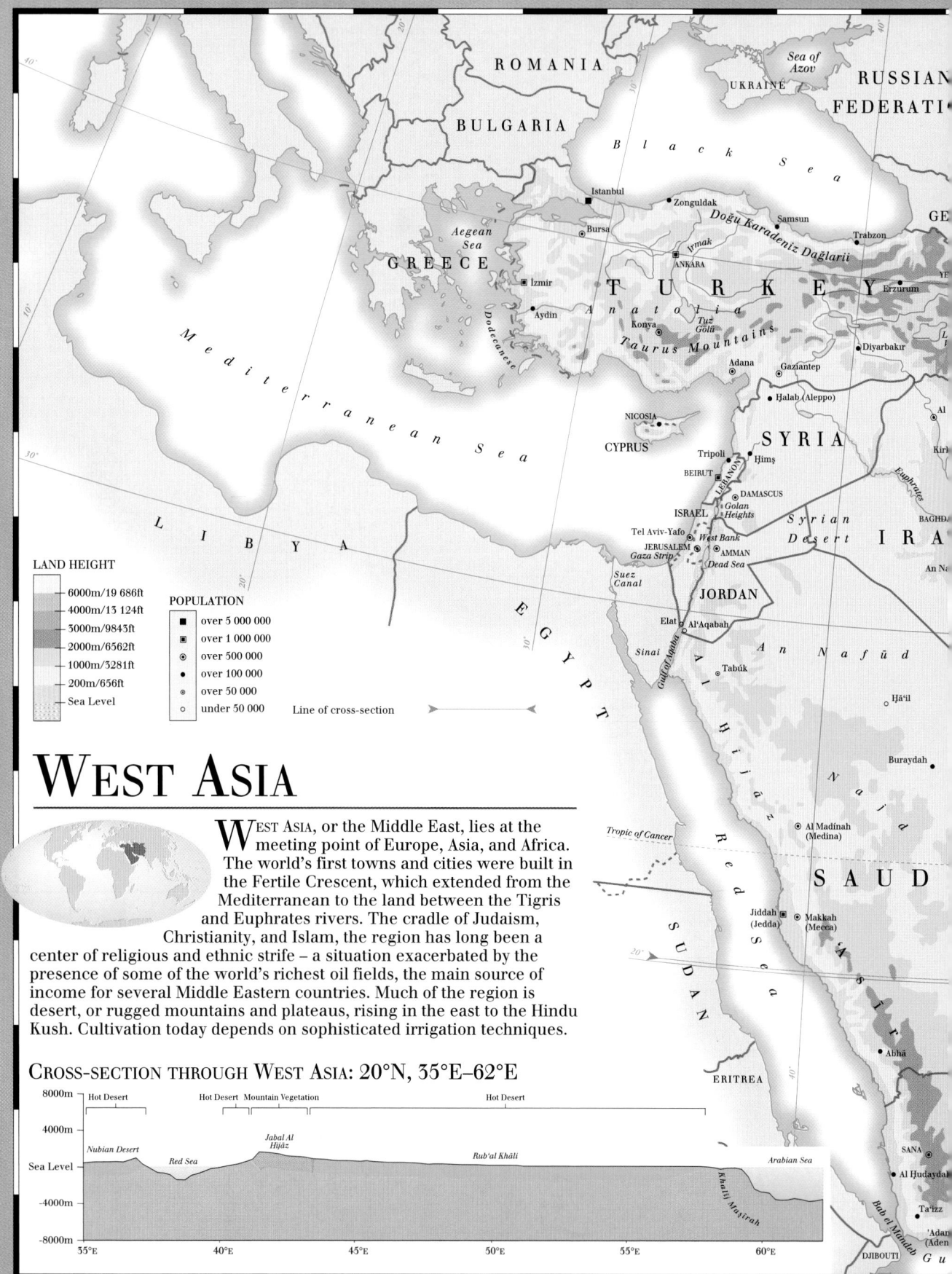

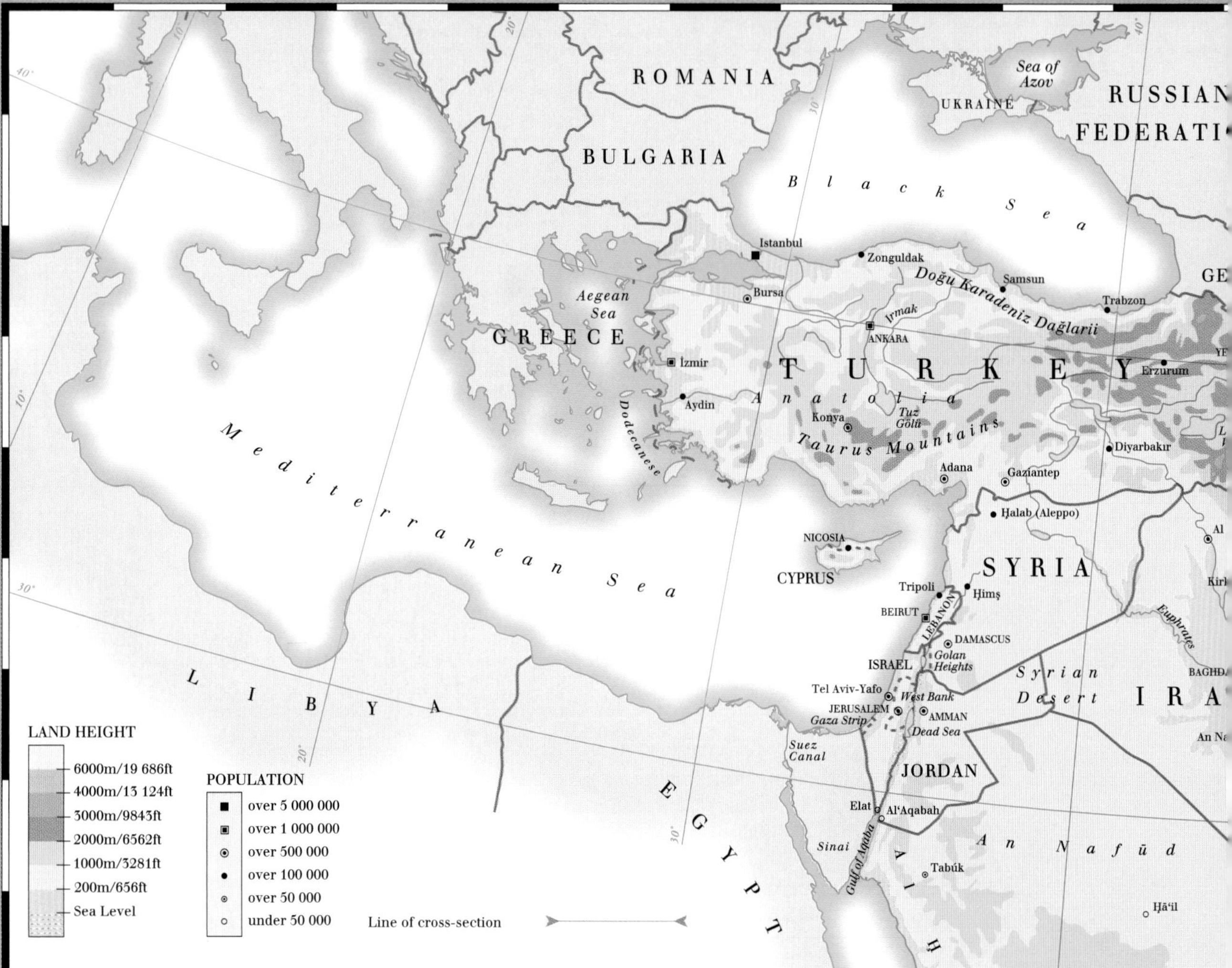
ROMANIA
Sea of Azov
UKRAINE
RUSSIAN FEDERATI
BULGARIA
Black Sea
Istanbul
Zonguldak
Doğu Karadeniz Dağlarii
Samsun
GE
Trabzon
Aegean Sea
Bursa
Irmak
ANKARA
GREECE
İzmir
TURKEY
Erzurum
Aydin
Anatolia
Dodecanese
Konya
Tuz Gölü
Taurus Mountains
Diyarbakır
Adana
Gaziantep
Mediterranean Sea
Ḥalab (Aleppo)
NICOSIA
CYPRUS
SYRIA
Tripoli
Ḥimş
BEIRUT
LEBANON
Euphrates
DAMASCUS
Golan Heights
ISRAEL
Syrian Desert
Tel Aviv-Yafo
West Bank
JERUSALEM
AMMAN
Gaza Strip
Dead Sea
LIBYA
Suez Canal
JORDAN
EGYPT
Elat
Al'Aqabah
Sinai
Gulf of Aqaba
An Nafūd
Tabūk
Ḥā'il
Al Ḥijāz
Buraydah
Najd
Tropic of Cancer
Al Madīnah (Medina)
Red Sea
SAUD
Jiddah (Jedda)
Makkah (Mecca)
SUDAN
'Asīr
Abhā
ERITREA
SANA
Al Ḥudaydah
Bab el Mandeb
Ta'izz
'Adan (Aden)
DJIBOUTI
LAND HEIGHT
6000m/19 686ft
4000m/13 124ft
3000m/9843ft
2000m/6562ft
1000m/3281ft
200m/656ft
Sea Level
POPULATION
over 5 000 000
over 1 000 000
over 500 000
over 100 000
over 50 000
under 50 000
Line of cross-section

WEST ASIA

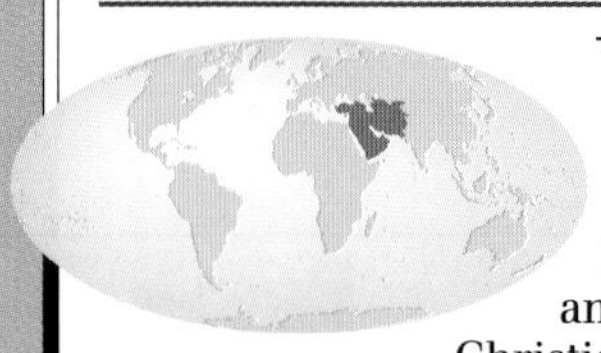

WEST ASIA, or the Middle East, lies at the meeting point of Europe, Asia, and Africa. The world's first towns and cities were built in the Fertile Crescent, which extended from the Mediterranean to the land between the Tigris and Euphrates rivers. The cradle of Judaism, Christianity, and Islam, the region has long been a center of religious and ethnic strife – a situation exacerbated by the presence of some of the world's richest oil fields, the main source of income for several Middle Eastern countries. Much of the region is desert, or rugged mountains and plateaus, rising in the east to the Hindu Kush. Cultivation today depends on sophisticated irrigation techniques.

CROSS-SECTION THROUGH WEST ASIA: 20°N, 35°E–62°E

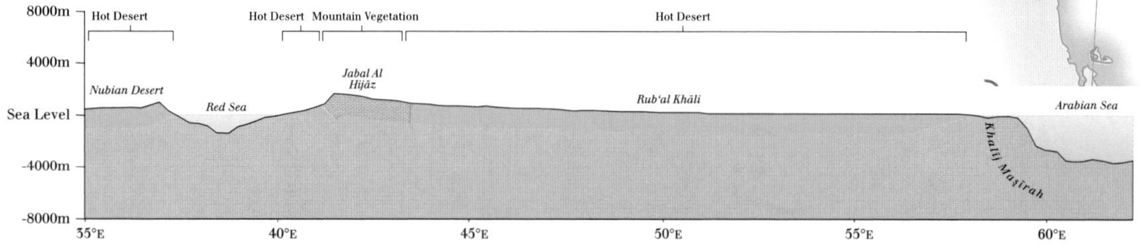
8000m
4000m
Sea Level
-4000m
-8000m
Hot Desert
Hot Desert
Mountain Vegetation
Hot Desert
Nubian Desert
Red Sea
Jabal Al Hijāz
Rub'al Khālī
Arabian Sea
Khalīj Maṣīrah
35°E
40°E
45°E
50°E
55°E
60°E

KAZAKHSTAN
Aral Sea
BISHKEK
Karakol
Ozero Issyk-Kul'
Kirghiz Range
Naryn
KYRGYZSTAN
Tien Shan
Caspian Sea
UZBEKISTAN
Qizilqum
TASHKENT
Namangan
Osh
Aydarko'l Ko'li
Daşoguz
Urganch
Khŭjand
CHINA
Garagum
Samarqand
AZERBAIJAN
BAKU
Türkmenbaçy
TAJIKISTAN
Pamirs
DUSHANBE
Qarshi
Balkanabat
Türkmenabat
TURKMENISTAN
Amyderya
Khorugh
Kŭlob
Länkäran
Köpetdag Gershi
AŞGABAT
Kurgan-Tyube
Karakoram Range
K2 8611m
Indus
Mary
Mazār-e-Sharīf
Rasht
Baghlān
Gorgān
Reshteh-ye Kuhhā-ye Alborz
Hindu Kush
Mashhad
TEHRĀN
Jalālābād
Peshāwar
ISLĀMĀBĀD
KĀBUL
Rāwalpindi
Hamadān
Qom
Herāt
Dasht-e-Kavīr
AFGHANISTAN
Gujrānwāla
Bākhtarān
Lahore
IRAN
Chenāb
Faisalābād
Eşfahān
Iranian Plateau
Kandahār
Hāmūn-e Şāberī
Helmand
Multān
Zagros Mountains
Ahvāz
Quetta
Başrah
Ābādān
Kermān
Zāhedān
Shīrāz
Thar Desert
Indus
KUWAIT
KUWAIT CITY
Sukkur
PAKISTAN
INDIA
The Gulf
Bandar-e 'Abbās
Strait of Hormuz
Hyderābād
BAHRAIN
MANAMA
Karāchi
Tropic of Cancer
DOHA
Sharjah
QATAR
Dubai
Al Hufūf
Gulf of Oman
Şuḩār
ABU DHABI
Arabian Sea
Ḩaraḑ
MUSCAT
UNITED ARAB EMIRATES
Ar Rustāq
ARABIA
Nizwa
Şūr
Scale : 1:17 000 000
0 200 400 km
0 200 400 miles
OMAN
Khalīj Maşīrah
Rub' al Khālī
INDIAN OCEAN
Şalālah
YEMEN
Hadhramaut
Al Mukallā
Socotra (to Yemen)
Aden

CONTINENTAL FACTS

PHYSICAL FEATURES

LARGEST LAKE: Caspian Sea 371,000 km² (143,243 mi²)

LONGEST RIVER: Euphrates, Turkey/Syria/Iraq 2815 km (1750 miles)

HIGHEST POINT: K2, Kashmir, India/Pakistan 8611m (28,253 ft)

LOWEST POINT: Dead Sea, Israel/Jordan 392 m (1286 ft) below sea level

POLITICAL FEATURES

TOTAL POPULATION: 484 million

LARGEST CITY AND ITS POPULATION: Karachi, Pakistan 13.6 million

COUNTRY WITH HIGHEST POPULATION DENSITY: Bahrain 1025 people/km² (2652 people/mi²)

LARGEST COUNTRY: Saudi Arabia 1,960,582 km² (756,981 mi²)

SMALLEST COUNTRY: Bahrain 620 km² (239 mi²)

UKRAINE
EUROPEAN RUSSIA
Karskoye More
Ostrov Komsomolets
Ostrov Oktyabr'skoy Revolyutsii
Ostrov Bol'shevik
Severnaya Zemlya
Poluostrov Taymyr
Ozero Taymyr
Severo-Sibirskaya Nizmennost'
Poluostrov Yamal
Gydanskiy Poluostrov
Arctic Circle
Salekhard
Nadym
Noril'sk
Ob'
Ural Mountains
Serov
Ural'sk
Ural
Yekaterinburg
Chelyabinsk
Tyumen'
Khanty-Mansiysk
Nizhnevartovsk
Zapadno-Sibirskaya Ravnina
RUSSIA
ASIATIC RUSSIA
Srednesibirskoye Ploskogor'ye
Yenisey
Nizhnyaya Tunguska
Podkamennaya Tunguska
Atyrau
Aktobe
Aktau
Caspian Sea
Kostanay
Irtysh
Ishim
Omsk
Ustyurt Plateau
KAZAKHSTAN
Aral Sea
Aral'sk
Syr Darya
ASTANA
Zhezkazgan
Karaganda
Novosibirsk
Tomsk
Barnaul
Krasnoyarsk
Bratsk
Bodaybo
TURKMENISTAN
UZBEKISTAN
Kyzylorda
Ozero Balkhash
Semipalatinsk
Rubtsovsk
Abakan
Lena
Ozero Baykal
Shymkent
Taraz
Ili
Ozero Zaysan
Uvs Nuur
Kyzyl
Irkutsk
Ulan-Ude
Chita
Yablonovyy
Taldykorgan
Almaty
Ölgiy
Hovd
Hyargas Nuur
Hövsgöl Nuur
AFGHANISTAN
TAJIKISTAN
KYRGYZSTAN
Yining
Altai Mountains
Erdenet
Darhan
ULAN BATOR
Choybalsan
Kerulen
Kashi
Tien Shan
Ürümqi
Altay
MONGOLIA
Tarim He
Turpan Hami
Hami
Bayanhongor
PAKISTAN
Hotan
Taklimakan Shamo
Saynshand
Gobi
Aksai Chin
Kunlun Shan
Altun Shan
Yumen
Qilian Shan
Qaidam Pendi
Baotou
Datong
BEIJING (PEKING)
Huang He
Qingzang Gaoyuan (Plateau of Tibet)
Golmud
Tianjin
INDIA
Himalayas
Qinghai Hu
Xining
Taiyuan
Shijiazhuang
TIBET
CHINA
Lanzhou
NEPAL
Brahmaputra
Mekong
Salween
Xi'an
Huang He (Yellow R.)
Zhengzhou
Xixabangma Feng 8012m
Lhasa
Tropic of Cancer
BHUTAN
Chengdu
Chang Jiang (Yangtze)
Wuhan
Chongqing
Dongting Hu
Poyang Hu
Nanchang
Changsha
Guiyang
Kunming
Xi Jiang
BURMA (MYANMAR)
Shantou
Nanning
Guangzhou
Hong Kong (Xianggang)
Macao (Aomen)
LAOS
VIETNAM
Gulf of Tongking
Haikou
Hainan Dao
South China Sea

Continental Facts

PHYSICAL FEATURES

Largest lake: Aral Sea, Kazakhstan/Uzbekistan 66,500 km² (25,700 mi²)

Longest river: Chang Jiang (Yangtze), China 6299 km (3915 miles)

Highest point: Xixabangma Feng, China 8012 m (26,286 ft)

Lowest point: Turpan Hami (Turfan Basin), China 154 m (505 ft) below sea level

POLITICAL FEATURES

Total population: 1572 million

Largest city and its population: Tokyo, Japan 33.9 million

Country with highest population density: Taiwan 701 people/km² (1815 people/mi²)

Largest country: Asiatic Russia 13,119,382 km² (5,065,394 mi²)

Smallest country: Taiwan 35,980 km² (13,892 mi²)

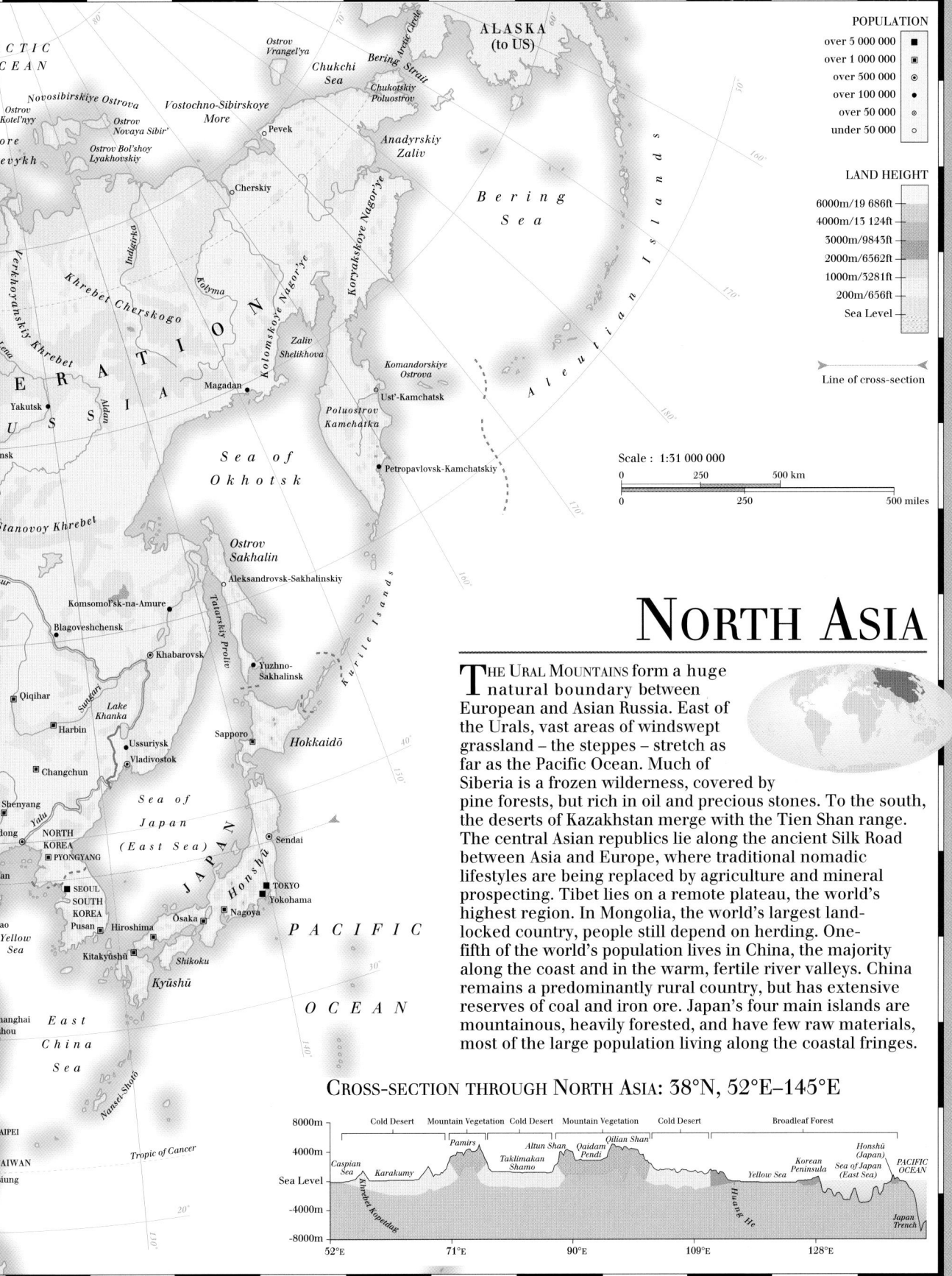

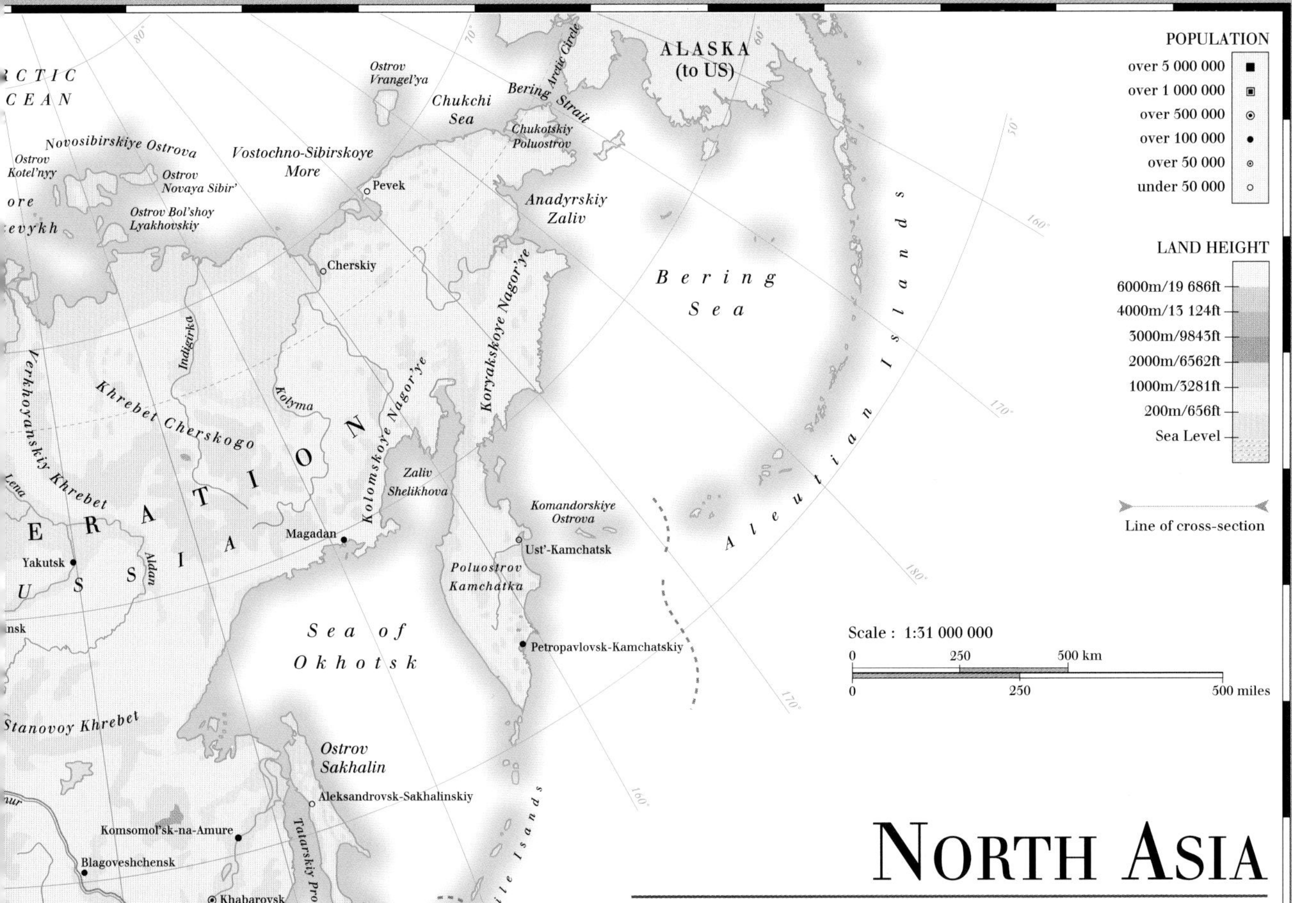
POPULATION
over 5 000 000
over 1 000 000
over 500 000
over 100 000
over 50 000
under 50 000
LAND HEIGHT
6000m/19 686ft
4000m/13 124ft
3000m/9843ft
2000m/6562ft
1000m/3281ft
200m/656ft
Sea Level
Line of cross-section
Scale : 1:31 000 000
0 250 500 km
0 250 500 miles
ALASKA (to US)
Ostrov Vrangel'ya
Chukchi Sea
Bering Strait
Arctic Circle
Chukotskiy Poluostrov
Novosibirskiye Ostrova
Ostrov Kotel'nyy
Ostrov Novaya Sibir'
Vostochno-Sibirskoye More
Ostrov Bol'shoy Lyakhovskiy
Pevek
Anadyrskiy Zaliv
Cherskiy
Bering Sea
Aleutian Islands
Koryakskoye Nagor'ye
Indigirka
Kolyma
Khrebet Cherskogo
Kolomskoye Nagor'ye
Verkhoyanskiy Khrebet
Lena
Zaliv Shelikhova
Komandorskiye Ostrova
Magadan
Ust'-Kamchatsk
Yakutsk
Aldan
RUSSIAN FEDERATION
Poluostrov Kamchatka
Sea of Okhotsk
Petropavlovsk-Kamchatskiy
Stanovoy Khrebet
Ostrov Sakhalin
Aleksandrovsk-Sakhalinskiy
Komsomol'sk-na-Amure
Tatarskiy Proliv
Blagoveshchensk
Khabarovsk
Kurile Islands
Yuzhno-Sakhalinsk
Qiqihar
Sungari
Lake Khanka
Harbin
Sapporo
Hokkaidō
Ussuriysk
Vladivostok
Changchun
Shenyang
Sea of Japan (East Sea)
Yalu
NORTH KOREA
PYONGYANG
Sendai
JAPAN
Honshū
SEOUL
SOUTH KOREA
TOKYO
Yokohama
Nagoya
Ōsaka
Pusan
Hiroshima
Yellow Sea
PACIFIC OCEAN
Kitakyūshū
Shikoku
Kyūshū
East China Sea
Nansei-Shotō
TAIWAN
Tropic of Cancer

NORTH ASIA

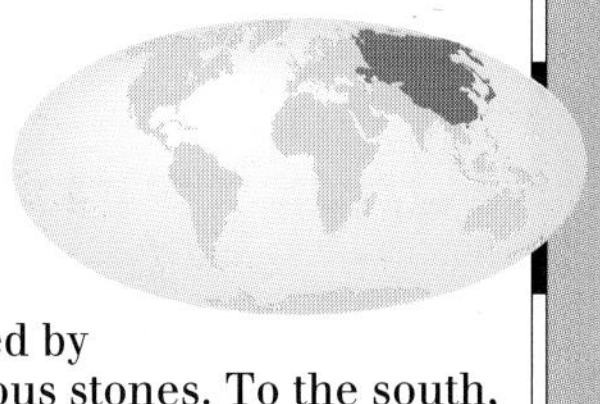

THE URAL MOUNTAINS form a huge natural boundary between European and Asian Russia. East of the Urals, vast areas of windswept grassland – the steppes – stretch as far as the Pacific Ocean. Much of Siberia is a frozen wilderness, covered by pine forests, but rich in oil and precious stones. To the south, the deserts of Kazakhstan merge with the Tien Shan range. The central Asian republics lie along the ancient Silk Road between Asia and Europe, where traditional nomadic lifestyles are being replaced by agriculture and mineral prospecting. Tibet lies on a remote plateau, the world's highest region. In Mongolia, the world's largest land-locked country, people still depend on herding. One-fifth of the world's population lives in China, the majority along the coast and in the warm, fertile river valleys. China remains a predominantly rural country, but has extensive reserves of coal and iron ore. Japan's four main islands are mountainous, heavily forested, and have few raw materials, most of the large population living along the coastal fringes.

CROSS-SECTION THROUGH NORTH ASIA: 38°N, 52°E–145°E

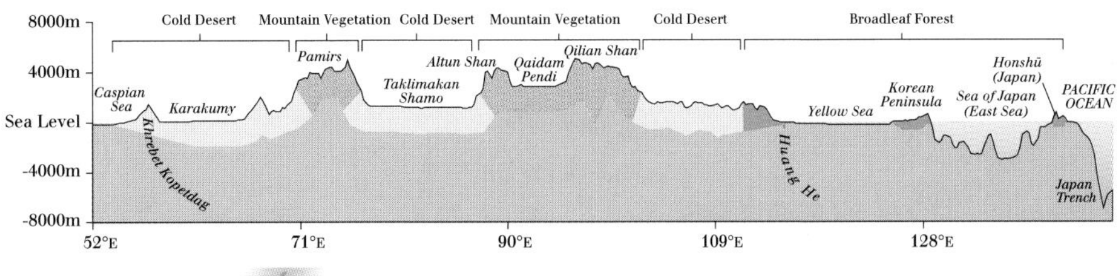
8000m
4000m
Sea Level
-4000m
-8000m
Cold Desert
Mountain Vegetation
Cold Desert
Mountain Vegetation
Cold Desert
Broadleaf Forest
Caspian Sea
Karakumy
Khrebet Kopetdag
Pamirs
Altun Shan
Taklimakan Shamo
Qaidam Pendi
Qilian Shan
Huang He
Yellow Sea
Korean Peninsula
Sea of Japan (East Sea)
Honshū (Japan)
PACIFIC OCEAN
Japan Trench
52°E
71°E
90°E
109°E
128°E

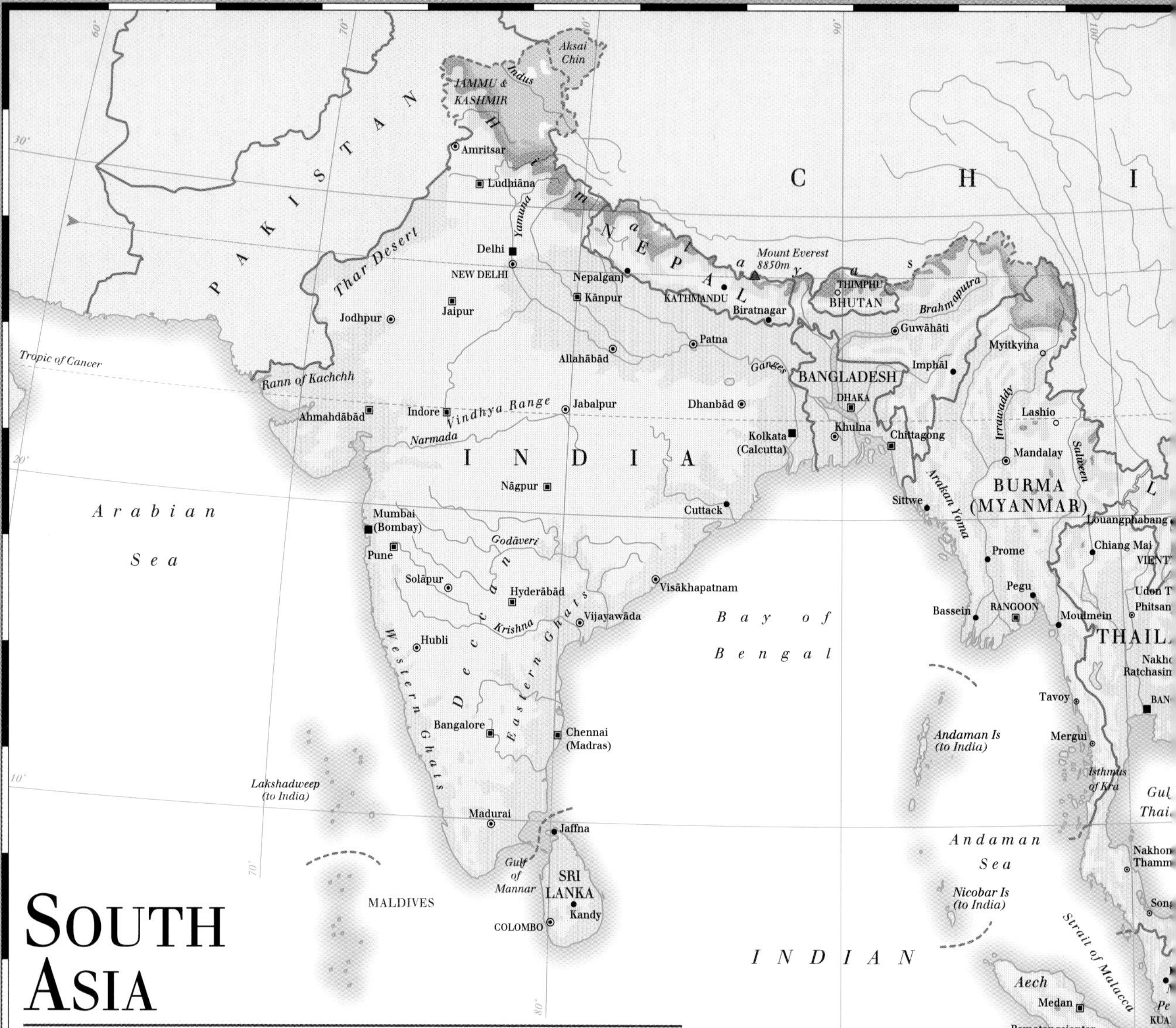
Aksai Chin
JAMMU & KASHMIR
Indus
P A K I S T A N
Amritsar
Ludhiāna
Yamuna
H i m a l a y a
C H I
Thar Desert
Delhi
NEW DELHI
Nepalganj
N E P A L
Mount Everest 8850m
THIMPHU
BHUTAN
Kānpur
KATHMANDU
Biratnagar
Brahmaputra
Jodhpur
Jaipur
Guwāhāti
Patna
Tropic of Cancer
Allahābād
Myitkyina
Ganges
Imphāl
Rann of Kachchh
BANGLADESH
Ahmadābād
Indore
Vindhya Range
Jabalpur
Dhanbād
DHAKA
Lashio
Narmada
Khulna
Chittagong
Irrawaddy
Kolkata (Calcutta)
Mandalay
I N D I A
Salween
Nāgpur
BURMA (MYANMAR)
Arabian Sea
Mumbai (Bombay)
Cuttack
Sittwe
Arakan Yoma
Louangphabang
Pune
Godāvari
Prome
Chiang Mai
Solāpur
Hyderābād
Visākhapatnam
Pegu
Bassein
RANGOON
Moulmein
Krishna
Vijayawāda
Bay of Bengal
THAIL
Hubli
Deccan
Western Ghats
Eastern Ghats
Tavoy
Bangalore
Chennai (Madras)
Andaman Is (to India)
Mergui
Isthmus of Kra
Lakshadweep (to India)
Madurai
Jaffna
Andaman Sea
Gulf of Mannar
SRI LANKA
MALDIVES
Kandy
COLOMBO
Nicobar Is (to India)
Strait of Malacca
INDIAN OCEAN
Aech
Medan
Pematangsiantar
Danau Toba
Pekanbaru
Equator

South Asia

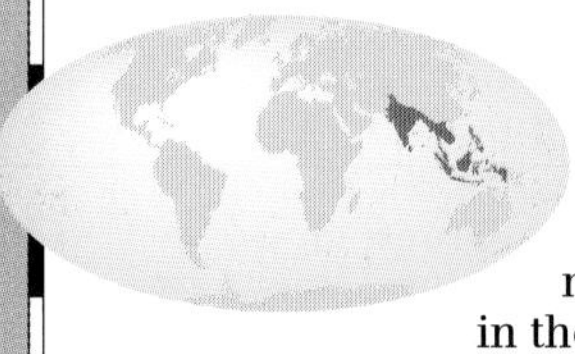

DOMINATED IN THE NORTH by the Himalayas, the highest mountain range in the world, India is isolated from the rest of Asia, forming a densely populated subcontinent. Its climate and topography range from the mountains of Kashmir in the north to coral beaches in the south. It is the birthplace of Hinduism, Buddhism, and Sikhism. Much of mainland southeast Asia is mountainous and forested, the people living in the river valleys and fertile coastal plains. Tropical rainforests, rich in species, cover much of the region. Indonesia forms a huge arc of over 13,000 volcanic islands. The Philippines, the region's only Christian country until 2002, comprises over 7000 mountainous islands.

Cross-section through South Asia: 28°N, 60°E–124°E

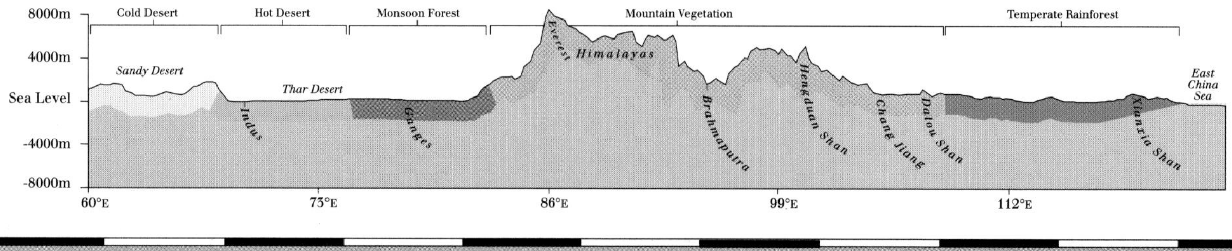
8000m
4000m
Sea Level
-4000m
-8000m
Cold Desert
Hot Desert
Monsoon Forest
Mountain Vegetation
Temperate Rainforest
Sandy Desert
Thar Desert
Everest
Himalayas
East China Sea
Indus
Ganges
Brahmaputra
Hengduan Shan
Chang Jiang
Dalou Shan
Xianzia Shan
60°E
73°E
86°E
99°E
112°E

CONTINENTAL FACTS

PHYSICAL FEATURES

LARGEST LAKE: Tônlé Sap, Cambodia 2850 km² (1000 mi²)

LONGEST RIVER: Mekong, China/Burma/Laos/Thailand/Cambodia/Vietnam 4425 km (2749 miles)

HIGHEST POINT: Mount Everest, Nepal 8850 m (29,035 ft)

LOWEST POINT: About half of Bangladesh lies between sea level and 8 m (25 ft)

POLITICAL FEATURES

TOTAL POPULATION: 1802 million

LARGEST CITY AND ITS POPULATION: Mumbai, India 19.2 million

COUNTRY WITH HIGHEST POPULATION DENSITY: Singapore 7049 people/km² (18,220 people/mi²)

LARGEST COUNTRY: India 3,287,590 km² (1,269,338 mi²)

SMALLEST COUNTRY: Maldives 300 km² (116 mi²)

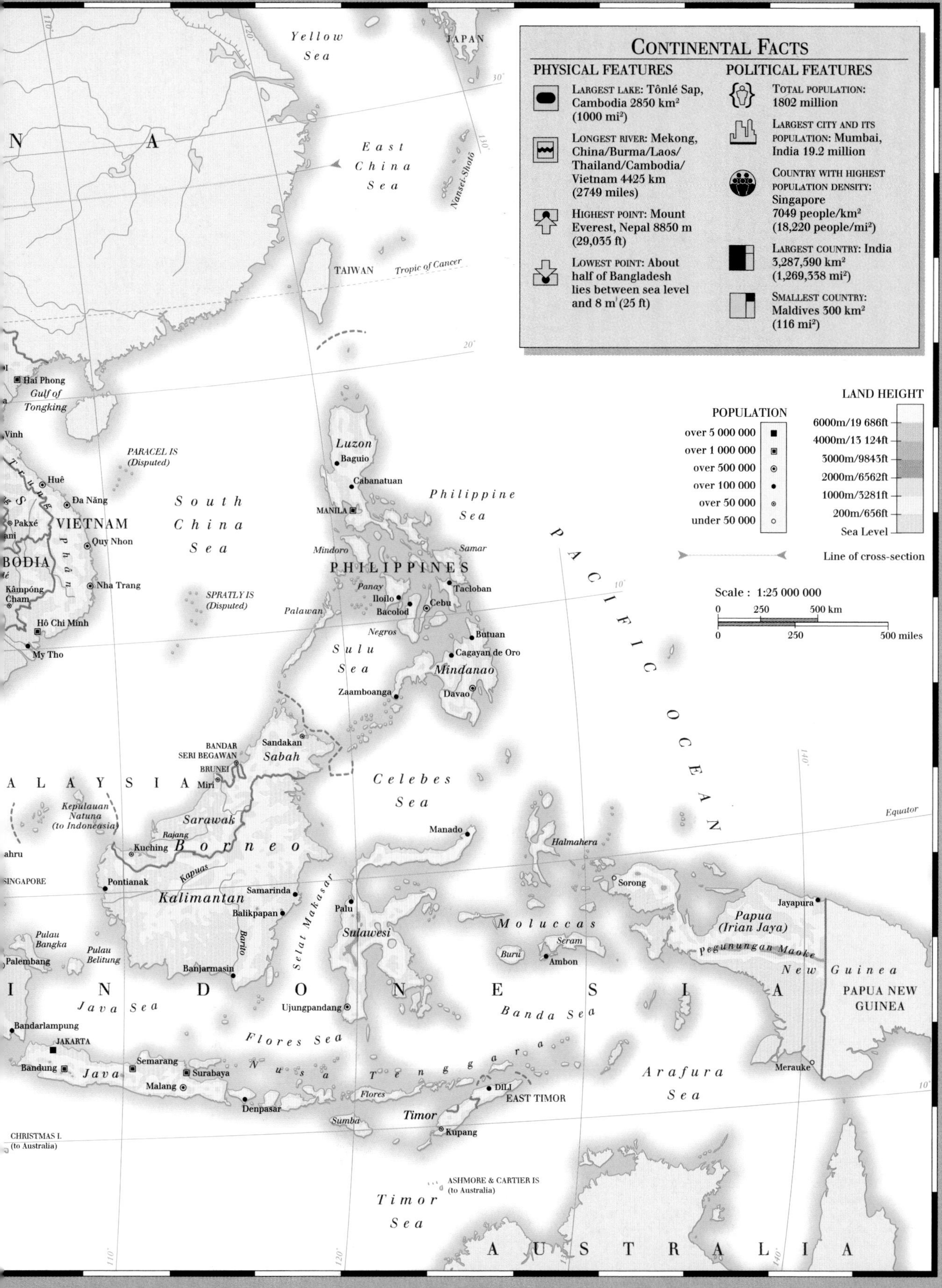
Yellow Sea
JAPAN
East China Sea
Nansei-Shotō
TAIWAN
Tropic of Cancer
Hai Phong
Gulf of Tongking
Vinh
Huê
Đa Năng
VIETNAM
Quy Nhon
Nha Trang
Pakxé
BODIA
Kâmpóng Cham
Hô Chi Minh
My Tho
PARACEL IS (Disputed)
South China Sea
SPRATLY IS (Disputed)
Luzon
Baguio
Cabanatuan
MANILA
Mindoro
PHILIPPINES
Philippine Sea
Samar
Panay
Iloilo
Bacolod
Cebu
Tacloban
Palawan
Negros
Butuan
Sulu Sea
Cagayan de Oro
Mindanao
Davao
Zaamboanga
PACIFIC OCEAN
Sandakan
Sabah
BANDAR SERI BEGAWAN
BRUNEI
Miri
MALAYSIA
Kepulauan Natuna (to Indonesia)
Sarawak
Rajang
Kuching
Borneo
Celebes Sea
Manado
Halmahera
Sorong
SINGAPORE
Pontianak
Kapuas
Kalimantan
Samarinda
Balikpapan
Barito
Selat Makasar
Palu
Sulawesi
Moluccas
Seram
Buru
Ambon
Jayapura
Papua (Irian Jaya)
Pegunungan Maoke
New Guinea
PAPUA NEW GUINEA
Pulau Bangka
Pulau Belitung
Palembang
Banjarmasin
INDONESIA
Java Sea
Ujungpandang
Banda Sea
Bandarlampung
JAKARTA
Flores Sea
Bandung
Java
Semarang
Surabaya
Malang
Nusa Tenggara
DILI
EAST TIMOR
Flores
Denpasar
Sumba
Timor
Kupang
Arafura Sea
Merauke
CHRISTMAS I. (to Australia)
ASHMORE & CARTIER IS (to Australia)
Timor Sea
AUSTRALIA
Equator
POPULATION
over 5 000 000
over 1 000 000
over 500 000
over 100 000
over 50 000
under 50 000
LAND HEIGHT
6000m/19 686ft
4000m/13 124ft
3000m/9843ft
2000m/6562ft
1000m/3281ft
200m/656ft
Sea Level
Line of cross-section
Scale : 1:25 000 000
0 250 500 km
0 250 500 miles

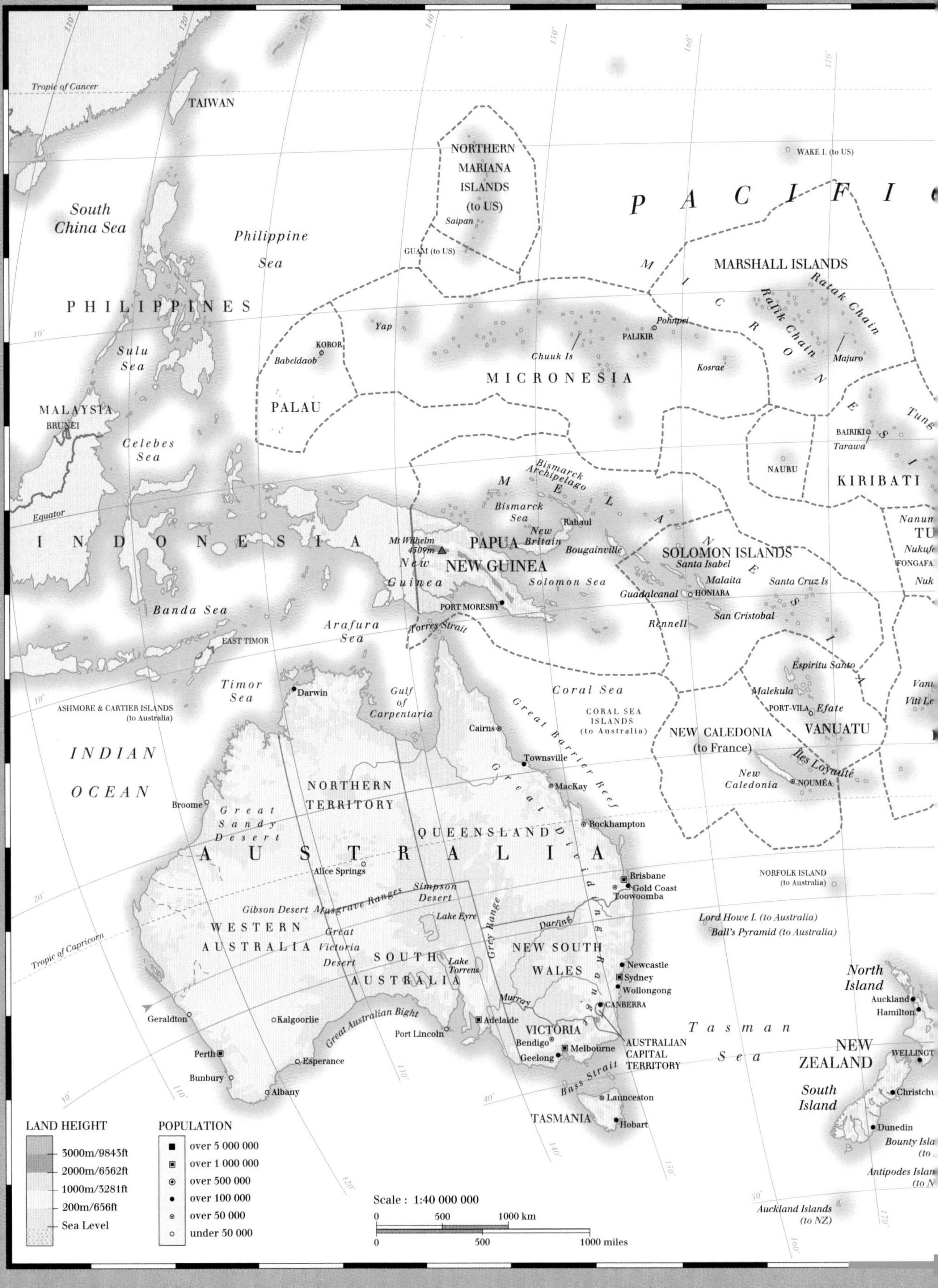
Tropic of Cancer
TAIWAN
South China Sea
Philippine Sea
NORTHERN MARIANA ISLANDS (to US)
Saipan
GUAM (to US)
WAKE I. (to US)
P A C I F I C
PHILIPPINES
Sulu Sea
MARSHALL ISLANDS
Ratak Chain
Ralik Chain
Majuro
M I C R O N E S I A
Yap
KOROR
Babeldaob
Pohnpei
PALIKIR
Chuuk Is
Kosrae
MICRONESIA
PALAU
MALAYSIA
BRUNEI
Celebes Sea
BAIRIKI
Tarawa
NAURU
KIRIBATI
Tung
Equator
Bismarck Archipelago
Bismarck Sea
M E L A N E S I A
Rabaul
New Britain
Bougainville
INDONESIA
Mt Wilhelm 4509m
PAPUA NEW GUINEA
New Guinea
Solomon Sea
SOLOMON ISLANDS
Santa Isabel
Malaita
Guadalcanal
HONIARA
Santa Cruz Is
San Cristobal
Rennell
PORT MORESBY
Banda Sea
Arafura Sea
Torres Strait
EAST TIMOR
Timor Sea
ASHMORE & CARTIER ISLANDS (to Australia)
Darwin
Gulf of Carpentaria
Coral Sea
CORAL SEA ISLANDS (to Australia)
Great Barrier Reef
Espiritu Santo
Malekula
PORT-VILA
Efate
VANUATU
NEW CALEDONIA (to France)
Îles Loyauté
New Caledonia
NOUMÉA
Cairns
Townsville
MacKay
Rockhampton
INDIAN OCEAN
Broome
Great Sandy Desert
NORTHERN TERRITORY
QUEENSLAND
Great Dividing Range
AUSTRALIA
Alice Springs
Simpson Desert
Brisbane
Gold Coast
Toowoomba
NORFOLK ISLAND (to Australia)
Gibson Desert
Musgrave Ranges
Lake Eyre
Grey Range
Darling
Lord Howe I. (to Australia)
Ball's Pyramid (to Australia)
Tropic of Capricorn
WESTERN AUSTRALIA
Great Victoria Desert
SOUTH AUSTRALIA
Lake Torrens
NEW SOUTH WALES
Newcastle
Sydney
Wollongong
CANBERRA
North Island
Auckland
Hamilton
Geraldton
Kalgoorlie
Great Australian Bight
Port Lincoln
Adelaide
Murray
VICTORIA
Bendigo
Melbourne
Geelong
AUSTRALIAN CAPITAL TERRITORY
Tasman Sea
NEW ZEALAND
WELLINGT
Perth
Esperance
Bunbury
Albany
Bass Strait
Launceston
TASMANIA
Hobart
South Island
Christchu
Dunedin
Bounty Isla
Antipodes Islan
Auckland Islands (to NZ)
LAND HEIGHT
3000m/9843ft
2000m/6562ft
1000m/3281ft
200m/656ft
Sea Level
POPULATION
over 5 000 000
over 1 000 000
over 500 000
over 100 000
over 50 000
under 50 000
Scale : 1:40 000 000
0
500
1000 km
0
500
1000 miles

AUSTRALASIA & OCEANIA

OCEANIA, A CONTINENT OF ISLANDS stretching across a vast area of the Pacific Ocean, is home to only 0.5% of the world's population. Dominated by Australia, it includes few other countries with significant land mass apart from New Zealand, Papua New Guinea, and Fiji, but myriad volcanic and coral islands in three main groups, Micronesia, Melanesia, and Polynesia. Australia, flat and dry, is sparsely populated, most people living along the coastal lowlands, especially in the southeast. Its first inhabitants, the Aboriginal peoples, retain some of their original lands in the interior, but the European and Asian settlers of recent centuries form most of the population. Australia is rich in minerals, such as gold, uranium, and iron ore, which are the basis of its prosperity. Mountainous Papua New Guinea is covered in tropical rainforest, while New Zealand is temperate, rugged, and volcanic in the north. Owing to their isolation, these countries' flora and fauna have evolved many unique species. The peoples of Oceania colonized the Pacific by 1100 CE, and the many insular farming and fishing communities have developed distinctive cultures, the Maoris of New Zealand being among the most notable.

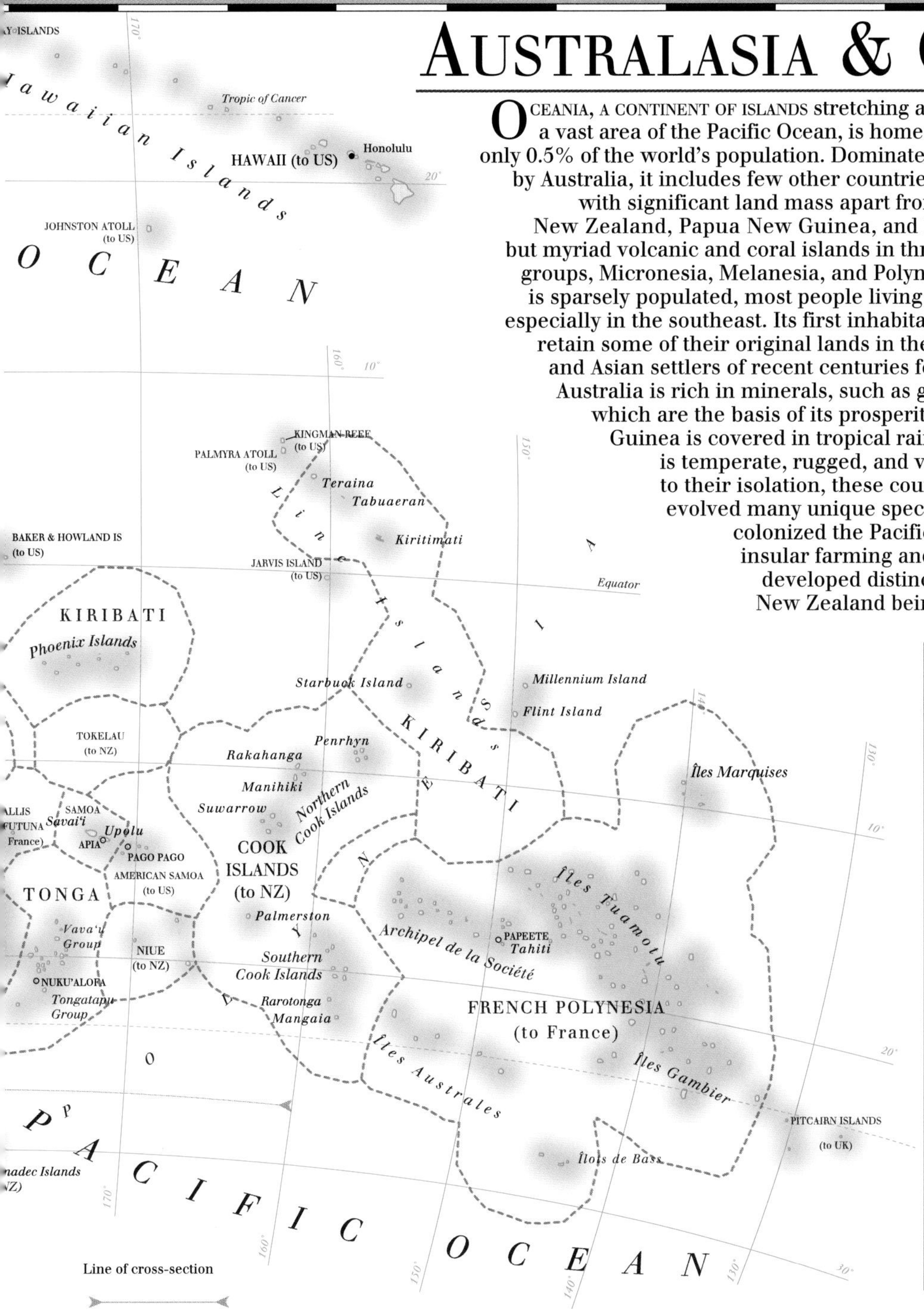
Hawaiian Islands
Tropic of Cancer
HAWAII (to US)
Honolulu
JOHNSTON ATOLL (to US)
OCEAN
KINGMAN REEF (to US)
PALMYRA ATOLL (to US)
Teraina
Tabuaeran
Line Islands
Kiritimati
BAKER & HOWLAND IS (to US)
JARVIS ISLAND (to US)
Equator
KIRIBATI
Phoenix Islands
Starbuck Island
Millennium Island
Flint Island
TOKELAU (to NZ)
Penrhyn
Rakahanga
Manihiki
Suwarrow
Northern Cook Islands
Îles Marquises
SAMOA
Savai'i
Upolu
APIA
PAGO PAGO
AMERICAN SAMOA (to US)
COOK ISLANDS (to NZ)
TONGA
Palmerston
Îles Tuamotu
Archipel de la Société
PAPEETE
Tahiti
Vava'u Group
NIUE (to NZ)
Southern Cook Islands
NUKU'ALOFA
Tongatapu Group
Rarotonga
Mangaia
FRENCH POLYNESIA (to France)
Îles Australes
Îles Gambier
PITCAIRN ISLANDS (to UK)
Îlots de Bass
PACIFIC OCEAN
Line of cross-section

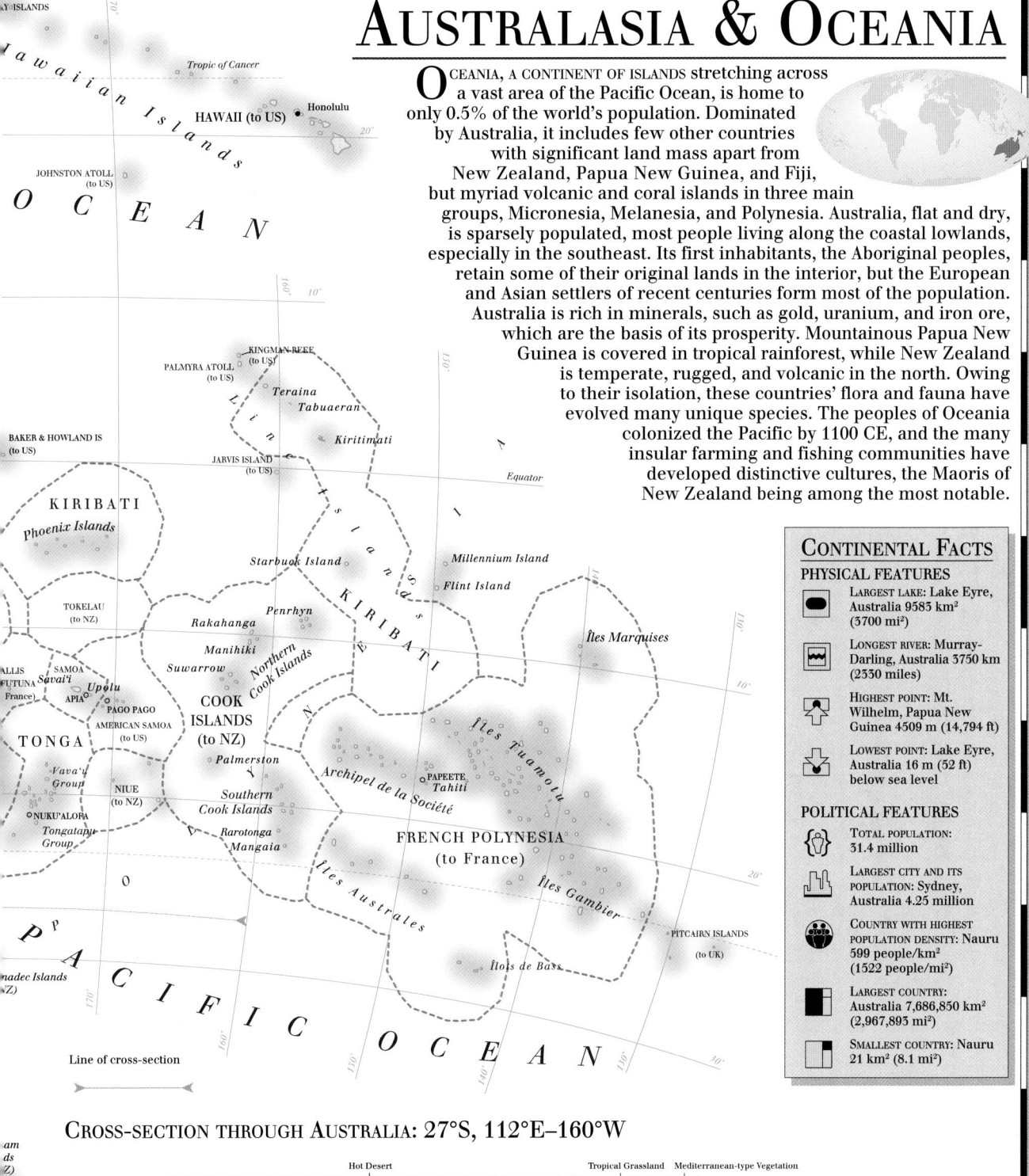

CONTINENTAL FACTS

PHYSICAL FEATURES

LARGEST LAKE: Lake Eyre, Australia 9583 km² (3700 mi²)

LONGEST RIVER: Murray-Darling, Australia 3750 km (2330 miles)

HIGHEST POINT: Mt. Wilhelm, Papua New Guinea 4509 m (14,794 ft)

LOWEST POINT: Lake Eyre, Australia 16 m (52 ft) below sea level

POLITICAL FEATURES

TOTAL POPULATION: 31.4 million

LARGEST CITY AND ITS POPULATION: Sydney, Australia 4.25 million

COUNTRY WITH HIGHEST POPULATION DENSITY: Nauru 599 people/km² (1522 people/mi²)

LARGEST COUNTRY: Australia 7,686,850 km² (2,967,893 mi²)

SMALLEST COUNTRY: Nauru 21 km² (8.1 mi²)

CROSS-SECTION THROUGH AUSTRALIA: 27°S, 112°E–160°W

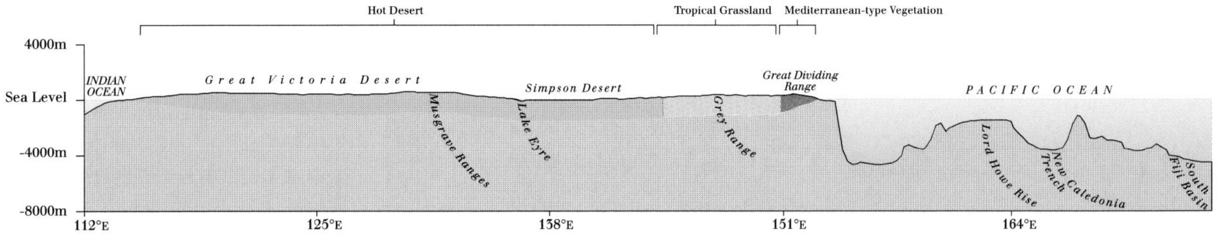
Hot Desert
Tropical Grassland
Mediterranean-type Vegetation
4000m
Sea Level
-4000m
-8000m
INDIAN OCEAN
Great Victoria Desert
Simpson Desert
Great Dividing Range
PACIFIC OCEAN
Musgrave Ranges
Lake Eyre
Grey Range
Lord Howe Rise
New Caledonia Trench
South Fiji Basin
112°E
125°E
138°E
151°E
164°E

CHRONOLOGY OF WORLD HISTORY

THIS TABLE PRESENTS A SUMMARY of the world's crucial historical events, from the first evidence of settlement and agriculture until 2002 CE. Each of the six columns is shaded a different color, with each color representing a particular continent. Reading across the columns, one can follow the development of cultures across the major landmasses of the world. By reading downward, each continent's particular cultural history can be seen, from its first steps toward civilization, through periods of migration, empire, and revolution, to its involvement in the global wars and political diplomacy of the 20th and 21st centuries.

NORTH AMERICA

- **15,000 BCE** Evidence of human settlement in North America
- **4000 BCE** Earliest cultivation of corn in Central America
- **100 CE** Teotihuacan becomes capital of largest state in Mesoamerica
- **c.300 CE** Start of classic Mayan civilization in Yucatan
- **900** Toltecs rise to power after Teotihuacan and Mayan states collapse
- **c.1000** Vikings colonize Greenland and discover America (Vinland)
- **1200** Aztecs enter Valley of Mexico
- **1325** Tenochtitlan founded by Aztecs
- **1492** Columbus reaches Caribbean
- **c.1500** Inuit peoples found throughout Arctic region
- **1502** Introduction of African slaves to Caribbean
- **1519** Cortes begins conquest of Aztec empire
- **1565** First African slaves arrive on mainland North America
- **1607** First permanent English settlement in North America (Jamestown, Virginia)
- **1608** French colonists found Québec
- **1620** Puritans on *Mayflower* land in New England
- **1759** British capture Québec
- **1776** American Declaration of Independence
- **1789** George Washington becomes first president of US
- **1791** Revolution in Haiti
- **1803** Louisiana Purchase nearly doubles size of US
- **1810** Revolution in Mexico
- **1819** US buys Florida from Spain
- **1821** Mexico gains independence
- **1828** Federalist–Centralist wars in Mexico (to 1859)
- **1845** Texas annexed by US
- **1846** US–Mexican War (to 1848)
- **1848** Californian Gold Rush

SOUTH AMERICA

- **c.20,000 BCE** First settlers arrive
- **c.11,000 BCE** Evidence of settlement at Monte Verde in present-day Chile
- **c.4500 BCE** Evidence of agriculture and herding in central Andes
- **c.2500 BCE** Masonry building and temple architecture on Pacific coast
- **c.1800 BCE** Ceremonial center of La Florida built in Peru
- **c.450 CE** Nazca culture flourishing; lines and giant figures drawn in desert
- **c.900 CE** Wari and Tiwanaku flourish as capitals of first competing empires
- **1100** Emergence of Chimu state on north coast of Peru
- **1380** Beginning of Inca empire in central highlands
- **1475** Chimu conquered by Incas
- **1494** Treaty of Tordesillas divides western hemisphere between Spain and Portugal
- **1500** Cabral sights Brazilian coast
- **1502** First expedition sent from Portugal to exploit coast of Brazil
- **c.1510** First African slaves brought to South America
- **1525** Civil war in Inca empire
- **1532** Pizarro begins defeat of Incas (to 1540)
- **1562** War and disease kill much of Amerindian population of Brazil (to 1563)
- **1630** Dutch establish New Holland, covering much of northern Brazil
- **1654** Portuguese regain control of Brazil
- **1663** Brazil becomes viceroyalty
- **1695** Gold discovered in Brazil
- **1739** Viceroyalty of New Granada established to defend Spanish interests on Caribbean coast
- **1750** Treaty of Madrid defines boundary between Spanish colonies and Brazil

EUROPE

- **c.6500 BCE** Farming spreads rapidly into central Europe
- **c.2800 BCE** Building of Stonehenge begins
- **c.1600 BCE** Minoan Palace civilization on Crete
- **c.750 BCE** Beginnings of Greek city-states
- **510 BCE** Roman Republic founded
- **431 BCE** Outbreak of Peloponnesian War between Sparta and Athens
- **218 BCE** Carthaginians invade Italy under command of Hannibal
- **49 BCE** Julius Caesar conquers Gaul
- **43 CE** Roman invasion of Britain
- **238 CE** Goths begin to invade borders of Roman Empire
- **330** Constantinople becomes new capital of Roman Empire
- **410** Invasion and pillage of Rome by Visigoths
- **711** Spain invaded by Muslims
- **793** Viking raids across Europe
- **800** Charlemagne becomes first Holy Roman Emperor
- **950** Harold Bluetooth consolidates the unification of Denmark
- **987** Feudal lords elect first Capetian king of France
- **1066** Norman conquest of England
- **1236** Russia invaded by Mongols
- **1337** Onset of Hundred Years War
- **1453** Byzantine Empire collapses as Ottoman Turks capture Constantinople
- **1478** Ivan III first czar of Russia
- **c.1500** Italian Renaissance
- **1521** Beginning of Protestant Reformation
- **1534** Henry VIII of England breaks with Rome
- **1588** Spanish Armada defeated by English
- **1618** Onset of Thirty Years War
- **1642** English Civil War (to 1649)
- **1756** Onset of Seven Years War
- **1789** French Revolution

AFRICA

- **c.400,000 BCE** First evidence of *Homo sapiens* (modern humans) in Rift Valley
- **3100 BCE** King Narmer unifies Upper and Lower Egypt and becomes first pharaoh
- **c.2650 BCE** Start of great pyramid building in Egypt
- **2040 BCE** Beginning of Middle Kingdom in Egypt
- **1352 BCE** Pharaoh Akhenaten promotes Aten (sun) worship in Egypt
- **814 BCE** Foundation of Phoenician colony of Carthage
- **146 BCE** Rome conquers Carthage
- **31 BCE** Cleopatra's death marks end of Ptolemaic dynasty in Egypt
- **c.600 CE** Kingdom of Ghana founded
- **641 CE** Muslims conquer Egypt
- **c.900 CE** Emergence of Great Zimbabwean state
- **1067** Almoravids destroy kingdom of Ghana
- **c.1300** Emergence of empire of Benin (Nigeria)
- **1390** Formation of kingdom of Kongo
- **1443** Portuguese begin mass export of slaves from Atlantic coast to Europe
- **1498** Vasco da Gama rounds Cape of Good Hope
- **1502** First slaves taken to New World
- **1570** Establishment of Portuguese colony of Angola
- **1652** Dutch establish colony at Cape of Good Hope
- **1787** British establish Sierra Leone for freed slaves
- **1795** British capture Cape of Good Hope from the Dutch
- **1798** Occupation of Egypt by Napoléon Bonaparte
- **1816** Shaka leads expansion of Zulu
- **1822** Freed black slaves found colony of Liberia
- **1830** French invasion of Algeria
- **1836** Start of Boer Great Trek
- **1848** Boers found Orange Free State
- **1853** Livingstone finds Victoria Falls (Musi-o-Tunya)
- **1869** Opening of Suez Canal
- **1875** Stanley establishes source of Nile

ASIA AND THE MIDDLE EAST

- **c.12,000 BCE** Beginnings of farming in Palestine
- **c.4800 BCE** 'Ubaid culture builds towns in Mesopotamia
- **c.3500 BCE** Fortified towns built throughout northern China
- **c.2800 BCE** Emergence of city-states in Indus Valley
- Wheel used in Mesopotamia
- **c.1750 BCE** Foundation of Old Babylonian Empire under Hammurabi
- **c.1200 BCE** Traditional date for exodus of the Jews from Egypt
- **c.1100 BCE** Phoenician civilization spreads throughout Mediterranean
- **c.660 BCE** Japanese empire founded
- **550 BCE** Persian Empire founded
- **c.480 BCE** Death – or *parinibbana* – of Gautama Buddha
- **334 BCE** Alexander the Great invades Asia Minor
- **332 BCE** Foundation of Mauryan empire in India
- **202 BCE** Han dynasty begins in China
- **c.112 BCE** "Silk Road" links China to West
- **c.30 CE** Crucifixion of Jesus of Nazareth, founder of Christianity
- **c.350 CE** Huns invade Persia and India
- **622** Mohammed, founder of Islam, flees Mecca; start of Muslim calendar
- **960** China united under Sung dynasty
- **1044** Foundation of Burma
- **1099** Jerusalem sacked in First Crusade
- **1185** Minamoto shoguns rule Japan
- **1206** Mongols begin to conquer Asia under Genghis Khan
- **1238** Foundation of first Thai kingdom
- **1258** Baghdad sacked by Mongols
- **1264** Yuan dynasty founded in China by Kublai Khan
- **1275** Marco Polo arrives in China
- **1333** Civil war in Japan
- **1368** Ming dynasty begins in China
- **1392** Korea proclaims independence
- **1498** Vasco da Gama completes first European voyage to India
- **1526** Foundation of Mughal empire in India
- **1600** Charter granted to East India Company
- **1609** Beginning of Tokugawa shogunate in Japan
- **1619** Dutch found Batavia (Jakarta)
- **1644** Manchus seize Peking

AUSTRALASIA AND OCEANIA

- **c.60,000 BCE** First people arrive in Australia
- **c.30,000 BCE** Aboriginal rock art begins to appear
- **c.8000–6000 BCE** Rising sea level covers New Guinea land bridge
- **c.6000 BCE** Migrations from southeast Asia give rise to Austronesian culture
- **c.4000 BCE** Austronesians reach southwestern Pacific islands
- **c.1000 BCE** Emergence of archaic Polynesian society in Fiji, Tonga, and Samoa
- **c.300 CE** Easter Island settled
- **c.600 CE** Polynesians arrive in Hawaii
- **1520** Magellan enters Pacific
- **1526** Jorge de Meneses first European to sight New Guinea
- **1606** Torres sails through strait that now bears his name; proves New Guinea is an island
- **1642** Tasman, searching for a southern continent, finds Tasmania and New Zealand
- **1688** Dampier first Englishman to visit Australia
- **1768** Cook's first voyage
- **1773** Cook crosses Antarctic Circle and explores Southern Ocean (to 1775)
- **1779** Cook killed in Hawaii on third voyage
- **1788** First penal settlement established at Port Jackson (Sydney)
- **1802** Flinders circumnavigates Australia (to 1803)
- **1818** Start of Maori "Musket Wars" in New Zealand
- **1819** Bellingshausen's expedition sights Antarctica
- **1829** Britain annexes western and final third of Australian continent
- **1830** A mere 200 foreigners, mostly British, permanently resident in New Zealand
- **1840** Treaty of Waitangi grants sovereignty over New Zealand to British
- **1841** New Zealand becomes a separate Crown colony
- **1845** Northern War in New Zealand (to 1846)

see pages 68–69 for CHRONOLOGY 2003–2004

North America (continued)

❑ **1861** US Civil War (to 1865)

❑ **1863** Emancipation Proclamation

❑ **1865** Lee surrenders to Grant at Appomattox
❑ Assassination of President Lincoln
❑ Slavery abolished in US

❑ **1867** US buys Alaska from Russia
❑ Dominion of Canada established

❑ **1869** 15th Amendment gives vote to freed slaves in US

❑ **1871** Start of Apache Wars

❑ **1876** Battle of Little Big Horn: Sioux warriors kill 250 US soldiers

❑ **1890** Massacre of Sioux warriors at Wounded Knee ends Amerindian wars

❑ **1896** Klondike Gold Rush, Alaska

❑ **1898** Spanish–American War

❑ **1899** Spain cedes Cuba and Puerto Rico to US

❑ **1910** Mexican Revolution begins

❑ **1921** US restricts immigration

❑ **1929** Wall Street Crash

❑ **1933** President Roosevelt introduces New Deal

❑ **1940s** Race riots in Harlem, Los Angeles, Detroit, and Chicago

❑ **1941** US enters war against Germany and Japan

❑ **1945** End of World War II

❑ **1949** Formation of NATO
❑ Cold War begins

❑ **1950** US supports south in Korean War (to 1953)

❑ **1959** Cuban Revolution

❑ **1962** Cuban missile crisis

❑ **1963** Martin Luther King leads march on Washington D.C.
❑ Assassination of President Kennedy

❑ **1964** US Congress approves sending first troops to Vietnam

❑ **1968** Assassination of Martin Luther King sparks riots in 124 US cities

❑ **1969** Neil Armstrong becomes first person on moon

❑ **1973** US withdraws from Vietnam

❑ **1974** President Nixon resigns over Watergate scandal

❑ **1979** Civil war in Nicaragua (to 1990)
❑ Civil war in El Salvador (to 1992)

❑ **1994** North American Free Trade Agreement (NAFTA) established

❑ **1999** President Clinton survives impeachment

❑ **2001** World's worst ever terrorist attack kills thousands in New York and Washington D.C.

❑ **2002** Telecommunications firm Worldcom files largest corporate bankruptcy in US history

South America (continued)

❑ **1811** Bolívar starts fight to liberate Venezuela
❑ Paraguay independent

❑ **1817** San Martin wins decisive victory over Spanish and liberates Chile

❑ **1821** Peru independent

❑ **1822** Brazil independent

❑ **1823** Slavery abolished in Chile

❑ **1825** Bolivia independent

❑ **1828** Uruguay independent

❑ **1830** Ecuador, Colombia, and Venezuela (formerly Gran Colombia) become separate states

❑ **1851** Slavery abolished in Colombia

❑ **1853** Slavery abolished in Ecuador, Argentina, and Uruguay

❑ **1854** Slavery abolished in Bolivia and Venezuela

❑ **1864** Paraguayan War: Brazil, Argentina, and Uruguay defeat Paraguay

❑ **1870** Slavery abolished in Paraguay

❑ **1888** Slavery abolished in Brazil

❑ **1900** Major Italian migration to Argentina

❑ **1914** Panama Canal opens

❑ **1930** Military revolution in Brazil

❑ **1932** Chaco War between Bolivia and Paraguay (to 1935); Paraguay defeats Bolivia

❑ **1937** "New State" in Brazil launched by Vargas

❑ **1946** Peron comes to power in Argentina

❑ **1955** Peron ousted by military coup; returns to power in 1973

❑ **1968** Tupamaros urban guerrilla group founded in Uruguay
❑ Military junta takes over Peru

❑ **1970** Allende elected president of Chile

❑ **1973** US backs Pinochet coup against elected government in Chile; Allende assassinated

❑ **1976** "Dirty War" of right-wing death squads in Argentina

❑ **1982** Falklands War between Argentina and UK

❑ **1983** Democracy restored in Argentina

❑ **1985** Democracy restored in Brazil and Uruguay

❑ **1989** Democracy restored in Chile

❑ **1999** Panama takes control of Panama Canal

❑ **2001–2002** Economic crisis in Argentina; five presidents in one month

Europe (continued)

❑ **1804** Napoléon becomes emperor of France

❑ **1815** Napoléon defeated
❑ Treaty of Vienna

❑ **1845** Beginning of Irish potato famine

❑ **1854** Crimean War (to 1856)

❑ **1861** Italy unified
❑ Emancipation of serfs in Russia

❑ **1870** Franco-Prussian War

❑ **1871** Germany unified

❑ **1914** World War I (to 1918)

❑ **1917** Russian Revolution

❑ **1922** Mussolini comes to power in Italy after Fascist "March on Rome"

❑ **1933** Nazis take power in Germany; Hitler is elected chancellor

❑ **1936** Spanish Civil War (to 1939)

❑ **1939** Germany invades Poland precipitating World War II

❑ **1941** German forces invade Russia

❑ **1944** British and US troops land in Normandy; Russians advance into eastern Europe

❑ **1945** Defeat of Germany

❑ **1949** Formation of NATO
❑ Cold War begins

❑ **1957** Treaties of Rome establish European Economic Community

❑ **1961** Building of the Berlin Wall
❑ Yuri Gagarin first person in space

❑ **1968** Troubles in Northern Ireland

❑ **1973** UK and Ireland join European Communities

❑ **1975** End of dictatorship in Spain with death of Gen. Franco

❑ **1986** Explosion at Chernobyl nuclear power reactor
❑ Soviet launch of *Mir* space station

❑ **1989** Democratic revolutions in eastern Europe
❑ Berlin Wall demolished

❑ **1990** Reunification of Germany

❑ **1991** The Soviet Union splits into its component countries
❑ Slovenia and Croatia claim their independence

❑ **1992** Civil war in Bosnia & Herzegovina (to 1995)

❑ **1993** Velvet Divorce: separation of Czech Republic and Slovakia

❑ **1994** Outbreak of war in Chechnya

❑ **1995** EU expands to 15 members

❑ **1999** "Ethnic cleansing" of Albanians in Kosovo leads to NATO air strikes against Yugoslavia

❑ **2000** President Milosevic is ousted in Yugoslavia (Serbia & Montenegro) in popular revolution

❑ **2002** Euro fully adopted in 12 EU states

AFRICA (CONTINUED)

❑ **1879** British defeat Zulus

❑ **1881** French occupy Tunisia

❑ **1882** Britain occupies Egypt

❑ **1883** France begins conquest of Madagascar

❑ **1889** Colonization of "Rhodesia"

❑ **1890** Land connection between Angola and Mozambique ended

❑ **1894** Britain occupies Uganda

❑ **1896** Ethiopian emperor Menelik II defeats Italians at Adawa

❑ **1899** Boer War (to 1902)

❑ **1910** Formation of Union of South Africa

❑ **1911** Italian conquest of Libya

❑ **1935** Second Italian invasion of Ethiopia

❑ **1942** British halt German advance at El Alamein

❑ **1948** Pro-apartheid National Party wins power in South Africa

❑ **1956** UK fails to block Egypt's nationalization of Suez Canal

❑ **1960** Outbreak of civil war in Belgian Congo
❑ Fifteen countries gain independence

❑ **1962** Algeria gains independence

❑ **1963** Zambia and Malawi granted independence
❑ Organization of African Unity (OAU) founded

❑ **1964** Nelson Mandela sentenced to life imprisonment

❑ **1974** Emperor Haile Selassie of Ethiopia deposed

❑ **1975** Angola and Mozambique gain independence; civil wars ensue

❑ **1980** Black majority rule established in Zimbabwe

❑ **1981** President Sadat of Egypt assassinated

❑ **1984** Worst recent famine in Ethiopia

❑ **1990** Mandela released: apartheid begins to be dismantled
❑ Namibia becomes independent

❑ **1991** Civil war in Sierra Leone (to 2001)

❑ **1994** South Africa holds first multiracial election; Mandela wins presidency
❑ Attempted genocide of Tutsis by Hutu in Rwanda

❑ **1997** Overthrow of Mobutu in Zaire (Democratic Republic of the Congo – DRC). Civil war starts in 1998

❑ **1999** Nigeria returns to democracy

❑ **2000** Ethiopia–Eritrea conflict ends

❑ **2002** End of 27-year Angolan civil war

ASIA AND THE MIDDLE EAST (CONTINUED)

❑ **1757** East India Company defeats Nawab of Bengal's forces at Plassey

❑ **1842** Opium Wars (to 1854), Britain compels China to open Treaty Ports and annexes Hong Kong

❑ **1851** Taiping rebellion in China (to 1864), 20 million killed

❑ **1868** Meiji Restoration in Japan

❑ **1877** Queen Victoria proclaimed empress of India

❑ **1911** Manchu dynasty overthrown in China, republic declared

❑ **1922** The last Ottoman sultan is deposed; Turkey proclaimed a republic

❑ **1932** Kingdom of Saudi Arabia founded

❑ **1937** Japanese forces invade China

❑ **1941** Pearl Harbor attacked by Japan

❑ **1945** Atom bombs dropped on Hiroshima and Nagasaki; c.210,000 killed, Japan surrenders

❑ **1947** Partition of India: Pakistan and India independent

❑ **1948** Burma and Ceylon (Sri Lanka) proclaim their independence
❑ Establishment of Israel

❑ **1949** People's Republic of China proclaimed
❑ Indonesia independent

❑ **1950** Korean War (until 1953)

❑ **1954** Laos, Cambodia, and Vietnam proclaim their independence

❑ **1959** China occupies Tibet

❑ **1965** US combat troops in Vietnam

❑ **1966** Cultural Revolution in China

❑ **1971** East Pakistan (Bangladesh) claims independence

❑ **1975** Fall of Saigon ends Vietnam War
❑ Civil war in Lebanon (to 1989)

❑ **1979** Overthrow of shah in Iran, Islamic Republic founded
❑ Vietnam pushes Khmer Rouge from Cambodia

❑ **1980** Iran–Iraq War (to 1988)

❑ **1982** Israeli invasion of Lebanon

❑ **1986** Marcos deposed in Philippines

❑ **1989** Massacre in Tiananmen Square

❑ **1990** Invasion of Kuwait by Iraq

❑ **1991** Gulf War

❑ **1996** *Taliban* take over in Afghanistan

❑ **1997** Hong Kong is returned to China
❑ Asian financial crisis

❑ **1998** India and Pakistan test nuclear weapons

❑ **2000** Palestinians begin new *intifada*

❑ **2001** US-led war ousts *taliban* regime in Afghanistan

❑ **2002** East Timor gains independence

AUSTRALASIA AND OCEANIA (CONTINUED)

❑ **c.1850** Migrant workers from China, Japan, and Philippines start arriving in Hawaii

❑ **1851** Gold discovered in New South Wales

❑ **1858** King Movement demands Maori state and opposes further land sales

❑ **1860** European settlers outnumber Maoris in New Zealand

❑ **1862** Second Maori War

❑ **1864** First French convict settlers in New Caledonia

❑ **1865** 1000 Chinese brought to Tahiti to work cotton plantation (to 1866)

❑ **1869** Last convict ship arrives in Australia

❑ **1870** Maori resistance crushed
❑ Germans start to buy up large tracts of Western Samoa

❑ **1874** Indian sugarcane workers arrive in Fiji

❑ **1888** Chile starts colonization of Easter Island

❑ **1890** Gold discovered in Western Australia

❑ **1898** US annexes Hawaii and seizes Guam from Spain

❑ **1901** Australia is self-governing federation within British Empire

❑ **1912** Amundsen's expedition reaches South Pole

❑ **1914** Over 60,000 Australian troops and more than 15,000 New Zealanders lose their lives in World War I (to 1918)

❑ **1930s** Australia hit hard by global Depression

❑ **1942** Australia under threat of invasion as Japanese bomb Darwin

❑ **1946** US begins nuclear tests at Eniwetok and Bikini atolls in Micronesia

❑ **1952** UK begins nuclear tests (to 1991) on mainland Australia

❑ **1966** France begins nuclear tests in Tuamotu Islands (to 1996)

❑ **1975** Restrictions imposed on immigrants to Australia

❑ **1985** South Pacific Forum declares nuclear-free Pacific

❑ **1988** Bicentennial celebrations in Australia occasion Aboriginal protests

❑ **1998** Ethnic conflict in Solomon Islands (to 2000)

❑ **1999** Australian referendum rejects proposal on becoming republic

❑ **2000** Coup in Fiji ousts first ethnic Indian government

❑ **2001** Peace accord signed in Bougainville, Papua New Guinea, ending 13 years of conflict

see pages 68–69 for CHRONOLOGY 2003–2004

THE FORMATION OF THE MODERN WORLD

THE WORLD AS WE KNOW IT today, like all of the species that inhabit it, is the product of many thousands of years of evolution. The political and cultural map of the globe bears the hallmark of many varied courses of human development the world over. Nevertheless, much of the modern human geography of the planet can be traced to developments in the relatively recent past. The following pages chart the rise and fall of the various states and empires of the early modern and modern ages. Beginning with the first great achievement of European exploration, the "discovery" of the Americas in 1492, the maps show the way in which various European and Asian powers expanded their cultural and political influence and control down to the present day. This process left indelible cultural imprints in the form of language, religion, education, and systems of government on every part of the planet.

MAJOR MIGRATIONS SINCE 1500

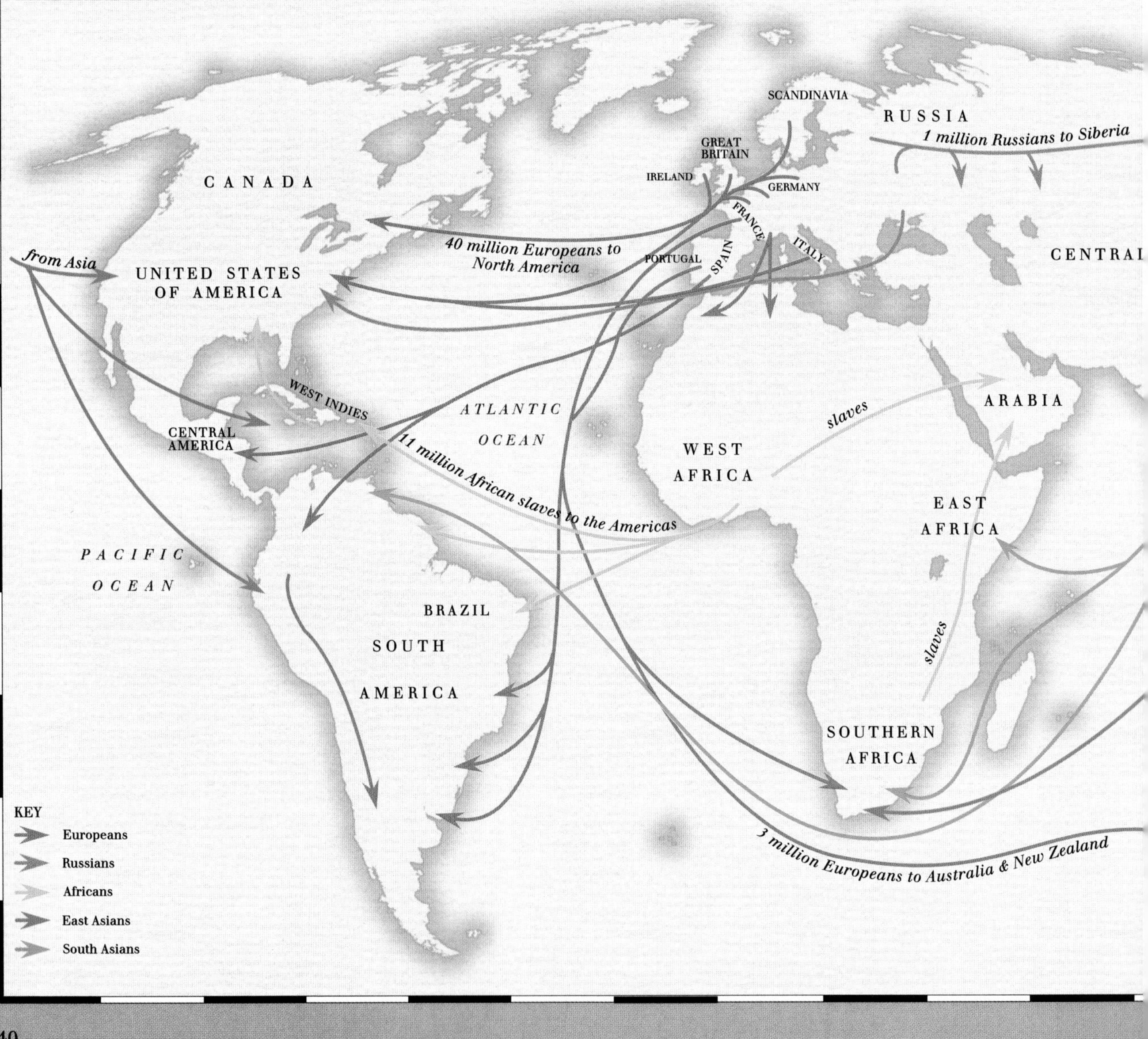
SCANDINAVIA
RUSSIA
1 million Russians to Siberia
GREAT BRITAIN
IRELAND
GERMANY
CANADA
FRANCE
ITALY
SPAIN
PORTUGAL
CENTRAL
from Asia
UNITED STATES OF AMERICA
40 million Europeans to North America
WEST INDIES
ATLANTIC OCEAN
ARABIA
slaves
CENTRAL AMERICA
WEST AFRICA
11 million African slaves to the Americas
EAST AFRICA
PACIFIC OCEAN
BRAZIL
SOUTH AMERICA
slaves
SOUTHERN AFRICA
3 million Europeans to Australia & New Zealand
KEY
Europeans
Russians
Africans
East Asians
South Asians

LANGUAGES OF THE WORLD

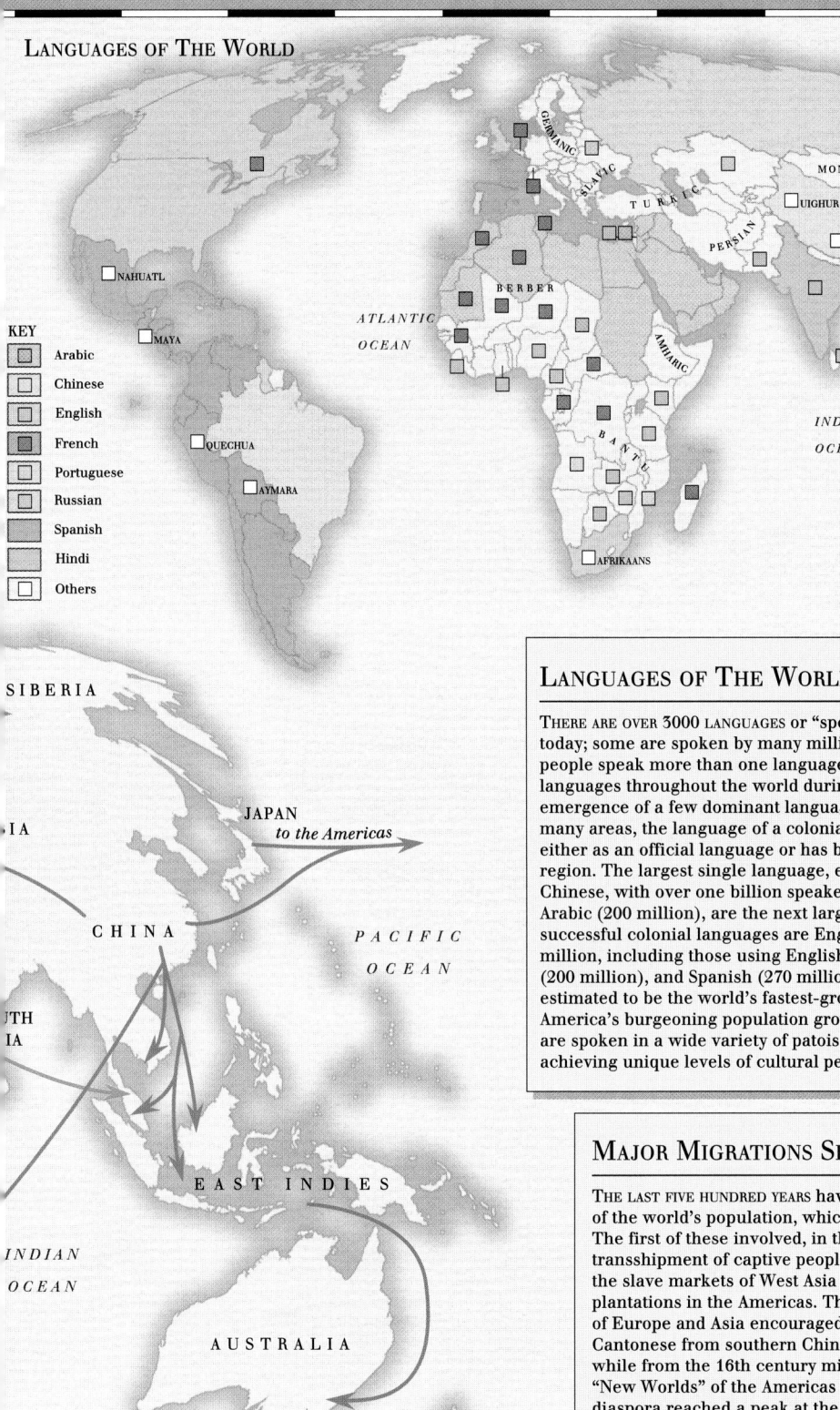

KEY
Arabic
Chinese
English
French
Portuguese
Russian
Spanish
Hindi
Others
GERMANIC
SLAVIC
TURKIC
PERSIAN
MONGOL
UIGHUR
MONGOL
KOREAN
JAPANESE
TIBETAN
AUSTRO-ASIATIC
FILIPINO, CEBUANO
AUSTRONESIAN
BERBER
AMHARIC
BANTU
AFRIKAANS
NAHUATL
MAYA
QUECHUA
AYMARA
ATLANTIC OCEAN
PACIFIC OCEAN
INDIAN OCEAN

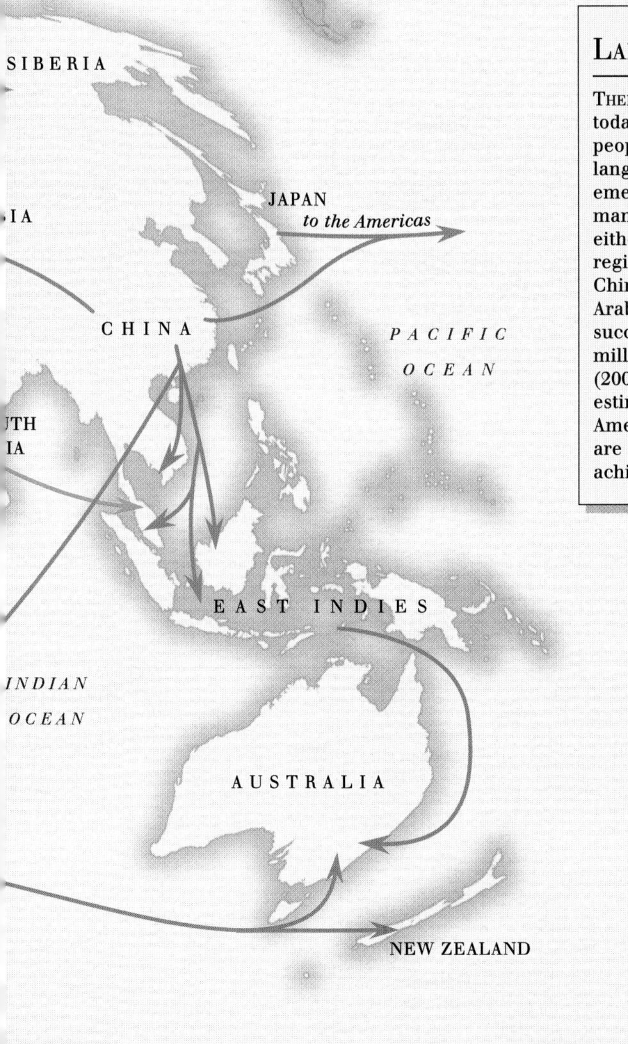
SIBERIA
JAPAN
to the Americas
CHINA
PACIFIC OCEAN
EAST INDIES
INDIAN OCEAN
AUSTRALIA
NEW ZEALAND

LANGUAGES OF THE WORLD

THERE ARE OVER 3000 LANGUAGES or "speech communities" in the world today; some are spoken by many millions, some by only dozens. Many people speak more than one language. The diffusion of the major languages throughout the world during the modern era has seen the emergence of a few dominant languages (shown on the map). In many areas, the language of a colonial power has been maintained either as an official language or has become the *lingua franca* of the region. The largest single language, encompassing many dialects, is Chinese, with over one billion speakers; Hindi (400 million) and Arabic (200 million), are the next largest first languages. The most successful colonial languages are English (estimated at up to 1500 million, including those using English as a second language), French (200 million), and Spanish (270 million). While the last is now estimated to be the world's fastest-growing language, owing to Latin America's burgeoning population growth, both English and French are spoken in a wide variety of patois, pidgins, and creoles, thus achieving unique levels of cultural penetration.

MAJOR MIGRATIONS SINCE 1500

THE LAST FIVE HUNDRED YEARS have witnessed a dramatic redistribution of the world's population, which occurred in a series of waves. The first of these involved, in the 16th–18th centuries, the mass transshipment of captive peoples from sub-Saharan Africa to supply the slave markets of West Asia and to work newly founded European plantations in the Americas. The rapidly growing populations of Europe and Asia encouraged a heavy flow of migration. The Cantonese from southern China spread throughout southeast Asia, while from the 16th century millions of Europeans emigrated to the "New Worlds" of the Americas and, later, Australasia. This European diaspora reached a peak at the end of the 19th century. Then, as the colonial empires coalesced in the early years of the 20th century, there was a final wave of global movement within them, when south and east Asians migrated to fill labor markets and exploit opportunities in Africa and the Americas. While homogeneous societies have developed in North America and Australia, many diverse ethnic communities remain scattered across the world.

The World in 1492

When Christopher Columbus sailed west from Europe, seeking a quicker route to Asia, he launched a process of discovery that was eventually to bring the disparate regions of the world into closer contact, to form the global map we know today. The largest political entity in the world at that time was the Chinese Ming empire. Culturally, the Islamic faith had forged a bond of religious unity which extended in a broad swathe from southeast Asia to the Atlantic coast of north Africa. Europe was a mêlée of rival monarchies; sub-Saharan Africa a patchwork of trading kingdoms; the Americas, a separate world of rich tribal cultures, with empires established only in Central America and the central Andes.

Global States and Territories

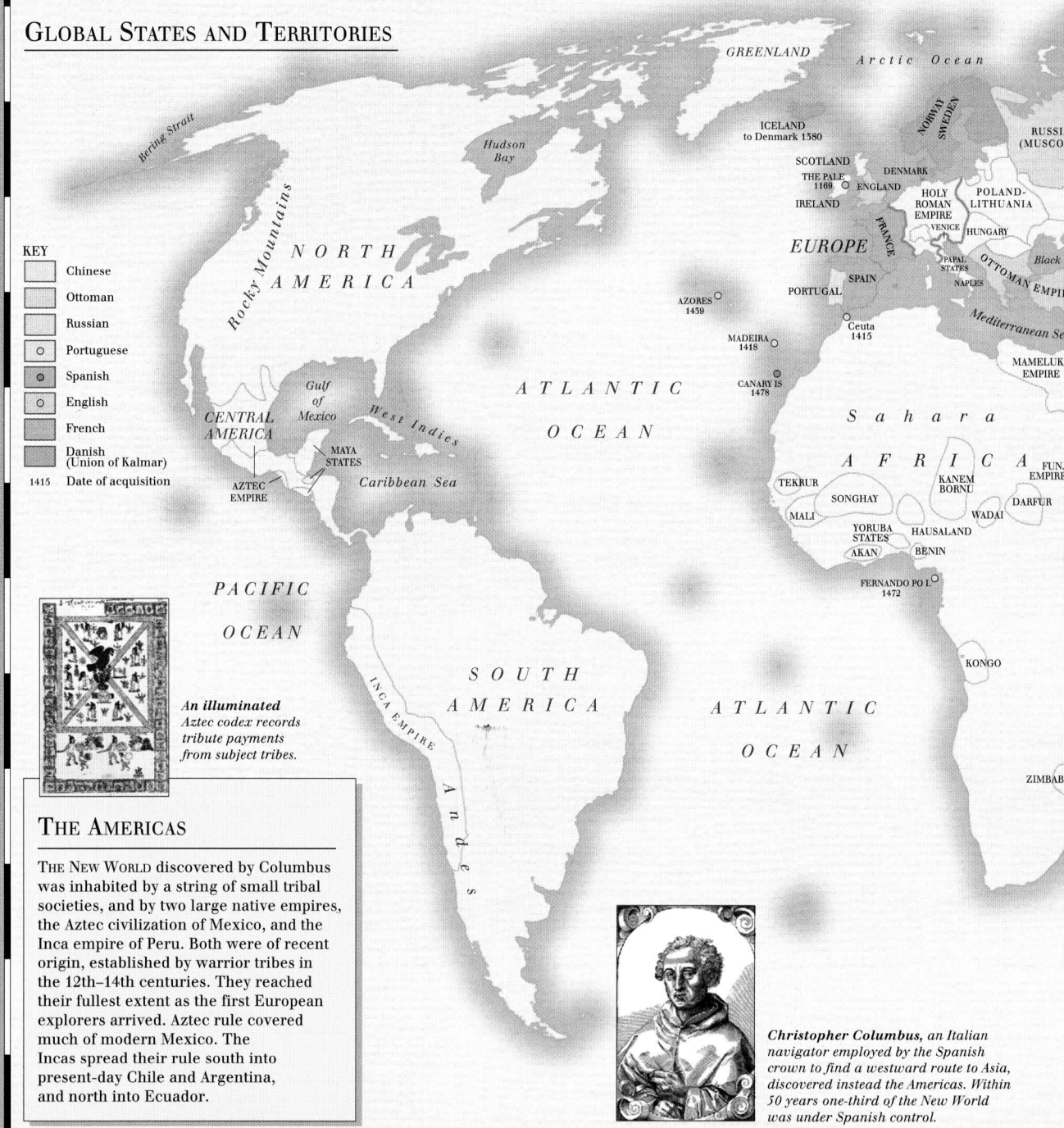

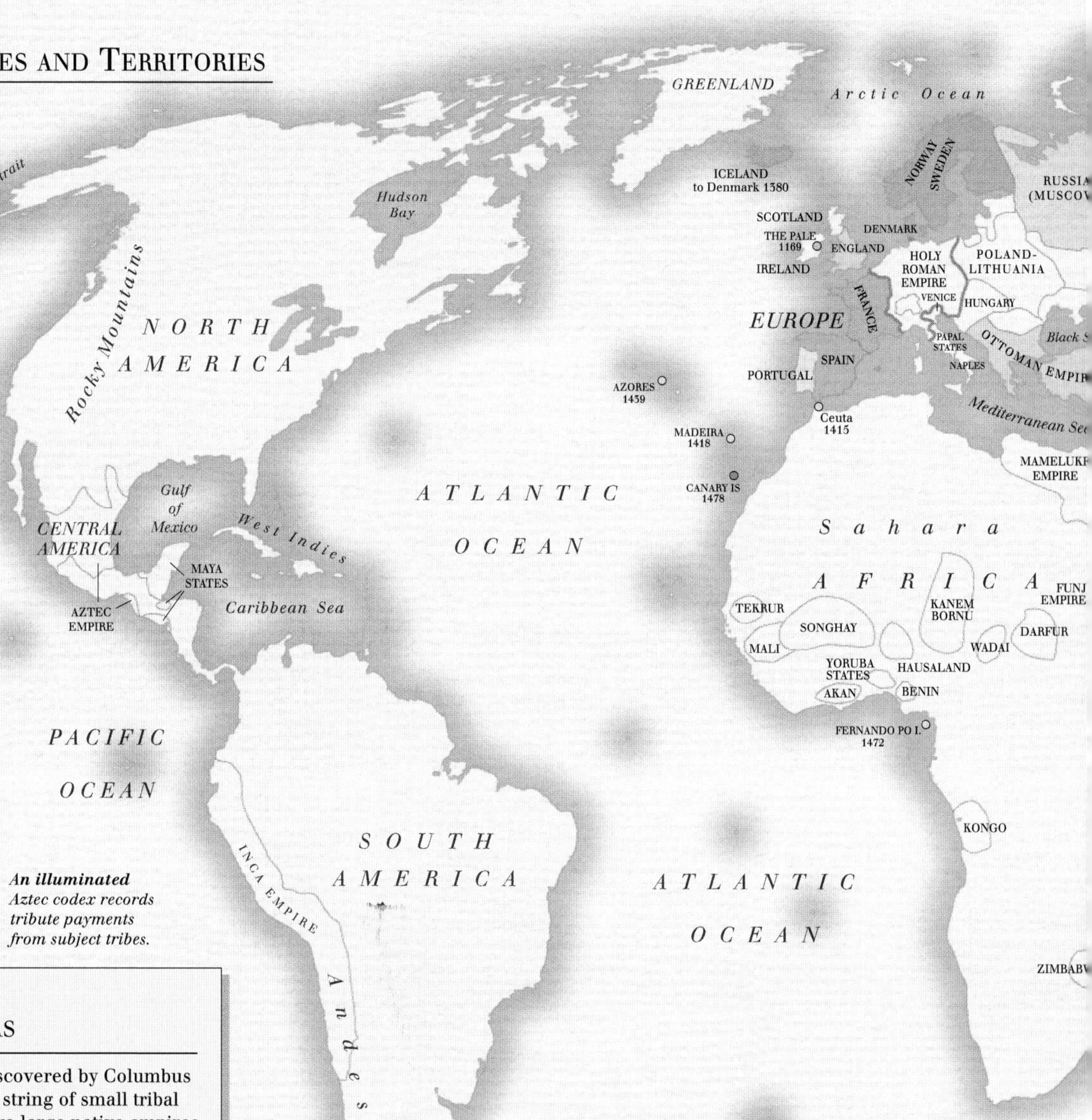
KEY
Chinese
Ottoman
Russian
Portuguese
Spanish
English
French
Danish (Union of Kalmar)
1415 Date of acquisition
GREENLAND
Arctic Ocean
Bering Strait
Hudson Bay
Rocky Mountains
NORTH AMERICA
ICELAND to Denmark 1380
NORWAY
SWEDEN
RUSSIA (MUSCOV
SCOTLAND
THE PALE 1169
ENGLAND
DENMARK
IRELAND
HOLY ROMAN EMPIRE
POLAND-LITHUANIA
VENICE
HUNGARY
FRANCE
EUROPE
PAPAL STATES
NAPLES
OTTOMAN EMPIR
Black S
SPAIN
PORTUGAL
AZORES 1459
Ceuta 1415
Mediterranean Se
MADEIRA 1418
MAMELUKE EMPIRE
CANARY IS 1478
Gulf of Mexico
West Indies
ATLANTIC OCEAN
CENTRAL AMERICA
MAYA STATES
AZTEC EMPIRE
Caribbean Sea
Sahara
AFRICA
FUNJ EMPIRE
TEKRUR
KANEM BORNU
SONGHAY
DARFUR
MALI
WADAI
YORUBA STATES
HAUSALAND
AKAN
BENIN
FERNANDO PO I. 1472
PACIFIC OCEAN
KONGO
SOUTH AMERICA
INCA EMPIRE
Andes
ATLANTIC OCEAN
ZIMBABW

An illuminated *Aztec codex records tribute payments from subject tribes.*

The Americas

The New World discovered by Columbus was inhabited by a string of small tribal societies, and by two large native empires, the Aztec civilization of Mexico, and the Inca empire of Peru. Both were of recent origin, established by warrior tribes in the 12th–14th centuries. They reached their fullest extent as the first European explorers arrived. Aztec rule covered much of modern Mexico. The Incas spread their rule south into present-day Chile and Argentina, and north into Ecuador.

Christopher Columbus, *an Italian navigator employed by the Spanish crown to find a westward route to Asia, discovered instead the Americas. Within 50 years one-third of the New World was under Spanish control.*

The Portuguese caravel, buoyant, sturdy, and lateen-rigged, was an ideal ocean-going vessel.

EUROPE

THOUGH CHRISTIAN EUROPE later transformed the exploration and settlement of the world, the Europe from which Columbus sailed was an unstable, violent continent, threatened by invaders from Asia to the east, and from the Ottoman Empire to the south. Civil wars and dynastic conflict resulted in shifting frontiers and small, militarily weak states. Only France, united by the late 15th century, Spain, a single monarchy from the 1490s, Portugal, and England were close to their modern forms.

EAST ASIA

THE MOST POWERFUL STATE in the world in 1492 was Ming China. Set up in 1386 after the collapse of Mongol power, the Ming dynasty ruled an area from Manchuria in the north to the borders of Vietnam in the south. Based on a traditional structure of bureaucratic control, the Ming emperors controlled their vast empire from Peking (Beijing), from where they launched punitive wars against the Mongols and Japanese pirates along the coast. Chinese culture and trade spread throughout east and southeast Asia, and Chinese navigators reached the Red Sea and the east African coast.

***Chinese junks** plied the China seas, and traded as far as the East Indies, Ceylon (Sri Lanka), and east Africa.*

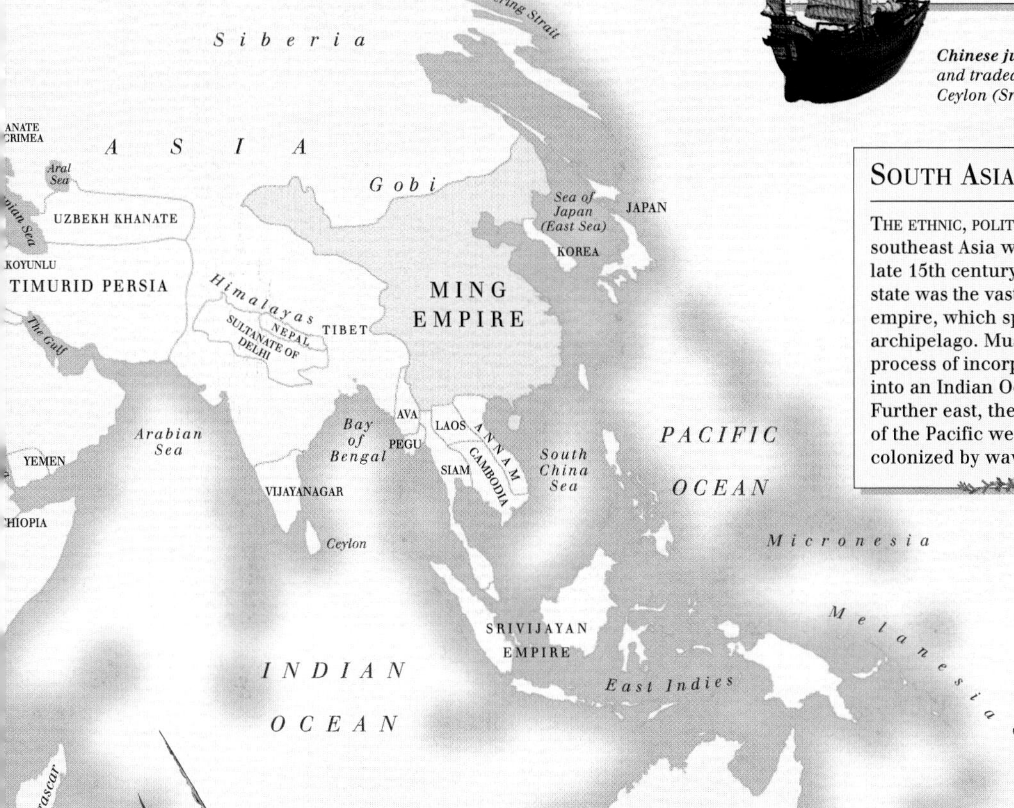

Bering Strait
Siberia
ASIA
Aral Sea
UZBEKH KHANATE
KOYUNLU
TIMURID PERSIA
The Gulf
Himalayas
NEPAL
SULTANATE OF DELHI
TIBET
Gobi
MING EMPIRE
Sea of Japan (East Sea)
JAPAN
KOREA
AVA
PEGU
LAOS
ANNAM
SIAM
CAMBODIA
Arabian Sea
Bay of Bengal
South China Sea
PACIFIC OCEAN
YEMEN
VIJAYANAGAR
Ceylon
Micronesia
Melanesia
SRIVIJAYAN EMPIRE
East Indies
INDIAN OCEAN
Madagascar
AUSTRALIA
NEW ZEALAND

SOUTH ASIA AND OCEANIA

THE ETHNIC, POLITICAL, and religious map of southeast Asia was largely in place by the late 15th century. However, the largest state was the vast Srivijayan Hindu–Buddhist empire, which spanned the East Indies archipelago. Muslim traders were in the process of incorporating this rich region into an Indian Ocean trading empire. Further east, the scattered island groups of the Pacific were being successively colonized by waves of Melanesians.

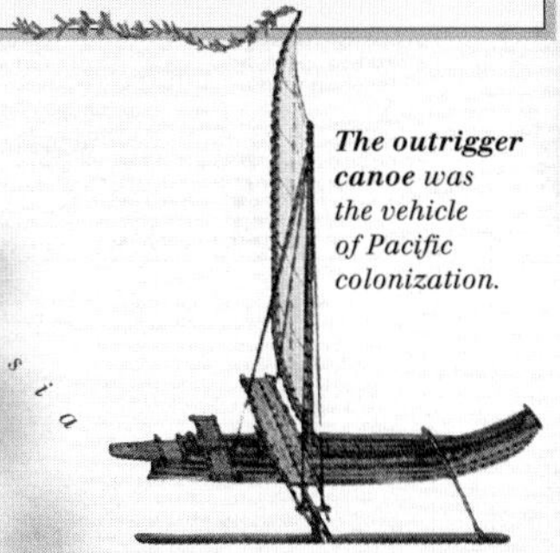

***The outrigger canoe** was the vehicle of Pacific colonization.*

***Arab dhows** built a trading network around the Indian Ocean.*

MIDDLE EAST AND AFRICA

AFTER CENTURIES OF INVASION from the Christian West and Asian nomadic empires, the Middle Eastern world stabilized around a revival of the Ottoman Empire. Vassal states extended across north Africa to Morocco, which linked the trading kingdoms of sub-Saharan Africa with the markets of Asia. The great cities of the Middle East surpassed those of Europe in wealth and learning.

***The magnetic compass,** in use since the 13th century, was a primary navigational tool for the first ocean-going explorers, although early compasses were not always reliable, and ships often went astray. Accurate navigation only came later with the invention of the chronometer.*

THE AGE OF DISCOVERY: 1492–1648

THE FIRST STATE to take advantage of the new age of exploration was Spain. By the middle of the 16th century, under the Emperor Charles V, Spain was established as the foremost European colonial power, and one of the richest and most powerful kingdoms in Europe. Spanish rule was extended over the whole of Central America, much of South America, Florida, and the Caribbean; in Asia, Spanish rule was established in the Philippines. Spain led the way in establishing European settler colonies overseas. By the middle of the 17th century, British, Dutch, and French colonists began to challenge Spanish dominance in the Americas and east Asia, while pirates around the world plundered Spain's wealthy merchant convoys.

GLOBAL STATES AND TERRITORIES

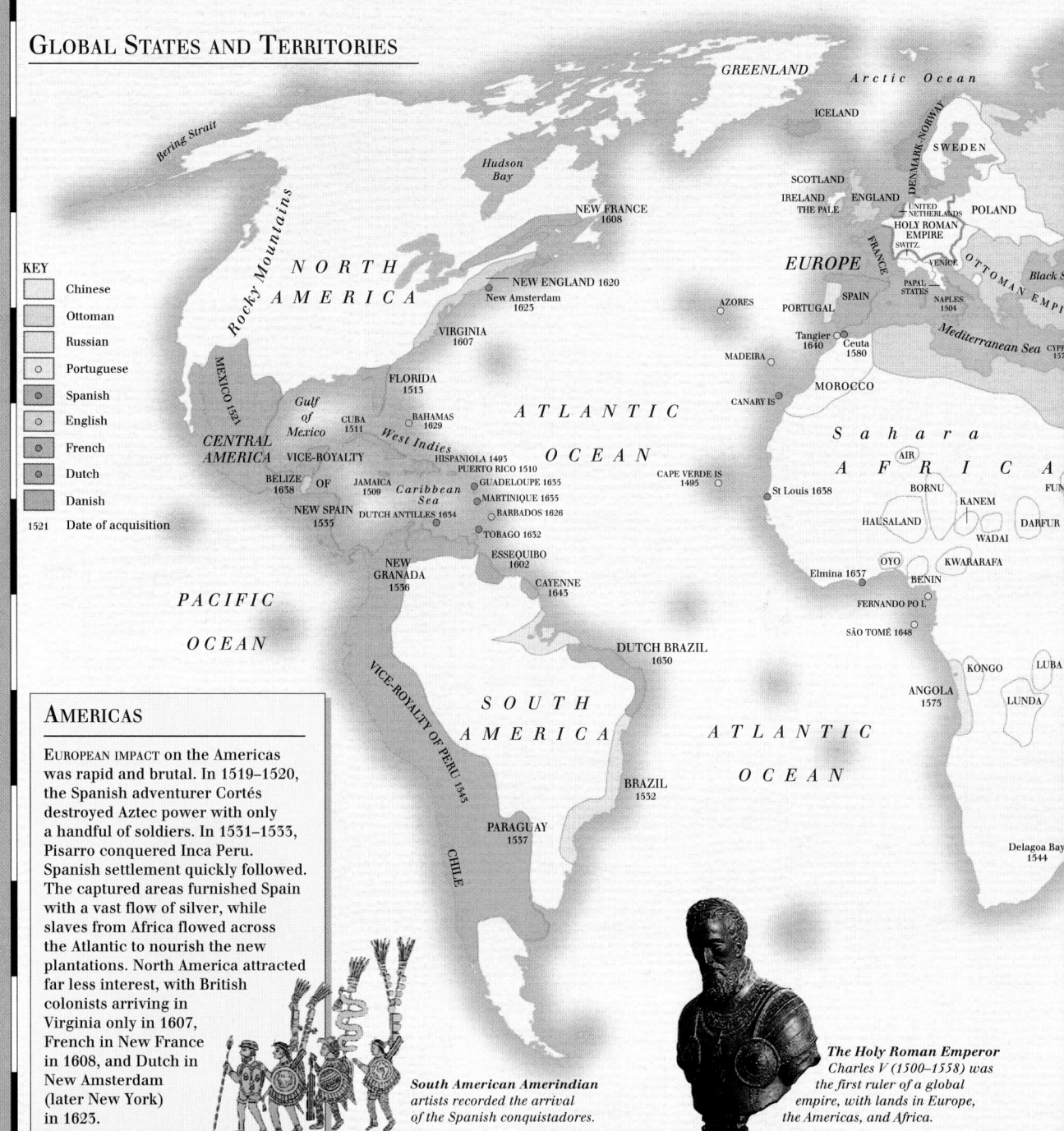

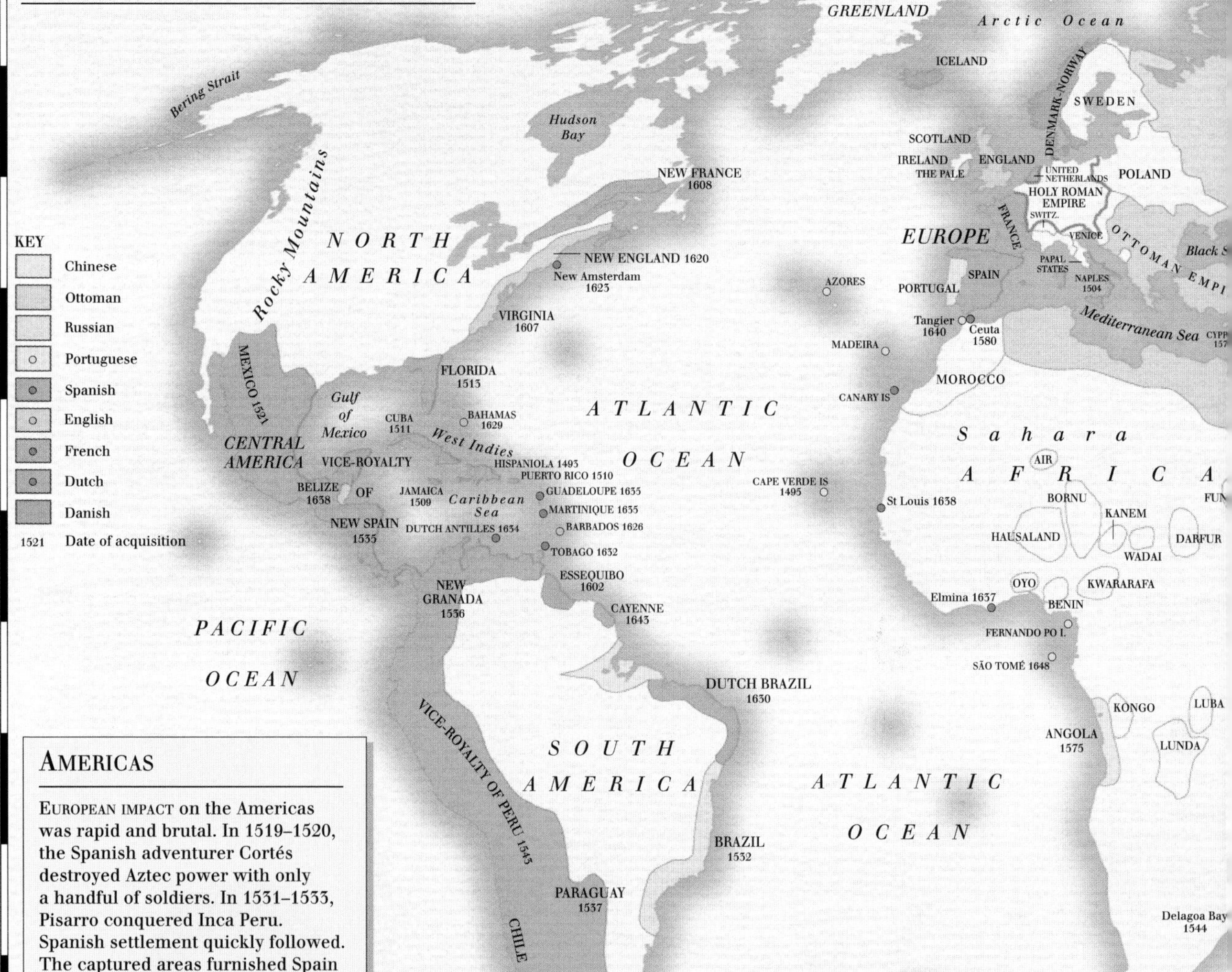
KEY
Chinese
Ottoman
Russian
Portuguese
Spanish
English
French
Dutch
Danish
1521 Date of acquisition
GREENLAND
Arctic Ocean
ICELAND
Bering Strait
Hudson Bay
DENMARK-NORWAY
SWEDEN
SCOTLAND
IRELAND
THE PALE
ENGLAND
UNITED NETHERLANDS
POLAND
HOLY ROMAN EMPIRE
SWITZ.
NEW FRANCE 1608
Rocky Mountains
NORTH AMERICA
EUROPE
FRANCE
VENICE
OTTOMAN EMPI
Black S
NEW ENGLAND 1620
New Amsterdam 1623
AZORES
PORTUGAL
SPAIN
PAPAL STATES
NAPLES 1504
VIRGINIA 1607
Tangier 1640
Ceuta 1580
Mediterranean Sea
CYPR 157
MADEIRA
MEXICO 1521
FLORIDA 1513
MOROCCO
CANARY IS
Gulf of Mexico
CUBA 1511
BAHAMAS 1629
ATLANTIC
West Indies
Sahara
CENTRAL AMERICA
VICE-ROYALTY
HISPANIOLA 1493
PUERTO RICO 1510
OCEAN
AIR
AFRICA
BELIZE 1638
OF
JAMAICA 1509
Caribbean Sea
GUADELOUPE 1635
MARTINIQUE 1635
CAPE VERDE IS 1495
St Louis 1638
BORNU
KANEM
FUN
NEW SPAIN 1535
DUTCH ANTILLES 1634
BARBADOS 1626
HAUSALAND
DARFUR
TOBAGO 1632
WADAI
ESSEQUIBO 1602
OYO
KWARARAFA
NEW GRANADA 1536
CAYENNE 1643
Elmina 1637
BENIN
PACIFIC OCEAN
FERNANDO PO I.
SÃO TOMÉ 1648
DUTCH BRAZIL 1630
KONGO
LUBA
ANGOLA 1575
LUNDA
VICE-ROYALTY OF PERU 1543
SOUTH AMERICA
ATLANTIC OCEAN
BRAZIL 1532
PARAGUAY 1537
CHILE
Delagoa Bay 1544

AMERICAS

EUROPEAN IMPACT on the Americas was rapid and brutal. In 1519–1520, the Spanish adventurer Cortés destroyed Aztec power with only a handful of soldiers. In 1531–1533, Pisarro conquered Inca Peru. Spanish settlement quickly followed. The captured areas furnished Spain with a vast flow of silver, while slaves from Africa flowed across the Atlantic to nourish the new plantations. North America attracted far less interest, with British colonists arriving in Virginia only in 1607, French in New France in 1608, and Dutch in New Amsterdam (later New York) in 1623.

***South American Amerindian** artists recorded the arrival of the Spanish conquistadores.*

***The Holy Roman Emperor** Charles V (1500–1558) was the first ruler of a global empire, with lands in Europe, the Americas, and Africa.*

EUROPE

FOR MORE THAN A CENTURY after Martin Luther inspired the Protestant Reformation in the 1520s, Europe was torn by religious wars. Scandinavia, England, and Scotland adopted the new beliefs, but elsewhere bitter civil conflicts led to the prolonged warfare and persecution known as the Thirty Years War. This ended in 1648; it destroyed wide areas of central Europe and decimated the German population, but resulted in a religious settlement which continues to the present. The Dutch Republic and northern Germany became Protestant while southern Germany, Poland, and southwest Europe remained Roman Catholic.

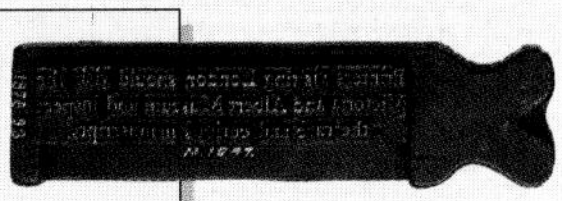

***Printing**, using movable type, was a key development in the dissemination of ideas, knowledge, and commerce in early modern Europe.*

ASIA

IN 1480, THE SMALL PRINCIPALITY OF MUSCOVY (Moscow) threw off Mongol control, and proceeded to expand Muscovite power over the whole of the area from the Arctic Ocean to the Caspian Sea. In the 1550s, the conquest of Kazan brought Russian power to the Urals, and over the next century it spread across Siberia, reaching the Pacific coast by 1649. Much of the area remained uninhabited, but to the south this new empire jostled uneasily with a string of central Asian Muslim khanates, and with the newly established Manchurian Ch'ing dynasty, which wrested control of China from the Ming in 1644.

***European navigators** and surveyors produced accurate maps and charts of their voyages.*

Bering Strait
RUSSIAN EMPIRE
Siberia
KAZAKHSTAN
ASIA
Aral Sea
KHWARIZM
KHOKAND KHANATE
KASHGAR KHANATE
UZBEKISTAN
Caspian Sea
SAFAVID PERSIA
The Gulf
Himalayas
TIBET
NEPAL
MUGHAL EMPIRE
MANCHU (CH'ING) EMPIRE
Sea of Japan (East Sea)
JAPAN
KOREA
Deshima 1641
PACIFIC OCEAN
OMAN 1508
Diu 1535
Surat 1608
Daman 1559
Bombay 1534
Hooghly 1640
ARAKAN
BURMA
Bay of Bengal
Arabian Sea
Goa 1510
Masulipatam 1611
Madras 1639
LAOS
ANNAM
SIAM
Macao 1557
FORMOSA 1624
South China Sea
PHILIPPINES from 1565
CEYLON 1505
Galle 1640
ETHIOPIA
Micronesia
Malacca 1641
MOLUCCAS from 1605
Melanesia
INDIAN OCEAN
PORTUGUESE EAST AFRICA from 1505
Makassar 1607
Batavia 1619
East Indies
1610
TIMOR
1618
Madagascar
AUSTRALIA
NEW ZEALAND

***The Indian Mughal** ruler Shahjahan (1592–1648), builder of the Taj Mahal.*

SOUTH ASIA AND OCEANIA

THE PORTUGUESE and the Spanish were the first European powers to open trade with the powerful Asian states of Mughal India and Ch'ing China. The Spanish opened trans-Pacific routes between Central America, the Philippines, and China. But the establishment of the Dutch and British East India companies in the early 17th century announced the advent of two new maritime powers.

***West African** trading kingdoms produced artifacts such as this bronze Portuguese soldier from Benin.*

AFRICA AND THE MIDDLE EAST

WHILE EUROPE WAS DIVIDED by the Reformation, Islam experienced a remarkable resurgence in the 16th century. The revival of the Ottoman Empire brought Islamic rule over much of southeast Europe. Islam spread along trade routes to sub-Saharan Africa. In east Africa, it spread south along the coast. Further east, Muslim rulers established new imperial states in Persia (Iran) and India.

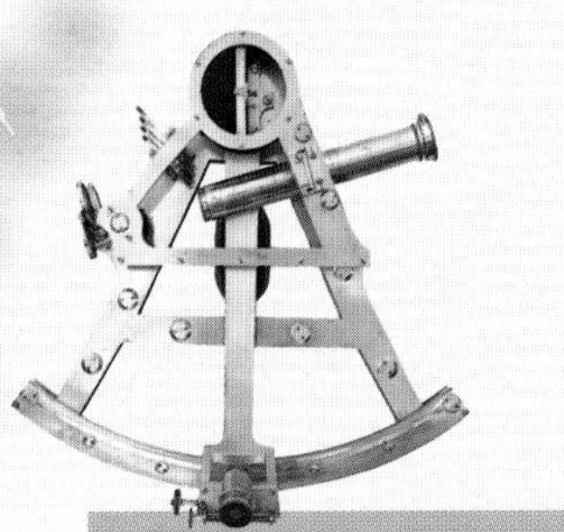

***The sextant** allowed navigators to take accurate measurements of heavenly bodies in relation to the horizon, thus allowing latitude to be calculated correctly. Early sextants had to be hand-held and were often used on shore rather than on board ship.*

THE AGE OF EXPANSION: 1648–1789

THE YEARS FROM the middle of the 17th century to the end of the 18th century saw a massive consolidation of European discovery and exploration, which took the form of colonial settlement and political expansion. This period also witnessed the beginning of a sharp rise in European population and in its economic strength, accompanied by rapid developments in the arts and sciences. All these factors powered European expansion – a process that would bring European culture to every part of the globe, gradually filling in the world map, and bringing it into often fatal contact with less robust indigenous cultures. By the last quarter of the 18th century, with Europe poised on the brink of political turmoil, only Africa and Australasia remained largely unmolested by European attentions.

GLOBAL STATES AND TERRITORIES

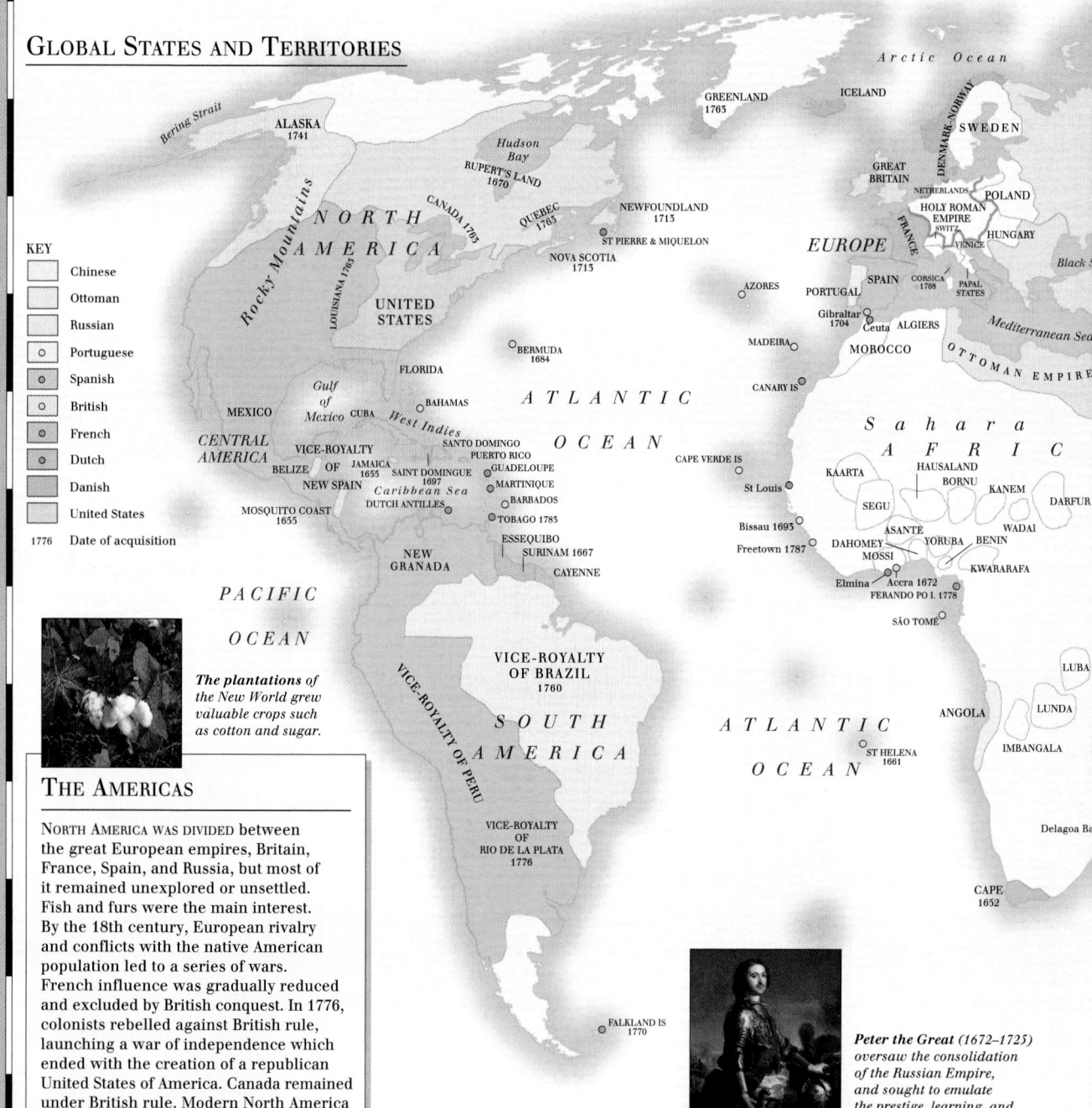

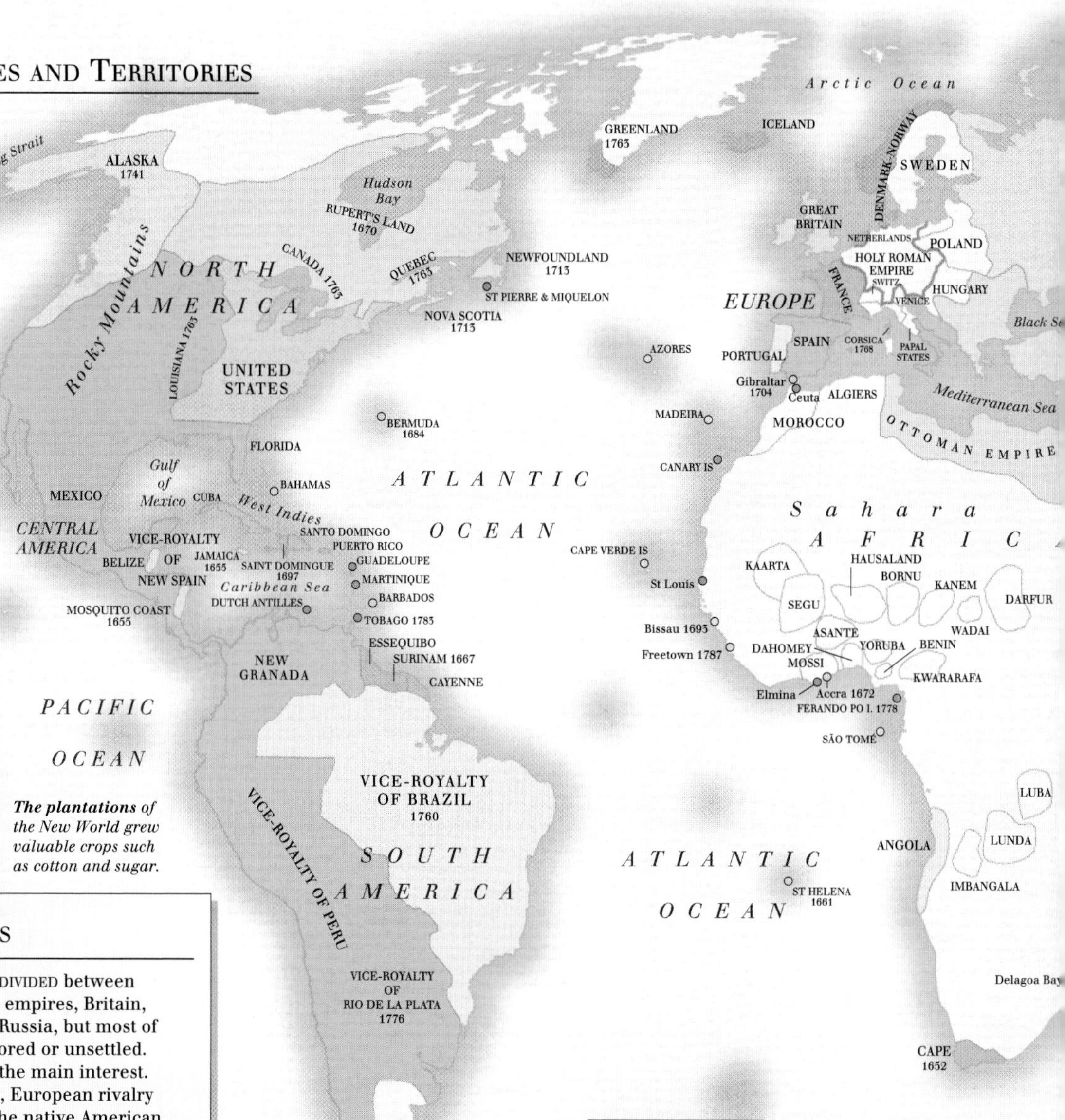
KEY
Chinese
Ottoman
Russian
Portuguese
Spanish
British
French
Dutch
Danish
United States
1776 Date of acquisition
Arctic Ocean
Bering Strait
ALASKA 1741
Hudson Bay
RUPERT'S LAND 1670
CANADA 1763
QUEBEC 1763
GREENLAND 1763
ICELAND
NEWFOUNDLAND 1713
ST PIERRE & MIQUELON
NOVA SCOTIA 1713
NORTH AMERICA
Rocky Mountains
LOUISIANA 1763
UNITED STATES
FLORIDA
Gulf of Mexico
MEXICO
CUBA
BAHAMAS
West Indies
BERMUDA 1684
CENTRAL AMERICA
VICE-ROYALTY OF NEW SPAIN
BELIZE
JAMAICA 1655
SANTO DOMINGO
PUERTO RICO
SAINT DOMINGUE 1697
GUADELOUPE
MARTINIQUE
BARBADOS
TOBAGO 1783
Caribbean Sea
DUTCH ANTILLES
MOSQUITO COAST 1655
ESSEQUIBO
SURINAM 1667
CAYENNE
NEW GRANADA
PACIFIC OCEAN
ATLANTIC OCEAN
VICE-ROYALTY OF BRAZIL 1760
VICE-ROYALTY OF PERU
SOUTH AMERICA
VICE-ROYALTY OF RIO DE LA PLATA 1776
FALKLAND IS 1770
SWEDEN
DENMARK-NORWAY
GREAT BRITAIN
NETHERLANDS
POLAND
HOLY ROMAN EMPIRE
SWITZ.
VENICE
HUNGARY
FRANCE
EUROPE
Black Sea
AZORES
PORTUGAL
SPAIN
CORSICA 1768
PAPAL STATES
Gibraltar 1704
Ceuta
ALGIERS
Mediterranean Sea
MADEIRA
MOROCCO
OTTOMAN EMPIRE
CANARY IS
Sahara
AFRICA
CAPE VERDE IS
St Louis
KAARTA
HAUSALAND
BORNU
KANEM
DARFUR
SEGU
WADAI
Bissau 1693
ASANTE
YORUBA
BENIN
Freetown 1787
DAHOMEY
MOSSI
KWARARAFA
Elmina
Accra 1672
FERANDO PO I. 1778
SÃO TOMÉ
LUBA
LUNDA
ANGOLA
IMBANGALA
ATLANTIC OCEAN
ST HELENA 1661
Delagoa Bay
CAPE 1652

***The plantations** of the New World grew valuable crops such as cotton and sugar.*

THE AMERICAS

NORTH AMERICA WAS DIVIDED between the great European empires, Britain, France, Spain, and Russia, but most of it remained unexplored or unsettled. Fish and furs were the main interest. By the 18th century, European rivalry and conflicts with the native American population led to a series of wars. French influence was gradually reduced and excluded by British conquest. In 1776, colonists rebelled against British rule, launching a war of independence which ended with the creation of a republican United States of America. Canada remained under British rule. Modern North America was gradually taking shape.

***Peter the Great** (1672–1725) oversaw the consolidation of the Russian Empire, and sought to emulate the prestige, learning, and sophistication of the western European monarchies.*

EUROPE

AFTER THE CRISIS of the Thirty Years War, Europe began to develop a more settled state system as successful dynastic houses imposed more centralized rule. The Habsburgs acquired control over Hungary and much of central Europe. Russia's frontiers pushed into Poland and the Ukraine. The French Bourbon monarchy became the most powerful in Europe. Its material wealth and culture made it a rival to the older empires of Asia. French became the common language of educated Europeans, and French philosophy led to the intellectual "Enlightenment."

***Isaac Newton** (1642–1727), the leading scientist of Europe's Age of Reason.*

ASIA

THE CH'ING DYNASTY forged the shape of modern China. By 1658 the whole of southern China was under Manchu control. Formosa (Taiwan) was occupied in 1683, outer Mongolia in 1697. A protectorate was established over Tibet in 1751. Over the course of this expansion, the population of China tripled and the economy boomed through trade in tea, porcelain, and silk with Russia and the West. Manchu China was powerful enough to resist incursions by the European empires, avoiding the fate of the crumbling Mughal empire in India, where Britain and France competed for trade and territory.

***Dutch and British** East Indiamen carried the vast European trade with Asia.*

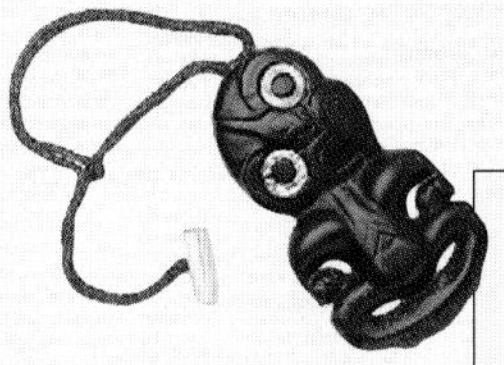

***Maori New Zealand** was one of the few indigenous cultures to remain untouched by European contact until the 19th century.*

OCEANIA

SOUTHEAST ASIA AND OCEANIA were areas of small, warring kingdoms, increasingly prey to the ambitions of European traders, first Spanish and Portuguese, then Dutch and British. Yet, by the late 18th century, there was still little formal colonization. Officially discovered by Europeans in the early 17th century, most of Australasia was still unexplored and unsettled, except for a number of small penal colonies set up by the British in New South Wales (1788) and Tasmania (1804).

USSIAN EMPIRE
Bering Strait
KAZAKHSTAN
ASIA
Aral Sea
MONGOLIA 1697
KHOKAND
SINKIANG 1760
TURKESTAN
MANCHU (CH'ING) EMPIRE
Sea of Japan (East Sea)
JAPAN
KOREA
PERSIA
AFGHANISTAN
Himalayas
TIBET 1751
NEPAL
Deshima
PACIFIC OCEAN
The Gulf
BALUCHISTAN
BENGAL 1757
MARATHA CONFEDERACY
BURMA
Chandernagore 1688
Surat
Diu
Daman
Bombay 1661
Bay of Bengal
FORMOSA 1683
Macao
Arabian Sea
NORTHERN CIRCARS 1756
SIAM
ANNAM
PHILIPPINES
Goa
South China Sea
MARIANAS 1668
ANDAMAN IS 1789
Mahé 1725
MADRAS
Pondicherry 1674
Karikal 1738
CAROLINE IS 1686
Micronesia
Galle
CEYLON 1658
Penang 1786
MALAYA
INDIAN OCEAN
MOLUCCAS
Melanesia
CHAGOS IS 1784
DUTCH EAST INDIES
TIMOR
GUESE AFRICA
Madagascar
RÉUNION 1662
Fort Dauphin 1766
AUSTRALIA
LORD HOWE I. 1788
NEW SOUTH WALES 1788
NEW ZEALAND

***African slavers** marched their human cargo from the interior to the coast for transshipment.*

AFRICA

DURING THE 17TH AND 18TH CENTURIES Africa was regarded by the rest of the world as a source of two things: gold and slaves. Some 13.5 million slaves were shipped in the 1700s, from the west coast and from Portuguese Angola. African dealers sold to European middlemen, who in turn sold on the surviving slaves. In northern and northeastern Africa, Arab slavers traded with the Ottoman Empire. But the rest of Africa remained isolated from the outside world.

***Harrison's chronometer,** invented in 1762, allowed navigators to measure time accurately, and thus calculate longitude correctly. This greatly reduced the risk of shipwreck and heralded the beginning of accurate mapping of the world.*

The Age of Revolution: 1789–1830

In 1789 royal power was shattered by the French Revolution. The collapse of the most powerful monarchy in Europe reverberated worldwide. The revolutions in France and America ushered in the idea of the modern nation state, and of popular representative government. Revolutionary outbreaks occurred elsewhere in Europe, and overseas colonies in Latin America won their independence. At the same time, an industrial revolution was taking place in Europe, transforming the old trading economy into a manufacturing base which would require a global supply of raw materials and a global market to fuel it. The revolutionary years thus marked the beginning of the modern political and economic world order.

Global States and Territories

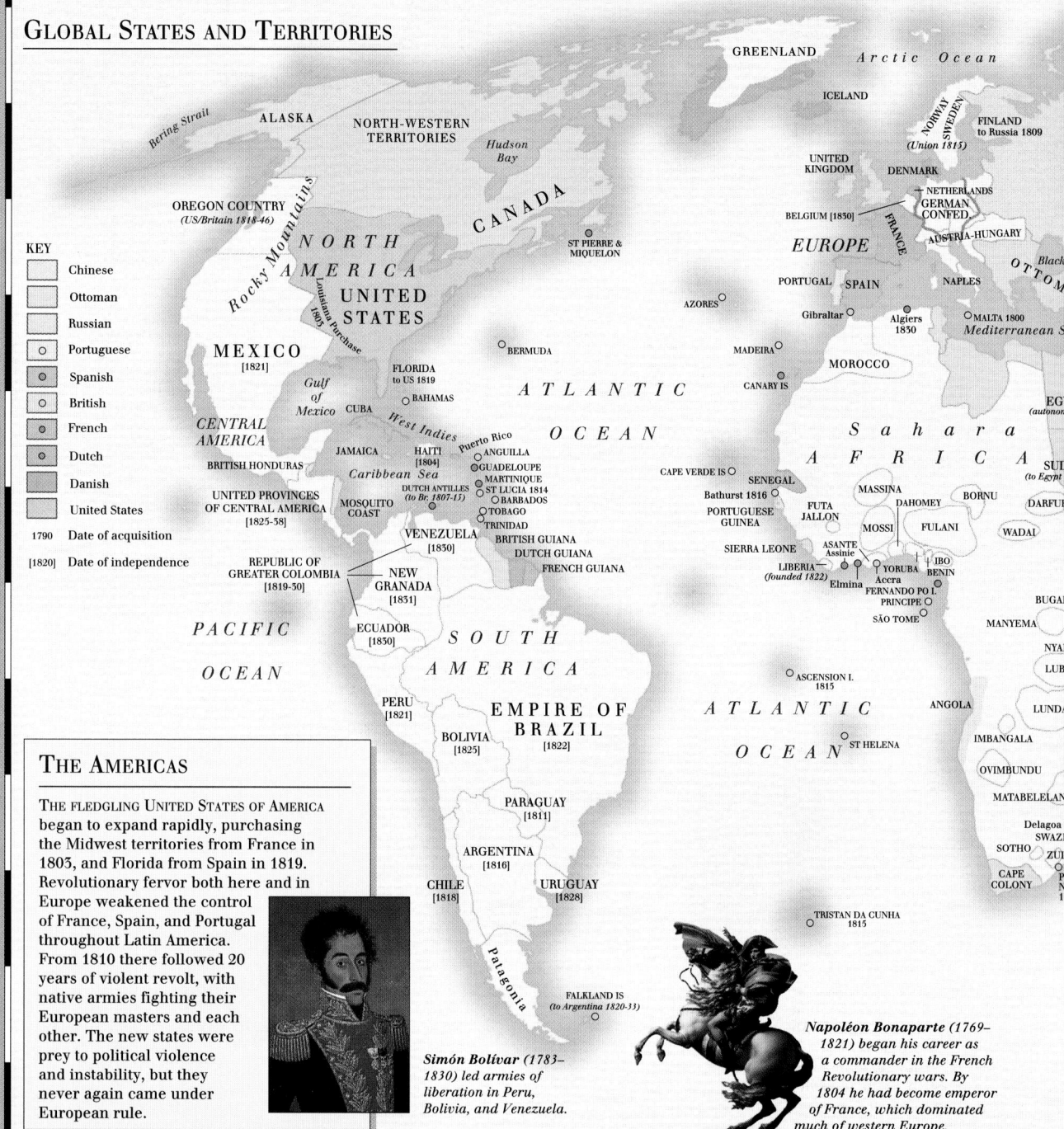

GREENLAND
Arctic Ocean
ICELAND
NORWAY
SWEDEN
(Union 1815)
FINLAND
to Russia 1809
UNITED KINGDOM
DENMARK
NETHERLANDS
GERMAN CONFED.
BELGIUM [1830]
FRANCE
AUSTRIA-HUNGARY
EUROPE
OTTOM
Black
PORTUGAL
SPAIN
NAPLES
Gibraltar
Algiers 1830
MALTA 1800
Mediterranean Se
AZORES
MADEIRA
MOROCCO
CANARY IS
EGY
(autonom
Sahara
AFRICA
SUD
(to Egypt 1
CAPE VERDE IS
SENEGAL
Bathurst 1816
PORTUGUESE GUINEA
FUTA JALLON
MASSINA
DAHOMEY
BORNU
DARFUR
MOSSI
FULANI
WADAI
SIERRA LEONE
ASANTE
Assinie
LIBERIA
(founded 1822)
Elmina
Accra
YORUBA
IBO
BENIN
FERNANDO PO I.
PRINCIPE
SÃO TOME
BUGAN
MANYEMA
NYAM
LUBA
ASCENSION I.
1815
ANGOLA
LUNDA
ATLANTIC OCEAN
ST HELENA
IMBANGALA
OVIMBUNDU
MATABELELANI
Delagoa B
SWAZI
SOTHO
ZULU
CAPE COLONY
TRISTAN DA CUNHA
1815
Bering Strait
ALASKA
NORTH-WESTERN TERRITORIES
Hudson Bay
CANADA
OREGON COUNTRY
(US/Britain 1818-46)
Rocky Mountains
NORTH AMERICA
UNITED STATES
Louisiana Purchase 1803
ST PIERRE & MIQUELON
KEY
Chinese
Ottoman
Russian
Portuguese
Spanish
British
French
Dutch
Danish
United States
1790 Date of acquisition
[1820] Date of independence
MEXICO
[1821]
BERMUDA
FLORIDA
to US 1819
BAHAMAS
Gulf of Mexico
CUBA
West Indies
ATLANTIC OCEAN
CENTRAL AMERICA
JAMAICA
HAITI
[1804]
Puerto Rico
ANGUILLA
GUADELOUPE
MARTINIQUE
ST LUCIA 1814
BARBADOS
TOBAGO
TRINIDAD
BRITISH HONDURAS
Caribbean Sea
DUTCH ANTILLES
(to Br. 1807-15)
UNITED PROVINCES OF CENTRAL AMERICA
[1825-38]
MOSQUITO COAST
VENEZUELA
[1830]
BRITISH GUIANA
DUTCH GUIANA
FRENCH GUIANA
REPUBLIC OF GREATER COLOMBIA
[1819-30]
NEW GRANADA
[1831]
PACIFIC OCEAN
ECUADOR
[1830]
SOUTH AMERICA
PERU
[1821]
EMPIRE OF BRAZIL
[1822]
BOLIVIA
[1825]
PARAGUAY
[1811]
ARGENTINA
[1816]
CHILE
[1818]
URUGUAY
[1828]
Patagonia
FALKLAND IS
(to Argentina 1820-33)

The Americas

The fledgling United States of America began to expand rapidly, purchasing the Midwest territories from France in 1803, and Florida from Spain in 1819. Revolutionary fervor both here and in Europe weakened the control of France, Spain, and Portugal throughout Latin America. From 1810 there followed 20 years of violent revolt, with native armies fighting their European masters and each other. The new states were prey to political violence and instability, but they never again came under European rule.

***Simón Bolívar** (1783–1830) led armies of liberation in Peru, Bolivia, and Venezuela.*

***Napoléon Bonaparte** (1769–1821) began his career as a commander in the French Revolutionary wars. By 1804 he had become emperor of France, which dominated much of western Europe.*

EUROPE

UNDER NAPOLÉON BONAPARTE, France subordinated a large part of Europe and destroyed the old feudal order. Napoléon helped to shape the new nation states that emerged in 19th-century Europe – Belgium, Italy, and Germany. He gave much of Europe its modern legal code and systems of measurement, education, and local government.

***Steam-powered engines** transformed the European industrial economy.*

ASIA

THE PRINCIPAL COLONIAL POWER in Asia was Russia, whose consolidation of its empire in northern and central Asia continued throughout the 19th century. But now the Dutch began to extend their control of the East Indies, while a bitter struggle between the British and the French was conducted in and around the Indian Ocean. France was gradually forced to concede many of its footholds in India, where the British East India Company rapidly extended its interests by a mixture of diplomacy and military force. But the elusive key to Asia's largest markets remained the slumbering giant of Ch'ing China, whose Manchu rulers, like the shoguns of Japan, remained unimpressed by European overtures.

***The spices of the East Indies,** such as pepper, were among the most highly valued trade commodities from Asia.*

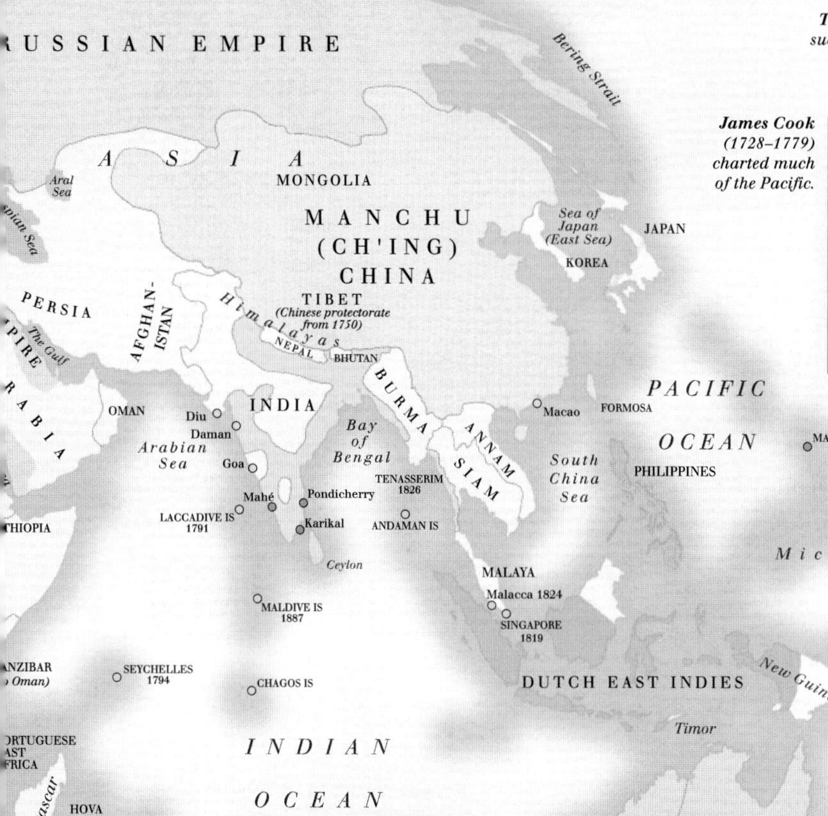
RUSSIAN EMPIRE
Bering Strait
ASIA
Aral Sea
MONGOLIA
MANCHU (CH'ING) CHINA
Sea of Japan (East Sea)
JAPAN
KOREA
PERSIA
AFGHANISTAN
TIBET (Chinese protectorate from 1750)
Himalayas
NEPAL
BHUTAN
The Gulf
ARABIA
OMAN
Diu
Daman
INDIA
Arabian Sea
Goa
Bay of Bengal
BURMA
ANNAM
SIAM
Macao
FORMOSA
PACIFIC OCEAN
MARIANAS
South China Sea
PHILIPPINES
TENASSERIM 1826
Mahé
Pondicherry
Karikal
LACCADIVE IS 1791
ANDAMAN IS
ETHIOPIA
Ceylon
CAROLINE IS
Micronesia
MALAYA
Malacca 1824
SINGAPORE 1819
MALDIVE IS 1887
Melanesia
New Guinea
SEYCHELLES 1794
CHAGOS IS
DUTCH EAST INDIES
Timor
INDIAN OCEAN
Madagascar
HOVA KINGDOM
MAURITIUS 1810
RÉUNION
WESTERN AUSTRALIA 1829
NEW SOUTH WALES
AUSTRALIA
LORD HOWE I.
NEW ZEALAND
CHATHAM IS 1791
TASMANIA (Van Diemen's Land)
AUCKLAND IS 1806
MACQUARIE IS 1811

***James Cook** (1728–1779) charted much of the Pacific.*

OCEANIA

THOUGH PORTUGUESE and Dutch explorers had confirmed the existence of Australasia in the 17th century, it was not until the voyages of Captain Cook in the 1770s that the geography of the Pacific was established, and the fertile eastern coast of Australia was explored and charted. Over the next 30 years, small settlements were established around the coast; by 1829, Britain had brought the whole of Australia under the British flag.

***The first European** migrants to Africa settled in Cape Colony.*

AFRICA

THE NORTHERN REGIONS OF AFRICA were part of the vast Islamic Ottoman Empire; from here Islam spread south to west Africa and the Horn of Africa. Holy wars (or *jihads*) in the late 18th and early 19th centuries completed the conversion to Islam of much of Saharan and sub-Saharan Africa. Large tribal kingdoms flourished in the Congo basin and southern Africa.

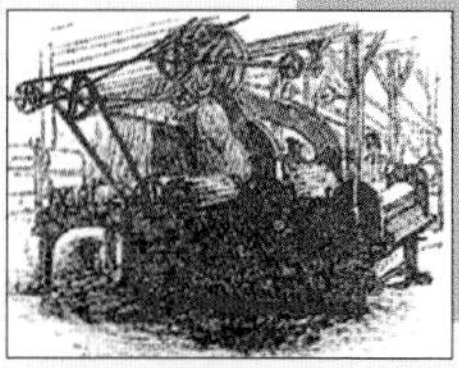

***The development** during the European industrial revolution of mechanized manufacturing plant and machinery, such as power looms, gave Europe effective control of a booming global trade in raw materials and mass-manufactured commodities.*

THE AGE OF EMPIRE: 1830–1914

THE 19TH CENTURY was dominated by the spread of modern industry and transportation, and the expansion of European trade and influence worldwide. Industry made Europe rich and powerful; its capital cities were monuments to the self-confidence of the new European age. Railroads and steamships revolutionized communications, bringing a stream of industrial goods, technical know-how, and European settlers across America, Africa, and Asia. Modern industry and weapons brought Europe to the summit of global influence. In these developments lay the origins of the division of the world into rich and poor regions; a developed, prosperous north and an underdeveloped, dependent south.

GLOBAL STATES AND TERRITORIES

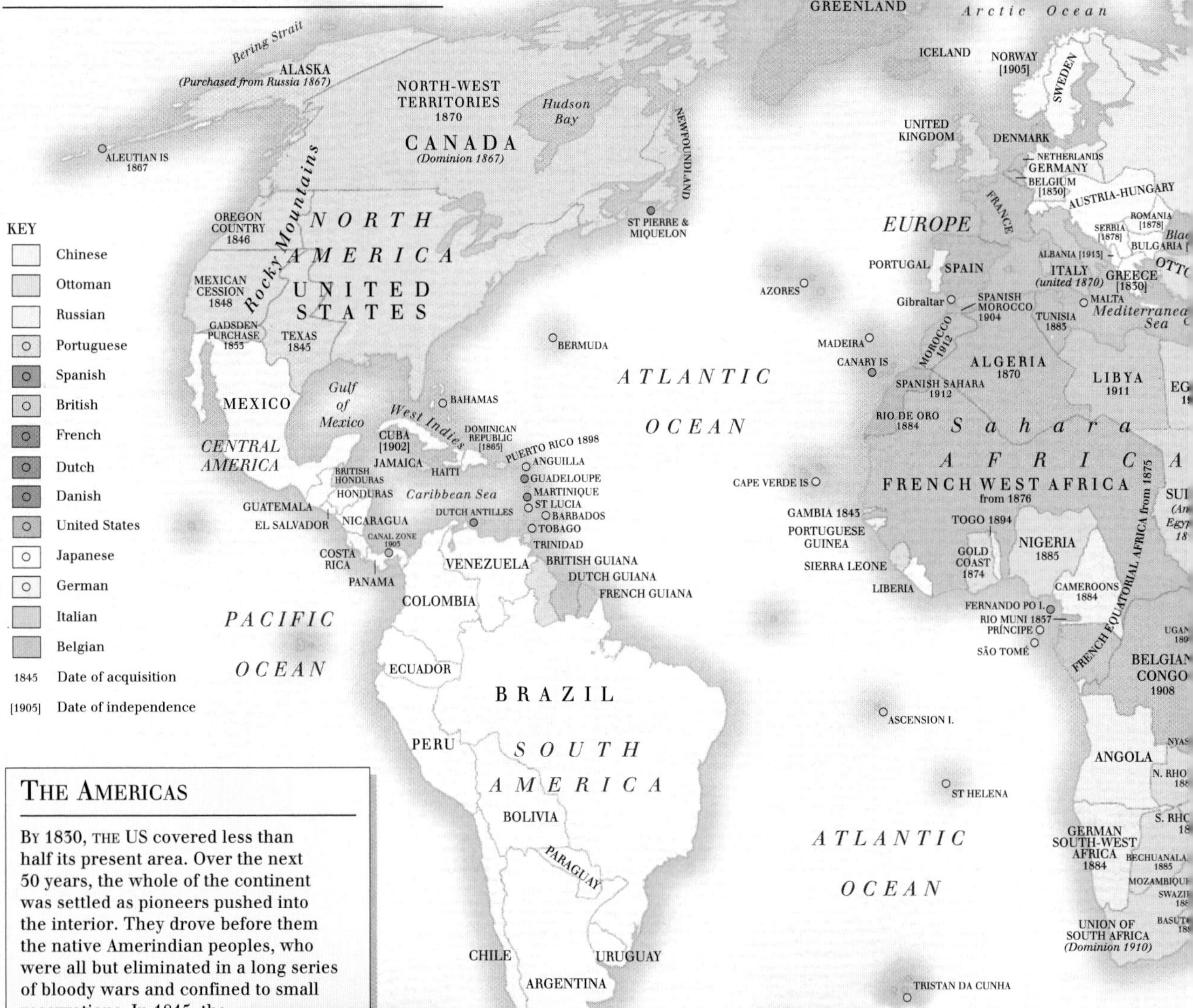

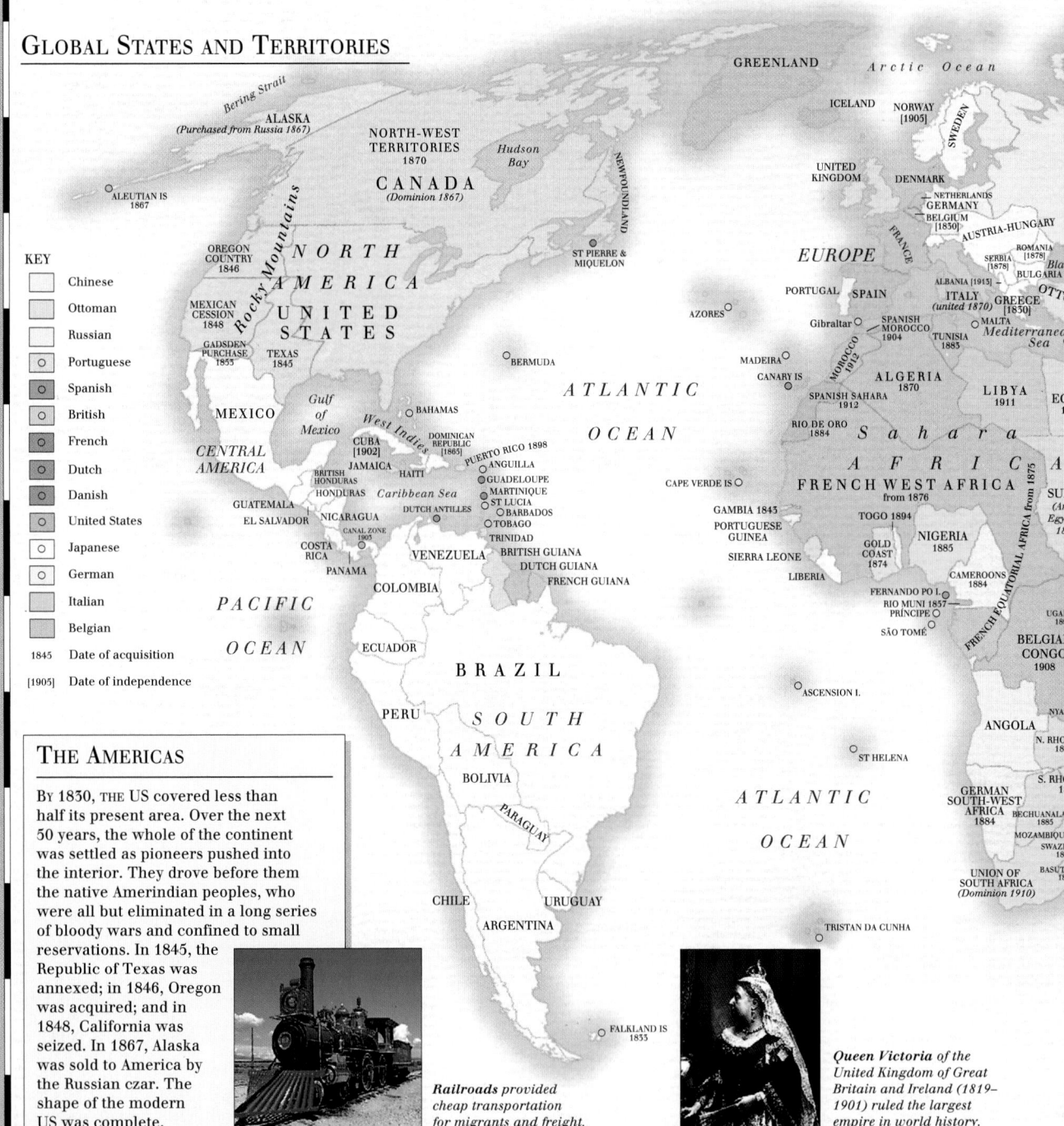

KEY
Chinese
Ottoman
Russian
Portuguese
Spanish
British
French
Dutch
Danish
United States
Japanese
German
Italian
Belgian
1845 Date of acquisition
[1905] Date of independence
Bering Strait
ALASKA
(Purchased from Russia 1867)
ALEUTIAN IS 1867
NORTH-WEST TERRITORIES 1870
CANADA
(Dominion 1867)
Hudson Bay
NEWFOUNDLAND
ST PIERRE & MIQUELON
Rocky Mountains
OREGON COUNTRY 1846
NORTH AMERICA
UNITED STATES
MEXICAN CESSION 1848
GADSDEN PURCHASE 1853
TEXAS 1845
MEXICO
Gulf of Mexico
BERMUDA
BAHAMAS
West Indies
CUBA [1902]
DOMINICAN REPUBLIC [1865]
PUERTO RICO 1898
HAITI
JAMAICA
ANGUILLA
GUADELOUPE
MARTINIQUE
ST LUCIA
BARBADOS
TOBAGO
TRINIDAD
CENTRAL AMERICA
BRITISH HONDURAS
HONDURAS
Caribbean Sea
DUTCH ANTILLES
GUATEMALA
EL SALVADOR
NICARAGUA
CANAL ZONE 1903
COSTA RICA
PANAMA
VENEZUELA
BRITISH GUIANA
DUTCH GUIANA
FRENCH GUIANA
COLOMBIA
PACIFIC OCEAN
ECUADOR
BRAZIL
PERU
SOUTH AMERICA
BOLIVIA
PARAGUAY
CHILE
URUGUAY
ARGENTINA
FALKLAND IS 1833
GREENLAND
Arctic Ocean
ICELAND
NORWAY [1905]
SWEDEN
UNITED KINGDOM
DENMARK
NETHERLANDS
GERMANY
BELGIUM [1830]
AUSTRIA-HUNGARY
FRANCE
EUROPE
SERBIA [1878]
ROMANIA [1878]
BULGARIA
PORTUGAL
SPAIN
ALBANIA [1913]
ITALY (united 1870)
GREECE [1830]
MALTA
Mediterranean Sea
AZORES
Gibraltar
SPANISH MOROCCO 1904
TUNISIA 1883
MADEIRA
MOROCCO 1912
CANARY IS
ALGERIA 1870
LIBYA 1911
SPANISH SAHARA 1912
ATLANTIC OCEAN
RIO DE ORO 1884
Sahara
AFRICA
CAPE VERDE IS
FRENCH WEST AFRICA from 1876
GAMBIA 1843
PORTUGUESE GUINEA
TOGO 1894
SIERRA LEONE
GOLD COAST 1874
NIGERIA 1885
LIBERIA
CAMEROONS 1884
FRENCH EQUATORIAL AFRICA from 1875
FERNANDO PO I.
RIO MUNI 1857
PRÍNCIPE
SÃO TOMÉ
BELGIAN CONGO 1908
ASCENSION I.
ANGOLA
ST HELENA
GERMAN SOUTH-WEST AFRICA 1884
BECHUANALAND 1885
MOZAMBIQUE
UNION OF SOUTH AFRICA (Dominion 1910)
TRISTAN DA CUNHA

THE AMERICAS

BY 1830, THE US covered less than half its present area. Over the next 50 years, the whole of the continent was settled as pioneers pushed into the interior. They drove before them the native Amerindian peoples, who were all but eliminated in a long series of bloody wars and confined to small reservations. In 1845, the Republic of Texas was annexed; in 1846, Oregon was acquired; and in 1848, California was seized. In 1867, Alaska was sold to America by the Russian czar. The shape of the modern US was complete.

***Railroads** provided cheap transportation for migrants and freight.*

***Queen Victoria** of the United Kingdom of Great Britain and Ireland (1819–1901) ruled the largest empire in world history.*

EUROPE

IN THE 19TH CENTURY, Europe was transformed into an industrial economy. In the new industrial cities, pressure developed for liberal reforms and parliamentary politics. Nationalists created new states in Germany, Italy, Greece, Serbia, and Belgium. While the modern map of Europe gradually began to take shape, European imperialists brought still more areas of the world under their control.

***Sailing ships** carried most oceanic trade until 1900.*

ASIA

BUILDING ON COLONIAL INTERESTS that stretched back into the 18th century, Britain and France transformed the political world of south Asia. Britain extended its rule in India and, in 1885, Burma was brought under British control. The Vietnamese and Chinese Empires were pressured by Europeans anxious to trade and to spread Christianity: the Ch'ing empire conceded areas of influence; the Vietnamese empire resisted and was brought under French domination by force. By the 1890s the whole of southern Asia except for Siam was dominated by Europe, which created the modern state structure of the region.

***The Japanese emperor Meiji** (1852–1912) opened Japan to Western trade and influence.*

***The colonization** of Australia and New Zealand was based on sheep farming.*

OCEANIA

DURING THE 19TH century, Australia and New Zealand remained closely tied to the British homeland. British settlers came to farm and later to prospect for gold and other valuable minerals. In 1840, New Zealand came under British rule and the native Maoris were forced off the land. Not until 1872 was the continent of Australia traversed, and not until 1901 was a single state, the Commonwealth of Australia, proclaimed.

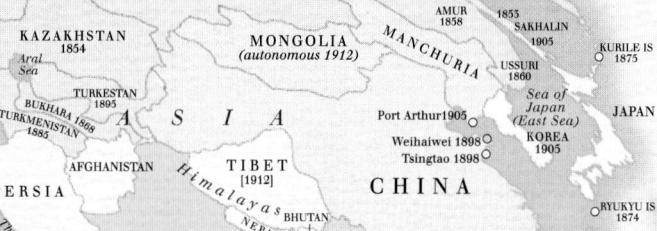

RUSSIAN EMPIRE
Bering Strait
KAZAKHSTAN 1854
Aral Sea
MONGOLIA (autonomous 1912)
MANCHURIA
AMUR 1858
1853 SAKHALIN 1905
KURILE IS 1875
USSURI 1860
TURKESTAN 1895
BUKHARA 1868
TURKMENISTAN 1885
ASIA
Port Arthur 1905
Weihaiwei 1898
Tsingtao 1898
Sea of Japan (East Sea)
KOREA 1905
JAPAN
AFGHANISTAN
TIBET [1912]
Himalayas
PERSIA
CHINA
NEPAL
BHUTAN
RYUKYU IS 1874
The Gulf
BAHRAIN 1861
ARABIA
OMAN
Chandernagore
INDIA
BURMA
Diu
Daman
Bay of Bengal
Arabian Sea
Goa
Macao
Hong Kong 1841
FORMOSA 1895
PACIFIC OCEAN
FRENCH INDO-CHINA 1887
SIAM
South China Sea
PHILIPPINES 1898
MARIANAS 1899
GUAM 1898
HADHRAMAUT 1888
Aden 1839
SOCOTRA 1886
Mahé
Pondicherry
LACCADIVE IS
Karikal
ANDAMAN IS
CEYLON
BRITISH SOMALILAND 1884
FRENCH SOMALILAND 1884
NICOBAR IS 1869
BRITISH NORTH BORNEO 1881
MALAYA
SARAWAK 1888
CAROLINE IS 1899
Micronesia
MALDIVE IS
BISMARCK ARCHIPELAGO 1884
NAURU 1888
Melanesia
SEYCHELLES
CHAGOS IS
DUTCH EAST INDIES
NEW GUINEA
PAPUA 1906
SOLOMON IS 1893
ZANZIBAR 1890
COMORO IS 1886
CHRISTMAS I. 1888
COCOS IS 1857
TIMOR
INDIAN OCEAN
MADAGASCAR 1882
MAURITIUS
RÉUNION
NEW CALEDONIA 1853
AUSTRALIA (Commonwealth 1901)
NORFOLK ISLAND
NEW ZEALAND 1840 (Dominion 1907)
CHATHAM IS.
TASMANIA
AUCKLAND IS
MACQUARIE IS

***Quinine** – the cure for malaria.*

***New medicines** made the colonization of Africa possible.*

AFRICA

THE POLITICAL STRUCTURE of independent Africa was torn up by encroaching European empires. As native societies reacted violently to European intrusion, so European military and political power was increased to secure European interests. In 1884, in Berlin, the European powers divided Africa between them. The "Partition of Africa" established the modern frontiers of many states.

***The Gatling gun**, the most successful of the hand-crank-operated machine guns of the 19th century.*

***The European** imperial powers maintained control of their often far-flung colonies by military superiority. Native forces were rarely a match for the large, highly trained armies, powerful navies, and technically advanced weaponry which the Europeans had at their disposal.*

THE AGE OF GLOBAL WAR: 1914–1945

IN 1914, IMPERIAL AND MILITARY rivalry in Europe provoked the first of two world wars, the largest and most destructive wars in human history. At the end of the first war, in 1918, the old international order was dead. The Russian Empire collapsed in revolution and was transformed by a communist minority into the Soviet Union. The German, Habsburg, and Ottoman empires were dismembered. A fragile peace ensued but the old equilibrium was gone. The rise of strident nationalism in Germany, Japan, and Italy destroyed the peace once again in 1939. The second war cost the lives of 50 million people and ravaged Europe and Asia. At its end, in 1945, the US and the Soviet Union had emerged as the new superpowers.

GLOBAL STATES AND TERRITORIES

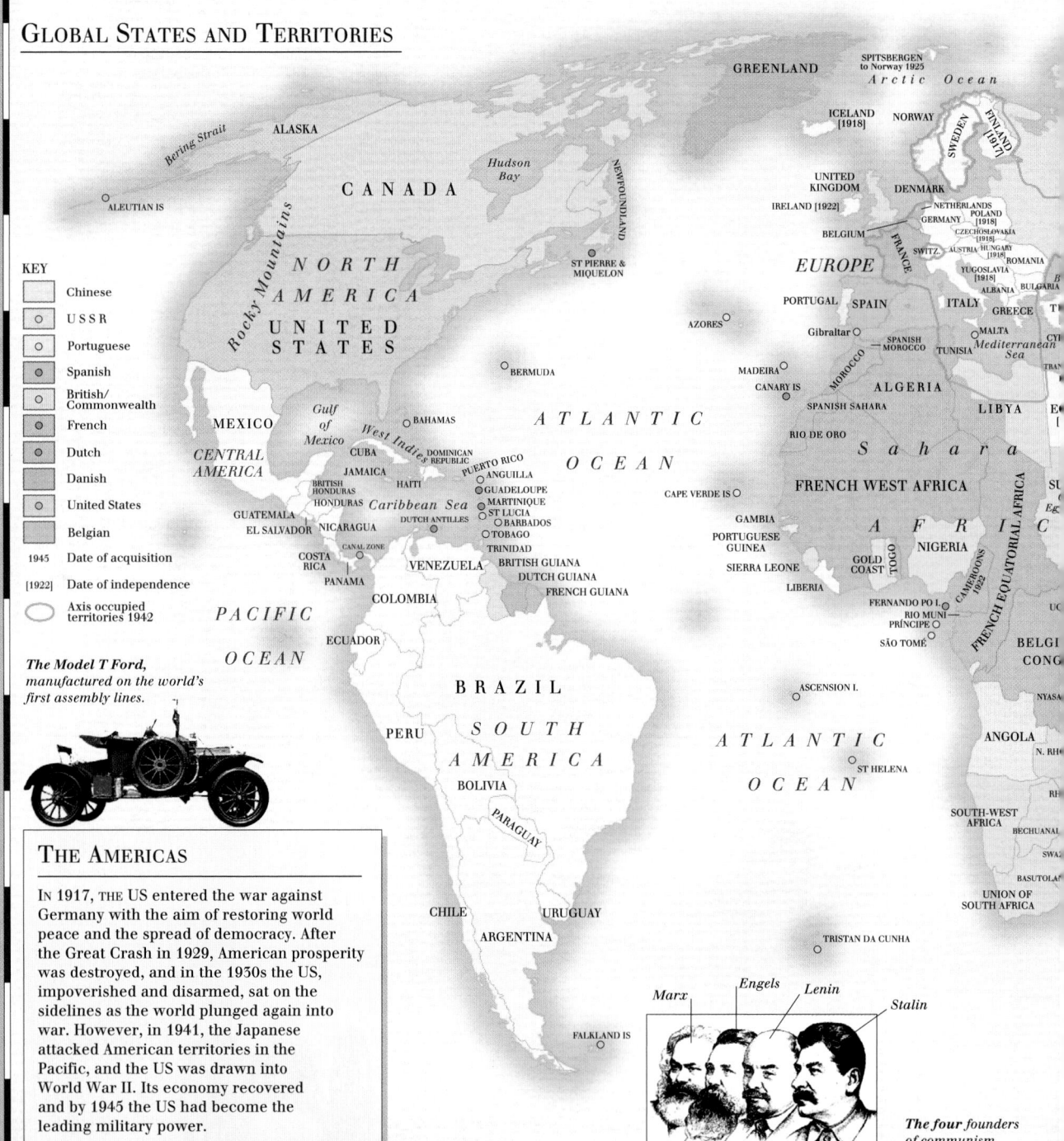

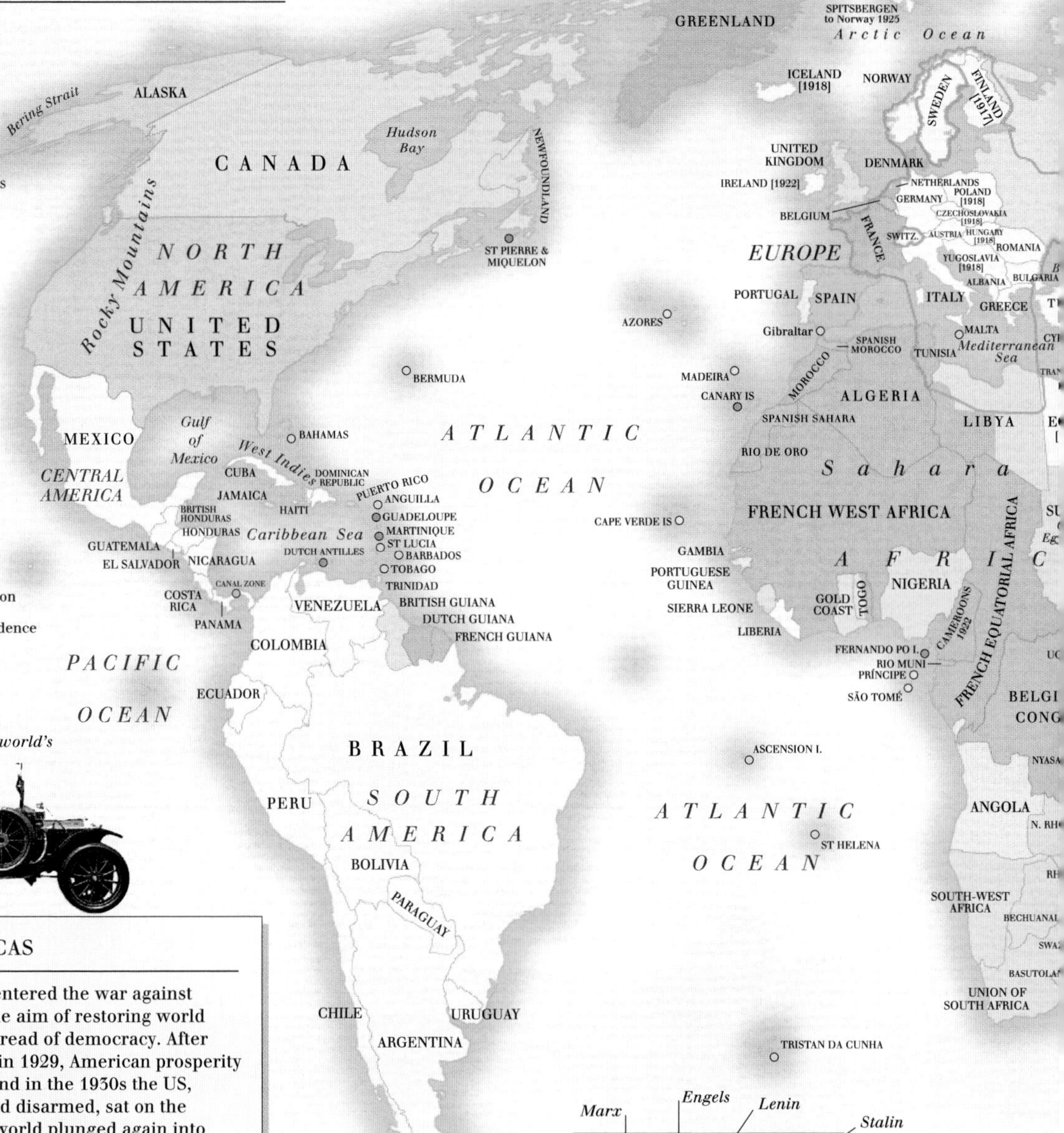
KEY
Chinese
USSR
Portuguese
Spanish
British/ Commonwealth
French
Dutch
Danish
United States
Belgian
1945 Date of acquisition
[1922] Date of independence
Axis occupied territories 1942
GREENLAND
SPITSBERGEN to Norway 1925
Arctic Ocean
ICELAND [1918]
NORWAY
SWEDEN
FINLAND [1917]
Bering Strait
ALASKA
ALEUTIAN IS
Hudson Bay
CANADA
NEWFOUNDLAND
UNITED KINGDOM
DENMARK
IRELAND [1922]
NETHERLANDS
POLAND [1918]
GERMANY
CZECHOSLOVAKIA [1918]
BELGIUM
FRANCE
SWITZ.
AUSTRIA
HUNGARY [1918]
ROMANIA
Rocky Mountains
NORTH AMERICA
UNITED STATES
ST PIERRE & MIQUELON
EUROPE
YUGOSLAVIA [1918]
ALBANIA
BULGARIA
PORTUGAL
SPAIN
ITALY
GREECE
AZORES
Gibraltar
SPANISH MOROCCO
TUNISIA
MALTA
Mediterranean Sea
BERMUDA
MADEIRA
CANARY IS
MOROCCO
ALGERIA
SPANISH SAHARA
LIBYA
MEXICO
Gulf of Mexico
BAHAMAS
West Indies
ATLANTIC OCEAN
RIO DE ORO
Sahara
CENTRAL AMERICA
CUBA
DOMINICAN REPUBLIC
PUERTO RICO
JAMAICA
ANGUILLA
HAITI
BRITISH HONDURAS
GUADELOUPE
HONDURAS
Caribbean Sea
MARTINIQUE
ST LUCIA
GUATEMALA
DUTCH ANTILLES
BARBADOS
EL SALVADOR
NICARAGUA
TOBAGO
TRINIDAD
CAPE VERDE IS
FRENCH WEST AFRICA
GAMBIA
AFRICA
PORTUGUESE GUINEA
TOGO
NIGERIA
SIERRA LEONE
GOLD COAST
CAMEROONS 1922
FRENCH EQUATORIAL AFRICA
LIBERIA
CANAL ZONE
COSTA RICA
PANAMA
VENEZUELA
BRITISH GUIANA
DUTCH GUIANA
FRENCH GUIANA
COLOMBIA
FERNANDO PO I.
RIO MUNI
PRÍNCIPE
SÃO TOMÉ
PACIFIC OCEAN
ECUADOR
BRAZIL
ASCENSION I.
PERU
SOUTH AMERICA
ATLANTIC OCEAN
ST HELENA
ANGOLA
BOLIVIA
PARAGUAY
SOUTH-WEST AFRICA
CHILE
URUGUAY
ARGENTINA
UNION OF SOUTH AFRICA
TRISTAN DA CUNHA
FALKLAND IS

The Model T Ford, manufactured on the world's first assembly lines.

THE AMERICAS

IN 1917, THE US entered the war against Germany with the aim of restoring world peace and the spread of democracy. After the Great Crash in 1929, American prosperity was destroyed, and in the 1930s the US, impoverished and disarmed, sat on the sidelines as the world plunged again into war. However, in 1941, the Japanese attacked American territories in the Pacific, and the US was drawn into World War II. Its economy recovered and by 1945 the US had become the leading military power.

Marx
Engels
Lenin
Stalin

The four founders of communism.

EUROPE

BOTH WORLD WARS had their origins in Europe. In 1914, Germany invaded Belgium; Britain, France, and Russia combined to defeat it, with US help. In 1918 new nation states were established in eastern Europe. But, by 1939, revived German nationalism started a second world war; much of western Europe came under a German "New Order" until the Soviet Union, Britain, and the US developed sufficient military strength to reconquer Europe and defeat Germany.

World War II *was decided by mechanical and industrial superiority.*

ASIA

THE COLLAPSE OF THE CHINESE EMPIRE in 1911, followed in 1917 by the disappearance of the Russian Empire, produced instability across Asia. Full-scale war broke out between Japan and China in 1937, with Japan trying to conquer China. The Soviet Union was the victim of German aggression from 1941. Both Japan and Germany were held at bay by communist forces which eventually succeeded in imposing stable politics on Asia. By 1945, the Soviet Union had reconquered its lost territories and dominated eastern Europe. In China, communist armies filled the vacuum left by the Japanese defeat.

Mahatma Gandhi *(1868–1948) led India to independence through peaceful noncooperation and protest.*

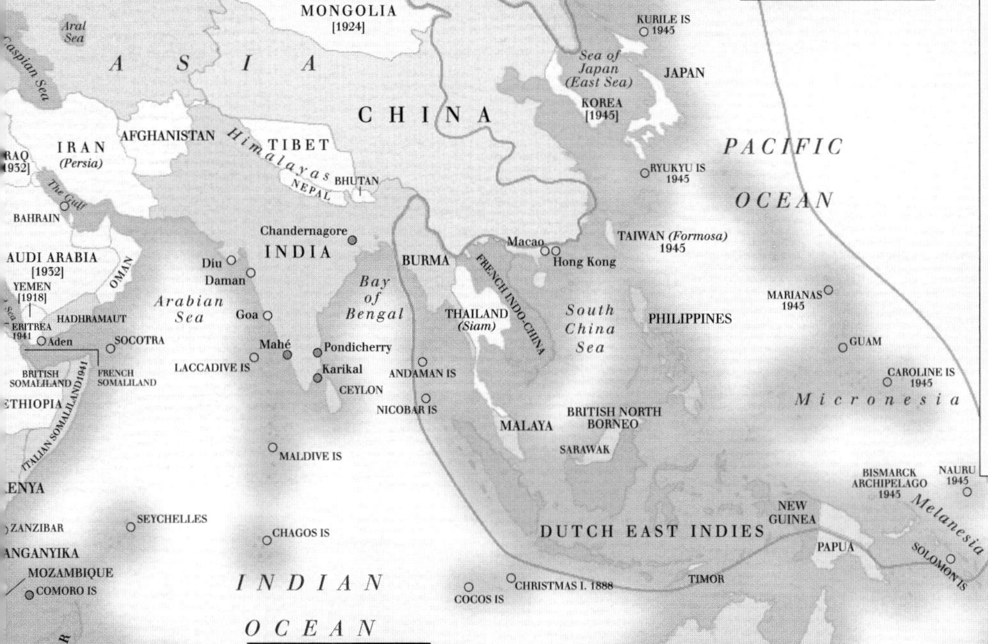
U S S R
Bering Strait
SAKHALIN 1945
MONGOLIA [1924]
Aral Sea
Caspian Sea
A S I A
KURILE IS 1945
Sea of Japan (East Sea)
JAPAN
KOREA [1945]
C H I N A
AFGHANISTAN
IRAN (Persia)
Himalayas
TIBET
BHUTAN
NEPAL
PACIFIC
OCEAN
RYUKYU IS 1945
The Gulf
BAHRAIN
Chandernagore
INDIA
Macao
Hong Kong
TAIWAN (Formosa) 1945
AUDI ARABIA [1932]
OMAN
Diu
Daman
BURMA
FRENCH INDO-CHINA
YEMEN [1918]
Arabian Sea
Bay of Bengal
Goa
THAILAND (Siam)
South China Sea
PHILIPPINES
MARIANAS 1945
HADHRAMAUT
ERITREA 1941
Aden
SOCOTRA
Mahé
Pondicherry
GUAM
BRITISH SOMALILAND
FRENCH SOMALILAND
LACCADIVE IS
Karikal
ANDAMAN IS
CAROLINE IS 1945
THIOPIA
ITALIAN SOMALILAND 1941
CEYLON
NICOBAR IS
BRITISH NORTH BORNEO
MALAYA
Micronesia
SARAWAK
MALDIVE IS
ENYA
BISMARCK ARCHIPELAGO 1945
NAURU 1945
SEYCHELLES
NEW GUINEA
Melanesia
ZANZIBAR
CHAGOS IS
DUTCH EAST INDIES
PAPUA
ANGANYIKA
SOLOMON IS
MOZAMBIQUE
COMORO IS
INDIAN
CHRISTMAS I. 1888
TIMOR
COCOS IS
OCEAN
MADAGASCAR
MAURITIUS
RÉUNION
NEW CALEDONIA
AUSTRALIA
(Dominion 1926)
LORD HOWE I.
NEW ZEALAND
CHATHAM IS
TASMANIA
AUCKLAND IS
MACQUARIE IS

OCEANIA

FOR THE ONLY TIME in its history, Australia was faced with the very real prospect of invasion. In World War II, Japanese armies reached the island of New Guinea, and bombed towns in northern Australia. Japanese submarines attacked Sydney harbor. The Battle of the Coral Sea, in May 1942, saved Australia, but it took almost three years to clear Japanese forces from the South Pacific, where they hung on grimly to the rich oil and mineral resources they had captured.

RISE OF ASIA

Japan promoted *itself as the liberator of Asia from the chains of European colonialism.*

Haile Selassie *(1892–1975), ruler of Ethiopia, the only independent empire in Africa.*

MIDDLE EAST

IN 1918, THE OTTOMAN EMPIRE disappeared after being in existence for 400 years. The modern map of north Africa and the Middle East was carved out of its ruins by the victors of World War I. The genocide of Europe's Jews by Nazi Germany during World War II accelerated the foundation of a new state of Israel in 1948, leading inexorably to conflict between displaced native Arabs and Jewish migrants.

The conquest *of the air was the most important technological achievement of the period. It added a devastating dimension to warfare, in the form of aerial bombing, while transforming civil transportation.*

A German Zeppelin *airship of the 1930s.*

The Modern Age: 1945–Present Day

TWO NUCLEAR EXPLOSIONS in Japan finally ended World War II and ushered in a new era of global rivalry. Total destruction by nuclear weapons was a real possibility as the two superpowers, the Soviet Union and the US, became locked with their allies in a fearful Cold War. Various side conflicts were staged in the ruins of the old empires where new nation states, with old colonial borders, were emerging. By 1991, communist power in the Soviet Union and Eastern Europe had crumbled, while the capitalism of the West had gained in strength.

The US is now the sole global superpower and has used its status to push Western goods and ideals to every corner of the globe, provoking often violent reactions among proud, conservative cultures. The age of globalization has begun.

Global States and Territories

KEY
Portuguese
Spanish
British
French
Dutch
Danish
US
[1972] Date of independence
GREENLAND
(Danish province 1953)
Arctic Ocean
ALASKA
(U S state 1959)
Bering Strait
ALEUTIAN IS
CANADA
Hudson Bay
Rocky Mountains
NORTH AMERICA
UNITED STATES
NEWFOUNDLAND
to Canada 1949
ST PIERRE & MIQUELON
ICELAND
NORWAY
SWEDEN
FINLAND
(Germany divided 1945 reunited 1989)
UNITED KINGDOM
IRELAND
DENMARK
NETHERLANDS
BELGIUM
FRANCE
EUROPE
PORTUGAL
SPAIN
ITALY
POLAND
ESTONIA [1991]
LATVIA [1991]
LITHUANIA [1991]
BELARUS [1991]
UKRAINE [1991]
MOLDOVA [1991]
SLOVAKIA [1993]
CZECH REP. [1993]
AUSTRIA
HUNGARY
ROMANIA
SLOVENIA [1991]
CROATIA [1991]
BULGARIA
ALBANIA
GREECE
MALTA [1964]
Mediterranean Sea
AZORES
Gibraltar
Ceuta
Melilla
MOROCCO [1956]
TUNISIA [1956]
MADEIRA
CANARY IS
ALGERIA [1962]
LIBYA [1951]
WESTERN SAHARA [1975] (occupied by Morocco from 1976)
Sahara
AFRICA
MAURITANIA [1960]
MALI [1960]
NIGER [1960]
CHAD [1960]
CAPE VERDE IS [1975]
SENEGAL [1960]
GAMBIA [1965]
GUINEA-BISSAU [1974]
GUINEA [1958]
SIERRA LEONE [1961]
LIBERIA
UPPER VOLTA [1960] (Burkina 1984)
IVORY COAST [1960]
GHANA [1957]
TOGO [1960]
DAHOMEY [1960] (Benin 1975)
NIGERIA [1960]
CAMEROON [1960]
CENTRAL AFRICAN REPUBLIC [1960]
EQUATORIAL GUINEA [1968]
SAO TOME & PRINCIPE [1975]
GABON [1960]
CONGO [1960]
RWANDA [1962]
BURUNDI [1962]
ANGOLA [1975]
NAMIBIA [1990] (formerly S.W. Africa, controlled by S. Africa)
BOTSWANA [1966]
SOUTH AFRICA (Republic 1961)
ASCENSION I.
ST HELENA
TRISTAN DA CUNHA
ATLANTIC OCEAN
BERMUDA
MEXICO
Gulf of Mexico
West Indies
BAHAMAS [1973]
CUBA
DOMINICAN REPUBLIC
PUERTO RICO
HAITI
JAMAICA [1962]
ANGUILLA
GUADELOUPE
MARTINIQUE
ST LUCIA [1979]
BARBADOS [1966]
TRINIDAD & TOBAGO [1962]
DUTCH ANTILLES
Caribbean Sea
CENTRAL AMERICA
BELIZE [1981]
HONDURAS
GUATEMALA
EL SALVADOR
NICARAGUA
COSTA RICA
PANAMA
PACIFIC OCEAN
VENEZUELA
GUYANA [1966]
SURINAME [1975]
FRENCH GUIANA
COLOMBIA
ECUADOR
PERU
BRAZIL
SOUTH AMERICA
BOLIVIA
PARAGUAY
Andes
CHILE
ARGENTINA
URUGUAY
FALKLAND IS

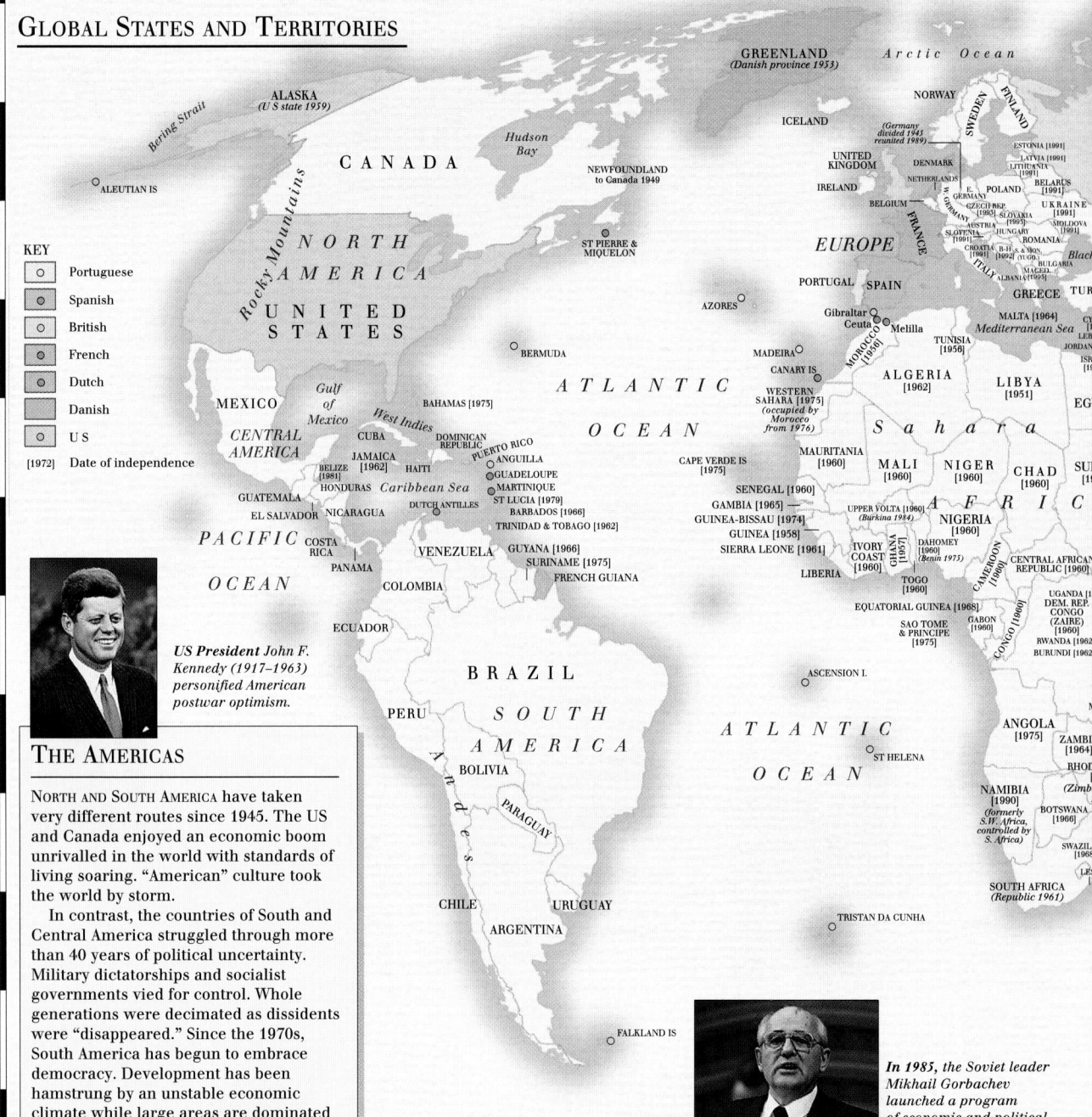

***US President** John F. Kennedy (1917–1963) personified American postwar optimism.*

The Americas

NORTH AND SOUTH AMERICA have taken very different routes since 1945. The US and Canada enjoyed an economic boom unrivalled in the world with standards of living soaring. "American" culture took the world by storm.

In contrast, the countries of South and Central America struggled through more than 40 years of political uncertainty. Military dictatorships and socialist governments vied for control. Whole generations were decimated as dissidents were "disappeared." Since the 1970s, South America has begun to embrace democracy. Development has been hamstrung by an unstable economic climate while large areas are dominated by the powerful narcotics trade.

***In 1985,** the Soviet leader Mikhail Gorbachev launched a program of economic and political reform which brought Soviet communism to an end.*

The Berlin Wall, symbol of the Cold War division of Europe, was demolished in 1989.

EUROPE

IN 1945, EUROPE LAY IN RUINS. The iron curtain descended to divide capitalist West from communist East. The West underwent an economic boom which restored widespread prosperity and political stability. It progressed toward economic and political unity under the EU. The East, meanwhile, labored under planned economies and quickly sought to catch up with the West after 1989, with many countries queuing to join the EU.

ASIA

IN SOUTHERN ASIA, popular nationalist movements came to power in India, Burma, Malaya, and Indonesia; in China and Indo-China, power passed to native communist movements whose roots went back to the 1920s. After 1949, China under Mao Zedong became, with its vast population and large military forces, a second communist superpower. Japan, meanwhile, was Asia's capitalist "miracle." Its economy and cities laid waste by bombing in 1945, it rebuilt with US aid so successfully that by the 1980s, it was the world's second-largest economy. China's potential economic growth, however, could put Japan's past achievements in the shade.

兵民是胜利之本

***Chinese communism,** based on the mobilization of peasants and workers, has nevertheless recognized the need for economic reforms.*

***A treaty** banning the testing of nuclear bombs in the Pacific was signed in 1986.*

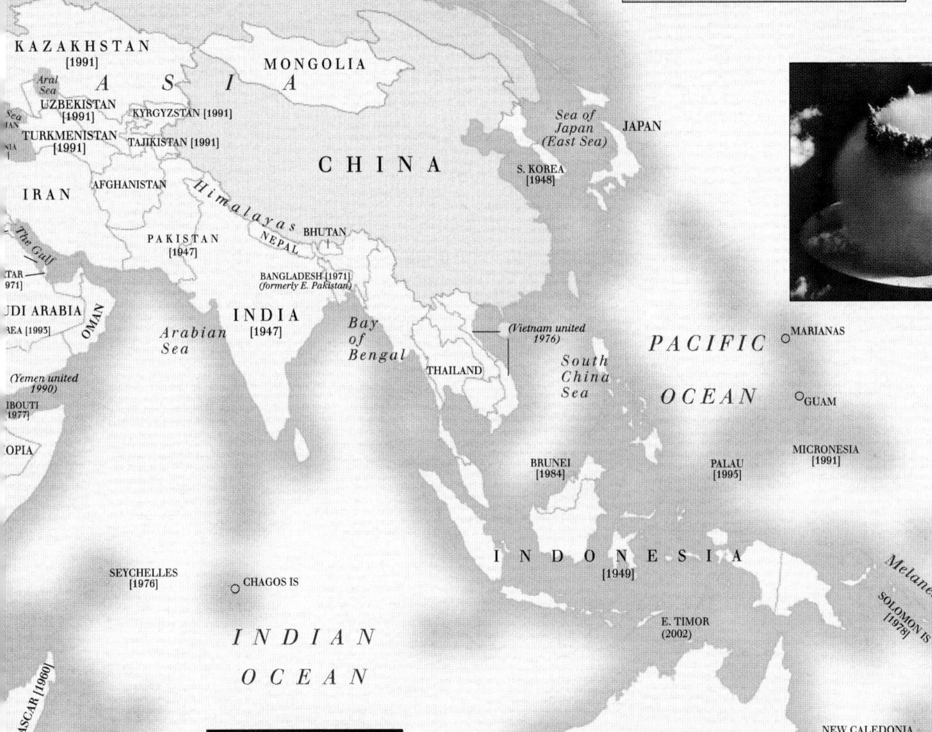
Bering Strait
KAZAKHSTAN [1991]
Aral Sea
A S I A
MONGOLIA
UZBEKISTAN [1991]
KYRGYZSTAN [1991]
TURKMENISTAN [1991]
TAJIKISTAN [1991]
CHINA
Sea of Japan (East Sea)
JAPAN
S. KOREA [1948]
IRAN
AFGHANISTAN
Himalayas
BHUTAN
NEPAL
PAKISTAN [1947]
The Gulf
BANGLADESH [1971] (formerly E. Pakistan)
OMAN
INDIA [1947]
Arabian Sea
Bay of Bengal
(Vietnam united 1976)
THAILAND
South China Sea
PACIFIC OCEAN
MARIANAS
GUAM
(Yemen united 1990)
MICRONESIA [1991]
BRUNEI [1984]
PALAU [1995]
INDONESIA [1949]
Melanesia
SEYCHELLES [1976]
CHAGOS IS
SOLOMON IS [1978]
E. TIMOR (2002)
INDIAN OCEAN
RÉUNION
AUSTRALIA
NEW CALEDONIA
NEW ZEALAND
AUCKLAND IS (to NZ)
MACQUARIE IS (to Australia)

OCEANIA

THE POSTWAR economies of Japan, the US, and Australia had by the 1990s created a new industrial and trading network around the Pacific Rim. Cheap labor and low overheads drew younger states – South Korea, Taiwan, Singapore, Malaysia, Indonesia – into the system and much of the world's manufacturing is now concentrated there, creating a consequent shift in the balance of the global economy.

***Gamal Abd al-Nasser** (1918–1970) of Egypt, galvanized the Arab states to resist the West.*

AFRICA AND THE MIDDLE EAST

THE COLONIAL POWERS, weakened by war, faced an irresistible wave of demands for self-determination. Between 1958 and 1975, 41 African countries gained independence. In north Africa and throughout the Middle East a new form of anti-imperialism emerged in the 1970s in the form of Islamic fundamentalism. In South Africa, white rule and the apartheid system ended in 1994.

***From the 1950s** to the 1970s, superpower rivalry focused on space exploration. The Soviets put the first man in space in 1961, and the Americans landed on the moon in 1969. Since then, both manned and unmanned missions have become almost everyday events.*

POPULATION

THE WORLD'S POPULATION – 6.4 billion in 2004 – is likely to reach nearly ten billion by 2050. Better nutrition, health care, and sanitation mean fewer infant deaths and longer life expectancy, though around 800 million people in the developing world are malnourished and over one billion live in extreme poverty. In much of Africa in particular, the AIDS epidemic is so severe that the population is set to fall significantly. Elsewhere it is lower birthrates, already familiar in most industrialized countries, that have slowed the rate of growth. The result is a rapidly aging population: it is thought that by 2050 there will be around two billion people over the age of 60. The distribution of population is very uneven, dependent on climate, terrain, natural resources, and economic factors. The great majority of people live in coastal zones and along river valleys. Urbanization is on the increase, and by 2003 just under half of the world's population lived in cities – most of them in Asia. The mass migration of people from rural areas in search of work has resulted in the growth of huge sprawling squatter camps on the edge of many Third World cities.

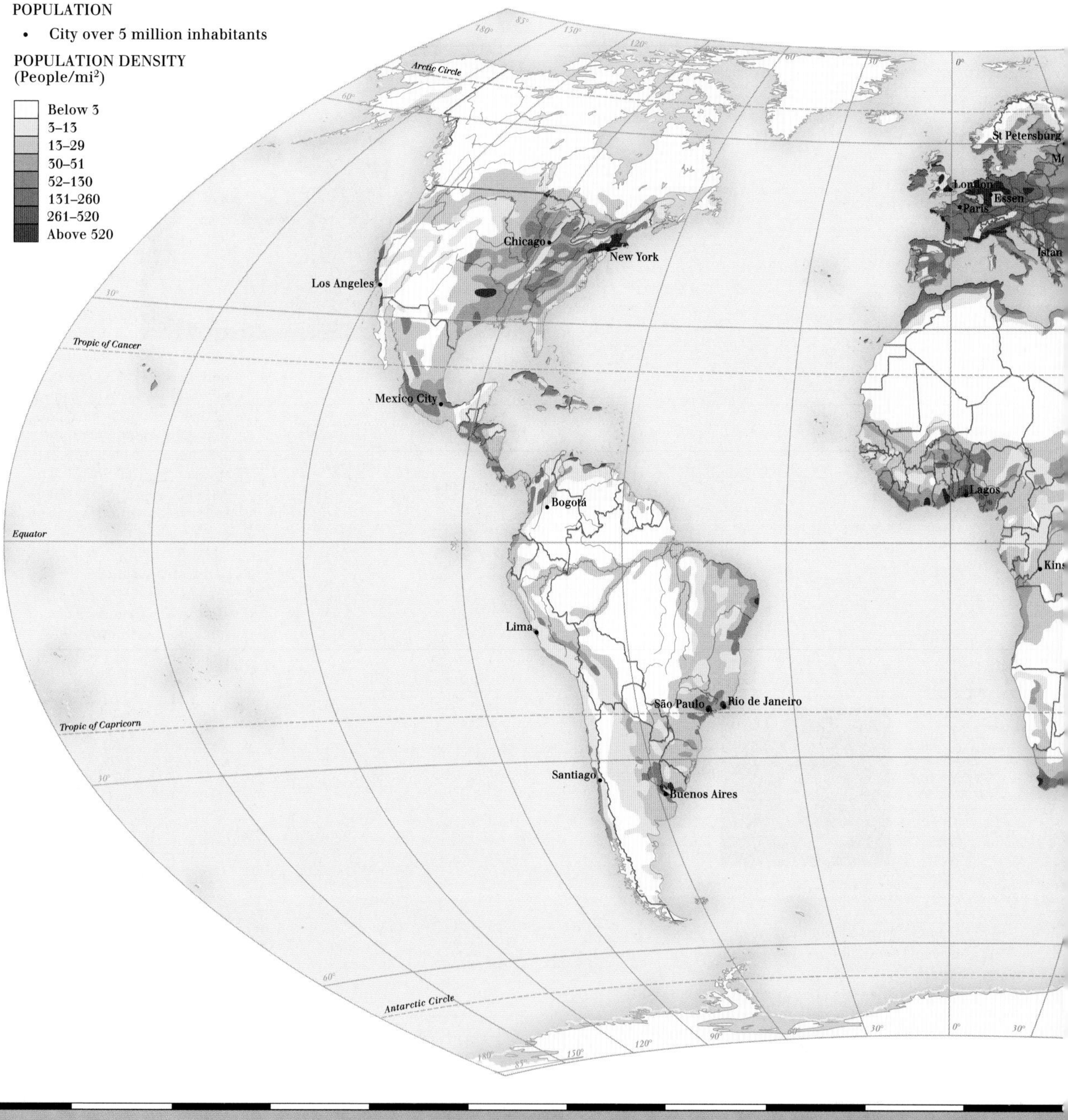
POPULATION
• City over 5 million inhabitants
POPULATION DENSITY
(People/mi²)
Below 3
3–13
13–29
30–51
52–130
131–260
261–520
Above 520
Arctic Circle
Tropic of Cancer
Equator
Tropic of Capricorn
Antarctic Circle
St Petersburg
London
Essen
Paris
Chicago
New York
Los Angeles
Mexico City
Bogotá
Lagos
Lima
São Paulo
Rio de Janeiro
Santiago
Buenos Aires

INFANT MORTALITY

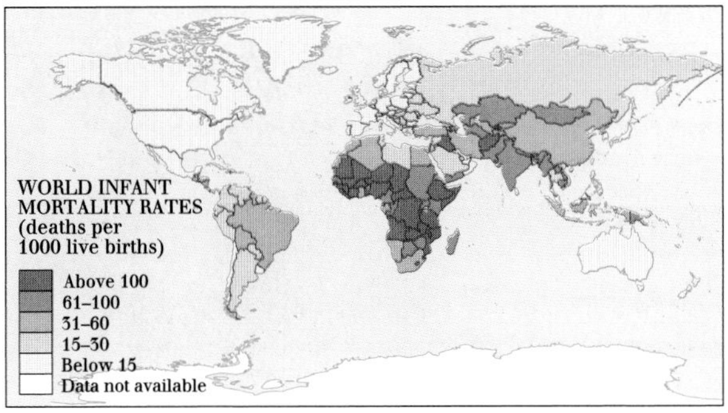
WORLD INFANT MORTALITY RATES (deaths per 1000 live births)
Above 100
61–100
31–60
15–30
Below 15
Data not available

Infant Mortality

INFANT MORTALITY RATES are highest in Africa, South America, and south Asia, where poverty and disease are rife, and where average standards of health care are not as good as in North America or Europe. The country with the highest infant mortality rate is Sierra Leone, where years of conflict have devastated communities.

LIFE EXPECTANCY

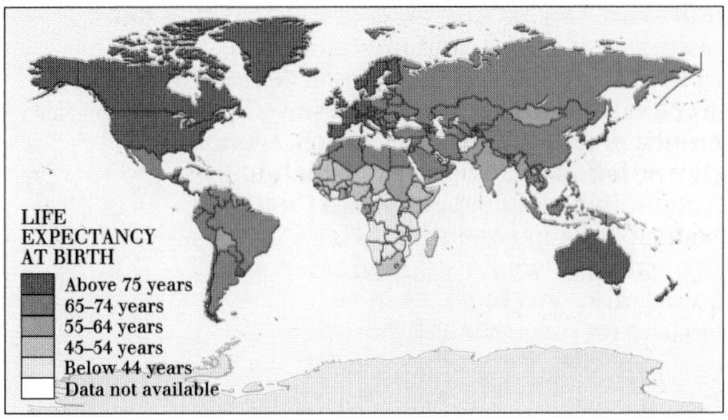
LIFE EXPECTANCY AT BIRTH
Above 75 years
65–74 years
55–64 years
45–54 years
Below 44 years
Data not available

Arctic Circle
Tehran
Lahore
Delhi
Karachi
Mumbai (Bombay)
Bangalore
Chennai (Madras)
Dhaka
Calcutta (Kolkata)
Tianjin
Beijing
Seoul
Tokyo
Osaka
Wuhan
Shanghai
Chongqing
Hong Kong
Bangkok
Manilla
Jakarta
Tropic of Cancer
Equator
Tropic of Capricorn
Antarctic Circle

Life Expectancy

LIFE EXPECTANCY IS poorest in Africa, for reasons similar to those noted above. In western Europe and North America, life expectancy is increasing at such a rate that each successive generation may expect to live longer than the last. In the developed world, people can now expect to live twice as long as they did a century ago.

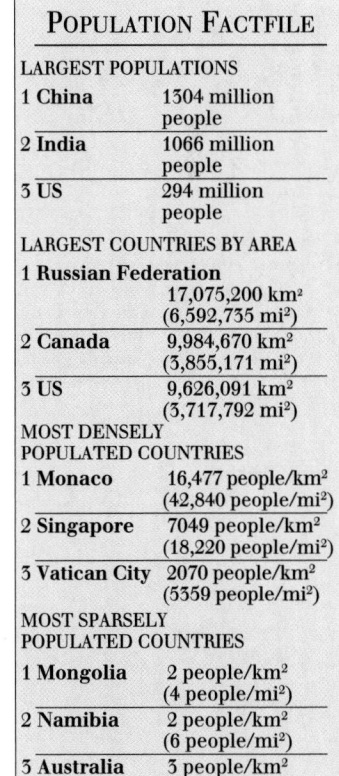

Population Factfile

LARGEST POPULATIONS

1 **China**	1304 million people
2 **India**	1066 million people
3 **US**	294 million people

LARGEST COUNTRIES BY AREA

1 **Russian Federation**	17,075,200 km² (6,592,735 mi²)
2 **Canada**	9,984,670 km² (3,855,171 mi²)
3 **US**	9,626,091 km² (3,717,792 mi²)

MOST DENSELY POPULATED COUNTRIES

1 **Monaco**	16,477 people/km² (42,840 people/mi²)
2 **Singapore**	7049 people/km² (18,220 people/mi²)
3 **Vatican City**	2070 people/km² (5359 people/mi²)

MOST SPARSELY POPULATED COUNTRIES

1 **Mongolia**	2 people/km² (4 people/mi²)
2 **Namibia**	2 people/km² (6 people/mi²)
3 **Australia**	3 people/km² (7 people/mi²)

World Economy

THE WEALTHY COUNTRIES of the developed world, with their aggressive, market-led economies and their access to productive new technologies and international markets, dominate the world economic system. At the other extreme, many of the countries of the developing world are locked in a cycle of unrepayable debt, rising populations, and unemployment. State-managed systems in the former communist bloc were dismantled in the 1990s, and China has emerged as a major 21st century economic power following decades of isolation. Technological advances mean that transactions between financial centers can occur at even greater speed, and new markets have sprung up throughout the world.

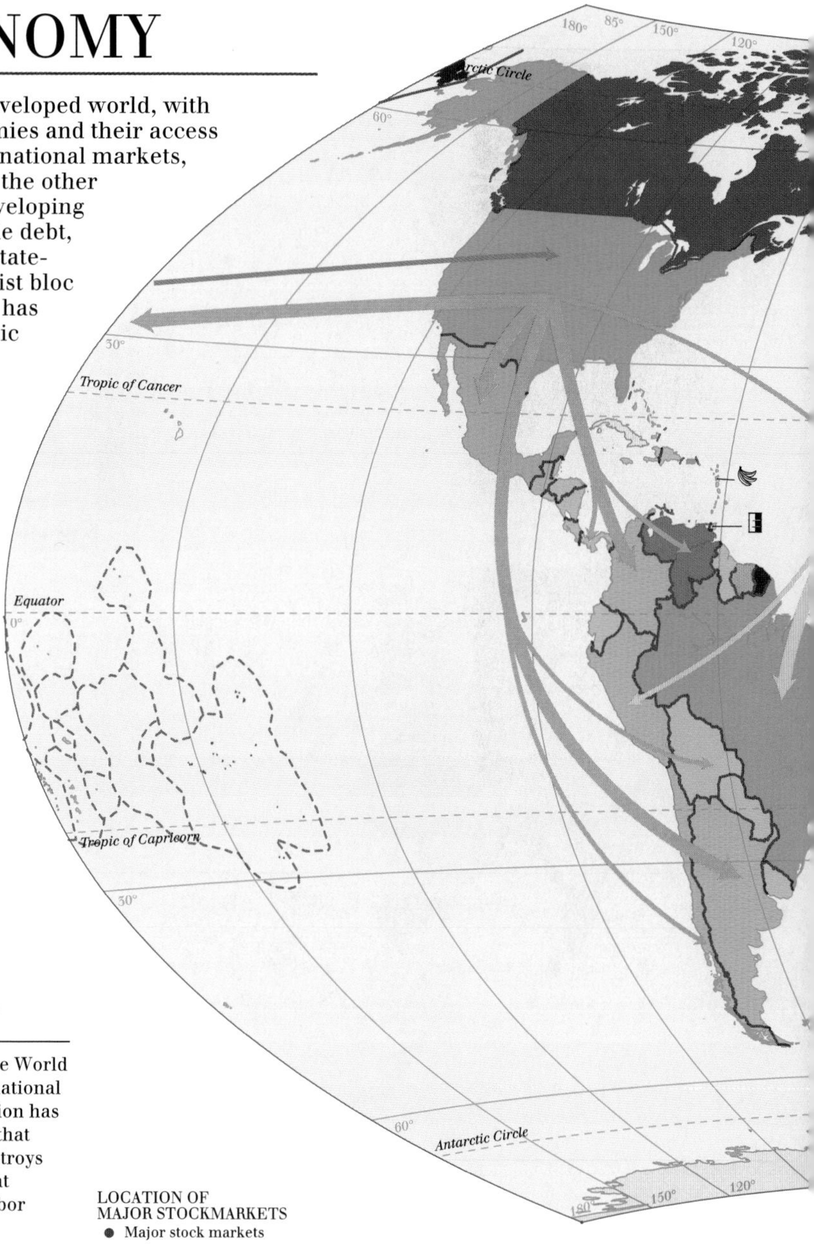

Arctic Circle
Tropic of Cancer
Equator
Tropic of Capricorn
Antarctic Circle

BALANCE OF TRADE (MILLIONS US $)

Surplus
- over 20,000
- 10,000–19,999
- 1000–9999
- 0-999

Deficit
- 0–999
- 1000-9999
- 10,000–19,999
- below 20,000

data unavailable

DIRECT INVESTMENT
- from US
- from Europe
- from Japan

COUNTRIES RELIANT ON A SINGLE EXPORT
- bananas
- coffee
- oil/petroleum
- copper

World Trade and Globalization

A basic tenet of liberal economics, embodied in the World Trade Organization, is that free trade stimulates national economies and encourages growth. Global recession has not shaken this faith, but its vocal critics contend that "globalization" undermines local cultures and destroys local economies. It is multinational companies that benefit, they say, by producing goods wherever labor costs and environmental standards are lowest.

LOCATION OF MAJOR STOCKMARKETS
- Major stock markets

INTERNATIONAL TRADE

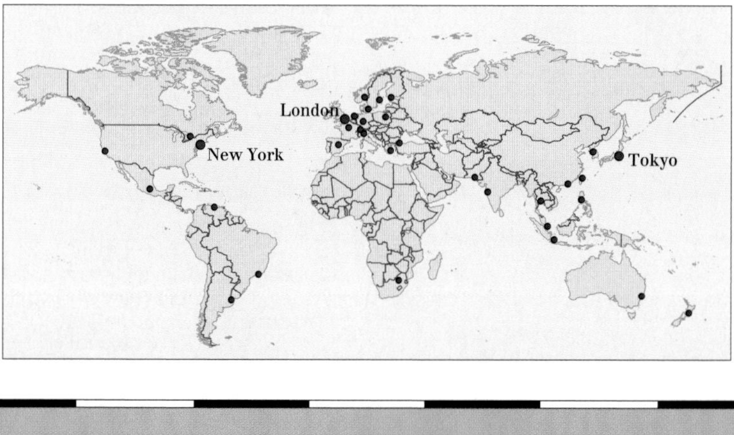

London
New York
Tokyo

World Economies

HIGHEST GNP PER CAPITA	
1 Liechtenstein	$50,000
2 Luxembourg	$39,470
3 Norway	$38,730
4 Switzerland	$36,170
5 US	$35,400

LOWEST GNP PER CAPITA	
1= Ethiopia	$100
1= Burundi	$100
1= Congo, Dem. Rep.	$100
4 Somalia	$120
5 Guinea-Bissau	$130

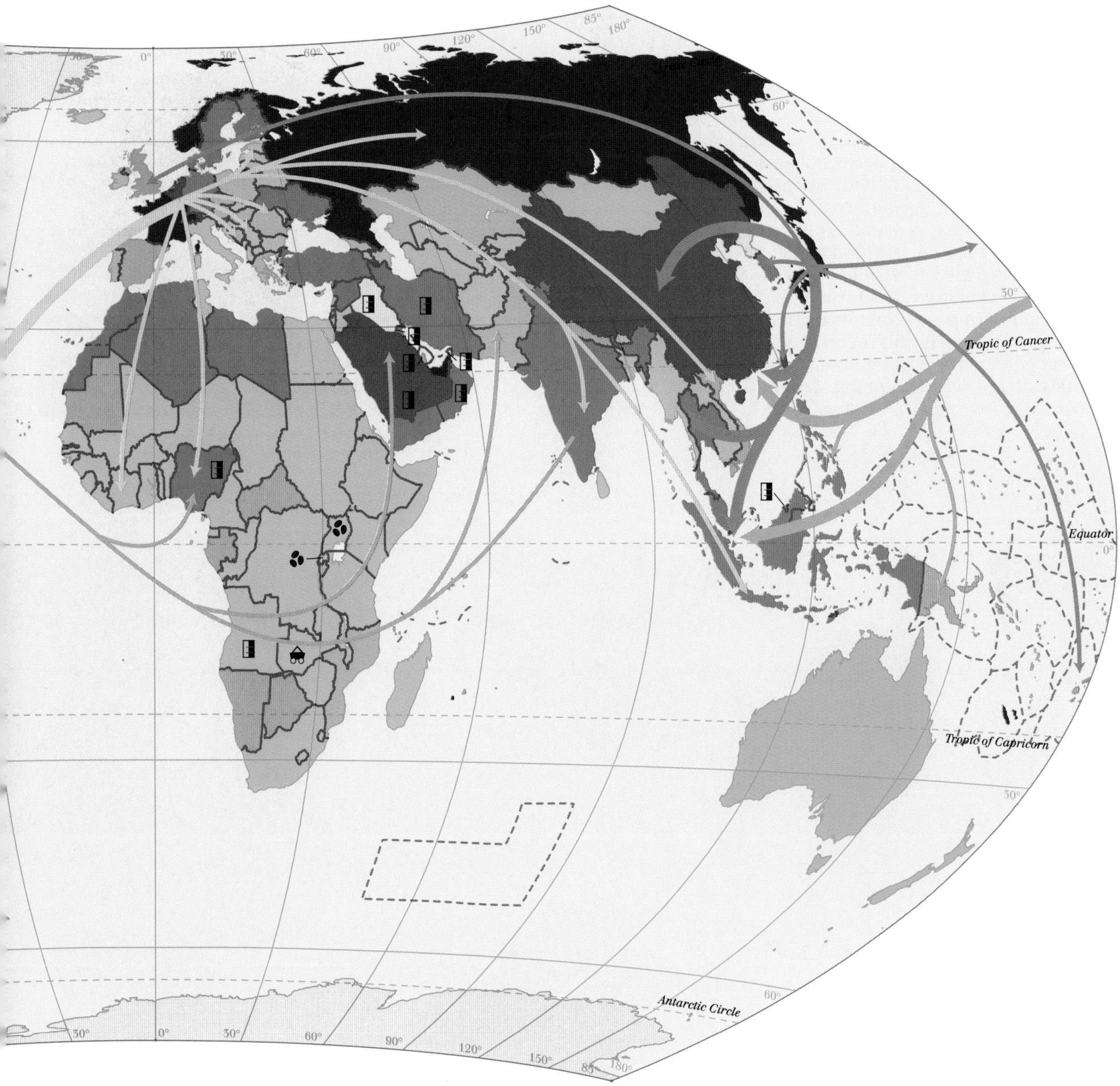
Arctic Circle
Tropic of Cancer
Equator
Tropic of Capricorn
Antarctic Circle
0°
30°
60°
90°
120°
150°
180°

TRADE BLOCS

INTERNATIONAL TRADE BLOCS are formed when groups of countries, often already enjoying close military and political ties, join together to offer mutually preferential terms of trade for both imports and exports. Global trade is dominated by three main blocs: the expanding EU, NAFTA, and ASEAN. They are supplanting older trade blocs such as the Commonwealth, a legacy of colonialism.

TRADE BLOCS

- EU
- ASEAN
- NAFTA
- SADC
- MERCOSUR
- ECOWAS

TRADE BLOCS

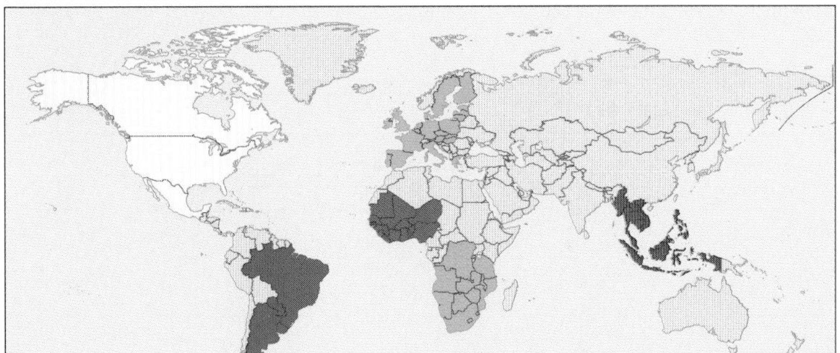

World Economy

THE SIZE OF A COUNTRY'S economy does not relate directly to its population or even its resources. Japan, for example, has a much "bigger" economy than China, India, Russia, or Latin America as a whole. Such imbalances usually occur because countries differ enormously in their living standards, the education and skills of their workforces, the productivity of their agriculture, and the value of their markets. A country's economic performance can be evaluated by calculating its gross national product (GNP). This is the total value of both the goods and the services (including so-called "invisible exports" – financial services, tourism, and so on) that it produces. Most trade (62% of the global total by value) is in manufactured goods, but during the last three decades the most rapidly growing sector has been services – banking, insurance, tourism, consultancy, accountancy, films, music and other cultural services, airlines, and shipping. Accounting for 20% of the total, services now exceed the value of trade in food and raw materials.

Comparative World Wealth

A global assessment of GNP by country reveals great disparities. The developed world, with only a quarter of the world's population, has 80% of the world's manufacturing income. This imbalance is maintained as war and political instability undermine poor countries' prospects.

***Mass-market tourism** is now an all-important source of revenue in many countries.*

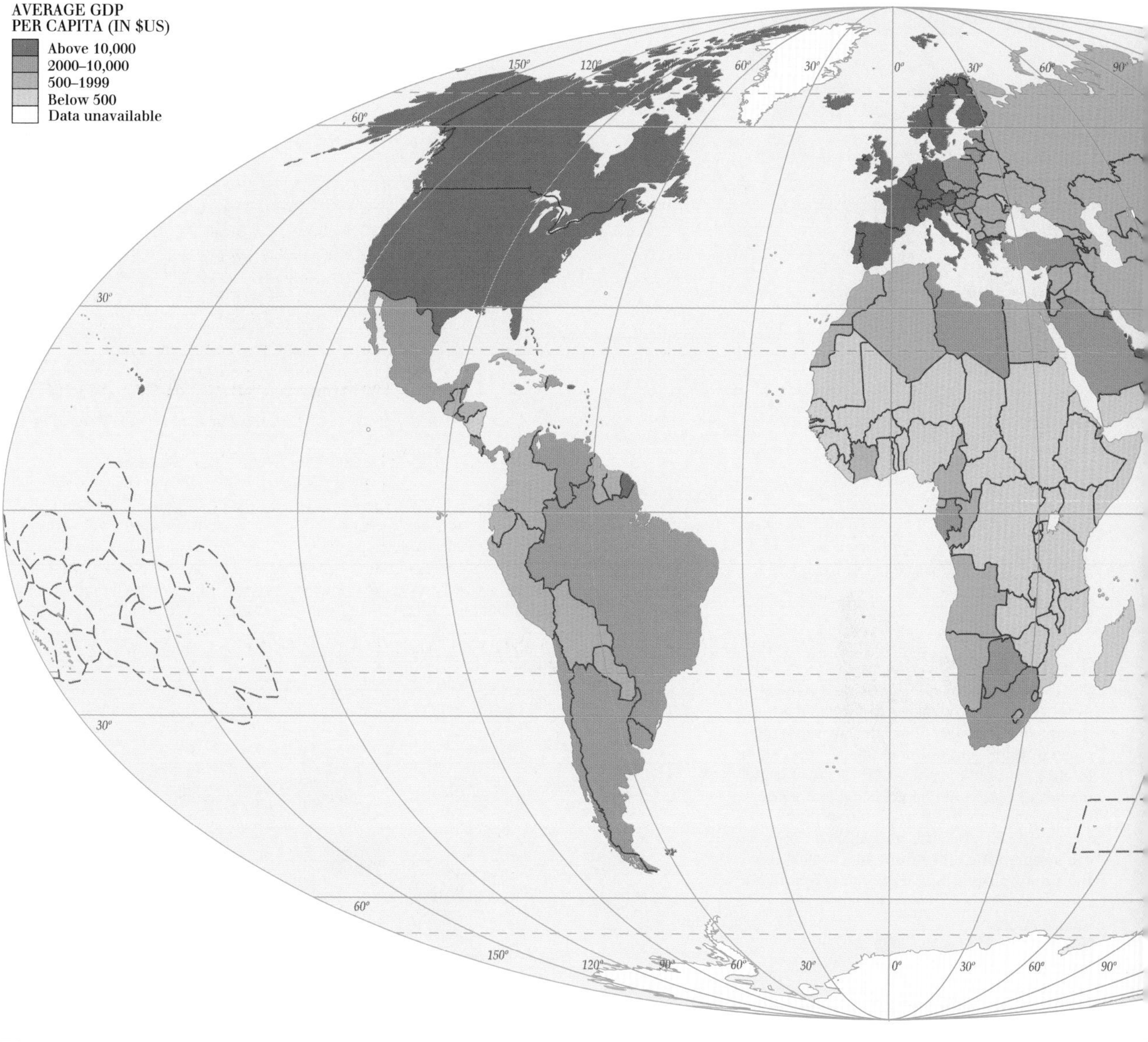
AVERAGE GDP
PER CAPITA (IN $US)
Above 10,000
2000–10,000
500–1999
Below 500
Data unavailable
150°
120°
60°
30°
0°
30°
60°
90°
60°
30°
30°
60°
150°
120°
90°
60°
30°
0°
30°
60°
90°

DEBT OF POOR AND MIDDLE-INCOME COUNTRIES

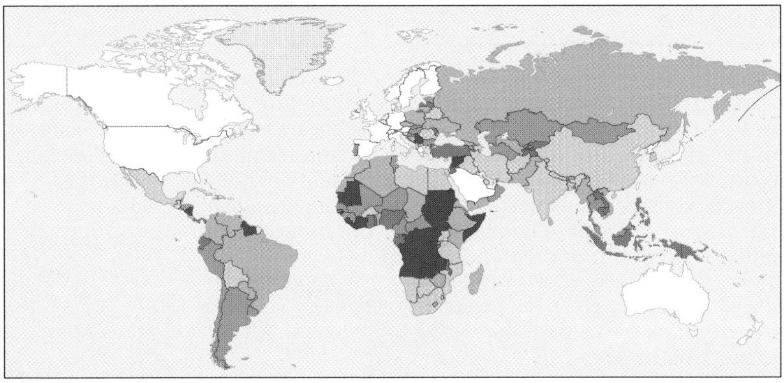

INTERNATIONAL DEBT (AS PERCENTAGE OF GNP)

over 100% · 70–100% · 50–69% · 30–49% · below 30 · negligible · not applicable · data unavailable

International Debt

In response to unsustainable levels of debt in the developing world, the IMF and World Bank have introduced a program to help heavily indebted poor countries (HIPCs) manage their repayments. The Jubilee 2000 campaign, advocating debt cancellation, won some qualified support among creditor countries.

World's 20 Largest Corporations

		2003, $ millions
1	**Wal-Mart Stores (US)**	$263,009
2	**British Petroleum (UK)**	$232,571
3	**Exxon Mobil (US)**	$222,883
4	**Royal Dutch/Shell Group (UK/Neth.)**	$201,728
5	**General Motors (US)**	$195,324
6	**Ford Motor Company (US)**	$164,505
7	**DaimlerChrysler (US/Germany)**	$156,602
8	**Toyota Motor Company (Japan)**	$153,111
9	**General Electric (US)**	$134,187
10	**Total Fina Elf (France)**	$118,441
11	**Allianz (Germany)**	$114,950
12	**ChevronTexaco (US)**	$112,937
13	**AXA (France)**	$111,912
14	**ConocoPhillips (US)**	$99,468
15	**Volkswagen (Germany)**	$98,637
16	**Nippon Telegraph and Telephone (Japan)**	$98,229
17	**ING Group (Neth.)**	$95,893
18	**Citigroup (US)**	$94,713
19	**Intl. Business Machines (US)**	$89,131
20	**American Intl. Group (US)**	$81,303

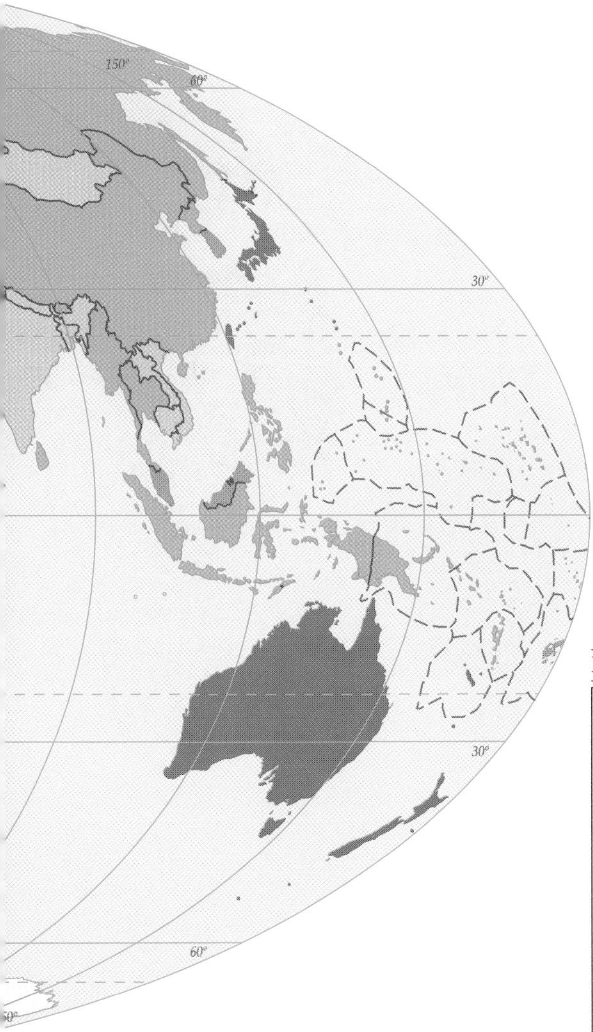

Newly Industrialized Countries

In the 1990s, the fast-growing export-oriented "Asian tiger" economies, such as Singapore, South Korea, and Taiwan, offered exciting prospects for foreign investors. The 1997–1998 Asian financial crisis came as a severe shock. Some countries quickly returned to growth, but investors became more cautious about their exposure in NICs around the world.

NEWLY INDUSTRIALIZED AND INDUSTRIALIZING COUNTRIES

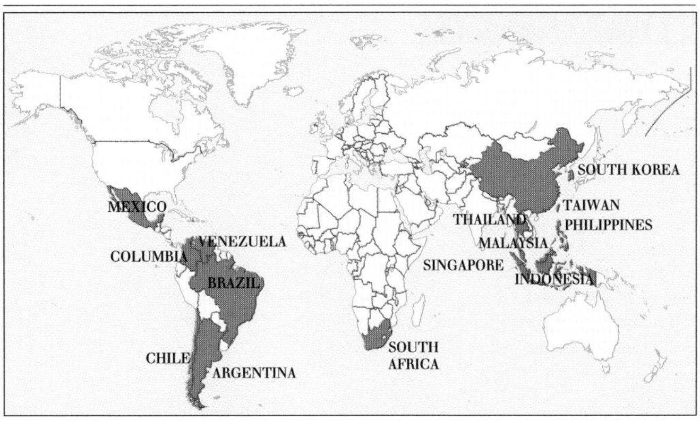
MEXICO
VENEZUELA
COLUMBIA
BRAZIL
CHILE
ARGENTINA
SOUTH AFRICA
THAILAND
MALAYSIA
SINGAPORE
INDONESIA
SOUTH KOREA
TAIWAN
PHILIPPINES

Global Tourism

TOURISM IS THE WORLD'S biggest industry. In 2002 there were a record 715 million tourists worldwide, a number expected to rise to over one billion by 2010. The industry had bounced back quickly from the global downturn in 2001, though world events continue to affect numbers. France is the most popular destination country, with 75 million visitors annually, but with cheaper flights, improved transportation, and increased leisure time, many of the countries of the developing world are rapidly becoming tourist meccas. Since the 1960s, mass tourism has become increasingly specialized, encompassing sport, adventure, and ecology. Tourism employs 200 million people – 8% of the workforce. However, the benefits of tourism are not always felt at a local level, where jobs are often low-paid and menial.

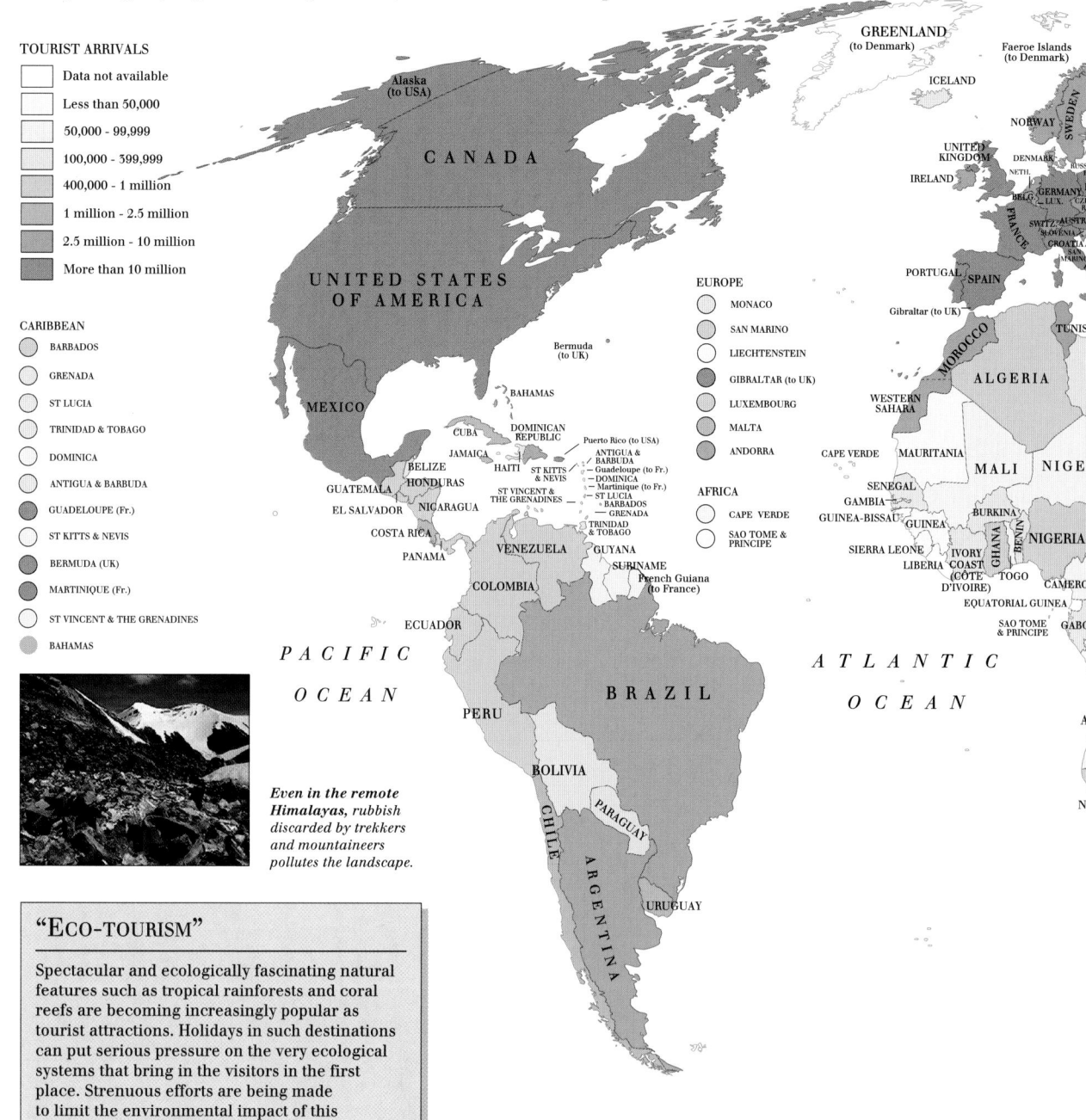

TOURIST ARRIVALS

- Data not available
- Less than 50,000
- 50,000 - 99,999
- 100,000 - 399,999
- 400,000 - 1 million
- 1 million - 2.5 million
- 2.5 million - 10 million
- More than 10 million

CARIBBEAN

- BARBADOS
- GRENADA
- ST LUCIA
- TRINIDAD & TOBAGO
- DOMINICA
- ANTIGUA & BARBUDA
- GUADELOUPE (Fr.)
- ST KITTS & NEVIS
- BERMUDA (UK)
- MARTINIQUE (Fr.)
- ST VINCENT & THE GRENADINES
- BAHAMAS

GREENLAND
(to Denmark)
Faeroe Islands
(to Denmark)
ICELAND
Alaska
(to USA)
CANADA
NORWAY
SWEDEN
UNITED KINGDOM
DENMARK
NETH.
IRELAND
BELG.
GERMANY
LUX.
FRANCE
SWITZ.
SLOVENIA
CROATIA
UNITED STATES OF AMERICA
EUROPE
MONACO
SAN MARINO
LIECHTENSTEIN
GIBRALTAR (to UK)
LUXEMBOURG
MALTA
ANDORRA
AFRICA
CAPE VERDE
SAO TOME & PRINCIPE
PORTUGAL
SPAIN
Gibraltar (to UK)
MOROCCO
TUNISIA
ALGERIA
WESTERN SAHARA
Bermuda
(to UK)
BAHAMAS
MEXICO
CUBA
DOMINICAN REPUBLIC
Puerto Rico (to USA)
JAMAICA
HAITI
ANTIGUA & BARBUDA
ST KITTS & NEVIS
Guadeloupe (to Fr.)
DOMINICA
Martinique (to Fr.)
ST LUCIA
BARBADOS
GRENADA
ST VINCENT & THE GRENADINES
TRINIDAD & TOBAGO
BELIZE
GUATEMALA
HONDURAS
EL SALVADOR
NICARAGUA
COSTA RICA
PANAMA
VENEZUELA
GUYANA
SURINAME
French Guiana
(to France)
COLOMBIA
ECUADOR
CAPE VERDE
MAURITANIA
MALI
SENEGAL
GAMBIA
GUINEA-BISSAU
GUINEA
BURKINA
SIERRA LEONE
LIBERIA
IVORY COAST (CÔTE D'IVOIRE)
GHANA
TOGO
BENIN
NIGERIA
EQUATORIAL GUINEA
SAO TOME & PRINCIPE
PACIFIC OCEAN
ATLANTIC OCEAN
BRAZIL
PERU
BOLIVIA
PARAGUAY
CHILE
ARGENTINA
URUGUAY

Even in the remote Himalayas, rubbish discarded by trekkers and mountaineers pollutes the landscape.

"Eco-tourism"

Spectacular and ecologically fascinating natural features such as tropical rainforests and coral reefs are becoming increasingly popular as tourist attractions. Holidays in such destinations can put serious pressure on the very ecological systems that bring in the visitors in the first place. Strenuous efforts are being made to limit the environmental impact of this so-called "eco-tourism."

The beautiful island *of Phuket, Thailand, has been taken over by tourist developments.*

A TOURIST PARADISE?

THE MOST REMOTE CORNERS of the world are now being penetrated by tourists in their quest for the exotic. In many parts of the developing world, tourism can be described as a form of "neocolonialism"; hotels and beaches are owned by multinational companies, and most of the profits are taken outside the country. Tourism frequently alienates local people from their own land, and has a negative impact on the local culture and environment.

RUSSIAN FEDERATION
KAZAKHSTAN
MONGOLIA
GEORGIA
ARM.
AZERB.
UZBEKISTAN
KYRGYZSTAN
TURKMENISTAN
TAJIKISTAN
AFGHANISTAN
NORTH KOREA
SOUTH KOREA
JAPAN
CHINA
SYRIA
IRAQ
IRAN
JORDAN
KUWAIT
PAKISTAN
NEPAL
BHUTAN
BAHRAIN
QATAR
UAE
SAUDI ARABIA
OMAN
BANGLADESH
INDIA
BURMA (MYANMAR)
LAOS
TAIWAN
PACIFIC OCEAN
ERITREA
YEMEN
DJIBOUTI
ETHIOPIA
SOMALIA
THAILAND
VIETNAM
CAMBODIA
PHILIPPINES
Guam (to USA)
MALDIVES
SRI LANKA
UGANDA
KENYA
MALAYSIA
SINGAPORE
TANZANIA
SEYCHELLES
INDONESIA
PAPUA NEW GUINEA
EAST TIMOR
COMOROS
MALAWI
MOZAMBIQUE
MADAGASCAR
MAURITIUS
INDIAN OCEAN
SWAZILAND
LESOTHO
AUSTRALIA
NEW ZEALAND
PACIFIC OCEAN
FIJI
MICRONESIA
NAURU
SOLOMON ISLANDS
VANUATU
SAMOA
TONGA
KIRIBATI
MIDDLE EAST
BAHRAIN
INDIAN OCEAN
COMOROS
MALDIVES
MAURITIUS
SEYCHELLES
ASIA
SINGAPORE

"Eco-tourists" *travel to the distant Antarctic, where they observe its rich wildlife.*

Global Security

THE ENDING OF THE COLD WAR in 1989 greatly reduced the risk of another global (and possibly nuclear) war, but did little to resolve localized tensions and conflicts. Since then territorial disputes, and particularly ethnic and religious tensions, have undermined peace and security around the world. In its efforts to bring together the international community the UN has become the accepted arbiter of world peace. It prefers to use economic sanctions, but will support military action as a last resort. However, slow decision-making processes and internal politicking have often left it unable to react quickly or effectively, as in the failure to halt the 1994 genocide in Rwanda. Perhaps its greatest contribution to global security has been the organization of peacekeeping missions which are frequently called into conflict situations to oversee peace treaties and aid postwar reconstruction. The September 11, 2001, attacks on the US prompted a shift in that country's foreign policy and it has now chosen to flex its muscles as the sole remaining superpower. Identifying terrorism as the greatest challenge to world security, and sidelining the UN if necessary, it has drawn on ad hoc coalitions of willing partners in its global "war on terrorism." It advocates the use of preemptive strikes to ensure future security.

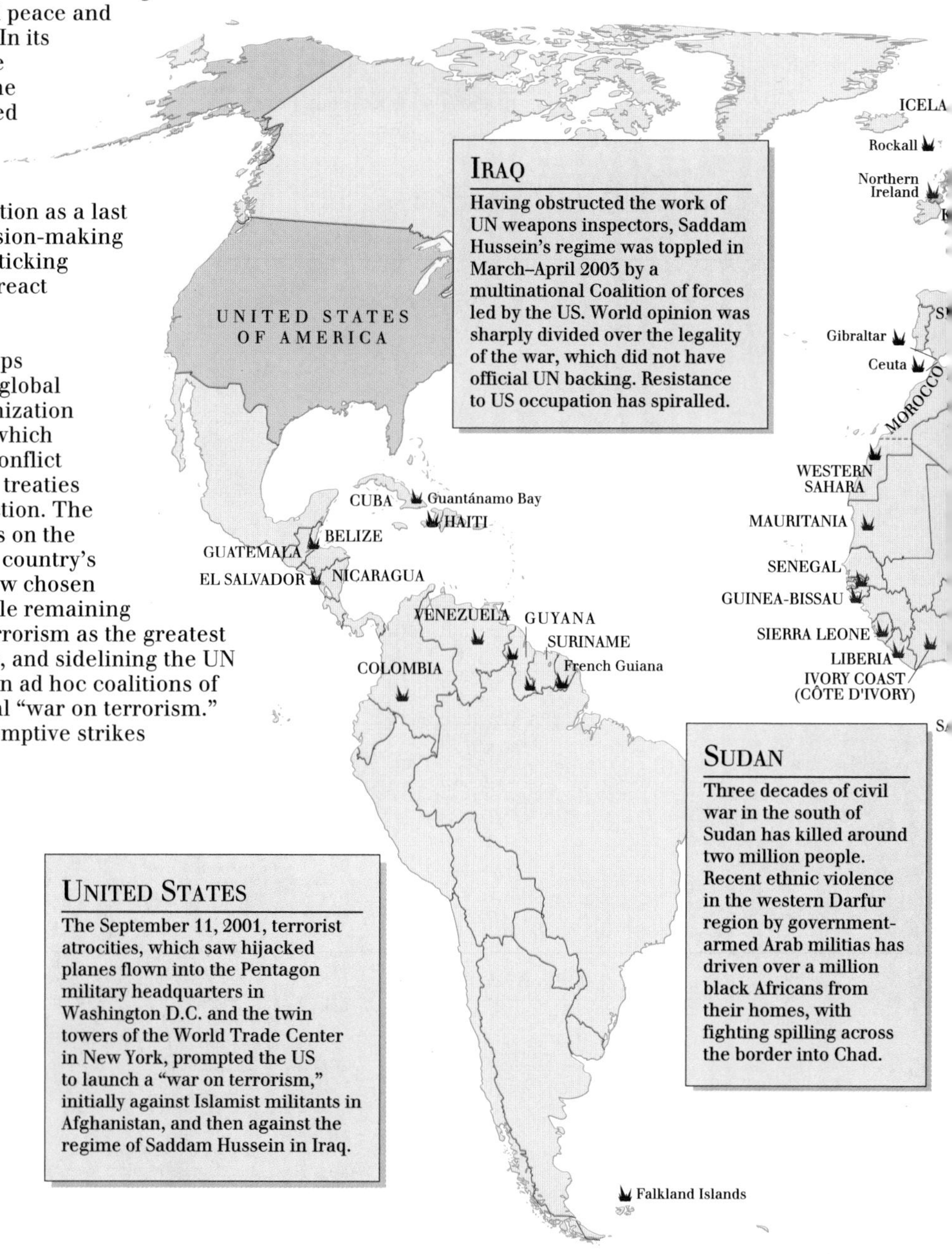
UNITED STATES OF AMERICA
Rockall
Northern Ireland
Gibraltar
Ceuta
MOROCCO
WESTERN SAHARA
MAURITANIA
SENEGAL
GUINEA-BISSAU
SIERRA LEONE
LIBERIA
IVORY COAST (CÔTE D'IVORY)
CUBA
Guantánamo Bay
HAITI
BELIZE
GUATEMALA
EL SALVADOR
NICARAGUA
VENEZUELA
GUYANA
SURINAME
French Guiana
COLOMBIA
Falkland Islands

Iraq

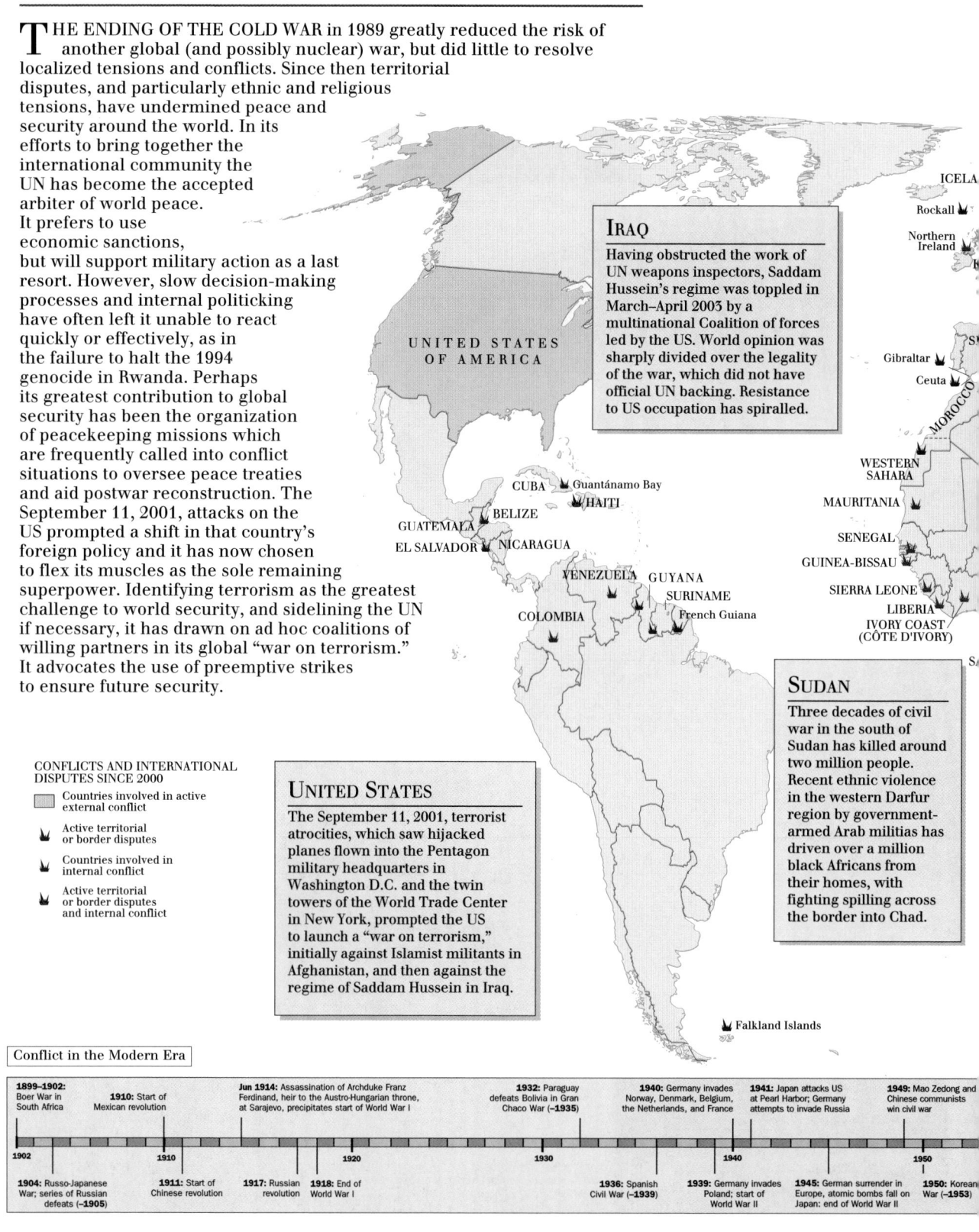

Having obstructed the work of UN weapons inspectors, Saddam Hussein's regime was toppled in March–April 2003 by a multinational Coalition of forces led by the US. World opinion was sharply divided over the legality of the war, which did not have official UN backing. Resistance to US occupation has spiralled.

Sudan

Three decades of civil war in the south of Sudan has killed around two million people. Recent ethnic violence in the western Darfur region by government-armed Arab militias has driven over a million black Africans from their homes, with fighting spilling across the border into Chad.

CONFLICTS AND INTERNATIONAL DISPUTES SINCE 2000

- Countries involved in active external conflict
- Active territorial or border disputes
- Countries involved in internal conflict
- Active territorial or border disputes and internal conflict

United States

The September 11, 2001, terrorist atrocities, which saw hijacked planes flown into the Pentagon military headquarters in Washington D.C. and the twin towers of the World Trade Center in New York, prompted the US to launch a "war on terrorism," initially against Islamist militants in Afghanistan, and then against the regime of Saddam Hussein in Iraq.

Conflict in the Modern Era

- **1899–1902:** Boer War in South Africa
- **1904:** Russo-Japanese War; series of Russian defeats (**–1905**)
- **1910:** Start of Mexican revolution
- **1911:** Start of Chinese revolution
- **Jun 1914:** Assassination of Archduke Franz Ferdinand, heir to the Austro-Hungarian throne, at Sarajevo, precipitates start of World War I
- **1917:** Russian revolution
- **1918:** End of World War I
- **1932:** Paraguay defeats Bolivia in Gran Chaco War (**–1935**)
- **1936:** Spanish Civil War (**–1939**)
- **1939:** Germany invades Poland; start of World War II
- **1940:** Germany invades Norway, Denmark, Belgium, the Netherlands, and France
- **1941:** Japan attacks US at Pearl Harbor; Germany attempts to invade Russia
- **1945:** German surrender in Europe, atomic bombs fall on Japan: end of World War II
- **1949:** Mao Zedong and Chinese communists win civil war
- **1950:** Korean War (**–1953**)

1902 1910 1920 1930 1940 1950

NEPAL

Maoist rebels launched a republican insurgency in 1999, gathering support in rural areas. Attempts to engage the rebels in the political process collapsed in 2001 and fighting intensified. In response the government has mounted a determined effort to defeat the rebels, leaving heavy casualties on both sides and damaging the country's all-important tourist industry.

CHECHNYA

Russian troops first entered the breakaway republic of Chechnya in 1994, launching a bloody war to crush Muslim separatists there. The capital, Grozny, was flattened and fighting has now been reduced to vicious guerrilla attacks in Chechnya and terrorist strikes in Russia proper by Chechen suicide bombers.

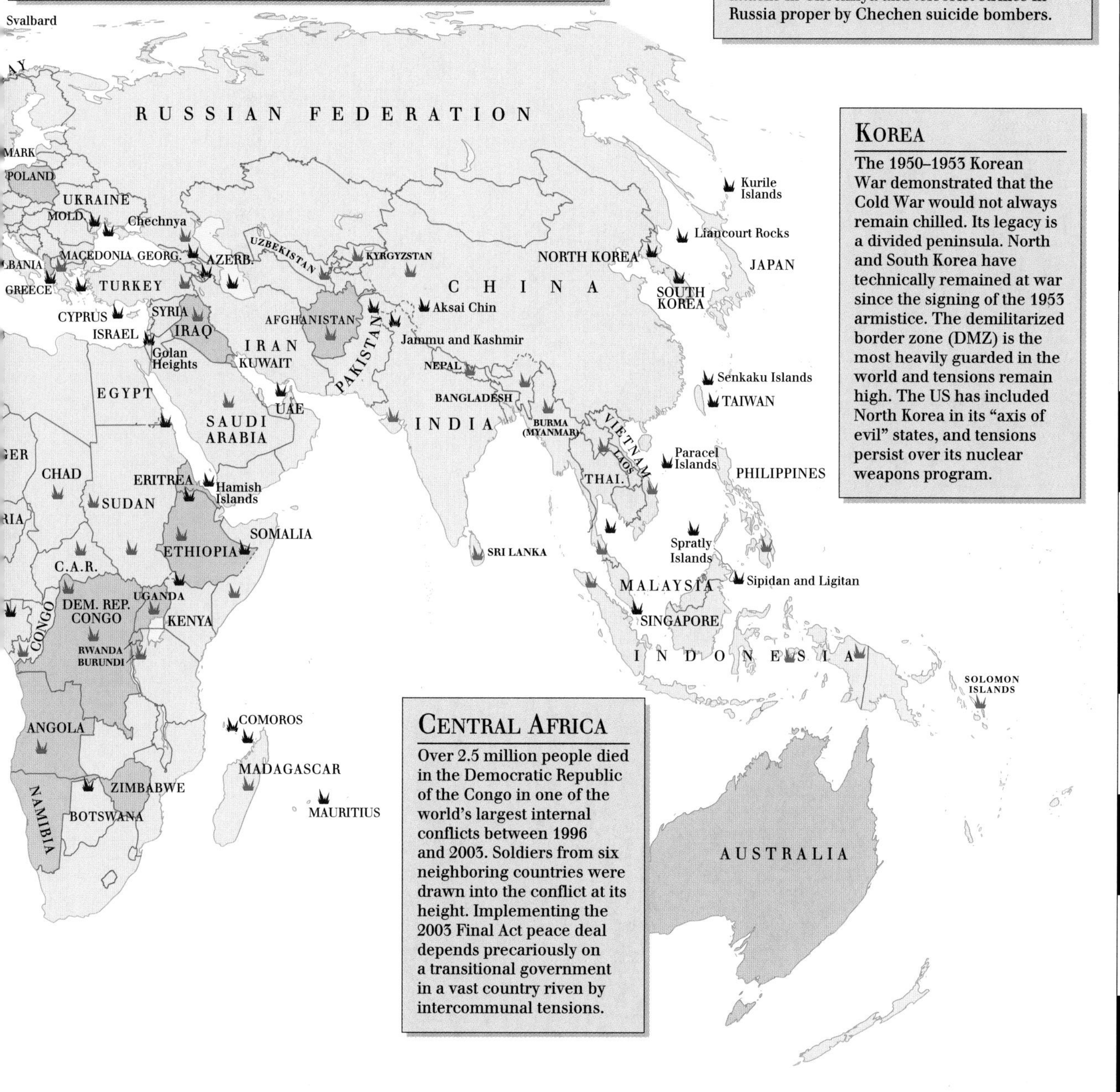

Svalbard
RUSSIAN FEDERATION
MARK
POLAND
UKRAINE
MOLD.
Chechnya
MACEDONIA
GEORG.
AZERB.
UZBEKISTAN
KYRGYZSTAN
GREECE
TURKEY
CYPRUS
SYRIA
IRAQ
ISRAEL
Golan Heights
AFGHANISTAN
IRAN
KUWAIT
PAKISTAN
Aksai Chin
Jammu and Kashmir
NEPAL
CHINA
NORTH KOREA
SOUTH KOREA
JAPAN
Kurile Islands
Liancourt Rocks
Senkaku Islands
TAIWAN
EGYPT
SAUDI ARABIA
UAE
BANGLADESH
INDIA
BURMA (MYANMAR)
VIETNAM
LAOS
THAI.
Paracel Islands
PHILIPPINES
CHAD
ERITREA
Hamish Islands
SUDAN
SOMALIA
ETHIOPIA
C.A.R.
SRI LANKA
Spratly Islands
MALAYSIA
Sipidan and Ligitan
SINGAPORE
INDONESIA
SOLOMON ISLANDS
UGANDA
DEM. REP. CONGO
KENYA
CONGO
RWANDA
BURUNDI
ANGOLA
COMOROS
MADAGASCAR
MAURITIUS
ZIMBABWE
NAMIBIA
BOTSWANA
AUSTRALIA

KOREA

The 1950–1953 Korean War demonstrated that the Cold War would not always remain chilled. Its legacy is a divided peninsula. North and South Korea have technically remained at war since the signing of the 1953 armistice. The demilitarized border zone (DMZ) is the most heavily guarded in the world and tensions remain high. The US has included North Korea in its "axis of evil" states, and tensions persist over its nuclear weapons program.

CENTRAL AFRICA

Over 2.5 million people died in the Democratic Republic of the Congo in one of the world's largest internal conflicts between 1996 and 2003. Soldiers from six neighboring countries were drawn into the conflict at its height. Implementing the 2003 Final Act peace deal depends precariously on a transitional government in a vast country riven by intercommunal tensions.

- **1954:** Algerian war of independence begins
- **1960:** Outbreak of civil war in Belgian Congo
- **1964:** US Congress approves war with Vietnam
- **1965:** India–Pakistan War over sovereignty of Kashmir
- **1968:** Troubles begin in Northern Ireland
- **1975:** US withdraws from Vietnam
- **1975:** Angola and Mozambique gain independence; civil wars ensue
- **1979:** Soviet Union invades Afghanistan (**–1989**) Civil war in Nicaragua (**–1990**) Civil war in El Salvador (**–1992**)
- **1980:** Iran–Iraq War (**–1988**)
- **1982:** Falklands War between UK and Argentina
- **1990:** Iraqi invasion of Kuwait and Gulf War (**–1991**)
- **1992:** Civil war in Bosnia & Herzegovina (**–1995**)
- **1994:** Massacre of Tutsis in Rwanda
- **1996:** Civil war in Dem. Rep. Congo (**–2003**)
- **1999:** "Ethnic cleansing" of Albanians in Kosovo by Serbs. Russian offensive in Chechnya
- **2001:** Terror attacks on US, US invasion of Afghanistan
- **2003:** US-led invasion of Iraq

1960 1970 1980 1990 2000

TIME ZONES

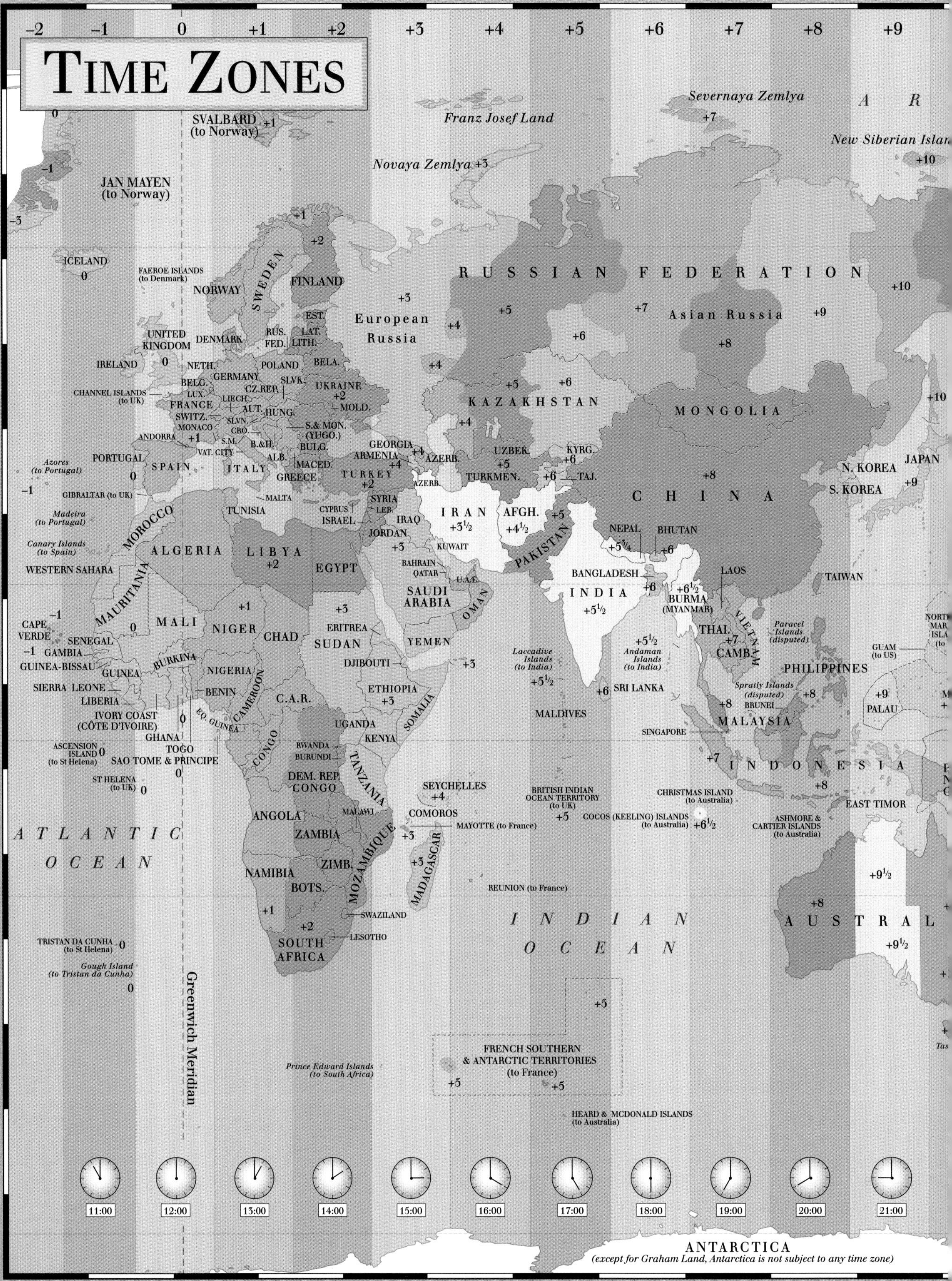

−2
−1
0
+1
+2
+3
+4
+5
+6
+7
+8
+9
SVALBARD (to Norway)
JAN MAYEN (to Norway)
Franz Josef Land
Severnaya Zemlya
New Siberian Islan
Novaya Zemlya
ICELAND
FAEROE ISLANDS (to Denmark)
NORWAY
SWEDEN
FINLAND
RUSSIAN FEDERATION
European Russia
Asian Russia
EST.
LAT.
LITH.
RUS. FED.
UNITED KINGDOM
IRELAND
DENMARK
NETH.
GERMANY
POLAND
BELA.
BELG.
LUX.
CZ.REP.
SLVK.
UKRAINE
CHANNEL ISLANDS (to UK)
FRANCE
LIECH.
AUT.
HUNG.
MOLD.
SWITZ.
MONACO
SLVN.
CRO.
S.& MON. (YUGO.)
ANDORRA
S.M.
B.&H.
BULG.
VAT. CITY
ALB.
MACED.
GEORGIA
ARMENIA
AZERB.
KAZAKHSTAN
MONGOLIA
UZBEK.
KYRG.
TURKMEN.
TAJ.
Azores (to Portugal)
PORTUGAL
SPAIN
ITALY
GREECE
TURKEY
GIBRALTAR (to UK)
MALTA
Madeira (to Portugal)
TUNISIA
CYPRUS
ISRAEL
SYRIA
LEB.
IRAQ
JORDAN
IRAN
AFGH.
PAKISTAN
NEPAL
BHUTAN
CHINA
N. KOREA
S. KOREA
JAPAN
Canary Islands (to Spain)
MOROCCO
ALGERIA
LIBYA
EGYPT
KUWAIT
BAHRAIN
QATAR
U.A.E.
SAUDI ARABIA
OMAN
BANGLADESH
INDIA
BURMA (MYANMAR)
LAOS
TAIWAN
WESTERN SAHARA
MAURITANIA
MALI
NIGER
CHAD
SUDAN
ERITREA
YEMEN
CAPE VERDE
SENEGAL
GAMBIA
GUINEA-BISSAU
GUINEA
BURKINA
NIGERIA
DJIBOUTI
Laccadive Islands (to India)
Andaman Islands (to India)
THAI.
CAMB.
VIETNAM
Paracel Islands (disputed)
PHILIPPINES
GUAM (to US)
SIERRA LEONE
LIBERIA
BENIN
CAMEROON
C.A.R.
ETHIOPIA
SOMALIA
SRI LANKA
Spratly Islands (disputed)
BRUNEI
PALAU
IVORY COAST (CÔTE D'IVOIRE)
GHANA
TOGO
EQ. GUINEA
UGANDA
KENYA
MALDIVES
MALAYSIA
SINGAPORE
ASCENSION ISLAND (to St Helena)
SAO TOME & PRINCIPE
CONGO
RWANDA
BURUNDI
TANZANIA
DEM. REP. CONGO
INDONESIA
ST HELENA (to UK)
SEYCHELLES
BRITISH INDIAN OCEAN TERRITORY (to UK)
CHRISTMAS ISLAND (to Australia)
COCOS (KEELING) ISLANDS (to Australia)
EAST TIMOR
ANGOLA
MALAWI
COMOROS
MAYOTTE (to France)
ASHMORE & CARTIER ISLANDS (to Australia)
ATLANTIC OCEAN
ZAMBIA
MOZAMBIQUE
MADAGASCAR
ZIMB.
NAMIBIA
BOTS.
REUNION (to France)
SWAZILAND
LESOTHO
SOUTH AFRICA
INDIAN OCEAN
AUSTRALIA
TRISTAN DA CUNHA (to St Helena)
Gough Island (to Tristan da Cunha)
Greenwich Meridian
FRENCH SOUTHERN & ANTARCTIC TERRITORIES (to France)
Prince Edward Islands (to South Africa)
HEARD & MCDONALD ISLANDS (to Australia)
11:00
12:00
13:00
14:00
15:00
16:00
17:00
18:00
19:00
20:00
21:00
ANTARCTICA
(except for Graham Land, Antarctica is not subject to any time zone)

+11
+12
–12
–11
–10
–9
–8
–7
–6
–5
–4
–3
–2
International Dateline
I C O C E A N
Queen Elizabeth Islands
No Time Zone
GREENLAND
(to Denmark)
0
–1
Baffin Island
Arctic Circle
Alaska
(to US)
CANADA
Newfoundland
–3½
ST PIERRE & MIQUELON
(to France)
UNITED STATES OF AMERICA
ATLANTIC OCEAN
PACIFIC OCEAN
BERMUDA
(to UK)
MIDWAY ISLANDS
(to US)
Hawaii
(to US)
JOHNSTON ATOLL (to US)
WAKE ISLAND
(to US)
MARSHALL ISLANDS
WALLIS & FUTUNA
(to France)
KINGMAN REEF (to US)
PALMYRA ATOLL (to US)
BAKER & HOWLAND ISLANDS (to US)
JARVIS ISLAND
(to US)
NAURU
KIRIBATI
+13
+14
TUVALU
TOKELAU
(to NZ)
COOK ISLANDS
(to NZ)
SOLOMON ISLANDS
VANUATU
FIJI
TONGA
SAMOA
NIUE (to NZ)
AMERICAN SAMOA
(to US)
FRENCH POLYNESIA
(to France)
Îles Marquises
–9½
PITCAIRN ISLANDS
(to UK)
NORFOLK ISLAND
(to Australia)
+11½
Kermadec Island
(to NZ)
NEW ZEALAND
Chatham Island
(to NZ)
+12¾
Bounty Island
(to NZ)
Campbell Island
(to NZ)
Macquarie Island (to Australia)
Clipperton Island
(to France)
Easter Island
(to Chile)
Galápagos Islands
(to Ecuador)
MEXICO
TURKS & CAICOS ISLANDS
(to UK)
DOM. REP.
CAYMAN ISLANDS
(to UK)
BAHAMAS
HONDURAS
BELIZE
CUBA
JAMAICA
NAVASSA I.
(to US)
HAITI
NETH. ANT.
(to Neth.)
ARUBA
(to Neth.)
GUATEMALA
EL SALVADOR
NICARAGUA
COSTA RICA
PANAMA
PUERTO RICO (to US)
BRITISH VIRGIN ISLANDS (to UK)
VIRGIN ISLANDS (to US)
ANGUILLA (to UK)
ST KITTS & NEVIS
ANTIGUA & BARBUDA
MONTSERRAT (to UK)
GUADELOUPE (to France)
DOMINICA
MARTINIQUE (to France)
ST LUCIA
BARBADOS
ST VINCENT & THE GRENADINES
GRENADA
TRINIDAD & TOBAGO
Tropic of Cancer
VENEZUELA
COLOMBIA
FRENCH GUIANA
(to France)
Equator
GUYANA
SURINAME
ECUADOR
PERU
BRAZIL
BOLIVIA
PARAGUAY
Tropic of Capricorn
San Felix Island
(to Chile)
San Ambrosia Island
(to Chile)
CHILE
Juan Fernandez Island
(to Chile)
ARGENTINA
URUGUAY
FALKLAND ISLANDS
(to UK)
23:00
24:00
01:00
02:00
03:00
04:00
05:00
06:00
07:00
08:00
09:00
10:00
Antarctic Circle
ANTARCTICA
Graham Land

CHRONOLOGY 2003–2004

BOTH CONSOLIDATION AND disintegration characterized the world in 2003–2004. Europe stretched its legs: the EU shifted its center of gravity to the east, while NATO also expanded to the borders of Russia, and a "rose revolution" in Georgia ended Shevardnadze's rule. Meanwhile, in the Middle East and Asia, terrorism and insurgency sent oil prices racing to record highs, brought fear and tragedy to southern Russia with the siege of a school in North Ossetia, and left US-led Coalition forces struggling to impose order in Iraq amid guerrilla attacks and uprisings in and around the holiest shrines of the Shi'a faith.

NORTH AMERICA

❑ **February 1, 2003** Seven astronauts are killed when the US space shuttle *Columbia* explodes on reentry.

❑ **April 13, 2003** The human genome is mapped, two years ahead of schedule, by international researchers.

❑ **April 15, 2003** After nine years in power, the separatist Partí Québécois is ousted from the Québec government.

❑ **December 12, 2003** Paul Martin becomes Canadian prime minister.

❑ **April 26, 2004** The US eases 20-year-old sanctions on Libya and allows US firms to buy Libyan oil.

❑ **April 29, 2004** Photographs are released of US reservists abusing prisoners at Abu Ghraib jail in Iraq.

❑ **July 1, 2004** Cuban exiles in US protest as tough new restrictions on travel to the island come into force.

❑ **July 23, 2004** Commission set up in US to probe 9/11 attacks cites "deep institutional failings" in US intelligence.

❑ **September 16, 2004** Hurricane Ivan hits US, after devastating Caribbean.

CENTRAL AND SOUTH AMERICA

❑ **January 1, 2003** Veteran left-wing leader "Lula" da Silva is inaugurated as president of Brazil.

❑ **March 18, 2003** A crackdown on prodemocracy activists begins in Cuba.

❑ **September 19, 2003** Argentina defaults on a $2.9 billion debt payment to the IMF.

❑ **October 17, 2003** Bolivian president Gonzalo Sánchez de Lozada resigns and flees the country amid violent protests over gas exports.

❑ **February 29, 2004** Haitian president Jean-Bertrand Aristide resigns and flees as rebels close in on the capital.

❑ **March 12, 2004** Congress votes to legalize divorce in Chile.

❑ **May 27, 2004** Floods in Haiti and the Dominican Republic kill 2000 people.

❑ **July 18, 2004** Bolivians vote in a referendum to allow the export of natural gas.

❑ **August 15, 2004** President Hugo Chávez of Venezuela wins a referendum on his rule.

EUROPE

❑ **February 4, 2003** The rump "Yugoslavia" ceases to exist and is replaced by Serbia & Montenegro.

❑ **February 14, 2003** Five million people demonstrate in Europe against the impending war on Iraq.

❑ **March 12, 2003** Serbian prime minister Zoran Djindjic is assassinated by members of the former Serbian secret service.

❑ **April 23, 2003** The Green Line which divides Cyprus is opened for the first time in 29 years.

❑ **August 29, 2003** Over 11,000 people are estimated to have died in a heatwave in France.

❑ **September 10, 2003** Swedish foreign minister Anna Lindh is stabbed to death in a department store.

❑ **October 19, 2003** The far-right Swiss People's Party becomes the largest party in Switzerland's National Council.

❑ **November 24, 2003** Georgia has its "rose revolution": President Eduard Shevardnadze steps down and flees to Russia after weeks of protests led by opposition leader Mikhail Saakashvili.

❑ **January 28, 2004** The Hutton Inquiry exonerates UK prime minister Tony Blair of lying about the readiness of Iraqi weapons of mass destruction.

❑ **February 11, 2004** France passes law banning Muslim headscarves and other religious symbols in schools.

❑ **March 7, 2004** Conservatives return to power in Greece for the first time in a decade.

❑ **March 11, 2004** Nearly 200 people are killed when bombs explode on packed commuter trains in Madrid. The opposition Spanish Socialist Workers' Party wins a surprise victory in the general election two days later.

❑ **March 29, 2004** NATO expands to 26 states, incorporating seven new members.

❑ **April 24, 2004** Turkish Cypriots vote "yes" in a referendum on a UN-backed plan to reunify the island; Greek Cypriots vote "no," thereby rejecting it.

❑ **May 1, 2004** The European Union expands to 25 members, including eight ex-communist states, Malta, and Cyprus.

❑ **September 3, 2004** Russian special forces end a school siege in which 1000 people were held hostage.

AFRICA

❑ **March 16, 2003** Veteran rebel Gen. François Bozizé leads a military coup in the Central African Republic.

❑ **April 2, 2003** The Final Act is signed outlining a definitive peace plan for the DRC. Rebel leaders are sworn in as vice presidents in July.

❑ **May 21, 2003** Over 2100 people die in a powerful earthquake in Algiers.

❑ **June 10, 2003** Three skulls from Herto, Ethiopia, are unveiled. At 160,000 years of age they are the oldest known human remains.

❑ **July 4, 2003** The civil war in Ivory Coast is declared over after almost ten months.

❑ **August 4, 2003** The first peacekeepers arrive in Liberia heralding an end to the civil war. A week later President Charles Taylor resigns and flees to Nigeria.

❑ **December 19, 2003** Libyan leader Col. Muammar al-Gaddafi announces that his regime will abandon the development of weapons of mass destruction.

❑ **January 28, 2004** Somali warlords and rival militias agree to the formation of a 275-member parliament.

❑ **January 30, 2004** Conflict in the Darfur region of western Sudan escalates; around 100,000 flee across the border to Chad.

❑ **March 9, 2004** A group of 70 suspected mercenaries is arrested in Zimbabwe, accused of traveling to Equatorial Guinea to take part in an alleged coup plot.

❑ **April 14, 2004** The African National Congress wins the South African general election by a landslide.

❑ **May 11, 2004** The Zimbabwean government declares that it expects a bumper harvest and refuses food aid.

❑ **June 3, 2004** Trials of suspected war criminals begin in Sierra Leone.

❑ **August 8, 2004** Mauritanian officials warn that as much as 80% of the harvest has been eaten by locusts.

❑ **August 15, 2004** African Union (AU) troops arrive in the Darfur region of Sudan to act as cease-fire monitors.

West Asia/Middle East

❑ **March 20, 2003** The invasion of Iraq by US, UK, and other "Coalition" forces begins. The regime of Saddam Hussein is toppled by April 9.

❑ **May 1, 2003** The US publishes its "roadmap" to peace in the Middle East. The plan is accepted by both Israel and the Palestinians, but is violated almost immediately.

❑ **June 2, 2003** Islamic *sharia* law is imposed in Pakistan's Northwest Frontier Province.

❑ **July 22, 2003** Uday and Qusay Hussein, the sons of the ousted Iraqi dictator, are killed in a six-hour seige.

❑ **November 11, 2003** At least 25 people are killed in Istanbul in suicide bombings against a bank and the British consulate.

❑ **December 13, 2003** Saddam Hussein is captured in Iraq by US soldiers.

❑ **December 26, 2003** Over 30,000 people die in an earthquake in the town of Bam in Iran.

❑ **June 6, 2004** The Israeli cabinet agrees to a withdrawal from Gaza.

❑ **June 28, 2004** The US-led Coalition Provisional Authority hands over power to an Iraqi interim government.

❑ **July 20, 2004** The UN General Assembly condemns Israel's West Bank barrier as illegal.

North and East Asia

❑ **February 18, 2003** 133 people die in an arson attack on the Seoul subway in South Korea.

❑ **May 15, 2003** Hu Jintao becomes president of China at the head of a new generation of Communist leaders.

❑ **June 1, 2003** The controversial Three Gorges Dam in China is flooded with the waters of the Yangtze River.

❑ **June 26, 2003** Beijing is declared free of Severe Acute Respiratory Syndrome (SARS): 191 people had died in the Chinese capital alone.

❑ **July 8, 2003** The Japanese House of Representatives votes to allow troops to serve abroad for the first time since 1945.

❑ **October 15, 2003** China becomes only the third country to launch a man into space.

❑ **March 21, 2004** Taiwanese president Chen Shui-bian is reelected by less than 1% of the vote, triggering a lengthy recount.

❑ **April 23, 2004** A train explosion in North Korea kills 150 people and injures thousands.

❑ **June 14, 2004** Loudspeakers on the North–South Korean border cease broadcasting propaganda.

South Asia

❑ **January 13, 2003** Leaders of the Naga independence movement declare their decades-long war with the Indian government over. Peace talks begin.

❑ **May 30, 2003** Burmese opposition leader Aung San Suu Kyi is rearrested once again following an attack on her motorcade. Her detention prompts widespread international condemnation.

❑ **August 27, 2003** A cease-fire between Maoist rebels and the Nepalese government collapses.

❑ **January 15, 2004** The first train from Pakistan for more than two years crosses into India.

❑ **March 18, 2004** Pakistan is named a "major non-NATO ally" by the US.

❑ **May 13, 2004** Congress (I) wins a stunning victory in Indian elections.

❑ **June 2, 2004** Sher Bahadur Deuba is reinstated as prime minister of Nepal, 18 months after his dismissal.

❑ **August 17, 2004** Maoist rebels in Nepal blockade Kathmandu for a week.

Southeast Asia

❑ **January 19, 2003** Anti-Thai riots erupt in the Cambodian capital of Phnom Penh.

❑ **May 19, 2003** The Indonesian government launches a major offensive against separatists in Aceh.

❑ **May 25, 2003** It is announced that over 2000 people have died during the Thai government's crackdown on the illegal narcotics trade.

❑ **October 31, 2003** Mahathir Mohamed steps down as Malaysian prime minister.

❑ **April 28, 2004** Around 127 people are killed in a series of gun battles in southern Thailand after police stations are attacked by militants.

Australia and Oceania

❑ **March 10, 2003** Bernard Dowiyogo, the veteran president of Nauru, dies in office.

❑ **May 25, 2003** Archbishop Peter Hollingworth, the governor-general of Australia, resigns amid scandal over child abuse in the Australian Church.

❑ **July 24, 2003** Peacekeepers arrive in the Solomon Islands to restore law and order, on invitation of the government.

❑ **February 15, 2004** Race riots are sparked in Australia by the death of an aboriginal boy in a Sydney suburb while being chased by police.

❑ **April 19, 2004** Fijian "founding father" Ratu Sir Kamisese Mara dies aged 83.

❑ **May 12, 2004** Australia pledges to double its annual aid budget to the south Pacific.

❑ **May 25, 2004** Opposition politicians take control of Nauru's parliament and pass several bills while the president and other government ministers are out of the country.

❑ **July 13, 2004** New Zealand imposes diplomatic sanctions on Israel over the alleged involvement of Mossad agents in a passport scandal.

see pages 36–39 for CHRONOLOGY OF WORLD HISTORY

INTERNATIONAL ORGANIZATIONS

THIS LISTING GIVES the full names of all international organizations referred to, often by acronym, in the World Desk Reference (political parties are to be found under the Politics heading within each country entry). The full names are followed by the date of the establishment or foundation, an indication of membership, where appropriate, and a summary of the organization's aims and functions.

ACC
Arab Cooperation Council
established 1989
members – Egypt, Iraq, Jordan, Yemen
Promotes Arab economic cooperation

ACP
African, Caribbean, and Pacific Countries
established 1976
members – 79 developing countries and territories
Preferential economic and aid relationship with the EU under the Lomé Convention

ACS
Association of Caribbean States
established 1994
members – 25 countries in the Caribbean region
Promotes economic, scientific, and cultural cooperation in the region

ADB
Asian Development Bank
established 1966
members – 45 Asia–Pacific countries and territories, 18 nonregional countries
Encourages regional development

AfDB
African Development Bank
established 1964
members – 53 African countries, 24 non-African countries
Encourages African economic and social development

AFESD
Arab Fund for Economic and Social Development
established 1968
members – 21 Arab countries (including Palestine)
Promotes social and economic development in Arab states

AL
League of Arab States (Arab League)
established 1945
members – 22 Arab countries (including Palestine)
Forum to promote Arab cooperation on social, political, and military issues

ALADI
Latin American Integration Association
established 1960
members – 12 Central and South American countries
Promotes trade and regional integration

AmCC
Amazonian Cooperation Council
established 1978
members – Bolivia, Brazil, Colombia, Ecuador, Guyana, Peru, Suriname, Venezuela
Promotes the harmonious development of the Amazon region

AMF
Arab Monetary Fund
established 1977
members – 22 Arab countries (including Palestine)
Promotes monetary and economic cooperation

AMU
Arab Maghreb Union
established 1989
members – Algeria, Libya, Mauritania, Morocco, Tunisia
Promotes integration and economic cooperation among north African Arab states

ANZUS
Australia–New Zealand–United States Security Treaty
established 1951
members – Australia, New Zealand, US
Trilateral security agreement. Security relations between the US and New Zealand were suspended in 1984 over the issue of US nuclear-powered or potentially nuclear-armed naval vessels visiting New Zealand ports. High-level contacts between the USA and New Zealand were resumed in 1994

AOSIS
Alliance of Small Island States
established 1991
members – 39 countries and dependencies
Promotes interests of small island states and low-lying coastal countries

AP
Andean Pact (Acuerdo de Cartegena), also known as Andean Community
established 1969
members – Bolivia, Colombia, Ecuador, Peru, Venezuela
Promotes development through integration

APEC
Asia–Pacific Economic Cooperation
established 1989
members – 21 Pacific Rim countries and Hong Kong
Promotes regional economic cooperation

ASEAN
Association of Southeast Asian Nations
established 1967
members – Brunei, Burma, Cambodia, Indonesia, Laos, Malaysia, Philippines, Singapore, Thailand, Vietnam
Promotes economic, social, and cultural cooperation

AU
African Union
established 2002
members – 52 African countries and Western Sahara
Promotes unity and cooperation in Africa (successor to the Organization of African Unity (OAU), established in 1963)

BADEA
Arab Bank for Economic Development in Africa
established 1973
members – 18 Arab countries (including Palestine)
Established as an agency of the Arab League to promote economic development in Africa

BDEAC
Central African States Development Bank
established 1975
members – Cameroon, Central African Republic, Chad, Congo, Equatorial Guinea, France, Gabon, Germany, Kuwait
Furthers economic development

Benelux
Benelux Economic Union
established 1960
members – Belgium, Luxembourg, Netherlands
Develops economic ties between member countries

BOAD
West African Development Bank
established 1973
members – Benin, Burkina, Guinea-Bissau, Ivory Coast, Mali, Niger, Senegal, Togo
Promotes economic development and integration in west Africa

BSEC
Organization of the Black Sea Economic Cooperation
established 1992
members – Albania, Armenia, Azerbaijan, Bulgaria, Georgia, Greece, Moldova, Romania, Russia, Turkey, Ukraine
Furthers regional stability through economic cooperation

CAEU
Council of Arab Economic Unity
established 1957
members – 12 Arab countries (including Palestine)
Encourages economic integration

Caricom
Caribbean Community and Common Market
established 1973
members – 14 Caribbean countries and Montserrat
Fosters economic ties in the Caribbean

CBSS
Council of the Baltic Sea States
established 1992
members – 11 Baltic Sea states and the European Commission
Promotes cooperation among Baltic Sea states

CDB
Caribbean Development Bank
established 1969
members – 17 Caribbean countries/dependencies, 8 non-Caribbean countries
Promotes regional development

CE
Council of Europe
established 1949
members – 45 European countries
Promotes unity and quality of life in Europe

CEFTA
Central European Free Trade Agreement
established 1992
members – Bulgaria, Czech Republic, Hungary, Poland, Romania, Slovakia, Slovenia
Promotes trade and cooperation

CEI
Central European Initiative
established 1989
members – 17 east and central European countries
Evolved from Quadrilateral Cooperation; promotes economic and political cooperation within the OSCE

CEMAC
Central African Economic and Monetary Community
established 1994
members – Cameroon, Central African Republic, Chad, Congo, Equatorial Guinea, Gabon
Aims to promote integration, by economic and monetary union (replaced UDEAC)

CEPGL
Economic Community of the Great Lakes Countries
established 1976
members – Burundi, Democratic Republic of the Congo, Rwanda
Promotes economic cooperation

CERN
European Organization for Nuclear Research
established 1954
members – 20 European countries
Provides for collaboration in nuclear research for peaceful purposes

CILSS
Permanent Interstate Committee for Drought Control in the Sahel
established 1973
members – 9 African countries in the Sahel region
Promotes prevention of drought and crop failure in the region

CIS
Commonwealth of Independent States
established 1991
members – 12 former republics of the Soviet Union
Promotes regional cooperation

CMCA
Central American Monetary Council
established 1960
members – Costa Rica, Dominican Republic, El Salvador, Guatemala, Honduras, Nicaragua
Now a subsystem of SICA. Furthers economic ties between its members; one of its institutions is the BCIE – Central American Bank for Economic Integration

COI
Indian Ocean Commission
established 1982
members – Comoros, France (representing Réunion), Madagascar, Mauritius, Seychelles
Promotes regional cooperation

COMESA
Common Market for Eastern and Southern Africa
established 1993
members – 20 African countries
Promotes economic development and cooperation (replaced PTA)

Comm
Commonwealth
established 1931
members – 53 countries. Members are chiefly former members of the British Empire
Develops relationships and contacts between members

CP
Colombo Plan
established 1950
members – Five donor countries: Australia, Japan, New Zealand, South Korea, US; and 20 Asia–Pacific countries
Encourages economic and social development in Asia–Pacific region

CPLP
Community of Portuguese-speaking Countries
established 1996
members – Portugal, Brazil, East Timor, and five Portuguese-speaking African countries – Angola, Cape Verde, Guinea-Bissau, Mozambique, São Tomé and Príncipe
To promote political and diplomatic links between member states, and cooperation on economic, social, cultural, judicial, and scientific development among Portuguese-speaking countries

Damasc
Damascus Declaration
established 1991
members – Bahrain, Egypt, Kuwait, Oman, Qatar, Saudi Arabia, Syria, United Arab Emirates
A loose association, formed after the 1991 Gulf War, which aims to secure the stability of the region

EAC
East African Community
established 2001
members – Kenya, Tanzania, Uganda
Promotes economic cooperation

EAPC
Euro-Atlantic Partnership Council
established 1991
members – The 26 members of NATO plus 20 other European countries
Forum for cooperation on political and security issues (successor to the North Atlantic Cooperation Council, NACC)

EBRD
European Bank for Reconstruction and Development
established 1991
members – 60 countries
Helps transition of former communist European states to market economies

ECO
Economic Cooperation Organization
established 1985
members – Afghanistan, Azerbaijan, Iran, Kazakhstan, Kyrgyzstan, Pakistan, Tajikistan, Turkey, Turkmenistan, Uzbekistan
Aims at cooperation in economic, social, and cultural affairs

ECOWAS
Economic Community of West African States
established 1975
members – 15 west African countries
Promotes regional economic cooperation

EEA
European Economic Area
established 1994
members – The 25 members of the EU, and Iceland, Liechtenstein, and Norway
Aims to include EFTA members in the EU single market

EEC
Eurasian Economic Community
established 2001
members – Belarus, Kazakhstan, Kyrgyzstan, Russia, Tajikistan
Coordinates regional trade

EFTA
European Free Trade Association
established 1960
members – Iceland, Liechtenstein, Norway, Switzerland
Promotes economic cooperation

ESA
European Space Agency
established 1973
members – 15 European countries, with Greece and Luxembourg as observers pending full membership on December 1, 2005
Promotes cooperation in space research for peaceful purposes

EU
European Union
established 1992
members – 25 European countries
Aims to integrate the economies of member states and promote cooperation and coordination of policies (successor to the European Communities (EC), established in 1957 by the Treaties of Rome)

FZ
Franc zone
established Not applicable
members – France (including overseas departments and territories) and 15 African countries
Aims to form monetary union among countries whose currencies are linked to that of France

G3
Group of 3
established 1987
members – Colombia, Mexico, Venezuela
Aims to ease trade restrictions

G7
Group of 7
established 1975
members – The seven major industrialized countries: Canada, France, Germany, Italy, Japan, UK, US
Summit meetings of the seven major industrialized countries, originally for economic purposes. For political purposes summit meetings are now held as the G8, including Russia

G8
Group of 8
established 1994
members – Canada, France, Germany, Italy, Japan, Russia, UK, US
Global forum of world's major powers, which holds regular summit meetings

G10
Group of 10
established 1962
members – 11 members: G7 members, plus Belgium, Netherlands, Sweden, and Switzerland
Ministers meet to discuss monetary issues

G15
Group of 15
established 1989
members – 19 developing countries
Meets annually to further cooperation among developing countries

G24
Group of 24
established Not applicable
members – 24 developing countries within the IMF
Promotes the interests of developing countries on monetary and development issues

GCC
Gulf Cooperation Council
established 1981
members – Bahrain, Kuwait, Oman, Qatar, Saudi Arabia, United Arab Emirates
Promotes cooperation in social, economic, and political affairs

Geplacea
Latin American and Caribbean Sugar Exporting Countries
established 1974
members – 23 countries
A forum for consultation on the production and sale of sugar

GGC
Gulf of Guinea Commission
established 2001
members – Angola, Cameroon, Congo, Democratic Republic of the Congo, Equatorial Guinea, Gabon, Nigeria, São Tomé and Príncipe
Promotes regional cooperation

IAEA
International Atomic Energy Agency
established 1957
members – 137 countries
Promotes and monitors peaceful use of atomic energy

IBRD
International Bank for Reconstruction and Development (also known as the World Bank)
established 1945
members – 184 countries
UN agency providing economic development loans

ICRC
International Committee of the Red Cross
established 1863
members – Up to 25 Swiss nationals form the international committee. Red Cross or Red Crescent societies exist in 178 countries
Coordinates all international humanitarian activities of the International Red Cross and Red Crescent Movement, giving legal and practical assistance to the victims of wars and disasters. It works through national committees of Red Cross or Red Crescent societies

IDB
Inter-American Development Bank
established 1959
members – 28 American countries and 18 nonregional countries
Promotes development in Latin America and the Caribbean through the financing of economic and social development projects and the provision of technical assistance

IGAD
Intergovernmental Authority on Development
established 1996
members – Djibouti, Eritrea, Ethiopia, Kenya, Somalia, Sudan, Uganda
Promotes cooperation on food security, infrastructure, and other development issues (supersedes IGADD, founded 1986, to promote cooperation on drought-related matters)

IMF
International Monetary Fund
established 1945
members – 184 countries. The voting rights of Liberia are currently suspended.
Promotes international monetary cooperation, the balanced growth of trade, and exchange-rate stability; provides credit resources to members experiencing balance-of-trade difficulties

IsDB
Islamic Development Bank
established 1975
members – 55 countries (including Palestine)
Promotes economic development on Islamic principles among Muslim communities (agency of the OIC)

IWC
International Whaling Commission
established 1946
members – 52 countries
Reviews conduct of whaling throughout world; coordinates and funds whale research

LCBC
Lake Chad Basin Commission
established 1964
members – Cameroon, Central African Republic, Chad, Niger, Nigeria
Encourages economic and environmental development in Lake Chad region

Mekong River
Mekong River Commission
established 1995
members – Cambodia, Laos, Thailand, Vietnam
Accord on the sustainable development of the Mekong River basin (replacing the 1958 interim Mekong Secretariat)

Mercosur
Southern Common Market
established 1991
members – Argentina, Brazil, Paraguay, Uruguay
Promotes economic integration, free trade, and common external tariffs

MRU
Mano River Union
established 1973
members – Guinea, Liberia, Sierra Leone
Aims to create customs and economic union in order to promote development

NAFTA
North American Free Trade Agreement
established 1994
members – Canada, Mexico, US
Free trade zone

NAM
Non-Aligned Movement
established 1961
members – 116 countries (including Palestine). Serbia and Montenegro was suspended in 1992, and is now an observer
Fosters political and military cooperation away from traditional Eastern or Western blocs

NATO
North Atlantic Treaty Organization
established 1949
members – 26 countries
Promotes mutual defense cooperation. Since January 1994, NATO's Partnership for Peace program has provided a loose framework for cooperation with former members of the Warsaw Pact and the ex-Soviet republics. A historic Founding Act signed between Russia and NATO in May 1997 allowed for the organization's eastward expansion: the Czech Republic, Hungary, and Poland joined in 1999, and seven more joined in 2004

NC
Nordic Council
established 1952
members – Denmark, Finland, Iceland, Norway, Sweden
Promotes cultural and environmental cooperation in Scandinavia

OAPEC
Organization of Arab Petroleum Exporting Countries
established 1968
members – Algeria, Bahrain, Egypt, Iraq, Kuwait, Libya, Qatar, Saudi Arabia, Syria, United Arab Emirates
Aims to promote the interests of member countries and increase cooperation in the petroleum industry

OAS
Organization of American States
established 1948
members – 35 American countries (though Cuba has been suspended since 1962)
Promotes security and economic and social development in the Americas

OAU
Organization of African Unity
Predecessor of the AU

OECD
Organization for Economic Cooperation and Development
established 1961
members – 30 industrialized democracies
Forum for coordinating economic policies among industrialized countries

OECS
Organization of Eastern Caribbean States
established 1981
members – Antigua and Barbuda, Dominica, Grenada, Montserrat, St. Kitts and Nevis, St. Lucia, St. Vincent and the Grenadines
Promotes political, economic, and defense cooperation

OIC
Organization of the Islamic Conference
established 1971
members – 57 countries (including Palestine)
Furthers Islamic solidarity and cooperation

OIF
International Organization of Francophony
established 1970
members – 47 countries and the governments of Québec, New Brunswick, and the French Community of Belgium
To promote cooperation and cultural and technical links among French-speaking countries and communities

OMVG
Gambia River Development Organization
established 1978
members – Gambia, Guinea, Guinea-Bissau, Senegal
Promotes integrated development of the Gambia River basin

Opanal
Agency for the Prohibition of Nuclear Weapons in Latin America and the Caribbean
established 1969
members – 33 countries
Aims to ensure compliance with the Treaty of Tlatelolco (banning nuclear weapons from South America and the Caribbean)

OPEC
Organization of the Petroleum Exporting Countries
established 1960
members – Algeria, Indonesia, Iran, Iraq, Kuwait, Libya, Nigeria, Qatar, Saudi Arabia, United Arab Emirates, Venezuela
Aims to coordinate oil policies to ensure fair and stable prices

OSCE
Organization for Security and Cooperation in Europe
established 1972
members – 55 countries
Aims to strengthen democracy and human rights, and settle disputes peacefully (formerly CSCE)

PC
Pacific Community
established 1948
members – 27 countries and territories
A forum for dialogue between Pacific countries and powers administering Pacific territories (formerly South Pacific Commission)

PfP
Partnership for Peace
see NATO
established Not applicable
members – 20 members: eastern European and former Soviet countries, Sweden, Finland, Malta, Austria, and Switzerland

PIF
Pacific Islands Forum
established 1971
members – 16 countries and self-governing territories
Develops regional political cooperation (formerly South Pacific Forum)

RG
Rio Group
established 1987
members – 19 Latin American and Caribbean countries
Forum for Latin American and Caribbean issues (evolved from Contadora Group, established 1948)

SAARC
South Asian Association for Regional Cooperation
established 1985
members – Bangladesh, Bhutan, India, Maldives, Nepal, Pakistan, Sri Lanka
Encourages economic, social, and cultural cooperation

SACU
Southern African Customs Union
established 1969
members – Botswana, Lesotho, Namibia, South Africa, Swaziland
Promotes cooperation in trade and customs matters among southern African states

SADC
Southern African Development Community
established 1992
members – 14 southern African countries
Promotes economic integration

San José
San José Group
established 1988
members – Costa Rica, El Salvador, Guatemala, Honduras, Nicaragua, Panama
A "complementary, voluntary, and gradual" economic union

SCO
Shanghai Cooperation Organization
established 1996
members – China, Kazakhstan, Kyrgyzstan, Russia, Tajikistan, Uzbekistan
Promotes regional security and cooperation (formerly Shanghai Five)

SELA
Latin American Economic System
established 1975
members – 27 countries
Promotes economic and social development through regional cooperation

SICA
Central American Integration System
established 1991
members – Belize, Costa Rica, El Salvador, Guatemala, Honduras, Nicaragua, Panama
Coordinates the political, economic, social, and environmental integration of the region

UEMOA
West African Economic and Monetary Union
established 1994
members – 8 west African countries
Aims for convergence of monetary policies and economic union

UN
United Nations
established 1945
members – 191 countries
Taiwan and the Vatican City do not belong to the UN
permanent members of the Security Council – China, France, Russia, UK, US
Aims to maintain international peace and security and to promote cooperation over economic, social, cultural, and humanitarian problems

Agencies include the regional commissions of the UN's Economic and Social Council:
ECA (Economic Commission for Africa – established 1958);
ECE (Economic Commission for Europe – established 1947);
ECLAC (Economic Commission for Latin America and the Caribbean – established 1948);
ESCAP (Economic and Social Commission for Asia and the Pacific – established 1947);
ESCWA (Economic and Social Commission for Western Asia – established 1973).

Other bodies of the UN, in which most members participate, include
IDA(the International Development Association);
UNCTAD (the UN Conference on Trade and Development);
UNDP (the UN Development Program);
UNFPA (the UN Population Fund);
UNHCR (the UN High Commissioner for Refugees);
UNICEF (the UN Children's Fund).

WEU
Western European Union
established 1955
members – 10 countries
A forum for European military cooperation

World Bank
see IBRD

WTO
World Trade Organization
established 1995
members – 143 countries and Hong Kong, Macao, and the EU
Aims to liberalize trade through multilateral trade agreements (successor to the General Agreement on Tariffs and Trade, GATT)

2

THE NATIONS OF THE WORLD

THE NATIONS OF THE WORLD

• AFGHANISTAN ~ ZIMBABWE

OVERSEAS TERRITORIES & DEPENDENCIES

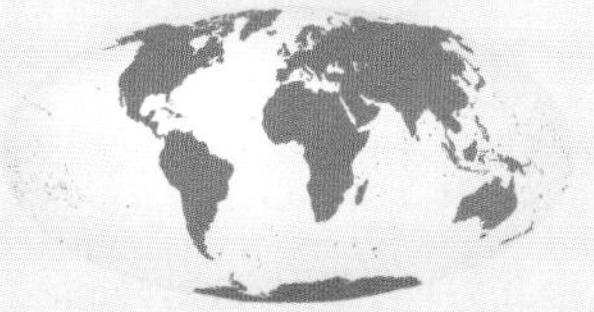

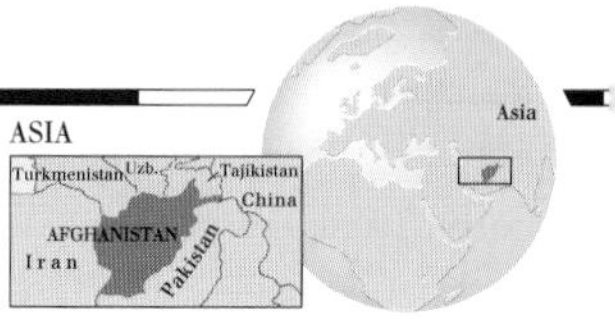
Asia
ASIA
Turkmenistan
Uzb.
Tajikistan
China
AFGHANISTAN
Iran
Pakistan

AFGHANISTAN

OFFICIAL NAME: Islamic State of Afghanistan **CAPITAL:** Kabul
POPULATION: 23.9 million **CURRENCY:** New afghani **OFFICIAL LANGUAGES:** Pashtu and Dari

1919
1919
Aug 19
AFG
+4.5
+93
.af

AFGHANISTAN LIES LANDLOCKED in central Asia, three-quarters of its territory inaccessible terrain. Its political system, economy, and infrastructure have been devastated by decades of armed conflict. In the 1980s Islamic *mujahideen* factions defeated the Soviet-backed communist regime, but rivalries undermined their fragile power-sharing agreement and the hard-line *taliban* militia swept to power in 1996. Islamic dress codes and behavior were vigorously enforced; women were left with few rights. The *taliban* regime crumbled in the face of the US-led "war on terrorism" launched in late 2001.

The Band-i-Amir River, *in the Hindu Kush. Afghanistan is mountainous and arid. Many Afghans are nomadic sheep farmers.*

CLIMATE

Mountain/cold desert

WEATHER CHART FOR KABUL

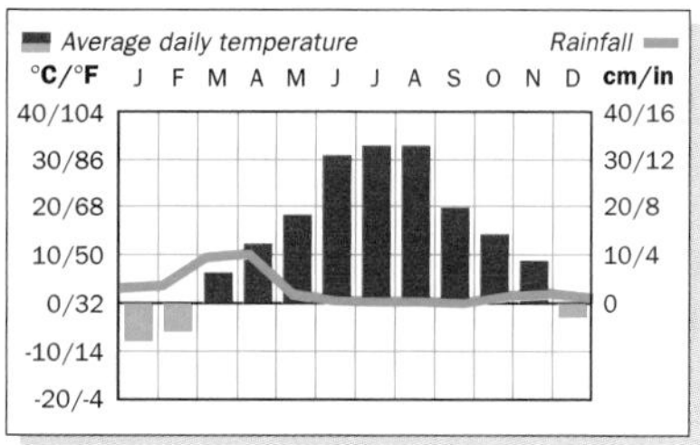
Average daily temperature
Rainfall
°C/°F
J F M A M J J A S O N D
cm/in
40/104
30/86
20/68
10/50
0/32
-10/14
-20/-4
40/16
30/12
20/8
10/4
0

Afghanistan has the world's widest temperature range, with lows of –50°C (–58°F) and highs of 53°C (127°F). Severe drought, a frequent problem, affected half the population in 2000.

TRANSPORTATION

Drive on right

Kabul International

Has no fleet

THE TRANSPORTATION NETWORK

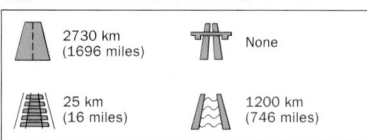

2730 km (1696 miles)

None

25 km (16 miles)

1200 km (746 miles)

The repair and reconstruction of the roads, severely damaged by war, and the modernization of the air traffic control system are the most urgent priorities. The rebuilding of roads is usually carried out by local communities. However, neighboring Pakistan has undertaken to rebuild a number of key routes, including the Kabul–Peshawar link, which will benefit its own trade with central Asia.

Securing key supply routes was a crucial factor in intra-*mujahideen* feuding and in the *taliban*'s efforts to gain control over the whole country. Anti-*taliban* forces relied heavily on supplies from the north. Much of Afghanistan's outlying territory is sown with landmines.

TOURISM

Visitors : Population 1:5975

4000 visitors

No change in 1995–1998

MAIN TOURIST ARRIVALS

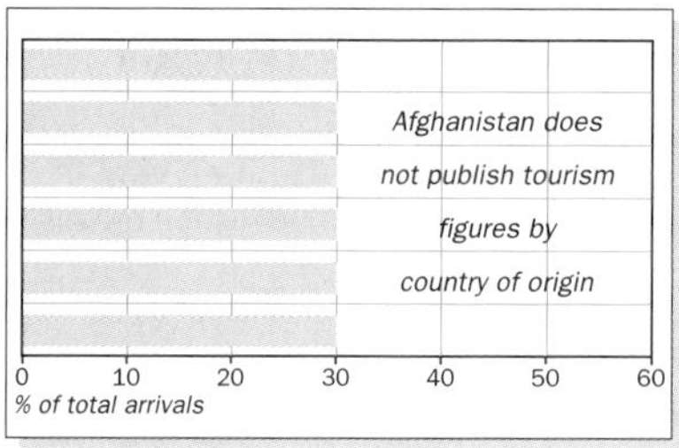
Afghanistan does
not publish tourism
figures by
country of origin
0
10
20
30
40
50
60
% of total arrivals

Afghanistan has yet to recover from decades of war. Few hotels are open in Kabul, and travel in the landmine-strewn and lawless interior is dangerous. The lack of a formal economy means that there are few visits from businessmen, and most expatriates left Kabul during the *taliban* period. Most major cultural treasures, such as the famous carvings of Buddha at Bamian, have been destroyed or looted, while Air Ariana, the national airline, lost six of its eight aircraft in the 2001 US bombing.

PEOPLE

Pop. density low

Pashtu, Tajik, Dari, Farsi, Uzbek, Turkmen

37/km² (95/mi²)

THE URBAN/RURAL POPULATION SPLIT

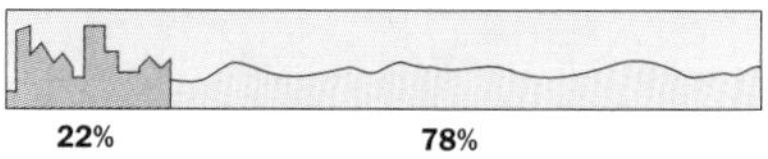
22%
78%

RELIGIOUS PERSUASION

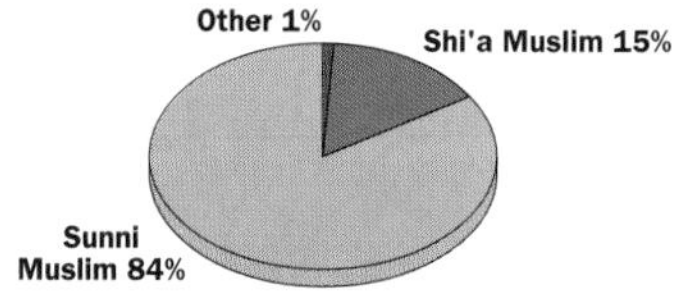
Other 1%
Shi'a Muslim 15%
Sunni Muslim 84%

ETHNIC MAKEUP

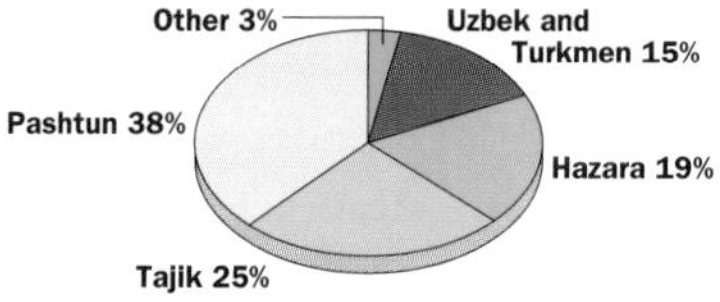
Other 3%
Uzbek and Turkmen 15%
Pashtun 38%
Hazara 19%
Tajik 25%

Ethnicity largely determined intra-*mujahideen* feuding after 1992. Pashtuns have traditionally been the rulers of Afghanistan, and dominated the *taliban*. The fall of that regime in 2001 provided the opportunity for the Tajik–Uzbek alliance to enforce a power-sharing agreement. Pashtuns have since faced reprisal attacks, particularly in the north, where they are a minority. Religious differences between Sunnis and Shi'as became acute under the Sunni *taliban* regime.

Some two million people were killed in the ten-year conflict which followed the invasion by Soviet Union forces in 1979 and in the post-1992 civil war. As many people again were maimed. A further six million people were forced to flee to Pakistan and Iran; many returned, but the US attacks in 2001 which ousted the *taliban* created a fresh wave of refugees and left hundreds of thousands more people internally displaced.

Women had few rights under the rigid Islamic regime of the *taliban*. The interim government has lifted the ban on women in employment and allowed girls to resume schooling, but social restrictions still exist.

POPULATION AGE BREAKDOWN

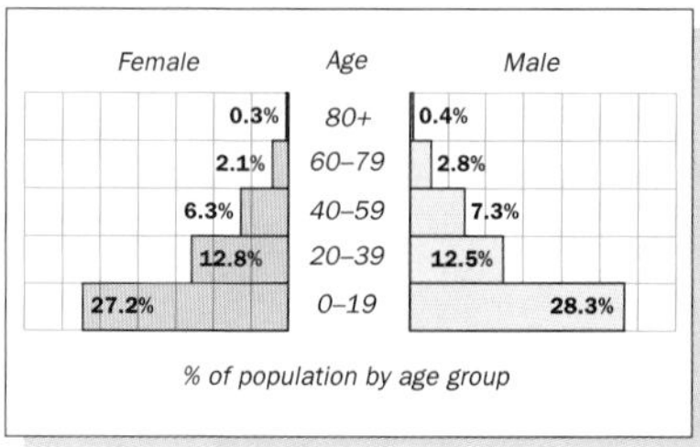
Female
Age
Male
0.3%
80+
0.4%
2.1%
60–79
2.8%
6.3%
40–59
7.3%
12.8%
20–39
12.5%
27.2%
0–19
28.3%
% of population by age group

POLITICS

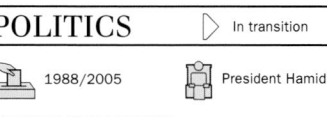

In transition

1988/2005

President Hamid Karzai

AT THE LAST ELECTION

House of Representatives (dissolved)

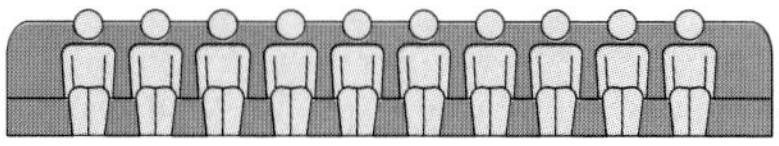

Following the downfall of Najibullah's regime in April 1992, both houses were dissolved and an interim *mujahideen* legislature formed.

Senate (dissolved)

Emerging from almost 30 years of constant war, in 2002 Afghanistan chose a transitional government through its Loya Jirga (grand council) as the foundation of a democratic, presidential system. Presidential elections were held in 2004.

Profile

Civil war was fueled from outside by Cold War rivalries. *Mujahideen* factions fought first against Soviet invaders, and then against each other, before a potent new force, the Islamist *taliban*, arose in 1995. After capturing Kabul in 1996 the *taliban* declared Afghanistan to be a "complete" Islamic state, and imposed a strict Islamic code.

After the 2001 terrorist attacks on the US, Afghanistan was targeted as a harborer of international Islamist terrorists. A full-scale bombing campaign tipped the balance in favor of the opposition Northern Alliance and the *taliban* were swiftly removed from power. In their place the US sponsored the formation of an interim government around the Pashtun leader Hamid Karzai, who was installed as transitional president in 2002. A new constitution, agreed in January 2004, outlines a strong presidency.

Main Political Issue

Political stability and central control

The control of the Kabul government, which was originally established upon the basis of the ad hoc unity of the Northern Alliance and the military might of the US, is precarious. Promised aid has been slow to arrive, its delivery complicated by the withdrawal of aid agencies as their workers became the target of terrorist attacks. The increased instability is blamed on both the reemergence of pro-*taliban* Islamist groups – particularly along the border with Pakistan – and the continuing ambitions and rivalries of regional warlords.

***Hamid Karzai** has struggled to exert power outside the capital Kabul.*

WORLD AFFAIRS

Joined UN in 1946

CP | ECO | IBRD | NAM | OIC

The nature of the Islamist *taliban* regime made Afghanistan a pariah state and the first target of the US-led "war on terrorism" in 2001. The new interim government is consequently heavily dependent on the countries which effectively installed it, making good relations with them essential for future aid. Pakistan was the last country to break off links with the *taliban* and remains Afghanistan's most delicately placed partner, with a history of religious as well as ethnic sympathies with the ousted, Pashtun-dominated, Islamist regime. Plans for a gas pipeline, carrying gas from Turkmenistan to south Asia, have been revived, and it is now a crucial economic issue.

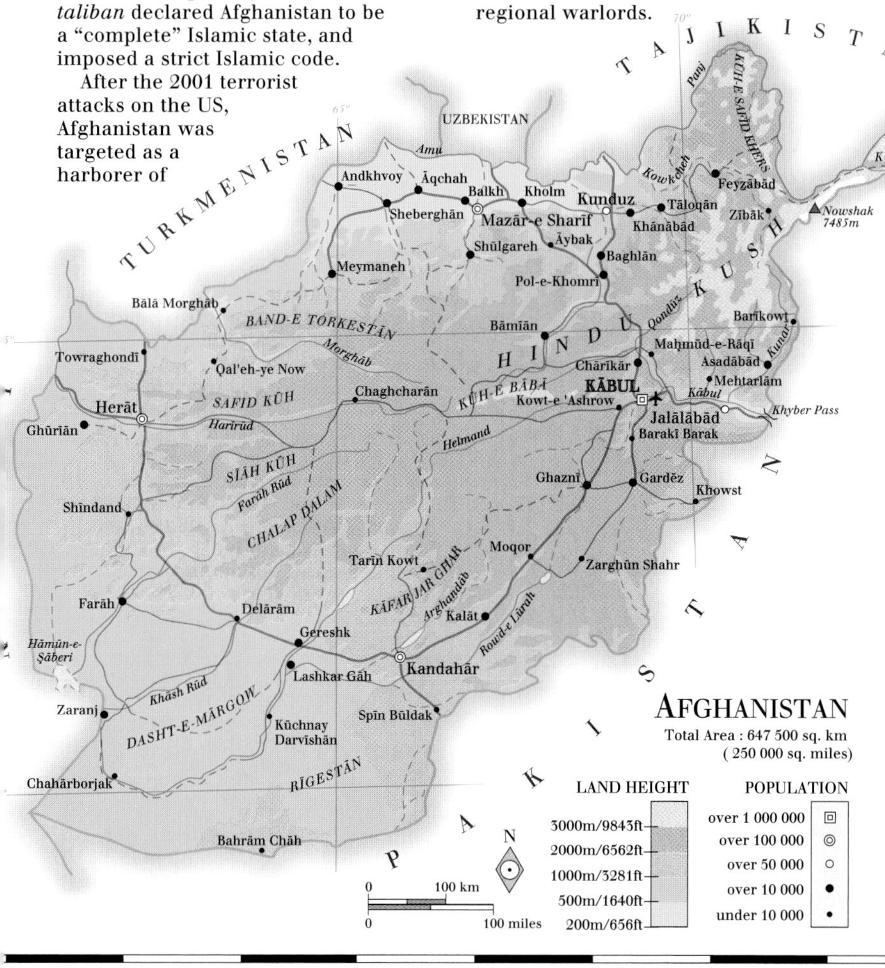
TAJIKISTAN
CHINA
UZBEKISTAN
TURKMENISTAN
PAKISTAN
Amu
Panj
KŪH-E SAFĪD KHERS
Kowkcheh
KŪH-E VAKHĀN
Nowshak 7485m
Andkhvoy
Āqchah
Balkh
Kholm
Kunduz
Tāloqān
Feyzābād
Sheberghān
Mazār-e Sharīf
Khānābād
Zībāk
Shūlgareh
Āybak
Baghlān
Meymaneh
Pol-e-Khomri
HINDU KUSH
Qonduz
Bārīkowt
Bālā Morghāb
BAND-E TORKESTĀN
Bāmīān
Morghāb
Maḩmūd-e-Rāqī
Towraghondī
Chārīkār
Asadābād
Qal'eh-ye Now
KŪH-E BĀBĀ
Kunar
Mehtarlām
KĀBUL
Kābul
Herāt
SAFĪD KŪH
Chaghcharān
Kowt-e 'Ashrow
Khyber Pass
Ghūrīān
Harīrūd
Jalālābād
Helmand
Barakī Barak
SĪĀH KŪH
Farāh Rūd
Ghaznī
Gardēz
Khowst
Shīndand
CHALAP DALAM
Tarīn Kowt
Moqor
Zarghūn Shahr
KĀFAR JAR GHAR
Arghandāb
Farāh
Delārām
Kalāt
Rowd-e Lurah
Hāmūn-e-Şāberi
Gereshk
Lashkar Gāh
Kandahār
Khāsh Rūd
Zaranj
DASHT-E-MĀRGOW
Kūchnay Darvīshān
Spīn Būldak
Chahārborjak
RĪGESTĀN
Bahrām Chāh
AFGHANISTAN
Total Area : 647 500 sq. km
(250 000 sq. miles)
LAND HEIGHT
3000m/9843ft
2000m/6562ft
1000m/3281ft
500m/1640ft
200m/656ft
POPULATION
over 1 000 000
over 100 000
over 50 000
over 10 000
under 10 000
N
0
100 km
0
100 miles
65°
70°

CHRONOLOGY

The foundations of an Afghan state of Pashtun peoples were laid in the mid-18th century, when Durrani Ahmad Shah became paramount chief of the Abdali Pashtun peoples.

- **1838–1842** First Anglo-Afghan war.
- **1878** Second British invasion of Afghan territory.
- **1879** Under Treaty of Gandmak signed with Amir Yaqub Ali Khan, various Afghan areas annexed by Britain. Yaqub Ali Khan later exiled. New treaty signed with Amir Abdul Rahman, establishing the Durand line, a contentious boundary between Afghanistan and Pakistan.
- **1919** Independence declared.
- **1933** Mohammed Zahir Shah ascends throne.
- **1953–1963** Mohammed Daud Khan prime minister; resigns after king rejects proposals for democratic reforms.

A

CHRONOLOGY *continued*

- **1965** Elections held, but monarchy retains power. Marxist Party of Afghanistan (PDPA) formed and banned. PDPA splits into the Parcham and Khalq factions.
- **1973** Daud mounts a coup, abolishes monarchy, and declares republic. *Mujahideen* rebellion begins. Refugees flee to Pakistan.
- **1978** Opposition to Daud from PDPA culminates in Saur revolution. Revolutionary Council under Mohammad Taraki takes power. Daud assassinated.
- **1979** Taraki ousted. Hafizullah Amin takes power. Amin killed in December coup backed by USSR. 80,000 Soviet troops invade Afghanistan. *Mujahideen* rebellion stepped up into full-scale guerrilla war, with US backing.
- **1980** Babrak Karmal, leader of Parcham PDPA, installed as head of Marxist regime.
- **1986** Mohammad Najibullah takes over from Karmal.
- **1989** Soviet Army withdraws.
- **1992** Najibullah hands over power to *mujahideen* factions.
- **1993** *Mujahideen* agree on formation of government.
- **1994** Power struggle between Burhanuddin Rabbani and Gulbuddin Hekmatyar.
- **1996** *Taliban* take power and impose strict Islamic regime.
- **1998** Earthquake in northern regions kills thousands.
- **1999** Power-sharing agreement between *taliban* and Northern Alliance breaks down.
- **2000** Worst drought in 30 years. UN imposes sanctions in response to *taliban* support for al-Qaida.
- **2001** *Taliban* government falls after intense US-led air strikes from October – first campaign in "war on terrorism." Interim government formed under Hamid Karzai; peacekeepers deployed in Kabul.
- **2002** Earthquakes kill thousands. Ex-king Zahir Shah returns from exile. Loya Jirga convenes, elects Karzai head of state.
- **2004** Approval of constitution. 90% of voters registered.

AID

Recipient

$1.28bn (receipts) — Up 215% in 2002

The fall of the *taliban* opened the way for massive inflows of aid. However, pledges by the US and its allies not to "forget" Afghanistan have been tested greatly as international priorities have shifted; only a fraction of the promised aid has arrived. Working conditions for aid personnel are extremely hazardous.

DEFENSE

No compulsory military service

Not available — Not available

AFGHAN ARMED FORCES

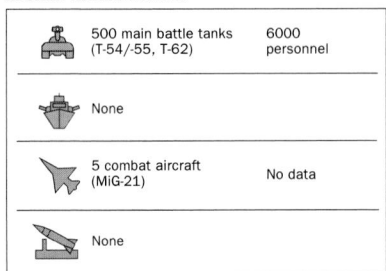

500 main battle tanks (T-54/-55, T-62)	6000 personnel
None	
5 combat aircraft (MiG-21)	No data
None	

The new regime is building a 60–70,000-strong national army and an air force of 8000. Private armies have been banned. An international peacekeeping force only extended its control beyond Kabul from late 2003. The US continues to launch offensives against the remaining al-Qaida and *taliban* forces.

Regional factions are heavily armed, thanks to decades of military assistance from the US and the USSR; warlords remain significant local power brokers. Though direct involvement by the superpowers came to an end in 1991, the arms supplied to rival groups remain. The US government is particularly concerned about the presence of hundreds of Stinger surface-to-air missiles; worried that they might be used against civilian airliners, it has frequently launched drives to buy them back.

Foreign Islamic militants have also helped to flood the country with arms. The bulk of these weapons originate in eastern Europe and the former Soviet Union. The movement of Islamist militants and weapons between Tajikistan and Afghanistan is now tackled by CIS troops.

ECONOMICS

Not available

$5.68bn — 43 new afghanis (43)

SCORE CARD

World GNP Ranking	110th
GNP per Capita	$250
Balance of Payments	–$132m
Inflation	56.7%
Unemployment	8%

ECONOMIC PERFORMANCE INDICATOR

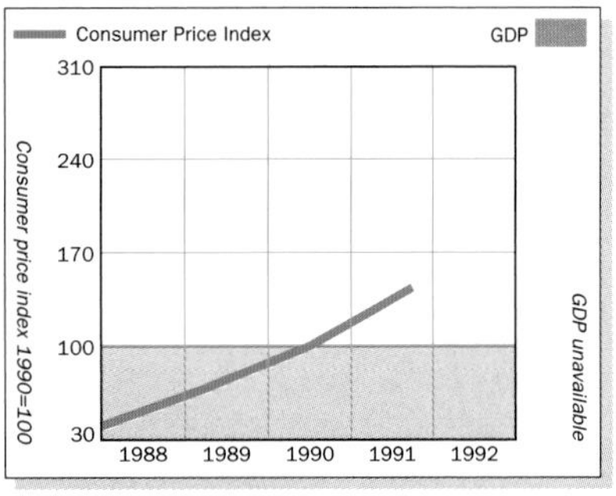

Consumer Price Index
GDP
310
240
170
100
30
1988
1989
1990
1991
1992
Consumer price index 1990=100
GDP unavailable

EXPORTS

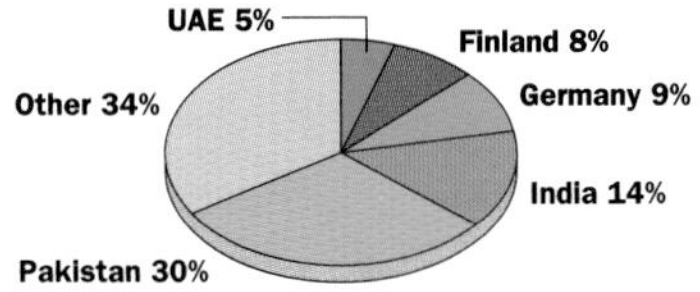

UAE 5%
Finland 8%
Germany 9%
India 14%
Pakistan 30%
Other 34%

IMPORTS

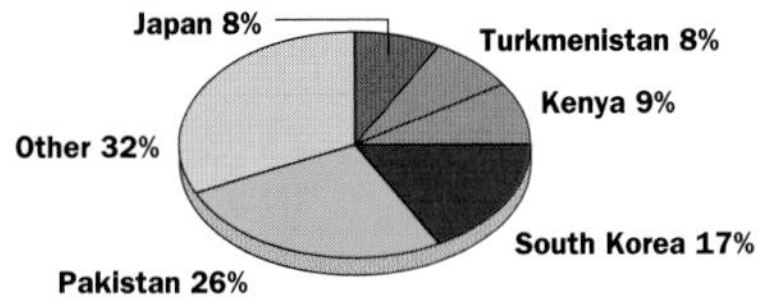

Japan 8%
Turkmenistan 8%
Kenya 9%
South Korea 17%
Pakistan 26%
Other 32%

Strengths

Very few, apart from illicit opium trade. Revalued currency issued in 2002. Overseas assets unfrozen from 2002.

Weaknesses

Decades of fighting: infrastructure, agriculture, and industry in ruins. Communication links damaged by earthquakes and devastated by bombing. Aid slow to materialize.

Profile

The protracted fighting has left Afghanistan one of the poorest and least developed countries in the world. It is estimated that some $15 billion is needed to rebuild the country and that over 80% of infrastructure has been destroyed. Agricultural activity is lower than the pre-1979 level; the Soviet "scorched earth" policy laid waste large areas, and much of the rural population fled to the cities. Many farmers turned back to growing poppies for opium production, but saw little profit, despite Afghanistan being one of the world's largest sources of opium. Though prohibited, poppy cultivation has increased under the new, less intimidating, regime.

Much of Afghanistan's infrastructure, already damaged by decades of civil war, was reduced to ruins by heavy US bombardment in 2001.

A

RESOURCES

Electric power 499,000 kW

800 tonnes

Not an oil producer and has no refineries

11m sheep, 5m goats, 2m cattle, 7m chickens

Natural gas, salt, coal, copper, lapis lazuli, barytes, talc

ELECTRICITY GENERATION

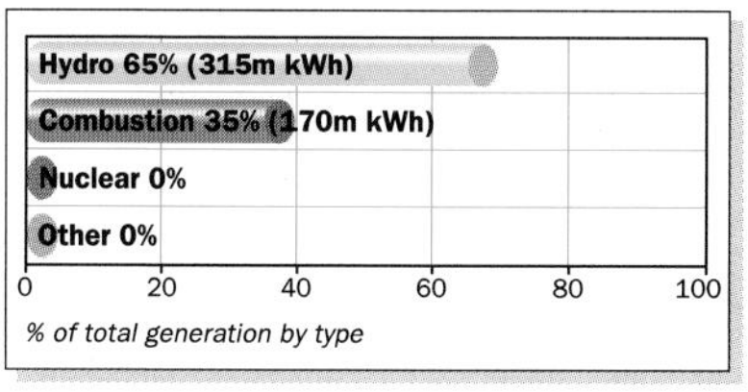

Hydro 65% (315m kWh)
Combustion 35% (170m kWh)
Nuclear 0%
Other 0%
0 20 40 60 80 100
% of total generation by type

Natural gas and coal are the most important strategic resources. In 2002 Afghanistan signed a gas agreement with Pakistan and Turkmenistan which could generate revenue estimated at $300 million. Restoring the power generation system is a government priority. The construction of dams on the Kunar and Laghman rivers is being considered. Coal production has fallen from prewar levels and mines are in urgent need of rehabilitation.

AFGHANISTAN : LAND USE

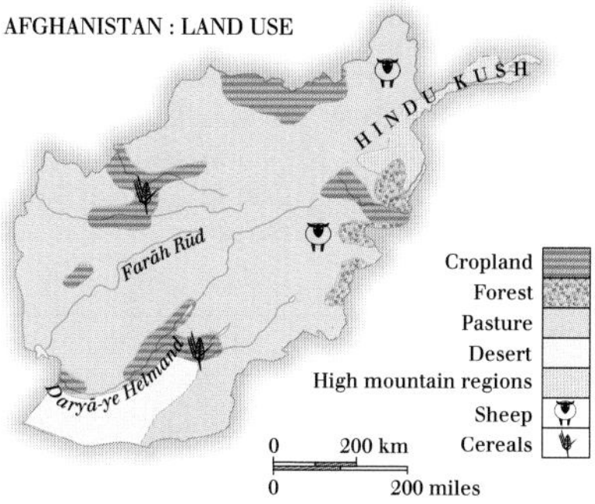

HINDU KUSH
Farāh Rūd
Daryā-ye Helmand
Cropland
Forest
Pasture
Desert
High mountain regions
Sheep
Cereals
0 200 km
0 200 miles

ENVIRONMENT

Not available

0.3% (0.2% partially protected)

0.05 tonnes per capita

ENVIRONMENTAL TREATIES

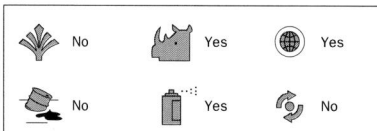

No Yes Yes

No Yes No

Environmental priorities are low. However, the country's lack of industry, even in Kabul, means that industrial pollution is minimal. The biggest problem facing Afghanistan is landmines: over ten million have been laid, and the UN estimates that it will take 100 years to make the country safe for civilians. Half the country's forests have been lost since 1977.

MEDIA

TV ownership low

Daily newspaper circulation 5 per 1000 people

PUBLISHING AND BROADCAST MEDIA

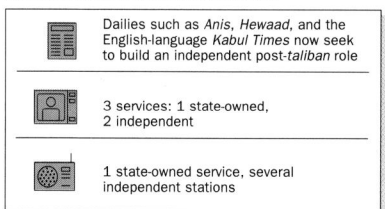

Dailies such as *Anis*, *Hewaad*, and the English-language *Kabul Times* now seek to build an independent post-*taliban* role

3 services: 1 state-owned, 2 independent

1 state-owned service, several independent stations

Various factions run newspapers and radio stations. The *taliban* banned television and the Internet, and though television broadcasts restarted in Kabul in 2001, the new Supreme Court in 2003 banned cable TV as un-Islamic.

The BBC, which produces radio programs in Pashtu and Persian (Dari), is popular, especially for its soap operas, which inform on welfare issues.

CRIME

Death penalty in use

Afghanistan does not publish prison figures

Levels of all crimes remain very high

CRIME RATES

Afghanistan does not publish statistics for murders, rapes, or thefts

Gun law operates widely. Journeys in rural areas are vulnerable to armed robbery. Cities vary according to which faction is dominant and the level of disruption caused by war. A new national police force is being trained.

EDUCATION

School leaving age: 12

36%

19,796 students

THE EDUCATION SYSTEM

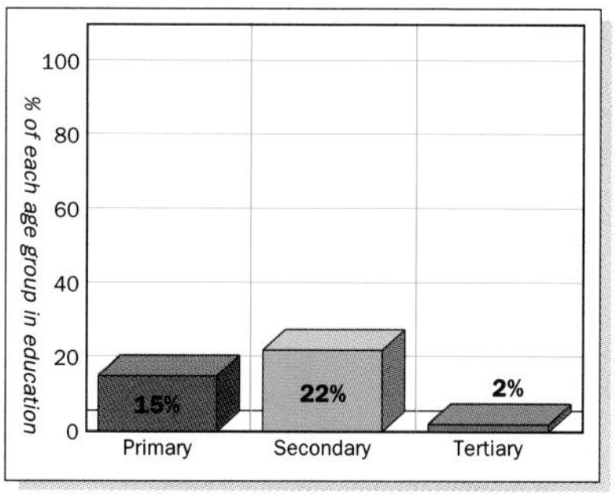

% of each age group in education
100
80
60
40
20
0
15%
22%
2%
Primary
Secondary
Tertiary

Under the *taliban* regime, education for women was extremely limited and segregation rigidly enforced; the literacy rate for women is the lowest in the world. The Northern Alliance announced the lifting of restrictions on female education in November 2001.

Kabul University, which had been closed in 1992, has now been partially reopened.

HEALTH

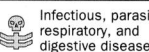

No welfare state health benefits

1 per 10,000 people

Infectious, parasitic, respiratory, and digestive diseases

The health service has collapsed completely and almost all medical professionals have left the country. Infant and maternal mortality rates are among the highest in the world, and life expectancy is very low.

Parasitic diseases and infections are a particular problem. The UN organized a program for the chlorination of well water, following an outbreak of cholera in Kabul, and launched a mass measles vaccination program in January 2002.

Under the *taliban* regime most women in Afghanistan had very little access to health care: their admission to hospital was strongly discouraged, as was the employment of female medical staff.

SPENDING

GDP/cap. decrease

CONSUMPTION AND SPENDING

0.2 per 1000 population

1 per 1000 population

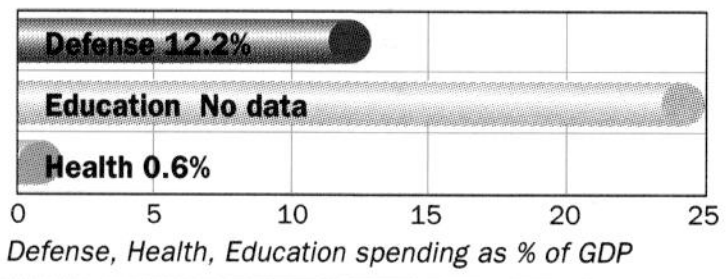

Defense 12.2%
Education No data
Health 0.6%
0 5 10 15 20 25
Defense, Health, Education spending as % of GDP

The vast majority of Afghans live in conditions of extreme poverty. The country does not have the resources to feed its people at present – a situation exacerbated by the severe drought of 2000, the 2001 fighting, and the 2002 earthquakes. The return of refugees from neighboring Pakistan and Iran makes Afghanistan even more dependent on outside assistance for its rehabilitation.

A number of *mujahideen* leaders accumulated personal fortunes during the civil war. These derive in part from the substantial foreign aid that was once available and, in some cases, from the trafficking of opium.

WORLD RANKING

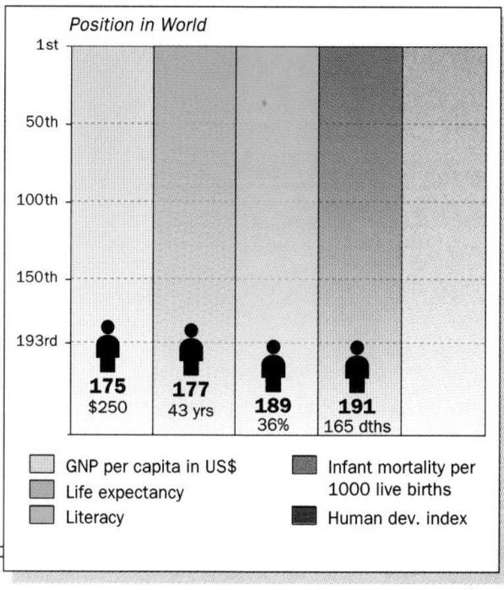

Position in World
1st
50th
100th
150th
193rd
175
$250
177
43 yrs
189
36%
191
165 dths
GNP per capita in US$
Life expectancy
Literacy
Infant mortality per 1000 live births
Human dev. index

A

ALBANIA

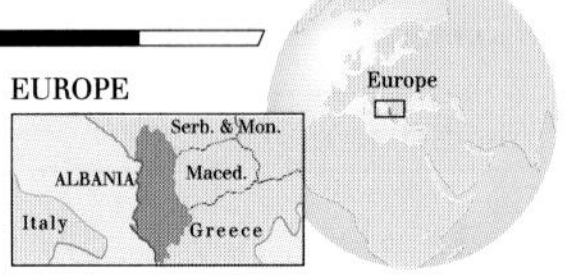
EUROPE
Europe
Serb. & Mon.
ALBANIA
Maced.
Italy
Greece

OFFICIAL NAME: Republic of Albania **CAPITAL:** Tirana
POPULATION: 3.2 million **CURRENCY:** Lek **OFFICIAL LANGUAGE:** Albanian

1912 | 1921 | Nov 28 | AL | +1 | +355 | .al

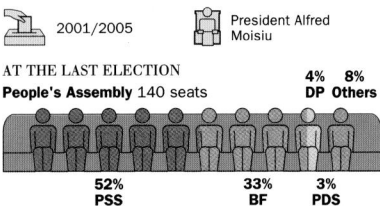

LYING AT THE SOUTHEASTERN end of the Adriatic Sea, opposite the heel of Italy, Albania is a poverty-stricken, mountainous country which became a one-party communist state in 1944. The "land of the eagles," as it is known by its people, became a multiparty democracy in 1991. It has struggled to progress from the economic collapse and regional strife which characterized the 1990s, and remains one of the poorest countries in Europe.

CLIMATE

Mediterranean/continental

WEATHER CHART FOR TIRANA

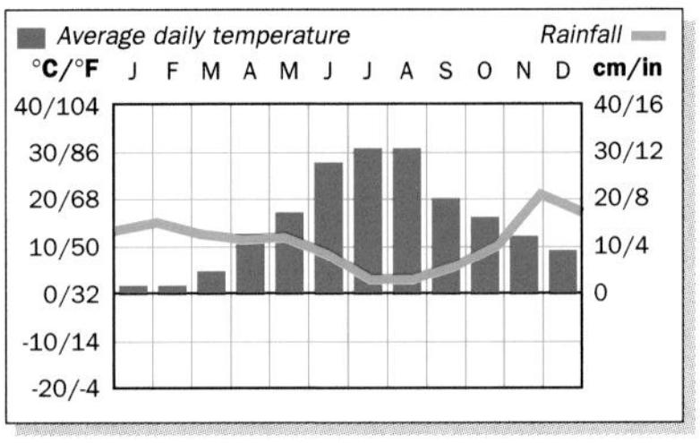
Average daily temperature
Rainfall
°C/°F J F M A M J J A S O N D cm/in
40/104
30/86
20/68
10/50
0/32
-10/14
-20/-4
40/16
30/12
20/8
10/4
0

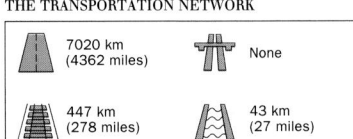

The coastal climate is Mediterranean, but rather wet in winter. Heavy rain or snow falls in winter in the mountains.

TRANSPORTATION

Drive on right

Rinas, Tirana 561,446 passengers

74 ships 48,700 grt

THE TRANSPORTATION NETWORK

7020 km (4362 miles)

None

447 km (278 miles)

43 km (27 miles)

The transportation infrastructure is poor: the rail network is limited and roads are in disrepair. Private cars were first allowed in 1991. Buses and private vans are the main means of transportation.

TOURISM

Visitors : Population 1:94

34,000 visitors

Down 13% in 2001

MAIN TOURIST ARRIVALS

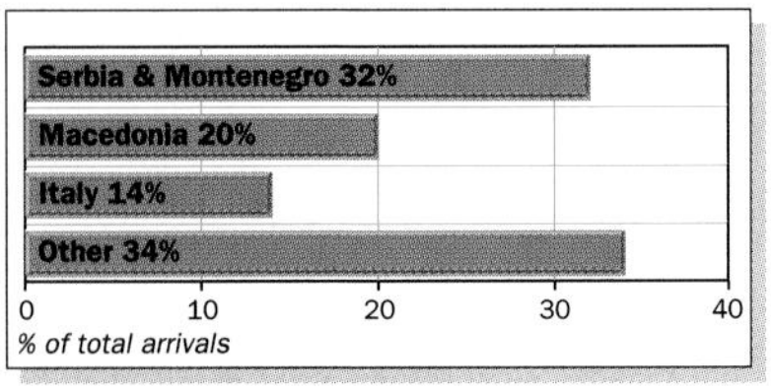
Serbia & Montenegro 32%
Macedonia 20%
Italy 14%
Other 34%
0
10
20
30
40
% of total arrivals

Instability and then the war in Kosovo upset plans to exploit Albania's scenic beauty. Facilities remain very limited, especially outside Tirana.

PEOPLE

Pop. density medium

Albanian, Greek

117/km² (302/mi²)

THE URBAN/RURAL POPULATION SPLIT

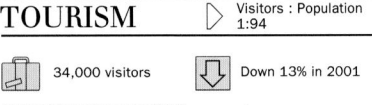

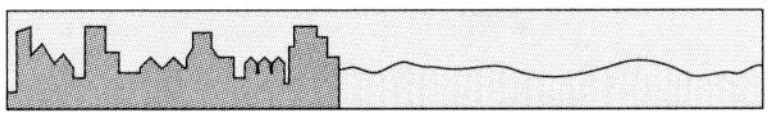
44%
56%

RELIGIOUS PERSUASION

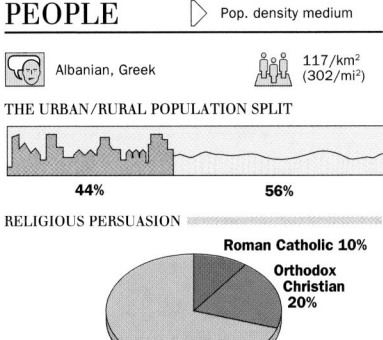

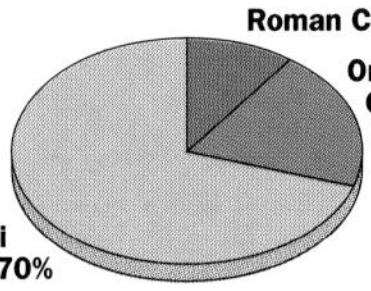
Roman Catholic 10%
Orthodox Christian 20%
Sunni Muslim 70%

The existence of ethnic minorities was only officially acknowledged in 1989. The Greek minority strongly contests official statistics, which state that 95% of the population are Albanian. Located mainly in the south, the Greeks claim to make up over 10% of the population. They suffer considerable discrimination.

Most Albanians converted to Islam under Ottoman suzerainty. Under communism, Albania was the only officially atheist state in the world. Religious practice has been permitted since 1991.

Society is traditional and male-dominated. Men are expected to be providers, and unemployment levels have decreased the chances of women finding work. Many women pay to be smuggled to the West, only to end up as prostitutes; Albania is a major transit point for human trafficking.

City of a thousand windows. *Berat was preserved as a museum while a new town was built further down the valley.*

POLITICS

Multiparty elections

2001/2005

President Alfred Moisiu

AT THE LAST ELECTION

People's Assembly 140 seats

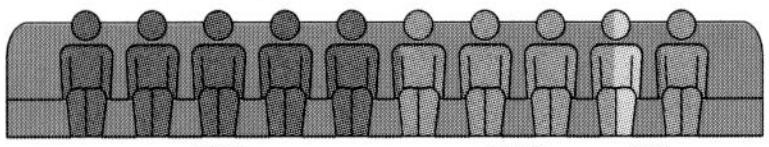
4% DP
8% Others
52% PSS
33% BF
3% PDS

PSS = Socialist Party of Albania **BF** = Union for Victory (led by the Democratic Party – **PD**) **DP** = Democrat Party (splinter from PD) **PDS** = Social Democratic Party

Albania was dominated for more than 40 years by communist ruler Enver Hoxha, who died in 1985. An exodus of Albanians in 1991 finally persuaded the regime to call multiparty elections, but the resulting center-right coalition failed to create a Western, liberal state.

Many people were ruined by investing in "pyramid" savings schemes which collapsed in 1997, prompting rebellion in the south and forcing the resignation of the government. A new coalition led by the former communist PSS was elected later that year, and won a further term in 2001, as Prime Minister Ilir Meta claimed credit for restoring a measure of security and hope. The PSS soon became divided by internal disputes. Veteran party leader Fatos Nano emerged victorious, and has since concentrated power in his own hands, becoming prime minister in July 2002.

WORLD AFFAIRS

Joined UN in 1955

WTO | CE | OSCE | OIC | PfP

The government has distanced itself from ethnic Albanian separatist movements in neighboring regions after crises in the Serbian province of Kosovo (in the late 1990s) and in Macedonia (in 2001). Membership of NATO and the EU is a long-term goal, but lack of progress with reforms delayed a Stabilization and Association Agreement with the EU until 2005.

AID

Recipient

$317m (receipts)

Up 17% in 2002

Since 1991 the West has provided aid. Food aid was stepped up in 1997, when anarchy swept the country, and again in 1999 to help cope with the hundreds of thousands of refugees arriving from Kosovo in Serbia. EU aid now focuses on helping structural reforms.

DEFENSE

Compulsory military service

$107m

Up 2% in 2002

Albania plans to reduce its military personnel by 2006 as part of a ten-year reconstruction program, aiming for a fully professional force and accession to NATO. In 2003, 70 commandos were sent to Iraq to help the US-led Coalition.

ECONOMICS

Inflation 34% p.a. (1990–2001)

$4.58bn

100.9 lekë (118.5)

SCORE CARD

❑ WORLD GNP RANKING	118th
❑ GNP PER CAPITA	$1450
❑ BALANCE OF PAYMENTS	–$408m
❑ INFLATION	7.8%
❑ UNEMPLOYMENT	23%

STRENGTHS

Oil and gas reserves. Remittances from expatriate Albanians. Progress with privatization. Strong agricultural sector.

WEAKNESSES

One of Europe's poorest countries. Rudimentary public services and infrastructure deter foreign investors.

EXPORTS

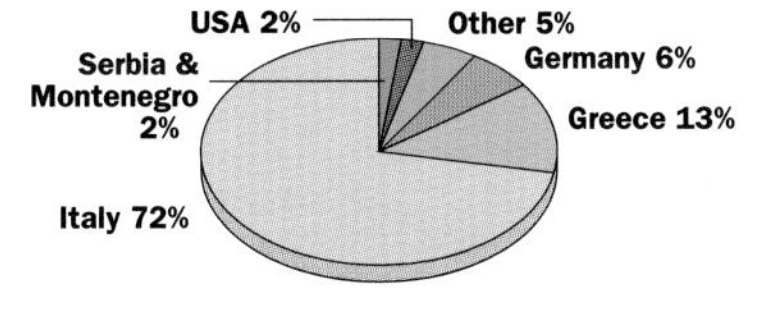
USA 2%
Other 5%
Germany 6%
Serbia & Montenegro 2%
Greece 13%
Italy 72%

IMPORTS

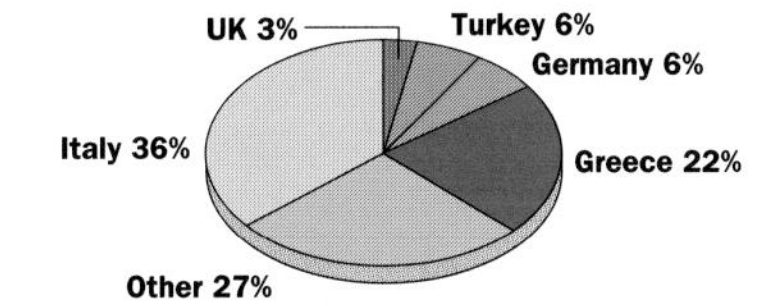
UK 3%
Turkey 6%
Germany 6%
Italy 36%
Greece 22%
Other 27%

ALBANIA

Total Area : 28 748 sq. km (11 100 sq. miles)

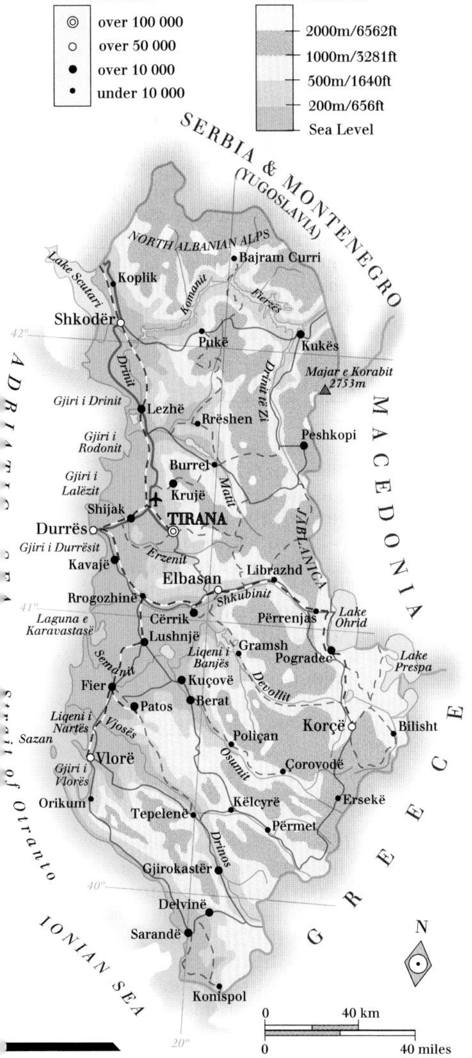
POPULATION
over 100 000
over 50 000
over 10 000
under 10 000
LAND HEIGHT
2000m/6562ft
1000m/3281ft
500m/1640ft
200m/656ft
Sea Level
SERBIA & MONTENEGRO (YUGOSLAVIA)
NORTH ALBANIAN ALPS
Bajram Curri
Lake Scutari
Koplik
Komanit
Shkodër
Pukë
Kukës
Drinit
Drinit të Zi
Majar e Korabit 2753m
Gjiri i Drinit
Lezhë
Rrëshen
Gjiri i Rodonit
Peshkopi
Burrel
Gjiri i Lalëzit
Krujë
Mat
Shijak
TIRANA
Durrës
Gjiri i Durrësit
Kavajë
Erzenit
Librazhd
Elbasan
Shkumbinit
JABLANICA
MACEDONIA
Rrogozhinë
Laguna e Karavastasë
Cërrik
Përrenjas
Lake Ohrid
Lushnjë
Gramsh
Semanit
Liqeni i Banjës
Pogradec
Lake Prespa
Fier
Kuçovë
Devollit
Patos
Berat
Liqeni i Nartës
Vjosës
Bilisht
Sazan
Korçë
Poliçan
Vlorë
Osumit
Çorovodë
Gjiri i Vlorës
Orikum
Ersekë
Tepelenë
Këlcyrë
Përmet
Drinos
Gjirokastër
Delvinë
Sarandë
Konispol
ADRIATIC SEA
Strait of Otranto
IONIAN SEA
GREECE
N
0 40 km
0 40 miles

RESOURCES

Electric power 1.9m kW

3596 tonnes

6356 b/d (reserves 183m barrels)

1.8m sheep, 1.02m goats, 4.3m chickens

Chromium, oil, coal, natural gas, copper, nickel

Albania needs huge capital investment to develop its minerals and to create a modern electricity supply system.

ENVIRONMENT

Sustainability rank: 24th

4% (2% partially protected)

0.9 tonnes per capita

Toxic waste pollution from communist-era heavy industry is among the worst in Europe. Years of shortages mean that most materials are recycled.

MEDIA

TV ownership high

Daily newspaper circulation 35 per 1000 people

PUBLISHING AND BROADCAST MEDIA

There are 12 daily newspapers, including *Rilindja Demokratike*, *Zëri i Popullit*, and *Koha Jonë*, the best-selling newspaper

1 state-run service, 75 private stations

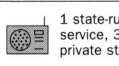

1 state-run service, 30 private stations

Though media freedom has greatly improved, overly critical papers face harassment. A 1998 law banned political or religious control of TV stations.

CRIME

Death penalty not used in practice

3053 prisoners

Down 11% in 2000–2002

Lawlessness is widespread; guns are easily available since the anarchy of 1997. Cannabis is widely grown.

CHRONOLOGY

Albania gained independence in 1912 for the first time in its history.

- ❑ **1924–1939** Ahmet Zogu in power; crowned King Zog in 1928.
- ❑ **1939–1943** Occupied by Italy.
- ❑ **1944** Communist state; led by Enver Hoxha until 1985.
- ❑ **1991** First multiparty elections.
- ❑ **1997** Economic chaos as failure of pyramid schemes causes revolt.
- ❑ **1999** Refugee influx from Kosovo.
- ❑ **2001** PSS wins second term.

EDUCATION

School leaving age: 13

99%

40,859 students

The communist-derived system is being reformed to European standards. Albania has eight universities.

HEALTH

Welfare state health benefits

1 per 714 people

Heart and respiratory diseases, cancers

The health service is rudimentary, and dependent on Western aid for most drugs and medical supplies.

SPENDING

GDP/cap. increase

CONSUMPTION AND SPENDING

43 per 1000 population

71 per 1000 population

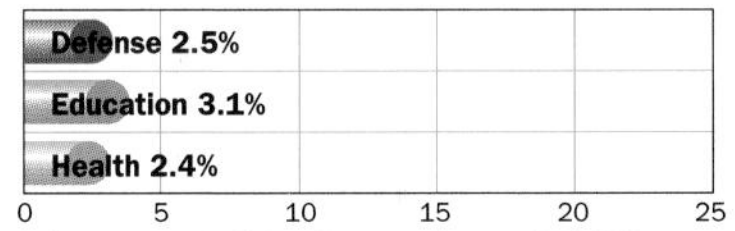
Defense 2.5%
Education 3.1%
Health 2.4%
0
5
10
15
20
25

Defense, Health, Education spending as % of GDP

Wealth is limited to a few private-sector entrepreneurs. Poverty is worst in northern rural areas but also acute in slum settlements around Tirana and other cities.

WORLD RANKING

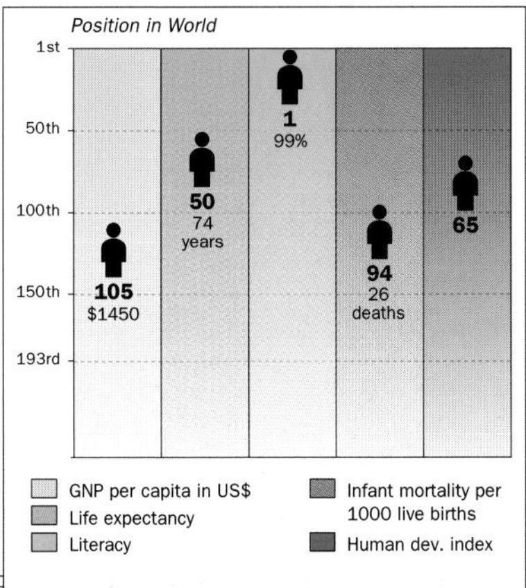
Position in World
1st
50th
100th
150th
193rd
105
$1450
50
74 years
1
99%
94
26 deaths
65
GNP per capita in US$
Life expectancy
Literacy
Infant mortality per 1000 live births
Human dev. index

A

ALGERIA

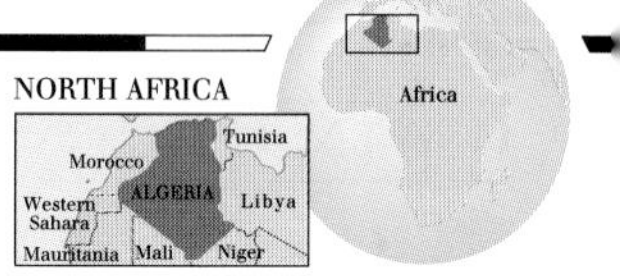
NORTH AFRICA
Africa
Morocco
Tunisia
ALGERIA
Libya
Western Sahara
Mauritania
Mali
Niger

OFFICIAL NAME: People's Democratic Republic of Algeria **CAPITAL:** Algiers
POPULATION: 31.8 million **CURRENCY:** Algerian dinar **OFFICIAL LANGUAGE:** Arabic

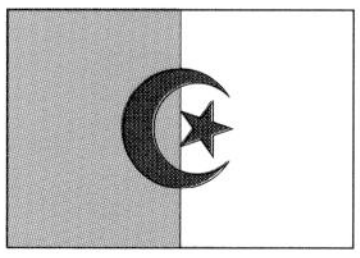

1962
1962
Nov 1
DZ
+1
+213
.dz

AFRICA'S SECOND-LARGEST country, which extends from a densely populated Mediterranean coast to the empty northern Sahara, Algeria won independence from France in 1962. The military blocked radical Islamists from taking power after winning elections in 1991, setting up a new civilian regime and fighting a bloody terrorist conflict ever since. Algeria has one of the youngest populations in the north African region.

CLIMATE

Hot desert/ Mediterranean

WEATHER CHART FOR ALGIERS

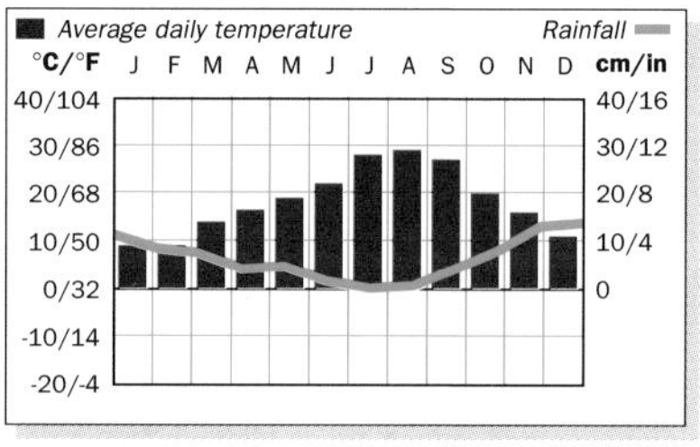
Average daily temperature
Rainfall
°C/°F
J F M A M J J A S O N D
cm/in
40/104
30/86
20/68
10/50
0/32
-10/14
-20/-4
40/16
30/12
20/8
10/4
0

Coastal areas have a warm, temperate climate. The whole area to the south of the Atlas Mountains is hot desert.

TRANSPORTATION

Drive on right

Houari Boumedienne, Algiers
3.35m passengers

141 ships
936,100 grt

THE TRANSPORTATION NETWORK

71,760 km (44,590 miles)

640 km (398 miles)

3572 km (2220 miles)

None

There are four international airports. Rail is the quickest way to travel between the main urban centers.

TOURISM

Visitors : Population 1:28

1.15m visitors

Up 16% in 2003

MAIN TOURIST ARRIVALS

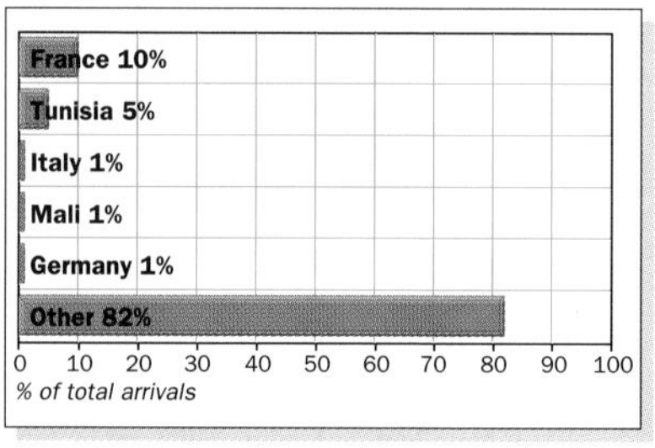
France 10%
Tunisia 5%
Italy 1%
Mali 1%
Germany 1%
Other 82%
0 10 20 30 40 50 60 70 80 90 100
% of total arrivals

The once-popular desert safaris are now rare. Tourists are a target for militant Islamist groups.

PEOPLE

Pop. density low

Arabic, Tamazight (Kabyle, Shawia, Tamashek), French

13/km² (35/mi²)

THE URBAN/RURAL POPULATION SPLIT

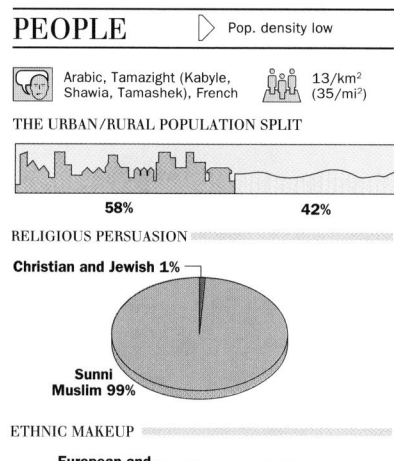

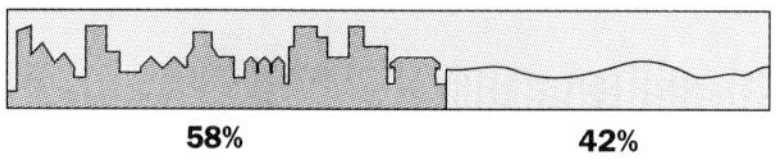
58%
42%

RELIGIOUS PERSUASION

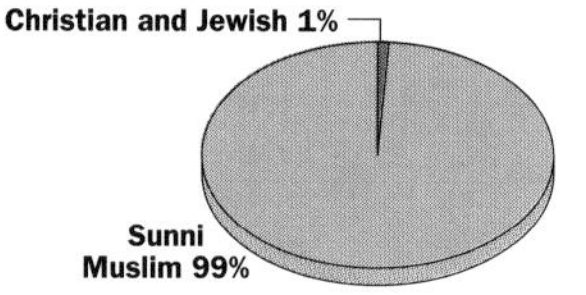
Christian and Jewish 1%
Sunni Muslim 99%

ETHNIC MAKEUP

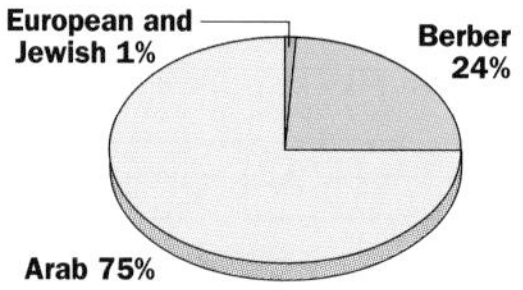
European and Jewish 1%
Berber 24%
Arab 75%

The population is predominantly Arab, under 30 years of age, and urban; some 24% are Berber. More than 85% speak Arabic and 99% are Sunni Muslim. Mosques provide social and medical services. Of the million or so French who settled before independence, only about 6000 remain. Most Berbers think of the mountainous Kabylia region as their homeland. Demonstrations there have met with violent police crackdowns, particularly in the Berber Spring of 1980, and since its anniversary in 2001. The Berber language, Tamazight, was recognized as a national, though not official, language in 2002.

POPULATION AGE BREAKDOWN

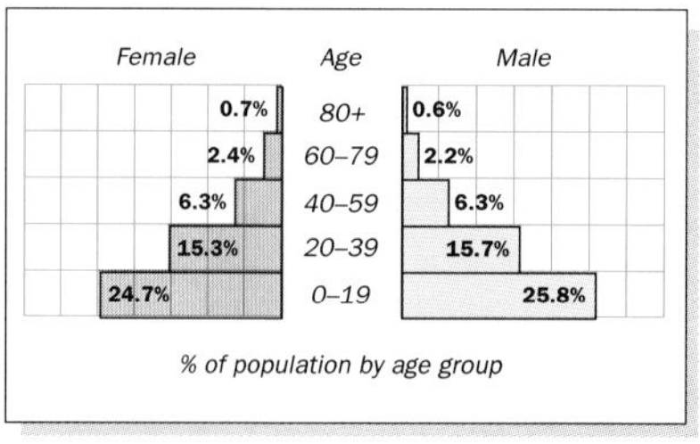
Female
Age
Male
0.7%
80+
0.6%
2.4%
60–79
2.2%
6.3%
40–59
6.3%
15.3%
20–39
15.7%
24.7%
0–19
25.8%
% of population by age group

POLITICS

Multiparty elections

L. House 2002/2007
U. House 2003/2006

President Abdelaziz Bouteflika

AT THE LAST ELECTION

National People's Assembly 389 seats

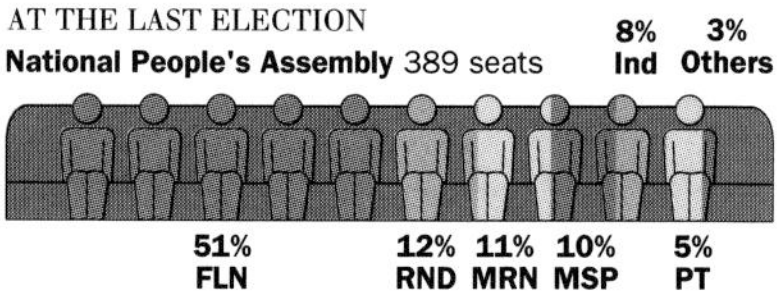
8% Ind
3% Others
51% FLN
12% RND
11% MRN
10% MSP
5% PT

FLN = National Liberation Front **RND** = National Democratic Rally **MRN** = Movement for National Reform **MSP** = Movement for a Peaceful Society **Ind** = Independents **PT** = Workers' Party **App** = Appointed **FFS** = Front of Socialist Forces

National Council 144 seats

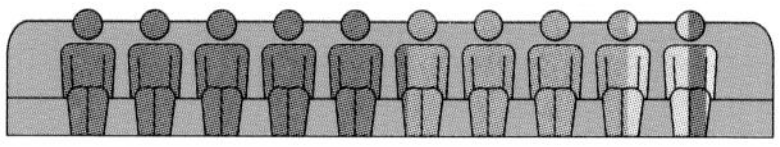

96 seats are indirectly elected by local assemblies, 48 are appointed by the president

Algeria is a multiparty democracy.

PROFILE

Until 1988, Algeria was a socialist single-party, secular regime. The subsequent adoption of privatization policies was strongly opposed by Islamist militants and the Islamic Salvation Front (FIS) won the first round of elections in late 1991. Fearing an Islamist victory, the military-dominated High Security Council canceled the second round in 1992. Islamist groups launched a bloody civil conflict, killing tens of thousands of people. Peace was brought a step closer in 1999 with the election of President Abdelaziz Bouteflika, despite an opposition boycott. The FIS's armed wing, the Islamic Salvation Army, voluntarily disarmed in January 2000, and other groups have followed suit. Bouteflika was resoundingly reelected in 2004, but low-level violence continues.

MAIN POLITICAL ISSUES

Islamic fundamentalism

Islamist militants want Algeria to become a theocracy. The steps taken in 1992 to prevent the FIS taking office unleashed violence spearheaded by the extremist Armed Islamic Group (GIA) and more recently the Salafist Group for Preaching and Combat. The annual death toll currently exceeds 1500.

Human rights and democracy

Agitation among Islamists and Berbers is fueled by poor living conditions and the lack of adequate representation. An official state of emergency has been in place since 1992; security forces have been accused of meeting insurrection with repression and violence.

WORLD AFFAIRS

Joined UN in 1962

AL | AMU | OIC | NAM | OPEC

Struggling against French rule from 1954 until 1962, Algeria's anticolonial credentials made it a leading figure in the developing and nonaligned worlds during the Cold War; its voice was prominent within the UN, the Arab League, and the Organization of African Unity. Meanwhile, its avowedly secular regime and the presence of significant oil and gas reserves made it an appealing economic partner for industrialized countries. In the 1980s in particular, Algeria was seen by the diplomatic community as a useful bridge between the West and Iran.

Algeria's influence, however, diminished in tandem with its political stability in the 1990s. Popular support for the fundamentalist FIS has raised concerns over the potential spread of Islamist militancy into neighbors in north Africa and further afield. Since 2001, the US has been keen to forge an alliance with the Algerian authorities as part of its "war on terrorism."

European governments are anxious to help stabilize the country to avoid the entry of refugees into France, Spain, and Italy. The EU has been calling for improvements in human rights and good governance and has given support to the Bouteflika regime; in 2003 Jacques Chirac became the first French president to visit Algiers since independence.

AID

Recipient

$361m (receipts) | Up 95% in 2002

As a major oil producer, Algeria receives relatively little aid. The collapse in the 1990s of the trade of eastern European goods in return for oil led Algeria to turn to the West for loans. The growing weight of Western economic involvement in turn fortified the regime against criticism of its hard-line methods against Islamist opponents. The EU and various Arab countries are now the largest donors, the bulk of funding going toward improving education facilities. After the 2003 earthquakes, aid for reconstruction became a priority.

***Saharan town,** showing the wide range of Algeria's scenery, from lush, irrigated gardens near water sources to barren dunes beyond. 80% of Algeria is desert.*

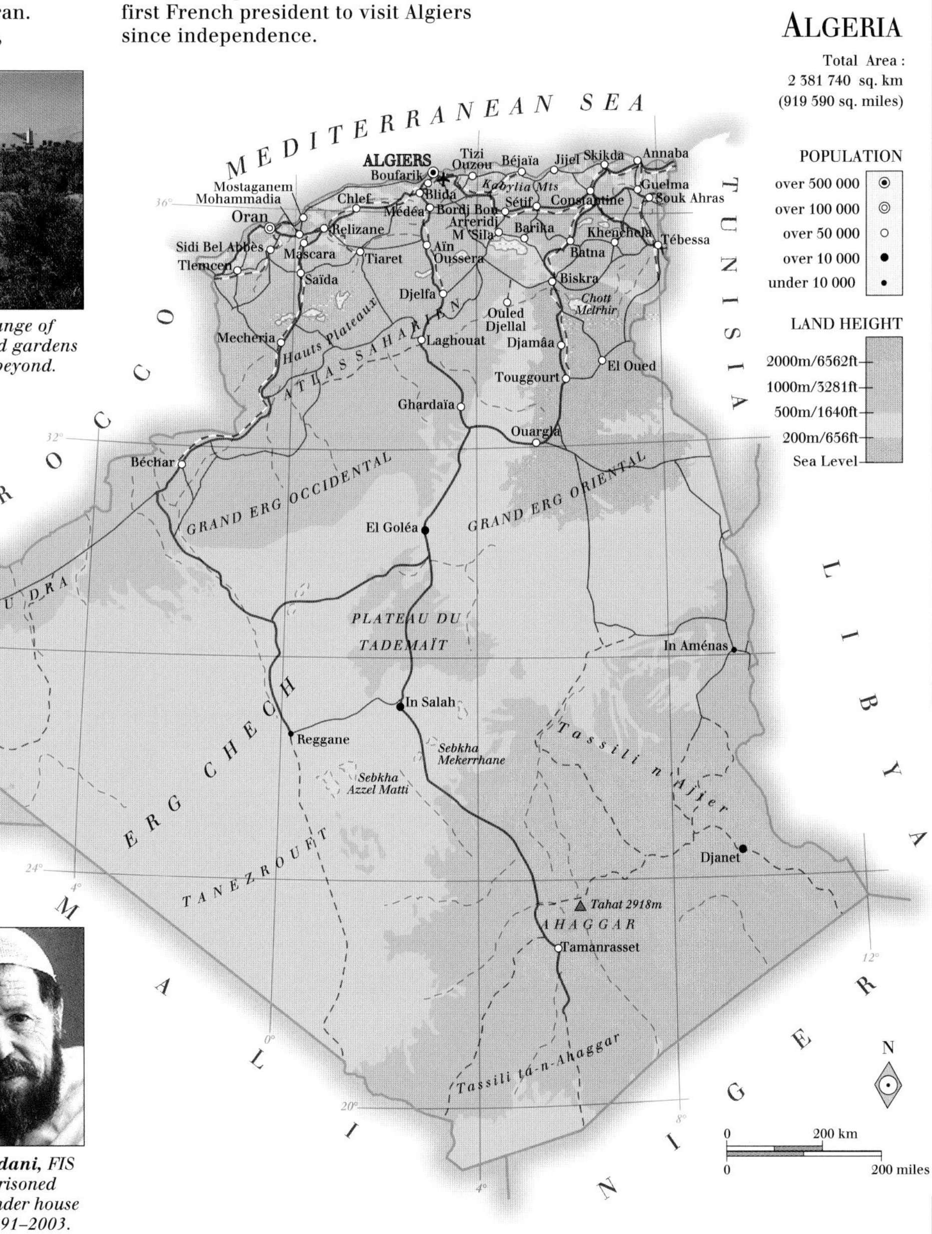
ALGERIA
Total Area: 2 381 740 sq. km (919 590 sq. miles)
POPULATION
over 500 000
over 100 000
over 50 000
over 10 000
under 10 000
LAND HEIGHT
2000m/6562ft
1000m/3281ft
500m/1640ft
200m/656ft
Sea Level
MEDITERRANEAN SEA
ALGIERS
Boufarik
Tizi Ouzou
Béjaïa
Jijel
Skikda
Annaba
Guelma
Souk Ahras
Mostaganem
Mohammadia
Oran
Chlef
Médéa
Blida
Kabylia Mts
Sétif
Constantine
Bordj Bou Arreridj
M'Sila
Barika
Khenchela
Tébessa
Batna
Sidi Bel Abbès
Tlemcen
Mascara
Relizane
Tiaret
Aïn Oussera
Saïda
Djelfa
Biskra
Chott Melrhir
Ouled Djellal
Mecheria
Hauts Plateaux
ATLAS SAHARIEN
Laghouat
Djamâa
El Oued
Touggourt
Ghardaïa
Ouargla
Béchar
GRAND ERG OCCIDENTAL
GRAND ERG ORIENTAL
El Goléa
HAMADA DU DRA
PLATEAU DU TADEMAÏT
Tindouf
In Aménas
In Salah
Reggane
ERG CHECH
Sebkha Mekerrhane
Sebkha Azzel Matti
Tassili n'Ajjer
Djanet
TANEZROUFT
Tahat 2918m
AHAGGAR
Tamanrasset
Tassili ta-n-Ahaggar
MOROCCO
WESTERN SAHARA
MAURITANIA
MALI
NIGER
LIBYA
TUNISIA
N
0 200 km
0 200 miles

***Abdelaziz Bouteflika,** who was elected president in 1999.*

***Abassi Madani,** FIS leader, imprisoned and then under house arrest in 1991–2003.*

A

CHRONOLOGY

The conquest of Algeria by France began in 1830. By 1900, French settlers occupied most of the best land. In 1954, war was declared on the colonial administration by the National Liberation Front (FLN).

- **1962** Cease-fire agreed, followed by independence of Algerian republic.
- **1965** Military junta topples government of Ahmed Ben Bella. Revolutionary council set up.
- **1966** Judiciary "Algerianized." Tribunals try "economic crimes."
- **1971** Oil industry nationalized. President Boumedienne continues with land reform, a national health service, and "socialist" management.
- **1976** Socialist state established.
- **1980** Ben Bella released after 15 years' detention. Agreement with France whereby latter gives incentives for return home of 800,000 Algerian immigrants.
- **1981** Algeria helps to negotiate release of hostages from US embassy in Tehran, Iran.
- **1985** Two most popular Kabyle (Berber) singers given three-year jail sentences for opposing regime.
- **1987** Limited economic liberalization. Cooperation agreement with Soviet Union.
- **1988** Anti-FLN violence; state of emergency. Algeria negotiates release of Kuwaiti hostages from aircraft; Shi'a hijackers escape.
- **1989** Constitutional reforms diminish power of FLN. New political parties founded, including FIS. AMU established.
- **1990** Political exiles able to return. FIS victorious in municipal elections.
- **1991** FIS leaders Abassi Madani and Ali Belhadj jailed. FIS wins most seats in first round of elections.
- **1992** Second round of elections canceled. Army overthrows President Chadli. President Boudiaf assassinated.
- **1994** Political violence led by GIA.
- **1995** Democratic presidential elections won by Liamine Zéroual.
- **1996** Murders continue, notably of Catholic clergy and GIA leader.
- **1997** Madani released, subsequently under house arrest.
- **1999** Abdelaziz Bouteflika elected president in poll boycotted by opposition candidates.
- **2001** Fresh investment in oil and gas benefits economy. Resurgence of Berber protests.
- **2002** Berber language Tamazight recognized as national language. FLN election victory.
- **2003** Over 2000 die in earthquakes. Madani and Belhadj released.
- **2004** Bouteflika reelected.

DEFENSE

Compulsory military service

$2.97bn

Down 6% in 2002

The National Liberation Army (NLA), armed mainly with former Soviet bloc weapons, is a dominant political power. There have been fears that parts of the army would forge an alliance with Muslim militants; the extreme rebel Armed Islamic Group (GIA), which has split from the FIS, is led by former army officers. However, the military are also suspected of taking part in reprisal killings of large numbers of Islamists.

ALGERIAN ARMED FORCES

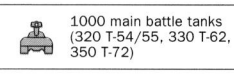

1000 main battle tanks (320 T-54/55, 330 T-62, 350 T-72)	110,000 personnel
2 submarines, 3 frigates, and 25 patrol boats	7500 personnel
175 combat aircraft (Su-24, MiG-23, MiG-25, MiG-29, MiG-21)	10,000 personnel
None	

ECONOMICS

Inflation 17% p.a. (1990–2001)

$53.8bn

70.65 Algerian dinars (78.38)

SCORE CARD

World GNP Ranking	47th
GNP per Capita	$1720
Balance of Payments	$7.06bn
Inflation	1.4%
Unemployment	30%

EXPORTS

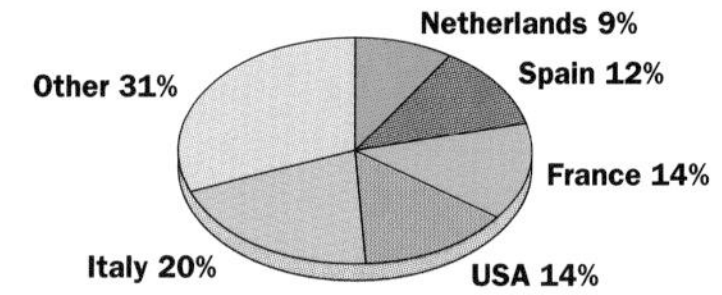
Netherlands 9%
Spain 12%
France 14%
USA 14%
Italy 20%
Other 31%

IMPORTS

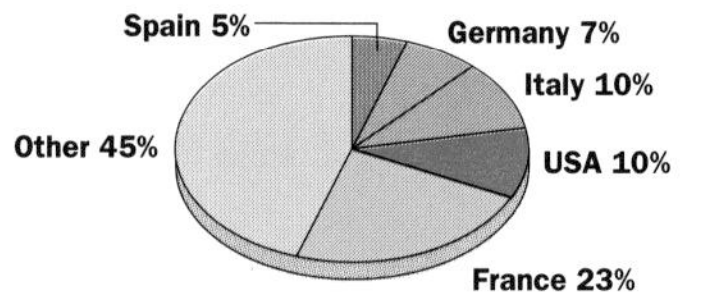
Spain 5%
Germany 7%
Italy 10%
USA 10%
France 23%
Other 45%

Strengths

Third-biggest exporter of natural gas, mainly to Europe: large reserves. Privatization program attracts significant foreign investment to energy sector. Potential for strong industrial base, notably electronics, petrochemicals, and food processing.

Weaknesses

Political instability. Lack of skilled labor coupled with high unemployment. Overdependence on oil and gas industries. Limited agriculture. Shortage of basic foodstuffs. Thriving black market.

Profile

Under the pro-Soviet National Liberation Front, centralized socialist planning dominated the Algerian economy. In the late 1980s, the economic collapse of the Soviet Union led to a change in policy, and Algeria began moving toward a market economy. These reforms were frozen following the military takeover in 1992, though many have since been resumed under pressure from the IMF and the World Bank. The majority of the economy's most productive sectors remain under state control, though private investment is encouraged in the oil industry and, since early 2001, in telecommunications. A number of Western oil companies have signed exploration contracts with Algeria since it has accepted more competitive production-sharing agreements. Investment levels are not likely rise, however, as long as the political situation is unstable. The government pledged $1.8 billion in 2003 for post-earthquake reconstruction.

ECONOMIC PERFORMANCE INDICATOR

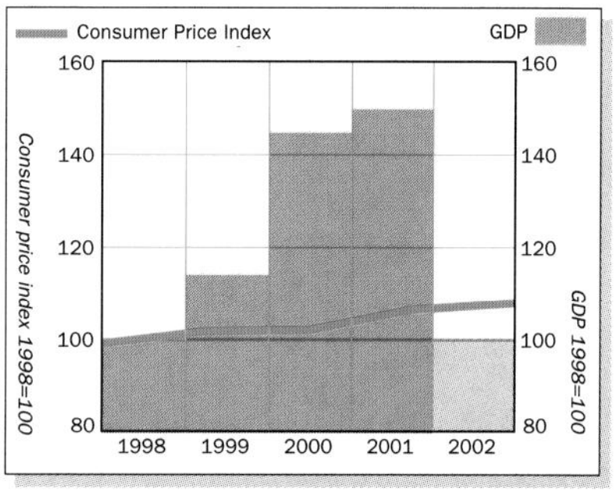
Consumer Price Index
GDP
Consumer price index 1998–100
GDP 1998–100
160
140
120
100
80
1998
1999
2000
2001
2002

ALGERIA : MAJOR BUSINESSES

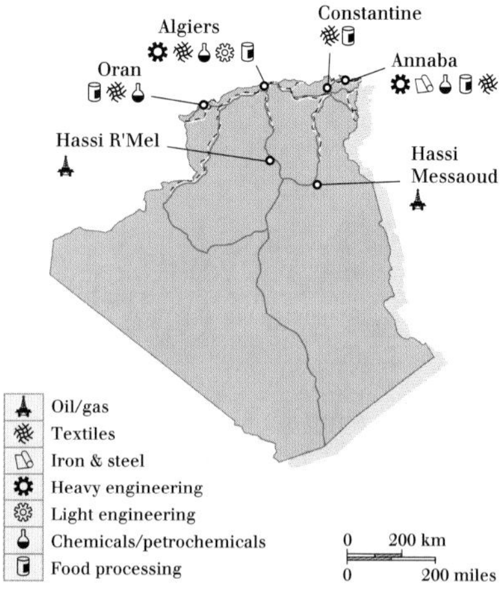
Algiers
Constantine
Oran
Annaba
Hassi R'Mel
Hassi Messaoud
Oil/gas
Textiles
Iron & steel
Heavy engineering
Light engineering
Chemicals/petrochemicals
Food processing
0 200 km
0 200 miles

RESOURCES

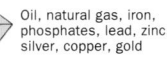

Electric power 6m kW

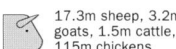

100,281 tonnes

1.86m b/d (reserves 11.3bn barrels)

17.3m sheep, 3.2m goats, 1.5m cattle, 115m chickens

Oil, natural gas, iron, phosphates, lead, zinc, silver, copper, gold

ELECTRICITY GENERATION

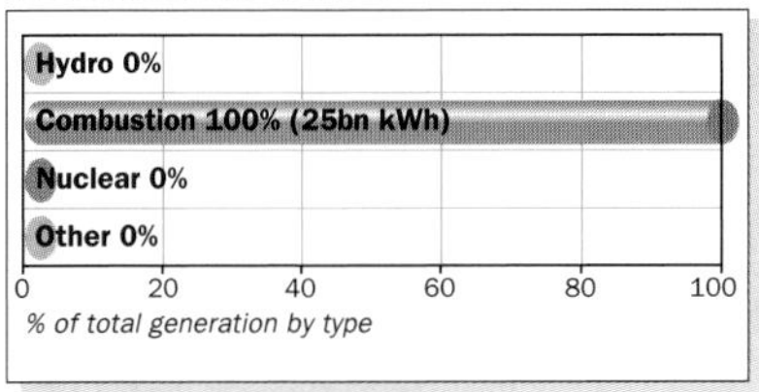
Hydro 0%
Combustion 100% (25bn kWh)
Nuclear 0%
Other 0%
0
20
40
60
80
100
% of total generation by type

Crude oil and natural gas, Algeria's main resources, have been produced since the 1950s. Algeria also has diverse minerals, including iron ore, zinc, silver, copper ore, lead, gold, and phosphates. In the 1960s and 1970s, Algeria sought to become a major manufacturer, with investments in building materials, refined products, and steel; none of these sectors are competitive on world markets.

Agriculture employs one-quarter of Algeria's workforce, but its importance to the economy is diminishing. Forests cover less than 1% of the land. Most are brushwood, but some areas include cork oak trees, Aleppo pine, evergreen oak, and cedar. Algeria has a large fishing fleet. Sardines, anchovies, tuna, and shellfish are the major commercial catches.

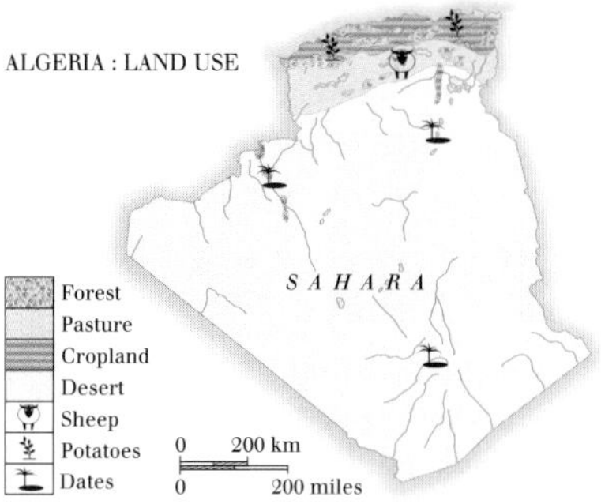
ALGERIA : LAND USE
SAHARA
Forest
Pasture
Cropland
Desert
Sheep
Potatoes
Dates
0 200 km
0 200 miles

ENVIRONMENT

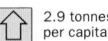

Sustainability rank: 70th

5% (0.1% partially protected)

2.9 tonnes per capita

ENVIRONMENTAL TREATIES

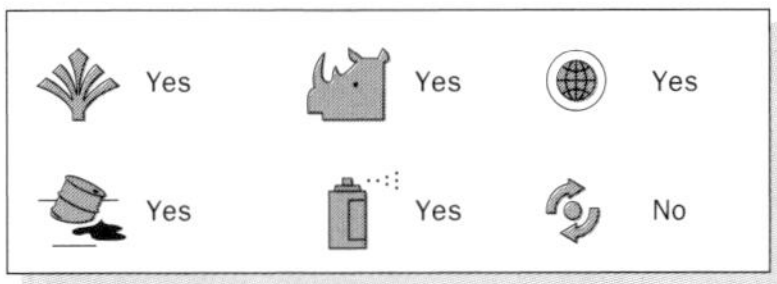
Yes
Yes
Yes
Yes
Yes
No

Since most of Algeria is desert or semidesert, over 90% of the population are forced to live on what remains – some 20% of the land. The desert is moving northward. Vegetation has been stripped for use as firewood and animal fodder, leaving fragile soils exposed which then require expensive specialist care to conserve them. Techniques for water purification are substandard, and rivers are being increasingly contaminated by untreated sewage, industrial effluent, and wastes from petroleum refining.

MEDIA

TV ownership medium

Daily newspaper circulation 27 per 1000 people

PUBLISHING AND BROADCAST MEDIA

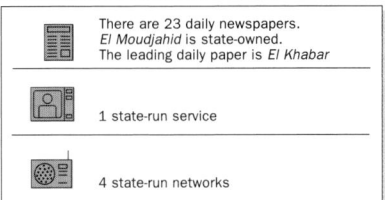

There are 23 daily newspapers. *El Moudjahid* is state-owned. The leading daily paper is *El Khabar*

1 state-run service

4 state-run networks

Newspapers, TV, and radio are mainly state-controlled and are cautious in reporting violence, but there is no overt censorship. TV is broadcast in Arabic, French, and Tamazight. The three main daily newspapers have a combined circulation of over one million. However, distribution is limited outside the major cities.

CRIME

Death penalty not used in practice

34,243 prisoners

Up 71% in 2000–2001

CRIME RATES

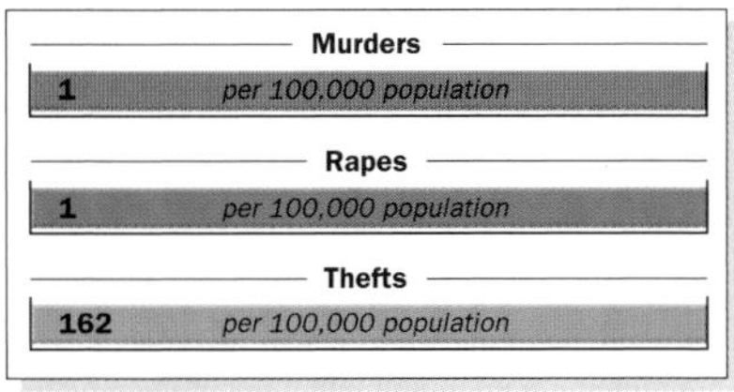
Murders
1 per 100,000 population
Rapes
1 per 100,000 population
Thefts
162 per 100,000 population

Thousands of people have been killed by radical Islamists since 1992, while human rights groups have accused progovernment death squads of brutal reprisal killings and of persecuting suspected Islamist militants.

EDUCATION

School leaving age: 15

69%

456,358 students

THE EDUCATION SYSTEM

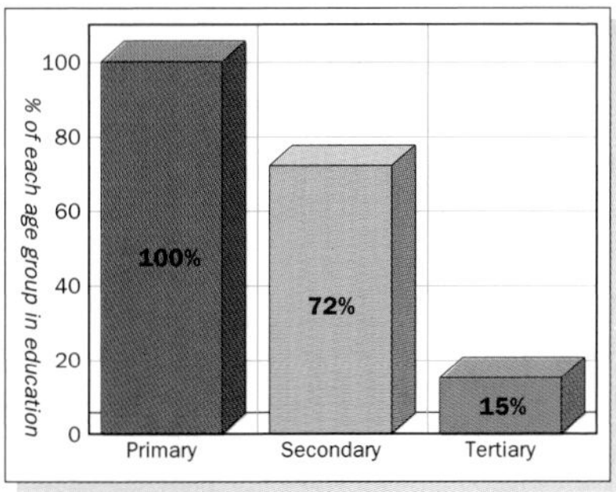
100
80
60
40
20
0
% of each age group in education
100%
72%
15%
Primary
Secondary
Tertiary

Over three-quarters of the school-age population receive a formal education, and the literacy rate is rising.

Since 1973, the curriculum has been Arabicized and the teaching of French restricted. Though the use of Arabic is enforced in public life, Tamazight was allowed in schools from 2003.

Ten main universities, and several polytechnics and technical colleges provide higher education.

HEALTH

Welfare state health benefits

1 per 1000 people

Respiratory, heart, and cerebrovascular diseases, malaria

Since 1974 all Algerians have had the right to free health care. Primary health care is rudimentary outside main cities. Because the formal health care system is overburdened, many people turn to alternative forms of medicine. The infant mortality rate has risen recently and is now the highest rate among the coastal states of north Africa.

SPENDING

GDP/cap. increase

CONSUMPTION AND SPENDING

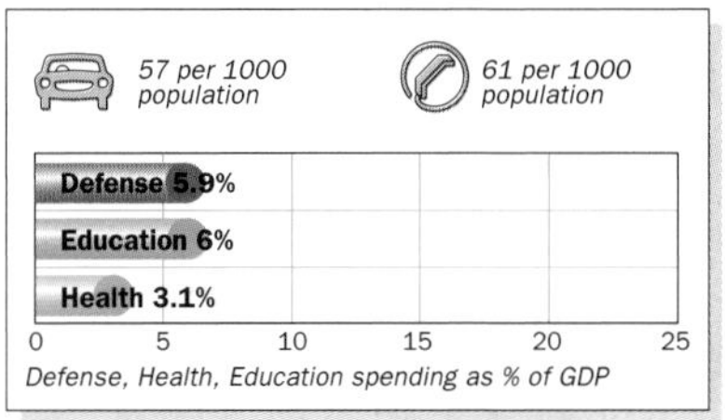
57 per 1000 population
61 per 1000 population
Defense 5.9%
Education 6%
Health 3.1%
0
5
10
15
20
25
Defense, Health, Education spending as % of GDP

There is great disparity in wealth between the political elite and the rest of the population. Those with military connections form the wealthiest group, while over 15% of people live in poverty and a majority struggles with soaring prices for basic necessities.

WORLD RANKING

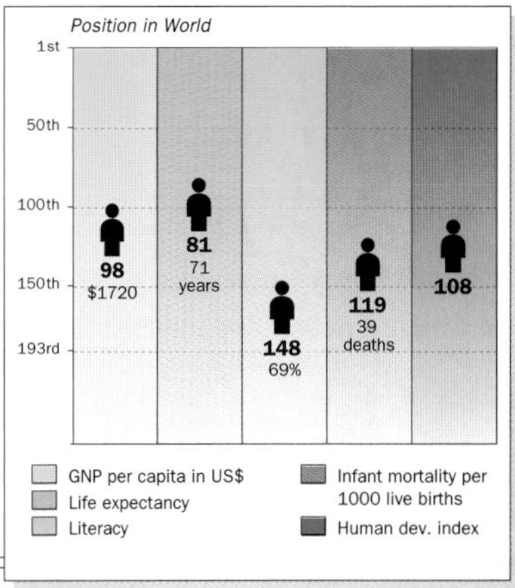
Position in World
1st
50th
100th
150th
193rd
98
$1720
81
71
years
148
69%
119
39
deaths
108
GNP per capita in US$
Life expectancy
Literacy
Infant mortality per 1000 live births
Human dev. index

A

ANDORRA

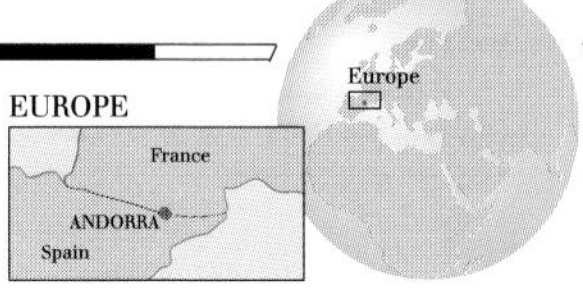
EUROPE
France
ANDORRA
Spain
Europe

OFFICIAL NAME: Principality of Andorra **CAPITAL:** Andorra la Vella
POPULATION: 69,150 **CURRENCY:** Euro **OFFICIAL LANGUAGE:** Catalan

1278 | 1278 | Sept 8 | AND | +1 | +376 | .ad

A TINY, LANDLOCKED principality between France and Spain, Andorra lies high in the eastern Pyrenees. From the 13th century, French and Spanish coprinces (today the President of France and the Bishop of Urgell) have ruled Andorra. In December 1993, the principality held its first full elections. Andorra's spectacular scenery, alpine climate, and duty-free shopping have made tourism, especially skiing, its main source of income.

***Andorra's outstanding mountain scenery** attracts skiers in winter, walkers in summer.*

CLIMATE

Mountain

WEATHER CHART FOR ANDORRA LA VELLA

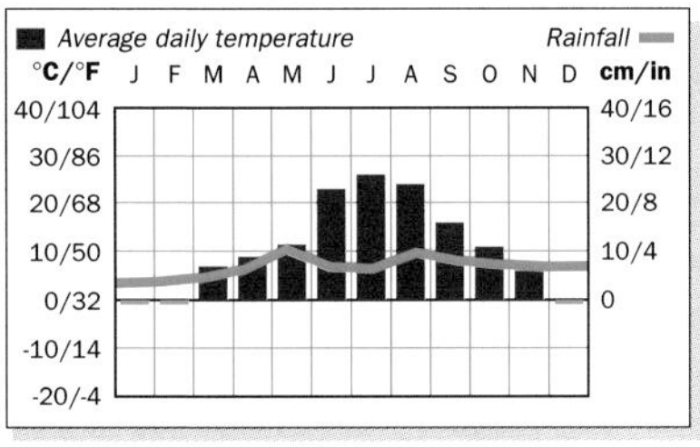
Average daily temperature
Rainfall
°C/°F J F M A M J J A S O N D cm/in
40/104 40/16
30/86 30/12
20/68 20/8
10/50 10/4
0/32 0
-10/14
-20/4

Springs are cool and wettest in May; summers are relatively dry and warm. Snowfalls in December and January provide snow for good skiing up to March. Andorra's climate supports an abundance of wild flowers.

TRANSPORTATION

Drive on right

None — Has no fleet

THE TRANSPORTATION NETWORK

198 km (123 miles)	None
None	None

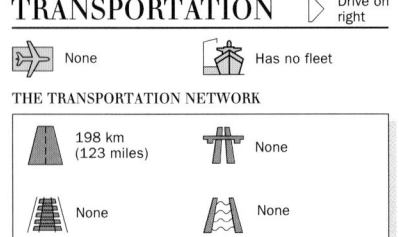

The road from France to Spain climbs to 2704 m (8875 ft) through one of the most dramatic mountain passes in Europe. Traffic congestion is a major problem in Andorra la Vella, especially in the summer. In 2001 plans for an overhead rail system were announced.

TOURISM

Visitors : Population 49:1

3.39m visitors — Down 4% in 2002

MAIN TOURIST ARRIVALS

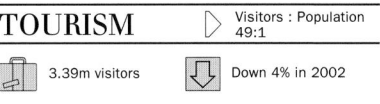

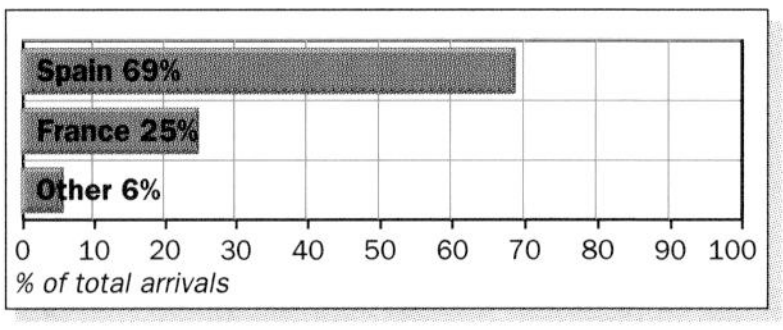
Spain 69%
France 25%
Other 6%
0 10 20 30 40 50 60 70 80 90 100
% of total arrivals

Most tourists visit Andorra to ski or shop. Traditionally there are a great many day-trippers from France and Spain, drawn by the many tax-free designer-label boutiques.

Five resorts offer Alpine skiing facilities, and specialize in Nordic skiing. In summer they cater instead for mountain hikers; Andorra's wild flowers attract many visitors, but there is also much for birdwatchers and entomologists to see.

Though not strongly promoted, wild boar and the goat-like chamois are hunted. Fishing is also very popular.

PEOPLE

Pop. density medium

Spanish, Catalan, French, Portuguese — 149/km² (384/mi²)

THE URBAN/RURAL POPULATION SPLIT

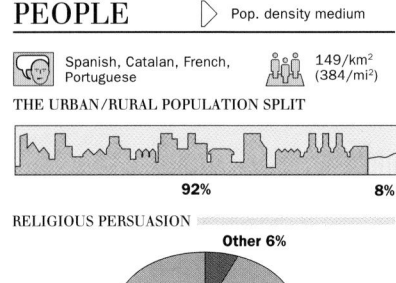

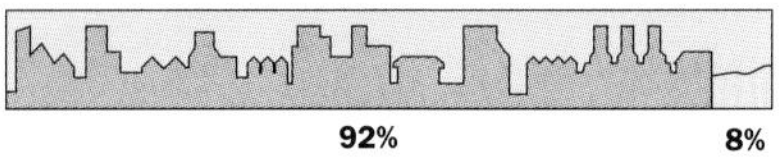
92%
8%

RELIGIOUS PERSUASION

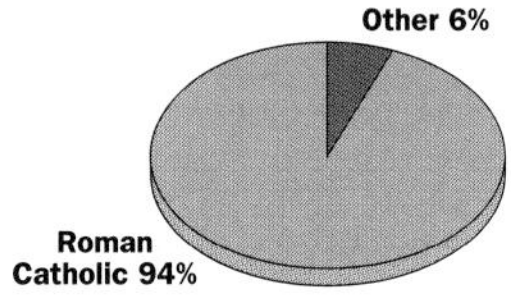
Other 6%
Roman Catholic 94%

While immigrant workers are vital, full residence is difficult to acquire. Many seasonal workers come from Argentina. Low taxes attract wealthy expatriates.

POLITICS

Multiparty elections

2001/2005 — Coprinces Jacques Chirac and Joan Enric Vives Sicília

AT THE LAST ELECTION

General Council of the Valleys 28 seats

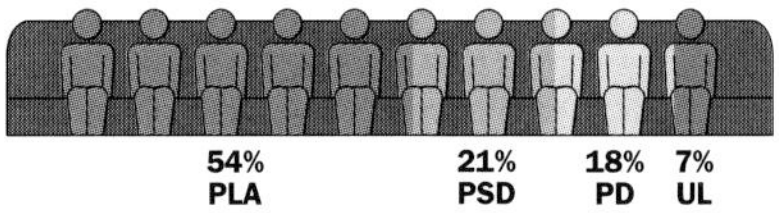
54% PLA
21% PSD
18% PD
7% UL

PLA = Liberal Party of Andorra **PSD** = Social Democratic Party **PD** = Democratic Party **UL** = Unió Laurediana

14 members are elected on a national list and 14 are elected in seven dual-member parishes

Andorra was a semifeudal state until 1993, when a referendum approved measures which legalized political parties and the right to strike, and altered relations with the coprinces. The ruling PLA, led by Marc Forné, has been returned to power twice.

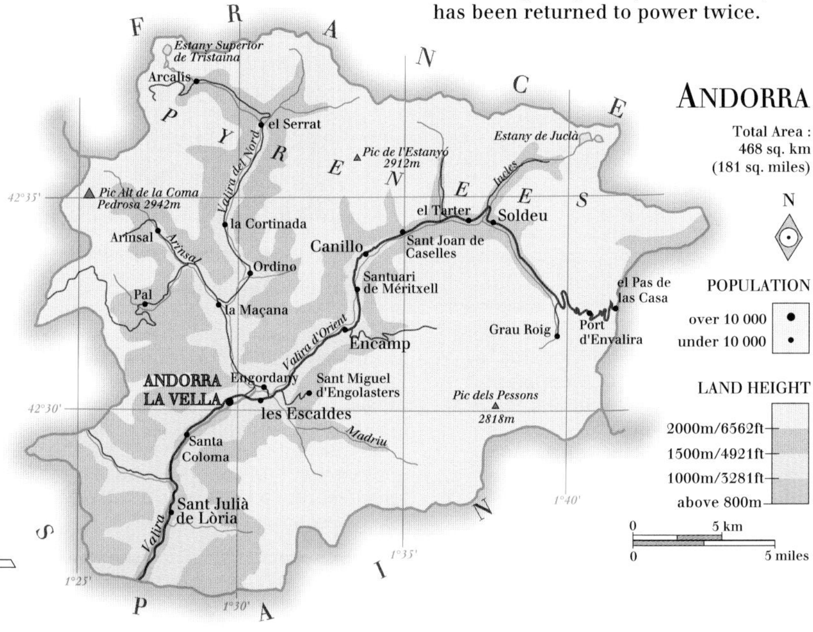
FRANCE
SPAIN
PYRENEES
Estany Superior de Tristaina
Arcalís
el Serrat
Valira del Nord
Pic de l'Estanyó 2912m
Estany de Juclà
Pic Alt de la Coma Pedrosa 2942m
la Cortinada
el Tarter
Soldeu
Arinsal
Canillo
Sant Joan de Caselles
Ordino
Santuari de Meritxell
Pal
la Maçana
Valira d'Orient
Encamp
Grau Roig
el Pas de las Casa
Port d'Envalira
ANDORRA LA VELLA
Engordany
Sant Miquel d'Engolasters
les Escaldes
Madriu
Pic dels Pessons 2818m
Santa Coloma
Sant Julià de Lòria
Valira
42°35'
42°30'
1°25'
1°30'
1°35'
1°40'
ANDORRA
Total Area : 468 sq. km (181 sq. miles)
N
POPULATION
over 10 000
under 10 000
LAND HEIGHT
2000m/6562ft
1500m/4921ft
1000m/3281ft
above 800m
0 5 km
0 5 miles

WORLD AFFAIRS

Joined UN in 1993

CE | OSCE

In 1991 Andorra became a member of the EU customs union and adopted the euro in 2002, having formerly used the French franc and Spanish peseta. Andorra's status as a tax haven has prompted criticism from the OECD.

AID

Not applicable

Andorra has no aid receipts or donations

Not applicable

The principality of Andorra neither receives nor provides aid, and has no plans to do so.

DEFENSE

No compulsory military service

Andorra has no defense budget

Not applicable

Andorra has no defense budget; France and Spain provide protection. The last military action was intervention by French *gendarmes* to restore order after a royalist coup in 1933.

ECONOMICS

Not available

$1.28bn

0.822 euros (0.871)

SCORE CARD

❑ WORLD GNP RANKING	150th
❑ GNP PER CAPITA	$19,368
❑ BALANCE OF PAYMENTS	Included in Spanish total
❑ INFLATION	4.3%
❑ UNEMPLOYMENT	Low unemployment

STRENGTHS

Tourism underpins the economy. Strict banking secrecy laws make Andorra attractive as a tax haven. Healthy luxury retail sector. Farming: cereals, potatoes, and tobacco are the major products.

WEAKNESSES

France and Spain effectively decide economic policy. Dependence on imported food and raw materials.

EXPORTS

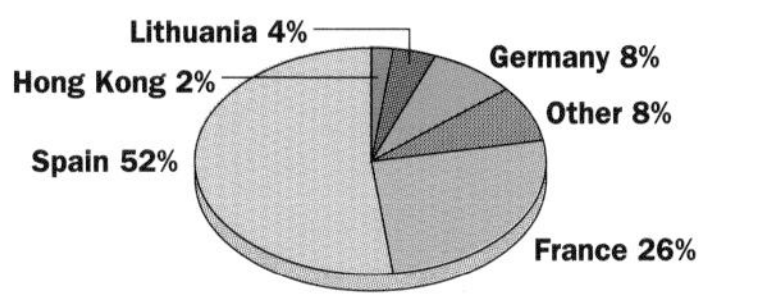
Lithuania 4%
Hong Kong 2%
Germany 8%
Other 8%
Spain 52%
France 26%

IMPORTS

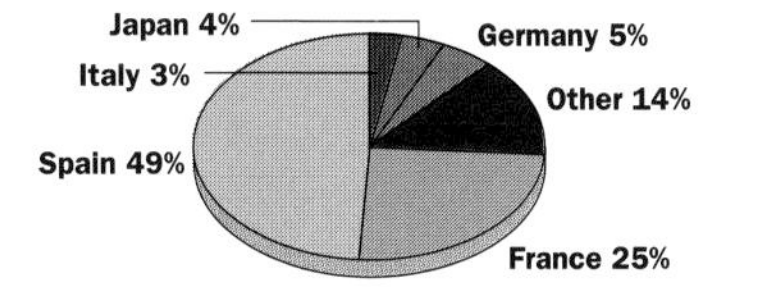
Japan 4%
Italy 3%
Germany 5%
Other 14%
Spain 49%
France 25%

RESOURCES

Not available

None

Not an oil producer and has no refineries

2683 sheep, 1194 cattle, 741 horses, 362 goats

None

Water is a major resource, hydropower providing most energy needs. However, Andorra has to import twice as much electricity as it produces, and plans to develop wind power. A third of the country is under forest cover.

ENVIRONMENT

Not available

None

Not available

The impact of millions of visitors each year on Andorra's alpine ecology is of great concern. The construction of hotels, ski resorts, and transportation links threaten to despoil the country's picturesque mountain landscape. Tourism development is also endangering the remarkable flora, and creates pressure to clear forested areas. Hunting is no longer promoted but remains a popular attraction; the wild boar and the Pyrenean chamois are particularly targeted. Some restrictions have been introduced to preserve rarer animal species.

MEDIA

TV ownership high

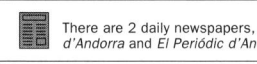

Daily newspaper circulation 60 per 1000 people

PUBLISHING AND BROADCAST MEDIA

There are 2 daily newspapers, *Diari d'Andorra* and *El Periódic d'Andorra*

1 independent commercial channel

6 independent commercial stations

Andorra has one domestic broadcaster, Radio i Televisio d'Andorra, and receives French and Spanish television channels. A Spanish TV company broadcasts one hour a day of programs for Andorra.

CRIME

No death penalty

55 prisoners

Up 20% in 2000

Tourists are natural targets for thieves, most of whom are not Andorran. Thefts of expensive cars for resale in France and Spain are on the increase.

Andorra's two criminal courts are known as the *Tribunals de Corts.*

EDUCATION

School leaving age: 14

99%

3180 students

There are around 30 schools in Andorra, with instruction in Catalan, French, and Spanish. The University of Andorra specializes in distance learning using the Internet.

CHRONOLOGY

Since 1278, Andorra has been autonomous, ruled by French and Spanish coprinces.

- ❑ **1970** Women get the vote.
- ❑ **1982** First constitution enshrines popular sovereignty.
- ❑ **1983** General Council votes in favor of income tax.
- ❑ **1984** Government resigns over attempt to introduce indirect taxes.
- ❑ **1991** EU customs union comes into effect.
- ❑ **1992** Political demonstrations demanding constitutional reform. Government resigns.
- ❑ **1993** Referendum approves new constitution.
- ❑ **1994** Government falls; replaced by center-right Liberal cabinet, which is reelected in 1997 and 2001.

HEALTH

Welfare state health benefits

1 per 385 people

Heart and cerebrovascular diseases

Andorra, with just one public hospital, has Europe's longest life expectancy. Health spas, such as the hot springs at les Escaldes, are popular.

SPENDING

GDP/cap. increase

CONSUMPTION AND SPENDING

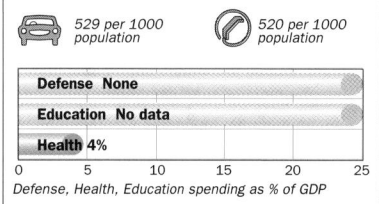

529 per 1000 population

520 per 1000 population

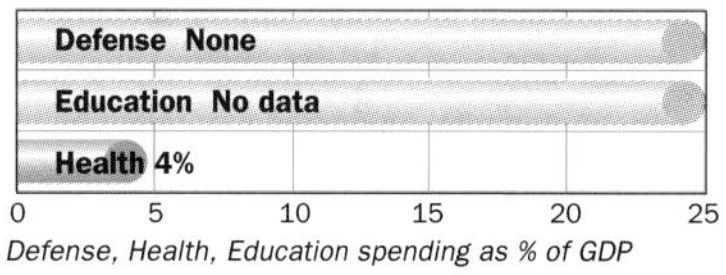
Defense None
Education No data
Health 4%
0
5
10
15
20
25
Defense, Health, Education spending as % of GDP

Hotel owners form the wealthiest group of citizens in Andorran society, though many of them choose to live across the border in neighboring Spain.

WORLD RANKING

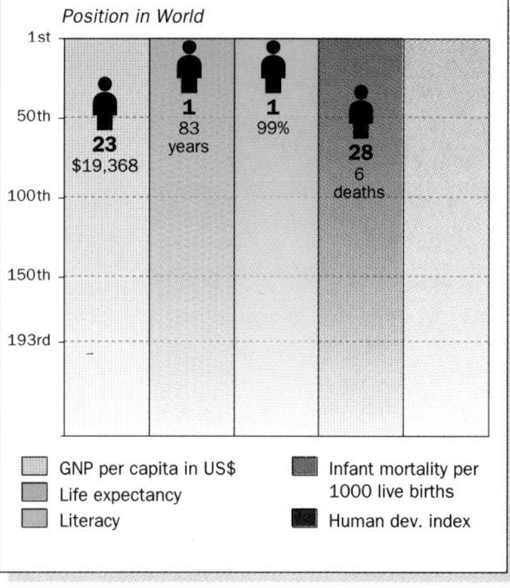
Position in World
1st
50th
100th
150th
193rd
23
$19,368
1
83
years
1
99%
28
6
deaths
GNP per capita in US$
Life expectancy
Literacy
Infant mortality per 1000 live births
Human dev. index

A

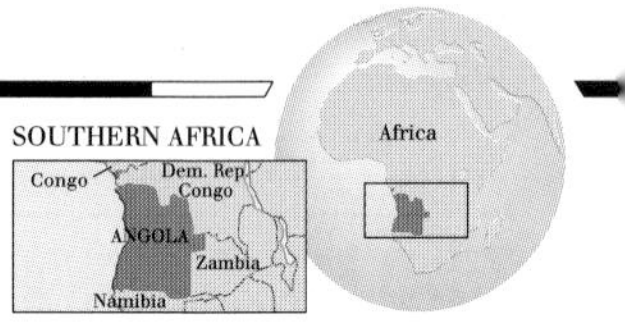
SOUTHERN AFRICA
Africa
Congo
Dem. Rep. Congo
ANGOLA
Zambia
Namibia

ANGOLA

OFFICIAL NAME: Republic of Angola **CAPITAL:** Luanda
POPULATION: 13.6 million **CURRENCY:** Readjusted kwanza **OFFICIAL LANGUAGE:** Portuguese

1975 | 1975 | Nov 11 | ANG | +1 | +244 | .ao

AN OIL-AND DIAMOND-RICH country in southwest Africa, Angola has suffered almost continuous civil war since independence from Portugal in 1975. During the Cold War the West supported UNITA rebels against the Soviet-backed MPLA government. After many failed peace initiatives, the latest, in 2002, has raised hopes yet again of a more permanent end to the violence.

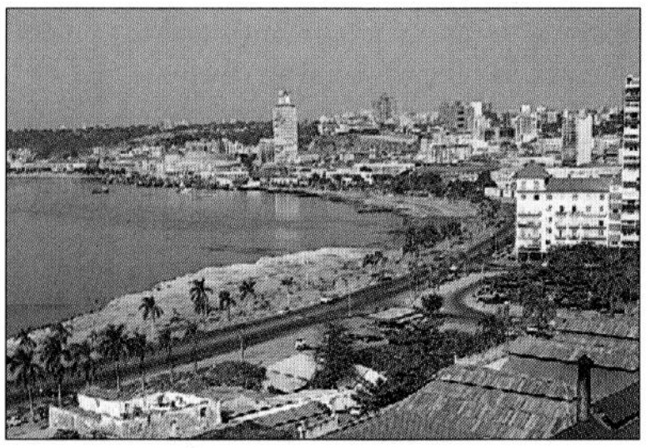

Angola's capital, Luanda. Founded in 1575 by the Portuguese, it became a transshipment point for slaves en route to Brazil.

CLIMATE

Tropical/steppe

WEATHER CHART FOR LUANDA

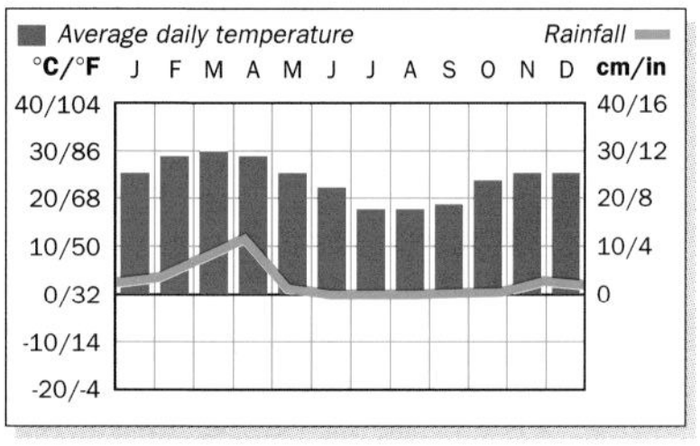
Average daily temperature
Rainfall
°C/°F
J F M A M J J A S O N D
cm/in
40/104
30/86
20/68
10/50
0/32
-10/14
-20/-4
40/16
30/12
20/8
10/4
0

The climate varies from temperate to tropical. Rainfall decreases from north to south. The Benguela Current makes the coast unusually cool and dry.

TRANSPORTATION

Drive on right

Luanda International (4 de Fevereiro) 777,350 passengers

124 ships 55,125 grt

THE TRANSPORTATION NETWORK

5143 km (3196 miles)

Much of this infrastructure has been destroyed by civil war.

2761 km (1716 miles)

1295 km (805 miles)

War has destroyed infrastructure, restricted movement of people and goods, and devastated port traffic. UN peacekeepers have tried to clear mines and repair roads, bridges, and railroads.

TOURISM

Visitors : Population 1:149

91,000 visitors

Up 36% in 2002

MAIN TOURIST ARRIVALS

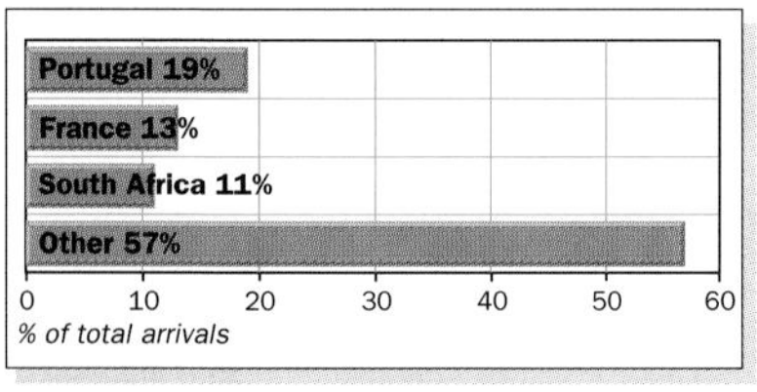
Portugal 19%
France 13%
South Africa 11%
Other 57%
0 10 20 30 40 50 60
% of total arrivals

A war zone since independence, Angola is only slowly starting to attract tourists. Most visitors are journalists or work for the oil multinationals in Cabinda.

PEOPLE

Pop. density low

Portuguese, Umbundu, Kimbundu, Kikongo

11/km² (28/mi²)

THE URBAN/RURAL POPULATION SPLIT

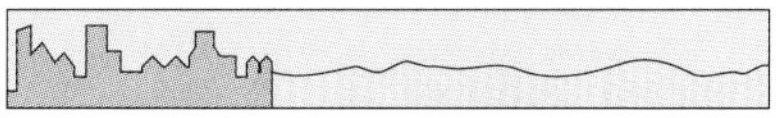
35%
65%

ETHNIC MAKEUP

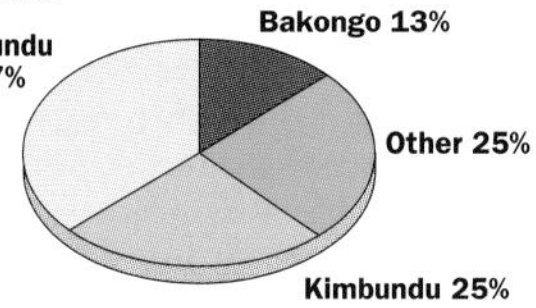
Ovimbundu 37%
Bakongo 13%
Other 25%
Kimbundu 25%

The predominantly rural-dwelling Ovimbundu and the mainly urban-based Kimbundu are the main ethnic groups; they generally supported UNITA or the MPLA respectively. The small mixed-race (Portuguese–African) community enjoys the highest standard of living. Christianity (mostly Roman Catholicism) is practiced alongside indigenous beliefs.

POLITICS

In transition

1992/1998 (postponed)

President José Eduardo dos Santos

AT THE LAST ELECTION

National Assembly 223 seats

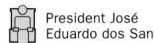

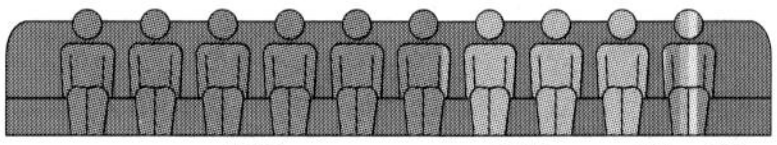
3% PRS
1% PLD
3% Others
58% MPLA–PT
32% UNITA
2% FNLA
1% Vacant

MPLA–PT = Popular Movement for the Liberation of Angola –Workers' Party **UNITA** = National Union for the Total Independence of Angola **PRS** = Social Renewal Party **FNLA** = Angolan National Liberation Front **PLD** = Liberal Democratic Party
The seats allotted to members from abroad remained vacant

In power since 1975, the MPLA in 1991 abandoned one-party rule and, under President José Eduardo dos Santos, won the first multiparty polls in 1992. Jonas Savimbi's defeated UNITA responded by restarting the civil war. A 1994 peace accord signed in Lusaka (Zambia) resulted in UNITA's joining a national unity government in 1997, but they left the government as fighting escalated once more in 1998. Savimbi's death in 2002 led to a renewed peace initiative, and the transformation of UNITA from a guerrilla group into a political party, but elections due in 1998 are still to be held.

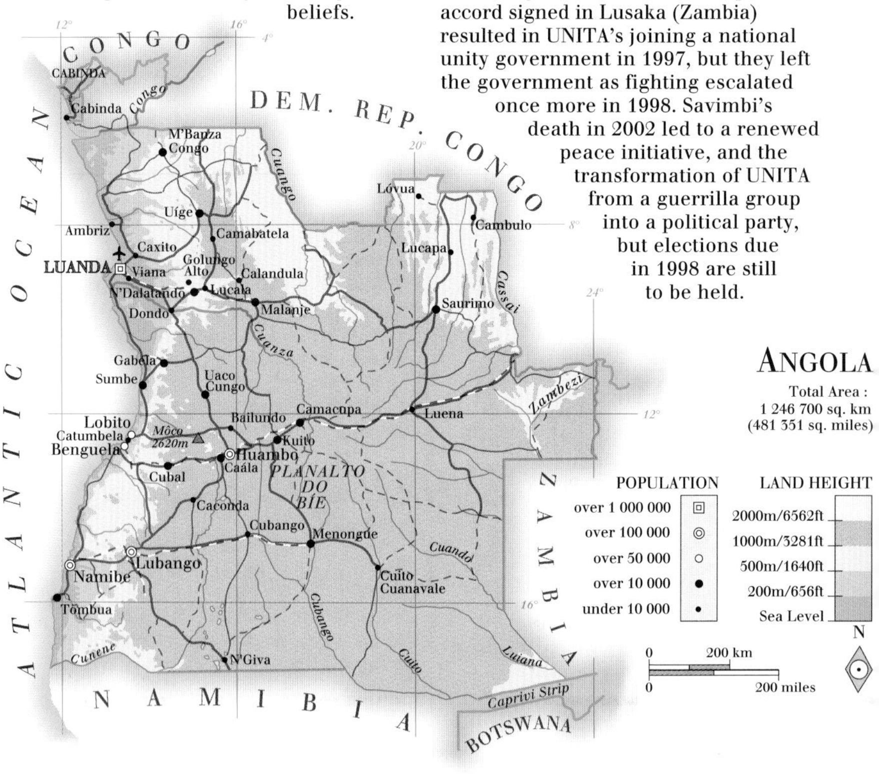
CONGO
CABINDA
Cabinda
Congo
DEM. REP. CONGO
ATLANTIC OCEAN
M'Banza Congo
Cuango
Uíge
Ambriz
Caxito
LUANDA
Viana
Golungo Alto
Camabatela
Calandula
N'Dalatando
Lucala
Dondo
Malanje
Cuanza
Lóvua
Cambulo
Lucapa
Cassai
Saurimo
Gabela
Sumbe
Uaco Cungo
Lobito
Catumbela
Benguela
Môco 2620m
Bailundo
Camacupa
Luena
Zambezi
Huambo
Kuito
Caála
PLANALTO DO BIÉ
Cubal
Caconda
Cubango
Menongue
Namibe
Lubango
Tômbua
Cuando
Cuito Cuanavale
Cunene
N'Giva
Cubango
Cuito
Luiana
Caprivi Strip
NAMIBIA
ZAMBIA
BOTSWANA
ANGOLA
Total Area : 1 246 700 sq. km (481 351 sq. miles)
POPULATION
over 1 000 000
over 100 000
over 50 000
over 10 000
under 10 000
LAND HEIGHT
2000m/6562ft
1000m/3281ft
500m/1640ft
200m/656ft
Sea Level
0 200 km
0 200 miles
N

WORLD AFFAIRS

Joined UN in 1976

COMESA IBRD NAM AU SADC

Peace and reconstruction are now supported by the US and Russia, though Angola has been a key frontier during the Cold War. Regional relations were also affected by the same global concerns, and when the civil war carried across local borders. Now, postapartheid South Africa is a key partner, while the end of hostilities in Angola eased tensions with Zambia.

There is international concern over who exactly profits from the country's lucrative diamond trade.

AID

Recipient

$421m (receipts) — Up 46% in 2002

Aid agencies and international donors have found it easier to offer assistance to Angola since the return of peace in 2002. The immediate focus was on the massive humanitarian crisis left by decades of war. Angola's ban on importing genetically modified produce is hindering the provision of food aid.

DEFENSE

No compulsory military service

$946m — Down 35% in 2002

By 2002 superior government forces had asserted control over more than 90% of the country. Under the cease-fire, some 5000 UNITA troops were integrated into the regular army. The remaining 80,000 were demobilized. Since then the army's main priority has been to tackle the separatist rebellion in the Cabinda exclave.

ECONOMICS

Inflation 659% p.a. (1990–2001)

$9.3bn — 79.03 readjusted kwanza (78.25)

SCORE CARD

- ❑ WORLD GNP RANKING..........................89th
- ❑ GNP PER CAPITA $710
- ❑ BALANCE OF PAYMENTS.................–$1.43bn
- ❑ INFLATION 103%
- ❑ UNEMPLOYMENT..................................50%

STRENGTHS

Oil. Diamonds. Rich mineral deposits. Large private sector. Lifting of wartime sanctions on UNITA territory.

WEAKNESSES

Damaged infrastructure. Subsistence agriculture. Drought. Landmines maim civilians, disrupt farming. Corruption. Continuing conflict in Cabinda.

EXPORTS

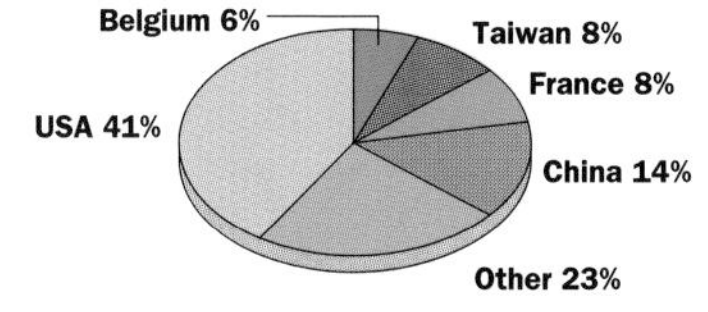
Belgium 6%
Taiwan 8%
France 8%
USA 41%
China 14%
Other 23%

IMPORTS

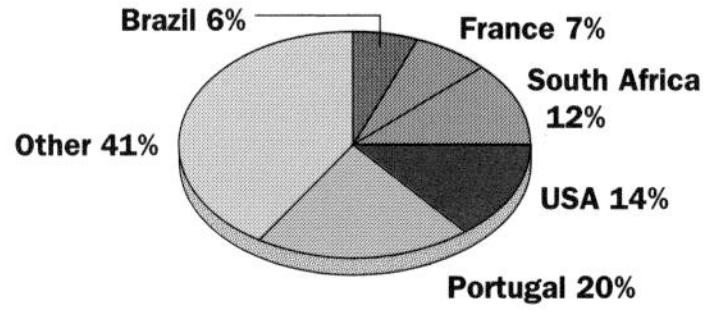
Brazil 6%
France 7%
South Africa 12%
Other 41%
USA 14%
Portugal 20%

RESOURCES

Electric power 460,000 kW

- 252,518 tonnes
- 885,000 b/d (reserves 8.9bn barrels)
- 4.15m cattle, 2.05m goats, 780,000 pigs, 6.8m chickens
- Oil, diamonds, iron, copper, lead, zinc, gold, manganese

Deepwater oil fields have been found. The rich alluvial diamond deposits were controlled by UNITA during the civil war.

ENVIRONMENT

Sustainability rank: 111th

7% (2% partially protected) — 0.5 tonnes per capita

Years of war have damaged the water supply. UNITA has been accused of widescale ivory poaching.

MEDIA

TV ownership medium

Daily newspaper circulation 11 per 1000 people.

PUBLISHING AND BROADCAST MEDIA

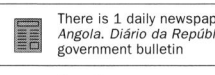

There is 1 daily newspaper, *O Jornal de Angola. Diário da República* is a daily government bulletin

2 services: 1 state-controlled, 1 independent

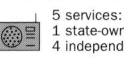

5 services: 1 state-owned, 4 independent

The news agency and *O Jornal de Angola* are state-owned. Independent media are critical but can face harassment.

CRIME

No death penalty

4975 prisoners — Down in 2000

Violent crime occurs frequently throughout Angola, and murder, theft, corruption, and diamond smuggling are commonplace. Street crime is especially common in Luanda. Rural areas are effectively controlled by gangs.

EDUCATION

School leaving age: 9

40% — 7845 students

A government-backed initiative, Adra, is making progress in reviving schooling in cities.

CHRONOLOGY

The Portuguese first established coastal forts in 1482.

- ❑ **1975** Independence. Civil war between MPLA and UNITA.
- ❑ **1979** José Eduardo dos Santos (MPLA) becomes president.
- ❑ **1991** UN-brokered peace.
- ❑ **1992** MPLA election victory provokes UNITA to resume fighting.
- ❑ **1994** Lusaka peace agreement.
- ❑ **1998** Civil war reerupts.
- ❑ **2000** Fighting spreads as UNITA increases guerrilla activity.
- ❑ **2002** UNITA leader Jonas Savimbi killed. April, cease-fire signed.

HEALTH

No welfare state health benefits

1 per 10,000 people — Malaria, diarrheal and respiratory diseases, severe malnutrition

Angola's health system is barely able to cope with casualties of war and the threat of epidemics. Angola has the greatest number of amputees (caused by landmines) in the world.

Immunization of three million children against polio began in 2002.

SPENDING

GDP/cap. increase

CONSUMPTION AND SPENDING

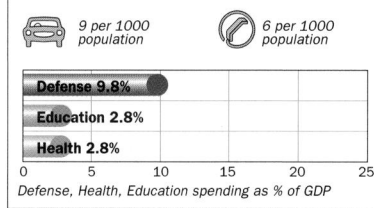

9 per 1000 population — *6 per 1000 population*

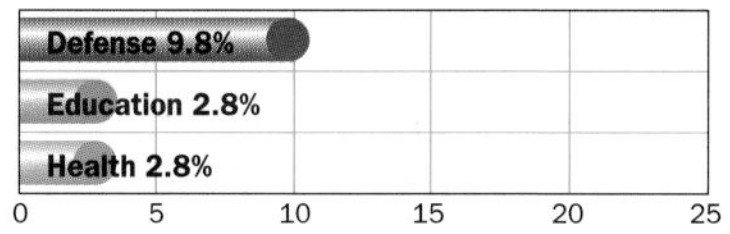
Defense 9.8%
Education 2.8%
Health 2.8%
0
5
10
15
20
25

Defense, Health, Education spending as % of GDP

State officials enjoy various luxuries, such as access to cars and other consumer goods, while the majority of people struggle to survive. The MPLA accuses its own generals of illicit diamond mining.

WORLD RANKING

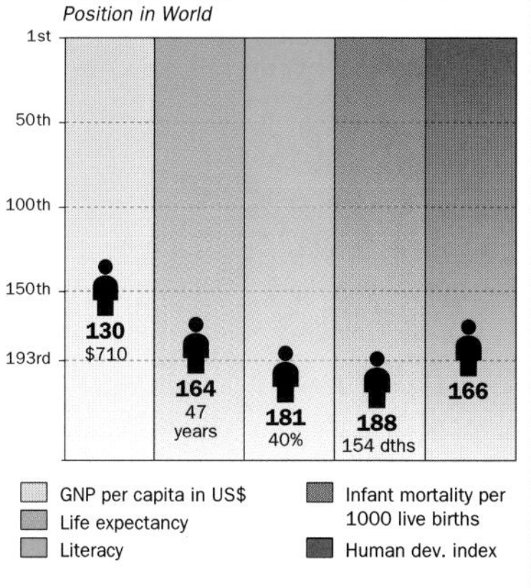
Position in World
1st
50th
100th
150th
193rd
130
$710
164
47 years
181
40%
188
154 dths
166
GNP per capita in US$
Life expectancy
Literacy
Infant mortality per 1000 live births
Human dev. index

A

ANTARCTICA

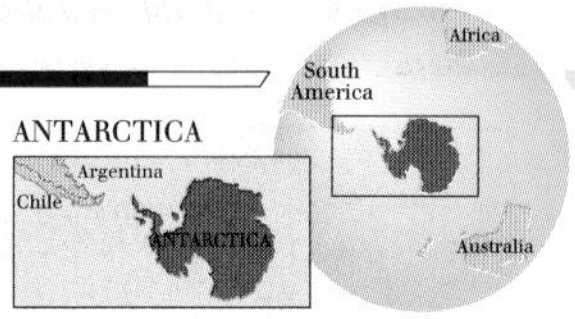
ANTARCTICA
Argentina
Chile
ANTARCTICA
South America
Africa
Australia

OFFICIAL NAME: Antarctica **CAPITAL:** None
POPULATION: None **CURRENCY:** None **OFFICIAL LANGUAGE:** None

1961 | 1961 | n/a | n/a | n/a | n/a | .aq

THE WORLD'S fifth-largest continent, Antarctica is almost entirely covered by ice over 2000 m (6560 ft) thick. The area sustains a varied wildlife, including seals, whales, and penguins. The Antarctic Treaty, signed in 1959 and in force since 1961, provides for international governance of Antarctica. To gain Consultative Status, countries have to set up a program of scientific research into the continent. Following a 1994 international agreement, a whale sanctuary was established around Antarctica.

CLIMATE

Freezing

WEATHER CHART

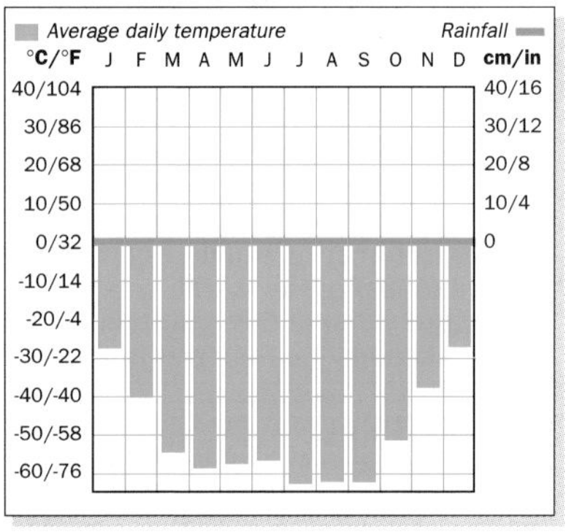
Average daily temperature
Rainfall
°C/°F
J F M A M J J A S O N D
cm/in
40/104
30/86
20/68
10/50
0/32
-10/14
-20/-4
-30/-22
-40/-40
-50/-58
-60/-76
40/16
30/12
20/8
10/4
0

Antarctica is the windiest as well as the coldest continent. Powerful winds create a narrow storm belt around the continent, which brings cloud, fog, and severe blizzards. Icebergs barricade more than 90% of the coastline, and climate change has seen an increase in their number and size in recent years. Antarctica contains over 80% of the world's fresh water.

TRANSPORTATION

Not applicable

Airstrips to some stations

Has no fleet

Ships are the main mode of transportation to Antarctica. They are also used for marine research projects. Several countries have built airstrips, used solely for governmental operations. Many aircraft are equipped with skis for rougher landings.

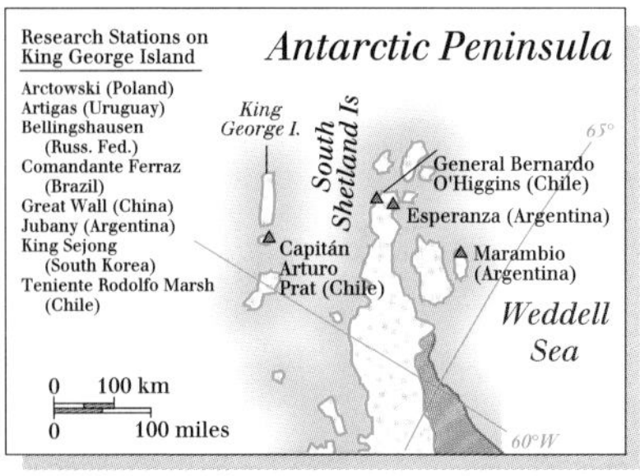
Research Stations on King George Island
Arctowski (Poland)
Artigas (Uruguay)
Bellingshausen (Russ. Fed.)
Comandante Ferraz (Brazil)
Great Wall (China)
Jubany (Argentina)
King Sejong (South Korea)
Teniente Rodolfo Marsh (Chile)
Antarctic Peninsula
King George I.
South Shetland Is
General Bernardo O'Higgins (Chile)
Esperanza (Argentina)
Capitán Arturo Prat (Chile)
Marambio (Argentina)
Weddell Sea
65°
60°W
0 100 km
0 100 miles

TOURISM

Not applicable

17,000 visitors

Up 81% in 2000–2002

Tourism in Antarctica has exploded since the late 1990s, and official regulation of the industry has become essential. Tour operators have replaced elderly ex-Soviet research vessels with cruise ships that can carry 1000 passengers, endangering the fragile ecosystem wherever they put ashore. Adventure sports such as skiing and kayaking are becoming popular. Several Antarctic bases now cater for tourists and even have souvenir shops.

PEOPLE

Not applicable

English, Spanish, French, Norwegian, Chinese, Polish, Russian, German, Japanese

Not applicable

ETHNIC MAKEUP

Antarctica has a transient population of Americans, British, French, Norwegians, Argentinians, Chileans, Chinese, Russians, Poles, and Japanese. Most are involved in research. Few stay more than two years.

Antarctica has no indigenous population. Around 80 Chilean settlers live at any one time in the continent's only permanent community on King George Island. The rest of the population are scientists and logistical staff working at the 40 permanent, and as many as 100 temporary, research stations. Most stations are too far apart for direct contact between different nationalities.

ANTARCTICA

Total Area : 14 000 000 sq. km (5 405 000 sq. miles)

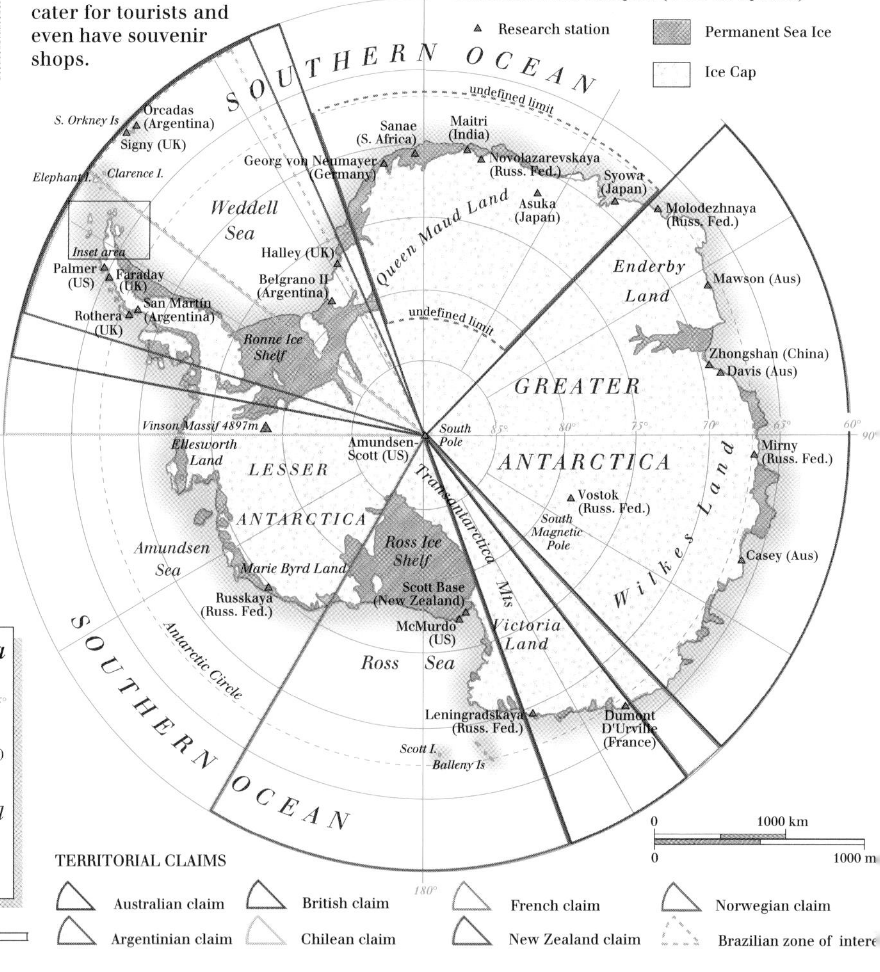
Research station
Permanent Sea Ice
Ice Cap
SOUTHERN OCEAN
undefined limit
S. Orkney Is
Orcadas (Argentina)
Signy (UK)
Elephant I.
Clarence I.
Inset area
Palmer (US)
Faraday (UK)
Rothera (UK)
San Martín (Argentina)
Weddell Sea
Georg von Neumayer (Germany)
Sanae (S. Africa)
Maitri (India)
Novolazarevskaya (Russ. Fed.)
Syowa (Japan)
Asuka (Japan)
Queen Maud Land
Halley (UK)
Belgrano II (Argentina)
Molodezhnaya (Russ. Fed.)
Enderby Land
Mawson (Aus)
Ronne Ice Shelf
Zhongshan (China)
Davis (Aus)
GREATER ANTARCTICA
Vinson Massif 4897m
Ellesworth Land
South Pole
Amundsen-Scott (US)
LESSER ANTARCTICA
Transantarctica Mts
Mirny (Russ. Fed.)
Vostok (Russ. Fed.)
South Magnetic Pole
Wilkes Land
Casey (Aus)
Amundsen Sea
Marie Byrd Land
Ross Ice Shelf
Russkaya (Russ. Fed.)
Scott Base (New Zealand)
McMurdo (US)
Victoria Land
Ross Sea
Antarctic Circle
Leningradskaya (Russ. Fed.)
Dumont D'Urville (France)
Scott I.
Balleny Is
0°
90°W
90°E
180°
0 1000 km
0 1000 miles
TERRITORIAL CLAIMS
Australian claim
British claim
French claim
Norwegian claim
Argentinian claim
Chilean claim
New Zealand claim
Brazilian zone of interest

Neumayer Channel, Antarctica. Many states are pressing for the whole of Antarctica to be protected as an international park.

POLITICS

Not applicable

Not applicable

Consultative Parties to Antarctic Treaty

NO LEGISLATIVE OR ADVISORY BODIES

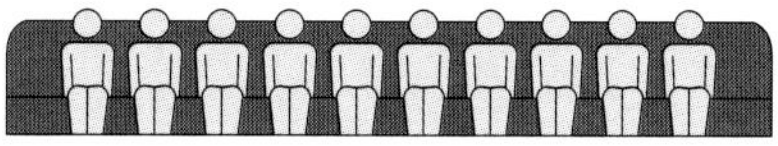

The Antarctic Treaty of 1959 was signed by 12 countries. Consultative meetings are held most years to discuss scientific, environmental, and political matters.

There are 27 parties to the Antarctic Treaty and 18 nations with observer status. There are territorial claims by Australia, France, New Zealand, and Norway, and overlapping claims in the Antarctic Peninsula by Argentina, Chile, and the UK. Other states do not recognize these claims.

Of main concern is the adoption of a wide range of environmental protection measures. Proposals include the monitoring of all scientific activities and also the prosecution of any country if it were demonstrated that its research would lead to detrimental global change.

WORLD AFFAIRS

Not a UN member

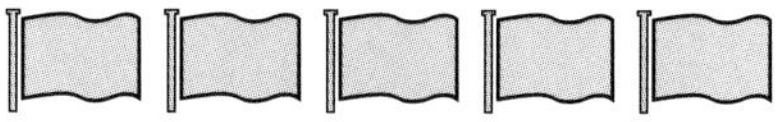

Rivalries exist between nations wishing to preserve Antarctica as a world park and those pursuing territorial claims.

AID

Recipient

Research is funded by governments

Subject to individual government budgets

Scientific programs in the Antarctic are almost entirely funded by government agencies in the home countries. Funding is occasionally provided by scientific institutions and universities.

DEFENSE

Not applicable

No defense force

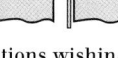

Not applicable

Under the Antarctic Treaty, Antarctica can be used only for peaceful purposes. Any military personnel present perform purely scientific or logistic roles.

ECONOMICS

Not applicable

Not applicable

Antarctica has no currency

Research is government-funded and is therefore subject to fluctuations. The exploitation of marine stocks provides no income for Antarctica.

RESOURCES

Not applicable

Included in national fish catch totals

Not an oil producer and has no refineries

None

Mineral extraction is banned

Antarctica's main resources are its marine stocks, including fin fish, seals, and whales. A campaign by environmental groups, supported by Australia and France, to ban mining and declare Antarctica a world park was rewarded with an agreement in 1991 to impose a 50-year ban on mining, and in 1994 by the approval of a whale sanctuary. Prospects for energy sources alternative to fossil fuels, such as solar power and wind generators, are being explored.

ENVIRONMENT

Not applicable

Most of Antarctica is protected

Not applicable

Antarctica is one of the Earth's last great wildernesses. Its layer of ice, 4000 m (13,120 ft) thick in places, has formed over thousands of years. Its ecosystem is such that a "footprint" will leave its mark for many years. Several species are unique to the continent, including king penguins. The blood of polar fish contains antifreeze agents. Ecological concerns include overfishing, particularly of krill, cod, and squid; the disintegration of ice shelves; the depletion of the ozone layer over Antarctica; and the various knock-on effects of global warming. In 1994 the IWC agreed to a French proposal to create an Antarctic whale sanctuary which, together with the Indian Ocean sanctuary, protects the feeding grounds of 90% of the world's whales.

MEDIA

Not applicable

There are no daily newspapers produced in Antarctica

A few bases publish newssheets for local consumption. Local radio stations are found at some of the larger bases.

CRIME

Not applicable

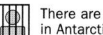

There are no prisons in Antarctica

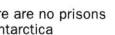

Crime is negligible

Each person in Antarctica is subject to their national laws. Occasional petty theft from stations is linked to visits from tourists.

CHRONOLOGY

The Russian explorer, Thaddeus von Bellingshausen, was the first to sight Antarctica, in 1820. The South Pole was first reached by the Norwegian, Roald Amundsen, in December 1911.

- **1957–1958** International Geophysical Year launches scientific exploration of Antarctica.
- **1959** Antarctic Treaty signed by 12 countries. Territorial claims frozen.
- **1978** Convention limiting seal hunting comes into force.
- **1985** Ozone depletion disclosed.
- **1994** Establishment of Antarctic whale sanctuary.
- **1998** Agreement on 50-year ban on mineral extraction comes into force.

EDUCATION

Not applicable

Not applicable

None

Schoolhouses exist on the Chilean base, Villa Las Estrellas, and the Argentinian base, Esperanza. Teaching is geared to the relevant national system. Some researchers' studies contribute to higher degrees.

Antarctic-based research has resulted in a number of scientific breakthroughs, including the discovery of the depletion of the ozone layer.

HEALTH

Not applicable

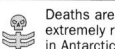

1 medical officer per station

Deaths are extremely rare in Antarctica

Each station has its own medical officer. The problems usually associated with polar conditions, such as frostbite and snow blindness, are very rare. All personnel are medically screened before arrival. If serious illnesses develop, patients have to be evacuated by air, including in recent years an acute case of gallstones and a doctor who self-diagnosed breast cancer.

SPENDING

Not applicable

US bases are the best-funded, while the budgets of other bases are subject to domestic politics. Most stations have TVs and video recorders. Telephone systems operate only within stations. Computers are supplied for scientific research. A 1670-km (1040-mile) fiber optic cable is set to provide Internet access to the South Pole by 2009.

WORLD RANKING

The UN Human Development Index conditions are not applicable to Antarctica.

A

ANTIGUA & BARBUDA

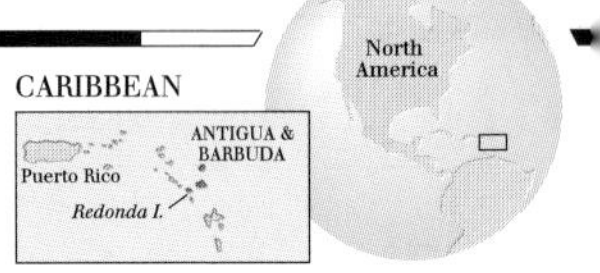
CARIBBEAN
North America
ANTIGUA & BARBUDA
Puerto Rico
Redonda I.

OFFICIAL NAME: Antigua and Barbuda **CAPITAL:** St. John's
POPULATION: 67,897 **CURRENCY:** Eastern Caribbean dollar **OFFICIAL LANGUAGE:** English

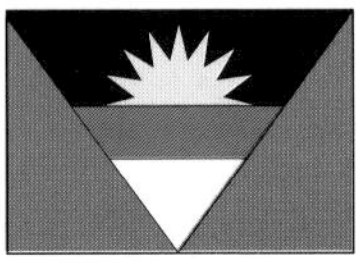

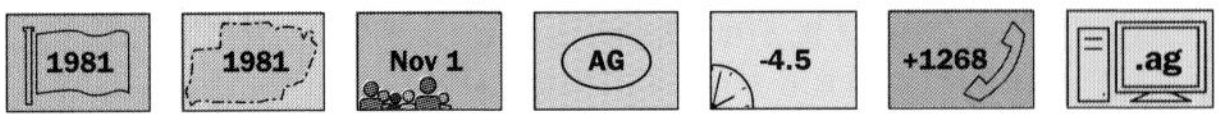
1981
1981
Nov 1
AG
-4.5
+1268
.ag

PART OF THE Leeward Islands chain, Antigua was in turn a Spanish, French, and British colony. British influence is still strong and most clearly revealed in the Antiguans' passion for cricket. Antigua has two dependencies: Barbuda, 50 km (30 miles) to the north, sporting a magnificent beach, and Redonda, 40 km (25 miles) west, an uninhabited rock with its own king.

CLIMATE

Tropical oceanic

WEATHER CHART FOR ST. JOHN'S

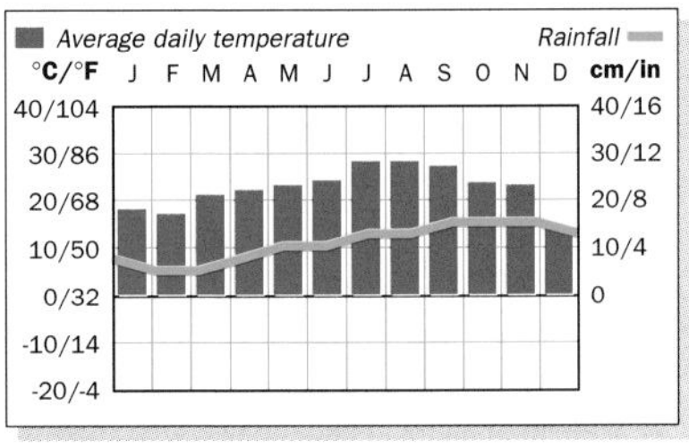
Average daily temperature
Rainfall
°C/°F
J F M A M J J A S O N D
cm/in
40/104
30/86
20/68
10/50
0/32
-10/14
-20/-4
40/16
30/12
20/8
10/4
0

Antigua is less humid than other Caribbean islands. Year-round trade winds moderate the heat.

TRANSPORTATION

Drive on left

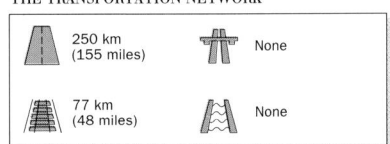

V. C. Bird International, St. John's 727,292 passengers

886 ships 5.07m grt

THE TRANSPORTATION NETWORK

250 km (155 miles)		None	
77 km (48 miles)		None	

Recent multimillion EC$ projects have expanded the international airport and provided a further 140 km (90 miles) of roads with all-weather surfaces.

TOURISM

Visitors : Population 2.9:1

198,085 visitors

Up 3% in 2002

MAIN TOURIST ARRIVALS

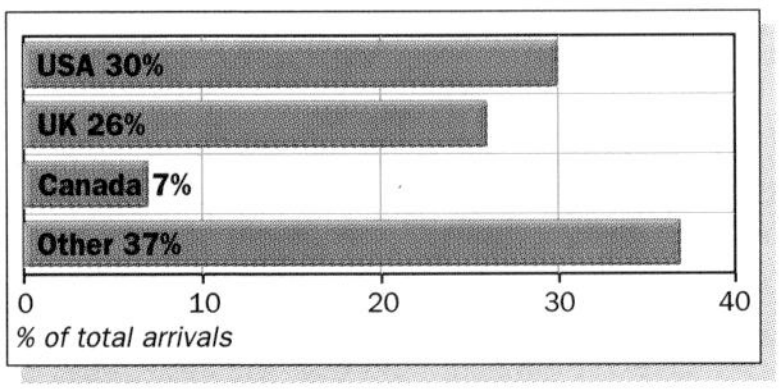
USA 30%
UK 26%
Canada 7%
Other 37%
0
10
20
30
40
% of total arrivals

Antigua is especially popular with US cruise ship tourists. Among other draws are the annual international tennis championship, the islands' three golf courses, and the attraction of large duty-free shopping malls.

PEOPLE

Pop. density medium

English, English patois

154/km² (399/mi²)

THE URBAN/RURAL POPULATION SPLIT

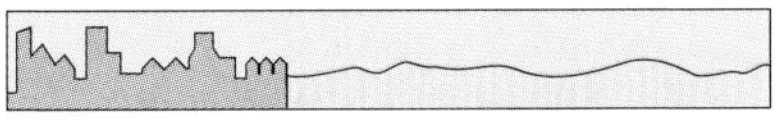
37%
63%

RELIGIOUS PERSUASION

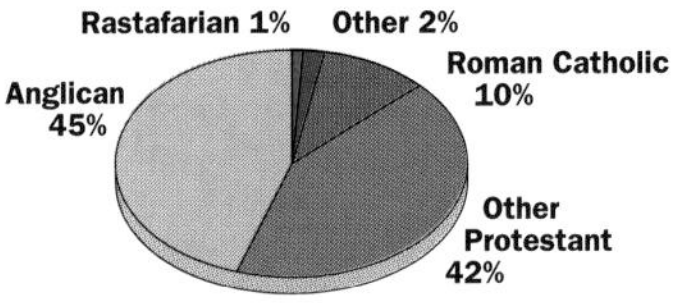
Rastafarian 1%
Other 2%
Roman Catholic 10%
Anglican 45%
Other Protestant 42%

Most of the population are descended from Africans, brought over between the 16th and 19th centuries. There are, in addition, a few Europeans and south Asians. Racial tension is rare. Some 4000–5000 Montserratians have been given shelter since the volcanic eruptions on Montserrat in the 1990s. Around 10% of the population are of Hispanic origin, mainly coming from the Dominican Republic. By Caribbean standards, wealth disparities are small.

POLITICS

Multiparty elections

L. House 2004/2009
U. House 2004/2009

H.M. Queen Elizabeth II

AT THE LAST ELECTION

House of Representatives 17 seats

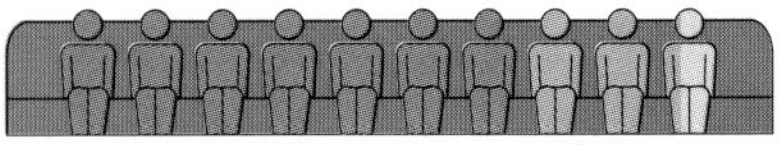
71% UPP
23% ALP
6% BPM

UPP = United Progressive Party **ALP** = Antigua Labour Party
BPM = Barbuda People's Movement

Senate 17 seats

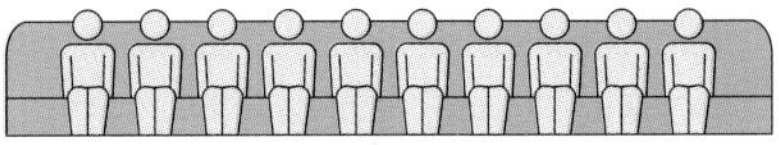

Eleven members of the Senate are appointed by the prime minister, four by the leader of the opposition, one by the governor-general, and one by the Barbuda Council

Vere Bird Sr., premier from 1960, retired in 1994 and was succeeded by his younger son Lester, who led the ALP into its sixth consecutive term in 1999. The family has been dogged by allegations of corruption. Vere Jr. was removed from public office in 1990 after accusations of gun-running, while Lester Bird was forced to deny a sex and narcotics scandal. The ALP lost the 2004 election to Baldwin Spencer and the UPP.

ANTIGUA & BARBUDA

Total Area : 442 sq. km (170 sq. miles)

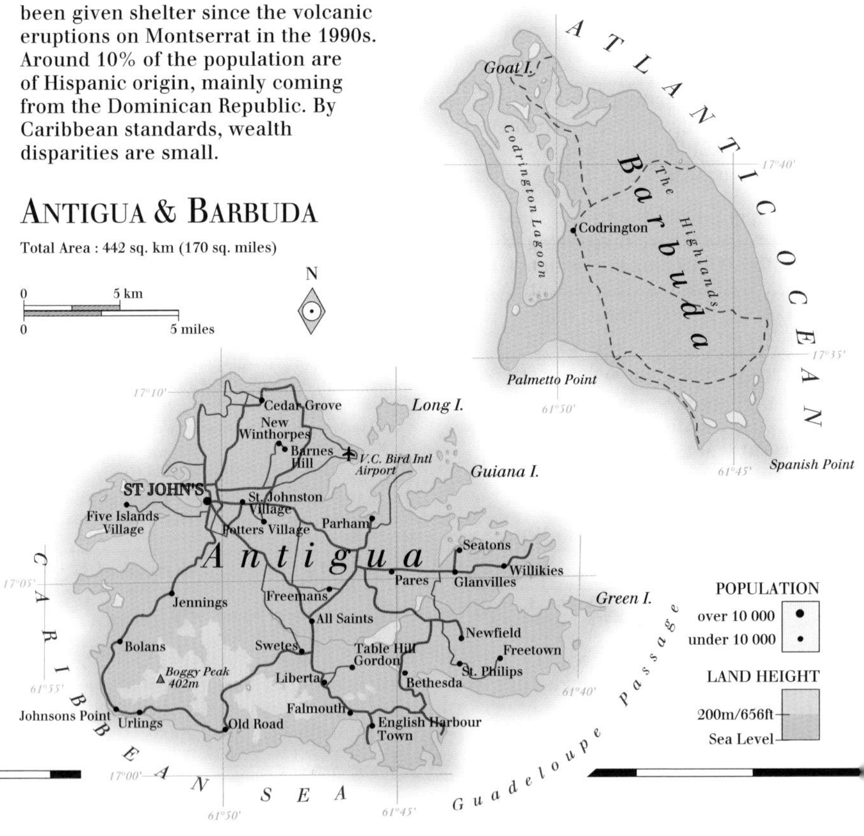
0
5 km
0
5 miles
N
ATLANTIC OCEAN
Goat I.
Codrington Lagoon
Barbuda
The Highlands
Codrington
Palmetto Point
Spanish Point
Long I.
Guiana I.
Cedar Grove
New Winthorpes
Barnes Hill
V.C. Bird Intl Airport
ST JOHN'S
St. Johnston Village
Five Islands Village
Potters Village
Parham
Antigua
Seatons
Willikies
Pares
Glanvilles
Green I.
Jennings
Freemans
All Saints
Newfield
Freetown
Bolans
Swetes
Table Hill Gordon
St. Philips
Boggy Peak 402m
Liberta
Bethesda
Falmouth
Johnsons Point
Urlings
Old Road
English Harbour Town
CARIBBEAN SEA
Guadeloupe Passage
POPULATION
over 10 000
under 10 000
LAND HEIGHT
200m/656ft
Sea Level

A

WORLD AFFAIRS

Joined UN in 1981

ACS | Caricom | Comm | OECS | OAS

While rejecting attempts by the OECD to regulate tax havens, Antigua has been internationally praised for its own efforts to combat money laundering.

AID

Recipient

US$14m (receipts) | Up 56% in 2002

Japan is Antigua's largest aid donor; in response, the government has supported Japan's pro-whaling stance. The UK gives some aid to help support refugees from Montserrat.

DEFENSE

No compulsory military service

US$4m | No change in 2002

There is a 170-strong defense force. The US suspended military aid in 2003 until Antigua signed an agreement exempting US citizens from being tried at the International Criminal Court.

ECONOMICS

Inflation 2.2% p.a. (1990–2001)

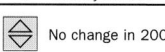

US$671m | 2.7 Eastern Caribbean dollars (2.67)

SCORE CARD

❑ World GNP Ranking	163rd
❑ GNP per Capita	US$9720
❑ Balance of Payments	–US$75m
❑ Inflation	1.3%
❑ Unemployment	11%

STRENGTHS

Tourism and construction of tourist hotels and infrastructure. Financial and communications services linked to offshore financial sector.

WEAKNESSES

High levels of debt, exceeding 80% of GDP. Overdependence on tourism, made more vulnerable by Antigua's promotion as an expensive destination. Lack of natural resources.

EXPORTS

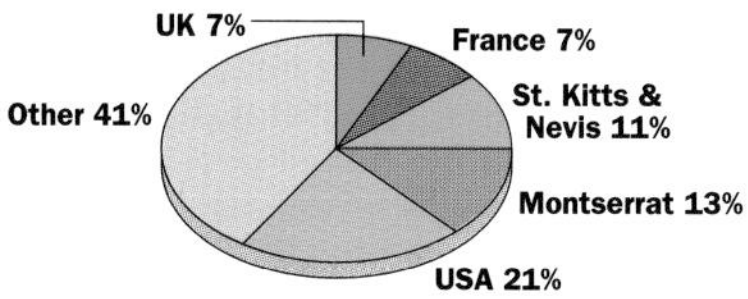
UK 7%
France 7%
St. Kitts & Nevis 11%
Other 41%
Montserrat 13%
USA 21%

IMPORTS

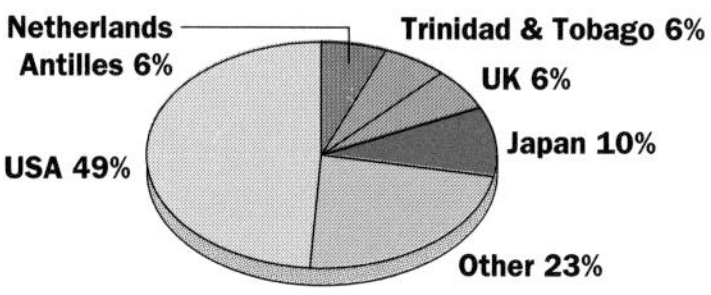
Netherlands Antilles 6%
Trinidad & Tobago 6%
UK 6%
Japan 10%
USA 49%
Other 23%

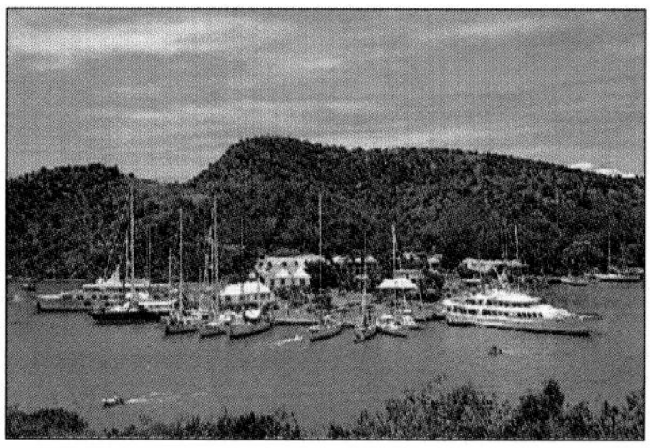

Nelson's Dockyard. *Luxury yachts fitted with state-of-the-art gadgetry contrast with the 18th-century St. John's harbor.*

RESOURCES

Electric power 27,000 kW

1583 tonnes | Not an oil producer

35,500 goats, 18,600 sheep, 100,000 chickens | None

Antigua has no strategic or commodity resources and has to import almost all its energy requirements.

ENVIRONMENT

Not available

15% | 5.1 tonnes per capita

Sewage from hotels causes major problems. Untreated effluent pollutes the sea, while uncontrolled disposal has killed valuable inshore fish stocks in the mangrove swamps; the whole swamp ecosystem is under threat from poorly planned hotel development.

MEDIA

TV ownership hgh

Daily newspaper circulation 91 per 1000 people

PUBLISHING AND BROADCAST MEDIA

There are 2 daily newspapers, the *Daily Observer* and the *Antigua Sun*. The leading paper is the twice-weekly *The Worker's Voice*

2 services: 1 state-owned, 1 independent | 6 services: 1 state-owned, 5 independent

In 2003 Antigua's state-owned radio and television stations, as well as its independent media outlets, reported extensively on charges of corruption against senior government figures.

CRIME

Death penalty in use

186 prisoners | Little change from year to year

Murder is rare. Rape, armed robbery, and burglary are main concerns, as is offshore money laundering.

EDUCATION

School leaving age: 16

87% | 631 students

Education is based on the former British selective system. Students go on to the University of the West Indies, or to study in the UK or the US.

CHRONOLOGY

In 1667, Antigua became a British colony. Barbuda, formerly owned privately by the Codrington family, was annexed in 1860.

- ❑ **1951** Universal adult suffrage introduced.
- ❑ **1981** Independence from UK; opposed by Barbudan secessionist movement.
- ❑ **1983** Supports US invasion of Grenada.
- ❑ **1994** Lester Bird elected prime minister succeeding his father.
- ❑ **1995** New taxes provoke protests.
- ❑ **1999** ALP wins sixth term.
- ❑ **2004** Baldwin Spencer and UPP oust ALP.

HEALTH

Welfare state health benefits

1 per 909 people | Heart and respiratory diseases, cancers

By Caribbean standards, the health system is efficient, with easy access to the state-run clinics and hospitals. A new hospital has been built in the capital, St. John's.

SPENDING

GDP/cap. increase

CONSUMPTION AND SPENDING

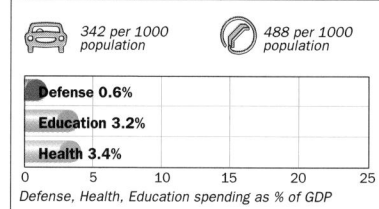

342 per 1000 population | *488 per 1000 population*

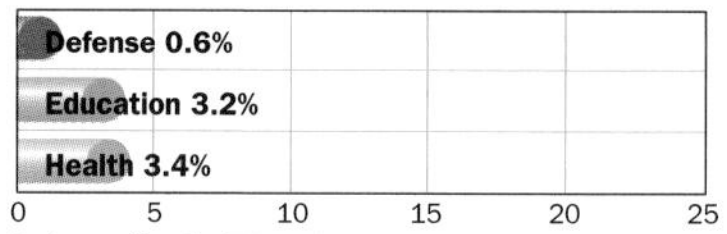
Defense 0.6%
Education 3.2%
Health 3.4%
0
5
10
15
20
25

Defense, Health, Education spending as % of GDP

Wealthy Antiguans are active in running the thriving tourist industry; some are allegedly also involved in money laundering. Unemployment is relatively low and the average per capita income is among the highest in the Caribbean.

WORLD RANKING

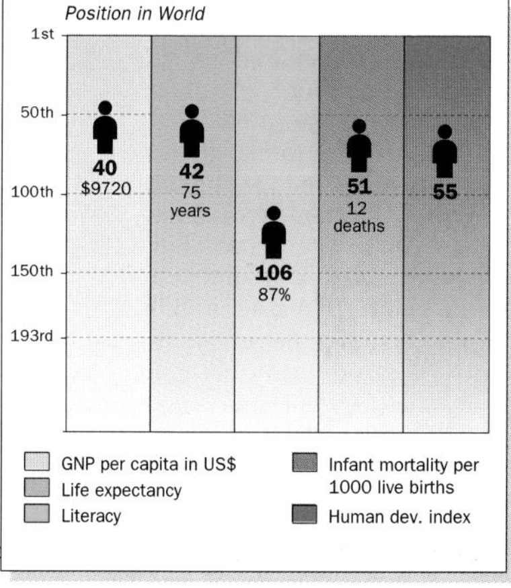
Position in World
1st
50th
100th
150th
193rd
40
$9720
42
75 years
106
87%
51
12 deaths
55
GNP per capita in US$
Life expectancy
Literacy
Infant mortality per 1000 live births
Human dev. index

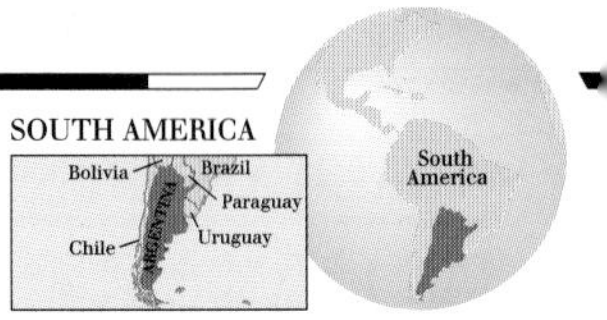
SOUTH AMERICA
Bolivia
Brazil
Paraguay
Chile
ARGENTINA
Uruguay
South America

ARGENTINA

OFFICIAL NAME: Republic of Argentina **CAPITAL:** Buenos Aires
POPULATION: 38.4 million **CURRENCY:** Argentine peso **OFFICIAL LANGUAGE:** Spanish

1816 | 1816 | May 25 | RA | -3 | +54 | .ar

OCCUPYING MOST OF THE southern portion of South America, Argentina extends 3460 km (2150 miles) from the Gran Chaco to Tierra del Fuego. The Andes mountains in the west run north–south, forming a natural border with Chile; their eastern flanks slope down to the fertile central Pampas, the region known as Entre Ríos. Agriculture, especially wheat, fruit, and beef, and energy resources are Argentina's main sources of wealth. Politics in Argentina was characterized in the past by periods of military rule, but in 1983 Argentina returned to a system of multiparty democracy.

Herding cattle *in the northeast, near Corrientes. Beef, Argentina's initial source of wealth, remains a major export.*

CLIMATE

Mountain/steppe/ subtropical

WEATHER CHART FOR BUENOS AIRES

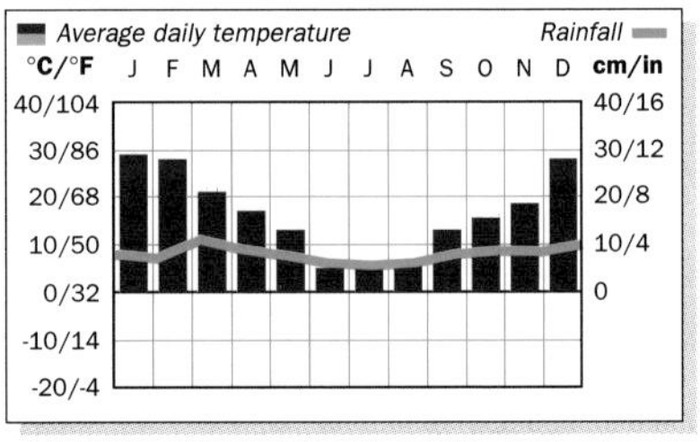
Average daily temperature
Rainfall
°C/°F J F M A M J J A S O N D cm/in
40/104
30/86
20/68
10/50
0/32
-10/14
-20/-4
40/16
30/12
20/8
10/4
0

The northeast of Argentina is near-tropical. The Andes are semiarid in the north and snowy in the south. The western lowlands are desert, while the Pampas have a mild climate with heavy summer rains.

TRANSPORTATION

Drive on right

Ezeiza International, Buenos Aires 4.89m passengers

481 ships 422,900 grt

THE TRANSPORTATION NETWORK

62,487 km (38,828 miles)

734 km (456 miles)

35,754 km (22,216 miles)

10,950 km (6804 miles)

Air travel is expensive, and inadequate connections between provinces frustrate business and tourism. The national airline, Aerolineas Argentinas, was privatized in 1990 but in 2000 was the subject of a rescue plan; airports are privately operated. The privatized railroad, one of the largest in the world, is primarily used for freight, but public rail lines in Buenos Aires have attracted strong investment and heavy use. Since 1990, thousands of kilometers of roads have been privatized, and tolls are among the highest in the world. The six main terminals in the port of Buenos Aires are privately run. A $20 billion national infrastructure program announced in 2001 has been stalled due to the economic crisis.

TOURISM

Visitors : Population 1:12

3.33m visitors

Up 18% in 2003

MAIN TOURIST ARRIVALS

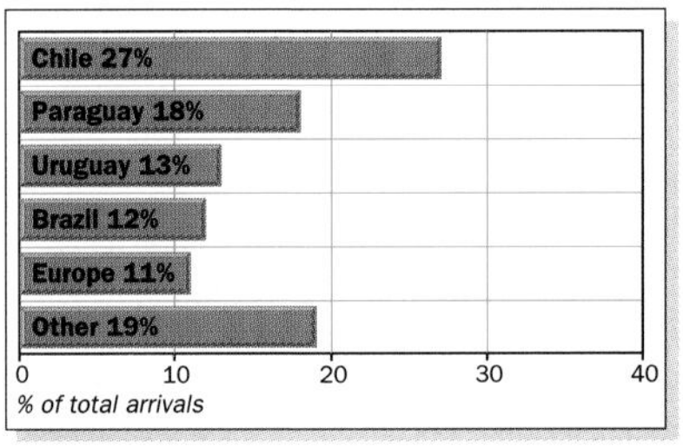
Chile 27%
Paraguay 18%
Uruguay 13%
Brazil 12%
Europe 11%
Other 19%
0 10 20 30 40
% of total arrivals

Tourism has been undersold, and the government, working with business, has launched a huge international marketing campaign. Visitors, still mostly from neighboring countries, are attracted by rich city life in Buenos Aires, the Atlantic coastal resort of Mar del Plata, ski stations such as Bariloche and Las Leñas in the Andes, and wineries around Mendoza; the fashion for tango is also a draw. Other major attractions are Antarctic cruises, the Iguazú National Park, and whale-watching off Peninsula Valdés, northeast of Trelew.

PEOPLE

Pop. density low

Spanish, Italian, Amerindian languages

14/km² (36/mi²)

THE URBAN/RURAL POPULATION SPLIT

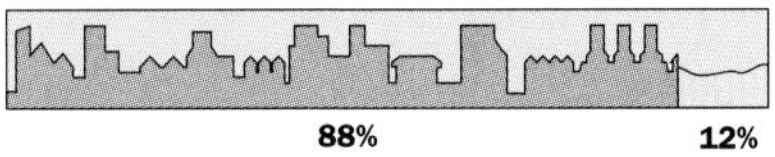
88%
12%

RELIGIOUS PERSUASION

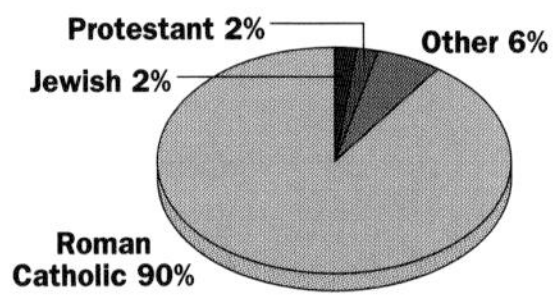
Protestant 2%
Jewish 2%
Other 6%
Roman Catholic 90%

ETHNIC MAKEUP

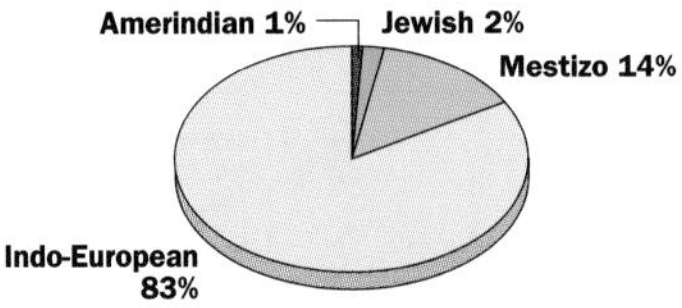
Amerindian 1%
Jewish 2%
Mestizo 14%
Indo-European 83%

Most Argentinians of European descent are from recent 20th-century migrations: over one-third are of Italian origin. Indigenous peoples now form a tiny minority, living mainly in Andean regions or in the Gran Chaco. Argentina also has communities of Welsh, Lebanese, Armenians, Syrians, Japanese, and Koreans.

POPULATION AGE BREAKDOWN

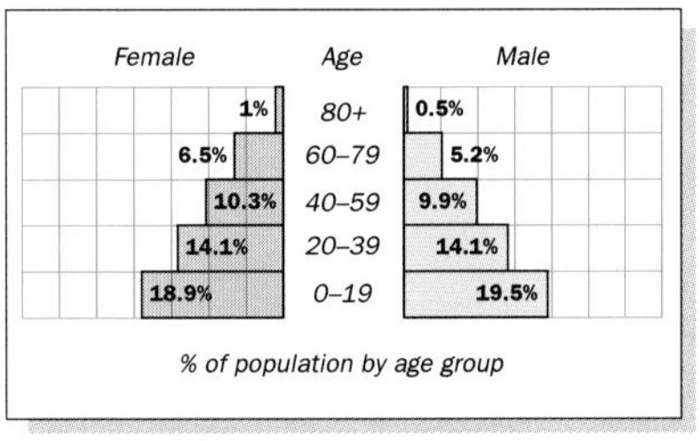
Female
Age
Male
1% 80+ 0.5%
6.5% 60–79 5.2%
10.3% 40–59 9.9%
14.1% 20–39 14.1%
18.9% 0–19 19.5%
% of population by age group

The vast majority of Argentinians are urban dwellers, with some 40% of the population living in Buenos Aires, one of the largest cities in Latin America.

Catholicism and the extended family remain strong in Argentina. In addition, the family forms the basis of many successful businesses.

Women have a higher profile than in most Latin American states, and were enfranchised in 1947. Today, many enter the professions and rise to positions of influence in service businesses such as the media, but are less prominent in party politics. Eva Perón, who inspired the musical *Evita*, helped to push women into a more active political role in the 1940s and 1950s, but this trend was reversed under military rule.

POLITICS

Multiparty elections

L. House 2003/2007
U. House 2003/2005

President Néstor Kirchner

Argentina is a multiparty democracy; the president is head of government.

PROFILE

The Peronists dominated politics from the 1940s. The party, founded on mass working-class and left-wing intellectual support, was inimical to the military and was finally overthrown in 1976 after a series of coups; the following seven-year junta left a legacy of human rights abuses. A protest vote saw the return of democracy under the UCR in 1983. President Carlos Menem (1989–1999) steered the Peronist party to the right, conquering hyperinflation but reaping strong public disapproval for his free-market policies.

UCR candidate Fernando de la Rúa claimed the presidency in 1999, with the support of the National Solidarity Front (Frepaso) but was brought down by the economic crisis of 2001, and was followed by four stopgap presidents. The much-vilified Menem won the first round of fresh elections in 2003, but withdrew as his support ebbed. Fellow Peronist Néstor Kirchner then won the contest by default.

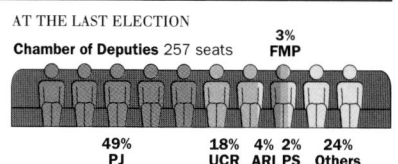

AT THE LAST ELECTION

Chamber of Deputies 257 seats

PJ	UCR	ARI	PS	FMP	Others
49%	18%	4%	2%	3%	24%

PJ = Justicialist Party (Peronists) **UCR** = Radical Civic Union–**UCR** **ARI** = Alternative for a Republic of Equals **FMP**= Popular Movement Front **PS** = Socialist Party

Senate 72 seats

PJ	UCR	Others
57%	19%	24%

MAIN POLITICAL ISSUES

Durability of government

The nature of Kirchner's electoral victory in 2003 raised the prospect of struggles within a Peronist party divided by rival loyalties, jeopardizing the passage of serious reforms. In the absence of a trusted opposition, the public remains deeply cynical of traditional party politics. Principal concerns are lack of governmental transparency, corruption, and ending the socially divisive free-market macroeconomics of the 1990s.

Recovery from economic collapse

A near cashless population was reduced to bartering in 2001–2002 by industrial collapse, fiscal austerity, and restrictions on bank withdrawals. Fragile signs of recovery emerged in early 2003. A long-awaited IMF agreement gave a temporary breathing space on debt repayments. Businesses responded well to a period of exchange-rate stability coupled with strong export earnings and the gradual recuperation of the crisis-ridden banking sector.

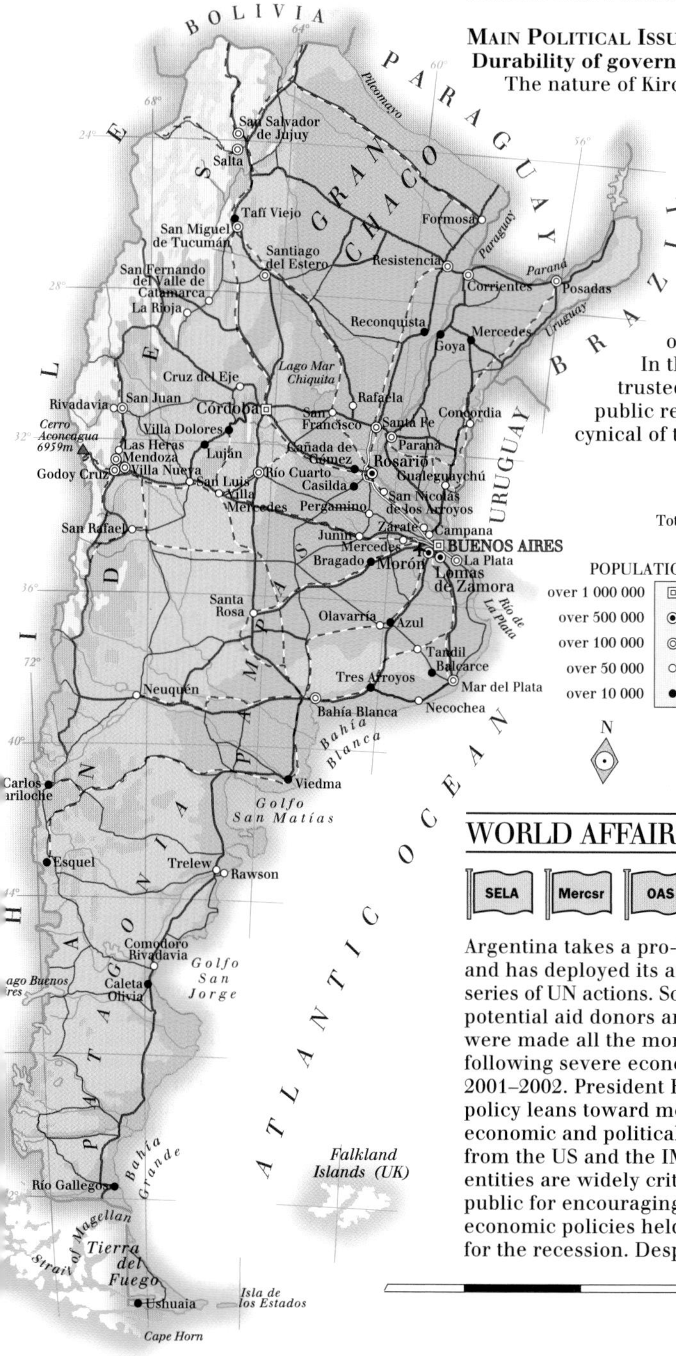
BOLIVIA
PARAGUAY
BRAZIL
URUGUAY
CHILE
ANDES
GRAN CHACO
PAMPAS
PATAGONIA
ATLANTIC OCEAN
San Salvador de Jujuy
Salta
Tafí Viejo
San Miguel de Tucumán
Santiago del Estero
Formosa
Resistencia
Corrientes
Posadas
Reconquista
Goya
Mercedes
Concordia
Córdoba
Rosario
Santa Fe
Paraná
Mendoza
San Juan
San Rafael
Río Cuarto
Santa Rosa
Neuquén
Bahía Blanca
Mar del Plata
BUENOS AIRES
La Plata
Viedma
Rawson
Trelew
Esquel
Comodoro Rivadavia
Río Gallegos
Ushuaia
Cape Horn
Falkland Islands (UK)
Tierra del Fuego
Strait of Magellan
Isla de los Estados
Golfo San Matías
Golfo San Jorge
Río de la Plata
Cerro Aconcagua 6959m
ARGENTINA
Total Area : 2 766 890 sq. km (1 068 296 sq. miles)
POPULATION
over 1 000 000
over 500 000
over 100 000
over 50 000
over 10 000
LAND HEIGHT
4000m/13124ft
2000m/6562ft
1000m/3281ft
200m/656ft
Sea Level
0 200 km
0 200 miles
N

Carlos Menem: authoritarian free-marketeer, now wanted for embezzlement.

Néstor Kirchner, Peronist victor in the 2003 presidential elections.

WORLD AFFAIRS

Joined UN in 1945

SELA | Mercsr | OAS | RG | G15

Argentina takes a pro-Western stance and has deployed its armed forces in a series of UN actions. Solid relations with potential aid donors and trade partners were made all the more essential following severe economic crisis in 2001–2002. President Kirchner's foreign policy leans toward more regional economic and political independence from the US and the IMF: both of these entities are widely criticized by the public for encouraging the very economic policies held responsible for the recession. Despite this, ties to the US remain strong, though US pressure for an open-skies agreement and issues of royalty payments on patented drugs have created tensions.

Friction with Brazil over trade rules complicates Argentina's membership of Mercosur. It wants Mercosur to be strengthened, and widened to include Chile as a full member.

The normalizing of relations with the UK in 1998 sidelined Argentina's claim to sovereignty over the Falkland Islands (known locally as Las Islas Malvinas), the focus of the 1982 war between the two countries. Direct flights between the islands and the mainland have been permitted since 2001.

A

AID

Recipient

No net receipts

Down 100% in 2002

Though one massive "financial shield" was agreed in 2001, the IMF's refusal of a further rescue package precipitated the crash in December that year.

CHRONOLOGY

The Spanish first established settlements in the Andean foothills in 1543. The indigenous Amerindians, who had stopped any Inca advance into their territory, also prevented the Spaniards from settling in the east until the 1590s.

- **1816** United Provinces of Río de la Plata declare independence; 70 years of civil war follow.
- **1835–1852** Dictatorship of Juan Manuel Rosas.
- **1853** Federal system set up.
- **1857** Europeans start settling the Pampas; six million by 1930.
- **1877** First refrigerated ship starts frozen beef trade to Europe.
- **1878–1883** War against Pampas Amerindians (almost exterminated).
- **1916** Hipólito Yrigoyen wins first democratic presidential elections.
- **1930** Military coup.
- **1943** New military coup. Gen. Juan Perón organizes trade unions.
- **1946** Perón elected president, with military and labor backing.
- **1952** Eva Perón, charismatic wife of Juan Perón, dies of leukemia.
- **1955** Military coup ousts Perón: inflation, strikes, unemployment.
- **1973** Perón reelected president.
- **1974** Perón dies; succeeded by his third wife "Isabelita," who is unable to exercise control.
- **1976** Military junta seizes power. Political parties are banned. Brutal repression during "dirty war" sees "disappearance" of over 15,000 "left-wing suspects."
- **1981** Gen. Galtieri president.
- **1982** Galtieri orders invasion of Falkland Islands. UK retakes them.
- **1983** Pro-human rights candidate Raúl Alfonsín (UCR) elected president. Hyperinflation.
- **1989** Carlos Menem (Peronist) president.
- **1992** Inflation down to 25%.
- **1998–1999** Argentina battered by Brazilian financial crisis. Economy enters recession.
- **1999** Fernando de la Rúa of UCR–Frepaso alliance elected president.
- **2001** December, Government is brought down by economic crisis.
- **2002** January, Eduardo Duhalde becomes fifth president in 12 days.
- **2003** Néstor Kirchner president by default after Menem pulls out of poll.

DEFENSE

No compulsory military service

$1.39bn

Down 68% in 2002

ARGENTINIAN ARMED FORCES

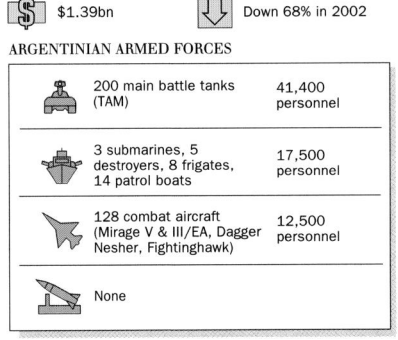

200 main battle tanks (TAM)	41,400 personnel
3 submarines, 5 destroyers, 8 frigates, 14 patrol boats	17,500 personnel
128 combat aircraft (Mirage V & III/EA, Dagger Nesher, Fightinghawk)	12,500 personnel
None	

The end of dictatorship led to trials and prison for the top brass, but subsequent immunity laws were meant to placate the military and close the chapter on the "dirty war" (1976–1983), during which some 15,000–30,000 people were killed or "disappeared." The military made public admissions of guilt in 1995. A 2001 ruling, however, said that such immunity was unconstitutional, clearing the way for further trials of military personnel. Former junta leader Gen. Leopoldo Galtieri was arrested in 2002, but died the following year before his trial was completed. The armed forces now participate in international peacekeeping and see themselves as modernized. Nonetheless, President Kirchner felt the need to initiate an overhaul of the military leadership in early 2003.

ECONOMICS

Inflation 4.3% p.a. (1990–2001)

$154bn

2.96 Argentine pesos (2.82)

SCORE CARD

World GNP Ranking	27th
GNP per Capita	$4220
Balance of Payments	$9.59bn
Inflation	25.9%
Unemployment	18%

EXPORTS

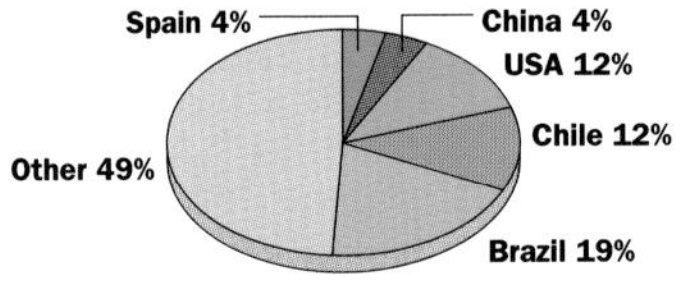
Spain 4%
China 4%
USA 12%
Chile 12%
Other 49%
Brazil 19%

IMPORTS

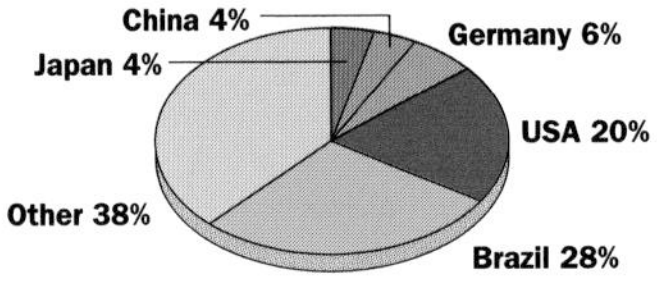
China 4%
Japan 4%
Germany 6%
USA 20%
Other 38%
Brazil 28%

Strengths

Rich agricultural base. Powerful agribusiness (mainly wheat, soybean, beef, fruit, and wine) and wealth of energy resources. Net exporter of oil. Weakened peso boosted exports.

Weaknesses

Vulnerability to external shocks, downturns in Brazil (largest single export market). Heavy debts, public and private, to refinance. Weak banking sector. Global fluctuations in prices of vital non-oil commodities. Energy shortages. High unemployment and risk of unrest. Endemic tax evasion. Subsidies and trade barriers bar agricultural produce from US and EU.

Profile

The "miracle" recovery of the 1990s was based on stabilizing the peso (by pegging it to the US dollar) and on a combination of neoliberal reforms and privatization. Argentina rode out the Mexican crisis of 1995, but was hit by damage to foreign investor confidence and a shrinking Brazilian market in 1998–1999. Regional recession in 2001 brought economic crisis, and the world's largest default on international debt. Agricultural exports and consumer spending were the base for a rapid revival, with GDP growing by 8.4% in 2003 but inflation soaring.

ECONOMIC PERFORMANCE INDICATOR

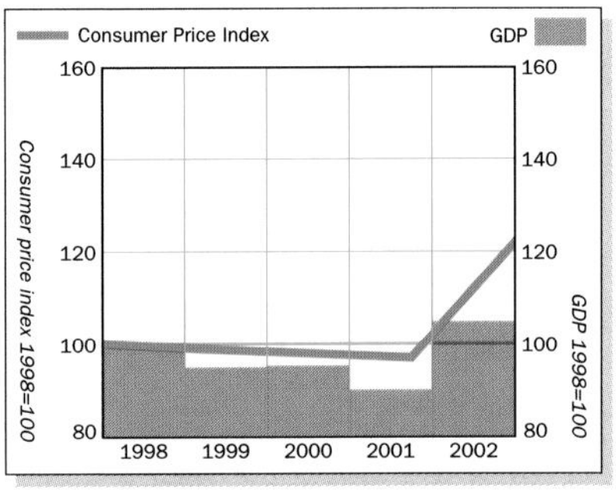
Consumer Price Index
GDP
Consumer price index 1998=100
GDP 1998=100
160
140
120
100
80
1998
1999
2000
2001
2002

ARGENTINA : MAJOR BUSINESSES

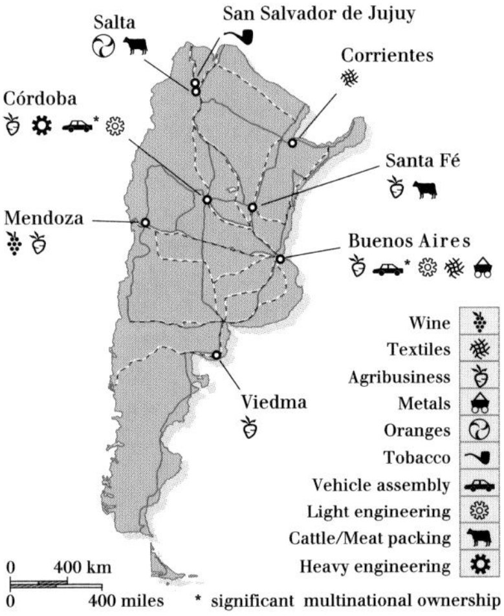
Salta
San Salvador de Jujuy
Corrientes
Córdoba
Santa Fé
Mendoza
Buenos Aires
Viedma
Wine
Textiles
Agribusiness
Metals
Oranges
Tobacco
Vehicle assembly
Light engineering
Cattle/Meat packing
Heavy engineering
0 400 km
0 400 miles
* significant multinational ownership

A

RESOURCES

Electric power 23.7m kW

924,662 tonnes

793,000 b/d (reserves 3.2bn barrels)

50.9m cattle, 12.4m sheep, 4.3m pigs, 111m chickens

Oil, natural gas, coal, iron, zinc, lead, uranium, tin, silver, copper, gold

ELECTRICITY GENERATION

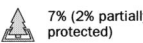

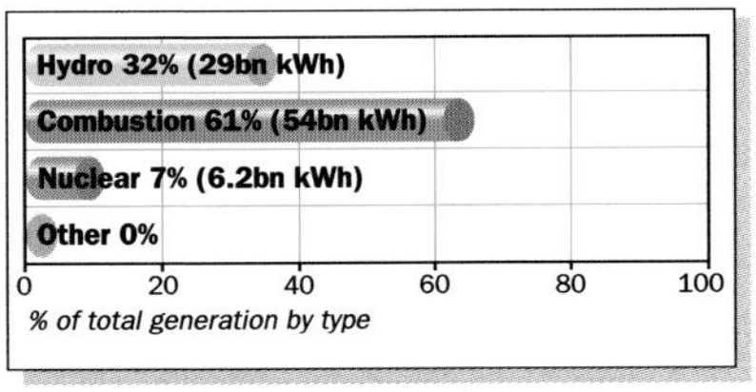
Hydro 32% (29bn kWh)
Combustion 61% (54bn kWh)
Nuclear 7% (6.2bn kWh)
Other 0%
0 20 40 60 80 100
% of total generation by type

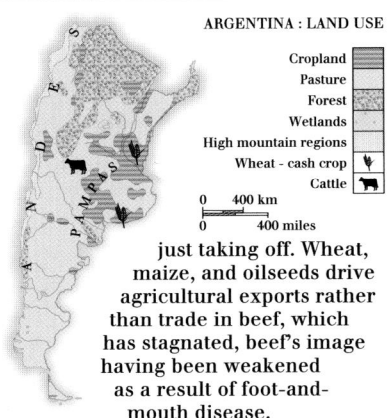

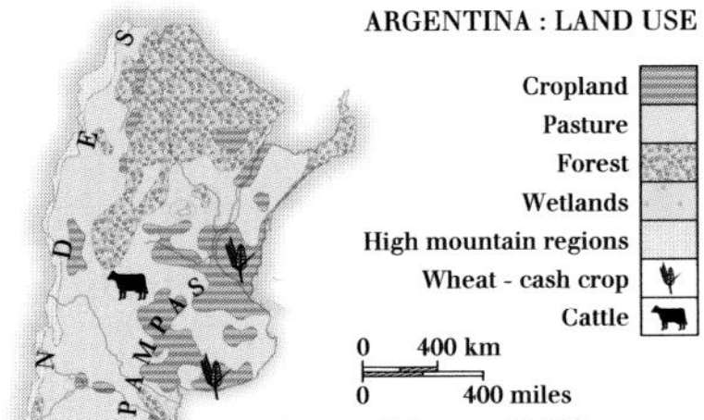
ARGENTINA : LAND USE
Cropland
Pasture
Forest
Wetlands
High mountain regions
Wheat - cash crop
Cattle
0 400 km
0 400 miles
ANDES
PAMPAS

Oil and gas are now major exports; reserves are increasingly being exploited. Copper and gold mining are just taking off. Wheat, maize, and oilseeds drive agricultural exports rather than trade in beef, which has stagnated, beef's image having been weakened as a result of foot-and-mouth disease.

HEALTH

Welfare state health benefits

1 per 370 people

Cancers, heart diseases, accidents

There are more than 1000 state-run hospitals, but free state provision suffers from underfunding, poorly paid staff, and long queues. Government-sponsored vaccination programs, mother-and-child schemes, feeding programs, and rural health projects barely tackle such problems as malnutrition, lack of decent sanitation, and threadbare medical cover in the poorest provinces. A health care deregulation bill was decreed in 2001 to dismantle the trade unions' monopoly of health insurance schemes.

ENVIRONMENT

Sustainability rank: 15th

7% (2% partially protected)

3.9 tonnes per capita

ENVIRONMENTAL TREATIES

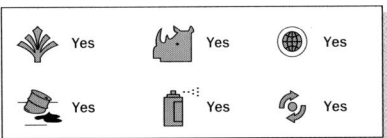

Yes Yes Yes

Yes Yes Yes

Environmental protection has low governmental priority. Legislation is weak and largely ignored by states, which retain a good deal of autonomy. Political parties typically shy away from the level of public spending needed to tackle major environmental problems, and a corrupt judiciary has meant poor enforcement of existing laws. Key problems are hazardous waste, poor urban water and air quality, inadequate sewerage, pesticide contamination due to agribusiness, deforestation, and illegal hunting.

CRIME

Death penalty not used in practice

33,007 prisoners

Up 61% in 2000–2001

CRIME RATES

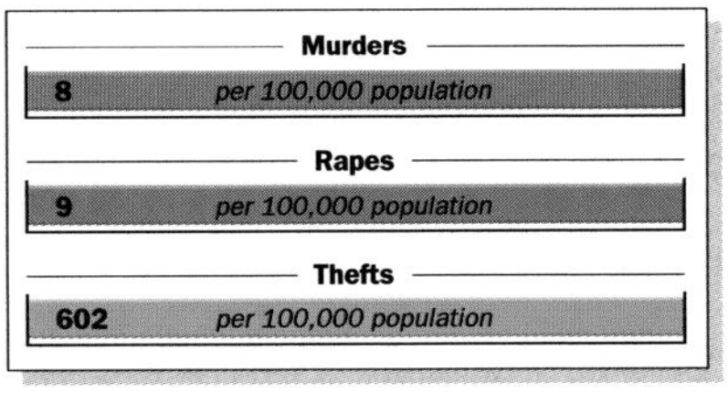
Murders
8 per 100,000 population
Rapes
9 per 100,000 population
Thefts
602 per 100,000 population

Economic collapse has led to increased violent crime and kidnapping. Ordinary people have responded by buying more guns. The judiciary and police command little respect. Overcrowded prisons lead to frequent riots, and criminal cases can take over a year to reach court.

SPENDING

GDP/cap. increase

CONSUMPTION AND SPENDING

145 per 1000 population

219 per 1000 population

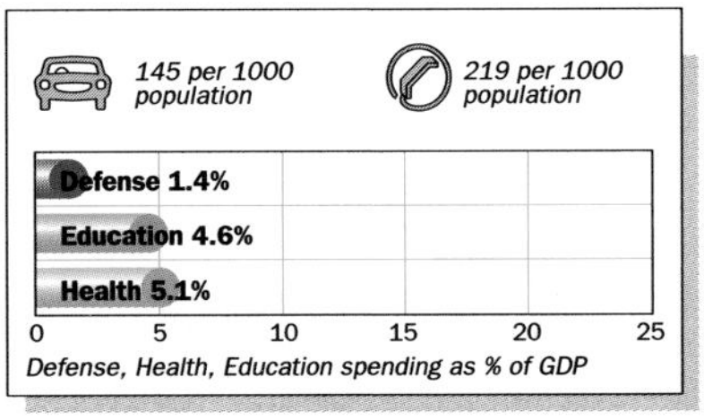
Defense 1.4%
Education 4.6%
Health 5.1%
0 5 10 15 20 25
Defense, Health, Education spending as % of GDP

Members of the wealthy elite, who travel in private jets to *estancias* (country estates), vacation in Europe and the US, and hold dollar accounts offshore to avoid tax, escaped the worst of the economic collapse in 2001–2002. Middle-income groups, squeezed after years of free-market reforms, lost out in the crisis which forced some 15 million below the poverty line, with four million in extreme poverty. Emergency government aid offered in 2002 to one million unemployed people with children under 18 was at a level below half the legal minimum salary. The precrisis figure of some 40% of workers in the low-wage black economy was set to balloon. Millions of cashless and poor people resorted to exchanging goods at barter clubs.

MEDIA

TV ownership high

Daily newspaper circulation 56 per 1000 people

PUBLISHING AND BROADCAST MEDIA

There are 181 daily newspapers. *Clarín* and *Crónica* are market leaders

15 stations owned by provincial or national authorities, 29 independent channels

122 stations: 37 state-controlled, 4 provincial, 3 university-run, 3 municipal, and 75 independent

Many journalists were murdered by the military in the 1970s, but the press was liberated under the UCR (1983–1989) and harries governments, especially on corruption. Intimidation can still occur, especially of investigative journalists.

The Internet had reached over 10% of the population by 2001.

EDUCATION

School leaving age: 14

97%

1.6m students

THE EDUCATION SYSTEM

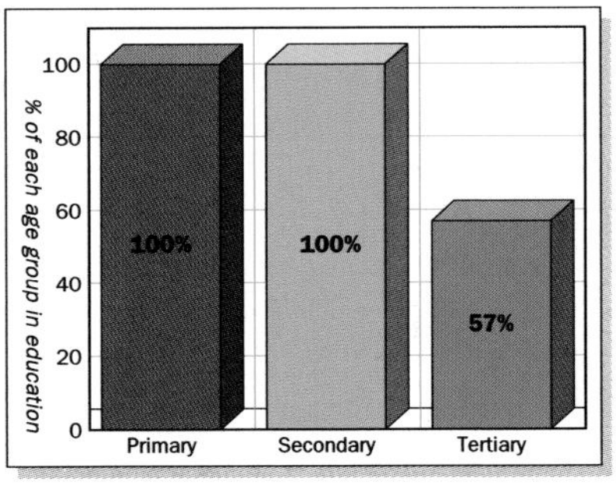
100
80
60
40
20
0
% of each age group in education
100%
100%
57%
Primary
Secondary
Tertiary

Public schooling is free and compulsory to the age of 14. Huge numbers of poor students drop out of the system near or after this age. Middle-class students began to enter the public system en masse as the economy faltered, forcing thousands of private schools to close. There are more private universities than state-run institutions.

WORLD RANKING

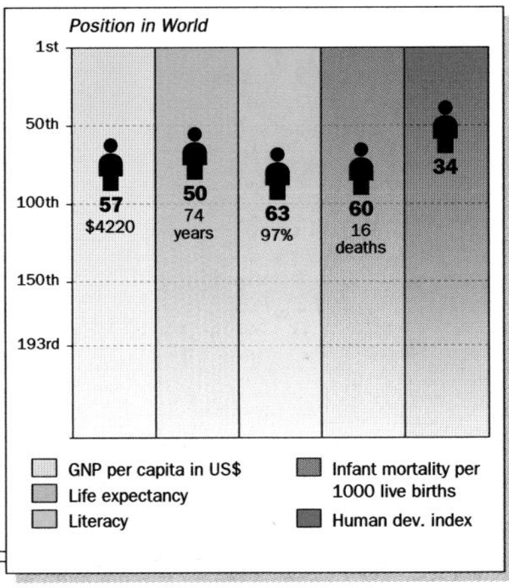
Position in World
1st
50th
100th
150th
193rd
57
$4220
50
74
years
63
97%
60
16
deaths
34
GNP per capita in US$
Life expectancy
Literacy
Infant mortality per 1000 live births
Human dev. index

A

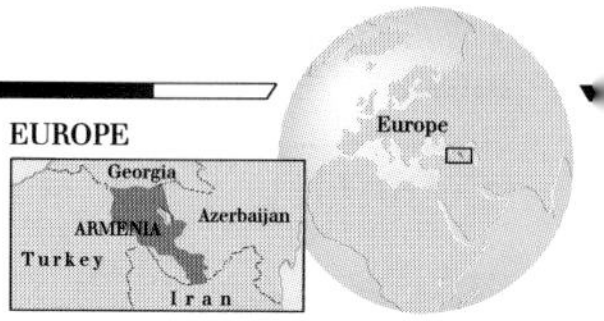
Europe
EUROPE
Georgia
ARMENIA
Azerbaijan
Turkey
Iran

ARMENIA

OFFICIAL NAME: Republic of Armenia **CAPITAL:** Yerevan
POPULATION: 3.1 million **CURRENCY:** Dram **OFFICIAL LANGUAGE:** Armenian

1991 | 1991 | Sept 21 | ARM | +4 | +374 | .am

LANDLOCKED IN THE Lesser Caucasus mountains, Armenia is the smallest of the former Soviet republics. It was the first country to adopt Christianity as its state religion, early in the 4th century. Keen to deepen links with the rest of the CIS, Armenia has kept to a path of radical economic reform, including privatization. The confrontation with Azerbaijan over the exclave of Nagorno Karabakh has dominated national life since 1988.

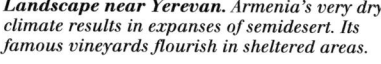

Landscape near Yerevan. *Armenia's very dry climate results in expanses of semidesert. Its famous vineyards flourish in sheltered areas.*

CLIMATE

Mountain

WEATHER CHART FOR YEREVAN

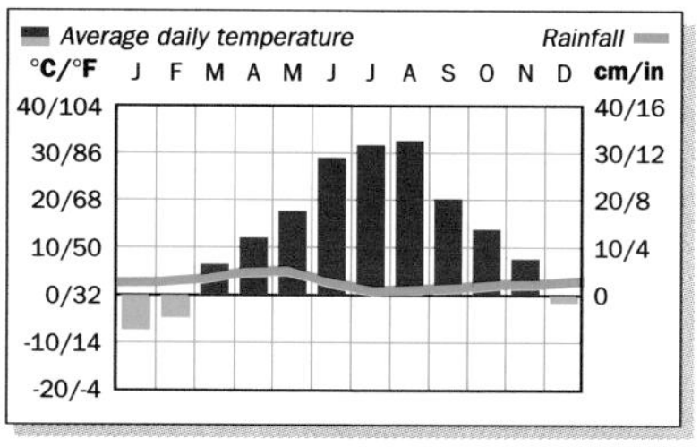
Average daily temperature
Rainfall
°C/°F
J F M A M J J A S O N D
cm/in
40/104
30/86
20/68
10/50
0/32
-10/14
-20/-4
40/16
30/12
20/8
10/4
0

Armenia has a continental climate, with little rainfall in the lowlands. Winters can be very cold.

TRANSPORTATION

Drive on right

Zvartnots, Yerevan 881,920 passengers

Has no fleet

THE TRANSPORTATION NETWORK

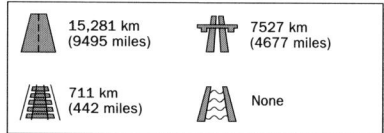

15,281 km (9495 miles)

7527 km (4677 miles)

711 km (442 miles)

None

Fuel prices are high due to a blockade imposed by neighboring Azerbaijan. Road and rail links with Georgia, connecting with the main east–west corridor, need upgrading.

TOURISM

Visitors : Population 1:19

162,089 visitors

Up 31% in 2002

MAIN TOURIST ARRIVALS

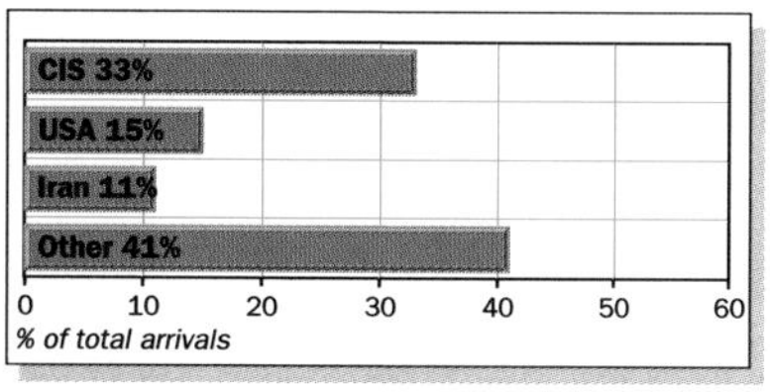
CIS 33%
USA 15%
Iran 11%
Other 41%
0
10
20
30
40
50
60
% of total arrivals

The 1700th anniversary of Armenian Christianity in 2001 boosted the war-damaged tourist industry. Most visitors are diaspora Armenians.

PEOPLE

Pop. density medium

Armenian, Azeri, Russian

104/km² (269/mi²)

THE URBAN/RURAL POPULATION SPLIT

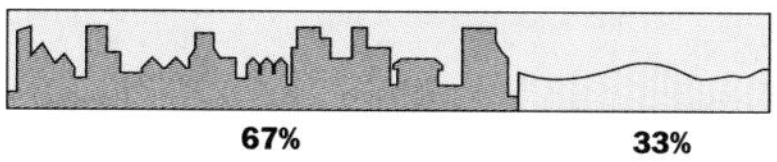
67%
33%

ETHNIC MAKEUP

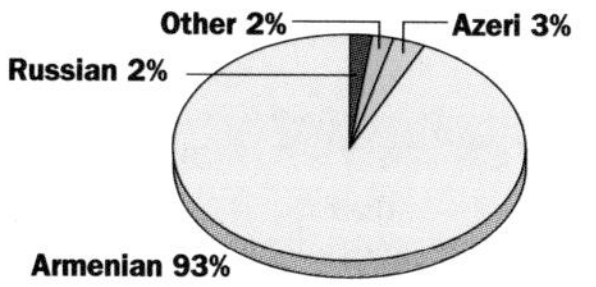
Other 2%
Azeri 3%
Russian 2%
Armenian 93%

Minority nationalities are well integrated in Armenia. There are strong contacts with the many Armenian emigrants, numbering over seven million, living principally in the US, France, and Syria.

Conflict with Azerbaijan forced the repatriation of 350,000 Armenians and 200,000 Azeris. The small Russian population is centered in Yerevan.

POLITICS

Multiparty elections

2003/2007

President Robert Kocharian

AT THE LAST ELECTION

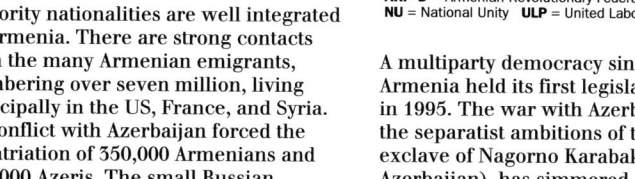

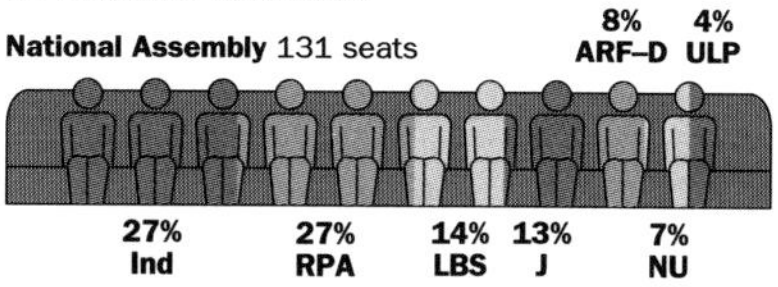
National Assembly 131 seats
8% ARF–D
4% ULP
27% Ind
27% RPA
14% LBS
13% J
7% NU

Ind = Independents **RPA** = Republican Party of Armenia
LBS = Law-based State **J** = Justice Bloc
ARF–D = Armenian Revolutionary Federation–Dashnaktsutyun
NU = National Unity **ULP** = United Labor Party

A multiparty democracy since 1991, Armenia held its first legislative elections in 1995. The war with Azerbaijan, over the separatist ambitions of the Armenian exclave of Nagorno Karabakh (inside Azerbaijan), has simmered since a 1994 cease-fire. Levon Ter-Petrossian, the country's first president, resigned in 1998 after parliament opposed his softer line in search of peace. He was succeeded by Robert Kocharian, a former premier and ex-governor of Nagorno Karabakh. In 1999, RPA prime minister Vazgen Sarkissian was shot dead in a dramatic attack in parliament. He was succeeded first by his brother Aram, then in 2000 by Andranik Markarian. Kocharian was reelected in a disputed ballot in early 2003. His authoritarian rule has provoked large-scale protests.

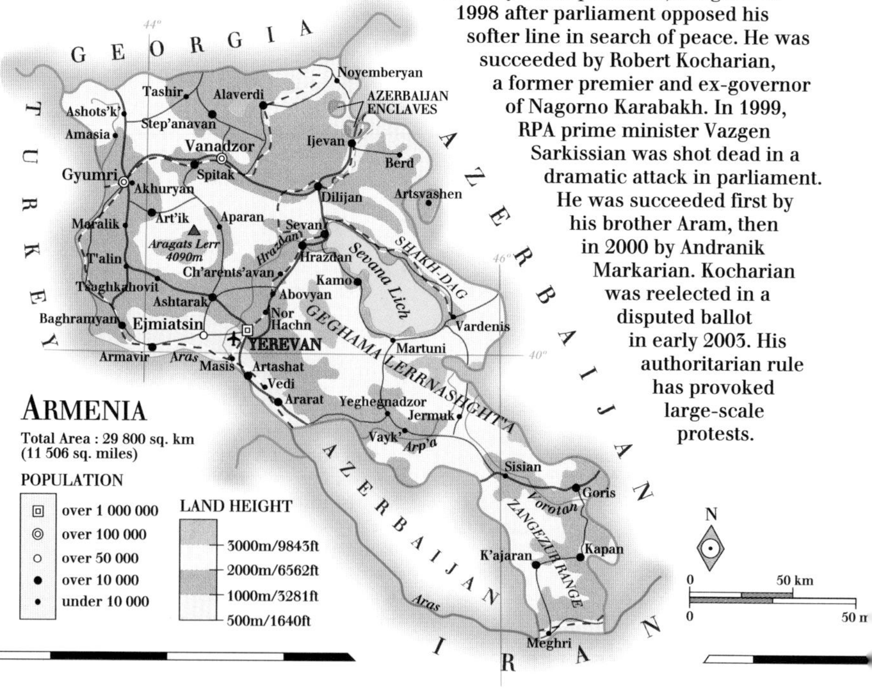
GEORGIA
TURKEY
AZERBAIJAN
IRAN
AZERBAIJAN ENCLAVES
Noyemberyan
Tashir
Alaverdi
Ashots'k'
Step'anavan
Amasia
Vanadzor
Ijevan
Berd
Gyumri
Spitak
Akhuryan
Dilijan
Artsvashen
Maralik
Art'ik
Aparan
Sevan
Aragats Lerr 4090m
T'alin
Hrazdan
Ch'arents'avan
Tsaghkahovit
Kamo
Sevana Lich
SHAKH-DAG
Ashtarak
Abovyan
Nor Hachn
Baghramyan
Ejmiatsin
YEREVAN
Vardenis
GEGHAMA LERRNASHGHTA
Armavir
Aras
Masis
Artashat
Martuni
Vedi
Ararat
Yeghegnadzor
Jermuk
Vayk'
Arp'a
Sisian
Goris
Vorotan
ZANGEZUR RANGE
K'ajaran
Kapan
Meghri
ARMENIA
Total Area : 29 800 sq. km (11 506 sq. miles)
POPULATION
over 1 000 000
over 100 000
over 50 000
over 10 000
under 10 000
LAND HEIGHT
3000m/9843ft
2000m/6562ft
1000m/3281ft
500m/1640ft
N
0
50 km

WORLD AFFAIRS

Joined UN in 1992

BSEC | CIS | CE | EAPC | OSCE

Continuing tension with Azerbaijan is diplomatically damaging; a Turkish trade embargo has been in place since 1988. Armenia joined the Council of Europe in 2001, but faces criticism for imprisoning, among others, Jehovah's Witnesses who refuse military service on religious grounds. It became a member of the WTO in 2003.

AID

Recipient

$293m (receipts)

Up 48% in 2002

Expatriates such as US billionaire Kirk Kerkorian are a major source of funds. Control of utilities has passed to Russia in lieu of debt payments.

DEFENSE

Compulsory military service

$615m

Down 3% in 2002

Fresh peace talks on Nagorno Karabakh, which were held in 1999–2000, proved to be inconclusive. Armenia receives military aid both from Russia, which stations a division in the country, and the NATO alliance, which staged war games in Armenia in 2003. The army includes conscripts on 24-month national service.

ECONOMICS

Inflation 172% p.a. (1990–2001)

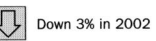

$2.43bn

533 drams (558.1)

SCORE CARD

❑ World GNP Ranking	136th
❑ GNP per Capita	$790
❑ Balance of Payments	–$148m
❑ Inflation	1.1%
❑ Unemployment	10%

STRENGTHS

Strong ties with Armenian emigrants. Deposits of rare metals, currently unexploited. Machine building and manufacturing – includes textiles and bottling mineral water. Development of private sector.

WEAKNESSES

Corruption. Energy, raw materials, and semifinished goods need to be imported. High unemployment.

EXPORTS

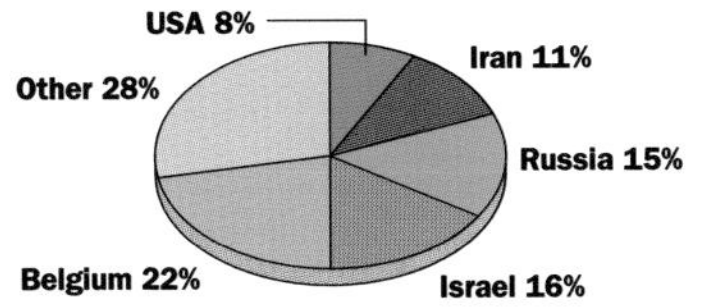
USA 8%
Iran 11%
Other 28%
Russia 15%
Belgium 22%
Israel 16%

IMPORTS

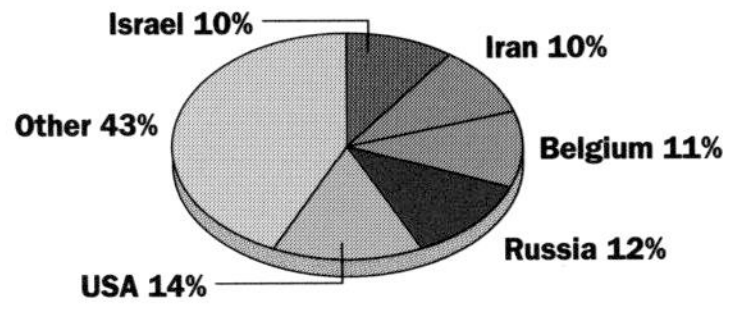
Israel 10%
Iran 10%
Other 43%
Belgium 11%
Russia 12%
USA 14%

RESOURCES

Electric power 3m kW

2197 tonnes

Not an oil producer

552,538 sheep, 514,200 cattle, 3.31m chickens

Copper, salt, molybdenum, silver, gold

Energy resources are negligible; EU funds to develop alternative energy sources depend on the closure of the sole nuclear power plant. Vegetables and fruit are grown in fertile lowlands, and grains in the hills; agriculture accounts for over a fifth of GDP.

ENVIRONMENT

Sustainability rank: 38th

8%

1.1 tonnes per capita

Environmental groups, backed by the EU, demand the closure of the Medzamor nuclear power plant, declared unsafe after the 1988 earthquake, but reopened in 1995 owing to the energy crisis. HEP generation near Lake Sevan has seriously lowered its water level.

MEDIA

TV ownership medium

Daily newspaper circulation 5 per 1000 people

PUBLISHING AND BROADCAST MEDIA

There are 12 daily newspapers, including *Azg*, *Haiastan*, and *Ankakhutiun*

1 state-controlled service, several independent stations

1 state-controlled service, several independent stations

Numerous TV and broadcasting stations assist media freedom. Independent journals and newspapers depend on the government-controlled paper industry.

CRIME

Death penalty not used in practice

4343 prisoners

Up 42% in 2000–2002

Reforms to the legal system introduced in 1999 included the replacement of the Supreme Court by an appeals court. Assassinations of political figures are common.

EDUCATION

School leaving age: 17

99%

68,704 students

The education system, previously conforming to that of the USSR, now emphasizes Armenian history and culture. One in eight adults have received higher education.

CHRONOLOGY

Armenia lost its autonomy in the 14th century. In 1639, Turkey took the west and Persia the east; Persia ceded its part to Russia in 1828.

- ❑ **1877–1878** Massacre of Armenians during Russo-Turkish war.
- ❑ **1915** Ottomans exile 1.75 million Turkish Armenians; most die.
- ❑ **1920** Independence.
- ❑ **1922** Becomes a Soviet republic.
- ❑ **1988** Earthquake kills 25,000. Conflict with Azerbaijan over Nagorno Karabakh begins.
- ❑ **1991** Independence from USSR.
- ❑ **1994** Cease-fire with Azerbaijan.
- ❑ **1995** First parliamentary elections.
- ❑ **1998** Kocharian elected president.
- ❑ **1999** Prime minister assassinated.
- ❑ **2003** Kocharian reelected.

HEALTH

No welfare state health benefits

1 per 328 people

Cerebrovascular and heart diseases, cancers

The well-developed network of hospitals and clinics is concentrated in urban areas. Primary health care is still free but it is often necessary to pay for nonbasic medication.

SPENDING

GDP/cap. decrease

CONSUMPTION AND SPENDING

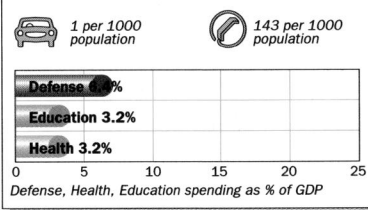

1 per 1000 population

143 per 1000 population

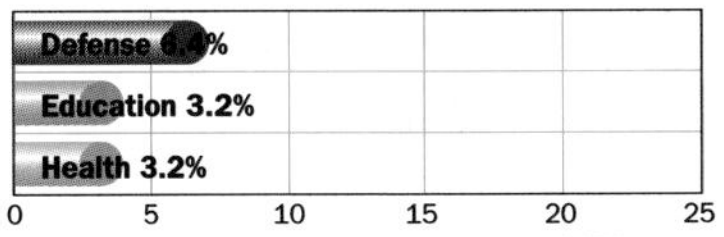
Defense 6.4%
Education 3.2%
Health 3.2%
0
5
10
15
20
25

Defense, Health, Education spending as % of GDP

The richest Armenian people are those living away from Armenia itself, particularly in the US and France. The many refugees from Baku, Azerbaijan, are the poorest.

WORLD RANKING

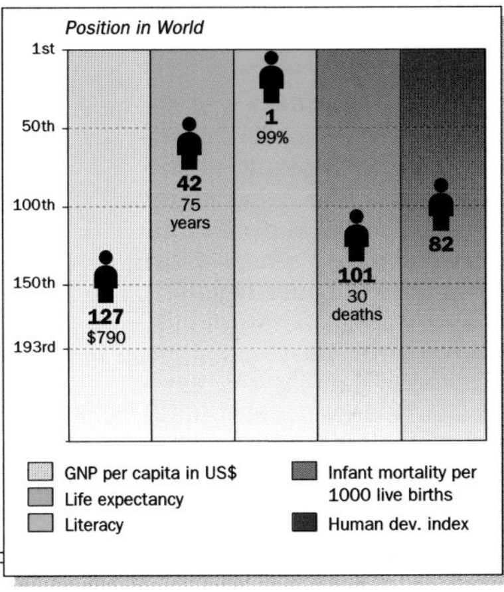
Position in World
1st
50th
100th
150th
193rd
127
$790
42
75
years
1
99%
101
30
deaths
82
GNP per capita in US$
Life expectancy
Literacy
Infant mortality per 1000 live births
Human dev. index

A

AUSTRALIA

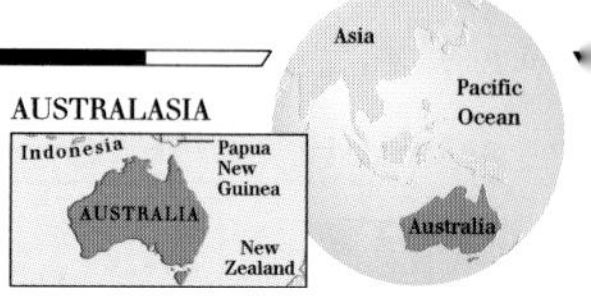
AUSTRALASIA
Indonesia
Papua New Guinea
AUSTRALIA
New Zealand
Asia
Pacific Ocean
Australia

OFFICIAL NAME: Commonwealth of Australia **CAPITAL:** Canberra
POPULATION: 19.7 million **CURRENCY:** Australian dollar **OFFICIAL LANGUAGE:** English

1901
1901
Jan 26
AUS
+8 to +11
+61
.au

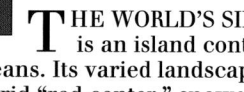

Uluru (Ayers Rock), Northern Territory.
The renaming of Ayers Rock reflects growing Aboriginal influence on Australian culture.

THE WORLD'S SIXTH-LARGEST country, Australia is an island continent located between the Indian and Pacific Oceans. Its varied landscapes include tropical rainforests, the deserts of the arid "red center," snowcapped mountains, rolling tracts of pastoral land, and magnificent beaches. Famous natural features include Uluru (Ayers Rock) and the Great Barrier Reef, while Sydney boasts the world-renowned Opera House. Most Australians live on the coast, and all the state capitals are coastal cities. Only Canberra, the national capital, lies inland. The vast interior is dotted with large nature reserves and some communities of the small Aboriginal population.

CLIMATE

Hot desert/steppe/tropical/Mediterranean

WEATHER CHART FOR CANBERRA

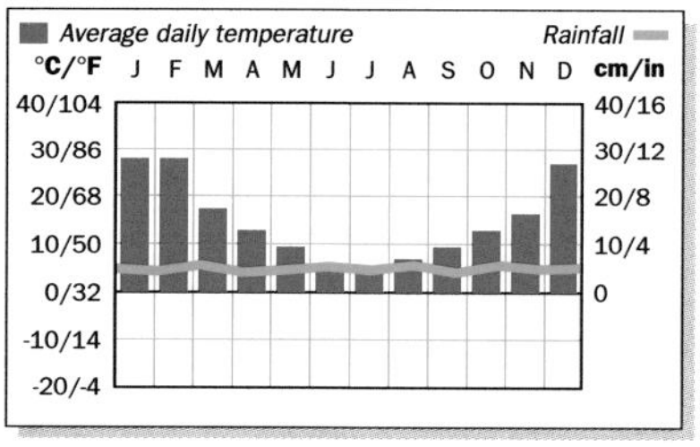
Average daily temperature
Rainfall
°C/°F J F M A M J J A S O N D cm/in
40/104
30/86
20/68
10/50
0/32
-10/14
-20/-4
40/16
30/12
20/8
10/4
0

The interior, west, and south are arid or semiarid and very hot in summer; central desert temperatures can reach 50°C (122°F). The north, around Darwin and Cape York Peninsula, is hot all year and humid during the summer monsoon. Only the east and southeast, within 400 km (250 miles) of the coast, and the southwest, around Perth, are temperate: most Australians live in these areas.

TRANSPORTATION

Drive on left

Kingsford Smith, Sydney 24.7m passengers

624 ships 1.86m grt

THE TRANSPORTATION NETWORK

329,100 km (204,493 miles)

18,619 km (11,569 miles)

9514 km (5912 miles)

8368 km (5200 miles)

Air transportation is well developed and vital to Australia's sparsely populated center and west. Sydney suffers from air congestion, but proposals for a second airport to service the city remain controversial. Most long-distance freight travels in massive trucks known as "road trains," though the long-planned rail link between Adelaide and Darwin, which opened in 2004, is expected to carry significant loads from north to south. Improvements in urban transportation are a priority.

TOURISM

Visitors : Population 1:4.5

4.42m visitors

Little change in 2002

MAIN TOURIST ARRIVALS

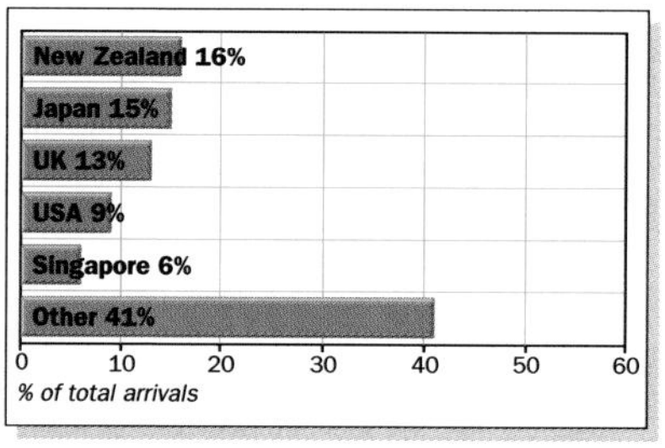
New Zealand 16%
Japan 15%
UK 13%
USA 9%
Singapore 6%
Other 41%
0 10 20 30 40 50 60
% of total arrivals

Tourism is now one of Australia's largest single foreign exchange earners. Many tourists have been attracted by faster, cheaper air travel and highly successful marketing campaigns, by both the national and state governments. The focus during the 1990s on drawing tourists from nearby Asian countries left the Australian tourist industry vulnerable after the Asian financial crisis of 1997–1998. In recent years New Zealanders have surpassed the Japanese as the largest category of visitors to Australia. However, tourists from southeast Asia continue to arrive in significant numbers.

The country's many attractions include wildlife, swimming and surfing off Pacific and Indian Ocean beaches, skin diving along the Great Barrier Reef, and skiing in the Australian Alps. Uluru, Aboriginal culture, and the town of Alice Springs are among the outback's attractions. The far north has tropical resorts, the northwest, pearl fishing. Visitors are also attracted by the vineyards of the south and southeast, the cultural life of Melbourne and Sydney, and the arts festivals held in state capitals. Sydney's famous landmarks and cosmopolitan feel, as well as the world-renowned Bondi Beach, make it a favorite.

The mid-1980s saw a phenomenal boom; tourist arrivals almost tripled in five years to reach two million in 1990. Even though growth slowed during the early 1990s, the number of visitors reached almost five million in 2000, boosted greatly by the celebrated Sydney Olympic Games.

INDIAN OCEAN
Bonaparte Archipelago
Derby
Broome
Port Hedland
GREAT SA DESER
Onslow
Hamersley Range
Newman
Paraburdoo
Lake Disappo
WESTERN
Lake Macleod
Carnarvon
Shark Bay
Dirk Hartog Island
AUSTRALIA
Lake Carnegie
Meekatharra
Mount Magnet
Geraldton
Kalgoorlie
Moora
Perth
Fremantle
Northam
Merredin
Norseman
Rockingham
Bunbury
Wagin
Collie
Bridgetown
Cape Leeuwin
Manjimup
Ravensthorpe
Albany

AUSTRALIA

Total Area : 7 686 850 sq. km (2 967 893 sq. miles)

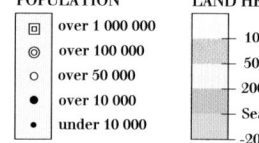

POPULATION
- over 1 000 000
- over 100 000
- over 50 000
- over 10 000
- under 10 000

LAND HEIGHT
- 1000m/3281ft
- 500m/1640ft
- 200m/656ft
- Sea Level
- -200m/-656ft

PEOPLE

Pop. density low

English, Italian, Cantonese, Greek, Arabic, Vietnamese, Aboriginal languages

3/km² (7/mi²)

THE URBAN/RURAL POPULATION SPLIT

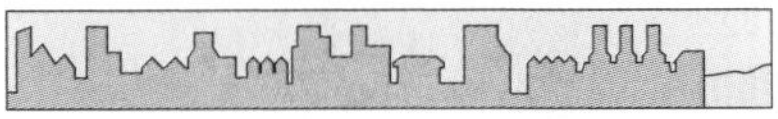
91%
9%

The first settlers arrived in Australia at least 100,000 years ago. Their modern descendants, the Aborigines, today make up less than 3% of the population. European settlement began in 1788 and was dominated by British and Irish immigrants – some of whom were convicts – until the gold rushes of the 1850s attracted people of other nationalities – including many Chinese – who then settled in the cities, especially Melbourne and Sydney. The federal government, installed in 1901, aimed to block non-European immigration through the Immigration Restriction Act. The act, known as the "White Australia" policy, was in force until 1958, while immigration drives after World War II brought many more British, Italian, and Greek settlers to Australia.

The White Australia policy was officially ended during the controversial 1972–1975 administration of ALP prime minister Gough Whitlam. Ever since, up to 50% of immigrants each year have come from Asia, transforming Australia into a multicultural society in which immigrant groups are encouraged to maintain connections with their own cultures and languages.

Aborigines, who number around 410,000, are the exception in an otherwise integrated society. Economically and socially marginalized, they face considerable discrimination. Until the mid-1960s, they were denied the vote and full social benefits. Their land had been occupied as *terra nullius* – land belonging to no one. Since the 1970s, Aborigines have made a more organized stand on land and civil rights. Native title to land was recognized in the 1993 Native Title Act (NTA), which followed the landmark "Mabo Judgment," though controversies continue over the pace of its application under the Liberal–National administration. The government has since amended the NTA, while some courts have favored modern leaseholders; the government's position was effectively summarized by the court in the Yorta Yorta case when it ruled in 1999 that native title in that instance had been "washed away" by the "tide of history."

Civil rights campaigns have also had to focus on areas such as health, housing, and education. Average life expectancy for Aborigines is still 20 years lower than the rest of the population while alcoholism is a pervasive problem both in towns and rural areas. Aborigines in urban areas may be relatively better housed but face particular problems in asserting their cultural identity. Discrimination is most prevalent in more conservative states such as Queensland, which in fact has the largest Aboriginal population.

RELIGIOUS PERSUASION

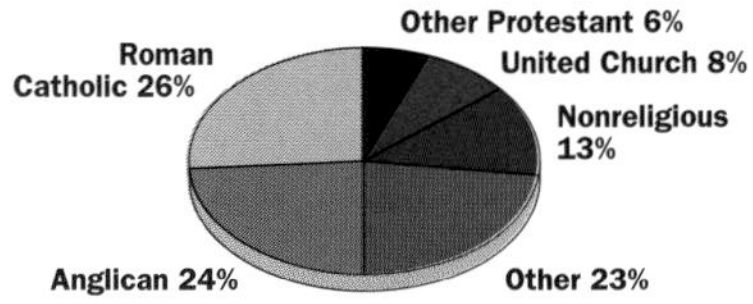
Other Protestant 6%
United Church 8%
Nonreligious 13%
Other 23%
Anglican 24%
Roman Catholic 26%

ETHNIC MAKEUP

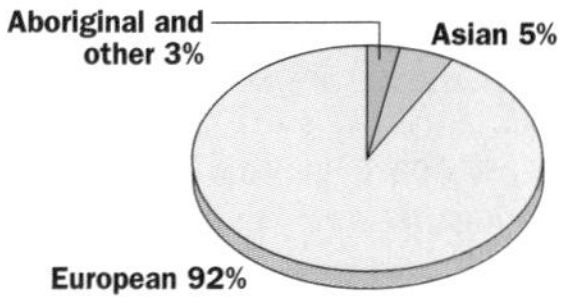
Aboriginal and other 3%
Asian 5%
European 92%

PAPUA NEW GUINEA
ARAFURA SEA
Torres Strait
Bamaga
Cape York
Melville Island
Bathurst Island
Wessel Islands
Darwin
Arnhem Land
Gulf of Carpentaria
Groote Eylandt
Katherine
Sir Edward Pellew Group
Wellesley Islands
Cape York Peninsula
Cooktown
Cairns
Karumba
Mitchell
Barkly Tableland
TANAMI DESERT
NORTHERN TERRITORY
Tennant Creek
Mount Isa
Cloncurry
Hughenden
Townsville
Flinders
Winton
Mackay
Longreach
Emerald
Rockhampton
Macdonnell Ranges
Alice Springs
QUEENSLAND
Great Artesian Basin
SIMPSON DESERT
Uluru (Ayers Rock)
Birdsville
Charleville
Bundaberg
Fraser I.
Maryborough
Gympie
Brisbane
Gold Coast
Surfers Paradise
Toowoomba
Ipswich
Lismore
Cunnamulla
Cooper Creek
SOUTH AUSTRALIA
Lake Eyre
Grey Range
Moree
Grafton
Bourke
Darling
Armidale
Coffs Harbour
Lake Torrens
Lake Frome
Flinders Ranges
NEW SOUTH WALES
Tamworth
Port Macquarie
Lake Gairdner
Port Augusta
Whyalla
Broken Hill
Dubbo
Taree
Maitland
Port Pirie
Orange
Newcastle
Gosford
Great Australian Bight
Eyre Peninsula
Spencer Gulf
Port Lincoln
Elizabeth
Adelaide
Mildura
Bathurst
Lithgow
Sydney
Griffith
Murrumbidgee
Goulburn
Wollongong
Wagga Wagga
Queanbeyan
CANBERRA
Lachlan
Kangaroo I.
VICTORIA
Murray
Albury
Mount Kosciuszko 2228m
AUST. CAPITAL TERRITORY
Shepparton
Horsham
Bendigo
Wangaratta
Australian Alps
Ballarat
Melbourne
Mount Gambier
Traralgon
Moe
Sale
Morwell
Cape Howe
TASMAN SEA
Warrnambool
Geelong
Bass Strait
King I.
Flinders I.
Furneaux Group
Burnie
Ulverstone
Devonport
Launceston
TASMANIA
Hobart
GREAT BARRIER REEF
CORAL SEA
GREAT DIVIDING RANGE
SOUTH PACIFIC OCEAN
N
0 400 km
0 400 miles

POPULATION AGE BREAKDOWN

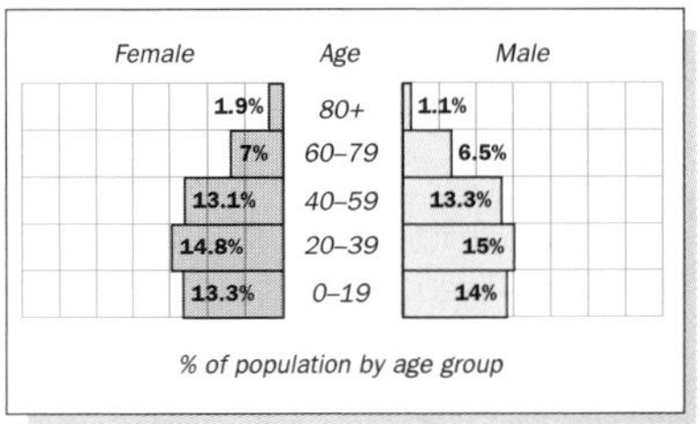
Female
Age
Male
1.9%
80+
1.1%
7%
60–79
6.5%
13.1%
40–59
13.3%
14.8%
20–39
15%
13.3%
0–19
14%
% of population by age group

A

CHRONOLOGY

Dutch, Portuguese, French, and – decisively – British incursions throughout the 17th and 18th centuries signaled the end of millennia of Aboriginal isolation. Governor Arthur Philip raised the British Union Flag at Sydney Cove on January 26, 1788.

- **1901** Inauguration of Commonwealth of Australia.
- **1915** Australian troops suffer heavy casualties at Gallipoli.
- **1939** Prime Minister Robert Menzies announces Australia will follow UK into war with Germany.
- **1942** Fall of Singapore to Japanese army. Japanese invasion of Australia seems imminent. Government turns to US for help.
- **1950** Australian troops committed to UN/US Korean War against North Korean communists.
- **1962** Menzies government commits Australian aid to war in Vietnam.
- **1966** Adopts decimal currency.
- **1972** Whitlam government elected. Aid to South Vietnam ceases.
- **1975** Whitlam government dismissed by Governor-General Sir John Kerr. Malcolm Fraser forms coalition government.
- **1983** Bob Hawke becomes prime minister of ALP administration.
- **1985** Corporate boom followed by deepening recession.
- **1992** Paul Keating defeats Hawke in leadership vote, becomes prime minister; announces "Turning toward Asia" policy. High Court's "Mabo Judgment" recognizes Aboriginal land rights.
- **1993** Against most predictions, Keating's ALP government reelected. Native Title Act provides compensation for Aboriginal rights extinguished by existing land title.
- **1996** Liberal John Howard prime minister. Shooting of 35 people in Tasmania prompts tightening of gun control laws. First death under Northern Territory's controversial euthanasia legislation; legislation later overruled at federal level.
- **1998** Elections: Howard's Liberal and National coalition retains power with reduced majority; fears of right-wing One Nation party breakthrough prove unfounded.
- **1999** Referendum rejects proposals to replace monarch as head of state by indirectly elected president.
- **2000** Olympic Games in Sydney.
- **2001** Surprise reelection of Liberal–National coalition.
- **2002** Bali bomb kills 88 Australians.
- **2003** Governor-general resigns amid church child abuse scandal.

POLITICS

Multiparty elections

L. House 2001/2004
U. House 2001/2004

H.M. Queen Elizabeth II

AT THE LAST ELECTION

House of Representatives 150 seats

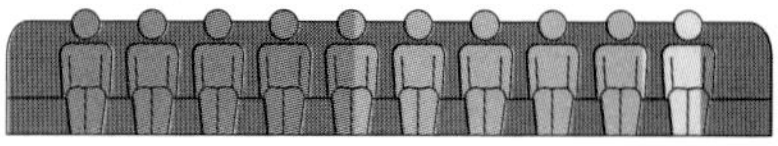

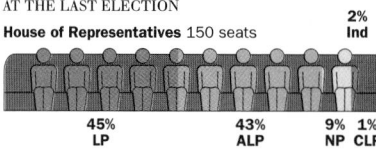

2% Ind
45% LP
43% ALP
9% NP
1% CLP

LP = Liberal Party **ALP** = Australian Labor Party **NP** = National Party **Ind** = Independents **CLP** = County–Liberal Party **AD** = Australian Democrats **G** = Greens

Senate 76 seats

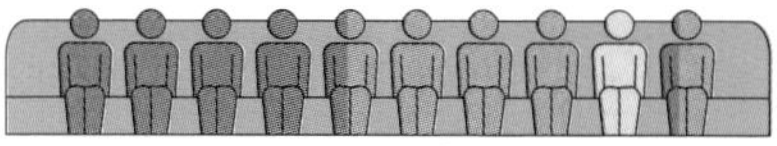

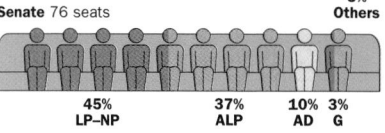

5% Others
45% LP–NP
37% ALP
10% AD
3% G

12 seats in the Senate are apportioned to each of the country's constituent states and two each to the Northern Territory and the Australian Capital Territory

Australia is a parliamentary democracy on the British model, incorporating a federal structure. There is a federal government, six state governments, and two self-governing territories.

Profile

The ALP and the Liberal and National parties have dominated Australian politics since 1945. The last two, politically to the right, work together in coalition and broadly represent big business and agricultural interests. The ALP gained some of this support in the 1980s, adopting free-market policies and blurring the differences between parties, but 13 years of ALP rule ended in 1996, when a Liberal–National coalition took office under John Howard. It has retained power in elections since then, but with a much reduced majority.

Main Political Issues

Political leadership

The election success of Prime Minister Howard in the 2001 polls took political analysts by surprise. It had been expected that the state of the economy and Howard's own unpopularity would be enough to guarantee victory for the ALP. Howard was saved in part by a successful campaign which capitalized on the two greatest fears of late 2001 – the apparent increase in the number of illegal immigrants and the specter of international terrorism – but also by the even lower popularity rating of his main adversary, the ALP's Kim Beazley. Despite clear grassroots support for the ALP – as attested in early 2002 when it took control of all regional governments – it has been unable to build on deep opposition to Howard's conservative policies, notably its commitment to the war on Iraq in 2003. Instead it is mired in factional infighting, and has had three leaders since 2001. The party hopes that the notably outspoken Mark Latham will revive its fortunes. For his part, Howard glossed over previous hints that he would retire in 2003, having reached 64 years of age, and has remained at the Liberal helm.

***Vineyards in South Australia.** Wine-making has been one of Australia's greatest agricultural success stories in recent years.*

Immigration

There is considerable concern at images of boatloads of would-be immigrants entering Australian waters and the dramatic attempts by asylum seekers to protest over the conditions in which they are housed. The Howard government has actively courted mistrust of refugees, focusing on "unacceptable" behavior. Its allegations that immigrants had thrown children overboard in an effort to secure asylum were proved groundless in 2002, and its notorious "Pacific solution" – using tiny Pacific states to house asylum applicants in exchange for aid – has been roundly criticized by the international community.

Rightward drift

The acceptance of right-wing policies in the political mainstream has been aided by the local success of the far-right xenophobic One Nation party. Even the ALP has conspicuously toned down its support for immigration and embraced market economics.

***Governor-General Michael Jeffrey.** His predecessor resigned amid scandal in 2003.*

***John Howard,** leader of the LP, was elected prime minister in 1996.*

***Mark Latham,** leader of the ALP since 2003.*

WORLD AFFAIRS

Joined UN in 1945

APEC | PC | Comm | OECD | PIF

Geopolitically Australia is in an ambiguous position. Isolated from its historic cultural and economic relatives in Europe and North America, it is seen as a Western outsider by the Asian states with which it has sought closer links. It views the US and EU as its main rivals in the lucrative Asian marketplace.

As membership of the EU eroded the UK's trade links with Australia, there was a determined effort in the 1990s to "turn toward Asia." Trade and aid ties were developed, though market liberalization slowed after the 1997–1998 Asian financial crisis.

Building on its role as the leading power in the south Pacific, Australia has championed the development of APEC (established in 1989) as a regional trading bloc. In order to boost stability, it has also made regional security a priority. In 1999 it led peacekeeping efforts in East Timor, and it played a pivotal role in securing peace in the Solomon Islands in 2000. In 2003 it pushed the concept of "cooperative intervention," particularly in relation to the Solomons, where it led a regional policing mission in an effort to restore law and order.

A serious concern since 2001 has been the perceived threat to Australian nationals from Islamist terrorists, highlighted by the Bali bombing in October 2002. To this end it has sought close cooperation from its neighbors and has strengthened ties with the US. In 2003 it agreed to participate in the US national missile defense project, and later, in a deeply unpopular move, supplied troops for the invasion of Iraq – though Australian soldiers are not involved in the reconstruction effort there. Prime Minister Howard has even backed the idea of preemptive strikes against terrorists and their supporters.

Australia has been strongly criticized for its treatment of the Aboriginal population and asylum seekers. The "Pacific Solution" to the immigration problem, adopted in late 2001, received international condemnation.

AID

Donor

US$989m (donations)

Up 13% in 2002

Australia spent only 0.26% of its GNP on aid programs in 2002. Nearly all is spent in the southeast Asia–Pacific region, the recipient of by far the most being Papua New Guinea, where Australian companies have major mining operations. The main focus in the Pacific region is on security. Trade barriers were dropped for 50 developing countries in 2002.

DEFENSE

No compulsory military service

US$7.55bn

Up 10% in 2002

Strategic ties with the US remain key: Australia committed 2000 troops to the Iraq invasion in 2003, its largest deployment since the Vietnam War. Australia sees itself as a major regional power, and in 2004 announced plans to spend US$320 million on long-range land-attack cruise missiles, drawing criticism from neighbors. Combating terrorism, especially in the Pacific region, has become a priority.

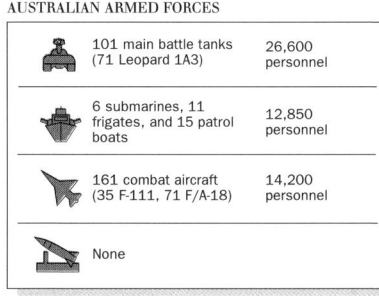

AUSTRALIAN ARMED FORCES

101 main battle tanks (71 Leopard 1A3)	26,600 personnel
6 submarines, 11 frigates, and 15 patrol boats	12,850 personnel
161 combat aircraft (35 F-111, 71 F/A-18)	14,200 personnel
None	

ECONOMICS

Inflation 1.7% p.a. (1990–2001)

US$384bn

1.44 Australian dollars (1.491)

SCORE CARD

❑ WORLD GNP RANKING	14th
❑ GNP PER CAPITA	US$19,530
❑ BALANCE OF PAYMENTS	–US$17.9bn
❑ INFLATION	3%
❑ UNEMPLOYMENT	6%

ECONOMIC PERFORMANCE INDICATOR

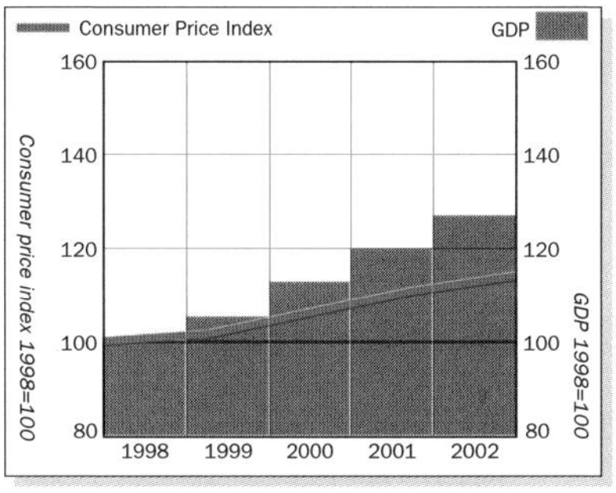
Consumer Price Index
GDP
160
140
120
100
80
Consumer price index 1998=100
GDP 1998=100
1998
1999
2000
2001
2002

EXPORTS

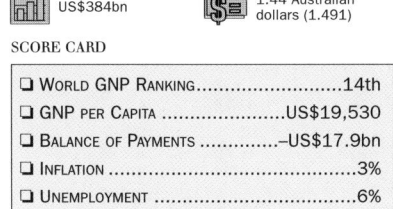

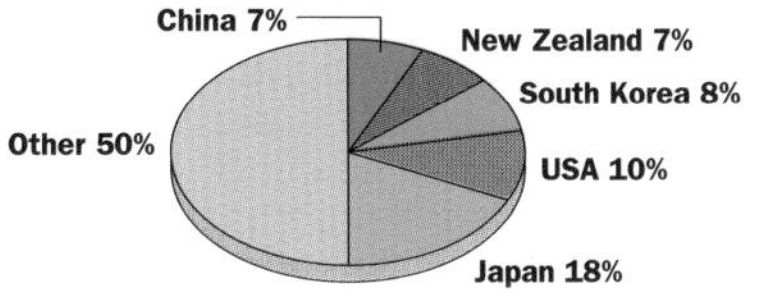
China 7%
New Zealand 7%
South Korea 8%
USA 10%
Japan 18%
Other 50%

IMPORTS

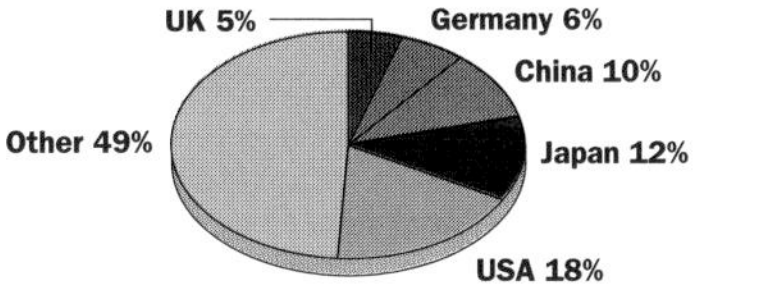
UK 5%
Germany 6%
China 10%
Japan 12%
USA 18%
Other 49%

STRENGTHS

Efficient agricultural and mining industries. Viticulture. Vast mineral deposits. Highly profitable tourist industry; record of dramatic growth. Good history regarding both economic growth and inflation. Budget surplus.

WEAKNESSES

Political and financial instability in export markets in southeast Asia. Competition from Asian economies with lower wage rates and less stringent working conditions. EU and NAFTA protectionist policies may hinder Australian exports. Balance-of-payments deficit.

PROFILE

Australian companies concentrated during the 1990s on the Asian market, which grew to take 60% of Australia's trade. They were hit hard when the 1997 Asian financial crisis tipped the region into recession. Japan remains the key export partner. In order to compete in Asia, the economy has been undergoing massive structural adjustment. The Howard government, like its ALP predecessor, has been dismantling the tariffs that had made Australia one of the OECD's most protected economies. Unemployment and the collapse of many businesses have resulted. However, recovery has been quick, with positive growth and lower unemployment in 2002, though progress was hampered in 2003 by serious drought and the global SARS epidemic.

AUSTRALIA : MAJOR BUSINESSES

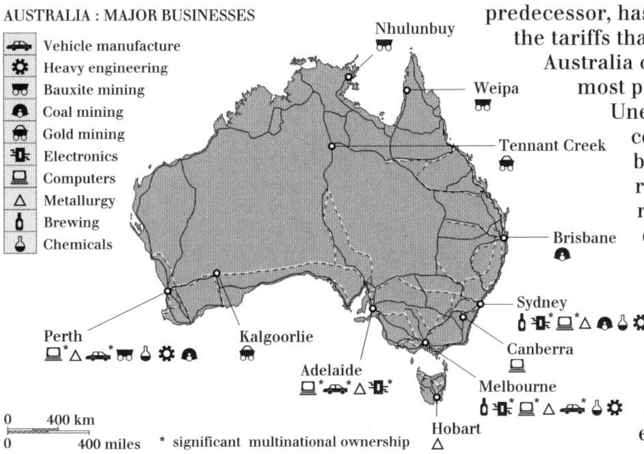
Vehicle manufacture
Heavy engineering
Bauxite mining
Coal mining
Gold mining
Electronics
Computers
Metallurgy
Brewing
Chemicals
Nhulunbuy
Weipa
Tennant Creek
Brisbane
Sydney
Canberra
Melbourne
Hobart
Adelaide
Kalgoorlie
Perth
0 400 km
0 400 miles
* significant multinational ownership

A

RESOURCES

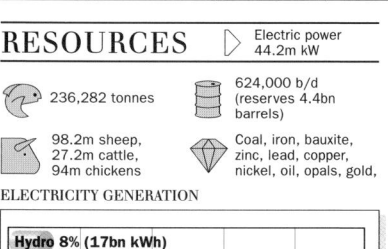

Electric power 44.2m kW

236,282 tonnes

624,000 b/d (reserves 4.4bn barrels)

98.2m sheep, 27.2m cattle, 94m chickens

Coal, iron, bauxite, zinc, lead, copper, nickel, oil, opals, gold,

ELECTRICITY GENERATION

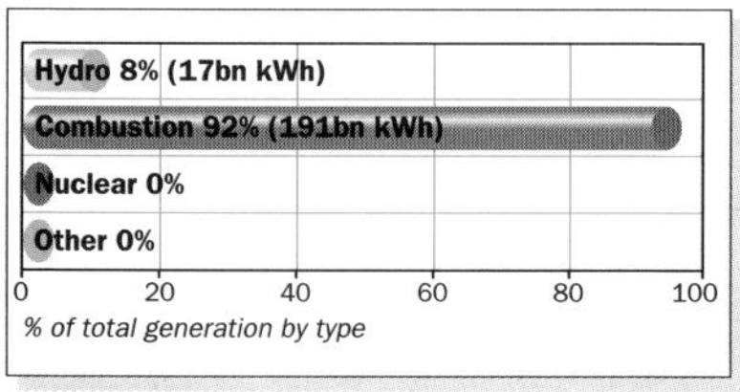
Hydro 8% (17bn kWh)
Combustion 92% (191bn kWh)
Nuclear 0%
Other 0%
0
20
40
60
80
100
% of total generation by type

Australia has one of the world's most important mining industries. It is a major exporter of coal, iron ore, gold, bauxite, and copper, and is self-sufficient in all minerals bar petroleum.

Since the first discoveries of coal in 1798, mineral production has risen every year; in the decade to 1992 it doubled. The share of minerals in the total economy is expected to continue growing, but, having benefited from Australia's location close to the markets of southeast Asia, it was left vulnerable following the regional crisis of 1997.

While minerals underpin much of Australia's wealth, there is growing concern at the environmental cost of extraction. There is also ongoing uncertainty over the possibility of Aboriginal claims to land holding valuable minerals. The 1992 "Mabo Judgment" recognized Aboriginal land rights predating European settlement, and was backed by later judgments, but legislation passed by the government in 1998, in deference to powerful mining interests, cut back Aborigines' rights to make such claims, and in 2002 the High Court ruled that land rights did not apply to minerals beneath the ground.

Viticulture is increasingly important and Australia is now the world's fourth-largest wine exporter, principally to the UK.

AUSTRALIA : LAND USE

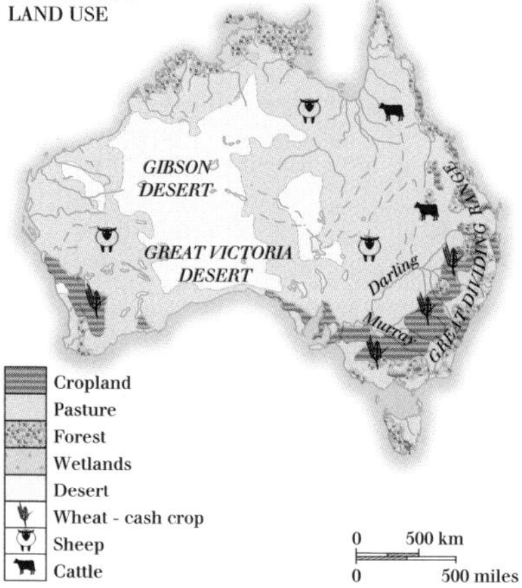
GIBSON DESERT
GREAT VICTORIA DESERT
Darling
Murray
GREAT DIVIDING RANGE
Cropland
Pasture
Forest
Wetlands
Desert
Wheat - cash crop
Sheep
Cattle
0 500 km
0 500 miles

Green Island in the far north of Queensland. It is part of the Great Barrier Reef which stretches 1995 km (1240 miles) down the coast.

ENVIRONMENT

Sustainability rank: 16th

13% (7% partially protected)

18 tonnes per capita

ENVIRONMENTAL TREATIES

Yes	Yes	Yes
Yes	Yes	No

Australia boasts a number of unique wildlife species, including the egg-laying duck-billed platypus and the iconic koala and kangaroo. Many native species have been adversely affected by the arrival of introduced species such as the dingo and the rabbit. The world famous Great Barrier Reef is at risk from rising sea temperatures. Fishing was banned in 2004 in one-third of the area of the reef, creating the world's largest marine reserve.

Despite a high degree of public awareness, green issues are dominated by NGOs such as Greenpeace, while the government has been criticized for favoring business and industry.

MEDIA

TV ownership high

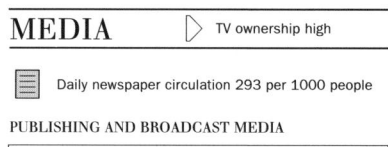

Daily newspaper circulation 293 per 1000 people

PUBLISHING AND BROADCAST MEDIA

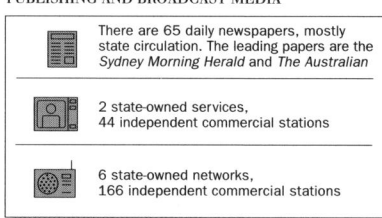

There are 65 daily newspapers, mostly state circulation. The leading papers are the *Sydney Morning Herald* and *The Australian*

2 state-owned services, 44 independent commercial stations

6 state-owned networks, 166 independent commercial stations

The printed press is firmly in the grip of "barons" such as Rupert Murdoch and Kerry Packer: four companies own 80% of papers. Private stations overshadow the state-funded Australian Broadcasting Corporation (ABC) and the multicultural Special Broadcasting Service (SBS). A 2002 High Court ruling enables Australians to sue foreign-based websites for defamation, on the basis that they can be read in Australia.

CRIME

No death penalty

22,492 prisoners

Up 3% in 2001

CRIME RATES

Murders
2 per 100,000 population

Rapes
Rape statistics are unavailable

Thefts
6653 per 100,000 population

Each state has its own police force and court system. The High Court and Family Court both have national jurisdiction. Since the 1970s, the legal system has been placing greater emphasis on individual rights. The disproportionate number of Aboriginal deaths in custody is of concern, as are rising narcotics-related offenses. Australia is active in narcotics control throughout southeast Asia. Increasingly strict gun laws helped to halve the number of gun-related deaths over the course of the 1990s. In 1997 the Wood inquiry uncovered widespread police corruption in New South Wales and led to sweeping reforms.

EDUCATION

School leaving age: 15/16

99%

845,132 students

THE EDUCATION SYSTEM

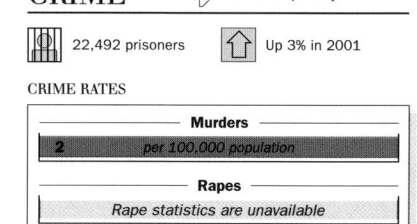

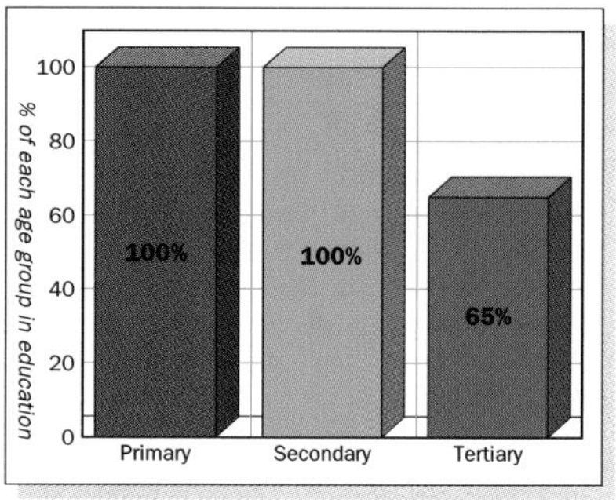
100
80
60
40
20
0
% of each age group in education
100%
100%
65%
Primary
Secondary
Tertiary

Education in Australia is a state responsibility, except in Canberra (where it is funded by the federal government). State education departments run the government schools and set the policies for educational practice and standards for all schools. Nongovernment schools, run by religious and other groups, exist in all states. Special provision is made for inaccessible outback areas, modern technologies bringing teaching to the bush.

Schooling is compulsory from age 5–6 to age 15–16 in all states. After their final year at school, students sit for the Higher School Certificate (HSC). Universities are independent of state control and are funded by the federal government.

POLICEMAN OF THE PACIFIC

AUSTRALIA'S FOREIGN policy has had to come to terms with the country's anomalous situation. Long seen as an outpost of the West in the East, it also belongs on the "global north" side of the developed–developing North–South divide, despite being located in the Southern Hemisphere between Asia and the South Pacific. After years of sticking closely to the UK, placing it at risk of invasion from Japan during World War II, Australia set its eyes on the markets of southeast Asia from the 1960s on, and now balances its geographic reality against its cultural heritage.

THE BACKYARD

Seeking to build a role as the main policing force in the south Pacific region, Australia led the peacekeeping effort in East Timor in 1999. In 2000 when civil conflict in the Solomon Islands escalated, Australia brokered a peace agreement, which nominally ended two years of warfare, but shied away from a longer-term commitment. The situation deteriorated, however, so in 2003 the Australian government convened a multinational taskforce, the Regional Assistance Mission for the Solomon Islands (RAMSI), choosing to maintain the initiative while spreading the burden of action.

Meanwhile, Australia's relative proximity to persecution, war, and poverty in other parts of the region had attracted the attention of those seeking escape to a better life. The "influx" of refugees, growing noticeably in recent years, prompted a panic among the Australian public, goaded by the sight of boatloads of desperate people heading for Australian shores. The government erected detention camps in unwelcoming outback locations to process the asylum applicants, causing many to complain violently at their treatment. It also pulled back the country's immigration zone in 2001, and eventually settled on the idea of farming out migrants to holding stations on neighboring Pacific islands in return for aid. The so-called "Pacific Solution" was widely criticized around the world, though other immigrant destinations are also now considering "outsourcing" the refugee "sorting" stations.

Refugees aboard the Norwegian-*registered ship, the* Tampa. *The arrival of the boat in Australian waters in 2001 prompted a hard-line response to immigration.*

NO WAR

***Demonstrators made** use of the iconic Sydney Opera House to voice their opposition to Australia's involvement in the Iraq invasion.*

AUSTRALIA IN THE WORLD

Casting its eyes further afield than the immediate backyard, Australia reconnected with its Western roots in the aftermath of the 2001 terrorist attacks on the US, pledging full support for the US "war on terrorism," and signing up to the US national missile defense system. Australia's active involvement in the war against the *taliban* in Afghanistan launched in October 2001 helped precipitate the arrival of significant numbers of Afghan refugees.

It also drew down militant Islamist anger on Australia, and the bombing on the Indonesian island of Bali on October 12, 2002, specifically targeted Australian holidaymakers: 88 Australians were among the 202 dead. Perhaps ironically, the outrage served to strengthen support for the tough stance of Prime Minister John Howard. Nonetheless, his decision not only to back, but to fight alongside the US and the UK in the 2003 invasion of Iraq prompted large-scale public anger in Australia; most of the country's servicemen were quickly withdrawn after the toppling of Saddam Hussein.

The recent alignment of Australia's foreign policy with the US is directly linked to the party of power, John Howard's conservative Liberals. The left-of-center Australian Labor Party, on the other hand, has openly attacked the policies of US Republican president George W. Bush, and has pledged to review Australia's position in the world if returned to power.

HEALTH

Welfare state health benefits

1 per 400 people

Cancers, heart diseases, accidents

Australia's extensive public health service has among the highest standards in the world, though hospital waiting lists are lengthening. Outback areas are serviced by the efficient Royal Flying Doctor Service. Vigilance continues in the areas of hygiene, nutrition, and general living standards; current priorities are heart disease, injury prevention, personal fitness, Aboriginal health, and the prevention of cancers. Despite the popular image of Australians as athletic, 21% of over-25-year-olds are obese. Government encouragement of private health insurance has raised concerns over public health funding and quality.

SPENDING

GDP/cap. increase

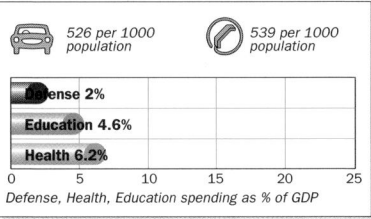

CONSUMPTION AND SPENDING

526 per 1000 population

539 per 1000 population

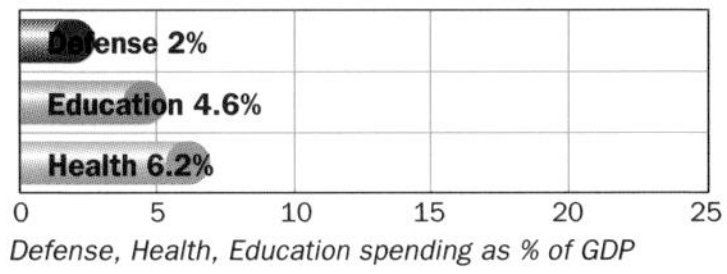
Defense 2%
Education 4.6%
Health 6.2%
0
5
10
15
20
25
Defense, Health, Education spending as % of GDP

Australians enjoy a relatively high standard of living. A benign climate and low population density allow for a comfortable life. Most people live in the cities along the southeast coast, in very large suburban areas. Recession in the late 1990s, however, upset the distribution of wealth, and by 2004 one in five people were living in what was defined as poverty, unable to maintain the average standard of living and earning less than the minimum wage. The unemployed, single-parent families, recent immigrants, and Aborigines fare worst.

WORLD RANKING

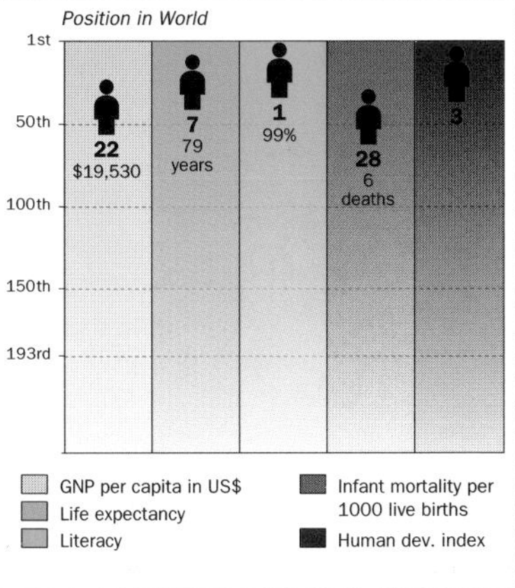
Position in World
1st
50th
100th
150th
193rd
22
$19,530
7
79
years
1
99%
28
6
deaths
3
GNP per capita in US$
Life expectancy
Literacy
Infant mortality per 1000 live births
Human dev. index

AUSTRIA

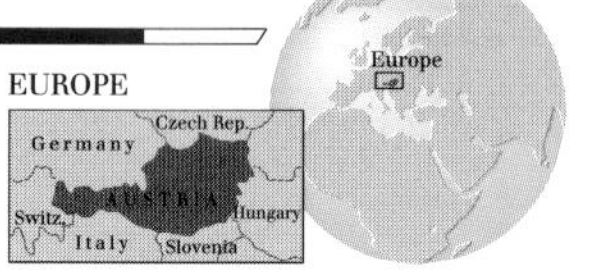
EUROPE
Europe
Germany
Czech Rep.
AUSTRIA
Switz.
Hungary
Italy
Slovenia

OFFICIAL NAME: Republic of Austria **CAPITAL:** Vienna
POPULATION: 8.1 million **CURRENCY:** Euro **OFFICIAL LANGUAGE:** German

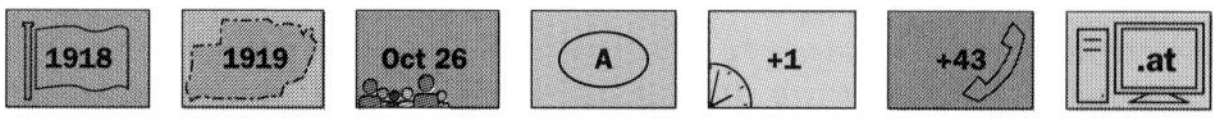
1918
1919
Oct 26
A
+1
+43
.at

LYING IN THE HEART OF EUROPE, Austria is dominated by the Alps in the west, while fertile plains make up the east and north. A separate republic after the collapse of the Austro-Hungarian Empire, Austria was absorbed into Hitler's Germany in 1938. It regained independence in 1955 after the departure of the last Soviet troops from the Allied Occupation Force. Its economy encompasses successful high-tech sectors, a tourist industry which attracts wealthier visitors, and a strong agricultural base. Having joined the EU in 1995, in 2002 it was one of 12 EU states to adopt the euro.

CLIMATE

Mountain/continental

WEATHER CHART FOR VIENNA

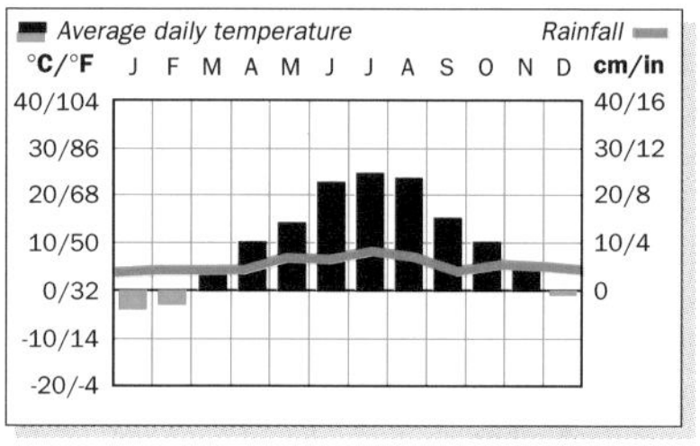
Average daily temperature
Rainfall
°C/°F
J F M A M J J A S O N D
cm/in
40/104
30/86
20/68
10/50
0/32
-10/14
-20/-4
40/16
30/12
20/8
10/4
0

Austria has a temperate continental climate. Alpine areas experience colder temperatures and higher precipitation.

TRANSPORTATION

Drive on right

Schwechat, Vienna 12.8m passengers

6 ships 29,900 grt

THE TRANSPORTATION NETWORK

200,000 km (124,274 miles)

1644 km (1022 miles)

5779 km (3591 miles)

358 km (222 miles)

Austria's central location in Europe has encouraged the development of a sophisticated communications and transportation network.

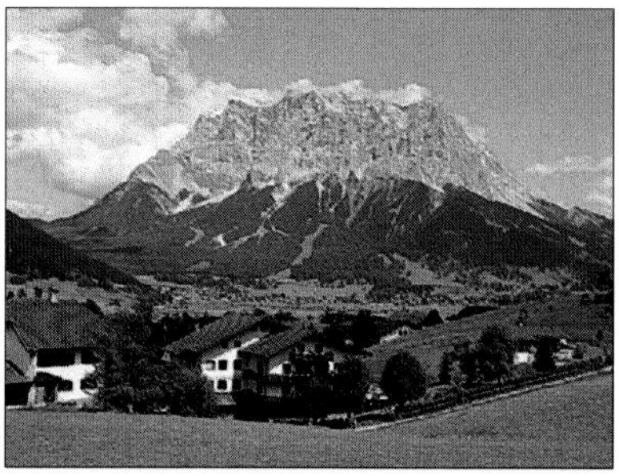

***The Tirol** is situated in the heart of Austria's Alps. It is the most mountainous region of all and attracts both winter and summer visitors.*

TOURISM

Visitors : Population 2.4:1

19.1m visitors

Up 3% in 2003

MAIN TOURIST ARRIVALS

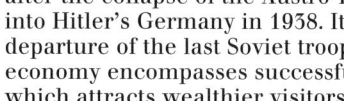

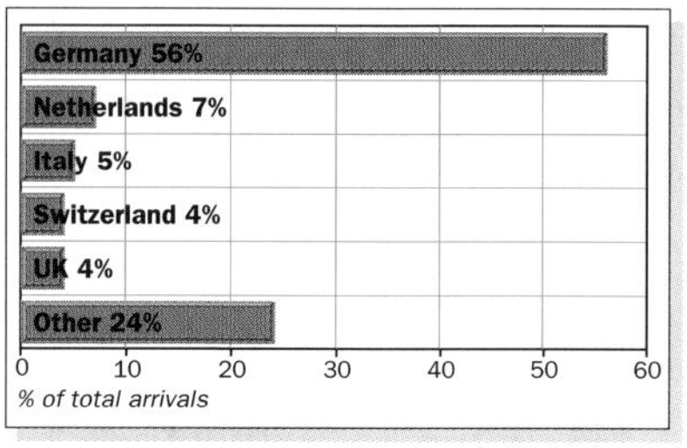
Germany 56%
Netherlands 7%
Italy 5%
Switzerland 4%
UK 4%
Other 24%
0
10
20
30
40
50
60
% of total arrivals

Well-developed Alpine skiing and winter sports resorts now attract over half of visitors. Many resorts, such as St. Anton and Kitzbühel, cater for the top end of the market. In the summer season, which peaks in July and August, tourists visit the scenic Tirol and the lakes around Bad Ischl. Year-round major attractions are Vienna, with its coffee houses and the Prater park (whose Ferris wheel was immortalized in *The Third Man*), and Salzburg, Austria's second city. The latter is internationally famous for its summer music festival and as the birthplace of Mozart.

AUSTRIA

Total Area : 83 858 sq. km (32 378 sq. miles)

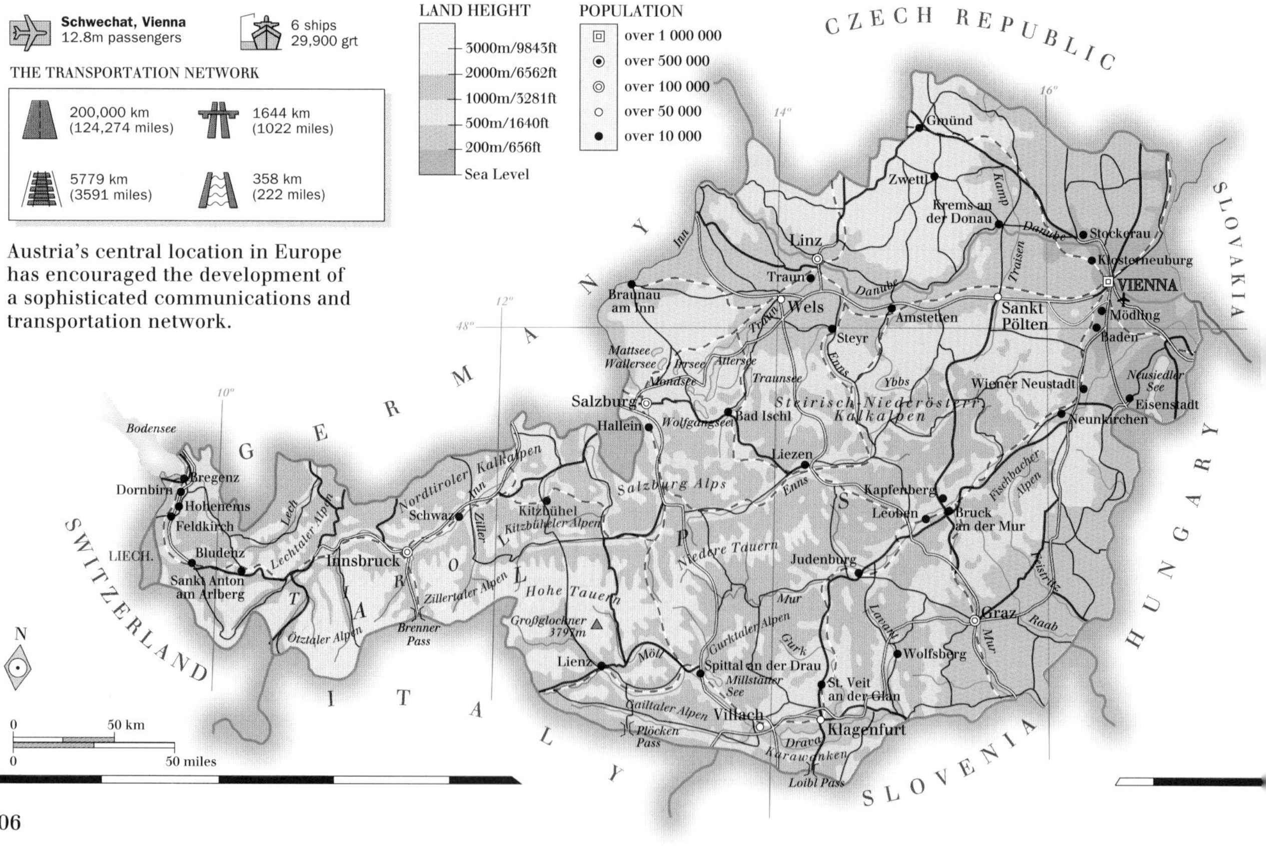
LAND HEIGHT
3000m/9843ft
2000m/6562ft
1000m/3281ft
500m/1640ft
200m/656ft
Sea Level
POPULATION
over 1 000 000
over 500 000
over 100 000
over 50 000
over 10 000
CZECH REPUBLIC
SLOVAKIA
HUNGARY
SLOVENIA
ITALY
SWITZERLAND
GERMANY
LIECH.
Bodensee
Gmünd
Zwettl
Krems an der Donau
Kamp
Danube
Stockerau
Klosterneuburg
VIENNA
Mödling
Baden
Linz
Traun
Wels
Braunau am Inn
Inn
Amstetten
Sankt Pölten
Traisen
Steyr
Enns
Ybbs
Mattsee
Wallersee
Irrsee
Attersee
Mondsee
Traunsee
Salzburg
Hallein
Wolfgangsee
Bad Ischl
Steirisch-Niederösterr. Kalkalpen
Wiener Neustadt
Neusiedler See
Eisenstadt
Neunkirchen
Liezen
Salzburg Alps
Kapfenberg
Leoben
Bruck an der Mur
Fischbacher Alpen
Bregenz
Dornbirn
Hohenems
Feldkirch
Bludenz
Sankt Anton am Arlberg
Lech
Lechtaler Alpen
Innsbruck
Nordtiroler Kalkalpen
Schwaz
Zillertal
Kitzbühel
Kitzbüheler Alpen
Zillertaler Alpen
Hohe Tauern
Niedere Tauern
Judenburg
Ötztaler Alpen
Brenner Pass
Großglockner 3797m
Mur
Gurktaler Alpen
Gurk
Lavant
Graz
Raab
Wolfsberg
Lienz
Möll
Spittal an der Drau
Millstätter See
St. Veit an der Glan
Gailtaler Alpen
Villach
Klagenfurt
Plöcken Pass
Drava
Karawanken
Loibl Pass
N
0
50 km
0
50 miles

PEOPLE

Pop. density medium

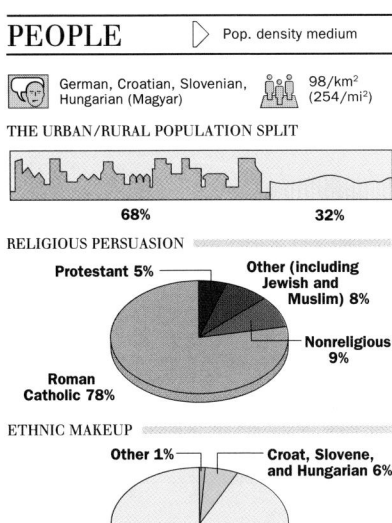

German, Croatian, Slovenian, Hungarian (Magyar)

98/km² (254/mi²)

THE URBAN/RURAL POPULATION SPLIT

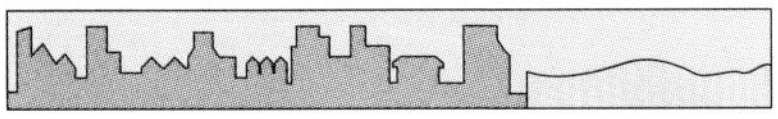
68%
32%

RELIGIOUS PERSUASION

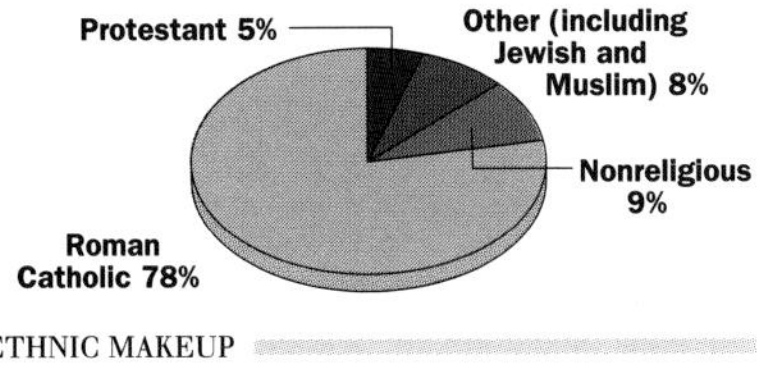
Protestant 5%
Other (including Jewish and Muslim) 8%
Nonreligious 9%
Roman Catholic 78%

ETHNIC MAKEUP

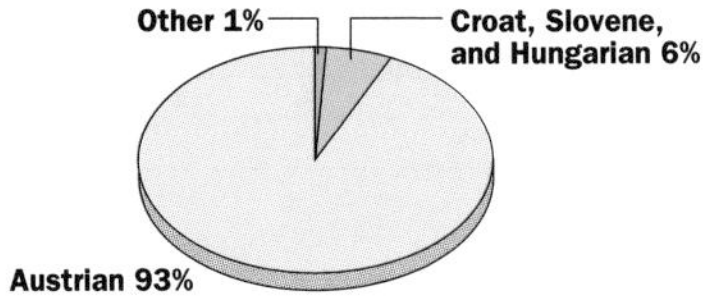
Other 1%
Croat, Slovene, and Hungarian 6%
Austrian 93%

Austrian society is homogeneous. Almost all Austrians are German speakers, though Austrians like to stress their distinctive identity in relation to Germany. Minorities are few; there are some ethnic Slovenes, Croats, and Hungarians in the south and east, as well as some Roma communities. These minorities have been augmented by large numbers of immigrants from eastern Europe and one-time refugees from the former Yugoslavia. The result has been a perceptible increase in ethnic tension, particularly as the far right claims that migrants are taking jobs from the local population.

The nuclear family is the norm, and it is common for both parents to work. While gender equality is enshrined in the constitution, in practice society is still strongly patriarchal.

Young Austrians tend to live in the parental home until they complete their higher education. This reflects the relatively long time taken to complete university degrees and the lack of maintenance grants from the state for students.

Austria is nominally a Roman Catholic country, but it is socially less conservative than the Catholic *Länder* (states) in Germany. Many marriages end in divorce; the proportion in 2002 was as high as 44 per 100.

POPULATION AGE BREAKDOWN

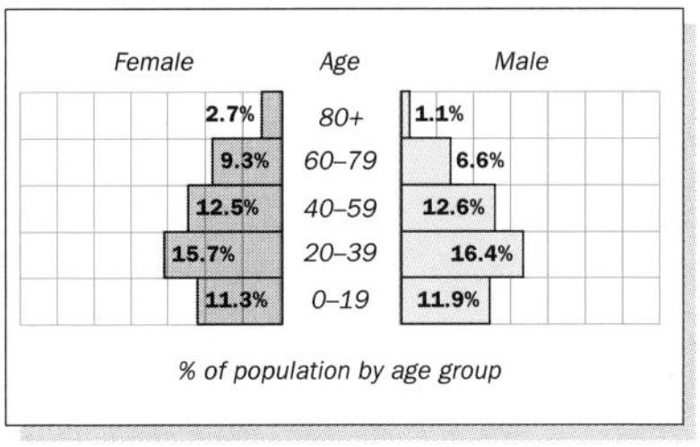
Female
Age
Male
2.7%
80+
1.1%
9.3%
60–79
6.6%
12.5%
40–59
12.6%
15.7%
20–39
16.4%
11.3%
0–19
11.9%
% of population by age group

POLITICS

Multiparty elections

L. House 2002/2006
U. House Varies by province

President Heinz Fischer

AT THE LAST ELECTION

National Council 183 seats

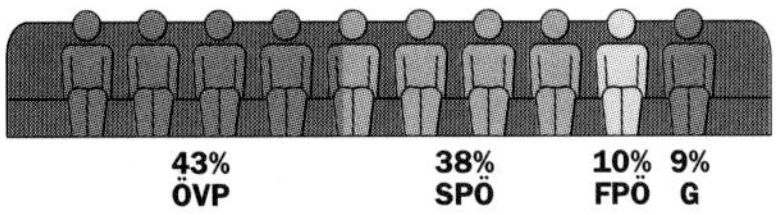
43% ÖVP
38% SPÖ
10% FPÖ
9% G

ÖVP = Austrian People's Party
SPÖ = Social Democratic Party of Austria
FPÖ = Freedom Party of Austria **G** = Greens

Federal Council 64 seats

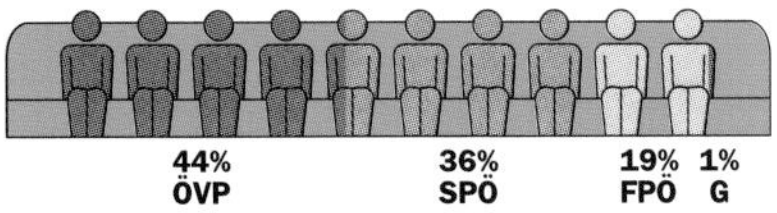
44% ÖVP
36% SPÖ
19% FPÖ
1% G

Austria is a federal, multiparty democracy. The chancellor (premier) holds real executive power.

PROFILE

The socialist SPÖ and the conservative ÖVP have dominated postwar politics. They governed Austria in coalition for 21 years until 1966, and then, in 1987, after a period when the SPÖ had dominated, formed the "grand coalition," in power until 1999. Their hold on power, with no real alternative, reached into all areas of public life. The far-right FPÖ achieved a breakthrough in elections in 1999, when it came equal second with the ÖVP. A new right-wing coalition of the ÖVP and the FPÖ, headed by ÖVP leader Wolfgang Schüssel, was met with regional and international criticism. FPÖ leader Jörg Haider drew strong condemnation, having openly expressed admiration for some of Hitler's policies. He remained a driving force behind the party, despite resigning formal leadership in 2000. In September 2002 the ruling coalition collapsed, prompting fresh elections. Though the ÖVP's popularity reached a 40-year high, and support for the FPÖ dwindled, the coalition was re-formed in 2003 when the ÖVP could find no other partner. Heinz Fischer (SPÖ) was elected president in April 2004.

The nine provincial assemblies and governments have considerable powers. Vienna, with provincial status, has long been dominated by the SPÖ.

MAIN POLITICAL ISSUE
Enlargement of the EU

With the accession to the EU of ten more states in May 2004, Austria moved from the edge of the EU toward the center. It shares a land border with four of the new members, and is well placed to take advantage of the opening up of the economies of the new member states. Concerns about an influx of cheap labor from eastern Europe led the government, like most other existing EU members, to impose a seven-year transitional period before workers from these countries can gain access to the Austrian labor market.

***Heinz Fischer,** of the opposition SPÖ, was elected president in 2004.*

***Wolfgang Schüssel,** ÖVP chancellor since 2000.*

WORLD AFFAIRS

Joined UN in 1955

EU | CE | PfP | OECD | OSCE

Despite the importance of relations with Germany, Austria's powerful northern neighbor and main trading partner, there has been a conscious policy of stressing Austria's independence and creating some diplomatic distance. Austria is keen to maintain its relationship with the US, which is reinforced by Austria's role as supplier of small arms to the US Army. The inclusion of the far-right FPÖ in the Austrian government in 2000 provoked the imposition of diplomatic sanctions by EU states for seven months.

Austria's status as a neutral state has begun to be questioned since it joined the EU and NATO's Partnership for Peace program. Austria is part of the Schengen Convention ending border controls between participating EU members. Its geopolitical position gives it considerable influence in eastern Europe, and exports to the region trebled in the 1990s. The ÖVP strongly supported the eastward enlargement of the EU which took place in May 2004.

AID

Donor

$520m (donations)

Down 2% in 2002

New projects are now assessed for their impact on the environment and on gender issues. Austria targets funds to its east European neighbors and the poorest developing countries. A major exporter to the former Yugoslavia before the wars there in the 1990s, Austria has since held a key role in regional reconstruction.

CHRONOLOGY

Austria came under the control of the Habsburgs in 1273. In 1867, the Dual Monarchy of Austria-Hungary was formed under Habsburg rule. Defeat in World War I in 1918 led to the breakup of the Habsburg empire and the formation of the Republic of Austria.

- ❑ **1934** Chancellor Dollfuss dismisses parliament and starts imprisoning social democrats, communists, and National Socialist (Nazi) Party members. Nazis attempt coup.
- ❑ **1938** The Anschluss – Austria incorporated into Germany by Hitler.
- ❑ **1945** Austria occupied by Soviet, British, US, and French forces. Elections result in ÖVP–SPÖ coalition.
- ❑ **1950** Attempted coup by Communist Party fails. Marshall Aid helps economic recovery.
- ❑ **1955** Occupying troops withdrawn. Austria recognized as a neutral sovereign state.
- ❑ **1971** SPÖ government formed under Chancellor Bruno Kreisky, who dominates Austrian politics for 12 years.
- ❑ **1983** Socialists and FPÖ form coalition government under Fred Sinowatz.
- ❑ **1986** Kurt Waldheim, former UN secretary-general, elected president, despite war crimes allegations. Franz Vranitzky replaces Sinowatz as federal chancellor. Nationalist Jörg Haider becomes FPÖ leader, prompting SPÖ to pull out of government. Elections produce stalemate
- ❑ **1987** January, "grand coalition" of SPÖ–ÖVP formed.
- ❑ **1990** ÖVP loses support in elections.
- ❑ **1992** Thomas Klestil (ÖVP) elected president. Elections confirm some traditional ÖVP supporters defecting to FPÖ.
- ❑ **1995** Austria joins EU. Early elections; SPÖ and ÖVP increase representation; "grand coalition" re-forms in early 1996.
- ❑ **1997** Vranitzky resigns; replaced by Viktor Klima.
- ❑ **1999** Haider's FPÖ wins 40% of votes in Carinthia regional poll, and is equal second with ÖVP in general election in October; SPÖ remains largest party.
- ❑ **2000** ÖVP accepts FPÖ into coalition: political crisis. EU imposes diplomatic sanctions, lifted after seven months.
- ❑ **2002** Euro fully adopted. FPÖ quits coalition. ÖVP wins fresh elections.
- ❑ **2003** ÖVP–FPÖ coalition re-formed.
- ❑ **2004** Heinz Fischer (SPÖ) president.

DEFENSE

▷ Compulsory military service

$1.7bn

Up 16% in 2002

The 1955 State Treaty, which restored Austria's independence, enshrined the country's neutrality. However, it has participated in NATO's Partnership for Peace program since 1995.

Despite the small size of Austria's armed forces, its arms industry is strong. It not only meets most of the hardware needs of its own army, but also exports arms to the US and other countries.

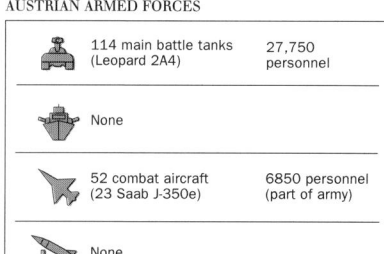

AUSTRIAN ARMED FORCES

114 main battle tanks (Leopard 2A4)	27,750 personnel
None	
52 combat aircraft (23 Saab J-350e)	6850 personnel (part of army)
None	

ECONOMICS

▷ Inflation 1.8% p.a. (1990–2001)

$192bn

0.822 euros (0.871)

SCORE CARD

❑ World GNP Ranking	21st
❑ GNP per Capita	$23,860
❑ Balance of Payments	$838m
❑ Inflation	1.8%
❑ Unemployment	4%

EXPORTS

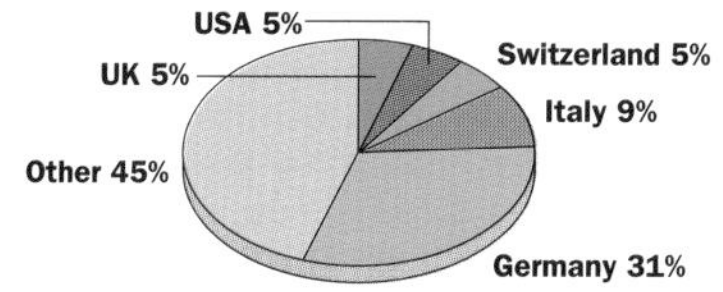

USA 5%
UK 5%
Switzerland 5%
Italy 9%
Other 45%
Germany 31%

IMPORTS

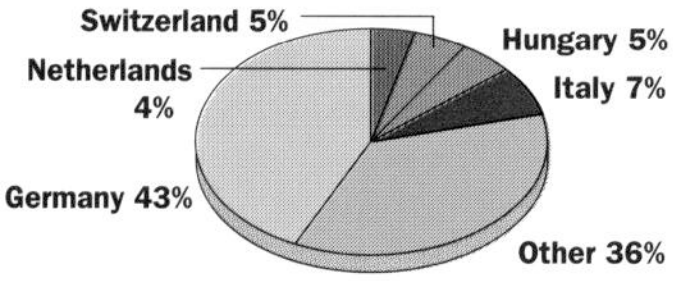

Switzerland 5%
Netherlands 4%
Hungary 5%
Italy 7%
Germany 43%
Other 36%

Strengths

Large manufacturing base. Strong chemical and petrochemical industries. Electrical engineering sector, textiles, and wood processing industries. Highly skilled labor force. Tourism is an important foreign currency earner.

Weaknesses

Lacks natural resources. Reliant on imported raw materials, particularly oil and gas. Process of introducing greater competition and deregulation has been slow.

Profile

Austria's industrial and high-tech sector is well developed and contributes over a quarter of GDP. Some services, notably tourism, are highly sophisticated and profitable, though tourism receipts have been down in recent years.

A recession in the early 1990s was reversed by a rapid increase in exports to eastern Europe and Germany and by rising domestic demand. The impact of

ECONOMIC PERFORMANCE INDICATOR

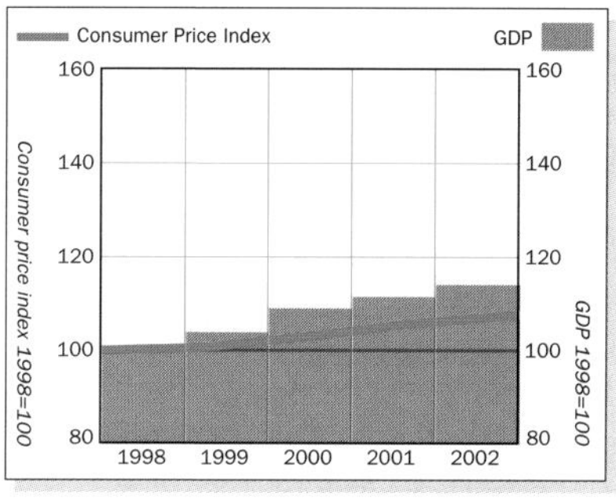

Consumer Price Index
GDP
160
140
120
100
80
Consumer price index 1998=100
GDP 1998=100
1998
1999
2000
2001
2002

EU membership has been largely positive. Foreign investment has increased, as more multinationals locate their headquarters for east European operations in Austria. Fiscal stabilization enabled Austria to meet the criteria necessary for it fully to adopt the euro in 2002. Since then, economic growth has been higher than in other eurozone countries, but not enough to reduce unemployment markedly, leading to concerns about the use of cheaper foreign labor. As in other countries in western Europe, the increasing age of the population obliged the government to reform the pension system, reducing payments and postponing retirement.

AUSTRIA : MAJOR BUSINESSES

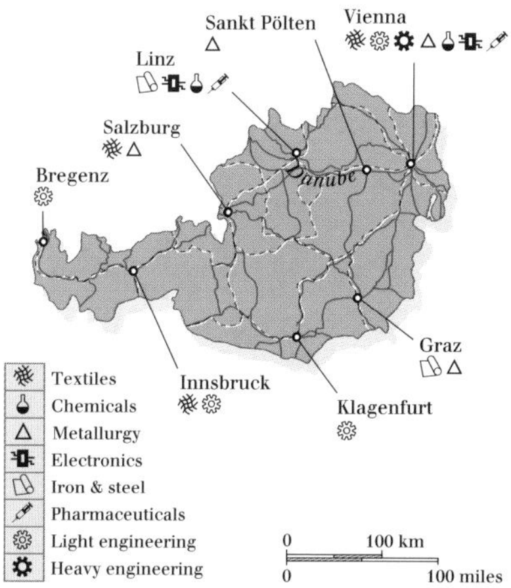

Sankt Pölten
Vienna
Linz
Salzburg
Bregenz
Danube
Graz
Innsbruck
Klagenfurt
Textiles
Chemicals
Metallurgy
Electronics
Iron & steel
Pharmaceuticals
Light engineering
Heavy engineering
0
100 km
0
100 miles

RESOURCES

Electric power 18.2m kW

2755 tonnes

19,328 b/d (reserves 78m barrels)

3.3m pigs, 2.07m cattle, 11m chickens

Iron, coal, magnesite, zinc, lead, oil, gas

ELECTRICITY GENERATION

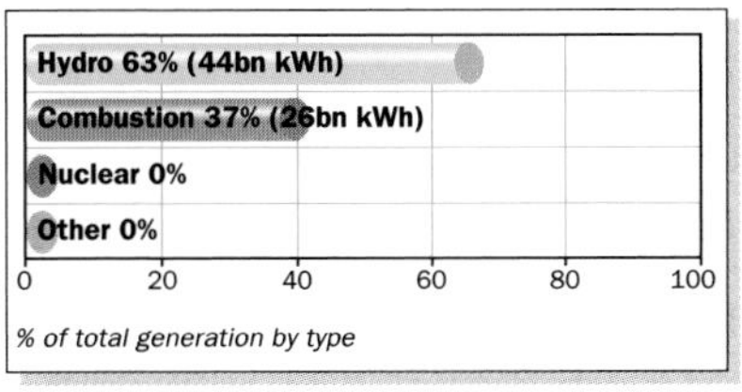

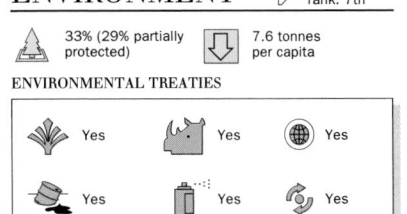

Hydro 63% (44bn kWh)
Combustion 37% (26bn kWh)
Nuclear 0%
Other 0%
0
20
40
60
80
100
% of total generation by type

AUSTRIA : LAND USE

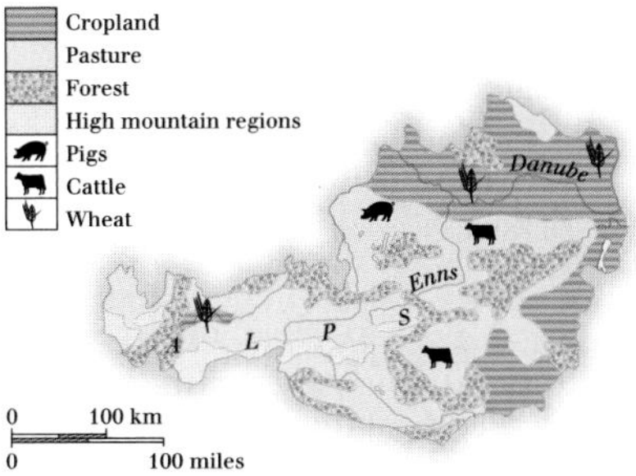

Cropland
Pasture
Forest
High mountain regions
Pigs
Cattle
Wheat
Danube
Enns
A
L
P
S
0 100 km
0 100 miles

Austria has few resources, and only iron ore is extracted for commercial purposes. It has to import a large amount of its energy. Russia is a key energy supplier, and gas is provided via pipelines running through the Czech Republic and Slovakia. The bulk of iron ore and raw steel for Austria's industry have traditionally come from Russia and Germany.

ENVIRONMENT

Sustainability rank: 7th

33% (29% partially protected)

7.6 tonnes per capita

ENVIRONMENTAL TREATIES

Yes	Yes	Yes
Yes	Yes	Yes

Environmental awareness is high and the government invests nearly 3% of GDP in environmental protection. Roughly half of all domestic waste is separated for recycling, with heavy fines for failing to observe regulations. The safety of nuclear reactors in the neighboring Czech Republic, Slovakia, and Slovenia is a major concern.

MEDIA

TV ownership high

Daily newspaper circulation 296 per 1000 people

PUBLISHING AND BROADCAST MEDIA

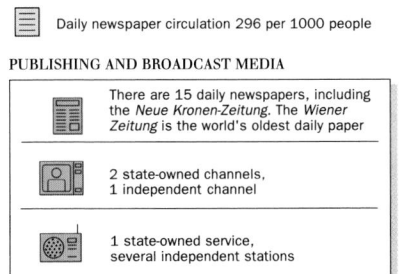

There are 15 daily newspapers, including the *Neue Kronen-Zeitung*. The *Wiener Zeitung* is the world's oldest daily paper

2 state-owned channels, 1 independent channel

1 state-owned service, several independent stations

TV and radio are dominated by the Austrian Broadcasting Company (ÖRF), though its monopoly is being eroded. Private radio stations began broadcasting in 1998 and the first commercial TV channel, ATV, was granted a national license in 2000. Regional newspapers are very popular. The government-run *Wiener Zeitung*, founded in 1703, claims to be the world's oldest daily.

CRIME

No death penalty

8114 prisoners

Down 7% in 2001

CRIME RATES

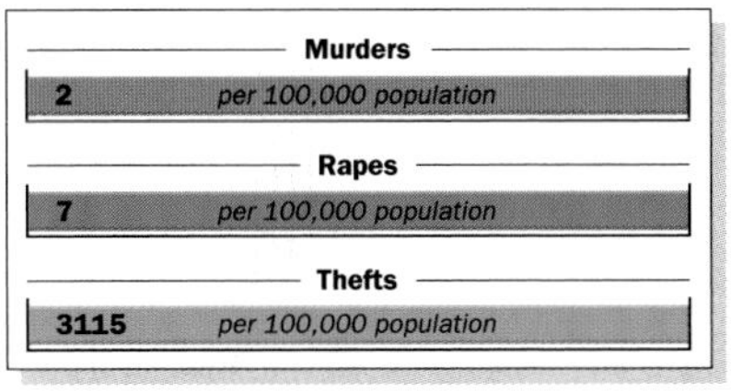

Murders
2 per 100,000 population
Rapes
7 per 100,000 population
Thefts
3115 per 100,000 population

Austria's crime rate is generally climbing, with the number of burglaries rising in particular. The arrival of the Russian mafia in Vienna has led to an increase in money laundering.

EDUCATION

School leaving age: 15

99%

254,341 students

THE EDUCATION SYSTEM

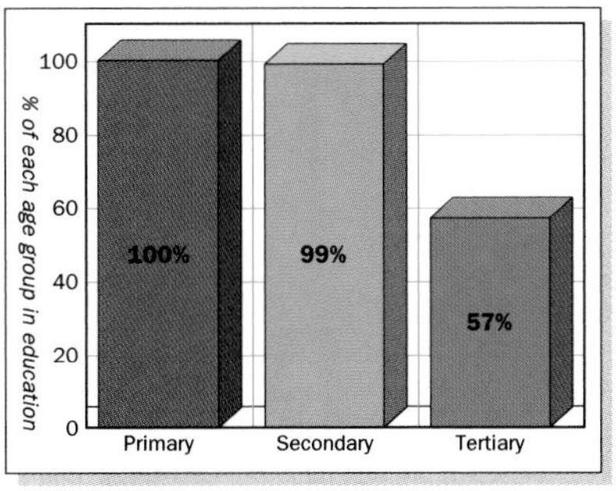

100
80
60
40
20
0
% of each age group in education
100%
99%
57%
Primary
Secondary
Tertiary

Some 9.5% of government spending is on education. Secondary education is divided between lower schools (11–15) and higher schools (15–18). Children showing early academic aptitude can attend a *Gymnasium* from age 11. Students hoping to study at university must pass the *Reifeprüfung* or *Matura*. An alternative vocational qualification, the *Berufsreifeprüfung*, was introduced for 18-year-olds in 1997.

HEALTH

Welfare state health benefits

1 per 312 people

Heart and cerebrovascular diseases, cancers

Funding for health has shifted to a more streamlined government budget. Private spending is becoming more significant and accounts for around a third of the total, as patients increasingly choose to use the private health sector to avoid waiting lists for operations. Control of hospitals and other facilities is being decentralized to the regional *Länder* (states).

SPENDING

GDP/cap. increase

CONSUMPTION AND SPENDING

495 per 1000 population

489 per 1000 population

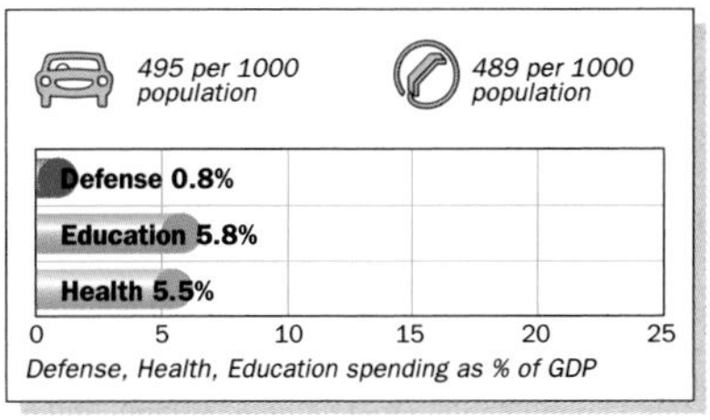

Defense 0.8%
Education 5.8%
Health 5.5%
0
5
10
15
20
25
Defense, Health, Education spending as % of GDP

Austria has retained many of its traditional social divisions. Inherited wealth is still respected above earned wealth, and there is less social mobility than in neighboring Germany.

Austrians have become less cautious with their money, and a previously high savings rate has fallen dramatically. Relatively few Austrians own stocks and shares, and most companies are dominated by a single shareholder. Legislation in 2000 banned anonymous savings accounts, a system unique in the EU to Austria which, it had been argued, encouraged money laundering and insider dealing. Government bonds offer low rates of interest and the property market is weak; many people, particularly in Vienna, tend to rent rather than buy their apartments. Asylum seekers, many from Afghanistan, Iraq, and the former Yugoslavia, form the poorest group in Austrian society.

WORLD RANKING

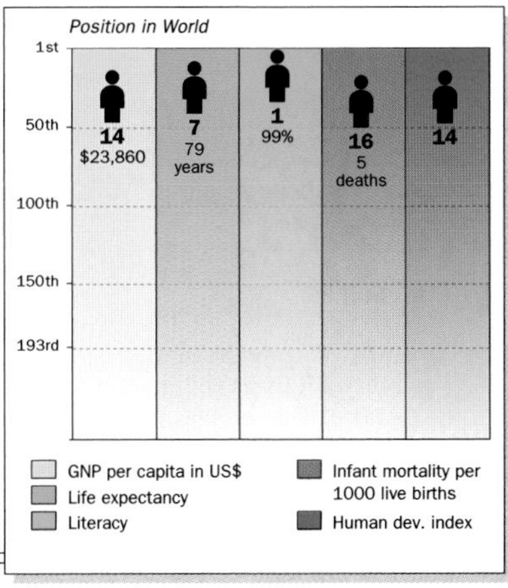

Position in World
1st
50th
100th
150th
193rd
14
$23,860
7
79 years
1
99%
16
5 deaths
14
GNP per capita in US$
Life expectancy
Literacy
Infant mortality per 1000 live births
Human dev. index

A

AZERBAIJAN

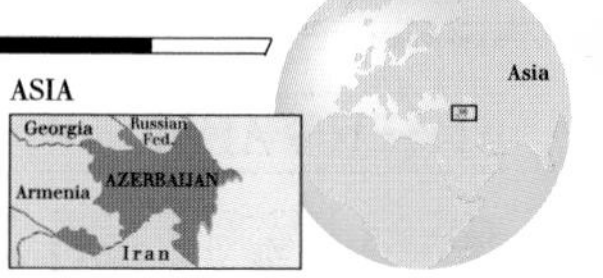
ASIA
Georgia
Russian Fed.
Armenia
AZERBAIJAN
Iran
Asia

OFFICIAL NAME: Republic of Azerbaijan **CAPITAL:** Baku
POPULATION: 8.4 million **CURRENCY:** Manat **OFFICIAL LANGUAGE:** Azeri

1991 | 1991 | May 28 | AZ | +4 | +994 | .az

Landscape typical of the Lesser Caucasus mountains near Qazax in the extreme northwest of Azerbaijan.

SITUATED ON THE WEST COAST of the Caspian Sea, Azerbaijan was the first Soviet republic to declare independence. The issue of the disputed enclave of Nagorno Karabakh, whose Armenian population seeks secession, led to full-scale war (1988–1994) and is still a dominant concern. Over 200,000 refugees, and more than twice as many internally displaced, added to the problems of the troubled economy. Azerbaijan's oil wealth, however, gives it long-term potential.

CLIMATE

Mountain/steppe

WEATHER CHART FOR BAKU

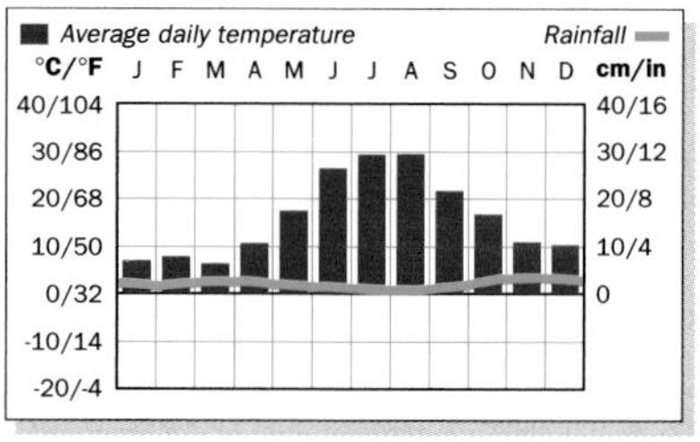
Average daily temperature
Rainfall
°C/°F J F M A M J J A S O N D cm/in
40/104
30/86
20/68
10/50
0/32
-10/14
-20/-4
40/16
30/12
20/8
10/4
0

Coastal areas are subtropical, but bitter winters inland have become a life-or-death issue for thousands of refugees.

TRANSPORTATION

Drive on right

Baku Bina

285 ships 633,200 grt

THE TRANSPORTATION NETWORK

23,012 km (14,299 miles)	None
2122 km (1319 miles)	None

Buses provide the most efficient public transportation. Access to the Naxçivan exclave is by air or via Iran.

TOURISM

Visitors : Population 1:10

834,000 visitors

Up 9% in 2002

MAIN TOURIST ARRIVALS

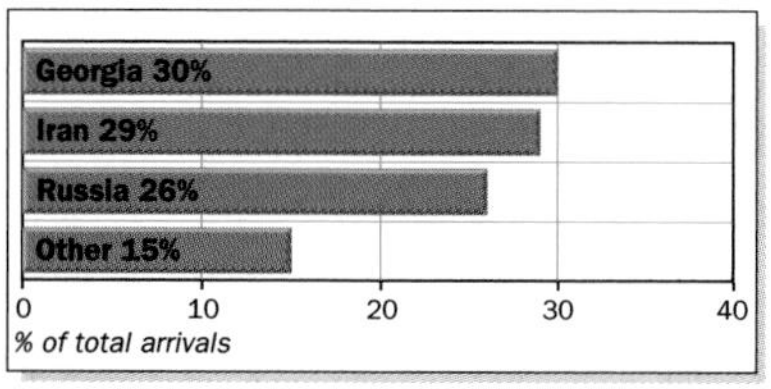
Georgia 30%
Iran 29%
Russia 26%
Other 15%
0
10
20
30
40
% of total arrivals

The Nagorno Karabakh conflict, and anti-Western feelings (Azerbaijan perceived the West as taking the Armenian side), kept tourist numbers low for many years, though arrivals have increased since 1999.

PEOPLE

Pop. density medium

Azeri, Russian

97/km² (251/mi²)

THE URBAN/RURAL POPULATION SPLIT

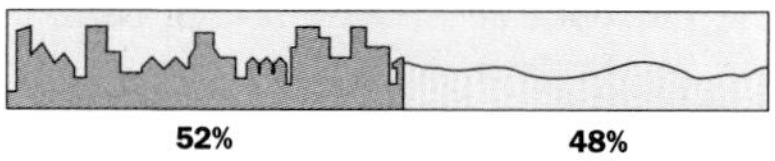
52%
48%

ETHNIC MAKEUP

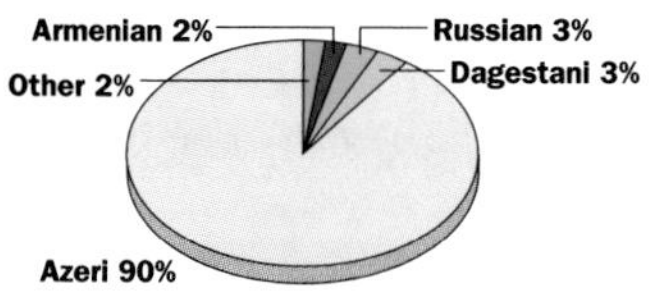
Armenian 2%
Russian 3%
Other 2%
Dagestani 3%
Azeri 90%

The Azeris are a Shi'a Muslim people with close ethnic links to the Turks. Before the collapse of the Soviet Union, and the violence of the 1990s, Orthodox Christian Armenians and Russians accounted for 11% of the population. Now ethnic Armenians are concentrated in the Nagorno Karabakh enclave and operate de facto independence.

Women, who were once prominent in the ruling party, lost political status after the fall of communism; they are slowly regaining their position.

POLITICS

Multiparty elections

2000/2005

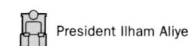

President Ilham Aliyev

AT THE LAST ELECTION

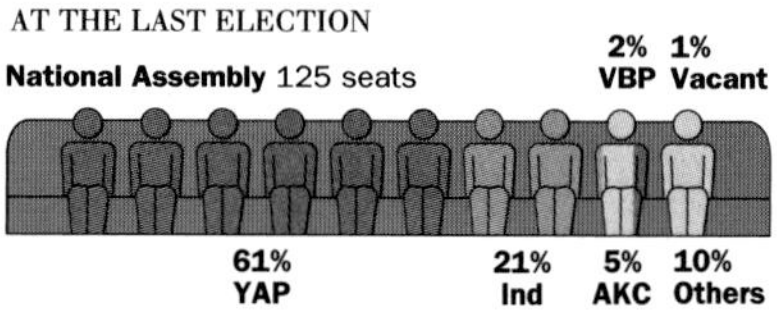
National Assembly 125 seats
2% VBP
1% Vacant
61% YAP
21% Ind
5% AKC
10% Others

YAP = New Azerbaijan Party **Ind** = Independents
AKC = Azerbaijan Popular Front **VBP** = Civic Solidarity Party
Vacant = Seat reserved for member from Nagorno Karabakh

Azerbaijan became an independent democracy amid war with Armenian forces in the early 1990s. A lasting solution to tensions is elusive. The YAP, in power since 1995, was controversially reelected in 2000. It supported the aging, and visibly ailing, President Heydar Aliyev, through two consecutive terms and backed the succession of his son Ilham in 2003. The latter's election was heavily criticized by the opposition and led to violent clashes.

AZERBAIJAN

Total Area : 86 600 sq. km (33 436 sq. miles)

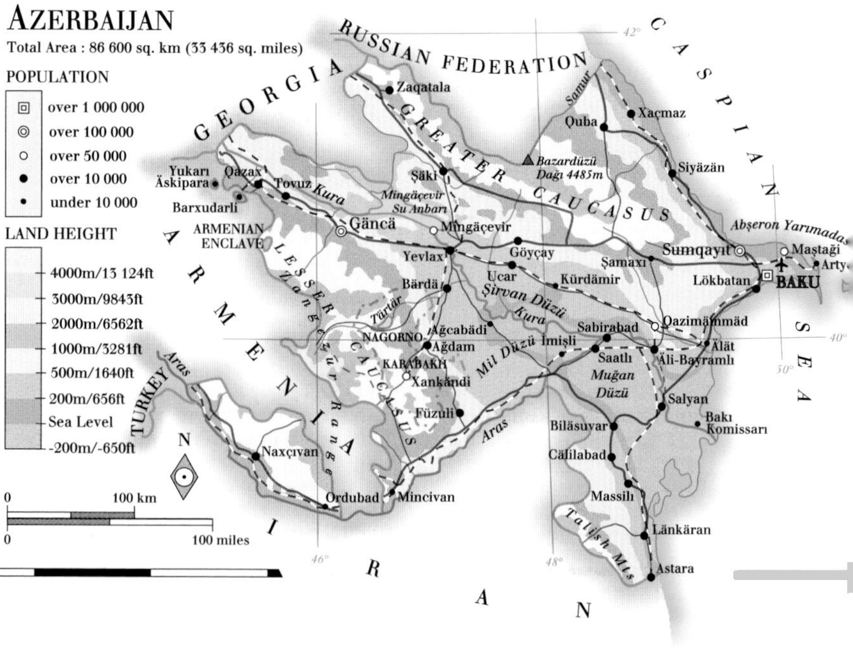
POPULATION
over 1 000 000
over 100 000
over 50 000
over 10 000
under 10 000
LAND HEIGHT
4000m/13 124ft
3000m/9843ft
2000m/6562ft
1000m/3281ft
500m/1640ft
200m/656ft
Sea Level
-200m/-650ft
0
100 km
0
100 miles
RUSSIAN FEDERATION
GEORGIA
CASPIAN SEA
ARMENIA
IRAN
TURKEY
ARMENIAN ENCLAVE
NAGORNO-KARABAKH
GREATER CAUCASUS
LESSER CAUCASUS
Zaqatala
Xaçmaz
Quba
Bazardüzü Dağı 4485m
Siyäzän
Şäki
Yukarı Äskipara
Qazax
Tovuz
Kura
Barxudarlı
Mingäçevir Su Anbarı
Gäncä
Mingäçevir
Göyçay
Abşeron Yarımadası
Sumqayıt
Maştağı
Artyom
Şamaxı
Yevlax
Bärdä
Ucar
Kürdämir
Lökbatan
BAKU
Şirvan Düzü
Qazimämmäd
Ağcabädi
Ağdam
Sabirabad
Älät
İmişli
Saatlı
Äli-Bayramlı
Xankändi
Mil Düzü
Muğan Düzü
Salyan
Füzuli
Bakı Komissarı
Aras
Biläsuvar
Cälilabad
Naxçıvan
Ordubad
Mincivan
Massılı
Länkäran
Astara
Talısh Mts
Tärtär
Samur
Zangezur Range

WORLD AFFAIRS

Joined UN in 1992

CIS | CE | EAPC | OIC | OSCE

Relations with Armenia remain the central issue. Azerbaijan, despite its Shi'a majority, sees Turkey as a bridge to the West. It wants to join NATO and has close ties to the EU. The West, Iran (which has a large, ethnically related Azari population), and Russia are interested in Caspian oil fields.

AID

Recipient

$349m (receipts)

Up 50% in 2002

Japan is the biggest donor. A pro-Armenia US Congress allowed only limited humanitarian aid in 1992–2002.

DEFENSE

Compulsory military service

$851m

Up 3% in 2002

Part of NATO's Partnership for Peace program since 1994, Azerbaijan has sent small peacekeeping contingents to Kosovo, Afghanistan, and Iraq.

ECONOMICS

Inflation 97% p.a. (1990–2000)

$5.8bn

4911 manats (4921)

SCORE CARD

❑ World GNP Ranking	108th
❑ GNP per Capita	$710
❑ Balance of Payments	–$768m
❑ Inflation	2.8%
❑ Unemployment	1%

Strengths

Extensive oil and natural gas reserves starting to come onstream. Oil pipeline to Turkey under construction. Iron, copper, lead, and salt deposits. Cotton and silk.

Weaknesses

Antiquated Soviet-era industry. Poor infrastructure; corruption. Fallout from Nagorno Karabakh conflict still drains state resources.

EXPORTS

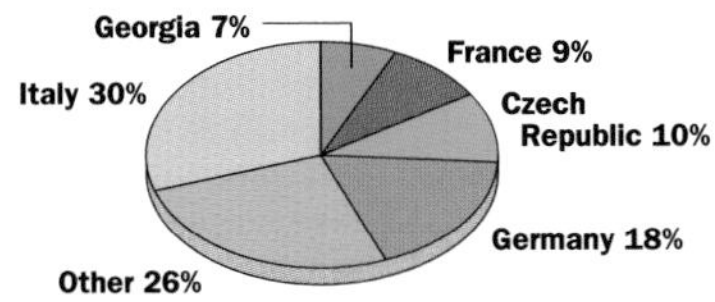
Georgia 7%
France 9%
Italy 30%
Czech Republic 10%
Germany 18%
Other 26%

IMPORTS

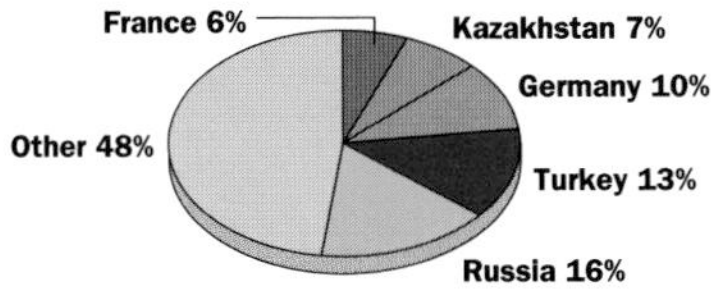
France 6%
Kazakhstan 7%
Germany 10%
Other 48%
Turkey 13%
Russia 16%

RESOURCES

Electric power 5.2m kW

11,063 tonnes

313,000 b/d (reserves 7bn barrels)

6.39m sheep, 2.18m cattle, 16.7m chickens

Iron, bauxite, copper, lead, zinc, limestone, salt, oil, gas

Relatively neglected in the Soviet period, Azerbaijan's Caspian Sea oil fields have attracted international interest. The shallow-water Guneshli field alone has over four million barrels of reserves. Offshore natural gas is also plentiful.

ENVIRONMENT

Sustainability rank: 114th

6% (3% partially protected)

3.6 tonnes per capita

Under the Soviet regime oil pollution devastated the Caspian Sea, and pesticides were massively overused in agriculture. Major rivers suffer heavy pollution from Georgia and Armenia. Lack of funds restricts action.

MEDIA

TV ownership high

Daily newspaper circulation 10 per 1000 people

PUBLISHING AND BROADCAST MEDIA

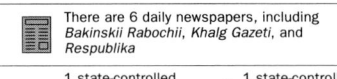

There are 6 daily newspapers, including *Bakinskii Rabochii*, *Khalg Gazeti*, and *Respublika*

1 state-controlled service, 5 independent stations

1 state-controlled service, 4 independent stations

From 2002, publications no longer required licenses from the state, but press intimidation still takes place.

CRIME

No death penalty

17,795 prisoners

Up 7% in 2000–2002

The judicial system returned to political control in 1993. Criminality is a particular problem in camps for those displaced in the Nagorno Karabakh conflict. Elsewhere, there is a low rate of violent crime, but assaults in the street have become less rare.

EDUCATION

School leaving age: 16

97%

163,305 students

When it came to power in the mid-1990s, the YAP began reversing communist influence over education policy, which had been particularly noticeable in the teaching of history. Baku State is the largest of an increasing number of universities.

HEALTH

Welfare state health benefits

1 per 278 people

Circulatory and heart diseases, cancers

The already poor health care system effectively collapsed as a result of war and the transition to a market economy.

CHRONOLOGY

Under consecutive Persian, Ottoman, and Russian influences, Azerbaijan, one of the world's major oil producers in 1900, attained independence in 1918.

- ❑ **1920** Red Army invades. Soviet republic established.
- ❑ **1922** Incorporated in Transcaucasian Soviet Federative Socialist Republic (TSFSR).
- ❑ **1930** Forced collectivization of agriculture.
- ❑ **1936** TSFSR disbanded; Azerbaijan a full union republic (ASSR).
- ❑ **1945** Attempted annexation of Azari region of Iran.
- ❑ **1985** Gorbachev tackles corruption in Communist Party of Azerbaijan.
- ❑ **1988** Nagorno Karabakh seeks unification with Armenia.
- ❑ **1990** Nagorno Karabakh attempts secession. Soviet troops move in.
- ❑ **1991** Independence.
- ❑ **1993** Heydar Aliyev president.
- ❑ **1994** Cease-fire with Armenia.
- ❑ **1995, 2000** General elections. Noncommunist YAP in power.
- ❑ **2004** Ilham Aliyev, son of Heydar, elected president.

SPENDING

GDP/cap. increase

CONSUMPTION AND SPENDING

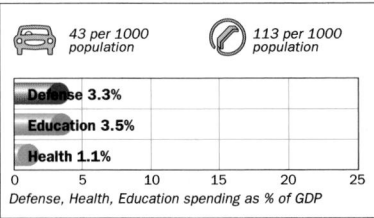

43 per 1000 population

113 per 1000 population

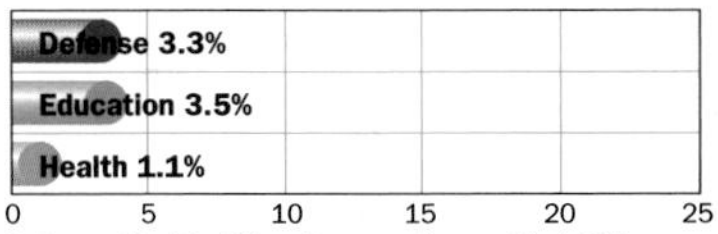
Defense 3.3%
Education 3.5%
Health 1.1%
0
5
10
15
20
25

Defense, Health, Education spending as % of GDP

New oil revenues are threatening to create a nouveau riche elite without reaching the 60% of Azerbaijan's population currently living in poverty.

WORLD RANKING

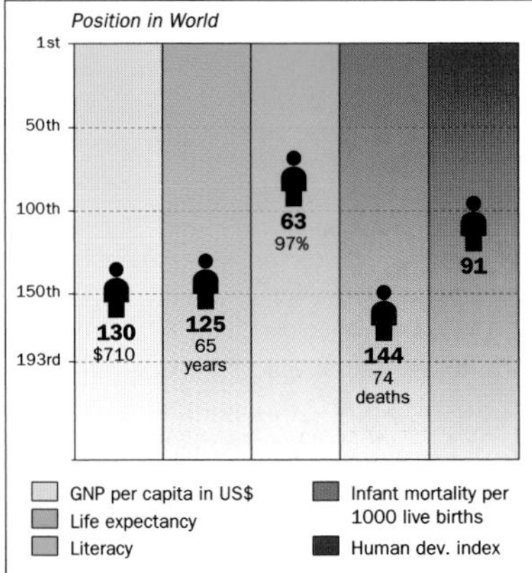
Position in World
1st
50th
100th
150th
193rd
130
$710
125
65 years
63
97%
144
74 deaths
91
GNP per capita in US$
Life expectancy
Literacy
Infant mortality per 1000 live births
Human dev. index

BAHAMAS

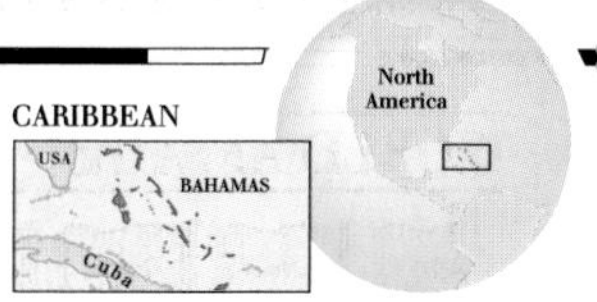
North America
CARIBBEAN
USA
BAHAMAS
Cuba

OFFICIAL NAME: Commonwealth of the Bahamas **CAPITAL:** Nassau
POPULATION: 314,000 **CURRENCY:** Bahamian dollar **OFFICIAL LANGUAGE:** English

1973 | 1973 | July 10 | BS | -5 | +1242 | .bs

THE BAHAMAS, THOUGH OFTEN bracketed with Caribbean countries, actually lies northeast of Cuba in the western Atlantic. The archipelago has 700 islands and 2400 cays: just 30 are inhabited. Long established as a tourist resort, the Bahamas today is also a major offshore financial center. It has one of the world's largest open-registry fleets; only a tiny fraction is owned by Bahamian nationals.

CLIMATE

Tropical oceanic

WEATHER CHART FOR NASSAU

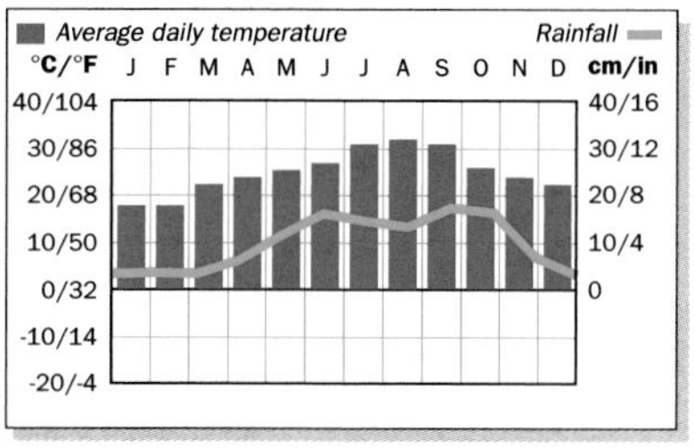
Average daily temperature
Rainfall
°C/°F
J F M A M J J A S O N D
cm/in
40/104
30/86
20/68
10/50
0/32
-10/14
-20/4
40/16
30/12
20/8
10/4
0

The whole of the Bahamas chain has a typically subtropical climate with consistently mild winters. Hurricanes may occur from July to December.

TRANSPORTATION

Drive on left

Nassau International

35.8m grt

THE TRANSPORTATION NETWORK

1535 km (954 miles)	None
None	None

While traveling around and between the major islands is relatively easy, transportation links for the many "Out Islands" are greatly restricted.

TOURISM

Visitors : Population 4.5:1

1.4m visitors

Down 9% in 2002

MAIN TOURIST ARRIVALS

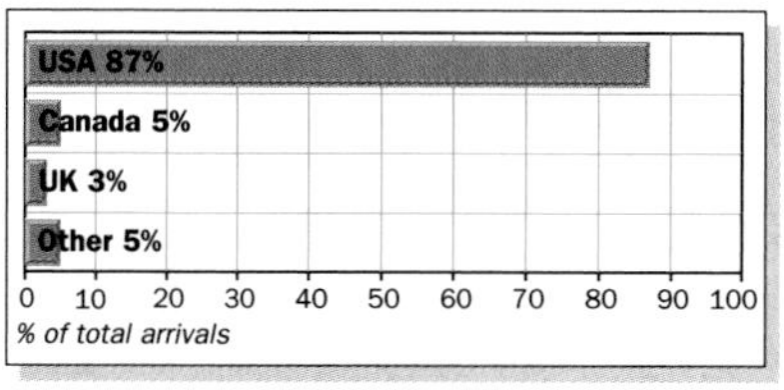
USA 87%
Canada 5%
UK 3%
Other 5%
0 10 20 30 40 50 60 70 80 90 100
% of total arrivals

The tourist industry, built around beaches, casinos, and cruise ships, employs over 40% of the population. Larger hotel complexes on the main islands compete with small, family-run guesthouses in the outlying destinations.

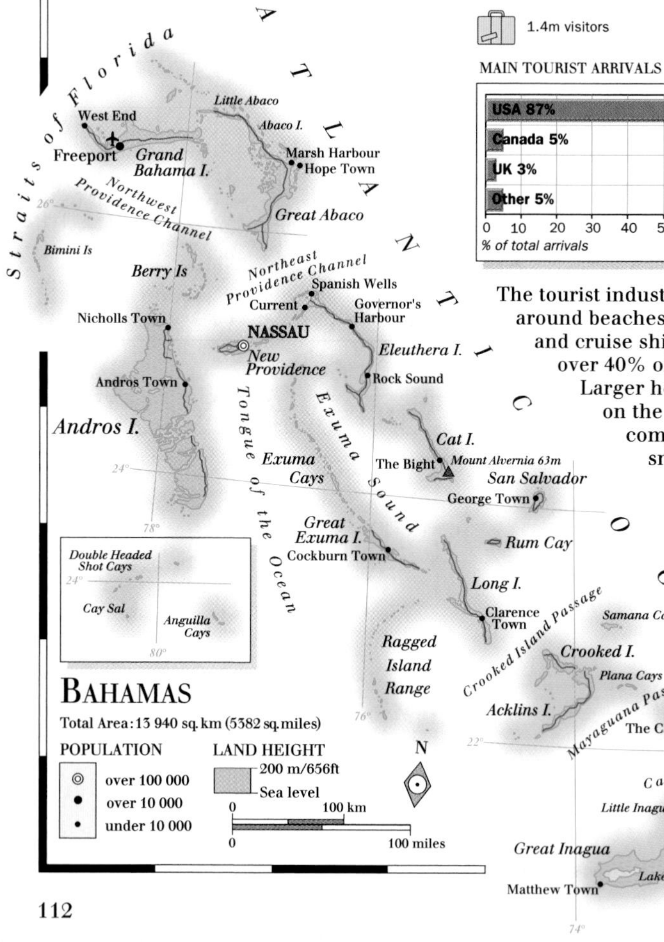
ATLANTIC OCEAN
Straits of Florida
West End
Freeport
Grand Bahama I.
Little Abaco
Abaco I.
Marsh Harbour
Hope Town
Northwest Providence Channel
Great Abaco
Bimini Is
Berry Is
Northeast Providence Channel
Spanish Wells
Current
Governor's Harbour
Nicholls Town
NASSAU
New Providence
Eleuthera I.
Rock Sound
Andros Town
Andros I.
Tongue of the Ocean
Exuma Sound
Exuma Cays
Cat I.
The Bight
Mount Alvernia 63m
San Salvador
George Town
Great Exuma I.
Cockburn Town
Rum Cay
Long I.
Clarence Town
Crooked Island Passage
Samana Cay
Crooked I.
Plana Cays
Ragged Island Range
Acklins I.
Mayaguana Passage
Mayaguana
The Carlton
Caicos Passage
Little Inagua
Great Inagua
Lake Rosa
Matthew Town
Double Headed Shot Cays
Cay Sal
Anguilla Cays
BAHAMAS
Total Area: 13 940 sq. km (5382 sq. miles)
POPULATION
over 100 000
over 10 000
under 10 000
LAND HEIGHT
200 m/656ft
Sea level
0 100 km
0 100 miles
N

PEOPLE

Pop. density low

English, English Creole, French Creole

31/km² (81/mi²)

THE URBAN/RURAL POPULATION SPLIT

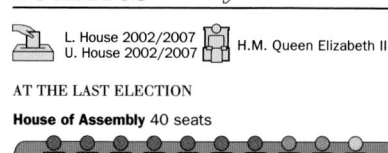

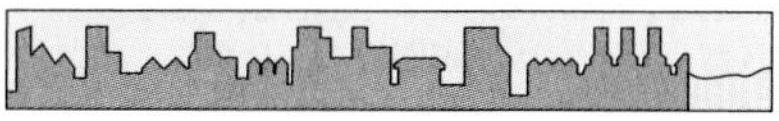
89%
11%

RELIGIOUS PERSUASION

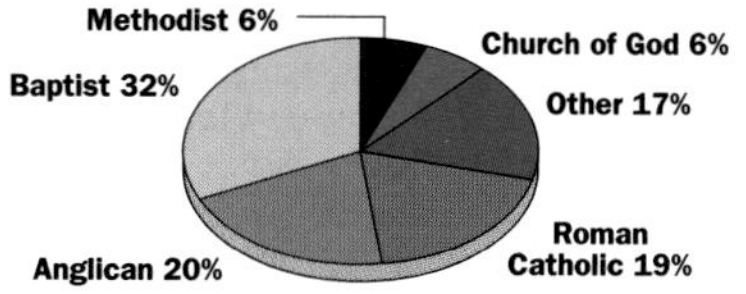
Methodist 6%
Church of God 6%
Baptist 32%
Other 17%
Roman Catholic 19%
Anglican 20%

Africans first arrived as slaves in the 16th century; their descendants constitute most of the population, alongside a rich white minority. About two-thirds of the population live on New Providence Island, and most of them in Nassau. More women are now entering the professions.

POLITICS

Multiparty elections

L. House 2002/2007
U. House 2002/2007

H.M. Queen Elizabeth II

AT THE LAST ELECTION

House of Assembly 40 seats

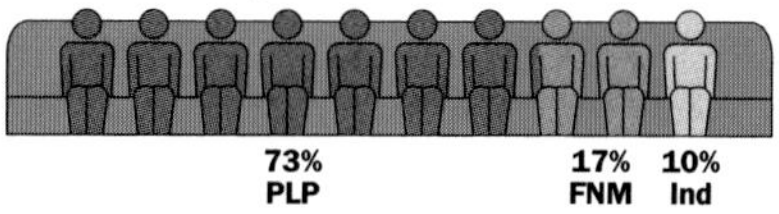
73% PLP
17% FNM
10% Ind

PLP = Progressive Liberal Party
FNM = Free National Movement
Ind = Independents

Senate 16 seats

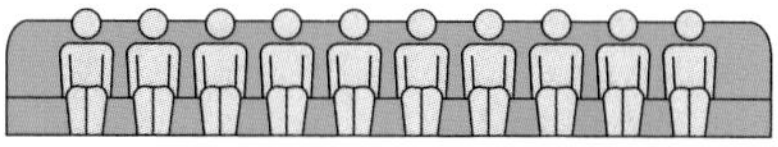

The members of the Senate are appointed by the governor-general on the recommendation of the prime minister and the leader of the opposition

Twenty-five years of unbroken rule by the PLP under Prime Minister Lynden Pindling were brought to an end by the 1992 elections. His legacy of steering the Bahamas to independence and ending white political domination was undermined by allegations of narcotics-related corruption. There followed a decade of FNM government under Hubert Ingraham, who emphasized tightening up ministerial accountability, introduced legislation to counter money laundering, and achieved relative economic success. However, his privatization drive proved deeply unpopular and the FNM was roundly defeated in 2002 by a resurgent PLP now led by Perry Christie.

WORLD AFFAIRS

Joined UN in 1973

ACS | Caricom | Comm | NAM | OAS

The Bahamas has made great progress in cleaning up its banking system following money-laundering allegations. Drugs trafficking and illegal migration from Haiti remain major problems and dominate regional relations.

AID

Recipient

US$5m (receipts) — Down 38% in 2002

Donations rose after Hurricane Floyd in 1999. The US has increased aid in return for action on money laundering linked to funding terrorism.

DEFENSE

No compulsory military service

US$25m — Down 14% in 2002

The UK is the main trainer of and supplier for the small naval defense force. The interception of narcotics and illegal immigrants is the force's main activity. There is no land army.

ECONOMICS

Inflation 2.7% p.a. (1990–2000)

US$4.53bn — 1 Bahamian dollar (1)

SCORE CARD

❑ World GNP Ranking	119th
❑ GNP per Capita	US$14,860
❑ Balance of Payments	–US$300m
❑ Inflation	2.2%
❑ Unemployment	7%

STRENGTHS

Major international financial services sector, including banking, insurance, and business trade center. Major tourism and cruise ship destination. Growing container port. International ship registration.

WEAKNESSES

Growing competition in financial services and tourism from neighboring states. Overdependence on US visitors.

EXPORTS

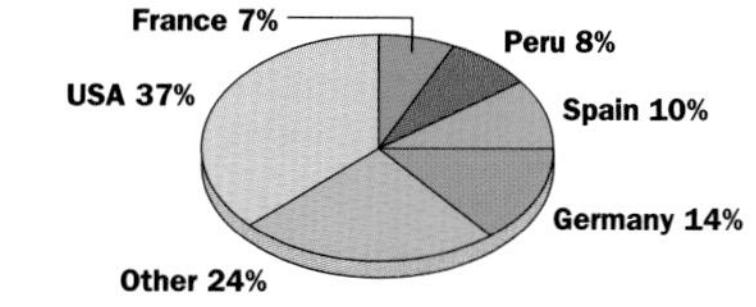
France 7%
Peru 8%
USA 37%
Spain 10%
Germany 14%
Other 24%

IMPORTS

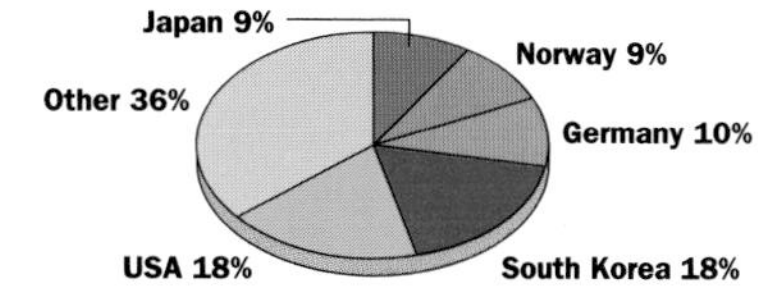
Japan 9%
Norway 9%
Other 36%
Germany 10%
USA 18%
South Korea 18%

***Archetypal island paradise.** Its natural beauty attracts more than four tourists per inhabitant to the Bahamas every year.*

RESOURCES

Electric power 401,000 kW

9303 tonnes — Not an oil producer

14,000 goats, 6450 sheep, 4950 pigs, 2.98m chickens — Salt, aragonite

The Bahamas has no strategic resources. A 13.5 MW electricity generating plant was opened in 1998.

ENVIRONMENT

Not available

11% (0.1% partially protected) — 5.7 tonnes per capita

As on many Caribbean islands, hotel overdevelopment is a major cause for concern. Environmental groups have also pointed out the potential for accidents posed by the Bahamas' enormous oil storage depots.

MEDIA

TV ownership medium

Daily newspaper circulation 99 per 1000 people

PUBLISHING AND BROADCAST MEDIA

There are 4 daily newspapers, the *Nassau Guardian*, the *Tribune*, the *Bahama Journal*, and the *Freeport News*

1 state-owned service — 5 services: 1 state-owned, 4 independent

The state-owned TV channel faces very stiff competition from Florida-based US broadcasters.

CRIME

Death penalty in use

1280 prisoners — Down 29% in 1999

The death penalty remains in force. Violent crime, ranging from narcotics-related murders to sexual assault, is on the increase. Tourists can be targets for petty thefts. Illegal weapons are readily available.

EDUCATION

School leaving age: 16

96% — 5305 students

Schooling follows the former British selective system. Tertiary students attend the University of the West Indies or colleges in the US.

B

CHRONOLOGY

Once an English pirate base, the Bahamas, whose first parliament sat in 1729, formally became a British colony in 1783.

- ❑ **1920–1933** US prohibition laws turn Bahamas into prosperous bootlegging center.
- ❑ **1959–1962** Introduction of full male suffrage; women gain the vote.
- ❑ **1973** Independence.
- ❑ **1983** Narcotics-smuggling scandals involving the government.
- ❑ **1992** FNM wins elections, ending 25 years of PLP rule.
- ❑ **2002** PLP returned to power.

HEALTH

Welfare state health benefits

1 per 667 people — Obstetric causes, heart diseases, cancers, murders, accidents

The health service combines state and private systems. In the outlying islands access to care relies on the Flying Doctor Service and around 50 local health centers. Three of the country's four hospitals are on New Providence.

SPENDING

GDP/cap. increase

CONSUMPTION AND SPENDING

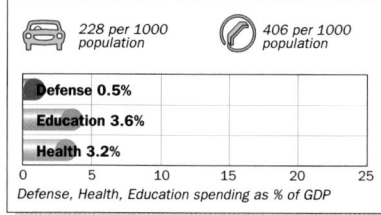

228 per 1000 population — *406 per 1000 population*

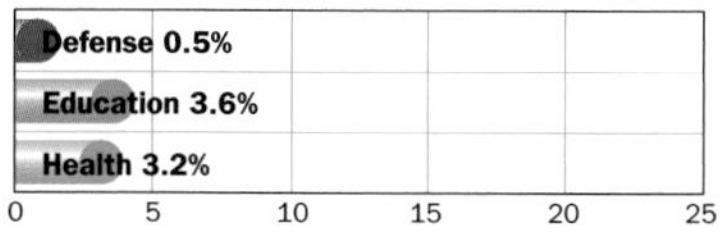
Defense 0.5%
Education 3.6%
Health 3.2%
0
5
10
15
20
25

Defense, Health, Education spending as % of GDP

There are marked wealth disparities: urban professionals who work in the financial sector are at one end of the scale, and the poor fishermen from the outlying islands are near the other. Cuban and Haitian refugees, who have no legal status, are the poorest group of all.

WORLD RANKING

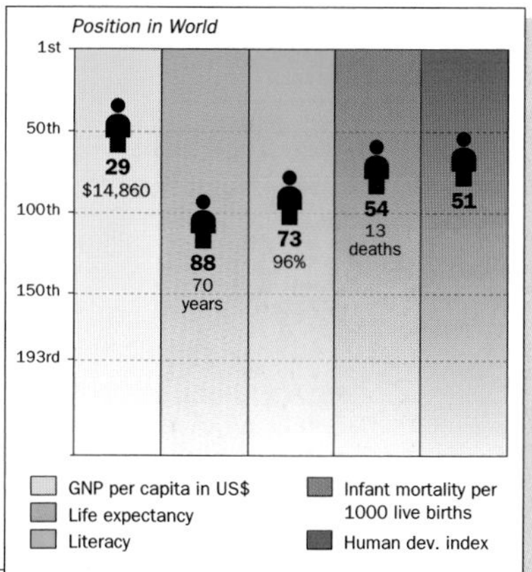
Position in World
1st
50th
100th
150th
193rd
29
$14,860
88
70
years
73
96%
54
13
deaths
51
GNP per capita in US$
Life expectancy
Literacy
Infant mortality per 1000 live births
Human dev. index

BAHRAIN

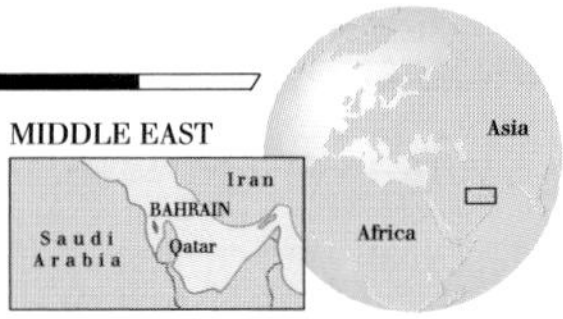
MIDDLE EAST
Asia
Iran
BAHRAIN
Saudi Arabia
Qatar
Africa

B

OFFICIAL NAME: Kingdom of Bahrain **CAPITAL:** Manama
POPULATION: 724,000 **CURRENCY:** Bahraini dinar **OFFICIAL LANGUAGE:** Arabic

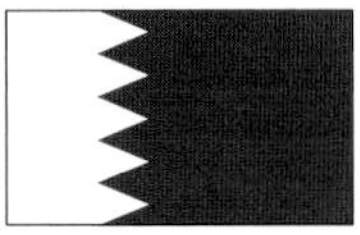

1971 | 1971 | Dec 16 | BRN | +3 | +973 | .bh

BAHRAIN IS AN ARCHIPELAGO state situated between the Qatar peninsula and the Saudi Arabian mainland. Only three of its islands are inhabited. Bahrain Island is connected to Saudi Arabia's Eastern Province by a causeway opened in 1986. Bahrain was the first Gulf emirate to export oil; its reserves are now almost depleted. Services such as offshore banking, insurance, and tourism are major employment sectors for skilled Bahrainis.

CLIMATE

Hot desert

WEATHER CHART FOR MANAMA

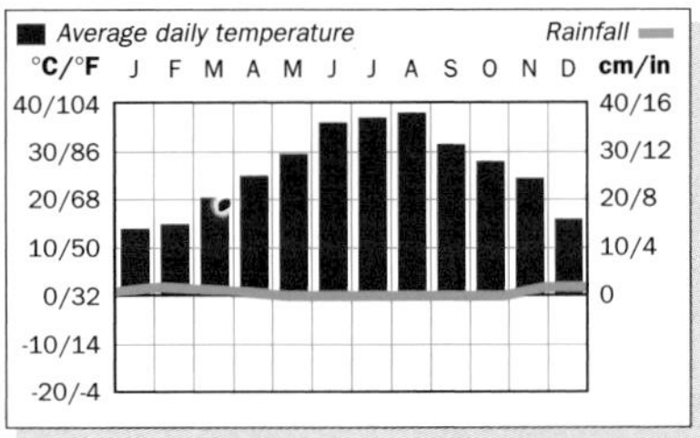
Average daily temperature
Rainfall
°C/°F
J F M A M J J A S O N D
cm/in
40/104
30/86
20/68
10/50
0/32
-10/14
-20/-4
40/16
30/12
20/8
10/4
0

Temperatures soar toward 40°C (104°F) in June–August. In December–March the weather is pleasantly warm.

TRANSPORTATION

Drive on right

Bahrain International, Manama
4.3m passengers

115 ships
287,740 grt

THE TRANSPORTATION NETWORK

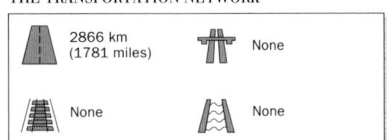

2866 km (1781 miles)

None

None

None

The King Fahd Causeway connects Bahrain to Saudi Arabia, and ferries travel regularly to Iran. Buses are the main form of public transportation.

TOURISM

Visitors : Population 4.4:1

3.17m visitors

Up 14% in 2002

MAIN TOURIST ARRIVALS

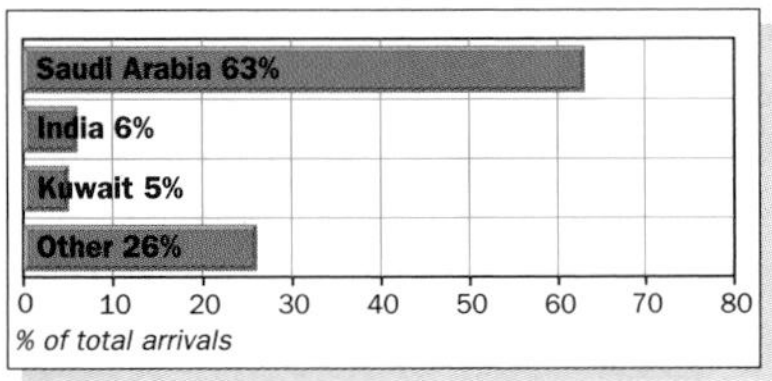
Saudi Arabia 63%
India 6%
Kuwait 5%
Other 26%
0 10 20 30 40 50 60 70 80
% of total arrivals

Bahrain's relatively liberal lifestyle has made it something of a magnet for visitors from neighboring Gulf states. It is a center for business conventions and has a new Formula 1 race course.

PEOPLE

Pop. density high

Arabic

1025/km² (2652/mi²)

THE URBAN/RURAL POPULATION SPLIT

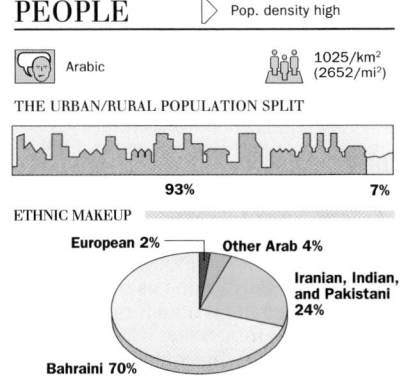

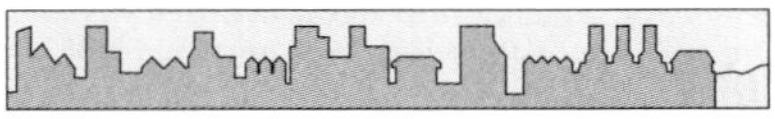
93%
7%

ETHNIC MAKEUP

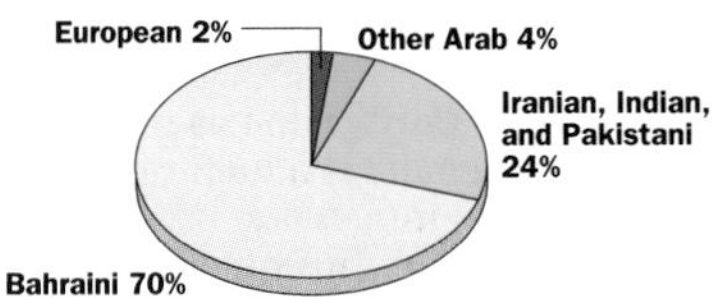
European 2%
Other Arab 4%
Iranian, Indian, and Pakistani 24%
Bahraini 70%

Bahrain is the smallest and most densely populated Arab state. The key division is between Sunni and Shi'a Muslims, about 30% and 70% of the population respectively. Sunnis hold the best jobs in business and government. Shi'a Muslims tend to do menial work and have a lower standard of living. The most impoverished Shi'as tend to be of Iranian descent.

Bahrain has a smaller expatriate population than many other Arab countries. The ruling al-Khalifa family has responded to declining oil reserves by diversifying the economy to provide service industry jobs for Bahrainis.

Bahrain is the most liberal of the Gulf states. Alcohol is freely available. Women have access to education and are not obliged to wear the veil. Since 2000 they have been entitled to participate in politics.

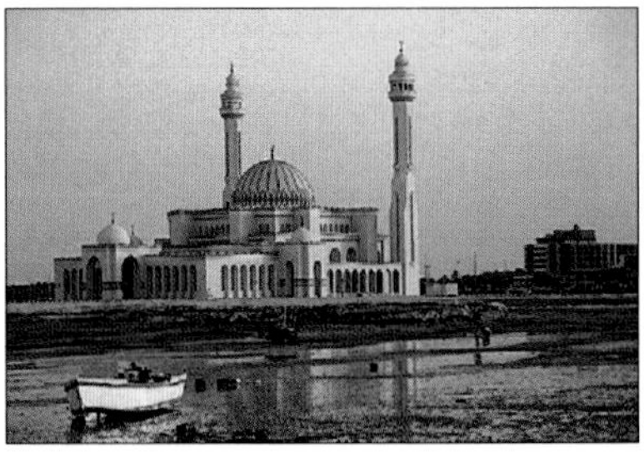

The Grand Mosque, Manama. *The largest building in Bahrain, it can accommodate 7000 people.*

POLITICS

Nonparty elections

L. House 2002/2006
U. House 2002/2006

H.M. Shaikh Hamad bin Isa al-Khalifa

AT THE LAST ELECTION

Chamber of Deputies 40 seats

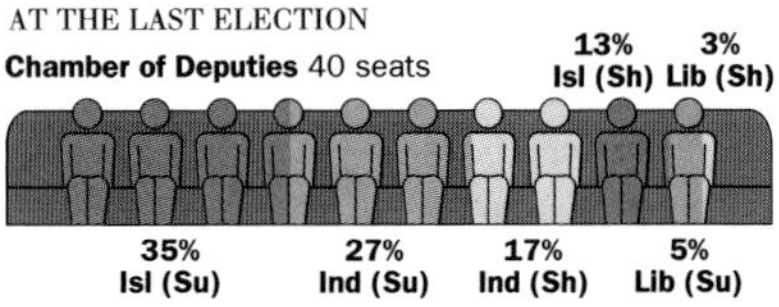
13% Isl (Sh)
3% Lib (Sh)
35% Isl (Su)
27% Ind (Su)
17% Ind (Sh)
5% Lib (Su)

Isl (Su) = Islamists (Sunni) **Ind (Su)** = Independents (Sunni)
Ind (Sh) = Independents (Shi'a) **Isl (Sh)** = Islamists (Shi'a)
Lib (Su) = Liberals (Sunni) **Lib (Sh)** = Liberals (Shi'a)

Consultative Council 40 seats

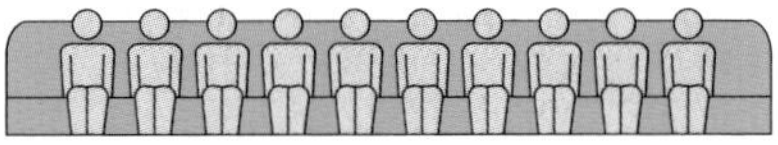

The Consultative Council is appointed by the king

The al-Khalifa family has been dominant since 1783. The amir was advised from 1993 by an appointed Consultative Council, and in 2002 Bahrain became a constitutional monarchy. That year it held the first legislative (albeit nonparty) elections since 1973: moderate Islamists gained the most seats, while radical candidates boycotted the poll. Shaikh Hamad bin Isa al-Khalifa, who has ruled since 1999, supports the economic liberalization initiated by his father. The repeal in 2001 of the State Security Law was welcomed by human rights groups.

WORLD AFFAIRS

Joined UN in 1971

AL | Damasc | GCC | OIC | OAPEC

Bahrain has good relations with the UK and the US. Though formally opposed to the 2003 war on Iraq, it hosted US forces. The International Court of Justice rejected Qatar's claim to the Hawar Islands in 2001. There is residual tension with Iran.

AID

Recipient

$71m (receipts)

Up 294% in 2002

Bahrain receives low levels of aid, but takes the lion's share from the offshore oil field shared with Saudi Arabia, effectively a subsidy from the latter.

DEFENSE

No compulsory military service

$314m

Down 3% in 2002

With only a small defense force, Bahrain hosts the US 5th Fleet and US air bases. The US has also used Bahrain as a test case in the region for the introduction of sophisticated weapons technology.

B

ECONOMICS

Inflation 0.8% p.a. (1990–2001)

$7.33bn

0.377 Bahraini dinars (0.377)

SCORE CARD

- WORLD GNP RANKING........100th
- GNP PER CAPITA........$10,500
- BALANCE OF PAYMENTS........–$516m
- INFLATION........1.2%
- UNEMPLOYMENT........6%

STRENGTHS

Oil and gas. Major offshore banking sector. Inward investment. Good infrastructure. Tourism. Aluminum production. Near self-sufficiency in food.

WEAKNESSES

Depleted oil reserves and water supplies. Insufficient diversification. High level of government borrowing.

EXPORTS

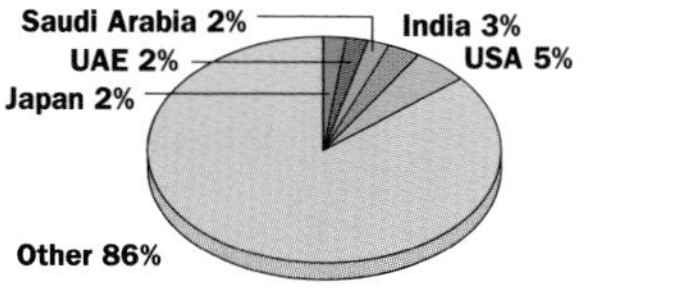
Saudi Arabia 2%
UAE 2%
Japan 2%
India 3%
USA 5%
Other 86%

IMPORTS

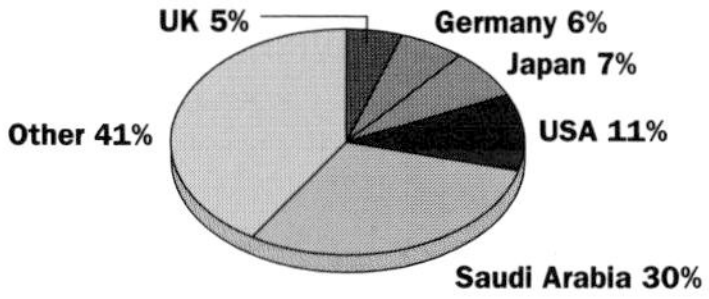
UK 5%
Germany 6%
Japan 7%
USA 11%
Other 41%
Saudi Arabia 30%

RESOURCES

Electric power 1.4m kW

11,230 tonnes

37,654 b/d (reserves 206m barrels)

17,500 sheep, 16,000 goats, 470,000 chickens

Oil, natural gas

Bahrain remains dependent on its oil and gas industry. Production of crude oil has declined sharply since the 1970s, and there are fears that reserves may run out by 2010. As oil has declined, so gas has assumed greater importance. Most is used to supply local industries, particularly the aluminum plant, which was established in 1972.

ENVIRONMENT

Not available

1% partially protected

27.9 tonnes per capita

Local marine life, particularly the dugong, is vulnerable to upstream oil pollution from the Gulf. Groundwater is deteriorating in quality and quantity, affecting plant life.

MEDIA

TV ownership high

Daily newspaper circulation 112 per 1000 people

PUBLISHING AND BROADCAST MEDIA

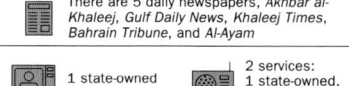

There are 5 daily newspapers, *Akhbar al-Khaleej*, *Gulf Daily News*, *Khaleej Times*, *Bahrain Tribune*, and *Al-Ayam*

1 state-owned service

2 services: 1 state-owned, 1 independent

Bahrain has a less authoritarian media regime than most of the Gulf, though government critics have been prosecuted. CNN and BBC satellite TV are freely available.

CRIME

Death penalty in use

911 prisoners

Down 62% in 1996–1998

Crime is minimal, and theft and muggings are rare. Suspected political dissidents are monitored by the police.

BAHRAIN

Total Area : 655 sq. km (253 sq. miles)

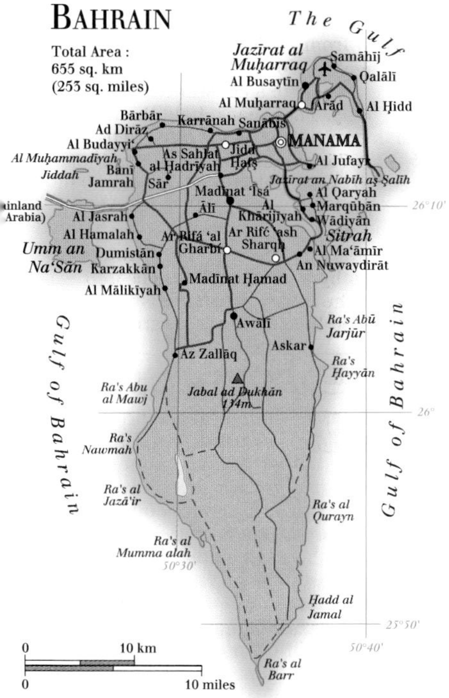
The Gulf
Jazīrat al Muḩarraq
Samāhīj
Qalālī
Al Busaytīn
Al Muḩarraq
Arād
Al Ḩidd
Bārbār
Ad Dirāz
Karrānah
Sanābis
Al Budayyi'
MANAMA
Al Muḩammadīyah
As Sahlah
Jidd Ḩafş
al Hadrīyah
Al Jufayr
Jiddah
Banī Jamrah
Sār
Jazīrat an Nabīh aş Şalīh
Madīnat 'Īsá
Al Qaryah
'Ālī
Marqūbān
Al Jasrah
Kharijīyah
Wādiyān
Al Hamalah
Ar Rifā' al Gharbī
Ar Rifā' ash Sharqī
Sitrah
Al Ma'āmīr
Umm an Na'Sān
Dumistān
Karzakkān
An Nuwaydirāt
Al Mālikīyah
Madīnat Ḩamad
Gulf of Bahrain
Ra's Abū Jarjūr
Awālī
Askar
Az Zallāq
Ra's Ḩayyān
Ra's Abu al Mawj
Jabal ad Dukhān 134m
Ra's Nawmah
Ra's al Jazā'ir
Ra's al Qurayn
Ra's al Mumma alah
Ḩadd al Jamal
Ra's al Barr
0 10 km
0 10 miles
N

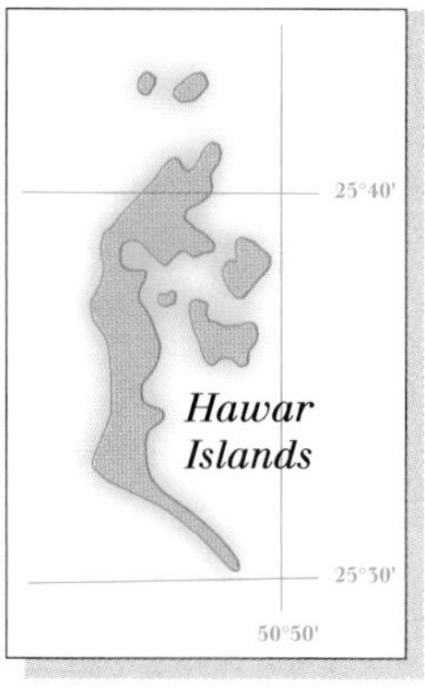
Hawar Islands

POPULATION

- ◎ over 100 000
- ○ over 50 000
- ● over 10 000
- • under 10 000

LAND HEIGHT

100m/328ft

Sea Level

CHRONOLOGY

Bahrain became a British Protected State in the 19th century.

- **1971** Independence from Britain.
- **1981** Founder member of GCC.
- **1991** Supports US-led action expelling Iraq from Kuwait.
- **1999** Accession of Shaikh Hamad.
- **2001** Referendum approves transition to democracy.
- **2002** Becomes a constitutional monarchy. Islamists win elections.

EDUCATION

School leaving age: 15

89%

11,048 students

Female literacy rates are among the highest in the Gulf. The University of Bahrain opened in 1986.

HEALTH

Welfare state health benefits

1 per 1000 people

Circulatory diseases, perinatal deaths, injury, poisonings

The high-quality health service is free to Bahraini nationals. Some go abroad for advanced care. The Muharraq Health Center was upgraded in 2001.

SPENDING

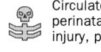

GDP/cap. increase

CONSUMPTION AND SPENDING

286 per 1000 population

261 per 1000 population

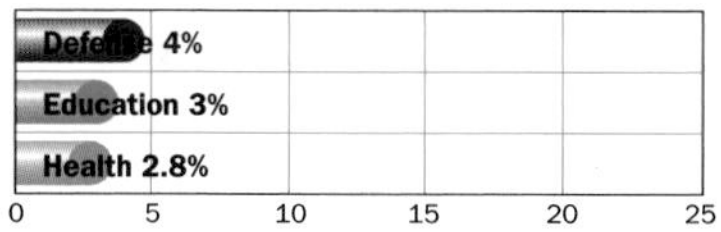
Defense 4%
Education 3%
Health 2.8%
0
5
10
15
20
25

Defense, Health, Education spending as % of GDP

Beneficiaries of the king's extensive patronage form the wealthiest group in society. Bahrain's largest religious community, the Shi'a Muslims, is also the poorest.

WORLD RANKING

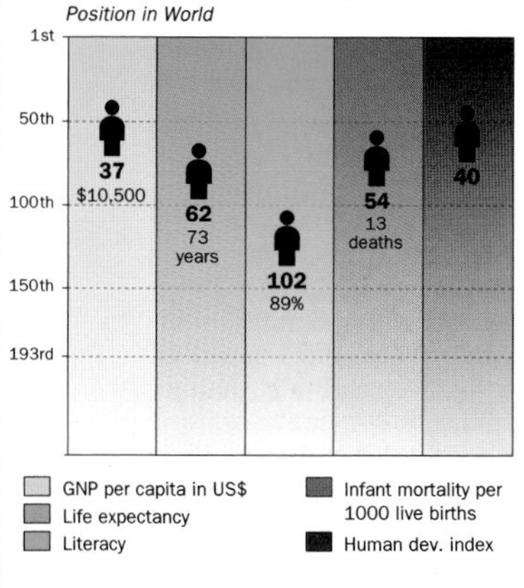
Position in World
1st
50th
100th
150th
193rd
37
$10,500
62
73 years
102
89%
54
13 deaths
40
GNP per capita in US$
Life expectancy
Literacy
Infant mortality per 1000 live births
Human dev. index

BANGLADESH

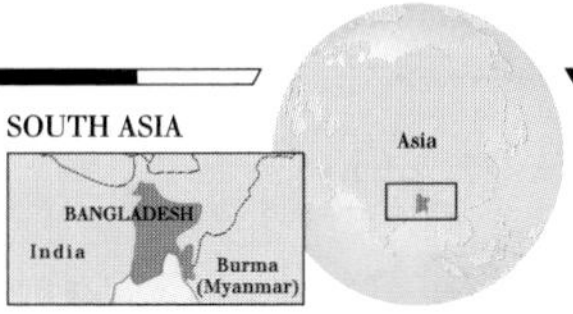
SOUTH ASIA
BANGLADESH
India
Burma (Myanmar)
Asia

OFFICIAL NAME: People's Republic of Bangladesh **CAPITAL:** Dhaka
POPULATION: 147 million **CURRENCY:** Taka **OFFICIAL LANGUAGE:** Bengali

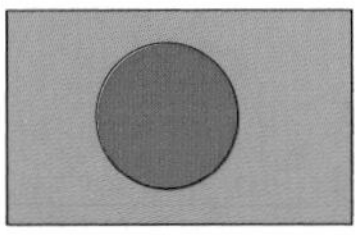

1971 | 1971 | March 26 | BD | +6 | +880 | .bd

LOCATED AROUND the confluence of the mighty Ganges and Jamuna rivers, Bangladesh is the eastern half of historic Bengal. Most of the country is composed of fertile alluvial plains; the north and northeast are mountainous, as is the Chittagong region in the southeast. After seceding from Pakistan in 1971, Bangladesh had a troubled history of political instability, with periods of emergency rule. Effective democracy was restored in 1991. Bangladesh's major economic sectors are jute production, textiles, and agriculture. Its climate can wreak havoc – in 1991 a massive cyclone killed more than 140,000 people.

CLIMATE

Tropical/subtropical

WEATHER CHART FOR DHAKA

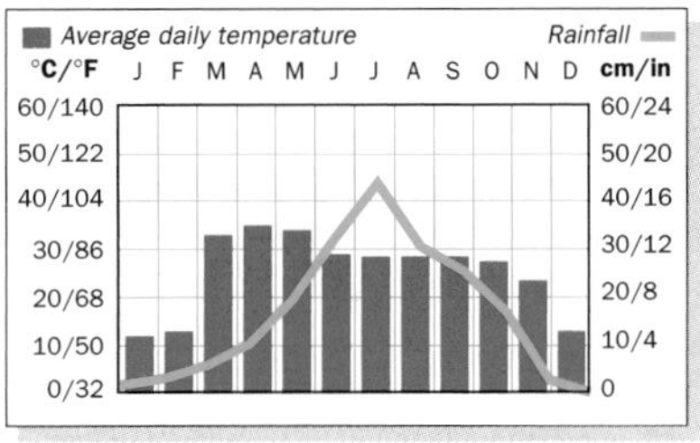
Average daily temperature
Rainfall
°C/°F J F M A M J J A S O N D cm/in
60/140
50/122
40/104
30/86
20/68
10/50
0/32
60/24
50/20
40/16
30/12
20/8
10/4
0

During the monsoon, the water level generally rises 6 m (20 ft) above normal, flooding up to two-thirds of the country. The floods are made much worse when the Ganges, Jamuna, and Meghna rivers, which converge in a huge delta in Bangladesh, are swollen by the melting of the Himalayan snows and heavy rain in India. Cyclones build up regularly in the Bay of Bengal, with sometimes devastating effects on the flat coastal region.

TRANSPORTATION

Drive on left

Zia International, Dhaka 2.95m passengers

325 ships 432,400 grt

THE TRANSPORTATION NETWORK

20,749 km (12,893 miles)

None

2706 km (1681 miles)

8046 km (5000 miles)

Most transportation in Bangladesh is by water, though government policy is now concentrating on developing road and rail links, including the reopening in mid-2000 of a passenger rail service into India. The 4.8-km (3-mile) Bangabandhu road and rail bridge across the Jamuna River at Sirajganj was finally inaugurated in 1998 and is now a major artery. Bangladesh's two major ports, Mungla and Chittagong, are being upgraded to take advanced container ships.

Begum Khaleda Zia, reelected as prime minister in 2001.

Sheikh Hasina Wajed, AL leader and former prime minister.

TOURISM

Visitors : Population 1:709

207,000 visitors

Little change in 2002

MAIN TOURIST ARRIVALS

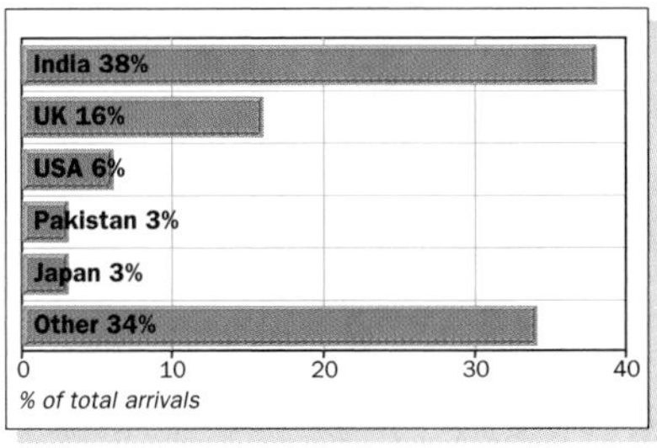
India 38%
UK 16%
USA 6%
Pakistan 3%
Japan 3%
Other 34%
0
10
20
30
40
% of total arrivals

The Mughal architecture in Dhaka and the Pala dynasty (7th–10th centuries) city of Sonargaon, just to the southeast, are major attractions, but tourists may be deterred by social and political unrest. Most visitors are Indian businessmen or Bangladeshis living overseas who return to visit relatives.

Traders on the Meghna River. Life is governed by the vast network of rivers. The floodplains are among the most fertile in the world.

PEOPLE

Pop. density high

Bengali, Urdu, Chakma, Marma (Magh), Garo, Khasi, Santhali, Tripuri, Mro

1096/km² (2837/mi²)

THE URBAN/RURAL POPULATION SPLIT

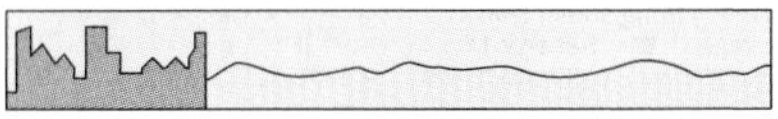
26%
74%

RELIGIOUS PERSUASION

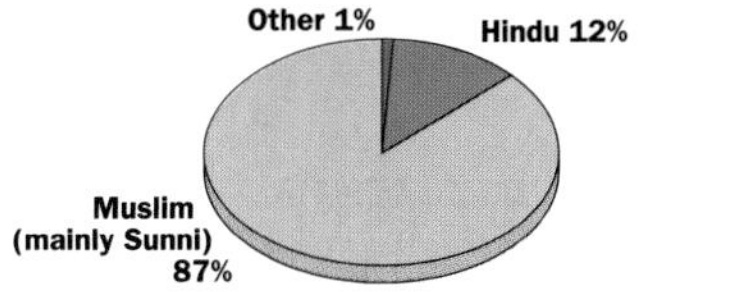
Other 1%
Hindu 12%
Muslim (mainly Sunni) 87%

ETHNIC MAKEUP

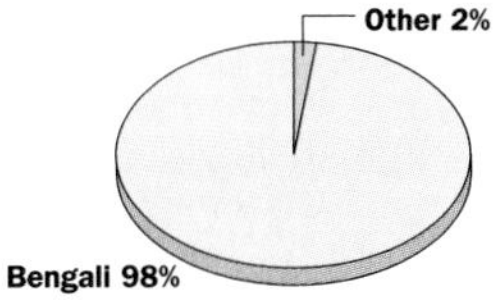
Other 2%
Bengali 98%

Bangladesh is one of the most densely populated countries in the world, despite the fact that three-quarters of the population is rural. As in India, there is considerable Muslim–Hindu tension; in 2001, thousands of Hindus and members of other religious minorities claimed persecution by the new nationalist government.

Though more than half of Bangladeshis, rural and urban, still live below the poverty line, there has been an improvement in living standards over the past decade.

The textile trade has been one factor in the growing emancipation of women, many of whom enjoy an independent income. They are now included in official employment statistics and are the main customers of the Grameen Bank, the most successful rural bank. They have led both the government and the opposition and, from 2004, 45 seats in the Parliament were reserved for women. Amnesty International, however, has repeatedly criticized the number of violent attacks against women, and the UN has estimated that nearly half of Bangladeshi women are victims of domestic violence.

POPULATION AGE BREAKDOWN

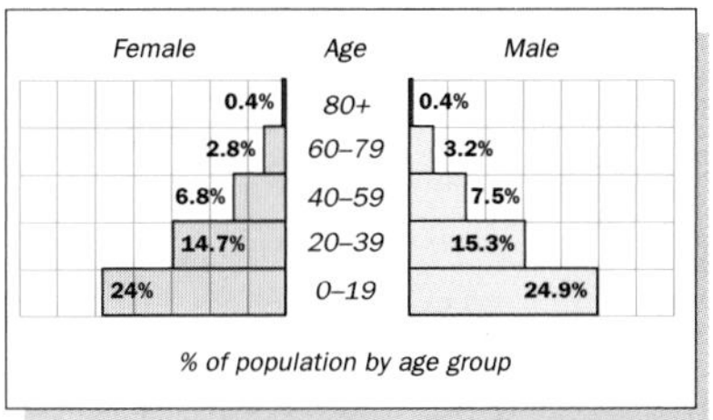
Female
Age
Male
0.4% 80+ 0.4%
2.8% 60–79 3.2%
6.8% 40–59 7.5%
14.7% 20–39 15.3%
24% 0–19 24.9%
% of population by age group

B

POLITICS

Multiparty elections

2001/2006

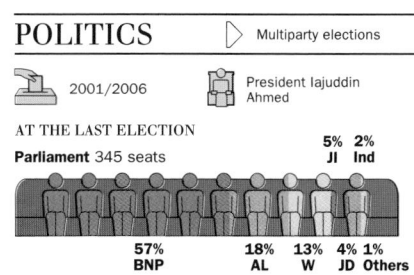

President Iajuddin Ahmed

AT THE LAST ELECTION

Parliament 345 seats

5% JI
2% Ind
57% BNP
18% AL
13% W
4% JD
1% Others

BNP = Bangladesh Nationalist Party and allies **AL** = Awami League **W** = Reserved for women **JI** = Jamaat-e-Islami **JD** = Jatiya Dal (Ershad) **Ind** = Independents

Bangladesh returned to multiparty democracy in 1991, following a period of military rule.

PROFILE

Between 1975 and 1990 the military was in power in Bangladesh. The overthrow of President Ershad in 1990 saw a return to multiparty politics; the army remains poised, however, to intervene in the event of a breakdown in internal order.

Bangladesh's first woman prime minister, Begum Khaleda Zia, head of the BNP, was elected in 1991. Constitutional changes soon replaced a presidential with a parliamentary system of government.

The AL, which had steered Bangladesh to independence in 1971, mounted a sustained campaign against Khaleda Zia's regime, in 1996 forcing a rerun of elections. It won the largest number of seats and its leader, Sheikh Hasina Wajed, went on to become the first prime minister to complete a full term. Khaleda Zia and her revived BNP returned to power in the 2001 poll, amid much electoral violence, forming a coalition with the Islamist JI.

MAIN POLITICAL ISSUES

The state sector

Bangladesh is coming under mounting pressure from multilateral lending institutions, which account for the vast majority of the country's capital inflows, to cut costs in the state sector. Simultaneously, state-sector workers are demanding wage increases in line with inflation.

Corruption

Bangladesh is consistently ranked among the most corrupt nations in the world. The misappropriation of public funds is endemic, while bribes are usually necessary to access basic services such as education, health care, and policing. In 2004, under pressure from donors, the government moved to fulfill its 2001 election pledge to set up an anticorruption commission.

BANGLADESH

Total Area : 144 000 sq. km (55 598 sq. miles)

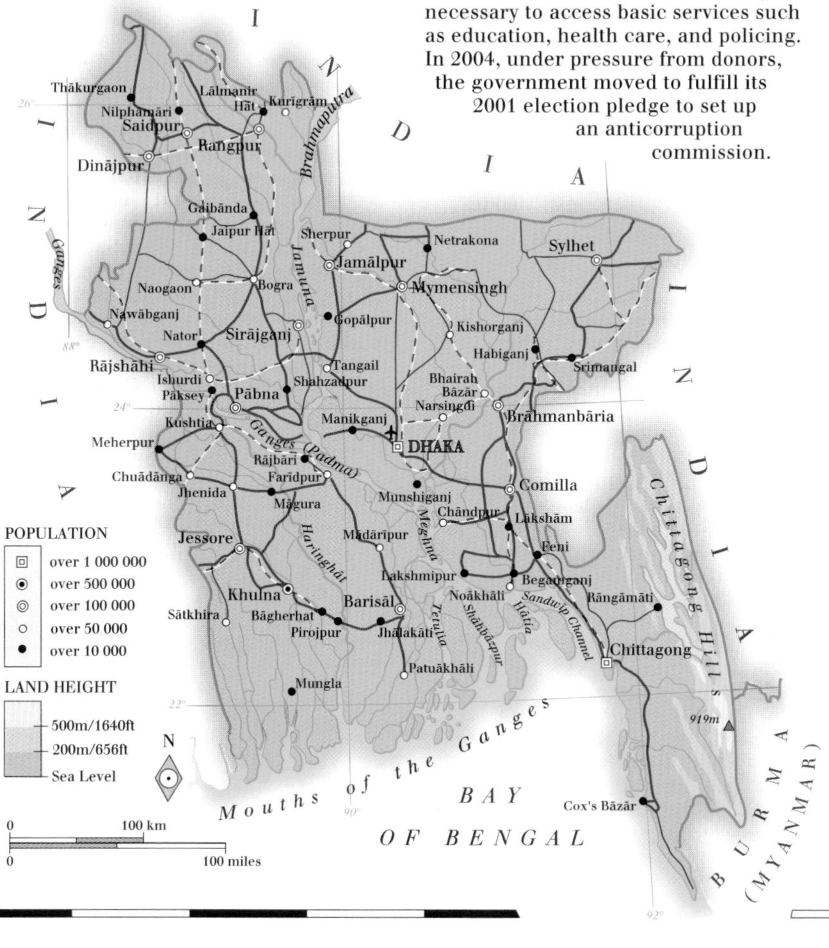
INDIA
INDIA
INDIA
Thākurgaon
Nilphāmāri
Saidpur
Lālmanir Hāt
Kurigrām
Rangpur
Brahmaputra
Dinājpur
Gaibānda
Jaipur Hāt
Sherpur
Netrakona
Sylhet
Jamālpur
Mymensingh
Naogaon
Bogra
Jamuna
Ganges
Nawābganj
Nator
Sirājganj
Gopālpur
Kishorganj
Habiganj
Rājshāhi
Ishurdi
Pāksey
Pābna
Tangail
Shahzadpur
Bhairab Bāzār
Narsingdi
Srimangal
Brāhmanbāria
Kushtia
Manikganj
DHAKA
Meherpur
Ganges (Padma)
Rājbāri
Farīdpur
Chuādānga
Jhenida
Māgura
Munshiganj
Comilla
Chāndpur
Lāksham
Meghna
Jessore
Mādāripur
Haringhāta
Feni
Lakshmipur
Noākhāli
Begamganj
Rāngāmāti
Khulna
Bāgherhat
Barisāl
Sātkhira
Pirojpur
Jhālakāti
Tetulia
Shāhbāzpur
Hātia
Sandwip Channel
Chittagong
Chittagong Hills
Patuākhāli
Mungla
919m
Mouths of the Ganges
BAY OF BENGAL
Cox's Bāzār
BURMA (MYANMAR)
POPULATION
over 1 000 000
over 500 000
over 100 000
over 50 000
over 10 000
LAND HEIGHT
500m/1640ft
200m/656ft
Sea Level
N
0
100 km
0
100 miles

WORLD AFFAIRS

Joined UN in 1974

Comm NAM OIC SAARC WTO

Good relations with the West, the main source of essential aid, are a priority. Relations with Pakistan have slowly improved since Pakistan's agreement in 1991 to accept the 250,000 pro-Pakistan Bihari Muslims living in Bangladeshi refugee camps since 1971. Relations with India are improving. The damaging effects of the construction of the Farakka Dam on the Ganges, which deprived Bangladesh of irrigation water, have been alleviated by a 30-year agreement signed in 1996 guaranteeing the right of both parties to share the Ganges' water. Tensions persist over the illegal migration of Bangladeshis into neighboring Indian states.

AID

Recipient

$913m (receipts)

Down 11% in 2002

Aid disbursements to Bangladesh each year are substantially greater than the annual value of foreign investment in the country. Aid also finances the bulk of state capital spending. One result of the level of aid is that Bangladesh has fallen into one of the traps of an aid-dependent economy: the large middle class has a vested interest in perpetuating a system which provides its members with lucrative contracts and access to external resources. Severe monsoon flooding in 2004 covered 60% of Bangladesh and resulted in food aid being needed for 20 million people.

CHRONOLOGY

Bengal was the first part of the Indian subcontinent to come under British rule when the East India Company was made the *diwani* (tax collector) by the Mughal emperor in 1765.

- **1905** Muslims persuade British rulers to partition state of Bengal, to create a Muslim-dominated East Bengal.
- **1906** Muslim League established in Dhaka.
- **1912** Partition of 1905 reversed.
- **1947** British withdrawal from India. Partition plans establish a largely Muslim state of East (present-day Bangladesh) and West Pakistan, separated by 1600 km (1000 miles) of Indian, and largely Hindu, territory.
- **1949** AL founded to campaign for autonomy from West Pakistan.
- **1968** Gen. Yahya Khan heads government in Islamabad.

B

CHRONOLOGY *continued*

- **1970** Elections give AL, under Sheikh Mujibur Rahman, clear majority. Rioting and guerrilla warfare following Yahya Khan's refusal to convene assembly. Year ends with worst recorded storms in Bangladesh's history – between 200,000 and 500,000 dead.
- **1971** Civil war, as Sheikh Mujib and AL declare unilateral independence. Ten million Bangladeshis flee to India. Pakistani troops defeated in 12 days by Mukhti Bahini – the Bengal Liberation Army.
- **1972** Sheikh Mujib elected prime minister. Nationalization of key industries, including jute and textiles. Bangladesh achieves international recognition and joins Commonwealth. Pakistan withdraws in protest.
- **1974** Severe floods damage rice crop.
- **1975** Sheikh Mujib assassinated. Military coups end with Gen. Ziaur Rahman taking power. Institution of single-party state.
- **1976** Banning of trade union federations.
- **1977** Zia assumes presidency. Islam adopted as first principle of constitution.
- **1981** Zia assassinated.
- **1982** Gen. Ershad takes over.
- **1983** Democratic elections restored by Ershad. Ershad assumes presidency.
- **1986** Elections. AL and BNP fail to unseat Ershad.
- **1987** Ershad announces state of emergency.
- **1988** Islam becomes constitutional state religion.
- **1990** Ershad resigns following demonstrations.
- **1991** Elections won by BNP. Khaleda Zia (widow of Zia) becomes prime minister. Ershad imprisoned. Role of the president reduced to ceremonial functions. Floods following cyclone kill 140,000 people.
- **1994** Author Taslima Nasreen, who is accused of blasphemy, escapes to Sweden.
- **1996** Election returns BNP to power. Results are rejected by opposition parties, which force fresh elections. Sheikh Hasina Wajed of AL then takes power.
- **2001** Supreme Court declares issuing of religious decrees (*fatawa*) to be a criminal offense. BNP returned to power following violence-marred elections.
- **2002** Privatization program begins.

DEFENSE

No compulsory military service

$638m

Up 4% in 2002

The military dominated politics between 1975 and 1990, and still has considerable influence. The army was mobilized to fight rising crime from 2002. The level of defense spending is controversial; some of the air force's Russian-built MiG-29 fighters were cut from the fleet in 2002, just two years after their purchase by the previous government. Bangladesh is the largest contributor to UN peacekeeping missions.

BANGLADESHI ARMED FORCES

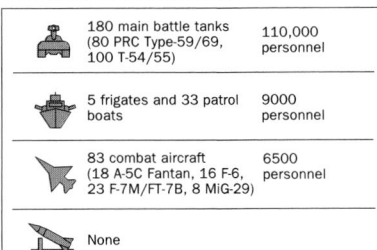

180 main battle tanks (80 PRC Type-59/69, 100 T-54/55)	110,000 personnel
5 frigates and 33 patrol boats	9000 personnel
83 combat aircraft (18 A-5C Fantan, 16 F-6, 23 F-7M/FT-7B, 8 MiG-29)	6500 personnel
None	

ECONOMICS

Inflation 3.9% p.a. (1990–2001)

$51.1bn

59.1 taka (58.41)

SCORE CARD

World GNP Ranking	50th
GNP per Capita	$380
Balance of Payments	$742m
Inflation	6.8%
Unemployment	3%

EXPORTS

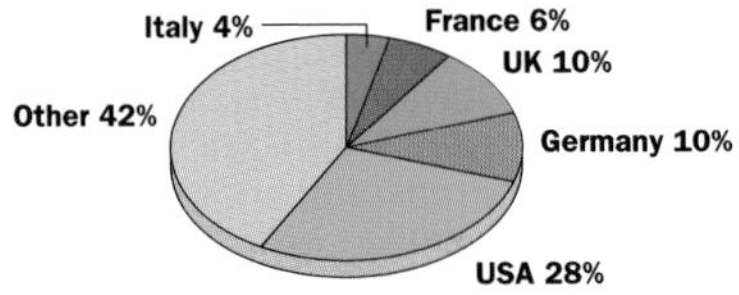
Italy 4%
France 6%
UK 10%
Other 42%
Germany 10%
USA 28%

IMPORTS

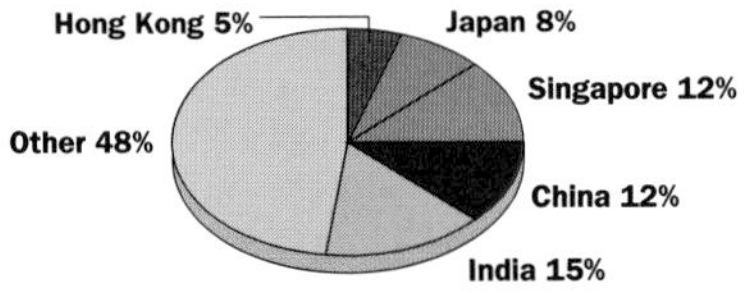
Hong Kong 5%
Japan 8%
Singapore 12%
Other 48%
China 12%
India 15%

Strengths

Over 80% of the world's jute fiber exports come from Bangladesh. Low wages ensure a competitive and expanding textile industry, which provides over three-quarters of manufacturing export earnings.

Weaknesses

The agricultural sector, employing the majority of Bangladeshis, is vulnerable to violent and unpredictable weather. Endemic corruption and poor infrastructure deter investment. Large and inefficient state sector.

Profile

Government ministers like to portray Bangladesh as an emerging NIC, but its economy is still overwhelmingly dependent on agriculture and large aid inflows. Agriculture, which provides jute and tobacco, is productive; Bangladesh's soils, fed by the Ganges, Jamuna, and Meghna rivers, are highly fertile. However, severe weather frequently destroys a whole crop.

ECONOMIC PERFORMANCE INDICATOR

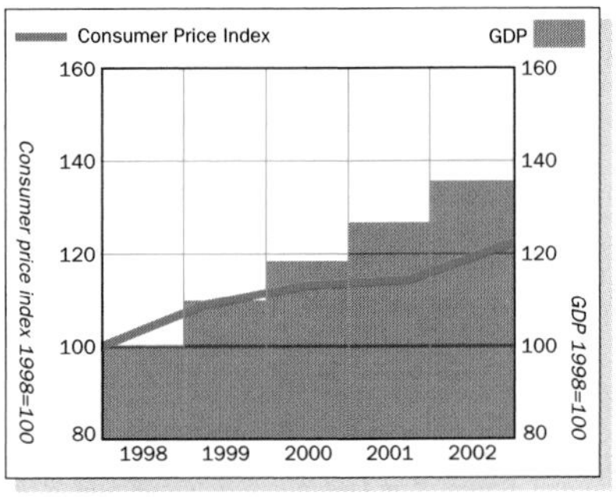
Consumer Price Index
GDP
160
140
120
100
80
Consumer price index 1998=100
GDP 1998=100
1998
1999
2000
2001
2002

Agricultural wages are among the lowest in the world.

The state sector, which owns large, inefficient, and massively loss-making companies, is in difficulty. The World Bank, the source of most aid, wishes to see loss-making concerns cut their workforces or close down. In 2002 a privatization program was announced.

Textiles and garments are currently the healthiest sectors. Economic zones (export processing zones) with special concessions have attracted foreign investment, as well as helping to promote a small indigenous electronics industry. Bangladesh receives generous textile import quotas from the EU and NAFTA.

BANGLADESH : MAJOR BUSINESSES

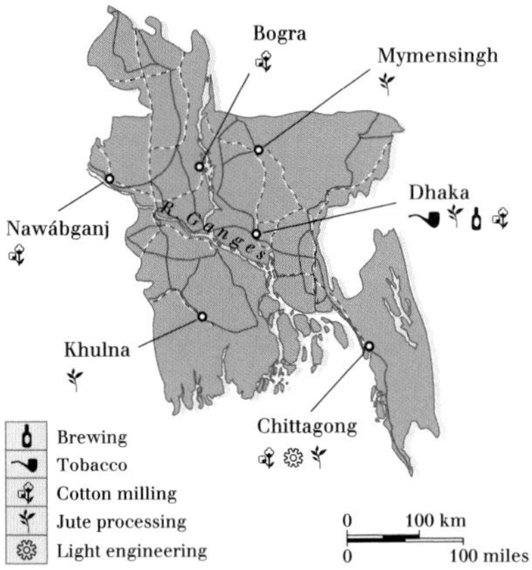
Bogra
Mymensingh
Dhaka
Nawábganj
R. Ganges
Khulna
Chittagong
Brewing
Tobacco
Cotton milling
Jute processing
Light engineering
0
100 km
0
100 miles

B

RESOURCES

Electric power 3.5m kW

1.69m tonnes

1444 b/d (reserves 70,000 barrels)

34.5m goats, 24.5m cattle, 13m ducks, 140m chickens

Salt, natural gas, oil, limestone

ELECTRICITY GENERATION

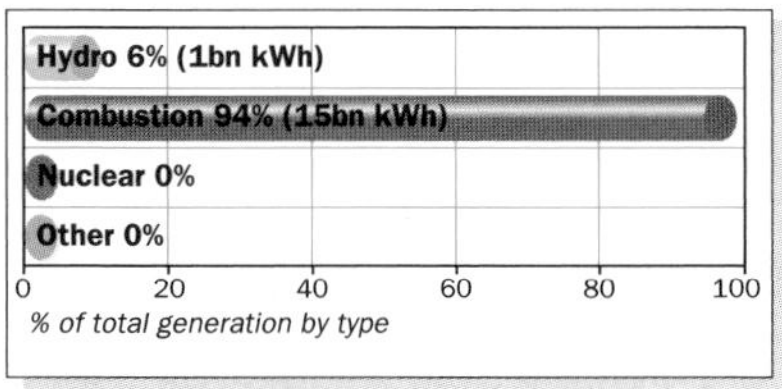
Hydro 6% (1bn kWh)
Combustion 94% (15bn kWh)
Nuclear 0%
Other 0%
0
20
40
60
80
100
% of total generation by type

BANGLADESH : LAND USE

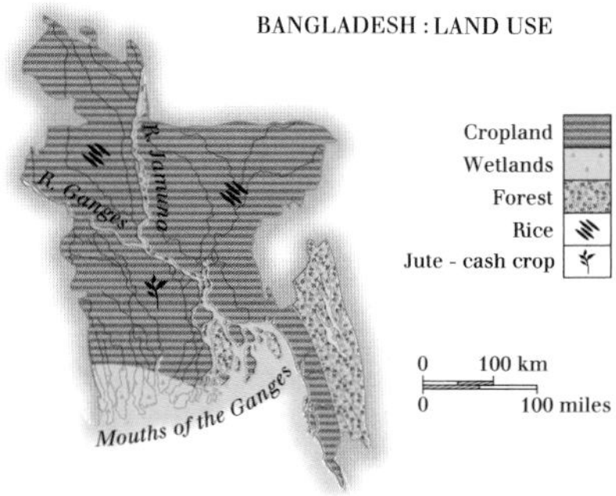
R. Jamuna
R. Ganges
Mouths of the Ganges
Cropland
Wetlands
Forest
Rice
Jute - cash crop
0
100 km
0
100 miles

Bangladesh is the world's major jute producer, accounting for almost 90% of world jute fiber exports and about 50% of world exports of jute products.

There are world-class gas reserves, estimated to last as long as 200 years at the present extraction rate. Gas exports are controversial; many demand greater domestic provision first. The first offshore oil field at Sangu came onstream in 1998.

ENVIRONMENT

Sustainability rank: 86th

0.8% (0.7% partially protected)

0.2 tonnes per capita

Bangladesh's climate gives rise to devastating floods and cyclones, with consequent huge death tolls and substantial damage to crops. The country is too poor to finance environmental initiatives.

ENVIRONMENTAL TREATIES

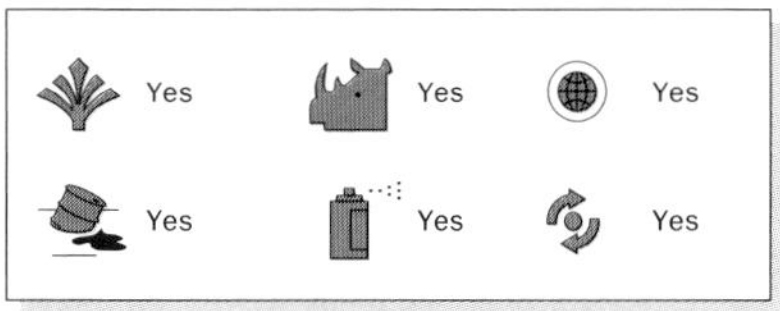
Yes
Yes
Yes
Yes
Yes
Yes

MEDIA

TV ownership medium

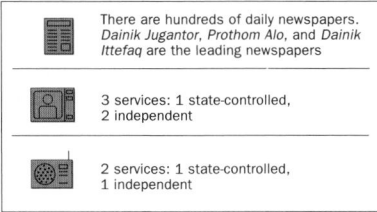

Daily newspaper circulation 53 per 1000 people

PUBLISHING AND BROADCAST MEDIA

There are hundreds of daily newspapers. *Dainik Jugantor, Prothom Alo,* and *Dainik Ittefaq* are the leading newspapers

3 services: 1 state-controlled, 2 independent

2 services: 1 state-controlled, 1 independent

With fewer than half of the population able to read, newspaper circulation is limited. English-language dailies appeal to the urban elite. Most TV programs are produced locally by the state-run service, though foreign satellite channels are increasingly available. Press freedom emerged briefly after President Ershad's fall in 1990 but has since been eroded, and violence or threats against journalists are a daily occurrence; Bangladesh has been named the world's most violent country for journalists.

HEALTH

Welfare state health benefits

1 per 4100 people

Parasitic, diarrheal, and communicable diseases

Though primary health care in rural areas improved in the 1990s, problems remain severe and are exacerbated by a shortage of medical staff and facilities. Sanitation is a major problem; drinking water is contaminated with disease and high levels of arsenic. Simple cloth filters could cut cholera infections by half. Priority for birth control programs has reduced the population growth rate dramatically in the last 20 years.

SPENDING

GDP/cap. increase

CONSUMPTION AND SPENDING

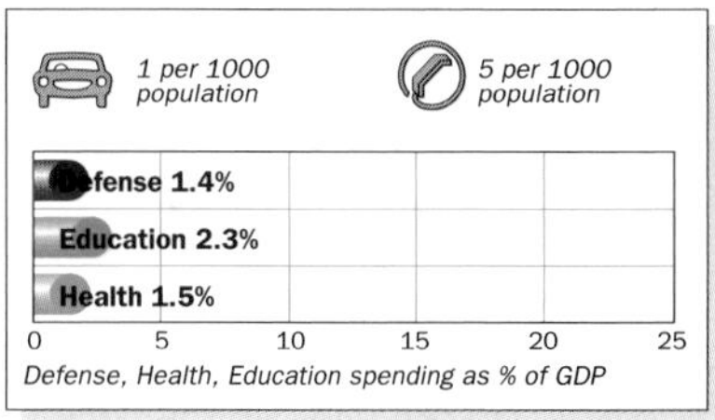
1 per 1000 population
5 per 1000 population
Defense 1.4%
Education 2.3%
Health 1.5%
0
5
10
15
20
25
Defense, Health, Education spending as % of GDP

Average incomes in Bangladesh remain very low, but wealth disparities are not quite as marked as in India. State officials tend to be among the better-off members of society.

CRIME

Death penalty in use

64,866 prisoners

Up 17% in 1996–1998

CRIME RATES

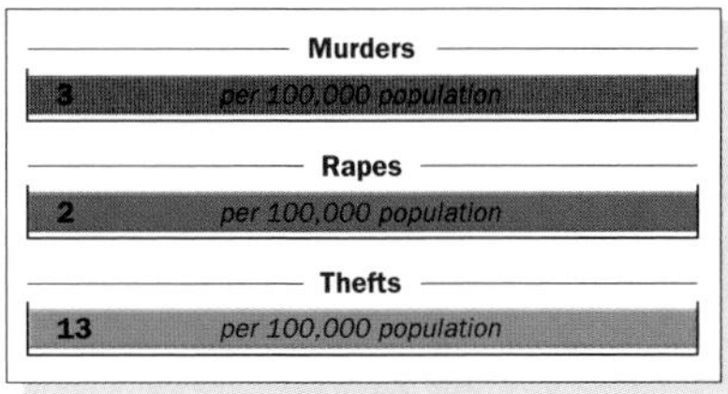
Murders
3 per 100,000 population
Rapes
2 per 100,000 population
Thefts
13 per 100,000 population

Rising levels of sectarian violence have led to the introduction of antiterrorism laws allowing summary justice and heavy penalties, including death. Deaths in prisons are common, and the human rights record of the security forces, especially the paramilitary Bangladesh Rifles, is questionable. From 2002, soldiers have been deployed to support police. Opposition activists have been targeted in crackdowns. Women are increasingly the victims of murder, rape, abduction, and acid attacks.

EDUCATION

School leaving age: 10

41%

878,537 students

THE EDUCATION SYSTEM

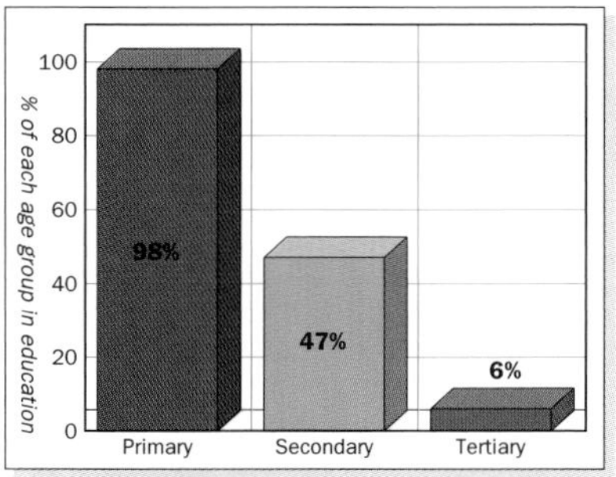
100
80
60
40
20
0
% of each age group in education
98%
47%
6%
Primary
Secondary
Tertiary

A dramatic reduction in the 1990s in the number of child workers meant an accompanying rise in school attendance. Islamic *madaris* are run parallel to the state system. There was an outcry from urban schools in 2002 when goat husbandry was put on the national curriculum. Exam cheating is a serious problem. Universities are frequently beset by political violence.

WORLD RANKING

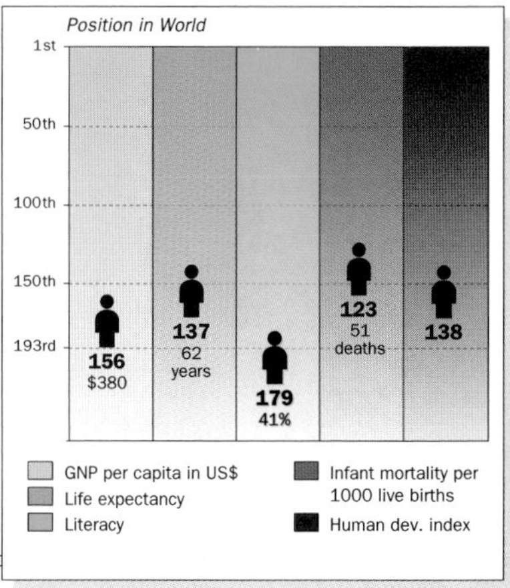
Position in World
1st
50th
100th
150th
193rd
156
$380
137
62
years
179
41%
123
51
deaths
138
GNP per capita in US$
Life expectancy
Literacy
Infant mortality per 1000 live births
Human dev. index

B

BARBADOS

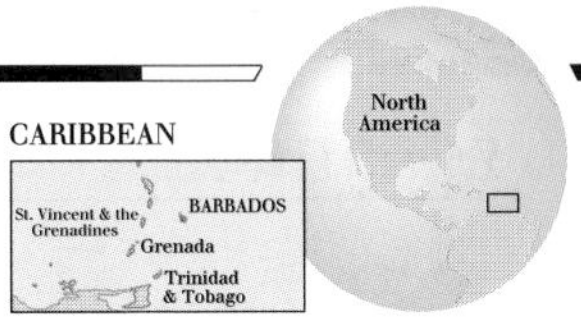
CARIBBEAN
North America
St. Vincent & the Grenadines
BARBADOS
Grenada
Trinidad & Tobago

OFFICIAL NAME: Barbados **CAPITAL:** Bridgetown
POPULATION: 270,000 **CURRENCY:** Barbados dollar **OFFICIAL LANGUAGE:** English

1966 | 1966 | Nov 30 | BDS | -4 | +1246 | .bb

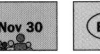

SITUATED TO THE NORTHEAST of Trinidad, Barbados is the most easterly of the West Indian Windward Islands. In the 16th century, the Portuguese were the first Europeans to reach the island, then inhabited by Arawak Indians. However, Barbados was not colonized until the 1620s, when British settlers arrived. Popularly referred to by its neighbors as "little England," Barbados now seeks to forge a new national identity for itself.

CLIMATE

Tropical oceanic

WEATHER CHART FOR BRIDGETOWN

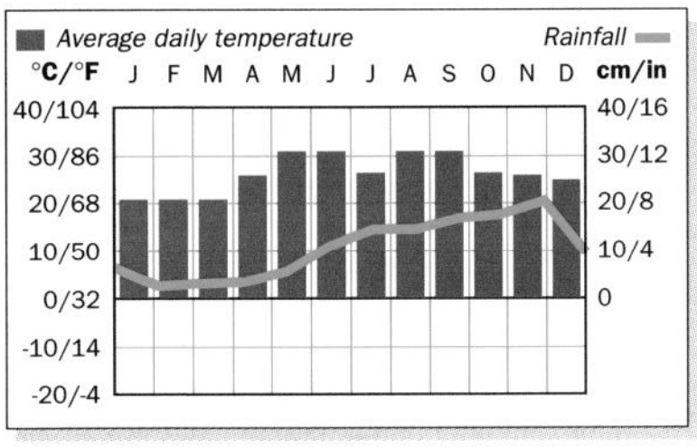
Average daily temperature
Rainfall
°C/°F J F M A M J J A S O N D cm/in
40/104
30/86
20/68
10/50
0/32
-10/14
-20/-4
40/16
30/12
20/8
10/4
0

Barbados has a moderate tropical climate and is sunnier and drier than its more mountainous Caribbean neighbors. Hurricanes may occur in the rainy season.

TRANSPORTATION

Drive on left

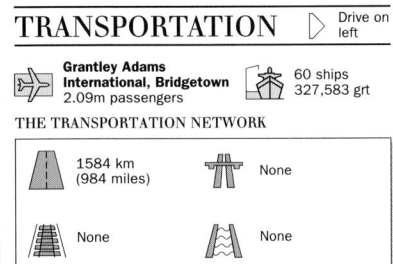

Grantley Adams International, Bridgetown
2.09m passengers

60 ships
327,583 grt

THE TRANSPORTATION NETWORK

1584 km (984 miles)	None
None	None

A multimillion dollar expansion program has upgraded facilities at the international airport. Piers at Bridgetown's port have been improved with foreign aid, as have the island's paved roads. There are bus routes over most of the island.

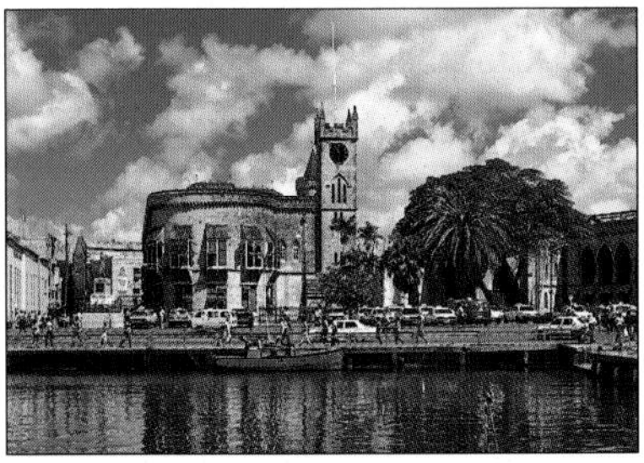

House of Assembly, Trafalgar Square, Bridgetown. Barbados's parliament, the third-oldest in the Commonwealth, dates from 1639.

TOURISM

Visitors : Population 1.8:1

498,000 visitors

Down 2% in 2002

MAIN TOURIST ARRIVALS

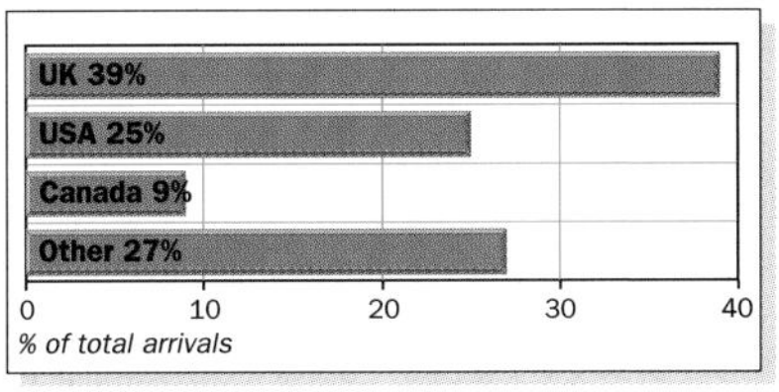
UK 39%
USA 25%
Canada 9%
Other 27%
0
10
20
30
40
% of total arrivals

Tourists, essential to the Barbadian economy, are attracted by the white sandy beaches and sporting activities, as well as the postcolonial ambience and the generally laid-back culture.

PEOPLE

Pop. density high

Bajan (Barbadian English), English

628/km² (1627/mi²)

THE URBAN/RURAL POPULATION SPLIT

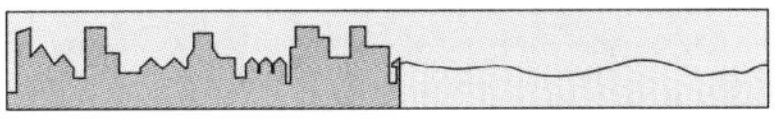
51%
49%

RELIGIOUS PERSUASION

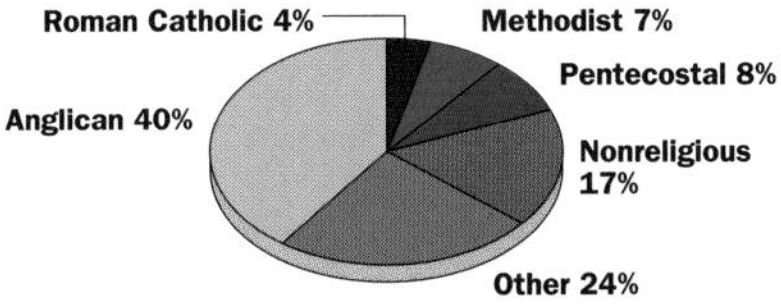
Roman Catholic 4%
Methodist 7%
Pentecostal 8%
Anglican 40%
Nonreligious 17%
Other 24%

Most Barbadians are descended from Africans brought to the island between the 16th and 19th centuries; there is also a small group of Europeans, mainly expatriates from the UK, many of whom take up residence on retirement. There is some latent tension between the white community and the majority black population, though this rarely spills over into violence. Increasing social mobility has allowed many black Barbadians to move into the professions and the civil service. The population has a low growth rate, partly due to high levels of emigration. Barbados enjoys a higher standard of living than most Caribbean countries.

POLITICS

Multiparty elections

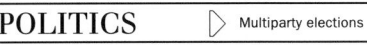

L. House 2003/2008
U. House 2003/2008

H.M. Queen Elizabeth II

AT THE LAST ELECTION

House of Assembly 30 seats

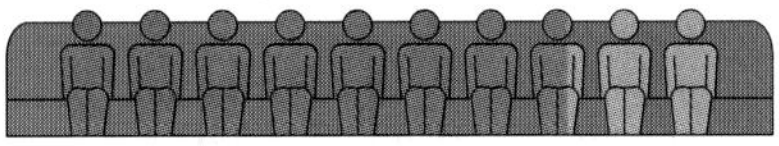
77% BLP
23% DLP

BLP = Barbados Labour Party
DLP = Democratic Labour Party

Senate 21 seats

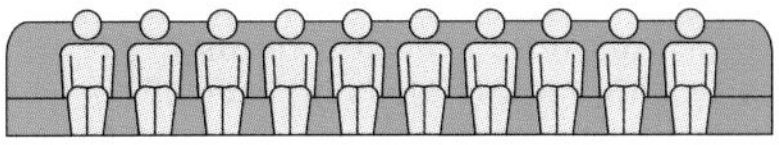

The members of the Senate are appointed. Twelve are chosen by the prime minister, two by the leader of the opposition, and seven independents by the governor-general

Barbados is a multiparty democracy. Owen Arthur, BLP leader and prime minister, prioritizes economic growth and international competitiveness. His party was swept to power in 1994 and won further victories in 1999 and 2003. However, the opposition DLP made significant gains in the 2003 poll as the government began to encounter economic difficulties. Arthur has previously pledged to transform Barbados into a republic.

WORLD AFFAIRS

Joined UN in 1966

ACS | Comm | Caricom | NAM | OAS

A fishing dispute with Trinidad & Tobago has developed into an issue over maritime borders.

AID

Recipient

US$3m (receipts)

Up in 2002

Most aid comes from the EU, the US, and the UN, mainly in the form of development project loans and balance-of-payments support.

DEFENSE

No compulsory military service

US$12m

Down 8% in 2002

The small Barbadian army and the constabulary benefit from financial support and training from the US and UK governments, which also supply equipment. Barbados is the headquarters of the Regional Security System, established in 1982 by the Windward and Leeward Islands, a body which acts as a multinational security force for its members.

B

ECONOMICS

Inflation 2.9% p.a. (1990–2001)

US$2.36bn

2 Barbados dollars (1.99)

SCORE CARD

- ❑ WORLD GNP RANKING........................137th
- ❑ GNP PER CAPITA ....US$8790
- ❑ BALANCE OF PAYMENTS................–US$171m
- ❑ INFLATION 0.1%
- ❑ UNEMPLOYMENT.................................10%

STRENGTHS

Well-developed tourism based on climate and accessibility. Information processing and financial services are important new growth sectors.

WEAKNESSES

Narrow economic base and an ailing sugar industry. Tourism industry vulnerable to global downturns. Relatively high manufacturing costs. Low population growth restricts labour supply.

EXPORTS

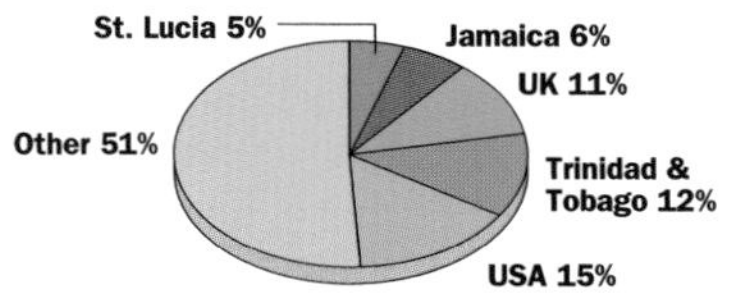
St. Lucia 5%
Jamaica 6%
UK 11%
Other 51%
Trinidad & Tobago 12%
USA 15%

IMPORTS

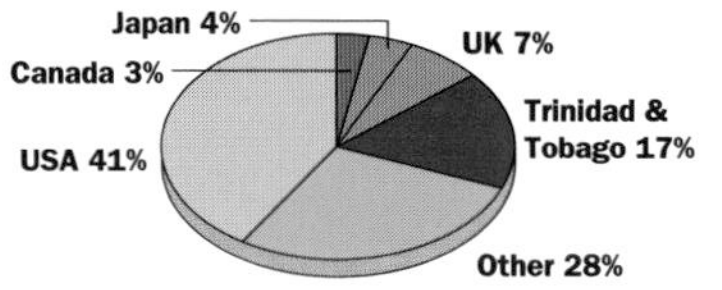
Japan 4%
UK 7%
Canada 3%
Trinidad & Tobago 17%
USA 41%
Other 28%

BARBADOS

Total Area : 430 sq. km (166 sq. miles)

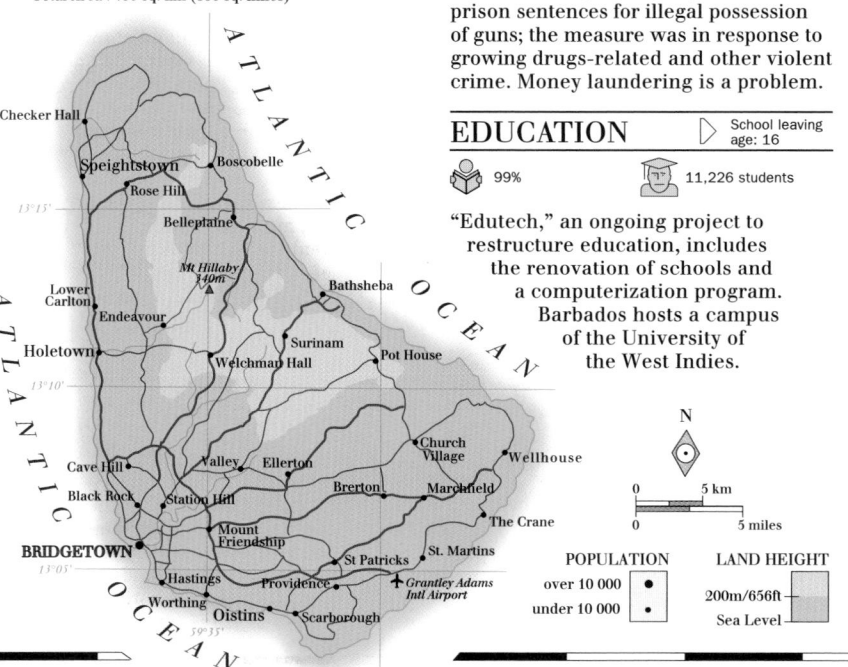

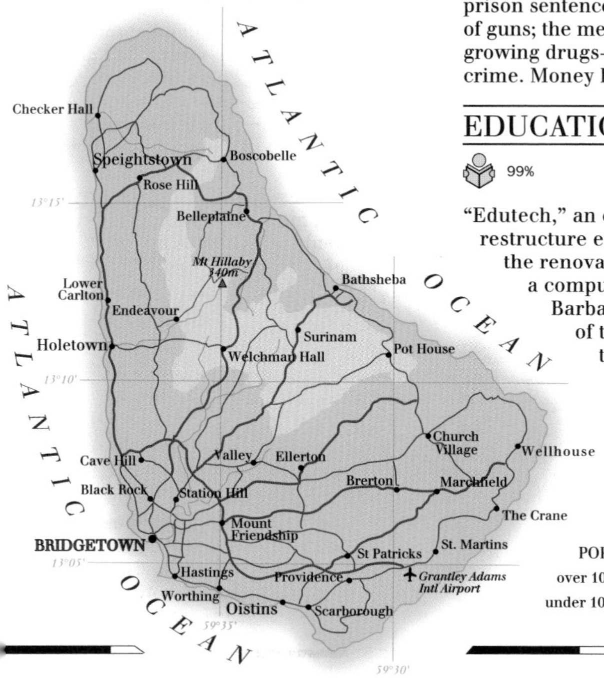
ATLANTIC
ATLANTIC OCEAN
ATLANTIC OCEAN
Checker Hall
Speightstown
Boscobelle
Rose Hill
13°15'
Belleplaine
Mt Hillaby 340m
Bathsheba
Lower Carlton
Endeavour
Holetown
Surinam
Welchman Hall
Pot House
13°10'
Church Village
Wellhouse
Cave Hill
Valley
Ellerton
Black Rock
Station Hill
Brereton
Marchfield
The Crane
Mount Friendship
BRIDGETOWN
St Patricks
St. Martins
13°05'
Hastings
Providence
Grantley Adams Intl Airport
Worthing
Oistins
Scarborough
59°35'
59°30'

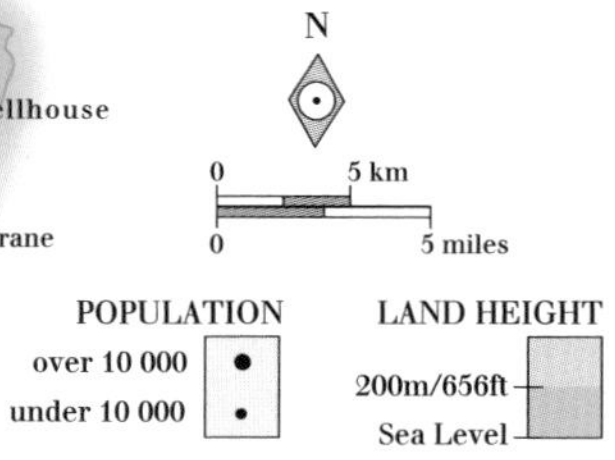
N
0
5 km
0
5 miles
POPULATION
over 10 000
under 10 000
LAND HEIGHT
200m/656ft
Sea Level

RESOURCES

Electric power 166,000 kW

2676 tonnes

1544 b/d (reserves 7.3m barrels)

57,000 turkeys, 27,000 sheep, 3.45m chickens

Oil, natural gas

Barbados has few strategic resources. Oil extracted by Barbados is refined in Trinidad & Tobago and then returned for domestic use.

ENVIRONMENT

Not available

0.5%

4.4 tonnes per capita

Oil slicks created by waste dumped from passing ships are polluting the encircling reef and adversely affecting the life cycle of the flying fish, Barbados's main fish stock.

MEDIA

TV ownership high

Daily newspaper circulation 200 per 1000 people

PUBLISHING AND BROADCAST MEDIA

There are 2 daily newspapers, the *Barbados Advocate* and the *Nation*

1 state-owned service with subscription option

3 services: 1 state-owned, 2 independent

There is no political interference in the media. The two daily newspapers are privately owned. Multichannel TV is available on subscription.

CRIME

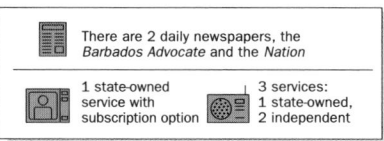

Death penalty in use

992 prisoners

Up 7% in 2000

An update in 2000 to firearms legislation imposed heavy fines and prison sentences for illegal possession of guns; the measure was in response to growing drugs-related and other violent crime. Money laundering is a problem.

EDUCATION

School leaving age: 16

99%

11,226 students

"Edutech," an ongoing project to restructure education, includes the renovation of schools and a computerization program. Barbados hosts a campus of the University of the West Indies.

CHRONOLOGY

Colonized by the British in 1627, Barbados grew rich in the 18th century from sugar produced using slave labor.

- ❑ **1951** Universal adult suffrage introduced.
- ❑ **1961** Full internal self-government.
- ❑ **1966** Independence from the UK.
- ❑ **1983** Barbados supports and provides a base for the US invasion of Grenada.
- ❑ **1994, 1999, 2003** BLP wins three successive general elections.

HEALTH

Welfare state health benefits

1 per 769 people

Heart and cerebrovascular diseases, cancers

The health system is based on subsidized government-run clinics and hospitals, supplemented by more expensive private clinics and private doctors. Facilities are within easy reach of all Barbadians.

SPENDING

GDP/cap. increase

CONSUMPTION AND SPENDING

233 per 1000 population

494 per 1000 population

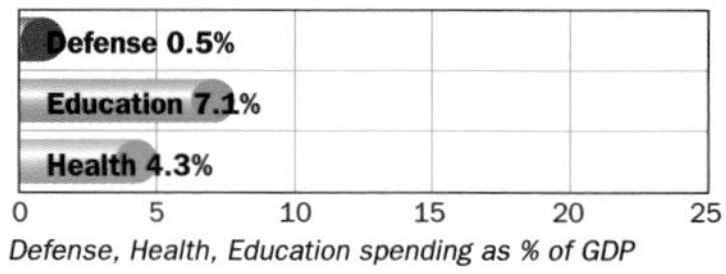
Defense 0.5%
Education 7.1%
Health 4.3%
0
5
10
15
20
25
Defense, Health, Education spending as % of GDP

A significant disparity exists between most Barbadians and a small affluent group, usually of European origin, which owns and controls business and industry, and parades status symbols such as yachts. Prime Minister Arthur stated in 1998 that "abject poverty" existed in the country.

WORLD RANKING

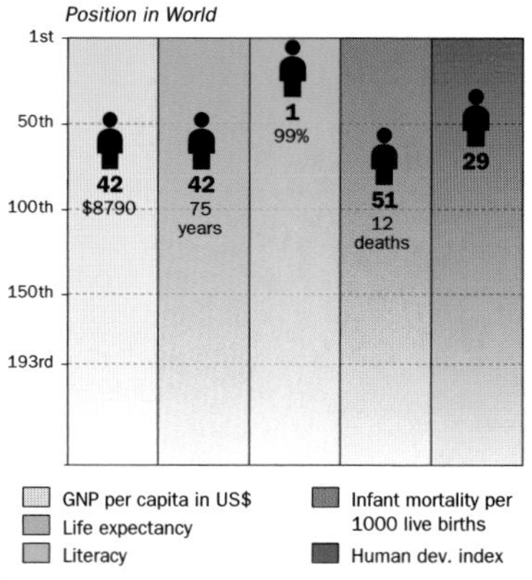
Position in World
1st
50th
100th
150th
193rd
42
$8790
42
75 years
1
99%
51
12 deaths
29
GNP per capita in US$
Life expectancy
Literacy
Infant mortality per 1000 live births
Human dev. index

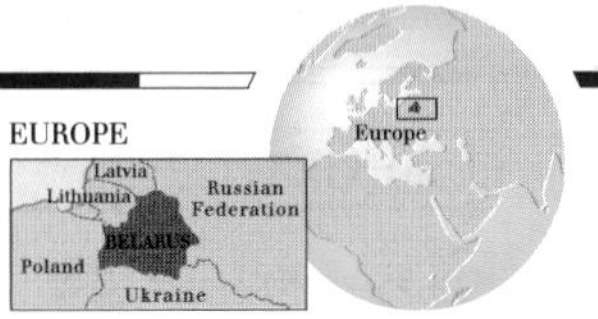
EUROPE
Europe
Latvia
Lithuania
Russian Federation
BELARUS
Poland
Ukraine

BELARUS

OFFICIAL NAME: Republic of Belarus **CAPITAL:** Minsk **POPULATION:** 9.9 million
CURRENCY: Belarussian rouble **OFFICIAL LANGUAGES:** Belarussian and Russian

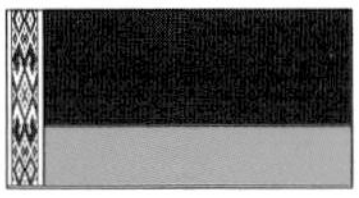

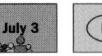

1991 | 1991 | July 3 | BY | +2 | +375 | .by

BELARUS LITERALLY MEANS "white Russia," a color associated in Slavic culture with freedom, and a reference to the fact that the country was never conquered by the Mongol Golden Horde. Devastated in World War II, and with few resources other than agriculture, Belarus only reluctantly became independent of Moscow in 1991; efforts to reunite the two countries have lost impetus in recent years. The Chernobyl nuclear disaster in Ukraine in 1986 has had lasting effects on the environment and on the health of Belarussians.

CLIMATE

Continental

WEATHER CHART FOR MINSK

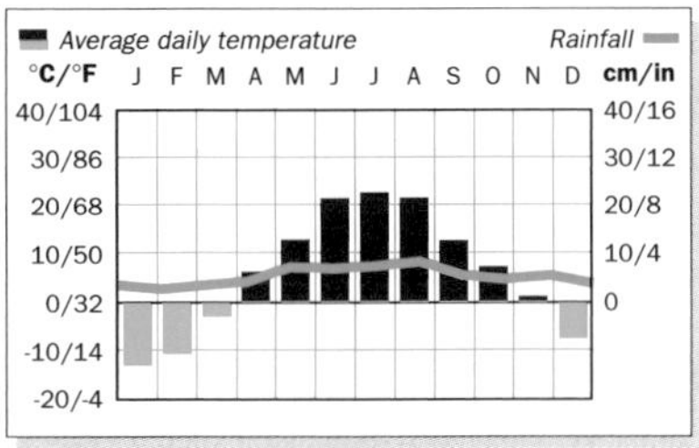
Average daily temperature
Rainfall
°C/°F
J F M A M J J A S O N D
cm/in
40/104
30/86
20/68
10/50
0/32
-10/14
-20/-4
40/16
30/12
20/8
10/4
0

Belarus has a continental climate somewhat moderated by the influence of the nearby Baltic Sea. Temperatures in winter drop well below freezing, however, while summers can be hot and humid. Summer is also the main season for rainfall.

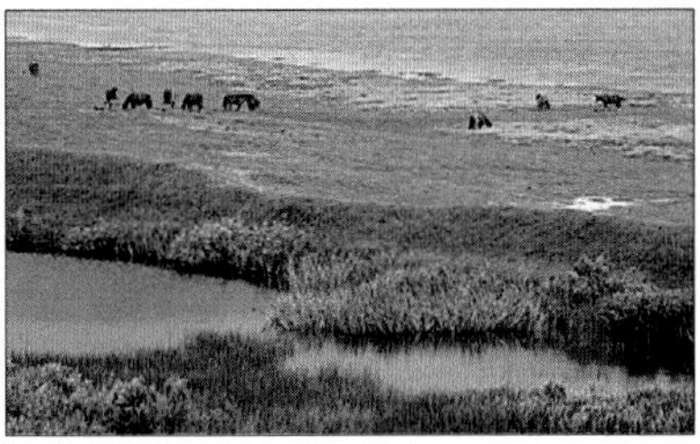

Much of southern Belarus is marshy and sparsely populated. It includes the vast Pripet Marshes and the Dnieper lowlands.

TRANSPORTATION

Drive on right

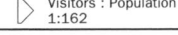

Minsk 421,954 passengers

Has no fleet

THE TRANSPORTATION NETWORK

67,019 km (41,644 miles)

None

5512 km (3425 miles)

Extensive canal and river systems

Belarus has no direct access to the sea, but is close to the Baltic ports. Railroad communications are good.

TOURISM

Visitors : Population 1:162

61,000 visitors

Down 83% in 1999–2001

MAIN OVERSEAS ARRIVALS

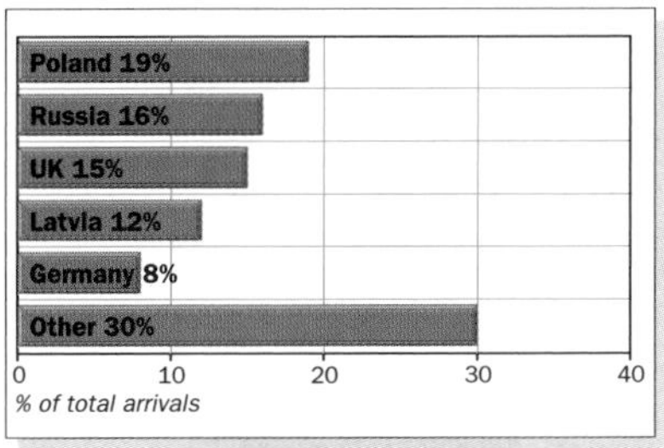
Poland 19%
Russia 16%
UK 15%
Latvia 12%
Germany 8%
Other 30%
0
10
20
30
40
% of total arrivals

Belarus has fewer tourists than its neighbors. Many of its historic buildings were destroyed during World War II. Minsk was totally flattened, and is now characterized by Stalinist and other high-rise buildings. There is little of mass appeal on which to build a tourist industry.

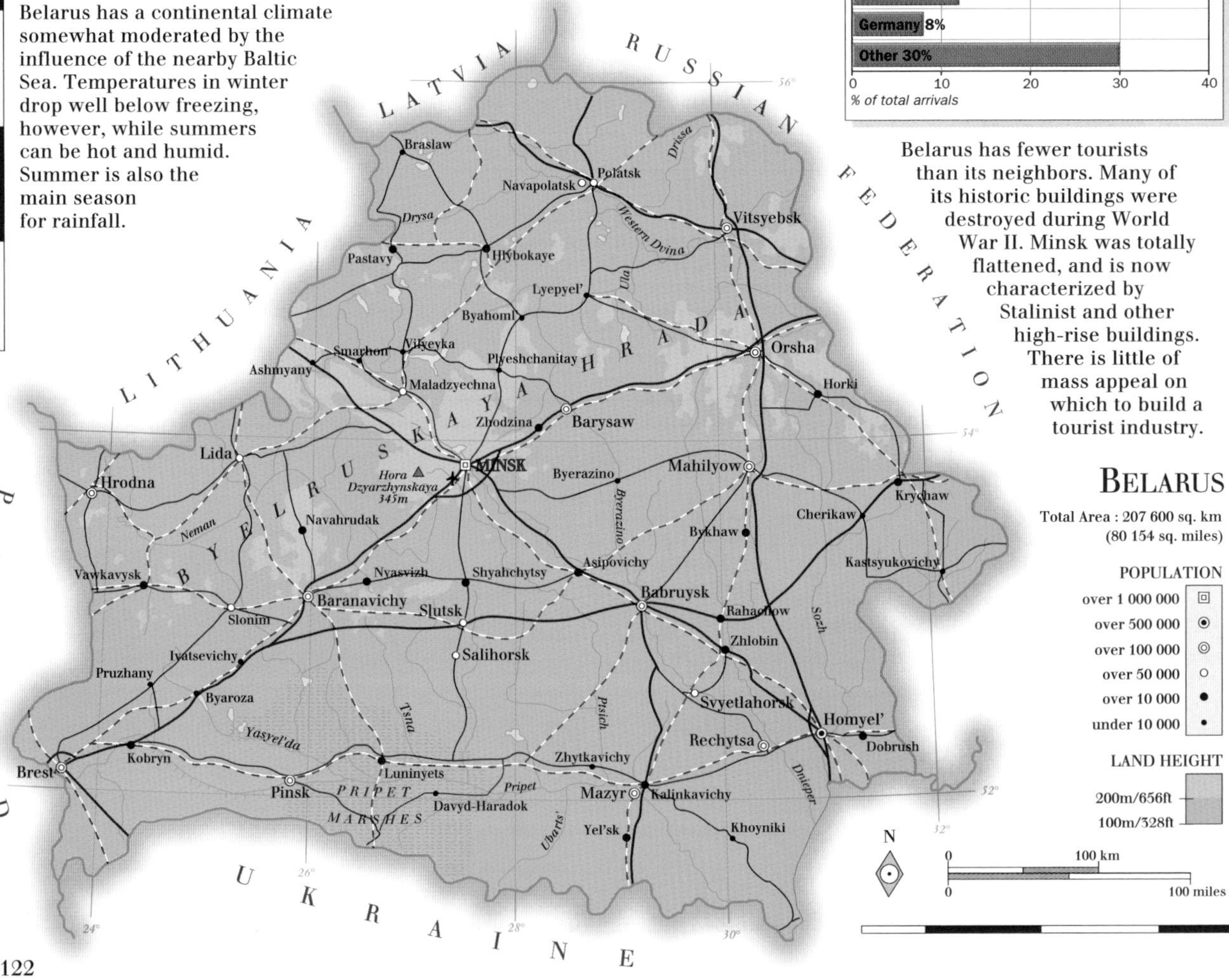
LATVIA
RUSSIAN FEDERATION
LITHUANIA
POLAND
UKRAINE
BYELARUSKAYA HRADA
Braslaw
Polatsk
Navapolatsk
Vitsyebsk
Pastavy
Hlybokaye
Lyepyel'
Byahoml'
Smarhon'
Vilyeyka
Pleshchanitsy
Orsha
Ashmyany
Maladzyechna
Horki
Zhodzina
Barysaw
Lida
MINSK
Hora Dzyarzhynskaya 345m
Byerazino
Mahilyow
Hrodna
Navahrudak
Krychaw
Cherikaw
Bykhaw
Kastsyukovichy
Vawkavysk
Nyasvizh
Shyahchytsy
Asipovichy
Baranavichy
Slutsk
Babruysk
Slonim
Rahachow
Salihorsk
Zhlobin
Ivatsevichy
Pruzhany
Byaroza
Svyetlahorsk
Homyel'
Dobrush
Rechytsa
Kobryn
Brest
Luninyets
Zhytkavichy
Pinsk
PRIPET MARSHES
Davyd-Haradok
Mazyr
Kalinkavichy
Khoyniki
Yel'sk
Drysa
Western Dvina
Ulla
Neman
Byerazino
Sozh
Dnieper
Pripet
Ptsich
Tsna
Yasyel'da
Ubarts'
BELARUS
Total Area : 207 600 sq. km (80 154 sq. miles)
POPULATION
over 1 000 000
over 500 000
over 100 000
over 50 000
over 10 000
under 10 000
LAND HEIGHT
200m/656ft
100m/328ft
N
0
100 km
0
100 miles

PEOPLE

Pop. density low

Belarussian, Russian

48/km² (124/mi²)

THE URBAN/RURAL POPULATION SPLIT

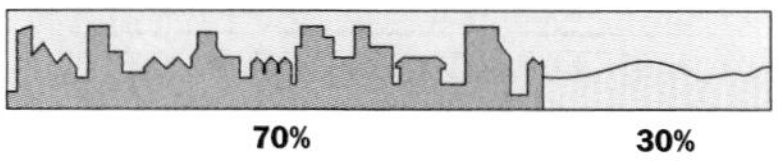
70%
30%

RELIGIOUS PERSUASION

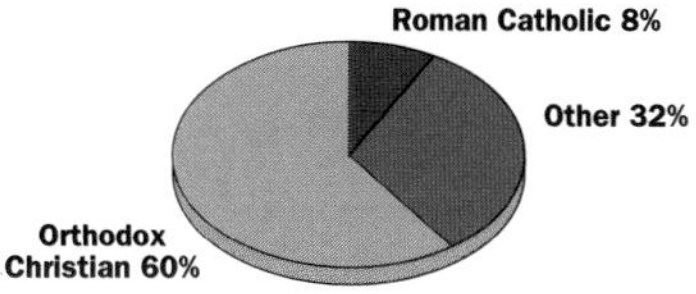
Roman Catholic 8%
Other 32%
Orthodox Christian 60%

ETHNIC MAKEUP

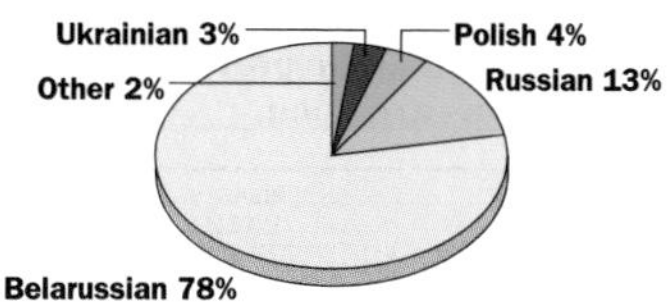
Ukrainian 3%
Polish 4%
Other 2%
Russian 13%
Belarussian 78%

Only 2% of the population are non-Slav and there is little ethnic tension. Most people speak Russian, and only 11% of the population are fluent in Belarussian, which is used mainly in rural areas; both languages have equal status. The social position of the Orthodox Church has increased since 1991 and was officially strengthened in 2002 at the expense of the growing number of Protestant churches.

POPULATION AGE BREAKDOWN

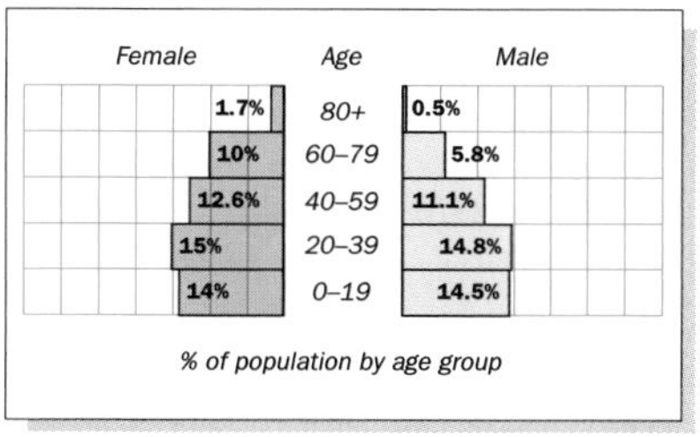
Female
Age
Male
1.7%
80+
0.5%
10%
60–79
5.8%
12.6%
40–59
11.1%
15%
20–39
14.8%
14%
0–19
14.5%
% of population by age group

POLITICS

Multiparty elections

L. House 2000/2004
U. House 2000/2004

President Aleksandr Lukashenka

AT THE LAST ELECTION

House of Representatives 110 seats

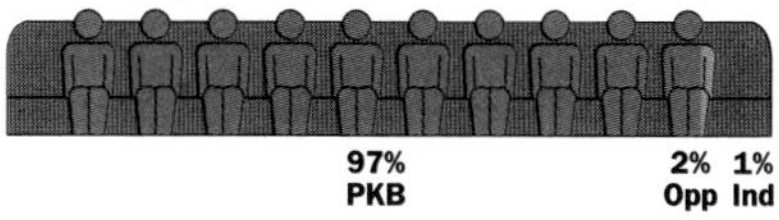
97% PKB
2% Opp
1% Ind

PKB = Party of Communists of Belarus and government supporters **Opp** = Minor opposition parties **Ind** = Independents

Council of the Republic 64 seats

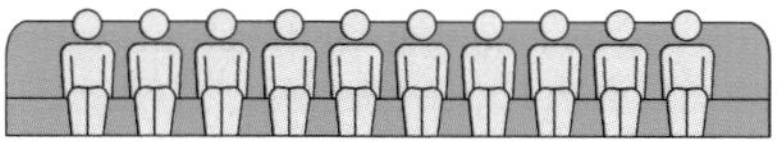

The Council of the Republic is indirectly elected

Belarus has a directly elected executive president, and a bicameral parliament.

Profile

Belarus, by far the slowest of the former Soviet states to implement political reform, has struggled to find an identity since 1991. A post-Soviet constitution was not adopted until 1994, and only in 1995 was the first fully fledged post-Soviet parliament elected, dominated by the PKB and its Agrarian Party ally. Aleksandr Lukashenka was unexpectedly elected Belarus's first president in 1994. He has since concentrated power in his own hands, drawing fierce criticism. A strong pluralist culture has yet to be established, however, opposition parties being hamstrung by internal divisions and easily outmaneuvered by the powerful presidency. A clampdown on political opponents effectively invalidated parliamentary elections in late 2000–early 2001. Lukashenka's reelection in late 2001 was immediately condemned by observers.

Main Political Issues

The relationship with Russia

In 1994 an accord (reinforced in 1999 and 2000) was signed on future monetary union with Russia. Lukashenka has sought ever closer relations, with the ultimate goal of a joint presidency. A union treaty was signed in late 1999, but it is more symbolic than practical. With Russian reticence and Belarus's declining enthusiasm for the union, the treaty has produced no significant developments toward joint state institutions or economic programs.

Powers of the presidency

Described as a dictator by his detractors, Lukashenka has an authoritarian style which has put him into conflict with his own government, let alone the international community, the domestic political opposition, and the public. His second term in office is due to expire in 2006. Some observers predict, however, that the current constitutional two-term limit is unlikely to stand in his way if he chooses to run for a third term; his first term was arbitrarily lengthened twice.

***President Aleksandr Lukashenka** has been accused of authoritarian rule.*

***Vladimir Goncharik**, Lukashenka's main rival in presidential elections in 2001.*

WORLD AFFAIRS

Joined UN in 1945

EAPC CIS IAEA CEI OSCE

Relations with Russia are paramount. Numerous bilateral agreements were signed after independence in 1991. Ties have been strengthened further by the pro-Russian stance of Lukashenka, though many in Russia fear that closer links will drain Moscow's resources for little strategic gain.

Concerns over human rights and authoritarianism damage relations with many other countries. A move to relax EU sanctions was hindered in 2001 by the closure of the OSCE office in Minsk. Lukashenka and members of his government were banned from entering any EU country from late 2002 until the office was reopened in April 2003.

AID

Recipient

$39m (receipts)

Little change in 2002

Though both the World Bank and the IMF provided loans for Belarus in the early 1990s, the lack of structural reforms since Lukashenka's administration came to power in 1994 has meant that further aid has been stalled. Some US bilateral aid continued, but the EU in particular has made it clear that support will depend on human rights improvements and the reversal of authoritarian threats to democracy.

Both the US and the EU extended credits to Belarus to assist in the conversion of the defense industry to nonmilitary production. Belarus also still requires aid to combat the effects of radiation pollution in the wake of the Chernobyl nuclear accident of 1986.

CHRONOLOGY

After forming part of medieval Kievan Rus, Belarus was ruled by three of its neighbors – Lithuania, Poland, and Russia – before incorporation into the USSR.

- **1918** Belarussian Bolsheviks stage coup. Independence as Belorussian Soviet Socialist Republic (BSSR).
- **1919** Invaded by Poland.
- **1920** Minsk retaken by Red Army. Eastern Belorussia reestablished as Soviet Socialist Republic.
- **1921** Treaty of Riga – Western Belorussia incorporated into Poland.
- **1922** BSSR merges with Soviet Russia and Ukraine to form USSR.
- **1929** Stalin implements collectivization of agriculture.
- **1939** Western Belorussia reincorporated into USSR when Soviet Red Army invades Poland.

B

CHRONOLOGY *continued*

- ❑ **1941–1944** Occupied by Germany during World War II.
- ❑ **1945** Founding member of UN.
- ❑ **1956–1980** Government dominated by wartime partisan leaders K. T. Mazurov (to 1965) and P. M. Masherov.
- ❑ **1986** Radioactive fallout after Chernobyl accident affects 70% of country.
- ❑ **1988** Evidence revealed of mass executions (over 300,000) by Soviet military between 1937 and 1941 near Minsk. Popular outrage fuels formation of nationalist Belorussian Popular Front (BPF), with Zyanon Paznyak as president. PKB authorities crush demonstration.
- ❑ **1989** Belarussian adopted as republic's official language.
- ❑ **1990** PKB prevents BPF from participating in elections to Supreme Soviet. BPF members join other opposition groups in Belorussian Democratic Bloc (BDB). BDB wins 25% of seats. PKB bows to opposition pressure and issues Declaration of the State Sovereignty of BSSR.
- ❑ **1991** March, 83% vote in referendum to preserve union with USSR. April, strikes against PKB and its economic policies. August, independence declared. Republic of Belarus adopted as official name. Stanislau Shushkevich elected chair of Supreme Soviet. December, Belarus, Russia, and Ukraine establish CIS.
- ❑ **1992** Supreme Soviet announces that Soviet nuclear weapons must be cleared from Belarus by 1999. Help promised from US.
- ❑ **1993** Belarussian parliament ratifies START-I and nuclear nonproliferation treaties.
- ❑ **1994** New presidential constitution approved; Aleksandr Lukashenka defeats conservative prime minister Vyacheslav Kebich in elections. Monetary union (reentry into rouble zone) agreed with Russia.
- ❑ **1995** First fully fledged post-Soviet parliament elected.
- ❑ **1996** Referendum approves changes to constitution strengthening Lukashenka's powers.
- ❑ **1997** Belarus and Russia ratify union treaty and Charter.
- ❑ **1998** Eviction from embassies sparks withdrawal of Western ambassadors.
- ❑ **1999** Signs union treaty with Russia.
- ❑ **2000–2001** Disputed parliamentary elections; clampdown on PKB's political opponents.
- ❑ **2001** Lukashenka reelected; observers label election seriously flawed.

DEFENSE

Compulsory military service

$1.89bn

Down 3% in 2002

BELARUSSIAN ARMED FORCES

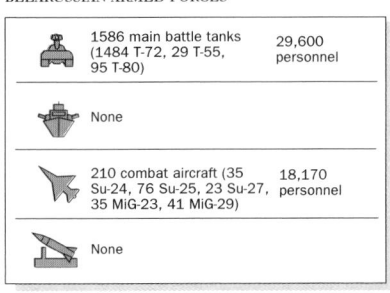

Army	1586 main battle tanks (1484 T-72, 29 T-55, 95 T-80)	29,600 personnel
Navy	None	
Air force	210 combat aircraft (35 Su-24, 76 Su-25, 23 Su-27, 35 MiG-23, 41 MiG-29)	18,170 personnel
Missiles	None	

After the breakup of the Soviet Union in 1991, Belarus briefly adopted a policy of neutrality. It also committed itself to disposing of its inherited nuclear capability. Tactical nuclear weapons were removed by 1993 and strategic nuclear weapons by 1996.

Despite joining the CIS collective security agreement in 1993, Belarus joined NATO's Partnership for Peace program in 1995. Lukashenka has not developed NATO ties further, preferring to establish stronger military links with Moscow. Under the Belarus–Russia union treaty defense policies in Belarus and Russia are to be harmonized. From 2002 Belarussian troops have been allowed to serve abroad, despite there theoretically being constitutional barriers.

ECONOMICS

Inflation 318% p.a. (1990–2001)

$13.5bn

2162 Belarussian roubles (2066)

SCORE CARD

- ❑ World GNP Ranking 80th
- ❑ GNP per Capita $1360
- ❑ Balance of Payments ....–$378m
- ❑ Inflation 42.5%
- ❑ Unemployment 3%

EXPORTS

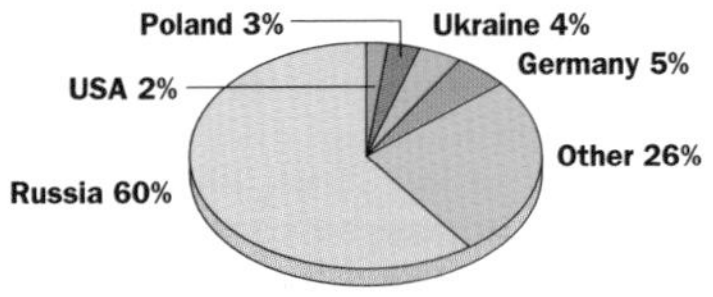
Poland 3%
Ukraine 4%
Germany 5%
USA 2%
Other 26%
Russia 60%

IMPORTS

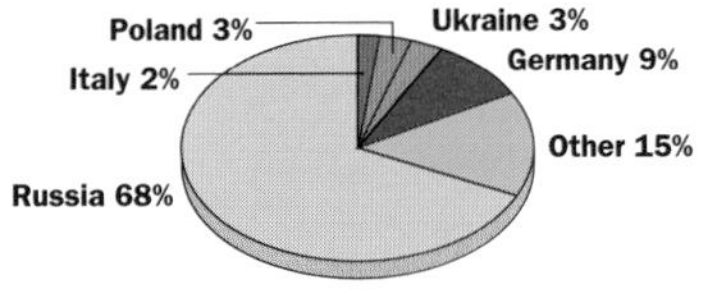
Poland 3%
Ukraine 3%
Germany 9%
Italy 2%
Other 15%
Russia 68%

Strengths

Low unemployment combined with relative social stability. Potential of forestry and agriculture.

Weaknesses

Lack of economic restructuring; support for outmoded businesses. Few natural resources. Dependence on Russia for energy and raw materials. Cleanup costs of Chernobyl. High inflation.

Profile

After 1991, Belarus adopted economic reform at a slower pace than other former Soviet states. Attempts to move more quickly to a market economy were thwarted by the largely Communist parliament. Upon election in 1994, Lukashenka suspended privatization moves, resuming them only halfheartedly in 1995, under a policy of "market socialism." The National Bank began to liberalize the exchange market in 2000 and is taking steps to ensure that money production is not increased.

A currency crisis in 1998, and rampant inflation, coincided with two successive bad harvests in 1998 and 1999. Inflation receded in 2000–2002, but the rate of economic growth has slowed.

ECONOMIC PERFORMANCE INDICATOR

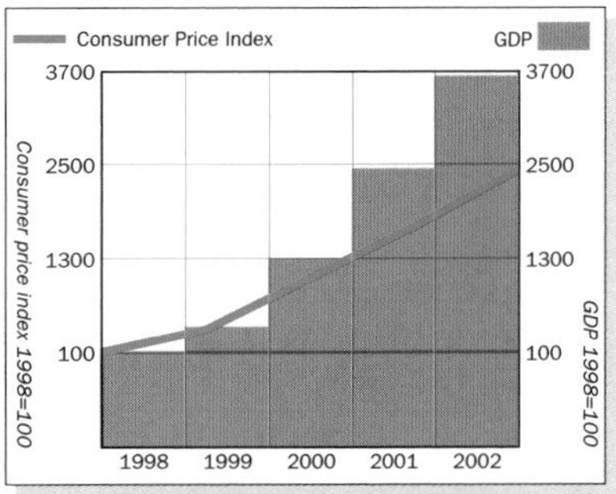
Consumer Price Index
GDP
3700
2500
1300
100
Consumer price index 1998=100
GDP 1998=100
1998
1999
2000
2001
2002

BELARUS : MAJOR BUSINESSES

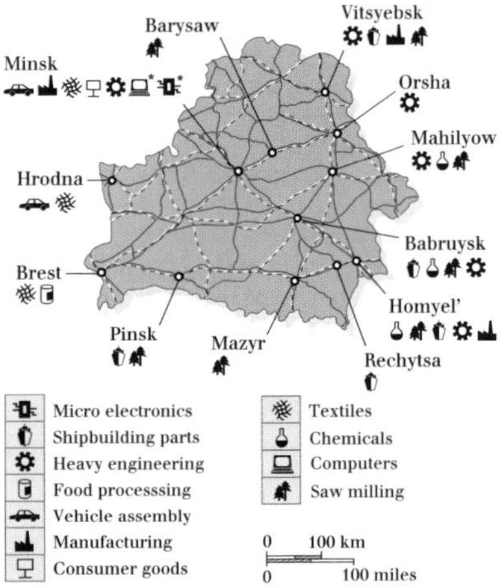
Barysaw
Vitsyebsk
Minsk
Orsha
Mahilyow
Hrodna
Babruysk
Brest
Homyel'
Pinsk
Mazyr
Rechytsa
Micro electronics
Shipbuilding parts
Heavy engineering
Food processsing
Vehicle assembly
Manufacturing
Consumer goods
Textiles
Chemicals
Computers
Saw milling
0 100 km
0 100 miles

* significant multinational ownership

B

RESOURCES

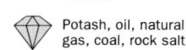

Electric power 7.8m kW

5609 tonnes

37,113 b/d (reserves 203m barrels)

4.01m cattle, 3.33m pigs, 30m chickens

Potash, oil, natural gas, coal, rock salt

ELECTRICITY GENERATION

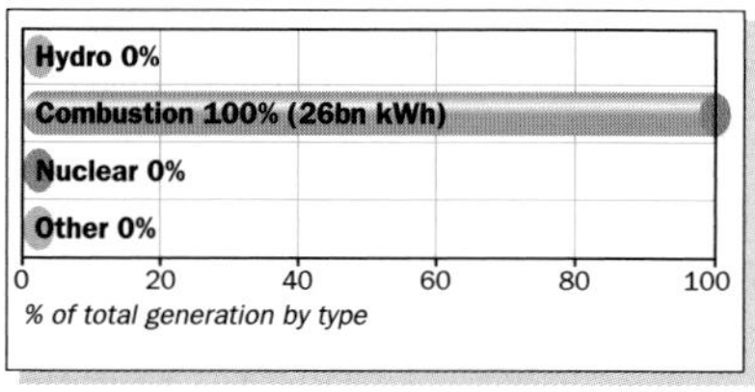
Hydro 0%
Combustion 100% (26bn kWh)
Nuclear 0%
Other 0%
0
20
40
60
80
100
% of total generation by type

Belarus is the world's third-largest producer of potash. Apart from this, there are no other significant strategic resources and the country is heavily dependent on Russia for fuel and energy supplies.

BELARUS : LAND USE

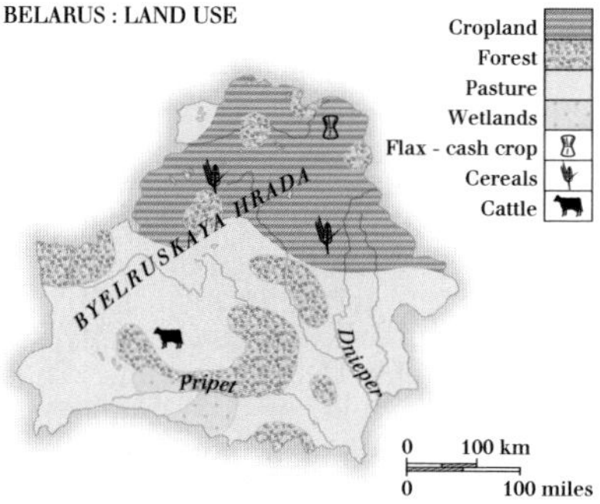
Cropland
Forest
Pasture
Wetlands
Flax - cash crop
Cereals
Cattle
BYELRUSKAYA HRADA
Dnieper
Pripet
0 100 km
0 100 miles

ENVIRONMENT

Sustainability rank: 49th

6% (3% partially protected)

5.9 tonnes per capita

ENVIRONMENTAL TREATIES

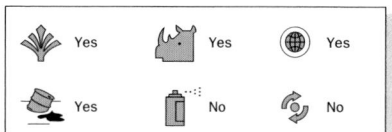

Yes | Yes | Yes

Yes | No | No

The massive leak from Ukraine's Chernobyl nuclear plant in 1986 released a huge cloud of radiation. Some 70% of the fallout fell on Belarus; 2.3 million people were immediately affected, and cases of leukemia and cancer continue to emerge. Farmland, forests, and water were all contaminated, including underwater streams feeding rivers in eastern Poland. Some areas in the fallout zone are still being farmed. The cleanup program swallows 20% of government finances, despite substantial Western aid, but the threat of further leaks has been removed by the closure in 2000 of Chernobyl's last reactor.

The Belavezhskaya Pushcha primeval forest, on the border with Poland, is one of Europe's largest nature reserves. It is now a habitat for the rare European bison or wisent.

MEDIA

TV ownership high

Daily newspaper circulation 152 per 1000 people

PUBLISHING AND BROADCAST MEDIA

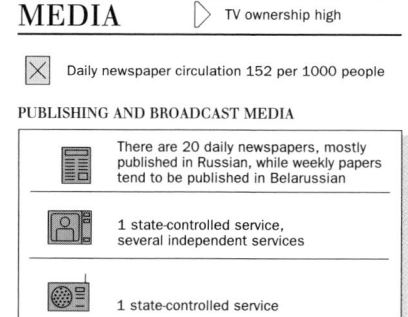

There are 20 daily newspapers, mostly published in Russian, while weekly papers tend to be published in Belarussian

1 state-controlled service, several independent services

1 state-controlled service

There are some independent media outlets, but government critics face harassment. Press freedom is curbed; state-backed publications predominate.

CRIME

Death penalty in use

55,156 prisoners

Up 4% in 2000–2002

CRIME RATES

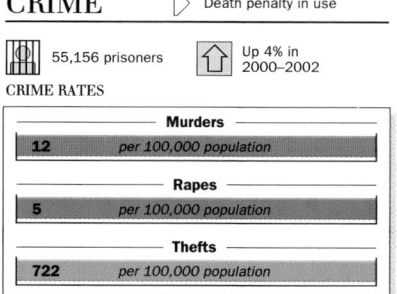

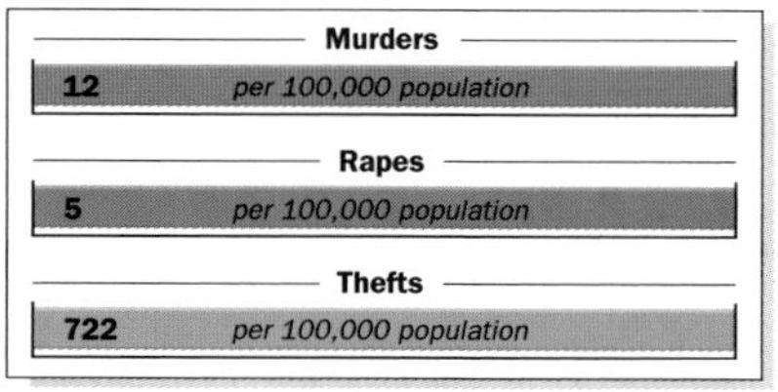
Murders
12 per 100,000 population
Rapes
5 per 100,000 population
Thefts
722 per 100,000 population

As elsewhere in the former Soviet Union, economic hardship and a general breakdown in law and order have resulted in a significant rise in crime. The prison population exceeds the intended capacity of 40,000. Belarus has become a transshipment point for illegal narcotics destined for western Europe, while locally produced opium supplies the internal market.

EDUCATION

School leaving age: 14

99%

437,995 students

THE EDUCATION SYSTEM

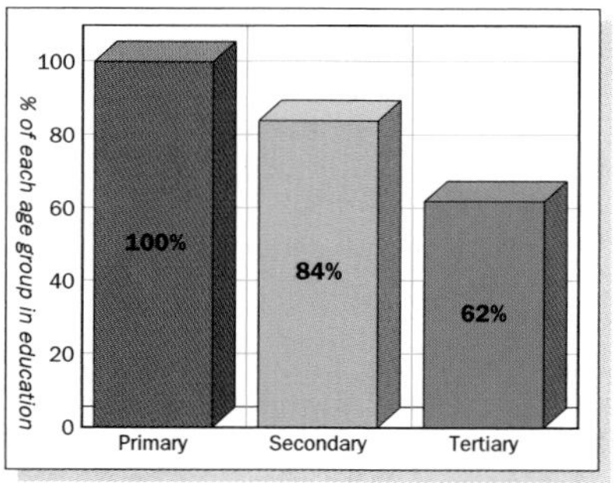
100
80
60
40
20
0
% of each age group in education
100%
84%
62%
Primary
Secondary
Tertiary

Education is officially compulsory for nine years, and teaching is mainly in Russian. Activists complain that because of political bias there is inadequate provision for the teaching of Belarussian. University education – taught in Russian – is of a fairly high standard.

HEALTH

Welfare state health benefits

1 per 222 people

Cerebrovascular and heart diseases, cancers, violence

Belarus's health service performs relatively well. It has been under particular strain, however, in coping with the long-term effects of the 1986 Chernobyl nuclear disaster. Assistance for victims of the accident is funded by a Chernobyl tax. The number of cancer and leukemia cases has soared, and extra wards and specialist units have had to be built. Many Belarussian doctors are being trained in the latest bone-marrow techniques in Europe and the US.

HIV/AIDS is a growing problem; most infections are via intravenous drug use.

SPENDING

GDP/cap. decrease

CONSUMPTION AND SPENDING

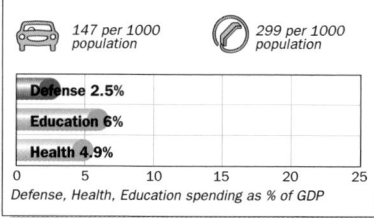

147 per 1000 population

299 per 1000 population

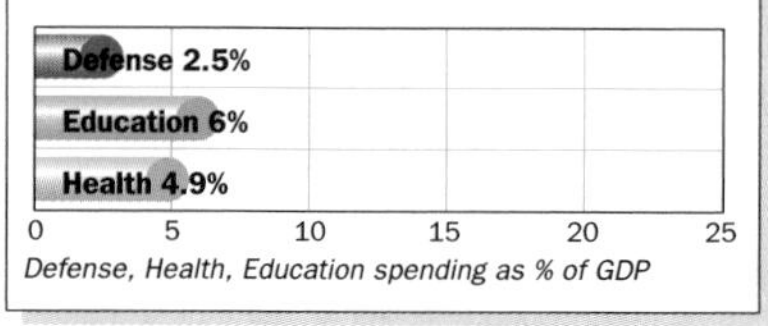
Defense 2.5%
Education 6%
Health 4.9%
0
5
10
15
20
25
Defense, Health, Education spending as % of GDP

The deteriorating economic situation has resulted in an overall drop in living standards. Wealth is concentrated among a small, communist elite which is opposed to market mechanisms. Since it has had the upper hand, its members have strengthened their grip on the state's resources. Thus far Belarus has not seen the expansion of entrepreneurial activity found in other former Soviet-bloc countries such as Poland or Russia.

Wage increases in 2001 – an election year – brought salaries to levels which were unaffordable, so that enterprise profitability and investment were severely affected.

WORLD RANKING

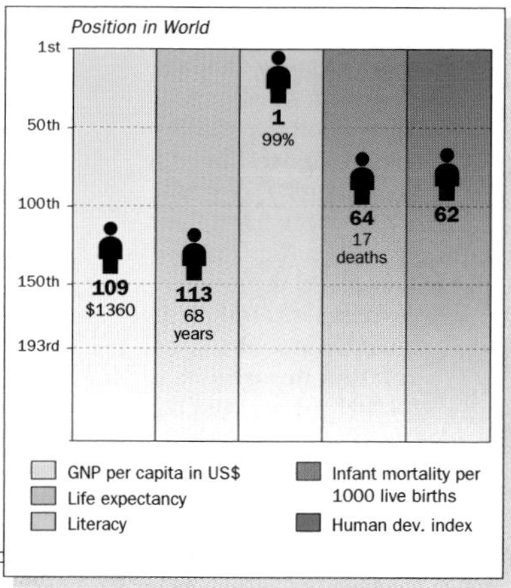
Position in World
1st
50th
100th
150th
193rd
109
$1360
113
68
years
1
99%
64
17
deaths
62
GNP per capita in US$
Life expectancy
Literacy
Infant mortality per 1000 live births
Human dev. index

BELGIUM

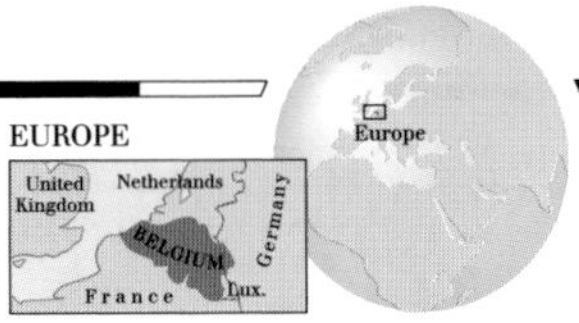
EUROPE
Europe
United Kingdom
Netherlands
Germany
BELGIUM
France
Lux.

OFFICIAL NAME: Kingdom of Belgium **CAPITAL:** Brussels **POPULATION:** 10.3 million
CURRENCY: Euro **OFFICIAL LANGUAGES:** Dutch, French, and German

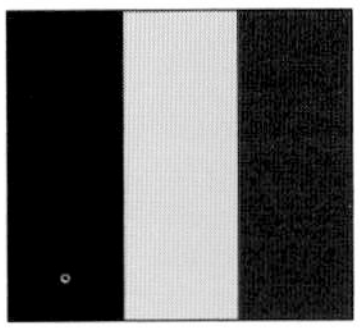

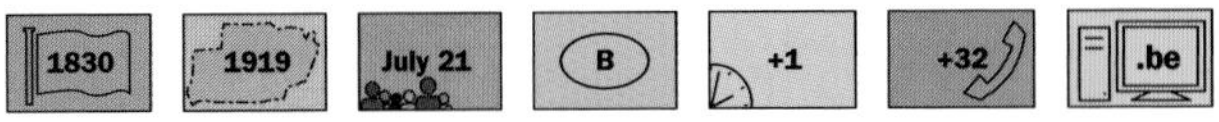
1830
1919
July 21
B
+1
+32
.be

LOCATED BETWEEN GERMANY, France, and the Netherlands, Belgium has a short coastline on the North Sea. The south includes the forested Ardennes region, while the north is crisscrossed by canals. Belgium has been fought over many times in its history; it was occupied by Germany in both world wars. Tensions have existed between the Dutch-speaking Flemings and French-speaking Walloons since the 1830s. These have been somewhat defused by Belgium's move to a federal political structure and the national consensus on the benefits of EU membership.

CLIMATE

Maritime

WEATHER CHART FOR BRUSSELS

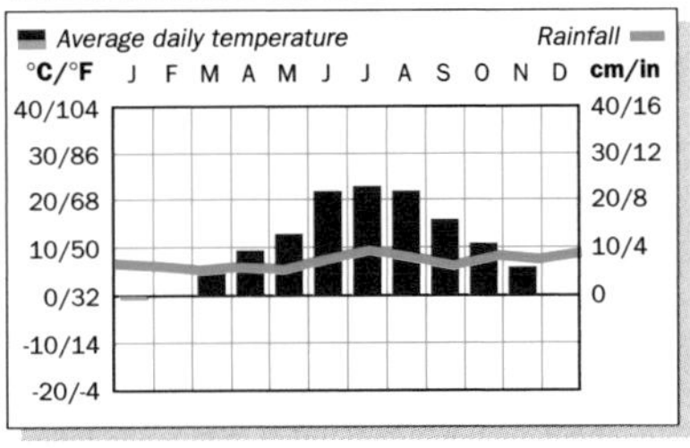
Average daily temperature
Rainfall
°C/°F
J F M A M J J A S O N D
cm/in
40/104
30/86
20/68
10/50
0/32
-10/14
-20/-4
40/16
30/12
20/8
10/4
0

Belgium has a typical maritime climate and is influenced by the Gulf Stream. Temperatures are mild, accompanied by heavy cloud cover and much rain. Widely fluctuating weather conditions, caused by cyclonic disturbances, can disrupt the climate on the coast. Summers tend to be short.

TRANSPORTATION

Drive on right

Brussels Zaventem
15.2m passengers

188 ships
186,700 grt

THE TRANSPORTATION NETWORK

116,242 km (72,229 miles)

1729 km (1074 miles)

3518 km (2186 miles)

1570 km (976 miles)

Belgium can be crossed within four hours by car or train. The expressway network is extensive, and though the railroad system has been reduced since 1970, it still constitutes one of the world's densest networks. Using high-speed TGV lines, Paris is just 80 minutes from Brussels, and London via the Channel Tunnel takes 2 hours 20 minutes.

In 2001 the national airline Sabena collapsed dramatically, amid a slump in the aviation industry. A section of it subsequently formed the basis for a new private airline, SN Brussels Airlines.

Antwerp is the second-largest port in Europe.

TOURISM

Visitors : Population 1:1.5

6.72m visitors

Up 4% in 2002

MAIN TOURIST ARRIVALS

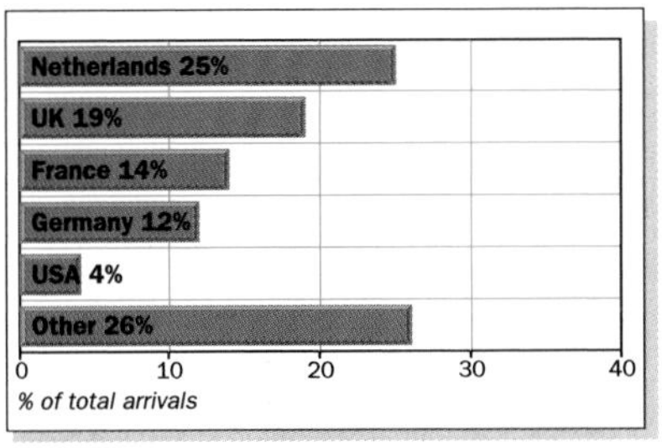
Netherlands 25%
UK 19%
France 14%
Germany 12%
USA 4%
Other 26%
0
10
20
30
40
% of total arrivals

Belgium's main attractions are its historic cities and the museums of Flemish art. Bruges, the capital of West Flanders, is often referred to as the "Venice of the North." With Gothic and Renaissance architecture and a complex canal system, it has become a favored destination for British weekend trippers and Japanese honeymooners. In Brussels, the famous Grande Place, a cluster of Gothic, Renaissance, and Baroque buildings in a cobbled square, survived bombing during World War II. Much of the rest of the old city center, however, was destroyed. Belgium has 15 resorts on its 62-km (38-mile) coastline, with a tramline running its entire length. Forests in the Ardennes to the southeast attract hikers.

The Ardennes plateau, *in the southeast, is famous for its scenery and cuisine. It is dissected by rivers, such as the Meuse and Semois.*

PEOPLE

Pop. density high

Dutch, French, German

314/km² (813/mi²)

THE URBAN/RURAL POPULATION SPLIT

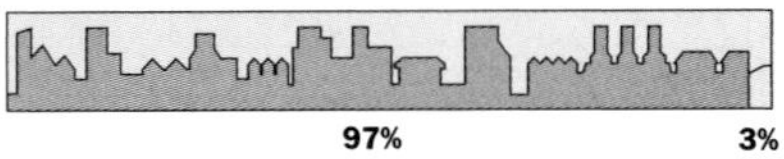
97%
3%

RELIGIOUS PERSUASION

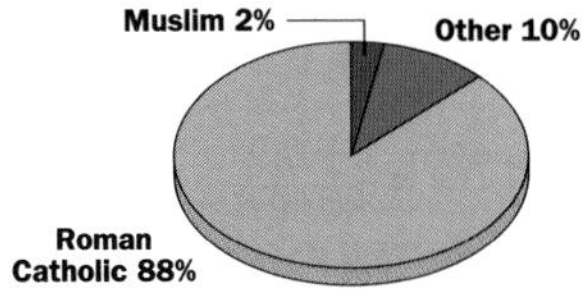
Muslim 2%
Other 10%
Roman Catholic 88%

ETHNIC MAKEUP

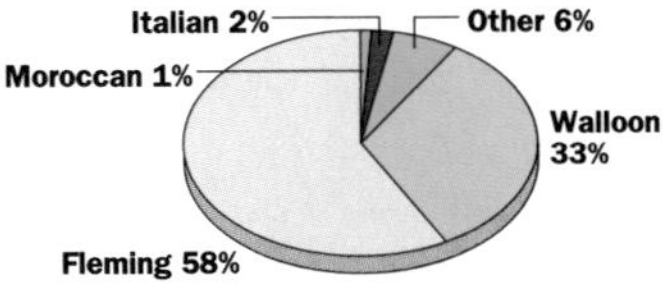
Italian 2%
Other 6%
Moroccan 1%
Walloon 33%
Fleming 58%

Belgium has been marked by the divisions between its Flemish and Walloon communities. The majority Dutch-speaking Flemings are concentrated in Flanders. Wallonia is French-speaking and Brussels is 85% francophone. Only rarely have tensions between Walloons and Flemings erupted into violence. French speakers were in the ascendancy for many years, their greater economic wealth reinforced by the dominance of the French language in public life. Since the 1960s, however, Wallonia's industries have declined and Flanders is now the wealthier region. Belgium began in 1970 to change from being one of Europe's most centralized states to one of its most federal states; each community now has control of much of its affairs and possesses its own government. A small German-speaking community in the east has extensive autonomy in educational and cultural matters. Belgium also has a sizable immigrant population.

Women make up two-fifths of the workforce; they only account, however, for one-fifth of the administrators and managers.

POPULATION AGE BREAKDOWN

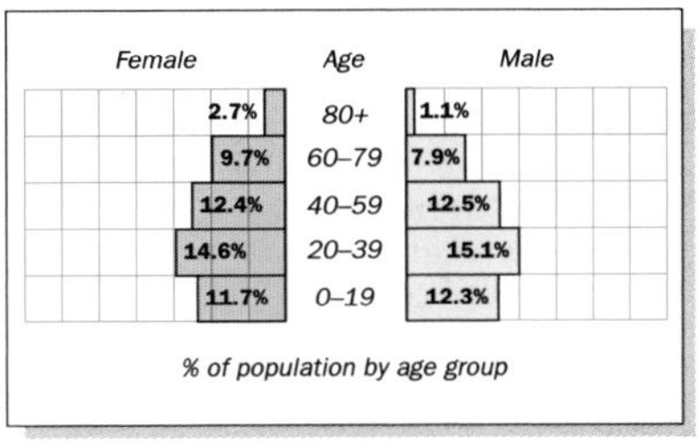
Female
Age
Male
2.7%
80+
1.1%
9.7%
60–79
7.9%
12.4%
40–59
12.5%
14.6%
20–39
15.1%
11.7%
0–19
12.3%
% of population by age group

BELGIUM

Total Area : 30 510 sq. km (11 780 sq. miles)

POPULATION

- ◻ over 1 000 000
- ◎ over 100 000
- ○ over 50 000
- ● over 10 000

LAND HEIGHT

- 500m/1640ft
- 200m/656ft
- Sea Level

N

0 40 km

0 40 miles

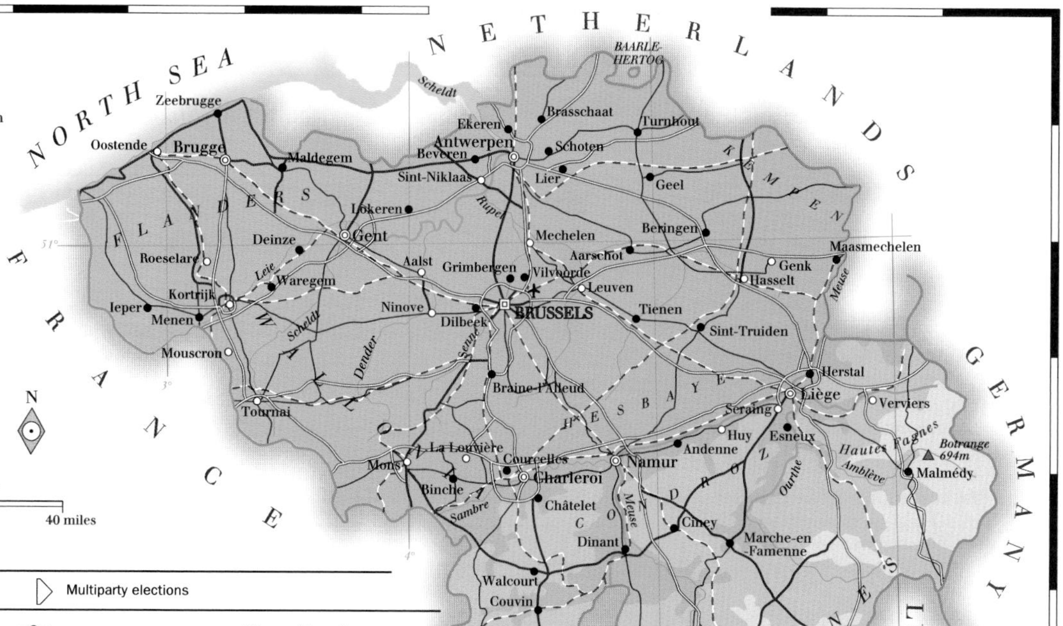
NORTH SEA
NETHERLANDS
FRANCE
GERMANY
LUXEMBOURG
FLANDERS
WALLONIA
HESBAYE
CONDROZ
ARDENNES
KEMPEN
BAARLE-HERTOG
Zeebrugge
Oostende
Brugge
Maldegem
Antwerpen
Ekeren
Beveren
Brasschaat
Schoten
Turnhout
Sint-Niklaas
Lier
Geel
Lokeren
Gent
Deinze
Roeselare
Kortrijk
Ieper
Menen
Waregem
Aalst
Mechelen
Beringen
Aarschot
Grimbergen
Vilvoorde
Leuven
Genk
Hasselt
Maasmechelen
Ninove
Dilbeek
BRUSSELS
Tienen
Sint-Truiden
Mouscron
Tournai
Braine-l'Alleud
Herstal
Liège
Seraing
Verviers
Huy
Esneux
Andenne
Namur
La Louvière
Courcelles
Charleroi
Mons
Binche
Châtelet
Dinant
Ciney
Marche-en-Famenne
Walcourt
Couvin
Bastogne
Arlon
Malmédy
Botrange 694m
Hautes Fagnes
Scheldt
Leie
Dender
Senne
Rupel
Meuse
Sambre
Ourthe
Amblève
Semois

POLITICS

▷ Multiparty elections

L. House 2003/2007
U. House 2003/2007

H.M. King Albert II

AT THE LAST ELECTION

Chamber of Representatives 150 seats

VLD	PS	MR	SPA–S	CD&V	VB	Ecolo	CDH	Others
17%	17%	16%	15%	14%	12%	3%	5%	1%

VLD = Flemish Liberals and Democrats **PS** = Socialist Party (francophone) **MR** = Reformist Movement (francophone) **SPA–S** = Socialist Party Different–Spirit coalition (Flemish) **CD&V** = Christian Democratic & Flemish **VB** = Flemish Block **CDH** = Humanist Democratic Center (francophone) **Ecolo** = Greens (francophone) **Co-op** = Co-opted members

Senate 71 seats

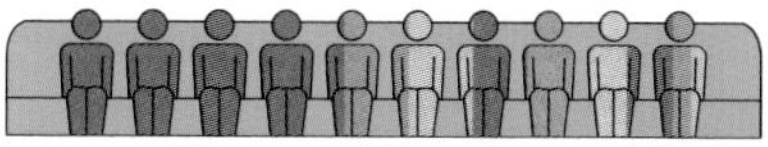

Co-op	VLD	SPA–S	CD&V	PS	VB	MR	CDH	Others
44%	10%	10%	8%	8%	7%	7%	3%	3%

The Senate has 40 directly elected members and 31 co-opted members

Successive constitutional reforms in the 1970s and 1980s culminated in the 1993 St. Michael Agreement, since when Belgium has been a federal monarchy. 2001 saw a further transfer of power from the center to Flanders, Wallonia, and Brussels.

PROFILE

Politics is largely defined along language lines. This apart, a high degree of consensus exists over the benefits of EU membership and monetary union.

In the late 1990s a centrist coalition of the Socialist and Christian Democrat parties had difficulty in securing the necessary majority for further constitutional reforms. A "rainbow" coalition composed of the Liberals, Socialists, and Greens, under the VLD's Guy Verhofstadt, came to power after the 1999 elections. The first government without Christian Democrats since 1958, it undertook a program of social liberalization, including the legalization of euthanasia and the decriminalization of cannabis. While the Liberals and Socialists increased their representation in 2003, the Greens saw their support more than halved as a consequence of political inexperience and their pursuit of unpopular policies such as banning tobacco advertising which cost Belgium its place on the Grand Prix circuit.

MAIN POLITICAL ISSUES

Language

Tensions between the two main language groups have been mitigated by progressive federalization, but Flemish groups in particular continue to demand further powers.

The far right

In recent years, support has increased for Flanders' far-right party, the VB, which modeled itself in the 1980s on the National Front in France. With a decidedly anti-immigration position and exploiting popular concern about unemployment, crime, and insecurity, the VB won 18% of the Flemish vote in the 2003 national elections, but it remains politically isolated.

King Albert II, *succeeded his brother King Baudouin, who died in 1993.*

Guy Verhofstadt, *youthful leader of the VLD and prime minister since 1999.*

WORLD AFFAIRS

▷ Joined UN in 1945

Benelux | CE | EU | OECD | NATO

Belgium's key concern is its role in the EU. It is a keen supporter of economic and monetary union. As a historic victim of wars between France and Germany, Belgium regards the EU as a guarantor of western European peace. The presence of the EU's key institutions in Brussels is also seen as economically attractive, and EU membership is an important foundation for Belgium's own federalist structure.

Belgium has little in the way of an independent foreign policy, but strongly favors the development of an EU foreign policy and a more assertive UN. Paying for just over 1% of all UN activities, Belgium is among its ten largest contributors.

AID

▷ Donor

$1.07bn (donations)

Up 24% in 2002

Some 0.43% of GNP was spent on overseas development aid in 2002. Belgian aid focuses on social projects and economic infrastructure in African countries; the former Belgian colony of the DRC is the top beneficiary.

CHRONOLOGY

Previously ruled by the French dukes of Burgundy, Belgium became a Habsburg possession in 1477. It passed from the Spanish to the Austrian branch of the Habsburgs in 1713. Belgium was incorporated into France in 1795.

- **1814–1815** Congress of Vienna; European powers decide to merge Belgium with the Netherlands under King William I of Orange.
- **1830** Revolt against Dutch; declaration of independence.
- **1831** European powers install Leopold Saxe Coburg as king.
- **1865** Leopold II crowned king.
- **1885** Berlin Conference gives Congo basin to Leopold as colony.
- **1914** German armies invade. Belgium occupied until 1918.
- **1921** Belgo-Luxembourg Economic Union formed. Belgian and Luxembourg currencies locked.
- **1932** Dutch language accorded equal official status with French.
- **1936** Belgium declares neutrality.
- **1940** Leopold III capitulates to Hitler. Belgium occupied till 1944.
- **1948** Customs union with Netherlands and Luxembourg (Benelux) formed.
- **1950** King abdicates in favor of son, Baudouin.
- **1957** Becomes one of six original signatories of Treaty of Rome, the principal foundation of what develops into the EU.
- **1992** Christian Democrat and Socialist government led by Jean-Luc Dehaene takes over federal government.
- **1993** Culmination of reforms creating federal state. Greater powers for regions and city governments. Death of Baudouin; succeeded by Albert II.
- **1995** Allegations of corruption and murder involving French-speaking PS force resignations of Walloon premier, federal deputy premier, and Willy Claes, NATO secretary-general.
- **1996** Murder and disappearance of young girls arouse fears of international kidnapping and pedophile ring.
- **1999** Claes found guilty of bribery in connection with defense contract. Liberals win general election. New coalition formed, including Greens for first time.
- **2001** Collapse of national airline Sabena.
- **2002** January, euro fully adopted – withdrawal of Belgian franc. May, legalization of euthanasia.
- **2003** Government reelected; Greens lose seats, VB makes gains.

DEFENSE

No compulsory military service

$3.44bn

Up 16% in 2002

BELGIAN ARMED FORCES

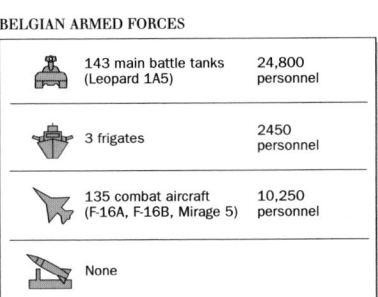

143 main battle tanks (Leopard 1A5)	24,800 personnel
3 frigates	2450 personnel
135 combat aircraft (F-16A, F-16B, Mirage 5)	10,250 personnel
None	

Belgium spends less on defense than the NATO average of 2% of GDP. In 1994, the government abolished conscription and undertook to cut troop levels. It also targeted all three military services for cuts as part of a program to reduce government debt; the defense budget was frozen for five years.

Spending on paratroops and transport aircraft, however, increased. The aim is to allow Belgian forces to fulfill their role in NATO's new rapid reaction force. It will also make Belgian forces more useful to the UN's worldwide operations. In 1996, the Belgian and Netherlands' navies came under a joint operational command, and in 2003 the government agreed in principle to the creation of a European Security and Defense Union.

ECONOMICS

Inflation 1.9% p.a. (1990–2001)

$237bn

0.822 euros (0.871)

SCORE CARD

World GNP Ranking	19th
GNP per capita	$22,940
Balance of payments	$11.5bn
Inflation	1.6%
Unemployment	7%

EXPORTS

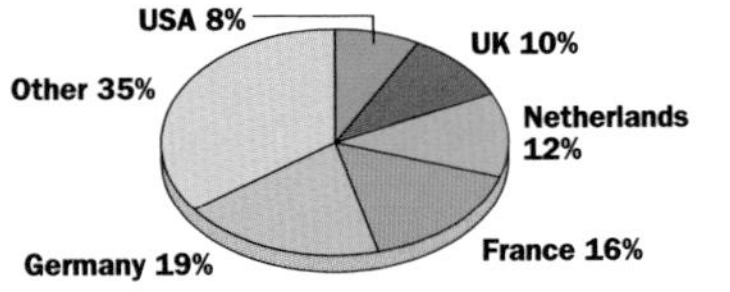
USA 8%
UK 10%
Other 35%
Netherlands 12%
France 16%
Germany 19%

IMPORTS

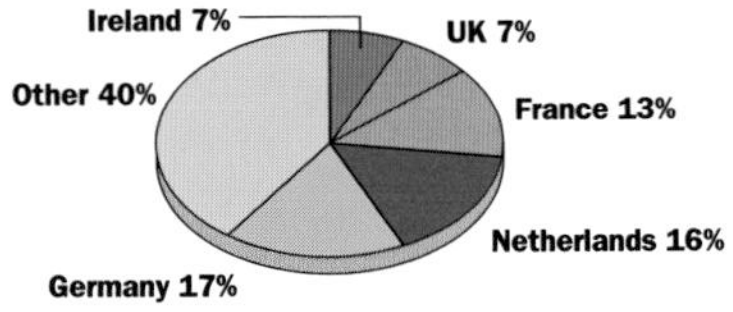
Ireland 7%
UK 7%
Other 40%
France 13%
Netherlands 16%
Germany 17%

ECONOMIC PERFORMANCE INDICATOR

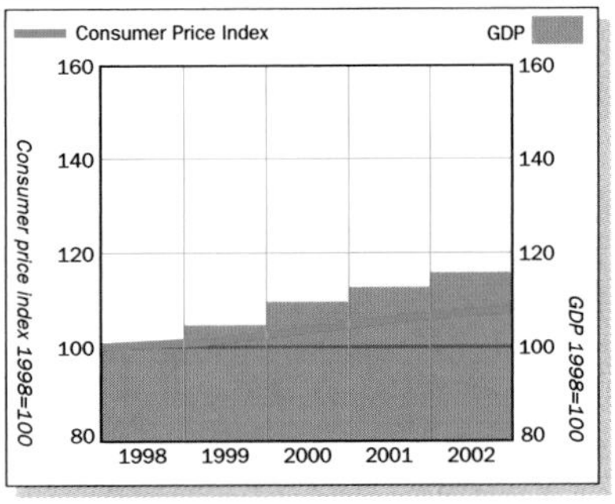
Consumer Price Index
GDP
160
140
120
100
80
1998
1999
2000
2001
2002
Consumer price index 1998=100
GDP 1998=100

Profile

Recession and rising unemployment in the early 1990s prompted the introduction of work-sharing schemes and benefit reforms. Unemployment and the massive public debt are declining gradually. Against a background of a downturn in the world economy, the government is committed to both greater fiscal stringency, in pursuit of a budget surplus, and reductions in taxation.

Strengths

One of world's most efficient producers of metal products and textiles. Flanders is a world leader in new high-tech industries. Successful chemicals industry. Highly educated and motivated multilingual workforce: estimates suggest productivity is 20% above that of Germany. Location attractive for US multinationals. Good sea outlets and access to Rhine inland waterway from Antwerp and Ghent.

Weaknesses

Public debt of around 100% of GDP, well over EU target of 60%. High long-term and low-skill joblessness with sharp local variations. Early retirement of large numbers of workers results in high state pension bill. Bureaucracy larger than European average.

BELGIUM : MAJOR BUSINESSES

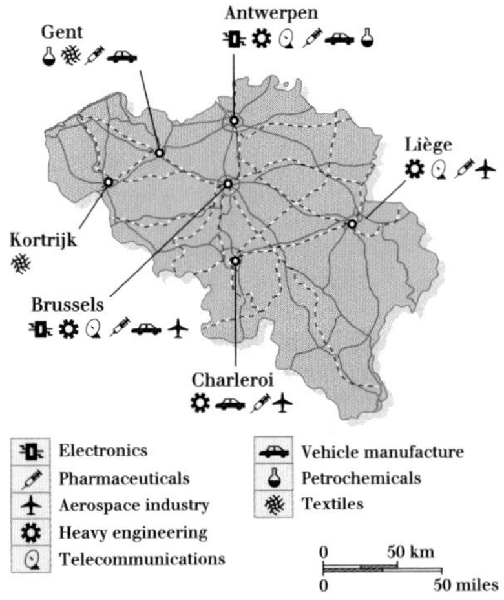
Gent
Antwerpen
Liège
Kortrijk
Brussels
Charleroi
Electronics
Pharmaceuticals
Aerospace industry
Heavy engineering
Telecommunications
Vehicle manufacture
Petrochemicals
Textiles
0
50 km
0
50 miles

RESOURCES

Electric power 15.7m kW

31,839 tonnes

Not an oil producer; refines 764,000 b/d

6.54m pigs, 2.78m cattle, 32m chickens

Coal, natural gas, shale, marble, sandstone, dolomite

ELECTRICITY GENERATION

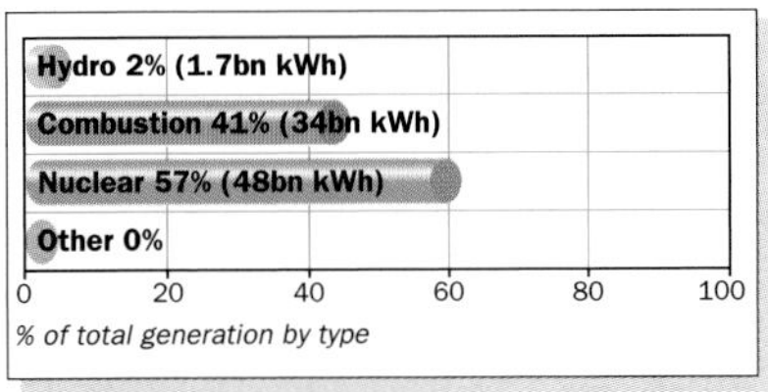

Hydro 2% (1.7bn kWh)
Combustion 41% (34bn kWh)
Nuclear 57% (48bn kWh)
Other 0%
0
20
40
60
80
100
% of total generation by type

Belgium has few natural resources and depends largely on the export of goods and services. The once-rich coal mines of Wallonia closed for good in 1992. There is some deciduous and conifer forestry in the Ardennes region.

BELGIUM : LAND USE

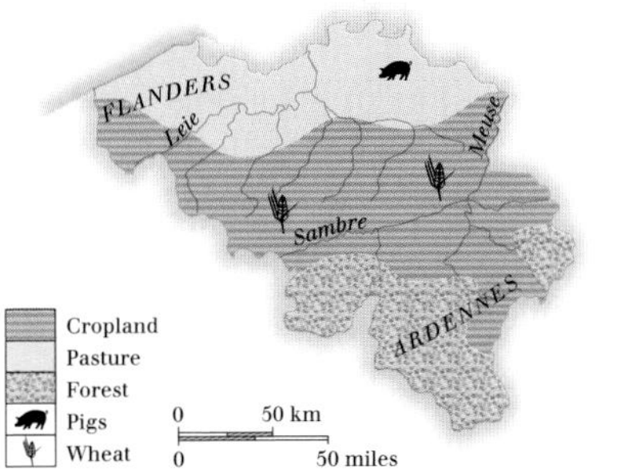

FLANDERS
Leie
Meuse
Sambre
ARDENNES
Cropland
Pasture
Forest
Pigs
Wheat
0
50 km
0
50 miles

ENVIRONMENT

Sustainability rank: 125th

3% partially protected

10 tonnes per capita

ENVIRONMENTAL TREATIES

Yes Yes Yes

Yes Yes Yes

Flanders is concerned about the pollution of groundwater supplies through acid rain, heavy metals, fertilizers, and pesticides. Its government operates an environmental management plan to raise standards. Wallonia has strict laws against illegal tipping of waste, and regulations on air quality and emissions. Awareness of environmental issues is reflected in the rise of the two green parties, which entered government for the first time in the coalition formed in 1999.

MEDIA

TV ownership high

Daily newspaper circulation 160 per 1000 people

PUBLISHING AND BROADCAST MEDIA

There are 30 daily newspapers, published in Dutch, French, and German, including *Het Laatste Nieuws* and *Le Soir*

3 state-owned services, broadcasting in Dutch, French, and German, and 5 independent commercial services

3 state-owned services, broadcasting in Dutch, French, and German, and numerous private stations

Newspapers tend to be regional and divided by language. Individual circulations are low: that of the most widely read paper is only 320,000. Control of broadcasting is divided along linguistic lines between two major corporations. Commercial TV only began in 1989, with the Flemish station VTM. Over 95% of Belgians have cable TV, receiving channels from all over Europe.

CRIME

No death penalty

9253 prisoners

Up 1% in 1999–2001

CRIME RATES

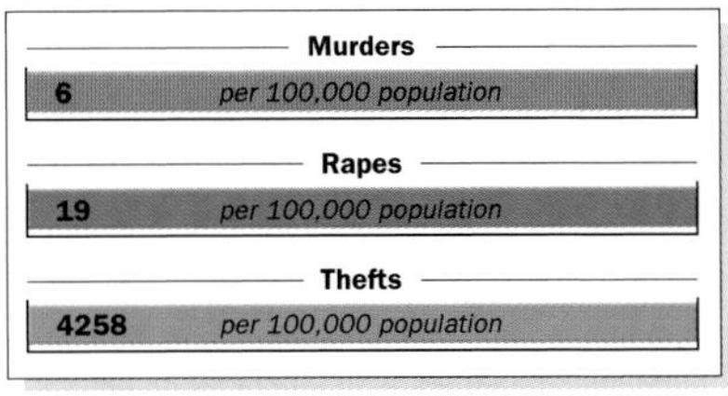

Murders
6 per 100,000 population
Rapes
19 per 100,000 population
Thefts
4258 per 100,000 population

Penalties for illegal narcotics use are strict. The "universal competence law," which had allowed the trial of non-Belgians for crimes against humanity, was watered down beyond use in 2003.

EDUCATION

School leaving age: 18

99%

298,387 students

THE EDUCATION SYSTEM

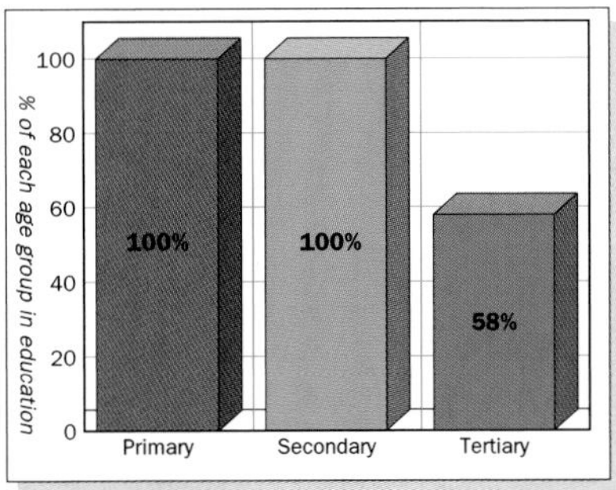

100
80
60
40
20
0
% of each age group in education
100%
100%
58%
Primary
Secondary
Tertiary

In Belgium, parents can choose between schooling provided by the two main language communities, by public authorities, or by private interests. Roman Catholic schools constitute the greatest number of "free" (privately organized) establishments. Since 1989 the system has been administered by the governments of the two main language groups. Some universities teach in French, others in Dutch.

HEALTH

Welfare state health benefits

1 per 256 people

Heart and respiratory diseases, cancers, accidents

The quality of health care is among the best in the world, and government spending is high. Belgium is a world leader in fertility treatment and heart and lung transplants. Treatment is not free, but Belgians are able to claim up to 75% of their costs.

Accidents rate unusually high in Belgium as a cause of death. In 2003 there were around 10,000 people living with HIV/AIDS.

In 2002 Belgium became the second country (after the Netherlands) to legalize euthanasia.

SPENDING

GDP/cap. increase

CONSUMPTION AND SPENDING

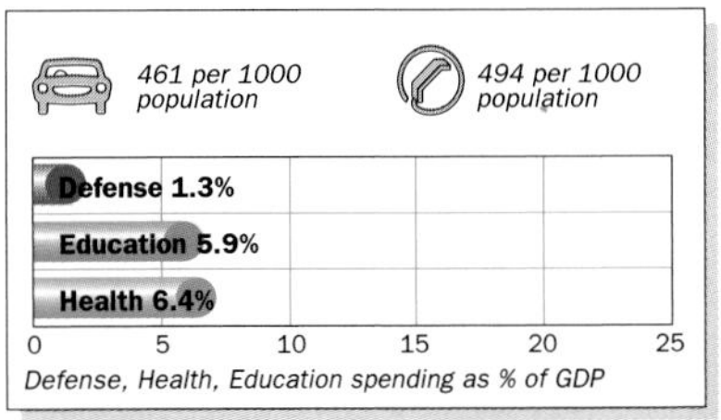

461 per 1000 population
494 per 1000 population
Defense 1.3%
Education 5.9%
Health 6.4%
0
5
10
15
20
25
Defense, Health, Education spending as % of GDP

Despite high levels of state debt and failing traditional industries, Belgium is one of Europe's richest countries. GNP per capita is lower than for the Netherlands, the UK, or Austria, but higher than for France or Germany. There are considerable regional differences, however: in Flanders the level of unemployment is only half that in Wallonia. The recession of the early 1990s prompted Belgians to save a higher proportion of their income, but the level of savings has fallen since then as consumer confidence has recovered.

The presence of highly paid EU officials and international company employees and bankers has made Brussels a distinctly wealthy, and expensive, city.

WORLD RANKING

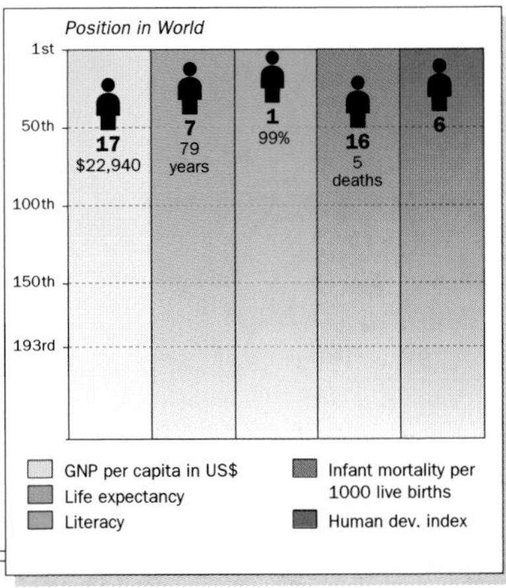

Position in World
1st
50th
100th
150th
193rd
17
$22,940
7
79 years
1
99%
16
5 deaths
6
GNP per capita in US$
Life expectancy
Literacy
Infant mortality per 1000 live births
Human dev. index

B

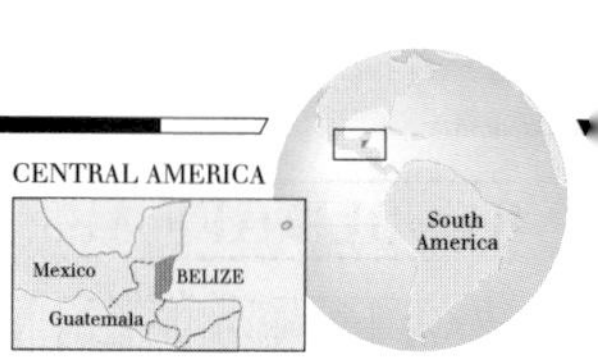
CENTRAL AMERICA
Mexico
BELIZE
Guatemala
South America

B

BELIZE

OFFICIAL NAME: Belize **CAPITAL:** Belmopan
POPULATION: 256,000 **CURRENCY:** Belizean dollar **OFFICIAL LANGUAGE:** English

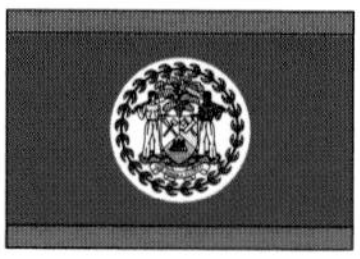

1981 | 1981 | Sept 21 | BZ | -6 | +501 | .bz

FORMERLY BRITISH HONDURAS, Belize was the last Central American country to gain its independence, in 1981. It lies on the southeastern shore of the Yucatán peninsula and shares a border with Mexico along the River Hondo. Belize is Central America's least populous country, and almost half of its land area is still forested. Its swampy coastal plains are protected from flooding by the world's second-largest barrier reef.

Small fishing village near Belize City. *About 500 tonnes of Caribbean spiny lobster, the main inshore species, are caught every year.*

CLIMATE

Tropical equatorial

WEATHER CHART FOR BELMOPAN

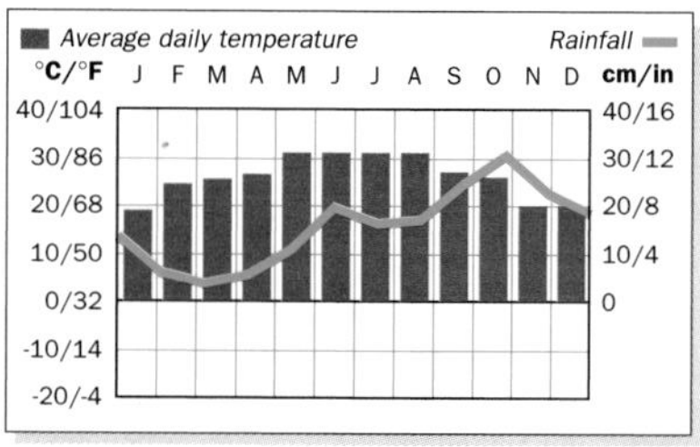
Average daily temperature
Rainfall
°C/°F
J F M A M J J A S O N D
cm/in
40/104
30/86
20/68
10/50
0/32
-10/14
-20/-4
40/16
30/12
20/8
10/4
0

Conditions are hot and humid. Coastal regions are affected by hurricanes, notably Hurricane Iris in late 2001.

TRANSPORTATION

Drive on right

Phillip S. W. Goldson, Belize City 272,000 passengers

1014 ships 1.47m grt

THE TRANSPORTATION NETWORK

488 km (303 miles)

None

None

825 km (513 miles)

A US$16 million IDB loan in 1998 helped improve the country's road network and its feeder roads. A terminal and a runway extension have been completed at the international airport near Belize City.

TOURISM

Visitors : Population 1:1.3

200,000 visitors

Up 2% in 2002

MAIN TOURIST ARRIVALS

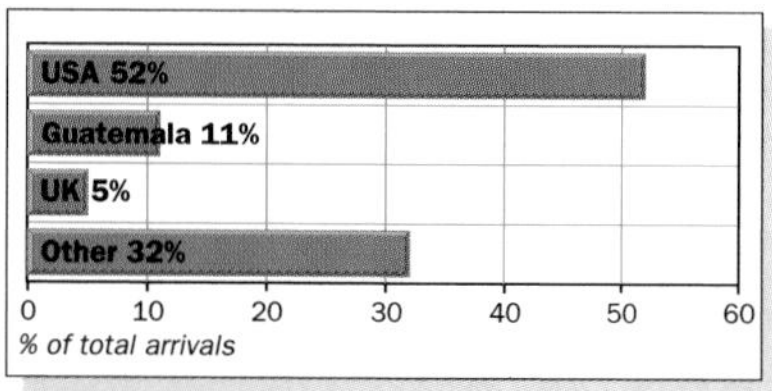
USA 52%
Guatemala 11%
UK 5%
Other 32%
0
10
20
30
40
50
60
% of total arrivals

The barrier reef, good beaches, and Mayan ruins draw visitors. "Eco" attractions need conservation.

PEOPLE

Pop. density low

English Creole, Spanish, English, Mayan, Garifuna (Carib)

11/km² (29/mi²)

THE URBAN/RURAL POPULATION SPLIT

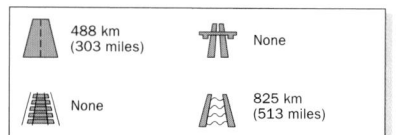

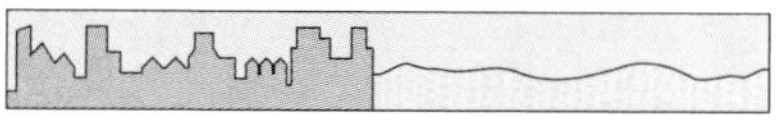
48%
52%

ETHNIC MAKEUP

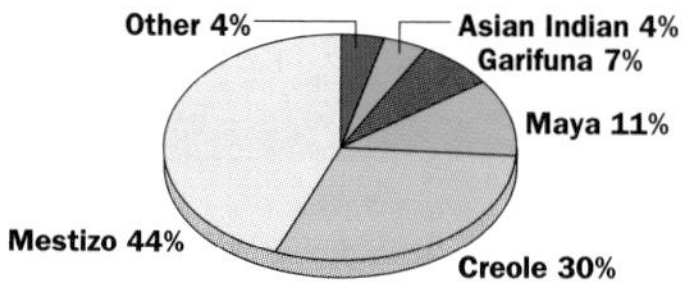
Other 4%
Asian Indian 4%
Garifuna 7%
Maya 11%
Mestizo 44%
Creole 30%

Along with the Spanish-speaking *mestizo* and English-speaking Creole there are the Maya Amerindians and the Afro-Carib *garifuna*, who have their own language. Around half the population is Roman Catholic. The number of Spanish speakers is rising, mostly through immigration from neighboring countries.

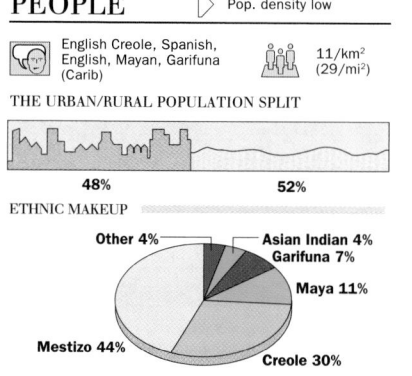

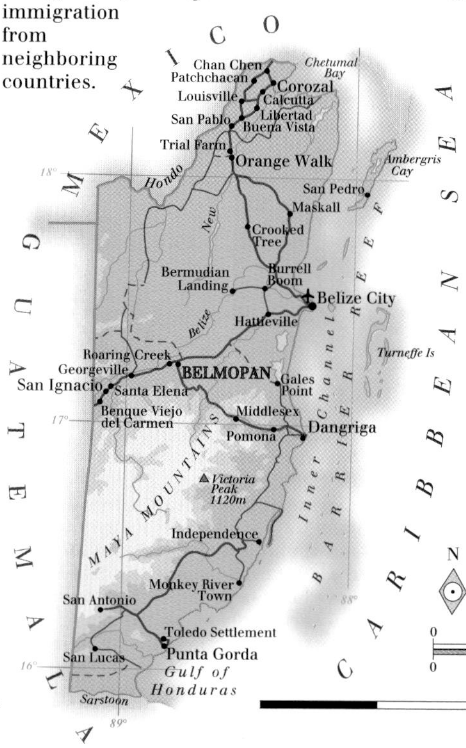
MEXICO
GUATEMALA
CARIBBEAN SEA
Chan Chen
Patchchacan
Chetumal Bay
Corozal
Louisville
Calcutta
San Pablo
Libertad
Buena Vista
Trial Farm
Orange Walk
Hondo
Ambergris Cay
San Pedro
Maskall
New
Crooked Tree
Bermudian Landing
Burrell Boom
Belize City
Hattieville
Belize
Turneffe Is
Roaring Creek
Georgeville
BELMOPAN
San Ignacio
Santa Elena
Gales Point
Benque Viejo del Carmen
Middlesex
Pomona
Dangriga
MAYA MOUNTAINS
Victoria Peak 1120m
Inner Channel
BARRIER REEF
Independence
Monkey River Town
San Antonio
Toledo Settlement
San Lucas
Punta Gorda
Gulf of Honduras
Sarstoon
18°
17°
16°
88°
89°

POLITICS

Multiparty elections

L. House 2003/2008
U. House 2003/2008

H.M. Queen Elizabeth II

AT THE LAST ELECTION

House of Representatives 29 seats

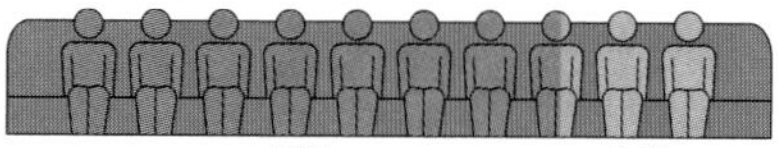
76% PUP
24% UDP

PUP = People's United Party
UDP = United Democratic Party

Senate 13 seats

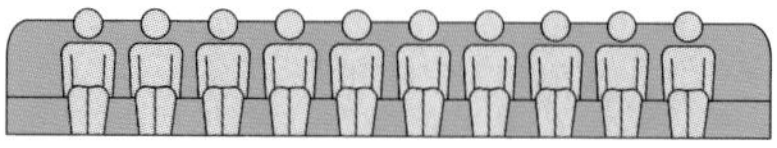

The members of the Senate are appointed by the governor-general

The PUP negotiated Belize's independence from the UK in 1981. Since then, control of the government has swung between the PUP and the UDP, in the absence of any major ideological or policy distinctions. The PUP, under Said Musa, won a crushing victory in 1998 and gained a historic second term in 2003, with a slightly reduced majority. Key political issues include addressing the rise in narcotics-related crimes and political corruption. The controversial practice of selling Belizean passports under the "economic citizenship" program was finally suspended in 2002.

BELIZE

Total Area : 22 966 sq. km (8867 sq. miles)

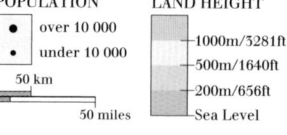

POPULATION
- over 10 000
- under 10 000

LAND HEIGHT
- 1000m/3281ft
- 500m/1640ft
- 200m/656ft
- Sea Level

N

0 50 km
0 50 miles

WORLD AFFAIRS

Joined UN in 1981

ACS | Comm | Caricom | NAM | OAS

Ties, traditionally to the Caribbean, are refocusing on Central America. The major concern is Guatemala's periodically restated claim to over half of Belize.

AID

Recipient

US$22m (receipts)

Little change in 2002

The US is the biggest aid donor, though this is mostly military assistance. With the help of a cheap loan from Taiwan, the government is spending US$50 million on building low-cost housing.

DEFENSE

No compulsory military service

US$17m

No change in 2002

The small Belize Defense Force took over full responsibility from the UK for the country's defense in 1994. The UK withdrew its garrison in the same year, but continues to maintain a jungle training school.

ECONOMICS

Inflation 1.8% p.a. (1990–2001)

US$750m

1.98 Belizean dollars (1.97)

SCORE CARD

❑ World GNP Ranking	160th
❑ GNP per Capita	US$2970
❑ Balance of Payments	–US$163m
❑ Inflation	2.2%
❑ Unemployment	9%

Strengths

Sugar, textile manufacture, agriculture, fishing, and considerable tourist potential. Sustainable public debt; fair access to concessionary foreign finance. Free trade zones and offshore banking.

Weaknesses

Narrow export base dependent on preferential market access; reliance on imports of processed foods. Hurricane damage.

EXPORTS

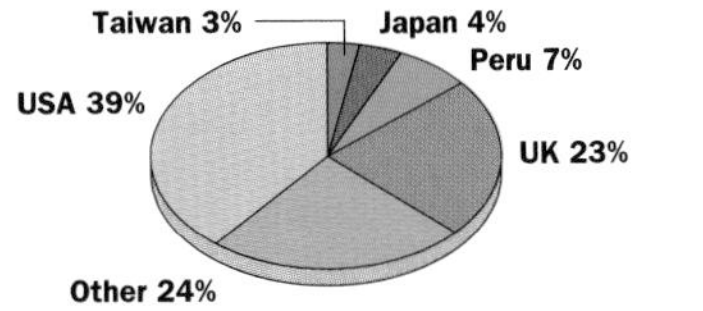
Taiwan 3%
Japan 4%
Peru 7%
USA 39%
UK 23%
Other 24%

IMPORTS

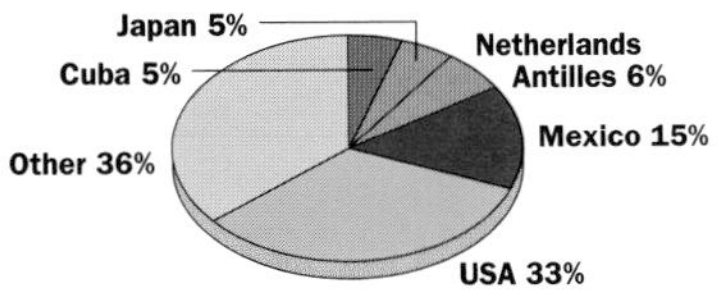
Japan 5%
Cuba 5%
Netherlands Antilles 6%
Mexico 15%
Other 36%
USA 33%

RESOURCES

Electric power 43,000 kW

18,830 tonnes

Reserves commercially unexploitable

58,380 cattle, 38,000 turkeys, 1.45m chickens

Oil

Belize relies on Mexico for half of its electricity. Oil deposits exist, but not in commercial quantities.

ENVIRONMENT

Not available

40% (31% partially protected)

3.1 tonnes per capita

Tourist developments and logging have depleted the dense tropical forests. Mahogany is endangered, and all exports and transshipments now require a certificate of origin. Global warming poses a major threat to the corals of the barrier reef.

MEDIA

TV ownership medium

There are no daily newspapers

PUBLISHING AND BROADCAST MEDIA

There are no daily newspapers. The leading papers are the weekly *Belize Times*, *Amandala*, and *Reporter*

3 independent services

14 independent services

Belize has not suffered the degree of press interference experienced in neighboring states, but successive governments have remained sensitive to even minor criticisms. The two radio stations of the public Broadcasting Corporation of Belize were sold in 1998 to two local stations, but the government has retained ownership of the transmitters. Two official newspapers compete with party-political and independent publications.

CRIME

Death penalty in use

1097 prisoners

Increase in narcotics- and gun-related crime

Belize is a major transit point to the US for cocaine, and narcotics-related crime is high. Armed robberies by criminal gangs based in neighboring Guatemala are also a major concern. The police force lacks resources and training, and a government ombudsman was appointed in 2000 to investigate police brutality and corruption.

EDUCATION

School leaving age: 14

77%

2853 students

Though most schools are run by the different churches, a handful are funded by the government, particularly those catering for special needs. The University College of Belize provides for higher education.

CHRONOLOGY

The Mayan heartland included what is now Belize. Between 1798 and 1981 it was effectively a British colony.

- ❑ **1919** Demands for more political rights by black Belizeans returning from World War I.
- ❑ **1936** New constitution.
- ❑ **1950** PUP formed. Voting age limit for women reduced from 30 to 21.
- ❑ **1954** Full adult suffrage.
- ❑ **1972** Guatemala threatens invasion. Britain sends troops.
- ❑ **1981** Full independence.
- ❑ **2000** Guatemala revives claim to half of Belize.
- ❑ **2001** Hurricane Iris hits Belize.
- ❑ **2003** PUP wins second term.

HEALTH

Welfare state health benefits

1 per 2000 people

Cancers, heart diseases, accidents, violence

The health service provided by the government includes seven hospitals, more than 30 regional health centers, and numerous mobile clinics. Water supplies and sanitation have been improved; most homes in Belmopan now have both.

SPENDING

GDP/cap. increase

CONSUMPTION AND SPENDING

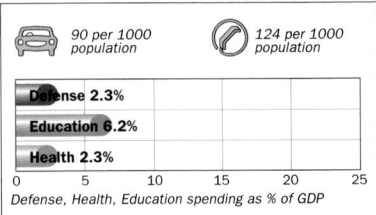

90 per 1000 population

124 per 1000 population

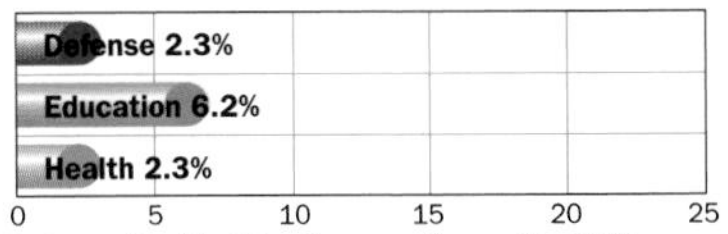
Defense 2.3%
Education 6.2%
Health 2.3%
0
5
10
15
20
25

Defense, Health, Education spending as % of GDP

The European Development Fund in 1999 granted 3.5 million Belizean dollars toward the reduction of rural poverty. Narcotics trading remains a source of wealth.

WORLD RANKING

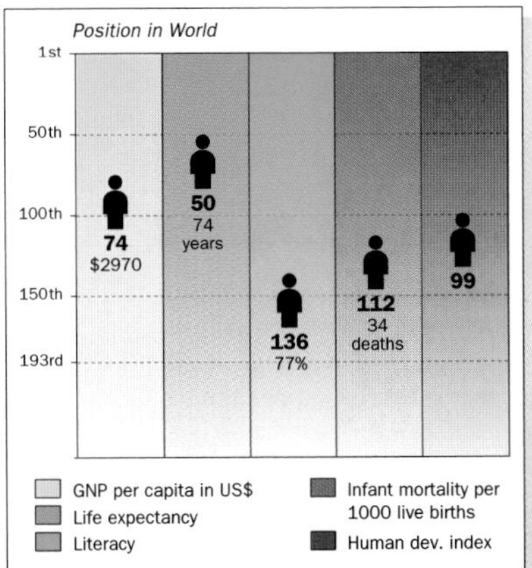
Position in World
1st
50th
100th
150th
193rd
74
$2970
50
74
years
136
77%
112
34
deaths
99
GNP per capita in US$
Life expectancy
Literacy
Infant mortality per 1000 live births
Human dev. index

B

BENIN

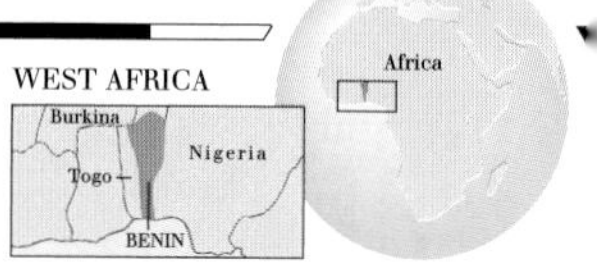

WEST AFRICA
Burkina
Togo
Nigeria
BENIN
Africa

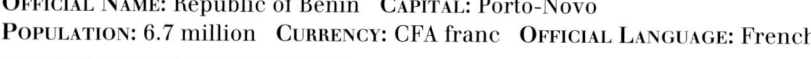

OFFICIAL NAME: Republic of Benin **CAPITAL:** Porto-Novo
POPULATION: 6.7 million **CURRENCY:** CFA franc **OFFICIAL LANGUAGE:** French

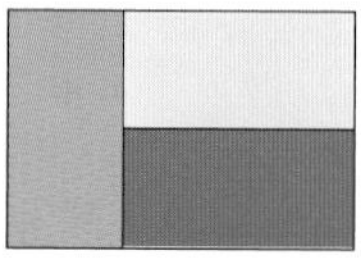

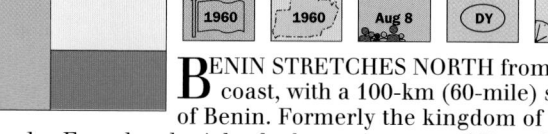

1960 | 1960 | Aug 8 | DY | +1 | +229 | .bj

BENIN STRETCHES NORTH from the west African coast, with a 100-km (60-mile) shoreline on the Bight of Benin. Formerly the kingdom of Dahomey, Benin was under French colonial rule, becoming part of French West Africa, until independence in 1960. In 1990 Benin was a pioneer of multipartyism in Africa, ending 17 years of one-party Marxist-Leninist rule. Benin's economy is based on well-diversified agriculture.

CLIMATE

Tropical wet and dry

WEATHER CHART FOR PORTO-NOVO

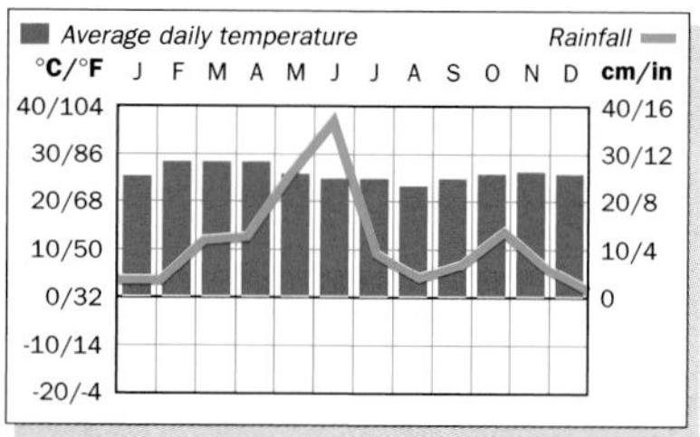

Average daily temperature
Rainfall
°C/°F J F M A M J J A S O N D cm/in
40/104
30/86
20/68
10/50
0/32
-10/14
-20/-4
40/16
30/12
20/8
10/4
0

There are two rainy seasons. The hot, dusty *harmattan* wind characterizes the December to February dry season.

TRANSPORTATION

Drive on right

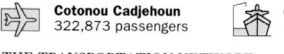

Cotonou Cadjehoun 322,873 passengers

6 ships 1000 grt

THE TRANSPORTATION NETWORK

1357 km (843 miles)

10 km (6 miles)

578 km (359 miles)

Sections of streams are navigable

The cofunded Benin–Niger railroad stops short at Parakou. The Cotonou–Porto-Novo line reopened in 1999.

TOURISM

Visitors : Population 1:93

72,000 visitors

Down 53% in 2002

MAIN TOURIST ARRIVALS

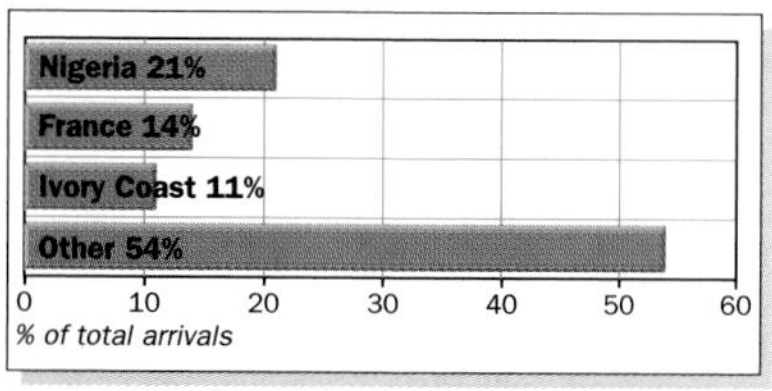

Nigeria 21%
France 14%
Ivory Coast 11%
Other 54%
0 10 20 30 40 50 60
% of total arrivals

Tourism is not well developed; there are plans to increase package vacations. There is some safari tourism in the north, particularly in the Atakora Mountains. Benin can be included as a short break for vacationers in Nigeria.

PEOPLE

Pop. density medium

Fon, Bariba, Yoruba, Adja, Houeda, Somba, French

61/km² (157/mi²)

THE URBAN/RURAL POPULATION SPLIT

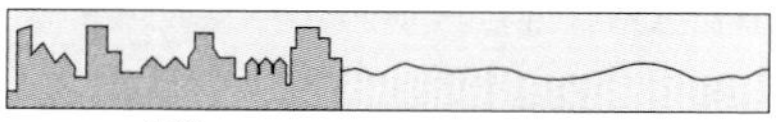

44%
56%

RELIGIOUS PERSUASION

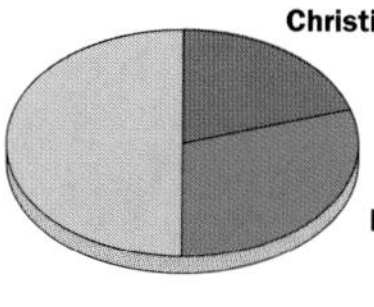

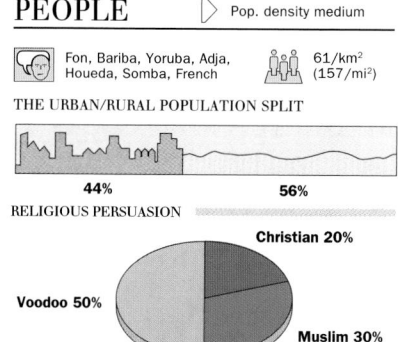

Christian 20%
Voodoo 50%
Muslim 30%

There are 42 different ethnic groups, the southern Fon tending to dominate politically and the south being better developed. Voodoo is thought to have originated here and been taken by slaves from Benin to Haiti. French culture is prized in urban areas.

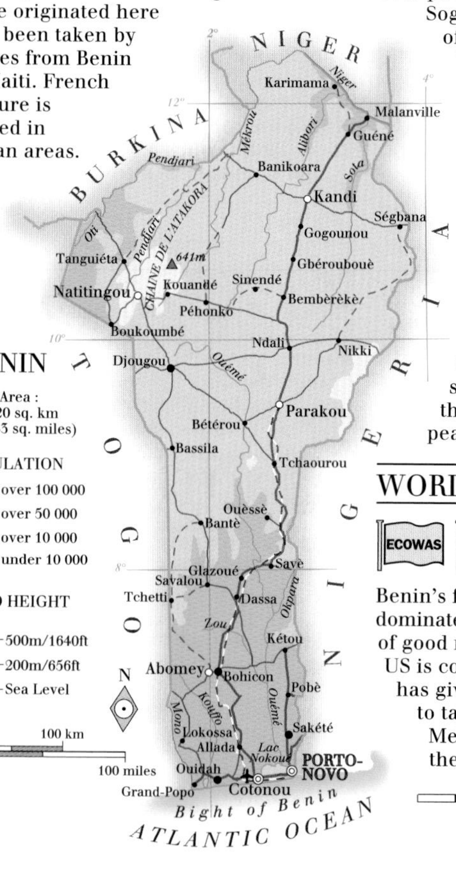

NIGER
BURKINA
TOGO
NIGERIA
BENIN
Total Area : 112 620 sq. km (43 483 sq. miles)
POPULATION
over 100 000
over 50 000
over 10 000
under 10 000
LAND HEIGHT
500m/1640ft
200m/656ft
Sea Level
0 100 km
0 100 miles
Karimama
Malanville
Guéné
Banikoara
Kandi
Ségbana
Gogounou
Gbéroubouè
Tanguiéta
Natitingou
Kouandé
Sinendé
Bembèrèkè
Péhonko
Boukoumbé
Ndali
Nikki
Djougou
Parakou
Bétérou
Bassila
Tchaourou
Ouèssè
Bante
Savè
Glazoué
Savalou
Tchetti
Dassa
Kétou
Abomey
Bohicon
Pobè
Sakété
Lokossa
Allada
PORTO-NOVO
Ouidah
Cotonou
Grand-Popo
Bight of Benin
ATLANTIC OCEAN
CHAINE DE L'ATAKORA
641m
Niger
Mékrou
Alibori
Sota
Pendjari
Oti
Ouémé
Zou
Couffo
Mono
Okpara
Lac Nokoué

POLITICS

Multiparty elections

2003/2007

President Mathieu Kérékou

AT THE LAST ELECTION

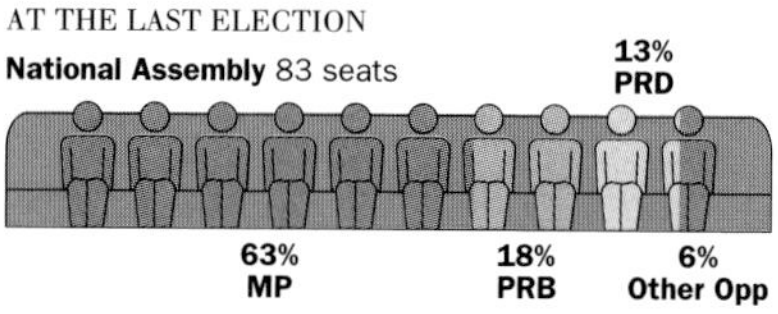

National Assembly 83 seats
13% PRD
63% MP
18% PRB
6% Other Opp

MP = Presidential Rally **PRB** = Benin Renaissance Party
PRD = Party of Democratic Renewal
Other Opp = Other opposition supporters

Benin's image as a leader in African democratization was tarnished by allegations of fraud over the 2001 presidential election, and may be further tainted should Mathieu Kérékou amend the constitution to permit a third term in 2006 (currently there is a two-term limit and an age restriction of 70, which he has already reached).

Democratization had begun at the National Conference of 1990, when Kérékou agreed to hold multiparty elections after years of failed Marxist-Leninist one-party military rule.

Kérékou became the first of the African one-party leaders to hand over power peacefully, to Nicéphore Soglo, a former World Bank official, after elections in 1991. The main issue became his World Bank-style deregulation of the economy, and he was defeated in a controversial election in 1996 which brought Kérékou back to power.

Kérékou dismissed claims of vote rigging in the 2001 presidential election, saying that democracy was "alive and kicking." Debate is now rife over whether Kérékou should be allowed a third term; a group of some small parties supports the idea as the key to peace, unity, and security.

WORLD AFFAIRS

Joined UN in 1960

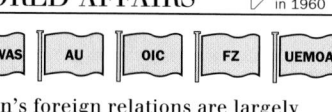

ECOWAS | AU | OIC | FZ | UEMOA

Benin's foreign relations are largely dominated by Nigeria. The continuation of good relations with France and the US is considered to be critical. The UN has given funds to Benin and Niger to take a border dispute over Mekrou and the River Niger to the International Court of Justice.

AID

Recipient

$220m (receipts) | Down 20% in 2002

Benin's poverty is such that the maintenance of aid is at the top of the political agenda. France, the main protector of Benin since independence in 1960, is the major aid donor. Other donors include the World Bank, the US, the EU, Germany, Denmark, and the African Development Bank. Almost all development finance comes from aid, and some has been used to finance debt servicing. There is the usual problem of finding suitable projects, though Benin has a large, well-educated (if top heavy) civil service, making implementation easier than in many parts of Africa.

DEFENSE

Compulsory military service

$46m | Up 12% in 2002

The 4300-strong army is involved in attempting to curb smuggling on the Nigerian border. Benin has sent troops to assist with peacekeeping in Liberia and Guinea-Bissau.

ECONOMICS

Inflation 8.2% p.a. (1990–2001)

$2.52bn | 539.2 CFA francs (571.2)

SCORE CARD

- ❑ World GNP Ranking 135th
- ❑ GNP per Capita $380
- ❑ Balance of Payments .... –$126m
- ❑ Inflation 2.5%
- ❑ Unemployment 2%

Strengths

Agriculture. Small but well-diversified manufacturing sector. Regional agreements support cotton trade. Weak CFA franc makes exports competitive. Growing services sector.

Weaknesses

Large-scale smuggling. Transportation and commerce greatly affected by fluctuations in Nigeria. Reliance on electricity imports from Ghana.

EXPORTS

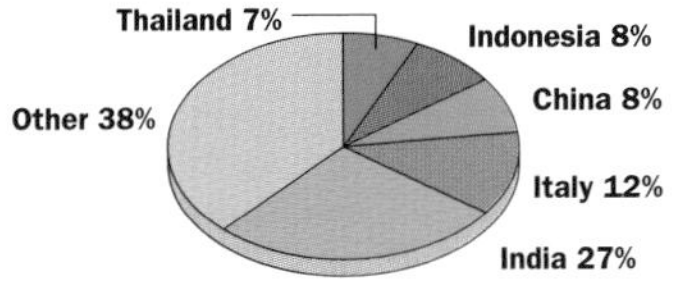
Thailand 7%
Indonesia 8%
China 8%
Other 38%
Italy 12%
India 27%

IMPORTS

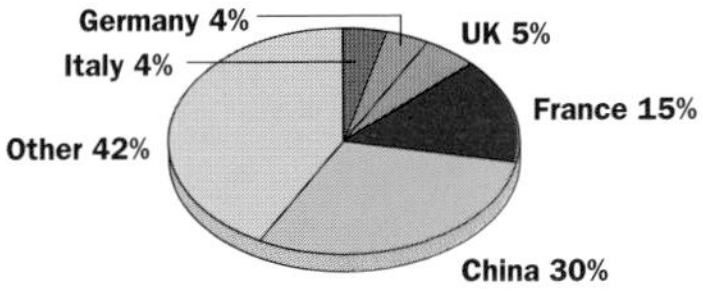
Germany 4%
Italy 4%
UK 5%
France 15%
Other 42%
China 30%

Flat landscape near Cotonou, characteristic of Benin's coastal region. Numerous lagoons lie behind its short coastline.

RESOURCES

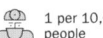

Electric power 55,000 kW

38,415 tonnes | 962 b/d (reserves 29m barrels)

1.6m cattle, 1.3m goats, 10m chickens | Oil, limestone, marble, gold

Most of Benin's electricity is derived from dams in nearby countries. Since a drought in Ghana in 1998 it has attempted to diversify its sources.

ENVIRONMENT

Sustainability rank: 95th

11% (4% partially protected) | 0.3 tonnes per capita

Desertification in the north is the major problem. Benin has been used in the past as a dumping ground for toxic waste.

MEDIA

TV ownership low

Daily newspaper circulation 5 per 1000 people

PUBLISHING AND BROADCAST MEDIA

There are 18 daily newspapers, including *Le Matinal* and *La Nation*

4 services: 1 state-owned, 3 independent | 19 services: 1 state-owned, 18 independent

Over 50 newspapers and periodicals are published, though circulation figures are tiny. The press has considerable freedom and a voluntary code of practice.

CRIME

Death penalty not used in practice

4961 prisoners | Up sharply in 1996–1998

Street robbery is a significant problem in the cities. Armed crime is rising. Child smuggling is a major issue and has affected relations with neighboring countries.

EDUCATION

School leaving age: 11

40% | 18,753 students

More is spent on education than on defense, and this is reinforced by Benin's active intellectual community, the "Latin Quarter of Africa." The university at Abomey-Calavi is rated highly in medicine and law.

CHRONOLOGY

In 1625 the Fon, indigenous slave traders, founded the kingdom of Dahomey. Dahomey in turn conquered the neighboring kingdoms of Dan, Allada, and the coast around Porto-Novo.

- ❑ **1857** French establish trading post at Grand-Popo.
- ❑ **1889** French defeat King Behanzin.
- ❑ **1892** French protectorate.
- ❑ **1904** Part of French West Africa.
- ❑ **1960** Full independence.
- ❑ **1975** Renamed Benin.
- ❑ **1989** Marxism-Leninism abandoned as official ideology.
- ❑ **1996** Former ruler Mathieu Kérékou defeats Nicéphore Soglo in controversial election.
- ❑ **2001** Kérékou reelected president amid claims of electoral fraud.

HEALTH

No welfare state health benefits

1 per 10,000 people | Communicable and diarrheal diseases, malaria

Outside the major towns, health services and doctors are scarce. It is forecast that by 2030 one million Beninese will have died from AIDS.

SPENDING

GDP/cap. increase

CONSUMPTION AND SPENDING

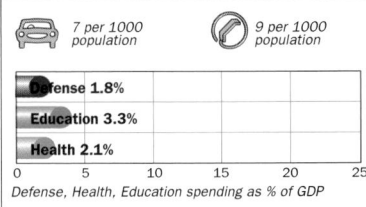

7 per 1000 population | *9 per 1000 population*

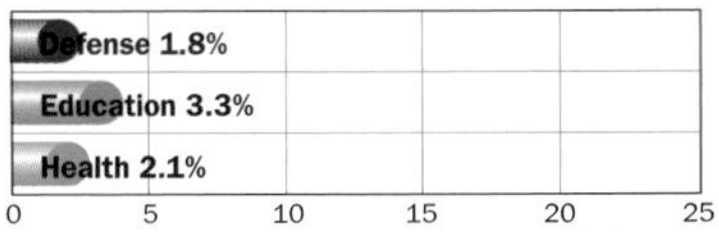
Defense 1.8%
Education 3.3%
Health 2.1%
0
5
10
15
20
25

Defense, Health, Education spending as % of GDP

Substantial differences in wealth reflect the strongly hierarchical nature of society, especially in the south. French cars are considered to be status symbols.

WORLD RANKING

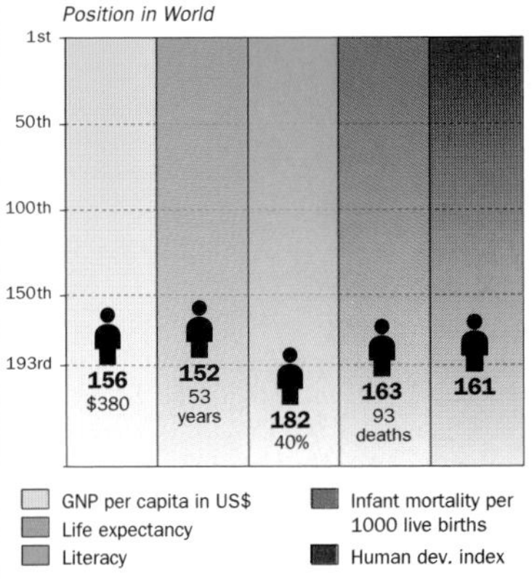
Position in World
1st
50th
100th
150th
193rd
156
$380
152
53 years
182
40%
163
93 deaths
161
GNP per capita in US$
Life expectancy
Literacy
Infant mortality per 1000 live births
Human dev. index

B

Bhutan

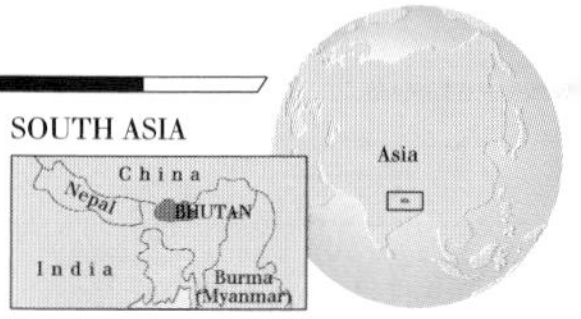
SOUTH ASIA
China
Nepal
BHUTAN
India
Burma (Myanmar)
Asia

OFFICIAL NAME: Kingdom of Bhutan **CAPITAL:** Thimphu
POPULATION: 2.3 million **CURRENCY:** Ngultrum **OFFICIAL LANGUAGE:** Dzongkha

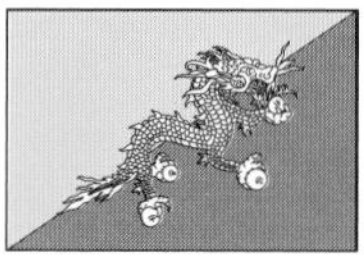

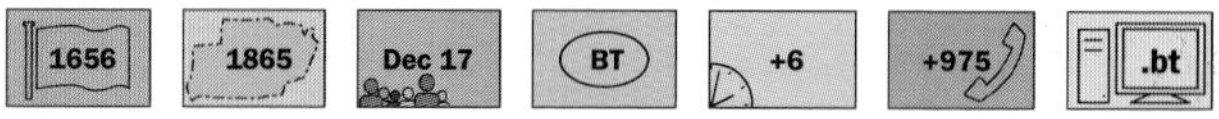
1656
1865
Dec 17
BT
+6
+975
.bt

PERCHED IN THE HIMALAYAS between India and China, Bhutan is 70% forested. The land rises from the low, tropical southern strip through the fertile central valleys to the high Himalayas, inhabited by seminomadic yak herders. Formally a Buddhist state where power is shared by the king and the government, Bhutan began modernizing in the 1960s, but has chosen to do so gradually, and remains largely closed to the outside world.

CLIMATE

Mountain/tropical monsoon

WEATHER CHART FOR THIMPHU

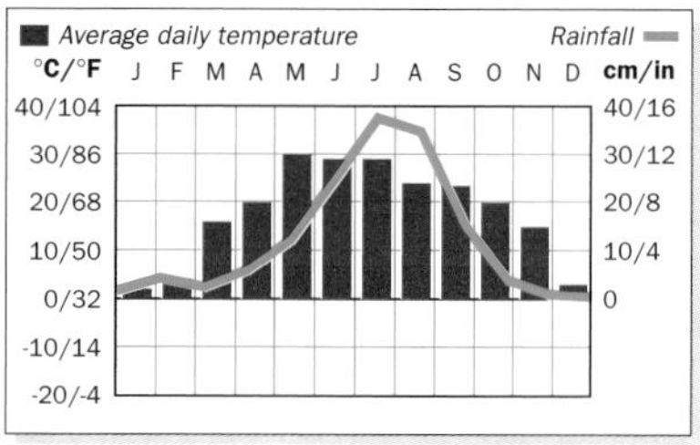
Average daily temperature
Rainfall
°C/°F J F M A M J J A S O N D cm/in
40/104
30/86
20/68
10/50
0/32
-10/14
-20/-4
40/16
30/12
20/8
10/4
0

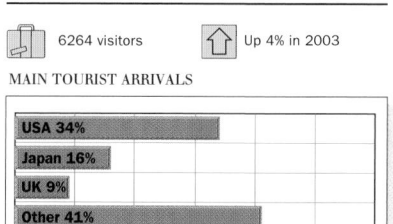

The south is tropical, the north alpine, cold, and harsh. The central valleys are warmer in the east than in the west. The summer monsoon affects all parts.

TRANSPORTATION

Drive on left

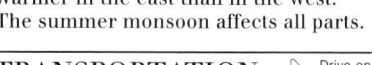

Paro International 19,939 passengers

Has no fleet

THE TRANSPORTATION NETWORK

2251 km (1399 miles)

None

None

None

The main surfaced road runs east–west across central Bhutan. Two others run south into India. Only the national airline, Druk Air, flies into Bhutan.

TOURISM

Visitors : Population 1:367

6264 visitors

Up 4% in 2003

MAIN TOURIST ARRIVALS

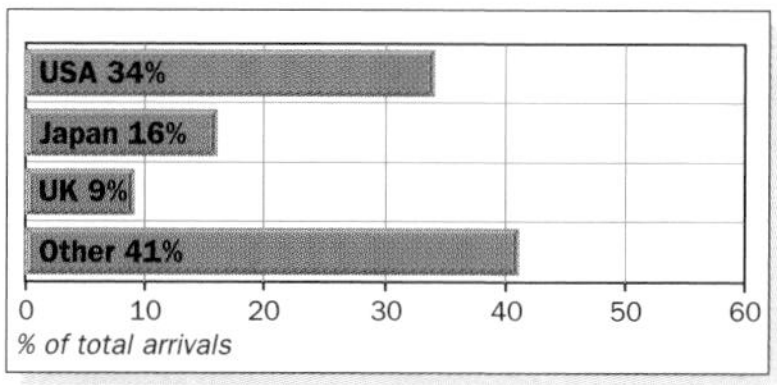
USA 34%
Japan 16%
UK 9%
Other 41%
0 10 20 30 40 50 60
% of total arrivals

To protect Bhutan's culture and natural environment, independent travel is not permitted. Guided visits cost a flat daily fee of $200; some monasteries are closed to tourists. In 1998, fire damaged the famous Taktsang monastery.

***Less than 10% of Bhutan is arable,** but its fertility allows almost any crop to grow. The diversity of wild plant species inspired its old name: Southern Valleys of the Medicinal Herbs.*

PEOPLE

Pop. density low

Dzongkha, Nepali, Assamese

49/km² (127/mi²)

THE URBAN/RURAL POPULATION SPLIT

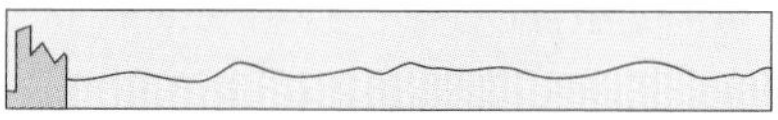
8%
92%

RELIGIOUS PERSUASION

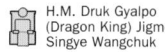

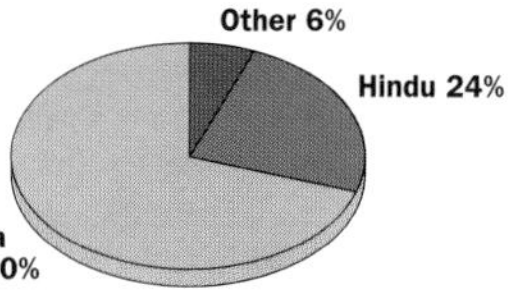
Other 6%
Hindu 24%
Mahayana Buddhist 70%

The majority of the population, the Drukpa peoples, originated from Tibet and are devoutly Buddhist. The Hindu minority is made up of Nepalese who settled in the south from 1910 to 1950. Bhutan has 20 languages. Dzongkha, the language of western Bhutan, native to less than a quarter of the population, was made the official language in 1988. The Nepalese community has reacted strongly, regarding this as "cultural imperialism."

POLITICS

Nonparty elections

Not applicable

H.M. Druk Gyalpo (Dragon King) Jigme Singye Wangchuk

LEGISLATIVE OR ADVISORY BODIES

National Assembly 150 seats

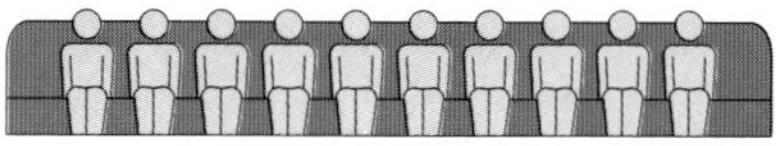

There are no legal political parties; members are indirectly elected individually to the National Assembly, to advise the king, who rules as an absolute monarch

The modernization of Bhutan's absolute monarchy began in 1961. Under further changes enacted in 1998, the king relinquished his right to appoint the government in favor of a cabinet elected by the National Assembly. The National Assembly was also empowered to pass a vote of no confidence against the king. These proposals came as a response to a prodemocracy movement fueled by ethnic Nepalese opposed to the Drukpa-dominated political system.

Bhutan

Total Area : 47 000 sq. km (18 147 sq. miles)

LAND HEIGHT

- 6000m/19686ft
- 4000m/13124ft
- 2000m/6562ft
- 1000m/3281ft
- 500m/1640ft
- 200m/656ft
- 160m/252ft

POPULATION

- over 10 000
- under 10 000

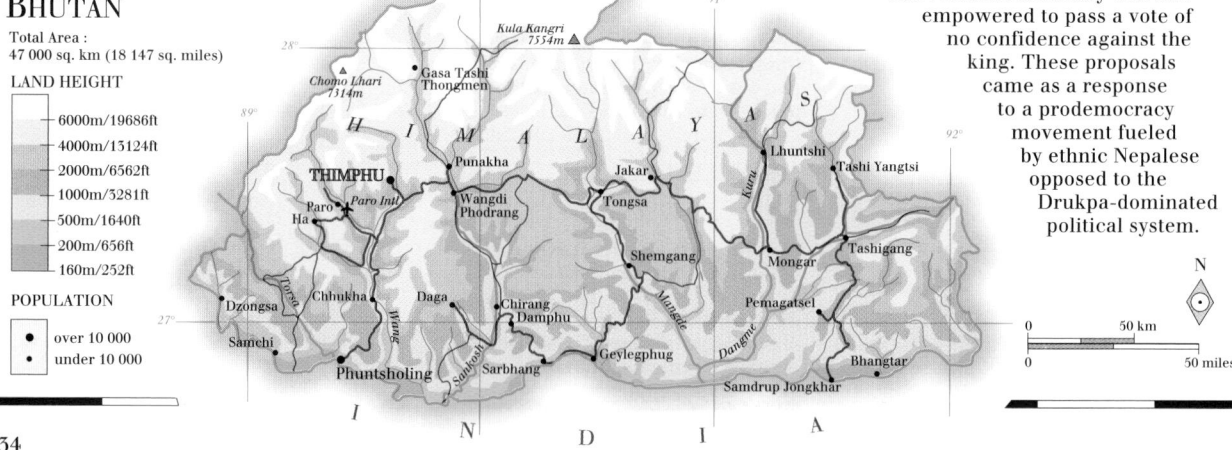

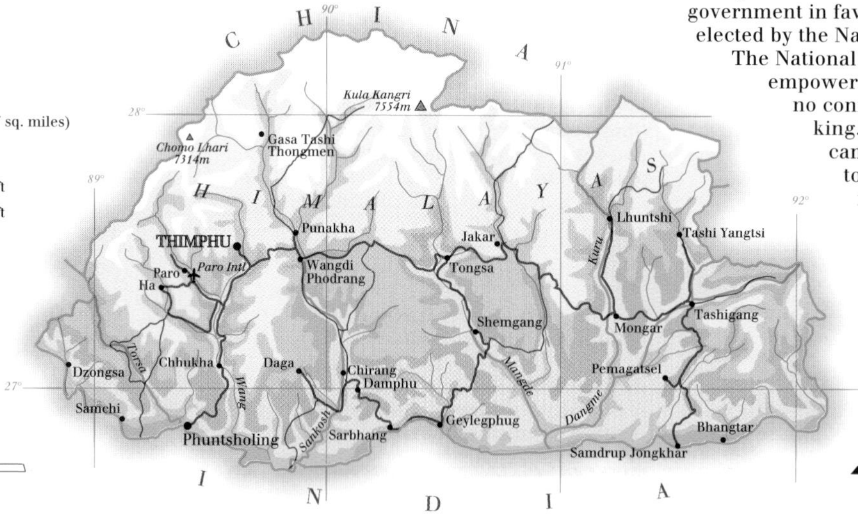
CHINA
INDIA
HIMALAYAS
Kula Kangri 7554m
Chomo Lhari 7314m
Gasa Tashi Thongmen
Punakha
THIMPHU
Paro
Paro Intl
Ha
Wangdi Phodrang
Jakar
Tongsa
Lhuntshi
Tashi Yangtsi
Tashigang
Mongar
Shemgang
Pemagatsel
Dzongsa
Chhukha
Daga
Chirang
Damphu
Samchi
Phuntsholing
Sarbhang
Geylegphug
Bhangtar
Samdrup Jongkhar
Torsa
Wang
Sankosh
Manas
Kuru
Dangme
28°
27°
89°
90°
91°
92°
N
0 50 km
0 50 miles

WORLD AFFAIRS

Joined UN in 1971

CP | IBRD | NAM | SAARC | ADB

Bhutan's closest links are with India. Relations with China are cordial, and negotiations to settle the China–Bhutan border have progressed smoothly since 1984. There is tension with Nepal over Bhutan's treatment of its ethnic Nepalese minority: a tentative agreement concerning those who had fled to Nepal was reached in 2003.

AID

Recipient

$73m (receipts)

Up 20% in 2002

Bhutan relies on foreign aid for half of its annual budget. The largest donors are Denmark and Japan.

DEFENSE

No compulsory military service

$18m

Down 5% in 2002

The army is under the command of the king, and is trained by Indian military instructors. India is committed to defending Bhutan against attack, and in 2004 pledged to modernize the army.

ECONOMICS

Inflation 9.3% p.a. (1990–2001)

$512m

45.98 ngultrum (46.47)

SCORE CARD

WORLD GNP RANKING	171st
GNP PER CAPITA	$600
BALANCE OF PAYMENTS	–$42m
INFLATION	2.5%
UNEMPLOYMENT	Low rate

STRENGTHS

New development of cash crops for Asian markets (cardamoms, apples, oranges, apricots). Hardwoods in south, especially teak, but exploitation currently tightly controlled. Large hydroelectric potential.

WEAKNESSES

Dependence on Indian workers for many public-sector jobs from road building to teaching. The majority of the population are dependent on agriculture. Cultivated land is extremely restricted because of steep mountain slopes. Very little industry. Few mineral resources.

EXPORTS

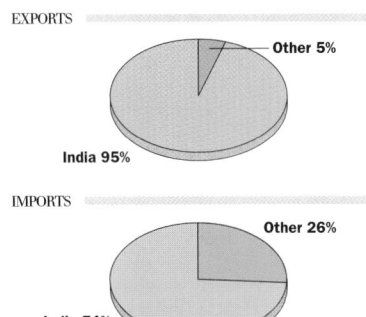

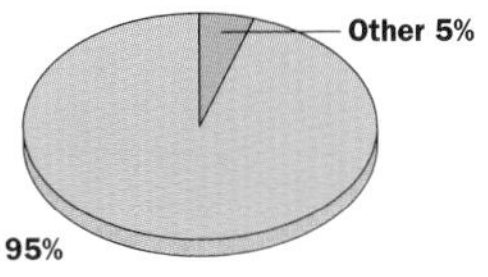
Other 5%
India 95%

IMPORTS

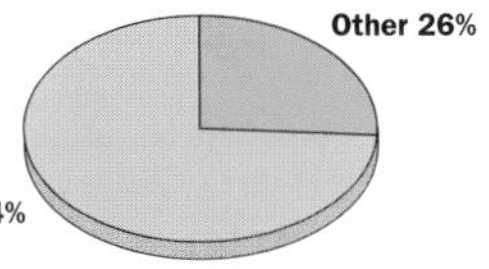
Other 26%
India 74%

RESOURCES

Electric power 362,000 kW

330 tonnes

Not an oil producer and has no refineries

340,000 cattle, 41,000 pigs, 220,000 chickens

Talc, gypsum, coal, limestone, slate, dolomite

Bhutan's forests remain largely intact, and logging is very strictly controlled. Hydroelectric potential is considerable, but few dams have been built. Power is sold to India from the Chhukha Dam, bringing in substantial foreign earnings.

ENVIRONMENT

Sustainability rank: 30th

21% (5% partially protected)

0.5 tonnes per capita

Bhutan's forests stabilize the steep mountainsides and supply the bulk of its fuel needs. Road building, begun in the 1960s, is the biggest cause of deforestation, which has led to topsoil erosion. The high northern pastures are at risk from overgrazing by yaks. Traditional Buddhist values instilling respect for nature and forbidding the killing of animals are still observed.

MEDIA

TV ownership low

There are no daily newspapers

PUBLISHING AND BROADCAST MEDIA

There are no daily newspapers. *Kuensel* is published weekly by the government in Dzongkha, English, and Nepali

1 state-owned service

1 state-owned service

Until 1999 TV was banned, in order to protect cultural values. An Internet café opened in Thimphu in 2000.

CRIME

No death penalty

Bhutan does not publish prison figures

Little variation from year to year

Violent crime and theft are rare. In 1991, *driglam namzha*, an ancient code of conduct including wearing traditional dress, was revived, with fines or imprisonment for noncompliance. The king abolished the death penalty in 2004.

EDUCATION

School leaving age: 16

47%

3251 students

Education is free. A small minority of children attend secondary school. Teaching is in English and Dzongkha. There are no universities.

CHRONOLOGY

The Drukpa, originally from Tibet, united Bhutan in 1656. In 1865 the Drukpa lost the Duars Strip to British India.

- **1907** Monarchy established.
- **1949** Indo-Bhutan Treaty of Friendship.
- **1953** National Assembly set up.
- **1968** King forms first cabinet.
- **1971** Bhutan joins UN.
- **1990** Ethnic Nepalese launch campaign for minority rights.
- **1998** King proposes to reform government.
- **1999** First TV service inaugurated.

HEALTH

Welfare state health benefits

1 per 6384 people

Diarrheal, respiratory diseases, tuberculosis, malaria, infant deaths

Free clinics, along with Thimphu's hospital, provide basic health care. Progress is being made in child immunization, and monks have been persuaded to teach hygiene. Infant mortality is high. Bhutanese, Tibetan, and Chinese traditional medicines are widely practiced.

SPENDING

GDP/cap. increase

CONSUMPTION AND SPENDING

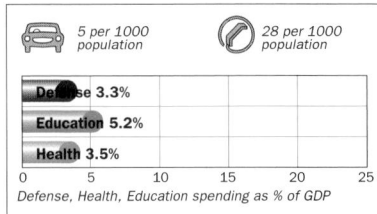

5 per 1000 population

28 per 1000 population

Defense 3.3%
Education 5.2%
Health 3.5%
0
5
10
15
20
25

Defense, Health, Education spending as % of GDP

Most of Bhutan's people are chronically poor, though starvation is virtually unknown. There is a small middle class, consisting of public employees and storekeepers.

WORLD RANKING

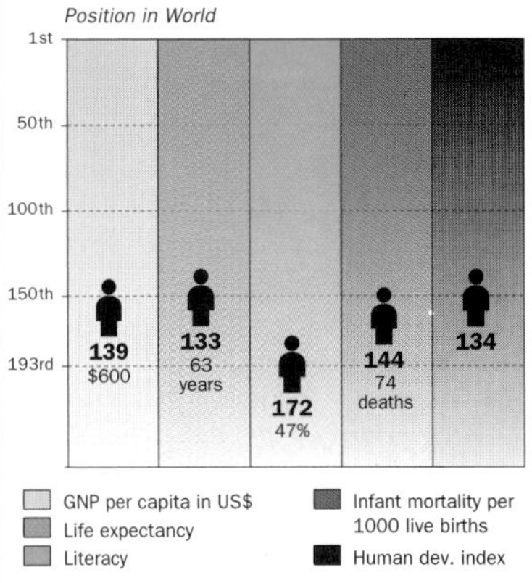
Position in World
1st
50th
100th
150th
193rd
139
$600
133
63
years
172
47%
144
74
deaths
134
GNP per capita in US$
Life expectancy
Literacy
Infant mortality per 1000 live births
Human dev. index

B

Bolivia

SOUTH AMERICA
Peru
Brazil
BOLIVIA
Chile
Paraguay
South America

Official Name: Republic of Bolivia **Capitals:** La Paz (administrative); Sucre (judicial)
Population: 8.8 million **Currency:** Boliviano **Official Languages:** Spanish, Quechua, and Aymara

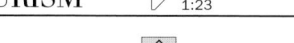

1825
1938
Aug 6
BOL
-4
+591
.bo

BOLIVIA LIES LANDLOCKED high in central South America, and is one of the continent's poorest nations. Over half of the population lives on the *altiplano*, the windswept plateau between two ranges of the Andes, 3500 m (11,500 ft) above sea level. La Paz, the highest capital in the world, has spawned a neighboring large twin, El Alto. Bolivia has the world's highest golf course, ski run, and soccer stadium. The eastern lowland regions are tropical and underdeveloped but are rapidly being colonized.

CLIMATE

Tropical/mountain

WEATHER CHART FOR LA PAZ

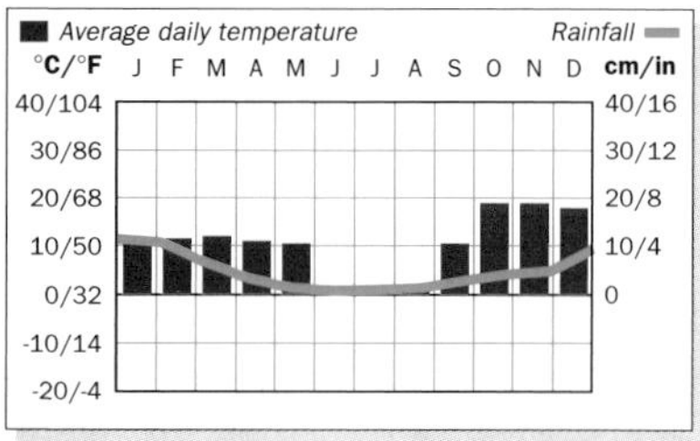
Average daily temperature
Rainfall
°C/°F J F M A M J J A S O N D cm/in
40/104
30/86
20/68
10/50
0/32
-10/14
-20/4
40/16
30/12
20/8
10/4
0

The Andean *altiplano* has an extreme tropical highland climate with winter night frosts. Annual rainfall in the west is only 25 cm (10 in). The hot eastern lowlands receive most rain in summer.

TRANSPORTATION

Drive on right

El Alto, La Paz

1 ship 15,800 dwt

THE TRANSPORTATION NETWORK

3765 km (2339 miles)	13 km (8 miles)
3698 km (2298 miles)	10,000 km (6214 miles)

Only 5% of roads in Bolivia are paved. Public transportation is inefficient. The national railroad was privatized in 1996, and passenger services were subsequently cut. Domestic airlines are generally unreliable.

***Potato harvest** on the* altiplano. *Migration to the more fertile lands in the east has been encouraged.*

***Copacabana** on the shores of Lake Titicaca. It lies on a large headland owned by Bolivia on the Peruvian side of the lake.*

TOURISM

Visitors : Population 1:23

382,185 visitors

Up 24% in 2002

MAIN TOURIST ARRIVALS

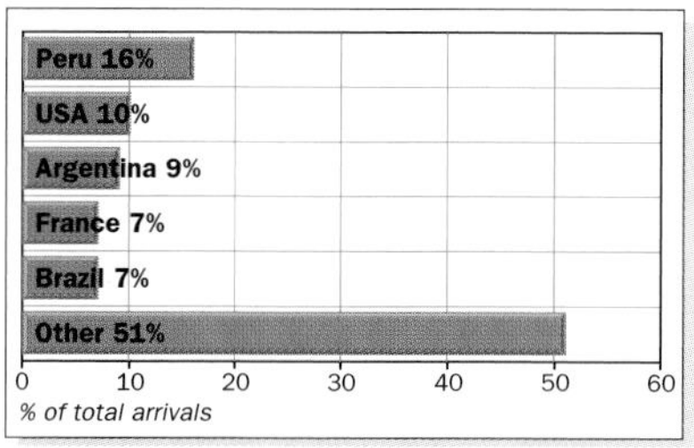
Peru 16%
USA 10%
Argentina 9%
France 7%
Brazil 7%
Other 51%
0 10 20 30 40 50 60
% of total arrivals

Foreign tourists are drawn by the traditional festivals, especially carnivals in February or March, the variety of Bolivia's scenery, and its Spanish colonial architecture. Major attractions include the Silver Mountain at Potosí, and Lake Titicaca, the highest navigable lake in the world, covering an area of 8970 sq. km (3463 sq. miles). Political instability has set tourism back in recent years, but potential is limited in any case by Bolivia's isolation, the rugged, inaccessible terrain, and the poor infrastructure.

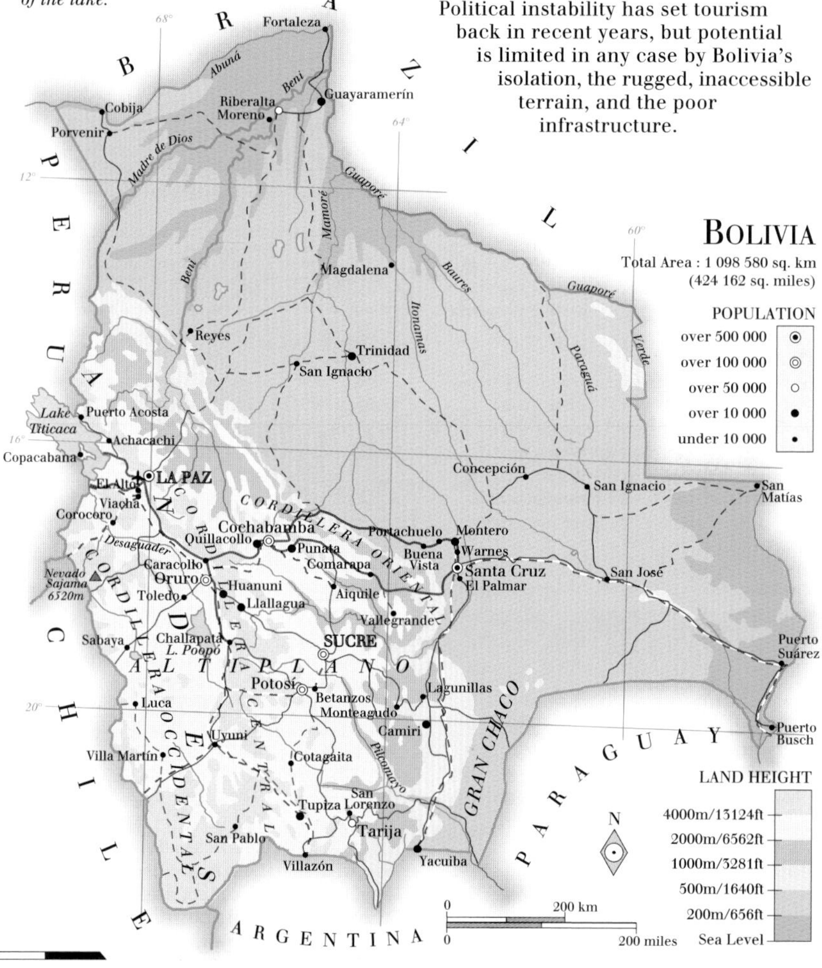
BOLIVIA
Total Area : 1 098 580 sq. km
(424 162 sq. miles)
POPULATION
over 500 000
over 100 000
over 50 000
over 10 000
under 10 000
LAND HEIGHT
4000m/13124ft
2000m/6562ft
1000m/3281ft
500m/1640ft
200m/656ft
Sea Level
0 200 km
0 200 miles
BRAZIL
PERU
CHILE
PARAGUAY
ARGENTINA
GRAN CHACO
ALTIPLANO
CORDILLERA OCCIDENTAL
CORDILLERA ORIENTAL
LA PAZ
SUCRE
El Alto
Cochabamba
Santa Cruz
Oruro
Potosí
Tarija
Trinidad
Cobija
Riberalta
Guayaramerín
Fortaleza
Porvenir
Magdalena
Reyes
San Ignacio
Concepción
San Matías
Puerto Acosta
Achacachi
Copacabana
Lake Titicaca
Viacha
Corocoro
Quillacollo
Punata
Montero
Warnes
Portachuelo
Buena Vista
Comarapa
El Palmar
San José
Caracollo
Huanuni
Llallagua
Toledo
Aiquile
Vallegrande
Sabaya
Challapata
L. Poopó
Nevado Sajama 6520m
Luca
Betanzos
Monteagudo
Lagunillas
Camiri
Uyuni
Villa Martín
Cotagaita
Tupiza
San Lorenzo
San Pablo
Villazón
Yacuiba
Puerto Suárez
Puerto Busch
Abuná
Beni
Madre de Dios
Mamoré
Guaporé
Itonamas
Baures
Paraguá
Verde
Pilcomayo
Desaguadero
N

PEOPLE

Pop. density low

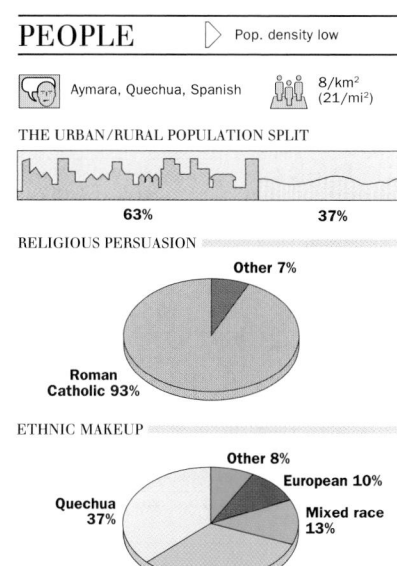

Aymara, Quechua, Spanish

8/km² (21/mi²)

THE URBAN/RURAL POPULATION SPLIT

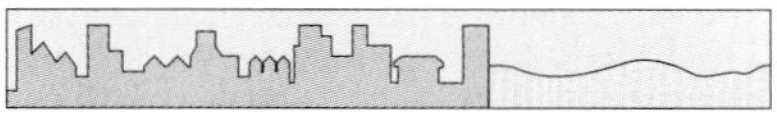
63%
37%

RELIGIOUS PERSUASION

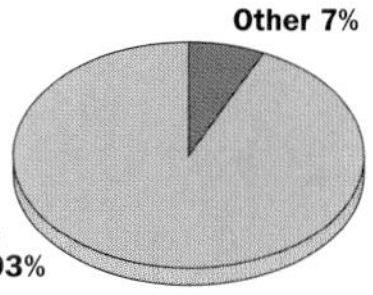
Other 7%
Roman Catholic 93%

ETHNIC MAKEUP

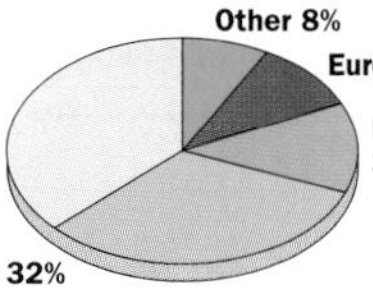
Other 8%
European 10%
Mixed race 13%
Quechua 37%
Aymara 32%

Two-thirds of Bolivians are Quechua and Aymara Amerindians who historically have been marginalized. In recent years, however, they have played a more active role in politics by supporting new populist parties.

Wealthy city elites, dating back to Spanish colonial rule, retain great influence, but new entrepreneurs with political ambitions have appeared. Most Bolivians are low-income earners (small traders, artisans, or miners) or subsistence farmers. Government schemes, spontaneous colonization, and the collapse of tin mining have led in the last few decades to large-scale migration from the Andes to lowland eastern regions. Some 130,000 lowland Amerindians live in highland cities in the western regions.

Family life tends to be close-knit; Amerindians practice Roman Catholicism mixed with their own traditions and culture. Women have low status.

POPULATION AGE BREAKDOWN

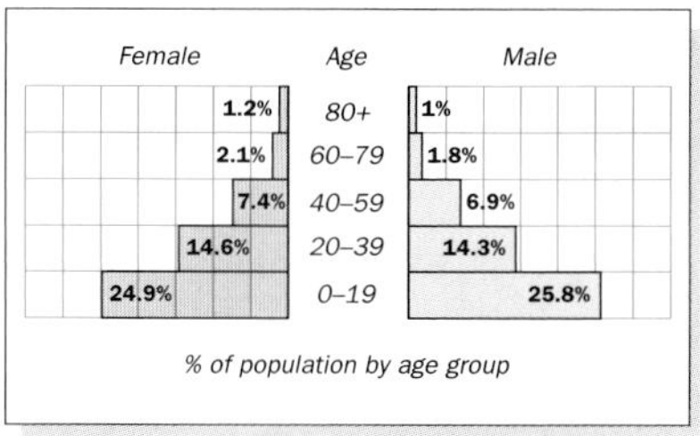
Female
Age
Male
1.2%
80+
1%
2.1%
60–79
1.8%
7.4%
40–59
6.9%
14.6%
20–39
14.3%
24.9%
0–19
25.8%
% of population by age group

POLITICS

Multiparty elections

L. House 2002/2007
U. House 2002/2007

President Carlos Mesa

AT THE LAST ELECTION

Chamber of Deputies 130 seats

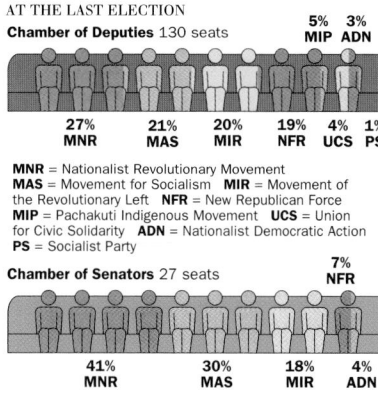

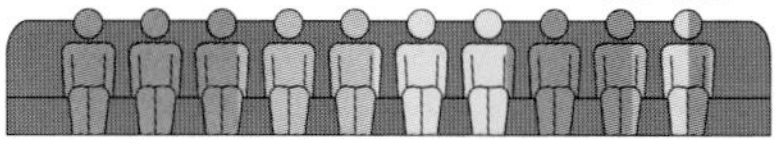
5% MIP
3% ADN
27% MNR
21% MAS
20% MIR
19% NFR
4% UCS
1% PS

MNR = Nationalist Revolutionary Movement **MAS** = Movement for Socialism **MIR** = Movement of the Revolutionary Left **NFR** = New Republican Force **MIP** = Pachakuti Indigenous Movement **UCS** = Union for Civic Solidarity **ADN** = Nationalist Democratic Action **PS** = Socialist Party

Chamber of Senators 27 seats

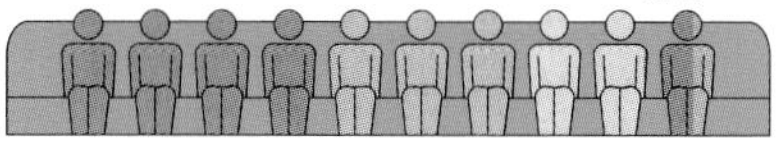
7% NFR
41% MNR
30% MAS
18% MIR
4% ADN

Bolivia is a multiparty democracy.

Profile

From 1825 to the early 1980s, Bolivia experienced, on average, more than one armed coup a year, punctuated by a national revolution in 1952 which delivered important reforms. The fragmented and drug-tainted military finally stepped down in 1982, but full elections were delayed until 1985.

New populist parties have emerged to challenge traditional politics and even the drift to free-market economics. Coalitions are unstable, nepotism is still rife, and the narcotics trade, the profits of which underpin the economy, is frequently implicated in political corruption scandals. The main trade union federation COB was traditionally the focus of opposition, but coca growers and other popular groups have now assumed this role; peasant leader Evo Morales was even a close second in presidential elections in 2002.

The unpopular austerity policies of the MNR were continued after its defeat in 1997. Gonzalo Sánchez de Lozada resumed the presidency in 2002, but he fled the country in October 2003 amid fierce public protest, and was replaced by his deputy Carlos Mesa.

Main Political Issues

Economic austerity

Violent demonstrations in 2003, ostensibly against gas exports, underlined vocal opposition to the IMF-backed austerity policies of the MNR, particularly among Amerindian groups. A referendum in 2004 backed Mesa's policy on exporting resources.

Coca growers

Poor farmers oppose the government's forced eradication of coca crops in an anticocaine drive to ensure more US aid. Serious clashes between farmers and government security forces have erupted sporadically since 2000. The *cocaleros* complain that modest subsidies to switch crops take no account of the low prices of other cash crops, such as bananas, pineapples, and palm hearts.

WORLD AFFAIRS

Joined UN in 1945

AP | AmCC | NAM | OAS | RG

Bolivia's overriding foreign policy concern has always been to recover access to the Pacific via Peru and Chile. Historic grievances fueled public opposition to a gas pipeline through Chile – the investors' choice – favoring instead a Peruvian route. Current gas export projects, coupled with the opening of the telecoms sector, and the extension of the Andean Trade Preference Act with the US are essential for growth. Current US aid is conditional on the Bolivian government taking measures to destroy the cocaine-producing and trafficking industry, involving military and police attacks on impoverished coca growers.

Bolivia is an associate member of the Mercosur economic trade bloc. This grouping, under the leadership of Brazil, will act as a strong negotiating bloc in upcoming talks for a Free Trade Area of the Americas (FTAA), due in 2005.

***Hugo Banzer Suárez**, former dictator, then elected president (1997–2001).*

***Carlos Mesa** took over as president in 2003 when his predecessor fled.*

CHRONOLOGY

The Aymara civilization was conquered by the Incas in the late 1400s. Fifty years later, the Incas were defeated by the *conquistadores*, and Upper Peru, as it became, was governed by Spain from Lima.

- **1545** Cerro Rico, the Silver Mountain, discovered at Potosí, providing Spain with vast wealth.
- **1776** Upper Peru becomes part of Viceroyalty of Río de la Plata centered on Buenos Aires.
- **1809** First abortive revolutionary uprisings in Latin America at Chuquisaca (Sucre), La Paz, and Cochabamba.
- **1824** Spaniards' final defeat by José de Sucre, Simon Bolívar's general.
- **1825** Independence.
- **1836–1839** Union with Peru fails. Internal disorder.
- **1864–1871** Ruthless rule of Mariano Melgarejo. Three Amerindian revolts over seizure of ancestral lands.

B

CHRONOLOGY *continued*

- **1879–1883** War of the Pacific, won by Chile. Bolivia left landlocked.
- **1880–1930** Period of stable governments. Exports from revived mining industry bring prosperity.
- **1903** Acre province ceded to Brazil.
- **1914** Republican Party founded.
- **1920** Amerindian rebellion.
- **1923** Miners bloodily suppressed.
- **1932–1935** Chaco War with Paraguay; in 1938 treaty Bolivia loses three-quarters of Chaco. Rise of radicalism and labor movement.
- **1951** Víctor Paz Estenssoro of MNR elected president. Military coup.
- **1952** Revolution. Paz Estenssoro and MNR brought back. Land reforms improve Amerindians' status. Education reforms, universal suffrage, tin mines nationalized.
- **1964** Military takes over in coup.
- **1967** Che Guevara killed while trying to initiate guerilla movement.
- **1969–1979** Military regimes rule with increasing severity. 1979 coup fails. Interim civilian rule.
- **1980** Military takes over again.
- **1982** President-elect Siles Zuazo finally heads leftist civilian MIR government. Inflation 24,000%.
- **1985** MNR wins elections. Austerity measures bring down inflation.
- **1986** Tin market collapses. 21,000 miners sacked.
- **1989** MIR takes power after close-run elections. President Paz Zamora makes pact with 1970s dictator Gen. Hugo Banzer, leader of ADN.
- **1990** 1.6 million hectares (4 million acres) of rainforest recognized as Amerindian territory.
- **1993** MNR back in power. Gonzalo Sánchez de Lozada president.
- **1997** Banzer wins presidency.
- **2001** Banzer resigns due to ill health.
- **2001–2003** Government program of coca eradication and bans on coca trading and marketing provoke clashes with peasant farmers.
- **2002** MNR wins elections. Sánchez de Lozada returns as president.
- **2003** Violent popular demonstrations. Sánchez de Lozada ousted: Carlos Mesa president.

AID

Recipient

$681m (receipts) | Down 7% in 2002

Aid accounts for 9% of GNP; most comes from Germany, the US, and the World Bank. US funds depend on progress in coca crop eradication. Poor rural areas get project aid from Western religious organizations, NGOs, and charities. The IDB provided emergency aid after flash floods destroyed infrastructure and badly damaged the historic center of La Paz in 2002.

DEFENSE

Compulsory military service

$119m | Down 12% in 2002

BOLIVIAN ARMED FORCES

36 light tanks (SK-105 Kuerassier)	25,000 personnel
60 riverine craft	3500 personnel
37 combat aircraft (18 AT-33AN)	3000 personnel
None	

Though the military has not actively interfered in politics for more than two decades, it is frequently used to quell internal dissent. The army is the major focus of defense spending, weaponry being bought mainly from the US. The Bolivian navy consists chiefly of gunboats on Lake Titicaca, which borders Peru, and on the Pilcomayo River. The army has worked with US forces against the cocaine business, though its integrity is questioned due to its past associations with narcotics trafficking. The main ambition of the military, apart from protecting its own interests and privileges, is the unrealizable aim of recapturing territory that would allow Bolivia access to the Pacific. Military service is selective and lasts for one year.

ECONOMICS

Inflation 8% p.a. (1990–2001)

$7.94bn | 7.939 bolivianos (7.659)

SCORE CARD

- World GNP Ranking.........................96th
- GNP per Capita $900
- Balance of Payments...................–$335m
- Inflation 0.9%
- Unemployment 5%

EXPORTS

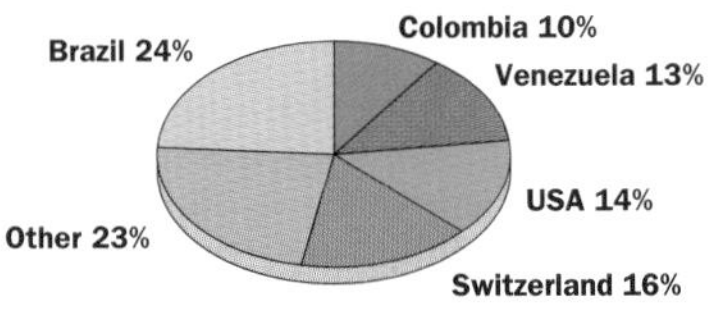
Brazil 24%
Colombia 10%
Venezuela 13%
USA 14%
Switzerland 16%
Other 23%

IMPORTS

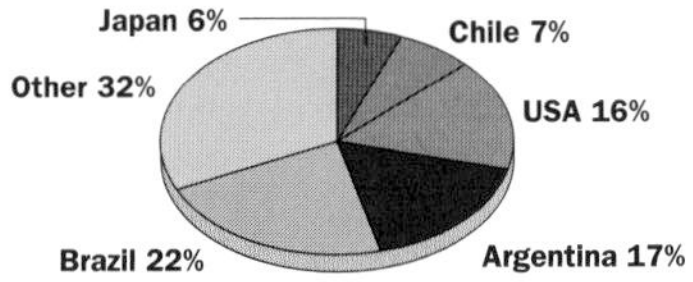
Japan 6%
Chile 7%
Other 32%
USA 16%
Brazil 22%
Argentina 17%

Strengths

Mineral riches: gold, silver, zinc, lead, tin. Newly discovered oil and natural gas deposits attracting foreign investment.

Weaknesses

Raw materials vulnerable to fluctuating world prices. Lack of processed or manufactured exports with higher added value. Lack of integration between economic sectors and regions. Poor infrastructure.

Profile

Traditionally, the state used earnings from the publicly owned state mining sector to control the economy. Years of deep recession in the 1980s, accompanied by accelerating inflation and a collapsing currency, saw the introduction of severe, IMF-approved,

ECONOMIC PERFORMANCE INDICATOR

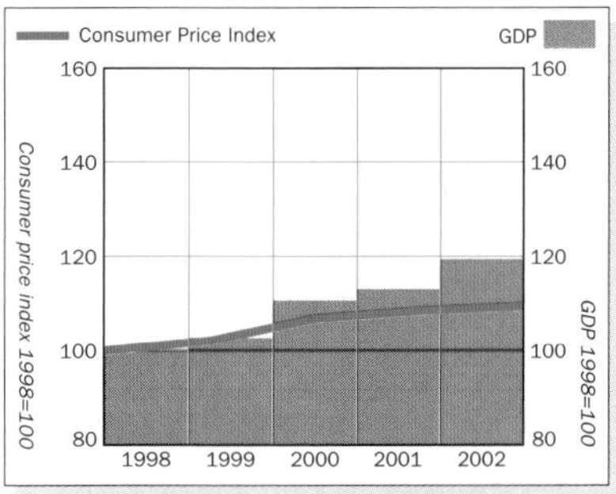
Consumer Price Index
GDP
160
140
120
100
80
Consumer price index 1998=100
GDP 1998=100
1998
1999
2000
2001
2002

austerity policies. These, along with the introduction of a new currency and tax reform, succeeded in curbing inflation, reducing public spending, and restoring international loans, but at the price of great social unrest. Growth was restored in the 1990s and stakes in state companies were offered to investors. A plan to reactivate the economy through public works has been financed by multilateral funding in return for austerity. Growth in oil and gas is needed for a sustained upturn.

BOLIVIA : MAJOR BUSINESSES

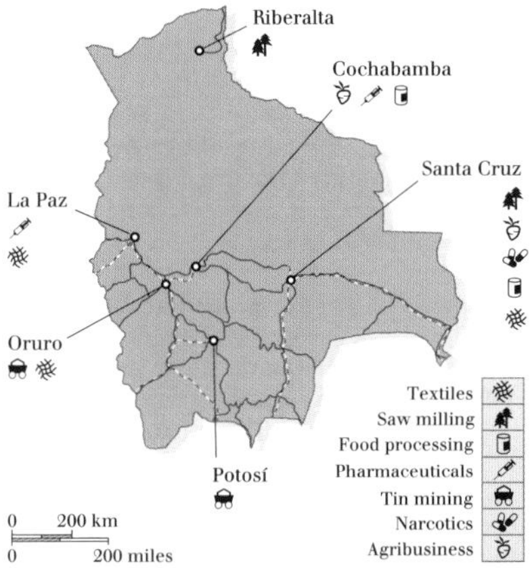
Riberalta
Cochabamba
Santa Cruz
La Paz
Oruro
Potosí
0 200 km
0 200 miles
Textiles
Saw milling
Food processing
Pharmaceuticals
Tin mining
Narcotics
Agribusiness

B

RESOURCES

Electric power 1.3m kW

6260 tonnes

30,215 b/d (reserves 110m barrels)

8.6m sheep, 6.68m cattle, 2.92m pigs, 75m chickens

Tin, natural gas, oil, zinc, tungsten, gold, antimony, silver, lead

ELECTRICITY GENERATION

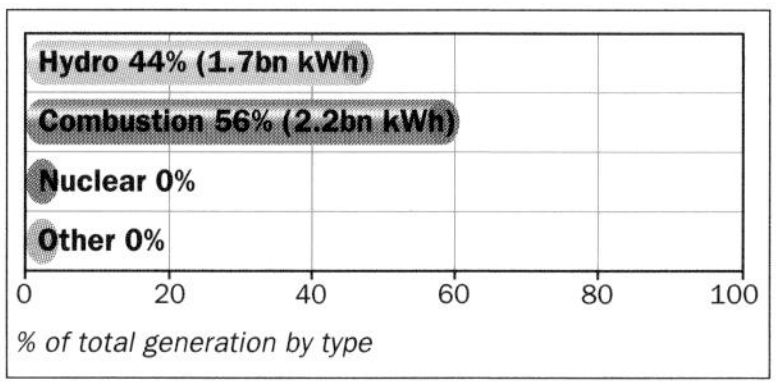
Hydro 44% (1.7bn kWh)
Combustion 56% (2.2bn kWh)
Nuclear 0%
Other 0%
0
20
40
60
80
100
% of total generation by type

Bolivia is rich in minerals, especially tin. A referendum in 2004 settled protests over how much of the country's oil and gas should be exported. A gas pipeline is to be built through Peru.

BOLIVIA : LAND USE

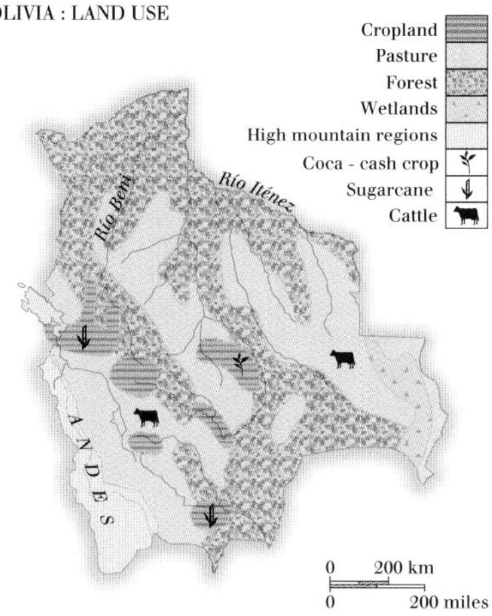
Cropland
Pasture
Forest
Wetlands
High mountain regions
Coca - cash crop
Sugarcane
Cattle
Río Beni
Río Iténez
ANDES
0 200 km
0 200 miles

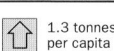

ENVIRONMENT

Sustainability rank: 21st

13% (7% partially protected)

1.3 tonnes per capita

ENVIRONMENTAL TREATIES

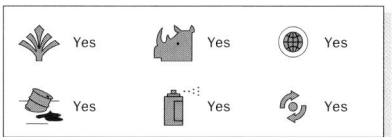

Yes Yes Yes

Yes Yes Yes

Deforestation is Bolivia's major ecological problem, as it is throughout the Amazon region. Land clearances are running at 150,000 hectares (370,000 acres) a year. Much of the cleared land is turned over to cattle ranching or the growing of coca. Pesticide and fertilizer overuse in the coca business is a concern. The industry is effectively uncontrolled, and rivers in Amazonia have high pollution levels.

Pollution problems are compounded by waste chemicals used in minerals industries. Mercury, used in the extraction of silver, has been found in dangerous quantities in river systems.

MEDIA

TV ownership medium

Daily newspaper circulation 55 per 1000 people

PUBLISHING AND BROADCAST MEDIA

There are 18 daily newspapers, including *Presencia*, *El Diario*, and *La Razón*

1 state-owned service with 9 stations, 36 independent stations

1 state-owned service, 145 independent stations

Bolivia has strict defamation laws and considerable self-censorship. One of the TV stations is university-run, providing mainly educational programs.

CRIME

Death penalty not used in practice

8315 prisoners

Down 18% in 1999–2000

CRIME RATES

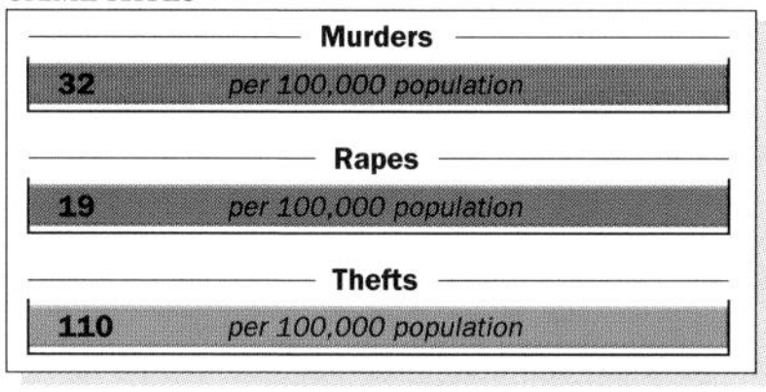
Murders
32 per 100,000 population
Rapes
19 per 100,000 population
Thefts
110 per 100,000 population

Violent crime is centered on narcotics-trafficking towns in the eastern lowlands, particularly Santa Cruz. Main cities are much safer for tourists, and have lower crime rates than cities in neighboring Peru. The police and army have a history of mistreating poor farmers and miners.

EDUCATION

School leaving age: 13

87%

278,763 students

THE EDUCATION SYSTEM

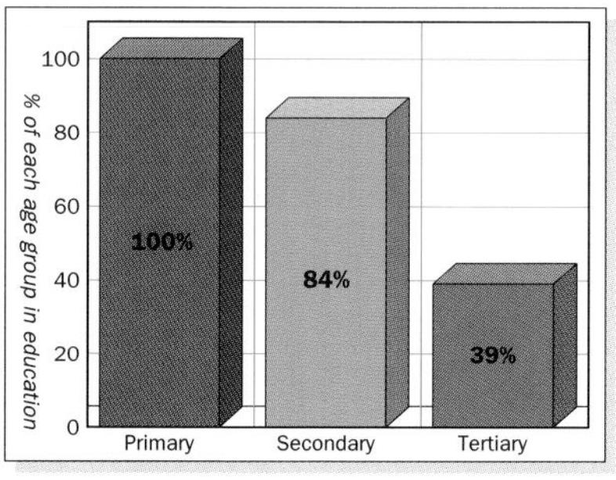
100
80
60
40
20
0
% of each age group in education
100%
84%
39%
Primary
Secondary
Tertiary

IMF targets for increased school attendance are being met, but education, based on a combination of the French and US systems, is seriously underfunded.

Though the majority of people speak indigenous languages, most teaching is in Spanish. Bolivia has one of the lowest literacy rates in South America. Reform and multilateral aid have led to some improvements.

HEALTH

No welfare state health benefits

1 per 769 people

Influenza, tuberculosis, other communicable diseases, malaria

Great disparities exist between rural and urban populations. Chronic malnutrition affects around 30% of children under three years of age in rural areas, 50% more than in urban centers. Overall Bolivia has one of the worst rates of infant mortality in the Western Hemisphere. Conditions are particularly acute among the Quechua Amerindians living in the highland areas. In 1994 the government decentralized the health system in an effort to redress the imbalance. Immunization drives have now reached most of the population. Traditional medicine and its practitioners are still widely used, especially midwives. Care for the elderly is still lacking.

SPENDING

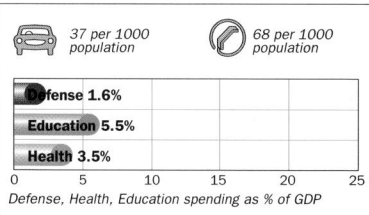

GDP/cap. increase

CONSUMPTION AND SPENDING

37 per 1000 population

68 per 1000 population

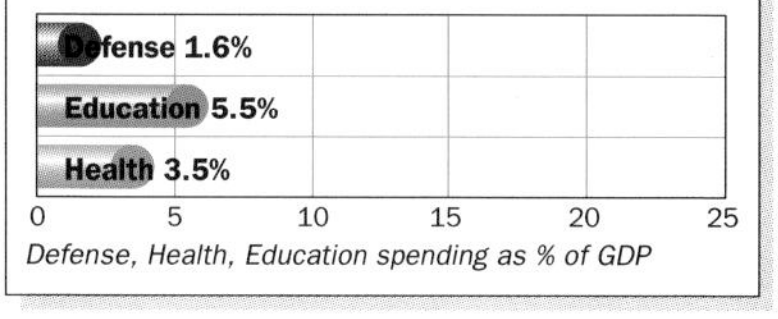
Defense 1.6%
Education 5.5%
Health 3.5%
0
5
10
15
20
25
Defense, Health, Education spending as % of GDP

Havoc created by economic reforms has widened the already huge gap between rich and poor. Generally, the indigenous population who form the rural poor are the worst off. The Andean highlands suffer from grinding poverty that has hardly changed in generations. Migrants to more prosperous eastern regions have faired better, but skewed land ownership remains a big problem. Poor housing, and the lack of utilities and a regular income are common to urban poverty. Most people do not have bank accounts.

WORLD RANKING

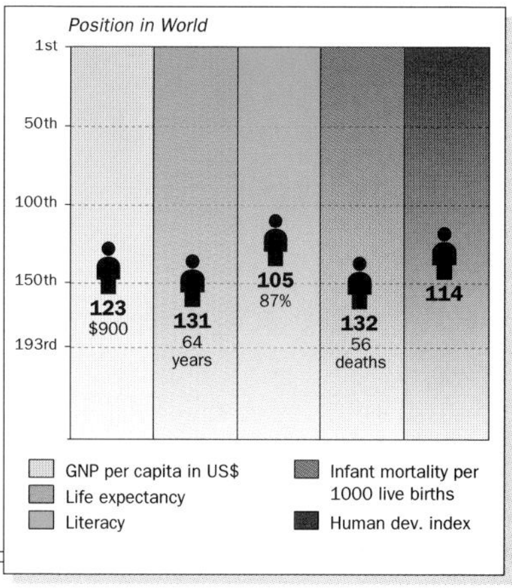
Position in World
1st
50th
100th
150th
193rd
123
$900
131
64
years
105
87%
132
56
deaths
114
GNP per capita in US$
Life expectancy
Literacy
Infant mortality per 1000 live births
Human dev. index

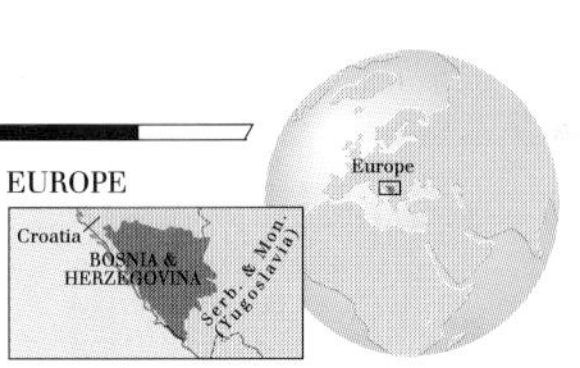
EUROPE
Europe
Croatia
BOSNIA & HERZEGOVINA
Serb. & Mon. (Yugoslavia)

BOSNIA & HERZEGOVINA

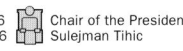

OFFICIAL NAME: Bosnia and Herzegovina **CAPITAL:** Sarajevo
POPULATION: 4.2 million **CURRENCY:** Marka **OFFICIAL LANGUAGE:** Serbo-Croat

1992 | 1992 | March 1 | BIH | +1 | +387 | .ba

A MOUNTAINOUS COUNTRY in southeast Europe, Bosnia & Herzegovina has access to the Adriatic Sea via a corridor south of Mostar. The collapse of the Socialist Federal Republic of Yugoslavia gave rise to fierce ethnic rivalries between the country's Bosniaks, Serbs, and Croats. Around 250,000 people died and more than two million were displaced before the 1995 Dayton peace accord ended three years of war. The country is now effectively an international protectorate.

CLIMATE

Continental

WEATHER CHART FOR SARAJEVO

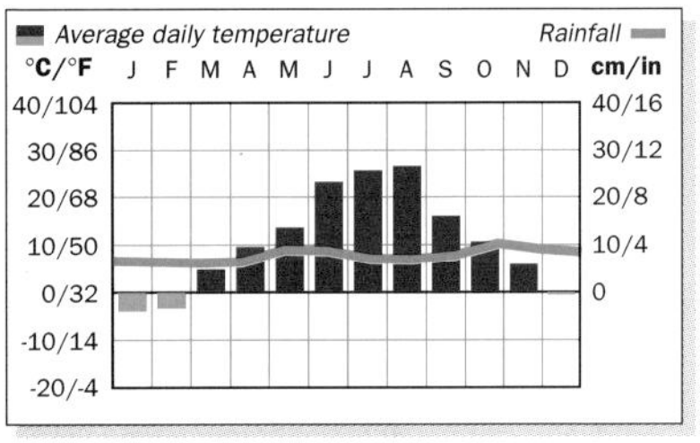
Average daily temperature
Rainfall
°C/°F
J F M A M J J A S O N D
cm/in
40/104
30/86
20/68
10/50
0/32
-10/14
-20/-4
40/16
30/12
20/8
10/4
0

Bosnia has a continental climate with warm summers and bitterly cold winters, often with heavy snow.

TRANSPORTATION

Drive on right

Sarajevo
331,711 passengers

Has no fleet

THE TRANSPORTATION NETWORK

11,360 km (7059 miles)

None

1032 km (641 miles)

Debris and silt block the Sava River

Though bridges, roads, and railroads were wrecked in the war, reconstruction and mine removal have enabled most main routes to be reopened. Sarajevo remains the hub of the communications network.

TOURISM

Visitors : Population 1:26

160,000 visitors

Up 45% in 2001–2002

MAIN TOURIST ARRIVALS

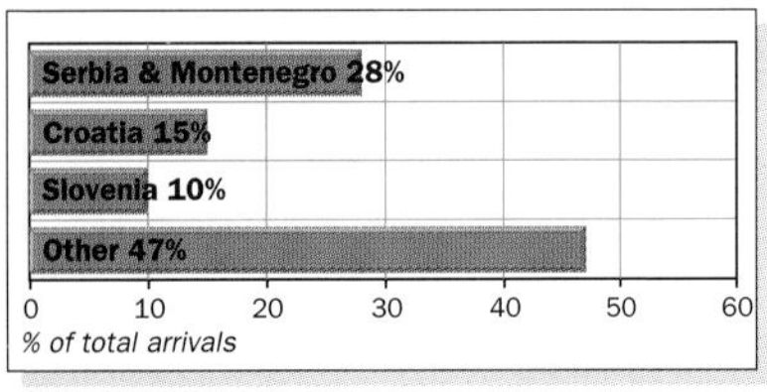
Serbia & Montenegro 28%
Croatia 15%
Slovenia 10%
Other 47%
0
10
20
30
40
50
60
% of total arrivals

Even before the war, Bosnia did not have much tourism infrastructure; only the adventurous have begun to visit.

PEOPLE

Pop. density medium

Serbo-Croat

82/km² (213/mi²)

THE URBAN/RURAL POPULATION SPLIT

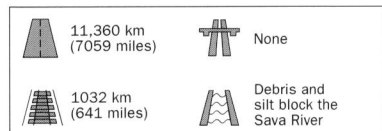

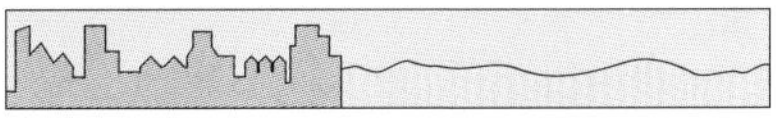
44%
56%

ETHNIC MAKEUP

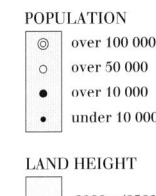

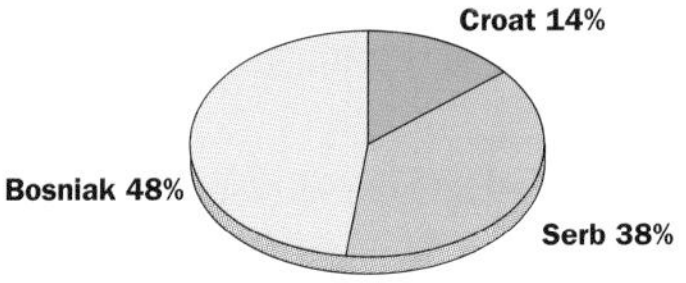
Croat 14%
Bosniak 48%
Serb 38%

Despite sharing the same origin and spoken language, Bosnia's population has been divided by history between Muslim Bosniaks, Orthodox Christian Serbs, and Roman Catholic Croats. Ethnic cleansing, practiced by all sides in the 1992–1995 civil war, left the once integrated communities sharply polarized and geographically redistributed. The process of returning refugees to their old homes has been slow.

POLITICS

Multiparty elections

L. House 2002/2006
U. House 2002/2006

Chair of the Presidency
Sulejman Tihic

AT THE LAST ELECTION

House of Representatives 42 seats

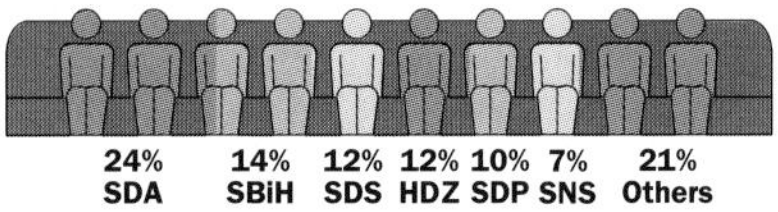
24% SDA
14% SBiH
12% SDS
12% HDZ
10% SDP
7% SNS
21% Others

SDA = Party of Democratic Action **SBiH** = Party for Bosnia & Herzegovina **SDS** = Serb Democratic Party **HDZ** = Croatian Democratic Union **SDP** = Social Democratic Party **SNS** = Independent Social Democrats

28 members are elected from the Federation of Bosnia-Herzegovina and 14 from the Republika Srpska

House of Peoples 15 seats

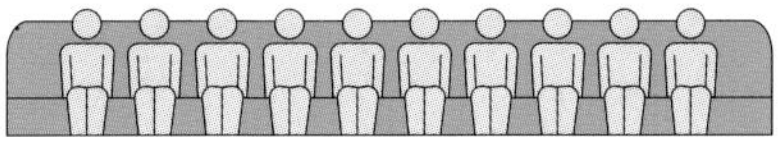

Ten members are appointed from the Federation of Bosnia-Herzegovina and five from the Republika Srpska

Bosnia is subdivided into the Muslim–Croat Federation and the Serb Republika Srpska (RS), plus the multiethnic district of Brčko. There are two levels of government: the overall Republic – with a rotating three-member collective presidency – and the constituent entities, with their own presidents, governments, and parliaments. A UN High Representative retains ultimate control. Legislative elections in October 2002 were the first to be organized by the Bosnian authorities: nationalist parties triumphed at all levels, overturning governments formed by more moderate parties.

BOSNIA & HERZEGOVINA

Total Area : 51 129 sq. km (19 741 sq. miles)

POPULATION
- over 100 000
- over 50 000
- over 10 000
- under 10 000

LAND HEIGHT
- 2000m/6562ft
- 1000m/3281ft
- 500m/1640ft
- 200m/656ft
- Sea Level

CROATIA
Bosanska Gradiška
Kozara
Sava
Vrbas
Bosanski Brod
Bosanski Šamac
Derventa
Modriča
Cazin
Prijedor
Brčko
Sava
Gradačac
Bihać
Banja Luka
Bijeljina
Grmeč
Sana
REPUBLIKA SRPSKA
Doboj
Gračanica
Teslić
Bosna
Maglaj
Tuzla
Ključ
Una
DINARIC ALPS
Jajce
Travnik
Zenica
Zvornik
Vlasenica
FEDERACIJA BOSNA I HERCEGOVINA
Bugojno
Srebrenica
Vranica
SARAJEVO
Livno
Treskavica
Konjic
Foča
Drina
Neretva
Mostar
Maglić 2387m
Trebinje
ADRIATIC SEA
SERBIA & MONTENEGRO
N
0 50 km
0 50 miles

WORLD AFFAIRS

Joined UN in 1992

CEI | EBRD | OSCE | IBRD | IAEA

International agencies maintain security. The Stabilization Force (SFOR) is NATO-led; its 35 participant countries include Russia. Policing came under the EU's mandate from 2003.

AID

Recipient

$587m (receipts) — Down 8% in 2002

Aid for reconstruction and refugee return, totaling several billion dollars, has come mainly from the EU and the US. Major objectives have included developing a market economy and job creation, housing, and infrastructure.

DEFENSE

Compulsory military service

$178m — Up 27% in 2002

Overall security is provided by SFOR. A single defense ministry and a 12,000-strong professional force were created in 2004, in response to a call for the separate armies to be integrated.

ECONOMICS

Inflation 2.7% p.a. (1992–2001)

$5.4bn — 1.53 maraka (1.71)

SCORE CARD

- ❑ WORLD GNP RANKING........113th
- ❑ GNP PER CAPITA........$1310
- ❑ BALANCE OF PAYMENTS........–$2.14bn
- ❑ INFLATION........0%
- ❑ UNEMPLOYMENT........40%

STRENGTHS

Potential to revive prewar industries and become a thriving market economy, with solid manufacturing base. Growth in 2000 of 10%. End of cross-border tariffs with Slovenia from 2002.

WEAKNESSES

War damage of $20–40 billion. Low foreign investment. Corruption. High unemployment and levels of poverty.

EXPORTS

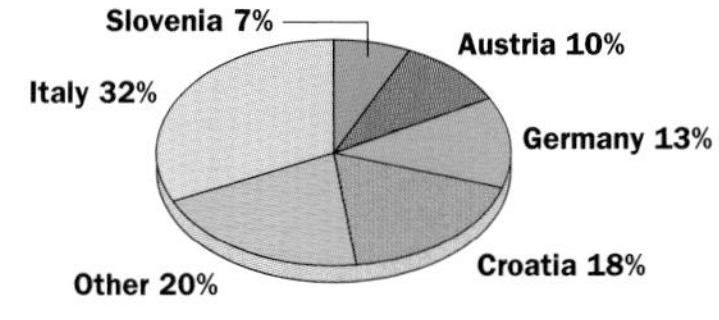
Slovenia 7%
Austria 10%
Italy 32%
Germany 13%
Croatia 18%
Other 20%

IMPORTS

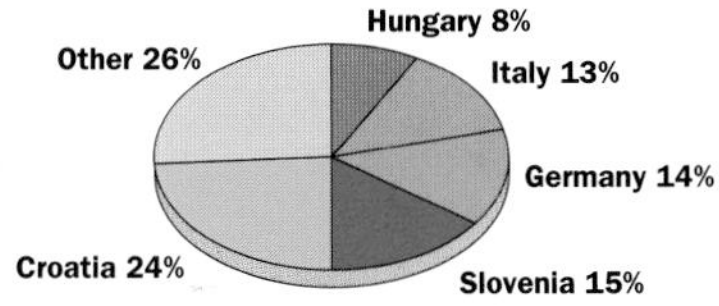
Hungary 8%
Other 26%
Italy 13%
Germany 14%
Croatia 24%
Slovenia 15%

RESOURCES

Electric power 2.7m kW

2500 tonnes — Not an oil producer

670,000 sheep, 440,000 cattle, 4.7m chickens — Coal, lignite, iron, bauxite, cement

Bosnia's land is not well suited to agriculture, but has mineral deposits, forests, and hydroelectric potential.

ENVIRONMENT

Sustainability rank: 57th

0.5% (0.2% partially protected) — 4.8 tonnes per capita

Apart from war damage, Bosnia faces the effects of industrial pollution incurred during the communist regime.

MEDIA

TV ownership medium

Daily newspaper circulation 152 per 1000 people

PUBLISHING AND BROADCAST MEDIA

There are 6 daily newspapers. *Oslobodjenje* (*Liberation*) was published daily throughout the war

29 services: 3 state-owned, 26 independent — 82 services: 3 state-owned, 79 independent

Constitutionally free, media outlets remain under pressure from government bodies and the danger of violence against journalists, and most are still highly partisan along ethnic lines.

CRIME

No death penalty

2283 prisoners — Crime is rising

All sides in the war, but especially the Serbs, have been accused of war crimes. The International Criminal Tribunal for the former Yugoslavia (ICTY) sits in The Hague, while a specific court for Bosnia is due to open in 2004. Serb leader Radovan Karadzic and around 20 others have evaded arrest. The RS finally passed laws on cooperating with the tribunal in 2001.

EDUCATION

School leaving age: 15

95% — 34,477 students

Ethnic bias and educational segregation are being combated by the development of a new coordinated curriculum.

The Muslim town of Mostar. *Its 16th-century bridge was destroyed in the 1992–1995 war, but has been painstakingly rebuilt.*

CHRONOLOGY

In 1945, Bosnia & Herzegovina became one of Yugoslavia's six constituent republics.

- ❑ **1990** Nationalists defeat communists in multiparty elections.
- ❑ **1991** Parliament announces republican sovereignty.
- ❑ **1992** EU and US recognize Bosnia. Serbs declare "Serbian Republic." Civil war begins.
- ❑ **1995** NATO air strikes on Serbs; US-brokered Dayton peace accord.
- ❑ **1996** First international war crimes trial since 1945 opens in The Hague. Elections held under Dayton accord.
- ❑ **2001** Ethnic Croats briefly establish autonomy in Herzegovina (in south).
- ❑ **2002** Elections: renewed support for nationalist parties.

B

HEALTH

No welfare state health benefits

1 per 714 people — Cholera and diphtheria epidemics, violence, deaths from war-stress

War strained health services severely and many died for lack of basic care. Reconstruction includes reform of the primary health care system.

SPENDING

GDP/cap. increase

CONSUMPTION AND SPENDING

27 per 1000 population — *237 per 1000 population*

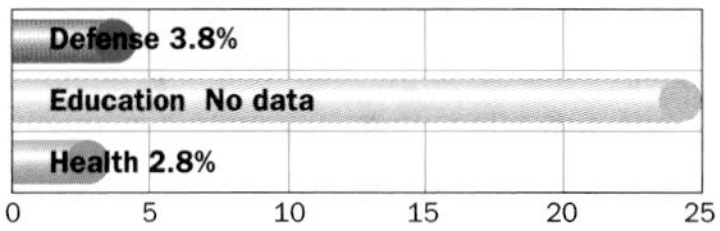
Defense 3.8%
Education No data
Health 2.8%
0
5
10
15
20
25

Defense, Health, Education spending as % of GDP

The war displaced 60% of the population. Housing, jobs, and reintegration are key challenges, while a lack of significant investment means that postwar poverty remains.

WORLD RANKING

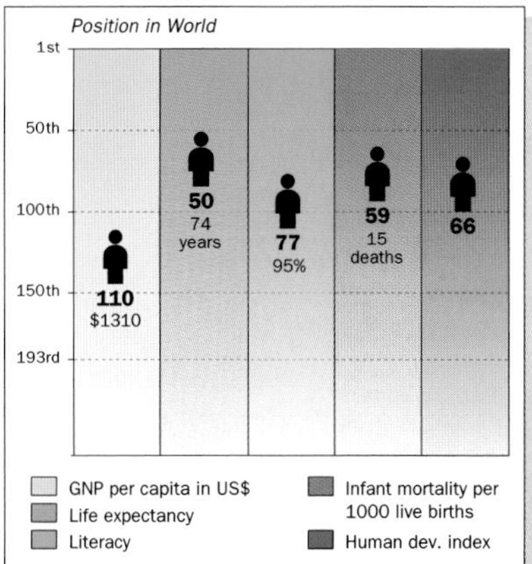
Position in World
1st
50th
100th
150th
193rd
110
$1310
50
74 years
77
95%
59
15 deaths
66
GNP per capita in US$
Life expectancy
Literacy
Infant mortality per 1000 live births
Human dev. index

B

BOTSWANA

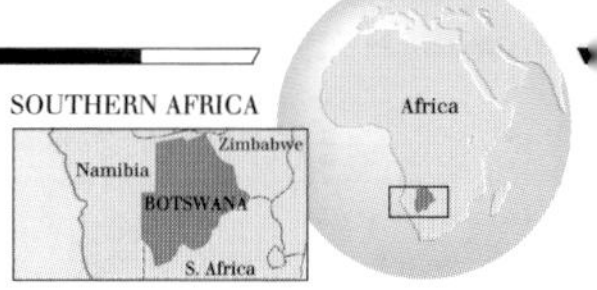
SOUTHERN AFRICA
Africa
Namibia
Zimbabwe
BOTSWANA
S. Africa

OFFICIAL NAME: Republic of Botswana **CAPITAL:** Gaborone
POPULATION: 1.8 million **CURRENCY:** Pula **OFFICIAL LANGUAGE:** English

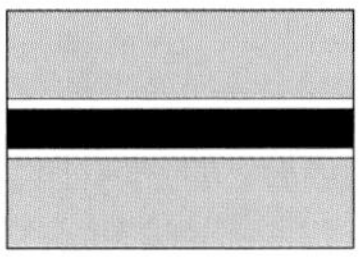

1966 | 1966 | Sept 30 | RB | +2 | +267 | .bw

BOTSWANA IS ARID and landlocked, its central plateau separating the populous eastern grasslands from the Kalahari Desert and the swamps of the Okavango Delta in the west. Diamonds provide Botswana with a prosperous economy, but rain is an even more precious resource, honored in the name of the currency, the pula. Botswana has one of the world's highest rates of HIV infection among adults.

The Okavango Delta, "jewel of the Kalahari," is the largest inland river delta in the world and home to a rich variety of wildlife.

CLIMATE

Steppe/hot desert

WEATHER CHART FOR GABORONE

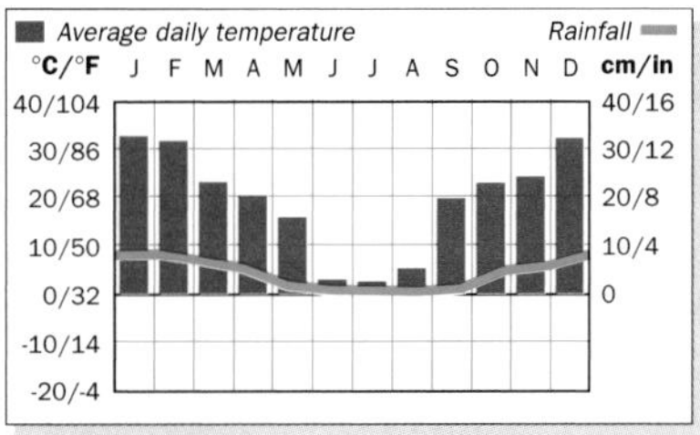
Average daily temperature
Rainfall
°C/°F J F M A M J J A S O N D cm/in
40/104 30/86 20/68 10/50 0/32 -10/14 -20/4
40/16 30/12 20/8 10/4 0

The subtropical climate is dry and prone to drought. Rainfall declines from 64 cm (25 in) in the north to under 10 cm (4 in) in the Kalahari Desert in the west.

TRANSPORTATION

Drive on left

Sir Seretse Khama International, Gaborone
473,794 passengers

Has no fleet

THE TRANSPORTATION NETWORK

5619 km (3491 miles)	None
888 km (552 miles)	None

The opening of the trans-Kalahari road to Namibia in 1998 has reduced Botswana's dependence on South African ports. Upgrading existing rail and road networks is a priority.

TOURISM

Visitors : Population 1:1.7

1.04m visitors

Up 4% in 2002

MAIN TOURIST ARRIVALS

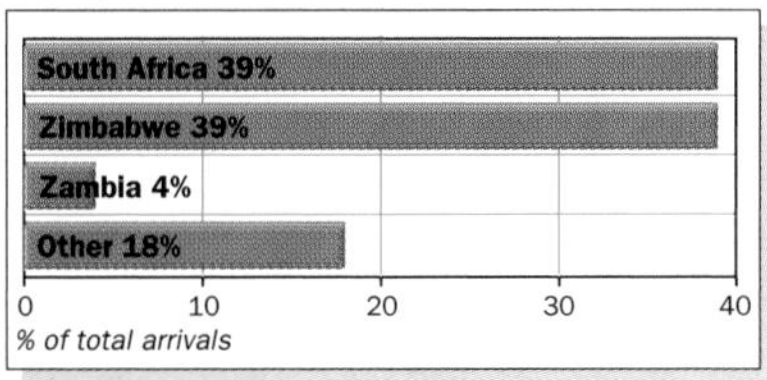
South Africa 39%
Zimbabwe 39%
Zambia 4%
Other 18%
0 10 20 30 40
% of total arrivals

Tourism is aimed at wealthy wildlife enthusiasts and focuses on safaris, especially to the Okavango Delta.

PEOPLE

Pop. density low

Setswana, English, Shona, San, Khoikhoi, isiNdebele

3/km² (8/mi)²

THE URBAN/RURAL POPULATION SPLIT

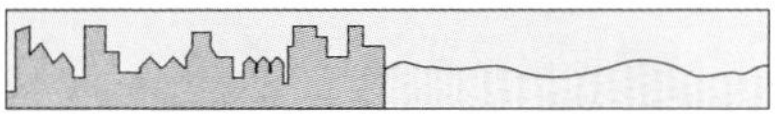
50%
50%

ETHNIC MAKEUP

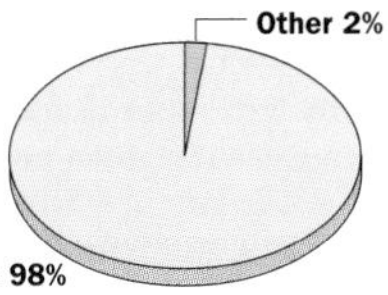
Other 2%
Tswana 98%

Botswana's stability reflects its ethnic homogeneity (98% Tswana) and the power of traditional authorities. The Bangwato form the largest clan. The indigenous San of the Kalahari were ordered to abandon their nomadic way of life in 2002, but are appealing against the order. A small white community still dominates the professions. Some 80% of people are Christian, but traditional beliefs are also widely practiced.

POLITICS

Multiparty elections

1999/2004

President Festus Mogae

AT THE LAST ELECTION

National Assembly 46 seats

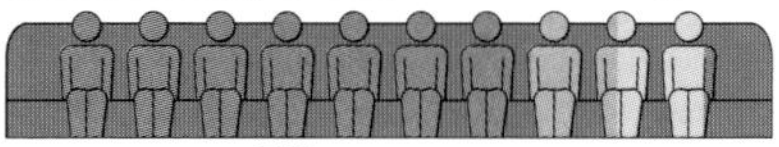
13%
App
72%
BDP
13%
BNF
2%
BCP

BDP = Botswana Democratic Party **BNF** = Botswana National Front **App** = Appointed **BCP** = Botswana Congress Party

In addition to 40 elected members, four are co-opted and the president and the attorney general are ex officio members

Botswana, formally a multiparty democracy, has been ruled since independence by the BDP. The party's majority was eroded in the mid-1990s, as corruption scandals and an economic dip boosted the opposition BNF.

Power was transferred smoothly from President Ketumile Masire to Festus Mogae in 1998, while Lt.-Gen. Seretse Ian Khama, the son of independence-era leader Sir Seretse Khama, was made vice president and heir apparent. The opposition BNF split in two, and the 1999 elections confirmed the BDP's hold on power.

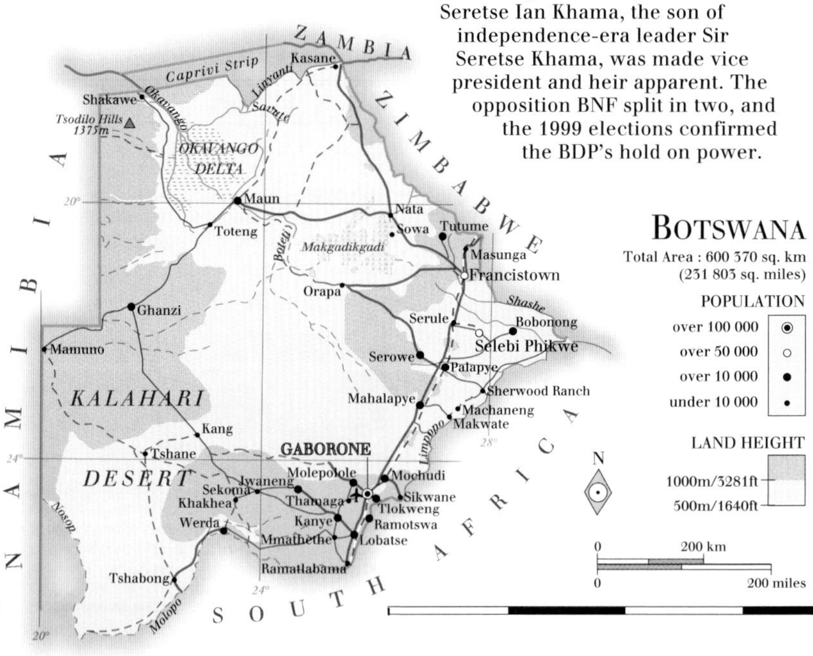
ZAMBIA
Caprivi Strip
Kasane
Linyanti
Savuti
Shakawe
Okavango
Tsodilo Hills 1375m
OKAVANGO DELTA
ZIMBABWE
NAMIBIA
Maun
Nata
Sowa
Tutume
Toteng
Boteti
Makgadikgadi
Masunga
Francistown
Orapa
Shashe
Ghanzi
Serule
Bobonong
Selebi Phikwe
Mamuno
Serowe
Palapye
KALAHARI
Mahalapye
Sherwood Ranch
Machaneng
Makwate
Limpopo
Kang
GABORONE
Tshane
Molepolole
Mochudi
DESERT
Sekoma
Jwaneng
Khakhea
Thamaga
Sikwane
Tlokweng
Kanye
Ramotswa
Werda
Mmathethe
Lobatse
Nossop
Tshabong
Ramatlabama
Molopo
SOUTH AFRICA
20°
24°
28°
N
BOTSWANA
Total Area : 600 370 sq. km (231 803 sq. miles)
POPULATION
over 100 000
over 50 000
over 10 000
under 10 000
LAND HEIGHT
1000m/3281ft
500m/1640ft
0 200 km
0 200 miles

WORLD AFFAIRS

Joined UN in 1966

Comm | NAM | AU | SADC | WTO

Botswana has strongly backed a politically and economically stable postapartheid South Africa. Though the headquarters of the SADC are in Gaborone, the potential for South Africa to dominate the community is a concern. Traditionally pro-Western in orientation, Botswana cherishes its relations with the UK and the US.

AID

Recipient

$38m (receipts) | Up 31% in 2002

Botswana's political and economic record has made it a favored recipient of aid, notably from Japan, Germany, the EU, the UK, and Norway. Some 90% of EU aid goes to projects which try to balance wildlife needs with rural development. Aid also targets transportation projects.

DEFENSE

No compulsory military service

$254m | Up 38% in 2002

The majority of officers in the Botswana Defense Force have been trained by the US. The force runs one of Africa's toughest antipoaching programs.

ECONOMICS

Inflation 9% p.a. (1990–2001)

$5.15bn | 4.647 pula (4.926)

SCORE CARD

- World GNP Ranking........................114th
- GNP per Capita $3010
- Balance of Payments..................–$47.2bn
- Inflation 8.1%
- Unemployment 16%

Strengths

Diamonds; party to Kimberley Process (curbs flow of gems from conflict areas). Recent economic growth among highest in world. Prudent management, large financial reserves, exchange control liberalization. Exports: copper, nickel, beef. Transportation links. Tourism potential. Relatively low corruption.

Weaknesses

AIDS. Overdependence on diamonds. Agriculture and industry weak. Small population. Water shortages. Impact of cattle farming on land. Unemployment. Economic migrants from Zimbabwe. High costs of transportation to coast.

EXPORTS

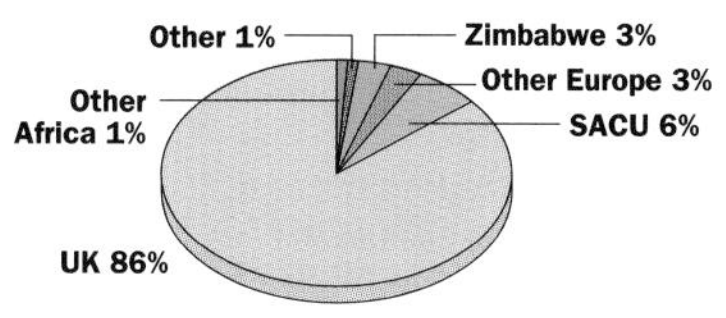
Other 1%
Zimbabwe 3%
Other Europe 3%
Other Africa 1%
SACU 6%
UK 86%

IMPORTS

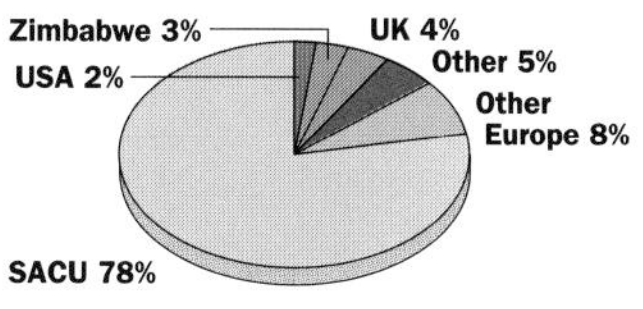
Zimbabwe 3%
UK 4%
USA 2%
Other 5%
Other Europe 8%
SACU 78%

RESOURCES

Electric power: Included in South African total

118 tonnes | Not an oil producer

2.25m goats, 1.7m cattle, 400,000 sheep, 4m chickens | Diamonds, copper, coal, nickel, soda ash, gold

Botswana is one of the world's top diamond producers. Large coal deposits are the basis of power grid expansion. Water is Botswana's scarcest resource.

ENVIRONMENT

Sustainability rank: 13th

19% (10% partially protected) | 2.3 tonnes per capita

Botswana is trying to help communities to earn a living from wildlife protection. A campaign has been launched to curb the use of agrochemicals.

MEDIA

TV ownership low

Daily newspaper circulation 27 per 1000 people

PUBLISHING AND BROADCAST MEDIA

There are 2 daily newspapers. *Dikgang tsa Gompieno* is published by the government

2 services: 1 state-owned, 1 independent | 3 services: 1 state-owned, 2 independent

A government-funded TV service was launched in 2000. The progovernment bias of radio and the main daily paper is offset in the many journals.

CRIME

Death penalty in use

5890 prisoners | Crime is rising

President Mogae warned of a "crime wave" in 1999. Diamond smuggling remains a major concern. Human rights are generally respected.

EDUCATION

School leaving age: 15

79% | 7651 students

Revenues from the diamond industry have helped to fund educational programs which have improved the country's literacy rate.

CHRONOLOGY

From 1600, Tswana migrations slowly displaced San people. In 1895, at local request, the UK set up the Bechuanaland Protectorate to preempt annexation by South Africa.

- **1965** BDP wins first, and all subsequent, general elections.
- **1966** Independence declared.
- **1980** Death of Sir Seretse Khama; succeeded by Vice President Quett (later Sir Ketumile) Masire.
- **1985–1986** South African raids.
- **1992–1993** Strikes and corruption scandals prompt resignations of senior BDP figures.
- **1994** Election: BDP support eroded.
- **1998** Masire retires; succeeded by Vice President Festus Mogae.
- **2001–2002** Botswana has world's highest rate of adult AIDS sufferers.

HEALTH

Welfare state health benefits

1 per 5000 people | AIDS, tuberculosis, heart diseases, pneumonia

In 2001 Botswana began to provide free antiretroviral drugs to people infected with HIV. At that time it had the world's highest infection rate (38.8%), but levels have dropped slightly since then.

SPENDING

GDP/cap. increase

CONSUMPTION AND SPENDING

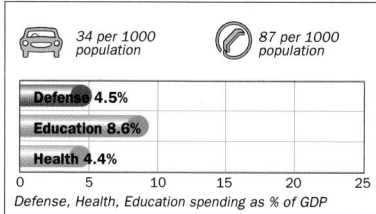

34 per 1000 population | *87 per 1000 population*

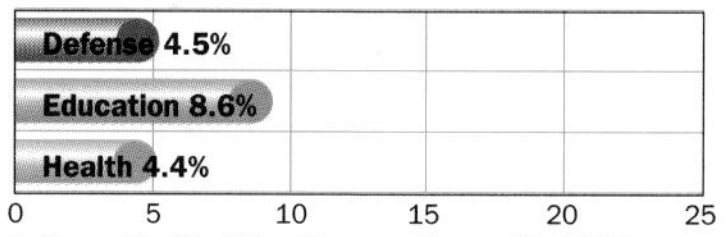
Defense 4.5%
Education 8.6%
Health 4.4%
0
5
10
15
20
25

Defense, Health, Education spending as % of GDP

GNP per capita is among Africa's highest, but about half the population live below the poverty line. Economic growth has exacerbated wealth inequalities.

WORLD RANKING

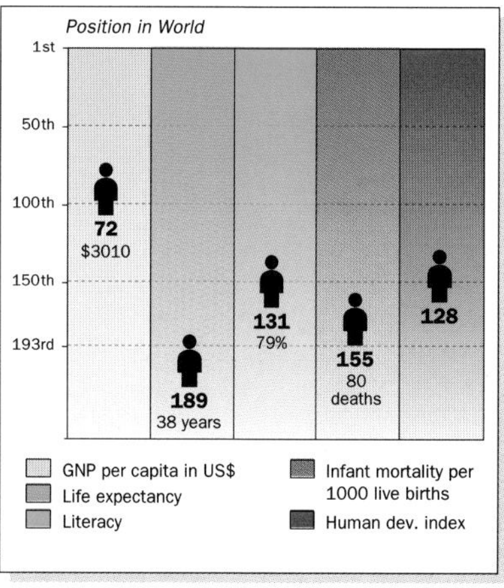
Position in World
1st
50th
100th
150th
193rd
72
$3010
189
38 years
131
79%
155
80 deaths
128
GNP per capita in US$
Life expectancy
Literacy
Infant mortality per 1000 live births
Human dev. index

BRAZIL

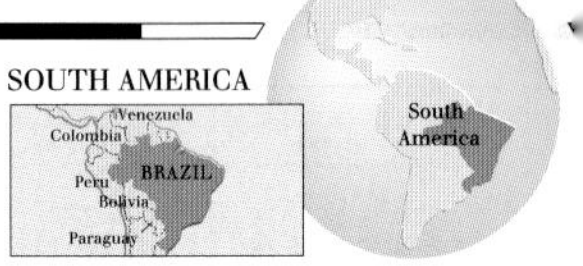
SOUTH AMERICA
Venezuela
Colombia
Peru
Bolivia
BRAZIL
Paraguay
South America

OFFICIAL NAME: Federative Republic of Brazil **CAPITAL:** Brasília
POPULATION: 179 million **CURRENCY:** Real **OFFICIAL LANGUAGE:** Portuguese

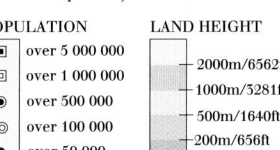

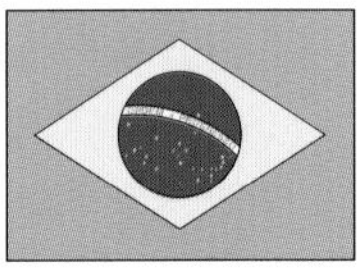

1822 | 1828 | Sept 7 | BR | -3 | +55 | .br

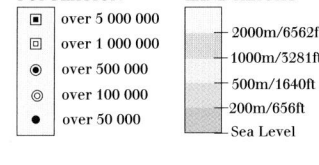

THE LARGEST COUNTRY in South America, Brazil became independent of Portugal in 1822. Today, it is renowned as the site of the world's largest tropical rainforest, the threat to which led to the UN's first international environment conference, held in Rio de Janeiro in 1992. Covering one-third of Brazil's total land area, the rainforest grows around the massive Amazon River and its delta. Apart from the basin of the River Plate in the south, the rest of the country consists of highlands. The mountainous northeast is part forested and part desert. Brazil is the world's leading coffee producer and also has rich reserves of gold, diamonds, oil, and iron ore. Cattle ranching is an expanding industry. The city of São Paulo is the world's fifth-biggest conurbation, with some 20 million inhabitants.

BRAZIL

Total Area : 8 511 965 sq. km
(3 286 470 sq. miles)

POPULATION	LAND HEIGHT
over 5 000 000	2000m/6562ft
over 1 000 000	1000m/3281ft
over 500 000	500m/1640ft
over 100 000	200m/656ft
over 50 000	Sea Level

VENEZUELA
COLOMBIA
SERRA PACARAIMA
Serra Parima
Boa Vista
RORAIMA
Pico da Neblina 3014m
GUIANA
Negro
Japurá
Içá
Solimões (Amazon)
AMAZONAS
Amazon Basin
Javari
Juruá
Purus
Madeira
Aripuanã
Porto Velho
ACRE
Rio Branco
RONDÔNIA
Roosevelt
Chapada dos Parecis
Guaporé
PERU
BOLIVIA
N
0
500 km
500 miles

CLIMATE

Tropical equatorial/hot and dry/subtropical/steppe

WEATHER CHART FOR BRASÍLIA

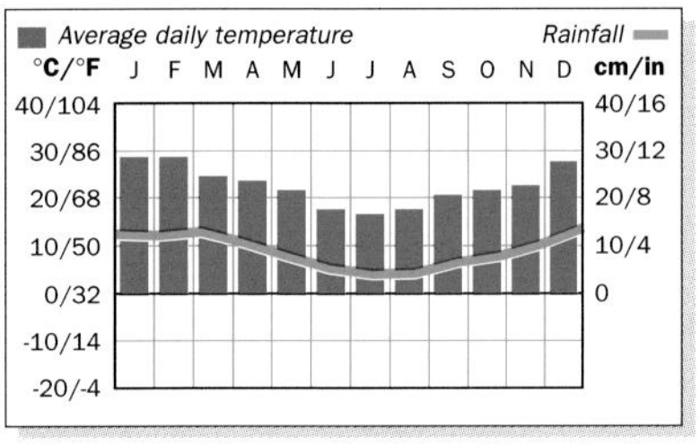
Average daily temperature
Rainfall
°C/°F
J F M A M J J A S O N D
cm/in
40/104
30/86
20/68
10/50
0/32
-10/14
-20/-4
40/16
30/12
20/8
10/4
0

Brazil's share of the Amazon basin, occupying half of the country, has a model equatorial climate. Its 150–200 cm (59–79 in) of rain are spread throughout the year. Temperatures are high, with almost no seasonal variation, but scarcely ever rise above 38°C (100°F).

The Brazilian plateau, occupying most of the rest of the country, has far greater temperature ranges. Rain falls mainly between October and April. The northeast, the least productive region of Brazil, is very dry and is frequently prone to severe drought. However, periodic bouts of torrential rain can devastate coastal regions, leading to severe flooding in recent years.

The southern states have hot summers and cool winters, when frost may occur.

TRANSPORTATION

Drive on right

Guarulhos International, São Paulo
12.5m passengers

476 ships
3.45m grt

THE TRANSPORTATION NETWORK

164,000 km (101,905 miles)	Trans-Amazonian Highway: 5300 km (3293 miles)
30,403 km (18,892 miles)	50,000 km (31,069 miles)

Brazil's size means that internal air travel is often essential. However, flights are expensive. Many Brazilians make use of the extensive if arduous bus routes. Urban roads are congested. Rail services have been cut back.

***Parati, in Rio state,** was one of Brazil's major gold-exporting ports in the 17th century. Its colonial architecture is well preserved.*

TOURISM

Visitors : Population
1:47

3.78m visitors

Down 21% in 2002

MAIN TOURIST ARRIVALS

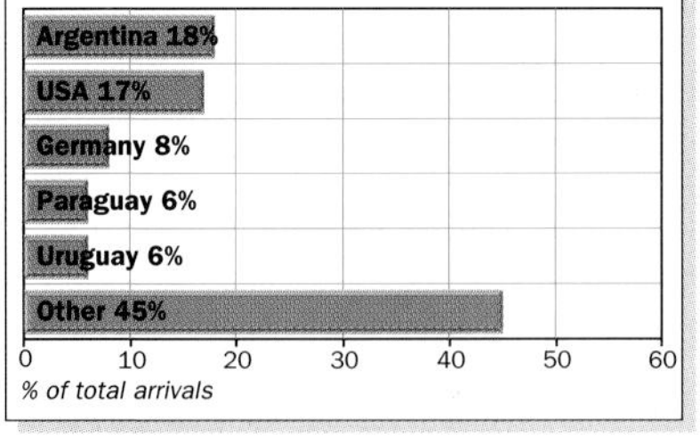
Argentina 18%
USA 17%
Germany 8%
Paraguay 6%
Uruguay 6%
Other 45%
0
10
20
30
40
50
60
% of total arrivals

Brazil is underperforming in tourism, with revenues falling to just over 0.5% of GDP in 2000, compared with a world average of over 10%.

Attractions are the celebrated beaches and world famous carnival of Rio de Janeiro – the center of the tourist trade – Brasília, the modern capital, Atlantic beaches stretching 2000 km (1250 miles), the Amazon River basin, the spectacular Iguaçu Falls, the Pantanal – the vast wetland region in the west – and the Afro-Brazilian culture of Salvador. They are offset by the limited availability of medium- to low-cost travel and budget hotels, which deters both domestic and foreign travelers.

In the virtual absence of low-cost charter flights, domestic air travel is expensive. This is blamed on high airport charges and inertia in Brazil's aviation department, which is controlled by the air force.

Average overnight hotel rates are higher than in Europe and the US, and the quality of service is generally poor. Basic infrastructure, such as sanitation and water supply, is also deficient.

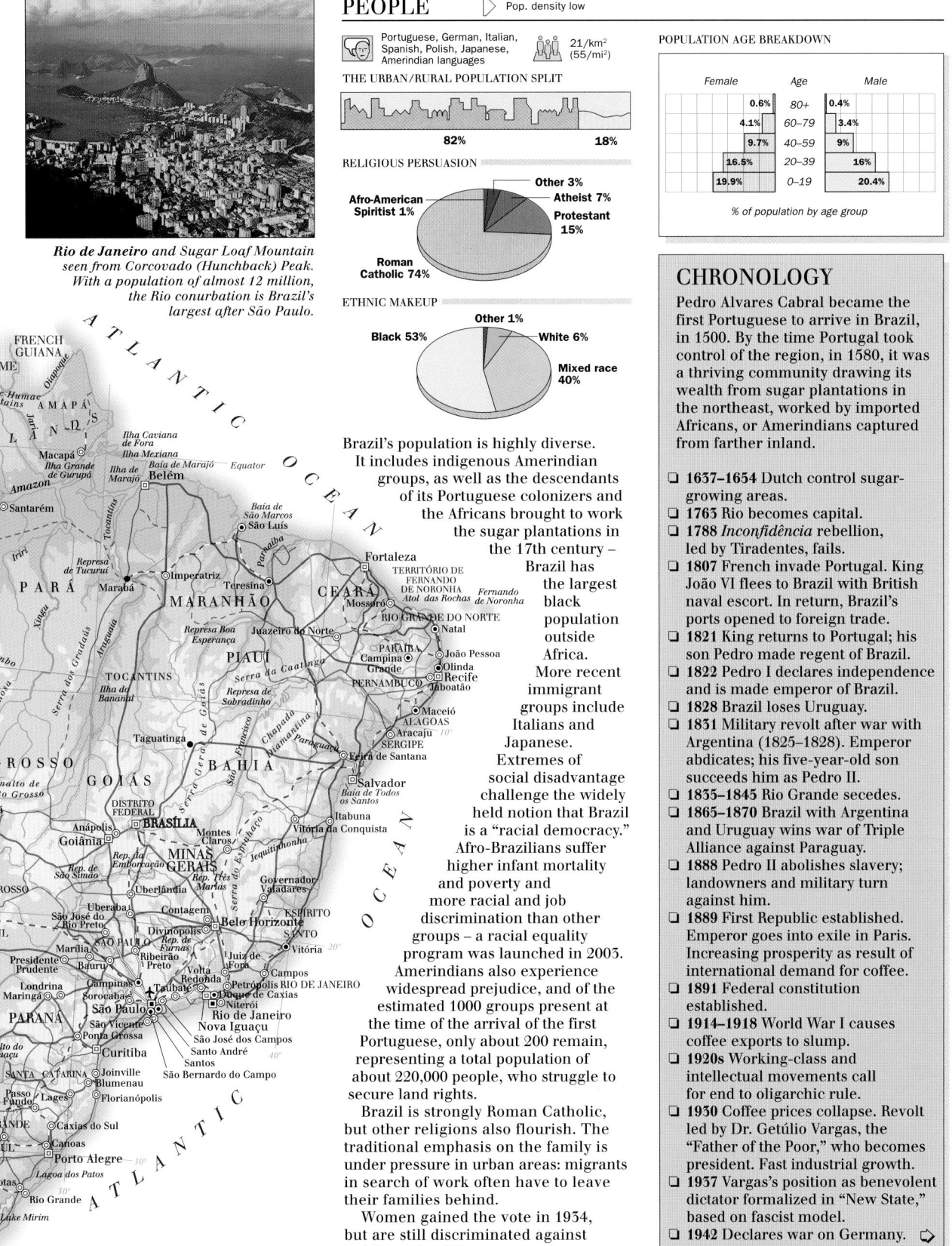

***Rio de Janeiro** and Sugar Loaf Mountain seen from Corcovado (Hunchback) Peak. With a population of almost 12 million, the Rio conurbation is Brazil's largest after São Paulo.*

PEOPLE

Pop. density low

Portuguese, German, Italian, Spanish, Polish, Japanese, Amerindian languages

21/km² (55/mi²)

THE URBAN/RURAL POPULATION SPLIT

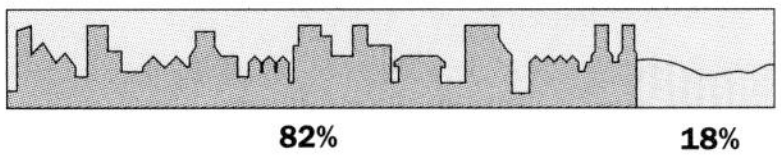
82%
18%

RELIGIOUS PERSUASION

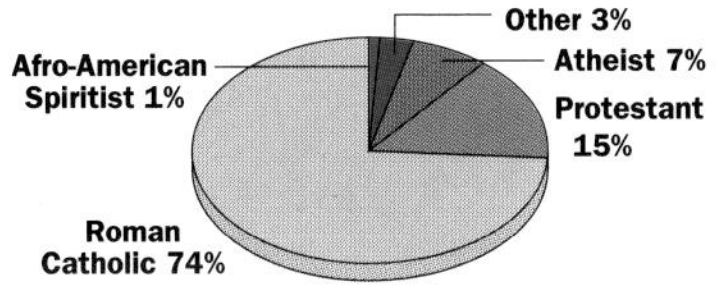
Other 3%
Atheist 7%
Protestant 15%
Afro-American Spiritist 1%
Roman Catholic 74%

ETHNIC MAKEUP

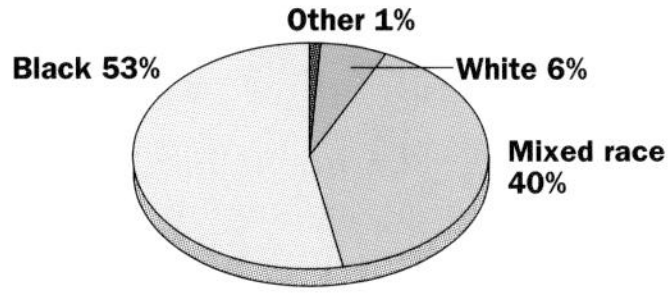
Other 1%
Black 53%
White 6%
Mixed race 40%

POPULATION AGE BREAKDOWN

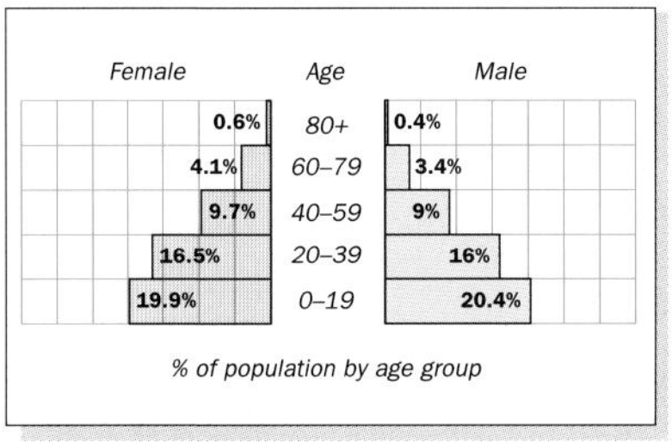
Female
Age
Male
0.6%
80+
0.4%
4.1%
60–79
3.4%
9.7%
40–59
9%
16.5%
20–39
16%
19.9%
0–19
20.4%
% of population by age group

Brazil's population is highly diverse. It includes indigenous Amerindian groups, as well as the descendants of its Portuguese colonizers and the Africans brought to work the sugar plantations in the 17th century – Brazil has the largest black population outside Africa. More recent immigrant groups include Italians and Japanese.

Extremes of social disadvantage challenge the widely held notion that Brazil is a "racial democracy." Afro-Brazilians suffer higher infant mortality and poverty and more racial and job discrimination than other groups – a racial equality program was launched in 2003. Amerindians also experience widespread prejudice, and of the estimated 1000 groups present at the time of the arrival of the first Portuguese, only about 200 remain, representing a total population of about 220,000 people, who struggle to secure land rights.

Brazil is strongly Roman Catholic, but other religions also flourish. The traditional emphasis on the family is under pressure in urban areas: migrants in search of work often have to leave their families behind.

Women gained the vote in 1934, but are still discriminated against in jobs and politics.

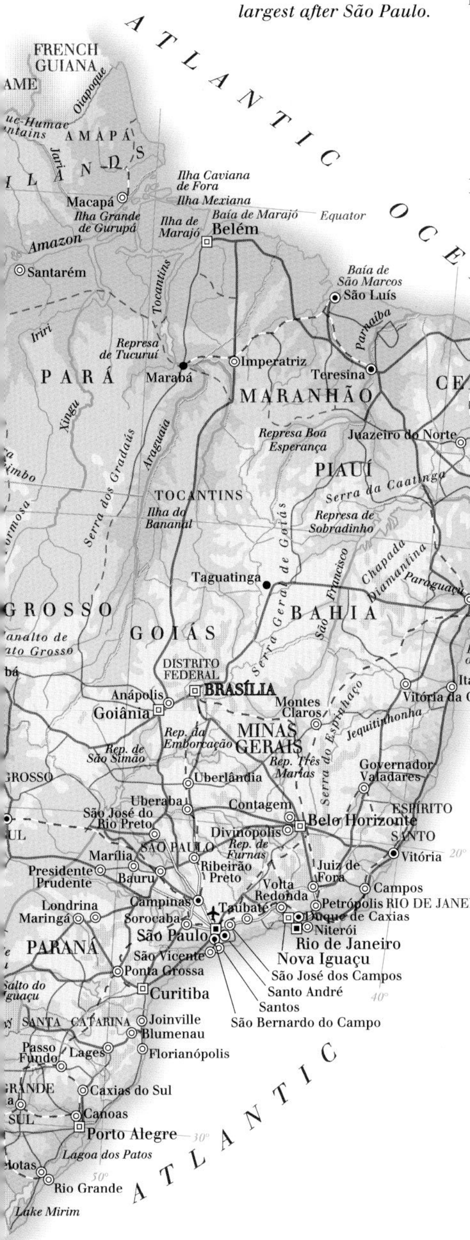
ATLANTIC OCEAN
FRENCH GUIANA
AMAPÁ
Macapá
Ilha Caviana de Fora
Ilha Mexiana
Ilha Grande de Gurupá
Ilha de Marajó
Baía de Marajó
Equator
Belém
Amazon
Santarém
Tocantins
Baía de São Marcos
São Luís
Represa de Tucuruí
Marabá
Imperatriz
PARÁ
Xingu
Teresina
MARANHÃO
Fortaleza
CEARÁ
Mossoró
RIO GRANDE DO NORTE
Natal
Represa Boa Esperança
Juazeiro do Norte
PIAUÍ
PARAÍBA
João Pessoa
Campina Grande
Olinda
Recife
PERNAMBUCO
Jaboatão
TOCANTINS
Ilha do Bananal
Represa de Sobradinho
Maceió
ALAGOAS
Aracaju
SERGIPE
Taguatinga
Feira de Santana
BAHIA
GOIÁS
Salvador
Baía de Todos os Santos
DISTRITO FEDERAL
BRASÍLIA
Anápolis
Goiânia
Montes Claros
Itabuna
Vitória da Conquista
MINAS GERAIS
Uberlândia
Governador Valadares
Uberaba
Contagem
Belo Horizonte
ESPÍRITO SANTO
Vitória
São José do Rio Preto
Divinópolis
SÃO PAULO
Marília
Ribeirão Preto
Juiz de Fora
Presidente Prudente
Bauru
Volta Redonda
Campos
Londrina
Maringá
Campinas
Taubaté
Petrópolis
RIO DE JANEIRO
Sorocaba
Duque de Caxias
São Paulo
Niterói
Rio de Janeiro
PARANÁ
Nova Iguaçu
São Vicente
Ponta Grossa
São José dos Campos
Santo André
Curitiba
Santos
São Bernardo do Campo
SANTA CATARINA
Joinville
Blumenau
Passo Fundo
Lages
Florianópolis
Caxias do Sul
Canoas
Porto Alegre
Lagoa dos Patos
Pelotas
Rio Grande
Lake Mirim

CHRONOLOGY

Pedro Alvares Cabral became the first Portuguese to arrive in Brazil, in 1500. By the time Portugal took control of the region, in 1580, it was a thriving community drawing its wealth from sugar plantations in the northeast, worked by imported Africans, or Amerindians captured from farther inland.

- **1637–1654** Dutch control sugar-growing areas.
- **1763** Rio becomes capital.
- **1788** *Inconfidência* rebellion, led by Tiradentes, fails.
- **1807** French invade Portugal. King João VI flees to Brazil with British naval escort. In return, Brazil's ports opened to foreign trade.
- **1821** King returns to Portugal; his son Pedro made regent of Brazil.
- **1822** Pedro I declares independence and is made emperor of Brazil.
- **1828** Brazil loses Uruguay.
- **1831** Military revolt after war with Argentina (1825–1828). Emperor abdicates; his five-year-old son succeeds him as Pedro II.
- **1835–1845** Rio Grande secedes.
- **1865–1870** Brazil with Argentina and Uruguay wins war of Triple Alliance against Paraguay.
- **1888** Pedro II abolishes slavery; landowners and military turn against him.
- **1889** First Republic established. Emperor goes into exile in Paris. Increasing prosperity as result of international demand for coffee.
- **1891** Federal constitution established.
- **1914–1918** World War I causes coffee exports to slump.
- **1920s** Working-class and intellectual movements call for end to oligarchic rule.
- **1930** Coffee prices collapse. Revolt led by Dr. Getúlio Vargas, the "Father of the Poor," who becomes president. Fast industrial growth.
- **1937** Vargas's position as benevolent dictator formalized in "New State," based on fascist model.
- **1942** Declares war on Germany. ➪

B

CHRONOLOGY *continued*

- **1945** Vargas forced out by military.
- **1950** Vargas reelected president.
- **1954** US opposes Vargas's socialist policies. The right, backed by the military, demands his resignation. Commits suicide.
- **1956–1960** President Juscelino Kubitschek, backed by Brazilian Labor Party (PTB), attracts foreign investment for new industries, especially from US.
- **1960–1961** Conservative Jânio da Silva Quadros president. Tries to break dependence on US trade.
- **1961** Brasília, built in three years, becomes new capital. PTB leader, João Goulart, elected president.
- **1961–1964** President's powers briefly curtailed as right wing reacts to presidential policies.
- **1964** Bloodless military coup under army chief Gen. Castelo Branco.
- **1965** Branco assumes dictatorship; bans existing political parties, but creates two official new ones. He is followed by a succession of military rulers. Fast-track economic development, the Brazilian Miracle, is counterbalanced by ruthless suppression of left-wing activists.
- **1974** World oil crisis marks end of economic boom. Brazil's foreign debt now largest in world.
- **1979** More political parties allowed.
- **1980** Huge migrations into Rondônia state begin.
- **1985** Civilian senator Tancredo Neves wins presidential elections as candidate of new liberal alliance, but dies before taking office. Illiterate adults granted the vote.
- **1987** Gold found on Yanomami lands in Roraima state; illegal diggers rush in by the thousand.
- **1988** New constitution promises massive social spending but fails to address land reform. Chico Mendes, rubber-tappers' union leader and environmentalist, murdered.
- **1989** First environmental protection plan. Yearly inflation reaches 1000%. Fernando Collor de Mello wins first presidential election held under completely free conditions.
- **1992** Earth Summit in Rio. Collor de Mello resigns and is impeached.
- **1994–1995** Plan Real ends hyperinflation. Congress resists constitutional reforms, but passes key privatizations of state monopolies.
- **1998–1999** Fernando Henrique Cardoso, in power since 1995, reelected president. Real devalued in economic crisis.
- **2001–2002** Recovery of economy threatened by crisis in Argentina.
- **2003** Lula da Silva takes office as president.

POLITICS

Multiparty elections

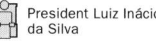

L. House 2002/2006
U. House 2002/2006

President Luiz Inácio da Silva

AT THE LAST ELECTION

Chamber of Deputies 513 seats

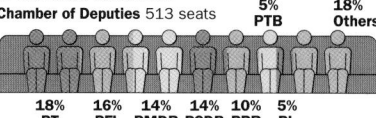

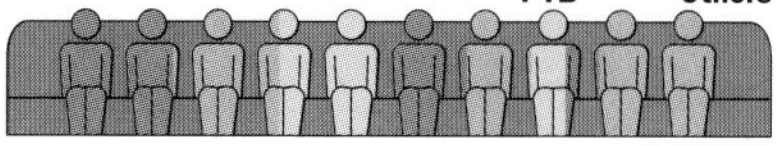
5% PTB
18% Others
18% PT
16% PFL
14% PMDB
14% PSDB
10% PPB
5% PL

PT = Workers' Party **PFL** = Liberal Front Party
PMDB = Brazilian Democratic Movement Party
PSDB = Brazilian Social Democracy Party
PPB = Brazilian Progressive Party
PTB = Brazilian Labor Party **PL** = Liberal Party

Federal Senate 81 seats

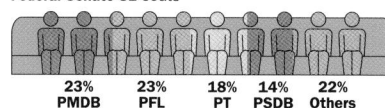

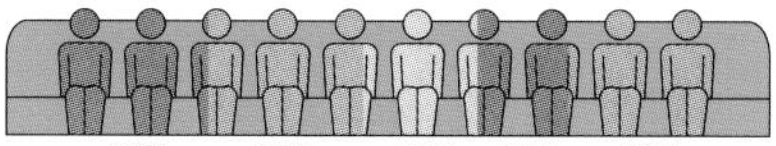
23% PMDB
23% PFL
18% PT
14% PSDB
22% Others

Brazil is a democratic federal republic with 27 regional parliaments and a national Congress. In 1993, Brazilians voted to retain the direct election of their president.

PROFILE

Military rule between 1964 and 1985 led to gross human rights abuses, against Amazon Amerindians in particular, and to economic mismanagement, which left Brazil with a legacy of huge debts and inefficient state industries.

Brazil's weak party system is centered on personalities. Parties do not have set ideological programs, but form shaky coalitions and engage in horse-trading to get legislation through the Congress. The preponderance of small parties and corruption adds to the problems. Former president Collor de Mello was impeached in 1992 on fraud charges.

Despite popular dissatisfaction with the center right in the 1990s, the left-wing PT, led by the charismatic Luiz Inácio "Lula" da Silva, was hindered by a lack of fresh ideas. Conservative Fernando Cardoso held the presidency from 1995. He kept a shaky coalition together, designing an anti-inflation plan for the real and emergency fiscal adjustments which saved Brazil from a return to persistent economic crisis. By 2002, the economic outlook had become less secure in the face of chaos in neighboring Argentina. With Cardoso constitutionally barred from seeking a third term, Lula, who had sufficiently toned down his socialism, was elected president in October – at his fourth successive attempt.

MAIN POLITICAL ISSUES

Political stability

President Lula was elected on a social platform, notably prioritizing the fight against hunger, and his government came to power with unprecedented public support. Nonetheless, he was not eager to stray too far from the successful policy mix promoted by his

Fernando Cardoso, *president from 1995 to 2002.*

Luiz Inácio "Lula" da Silva, *left-wing leader, elected president in 2002.*

predecessor, President Cardoso, which had provided stability and boosted consumer and investor confidence. Maintaining fiscal discipline while fulfilling his election promises is likely to prove difficult. Early signs of frustration with his commitment to the existing center-right policies materialized in early 2003 from the left wing of his own PT party, trade unions, and the landless peasant movement.

Economic management

Rapid recovery from the 1999 currency crisis relied on a tight monetary and fiscal regime backed by a sound macroeconomic policy. This permitted modest growth in 2001 and 2002, despite the global downturn and energy rationing at home. Plaudits from the IMF separated Brazil in investors' minds from the economic turmoil in Argentina. Efforts to manipulate the constitution in order to secure further reforms will require delicate consensus politics in a Congress eager to review the state-funding arrangements established under Cardoso.

Land redistribution

Brazil has up to five million landless families. An active campaign by the Landless Workers' Movement (MST) aims to redistribute vast tracts of private and often fallow land through illegal invasions, provoking occasional violent confrontations with security forces. The movement stepped up its campaign in 2003, despite the inauguration of the left-leaning President Lula.

Coffee plantation, *São Paulo state. Coffee was introduced into Brazil in the early 18th century. It is declining in importance and now accounts for less than 4% of export revenues.*

B

WORLD AFFAIRS

Joined UN in 1945

AmCC | G24 | Mercosr | OAS | RG

Brazil has ambitions to act as main broker in future talks with the US on the Free Trade Area of the Americas (FTAA), which is due to be signed in 2005. It hosted a conference in 2002 of the FTAA candidate countries and has strengthened ties with Mexico, its chief rival for regional leadership. Free trade talks with the EU and Mercosur have raised the prospect of compromise by Europe on agriculture, long the main bone of contention between the two regions. Though pragmatic in his relations with the US, President Lula has supported left-wing president Hugo Chávez in Venezuela's domestic crisis and has offered to mediate in Colombia, despite protests about apparent support in Brazil for left-wing Colombian guerrillas.

AID

Recipient

$376m (receipts) | Up 8% in 2002

Aid, mainly from Japan and EU states, funds environmental, basic sanitation, road-building, and antipoverty projects. As a consequence of the Argentine economic crisis, the IMF loaned Brazil $10 billion in 2002, and promised $30 billion more in the following years.

DEFENSE

Compulsory military service

$9.65bn | Up 1% in 2002

BRAZILIAN ARMED FORCES

178 main battle tanks (87 Leopard 1, 91 M-60A3)	189,000 personnel
4 submarines, 1 carrier, 14 frigates, 5 corvettes, and 47 patrol boats	48,600 personnel
254 combat aircraft (68 AT-26, 68 AT-27, 47 F-5E/F, 15 Mirage F-103E/D)	50,000 personnel
None	

The military still has an important internal security role, particularly in the north. The arms industry is large, but Brazil states that it has no intention of using its nuclear energy for military purposes: the Comprehensive Test Ban and Nuclear Non-Proliferation treaties were signed in 1998.

Membership of the Mercosur trade bloc has led to increased regional cooperation. Brazilian troops participate in UN peacekeeping, leading the mission in Haiti from June 2004. A $750 million order for US fighter aircraft was suspended in 2003, preference being given to social initiatives.

ECONOMICS

Inflation 168% p.a. (1990–2001)

$495bn | 3.097 reals (2.869)

SCORE CARD

❑ WORLD GNP RANKING	12th
❑ GNP PER CAPITA	$2830
❑ BALANCE OF PAYMENTS	–$7.7bn
❑ INFLATION	8.4%
❑ UNEMPLOYMENT	9%

EXPORTS

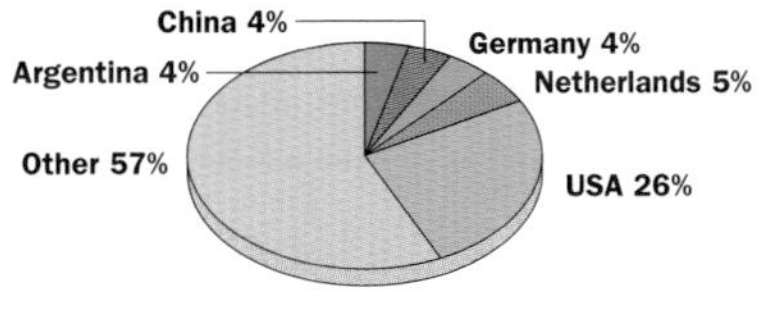
China 4%
Germany 4%
Argentina 4%
Netherlands 5%
Other 57%
USA 26%

IMPORTS

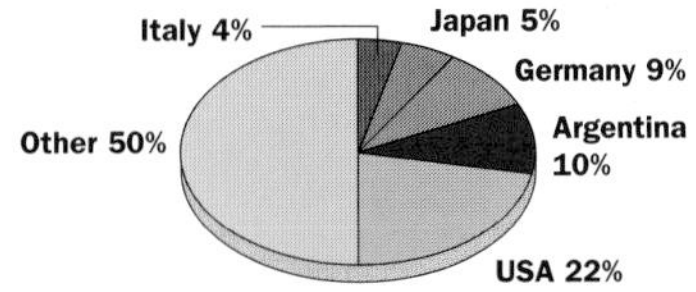
Italy 4%
Japan 5%
Germany 9%
Argentina 10%
Other 50%
USA 22%

STRENGTHS

Dominant economy in region. Strong foreign direct investment flows. Huge growth potential: immense natural resources; major producer of coffee, soybeans, sugar, oranges; large deposits of gold, silver, and iron; major steel producer; expanding oil industry. Development aided by cross-border infrastructural projects and modernization of telecoms.

WEAKNESSES

Expensive domestic borrowing. Weak local capital markets. Vulnerability to external shocks and commodity price fluctuations. Modest productivity. Heavy debt burden. Social inequalities threaten unrest. High cost of crime. Electricity blackouts caused by badly maintained transmission network or failure of hydropower supply due to drought.

PROFILE

Brazil is the world's 12th-largest economy. Average growth from the start of the 20th century to the early 1970s was over 5%, second only to Japan over a comparable period. Diversification and industrialization transformed Brazil into a producer of cars, computers, and aircraft, but profligate spending produced heavy debts in the 1980s. International lenders demanded belt tightening in return for rescheduling, and a steep recession followed in 1990–1992.

The launching of the new currency, the real, in 1994, was the fifth attempt at monetary stabilization since 1986; it contributed to a dramatic fall in inflation. Economic growth in 1994

ECONOMIC PERFORMANCE INDICATOR

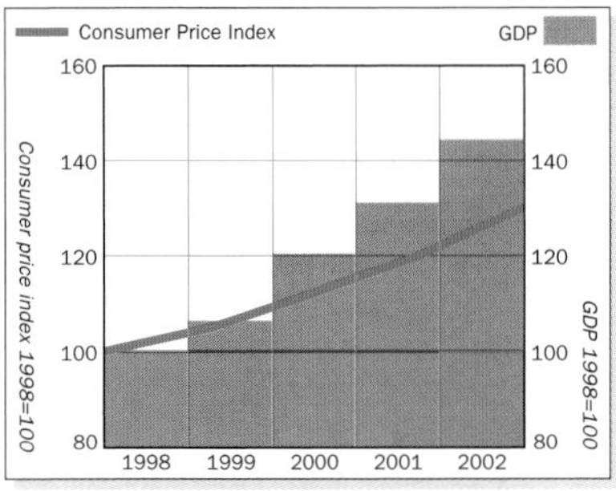
Consumer Price Index
GDP
Consumer price index 1998=100
GDP 1998=100
160
140
120
100
80
1998
1999
2000
2001
2002

boosted regional confidence and facilitated the launch of Mercosur. In 1995 a fractious Congress blocked reforms of the tax and social security systems, but finally agreed to end state monopolies in such sectors as telecommunications and oil, thus reviving the privatization program.

The economy grew strongly through 1996 and 1997, but was seriously threatened in 1998 by an international financial crisis. A $41.5 billion rescue package was arranged by the IMF, but foreign currency reserves were heavily depleted in a bid to support the real, which was devalued in 1999 due to speculative pressures. A deep recession was avoided, however, by the successful application over 18 months of tight fiscal and monetary policies, restoring domestic and international confidence.

Modest growth was posted in 2001, but the economic meltdown in Argentina and the effects of global downturn brought the value of the real down in 2002. The IMF calmed market jitters when it approved a billion-dollar credit line. It expressed confidence that President Lula's administration would keep macroeconomic discipline, even though the economy remains sluggish, notwithstanding an increase in exports.

BRAZIL : MAJOR BUSINESSES

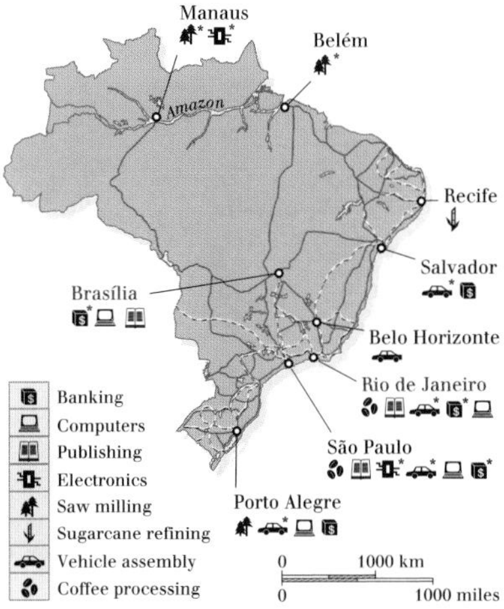
Manaus
Belém
Amazon
Recife
Salvador
Brasília
Belo Horizonte
Rio de Janeiro
São Paulo
Porto Alegre
Banking
Computers
Publishing
Electronics
Saw milling
Sugarcane refining
Vehicle assembly
Coffee processing
0
1000 km
0
1000 miles

* significant multinational ownership

B

RESOURCES

Electric power 73.1m kW

980,000 tonnes

1.55m b/d (reserves 10.6bn barrels)

190m cattle, 32.6m pigs, 14.2m sheep, 1.05bn chickens

Iron, manganese, coal, bauxite, nickel, oil, tin, silver, diamonds, gold, natural gas, uranium

ELECTRICITY GENERATION

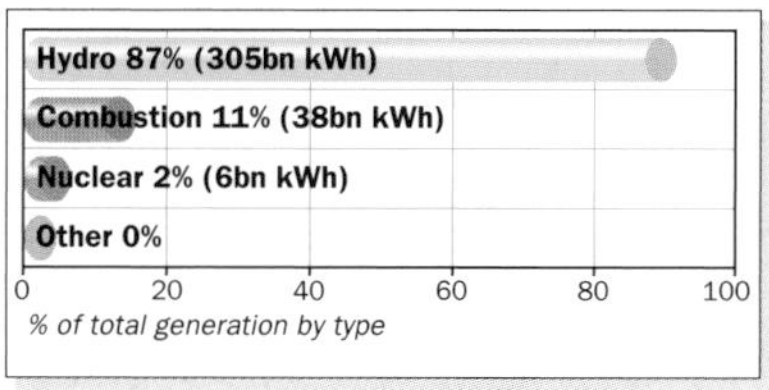
Hydro 87% (305bn kWh)
Combustion 11% (38bn kWh)
Nuclear 2% (6bn kWh)
Other 0%
0
20
40
60
80
100
% of total generation by type

Brazil imports gas from Argentina and Bolivia, and has similar plans with Uruguay. Nuclear power has been dogged by controversy and high costs. Hydropower, accounting for almost 90% of electricity generation, is extremely vulnerable to drought, which forced energy rationing in 2001–2002. Efforts to reduce this dependency include the use of domestically enriched uranium as a fuel. Brazil is the world's largest producer of ethanol from sugar, used as an alternative to gasoline. It is a leading regional producer of many minerals. Exploration of the Amazon's biodiversity was brought under government control in mid-2000, with all new ventures involving any living thing requiring official approval.

Amazon
AMAZON BASIN
BRAZIL : LAND USE
Cropland
Forest
Pasture
Cattle
Coffee – cash crop
Oranges
0 1000 km
0 1000 miles

Some 200 indigenous groups remain in the disappearing rainforest.

ENVIRONMENT

Sustainability rank: 20th

7% (4% partially protected)

1.8 tonnes per capita

ENVIRONMENTAL TREATIES

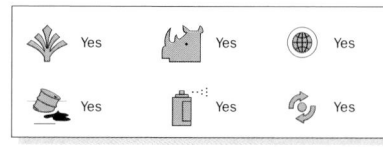

Yes Yes Yes

Yes Yes Yes

Federal agencies charged with protecting the Amazon Rainforest are underfunded, understaffed, and accused of corruption.

The forest contains an estimated 30% of all the world's plant and animal species. However, 38 million animals a year are smuggled out of the region, and irreplaceable genetic diversity is being lost year by year with the forest's continuing destruction for the sake of cattle pasture, logging, and soybean farming. In 2002 the world's largest tropical forest reserve was created in northern Brazil.

Opencast bauxite mines pollute rivers and threaten indigenous Amerindians, while in 2000 the worst oil spill in 25 years devastated the Iguaçu River. Urban industrial pollution and untreated sewage are also major problems.

MEDIA

TV ownership high

Daily newspaper circulation 46 per 1000 people

PUBLISHING AND BROADCAST MEDIA

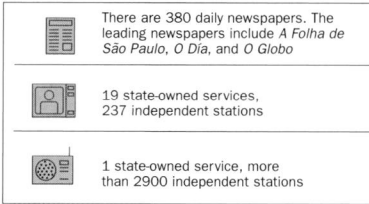

There are 380 daily newspapers. The leading newspapers include *A Folha de São Paulo*, *O Día*, and *O Globo*

19 state-owned services, 237 independent stations

1 state-owned service, more than 2900 independent stations

TV and radio licenses have been notoriously awarded as political favors. The huge Globo group dominates the home market, with radio, press, and online interests: its TV network is one of the largest in the world. However, it is being challenged by the Internet and the growth of new media companies, involving foreign multinationals. A constitutional amendment in 2002 allowed foreign groups to take 30% stakes in TV, radio, and the press.

CRIME

Death penalty not used in practice

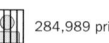

284,989 prisoners

Up 19% in 2000–2001

CRIME RATES

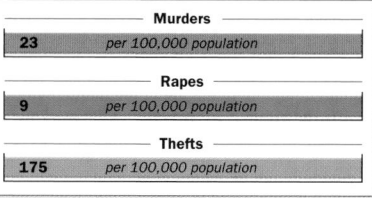

Murders	23	per 100,000 population
Rapes	9	per 100,000 population
Thefts	175	per 100,000 population

In cities, crime levels are among the world's highest, with armed robbery and narcotics-related organized crime uppermost. Badly paid police are frequently accused of extortion, violence, and murder. Death squads, thought to be linked to the police, have targeted street children in major cities. A combination of atrocious conditions and overcrowding means that violent disturbances in prisons are common. A strict gun-control law, banning private gun ownership, came into force in 2004.

In the countryside, landless squatters and indigenous peoples have been wounded and murdered in the process of being driven off land by gunmen funded by large landowners. In Roraima state, the discovery of large gold deposits has led to the homelands of Brazil's largest tribe, the Yanomami, being invaded by thousands of gun-toting prospectors, *garimpeiros*.

EDUCATION

School leaving age: 14

86%

2.78m students

THE EDUCATION SYSTEM

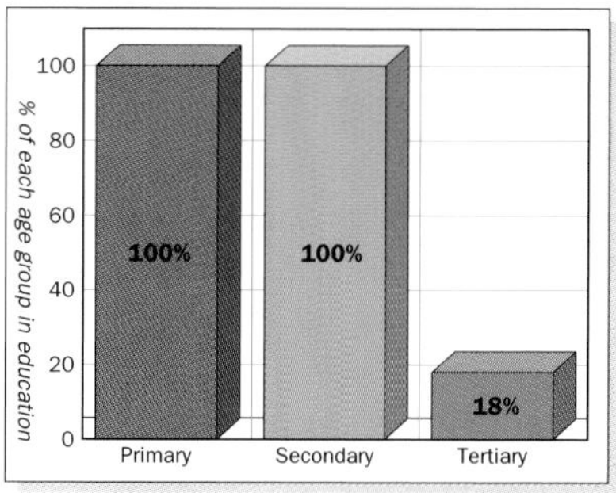
100
80
60
40
20
0
% of each age group in education
100%
100%
18%
Primary
Secondary
Tertiary

The average time spent at school is less than that in other South American countries. The portion of GDP spent on education is comparable to that of European countries, but it is misapplied, so that basic primary education remains weak, while many children of wealthy families receive excellent tuition at free public universities. Of Brazil's 150 universities, 77 are administered by the state. Children living in remote communities in Amazonia and in the slums around major cities, and urban street children, have limited access to mainstream education. Classes frequently include children older than the expected age range. Despite an anti-illiteracy campaign, begun in 1971, the adult illiteracy rate is still over 10%.

BRAZIL'S THREATENED AMAZON REGION

DEFORESTATION IN the Brazilian Amazon has accelerated alarmingly, with rainforest loss since 2001 amounting to some 23,000–25,000 sq. km (9000–10,000 sq. miles) a year. These official statistics are the second worst on record, and a 30–40% increase over the late 1990s.

Despite 30 years of destruction, 86% of the Amazon region remains intact, but its continuing decline is a matter of global concern. It is vital as a "carbon sink," as its plant growth absorbs carbon dioxide to reduce the buildup in the atmosphere of this "greenhouse gas" and helps counteract the climate-altering effects of emissions from the world's industrial activity and fossil fuel energy use.

KNOWLEDGE IN DANGER

Brazil has the greatest biodiversity on earth. The loss of habitat compromises future knowledge ranging from medical treatments and possible food crops to information about evolution, adaptation, and survival strategies. The Amazon alone contains some 30% of all the world's known animal and plant species, besides possibly millions of uncatalogued insects; it has about 80,000 species of trees and flowering plants, more than 2000 bird species, a similar diversity of freshwater fish and more than 3000 species of mammals.

To preserve the genetic codes of some 381 threatened Brazilian plant species (not only in the rainforest but in other major "biomes" including the Atlantic temperate forests and the Pantanal floodplains), Rio de Janeiro's Botanic Gardens in June 2004 opened a DNA bank, with two new laboratories for work on conservation and the development of plant-based drug treatments.

INFRASTRUCTURE AND EXPLOITATION

Some 85% of deforestation is estimated to occur within 50 km (30 miles) of a road, where it is relatively easy and profitable to extract timber and create pasture. According to government figures, 80% of rainforest destruction is attributable to the growth in cattle ranching for beef production.

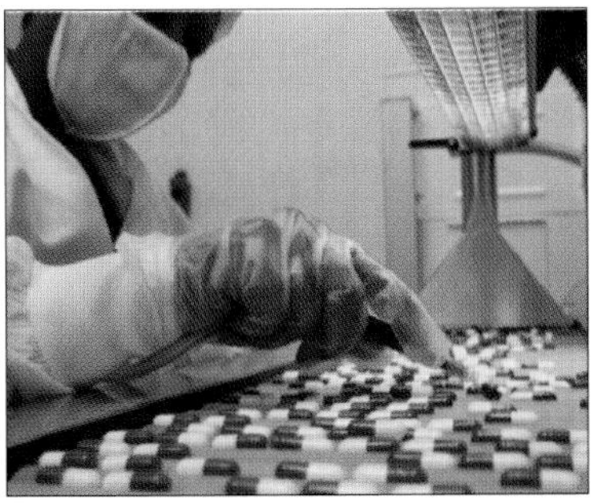

***Much medicine** depends on research for which biodiversity is vital.*

Conservationists fear that the planned paving of the BR-163 highway by 2008, replacing a dirt road with a 1765-km (1097-mile) superhighway to the port of Santarém, will accelerate forest destruction in the heart of the region and hugely expand soybean farming. This industry is already moving rapidly into Para and Mato Grosso states on the back of a boom which has seen Brazil net 34% of world sales (largely at the expense of the US, whose genetically modified soybeans are rejected by European consumers).

The election in 2002 of the da Silva administration put in doubt the previous government's "Plan Brasil" for the investment of over $40 billion in new infrastructure for the Amazon. New environment minister Marina Silva, herself a former Amazonian rubber tapper and environmental activist, has pledged better protection of the region. Under the Amazon Regional Protected Areas programme (ARPA) the Tumucumaque National Park, covering more than 38,000 sq. km (14,672 sq. miles), was declared a protected area, and in August 2004 a new Biodiversity Conservation Program was launched, with UNESCO backing, to cover the country's seven World Natural Patrimony Sites. However, a 1998 pledge to set aside at least 12% of the Amazon for conservation by 2013 remains a distant goal, and environmentalists remain skeptical about the latest in a series of new initiatives to clamp down on illegal logging and forest clearance. Announced with great fanfare in March 2004, this involved giving action plans and targets to 12 federal agencies and providing for the deployment of helicopter-based intervention teams.

***Equatorial vegetation near Manaus** in the center of Amazonas state. The brown waters of the Rio Solimões and the black waters of the Rio Negro meet near Manaus.*

HEALTH

Welfare state health benefits

1 per 769 people

Heart diseases, cancers, accidents, violence

Federal health is underfunded. Fewer than 20% of hospitals are state-run, and they need modernization, while private care is beyond the means of the majority. On average only 15% of the health budget goes to child health, immunization, and other preventive programs. However, infant mortality, at 95 per 1000 children in 1970, had dropped to one-third of that level by 2000; access to potable water increased from 74% of the population in 1992 to 87%. In 2001 international drug companies and the US dropped patent infringement claims against Brazil for distributing anti-AIDS drugs free to more than 100,000 HIV patients.

SPENDING

GDP/cap. increase

CONSUMPTION AND SPENDING

137 per 1000 population *223 per 1000 population*

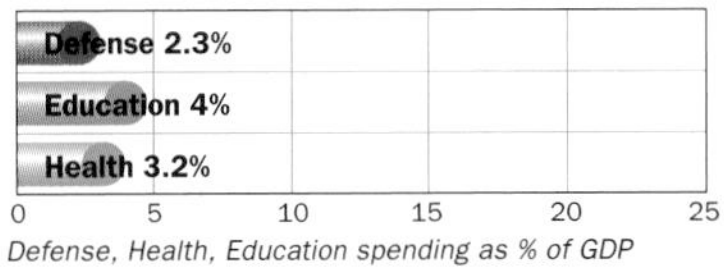
Defense 2.3%
Education 4%
Health 3.2%
0
5
10
15
20
25
Defense, Health, Education spending as % of GDP

Brazil's income distribution is among the most skewed in the world. The richest 10% of the population take almost 50% of the income and the poorest 50% only 10%. Up to five million families remain landless, while nearly 66% of arable land is owned by just 3% of the population. Vast tracts of disputed land are marked for redistribution, but invasions by landless workers continue. In 2003 President Lula launched a Zero Hunger campaign to provide benefits to the poorest families, and pledged to end economic slavery, by which 25,000 people are forced to work in order to pay largely invented debts.

WORLD RANKING

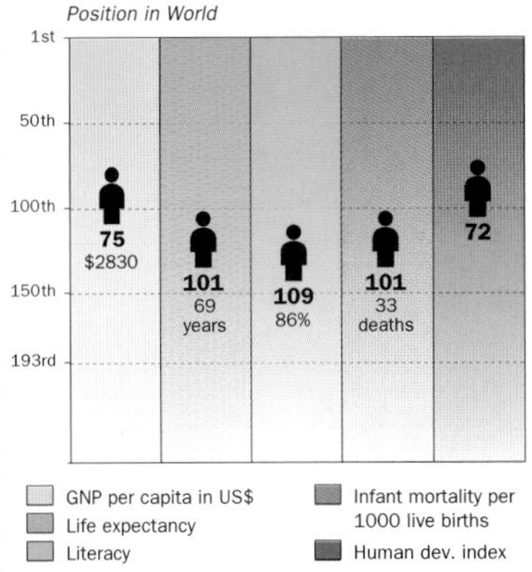
Position in World
1st
50th
100th
150th
193rd
75
$2830
101
69
years
109
86%
101
33
deaths
72
GNP per capita in US$
Life expectancy
Literacy
Infant mortality per 1000 live births
Human dev. index

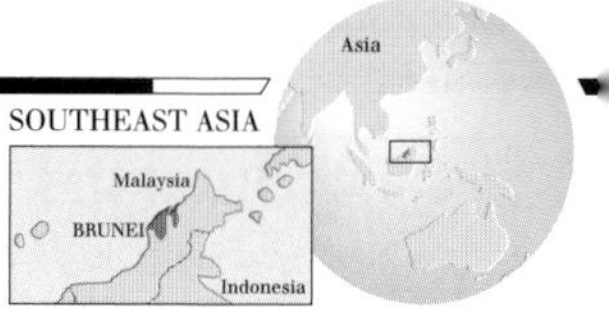
Asia
SOUTHEAST ASIA
Malaysia
BRUNEI
Indonesia

BRUNEI

OFFICIAL NAME: Sultanate of Brunei **CAPITAL:** Bandar Seri Begawan
POPULATION: 358,000 **CURRENCY:** Brunei dollar **OFFICIAL LANGUAGE:** Malay

1984 | 1984 | Feb 23 | BRU | +8 | +673 | .bn

LYING ON THE NORTHWESTERN coast of the island of Borneo, Brunei is divided in two by a strip of the surrounding Malaysian state of Sarawak. The interior is mostly rainforest. Independent from the UK since 1984, Brunei is ruled by decree of the sultan. It is undergoing increasing Islamization. Oil and gas revenues have brought one of the world's highest standards of living.

CLIMATE

Tropical equatorial

WEATHER CHART FOR BANDAR SERI BEGAWAN

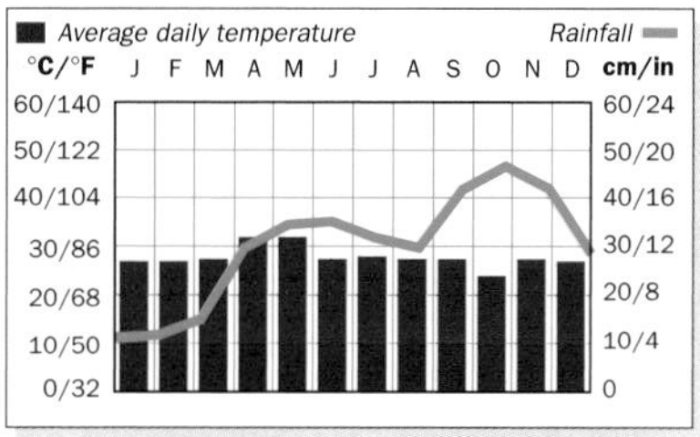
Average daily temperature
Rainfall
°C/°F
J F M A M J J A S O N D
cm/in
60/140
50/122
40/104
30/86
20/68
10/50
0/32
60/24
50/20
40/16
30/12
20/8
10/4
0

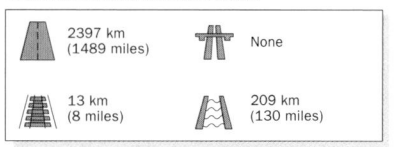

Just 480 km (300 miles) north of the equator, Brunei has a long rainy season with extremely high humidity.

TRANSPORTATION

Drive on left

Bandar Seri Begawan 1.28m passengers

482,600 grt

THE TRANSPORTATION NETWORK

2397 km (1489 miles)

None

13 km (8 miles)

209 km (130 miles)

Interest-free loans for civil servants, subsidized gasoline, and limited public transportation account for the high rates of car ownership.

TOURISM

Visitors : Population 2.7:1

984,093 visitors

Up 2% in 1999–2000

MAIN TOURIST ARRIVALS

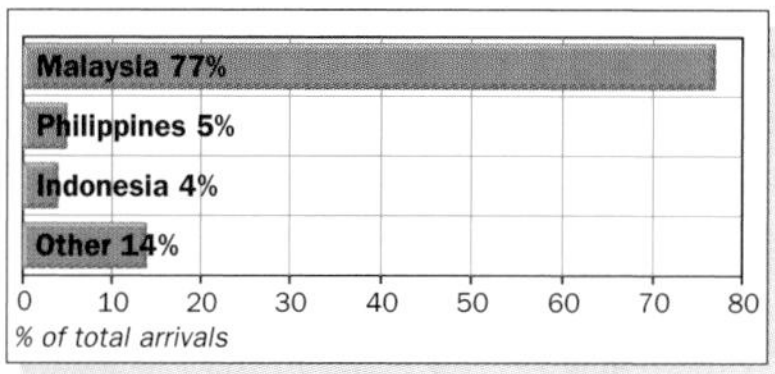
Malaysia 77%
Philippines 5%
Indonesia 4%
Other 14%
0 10 20 30 40 50 60 70 80
% of total arrivals

Though the government is keen to protect Bruneians from Western influence, it wants to encourage quality tourism as part of its diversification program. Promoted as the "Gateway to Borneo," Brunei's rainforests could be developed for tourism. The Winston Churchill Museum, founded by the late Sultan Omar Ali Saifuddin, has now been superseded by the Museum of Royal Regalia.

PEOPLE

Pop. density medium

Malay, English, Chinese

68/km² (176/mi²)

THE URBAN/RURAL POPULATION SPLIT

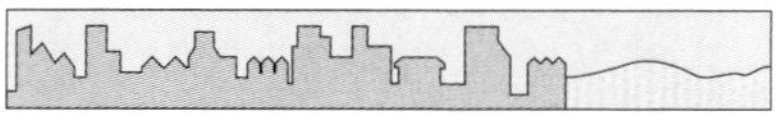
73%
27%

ETHNIC MAKEUP

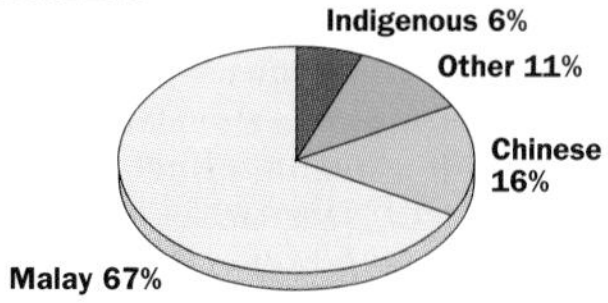
Indigenous 6%
Other 11%
Chinese 16%
Malay 67%

Malays are the beneficiaries of positive discrimination; many in the Chinese community are either stateless or hold British protected person passports. Among indigenous groups, the Murut and Dusuns are favored over the Ibans. Women, less restricted than in some Muslim states, are obliged to wear headscarves but not the veil. Many hold influential posts in the civil service.

POLITICS

No multiparty elections

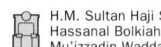

No date set for elections

H.M. Sultan Haji Sir Hassanal Bolkiah Mu'izzadin Waddaulah

LEGISLATIVE OR ADVISORY BODIES

Legislative Council 21 seats

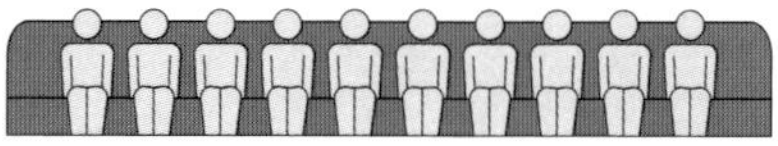

The appointed Legislative Council was reconvened in 2004 for the first time since 1984. There are also four advisory councils. Political parties were banned in 1988

A state of emergency has been in force since a failed rebellion in 1962. "Malay Muslim Monarchy" was introduced in 1990, promoting Islamic values as the state ideology. This further alienated the large Chinese and expatriate communities. Power is closely tied to the royal family; the sultan and his brother hold the defense, finance, and foreign affairs portfolios. The Legislative Council was reconvened in 2004 for the first time in 20 years; partial elections are promised, though parties remain banned.

WORLD AFFAIRS

Joined UN in 1984

APEC | ASEAN | Comm | OIC | WTO

Brunei leads calls for a regional free trade area. Political exiles opposed to the government and based in Malaysia are a main concern. Relations with the UK, the ex-colonial power, are good.

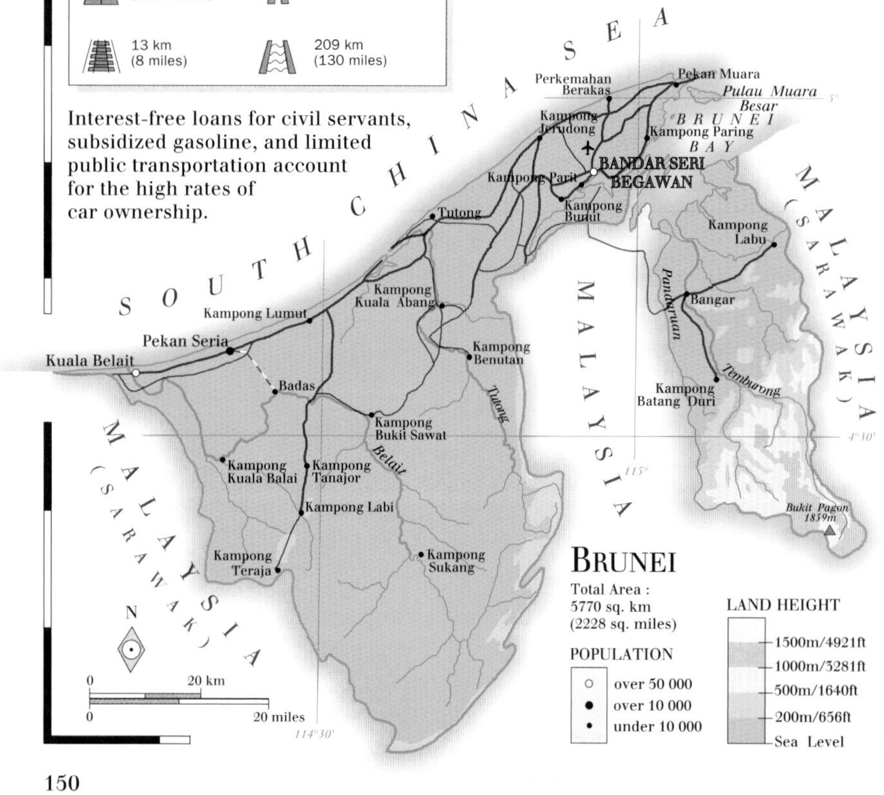
SOUTH CHINA SEA
Perkemahan Berakas
Pekan Muara
Pulau Muara Besar
BRUNEI BAY
Kampong Jerudong
Kampong Paring
Kampong Parit
BANDAR SERI BEGAWAN
Kampong Bunut
Tutong
Kampong Labu
Pandaruan
Bangar
Kampong Kuala Abang
Kampong Lumut
Pekan Seria
Kuala Belait
Kampong Benutan
Badas
Tutong
Temburong
Kampong Batang Duri
MALAYSIA
MALAYSIA (SARAWAK)
Kampong Bukit Sawat
Belait
Kampong Kuala Balai
Kampong Tanajor
Kampong Labi
Bukit Pagon 1850m
Kampong Teraja
Kampong Sukang
N
0 20 km
0 20 miles
BRUNEI
Total Area : 5770 sq. km (2228 sq. miles)
POPULATION
over 50 000
over 10 000
under 10 000
LAND HEIGHT
1500m/4921ft
1000m/3281ft
500m/1640ft
200m/656ft
Sea Level

The magnificent Omar Ali Saifuddin Mosque is surrounded by an artificial lagoon.

AID

Donor

Ad hoc handouts from the sultan

Not applicable

Aid spending is largely ad hoc. It has included donations to the Contras in Nicaragua, the Bosnian Muslims, and the homeless of New York.

DEFENSE

No compulsory military service

US$253m

Down 9% in 2002

In 2003 there was a brief stand-off with Malaysia over oil exploration. The UK maintains over 1000 troops in Brunei and runs a jungle warfare training school. Singapore is also an ally.

ECONOMICS

Inflation 1.1% p.a. (1990–1999)

US$7.75bn

1.722 Brunei dollars (1.761)

SCORE CARD

- WORLD GNP RANKING....................99th
- GNP PER CAPITA....................US$24,100
- BALANCE OF PAYMENTS....................US$3.9bn
- INFLATION....................–2%
- UNEMPLOYMENT....................10%

STRENGTHS

Nearly 15 years of known oil reserves and 30 years of gas. Earnings from massive overseas investments, mainly in the US and Europe, now exceed oil and gas revenues.

WEAKNESSES

Single-product economy. Failure of diversification programs could lead to problems in the future.

EXPORTS

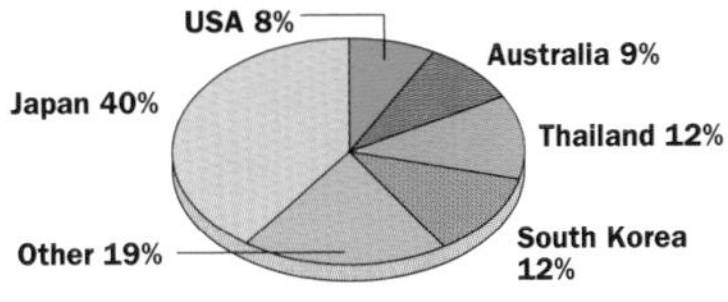
USA 8%
Australia 9%
Japan 40%
Thailand 12%
Other 19%
South Korea 12%

IMPORTS

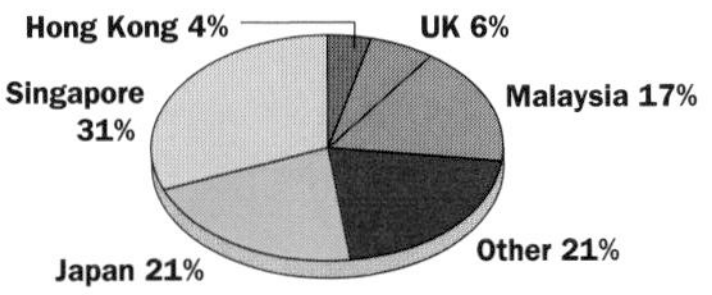
Hong Kong 4%
UK 6%
Singapore 31%
Malaysia 17%
Other 21%
Japan 21%

RESOURCES

Electric power 483,000 kW

1591 tonnes

214,000 b/d (reserves 1.1bn barrels)

70,000 ducks, 6000 buffaloes, 4000 sheep, 11m chickens

Oil, natural gas

Oil and gas are the major resources. Energy policy is now focused on regulating output in order to conserve stocks, since reserves are of limited duration. Almost all food is imported.

ENVIRONMENT

Not available

21% (0.2% partially protected)

14.3 tonnes per capita

The Forestry Strategic Plan aims to protect Brunei's forests (which take up 80% of its land area). It has allocated 64% of their area for protection, recreation, and the prevention of soil erosion. However, Brunei's mangrove swamps, the largest on the island of Borneo, remain unprotected.

MEDIA

TV ownership high

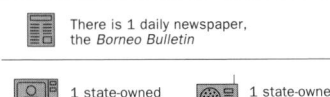

Daily newspaper circulation 69 per 1000 people

PUBLISHING AND BROADCAST MEDIA

There is 1 daily newspaper, the *Borneo Bulletin*

1 state-owned service

1 state-owned service

State controls were relaxed somewhat in 2000, but self-censorship on political and religious content continues.

CRIME

Death penalty not used in practice

454 prisoners

Down 21% in 2000–2001

Crime levels are low. Most crime involves petty theft or is linked to alcohol and narcotics (both banned). A stolen car often makes TV news headlines. The state of emergency enables the government to detain without charge or trial for indefinitely renewable two-year periods.

EDUCATION

School leaving age: 16

94%

3984 students

Free schooling is available to the entire population, with the exception of the stateless Chinese, who do not qualify. The University of Brunei Darussalam was opened in 1985.

HEALTH

Welfare state health benefits

1 per 929 people

Heart diseases, cancers

The health service is free, though if major surgery is required Bruneians tend to travel to Singapore.

CHRONOLOGY

Under British control since 1841, Brunei became a formal British Protectorate in 1888.

- **1929** Oil extraction begins.
- **1959** First constitution enshrines Islam as state religion. Internal self-government.
- **1962** Prodemocracy rebellion. State of emergency; sultan rules by decree.
- **1984** Independence from Britain. Brunei joins ASEAN.
- **1990** Ideology of "Malay Muslim Monarchy" introduced.
- **1991** Imports of alcohol banned.
- **1992** Joins Non-Aligned Movement.
- **1998** Sultan's son, Prince Al-Muhtadee Billah, made crown prince.
- **2004** Legislature reconvened.

SPENDING

GDP/cap. decrease

CONSUMPTION AND SPENDING

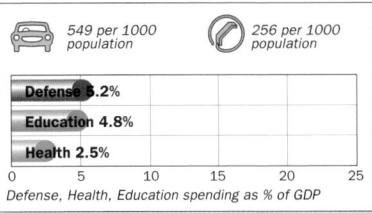

549 per 1000 population

256 per 1000 population

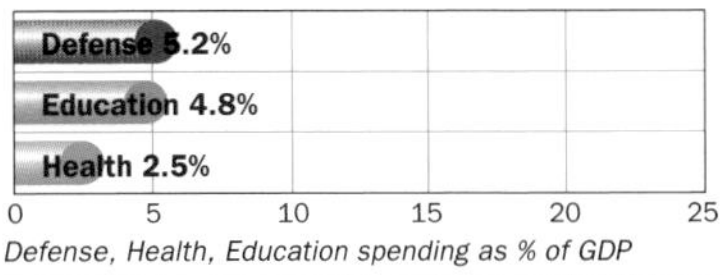
Defense 5.2%
Education 4.8%
Health 2.5%
0
5
10
15
20
25

Defense, Health, Education spending as % of GDP

The wealthiest people in Brunei are those close to the sultan, one of the world's richest men. A generally high standard of living, along with a degree of social mobility among Malays, keeps discontent to a minimum. Bruneians are major consumers of high-tech hi-fi and video equipment, designer-label watches, and Western designer clothes. The sultan's younger brother, Prince Jefri, in 2001 auctioned his possessions, ranging from fire engines to marble baths, after the failure of his business left him with debts of US$3 billion.

WORLD RANKING

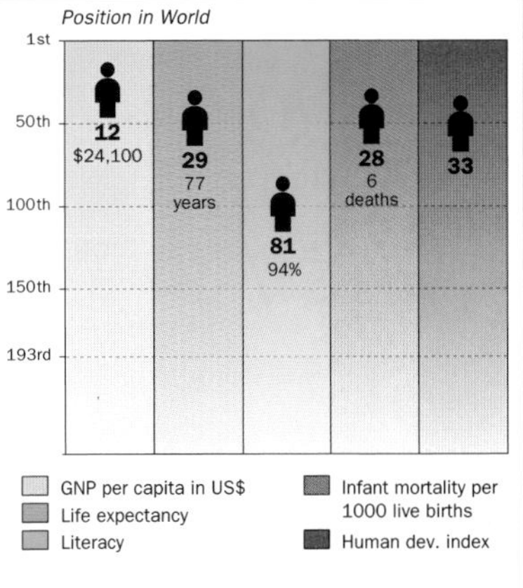
Position in World
1st
50th
100th
150th
193rd
12
$24,100
29
77 years
81
94%
28
6 deaths
33
GNP per capita in US$
Life expectancy
Literacy
Infant mortality per 1000 live births
Human dev. index

BULGARIA

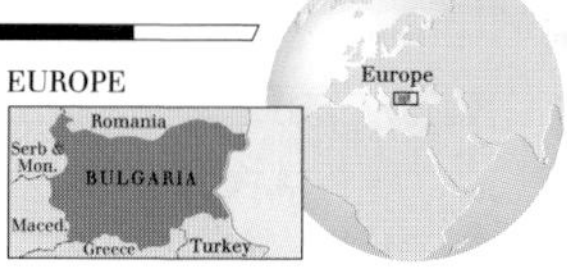
EUROPE
Europe
Romania
Serb & Mon.
BULGARIA
Maced.
Greece
Turkey

OFFICIAL NAME: Republic of Bulgaria **CAPITAL:** Sofia
POPULATION: 7.9 million **CURRENCY:** Lev **OFFICIAL LANGUAGE:** Bulgarian

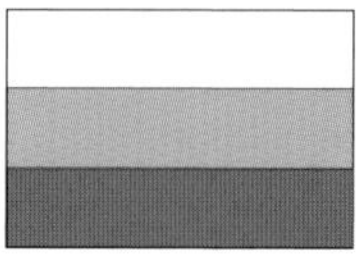

1908 | 1947 | March 3 | BG | +2 | +359 | .bg

EXTENDING SOUTH FROM the River Danube, Bulgaria has a mountainous interior, with the popular resorts of the Black Sea to the east. The most populated areas are around Sofia in the west, Plovdiv in the south, and along the Danube plain. Bulgaria was directly ruled by the Ottomans until 1878; Communists overthrew the monarchy in 1946 and, under General Secretary Todor Zhivkov from 1954, Bulgaria was one of the Soviet Union's most loyal allies. Economic and political reform after 1989 was slow, but Bulgaria now hopes to build its future as an integral part of Europe.

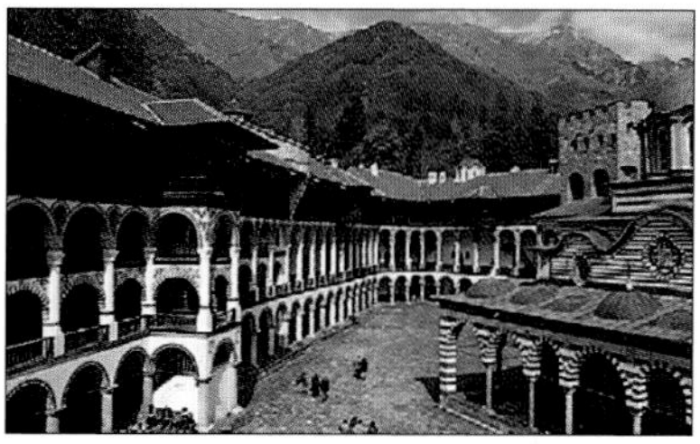

***Rila Monastery** in the Rila Mountains. It is famous for its 1200 National Revival period frescoes dating from the mid-19th century.*

CLIMATE

Mediterranean/ continental

WEATHER CHART FOR SOFIA

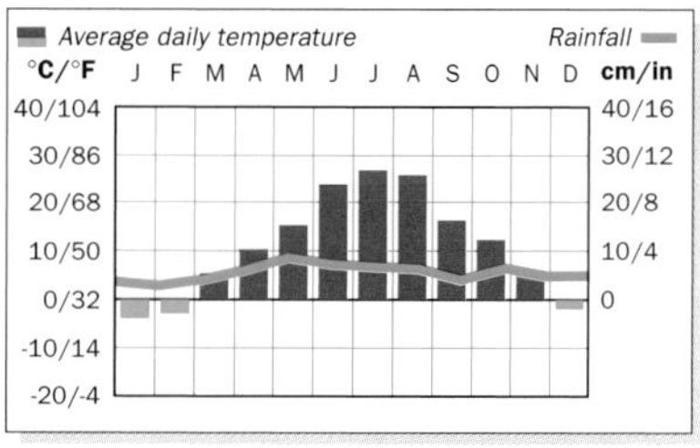
Average daily temperature
Rainfall
°C/°F
J F M A M J J A S O N D
cm/in
40/104
30/86
20/68
10/50
0/32
-10/14
-20/-4
40/16
30/12
20/8
10/4
0

The central valley and the lowlands have warm summers and cold, snowy winters, but hot or cold winds from Russia can bring spells of more extreme weather. The hotter summers on the Black Sea coast have encouraged the growth of tourist resorts. Snow may lie on the high mountain peaks until June.

TRANSPORTATION

Drive on right

Sofia 1.36m passengers

165 ships 889,300 grt

THE TRANSPORTATION NETWORK

35,049 km (21,778 miles)

324 km (201 miles)

4318 km (2683 miles)

470 km (292 miles)

At the crossroads between Europe and Asia, Bulgarian railroads and expressways were underfunded under Zhivkov (when north–south routes were left undeveloped) and in the economically uncertain 1990s. Funding for modernizing key routes is now in place. Ferries are used for most cross-Danube traffic. In 2000 agreement was reached with Romania on building a second bridge across the river, scheduled to open in 2005.

TOURISM

Visitors : Population 1:2

4.05m visitors

Up 18% in 2003

MAIN TOURIST ARRIVALS

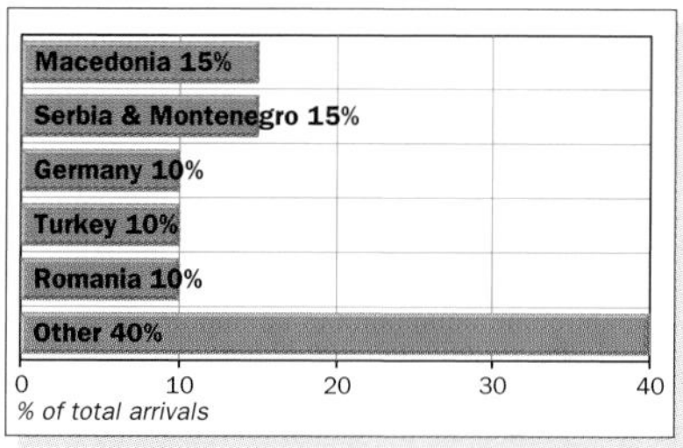
Macedonia 15%
Serbia & Montenegro 15%
Germany 10%
Turkey 10%
Romania 10%
Other 40%
0
10
20
30
40
% of total arrivals

The tourist industry formerly catered for the east European mass market. Western tourists are attracted by low prices for skiing and beach vacations. Bulgaria is now privatizing the industry and seeks to move it upmarket by stressing the country's heritage. Since the mid-1990s a slump in earnings has been reversed: Russians are returning in larger numbers and there are more tours from western Europe, especially from Germany.

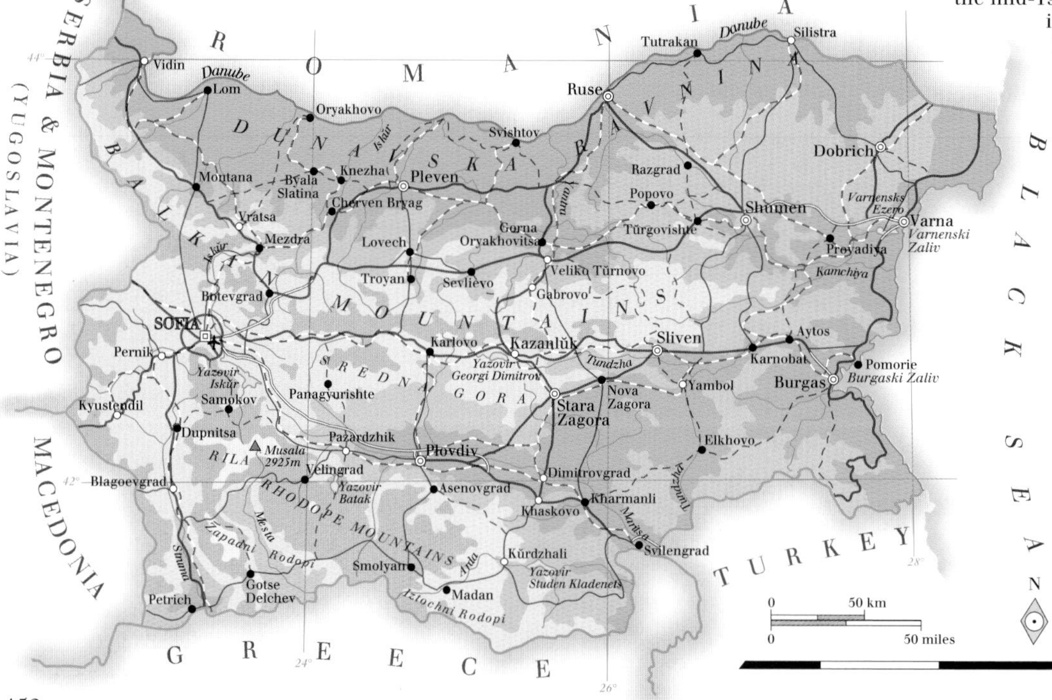
ROMANIA
SERBIA & MONTENEGRO (YUGOSLAVIA)
MACEDONIA
GREECE
TURKEY
BLACK SEA
Danube
Vidin
Lom
Oryakhovo
Svishtov
Ruse
Tutrakan
Silistra
Dobrich
Varna
Varnenski Zaliv
Shumen
Razgrad
Popovo
Türgovishte
Provadiya
Pleven
Knezha
Byala Slatina
Montana
Vratsa
Mezdra
Cherven Bryag
Lovech
Gorna Oryakhovitsa
Veliko Türnovo
Troyan
Sevlievo
Gabrovo
Botevgrad
SOFIA
Pernik
Kyustendil
Samokov
Dupnitsa
Blagoevgrad
Petrich
Gotse Delchev
Karlovo
Kazanlŭk
Sliven
Aytos
Karnobat
Pomorie
Burgas
Burgaski Zaliv
Yambol
Nova Zagora
Stara Zagora
Panagyurishte
Pazardzhik
Plovdiv
Velingrad
Asenovgrad
Dimitrovgrad
Khaskovo
Kharmanli
Svilengrad
Elkhovo
Kŭrdzhali
Smolyan
Madan
Musala 2925m
RILA
RHODOPE MOUNTAINS
SREDNA GORA
BALKAN MOUNTAINS
DUNAVSKA RAVNINA
Yazovir Iskŭr
Yazovir Georgi Dimitrov
Yazovir Batak
Yazovir Studen Kladenets
Zapadni Rodopi
Iztochni Rodopi
Iskŭr
Tundzha
Maritsa
Arda
Mesta
Struma
Kamchiya
Yantra
Varnensko Ezero
0 50 km
0 50 miles
N

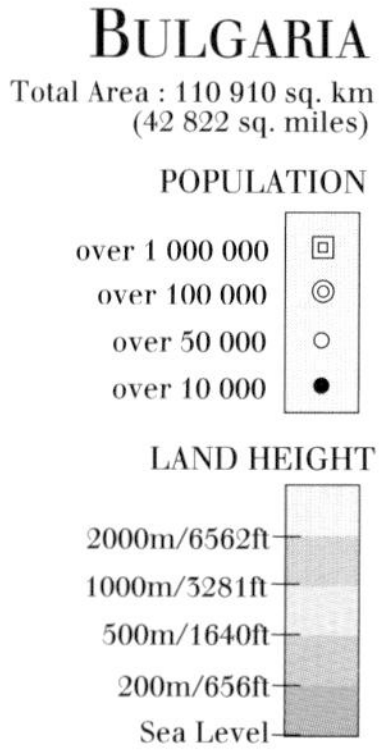
BULGARIA
Total Area : 110 910 sq. km (42 822 sq. miles)
POPULATION
over 1 000 000
over 100 000
over 50 000
over 10 000
LAND HEIGHT
2000m/6562ft
1000m/3281ft
500m/1640ft
200m/656ft
Sea Level

B

PEOPLE

Pop. density medium

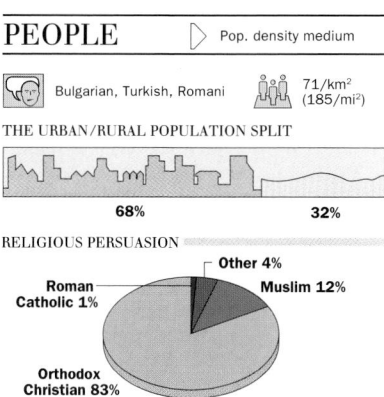

Bulgarian, Turkish, Romani

71/km² (185/mi²)

THE URBAN/RURAL POPULATION SPLIT

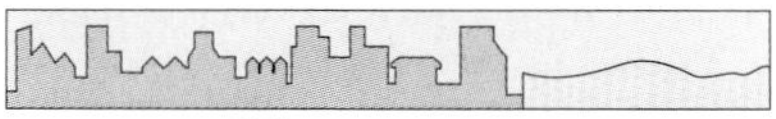
68%
32%

RELIGIOUS PERSUASION

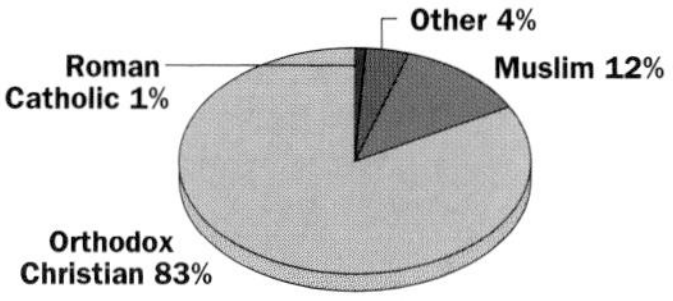
Other 4%
Roman Catholic 1%
Muslim 12%
Orthodox Christian 83%

ETHNIC MAKEUP

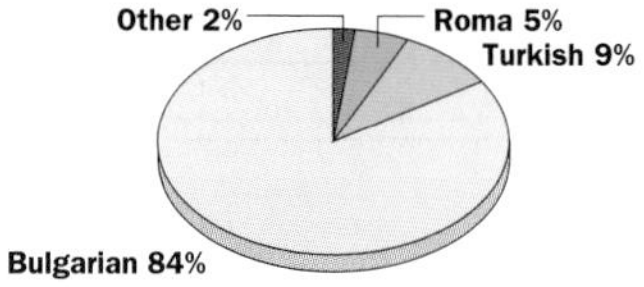
Other 2%
Roma 5%
Turkish 9%
Bulgarian 84%

The Communist era was marked by the active suppression of minority cultural identities. In the 1970s, Bulgarian Muslims, or Pomaks, were forced to change Muslim names to Bulgarian ones. Bulgarian Turks were particularly targeted in the 1980s. Linguistic and religious freedom was granted in 1989, but 300,000 Turks, or 40%, still left for Turkey – an option denied to Pomaks. The farming skills of the Turkish community have traditionally been important, but many Turks have been left landless by recent privatizations, causing new waves of emigration.

Roma suffer discrimination at all levels. It is thought that the number of Roma is much higher than officially recognized, since many disguise their ethnicity in an effort to avoid persecution. Other minorities include Russians, Armenians, and Vlachs.

Women have equal rights in theory, but society remains patriarchal, especially among Turks.

POPULATION AGE BREAKDOWN

Female
Age
Male
1.4%
80+
0.9%
10.5%
60–79
8.6%
13.5%
40–59
12.9%
13.7%
20–39
14%
11.9%
0–19
12.6%
% of population by age group

WORLD AFFAIRS

Joined UN in 1955

BSEC CE NATO CEFTA OSCE

Bulgaria became a member of NATO in March 2004. Not included in the 2004 expansion of the EU, it has been told that membership is likely in 2007.

Bulgaria conscientiously adhered to UN sanctions against Yugoslavia, despite the costs of lost trade. Relations with Russia are no longer close, but are maintained carefully because of dependence on Russia for oil and gas. Relations with Turkey have greatly improved since the tensions of the final years of communist rule.

AID

Recipient

$381m (receipts)

Up 10% in 2002

Loans from the IMF, the World Bank, and the EBRD are mainly intended for infrastructure improvements. The EU is by far the largest single donor, with funds aiding reforms in preparation for Bulgaria's eventual membership of the EU. Humanitarian aid focuses mainly on medical provision and children's homes.

POLITICS

Multiparty elections

2001/2005

President Georgi Purvanov

AT THE LAST ELECTION

National Assembly 240 seats

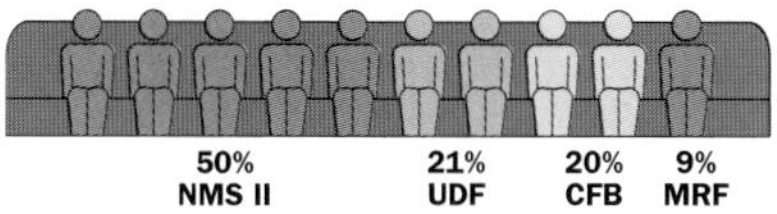
50% NMS II
21% UDF
20% CFB
9% MRF

NMS II = National Movement Simeon II
UDF = United Democratic Forces (led by the Union of Democratic Forces–**UDF**) **CFB** = Coalition for Bulgaria (led by the Bulgarian Socialist Party–**BSP**)
MRF = Movement for Rights and Freedoms

Bulgaria is a multiparty democracy.

PROFILE

Having moved falteringly to a pluralist democratic system after the fall of the communist Zhivkov regime in 1989, Bulgaria suffered during the 1990s from successive weak governments, each brought down by no-confidence votes.

The UDF, a broad anticommunist alliance, fell from office in 1992, and by the time of the 1994 general election the former communist BSP appeared to be firmly in the ascendant, winning an overall majority. The BSP government resisted political and economic change; the result was one of the slowest privatization programs in eastern Europe, with the old communist web of patronage still intact.

A new UDF government in 1997 launched free-market reforms backed by the IMF. Its considerable success, and reorientation of policy toward the goals of EU and NATO membership, allowed the UDF to approach the June 2001 elections with some confidence, despite a surge in support for a monarchist party launched by ex-king Simeon II (who had left Bulgaria as a small child in 1946). The poll, however, left the UDF with fewer than a quarter of the National Assembly seats, exactly half of which went to the NMS II.

Bulgarianizing his family name, Prime Minister Simeon Saxecoburggotski formed a coalition with the MRF (which traditionally represents the ethnic Turkish minority) and in 2002 secured cooperation from the BSP and the UDF. However, the government's popularity has declined as its promised "spiritual and economic revival" has been slow to unfold. Divisions within the ideologically vague NMS II and revitalized opposition from the BSP and UDF threaten the government's survival.

Ex-king Simeon II (Saxecoburggotski) returned as prime minister in 2001.

Georgi Purvanov, of the BSP, elected president against expectations in 2001.

CHRONOLOGY

Part of the Ottoman Empire from 1396, Bulgaria gained autonomy in 1878 and independence in 1908. Under King Ferdinand, it sided with Germany during World War I, and subsequently lost valuable territory to Greece and Serbia. Under King Boris, Bulgaria once again sided with Germany in World War II.

- **1943** Child king Simeon II accedes.
- **1944** Allies firebomb Sofia. Soviet army invades. Antifascist Fatherland Front coalition, including Agrarian Party and Bulgarian Communist Party (BCP), takes power in bloodless coup. Kimon Georgiev prime minister.
- **1946** September, referendum abolishes monarchy. Republic proclaimed. October, general election results in BCP majority.
- **1947** Prime Minister Georgi Dmitrov discredits Agrarian Party leader Nikola Petkov. Petkov arrested and sentenced to death. International recognition of Dmitrov government. Soviet-style constitution adopted; one-party state established. Country renamed People's Republic of Bulgaria. Nationalization of economy begins.
- **1949** Dmitrov dies, succeeded as prime minister by Vasil Kolarov.
- **1950** Kolarov dies. "Little Stalin" Vulko Chervenkov replaces him ⇨

B

CHRONOLOGY *continued*

and begins BCP purge and collectivization.

- **1953** Stalin dies; Chervenkov's power begins to wane.
- **1954** Chervenkov yields power to Todor Zhivkov. Zhivkov sets out to make Bulgaria an inseparable part of the Soviet system.
- **1955–1960** Zhivkov exonerates victims of Chervenkov's purges.
- **1965** Plot to overthrow Zhivkov discovered by Soviet agents.
- **1968** Bulgarian troops aid Soviet army in invasion of Czechoslovakia.
- **1971** New constitution. Zhivkov becomes president of State Council and resigns as premier.
- **1978** Purge of BCP: 30,000 members expelled.
- **1984** Turkish minority forced to take Slavic names.
- **1989** June–August, exodus of 300,000 Bulgarian Turks. November, Zhivkov ousted as BCP leader and head of state. Replaced by Petur Mladenov. Mass protest in Sofia for democratic reform. December, Union of Democratic Forces (UDF) formed.
- **1990** Economic collapse. Zhivkov arrested. BCP loses constitutional role as leading political party, changes name to Bulgarian Socialist Party (BSP). Elections: BSP victory. Parliament chooses Zhelyu Zhelev, UDF leader, as president. Country renamed Republic of Bulgaria; communist symbols removed from national flag.
- **1991** February, price controls abolished; steep price rises. July, new constitution adopted. October, UDF wins elections.
- **1992** Continued political and social unrest. October, UDF resigns after losing vote of confidence. December, MRF forms government. Zhivkov convicted of corruption and human rights abuses.
- **1993** Ambitious privatization program begins, but progress slow.
- **1994** General elections return BSP to power.
- **1995** BSP leader, Zhan Videnov, heads coalition government.
- **1996** Financial crisis and collapse of lev. Presidential elections won by opposition UDF candidate, Peter Stoyanov.
- **1997** General election won by UDF, whose leader Ivan Kostov becomes prime minister.
- **2001** Despite economic upturn, voters turn to new party headed by ex-king, who, as Simeon Saxecoburggotski, becomes prime minister. November, BSP leader Georgi Purvanov elected president.
- **2004** Joins NATO.

DEFENSE

Compulsory military service

$378m

Up 4% in 2002

BULGARIAN ARMED FORCES

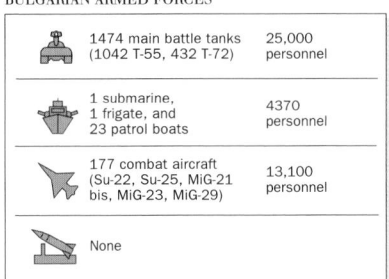

1474 main battle tanks (1042 T-55, 432 T-72)	25,000 personnel
1 submarine, 1 frigate, and 23 patrol boats	4370 personnel
177 combat aircraft (Su-22, Su-25, MiG-21 bis, MiG-23, MiG-29)	13,100 personnel
None	

Defense spending has fallen, from 14% of GDP in 1985 to 2.5% in 2002.

Preparing to join NATO, a long-held ambition realized in March 2004 after seven years of negotiations, involved a major reorientation in defense thinking.

In 1999 the crisis in Kosovo had prompted Bulgaria to make its airspace available to NATO.

In late 1999 the government adopted "Plan 2004," which embodied a radical acceleration of its previous plans to restructure the armed forces. The new plan aimed to downsize from 75,000 to 45,000 personnel, including central staff, and focused on rapid reaction capabilities. It was considered that this smaller but combat-ready force would be less costly to maintain in the long run than a larger force.

ECONOMICS

Inflation 93% p.a. (1990–2001)

$14.1bn

1.608 leva (1.695)

SCORE CARD

World GNP Ranking	78th
GNP per capita	$1770
Balance of payments	–$677m
Inflation	5.8%
Unemployment	17%

EXPORTS

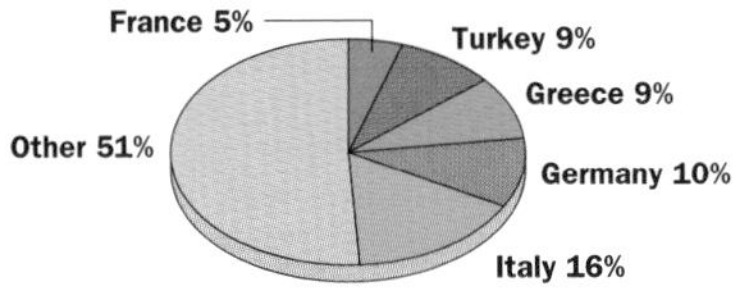
France 5%
Turkey 9%
Greece 9%
Germany 10%
Italy 16%
Other 51%

IMPORTS

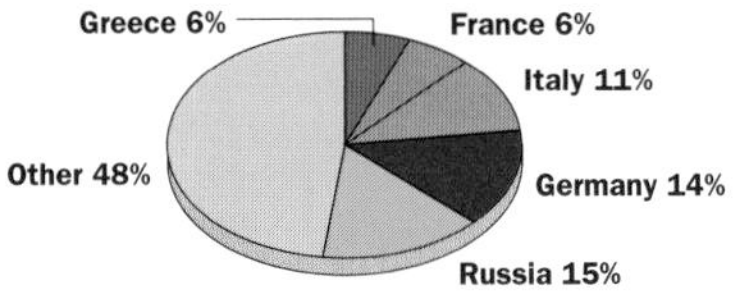
Greece 6%
France 6%
Italy 11%
Germany 14%
Russia 15%
Other 48%

Strengths

Coal and natural gas. Good agricultural production, especially grapes for well-developed wine industry, and tobacco. Increased ties with EU. Strong expertise in computer software.

Weaknesses

Outdated infrastructure and equipment, and outstanding debt throughout industry. High unemployment.

Profile

Restructuring the economy is linked to privatization – a process delayed for political and technical reasons until the late 1990s. A financial crisis in 1996 triggered the collapse of the national currency, the lev. Foreign investment is still low, despite laws that since 1992 have allowed foreign firms to own companies outright. Trade has shifted toward the EU, while that with the former Soviet Union has fallen sharply. The UDF government which was returned in 1997 followed IMF advice and made free-market reforms, backed by foreign loans, successfully bringing inflation under control. These policies have been continued under Saxecoburggotski, with the stated aim of joining the EU, which confirmed Bulgaria as a market economy in 2002. Growth has been steady.

ECONOMIC PERFORMANCE INDICATOR

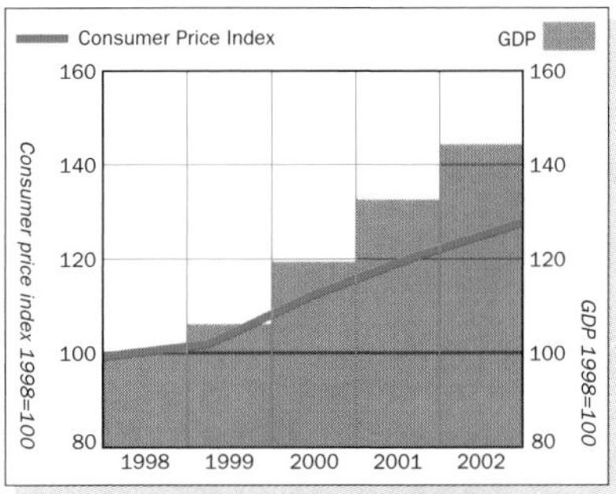
Consumer Price Index
GDP
160
140
120
100
80
Consumer price index 1998=100
GDP 1998=100
1998
1999
2000
2001
2002

BULGARIA : MAJOR BUSINESSES

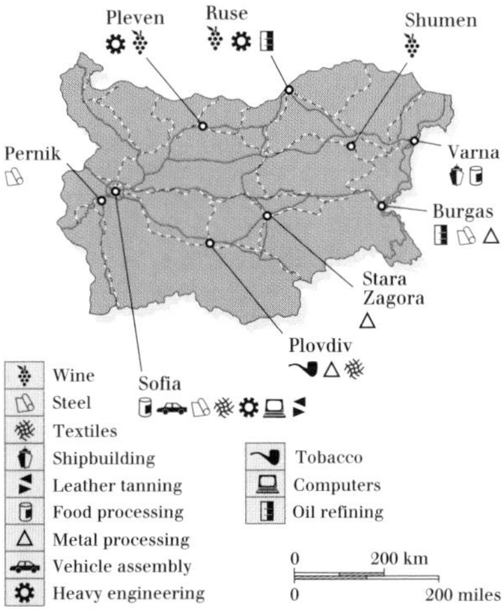
Pleven
Ruse
Shumen
Pernik
Varna
Burgas
Stara Zagora
Plovdiv
Sofia
Wine
Steel
Textiles
Shipbuilding
Leather tanning
Food processing
Metal processing
Vehicle assembly
Heavy engineering
Tobacco
Computers
Oil refining
0
200 km
0
200 miles

RESOURCES

Electric power 11m kW

8140 tonnes

842 b/d (reserves 15m barrels)

1.73m sheep, 1m pigs, 900,000 goats, 18m chickens

Coal, iron, copper, lead, zinc, natural gas, oil, manganese

ELECTRICITY GENERATION

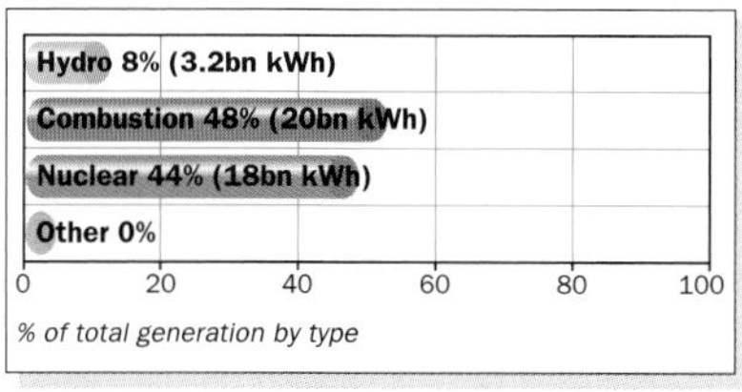

Hydro 8% (3.2bn kWh)
Combustion 48% (20bn kWh)
Nuclear 44% (18bn kWh)
Other 0%
0
20
40
60
80
100
% of total generation by type

Improvements in the production of coal – its chief fossil fuel – and the increasing efficiency of the Kozloduy nuclear power plant have made Bulgaria a major regional energy exporter.

The EU is providing aid to upgrade two nuclear reactors at Kozloduy, in return for the closure of old reactors there which pose particular safety risks. A new plant north of Pleven is planned to open in 2008. Bulgaria's strategic position between the rest of Europe and oil-producers in Russia and the Middle East has raised the possibility of lucrative deals for oil and gas transit, particularly as it can offer routes which avoid the relatively precarious Bosphorus. HEP, produced primarily by the Belmekan–Sestrimo facility in the Rila Mountains, is diminishing in importance.

BULGARIA : LAND USE

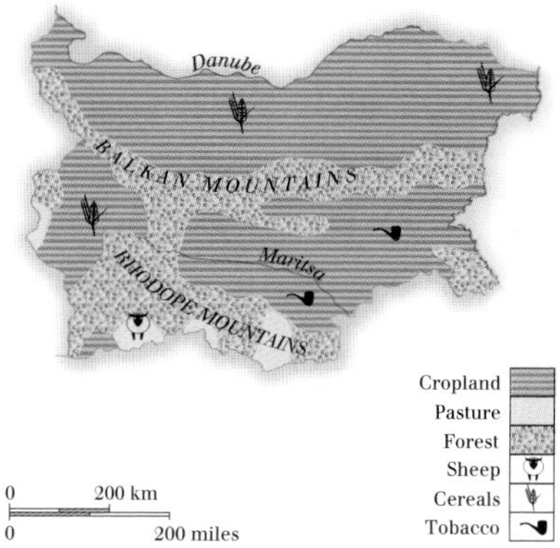

Danube
BALKAN MOUNTAINS
Maritsa
RHODOPE MOUNTAINS
Cropland
Pasture
Forest
Sheep
Cereals
Tobacco
0
200 km
0
200 miles

ENVIRONMENT

Sustainability rank: 71st

5% (2% partially protected)

5.2 tonnes per capita

ENVIRONMENTAL TREATIES

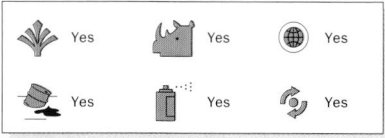

Yes	Yes	Yes
Yes	Yes	Yes

Environmental degradation led to the foundation in 1989 of the Ecoglasnost party. It circulated information on pollution and nuclear waste dump locations, and brought polluters to court. The Kozloduy nuclear complex, east of Lom, was restarted in 1995 despite safety concerns. It is in the process of closing its oldest reactors. Air pollution has diminished, but problems remain. NATO bombing of Serbian chemical and oil refineries on the Danube in 1999 led to downriver pollution in Bulgaria.

MEDIA

TV ownership high

Daily newspaper circulation 116 per 1000 people

PUBLISHING AND BROADCAST MEDIA

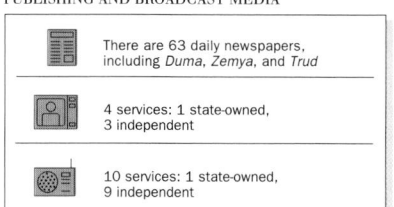

There are 63 daily newspapers, including *Duma*, *Zemya*, and *Trud*

4 services: 1 state-owned, 3 independent

10 services: 1 state-owned, 9 independent

State-run broadcasters retained an effective monopoly until the 2000 launch of a national commercial channel, bTV, owned by the international giant News Corporation. One group dominates the newspaper market, while political parties own much of the remainder. Internet providers are regulated. Journalists complain of the tough libel laws.

CRIME

No death penalty

10,500 prisoners

Up 5% in 2000–2002

CRIME RATES

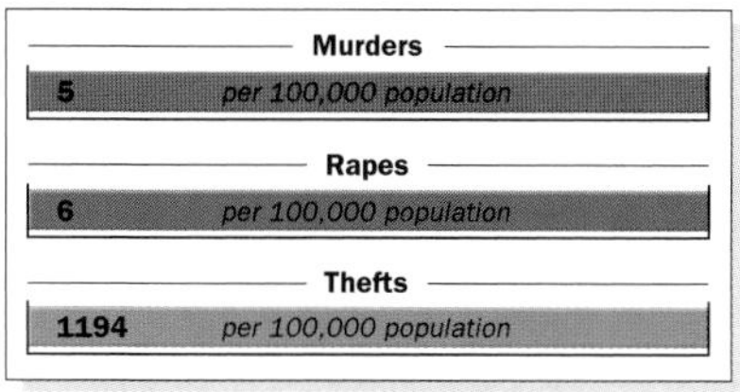

Murders
5
per 100,000 population
Rapes
6
per 100,000 population
Thefts
1194
per 100,000 population

In the 1990s Bulgaria became a key narcotics trafficking route to western Europe. Former security agents, party officials, and prestigious ex-athletes moved into protection rackets, counterfeiting, and similar activities. Violations of minority rights are a sensitive political issue.

EDUCATION

School leaving age: 15

99%

233,678 students

THE EDUCATION SYSTEM

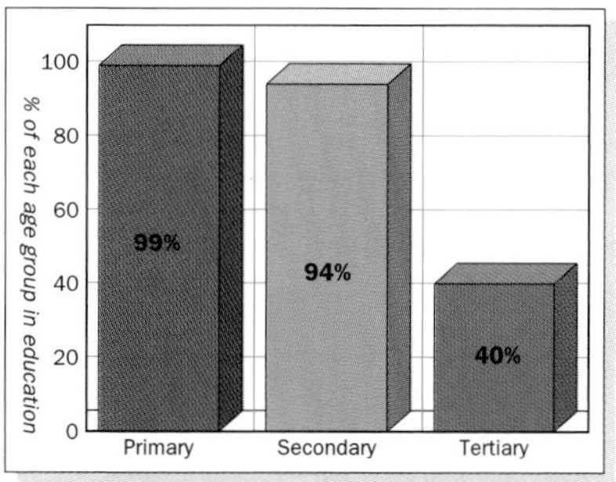

100
80
60
40
20
0
% of each age group in education
99%
94%
40%
Primary
Secondary
Tertiary

Education is free and compulsory between the ages of seven and 15. The system has been changed from a Soviet-inspired to a west European-style model. Over 10,000 teachers were dismissed in 2002 as part of a restructuring of the sector. Standards continue to be lowest in the rural and Turkish communities.

HEALTH

Welfare state health benefits

1 per 294 people

Cerebrovascular and heart diseases, cancers

Hospital facilities have kept pace with population growth, but the 1997 economic crisis brought the health service to the brink of collapse. A new health policy was formulated in 1999, the plan of action emphasizing primary care. The Bulgarian Red Cross assists in health administration.

SPENDING

GDP/cap. decrease

CONSUMPTION AND SPENDING

260 per 1000 population

368 per 1000 population

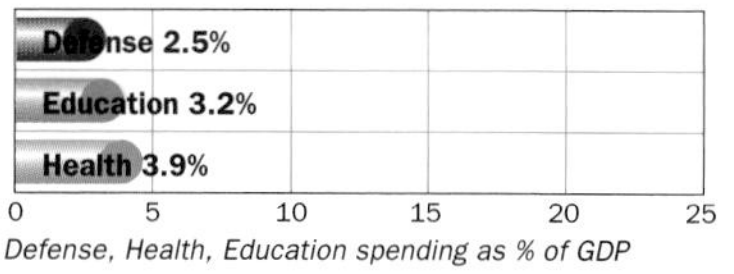

Defense 2.5%
Education 3.2%
Health 3.9%
0
5
10
15
20
25
Defense, Health, Education spending as % of GDP

The benefits of economic growth have not been evenly distributed. Pockets of serious poverty remain in rural areas and among ethnic minorities, notably the Roma, and the unemployed.

WORLD RANKING

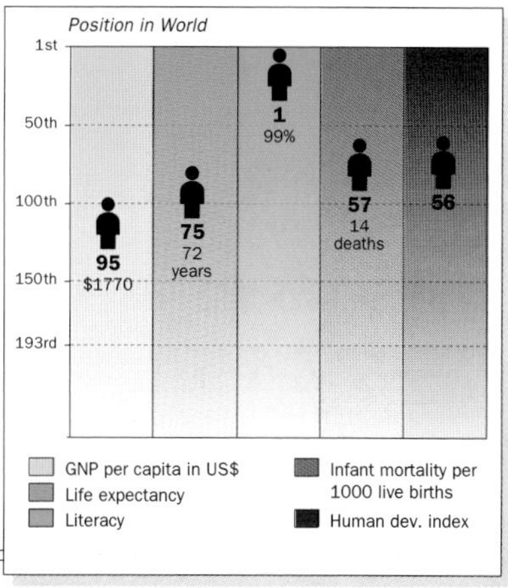

Position in World
1st
50th
100th
150th
193rd
95
$1770
75
72
years
1
99%
57
14
deaths
56
GNP per capita in US$
Life expectancy
Literacy
Infant mortality per 1000 live births
Human dev. index

BURKINA

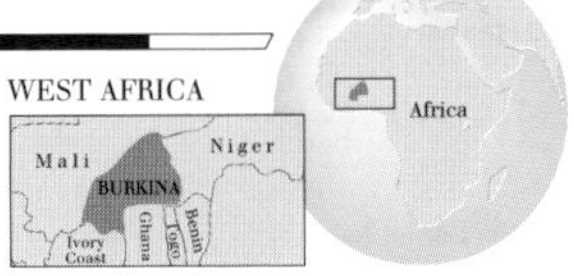
WEST AFRICA
Africa
Mali
Niger
BURKINA
Ivory Coast
Ghana
Togo
Benin

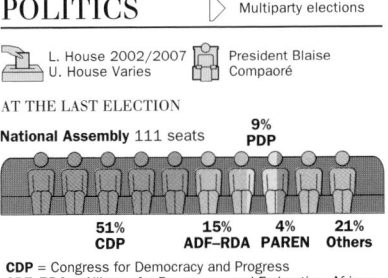

OFFICIAL NAME: Burkina Faso **CAPITAL:** Ouagadougou
POPULATION: 13 million **CURRENCY:** CFA franc **OFFICIAL LANGUAGE:** French

1960 | 1960 | Dec 11 | BF | 0 | +226 | .bf

LANDLOCKED IN WEST AFRICA, Burkina (formerly Upper Volta) gained independence from France in 1960. The majority of Burkina lies in the arid fringe of the Sahara known as the Sahel. Ruled by military dictators for much of its postindependence history, Burkina became a multiparty state in 1991. However, much power still rests with President Blaise Compaoré. Burkina's economy remains largely based on agriculture.

CLIMATE

Tropical/steppe

WEATHER CHART FOR OUAGADOUGOU

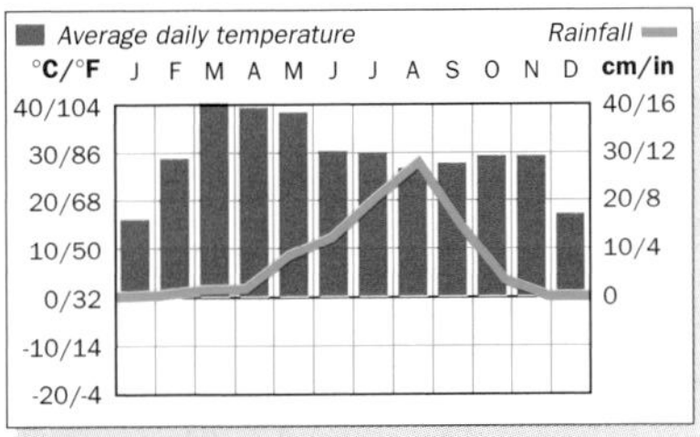
Average daily temperature
Rainfall
°C/°F
J F M A M J J A S O N D
cm/in
40/104
30/86
20/68
10/50
0/32
-10/14
-20/-4
40/16
30/12
20/8
10/4
0

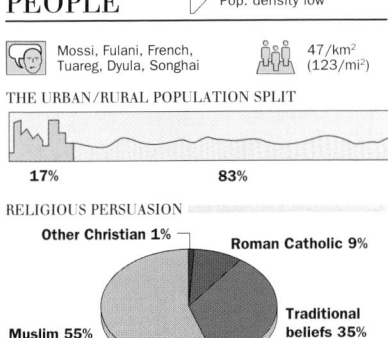

The tropical climate comprises two seasons – unreliable rains from June to October, and a long dry season.

TRANSPORTATION

Drive on right

Ouagadougou 193,283 passengers

Has no fleet

THE TRANSPORTATION NETWORK

2001 km (1243 miles)

None

622 km (386 miles)

None

The railroad to the port of Abidjan in Ivory Coast provides the main commercial route to the sea. Roads through Benin, Togo, and Ghana provide alternative access.

TOURISM

Visitors : Population 1:87

149,000 visitors

Up 18% in 2001–2002

MAIN TOURIST ARRIVALS

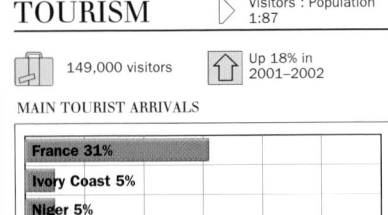

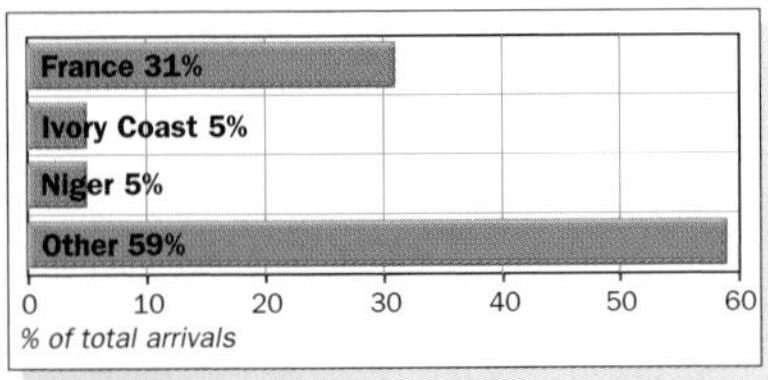
France 31%
Ivory Coast 5%
Niger 5%
Other 59%
0
10
20
30
40
50
60
% of total arrivals

Some potential exists for safari tourism, and the cities offer an attractive mix of colonial and African architecture. Big game hunting is allowed in some areas.

PEOPLE

Pop. density low

Mossi, Fulani, French, Tuareg, Dyula, Songhai

47/km² (123/mi²)

THE URBAN/RURAL POPULATION SPLIT

17%
83%

RELIGIOUS PERSUASION

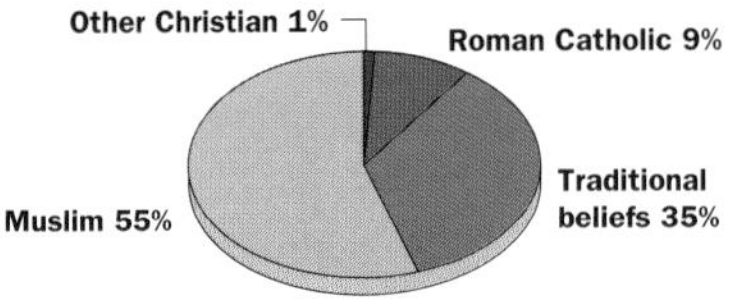
Other Christian 1%
Roman Catholic 9%
Traditional beliefs 35%
Muslim 55%

No ethnic group is dominant, though the Mossi people who live in the area of their old empire around Ouagadougou are the most numerous and play a key political role. The first president, Maurice Yameogo, and the incumbent Blaise Compaoré are both Mossi. The communities in the west are the most ethnically mixed. Extreme poverty has led to a strong sense of egalitarianism within society, but has, along with population pressure, prompted mass emigration, mostly to Ghana and Ivory Coast. The 200,000 or so Burkinabes in Ivory Coast have been caught up in the ongoing conflict there.

The extended family is important. The absence of women in public life belies their real power and social influence. However, most women are still denied access to education and the professions.

Camel plowing. Burkina's poor soils and frequent droughts lead many young men to emigrate seasonally in search of work.

POLITICS

Multiparty elections

L. House 2002/2007
U. House Varies

President Blaise Compaoré

AT THE LAST ELECTION

National Assembly 111 seats

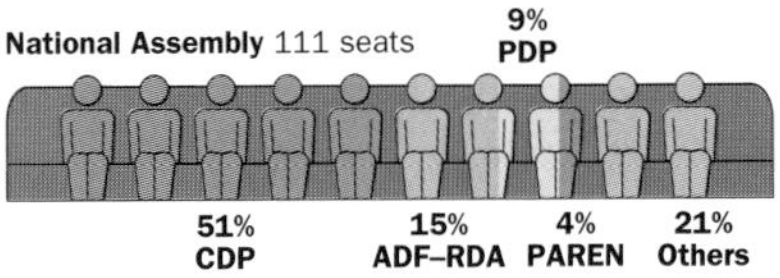
9% PDP
51% CDP
15% ADF–RDA
4% PAREN
21% Others

CDP = Congress for Democracy and Progress **ADF–RDA** = Alliance for Democracy and Federation–African Democratic Rally **PDP** = Party for Democracy and Progress **PAREN** = Party for National Renewal

House of Representatives 178 seats

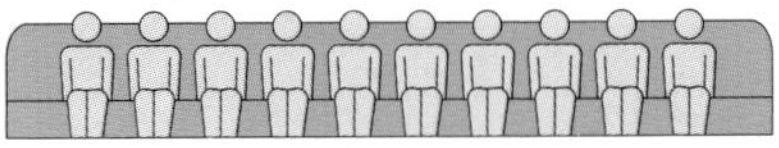

Members of the House of Representatives are appointed or indirectly elected on a nonparty basis by provincial councils and various communities

A multiparty democracy in theory, Burkina is dominated by former military dictator Blaise Compaoré, who has been in power since Capt. Thomas Sankara, his former superior, was assassinated in 1987. Several of Compaoré's close military colleagues have also been killed. His grip on power appears to be solid, and he was reelected president in 1998 with almost 90% of the vote.

The CDP and the government came under pressure in 1998 and 1999 after the assassination of a newspaper editor in which leading establishment figures were implicated. Most opposition leaders still live in exile, but opposition parties made unexpected gains in the 2002 polls. This led to a change to the electoral system which the opposition claims will give the government unfair advantage in future polls.

WORLD AFFAIRS

Joined UN in 1960

CILSS | ECOWAS | AU | OIC | FZ

Being landlocked means that relations with neighbors are vitally important. Burkina, however, has accused Ivory Coast of backing a coup attempt, while Ivory Coast claims that Burkina supports its northern rebels.

AID

Recipient

$473m (receipts)

Up 21% in 2002

External aid, mostly from the World Bank and France, is important to the economy. The large number of NGOs has caused organizational problems; there is often difficulty in finding suitable projects for all the prospective donors.

BURKINA

Total Area : 274 200 sq. km (105 869 sq. miles)

POPULATION

- over 100 000
- over 50 000
- over 10 000
- under 10 000

LAND HEIGHT

- 500m/1640ft
- 200m/656ft
- Sea Level

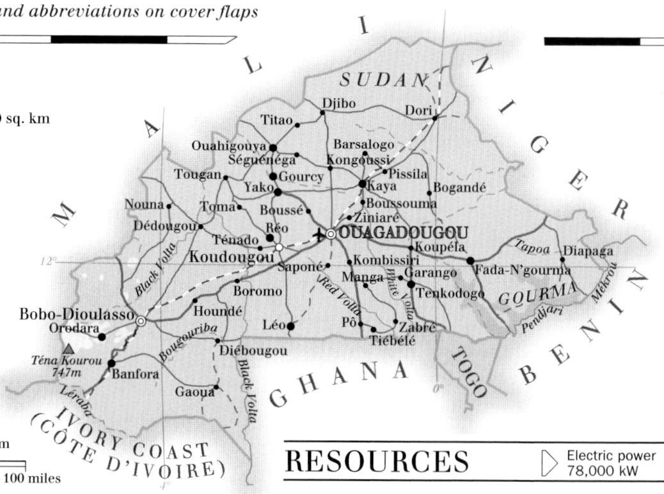
MALI
NIGER
BENIN
TOGO
GHANA
IVORY COAST (CÔTE D'IVOIRE)
SUDAN
GOURMA
Djibo
Dori
Titao
Ouahigouya
Séguénéga
Barsalogo
Kongoussi
Tougan
Gourcy
Pissila
Yako
Kaya
Bogandé
Nouna
Toma
Boussé
Boussouma
Ziniaré
Dédougou
Réo
OUAGADOUGOU
Koupéla
Ténado
Koudougou
Saponé
Kombissiri
Manga
Garango
Tenkodogo
Fada-N'gourma
Diapaga
Tapoa
Mékrou
Pendjari
Boromo
Black Volta
Red Volta
White Volta
Bobo-Dioulasso
Houndé
Orodara
Bougouriba
Léo
Pô
Zabré
Tiébélé
Diébougou
Téna Kourou 747m
Banfora
Gaoua
Léraba
N
0 100 km
0 100 miles

DEFENSE

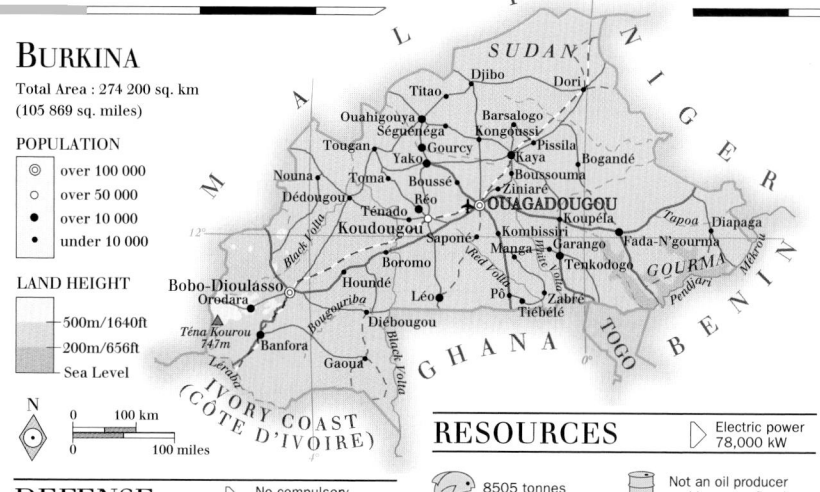

No compulsory military service

$41m

Up 8% in 2002

The main role of the 6400-strong army has been maintaining internal security. Burkina is reliant on France for most equipment and training.

ECONOMICS

Inflation 4.5% p.a. (1990–2001)

$2.91bn

539.2 CFA francs (571.2)

SCORE CARD

- ❑ WORLD GNP RANKING........................132nd
- ❑ GNP PER CAPITA...............................$250
- ❑ BALANCE OF PAYMENTS....................–$324m
- ❑ INFLATION..2.2%
- ❑ UNEMPLOYMENT.....................................1%

STRENGTHS

Remittances from plantation workers in Ghana and Ivory Coast. Strongly improved economic management. Low debt burden. Ability to attract foreign aid. Cotton. Potential for exploitation of mineral resources.

WEAKNESSES

Landlocked. Poor soil quality. Food crop fluctuations. Overseas remittances have dropped. Access to Abidjan port affected by instability in Ivory Coast. Drought and desertification in the Sahel.

EXPORTS

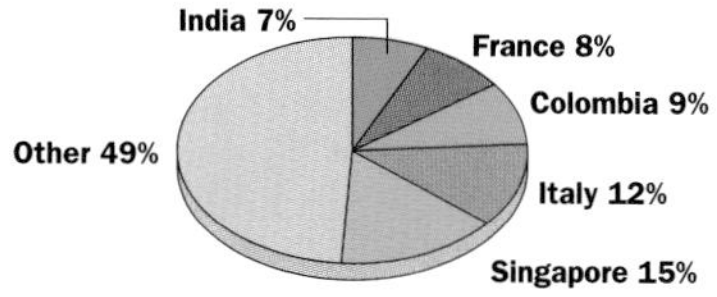
India 7%
France 8%
Colombia 9%
Other 49%
Italy 12%
Singapore 15%

IMPORTS

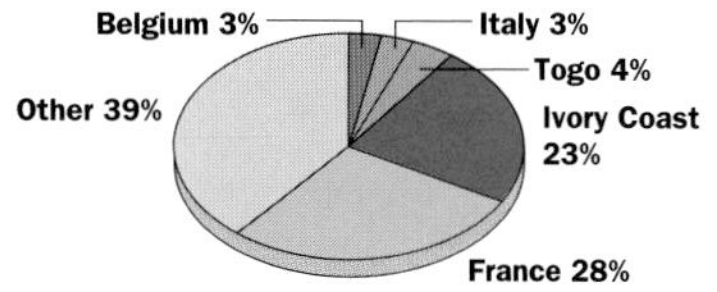
Belgium 3%
Italy 3%
Togo 4%
Other 39%
Ivory Coast 23%
France 28%

RESOURCES

Electric power 78,000 kW

8505 tonnes

Not an oil producer and has no refineries

8.8m goats, 6.9m sheep, 5m cattle, 24m chickens

Gold, antimony, marble, manganese, silver, zinc

Burkina has substantial mineral wealth, though falling world prices led to the largest gold mine closing in 1999. The completion of two new dams will reduce dependence on diesel power generators and ease pressure on water supplies.

ENVIRONMENT

Sustainability rank: 101st

12% (8% partially protected)

0.1 tonnes per capita

As for other countries on the southern rim of the Sahara, desertification is the main issue. A ten-year reforestation program was launched in 2003.

MEDIA

TV ownership medium

Daily newspaper circulation 1 per 1000 people

PUBLISHING AND BROADCAST MEDIA

There are 6 daily newspapers, including *Sidwaya*, *Le Pays*, *Le Journal de Soir*, and *L'Observateur Paalga*

4 services: 1 state-owned, 3 independent

1 state-owned service, 46 independent stations

There are a number of small independent newspapers funded by opposition groups. A code of practice was introduced in 1999.

CRIME

Death penalty not used in practice

2800 prisoners

Crime is rising

Crime levels have traditionally been low. However, the urbanization of society and the increase in political violence have seen levels increase.

EDUCATION

School leaving age: 16

25%

9900 students

Education is based on the French system. Recently, practical subjects have received more emphasis.

CHRONOLOGY

Ruled by Mossi kings from the 16th century, Upper Volta, a province of French West Africa in the late 19th century, gained independence in 1960.

- ❑ **1980** Ousting of military ruler; Col. Saye Zerbo becomes president.
- ❑ **1982** Capt. Thomas Sankara takes power. People's Salvation Council (PSC) begins radical reforms.
- ❑ **1984** Renamed Burkina.
- ❑ **1987** Sankara assassinated, Capt. Blaise Compaoré takes power.
- ❑ **1991** New constitution. Compaoré elected president.
- ❑ **1999** Biggest gold mine closed. General strike.
- ❑ **2001** HIV infection rate second-highest in west Africa.
- ❑ **2001–2003** Meningitis kills thousands.
- ❑ **2002** CDP narrowly wins elections.

HEALTH

No welfare state health benefits

1 per 33,333 people

Malaria, diarrheal and respiratory diseases

Health spending focuses on primary health care and vaccination. The rate of HIV infection had fallen to 4.2% by 2004.

SPENDING

GDP/cap. increase

CONSUMPTION AND SPENDING

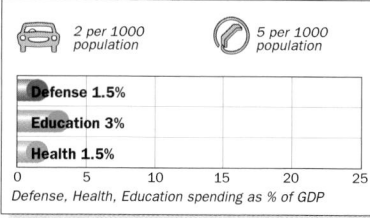

2 per 1000 population

5 per 1000 population

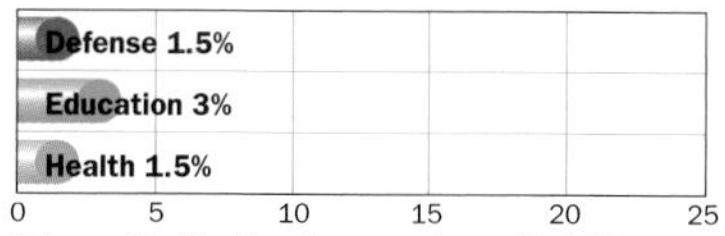
Defense 1.5%
Education 3%
Health 1.5%
0
5
10
15
20
25

Defense, Health, Education spending as % of GDP

Burkina is a country of extreme, almost universal, poverty. Displays of wealth are rare and ownership of high-tech items is limited to a small elite.

WORLD RANKING

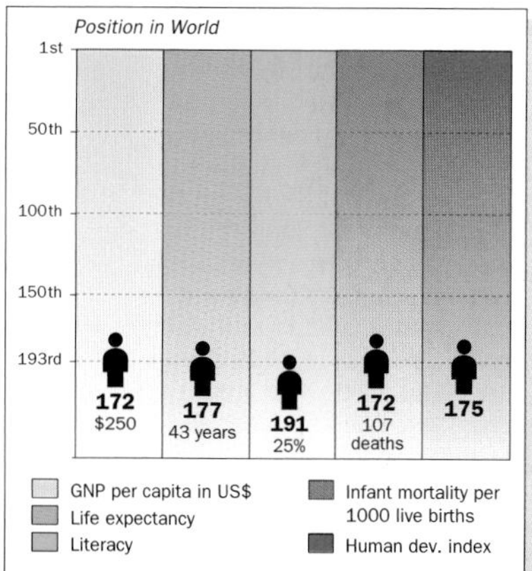
Position in World
1st
50th
100th
150th
193rd
172
$250
177
43 years
191
25%
172
107 deaths
175
GNP per capita in US$
Life expectancy
Literacy
Infant mortality per 1000 live births
Human dev. index

B

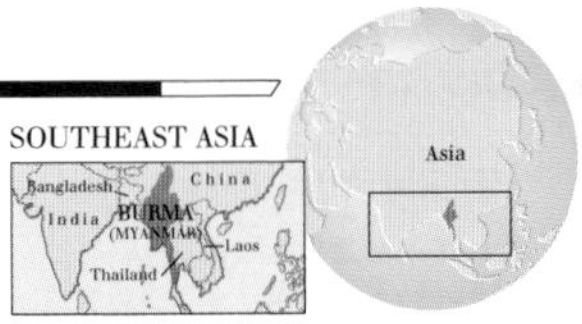
SOUTHEAST ASIA
Bangladesh
China
India
BURMA (MYANMAR)
Laos
Thailand
Asia

B

BURMA (MYANMAR)

OFFICIAL NAME: Union of Myanmar **CAPITAL:** Rangoon (Yangon)
POPULATION: 49.5 million **CURRENCY:** Kyat **OFFICIAL LANGUAGE:** Burmese (Myanmar)

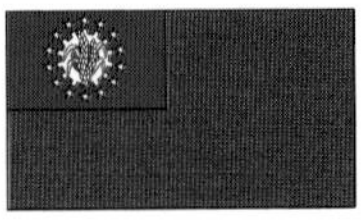

1948
1948
Jan 4
BUR
+6.5
+95
.mm

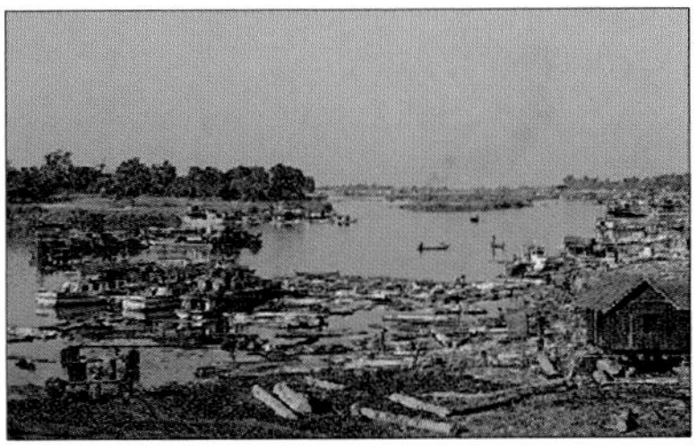

Transporting timber on the Irrawaddy River near Mandalay. Burma once had the world's largest reserves of teak.

A PREDOMINANTLY BUDDHIST country on the northeastern shores of the Indian Ocean, Burma is mountainous in the north and east, while the fertile Irrawaddy basin occupies most of the country. Rocked by ethnic conflict ever since gaining independence from the UK in 1948, Burma has been ruled by repressive military regimes since 1962. The National League for Democracy (NLD) gained a majority in free elections in 1990, but has been prevented from taking power by the military. Rich in natural resources, which include fisheries and teak forests, Burma remains a mostly agricultural economy.

CLIMATE

Tropical/mountain

WEATHER CHART FOR RANGOON

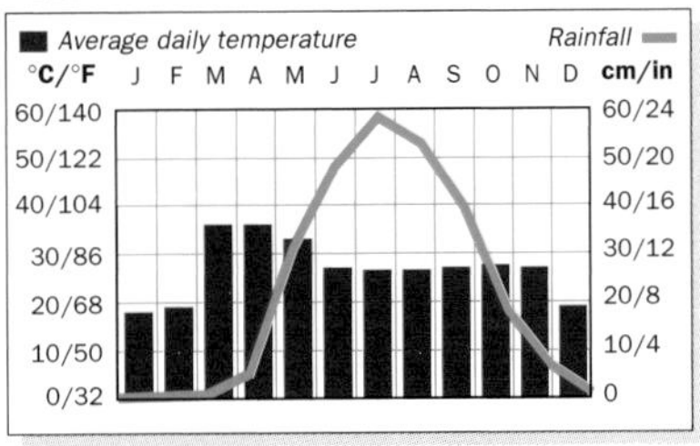
Average daily temperature
Rainfall
°C/°F
J F M A M J J A S O N D
cm/in
60/140
50/122
40/104
30/86
20/68
10/50
0/32
60/24
50/20
40/16
30/12
20/8
10/4
0

There are three seasons: the wet season, when rainfall in the far south Tenasserim region and Irrawaddy delta can reach 500 cm (197 in); summer, when northern Burma experiences 50°C (122°F) and 100% humidity; and winter, when it is rarely cooler than 15°C (59°F) except in the northern mountains.

TRANSPORTATION

Drive on right

Mingaladon, Rangoon
580,000 passengers

124 ships
402,159 grt

THE TRANSPORTATION NETWORK

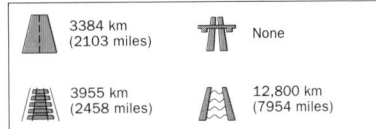

3384 km (2103 miles)

None

3955 km (2458 miles)

12,800 km (7954 miles)

Burma's main transportation corridors run north–south. Most traffic is concentrated between Rangoon and Mandalay. A daily express train runs between these two cities, though visitors are urged to take internal flights on the state-owned carriers. The Irrawaddy River and its tributaries also provide an important artery for travel.

Beyond the Irrawaddy basin, transportation is limited and hazardous. The vast majority of roads remain unpaved, and access to neighboring countries is restricted. At certain points on the Chinese border, access is one-way only: out of China.

TOURISM

Visitors : Population 1:228

217,000 visitors

Up 6% in 2002

MAIN TOURIST ARRIVALS

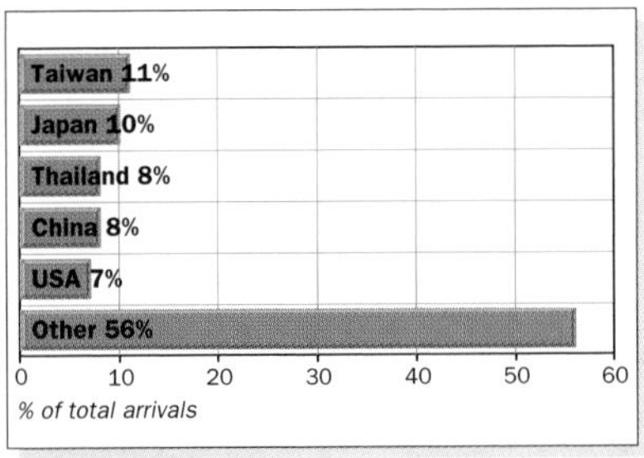
Taiwan 11%
Japan 10%
Thailand 8%
China 8%
USA 7%
Other 56%
0
10
20
30
40
50
60
% of total arrivals

Since 1988 the military authorities have courted tourists for their economic value. The previous one-week restriction for visitors arriving to marvel at Burma's stunning Buddhist heritage was increased to 28 days. The state-run tourist agency is heavily promoted, while independent travelers are required to spend a minimum of $200 during their stay. However, whole provinces remain entirely off-limits, and elsewhere official guides are often required. Opposition groups wish to discourage people from traveling to Burma at all.

PEOPLE

Pop. density medium

Burmese, Shan, Karen, Rakhine, Chin, Yangbye, Kachin, Mon

75/km² (195/mi²)

THE URBAN/RURAL POPULATION SPLIT

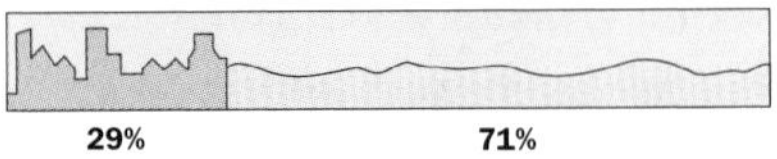
29%
71%

RELIGIOUS PERSUASION

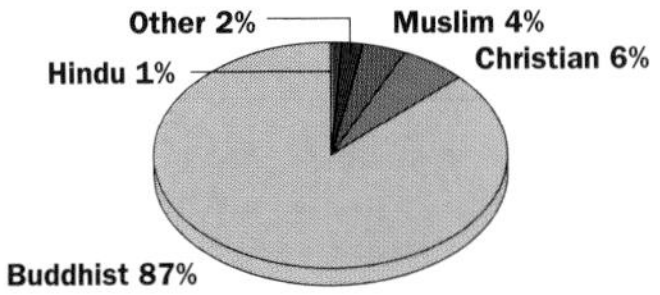
Other 2%
Muslim 4%
Hindu 1%
Christian 6%
Buddhist 87%

ETHNIC MAKEUP

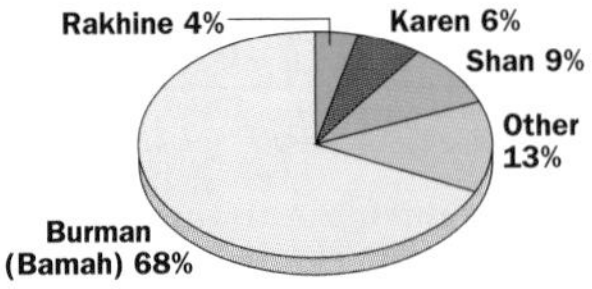
Rakhine 4%
Karen 6%
Shan 9%
Other 13%
Burman (Bamah) 68%

A savage history of ethnic repression at the hands of the Burman majority still plays a large part in the mistrust felt by the smaller minority communities. Each group maintains a distinct cultural identity. At independence the Chin, Kachin, Karen, Karenni, Mon, and Shan all unsuccessfully demanded their own state within a federation. Despite uniting against the military dictatorship in 1988, most factions had by 1996 signed peace agreements. The Karen National Union, the last major separatist group fighting government forces, began peace talks with the government in 2004. While the Burman claim racial purity, many of them are in fact of mixed blood or ethnically Chinese.

Accusations of forced labor lie at the heart of international criticism of the military regime, with ethnic minorities apparently at highest risk.

Domestic life in Burma is still based around the extended family. Women have a prominent role, and access to education. Many run or own businesses in their own right. However, top jobs in government are still held almost exclusively by men.

POPULATION AGE BREAKDOWN

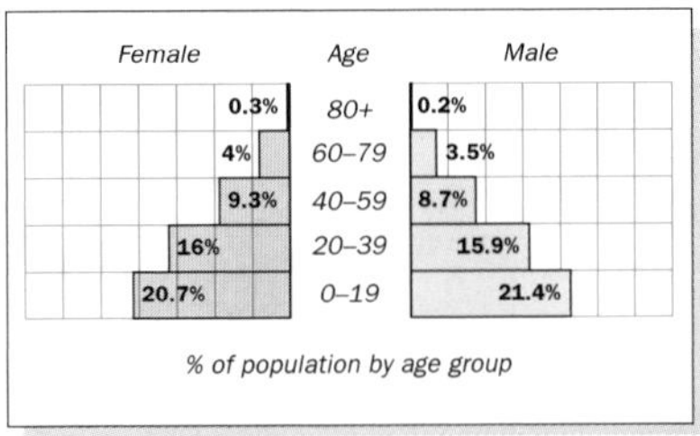
Female
Age
Male
0.3%
80+
0.2%
4%
60–79
3.5%
9.3%
40–59
8.7%
16%
20–39
15.9%
20.7%
0–19
21.4%
% of population by age group

B

POLITICS

No legislative elections

1990/suspended

Chairman Than Shwe

AT THE LAST ELECTION

Constituent Assembly 485 seats

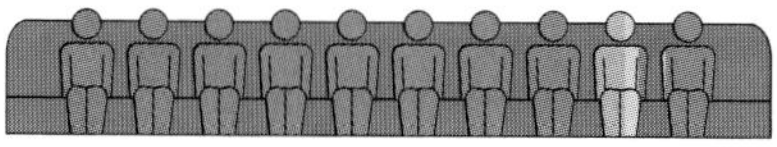
2% RDL
1% MNDF
1% NDP
81% NLD
5% SNLD
2% NUP
8% Others

NLD = National League for Democracy
SNLD = Shan National League for Democracy
RDL = Rakhine Democracy League
NUP = National Unity Party
MNDF = Mon National Democratic Front
NDP = National Democratic Party for Human Rights

A Constituent Assembly, responsible for the drafting of a new constitution and with no legislative power, was elected in 1990, but prevented from convening by the regime

Burma is ruled by the military-backed State Peace and Development Council (SPDC), under Gen. Than Shwe.

PROFILE

The military has ruled since 1962. Gen. Saw Maung seized power amid mass prodemocracy protests in 1988.

The regime has never recognized the NLD's 1990 electoral victory and has suppressed all democratic opposition. Recent moves toward negotiation have produced few tangible results.

Ethnic rebellion in outer regions degenerated into cross-border guerrilla activity after a concerted government offensive in 1996.

MAIN POLITICAL ISSUES

Restoring democracy

In a nod to international pressure and the popularity of the prodemocracy movement, the junta has talked openly of steering Burma toward "disciplined democracy." In reality there has been little progress toward ending the dictatorship. The opposition NLD is led by the charismatic Aung San Suu Kyi who has been intermittently under house arrest since 1990. Her latest detention, in 2003, followed violence in the north.

Aung San Suu Kyi, *leader of the pro-democracy movement.*

Gen. Than Shwe, *leader of the military junta since 1992.*

BURMA

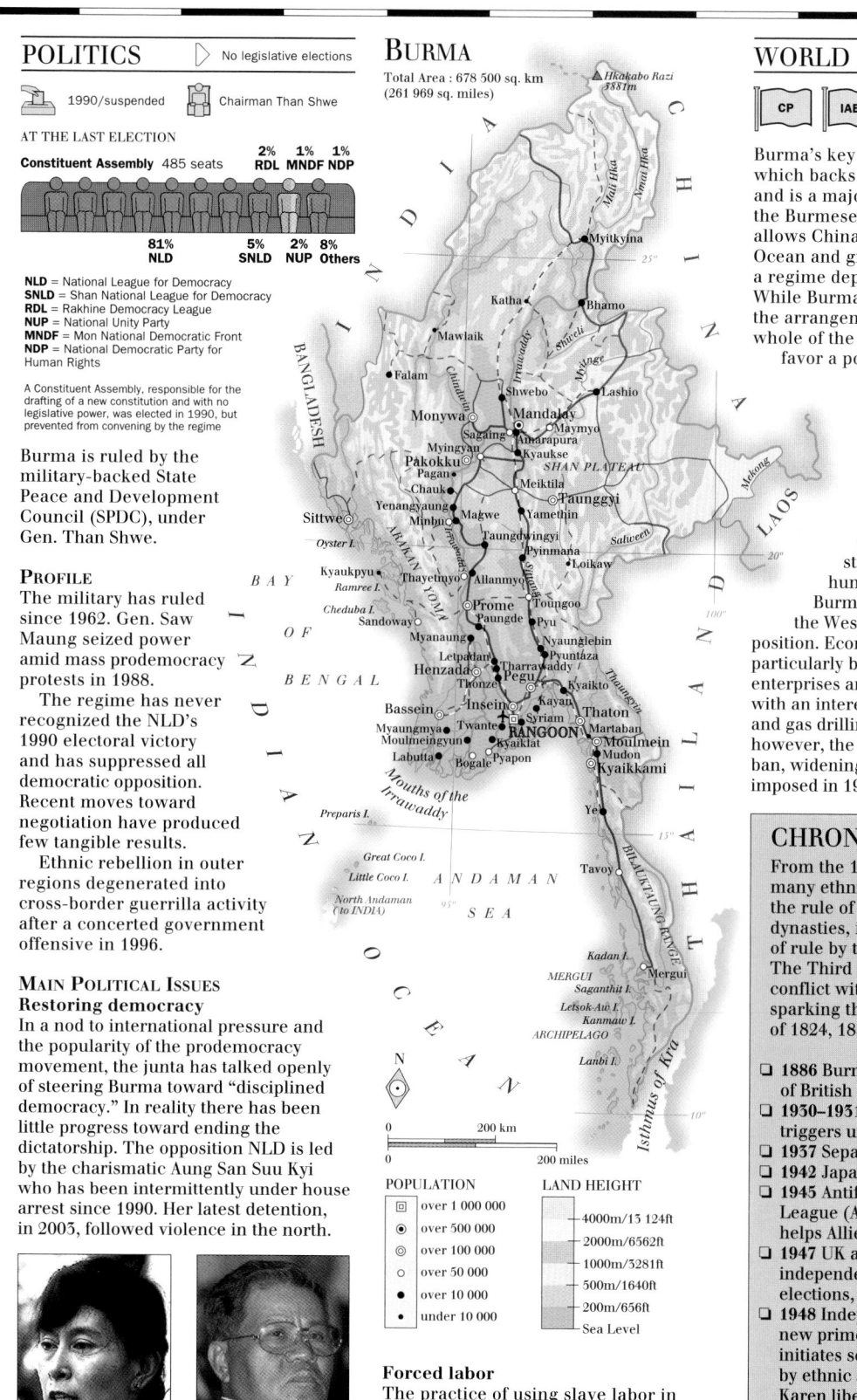

Total Area : 678 500 sq. km (261 969 sq. miles)

Hkakabo Razi 5881m
INDIA
CHINA
BANGLADESH
LAOS
THAILAND
BAY OF BENGAL
INDIAN OCEAN
ANDAMAN SEA
Myitkyina
Bhamo
Katha
Mawlaik
Falam
Shwebo
Lashio
Monywa
Mandalay
Sagaing
Maymyo
Amarapura
Myingyan
Pakokku
Kyaukse
SHAN PLATEAU
Pagan
Chauk
Meiktila
Taunggyi
Yenangyaung
Sittwe
Minbu
Magwe
Yamethin
Oyster I.
Taungdwingyi
Pyinmana
Loikaw
Salween
Kyaukpyu
Ramree I.
Thayetmyo
Allanmyo
Cheduba I.
Prome
Toungoo
Sandoway
Paungde
Pyu
Myanaung
Nyaunglebin
Letpadan
Pyuntaza
Henzada
Tharrawaddy
Thonze
Pegu
Kyaikto
Bassein
Insein
Kayan
Thaton
Syriam
Myaungmya
Twante
RANGOON
Martaban
Moulmeingyun
Kyaiklat
Moulmein
Mudon
Labutta
Bogale
Pyapon
Kyaikkami
Mouths of the Irrawaddy
Preparis I.
Ye
Great Coco I.
Little Coco I.
North Andaman (to INDIA)
Tavoy
BILAUKTAUNG RANGE
Kadan I.
Mergui
MERGUI ARCHIPELAGO
Saganthit I.
Letsok-Aw I.
Kanmaw I.
Lanbi I.
Isthmus of Kra
Mali Hka
Nmai Hka
Chindwin
Irrawaddy
Shweli
Myitnge
Mekong
Sittang
Thaungyin
ARAKAN YOMA
N
0 200 km
0 200 miles

POPULATION

- over 1 000 000
- over 500 000
- over 100 000
- over 50 000
- over 10 000
- under 10 000

LAND HEIGHT

- 4000m/13 124ft
- 2000m/6562ft
- 1000m/3281ft
- 500m/1640ft
- 200m/656ft
- Sea Level

Forced labor

The practice of using slave labor in rural areas was officially banned in 2000. However, many groups, including the International Labor Organization, insist that the military authorities still regularly make use of slave laborers.

WORLD AFFAIRS

Joined UN in 1948

CP | IAEA | ASEAN | NAM | WTO

Burma's key relationship is with China, which backs the SPDC military regime and is a major supplier of weapons to the Burmese army. The relationship allows China access to the Indian Ocean and gives it influence over a regime dependent on its support. While Burma's neighbors fear that the arrangement could destabilize the whole of the Asia–Pacific region, many favor a policy of "constructive engagement" with the SPDC. In 1997, Burma was admitted to ASEAN, despite continuing concerns about its human rights record.

The EU and Western members of the UN have strongly condemned the human rights violations in Burma. In practice, however, the West has held an ambivalent position. Economic ties have expanded, particularly between SPDC-owned state enterprises and Western multinationals with an interest in Burmese offshore oil and gas drilling sectors. In mid-2003, however, the US imposed an import ban, widening the economic sanctions imposed in 1997.

CHRONOLOGY

From the 11th century, Burma's many ethnic groups came under the rule of three Tibeto-Burman dynasties, interspersed with periods of rule by the Mongols and the Mon. The Third Dynasty came into conflict with the British in India, sparking the Anglo-Burmese wars of 1824, 1852, and 1885.

- **1886** Burma becomes a province of British India.
- **1930–1931** Economic depression triggers unrest.
- **1937** Separation from India.
- **1942** Japan invades.
- **1945** Antifascist People's Freedom League (AFPFL), led by Aung San, helps Allies reoccupy country.
- **1947** UK agrees to Burmese independence. Aung San wins elections, but is assassinated.
- **1948** Independence under new prime minister, U Nu, who initiates socialist policies. Revolts by ethnic separatists, notably Karen liberation struggle.
- **1958** Ruling AFPFL splits into two. Shan liberation struggle begins.
- **1960** U Nu's faction wins elections.
- **1961** Kachin rebellion begins.

B

CHRONOLOGY *continued*

- **1962** Gen. Ne Win stages military coup. "New Order" policy of "Buddhist Socialism" deepens international isolation. Mining and other industries nationalized. Free trade prohibited.
- **1964** Socialist Program Party declared sole legal party.
- **1976** Social unrest. Attempted military coup. Ethnic liberation groups gain control of 40% of country.
- **1982** Nonindigenous people barred from public office.
- **1988** Thousands die in student riots. Ne Win resigns. Martial law. Aung San Suu Kyi, daughter of Aung San, and others form NLD. Gen. Saw Maung leads military coup. State Law and Order Restoration Council (SLORC) takes power. Ethnic resistance groups form Democratic Alliance of Burma.
- **1989** Army arrests NLD leaders and steps up antirebel activity. Country officially renamed Union of Myanmar.
- **1990** Elections permitted. NLD wins landslide. SLORC remains in power, however. More NLD leaders arrested.
- **1991** Aung San Suu Kyi awarded Nobel Peace Prize.
- **1992** Gen. Than Shwe takes over as SLORC leader.
- **1996** Student agitation over renewed repression of NLD.
- **1997** Ruling SLORC renamed State Peace and Development Council (SPDC). Burma joins ASEAN. US imposes sanctions and bans further investment.
- **1998** NLD sets deadline for convening parliament; junta refuses.
- **1999** Aung San Suu Kyi rejects conditions set by SPDC for visiting the UK to see her husband, Michael Aris, who dies of cancer.
- **2000** Junta and NLD begin talks.
- **2003** Aung San Suu Kyi detained once more, after a year's freedom. US bans imports from Burma.

AID

Recipient

$121m (receipts) | Down 5% in 2002

Moves in 2000 to begin talks with the democratic opposition were welcomed by the UN, but were not enough to lift the sanctions on aid imposed in 1988. Some humanitarian assistance is provided through agencies such as WHO. Japan led the way in rewarding Burma's conciliatory gestures and became the largest single donor, but in 2003 joined countries suspending aid when Aung San Suu Kyi was rearrested.

DEFENSE

No compulsory military service

$2.84bn | Up 27% in 2002

BURMESE ARMED FORCES

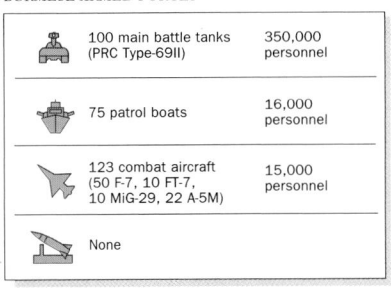

100 main battle tanks (PRC Type-69II)	350,000 personnel
75 patrol boats	16,000 personnel
123 combat aircraft (50 F-7, 10 FT-7, 10 MiG-29, 22 A-5M)	15,000 personnel
None	

The military authorities have steadily increased the country's military power, doubling the size of the army and obtaining modern weapons and military technology from around the world, primarily from China, which since 1989 has delivered arms worth over $1 billion to Burma, including tanks and jet fighters.

Burma's growing military capability is used mainly to control internal dissent, and the army has suppressed most ethnic insurgent campaigns by utilizing its military superiority and cutting numerous deals with rebel leaders. Neighboring states now assist in combating the remaining militant groups. The army is accused of human rights abuses and of forcibly recruiting underage soldiers.

ECONOMICS

Inflation 25% p.a. (1990–2001)

$46bn | 6.42 kyats (6.201)

SCORE CARD

- World GNP Ranking 52nd
- GNP per Capita $1000
- Balance of Payments ....–$309m
- Inflation 57.1%
- Unemployment 5%

EXPORTS

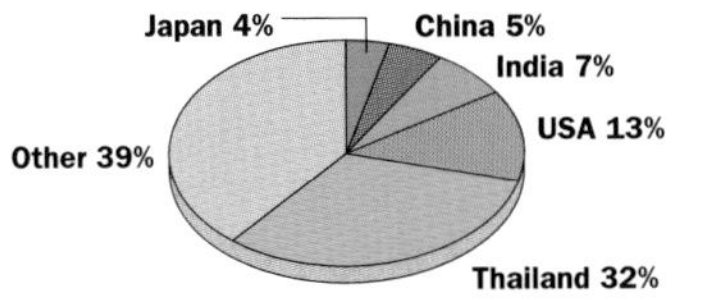
Japan 4%
China 5%
India 7%
USA 13%
Other 39%
Thailand 32%

IMPORTS

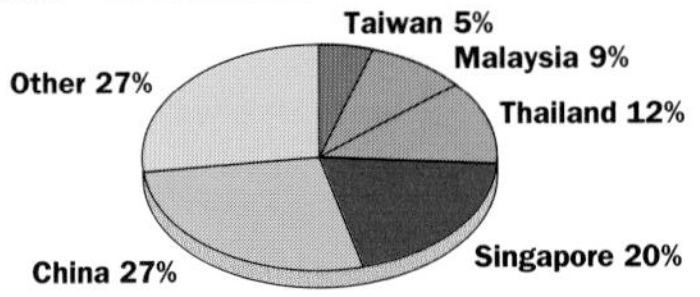
Taiwan 5%
Malaysia 9%
Other 27%
Thailand 12%
China 27%
Singapore 20%

Strengths

Very rich in natural resources: fertile soil, rich fisheries, timber including diminishing teak reserves, gems, offshore natural gas, and oil.

Weaknesses

Shortage of skilled workforce. Huge external debt. Rudimentary financial systems and institutions. Nationwide black market. Dependence on imported manufactures. Economic sanctions.

Profile

Burma's economy is agriculture-based and functions mainly on a cash and barter system. Its key industries are controlled by military-run state enterprises. Every aspect of economic life is permeated by a black market, where prices are rocketing – a reaction to official price controls.

ECONOMIC PERFORMANCE INDICATOR

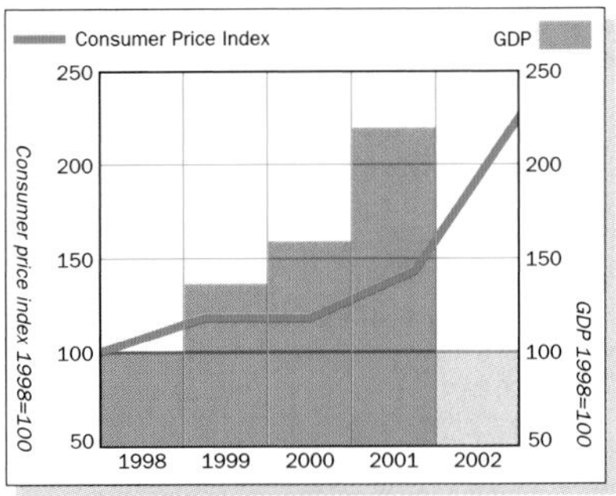
Consumer Price Index
GDP
Consumer price index 1998=100
GDP 1998=100
250
200
150
100
50
1998
1999
2000
2001
2002

The SPDC's open-door market-economy policy since 1989 has brought a flood of foreign investment in oil and gas (by Western companies), and in forestry, tourism, and mining (by Asian companies). The resulting boom in trade with China has turned less developed Upper Burma into a thriving business center. The northeastern border states account for about 60% of the world's heroin; a narcotics-eradication program is encouraging farmers to grow food crops instead of opium poppies. The US banned imports from Burma in 2003, particularly affecting the textile and garment industries.

BURMA : MAJOR BUSINESSES

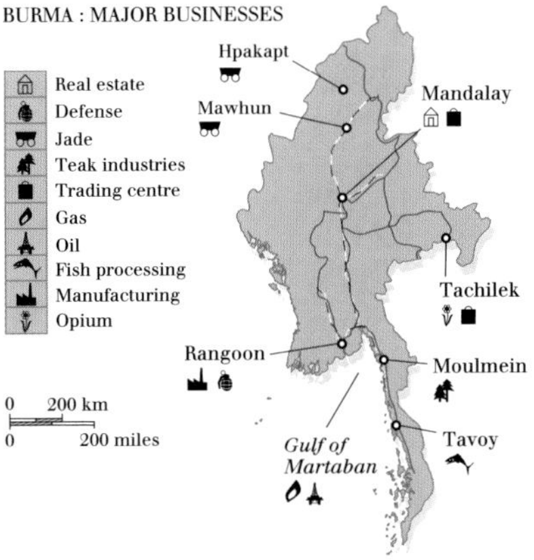
Real estate
Defense
Jade
Teak industries
Trading centre
Gas
Oil
Fish processing
Manufacturing
Opium
Hpakapt
Mawhun
Mandalay
Tachilek
Rangoon
Moulmein
Tavoy
Gulf of Martaban
0 200 km
0 200 miles

B

RESOURCES

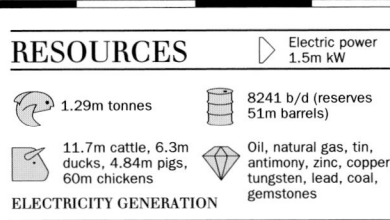

Electric power 1.5m kW

1.29m tonnes

8241 b/d (reserves 51m barrels)

11.7m cattle, 6.3m ducks, 4.84m pigs, 60m chickens

Oil, natural gas, tin, antimony, zinc, copper, tungsten, lead, coal, gemstones

ELECTRICITY GENERATION

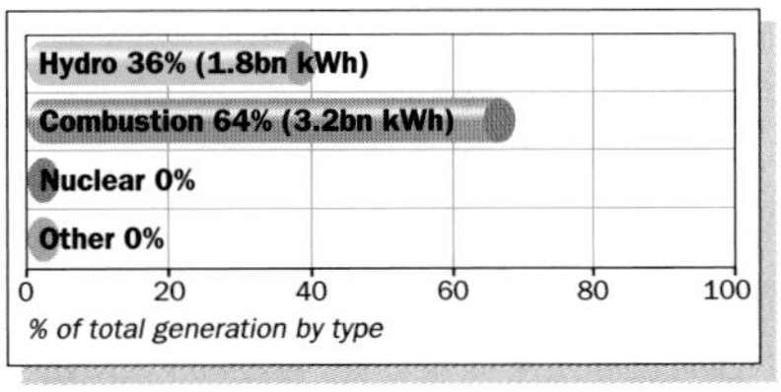
Hydro 36% (1.8bn kWh)
Combustion 64% (3.2bn kWh)
Nuclear 0%
Other 0%
0
20
40
60
80
100
% of total generation by type

Burma is one of the world's largest teak exporters. It is also a producer of pearls, rubies, and other gems. Extraction of oil and gas desposits is mostly funded from abroad, though public pressure in the West has seen a fall in investment in Burma.

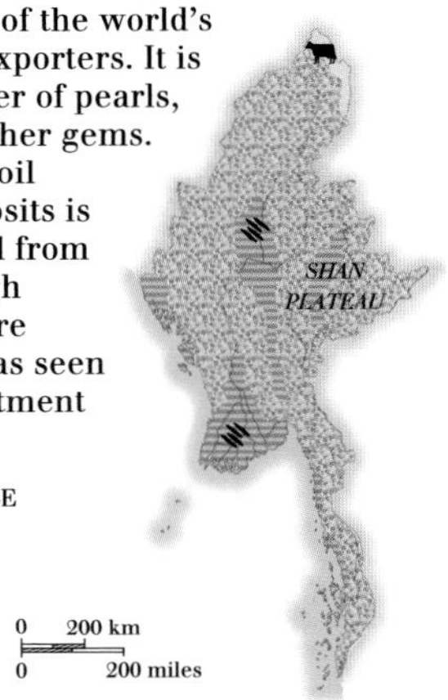
SHAN PLATEAU
0 200 km
0 200 miles

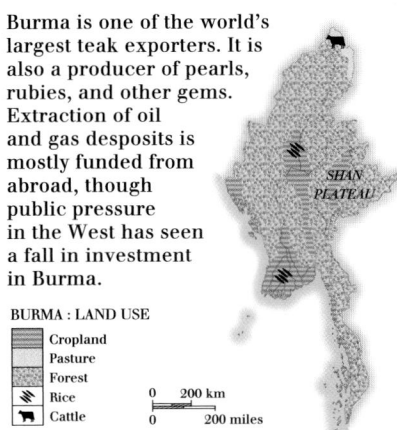

BURMA : LAND USE

Cropland
Pasture
Forest
Rice
Cattle

ENVIRONMENT

Sustainability rank: 90th

0.3%

0.2 tonnes per capita

ENVIRONMENTAL TREATIES

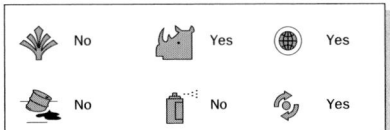

No · Yes · Yes

No · No · Yes

Deforestation is a major issue; Chinese firms have open logging concessions. The world's largest tiger reserve was created in 2004 in northern Burma.

MEDIA

TV ownership low

Daily newspaper circulation 9 per 1000 people

PUBLISHING AND BROADCAST MEDIA

There are 5 daily newspapers, including *Myanma Alin* and *New Light of Myanmar*

2 state-controlled services

1 state-controlled service

Political dissent of any kind is a criminal offense. An underground prodemocracy press produces antigovernment material.

CRIME

Death penalty in use

53,195 prisoners

Down in 1999

CRIME RATES

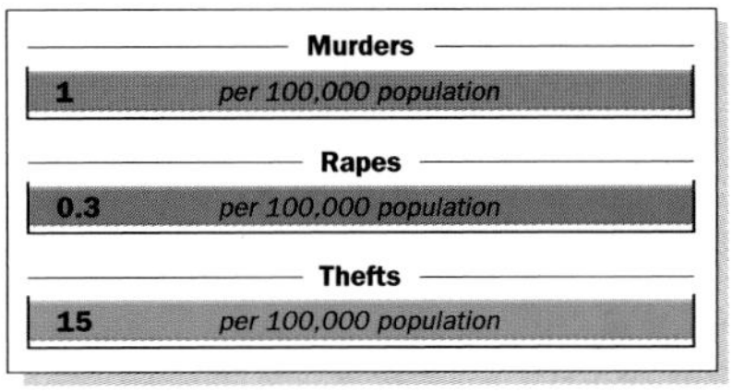
Murders
1 per 100,000 population
Rapes
0.3 per 100,000 population
Thefts
15 per 100,000 population

Even compared with similar totalitarian regimes, levels of bribery, corruption, embezzlement, and black marketeering are high. The state is guilty of illegal activity. The UN reports regularly on human rights abuses against civilians, and the murder of innocent civilians including children, women, Buddhist monks, students, members of ethnic minorities, and political dissidents.

There is a nominal civilian judicial system in Burma, but in practice all judges and lawyers are appointed by the junta and all legal functions are executed by the SPDC. The most common charge is that of sedition against the state or the army under the 1975 "Law to Protect the State from Destructionists." Among the SPDC's frequent arbitrary "notices" is Order 2/88, prohibiting assemblies of more than five persons. Most detainees have no legal rights of representation and are either jailed, used as forced labor, or put under house arrest without public trial. Amnesty International is banned.

EDUCATION

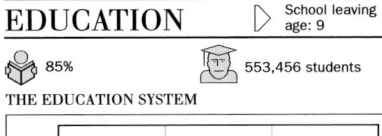

School leaving age: 9

85%

553,456 students

THE EDUCATION SYSTEM

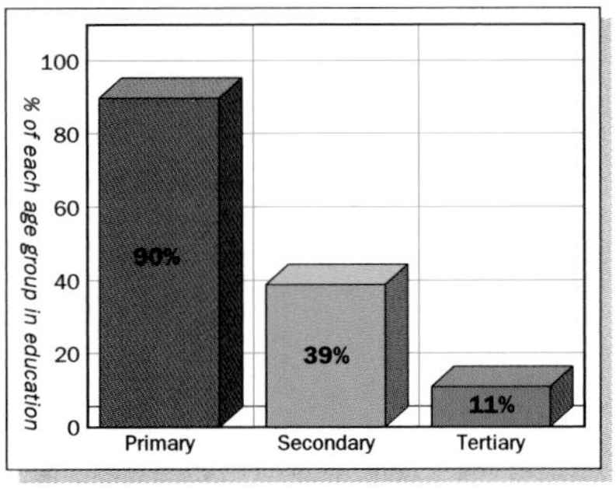
100
80
60
40
20
0
% of each age group in education
90%
39%
11%
Primary
Secondary
Tertiary

The education system offers 11 years of schooling; the first five are compulsory. A shortage of teachers, many of whom have left or are in jail, has disrupted education. Ethnic-language schools are discouraged. All but two universities were closed in the late 1990s by the regime, but quietly reopened in 2000. The NLD has criticized the shortened and "sanitized" courses on offer.

HEALTH

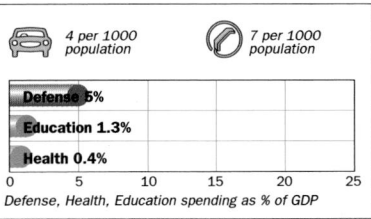

Welfare state health benefits

1 per 3241 people

Malaria, fevers, heart and diarrheal diseases

Health services are well developed and staff well trained, but provision is not comprehensive. Leprosy has a high prevalence in Burma, though programs to target the disease have helped bring the level down dramatically since the 1970s. It still has the third-highest rate of infection in Asia. The growing number of AIDS cases is largely due to migrant prostitution across the Thai–Burmese border, putting an additional strain on health facilities.

SPENDING

GDP/cap. increase

CONSUMPTION AND SPENDING

4 per 1000 population

7 per 1000 population

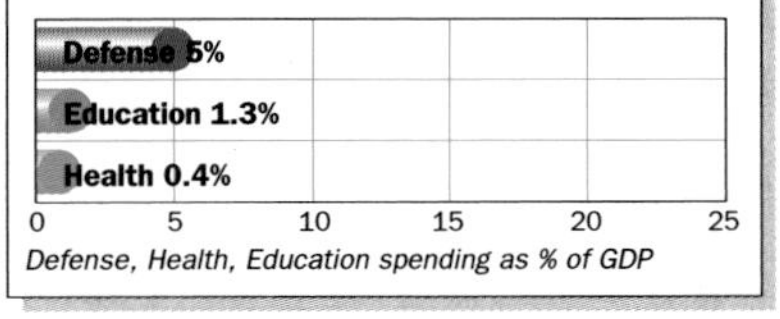
Defense 5%
Education 1.3%
Health 0.4%
0
5
10
15
20
25
Defense, Health, Education spending as % of GDP

The state monopoly of the production and distribution of goods by rationing under Gen. Ne Win's administration led to an increase in corruption and the rise of a nationwide black market, with huge disparities between official and unofficial prices. Only the military elite and their supporters could afford to live well. The situation has not changed significantly since 1988. Giant military enterprises grouped under a Defense Services holding company now reap wealth and distribute privileges for a minority. Nevertheless, traditional social and economic mobility still exists. Climbing the socioeconomic ladder is mainly a matter of loyalty to the military. Dissidents forced out of their jobs and hill tribes form the poorest groups. Officially, 23% of the population live in poverty.

WORLD RANKING

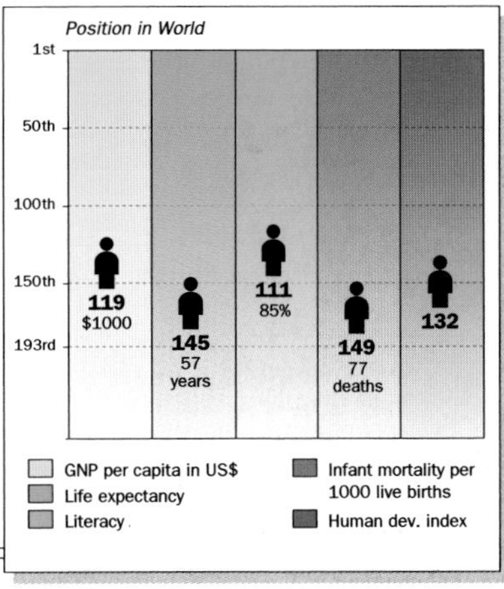
Position in World
1st
50th
100th
150th
193rd
119
$1000
145
57
years
111
85%
149
77
deaths
132
GNP per capita in US$
Life expectancy
Literacy
Infant mortality per 1000 live births
Human dev. index

BURUNDI

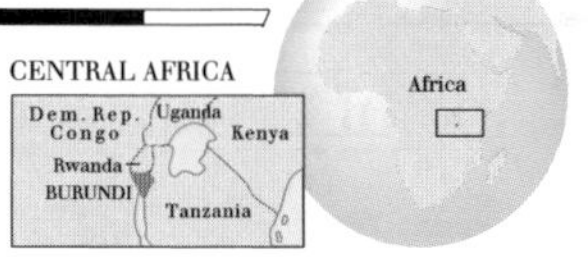

CENTRAL AFRICA
Dem. Rep. Congo
Uganda
Kenya
Rwanda
BURUNDI
Tanzania
Africa

B

OFFICIAL NAME: Republic of Burundi **CAPITAL:** Bujumbura
POPULATION: 6.8 million **CURRENCY:** Burundi franc **OFFICIAL LANGUAGES:** French and Kirundi

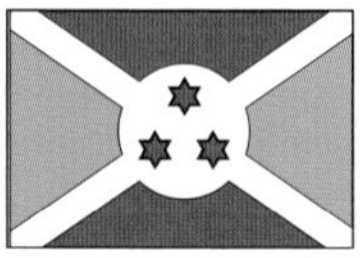

1962
1962
July 1
RU
+2
+257
.bi

LANDLOCKED BURUNDI lies just south of the equator on the Nile–Congo watershed. Lake Tanganyika forms part of its border with the Democratic Republic of the Congo (DRC). Tension between the Hutu majority and the dominant Tutsi minority remains the main factor in politics. The current political unrest dates from October 1993, when the assassination of the first Hutu president in a coup by the Tutsi-dominated army sparked terrible violence.

Pig farming and fish ponds. *Much of the population depends on subsistence farming.*

CLIMATE

Tropical wet and dry

WEATHER CHART FOR BUJUMBURA

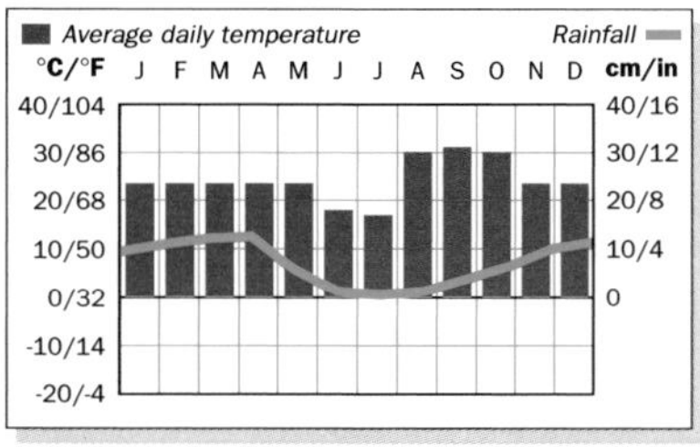

Average daily temperature
Rainfall
°C/°F J F M A M J J A S O N D cm/in
40/104
30/86
20/68
10/50
0/32
-10/14
-20/-4
40/16
30/12
20/8
10/4
0

Burundi is temperate with high humidity, much cloud, and frequent heavy rain. The highlands have frost.

TRANSPORTATION

Drive on right

Bujumbura International 69,191 passengers

Has no fleet

THE TRANSPORTATION NETWORK

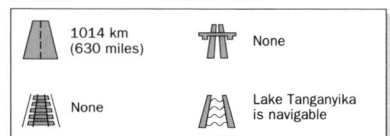

1014 km (630 miles)	None
None	Lake Tanganyika is navigable

The dense road network has been rehabilitated. There are plans for a railroad to link Burundi with Rwanda, Uganda, and Tanzania.

TOURISM

Visitors : Population 1:189

36,000 visitors

Up 20% in 2001

MAIN TOURIST ARRIVALS

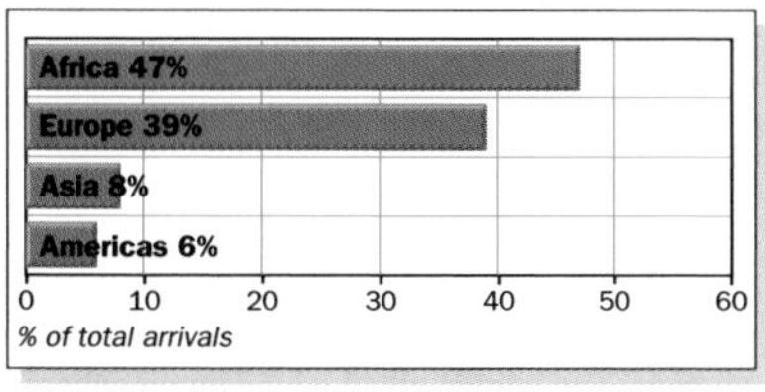

Africa 47%
Europe 39%
Asia 8%
Americas 6%
0 10 20 30 40 50 60
% of total arrivals

A lack of basic infrastructure and violent political strife have deterred tourists. The industry has limited potential, since Burundi lacks its neighbors' spectacular scenery and game parks.

PEOPLE

Pop. density high

Kirundi, French, Kiswahili

265/km² (687/mi²)

THE URBAN/RURAL POPULATION SPLIT

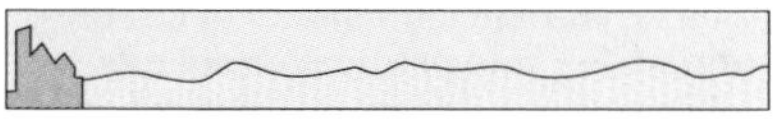

10%
90%

ETHNIC MAKEUP

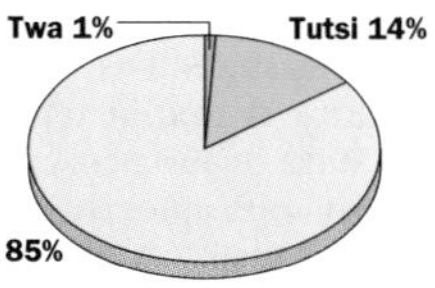

Twa 1%
Tutsi 14%
Hutu 85%

Burundi's history has been marked by violent conflict between the majority Hutu and the Tutsi, formerly the political elite, who still control the army. Large-scale massacres have occurred repeatedly over the past few decades. Hundreds of thousands of people, mostly Hutu, have been killed in political and ethnic conflict since 1993. The Twa pygmy minority, however, has not been greatly affected.

Most Burundians are subsistence farmers. The vast majority of the population are Roman Catholic.

POLITICS

In transition

L. House 2002/2004
U. House 2002/2004

President Domitien Ndayizeye

AT THE LAST ELECTION

Transitional National Assembly 170 seats

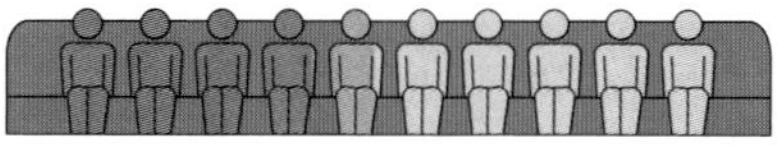

38% Frodebu **10% Uprona** **52% Others**

Frodebu = Front for Democracy in Burundi
Uprona = Union for National Progress

The Transitional National Assembly consists of members of all parties that signed the Arusha peace accord, and members of "civil society."

Transitional Senate 51 seats

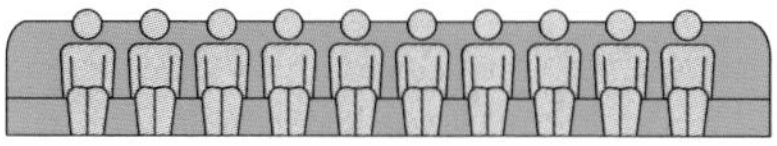

The indirectly elected Transitional Senate comprises 24 Hutus, 24 Tutsis, and three Twas, as formulated under the 2000 Arusha peace accord.

After a series of coups, the imposition of a one-party state in 1981, and widespread ethnic violence, Burundi adopted a multiparty system in 1992 under Tutsi coup leader Pierre Buyoya. The first Hutu president, Melchior Ndadaye of Frodebu, was assassinated in 1993, and by 1994 Burundi had plunged into a vicious civil war between Hutu militias and the Tutsi-dominated army. Buyoya staged another coup in 1996, agreeing in 1998 to a transitional constitution. A joint Hutu–Tutsi transitional government was installed in 2001 amid ongoing fighting. Two years later Buyoya handed over to his Hutu deputy Domitien Ndayizeye. Sporadic fighting continues, exacerbated by ethnic conflict in the DRC, with various cease-fire attempts.

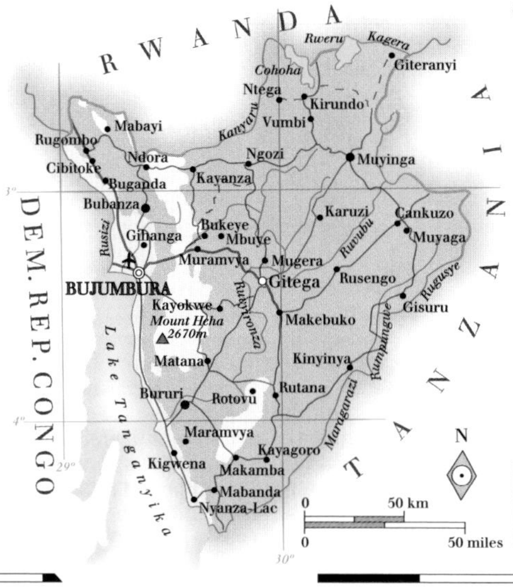

RWANDA
TANZANIA
DEM. REP. CONGO
Lake Tanganyika
Rweru
Kagera
Giteranyi
Cohoha
Ntega
Kirundo
Vumbi
Mabayi
Kanyaru
Rugombo
Ngozi
Muyinga
Cibitoke
Ndora
Bugända
Kayanza
Bubanza
Karuzi
Cankuzo
Gihanga
Bukeye
Mbuye
Muyaga
Rusizi
Muramvya
Mugera
BUJUMBURA
Gitega
Rusengo
Kayokwe
Mount Heha 2670m
Ruvyironza
Makebuko
Gisuru
Matana
Kinyinya
Rutana
Bururi
Rotovu
Maramvya
Kayagoro
Kigwena
Makamba
Mabanda
Nyanza-Lac
N
0 50 km
0 50 miles

BURUNDI

Total Area : 27 830 sq. km (10 745 sq. miles)

LAND HEIGHT

2000m/6562ft
1000m/3281ft
500m/1640ft

POPULATION

over 100 000
over 50 000
over 10 000
under 10 000

B

WORLD AFFAIRS

Joined UN in 1962

ACP | CEPGL | COMESA | OIF | AU

In 2003 the warring factions agreed to the formation of an African peacekeeping force for Burundi.

AID

Recipient

$172m (receipts) | Up 26% in 2002

Years of war have left Burundi dependent on international aid. In 2004 donors headed by the EU pledged $1 billion; most of this will relieve debt.

DEFENSE

No compulsory military service

$38m | Up 9% in 2002

The 45,000-strong army is run by Tutsi; the promotion of Hutu as officers helped cause the 1993 coup. Under recent peace deals rebel Hutu militias have from 2003 been integrated into the regular army. UNICEF began a program to remove child soldiers from these militias in 2001, but 8000 remained in 2004.

ECONOMICS

Inflation 13% p.a. (1990–2001)

$704m | 1060 Burundi francs (1075)

SCORE CARD

- World GNP Ranking 162nd
- GNP per Capita $100
- Balance of Payments .... –$3m
- Inflation .... –1.4%
- Unemployment 14%

STRENGTHS

Small quantities of gold and tungsten. Potential of massive nickel reserves and oil in Lake Tanganyika.

WEAKNESSES

Harsh regional sanctions since 1996 coup. Agricultural economy under pressure from high birthrate, war damage, and displacement. Little prospect of lasting political stability.

EXPORTS

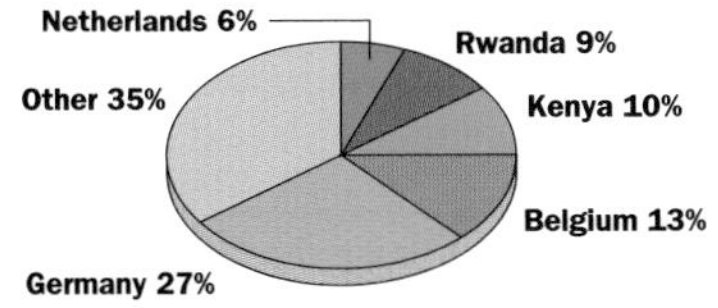
Netherlands 6%
Rwanda 9%
Other 35%
Kenya 10%
Belgium 13%
Germany 27%

IMPORTS

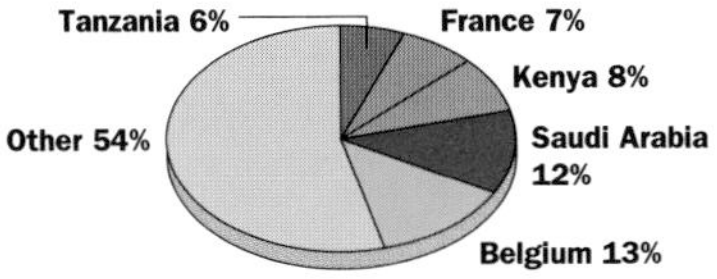
Tanzania 6%
France 7%
Kenya 8%
Other 54%
Saudi Arabia 12%
Belgium 13%

RESOURCES

Electric power 44,000 kW

9064 tonnes | Oil reserves not yet exploited

750,000 goats, 325,000 cattle, 4.3m chickens | Gold, tungsten, nickel, vanadium, uranium, oil

Burundi has around 5% of the world's nickel reserves. Extraction, however, is not economically viable. There are also deposits of gold and vanadium. Surveys in the 1980s detected oil reserves below Lake Tanganyika, but production has yet to begin. Burundi used to import gasoline from Iran and electricity from the DRC. New HEP plants at Mugera and Rwegura, in the north, are intended to meet most domestic electricity requirements.

ENVIRONMENT

Sustainability rank: 115th

6% (5% partially protected) | 0.04 tonnes per capita

Only 2% of Burundi is forest, and even this is under pressure from one of Africa's highest birthrates. Burundi suffers from the problems associated with deforestation, particularly soil erosion. Some soils are also being exhausted from overuse. Several tree-planting programs have been introduced. UNESCO is also running ecological education initiatives at village level, aimed at women farmers.

MEDIA

TV ownership low

Daily newspaper circulation 2 per 1000 people

PUBLISHING AND BROADCAST MEDIA

Le Renouveau du Burundi is published three times a week by the government

1 state-controlled service | 1 state-controlled service, some independent stations

Pro-Hutu/anti-Tutsi radio stations have been broadcasting since 1994. Radio Umwizero, an EU-funded station promoting peace, was launched in 1996.

CRIME

Death penalty in use

8647 prisoners | Crime is rising

Burundi has an appalling human rights record. There have been frequent massacres of Hutu by the army. The worst pogroms occurred in 1972, 1988, 1993, and 1994.

EDUCATION

School leaving age: 12

50% | 6289 students

Elementary schooling begins at six, and is compulsory to age 12. Civil war has prevented thousands of children from attending school. There is one state-run university.

CHRONOLOGY

From the 16th century, Burundi (formerly Urundi) was ruled by the minority Tutsi with the majority Hutu as their serfs. Merged with Rwanda, Burundi was controlled by Germany from 1884 and by Belgium from 1919.

- **1959** Split from Rwanda.
- **1962** Independence.
- **1966** Army overthrows monarchy.
- **1972** 150,000 Hutu massacred.
- **1993** Ndadaye wins first free elections; killed four months later.
- **1996** Pierre Buyoya retakes power.
- **2000** Renewed violence. Arusha peace accord signed by most groups.
- **2001** Multiethnic transitional government appointed.
- **2003** Domitien Ndayizeye becomes president in peaceful transfer.

HEALTH

No welfare state health benefits

1 per 10,000 people | Communicable infections, parasitic diseases, AIDS

Over half of the population of Burundi are underfed, and over 30% do not have access to health services. By 2004, 6% of adults were living with HIV/AIDS.

SPENDING

GDP/cap. decrease

CONSUMPTION AND SPENDING

1 per 1000 population | *3 per 1000 population*

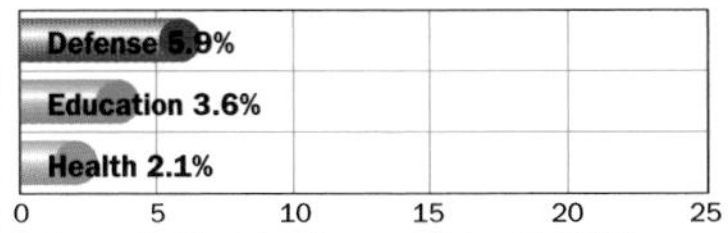
Defense 5.9%
Education 3.6%
Health 2.1%
0
5
10
15
20
25

Defense, Health, Education spending as % of GDP

Wealth is concentrated within the Tutsi political and business elite. Most of Burundi's people live at the level of subsistence farming.

WORLD RANKING

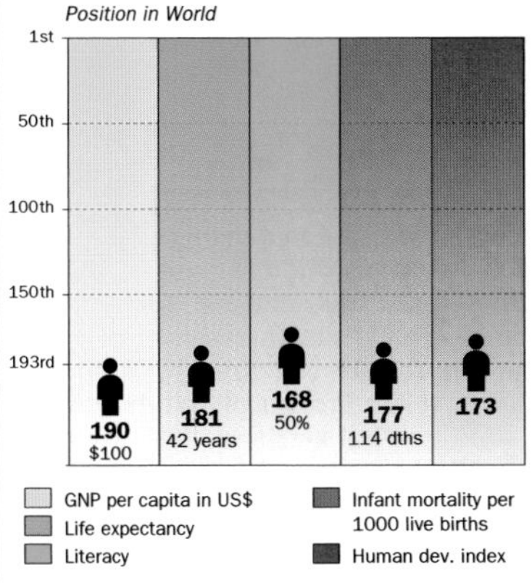
Position in World
1st
50th
100th
150th
193rd
190
$100
181
42 years
168
50%
177
114 dths
173
GNP per capita in US$
Life expectancy
Literacy
Infant mortality per 1000 live births
Human dev. index

CAMBODIA

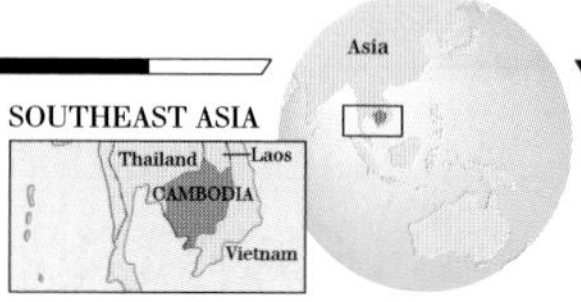

Asia
SOUTHEAST ASIA
Thailand
Laos
CAMBODIA
Vietnam

OFFICIAL NAME: Kingdom of Cambodia **CAPITAL:** Phnom Penh
POPULATION: 14.1 million **CURRENCY:** Riel **OFFICIAL LANGUAGE:** Khmer

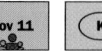

1953 | 1953 | Nov 11 | K | +7 | +855 | .kh

THE ANCIENT KINGDOM of Cambodia emerged from French colonial rule in 1953, only to be plunged into violent civil conflict. Under the extremist Khmer Rouge, headed by the infamous Pol Pot, the country endured one of the world's most brutal totalitarian regimes. Since the withdrawal of Vietnamese troops in 1989 the country has gradually returned to relative stability. The dominating geographic feature is the Tônlé Sap, or Great Lake, which drains into the Mekong River. Over three-quarters of Cambodia is forested, with mangroves lining the coast.

CLIMATE

Tropical monsoon

WEATHER CHART FOR PHNOM PENH

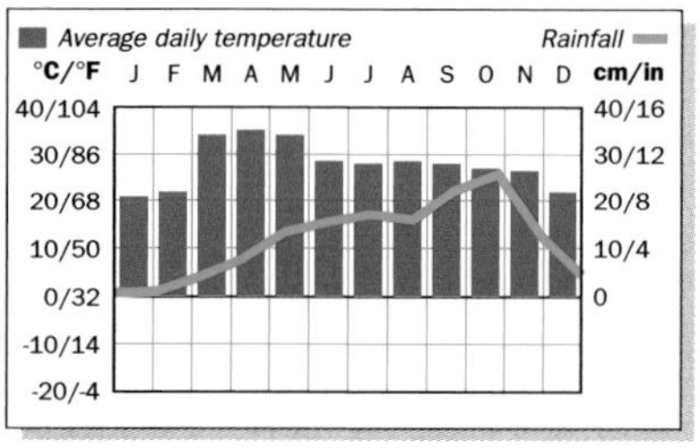

Average daily temperature
Rainfall
°C/°F J F M A M J J A S O N D cm/in
40/104 40/16
30/86 30/12
20/68 20/8
10/50 10/4
0/32 0
-10/14
-20/4

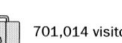

Cambodia has a varied climate. Low-lying regions have moderate rainfall and the most consistent year-round temperatures. The dry season from December to April is characterized by high temperatures and an average of eight hours of sunshine a day. From May to September, winds are southeasterly, while from October to April they are north or northeasterly. During the rainy season, Cambodia is sultry and humid. The monsoons in 2000 caused severe flooding of the Mekong River, which inundated Phnom Penh.

TRANSPORTATION

Drive on right

Pochentong, Phnom Penh 867,190 passengers

727 ships 2.43m grt

THE TRANSPORTATION NETWORK

1972 km (1225 miles)	None
603 km (375 miles)	3700 km (2299 miles)

Years of war led to a near-collapse of Cambodia's rail and road systems. Though international aid has helped fund key projects, the state of the country's roads remains appalling. The government has pledged to make reconstruction a priority. The Mekong River is vital for accessing the interior. Taxi-mopeds, bicycles, and rickshaws dominate urban transportation.

***Angkor Wat** stands in the ruins of the ancient city of Angkor, once the capital of the Khmer empire. It is now one of Cambodia's leading tourist attractions.*

TOURISM

Visitors : Population 1:20

701,014 visitors

Down 11% in 2003

MAIN TOURIST ARRIVALS

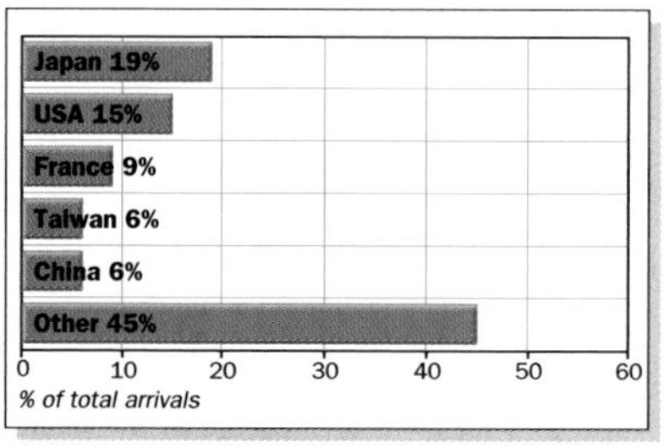

Japan 19%
USA 15%
France 9%
Taiwan 6%
China 6%
Other 45%
0 10 20 30 40 50 60
% of total arrivals

Cambodia, the center of the Khmer empire between 800 and 1400 CE, has some of the most impressive temples in southeast Asia. The most famous is Angkor Wat, near Siem Reap (Siemreab), which is now largely safe for tourists after the Khmer Rouge relinquished control of the area in 1998. Kidnappings and murders of tourists by the Khmer Rouge kept Cambodia off the backpacker circuit in the mid-1990s. Once the political situation is fully stabilized and landmines have been cleared, there is considerable potential, not just for adventurous independent travelers.

PEOPLE

Pop. density medium

Khmer, French, Chinese, Vietnamese, Cham

80/km² (207/mi²)

THE URBAN/RURAL POPULATION SPLIT

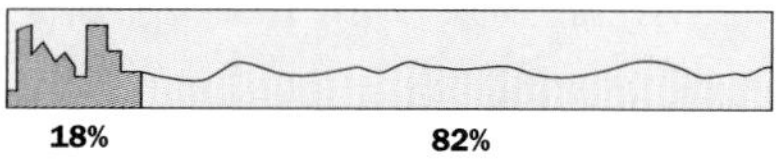

18%
82%

RELIGIOUS PERSUASION

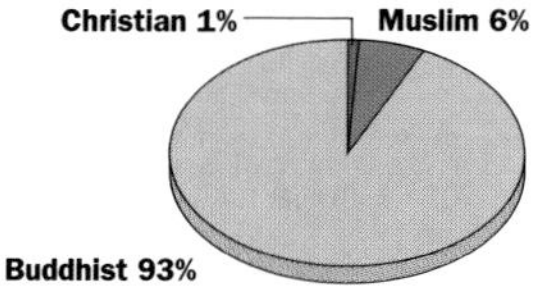

Christian 1%
Muslim 6%
Buddhist 93%

ETHNIC MAKEUP

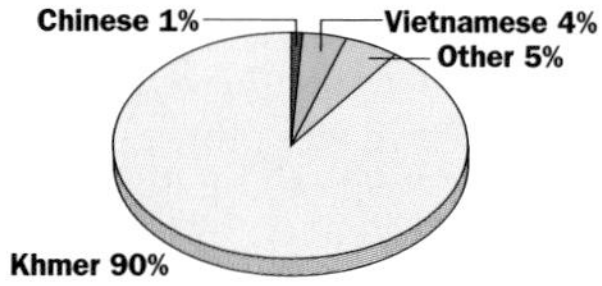

Chinese 1%
Vietnamese 4%
Other 5%
Khmer 90%

Cambodia underwent one of the 20th century's most horrific experiments in social transformation between 1975 and 1979 under Pol Pot's Khmer Rouge regime. Warfare, starvation, exhaustion, or execution killed one in eight of the population. Half a million more fled to Thailand. The Pol Pot regime's extreme radical beliefs led to the scrapping of money, possessions, and hierarchy. "Bourgeois" learning was despised, whereas peasants, soldiers of the revolution, and some industrial workers were officially given higher status. Boys and girls of 13 and 14 were taken from their homes, indoctrinated in the tenets of revolution, and allowed to kill those held guilty of bourgeois crimes. Violence at all levels was sanctioned in the name of revolution. The legacies of the regime are both the emigration of surviving professionals, and one of the world's highest rates of orphans and widows.

Religious and ethnic tensions are minimal, though there is a traditional hostility in Khmer culture toward ethnic Vietnamese.

POPULATION AGE BREAKDOWN

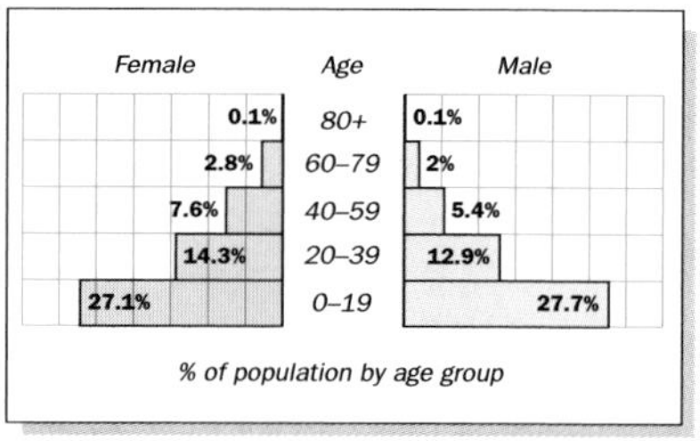

Female
Age
Male
0.1% 80+ 0.1%
2.8% 60–79 2%
7.6% 40–59 5.4%
14.3% 20–39 12.9%
27.1% 0–19 27.7%
% of population by age group

C

POLITICS

Multiparty elections

L. House 2003/2008
U. House 1999/2005

H.M. King Norodom Sihamoni

AT THE LAST ELECTION

National Assembly 123 seats

59% CPP | 21% Funcinpec | 20% SRP

CPP = Cambodian People's Party
Funcinpec = United National Front for an Independent Neutral Peaceful and Cooperative Cambodia
SRP = Sam Rainsy Party

Senate 61 seats

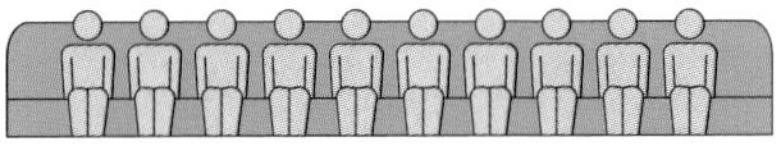

The membership of the Senate, first established in March 1999, was determined in proportion to the results of the 1998 elections: 53% CPP, 35% Funcinpec, 12% SRP

Cambodia is a constitutional monarchy.

Profile

Pol Pot and his Maoist extremist and murderous Khmer Rouge regime were ousted in 1979 by a Vietnamese invasion. The Khmer Rouge then joined a Western-backed anti-Vietnamese exile coalition with the supporters of the then Prince Sihanouk and the Khmer People's National Liberation Front (KPNLF), gaining UN recognition against the Vietnam-backed regime in Phnom Penh. In 1989 Vietnam withdrew its forces, paving the way for UN-supervised elections in 1993. The royalist Funcinpec were the main winners and King Sihanouk formed a coalition government; the Khmer Rouge remained outside this coalition, resuming armed resistance until its surrender in 1998. The strife-torn coalition meanwhile had descended into open hostility in 1997, when Hun Sen of the communist CPP ousted his co-prime minister Prince Ranariddh. Since then the CPP has failed to win the necessary two-thirds majority, forcing it to remain in coalition with Funcinpec. Postelection wrangling in 2003 led to political deadlock until the two parties struck a new deal in June 2004. King Sihanouk triggered a further crisis in October when he stated his desire to abdicate.

Main Political Issues

Settling accounts with Khmer Rouge
The Khmer Rouge, which had resumed its armed struggle in 1993, surrendered in 1998, after mass defections and the death of Pol Pot earlier that year. In 2004 parliament ratified a UN-backed plan for a tribunal to try Khmer Rouge leaders for crimes against humanity.

Political violence and intimidation
A high level of political violence and intimidation followed inconclusive legislative elections in 2003, with opposition figures targeted for assassination. The situation has been made worse by the lamentable state of the judicial system.

Prime Minister Hun Sen, who ousted his co-prime minister in 1997.

Norodom Sihanouk, a pivotal figure in society and politics, abdicated in 2004.

WORLD AFFAIRS

Joined UN in 1955

ASEAN | CP | OIF | Mekong River | NAM

During the civil war that followed the Vietnamese invasion of 1979, Cambodia was reduced to an international pariah. The Vietnam-puppet government was recognized by few countries outside the Soviet bloc, and its seat at the UN was allotted to the exiled resistance coalition, despite one of the components being the Khmer Rouge, which had inflicted appalling violence and suffering on Cambodians. The 1993 constitution aims to make the country a nonaligned "island of peace" with a neutral foreign policy.

Cambodia's relations with Vietnam remain problematic, fueled in part by the historic animosity between the two countries. The situation has improved since the late 1990s, and Cambodia's membership of ASEAN was confirmed in 1999.

Relations with Thailand were greatly affected by anti-Thai rioting in Phnom Penh in early 2003, after a Thai actress was (falsely) reported to have claimed that the Angkor Wat temples had been stolen from Thailand.

AID

Recipient

$487m (receipts) | Up 16% in 2002

Aid is crucial to Cambodia's economy, providing the bulk of government revenues. Widespread corruption and political instability prompted some countries to withhold assistance in the late 1990s, but NGOs continued working in the country, and Western donors made fresh pledges in 2000.

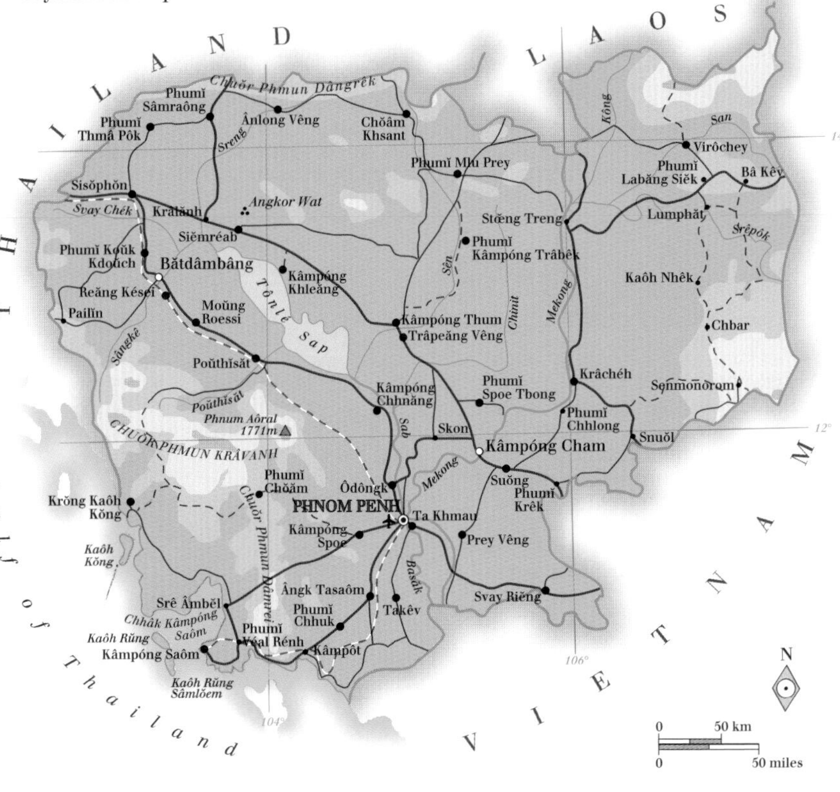
THAILAND
LAOS
VIETNAM
Gulf of Thailand
Sisŏphŏn
Bătdâmbâng
Angkor Wat
Siĕmréab
Tônle Sap
Pouŭthĭsăt
Phnum Aôral 1771m
CHUŎR PHNUM KRÂVANH
PHNOM PENH
Kâmpóng Cham
Krâchéh
Stœng Treng
Mekong
Kâmpóng Saôm
Kâmpôt
Ta Khmau
Prey Vêng
Svay Riĕng
Takêv
Snuŏl
Sênmonoŭrôm
Lumphăt
Vîrôchey
Bâ Kêv
Kaôh Nhêk
Chbar
Krŏng Kaôh Kŏng
Pailĭn
Ânlong Vêng
Chŏâm Khsant
Phumĭ Sâmraông
Phumĭ Thmâ Pŏk
Kâmpóng Thum
Kâmpóng Chhnăng
Kâmpóng Spœ
Ŏdôngk
Skon
Suŏng
Sab
Basăk
Chinit
Sên
Sân
Kông
Srêpŏk
Sângkê
Srê Âmbĕl
Ângk Tasaôm
Kaôh Kŏng
Kaôh Rŭng
Kaôh Rŭng Sâmlœm
Chuŏr Phnum Dângrêk
14°
12°
104°
106°
N
0 50 km
0 50 miles

Cambodia

Total Area : 181 040 sq. km (69 900 sq. miles)

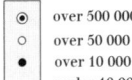

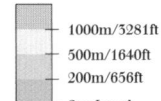

POPULATION	LAND HEIGHT
over 500 000	1000m/3281ft
over 50 000	500m/1640ft
over 10 000	200m/656ft
under 10 000	Sea Level

C

CHRONOLOGY

A former French protectorate, Cambodia gained independence in 1953 as a constitutional monarchy with Norodom Sihanouk as king.

- **1955** Sihanouk abdicates to pursue political career; takes title "prince."
- **1960** Sihanouk head of state.
- **1970** Right-wing coup led by Prime Minister Lon Nol deposes Sihanouk. Exiled Sihanouk forms Royal Government of National Union of Cambodia (GRUNC), backed by communist Khmer Rouge. Lon Nol proclaims Khmer Republic.
- **1975** GRUNC troops capture Phnom Penh. Prince Sihanouk head of state, Khmer Rouge assumes power. Huge numbers die under radical extremist regime.
- **1976** Country renamed Democratic Kampuchea. Elections. Sihanouk resigns; GRUNC dissolved. Khieu Samphan head of state; Pol Pot prime minister.
- **1978** December, Vietnam invades, supported by Cambodian communists opposed to Pol Pot.
- **1979** Vietnamese capture Phnom Penh. Khmer Rouge ousted by Kampuchean People's Revolutionary Party (KPRP), led by Pen Sovan. Khmer Rouge starts guerrilla war. Pol Pot held responsible for genocide and sentenced to death in absentia.
- **1982** Government-in-exile including Khmer Rouge and Khmer People's National Liberation Front, headed by Prince Sihanouk, is recognized by UN.
- **1989** Vietnamese troops withdraw.
- **1990** UN Security Council approves plan for UN-monitored cease-fire and elections.
- **1991** Signing of Paris peace accords. Sihanouk reinstated as head of state of Cambodia.
- **1993** UN-supervised elections won by royalist Funcinpec. Sihanouk takes title of "king."
- **1994** Khmer Rouge refuses to join peace process.
- **1996** Leading Khmer Rouge member Ieng Sary defects.
- **1997** Joint prime minister Hun Sen mounts coup against royalist copremier Prince Ranariddh.
- **1998** April, death of Pol Pot; June, Khmer Rouge surrender; July, elections; November, Hun Sen heads coalition with Funcinpec.
- **2001** Law approved on trials of Khmer Rouge leaders for atrocities committed by regime.
- **2003** Relatively peaceful elections won by CPP; coalition talks begin.
- **2004** CPP–Funcinpec coalition re-formed after 11-month stalemate.

DEFENSE

No compulsory military service

$87m

Up 5% in 2002

CAMBODIAN ARMED FORCES

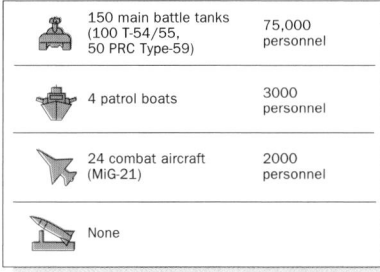

150 main battle tanks (100 T-54/55, 50 PRC Type-59)	75,000 personnel
4 patrol boats	3000 personnel
24 combat aircraft (MiG-21)	2000 personnel
None	

The defense priority in the early 1990s was to unify the command structures of the various armies. The surrender of Khmer Rouge forces in mid-1998 and the disintegration of remaining pockets of Khmer resistance later that year improved the prospects for a unified national army. Plans for demobilizing and rehabilitating 30,000 soldiers have been hindered by evidence of corruption.

Under the nominal overall structure of the Royal Cambodian Armed Forces, there remain in existence three main armies – the CPP's Cambodian People's Armed Forces, Funcinpec's Armée Nationale Sihanoukiste, and the KPNLF's Khmer People's National Liberation Armed Forces. The rivalries between them are still intense, with the first two in open conflict as recently as 1997–1998. Though well equipped, their soldiers are poorly paid. A conscription system exists, but it is not implemented.

Cambodia is leading the region in destroying surplus stocks of weapons to prevent their falling into the hands of terrorists.

ECONOMICS

Inflation 22% p.a. (1990–2001)

$3.76bn

3990 riels (3835)

SCORE CARD

World GNP Ranking	123rd
GNP per Capita	$300
Balance of Payments	–$64m
Inflation	3.2%
Unemployment	2%

EXPORTS

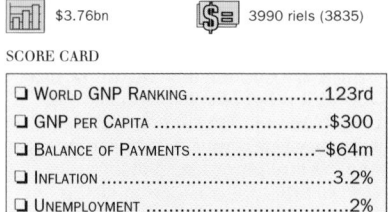

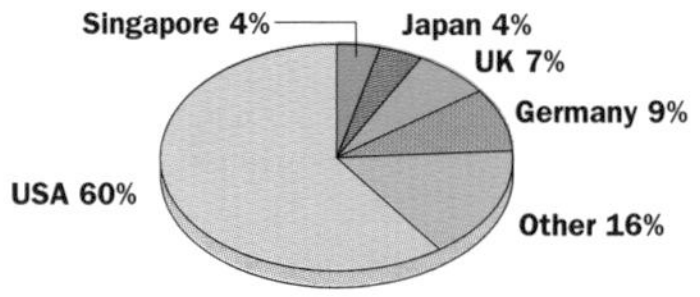
Singapore 4%
Japan 4%
UK 7%
Germany 9%
USA 60%
Other 16%

IMPORTS

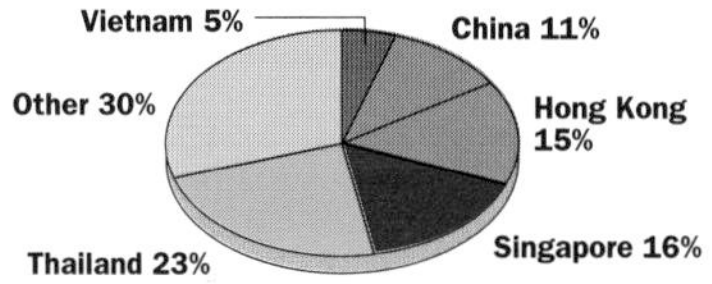
Vietnam 5%
China 11%
Other 30%
Hong Kong 15%
Thailand 23%
Singapore 16%

Strengths

Currently very few, as economy still recovering from long-running conflicts. Considerable future potential. Growth in tourism. Relatively unbureaucratic mentality. Self-sufficiency in rice achieved by 1999. Gems, especially sapphires. Possible offshore oil wealth. Export-oriented garment industry.

Weaknesses

Tiny tax base makes economic reform hard to implement. Deflation in 2001. Dependence on overseas aid: corruption at most levels of government limits its effectiveness. Disputes over land ownership rights.

ECONOMIC PERFORMANCE INDICATOR

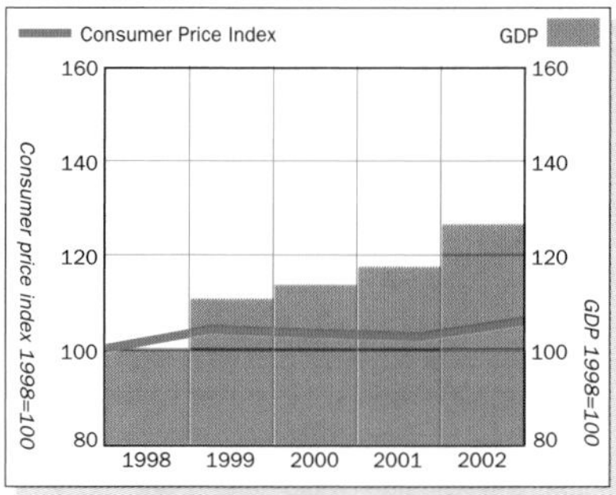
Consumer Price Index
GDP
160
140
120
100
80
Consumer price index 1998=100
GDP 1998=100
1998
1999
2000
2001
2002

Profile

A switch was made in the 1990s from Vietnamese-inspired central planning to encouragement of the private sector. The Asian financial crisis and internal turmoil affected funding after 1997. The country remains dependent on imports and growth has been slow. A period of deflation affected the country in 2001.

CAMBODIA : MAJOR BUSINESSES

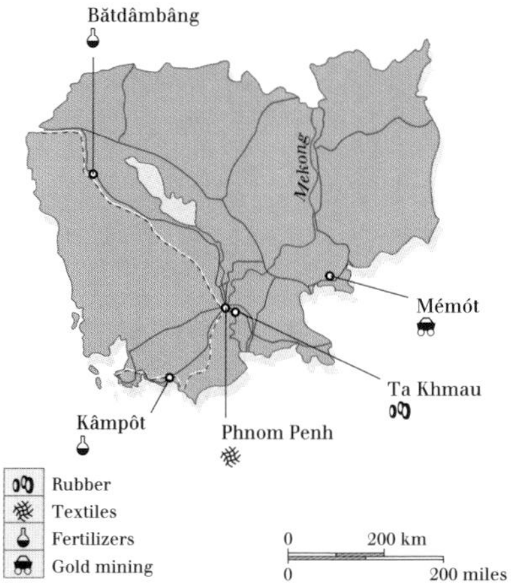
Bătdâmbâng
Mekong
Mémót
Ta Khmau
Kâmpôt
Phnom Penh
Rubber
Textiles
Fertilizers
Gold mining
0
200 km
0
200 miles

RESOURCES

Electric power 35,000 kW

412,700 tonnes

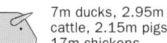

Not an oil producer

7m ducks, 2.95m cattle, 2.15m pigs, 17m chickens

Salt, phosphates, gemstones

Few resources are currently exploited, apart from tropical rainforest timber, particularly teak and rosewood, much of which is felled illegally.

ELECTRICITY GENERATION

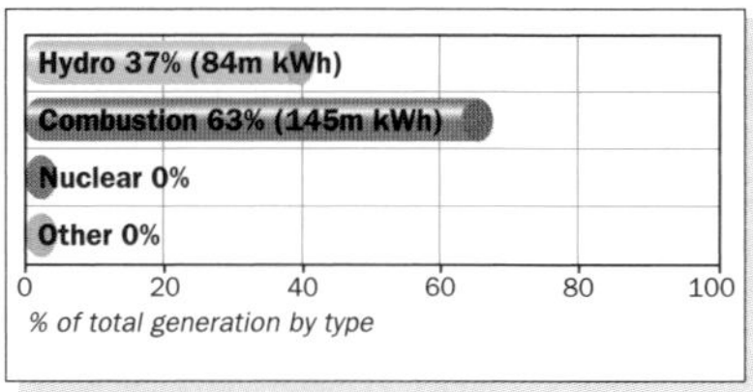
Hydro 37% (84m kWh)
Combustion 63% (145m kWh)
Nuclear 0%
Other 0%
0
20
40
60
80
100
% of total generation by type

CAMBODIA : LAND USE

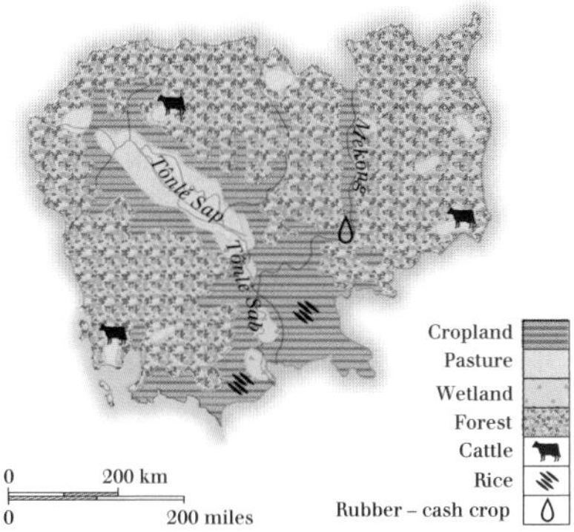
Tonle Sap
Tonle Sap
Mekong
Cropland
Pasture
Wetland
Forest
Cattle
Rice
Rubber – cash crop
0
200 km
0
200 miles

ENVIRONMENT

Sustainability rank: 97th

19% (14% partially protected)

0.05 tonnes per capita

ENVIRONMENTAL TREATIES

Yes	Yes	Yes
Yes	No	Yes

Deforestation is one of the most serious problems facing Cambodia. Illegal logging is the main culprit. Timber, one of the country's most valuable assets, was sold in huge quantities by all Cambodian factions to finance their war efforts. A moratorium on logging was declared at the end of 1992, but was largely ignored. Despite international pressure and efforts from 2000 to tighten controls, in many parts of the country logging is impossible to police. Tropical hardwoods extracted illegally from Cambodia find lucrative outlets through Thailand in particular. The environmental consequences – topsoil erosion and increased risk of flooding – are enormous and will hold back Cambodia's reconstruction.

MEDIA

TV ownership low

Daily newspaper circulation 2 per 1000 people

Phnom Penh has several independent TV stations in addition to the national network. Many, however, are reliant on party political support, which compromises their independence. King Sihanouk backs press freedoms, though they are not guaranteed by the state. Foreign radio can be received.

CRIME

No death penalty

6128 prisoners

Narcotics-related crime is rising

CRIME RATES

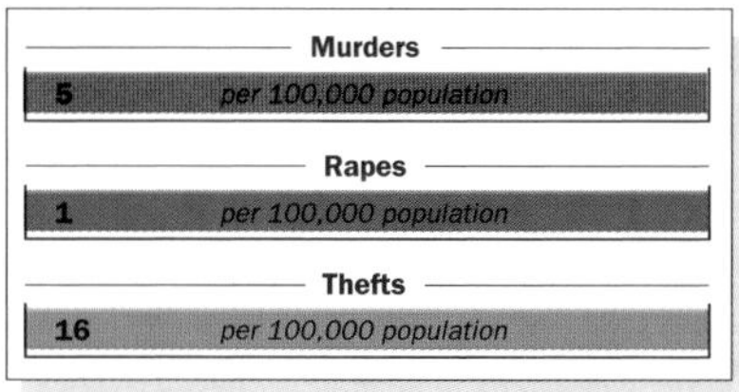
Murders
5 per 100,000 population
Rapes
1 per 100,000 population
Thefts
16 per 100,000 population

It is claimed that there has been a proliferation of narcotics trading, money laundering, and illegal banking operations. Mob killings go largely unremarked. Corruption in business is a major issue. Phnom Penh witnessed an increase in violent crime in the aftermath of the 1997 coup, owing to the spread of illegally owned firearms. Until the surrender of the Khmer Rouge in 1998, areas under its command, especially in the west around Pailin and Battambang, were particularly dangerous. Banditry remains rife and policing virtually nonexistent.

EDUCATION

School leaving age: 12

69%

25,416 students

THE EDUCATION SYSTEM

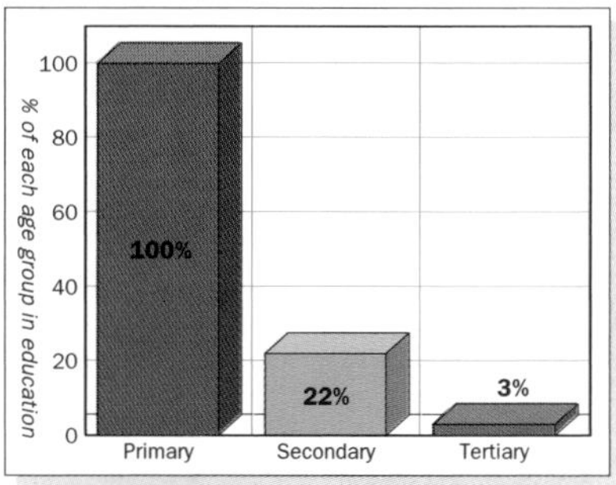
100
80
60
40
20
0
% of each age group in education
100%
22%
3%
Primary
Secondary
Tertiary

The government aims to provide a complete education system from primary to tertiary. Currently primary education is compulsory, and lasts for six years between the ages of six and 12. Only 5000 of Cambodia's 20,000 teachers survived the Pol Pot period; the Vietnamese-installed government trained or retrained about 40,000.

PUBLISHING AND BROADCAST MEDIA

There are 2 daily newspapers; only 10 newspapers and magazines publish regularly

6 services: 1 state-run, 5 independent

9 services: 1 state-run, 8 independent

HEALTH

No welfare state health benefits

1 per 3333 people

Circulatory and infectious diseases, cancers

The Cambodian health system was effectively destroyed in the Pol Pot period; only 50 doctors survived, and Cambodia's health indicators were among the worst in the world.

Conditions have since improved, but AIDS is widespread, affecting even children in rural areas. Infant mortality remains high, and malaria and cholera are endemic. In 2000, UNICEF helped mount an immunization campaign against tetanus, a major cause of neonatal mortality.

SPENDING

GDP/cap. increase

CONSUMPTION AND SPENDING

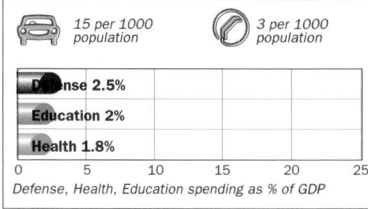

15 per 1000 population

3 per 1000 population

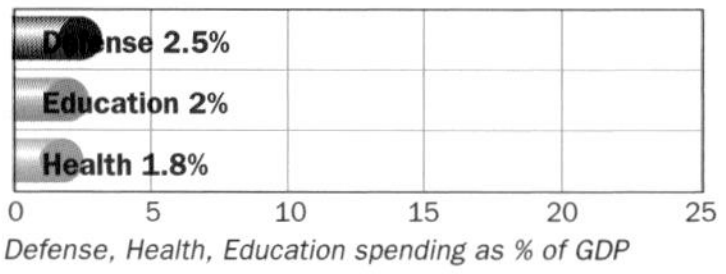
Defense 2.5%
Education 2%
Health 1.8%
0
5
10
15
20
25
Defense, Health, Education spending as % of GDP

New industries such as textiles, in which female garment workers may earn around $40 a month in vast workshops, help to attract migrants to the towns, though they risk unemployment and homelessness. Cambodians in rural areas face more severe poverty, exacerbated by land shortage.

WORLD RANKING

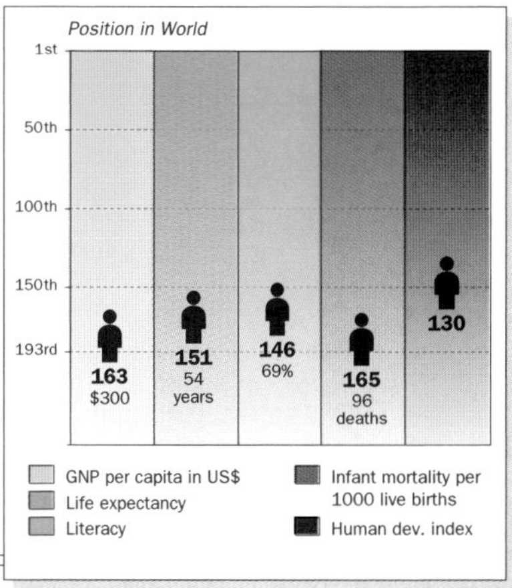
Position in World
1st
50th
100th
150th
193rd
163
$300
151
54
years
146
69%
165
96
deaths
130
GNP per capita in US$
Life expectancy
Literacy
Infant mortality per 1000 live births
Human dev. index

C

CAMEROON

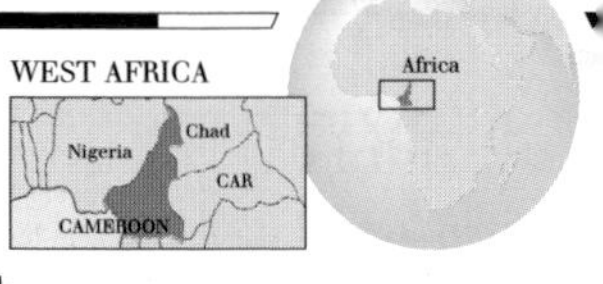
WEST AFRICA
Africa
Nigeria
Chad
CAR
CAMEROON

OFFICIAL NAME: Republic of Cameroon **CAPITAL:** Yaoundé
POPULATION: 16 million **CURRENCY:** CFA franc **OFFICIAL LANGUAGES:** French and English

1960 | 1961 | May 20 | CAM | +1 | +237 | .cm

LOCATED ON THE CENTRAL west African coast, over half of Cameroon is forested, with equatorial rainforest to the south and evergreen forest and wooded savanna north of the Sanaga River. Most cities are located in the south, though there are densely populated areas around Mount Cameroon, a dormant volcano. For 30 years Cameroon was effectively a one-party state. Democratic elections in 1992 returned the former ruling party to power.

Savanna landscape below Mindif Pic in Cameroon's far north. From here, the land slopes down to the hot, arid Lake Chad basin.

CLIMATE

Tropical equatorial

WEATHER CHART FOR YAOUNDÉ

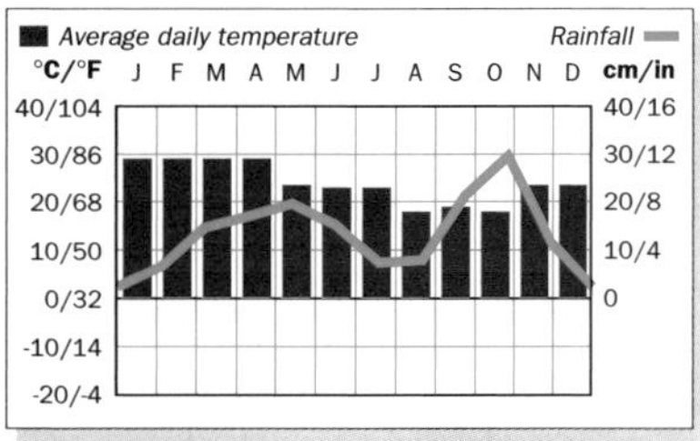
Average daily temperature
Rainfall
°C/°F J F M A M J J A S O N D cm/in
40/104
30/86
20/68
10/50
0/32
-10/14
-20/4
40/16
30/12
20/8
10/4
0

Climate varies from the equatorial south, with 500 cm (200 in) of rain a year, to the drought-beset Sahelian north.

TRANSPORTATION

Drive on right

Douala International 570,246 passengers

59 ships 16,700 grt

THE TRANSPORTATION NETWORK

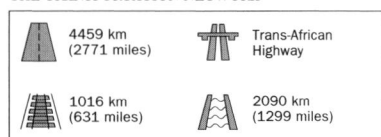

4459 km (2771 miles)

Trans-African Highway

1016 km (631 miles)

2090 km (1299 miles)

Major projects are the east–west Trans-African Highway and the realigning of the Douala–Nkongsamba railroad.

TOURISM

Visitors : Population 1:72

221,000 visitors

Up 275% in 2001

MAIN TOURIST ARRIVALS

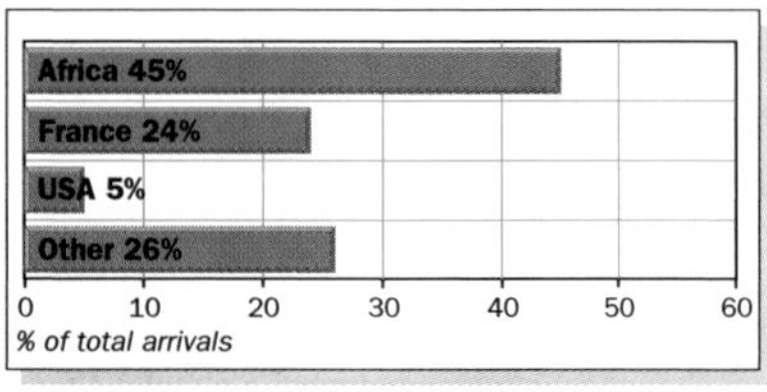
Africa 45%
France 24%
USA 5%
Other 26%
0 10 20 30 40 50 60
% of total arrivals

The government and Commonwealth are trying to boost visitor numbers, with a target of 500,000 a year. There are beach hotels near Kribi and package tours to northern game parks, but high levels of crime and corruption still deter many.

PEOPLE

Pop. density low

Bamileke, Fang, Fulani, French, English

34/km² (89/mi²)

THE URBAN/RURAL POPULATION SPLIT

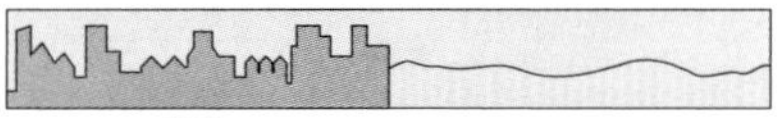
50%
50%

RELIGIOUS PERSUASION

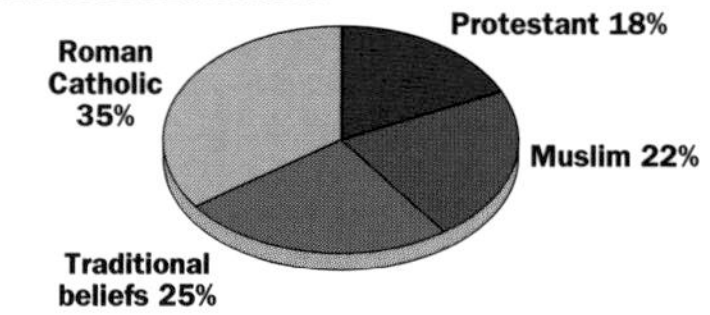
Protestant 18%
Roman Catholic 35%
Muslim 22%
Traditional beliefs 25%

Cameroon is ethnically diverse – there are 230 groups, no single group being dominant. The largest is the Bamileke of the center southwest, but it has never held political power. When President Ahidjo, a northern Fulani, retired, he was replaced by Paul Biya of the southeastern Bulu-Beti group. The north–south enmity which affects many other west African states is also present here, albeit diminished by the great ethnic diversity. There is growing tension between the French- and minority English-speaking communities over identity and related issues of exclusion.

POLITICS

Multiparty elections

2002/2007

President Paul Biya

AT THE LAST ELECTION

National Assembly 180 seats

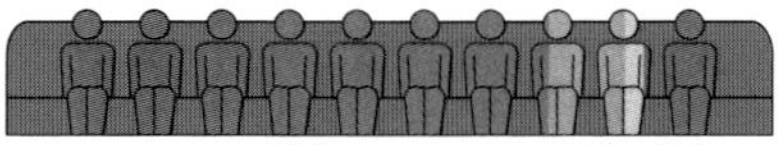
2% CDU
74% RDPC
12% SDF
12% Others

RDPC = Cameroon People's Democratic Rally **SDF** = Social Democratic Front **CDU** = Cameroon Democratic Union

A Senate is to be created under the 1995 constitution

Incumbent president Paul Biya's RDPC narrowly won control of the new parliament in multiparty elections in 1992 boycotted by the main opposition SDF. It has held on to power in the face of SDF claims of corruption, steadily increasing its majority in 1997 and again in 2002. Similarly, Biya's own reelections in 1992 and 1997 were condemned as the products of fraud and intimidation by SDF candidate John Fru Ndi.

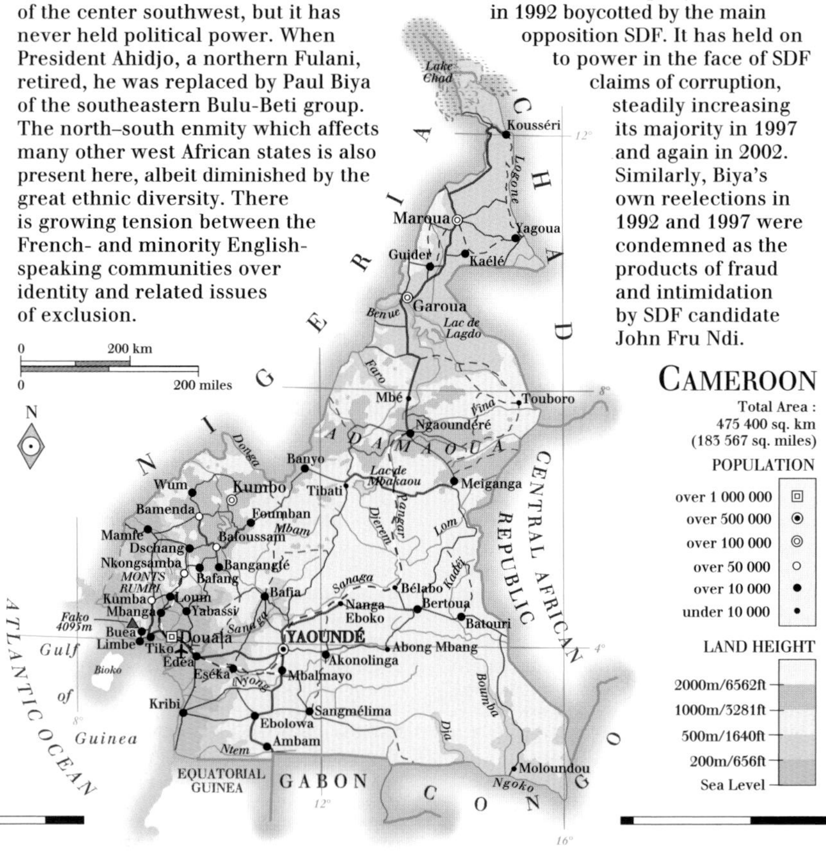
Lake Chad
CHAD
NIGERIA
Kousséri
Logone
Maroua
Yagoua
Guider
Kaélé
Benue
Garoua
Lac de Lagdo
Faro
Mbé
Touboro
Vina
Ngaoundéré
ADAMAOUA
Donga
Banyo
Lac de Mbakaou
Meiganga
Tibati
Wum
Kumbo
Bamenda
Foumban
Mbam
Mamfe
Bafoussam
Dschang
Nkongsamba
Bangangté
MONTS RUMPI
Bafang
Kumba
Loum
Mbanga
Yabassi
Fako 4095m
Buea
Limbe
Tiko
Douala
Edea
Bafia
Sanaga
Nanga Eboko
Bélabo
Kadei
Bertoua
Batouri
YAOUNDÉ
Abong Mbang
Akonolinga
Eséka
Nyong
Mbalmayo
Sangmélima
Kribi
Ebolowa
Ambam
Ntem
Dja
Boumba
Moloundou
Ngoko
Djerem
Mbéré
Lom
CENTRAL AFRICAN REPUBLIC
EQUATORIAL GUINEA
GABON
CONGO
Bioko
Gulf of Guinea
ATLANTIC OCEAN
0 200 km
0 200 miles
N
CAMEROON
Total Area : 475 400 sq. km (183 567 sq. miles)
POPULATION
over 1 000 000
over 500 000
over 100 000
over 50 000
over 10 000
under 10 000
LAND HEIGHT
2000m/6562ft
1000m/3281ft
500m/1640ft
200m/656ft
Sea Level

C

WORLD AFFAIRS

Joined UN in 1960

BDEAC | Comm | OIC | LCBC | FZ

Cameroon's most important relationship is with France, but it is fast becoming a regional center for oil exploitation.

A territorial dispute with Nigeria over the (largely anglophone) oil-rich Bakassi peninsula, where there were clashes in 1996 and 1998, remains an issue, despite there having been an international ruling in Cameroon's favor in 2002.

AID

Recipient

$632m (receipts)

Up 56% in 2002

France is by far the most important donor; it has twice paid Cameroon's back debts to the IMF to prevent its being blacklisted. The IMF agreed in 2000 to cancel $2 billion of debt if aid projects, many of which have been abandoned due to lack of funds, are completed.

DEFENSE

No compulsory military service

$122m

Up 3% in 2002

The 12,500-strong army has been active in supporting the regime and maintaining order in the face of prodemocratic protests since before independence. Military equipment and training come mainly from France. There is also a 9000-strong paramilitary gendarmerie.

ECONOMICS

Inflation 4.9% p.a. (1990–2001)

$8.75bn

539.2 CFA francs (571.2)

SCORE CARD

❑ WORLD GNP RANKING	93rd
❑ GNP PER CAPITA	$550
❑ BALANCE OF PAYMENTS	–$147m
❑ INFLATION	2.8%
❑ UNEMPLOYMENT	30%

STRENGTHS

US companies exploiting oil reserves. Chad–Cameroon oil pipeline project. Very diversified agriculture includes timber, cocoa, bananas, and coffee. Self-sufficiency in food. Strong informal sector. Private sector in relatively good state. Electricity production is 97% HEP.

WEAKNESSES

Massive fuel smuggling from Nigeria affects refinery profits. Inflated civil service. Widespread corruption.

EXPORTS

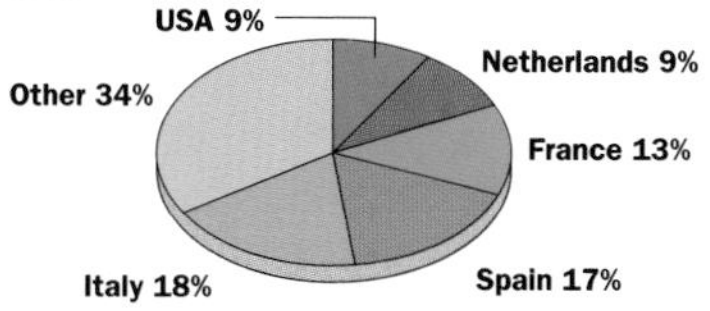
USA 9%
Netherlands 9%
France 13%
Spain 17%
Italy 18%
Other 34%

IMPORTS

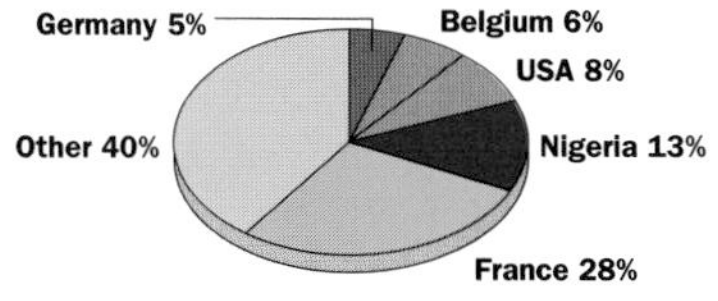
Germany 5%
Belgium 6%
USA 8%
Nigeria 13%
France 28%
Other 40%

RESOURCES

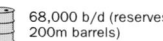

Electric power 900,000 kW

111,081 tonnes

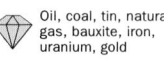

68,000 b/d (reserves 200m barrels)

5.9m cattle, 4.4m goats, 3.8m sheep, 31m chickens

Oil, coal, tin, natural gas, bauxite, iron, uranium, gold

New oil discoveries may bolster declining extraction rates. In spite of large bauxite deposits, much is imported for the Edea aluminum smelter, which uses a large share of electricity output.

ENVIRONMENT

Sustainability rank: 93rd

5% (2% partially protected)

0.4 tonnes per capita

The rate of commercial logging and the Cameroon–Chad oil pipeline constitute major threats to Cameroon's environment.

MEDIA

TV ownership medium

Daily newspaper circulation 0.5 per 1000 people

PUBLISHING AND BROADCAST MEDIA

There are 2 daily newspapers, the bilingual *Le Tribune du Cameroun* and *Le Quotidien*

3 services: 1 state-owned, 2 independent

2 services: 1 state-owned, 1 independent

There are frequent allegations of censorship and violence against journalists. English-language media are generally more outspoken.

CRIME

Death penalty in use

20,000 prisoners

Up sharply in 1996–1998

Armed robbery and burglary in Douala and Yaoundé are rising fast. The police are known to use torture.

EDUCATION

School leaving age: 12

68%

68,495 students

The French-speaking majority has failed in its attempt to take over the bilingual system. Cameroon has a high literacy rate compared with much of the rest of west and central Africa.

CHRONOLOGY

One of the great trading emporia of west Africa, Cameroon was divided between the French and British in 1919, after 30 years of German rule.

- ❑ **1955** Revolt; French kill 10,000.
- ❑ **1960** French sector independent.
- ❑ **1961** British south joins Cameroon (north joins Nigeria).
- ❑ **1982** Ahmadou Ahidjo, first president, dies; succeeded by Biya.
- ❑ **1983–1984** Coup attempts. Heavy casualties; 50 plotters executed.
- ❑ **1990** Declaration of multiparty state.
- ❑ **1992** Multiparty elections.
- ❑ **1997** President and ruling RDPC returned in disputed elections.
- ❑ **2000** World Bank funds pipeline project, despite environmental fears.
- ❑ **2001** Over 80% of indigenous forests allocated for logging.
- ❑ **2002** RDPC increases its majority.

HEALTH

No welfare state health benefits

1 per 10,000 people

Malaria, diarrheal and respiratory diseases, AIDS

A sharp fall in government health provision means that more people are using the private health sector or traditional practitioners.

SPENDING

GDP/cap. increase

CONSUMPTION AND SPENDING

8 per 1000 population

7 per 1000 population

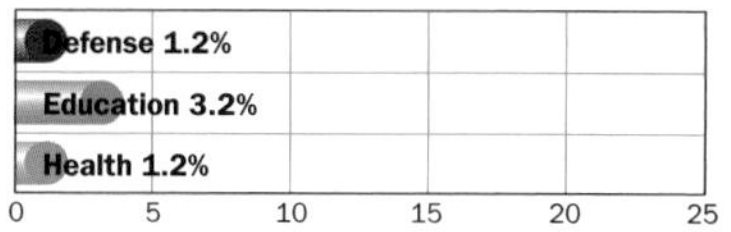
Defense 1.2%
Education 3.2%
Health 1.2%
0
5
10
15
20
25

Defense, Health, Education spending as % of GDP

Wealth is unevenly distributed and has been declining since the end of the 1980s oil boom. There is still a very wealthy, albeit small, sector of the population.

WORLD RANKING

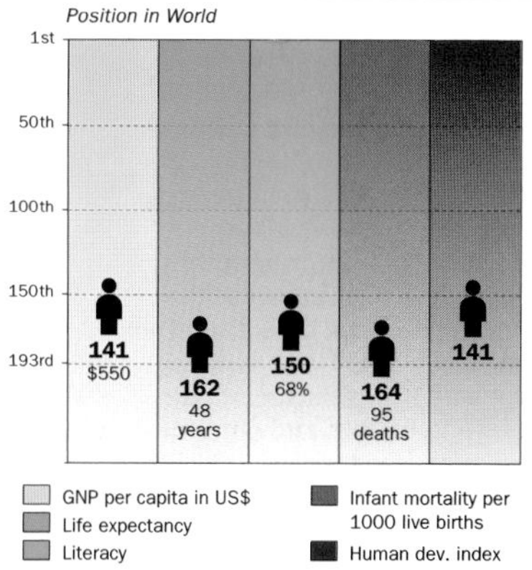
Position in World
1st
50th
100th
150th
193rd
141
$550
162
48
years
150
68%
164
95
deaths
141
GNP per capita in US$
Life expectancy
Literacy
Infant mortality per 1000 live births
Human dev. index

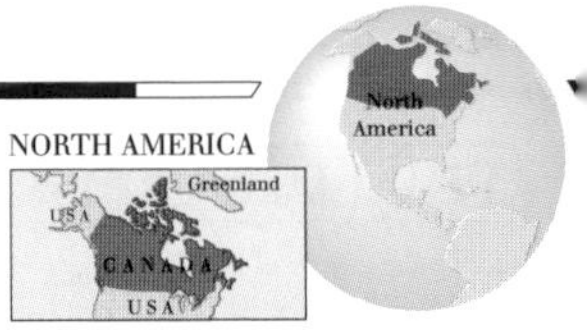
NORTH AMERICA
North America
Greenland
USA
CANADA
USA

CANADA

OFFICIAL NAME: Canada **CAPITAL:** Ottawa **POPULATION:** 31.5 million
CURRENCY: Canadian dollar **OFFICIAL LANGUAGES:** English and French

1867 | 1949 | July 1 | CDN | -3.5 to -8 | +1 | .ca

CANADA IS THE WORLD'S second-largest country, stretching north to Cape Columbia on Ellesmere Island, south to Lake Erie, and across six time zones from Newfoundland to the Pacific seaboard. The interior lowlands around Hudson Bay form part of the vast Canadian Shield. The lowlands give way to the Great Plains and the Rocky Mountains are to the west. The Great Lakes–St. Lawrence River lowlands to the southeast are the most populous areas. The St. Lawrence, Yukon, Mackenzie, and Fraser Rivers are among the world's 40 largest. An Inuit homeland, Nunavut, formerly the eastern part of the Northwest Territories, was created in 1999, covering nearly a quarter of Canada's land area. French-speaking Québec's relationship with the rest of the country has been a source of constitutional wrangling.

CLIMATE

Continental/subarctic/mountain

WEATHER CHART FOR OTTAWA

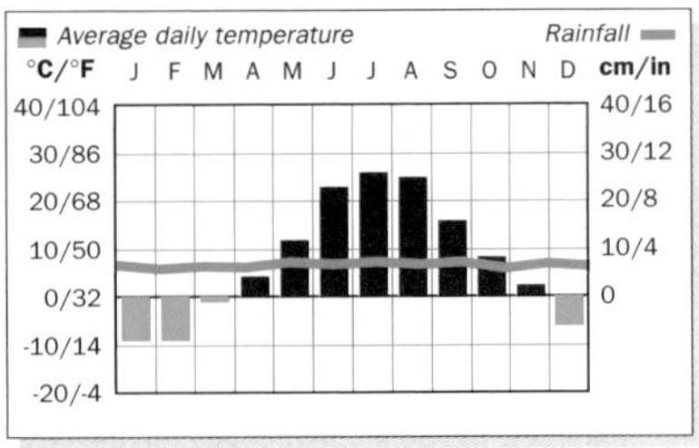
Average daily temperature
Rainfall
°C/°F
J F M A M J J A S O N D
cm/in
40/104
30/86
20/68
10/50
0/32
-10/14
-20/-4
40/16
30/12
20/8
10/4
0

Canada's climate ranges from polar and subpolar in the north, to cool in the south. Summers in the interior are hotter, and winters colder and longer than on the coast, with temperatures well below freezing and deep snow. The Pacific coast around Vancouver has the warmest winters, where temperatures rarely fall below zero.

TRANSPORTATION

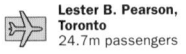

Drive on right

Lester B. Pearson, Toronto
24.7m passengers

902 ships
2.8m grt

THE TRANSPORTATION NETWORK

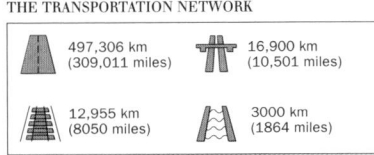

497,306 km (309,011 miles)

16,900 km (10,501 miles)

12,955 km (8050 miles)

3000 km (1864 miles)

The emergence of a national economy depended on the development of an efficient system of transportation. The Trans-Canada Highway and two transcontinental rail systems are the east–west backbones of the road and rail networks, which also reach into the far north. The Great Lakes–St. Lawrence Seaway system's cheap transportation helped Ontario and Québec dominate the economy for most of the 20th century. Air Canada, now privatized, remains the largest airline.

CANADA

Total Area : 9 984 670 sq. km (3 855 171 sq. miles)

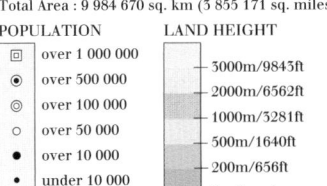

POPULATION
- over 1 000 000
- over 500 000
- over 100 000
- over 50 000
- over 10 000
- under 10 000

LAND HEIGHT
- 3000m/9843ft
- 2000m/6562ft
- 1000m/3281ft
- 500m/1640ft
- 200m/656ft
- Sea Level

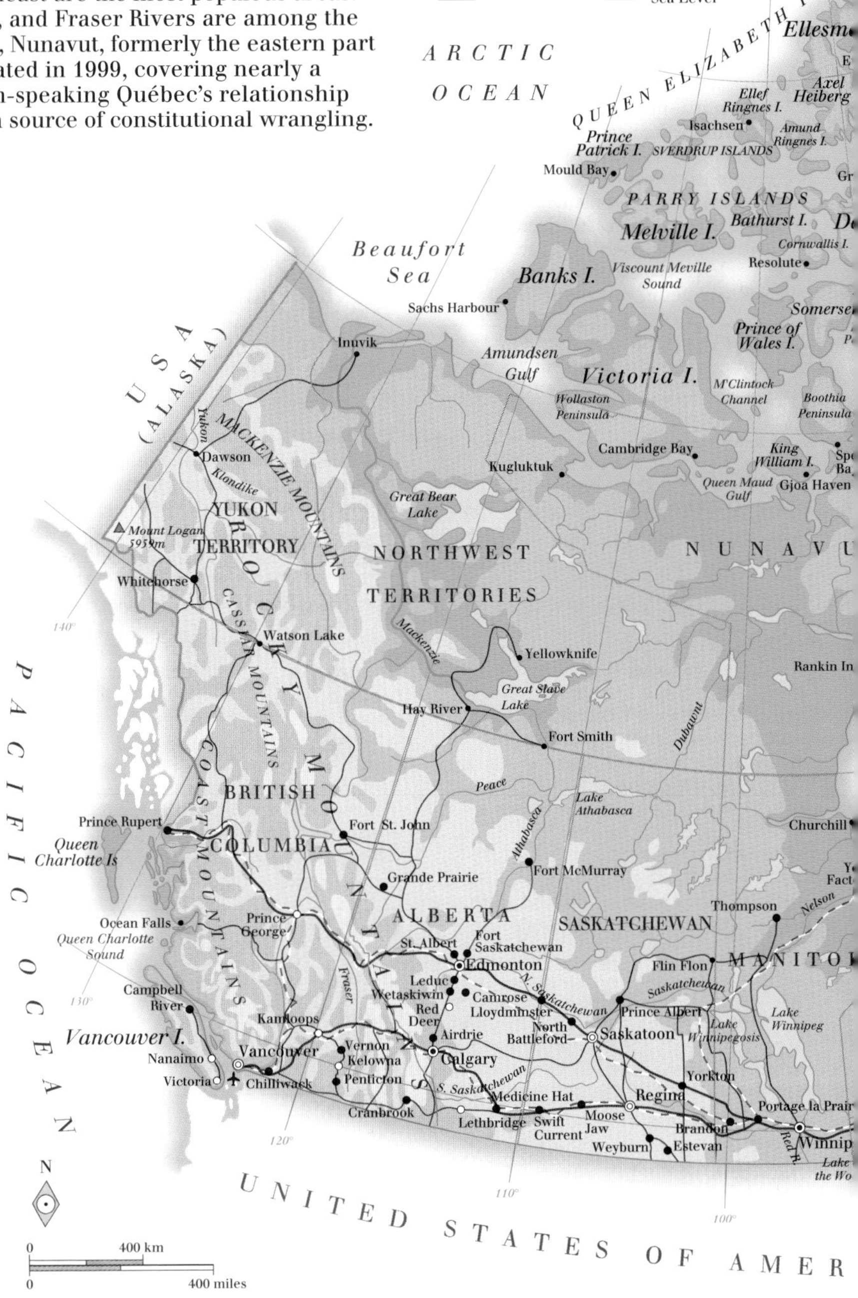
ARCTIC OCEAN
QUEEN ELIZABETH ISLANDS
Ellesmere
Axel Heiberg
Ellef Ringnes I.
Amund Ringnes I.
Isachsen
Prince Patrick I.
SVERDRUP ISLANDS
Mould Bay
PARRY ISLANDS
Melville I.
Bathurst I.
Cornwallis I.
Resolute
Beaufort Sea
Banks I.
Viscount Meville Sound
Sachs Harbour
Somerset
Prince of Wales I.
Inuvik
Amundsen Gulf
Victoria I.
M'Clintock Channel
Boothia Peninsula
Wollaston Peninsula
USA (ALASKA)
Yukon
MACKENZIE MOUNTAINS
Dawson
Klondike
Cambridge Bay
King William I.
Kugluktuk
Queen Maud Gulf
Gjoa Haven
Great Bear Lake
YUKON TERRITORY
Mount Logan 5959m
NORTHWEST TERRITORIES
NUNAVUT
Whitehorse
ROCKY MOUNTAINS
CASSIAR MOUNTAINS
Watson Lake
Mackenzie
Yellowknife
Rankin Inlet
Great Slave Lake
Hay River
Fort Smith
Dubawnt
PACIFIC OCEAN
COAST MOUNTAINS
BRITISH COLUMBIA
Peace
Lake Athabasca
Prince Rupert
Fort St. John
Churchill
Queen Charlotte Is
Athabasca
Fort McMurray
Grande Prairie
ALBERTA
SASKATCHEWAN
Thompson
Nelson
Ocean Falls
Prince George
Queen Charlotte Sound
St. Albert
Fort Saskatchewan
Edmonton
Flin Flon
MANITOBA
Leduc
Wetaskiwin
Camrose
Lloydminster
N. Saskatchewan
Saskatchewan
Campbell River
Fraser
Red Deer
Prince Albert
Lake Winnipegosis
Lake Winnipeg
Kamloops
North Battleford
Saskatoon
Vancouver I.
Vernon
Kelowna
Airdrie
Nanaimo
Vancouver
Calgary
Victoria
Chilliwack
Penticton
S. Saskatchewan
Yorkton
Medicine Hat
Regina
Portage la Prairie
Cranbrook
Lethbridge
Swift Current
Moose Jaw
Brandon
Weyburn
Estevan
Winnipeg
Red R.
Lake of the Woods
UNITED STATES OF AMERICA
N
0 400 km
0 400 miles
140°
130°
120°
110°
100°

TOURISM

Visitors : Population 1:1.8

17.5m visitors

Down 13% in 2003

MAIN TOURIST ARRIVALS

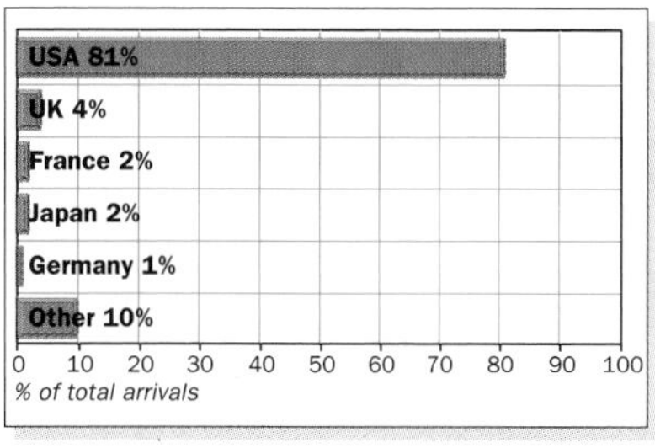
USA 81%
UK 4%
France 2%
Japan 2%
Germany 1%
Other 10%
0 10 20 30 40 50 60 70 80 90 100
% of total arrivals

Most tourist visitors come from the US, often on short tours. Efforts to attract European visitors center on campaigns emphasizing Canada's unpolluted natural beauty. Bizarrely, the fictional home of the eponymous heroine of *Anne of Green Gables* on Prince Edward Island is a magnet for tourists from Japan, where the novels about her by L. M. Montgomery enjoy enormous popularity.

PEOPLE

Pop. density low

English, French, Chinese, Italian, German, Ukrainian, Portuguese, Inuktitut, Cree

3/km²
9/mi²

THE URBAN/RURAL POPULATION SPLIT

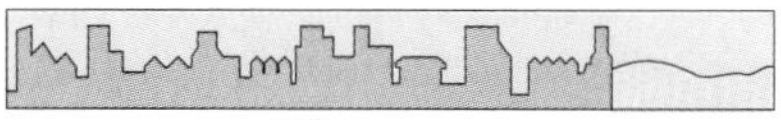
79%
21%

ETHNIC MAKEUP

Most Canadians are descended from immigrants from Britain, France, Ireland, and other European countries. Many now identify themselves simply as Canadian. In the 2001 census, which allowed multiple ethnic-origin answers, 6.7 million people chose only "Canadian" and 5 million more included it among their choices. Other responses included 14.3 million English, Scots, Irish, or Welsh, 4.7 million French, 8.7 million other European, 3 million Asian, and 1.3 million Amerindian, Métis, or Inuit.

RELIGIOUS PERSUASION

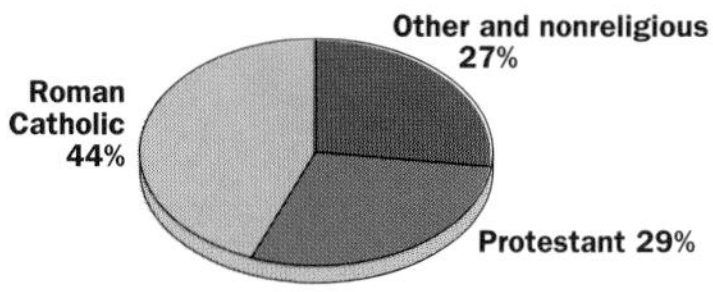
Other and nonreligious 27%
Roman Catholic 44%
Protestant 29%

Two-thirds of the population live in the 5% of land area taken up by the Great Lakes–St. Lawrence lowlands. Relations between the French-speaking Québécois and the English-speaking majority have been the dominant ethnic issue of the past 40 years. The issue was championed in mainstream politics by the Parti Québécois and, at federal level, the Bloc Québécois. Full independence was only narrowly defeated in two referenda (1980 and 1995), but support for secessionism has since waned as the dominance of the French language has been written into Québec law and living standards have been raised generally.

A dude ranch in British Columbia. *Many tourists are attracted by Canada's wide choice of outdoor pursuits.*

POPULATION AGE BREAKDOWN

Female
Age
Male
80+ 1.8% 1%
60–79 7.2% 6.2%
40–59 12.6% 12.6%
20–39 15.8% 16.1%
0–19 13% 13.7%
% of population by age group

Canada's ethnic mix has changed significantly since the 1970s as immigration policy was relaxed to welcome those with money or skills. The government promotes a policy which encourages each group to maintain its own culture, creating a "mosaic" or a "community of communities."

The largest element of the indigenous population is the one millon people of native Amerindian descent, known in Canada as First Nations. There are also 300,000 Métis (French-Amerindians) and an Inuit population of some 56,000 in the north. In 1992 the Inuit successfully settled their long-standing land claim, and in 1999 the Nunavut area, with only 27,000 mainly Inuit inhabitants, gained the status of a territory, the first part of Canada to be governed by indigenous Canadians in modern history. A Supreme Court land rights ruling in 1997, establishing the principle of "Aboriginal title," opened the way for the return of ancestral lands claimed by native Amerindian nations, and in 1998 the federal government formally apologized for past mistreatment. Claims for extra fishing and land rights and challenges to existing treaties continue.

Canada has a long tradition of state welfare more akin to Scandinavia than the US. Unemployment provision and health care, supported by high taxes, are still generous, despite recent cutbacks.

The government has sought to end inequalities. Measures include the "pay-equity" laws, which aim to specify pay rates for jobs done by men or women requiring a similar level of skill. Women are well represented at most levels of business and government.

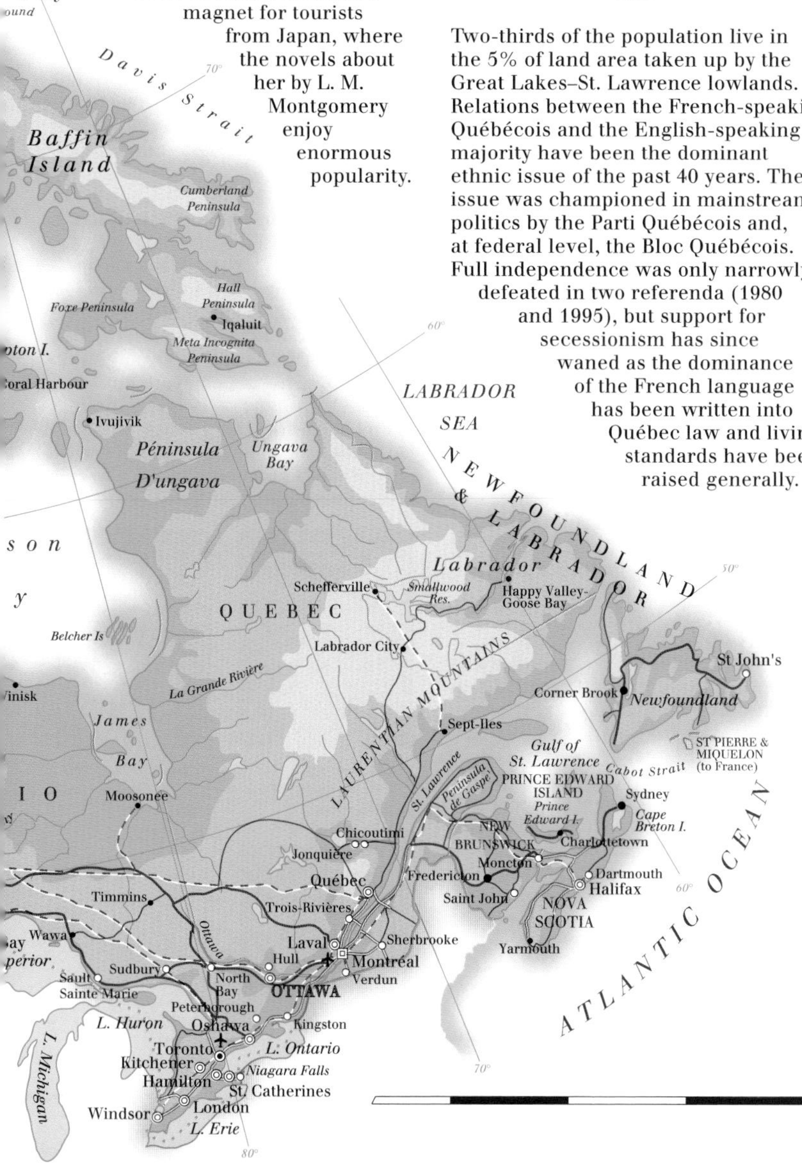
Davis Strait
Baffin Island
Cumberland Peninsula
Hall Peninsula
Iqaluit
Meta Incognita Peninsula
Foxe Peninsula
Coral Harbour
Ivujivik
Péninsula D'ungava
Ungava Bay
LABRADOR SEA
NEWFOUNDLAND & LABRADOR
Labrador
Smallwood Res.
Happy Valley-Goose Bay
Schefferville
QUEBEC
Belcher Is
Labrador City
La Grande Rivière
LAURENTIAN MOUNTAINS
St John's
Corner Brook
Newfoundland
James Bay
Sept-Iles
ST PIERRE & MIQUELON (to France)
Gulf of St. Lawrence
Cabot Strait
PRINCE EDWARD ISLAND
Prince Edward I.
Sydney
Cape Breton I.
Moosonee
Chicoutimi
Jonquière
NEW BRUNSWICK
Charlottetown
Moncton
Fredericton
Dartmouth
Halifax
Québec
Saint John
NOVA SCOTIA
Timmins
Trois-Rivières
Wawa
Laval
Sherbrooke
Yarmouth
Hull
Montréal
Sudbury
Verdun
Sault Sainte Marie
North Bay
OTTAWA
Peterborough
L. Huron
Oshawa
Kingston
Toronto
L. Ontario
Kitchener
Hamilton
Niagara Falls
St Catherines
L. Michigan
London
Windsor
L. Erie
ATLANTIC OCEAN

CHRONOLOGY

Peopled for centuries by indigenous Amerindians and Inuit, Canada began to be settled by Europeans in the first half of the 17th century, following the English expedition led by John Cabot in 1497 and the landing of Frenchman Jacques Cartier in 1534.

- ❑ **1754–1760** British defeat French and Amerindian allies in Canada.
- ❑ **1763** Under Treaty of Paris, France cedes its St. Lawrence and Québec settlements to Britain.
- ❑ **1774** Act of Québec recognizes Roman Catholicism, French language, culture, and traditions.
- ❑ **1775–1783** American War of Independence. Canada becomes refuge for loyalists to British crown.
- ❑ **1867** Dominion of Canada created under British North America Act.
- ❑ **1897** Klondike gold rush begins.
- ❑ **1914–1918, 1939–1945** Canada supports Allies in both world wars.
- ❑ **1931** Autonomy within Commonwealth.
- ❑ **1949** Founder member of NATO. Newfoundland joins Canada.
- ❑ **1968** Liberal Party under Pierre Trudeau in power. Separatist Parti Québécois (PQ) formed.
- ❑ **1970s** Québec secessionist movement grows, accompanied by terrorist attacks.
- ❑ **1976** PQ wins Québec elections.
- ❑ **1977** French made official language in Québec.
- ❑ **1980** Referendum rejects secession of Québec. Trudeau prime minister.
- ❑ **1982** UK transfers all powers relating to Canada in British law.
- ❑ **1984** Trudeau resigns. Elections won by PCP. Brian Mulroney prime minister until 1993.
- ❑ **1987** Meech Lake Accord on provincial–federal relationship.
- ❑ **1989** Canadian–US Free Trade Agreement.
- ❑ **1992** Charlottetown Agreement on provincial–federal issues rejected in referendum. Canada, Mexico, and US finalize terms for NAFTA.
- ❑ **1993** Crushing election defeat of PCP, rise of regional parties. Liberal Jean Chrétien prime minister.
- ❑ **1994** PQ regains power in Québec. NAFTA takes effect.
- ❑ **1995** Narrow "no" vote in second Québec sovereignty referendum.
- ❑ **1995** Fishing dispute with EU.
- ❑ **1997** Regionalism dominates federal election; Liberals retain power based on support in Ontario.
- ❑ **2003** PQ ousted by Liberals in Québec after nine years in power. Chrétien stands down in favor of Paul Martin.
- ❑ **2004** Early elections: Liberals again retain power.

POLITICS

Multiparty elections

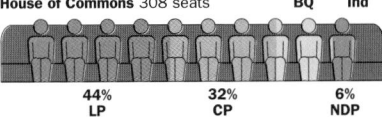

L. House 2004/2009 | H.M. Queen Elizabeth II

AT THE LAST ELECTION

House of Commons 308 seats

17% BQ
1% Ind
44% LP
32% CP
6% NDP

LP = Liberal Party **CP** = Conservative Party
BQ = Bloc Québécois **NDP** = New Democratic Party
Ind = Independents **PCP** = Progressive Conservative Party

Senate 105 seats

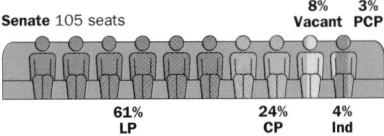

8% Vacant
3% PCP
61% LP
24% CP
4% Ind

Senators are appointed by the governor-general on the recommendation of the prime minister, to a usual maximum of 105; the prime minister may also appoint an extra seven senators. Senators retain their seats until the age of 75

Canada is a federal multiparty democracy.

Profile

The collapse of the Progressive Conservative Party (PCP) in 1993 ushered in an era of left-of-center dominance under the LP and Jean Chrétien. Other parties began to focus on regional, rather than pan-Canadian, issues, leading to the hopeless dissipation of the right wing; after the 1993 election the BQ had become the second-largest party in parliament. Over the next decade the conservatives worked to reconnect with voters, and merged in 2003 to form the CP under Stephen Harper.

Chrétien stepped down in 2003, in favor of former finance minister Paul Martin. A funding scandal in Québec damaged the LP in the run-up to the 2004 election, with late opinion polls showing the CP to be in the lead. The LP scraped a surprise win to form a minority government, Martin relying on the somewhat ambivalent support of the BQ and NDP to maintain power.

Main Political Issues

The unity of the state

Opposition to federal government is not confined to Québec – recent federal elections have confirmed support for greater autonomy for Canada's western provinces – but Canada has agonized over separatist tendencies in francophone Québec almost since the foundation of the state. Québec did not take part in the 1997 Calgary conference, where a Canadian unity framework was agreed by the other provinces, together with recognition of Québec's "unique character." A series of earlier proposals, to recognize Québec as a distinct society and strengthen the powers of all the federal provinces, had failed to gain ratification or been rejected by the electorate.

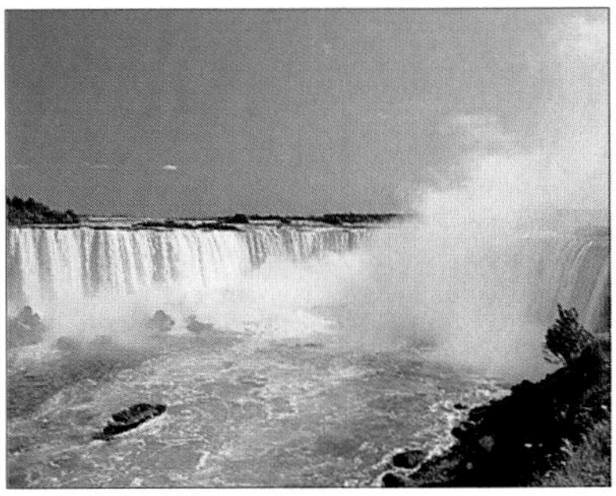

***The Niagara Falls** are situated between Lakes Erie and Ontario on the Canada–US border. Horseshoe Falls, in Canada, are 49 m (160 ft) high and 790 m (2591 ft) across.*

The ambition of the Parti Québécois (PQ) to hold yet another referendum on separatism, despite losing those held in 1980 and 1995, was derailed when the party lost provincial elections to the LP in 2003. The popularity of the PQ suffered as voters were keen to focus on everyday issues, rather than the promise of more constitutional wrangling. Any future vote on secession will anyway require federal approval and the agreement of at least seven of the ten provinces, while the 2000 Clarity Act set strict criteria for the validation of any prosecession referendum.

Health care

The publicly funded "medicare" health care system is highly popular but widely criticized. All political parties recognize the need to address problems of staff shortages, long waiting times, and the lack of new technologies. The cost of reforms, however, is potentially large. Market-oriented economic reforms have left few revenue options open to government. Though some politicians see hope in the public–private partnerships pioneered in the UK, full private care remains illegal in Canada.

***Jean Charest,** Liberal premier of Québec since 2003.*

***Paul Martin,** heir to Chrétien: prime minister from 2003.*

***Jean Chrétien,** Liberal prime minister 1993–2003.*

C

WORLD AFFAIRS

Joined UN in 1945

Comm | G8 | OECD | NAFTA | NATO

Canada's most important relationship is with the US. Though relations are on the whole good, there are tensions. Canada has protested over US duties on its timber and a ban on beef products, and many worry about the increase in labor competition from Mexico since the creation of NAFTA in 1994. At a more basic level Canadians are wary of the encroachment of US culture and of its concurrent social ills. There are also concerns over the transportation of Alaskan oil and US resistance to treaties such as the Kyoto Protocol, signed by Canada in 2002. Canada backed the US-led "war on terrorism," but refused to support the 2003 attack on Iraq.

In the forefront on debt relief for the poorest countries, Canada has also led the world campaign against antipersonnel mines.

AID

Donor

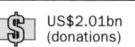

US$2.01bn (donations)

Up 31% in 2002

Canada's aid budget, earmarked for cuts in the 1990s, was given extra funding again into the new century. NGOs supported by the Canadian International Development Agency (CIDA) are prominent on global development issues, and most Canadians approve of giving aid.

Aid now aims to provide know-how skills, rather than funding for large-scale development projects. CIDA has pioneered a theme-based approach, stressing health and nutrition, basic education, AIDS, and child protection. The regional focus of aid has gradually shifted, with less emphasis on Africa. Programs in the 1990s supported recovery and reform in former communist countries. Aid is now given to a range of countries; eastern Europe remains a particular focus.

DEFENSE

No compulsory military service

US$7.77bn

Down 7% in 2002

CANADIAN ARMED FORCES

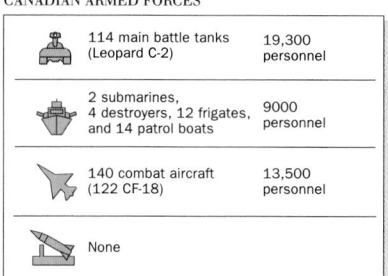

114 main battle tanks (Leopard C-2)	19,300 personnel
2 submarines, 4 destroyers, 12 frigates, and 14 patrol boats	9000 personnel
140 combat aircraft (122 CF-18)	13,500 personnel
None	

Canada cooperates closely with the US on North American defense and security issues.

Canadian troops have served in many UN peacekeeping operations, most recently in Kosovo, East Timor, Sierra Leone and Haiti. Their involvement in Somalia, however, which ended in 1993, was tarnished by a scandal over racism, torture, and murder which shocked Canadian society. International commitments have stretched the armed forces: in 2004 the government announced plans to increase troop strength by 5000. The focus of planning is now the creation of rapid reaction forces.

ECONOMICS

Inflation 1.5% p.a. (1990–2001)

US$702bn

1.341 Canadian dollars (1.359)

SCORE CARD

❑ WORLD GNP RANKING	8th
❑ GNP PER CAPITA	US$22,390
❑ BALANCE OF PAYMENTS	US$14.9bn
❑ INFLATION	2.2%
❑ UNEMPLOYMENT	8%

EXPORTS

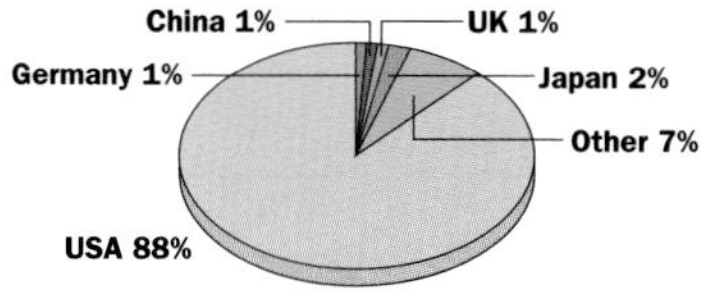
China 1%
UK 1%
Germany 1%
Japan 2%
Other 7%
USA 88%

IMPORTS

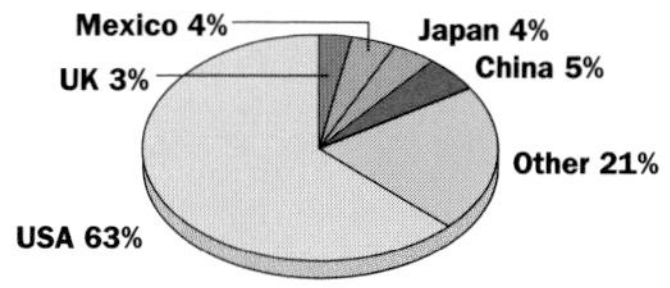
Mexico 4%
Japan 4%
UK 3%
China 5%
Other 21%
USA 63%

STRENGTHS

A broad and rich resource base. Provides exports, raw materials for manufacturing sector, and massive cheap energy, notably HEP; also large oil and gas reserves. Agriculture and forestry contribute 2% of GDP, mining 4%. Successful manufacturing sector, employing 15% of the workforce: forestry products, transportation equipment, and chemicals. Budget surplus. Access to huge US and Mexican markets through NAFTA. Low inflation.

WEAKNESSES

Problems of competitiveness: higher taxes, lower productivity, more regulations, relative to NAFTA; other threats from globalization. Vulnerable to price fluctuations for raw material exports. Brain drain of professionals heading south.

ECONOMIC PERFORMANCE INDICATOR

Consumer Price Index
GDP
160
140
120
100
80
Consumer price index 1998=100
GDP 1998=100
1998
1999
2000
2001
2002

PROFILE

Canada has an enormous resource base, and it has one of the highest standards of living in the world. Since the mid-1980s, however, manufactured exports have faced increasing competition, while prices for its primary exports fluctuate. Real growth averaged 3.5% a year for most of the 1980s, but then stagnated for five years, while budget deficits rose, forcing restructuring at both federal and provincial levels. Many welfare programs were cut back; the defense budget was sharply reduced. Growth resumed after 1993 and an unwieldy budget deficit was turned into a record surplus by 1997. Within NAFTA, Canadian firms have had to become more competitive to maintain exports. Most have been successful, with better productivity and a high-tech shift. Unemployment, at almost 10% in the mid-1990s, has "stabilized" below 8%. Canada's close ties to the US left it hard hit by the 2001 slowdown.

CANADA : MAJOR BUSINESSES

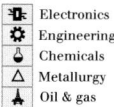

- Aerospace industry
- Vehicle manufacture
- Timber industries
- Pulp & paper
- Food processing
- Fish processing
- Electronics
- Engineering
- Chemicals
- Metallurgy
- Oil & gas

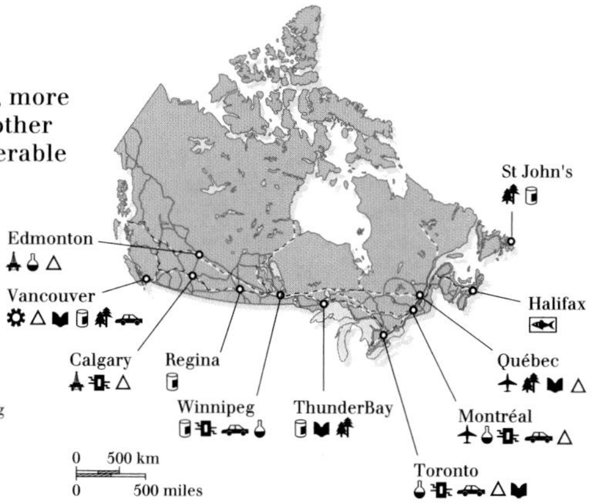
St John's
Edmonton
Vancouver
Halifax
Calgary
Regina
Québec
Winnipeg
ThunderBay
Montréal
Toronto
0 500 km
0 500 miles

C

RESOURCES

Electric power 118m kW

1.2m tonnes

2.99m b/d (reserves 16.9bn barrels)

14.7m pigs, 13.5m cattle, 6m turkeys, 160m chickens

Coal, oil, gas, gold, zinc, uranium, nickel, potash, asbestos, gypsum

ELECTRICITY GENERATION

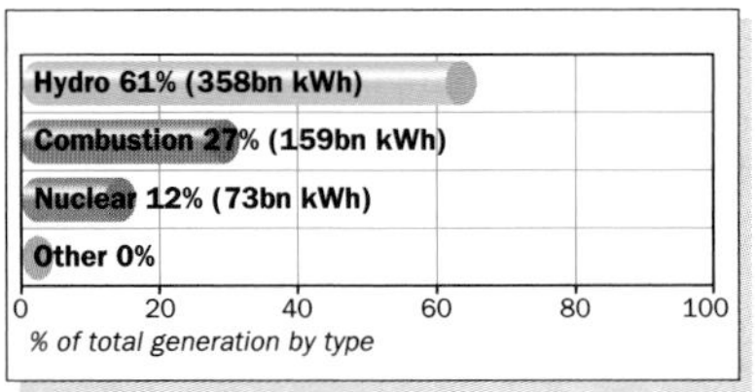
Hydro 61% (358bn kWh)
Combustion 27% (159bn kWh)
Nuclear 12% (73bn kWh)
Other 0%
0
20
40
60
80
100
% of total generation by type

Canada is a country of enormous natural resources. It is the world's largest exporter of forest products and a top exporter of fish, furs, and wheat. Minerals have played a key role in Canada's transformation into an urban–industrial economy. Alberta, British Columbia, Québec, and Saskatchewan are the principal mining regions. Ontario and the Northwest (NWT) and Yukon Territories are also significant producers. Canada is the world's largest producer of uranium and potash, the third-largest of asbestos, gypsum, and nickel, and the fourth-largest of zinc. Oil and gas are exploited in Alberta, off the Atlantic coast, and in the northwest – huge additional reserves are thought to exist in the high Arctic. Most exports go to the US. Canada is also one of the world's top hydroelectricity producers.

CANADA : LAND USE

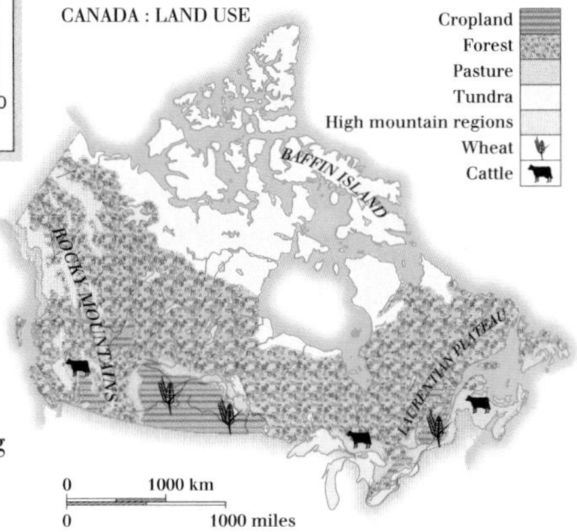
Cropland
Forest
Pasture
Tundra
High mountain regions
Wheat
Cattle
BAFFIN ISLAND
ROCKY MOUNTAINS
LAURENTIAN PLATEAU
0
1000 km
0
1000 miles

ENVIRONMENT

Sustainability rank: 4th

11% (5% partially protected)

14.2 tonnes per capita

ENVIRONMENTAL TREATIES

Yes	Yes	Yes
Yes	Yes	Yes

With a population of only just over 30 million living in the world's second-largest country, Canada is justly renowned for vast tracts of wilderness untroubled by pollution either from industry or from intensive farming methods. A major conservation issue is the battle to stop the logging of virgin forest in northern Ontario and on the west coast. Notable successes were achieved in the late 1990s, pressuring timber companies to adopt more sustainable policies, and a landmark agreement in early 2001 promised protection for British Columbia's coastal Great Bear Rainforest.

Canadians have tighter pollution controls than the neighboring US. Ontario, the most polluted province, has imposed stricter limits on oil refineries and (from 2001) on electricity-generating plants. Carbon dioxide emissions (mainly from cars) are among the highest in the world per capita. Canada has accepted a target of a 6% cut by 2010. Production of hazardous waste is also higher than the European average.

MEDIA

TV ownership high

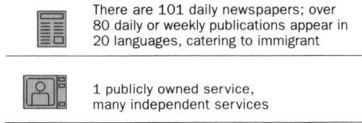

Daily newspaper circulation 159 per 1000 people

PUBLISHING AND BROADCAST MEDIA

There are 101 daily newspapers; over 80 daily or weekly publications appear in 20 languages, catering to immigrant

1 publicly owned service, many independent services

1 publicly owned service, many independent services

The public Canadian Broadcasting Corporation (CBC) runs two national TV channels, in English and French; the conservative opposition has called for its privatization. Local cable services often include multilingual or ethnic channels. Canadian TV is renowned for its news and sports coverage. *La Presse* is a leading French daily and the *Globe and Mail* is the leading national newspaper in English.

***Black spruce in fall** in northern Canada. Whether due to global warming or localized temperature cycles, the tundra is retreating across Arctic Canada.*

CRIME

No death penalty

36,024 prisoners

Up 2% in 2001

CRIME RATES

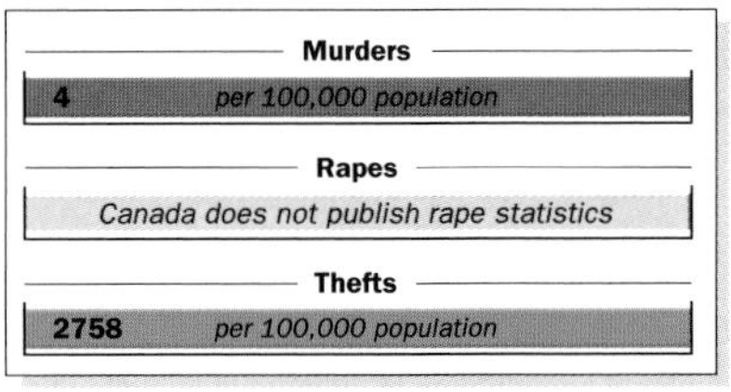
Murders
4 per 100,000 population
Rapes
Canada does not publish rape statistics
Thefts
2758 per 100,000 population

Rates for serious crime are lower in Canada than in the US. Canadians ascribe this to their far stricter gun control laws, which were further tightened in the 1990s. Newfoundland police began carrying guns routinely only in 1998, the last force in North America to do so. There have been careful efforts to maintain the inner cities as crime-free zones.

Innovative "drug treatment courts" in Toronto and Vancouver link criminal justice with treatment and social care.

Federal prisoners were allowed to vote from 2004.

EDUCATION

School leaving age: 16

99%

1.21m students

THE EDUCATION SYSTEM

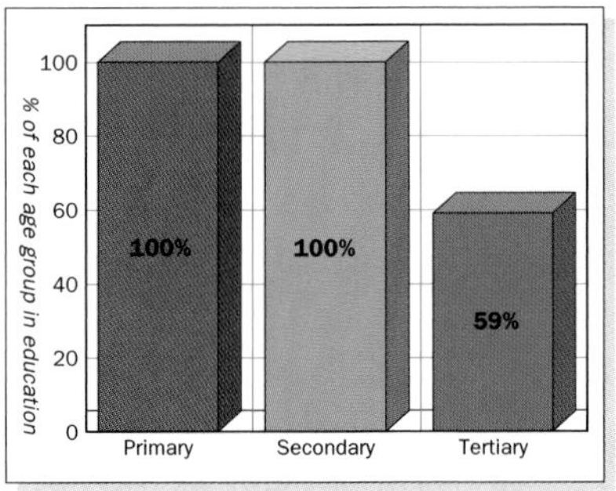
100
80
60
40
20
0
% of each age group in education
100%
100%
59%
Primary
Secondary
Tertiary

Education is a responsibility of the individual provinces, rather than the federal government, and is accorded a very high priority. The period of free compulsory school attendance varies, but is a minimum of nine years.

The prime medium of instruction is English in all provinces except francophone Québec. In several other provinces, French-speaking students are entitled to be taught in French. Multicultural education also helps maintain the cultural identity of immigrant groups.

Canada has 58 universities and some 200 other higher education institutions. Nearly all high school graduates go on to some form of tertiary or further education, one of the highest proportions in the industrialized world.

C

THE CANADIAN WAY

CANADA IS ALWAYS near the top of international quality-of-life surveys. With a healthy economy, a modern infrastructure, and stunning natural scenery, it also wins acclaim for exciting urban living; five Canadian cities ranked among the world's top 30 cities in which to live in the Mercer Human Resource Consulting 2004 listings (Vancouver [3], Toronto [15], Ottawa [20], Calgary [24=], and Montréal [24=]).

TRUTH

In the 19th century the UK extended the transportation, communications, and industrial infrastructure across the continent, in order to exploit Canada's abundant natural resources, and thus benefit from its vast colony. While agriculture and mining remain important, they have been overtaken in recent decades by services and manufacturing. Since the mid-20th century, Canada has experienced a period of relative economic boom.

A significant economic factor is the moderate size of the population. Canada's wealth is shared between a relatively small number of people, with the effect of raising the average income. Despite comprising around 40% of the territory of North America, it is home to less than 7% of North Americans; there are just three Canadians to every square kilometer of Canada. This statistic is, of course, somewhat misleading; four-fifths of the population live in urban areas, though only Montréal can boast more than one million inhabitants. In general, Canadian cities are uncluttered, blessed with abundant green space, and far from crowded.

Quality of life has also been aided by good social services, in particular a health service that is free at source. Liberal values in political life extend to society at large; many thousands of immigrants are welcomed into the country, and their different cultures respected and cherished by the state.

Vancouver on Canada's western seaboard is reputedly the country's most desirable city.

***Adrienne Clarkson** (governor-general 1999–2005) being escorted by Mounties.*

Equality for women has become an expected norm. Vietnamese-born television celebrity Adrienne Clarkson served as governor-general from 1999 to 2005, proving that race and gender are not limitations to success.

In real terms all this translates to high levels of participation and success in education (largely unaffected by social background), sustainable levels of unemployment, low crime rates, a strong awareness of the environment, and pride in social tolerance.

JUSTICE

Inevitably, Canada is not unmitigated paradise. In 2001, the government produced a *Citizens' Report Card*, which, while it confirmed a general satisfaction with life, highlighted a number of areas of concern for ordinary Canadians.

Foremost was a fear that racial and community discrimination were growing. It was noted that intolerance, though still low, had become more widespread. There is also concern over lengthening hospital waiting lists and an apparent lack of access to the specialist treatment so flaunted in the US health care system. The rising cost of further education also featured, as did the environment, with Canadians noting a fall in air and water quality in recent years.

The least pressing worry for most, but perhaps a sign of trouble to come, was the increasing gap between rich and poor. The previously even distribution of wealth is showing signs of breaking down as levels of poverty grow. Future governments will have to close the gap and focus on these concerns if they are to protect the Canadian way of life that most now expect.

HEALTH

▷ Welfare state health benefits

1 per 476 people

Cancers, heart and respiratory diseases

The comprehensive state health service is funded from national insurance.

Rising costs are the result of an aging population and the spread of more sophisticated and expensive treatments. Health care is a dominant electoral issue. Popular backing for retaining the present publicly funded system has encouraged the LP government to restore spending to earlier levels, after a period of cuts made to reverse the budget deficit. There is fierce debate over the possibility of privatization.

SPENDING

▷ GDP/cap. increase

CONSUMPTION AND SPENDING

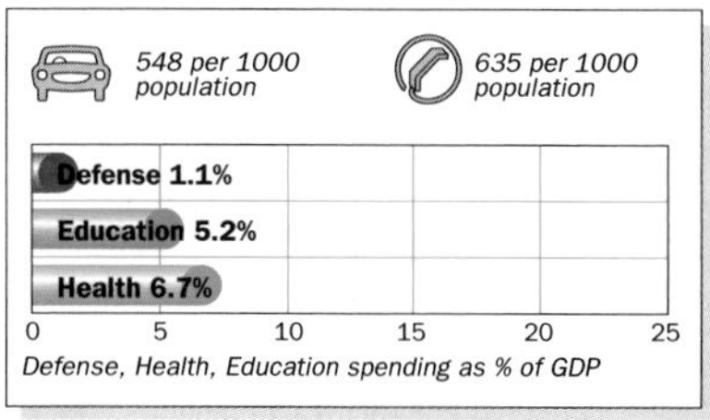
548 per 1000 population
635 per 1000 population
Defense 1.1%
Education 5.2%
Health 6.7%
0 5 10 15 20 25
Defense, Health, Education spending as % of GDP

Life for most Canadians is very good, despite strains caused by recession during the early 1990s – including a peak in unemployment at over 10%.

The UN ranks Canada as one of the best countries in the world in which to live. In its overall assessment of human development indicators such as income, education, and life expectancy, Canada was consistently top in the 1990s, but has now slipped to fourth.

However, disadvantaged groups do exist, in particular among indigenous Canadians. Unemployment, poor housing, and mortality rates for Amerindians and Inuit are well above those for other Canadians; the Inuit suicide rate is three times higher. Those Amerindians who live on reserves are the poorest group.

WORLD RANKING

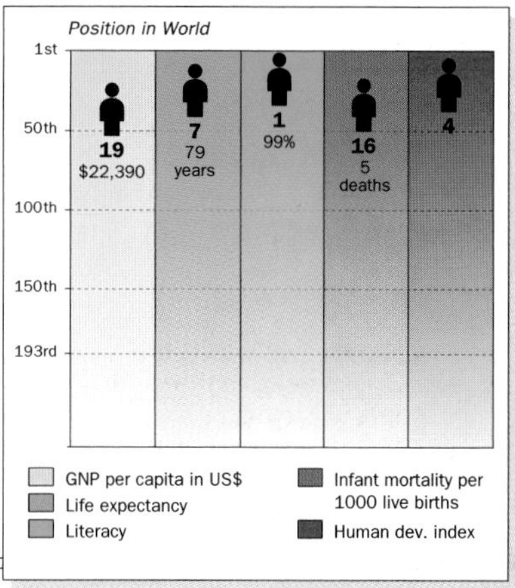
Position in World
1st
50th
100th
150th
193rd
19 $22,390
7 79 years
1 99%
16 5 deaths
4
GNP per capita in US$
Life expectancy
Literacy
Infant mortality per 1000 live births
Human dev. index

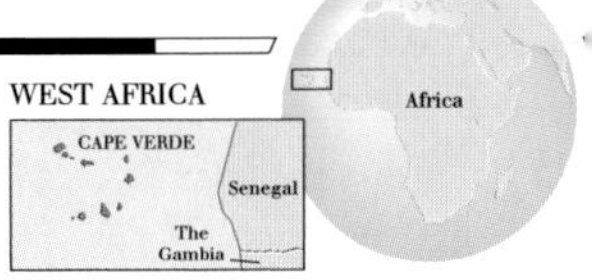
WEST AFRICA
CAPE VERDE
Senegal
The Gambia
Africa

Cape Verde

Official Name: Republic of Cape Verde **Capital:** Praia
Population: 463,000 **Currency:** Cape Verde escudo **Official Language:** Portuguese

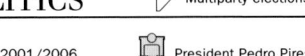

1975 | 1975 | July 5 | CV | -1 | +238 | .cv

The Cape Verde archipelago off the west coast of Africa became independent of Portugal in 1975. Most of the islands are mountainous and volcanic; the low-lying islands of Sal, Boa Vista, and Maio have agricultural potential, though they are prone to debilitating droughts. Around 50% of the population live on Santiago. Cape Verde has been one of Africa's most stable democracies since multiparty elections were first held in 1991.

Climate

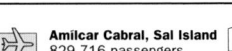

Tropical oceanic

WEATHER CHART FOR PRAIA

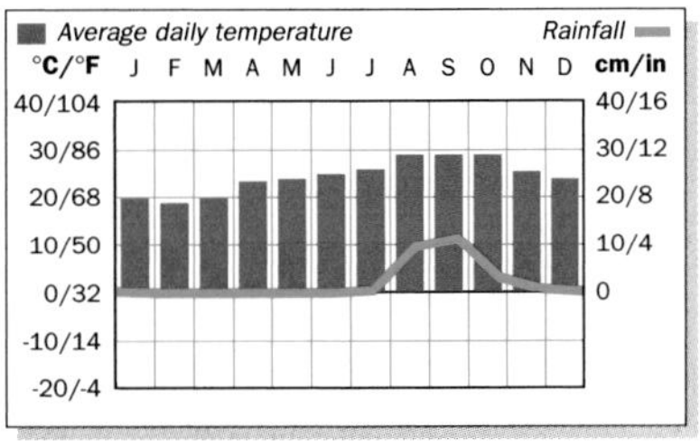
Average daily temperature
Rainfall
°C/°F
J F M A M J J A S O N D
cm/in
40/104
30/86
20/68
10/50
0/32
-10/14
-20/-4
40/16
30/12
20/8
10/4
0

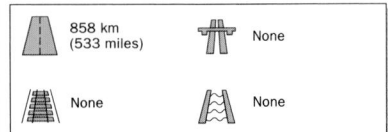

Cape Verde has a very dry climate, subject to droughts that sometimes last for years at a time.

Transportation

Drive on right

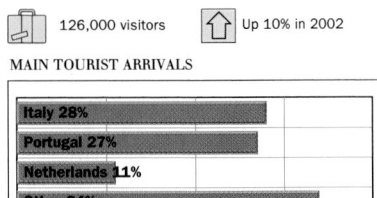

Amílcar Cabral, Sal Island 829,716 passengers

39 ships 16,400 grt

THE TRANSPORTATION NETWORK

858 km (533 miles)

None

None

None

Travel between the islands is either by ferry or the more expensive daily flights run by Cabo Verde Airlines.

Tourism

Visitors : Population 1:3.7

126,000 visitors

Up 10% in 2002

MAIN TOURIST ARRIVALS

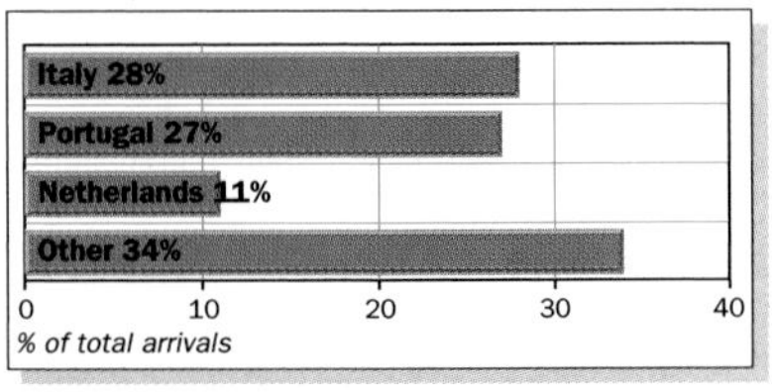
Italy 28%
Portugal 27%
Netherlands 11%
Other 34%
0
10
20
30
40
% of total arrivals

Tourism is generally on a modest scale; package tourism has gained a foothold. The islands of Santiago, Santo Antão, Fogo, and Brava have tourist potential, offering a combination of mountain scenery and extensive beaches.

People

Pop. density medium

Portuguese Creole, Portuguese

115/km² (298/mi²)

THE URBAN/RURAL POPULATION SPLIT

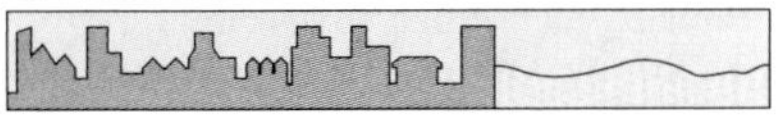
64%
36%

RELIGIOUS PERSUASION

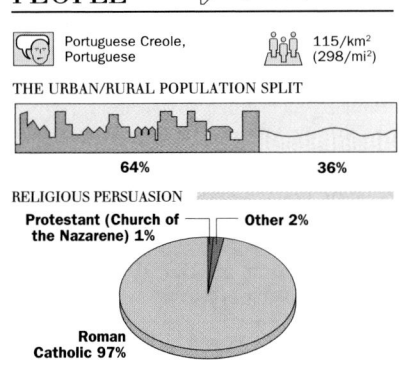

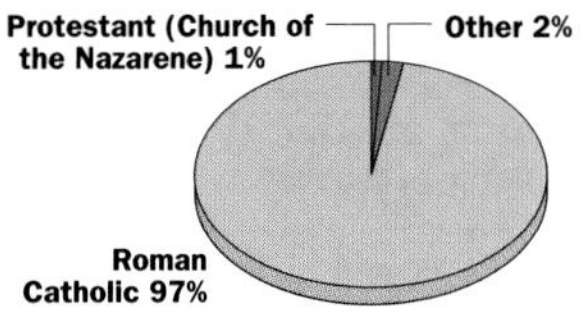
Protestant (Church of the Nazarene) 1%
Other 2%
Roman Catholic 97%

The majority of the population is Portuguese–African *mestiço*; the remainder is largely African, descended either from slaves or from more recent immigrants from the mainland. The Creolization of the culture has led to a relative lack of ethnic tension. African culture is influential on Santiago Island.

The extended family, as well as the Roman Catholic Church, have helped to ensure the vitality of family life. Some 600,000 Cape Verdean emigrants now live abroad, especially in Portugal and the US: overseas remittances are an important part of the economy.

Politics

Multiparty elections

2001/2006

President Pedro Pires

AT THE LAST ELECTION

National Assembly 72 seats

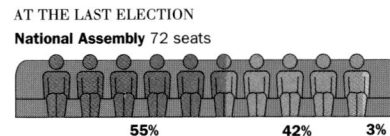

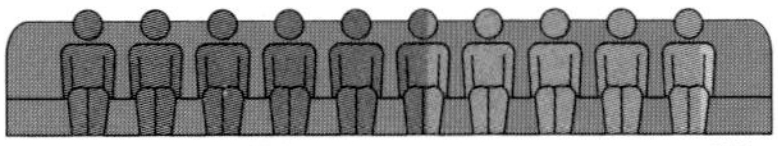
55% PAICV
42% MPD
3% ADM

PAICV = African Party for the Independence of Cape Verde
MPD = Movement for Democracy
ADM = Democratic Alliance for Change

Cape Verde experienced a peaceful transition to multipartyism in 1991, when elections brought the MPD to power. Though there had previously been a decade of single-party rule under the PAICV, it had in fact operated a liberal system in which opposition and dissent were tolerated. The large Cape Verdean diaspora had an important influence in effecting the transition to multiparty politics.

The MPD was defeated in legislative elections in January 2001, when the PAICV was returned to power with an absolute majority. Pedro Pires of the PAICV was elected president the following month, beating his MPD rival by just 17 votes. The main issues for the government are economic development, forging new international partnerships, and responding to drought.

World Affairs

Joined UN in 1975

CPLP | ECOWAS | OIF | NAM | AU

Cape Verde wishes to diversify its international contacts to secure aid and foreign investment, while maintaining good relations with Portugal. Regionally, it has improved relations with Guinea-Bissau, after withdrawing from a proposed union in 1980.

Ties to other lusophone countries, including Angola and Brazil, are important, as are links with nearby Senegal and Gambia.

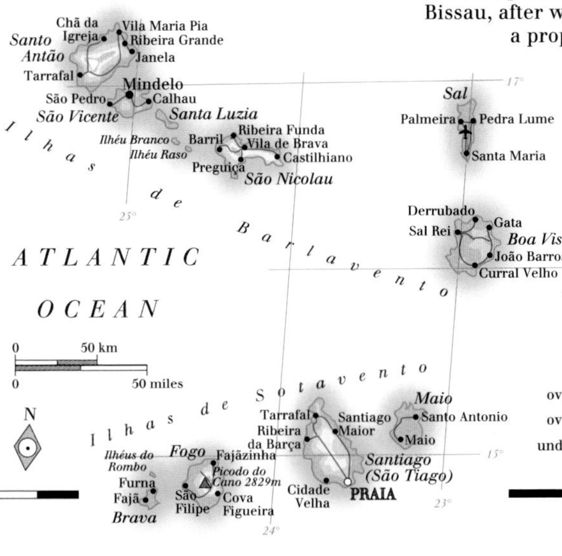
Santo Antão
Chã da Igreja
Vila Maria Pia
Ribeira Grande
Janela
Tarrafal
Mindelo
São Pedro
Calhau
São Vicente
Santa Luzia
Ilhéu Branco
Ilhéu Raso
Barril
Ribeira Funda
Vila de Brava
Castilhiano
Preguiça
São Nicolau
Ilhas de Barlavento
Sal
Palmeira
Pedra Lume
Santa Maria
Derrubado
Gata
Sal Rei
Boa Vista
João Barrosa
Curral Velho
ATLANTIC OCEAN
0 50 km
0 50 miles
N
Ilhas de Sotavento
Ilhéus do Rombo
Fogo
Fajãzinha
Pico do Cano 2829m
Furna
Fajã
Brava
São Filipe
Cova Figueira
Tarrafal
Ribeira da Barça
Santiago Maior
Cidade Velha
PRAIA
Santiago (São Tiago)
Maio
Santo Antonio
Maio

Cape Verde

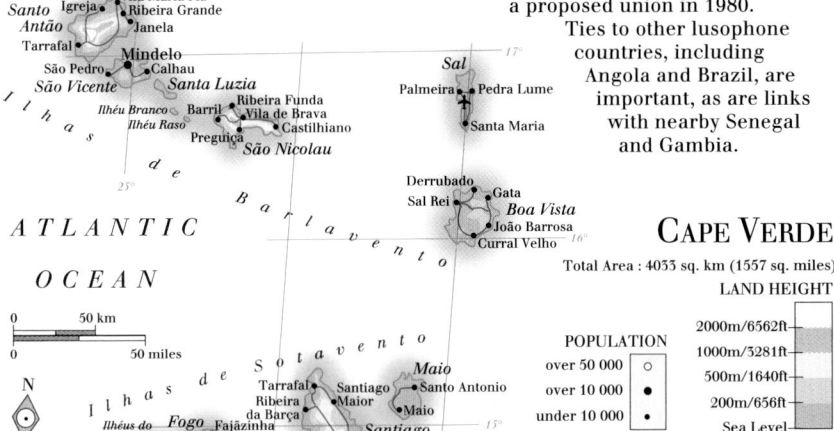

Total Area : 4033 sq. km (1557 sq. miles)

LAND HEIGHT

2000m/6562ft
1000m/3281ft
500m/1640ft
200m/656ft
Sea Level

POPULATION

over 50 000
over 10 000
under 10 000

C

AID

Recipient

$92m (receipts)

Up 19% in 2002

Aid finances almost all development in Cape Verde, which is one of the least industrialized countries in the world and is vulnerable to food shortages. The World Bank is the main source of aid followed by Portugal. Remittances from Cape Verdeans abroad account for 20% of GDP. The AfDB loaned $8 million in 2002 to finance a food security and environmental project.

DEFENSE

Compulsory military service

$8m

Up 14% in 2002

After independence, armed forces were established, now consisting of a 1000-strong army, a small air force, and a naval coast guard. They have never been called upon to play a political role; their main duties are to protect territorial waters against illegal fishing and to curb smuggling.

ECONOMICS

Inflation 4.8% p.a. (1990–2001)

$572m

108.9 Cape Verde escudos (109)

SCORE CARD

❑ World GNP Ranking	168th
❑ GNP per Capita	$1250
❑ Balance of Payments	–$71m
❑ Inflation	1.9%
❑ Unemployment	21%

Strengths

Strategic location close to the mid-Atlantic where Africa is nearest to Latin America: military and economic advantages, including shipping maintenance and air travel. Low debt-servicing costs. Tourism and fishing. Privatization program.

Weaknesses

Permanent threat of drought and water supply problems, despite desalination plants. Lack of agricultural land and dependence on food aid. Difficulties of communications between islands.

EXPORTS

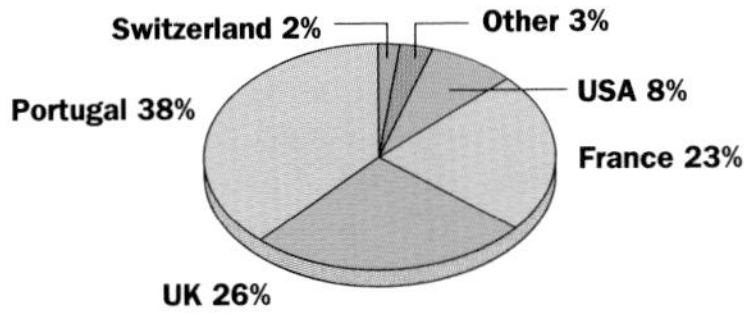
Switzerland 2%
Other 3%
USA 8%
Portugal 38%
France 23%
UK 26%

IMPORTS

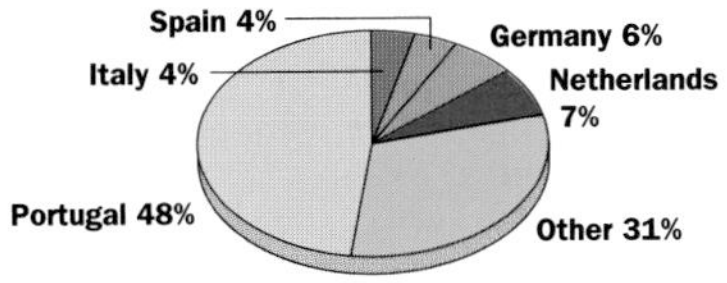
Spain 4%
Germany 6%
Italy 4%
Netherlands 7%
Portugal 48%
Other 31%

Portuguese colonial-style architecture *on Fogo, one of the larger islands. The volcano at its center is the highest point in Cape Verde.*

RESOURCES

Electric power 7000 kW

9653 tonnes

Not an oil producer

200,000 pigs, 112,337 goats, 417,000 chickens

Salt, limestone, pozzolana

Cape Verde has no known strategic resources. With no oil or gas and no possibility of hydroelectric power, it depends on imported petroleum for energy. There is a permanent shortfall in food production due to poverty of soil and lack of rain. Cereal production meets just one-quarter of requirements.

ENVIRONMENT

Not available

None

0.3 tonnes per capita

Cape Verde has recently suffered several years of persistent drought, which have affected food production and reduced livestock herds. It is a very active member of CILSS, which struggles against drought in the Sahel region. Environmental initiatives include reforestation, soil conservation, and a water resources program.

MEDIA

TV ownership medium

There are no daily newspapers

PUBLISHING AND BROADCAST MEDIA

There are no daily newspapers. Independent publications suffer from financial pressures

1 state-controlled service

3 services: 1 state-controlled, 2 independent

The government publishes three weeklies. Press freedom is guaranteed by law; private radio is the main outlet for opposition to the government. Broadcasting is in Portuguese and Creole, with the cooperation of the Portuguese service RTPI.

CRIME

No death penalty

755 prisoners

Little change from year to year

Crime is not a serious problem, even in urban centers, though narcotics trafficking is increasing.

CHRONOLOGY

Cape Verde was a Portuguese colony from 1462 until 1975, and was ruled jointly with Guinea-Bissau.

- ❑ **1961** Joint struggle for independence of Cape Verde and Guinea-Bissau begins.
- ❑ **1974** Guinea-Bissau independent.
- ❑ **1975** Cape Verde independent.
- ❑ **1981** Final split from Guinea-Bissau.
- ❑ **1991** MPD wins first multiparty poll.
- ❑ **2001** General election returns PAICV to power.

EDUCATION

School leaving age: 12

76%

Not available

At independence, education became a priority; 99% of children now attend elementary school, though only half go on to secondary education.

HEALTH

No welfare state health benefits

1 per 5000 people

Heart disease, tuberculosis, typhoid, and accidents

Health care has improved since the colonial period, though there was an outbreak of polio in 2000.

SPENDING

GDP/cap. increase

CONSUMPTION AND SPENDING

32 per 1000 population

160 per 1000 population

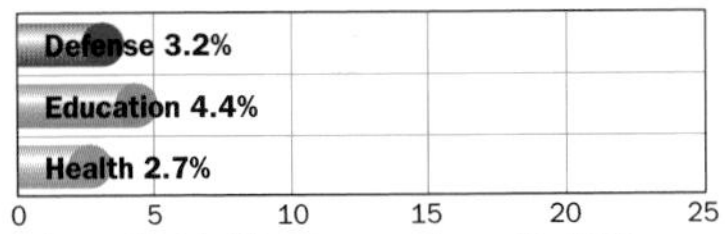
Defense 3.2%
Education 4.4%
Health 2.7%
0
5
10
15
20
25

Defense, Health, Education spending as % of GDP

Around 90% of the population of Cape Verde is engaged in primary production; by comparison, the small business class in Praia is well-off.

WORLD RANKING

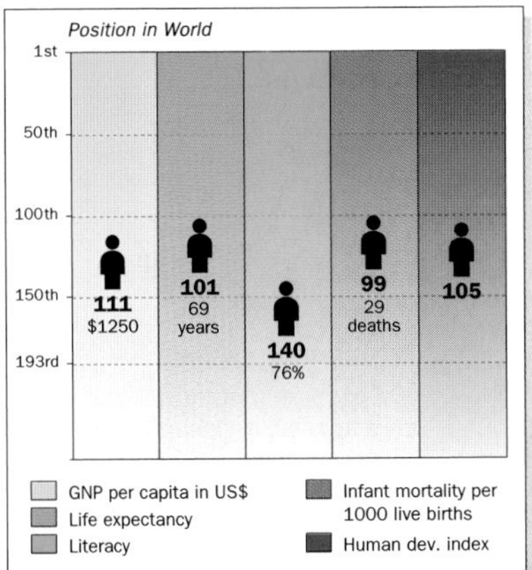
Position in World
1st
50th
100th
150th
193rd
111
$1250
101
69
years
140
76%
99
29
deaths
105
GNP per capita in US$
Life expectancy
Literacy
Infant mortality per 1000 live births
Human dev. index

CENTRAL AFRICAN REPUBLIC

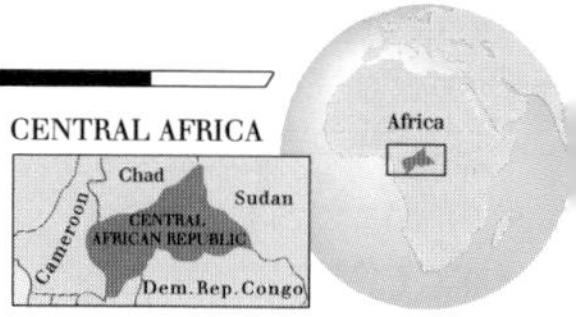
CENTRAL AFRICA
Africa
Chad
Sudan
CENTRAL AFRICAN REPUBLIC
Cameroon
Dem. Rep. Congo

OFFICIAL NAME: Central African Republic **CAPITAL:** Bangui
POPULATION: 3.9 million **CURRENCY:** CFA franc **OFFICIAL LANGUAGE:** French

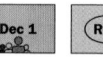

1960 | 1960 | Dec 1 | RCA | +1 | +236 | .cf

LANDLOCKED AT THE EASTERN end of the Sahel, the Central African Republic (CAR) is a low plateau stretching north from the Ubangi River. Almost all the population lives in the equatorial, rainforested south. "Emperor" Bokassa's eccentric rule from 1965 to 1979 was followed by military dictatorship. Democracy was restored in 1993. Any hopes for political stability have been shattered by a string of mutinies and coups since 1996.

CLIMATE

Tropical equatorial

WEATHER CHART FOR BANGUI

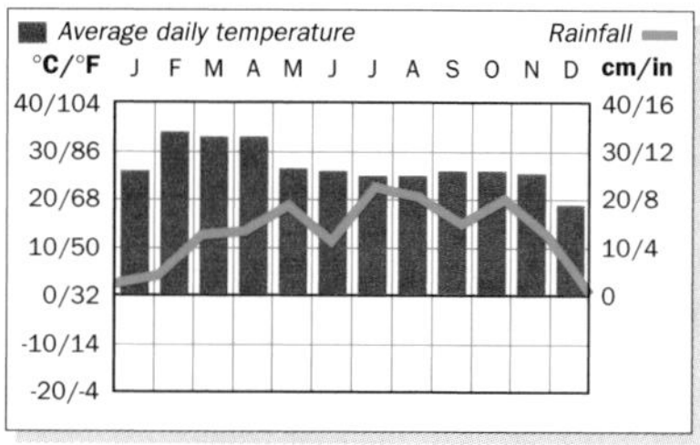
Average daily temperature
Rainfall
°C/°F
J F M A M J J A S O N D
cm/in
40/104
30/86
20/68
10/50
0/32
-10/14
-20/-4
40/16
30/12
20/8
10/4
0

The south is equatorial, the north has a savanna-type climate, and the far north lies within the Sahel.

TRANSPORTATION

Drive on right

Mpoko, Bangui 43,174 passengers

Has no fleet

THE TRANSPORTATION NETWORK

729 km (453 miles)

Trans-African Highway

None

900 km (559 miles)

The CAR has a limited transportation system, depending on the river link to Brazzaville, Congo, and rail from there to Pointe-Noire and the Congo River ports.

TOURISM

Visitors : Population 1:390

10,000 visitors

Little change in 2000

MAIN TOURIST ARRIVALS

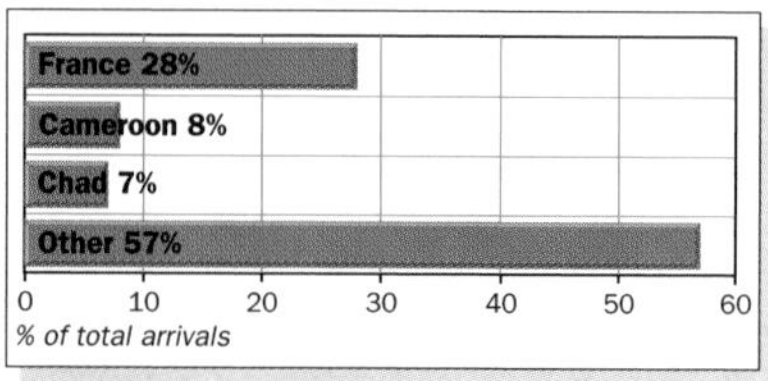
France 28%
Cameroon 8%
Chad 7%
Other 57%
0 10 20 30 40 50 60
% of total arrivals

High levels of insecurity and crime, particularly in recent years, have prevented the CAR from promoting tourism, despite the abundance of scenery and big game wildlife.

PEOPLE

Pop. density low

Sango, Banda, Gbaya, French

6/km² (16/mi²)

THE URBAN/RURAL POPULATION SPLIT

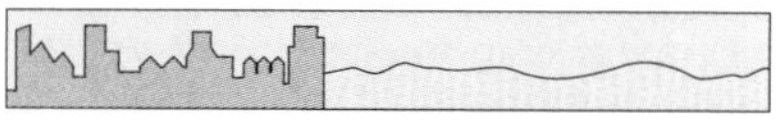
42%
58%

ETHNIC MAKEUP

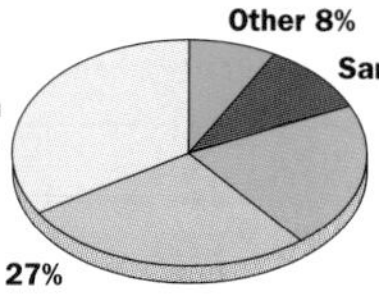
Other 8%
Sara 10%
Baya 34%
Mandjia 21%
Banda 27%

The Baya and Banda are the largest ethnic groups, but the lingua franca is Sango, a trading creole originating among the southern riverine minorities which provided the political leaders from independence until 1993 (Presidents Dacko and Kolingba and "Emperor" Bokassa). Resentment against the river peoples occasionally flares up, as happened after the coup attempt in 2001. As in other non-Muslim African countries, women have considerable power. Elizabeth Domitien was prime minister from 1975 to 1976 and Ruth Rolland ran for president in 1993.

WORLD AFFAIRS

Joined UN in 1960

BDEAC | CEMAC | FZ | LCBC | AU

Regional relations were altered by Gen. Bozizé's 2003 coup. While Chad had given him active support, Libya and factions from the neighboring DRC had emerged as the major allies of Patassé, becoming directly involved in the precoup conflicts. Bozizé is now keen to normalize relations, especially with other CEMAC countries and the DRC, but the AU is reluctant to recognize his regime.

AID

Recipient

$60m (receipts)

Down 10% in 2002

Almost all development projects are funded from external aid. France, the former colonial power, provides one-third of the total. Japan and the EU are other major donors. The CAR receives assistance from the World Bank and the IMF, which have provided funds to support its economic program. The Paris Club of creditor countries in 1998 rescheduled and reduced its debt.

DEFENSE

Compulsory military service

$20m

Up 33% in 2002

The well-equipped, 1400-strong army drains the budget and has frequently intervened in politics. Military rebellion resurfaced in 2001, a year after the withdrawal of a UN force. In 2001 and 2002 progovernment soldiers were supported by forces from Libya and Chad and rebel fighters from the DRC, but were unable to halt the 2003 coup.

POLITICS

In transition

1998/2005

President François Bozizé

AT THE LAST ELECTION

National Assembly (dissolved) 109 seats

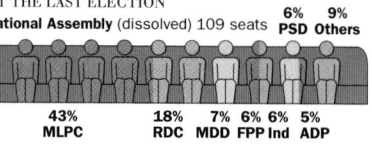

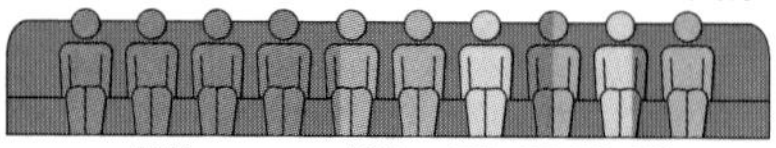
6% PSD
9% Others
43% MLPC
18% RDC
7% MDD
6% FPP
6% Ind
5% ADP

MLPC = Central African People's Liberation Movement **RDC** = Central African Democratic Rally **MDD** = Movement for Democracy and Development **FPP** = Patriotic Front for Progress **Ind** = Independents **PSD** = Social Democratic Party **ADP** = Alliance for Democracy and Progress

Elections in 1993 ended 12 years of single-party rule under Gen. André Kolingba. Former prime minister-turned-dissident Ange-Félix Patassé became president. His decade in power was dogged by army mutinies. The first major rebellion, in 1996, was only calmed after the intervention of a French-led multinational force in 1997. His party, the MLPC, remained the largest in parliament after the 1998 elections, but he was faced with yet more rebellion in 2001. Kolingba led a failed coup in May and was later supported by army chief Gen. François Bozizé. Patassé was kept in power with the assistance of Libyan and Congolese fighters in 2001, and again in 2002, but was finally toppled in a coup led by Gen. Bozizé in 2003. Bozizé appointed an independent commission to supervise elections in 2005, when, he said, he would not contest the presidency.

CENTRAL AFRICAN REPUBLIC

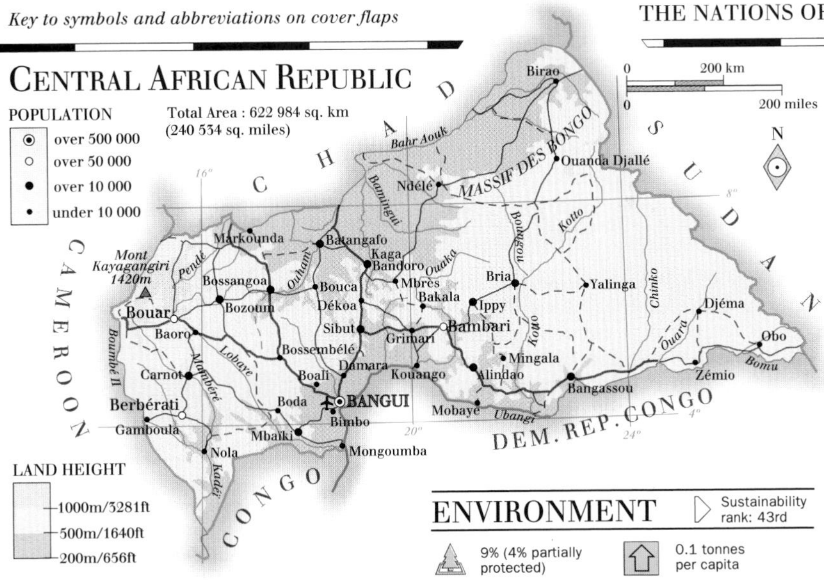
POPULATION
over 500 000
over 50 000
over 10 000
under 10 000
Total Area : 622 984 sq. km
(240 534 sq. miles)
0 200 km
0 200 miles
N
LAND HEIGHT
1000m/3281ft
500m/1640ft
200m/656ft
CHAD
SUDAN
CAMEROON
CONGO
DEM. REP. CONGO
Birao
Bahr Aouk
MASSIF DES BONGO
Ouanda Djallé
Ndélé
Bamingui
Kotto
Bongou
Markounda
Batangafo
Kaga Bandoro
Ouaka
Mont Kayagangiri 1420m
Pendé
Bossangoa
Ouham
Bouca
Mbrès
Bakala
Bria
Yalinga
Chinko
Bouar
Bozoum
Dékoa
Ippy
Djéma
Baoro
Sibut
Grimari
Bambari
Ouarra
Obo
Bossembélé
Mingala
Bomu
Boumbé II
Lobaye
Damara
Kouango
Alindao
Zémio
Carnot
Mambéré
Boali
Bangassou
Berbérati
Boda
BANGUI
Mobaye
Ubangi
Gamboula
Mbaïki
Bimbo
Nola
Mongoumba
Kadéï

CHRONOLOGY

The French colony of Ubangi-Chari gained autonomy as the CAR in 1958.

- **1960** Independence under David Dacko; one-party state.
- **1965** Coup by Jean-Bédel Bokassa.
- **1977** Bokassa crowned "emperor."
- **1979** French help reinstate Dacko.
- **1981** Gen. Kolingba ousts Dacko.
- **1993** Democracy restored. Ange-Félix Patassé president.
- **1996–1997** Army rebellion.
- **2001–2003** Further mutinies.
- **2003** Gen. Bozizé leads coup.

C

ECONOMICS

Inflation 4.2% p.a. (1990–2001)

$969m

539.2 CFA francs (571.2)

SCORE CARD

- World GNP Ranking 155th
- GNP per Capita $250
- Balance of Payments $16m
- Inflation 3.4%
- Unemployment 8%

Strengths
Self-sufficiency in food. Some diversity of export earnings (diamonds, cotton, timber, iron, coffee). Transit zone in central Africa.

Weaknesses
Instability. Landlocked. Government mismanagement. Poor infrastructure. Shortage of trained workers.

EXPORTS

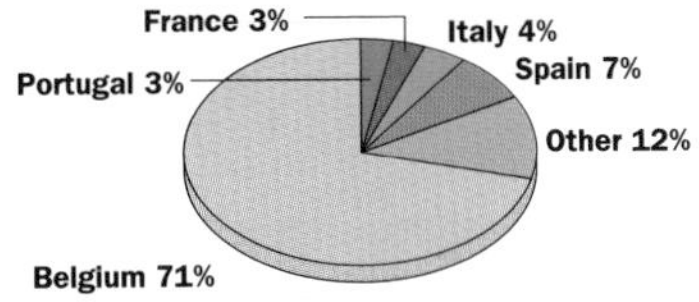
France 3%
Italy 4%
Spain 7%
Portugal 3%
Other 12%
Belgium 71%

IMPORTS

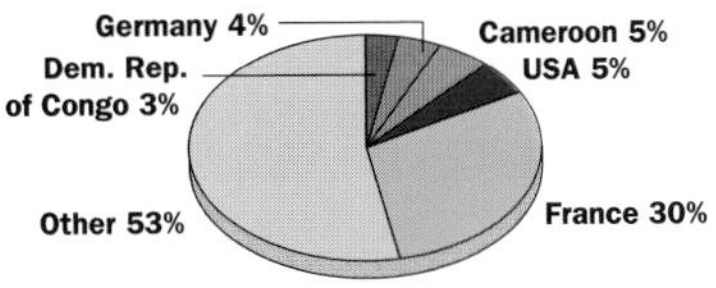
Germany 4%
Cameroon 5%
Dem. Rep. of Congo 3%
USA 5%
Other 53%
France 30%

RESOURCES

Electric power 43,000 kW

15,125 tonnes

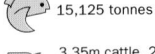

Not an oil producer and has no refineries

3.35m cattle, 2.92m goats, 771,000 pigs, 4.58m chickens

Diamonds, gold, uranium, iron, copper, manganese

Very little of the country's territory has been explored, and there is great potential for hidden resources.

ENVIRONMENT

Sustainability rank: 43rd

9% (4% partially protected)

0.1 tonnes per capita

Hunting elephants was banned in 1985, as numbers had fallen by 84% in a decade. The government empowered private antipoaching militias in 2002 to tackle the trade in bushmeat.

MEDIA

TV ownership low

Daily newspaper circulation 2 per 1000 people

PUBLISHING AND BROADCAST MEDIA

There are 3 daily newspapers, *E Le Songo*, *Le Citoyen*, and *Le Novateur*

1 state-owned service

4 services: 1 state-owned, 3 independent

The three weeklies and three daily newspapers have only limited circulation. A small opposition press has developed with multipartyism, but is inhibited by lack of resources.

CRIME

Death penalty not used in practice

4168 prisoners

Crime is rising

Human rights abuses were rampant during the Bokassa years and are again on the rise. While Bangui retains a fragile calm, rural areas are virtually lawless. Roaming militias made up of demobilized Chadian fighters who backed Gen. Bozizé in 2003 are blamed for much of the increase in crime.

***Baskets of cotton,** Meme village. Cotton is one of the Central African Republic's most significant export crops.*

EDUCATION

School leaving age: 14

49%

6323 students

Schooling, on the French model, is compulsory, but in practice is only received by 55% of 6–14-year-olds.

HEALTH

No welfare state health benefits

1 per 25,000 people

Communicable and parasitic diseases, malnutrition, AIDS

The health system has all but collapsed. Much of the population now relies on traditional medicine.

SPENDING

GDP/cap. increase

CONSUMPTION AND SPENDING

1 per 1000 population

2 per 1000 population

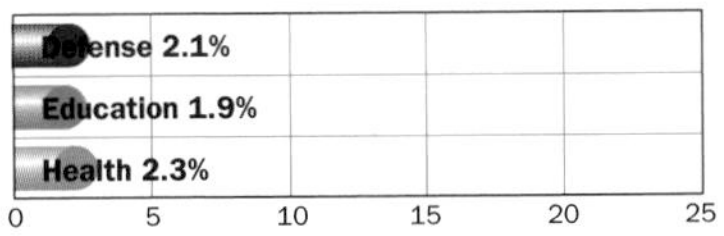
Defense 2.1%
Education 1.9%
Health 2.3%
0
5
10
15
20
25

Defense, Health, Education spending as % of GDP

There is a small political–military elite in the CAR, which came into being only in postcolonial days. For its members, Paris is the chosen destination and source of style.

WORLD RANKING

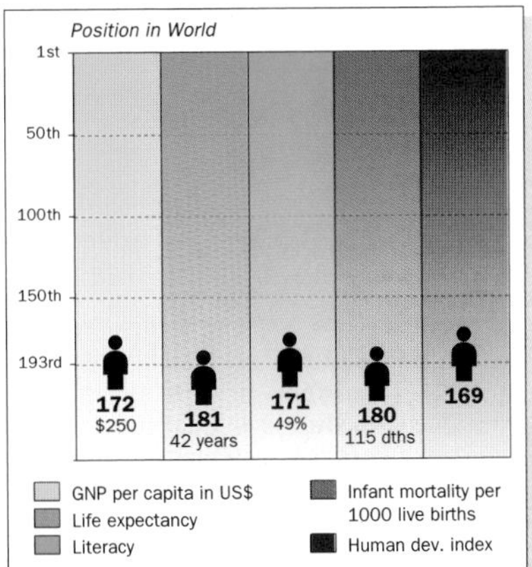
Position in World
1st
50th
100th
150th
193rd
172
$250
181
42 years
171
49%
180
115 dths
169
GNP per capita in US$
Life expectancy
Literacy
Infant mortality per 1000 live births
Human dev. index

CHAD

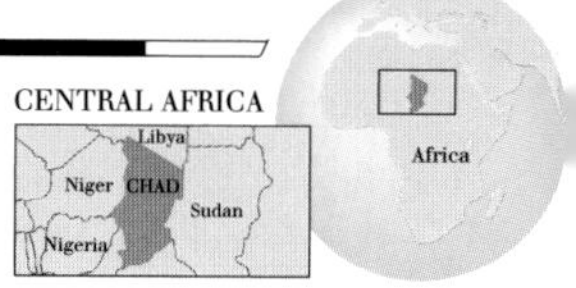

CENTRAL AFRICA
Libya
Niger
CHAD
Sudan
Nigeria
Africa

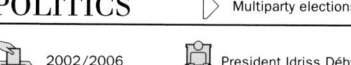

OFFICIAL NAME: Republic of Chad **CAPITAL:** N'Djamena **POPULATION:** 8.6 million
CURRENCY: CFA franc **OFFICIAL LANGUAGES:** Arabic and French

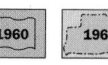

C

1960 | 1960 | Aug 11 | TCH | +1 | +235 | .td

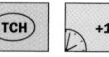

LANDLOCKED IN NORTH central Africa, Chad has had a turbulent history since independence from France in 1960. Intermittent periods of civil war, involving French and Libyan troops, followed a coup in 1975. Another coup in 1990 preceded a transition to multipartyism, enshrined in a new constitution. The tropical, cotton-producing south is the most populous region. The discovery of large oil reserves could potentially have a dramatic impact on the economy.

CLIMATE

Hot desert/steppe/ tropical

WEATHER CHART FOR N'DJAMENA

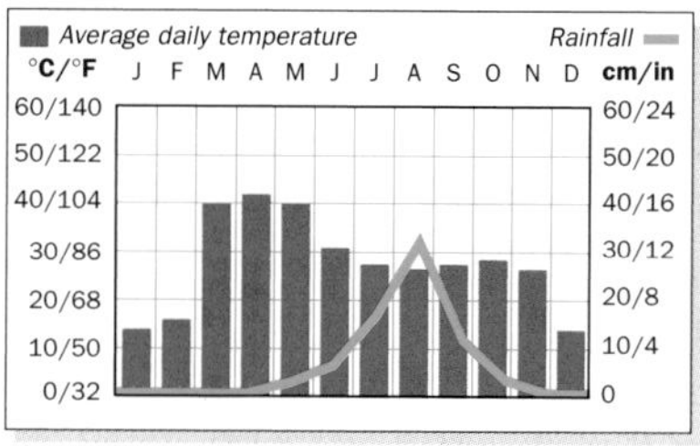

Average daily temperature
Rainfall
°C/°F
J F M A M J J A S O N D
cm/in
60/140
50/122
40/104
30/86
20/68
10/50
0/32
60/24
50/20
40/16
30/12
20/8
10/4
0

There are three distinct zones: the tropical south, the central semiarid Sahelian belt, and the desert north.

TRANSPORTATION

Drive on right

N'Djamena International 16,861 passengers

Has no fleet

THE TRANSPORTATION NETWORK

334 km (208 miles)	None
None	2000 km (1243 miles)

Chad has a limited transportation infrastructure. The nearest rail links are in Nigeria and Cameroon.

TOURISM

Visitors : Population 1:269

32,000 visitors

Down 43% in 2002

MAIN TOURIST ARRIVALS

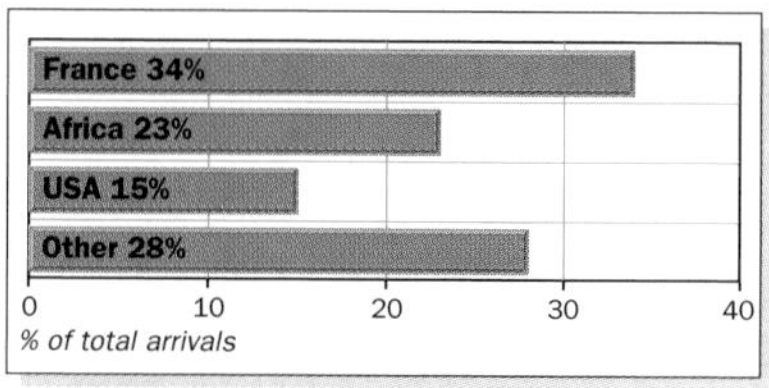

France 34%
Africa 23%
USA 15%
Other 28%
0
10
20
30
40
% of total arrivals

Tourism is virtually nonexistent due to poverty and years of war. Among potential attractions are national parks and game reserves, prehistoric rock painting in the Tibesti plateau, and the Muslim cities of the Sahara.

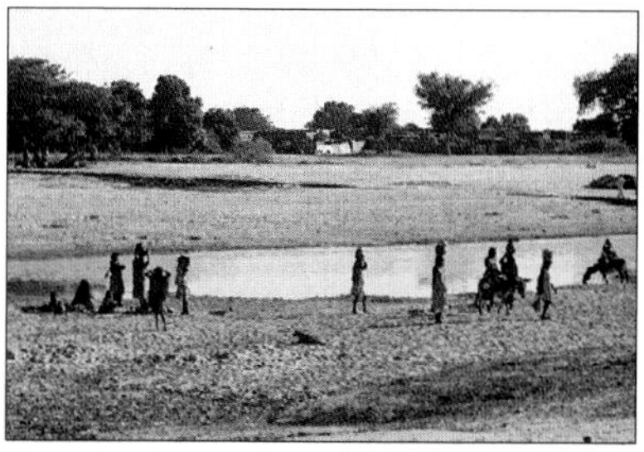

***Watering hole at Oum Hadjer**, a village on the Batha watercourse in central Chad, 145 km (90 miles) east of Ati.*

PEOPLE

Pop. density low

French, Sara, Arabic, Maba

7/km² (18/mi²)

THE URBAN/RURAL POPULATION SPLIT

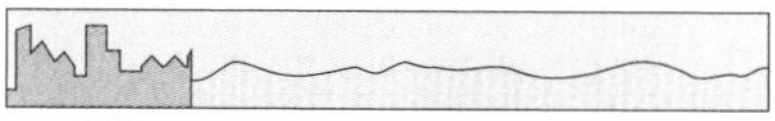

25%
75%

RELIGIOUS PERSUASION

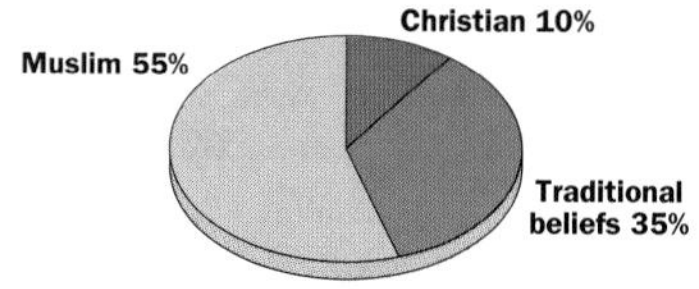

Christian 10%
Muslim 55%
Traditional beliefs 35%

About half the population, mainly the Sara-speaking and related peoples, is concentrated in the south in one-fifth of the national territory. Most of the rest are located in the central sultanates. The northern third of Chad has a population of only 100,000 people, mainly nomadic Muslim Toubou.

POLITICS

Multiparty elections

2002/2006

President Idriss Déby

AT THE LAST ELECTION
National Assembly 155 seats

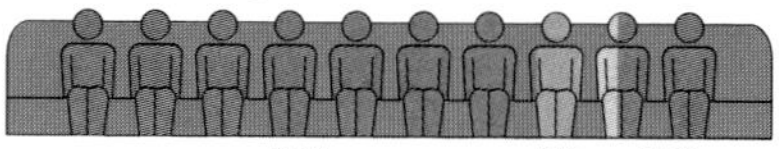

6% FAR
72% MPS
7% RDP
15% Others

MPS = Patriotic Salvation Movement
RDP = Rally for Democracy and Progress
FAR = Front of Action Forces for the Republic

Idriss Déby overthrew President Hissène Habré in 1990 after an armed invasion from Sudan. He promised multipartyism, and in 1992 – for the first time since the early 1960s – political parties were legalized. A referendum in 1996 approved a new constitution based on the French model. President Déby was confirmed in office in elections in 1996 and again in 2001. In 2004, amid an opposition boycott, Déby and his ruling MPS amended the constitution to allow him to run again in 2006. Critics suggest that the discovery of oil may have influenced Déby's decision. A peace deal with northern rebels was struck in 2003.

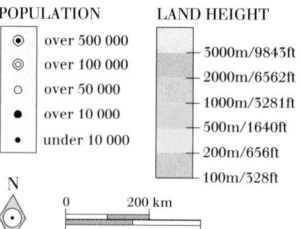

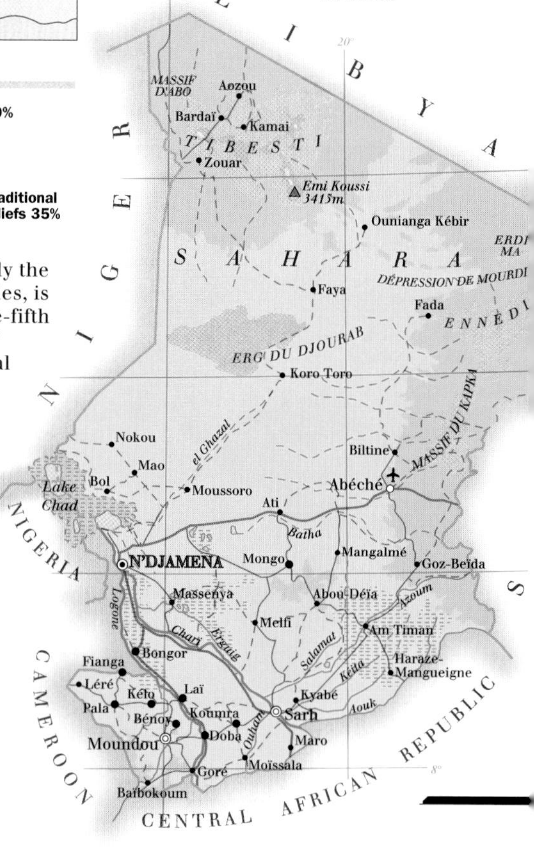

LIBYA
NIGER
NIGERIA
CAMEROON
CENTRAL AFRICAN REPUBLIC
MASSIF D'ABO
Aozou
Bardaï
Kamai
TIBESTI
Zouar
Emi Koussi 3415m
Ouinanga Kébir
SAHARA
ERDI MA
DÉPRESSION DE MOURDI
Faya
Fada
ENNEDI
ERG DU DJOURAB
Koro Toro
MASSIF DU KAPKA
Nokou
Mao
Lake Chad
Bol
el Ghazal
Moussoro
Biltine
Abéché
Ati
Batha
Mangalmé
N'DJAMENA
Mongo
Goz-Beïda
Massenya
Abou-Déïa
Azoum
Logone
Melfi
Chari
Erguig
Salamat
Am Timan
Bongor
Fianga
Haraze-Mangueigne
Léré
Kélo
Laï
Keïta
Pala
Béboy
Koumra
Kyabé
Sarh
Aouk
Moundou
Doba
Ouham
Maro
Goré
Moïssala
Baïbokoum

CHAD

Total Area : 1 284 000 sq. km (495 752 sq. miles)

POPULATION	LAND HEIGHT
over 500 000	3000m/9843ft
over 100 000	2000m/6562ft
over 50 000	1000m/3281ft
over 10 000	500m/1640ft
under 10 000	200m/656ft
	100m/328ft

N

0 200 km
0 200 miles

C

WORLD AFFAIRS

Joined UN in 1960

CILSS | FZ | LCBC | AU | OIC

Chad's most important relationship is with France. Relations with Sudan are strained by cross-border skirmishes.

AID

Recipient

$233m (receipts)

Up 25% in 2002

In return for financial support for the new oil pipeline, Chad has entered into a partnership agreement with the World Bank under which the vast majority of oil revenue is kept in a trust and must be spent on development.

DEFENSE

Compulsory military service

$14m

Up 8% in 2002

On seizing power, Déby swelled the existing army with irregulars, a policy now reversed and the army reduced to 25,000, including former rebels. Chadian forces are fighting Islamist militant groups with US backing.

ECONOMICS

Inflation 6.7% p.a. (1990–2001)

$1.78bn

539.2 CFA francs (571.2)

SCORE CARD

❑ WORLD GNP RANKING	141st
❑ GNP PER CAPITA	$210
❑ BALANCE OF PAYMENTS	–$660m
❑ INFLATION	5.2%
❑ UNEMPLOYMENT	Widespread underemployment

STRENGTHS

Discovery of large oil deposits and Chad–Cameroon pipeline could transform economy. Cotton industry; potential for other agriculture in south. Strategic trading location in heart of Africa. Natron and uranium deposits.

WEAKNESSES

Underdevelopment and poverty. Lack of transportation infrastructure. Political instability. Frequent droughts.

EXPORTS

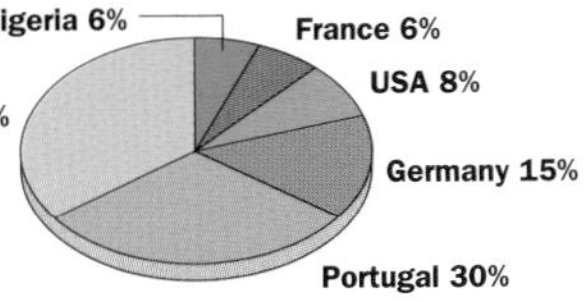
Nigeria 6%
France 6%
USA 8%
Other 35%
Germany 15%
Portugal 30%

IMPORTS

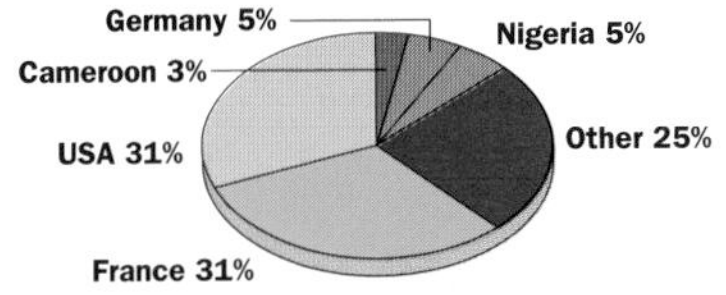
Germany 5%
Nigeria 5%
Cameroon 3%
USA 31%
Other 25%
France 31%

RESOURCES

Electric power 29,000 kW

84,000 tonnes

225,000 b/d (reserves 1bn barrels)

6.27m cattle, 5.59m goats, 2.51m sheep, 5m chickens

Natron, uranium, oil, kaolin, soda, rock salt

The opening in 2003 of a pipeline to take oil from newly found reserves in the southern Doba region to the coast of Cameroon has made Chad a net oil exporter. Natron, a type of salt, is the only other resource currently exploited. There is uranium in the Aozou strip.

ENVIRONMENT

Sustainability rank: 96th

9% (8.6% partially protected)

0.02 tonnes per capita

President Déby's government has made protection of the environment a priority, with antidesertification measures such as tree-planting campaigns and aid-funded irrigation schemes. There is concern that environmental damage may result from oil production and from the Chad–Cameroon oil pipeline.

MEDIA

TV ownership low

Daily newspaper circulation 0.2 per 1000 people

PUBLISHING AND BROADCAST MEDIA

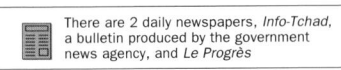

There are 2 daily newspapers, *Info-Tchad*, a bulletin produced by the government news agency, and *Le Progrès*

1 state-controlled service

8 services: 1 state-controlled, 7 independent

Broadcasting is controlled by the government, which sometimes allows the airing of opposition views. There are a few independent publications, of which the best known is the weekly *N'Djamena-Hebdo*.

CRIME

Death penalty in use

3883 prisoners

Crime is rising

The judicial system is corrupt and controlled by the president. The easy availability of weapons for the past two decades has meant that local disputes often now lead to gun battles. Armed robbery, smuggling, and vandalism are widespread. Crime has worsened markedly in towns near the oil fields.

EDUCATION

School leaving age: 11

46%

5901 students

All schools are underfunded and suffer from a lack of trained teachers. Chad has the lowest ratio of female enrollment in schools in Africa. Overall, only 55% of children attend classes and barely a third of them are girls.

CHRONOLOGY

France extended its domination of the area now known as Chad after ousting the last Arab ruler in 1900.

- ❑ **1960** Independence. One-party state.
- ❑ **1973–1994** Libyans occupy uranium-rich Aozou strip.
- ❑ **1975** Coup by Gen. Félix Malloum.
- ❑ **1979–1982** North–south civil war.
- ❑ **1980** Goukouni Oueddei in power.
- ❑ **1982** Hissène Habré (northerner) defeats Oueddei.
- ❑ **1990** Idriss Déby overthrows Habré, who flees to Senegal.
- ❑ **1996** National cease-fire; new constitution.
- ❑ **1997** Déby's MPS wins elections.
- ❑ **1999** Rebellion breaks out in north.
- ❑ **2001** Déby reelected.
- ❑ **2002** MPS increases its majority.
- ❑ **2003** Oil production begins.

HEALTH

Welfare state health benefits

1 per 33,333 people

Diarrheal, parasitic, and communicable diseases

There are a few city hospitals and over 300 smaller health centers. One in five children die before the age of five.

SPENDING

GDP/cap. increase

CONSUMPTION AND SPENDING

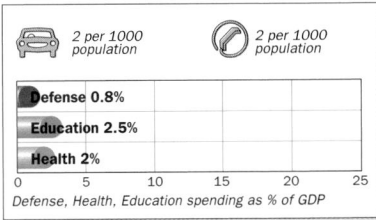

2 per 1000 population

2 per 1000 population

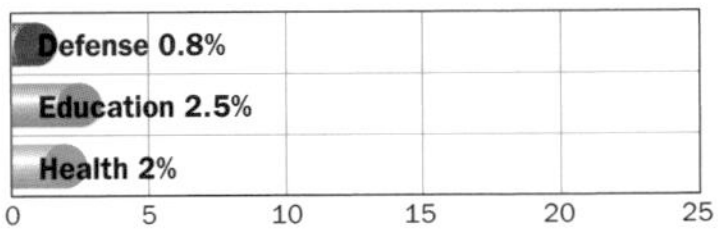
Defense 0.8%
Education 2.5%
Health 2%
0
5
10
15
20
25

Defense, Health, Education spending as % of GDP

Poverty is almost universal in Chad; the middle class is very small. There are few wealthy individuals. It remains to be seen whether new income from oil will affect most people's daily lives.

WORLD RANKING

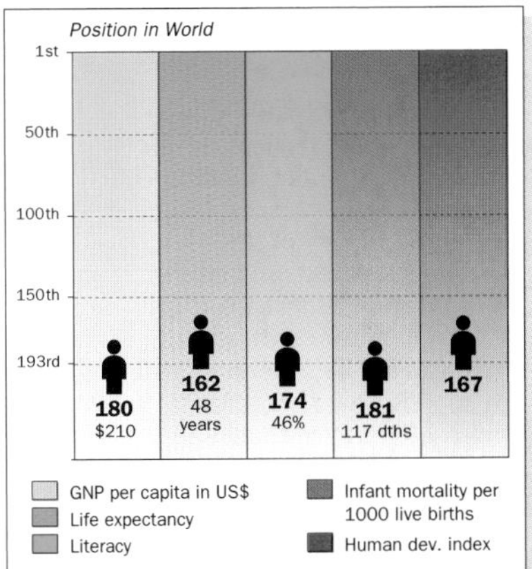
Position in World
1st
50th
100th
150th
193rd
180
$210
162
48 years
174
46%
181
117 dths
167
GNP per capita in US$
Life expectancy
Literacy
Infant mortality per 1000 live births
Human dev. index

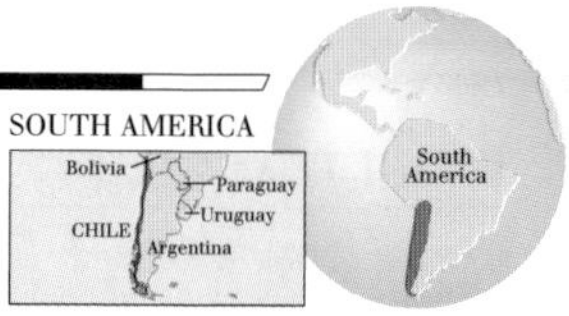
SOUTH AMERICA
Bolivia
Paraguay
Uruguay
CHILE
Argentina
South America

CHILE

OFFICIAL NAME: Republic of Chile **CAPITAL:** Santiago
POPULATION: 15.8 million **CURRENCY:** Chilean peso **OFFICIAL LANGUAGE:** Spanish

C

1818 | 1883 | Sept 18 | RCH | -4 | +56 | .cl

CHILE EXTENDS IN A narrow ribbon 4350 km (2700 miles) down the Pacific coast of South America. Its extraordinary shape means that its physical geography ranges from the deserts of the High Andes in the north to fertile valleys in the center, while in the south are the fjords, lakes, and deep sea channels of the Southern Andes. In 1989, Chile returned to elected civilian rule, following a popular rejection of the Pinochet dictatorship. A collapse in copper prices, coupled with weaker export markets, has interrupted the high economic growth seen in the 1990s.

General Pinochet, *a dictatorial president rejected by popular referendum in 1988.*

Ricardo Lagos *was narrowly elected president in 2000.*

CLIMATE

Desert/mountain/maritime

WEATHER CHART FOR SANTIAGO

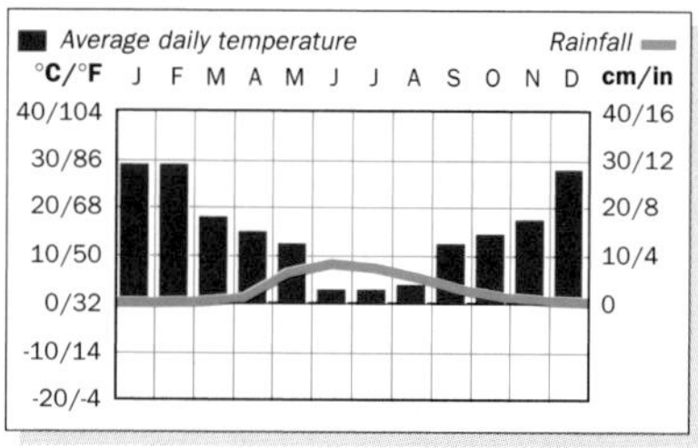
Average daily temperature
Rainfall
°C/°F
J F M A M J J A S O N D
cm/in
40/104
30/86
20/68
10/50
0/32
-10/14
-20/-4
40/16
30/12
20/8
10/4
0

Chile has an immensely varied climate. The north, which includes the world's driest desert, the Atacama, is frequently cloudy and cool for its latitude. The central regions have an almost Mediterranean climate, with changeable winters and hot, dry summers. The higher reaches of the Andes have a typically alpine climate, with glaciers and year-round snow. The south is the wettest region.

TRANSPORTATION

Drive on right

Comodoro Arturo Merino Benítez, Santiago 5.75m passengers

525 ships 879,600 grt

THE TRANSPORTATION NETWORK

15,921 km (9893 miles)

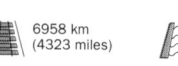

Pan-American Highway, 3455 km (2147 miles)

6958 km (4323 miles)

725 km (450 miles)

Chile's shape dictates a north–south perspective for transportation links. Roads are the most important arteries; rail services have been largely neglected in recent decades. Chile has been given strong regional and international links by the 1999 open skies agreement with the US, its first with a South American country. Well-used routes servicing Santiago are a priority for upgrading. The IDB is part-funding a six-year Urban Transit Plan for the capital, which aims to improve services and cut pollution by 2006.

TOURISM

Visitors : Population 1:9.9

1.6m visitors

Up 13% in 2003

MAIN TOURIST ARRIVALS

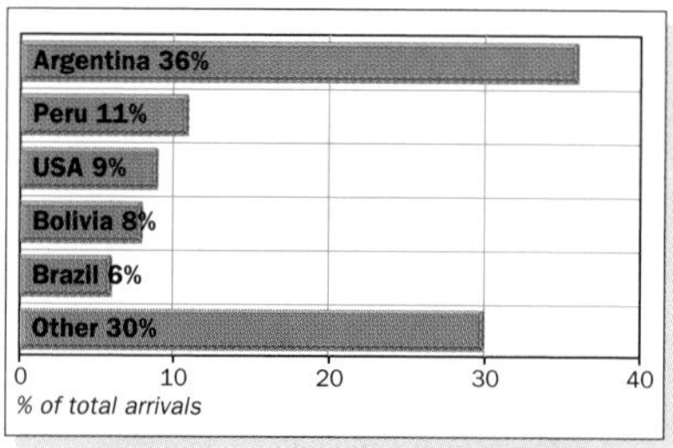
Argentina 36%
Peru 11%
USA 9%
Bolivia 8%
Brazil 6%
Other 30%
0
10
20
30
40
% of total arrivals

The Pinochet years saw a dramatic decline in tourists from the US and Europe, though the numbers from neighboring countries held up. Since 1989, visitors have returned, but over half of them still come from South America, mainly Argentina.

Chile's attractions include its stunning Andean scenery, its immensely long coastline, and a number of exceptional sites, such as Chuquicamata, the world's largest copper mine, the Elqui Valley wine-growing region, and the spectacular glaciers and fjords of the south. Many tourists are specifically drawn to the wide range of adventure sports available. Easter Island in the Pacific, with its mysterious, massive stone statues, is another major attraction.

Peaks in the Paine range, southern Chile. *Fjords, glaciers, and myriad islands typify Chile's very wet, wild, and stormy south.*

PEOPLE

Pop. density low

Spanish, Amerindian languages

21/km² (55/mi²)

THE URBAN/RURAL POPULATION SPLIT

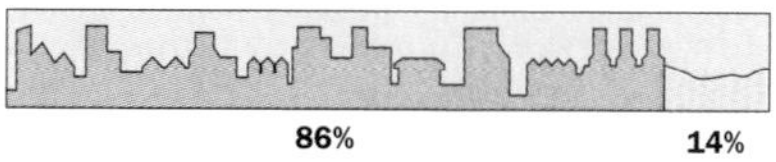
86%
14%

RELIGIOUS PERSUASION

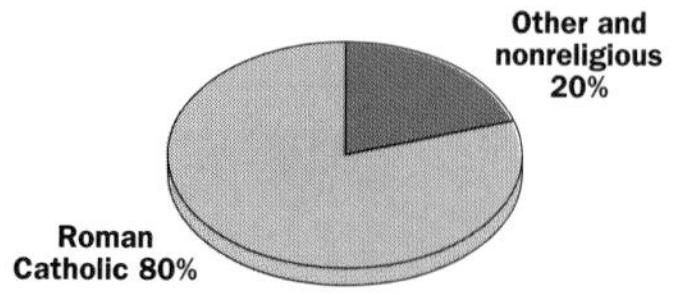
Other and nonreligious 20%
Roman Catholic 80%

ETHNIC MAKEUP

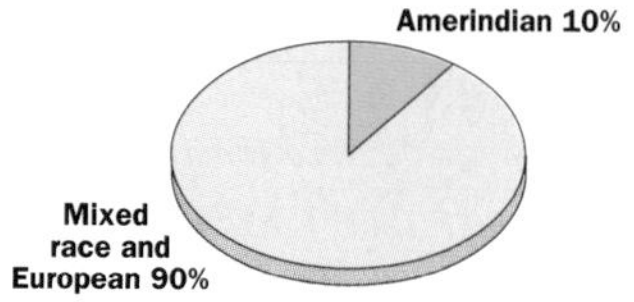
Amerindian 10%
Mixed race and European 90%

One-third of the population live in Santiago, where there are large slums. Most people are of mixed Spanish–Amerindian descent; Chile has relatively few immigrants. There are some 80,000 Mapuche Amerindians around Temuco in the south, 20,000 Aymara in the High Andes, and 2000 Rapa Nui on Easter Island. Ethnic issues highlighted by a Commission for Historic Truth, set up in 2000, have yet to be addressed.

Over 25% of working women are employed in domestic service. Divorce was legalized in 2004.

POPULATION AGE BREAKDOWN

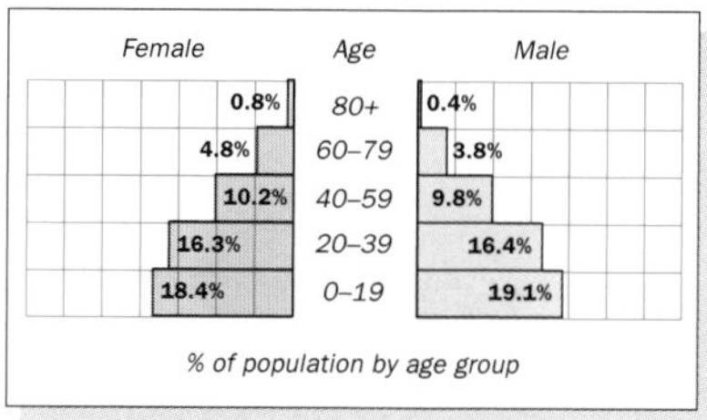
Female
Age
Male
0.8%
80+
0.4%
4.8%
60–79
3.8%
10.2%
40–59
9.8%
16.3%
20–39
16.4%
18.4%
0–19
19.1%
% of population by age group

Juan Fernández Is
I. Alejandro Selkirk
San Juan Bautista
I. Robinson Crusoe
100 km
100 miles
Easter I.
Terevaka
Hanga Roa
10 km
10 miles
PERU
BOLIVIA
ARGENTINA
PACIFIC OCEAN
Arica
Iquique
Atacama Desert
Chuquicamata
Calama
Antofagasta
Chañaral
Nevado Ojos del Salado 6880m
Copiapó
Vallenar
La Serena
Coquimbo
Elqui
Ovalle
Illapel
Los Andes
Viña del Mar
Valparaíso
Quilpué
SANTIAGO
Llolleo
San Bernardo
Puente Alto
Rancagua
Curicó
Rengo
Talca
San Javier de Loncomilla
Linares
Parral
San Carlos
Talcahuano
Concepción
Chillán
Los Ángeles
Curanilahue
Bío Bío
Mulchén
Traiguén
Victoria
Temuco
Lautaro
Valdivia
La Unión
Puerto Varas
Puerto Montt
Isla de Chiloé
Castro
Puerto Aisén
Coihaique
Lago General Carrera
Chile Chico
Isla Wellington
Cerro Paine
Puerto Natales
Punta Arenas
Porvenir
Strait of Magellan
Beagle Channel
I. Picton
I. Nueva
I. Lennox
Cape Horn
Drake Passage
CHILE
Total Area : 756 950 sq. km (292 258 sq. miles)
POPULATION
over 1 000 000
over 100 000
over 50 000
over 10 000
under 10 000
LAND HEIGHT
4000m/13124ft
2000m/6562ft
1000m/3281ft
200m/656ft
Sea Level
N
0 300 km
0 300 miles

POLITICS

Multiparty elections

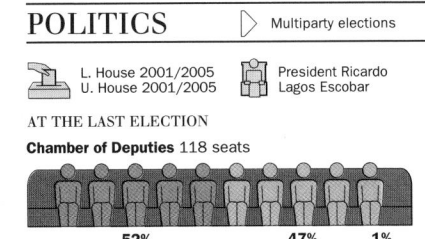

L. House 2001/2005
U. House 2001/2005

President Ricardo Lagos Escobar

AT THE LAST ELECTION

Chamber of Deputies 118 seats

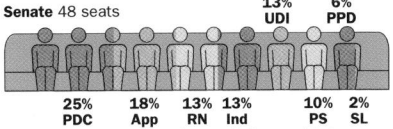

52% CPD **47% APC** **1% Ind**

CPD = Concertación – Coalition of Parties for Democracy (Christian Democratic Party–**PDC**, Party for Democracy–**PPD**, and Socialist Party of Chile–**PS**) **APC** = Alliance for Chile (Independent Democratic Union–**UDI** and National Renewal Party–**RN**) **Ind** = Independents **App** = Appointed **SL** = Senator-for-Life

Senate 48 seats

13% UDI **6% PPD**

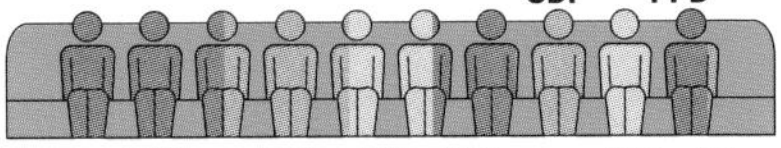

25% PDC **18% App** **13% RN** **13% Ind** **10% PS** **2% SL**

There are 38 elected members and nine appointed senators. Former president Frei is a senator-for-life

After 16 years of military rule under Gen. Augusto Pinochet, Chile returned to multiparty democracy in 1989.

PROFILE

Chilean politics is still strongly affected by the legacy of the military dictatorship of 1973–1989, which began when Pinochet's coup overthrew the elected Marxist government of Salvador Allende.

The CIA backed the Pinochet coup, anxious to halt Allende's program of nationalization of the largely US-owned copper mines. As a result, thousands of Chileans were killed by the military or "disappeared," and a further 80,000 were taken as political prisoners.

Pinochet's nationalist politics drew on the example of Franco's Spain, while his economic policy was one of the first experiments in the free-market Chicago School of monetarism. Chile's business and middle classes prospered, while opposition, which was brutally suppressed by the DINA secret police, came most visibly from the Church and the urban poor.

In 1988 Pinochet, attempting to secure a popular mandate for continuing his regime, was surprised when the population emphatically voted for democracy. Patricio Aylwin won presidential elections held in 1989, heading Concertación, a center-left coalition. Pinochet stepped down, but remained head of the army.

Under Aylwin, politics became more stable, partly as a result of a cross-party consensus on economic policy. Continued growth and some progressive social measures attracted the support of the trade unions. These policies were continued under Eduardo Frei of the PS, who was elected president in 1993.

When Pinochet retired as army chief in 1998, heated disagreements over his entry to the Senate as a senator-for-life split Concertación along broadly left and right lines. Disagreements over Pinochet's subsequent arrest and detention in Europe on human rights charges further complicated the picture. Judged too ill to face trial, however, he resigned from the Senate in 2002.

Ricardo Lagos of the PS emerged as front-runner for the 1999 presidential elections, in which both the PS and the PDC presented themselves as the guarantors of peace and democracy. Right-wing opposition parties, however, also began to downplay their past links with Pinochet to broaden their electoral appeal. Lagos narrowly won a run-off poll in 2000. Facing a better organized opposition than hitherto, the ruling center-left Concertación performed reasonably well in the 2001 elections retaining its majority in the Chamber of Deputies but losing it in the Senate.

MAIN POLITICAL ISSUES

Future of the ruling alliance

Corruption scandals involving officials of all the member parties of the ruling Concertación coalition have threatened to cause its dissolution or renegotiation. Despite bills on probity, transparency, and modernization promoted by the government of the still popular President Lagos, observers have suggested that Concertación has outlived its political usefulness now that democracy is maturing. A new understanding between the PDC and PS is one possible outcome, and fragmentation into right, center, and left parties, as before, is another.

Reform of the military

The resignation in 2002 of Gen. Patricio Ríos, the air force commander accused of covering up human rights abuses committed by some of his senior officers during military rule in the 1970s and 1980s, enhanced presidential authority and refocused attention on the efforts to reform the 1980 constitution drafted by the military.

CHRONOLOGY

Spanish *conquistadores* were repelled by the fierce indigenous Araucanian people in 1536. Conquest began in 1540, and Santiago was founded in 1541. Chile was under Spanish rule until independence in 1818.

- **1817–1818** Bernardo O'Higgins leads republican Army of the Andes in victories against royalist forces.
- **1879–1883** War of the Pacific with Bolivia and Peru. Chile gains valuable nitrate regions.
- **1891–1924** Parliamentary republic ends with growing political chaos. ⇨

C

C

CHRONOLOGY *continued*

- 1936–1946 Communist, Radical, and Socialist parties form influential Popular Front coalition.
- 1943 Chile backs US in World War II.
- 1946–1964 Right-wing Chilean presidents follow US McCarthy policy and marginalize the left.
- 1970 Salvador Allende elected president. Socialist reforms provoke strong reaction from the right.
- 1973 Allende killed in army coup. Brutal dictatorship of Gen. Pinochet begins.
- 1988 Referendum votes "no" to Pinochet staying in power.
- 1989 Democracy peacefully restored; Pinochet steps down after Aylwin election victory.
- 1998 Pinochet detained in UK pending extradition to Spain on human rights charges.
- 2000 Ricardo Lagos (PS) sworn in as president. Pinochet, deemed unfit to face trial, returns to Chile, where charges are suspended in 2001.

WORLD AFFAIRS

Joined UN in 1945

APEC | G15 | NAM | OAS | RG

During the Allende period in the early 1970s, the US actively worked against the government, fearing that the spread of socialism would jeopardize its investments in Latin America. The subsequent Pinochet regime's human rights record eventually became an embarrassment. In 1999, in response to Pinochet's detention in the UK and planned extradition to Spain to stand trial on human rights charges, Chile argued that this amounted to an infringement of its sovereignty. Relations with Spain and the UK improved in 2000 following Pinochet's return to Chile.

A nonpermanent member of the UN Security Council in 2003, Chile expressed reservations over war in Iraq and came under strong diplomatic pressure from the US and UK governments before efforts to gain a second UN resolution authorizing action ceased.

An associate member of Mercosur, Chile has free trade agreements with the EU, South Korea, and the US – its chief export market. Border disputes with Bolivia and Peru are ongoing.

AID

Recipient

No net receipts

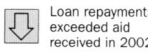

Loan repayments exceeded aid received in 2002

Foreign aid is small-scale and mostly from Japan and Germany. Projects focus on economic infrastructure.

DEFENSE

Compulsory military service

$2.56bn

Down 9% in 2002

CHILEAN ARMED FORCES

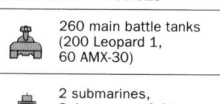

260 main battle tanks (200 Leopard 1, 60 AMX-30)	47,700 personnel
2 submarines, 3 destroyers, 3 frigates, and 27 patrol boats	19,000 personnel
79 combat aircraft (19 F-5, 34 Mirage, 14 A-37B, 12 A-36)	10,600 personnel
None	

Most of the officers linked to human rights abuses under the 1973–1989 dictatorship are now retired, but dozens still face investigation and possible trial. The army now has a moderate chief, and in 2002, for the first time, a woman and a member of the PS – Michelle Bachelet – was appointed defense minister. The defense budget is supplemented by around $200 million each year from the copper industry under a rule from the era of military government. Despite pressure from the army high command, the government is prioritizing modernization of the air force and navy, though purchase of F-16 fighter aircraft has been held up by financing problems. The deal has also provoked concerns over the pressing need for greater social spending.

ECONOMICS

Inflation 7.5% p.a. (1990–2001)

$66.3bn

636.3 Chilean pesos (700.8)

SCORE CARD

- World GNP Ranking....................43rd
- GNP per Capita....................$4250
- Balance of Payments....................–$553m
- Inflation....................2.5%
- Unemployment....................8%

EXPORTS

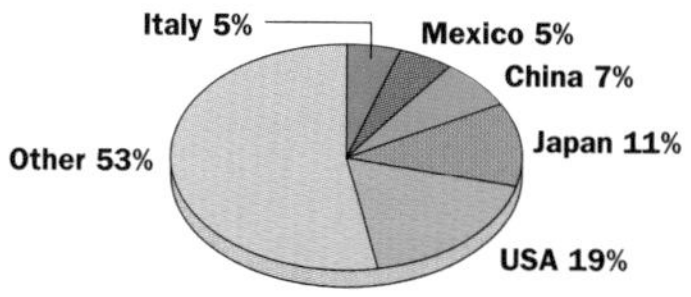
Italy 5%
Mexico 5%
China 7%
Japan 11%
USA 19%
Other 53%

IMPORTS

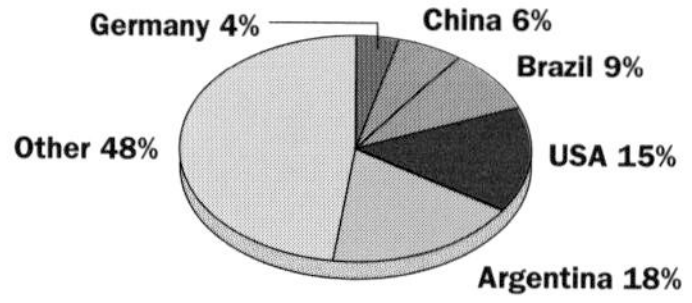
Germany 4%
China 6%
Brazil 9%
USA 15%
Argentina 18%
Other 48%

Strengths

World's largest copper producer. Fresh fruit exports. Strong investment inflows allowing steady economic growth. Highest level of credit rating due to fiscal and monetary stability and highly liquid financial system. Development of nontraditional industries such as wine and fresh and prepared fish.

Weaknesses

Vulnerability of copper revenues (representing 30% of exports) and oil imports (94% of fuel consumed) to world price fluctuations. Dependence on US as single largest trading partner. Vulnerable peso.

Profile

Competing ideologies have battled over Chile's economy. Allende's socialism brought huge corporations into the state sector. Pinochet introduced radical monetarist policies. The selling-off of state enterprises at below market value led to large profits for investors and speculators. Tough economic measures, irrespective of the social consequences, brought Chile's inflation rate down from 400%.

The Aylwin and Frei governments continued with neoliberal policies, including privatizing the pension system. However, some 30 companies, including the large Codelco copper company, remain in the state sector.

Avoiding the worst of the Argentine crisis, domestic activity rose in 2003, but oil and copper prices remained a worry.

ECONOMIC PERFORMANCE INDICATOR

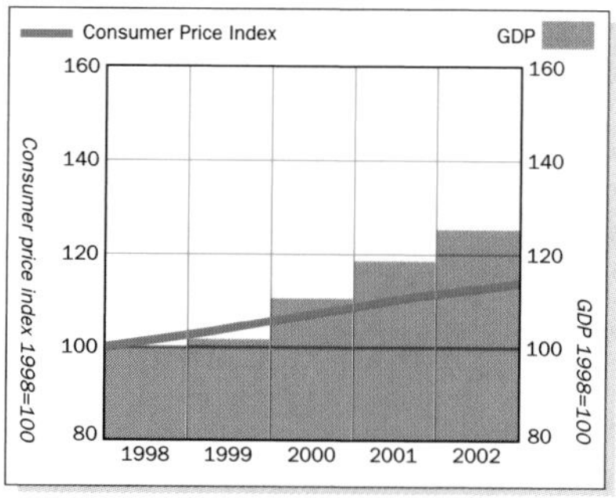
Consumer Price Index
GDP
160
140
120
100
80
Consumer price index 1998=100
GDP 1998=100
1998
1999
2000
2001
2002

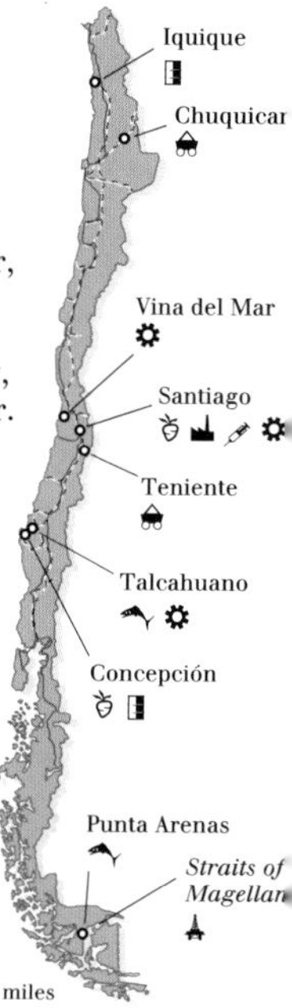
Iquique
Chuquicamata
Vina del Mar
Santiago
Teniente
Talcahuano
Concepción
Punta Arenas
Straits of Magellan
0 300 km
0 300 miles

CHILE : MAJOR BUSINESSES

- Oil
- Oil refining
- Copper mining
- Manufacturing
- Pharmaceuticals
- Heavy engineering
- Fish processing
- Agribusiness

C

RESOURCES

Electric power 8.7m kW

4.36m tonnes

5414 b/d (reserves 289m barrels)

18.5m turkeys, 4.1m sheep, 3.93m cattle, 80m chickens

Coal, copper, gold, silver, iron, lithium, molybdenum, iodine, natural gas, oil

ELECTRICITY GENERATION

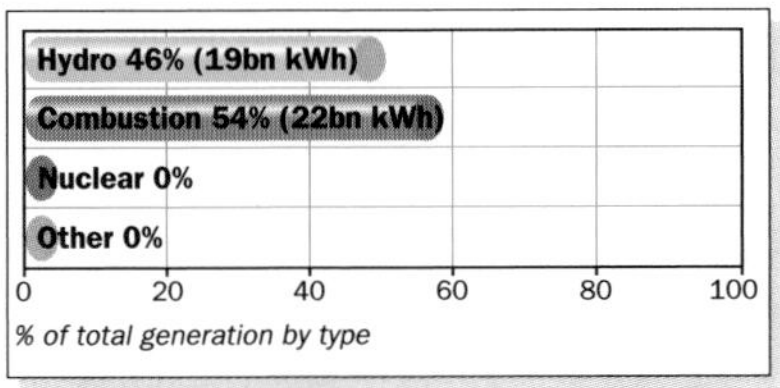
Hydro 46% (19bn kWh)
Combustion 54% (22bn kWh)
Nuclear 0%
Other 0%
0
20
40
60
80
100
% of total generation by type

Chile is the world's largest producer of copper, which accounts for almost 30% of its export revenues. There are important deposits of lithium, molybdenum, and especially of gold. Chile also has reserves of natural gas, oil, and coal, and plenty of hydroelectric potential. In addition, it is a leading producer of fishmeal, and has a flourishing wine industry.

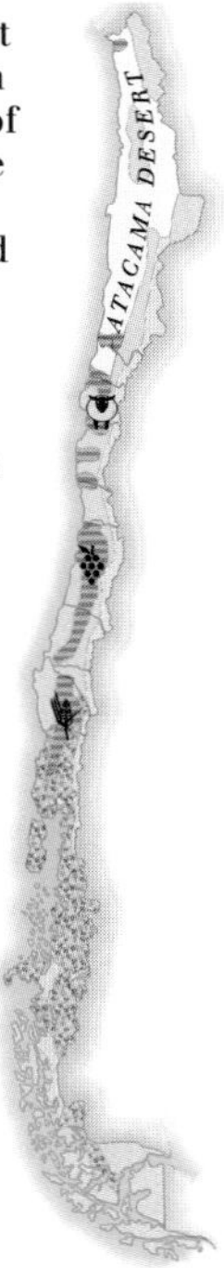
ATACAMA DESERT

CHILE : LAND USE

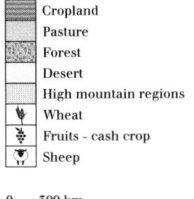

Cropland
Pasture
Forest
Desert
High mountain regions
Wheat
Fruits - cash crop
Sheep

0 300 km
0 300 miles

ENVIRONMENT

Sustainability rank: 35th

19% (7% partially protected)

3.9 tonnes per capita

ENVIRONMENTAL TREATIES

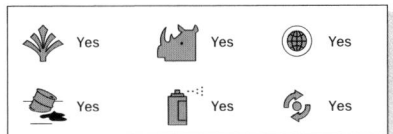

Yes	Yes	Yes
Yes	Yes	Yes

Environmental concerns do not rank high on the political agenda. Severe smogs still cover Santiago, due in part to diesel fumes from the city's tens of thousands of buses. The chief concern is logging in the south by Japanese and other foreign companies. The huge growth of the salmon industry, which fences off sea lakes, is resulting in dolphins losing their natural habitats. Overfishing of swordfish by the EU has led to friction, particularly with Spain.

MEDIA

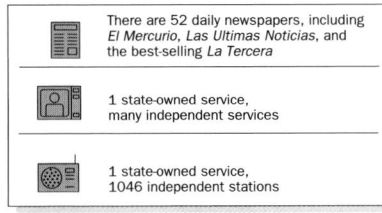

TV ownership high

Daily newspaper circulation 98 per 1000 people

PUBLISHING AND BROADCAST MEDIA

There are 52 daily newspapers, including *El Mercurio, Las Ultimas Noticias*, and the best-selling *La Tercera*

1 state-owned service, many independent services

1 state-owned service, 1046 independent stations

A long-delayed liberalized press law was finally introduced in 2001. Military courts are no longer be able to try journalists, and political authorities can't use the former special procedures to sue reporters for slander.

CRIME

Death penalty not used in practice

33,098 prisoners

Up 12% in 2000

CRIME RATES

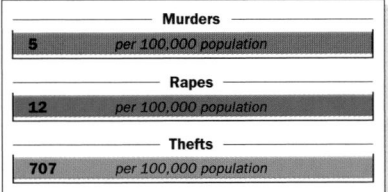

Murders: 5 per 100,000 population

Rapes: 12 per 100,000 population

Thefts: 707 per 100,000 population

The judiciary has been slow to pursue human rights cases from the Pinochet regime, despite the discoveries during the 1990s of mass graves of victims of the DINA (secret police). Mapuche leaders were among the "disappeared." Levels of child abuse are exceptionally high, though now starting to fall.

EDUCATION

School leaving age: 14

96%

452,177 students

THE EDUCATION SYSTEM

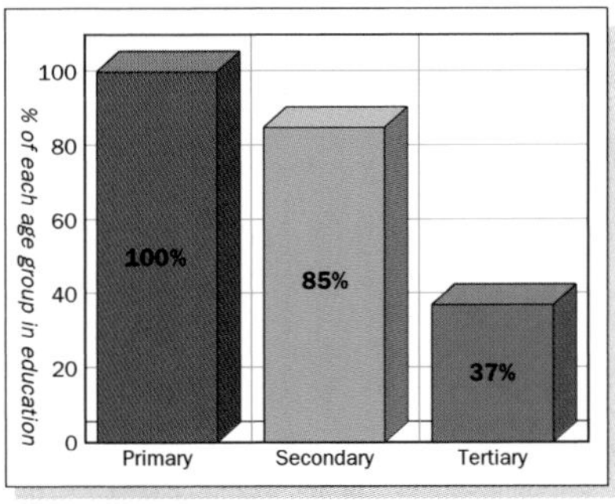
100
80
60
40
20
0
% of each age group in education
100%
85%
37%
Primary
Secondary
Tertiary

Economic growth has permitted public spending on education to increase substantially, but the sector suffers from budgetary cuts. Free primary education is officially compulsory for eight years. Human rights issues now appear in school curricula.

HEALTH

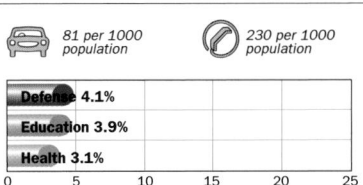

Welfare state health benefits

1 per 909 people

Cancers, respiratory, cerebrovascular, and heart diseases

Recent growth has meant increased public spending on health, but 2002 saw cuts. The public health service covers 80% of people, but is mostly found in urban areas. There is private care for the rich. Infant mortality has fallen below one-third of the 1980 level of 33 deaths per 1000.

SPENDING

GDP/cap. increase

CONSUMPTION AND SPENDING

81 per 1000 population

230 per 1000 population

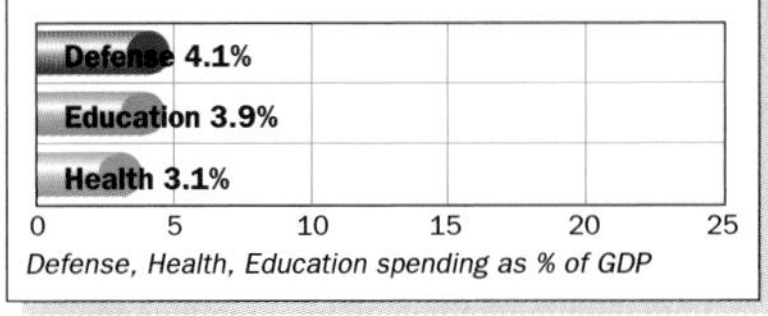
Defense 4.1%
Education 3.9%
Health 3.1%
0
5
10
15
20
25
Defense, Health, Education spending as % of GDP

Chile's traditionally large middle class did well under Pinochet and the economic policies of the Chicago School. The wealthiest sections benefited considerably from the sale of state assets at 40–50% of their true market value. Five years into the regime, wealth had become highly concentrated, with just nine economic conglomerates controlling the assets of the top 250 businesses, 82% of banking, and 64% of all financial loans. The regime's artificially high domestic interest rates enabled those with access to international finance to earn an estimated $800 million between 1977 and 1980, simply by borrowing abroad and lending at home. These groups have retained their position.

The poor, by contrast, are over 15% worse off than in 1970, with millions of people living just above the UN poverty line and over 1.3 million below it. Poverty is concentrated among the native Amerindian community.

WORLD RANKING

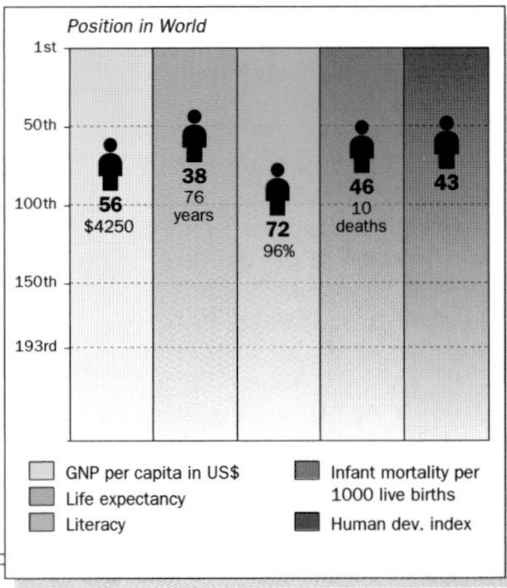
Position in World
1st
50th
100th
150th
193rd
56
$4250
38
76
years
72
96%
46
10
deaths
43
GNP per capita in US$
Life expectancy
Literacy
Infant mortality per 1000 live births
Human dev. index

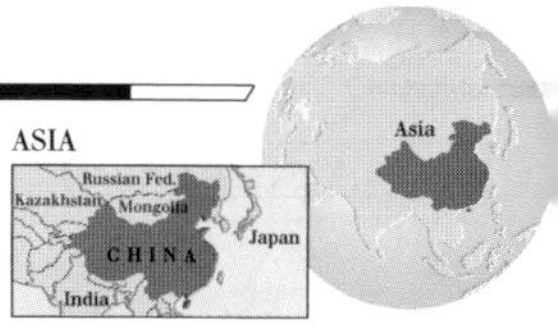
ASIA
Russian Fed.
Kazakhstan
Mongolia
CHINA
Japan
India
Asia

CHINA

OFFICIAL NAME: People's Republic of China **CAPITAL:** Beijing
POPULATION: 1.3 billion **CURRENCY:** Renminbi (known as yuan) **OFFICIAL LANGUAGE:** Mandarin

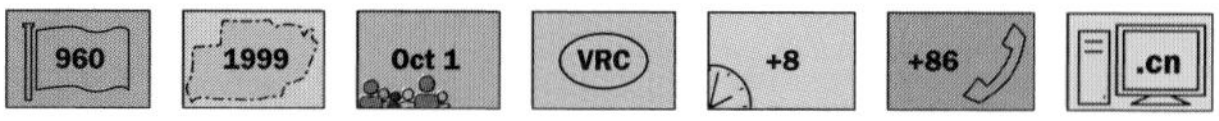
960
1999
Oct 1
VRC
+8
+86
.cn

COVERING A VAST AREA of eastern Asia and home to one-fifth of the world's population, China is bordered by 14 countries. Two-thirds of China is uplands: the southwestern mountains include the Tibetan Plateau; in the northwest, the Tien Shan Mountains separate the Tarim and Dzungarian basins. Two-thirds of the population live in the low-lying east. China was dominated by Chairman Mao Zedong from the founding in 1949 of the Communist People's Republic until his death in 1976. Despite the major disasters of the 1950s Great Leap Forward and the 1960s Cultural Revolution, it became an industrial and nuclear power. Today, China is rapidly developing a market-oriented economy. The current leadership remains set on achieving this without political liberalization, instead enforcing single-party rule as was advocated by "elder statesman" Deng Xiaoping, who died in 1997.

***Li River (Xi Jiang), Guangxi,** China's most beautiful region. Its spectacular scenery has encouraged large-scale tourist development.*

CLIMATE

Mountain/tropical/continental/steppe

WEATHER CHART FOR BEIJING

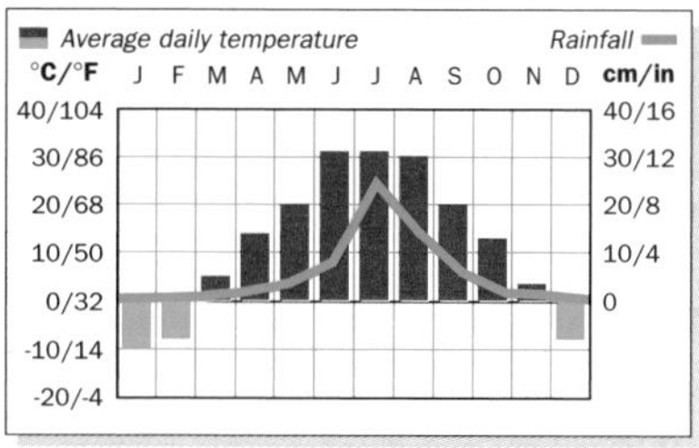
Average daily temperature
Rainfall
°C/°F
J F M A M J J A S O N D
cm/in
40/104
30/86
20/68
10/50
0/32
-10/14
-20/-4
40/16
30/12
20/8
10/4
0

China is divided into two main climatic regions. The north and west are semiarid or arid, with extreme temperature variations. The south and east are warmer and more humid, with year-round rainfall.

Winter temperatures vary with latitude and are warmest on the subtropical southeast coast, where they average about 16°C (60°F). Summer temperatures are more uniform, rising above 21°C (70°F) throughout China; on the southeast coast, the July average is about 30°C (86°F). In the north and west, temperate summers contrast with harsh winters. In northern Manchuria, rivers freeze for five months and temperatures can fall to –25°C (–13°F). In the deserts of Xinjiang province, temperatures range from –11°C (12°F) in winter to 33°C (91°F) in summer.

Summer and autumn are China's wettest seasons. Winds from the Pacific during the summer monsoon bring rains to most of the country. The south and east also have wet winters, but elsewhere the winter monsoon brings cold, dry air from Siberia.

Floods are frequent and sometimes catastrophic, as in 1998. Droughts can be even more devastating: that of 1959–1961 contributed to a famine which killed millions.

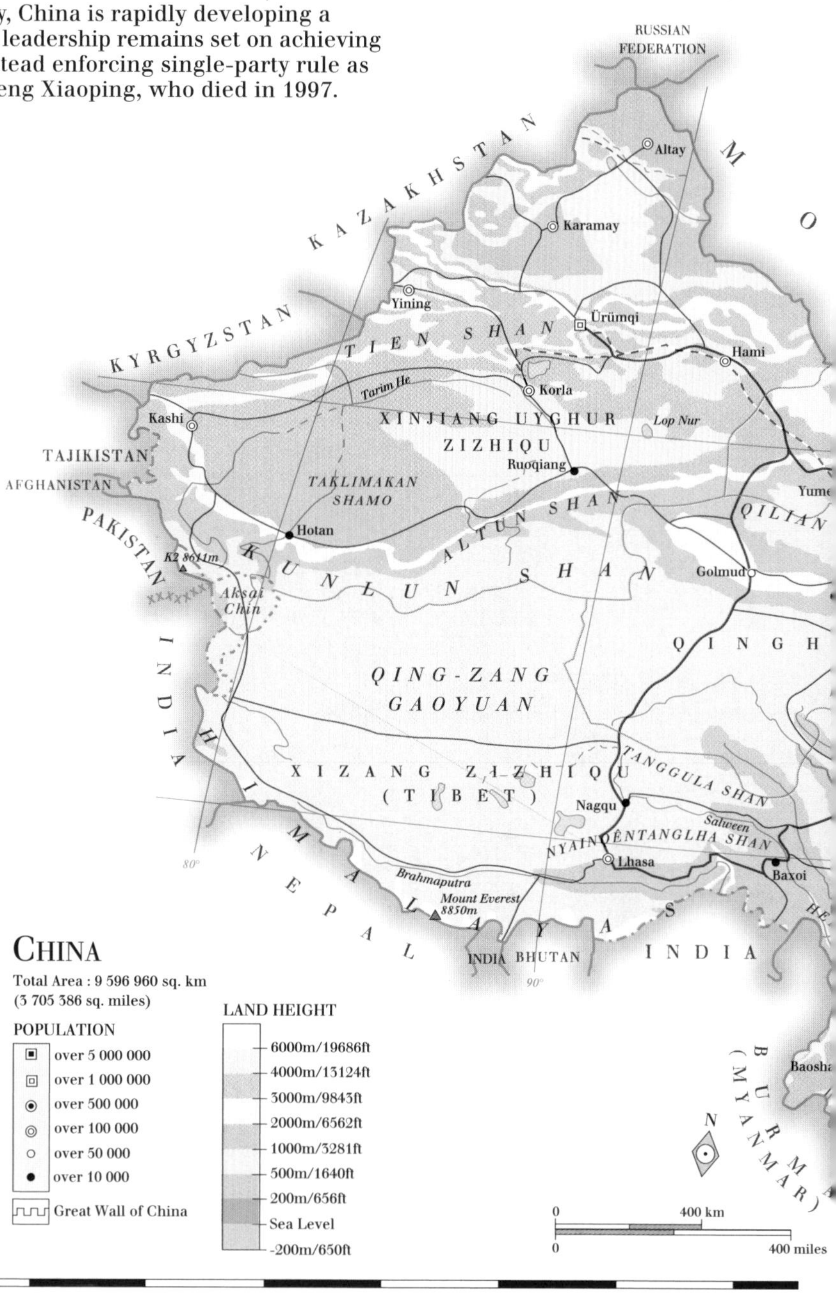
RUSSIAN FEDERATION
KAZAKHSTAN
Altay
Karamay
Yining
Ürümqi
Hami
KYRGYZSTAN
TIEN SHAN
Tarim He
Korla
Kashi
XINJIANG UYGHUR ZIZHIQU
Lop Nur
Ruoqiang
TAJIKISTAN
AFGHANISTAN
PAKISTAN
TAKLIMAKAN SHAMO
Hotan
ALTUN SHAN
QILIAN
K2 8611m
KUNLUN SHAN
Golmud
Aksai Chin
INDIA
QING-ZANG GAOYUAN
QINGH
TANGGULA SHAN
XIZANG ZIZHIQU (TIBET)
Nagqu
Salween
NYAINQÊNTANGLHA SHAN
Lhasa
Baxoi
Brahmaputra
Mount Everest 8850m
NEPAL
HIMALAYAS
INDIA
BHUTAN
INDIA
BURMA (MYANMAR)
Baosha
CHINA
Total Area : 9 596 960 sq. km (3 705 386 sq. miles)
POPULATION
over 5 000 000
over 1 000 000
over 500 000
over 100 000
over 50 000
over 10 000
Great Wall of China
LAND HEIGHT
6000m/19686ft
4000m/13124ft
3000m/9843ft
2000m/6562ft
1000m/3281ft
500m/1640ft
200m/656ft
Sea Level
-200m/650ft
0 400 km
0 400 miles

C

TOURISM

Visitors : Population 1:40

33m visitors

Down 10% in 2003

MAIN TOURIST ARRIVALS

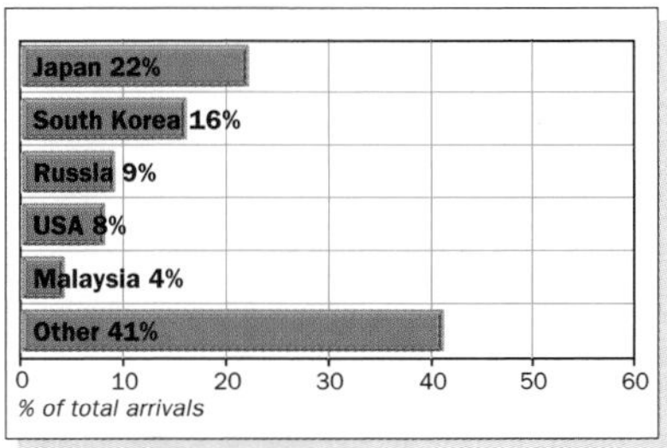
Japan 22%
South Korea 16%
Russia 9%
USA 8%
Malaysia 4%
Other 41%
0
10
20
30
40
50
60
% of total arrivals

The easing of restrictions since the 1980s led to the rapid growth of all kinds of tourism, from luxury tours to budget packages and backpacking. Most of China is now open to visitors, and tourists are allowed into Tibet, though access to Xinjiang in western China, and other areas, is sometimes impossible. The Forbidden City and Tiananmen Square in Beijing, the modern splendor of Shanghai and Hong Kong, the Great Wall, and the terracotta warriors at Xi'an remain among the top attractions. The number of Chinese able to travel abroad now exceeds ten million.

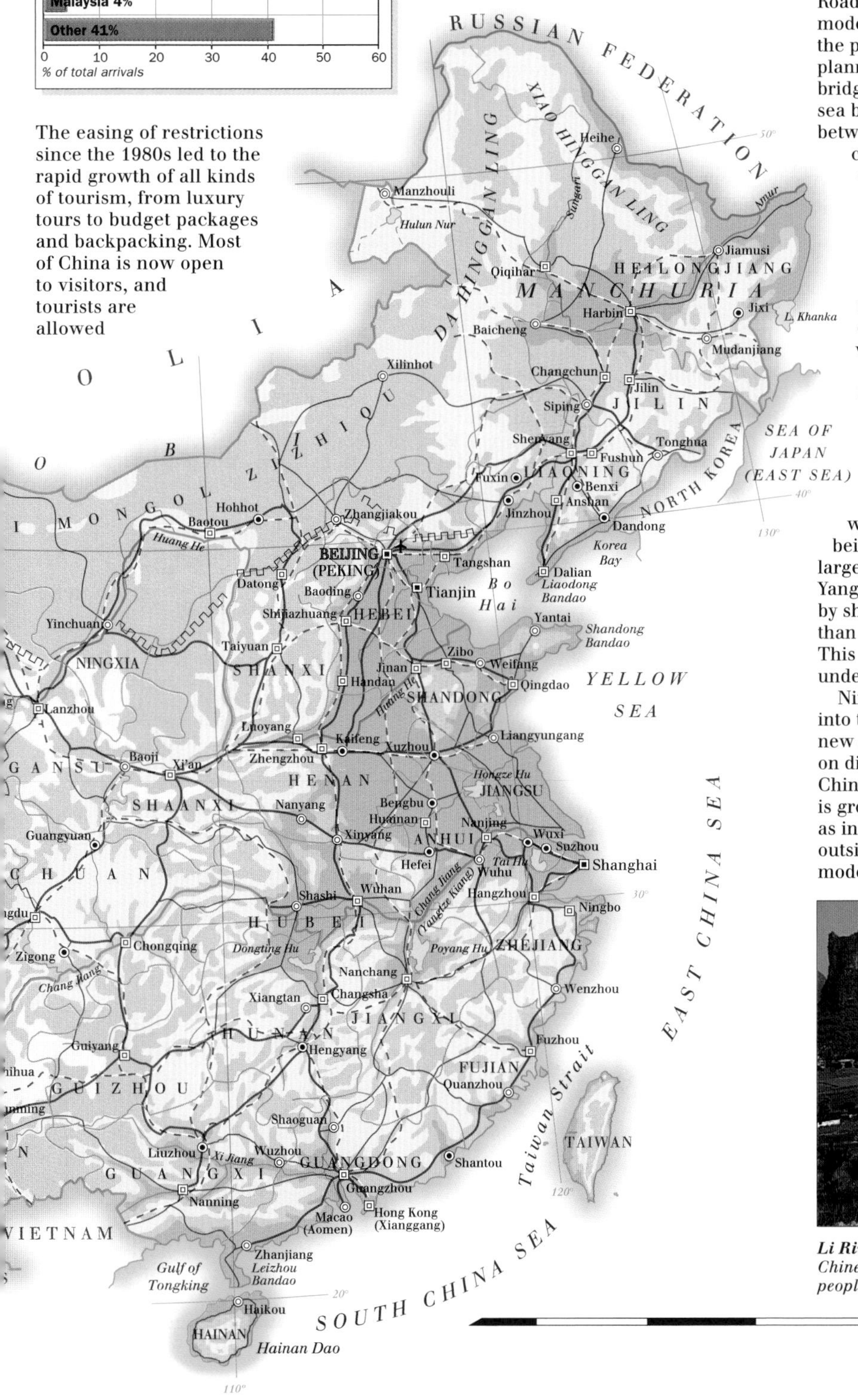
RUSSIAN FEDERATION
XIAO HINGGAN LING
DA HINGGAN LING
Heihe
Manzhouli
Hulun Nur
Amur
Jiamusi
Qiqihar
HEILONGJIANG
MANCHURIA
Harbin
Jixi
L. Khanka
Baicheng
Mudanjiang
MONGOLIA
Xilinhot
Changchun
Jilin
Siping
JILIN
NEI MONGOL ZIZHIQU
Shenyang
Fushun
Tonghua
SEA OF JAPAN (EAST SEA)
Fuxin
LIAONING
Benxi
NORTH KOREA
Hohhot
Baotou
Zhangjiakou
Jinzhou
Anshan
Dandong
Huang He
BEIJING (PEKING)
Tangshan
Korea Bay
Datong
Baoding
Tianjin
Bo Hai
Dalian
Liaodong Bandao
Shijiazhuang
HEBEI
Yantai
Shandong Bandao
Yinchuan
Taiyuan
Zibo
Weifang
NINGXIA
SHANXI
Jinan
Handan
Qingdao
YELLOW SEA
Lanzhou
SHANDONG
Luoyang
Kaifeng
Liangyungang
Baoji
Xi'an
Zhengzhou
Xuzhou
GANSU
HENAN
Hongze Hu
JIANGSU
SHAANXI
Nanyang
Bengbu
Huainan
Nanjing
Guangyuan
Xinyang
ANHUI
Wuxi
Suzhou
Shanghai
Hefei
Tai Hu
Wuhu
SICHUAN
Wuhan
Shashi
Chang Jiang (Yangtze Kiang)
Hangzhou
Ningbo
HUBEI
EAST CHINA SEA
Zigong
Chongqing
Dongting Hu
Poyang Hu
ZHEJIANG
Nanchang
Wenzhou
Xiangtan
Changsha
JIANGXI
HUNAN
Hengyang
Fuzhou
Guiyang
FUJIAN
Quanzhou
GUIZHOU
Taiwan Strait
Shaoguan
TAIWAN
Liuzhou
Xi Jiang
Wuzhou
GUANGDONG
Shantou
GUANGXI
Guangzhou
Nanning
Macao (Aomen)
Hong Kong (Xianggang)
VIETNAM
Zhanjiang
Leizhou Bandao
Gulf of Tongking
SOUTH CHINA SEA
Haikou
HAINAN
Hainan Dao

TRANSPORTATION

Drive on right

Chek Lap Kok, Hong Kong 26.8m passengers

3326 ships 17.3m grt

THE TRANSPORTATION NETWORK

1.23m km (764,309 miles)	16,314 km (10,137 miles)
59,530 km (36,990 miles)	110,000 km (68,351 miles)

Road and railroad networks are being modernized and expanded to support the push for economic growth. The planned 36-km (23-mile) Hangzhou Bay bridge, which will be the world's longest sea bridge, will slash transit times between Ningbo and Shanghai when it is completed in 2009. The world's first commercial maglev (magnetic train) route was opened in Shanghai in 2002. Plans have been announced to connect the Tibetan capital, Lhasa, to the railroad system by extending the track from Golmud. If and when it is completed, it will be one of the world's highest railroads.

Container shipping is growing fast. Shanghai handled one-third of all Chinese container traffic before the reversion of Hong Kong (which is the world's biggest container port) to Chinese rule in 1997. The inland waterway system, which was hitherto in a state of disrepair, is being upgraded and now handles a large share of internal freight. The Yangtze River (Chang Jiang) is navigable by ships of over 1000 tonnes for more than 1000 km (620 miles) from the coast. This capacity is planned to increase under the Three Gorges Dam project.

Nine small airlines were consolidated into three carriers in 2002. Hong Kong's new airport opened in 1999. Restrictions on direct flights between the US and China were lifted in 2004. Air travel is growing rapidly, like car ownership, as individual wealth increases, but outside cities bicycles still form the main mode of personal transportation.

Li River (Xi Jiang) valley. *Irrigation helps Chinese farmers to feed 20% of the world's people, using only 7% of the world's farmland.*

C

PEOPLE

Pop. density medium

Mandarin, Wu, Cantonese, Hsiang, Min, Hakka, Kan

140/km² (362/mi²)

THE URBAN/RURAL POPULATION SPLIT

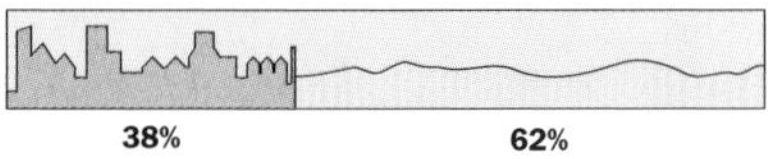

38%
62%

RELIGIOUS PERSUASION

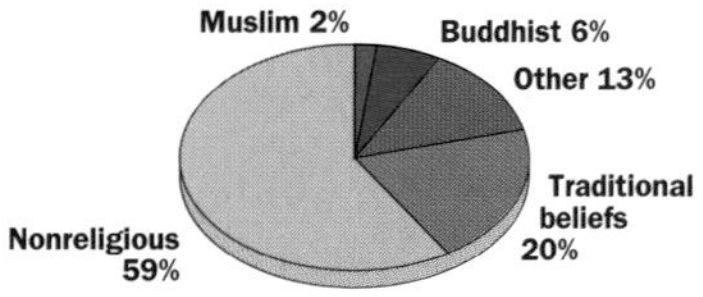

Muslim 2%
Buddhist 6%
Other 13%
Traditional beliefs 20%
Nonreligious 59%

ETHNIC MAKEUP

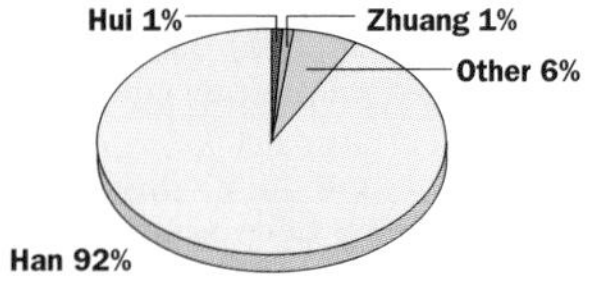

Hui 1%
Zhuang 1%
Other 6%
Han 92%

The vast majority of China's population is Han Chinese. The rest belong to one of 55 minority nationalities, or recognized ethnic groups. The minorities have disproportionate political significance because many, like the Mongolians, Tibetans, or Muslim Uyghurs, live in strategic border areas. The policy of resettling Han in these regions is bitterly resented. The 16 million Zhuang people, centered on the southeastern Guanxi Zhuang autonomous region form the largest single ethnic minority. There are more Mongolians in China than in Mongolia itself, though any thought of reuniting the populations has long been abandoned.

A one-child policy was adopted in 1979. Most Han Chinese still face strict family-planning controls, though these are widely flouted. Cases of female infanticide have produced a serious demographic imbalance, and rules were relaxed for minorities after some small groups came near to extinction.

Chinese society is patriarchal in practice, and generations tend to live together. However, economic change is putting pressure on family life, breaking down the social controls of the Mao era. Divorce and unemployment are rising; materialism has replaced the puritanism of the past. The Falun Gong spiritual movement, perceived as a rival to CCP authority, was banned in 1999.

POPULATION AGE BREAKDOWN

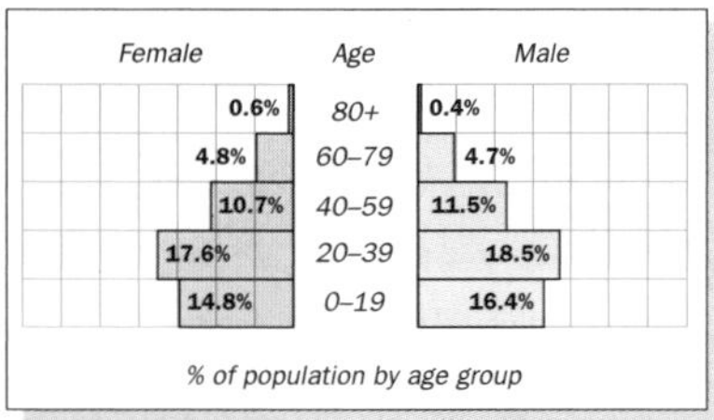

Female
Age
Male
0.6%
80+
0.4%
4.8%
60–79
4.7%
10.7%
40–59
11.5%
17.6%
20–39
18.5%
14.8%
0–19
16.4%
% of population by age group

POLITICS

No multiparty elections

2003/2008

President Hu Jintao

AT THE LAST ELECTION

National People's Congress 2979 seats

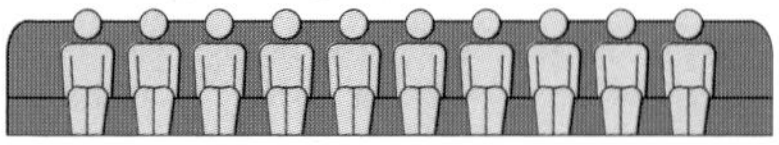

The Communist Party of China (CCP) is the only permitted party

China is a single-party state, dominated by the CCP, the world's largest political party. The National People's Congress, indirectly elected every five years, is theoretically the supreme organ of state power. It appoints the president and executive State Council, headed by the prime minister. The real focus of power, however, is the 22-member Politburo of the CCP and, in particular, its Standing Committee of seven.

Profile

The death in 1997 of Deng Xiaoping marked the passing of the dominance of the "Immortals" – those who took part with Mao in the 1934–1935 Long March. Deng, the architect of China's economic reforms, had worked hard behind the scenes forming alliances to promote his ideas and followers. His successor Jiang Zemin consolidated his position as president and CCP general secretary after Deng's death. A "fourth generation" leadership emerged at the 2002 party congress, with the new general secretary Hu Jintao appointed as China's president in 2003.

Main Political Issues

Economic change and CCP authority

After the death of Mao in 1976, China embarked on economic reform, while seeking to secure the dominance of the CCP and avoid political upheaval. The "great helmsman" of this process for two decades was Deng, China's paramount leader even after he had relinquished all official posts. Advocating a fast-track move to a "socialist market economy," he looked to South Korea and Taiwan as achieving high growth without political reform. At the 1997 party congress the reformers, led by Jiang, took their opportunity to realign formal party policy with their desire to privatize large areas of state-run industry. The transfer of much of the huge state economic system into private ownership has been a challenge to the CCP monopoly on power. The 22 provinces, particularly those in the southeast, are increasingly acting independently of Beijing. At a popular level, there is growing rural discontent over a widening wealth gap. However, the party has allowed no political opposition to surface.

Nanjing Donglu (Nanking Road), in central Shanghai, is one of China's most famous shopping streets. A magnet for foreign investment, Shanghai is China's largest city.

Shifting balances in the top leadership

The prodemocracy protests of 1989, culminating in the Tiananmen Square massacre, enabled conservatives within the party to gain the upper hand until Deng moved to restore the balance. His own longevity shifted the advantage toward his heir apparent, Jiang, who subsequently strengthened his own power base and international stature. A major overhaul of party ideology in 2001, under Jiang's "Three Represents" doctrine, encouraged the promotion equally of business, culture, and the rural masses. Jiang and his prime minister Zhu Rongji stood down from the Politburo at the 2002 party congress, handing over to the new generation of leaders, headed by Hu Jintao and Wen Jiabao (later premier). Jiang retains considerable influence, but constitutional changes approved in 2004 – including formal guarantees of private property and human rights – underlined Hu's increasing authority.

***Deng Xiaoping** was China's paramount leader until his death in 1997.*

***Jiang Zemin,** president until 2003, retains significant influence.*

***Wen Jiabao,** premier of the State Council, appointed in 2003.*

***President Hu Jintao** represents a "fourth generation" of leaders.*

THE CHINESE WILD WEST

HISTORIC CHINA IS CENTERED around the lowland provinces south of Beijing, mostly inhabited by the country's largest ethnic group, the Han. The surrounding territory has, nonetheless, stayed for the most part firmly within the Chinese sphere of influence. More contentious is Beijing's control of the far west. The province of Xizang Zizhiqu (Tibet), often within the Chinese imperial orbit, was brought under direct Communist control under Chairman Mao Zedong following the 1949 revolution. Efforts within both Tibet and neighboring Xinjiang to restore autonomy or independence have been sternly repressed.

***The Kumbum dagoba** at the Palkhor Tschöde monastery, Gyangze (Chiang-tzu), Tibet. At the tip of this 15th-century structure is a Buddhist chapel.*

TIBET

Covering 1,221,600 sq. km (472,000 sq. miles) across the "roof of the world," modern Tibet has China's lowest population density, at only two inhabitants per sq. km (five per sq. mile). The ancient Buddhist city of Lhasa is its capital. Tibetans were officially recorded as making up 2.41 million of the province's total population of 2.62 million at the 2000 census.

An independent kingdom from the 7th century, Tibet was effectively subjugated by Chinese imperial leaders from 1254. The traditional territory of Tibet extended north and eastward across twice as much land as covered by the modern province. Following the first Chinese revolution in 1911, Tibet briefly enjoyed the status of a fully autonomous state under nominal Chinese control, until Chinese Communist forces invaded in 1950. Though the Chinese government insists that the "peaceful liberation" was warmly welcomed by the Tibetan people, discontent erupted in a full-scale revolt in 1959. The rebellion, or "National Uprising," was ruthlessly crushed; between 87,000 and 430,000 people were killed, and the Dalai Lama, spiritual head of Tibetan Buddhism, fled to India amid an exodus of refugees. In 1964 Tibet was made an integral part of China, known as Xizang Zizhiqu; opponents of Chinese rule were imprisoned or executed and many Buddhist monasteries were damaged.

The Dalai Lama established a government-in-exile based in Dharamsala, and has achieved considerable international support. Seeking a peaceful end to the dispute with China, he has recently come close to accepting Chinese rule – reestablishing direct relations with Beijing in 2002 after a nine-year break – in an effort to win greater real self-government and cultural freedom for the Tibetan people. The Dalai Lama's insistence on a nonviolent campaign has helped gain backing abroad, but has frustrated many within Tibet.

In addition to its use of political violence, China's control of Tibet has changed the landscape in other ways. Han Chinese colonists have been offered economic incentives to establish businesses in Tibet, drawing thousands to the wild west where the Communist authorities have been keen to "develop" the region with great architectural, infrastructure, and industrial projects. Tibetan activists accuse these developments of scarring the Buddhist face of Tibet and causing serious environmental damage.

Culturally, the onslaught has included the official marginalization of Tibetan teaching in favor of secular Communist ideology. Religious practice is allowed to continue, but only under strict central control. Since 1995, the Chinese authorities have detained a young boy recognized by Tibetan Buddhists as the latest incarnation of their second-ranking spiritual leader, the Panchen Lama, instead naming their own candidate to this office. Tibetans see this as an unwarranted interference in their religious life.

XINJIANG (EAST TURKESTAN)

The Muslim Uyghurs are a Turkic people who identify closely with the ethnic groups of neighboring central Asia. Uyghur separatists refer to Xinjiang (once more commonly known in the West as Sinkiang) as East Turkestan, promoting their connection with the Kazakhs and Kyrgyz of "West Turkestan." However, the migration of Han Chinese to the province means that Uyghurs are now in the minority of its population of 19.25 million.

***The Dalai Lama,** heads a Tibetan government-in-exile from the northern Indian city of Dharamsala where he receives visits from many religious and political pilgrims.*

Xinjiang Uyghur Zizhiqu, to give the province its full name, has a total area of 1,646,900 sq. km (636,000 sq. miles), or nearly 18% of China's total land mass. It consists largely of desert, but the regional capital, Urumqi, is an industrial city noted for iron and steel, oil, and chemicals.

Divorced from Buddhism since embracing Islam in the 10th century, Uyghurs do not pursue their struggle for separatism under the same pacifist ideology that is dominant in Tibet. The main pro-independence group, the East Turkestan Islamic Movement (ETIM), has led a low-level campaign against the Chinese authorities in the province. The Communist government has responded with strict security measures, which were strengthened after the 2001 terrorist attacks on the US, when ETIM activists were designated "terrorists," allowing the government to pursue a crackdown on the group and its supporters with tacit international approval.

***Uyghur dancers** in traditional dress. The styles closely resemble those of central Asia.*

CHINA'S REGIONAL DISPARITIES

In early 2004, the Chinese government was praised by the international community for lifting 400 million Chinese out of poverty since liberal economic reforms were begun in 1978. China's unprecedented economic growth in recent years, however, has failed to catch all the massive population in its net. China's own

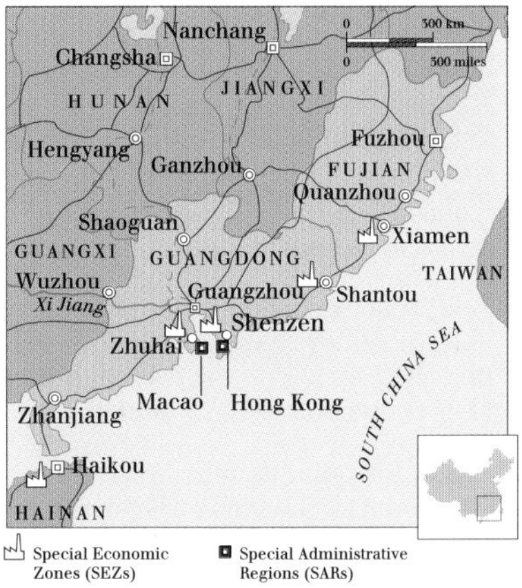
Nanchang
Changsha
HUNAN
JIANGXI
0 300 km
0 300 miles
Fuzhou
Hengyang
Ganzhou
FUJIAN
Quanzhou
Shaoguan
Xiamen
GUANGXI
GUANGDONG
TAIWAN
Wuzhou
Xi Jiang
Guangzhou
Shantou
Shenzen
Zhuhai
SOUTH CHINA SEA
Macao
Hong Kong
Zhanjiang
Haikou
HAINAN
Special Economic Zones (SEZs)
Special Administrative Regions (SARs)

Poverty Alleviation Office has now admitted an increase in the number of people living in "abject poverty"; 85 million Chinese struggle to survive on less than 637 yuan ($77) a year, or $0.20 a day – one-tenth of the UN's international poverty rate of $2 a day.

China's cities

The reabsorption of the former British colony of Hong Kong into China in 1997 brought one of the world's most modern and successful capitalist cities into the Communist fold. Pledging to leave the local economy untouched as a special administrative region (SAR), and doing the same with Macao which rejoined China from Portuguese control in 1999, the government confirmed its commitment to striving for a "socialist market economy," focused on modern, urban-based service industries. Massive domestic, and more recently foreign, investment has helped develop other cities such as Beijing and Shanghai.

Life in these thoroughly modern metropolises bears no resemblance to the rural China known by Chairman Mao. Hong Kong, Beijing, and Shanghai were even listed among the 16 most expensive places in which to live in the world by Mercer Human Resource Consulting in 2004. Consumerism and the information revolution have been embraced wholeheartedly, while the outside world drools at the prospect of such an enormous market for its high-tech goods. Mobile phone use has soared, with almost 300 million handsets ringing away, and Internet access has become increasingly popular, despite government efforts to maintain its tight control over information and ideas.

Foreign investment

Much of this success is based on foreign direct investment which after a dip in the 1990s reached $52.7 billion in 2002. In that year China overtook the US as the world's strongest magnet for investment; most is in the coastal cities and the special economic zones (SEZs) around those in the south; 14 cities were picked in the mid-1980s for the dual role of "windows" (opening to the outside world) and "radiators" (spreading the development of an export-oriented economy).

Foreign investors in Shanghai's Pudong New Zone, on the east bank of the Huangpu River, enjoy more preferential conditions than in the SEZs, including the right to sell goods and financial services. Pudong has attracted major foreign companies keen to establish a foothold in the potentially massive Chinese market, including General Motors, NEC, Sharp, Hitachi, Siemens, Unilever, BASF, and Pilkington. Pudong also forms the "dragon head" for a chain of open cities, extending up the Yangtze River (Chang Jiang), where foreign investment has been encouraged since 1990. A new set of open cities has been designated since 1992, this time in borderlands adjoining Russia, Mongolia, Kazakhstan, Burma, and Vietnam, to develop infrastructure and promote trade and the growth of export-oriented industries.

The impoverished interior

In contrast, the rural areas which provided the base for the People's Liberation Army during the revolution, and for which Mao formulated his version of agrarian Communism, have now been left far behind. It is here that abject poverty is found. The Chinese Academy of Sciences calculated in early 2004 that average urban incomes now outstripped rural wages by a factor of three.

Outmoded agricultural and heavy industrial practices are inefficient, and in some cases just plain dangerous. Investment is mostly taken up by grand industrial schemes such as the Three Gorges Dam, while government-funded drives to alleviate poverty have been hit by large-scale corruption; the National Audit Association claimed that as much as 10% of the 48.8 billion yuan spent on antipoverty schemes has been embezzled by local officials.

Blaming nature

While the high level of corruption is acknowledged by the government, it continues to blame the country's inequalities mainly on natural disasters. Serious flooding and earthquakes have certainly taken their toll on the rural landscape, but their effects have been made much worse by the environmental degradation wrought by industrial projects and the water-hungry cities, while poor infrastructure in remote areas can only be blamed on a lack of successful investment.

With the socialist ideal steadily weakening, the government has rightly become wary of the disparities in its regions. A "war" on poverty has been declared, but will prove logistically much harder to pursue than the "war" on corruption fought in recent years. Meanwhile, some analysts point out that wealth disparities between town and country, and high levels of bureaucratic corruption, have traditionally been at the root of revolution and chaos throughout Chinese history. Many wonder if the Communist dynasty will have to face more than unhappy statistics in the decades to come.

PHILIPS

***Hong Kong's** return to Chinese sovereignty, after 157 years of British rule, took place at midnight on June 30, 1997.*

C

WORLD AFFAIRS

Joined UN in 1945

APEC | IAEA | WTO | ADB | SCO

The push for economic modernization and concerns about regional stability dominate. Investment, technology, and trade considerations outweigh ideology.

Despite lingering concerns over human rights, relations with the West have rebounded from the low of the 1989 Tiananmen Square massacre. China was awarded Most Favored Nation trading status by the US in 2000 and entered the WTO in 2001 (with Hong Kong retaining its separate membership). Despite initial tensions with the new US administration in 2001, the two countries had reached a "common understanding" by the end of the year on the issue of terrorism.

Regionally, ties have been normalized with Vietnam, and Himalayan territorial disputes with India were shelved in 2003, enabling the reopening of lucrative cross-border routes. China has strengthened ties with South Korea while maintaining a paternalistic relationship with North Korea. Relations with Russia have improved steadily on the basis of shared opposition to certain US policies. Closer cooperation with the EU was pledged in 2003.

Taiwan remains a dark spot. Beijing strongly rejects any moves to recognize even de facto independence for the island. Closer links have been forged since 2000, with an increase in tourist traffic and direct trade, but ties are frequently damaged by displays of military might and repetitive threats.

AID

Recipient

$1.48bn (receipts) — Little change in 2002

In the 1970s aid was an important part of Chinese diplomacy, going mostly to Africa, but other communist and southeast Asian states were also beneficiaries. Outward aid flows almost ceased in the late 1970s, as the economic reform process turned China itself into a major aid recipient. Japan is the biggest bilateral donor, but the potential of the Chinese market means that most developed states provide aid. A significant portion of funding is linked to donor countries' interests in opportunities created by China's huge infrastructure problems, and is used to finance high-tech imports.

DEFENSE

Compulsory military service

$48.4bn — Up 14% in 2002

CHINESE ARMED FORCES

7180 main battle tanks (T-59I/II, T-79, T-88B/C, T-98, T-96)	1.7m personnel
68 submarines, 21 destroyers, 42 frigates, and 368 patrol boats	250,000 personnel
1900 combat aircraft (300 Q-5, 350 J-6, 674 J-7, 184 J-8, 180 H-5/6, 90 Su-26)	400,000 personnel
ICBM (24 DF-5A, 8 DF-31), IRBM (20 DF-4, 32 DF-3A, 60 DF-21), SLBM (12 CSS-N-3) in 1 SSBN, SRBM (24 DF-15, 32 DF-11A)	

The People's Liberation Army (PLA) is the basis of CCP control and is intimately entwined with the one-party state. It was used in 1967 to restore order during the chaos of the Cultural Revolution, and in 1989 to suppress prodemocracy protests in Tiananmen Square, as well as to stamp out dissent in Tibet. From a 1990s peak of three million personnel it is now being cut back as part of a modernization process, reducing both its numbers and its involvement in the economy through army-run industries.

China has a large weapons production and export industry, and has extended its nuclear weapons capability to include the neutron bomb. China put its first manned spacecraft into orbit in 2003, only the third country ever to do so.

ECONOMICS

Inflation 6.2% p.a. (1990–2001)

$1234bn — 8.2765 yuan (8.2775)

SCORE CARD

- ❑ WORLD GNP RANKING.............6th
- ❑ GNP PER CAPITA.............$960
- ❑ BALANCE OF PAYMENTS.............$35.4bn
- ❑ INFLATION.............–0.8%
- ❑ UNEMPLOYMENT.............2% (official)

STRENGTHS

Huge domestic market. Food self-sufficiency. Mineral reserves. Diversified industrial sector. Low wage costs. Rapid sustained growth. Growing export sector. Hong Kong as financial center. Heavy investment in communications and IT.

ECONOMIC PERFORMANCE INDICATOR

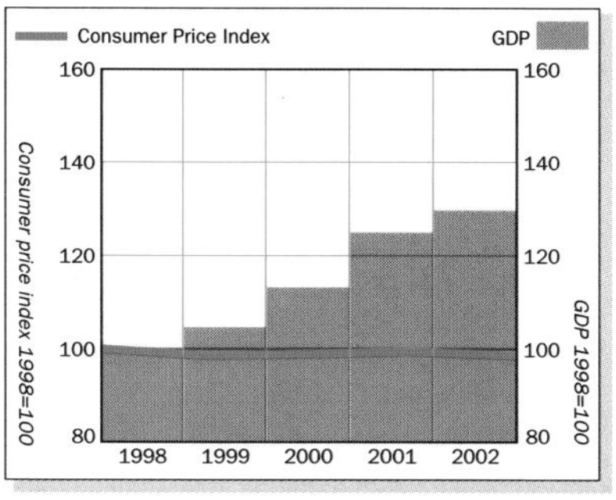
Consumer Price Index
GDP
160
140
120
100
80
1998
1999
2000
2001
2002
Consumer price index 1998=100
GDP 1998=100

EXPORTS

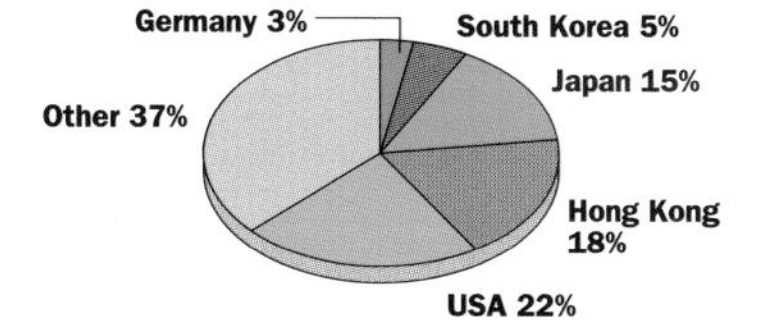
Germany 3%
South Korea 5%
Japan 15%
Other 37%
Hong Kong 18%
USA 22%

IMPORTS

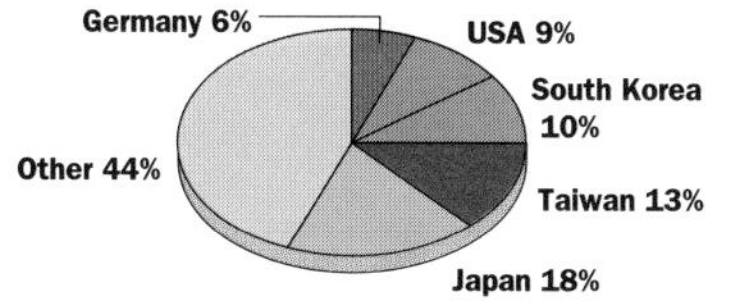
Germany 6%
USA 9%
South Korea 10%
Other 44%
Taiwan 13%
Japan 18%

WEAKNESSES

Corruption. Huge underemployment, rising unemployment. Geographical and income disparities. Poor transportation. Unevenly distributed resources.

CHINA : MAJOR BUSINESSES

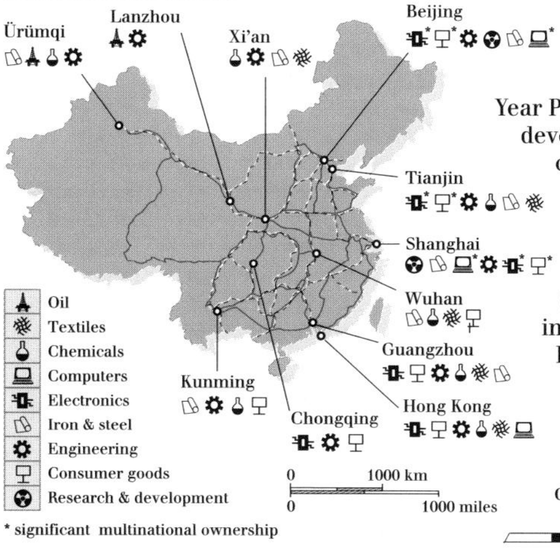
Ürümqi
Lanzhou
Xi'an
Beijing
Tianjin
Shanghai
Wuhan
Guangzhou
Hong Kong
Chongqing
Kunming
Oil
Textiles
Chemicals
Computers
Electronics
Iron & steel
Engineering
Consumer goods
Research & development
0
1000 km
0
1000 miles

* significant multinational ownership

PROFILE

China has shifted from a centrally planned to a market-oriented economy; liberalization has gone furthest in the south. In the Ninth Five-Year Plan (1996– 2000) the government retained strict controls, promoting intensive growth and boosting privatization of the huge state-owned sector. The Tenth Five-Year Plan (2001–2005) emphasizes rapid development, reforms, and improving competitiveness. The government now runs a record deficit of almost $40 billion. GDP growth passed 9% in 2003.

Trade entered a new era in 2000–2001. A substantial growth in imports followed a deal with the EU and the normalization of US trade relations, while a boost in exports has aided the high growth rate in 2002. Even Taiwan has dropped its ban on direct trade with the mainland.

C

RESOURCES

Electric power 235m kW

44.1m tonnes

3.4m b/d (reserves 23.7bn barrels)

660m ducks, 470m pigs, 228m geese, 3.98bn chickens

Coal, oil, natural gas, salt, iron, molybdenum, titanium, tungsten

ELECTRICITY GENERATION

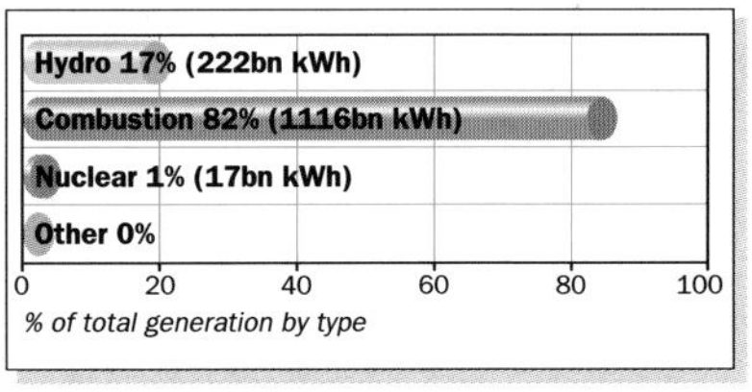
Hydro 17% (222bn kWh)
Combustion 82% (1116bn kWh)
Nuclear 1% (17bn kWh)
Other 0%
0
20
40
60
80
100
% of total generation by type

The world's biggest producer of steel and tungsten, with the world's largest deposits of more than a dozen minerals, and commercial deposits of most others, China plays a dominant role in the world mineral trade.

China is the world's largest producer and consumer of coal, though it has only 12% of world reserves. Annual output (around one billion tonnes) considerably exceeds demand; this and appalling safety records are forcing the closure of many mines.

Power provision was decentralized and opened to foreign investment in 2002. Nuclear power capacity in 2003 leapt to 5400 MW with the installation of new reactors, with planned major expansion to 50,000 MW by 2020. The world's largest HEP plant, the highly controversial Three Gorges Dam on the Yangtze River, began generating power in June 2003. However, demand has increased 10% per month since September 2003, outstripping supply.

Crude oil production has risen only slightly since reaching 160 million tonnes a year in 1997. Eastern oil fields are depleted, and hopes now center on enormous reserves in the Tarim basin in the far west. A 4000-km (2500-mile) pipeline is due to be on line by 2005.

CHINA : LAND USE

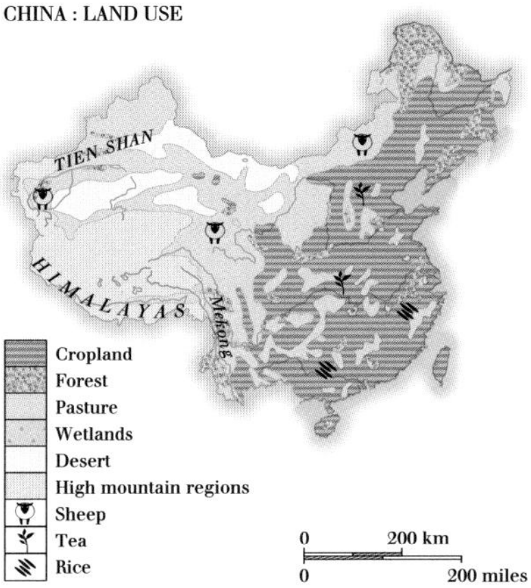
TIEN SHAN
HIMALAYAS
Mekong
Cropland
Forest
Pasture
Wetlands
Desert
High mountain regions
Sheep
Tea
Rice
0
200 km
0
200 miles

ENVIRONMENT

Sustainability rank: 129th

8% (2% partially protected)

2.2 tonnes per capita

ENVIRONMENTAL TREATIES

Yes	Yes	Yes
Yes	Yes	Yes

Climate and geology cause frequent natural disasters; their impact is often made worse by human actions. The economic policies of the 1950s turned drought into a devastating famine, while poor building standards pushed the death toll in the 1976 Tangshan earthquake to over 500,000.

Widespread industrial pollution and environmental degradation increase as China's leaders seek economic growth. However, the environment is a growing concern among educated Chinese. Becoming less suspicious of Western pressure, the government is taking steps to respond to acute problems of urban air pollution, deforestation, and water quality in particular. Nonetheless, grand schemes such as the Three Gorges Dam, and the diversion of Yangtze water to the parched north, continue to be pursued with devastating effects on existing ecosystems.

MEDIA

TV ownership high

Daily newspaper circulation 40 per 1000 people

PUBLISHING AND BROADCAST MEDIA

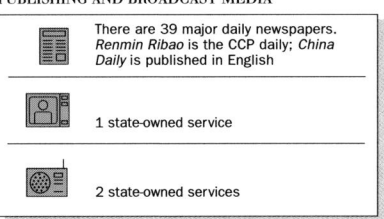

There are 39 major daily newspapers. *Renmin Ribao* is the CCP daily; *China Daily* is published in English

1 state-owned service

2 state-owned services

China's more open, market-oriented economy has created access to nonofficial sources of information. TV ownership is rising and those with satellite dishes can choose what to view, while growing Internet usage makes central control even more difficult. Since 2000, Internet sites have had to obtain official approval and have been held responsible for their content. Many Internet cafés were closed in 2001, and new rules in 2002 restricted the media's use of Internet sources.

The ideological influence of the huge-circulation party newspaper *Renmin Ribao* (*People's Daily*) and the trade union *Gongren Ribao* (*Workers' Daily*) is much diminished; unprofitable state-run newspapers have been closed. "Undesirable" papers also have their licenses removed, in periodic cleanups.

CHRONOLOGY

China's recorded history began 4000 years ago with the Shang dynasty, founded in 1766 BCE; succeeding dynasties expanded its boundaries. The empire was reunified by the Sung dynasty in 960 CE after a period of dispersal, and reached its greatest extent under the Qing (Manchu) dynasty in the 18th century. For 3000 years China had been one of the world's most advanced nations, but, having fallen behind the industrializing West, its resistance to European trade was broken in a series of wars in the 19th century.

- **1839–1860** Opium Wars with Britain. China defeated; forced to open ports to foreigners.
- **1850–1873** Internal rebellions against Qing dynasty, including the large-scale Taiping rebellion.
- **1895** Defeat by Japan in war over Korean peninsula.
- **1900** Boxer Rebellion to expel all foreigners suppressed.
- **1911** Qing dynasty overthrown by nationalists led by Sun Yat-sen. Republic of China declared.
- **1912** Sun Yat-sen forms National People's Party (Guomindang).
- **1916** Nationalists factionalize. Sun Yat-sen sets up government in Guangdong. Rest of China under control of rival warlords.
- **1921** CCP founded in Shanghai.
- **1923** CCP joins Soviet-backed Guomindang to fight warlords.
- **1925** Chiang Kai-shek becomes Guomindang leader on death of Sun Yat-sen.
- **1927** Chiang turns on CCP. CCP leaders escape to rural south.
- **1930–1934** Mao Zedong formulates strategy of peasant-led revolution.
- **1931** Japan invades Manchuria.
- **1934** Chiang forces CCP out of its southern bases. Start of 12,000-km (7450-mile) Long March north.
- **1935** Long March ends. Mao becomes CCP leader.
- **1937–1945** War against Japan: CCP Red Army in north, Guomindang in south. Japan defeated.
- **1945–1949** War between Red Army and Guomindang. US-backed Guomindang retreats to Taiwan.
- **1949** October 1, Mao proclaims People's Republic of China.
- **1950** Invasion of Tibet. Mutual assistance treaty with USSR.
- **1950–1958** Land reform; culminates in setting up of communes. First Five-Year Plan (1953–1957) fails.
- **1958** "Great Leap Forward" fails; contributes to millions of deaths during 1959–1961 famine. Mao resigns as CCP chairman; succeeded by Liu Shaoqi.

C

CHRONOLOGY *continued*

- **1960** Sino-Soviet split.
- **1961–1965** More pragmatic economic approach led by Liu and Deng Xiaoping.
- **1966** Cultural Revolution initiated by Mao to restore his supreme power. Youthful Red Guards attack all authority. Mao rules, with Military Commission under Lin Biao and State Council under Zhou Enlai.
- **1967** Army intervenes to restore order amid countrywide chaos. Liu and Deng purged from party.
- **1969** Mao regains chair of CCP. Lin Biao designated his successor, but quickly attacked by Mao.
- **1971** Lin dies in plane crash.
- **1972** US president Nixon visits. More open foreign policy initiated.
- **1973** Mao's wife Jiang Qing, Zhang Chunqiao, and other "Gang of Four" members elected to CCP Politburo. Deng Xiaoping rehabilitated.
- **1976** Zhou Enlai dies. Mao strips Deng of posts. September, Mao dies. October, Gang of Four arrested.
- **1977** Deng regains party posts, begins to extend power base.
- **1978** Decade of economic modernization launched. Open door policy to foreign investment; farmers allowed to farm for profit.
- **1980** Deng emerges as China's paramount leader. Economic reform gathers pace, but hopes for political change suppressed.
- **1983–1984** Conservative elderly leaders attempt to slow reform.
- **1984** Industrial reforms announced.
- **1989** Prodemocracy demonstrations in Tiananmen Square crushed by army; 1000–5000 dead.
- **1992–1995** Trials of prodemocracy activists continue. Plans for market economy accelerated.
- **1993** Jiang Zemin president.
- **1997** February, Deng Xiaoping dies at 92. June 30, UK hands back Hong Kong. September, party congress confirms reformist policies.
- **1998** Severe flooding: 3000 killed.
- **1999** China develops neutron bomb. Friction with Taiwan. Clampdown on Falun Gong sect. December 19, Portugal hands back Macao.
- **2000** US normalizes trade relations.
- **2001** Major diplomatic incident over downed US spy plane. "Strike Hard" campaign against corruption. December, accession to WTO.
- **2002** Crackdown on Uyghur separatism.
- **2003** Hu Jintao president. SARS outbreak. June, Three Gorges Dam flooded. October, first manned spacecraft launched.
- **2004** Rising demand for electricity leads to brownouts.

CRIME

Death penalty in use

1.51m prisoners

Up 60% in 2000

CRIME RATES

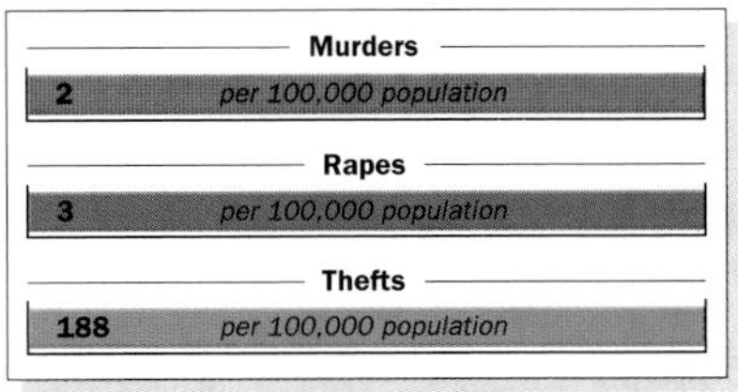
Murders
2
per 100,000 population
Rapes
3
per 100,000 population
Thefts
188
per 100,000 population

China's legal system is a mix of custom and statute. Judges have been required to hold law degrees only since 2002. A rise in corruption and violent crime has paralleled economic reform and social changes. In 2000 many party officials were convicted in the largest ever corruption trial. A crackdown on human trafficking followed the breaking up of rings smuggling Chinese into Europe. The death penalty is used extensively – at a peak in 2001 China carried out over 80% of the world's executions. Since a clampdown on dissent after the 1989 Tiananmen Square massacre many detainees have been released, but many more remain incarcerated.

EDUCATION

School leaving age: 14

91%

15.1m students

THE EDUCATION SYSTEM

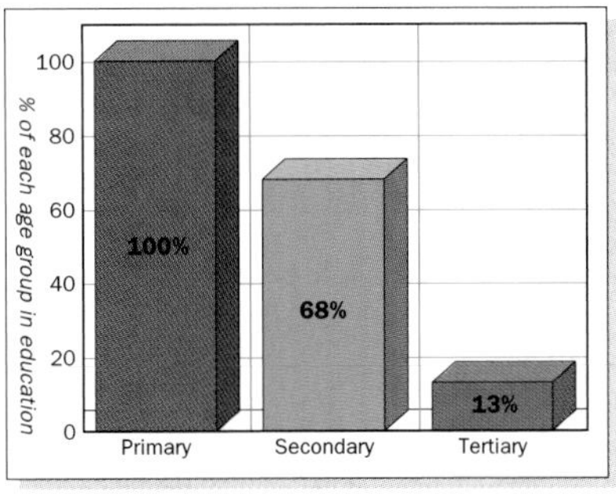
100
80
60
40
20
0
% of each age group in education
100%
68%
13%
Primary
Secondary
Tertiary

Despite the expansion of education since 1949, illiteracy and semiliteracy are still widespread. School attendance fell when fees at all levels were introduced in the 1980s, but now most children of secondary school age are in school – including those catching up with primary education.

Selection for higher education is now based on academic rather than political criteria, though fees can be prohibitive. Internet-based distance learning degrees, first allowed in 1998, are increasingly popular. In May 2001, the government legalized private schools (which have been tacitly permitted since the early 1980s) in an effort to regulate and profit from them. About seven million pupils are thought to attend them.

HEALTH

Welfare state health benefits

1 per 714 people

Cardiovascular and diarrheal diseases, cancers, tuberculosis

Primary health care combines Western and traditional medicine and extends to the remotest areas. For decades, free health care accompanied full state employment, and life expectancy was on a par with many richer countries. The change to a market-oriented economy, however, has produced a gaping divide between city and rural provision, and fees for treatment are rising. The UN estimated in 2002 that there would be over ten million HIV/AIDS sufferers in China by 2010. The outbreak of acute pneumonia (SARS) strained facilities in 2003. Suicide is a leading cause of death among the young.

SPENDING

GDP/cap. increase

CONSUMPTION AND SPENDING

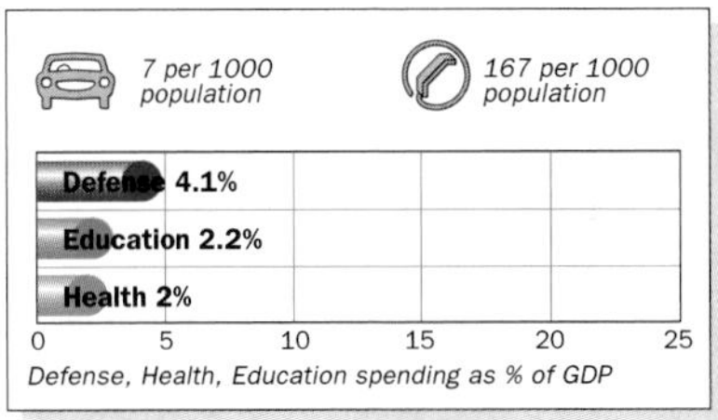
7 per 1000 population
167 per 1000 population
Defense 4.1%
Education 2.2%
Health 2%
0
5
10
15
20
25
Defense, Health, Education spending as % of GDP

Economic change has widened wealth disparities. Most Chinese are farmers, whose living standards compare unfavorably with urban dwellers. Many people have migrated to the cities in search of jobs. The number of people living in "abject poverty" actually rose in 2004; the government has pledged to remove agricultural taxes by 2009. The burgeoning small-business class and employees of foreign-funded companies have benefited most. They mainly live in the east where there are a number of dollar millionaires. One sign of increased wealth is the spread of mobile phones – more numerous than in the US by 2001 and by 2003 outnumbering landlines.

WORLD RANKING

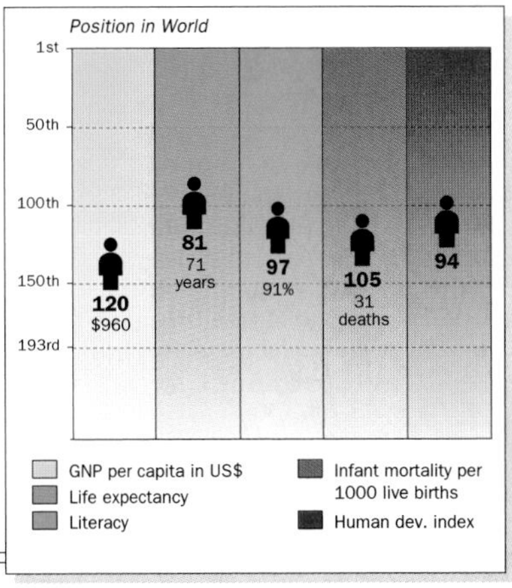
Position in World
1st
50th
100th
150th
193rd
120
$960
81
71
years
97
91%
105
31
deaths
94
GNP per capita in US$
Life expectancy
Literacy
Infant mortality per 1000 live births
Human dev. index

C

COLOMBIA

SOUTH AMERICA
Panama
Venezuela
COLOMBIA
Ecuador
Peru
Brazil
South America

OFFICIAL NAME: Republic of Colombia **CAPITAL:** Bogotá
POPULATION: 44.2 million **CURRENCY:** Colombian peso **OFFICIAL LANGUAGE:** Spanish

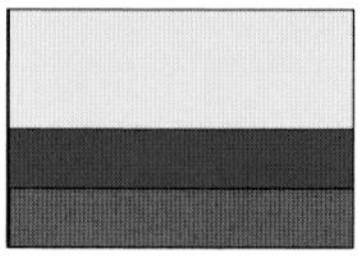

1819
1903
July 20
CO
-5
+57
.co

LYING IN NORTHWEST South America, Colombia has coastlines on both the Caribbean and the Pacific. The east is densely forested and sparsely populated, and separated from the western coastal plains by the Andes mountains. The Andes divide into three ranges (cordilleras) in Colombia. The eastern range is divided from the two western ranges by the densely populated Magdalena River valley. The Colombian lowlands are very wet, hot, and fertile, supporting two harvests and allowing many crops to be planted at any time of year. A state plagued by instability and violence, Colombia is noted for its coffee, emeralds, gold, and narcotics trafficking.

CLIMATE

Tropical/mountain

WEATHER CHART FOR BOGOTÁ

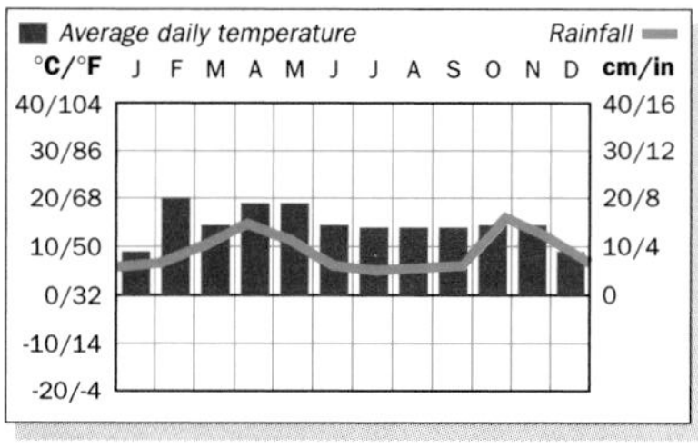
Average daily temperature
Rainfall
°C/°F
J F M A M J J A S O N D
cm/in
40/104
30/86
20/68
10/50
0/32
-10/14
-20/-4
40/16
30/12
20/8
10/4
0

Most of Colombia is wet, and the hot Pacific coastal areas receive up to 500 cm (200 in) of rain a year. The Caribbean coast is a little drier. The Andes have three climatic regions: the *tierra caliente* (hot lowlands), *tierra templada* (temperate uplands), and *tierra fría* (cold highlands); the last has year-round springlike conditions such as those found in Bogotá. The equatorial east has two wet seasons.

TRANSPORTATION

Drive on right

El Dorado, Bogotá
4.66m passengers

109 ships
67,800 grt

THE TRANSPORTATION NETWORK

15,818 km (9829 miles)

Caribbean Trunk Highway

3154 km (1960 miles)

18,140 km (11,272 miles)

Roads in the north are in reasonable condition. Those in the south and east tend to be rutted and badly affected by the frequent rains. Continuing instability means that roads are frequently blocked by the guerrillas and the military. Most of the railroad is closed. Rivers are an important means of transportation; the Magdalena, Orinoco, Atrato, and Amazon river systems are all extensively navigable. Colombia's Avianca, the second-oldest airline in the world, is in financial trouble.

TOURISM

Visitors : Population 1:71

620,600 visitors

Up 15% in 2003

MAIN TOURIST ARRIVALS

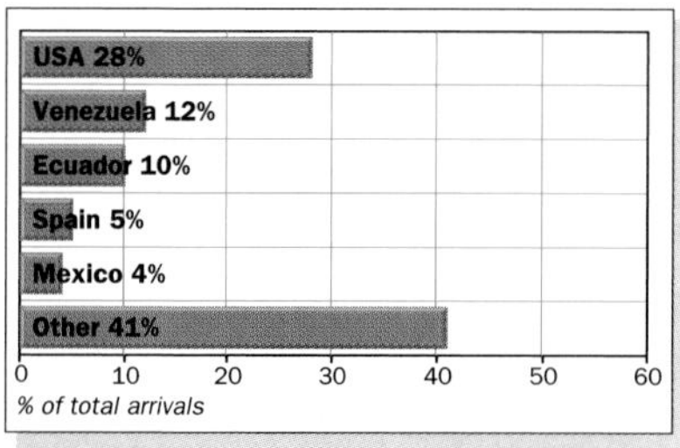
USA 28%
Venezuela 12%
Ecuador 10%
Spain 5%
Mexico 4%
Other 41%
0
10
20
30
40
50
60
% of total arrivals

Tourism in Colombia is largely limited to the beaches of the Caribbean coast. Cartagena, Barranquilla, and Santa Marta are the main resorts. Cartagena has also been developed as a major Latin American conference center.

The expansion of tourism has been limited by Colombia's political instability and the prevalence of narcotics-related crime. The well-publicized activities of drugs cartels in Medellín and Cali, and instances of kidnappings in Bogotá, are major deterrents for travelers.

Limited infrastructure makes many regions of the country, particularly Amazonia to the east of the Andes, almost inaccessible. The Pacific coast is also barely exploited.

***Simón Bolívar and Cristóbal Colón,** twin peaks with a height of 5775 m (18,947 ft), are the highest in the Colombian Andes.*

PEOPLE

Pop. density low

Spanish, Wayuu, Páez, and other Amerindian languages

43/km² (110/mi²)

THE URBAN/RURAL POPULATION SPLIT

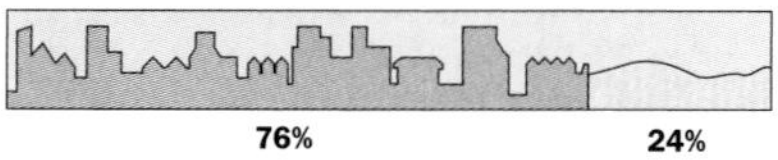
76%
24%

RELIGIOUS PERSUASION

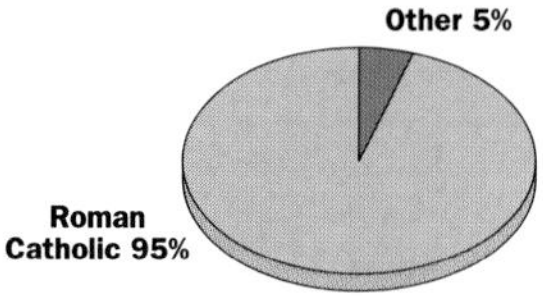
Other 5%
Roman Catholic 95%

ETHNIC MAKEUP

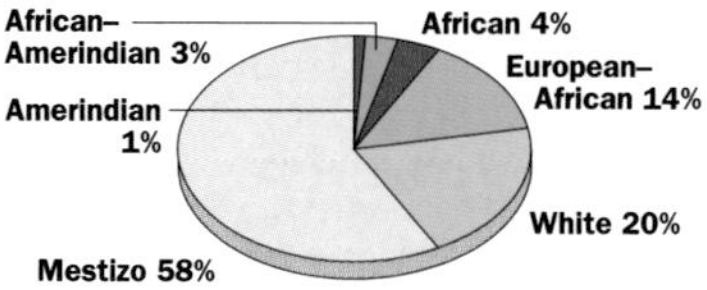
African–Amerindian 3%
African 4%
European–African 14%
Amerindian 1%
White 20%
Mestizo 58%

Most Colombians are of mixed blood. An estimated 450,000 indigenous Amerindians live mainly in Amazonia, the southwest, and the northernmost tip of the country. An underrepresented small black population lives along the coasts, particularly in the western Chocó region – Colombia's poorest.

Some progress has been made in giving Amerindians a greater political voice. Since 1991, two seats in the Senate have been reserved for indigenous representatives, and pressure groups are increasingly active. Harassment by landowners and narcotics traffickers continues in Amazonia, and very few investigations into suspected human rights violations against Amerindians have led to prosecutions.

Women have a higher profile than in much of the rest of Latin America. Many are prominent in the professions, though few reach the top in politics. The traditional Roman Catholic extended family is still the norm.

NGOs estimate that civil conflict has killed 300,000 Colombians, displaced three million, and seen two million emigrate since 1985.

POPULATION AGE BREAKDOWN

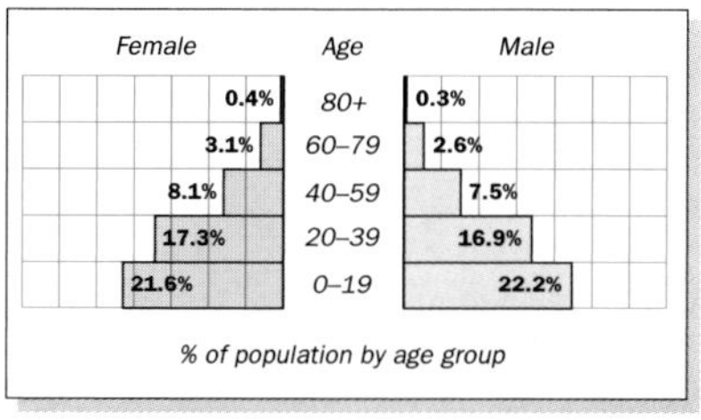
Female
Age
Male
0.4%
80+
0.3%
3.1%
60–79
2.6%
8.1%
40–59
7.5%
17.3%
20–39
16.9%
21.6%
0–19
22.2%
% of population by age group

POLITICS

Multiparty elections

L. House 2002/2006
U. House 2002/2006

President Alvaro Uribe Velez

AT THE LAST ELECTION

House of Representatives 166 seats

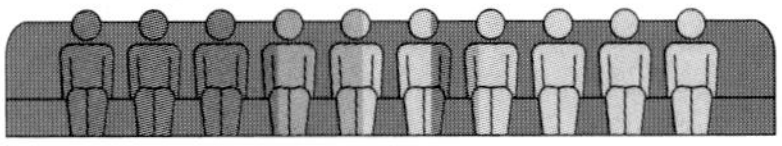
33% PL
13% PCC
10% C
4% CR
3% AL
37% Others

PL = Liberal Party **PCC** = Colombian Conservative Party **C** = Coalition **CR** = Radical Change **AL** = Liberal Opening **MN** = National Movement

Senate 102 seats

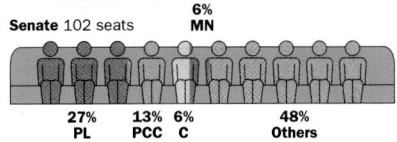

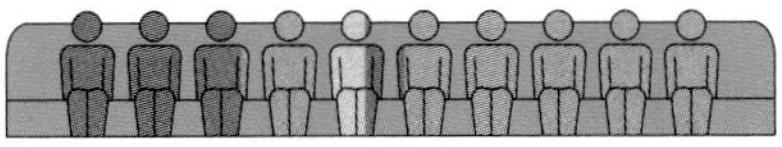
27% PL
13% PCC
6% C
6% MN
48% Others

Two seats are reserved for special representatives of the Amerindian communities

Colombia is a presidential democracy, with a bicameral Congress.

PROFILE

The two-party system which had held sway from the late 1950s appeared to have fractured by the 21st century. The dominance of the PCC and the PL, with few ideological differences, was undermined by electoral breakthroughs by new, smaller parties, culminating in the presidential victory of right-wing independent Alvaro Uribe Velez in 2002. Uribe is trying to amend the constitution to allow him to stand for reelection.

Pervasive corruption and the violence associated with drugs cartels, guerrillas, paramilitaries, and the military have weakened confidence in the state and the government, and have deterred foreign investors.

MAIN POLITICAL ISSUES

Elusive peace

Peace efforts were abandoned in February 2002 as the country returned to full-scale civil conflict against the left-wing Armed Revolutionary Forces of Colombia (FARC) and the National Liberation Army (ELN). Uribe, accused by the FARC of having connections to right-wing militias, has continued the offensive with the aid of US military advisers. However, in 2004 Uribe offered to halt offensive operations against the ELN if it called a cease-fire.

Reforms

IMF-sponsored labor, pension, and tax reforms, which were designed to reactivate the economy and increase investment, were pushed through Congress but failed to gain popular approval in a referendum in 2003, undermining Uribe's position.

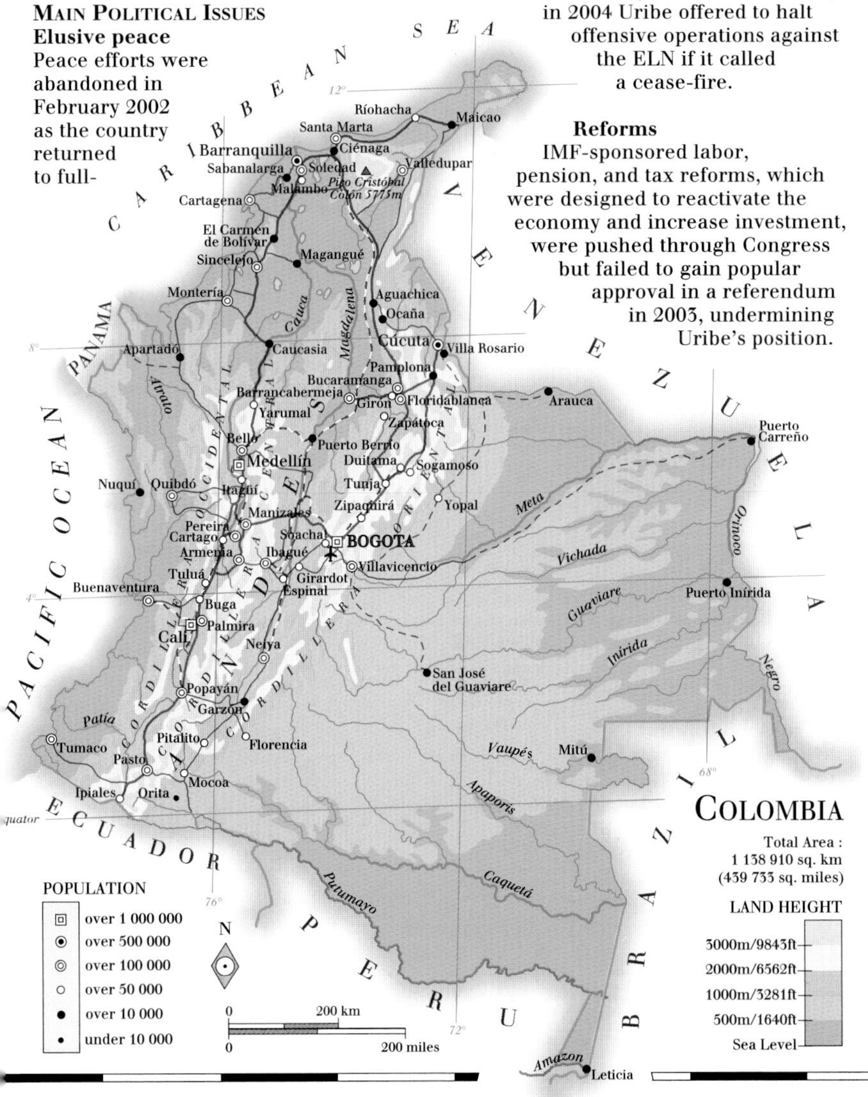
CARIBBEAN SEA
PACIFIC OCEAN
PANAMA
VENEZUELA
ECUADOR
PERU
BRAZIL
Ríohacha
Maicao
Santa Marta
Barranquilla
Ciénaga
Sabanalarga
Soledad
Valledupar
Malambo
Pico Cristóbal Colón 5775m
Cartagena
El Carmen de Bolívar
Sincelejo
Magangué
Montería
Aguachica
Ocaña
Cúcuta
Villa Rosario
Caucasia
Apartadó
Pamplona
Bucaramanga
Barrancabermeja
Girón
Floridablanca
Arauca
Yarumal
Zapatoca
Puerto Carreño
Bello
Puerto Berrío
Medellín
Duitama
Sogamoso
Nuquí
Quibdó
Tunja
Itagüí
Zipaquirá
Yopal
Manizales
Pereira
Cartago
Soacha
BOGOTA
Armenia
Ibagué
Villavicencio
Tuluá
Girardot
Espinal
Buenaventura
Buga
Puerto Inírida
Cali
Palmira
Neiva
San José del Guaviare
Popayán
Garzón
Pitalito
Florencia
Tumaco
Pasto
Mitú
Mocoa
Ipiales
Orita
Leticia
Cauca
Magdalena
Atrato
Meta
Vichada
Orinoco
Guaviare
Inírida
Negro
Patía
Vaupés
Apaporis
Caquetá
Putumayo
Amazon
COLOMBIA
Total Area : 1 138 910 sq. km (439 733 sq. miles)
LAND HEIGHT
3000m/9843ft
2000m/6562ft
1000m/3281ft
500m/1640ft
Sea Level
POPULATION
over 1 000 000
over 500 000
over 100 000
over 50 000
over 10 000
under 10 000
N
0 200 km
0 200 miles

Alvaro Uribe Velez, *the right-leaning independent elected president in 2002.*

Andres Pastrana Arango *launched "Plan Colombia" in 2000 while president.*

WORLD AFFAIRS

Joined UN in 1945

ACS | AP | AmCC | OAS | RG

Good relations with the US are conditional on tough measures to fight the narcotics trade. A $1.3 billion military aid package, approved in 2000, provided training, intelligence, and hardware, ostensibly to assist the "Plan Colombia" antidrugs program. The boundary between this aim and the targeting of guerrilla groups was always blurred. The army's invasion in 2002 of the demilitarized haven, granted to the FARC as part of peace efforts, was reportedly assisted by US military advisers. The US administration fought shy of describing events as a chapter in the US-led "war on terrorism," however, insisting that it was operating within legal limits set down by the Congress. Colombia's neighbors fear a "spillover" of violence and refugees.

AID

Recipient

$441m (receipts) | Up 16% in 2002

US military "antinarcotics aid" forms some 75% of total US aid. The IMF approved a standby loan of $2.1 billion in 2003 to act as security for other loans from international institutions.

CHRONOLOGY

In 1525, Spain began the conquest of Colombia, which became its chief source of gold.

- **1819** Simón Bolívar defeats the Spanish at Boyacá. Republic of Gran Colombia formed with Venezuela, Ecuador, and Panama.
- **1830** Venezuela and Ecuador split away during revolts and civil wars.
- **1849** The centralist Conservative and federalist Liberal parties are established.
- **1861–1886** Liberals hold monopoly on power.
- **1886–1930** Conservative rule.
- **1899–1903** Liberal "War of 1000 Days" revolt fails; 120,000 die.

CHRONOLOGY *continued*

- ❑ **1903** Panama secedes, but is not recognized by Colombia until 1921.
- ❑ **1930** Liberal President Olaya Herrera elected by coalition in first peaceful change of power.
- ❑ **1946** Conservatives take over.
- ❑ **1948** Shooting of Liberal mayor of Bogotá and riot – El Bogotazo – spark civil war – La Violencia – lasting until 1957; 300,000 killed.
- ❑ **1953–1957** Military dictatorship of Rojas Pinilla.
- ❑ **1958** Conservatives and Liberals agree to alternate government in a National Front until 1974. Other parties banned.
- ❑ **1965** Left-wing guerrilla National Liberation Army and Maoist Popular Liberation Army founded.
- ❑ **1966** Pro-Soviet FARC guerrilla group formed.
- ❑ **1968** Constitutional reform allows new parties, but two-party parity continues. Guerrilla groups proliferate from now on.
- ❑ **1984** Minister of justice assassinated for attempting to enforce antinarcotics campaign.
- ❑ **1985** M-19 guerrillas blast their way into ministry of justice; 11 judges and 90 others killed. Patriotic Union (UP) party formed.
- ❑ **1986** Liberal Virgilio Barco Vargas wins presidential elections, ending power-sharing. UP wins ten seats in parliament. Right-wing paramilitary start murder campaign against UP politicians. Violence by both left-wing groups and death squads run by narcotics cartels continues.
- ❑ **1989** M-19 reaches peace deal with government, including full pardon. Becomes legal party.
- ❑ **1990** Presidential candidates of UP and PL murdered during campaign. Liberal César Gaviria elected on antidrugs platform.
- ❑ **1991** New constitution legalizes divorce, prohibits extradition of Colombian nationals. Indigenous peoples' democratic rights guaranteed, but territorial claims are not addressed.
- ❑ **1992–1993** Medellín drugs cartel leader, Pablo Escobar, captured, escapes, and shot dead by police.
- ❑ **1995–1996** President Ernesto Samper cleared of charges of receiving drug funds for elections.
- ❑ **1999** Earthquake kills thousands.
- ❑ **2001** US-backed spraying of coca plantations and destruction of food crops by herbicides ("Plan Colombia") provokes resentment.
- ❑ **2002** Peace talks abandoned. Renewed military offensive. Independent candidate Alvaro Uribe Velez elected president.
- ❑ **2004** ELN offered cease-fire.

DEFENSE

▷ Compulsory military service

$2.84bn

No change in 2002

COLOMBIAN ARMED FORCES

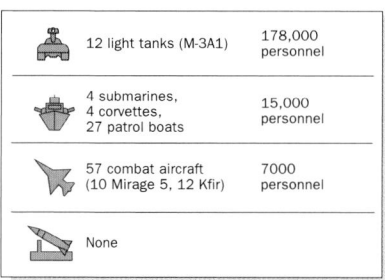

12 light tanks (M-3A1)	178,000 personnel
4 submarines, 4 corvettes, 27 patrol boats	15,000 personnel
57 combat aircraft (10 Mirage 5, 12 Kfir)	7000 personnel
None	

The military is powerful, but rarely intervenes directly in politics. Human rights groups accuse the armed forces and their paramilitary allies of gross and systematic abuses, involving torture and murder, in their fight against guerrilla groups and the production of narcotics. Though restructured in 1998, the army high command remains suspicious of peace negotiations and supports a tougher stance against the rebels, successfully exploiting tensions to expand the army substantially under President Pastrana, with numbers set to rise still more. Orders were given in 2002 to retake the FARC "safe haven." Colombia participates in the joint Latin American Defense Force. The US supplies most arms and training, especially through "Plan Colombia."

ECONOMICS

▷ Inflation 20% p.a. (1990–2001)

$79.6bn

2693 Colombian pesos (2817)

SCORE CARD

❑ World GNP Ranking	42nd
❑ GNP per Capita	$1820
❑ Balance of Payments	–$1.58bn
❑ Inflation	6.3%
❑ Unemployment	18%

EXPORTS

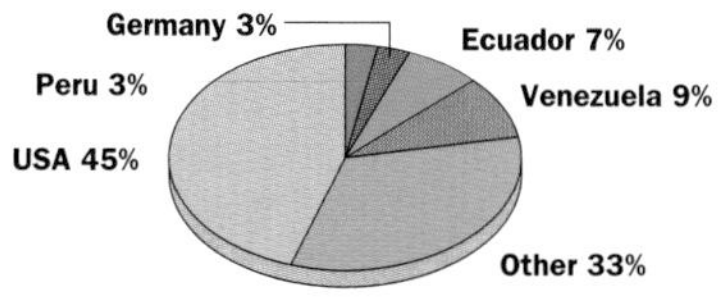

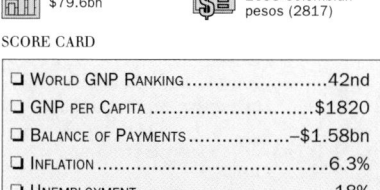

Germany 3%
Ecuador 7%
Peru 3%
Venezuela 9%
USA 45%
Other 33%

IMPORTS

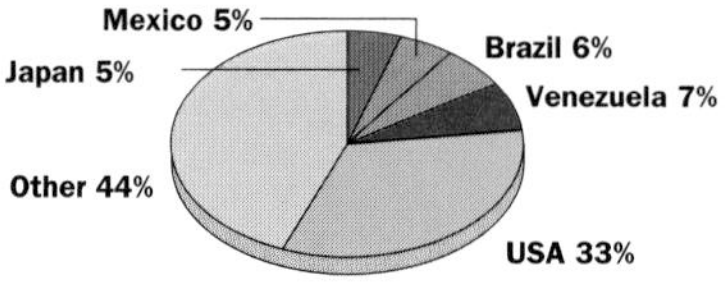

Mexico 5%
Brazil 6%
Japan 5%
Venezuela 7%
Other 44%
USA 33%

Strengths

Substantial oil and coal deposits, well-developed hydroelectric power: Colombia almost energy self-sufficient. Diversified exports including coffee and flowers. Light manufactures. Highly successful, if illegal, narcotics trade injects cash into the economy.

Weaknesses

Foreign investors discouraged by narcotics-related violence, corruption, and political instability. Domestic industry uncompetitive. High unemployment. Coffee and oil subject to world price fluctuations.

Profile

Of all the Latin American economies, Colombia's is probably the closest to the US model. The state has traditionally played a relatively minor role and

ECONOMIC PERFORMANCE INDICATOR

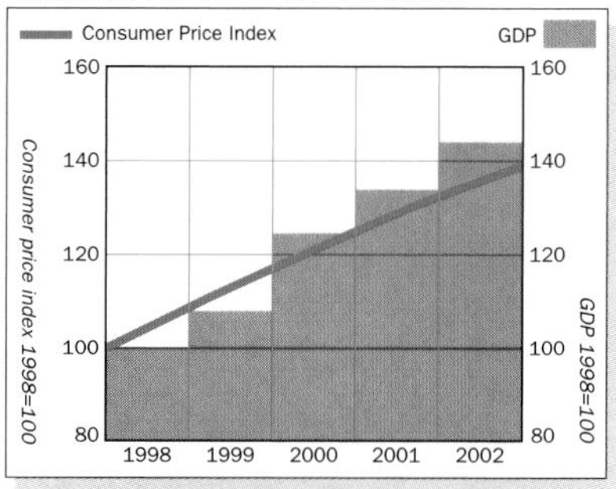

Consumer Price Index
GDP
160
140
120
100
80
1998
1999
2000
2001
2002
Consumer price index 1998=100
GDP 1998=100

Colombia has a successful private export sector. Reforms and austerity measures secured an IMF standby agreement in 2003 and $9 billion in multilateral pledges.

Regional disparities remain marked. Most wealth is found in the Bogotá, Medellín, and Cali regions. Rural areas are largely underdeveloped. The main obstacle to growth is the instability caused by the narcotics business and protracted conflict. Given stability and investment, Colombia's potential for growth is considerable.

COLOMBIA : MAJOR BUSINESSES

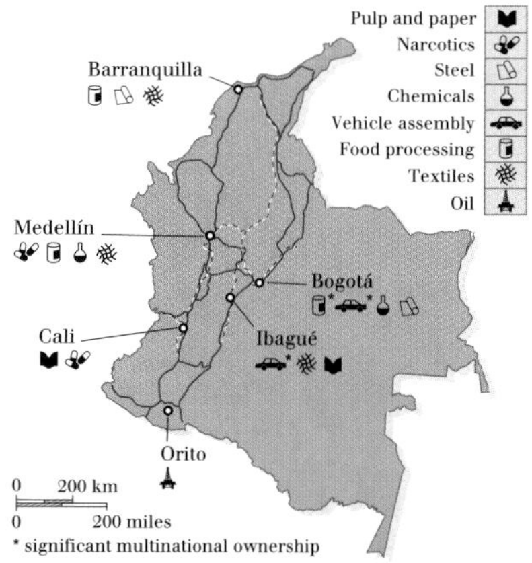

Pulp and paper
Narcotics
Steel
Chemicals
Vehicle assembly
Food processing
Textiles
Oil
Barranquilla
Medellín
Bogotá
Ibagué
Cali
Orito
0 200 km
0 200 miles
* significant multinational ownership

RESOURCES

Electric power 12.7m kW

190,000 tonnes

564,000 b/d (reserves 1.5bn barrels)

25m cattle, 2.7m horses, 2.3m pigs, 118m chickens

Oil, coal, natural gas, silver, emeralds, gold, platinum

ELECTRICITY GENERATION

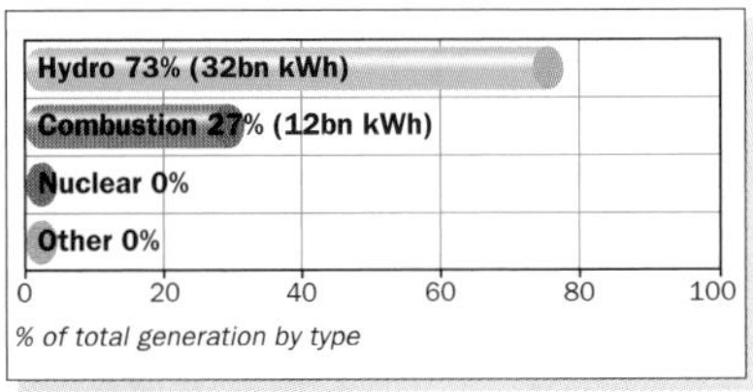
Hydro 73% (32bn kWh)
Combustion 27% (12bn kWh)
Nuclear 0%
Other 0%
0
20
40
60
80
100
% of total generation by type

Colombia has substantial oil reserves but needs increasing investment to maintain production. Coal and gas are important, and it is a major producer of gold, platinum, silver, and emeralds.

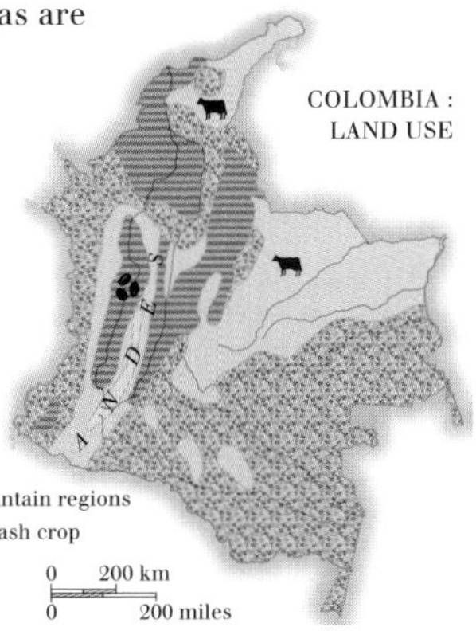
ANDES
Cropland
Pasture
Forest
High mountain regions
Coffee - cash crop
Cattle
0 200 km
0 200 miles

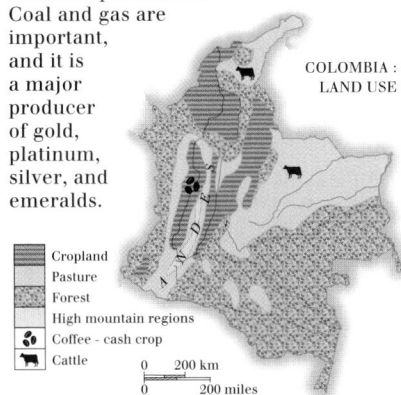

COLOMBIA : LAND USE

ENVIRONMENT

Sustainability rank: 22nd

10% (0.3% partially protected)

1.4 tonnes per capita

ENVIRONMENTAL TREATIES

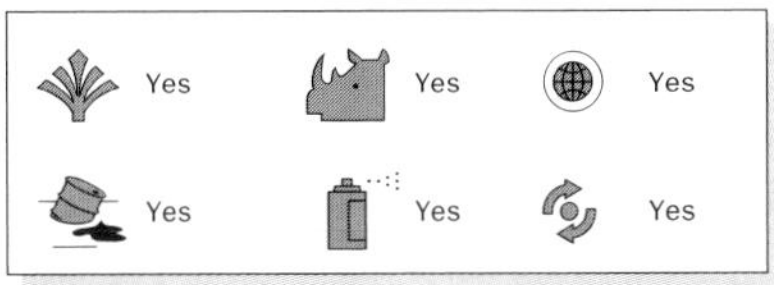
Yes
Yes
Yes
Yes
Yes
Yes

The government calculated in 2002 that 56% of the world's cocaine is produced in former Colombian rainforest.

MEDIA

TV ownership high

Daily newspaper circulation 26 per 1000 people

PUBLISHING AND BROADCAST MEDIA

There are 37 daily newspapers. *El Tiempo* and *El Espectador* have the largest circulations

4 services: 1 state-owned, 3 independent

589 stations: 31 state-owned, 558 independent

The independent press is very small. Journalists have been murdered by paramilitaries and held by guerrillas.

CRIME

No death penalty

54,034 prisoners

Down 6% in 2000

CRIME RATES

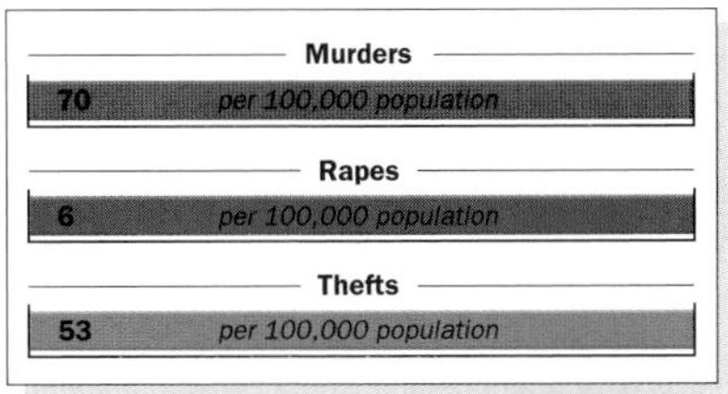
Murders
70 per 100,000 population
Rapes
6 per 100,000 population
Thefts
53 per 100,000 population

Colombia is one of the most violent countries in the world. Armed groups assassinated 20 mayoral candidates and 20 mayors, and kidnapped 200 other candidates in regional and local elections in 2000. The local monitoring group Fundación País Libre reported 2856 cases of kidnapping in 2001, mostly by guerrillas and paramilitaries, the rest blamed on other criminal groups. In 2002 anonymous gunmen murdered the Archbishop of Cali. Homicide is the main cause of death among young men in cities; overall, it rates second in the mortality stakes. Much of the violence is narcotics-related; the army, police, paramilitaries, and guerrillas are all accused of being involved. Police were empowered in 2002 to create "zones of rehabilitation and consolidation" and, in conjunction with the US-backed "Plan Colombia," coca production fell by 30% that year.

The deplorable phenomenon of "social cleansing" involves the murder of street children and beggars by armed gangs, some in Bogotá funded by businesses.

Frequent armed robberies and kidnappings make wealthy residents extremely security conscious.

EDUCATION

School leaving age: 14

92%

934,085 students

THE EDUCATION SYSTEM

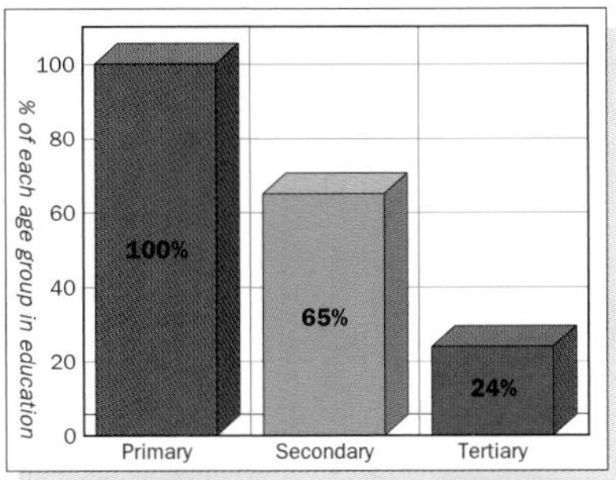
100
80
60
40
20
0
% of each age group in education
100%
65%
24%
Primary
Secondary
Tertiary

Education in Colombia is free and compulsory, and is a mix of French and US models, with a *baccalauréat*-style examination taken at the end of secondary school. A voucher system grants half the cost of private school fees to poor pupils. Where provided, public and university education is generally of a high standard, but the resources available to public education have decreased due to budget cuts. The rich send their children to private schools and universities in the US.

HEALTH

Welfare state health benefits

1 per 833 people

Heart diseases, murders, accidents, cancers

Health care reforms in 1993 aimed to provide universal access via a contributory system with subsidies for the poor. By 2003, however, only 54% of people were covered, and around half of those were being subsidized. Rural areas have little health provision. A polio vaccination campaign has largely eradicated the virus. By 2004 Colombia had the fourth-highest rate of landmine injuries in the world.

SPENDING

GDP/cap. increase

CONSUMPTION AND SPENDING

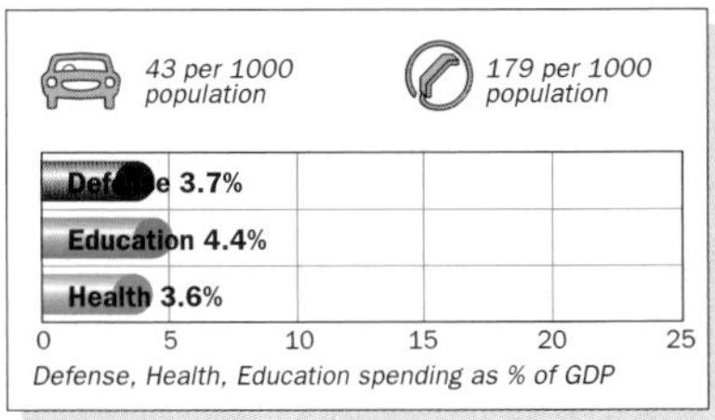
43 per 1000 population
179 per 1000 population
Defense 3.7%
Education 4.4%
Health 3.6%
0
5
10
15
20
25
Defense, Health, Education spending as % of GDP

There is little social mobility; the historically wealthy Spanish families are still dominant in political and business life, but the entry of narcotics-related money has created new elites in cities and among landowners. Drug money also finances the import of consumer goods such as TV sets, computers, and perfume. The wealthy go to the US for medical treatment and educate their children overseas. The rural poor are mostly landless. The inhabitants of shanty towns in Barranquilla, Buenaventura, Cali, and Cartagena form the poorest groups.

WORLD RANKING

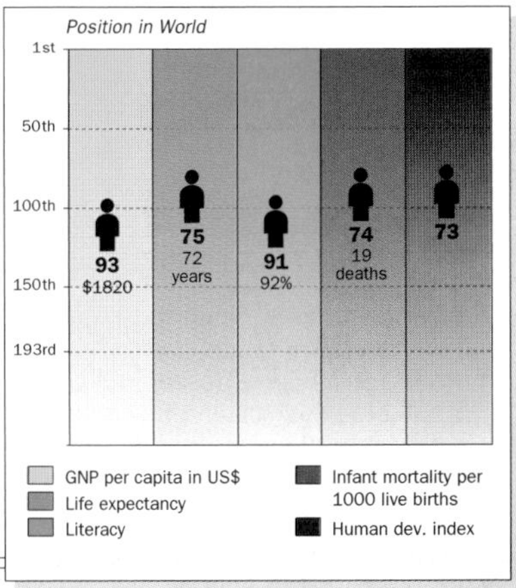
Position in World
1st
50th
100th
150th
193rd
93
$1820
75
72 years
91
92%
74
19 deaths
73
GNP per capita in US$
Life expectancy
Literacy
Infant mortality per 1000 live births
Human dev. index

COMOROS

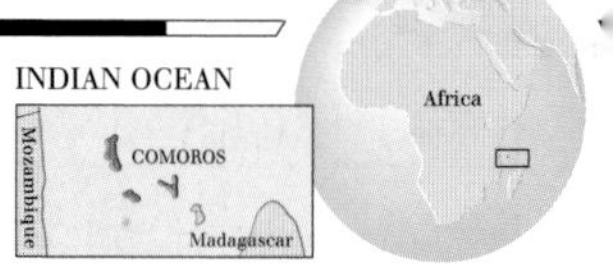
INDIAN OCEAN
Mozambique
COMOROS
Madagascar
Africa

OFFICIAL NAME: Union of the Comoros **CAPITAL:** Moroni
POPULATION: 768,000 **CURRENCY:** Comoros franc **OFFICIAL LANGUAGES:** Arabic, French, and Comoran

1975 | 1975 | July 6 | COM | +3 | +269 | .km

THE ARCHIPELAGO republic of the Comoros lies off the east African coast, between Mozambique and Madagascar. It consists of three main islands and a number of islets. Most of the population are subsistence farmers. In 1975, the Comoros islands, except for Mayotte, became independent of France. Since then instability has plagued this poor country, with countless coups and countercoups, and repeated attempts at secession by smaller islands.

Moroni, the capital, on Grande Comore. The Comoros islands are fertile and heavily forested. Many are ringed by coral reefs.

CLIMATE

Tropical oceanic

WEATHER CHART FOR MORONI

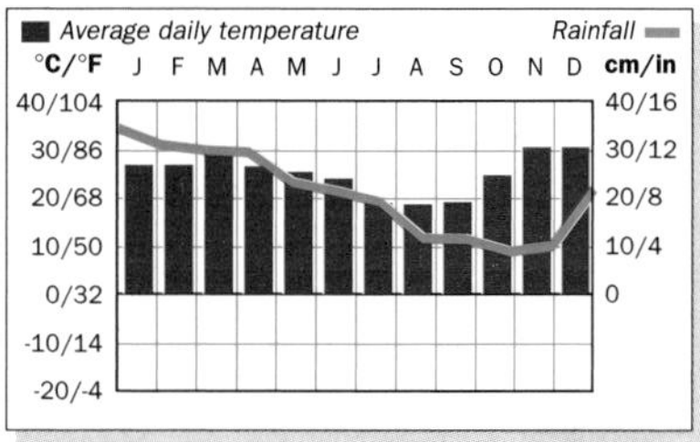
Average daily temperature
Rainfall
°C/°F
J F M A M J J A S O N D
cm/in
40/104
30/86
20/68
10/50
0/32
-10/14
-20/-4
40/16
30/12
20/8
10/4
0

The islands are tropical; it is hot and humid on the coasts and cooler higher up, notably on Mount Kartala.

TRANSPORTATION

Drive on right

Moroni International Prince Said Ibrahim, Grande Comore 101,015 passengers

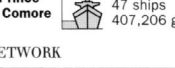

47 ships 407,206 grt

THE TRANSPORTATION NETWORK

678 km (421 miles)

None

None

None

Ferries travel between the islands and also compensate for poor roads on Mohéli. Each island has an airfield.

TOURISM

Visitors : Population 1:41

18,936 visitors

Down 2% in 2002

MAIN TOURIST ARRIVALS

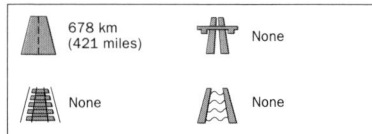

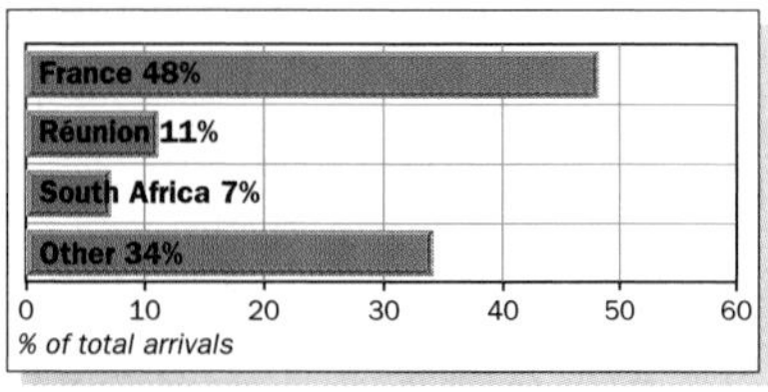
France 48%
Réunion 11%
South Africa 7%
Other 34%
0
10
20
30
40
50
60
% of total arrivals

Plans for tourism to take advantage of the islands' beautiful scenery, magnificent beaches, and fascinating history are fundamentally undermined by the country's chronic instability. Some cruise ships have begun to visit.

PEOPLE

Pop. density high

Arabic, Comoran, French

344/km² (892/mi²)

THE URBAN/RURAL POPULATION SPLIT

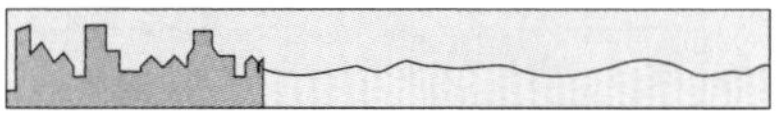
34%
66%

RELIGIOUS PERSUASION

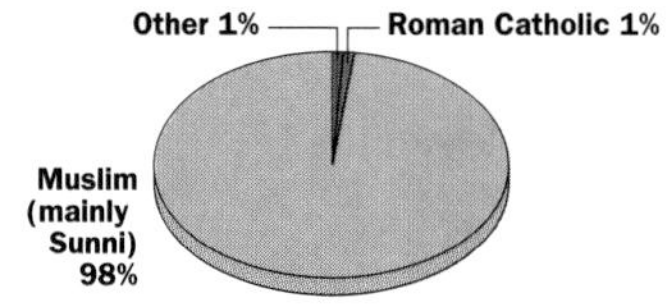
Other 1%
Roman Catholic 1%
Muslim (mainly Sunni) 98%

The Comoros has absorbed Polynesians, Africans, Indonesians, Persians, and Arabs over time, as well as immigrants from Portugal, the Netherlands, France, and India. Each island is named in French and Comoran – a mix of Kiswahili and Arabic. Some communities retain their individual character: Mohéli is still primarily African. Ethnic tension is rare; a more potent divisive factor, especially on Anjouan, is regionalism.

POLITICS

Multiparty elections

2004/2009

President Assoumani Azali

AT THE LAST ELECTION

Assembly of the Union 33 seats

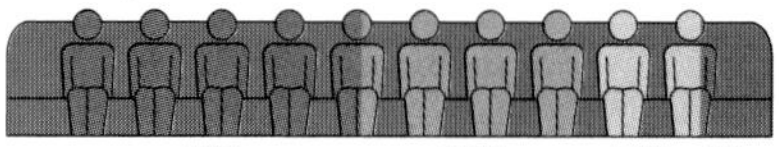
46% App
33% Opp
18% Supp
3% Ind

App = Appointed by regional assemblies
Opp = Opposition alliance of regional parties
Supp = Supporters of President Azali **Ind** = Independent

Comoran politics is characterized by chaos. Coups and countercoups have plagued the islands since independence. The key issue is the balance of power between the islands and the overarching government based on Grande Comore. Unrest followed declarations of independence on Anjouan and Mohéli in 1997 and renewed violence in 1999 prompted Col. Assoumani Azali to assume power. In 2002 he forged a new loose "Union of the Comoros," of which he was elected president unopposed. All the island governments contest Azali's authoritarian use of his new constitutional powers, and the 2004 legislative elections showed an increase in support for regional parties.

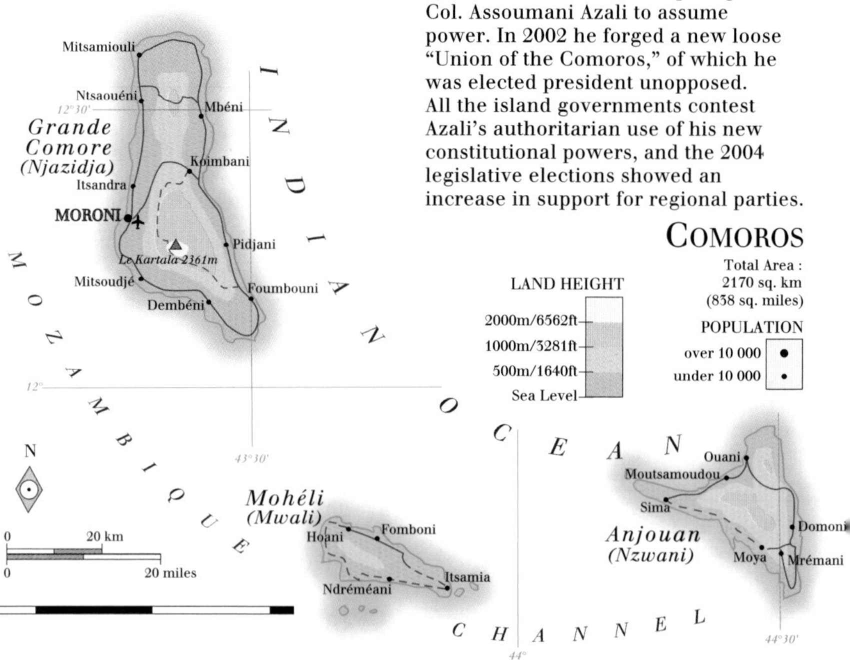
Mitsamiouli
Ntsaouéni
Mbéni
Grande Comore (Njazidja)
Koimbani
Itsandra
MORONI
Pidjani
Le Kartala 2361m
Mitsoudjé
Foumbouni
Demběni
INDIAN OCEAN
MOZAMBIQUE CHANNEL
N
0 20 km
0 20 miles
Mohéli (Mwali)
Hoani
Fomboni
Itsamia
Ndréméani
Ouani
Moutsamoudou
Sima
Domoni
Anjouan (Nzwani)
Moya
Mrémani
COMOROS
Total Area : 2170 sq. km (838 sq. miles)
LAND HEIGHT
2000m/6562ft
1000m/3281ft
500m/1640ft
Sea Level
POPULATION
over 10 000
under 10 000

C

WORLD AFFAIRS

Joined UN in 1975

AL OIC AU COI FZ

France remains the main aid donor, though economic ties with South Africa are strong. The turbulent situation on the war-torn islands forced a visiting OAU assessment team to flee Anjouan in 1999. An army of European mercenaries attempted to take over Mohéli in December 2001. The Comoros still claims sovereignty over Mayotte.

AID

Recipient

$32m (receipts) | Up 19% in 2002

Foreign aid, mainly from France, the World Bank, the EU, and the UN, accounts for over 40% of GDP. Because of its Islamic links, the Comoros also gets aid from Arab states and OPEC. In 1998, major donors attacked the government for spending more than 70% on "political superstructure."

DEFENSE

No compulsory military service

$3m (estimate) | No significant change

France and South Africa finance the small presidential guard, the principal security force. Mauritian aid was also sought after clashes on Anjouan.

ECONOMICS

Inflation 3.6% p.a. (1990–2001)

$228m | 404.4 Comoros francs (454.3)

SCORE CARD

❑ World GNP Ranking	182nd
❑ GNP per Capita	$390
❑ Balance of Payments	–$1m
❑ Inflation	7.1%
❑ Unemployment	20%

Strengths

Main cash crops are vanilla, ylang-ylang, and cloves.

Weaknesses

Subsistence-level farming. Most food requirements imported. Lack of basic infrastructure, notably electricity and transportation. Poor education provision. Alleged financial mismanagement. Political instability – hinders growth of tourism. Dependence on aid.

EXPORTS

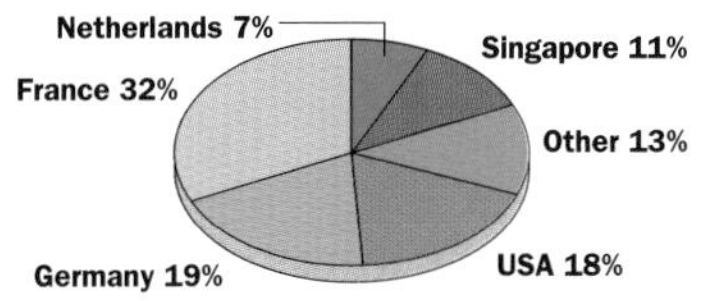
Netherlands 7%
Singapore 11%
France 32%
Other 13%
Germany 19%
USA 18%

IMPORTS

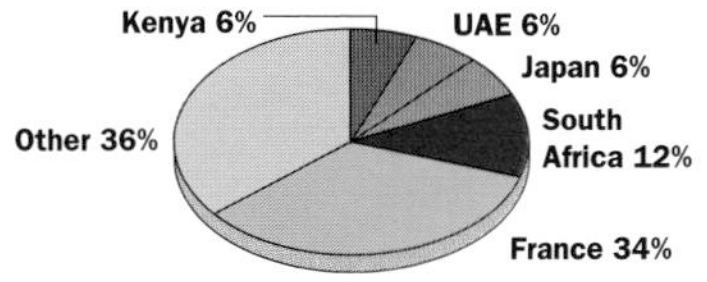
Kenya 6%
UAE 6%
Japan 6%
Other 36%
South Africa 12%
France 34%

RESOURCES

Electric power 6000 kW

12,180 tonnes | Not an oil producer

115,000 goats, 52,000 cattle, 490,000 chickens | None

There are few strategic resources. Most fuel for energy is imported, though there is potential for geothermal generation and HEP, and trials for the utilization of solar energy have begun.

ENVIRONMENT

Not available

None | 0.1 tonnes per capita

Comorans have become more aware of environmental issues, partly in response to international pressure. While tourism is promoted, the government recognizes the long-term commercial value of imposing environmental controls on new developments. It has also set up protection schemes for native fauna, including the rare coelocanth.

MEDIA

TV ownership low

There are no daily newspapers

PUBLISHING AND BROADCAST MEDIA

There are 2 weekly newspapers, the state-owned *Al Watwan* and the independent *La Gazette des Comores*

1 state-owned service | 1 state-controlled service, some independent services

China helped to fund the islands' first national TV station. There are several radio stations and newspapers which are critical of the government.

CRIME

Death penalty in use

200 prisoners | Crime is rising

A climate of lawlessness has been created by the continuing power struggles between rival militias – particularly on the island of Anjouan since 1997.

EDUCATION

School leaving age: 14

56% | 714 students

The first university was inaugurated in 2003. Nearly all children attend elementary school, though the ratio of pupils to teachers is high. Many children also attend Koranic school.

CHRONOLOGY

The Comoros was ruled by matrilineally inherited sultanates until shortly before becoming a French protectorate in 1886.

- ❑ **1961** Internal self-government.
- ❑ **1975** Independence.
- ❑ **1978** Mercenaries restore Ahmed Abdallah to power.
- ❑ **1989** Abdallah assassinated.
- ❑ **1992** Chaotic first multiparty polls.
- ❑ **1997** Anjouan separatists beat off government troops.
- ❑ **1999** Col. Azali seizes power. Anjouan militias clash.
- ❑ **2000** Fomboni declaration signed with Anjouan.
- ❑ **2001** Successive coups on Anjouan.
- ❑ **2002** New constitution. Azali returned to office.
- ❑ **2004** Regional parties win majority in legislative elections.

HEALTH

No welfare state health benefits

1 per 10,000 people | Malaria, infectious intestinal and bacterial diseases

Though there are a good number of regional health centers, poor facilities deter potential patients.

SPENDING

GDP/cap. decrease

CONSUMPTION AND SPENDING

13 per 1000 population | *13 per 1000 population*

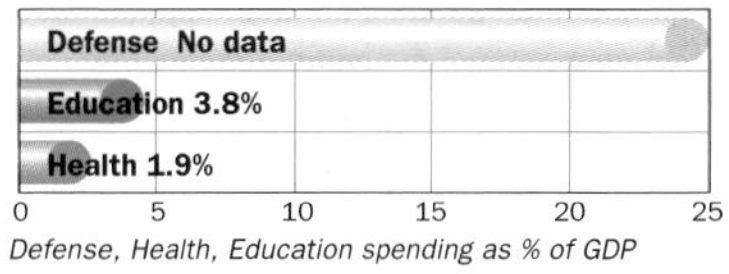
Defense No data
Education 3.8%
Health 1.9%
0
5
10
15
20
25

Defense, Health, Education spending as % of GDP

A political and business elite controls most of the wealth. Bridegrooms win social status according to the size of their wedding. Government workers often suffer from wage arrears.

WORLD RANKING

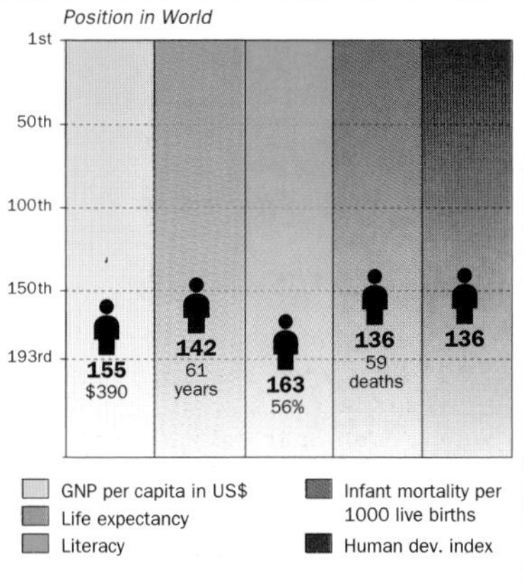
Position in World
1st
50th
100th
150th
193rd
155
$390
142
61
years
163
56%
136
59
deaths
136
GNP per capita in US$
Life expectancy
Literacy
Infant mortality per 1000 live births
Human dev. index

CONGO

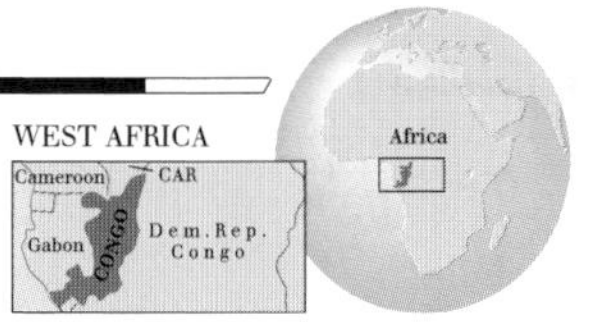
WEST AFRICA
Africa
Cameroon
CAR
Gabon
CONGO
Dem. Rep. Congo

OFFICIAL NAME: Republic of the Congo **CAPITAL:** Brazzaville
POPULATION: 3.7 million **CURRENCY:** CFA franc **OFFICIAL LANGUAGE:** French

C

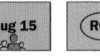

1960 | 1960 | Aug 15 | RCB | +1 | +242 | .cg

STRADDLING THE EQUATOR in west central Africa, Congo achieved independence from France in 1960, soon falling under a Marxist-Leninist form of government which discouraged much foreign investment. Multiparty democracy was achieved in 1991, but was soon overshadowed by years of violence.

CLIMATE

Tropical equatorial

WEATHER CHART FOR BRAZZAVILLE

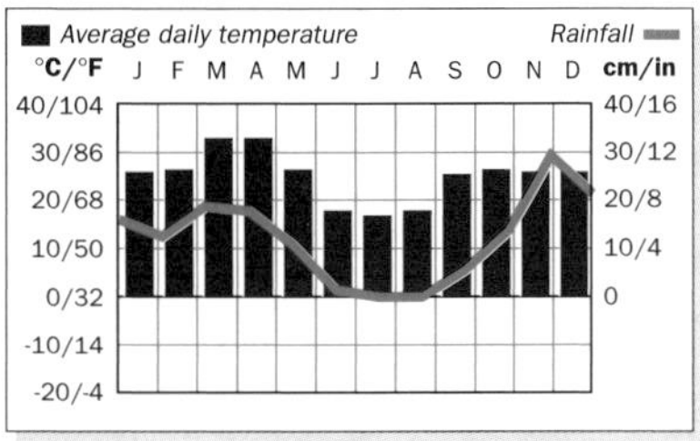
Average daily temperature
Rainfall
°C/°F
J F M A M J J A S O N D
cm/in
40/104
30/86
20/68
10/50
0/32
-10/14
-20/-4
40/16
30/12
20/8
10/4
0

In most years there is a dry season and a wet season with two peaks in Congo. The rainfall is heaviest in the coastal regions.

TRANSPORTATION

Drive on right

Maya Maya, Brazzaville 454,392 passengers

18 ships 3400 grt

THE TRANSPORTATION NETWORK

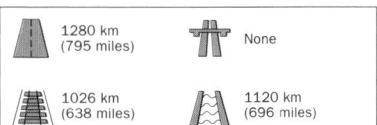

1280 km (795 miles)

None

1026 km (638 miles)

1120 km (696 miles)

Pointe-Noire is a major port, used by the Central African Republic, Chad, and Cameroon. The Congo Ocean Railroad (to Brazzaville) reopened in 2000. There are plans for a second, and larger, international airport near Ewo.

TOURISM

Visitors : Population 1:195

19,000 visitors

Down 27% in 2001

MAIN TOURIST ARRIVALS

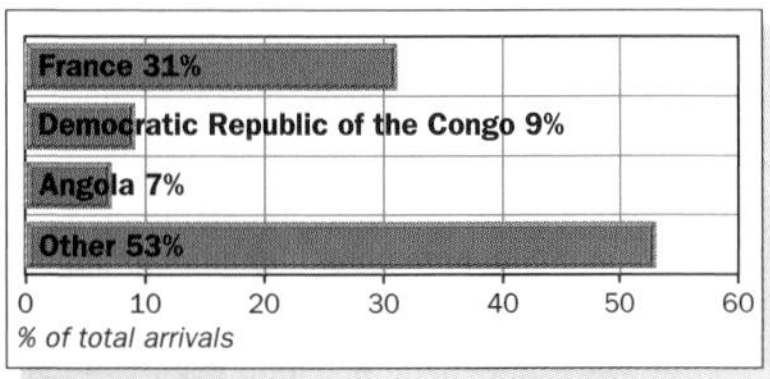
France 31%
Democratic Republic of the Congo 9%
Angola 7%
Other 53%
0 10 20 30 40 50 60
% of total arrivals

The Marxist-Leninist regime did not seek to develop tourism, and visitors, mostly on safaris and business-related trips, are still rare.

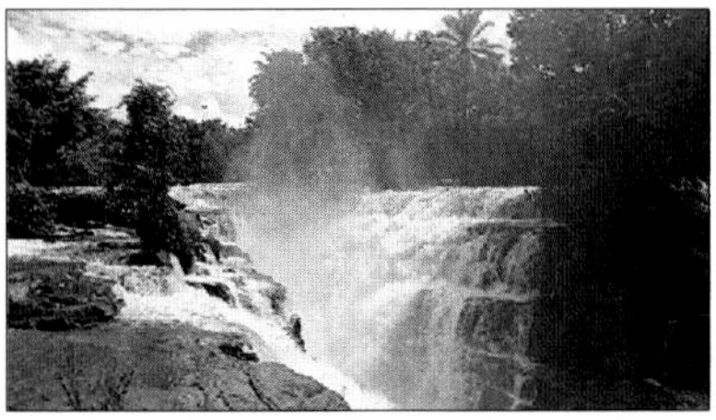

The Loufoulakari Falls, near Brazzaville. The Congo River is a key transportation artery for the region.

PEOPLE

Pop. density low

Kongo, Teke, Lingala, French

11/km² (28/mi²)

THE URBAN/RURAL POPULATION SPLIT

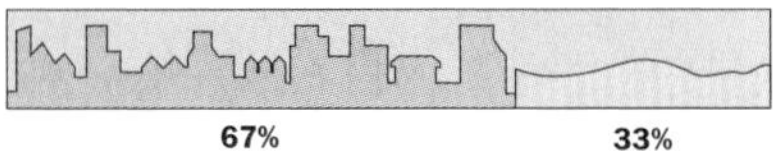
67%
33%

ETHNIC MAKEUP

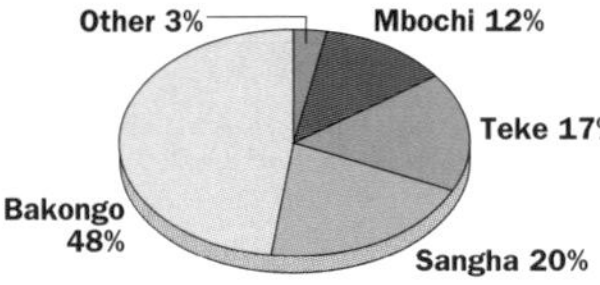
Other 3%
Mbochi 12%
Teke 17%
Bakongo 48%
Sangha 20%

Congo is one of the most tribally conscious countries in Africa. It is also one of the most urbanized in the region, most people living in Brazzaville, Pointe-Noire, and the area in between; to the north the country is dense jungle. Women have achieved considerable freedom since the 1950s.

POLITICS

Multiparty elections

L. House 2002/2007
U. House 2002/2008

President Denis Sassou-Nguesso

AT THE LAST ELECTION

National Assembly 137 seats

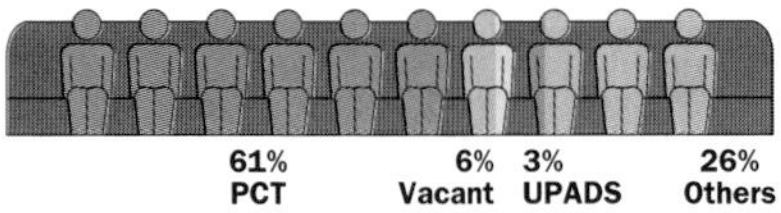
4% UDR
61% PCT
6% Vacant
3% UPADS
26% Others

PCT = Congolese Labor Party and allies
UDR = Union for Democracy and the Republic
UPADS = Pan-African Union for Social Democracy

Senate 66 seats

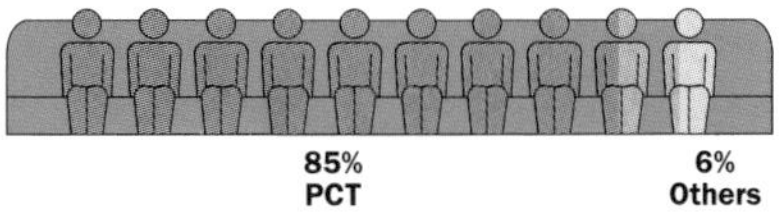
9% Vacant
85% PCT
6% Others

Former Marxist dictator Denis Sassou-Nguesso seized power in 1997, amid intense fighting which left thousands dead. Relative peace was secured in 1999. A new constitution giving greater power to the presidency was approved in 2002, and Sassou-Nguesso was easily elected. Fighting broke out again later that year, but legislative elections were eventually held and were won by Sassou-Nguesso's supporters.

CONGO

Total Area : 342 000 sq. km (132 046 sq. miles)

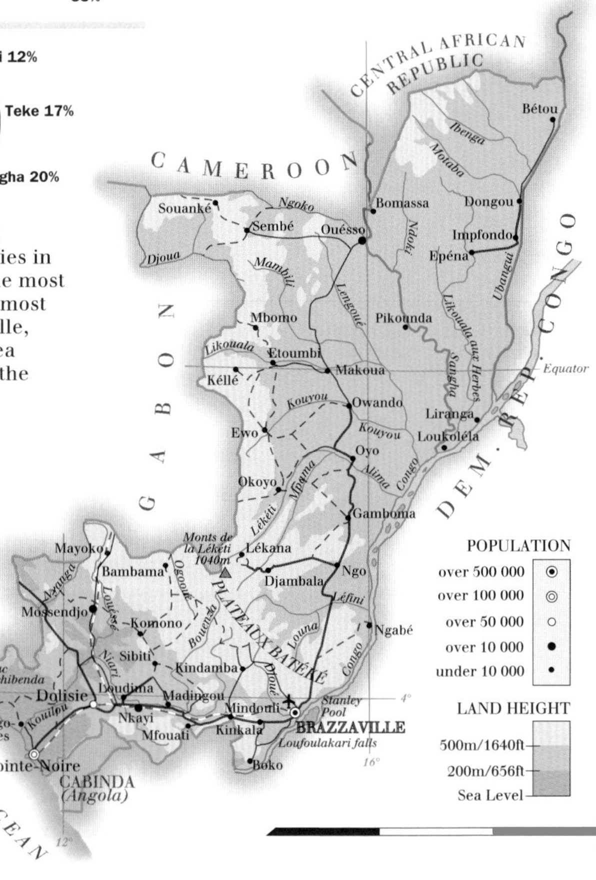
CENTRAL AFRICAN REPUBLIC
CAMEROON
GABON
DEM. REP. CONGO
ATLANTIC OCEAN
CABINDA (Angola)
Bétou
Souanké
Sembé
Ouésso
Bomassa
Dongou
Impfondo
Epéna
Mbomo
Pikounda
Etoumbi
Makoua
Kéllé
Owando
Liranga
Loukoléla
Ewo
Oyo
Okoyo
Gamboma
Mayoko
Lékana
Bambama
Djambala
Ngo
Mossendjo
Komono
Ngabé
Sibiti
Kindamba
Nzambi
Dolisie
Loudima
Madingou
Mindouli
Madingo-Kayes
Nkayi
Mfouati
Kinkala
BRAZZAVILLE
Pointe-Noire
Boko
Loufoulakari falls
Stanley Pool
PLATEAUX BATÉKÉ
Monts de la Lékéti 1040m
Lac Tchibenda
Equator
N
0 100 km
0 100 miles
POPULATION
over 500 000
over 100 000
over 50 000
over 10 000
under 10 000
LAND HEIGHT
500m/1640ft
200m/656ft
Sea Level

WORLD AFFAIRS

Joined UN in 1960

BDEAC | CEMAC | FZ | NAM | ACP

Balancing relations with France and the US is a priority, since both seek to extend their stakes in the oil industry. Congo has been susceptible in recent years to political instability and wars in neighboring countries. It has hosted refugees from Angola, the DRC, the CAR, Chad, and Rwanda. Angola has been a key regional ally for Sassou-Nguesso.

AID

Recipient

$420m (receipts) — Up 460% in 2002

Congo is chronically indebted and at odds with the IMF, which says that $102.3 million in oil earnings evaporated in 2003. It is often overlooked by donors in favor of its larger neighbor, the DRC.

DEFENSE

No compulsory military service

$88m — Up 10% in 2002

A peace deal signed in 2003 provides for the demobilization, disarmament, and reintegration of "Ninja" rebels – the fittest – into the national army. The air force numbers 1200, and is equipped with 12 MiG-21s.

ECONOMICS

Inflation 8.8% p.a. (1990–2001)

$2.23bn — 539.2 CFA francs (571.2)

SCORE CARD

- ❑ WORLD GNP RANKING........................138th
- ❑ GNP PER CAPITA $610
- ❑ BALANCE OF PAYMENTS......................–$34m
- ❑ INFLATION 4.4%
- ❑ UNEMPLOYMENT.......Widespread underemployment

STRENGTHS

Increase in importance of oil, now providing 95% of export revenues. Significant timber supplies. Skilled and well-trained workforce helps sustain substantial industrial base in the capital and Pointe-Noire.

WEAKNESSES

Massive debt burden. Top-heavy bureaucracy. Overdependence on oil. Political instability. Large refugee population.

EXPORTS

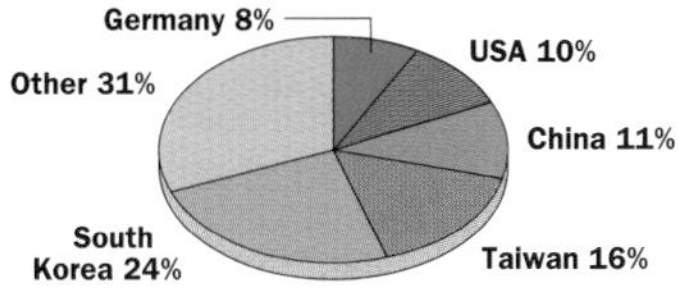
Germany 8%
USA 10%
Other 31%
China 11%
South Korea 24%
Taiwan 16%

IMPORTS

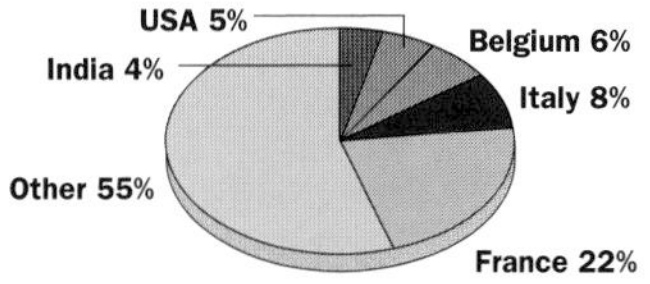
USA 5%
Belgium 6%
India 4%
Italy 8%
Other 55%
France 22%

RESOURCES

Electric power 121,000 kW

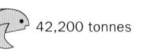

42,200 tonnes — 243,000 b/d (reserves 1.5bn barrels)

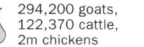

294,200 goats, 122,370 cattle, 2m chickens — Oil, natural gas, zinc, gold, copper, potash, diamonds

Oil is by far the most important resource, the majority of which is exported. Known natural gas reserves are not exploited due to a lack of dedicated facilities. Congo is a net importer of electricity, mostly from the neighboring DRC, despite an estimated HEP potential of 3000 MW. Plans for several new dams are being considered; the Imboulou Dam, the largest so far, is being built on the Lefini River by a Chinese consortium.

ENVIRONMENT

Sustainability rank: 40th

7% (4% partially protected) — 0.5 tonnes per capita

The 1999 Yaoundé Declaration should help control exploitation of tropical timber. Congo has been used in the past as a dumping ground for dangerous toxic waste from the West.

MEDIA

TV ownership low

Daily newspaper circulation 8 per 1000 people

PUBLISHING AND BROADCAST MEDIA

There are 64 daily newspapers, including *Mweti* and *Aujourd'hui*

1 state-controlled service — 4 services: 2 state-controlled, 2 independent

With only moderate media control, the press often takes an antigovernment stance. During World War II, Radio Brazzaville, still the official state radio, was vital to de Gaulle's French forces.

CRIME

Death penalty not used in practice

918 prisoners — Crime is rising

In 2003 the government launched a crackdown on crime in Brazzaville. Instability in neighboring countries means that guns are easily available.

EDUCATION

School leaving age: 15

83% — 13,403 students

Congo has one of the highest rates of literacy in Africa. There is one university, Marien Ngouabi, in Brazzaville.

CHRONOLOGY

The kingdoms of Teke and Loango were incorporated as the Middle Congo (part of French Equatorial Africa) between 1880 and 1883.

- ❑ **1960** Independence.
- ❑ **1964** Marxist-Leninist National Revolution Movement (MNR) sole legal party.
- ❑ **1977** Yhompi-Opango head of state after President Ngoumbi's murder.
- ❑ **1979** Col. Denis Sassou-Nguesso president.
- ❑ **1991** Multiparty democracy.
- ❑ **1992** Pascal Lissouba president.
- ❑ **1993** Elections: Lissouba's UPADS party gains majority.
- ❑ **1997** Sassou-Nguesso ousts Lissouba.
- ❑ **1999** Cease-fire signed.
- ❑ **2001** IMF starts to clear debt.
- ❑ **2002** New constitution approved. Sassou-Nguesso wins elections.

HEALTH

Welfare state health benefits

1 per 3333 people — Diarrheal, parasitic, and respiratory diseases, malaria

The health service, set up by French military doctors at the start of the 20th century, has been devastated by civil war.

SPENDING

GDP/cap. increase

CONSUMPTION AND SPENDING

8 per 1000 population — *7 per 1000 population*

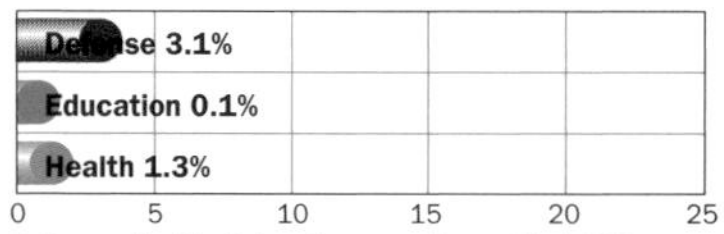
Defense 3.1%
Education 0.1%
Health 1.3%
0
5
10
15
20
25

Defense, Health, Education spending as % of GDP

Wealth generated from oil extraction has sustained an active and confident middle class. French-label products are considered to be status symbols.

WORLD RANKING

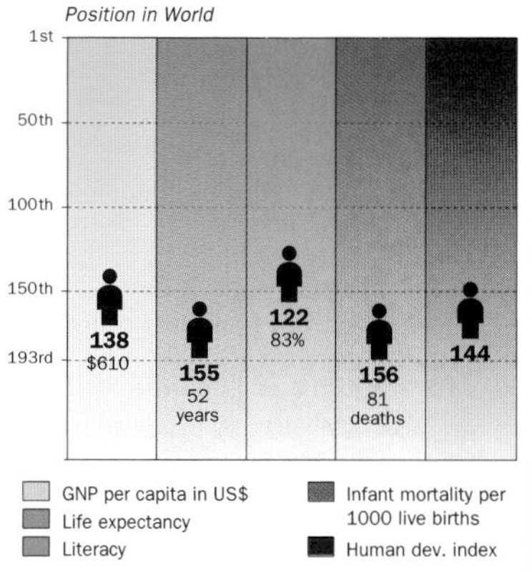
Position in World
1st
50th
100th
150th
193rd
138
$610
155
52 years
122
83%
156
81 deaths
144
GNP per capita in US$
Life expectancy
Literacy
Infant mortality per 1000 live births
Human dev. index

CONGO (DEMOCRATIC REPUBLIC)

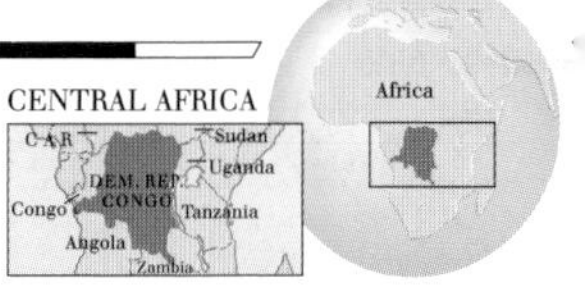
CENTRAL AFRICA
C.A.R.
Sudan
Uganda
DEM. REP. CONGO
Congo
Tanzania
Angola
Zambia
Africa

OFFICIAL NAME: Democratic Republic of the Congo **CAPITAL:** Kinshasa
POPULATION: 52.8 million **CURRENCY:** Congolese franc **OFFICIAL LANGUAGE:** French

1960 | 1960 | June 6 | CGO | +1 | +243 | .zr

LYING IN EAST CENTRAL AFRICA, the Democratic Republic of the Congo (DRC), known as Zaire from 1971 to 1997, is Africa's third-largest country. The rainforested basin of the Congo River occupies 60% of the land area. The notoriously corrupt Marshal Mobutu ruled from 1965 until his overthrow in 1997 by Laurent-Désiré Kabila. A rebellion launched in 1998 plunged the country into renewed chaos, and spiraled into regional conflict. Peace tentatively arrived two years after Joseph Kabila's succession in January 2001.

The Congo River is navigable for 1357 km (848 miles), and provides one of the most convenient ways of traveling in the country.

CLIMATE

Tropical equatorial/ wet and dry

WEATHER CHART FOR KINSHASA

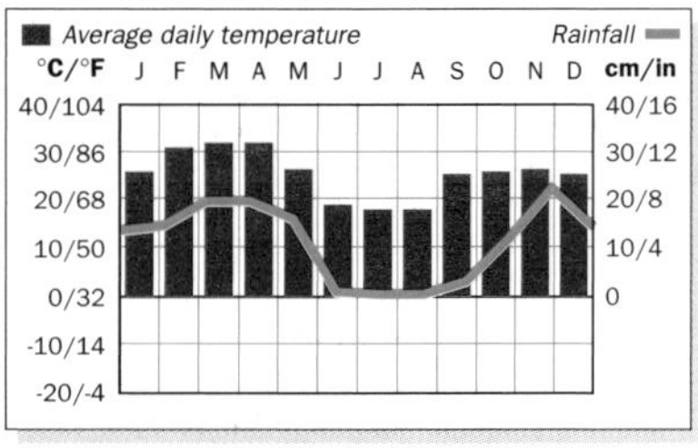
Average daily temperature
Rainfall
°C/°F
J F M A M J J A S O N D
cm/in
40/104
30/86
20/68
10/50
0/32
-10/14
-20/-4
40/16
30/12
20/8
10/4
0

The climate is tropical and humid. Temperatures average 25°C (77°F) and vary little through the year. Annual rainfall is around 150–200 cm (60–80 in); mountainous areas are wetter. The equator passes through the north of the country, causing marked regional variations. To its south, well-differentiated wet and dry seasons are October–May and June–September respectively. North of the equator, a short dry season lasts from December to February; the rest of the year is wet.

TRANSPORTATION

Drive on right

N'Djili, Kinshasa
437,852 passengers

20 ships
12,900 grt

THE TRANSPORTATION NETWORK

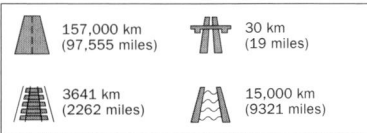

157,000 km (97,555 miles)

30 km (19 miles)

3641 km (2262 miles)

15,000 km (9321 miles)

The Congo River and its many tributaries provide the main means of communication. The size of the country and the fact that most of it is covered by dense rainforest have severely limited the development of road and rail networks. Many forest settlements are inaccessible except by air. Road maintenance, always poor, has virtually ceased outside the main towns since 1990, isolating even more settlements situated away from the main rivers.

TOURISM

Visitors : Population 1:513

103,000 visitors

Up 94% in 2000

MAIN TOURIST ARRIVALS

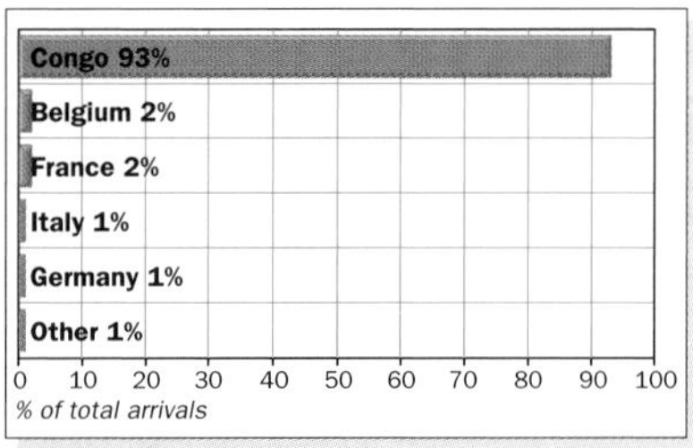
Congo 93%
Belgium 2%
France 2%
Italy 1%
Germany 1%
Other 1%
0 10 20 30 40 50 60 70 80 90 100
% of total arrivals

Political turmoil and widespread anarchy since early 1997 ensure that the country remains off the itinerary for most tourists and businessmen.

Potential tourist attractions consist mainly of scenery – mountains and lakes – and wildlife, but there are few facilities for tourists even in the capital. The Congo, 16 km (10 miles) wide in places, is Africa's second-longest river after the Nile. Visitors were formerly also attracted by the vibrant music of Kinshasa's many bands.

PEOPLE

Pop. density low

Kiswahili, Tshiluba, Kikongo, Lingala, French

23/km² (60/mi²)

THE URBAN/RURAL POPULATION SPLIT

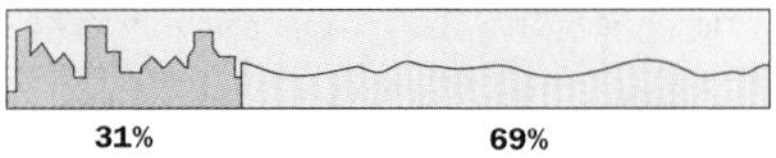
31%
69%

RELIGIOUS PERSUASION

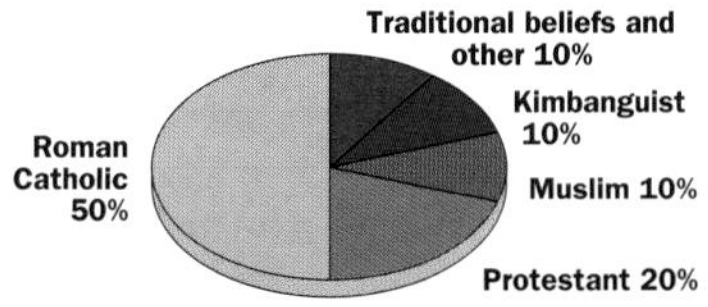
Traditional beliefs and other 10%
Kimbanguist 10%
Muslim 10%
Protestant 20%
Roman Catholic 50%

ETHNIC MAKEUP

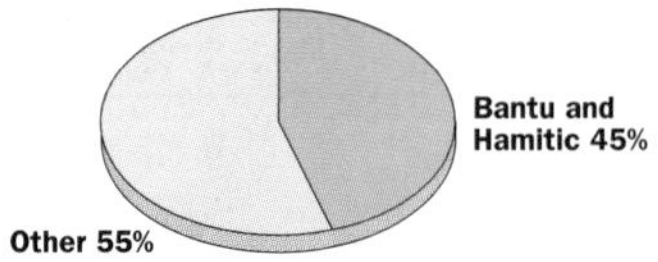
Bantu and Hamitic 45%
Other 55%

The southern Shaba mining area and major urban centers are densely populated, while the rainforests are relatively empty. There is great ethnic diversity, with more than 12 main groups and around 190 smaller ones. The majority are of Bantu origin, but there are also large Hamitic and Nilotic populations, mainly in the north and northeast. The original inhabitants, the forest pygmies, today form a tiny and marginalized group.

War and consequent hunger, poverty, and disease have killed thousands of people. Much violence has an ethnic basis, exacerbated by Mobutu's use of the nationality law. In 1994 a Hutu refugee influx from Rwanda caused serious tension among Tutsis in eastern areas; revenge killings became common. Regarded by Mobutu as foreigners, Tutsis were the backbone of the 1996–1997 insurgency that overthrew him, and then turned against rebel leader-turned-president Laurent Kabila. Severe violence between Hema and Lendu tribes broke out in the northeast after the withdrawal of Ugandan and Rwandan troops in 2003 and conflict continued in 2004, especially in the east.

POPULATION AGE BREAKDOWN

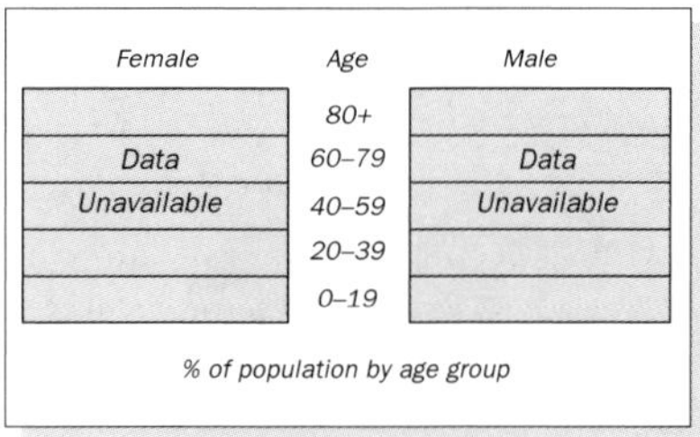
Female
Age
Male
80+
60–79
40–59
20–39
0–19
Data Unavailable
Data Unavailable
% of population by age group

CONGO, DEMOCRATIC REPUBLIC

Total Area : 2 345 410 sq. km
(905 563 sq. miles)

POPULATION

- over 1 000 000
- over 500 000
- over 100 000
- over 50 000
- over 10 000
- under 10 000

LAND HEIGHT

- 2000m/6562ft
- 1000m/3281ft
- 500m/1640ft
- 200m/656ft
- Sea Level

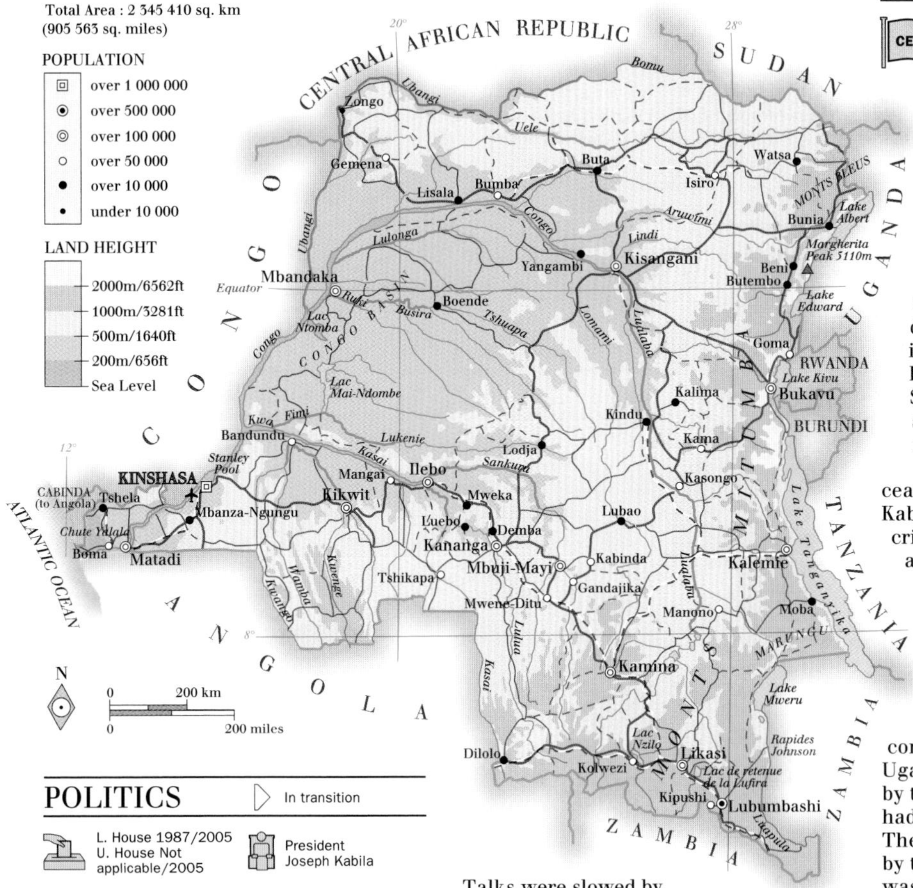
CENTRAL AFRICAN REPUBLIC
SUDAN
UGANDA
RWANDA
BURUNDI
TANZANIA
ZAMBIA
ANGOLA
CONGO
CABINDA (to Angola)
ATLANTIC OCEAN
KINSHASA
Zongo
Gemena
Lisala
Bumba
Buta
Isiro
Watsa
Bunia
Lake Albert
Margherita Peak 5110m
Beni
Butembo
Lake Edward
Goma
Lake Kivu
Bukavu
Kisangani
Yangambi
Mbandaka
Equator
Boende
Lac Ntomba
Lac Mai-Ndombe
Bandundu
Stanley Pool
Mangai
Ilebo
Lodja
Kikwit
Tshela
Mbanza-Ngungu
Boma
Matadi
Chute Yelala
Mweka
Luebo
Demba
Kananga
Tshikapa
Mbuji-Mayi
Kabinda
Gandajika
Mwene-Ditu
Lubao
Kasongo
Kindu
Kalima
Kama
Kalemie
Manono
Moba
Kamina
Lake Mweru
Dilolo
Kolwezi
Likasi
Kipushi
Lubumbashi
Rapides Johnson
Lac de retenue de la Lufira
Lac Nzilo
MONTS BLEUS
MITUMBA
MARUNGU
Lake Tanganyika
Congo
Ubangi
Uele
Bomu
Aruwimi
Lindi
Lulonga
Ruki
Busira
Tshuapa
Lomami
Lualaba
Lukenie
Kasai
Sankuru
Kwa
Fimi
Kwango
Kwenge
Wamba
Lulua
Luapula
N
200 km
200 miles

POLITICS

In transition

L. House 1987/2005
U. House Not applicable/2005

President Joseph Kabila

LEGISLATIVE OR ADVISORY BODIES

National Assembly 500 seats

The last legislative poll was in 1987 when members were chosen from Mobutu's Popular Revolutionary Movement (**MPR**). A bicameral interim legislature was appointed in July/August 2003 by political parties, rebel groups, and representatives of the government, superseding the 300-member Constituent Legislative Assembly appointed by Laurent Kabila in 2000.

Senate 120 seats

Laurent-Désiré Kabila's regime has been liberalized only slightly by his son.

PROFILE

The democratic credentials of Laurent Kabila, who in 1997 overthrew Mobutu's 32-year dictatorial regime, came under question as he dissolved parliament and scrapped the constitution. A constituent assembly did not convene until 2000. Meanwhile, in 1998 Kabila's ethnic Tutsi supporters, backed by Uganda and Rwanda, had risen against him. His murder in 2001 left a vacuum exposing the true extent of his grip on power. His son Joseph, the armed forces' head, was rapidly appointed as his successor. Talks were slowed by continued fighting, but a UN peacekeeping force eventually arrived and cease-fires and troop withdrawals began. In 2003 a Final Act providing for a transitional power-sharing government was agreed and elections planned for 2005. Localized violence continued.

MAIN POLITICAL ISSUE

Identity and the struggle for resources

Conflict is closely tied to issues of land and resources, with ethnicity being used to justify inclusion or exclusion. Army and political players all seek power in the transitional government. How to reclaim and distribute fairly the DRC's rich mineral resources and potential wealth is a major challenge.

***Joseph Kabila,** who succeeded his father as president in 2001.*

***Mobutu,** the ousted dictator, held power from 1965 to 1997.*

WORLD AFFAIRS

Joined UN in 1960

CEPGL | COMESA | OIF | G24 | AU

Civil war, which has devastated the country, has irrevocably muddied the DRC's international relations. While the West grew frustrated with the slow pace of peace, neighboring countries were drawn into one of the continent's largest conflicts.

The vast potential wealth of the Congolese forests and mineral deposits saw civil war quickly spiral into regional war by 1998. Angola, Burundi, Chad, Namibia, Rwanda, Sudan, Uganda, and Zimbabwe all sent troops. Relations with Rwanda remain especially volatile.

Fighting continued despite a 1999 cease-fire signed in Lusaka. Laurent Kabila attracted intense international criticism in 2000 for suspending the accords, for taking an autocratic approach to a new transitional assembly, and for obstructing the arrival of the UN peacekeeping mission, MONUC. The accession in 2001 of Kabila's son Joseph reinvigorated the peace process; though fighting continued into 2002, with Rwanda and Uganda even reinforcing their troops, by the end of that year foreign forces had withdrawn to a significant extent. The vacuum created in the northeast by the departure of Ugandan forces was filled by intercommunal violence. French-led international forces spearheaded a limited peacekeeping mission there in 2003 amid rising concern about the worsening humanitarian situation. In 2004 the UN came under increasing criticism for failing to prevent widespread violence in the east and the capture by renegade soldiers of the town of Bukavu.

AID

Recipient

$807m (receipts) | Up 207% in 2002

The regime's importance to the West during the Cold War brought in aid on a large scale. Between 1970 and 1989, it received $8.3 billion in economic aid and large-scale military assistance.

By 1990, changing political priorities prompted the US to act on long-deferred problems of human rights abuses and misappropriation of aid. It suspended all but humanitarian aid; most other donors followed suit, and the IMF declared the government to be "noncooperative" over its foreign debt. Joseph Kabila's accession in early 2001 improved the country's international standing; aid was resumed and debt cancellations followed: $10 billion (80% of the total) was forgiven in 2003.

C

CHRONOLOGY

The modern Congo was the site of the Kongo and other powerful African kingdoms, and a focus of the slave trade. Belgium's King Leopold II claimed most of the Congo basin after 1876 as his personal possession.

- **1885** Brutal colonization of Congo Free State (CFS) as Leopold's private fief.
- **1908** Belgium takes over CFS after international outcry.
- **1960** Independence as Republic of Congo (Democratic Republic of the Congo from 1964). Katanga (Shaba) province secedes. UN intervenes.
- **1963** Katanga secession collapses.
- **1965** Marshal Joseph-Désiré Mobutu seizes power.
- **1970** Mobutu elected president; his MPR becomes sole legal party.
- **1971** Country renamed Zaire.
- **1977–1978** Two invasions by former Katanga separatists repulsed with Western help.
- **1982** Opposition parties set up Union for Democracy and Social Progress (UDPS).
- **1986–1990** Civil unrest and foreign criticism of human rights abuses.
- **1990** Belgium suspends aid after security forces kill prodemocracy demonstrators. Mobutu announces transition to multiparty rule.
- **1991** Opposition leader Etienne Tshisekedi heads short-lived "crisis government" formed by Mobutu.
- **1992–1993** Rival governments claim legitimacy.
- **1994** Combined High Council of the Republic–Transitional Parliament established.
- **1995** Regime demands international assistance to support a million Rwandan Hutu refugees.
- **1996** Major insurgency launched in east by Alliance of Democratic Forces for the Liberation of the Congo (AFDL) including Laurent Kabila's Popular Revolutionary Party (PRP), with disaffected ethnic Tutsi Banyamulunge.
- **1997** Forces led by Kabila sweep south and west. Kabila takes power. Country renamed DRC. Mobutu dies in exile.
- **1998** Banyamulunge join Kabila's opponents and launch rebellion in the east, backed by Rwanda and Uganda. Southern African states, give military backing to Kabila.
- **2000** UN approves peacekeeping mission; arrival stalled by Kabila.
- **2001** Kabila assassinated; succeeded by son Joseph. Peace talks restarted.
- **2003** April, Final Act peace accord signed. Hundreds massacred at Drodro in northeast during tribal conflict.

DEFENSE

No compulsory military service

$946m

Down 3% in 2002

The military strongly backed Mobutu's regime, but offered no real resistance when Laurent Kabila's insurgents swept the country in 1996–1997. His troops, poorly paid and undisciplined, but supported by foreign allies, then fought rebels in the 1998–2003 civil war. The UN peacekeeping force, MONUC, was in 2002 doubled in size to 10,800 personnel. Rebel forces have largely been integrated into a new national army.

CONGOLESE ARMED FORCES

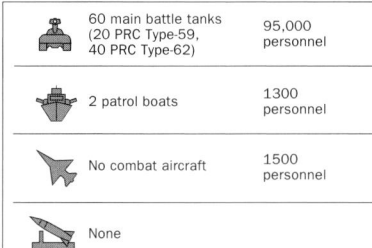

60 main battle tanks (20 PRC Type-59, 40 PRC Type-62)	95,000 personnel
2 patrol boats	1300 personnel
No combat aircraft	1500 personnel
None	

ECONOMICS

Inflation 846% p.a. (1990–2001)

$5.05bn

378 Congolese francs (421.5)

SCORE CARD

World GNP Ranking	115th
GNP per Capita	$100
Balance of Payments	–$159m
Inflation	32%
Unemployment	Very high

EXPORTS

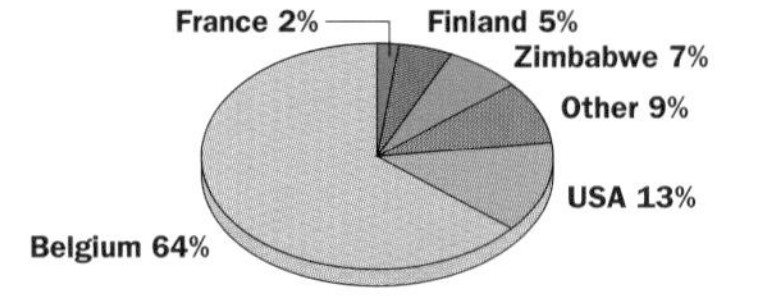
France 2%
Finland 5%
Zimbabwe 7%
Other 9%
USA 13%
Belgium 64%

IMPORTS

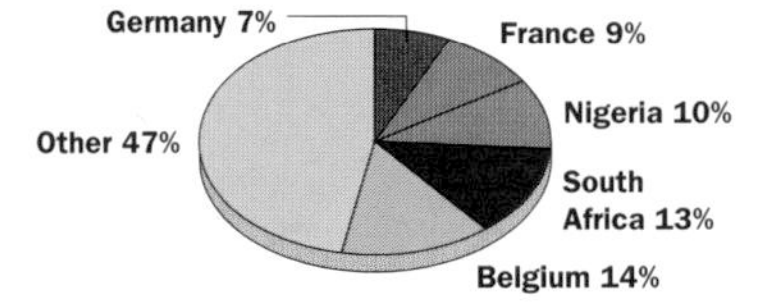
Germany 7%
France 9%
Nigeria 10%
South Africa 13%
Belgium 14%
Other 47%

ECONOMIC PERFORMANCE INDICATOR

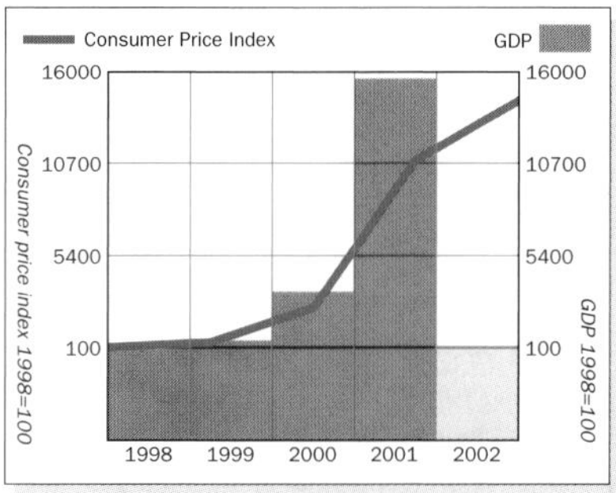
Consumer Price Index
GDP
16000
10700
5400
100
Consumer price index 1998=100
GDP 1998=100
1998
1999
2000
2001
2002

Strengths

Rich resource base. Minerals – notably copper, cobalt, diamonds – provide 85% of export earnings. 80% of debt canceled in 2003. Energy: oil; possibly Africa's largest hydropower potential. Rich soil; much unutilized arable land.

Weaknesses

Decades of mismanagement and corruption: inadequate, disintegrating infrastructure; not self-sufficient in food. Political instability. Hyperinflation. Loss of export income. Mineral resources plundered by foreign powers.

Profile

Corruption, instability, long-term mismanagement, and civil war have brought what is potentially a leading African economy to a state of collapse.

By the mid-1990s real GDP was falling by 10% or more each year. The government budget ran record deficits, and inflation spiraled virtually out of control from 1994 onward. Lack of spares and power cuts have halted most industry and closed many mines. Strikes and riots over plummeting living standards hastened the flight of foreign capital. Subsistence farming and petty trade keep most people going. Restructuring state-owned enterprises in 2001 was aimed at attracting back foreign investment.

While espousing the desire for a free-market economy, the Kabila regime has urgent need for aid and disaster relief in the east. It is seeking new partnerships to rejuvenate the neglected but considerable mining industry. However, any real recovery will require tackling outstanding debt, initiating reforms, and democratization.

CONGO, DEM. REP. : MAJOR BUSINESSES

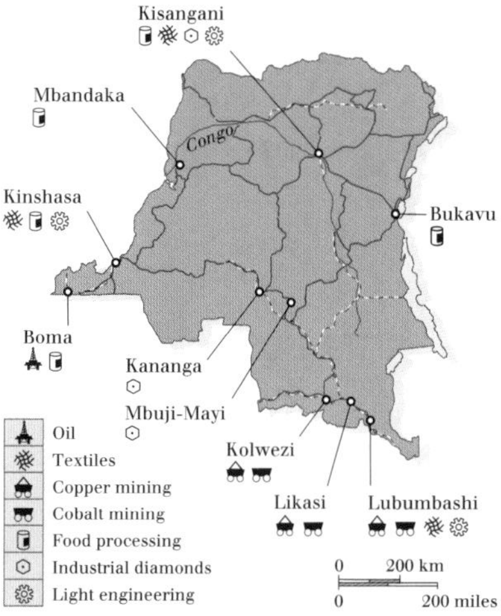
Kisangani
Mbandaka
Congo
Kinshasa
Bukavu
Boma
Kananga
Mbuji-Mayi
Kolwezi
Likasi
Lubumbashi
Oil
Textiles
Copper mining
Cobalt mining
Food processing
Industrial diamonds
Light engineering
0
200 km
0
200 miles

C

RESOURCES

Electric power 3.2m kW

208,848 tonnes

26,165 b/d (reserves 191m barrels)

4m goats, 953,100 pigs, 19.6m chickens

Copper, diamonds, oil, coltan, cobalt, zinc, uranium, manganese

ELECTRICITY GENERATION

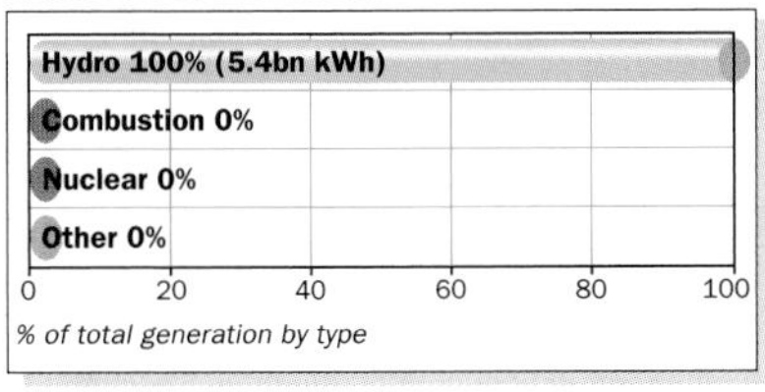

Hydro 100% (5.4bn kWh)
Combustion 0%
Nuclear 0%
Other 0%
0
20
40
60
80
100
% of total generation by type

What should be a prosperous country, with its rich resources, is instead one of the world's poorest states, exploited and mismanaged by its rulers for decades and plundered further by foreign forces during the civil war. In the 1980s, the country was the world's largest cobalt exporter and second-largest industrial diamond exporter. Since 1990, copper and cobalt output have collapsed and diamond smuggling is booming. There are oil reserves and hydroelectric installations with sufficient potential capacity to export power, but instead lack of maintenance has shut down many turbines and most urban areas face power cuts. Despite rich soils and the fact that 60% of people are involved in farming, the DRC is not even self-sufficient in food.

CONGO, DEM. REP. : LAND USE

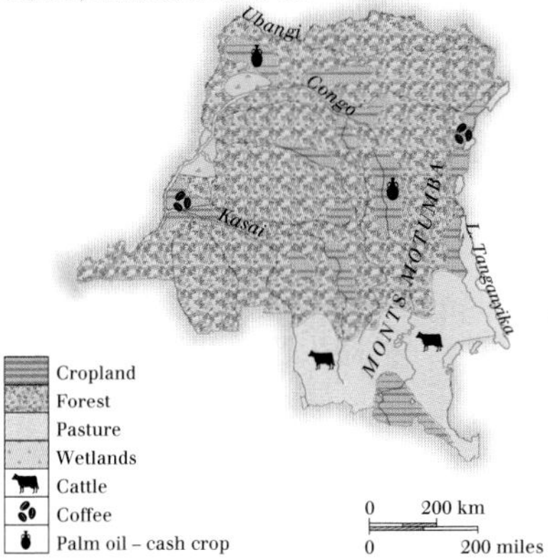

Ubangi
Congo
Kasai
MONTS MITUMBA
L. Tanganyika
Cropland
Forest
Pasture
Wetlands
Cattle
Coffee
Palm oil – cash crop
0 200 km
0 200 miles

ENVIRONMENT

Sustainability rank: 109th

5% (2% partially protected)

0.1 tonnes per capita

ENVIRONMENTAL TREATIES

Yes	Yes	Yes
Yes	Yes	No

Rainforests cover over 60% of the country, representing almost 6% of the world's and 50% of Africa's remaining woodlands. They are home to several endangered species. The poor transportation network has so far prevented large-scale commercial exploitation of timber, but clearance for fuelwood is a problem. The collapse of many urban refuse and sewage disposal systems has led to major health and pollution problems. Environmental damage caused by the civil war is estimated at $320 million.

MEDIA

TV ownership low

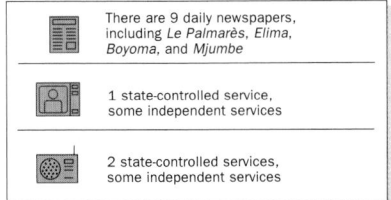

Daily newspaper circulation 3 per 1000 people

PUBLISHING AND BROADCAST MEDIA

There are 9 daily newspapers, including *Le Palmarès*, *Elima*, *Boyoma*, and *Mjumbe*

1 state-controlled service, some independent services

2 state-controlled services, some independent services

Fighting makes services less accessible outside the capital. Unlike the broadcast media, press outlets are privately owned, and many newspapers openly criticize the authorities, though self-preservation requires a degree of self-censorship. A ban on foreign radio broadcasts was lifted in 2001. MONUC operates the only countrywide radio station, Radio Okapi.

CRIME

Death penalty in use

The DRC does not publish prison figures

Violence and crime are rising rapidly

CRIME RATES

All types of crime are on the increase in the DRC

Civil war and remaining insecurity exacerbate long-standing problems of corruption and human rights abuses. Extortion, robbery, rape, and murder are widespread and on the increase. Ethnic violence, suppressed after 1965, resurfaced in the south and between the Hema and Lendu tribes in the northeast, leading to some gruesome atrocities. Crimes committed during combat in the civil war were pardoned in 2003. Prison conditions are atrocious; deaths are frequent from disease and malnutrition.

EDUCATION

School leaving age: 14

63%

60,341 students

THE EDUCATION SYSTEM

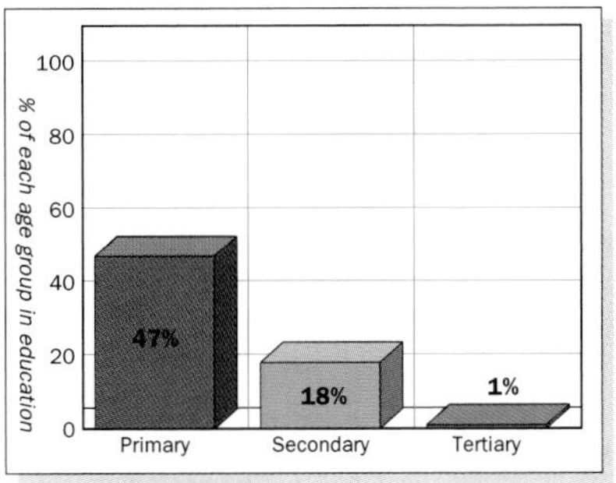

100
80
60
40
20
0
% of each age group in education
47%
18%
1%
Primary
Secondary
Tertiary

In 1997, just over 37% of secondary-age children were attending classes, but this figure dropped sharply during the civil war and has yet to recover. State provision, as with health care, is patchy and has faced sharp budget cuts since 1980. Most private schools are run by the Roman Catholic Church.

HEALTH

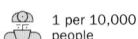

No welfare state health benefits

1 per 10,000 people

Malaria, respiratory and diarrheal diseases

State services have now virtually collapsed. Disease and death rates are rising, especially in rural areas. A new health insurance plan was announced in 2001, designed to enable greater access to health care. As of December 2003, over one million people were estimated to be HIV/AIDS infected.

SPENDING

GDP/cap. decrease

CONSUMPTION AND SPENDING

4 per 1000 population

Under 0.5 per 1000 population

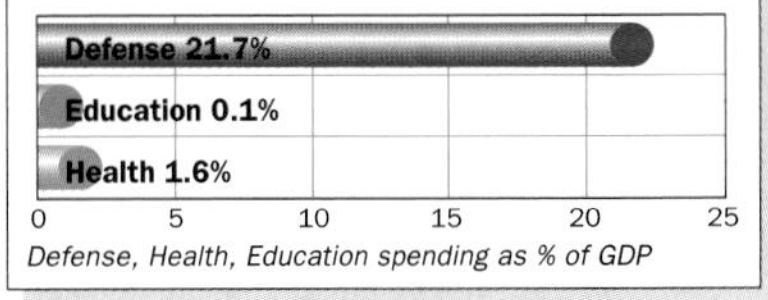

Defense 21.7%
Education 0.1%
Health 1.6%
0
5
10
15
20
25
Defense, Health, Education spending as % of GDP

Before his death in exile in 1997, ex-dictator Mobutu was one of the world's richest men, worth an estimated $4 billion. Most of his former subjects live in poverty exacerbated by civil war.

WORLD RANKING

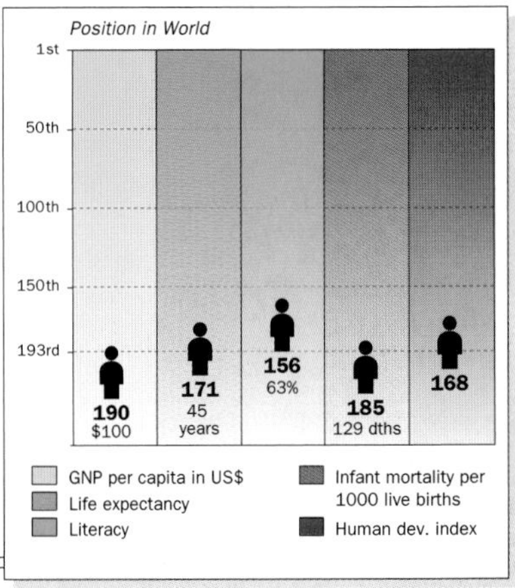

Position in World
1st
50th
100th
150th
193rd
190
$100
171
45
years
156
63%
185
129 dths
168
GNP per capita in US$
Life expectancy
Literacy
Infant mortality per 1000 live births
Human dev. index

COSTA RICA

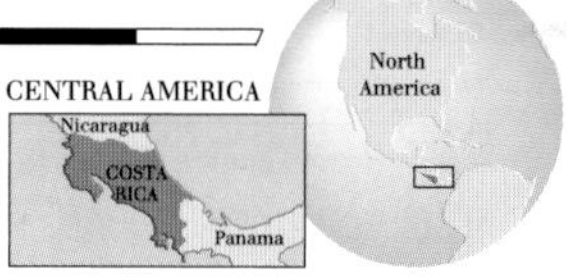
CENTRAL AMERICA
Nicaragua
COSTA RICA
Panama
North America

OFFICIAL NAME: Republic of Costa Rica **CAPITAL:** San José
POPULATION: 4.2 million **CURRENCY:** Costa Rican colón **OFFICIAL LANGUAGE:** Spanish

C

1838 | 1838 | Sept 15 | CR | -6 | +506 | .cr

SPANNING THE CENTRAL AMERICAN isthmus and wedged between Nicaragua and Panama, Costa Rica was under Spanish rule until 1821 and gained full independence in 1838. From 1948 until the end of the 1980s, it had the most developed welfare state in Central America. Costa Rica is nominally a multiparty democracy, but two parties dominate. Its army was abolished in 1948; the 1949 constitution then forbade national armies.

CLIMATE

Tropical wet & dry

WEATHER CHART FOR SAN JOSÉ

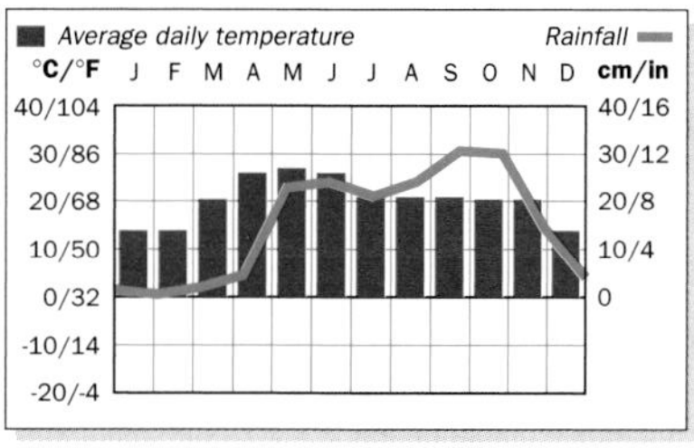
Average daily temperature
Rainfall
°C/°F J F M A M J J A S O N D cm/in
40/104 40/16
30/86 30/12
20/68 20/8
10/50 10/4
0/32 0
-10/14
-20/-4

The Caribbean coast has heavy rainfall, while the Pacific coast is much drier. The central uplands are temperate.

TRANSPORTATION

Drive on right

Juan Santamaría, San José
988,000 passengers

13 ships
4000 grt

THE TRANSPORTATION NETWORK

7894 km (4905 miles)	Pan-American Highway, 663 km (412 miles)
848 km (527 miles)	730 km (454 miles)

San José is the hub of a well-used bus network. Rail services have not recovered from an earthquake in 1991.

TOURISM

Visitors : Population 1:3.8

1.11m visitors

Down 2% in 2002

MAIN TOURIST ARRIVALS

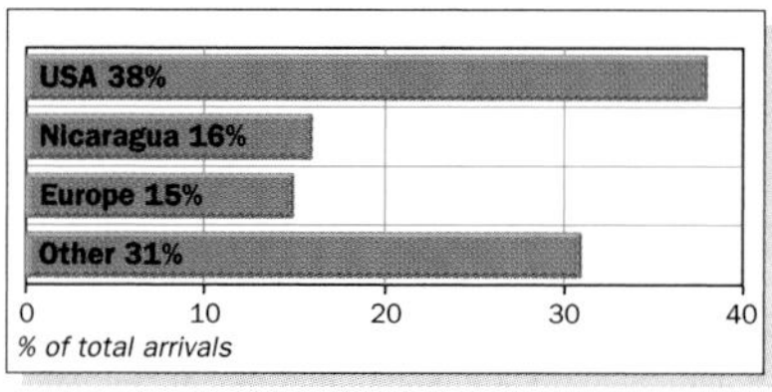
USA 38%
Nicaragua 16%
Europe 15%
Other 31%
0 10 20 30 40
% of total arrivals

Tourism has brought in over $1 billion each year since 1999, and has expanded with the help of both domestic and foreign investment. The country's tropical scenery and wildlife are promoted heavily for "eco-tourists."

PEOPLE

Pop. density medium

Spanish, English Creole, Bribri, Cabecar

82/km² (213/mi²)

THE URBAN/RURAL POPULATION SPLIT

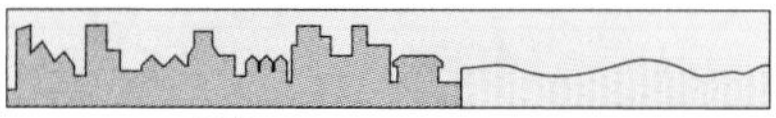
60%
40%

RELIGIOUS PERSUASION

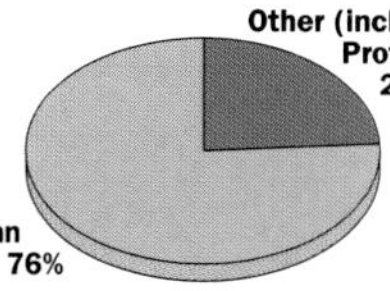
Other (including Protestant) 24%
Roman Catholic 76%

Most of the population is *mestizo*, of partly Spanish origin. One-third of people in the Limón area are black and often English-speaking. There are only about 5000 indigenous Amerindians.

POLITICS

Multiparty elections

2002/2006

President Abel Pacheco de la Espriella

AT THE LAST ELECTION

Legislative Assembly 57 seats

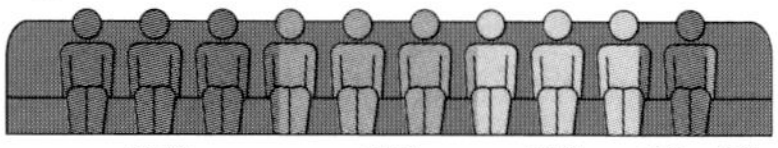
33% PUSC
30% PLN
25% PRC
10% ML
2% PAC

PUSC = Social Christian Unity Party **PLN** = National Liberation Party **PRC** = Costa Rican Renewal Party **ML** = Liberty Movement **PAC** = Citizens' Action Party

Politics has long been dominated by the PUSC and PLN, both of which have close ties to major banana- and coffee-growing families. Historically the US has exercised a very powerful influence on politics.

The PLN in 1994 promised reforms to its previous austerity policies, but soon came under pressure from international financial organizations to reduce the budget deficit. Harsh structural adjustment measures proved highly unpopular.

In 1998 the PUSC regained power. President Miguel Angel Rodríguez launched a three-year plan to reduce inflation and poverty, create thousands of jobs, and stimulate foreign investment in state companies. His chosen successor, Abel Pacheco, needed an unprecedented second round to clinch the presidency in 2002, when voter turnout hit an all-time low.

WORLD AFFAIRS

Joined UN in 1945

ACS | Geplac | RG | OAS | San José

Trade ties with the US and protection of prices for coffee and bananas are priorities. Trade ties have also been agreed with Canada and Chile. Tensions with Nicaragua over their mutual border were resolved in 2000, but illegal immigrants remain an issue.

NICARAGUA
CARIBBEAN SEA
PACIFIC OCEAN
PANAMA
La Cruz
Los Chiles
Upala
San Rafael
Liberia
Bagaces
Tilarán
Filadelfia
Cañas
Santa Cruz
Quesada
Puerto Viejo
Nicoya
Juntas
Guápiles
Guácimo
Hojancha
Zarcero
Siquirres
Carmona
San Ramón
Heredia
Matina
Puntarenas
Alajuela
SAN JOSÉ
Limón
Paquera
Orotina
Cartago
Turrialba
Paraíso
Península de Nicoya
San Marcos
Jacó
Santa María
Parrita
Bribrí
Cerro Chirripó Grande 3819m
Quepos
San Isidro
CORDILLERA DE TALAMANCA
Buenos Aires
Cortés
Palmar Norte
San Vito
Golfito
Neily
Península de Osa
Isla del Coco
0 5 km
0 5 miles
N

COSTA RICA

Total Area : 51 100 sq. km (19 730 sq. miles)

POPULATION		LAND HEIGHT
over 100 000	◎	3000m/9843ft
over 50 000	○	2000m/6562ft
over 10 000	●	1000m/3281ft
under 10 000	•	500m/1640ft
		200m/656ft
		Sea level

0 50 km
0 50 miles

Pineapple plantation in the south, crossed by the Pan-American Highway which runs for 663 km (412 miles) through Costa Rica.

AID

Recipient

$5m (receipts) Up 150% in 2002

During the 1980s Costa Rica was a large recipient of US aid designed to inoculate it against left-wing insurgencies such as those in El Salvador, Guatemala, and neighboring Nicaragua. Peace in the region has led to a sharp decline in such aid, especially given the country's relatively high per capita income. World Bank aid has helped to modernize Juan Santamaría international airport.

DEFENSE

No compulsory military service

$89m Up 17% in 2002

Costa Rica emerged from the 1948 civil war as a neutral, demilitarized modern state. A 4400-strong Civil Guard is complemented by a largely military-trained police force. Spending on security as a percentage of GDP has long been the lowest in the isthmus. Lack of a common command structure hinders the influence of the security forces but also renders them less open to public control. Right-wing paramilitary groups are known to exist.

ECONOMICS

Inflation 16% p.a. (1990–2001)

$16.1bn 437.7 Costa Rican colones (398.7)

SCORE CARD

❑ WORLD GNP RANKING	75th
❑ GNP PER CAPITA	$4070
❑ BALANCE OF PAYMENTS	–$946m
❑ INFLATION	9.2%
❑ UNEMPLOYMENT	6%

EXPORTS

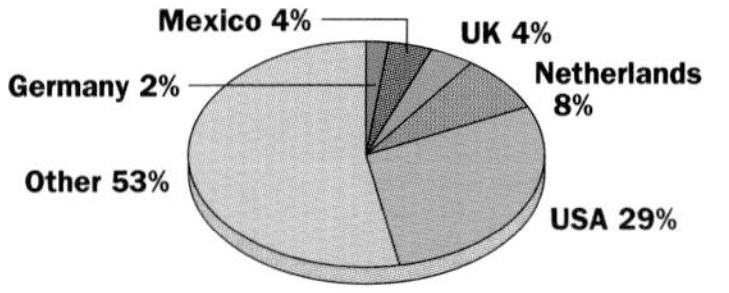
Mexico 4%
UK 4%
Germany 2%
Netherlands 8%
Other 53%
USA 29%

IMPORTS

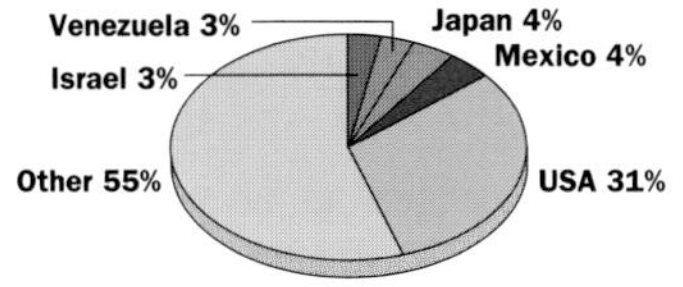
Venezuela 3%
Japan 4%
Mexico 4%
Israel 3%
Other 55%
USA 31%

STRENGTHS

Major coffee, beef, and banana exports. Expanding tourism also fueling construction. Strong inward investment. Favorable WTO ruling on access to EU market for bananas.

WEAKNESSES

Coffee, beef, and bananas all vulnerable to falling prices. History of high inflation. Dependence on imported oil. Large domestic debt. Competitiveness hindered by insufficient investment in infrastructure. State monopolies have deterred investment in energy, telecommunications, and insurance sectors. Inefficient management.

RESOURCES

Electric power 1.7m kW

45,253 tonnes

Not an oil producer; refines 360 b/d

1.15m cattle, 500,000 pigs, 18.5m chickens

Bauxite, gold, silver, manganese, mercury

Costa Rica has large bauxite deposits in the south – aluminum smelting is an important industry. Small quantities of gold, silver, manganese, and mercury are also mined. Self-sufficiency in energy is being pursued through the development of hydroelectric power, which now provides almost all energy.

MEDIA

TV ownership medium

Daily newspaper circulation 91 per 1000 people

PUBLISHING AND BROADCAST MEDIA

There are 8 daily newspapers, including *La Nación, La República, La Prensa Libre,* and *Diario Extra*

18 stations: 1 state-owned, 17 independent

Around 35 state-owned and independent stations

The media are free but dominated by conservative opinion. Entry into journalism is strictly licensed.

ENVIRONMENT

Sustainability rank: 9th

23% (12% partially protected)

1.4 tonnes per capita

Despite good environmental regulation, reckless economic development has contributed to extensive deforestation. Forests now cover less than a third of the country. Pesticide abuse by agribusiness has poisoned rivers and threatened species. Urban sprawl has degraded the fertile central valley.

CRIME

No death penalty

8526 prisoners

Up 3% in 1999

Costa Rica is the least violent Central American country. Attacks on and kidnappings of tourists are rare but have dented its image as a safe haven. Narcotics smuggling and money laundering are increasing problems, and Costa Rica cooperates closely with US law enforcement agencies in these areas.

CHRONOLOGY

Costa Rica, ruled since the 16th century by Spain, became an independent state in 1838.

- ❑ 1948 Disputed elections lead to civil war; ended by Social Democratic Party (later the PLN) forming provisional government under José Ferrer. Army abolished.
- ❑ 1949 New constitution promulgated.
- ❑ 1987 Central American Peace Plan initiated by President Arias.
- ❑ 1998 PUSC returns to power.

C

EDUCATION

School leaving age: 15

96% 61,654 students

Costa Rica has the highest literacy rate in the isthmus, and is home to the University of Central America.

HEALTH

Welfare state health benefits

1 per 1111 people

Cancers, respiratory diseases, accidents

The public health system is one of the most developed in Latin America. Some private clinics offer cosmetic surgery vacations.

SPENDING

GDP/cap. increase

CONSUMPTION AND SPENDING

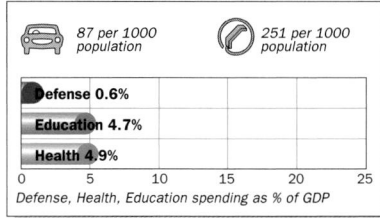

87 per 1000 population *251 per 1000 population*

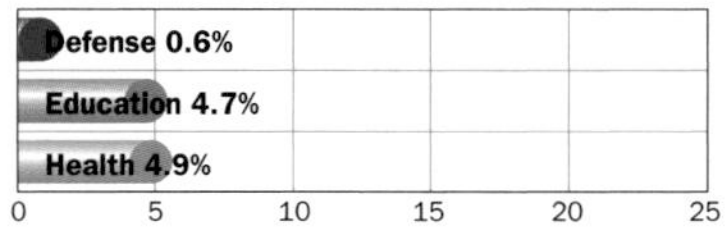
Defense 0.6%
Education 4.7%
Health 4.9%
0
5
10
15
20
25

Defense, Health, Education spending as % of GDP

Plantation-owners are the wealthiest group; over 20% of the population live in poverty. Nonetheless, Costa Rica has the region's highest standard of living.

WORLD RANKING

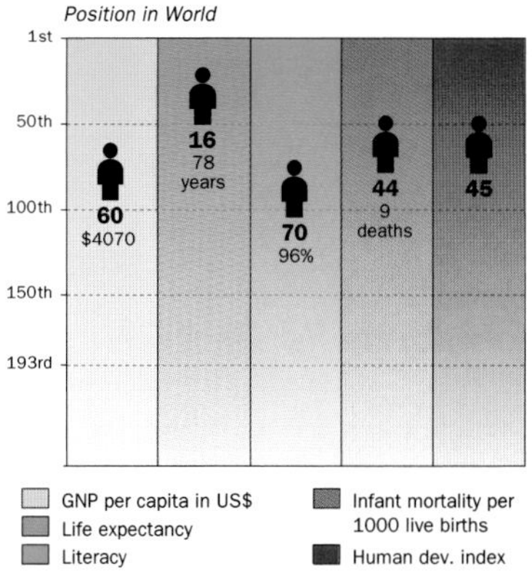
Position in World
1st
50th
100th
150th
193rd
60
$4070
16
78 years
70
96%
44
9 deaths
45
GNP per capita in US$
Life expectancy
Literacy
Infant mortality per 1000 live births
Human dev. index

EUROPE
Europe
Slovenia
Hungary
CROATIA
Bosnia & Herzegovina
Serb. & Mon.

CROATIA

OFFICIAL NAME: Republic of Croatia **CAPITAL:** Zagreb
POPULATION: 4.4 million **CURRENCY:** Kuna **OFFICIAL LANGUAGE:** Croatian

1991 | 1991 | May 30 | HR | +1 | +385 | .hr

THOUGH IT WAS CONTROLLED by Hungary from medieval times and was a part of the Yugoslav state for much of the 20th century, Croatia still has a strong national identity. It includes the historic provinces of Slavonia, Istria, and Dalmatia (Dinara). Actively involved in the conflicts which broke up Yugoslavia in the early 1990s, Croatia only regained full control of Serb-occupied Eastern Slavonia, around Vukovar, in 1998.

Dubrovnik, Dalmatia. This historic city on the Adriatic coast was shelled and besieged by the Yugoslav federal army in 1991.

CLIMATE

Mediterranean/ continental

WEATHER CHART FOR ZAGREB

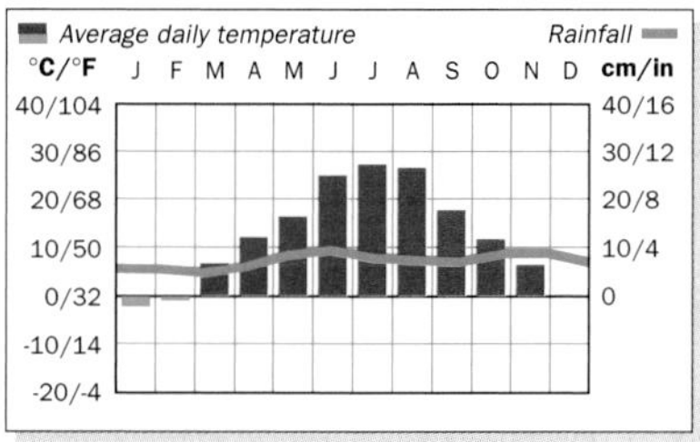
Average daily temperature
Rainfall
°C/°F
J F M A M J J A S O N D
cm/in
40/104
30/86
20/68
10/50
0/32
-10/14
-20/-4
40/16
30/12
20/8
10/4
0

Northern Croatia has a temperate continental climate. Its Adriatic coast has a Mediterranean climate.

TRANSPORTATION

Drive on right

Pleso International, Zagreb
1.31m passengers

256 ships
834,700 grt

THE TRANSPORTATION NETWORK

23,808 km (14,794 miles)

410 km (255 miles)

2726 km (1694 miles)

785 km (488 miles)

Zagreb has recovered from the effects of war, and of sanctions against Yugoslavia, and is once again an important regional road and rail hub. The Adriatic Highway affords fantastic views along the Dalmatian coast.

TOURISM

Visitors : Population 1.7:1

7.4m visitors

Up 7% in 2003

MAIN TOURIST ARRIVALS

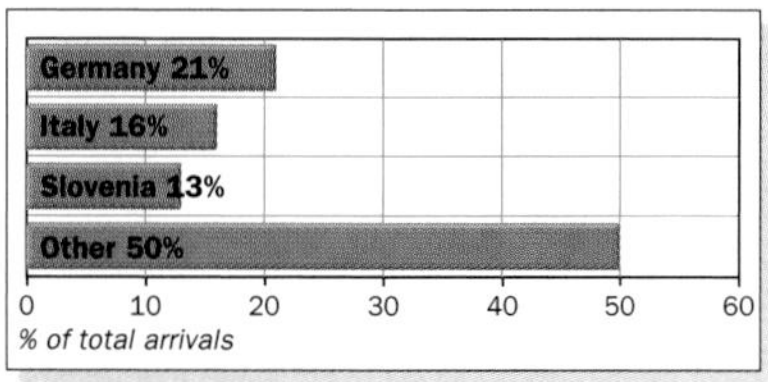
Germany 21%
Italy 16%
Slovenia 13%
Other 50%
0 10 20 30 40 50 60
% of total arrivals

The Adriatic coast is regaining its popularity as a tourist destination. There are also many historical sites.

PEOPLE

Pop. density medium

Croatian

78/km² (202/mi²)

THE URBAN/RURAL POPULATION SPLIT

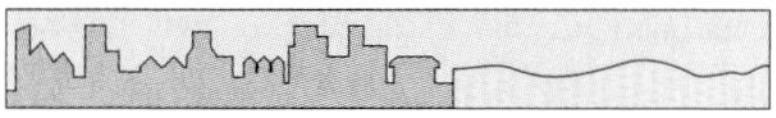
59%
41%

RELIGIOUS PERSUASION

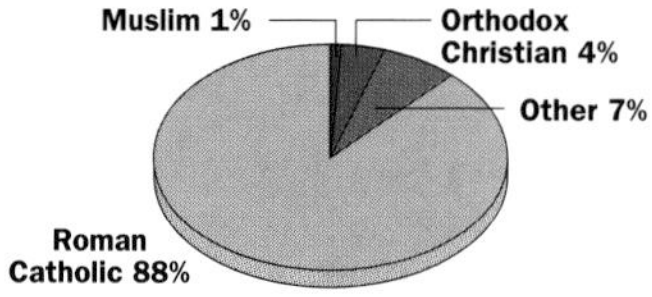
Muslim 1%
Orthodox Christian 4%
Other 7%
Roman Catholic 88%

War greatly altered the ethnic makeup. The Orthodox Christian Serb minority once constituted 12% of the population and had been based along the borders with Bosnia and Serbia. Alienated by Croatian nationalism, they established the Republic of Serbian Krajina in 1991. It was overrun by the Croatian army in 1995 and hundreds of thousands of Serbs were forced to flee east. Those who remained now make up just 4% of the population – not enough to warrant "minority rights" under the constitution. There was an influx of Croats and Bosniaks from Bosnia in the 1990s.

POLITICS

Multiparty elections

2003/2007

President Stipe Mesic

AT THE LAST ELECTION

House of Representatives 152 seats

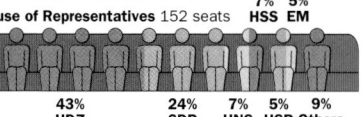

7% HSS
5% EM
43% HDZ
24% SDP
7% HNS
5% HSP
9% Others

HDZ = Croatian Democratic Union **SDP** = Social Democratic Party **HNS** = Croatian People's Party
HSS = Croatian Peasant Party
HSP = Croatian Party of Rights **EM** = Ethnic minorities

Four seats are reserved for representatives of Croats living abroad (all are currently held by the HDZ). Eight seats are reserved for ethnic minorities (one is held by the HSS)

The nationalist HDZ, which had been in power from independence, was left rudderless in 1999 by the death of President Franjo Tudjman. Mired in corruption and spying scandals, the party was defeated in elections in 2000 by a center-left coalition headed by the SDP, whose candidate Stipe Mesic was elected president. The popularity of the SDP government, however, proved short-lived and it was defeated by a resurgent HDZ under Ivo Sanader in elections in 2003. Toning down its nationalist rhetoric, the HDZ pledged to continue Croatia's pro-Western course.

Croatia had been internationally isolated for Tudjman's refusal to bring alleged war criminals to justice. The SDP government appeased the international community by making some arrests, but balked at extraditing the country's most popular "war heroes."

WORLD AFFAIRS

Joined UN in 1992

CE | WTO | PfP | CEI | OSCE

The end of the Tudjman era cleared the way for a rapprochement with the international community and Croatia's neighbors, but it took four years for the issue of the extradition of high-profile suspected war criminals to be resolved. A dispute with Montenegro over the Prevlaka Peninsula ended in 2002. Croatia applied in 2003 to join the EU.

AID

Recipient

$166m (receipts)

Up 47% in 2002

Aid has increased dramatically in recent years; the US is the largest donor.

DEFENSE

Compulsory military service

$517m

Up 2% in 2002

Under 2002 proposals the army will be reduced by half by 2005. Croatia sent troops to Iraq, and is well placed to join NATO in the next wave of expansion.

ECONOMICS

Inflation 72% p.a. (1990–2001)

$20.3bn

6.036 kuna (6.531)

SCORE CARD

- ❑ WORLD GNP RANKING..........................64th
- ❑ GNP PER CAPITA $4540
- ❑ BALANCE OF PAYMENTS ....–$1.55bn
- ❑ INFLATION 2.8%
- ❑ UNEMPLOYMENT..................................15%

EXPORTS

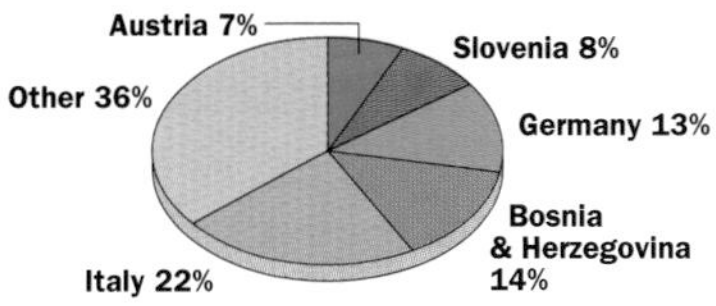

Austria 7%
Slovenia 8%
Other 36%
Germany 13%
Bosnia & Herzegovina 14%
Italy 22%

IMPORTS

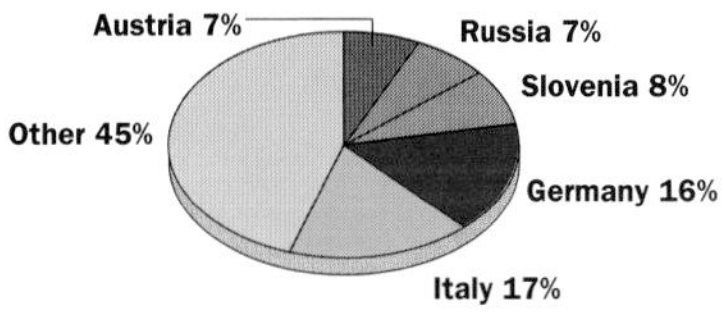

Austria 7%
Russia 7%
Slovenia 8%
Other 45%
Germany 16%
Italy 17%

STRENGTHS
Steady growth. Progress in reducing government overspending, backed by IMF. Recovery in tourism. Inflation brought under control.

WEAKNESSES
Slow privatization, until 2001. Lack of inward investment. War damage estimated at $50 billion. Persistent high unemployment.

RESOURCES

Electric power 3.8m kW

28,256 tonnes

22,316 b/d (reserves 49m barrels)

1.35m pigs, 710,000 turkeys, 11.8m chickens

Coal, bauxite, iron, oil, china clay, natural gas

Croatia generates just over half of its electricity from HEP and the remainder from combustion. It has very few minerals, though it does have oil and gas fields. The rich fishing grounds of the Adriatic are a major resource.

ENVIRONMENT

Sustainability rank: 12th

8% (5% partially protected)

4.4 tonnes per capita

Croatia was the first Yugoslav republic to create reserves in order to protect endangered and unique wetlands.

MEDIA

TV ownership medium

Daily newspaper circulation 114 per 1000 people

PUBLISHING AND BROADCAST MEDIA

There are 12 daily newspapers, published locally, including *Vecernji List* in Zagreb and *Slobodna Dalmacija* in Split

2 services: 1 state-controlled, 1 independent

4 stations: 1 state-controlled, 3 independent

Media freedoms have gradually been improving since 2000. The independent Nova TV channel was licensed in 1999.

CRIME

No death penalty

2584 prisoners

Up 44% in 2000–2002

War crimes trials are not always unbiased; ethnic Serbs can be at a disadvantage. Narcotics trafficking and people smuggling are growing problems.

CHRONOLOGY

Between 1945 and 1991 Croatia was a republic of the Yugoslav federation.

- ❑ **1991** Independence. Rebel Croatian Serb republic of Krajina proclaimed.
- ❑ **1992** Franjo Tudjman president. Involvement in Bosnian civil war.
- ❑ **1995** Krajina and Western Slavonia recaptured. Dayton peace accord.
- ❑ **1998** Eastern Slavonia reintegrated.
- ❑ **1999** Death of Tudjman.
- ❑ **2000** SDP beats HDZ in elections.
- ❑ **2003** HDZ regains primacy in polls.

C

EDUCATION

School leaving age: 15

98%

116,434 students

The education system is well developed. There are four universities, at Zagreb, Rijeka, Osijek, and Split.

HEALTH

Welfare state health benefits

1 per 417 people

Cancers, heart and cerebrovascular diseases

Most Croats are covered by a health insurance scheme. However, an extra strain on already scarce funds was created by the demands of refugees and disabled war veterans.

SPENDING

GDP/cap. increase

CONSUMPTION AND SPENDING

265 per 1000 population

417 per 1000 population

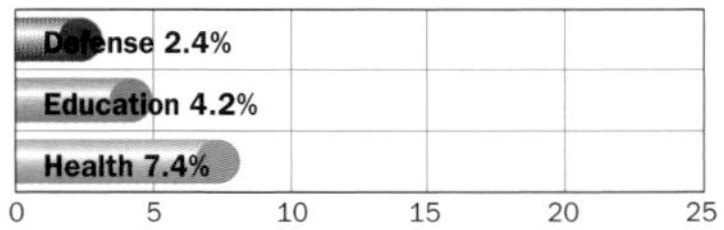

Defense 2.4%
Education 4.2%
Health 7.4%
0
5
10
15
20
25

Defense, Health, Education spending as % of GDP

Wage rises in the mid-1990s and again in 1999 led to spending booms. Consumers' high expectations were reined in by tighter wage policies.

WORLD RANKING

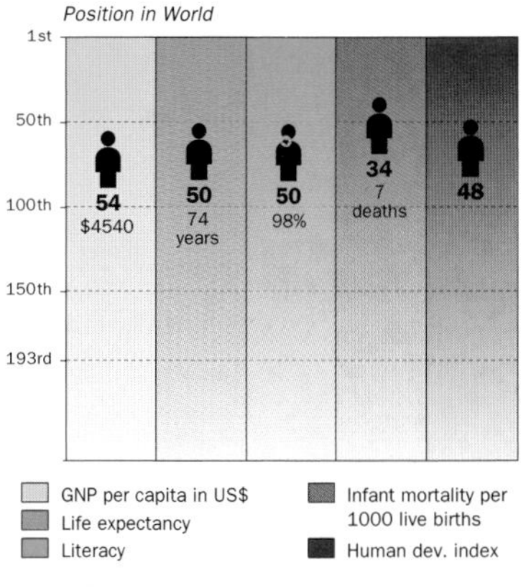

Position in World
1st
50th
100th
150th
193rd
54
$4540
50
74
years
50
98%
34
7
deaths
48
GNP per capita in US$
Life expectancy
Literacy
Infant mortality per 1000 live births
Human dev. index

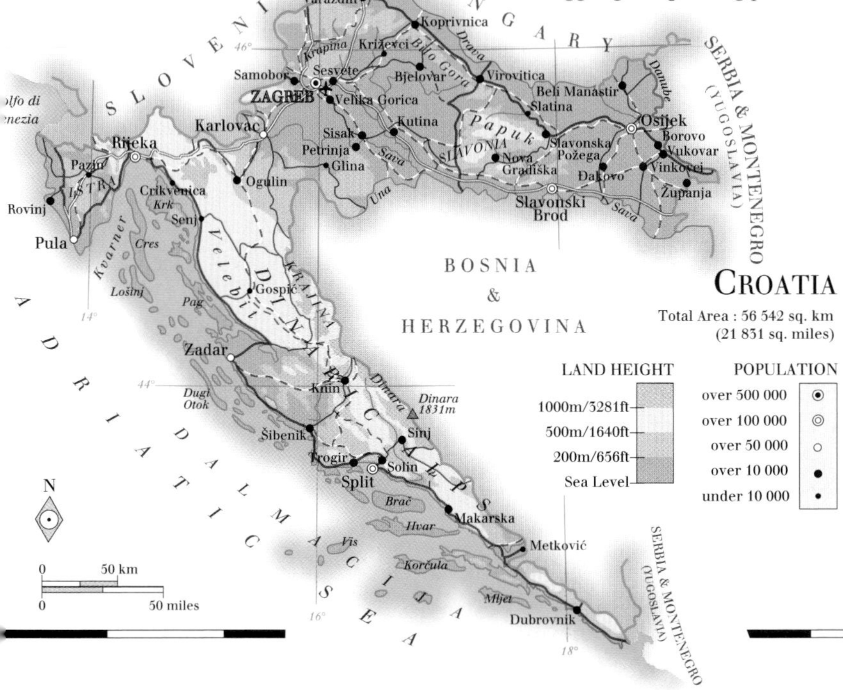

HUNGARY
SLOVENIA
SERBIA & MONTENEGRO (YUGOSLAVIA)
BOSNIA & HERZEGOVINA
ADRIATIC SEA
ČAkovec
Varaždin
Koprivnica
Krapina
Križevci
Bjelovar
Virovitica
Samobor
Sesvete
ZAGREB
Velika Gorica
Beli Manastir
Slatina
Osijek
Borovo
Vukovar
Vinkovci
Županja
Karlovac
Sisak
Petrinja
Glina
Kutina
Nova Gradiška
Slavonska Požega
Đakovo
Slavonski Brod
Rijeka
Pazin
ISTRA
Rovinj
Pula
Crikvenica
Krk
Senj
Cres
Lošinj
Ogulin
Gospić
Pag
Zadar
Dugi Otok
Knin
Dinara 1831m
Šibenik
Sinj
Trogir
Solin
Split
Brač
Hvar
Vis
Korčula
Makarska
Metković
Mljet
Dubrovnik
Drava
Sava
Una
Danube
Papuk
Velebit
Kvarner
DINARIC ALPS
DALMACIJA
KRAJINA
CROATIA
Total Area : 56 542 sq. km (21 831 sq. miles)
LAND HEIGHT
1000m/3281ft
500m/1640ft
200m/656ft
Sea Level
POPULATION
over 500 000
over 100 000
over 50 000
over 10 000
under 10 000
N
50 km
50 miles

CUBA

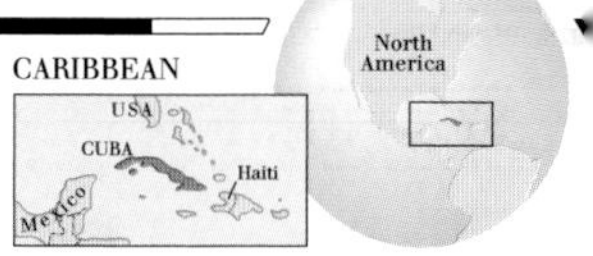
CARIBBEAN
USA
CUBA
Mexico
Haiti
North America

OFFICIAL NAME: Republic of Cuba **CAPITAL:** Havana
POPULATION: 11.3 million **CURRENCY:** Cuban peso **OFFICIAL LANGUAGE:** Spanish

C

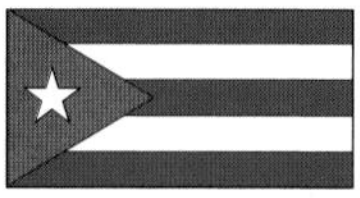

1902 | 1902 | Jan 1 | C | -5 | +53 | .cu

Valle de Viñales, Pinar del Río province. Cuba's undulating countryside is ideal for growing the main export crop, sugar.

THE CARIBBEAN'S LARGEST ISLAND, Cuba has widely cultivated lowlands which fall between three mountainous areas. The fertile soil of the lowlands supports the sugarcane, rice, and coffee plantations. Sugar, the country's major export, suffers from underinvestment, low yields, and fluctuating world prices. A former Spanish colony, Cuba in 1959 became the only communist state in the Americas. In 1962, the deployment of Soviet nuclear missiles on the island shocked the US and brought the two superpowers close to war. Veteran president Fidel Castro is still very much in control, but, since the collapse of the USSR, the US sees Cuba as less of a threat.

CLIMATE

Tropical oceanic

WEATHER CHART FOR HAVANA

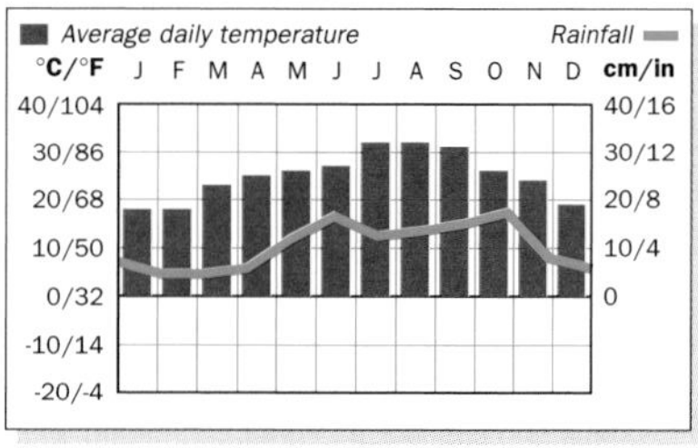
Average daily temperature
Rainfall
°C/°F J F M A M J J A S O N D cm/in
40/104
30/86
20/68
10/50
0/32
-10/14
-20/-4
40/16
30/12
20/8
10/4
0

Cuba's subtropical climate is hot all year round and very hot in the summer. Rainfall is heaviest in the mountains, which receive up to 250 cm (98 in) a year. Generally, the north is wetter than the south; the Guantánamo area receives only 20 cm (8 in) of rainfall annually. In winter, the west is affected sometimes by cold air from the US, but only for a day or two at a time.

TRANSPORTATION

Drive on right

José Martí, Havana
2.4m passengers

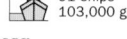

91 ships
103,000 grt

THE TRANSPORTATION NETWORK

29,820 km (18,529 miles)

638 km (396 miles)

4382 km (2723 miles)

240 km (149 miles)

Public transportation in Cuba has been extremely cheap, though fuel shortages have made it increasingly erratic and unreliable. Cubans rely mostly on traditional black bicycles, imported by the thousand from China. Havana owes much of its charm to the number of 50-year-old Chevrolets and Oldsmobiles still being driven around. This is another result of sanctions, but keeps the many inventive local spare-parts workshops in business.

TOURISM

Visitors : Population 1:6

1.87m visitors

Up 13% in 2003

MAIN TOURIST ARRIVALS

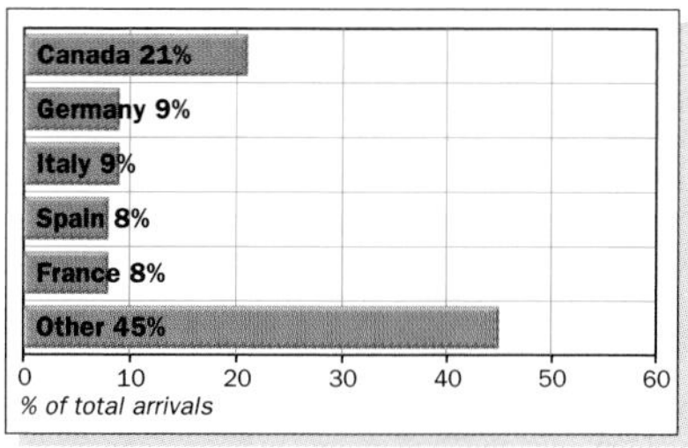
Canada 21%
Germany 9%
Italy 9%
Spain 8%
France 8%
Other 45%
0 10 20 30 40 50 60
% of total arrivals

Tourism began to develop after 1977 (when the US briefly relaxed some travel restrictions), and Cuba is now among the Caribbean's most popular tourist destinations. Tourism has supplanted sugar as the most important motor of the economy and a key generator of foreign exchange, but official estimates that the annual number of arrivals will exceed five million by 2010 appear optimistic. The government seeks to promote family tourism by cracking down on prostitutes who target Havana's main hotels.

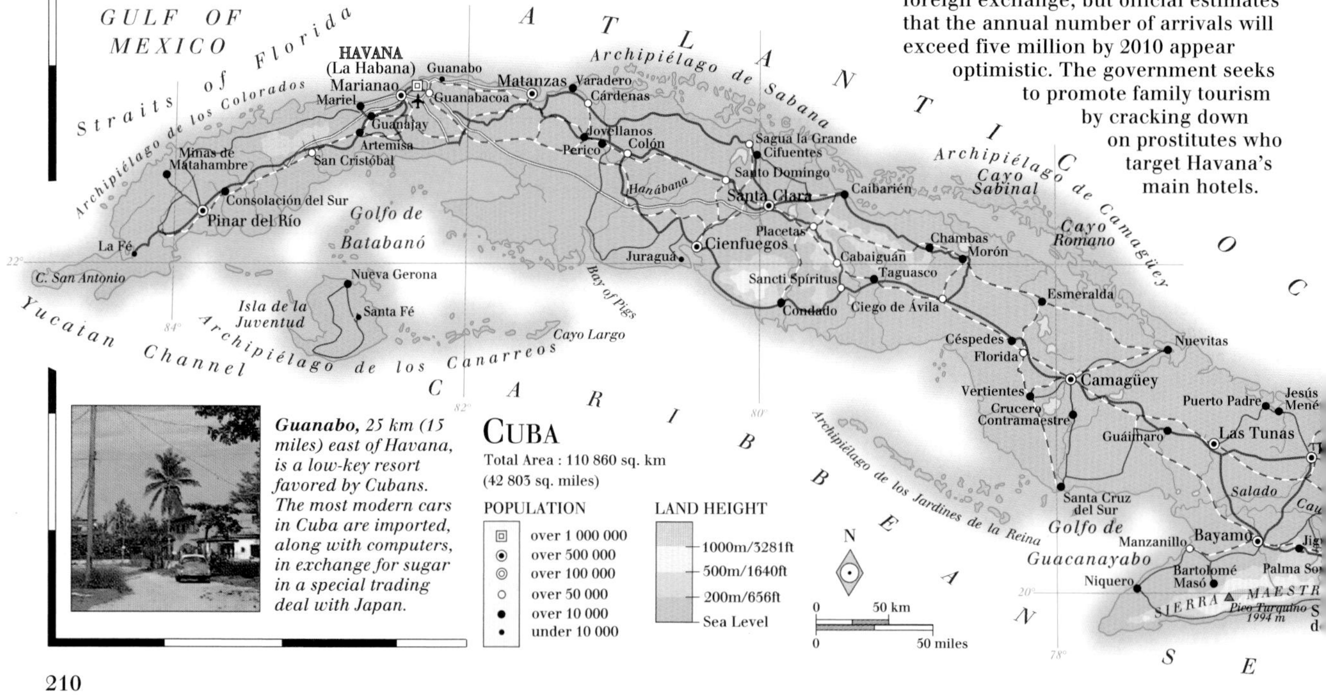
GULF OF MEXICO
Straits of Florida
Archipiélago de los Colorados
HAVANA (La Habana)
Guanabo
Marianao
Mariel
Guanabacoa
Guanajay
Artemisa
Matanzas
Varadero
Cárdenas
Jovellanos
Perico
Colón
Minas de Matahambre
San Cristóbal
Consolación del Sur
Pinar del Río
La Fé
C. San Antonio
Golfo de Batabanó
Nueva Gerona
Isla de la Juventud
Santa Fé
Yucatan Channel
Archipiélago de los Canarreos
Cayo Largo
Bay of Pigs
Jaragua
Cienfuegos
Hanábana
Santa Clara
Sagua la Grande
Cifuentes
Santo Domingo
Placetas
Caibarién
Archipiélago de Sabana
Archipiélago de Camagüey
Cayo Sabinal
Cayo Romano
Chambas
Morón
Cabaiguán
Taguasco
Sancti Spíritus
Condado
Ciego de Ávila
Esmeralda
Céspedes
Florida
Nuevitas
Camagüey
Vertientes
Cruce de Contramaestre
Puerto Padre
Jesús Mené
Guáimaro
Las Tunas
Salado
Santa Cruz del Sur
Archipiélago de los Jardines de la Reina
Golfo de Guacanayabo
Manzanillo
Bayamo
Bartolomé Masó
Niquero
Pico Turquino 1994 m
SIERRA MAESTRA
ATLANTIC OCEAN
CARIBBEAN SEA
CUBA
Total Area : 110 860 sq. km (42 803 sq. miles)
POPULATION
over 1 000 000
over 500 000
over 100 000
over 50 000
over 10 000
under 10 000
LAND HEIGHT
1000m/3281ft
500m/1640ft
200m/656ft
Sea Level
N
0 50 km
0 50 miles

Guanabo, 25 km (15 miles) east of Havana, is a low-key resort favored by Cubans. The most modern cars in Cuba are imported, along with computers, in exchange for sugar in a special trading deal with Japan.

C

PEOPLE

Pop. density medium

Spanish

102/km² (264/mi²)

THE URBAN/RURAL POPULATION SPLIT

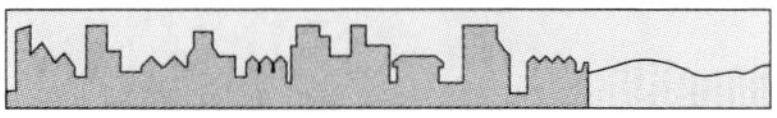
76%
24%

RELIGIOUS PERSUASION

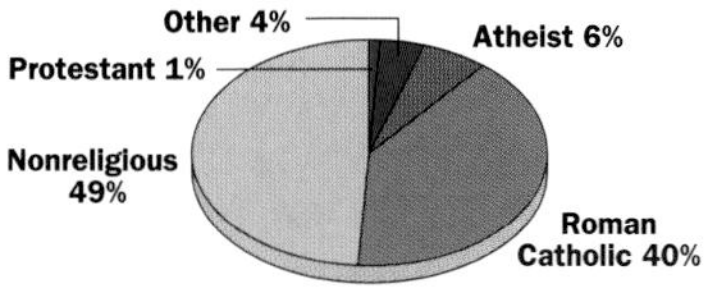
Other 4%
Protestant 1%
Atheist 6%
Nonreligious 49%
Roman Catholic 40%

ETHNIC MAKEUP

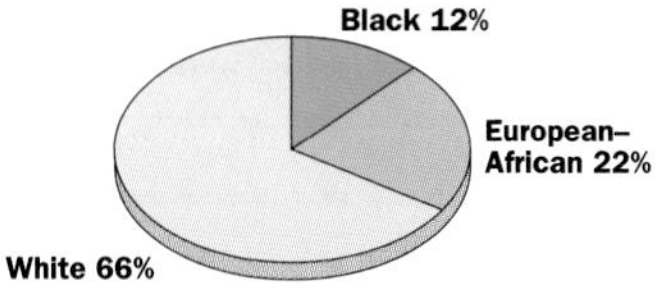
Black 12%
European–African 22%
White 66%

Ethnic tension in Cuba is minimal. About 70% of Cubans are of Spanish descent, mainly from the settlers, but also from the more recent influx of exiles from Franco's Spain. The black population is descended from the slaves and from migrants from neighboring states, in particular Jamaica.

Living standards in Cuba fell dramatically in the early 1990s after the collapse of the east European communist bloc, previously its main trading partner, and rationing for most basic foodstuffs was subsequently introduced. The "dollarization" of the economy in recent years has led to great divisions between those who survive on pesos and those who have access to dollars and thus a much wider range of goods. Since the early 1990s the number of those trying to leave, legally or otherwise, has risen markedly.

An increasing number of women are playing a prominent role in politics, the professions, and the armed forces. Child-care facilities are widespread.

POPULATION AGE BREAKDOWN

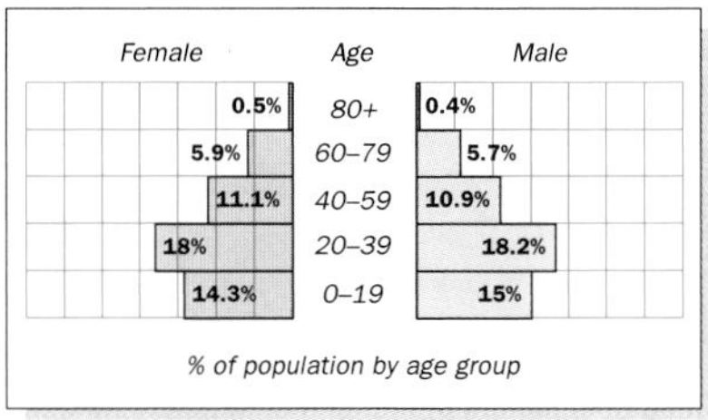
Female
Age
Male
0.5%
80+
0.4%
5.9%
60–79
5.7%
11.1%
40–59
10.9%
18%
20–39
18.2%
14.3%
0–19
15%
% of population by age group

WORLD AFFAIRS

Joined UN in 1945

ACP | IAEA | SELA | NAM | ACS

Since the 1959 revolution, and particularly after the 1962 stand-off over Soviet missiles, the US has considered Cuba a danger. The US trade blockade, first imposed in 1961, has left Cuba economically isolated despite regular votes in the UN condemning sanctions. The end of Soviet aid in the 1990s was another serious blow to Castro's embattled regime. The search for alternative sources of support led to better relations with the EU and Latin America, but Castro's refusal to countenance reform has caused a recent deterioration of relations with both regions. Castro's closest ally is the Chávez government in Venezuela.

Ties to Russia have been weakened further, but relations with the US remain fraught, despite the arrival in 2001 of the first direct trade between the two countries' governments, in the form of emergency aid. In 2002 the US included Cuba in its list of "axis of evil" terrorist-sponsoring states, and further sanctions were imposed in 2004 by the Bush administration.

POLITICS

No multiparty elections

2003/2008

President Fidel Castro Ruz

AT THE LAST ELECTION

National Assembly of the People's Power 609 seats

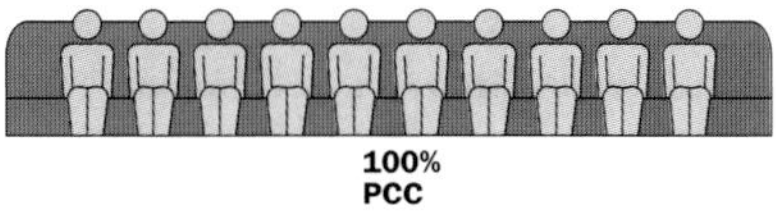
100%
PCC

PCC = Cuban Communist Party

Fidel Castro has led Cuba since 1959. The country's one-party communist system, set out in the 1976 constitution, was designated "untouchable" in 2002.

PROFILE

The 1959 popular revolution, led by Castro, toppled the corrupt Batista dictatorship and launched a far-reaching program of social, economic, and political reforms.

In the 1990s the revolution seemed under siege in the wake of the collapse of the Soviet Union and tightened trade sanctions by the US. Supporters continue to see Cuba as living proof of the triumph of socialist development over adversity, but critics offer the view that the Castro administration is an intolerant dictatorship.

MAIN POLITICAL ISSUES

Prosecution of dissidents

The communist regime does not tolerate dissent. The most recent crackdown on prodemocracy activists – the arrest and summary trial of 75 people in 2003 – attracted considerable international criticism. The US and the EU reacted by hardening diplomatic sanctions.

The succession

The aging Castro remains firmly in place, and debate about his successor is somewhat muted. While some predict that a younger, collective, and reform-minded leadership would normalize relations with the US and steer Cuba toward democracy, others warn of a period of unrest as reformers and communist hard-liners compete to fill the likely power vacuum.

Raúl Castro, *brother of Fidel and the minister of defense.*

Fidel Castro, *Cuba's charismatic communist leader since 1959.*

N
Moa
Baracoa
El Salvador
Guantánamo
GUANTÁNAMO BAY (to US)
Windward Passage

AID

Recipient

$61m (receipts)

Up 13% in 2002

Spain, the EU, and UNICEF have given aid, and China loaned $400 million in 2001. The US offered $50,000 in aid after Hurricane Charley in 2004, but Cuba rejected it as hypocritical.

CHRONOLOGY

Originally inhabited by the Arawak people, Cuba was claimed for Spain by Columbus in 1492. Development of the sugar industry from the 18th century, using imported slave labor, made Cuba the world's third-largest producer by 1860.

- **1868** End of the slave trade.
- **1868–1878** Ten Years' War for independence from Spain.
- **1895** Second war of independence. Thousands die in Spanish concentration camps.
- **1898** In support of Cuban rebels US declares war on Spain to protect strong American financial interests in Cuba.
- **1899** US takes Cuba and installs military interim government.
- **1901** US is granted intervention rights and military bases, including Guantánamo Bay naval base.

C

CHRONOLOGY *continued*

- **1902** Tomás Estrada Palma takes over as first Cuban president. US leaves Cuba, but intervenes in 1906–1909 and 1919–1924.
- **1909** Liberal presidency of José Miguel Goméz. Economy prospers; US investment in tourism, gambling, and sugar.
- **1925–1933** Dictatorship of President Gerardo Machado.
- **1933** Years of guerrilla activity end in revolution. Sgt. Fulgencio Batista takes over; military dictatorship.
- **1955** Fidel Castro exiled after two years' imprisonment for subversion.
- **1956–1958** Castro returns to lead a guerrilla war in the Sierra Maestra.
- **1959** Batista flees. Castro takes over. Wholesale nationalizations; Cuba reorganized on Soviet model.
- **1960** US breaks off relations.
- **1961** US-backed invasion of Bay of Pigs by anti-Castro Cubans fails. Cuba declares itself Marxist-Leninist. US economic and political blockade.
- **1962** Missile crisis: Soviet deployment of nuclear weapons in Cuba leads to extreme Soviet–US tension; war averted by Khrushchev ordering withdrawal of weapons.
- **1965** One-party state formalized.
- **1972** Cuba joins COMECON (communist economic bloc).
- **1976** New socialist constitution. Cuban troops in Angola until 1991.
- **1977** Sends troops to Ethiopia.
- **1980** 125,000 Cubans, including "undesirables," flee to US.
- **1982** US tightens sanctions and bans flights and tourism to Cuba.
- **1983** US invasion of Grenada. Cuba involved in clashes with US forces.
- **1984** Agreement with US on Cuban emigration and repatriation of "undesirables" is short-lived.
- **1988** UN's second veto of US attempt to accuse Cuba of human rights violations. Diplomatic relations established with the European Communities.
- **1989** Senior military executed for arms and narcotics smuggling.
- **1991** Preferential trade agreement with USSR ends. Severe rationing.
- **1992–1993** US tightens blockade. All former Soviet military leave.
- **1994–1995** Economic reforms to boost foreign trade and investment.
- **1996** US Helms-Burton Act tightens sanctions.
- **1998** Visit of Pope John Paul II.
- **1999** Leading moderate dissidents put on trial.
- **2001** Hurricane Michelle hits Cuba.
- **2002** Guantánamo Bay used as high-security prison for captives from US "war on terrorism."
- **2003** Major crackdown on dissidents.

DEFENSE

Compulsory military service

$1.04bn

Down 3% in 2002

CUBAN ARMED FORCES

900 main battle tanks (T-34, T-54/55, T-62)	35,000 personnel
5 patrol boats	3000 personnel
130 combat aircraft (MiG-21/23/29)	8000 personnel
None	

From 1959 to the 1980s, Cuba's efficient military, well represented in the Council of Ministers and the Politburo, was one of the achievements of the revolution. Under Castro's brother Raúl, it succeeded in repelling the US-sponsored Bay of Pigs invasion in 1961, and saw effective action in Africa in the 1970s, preventing South Africa from taking control of Angola, and Somalia from occupying the Ogaden region in Ethiopia.

Since the worldwide collapse of communist regimes, the Cuban army has lost much of its prestige. Russia is still the main source of arms.

A siege mentality associated with the US economic embargo keeps the military on the alert for perceived internal and external threats.

ECONOMICS

Inflation 1.1% p.a. (1990–1999)

$18bn

1 Cuban peso (21)

SCORE CARD

- World GNP Ranking 71st
- GNP per Capita $1600
- Balance of Payments .... In deficit
- Inflation 7.1%
- Unemployment 3%

EXPORTS

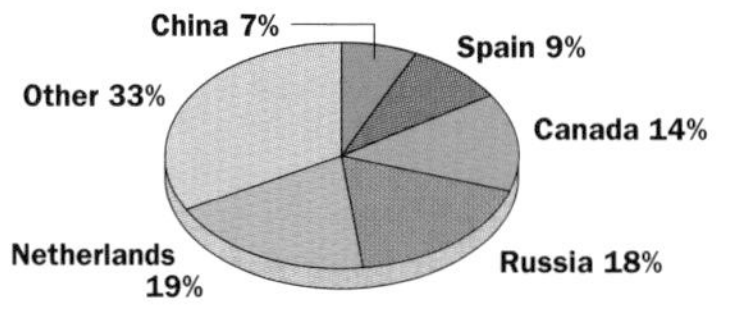
China 7%
Spain 9%
Other 33%
Canada 14%
Netherlands 19%
Russia 18%

IMPORTS

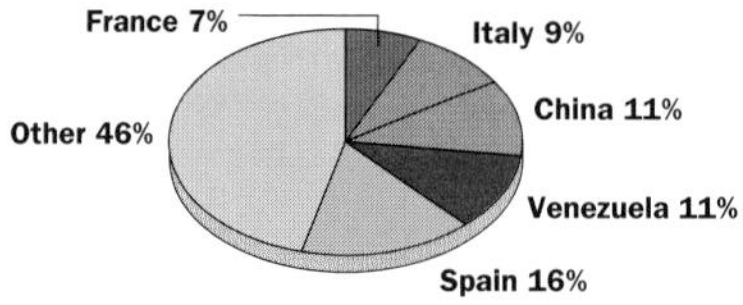
France 7%
Italy 9%
Other 46%
China 11%
Venezuela 11%
Spain 16%

ECONOMIC PERFORMANCE INDICATOR

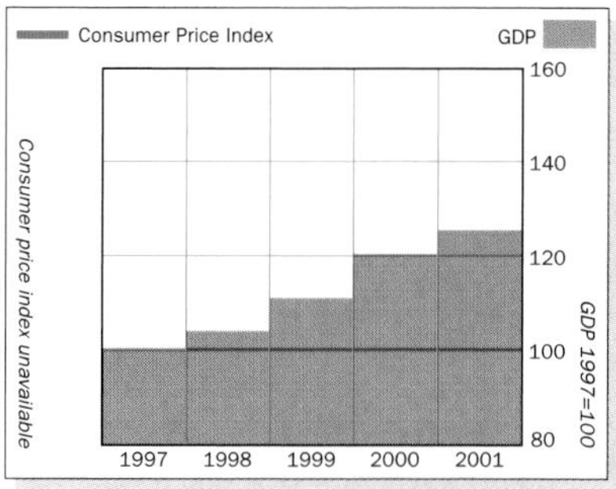
Consumer Price Index
GDP
Consumer price index unavailable
GDP 1997=100
160
140
120
100
80
1997
1998
1999
2000
2001

Strengths

Tourism remains major growth sector, though ambitious targets are not being met. Nickel and cigars. Biotechnologies and pharmaceuticals. Non-US foreign investment in oil and gas.

Weaknesses

Denied major market and investment capital by US trade embargo. Acute shortage of hard currency. Vulnerability of nickel to world price fluctuations. Collapse of sugar industry. Difficult terms of trade and weak legal framework deter investment. Infrastructure is deficient. Shortages of fuel, fertilizers, spare parts, and other inputs.

Profile

The collapse of the USSR meant the loss of some $5 billion in annual aid and led to a deep recession. A cautious adoption of some capitalist-style reforms in the mid-1990s, including the free use of the US dollar, stimulated the growth of a dollarized sector centered on tourism, which has attracted strong foreign investment. Tourism now dominates the economy, and benefits some 160,000 self-employed and small businesses. However, the once important sugar industry has collapsed, with the loss of around 100,000 jobs in recent years. Foreign companies are involved in joint ventures in banking and the oil and gas sectors. There is a very large informal sector. The government lost a significant source of revenue in 2001, when Russia terminated the lease on its information-gathering center.

CUBA : MAJOR BUSINESSES

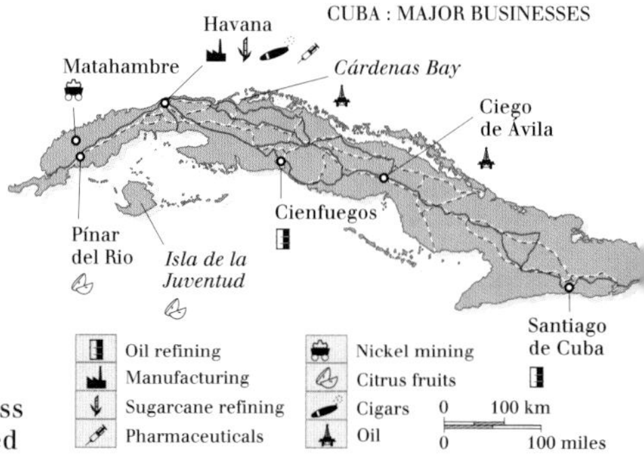
Havana
Matahambre
Cárdenas Bay
Ciego de Ávila
Cienfuegos
Pínar del Rio
Isla de la Juventud
Santiago de Cuba
Oil refining
Manufacturing
Sugarcane refining
Pharmaceuticals
Nickel mining
Citrus fruits
Cigars
Oil
0 100 km
0 100 miles

C

RESOURCES

Electric power 4.3m kW

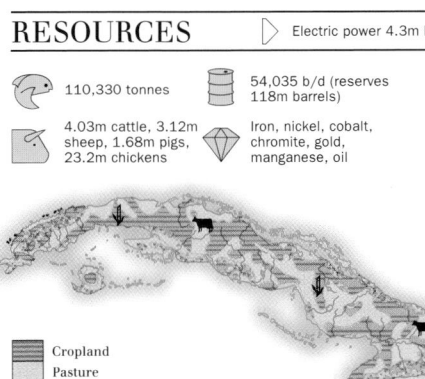

110,330 tonnes

54,035 b/d (reserves 118m barrels)

4.03m cattle, 3.12m sheep, 1.68m pigs, 23.2m chickens

Iron, nickel, cobalt, chromite, gold, manganese, oil

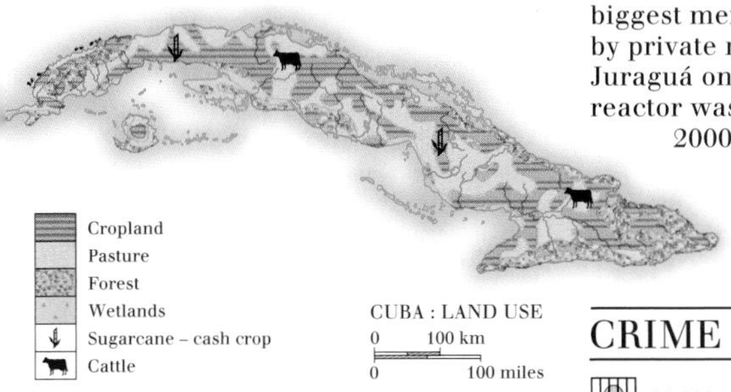
Cropland
Pasture
Forest
Wetlands
Sugarcane – cash crop
Cattle
CUBA : LAND USE
0
100 km
0
100 miles

ELECTRICITY GENERATION

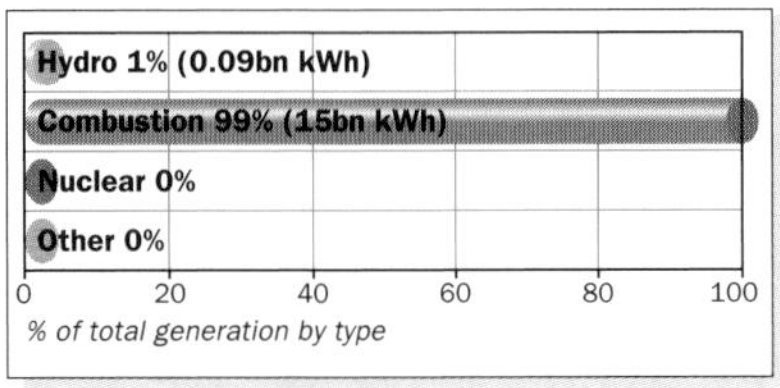
Hydro 1% (0.09bn kWh)
Combustion 99% (15bn kWh)
Nuclear 0%
Other 0%
0
20
40
60
80
100
% of total generation by type

The collapse of the USSR precipitated a steep decline in demand for sugar; production hit a 50-year low in 1998.

Cuba seeks to expand nickel and cobalt production, traditionally its biggest merchandise exports, assisted by private mining ventures. Work at Juraguá on a Russian-built nuclear reactor was abandoned in December 2000. The government intends to expand crude oil production until Cuba is self-sufficient in energy. It currently imports Venezuelan oil.

ENVIRONMENT

Sustainability rank: 58th

69% (15% partially protected)

2.8 tonnes per capita

ENVIRONMENTAL TREATIES

Yes	Yes	Yes
Yes	Yes	Yes

At the time of the revolution in 1959, only 14% of the country's forest cover remained, but a strong drive to replant has raised the tree cover level to over 20%. The intensive use of irrigation without adequate drainage has caused salinization and waterlogging. The government's pro-environmental stance contrasts with that of the US.

MEDIA

TV ownership medium

Daily newspaper circulation 118 per 1000 people

PUBLISHING AND BROADCAST MEDIA

There are 18 regional daily newspapers. *Granma*, published by the government, has the biggest circulation

1 state-owned service

1 state-owned service

A catch-all anticrime law restricts and penalizes investigative reporting by independent journalists which is judged to be assisting the US foreign policy against Cuba.

CRIME

Death penalty in use

33,000 prisoners

Crime is rising

CRIME RATES

Cuba does not publish official statistics for murders, rapes, or thefts

Violent crime is officially viewed as a threat to national stability. In 1999 the death penalty was extended to certain narcotics offenses, robbery involving firearms, attacks on security officers, and sexual corruption of minors. In the biggest crackdown in a decade, 75 prodemocracy activists were arrested in March 2003 and summarily tried. Shortly afterward a de facto three-year moratorium on executions was ended by the execution of three ferry hijackers.

EDUCATION

School leaving age: 14

97%

192,000 students

THE EDUCATION SYSTEM

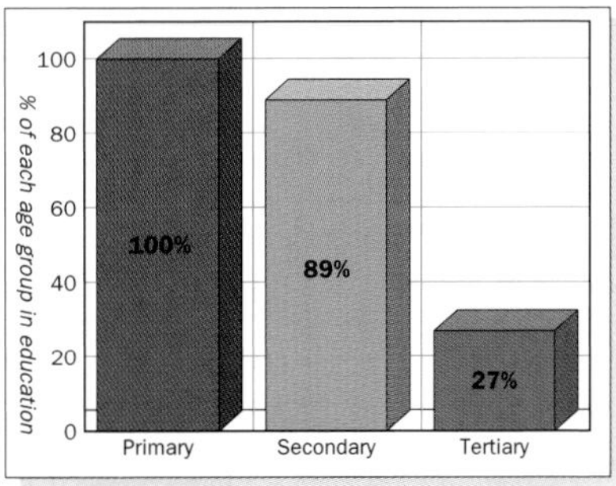
100
80
60
40
20
0
% of each age group in education
100%
89%
27%
Primary
Secondary
Tertiary

Education, which is universal and free at all levels, combines academic with manual work, in line with Marxist-Leninist principles. The importance given to education under Castro, which is reflected in the high literacy rate, is now being promoted to attract foreign investment in high-tech industries, particularly biotechnology. There are three large universities and more than 40 smaller tertiary institutions.

HEALTH

Welfare state health benefits

1 per 189 people

Cancers, heart and cerebrovascular diseases, pneumonia

Average life expectancy in Cuba is among the highest in Latin America, which is a reflection of its efficient, countrywide health service. The US trade embargo has led to shortages of hospital equipment and of raw materials for drugs, normally supplied by Havana's sizable pharmaceuticals industry. Cuba's advanced surgery techniques attract patients from overseas. The government's AIDS program has helped keep the mortality of sufferers low and curtailed the spread of infection.

SPENDING

GDP/cap. increase

CONSUMPTION AND SPENDING

16 per 1000 population

51 per 1000 population

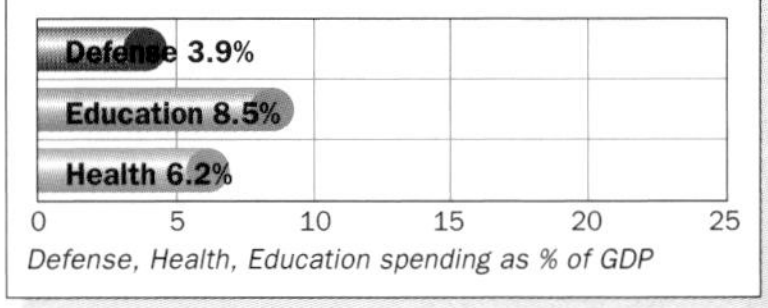
Defense 3.9%
Education 8.5%
Health 6.2%
0
5
10
15
20
25
Defense, Health, Education spending as % of GDP

Under Batista there were huge wealth disparities, and Cuba was a playground for the rich. The 1959 revolution succeeded in reducing the disparities, partly by taking over all businesses, from oil companies to barbershops, and partly by prescribing not only minimum but also maximum wages. Economic regulations have varied since then; for a brief period in 1985, different wage rates were allowed in an attempt to provide incentives for those who work hard, but this decision was reversed in 1986. Economic liberalization in the mid-1990s has created a large gulf between that section of the population with access to US dollars and those left in the peso economy who have to subsist on lower salaries.

WORLD RANKING

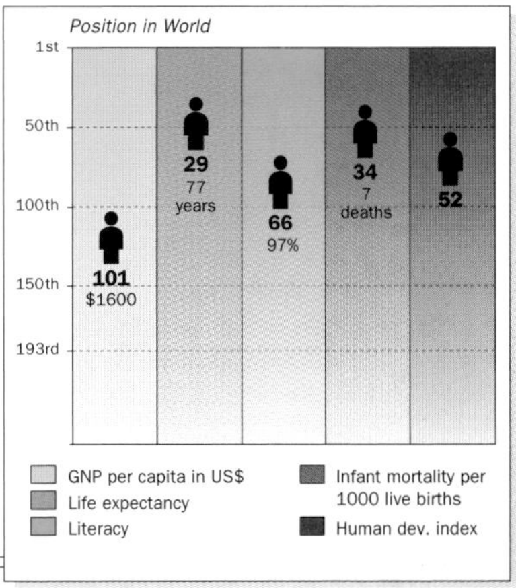
Position in World
1st
50th
100th
150th
193rd
101
$1600
29
77
years
66
97%
34
7
deaths
52
GNP per capita in US$
Life expectancy
Literacy
Infant mortality per 1000 live births
Human dev. index

CYPRUS

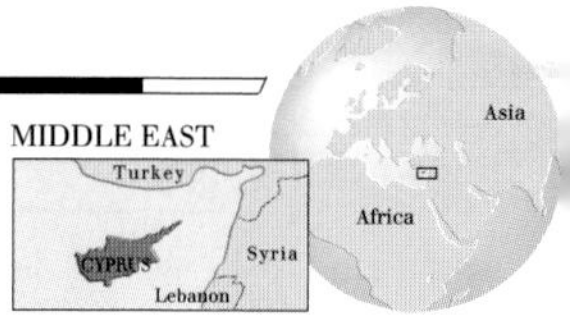
MIDDLE EAST
Turkey
CYPRUS
Syria
Lebanon
Asia
Africa

OFFICIAL NAME: Republic of Cyprus **CAPITAL:** Nicosia **POPULATION:** 802,000
CURRENCY: Cyprus pound (Turkish lira in TRNC) **OFFICIAL LANGUAGES:** Greek and Turkish

C

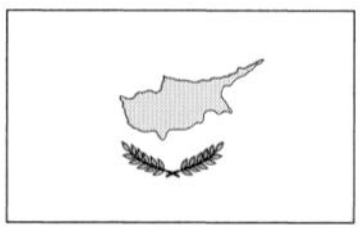

1960 | 1960 | Oct 1 | CY | +2 | +357 | .cy

THE ISLAND OF Cyprus, which rises from a central plateau to a high point at Mount Olympus, lies south of Turkey in the eastern Mediterranean. It was partitioned in 1974, following an invasion by Turkish troops. The south of the island is the Greek Cypriot Republic of Cyprus (Cyprus); the self-proclaimed Turkish Republic of Northern Cyprus (TRNC) is recognized only by Turkey.

CLIMATE

Mediterranean

WEATHER CHART FOR NICOSIA

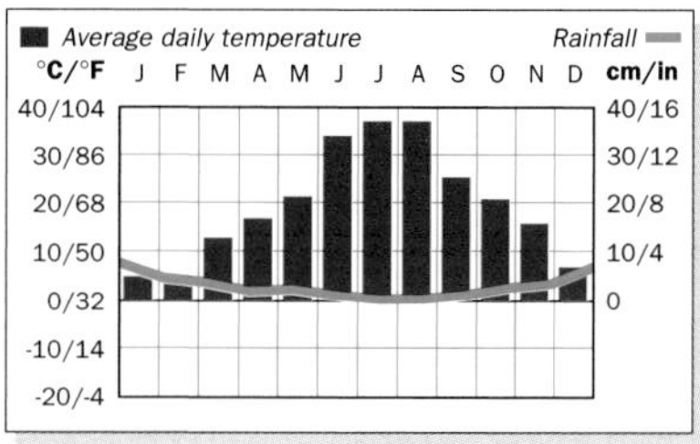
Average daily temperature
Rainfall
°C/°F
J F M A M J J A S O N D
cm/in
40/104
30/86
20/68
10/50
0/32
-10/14
-20/-4
40/16
30/12
20/8
10/4
0

The climate is typically Mediterranean: summers are hot and dry, and winters mild, though there is mountain snow.

TRANSPORTATION

Drive on left

Larnaca 4.8m passengers

1325 ships 23m grt

THE TRANSPORTATION NETWORK

6959 km (4324 miles)

178 km (111 miles)

None

None

Cyprus views flights to the TRNC as illegal. People were allowed to cross the Green Line for the first time in 2003.

TOURISM

Visitors : Population 2.9:1

2.3m visitors

Down 5% in 2003

MAIN TOURIST ARRIVALS

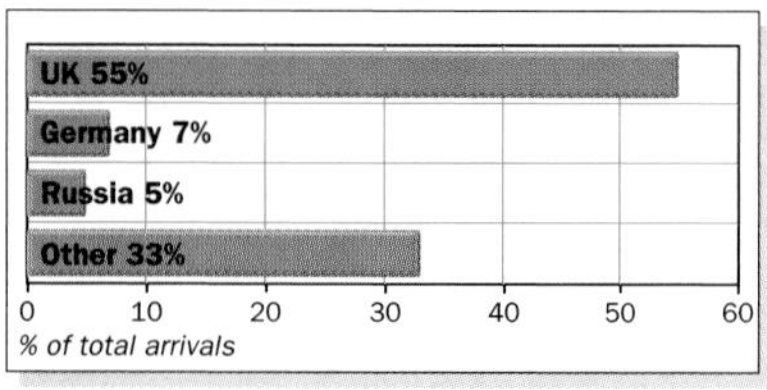
UK 55%
Germany 7%
Russia 5%
Other 33%
0
10
20
30
40
50
60
% of total arrivals

Tourists come for beaches, archaeology, or the abundant wildlife, notably on the Akamas peninsula and in the Troodos Mountains. A ten-year plan aims to double the number of visitors by 2010, though the industry was hit by a slump in 2002–2003.

PEOPLE

Pop. density medium

Greek, Turkish

87/km² (225/mi²)

THE URBAN/RURAL POPULATION SPLIT

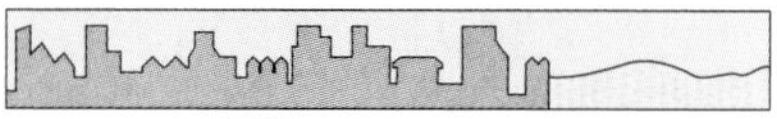
71%
29%

ETHNIC MAKEUP

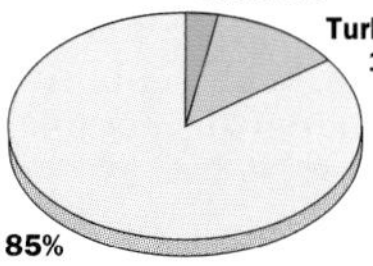
Other 3%
Turkish 12%
Greek 85%

Cyprus's Greek majority are Orthodox Christian. The Turkish minority are Muslim. They first arrived on the island as settlers in the 16th century, under the rule of the Ottoman Empire. Both Cypriot communities have suffered great upheavals: in 1974 the island was partitioned along what became the Green Line and 200,000 Greek Cypriots were forced to flee to the south, while 65,000 Turkish Cypriots fled in the other direction. Northern Cyprus is officially recognized as an independent entity only by Turkey. Over 100,000 mainland Turks have settled there and now outnumber indigenous Turkish Cypriots.

Contract labor, mainly from eastern Europe, is brought in to staff hotels in the south, where wage levels are at least three times higher than in the north. Unemployment levels in the north, meanwhile, are rising.

***The 2nd-century theater** at Curium, 14 km (19 miles) west of Limassol. Curium was the site of a flourishing Mycenaean colony before 1100 BCE.*

POLITICS

Multiparty elections

Cyprus 2001/2006
TRNC 2003/2008

President Tassos Papadopoulos (Cyprus)
President Rauf Denktash (TRNC)

AT THE LAST ELECTION

House of Representatives 80 seats

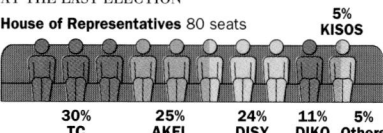

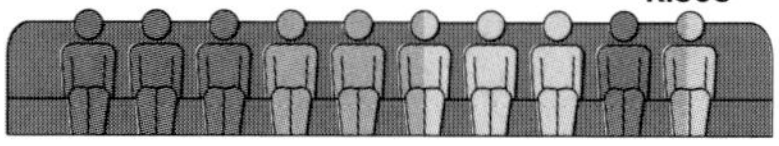
5% KISOS
30% TC
25% AKEL
24% DISY
11% DIKO
5% Others

TC = Reserved for Turkish Cypriots **AKEL** = Progressive Party of the Working People **DISY** = Democratic Rally **DIKO** = Democratic Party **KISOS** = Movement of Social Democrats

The 24 seats reserved for Turkish Cypriots have not been occupied since December 1963

Assembly (TRNC) 50 seats

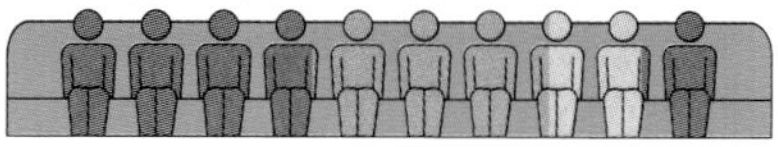
38% CTP
36% UBP
14% DP
12% BDH

CTP = Republican Turkish Party
UBP = National Unity Party **DP** = Democrat Party
BDH = Peace and Democracy Movement

The UN-backed unification plan proposed two communities sharing several government functions. Greek Cypriots feared too much influence over their affairs by the small Turkish minority. From 2003, hard-line leaders Tassos Papadopoulos and Rauf Denktash refused to make progress, but with Cyprus's EU accession imminent, the plan was put to a referendum. The Turkish Cypriot minority voted in favor, anxious to end their isolation and gain the benefits of EU membership, but the Greek Cypriots overwhelmingly rejected the plan. Without a "yes" from both sides, effectively only the Greek part of the island could accede in May 2004.

WORLD AFFAIRS

Joined UN in 1960

CE | Comm | EU | NAM | OSCE

Over 1000 UN troops patrol the Green Line, though the opening of the border in 2003 saw large numbers of people cross in both directions. The Greek Cypriot rejection of a UN settlement in 2004 saw EU funds that had been set aside for reunification channeled instead to the impoverished Turkish zone.

AID

Recipient

$50m (receipts)

Little change in 2002

The TRNC's exclusion from EU membership due to Greek Cypriot rejection of unification was followed by pledges of international funds to combat its isolation and dependence on Turkey.

CYPRUS

Total Area : 9250 sq. km (3571 sq. miles)

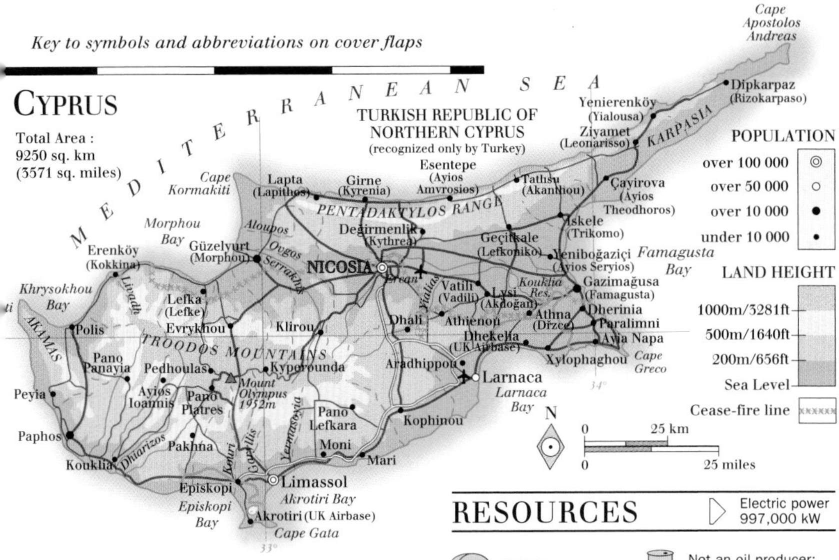

MEDITERRANEAN SEA
TURKISH REPUBLIC OF NORTHERN CYPRUS (recognized only by Turkey)
Cape Apostolos Andreas
Dipkarpaz (Rizokarpaso)
Yenierenköy (Yialousa)
Ziyamet (Leonarisso)
KARPASIA
Esentepe (Ayios Amvrosios)
Cape Kormakiti
Lapta (Lapithos)
Girne (Kyrenia)
Tatlısu (Akanthou)
Çayirova (Ayios Theodhoros)
PENTADAKTYLOS RANGE
Morphou Bay
Aloupos
Değirmenlik (Kythrea)
İskele (Trikomo)
Erenköy (Kokkina)
Güzelyurt (Morphou)
Ovgos
Serrakhis
NICOSIA
Geçitkale (Lefkoniko)
Yeniboğaziçi (Ayios Seryios)
Famagusta Bay
Khrysokhou Bay
Livadhi
Lefka (Lefke)
Pedieos
Vatili (Vadili)
Lysi (Akdoğan)
Koukhia Res.
Gazimağusa (Famagusta)
AKAMAS
Polis
Evrykhou
Klirou
Yialias
Dhali
Athna (Dirze)
Athienon
Dherinia
Paralimni
Dhekelia (UK Airbase)
Ayia Napa
TROODOS MOUNTAINS
Pano Panayia
Pedhoulas
Kyperounda
Xylophaghou
Cape Greco
Aradhippou
Larnaca
Larnaca Bay
Peyia
Ayios Ioannis
Pano Platres
Mount Olympus 1952m
Yermasoyia
Pano Lefkara
Kophinou
Paphos
Pakhna
Moni
Mari
Koukha
Dhiarizos
Kouris
Garyllis
Limassol
Episkopi
Episkopi Bay
Akrotiri Bay
Akrotiri (UK Airbase)
Cape Gata
POPULATION
over 100 000
over 50 000
over 10 000
under 10 000
LAND HEIGHT
1000m/3281ft
500m/1640ft
200m/656ft
Sea Level
Cease-fire line
N
0 25 km
0 25 miles

CHRONOLOGY

Cyprus was dominated, in turn, by Egypt, Greece, the Byzantines, the Ottomans, and the UK, before independence in 1960.

- ❑ **1974** President Makarios deposed by Greek military junta. Turkey invades. Partition.
- ❑ **1983** Self-proclamation of TRNC.
- ❑ **1993** Glafcos Clerides president.
- ❑ **2003** Tassos Papadopoulos elected president. Green Line opened.
- ❑ **2004** Referendum rejects plan for reunification. Cyprus joins EU.

DEFENSE

▷ Compulsory military service

$227m — Up 2% in 2002

In addition to two sovereign British bases and UN forces, there are 36,000 Turkish troops in northern Cyprus and 1250 Greek troops in the buffer zone. The 10,000-strong Greek Cypriot army and the 5000-strong Turkish Cypriot army both rely heavily on conscripts.

ECONOMICS

▷ Inflation 3.4% p.a. (1990–2001)

$9.37bn — 0.4778 Cyprus pounds (0.5101)

SCORE CARD

❑ World GNP Ranking	88th
❑ GNP per Capita	$12,320
❑ Balance of Payments	-$517m
❑ Inflation	2.8%
❑ Unemployment	4%

Strengths

Large tourism industry, accounting for over 20% of GDP. Integration with EU. Manufacturing sector and provision of services to Middle Eastern countries.

Weaknesses

Pressure for tighter supervision of offshore finance. Slow pace of liberalization. TRNC starved of foreign investment for many years.

EXPORTS

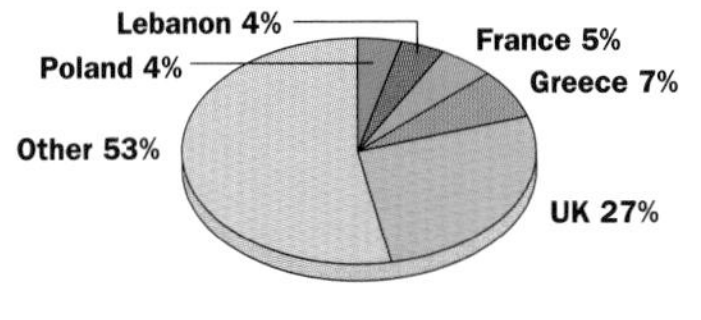

Lebanon 4%
Poland 4%
France 5%
Greece 7%
Other 53%
UK 27%

IMPORTS

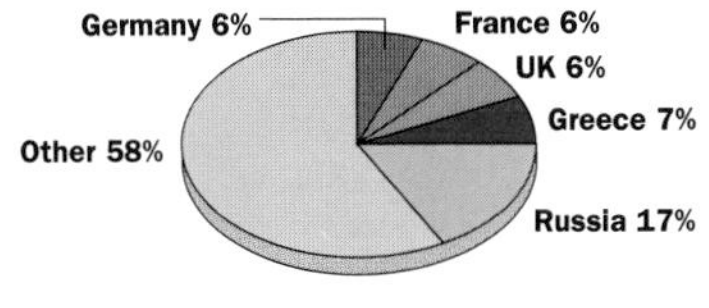

Germany 6%
France 6%
UK 6%
Greece 7%
Other 58%
Russia 17%

RESOURCES

▷ Electric power 997,000 kW

77,686 tonnes — Not an oil producer; refines 23,700 b/d

451,000 pigs, 450,000 goats, 3.5m chickens — Asbestos, gypsum, iron, bentonite, copper

Cyprus stopped supplying free electricity to the TRNC in 1994. The possibility of offshore oil and gas to the south has attracted interest. Water is precious; desalinization plants and new reservoirs have boosted supplies.

ENVIRONMENT

▷ Not available

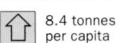

8% (7% partially protected) — 8.4 tonnes per capita

Campaigners demand that the 155 sq. km (60 sq. miles) of the Akamas peninsula be fully protected from the threat of being sold for tourist development. Akamas is home to an unusual variety of plant and bird life, and contains breeding sites of the rare green turtle.

MEDIA

▷ TV ownership high

Daily newspaper circulation 111 per 1000 people

PUBLISHING AND BROADCAST MEDIA

There are 9 daily newspapers. *Phileleftheros* has the largest circulation; others include *Haravgi*, *Simerini*, and *Alithia*

6 services: 1 state-controlled, 5 independent — 5 services: 1 state-controlled, 4 independent

The media in Cyprus are lively and tend to be highly politicized. In the TRNC, independent papers have faced harassment from the authorities.

CRIME

▷ No death penalty

345 prisoners — Up 4% in 2001

Crime rates are low and violence is rare. The unruly and sometimes violent behavior of foreign forces has on occasion led Cypriots to object to their presence. The arrest of a Cypriot politician during protests at a UK military base in 2001 provoked riots.

EDUCATION

▷ School leaving age: 15

97% — 11,934 students

Education is free and enrollment is high. The University of Cyprus opened in 1992, but many Cypriots study abroad.

HEALTH

▷ Welfare state health benefits

1 per 381 people — Heart diseases, accidents, cancers

Health care is more advanced in the south; sophisticated surgery is carried out at Lefkosia General Hospital.

SPENDING

▷ GDP/cap. increase

CONSUMPTION AND SPENDING

348 per 1000 population — 688 per 1000 population

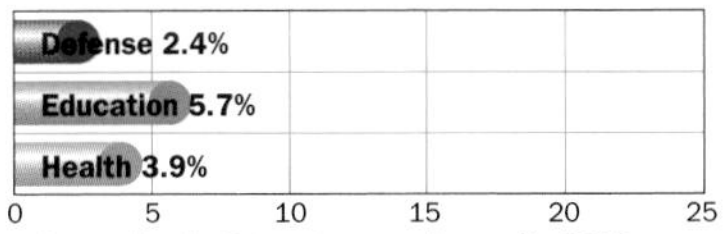

Defense 2.4%
Education 5.7%
Health 3.9%
0 5 10 15 20 25

Defense, Health, Education spending as % of GDP

Average per capita income in the south is greater than in Greece or Portugal, and over three times higher than in the Turkish Cypriot north.

WORLD RANKING

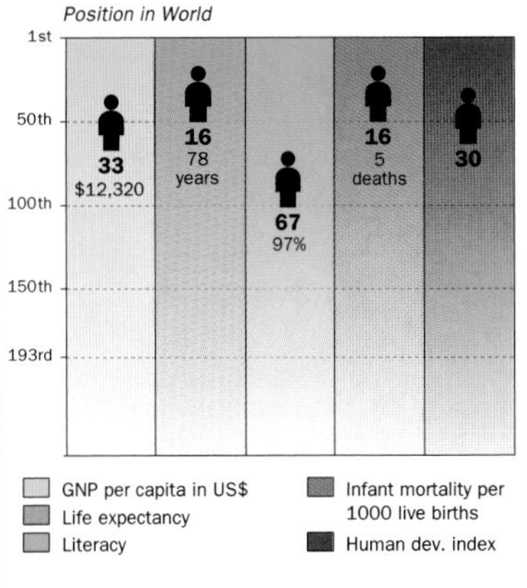

Position in World
1st
50th
100th
150th
193rd
33 $12,320
16 78 years
67 97%
16 5 deaths
30
GNP per capita in US$
Life expectancy
Literacy
Infant mortality per 1000 live births
Human dev. index

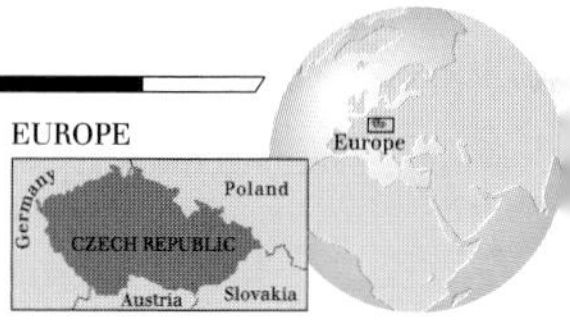
EUROPE
Europe
Germany
Poland
CZECH REPUBLIC
Austria
Slovakia

CZECH REPUBLIC

OFFICIAL NAME: Czech Republic **CAPITAL:** Prague
POPULATION: 10.2 million **CURRENCY:** Czech koruna **OFFICIAL LANGUAGE:** Czech

C

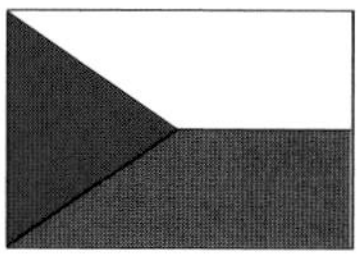

1993 | 1993 | Oct 28 | CZ | +1 | +420 | .cz

LANDLOCKED IN CENTRAL Europe, the Czech Republic comprises the territories of Bohemia and Moravia, and for most of the 20th century it was part of Czechoslovakia. In 1989, the "Velvet Revolution" ended four decades of communist rule, and free elections followed in 1990. In 1993 the Czech Republic and Slovakia peacefully dissolved their federal union to become two independent states.

CLIMATE

Continental

WEATHER CHART FOR PRAGUE

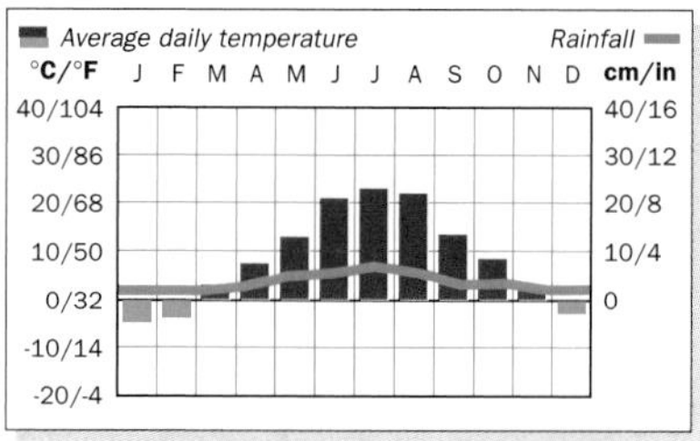
Average daily temperature
Rainfall
°C/°F J F M A M J J A S O N D cm/in
40/104 40/16
30/86 30/12
20/68 20/8
10/50 10/4
0/32 0
-10/14
-20/-4

The Czech climate is more moderate than that of Slovakia, though easterly winds bring low temperatures in winter.

TRANSPORTATION

Drive on right

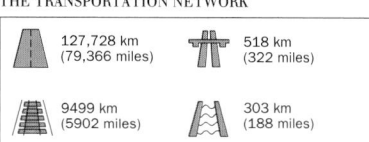

Ruzyné, Prague
7.46m passengers

Has no fleet

THE TRANSPORTATION NETWORK

127,728 km (79,366 miles)	518 km (322 miles)
9499 km (5902 miles)	303 km (188 miles)

There are new expressways and rail links to Germany. Prague is a busy regional center for passenger air traffic.

TOURISM

Visitors : Population 1:2.1

4.97m visitors

Up 5% in 2003

MAIN TOURIST ARRIVALS

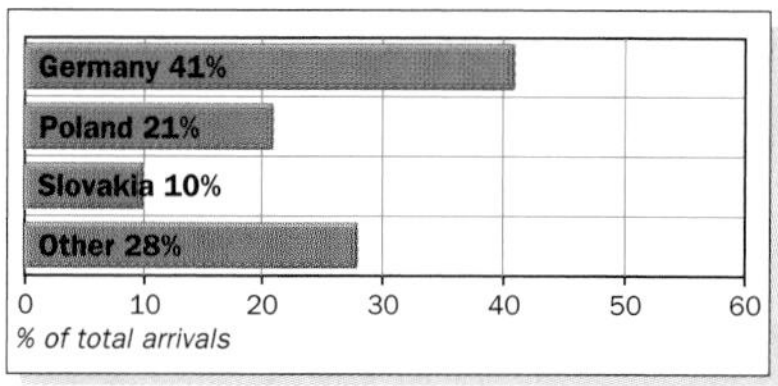
Germany 41%
Poland 21%
Slovakia 10%
Other 28%
0 10 20 30 40 50 60
% of total arrivals

Revenue from tourism amounts to nearly $3 billion a year, and tourism is an invaluable source of foreign earnings for the Czech economy. Germans are the most numerous among the millions of visiting tourists, who are mainly from Europe. Prague, which rivals Paris as the most beautiful capital in Europe, is still the main destination for visitors, though a growing proportion now seek other attractions such as spa towns and skiing.

PEOPLE

Pop. density medium

Czech, Slovak, Hungarian (Magyar)

129/km² (335/mi²)

THE URBAN/RURAL POPULATION SPLIT

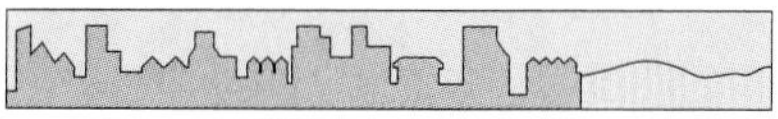
75%
25%

RELIGIOUS PERSUASION

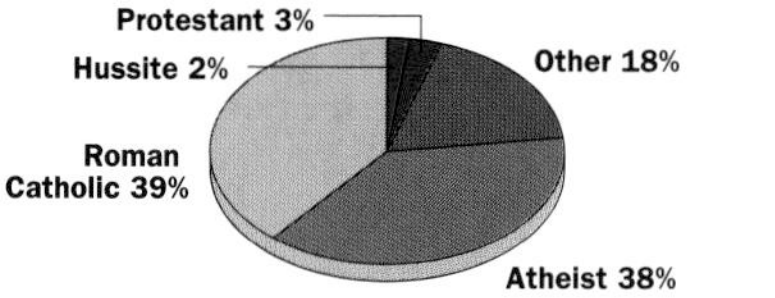
Protestant 3%
Hussite 2%
Other 18%
Roman Catholic 39%
Atheist 38%

Czechs make up over 80% of the population; Moravians are the next largest group. Some 300,000 Slovaks were left in the country after partition, and dual citizenship is now permitted. Ethnic tensions are few, except that the Roma community faces serious discrimination. Divorce rates are high.

POLITICS

Multiparty elections

L. House 2002/2006
U. House 2002/2004

President Vaclav Klaus

AT THE LAST ELECTION

Chamber of Deputies 200 seats

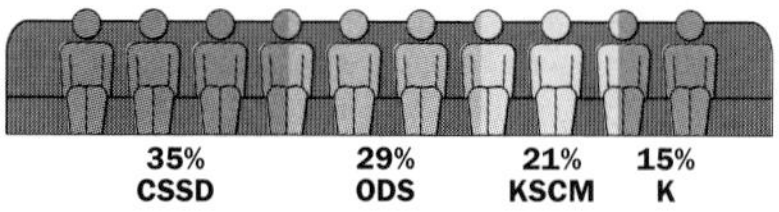
35% CSSD
29% ODS
21% KSCM
15% K

CSSD = Czech Social Democratic Party
ODS = Civic Democratic Party
KSCM = Communist Party of Bohemia and Moravia
K = Coalition of the Christian Democratic Union–Czech People's Party (**KDU–CSL**) and the Freedom Union (**US**)

Senate 81 seats

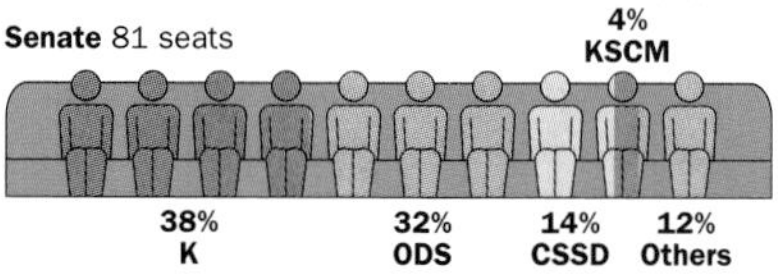
4% KSCM
38% K
32% ODS
14% CSSD
12% Others

The prodemocratic solidarity of 1989–1990, which saw the election of the Civic Forum and dissident playwright Vaclav Havel as president, soon gave way to a two-party system. The right-of-center ODS pursued market economics, and oversaw the split with the Slovak Republic in 1993. It then gave tacit support to the social-democratic CSSD's minority government from 1998. The CSSD under Vladimir Spidla was able to form a slender majority government, without ODS backing, in 2002. Havel retired in 2003 with no obvious successor, eventually being replaced by former prime minister Vaclav Klaus. Spidla resigned in 2004 amid turmoil within the CSSD. He was replaced by Stanislav Gross.

CZECH REPUBLIC

Total Area : 78 866 sq. km (30 450 sq. miles)

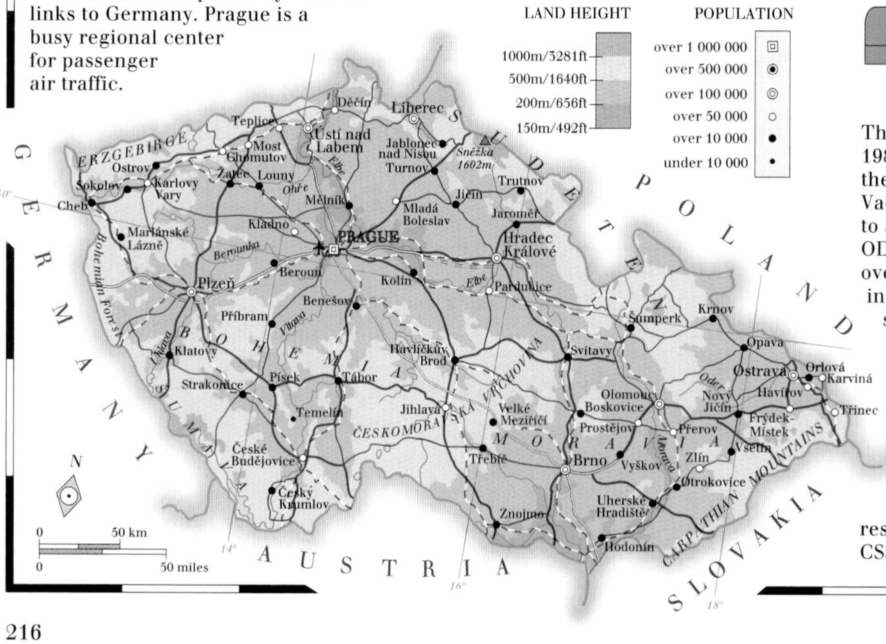
LAND HEIGHT
1000m/3281ft
500m/1640ft
200m/656ft
150m/492ft
POPULATION
over 1 000 000
over 500 000
over 100 000
over 50 000
over 10 000
under 10 000
PRAGUE
Plzeň
Brno
Ostrava
Olomouc
Liberec
Ústí nad Labem
Hradec Králové
Pardubice
České Budějovice
Karlovy Vary
Cheb
Děčín
Teplice
Most
Chomutov
Kladno
Kolín
Jihlava
Zlín
Opava
Karviná
Havířov
Třinec
Znojmo
Hodonín
Tábor
Písek
Příbram
G E R M A N Y
P O L A N D
A U S T R I A
S L O V A K I A
B O H E M I A
M O R A V I A
ERZGEBIRGE
SUDETEN
CARPATHIAN MOUNTAINS
Bohemian Forest
ČESKOMORAVSKÁ VRCHOVINA
Sněžka 1602m
Elbe
Vltava
Morava
Oder
N
0 50 km
0 50 miles

WORLD AFFAIRS

Joined UN in 1993

CE | EU | NATO | OECD | OSCE

The Czech Republic joined the EU as part of the organization's major wave of expansion in 2004. It had already joined NATO in 1999, and was a founding member of the Visegrad Group, which works to promote regional ties. Austria and Germany strongly opposed the opening of the Temelín nuclear plant in 2000.

AID

Recipient

$393m (receipts)

Up 25% in 2002

Aid for economic restructuring has been crucial to upgrading infrastructure such as telecommunications.

DEFENSE

Phasing out conscription

$1.4bn

Up 21% in 2002

The split with Slovakia left an oversized, expensive army: professional soldiers with a communist past were the first to be demobilized. The last conscripts signed up in 2004. The country's security was handed over to the US for the duration of a NATO summit in 2002. The Czech Republic is among the world's 20 largest arms exporters.

ECONOMICS

Inflation 11% p.a. (1990–2001)

$56bn

26.17 Czech koruny (27.5)

SCORE CARD

- World GNP Ranking.......45th
- GNP per Capita.......$5480
- Balance of Payments.......–$4.48bn
- Inflation.......1.8%
- Unemployment.......7%

Strengths
Skilled industrial labor force. Good industrial base. Speed of privatization of state industries. Attractive to German investors. Draw of Prague for tourists.

Weaknesses
Lack of diversification. Limited restructuring, excessive bureaucracy. Pressure to cut government expenditure to reduce growing budget deficit. Rising unemployment.

EXPORTS

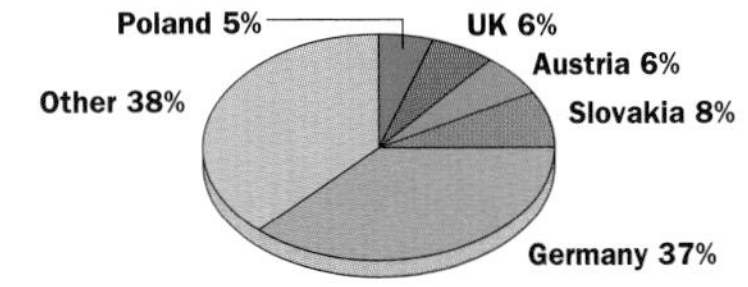
Poland 5%
UK 6%
Austria 6%
Other 38%
Slovakia 8%
Germany 37%

IMPORTS

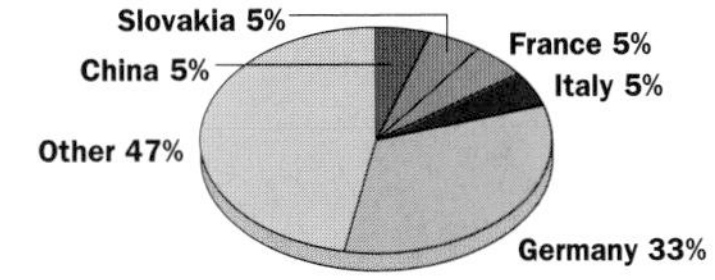
Slovakia 5%
France 5%
China 5%
Italy 5%
Other 47%
Germany 33%

RESOURCES

Electric power 15.2m kW

24,744 tonnes

3509 b/d (reserves 88m barrels)

3.36m pigs, 1.47m cattle, 12.4m chickens

Oil, natural gas, copper, lead, zinc, coal, uranium

The Czech Republic now imports all metals. Brown coal is still exported. The government is aiming to phase out the worst-polluting coal-fired power plants. Opposition to a planned 2000 MW Soviet-designed nuclear power plant at Temelín delayed its completion until late 2000.

ENVIRONMENT

Sustainability rank: 64th

16% (15% partially protected)

11.6 tonnes per capita

Pollution from the power, chemical, and cement industries and the new Temelín nuclear plant are key concerns.

MEDIA

TV ownership high

Daily newspaper circulation 254 per 1000 people

PUBLISHING AND BROADCAST MEDIA

There are 21 daily newspapers. *Mladá Fronta Dnes* has the largest circulation

4 services: 1 state-owned, 3 independent

1 state-owned service, over 70 independent services

Government-influenced appointments of senior media officials provoked mass protests and a change in the law in 2001.

CRIME

No death penalty

17,360 prisoners

Down 8% in 2001

Prostitution is becoming a growing problem, especially in regions bordering Austria and Germany.

EDUCATION

School leaving age: 15

99%

242,687 students

Schooling has reverted to the pre-1945 system. Charles University in Prague was founded in the 13th century.

HEALTH

Welfare state health benefits

1 per 294 people

Cancers, heart and cerebrovascular diseases

Government spending is high, and only a few hospitals are entirely privately owned. Wealthy Czechs travel to Germany for complex surgery.

***The Vltava River** in Prague. Millions of tourists, mainly from Europe, visit the beautiful city of Prague every year.*

CHRONOLOGY

Once part of the Austro-Hungarian Empire, Czechoslovakia was established in 1918.

- **1968** "Prague Spring." Invasion by Warsaw Pact countries.
- **1989** "Velvet Revolution."
- **1990** Free elections won by Civic Forum; Vaclav Havel president.
- **1993** Split with Slovakia.
- **1998** Elections: CSSD forms minority government.
- **1999** Joins NATO.
- **2002** CSSD reelected. Serious floods.
- **2003** Vaclav Klaus president.
- **2004** Joins EU.

SPENDING

GDP/cap. increase

CONSUMPTION AND SPENDING

354 per 1000 population

362 per 1000 population

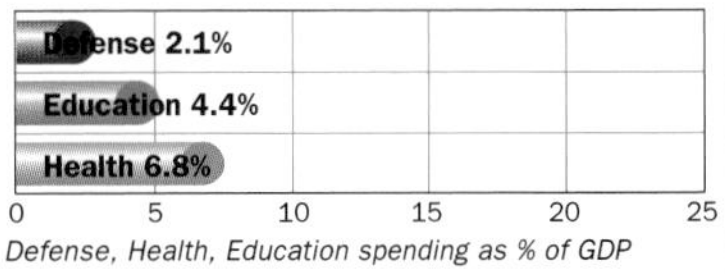
Defense 2.1%
Education 4.4%
Health 6.8%
0
5
10
15
20
25
Defense, Health, Education spending as % of GDP

An entrepreneurial class has emerged since 1989. Rapid privatization in the 1990s was achieved by offering ordinary Czechs coupons for shares.

WORLD RANKING

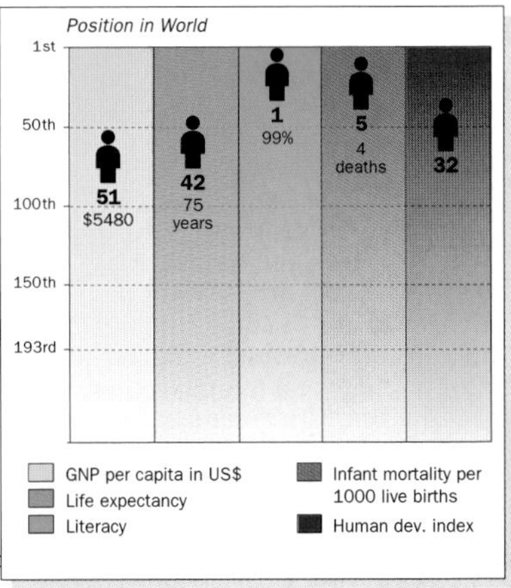
Position in World
1st
50th
100th
150th
193rd
51
$5480
42
75
years
1
99%
5
4
deaths
32
GNP per capita in US$
Life expectancy
Literacy
Infant mortality per 1000 live births
Human dev. index

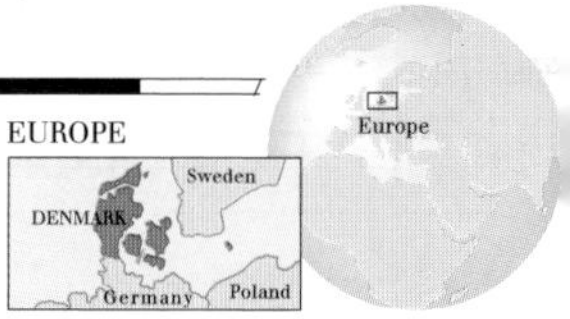
EUROPE
Europe
Sweden
DENMARK
Germany
Poland

DENMARK

OFFICIAL NAME: Kingdom of Denmark **CAPITAL:** Copenhagen
POPULATION: 5.4 million **CURRENCY:** Danish krone **OFFICIAL LANGUAGE:** Danish

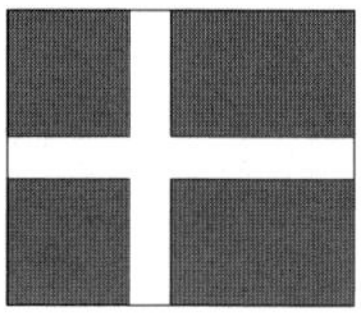

950
1944
April 16
DK
+1
+45
.dk

THE MOST SOUTHERLY COUNTRY in Scandinavia, Denmark occupies the Jutland (Jylland) peninsula, the islands of Sjælland, Fyn, Lolland, and Falster, and more than 400 smaller islands. Its terrain is among the flattest in the world. The Faeroe Islands and Greenland in the North Atlantic are self-governing associated territories. Politically, Denmark is stable, despite a preponderance of minority governments since 1945. It possesses a long liberal tradition and was one of the first countries to establish a welfare system, in the 1930s.

CLIMATE

Maritime

WEATHER CHART FOR COPENHAGEN

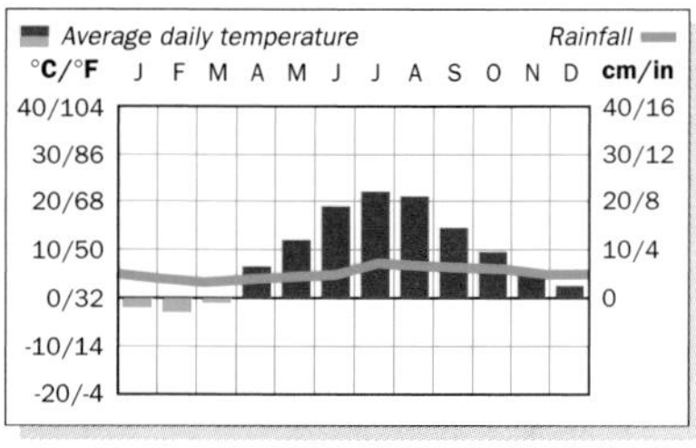
Average daily temperature
Rainfall
°C/°F
J F M A M J J A S O N D
cm/in
40/104
30/86
20/68
10/50
0/32
-10/14
-20/-4
40/16
30/12
20/8
10/4
0

Denmark's temperate, damp climate is one of the keys to its agricultural success. The Faeroes are windy, foggy, and cool. Greenland's climate ranges north–south from arctic to subarctic.

TRANSPORTATION

Drive on right

Kastrup, Copenhagen 17.6m passengers

857 ships 7.4m grt

THE TRANSPORTATION NETWORK

71,622 km (44,504 miles)

1010 km (628 miles)

2273 km (1412 miles)

417 km (259 miles)

There is an extensive, well-integrated transportation network of bus, rail, and ferry services. State-owned companies predominate, though privatization of some ferry and rail services has been mooted. Denmark wishes to reduce significant state transportation subsidies. A few private companies operate in the Faeroes and Greenland with state support.

Major new construction projects focus on bridge and tunnel links, such as the Storebælt project connecting the islands of Fyn and Sjælland. A 16-km (10-mile) Øresund road and rail link by bridge and tunnel, connecting Copenhagen with Malmö in Sweden, opened in July 2000. Copenhagen's new Metro light rail system has now been completed.

The island of Fyn, like the rest of Denmark, is flat and depends on coastal defenses to prevent flooding by the sea.

TOURISM

Visitors : Population 1:2.7

2.02m visitors

Up 1% in 2003

MAIN TOURIST ARRIVALS

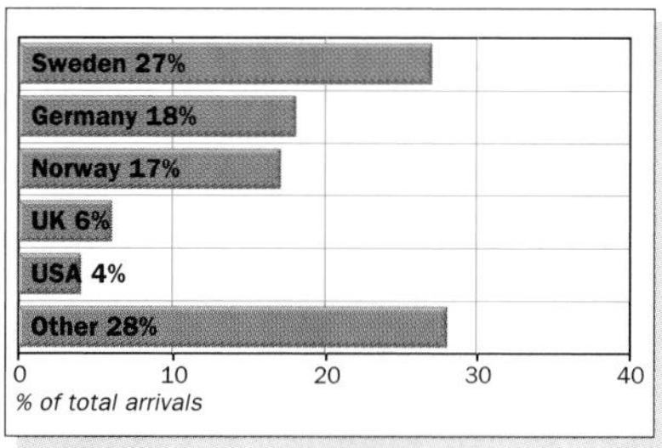
Sweden 27%
Germany 18%
Norway 17%
UK 6%
USA 4%
Other 28%
0
10
20
30
40
% of total arrivals

Principal attractions for tourists are Copenhagen (with its Tivoli Gardens and 18th-century architecture), Legoland, the countryside, and seaside resorts. Since 1959, only Danes have been allowed to own vacation homes.

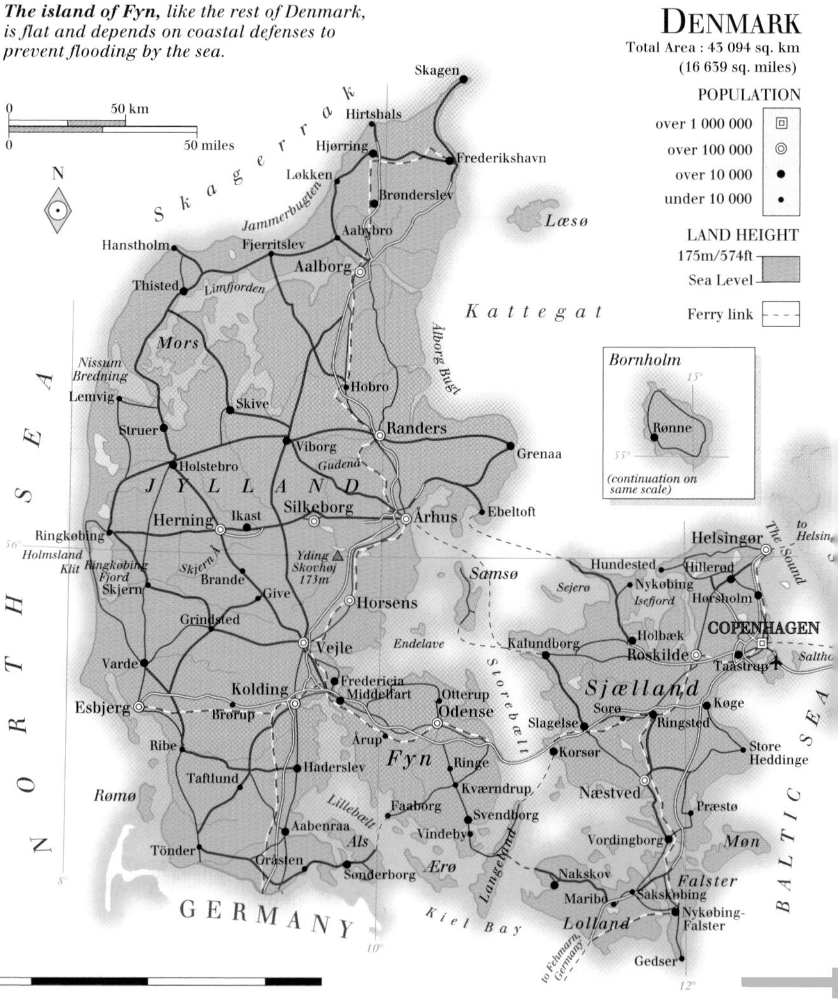
DENMARK
Total Area : 43 094 sq. km
(16 639 sq. miles)
POPULATION
over 1 000 000
over 100 000
over 10 000
under 10 000
LAND HEIGHT
175m/574ft
Sea Level
Ferry link
0
50 km
50 miles
N
Skagerrak
Kattegat
NORTH SEA
BALTIC SEA
GERMANY
Kiel Bay
Skagen
Hirtshals
Hjørring
Frederikshavn
Løkken
Brønderslev
Jammerbugten
Læsø
Hanstholm
Fjerritslev
Aabybro
Aalborg
Thisted
Limfjorden
Mors
Ålborg Bugt
Nissum Bredning
Lemvig
Hobro
Skive
Struer
Randers
Holstebro
Viborg
Grenaa
Gudenå
JYLLAND
Silkeborg
Ebeltoft
Herning
Ikast
Århus
Ringkøbing
Holmsland Klit
Ringkøbing Fjord
Skjern
Skjern Å
Brande
Yding Skovhøj 173m
Give
Horsens
Samsø
Sejerø
Grindsted
Vejle
Endelave
Varde
Fredericia
Middelfart
Kolding
Esbjerg
Brørup
Odense
Otterup
Ribe
Årup
Fyn
Haderslev
Ringe
Taftlund
Rømø
Kværndrup
Faaborg
Svendborg
Lillebælt
Aabenraa
Als
Vindeby
Tønder
Gråsten
Sønderborg
Ærø
Langeland
Storebælt
Kalundborg
Sjælland
Slagelse
Sorø
Ringsted
Korsør
Næstved
Helsingør
Hundested
Hillerød
Nykøbing
Isefjord
Hørsholm
COPENHAGEN
Holbæk
Roskilde
Taastrup
Køge
Store Heddinge
Præstø
Vordingborg
Møn
Nakskov
Maribo
Falster
Sakskøbing
Lolland
Nykøbing-Falster
Gedser
to Fehmarn, Germany
to Helsingborg
The Sound
Saltholm
Bornholm
Rønne
(continuation on same scale)

D

PEOPLE

Pop. density medium

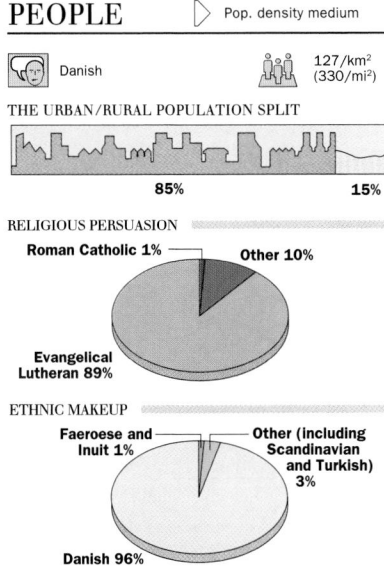

Danish

127/km² (330/mi²)

THE URBAN/RURAL POPULATION SPLIT

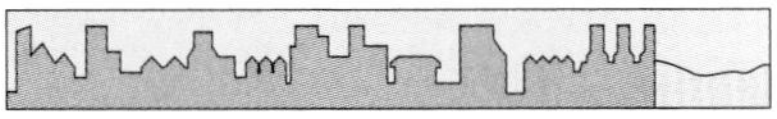
85%
15%

RELIGIOUS PERSUASION

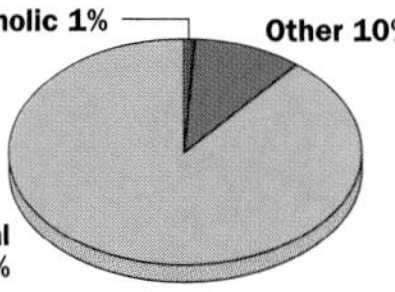
Roman Catholic 1%
Other 10%
Evangelical Lutheran 89%

ETHNIC MAKEUP

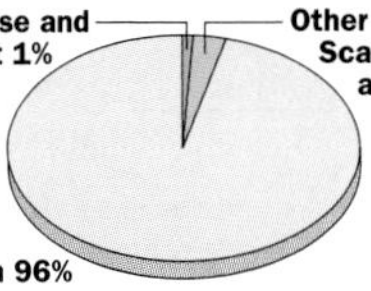
Faeroese and Inuit 1%
Other (including Scandinavian and Turkish) 3%
Danish 96%

Danish society is homogeneous, but the small population of foreign citizens doubled between 1984 and 1999, and the current right-leaning government has pledged to curb immigration. The most visible minority groups are the Inuit, Greenland's indigenous inhabitants, and the Turkish community. Rising unemployment has engendered some ethnic tension, though racially motivated attacks are still rare.

Helped by Denmark's extensive social and educational provision, almost all women now work in part-time or full-time jobs. Consequently, attendance at day nurseries is exceptionally high; 90% of three- to five-year-olds were enrolled in 2000.

Danish living arrangements have changed dramatically since the 1960s. Divorce rates are high and fewer people now live in extended families, while single-person households are increasing. Marriage is becoming less common and occurring later in life. Cohabiting couples now have equivalent legal rights. However, couples tend to marry when they have children, and 75% of children are raised by both parents. In 1989, Denmark became the first country to offer homosexual couples registered partnerships, effectively granting them the same legal status as heterosexual couples, though few have taken advantage of this.

POPULATION AGE BREAKDOWN

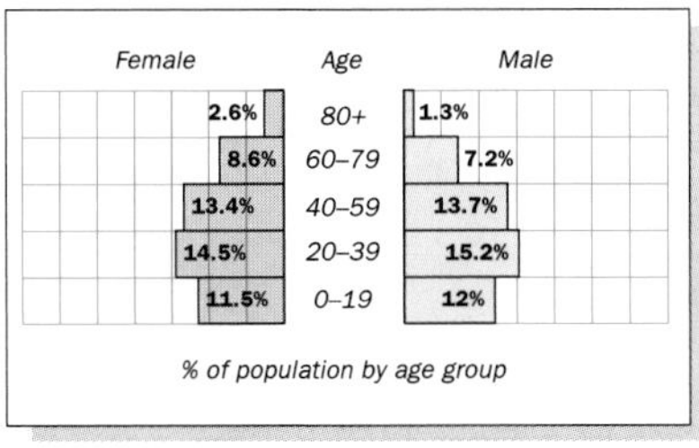
Female
Age
Male
2.6%
80+
1.3%
8.6%
60–79
7.2%
13.4%
40–59
13.7%
14.5%
20–39
15.2%
11.5%
0–19
12%
% of population by age group

POLITICS

Multiparty elections

2001/2005

H.M. Queen Margrethe II

AT THE LAST ELECTION

Parliament 179 seats

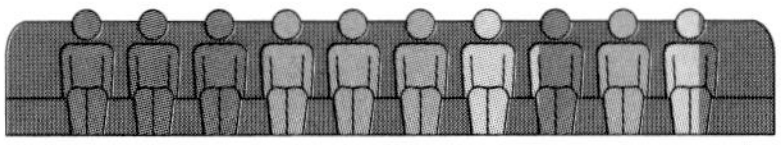
12% DFP
9% KF
7% SF
31% V
29% SD
9% Other CL
3% Other CR

V = Liberal Party (Venstre) **SD** = Social Democrats **DFP** = Danish People's Party **KF** = Conservative People's Party **Other CL** = Other Center Left **SF** = Socialist People's Party **Other CR** = Other Center Right

Greenland and the Faeroe Islands send two members each to the Parliament

Anders Fogh Rasmussen, heads a right-wing, minority coalition.

Queen Margrethe II, who succeeded to the throne in 1972.

Denmark is a constitutional monarchy and a multiparty democracy. The associated territories of Greenland and the Faeroe Islands have home rule. The latter is divided over the issue of independence.

PROFILE

The intricate proportional electoral system ensures a truly representative Parliament, but also tends to lead to minority governments. After a decade of Conservative–Liberal rule, the SD from 1993 headed a center-left coalition under Poul Nyrup Rasmussen. The pendulum swung back with a victory in 2001 for the Liberals and Anders Fogh Rasmussen. The Danish Confederation of Trade Unions voted in 2003 to cut its historic ties to the SD, ending over 100 years of political and financial support.

Major policy differences between the two main political groups are few; tax and immigration are important issues.

MAIN POLITICAL ISSUES

Relations with the EU

Denmark is a somewhat reluctant member of the EU. Left-of-center parties have grown suspicious of further integration and voters have previously rejected the Maastricht Treaty (1992) and membership of the eurozone (2000). Many voters are wary of monetary union, a common defense force, and local election voting rights for European citizens living in Denmark. Nonetheless, the Liberal government has championed Denmark's commitment to the Union, and Prime Minister Rasmussen has suggested that another referendum on the euro should be held once the new EU constitution is ironed out. Denmark held the EU presidency from July to December 2003.

Immigration

Despite Danish liberal traditions, the position and integration into society of immigrants and refugees, who account for under 5% of the population, is a controversial issue. The election of a right-wing government in 2001 signaled support for an overtly restrictive policy and a greater emphasis on integration for those immigrants already there. The ruling coalition relies for support on the far-right, anti-immigrant DFP, which almost doubled its representation in the 2001 election. Legislation passed in 2002 prevents the foreign (non-EU) spouse of a Danish citizen living in or emigrating to Denmark.

WORLD AFFAIRS

Joined UN in 1945

CE | EU | NATO | OECD | OSCE

Relations with the rest of Europe are the major foreign policy concern, notably the issues of a common defense policy and monetary union. Denmark has decided against introducing the euro, but the krone is pegged to it and economic policies follow those of the participating states. Promoting economic ties with Norway, Sweden, and Finland is a priority, as is improving links with former Eastern bloc states, especially those on the Baltic – not least to assist pollution reduction, a serious concern. Denmark is also a strong supporter of Third World development, especially in Africa.

CHRONOLOGY

Founded in the 10th century, Denmark's monarchy is Europe's oldest. It was the dominant Baltic power until the 17th century, when it was eclipsed by Sweden.

- **1815** Denmark forced to cede Norway to Swedish rule.
- **1849** Creation of first Danish democratic constitution.
- **1864** Denmark forced to cede provinces of Schleswig and Holstein after losing war with Prussia.
- **1914–1918** Denmark neutral in World War I.
- **1915** Universal adult suffrage introduced. Rise of SD.
- **1920** Northern Schleswig votes to return to Danish rule.

D

CHRONOLOGY *continued*

- **1929** First full SD government, Thorvald Stauning prime minister.
- **1930s** Implementation of advanced social welfare legislation and other liberal reforms under SD.
- **1939** Outbreak of World War II; Denmark reaffirms neutrality.
- **1940** Nazi occupation. National coalition government formed.
- **1943** Danish Resistance successes lead Nazis to take full control.
- **1944** Iceland declares independence from Denmark.
- **1945** Denmark recognizes Icelandic independence. After defeat of Nazi Germany, SD leads postwar coalition governments.
- **1948** Faeroes granted home rule.
- **1952** Founder member of the Nordic Council.
- **1953** Constitution reformed; single-chamber, proportionally elected parliament created.
- **1959** Denmark joins EFTA.
- **1972** Margrethe becomes queen.
- **1973** Denmark joins European Communities.
- **1979** Greenland granted home rule.
- **1975–1982** SD's Anker Jorgensen heads series of coalitions. Final coalition collapses over economic policy differences.
- **1982** Poul Schlüter first Conservative prime minister since 1894, in coalition with Liberals.
- **1992** Referendum rejects Maastricht Treaty on European Union.
- **1993** Schlüter resigns over "Tamilgate" scandal. Center-left government led by Poul Nyrup Rasmussen of SD. Danish voters ratify revised Maastricht Treaty.
- **1994, 1998** Elections: Rasmussen heads SD-led minority coalition.
- **2000** Referendum rejects joining eurozone.
- **2001** Elections: Liberals regain power. Anders Fogh Rasmussen appointed prime minister.

AID

Donor

$1.64bn (donations)

Up 1% in 2002

During the 1990s, Denmark was the world's leading aid donor in GNP terms, contributing on average 1% of national income. It supports both economic and social development projects and policy reforms. The Liberal government which came to power in 2001 has cut the foreign aid budget.

Denmark provides aid to Asia and Latin America, but its closest ties are with Africa. Tanzania is the largest single aid recipient. Denmark has also provided considerable support to other southeast African states.

DEFENSE

Compulsory military service

$2.56bn

Up 4% in 2002

Apart from NATO commitments, defense has a low priority; spending consitituted 1.6% of GDP in 2002, well below the NATO average of 2%. Denmark provides troops for the NATO-led forces in the former Yugoslavia and observers for other UN peacekeeping operations. One-quarter of its armed forces are conscripts, and its reserves include a Home Guard. Denmark has observer status at the WEU.

DANISH ARMED FORCES

238 main battle tanks (220 Leopard 1A5, 18 Leopard 2A4)	14,700 personnel
4 submarines, 3 corvettes, and 27 patrol boats	4000 personnel
68 combat aircraft (F-16A/B)	3500 personnel
None	

ECONOMICS

Inflation 2.2% p.a. (1990–2001)

$163bn

6.109 Danish kroner (6.47)

SCORE CARD

World GNP Ranking	26th
GNP per Capita	$30,260
Balance of Payments	$4.92bn
Inflation	2.4%
Unemployment	4%

EXPORTS

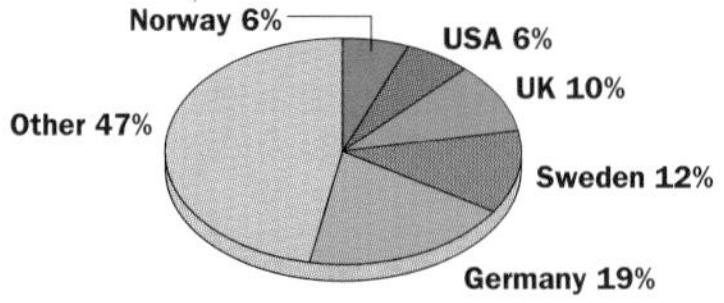
Norway 6%
USA 6%
UK 10%
Other 47%
Sweden 12%
Germany 19%

IMPORTS

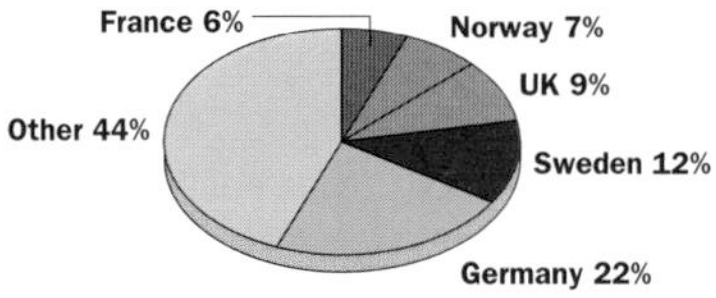
France 6%
Norway 7%
UK 9%
Other 44%
Sweden 12%
Germany 22%

Strengths

Low inflation; unemployment low, but rising. Substantial balance-of-payments surplus. Gas and oil reserves. Strong high-tech, high-profit manufacturing sector. Skilled workforce.

Weaknesses

Heavy tax burden. Labor costs and historically strong currency affect competitiveness.

Profile

Denmark's mix of a large state sector and a private sector has been successful. GDP per capita is one of the highest among the OECD countries. However, total taxation, at about 50%, is also among the world's highest. In 2001 the Liberal government promised to fund increased welfare spending and lower taxation by extending privatization and reducing development aid.

In the 1980s the government stabilized the exchange rate and tightened budget controls in order to reduce inflation and reverse the

ECONOMIC PERFORMANCE INDICATOR

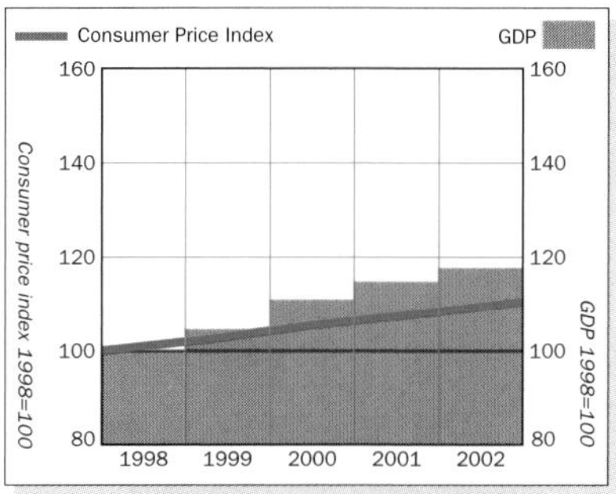
Consumer Price Index
GDP
160
140
120
100
80
Consumer price index 1998=100
GDP 1998=100
1998
1999
2000
2001
2002

balance-of-payments deficit. Growth slowed in the early 1990s, but an economic upturn between 1993 and 2000 was first led by private consumption and then buoyed by exports and business investment. Growth slowed significantly in 2001, but had regained momentum by mid-2002.

Voters have refused to accept EU monetary union, most recently in a "no" vote in 2000 in a referendum on the euro. However, Denmark meets the EU's convergence criteria for monetary union, the krone is pegged to the euro, and economic policies follow those of the participating states.

DENMARK : MAJOR BUSINESSES

Hirtshals
Ålborg
Århus
Copenhagen
Korsar
Esbjerg
Fredericia
Odense
Oil & gas
Brewing
Textiles
Chemicals
Agribusiness
Electronics
Transportation services
Light engineering
Trading center
Fish processing
0 100 km
0 100 miles

RESOURCES

Electric power 13.6m kW

1.55m tonnes

368,000 b/d (reserves 1.3bn barrels)

12.9m pigs, 1.72m cattle, 19.7m chickens

Natural gas, oil

ELECTRICITY GENERATION

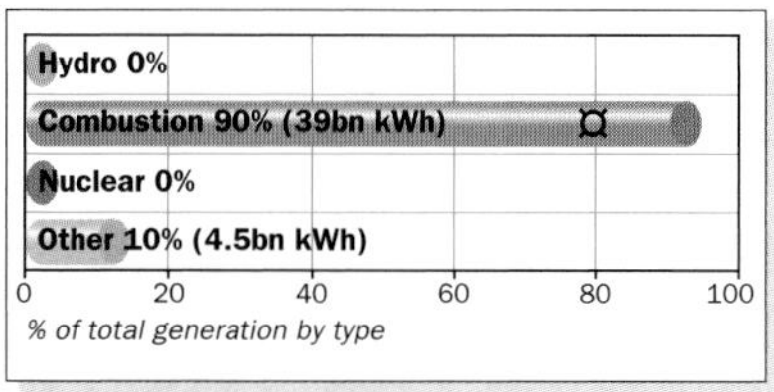

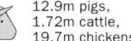

Hydro 0%
Combustion 90% (39bn kWh)
Nuclear 0%
Other 10% (4.5bn kWh)
0
20
40
60
80
100
% of total generation by type

The expansion of North Sea oil and gas output has made Denmark a net exporter of energy. The use of wind power is expanding rapidly; Denmark is a world leader in this technology. Agriculture is highly efficient, and Denmark is the world's biggest exporter of pork.

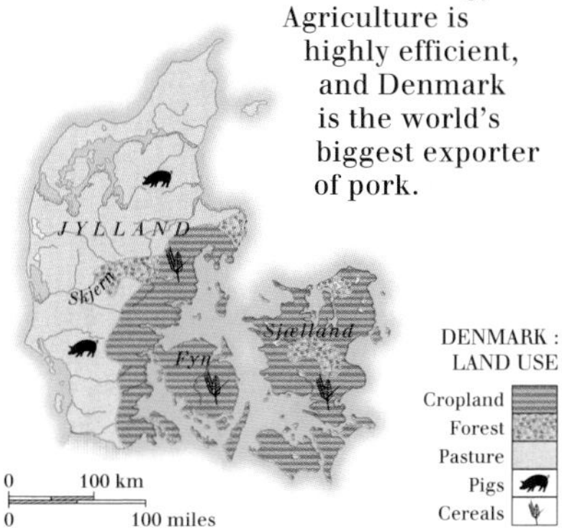

JYLLAND
Skjern
Fyn
Sjælland
DENMARK : LAND USE
Cropland
Forest
Pasture
Pigs
Cereals
0
100 km
0
100 miles

ENVIRONMENT

Sustainability rank: 31st

34% (31% partially protected)

8.4 tonnes per capita

ENVIRONMENTAL TREATIES

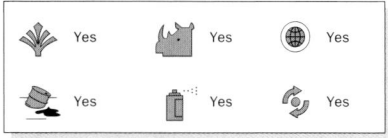

Yes Yes Yes

Yes Yes Yes

Denmark has some of the strictest regulations in Europe, including those aimed at reducing ozone-destroying emissions and water pollution, and met its 2000 recycling target – 54% of all waste – a year early. There was a marked change in policy under the incoming Liberal government of 2001. The bans on house-building in state forests and on the sale of beer in cans were lifted, three planned wind power plants were shelved, and the environment ministry's budget was cut by one-third.

MEDIA

TV ownership high

Daily newspaper circulation 283 per 1000 people

PUBLISHING AND BROADCAST MEDIA

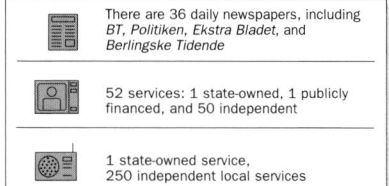

There are 36 daily newspapers, including *BT, Politiken, Ekstra Bladet,* and *Berlingske Tidende*

52 services: 1 state-owned, 1 publicly financed, and 50 independent

1 state-owned service, 250 independent local services

The media have a long history of political independence, and objectivity is prized. The tone of both TV and the press is serious; there is no scandal-mongering tabloid press as found in the US, the UK, and Germany. Invasion of privacy laws are strict. Proposed legislation would extend competition in broadcasting and prepare for the privatization of TV2.

CRIME

No death penalty

3439 prisoners

Down 6% in 2001

CRIME RATES

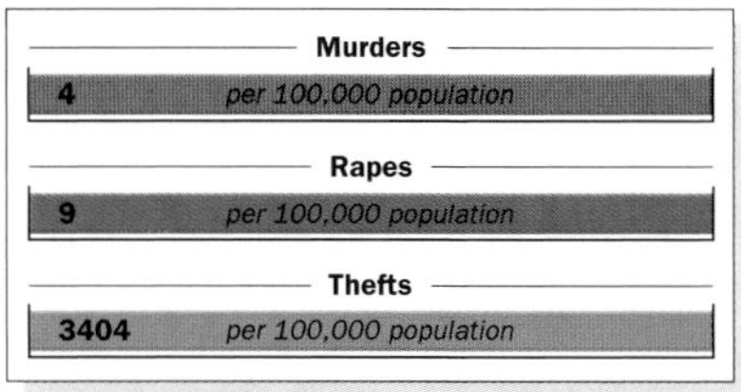

Murders
4 per 100,000 population
Rapes
9 per 100,000 population
Thefts
3404 per 100,000 population

The potential importing of Mafia-style organized crime from eastern Europe, computer hacking, and drug trafficking are problems. In 2001, stricter penalties for violence and rape were promised.

EDUCATION

School leaving age: 16

99%

191,645 students

THE EDUCATION SYSTEM

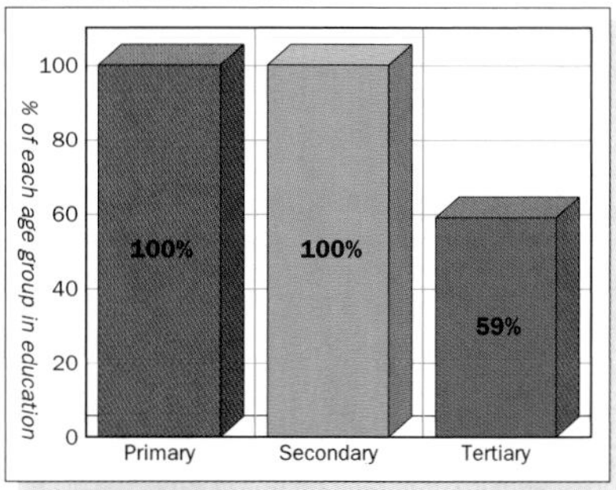

100
80
60
40
20
0
% of each age group in education
100%
100%
59%
Primary
Secondary
Tertiary

The educational level is generally high, in part reflecting the need for a skilled workforce. Formal schooling begins at age seven and is mandatory for nine years. However, most children receive preschool education, and around 90% of pupils go on at the age of 16 to further academic or vocational training. There are five main universities and six specialist institutions. The University of Copenhagen was founded in 1479.

HEALTH

Welfare state health benefits

1 per 294 people

Cancers, heart and cerebrovascular diseases, bronchitis

Denmark was one of the first countries to introduce a state social welfare system. The national health service, which still provides free treatment for almost everything, is the main reason for high taxes – in 2001 almost a quarter of government spending was allocated to social services. Any attempts to reduce expenditure will meet with strong opposition. Repeated surveys show that most Danes prefer their system to those based on private health insurance. In the early 1980s, Denmark had the highest incidence of AIDS in Europe, but after peaking in 1993, the rate has dropped markedly; drug therapies are freely available.

SPENDING

GDP/cap. increase

CONSUMPTION AND SPENDING

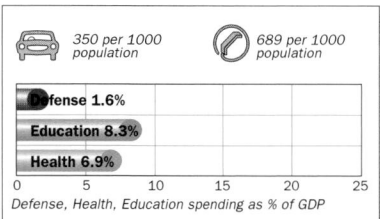

350 per 1000 population

689 per 1000 population

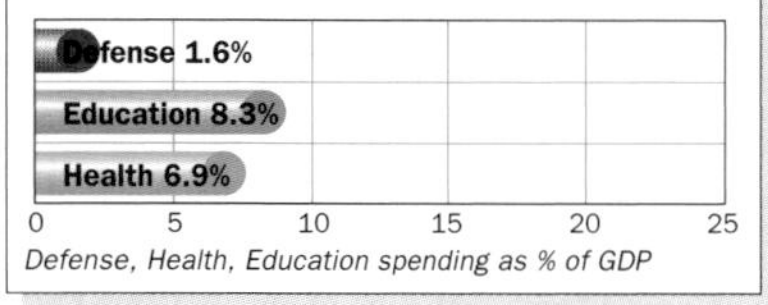

Defense 1.6%
Education 8.3%
Health 6.9%
0
5
10
15
20
25
Defense, Health, Education spending as % of GDP

Denmark forms one of the world's most egalitarian societies. Most Danes are comfortably off. Income distribution is the most even among Western countries and social mobility is high. Free higher education means that access to the professions is more a question of ability than wealth or connections. The generous social security system means that Danes suffer little from social deprivation. The SD government of 1994–2001 created more kindergarten places and increased time off for those with young children. Refugees and recent immigrants tend to be the most disadvantaged members of Danish society.

WORLD RANKING

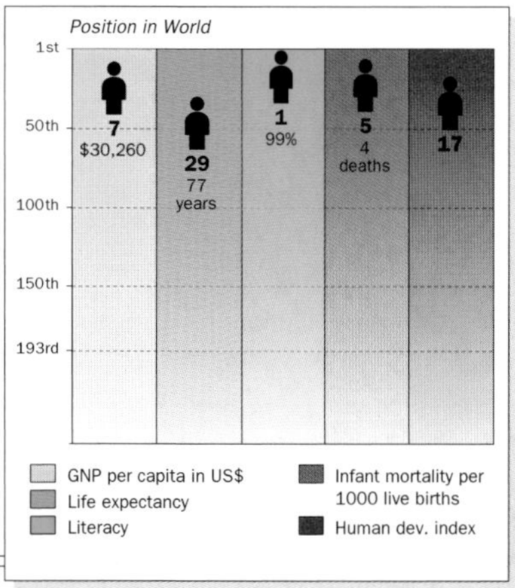

Position in World
1st
50th
100th
150th
193rd
7
$30,260
29
77 years
1
99%
5
4 deaths
17
GNP per capita in US$
Life expectancy
Literacy
Infant mortality per 1000 live births
Human dev. index

See also OVERSEAS TERRITORIES *p.640*

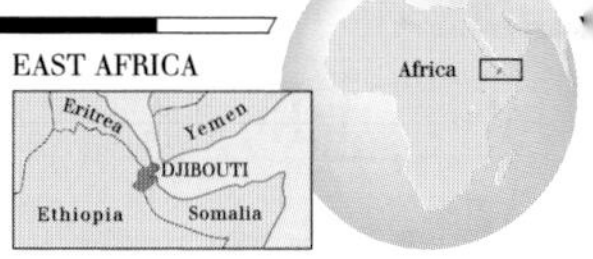
EAST AFRICA
Africa
Eritrea
Yemen
DJIBOUTI
Ethiopia
Somalia

DJIBOUTI

OFFICIAL NAME: Republic of Djibouti **CAPITAL:** Djibouti
POPULATION: 703,000 **CURRENCY:** Djibouti franc **OFFICIAL LANGUAGES:** Arabic and French

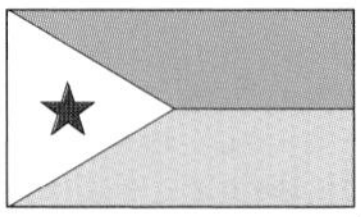

1977 | 1977 | June 27 | DJI | +3 | +253 | .dj

A CITY WITH A DESERT HINTERLAND, Djibouti lies in northeast Africa on the strait linking the Red Sea and the Indian Ocean. Known from 1967 as the French Territory of the Afars and Issas, Djibouti became independent in 1977. Its economy relies on the main port, the railroad to Addis Ababa, and French aid. A guerrilla war which erupted in 1991 as a result of tension between the Issas in the south and the Afars in the north has largely been resolved.

CLIMATE

Hot desert

WEATHER CHART FOR DJIBOUTI

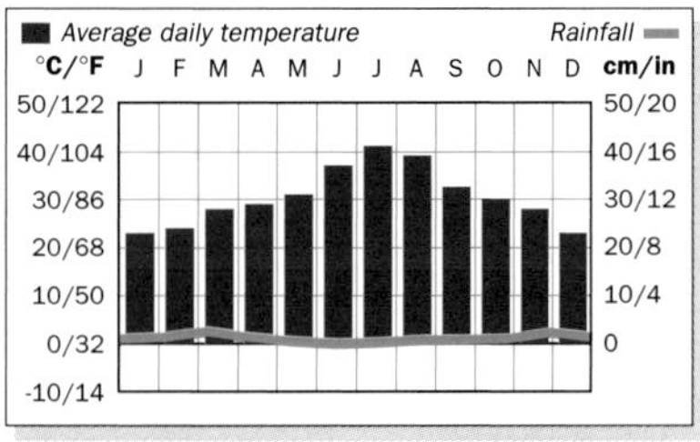
Average daily temperature
Rainfall
°C/°F
J F M A M J J A S O N D
cm/in
50/122
40/104
30/86
20/68
10/50
0/32
-10/14
50/20
40/16
30/12
20/8
10/4
0

Despite extremely low rainfall, the monsoon season is characterized by very humid conditions. Even locals find the heat in June–August hard to bear.

TRANSPORTATION

Drive on right

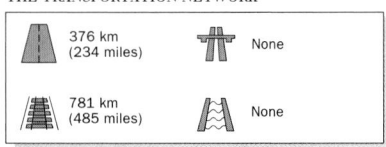

Djibouti 180,452 passengers

11 ships 2691 grt

THE TRANSPORTATION NETWORK

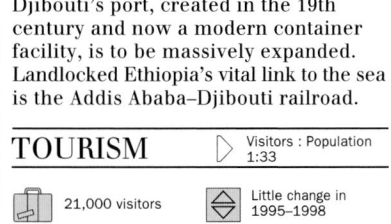

376 km (234 miles)

None

781 km (485 miles)

None

Djibouti's port, created in the 19th century and now a modern container facility, is to be massively expanded. Landlocked Ethiopia's vital link to the sea is the Addis Ababa–Djibouti railroad.

TOURISM

Visitors : Population 1:33

21,000 visitors

Little change in 1995–1998

MAIN TOURIST ARRIVALS

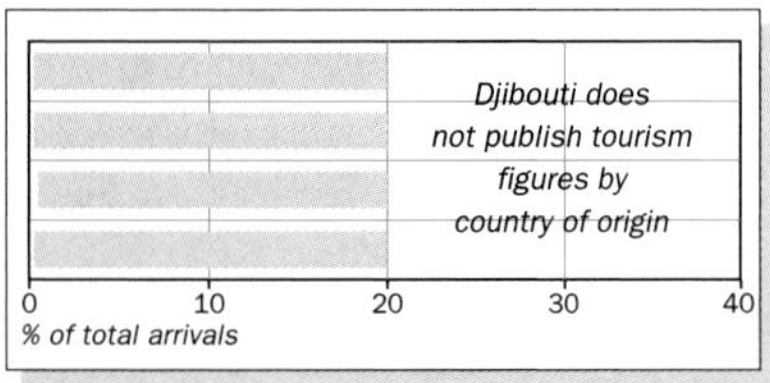
Djibouti does not publish tourism figures by country of origin
0
10
20
30
40
% of total arrivals

Most visitors are passing through on their way to Ethiopia, or coming to see relatives working in Djibouti port.

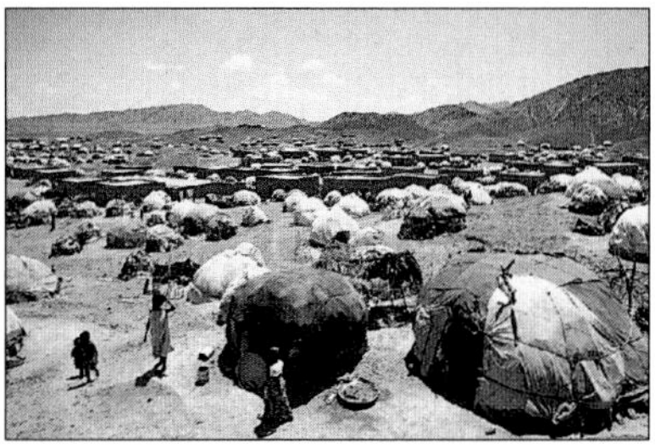

Nomadic Djiboutian village. Nomads form the poorest group in society.

PEOPLE

Pop. density low

Somali, Afar, French, Arabic

30/km² (79/mi²)

THE URBAN/RURAL POPULATION SPLIT

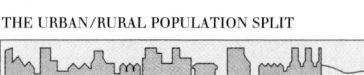

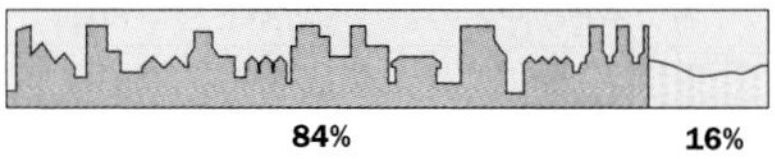
84%
16%

ETHNIC MAKEUP

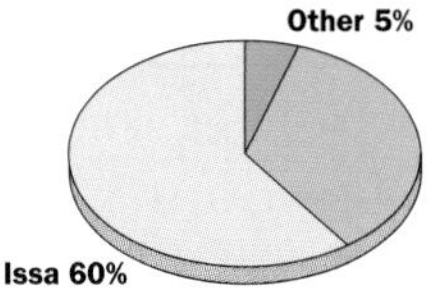
Other 5%
Afar 35%
Issa 60%

The main ethnic groups are the Afars and Issas; tension between these groups developed in 1991 into a guerrilla war. In 2003, 100,000 illegal immigrants were forced to leave. The small rural population is mostly nomadic.

POLITICS

Multiparty elections

2003/2008

President Ismael Omar Guelleh

AT THE LAST ELECTION

National Assembly 65 seats

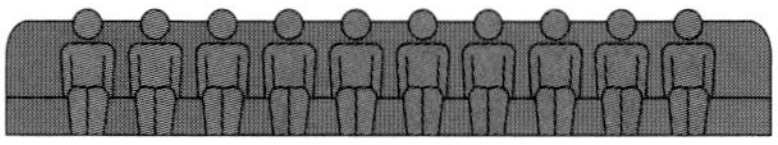

100% UMP

UMP = Union for a Presidential Majority, composed of the Popular Rally for Progress (**RPP**), the Front for the Restoration of Unity and Democracy (**FRUD**), and two other parties

President Hassan Gouled Aptidon, an Issa, backed by France, dominated politics from independence in 1977 until his retirement in 1999. The Afar guerrilla group FRUD took control of much of the country in 1991. The French intervened militarily, and forced Gouled to hold multiparty elections in 1992. FRUD became a legal party after a 1994 peace deal. An alliance of the ruling RPP and FRUD won all seats in elections in 1997, and again within the UMP coalition in 2003, despite competition from recently unbanned opposition parties. Presidential elections in 1999 were won by Ismael Omar Guelleh, a former close aide of Gouled, amid opposition claims of electoral fraud.

DJIBOUTI

Total Area : 23 000 sq. km (8,880 sq. miles)

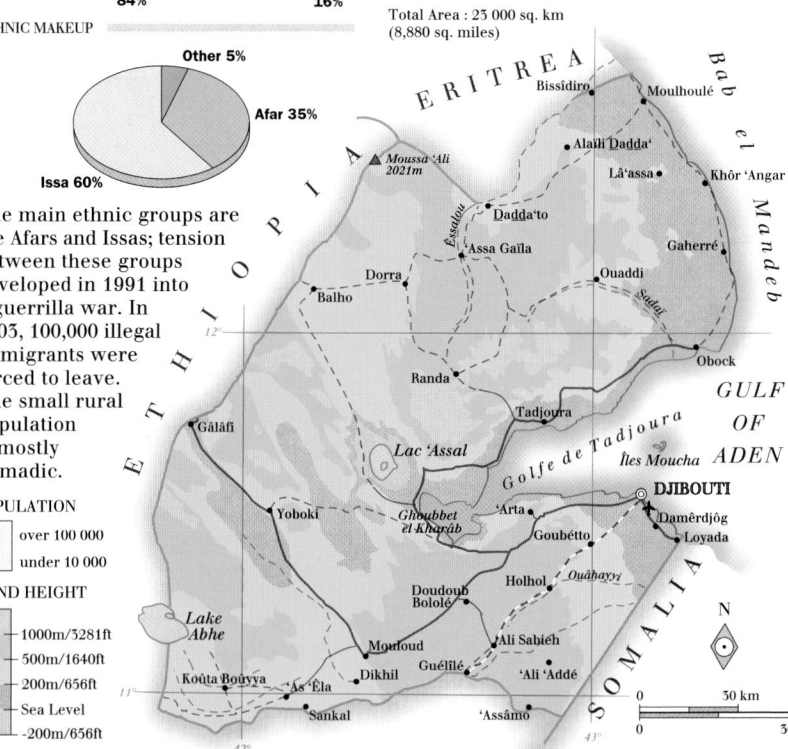

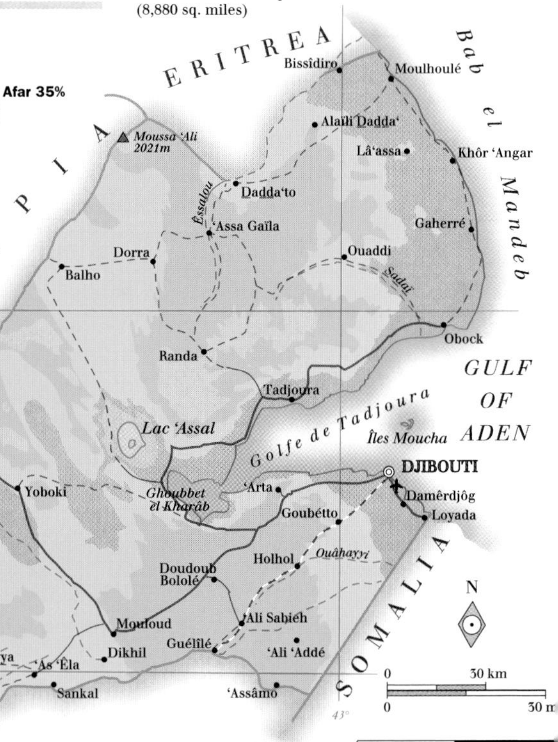
ERITREA
ETHIOPIA
SOMALIA
Bab el Mandeb
GULF OF ADEN
Golfe de Tadjoura
Bissîdiro
Moulhoulé
Alaili Dadda'
Lâ'assa
Khôr 'Angar
Moussa 'Ali 2021m
Dadda'to
Assa Gaïla
Gaherré
Dorra
Ouaddi
Balho
Obock
Randa
Tadjoura
Gâlâfi
Lac 'Assal
Îles Moucha
DJIBOUTI
Yoboki
Ghoubbet el Kharâb
'Arta
Damêrdjôg
Loyada
Goubétto
Holhol
Doudoub Bololé
Lake Abhe
Mouloud
'Ali Sabîeh
Dikhil
Guélîlé
'Ali 'Addé
Koûta Boûyya
As 'Ela
Sankal
'Assâmo
N
0
30 km
POPULATION
over 100 000
under 10 000
LAND HEIGHT
1000m/3281ft
500m/1640ft
200m/656ft
Sea Level
-200m/656ft

WORLD AFFAIRS

Joined UN in 1977

AL | OIF | IGAD | AU | OIC

Djibouti offers Ethiopia its main access to the sea. Links to Eritrea were restored in 2000. Djibouti is active in the Somali reconciliation process. It was quick to support the US "war on terrorism." Ties to France remain important.

AID

Recipient

$78m (receipts) | Up 34% in 2002

Djibouti is reliant on international aid, of which almost half is provided by France. Recent antipoverty projects have been funded by the AfDB.

DEFENSE

No compulsory military service

$21m | Down 5% in 2002

The size of the armed forces is a state secret, but is estimated at 9850 personnel. Up to 2000 US troops are stationed in the country, and there is a 2800-strong French garrison.

ECONOMICS

Inflation 3.6% p.a. (1990–2001)

$590m | 175 Djibouti francs (175)

SCORE CARD

- World GNP Ranking 167th
- GNP per Capita $850
- Balance of Payments .... –$13m
- Inflation 2%
- Unemployment 50%

Strengths

Important location on Red Sea; continuing upgrading of Djibouti and Tadjoura port facilities. Development of information technology infrastructure.

Weaknesses

High poverty and unemployment levels. Dependence on French and US aid and military bases. Regional instability. Stiff competition from other ports on Red Sea.

EXPORTS

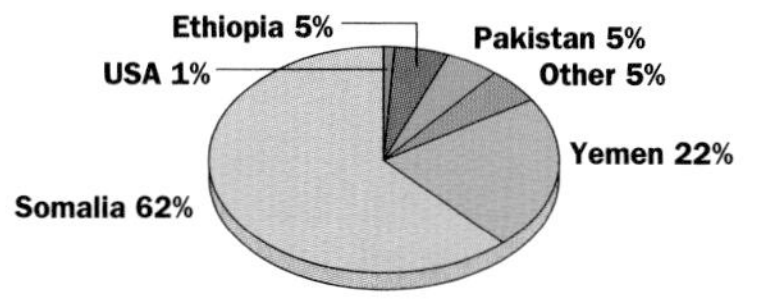
Ethiopia 5%
Pakistan 5%
USA 1%
Other 5%
Yemen 22%
Somalia 62%

IMPORTS

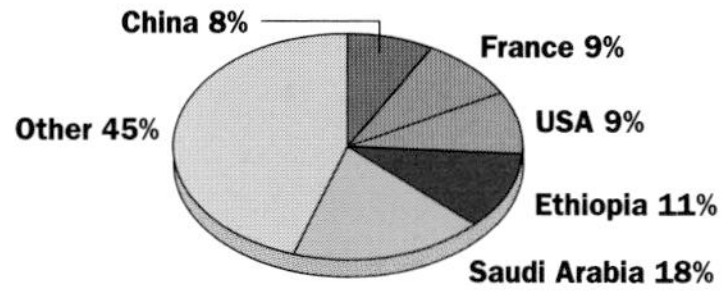
China 8%
France 9%
Other 45%
USA 9%
Ethiopia 11%
Saudi Arabia 18%

RESOURCES

Electric power 88,000 kW

350 tonnes | Not an oil producer

512,000 goats, 466,000 sheep, 297,000 cattle | Gypsum, mica, amethyst, sulfur, natural gas

The few mineral resources are scarcely exploited. Geothermal energy is being developed and natural gas has recently been found. The guerrilla war delayed attempts to develop underground water supplies for agriculture.

ENVIRONMENT

Not available

0.4% | 0.6 tonnes per capita

The concentration of business around Djibouti port means that inland desert areas are largely untouched. Pollution from container ships is of concern.

MEDIA

TV ownership medium

There are no daily newspapers

PUBLISHING AND BROADCAST MEDIA

There are no daily newspapers. The weekly *La Nation de Djibouti* is published by the government

1 state-controlled service | 1 state-controlled service

Djibouti is a member of the Arab Satellite Communications Organization. The media are largely state-controlled, but there is one opposition newspaper.

CRIME

No death penalty

384 prisoners | Up 74% in 1996–1998

The government's human rights record is poor, while FRUD was accused of guerrilla war atrocities. Though narcotics smuggling and prostitution are rife, nonviolent petty crime is more common.

EDUCATION

School leaving age: 11

66% | 496 students

Schooling is mostly in French, while there is a growing emphasis on Islamic teaching. In 2000–2001 higher education was reorganized, with the creation of the core of a future University of Djibouti in association with French universities.

HEALTH

Welfare state health benefits

1 per 10,000 people | Respiratory and heart diseases

AIDS is a growing problem in Djibouti port, with its large prostitute population. At the end of 2003 the UN estimated that there were some 9100 HIV/AIDS sufferers. Small French-financed hospitals cater for the urban elite.

CHRONOLOGY

The French set up a coaling station at Djibouti in the 1880s, to balance the British presence in Aden.

- **1917** Railroad from Addis Ababa reaches Djibouti port.
- **1977** Independence.
- **1981–1992** One-party state.
- **1989** Eruption of violence between Afars and Issas.
- **1991** FRUD launches insurrection against Issa-dominated government.
- **1994** Peace agreement with FRUD.
- **1999** Ismael Omar Guelleh becomes president.
- **2000** Unsuccessful coup attempt by police officers.

SPENDING

GDP/cap. decrease

CONSUMPTION AND SPENDING

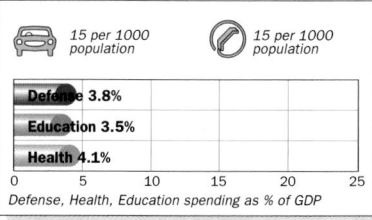

15 per 1000 population | *15 per 1000 population*

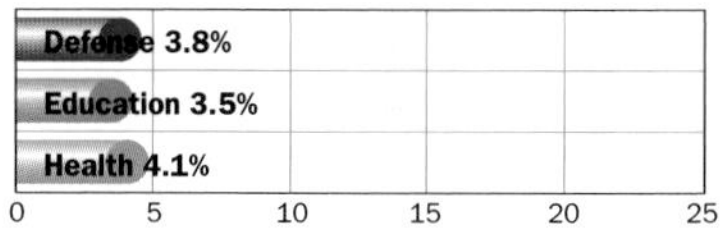
Defense 3.8%
Education 3.5%
Health 4.1%
0
5
10
15
20
25

Defense, Health, Education spending as % of GDP

As happens in many African states, the wealth in Djibouti tends to be concentrated among those closest to government. Djiboutians working in the ports also do well, though much port labor is expatriate. The nomads of the interior are the poorest group. The deployment of US troops to Djibouti is beginning to make a difference: the two biggest employers after the government are the French and US garrisons.

Trade in the mild narcotic qat, or "green gold," which is grown in Ethiopia and shipped through Djibouti, is highly lucrative, to the extent that the state is now taking its share of the profits. In Djibouti, qat chewing is an age-old social ritual.

WORLD RANKING

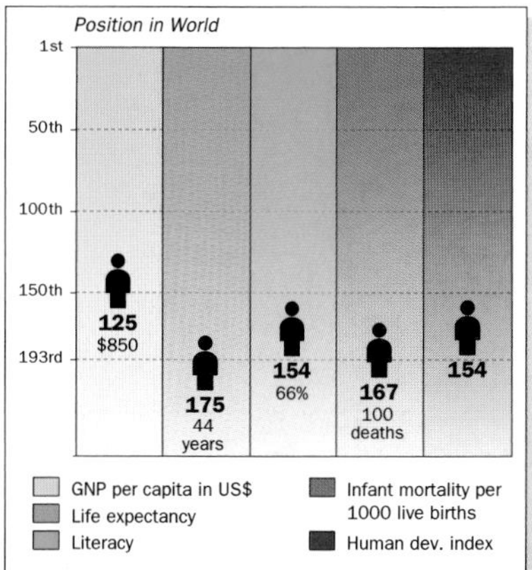
Position in World
1st
50th
100th
150th
193rd
125
$850
175
44
years
154
66%
167
100
deaths
154
GNP per capita in US$
Life expectancy
Literacy
Infant mortality per 1000 live births
Human dev. index

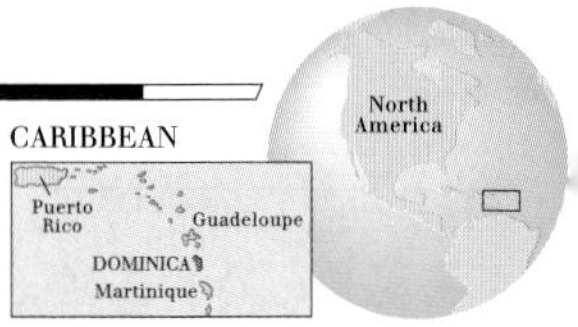
CARIBBEAN
North America
Puerto Rico
Guadeloupe
DOMINICA
Martinique

DOMINICA

OFFICIAL NAME: Commonwealth of Dominica **CAPITAL:** Roseau
POPULATION: 69,655 **CURRENCY:** Eastern Caribbean dollar **OFFICIAL LANGUAGE:** English

1978 | 1978 | Nov 3 | WD | -4 | +1767 | .dm

DOMINICA IS RENOWNED as the Caribbean island that resisted European colonization until the 18th century, when it came under French control, passing to the UK in 1759. It is known as the "Nature Island" because of its spectacular, lush, and abundant flora and fauna, protected by extensive national parks. The most mountainous of the Lesser Antilles, Dominica is located between Guadeloupe and Martinique in the West Indian Windward Islands group. Its volcanic origin has given it very fertile soils and the second-largest boiling lake in the world.

CLIMATE

Tropical oceanic

WEATHER CHART FOR ROSEAU

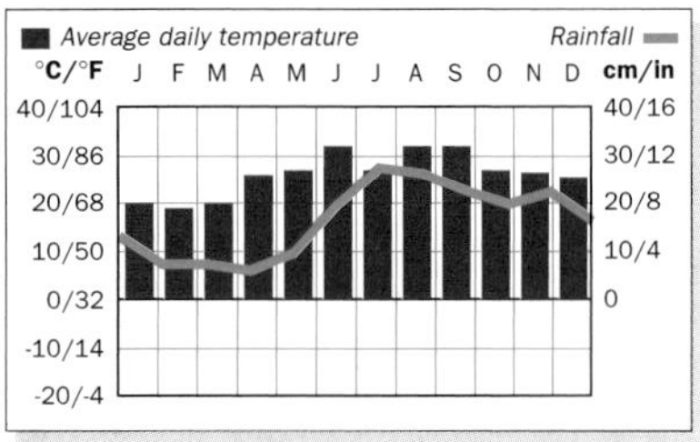
Average daily temperature
Rainfall
°C/°F J F M A M J J A S O N D cm/in
40/104
30/86
20/68
10/50
0/32
-10/14
-20/-4
40/16
30/12
20/8
10/4
0

Like the other Windward Islands in the eastern Caribbean, Dominica is subject to constant trade winds. The rainy season is in the summer, and tropical depressions and hurricanes are likely between June and November. Short, thundery showers in the late afternoon and evening are common throughout the year.

TRANSPORTATION

Drive on left

Canefield, Roseau 108,179 passengers

8 ships 3994 grt

THE TRANSPORTATION NETWORK

390 km (242 miles)

None

None

None

Both airports take only small propeller aircraft. Roads are well maintained. There is no speed limit in rural areas.

TOURISM

Visitors : Population 1:1

69,000 visitors

Up 4% in 2002

MAIN TOURIST ARRIVALS

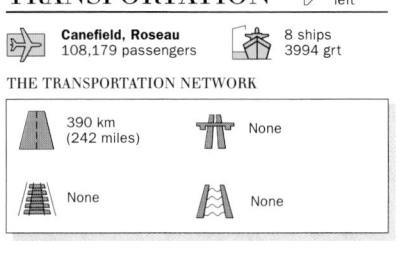

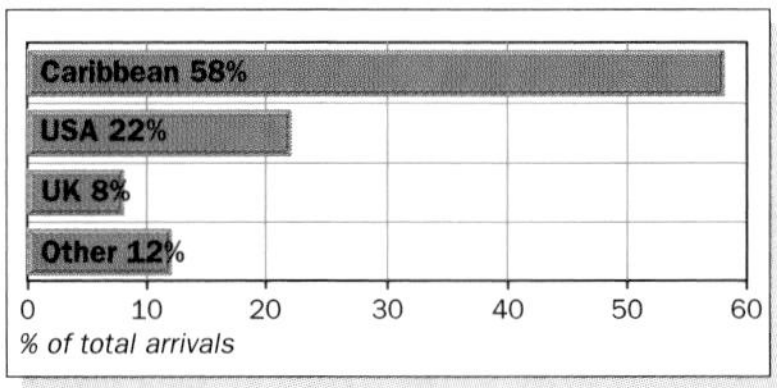
Caribbean 58%
USA 22%
UK 8%
Other 12%
0 10 20 30 40 50 60
% of total arrivals

The national parks, with their rare indigenous birds, hot springs, and sulfur pools, are a major attraction for tourists. However, the lack of an airport able to take commercial jetliners (visitors use connecting flights from Barbados or Antigua) has made Dominica less accessible to mass-market tourism than its neighbors.

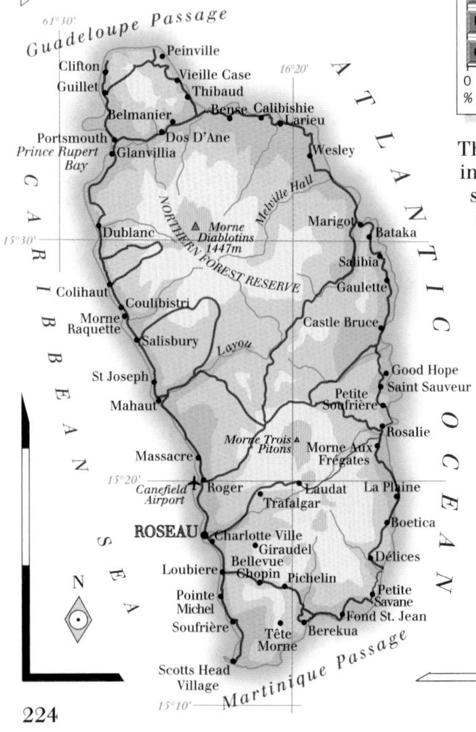
Guadeloupe Passage
Peinville
Clifton
Guillet
Vieille Case
Thibaud
Belmanier
Bense
Calibishie
Larieu
Portsmouth
Prince Rupert Bay
Dos D'Ane
Glanvillia
Wesley
ATLANTIC OCEAN
CARIBBEAN SEA
Melville Hall
NORTHERN FOREST RESERVE
Morne Diablotins 1447m
Dublanc
Marigot
Bataka
Salibia
Colihaut
Gaulette
Coulibistri
Morne Raquette
Castle Bruce
Salisbury
Layou
St Joseph
Good Hope
Saint Sauveur
Mahaut
Petite Soufrière
Rosalie
Morne Trois Pitons
Morne Aux Frégates
Massacre
Canefield Airport
Roger
Laudat
La Plaine
Trafalgar
ROSEAU
Charlotte Ville
Giraudel
Boetica
Bellevue Chopin
Délices
Loubiere
Pichelin
Pointe Michel
Petite Savane
Fond St. Jean
Soufrière
Tête Morne
Berekua
Scotts Head Village
Martinique Passage

DOMINICA

Total Area : 754 sq. km (291 sq. miles)

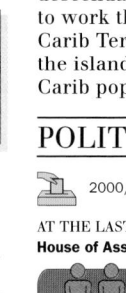

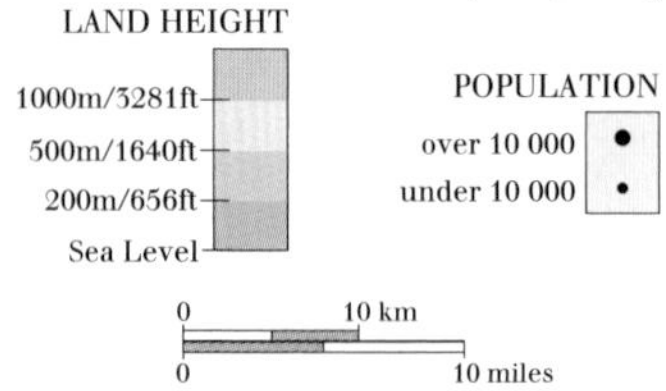
LAND HEIGHT
1000m/3281ft
500m/1640ft
200m/656ft
Sea Level
POPULATION
over 10 000
under 10 000
0 10 km
0 10 miles

PEOPLE

Pop. density medium

French Creole, English

93/km² (240/mi²)

THE URBAN/RURAL POPULATION SPLIT

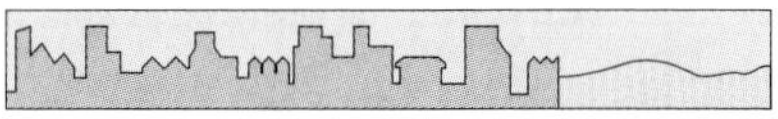
72%
28%

RELIGIOUS PERSUASION

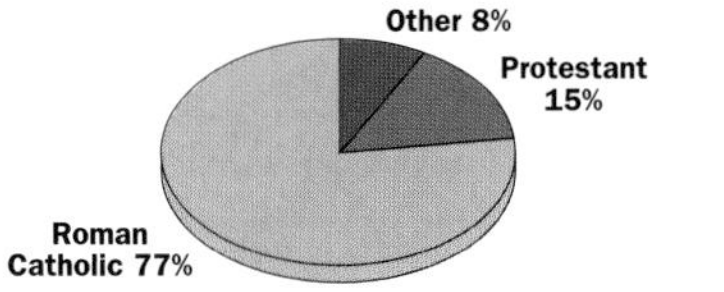
Other 8%
Protestant 15%
Roman Catholic 77%

The majority of Dominicans are descendants of Africans brought over to work the banana plantations. The Carib Territory on the northeast of the island contains the only surviving Carib population in the Caribbean.

POLITICS

Multiparty elections

2000/2005

President Nicholas Liverpool

AT THE LAST ELECTION

House of Assembly 30 seats

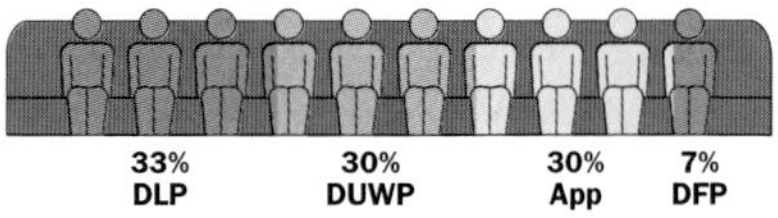
33% DLP
30% DUWP
30% App
7% DFP

DLP = Dominica Labour Party **DUWP** = Dominica United Workers' Party **App** = Appointed **DFP** = Dominica Freedom Party

Nine senators are appointed to the House of Assembly by the head of state

Politicians tend to come from the professional classes – usually young lawyers and doctors. The center-left DUWP narrowly won the 1995 elections, ending 15 years of rule by the right-wing DFP. A further swing to the left produced a DLP victory in 2000. Economic recession has led to a standby agreement with the IMF and subsequent austerity budgets: cutbacks in the public sector have provoked widespread political protest. Prime Minister Pierre Charles died suddenly in January 2004; Roosevelt Skerrit became the world's youngest premier on taking office at the age of 31.

WORLD AFFAIRS

Joined UN in 1978

ACS | Comm | Caricom | OAS | OECS

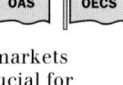

Preferential access to EU markets for Caribbean bananas, crucial for Dominica's economy, was lost after a successful protest to the WTO in 1999 by the US. Dominica maintains close links with France and the UK.

***Inshore fishing boats,** which mostly supply the domestic market, on a typical beach.*

AID

Recipient

US$30m (receipts) | Up 50% in 2002

Dominica is increasingly aid-dependent. Japanese aid "buys" support for whaling, while Chinese aid followed diplomatic recognition in 2004.

DEFENSE

No compulsory military service

Defense forces were officially disbanded in 1981 | Not applicable

Dominica has no armed forces, but it does participate in the US-sponsored Regional Security System.

ECONOMICS

Inflation 2.8% p.a. (1990–2001)

US$216m | 2.7 Eastern Caribbean dollars (2.67)

SCORE CARD

❑ World GNP Ranking	184th
❑ GNP per capita	US$3000
❑ Balance of payments	–US36m
❑ Inflation	0.2%
❑ Unemployment	23%

Strengths

Bananas, though this sector has declined since the loss of EU preferential access. Growing services sector and "eco-tourism." IMF standby credit approved in 2002.

Weaknesses

Dependence on US and EU markets for its banana crop; access threatened by WTO ruling. Low productivity in public sector. Poor infrastructure.

EXPORTS

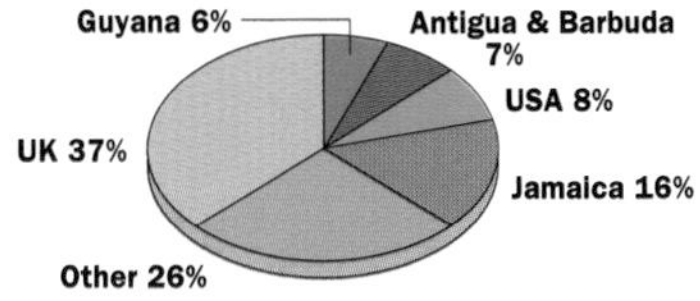
Guyana 6%
Antigua & Barbuda 7%
USA 8%
Jamaica 16%
UK 37%
Other 26%

IMPORTS

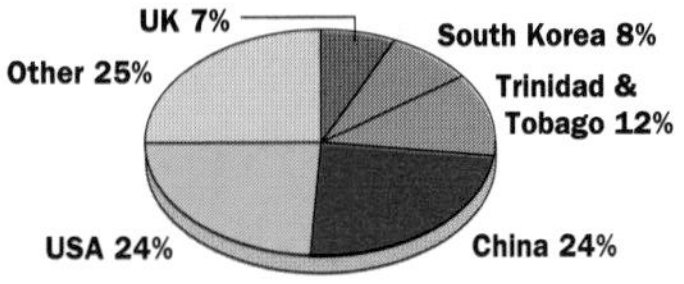
UK 7%
South Korea 8%
Other 25%
Trinidad & Tobago 12%
USA 24%
China 24%

RESOURCES

Electric power 13,000 kW

1157 tonnes | Not an oil producer

13,400 cattle, 9700 goats, 7600 sheep, 190,000 chickens | None

Dominica has no natural resources. A hydroelectric power plant in the Morne Trois Pitons national park provides half the island's power.

ENVIRONMENT

Not available

23% (13% partially protected) | 1.4 tonnes per capita

Increased agriculture and timber harvesting is threatening Dominica's rainforest; already there is more land under cultivation than planned by the government. The current promotion of the rainforest as a tourist attraction poses a threat, as does a possible expansion in HEP generators. Two species of parrot – the imperial, or sisserou, and the red-necked – are threatened, despite conservation orders. Endangered hawksbill turtles, living on coral reefs off the island, are traditionally hunted.

MEDIA

TV ownership medium

There are no daily newspapers

PUBLISHING AND BROADCAST MEDIA

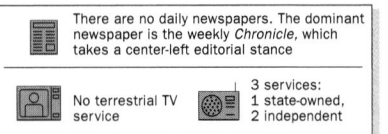

There are no daily newspapers. The dominant newspaper is the weekly *Chronicle*, which takes a center-left editorial stance

No terrestrial TV service | 3 services: 1 state-owned, 2 independent

Two local franchises offer cable TV on a total of 12 channels with selected US programming. Broadcasts from other Caribbean states can also be received. There are four weekly newspapers.

CRIME

Death penalty in use

402 prisoners | Up 13% in 2000

Burglary and armed robbery are the major concerns in Dominica; rates rose notably in 2002, and burglaries account for three-quarters of all crimes. Justice is based on British common law and administered by the Eastern Caribbean Supreme Court, which is based on the island of St. Lucia.

EDUCATION

School leaving age: 17

76% | 461 students

Education is partly based on the old British model, and retains the selective 11-plus exam for entrance into high school. Students go on to the University of the West Indies or, increasingly, to colleges in the US and the UK.

CHRONOLOGY

Colonized first by the French, Dominica came under British control in 1759.

- ❑ **1975** Morne Trois Pitons national park established.
- ❑ **1978** Independence from UK. Patrick John first prime minister.
- ❑ **1980** Eugenia Charles becomes Caribbean's first woman prime minister.
- ❑ **1981** Two coup attempts, backed by Patrick John, foiled.
- ❑ **1995** Opposition DUWP defeats DFP. Dame Eugenia Charles retires after 27 years in politics.
- ❑ **1999** WTO ruling on preferential access for bananas to EU market.
- ❑ **2000** DLP wins elections.

D

HEALTH

Welfare state health benefits

1 per 2000 people | Cancers, heart, cerebrovascular, and infectious diseases

There are four hospitals, but surgery is carried out in only one. Difficult communications hamper emergency access in the interior.

SPENDING

GDP/cap. increase

CONSUMPTION AND SPENDING

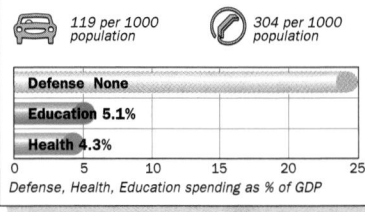

119 per 1000 population | *304 per 1000 population*

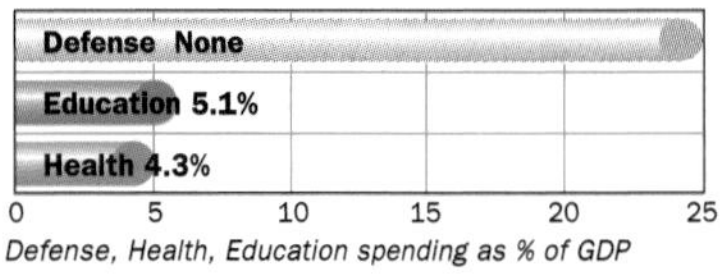
Defense None
Education 5.1%
Health 4.3%
0
5
10
15
20
25
Defense, Health, Education spending as % of GDP

Wealth disparities are not as marked in Dominica as they are on the larger Caribbean islands, but the alleviation of poverty has become a major plank of government policy. Measures taken include increased benefits and help for the country's pensioners.

WORLD RANKING

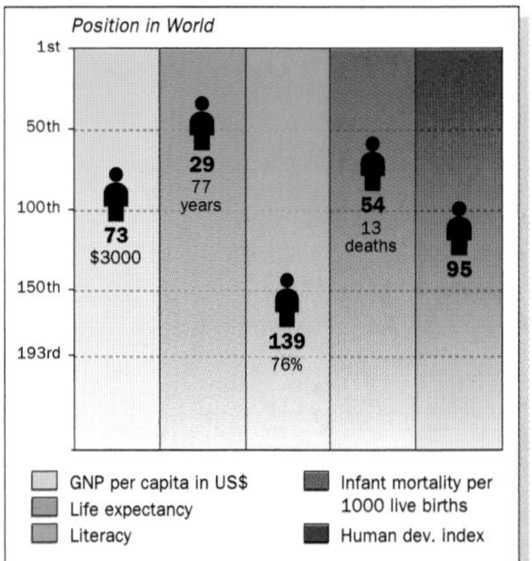
Position in World
1st
50th
100th
150th
193rd
73
$3000
29
77
years
139
76%
54
13
deaths
95
GNP per capita in US$
Life expectancy
Literacy
Infant mortality per 1000 live births
Human dev. index

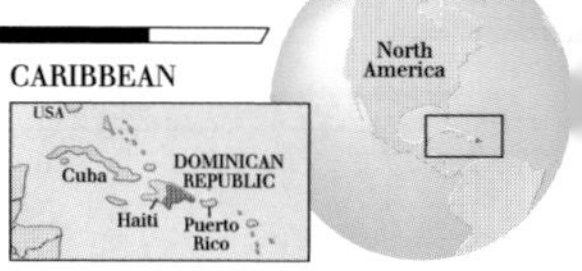

CARIBBEAN
North America
USA
Cuba
DOMINICAN REPUBLIC
Haiti
Puerto Rico

DOMINICAN REPUBLIC

OFFICIAL NAME: Dominican Republic **CAPITAL:** Santo Domingo
POPULATION: 8.7 million **CURRENCY:** Dominican Republic peso **OFFICIAL LANGUAGE:** Spanish

1865 | 1865 | Feb 27 | DOM | -4 | +1809 | .do

THE MOST POPULAR tourist destination in the Caribbean, the Dominican Republic lies 970 km (600 miles) southeast of Florida. Once ruled by Spain, it occupies the eastern two-thirds of the island of Hispaniola and boasts both the region's highest point (Pico Duarte, 3088 m – 10,131 ft) and its lowest (Lake Enriquillo, 44 m – 144 ft – below sea level). Spanish-speaking, it seeks closer ties with the anglophone West Indies.

View south from Pico Duarte along the fertile banks of the Río Yaque del Norte.

CLIMATE

Tropical equatorial/oceanic

WEATHER CHART FOR SANTO DOMINGO

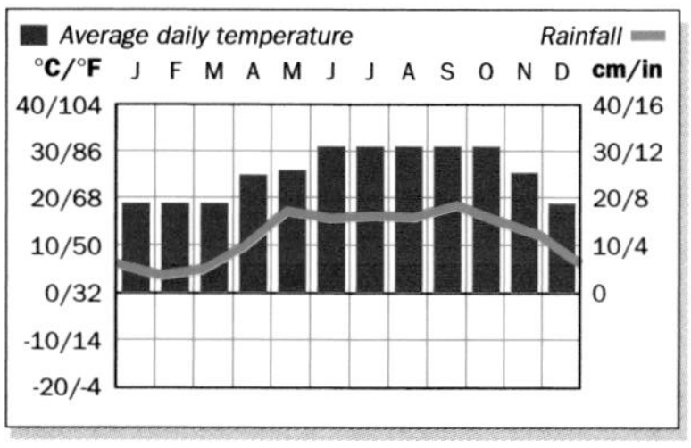

Average daily temperature
Rainfall
°C/°F J F M A M J J A S O N D cm/in
40/104
30/86
20/68
10/50
0/32
-10/14
-20/-4
40/16
30/12
20/8
10/4
0

The trade winds blow all year round, providing relief from the tropical heat and humidity. The hurricane season runs from June until November.

TRANSPORTATION

Drive on right

Punta Cana International, Higüey 2.58m passengers

19 ships 9200 grt

THE TRANSPORTATION NETWORK

3174 km (1972 miles)	None
517 km (321 miles)	None

Urban and rural transportation is poor; railroads are mainly for transporting sugarcane and ores. An international consortium in 1999 won a 30-year concession to operate four airports.

TOURISM

Visitors : Population 1:2.6

3.32m visitors

Up 18% in 2003

MAIN TOURIST ARRIVALS

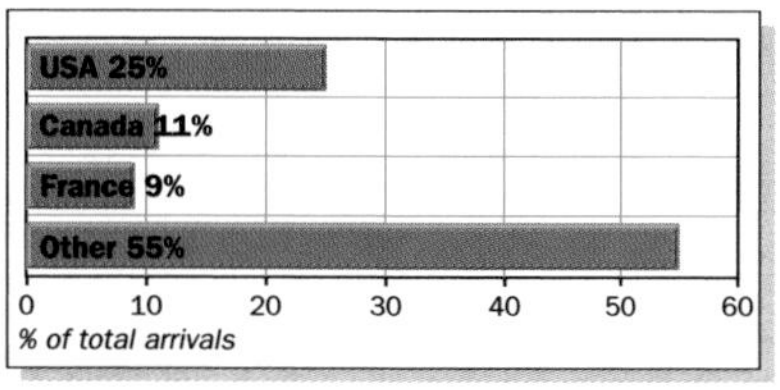

USA 25%
Canada 11%
France 9%
Other 55%
0 10 20 30 40 50 60
% of total arrivals

Ample accommodation and excellent beaches attract many tourists each year, mainly from Europe and North America.

PEOPLE

Pop. density medium

Spanish, French Creole

180/km² (466/mi²)

THE URBAN/RURAL POPULATION SPLIT

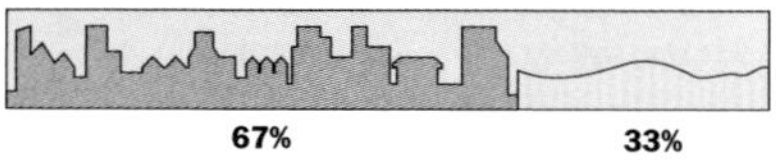

67%
33%

RELIGIOUS PERSUASION

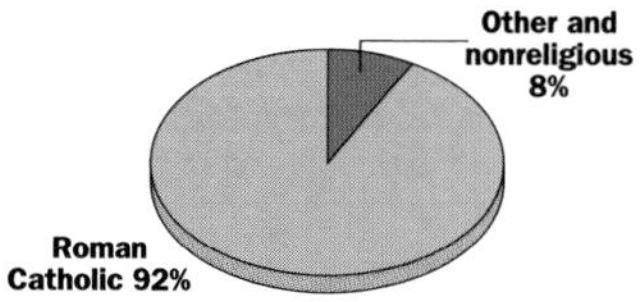

Other and nonreligious 8%
Roman Catholic 92%

The white population, primarily the descendants of Spanish settlers, still own most of the land. The mixed race majority – about 73% – controls much of the republic's commerce, and forms the bulk of the professional middle classes. Blacks, the descendants of Africans, are mainly small-scale farmers and often the victims of latent racism, especially if of Haitian origin. Women in the black community work the farms; in the white and mixed race communities women are starting to make professional careers.

POLITICS

Multiparty elections

L. House 2002/2006
U. House 2002/2006

President Leonel Fernández

AT THE LAST ELECTION

Chamber of Deputies 150 seats

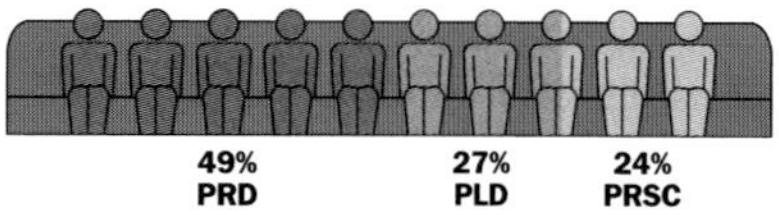

49% PRD
27% PLD
24% PRSC

PRD = Dominican Revolutionary Party **PLD** = Dominican Liberation Party **PRSC** = Christian Social Reform Party

Senate 32 seats

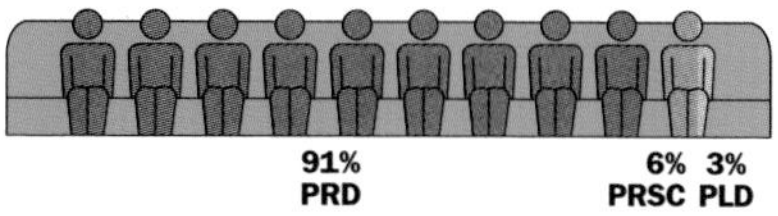

91% PRD
6% PRSC
3% PLD

Decades of conservative rule under Joaquín Balaguer ended in 1996 with the election of Leonel Fernández of the moderate PLD. Hipolito Mejía of the center-left PRD won the presidency in 2000, but his initial popularity was eroded by spiraling living costs, high unemployment, chronic electricity shortages, and major bank collapses. Internal disputes within the PRD, street protests over the terms of an IMF loan, and continuing allegations of corruption led to his defeat and the reelection of Fernández in 2004.

DOMINICAN REPUBLIC

Total Area : 48 730 sq. km (18 815 sq. miles)

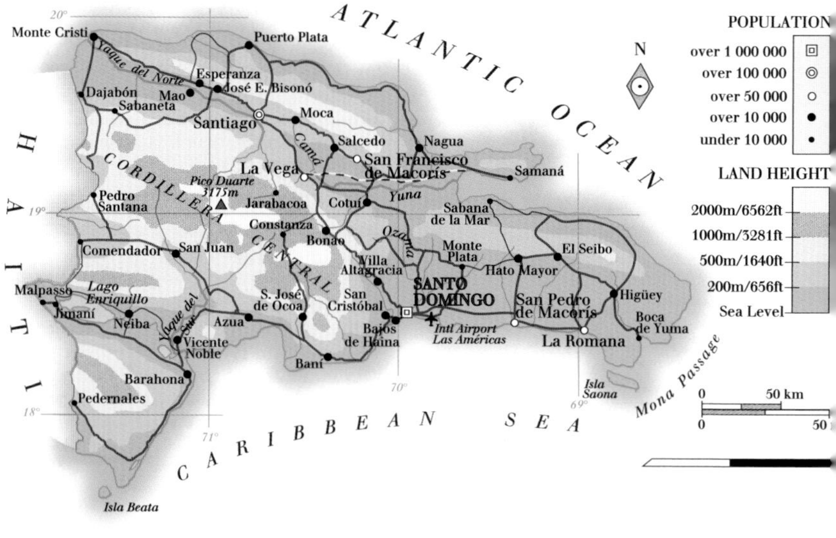

ATLANTIC OCEAN
CARIBBEAN SEA
HAITI
CORDILLERA CENTRAL
Monte Cristi
Puerto Plata
Yaque del Norte
Esperanza
Mao
José E. Bisonó
Dajabón
Sabaneta
Santiago
Moca
Salcedo
Nagua
San Francisco de Macorís
Samaná
La Vega
Pico Duarte 3175m
Jarabacoa
Cotuí
Yuna
Pedro Santana
Sabana de la Mar
Constanza
Bonao
Comendador
San Juan
Monte Plata
El Seibo
Hato Mayor
Villa Altagracia
SANTO DOMINGO
Malpasso
Lago Enriquillo
Jimaní
Neiba
S. José de Ocoa
San Cristóbal
San Pedro de Macorís
Higüey
Azua
Bajos de Haina
Intl Airport Las Américas
La Romana
Boca de Yuna
Vicente Noble
Baní
Barahona
Pedernales
Isla Saona
Mona Passage
Isla Beata
N
POPULATION
over 1 000 000
over 100 000
over 50 000
over 10 000
under 10 000
LAND HEIGHT
2000m/6562ft
1000m/3281ft
500m/1640ft
200m/656ft
Sea Level
0 50 km
0 50

WORLD AFFAIRS

Joined UN in 1945

ACS | Geplac | IBRD | OAS | SELA

Relations with Haiti, with which it shares the island of Hispaniola, are the dominant regional issue: there are some 300,000 Haitian illegal immigrants in the Dominican Republic.

AID

Recipient

$157m (receipts) | Up 45% in 2002

Japan and the US are the largest donors. The IMF reluctantly approved a $657 million loan package in 2004.

DEFENSE

No compulsory military service

$153m | Down 1% in 2002

The Dominican Republic military is the second-largest in the region after Cuba. It focuses on illegal immigration from Haiti and narcotics smuggling. The main arms supplier is the US.

ECONOMICS

Inflation 9.1% p.a. (1990–2001)

$20bn | 45 Dominican Republic pesos (30.6)

SCORE CARD

❑ World GNP Ranking	65th
❑ GNP per Capita	$2320
❑ Balance of Payments	–$875m
❑ Inflation	5.2%
❑ Unemployment	16%

Strengths

Sustained tourism growth. Mining – mainly of nickel and gold – and sugar major sectors. Hand-made cigars, which are biggest sellers in US. Large hidden economy based on transshipment of narcotics to US.

Weaknesses

Peso falling in value. Massive bank fraud exposed in 2003 – $2.2 billion embezzled. Electricity shortages. Rising unemployment. Tourism vulnerable to global slumps.

EXPORTS

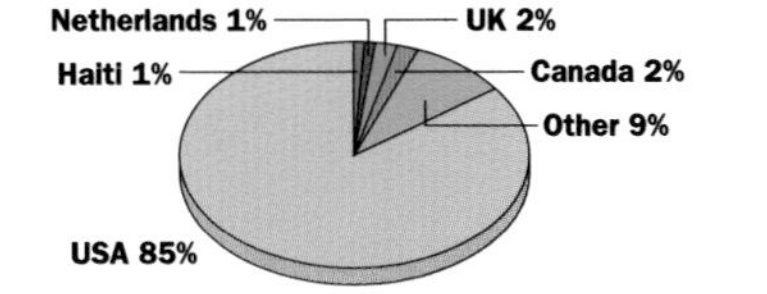
Netherlands 1%
UK 2%
Haiti 1%
Canada 2%
Other 9%
USA 85%

IMPORTS

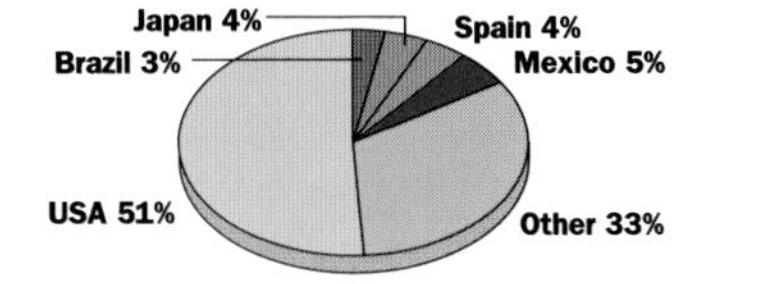
Japan 4%
Spain 4%
Brazil 3%
Mexico 5%
USA 51%
Other 33%

RESOURCES

Electric power 3.6m kW

15,864 tonnes | Not an oil producer; refines 37,300 b/d

2.16m cattle, 577,500 pigs, 46.5m chickens | Ferro-nickel, bauxite, copper, gold, silver

The Dominican Republic is a net energy importer: hydroelectric generators are the only domestic source of power, and electricity blackouts can be a major problem. Oil prospecting has been unsuccessful, and oil is imported from Mexico and Venezuela on preferential terms under the San José Agreement. The Dominican Republic's quota from Venezuela was increased under the 2000 Caracas Accord.

ENVIRONMENT

Sustainability rank: 79th

174% (154% partially protected) including marine areas | 3 tonnes per capita

Forests are threatened by destructive agricultural practices and also by the use of wood as fuel by rural communities. Deforestation has accelerated soil erosion, exacerbating floods in 2004.

MEDIA

TV ownership medium

Daily newspaper circulation 27 per 1000 people

PUBLISHING AND BROADCAST MEDIA

There are 11 daily newspapers, including *Listín Diario*, *Ultima Hora*, *El Nacional*, and *El Caribe*

7 services: 2 state-owned, 5 independent | 131 services: 1 state-owned, 130 independent

Television broadcasts from both Mexico and the US can easily be received in the Dominican Republic.

CRIME

No death penalty

16,789 prisoners | Narcotics-related crime is rising

The Dominican Republic is increasingly used by narcotics cartels as a transit point to the US. Narcotics trafficking and arms smuggling are linked to the high levels of violent crime.

EDUCATION

School leaving age: 17

84% | 176,995 students

State schools are badly underfunded. The state university in Santo Domingo is the oldest university in the Western Hemisphere; the rich send their children to study in the US and Spain.

HEALTH

Welfare state health benefits

1 per 455 people | Heart attacks, infectious and parasitic diseases

Wealthy Dominicans fly to Cuba and the US for treatment. The poor rely on a basic public service, inadequately provided by over 120 state hospitals.

CHRONOLOGY

The 1697 Franco-Spanish partition of Hispaniola left Spain with the eastern two-thirds of the island, now the Dominican Republic.

- ❑ **1865** Independence from Spain.
- ❑ **1930–1961** Gen. Trujillo dictator.
- ❑ **1965** Civil war. US intervention.
- ❑ **1966–1996** Conservative Joaquín Balaguer holds presidency.
- ❑ **1996** Leonel Fernández of moderate PLD succeeds Balaguer.
- ❑ **1998** Major hurricane damage.
- ❑ **2000** Hipolito Mejía of center-left PRD wins presidency.
- ❑ **2004** Fernández reelected.

SPENDING

GDP/cap. increase

CONSUMPTION AND SPENDING

66 per 1000 population | *110 per 1000 population*

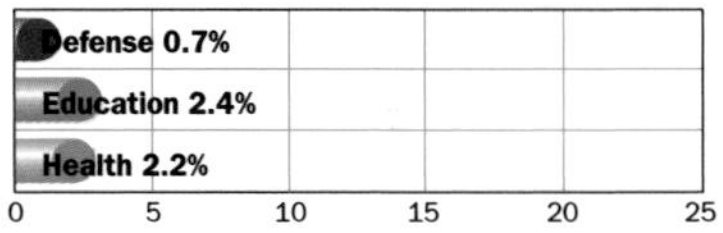
Defense 0.7%
Education 2.4%
Health 2.2%
0
5
10
15
20
25

Defense, Health, Education spending as % of GDP

Great disparities exist between rich and poor. Black Dominicans, accounting for the major proportion of small farmers and unemployed, remain at the bottom of the economic and social ladder. Haitian immigrants are poorly paid, badly treated, and liable to be deported at short notice. Those of mixed race have shown most upward mobility in recent years, but, nevertheless, the old Spanish families still form the wealthiest section of society and retain their grip on valuable estates. In 2003 the collapse of three major banks, through widespread fraud, led the government to agree to a $5 billion bailout which crippled the economy and saw living standards plummet.

WORLD RANKING

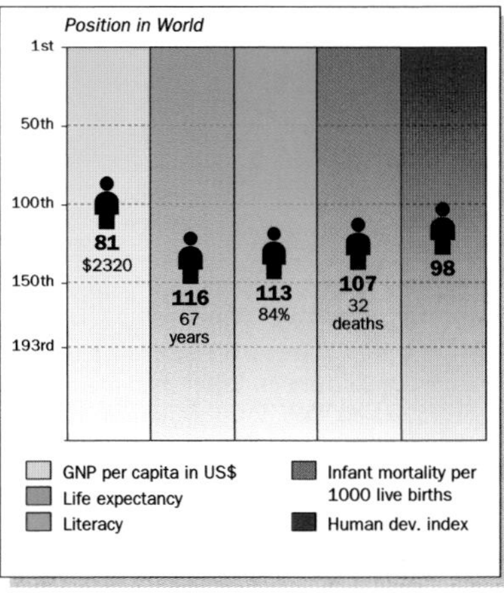
Position in World
1st
50th
100th
150th
193rd
81
$2320
116
67 years
113
84%
107
32 deaths
98
GNP per capita in US$
Life expectancy
Literacy
Infant mortality per 1000 live births
Human dev. index

East Timor

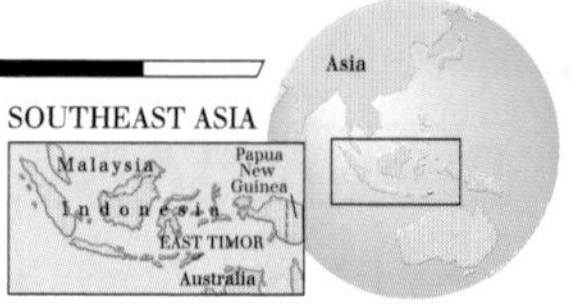
SOUTHEAST ASIA
Asia
Malaysia
Papua New Guinea
Indonesia
EAST TIMOR
Australia

Official Name: Democratic Republic of Timor-Leste **Capital:** Dili **Population:** 778,000
Currency: US dollar **Official Languages:** Tetum (Portuguese/Austronesian) and Portuguese

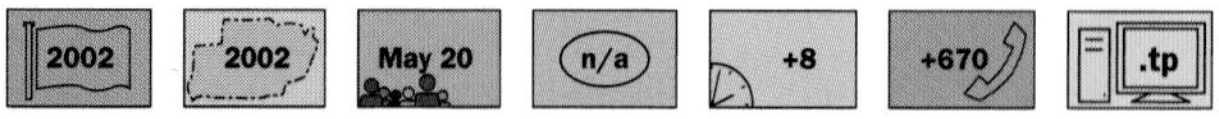
2002
2002
May 20
n/a
+8
+670
.tp

LYING NORTH OF Australia across the Timor Sea, the island of Timor has a narrow coastal plain giving way to forested highlands. Its mountainous backbone rises to 2963 m (9715 ft). The eastern half was colonized for over 400 years by Portugal, then occupied from 1975 by Indonesia, whose forces hunted down all resistance. A referendum in 1999 launched a turbulent transition to independence in May 2002.

CLIMATE

Tropical equatorial

WEATHER CHART FOR DILI

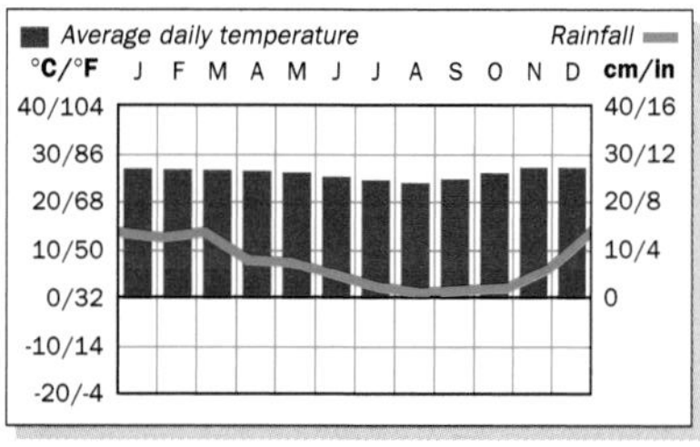
Average daily temperature
Rainfall
°C/°F
J F M A M J J A S O N D
cm/in
40/104
30/86
20/68
10/50
0/32
-10/14
-20/-4
40/16
30/12
20/8
10/4
0

The climate is tropical, with heavy rain from December to March, then dry and increasingly hot weather for the rest of the year, especially in the north.

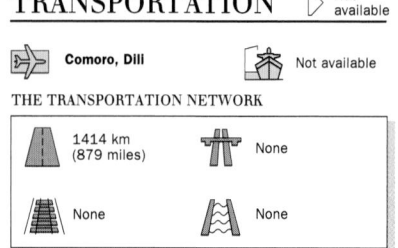

TRANSPORTATION

Not available

Comoro, Dili

Not available

THE TRANSPORTATION NETWORK

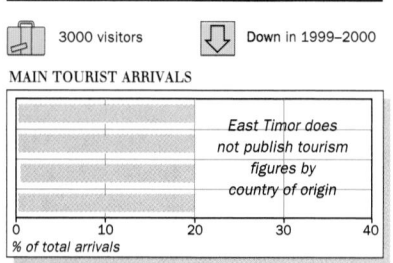

1414 km (879 miles)

None

None

None

Roads are of poor quality and public transportation beyond Dili is unreliable and sparse. There is no railroad.

TOURISM

Visitors : Population 1:259

3000 visitors

Down in 1999–2000

MAIN TOURIST ARRIVALS

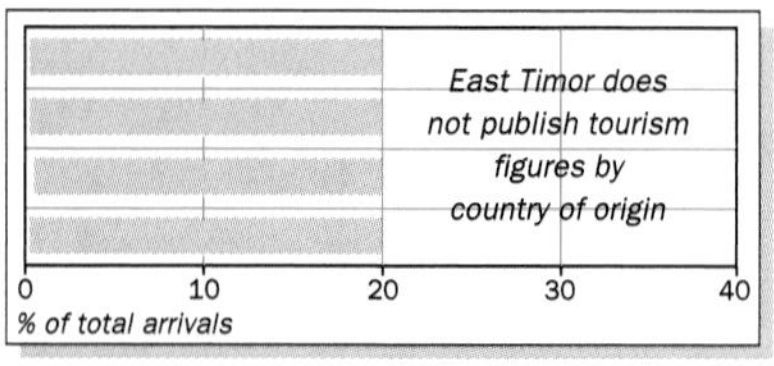
East Timor does not publish tourism figures by country of origin
0
10
20
30
40
% of total arrivals

The number of tourists fell dramatically after the preindependence violence in the region. The country is now trying to market itself as a tourist destination, but infrastructure and accommodation remain poor.

PEOPLE

Pop. density medium

Tetum (Portuguese/Austronesian), Bahasa Indonesia, and Portuguese

53/km² (138/mi²)

THE URBAN/RURAL POPULATION SPLIT

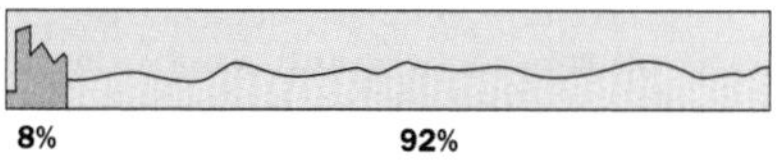
8%
92%

RELIGIOUS PERSUASION

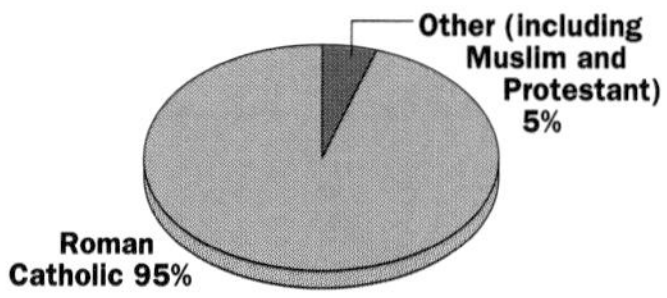
Other (including Muslim and Protestant) 5%
Roman Catholic 95%

East Timor is almost entirely Roman Catholic. The Timorese are a mix of Malay and Papuan peoples, and many indigenous Papuan tribes survive. There is an urban Chinese minority, and ethnic Indonesian settlers became numerous after annexation, constituting 20% of the population by 1999. Preindependence violence was politically rather than ethnically motivated.

Women do not enjoy a high profile in public life. The incidence of domestic violence is notably high.

East Timor

Total Area : 15,007 sq. km (5794 sq. miles)

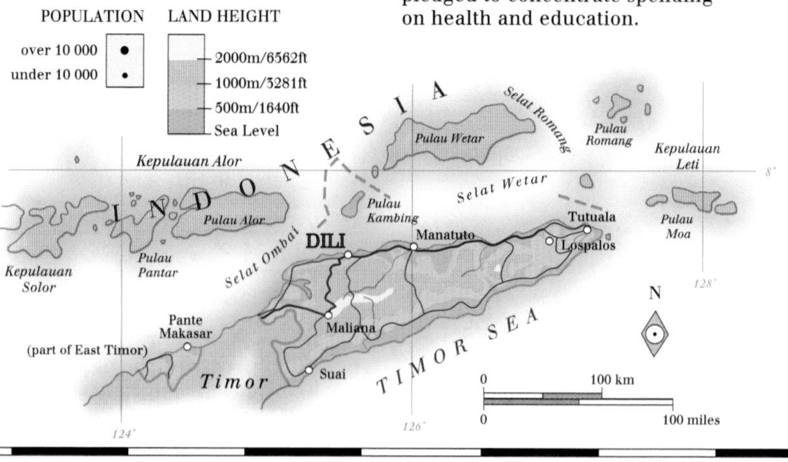
POPULATION
over 10 000
under 10 000
LAND HEIGHT
2000m/6562ft
1000m/3281ft
500m/1640ft
Sea Level
INDONESIA
Selat Romang
Pulau Wetar
Pulau Romang
Kepulauan Leti
Kepulauan Alor
Selat Wetar
Pulau Kambing
Pulau Alor
Tutuala
Lospalos
Manatuto
DILI
Selat Ombai
Pulau Pantar
Kepulauan Solor
Pulau Moa
Pante Makasar
(part of East Timor)
Maliana
Suai
Timor
TIMOR SEA
N
0
100 km
100 miles
124°
126°
128°
8°

POLITICS

Multiparty elections

2001/2006

President Xanana Gusmão

AT THE LAST ELECTION

National Parliament 88 seats

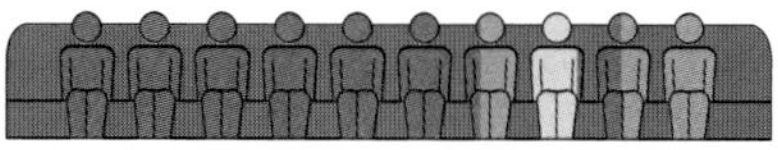
7% PSD
63% Fretilin
8% PD
7% ASDT
15% Others

Fretilin = Revolutionary Front of an Independent East Timor
PD = Democratic Party **PSD** = Social-Democratic Party
ASDT = Timorese Social-Democratic Association

East Timor is an emerging multiparty democracy. The Fretilin movement was the leading voice in the long struggle for independence. Turnout at recent elections was high.

After years of unrest and human rights abuses committed by the Indonesian army, the Indonesian government in 1999 conceded a referendum on East Timor's future. Pro-Indonesian militias went on the rampage, murdering hundreds of people in indiscriminate attacks, and forcing thousands into the Indonesian-controlled western half of the island. An Australian-led international peacekeeping force eventually secured relative calm and organized the promised vote on August 30, 1999. An overwhelming 80% of voters endorsed independence.

The UN Mission in East Timor was given full power over the territory in October 1999. Fretilin emerged as the outright victor in elections in late 2001 to the new Constituent Assembly. Its popular leader, Xanana Gusmão, reversed his decision to retire from politics and was duly elected president in 2002. Independence took effect on May 20 that year.

The new government, headed by Prime Minister Mari Alkatiri, pledged to concentrate spending on health and education.

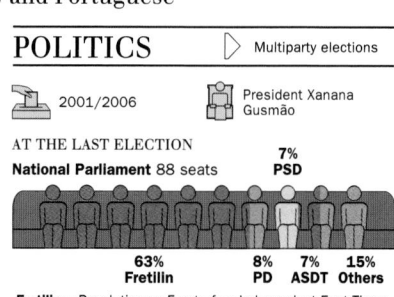

WORLD AFFAIRS

Joined UN in 2002

ACP | ADB | IBRD | CPLP | NAM

Relations with Indonesia remain strained over the issue of justice for past human rights abuses. Australia, one of the few Western countries to recognize Indonesia's annexation of East Timor (while Portugal, the former colonial power, had opposed it), later swung vital support behind the cause of independence. While the Timor Sea Treaty, ratified by Australia in 2003, allows for a joint petroleum development area, the maritime boundary is hotly disputed.

East Timor has joined the UN and the ADB, and has applied to join ASEAN.

AID

Recipient

$220m (receipts) — Up 13% in 2002

International aid provides the backbone of East Timor's GDP. Donors pledged $220 million in 2002. Australia and Portugal are by far the biggest donors.

DEFENSE

No compulsory military service

Not available — Not available

The East Timorese Defense Force was established in 2001, formed from the remnants of proindependence militia. Its role in providing security is likely to expand with the gradual withdrawal of UN peacekeeping forces.

ECONOMICS

Not available

$402m — Currency is US dollar

SCORE CARD

❑ World GNP Ranking	173rd
❑ GNP per Capita	$520
❑ Balance of Payments	$37m
❑ Inflation	0.2%
❑ Unemployment	17%

Strengths

Potential from oil and natural gas reserves in Timor Sea. Traditional agricultural base; coffee exports.

Weaknesses

Infrastructure devastated by 1999 violence. Insecurity deterred investment. Questions over allocation of revenues from disputed Timor Sea.

EXPORTS/IMPORTS

Export and import figures are not available for East Timor. Indonesia is the main trading partner.

***Despite its young age,** East Timor has a strong national identity, based largely on the domination of Roman Catholicism.*

RESOURCES

Electric power 14,400 kW

356 tonnes — Oil figures not available

345,000 pigs, 170,000 cattle, 1.3m chickens — Oil, natural gas, gold, manganese, marble

East Timor has few natural resources. Oil reserves in the Timor Sea are in part claimed by Australia, which has begun drilling in some disputed regions.

ENVIRONMENT

Not available

Not available — 0.2 tonnes per capita

Unrestricted logging under Indonesian rule has greatly diminished important species and contributed to erosion of the country's poor-quality soil.

MEDIA

TV ownership low

Daily newspaper circulation figures are not available

PUBLISHING AND BROADCAST MEDIA

There are 2 daily newspapers, the *Timor Post* and *Suara Timor Lorosae*. The UN Mission publishes the biweekly *Tais Timor*

1 state-controlled service — 4 stations: 1 state-run, 1 run by the Catholic Church, 2 independent

Official newsletters have the highest circulation. Two independent daily papers were established in 2000, the *Timor Post* and *Suara Timor Lorosae*, both partly run by staff of *Suara Timor Timur*, the main preindependence daily.

CRIME

No death penalty

East Timor does not publish prison figures — Crime is rising

Petty and violent crimes are common. Most of the perpetrators of violence in 1999 have yet to be brought to justice.

EDUCATION

Not available

59% — 7500 students

During Indonesian domination, classes were taught in Bahasa Indonesia. The number of students attending school and university has almost recovered from the sharp decline in 1999.

CHRONOLOGY

The Portuguese arrived in Timor in the 1520s. It was formally divided by Portugal and the Netherlands in 1859.

- ❑ **1949** Dutch west Timor becomes part of Indonesia.
- ❑ **1975** Fretilin declares East Timor independent; Indonesia invades.
- ❑ **1991** Massacre of proindependence demonstrators in Dili.
- ❑ **1996** Timorese leaders receive Nobel Peace Prize, raising global awareness.
- ❑ **1999** Indonesian government agrees to hold referendum; resulting violence quelled by UN force.
- ❑ **2001** Elections to new Constituent Assembly; Fretilin wins majority.
- ❑ **2002** Xanana Gusmão elected president. Independence.

HEALTH

Not available

1 per 40,000 people — Not available

Life expectancy in East Timor has historically been lower than in the rest of the Indonesian archipelago. There is a shortage of doctors and midwives.

SPENDING

Not available

CONSUMPTION AND SPENDING

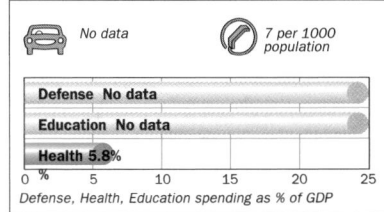

No data — *7 per 1000 population*

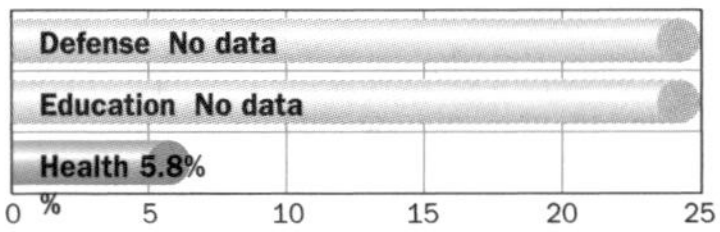
Defense No data
Education No data
Health 5.8%
0 %
5
10
15
20
25

Defense, Health, Education spending as % of GDP

Living standards, already relatively low for the region, were made worse by the events of 1999. Thousands were left homeless. Well-paid UN staff enjoyed a sharply contrasting lifestyle.

WORLD RANKING

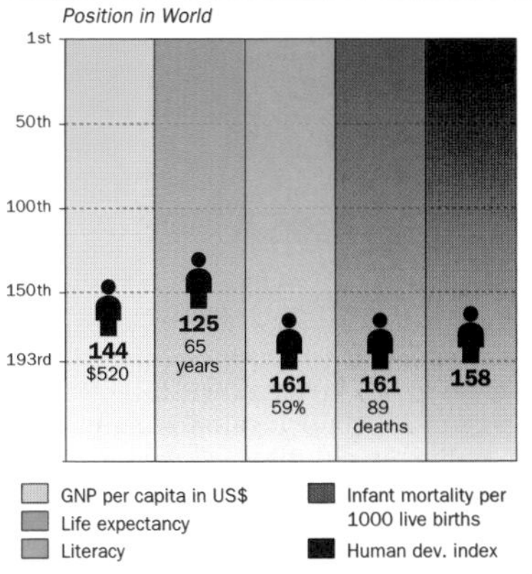
Position in World
1st
50th
100th
150th
193rd
144
$520
125
65
years
161
59%
161
89
deaths
158
GNP per capita in US$
Life expectancy
Literacy
Infant mortality per 1000 live births
Human dev. index

E

ECUADOR

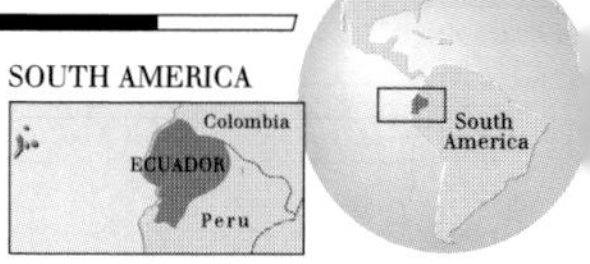
SOUTH AMERICA
Colombia
ECUADOR
Peru
South America

OFFICIAL NAME: Republic of Ecuador **CAPITAL:** Quito
POPULATION: 13 million **CURRENCY:** US dollar **OFFICIAL LANGUAGE:** Spanish

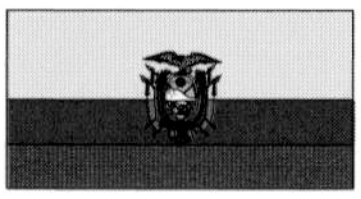

1830 | 1942 | Aug 10 | EC | -5 | +593 | .ec

ONCE PART OF THE INCA heartland, Ecuador lies on the western coast of South America. It was ruled by Spain from 1533, when the last Inca emperor was executed, until independence in 1830. Most Ecuadorians live either in the lowland coastal region or in the Andean Sierra. The Amerindian community is deeply involved in politics. Massive depreciation of the national currency, the sucre, forced the government to adopt the US dollar in 2000.

CLIMATE

Tropical/mountain

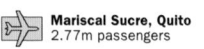

WEATHER CHART FOR QUITO

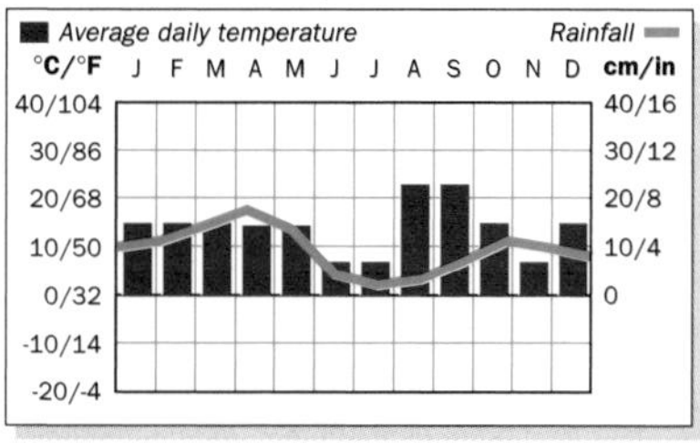
Average daily temperature
Rainfall
°C/°F J F M A M J J A S O N D cm/in
40/104
30/86
20/68
10/50
0/32
-10/14
-20/-4
40/16
30/12
20/8
10/4
0

Climate varies from hot equatorial in the Amazon forests, to dry heat in the south and "perpetual spring" in Quito.

TRANSPORTATION

Drive on right

Mariscal Sucre, Quito 2.77m passengers

182 ships 313,100 grt

THE TRANSPORTATION NETWORK

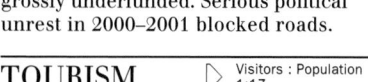

8207 km (5100 miles)

Pan-American Highway

966 km (600 miles)

1500 km (932 miles)

The road network and railroad are grossly underfunded. Serious political unrest in 2000–2001 blocked roads.

TOURISM

Visitors : Population 1:17

759,950 visitors

Up 16% in 2003

MAIN TOURIST ARRIVALS

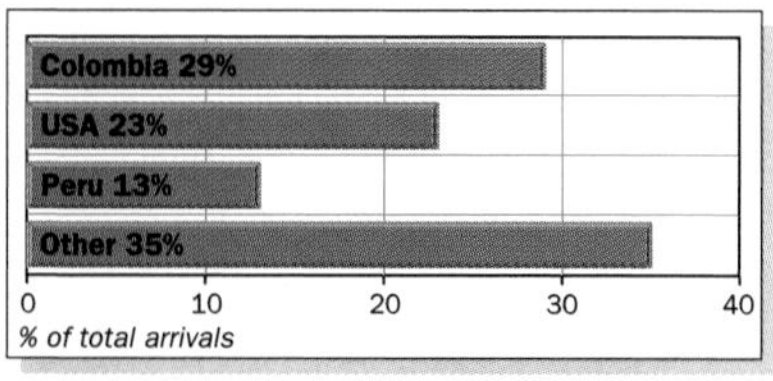
Colombia 29%
USA 23%
Peru 13%
Other 35%
0
10
20
30
40
% of total arrivals

Tourism is growing. Quito, once the capital of the Inca empire, has restored many of its Spanish colonial buildings, including 86 churches. Access to the unique wildlife on the Galapagos Islands is restricted to 60,000 visitors a year.

PEOPLE

Pop. density low

Spanish, Quechua, other Amerindian languages

47/km² (122/mi²)

THE URBAN/RURAL POPULATION SPLIT

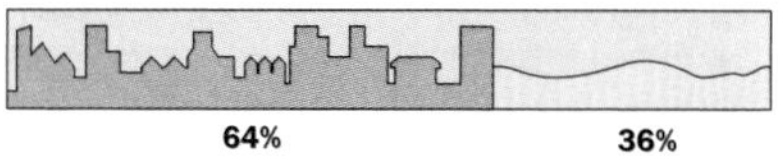
64%
36%

RELIGIOUS PERSUASION

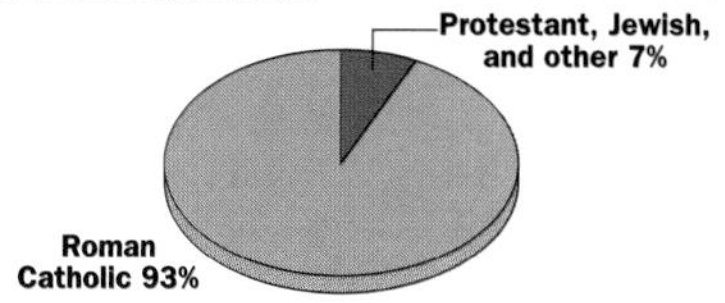
Protestant, Jewish, and other 7%
Roman Catholic 93%

Over half of the population is of Amerindian–Spanish extraction (*mestizo*). Black communities exist on the coast. The Amerindians, who make up about one-quarter of the population, are pressing for Ecuador to be described as a plurinational state, within which the different indigenous communities are recognized as distinct nationalities. The strong and largely unified Amerindian movement is at the forefront of social protests.

POLITICS

Multiparty elections

2002/2006

President Lucio Gutiérrez

AT THE LAST ELECTION

National Congress 100 seats

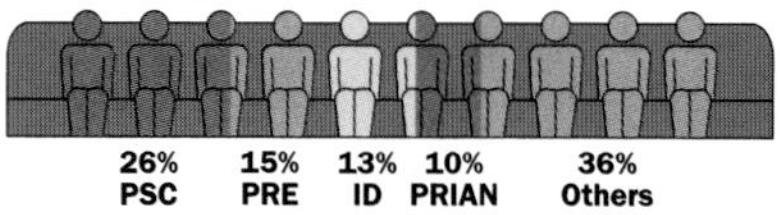
26% PSC
15% PRE
13% ID
10% PRIAN
36% Others

PSC = Social Christian Party
PRE = Ecuadorian Roldosist Party **ID** = Democratic Left
PRIAN = Institutional Renewal Party of Democratic Action

Attempts to rescue the economy through austerity reforms and dollarization since the late 1990s have provoked violent and widespread popular protests; Amerindian groups, headed by the National Indigenous Confederation (CONAIE), form the main opposition. In 2000 the army backed protestors, overthrowing the government. The coup leader, Col. Lucio Gutiérrez, went on to win the presidency in 2002. His market-friendly policies quickly faced opposition from the Congress and CONAIE.

WORLD AFFAIRS

Joined UN in 1945

AP | AmCC | NAM | OAS | RG

Oil prices and access to US and EU markets for bananas are major concerns. There are serious security problems on the border with Colombia.

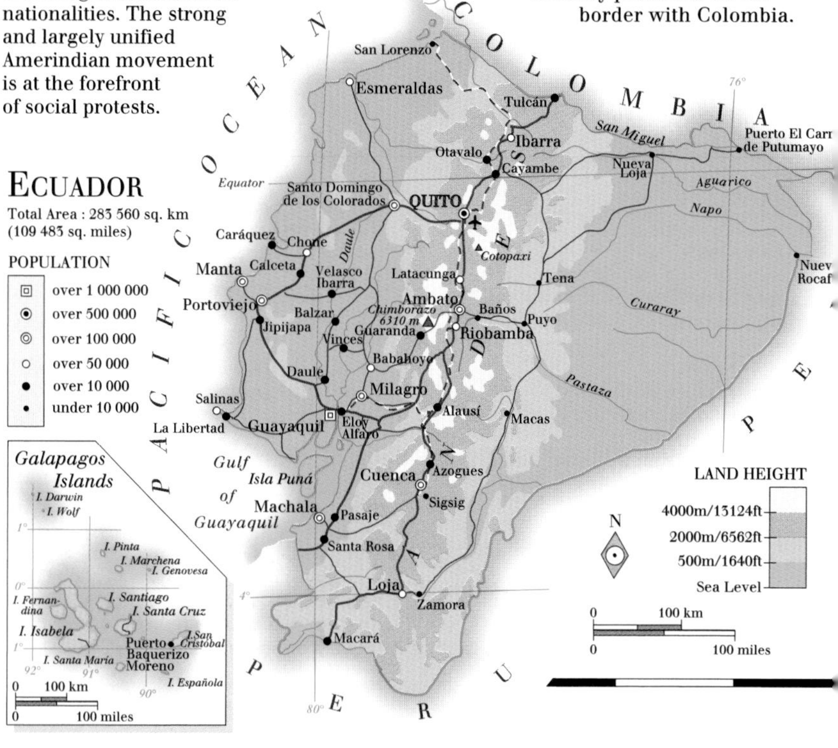
ECUADOR
Total Area : 283 560 sq. km (109 483 sq. miles)
POPULATION
over 1 000 000
over 500 000
over 100 000
over 50 000
over 10 000
under 10 000
COLOMBIA
PACIFIC OCEAN
PERU
San Lorenzo
Esmeraldas
Tulcán
San Miguel
Puerto El Carmen de Putumayo
Ibarra
Otavalo
Cayambe
Nueva Loja
Aguarico
Napo
Equator
Santo Domingo de los Colorados
QUITO
Caráquez
Chone
Cotopaxi
Manta
Calceta
Velasco Ibarra
Latacunga
Tena
Portoviejo
Ambato
Baños
Jipijapa
Balzar
Chimborazo 6310 m
Guaranda
Riobamba
Puyo
Curaray
Vinces
Babahoyo
Daule
Milagro
Pastaza
Salinas
La Libertad
Guayaquil
Eloy Alfaro
Alausí
Macas
Gulf of Guayaquil
Isla Puná
Cuenca
Azogues
Sigsig
Machala
Pasaje
Santa Rosa
Loja
Zamora
Macará
Galapagos Islands
I. Darwin
I. Wolf
I. Pinta
I. Marchena
I. Genovesa
I. Fernandina
I. Santiago
I. Santa Cruz
I. Isabela
I. San Cristóbal
Puerto Baquerizo Moreno
I. Santa María
I. Española
100 km
100 miles
LAND HEIGHT
4000m/13124ft
2000m/6562ft
500m/1640ft
Sea Level
N
0
100 km
100 miles

***Quito is the second-highest** capital in the world, after La Paz in Bolivia. It lies in an Andean valley lined with 30 volcanoes.*

AID

Recipient

$216m (receipts)

Up 25% in 2002

Aid from the US, Japan, Spain, and the IDB alleviates the heavy foreign debt burden. The Galapagos Islands receive generous grants from UNESCO.

DEFENSE

Compulsory military service

$685m

Up 36% in 2002

The army kept out of politics from 1979 until its intervention in 2000. A subsequent change in budgetary processes means that the military is no longer funded directly from oil revenues.

ECONOMICS

Inflation 37% p.a. (1990–2001)

$19.1bn

Currency is US dollar

SCORE CARD

❑ World GNP Ranking	69th
❑ GNP per Capita	$1490
❑ Balance of Payments	–$1.22bn
❑ Inflation	12.5%
❑ Unemployment	11%

Strengths

Net oil exporter. World's biggest banana producer. Fishing industry. US dollar offers stability, but removes control.

Weaknesses

Oil accounts for 50% of exports. Energy crises. High inflation. Financial instability. Poor infrastructure and land productivity.

EXPORTS

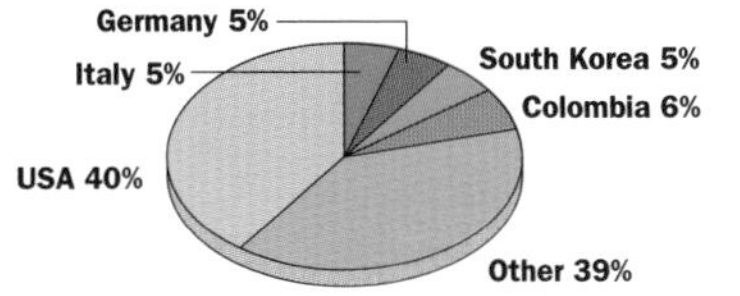
Germany 5%
Italy 5%
South Korea 5%
Colombia 6%
USA 40%
Other 39%

IMPORTS

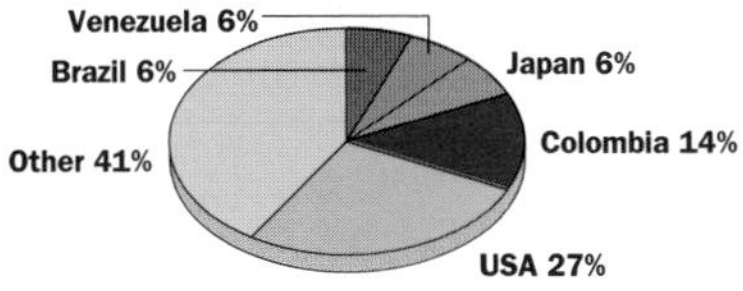
Venezuela 6%
Brazil 6%
Japan 6%
Colombia 14%
Other 41%
USA 27%

RESOURCES

Electric power 3.5m kW

654,539 tonnes

427,000 b/d (reserves 4.6bn barrels)

4.98m cattle, 3.01m pigs, 2.64m sheep, 142m chickens

Oil, natural gas, gold, silver, copper, zinc

The government is encouraging faster oil exploration and higher output. Ecuador left OPEC in 1992. Overfishing is threatening mackerel and squid stocks.

ENVIRONMENT

Sustainability rank: 41st

46% (25% partially protected)

2 tonnes per capita

Oil drilling in new areas of Amazonia threatens indigenous tribes. Tourism, some of it illegal, has upset the delicate ecosystems of the Galapagos Islands; the land iguana is endangered, and black coral is stolen in quantity for souvenirs. The breaching of the *Jessica* oil tanker just offshore in 2001 raised concerns about shipping oil through ecologically sensitive areas.

MEDIA

TV ownership medium

Daily newspaper circulation 96 per 1000 people

PUBLISHING AND BROADCAST MEDIA

There are 29 daily newspapers. The leading papers include *El Commercio* and *Hoy*

67 independent services

321 stations: 1 state-owned, 320 independent

The largely independent press is highly regionalized, based either in the Quito region or around Guayaquil on the coast, which is also a center for commercially run radio stations. There are ten cultural and ten religious radio stations.

CRIME

No death penalty

7716 prisoners

Up 1% in 1999

Right-wing paramilitaries, rumored to be supported by Colombians, were blamed for high-profile murders in the late 1990s. Unprecedented numbers of citizens are applying for arms permits, while the illegal arms trade is thriving. Ecuador's 34 prisons are extremely overcrowded and conditions are poor; protests by prisoners are common. In 2004 prison guards went on strike.

EDUCATION

School leaving age: 14

91%

206,541 students

The government has launched programs to combat high levels of adult illiteracy in rural areas of Ecuador. Secondary schools are badly underfunded.

There are 54 universities, many of them private. Public universities have an open admissions policy.

CHRONOLOGY

Alternating republican and military governments ruled Ecuador from independence in 1830 to 1979.

- ❑ **1941–1942** War with Peru. Loss of mineral-rich El Oro region.
- ❑ **1948–1960** Prosperity from bananas.
- ❑ **1972** Oil production starts.
- ❑ **1979** Return to democracy.
- ❑ **1992** Amerindians win land in Amazonia.
- ❑ **1996–1997** Abdalá Bucarám Ortíz removed from presidency on grounds of mental incapacity.
- ❑ **1998–1999** Economic crisis.
- ❑ **2000** Army sides with Amerindian protestors. Vice President Gustavo Noboa replaces president.
- ❑ **2002** Lucio Gutiérrez, leader of 2000 coup, elected president.

E

HEALTH

Welfare state health benefits

1 per 588 people

Cancers, accidents, heart and infectious diseases

Health care is seriously underfunded. Some services exist in poor urban districts but are still unavailable in many rural areas. Severe budget cuts mean that any improvement will depend on more outside aid.

SPENDING

GDP/cap. increase

CONSUMPTION AND SPENDING

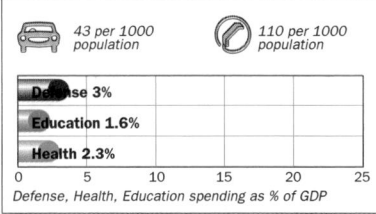

43 per 1000 population

110 per 1000 population

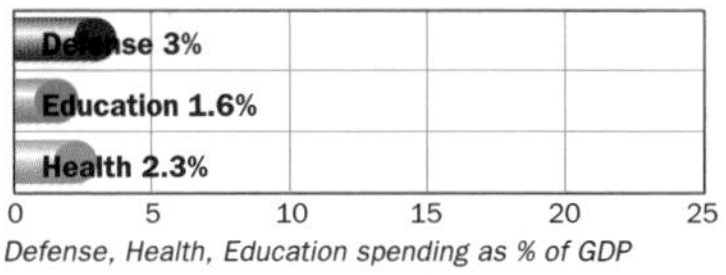
Defense 3%
Education 1.6%
Health 2.3%
0
5
10
15
20
25
Defense, Health, Education spending as % of GDP

The US state aid agency estimates that as much as 70% of the population lives in poverty. Most of these people are concentrated in urban areas.

WORLD RANKING

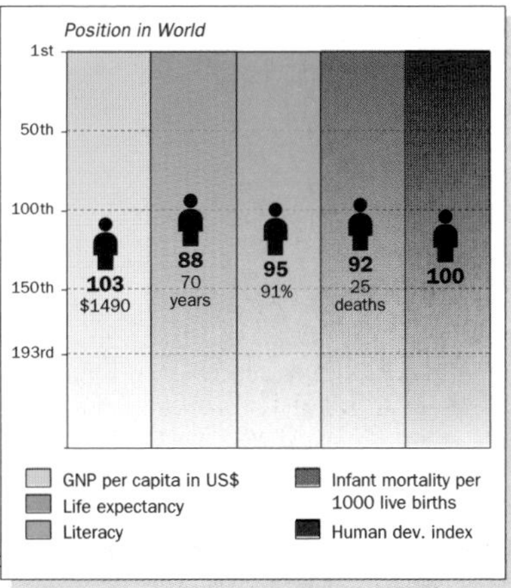
Position in World
1st
50th
100th
150th
193rd
103
$1490
88
70 years
95
91%
92
25 deaths
100
GNP per capita in US$
Life expectancy
Literacy
Infant mortality per 1000 live births
Human dev. index

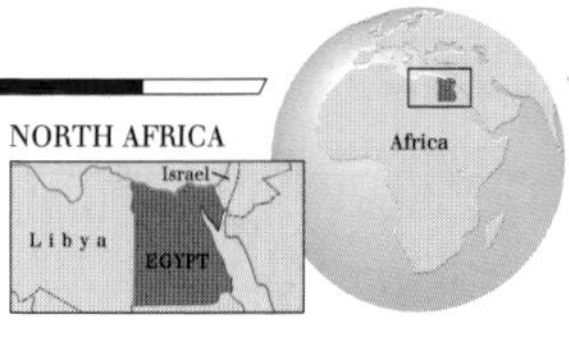
NORTH AFRICA
Israel
Libya
EGYPT
Africa

EGYPT

OFFICIAL NAME: Arab Republic of Egypt **CAPITAL:** Cairo
POPULATION: 71.9 million **CURRENCY:** Egyptian pound **OFFICIAL LANGUAGE:** Arabic

1936
1982
July 23
ET
+2
+20
.eg

OCCUPYING THE NORTHEAST corner of Africa, Egypt is divided by the highly fertile Nile valley separating the arid western desert from the smaller semiarid eastern desert. Egypt's 1979 peace treaty with Israel brought security, the return of the Sinai, and large injections of US aid. Its essentially pro-Western military-backed regime is now being challenged by an increasingly influential Islamic fundamentalist movement.

***18th-Dynasty Temple of Queen Hatshepsut** dating from the Middle Kingdom, c.1480 BCE. It is at Deir el-Bahri on the west bank of the Nile opposite Thebes, Egypt's capital at the time.*

CLIMATE

Hot desert/ Mediterranean

WEATHER CHART FOR CAIRO

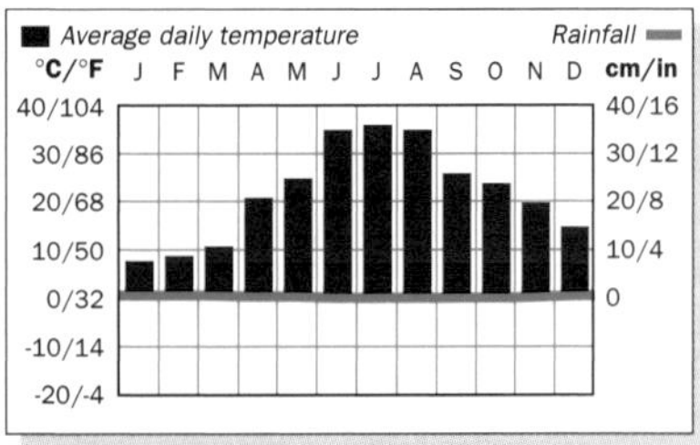
Average daily temperature
Rainfall
°C/°F
J F M A M J J A S O N D
cm/in
40/104
30/86
20/68
10/50
0/32
-10/14
-20/-4
40/16
30/12
20/8
10/4
0

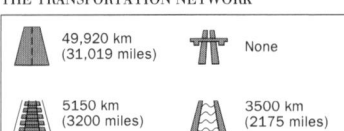

Summers are very hot, especially in the south, but winters are cooler. The only significant rain falls in winter along the Mediterranean coast.

TRANSPORTATION

Drive on right

Cairo International 8.34m passengers

361 ships 1.28m grt

THE TRANSPORTATION NETWORK

49,920 km (31,019 miles)

None

5150 km (3200 miles)

3500 km (2175 miles)

Cities are linked by adequate roads, but the Nile and railroads are the main transportation arteries. Trains are frequently overcrowded. The Suez Canal is a vital international shipping lane.

TOURISM

Visitors : Population 1:13

5.74m visitors

Up 17% in 2003

MAIN TOURIST ARRIVALS

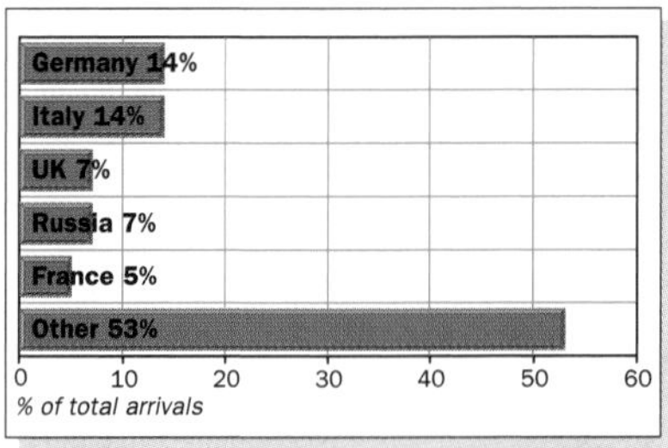
Germany 14%
Italy 14%
UK 7%
Russia 7%
France 5%
Other 53%
0
10
20
30
40
50
60
% of total arrivals

Egypt's wealth of antiquities from its ancient civilizations have made it a key tourist destination since the 1880s. Today, it also offers Nile cruises and some of the world's best scuba diving, notably on the coral reefs near Hurghada on the Red Sea.

Visitor numbers have more than doubled since 1990, though annual trends fluctuated as militant Islamists began targeting Western tourists in the mid-1990s; in an attack in Luxor in November 1997, 58 tourists were killed. Heightened security measures allowed a brief recovery, but the September 2001 terrorist attacks in the US caused a brief contraction in the global tourism industry that affected Islamic countries in particular.

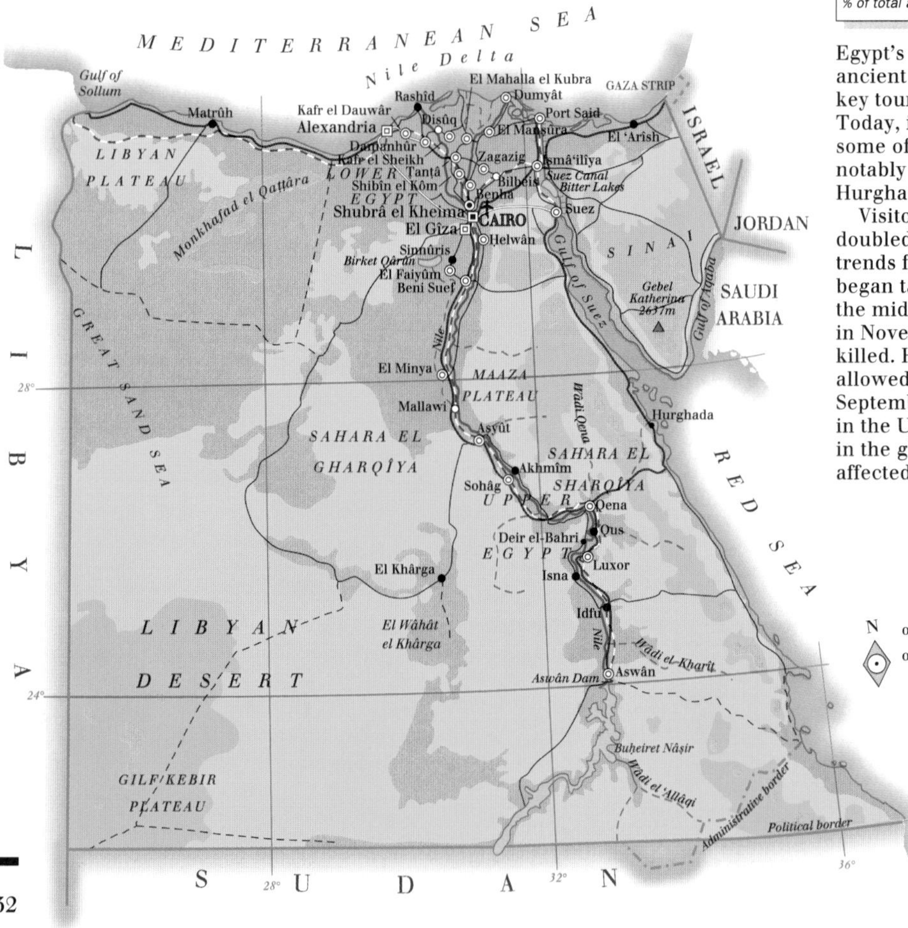
MEDITERRANEAN SEA
Nile Delta
Gulf of Sollum
Matrûh
Rashîd
El Mahalla el Kubra
Dumyât
GAZA STRIP
Kafr el Dauwâr
Alexandria
Disûq
Port Said
El Mansûra
El 'Arîsh
ISRAEL
LIBYAN PLATEAU
Damanhûr
Kafr el Sheikh
Tanta
Zagazig
Ismâ'ilîya
Shibîn el Kôm
LOWER EGYPT
Bilbeis
Suez Canal
Bitter Lakes
Monkhafad el Qattâra
Benha
Shubrâ el Kheima
CAIRO
Suez
JORDAN
El Gîza
Helwân
SINAI
Sinnûris
Birket Qârûn
El Faiyûm
Beni Suef
Gulf of Suez
Gebel Katherina 2637m
Gulf of Aqaba
SAUDI ARABIA
LIBYA
GREAT SAND SEA
Nile
El Minya
MAAZA PLATEAU
Mallawi
Wâdi Qena
Hurghada
SAHARA EL GHARQÎYA
Asyût
SAHARA EL SHARQÎYA
Akhmîm
RED SEA
Sohâg
UPPER EGYPT
Qena
Deir el-Bahri
Qus
Luxor
El Khârga
Isna
Idfu
El Wâhât el Khârga
LIBYAN DESERT
Wâdi el-Kharît
Aswân
Aswân Dam
Buheiret Nâsir
Wâdi el-'Allâqi
GILF KEBIR PLATEAU
Administrative border
Political border
SUDAN
28°
24°
32°
36°

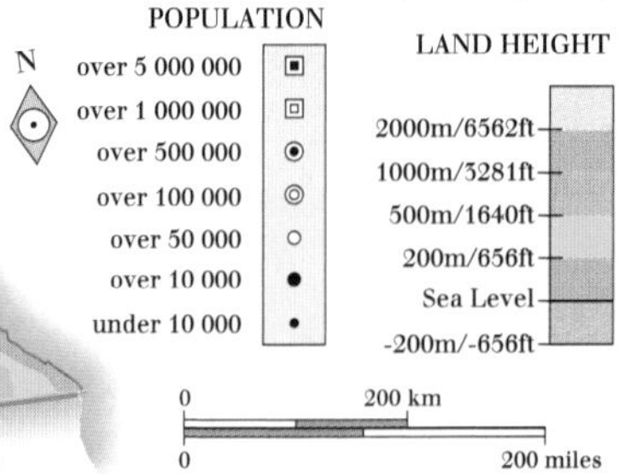
EGYPT
Total Area : 1 001 450 sq. km (386 660 sq. miles)
POPULATION
over 5 000 000
over 1 000 000
over 500 000
over 100 000
over 50 000
over 10 000
under 10 000
N
LAND HEIGHT
2000m/6562ft
1000m/3281ft
500m/1640ft
200m/656ft
Sea Level
-200m/-656ft
0
200 km
0
200 miles

PEOPLE

Pop. density medium

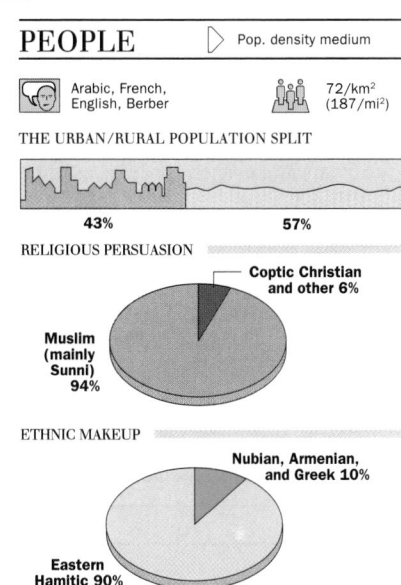

Arabic, French, English, Berber

72/km² (187/mi²)

THE URBAN/RURAL POPULATION SPLIT

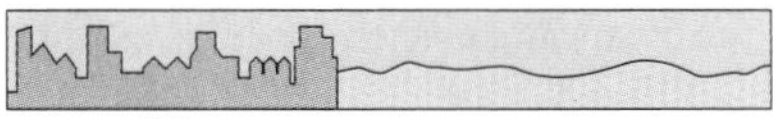
43%
57%

RELIGIOUS PERSUASION

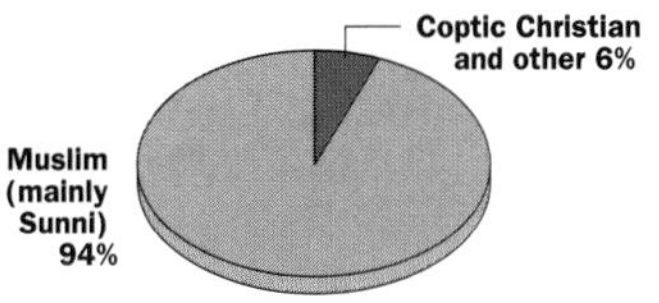
Coptic Christian and other 6%
Muslim (mainly Sunni) 94%

ETHNIC MAKEUP

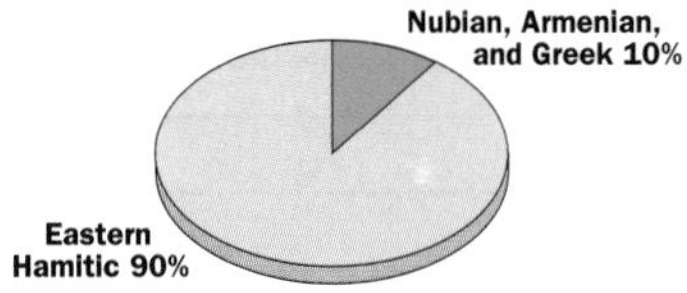
Nubian, Armenian, and Greek 10%
Eastern Hamitic 90%

Most Egyptians speak Arabic, and many also have French or English as a second language. There is a long tradition of ethnic and religious tolerance, though the rise in Islamic fundamentalism has sparked sectarian clashes between Muslims and Copts (Coptic Christianity is one of the earliest branches of Christianity). Berber-speaking communities are found in the western oases; small colonies of Greeks and Armenians live in the larger towns. Many Jews left Egypt for Israel after 1948, but a small community remains in Cairo.

Cairo is the second most populous city in Africa, and Egypt's high birthrate has spawned profound social problems. In 1985 the government set up the National Population Council, which made birth control readily available. Since then, the birthrate has dropped from 39 to 24 per 1000 people, one of the lowest rates in Africa. Despite this decrease, the population is still predicted to reach almost 100 million by 2025. With the growing influence of Islamic fundamentalists, who oppose contraception, the birthrate may accelerate once more.

Egyptian women have been among the most liberated in the Arab world; a 2000 law allows them to initiate divorce proceedings. Islamic fundamentalism may threaten their position, however, particularly in rural areas.

POPULATION AGE BREAKDOWN

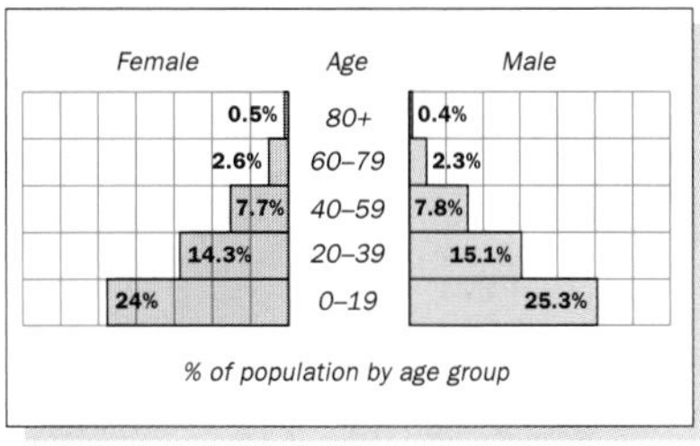
Female
Age
Male
0.5%
80+
0.4%
2.6%
60–79
2.3%
7.7%
40–59
7.8%
14.3%
20–39
15.1%
24%
0–19
25.3%
% of population by age group

POLITICS

Multiparty elections

2000/2005

President Mohammed Hosni Mubarak

AT THE LAST ELECTION

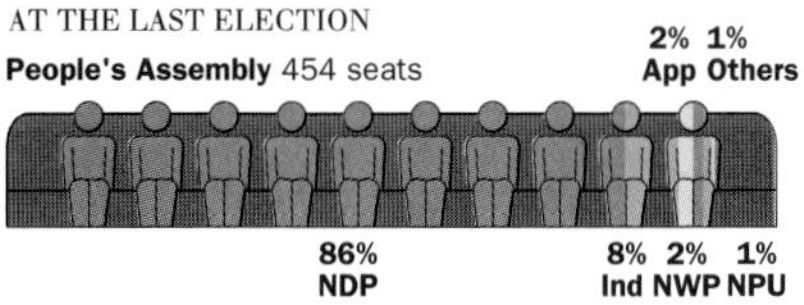
People's Assembly 454 seats
2% App
1% Others
86% NDP
8% Ind
2% NWP
1% NPU

NDP = National Democratic Party **Ind** = Independents **App** = Appointed **NWP** = New Wafd Party **NPU** = National Progressive Unionist Party

Ten members are appointed by the head of state

Egypt is a multiparty system in theory; the monolithic NDP, however, is backed by the military and the all-powerful presidency.

PROFILE

Egypt has had just three leaders since 1954, when Gemal Abdel Nasser, the power behind a military coup in 1952, assumed the presidency. In 1981 President Anwar Sadat was assassinated, but was immediately replaced by Hosni Mubarak, a man of the same mold. The NDP dominates the political process by means of the state of emergency. Elections in 2000 were more transparent than before and candidates associated with the Islamic opposition fared slightly better, though many independents later joined the NDP.

While Nasser promoted Arab socialism along Soviet lines, Sadat and Mubarak (whose fourth six-year term began in 1999) encouraged private enterprise. There has been little parallel liberalization in politics.

MAIN POLITICAL ISSUES

Islamic fundamentalism

Islamist terrorist groups have launched numerous attacks since 1994 on police and tourists, and in 1995 attempted to assassinate Mubarak. Fundamentalists attract both urban and rural poor with promises of improved conditions. Mosques are often the main providers of education and health services that parallel those of the state. Draconian measures are used by the government to counter the terrorist threat, and the only legal Islamic party, the Labor Party, was banned in 2000. Yet religious organizations, especially the long-banned but relatively moderate Muslim Brotherhood, are still allowed to pursue social programs. A 1999 truce between the government and radicals from the Gamaat Islamiya and a wing of Islamic Jihad still holds, though other Egyptian Islamists have become more active in global terrorism, especially since the 2001 terrorist attacks on the US.

Hosni Mubarak, *president since the assassination of Anwar Sadat in 1981.*

Gemal Abdel Nasser, *pan-Arab nationalist, president from 1954 to 1970.*

The state of emergency

In force since the assassination of Sadat by Islamist terrorists in 1981, the national state of emergency has been repeatedly extended by the NDP, most recently in 2003 for a further three years. Emergency laws have been invoked to justify the ban on religious parties, some human rights organizations, and groupings like the Muslim Brotherhood. Human rights groups claim that emergency powers are routinely applied to silence political opponents.

WORLD AFFAIRS

Joined UN in 1945

AL | Damasc | OAPEC | AU | OIC

Egypt has close relations with the West, particularly the US. Its crucial support for the 1991 Gulf War won it a massive economic reward from Saudi Arabia. It is also one of only two Arab countries technically at peace with Israel, for which it faces criticism from hard-line Muslims. Egypt still backs Palestinian autonomy and the US-led "roadmap" for peace, and has worked closely with liberals in the Palestinian National Authority; it brokered a brief cease-fire in 2003 and expects to oversee security in an Israeli-free Gaza from 2006. Israeli military action, however, caused Egypt to downgrade ties with Israel in 2002.

Relations with Iran remain tense: Iran actively supports the Islamist groups operating against the NDP government, and characterizes Egypt as a corrupt state under US influence.

Egypt expressed concern over international treatment of Saddam Hussein's Iraq, Mubarak advocating a diplomatic solution. He has also urged restraint in the "war on terrorism."

Egypt's diplomatic service is the Arab world's largest, and many Egyptians have served on international bodies.

AID

Recipient

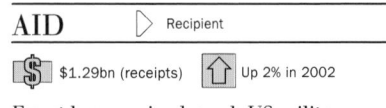

$1.29bn (receipts)

Up 2% in 2002

Egypt has received much US military aid since the late 1970s, and was the top recipient of US aid in 2001–2002, receiving almost twice as much as Israel. Aid was pledged in 2002 to make up for lost tourism revenue.

E

CHRONOLOGY

Egypt's centuries-long Ottoman occupation ended in 1914 when it came under direct British rule. It became fully independent in 1936. Army officers led by Lt. Col. Gemal Abdel Nasser seized power in 1952.

- **1953** Political parties dissolved, monarchy abolished. Republic proclaimed with Gen. Mohammed Neguib as president.
- **1954** Nasser deposes Neguib to become president.
- **1956** Suez Crisis following nationalization of Suez Canal. Israeli, British, and French forces invade, but withdraw after pressure from UN and US.
- **1958** Egypt merges with Syria as United Arab Republic.
- **1960–1970** Aswan High Dam built.
- **1961** Syria breaks away from union with Egypt.
- **1967** Six-Day War with Israel; loss of Sinai.
- **1970** Nasser dies; succeeded by Anwar Sadat.
- **1971** Readopts the name Egypt. Islam becomes state religion.
- **1972** Soviet military advisers dismissed from Egypt.
- **1974–1975** US brokers partial Israeli withdrawal from Sinai.
- **1977** Sadat visits Jerusalem: first ever meeting between Egyptian president and Israeli prime minister.
- **1978** Camp David accords, brokered by US, signed by Egypt and Israel.
- **1979** Egypt and Israel sign peace treaty, alienating most Arab states.
- **1981** Sadat assassinated; succeeded by Lt. Gen. Hosni Mubarak.
- **1982** Last Israeli troops leave Sinai.
- **1986** President Mubarak meets Israeli prime minister Shimon Peres to discuss Middle East peace.
- **1989** After 12-year rift, Egypt and Syria resume diplomatic relations.
- **1990–1991** Egypt participates in UN operation to liberate Kuwait.
- **1991** Damascus Declaration provides for a defense pact between Egypt, Syria, and GCC countries against Iraq.
- **1994–1998** Islamist extremists begin campaign of terrorism, killing civilians and tourists. Government steps up countermeasures.
- **1999** Banned Gamaat Islamiya ends campaign to overthrow government.
- **2000** Egypt recalls ambassador to Israel because of escalating Israeli aggression against Palestinians.
- **2001** Heavy decline in tourist numbers following September 2001 attack on US.
- **2003** State of emergency extended for further three years.

DEFENSE

Compulsory military service

$3.12bn

No change in 2002

EGYPTIAN ARMED FORCES

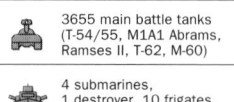

3655 main battle tanks (T-54/55, M1A1 Abrams, Ramses II, T-62, M-60)	320,000 personnel
4 submarines, 1 destroyer, 10 frigates, and 47 patrol boats	20,000 personnel
579 combat aircraft (F-16, Alpha Jet, PRC J-6/7, F-4E, Mirage 5, MiG-21)	30,000 personnel
None	

Egypt's armed forces, the largest in the Arab world, have not seen serious action since the 1991 liberation of Kuwait. Egypt has made modest contributions to peacekeeping missions since then. More than 400,000 reservists augment the regular troops.

After the 1978 Camp David framework agreements were reached with Israel, Egypt stopped buying Soviet weapons and aircraft, and turned instead to Western suppliers. Cooperation with the US has reaped dividends in the form of access to more sophisticated defense equipment and improved training. Egypt has a small arms industry and sells light weapons, notably its version of the Soviet-developed AK-47 assault rifle, to other developing countries.

ECONOMICS

Inflation 7.8% p.a. (1990–2001)

$97.6bn

6.1899 Egyptian pounds (6.056)

SCORE CARD

- WORLD GNP RANKING....................37th
- GNP per Capita....................$1470
- BALANCE OF PAYMENTS....................$470m
- INFLATION....................2.7%
- UNEMPLOYMENT....................9%

EXPORTS

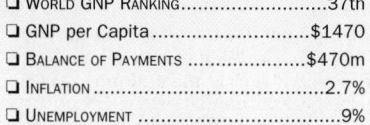

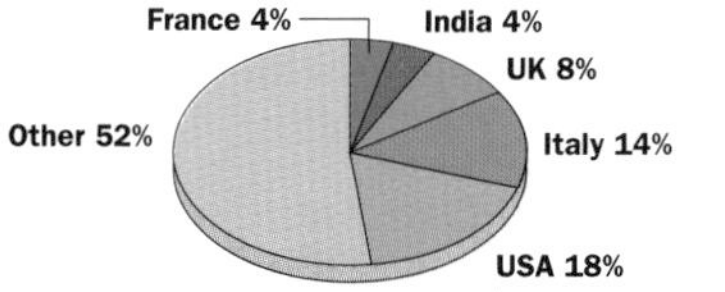
France 4%
India 4%
UK 8%
Italy 14%
USA 18%
Other 52%

IMPORTS

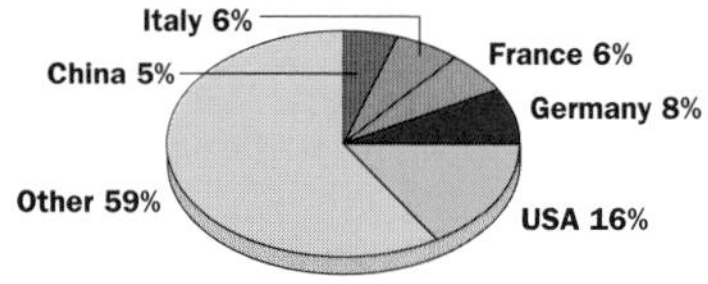
Italy 6%
China 5%
France 6%
Germany 8%
USA 16%
Other 59%

STRENGTHS

Oil and gas revenues. Well-developed tourist infrastructure. Agriculture, especially cotton. Overseas remittances. Light industry and manufacturing. Fiscal and structural reforms: inflation and deficit down, investment up. Planned gas pipeline to Lebanon.

WEAKNESSES

Tourism hit by "war on terrorism." Dependence on imported technology. Rural poverty. Currency devaluations.

PROFILE

The Soviet-inspired economic model pursued by Nasser was rigid and highly centralized. It gave Egypt one of the largest public sectors of all developing countries. Economic restrictions were first relaxed in 1974. President Sadat's "open-door" policy (*infitah*) allowed joint ventures with foreign partners for the first time, though only business classes profited. Most Egyptians suffered from new austerity measures.

Under President Mubarak, economic reform has quickened and there is more awareness of poverty and unemployment. Priorities now are to encourage manufacturing, sustain economic growth, and reduce the gap between rich and poor.

ECONOMIC PERFORMANCE INDICATOR

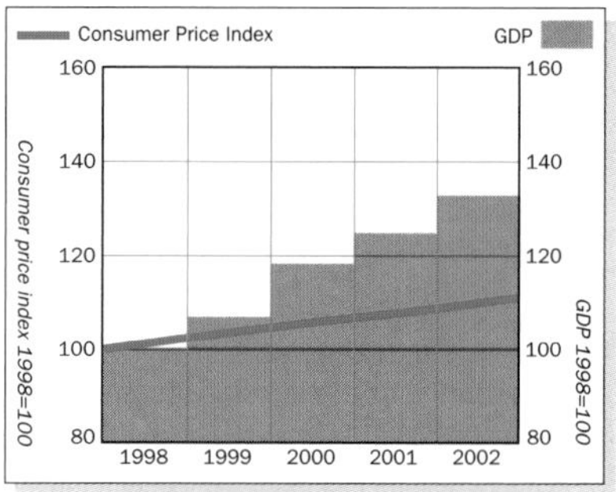
Consumer Price Index
GDP
160
140
120
100
80
Consumer price index 1998=100
GDP 1998=100
1998
1999
2000
2001
2002

EGYPT : MAJOR BUSINESSES

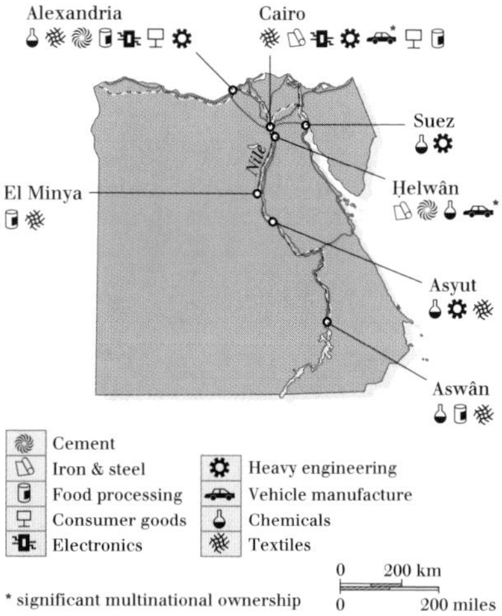
Alexandria
Cairo
Suez
Helwân
El Minya
Asyut
Aswân
Nile
Cement
Iron & steel
Food processing
Consumer goods
Electronics
Heavy engineering
Vehicle manufacture
Chemicals
Textiles
* significant multinational ownership
0
200 km
0
200 miles

RESOURCES

Electric power 17.7m kW

771,515 tonnes

750,000 b/d (reserves 3.6bn barrels)

9.2m ducks, 9.1m geese, 4.7m sheep, 92m chickens

Natural gas, oil, phosphates, manganese, uranium

ELECTRICITY GENERATION

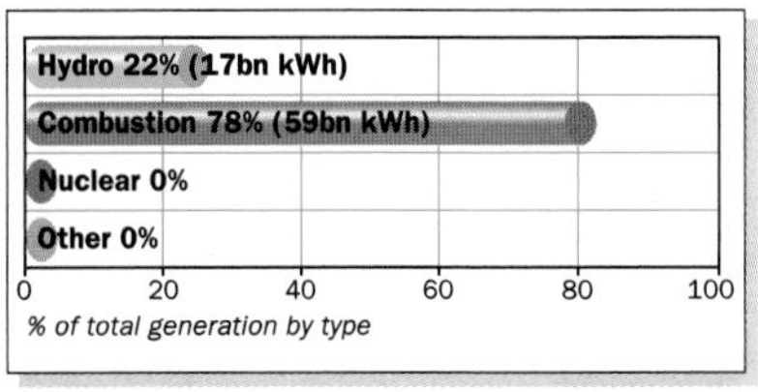

Hydro 22% (17bn kWh)
Combustion 78% (59bn kWh)
Nuclear 0%
Other 0%
0 20 40 60 80 100
% of total generation by type

Oil and gas are Egypt's most valuable resources. Oil multinationals are involved in new explorations, but more competitive oil-rich countries, such as Algeria and Yemen, are more profitable; three-quarters of Egypt's oil production is consumed locally.

Most electricity is derived from gas and hydroelectric power. The Aswan High Dam, built between 1960 and 1970 and with a maximum output of 10 billion kWh, provides the bulk of hydroelectricity. Within four years, revenue from the dam had covered its construction costs. A contract to upgrade the turbines has been awarded to a Russian company.

EGYPT : LAND USE

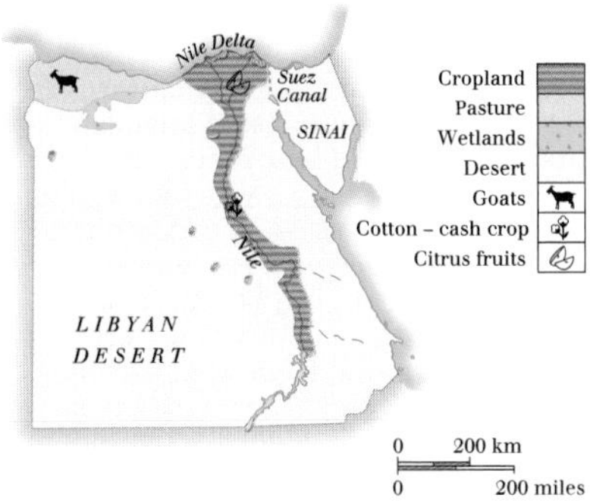

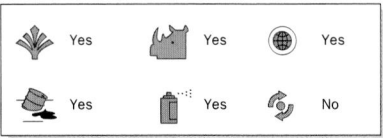

Nile Delta
Suez Canal
SINAI
Nile
LIBYAN DESERT
Cropland
Pasture
Wetlands
Desert
Goats
Cotton – cash crop
Citrus fruits
0 200 km
0 200 miles

ENVIRONMENT

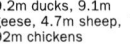

Sustainability rank: 74th

10% (0.7% partially protected)

2.2 tonnes per capita

ENVIRONMENTAL TREATIES

Yes	Yes	Yes
Yes	Yes	No

Egypt suffers from a chronic lack of water. The Nile, the only perennial source, is increasingly saline because of its much-reduced flow, due to irrigation use and the Aswan High Dam. The main cities suffer heavy industrial pollution, and environmental controls are few. In Cairo a sewerage system has improved sanitary conditions.

MEDIA

TV ownership medium

Daily newspaper circulation 31 per 1000 people

Pressure from Islamists has resulted in more airtime for Islamic sermons. Nilesat 101 was the Arab world's first satellite, and Egypt is now a center for satellite TV. A "free media zone" was launched in 2000 to attract foreign companies. Mubarak repealed harsh penalties against journalists in 2004.

PUBLISHING AND BROADCAST MEDIA

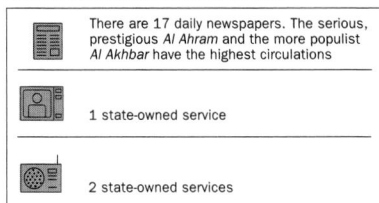

There are 17 daily newspapers. The serious, prestigious *Al Ahram* and the more populist *Al Akhbar* have the highest circulations

1 state-owned service

2 state-owned services

CRIME

Death penalty in use

80,000 prisoners

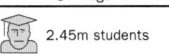

Down 5% in 1994

CRIME RATES

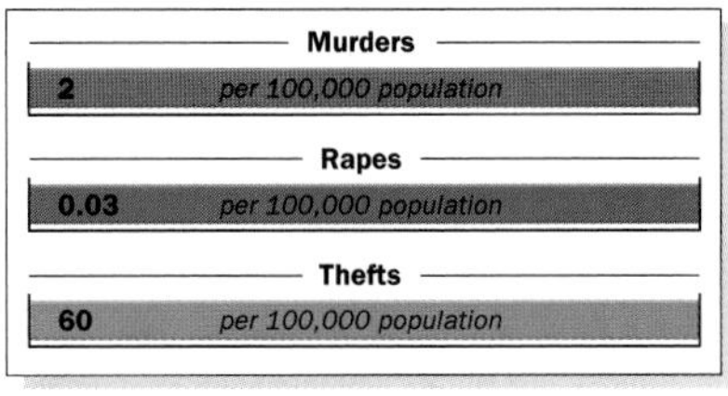

Murders
2 per 100,000 population
Rapes
0.03 per 100,000 population
Thefts
60 per 100,000 population

Terrorist attacks have tarnished Egypt's reputation as a law-abiding country. Street crime and muggings, previously rare, are increasing.

Intercommunity violence – in particular between Muslims and Christians – has become more common, as have attacks on Western tourists by Islamic extremists. Human rights groups have criticized the police for their abuse of current emergency laws, which results in the routine torture and/or death in police custody of scores of political prisoners.

EDUCATION

School leaving age: 14

56%

2.45m students

THE EDUCATION SYSTEM

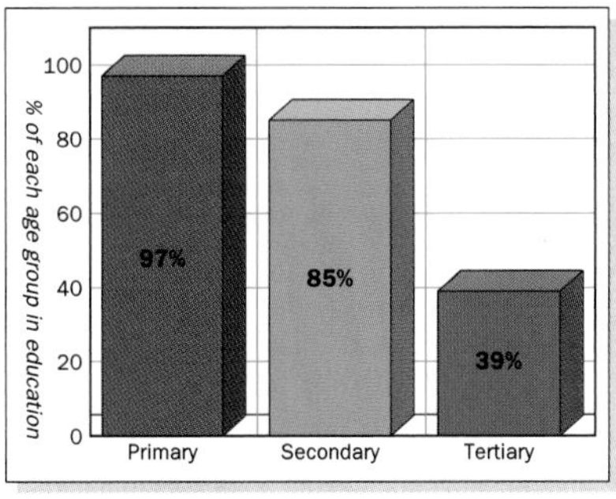

100
80
60
40
20
0
% of each age group in education
97%
85%
39%
Primary
Secondary
Tertiary

Most Egyptians attend elementary school until the age of 11, but not many complete secondary education. Two-thirds of men, but only a minority of women, are literate. A government initiative to improve girls' primary education was launched in 2000. The quality of the education given by Egyptian universities is widely respected in the Arab world.

HEALTH

Welfare state health benefits

1 per 625 people

Digestive, respiratory, and heart diseases, perinatal deaths

Health care, though improved, remains basic – there is only one hospital bed for every 500 people. Islamic medical centers based on the mosque organization are spreading, and are replacing the state system. In 1996 the government banned Pharaonic circumcision (female infibulation), a move upheld in 1997 by the Supreme Constitutional Court after being overturned by a lower court.

SPENDING

GDP/cap. increase

CONSUMPTION AND SPENDING

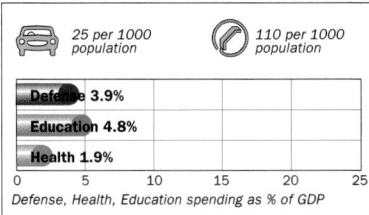

25 per 1000 population

110 per 1000 population

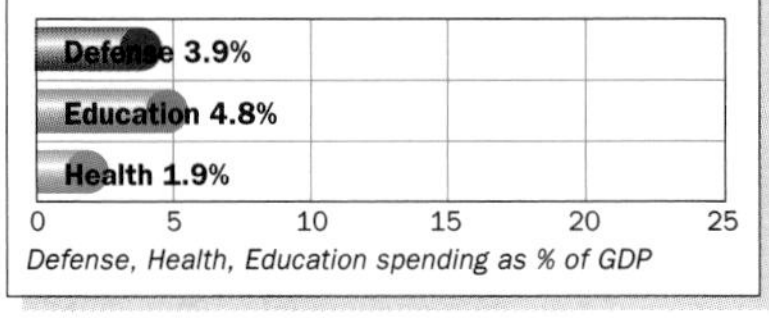

Defense 3.9%
Education 4.8%
Health 1.9%
0 5 10 15 20 25
Defense, Health, Education spending as % of GDP

A rapidly growing population and the introduction of market economics have combined to produce widespread poverty, particularly in the south, while concentrating wealth in the hands of a small urban elite. Poverty levels are highest in rural areas. Urban unemployment and internal migration have led to the creation of enormous slums around Cairo and other cities.

WORLD RANKING

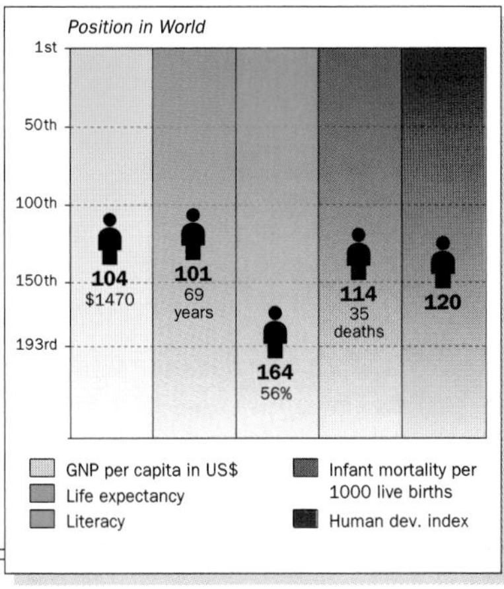

Position in World
1st
50th
100th
150th
193rd
104
$1470
101
69 years
164
56%
114
35 deaths
120
GNP per capita in US$
Life expectancy
Literacy
Infant mortality per 1000 live births
Human dev. index

E

EL SALVADOR

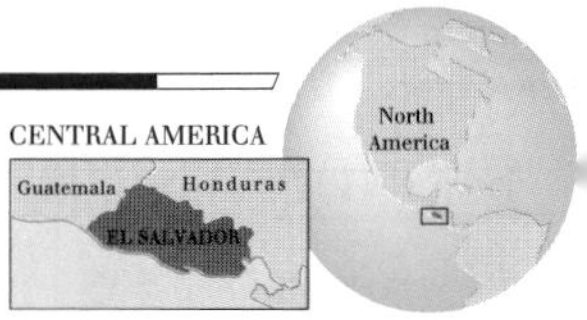
CENTRAL AMERICA
Guatemala
Honduras
EL SALVADOR
North America

OFFICIAL NAME: Republic of El Salvador **CAPITAL:** San Salvador
POPULATION: 6.5 million **CURRENCIES:** Salvadorean colón & US dollar **OFFICIAL LANGUAGE:** Spanish

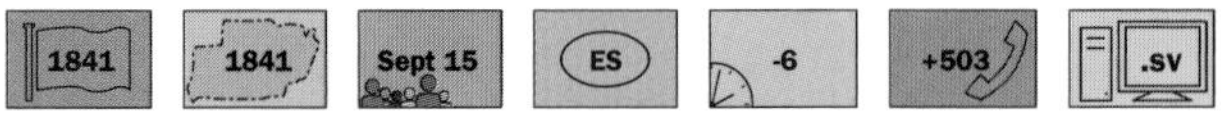
1841
1841
Sept 15
ES
-6
+503
.sv

THE SMALLEST AND MOST densely populated Central American republic, El Salvador won full independence in 1841. Located on the Pacific coast, it lies within a zone of seismic activity. Between 1981 and 1991, El Salvador was engulfed in a civil war between US-backed right-wing government forces and left-wing FMLN guerrillas. Since the UN-brokered peace agreement, the country has been concentrating on rebuilding its shattered economy.

View over the capital, San Salvador. It lies in a depression in the southern and higher of El Salvador's two mountain ranges, which is punctuated by more than 20 volcanoes.

CLIMATE

Tropical wet and dry

WEATHER CHART FOR SAN SALVADOR

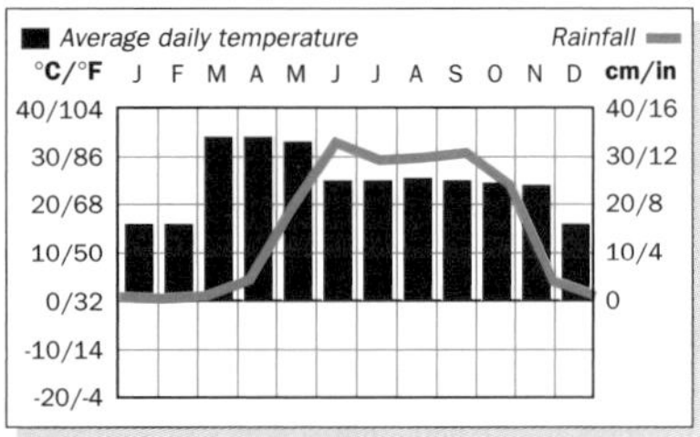
Average daily temperature
Rainfall
°C/°F
J F M A M J J A S O N D
cm/in
40/104
30/86
20/68
10/50
0/32
-10/14
-20/-4
40/16
30/12
20/8
10/4
0

The tropical coastal *tierra caliente* is very hot, with seasonal rains. The low hills are cooler at night; the higher *tierra templada* is drier and also cooler.

TRANSPORTATION

Drive on right

San Salvador 1.4m passengers

14 ships 5600 grt

THE TRANSPORTATION NETWORK

2006 km (1246 miles)

Pan-American Highway: 327 km (203 miles)

283 km (176 miles)

Rio Lempa partly navigable

Earthquakes in 2001 further damaged the already war-ravaged road and rail networks. Reconstruction will take many years.

TOURISM

Visitors : Population 1:6.8

951,000 visitors

Up 30% in 2002

MAIN TOURIST ARRIVALS

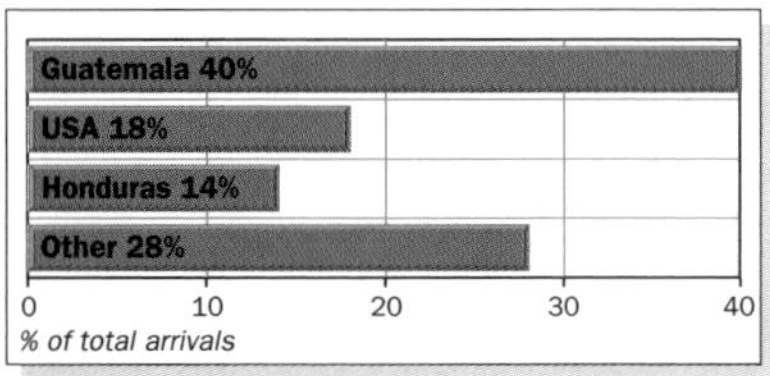
Guatemala 40%
USA 18%
Honduras 14%
Other 28%
0
10
20
30
40
% of total arrivals

Peace has brought visitors back to the unspoiled beach resorts, but crime, earthquakes, and high prices for rooms and air travel hinder tourist expansion.

PEOPLE

Pop. density high

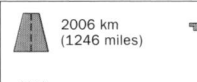

Spanish

314/km² (812/mi²)

THE URBAN/RURAL POPULATION SPLIT

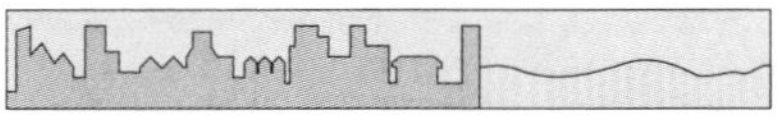
62%
38%

RELIGIOUS PERSUASION

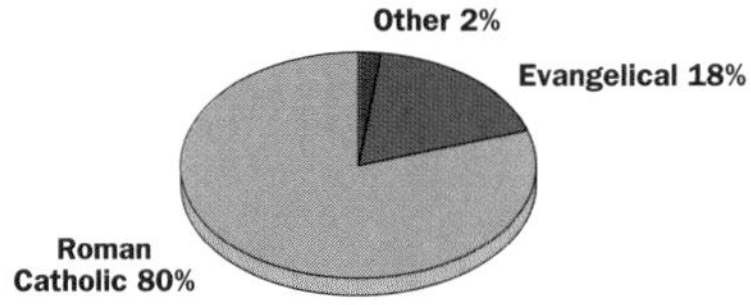
Other 2%
Evangelical 18%
Roman Catholic 80%

Salvadorans are largely *mestizo* (mixed race); there are few ethnic tensions. The civil war was fought over gross economic disparities, which still exist.

POLITICS

Multiparty elections

2003/2006

President Antonio Saca

AT THE LAST ELECTION

Legislative Assembly 84 seats

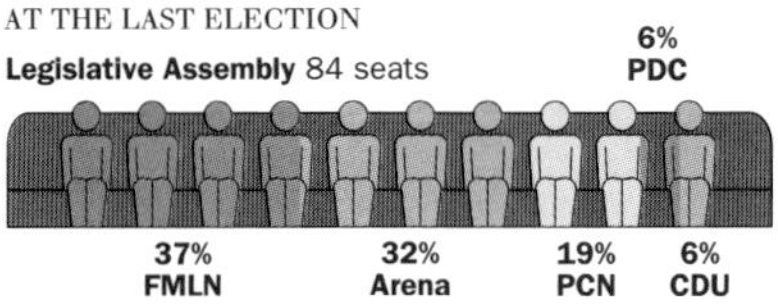
6%
PDC
37%
FMLN
32%
Arena
19%
PCN
6%
CDU

FMLN = Farabundo Martí National Liberation Front **Arena** = Nationalist Republican Alliance **PCN** = National Conciliation Party **PDC** = Christian Democratic Party **CDU** = United Democratic Center

El Salvador was dominated by the centrist PDC and right-wing Arena until the rise in the late 1990s of the FMLN, the leftist former guerrillas. In 1997 the FMLN won the mayorship of San Salvador and half the state capitals.

In the 1999 presidential election a divided FMLN came a poor second to Arena's Francisco Flores, who promised reduced poverty and the redistribution of income. With the economy in difficulties, Arena lost Assembly elections to the FMLN, but emerged victorious from the 2004 presidential poll, won by popular former sports commentator Tony Saca.

Crime is a major issue as are the human rights abuses of the civil war.

WORLD AFFAIRS

Joined UN in 1945

ACS | Geplac | IBRD | OAS | San José

El Salvador was an international pariah in the 1980s because of the human rights abuses committed by military death squads. Today it cooperates with its neighbors in pressing the US on key issues such as trade and immigration. It relied heavily on US aid in 2001 after three devastating earthquakes. In 2000 it cosigned a free trade treaty with Guatemala, Honduras, and Mexico. Long-standing border disputes exist with Honduras, and El Salvador contests the sovereignty of islands in the Gulf of Fonseca.

AID

Recipient

$233m (receipts)

Down 2% in 2002

Post–civil-war aid focused on efforts to secure peace and achieve national reconciliation by funding rebuilding and refugee resettlement programs. The current emphasis is toward supporting growth.

The UN received a slow international response in 2001 to its appeal for $34.8 million in emergency housing, medicine, and disaster prevention programs after El Salvador's devastating earthquakes.

DEFENSE

Compulsory military service

$155m

Down 5% in 2002

Between 1979 and 1991, the role of the US-backed military was to fight an unrestricted war against left-wing groups; governments that opposed the military were overthrown. US military aid dropped drastically in the 1990s before recovering after 2001. The armed forces are a quarter of the size they were in 1991, but are being drawn back into an internal security role.

E

ECONOMICS

Inflation 6.8% p.a. (1990–2001)

$13.6bn

8.752 Salvadorean colones (8.752)

SCORE CARD

❑ WORLD GNP RANKING	79th
❑ GNP PER CAPITA	$2110
❑ BALANCE OF PAYMENTS	–$384m
❑ INFLATION	1.9%
❑ UNEMPLOYMENT	6%

STRENGTHS

Coffee. Foreign investment. Family remittances from US. Dollarization.

WEAKNESSES

Exports uncompetitive. High tax evasion. Low savings. Vast reconstruction needed after earthquakes in 2001. International concern over conditions in *maquilas* (assembly plants).

EXPORTS

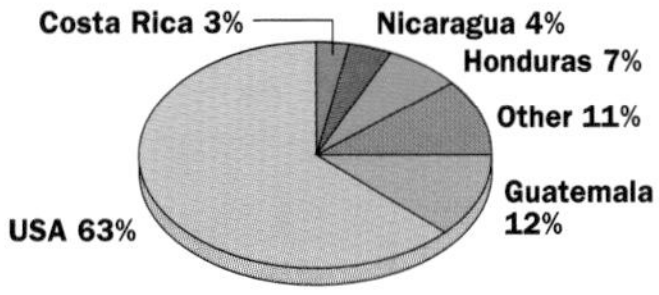

Costa Rica 3%
Nicaragua 4%
Honduras 7%
Other 11%
Guatemala 12%
USA 63%

IMPORTS

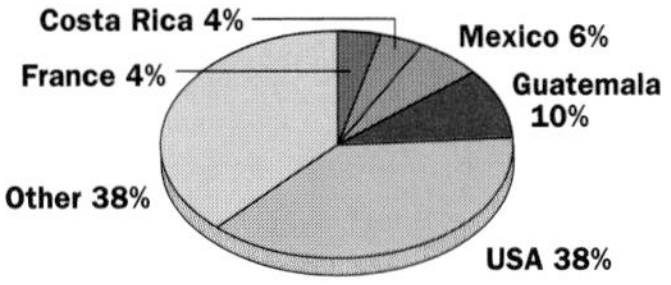

Costa Rica 4%
Mexico 6%
France 4%
Guatemala 10%
Other 38%
USA 38%

RESOURCES

Electric power 601,000 kW

18,142 tonnes

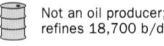

Not an oil producer; refines 18,700 b/d

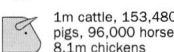

1m cattle, 153,480 pigs, 96,000 horses, 8.1m chickens

Salt, limestone, gypsum

No significant resources. Several volcanoes facilitate abundant and relatively cheap geothermal energy.

ENVIRONMENT

Sustainability rank: 75th

0.4% (0.2% partially protected)

1.1 tonnes per capita

Deforestation has led to erosion and desertification – worsening landslides during the earthquakes of 2001. Overuse of pesticides is a major problem.

MEDIA

TV ownership medium

Daily newspaper circulation 28 per 1000 people

PUBLISHING AND BROADCAST MEDIA

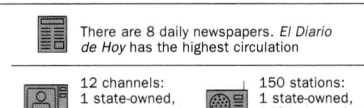

There are 8 daily newspapers. *El Diario de Hoy* has the highest circulation

12 channels: 1 state-owned, 11 independent

150 stations: 1 state-owned, 149 independent

The media are constitutionally free, but are mainly owned by powerful groups such as the Dutriz family.

CRIME

Death penalty not used in practice

10,278 prisoners

Down 43% in 2000–2001

A corrupt judiciary and police force failed to stem a postwar crime wave fueled by readily available arms; armed robberies, kidnappings, and murders deter investment and tourism. Many gang members were deported from the US in the 1990s; the Mara Salvatrucha gang alone has 17,000 members.

EDUCATION

School leaving age: 15

80%

118,491 students

Education is based on the US system and is limited in rural areas. During the civil war, state universities were closed, prompting the creation of private universities which continue to thrive despite their low standards. A 1995 reform bill tried to address the negative impact of deregulation.

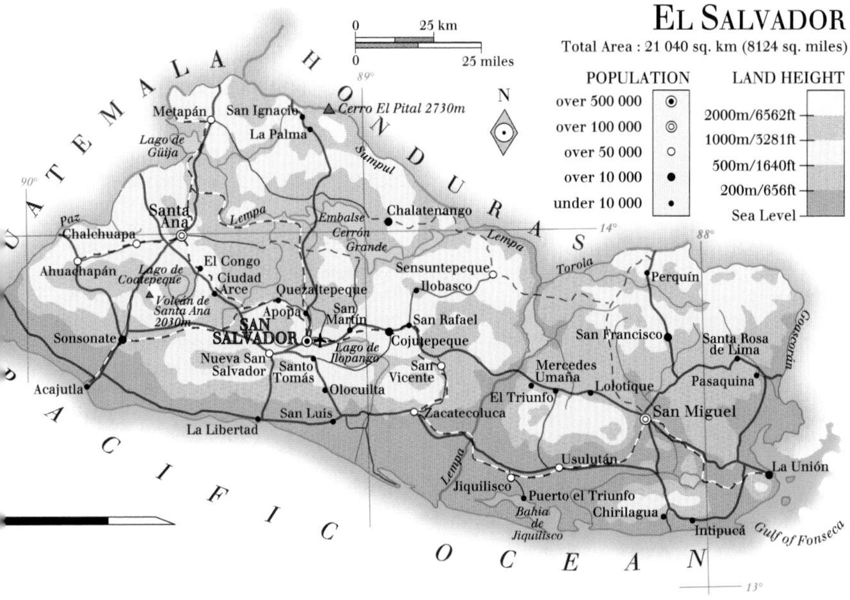

EL SALVADOR
Total Area : 21 040 sq. km (8124 sq. miles)
POPULATION
over 500 000
over 100 000
over 50 000
over 10 000
under 10 000
LAND HEIGHT
2000m/6562ft
1000m/3281ft
500m/1640ft
200m/656ft
Sea Level
0 25 km
0 25 miles
GUATEMALA
HONDURAS
PACIFIC OCEAN
Metapán
San Ignacio
La Palma
Cerro El Pital 2730m
Lago de Güija
Santa Ana
Chalatenango
Chalchuapa
Ahuachapán
El Congo
Ciudad Arce
Lago de Coatepeque
Volcán de Santa Ana 2030m
Quezaltepeque
Apopa
San Martín
SAN SALVADOR
Sonsonate
Nueva San Salvador
Santo Tomás
Lago de Ilopango
Olocuilta
Acajutla
La Libertad
San Luis
Sensuntepeque
Ilobasco
San Rafael
Cojutepeque
San Vicente
Zacatecoluca
Embalse Cerrón Grande
Lempa
Sumpul
Torola
Perquín
San Francisco
Santa Rosa de Lima
Mercedes Umaña
El Triunfo
Lolotique
Pasaquina
San Miguel
Usulután
Jiquilisco
Puerto el Triunfo
Bahía de Jiquilisco
Chirilagua
Intipucá
La Unión
Goascorán
Gulf of Fonseca

CHRONOLOGY

El Salvador was a Spanish colony until 1821. Part of the United Provinces of Central America in 1823–1839, it became fully independent in 1841.

- ❑ **1932** Army crushes popular insurrection led by Farabundo Martí.
- ❑ **1944–1979** Army rules through PCN.
- ❑ **1979** Reformist officers overthrow PCN government.
- ❑ **1981** FMLN launches civil war.
- ❑ **1989** Arena wins presidency.
- ❑ **1991** UN-brokered peace. FMLN recognized as a political party.
- ❑ **2000, 2003** FMLN wins Assembly elections.
- ❑ **2001** Devastating earthquakes kill hundreds. Dollarization of economy.
- ❑ **2004** Arena retains presidency.

HEALTH

Welfare state health benefits

1 per 909 people

Heart disease, cancers, homicide, infectious diseases

Health problems worsened after the 2001 earthquakes. Plans to privatize the health service are unpopular.

SPENDING

GDP/cap. increase

CONSUMPTION AND SPENDING

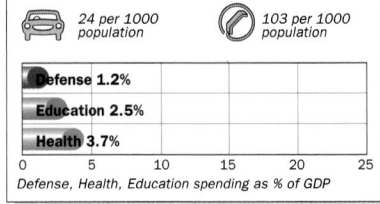

24 per 1000 population

103 per 1000 population

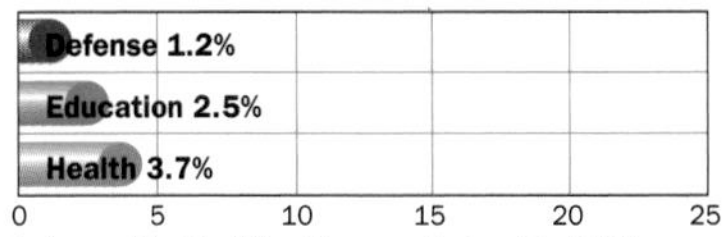

Defense 1.2%
Education 2.5%
Health 3.7%
0
5
10
15
20
25

Defense, Health, Education spending as % of GDP

Though there is a growing middle class, much of the country's wealth is controlled by just a few hundred families. Land distribution remains highly skewed, and nearly half the population live in poverty.

WORLD RANKING

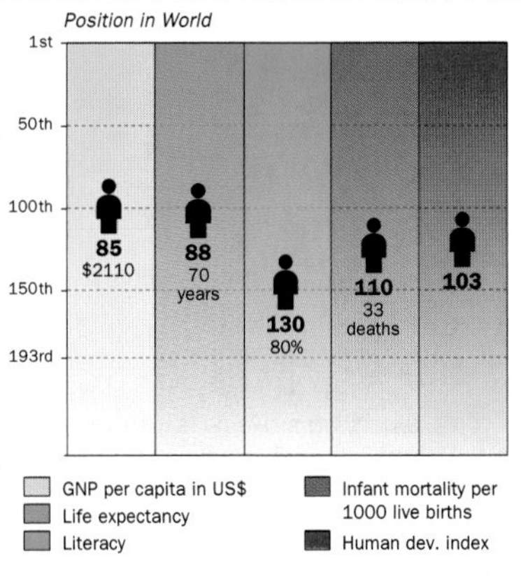

Position in World
1st
50th
100th
150th
193rd
85
$2110
88
70 years
130
80%
110
33 deaths
103
GNP per capita in US$
Life expectancy
Literacy
Infant mortality per 1000 live births
Human dev. index

EQUATORIAL GUINEA

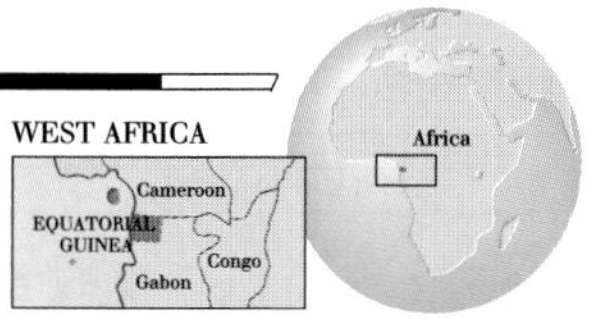
WEST AFRICA
Africa
Cameroon
EQUATORIAL GUINEA
Gabon
Congo

OFFICIAL NAME: Republic of Equatorial Guinea **CAPITAL:** Malabo
POPULATION: 494,000 **CURRENCY:** CFA franc **OFFICIAL LANGUAGES:** Spanish and French

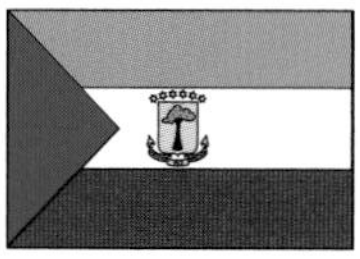

1968 | 1968 | Oct 12 | GQ | +1 | +240 | .gq

COMPRISING FIVE ISLANDS and the territory of Río Muni on the west coast of Africa, Equatorial Guinea lies just north of the equator. Mangrove swamps border the mainland coast. The republic gained its independence in 1968 after 190 years of Spanish rule. Multipartyism was accepted in 1991, but the fairness of subsequent general elections has been questioned.

Bioko, formerly Fernando Po. Though the volcanic land is very fertile, cocoa production fell by 90% during the Macías years.

CLIMATE

Tropical equatorial

WEATHER CHART FOR MALABO

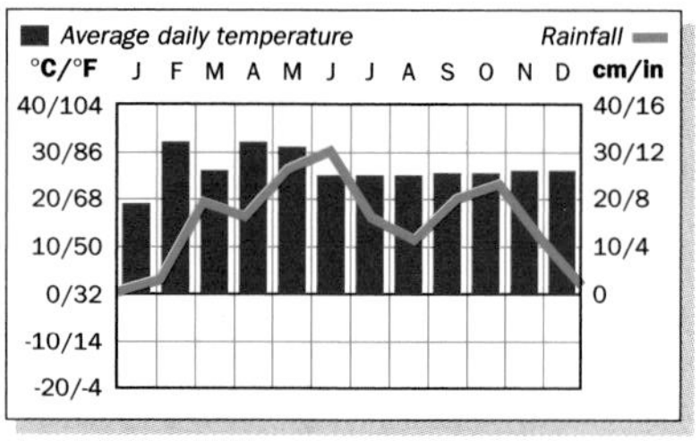
Average daily temperature
Rainfall
°C/°F
J F M A M J J A S O N D
cm/in
40/104
30/86
20/68
10/50
0/32
-10/14
-20/-4
40/16
30/12
20/8
10/4
0

The island of Bioko is extremely wet and humid, with an annual rainfall of 200 cm (80 in), while the mainland is only marginally drier and cooler.

TRANSPORTATION

Drive on right

Malabo International 187,474 passengers

43 ships 28,546 grt

THE TRANSPORTATION NETWORK

508 km (316 miles)

None

None

None

There are six flights a week between Malabo and Bata. Mainland public transportation is restricted to minibuses. There is only one properly paved road, serving the president's hometown.

TOURISM

Not available

Tourism receipts totaled $2m in 1998

Numbers are increasing slowly

MAIN TOURIST ARRIVALS

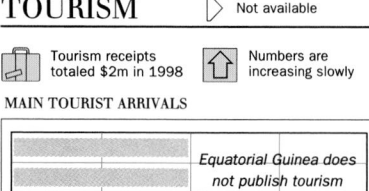

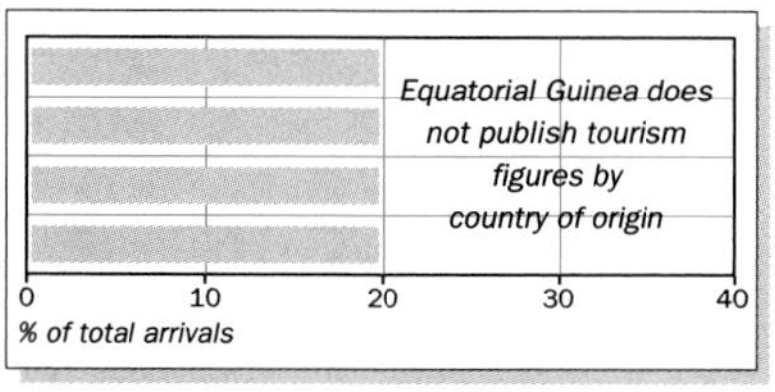
Equatorial Guinea does not publish tourism figures by country of origin
0
10
20
30
40
% of total arrivals

Equatorial Guinea is only of interest to the adventurous, independent tourist, despite the potential attraction of its beaches and the island of Bioko's spectacular mountain scenery.

PEOPLE

Pop. density low

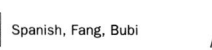

Spanish, Fang, Bubi

18/km² (46/mi²)

THE URBAN/RURAL POPULATION SPLIT

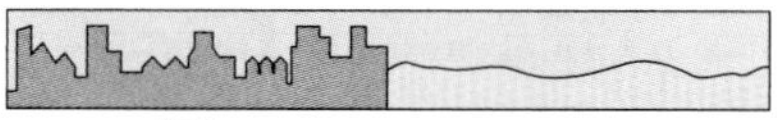
50%
50%

RELIGIOUS PERSUASION

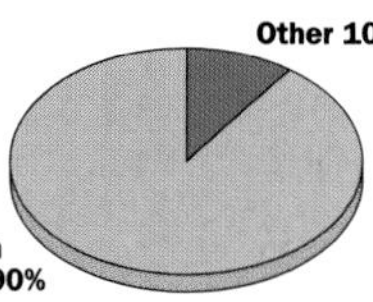
Other 10%
Roman Catholic 90%

Equatorial Guinea is the only Spanish-speaking country in Africa. The mainland has a majority of Fang, a people also found in Cameroon and north Gabon. The Fang dominated politically under the Macías dictatorship. Bioko is populated by a majority of Bubi and a minority of Creoles, known as Fernandinos. Tensions between the mainland and Bioko have been reignited since the discovery of oil reserves off Bioko. The extended family has maintained its importance.

POLITICS

Multiparty elections

2004/2009

President Teodoro Obiang Nguema Mbasogo

AT THE LAST ELECTION

House of Representatives of the People 100 seats

68% PDGE
30% C
2% CPDS

PDGE = Equatorial Guinea Democratic Party
C = Coalition of the "democratic opposition" (allies of the PDGE) **CPDS** = Convergence for Social Democracy

The ruling PDGE was set up in 1987 by Teodoro Obiang Nguema Mbasogo, nephew of the dictator Francisco Macías Nguema, whom he had overthrown in 1979. It replaced Macías's National Workers' Party (PUNT).

The gradual movement toward multipartyism – which was initiated in 1988 following the first elections for 20 years – has been marked by instability. Opposition parties boycotted the 1993 elections, while Obiang Nguema was the only effective candidate in the 1996 and 2002 polls, declared farcical by international observers. Dozens of opposition figures were detained in 2002–2003 over a 1997 plot to overthrow the government. Many others are still in exile.

A further coup plot was thwarted in early 2004 when a mercenary group was intercepted in Zimbabwe en route to Malabo to install the government-in-exile of Severo Moto Nsa. Recent legislative elections were won easily by the PDGE, but again denounced by the opposition and observers.

EQUATORIAL GUINEA

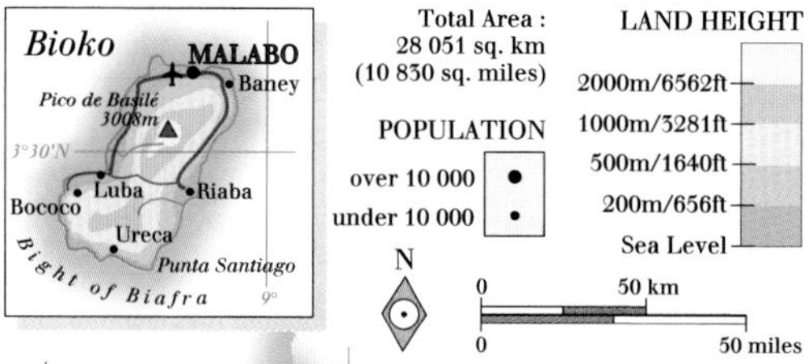
Bioko
MALABO
Baney
Pico de Basilé 3008m
3°30'N
Luba
Riaba
Bococo
Ureca
Punta Santiago
Bight of Biafra
9°
Total Area : 28 051 sq. km (10 830 sq. miles)
POPULATION
over 10 000
under 10 000
LAND HEIGHT
2000m/6562ft
1000m/3281ft
500m/1640ft
200m/656ft
Sea Level
N
0
50 km
0
50 miles

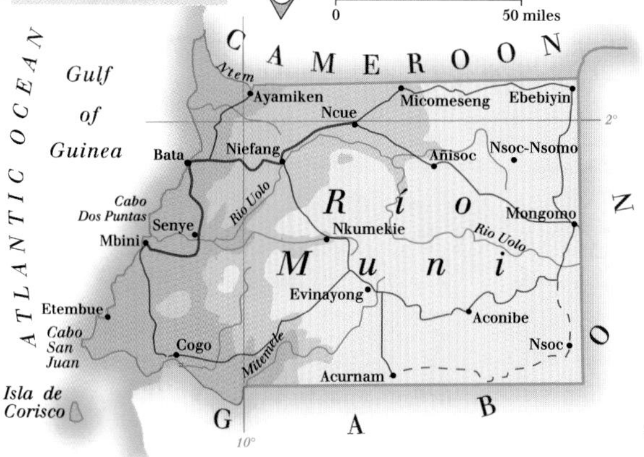
CAMEROON
ATLANTIC OCEAN
Gulf of Guinea
Ntem
Ayamiken
Ncue
Micomeseng
Ebebiyin
2°
Bata
Niefang
Añisoc
Nsoc-Nsomo
Río Uolo
Río Muni
Mongomo
Cabo Dos Puntas
Senye
Nkumekie
Mbini
Evinayong
Aconibe
Etembue
Cabo San Juan
Cogo
Mitemele
Nsoc
Acurnam
Isla de Corisco
GABON
10°

WORLD AFFAIRS

Joined UN in 1968

BDEAC ACP FZ NAM AU

A maritime border dispute with Nigeria was settled in 2000, paving the way for the exploitation of large oil reserves in the Gulf of Guinea. Oil potential has stimulated US interest, quietened human rights concerns, and prompted the appointment of a UN mediator to resolve the dispute with Gabon over islands in Corisco Bay which may control undiscovered oil reserves. Oil production in Equatorial Guinea has now overtaken that of Gabon.

AID

Recipient

$20m (receipts)

Up 54% in 2002

Equatorial Guinea is poorly developed, but with the increase in oil revenues many aid programs have ceased altogether or are substantially reduced. Inefficiency, corruption, and a shortage of skilled people hinder the planning and implementation of projects. An IMF program was suspended in 1997 after the government failed to implement reforms. The World Bank originally severed its links with the country in 1993, but resumed lending in 2002.

DEFENSE

No compulsory military service

$4m

No change in 2002

The main concern is internal security. Cuba and North Korea provided Macías with a presidential guard, while Obiang Nguema has been protected by Moroccan troops. A long-running dispute with Gabon over islands in Corisco Bay is unresolved. Spain has provided military training, as has the US.

RESOURCES

Electric power 18,000 kW

3500 tonnes

249,000 b/d (reserves 71m barrels)

37,600 sheep, 30,000 ducks, 320,000 chickens

Oil, natural gas, gold

Oil production levels are expected to double between 2002 and 2005. Obiang Nguema has pledged to use income from oil to promote development. The region around Bata is served by a 3.2 MW hydropower plant.

ENVIRONMENT

Not available

None

0.4 tonnes per capita

The government has failed to impose any serious measures to stop timber companies depleting the rainforest.

MEDIA

TV ownership medium

Daily newspaper circulation 5 per 1000 people

PUBLISHING AND BROADCAST MEDIA

There is no regular daily press. The formerly daily newspaper *Poto Poto* now appears irregularly

1 state-owned service

2 services: 1 state-owned, 1 independent

The press remains tightly controlled, despite the state's adoption of multipartyism. In 2003, state radio declared Obiang Nguema to be "like God in Heaven."

CRIME

Death penalty in use

Equatorial Guinea does not publish prison figures

Little change from year to year

The level of recorded crime is relatively low, but many offenses are not reported. Many human rights abuses still occur.

CHRONOLOGY

Equatorial Guinea remained a backwater of Spanish colonialism until development began after 1939.

- **1968** Independence. President Macías begins reign of terror.
- **1979** Coup puts nephew in power.
- **1991** Multiparty constitution.
- **2001** Corruption scandal.
- **2002** Obiang Nguema reelected in disputed vote.
- **2004** PDGE wins denounced poll. Coup attempt foiled.

E

EDUCATION

School leaving age: 11

84%

1003 students

Education declined in the Macías years, when attendance rates fell from 90% to 55%. Though education is declared the state's first priority, funding is poor.

HEALTH

No welfare state health benefits

1 per 5000 people

Diarrheal and respiratory diseases, malaria

Life expectancy – just 37 years in 1960 – has risen substantially. There are 20 doctors to every 100,000 people.

SPENDING

GDP/cap. increase

CONSUMPTION AND SPENDING

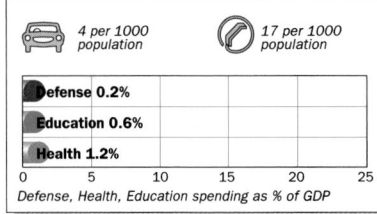

4 per 1000 population

17 per 1000 population

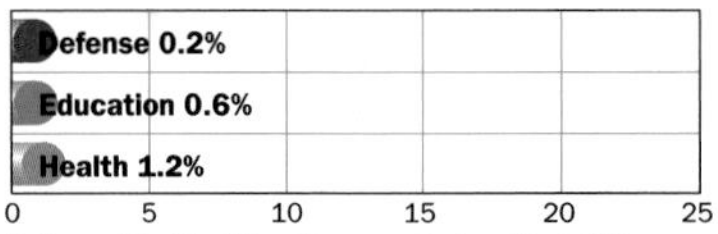
Defense 0.2%
Education 0.6%
Health 1.2%
0
5
10
15
20
25

Defense, Health, Education spending as % of GDP

What wealth there is in Equatorial Guinea tends to be concentrated in the ruling clan. There is also a remnant of the former Spanish plutocracy.

ECONOMICS

Inflation 17% p.a. (1990–2001)

$327m

539.2 CFA francs (571.2)

SCORE CARD

World GNP Ranking	177th
GNP per capita	$700
Balance of Payments	–$344m
Inflation	11.8%
Unemployment	30%

STRENGTHS

Fertile soils. Timber. Cocoa and coffee. Extensive territorial waters, with potential for fisheries. The economy is strengthening as oil and gas reserves are exploited.

WEAKNESSES

Lasting effects of economic regression under Macías dictatorship. Maladministration and ideological attacks on the educated have restricted growth; under Macías, cocoa production slumped by 90%. Government complaints that oil exploitation contracts favor foreign corporations. High unemployment.

EXPORTS

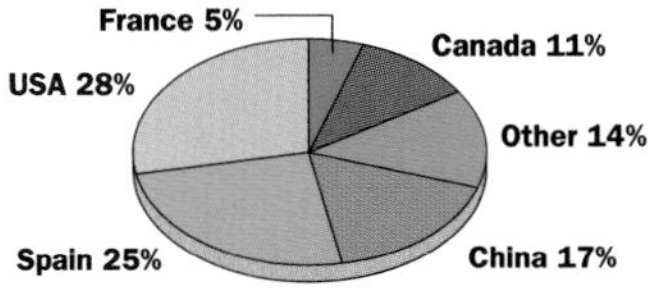
France 5%
Canada 11%
USA 28%
Other 14%
Spain 25%
China 17%

IMPORTS

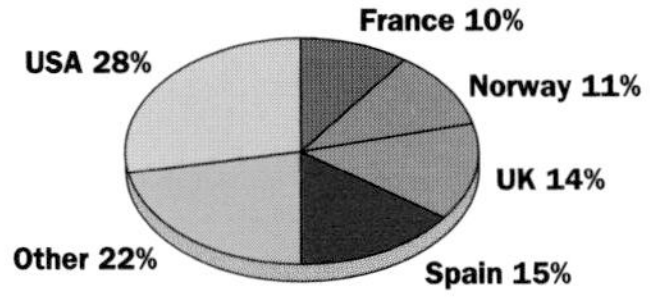
France 10%
USA 28%
Norway 11%
UK 14%
Other 22%
Spain 15%

WORLD RANKING

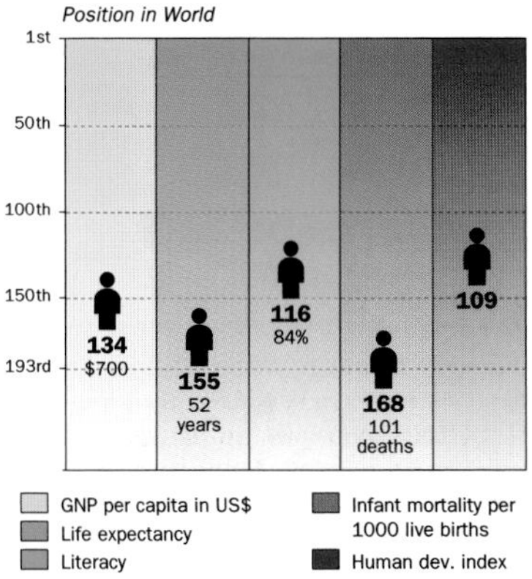
Position in World
1st
50th
100th
150th
193rd
134
$700
155
52
years
116
84%
168
101
deaths
109
GNP per capita in US$
Life expectancy
Literacy
Infant mortality per 1000 live births
Human dev. index

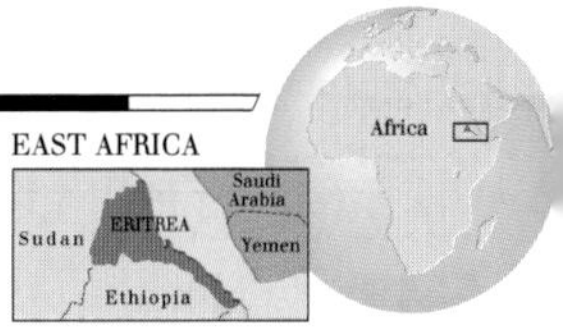
EAST AFRICA
Africa
Saudi Arabia
Sudan
ERITREA
Yemen
Ethiopia

ERITREA

OFFICIAL NAME: State of Eritrea **CAPITAL:** Asmara **POPULATION:** 4.1 million
CURRENCY: Nakfa **OFFICIAL LANGUAGE:** Tigrinya, English, and Arabic

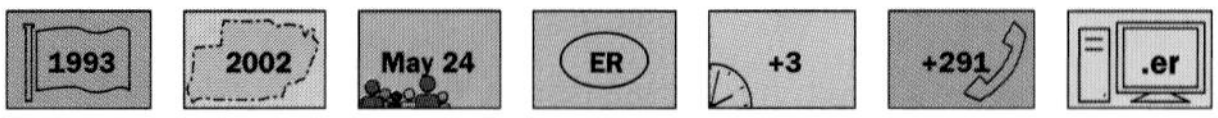
1993
2002
May 24
ER
+3
+291
.er

LYING ALONG THE SHORE of the Red Sea, Eritrea has a landscape of rugged mountains, bush, and desert. A former Italian colony later annexed by Ethiopia, Eritrea fought a long war to win independence in 1993. It is the only country successfully to have seceded in postcolonial Africa. Like its southern neighbor, Eritrea is prone to recurring droughts and the threat of famine. War with Ethiopia in 1998–2000 brought heavy losses on both sides.

CLIMATE

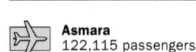

Hot desert/mountain

WEATHER CHART FOR ASMARA

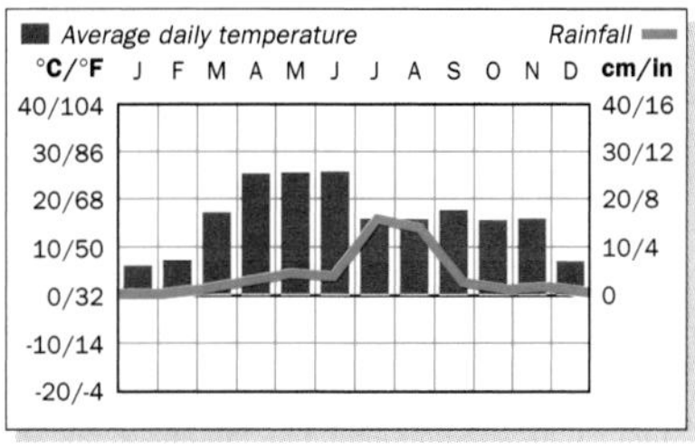
Average daily temperature
Rainfall
°C/°F J F M A M J J A S O N D cm/in
40/104 40/16
30/86 30/12
20/68 20/8
10/50 10/4
0/32 0
-10/14
-20/-4

Eritrea's harvest is dependent on mid-year rainfall in the highlands. Lowland temperatures may exceed 50°C (122°F).

TRANSPORTATION

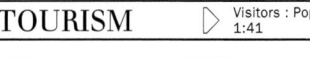

Drive on right

Asmara
122,115 passengers

12 ships
20,686 grt

THE TRANSPORTATION NETWORK

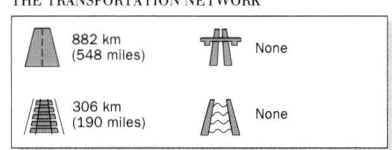

882 km (548 miles)

None

306 km (190 miles)

None

All transportation infrastructure requires massive investment. Ethiopian access to Eritrea's ports is a source of friction.

TOURISM

Visitors : Population 1:41

101,000 visitors

Down 11% in 2002

MAIN TOURIST ARRIVALS

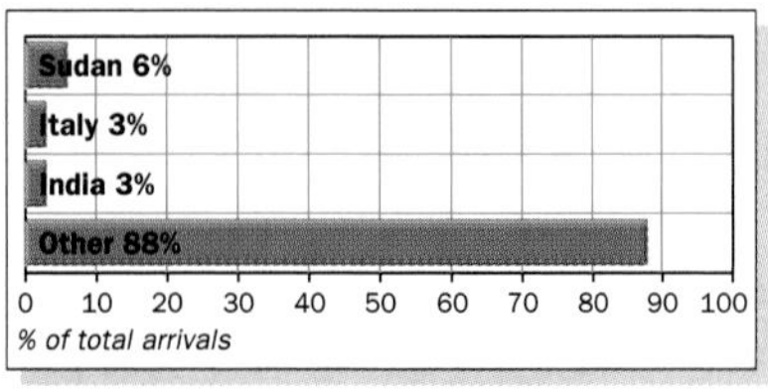
Sudan 6%
Italy 3%
India 3%
Other 88%
0 10 20 30 40 50 60 70 80 90 100
% of total arrivals

There is currently very little tourism, but Eritrea has considerable long-term potential, especially along the Red Sea coast, with its underwater attractions, and in the spectacular Danakil depression. Guides are essential.

PEOPLE

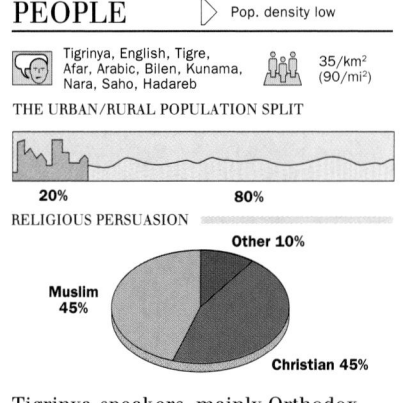

Pop. density low

Tigrinya, English, Tigre, Afar, Arabic, Bilen, Kunama, Nara, Saho, Hadareb

35/km² (90/mi²)

THE URBAN/RURAL POPULATION SPLIT

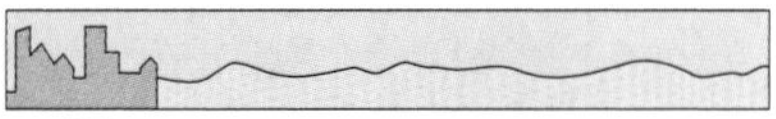
20%
80%

RELIGIOUS PERSUASION

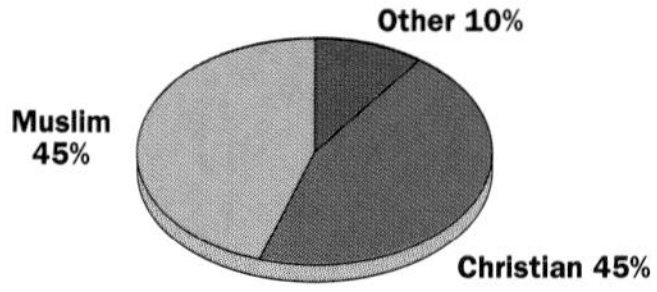
Other 10%
Muslim 45%
Christian 45%

Tigrinya-speakers, mainly Orthodox Christians, form the largest of Eritrea's nine main ethnic groups. A strong sense of nationhood has been forged by the three-decade struggle for independence. Women played an important role in the war; from 1973, 30,000 fought alongside men, some in positions of command. The nomadic peoples of the Danakil desert remain fiercely independent. Subsistence farmers account for 80% of the population.

ERITREA

Total Area : 121 320 sq. km
(46 842 sq. miles)

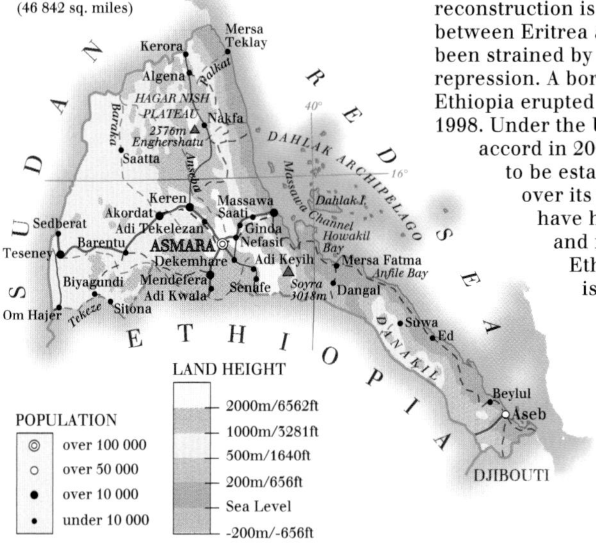
Mersa Teklay
Kerora
Algena
HAGAR NISH PLATEAU
2576m
Nakfa
Enghershatu
Saatta
Keren
Massawa
Saati
Akordat
Adi Tekelezan
Ginda
Sedberat
Barentu
ASMARA
Nefasit
Teseney
Dekemhare
Adi Keyih
Biyagundi
Mendefera
Adi Kwala
Senafe
Soyra 3018m
Mersa Fatma
Anfile Bay
Dangal
Om Hajer
Sitona
Suwa
Ed
Beylul
Aseb
DJIBOUTI
SUDAN
ETHIOPIA
RED SEA
DAHLAK ARCHIPELAGO
Dahlak I.
Massawa Channel
Howakil Bay
DANAKIL
Barka
Anseba
Tekeze
POPULATION
over 100 000
over 50 000
over 10 000
under 10 000
LAND HEIGHT
2000m/6562ft
1000m/3281ft
500m/1640ft
200m/656ft
Sea Level
-200m/-656ft

POLITICS

No legislative elections

Elections not yet held

President Issaias Afewerki

LEGISLATIVE OR ADVISORY BODIES

National Assembly 150 seats

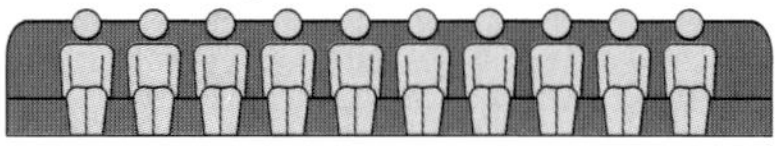

The National Assembly comprises 75 People's Front for Democracy and Justice (**PFDJ**) central committee members and 75 directly elected members, including 11 seats reserved for women. Elections expected in 1997 under the new constitution have not yet taken place

A former Italian colony, Eritrea was dominated by Ethiopia in a federation set up in 1952. Within ten years Ethiopia had reduced Eritrea to a province, prompting a long secessionist struggle. The Eritrean People's Liberation Front (EPLF) and its Tigrean allies helped defeat the Ethiopian regime in 1991. In 1993 a referendum gave overwhelming support to independence.

Pending elections, the country is run by a core leadership from the EPLF (now the PFDJ), with the National Assembly convening rarely. The 1997 constitution forbids parties based on religious or ethnic affiliations. President Issaias Afewerki, a Christian, has been careful to include Muslims in his cabinet. He lashed out at opponents in 2001 and faced unprecedented criticism, even from within the PFDJ.

WORLD AFFAIRS

Joined UN in 1993

COMESA
IAEA
IGAD
NAM
AU

Attracting Western and Arab aid for reconstruction is a priority. Relations between Eritrea and aid donors have been strained by accusations of political repression. A border conflict with Ethiopia erupted into open warfare in 1998. Under the UN-sponsored peace accord in 2000, a new border was to be established, but disputes over its physical demarcation have hindered the process and reawoken tensions; Ethiopia's main concern is access to the sea.

AID

Recipient

$230m (receipts) — Down 18% in 2002

The economy is highly aid-dependent, and millions of Eritreans survive on food aid. This is an obvious and pressing need, given the country's vulnerability to famine, but donors have been less generous with aid for the $2 billion cost of reconstruction. Emergency UN aid was requested in 2000 to assist over a million people displaced by the Ethiopian incursion. $100 million of food aid was needed in 2004.

DEFENSE

Compulsory military service

$100m — Down 42% in 2002

Defense expenditure is massive. Vast numbers of conscripts swell the 50,000-strong permanent army. During the independence struggle a third of soldiers were women. Troops were being rehabilitated on "food for work" schemes until the latest war with Ethiopia, which inflicted heavy losses. Mass demobilization was restarted in 2002.

ECONOMICS

Inflation 9% p.a. (1993–2001)

$796m — 13.55 nakfa (13.552)

SCORE CARD

- ❑ WORLD GNP RANKING........158th
- ❑ GNP PER CAPITA........$190
- ❑ BALANCE OF PAYMENTS........–$85m
- ❑ INFLATION........1.1%
- ❑ UNEMPLOYMENT........Widespread underemployment

STRENGTHS

Strategic Red Sea position: transportation and tourism potential. Asmara–Massawa railroad reopened in 2003. Potential for mining and oil industry. Commitment to cutting food aid dependence.

WEAKNESSES

Destruction of infrastructure and equipment; port of Massawa heavily bombed. Dependent on aid. Most of population living at subsistence level. Susceptibility to drought and famine. Return of some 750,000 refugees.

EXPORTS

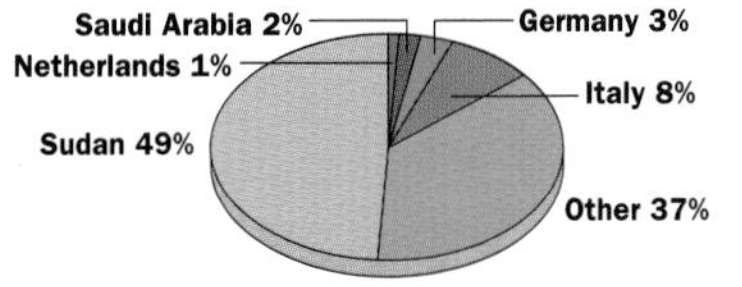
Saudi Arabia 2%
Germany 3%
Netherlands 1%
Italy 8%
Sudan 49%
Other 37%

IMPORTS

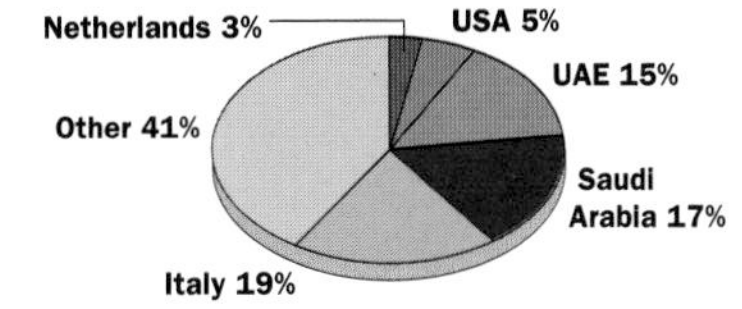
Netherlands 3%
USA 5%
UAE 15%
Other 41%
Saudi Arabia 17%
Italy 19%

RESOURCES

Electric power 172,000 kW

8820 tonnes — Not an oil producer; oil refinery at Assab

2.1m sheep, 1.93m cattle, 1.7m goats, 1.37m chickens — Copper, potash, gold, iron, silver, zinc, oil, silica, granite, marble

Eritrea has substantial copper reserves, and lesser ones of silver, zinc, and gold. Building materials are exported. Onshore and offshore oil deposits are believed to exist. There is potential for power generation from geothermal sources, though most now comes from a new diesel-powered plant in Massawa.

ENVIRONMENT

Not available

4% — 0.1 tonnes per capita

Deforestation and soil erosion are major problems. During the struggle for independence, the Ethiopian army uprooted trees to destroy cover for Eritrean soldiers. Since 1991, around 70 million seedlings have been grown in a replanting scheme. The Red Sea coast is a conservation priority.

MEDIA

TV ownership low

There are no daily newspapers

PUBLISHING AND BROADCAST MEDIA

New Eritrea, owned by the PFDJ, is published every 3 days in English, Tigrinya, and Arabic

1 state-controlled service — 2 state-controlled services

The media are largely controlled by the PFDJ, which runs both the radio and TV services. Independent newspapers are not encouraged.

CRIME

Death penalty in use

Eritrea does not publish prison figures — Crime levels remain low

Crime is not a major problem, but Islamist terrorist groups are active. The police answer to the PFDJ. There are several political prisoners.

EDUCATION

School leaving age: 13

57% — 5505 students

Enrollment is recovering from low levels during the war. There is one university. In an attempt to reduce potential ethnic tension, all children above the age of 11 are taught in English or Arabic.

HEALTH

No welfare state health benefits

1 per 20,000 people — Malaria, potential risk of famine

The risk of famine overrides normal health concerns. Eritreans built their own hospitals during the independence struggle. Health provision is basic.

***Seasonal river beds** carry rain from the Ethiopian highlands into Eritrea, providing essential irrigation for agriculture.*

CHRONOLOGY

British military rule replaced Italian colonial authority in 1941.

- ❑ **1952** Ethiopia absorbs Eritrea.
- ❑ **1961** Beginning of armed struggle.
- ❑ **1987** EPLF refuses offer of autonomy; fighting intensifies.
- ❑ **1991** EPLF takes Asmara.
- ❑ **1993** Formal independence.
- ❑ **1998** Border war with Ethiopia.
- ❑ **2000** OAU peace treaty signed.
- ❑ **2001** Ethiopia completes troop withdrawal.
- ❑ **2002** Border demarcation begins.

SPENDING

GDP/cap. increase

CONSUMPTION AND SPENDING

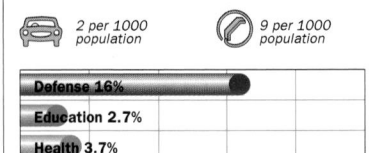

2 per 1000 population — *9 per 1000 population*

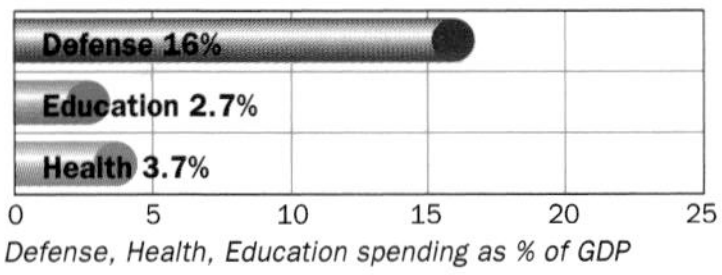
Defense 16%
Education 2.7%
Health 3.7%
0
5
10
15
20
25
Defense, Health, Education spending as % of GDP

Some 80% of Eritrea's population are subsistence farmers. A few of the many thousands of refugees who fled to Arab and Western countries have built up some personal savings.

WORLD RANKING

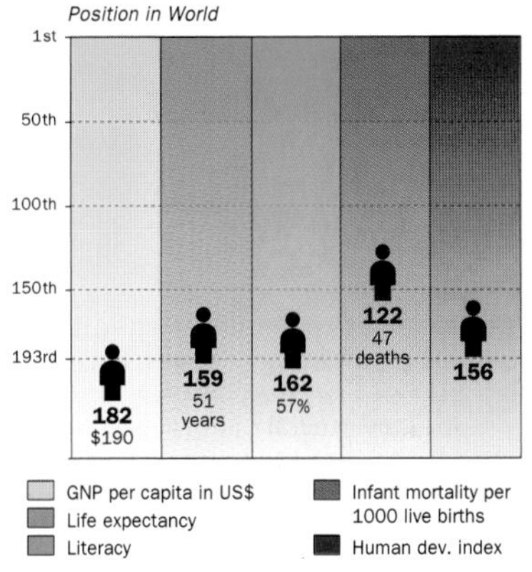
Position in World
1st
50th
100th
150th
193rd
182
$190
159
51
years
162
57%
122
47
deaths
156
GNP per capita in US$
Life expectancy
Literacy
Infant mortality per 1000 live births
Human dev. index

E

E

ESTONIA

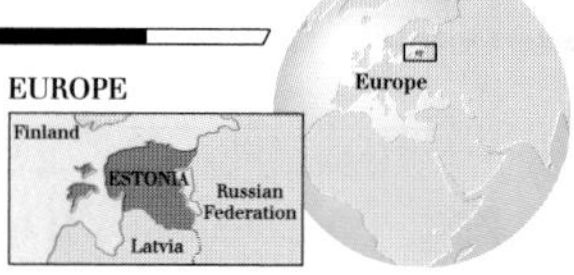
EUROPE
Europe
Finland
ESTONIA
Russian Federation
Latvia

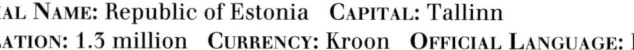

OFFICIAL NAME: Republic of Estonia **CAPITAL:** Tallinn
POPULATION: 1.3 million **CURRENCY:** Kroon **OFFICIAL LANGUAGE:** Estonian

1991
1991
Feb 24
EST
+2
+372
.ee

TRADITIONALLY THE MOST Western-oriented of the Baltic states, Estonia is bordered by Latvia and the Russian Federation. Its terrain is flat, boggy, and partly wooded, and includes more than 1500 islands. Estonia formally regained its independence as a multiparty democracy in 1991. In contrast to the peoples of Latvia and Lithuania, Estonians are Finno-Ugric, speaking a language related to Finnish.

CLIMATE

Continental

WEATHER CHART FOR TALLINN

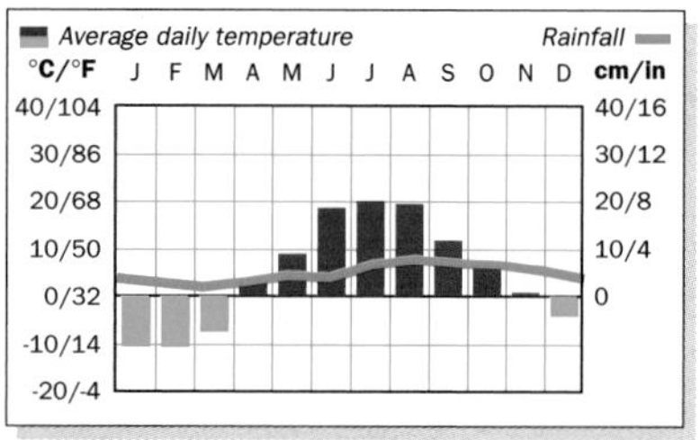
Average daily temperature
Rainfall
°C/°F
J F M A M J J A S O N D
cm/in
40/104
30/86
20/68
10/50
0/32
-10/14
-20/4
40/16
30/12
20/8
10/4
0

Estonia's coastal location gives it cool summers, and cold winters when the Baltic Sea freezes.

TRANSPORTATION

Drive on right

Tallinn 716,199 passengers

181 ships 357,400 grt

THE TRANSPORTATION NETWORK

10,408 km (6467 miles)	94 km (58 miles)
967 km (601 miles)	320 km (199 miles)

Railroads have improved and buses are reliable. Baltic ferries link Tallinn with Finland, Sweden, and Germany.

TOURISM

Visitors : Population 1:1

1.36m visitors

Up 3% in 2002

MAIN TOURIST ARRIVALS

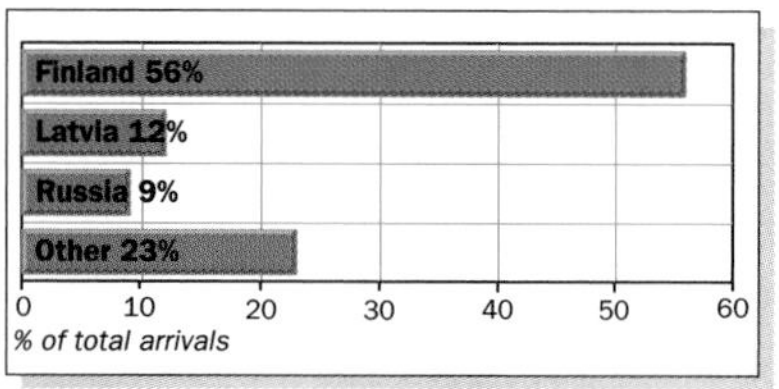
Finland 56%
Latvia 12%
Russia 9%
Other 23%
0 10 20 30 40 50 60
% of total arrivals

Estonia is particularly popular with Finns. Water sports, winter sports, folk and architectural heritage, and nature tours are the main attractions. Tallinn's medieval center draws tourists on short visits and Baltic cruises.

PEOPLE

Pop. density low

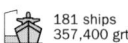

Estonian, Russian

29/km² (75/mi²)

THE URBAN/RURAL POPULATION SPLIT

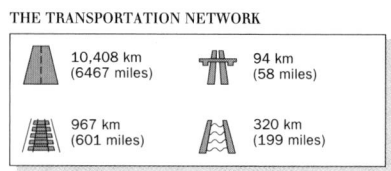

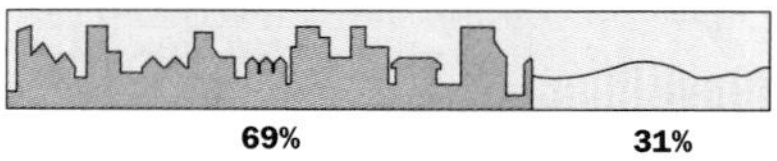
69%
31%

ETHNIC MAKEUP

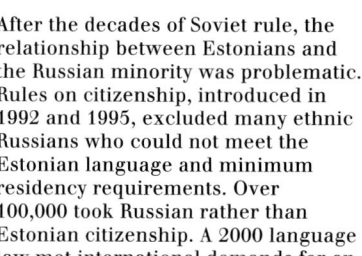

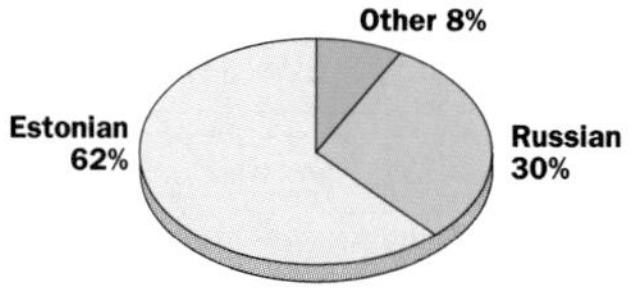
Other 8%
Estonian 62%
Russian 30%

After the decades of Soviet rule, the relationship between Estonians and the Russian minority was problematic. Rules on citizenship, introduced in 1992 and 1995, excluded many ethnic Russians who could not meet the Estonian language and minimum residency requirements. Over 100,000 took Russian rather than Estonian citizenship. A 2000 language law met international demands for an end to discrimination against the Russian-speaking minority. Estonians are predominantly Lutheran. Families are small; divorce rates are high.

POLITICS

Multiparty elections

2003/2007

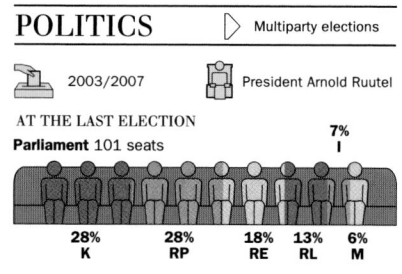

President Arnold Ruutel

AT THE LAST ELECTION

Parliament 101 seats

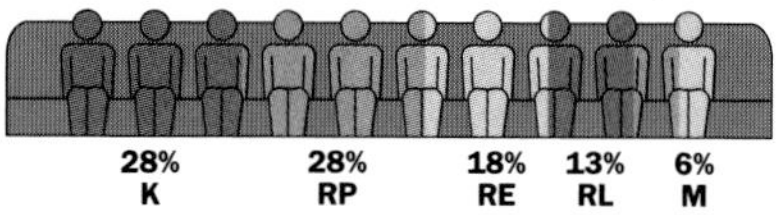
7%
I
28%
K
28%
RP
18%
RE
13%
RL
6%
M

K = Center Party **RP** = Union for the Republic
RE = Reform Party **RL** = Estonian People's Union
I = Pro Patria Union **M** = Moderates

Coalitions have been the norm since the end of communist rule. The left-wing Center Party dominated parliament from 1999, but was initially kept from power. Instead Mart Laar, of the center-right Pro Patria Union, became prime minister. Though hindered by a slim majority, his efforts to pursue free-market reforms became easier as the economy grew strongly from the beginning of 2000. However, cracks in his coalition led to its collapse in 2002, enabling the Center Party to enter the RE-led government. The 2003 elections resulted in a tie between the Center Party and the new right-wing RP, whose leader Juhan Parts became prime minister. He formed a new center-right coalition with the RE and the RL.

ESTONIA

Total Area : 45 226 sq. km (17 462 sq. miles)

LAND HEIGHT

200m/565ft

Sea Level

POPULATION

- over 500 000
- over 100 000
- over 50 000
- over 10 000
- under 10 000

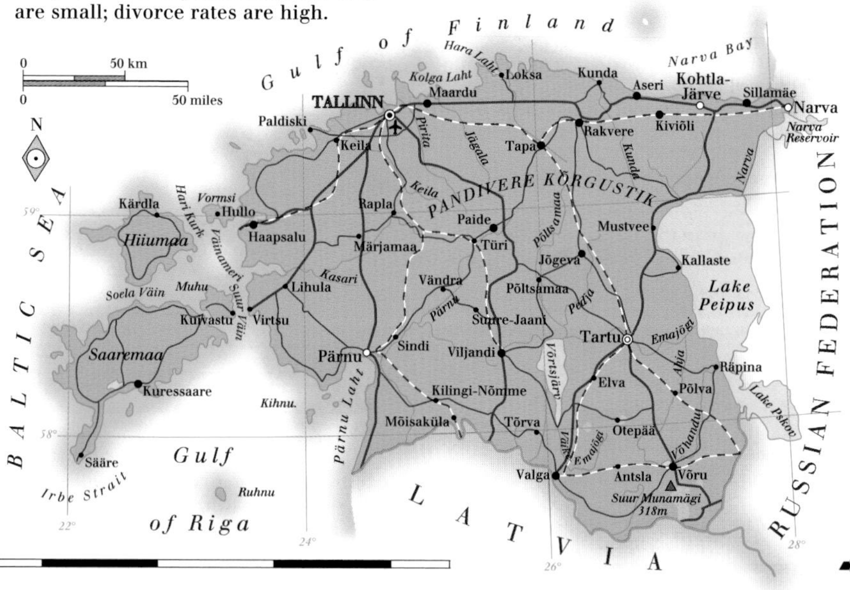
Gulf of Finland
Narva Bay
0 50 km
0 50 miles
TALLINN
Paldiski
Keila
Maardu
Kolga Laht
Hara Laht
Loksa
Kunda
Aseri
Kohtla-Järve
Sillamäe
Narva
Narva Reservoir
Rakvere
Kiviõli
Tapa
Pirita
Jägala
Kunda
Narva
Keila
PANDIVERE KÕRGUSTIK
Rapla
Paide
Mustvee
Türi
Märjamaa
Jõgeva
Kallaste
Vormsi
Hullo
Kärdla
Hiiumaa
Hari Kurk
Väinameri
Haapsalu
Kasari
Lihula
Vändra
Põltsamaa
Lake Peipus
Soela Väin
Muhu
Suur Väin
Kuivastu
Virtsu
Pärnu
Sindi
Viljandi
Suure-Jaani
Tartu
Emajõgi
Räpina
Saaremaa
Kuressaare
Kilingi-Nõmme
Elva
Põlva
Võrtsjärv
Kihnu
Pärnu Laht
Mõisaküla
Tõrva
Otepää
Lake Pskov
Sääre
Gulf of Riga
Irbe Strait
Ruhnu
Valga
Antsla
Võru
Võhandu
Suur Munamägi 318m
BALTIC SEA
LATVIA
RUSSIAN FEDERATION

WORLD AFFAIRS

Joined UN in 1991

CBSS | CE | EU | OSCE | NATO

Estonia's trade with the West has been growing, and ties with other Baltic states and Scandinavia have been particularly emphasized. Integration with the EU and NATO is the top priority; membership of NATO came in March 2004, while EU accession followed in May.

Estonia has now accepted the de facto border with Russia, having effectively ceded a portion of its territory during the Soviet period.

AID

Recipient

$69m (receipts)

Little change in 2002

Though an aid recipient, since 1997 Estonia has also been an aid donor, mainly through technical assistance.

DEFENSE

Compulsory military service

$93m

Up 43% in 2002

The government agreed in 2000 to shorten compulsory military service from 12 to eight months. Initial US opposition to full membership of NATO eventually changed to support for the Baltic states' entry into the organization, achieved in 2004.

ECONOMICS

Inflation 46% p.a. (1990–2001)

$5.69bn

12.86 kroons (13.62)

SCORE CARD

- WORLD GNP RANKING........................109th
- GNP PER CAPITA $4190
- BALANCE OF PAYMENTS....................–$802m
- INFLATION 3.6%
- UNEMPLOYMENT.................................10%

STRENGTHS

Improved productivity and stable currency are pegged to the euro. Simplicity of tax regime. More advantage is being taken of natural resources, including timber and oil shale. Transportation infrastructure has been upgraded. Exports growing.

WEAKNESSES

Poor raw materials base. Dependence on imported energy supplies.

EXPORTS

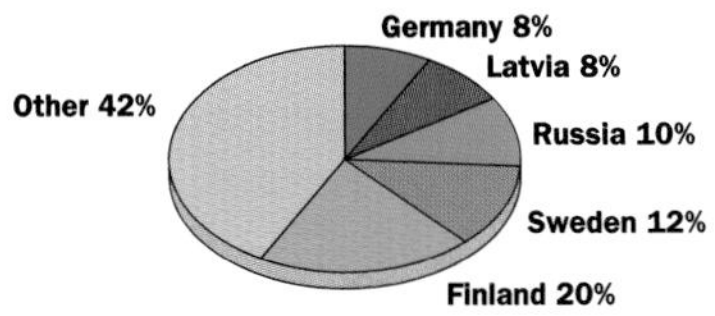
Germany 8%
Latvia 8%
Other 42%
Russia 10%
Sweden 12%
Finland 20%

IMPORTS

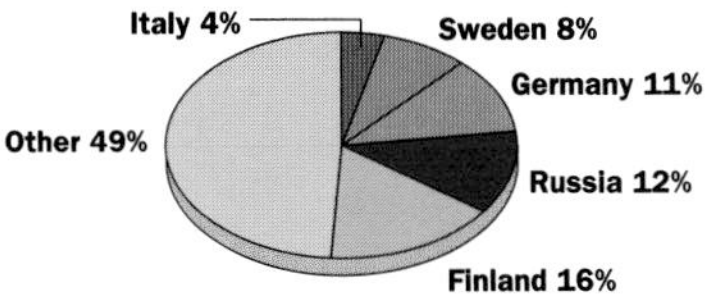
Italy 4%
Sweden 8%
Germany 11%
Other 49%
Russia 12%
Finland 16%

RESOURCES

Electric power 2.6m kW

105,634 tonnes

5000 b/d

340,800 pigs, 253,900 cattle, 2.1m chickens

Oil shale, coal, peat, phosphorite

The chief energy resource is oil shale. Phosphorite mining has been stopped. Half of all timber production is illegal.

ENVIRONMENT

Sustainability rank: 18th

12% (8% partially protected)

11.7 tonnes per capita

Industrial pollution comes especially from power plants burning oil shale. Danger of radioactive leaks from former Soviet bases remains. Water supply and sewage treatment have improved.

MEDIA

TV ownership high

Daily newspaper circulation 176 per 1000 people

PUBLISHING AND BROADCAST MEDIA

There are 17 daily newspapers. The main daily newspapers are *Eesti Ekspress*, *Maaleht*, and *Postimees*

3 services: 1 state-owned, 2 independent

30 services: 1 state-owned, 29 independent

The mass media are not harassed, but tend to reflect the view of the government. Almost half of all households have cable TV, available in Finnish, Swedish, Russian, and Latvian.

CRIME

No death penalty

4874 prisoners

Up 1% in 2001

Robbery and narcotics are the main crime problems. Generally, however, crime levels are still relatively low.

EDUCATION

School leaving age: 15

99%

63,625 students

Education is becoming increasingly Westernized. There are six public universities; the oldest is in Tartu.

HEALTH

Welfare state health benefits

1 per 323 people

Ischemic heart and cerebrovascular diseases, cancers

The health system, improved since the collapse of communism, is better than in most other former Soviet republics.

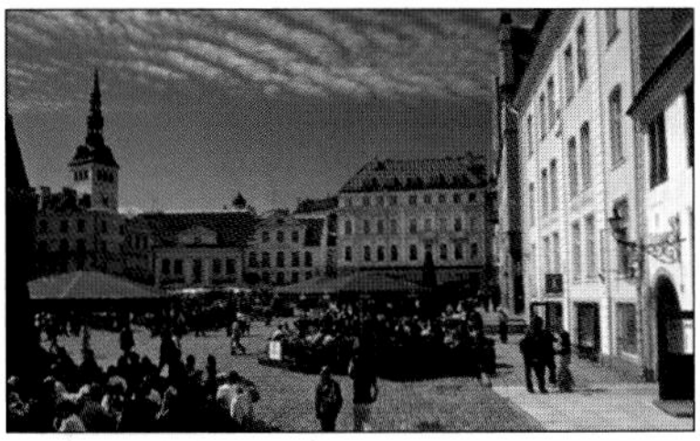

***The historical center** of Tallinn was restored after much of the city was destroyed during World War II.*

E

CHRONOLOGY

After Swedish and then Russian rule, Estonia briefly enjoyed independence from 1921 until its incorporation into the Soviet Union in 1940.

- **1990** Unilateral declaration of independence; achieved in 1991.
- **1992** First multiparty elections: center-right government formed.
- **1992–2001** Lennart Meri president.
- **1999** Left-wing K wins elections, but center-right forms new coalition.
- **2001** Communist-era leader Arnold Ruutel elected president.
- **2002** K joins new ruling coalition.
- **2003** K and RP tie in elections.
- **2004** Joins NATO and EU.

SPENDING

GDP/cap. increase

CONSUMPTION AND SPENDING

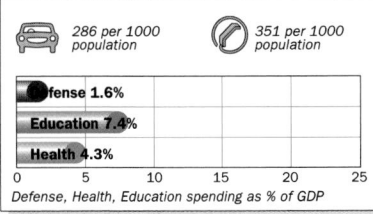

286 per 1000 population

351 per 1000 population

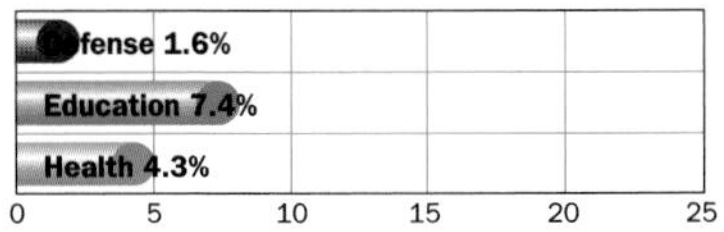
fense 1.6%
Education 7.4%
Health 4.3%
0
5
10
15
20
25

Defense, Health, Education spending as % of GDP

Market reforms have led to increased prosperity. A few people have become very rich. Average wages are higher than in other Baltic states.

WORLD RANKING

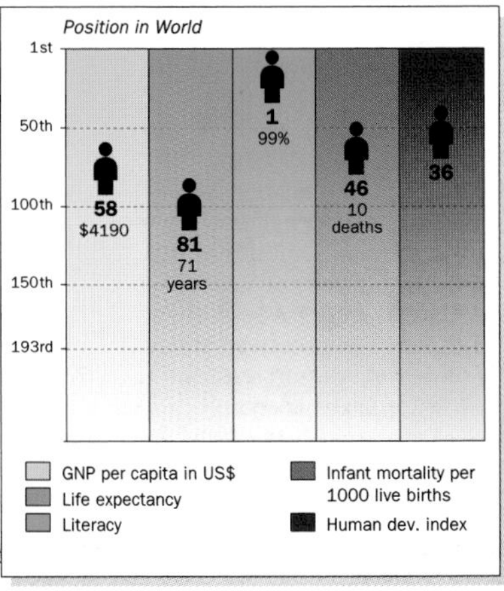
Position in World
1st
50th
100th
150th
193rd
58
$4190
81
71
years
1
99%
46
10
deaths
36
GNP per capita in US$
Life expectancy
Literacy
Infant mortality per 1000 live births
Human dev. index

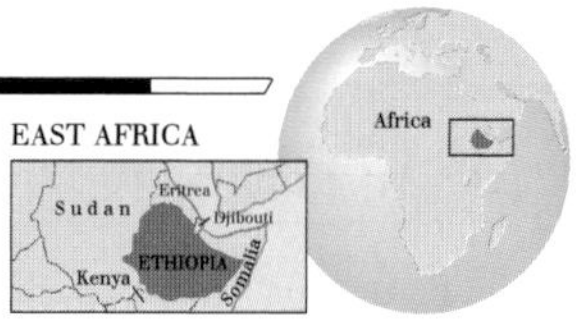
EAST AFRICA
Africa
Sudan
Eritrea
Djibouti
ETHIOPIA
Kenya
Somalia

ETHIOPIA

OFFICIAL NAME: Federal Democratic Republic of Ethiopia **CAPITAL:** Addis Ababa
POPULATION: 70.7 million **CURRENCY:** Ethiopian birr **OFFICIAL LANGUAGE:** Amharic

1896 | 2002 | May 28 | ETH | +3 | +251 | .et

THE FORMER EMPIRE OF Ethiopia, the only African country to escape colonization, is the cradle of an ancient civilization which adopted Orthodox Christianity in the 4th century. It has been landlocked since 1993, when Eritrea seceded. Ethiopia is mountainous except for desert lowlands in the northeast and southeast, and is prone to devastating drought and famine. A long civil war ended in 1991 with the defeat of the Stalinist military dictatorship that had ruled since 1974. A free-market, multiparty democratic system now provides substantial regional autonomy. War with Eritrea in 1998–2000 brought heavy losses on both sides before a peace agreement was signed in December 2000. Arbitrators began redefining the border in spring 2002.

CLIMATE

Mountain/steppe

WEATHER CHART FOR ADDIS ABABA

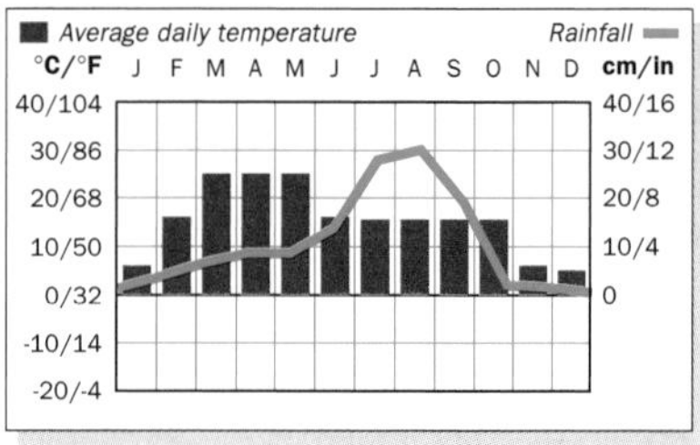
Average daily temperature
Rainfall
°C/°F
J F M A M J J A S O N D
cm/in
40/104
30/86
20/68
10/50
0/32
-10/14
-20/-4
40/16
30/12
20/8
10/4
0

In general, the climate is moderate, except in the lowlands of the Danakil and the Ogaden deserts, which are hot all year round and can suffer severe drought. The highlands are temperate, with night frost in the mountains. The single rainy season in the west brings twice as much rain as do the two wet seasons in the east. During these cloudy periods, thunderstorms occur almost daily.

TRANSPORTATION

Drive on right

Bole International, Addis Ababa
1.32m passengers

9 ships
81,933 grt

THE TRANSPORTATION NETWORK

3789 km (2354 miles)

Trans-East Africa Highway

681 km (423 miles)

None

Ethiopia's main access to the sea by road has been through the Red Sea ports of Assab and Massawa, now part of an independent Eritrea. The single railroad linking Addis Ababa with Djibouti has grown in strategic importance due to tensions with Eritrea. Inland, pack mules and donkeys are widely used. Ethiopian Airlines has good services to much of Africa, and to major cities around the world.

TOURISM

Visitors : Population 1:405

174,560 visitors

Up 12% in 2003

MAIN TOURIST ARRIVALS

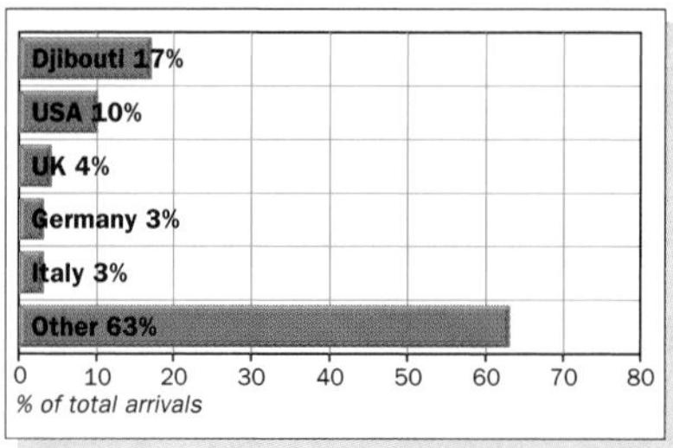
Djibouti 17%
USA 10%
UK 4%
Germany 3%
Italy 3%
Other 63%
0 10 20 30 40 50 60 70 80
% of total arrivals

Despite Ethiopia's unique attractions, tourism is on a small scale, though since 1991 there has been a sizable increase in the number of visitors, mostly on organized tours. Several new hotels are being built. The Rift Valley lakes, Lake Tana, the Gonder castles, and the Blue Nile gorge, with its spectacular scenery, are popular destinations, but guides are essential. Ancient rock-hewn churches, and cities such as Aksum, the royal capital of the first Ethiopian kingdom, are now accessible. There are nine national parks.

***Lalibela** lies 120 km (75 miles) northwest of Desē in Ethiopia's plateau region, and is famous for the rock-hewn churches created by King Lalibela of the Zagwe dynasty.*

PEOPLE

Pop. density medium

Amharic, Tigrinya, Galla, Sidamo, Somali, English, Arabic

64/km² (165/mi²)

THE URBAN/RURAL POPULATION SPLIT

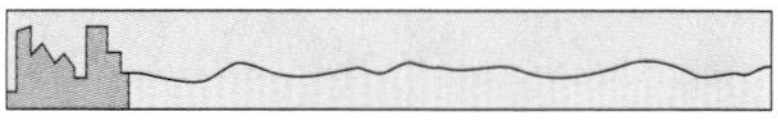
16%
84%

RELIGIOUS PERSUASION

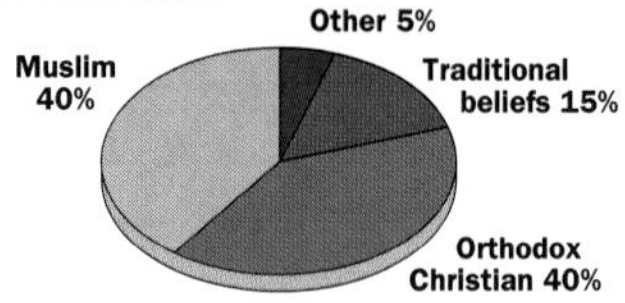
Other 5%
Muslim 40%
Traditional beliefs 15%
Orthodox Christian 40%

ETHNIC MAKEUP

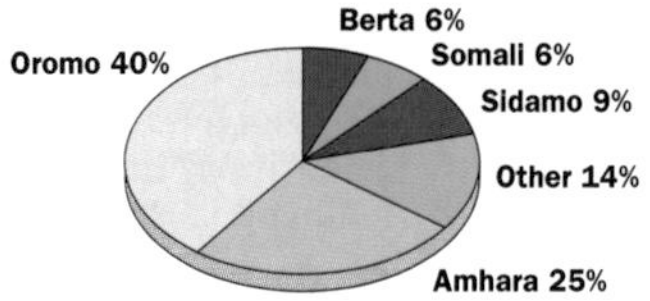
Berta 6%
Oromo 40%
Somali 6%
Sidamo 9%
Other 14%
Amhara 25%

Ethiopia has 76 ethnic nations, speaking 286 languages. Oromos (or Gallas) form the largest group, while less than 5% of the population are Tigreans, who dominate politics.

Civil war was sparked by fighting between different ethnic groups, but they later united in opposition to the Mengistu regime. Ethnic tensions are still near the surface in spite of the post-1995 federal structure, and there have been reports of boundary disputes in several regions. The Oromos withdrew from the Tigrean-dominated government in 1992. Hostility to the government has also been voiced by disaffected Amharas, who had been dominant for several centuries, and by the Orthodox Church. The aspirations of ethnic Somalis in the southeast are another source of tension.

Most of the small Jewish community, which had lived in Ethiopia for 2000 years, was evacuated to Israel in 1991. Israel pledged in 2004 to accept the remaining 20,000.

The participation of women in rural organizations is increasing, reflecting the key role women played in the war.

POPULATION AGE BREAKDOWN

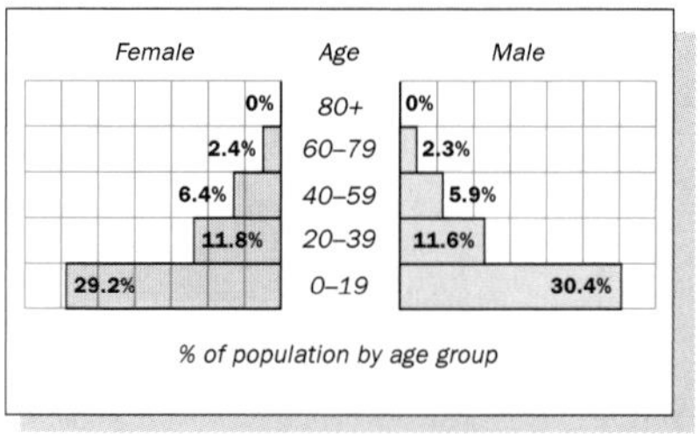
Female
Age
Male
0%
80+
0%
2.4%
60–79
2.3%
6.4%
40–59
5.9%
11.8%
20–39
11.6%
29.2%
0–19
30.4%
% of population by age group

Key to symbols and abbreviations on cover flaps

ETHIOPIA

Total Area :
1 127 127 sq. km
(435 184 sq. miles)

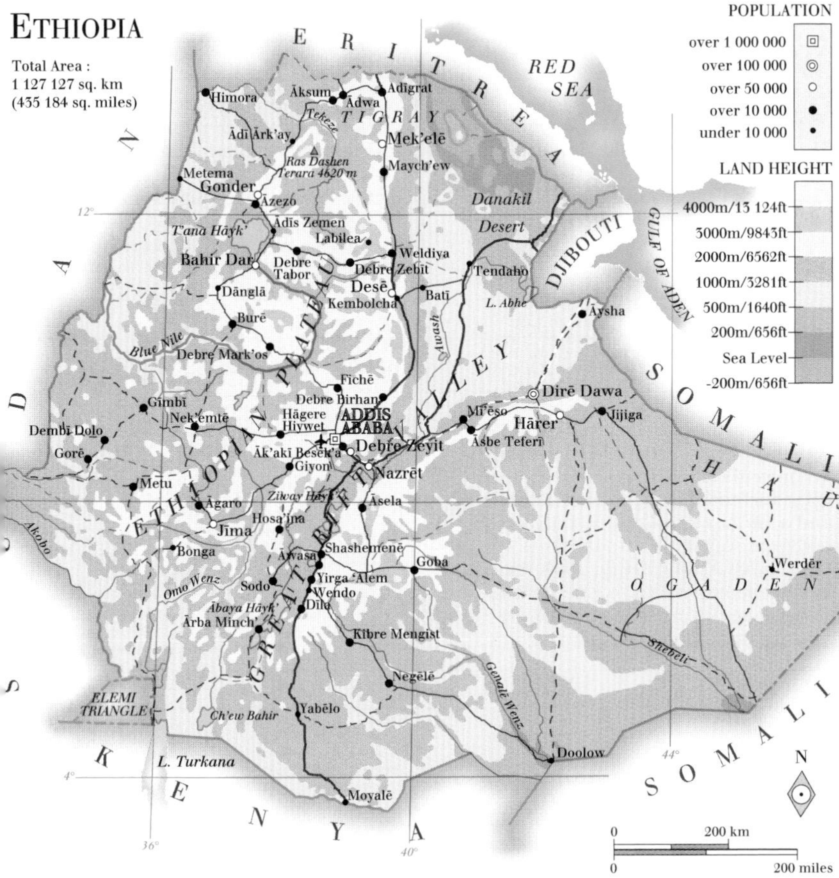

POPULATION
over 1 000 000
over 100 000
over 50 000
over 10 000
under 10 000
LAND HEIGHT
4000m/13 124ft
3000m/9843ft
2000m/6562ft
1000m/3281ft
500m/1640ft
200m/656ft
Sea Level
-200m/656ft
ERITREA
RED SEA
SUDAN
DJIBOUTI
GULF OF ADEN
SOMALIA
KENYA
TIGRAY
Danakil Desert
ETHIOPIAN PLATEAU
GREAT RIFT VALLEY
HAUD
OGADEN
ELEMI TRIANGLE
Himora
Āksum
Ādwa
Ādīgrat
Ādī Ārk'ay
Tekezē
Ras Dashen Terara 4620 m
Mek'elē
Maych'ew
Metema
Gonder
Āzezo
T'ana Hāyk'
Ādīs Zemen
Labilea
Bahir Dar
Debre Tabor
Weldiya
Debre Zebīt
Dese
Kembolcha
Batī
Tendaho
L. Abhe
Āysha
Awash
Dānglā
Burē
Blue Nile
Debre Mark'os
Fichē
Debre Birhan
Hāgere Hiywet
ADDIS ABABA
Gīmbī
Nek'emtē
Dembī Dolo
Gorē
Āk'ak'ī Besek'a
Debre Zeyit
Giyon
Nazrēt
Mī'ēso
Dirē Dawa
Hārer
Jijiga
Āsbe Teferī
Metu
Āgaro
Jīma
Ziway Hāyk'
Hosa'ina
Āsela
Bonga
Āwasa
Shashemenē
Goba
Yirga 'Alem
Wendo
Omo Wenz
Sodo
Ābaya Hāyk'
Ārba Minch'
Dila
Kibre Mengist
Negēlē
Genalē Wenz
Shebelē
Werdēr
Ch'ew Bahir
Yabēlo
L. Turkana
Moyalē
Doolow
Akobo
N
0 200 km
0 200 miles

WORLD AFFAIRS

Joined UN in 1945

COMESA | G24 | IGAD | NAM | AU

Landlocked since the secession of Eritrea, Ethiopia needs continued access to the Red Sea ports of Massawa and Assab. Relations with Eritrea remained cordial until a border dispute escalated into armed conflict in 1998. A peace accord reached two years later allowed for the demarcation of a new boundary, but progress has been hindered by disputes over border towns.

Addis Ababa is the headquarters of the AU and of the UN Economic Commission for Africa. Ethiopia is active in regional diplomacy, including numerous attempts at brokering peace in Somalia, though tension with Somali factions has escalated into armed intervention by Ethiopia, provoking considerable resentment in Somalia.

The Ethiopian government's official policy is one of noninterference in the affairs of neighboring countries, though both Sudan and Somalia have accused Ethiopia of supporting rebels. Links with other African states have been strengthened, as have those with the US, the EU, and Israel.

POLITICS

Multiparty elections

L. House 2000/2005
U. House 2000/2005

President Girma Wolde Giorgis

AT THE LAST ELECTION

House of People's Representatives 550 seats

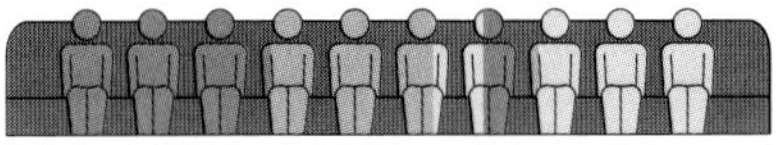

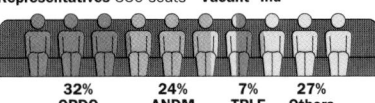

8% Vacant
2% Ind
32% OPDO
24% ANDM
7% TPLF
27% Others

OPDO = Oromo People's Democratic Organization
ANDM = Amhara National Democratic Movement
TPLF = Tigre People's Liberation Front **Ind** = Independents

The Ethiopian People's Revolutionary Democratic Front (**EPRDF**) includes all the main parties and controls over 90% of the lower house

House of the Federation 108 seats

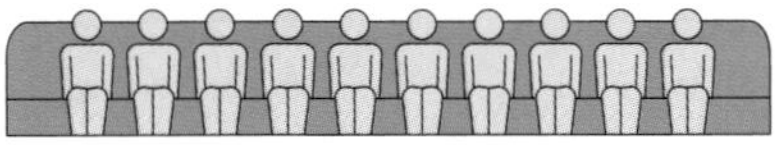

The upper house is elected indirectly on a nonparty basis

The transitional period which followed the collapse of the Mengistu military dictatorship in 1991 ended in 1995 with multiparty elections.

PROFILE

The current government, first elected in 1995, succeeded that set up in 1991 by the EPRDF, the strongest of the groups that fought Mengistu's Marxist regime and chiefly responsible for winning the civil war. Prime Minister Meles Zenawi is the leader of the Tigrean People's Liberation Front, the largest group within the EPRDF. There is growing opposition from the Oromos and Amharas to the dominance of Tigreans. The nine states are run by elected governments mainly headed by local liberation movements.

MAIN POLITICAL ISSUE

Interethnic and postwar reconciliation

Achieving stability is a key priority. The 1995 constitution which provides a great deal of local autonomy was intended to appease the demands of the various ethnic groups, but tensions remain. Looking north, the administration is keen to keep the slow-paced peace process with Eritrea on track, albeit under strong UN pressure.

Prime Minister Meles Zenawi, *leader of the EPRDF, which ousted the Mengistu regime.*

Haile Selassie, *emperor until 1974, revered by Rastafarians.*

CHRONOLOGY

After repelling a devastating Muslim invasion in 1523, Ethiopia developed as an isolated empire until Egyptian and Sudanese incursions in the 1850s led to its renewed political power under Emperor Teodros. His successor, Menelik II, doubled the empire southward and eastward.

- **1896** Italian invasion of Tigre defeated. Europeans recognize Ethiopia's independence.
- **1913** Menelik II dies.
- **1916** His son, Lij Iyasu, is deposed for his conversion to Islam and a proposed alliance with Turkey. Menelik's daughter, Zauditu, becomes empress with Ras (Prince) Tafari as regent.
- **1923** Joins League of Nations.
- **1930** Zauditu dies. Ras Tafari crowned Emperor Haile Selassie.
- **1936** Italians occupy Ethiopia. League of Nations fails to react.
- **1941** British oust Italians and restore Haile Selassie, who sets up a constitution, parliament, and cabinet, but retains personal power and the feudal system.
- **1952** Eritrea, ruled by Italy until 1941, then under British mandate, federated with Ethiopia. ⇨

CHRONOLOGY *continued*

- **1962** Unitary state created; Eritrea loses its autonomy despite demands of secessionists.
- **1972–1974** Famine kills 200,000.
- **1974** Strikes and army mutinies at Haile Selassie's autocratic rule and country's economic decline. Dergue (Military Committee) stages coup.
- **1975** Becomes socialist state: nationalizations, worker cooperatives, and health reforms.
- **1977** Col. Mengistu Haile Mariam takes over. Somali invasion of Ogaden defeated with Soviet and Cuban help.
- **1978–1979** Thousands of political opponents killed or imprisoned.
- **1984** Workers' Party of Ethiopia (WPE) set up on Soviet model. One million die in famine after drought and years of war. Live Aid concert raises funds for relief.
- **1986** Eritrean rebels now control entire northeastern coast.
- **1987** Serious drought again threatens famine.
- **1988** Eritrean and Tigrean People's Liberation Fronts (EPLF and TPLF) begin new offensives. Mengistu's budget is for "Everything to the War Front." Diplomatic relations with Somalia restored.
- **1989** Military coup attempt fails. TPLF controls most of Tigre. TPLF and Ethiopian People's Revolutionary Movement form alliance – EPRDF.
- **1990** Military gains by opponents of Mengistu regime. Moves toward market economy and restructuring of ruling party to include non-Marxists. Distribution of food aid for victims of new famine is hampered by government and rebel forces.
- **1991** Mengistu accepts military defeat and flees country. EPRDF enters Addis Ababa, sets up provisional government, promising representation for all ethnic groups. Outbreaks of fighting continue, between mainly Tigrean EPRDF and opposing groups.
- **1993** Eritrean independence recognized following referendum.
- **1995** Transitional rule ends. EPRDF wins landslide in multiparty elections, sets up first democratic government. New nine-state federation is formed.
- **1998–2000** Border war with Eritrea.
- **2000** OAU peace treaty signed. Haile Selassie's remains buried in Trinity Cathedral, Addis Ababa.
- **2001** Ethiopia completes troop withdrawal from Eritrea.
- **2002** Over 120 human rights demonstrators killed by police.

AID

Recipient

$1.31bn (receipts) — Up 17% in 2002

Aid plays an increasingly important role in the economy. The World Bank, the US, and the EU are the largest sources of assistance. The World Bank donated $3.6 billion in 2002 toward tackling poverty. However, emphasis has shifted from infrastructure development back to straightforward food aid since recurring and prolonged droughts hit the country from 2000. Contributions have consistently fallen short of the country's needs, and failed to prevent a new famine in early 2003, despite months of warnings.

DEFENSE

No compulsory military service

$442m — Down 23% in 2002

Ethiopia is one of the most heavily militarized states in Africa. Its sizable standing army is boosted by conscription at times of crisis. Heavy losses have been sustained in fighting with Eritrea, and a 12-month international arms embargo was imposed following the Ethiopian advance in 2000. The government is trying to gain control of the many ethnic and clan-based militias throughout the country.

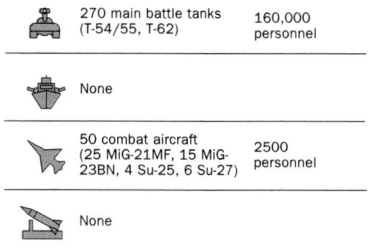

ETHIOPIAN ARMED FORCES

270 main battle tanks (T-54/55, T-62)	160,000 personnel
None	
50 combat aircraft (25 MiG-21MF, 15 MiG-23BN, 4 Su-25, 6 Su-27)	2500 personnel
None	

ECONOMICS

Inflation 6.1% p.a. (1990–2001)

$6.52bn — 8.6 Ethiopian birr (8.575)

SCORE CARD

World GNP Ranking	102nd
GNP per capita	$100
Balance of payments	–$150m
Inflation	1.6%
Unemployment	8%

EXPORTS

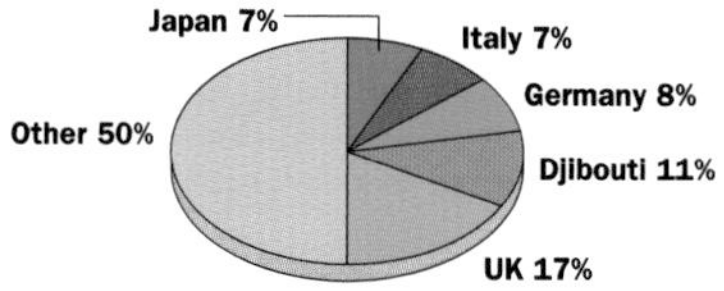

Japan 7%
Italy 7%
Germany 8%
Djibouti 11%
UK 17%
Other 50%

IMPORTS

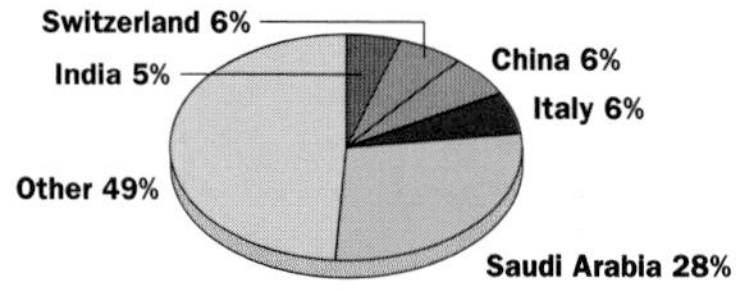

Switzerland 6%
India 5%
China 6%
Italy 6%
Other 49%
Saudi Arabia 28%

Strengths

Increased economic aid in 1990s. End of total state control. Coffee production.

Weaknesses

Overwhelming dependence on agriculture. Periodic serious droughts and famine. Massive displacement of population by war and drought. Steep projected growth in HIV/AIDS cases. War-damaged infrastructure. Small industrial base. Lack of skilled workers.

Profile

After the end of the civil war in 1991, Ethiopia began moving toward a market economy by encouraging foreign investment and reforming land tenure. Economic decline was reversed in 1993 as agricultural and industrial output grew, with foreign aid used to fund the purchase of parts and raw materials for manufacturing. These gains were undermined by war with Eritrea in 1998–2000 and the renewed danger of severe drought-related famine from 2000.

ECONOMIC PERFORMANCE INDICATOR

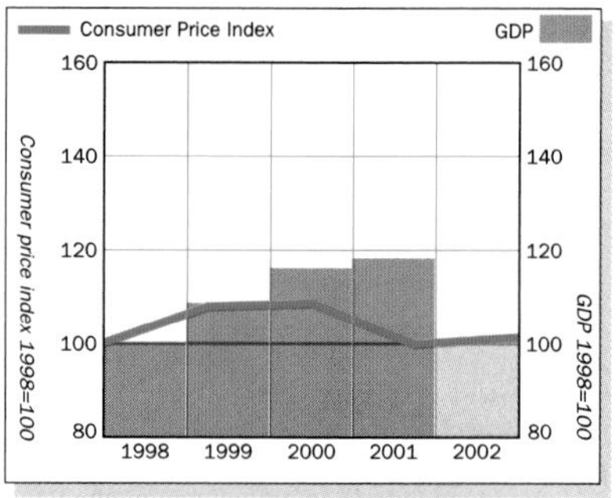

Consumer Price Index
GDP
160
140
120
100
80
Consumer price index 1998=100
GDP 1998=100
1998
1999
2000
2001
2002

ETHIOPIA : MAJOR BUSINESSES

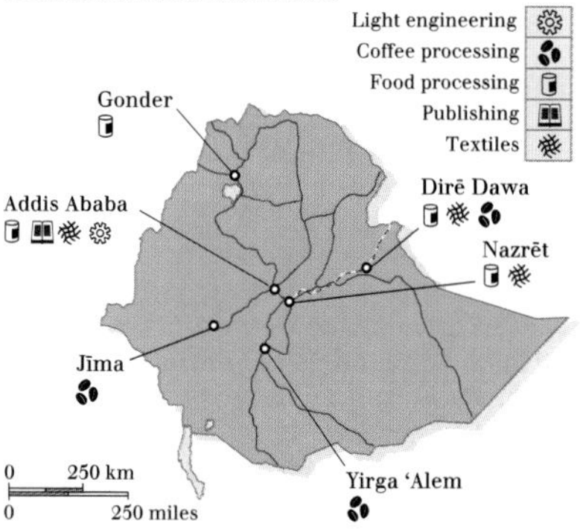

Light engineering
Coffee processing
Food processing
Publishing
Textiles
Gonder
Addis Ababa
Dirē Dawa
Nazrēt
Jīma
Yirga 'Alem
0 250 km
0 250 miles

RESOURCES

Electric power 469,000 kW

15,390 tonnes

Oil reserves not yet exploited; refines 12,300 b/d

35.5m cattle, 11.4m sheep, 9.62m goats, 39m chickens

Oil, gold, platinum, copper, potash, iron, natural gas

ELECTRICITY GENERATION

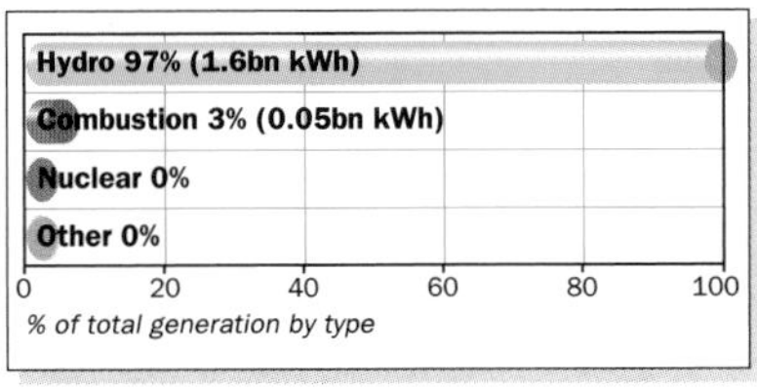
Hydro 97% (1.6bn kWh)
Combustion 3% (0.05bn kWh)
Nuclear 0%
Other 0%
0 20 40 60 80 100
% of total generation by type

Manpower and financial constraints have prevented a systematic survey of mineral resources. Mining contributes barely 0.5% of GDP. Domestic reliance on fuelwood is causing slow massive deforestation and soil erosion; potential for expanding HEP could reduce fuel needs. Construction of the 300 MW Tekeze Dam began in 2002 and is expected to be completed by 2007. The potential for geothermal energy production along the Rift Valley is estimated at 700 MW. The Malaysian oil firm Petronas won exploration rights in western Ethiopia in 2003.

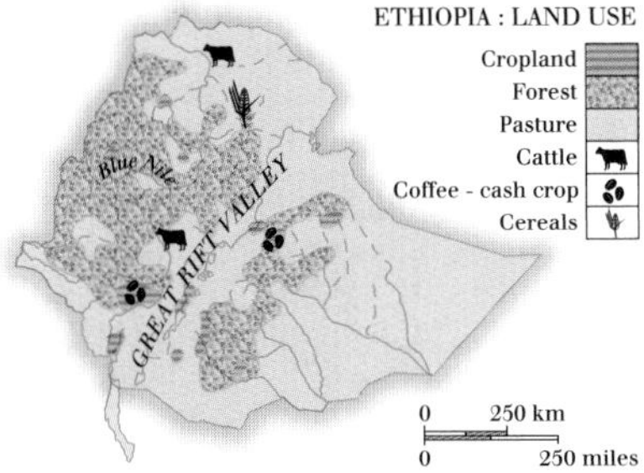
ETHIOPIA : LAND USE
Cropland
Forest
Pasture
Cattle
Coffee - cash crop
Cereals
Blue Nile
GREAT RIFT VALLEY
0 250 km
0 250 miles

ENVIRONMENT

Sustainability rank: 113th

17% (14% partially protected)

0.1 tonnes per capita

ENVIRONMENTAL TREATIES

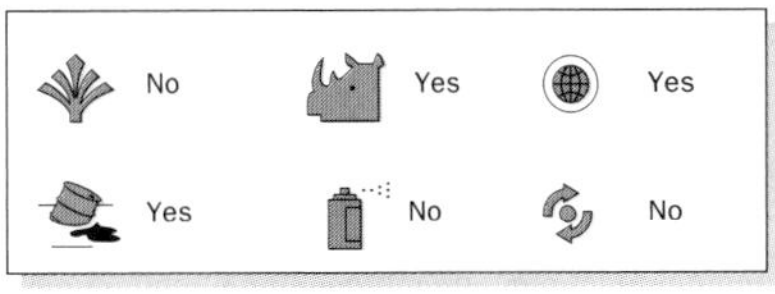
No
Yes
Yes
Yes
No
No

The gathering of wood for fuel has caused deforestation and rapid soil erosion, particularly in the highlands. Forest cover has fallen from 40% in 1900 to only 5% today. Dung is being used for fuel, instead of as a fertilizer. Local projects include terracing hillsides to prevent soil and water run-off – 36,000 km (22,370 miles) of terraces were built in Tigre in 1992. Thousands of people invaded the Bale Mountains National Park in 2002 in search of water, threatening its delicate ecosystem.

MEDIA

TV ownership low

Daily newspaper circulation 0.4 per 1000 people

The independent press has become prolific and critical, though legal action has been taken to silence several publications. Circulations remain small. All main newspapers and the TV broadcasting station are government-owned and operated. Private radio licenses are to be issued from 2005.

PUBLISHING AND BROADCAST MEDIA

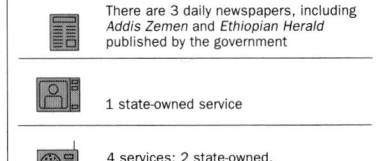

There are 3 daily newspapers, including *Addis Zemen* and *Ethiopian Herald* published by the government

1 state-owned service

4 services: 2 state-owned, 2 independent

CRIME

Death penalty in use

13,585 prisoners

Up 12% in 2000–2001

CRIME RATES

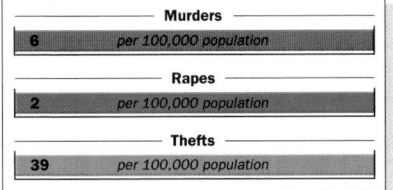

Murders	6	per 100,000 population
Rapes	2	per 100,000 population
Thefts	39	per 100,000 population

A number of human rights abuses by the transitional government have been documented by the independent Ethiopian Human Rights Council. These include detention without trial, "disappearances," and extrajudicial killings. There is some concern over indiscipline among EPRDF forces, who provide a de facto police force in many regions. In rural areas the state system has yet to replace traditional forms of justice.

EDUCATION

School leaving age: 13

42%

87,431 students

THE EDUCATION SYSTEM

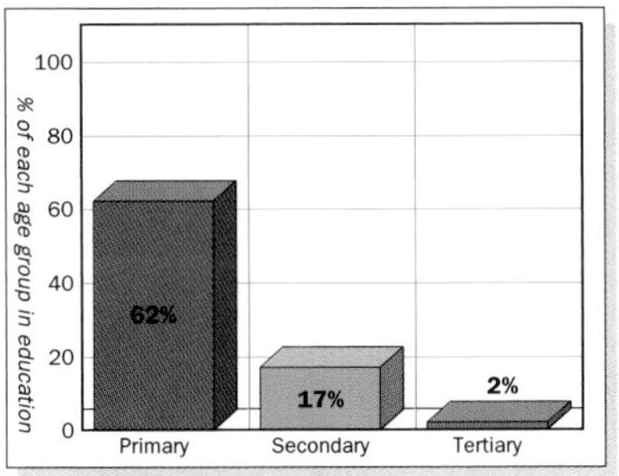
100
80
60
40
20
0
% of each age group in education
62%
17%
2%
Primary
Secondary
Tertiary

Education is free, but classes are crowded and schooling has been severely disrupted by war. Only a small minority of children attend secondary school. Addis Ababa University, a center of political activity (usually anti-EPRDF), suffers periodic closures and the dismissal of leading academics.

HEALTH

No welfare state health benefits

1 per 33,333 people

Diarrheal and respiratory diseases, tuberculosis, malaria

Starvation after severe drought is the principal concern. Malnutrition is increasingly widespread, causing growth problems and allowing the rapid spread of infectious diseases among the weakened. HIV affects 4.4% of adults – almost one and a half million people. Fewer than one in four Ethiopians have access to clean water. The use of traditional remedies is widespread.

SPENDING

GDP/cap. increase

CONSUMPTION AND SPENDING

1 per 1000 population

5 per 1000 population

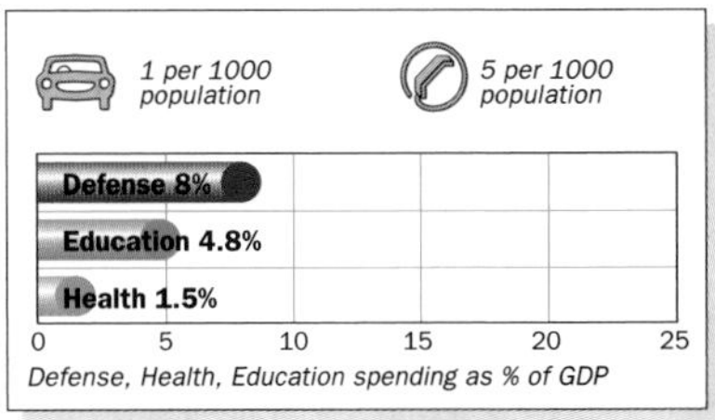
Defense 8%
Education 4.8%
Health 1.5%
0 5 10 15 20 25
Defense, Health, Education spending as % of GDP

Most Ethiopians are extremely poor, many of the country's wealthier families having fled into exile in recent years. Ethiopian Christian culture places more value on maintaining traditional social structures than on realizing individual ambition. Living at subsistence level and a reliance on traditional agriculture remain the general expectation.

WORLD RANKING

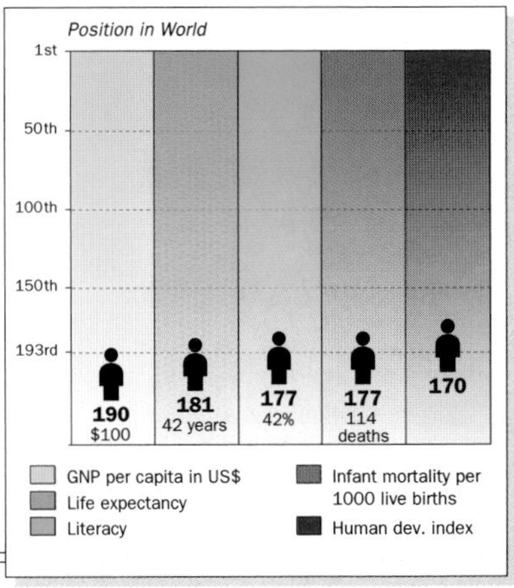
Position in World
1st
50th
100th
150th
193rd
190
$100
181
42 years
177
42%
177
114
deaths
170
GNP per capita in US$
Life expectancy
Literacy
Infant mortality per 1000 live births
Human dev. index

E

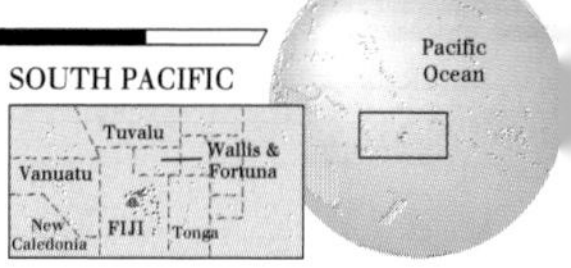
SOUTH PACIFIC
Tuvalu
Wallis & Fortuna
Vanuatu
New Caledonia
FIJI
Tonga
Pacific Ocean

FIJI

OFFICIAL NAME: Republic of the Fiji Islands **CAPITAL:** Suva
POPULATION: 839,000 **CURRENCY:** Fiji dollar **OFFICIAL LANGUAGE:** English

1970 | 1970 | Oct 10 | FJI | +12 | +679 | .fj

FIJI IS A VOLCANIC archipelago in the southern Pacific Ocean, comprising two main islands and nearly 900 smaller islands and islets. The Melanesian Fijian population was outnumbered in the post-1945 period by ethnic Indians, descended from workers brought over by the British in 1879–1916. Coups led by Fijian supremacists between 1987 and 2000 led to a mass exodus of Indo-Fijians, reversing the ethnic balance and seriously damaging the economy.

CLIMATE

Tropical oceanic

WEATHER CHART FOR SUVA

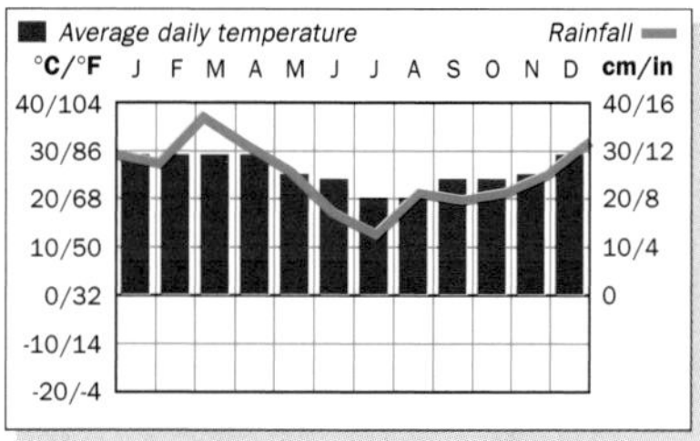
Average daily temperature
Rainfall
°C/°F
J F M A M J J A S O N D
cm/in
40/104
30/86
20/68
10/50
0/32
-10/14
-20/-4
40/16
30/12
20/8
10/4
0

The eastern sides of the main islands are wettest, having more than twice the annual rainfall of the western flanks. Fiji lies in a cyclone path.

TRANSPORTATION

Drive on left

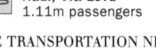

Nadi, Viti Levu 1.11m passengers

51 ships 27,200 grt

THE TRANSPORTATION NETWORK

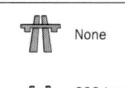

1686 km (1048 miles)	None
597 km (371 miles)	203 km (126 miles)

On the axis of Australian–west coast US air routes, Fiji is well served by international flights. An international airport is proposed for Vanua Levu.

TOURISM

Visitors : Population 1:2.1

398,000 visitors

Up 14% in 2002

MAIN TOURIST ARRIVALS

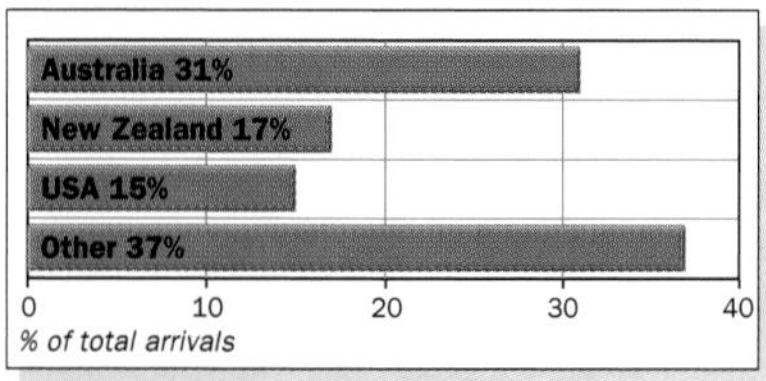
Australia 31%
New Zealand 17%
USA 15%
Other 37%
0
10
20
30
40
% of total arrivals

Tourism – Fiji's largest earner – is greatly affected by political instability: 7500 jobs were lost in 2000 alone. Recovery has been rapid.

PEOPLE

Pop. density low

Fijian, English, Hindi, Urdu, Tamil, Telugu

46/km² (119/mi²)

THE URBAN/RURAL POPULATION SPLIT

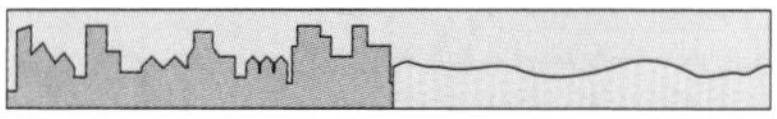
51%
49%

RELIGIOUS PERSUASION

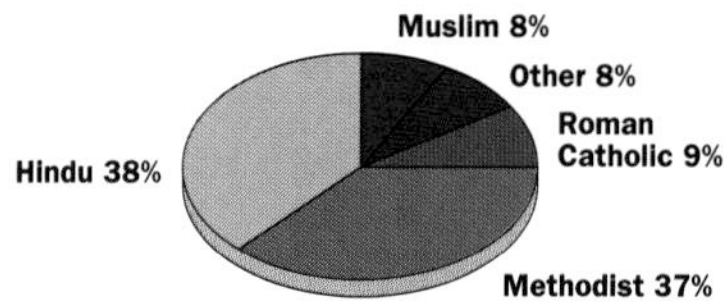
Muslim 8%
Other 8%
Roman Catholic 9%
Hindu 38%
Methodist 37%

A delicate ethnic balance was shattered by the exodus of Indo-Fijians in 1987–1989 and again in 2000–2001. The lawlessness accompanying the recent upheavals exaggerated ethnic tensions and brought racist rhetoric back to the political mainstream. A substantial population of Polynesians live on Rotuma and have a great degree of autonomy. Women are lobbying for more rights.

POLITICS

Multiparty elections

L. House 2001/2006
U. House 2001/2006

President Ratu Josefa Iloilo

AT THE LAST ELECTION

House of Representatives 71 seats

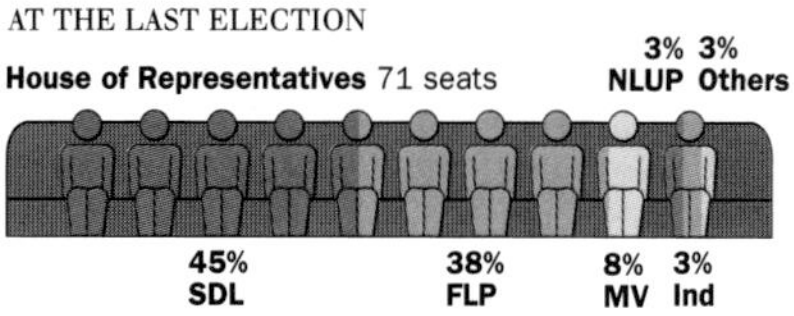
3% NLUP
3% Others
45% SDL
38% FLP
8% MV
3% Ind

SDL = Fijian People's Party **FLP** = Fiji Labor Party
MV = Conservative Alliance **NLUP** = New Labor Unity Party
Ind = Independents

Senate 32 seats

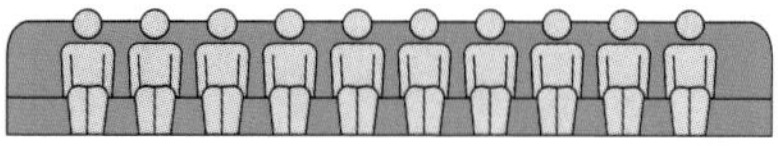

The Senate is appointed by the president

The Great Council of Chiefs emerged as the power broker after the 2000 coup, preventing the FLP from returning to power and upholding the ban on the multiethnic 1997 constitution. The new Fijian-nationalist SDL government, led by Laisenia Qarase, refused to let the FLP join the cabinet, despite its right to do so after winning over 10% of votes in new elections in 2001. Former FLP prime minister Mahendra Chaudhry rejected the role of opposition leader. The courts have backed the FLP, ruling in 2003 that it must be given cabinet seats.

FIJI

Total Area : 18 270 sq. km (7054 sq. miles)

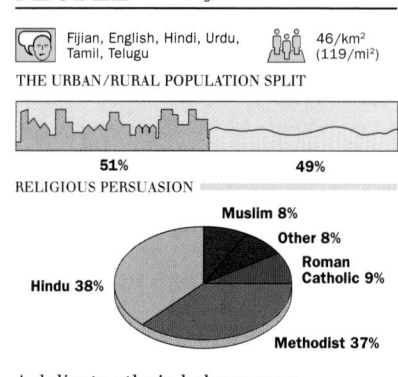

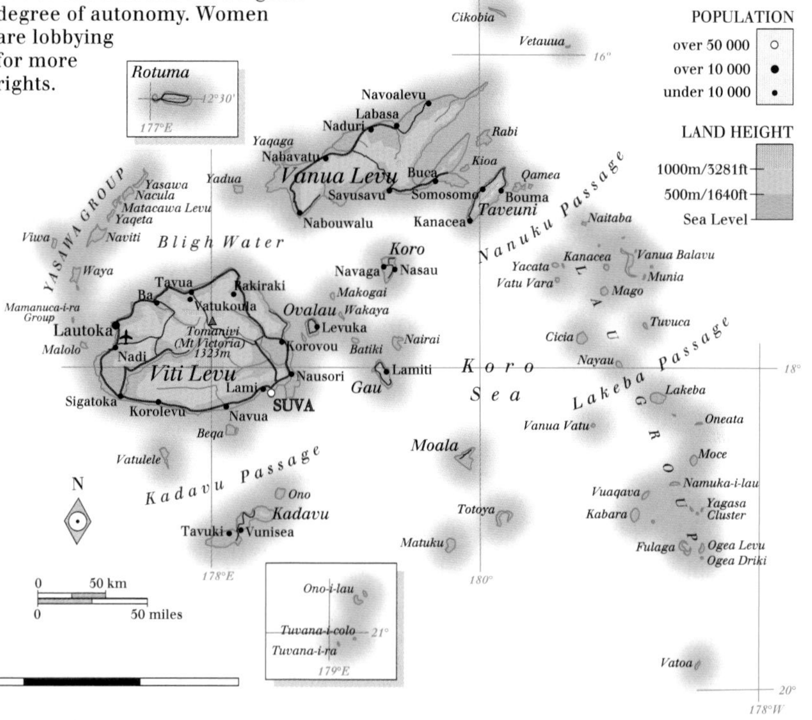
POPULATION
over 50 000
over 10 000
under 10 000
LAND HEIGHT
1000m/3281ft
500m/1640ft
Sea Level
Rotuma
177°E
Cikobia
Vetauua
Navoalevu
Labasa
Naduri
Rabi
Yaqaga
Nabavatu
Vanua Levu
Buca
Kioa
Qamea
Savusavu
Somosomo
Bouma
Taveuni
Nabouwalu
Kanacea
Naitaba
Yasawa
Nacula
Matacawa Levu
Yaqeta
Yadua
Naviti
Viwa
Bligh Water
Waya
Koro
Navaga
Nasau
Makogai
Wakaya
Ovalau
Levuka
Nairai
Batiki
Tavua
Rakiraki
Ba
Vatukoula
Tomanivi (Mt Victoria) 1323m
Lautoka
Nadi
Viti Levu
Korovou
Nausori
Lami
SUVA
Sigatoka
Korolevu
Navua
Beqa
Mamanuca-i-ra Group
Malolo
Gau
Lamiti
Koro Sea
Nanuku Passage
Kanacea
Vanua Balavu
Munia
Yacata
Vatu Vara
Mago
Tuvuca
Cicia
Nayau
Lakeba Passage
Lakeba
Oneata
Vanua Vatu
Moala
Moce
Namuka-i-lau
Vuaqava
Kabara
Yagasa Cluster
Totoya
Matuku
Fulaga
Ogea Levu
Ogea Driki
Vatulele
Kadavu Passage
Ono
Kadavu
Tavuki
Vunisea
N
0 50 km
0 50 miles
Ono-i-lau
Tuvana-i-colo
Tuvana-i-ra
179°E
178°E
180°
Vatoa
178°W
16°
18°
20°
21°

WORLD AFFAIRS

Joined UN in 1970

ACP | CP | Comm | PC | PIF

Fiji's international reputation has been severely damaged by its discrimination against Indo-Fijians and the recent coups. Fiji has been intermittently suspended from the Commonwealth.

AID

Recipient

US$34m (receipts) | Up 31% in 2002

International reaction to the 2000 coup prompted drastic cuts in aid donations. EU aid was restored in 2003.

DEFENSE

No compulsory military service

US$26m | No change in 2002

Of the almost entirely ethnic Fijian military, significant numbers – around 20% – are assigned to UN duties and have served in Lebanon and Egypt.

ECONOMICS

Inflation 3.1% p.a. (1990–2001)

US$1.75bn | 1.798 Fiji dollars (1.873)

SCORE CARD

❑ World GNP Ranking	142nd
❑ GNP per Capita	US$2130
❑ Balance of Payments	US$13m
❑ Inflation	0.8%
❑ Unemployment	12%

Strengths

Diversification. Strong and resilient tourist infrastructure. Location on Pacific air routes. Remittances from overseas Fijians growing. Many NGOs located in Suva.

Weaknesses

2000 coup caused dramatic contraction in economy – 12.5%. Migration of many Indo-Fijian professionals. Sugar crops vulnerable to drought. Major exports – sugar, copra, and gold – subject to large fluctuations in world prices.

EXPORTS

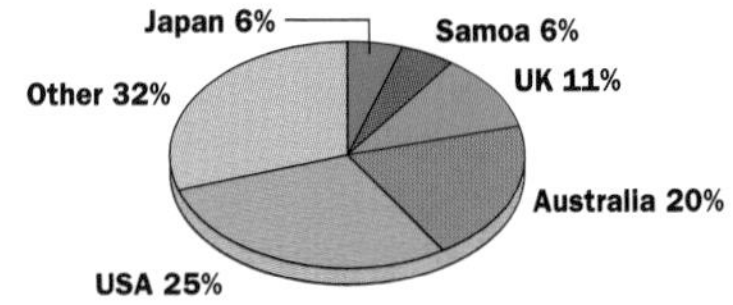
Japan 6%
Samoa 6%
UK 11%
Other 32%
Australia 20%
USA 25%

IMPORTS

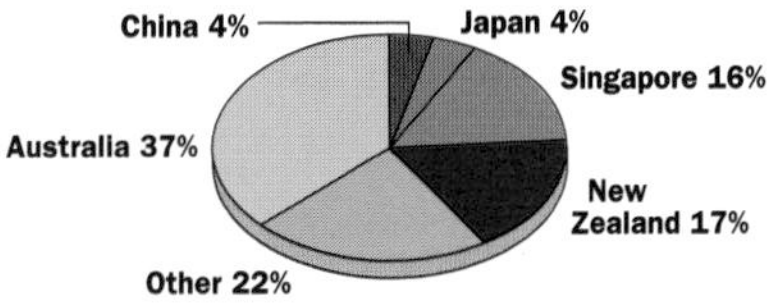
China 4%
Japan 4%
Singapore 16%
Australia 37%
New Zealand 17%
Other 22%

Cane field on the west side of Viti Levu, between Nadi and Lautoka. Sugar accounts for just over a fifth of Fiji's exports.

RESOURCES

Electric power 200,000 kW

44,689 tonnes | Not an oil producer

320,000 cattle, 248,000 goats, 3.8m chickens | Gold, silver

The varied terrain allows diversified agriculture. Gold and minerals are mined. A hydroelectric plant at Monasavu provides 79% of electricity.

ENVIRONMENT

Not available

1.1% | 0.9 tonnes per capita

Environmental awareness is high. Tourism is damaging coral reefs and fertilizers are overused. Fiji was downwind of French nuclear tests.

MEDIA

TV ownership medium

Daily newspaper circulation 52 per 1000 people

PUBLISHING AND BROADCAST MEDIA

There are 2 English-language dailies, *Fiji Times* and *Fiji Daily Post*. *Nai Lalakai* and *Shanti Dut* are Fijian and Indian weeklies

2 services: 1 state-owned, 1 independent | 4 services: 1 state-controlled, 3 independent

Freedom of the press is championed by the government, and cases of corruption are often reported in the media. However, the police have blocked politically sensitive broadcasts.

CRIME

Death penalty not used in practice

897 prisoners | Down 30% in 2003

Usually theft and drink-related violence top the crime list. US$500 million of narcotics were seized near Suva in 2004.

EDUCATION

School leaving age: 15

93% | 9208 students

Education, originally modeled on the British system, is now mostly run by local committees and is increasingly racially segregated. The use of the birch in schools was banned in 2002.

CHRONOLOGY

The British decision to import Indian sugar workers in 1879–1916 dramatically changed Fijian society.

- ❑ **1970** Independence from Britain.
- ❑ **1987** Election win for Indo-Fijian coalition. Sitiveni Rabuka's coups secure minority ethnic Fijian rule. Ejected from Commonwealth.
- ❑ **1989** Mass Indo-Fijian emigration.
- ❑ **1990** Constitution discriminating against Indo-Fijians introduced.
- ❑ **1992** Rabuka wins legislative polls.
- ❑ **1997** Census shows ethnic Fijians outnumber Indo-Fijians. Fiji rejoins Commonwealth. New constitution.
- ❑ **1999** General election won by FLP. First Indo-Fijian prime minister.
- ❑ **2000** Civilian-led coup; new ethnic Fijian government.
- ❑ **2001** Nationalists win elections.

HEALTH

Welfare state health benefits

1 per 2974 people | Cerebrovascular and heart diseases, cancers, accidents

Medical treatment is provided for all at a nominal charge. There is a shortfall of native health workers. Suicide is rising, particularly among ethnic Indians.

SPENDING

GDP/cap. increase

CONSUMPTION AND SPENDING

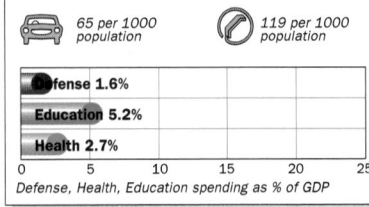

65 per 1000 population | 119 per 1000 population

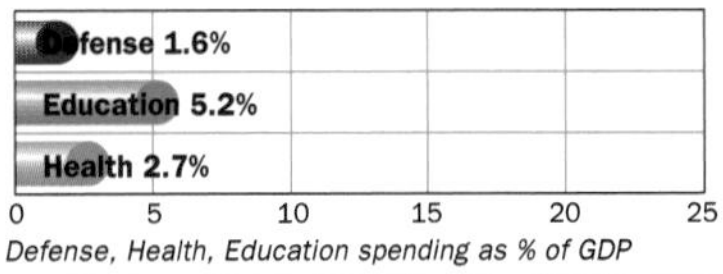
Defense 1.6%
Education 5.2%
Health 2.7%
0
5
10
15
20
25
Defense, Health, Education spending as % of GDP

Ostentatious displays of wealth are rare in Fiji; prestige derives from family and landholdings. The professional middle class, traditionally dominated by Indo-Fijians, is becoming more mixed.

WORLD RANKING

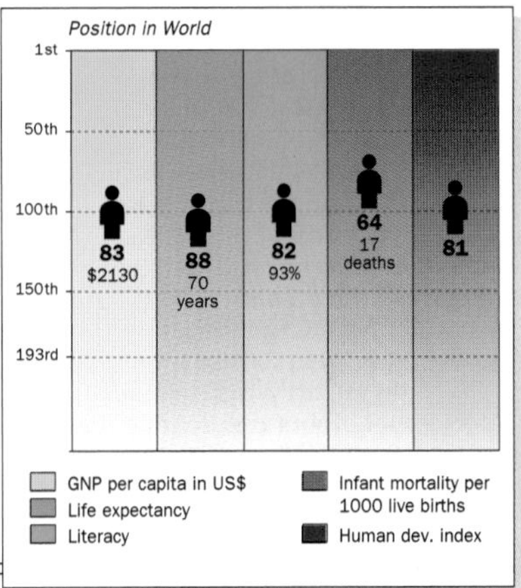
Position in World
1st
50th
100th
150th
193rd
83
$2130
88
70 years
82
93%
64
17 deaths
81
GNP per capita in US$
Life expectancy
Literacy
Infant mortality per 1000 live births
Human dev. index

F

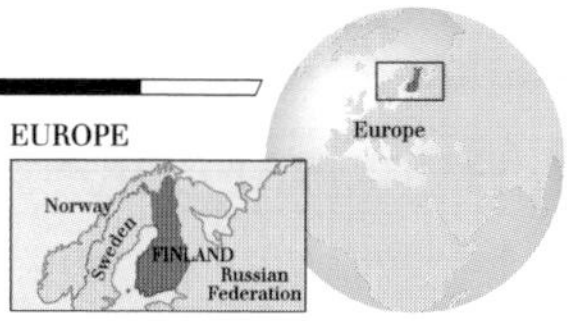
Europe
EUROPE
Norway
Sweden
FINLAND
Russian
Federation

FINLAND

OFFICIAL NAME: Republic of Finland **CAPITAL:** Helsinki
POPULATION: 5.2 million **CURRENCY:** Euro **OFFICIAL LANGUAGES:** Finnish and Swedish

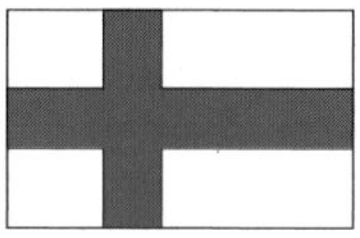

1917
1947
Dec 6
FIN
+2
+358
.fi

BORDERED TO THE north and west by Norway and Sweden and to the east by Russia, Finland is a low-lying country of forests and 187,888 lakes. Politics is based on consensus, and the country has been stable despite successive short-lived coalitions. Russia annexed Finland in 1809, ruling it until 1917. After two wars against the USSR, Finland accepted a close relationship with its eastern neighbor in exchange for peace. It joined the European Union in 1995 and, despite popular suspicion of Brussels bureaucracy, Finland was among the 12 EU states to adopt the euro from 2002.

CLIMATE

Subarctic/continental

WEATHER CHART FOR HELSINKI

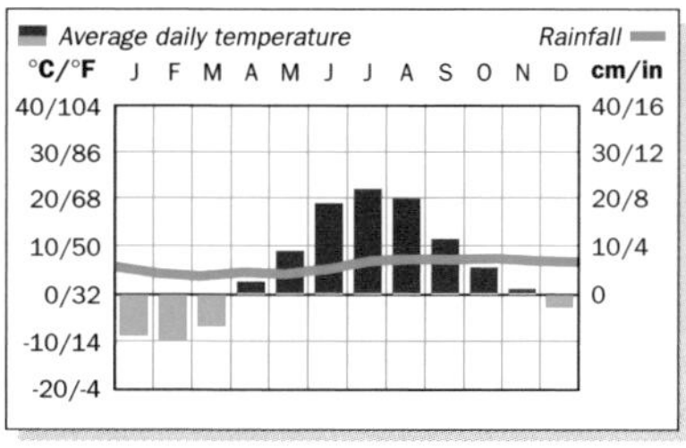
Average daily temperature
Rainfall
°C/°F
J F M A M J J A S O N D
cm/in
40/104
30/86
20/68
10/50
0/32
-10/14
-20/-4
40/16
30/12
20/8
10/4
0

North of the Arctic Circle the climate is extreme. Temperatures fall to –30°C (–22°F) in the six-month winter and rise to 27°C (81°F) during the 73 days of summer midnight sun. In the south, summers are mild and short, winters are cold.

TRANSPORTATION

Drive on right

Helsinki–Vantaa, 9.7m passengers

283 ships 1.55m grt

THE TRANSPORTATION NETWORK

50,635 km (31,463 miles)

591 km (367 miles)

5850 km (3635 miles)

6675 km (4148 miles)

The transportation system is well integrated. The railroad connects with the Swedish and Russian networks. There are frequent air services to most neighboring states, and links with Baltic states are being expanded. With one of the densest domestic networks in Europe, internal air travel is important, particularly north of the Arctic Circle. Finland has Europe's largest inland waterway system, now used mainly for recreation. Its international ports handle around 80 million tonnes a year. Kotka is the chief export port. Helsinki's specialized harbors handle most imports, but construction of a new harbor at Vuosaari is under way, and cargo traffic is due to move there in 2008.

TOURISM

Visitors : Population 1:1.8

2.88m visitors

Up 2% in 2002

MAIN TOURIST ARRIVALS

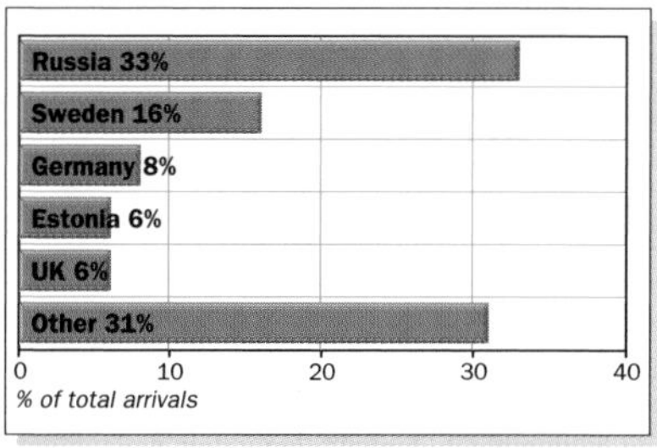
Russia 33%
Sweden 16%
Germany 8%
Estonia 6%
UK 6%
Other 31%
0
10
20
30
40
% of total arrivals

The scenery of the southern lakes and the vast forests of its Arctic north are Finland's main attractions. Helsinki, with many first-class restaurants, is an important cultural center; its opera house has an international reputation. Annual events such as the Helsinki arts festival, and the July wife-carrying championships, also attract visitors. Most tourists try a sauna – a Finnish tradition – and the local vodka, which is reputedly among the world's finest.

In 2001 Finland was ranked the seventh most popular European destination for employers offering vacations as an incentive to their workforce.

A summer's night at Kilpisjärvi, "The Way of the Four Winds," which lies at the point where Finland, Sweden, and Norway meet.

PEOPLE

Pop. density low

Finnish, Swedish, Sámi

17/km² (44/mi²)

THE URBAN/RURAL POPULATION SPLIT

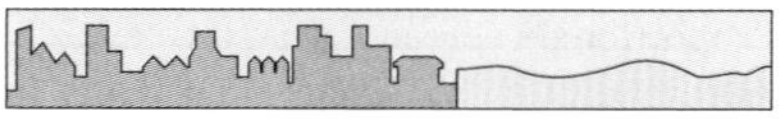
59%
41%

RELIGIOUS PERSUASION

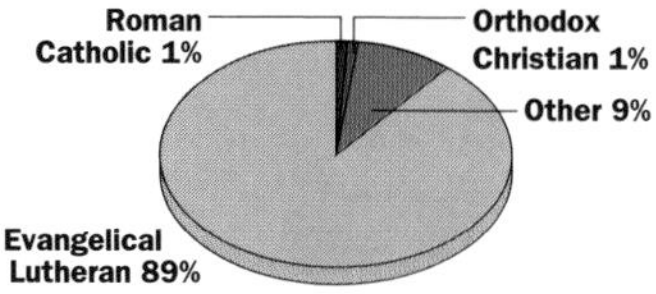
Roman Catholic 1%
Orthodox Christian 1%
Other 9%
Evangelical Lutheran 89%

ETHNIC MAKEUP

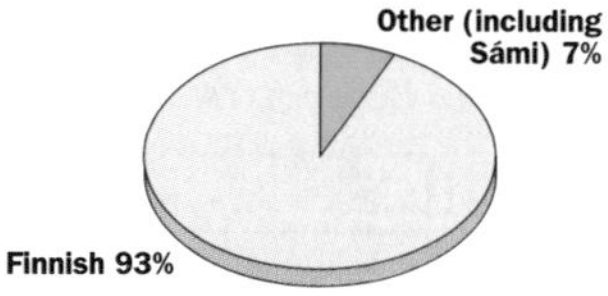
Other (including Sámi) 7%
Finnish 93%

Most Finns are of Indo-European extraction. Finnish, part of the small Finno-Ugric linguistic group, is a legacy of the country's early Finno-Ugrian settlers. An influx of European peoples integrated with these tribes and adopted their distinct language. Sámi, also a Finno-Ugric language, is spoken by the small Sámi population which lives within the Arctic Circle. Swedish speakers make up around 6% of the population and mostly live in the southwest coastal regions and on the Åland Islands.

More than half of Finns live in the five southernmost districts around Helsinki. Families tend to be close-knit, though divorce rates are high. The sauna is an integral part of everyday life; there are 1.5 million saunas among 5.2 million Finns.

Finnish women have a long tradition of political and economic participation. They were the first in Europe to get the vote, in 1906, and the first in the world able to stand for parliament. In 2003 Finland became for a short time the only European country to have both a female president and prime minister.

POPULATION AGE BREAKDOWN

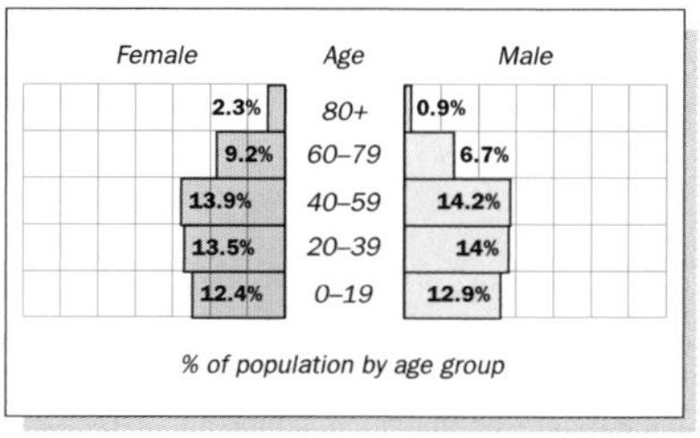
Female
Age
Male
2.3%
80+
0.9%
9.2%
60–79
6.7%
13.9%
40–59
14.2%
13.5%
20–39
14%
12.4%
0–19
12.9%
% of population by age group

F

POLITICS

Multiparty elections

2003/2007

President Tarja Halonen

Finland's constitution combines parliamentary government with a strong presidency. The Swedish-speaking Åland Islands external territory is self-governing.

AT THE LAST ELECTION

Parliament 200 seats

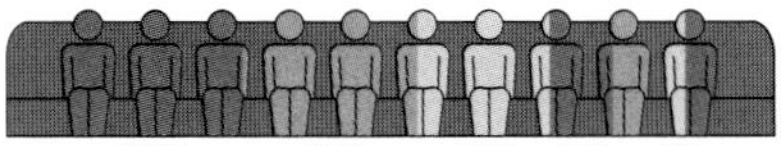
7% G
5% Others
28% KESK
27% SDP
20% KOK
9% VL
4% SFP

KESK = Center Party **SDP** = Social Democratic Party **KOK** = National Coalition Party **VL** = Left-wing Alliance **G** = Greens **SFP** = Swedish People's Party

PROFILE

Proportional representation has led to government by coalition, usually dominated by the SDP or KESK. The emphasis on consensus favors stability but slows decision-making. The KESK led a new coalition from 2003. KESK leader Anneli Jäätteenmäki became the country's first female premier, but resigned after only two months in office, and was replaced by Matti Vanhanen.

MAIN POLITICAL ISSUES

EU membership

Finland joined the EU in 1995. The small but influential farming community was hostile to membership, while others feared that welfare cuts would be more far-reaching if the economy was liberalized in line with EU expectations. In the event, after a dose of austerity, EU membership became associated with greater prosperity from the late 1990s. However, public opinion regarding the EU remains evenly divided between its supporters and detractors. Finland's decision to join the eurozone was in contrast to the nonmembership of its closest EU neighbor, Sweden.

Nuclear power

In 2002 parliament narrowly approved the construction of a fifth nuclear reactor. It will be the first to be built in Scandinavia or western Europe since 1991 and the first in Finland for 30 years. The vote was divisive, and the Green Party, a junior coalition partner, pulled out of the SDP-led government in protest. KESK Prime Minister Vanhanen has previously expressed his opposition to the plan.

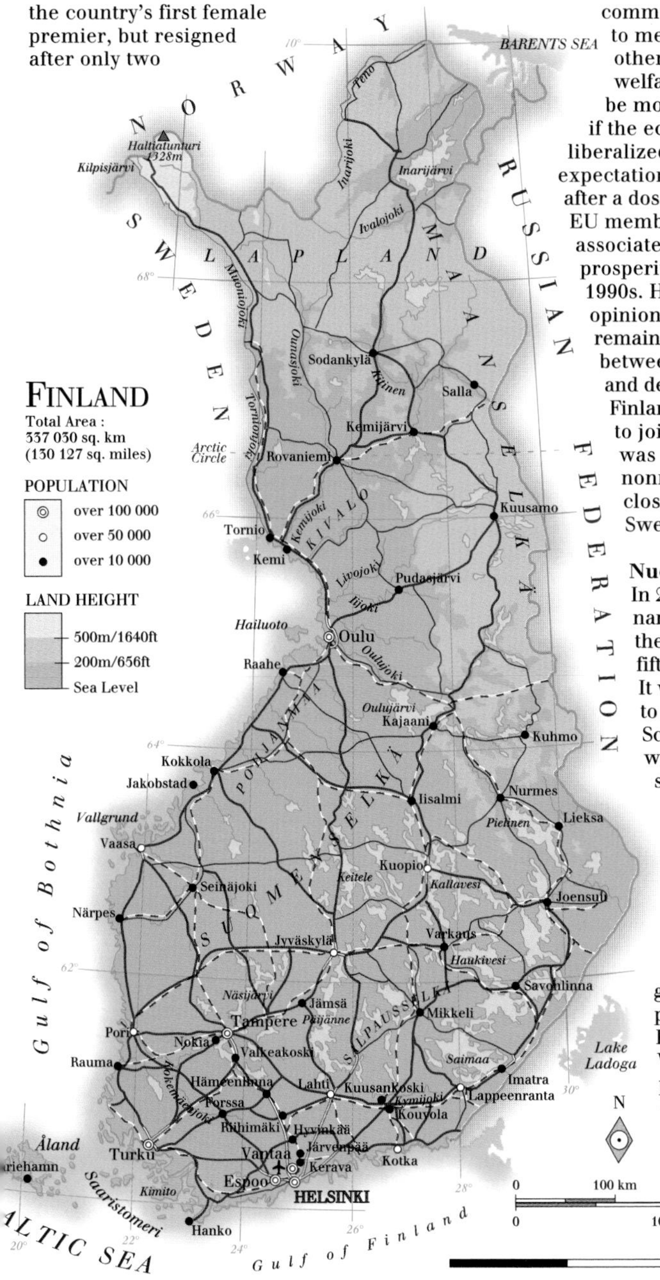
NORWAY
BARENTS SEA
Haltiatunturi 1328m
Kilpisjärvi
Inarijoki
Inarijärvi
Ivalojoki
Teno
SWEDEN
LAPLAND
MAANSELKÄ
RUSSIAN FEDERATION
Sodankylä
Salla
Kemijärvi
Rovaniemi
Arctic Circle
Muonionjoki
Ounasjoki
Tornionjoki
Kitinen
KIVALO
Kemijoki
Kuusamo
Tornio
Kemi
Iijoki
Livojoki
Pudasjärvi
Hailuoto
Oulu
Oulujoki
Raahe
Oulujärvi
Kajaani
Kuhmo
POHJANMAA
Kokkola
Jakobstad
Vallgrund
Vaasa
Iisalmi
Nurmes
Pielinen
Lieksa
Kuopio
Keitele
Kallavesi
Joensuu
Seinäjoki
SUOMENSELKÄ
Närpes
Varkaus
Haukivesi
Jyväskylä
Savonlinna
Näsijärvi
Jämsä
Mikkeli
SALPAUSSELKÄ
Tampere
Päijänne
Pori
Nokia
Valkeakoski
Rauma
Saimaa
Lake Ladoga
Imatra
Hämeenlinna
Lahti
Kuusankoski
Lappeenranta
Kokemäenjoki
Forssa
Kymijoki
Kouvola
Riihimäki
Hyvinkää
Järvenpää
Åland
Turku
Vantaa
Kerava
Kotka
Espoo
HELSINKI
Kimito
Saaristomeri
Hanko
Gulf of Bothnia
Gulf of Finland
BALTIC SEA
N
0 100 km
0 100 miles

FINLAND

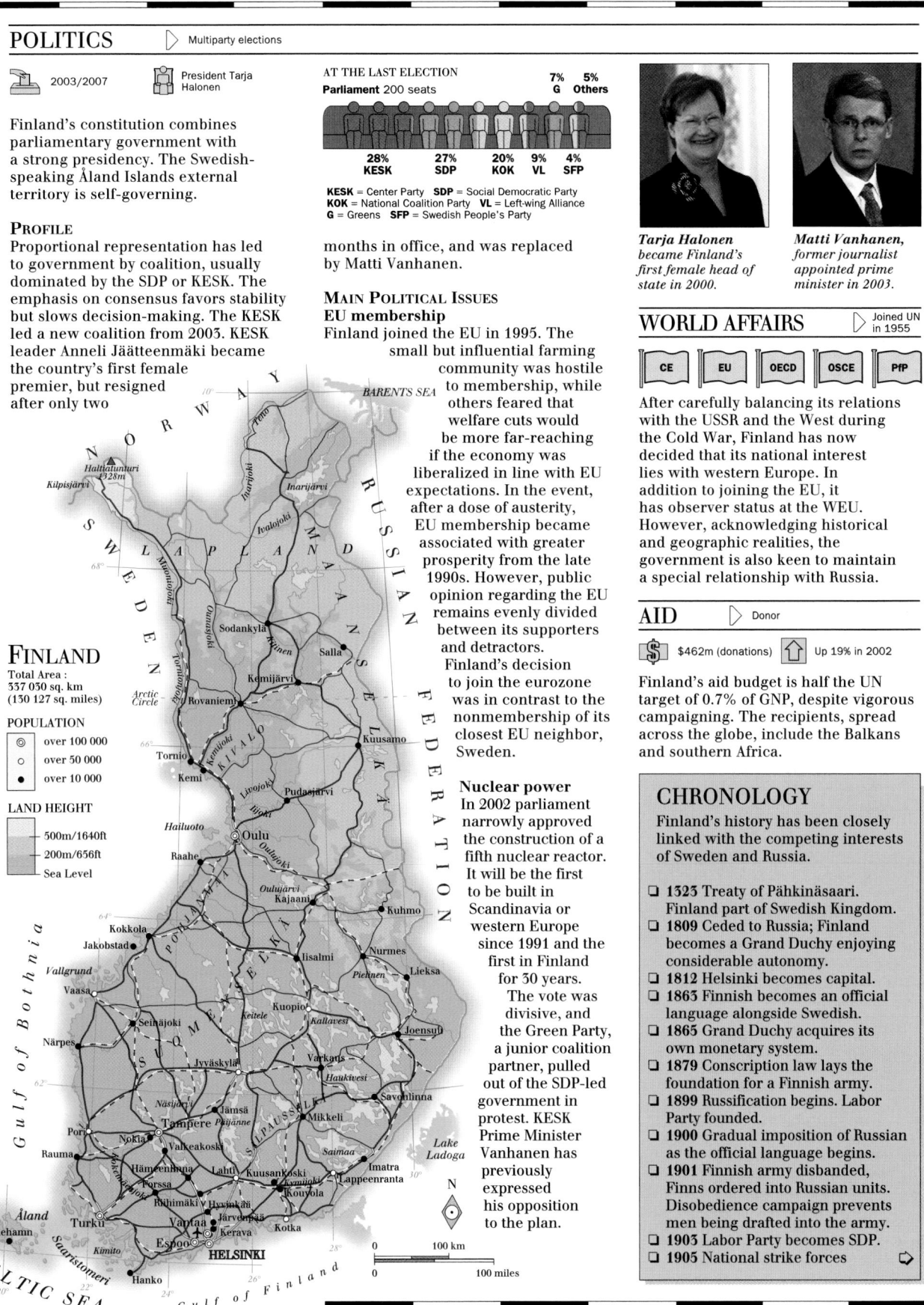

Total Area : 337 030 sq. km (130 127 sq. miles)

POPULATION

- over 100 000
- over 50 000
- over 10 000

LAND HEIGHT

- 500m/1640ft
- 200m/656ft
- Sea Level

Tarja Halonen became Finland's first female head of state in 2000.

Matti Vanhanen, former journalist appointed prime minister in 2003.

WORLD AFFAIRS

Joined UN in 1955

CE EU OECD OSCE PfP

After carefully balancing its relations with the USSR and the West during the Cold War, Finland has now decided that its national interest lies with western Europe. In addition to joining the EU, it has observer status at the WEU. However, acknowledging historical and geographic realities, the government is also keen to maintain a special relationship with Russia.

AID

Donor

$462m (donations) Up 19% in 2002

Finland's aid budget is half the UN target of 0.7% of GNP, despite vigorous campaigning. The recipients, spread across the globe, include the Balkans and southern Africa.

CHRONOLOGY

Finland's history has been closely linked with the competing interests of Sweden and Russia.

- **1323** Treaty of Pähkinäsaari. Finland part of Swedish Kingdom.
- **1809** Ceded to Russia; Finland becomes a Grand Duchy enjoying considerable autonomy.
- **1812** Helsinki becomes capital.
- **1863** Finnish becomes an official language alongside Swedish.
- **1865** Grand Duchy acquires its own monetary system.
- **1879** Conscription law lays the foundation for a Finnish army.
- **1899** Russification begins. Labor Party founded.
- **1900** Gradual imposition of Russian as the official language begins.
- **1901** Finnish army disbanded, Finns ordered into Russian units. Disobedience campaign prevents men being drafted into the army.
- **1903** Labor Party becomes SDP.
- **1905** National strike forces

F

CHRONOLOGY *continued*

restoration of 1899 status quo.
- **1906** Parliamentary reform. Universal suffrage introduced.
- **1910** Responsibility for important legislation passed to Russian parliament.
- **1917** Russian revolution allows Finland to declare independence.
- **1918** Civil war between Bolsheviks and right-wing government. Gen. Gustav Mannerheim leads government to victory at Battle of Tampere.
- **1919** Finland becomes republic. Kaarlo Ståhlberg elected president with wide political powers.
- **1920** Treaty of Tartu: Russia recognizes Finland's borders.
- **1921** London Convention. Åland Islands become part of Finland.
- **1939** August, Hitler–Stalin nonaggression pact gives USSR a free hand in Finland. November, Soviet invasion; strong Finnish resistance in ensuing Winter War.
- **1940** Treaty of Moscow. Finland cedes a tenth of national territory.
- **1941** Finnish troops join Germany in its invasion of USSR.
- **1944** June, Red Army invades. August, President Risto Ryti resigns. September, Finland, led by Marshal Mannerheim, signs armistice.
- **1946** President Mannerheim resigns, Juho Paasikivi president.
- **1948** Signs friendship treaty with USSR. Agrees to resist any attack on USSR made through Finland by Germany or its allies.
- **1952** Payment of $570 million in war reparations completed.
- **1956** Uhro Kekkonen, leader of the Agrarian Party, becomes president.
- **1956–1991** A series of coalition governments involving SDP and Agrarians (renamed KESK in 1965).
- **1981** President Kekkonen resigns.
- **1982** Mauno Koivisto president.
- **1989** USSR recognizes Finnish neutrality for first time.
- **1991** Non-SDP government elected. Austerity measures.
- **1992** Signs ten-year agreement with Russia which, for first time since World War II, involves no military agreement.
- **1994** SDP candidate Martti Ahtisaari elected president.
- **1995** Finland joins EU. General election returns SDP-led coalition under Paavo Lipponen (reelected in 1999).
- **2000** Tarja Halonen elected as first woman president.
- **2002** Euro fully adopted. Fifth nuclear power plant approved.
- **2003** KESK wins elections. Anneli Jäätteenmäki, first female prime minister, resigns after two months.

DEFENSE

Compulsory military service

$1.97bn

Up 39% in 2002

Finland is a neutral country. Its armed forces, the majority of whom are conscripts, are backed up by over 300,000 reservists and 3100 border guards. Russia's relative instability in the 1990s reinforced concern about border security, the main defense issue. Finland participates in NATO's Partnership for Peace program and has WEU observer status. Military service lasts for up to 12 months.

FINNISH ARMED FORCES

235 main battle tanks (74 T-55, 161 T-72)	19,200 personnel
9 patrol boats	5000 personnel
63 combat aircraft (F/A-18C/D)	2800 personnel
None	

ECONOMICS

Inflation 1.9% p.a. (1990–2001)

$124bn

0.822 euros (0.871)

SCORE CARD

- World GNP Ranking 29th
- GNP per Capita $23,890
- Balance of Payments $9.89bn
- Inflation 1.7%
- Unemployment 9%

EXPORTS

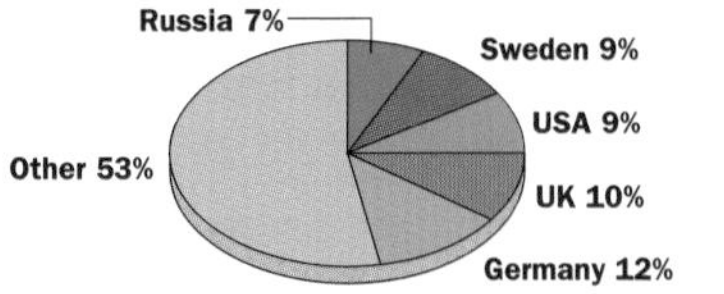

Russia 7%
Sweden 9%
USA 9%
UK 10%
Germany 12%
Other 53%

IMPORTS

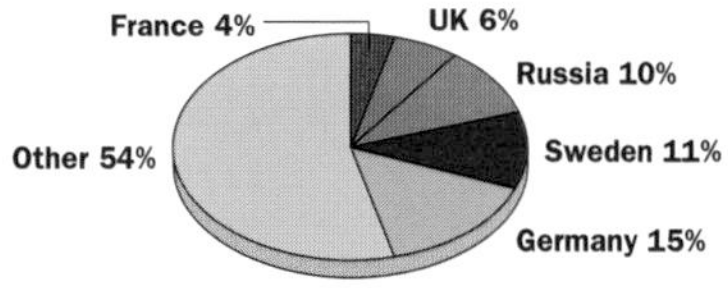

France 4%
UK 6%
Russia 10%
Sweden 11%
Germany 15%
Other 54%

Strengths

Industry export- and quality-oriented. Large high-tech sector, especially Nokia mobile phones and Internet services. World leader in pulp and paper. Exports quick to recover from recession. Relatively low inflation. Improved foreign investment incentives. Gateway to Russian and Baltic economies. Membership of eurozone. Competitive economy.

Weaknesses

Slowdown in economy from 2001; telecommunications industry hit particularly badly by global slump. Rapidly aging population and low retirement age. High level of public and foreign debt. High unemployment. Small domestic market. Peripheral position in Europe. High taxation.

Profile

Finland is a wealthy market economy. In the early 1990s it experienced the worst recession in 60 years, chiefly as a result of the collapse of the former

ECONOMIC PERFORMANCE INDICATOR

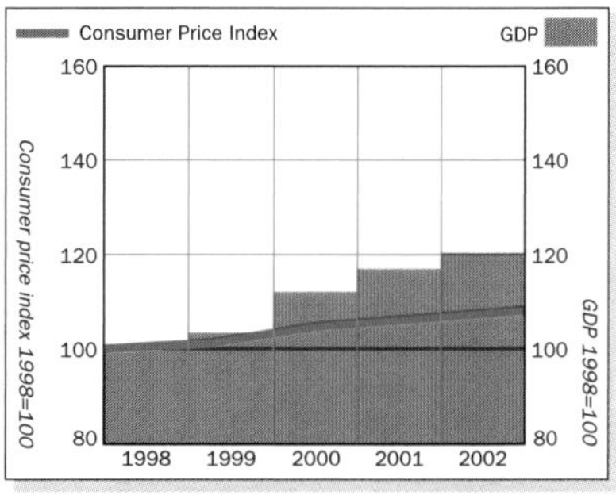

Consumer Price Index
GDP
160
140
120
100
80
Consumer price index 1998=100
GDP 1998=100
1998
1999
2000
2001
2002

Soviet Union. Russia took only 7% of Finland's exports in 2002, compared with over 25% to the Soviet Union before 1990.

A rapid rise in unemployment and business failures after 1990 pushed up government spending. The floating of the markka in 1992 and austerity measures improved competitiveness, overturned substantial fiscal deficits, and allowed tax cuts in 2002. Though it has fallen, unemployment is still around 9%. Rapid growth in 2000 was followed by a slowdown in 2001. Finland fully adopted the euro in 2002, and in 2003 was named the world's most competitive economy.

FINLAND : MAJOR BUSINESSES

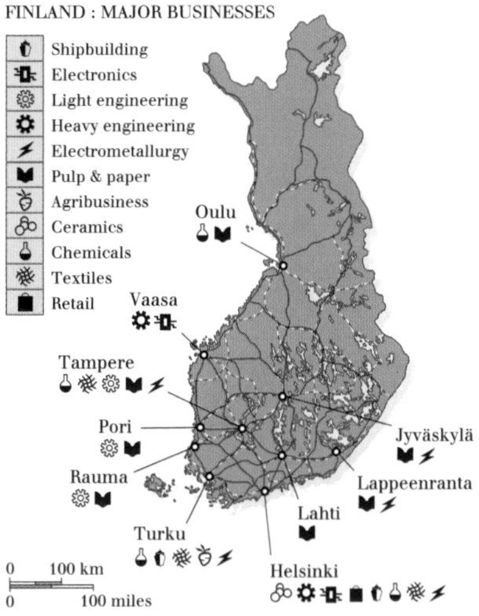

Shipbuilding
Electronics
Light engineering
Heavy engineering
Electrometallurgy
Pulp & paper
Agribusiness
Ceramics
Chemicals
Textiles
Retail
Oulu
Vaasa
Tampere
Pori
Jyväskylä
Rauma
Lappeenranta
Lahti
Turku
Helsinki
0 100 km
0 100 miles

RESOURCES

Electric power 16.5m kW

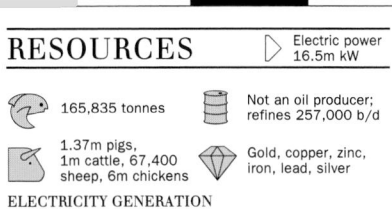

165,835 tonnes

Not an oil producer; refines 257,000 b/d

1.37m pigs, 1m cattle, 67,400 sheep, 6m chickens

Gold, copper, zinc, iron, lead, silver

ELECTRICITY GENERATION

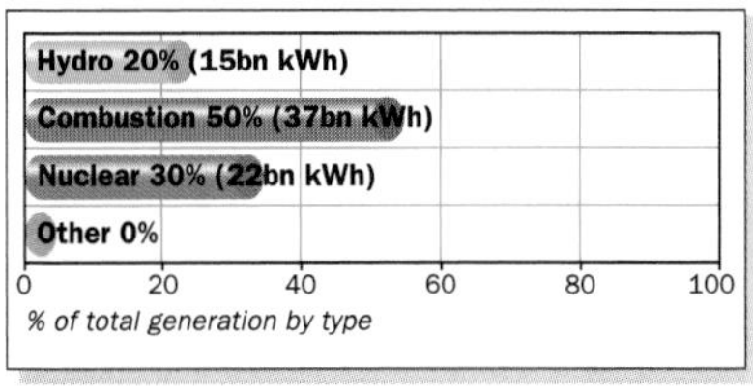
Hydro 20% (15bn kWh)
Combustion 50% (37bn kWh)
Nuclear 30% (22bn kWh)
Other 0%
0
20
40
60
80
100
% of total generation by type

Finland's trees are its prime natural resource. Commercial forests cover 65% of the land, and wood products account for over 20% of exports. Finland has no oil, but has significant hydroelectric resources. Oil import costs have risen since 1990, when the collapse of the USSR ended a 42-year agreement on the exchange of Finnish manufactured goods for Soviet oil. The high energy demands of industry are now met chiefly by combustion and nuclear power. A fifth nuclear power plant was approved in 2002.

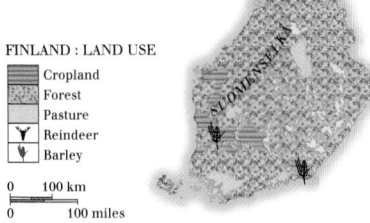

FINLAND : LAND USE

LAPLAND
MAANSELKÄ
SUOMENSELKÄ

Cropland
Forest
Pasture
Reindeer
Barley

0 100 km
0 100 miles

ENVIRONMENT

Sustainability rank: 1st

9% (5% partially protected)

10.3 tonnes per capita

ENVIRONMENTAL TREATIES

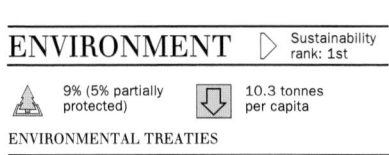

Yes Yes Yes
Yes Yes Yes

Finland has strict laws on industrial emissions. Energy efficiency is a priority; nearly half of all homes are connected to district heating systems. Though there is opposition to the fifth nuclear plant, proponents argue that it will help the country meet its target emissions for greenhouse gases. The government is funding nuclear safety programs in Russia. Rising levels of pollution in the Baltic have given rise to concern.

MEDIA

TV ownership high

Daily newspaper circulation 445 per 1000 people

PUBLISHING AND BROADCAST MEDIA

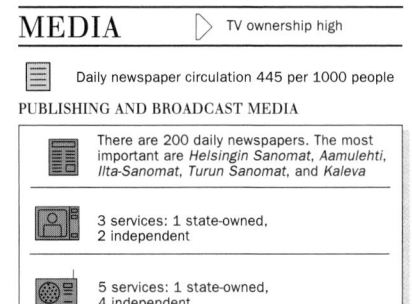

There are 200 daily newspapers. The most important are *Helsingin Sanomat, Aamulehti, Ilta-Sanomat, Turun Sanomat*, and *Kaleva*

3 services: 1 state-owned, 2 independent

5 services: 1 state-owned, 4 independent

Nine out of ten adult Finns read a daily newspaper, one of the world's highest per capita ratios. The independent *Helsingin Sanomat* has the highest circulation. There is no censorship, but the press shows restraint in criticizing the government.

CRIME

No death penalty

3617 prisoners

Down 6% in 2001

CRIME RATES

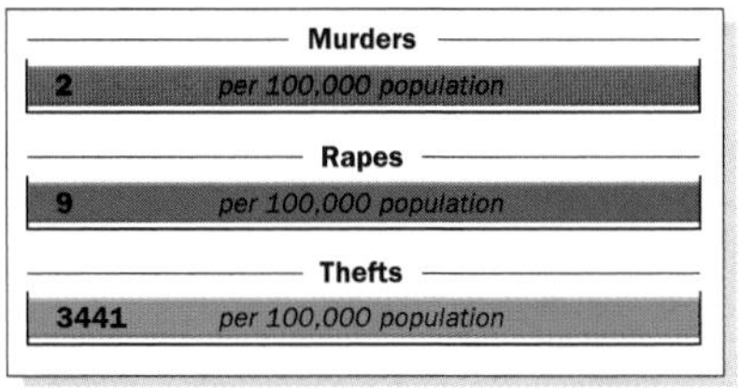
Murders
2 per 100,000 population
Rapes
9 per 100,000 population
Thefts
3441 per 100,000 population

The jump in unemployment in the early 1990s was seen as one of the causes of rising crime. There is concern about links with organized crime in Russia.

EDUCATION

School leaving age: 16

99%

291,089 students

THE EDUCATION SYSTEM

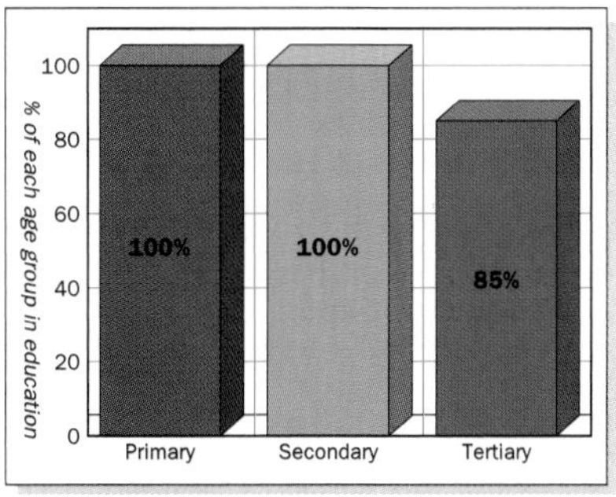
100
80
60
40
20
0
% of each age group in education
100%
100%
85%
Primary
Secondary
Tertiary

Compulsory education, introduced in 1921, lasts from seven to 16 years of age. The comprehensive system dates from the 1970s. Almost all children receive preschool education and also go on to three years of upper secondary education. Tough examinations mean that only around 40% of entrants qualify to attend one of the 20 universities. There are also 25 polytechnics.

HEALTH

Welfare state health benefits

1 per 323 people

Heart diseases, cancers, cerebro-vascular diseases

Of total government expenditure, around 20% is spent on Finland's well-developed health system. Every Finn is legally guaranteed access to a local health center which is staffed by up to four doctors, as well as nurses and a midwife. Most nonhospital medical costs are covered by national health insurance; hospital fees are moderate. Diabetes and osteoporosis are increasing, and obesity is a growing health problem.

SPENDING

GDP/cap. increase

CONSUMPTION AND SPENDING

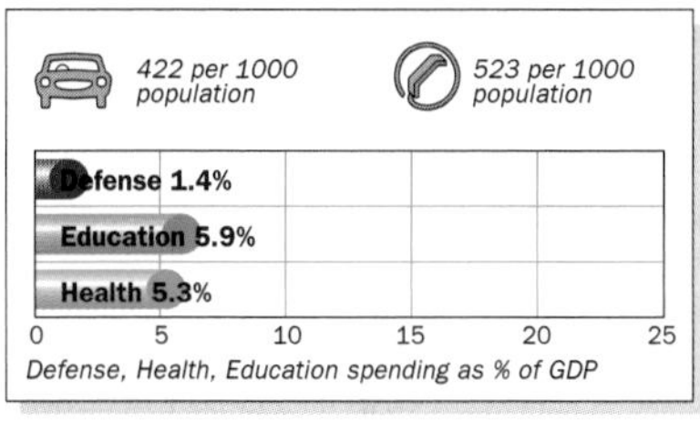
422 per 1000 population
523 per 1000 population
Defense 1.4%
Education 5.9%
Health 5.3%
0
5
10
15
20
25
Defense, Health, Education spending as % of GDP

The economic boom and labor shortages of the 1980s helped living standards to soar. Personal consumption reached Swedish levels, and many families were able to take two vacations a year. Social security benefits were extended.

During the deep recession which began in 1990, this improvement was reversed. Wealth disparities widened and expenditure cuts led to lower social security benefits for the jobless. Those in work had to accept lower pay rises and higher taxes. Average real disposable incomes dropped sharply. The situation started to improve in 2000, with a temporary downturn in 2001. Income disparities fell again and are now as low as in other Scandinavian countries.

Ethnic Ingrian immigrants from the former USSR were the poorest group in Finnish society in the 1990s.

WORLD RANKING

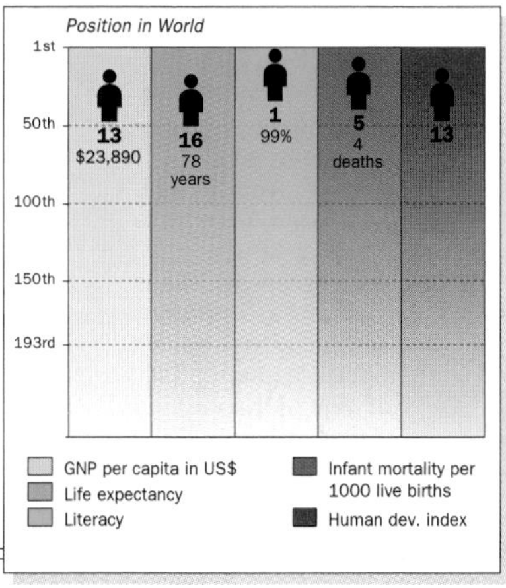
Position in World
1st
50th
100th
150th
193rd
13
$23,890
16
78 years
1
99%
5
4 deaths
13
GNP per capita in US$
Life expectancy
Literacy
Infant mortality per 1000 live births
Human dev. index

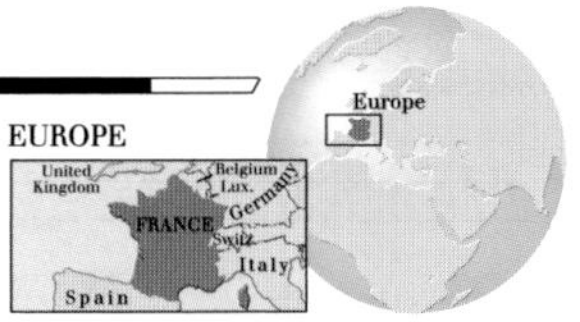
Europe
EUROPE
United Kingdom
Belgium
Lux.
Germany
FRANCE
Switz.
Italy
Spain

FRANCE

OFFICIAL NAME: French Republic **CAPITAL:** Paris
POPULATION: 60.1 million **CURRENCY:** Euro **OFFICIAL LANGUAGE:** French

987 1919 July 14 F +1 +33 .fr

STRADDLING WESTERN EUROPE from the English Channel (la Manche) to the Mediterranean, France was Europe's first modern republic, and possessed a colonial empire second only to that of the UK. Today, it is one of the world's major industrial powers and its fourth-largest exporter. Industry is the leading economic sector, but the agricultural lobby remains powerful – French farmers will mount the barricades in defense of their interests. France's focus is very much on Europe. Together with Germany it was a founder member of the European Economic Community (EEC), and has supported successive steps to build a more closely integrated European Union. Paris, the French capital, is generally considered to be one of the world's most beautiful cities. Some of the most influential artists, writers, and filmmakers of the modern era have lived there.

Le Plessis-Bourré, Loire Valley. *The region is famous for its many chateaux, which attract thousands of visitors every year.*

CLIMATE

Maritime/Mediterranean/mountain/continental

WEATHER CHART FOR PARIS

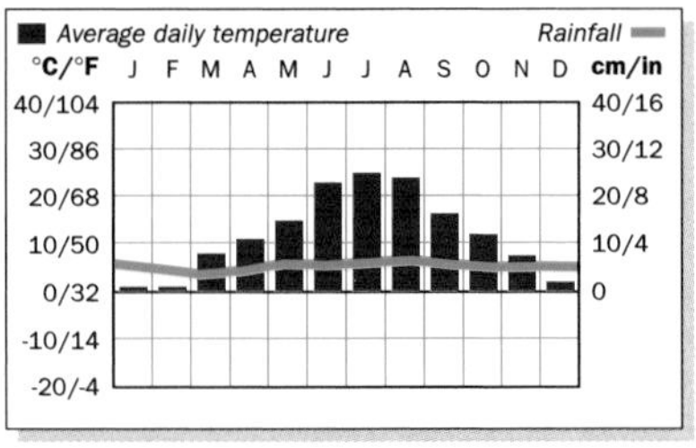
Average daily temperature
Rainfall
°C/°F
J F M A M J J A S O N D
cm/in
40/104
30/86
20/68
10/50
0/32
-10/14
-20/-4
40/16
30/12
20/8
10/4
0

France's climate differs significantly from region to region. The northwest, in particular Brittany, is mild but damp. The east has hot summers and stormy winters, while in the south summers are dry and hot, and forest fires are a frequent occurrence.

TRANSPORTATION

Drive on right

Charles de Gaulle, Paris 48.1m passengers

707 ships 1.54m grt

THE TRANSPORTATION NETWORK

894,000 km (555,505 miles)

10,068 km (6256 miles)

29,352 km (18,238 miles)

14,932 km (9278 miles)

France led Europe in high-speed train technology in 1981 with the TGV (*train à grande vitesse*) from Paris to Lyon. TGV lines now link up with the Channel Tunnel, Belgium, Italy, Spain, and the Mediterranean. Plans for a third airport for Paris at Chaulnes, 130 km (80 miles) to the north, have become a political football, while the collapse of part of the new terminal at Charles de Gaulle in 2004 has set back plans to make Paris the major transportation hub in Europe.

TOURISM

Visitors : Population 1.2:1

75m visitors

Down 3% in 2003

MAIN TOURIST ARRIVALS

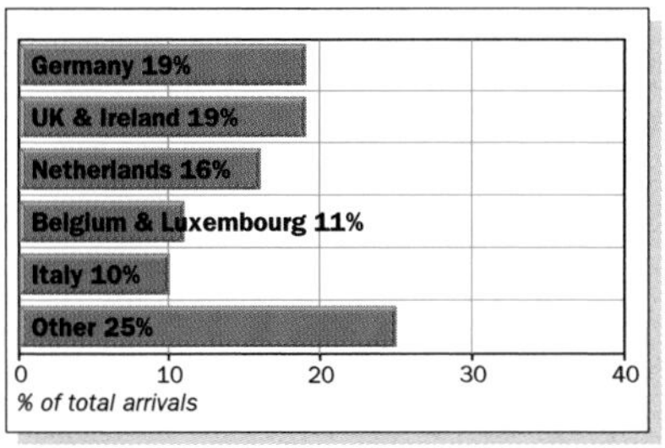
Germany 19%
UK & Ireland 19%
Netherlands 16%
Belgium & Luxembourg 11%
Italy 10%
Other 25%
0
10
20
30
40
% of total arrivals

France is the world's leading tourist destination, with about 75 million visitors a year. It ranks high as a destination for visitors from neighboring countries, particularly Germany and the UK. Most French people also prefer to take vacations in their own country, though many do visit Spain and Italy.

Paris is the most visited city in Europe. Its attractions include the Eiffel Tower, Nôtre Dame cathedral, Eurodisney, the Pompidou Center, and the Louvre, the world's most popular art museum.

The Côte d'Azur in the southeast became a byword for fashionable tourism when royalty and other notables flocked to resorts such as Nice at the end of the 19th century. Today Cannes hosts the world's leading film festival, and has a growing business convention trade. Other destinations throughout the country attract tourists for a variety of reasons such as wine production, historic and archaeological sites, and good beaches. There are resorts for skiing and hiking in the Alps and Pyrenees, and sailing off the varied coastline is also popular.

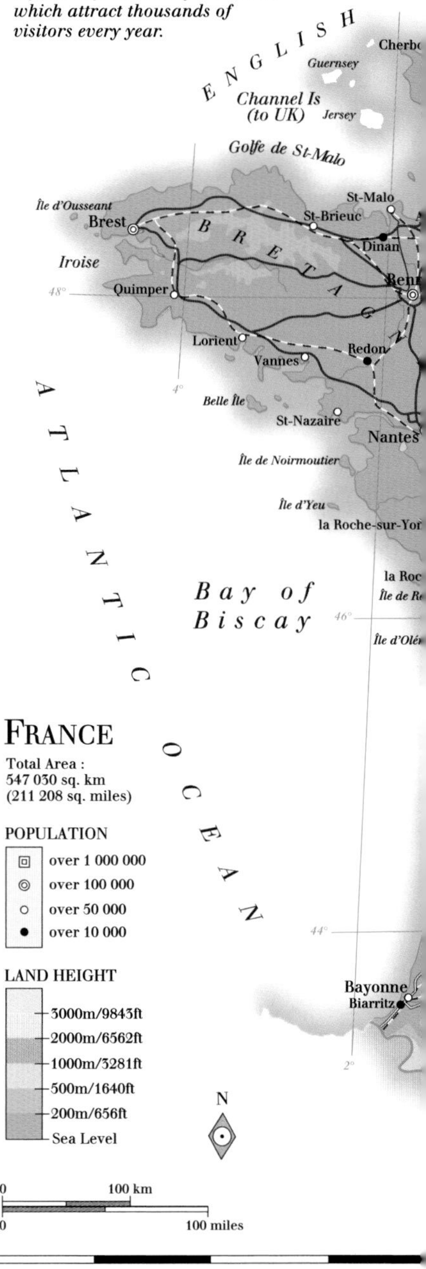
ENGLISH
Cherbo
Guernsey
Channel Is (to UK)
Jersey
Golfe de St-Malo
St-Malo
St-Brieuc
Île d'Ouessant
Brest
BRETAGNE
Dinan
Iroise
Quimper
Renn
Lorient
Redon
Vannes
Belle Île
St-Nazaire
Nantes
Île de Noirmoutier
Île d'Yeu
la Roche-sur-Yor
ATLANTIC OCEAN
Bay of Biscay
la Roc
Île de Ré
Île d'Olér
Bayonne
Biarritz
FRANCE
Total Area :
547 030 sq. km
(211 208 sq. miles)
POPULATION
over 1 000 000
over 100 000
over 50 000
over 10 000
LAND HEIGHT
3000m/9843ft
2000m/6562ft
1000m/3281ft
500m/1640ft
200m/656ft
Sea Level
N
0
100 km
0
100 miles

PEOPLE

Pop. density medium

French, Provençal, German, Breton, Catalan, Basque

109/km² (283/mi²)

THE URBAN/RURAL POPULATION SPLIT

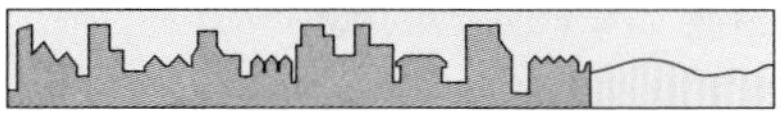
76%
24%

POPULATION AGE BREAKDOWN

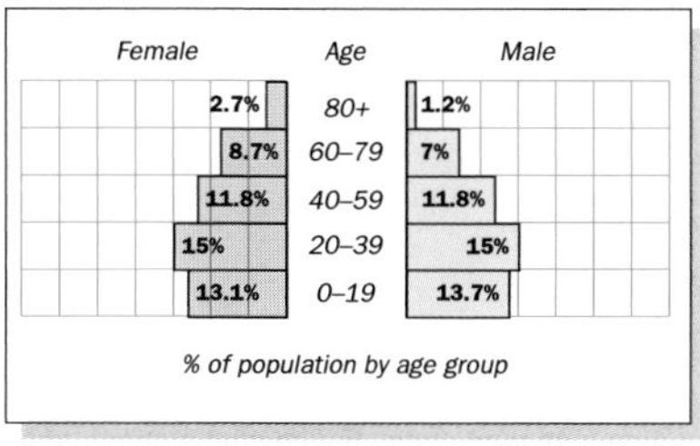
Female
Age
Male
2.7%
80+
1.2%
8.7%
60–79
7%
11.8%
40–59
11.8%
15%
20–39
15%
13.1%
0–19
13.7%
% of population by age group

RELIGIOUS PERSUASION

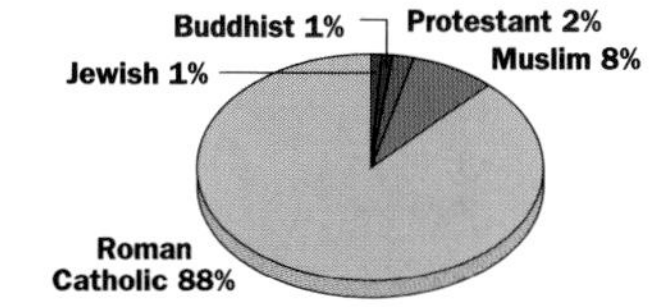
Buddhist 1%
Protestant 2%
Jewish 1%
Muslim 8%
Roman Catholic 88%

ETHNIC MAKEUP

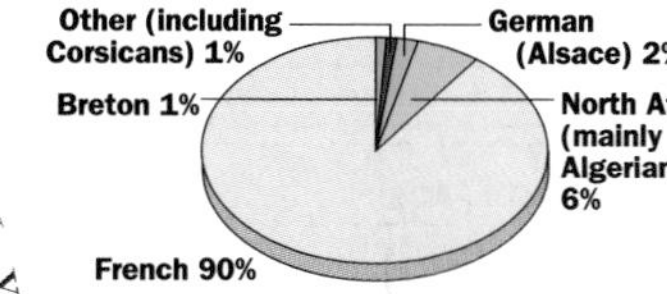
Other (including Corsicans) 1%
German (Alsace) 2%
Breton 1%
North African (mainly Algerian) 6%
French 90%

There is a strong sense of national identity, and compulsory use of French has traditionally been promoted as a unifying force. The cultural traditions of Bretons, Flemings, Alsatians, Basques, Occitans, Catalans, and Corsicans are now also valued, but the Constitutional Court has struck down legislation on the use of regional language in government.

The Roman Catholic Church is still dominant, but there are sizable Muslim, Protestant, Buddhist, and Jewish minorities. The secular state is a strong republican principle which is rigorously applied.

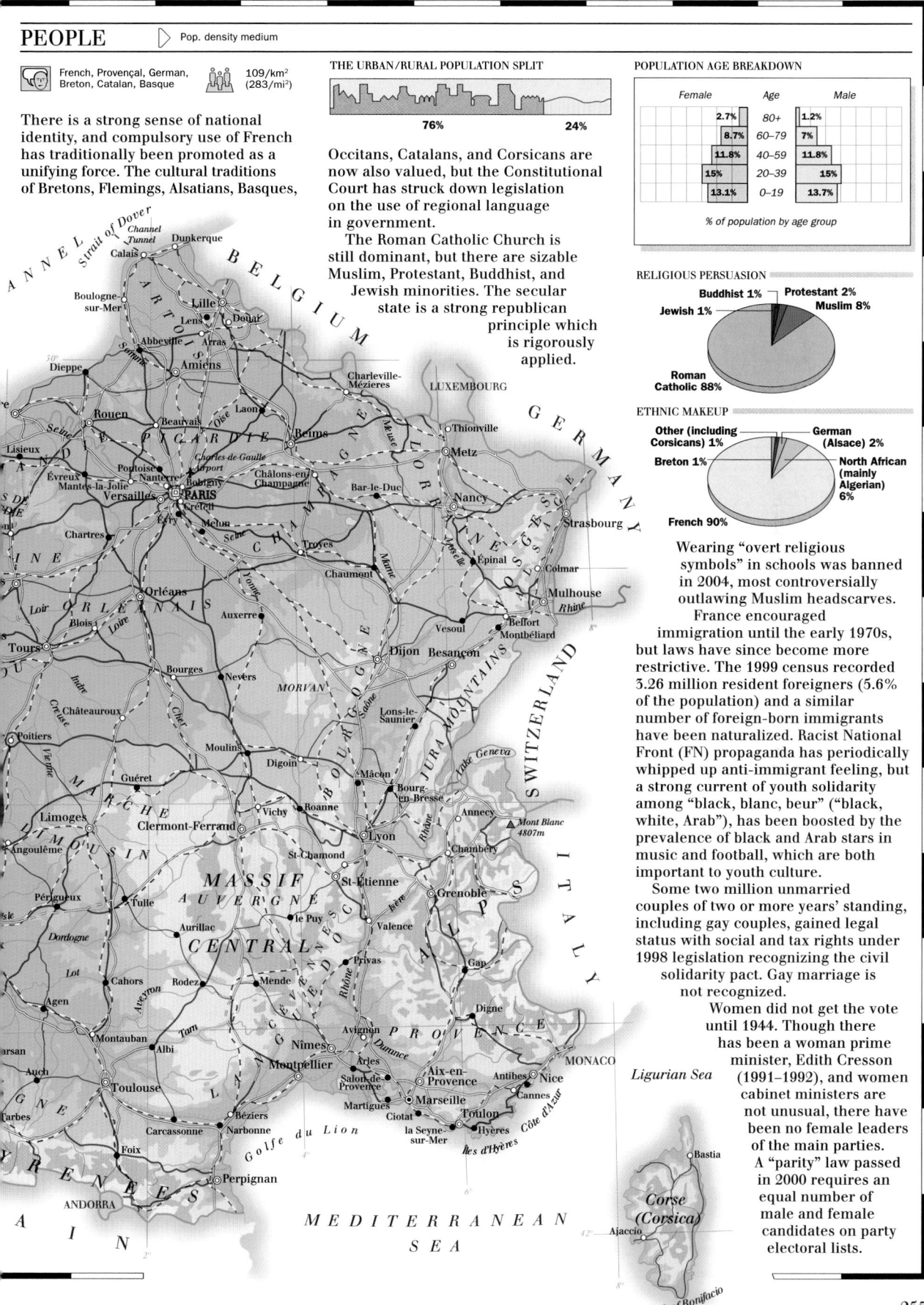

Wearing "overt religious symbols" in schools was banned in 2004, most controversially outlawing Muslim headscarves.

France encouraged immigration until the early 1970s, but laws have since become more restrictive. The 1999 census recorded 3.26 million resident foreigners (5.6% of the population) and a similar number of foreign-born immigrants have been naturalized. Racist National Front (FN) propaganda has periodically whipped up anti-immigrant feeling, but a strong current of youth solidarity among "black, blanc, beur" ("black, white, Arab"), has been boosted by the prevalence of black and Arab stars in music and football, which are both important to youth culture.

Some two million unmarried couples of two or more years' standing, including gay couples, gained legal status with social and tax rights under 1998 legislation recognizing the civil solidarity pact. Gay marriage is not recognized.

Women did not get the vote until 1944. Though there has been a woman prime minister, Edith Cresson (1991–1992), and women cabinet ministers are not unusual, there have been no female leaders of the main parties.

A "parity" law passed in 2000 requires an equal number of male and female candidates on party electoral lists.

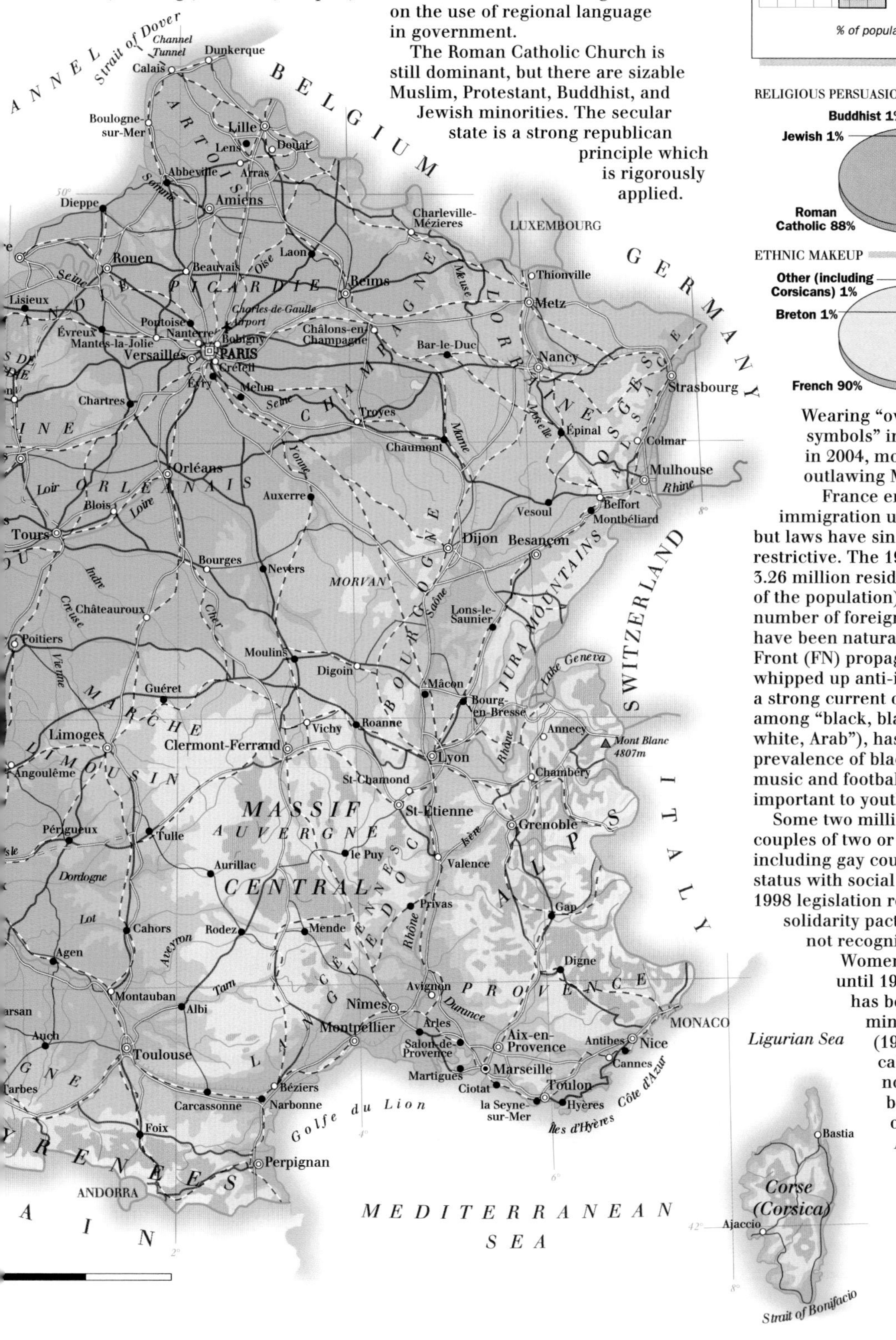
Strait of Dover
Channel Tunnel
Dunkerque
Calais
BELGIUM
Boulogne-sur-Mer
ARTOIS
Lille
Lens
Douai
Arras
Abbeville
Somme
Amiens
Dieppe
Charleville-Mézieres
LUXEMBOURG
Rouen
Beauvais
Oise
Laon
PICARDIE
Reims
Seine
Lisieux
Thionville
Metz
GERMANY
Charles-de-Gaulle Airport
Pontoise
Nanterre
Évreux
Mantes-la-Jolie
Bobigny
Versailles
PARIS
Créteil
Évry
Melun
Châlons-en-Champagne
Bar-le-Duc
Nancy
Strasbourg
Chartres
CHAMPAGNE
LORRAINE
VOSGES
ALSACE
Troyes
Épinal
Moselle
Marne
Meuse
Chaumont
Colmar
Orléans
ORLÉANAIS
Yonne
Mulhouse
Rhine
Loir
Blois
Loire
Auxerre
Belfort
Vesoul
Montbéliard
Tours
Dijon
Besançon
Bourges
Nevers
MORVAN
Indre
Châteauroux
Creuse
Cher
Lons-le-Saunier
JURA MOUNTAINS
SWITZERLAND
Poitiers
Vienne
Moulins
Digoin
Saône
BOURGOGNE
Lake Geneva
Guéret
MARCHE
Mâcon
Bourg-en-Bresse
Vichy
Roanne
Annecy
Limoges
LIMOUSIN
Clermont-Ferrand
Mont Blanc 4807m
Angoulême
Lyon
Rhône
Chambéry
St-Chamond
St-Étienne
MASSIF CENTRAL
AUVERGNE
Périgueux
Tulle
Le Puy
Isère
Grenoble
ALPS
ITALY
Aurillac
Valence
Dordogne
CÉVENNES
LANGUEDOC
Privas
Gap
Lot
Cahors
Rodez
Aveyron
Mende
Agen
Digne
Montauban
Tarn
Albi
Avignon
PROVENCE
Durance
Nîmes
Arles
Montpellier
Aix-en-Provence
MONACO
Auch
Toulouse
Salon-de-Provence
Antibes
Nice
Ligurian Sea
Marseille
Cannes
Martigues
Ciotat
Toulon
Côte d'Azur
Tarbes
Béziers
Carcassonne
Narbonne
Golfe du Lion
la Seyne-sur-Mer
Hyères
Îles d'Hyères
Foix
Bastia
PYRENEES
Perpignan
ANDORRA
Corse (Corsica)
MEDITERRANEAN SEA
Ajaccio
Strait of Bonifacio

F

F

CHRONOLOGY

The French Revolution of 1789–1794 overthrew a monarchy that had lasted for more than 800 years. It ushered in successive periods of republicanism, Napoleonic imperialism, and monarchism. In 1870 the founding of the Third Republic established France firmly in the republican tradition.

- **1914–1918** 1.4 million Frenchmen killed in World War I.
- **1918–1939** Economic recession and political instability: 20 prime ministers and 44 governments.
- **1940** Capitulation to Germany. Puppet Vichy regime. Abroad, Gen. de Gaulle leads "Free French."
- **1944** Liberation of France.
- **1946–1958** Fourth Republic. Political instability: 26 governments. Nationalizations. France takes leading role in EEC formation.
- **1958** Fifth Republic. De Gaulle president with strong powers.
- **1960** Most French colonies gain independence.
- **1962** Algerian independence after bitter war with France.
- **1966** France withdraws from NATO military command.
- **1968** General strike and riots over education policy and low wages. National Assembly dissolved; Gaullist victory in June elections.
- **1969** De Gaulle resigns after defeat in referendum on regional reform; replaced by Georges Pompidou.
- **1974** Valéry Giscard d'Estaing president. Center-right coalition.
- **1981** Left wins elections; François Mitterrand president.
- **1983–1986** Government U-turn on economic policy.
- **1986** Cohabitation between socialist president and new right-wing government led by Jacques Chirac. Privatization program introduced.
- **1988** Mitterrand wins second term. PS-led coalition returns.
- **1993** Center right wins elections. Second period of cohabitation.
- **1995** Jacques Chirac president.
- **1995–1996** Controversial series of Pacific nuclear tests.
- **1996** Unpopular austerity measures to prepare for adopting euro.
- **1997** PS-led government takes office in reversed cohabitation.
- **1999** France introduces euro.
- **2000** 35-hour week becomes law.
- **2002** January, euro fully adopted. April–June, center-right victory in presidential and legislative elections.
- **2003** Strikes over pension reform. Heatwave kills 15,000 people.
- **2004** Regional polls dent center-right ascendancy.

POLITICS

Multiparty elections

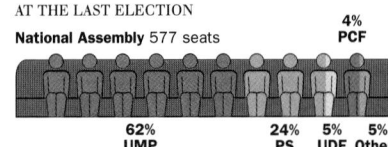

L. House 2002/2007
U. House 2004/2007

President Jacques Chirac

AT THE LAST ELECTION

National Assembly 577 seats

4% **PCF**

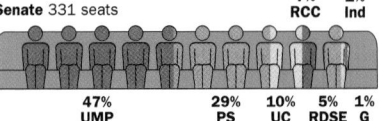

62% **UMP** | 24% **PS** | 5% **UDF** | 5% **Others**

UMP = Union for a Popular Movement (formerly the Union for a Presidential Majority, a coalition of the Rally for the Republic – **RPR** and Liberal Democracy – **DL**)
PS = Socialist Party **UDF** = Union for French Democracy
PCF = Communist Party of France **UC** = Centrist Union
RCC = Republicans, Communists, and Citizens
RDSE = European Democratic and Social Rally
Ind = Independents **G** = Greens

Senate 331 seats

7% **RCC** | 1% **Ind**

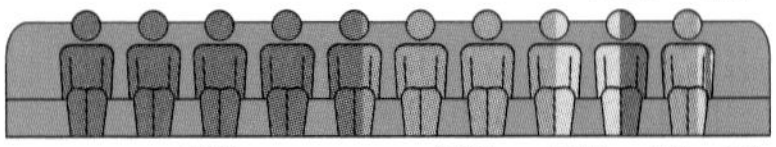

47% **UMP** | 29% **PS** | 10% **UC** | 5% **RDSE** | 1% **G**

France is a multiparty democracy. The constitution of the Fifth Republic, framed by Charles de Gaulle in 1958, ensures that the president has strong executive powers, but rules in tandem with a government and prime minister chosen by the National Assembly. Under changes agreed in 2000, the president and parliament are no longer elected according to separate timetables; the 2002 elections chose both for a five-year term. Traditionally the president focuses more on foreign policy and defense issues than on domestic and economic policy.

Profile

Apart from François Mitterrand of the PS (1981–1995), French presidents of the Fifth Republic have all been right-of-center. Until the electoral reforms of 2000, French presidents were frequently encumbered with opposition-dominated parliaments, forcing periods of so-called cohabitation with an opposition cabinet. President Jacques Chirac was able to overcome this obstacle in 2002 when his reelection was backed by the UMP's victory in parliamentary elections.

Economic reforms introduced under Chirac and aimed at reversing the budget deficit have proved very unpopular. Crushing defeat for the UMP in the 2004 regional and European parliamentary polls weakened Prime Minister Jean-Pierre Raffarin who nonetheless retained the leadership of a reshuffled government. The opposition PS emerged much strengthened, recovering from defeat in 2002.

The racist National Front (FN) shocked the world when its leader Jean-Marie Le Pen finished second in the first round of the 2002 presidential poll, though it failed to win any seats in that year's legislative elections. Subsequent regional and local elections have seen the FN and other far-right parties winning some 16% of the vote.

Main Political Issues

Liberal economic reform

The center right elected in 2002 promised immediate income tax cuts and probusiness measures. In 2003 a controversial cost-cutting pension reform, effectively delaying retirement by two years, was implemented despite a wave of protest strikes. Voters voiced their discontent in 2004, handing all but one of the 22 regional councils to the PS.

Racism and "exclusion"

Inner-city deprivation and "exclusion" of the unemployed and homeless are widely recognized as divisive, but they remain very difficult to tackle effectively. Exploiting concerns about crime, urban violence, and unemployment, the racist right has turned such fears to its political advantage on several occasions. Legislation on immigration has been tightened, and the center-right government, in power from 2002, has taken a particularly uncompromising line.

European integration and globalization

A current of opposition to European integration grew in the 1990s, fueled by fears that French sovereignty was compromised by it. Opponents of "globalization" tap into similar concerns that French jobs and culture are under threat. When France joined the eurozone, many saw giving up the franc as losing a symbolic part of their national identity. The most strident opponent of EU integration is the FN, but the center right is also a stout defender of French interests, notably over agricultural reform and in backing French economic interests abroad.

Jacques Chirac, *president of France since 1995.*

Jean-Marie Le Pen, *leader of the far-right FN and presidential runner-up in 2002.*

Jean-Pierre Raffarin *was appointed prime minister by Chirac in 2002.*

WORLD AFFAIRS

Joined UN in 1945

EU | G8 | NATO | OECD | OSCE

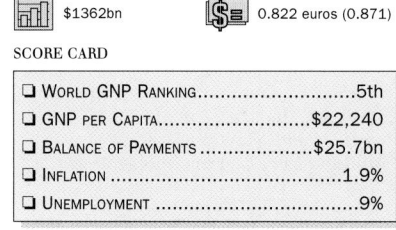

There have been two strands to foreign policy since World War II – strong independence and furtherance of French interests in a united Europe. France's role in the EU is seen as a way of combining them; many smaller EU states are angered by France's disregard for EU constraints, particularly as regards its budget deficit. France maintains its influence over francophone Africa.

A Franco–German alliance has long been a core element of the expanding EU, and there are plans to harmonize laws across the two states. Relations with the UK are more troublesome. Periodic friction arises over agricultural imports and the passage of immigrants across the Channel, but the central issue remains the UK's closeness to the US.

France has long been concerned with US dominance in both foreign affairs and culture. It maintained an independent nuclear deterrent throughout the Cold War. More recently, France vocally opposed war on Iraq in 2003, threatening to use its veto in the UN Security Council. France (and Germany) were dismissed by the US as "old Europe" over this issue, whereas most other European countries were more supportive of the US at the time.

AID

Donor

$5.49bn (donations)

Up 31% in 2002

France's motives as a major global donor are not simply commercial: it also wishes to maintain the influence of the French language, particularly in Africa, though its overseas territories remain main aid recipients. Médecins sans Frontières is part of a tradition of active involvement through NGOs.

ECONOMICS

Inflation 1.5% p.a. (1990–2001)

$1362bn

0.822 euros (0.871)

SCORE CARD

❑ WORLD GNP RANKING	5th
❑ GNP PER CAPITA	$22,240
❑ BALANCE OF PAYMENTS	$25.7bn
❑ INFLATION	1.9%
❑ UNEMPLOYMENT	9%

EXPORTS

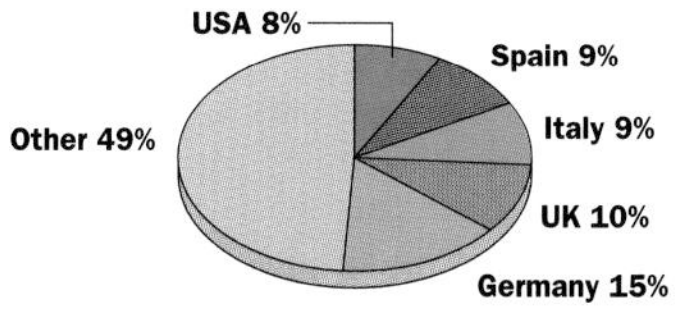
USA 8%
Spain 9%
Italy 9%
UK 10%
Germany 15%
Other 49%

IMPORTS

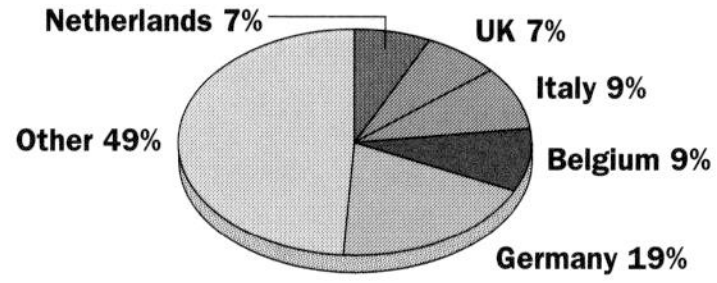
Netherlands 7%
UK 7%
Italy 9%
Belgium 9%
Germany 19%
Other 49%

STRENGTHS

Engineering, reflected in TGV and nuclear industries. Specializations: cars (Citroën, Peugeot, and Renault), water and other utility companies, and telecommunications. Major exporter: defense sector, chemicals, pharmaceuticals, food products. World's leading tourist destination. Success in attracting inward investment. Strong technocratic traditions: unlike in US or UK, top graduates are attracted into engineering. Luxury goods, cosmetics, perfumes, and quality wines. Most agriculture well modernized; France is Europe's leading agricultural producer.

WEAKNESSES

High taxes, social charges, and labor costs. Persistent high unemployment. France has lost its positions in traditional industries such as iron and steel, metallurgy, and textiles. Some major high-tech industries are run partly to further national pride rather than strictly on a commercial basis; France Telecom has faced major financial difficulties.

ECONOMIC PERFORMANCE INDICATOR

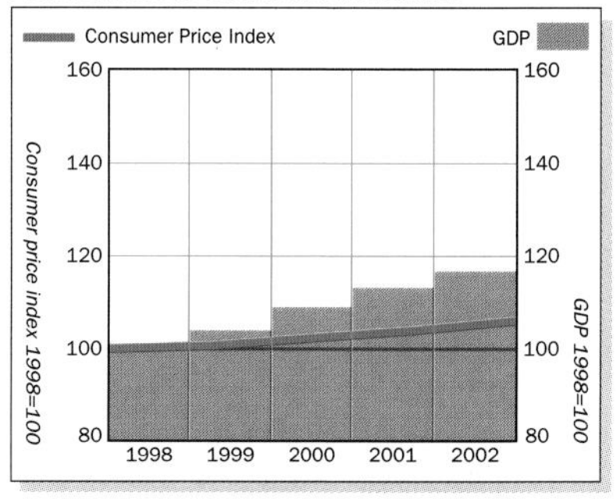
Consumer Price Index
GDP
Consumer price index 1998=100
GDP 1998=100
160
140
120
100
80
1998
1999
2000
2001
2002

PROFILE

Integration in western Europe, starting with coal and steel in the 1950s, placed France at the heart of the EU. It was one of the 12 EU countries to adopt the euro in 2002 (though it has ignored restrictions on the size of its budget deficit).

France has a long tradition of state involvement in running the economy, but for the last 20 years both right-of-center and socialist governments have vigorously pursued privatization. Regional hubs are of growing economic significance. France is the EU's largest agricultural producer; its farmers form a powerful political lobby. Unemployment is a major issue. Active trade unions lost a major battle over pension reform in 2003, while their earlier victory in securing a 35-hour week in 2000 is now widely challenged, with its critics complaining of an erosion in the competitiveness of French business.

FRANCE : MAJOR BUSINESSES

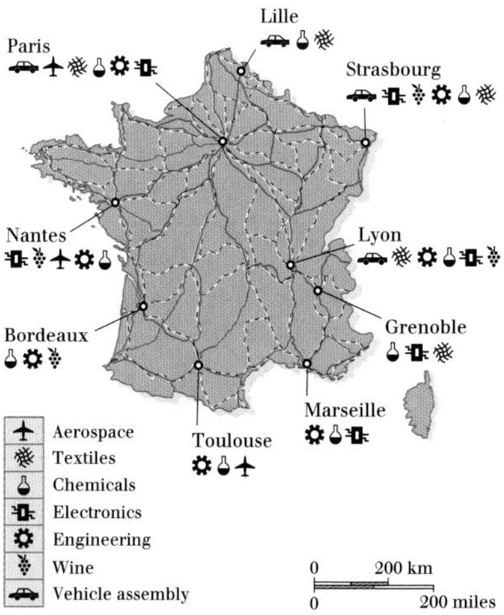
Lille
Paris
Strasbourg
Nantes
Lyon
Bordeaux
Grenoble
Marseille
Toulouse
Aerospace
Textiles
Chemicals
Electronics
Engineering
Wine
Vehicle assembly
0
200 km
0
200 miles

DEFENSE

No compulsory military service

$38bn

Up 17% in 2002

FRENCH ARMED FORCES

614 main battle tanks (244 AMX-30B2, 370 Leclerc)	137,000 personnel
1 carrier, 6 submarines, 1 cruiser, 12 destroyers, 20 frigates, 35 patrol boats	44,250 personnel
478 combat aircraft (340 Mirage F-1B/1CR/2000B/C/5F/N/D)	64,000 personnel
64 SLBM in 4 SSBN	

France was a founder member of NATO, but left its military command in 1966 in opposition to US domination. It maintained an independent nuclear deterrent through the Cold War, but went through a rapprochement with NATO in the 1990s. Joint participation with Germany in European army units is partly symbolic of reconciliation, as well as an expression of the need for an EU defense structure.

The influence of the army, which was once very strong, is now much diminished. Compulsory military service ended in 2001.

France has one of the world's largest and most export-oriented defense industries, producing its own tanks, jet fighter aircraft, and missiles.

F

RESOURCES

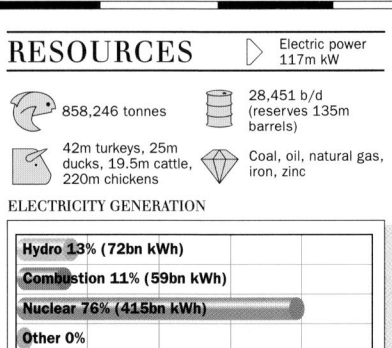

Electric power 117m kW

858,246 tonnes

28,451 b/d (reserves 135m barrels)

42m turkeys, 25m ducks, 19.5m cattle, 220m chickens

Coal, oil, natural gas, iron, zinc

ELECTRICITY GENERATION

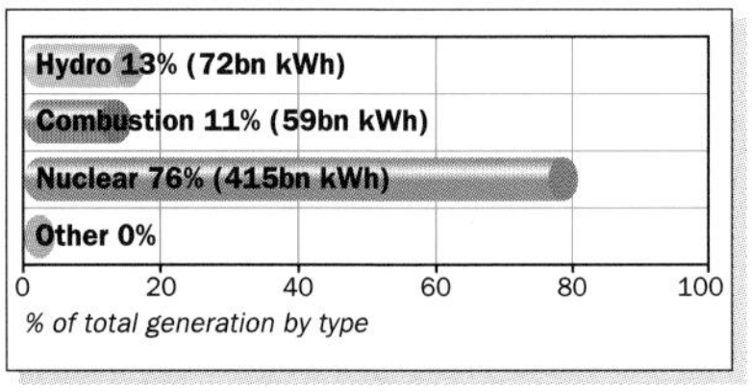
Hydro 13% (72bn kWh)
Combustion 11% (59bn kWh)
Nuclear 76% (415bn kWh)
Other 0%
0
20
40
60
80
100
% of total generation by type

France is the world's most committed user of nuclear energy, which provides around three-quarters of its electricity requirements. The policy reflects a desire for national energy self-sufficiency. Coal is still plentiful in the north and Lorraine, but the last coal mine closed in 2004. Gas fields off the southwest coast are also near exhaustion.

FRANCE : LAND USE

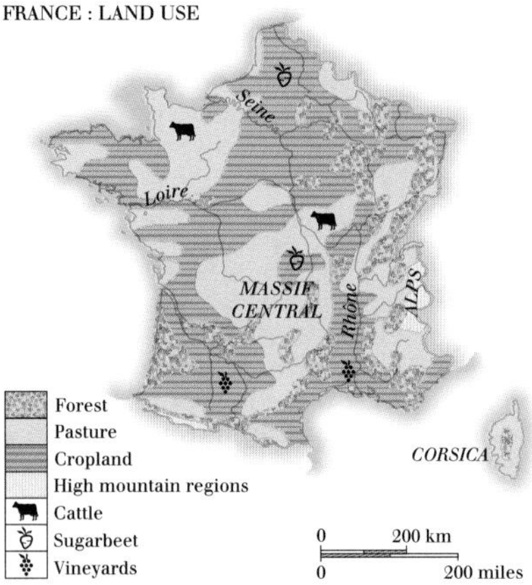
Seine
Loire
MASSIF CENTRAL
Rhône
ALPS
CORSICA
Forest
Pasture
Cropland
High mountain regions
Cattle
Sugarbeet
Vineyards
0
200 km
0
200 miles

ENVIRONMENT

Sustainability rank: 33rd

13% (9% partially protected)

6.2 tonnes per capita

ENVIRONMENTAL TREATIES

Yes | Yes | Yes

Yes | Yes | Yes

Awareness of "green" issues has risen with a series of campaigns against major infrastructure projects. Nuclear power's importance, however, puts the environmentalist lobby in perspective. Transportation of oil by sea poses the threat of pollution of the Atlantic coast. Brittany's beaches and fisheries were badly affected by the wreck of the *Erika* in 1999. The severe storms, floods, droughts, and forest fires in recent years highlight vulnerability to global climate change.

— MILITANT ISLAM AND THE SECULAR TRADITION —

LIKE OTHER WESTERN countries challenged by radical Islam both within and beyond their national borders, France is preoccupied with tackling the perceived threat of terrorism and with issues of multiculturalism and integration.

OPERATION VIGIPIRATE

The most visible antiterrorist response, the so-called "Operation Vigipirate," was launched in 1995 after a spate of bombings on the Paris metro. Its main target has been militant Algerian groups who denounce French support for the regime in that country, a former French colony and source of the largest numbers of France's minority of north African immigrant origin. Strengthened after the September 2001 terrorist attacks in the US, Vigipirate has four levels of alert. It gives exceptional powers to police and heavily armed security forces, who are much in evidence in locations such as airports and main railways stations.

GHETTOIZATION

The city suburbs, where the main concentrations of French citizens of north African ethnic origin live in high-density housing, have worse problems of unemployment, crime, and violence than the national average. Official crime statistics do not record racial information, but it is widely accepted – and played upon to political effect by the far-right National Front – that a disproportionate amount of crime is committed by young men of north African origin. Heavy-handed policing of the suburbs, ranging from frequent demands for identity documents to alleged brutality, has increased the sense of exclusion and alienation among young people in particular.

Immigration from France's ex-colonies in north Africa took place mainly in the 1960s and 1970s. The new arrivals generally kept a relatively low profile,

EGALITE-FRATERNITE

***Headscarves, worn to symbolize** Islamic identity, challenged the secular nature of French state schools.*

***Immigration can produce** a multiethnic mix, but social exclusion is creating Islamic ghettos in many urban areas.*

but in the 1980s a second (largely French-born) generation demanded equal rights. Many in the third generation, though now secure in their French citizenship, have real issues with social integration, and challenge mainstream French society to accept and respect their distinct identity.

The government proposed in mid-2004 a five-year plan to improve social cohesion, after a study of 630 city suburbs concluded that at least half had already become separate ethnic communities where young people were even turning against the French language. Islamic radicalization included condemnation of young Muslim women who wore Western clothing.

THE HEADSCARVES ISSUE

A law banning Islamic headscarves and other religious symbols from state schools, with effect from the 2004/2005 school year, made this simmering issue a major point of confrontation. Opponents denounced the ban as an assault on the rights of young women to proclaim their Islamic values. Its advocates presented themselves as defenders of the secular principles of the French republic, and stressed that the law applied to all religious symbols, including Jewish skullcaps and Christian crucifixes.

The 1905 law on separation of church and state prohibits proselytizing in public buildings. In 1989 a ban on religious symbols in schools was ruled illegal by the French courts, but it was accepted that a pupil could be expelled for wearing a sign that amounted to proselytizing. President Chirac supported the 2004 law as clarifying the position of school authorities wishing to act against "ostentatious" religious symbols – headscarves in particular being widely seen as symbolizing an intolerant version of Islam and the oppression of women.

MEDIA

TV ownership high

Daily newspaper circulation 201 per 1000 people

PUBLISHING AND BROADCAST MEDIA

There are 117 daily newspapers, including *Le Monde, Libération,* and *Le Figaro. Ouest-France* has the highest circulation

10 services: 3 state-controlled, 7 independent

7 services: 3 state-controlled, 4 independent

TV and radio were freed from direct state influence in the 1980s. Two of the main TV channels are still state-owned, but TF1 was privatized in 1987. Canal Plus mixes pay-per-view and advertising-backed services. A Breton-language station started up in 2000. Commercial channels have multiplied with the growth of satellite and cable.

The once-innovative Minitel electronic communications system is now overshadowed by the Internet. Circulation of prestigious national newspapers has dwindled and regional papers too have suffered from a gradual shift to electronic media.

CRIME

No death penalty

59,155 prisoners

Up 14% in 2000–2002

CRIME RATES

Murders
4 *per 100,000 population*

Rapes
18 *per 100,000 population*

Thefts
4225 *per 100,000 population*

The Code Napoléon, enacted in 1804, still forms the basis of French law. Criminal justice is based on inquisitorial rather than adversarial principles: the judge has considerable powers to examine witnesses and assess evidence. There are no *sub judice* restrictions on reporting trials. Political corruption cases, reaching into government, attract much attention.

Public concern about rising petty crime and violence has encouraged tough policing. Harsh laws targeting beggars, prostitutes, and squatters were introduced in 2002, and have been held responsible for a sudden increase in the prison population.

EDUCATION

School leaving age: 16

99%

2.03m students

THE EDUCATION SYSTEM

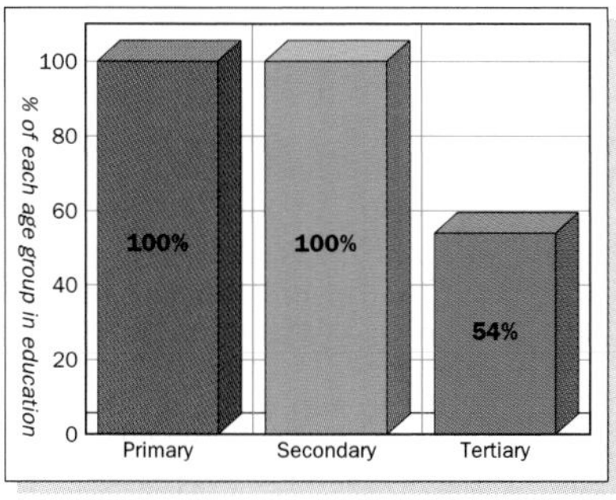

% of each age group in education
100
80
60
40
20
0
100%
100%
54%
Primary
Secondary
Tertiary

Education is highly centralized, a situation which is slowly generating a desire for greater flexibility. The education ministry organizes the curriculum, sets examinations, and decides staffing issues. Roman Catholic schools, which take most of the 17% of privately educated children (but which are not fee paying and receive large state subsidies), are the exception. However, they are still obliged to follow the national curriculum.

The focus in the classroom remains the acquisition of a broad range of knowledge. Pupils' academic records are impressive, despite frequent staff strikes.

France has more than 70 universities and higher education bodies, with 1.2 million students. The famous Sorbonne in Paris was split into 13 separate universities in 1971. Entry is not competitive, but based on passing the secondary-level exam, the *baccalauréat*. Most students attend the university nearest to home. The universities have been given neither the funds nor the staff to cope with the huge increase in student numbers in recent years. The Grandes Ecoles, the most influential tertiary institutions, are outside the university system, and each takes just a few hundred carefully selected students. They groom the future governing elite, opening the way for their successful graduates to gain the top civil service and professional jobs.

Massif Central, Auvergne. *The Massif's lonely granite plateaus and extinct volcanoes are France's oldest rock formations.*

HEALTH

Welfare state health benefits

1 per 303 people

Cancers, heart and cerebrovascular diseases, accidents

The French consume more medicines per capita than any other nation, and a significant number take medically approved, and prescribed, cures at health spas. Patients pay for treatment, and then get the majority of the cost reimbursed by an insurance company paid by the social services. The national health system is widely praised, but has been criticized as "profoundly disorganized" and faces mounting debt. Though health awareness has risen in recent years, drinking and smoking are ingrained in social behavior. Cirrhosis of the liver is not uncommon as a cause of death. In 2003 a major, controversial antismoking campaign was launched.

SPENDING

GDP/cap. increase

CONSUMPTION AND SPENDING

473 per 1000 population

569 per 1000 population

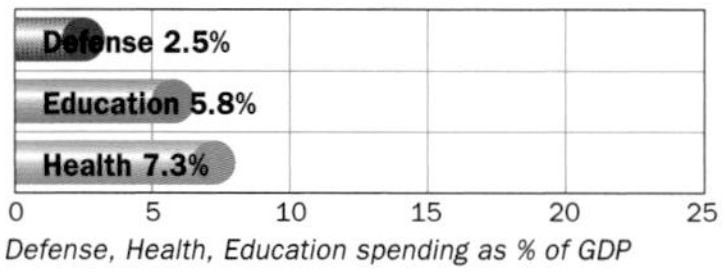

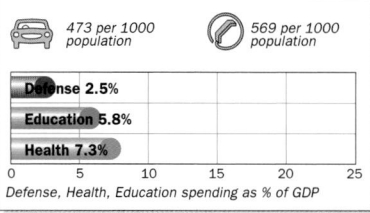

Defense 2.5%
Education 5.8%
Health 7.3%
0
5
10
15
20
25
Defense, Health, Education spending as % of GDP

Wealth and income disparities in France are higher than in most OECD states. The Socialists narrowed the gap a little in the 1980s with the introduction of the legal minimum wage (*le SMIC*). Most tax is indirect – a result of a long French tradition of income-tax evasion. Substantial tax cuts announced in 2000 aimed to redress the imbalance of income tax on the rich and poor. The wealthy take exotic vacations in the Himalayas, the Andes, and Polynesia. The French lagged behind their neighbors in taking up the Internet, but by 2003 this was changing, with high-speed connectivity widely available.

WORLD RANKING

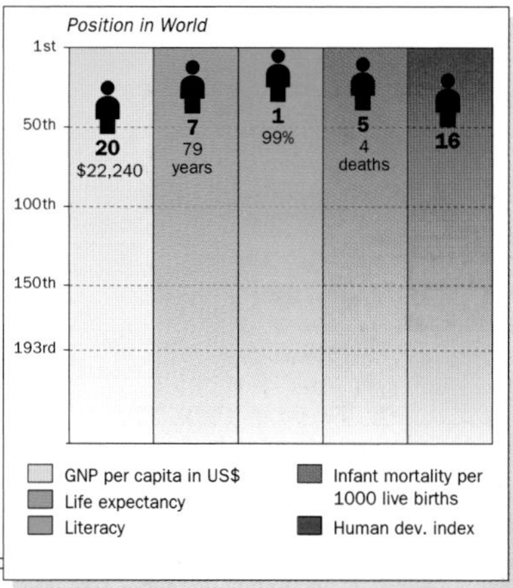

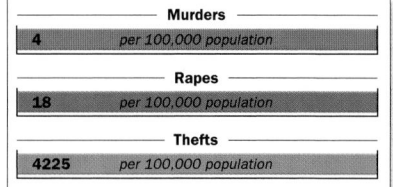

Position in World
1st
50th
100th
150th
193rd
20
$22,240
7
79
years
1
99%
5
4
deaths
16
GNP per capita in US$
Life expectancy
Literacy
Infant mortality per 1000 live births
Human dev. index

F

GABON

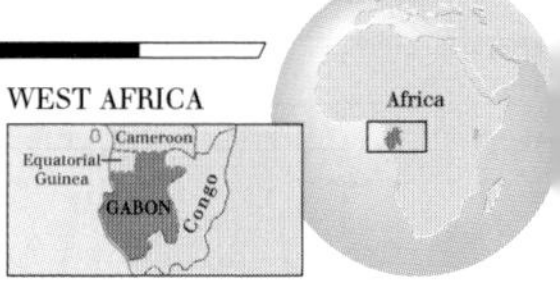
WEST AFRICA
Africa
Cameroon
Equatorial Guinea
GABON
Congo

OFFICIAL NAME: Gabonese Republic **CAPITAL:** Libreville
POPULATION: 1.3 million **CURRENCY:** CFA franc **OFFICIAL LANGUAGE:** French

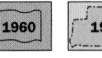

1960 | 1960 | Aug 17 | G | +1 | +241 | .ga

AN EQUATORIAL COUNTRY on the west coast of Africa, Gabon has an economy based on the production of oil. Only a small area of Gabon is cultivated, and more than two-thirds of it constitutes one of the world's finest virgin rainforests. Gabon became independent of France in 1960. A single-party state from 1968, it returned to multiparty democracy in 1990. Gabon's population is small, and the government is encouraging its increase.

CLIMATE

Tropical equatorial

WEATHER CHART FOR LIBREVILLE

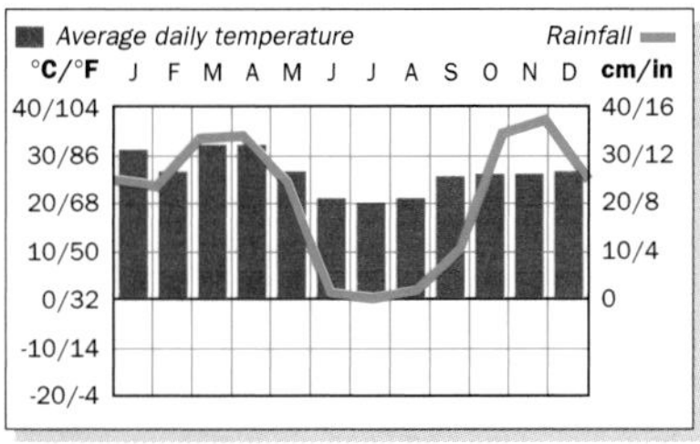
Average daily temperature
Rainfall
°C/°F J F M A M J J A S O N D cm/in
40/104 30/86 20/68 10/50 0/32 -10/14 -20/-4
40/16 30/12 20/8 10/4 0

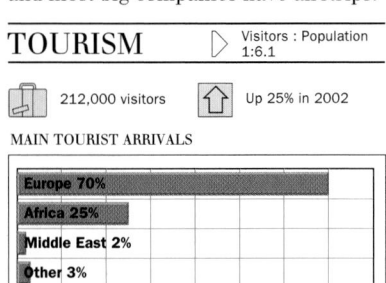

The climate is heavily equatorial – hot all year round with a long rainy season from October to May. The cold Benguela current lowers coastal temperatures.

TRANSPORTATION

Drive on right

Libreville 854,776 passengers | 44 ships 12,500 grt

THE TRANSPORTATION NETWORK

846 km (526 miles) | 30 km (19 miles)
731 km (454 miles) | 1600 km (994 miles)

The Trans-Gabon Railroad from Owendo port near Libreville to Massoukou is the key transportation link.

Air transportation is well developed, and most big companies have airstrips.

TOURISM

Visitors : Population 1:6.1

212,000 visitors | Up 25% in 2002

MAIN TOURIST ARRIVALS

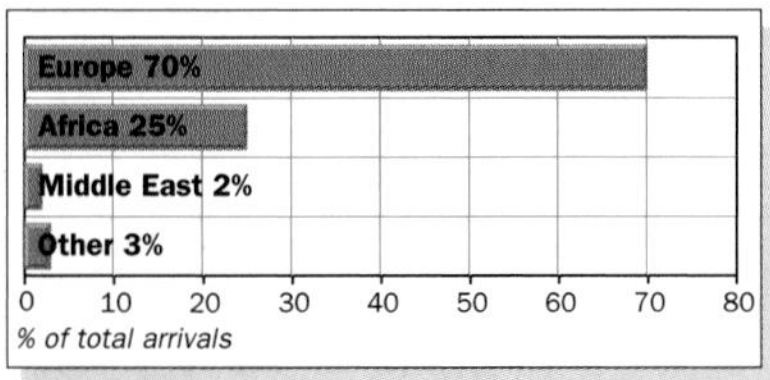
Europe 70%
Africa 25%
Middle East 2%
Other 3%
0 10 20 30 40 50 60 70 80
% of total arrivals

Gabon's tourist industry is growing, but is hampered by visa restrictions and high prices, especially in Libreville.

PEOPLE

Pop. density low

Fang, French, Punu, Sira, Nzebi, Mpongwe | 5/km² (13/mi²)

THE URBAN/RURAL POPULATION SPLIT

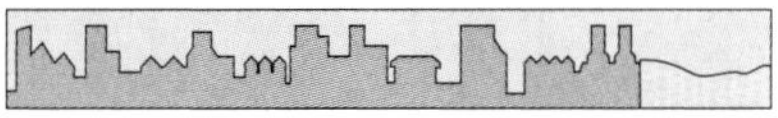
83%
17%

ETHNIC MAKEUP

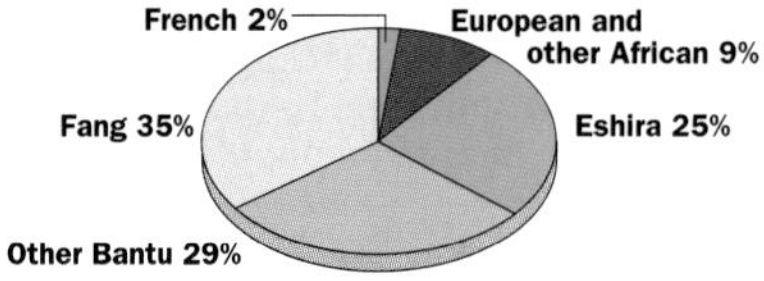
French 2%
European and other African 9%
Fang 35%
Eshira 25%
Other Bantu 29%

The largest ethnic group in Gabon is the Fang, who live mainly in the north. President Omar Bongo, from a subgroup of the Bateke in the southeast, has artfully united the common interests of other ethnic groups to keep the Fang from government. The Myene group around Port-Gentil consider themselves the aristocrats of Gabonese society owing to their long-standing ex-colonial contacts. Oil wealth has led to the growth of a distinct bourgeoisie. Gabon is one of Africa's most urbanized countries.

POLITICS

Multiparty elections

L. House 2001/2006
U. House 2003/2009
President Omar Bongo

AT THE LAST ELECTION

National Assembly 120 seats

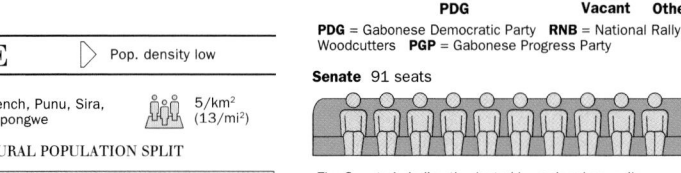

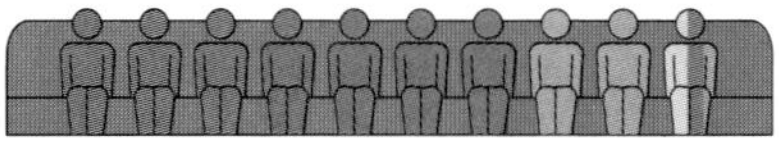
5% RNB
2% PGP
71% PDG
19% Vacant
3% Others

PDG = Gabonese Democratic Party **RNB** = National Rally of Woodcutters **PGP** = Gabonese Progress Party

Senate 91 seats

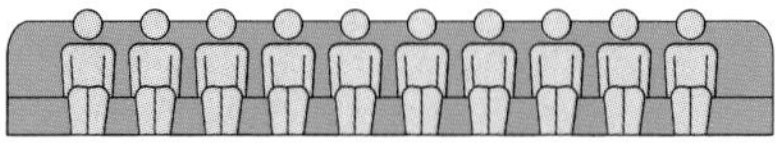

The Senate is indirectly elected by regional councils

Omar Bongo has been in power since 1967, running a single-party state from 1968 until a multiparty system was introduced in 1990. Elections since then have confirmed Bongo in power, along with the former sole ruling party, the PDG. The fairness of the polls has been widely disputed. The opposition accuses Bongo of attempting to prolong his term in office indefinitely; in 1997 presidential terms were extended to seven years, and the constitutional restriction on the permitted number of terms was dropped in 2003.

WORLD AFFAIRS

Joined UN in 1960

FZ | G24 | AU | OIC | ACP

Gabon remains influential regionally (the Gulf of Guinea Commission was launched in Libreville in 2001), and relations further afield, particularly with OPEC, are also important. Dwindling oil production has led Gabon to look as far as China to attract investment for new exploration.

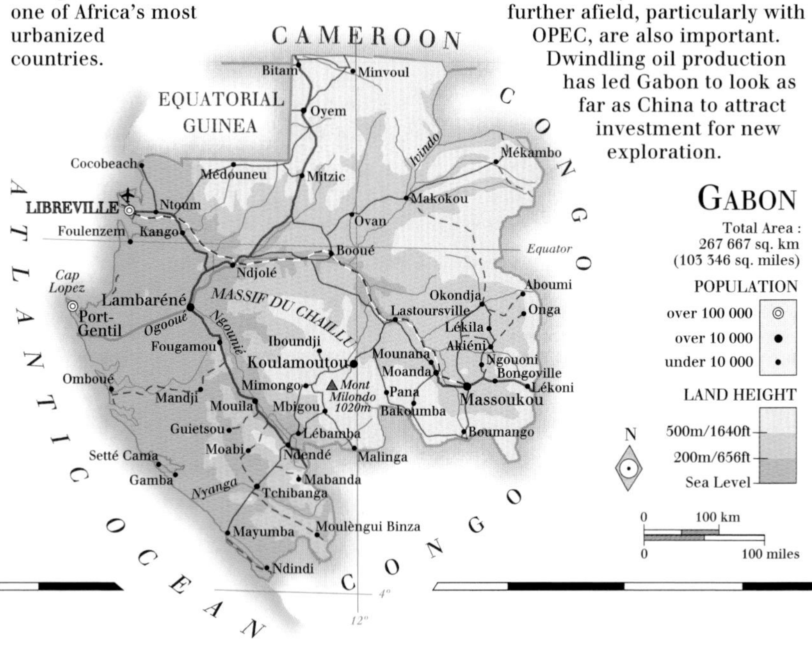
CAMEROON
EQUATORIAL GUINEA
CONGO
ATLANTIC OCEAN
Bitam
Minvoul
Oyem
Cocobeach
Médouneu
Mitzic
Mékambo
LIBREVILLE
Ntoum
Makokou
Foulenzem
Kango
Ovan
Booué
Equator
Ndjolé
Cap Lopez
Port-Gentil
Lambaréné
MASSIF DU CHAILLU
Okondja
Aboumi
Onga
Lastoursville
Lékila
Akiéni
Ngouoni
Bongoville
Léconi
Fougamou
Iboundji
Koulamoutou
Mounana
Moanda
Omboué
Mimongo
Mont Milondo 1020m
Pana
Massoukou
Mandji
Mouila
Mbigou
Bakoumba
Guietsou
Lébamba
Boumango
Sette Cama
Moabi
Ndendé
Malinga
Gamba
Mabanda
Tchibanga
Mayumba
Moulèngui Binza
Ndindi
Ogooué
Ngounié
Ivindo
Nyanga
GABON
Total Area : 267 667 sq. km (103 346 sq. miles)
POPULATION
over 100 000
over 10 000
under 10 000
LAND HEIGHT
500m/1640ft
200m/656ft
Sea Level
0 100 km
0 100 miles

AID

Recipient

$72m (receipts)

Up 700% in 2002

France is by far the major aid donor, providing over two-thirds of total receipts. For a middle-income country with one of the highest GNPs per capita in the developing world, Gabon has benefited from considerable aid. Its indebtedness is the result of excessive borrowing, which was encouraged by Western banks in the 1970s. Much aid goes to servicing this debt.

DEFENSE

No compulsory military service

$75m

Up 9% in 2002

Bongo's background in the military is reflected in Gabon's large defense budget and prestige weaponry, which includes French Mirage jets. France guarantees the country's security and keeps a small garrison in Libreville. Gabon receives a small amount of military aid from the US. It led the 1998–2000 UN peacekeeping mission in the Central African Republic.

CHRONOLOGY

Gabon became a French colony in 1886, administered as part of French Equatorial Africa.

- **1960** Independence. Léon M'ba president.
- **1967** Albert-Bernard (later Omar) Bongo president.
- **1968** Single-party state instituted.
- **1990** Multiparty democracy.
- **1998** Bongo reelected president.
- **2001** Elections: ruling PDG retains majority.

G

ECONOMICS

Inflation 5.6% p.a. (1990–2001)

$4.03bn

539.2 CFA francs (571.2)

SCORE CARD

- World GNP Ranking........................120th
- GNP per Capita $3060
- Balance of Payments $584m
- Inflation 5.9%
- Unemployment..................................21%

Strengths
Oil and relatively small population: high per capita GNP. Abundant resources – including some of the world's best tropical hardwoods.

Weaknesses
Large debt burden incurred in the 1970s. Continuing dependence on French technical assistance. Existing oil reserves becoming depleted. High unemployment and levels of HIV.

EXPORTS

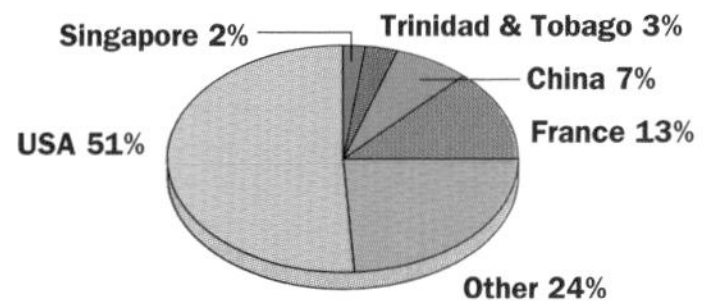
Singapore 2%
Trinidad & Tobago 3%
China 7%
USA 51%
France 13%
Other 24%

IMPORTS

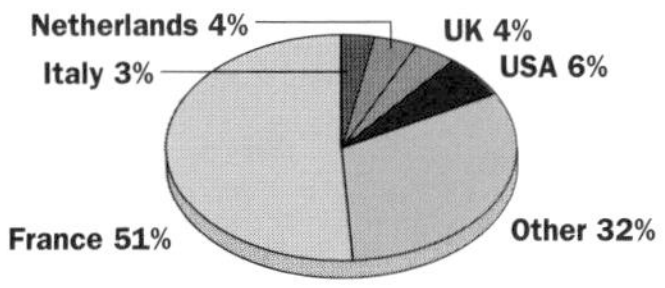
Netherlands 4%
UK 4%
Italy 3%
USA 6%
France 51%
Other 32%

RESOURCES

Electric power 410,000 kW

40,559 tonnes

240,000 b/d (reserves 2.4bn barrels)

212,000 pigs, 195,000 sheep, 3.1m chickens

Oil, manganese, uranium, gold, iron, natural gas

Oil is the major export earner. Gabon also has large deposits of uranium and over 100 years' reserves of manganese. The unexploited iron ore deposits at Bélinga are among the world's largest.

ENVIRONMENT

Sustainability rank: 36th

10% partially protected

2.8 tonnes per capita

The Trans-Gabon Railroad sliced through one of the world's finest virgin rainforests. Gabon created a system of 13 national parks covering 10% of its land in 2002. An outbreak of the Ebola virus that year contributed to the loss of huge numbers of great apes.

MEDIA

TV ownership high

Daily newspaper circulation 30 per 1000 people

PUBLISHING AND BROADCAST MEDIA

There are 2 daily newspapers, *L'Union* and *Gabon-Matin*

3 services: 1 state-owned, 2 independent

7 services: 2 state-controlled, 5 independent

The media are mostly government-controlled. There was a crackdown in 1998 on independent media – which in the 1990s had become quite diverse – raising concerns about freedom of expression.

CRIME

Death penalty in use

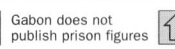

Gabon does not publish prison figures

Crime is rising

Gabon's human rights record has improved in recent years, though urban crime rates are rising. The government launched a campaign to combat child trafficking in 2001.

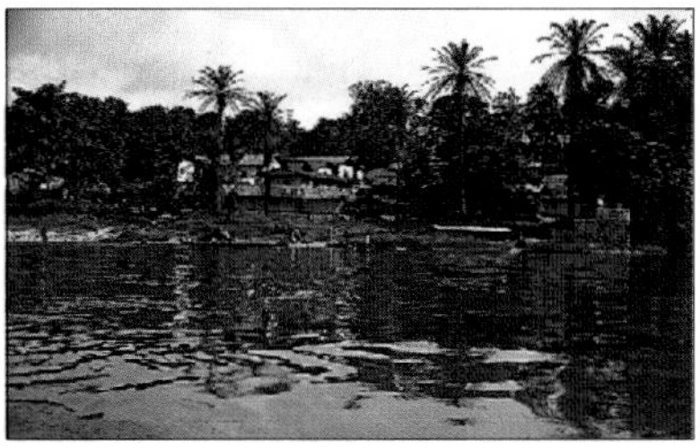

***Albert Schweitzer Hospital,** Lambaréné, on the lower Ogooué River. Schweitzer won the Nobel Peace Prize in 1952.*

EDUCATION

School leaving age: 16

71%

7473 students

Education follows the French system. Primary school enrollment is high. There are three universities, all public, which have a fair degree of autonomy.

HEALTH

No welfare state health benefits

1 per 5000 people

Heart and diarrheal diseases, pneumonia, accidents, AIDS

Oil revenues have allowed substantial investment in the health service, which is now among the best in Africa.

SPENDING

GDP/cap. increase

CONSUMPTION AND SPENDING

22 per 1000 population

25 per 1000 population

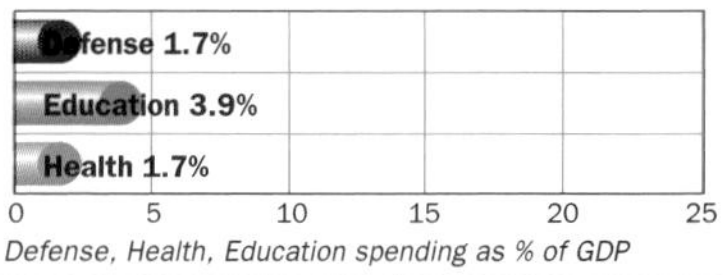
Defense 1.7%
Education 3.9%
Health 1.7%
0
5
10
15
20
25
Defense, Health, Education spending as % of GDP

Oil wealth has created an affluent bourgeoisie. Immigrants take on low-income and menial jobs. The cost of living in Libreville is surprisingly high.

WORLD RANKING

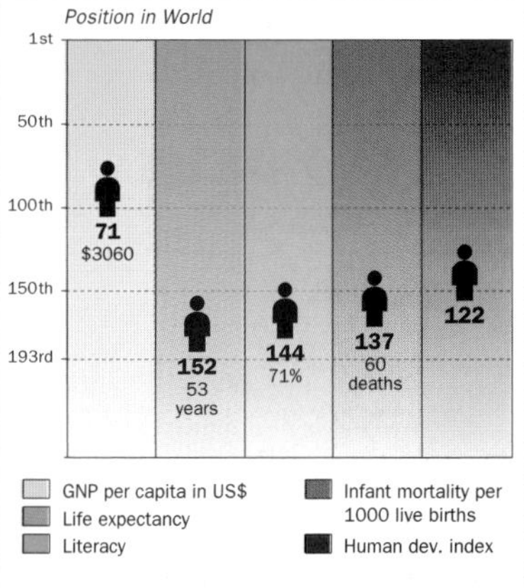
Position in World
1st
50th
100th
150th
193rd
71
$3060
152
53 years
144
71%
137
60 deaths
122
GNP per capita in US$
Life expectancy
Literacy
Infant mortality per 1000 live births
Human dev. index

GAMBIA

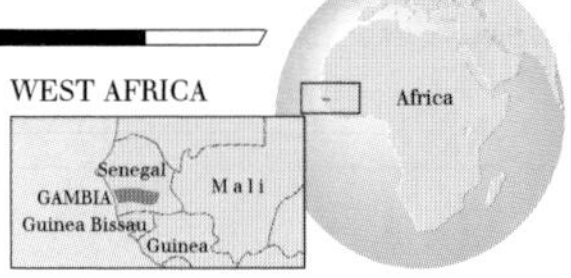
WEST AFRICA
Africa
Senegal
GAMBIA
Mali
Guinea Bissau
Guinea

OFFICIAL NAME: Republic of the Gambia **CAPITAL:** Banjul
POPULATION: 1.4 million **CURRENCY:** Dalasi **OFFICIAL LANGUAGE:** English

1965 | 1965 | Feb 18 | WAG | 0 | +220 | .gm

A NARROW COUNTRY on the western coast of Africa, Gambia was renowned as a stable democracy until an army coup in 1994. Agriculture accounts for 65% of GDP, yet many Gambians are leaving rural areas for the towns, where average incomes are four times higher. Its position as an enclave within Senegal seems likely to endure, following the failure of an experiment in federation in the 1980s.

CLIMATE

Tropical wet and dry

WEATHER CHART FOR BANJUL

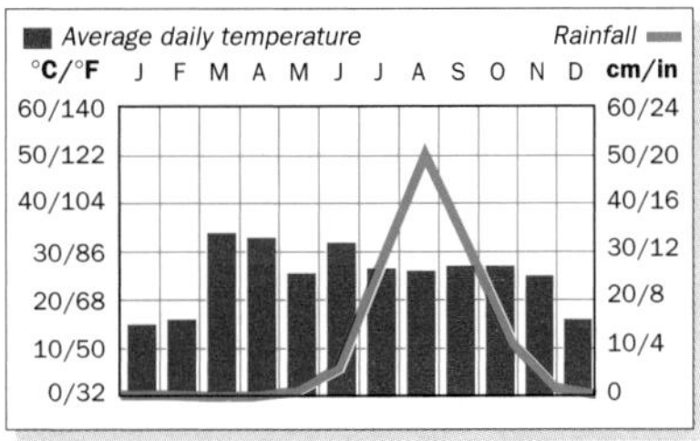
Average daily temperature
Rainfall
°C/°F
J F M A M J J A S O N D
cm/in
60/140
50/122
40/104
30/86
20/68
10/50
0/32
60/24
50/20
40/16
30/12
20/8
10/4
0

The subtropical and sunny dry season is punctuated by intermittent hot *harmattan* winds.

TRANSPORTATION

Drive on right

Yundum International, Banjul 355,944 passengers

9 ships 2183 grt

THE TRANSPORTATION NETWORK

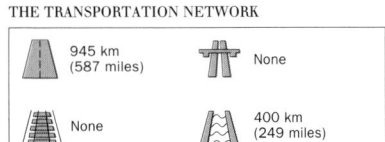

945 km (587 miles)

None

None

400 km (249 miles)

Roads, rather than the Gambia River, are now the primary means of inland transportation. The Trans-Gambia Highway and Kombo coastal roads are currently being upgraded.

TOURISM

Visitors : Population 1:18

79,000 visitors

Up 5% in 2002

MAIN TOURIST ARRIVALS

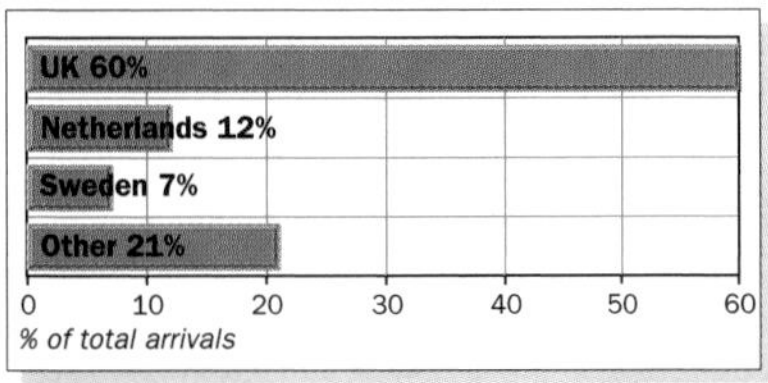
UK 60%
Netherlands 12%
Sweden 7%
Other 21%
0
10
20
30
40
50
60
% of total arrivals

"Eco-tourism" is being developed, but most of those enjoying the beaches and resort hotel life are Europeans escaping winter, including many single women.

PEOPLE

Pop. density medium

Mandinka, Fulani, Wolof, Jola, Soninke, English

140/km² (363/mi²)

THE URBAN/RURAL POPULATION SPLIT

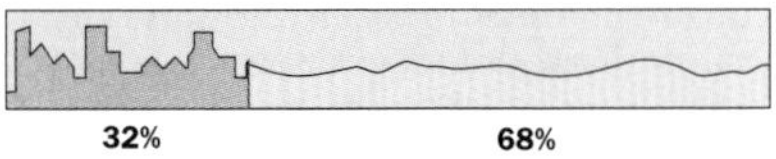
32%
68%

ETHNIC MAKEUP

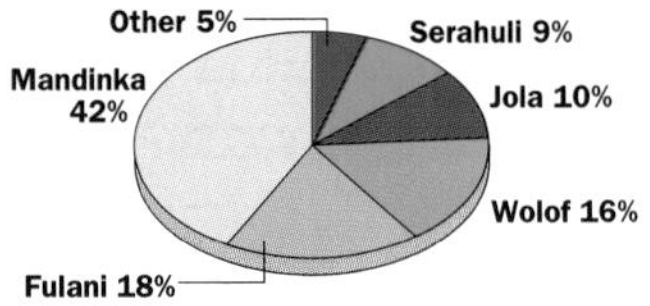
Other 5%
Serahuli 9%
Mandinka 42%
Jola 10%
Wolof 16%
Fulani 18%

The Mandinka have traditionally dominated politically. Potential resentment among the smaller ethnic groups was offset under the regime of President Sir Dawda Jawara by the distribution of political offices fairly according to ethnic origins. President Jammeh, a fervent Muslim, is from the minority Jola (or Diola) community, numerous across the border in Senegal, where they are active in a local rebellion. About 85% of Gambians follow Islam, though there is no official state religion. There is a yearly influx of migrants, who come from Senegal, Guinea, and Mali to trade in groundnuts, and a small UK expatriate community along the coast. Gambia is still a poor country, with 80% of the labor force engaged in agriculture. Women are active as traders in an otherwise male-dominated society.

Fishing village. *Overfishing in the waters off Gambia and Senegal, mainly by foreign vessels, is a growing problem.*

POLITICS

Multiparty elections

2002/2007

President Yahya Jammeh

AT THE LAST ELECTION

National Assembly 53 seats

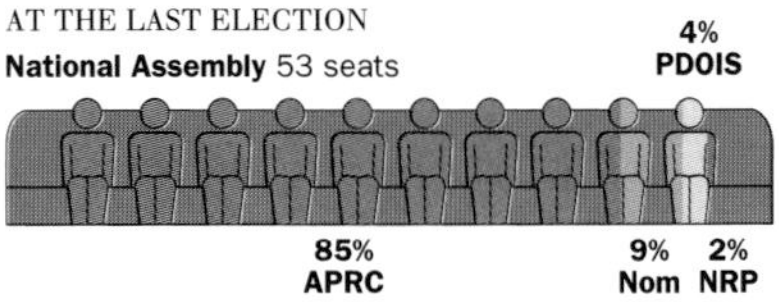
4% PDOIS
85% APRC
9% Nom
2% NRP

APRC = Alliance for Patriotic Reorientation and Construction
Nom = Nominated **PDOIS** = People's Democratic Organization for Independence and Socialism
NRP = National Reconciliation Party

Sir Dawda Jawara ruled under the People's Progressive Party (PPP) from 1962 until a coup in 1994, for most of which time Gambia was one of Africa's few democracies. The coup leaders claimed that it had been initiated to end corruption and preserve democracy. Jawara went into exile in the UK, and several portfolios in the new government went to civil servants who had served previously. Military leader Yahya Jammeh was elected president in controversial elections in 1996, and the following January his APRC won a majority of seats in the legislative election.

Though the ban on opposition parties was lifted in 2001, Jammeh and the APRC were reelected in 2001 and 2002 respectively. Opposition leader Lamine Waa Juwara, in and out of prison since 1994 and again facing trial, recently formed the National Democratic Action Movement and resigned from the main opposition United Democratic Party.

WORLD AFFAIRS

Joined UN in 1965

CILSS | Comm | ECOWAS | AU | OIC

International criticism of the 1994 coup which brought President Jammeh to power has softened in recent years, but an apparent crackdown on opponents following Jammeh's reelection in 2001 reawakened concern. Relations with Senegal have been strained by the rebellion of the Jola community in the province of Casamance.

AID

Recipient

$61m (receipts)

Up 13% in 2002

Western aid flows, suspended after the 1994 coup, have largely resumed. International agencies are the major donors. 2002/2003 was officially declared a year of crop failure in an effort to attract emergency food aid.

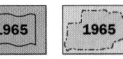

GAMBIA

Total Area : 11 300 sq. km (4363 sq. miles)

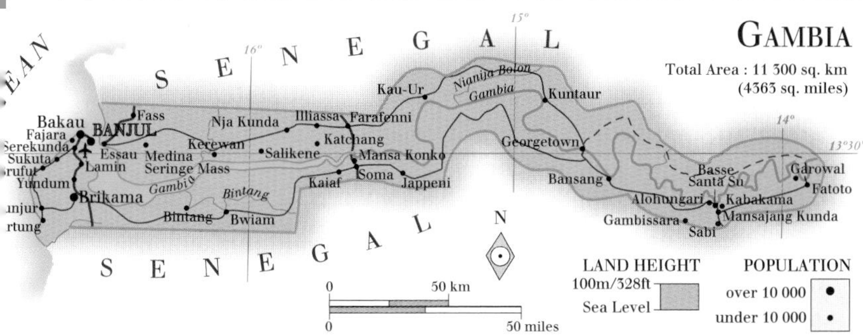
SENEGAL
SENEGAL
Bakau
Fajara
Serekunda
Sukuta
BANJUL
Fass
Essau
Lamin
Medina
Seringe Mass
Kerewan
Nja Kunda
Illiassa
Farafenni
Salikene
Katchang
Mansa Konko
Soma
Kaiaf
Jappeni
Kau-Ur
Niamja Bolon
Gambia
Kuntaur
Georgetown
Bansang
Basse Santa Su
Garowal
Fatoto
Alohungari
Kabakama
Mansajang Kunda
Gambissara
Sabi
Yundum
Brikama
Bintang
Bwiam
N
0
50 km
50 miles
LAND HEIGHT
100m/328ft
Sea Level
POPULATION
over 10 000
under 10 000

CHRONOLOGY

Mandinka traders brought Islam in the 13th century and were the main influence until the 18th century. The 1700s and 1800s saw colonial rivalry between Britain and France.

- 1888 British possession.
- 1959 Dawda Jawara founds PPP.
- 1965 Independence from Britain.
- 1970 Republic; Jawara president.
- 1982–1989 Federation with Senegal.
- 1994 Jawara ousted in army coup.
- 1996 Yahya Jammeh wins presidential election.
- 2000 Military coup foiled.
- 2001 $2 million antipoverty program launched by government.
- 2002 Jammeh's party sweeps parliamentary elections.

DEFENSE

No compulsory military service

$3m

Down 25% in 2002

The 800-strong Gambia National Army includes a small marine unit, with three patrol boats, and a presidential guard. Most arms are bought from the UK, though supplies are now increasingly coming from Nigeria too. The Gambian armed forces have taken part in peacekeeping missions to Liberia and elsewhere in the region.

ECONOMICS

Inflation 4.1% p.a. (1990–2001)

$375m

29.75 dalasis (26)

SCORE CARD

- WORLD GNP RANKING........................174th
- GNP PER CAPITA..............................$270
- BALANCE OF PAYMENTS.....................–$53m
- INFLATION....................................16.9%
- UNEMPLOYMENT ....Widespread underemployment

STRENGTHS

Low tariffs promote regional trade. Natural deepwater harbor at Banjul, one of the finest on the west African coast. Well-managed economy, favorably viewed by donors. Agriculture, especially livestock. Tourism. Oil potential.

WEAKNESSES

Small market inhibits investment. Smuggling. Lack of resources, little agricultural diversification; consequent overreliance on groundnuts. Decline of fish stocks. Major crop failure in 2002.

EXPORTS

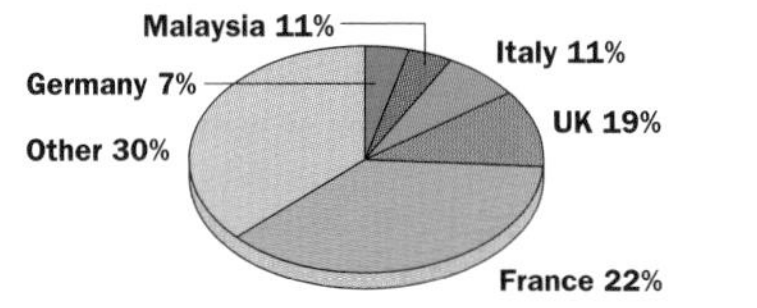
Malaysia 11%
Italy 11%
Germany 7%
UK 19%
Other 30%
France 22%

IMPORTS

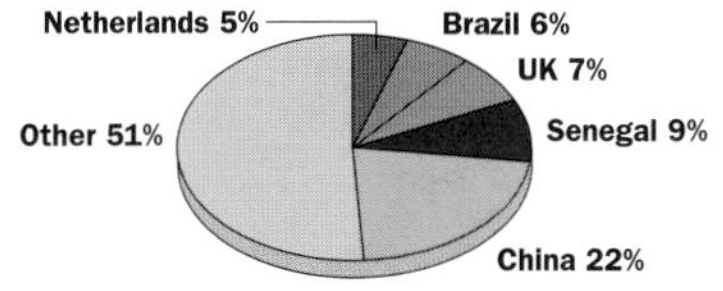
Netherlands 5%
Brazil 6%
UK 7%
Other 51%
Senegal 9%
China 22%

RESOURCES

Electric power 29,000 kW

34,527 tonnes

327,000 cattle, 262,000 goats, 600,000 chickens

Oil reserves not currently exploited

Ilmenite, zirconium, rutile, kaolin, tin, oil

The Gambia River is one of Africa's few good waterways, but it is underused owing to its separation from its natural hinterland by the Gambia–Senegal border. Irrigation is at present provided by a single dam; plans for further dams for power generation have met with opposition. Offshore oil deposits were discovered in 2004.

ENVIRONMENT

Sustainability rank: 103rd

2% (0.4% partially protected)

0.2 tonnes per capita

The impact of tourism and of overfishing in Gambian waters are major concerns, as are desertification and deforestation.

MEDIA

TV ownership low

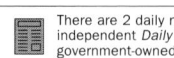

Daily newspaper circulation 2 per 1000 people

PUBLISHING AND BROADCAST MEDIA

There are 2 daily newspapers, the independent *Daily Observer* and the government-owned *Gambia Daily*

1 state-owned service

9 services: 1 state-owned, 8 independent

The independent media are restricted. Radio news broadcasts are dominated by state-controlled Radio Gambia, and the government runs the only national television station.

CRIME

Death penalty not used in practice

450 prisoners

General crime levels are low, but rising

Crime levels are relatively low in what is a peaceful society compared with many other states in the region.

EDUCATION

Schooling is not compulsory

38%

1702 students

Efforts to increase enrollment have been successful. Levels are now over 80% for primary and over 35% for secondary. A university was established in 1998.

HEALTH

No welfare state health benefits

1 per 25,000 people

Malaria, tuberculosis, parasitic diseases

Most people have access to basic medicines, but these are no longer free. Advanced medical care in the public sector is limited. An HIV/AIDS awareness campaign was launched in 2002.

SPENDING

GDP/cap. increase

CONSUMPTION AND SPENDING

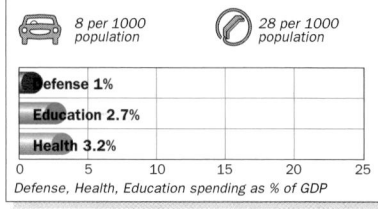

8 per 1000 population

28 per 1000 population

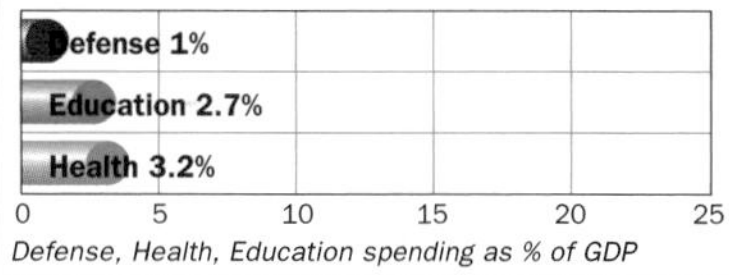
Defense 1%
Education 2.7%
Health 3.2%
0
5
10
15
20
25
Defense, Health, Education spending as % of GDP

Public service and the professions have created wealth and some people are comfortably off, but great wealth is not a feature of Gambian life. Unemployed young men in Banjul are regarded as the underclass.

WORLD RANKING

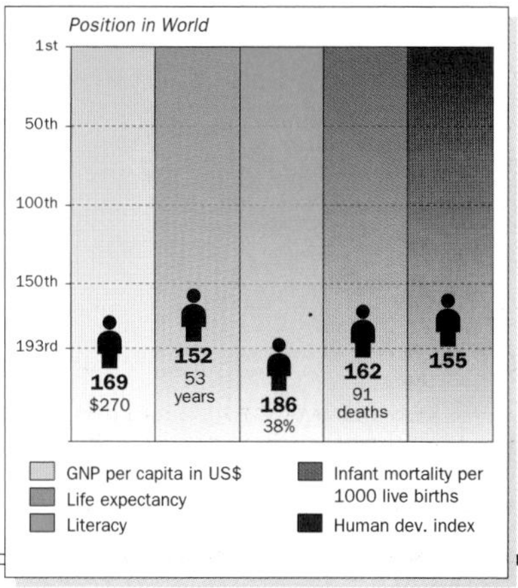
Position in World
1st
50th
100th
150th
193rd
169
$270
152
53 years
186
38%
162
91 deaths
155
GNP per capita in US$
Life expectancy
Literacy
Infant mortality per 1000 live births
Human dev. index

G

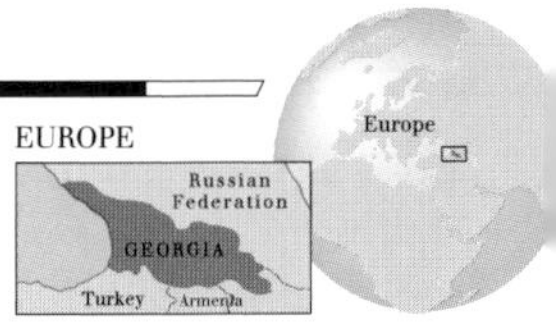
EUROPE
Europe
Russian Federation
GEORGIA
Turkey
Armenia

GEORGIA

OFFICIAL NAME: Georgia **CAPITAL:** Tbilisi
POPULATION: 5.1 million **CURRENCY:** Lari **OFFICIAL LANGUAGE:** Georgian; Abkhazian (in Abkhazia)

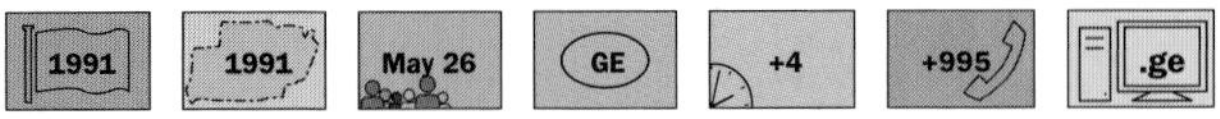
1991
1991
May 26
GE
+4
+995
.ge

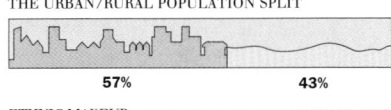

SANDWICHED BETWEEN the Greater and Lesser Caucasus, Georgia is a mountainous country, with a Black Sea coastline running north–south from Abkhazia to Ajaria. Georgia was one of the first republics to demand independence from the Soviet Union. It has been plagued by civil war, ethnic disputes in Abkhazia and South Ossetia, and, in 2004, by a defiant local chief in Ajaria. Georgia is a primarily agricultural country, and is noted for its wine.

CLIMATE

Mountain/subtropical

WEATHER CHART FOR TBILISI

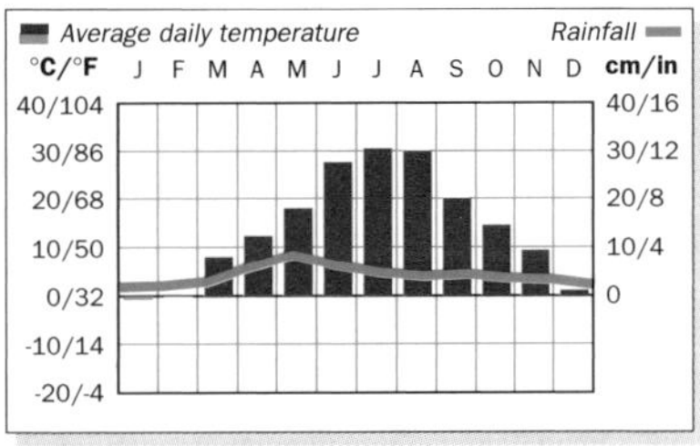
Average daily temperature
Rainfall
°C/°F
J F M A M J J A S O N D
cm/in
40/104
30/86
20/68
10/50
0/32
-10/14
-20/-4
40/16
30/12
20/8
10/4
0

Georgia's climate is continental inland and subtropical along the coast, where grapes, citrus fruit, and tea are grown.

***Tbilisi, Georgia's capital** since the 5th century. Its buildings rise in steep terraces from both banks of the Kura River.*

TRANSPORTATION

Drive on right

Tbilisi
270,505 passengers

261 ships
569,300 grt

THE TRANSPORTATION NETWORK

19,015 km
(11,815 miles)

None

1565 km
(972 miles)

None

Fragile relations with Russia affect transportation. An oil pipeline and rail link from Baku, Azerbaijan, to Georgia's Black Sea ports was opened in 1999.

TOURISM

Visitors : Population
1:17

298,000 visitors

Down 1% in 2002

MAIN TOURIST ARRIVALS

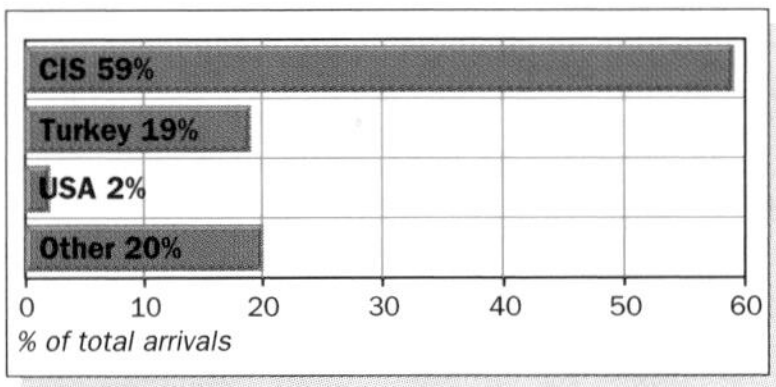
CIS 59%
Turkey 19%
USA 2%
Other 20%
0
10
20
30
40
50
60
% of total arrivals

The volatile political situation has discouraged the growth of tourism. Most tourists still come from former Soviet states.

PEOPLE

Pop. density medium

Georgian, Russian, Azeri, Armenian, Mingrelian, Ossetian, Abkhazian

73/km² (190/mi²)

THE URBAN/RURAL POPULATION SPLIT

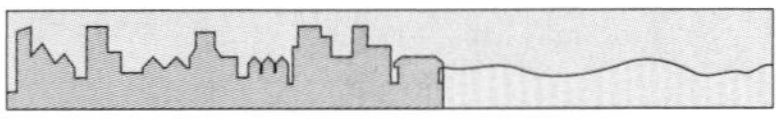
57%
43%

ETHNIC MAKEUP

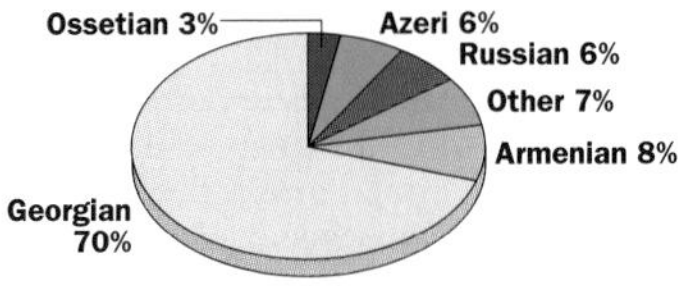
Ossetian 3%
Azeri 6%
Russian 6%
Other 7%
Armenian 8%
Georgian 70%

Georgia was converted to (Orthodox) Christianity in 326 CE. Conflict with the Abkhaz and Ossets in the 1990s displaced over 300,000 people. The Muslim–Georgian Ajarians enjoyed a level of autonomy under Shevardnadze. The Armenians of Javakheti, in the south, are the poorest group.

POLITICS

Multiparty elections

2004/2008

President Mikhail Saakashvili

AT THE LAST ELECTION

Parliament of Georgia 235 seats

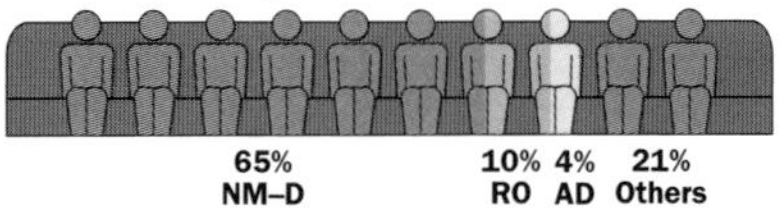
65% NM–D
10% RO
4% AD
21% Others

NM–D = National Movement – Democrats
RO = Rightist Opposition **AD** = Abkhazian deputies

Georgia has a strong presidency; party allegiances are fluid. President Eduard Shevardnadze, a former Soviet foreign minister, came to power amid civil war in 1992. His authoritarian manner drew increasing criticism, and attempts to rig legislative elections in 2003 prompted a popular revolution, after which he fled to Russia. Opposition leader Mikhail Saakashvili was elected president with a massive majority in January 2004. He has stated his determination to see a united Georgia, which threatens to upset the armed stalemates in the self-declared republics of Abkhazia and South Ossetia. Central control over Ajaria was reimposed in 2004.

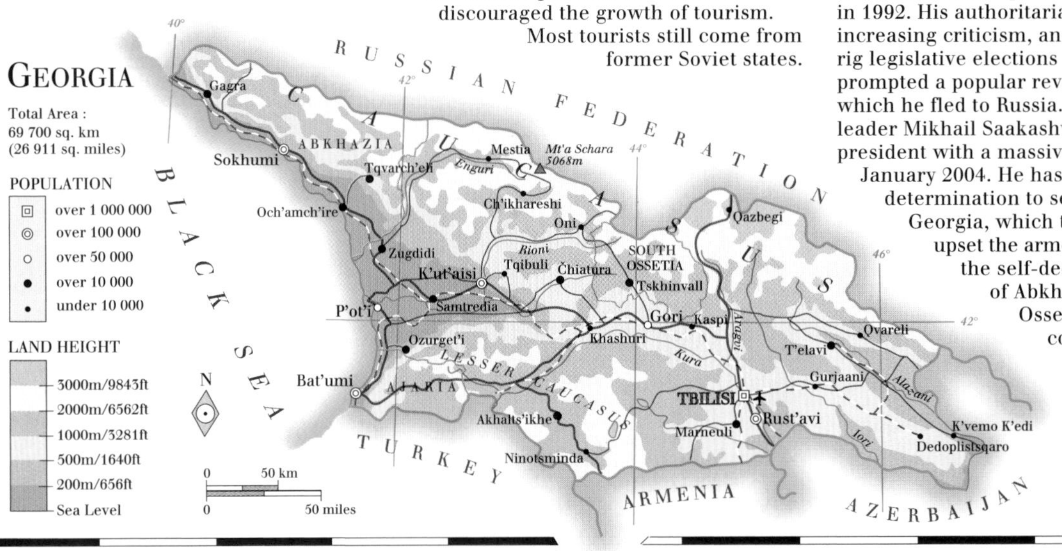
GEORGIA
Total Area :
69 700 sq. km
(26 911 sq. miles)
POPULATION
over 1 000 000
over 100 000
over 50 000
over 10 000
under 10 000
LAND HEIGHT
3000m/9843ft
2000m/6562ft
1000m/3281ft
500m/1640ft
200m/656ft
Sea Level
N
0 50 km
0 50 miles
RUSSIAN FEDERATION
BLACK SEA
TURKEY
ARMENIA
AZERBAIJAN
CAUCASUS
LESSER CAUCASUS
ABKHAZIA
AJARIA
SOUTH OSSETIA
Gagra
Sokhumi
Och'amch'ire
Zugdidi
Tqvarch'eli
Mestia
Mt'a Schara 5068m
Enguri
Ch'ikhareshi
Oni
Rioni
Tqibuli
Chiatura
K'ut'aisi
P'ot'i
Samtredia
Tskhinvali
Gori
Kaspi
Qazbegi
Khashuri
Ozurget'i
Bat'umi
Akhalts'ikhe
Ninotsminda
Kura
Aragvi
TBILISI
Rust'avi
Marneuli
T'elavi
Qvareli
Gurjaani
Alazani
Iori
K'vemo K'edi
Dedoplists'qaro
40°
42°
44°
46°
42°

WORLD AFFAIRS

Joined UN in 1992

BSEC | CIS | CE | OSCE | PfP

The US and Russia struggle for influence over Georgia. Saakashvili believes that Georgia will join both NATO and the EU.

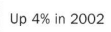

AID

Recipient

$313m (receipts) | Up 4% in 2002

In 2001 aid rose sharply, and this level has been maintained. The US is the largest donor, trailed by the World Bank.

DEFENSE

Compulsory military service

$236m | Down 10% in 2002

US concerns over the presence of Islamist terrorists prompted the arrival in 2002 of US forces to train the regular Georgian army; the security service is already CIA-trained. The security forces did not intervene when Shevardnadze was overthrown in 2003. Fighting broke out in South Ossetia in 2004.

ECONOMICS

Inflation 279% p.a. (1990–2001)

$3.36bn | 2.12 lari (2.155)

SCORE CARD

❑ WORLD GNP RANKING	130th
❑ GNP PER CAPITA	$650
❑ BALANCE OF PAYMENT	–$258m
❑ INFLATION	5.6%
❑ UNEMPLOYMENT	11%

STRENGTHS

Gateway to West for Azeri oil through pipelines to Black Sea and Mediterranean ports. Traditional and well-established wine industry providing exports, mainly to Russia. Healthy industrial and agricultural sectors.

WEAKNESSES

Political instability deters investment. Large black economy and influential Mafia. Serious budget deficit problems. Negative trade balance.

EXPORTS

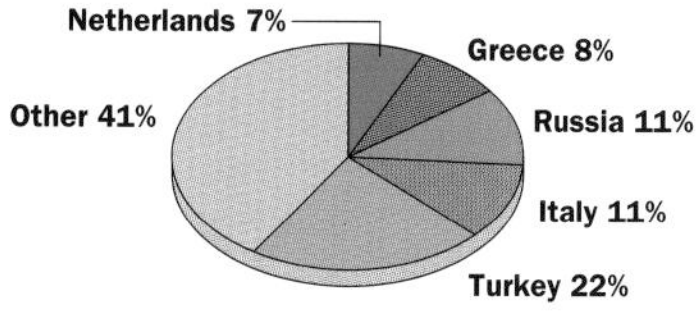
Netherlands 7%
Greece 8%
Other 41%
Russia 11%
Italy 11%
Turkey 22%

IMPORTS

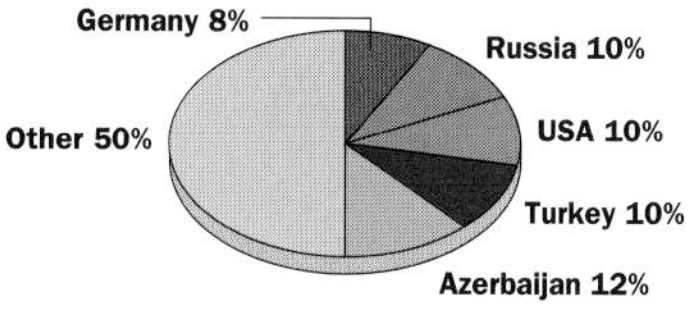
Germany 8%
Russia 10%
Other 50%
USA 10%
Turkey 10%
Azerbaijan 12%

RESOURCES

Electric power 4.6m kW

1910 tonnes | 2206 b/d (reserves 36m barrels)

1.22m cattle, 611,200 sheep, 9.95m chickens | Manganese, coal, oil, natural gas, zinc, copper

Known oil reserves are as yet barely developed. Georgia is dependent on Russia for much of its energy supply, though a new US–Georgian oil refinery was opened in eastern Georgia in 1998. Georgia is a predominantly agricultural country; food processing and wine and beer production continue to be the major industries. Manganese and small quantities of zinc, copper, and semiprecious stones are mined.

ENVIRONMENT

Not available

2% | 1.2 tonnes per capita

Radiation from materials left by departing Russian soldiers is a growing problem, as is Black Sea pollution and ensuring protection of upland pastures.

MEDIA

TV ownership high

Daily newspaper circulation 5 per 1000 people

PUBLISHING AND BROADCAST MEDIA

There are 3 daily newspapers: *Rezonansi* published in Georgian; *Georgian Messenger* and *Georgian Times* published in English

8 services: 1 state-controlled, 7 independent | 12 services: 1 state-controlled, 11 independent

Government newspapers are subsidized. The independent TV channel, Rustavi–2, was permitted to reopen in 1998, but faced harassment under Shevardnadze.

CRIME

No death penalty

7343 prisoners | Up 5% in 1999–2001

Organized crime under the control of Mafia-style groups has flourished since independence in 1991. The police force, accused of corruption and human rights abuses, was purged in 2002.

EDUCATION

School leaving age: 14

99% | 140,627 students

Since independence, education has stressed Georgian language and history. All levels of education are seriously underfunded. Tbilisi University was formerly of a high standard.

HEALTH

Welfare state health benefits

1 per 256 people | Cerebrovascular and heart diseases, cancers, liver disease

The health system was limited under the control of the Soviet Union. Internal strife and a lack of resources have prevented any recent investment.

CHRONOLOGY

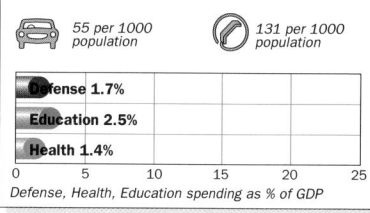

A Russian protectorate from 1763, Georgia was absorbed into the Russian Empire in 1801. It was established as an independent state under a Menshevik socialist government in 1918.

- ❑ **1921** Soviet Red Army invades. Effectively part of USSR.
- ❑ **1922–1936** Incorporated into Transcaucasian Soviet Federative Socialist Republic (TSFSR).
- ❑ **1989** Proindependence riots.
- ❑ **1990** Declares sovereignty.
- ❑ **1991** Independence. Zviad Gamsakhurdia elected president.
- ❑ **1992** Gamsakhurdia flees Tbilisi. Shevardnadze elected chair of Supreme Soviet and State Council.
- ❑ **1992–1993** Abkhazia conflict.
- ❑ **1995** Shevardnadze narrowly survives assassination attempt, subsequently elected president.
- ❑ **1999** Opening of pipeline from Caspian to Black Sea.
- ❑ **2000** Shevardnadze reelected. Russian troop withdrawal begins.
- ❑ **2003** Shevardnadze ousted in "velvet revolution."
- ❑ **2004** Mikhail Saakashvili president.

G

SPENDING

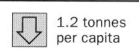

GDP/cap. decrease

CONSUMPTION AND SPENDING

55 per 1000 population | *131 per 1000 population*

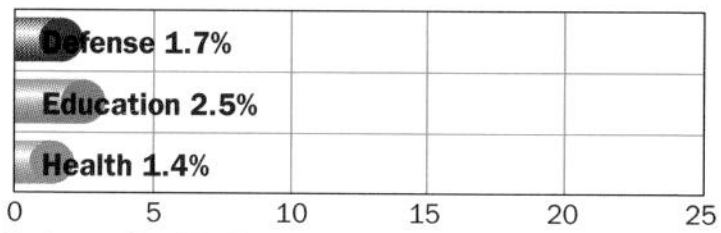
Defense 1.7%
Education 2.5%
Health 1.4%
0
5
10
15
20
25

Defense, Health, Education spending as % of GDP

There is a wealthy and extravagant urban elite, but most depend on small incomes from agriculture. Wages and welfare payments are often in arrears.

WORLD RANKING

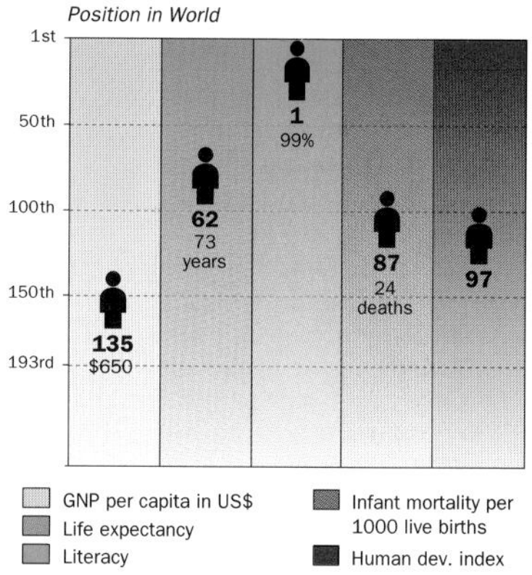
Position in World
1st
50th
100th
150th
193rd
135
$650
62
73 years
1
99%
87
24 deaths
97
GNP per capita in US$
Life expectancy
Literacy
Infant mortality per 1000 live births
Human dev. index

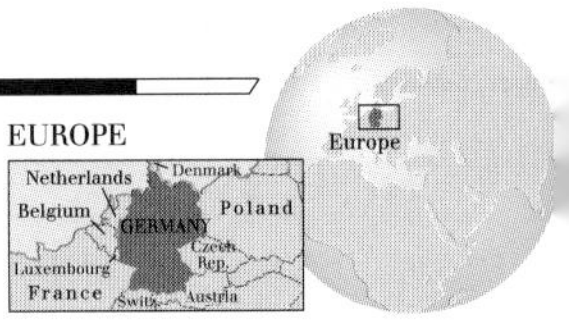
EUROPE
Europe
Netherlands
Denmark
Belgium
GERMANY
Poland
Czech Rep.
Luxembourg
France
Switz.
Austria

GERMANY

OFFICIAL NAME: Federal Republic of Germany **CAPITAL:** Berlin
POPULATION: 82.5 million **CURRENCY:** Euro **OFFICIAL LANGUAGE:** German

1871 | 1990 | Oct 3 | D | +1 | +49 | .de

WITH COASTLINES on both the Baltic and North Seas, Germany is bordered by nine countries. Plains and rolling hills in the north give way to more mountainous terrain in the south. Europe's foremost industrial power, and its most populous country apart from Russia, Germany is the world's second-biggest exporter. Unified in the 1870s, it was divided after the defeat of the Nazi regime in 1945. The communist-ruled east was part of the Soviet bloc until the collapse of the East German regime in 1989, which paved the way for reunification in 1990. Tensions created by wealth differences between east and west were then exacerbated by record levels of unemployment. The government committed itself to European union and adopted the single currency, the euro, even though the stable deutsche mark had been a symbol of German pride.

CLIMATE

Continental/maritime

WEATHER CHART FOR BERLIN

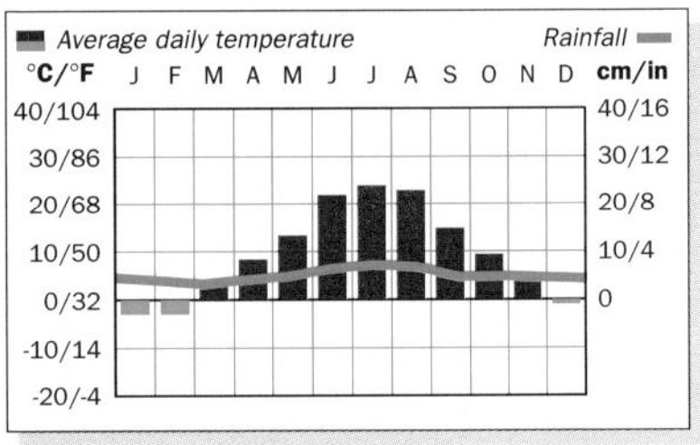
Average daily temperature
Rainfall
°C/°F
J F M A M J J A S O N D
cm/in
40/104
30/86
20/68
10/50
0/32
-10/14
-20/-4
40/16
30/12
20/8
10/4
0

Germany has a broad climatic range. The upper Rhine valley is very mild and suitable for wine making. The Bavarian Alps, the Harz Mountains, and the Black Forest are by contrast cold, with heavy falls of snow in winter.

TRANSPORTATION

Drive on right

Frankfurt/Main International 48.4m passengers

857 ships 6.55m grt

THE TRANSPORTATION NETWORK

649,515 km (403,589 miles)

11,786 km (7323 miles)

35,868 km (22,287 miles)

7500 km (4660 miles)

Germany virtually invented the modern highway with the first *Autobahnen* in the 1930s. These have since become Europe's most elaborate highway network; there are generally no tolls and few speed limits, despite protests from environmentalists. The efficient railroad system has been restructured as a first step toward privatization. Germany's high-speed ICE railroad opened its main north–south routes in 1991 and has expanded greatly since then. Urban transportation systems are highly efficient.

TOURISM

Visitors : Population 1:4.5

18.4m visitors

Up 2% in 2003

MAIN TOURIST ARRIVALS

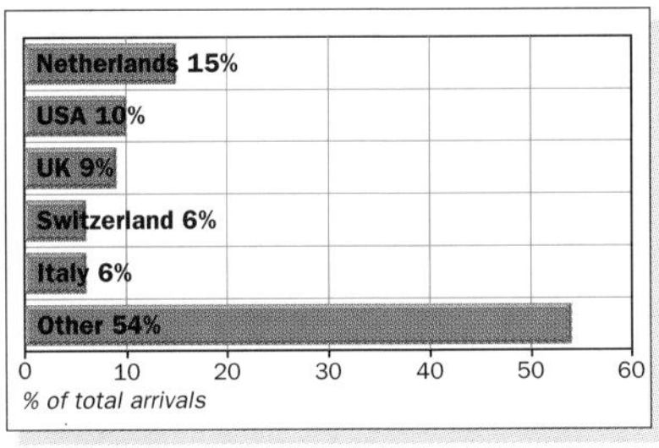
Netherlands 15%
USA 10%
UK 9%
Switzerland 6%
Italy 6%
Other 54%
0 10 20 30 40 50 60
% of total arrivals

Northerly beaches and a colder climate make Germany less of a tourist destination than France or Italy. Skiing in the Bavarian Alps, the historic castles of the Rhine valley, the Black Forest, and Germany's excellent beer all attract visitors. Berlin, even before 1989, drew tourists with its rich cultural life and its Wall separating capitalist West and communist East. Now capital of the reunified Germany, and with a dynamic and vibrant atmosphere, it has undergone massive reconstruction.

The Stillach Valley, Allgäu Alps, *Bavaria (Bayern). Alarm at acid rain damage to Germany's forests sparked off the rise of the Greens, who joined the government in 1998.*

GERMANY
Total Area : 357 021 sq. km
(137 846 sq. miles)
POPULATION
over 1 000 000
over 500 000
over 100 000
over 10 000
0 50 km
0 50 miles
N
LAND HEIGHT
2000m/6562ft
1000m/3281ft
500m/1640ft
200m/656ft
Sea Level
NORTH SEA
Nordfriesische Inseln
Helgoland
German Bight
Helgoländer Bucht
Ostfriesische Inseln
Cuxhaven
Wilhelmshaven
Emden
Weser
Oldenburg
NETHERLANDS
Ems
Osnabrück
Münster
NORDRHEIN-WESTFALEN
Hamm
Rhine
Recklinghausen
Herne
Gelsenkirchen
Bochum
Oberhausen
Dortmund
Duisburg
Essen
Hagen
RUHR
Mülheim
Wuppertal
Mönchengladbach
Düsseldorf
Solingen
VALLEY
Leverkusen
Köln
Siegen
Aachen
Bonn
SCHIEFERGEBIRGE
RHEINISCHES
Koblenz
EIFEL
BELGIUM
LUXEMBOURG
Wiesbaden
Mainz
Mosel
RHEINLAND-PFALZ
Trier
Kaiserslautern
SAARLAND
Ludwigshafen
Saarbrücken
Karlsruhe
Baden-Baden
FRANCE
Offenburg
Freiburg im Breisgau
BLACK FOREST
SCHWARZWALD
SWITZERLAND

PEOPLE

Pop. density high

German, Turkish

236/km² (611/mi²)

THE URBAN/RURAL POPULATION SPLIT

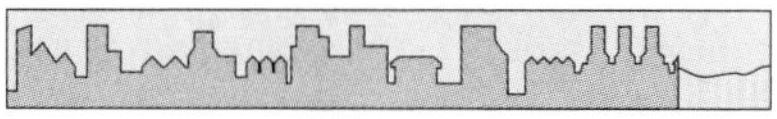
88%
12%

RELIGIOUS PERSUASION

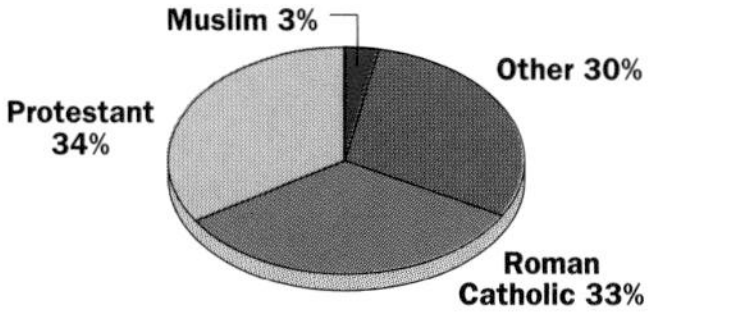
Muslim 3%
Other 30%
Protestant 34%
Roman Catholic 33%

ETHNIC MAKEUP

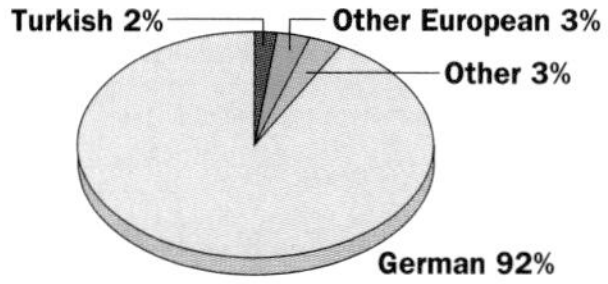
Turkish 2%
Other European 3%
Other 3%
German 92%

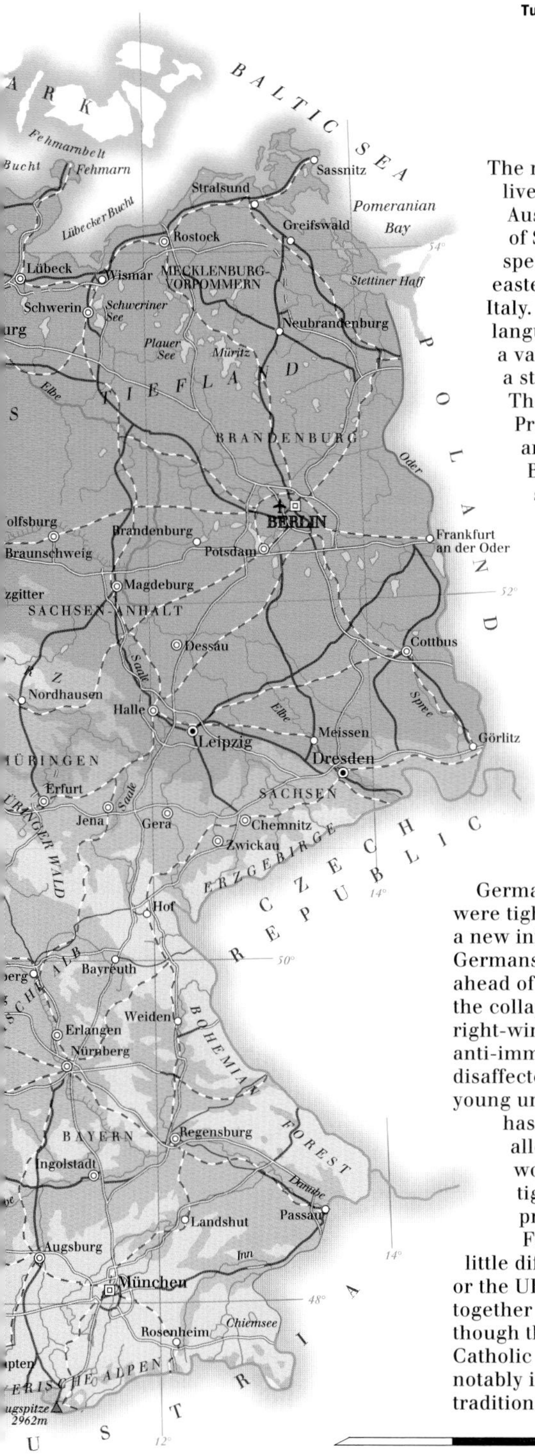
BALTIC SEA
Fehmarn
Sassnitz
Stralsund
Pomeranian Bay
Rostock
Greifswald
Lübeck
Wismar
MECKLENBURG-VORPOMMERN
Stettiner Haff
Schwerin
Schweriner See
Neubrandenburg
Plauer See
Müritz
BRANDENBURG
BERLIN
Brandenburg
Potsdam
Frankfurt an der Oder
Braunschweig
Magdeburg
SACHSEN-ANHALT
Dessau
Cottbus
Nordhausen
Halle
Leipzig
Meissen
Görlitz
Dresden
SACHSEN
Erfurt
Jena
Gera
Chemnitz
Zwickau
CZECH REPUBLIC
Hof
Bayreuth
Weiden
Erlangen
Nürnberg
BOHEMIAN FOREST
BAYERN
Regensburg
Ingolstadt
Landshut
Passau
Augsburg
München
Rosenheim
Chiemsee

The majority of German-speakers live in Germany itself, though Austria and the greater part of Switzerland are German-speaking, as are parts of eastern France and northern Italy. Germans share a common language, but they speak it in a variety of dialects, reflecting a strong sense of regionalism. The north is still largely Protestant, while the south and southwest, particularly Bavaria (Bayern), have strong Catholic traditions.

The large immigrant population now totals some 7.3 million, the 2.1 million Turks forming the largest single group. *Gastarbeiter* (guest workers) recruited from the mid-1950s to mid-1970s provided part of the labor on which the former West Germany's economic recovery was built. Legislation in 1999 improved the rights of their children to obtain German nationality. Germany's once liberal asylum laws were tightened in 1993 in response to a new influx of migrants. Ethnic Germans enjoyed privileged access ahead of others fleeing westward after the collapse of communism. Extreme right-wing parties sought to exploit anti-immigrant feeling among disaffected groups including the young unemployed. The government has made special provisions to allow immigration by skilled workers while concurrently tightening the asylum procedure.

Family ties in Germany are little different from those in the US or the UK. Millions of couples live together in common-law arrangements, though this is frowned on by the Roman Catholic Church. In rural districts, notably in Bavaria (Bayern), more traditional habits are still observed.

The birthrate is one of Europe's lowest, and the population would have fallen were it not for the influx of immigrants since the 1950s.

Germany has a tradition of strong feminism. Women have full rights under the law and play a bigger role in politics than in most other European countries. Over 30% of Bundestag (Federal Assembly) members elected in 2002 were women, and women ministers occupy several top cabinet posts. From 2001, women were permitted to take on combat roles in the armed forces. However, they are underrepresented in top jobs in business and industry. Abortion remains a charged issue. Women in the former East Germany had the right to abortion on demand, but the Constitutional Court, after strong Catholic lobbying, overruled a relatively liberal 1992 compromise law for the whole country. The current regulations, dating from mid-1995, allow abortions (but only after counseling) within three months of conception.

G

POPULATION AGE BREAKDOWN

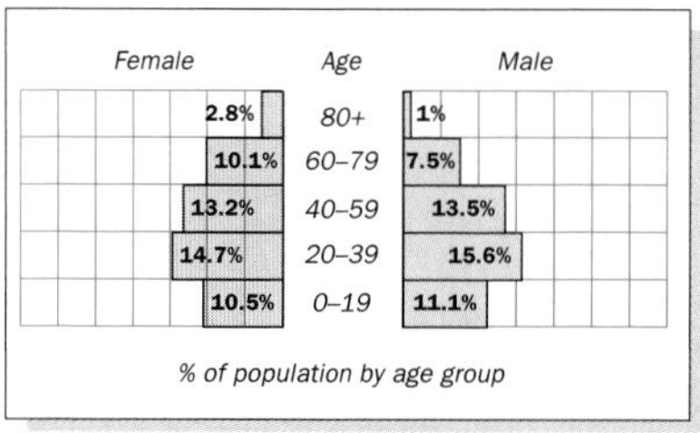
Female
Age
Male
2.8%
80+
1%
10.1%
60–79
7.5%
13.2%
40–59
13.5%
14.7%
20–39
15.6%
10.5%
0–19
11.1%
% of population by age group

CHRONOLOGY

German unification in the 19th century brought together a mosaic of states with a common linguistic, but varied cultural, heritage.

- ❑ **1815** German Confederation under nominal Austrian leadership.
- ❑ **1834** Zollverein Customs Union of 18 states, including Prussia.
- ❑ **1862** Otto von Bismarck appointed Prussian chancellor.
- ❑ **1864–1870** Prussia defeats Austrians, Danes, and French; north German states under Prussian control.
- ❑ **1871** Southern states join Prussian-led unified German Empire under Wilhelm I.
- ❑ **1870s** Rapid industrialization.
- ❑ **1890** Kaiser Wilhelm II accedes, with aspirations to German world role. Bismarck sacked.
- ❑ **1914–1918** World War I.
- ❑ **1918** Germany signs armistice; Weimar Republic created.
- ❑ **1919** Treaty of Versailles: colonies lost and reparations paid. Rhineland demilitarized.

⇨

G

CHRONOLOGY *continued*

- **1923** France occupies Ruhr; financial collapse, hyperinflation.
- **1933** Adolf Hitler chancellor after Nazis elected largest party. One-party rule; rearmament.
- **1935** Nuremberg Laws; official persecution of Jews begins.
- **1936** German entry into Rhineland. Axis alliance with Italy.
- **1938** Annexation of Austria and Sudetenland.
- **1939** Invasion of Poland starts World War II.
- **1940** France, Belgium, Netherlands, and Norway invaded.
- **1941** USSR invaded.
- **1942–1943** Germans defeated by Red Army at Stalingrad.
- **1945** German surrender; Allies control four occupation zones.
- **1949** Germany divided: communist East led by Walter Ulbricht 1951–1971, Erich Honecker 1971–1989; liberal democratic West led by CDU's Konrad Adenauer, 1949–1963.
- **1955** West Germany joins NATO.
- **1961** Berlin Wall built.
- **1966–1969** West German "grand coalition" of CDU and SPD.
- **1969–1982** SPD-led West German governments under Willy Brandt until 1974, then Helmut Schmidt.
- **1973** Both Germanies join UN.
- **1982** Helmut Kohl West German chancellor, CDU–FDP coalition.
- **1989** Fall of Berlin Wall.
- **1990** Reunification of Germany. First all-German elections since 1933; Kohl heads government.
- **1998** Gerhard Schröder heads coalition of SPD and Greens.
- **2000** Disgrace of Kohl in party funding scandal.
- **2001** Coalition of SPD and former communist PDS in city of Berlin.
- **2002** Euro fully adopted. SPD–Green coalition reelected.
- **2003** Economy enters recession.
- **2004** Horst Köhler of CDU elected president.

***The Messeturm**, Frankfurt, is the second-tallest office building in Europe. Frankfurt is Germany's financial services center, and many leading companies are located there.*

POLITICS

Multiparty elections

L. House 2002/2006
U. House varying

President Horst Köhler

AT THE LAST ELECTION

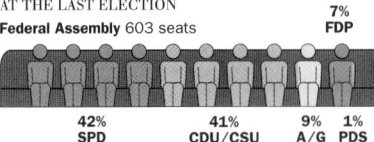

Federal Assembly 603 seats

7% **FDP**

42% **SPD** | 41% **CDU/CSU** | 9% **A/G** | 1% **PDS**

SPD = Social Democratic Party of Germany **CDU/CSU** = Christian Democratic Union/Christian Social Union
A/G = Alliance 90/Greens **FDP** = Free Democratic Party
PDS = Party of Democratic Socialism

Federal Council 69 seats

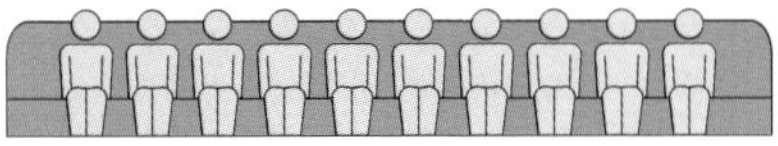

Each of the 16 states (*Länder*) is represented by between three and six members in the Federal Council (Bundesrat), who are appointed after the elections in each *Land*

Germany is a federal democratic republic of 16 *Länder* (states). The government is led by the federal chancellor, elected by the Bundestag (Federal Assembly). The president's role is largely ceremonial. The "Basic Law" of West Germany, drawn up in 1948, became the 1990 federal constitution of reunified Germany.

Profile

Germany's politics are now strongly democratic, with a long tradition of federative association. Before 1871, Germany was a mass of separate principalities, kingdoms, and city-states, a situation largely respected by Bismarck's unification constitution. The 1933–1945 Nazi period, during which the federal system was abolished, was very much a hiatus. The Allies reestablished the federal system in West Germany in 1949; in the east, the *Länder* were restored after reunification in 1990. In many ways, the *Länder* are at the heart of German political life, each with its own elected parliament and largely controlling its finances. By general consensus the system delivers efficient and commercially astute government. There have been few major differences on domestic policy between the postwar ruling coalitions. All parties support the social market economy on which prosperity was built.

Germany has enjoyed stable governments, with center-left and center-right coalitions each holding sway since the "grand coalition" of 1966–1969. In 1998 the electorate chose moderate SPD leader Gerhard Schröder in a vote for change, ousting long-serving CDU chancellor Helmut Kohl. In opposition the CDU was beset by party-funding scandal. Kohl was disgraced. Edmund Stoiber, leader of the CDU's Bavarian-based sister party, the CSU, challenged Schröder for the chancellorship in 2002, but he fell short of toppling the "red–green" coalition. However, economic problems, high unemployment, and the "Agenda 2010" package that Schröder introduced in response caused him to lose popularity rapidly thereafter. He stepped down as SPD leader in 2004.

Main Political Issues

The economy

Recession was a shock to Germany, used to constant growth since the 1950s. Spending was reined in to meet targets for European monetary union in the late 1990s. Unrest ensued as unemployment topped four million. A brief return to growth enabled the SPD to start tackling pension reform, but economic weakness still dominates the political agenda.

East and west

Most Germans supported reunification after the fall of the Berlin Wall in 1989, but feelings soured as the true cost became clear. Many billions of euros have been spent on reconstruction in the east, financed partly by a "solidarity surcharge" on income tax, but the tenth anniversary of reunification in 2000 was less a celebration than a reflection on past mistakes. The east remains poorer, and people moving west, still seen as "Ossis," may find it hard to fit in. Support for the former communist PDS is strong in, but confined almost entirely to, the east.

Far-right violence

Unemployment and resentment of "foreigners" led to a rise in support for far-right parties. Foreign workers, particularly Turks, and asylum seekers have been subject to shocking attacks. The problem of racism, even if no worse than in many other European states, is particularly sensitive, given Germany's history.

***Horst Köhler,** conservative elected president in 2004.*

***Gerhard Schröder,** chancellor from 1998, reelected in 2002.*

***Joschka Fischer,** leading Green politician and a popular foreign minister from 1998.*

WORLD AFFAIRS

Joined UN in 1973

EU | G8 | NATO | OECD | OSCE

During the Cold War, a Germany divided since the end of World War II was inevitably forced to play a subservient role in international affairs. West Germany closely adhered to US interests, while East Germany took its orders directly from the Soviet Union. After reunification in 1990 the emphasis changed, and Germany began to voice a foreign policy which reflects its position as the most powerful country in Europe.

In 2001 Germany was given command of the NATO peacekeeping mission in Macedonia, and German troops were involved in the "war on terrorism" in Afghanistan. Extremely critical of the US-led assault on Iraq in 2003, Germany continues to champion EU enlargement, and, because of large-scale investment, has considerable influence in eastern Europe.

AID

Donor

$5.32bn (donations)

Up 7% in 2002

Unlike the US and France, Germany's aid programs are not directly motivated by its desire for political influence in the world's poorer regions. Most are multilateral, though there is also a strong tradition of direct aid. Much comes from church organizations such as the Protestant Brot für die Welt. Many German volunteers and missionaries work overseas on aid programs.

DEFENSE

Compulsory military service

$31.5bn

Up 18% in 2002

The armed forces are being streamlined, to focus more on mobility and provide support to allied states; Germany backs the concept of an EU force. In 1994 the Constitutional Court ruled that military units could take part in collective defense activities abroad: participation in the 1999 NATO action against Serbia was a landmark. In 2002–2003 Germany led the peacekeeping force in Afghanistan.

GERMAN ARMED FORCES

2398 main battle tanks (670 Leopard 1A1/A3/A4/A5, 1728 Leopard 2)	191,350 personnel
12 submarines, 1 destroyer, 12 frigates, and 20 patrol boats	25,650 personnel
376 combat aircraft (152 F-4, 262 Tornado, 3 MiG-21/23, 1 Su-22)	67,500 personnel
None	

ECONOMICS

Inflation 1.8% p.a. (1990–2001)

$1876bn

0.822 euros (0.871)

SCORE CARD

- World GNP Ranking....................3rd
- GNP per capita....................$22,740
- Balance of payments....................$46.6bn
- Inflation....................1.3%
- Unemployment....................9%

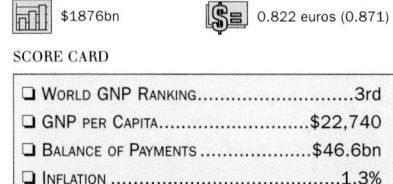

EXPORTS

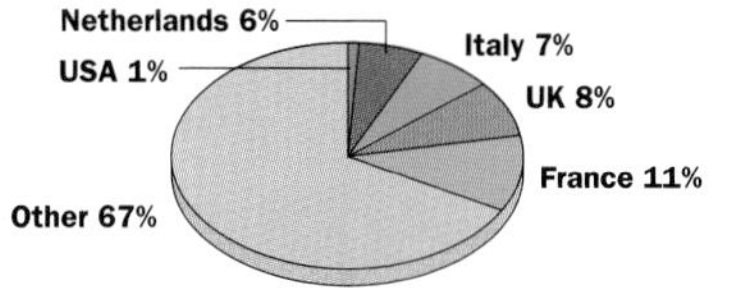
Netherlands 6%
USA 1%
Italy 7%
UK 8%
France 11%
Other 67%

IMPORTS

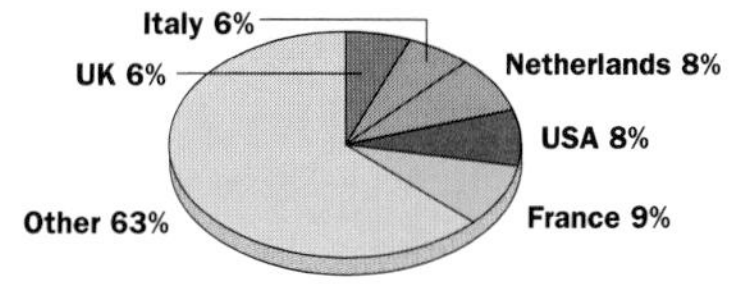
Italy 6%
UK 6%
Netherlands 8%
USA 8%
France 9%
Other 63%

STRENGTHS

Europe's major industrial power. Cars, heavy engineering, electronics, and chemicals. Efficient industry benefits from low inflation. Strong work ethic.

WEAKNESSES

Underestimation of costs of updating inefficient east German economy. High welfare costs and potentially crippling pension obligations (despite reforms in 2001) with an aging population. High unemployment. Relatively few small firms, short working week in terms of hours, poorly developed service sector.

ECONOMIC PERFORMANCE INDICATOR

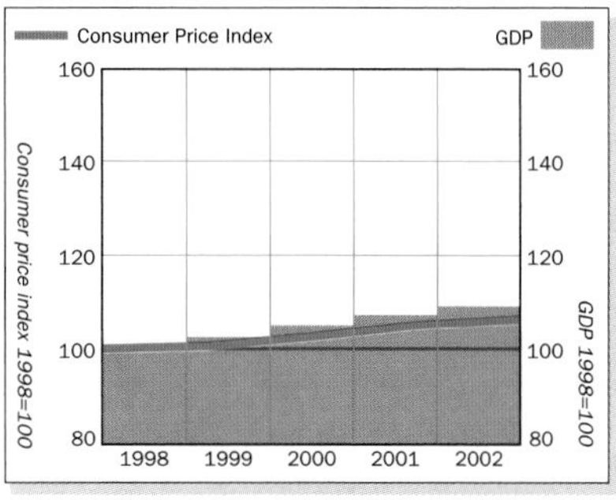
Consumer Price Index
GDP
160
140
120
100
80
Consumer price index 1998=100
GDP 1998=100
1998
1999
2000
2001
2002

PROFILE

West Germany's remarkable postwar recovery, to become the world's third-strongest economy, was based on the concept of a social market economy, under which the state provided welfare and ensured workers' rights, while the economy was largely in private hands. Major banks and businesses are privately owned, except for the partly state-owned Volkswagen. After reunification in 1990, massive investment went into the former East Germany, where state concerns were sold off.

Germany was one of the 12 EU states to adopt the euro in 2002. The SPD-led government elected in 1998 undertook to tackle unemployment and to maintain growth, which reached a ten-year high of 3.1% in 2000. Major tax reforms aimed to balance the budget by 2006. The government received $46 billion from the sale of "third generation" mobile phone operators' licenses in 2001, but global economic slowdown hit employment levels hard. The jobless figure rose again, exceeding four million in late 2002. Tax cuts were brought forward in an attempt to boost consumer spending. The economy went into recession in 2003, and Germany narrowly escaped threatened EU sanctions over its rising budget deficit.

GERMANY : MAJOR BUSINESSES

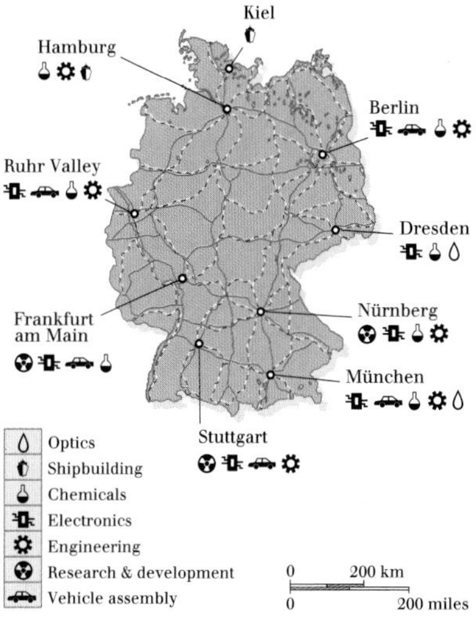
Kiel
Hamburg
Berlin
Ruhr Valley
Dresden
Frankfurt am Main
Nürnberg
München
Stuttgart
Optics
Shipbuilding
Chemicals
Electronics
Engineering
Research & development
Vehicle assembly
0 200 km
0 200 miles

***Potsdamer Platz, Berlin,** was rapidly reconstructed after reunification and is once again the commercial center of the capital.*

G

RESOURCES

Electric power 119m kW

264,691 tonnes

63,478 b/d (reserves 209m barrels)

26.3m pigs, 13.7m cattle, 9m turkeys, 110m chickens

Coal, oil, natural gas, copper, salt, potash, tin, nickel

ELECTRICITY GENERATION

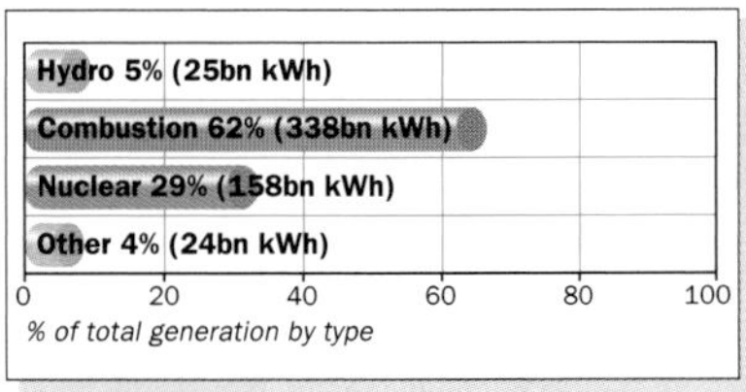
Hydro 5% (25bn kWh)
Combustion 62% (338bn kWh)
Nuclear 29% (158bn kWh)
Other 4% (24bn kWh)
0 20 40 60 80 100
% of total generation by type

With relatively few natural resources, Germany imports over 60% of its energy needs, mainly oil and gas. Coal, the basis of industrialization, now accounts for under a quarter of energy consumption. West Germany invested less heavily than France in nuclear power, and Soviet-built plants in the east have been shut down. The "red–green" coalition government decided in mid-2000 to phase out nuclear power. Renewable resources, particularly wind, account for 4% of primary energy consumption (with a target of 50% by 2050); Germany is the world's leading user of wind power.

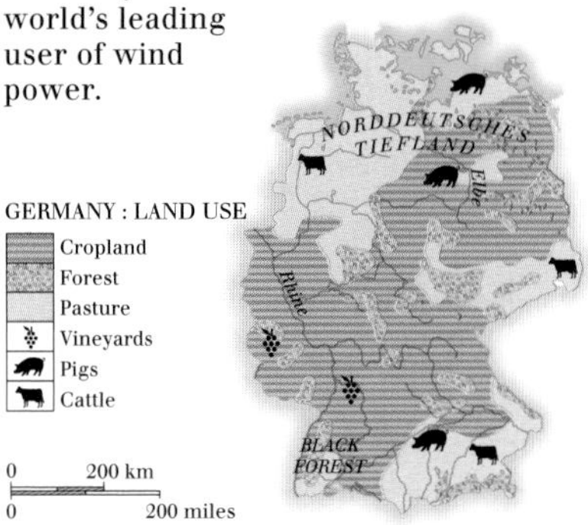
GERMANY : LAND USE
Cropland
Forest
Pasture
Vineyards
Pigs
Cattle
0 200 km
0 200 miles
NORDDEUTSCHES TIEFLAND
Elbe
Rhine
BLACK FOREST

ENVIRONMENT

Sustainability rank: 50th

32% (27% partially protected)

9.6 tonnes per capita

ENVIRONMENTAL TREATIES

Yes	Yes	Yes
Yes	Yes	Yes

Germans are among the world's most environmentally conscious people. Campaigns led by the Green Party, which emerged as a powerful political force in the 1980s, have influenced the policies of all major parties. The Greens are a significant force in the Bundestag; they joined the SPD-led federal government coalition in 1998, and are strongly represented in *Land* parliaments and local councils.

Germany has some of the strictest pollution controls in the world, with ambitious targets for reducing carbon dioxide emissions, compelling businesses to become more energy-efficient. Germans recycle around 80% of their waste paper and glass, and three-quarters of their used tires.

The nuclear debate has been vigorously fought and won by the Greens; a gradual program of closing existing nuclear power plants was approved in 2001, though waste disposal is still an issue. Fears in the 1980s that up to 50% of trees were sick or dying because of car fumes and industrial pollution led to Germany becoming the first European country to insist that new cars be fitted with catalytic converters. The east had the highest per capita rate of sulfur emissions in the world, but these have been reduced by the closure of industrial plants and the elimination of the noxious Trabant cars.

MEDIA

TV ownership high

Daily newspaper circulation 300 per 1000 people

PUBLISHING AND BROADCAST MEDIA

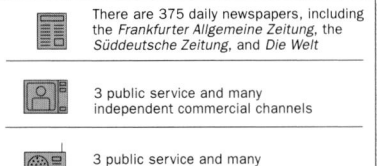

There are 375 daily newspapers, including the *Frankfurter Allgemeine Zeitung*, the *Süddeutsche Zeitung*, and *Die Welt*

3 public service and many independent commercial channels

3 public service and many independent networks

TV is supervised by the political parties to ensure a balance of views. Satellite and cable TV have taken much of the audience once shared between the main public service channels, ARD and ZDF. Media conglomerates such as Bertelsmann are major international players. Newspapers are mostly regional and serious. An exception is *Bild*, a right-wing, sensationalist tabloid, which sells 4.4 million copies daily.

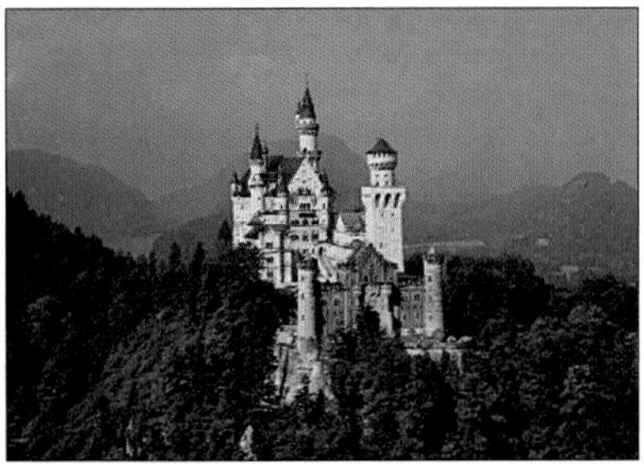

Neuschwanstein Castle, Bavaria (Bayern), one of Germany's major tourist attractions. It was built for the eccentric King Ludwig II.

EDUCATION

School leaving age: 18

99%

1.8m students

THE EDUCATION SYSTEM

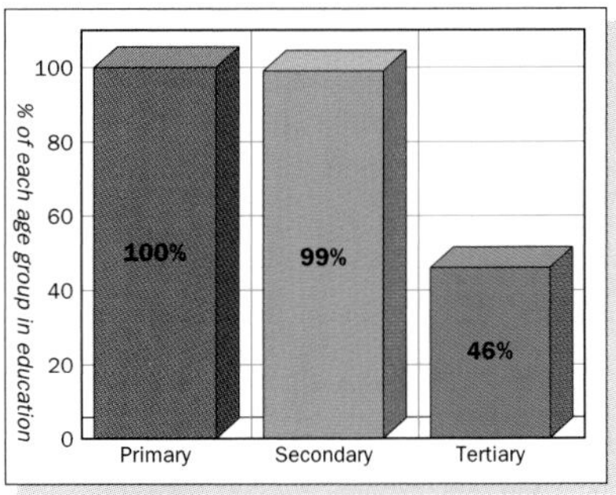
100
80
60
40
20
0
% of each age group in education
100%
99%
46%
Primary
Secondary
Tertiary

Nearly one-tenth of total government expenditure goes on education, which is run by the *Länder*. They coordinate teaching policies, but have autonomy within their borders. The German approach to education stresses academic and vocational achievement. Sporting or cultural activities tend to be organized informally. Nearly all schools have Internet access.

Young people wanting to leave school must continue studying at least part-time until 18. Those who wish to go to university attend the upper-secondary *Gymnasien* to prepare for the *Abitur* exam. Students were taking an average of seven years to complete degrees, until new legislation added shorter bachelor's and master's degrees as in other countries. Research is done as much by major companies as by the universities.

CRIME

No death penalty

81,176 prisoners

Up 3% in 2000–2002

CRIME RATES

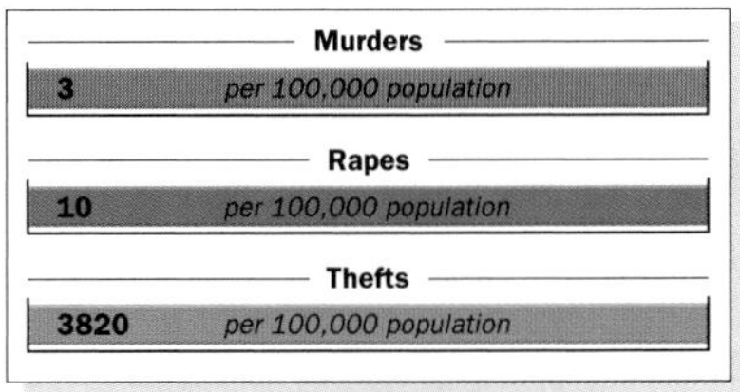
Murders
3 per 100,000 population
Rapes
10 per 100,000 population
Thefts
3820 per 100,000 population

Crime rates are lower than in most European countries, and reporting is high. This is largely the result of a genuine respect for the law, coupled with a strong police force. Recently, however, higher unemployment has led to an increase in petty theft and a wave of violence, notably against immigrants.

German politicians, once with an enviably clean reputation, have suffered several corruption scandals. Civil service corruption remains rare. People convicted under environmental laws can face ten-year jail sentences.

GERMANY, EUROPE, AND THE WORLD

SINCE THE CREATION of the European Coal and Steel Community and then the European Economic Community in the 1950s, Germany (at that time West Germany) has been at the heart of European integration. Backing enlargement of the Community and ever closer integration in what became the European Union, it has grown to become by some distance the most economically important member of the EU. It has put its weight behind monetary union, and in addition has achieved a growing military weight.

RAPID REACTION FORCE

One of the most striking aspects of Germany's involvement in the EU in recent years has been its military rehabilitation under the auspices of the EU's planned Rapid Reaction Force (ERRF). This was effectively agreed under the joint European foreign and defense policy at the inception of the EU at the Maastricht conference in 1991. The military staff of the ERRF finally became operational in June 2001. It is designed to provide security for Europe's overseas interests and to protect the Union's own borders, with a deployment time of just 60 days. In theory it is guided by the basic principles of the UN and defers operations in the first instance to NATO. The first chief of staff is a German officer, Lt. Gen. Rainer Schuwirth.

Germany's commitment to the ERRF is more comprehensive than that of any other EU member state. The government agreed in May 2003 to increase its contribution from 30,000 to 33,000 troops, thereby providing over half of the 60,000 permanent personnel. Though Germany provided just 70 soldiers to the EU's first peacekeeping mission, the Concordia mission in Macedonia in 2003, that too was headed by a German officer, Adm. Rainer Feist. While the contributions and involvement in control of the EU's military activities was a big step for Germany itself, it also represented a significant step for the EU.

***The dome of the Reichstag**, in Berlin, represents the economic and political strength of the united Germany.*

EUROPE IN THE WORLD

The 2003 invasion of Iraq by the US, the UK, and their allies proved an important test of EU–US relations ahead of the EU's expansion in 2004. Neither Germany nor France backed this action. In a much quoted remark in January 2003, US defense secretary Donald Rumsfeld stated that to think of Europe as France and Germany was to think of "old Europe." The smaller EU nations and many of the ten new post-2004 members were seen as more supportive of the US line, whereas these two countries were at the heart of attempts to strengthen a European position in the world that would not necessarily favor automatic recourse to the US. The French and German stance also placed added emphasis on the role of the UN. This was somewhat ironic for Germany; as the vanquished in World War II, it does not have a seat on the UN Security Council, though many argue that this is out of step with modern geopolitical realities.

***German troops** board a transport plane bound for a tour of duty in Macedonia.*

HEALTH

Welfare state health benefits

1 per 303 people

Cancers, heart, cerebrovascular, and respiratory

The German social security system, pioneered by Bismarck, is one of the most comprehensive in the world. Health insurance is compulsory, and employer and employee contributions are high. Though most hospitals are run by the *Länder*, some are still owned by Germany's wealthy churches. Almost one-quarter of health spending is now private.

Germans are increasingly health-conscious, paying great attention to diet. Nearly a million people go on cures every year to the country's 200-plus spas. In the east there is a higher incidence of lung diseases, the legacy of industrial pollution.

G

SPENDING

GDP/cap. increase

CONSUMPTION AND SPENDING

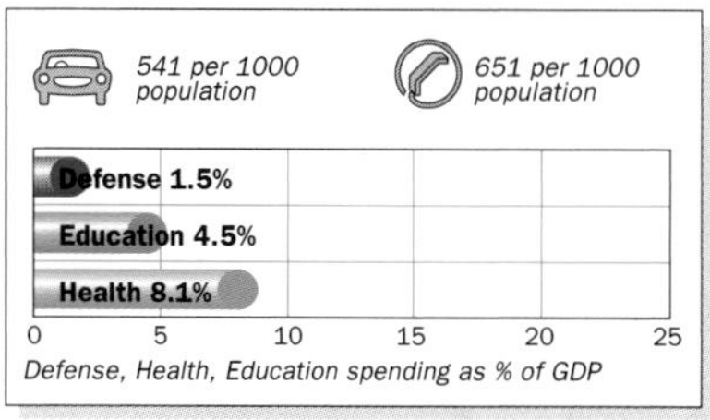
541 per 1000 population
651 per 1000 population
Defense 1.5%
Education 4.5%
Health 8.1%
0
5
10
15
20
25
Defense, Health, Education spending as % of GDP

The effects of the Nazi period, which discredited many of the ruling class, and the destruction of the property of millions of families in the war, explain the relatively classless nature of society. Status is now more closely linked to wealth than to birth. In the west, there are fewer disparities than in most of Europe; workers are generally well paid and social security is generous. Wages in the east, however, are 10% below western rates, and unemployment is higher. Proposals in 2004 to means-test benefits led to street protests. Most Germans own a mobile phone, and over half had direct Internet access by 2003.

WORLD RANKING

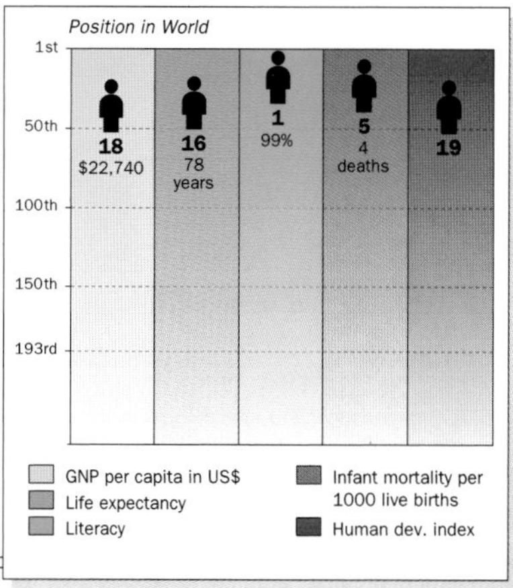
Position in World
1st
50th
100th
150th
193rd
18
$22,740
16
78
years
1
99%
5
4
deaths
19
GNP per capita in US$
Life expectancy
Literacy
Infant mortality per 1000 live births
Human dev. index

GHANA

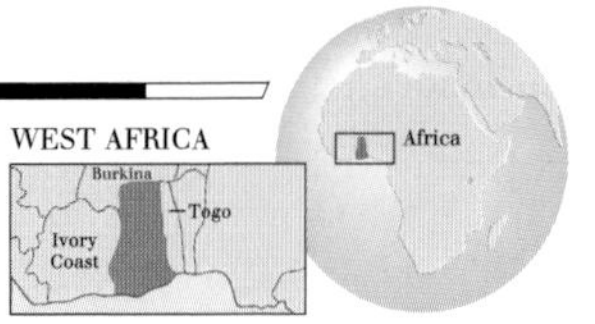
WEST AFRICA
Burkina
Togo
Ivory Coast
Africa

OFFICIAL NAME: Republic of Ghana **CAPITAL:** Accra
POPULATION: 20.9 million **CURRENCY:** Cedi **OFFICIAL LANGUAGE:** English

1957 | 1957 | March 6 | GH | 0 | +233 | .gh

THE HEARTLAND OF THE ancient Ashanti kingdom, modern Ghana is a union of the former British colony of the Gold Coast and the British-administered part of the UN Trust Territory of Togoland. Ghana gained independence in 1957, the first west African colony to do so. Multiparty democracy was embraced in 1992, and the handover of power to the main opposition party in 2000 confirmed the shift from a recent history of intermittent military rule.

CLIMATE

Tropical wet and dry/ equatorial

WEATHER CHART FOR ACCRA

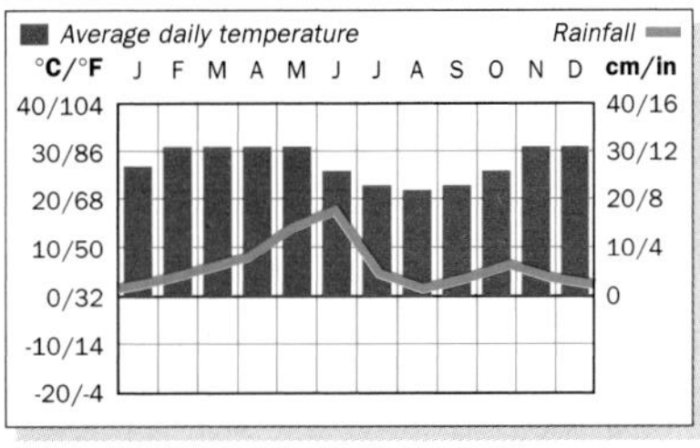
Average daily temperature
Rainfall
°C/°F J F M A M J J A S O N D cm/in
40/104
30/86
20/68
10/50
0/32
-10/14
-20/-4
40/16
30/12
20/8
10/4
0

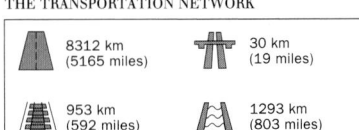

Southern Ghana has two rainy seasons: from April to July and September to November. The drier north has just one, from April to September.

TRANSPORTATION

Drive on right

Kotoka, Accra 741,622 passengers

213 ships 126,200 grt

THE TRANSPORTATION NETWORK

8312 km (5165 miles)	30 km (19 miles)
953 km (592 miles)	1293 km (803 miles)

Transportation infrastructure, having deteriorated in the 1960s and 1970s, has largely been renewed; roads, rail, and airports are all in good condition.

TOURISM

Visitors : Population 1:43

483,000 visitors

Up 10% in 2002

MAIN TOURIST ARRIVALS

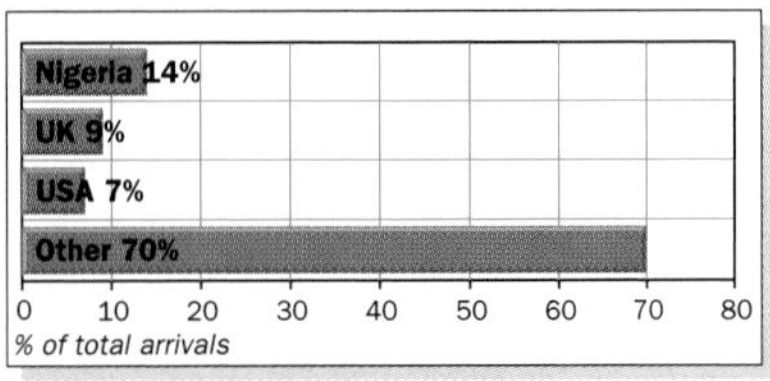
Nigeria 14%
UK 9%
USA 7%
Other 70%
0 10 20 30 40 50 60 70 80
% of total arrivals

Tourism is now the third-biggest foreign currency earner. Good beaches and old coastal forts are among the attractions. "Eco-tourism" is growing rapidly.

PEOPLE

Pop. density medium

Twi, Fanti, Ewe, Ga, Adangbe, Gurma, Dagomba (Dagbani)

91/km² (235/mi²)

THE URBAN/RURAL POPULATION SPLIT

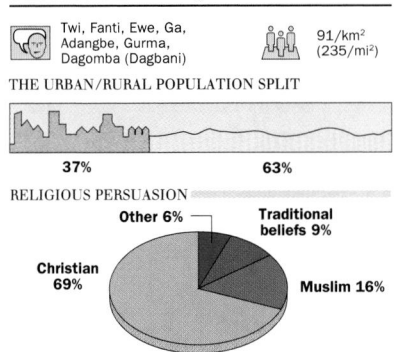

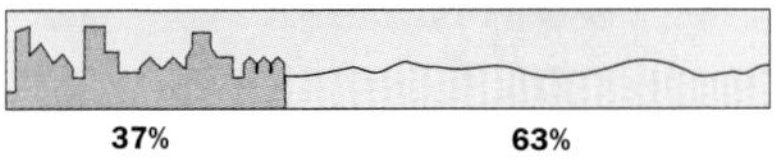
37%
63%

RELIGIOUS PERSUASION

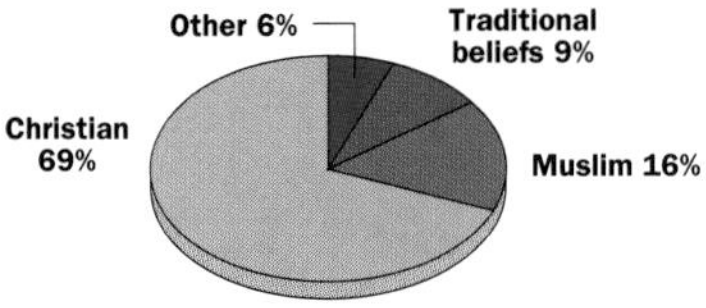
Other 6%
Traditional beliefs 9%
Christian 69%
Muslim 16%

The largest ethnic group is the coastal Akan, who include the Ashanti and Fanti peoples. Other important groups are the Mole-Dagbani in the north, Ga-Adangbe around Accra, and Ewe in the southeast. Though the north is less developed than the south, ethnic tensions are relatively rare.

POLITICS

Multiparty elections

2000/2004

President John Kufuor

AT THE LAST ELECTION

Parliament 200 seats

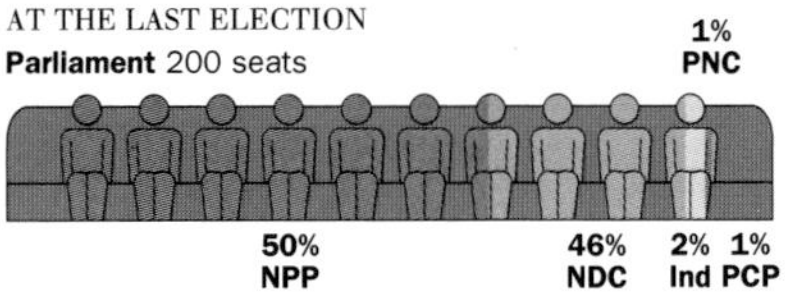
1% PNC
50% NPP
46% NDC
2% Ind
1% PCP

NPP = New Patriotic Party **NDC** = National Democratic Congress **Ind** = Independents **PNC** = People's National Convention **PCP** = People's Convention Party

Ghana's return to multiparty rule in 1992 marked the legitimization of the military government of Jerry Rawlings. An air force flight-lieutenant of Ewe–Scottish descent and one of the great survivors of African politics, Rawlings staged coups in 1979 and 1981, and led the 1981–1992 Provisional National Defense Council (PNDC) military government. As the NDC candidate, Rawlings won 58% of the vote in the 1992 presidential election. Opposition parties boycotted the following parliamentary elections, which the NDC won easily. Elections in 1996 gave Rawlings a further and final term of office. In December 2000 the opposition NPP gained a historic victory when it stripped the NDC of its parliamentary majority and NPP candidate John Kufuor won the presidency.

WORLD AFFAIRS

Joined UN in 1957

Comm | ECOWAS | G24 | IAEA | AU

Good relations with the West, which provides the bulk of Ghana's military and development aid, are a priority. Ghana has played a significant part in UN peacekeeping operations. It has also been the main contributor, after Nigeria, to ECOMOG, the ECOWAS peacekeeping forces, in war-torn Liberia and Ivory Coast. Ghana maintains good relations with its French-speaking neighbors, despite periods of strain with Togo.

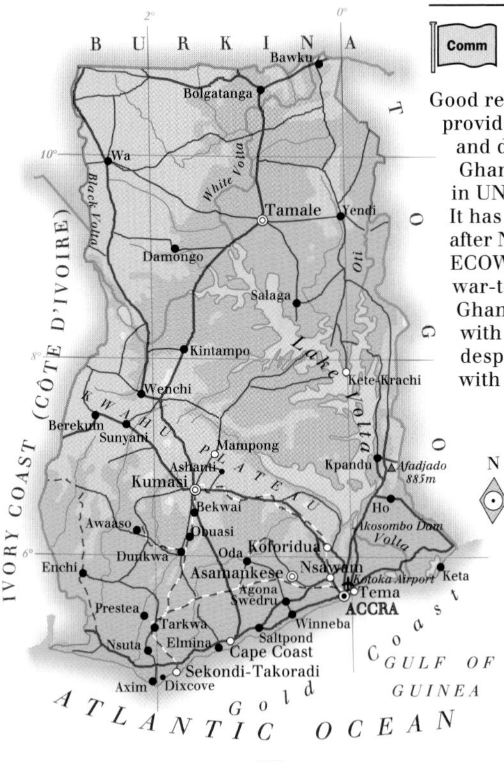
BURKINA
TOGO
IVORY COAST (CÔTE D'IVOIRE)
Bawku
Bolgatanga
Wa
White Volta
Black Volta
Tamale
Yendi
Damongo
Oti
Salaga
Kintampo
Lake Volta
Kete-Krachi
Wenchi
Berekum
Sunyani
KWAHU PLATEAU
Mampong
Ashanti
Kumasi
Kpandu
Afadjado 885m
Bekwai
Ho
Awaaso
Obuasi
Akosombo Dam
Volta
Dunkwa
Oda
Koforidua
Enchi
Asamankese
Nsawam
Kotoka Airport
Keta
Agona Swedru
Tema
ACCRA
Prestea
Tarkwa
Winneba
Nsuta
Elmina
Saltpond
Cape Coast
Sekondi-Takoradi
Axim
Dixcove
Gold Coast
GULF OF GUINEA
ATLANTIC OCEAN

GHANA

Total Area : 239 460 sq. km (92 455 sq. miles)

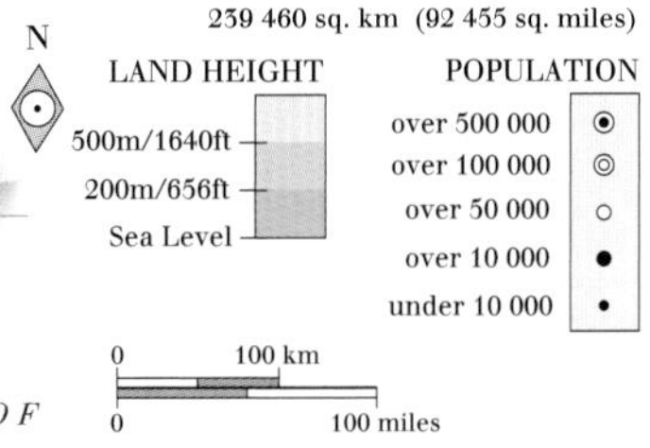
N
LAND HEIGHT
500m/1640ft
200m/656ft
Sea Level
POPULATION
over 500 000
over 100 000
over 50 000
over 10 000
under 10 000
0 100 km
0 100 miles

AID

Recipient

$653m (receipts) | Little change in 2002

Ghana receives most of its aid from the World Bank, which has supported a largely successful economic recovery program which began in 1983. In 2004 it pledged $1 billion over the next four years. Aid is now channeled toward infrastructure development.

DEFENSE

No compulsory military service

$30m | Down 3% in 2002

Ghana has a history of coups and of military involvement in politics. The civilian component of the armed forces is being increased in order to bring the military more firmly under civil control, and membership of quasipolitical associations has been banned. The 5000-strong army has been deployed to assist in UN and ECOWAS operations.

ECONOMICS

Inflation 27% p.a. (1990–2001)

$5.5bn | 9020 cedis (8675)

SCORE CARD

❑ World GNP Ranking	112th
❑ GNP per capita	$270
❑ Balance of Payments	–$31m
❑ Inflation	14.8%
❑ Unemployment	20%

Strengths

Relatively well-developed industrial base. Second-largest gold producer in Africa – Ashanti Goldfields Company: multinational active in 12 African countries. Cocoa production accounts for around 14% of world total. Steady economic growth during 1990s.

Weaknesses

High budget deficits and debt repayments; the cedi has generally declined in value since devaluation in 1983. Foreign investment largely restricted to gold mining. High inflation levels. Underdevelopment in north. High unemployment.

EXPORTS

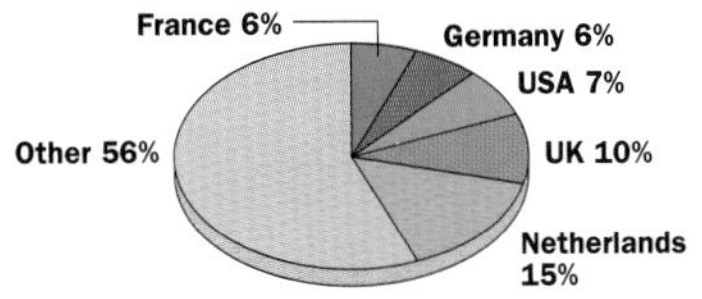
France 6%
Germany 6%
USA 7%
UK 10%
Other 56%
Netherlands 15%

IMPORTS

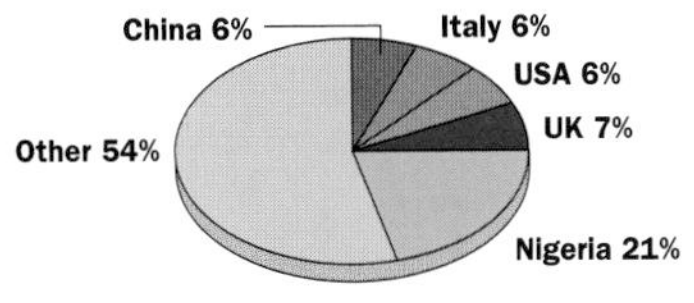
China 6%
Italy 6%
USA 6%
UK 7%
Other 54%
Nigeria 21%

Dixcove harbor, close to Ghana's most southerly cape. The majority of Ghanaians lead a traditional subsistence existence.

RESOURCES

Electric power 1.2m kW

451,287 tonnes | 241 b/d (reserves 15m barrels)

3.26m goats, 3.1m sheep, 1.35m cattle, 26.7m chickens | Gold, diamonds, oil, bauxite, manganese

Gold production has expanded strongly since the mid-1980s; by 1993, gold had overtaken cocoa as the major export. Diamonds, bauxite, and manganese are also exported. Hydropower from the Volta Dam is exported to Togo and Benin, but is hit by periodic droughts.

ENVIRONMENT

Sustainability rank: 65th

6% (0.7% partially protected) | 0.3 tonnes per capita

Cutting wood for fuel, timber, and farming has destroyed 70% of Ghana's forests since 1981. Devastation caused by mining is now being tackled under a World Bank project.

MEDIA

TV ownership medium

Daily newspaper circulation 14 per 1000 people

PUBLISHING AND BROADCAST MEDIA

There are 2 daily newspapers, the *Ghanaian Times* and the *Daily Graphic*

3 services: 1 state-controlled, 2 independent | 1 state-controlled service, many independent stations

There is an increasing degree of media freedom, and the many private weeklies and independent radio stations are often critical of government policy.

CRIME

Death penalty in use

11,624 prisoners | Up 61% in 2000–2001

Several former government ministers are being tried on corruption charges. Street crime can be a problem in Accra and at tourist attractions.

EDUCATION

School leaving age: 14

74% | 64,098 students

The "Vision 2020" program aims to improve access to education and to redress existing gender imbalances. There are five universities.

CHRONOLOGY

In 1874 Kumasi, capital of the Ashanti kingdom, was sacked by a British force to create the Gold Coast colony.

- ❑ **1957** Independence under Kwame Nkrumah.
- ❑ **1964** Single-party state.
- ❑ **1966** Army coup.
- ❑ **1972–1979** "Kleptocracy" of Gen. Acheampong. Executed 1979.
- ❑ **1979** Flt. Lt. Jerry Rawlings leads coup. Civilian Hilla Limann wins elections.
- ❑ **1981** Rawlings takes power again.
- ❑ **1992, 1996** Rawlings and NDC win multiparty elections.
- ❑ **2000** Opposition NPP wins elections; John Kufuor wins presidency.

G

HEALTH

Welfare state health benefits

1 per 10,000 people | Malaria, diarrheal diseases, tuberculosis

In 2004 a government-subsidized health insurance scheme to provide care for the whole population was launched. Private health care is available.

SPENDING

GDP/cap. increase

CONSUMPTION AND SPENDING

23 per 1000 population | *13 per 1000 population*

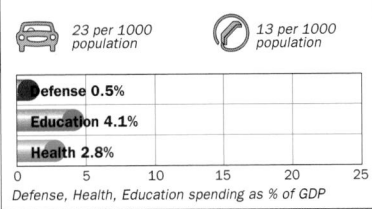

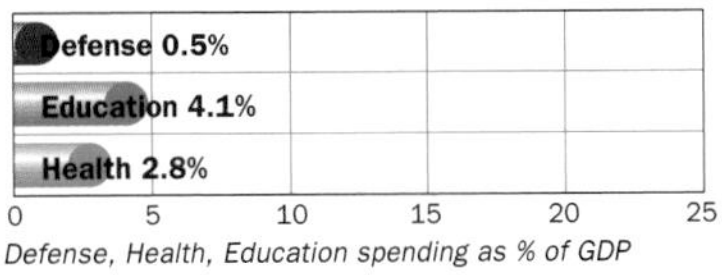
Defense 0.5%
Education 4.1%
Health 2.8%
0
5
10
15
20
25
Defense, Health, Education spending as % of GDP

Political uncertainty brought few opportunities for advancement, and many Ghanaians emigrated, but the situation is now improving. The main economic disparity is still between the poorer rural north and the richer, more urban, south.

WORLD RANKING

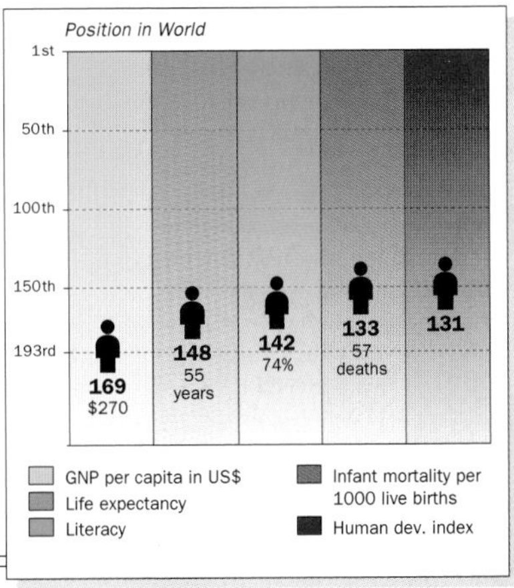
Position in World
1st
50th
100th
150th
193rd
169
$270
148
55
years
142
74%
133
57
deaths
131
GNP per capita in US$
Life expectancy
Literacy
Infant mortality per 1000 live births
Human dev. index

GREECE

EUROPE
Maced.
Bulgaria
Albania
Turkey
GREECE
Europe

OFFICIAL NAME: Hellenic Republic **CAPITAL:** Athens
POPULATION: 11 million **CURRENCY:** Euro **OFFICIAL LANGUAGE:** Greek

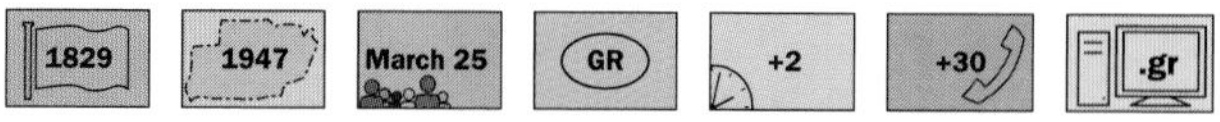
1829
1947
March 25
GR
+2
+30
.gr

THE SOUTHERNMOST COUNTRY of the Balkans, Greece is embraced by the Aegean, Ionian, and Cretan Seas. Its mainly mountainous territory includes more than 2000 islands. Only one-third of the land is cultivated. There is a strong seafaring tradition, and some of the world's biggest shipowners are Greek. Greece is rich in minerals – including chromium, whose occurrence is rare. Relations with Turkey, marked by conflict and territorial disputes, have improved in recent years. To the north, however, upheavals in Albania and the conflicts in former Yugoslavia have made for greater instability.

CLIMATE

Mediterranean

WEATHER CHART FOR ATHENS

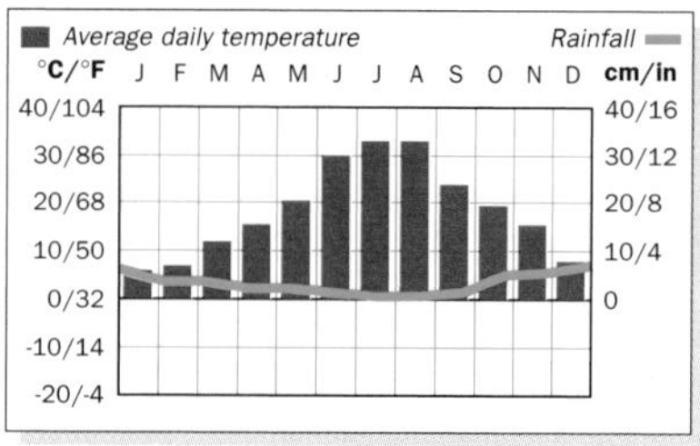
Average daily temperature
Rainfall
°C/°F J F M A M J J A S O N D cm/in
40/104
30/86
20/68
10/50
0/32
-10/14
-20/-4
40/16
30/12
20/8
10/4
0

The climate varies from region to region. The northwest is alpine, while parts of Crete border on the subtropical. The large central plain experiences high summer temperatures. Water is a problem, particularly on the many barren Aegean islands.

TRANSPORTATION

Drive on right

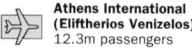

Athens International (Eliftherios Venizelos)
12.3m passengers

1548 ships
28.8m grt

THE TRANSPORTATION NETWORK

107,640 km (66,884 miles)

470 km (292 miles)

2383 km (1481 miles)

80 km (50 miles)

The easiest and cheapest method of transportation between the islands and the mainland is by boat or hovercraft. A major ferry disaster in 2000 prompted government moves to improve standards. Greece has 444 ports, of which Piraeus is the main one, and 123 are large enough to handle passenger or freight traffic. A new airport at Spata, 30 km east of Athens, opened in 2001. Greece has a good, if increasingly congested, road network. Expressway routes have been upgraded and two lines have been added to the Athens metro with the help of EU funds. An interurban bus system and a fleet of air-conditioned tourist Pullmans offer an extensive service.

TOURISM

Visitors : Population 1.3:1

14.2m visitors

Up 8% in 2001–2002

MAIN TOURIST ARRIVALS

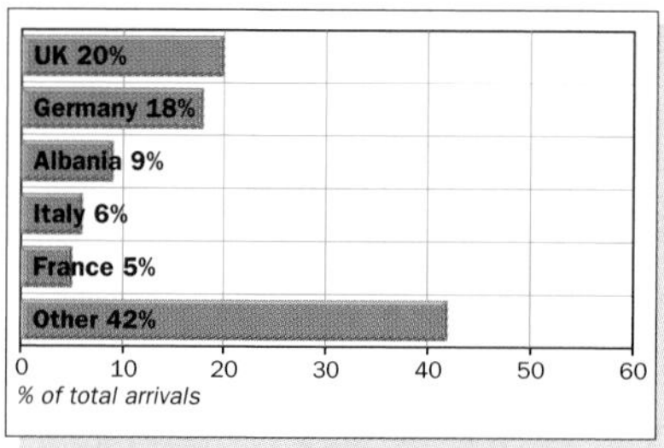
UK 20%
Germany 18%
Albania 9%
Italy 6%
France 5%
Other 42%
0 10 20 30 40 50 60
% of total arrivals

Tourism is a mainstay of the Greek economy, with an annual turnover of almost $10 billion, and is a major source of foreign exchange. Until recently, the state gave grants for hotel development and many third-grade hotels were built, especially on Crete and Rhodes. Smaller islands often lack sufficient water supplies or sandy beaches. To offset falling visitor numbers in the mid-1990s the industry has been encouraged to move upmarket, and is also promoting year-round activity vacations and conference tourism. The 2004 Athens Olympics have been a stimulus to upgrade the city's facilities. A museum is planned to house the Parthenon Marbles, currently held in the British Museum in London.

The theater at Dodona. *Classical sites, such as this theater in northwestern Greece, have helped to make tourism one of the country's most important industries.*

PEOPLE

Pop. density medium

Greek, Turkish, Macedonian, Albanian

84/km² (218/mi²)

THE URBAN/RURAL POPULATION SPLIT

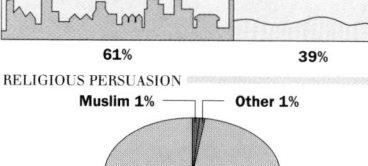

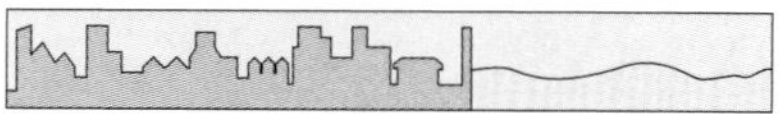
61%
39%

RELIGIOUS PERSUASION

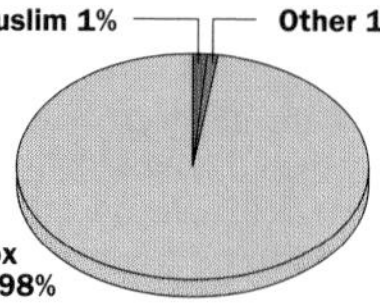
Muslim 1%
Other 1%
Orthodox Christian 98%

ETHNIC MAKEUP

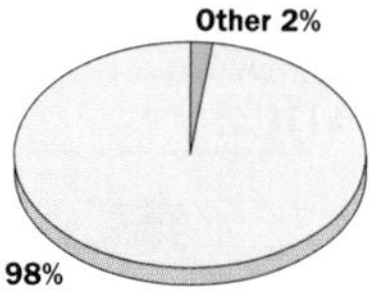
Other 2%
Greek 98%

The Greeks were for many centuries a largely agrarian and seafaring nation. The German occupation during World War II, and the civil war that followed, destroyed much of the fabric of rural life and there was rapid urbanization from the 1950s. There was also extensive emigration in the 1950s and 1960s to northern Europe, Australia, the US, Canada, and southern Africa. However, many people returned to Greece in the 1980s, putting pressure on the labor market. The socialist PASOK governments of 1981–1989 spent large sums, mostly from EU sources, on developing the infrastructure and business life of the rural regions with a view to halting migration to the cities. The policy was partly successful, but a majority still lives in or near the capital, Athens, and Thessaloníki in the north.

Some 98% of the population belong to the Greek Orthodox Church. Civil marriage and divorce only became legal in 1982. There are minorities of Muslims, Roman Catholics, and Jews, and a recent influx of illegal immigrants, mainly from Albania.

POPULATION AGE BREAKDOWN

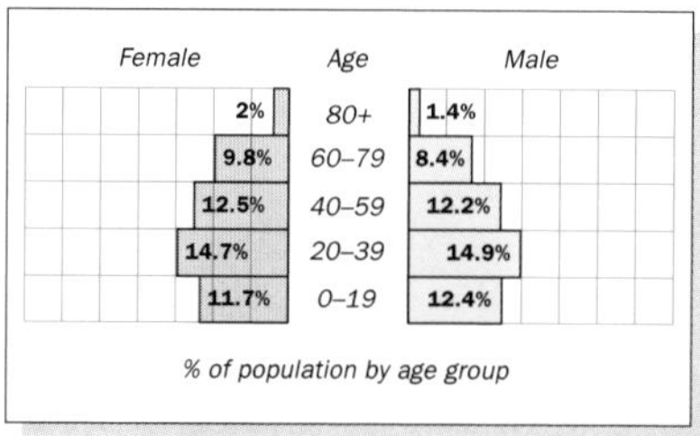
Female
Age
Male
2% 80+ 1.4%
9.8% 60–79 8.4%
12.5% 40–59 12.2%
14.7% 20–39 14.9%
11.7% 0–19 12.4%
% of population by age group

POLITICS

Multiparty elections

2004/2008

President Costas Stephanopoulos

AT THE LAST ELECTION

Parliament 300 seats

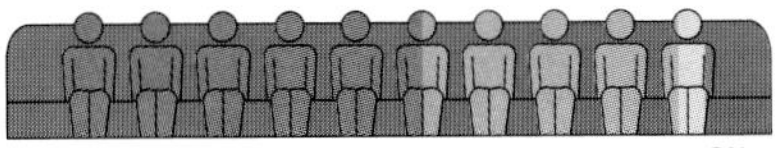
39%
PASOK
4%
KKE
55%
ND
2%
Synaspismos

ND = New Democracy **PASOK** = Pan-Hellenic Socialist Movement **KKE** = Communist Party of Greece **Synaspismos** = Coalition of the Left and Progress

Greece is a multiparty democracy. A military regime held power in 1967–1974.

PROFILE

PASOK founder Andreas Papandreou headed the first socialist government in 1981–1989. When returned to power in 1993, PASOK adopted the economic policies of the outgoing conservatives. Power passed to Costas Simitis in 1996. The ND, headed by Costas Karamanlis, nephew of the former president, in 2004 campaigned on the deficient organization of the Olympic Games, defeating PASOK and its new leader George Papandreou, son of the former prime minister.

MAIN POLITICAL ISSUES

Closer European union

Greece joined the eurozone in 2001, but only after stringent austerity policies which evoked widespread protests. Greece supported EU enlargement, even though it was the poorest of the existing members and will lose funding to new members from 2007.

Turkey and Cyprus

Greece has pursued rapprochement with Turkey since 1999, but progress has been uneven, particularly because of the unresolved Cyprus question. Greece's aim that a reunified Cyprus should join the EU in 2004 was thwarted by the Greek Cypriot rejection of a UN settlement plan.

Albanian refugees

Thousands of Albanians of Greek descent entered Greece illegally after 1990. Willing to work for very low wages, they swelled the thriving black economy. A legalization program was implemented from 1998, which has resulted in the registration of 375,000 Albanians.

Costas Karamanlis, *prime minister since March 2004.*

President Costas Stephanopoulos, *elected with right- and left-wing support.*

G

WORLD AFFAIRS

Joined UN in 1945

EU NATO OECD OSCE CE

Though part of the Western alliance, Greece has sympathies with Russians and Serbs, who share its Orthodox heritage. Friction with its northern neighbor over the use of the name "Macedonia" (also the name of a province in Greece) eased after Greece agreed in 1995 to recognize its neighbor's sovereignty as the Former Yugoslav Republic of Macedonia (FYRM). The current priority is Greece's role within the EU, and the impact of the latter's eastward expansion – and possible eventual inclusion of Turkey.

AID

Donor

$276m (donations) Up 37% in 2002

Greece's contribution to overseas development aid is the lowest per capita among major donors; it totaled just $19 a head in 2001, but is growing. The vast majority of aid is channeled toward neighboring Balkan countries. Greece receives regional development assistance from the EU, especially from the EU's structural and cohesion funds. Some of the money has been used to reverse the decline of northeast Greece, the country's least developed region.

In recent years, emergency humanitarian aid has been given to Turkey after natural disasters, most notably after the severe earthquake near Istanbul in 1999.

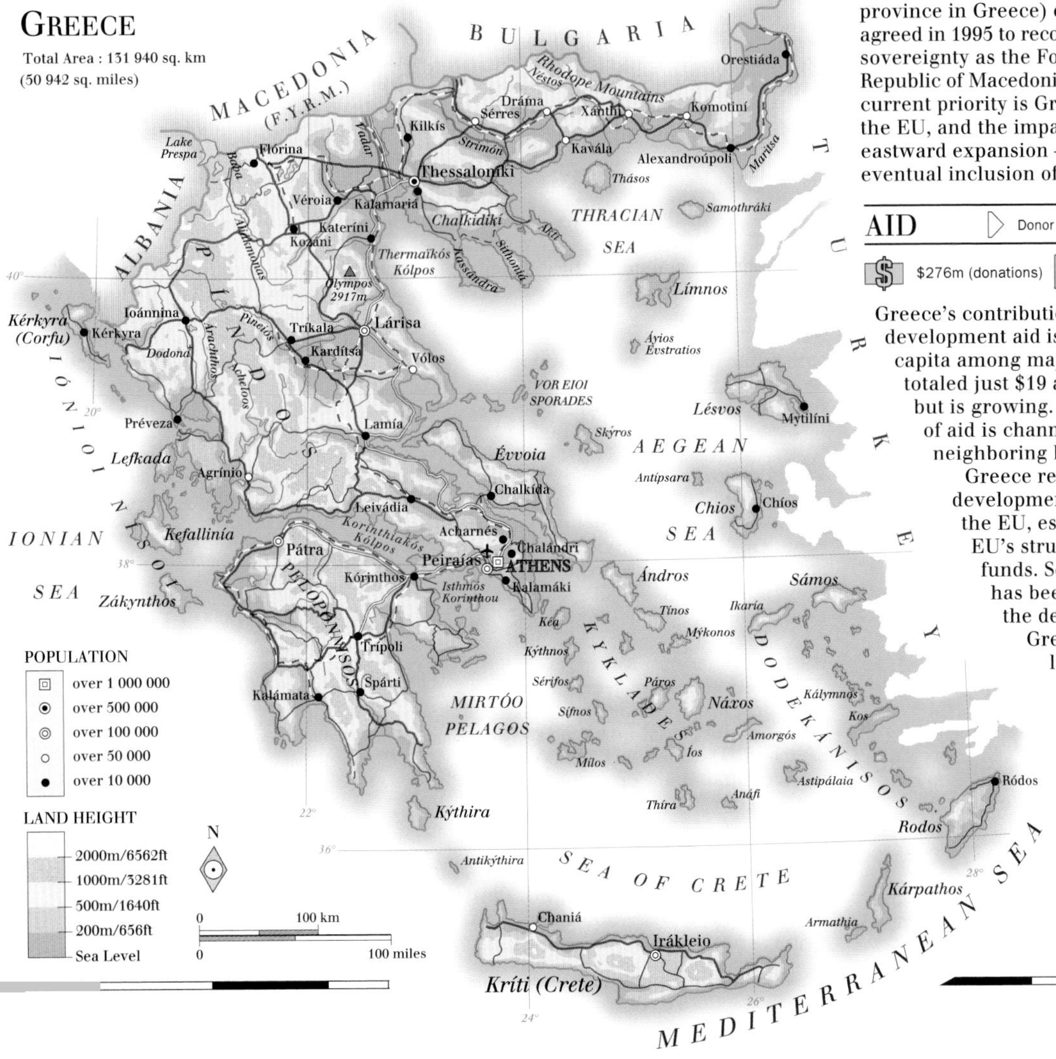
GREECE
Total Area : 131 940 sq. km
(50 942 sq. miles)
BULGARIA
MACEDONIA (F.Y.R.M.)
ALBANIA
TURKEY
Orestiáda
Rhodope Mountains
Néstos
Dráma
Sérres
Xánthi
Komotiní
Kilkís
Strimón
Kavála
Alexandroúpoli
Maritsa
Lake Prespa
Flórina
Thessaloníki
Thásos
Véroia
Kalamariá
Samothráki
Kateríni
Kozáni
Chalkidikí
THRACIAN SEA
Thermaïkós Kólpos
Olympos 2917m
Límnos
Ioánnina
Lárisa
Kérkyra (Corfu)
Kérkyra
Tríkala
Kardítsa
Vólos
Dodoní
Áyios Evstrátios
VOR EIOI SPORADES
Lésvos
Mytilíni
Préveza
Lamía
Skýros
AEGEAN SEA
Lefkada
Évvoia
Agrínio
Chalkída
Antípsara
Chíos
Leivádia
IONIAN SEA
Kefallinía
Acharnés
Pátra
Chalándri
Peiraías
ATHENS
Kórinthos
Kalamáki
Ándros
Sámos
Zákynthos
Ikaría
Tínos
Kéa
Mýkonos
Trípoli
Kýthnos
Sérifos
Páros
Spárti
Kalámata
Sífnos
Náxos
Kálymnos
Kos
MIRTÓO PELAGOS
Amorgós
Íos
Mílos
Astipálaia
Ródos
Anáfi
Thíra
Kýthira
Rodos
Antikýthira
SEA OF CRETE
Kárpathos
Chaniá
Armathia
Iráklеio
Kríti (Crete)
MEDITERRANEAN SEA
POPULATION
over 1 000 000
over 500 000
over 100 000
over 50 000
over 10 000
LAND HEIGHT
2000m/6562ft
1000m/3281ft
500m/1640ft
200m/656ft
Sea Level
N
100 km
100 miles

CHRONOLOGY

Greece was occupied by Nazi Germany between 1941 and 1944. After liberation by the Allies, communists and royalists fought a five-year civil war. This ended with communist defeat, and King Paul became the constitutional monarch.

- ❑ **1964** King Constantine succeeds his father, King Paul.
- ❑ **1967** Military coup. King in exile. Col. Giorgios Papadopoulos premier.
- ❑ **1973** Greece declared a republic, with Papadopoulos as president. Papadopoulos overthrown in military coup. Lt. Gen. Ghizikis becomes president, Adamantios Androutsopoulos prime minister.
- ❑ **1974** Greece leaves NATO in protest at Turkish occupation of northern Cyprus. "Colonels' regime" falls. Constantinos Karamanlis becomes premier; his ND wins elections.
- ❑ **1975** Konstantinos Tsatsou becomes president.
- ❑ **1977** Elections: ND reelected.
- ❑ **1980** Karamanlis president. Georgios Rallis prime minister. Greece rejoins NATO.
- ❑ **1981** PASOK wins elections. Andreas Papandreou first socialist premier. Greece joins European Communities.
- ❑ **1985** Proposals to limit power of president. Karamanlis resigns. Christos Sartzetakis president. Greece and Albania reopen borders, closed since 1940.
- ❑ **1985–1989** Civil unrest caused by economic austerity program.
- ❑ **1988** Cabinet implicated in financial scandal. Leading members resign.
- ❑ **1989** Defense agreement with US. Two inconclusive elections lead to formation of all-party coalition.
- ❑ **1990** Coalition government collapses. ND wins elections. Konstantinos Mitsotakis prime minister, Karamanlis president.
- ❑ **1990–1992** Strikes against economic reform.
- ❑ **1992** EU persuaded not to recognize independent Macedonia.
- ❑ **1993** PASOK wins election, Andreas Papandreou premier.
- ❑ **1995** Costas Stephanopoulos elected president; recognition of sovereignty of Former Yugoslav Republic of Macedonia (FYRM).
- ❑ **1996** Andreas Papandreou resigns as prime minister; succeeded by Costas Simitis.
- ❑ **1999** Earthquakes in Greece and Turkey. Sympathetic response shows improvement in relations.
- ❑ **2001** Armed conflict in FYRM.
- ❑ **2002** Euro fully adopted.
- ❑ **2004** ND wins general election. Athens hosts centennial Olympics.

G

DEFENSE

▷ Compulsory military service

$6.15bn

Up 17% in 2002

Greece spends a higher percentage of GDP on defense than any other NATO country except Turkey, whose perceived threat is its main concern, though tensions with that country are now less acute. In 1998 a law was passed on the conscription of women (for four days a year) for the defense of border regions. The security operation mounted for the 2004 Olympics was the biggest in the Games' history.

GREEK ARMED FORCES

1723 main battle tanks (683 M-48, 628 M-60, 412 Leopard 1)	114,000 personnel
8 submarines, 2 destroyers, 12 frigates, and 40 patrol boats	19,000 personnel
418 combat aircraft (A-7, F-5, F-4E, F-16, Mirage F-1, Mirage 2000)	33,000 personnel
None	

ECONOMICS

▷ Inflation 8.5% p.a. (1990–2001)

$124bn

0.822 euros (0.871)

SCORE CARD

- ❑ World GNP Ranking......30th
- ❑ GNP per Capita......$11,660
- ❑ Balance of Payments......–$10.4bn
- ❑ Inflation......3.6%
- ❑ Unemployment......10%

EXPORTS

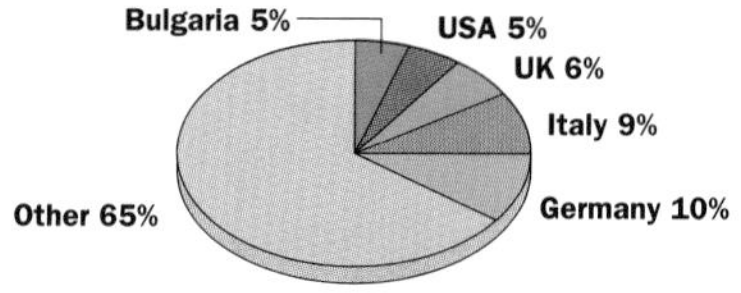
Bulgaria 5%
USA 5%
UK 6%
Italy 9%
Germany 10%
Other 65%

IMPORTS

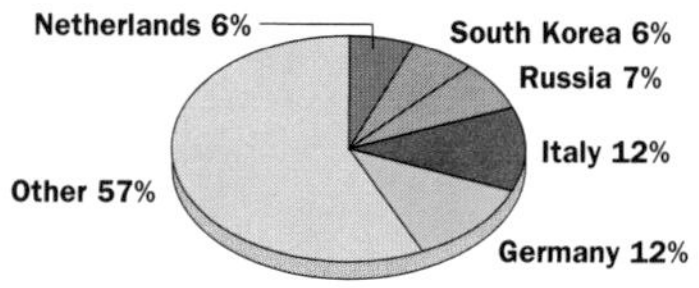
Netherlands 6%
South Korea 6%
Russia 7%
Italy 12%
Germany 12%
Other 57%

Strengths

One of the major tourist destinations in Europe. Efficient agricultural exporter. Shipping: the world's largest beneficially owned fleet.

Weaknesses

High levels of public debt. Until recently, interest rates and bureaucratic banking system discouraged private initiative. State-owned sector, like black economy, remains large. Loss of jobs to low-wage ex-communist neighboring states.

Profile

Greek recovery from World War II was slow; it was not until the 1960s that any substantial investment occurred. The Colonels' dictatorship curbed inflationary pressures with a wage freeze. When civilian government was restored in 1974, a spate of high wage settlements and the oil price shocks of 1973 and 1979 drove inflation over 20%. EU membership from 1981 brought large subsidies to what was then the poorest member state.

ECONOMIC PERFORMANCE INDICATOR

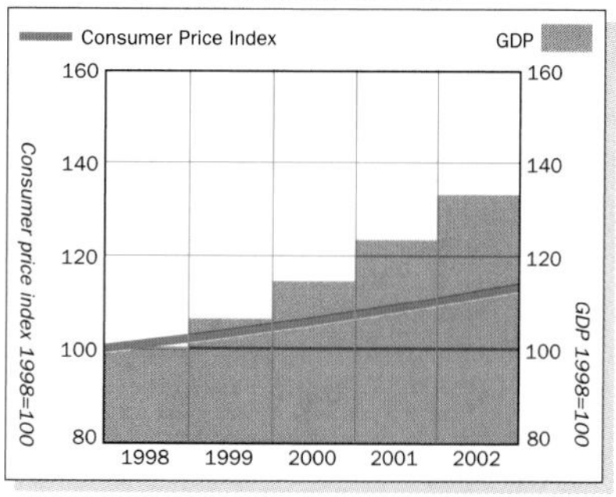
Consumer Price Index
GDP
160
140
120
100
80
Consumer price index 1998=100
GDP 1998=100
1998
1999
2000
2001
2002

Greece's largest companies made substantial losses until the socialists' controversial austerity program of 1986–1987 reined in labor costs.

Greece failed in 1999 to meet the economic convergence criteria for introducing the euro. It then tackled the problems with determination, balancing the budget and bringing inflation under control, though public-sector debt remains high. In 2001 Greece became the 12th member of the eurozone. The Olympic Games caused a huge budget deficit in 2004.

GREECE : MAJOR BUSINESSES

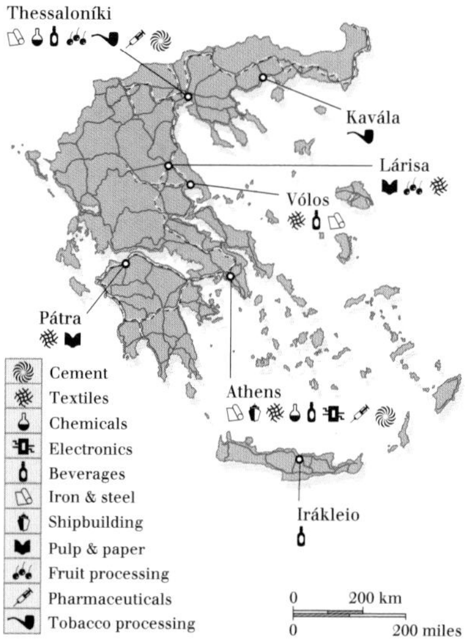
Thessaloníki
Kavála
Lárisa
Vólos
Pátra
Athens
Irákleio
Cement
Textiles
Chemicals
Electronics
Beverages
Iron & steel
Shipbuilding
Pulp & paper
Fruit processing
Pharmaceuticals
Tobacco processing
0
200 km
0
200 miles

RESOURCES

Electric power 11.1m kW

192,190 tonnes

5133 b/d (reserves 19m barrels)

9.1m sheep, 5m goats, 903,000 pigs, 28m chickens

Oil, gas, coal, iron, bauxite, marble, nickel, magnesite, chromium

ELECTRICITY GENERATION

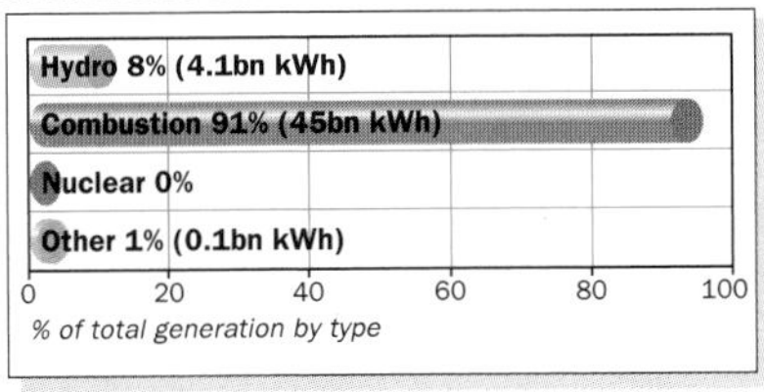

Hydro 8% (4.1bn kWh)
Combustion 91% (45bn kWh)
Nuclear 0%
Other 1% (0.1bn kWh)
0
20
40
60
80
100
% of total generation by type

There is an oil and gas field off the coast of the island of Thasos. There may also be exploitable reserves in eastern waters, whose ownership is contested by Turkey. Coal, iron, and other mining contribute less than 1% to GDP. Greece is a leading producer of marble.

GREECE : LAND USE

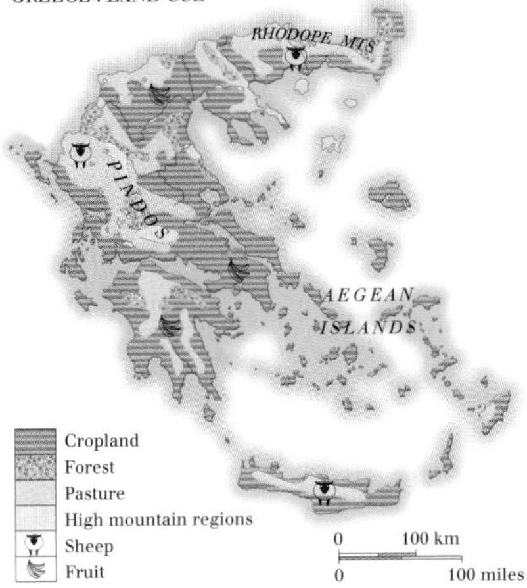

RHODOPE MTS
PINDOS
AEGEAN ISLANDS
Cropland
Forest
Pasture
High mountain regions
Sheep
Fruit
0 100 km
0 100 miles

ENVIRONMENT

Sustainability rank: 60th

4% (1% partially protected)

8.5 tonnes per capita

ENVIRONMENTAL TREATIES

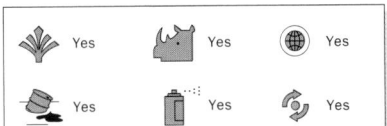

Yes Yes Yes

Yes Yes Yes

Local fishing interests have formed a successful antipollution organization, HELMEPA. Smog in Athens is irritating to the eyes and throat and highly damaging to ancient monuments: the Parthenon in Athens has suffered more erosion in the last two decades than in the previous two millennia. Forest fires regularly cause havoc, damaging flora and fauna.

CRIME

Death penalty not used in practice

8500 prisoners

Up 19% in 2001

CRIME RATES

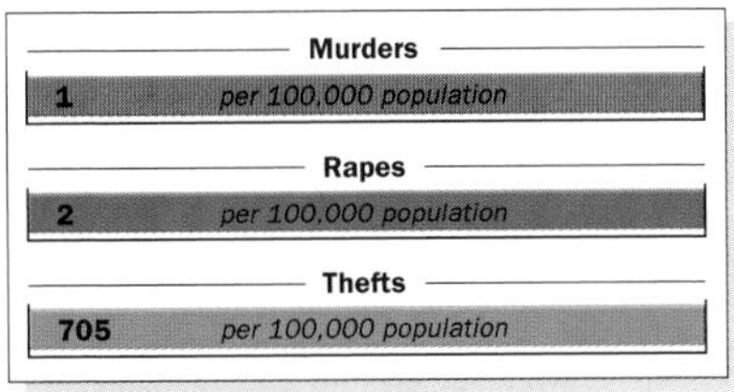

Murders
1 per 100,000 population
Rapes
2 per 100,000 population
Thefts
705 per 100,000 population

An influx of migrants is blamed for an increase in violent crime. The terrorist group November 17, which had carried out high-profile assassinations, was finally tracked down in 2002.

MEDIA

TV ownership high

Daily newspaper circulation 64 per 1000 people

PUBLISHING AND BROADCAST MEDIA

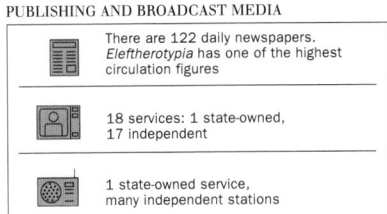

There are 122 daily newspapers. *Eleftherotypia* has one of the highest circulation figures

18 services: 1 state-owned, 17 independent

1 state-owned service, many independent stations

After the state broadcasting monopoly ended in 1990, many private TV and radio networks emerged. Commercial broadcasting has made politicians more answerable to the public, and has also had a cultural impact, with the import of more foreign programs, particularly from the US. Many private radio and TV broadcasters are unlicensed.

EDUCATION

School leaving age: 14

97%

478,205 students

THE EDUCATION SYSTEM

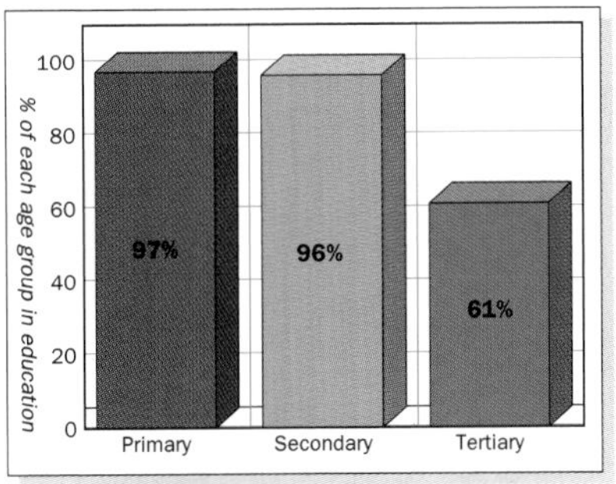

100
80
60
40
20
0
% of each age group in education
97%
96%
61%
Primary
Secondary
Tertiary

Some 10% of total government spending is on education, which is free and officially compulsory for nine years. The use of informal Greek (*demotiki*) replaced the formal *katharevoussa* in Greek schools when it became the country's official language in 1976. There are 18 universities and 74 other institutions of higher education.

HEALTH

Welfare state health benefits

1 per 227 people

Cerebrovascular and heart diseases, cancers

The first PASOK government introduced a national health service and a national pharmaceuticals industry. Some 14% of government expenditure goes on health, and every Greek is entitled to sickness benefit. Greece now has one of the highest numbers of doctors per head of population in the EU. In the early 1990s the ND attempted to upgrade private medicine and to incorporate its activities with those in state hospitals. Overall, provision has improved greatly, but private clinics now offer better facilities than state-run centers.

G

SPENDING

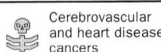

GDP/cap. increase

CONSUMPTION AND SPENDING

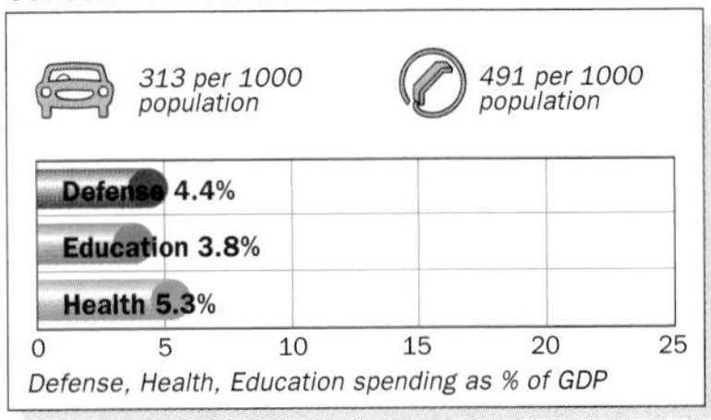

313 per 1000 population
491 per 1000 population
Defense 4.4%
Education 3.8%
Health 5.3%
0
5
10
15
20
25
Defense, Health, Education spending as % of GDP

Greek society changed dramatically in the postwar period. Formerly a largely agricultural society living in isolated communities, it was rapidly urbanized in the 1950s. Former agricultural workers made fortunes, many by grabbing opportunities presented by the shipping industry. Among these were the now prominent Niarchos and Onassis families.

The advent of the republic in 1975 reflected the social changes which had occurred since the war. New wealth and success became more admired than aristocratic birth or prestige. Greece is now a socially mobile society. Living standards have improved universally since the 1950s.

WORLD RANKING

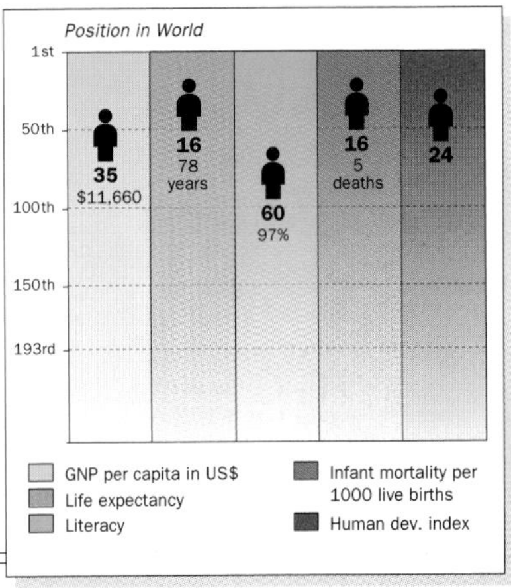

Position in World
1st
50th
100th
150th
193rd
35
$11,660
16
78 years
60
97%
16
5 deaths
24
GNP per capita in US$
Life expectancy
Literacy
Infant mortality per 1000 live births
Human dev. index

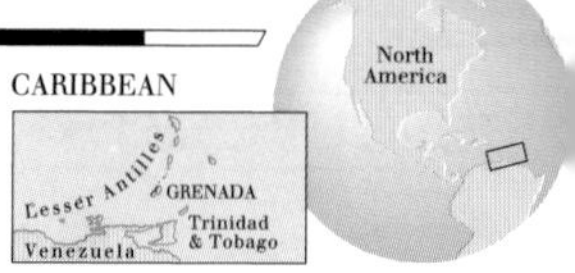
CARIBBEAN
North America
Lesser Antilles
GRENADA
Trinidad & Tobago
Venezuela

GRENADA

OFFICIAL NAME: Grenada **CAPITAL:** St. George's
POPULATION: 89,258 **CURRENCY:** Eastern Caribbean dollar **OFFICIAL LANGUAGE:** English

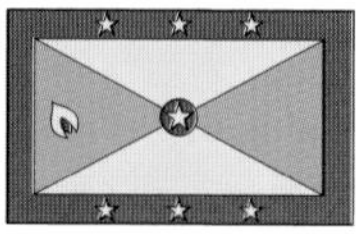

1974
1974
Feb 7
WG
-4
+1473
.gd

St. George's harbor. The newest hotel developments are on the beaches to the south.

THE MOST SOUTHERLY of the Windward Islands, Grenada also includes the southern Grenadine islands of Carriacou and Petite Martinique. It became a focus of international attention in 1983 when the US, with token backing from several Caribbean states, mounted an invasion to sever its growing links with Castro's Cuba. It is the world's second-largest nutmeg producer, but the crop was devastated by Hurricane Ivan in 2004.

G

CLIMATE

Tropical oceanic

WEATHER CHART FOR ST. GEORGE'S

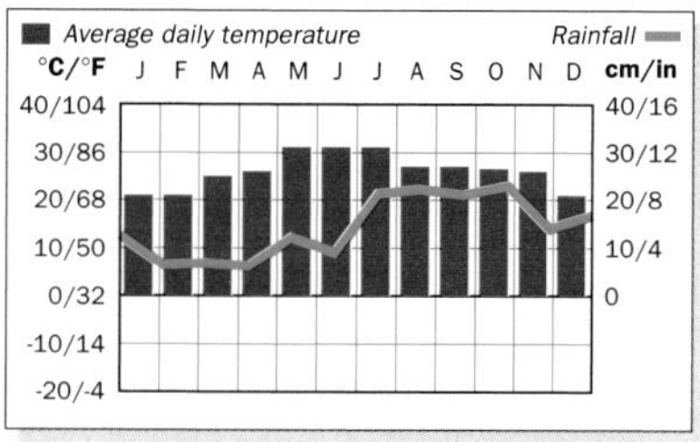
Average daily temperature
Rainfall
°C/°F J F M A M J J A S O N D cm/in
40/104 40/16
30/86 30/12
20/68 20/8
10/50 10/4
0/32 0
-10/14
-20/-4

Rainfall totals 150 cm (60 in) on the coast, and twice that in the mountains. Hurricanes occur in the rainy season.

TRANSPORTATION

Drive on left

Point Salines, St. George's 441,808 passengers

6 ships 1009 grt

THE TRANSPORTATION NETWORK

634 km (394 miles)	None
None	None

Roads in the interior are poor. Catamarans provide the fastest link between Grenada and Carriacou.

TOURISM

Visitors : Population 1.5:1

132,000 visitors

Up 7% in 2002

MAIN TOURIST ARRIVALS

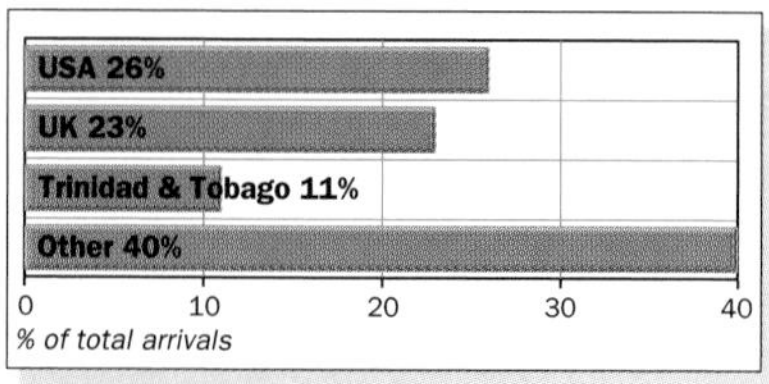
USA 26%
UK 23%
Trinidad & Tobago 11%
Other 40%
0 10 20 30 40
% of total arrivals

Tourism has developed since the 1984 completion of the international airport, though there has been a concurrent decline in cruise ship arrivals. A ten-year development plan aims to increase hotel capacity to 2500 rooms by 2007.

PEOPLE

Pop. density high

English, English Creole

263/km² (681/mi²)

THE URBAN/RURAL POPULATION SPLIT

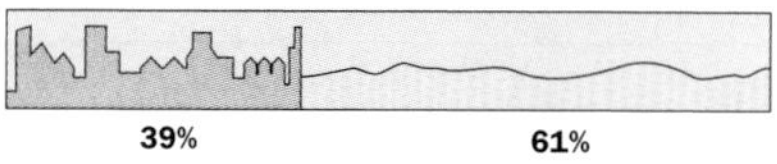
39%
61%

RELIGIOUS PERSUASION

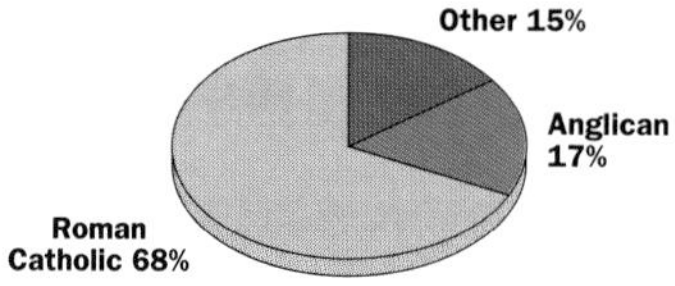
Other 15%
Anglican 17%
Roman Catholic 68%

Most Grenadians are descendants of Africans brought over to work sugar plantations in the 16th to 19th centuries, though there are also a few East Indians and descendants of European settlers. As in other Caribbean states, extended families with absentee fathers are not uncommon. Around half of the population is under the age of 30.

POLITICS

Multiparty elections

L. House 2003/2008
U. House 2003/2008

H.M. Queen Elizabeth II

AT THE LAST ELECTION

House of Representatives 15 seats

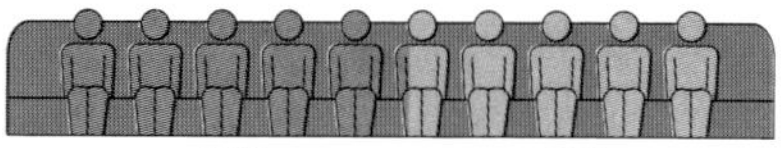
53% NNP
47% NDC

NNP = New National Party
NDC = National Democratic Congress

Senate 13 seats

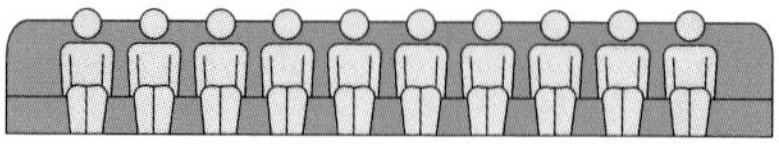

The members of the Senate are appointed by the prime minister and the leader of the opposition

Sir Eric Gairy dominated politics as prime minister until his overthrow in 1979. The charismatic socialist Maurice Bishop, who succeeded him, was in turn deposed and then executed in 1983. This latter coup was the pretext for a US invasion, the primary motive of which was to end the perceived Cuban influence in Grenada. Politics has since been center right, and there is little to choose ideologically between the major parties. The NNP, led by Keith Mitchell, gained power in 1995, and in 1999 took all 15 seats in an unparalleled victory over a divided opposition. in the 2003 elections, however, its majority was reduced to a single seat.

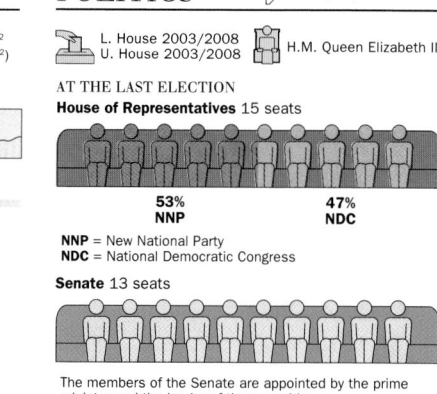

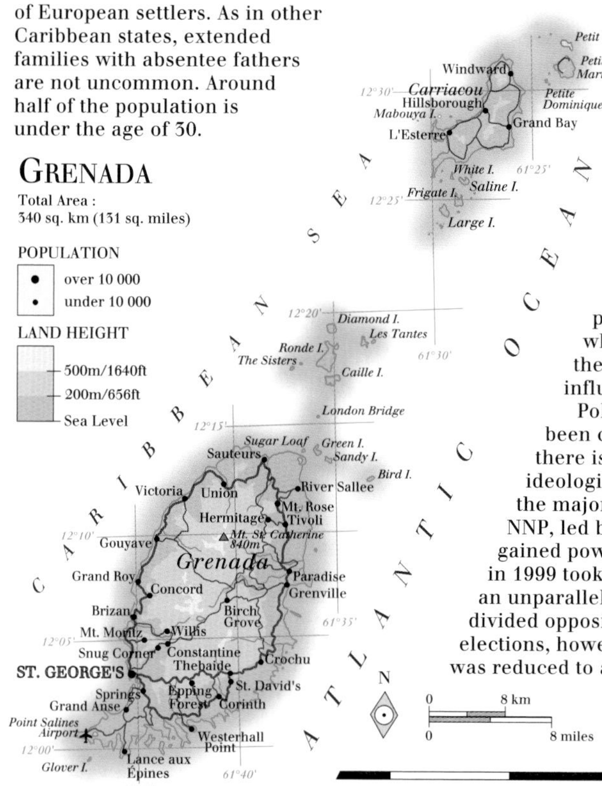
GRENADA
Total Area :
340 sq. km (131 sq. miles)
POPULATION
over 10 000
under 10 000
LAND HEIGHT
500m/1640ft
200m/656ft
Sea Level
CARIBBEAN SEA
ATLANTIC OCEAN
Petit St Vincent I.
Petite Martinique
Windward
Carriacou
Hillsborough
Mabouya I.
Petite Dominique
Grand Bay
L'Esterre
White I.
Saline I.
Frigate I.
Large I.
Diamond I.
Les Tantes
Ronde I.
The Sisters
Caille I.
London Bridge
Sugar Loaf
Green I.
Sandy I.
Sauteurs
Bird I.
Victoria
Union
River Sallee
Hermitage
Mt. Rose
Tivoli
Mt. St Catherine 840m
Gouyave
Grenada
Grand Roy
Paradise
Grenville
Concord
Brizan
Birch Grove
Mt. Moritz
Willis
Snug Corner
Constantine
Thebaide
Crochu
ST. GEORGE'S
Springs
Epping Forest
St. David's
Grand Anse
Corinth
Point Salines Airport
Westerhall Point
Glover I.
Lance aux Epines
0 8 km
0 8 miles
N

WORLD AFFAIRS

Joined UN in 1974

ACS | Caricom | Comm | OAS | OECS

Key priorities are relations with the rest of the Windward Islands group, promoting Grenada as a tourist destination, and maintaining close links with the EU. Since 1983, Grenada has supported US policy, but it restored links with Cuba in 2002.

AID

Recipient

US$9m (receipts)

Down 25% in 2002

Main aid sources are Japan and the Caribbean Development Bank. Humanitarian and reconstruction aid was promised after Hurricane Ivan in 2004.

DEFENSE

No compulsory military service

Minimal expenditure

Defense spending is falling

The People's Revolutionary Army, created by Maurice Bishop in the wake of his 1979 coup, was replaced in 1983 by a paramilitary defense unit trained by the US and the UK.

ECONOMICS

Inflation 2.3% p.a. (1990–2001)

US$361m

2.7 Eastern Caribbean dollars (2.67)

SCORE CARD

- ❑ WORLD GNP RANKING........................175th
- ❑ GNP PER CAPITA.........................US$3530
- ❑ BALANCE OF PAYMENTS................–US$121m
- ❑ INFLATION..4.5%
- ❑ UNEMPLOYMENT................................13%

STRENGTHS

Second-largest producer of nutmeg after Indonesia. Other important sectors are tourism, cocoa, bananas, construction, and financial services.

WEAKNESSES

Weak tax base, lack of diversification. Hurricane Ivan destroyed much infrastructure in 2004. Global nutmeg price fluctuates. High unemployment.

EXPORTS

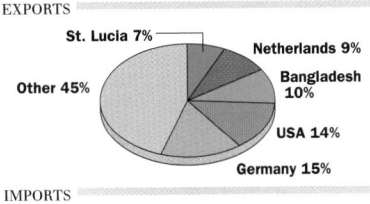

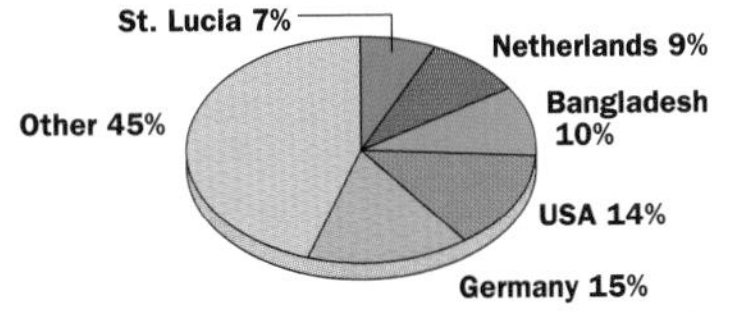
St. Lucia 7%
Netherlands 9%
Bangladesh 10%
Other 45%
USA 14%
Germany 15%

IMPORTS

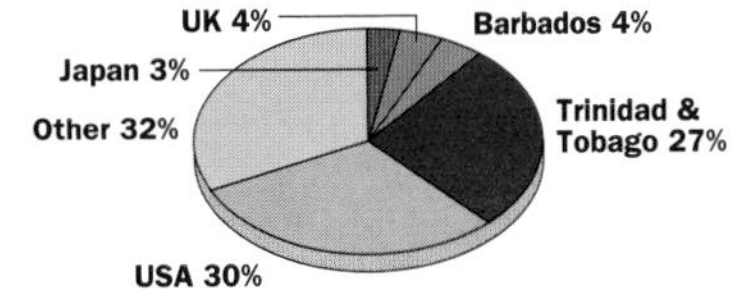
UK 4%
Barbados 4%
Japan 3%
Other 32%
Trinidad & Tobago 27%
USA 30%

RESOURCES

Electric power 27,000 kW

2247 tonnes

Not an oil producer

13,200 sheep, 7200 goats, 5850 pigs, 268,000 chickens

None

Grenada has no strategic resources and has to import most of its energy. The major asset is Grenadian nutmeg, which is highly prized for its quality, but production levels fluctuate.

ENVIRONMENT

Not available

1.7% partially protected

2.1 tonnes per capita

Tourism threatens some key environmental sites, including a remnant of rainforest. Resort projects have caused serious beach erosion, in turn requiring costly coastal defenses. An environmental levy on visitors was opposed by cruise companies.

MEDIA

TV ownership high

There are no daily newspapers

PUBLISHING AND BROADCAST MEDIA

There are no daily newspapers. The *Grenadian Voice* and the *Grenada Guardian* are published weekly

2 services: 1 partly state-owned, 1 independent

4 services: 1 partly state-owned, 3 independent

There are many weekly newspapers, often critical of government policy. The government owns a minority share in the Grenada Broadcasting Network.

CRIME

Death penalty not used in practice

297 prisoners

Crime is rising

The doubling of poverty during the 1990s and high unemployment have contributed to a rising crime rate. Narcotics trafficking is also a growing problem. However, while there is street crime, the level of violence is low.

EDUCATION

School leaving age: 16

94%

651 students

Education follows the former British selective 11-plus system. Many students go on to the University of the West Indies, or to college in the US.

HEALTH

Welfare state health benefits

1 per 2000 people

Heart diseases, cancers, nutritional disorders

After 1979, Cuban physicians provided a basic health care system. There are free weekly clinics in each district, and treatment in subsidized state hospitals now matches the Caribbean average. In 1999 Cuba began its promised expansion of the general hospital.

CHRONOLOGY

Sighted, and named, by Columbus in 1498, Grenada was a French colony from 1650. Captured by the British in 1762, it formally became a part of the British Empire in 1783.

- ❑ **1885–1958** Grenada acts as administrative center for the Windward Islands.
- ❑ **1950** Eric Gairy founds Grenada United Labour Party.
- ❑ **1951** Universal suffrage introduced.
- ❑ **1967** Internal self-government.
- ❑ **1974** Full independence. Gairy prime minister.
- ❑ **1979** Coup. Maurice Bishop prime minister. Growing links with Cuba.
- ❑ **1983** After improving ties with US, Bishop is ousted and executed by former allies. US invasion establishes pro-US administration.
- ❑ **1995** Keith Mitchell of NNP becomes prime minister.
- ❑ **1999** NNP reelected, taking all 15 seats in House of Representatives.
- ❑ **2001–2002** Blacklisted as tax haven.
- ❑ **2002** Relations with Cuba restored.
- ❑ **2003** NNP reelected.
- ❑ **2004** Hurricane Ivan damages 90% of buildings.

G

SPENDING

GDP/cap. increase

CONSUMPTION AND SPENDING

196 per 1000 population

316 per 1000 population

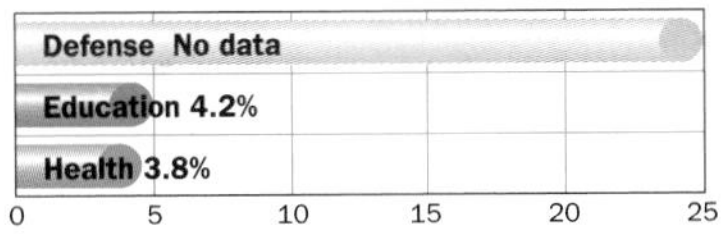
Defense No data
Education 4.2%
Health 3.8%
0
5
10
15
20
25

Defense, Health, Education spending as % of GDP

Wealth disparities in Grenada are less marked than in most Caribbean states, but poverty is growing. The wealthiest groups are those in control of the nutmeg trade.

WORLD RANKING

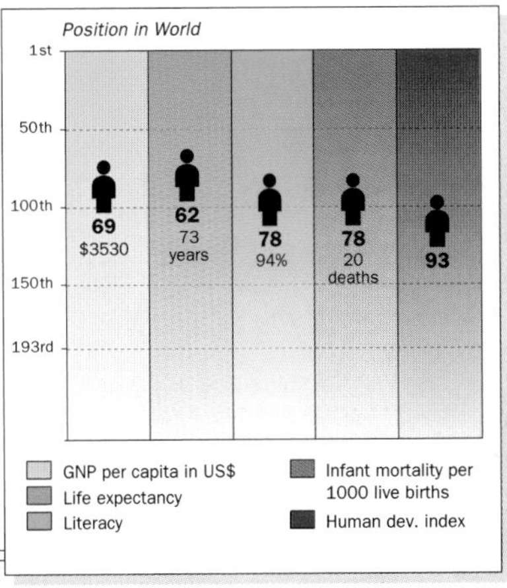
Position in World
1st
50th
100th
150th
193rd
69
$3530
62
73 years
78
94%
78
20 deaths
93
GNP per capita in US$
Life expectancy
Literacy
Infant mortality per 1000 live births
Human dev. index

GUATEMALA

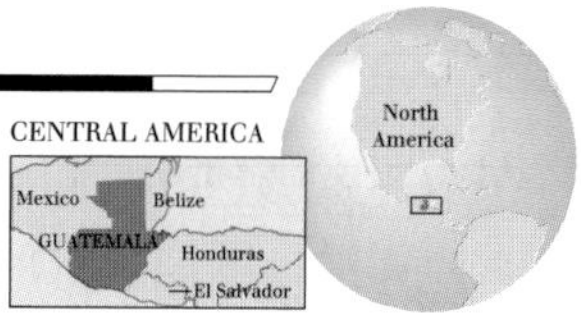

North America
CENTRAL AMERICA
Mexico
Belize
GUATEMALA
Honduras
El Salvador

OFFICIAL NAME: Republic of Guatemala **CAPITAL:** Guatemala City
POPULATION: 12.3 million **CURRENCY:** Quetzal **OFFICIAL LANGUAGE:** Spanish

1838
1838
Sept 15
GCA
-6
+502
.gt

THE LARGEST AND MOST POPULOUS of the states of the Central American isthmus, Guatemala was home to the ancient Mayan civilization. Its fertile Pacific and Caribbean coastal lowlands give way to the highlands which dominate the country. Independent since 1838, Guatemala was governed by a military regime from 1954. Civilian rule was not restored until 1986, and civil war continued for another decade. Almost 40% of people live on less than $2 a day.

CLIMATE

Tropical equatorial/ wet and dry

WEATHER CHART FOR GUATEMALA CITY

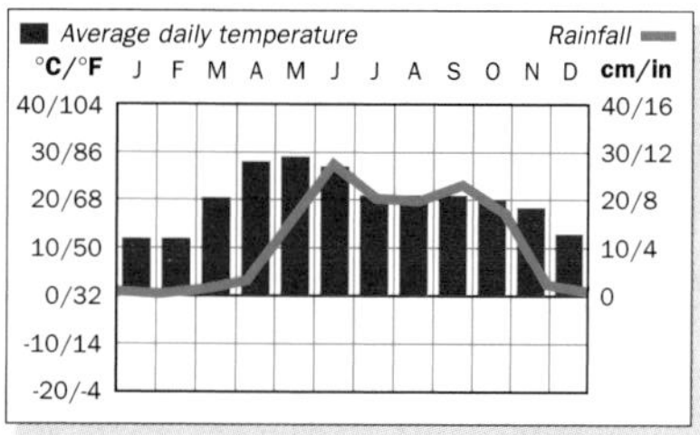

Average daily temperature
Rainfall
°C/°F J F M A M J J A S O N D cm/in
40/104
30/86
20/68
10/50
0/32
-10/14
-20/4
40/16
30/12
20/8
10/4
0

The climate varies with altitude: daytime temperatures average 28°C (82°F) in tropical coast areas and 20°C (68°F) in the more temperate central highlands.

TRANSPORTATION

Drive on right

La Aurora, Guatemala City 939,000 passengers

11 ships 8900 grt

THE TRANSPORTATION NETWORK

4941 km (3070 miles)

74 km (46 miles)

886 km (551 miles)

990 km (615 miles)

Good roads link the major towns. The railroad and two international airports are attracting foreign investment.

TOURISM

Visitors : Population 1:14

880,464 visitors

Little change in 2003

MAIN TOURIST ARRIVALS

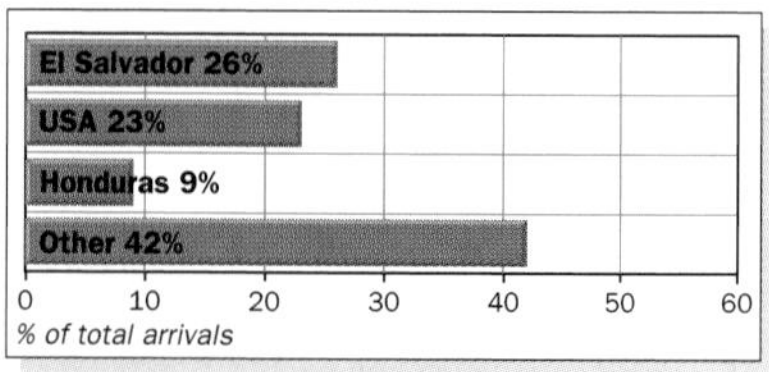

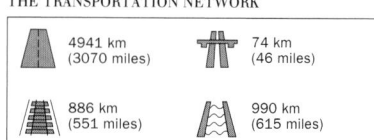

El Salvador 26%
USA 23%
Honduras 9%
Other 42%
0 10 20 30 40 50 60
% of total arrivals

Tourism rapidly revived after the military excesses in the 1980s, but postwar crime, including an increase in mob violence, deters visitors. Mayan ruins are the top attractions.

PEOPLE

Pop. density medium

Quiché, Mam, Cakchiquel, Kekchí, Spanish

113/km² (294/mi²)

THE URBAN/RURAL POPULATION SPLIT

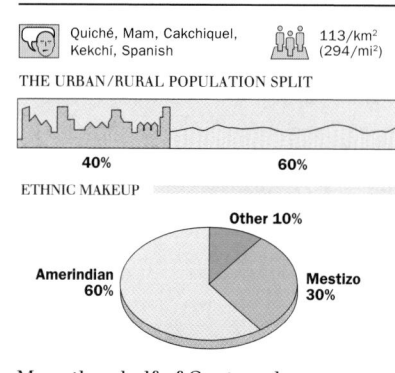

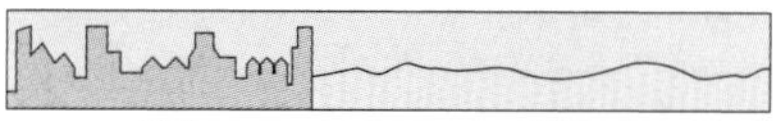

40%
60%

ETHNIC MAKEUP

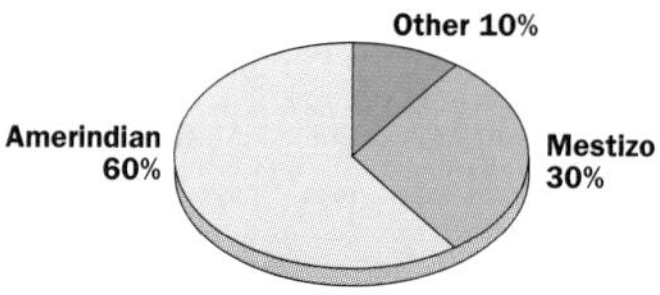

Other 10%
Amerindian 60%
Mestizo 30%

More than half of Guatemalans are Amerindians, descendants of the original Mayas. Culture and language distinguish them from *ladino* groups. *Ladinos* include a white elite, a large mixed-race group, and also Amerindians rejecting traditional dress and language to avoid discrimination. Political power and 65% of land are held by a few *ladino* families. Amerindians mainly live in the highlands, by subsistence farming. In a 1999 plebiscite, *ladinos* rejected proposed reforms recognizing 23 Amerindian languages and the right of Amerindians to have judicial hearings in their own languages.

POLITICS

Multiparty elections

2003/2007

President Oscar Berger Perdomo

AT THE LAST ELECTION

Congress of the Republic 158 seats

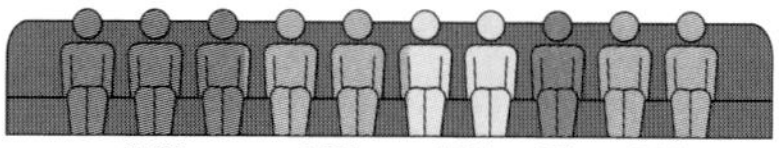

28% GANA
24% FRG
18% UNE
9% PAN
21% Others

GANA = Grand National Alliance **FRG** = Guatemalan Republican Front **UNE** = National Union of Hope **PAN** = National Advancement Party

The military government which came to power in 1954 with US backing brutally suppressed opposition and persecuted the highland Amerindians, until the return of democracy in 1986. Civil war effectively continued until President Arzú of the PAN concluded a peace agreement with the Guatemalan National Revolutionary Unity (URNG) guerrillas in 1996. The 36-year war had claimed 200,000 lives, mostly innocent civilians. Right-wing candidates have performed well in presidential elections since, with Alfonso Portillo of the FRG winning in 1999 and Oscar Berger, the conservative mayor of Guatemala City, in 2003. Efraín Ríos Montt, military ruler in 1982–1986, remains a force in politics, despite being investigated by a Spanish court on charges of genocide. He came a distant third, however, in the 2003 elections.

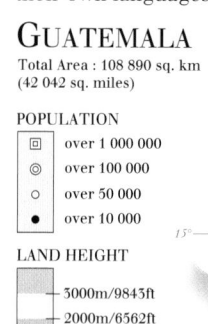

GUATEMALA

Total Area : 108 890 sq. km (42 042 sq. miles)

POPULATION

- over 1 000 000
- over 100 000
- over 50 000
- over 10 000

LAND HEIGHT

- 3000m/9843ft
- 2000m/6562ft
- 1000m/3281ft
- 500m/1640ft
- 200m/656ft
- Sea Level

MEXICO
BELIZE
CARIBBEAN SEA
Gulf of Honduras
HONDURAS
EL SALVADOR
PACIFIC OCEAN
San Pedro
Tikal
Lago Petén Itzá
Flores
La Libertad
Usumacinta
Pasión
Dolores
San Luis
Santa Isabel
Barillas
Chixoy
Cobán
San Pedro Carchá
Cahabón
Polochic
Panzós
Santo Tomás de Castilla
Puerto Barrios
Livingston
Sarstún
Bahía de Amatique
Lago de Izabal
Motagua
Morales
Los Amates
Gualán
Huehuetenango
Rabinal
Salamá
Volcán Tajumulco 4220m
SIERRA MADRE
San Marcos
Totonicapán
Chichicastenango
Quezaltenango
Sololá
Lago de Atitlán
Chimaltenango
Coatepeque
Retalhuleu
Mazatenango
Antigua Guatemala
GUATEMALA CITY
El Progreso
Zacapa
Jalapa
Chiquimula
Esquipulas
Santa Lucía Cotzumalguapa
Pueblo Nuevo Tiquisate
Escuintla
Cuilapa
Jutiapa
Asunción Mita
Chiquimulilla
Nueva Concepción
Moyuta
Puerto San José
91°
90°
89°
92°
17°
16°
15°
14°
N
0 50 km
0 50 miles

WORLD AFFAIRS

Joined UN in 1945

ACS | Geplac | NAM | OAS | San José

Economic relations with the US and neighboring states are priorities. A UN mission was deployed for six months to oversee the 1996 peace accord. Guatemala lays claim to half of Belize.

AID

Recipient

$249m (receipts) | Up 10% in 2002

International aid in recent years has responded to the needs of postwar reconstruction and hurricane relief. In 2004 the government sought to focus donations on tackling the worst cases of malnutrition and poverty.

DEFENSE

Compulsory military service

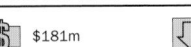

$181m | Down 2% in 2002

A damning "truth commission" report in 1999 found the armed forces and their allies guilty of 93% of human rights violations during the civil war. President Berger is cutting troop numbers by almost half, to 15,500.

ECONOMICS

Inflation 9.9% p.a. (1990–2001)

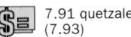

$21bn | 7.91 quetzales (7.93)

SCORE CARD

- WORLD GNP RANKING 62nd
- GNP PER CAPITA $1760
- BALANCE OF PAYMENTS ....–$1.19bn
- INFLATION 8%
- UNEMPLOYMENT 3%

STRENGTHS

Main exports are coffee, sugar, beef, bananas, and cardamom. Privatizations boost foreign investor confidence.

WEAKNESSES

Exports affected by world price changes. Domestic market limited by inequality. Tax evasion. Shaky financial system. Natural disasters. Corruption.

EXPORTS

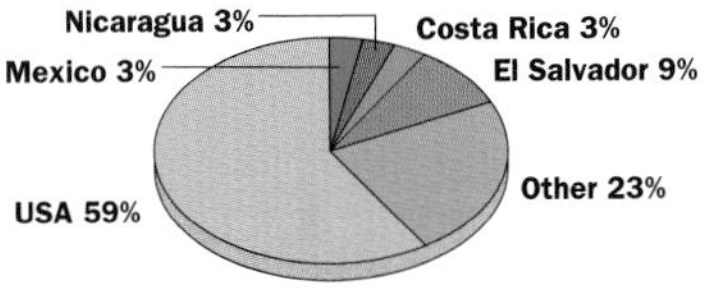
Nicaragua 3%
Costa Rica 3%
Mexico 3%
El Salvador 9%
Other 23%
USA 59%

IMPORTS

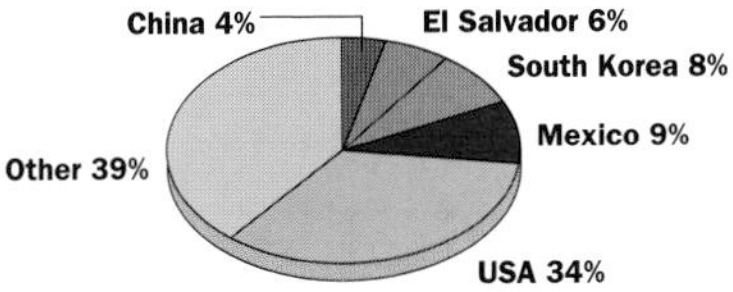
China 4%
El Salvador 6%
South Korea 8%
Mexico 9%
Other 39%
USA 34%

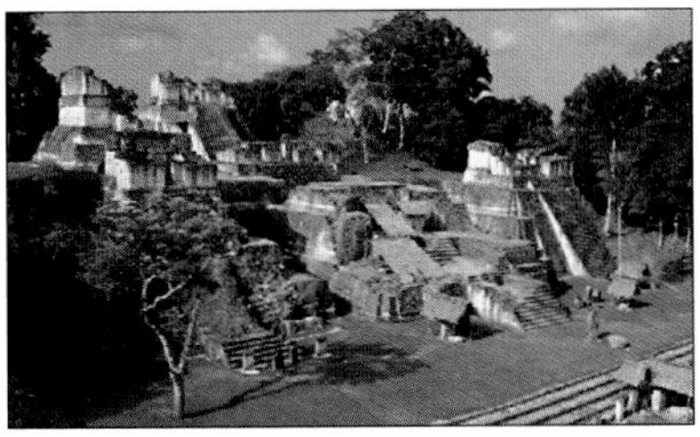

North Acropolis, Tikal, Petén. *One of the largest lowland Mayan cities, Tikal was virtually abandoned by about 900 CE.*

RESOURCES

Electric power 1.3m kW

14,300 tonnes | 20,752 b/d (reserves 197m barrels)

2.5m cattle, 780,000 pigs, 260,000 sheep, 27m chickens | Oil, antimony, lead, tungsten, nickel, copper

Agriculture provides over 20% of GDP and over 50% of export earnings. Cash crops such as coffee are prone to price fluctuations. Nearly four decades of civil war held back the development of oil reserves and hydroelectric potential.

ENVIRONMENT

Sustainability rank: 67th

20% (3% partially protected) | 0.9 tonnes per capita

Forest cover has fallen dramatically since 1954 to 26%, due to intensive agriculture. The excessive use of pesticides, many banned in the US, threatens health. In rural areas indoor pollution from traditional wood-burning, open-fire stoves is a major concern.

MEDIA

TV ownership medium

Daily newspaper circulation 33 per 1000 people

PUBLISHING AND BROADCAST MEDIA

There are 7 daily newspapers, including *Prensa Libre, Siglo Veintiuno, El Periódico,* and the state *Diario de Centroamérica*

5 services: 1 state-owned (currently off air), 4 independent | 1 state-owned service, many independent stations

Powerful groups own the media, but newspapers can be hard-hitting. The four independent TV stations are controlled by a single owner.

CRIME

Moratorium on death penalty

6974 prisoners | Up 20% in 2000

Violence is high. The UN has been allowed to investigate organized crime and human rights abuses from 2004.

EDUCATION

School leaving age: 15

70% | 174,750 students

Education is only for the privileged. Guatemala has one of the lowest literacy rates in Latin America; only 62% of women are literate.

CHRONOLOGY

The site of the Mayan civilization, Guatemala declared independence from Spain in 1821. It became a fully independent nation in 1838.

- **1954** US-backed coup topples reformist government.
- **1966–1984** Counterinsurgency war; highlands "pacification."
- **1986–1993** Return of civilian rule; President Jorge Serrano flees country after abortive "self-coup."
- **1996** Peace deal with URNG guerrillas ends 36 years of civil war.
- **1998** Bishop Juan Gerardi, human rights campaigner, murdered.
- **1999** "Truth Commission" blames army for most human rights abuses.
- **2004** Oscar Berger takes office as president.

G

HEALTH

Welfare state health benefits

1 per 1111 people | Gastrointestinal infections, tuberculosis, heart disease, violence

Health spending is a budget priority as a result of pressure from the UN and multilateral lenders. Gastrointestinal and other infections directly linked to poverty remain the main causes of death.

SPENDING

GDP/cap. increase

CONSUMPTION AND SPENDING

52 per 1000 population | *71 per 1000 population*

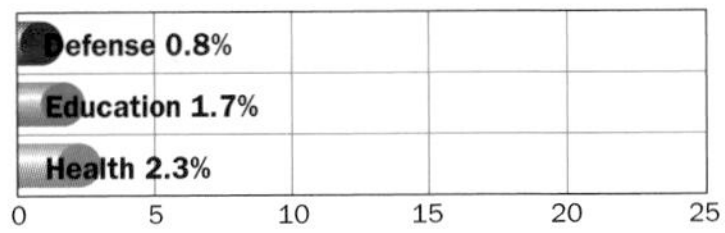
Defense 0.8%
Education 1.7%
Health 2.3%
0
5
10
15
20
25

Defense, Health, Education spending as % of GDP

Poverty in Guatemala has risen since 1980: over half the population now live below the national poverty line. The richest 10% control an estimated 46% of the national wealth.

WORLD RANKING

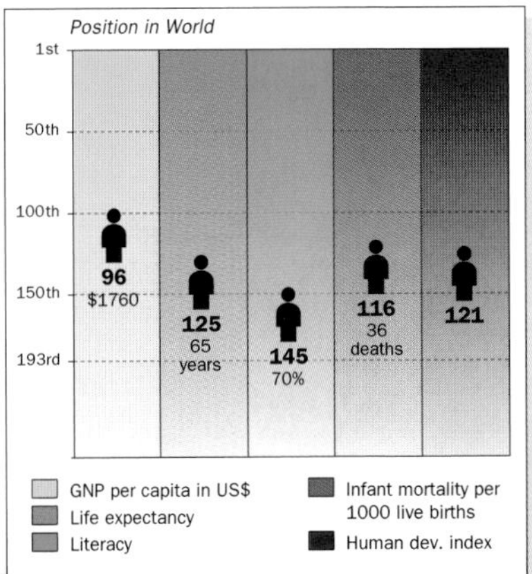
Position in World
1st
50th
100th
150th
193rd
96
$1760
125
65 years
145
70%
116
36 deaths
121
GNP per capita in US$
Life expectancy
Literacy
Infant mortality per 1000 live births
Human dev. index

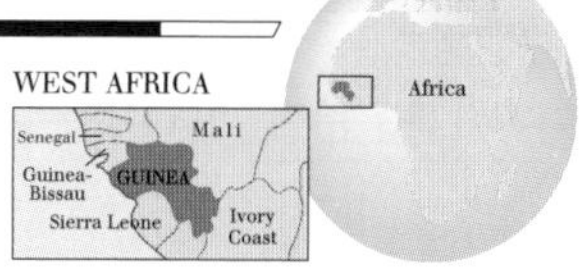
WEST AFRICA
Africa
Senegal
Mali
Guinea-Bissau
GUINEA
Sierra Leone
Ivory Coast

GUINEA

OFFICIAL NAME: Republic of Guinea **CAPITAL:** Conakry
POPULATION: 8.5 million **CURRENCY:** Guinea franc **OFFICIAL LANGUAGE:** French

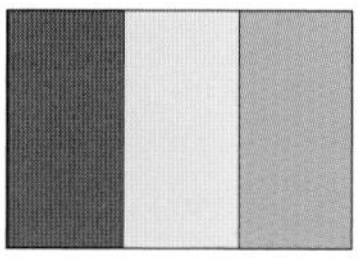

1958 | 1958 | April 3 | RG | 0 | +224 | .gn

GUINEA LIES ON the western coast of Africa. Central highlands, either densely forested or savanna covered, slope down to coastal plains and swamps; the north is semidesert. Military rule from 1984 ended with disputed elections in 1995. Neighboring civil wars have spilled over into domestic conflict in Guinea.

CLIMATE

Tropical monsoon

WEATHER CHART FOR CONAKRY

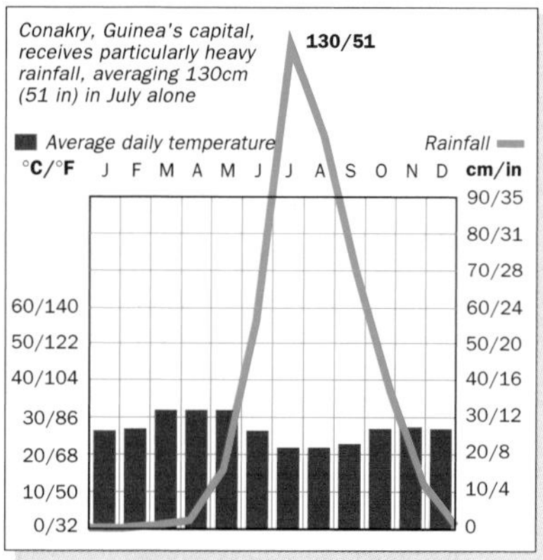
Conakry, Guinea's capital, receives particularly heavy rainfall, averaging 130cm (51 in) in July alone
130/51
Average daily temperature
Rainfall
°C/°F
J F M A M J J A S O N D
cm/in
90/35
80/31
70/28
60/24
50/20
40/16
30/12
20/8
10/4
0
60/140
50/122
40/104
30/86
20/68
10/50
0/32

Dusty *harmattan* winds govern the dry season. A six-month rainy season begins in April.

TRANSPORTATION

Drive on right

Conakry 299,555 passengers

35 ships 11,800 grt

THE TRANSPORTATION NETWORK

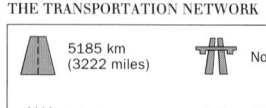

5185 km (3222 miles)

None

1115 km (693 miles)

1295 km (805 miles)

Guinea has no public transportation; most roads are underdeveloped. Trains no longer run; tracks are in disrepair. Domestic airlines use dirt landing strips.

A small mosque in Conakry. *Muslims make up 85% of the population; 8% are Christian. The remainder follow traditional beliefs.*

TOURISM

Visitors : Population 1:198

43,000 visitors

Up 16% in 2002

MAIN TOURIST ARRIVALS

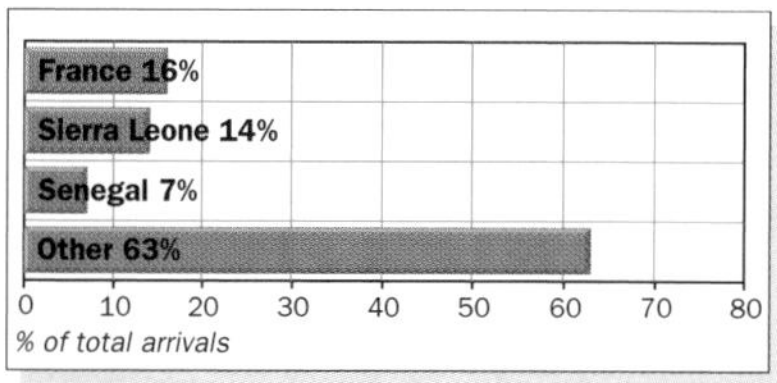
France 16%
Sierra Leone 14%
Senegal 7%
Other 63%
0 10 20 30 40 50 60 70 80
% of total arrivals

Limited infrastructure means that Guinea struggles to exploit the tourist potential of its beaches, scenery, and rich culture.

PEOPLE

Pop. density low

Fulani, Malinke, Soussou, French

35/km² (90/mi²)

THE URBAN/RURAL POPULATION SPLIT

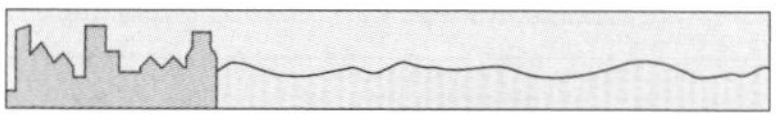
28%
72%

ETHNIC MAKEUP

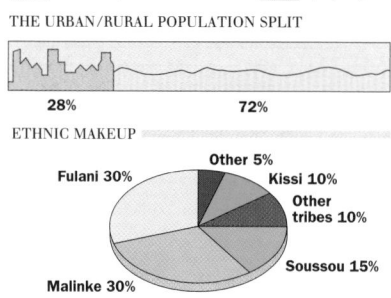

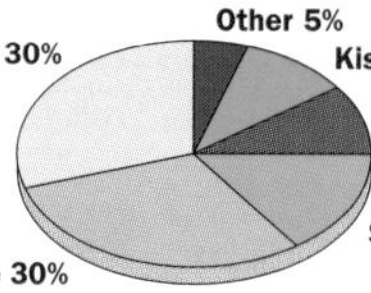
Other 5%
Fulani 30%
Kissi 10%
Other tribes 10%
Soussou 15%
Malinke 30%

Since the death of Marxist dictator Sekou Touré in 1984, traditional rivalries have reemerged between ethnic groups. The two largest groups are the Fulani, based in the highland region of Fouta Djallon, and the Malinke, who lost the power they had held under Touré, and have suffered reprisals.

The extended family system survived the climate of suspicion generated by paid informers under Sekou Touré. Women acquired influence within his Marxist party, but a Muslim revival since 1984 has reversed this trend.

Thousands of refugees, fleeing from conflicts in Liberia and Ivory Coast, are now caught up in fighting in the southern border region; armed Liberian rebels have exacerbated the crisis, along with growing tensions between the Malinke and Guerze ethnic groups.

POLITICS

Multiparty elections

2002/2007

President Lansana Conté

AT THE LAST ELECTION

National Assembly 114 seats

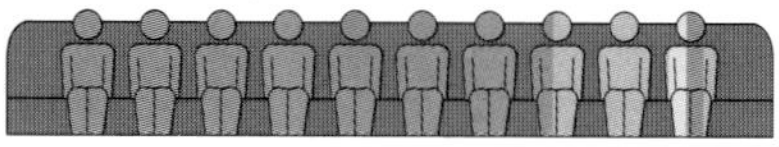
3% PDG
74% PUP
17% UPR
3% UPG
3% Others

PUP = Party of Unity and Progress **UPR** = Union for Progress and Renewal **UPG** = Union for the Progress of Guinea **PDG** = Democratic Party of Guinea

The transition to democracy following the death in 1984 of Marxist dictator Sekou Touré was postponed by the military until 1993. Serious violence broke out that year following the presidential election, amid accusations of vote rigging leveled at the incumbent junta, headed by Gen. Lansana Conté. A disputed victory for Conté's PUP in the 1995 legislative elections was followed by his own reelection in 1998. Fighting escalated into civil war in 2000, with incursions from rebels based in Sierra Leone and Liberia.

The PUP increased its majority in much-delayed legislative polls in July 2002. A prodemocracy conference was outlawed and Conté changed the constitution, enabling his reelection in 2003 in a poll boycotted by the opposition. The PUP is consistently accused of repression and the harassment of opposition politicians. Prime Minister François Fall resigned in 2004, claiming that Conté was blocking all attempts at reform.

WORLD AFFAIRS

Joined UN in 1958

ECOWAS | OIF | AU | OIC | OMVG

Guinea has been deeply involved in regional crises in neighboring Sierra Leone, Liberia, and Ivory Coast. Though relations were symbolically patched up in 2002, tensions remain over the region's porous borders.

AID

Recipient

$250m (receipts)

Down 11% in 2002

In 1969, the World Bank funded the Boké bauxite project, then one of its most ambitious projects. Since 1986, Western aid has grown to finance over 85% of all development projects. The 1997–2000 World Bank/IMF structural reform program foresees an annual growth rate of 5%.

GUINEA

Total Area :
245 857 sq. km
(94 925 sq. miles)

POPULATION

- ⦿ over 500 000
- ○ over 50 000
- ● over 10 000
- • under 10 000

LAND HEIGHT

- 1000m/3281ft
- 500m/1640ft
- 200m/656ft
- Sea Level

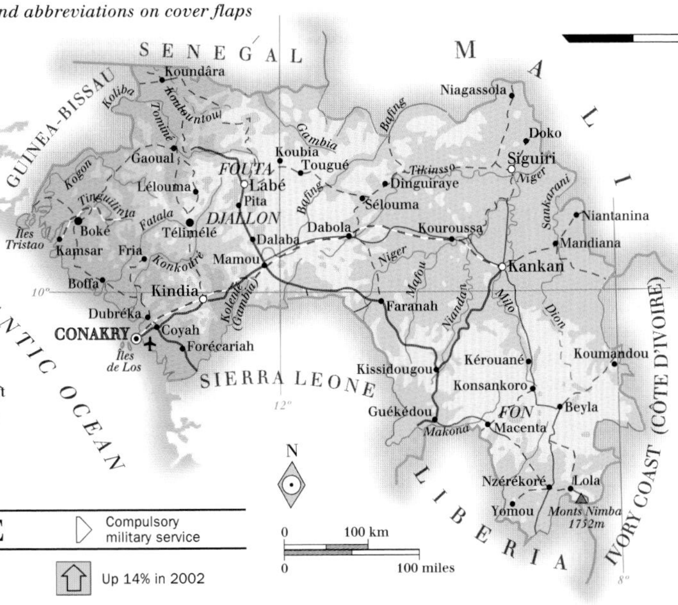
SENEGAL
MALI
GUINEA-BISSAU
ATLANTIC OCEAN
SIERRA LEONE
LIBERIA
IVORY COAST (CÔTE D'IVOIRE)
Koundâra
Niagassola
Doko
Siguiri
Koubia
Tougué
Gaoual
Labé
Pita
Dinguiraye
Séiouma
Lélouma
Boké
Télimélé
Dalaba
Dabola
Kouroussa
Niantanina
Mandiana
Kankan
Kamsar
Fria
Mamou
Boffa
Kindia
Dubréka
CONAKRY
Coyah
Forécariah
Faranah
Kérouané
Koumandou
Kissidougou
Konsankoro
Beyla
Guékédou
Macenta
Nzérékoré
Lola
Yomou
Monts Nimba 1752m
FOUTA DJALLON
FON
Îles Tristao
Îles de Los
Niger
Milo
Niandan
Sankarani
Bafing
Gambia
Konkouré
Tinguilinta
N
0 100 km
0 100 miles

DEFENSE

Compulsory military service

$57m — Up 14% in 2002

The 8500-strong army is the largest branch of the armed forces. Weaponry is supplied by France and the US; the US also operates a military training and assistance program. Guinea channeled arms from Iran to rebel forces in Liberia in 2002–2003.

ECONOMICS

Inflation 5.1% p.a. (1990–2001)

$3.15bn — 2055 Guinea francs (1990)

SCORE CARD

❑ WORLD GNP RANKING	131st
❑ GNP PER CAPITA	$410
❑ BALANCE OF PAYMENTS	–$46m
❑ INFLATION	2.4%
❑ UNEMPLOYMENT	Widespread underemployment

STRENGTHS

Natural resources including bauxite, gold, and diamonds. Major iron ore deposits at Mount Nimba. Good soil and climate give high cash-crop yields.

WEAKNESSES

Chronic instability. Poor infrastructure. Conflict in Liberia has set back major joint projects. Refugee influx a drain on resources. Electricity shortages. Widespread corruption. Falling bauxite revenue and increasing food prices.

EXPORTS

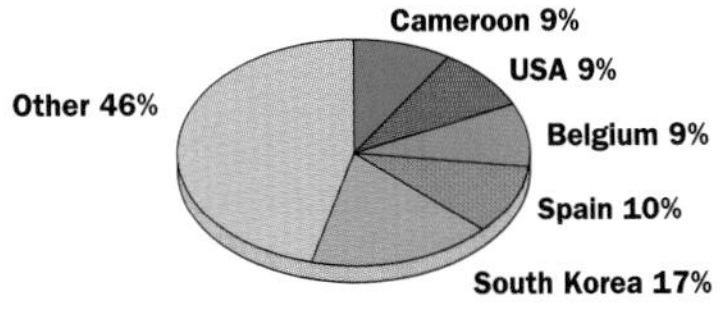
Cameroon 9%
USA 9%
Belgium 9%
Spain 10%
South Korea 17%
Other 46%

IMPORTS

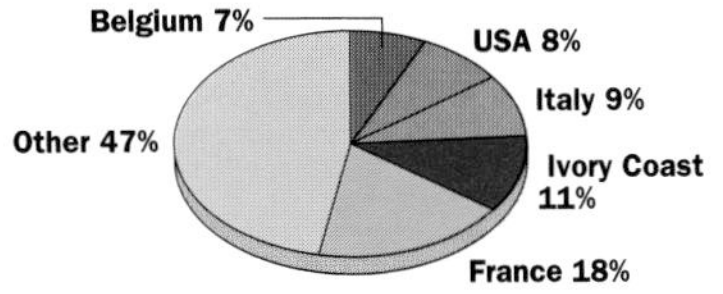
Belgium 7%
USA 8%
Italy 9%
Ivory Coast 11%
France 18%
Other 47%

RESOURCES

Electric power 197,000 kW

- 90,000 tonnes
- Not an oil producer
- 3.28m cattle, 1.2m goats, 1m sheep, 13.5m chickens
- Bauxite, diamonds, gold, iron

Bauxite provides the majority of export earnings, though gold production has increased significantly. Guinea, with 30% of the world's known bauxite reserves, is the world's largest producer after Australia. Demand for electricity for bauxite processing is high.

ENVIRONMENT

Sustainability rank: 98th

0.7% — 0.2 tonnes per capita

Uncontrolled deforestation, particularly of large areas of rainforest, is the major long-term problem.

MEDIA

TV ownership low

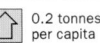

Daily newspaper circulation 2 per 1000 people

PUBLISHING AND BROADCAST MEDIA

There is 1 daily newspaper, the state-owned *Horoya*

1 state-owned service — 1 state-owned service

Guinea's limited broadcast media are state-owned. Private newspapers can be critical of the government, but high printing costs deter publishing.

CRIME

Death penalty in use

3070 prisoners — Crime is rising

The death penalty was reintroduced in 2001 in an attempt to crack down on spiraling crime. Prison conditions are very poor. The unregulated mining industry facilitates money laundering.

CHRONOLOGY

France colonized Guinea in 1890, strongly opposed by the Fulani Muslim empire of Fouta Djallon.

- ❑ **1958** Full independence under Sekou Touré.
- ❑ **1984** Touré dies. Army coup.
- ❑ **1993–1995** Disputed elections.
- ❑ **2000** Cross-border rebel attacks place Guinea in a state of civil war.
- ❑ **2002** PUP wins delayed elections.
- ❑ **2003** Conté reelected president.

EDUCATION

School leaving age: 12

41% — 8151 students

Access to education has improved since the late 1990s, especially for boys. There are two public universities.

HEALTH

No welfare state health benefits

1 per 10,000 people — Malaria, diarrheal and respiratory diseases, tuberculosis

Despite two decades of programs to improve health care, provision is still poor, especially in rural areas. HIV infection is low for sub-Saharan Africa.

SPENDING

GDP/cap. increase

CONSUMPTION AND SPENDING

2 per 1000 population — *3 per 1000 population*

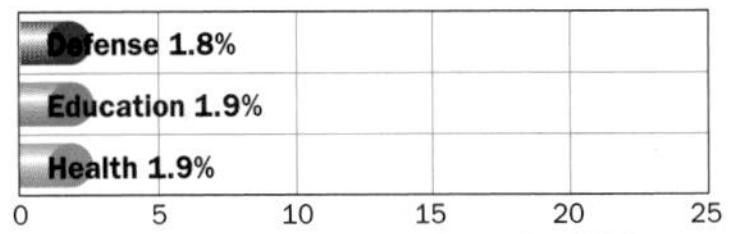
Defense 1.8%
Education 1.9%
Health 1.9%
0
5
10
15
20
25

Defense, Health, Education spending as % of GDP

Private enterprise has brought with it a new business class and Guinea now has some wealthy exiles, but much of the country remains poor and underdeveloped; GNP is only just over $400 per capita.

WORLD RANKING

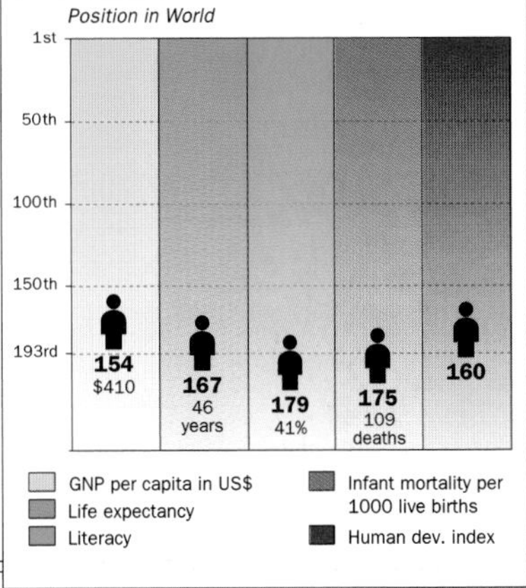
Position in World
1st
50th
100th
150th
193rd
154
$410
167
46 years
179
41%
175
109 deaths
160
GNP per capita in US$
Life expectancy
Literacy
Infant mortality per 1000 live births
Human dev. index

G

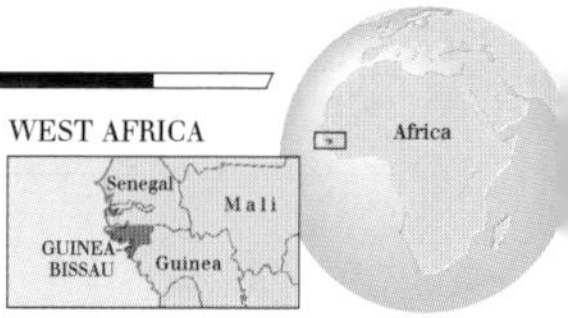
WEST AFRICA
Africa
Senegal
Mali
GUINEA-BISSAU
Guinea

GUINEA-BISSAU

OFFICIAL NAME: Republic of Guinea-Bissau **CAPITAL:** Bissau
POPULATION: 1.5 million **CURRENCY:** CFA franc **OFFICIAL LANGUAGE:** Portuguese

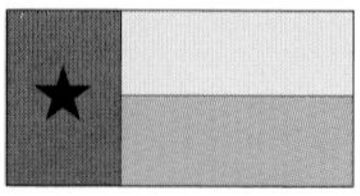

1974 | 1974 | Sept 24 | GNB | 0 | +245 | .gw

LYING ON AFRICA'S west coast, impoverished Guinea-Bissau is a former Portuguese territory. Apart from savanna highlands in the northeast, the country is low-lying. The PAIGC initiated a process of transition to multiparty democracy in 1990, and elections were held in 1994. Since then, the democratic process has been interrupted by a series of army rebellions and military coups, the latest in 2003. Guinea-Bissau remains one of the world's poorest countries.

G

CLIMATE

Tropical monsoon

WEATHER CHART FOR BISSAU

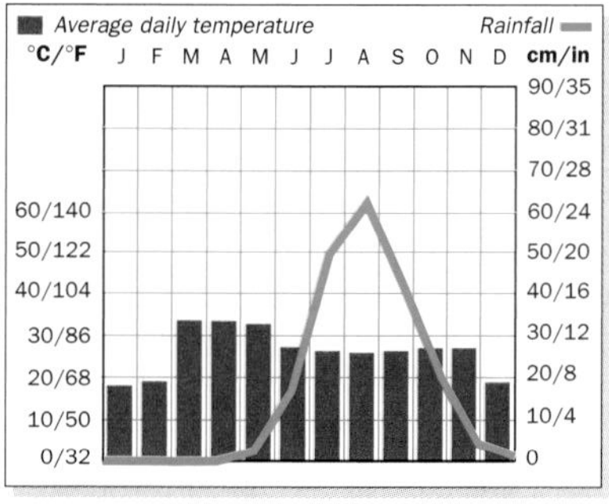
Average daily temperature
Rainfall
°C/°F J F M A M J J A S O N D cm/in
90/35
80/31
70/28
60/140 60/24
50/122 50/20
40/104 40/16
30/86 30/12
20/68 20/8
10/50 10/4
0/32 0

The climate is tropical. The north is affected by the Sahel, the wetter south by the Atlantic. Droughts can occur.

TRANSPORTATION

Drive on right

Bissalanca, Bissau

24 ships
6459 grt

THE TRANSPORTATION NETWORK

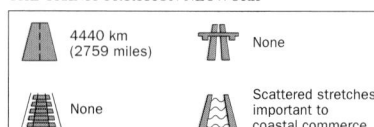

4440 km (2759 miles)

None

None

Scattered stretches important to coastal commerce

The many waterways and islands make water transportation as vital as the roads. Both are being improved.

TOURISM

Visitors : Population 1:188

8000 visitors

No significant change from year to year

MAIN TOURIST ARRIVALS

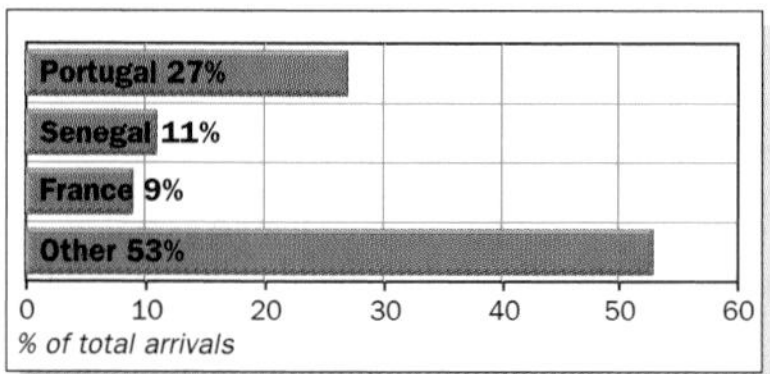
Portugal 27%
Senegal 11%
France 9%
Other 53%
0 10 20 30 40 50 60
% of total arrivals

The lack of tourist facilities means that the country remains a destination for only the most adventurous of travelers.

PEOPLE

Pop. density medium

Portuguese Creole, Balante, Fulani, Malinke, Portuguese

53/km² (138/mi²)

THE URBAN/RURAL POPULATION SPLIT

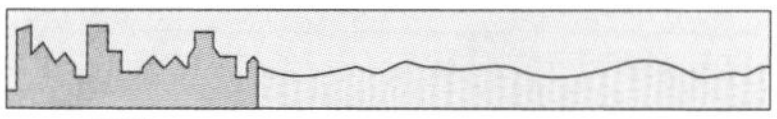
33%
67%

RELIGIOUS PERSUASION

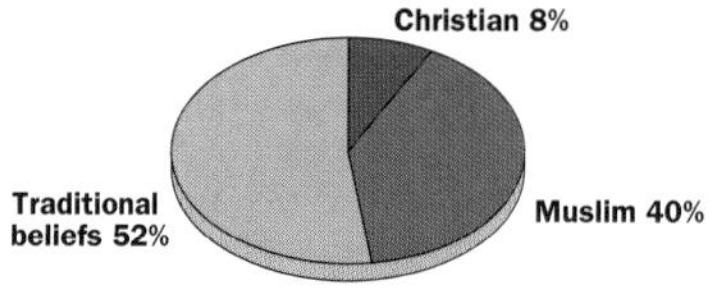
Christian 8%
Traditional beliefs 52%
Muslim 40%

The largest ethnic group is the southern Balante, which forms almost one-third of the population. Mixed-race *mestiço* and European minorities make up just 2% of the population. Though small in number, the *mestiços* – many of whom derive from Cape Verde, Portugal's other former west African colony – still dominate the bureaucracy. Resentment at this, especially among the Balante, who provided most of the PAIGC troops in the independence war, was one cause of the 1980 coup. The majority of the population live and work on small family farms, grouped in self-contained villages. Most of the urban population live in the capital, Bissau, where they face economic hardship and increasing political instability.

POLITICS

Multiparty elections

2004/2008

Interim President Henrique Rosa

AT THE LAST ELECTION

National People's Assembly 102 seats

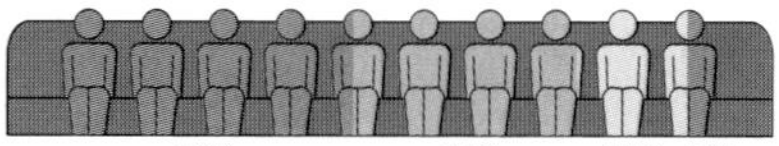
44% PAIGC
34% PRS
17% PUSD
5% Others

PAIGC = African Party for the Independence of Guinea and Cape Verde **PRS** = Party for Social Renewal **PUSD** = United Social Democratic Party

Twenty years of one-party rule ended in 1994 with the holding of multiparty elections. However, opposition groups disputed the ruling PAIGC's victory.

A period of instability led to an army rebellion in 1998 and eight months of fighting between those loyal to President João Bernardo Vieira and to the army chief, Gen. Ansumane Mane; about half the population was displaced as a result. ECOWAS troops intervened and a national unity government was formed, only to be overthrown by an army coup in 1999.

Fresh elections were won by the PRS, and its candidate Kumba Yalla won the presidency in 2000. The erratic Yalla persistently postponed the next set of elections and was overthrown in a coup in 2003. The new military authorities appointed businessman Henrique Rosa interim president. Legislative elections held in 2004 were won by the PAIGC.

WORLD AFFAIRS

Joined UN in 1974

ECOWAS | CPLP | OIF | AU | OIC

Relations with neighboring states are extremely tense due to the activities of various rebel militias on the borders. There is mounting international concern over the lack of effective democracy and reports of repression.

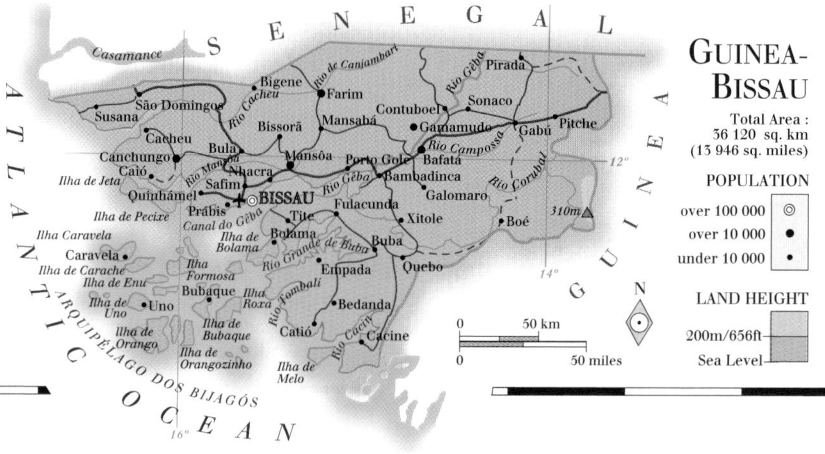
SENEGAL
GUINEA
ATLANTIC OCEAN
ARQUIPÉLAGO DOS BIJAGÓS
Casamance
São Domingos
Susana
Cacheu
Bigene
Farim
Pirada
Sonaco
Contuboel
Gamamudo
Gabú
Pitche
Bissorã
Mansabá
Mansôa
Porto Gole
Bafatá
Bambadinca
Galomaro
Canchungo
Caió
Bula
Nhacra
Safim
BISSAU
Quinhámel
Prábis
Fulacunda
Xitole
Boé
310m
Tite
Bolama
Buba
Empada
Quebo
Bedanda
Catió
Cacine
Ilha de Jeta
Ilha de Pecixe
Ilha Caravela
Caravela
Ilha de Carache
Ilha de Enu
Ilha de Uno
Uno
Ilha de Orango
Ilha Formosa
Bubaque
Ilha Roxa
Ilha de Bubaque
Ilha de Orangozinho
Ilha de Meio
Ilha de Bolama
Canal do Gêba
Rio Cacheu
Rio Gêba
Rio Corubal
Rio Grande de Buba
Rio Tombali
Rio Cacine
Rio Mansôa
Rio Campossa
Rio de Canjambari
12°
14°
16°
GUINEA-BISSAU
Total Area : 36 120 sq. km (13 946 sq. miles)
POPULATION
over 100 000
over 10 000
under 10 000
LAND HEIGHT
200m/656ft
Sea Level
0 50 km
0 50 miles
N

AID

Recipient

$59m (receipts)

Little change in 2002

After the EU, Portugal is the most important single aid donor. Balance-of-payments support is critical to the economy. Export earnings are small compared with the costs of imports and debt servicing. Donor support was frozen in 1991 because of the country's World Bank arrears, but the government pushed ahead with economic reforms begun in the mid-1980s, and the World Bank and the IMF agreed a $790 million debt-relief package in 2001. Education, infrastructure, and health care are the main targets of project aid.

DEFENSE

Compulsory military service

$3m

No change in 2002

There are around 9000 troops. The army led coups in 1980, 1999, and 2003, and suffered internal rebellions in 1998 and 2000, continuing a history of military interference in politics. ECOWAS soldiers have intervened to restore order on a number of occasions.

ECONOMICS

Inflation 29% p.a. (1990–2001)

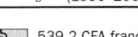

$186m

539.2 CFA francs (571.2)

SCORE CARD

- WORLD GNP RANKING 185th
- GNP PER CAPITA $130
- BALANCE OF PAYMENTS .... –$35m
- INFLATION 0.9%
- UNEMPLOYMENT ....Widespread underemployment

STRENGTHS

Minimal at present, but good potential in fisheries and timber, and for hydropower and offshore oil.

WEAKNESSES

Instability. Lack of sufficiency in rice staple. Fish stocks depleted by poaching. Few exports, mainly cashew nuts, groundnuts. Minimal industry. High illiteracy. Poor state economic management.

EXPORTS

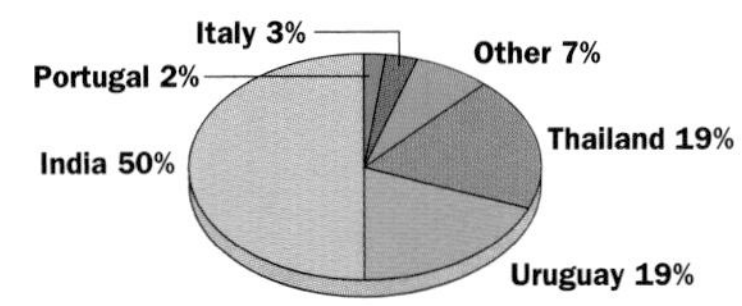
Italy 3%
Portugal 2%
Other 7%
Thailand 19%
India 50%
Uruguay 19%

IMPORTS

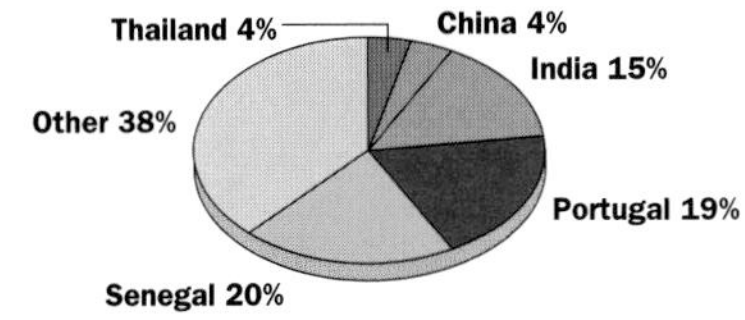
Thailand 4%
China 4%
India 15%
Other 38%
Portugal 19%
Senegal 20%

***Bafatá, the chief town** in central Guinea-Bissau. It lies on the Gêba River and is also an important inland port.*

RESOURCES

Electric power 21,000 kW

5000 tonnes

Oil reserves not yet exploited

520,000 cattle, 360,000 pigs, 1.5m chickens

Bauxite, phosphates, oil

Fish and timber are the main natural resources, but local exploitation is only a tiny proportion of the sustainable levels. There is considerable potential for developing hydropower and for offshore oil production.

ENVIRONMENT

Sustainability rank: 127th

None

0.2 tonnes per capita

Drought and locust plagues are serious natural hazards. A small population and minimal industry mean that there are few serious environmental problems.

MEDIA

TV ownership low

Daily newspaper circulation 5 per 1000 people

PUBLISHING AND BROADCAST MEDIA

There is one daily newspaper, *Nô Printcha*, published by the government

1 state-owned service

2 services: 1 state-owned, 1 independent

Three independent newspapers publish intermittently due to high costs. There is one state-owned TV channel. The Portuguese-run RTP-Africa broadcasts two hours of programming a day.

CRIME

No death penalty

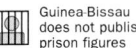

Guinea-Bissau does not publish prison figures

Crime is rising

Human rights abuses increased during the late 1990s, but reported crime levels are relatively low. Separatist conflict in neighboring Senegal makes the border region dangerous.

EDUCATION

School leaving age: 12

40%

463 students

War damaged schools and cut teacher numbers. Female education is a priority. The first universities opened in 2003.

CHRONOLOGY

Explored by the Portuguese in the 15th century, Portuguese Guinea was established in 1879. A war for independence began in the 1960s.

- **1974** Independence. PAIGC rules.
- **1980** Military coup.
- **1990** Multiparty politics accepted.
- **1994** Multiparty elections.
- **1998** Army rebellion led by Gen. Mane. ECOWAS intervention.
- **1999** Transitional government. May, army seizes power. November, PRS defeats PAIGC in elections.
- **2003** President Kumba Yalla overthrown in military coup.
- **2004** PAIGC returns to power.

G

HEALTH

No welfare state health benefits

1 per 5000 people

Parasitic, diarrheal, and communicable diseases, malaria

Guinea-Bissau's health statistics are among the world's worst, due partly to the minimal medical facilities. What had been available was severely affected by civil war, leading to outbreaks of diseases such as meningitis. In mid-2000 the AfDB provided $500,000 in funding for an emergency health program.

SPENDING

GDP/cap. increase

CONSUMPTION AND SPENDING

6 per 1000 population

9 per 1000 population

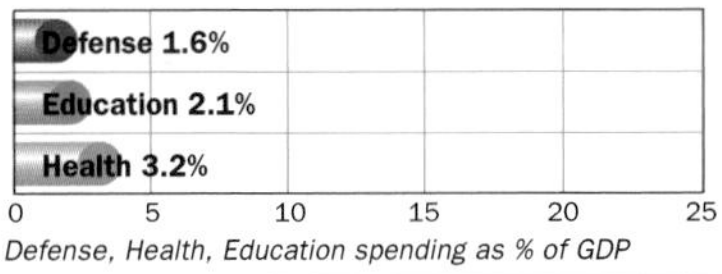
Defense 1.6%
Education 2.1%
Health 3.2%
0
5
10
15
20
25

Defense, Health, Education spending as % of GDP

Living conditions for the majority of Guinea-Bissau's people are extremely poor; around 50% of the population are unable to meet their basic needs. The tiny elite is mainly *mestiço*.

WORLD RANKING

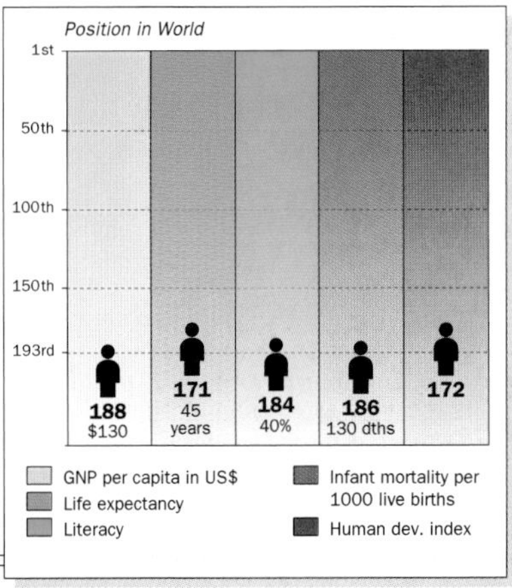
Position in World
1st
50th
100th
150th
193rd
188
$130
171
45
years
184
40%
186
130 dths
172
GNP per capita in US$
Life expectancy
Literacy
Infant mortality per 1000 live births
Human dev. index

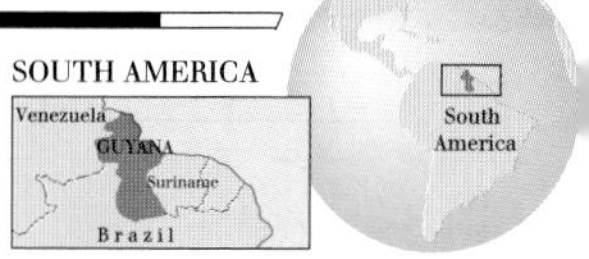
SOUTH AMERICA
Venezuela
GUYANA
Suriname
Brazil
South America

GUYANA

OFFICIAL NAME: Cooperative Republic of Guyana **CAPITAL:** Georgetown
POPULATION: 765,000 **CURRENCY:** Guyana dollar **OFFICIAL LANGUAGE:** English

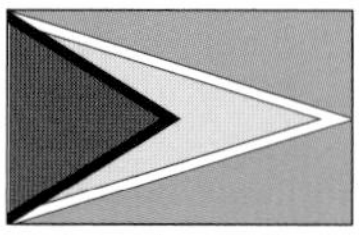

1966 | 1966 | Feb 23 | GUY | -4 | +592 | .gy

LYING ON THE NORTHERN EDGE of South America, Guyana stretches 600 km (375 miles) from dense tropical rainforests, through broad savanna and mountains dotted with waterfalls, to the narrow Atlantic coastal plain where most of the population lives. A British colony from 1814 until independence in 1966, Guyana has closer ties with the mostly anglophone Caribbean than with its Spanish-, Portuguese-, and Dutch-speaking neighbors.

POLITICS

Multiparty elections

2001/2006

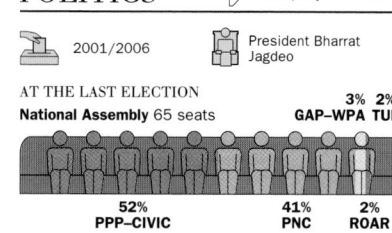

President Bharrat Jagdeo

AT THE LAST ELECTION

National Assembly 65 seats

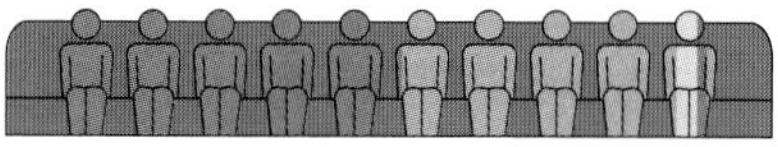
3% GAP–WPA
2% TUF
52% PPP–CIVIC
41% PNC
2% ROAR

PPP–CIVIC = People's Progressive Party–CIVIC
PNC = People's National Congress
GAP–WPA = Guyana Action Party–Working People's Alliance
ROAR = Rise, Organize, and Rebuild **TUF** = The United Force

The success of the PPP in 1992, in what was widely seen as the first fair poll since independence, ended PNC dominance. Politics since has been characterized by serious animosity between the two main parties. The PNC violently contested the succession of Janet Jagan as president in 1997 on the death of her husband, veteran PPP leader Cheddi; open hostility erupted once again in 2001 when Bharrat Jagdeo won the presidency. Tensions eased after the death of PNC leader and ex-president Desmond Hoyte in 2003, but significant divisions remain.

G

CLIMATE

Tropical equatorial

WEATHER CHART FOR GEORGETOWN

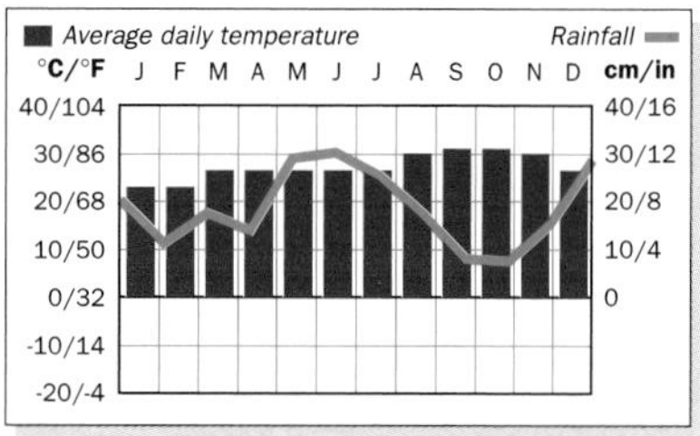
Average daily temperature
Rainfall
°C/°F J F M A M J J A S O N D cm/in
40/104 40/16
30/86 30/12
20/68 20/8
10/50 10/4
0/32 0
-10/14
-20/-4

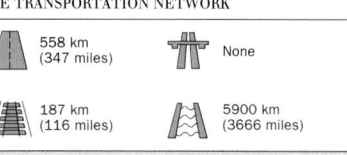

The lowlands are very humid, with a constant temperature. The highlands are a little cooler, especially at night.

TRANSPORTATION

Drive on left

Cheddi Jagan International, Georgetown 270,500 passengers

59 ships 15,169 grt

THE TRANSPORTATION NETWORK

558 km (347 miles)	None
187 km (116 miles)	5900 km (3666 miles)

Travel to the interior is best by air or river; most paved roads are coastal. There is only one international airport.

TOURISM

Visitors : Population 1:7.4

104,000 visitors

Up 10% in 2002

MAIN TOURIST ARRIVALS

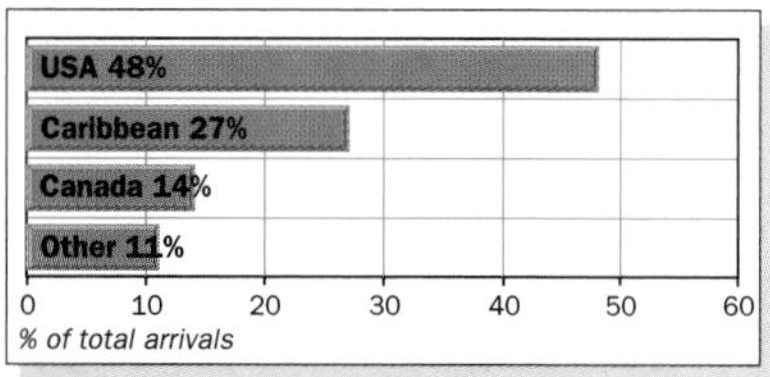
USA 48%
Caribbean 27%
Canada 14%
Other 11%
0 10 20 30 40 50 60
% of total arrivals

The government promotes tourism, but the number of tourists is modest. "Guyana" means "Land of Many Waters"; the Kaieteur Falls are among the world's most impressive. Old Dutch wooden architecture characterizes Georgetown.

Modest homes, Georgetown. *Most buildings are made of wood. The cathedral is one of the world's tallest freestanding wooden buildings.*

PEOPLE

Pop. density low

English Creole, Hindi, Tamil, Amerindian languages, English

4/km² (10/mi²)

THE URBAN/RURAL POPULATION SPLIT

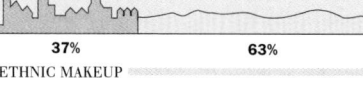

37%
63%

ETHNIC MAKEUP

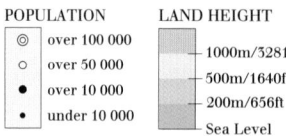

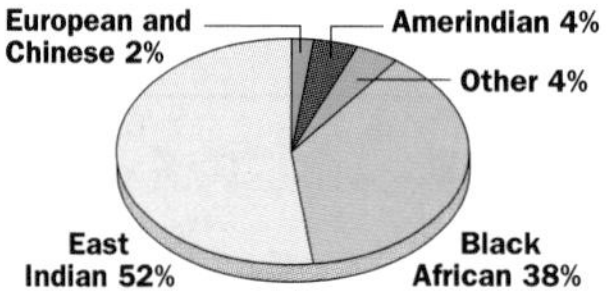
European and Chinese 2%
Amerindian 4%
Other 4%
East Indian 52%
Black African 38%

Guyana is a complex multiracial society. Tension exists between the Afro-Guyanese, descended from slaves brought over in the 17th to 19th centuries, and the Indo-Guyanese, descendants of laborers brought from India in the 19th century. This is currently displayed in the hostility existing between the PNC, representing Afro-Guyanese, and the PPP, traditionally representing the Indo-Guyanese.

GUYANA

Total Area : 214 970 sq. km (83 000 sq. miles)

POPULATION	LAND HEIGHT
over 100 000	1000m/3281ft
over 50 000	500m/1640ft
over 10 000	200m/656ft
under 10 000	Sea Level

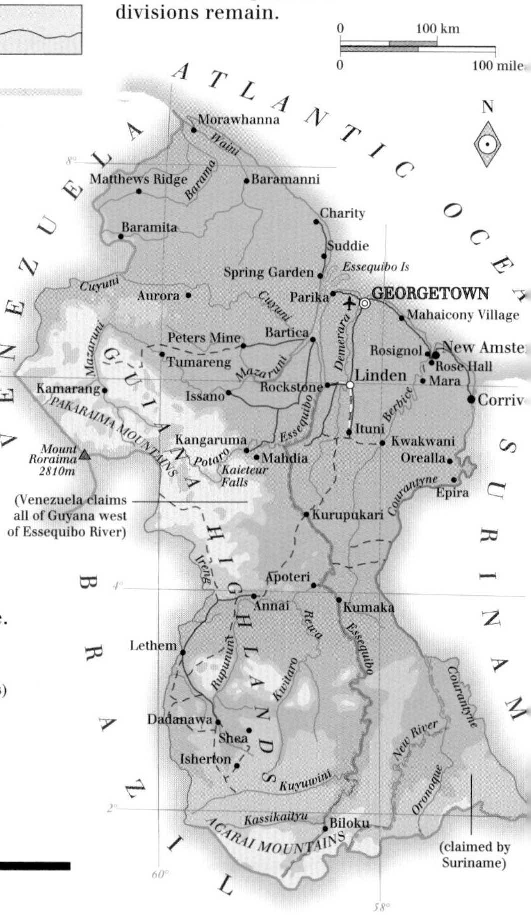
0 100 km
0 100 miles
ATLANTIC OCEAN
N
Morawhanna
Waini
Matthews Ridge
Barama
Baramanni
Charity
Baramita
Suddie
Essequibo Is
Spring Garden
VENEZUELA
Cuyuni
Aurora
Parika
GEORGETOWN
Mahaicony Village
Peters Mine
Bartica
Tumareng
Mazaruni
Demerara
Rosignol
New Amsterdam
Rose Hall
Linden
Mara
Kamarang
Issano
Rockstone
Corriverton
PAKARAIMA MOUNTAINS
GUIANA HIGHLANDS
Ituni
Berbice
Kangaruma
Kwakwani
Mount Roraima 2810m
Potaro
Mahdia
Oreallia
Kaieteur Falls
Epira
Courantyne
(Venezuela claims all of Guyana west of Essequibo River)
Kurupukari
SURINAME
Ireng
Apoteri
BRAZIL
Annai
Kumaka
Rewa
Lethem
Rupununi
Kwitaro
Essequibo
Courantyne
Dadanawa
Shea
New River
Isherton
Kuyuwini
Oronoque
Kassikaityu
Biloku
ACARAI MOUNTAINS
(claimed by Suriname)
60°
58°

WORLD AFFAIRS

Joined UN in 1966

ACS | OIC | Caricom | Comm | OAS

Guyana has long-standing territorial disputes with Venezuela and Suriname, both of which flared up in 1999–2000. Closer integration with the Caribbean is also a major concern.

AID

Recipient

US$65m (receipts)

Down 33% in 2002

Most aid comes from the IDB, the UK, and the US. Recent grants covered public health projects, business development, and protection of the rainforest.

DEFENSE

No compulsory military service

US$5m

Down 17% in 2002

The security forces, which include a small land army, benefit from financial support and training provided by the US and UK governments.

ECONOMICS

Inflation 12% p.a. (1990–2001)

US$656m

179 Guyana dollars (179)

SCORE CARD

❑ World GNP Ranking	164th
❑ GNP per Capita	US$860
❑ Balance of Payments	–US$111m
❑ Inflation	5.3%
❑ Unemployment	9%

Strengths

Diverse exports: gold, rice, sugar, diamonds, bauxite, and timber production. Debt reduction agreed with multilateral agencies.

Weaknesses

Political instability dents investor confidence. Bauxite industry weakened by departure of major US investor, Alcoa. Sugar exports threatened by end of preferential access to EU markets. High unemployment. Narcotics trade and rising crime.

EXPORTS

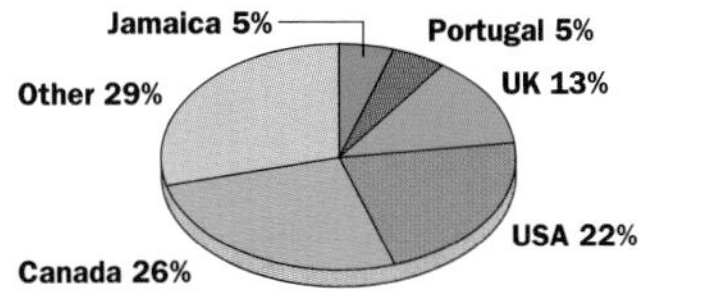

Jamaica 5%
Portugal 5%
Other 29%
UK 13%
USA 22%
Canada 26%

IMPORTS

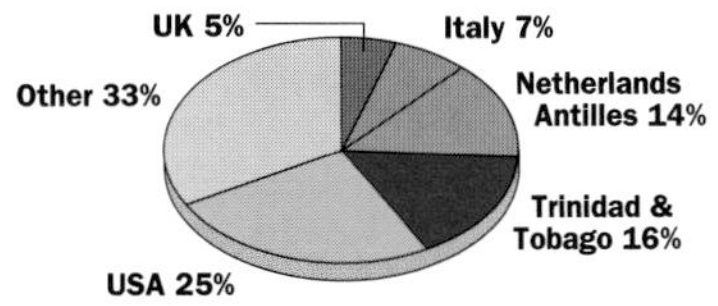

UK 5%
Italy 7%
Other 33%
Netherlands Antilles 14%
Trinidad & Tobago 16%
USA 25%

RESOURCES

Electric power 302,000 kW

54,013 tonnes

Minimal oil production

130,000 sheep, 110,000 cattle, 21.3m chickens

Gold, diamonds, bauxite, gemstones, oil, manganese, uranium

Gold, diamonds, bauxite, and timber are major resources. Despite oil prospecting and HEP potential, most energy comes from petroleum imports. The erratic power supply has improved, but the loss-making privatized electricity firm was renationalized after four years in 2003.

ENVIRONMENT

Not available

0.3%

2.1 tonnes per capita

The state of disrepair of the 18th-century sea defense system endangers the urbanized coastline that lies below sea level. Commercial logging threatens to deplete the rainforest. The pollution of rivers caused by mining activities is now a serious problem.

MEDIA

TV ownership medium

Daily newspaper circulation 75 per 1000 people

PUBLISHING AND BROADCAST MEDIA

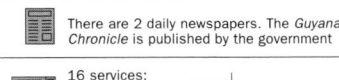

There are 2 daily newspapers. The *Guyana Chronicle* is published by the government

16 services: 1 state-owned, 15 independent

1 state-owned service

The government owns a TV service and the sole radio station, and publishes a daily newspaper. Many private newspapers and TV channels exist.

CRIME

Death penalty in use

1507 prisoners

Thefts increased in 2000–2001

The police are strongly criticized for corruption and ineffectiveness in the face of rising urban crime. Serious violence between PNC and PPP–CIVIC supporters erupted in 1998, 1999, and 2001.

EDUCATION

School leaving age: 15

97%

9100 students

Education is based on the former British system. Entry to high schools is by examination at 11 years. There is a state-financed university, though many students go to the US or the UK.

HEALTH

Welfare state health benefits

1 per 5000 people

Heart diseases, violence, accidents, cancers

Nearly all of the population have access to the mainly state-run health service, though this is hindered by poor transportation links.

CHRONOLOGY

During the 17th and 18th centuries, the Dutch founded three colonies, Essequibo, Demerara, and Berbice, in the region. In 1814, these came under British control, and were later combined to form British Guiana.

- ❑ **1953** First universal elections won by PPP under Cheddi Jagan; parliament later suspended by UK.
- ❑ **1966** Independence from UK.
- ❑ **1973** PPP boycotts parliament, accusing PNC of electoral fraud.
- ❑ **1992** Fair elections won by PPP. Cheddi Jagan president.
- ❑ **1997–1998** Jagan dies in office; PNC rejects his widow's election victory. Political crisis.
- ❑ **1999** Caricom-brokered peace deal. Janet Jagan resigns; Bharrat Jagdeo takes over as president.
- ❑ **2001** Jagdeo and PPP reelected. Political violence flares again.

SPENDING

GDP/cap. increase

CONSUMPTION AND SPENDING

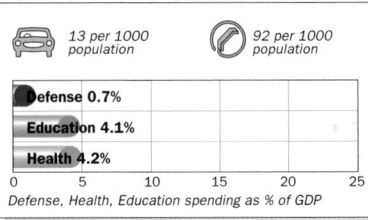

13 per 1000 population

92 per 1000 population

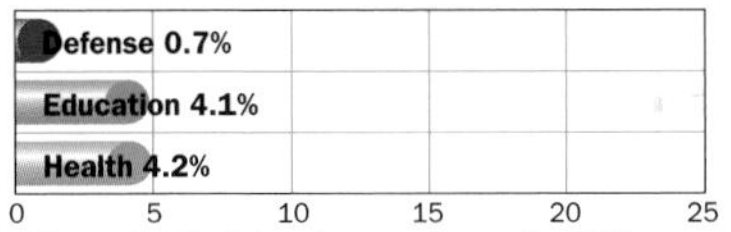

Defense 0.7%
Education 4.1%
Health 4.2%
0
5
10
15
20
25

Defense, Health, Education spending as % of GDP

Significant urban and rural poverty in Guyana has forced the government to make provision in the budget for poverty alleviation. Redundancies in the public sector exacerbate the problem. The poorest group in society are Amerindian subsistence farmers. There are a few very affluent urban families who derive their wealth not only from business but also from rural farming interests.

WORLD RANKING

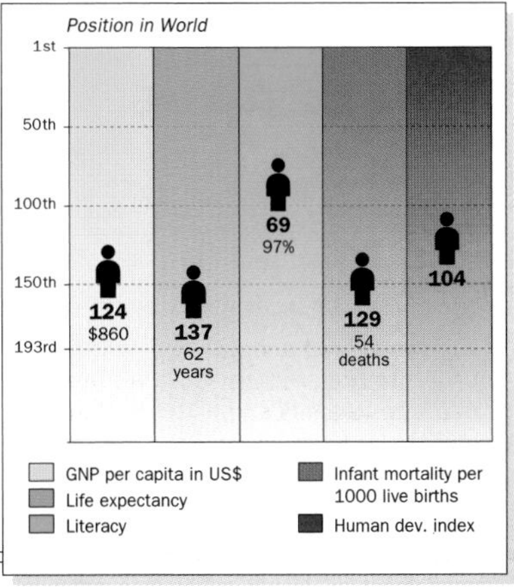

Position in World
1st
50th
100th
150th
193rd
124
$860
137
62
years
69
97%
129
54
deaths
104
GNP per capita in US$
Life expectancy
Literacy
Infant mortality per 1000 live births
Human dev. index

G

HAITI

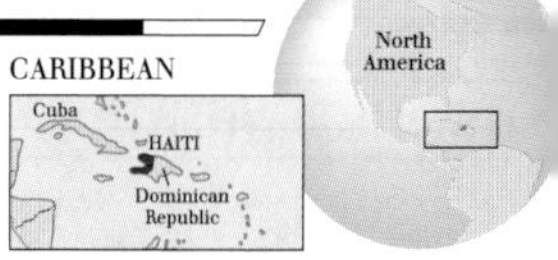
North America
CARIBBEAN
Cuba
HAITI
Dominican Republic

OFFICIAL NAME: Republic of Haiti **CAPITAL:** Port-au-Prince **POPULATION:** 8.3 million
CURRENCY: Gourde **OFFICIAL LANGUAGES:** French and French Creole

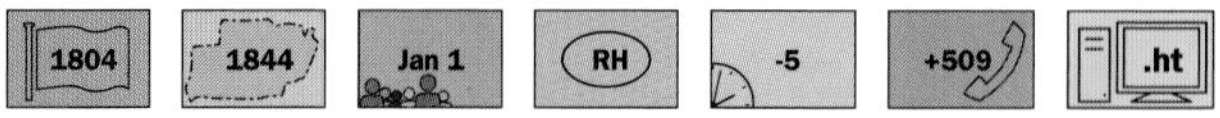
1804
1844
Jan 1
RH
-5
+509
.ht

HAITI OCCUPIES the western third of the Caribbean island of Hispaniola. A colony of Spain and then of France, in 1804 it was the first Caribbean state to become independent, and has been in a state of political chaos virtually ever since. Democracy did not materialize with the exile of the dictator Jean-Claude Duvalier in 1986. Since then, a series of coups, US military intervention, and popular uprisings have resulted in periodic anarchy and endemic poverty.

CLIMATE

Tropical equatorial/oceanic

WEATHER CHART FOR PORT-AU-PRINCE

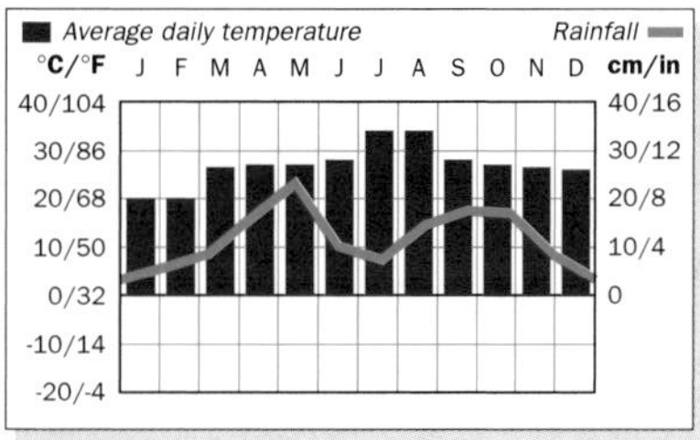
Average daily temperature
Rainfall
°C/°F
J F M A M J J A S O N D
cm/in
40/104
30/86
20/68
10/50
0/32
-10/14
-20/-4
40/16
30/12
20/8
10/4
0

Humidity is lower than the Caribbean average, as Haiti lies in the rain shadow of Hispaniola's central mountains.

TRANSPORTATION

Drive on right

Mais Gaté, Port-au-Prince 991,912 passengers

5 ships 1300 grt

THE TRANSPORTATION NETWORK

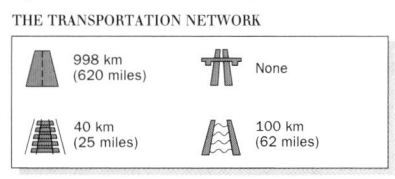

998 km (620 miles)	None
40 km (25 miles)	100 km (62 miles)

Roads are poor, especially in the interior. Ferries provide the easiest access to the southern peninsula.

TOURISM

Visitors : Population 1:58

142,000 visitors

Up 1% in 2001

MAIN TOURIST ARRIVALS

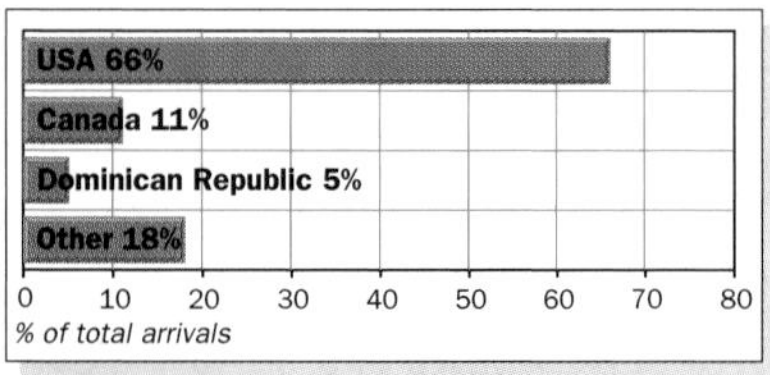
USA 66%
Canada 11%
Dominican Republic 5%
Other 18%
0 10 20 30 40 50 60 70 80
% of total arrivals

Haiti's location, history, and culture provided much of its attraction for tourists in the 1960s and 1970s. Political instability and violence since the 1980s, however, have led to the near collapse of the industry.

PEOPLE

Pop. density high

French Creole, French

301/km² (780/mi²)

THE URBAN/RURAL POPULATION SPLIT

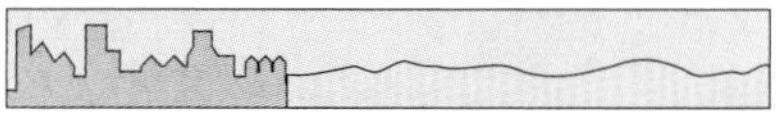
37%
63%

RELIGIOUS PERSUASION

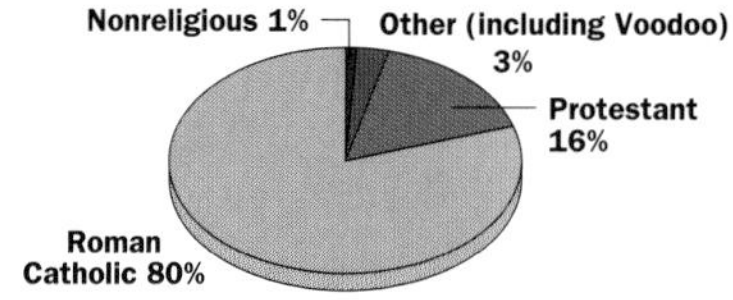
Nonreligious 1%
Other (including Voodoo) 3%
Protestant 16%
Roman Catholic 80%

Most Haitians are of African descent; a few have European roots, primarily French. Haiti is the poorest country in the Americas. Social tensions run high, and political repression and a collapsing economy have led many to emigrate legally, or illegally, to North America or elsewhere in the Caribbean, particularly the Dominican Republic; one in eight Haitians lives abroad. As well as being Christians, a majority of Haitians practice voodoo, which was given the status of an official religion only in 2003.

POLITICS

Multiparty elections

L. House 2000/2005
U. House 2000/2005

Interim President Boniface Alexandre

AT THE LAST ELECTION

Chamber of Deputies 83 seats

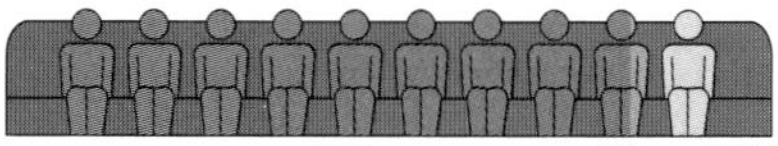
87% Lavalas coalition
2% Vacant
11% Others

Senate 27 seats

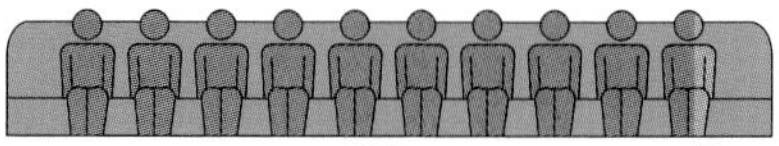
96% Lavalas coalition
4% Others

A wealthy elite, backed by the military, supported the Duvalier dictatorships and regularly financed coups after "Baby Doc" Duvalier's overthrow in 1986. Jean-Bertrand Aristide won the first democratic elections in 1990, but was overthrown by a coup in 1991. US forces intervened to restore him in 1994. His chief adviser René Préval, who held the presidency in 1996–2000, became mired in conflict with the legislature. Aristide's reelection in 2000 was disputed by the opposition and a period of political stalemate ensued; mediation by the OAS and Caricom failed. Mounting protests in 2003 led to armed uprising in 2004; Aristide resigned the presidency and order was only restored by the arrival of a multinational force headed by the US and France. Gerard Latortue was appointed as interim prime minister and Boniface Alexandre as interim president.

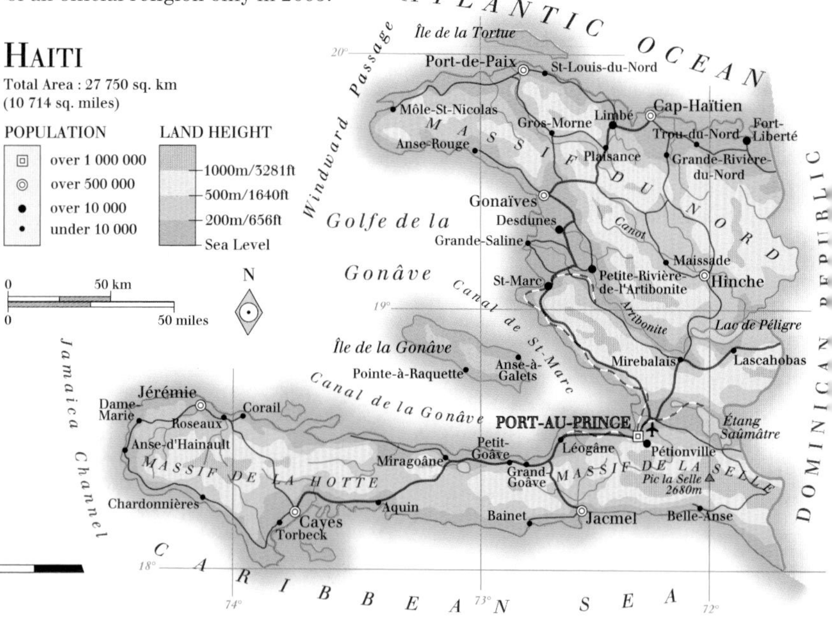
HAITI
Total Area : 27 750 sq. km
(10 714 sq. miles)
POPULATION
over 1 000 000
over 500 000
over 10 000
under 10 000
LAND HEIGHT
1000m/3281ft
500m/1640ft
200m/656ft
Sea Level
0 50 km
0 50 miles
N
ATLANTIC OCEAN
Île de la Tortue
Windward Passage
Port-de-Paix
St-Louis-du-Nord
Môle-St-Nicolas
Cap-Haïtien
Fort-Liberté
Limbé
Gros-Morne
Trou-du-Nord
Anse-Rouge
Plaisance
Grande-Rivière-du-Nord
MASSIF DU NORD
Gonaïves
Desdunes
Golfe de la Gonâve
Grande-Saline
Maïssade
St-Marc
Petite-Rivière-de-l'Artibonite
Hinche
Canal de St-Marc
Lac de Péligre
Île de la Gonâve
Mirebalais
Lascahobas
Pointe-à-Raquette
Anse-à-Galets
Canal de la Gonâve
Jamaica Channel
Jérémie
Dame-Marie
Corail
Roseaux
PORT-AU-PRINCE
Étang Saumâtre
Anse-d'Hainault
Pétionville
MASSIF DE LA HOTTE
Miragoâne
Petit-Goâve
Léogâne
Grand-Goâve
MASSIF DE LA SELLE
Pic la Selle 2680m
Chardonnières
Aquin
Cayes
Torbeck
Bainet
Jacmel
Belle-Anse
CARIBBEAN SEA
DOMINICAN REPUBLIC

WORLD AFFAIRS

Joined UN in 1945

ACS | ACP | Caricom | OAS | WTO

A long history of political instability has led to Haiti's isolation in world affairs. The US has intervened militarily on several occasions to impose order. UN peacekeepers arrived in June 2004.

AID

Recipient

$156m (receipts) — Down 9% in 2002

Initial donations for Haiti's reconstruction were reluctant, but at a second donor conference in July 2004 pledges were dramatically increased to a total of $1.5 billion over the next two years.

DEFENSE

No compulsory military service

$31m — Down 14% in 2002

The military frequently interfered in politics until it was disbanded following the return of democracy in 1994. A 5300-strong national police force, funded and trained by the US, was formed in its place. It offered little resistance to rebel forces in 2004.

ECONOMICS

Inflation 20% p.a. (1990–2001)

$3.61bn — 32.35 gourdes (39.15)

SCORE CARD

- ❑ WORLD GNP RANKING 126th
- ❑ GNP PER CAPITA $440
- ❑ BALANCE OF PAYMENTS .... –$177m
- ❑ INFLATION 9.9%
- ❑ UNEMPLOYMENT 70%

STRENGTHS

Few. Coffee exports. Remittances from Haitians living abroad. Large profits from transshipment of narcotics to US.

WEAKNESSES

Many. Poverty, political instability, dictatorship, and coups have destroyed investor confidence and held back infrastructural development.

EXPORTS

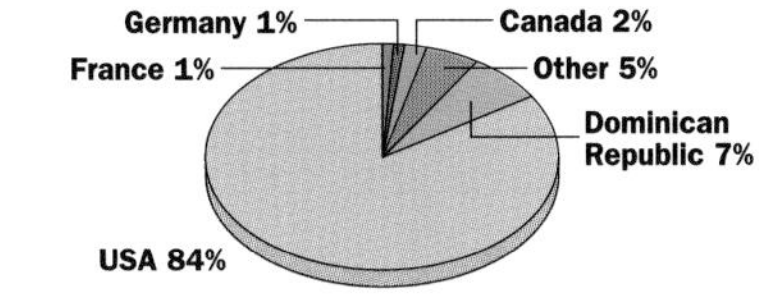
Germany 1%
Canada 2%
France 1%
Other 5%
Dominican Republic 7%
USA 84%

IMPORTS

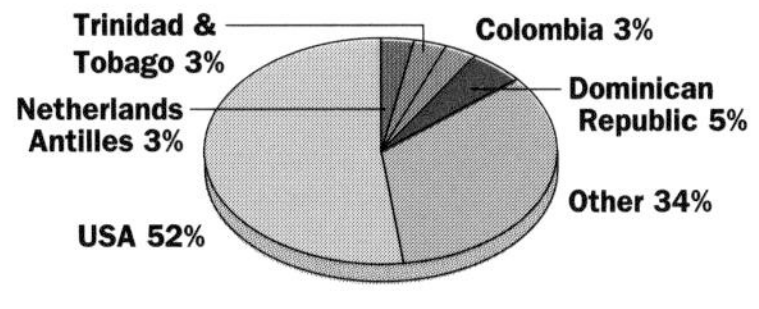
Trinidad & Tobago 3%
Colombia 3%
Dominican Republic 5%
Netherlands Antilles 3%
Other 34%
USA 52%

***In remote villages in Haiti** most houses are made of earth and do not have glass in their windows.*

RESOURCES

Electric power 260,000 kW

5000 tonnes — Not an oil producer

1.94m goats, 1.46m cattle, 1m pigs, 5.65m chickens — Marble, limestone, clay, silver, gold, natural asphalt

Haiti has no strategic resources. Under prolonged economic sanctions, it had to find unofficial sources of oil; much was imported from Europe.

ENVIRONMENT

Sustainability rank: 137th

0.4% (0.1% partially protected) — 0.2 tonnes per capita

Forests now cover only 3.2% of land area; severe soil erosion exacerbated floods in 2004. The removal of 4000 tonnes of toxic waste, illegally dumped near Gonaïves in 1988, finally began in 1998.

MEDIA

TV ownership low

Daily newspaper circulation 3 per 1000 people

PUBLISHING AND BROADCAST MEDIA

There are 2 daily newspapers, *Le Nouvelliste* and *Le Matin*

5 services: 1 state-owned, 4 independent — More than 250 services: 1 state-owned, the rest independent

Radio is the main broadcast medium, with more than 250 stations, though many studios were destroyed in the chaos of Aristide's downfall in 2004.

CRIME

No death penalty

4152 prisoners — Crime is rising

Most of the 5300-strong police force fled during the 2004 revolt and the security situation remains extremely dangerous; many rebels have failed to disarm. Narcotics trafficking has slowed since Aristide's departure.

EDUCATION

School leaving age: 11

52% — 6288 students

The 2004 uprising badly damaged what remained of the desperately underfunded education system: at least 50 schools were completely destroyed.

CHRONOLOGY

In 1697, Spain ceded the west of Hispaniola to France. Ex-slave Toussaint Louverture's rebellion in 1791 led to independence in 1804.

- ❑ **1915–1934** US occupation.
- ❑ **1957–1971** François "Papa Doc" Duvalier's brutal dictatorship.
- ❑ **1971–1986** His son Jean-Claude, "Baby Doc," rules; eventually flees.
- ❑ **1986–1988** Military rule.
- ❑ **1990** Jean-Bertrand Aristide elected; exiled in 1991 coup.
- ❑ **1994–1995** US forces oust military. Aristide reinstated; elections.
- ❑ **1997–1999** Political deadlock.
- ❑ **2000** Lavalas and Aristide reelected.
- ❑ **2004** Aristide resigns and flees.

H

HEALTH

No welfare state health benefits

1 per 5000 people — Malaria, other parasitic diseases, tuberculosis

Most Haitians cannot afford health care. In rural areas, help is often sought from voodoo priests.

SPENDING

GDP/cap. decrease

CONSUMPTION AND SPENDING

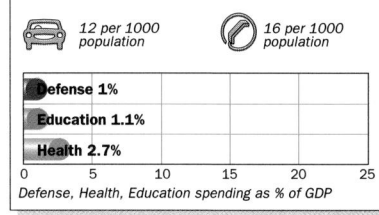

12 per 1000 population — *16 per 1000 population*

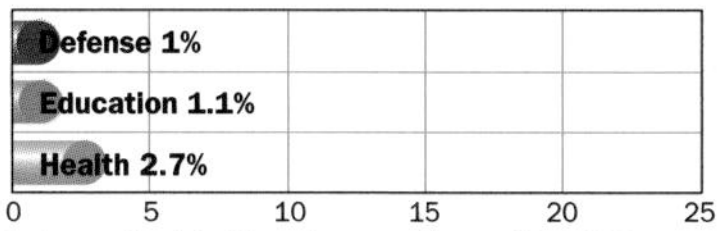
Defense 1%
Education 1.1%
Health 2.7%
0
5
10
15
20
25

Defense, Health, Education spending as % of GDP

Haiti's rigid class structure maintains extreme disparities of wealth between a few affluent families and the mass of the population, who live in slums without running water or proper sanitation. The World Bank has estimated that 80% of the rural population live below the poverty line.

WORLD RANKING

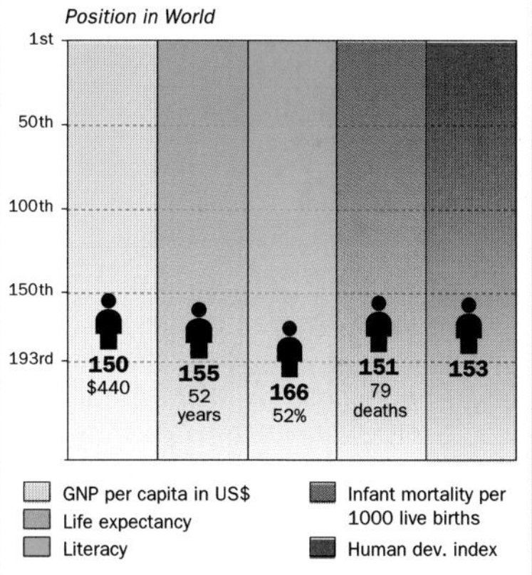
Position in World
1st
50th
100th
150th
193rd
150
$440
155
52 years
166
52%
151
79 deaths
153
GNP per capita in US$
Life expectancy
Literacy
Infant mortality per 1000 live births
Human dev. index

HONDURAS

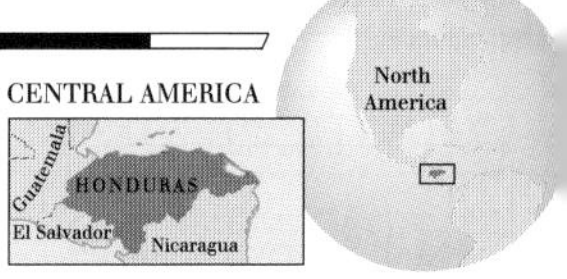
CENTRAL AMERICA
North America
Guatemala
HONDURAS
El Salvador
Nicaragua

OFFICIAL NAME: Republic of Honduras **CAPITAL:** Tegucigalpa
POPULATION: 6.9 million **CURRENCY:** Lempira **OFFICIAL LANGUAGE:** Spanish

1838 | 1838 | Sept 15 | HN | -6 | +504 | .hn

MOST OF HONDURAS is mountainous terrain, with a small sheltered Pacific coast to the south and a broad Caribbean shoreline to the north, including part of the virtually uninhabited Mosquito Coast. After a succession of military governments it returned to full civilian rule in 1984. In 1998 Honduras was devastated by Hurricane Mitch, which resulted in the death of at least 5600 people and damage estimated at some $3 billion.

CLIMATE

Tropical equatorial

WEATHER CHART FOR TEGUCIGALPA

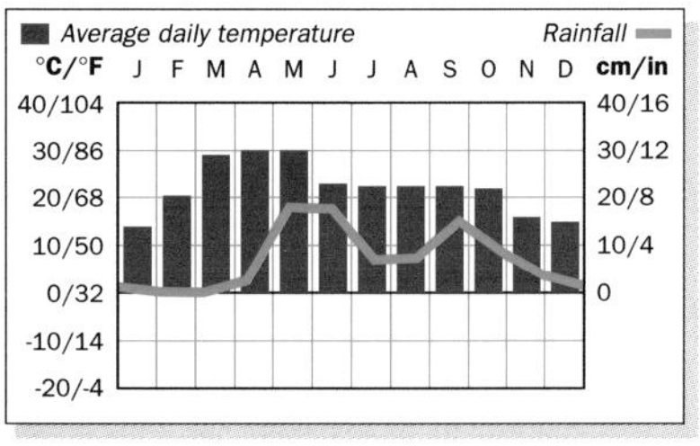
Average daily temperature
Rainfall
°C/°F J F M A M J J A S O N D cm/in
40/104
30/86
20/68
10/50
0/32
-10/14
-20/-4
40/16
30/12
20/8
10/4
0

Honduras's Caribbean coastline is generally extremely hot. The rest of the country is much cooler.

TRANSPORTATION

Drive on right

Dr. Ramón Villeda Morales, San Pedro Sula 522,452 passengers

1155 ships 933,200 grt

THE TRANSPORTATION NETWORK

2721 km (1691 miles)

None

699 km (434 miles)

465 km (289 miles)

Domestic air travel has blossomed in recent years, and is more convenient than the partly unpaved road system.

TOURISM

Visitors : Population 1:11

624,250 visitors

Up 14% in 2003

MAIN TOURIST ARRIVALS

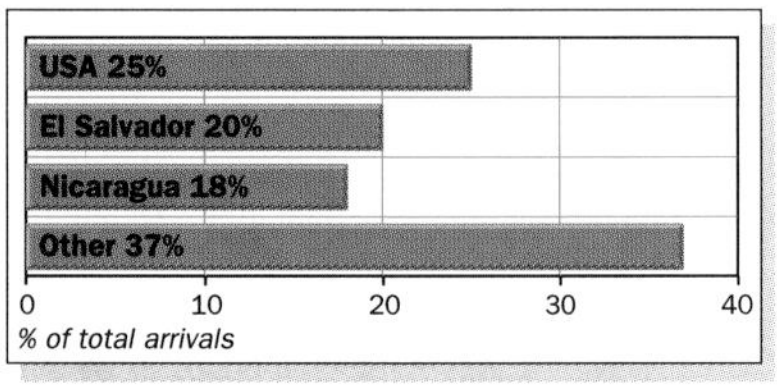
USA 25%
El Salvador 20%
Nicaragua 18%
Other 37%
0
10
20
30
40
% of total arrivals

Caribbean coast resorts and the Bay Islands are popular, while exploring the remote region inland from the Mosquito Coast and jungle rafting appeal to the adventurous. The ruined Mayan temples of Copán are a major draw.

PEOPLE

Pop. density medium

Spanish, Garífuna (Carib), English Creole

62/km² (160/mi²)

THE URBAN/RURAL POPULATION SPLIT

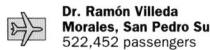

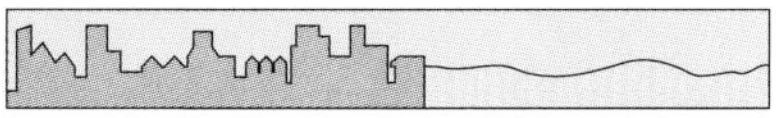
55%
45%

ETHNIC MAKEUP

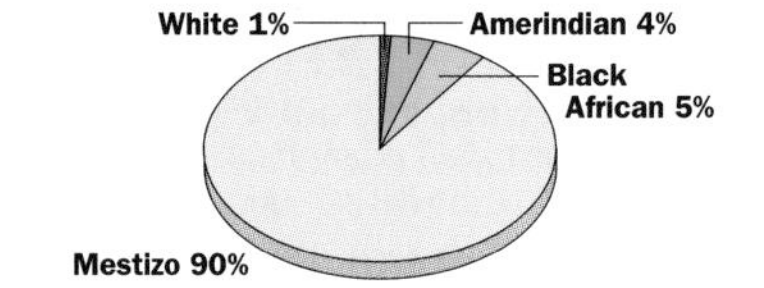
White 1%
Amerindian 4%
Black African 5%
Mestizo 90%

As in most of Central America, very few pure indigenous groups remain. The estimated 45,000 Miskito Amerindians, and the English-speaking *garífuna* (black) population on the Caribbean coast united in 1999 to oppose a constitutional amendment allowing foreigners to buy land in coastal areas, traditionally their communal lands. Poverty is at the root of social tension; whites still have the best opportunities.

Rural poverty and strong Roman Catholicism (97% are Roman Catholic) mean that the family is a powerful unifying force. The status of women is low; many work in domestic service.

POLITICS

Multiparty elections

2001/2005

President Ricardo Maduro

AT THE LAST ELECTION

National Congress 128 seats

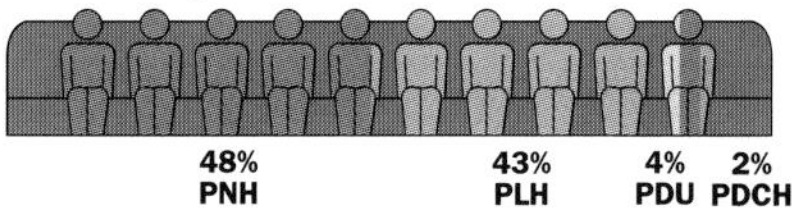
3% PINU–SD
48% PNH
43% PLH
4% PDU
2% PDCH

PNH = National Party of Honduras **PLH** = Liberal Party of Honduras **PDU** = Party of Democratic Unification **PINU–SD** = Innovation and Unity Party–Social Democracy **PDCH** = Honduran Christian Democratic Party

The traditional power brokers have been the military, the US embassy, and the United Fruit Company (now called Chiquita), the country's biggest banana producer. The military held power intermittently from the mid-1950s, until pressure from the US government forced it to restore civilian rule in 1984. During the 1980s, US military aid and political influence increased sharply. The armed forces retained a strong political hold. Attempts continue to bring human rights cases from the 1980s to trial.

The PNH and PLH have few real ideological differences. Presidents, able to serve only one four-year term, have tended to be weak. The PLH introduced unpopular austerity measures in 1994, but also began reducing the autonomy of the military by abolishing conscription. President Carlos Flores of the PLH, elected in 1997, continued this "demilitarization" process by naming a civilian defense minister in 1999. The presidency was won back by the PNH when Ricardo Maduro was elected in 2001.

Reconstruction after the devastation of Hurricane Mitch in 1998 is a long-term undertaking.

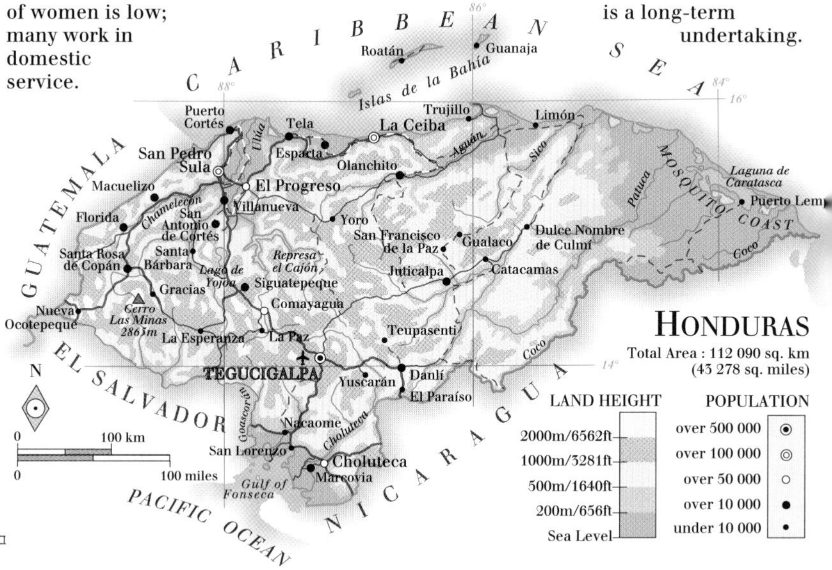
CARIBBEAN SEA
Roatán
Guanaja
Islas de la Bahía
Puerto Cortés
Tela
La Ceiba
Trujillo
Limón
San Pedro Sula
Esparta
Olanchito
El Progreso
Macuelizo
Villanueva
Florida
San Antonio de Cortés
Yoro
San Francisco de la Paz
Gualaco
Dulce Nombre de Culmí
Santa Rosa de Copán
Santa Bárbara
Represa el Cajón
Juticalpa
Catacamas
Gracias
Siguatepeque
Comayagua
Nueva Ocotepeque
Cerro Las Minas 2863m
La Esperanza
La Paz
Teupasenti
TEGUCIGALPA
Yuscarán
Danlí
El Paraíso
Nacaome
San Lorenzo
Choluteca
Marcovia
Gulf of Fonseca
PACIFIC OCEAN
GUATEMALA
EL SALVADOR
NICARAGUA
MOSQUITO COAST
Laguna de Caratasca
Puerto Lempira
Patuca
Coco
Aguán
Sico
Ulúa
Chamelecón
Lago de Yojoa
Goascorán
Choluteca
N
0 100 km
0 100 miles
HONDURAS
Total Area : 112 090 sq. km (43 278 sq. miles)
LAND HEIGHT
2000m/6562ft
1000m/3281ft
500m/1640ft
200m/656ft
Sea Level
POPULATION
over 500 000
over 100 000
over 50 000
over 10 000
under 10 000

WORLD AFFAIRS

Joined UN in 1945

ACS | IAEA | NAM | OAS | San José

Relations with the US are key. In 2001 free trade was agreed with El Salvador, Guatemala, and Mexico. Border disputes exist with El Salvador and Nicaragua.

AID

Recipient

$435m (receipts)

Down 36% in 2002

Most aid to Honduras comes from the US. Aid under the Heavily Indebted Poor Countries' Initiative was delayed in 2003 for failure to meet IMF goals.

DEFENSE

No compulsory military service

$108m

Up 15% in 2002

Until 1994, the military operated with virtual impunity. The first civilian defense minister was appointed in 1999, consolidating the transition to civilian rule, though the military is still used to bolster internal security.

ECONOMICS

Inflation 18% p.a. (1990–2001)

$6.32bn

18.2 lempiras (17.33)

SCORE CARD

- ❏ WORLD GNP RANKING........................104th
- ❏ GNP PER CAPITA $930
- ❏ BALANCE OF PAYMENTS....................–$266m
- ❏ INFLATION 7.7%
- ❏ UNEMPLOYMENT 4%

STRENGTHS

Coffee, flowers, fruit. Economic boost due to hurricane reconstruction. Overseas remittances. Barely exploited mineral deposits. Hardwoods.

WEAKNESSES

Foreign debt. Coffee vulnerable to world price changes. Banana industry affected by hurricane damage. Lack of land reform. Crime deters investment. High underemployment. Corruption. Weak industrial base. Overreliance on HEP.

EXPORTS

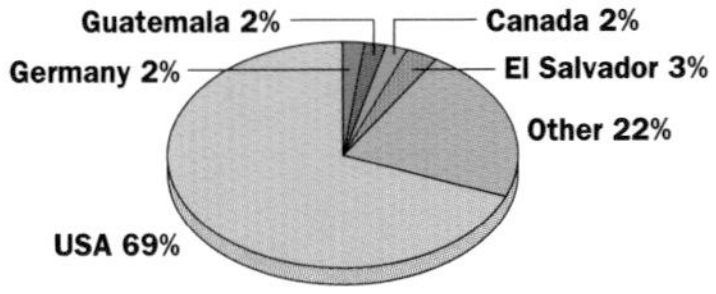
Guatemala 2%
Canada 2%
Germany 2%
El Salvador 3%
Other 22%
USA 69%

IMPORTS

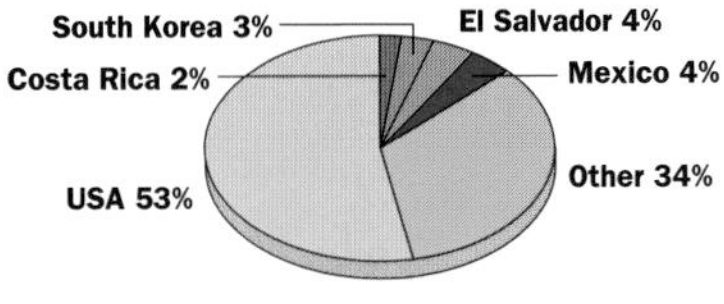
South Korea 3%
El Salvador 4%
Costa Rica 2%
Mexico 4%
Other 34%
USA 53%

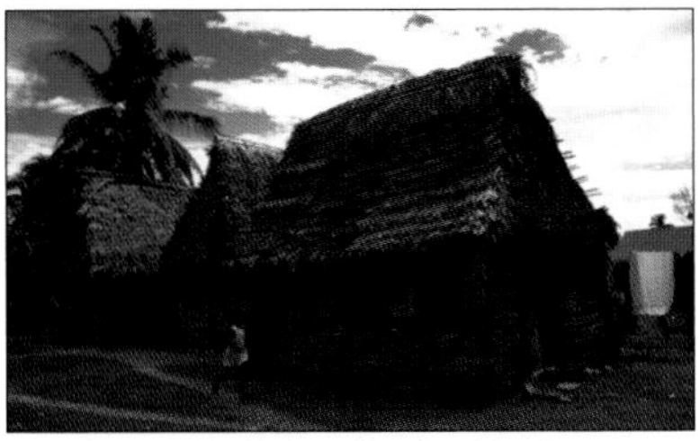

***A garífuna settlement** on Honduras's long Caribbean coast.*

RESOURCES

Electric power 912,000 kW

16,451 tonnes

Not an oil producer

2.4m cattle, 478,000 pigs, 181,000 horses, 18.7m chickens

Lead, zinc, silver, gold, copper, iron, tin, coal

Coffee exports dropped dramatically in 2001, due to low world prices. Oil exploration is under way. Most energy is produced from hydroelectric power.

ENVIRONMENT

Sustainability rank: 47th

6% (4% partially protected)

0.7 tonnes per capita

Complete lack of regulation has led to ecological crisis. Coastal areas suffer the effects of shrimp farming.

MEDIA

TV ownership medium

Daily newspaper circulation 55 per 1000 people

PUBLISHING AND BROADCAST MEDIA

There are 9 daily newspapers, including *La Prensa, El Heraldo,* and *La Tribuna*

6 independent services

1 state-owned service, over 280 independent stations

Self-censorship, dependence on US sources, corruption, and intimidation guarantee a largely compliant media.

CRIME

No death penalty

11,502 prisoners

Violent crime is rising

Overzealous security forces are frequently accused of murdering child members of violent street gangs.

EDUCATION

School leaving age: 13

80%

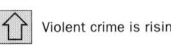

90,620 students

The drop-out rate of students is very high: one-third of all children do not complete primary school.

HEALTH

Welfare state health benefits

1 per 1250 people

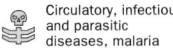

Circulatory, infectious, and parasitic diseases, malaria

A third of Hondurans have no access to health services. Honduras has 60% of Central America's AIDS cases.

CHRONOLOGY

Honduras was a Spanish possession until 1821. In 1823, it formed the United Provinces of Central America with four neighboring nations.

- ❏ **1838** Declares full independence.
- ❏ **1890s** US banana plantations set up.
- ❏ **1932–1949** Dictatorship of Gen. Tiburcio Carías Andino of PNH.
- ❏ **1954–1957** Elected PLH president Villeda Morales deposed, reelected.
- ❏ **1963** Military coup.
- ❏ **1969** 13-day Soccer War with El Salvador.
- ❏ **1980–1983** PLH wins elections but Gen. Gustavo Alvarez holds real power. Trades unionists arrested; death squads operate.
- ❏ **1984** Return to democracy.
- ❏ **1988** 12,000 Contra rebels forced out of Nicaragua into Honduras.
- ❏ **1995** Military defies human rights charges.
- ❏ **1998** Hurricane Mitch wreaks havoc.
- ❏ **1999** First civilian defense minister.
- ❏ **2002** Ricardo Maduro takes office as president.

H

SPENDING

GDP/cap. increase

CONSUMPTION AND SPENDING

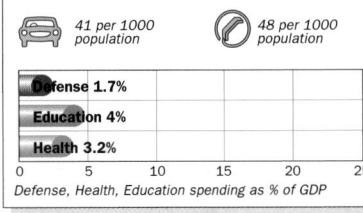

41 per 1000 population

48 per 1000 population

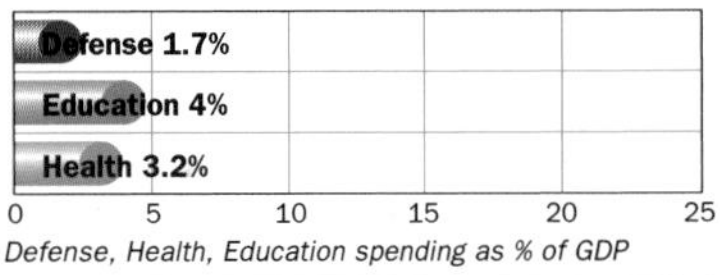
Defense 1.7%
Education 4%
Health 3.2%
0
5
10
15
20
25
Defense, Health, Education spending as % of GDP

Honduran society is characterized by great inequalities: the richest 5% own two-thirds of the land. As many as 85% of the population were thrown into poverty in 1998 by Hurricane Mitch. Some 45% are still existing on less than $2 a day.

WORLD RANKING

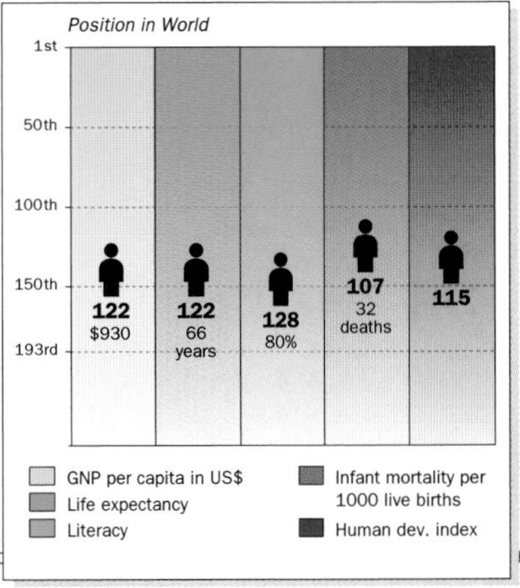
Position in World
1st
50th
100th
150th
193rd
122
$930
122
66
years
128
80%
107
32
deaths
115
GNP per capita in US$
Life expectancy
Literacy
Infant mortality per 1000 live births
Human dev. index

Hungary

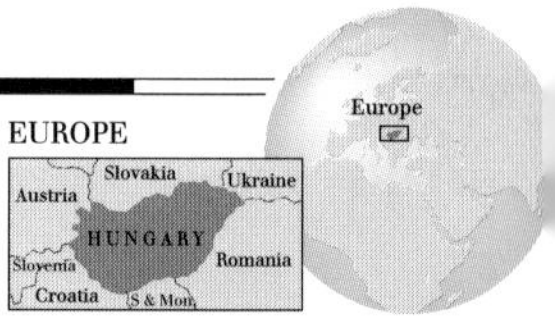
Europe
EUROPE
Slovakia
Ukraine
Austria
HUNGARY
Slovenia
Romania
Croatia
S & Mon.

Official Name: Republic of Hungary **Capital:** Budapest
Population: 9.9 million **Currency:** Forint **Official Language:** Hungarian (Magyar)

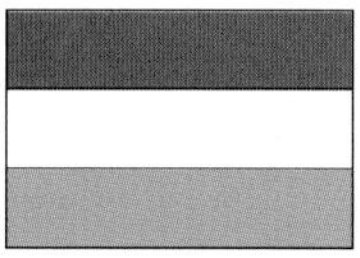

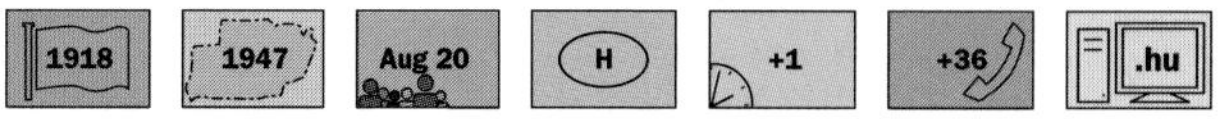
1918
1947
Aug 20
H
+1
+36
.hu

Lying at the heart of central Europe, Hungary is landlocked and has borders with seven states. Historically, Hungary has been a cosmopolitan cultural center, and during its years of market socialism was more prosperous than the other Eastern Bloc countries. Economic and political reforms in the post-1989 era brought it closer to the EU, which it joined in the major wave of enlargement in 2004; Hungary had already become a member of NATO in 1999. In foreign policy it is particularly sensitive about the treatment of Hungarian minorities in neighboring states.

CLIMATE

Continental

WEATHER CHART FOR BUDAPEST

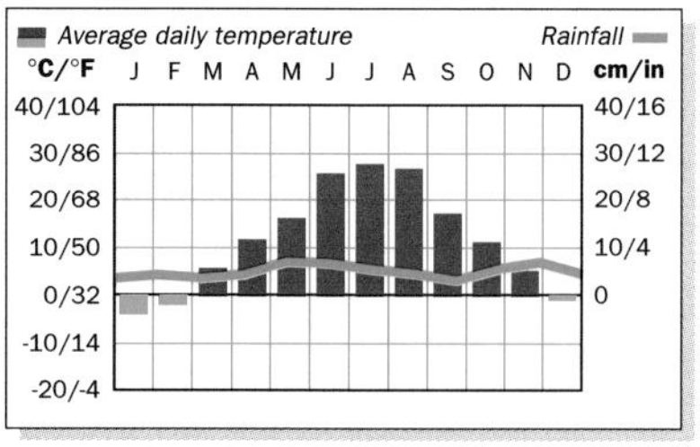
Average daily temperature
Rainfall
°C/°F J F M A M J J A S O N D cm/in
40/104 40/16
30/86 30/12
20/68 20/8
10/50 10/4
0/32 0
-10/14
-20/-4

Hungary has a continental climate, with wet springs, late summers, and cold, cloudy winters. There are no great differences of weather and climate within the country. Conditions in summer and winter may, however, differ greatly from one year to the next. The transition between seasons tends to be sudden.

TRANSPORTATION

Drive on right

Budapest Ferihegy
5.01m passengers

1 ship
3784 grt

THE TRANSPORTATION NETWORK

73,849 km (45,888 miles)

448 km (278 miles)

7949 km (4939 miles)

1373 km (853 miles)

Freight travels mainly via the rail link from Budapest to the Austrian border. Most foreign investment is located along this corridor. A direct link to Slovenia opened in mid-2001. The Budapest–Vienna expressway was the first of four big EU-backed road projects to be completed.

TOURISM

Visitors : Population 1.6:1

15.9m visitors

Up 4% in 2002

MAIN TOURIST ARRIVALS

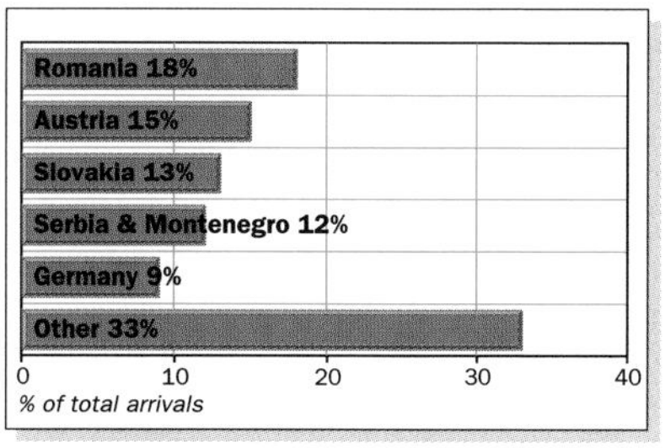
Romania 18%
Austria 15%
Slovakia 13%
Serbia & Montenegro 12%
Germany 9%
Other 33%
0 10 20 30 40
% of total arrivals

Lake Balaton, the traditional summer vacation destination, was a magnet for east European visitors during the communist period. Since then, Hungary has invested heavily in its tourist facilities, and the number of travel agents and hotels has risen dramatically. Austrians and Romanians are most numerous among those who travel to Hungary, many on business. Budapest's baths, some of which date from the Ottoman period, are a distinctive feature, and the capital also promotes itself as an international business convention center.

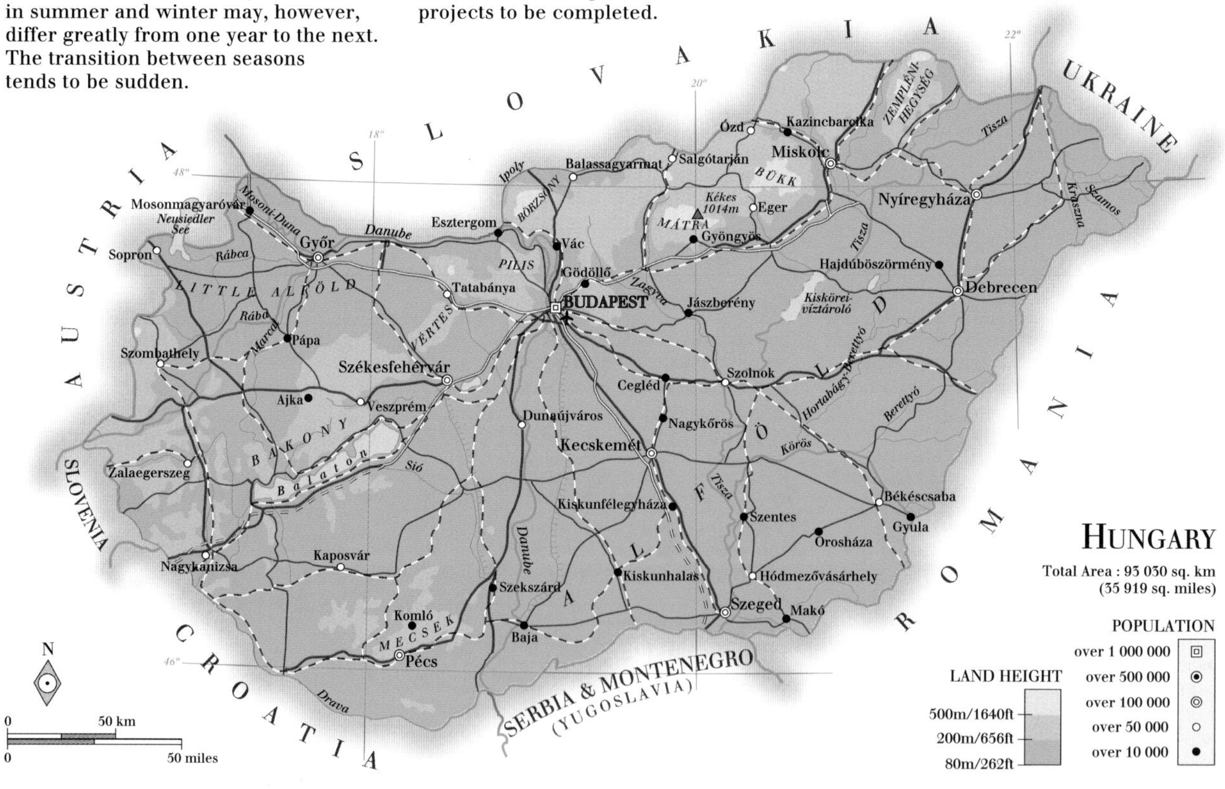
SLOVAKIA
UKRAINE
AUSTRIA
SLOVENIA
CROATIA
SERBIA & MONTENEGRO (YUGOSLAVIA)
ROMANIA
BUDAPEST
Miskolc
Nyíregyháza
Debrecen
Győr
Sopron
Mosonmagyaróvár
Neusiedler See
Esztergom
Balassagyarmat
Salgótarján
Ózd
Kazincbarcika
Eger
Kékes 1014m
MÁTRA
BÜKK
Gyöngyös
Vác
Gödöllő
Tatabánya
Pápa
Szombathely
Székesfehérvár
Veszprém
Ajka
Zalaegerszeg
Nagykanizsa
Kaposvár
Pécs
Komló
Szekszárd
Baja
Dunaújváros
Kecskemét
Cegléd
Nagykőrös
Szolnok
Jászberény
Hajdúböszörmény
Kiskörei-víztároló
Kiskunfélegyháza
Kiskunhalas
Szeged
Makó
Szentes
Hódmezővásárhely
Orosháza
Békéscsaba
Gyula
LITTLE ALFÖLD
ALFÖLD
BAKONY
MECSEK
PILIS
VÉRTES
BÖRZSÖNY
ZEMPLÉNI-HEGYSÉG
Balaton
Danube
Tisza
Drava
Rába
Rábca
Marcal
Sió
Zagyva
Ipoly
Mosoni-Duna
Körös
Berettyó
Hortobágy-Berettyó
Kraszna
Szamos
Sajó
48°
46°
18°
20°
22°
N
0 50 km
0 50 miles
HUNGARY
Total Area : 93 030 sq. km (35 919 sq. miles)
POPULATION
over 1 000 000
over 500 000
over 100 000
over 50 000
over 10 000
LAND HEIGHT
500m/1640ft
200m/656ft
80m/262ft

PEOPLE

Pop. density medium

Hungarian (Magyar)

107/km² (278/mi²)

THE URBAN/RURAL POPULATION SPLIT

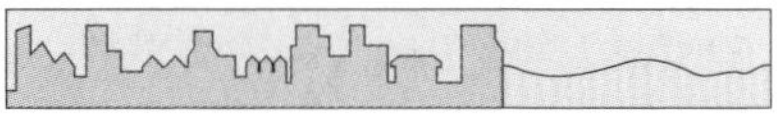
65%
35%

RELIGIOUS PERSUASION

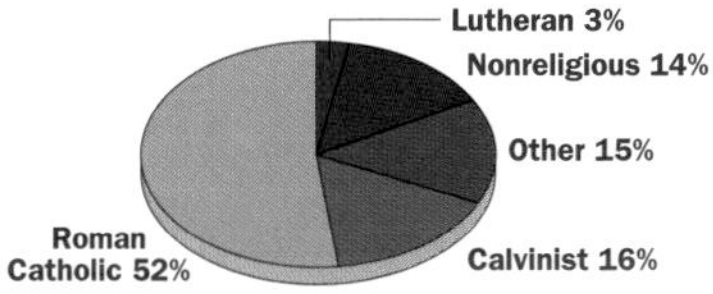
Lutheran 3%
Nonreligious 14%
Other 15%
Calvinist 16%
Roman Catholic 52%

ETHNIC MAKEUP

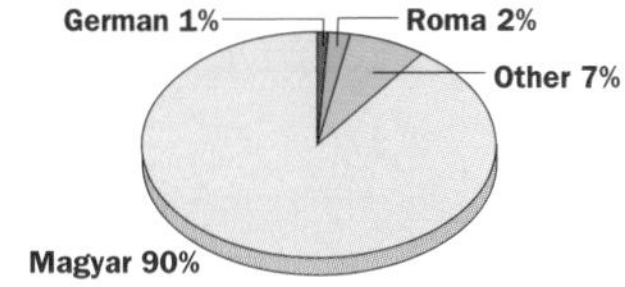
German 1%
Roma 2%
Other 7%
Magyar 90%

Hungary's population is shrinking, having reached a peak of just under 11 million in 1980.

An almost ethnically homogeneous society means that tensions are rare. There are small minorities of Roma, Germans, Jews, Romanians, Serbs, Slovaks, and Croats. The government is greatly concerned about the treatment of more than three million Hungarians in Romanian Transylvania, Serbian Vojvodina, and Slovakia. New legislation gave them special status in Hungary from 2002, including the right to work there for three months a year. Prejudice against Roma is widespread, despite official drives to stamp it out. Over two-thirds of the prewar Jewish community were murdered by the Nazis; antisemitism has reemerged since 1989. Overall, religious adherence is falling and the 2001 census showed an increase in the numbers of the nonreligious. A new bourgeoisie has emerged, but for the unskilled and unemployed life is often tougher than under communism.

POPULATION AGE BREAKDOWN

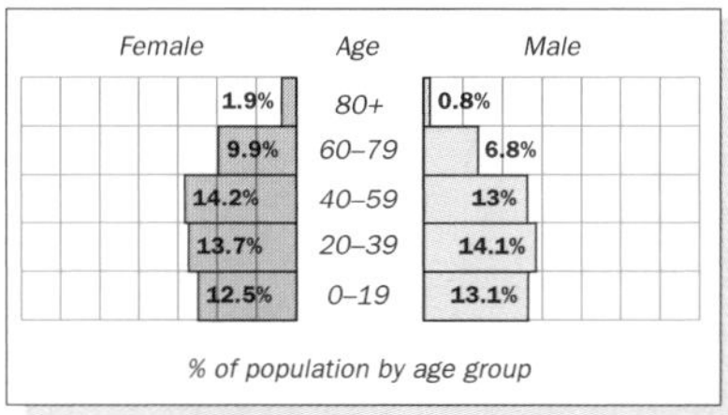
Female
Age
Male
1.9%
80+
0.8%
9.9%
60–79
6.8%
14.2%
40–59
13%
13.7%
20–39
14.1%
12.5%
0–19
13.1%
% of population by age group

POLITICS

Multiparty elections

2002/2006

President Ferenc Mádl

AT THE LAST ELECTION

National Assembly 386 seats

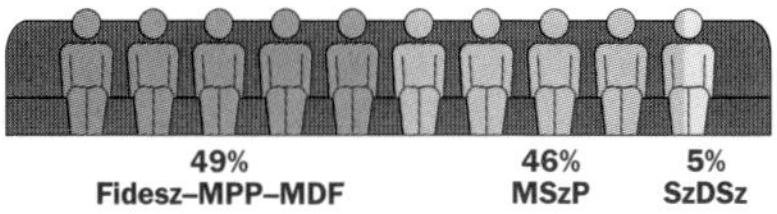
49% Fidesz–MPP–MDF
46% MSzP
5% SzDSz

Fidesz–MPP–MDF = Federation of Young Democrats–Hungarian Civic Party and Hungarian Democratic Forum
MSzP = Hungarian Socialist Party
SzDSz = Alliance of Free Democrats

Hungary has been a multiparty democracy since 1990.

Profile

Since 1990, the electoral pendulum has swung at four-yearly intervals between relatively stable coalitions of right and left, though the distinction has lessened.

Party splits and poor economic results increased apathy in the early 1990s against the Christian-democratic nationalist MDF; power shifted to the former communist MSzP in 1994. The right-of-center Fidesz–MPP coalition led by Viktor Orbán, which took office in 1998, drove the country further toward a market economy and approved the controversial Status Law covering Hungarian communities abroad. While the economy improved overall, disparities widened. Fidesz–MPP–MDF was narrowly defeated in 2002 by a coalition of the MSzP and the SzDSz. Prime Minister Peter Medgyessy steered the country into the EU in 2004 but dispute over a reshuffle in August led to his resignation; business tycoon Ferenc Gyurcsany was nominated to replace him.

Main Political Issues

Free-market economics

Market-economy-oriented reforms have led to strong economic recovery in Budapest and the west. Widening income differentials between young, skilled workers in the private sector and those in education, health, and other state sectors have provoked protests and strikes.

Status Law

Legislation granting special rights to expatriate Hungarians was passed in 2001. Hungary's neighbors have complained bitterly of interference and have warned of a link to expansionist sentiment among Hungary's far right.

***Ferenc Mádl,** known as "Mr. Professor," was elected president in 2000.*

***Peter Medgyessy** oversaw EU accession while prime minister.*

***The majestic Danube River** divides the modern city of Budapest, flowing between the ancient towns of Buda (foreground) and Pest.*

WORLD AFFAIRS

Joined UN in 1955

CE | EU | NATO | OECD | OSCE

Hungary gained WEU associate status in 1994. In a 1997 referendum 85% of voters endorsed joining NATO, and in 1999 Hungary became a full member. Joining the EU was a slower process, from an association agreement in 1994 to membership in 2004.

Hungary has a cooperation and friendship treaty with Russia, but relations have been strained by Hungary's open courting of the West. Difficult relations with Slovakia and Romania were eased by friendship treaties concluded in the mid-1990s, but were troubled again by the controversial Status Law which provides benefits to ethnic Hungarians resident abroad.

CHRONOLOGY

The region today occupied by Hungary was first settled by the Finno-Ugrian Magyar peoples from the 8th century. In the 16th century, it was divided between Austria and the Ottoman Empire, and was controlled by Austria until 1867, when Austria-Hungary was formed.

- **1918** Hungarian Republic created as successor state to Austria-Hungary.
- **1919** Béla Kún leads a short-lived communist government. Romania intervenes militarily and hands power to Adm. Horthy.
- **1938–1941** Hungary gains territory from Czechoslovakia, Yugoslavia, and Romania in return for supporting Nazi Germany.
- **1941** Hungary drawn into World War II on Axis side when Hitler attacks Soviet Union.
- **1944** Nazi Germany preempts Soviet advance on Hungary by invading. Deportation of Hungarian Jews and Roma to extermination camps begins. Soviet Red Army enters in October. Horthy forced to resign.
- **1945** Liberated by Red Army. Soviet-formed provisional government

H

H

CHRONOLOGY *continued*

installed. Imre Nagy introduces land reform.

- ❑ **1947** Communists emerge as largest party in second postwar election.
- ❑ **1948** Forcible merger of Social Democrats with communists; known as Hungarian Socialist Workers' Party (HSWP) from 1956.
- ❑ **1949** New constitution; formally becomes People's Republic.
- ❑ **1950–1951** First Secretary Mátyás Rákosi uses authoritarian powers to collectivize agriculture and industrialize the economy.
- ❑ **1953** Nagy, Rákosi's rival, becomes premier and reduces political terror.
- ❑ **1955** Nagy deposed by Rákosi.
- ❑ **1956** Rákosi out. Student demonstrations, demanding withdrawal of Soviet troops and Nagy's return, become popular uprising. Nagy appointed premier and János Kádár First Secretary. Nagy announces Hungary will leave Warsaw Pact. Three days later, Soviet forces suppress protests. About 25,000 killed. Kádár becomes premier.
- ❑ **1958** Nagy executed.
- ❑ **1968** Kádár introduces New Economic Mechanism to bring market elements to socialism.
- ❑ **1986** Police suppress commemoration of 1956 uprising. Democratic opposition demands Kádár's resignation.
- ❑ **1987** Party reformers establish MDF as a political movement.
- ❑ **1988** Kádár ousted. Protests force suspension of plans for Nagymaros Dam on the Danube.
- ❑ **1989** Parliament votes to allow independent parties. Posthumous rehabilitation of Nagy, who is given state funeral. Round table talks between HSWP and opposition.
- ❑ **1990** József Antall's MDF wins multiparty elections decisively. Speed of economic reform hotly debated. Árpád Göncz president.
- ❑ **1991** Warsaw Pact dissolved. Last Soviet troops leave.
- ❑ **1994** Hungary joins NATO's Partnership for Peace program. Former communist MSzP wins general election. Austerity program prompts protests.
- ❑ **1998** Elections: Viktor Orbán (Fidesz–MPP) forms right-of-center coalition.
- ❑ **1999** Joins NATO. Airspace used in NATO bombing of Serbia.
- ❑ **2000** Ferenc Mádl succeeds Göncz as president.
- ❑ **2002** Elections won by socialist and free democrat alliance. Peter Medgyessy prime minister.
- ❑ **2004** Joins EU. Medgyessy resigns.

AID

Recipient

$471m (receipts) | Up 13% in 2002

Hungary received substantial Western aid in 1990–1996, but by the end of the decade was considered able to attract investment mainly on commercial terms. Assistance from the EU continued in the runup to accession. Main focuses are health infrastructure, education programs, and other social initiatives.

DEFENSE

Phasing out conscription

$1.08bn | Up 20% in 2002

Troop numbers were more than halved and conventional arms and the military hierarchy were modernized in advance of NATO membership in 1999. The emphasis has switched toward more flexibility and rapid response. Almost immediately upon accession, Hungary permitted NATO to use its airspace to bomb Serbia. Military service, already shortened to six months, is to be phased out by 2006.

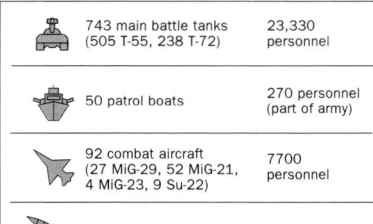

HUNGARIAN ARMED FORCES

743 main battle tanks (505 T-55, 238 T-72)	23,330 personnel
50 patrol boats	270 personnel (part of army)
92 combat aircraft (27 MiG-29, 52 MiG-21, 4 MiG-23, 9 Su-22)	7700 personnel
None	

ECONOMICS

Inflation 18% p.a. (1990–2001)

$53.7bn | 206.1 forint (231.9)

SCORE CARD

❑ World GNP Ranking	48th
❑ GNP per capita	$5290
❑ Balance of Payments	–$2.64bn
❑ Inflation	5.3%
❑ Unemployment	6%

EXPORTS

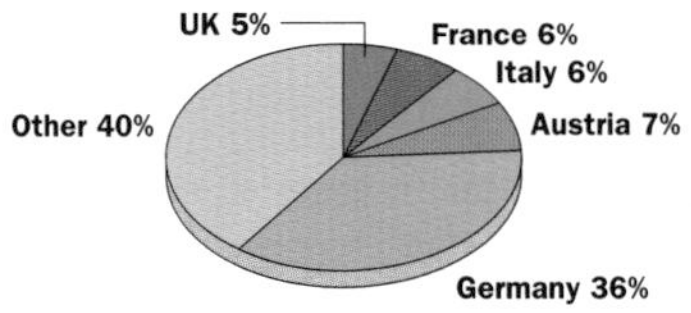
UK 5%
France 6%
Italy 6%
Austria 7%
Other 40%
Germany 36%

IMPORTS

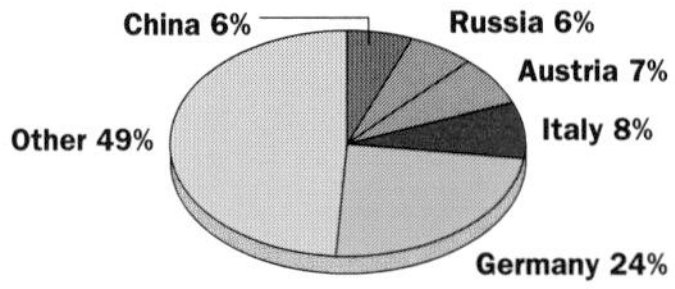
China 6%
Russia 6%
Austria 7%
Italy 8%
Other 49%
Germany 24%

Strengths

Openness to foreign direct investment. Favorable tax regime, streamlined bureaucracy. Strong export-led growth since late 1990s. High industrial production: new, state-of-the-art factories. Currency fully convertible from mid-2001. Inflation dropping.

Weaknesses

Low energy efficiency. Development bypassing rural eastern areas. Large budget deficit. Widening, though small, income differentials. Money laundering.

Profile

The collapse of COMECON (communist economic bloc) caused a reorientation of trade toward western Europe; by 2002 three-quarters of exports went to EU countries. The economy did not recover to its pre-1989 level, however, until 1999. Privatization has reduced the state-owned share of the economy from 85% to 15%, and has helped to cut external debt. A move toward services has caused agriculture to suffer.

ECONOMIC PERFORMANCE INDICATOR

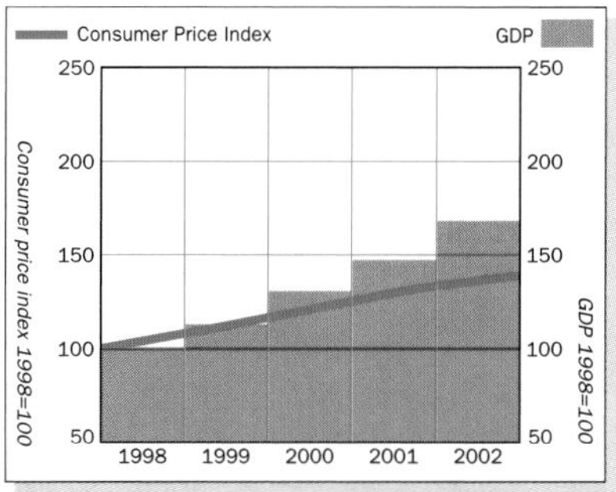
Consumer Price Index
GDP
250
200
150
100
50
Consumer price index 1998=100
GDP 1998=100
1998
1999
2000
2001
2002

HUNGARY : MAJOR BUSINESSES

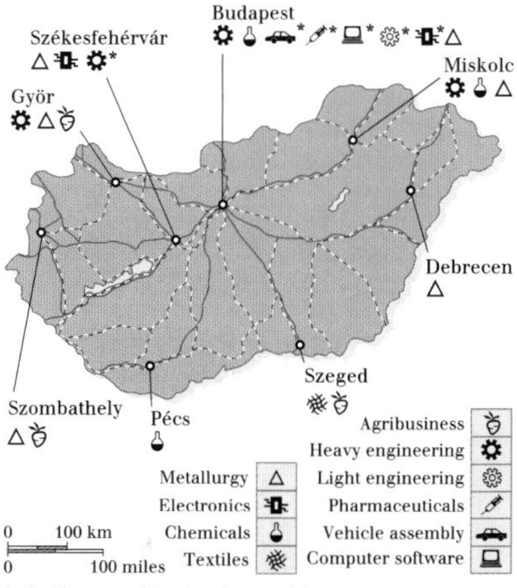
Budapest
Székesfehérvár
Miskolc
Györ
Debrecen
Szeged
Szombathely
Pécs
Agribusiness
Heavy engineering
Light engineering
Pharmaceuticals
Vehicle assembly
Computer software
Metallurgy
Electronics
Chemicals
Textiles
0 100 km
0 100 miles

* significant multinational ownership

RESOURCES

Electric power 8.3m kW

19,694 tonnes

22,777 b/d (reserves 58m barrels)

5.08m pigs, 3.44m ducks, 32.2m chickens

Bauxite, coal, oil, natural gas, lignite

ELECTRICITY GENERATION

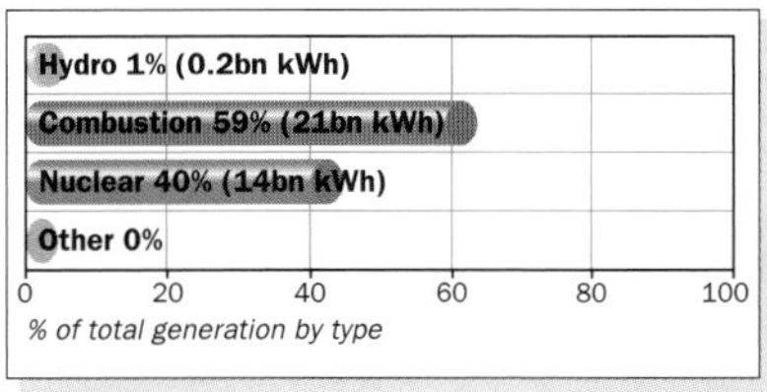
Hydro 1% (0.2bn kWh)
Combustion 59% (21bn kWh)
Nuclear 40% (14bn kWh)
Other 0%
0
20
40
60
80
100
% of total generation by type

HUNGARY : LAND USE

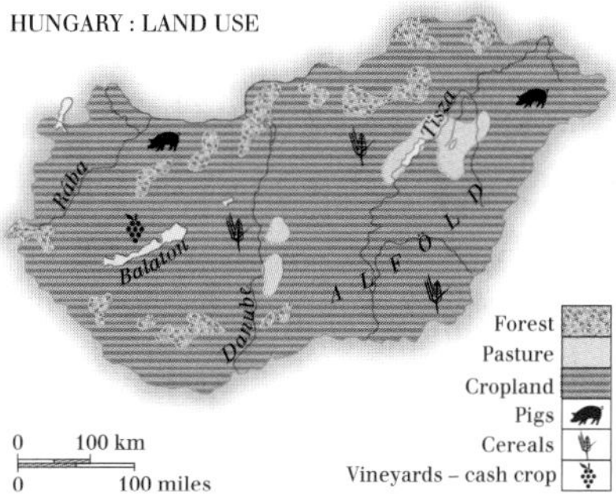
Rába
Balaton
Duna
Tisza
A L F Ö L D
Forest
Pasture
Cropland
Pigs
Cereals
Vineyards – cash crop
0
100 km
0
100 miles

Hungary has bauxite, brown coal, lignite, oil, and natural gas reserves. It depends for about 40% of its electricity on nuclear energy from the Paks complex, north of Baja. Fertile farmlands provide grains, sugar beet, and potatoes. Wine production is also important.

HEALTH

Welfare state health benefits

1 per 345 people

Cancers, heart and cerebrovascular diseases, accidents

Medical treatment has traditionally been free to all, though there is a contribution to prescription costs. State sickness benefits remain relatively generous. Spending on the health service has fallen in recent years in real terms; at around $840 per capita, it is the lowest in the OECD, and there is concern that Hungary's health care sector is among the least developed of OECD countries. The ratio of doctors to patients is high, but there is a shortage of nurses. Family physician services are being privatized rapidly under a law passed in 2000.

ENVIRONMENT

Sustainability rank: 11th

7% (5% partially protected)

5.4 tonnes per capita

ENVIRONMENTAL TREATIES

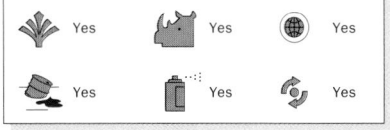

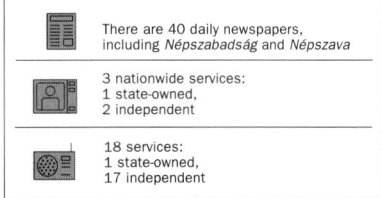

Yes	Yes	Yes
Yes	Yes	Yes

A high sulfur content in Hungary's fossil fuels exacerbates the serious air pollution in industrial zones. A "green card" system favors the use of cars with catalytic converters, reducing the serious levels of pollution from older vehicles.

The ecologically sensitive wetlands and lake systems of the Tisza River were contaminated with cyanide by a factory in Romania in 2000. An EU-sponsored program now oversees the river's management.

CRIME

No death penalty

16,700 prisoners

Up 3% in 2001

CRIME RATES

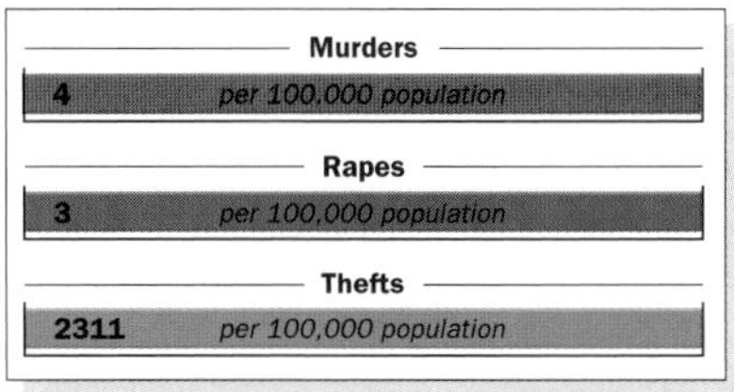
Murders
4
per 100,000 population
Rapes
3
per 100,000 population
Thefts
2311
per 100,000 population

An alarming trend in the late 1990s was the increase in murders of elderly people for financial gain. Organized crime, money laundering, and smuggling of illegal immigrants are rising.

SPENDING

GDP/cap. increase

CONSUMPTION AND SPENDING

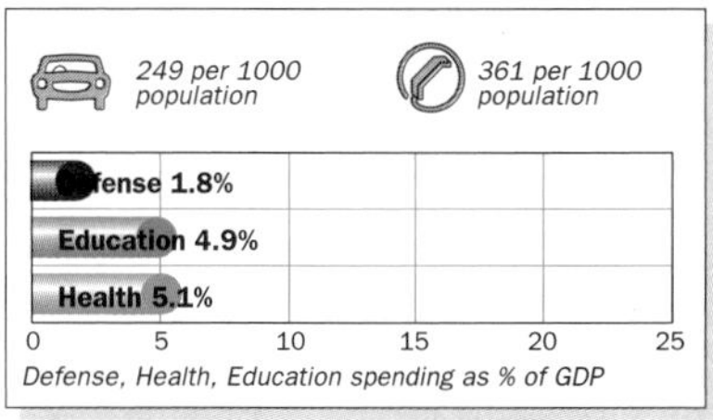
249 per 1000 population
361 per 1000 population
Defense 1.8%
Education 4.9%
Health 5.1%
0
5
10
15
20
25
Defense, Health, Education spending as % of GDP

Hungary enjoys one of the highest standards of living among the former communist countries and still has the most even distribution of wealth in the world. Mobile phone and Internet access is relatively high. Real wages, which fell by 15% in the mid-1990s, had largely regained ground by 2000. To earn enough to buy basic consumer goods, Hungarians still have to work longer hours than workers in western Europe. Public services pay has not kept pace with the rising cost of living, and there is a growing disparity with the private sector. The Roma minority suffers particularly over access to housing and has a life expectancy 10–15 years lower than the average.

MEDIA

TV ownership high

Daily newspaper circulation 465 per 1000 people

PUBLISHING AND BROADCAST MEDIA

There are 40 daily newspapers, including *Népszabadság* and *Népszava*

3 nationwide services:
1 state-owned,
2 independent

18 services:
1 state-owned,
17 independent

Newspapers and magazines are fiercely independent and critical of government policy. In 1994, the Constitutional Court declared that state interference in the media was unlawful, but allegations of interference persist. The boards controlling state TV and radio must have equal representation from government and opposition under a 1996 media law, but the Orbán government was accused of bending, if not ignoring, the rules.

EDUCATION

School leaving age: 16

99%

330,549 students

THE EDUCATION SYSTEM

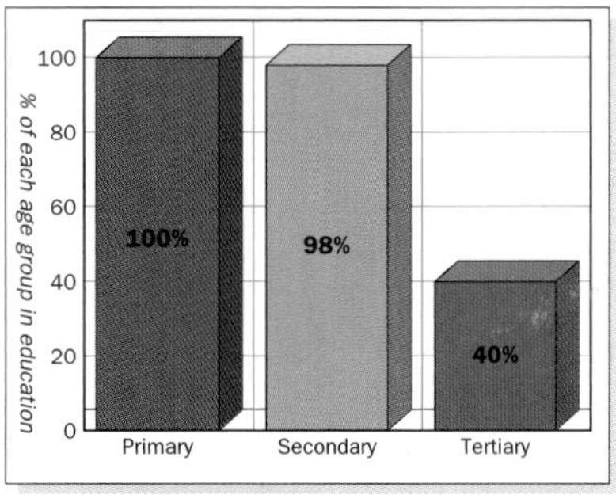
100
80
60
40
20
0
% of each age group in education
100%
98%
40%
Primary
Secondary
Tertiary

Education is free and compulsory from the age of six to 16. Bilingual schools have been established in southern Hungary to promote the languages of the national minorities. In 1999–2000 a major transformation of the education system took place, as a result of which there are 30 universities and colleges run by the state and 26 run by the Roman Catholic Church; a further six colleges are run by various foundations.

WORLD RANKING

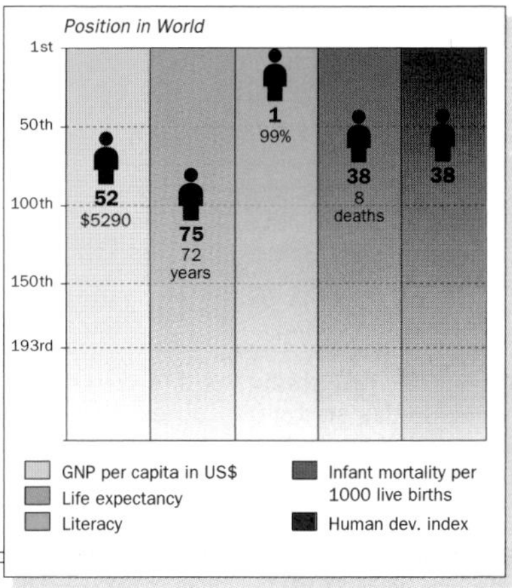
Position in World
1st
50th
100th
150th
193rd
52
$5290
75
72
years
1
99%
38
8
deaths
38
GNP per capita in US$
Life expectancy
Literacy
Infant mortality per 1000 live births
Human dev. index

H

ICELAND

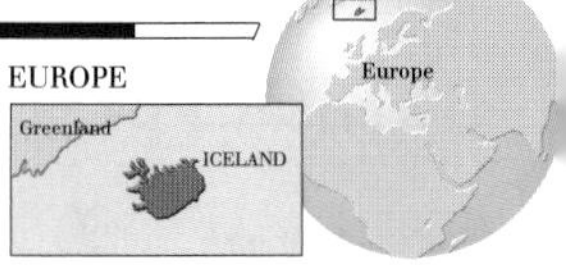
EUROPE
Europe
Greenland
ICELAND

OFFICIAL NAME: Republic of Iceland **CAPITAL:** Reykjavík
POPULATION: 290,000 **CURRENCY:** Icelandic króna **OFFICIAL LANGUAGE:** Icelandic

1944 | 1944 | June 17 | IS | 0 | +354 | .is

EUROPE'S WESTERNMOST country, Iceland has a strategic location in the North Atlantic, just south of the Arctic Circle. Its position, on the rift where the North American and European continental plates are pulling apart, accounts for its 200 volcanoes and its numerous geysers and solfataras. Previously a Danish possession, Iceland became fully independent in 1944. Most settlements are along the coast, where ports remain ice-free in winter.

CLIMATE

Subarctic

WEATHER CHART FOR REYKJAVÍK

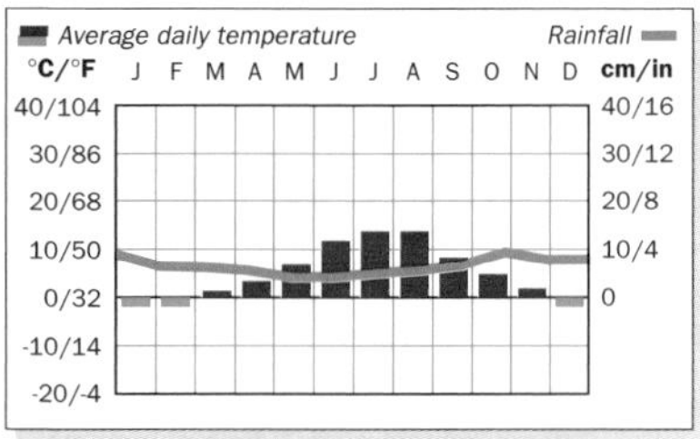
Average daily temperature
Rainfall
°C/°F
J F M A M J J A S O N D
cm/in
40/104
30/86
20/68
10/50
0/32
-10/14
-20/-4
40/16
30/12
20/8
10/4
0

Iceland sits in the Gulf Stream, making winters relatively mild. Summers are cool, with fine, long sunny days.

TRANSPORTATION

Drive on right

Keflavík International, Reykjavík 1.37m passengers

1127 ships 233,126 grt

THE TRANSPORTATION NETWORK

4029 km (2503 miles) | None
None | None

During winter Icelanders rely on internal flights to cross the country. Most freight moves by sea. The only main road circles the island.

TOURISM

Visitors : Population 1:1

278,000 visitors

Down 8% in 2001–2002

MAIN TOURIST ARRIVALS

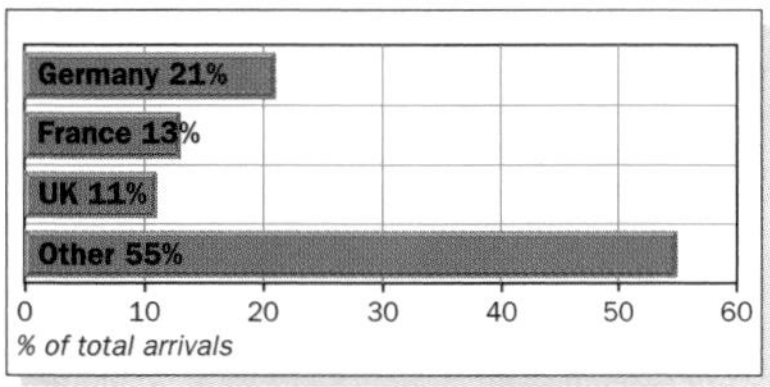
Germany 21%
France 13%
UK 11%
Other 55%
0 10 20 30 40 50 60
% of total arrivals

Iceland is promoting itself, especially in Japan, as an upmarket destination with spectacular scenery – glaciers, green valleys, fjords, and hot springs – and whale-watching.

PEOPLE

Pop. density low

Icelandic

3/km² (7/mi²)

THE URBAN/RURAL POPULATION SPLIT

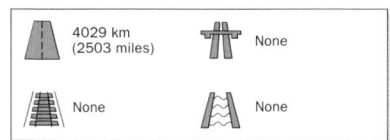

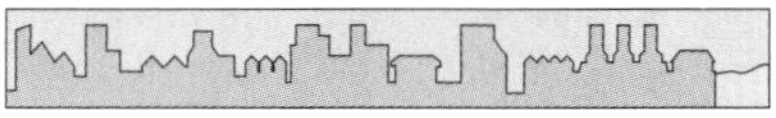
93%
7%

RELIGIOUS PERSUASION

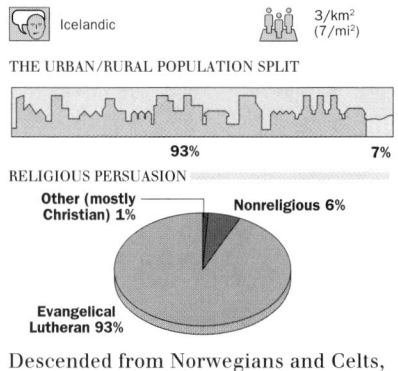

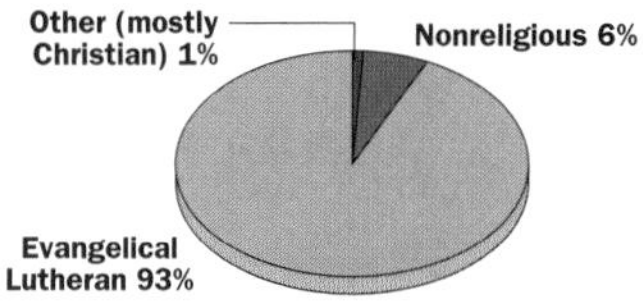
Other (mostly Christian) 1%
Nonreligious 6%
Evangelical Lutheran 93%

Descended from Norwegians and Celts, Icelanders are ethnically homogeneous. Almost all belong to the Evangelical Lutheran Church. More than half the population live in or near Reykjavík. Living standards are high, and there are few social tensions. The Icelandic language has changed little in 700 years, in part due to Iceland's isolation.

POLITICS

Multiparty elections

2003/2007

President Olafur Ragnar Grimsson

AT THE LAST ELECTION

Parliament 63 seats

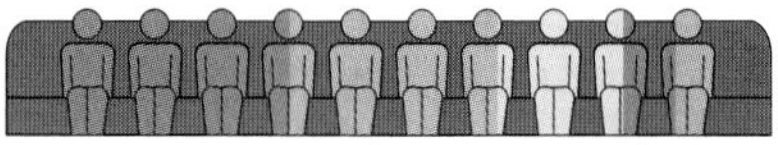
35% SSF
32% SF
19% FSF
8% VG
6% FF

SSF = Independence Party **SF** = Alliance
FSF = Progressive Party **VG** = Left-Green Alliance
FF = Liberal Party

Iceland has always been ruled by coalitions, but the traditional four-party system began to splinter in the 1980s. Arguments over whether or not to join the EU were defused in 1992 with the successful negotiation of the EEA, giving Iceland access to the key EU market.

David Oddsson became leader of the Independence Party and prime minister in 1991. He switched in 1995 from a center-left to a center-right coalition, with the Progressive Party, and was reelected in 1999 and 2003. Oddsson, by then Europe's longest-serving prime minister in office, successfully built on an economic recovery based on market-led reforms. As announced after the 2003 poll, he handed over to Foreign Minister Halldor Asgrimsson in late 2004.

ICELAND

Total Area : 103 000 sq. km (39 768 sq. miles)

POPULATION
- over 50 000
- over 10 000
- under 10 000

LAND HEIGHT
- 1000m/3281ft
- 500m/1640ft
- 200m/656ft
- Sea Level
- Ice Cap

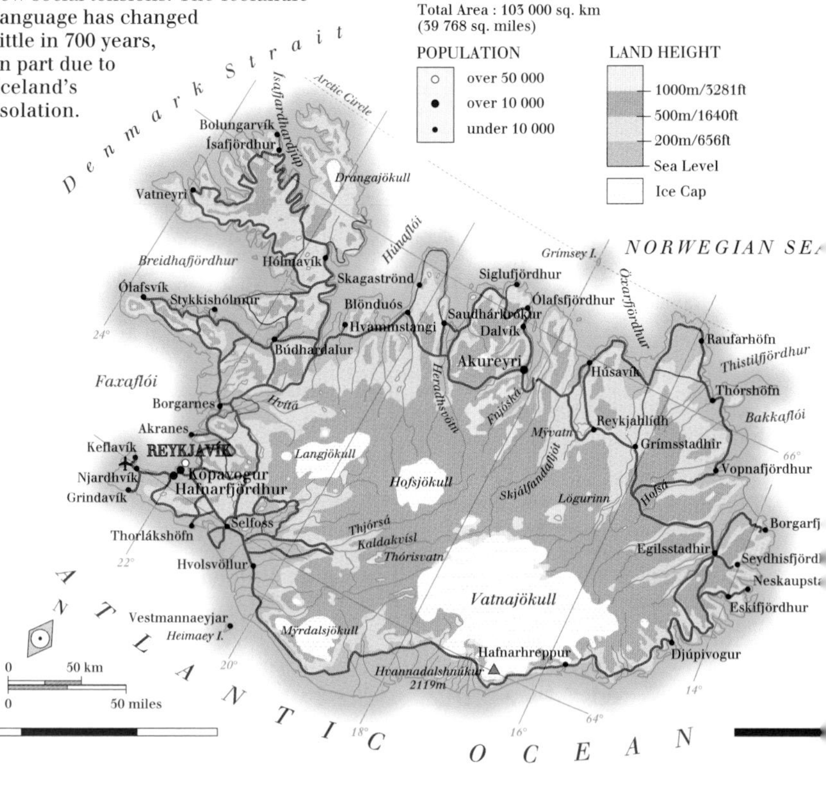
Denmark Strait
Arctic Circle
NORWEGIAN SEA
ATLANTIC OCEAN
Bolungarvík
Ísafjördhur
Ísafjardhardjúp
Drangajökull
Vatneyri
Breidhafjördhur
Hólmavík
Húnaflói
Ólafsvík
Stykkishólmur
Skagaströnd
Blönduós
Hvammstangi
Búdhardalur
Grímsey I.
Siglufjördhur
Ólafsfjördhur
Saudhárkrókur
Dalvík
Akureyri
Eyjafjördhur
Öxarfjördhur
Raufarhöfn
Thistilfjördhur
Húsavík
Thórshöfn
Bakkaflói
Reykjahlídh
Grímsstadhir
Vopnafjördhur
Faxaflói
Borgarnes
Akranes
Keflavík
REYKJAVÍK
Njardhvík
Kópavogur
Hafnarfjördhur
Grindavík
Selfoss
Thorlákshöfn
Hvolsvöllur
Vestmannaeyjar
Heimaey I.
Langjökull
Hofsjökull
Hvítá
Heradhsvötn
Fnjóská
Mývatn
Skjálfandafljót
Lögurinn
Hofsá
Thjórsá
Kaldakvísl
Thórisvatn
Vatnajökull
Mýrdalsjökull
Hafnarhreppur
Hvannadalshnúkur 2119m
Djúpivogur
Egilsstadhir
Borgarfj
Seydhisfjördh
Neskaupst
Eskifjördhur
0 50 km
0 50 miles
24°
22°
20°
18°
16°
14°
64°
66°

WORLD AFFAIRS
Joined UN in 1946

CE | NATO | OECD | OSCE | EFTA

As a member of EFTA, Iceland has access to European markets through the EEA, undermining the need to join the EU. Dispute with the UK over Iceland's enlargement of its fishing zone to 200 nautical miles, were resolved in 1976. Iceland's desire to restart large-scale whaling provokes much international criticism.

AID
Donor

$13m (donations) | Up 30% in 2002

Aid donations are modest, and form a smaller proportion of the budget than in other Scandinavian states.

DEFENSE
No compulsory military service

Coast guard is only military force | Not applicable

Despite being a member of NATO, Iceland has no armed forces. The US is keen to reduce the presence of its forces.

ECONOMICS
Inflation 3.4% p.a. (1990–2001)

$7.94bn | 72.64 Icelandic krónur (76.28)

SCORE CARD

- WORLD GNP RANKING........................97th
- GNP PER CAPITA $27,960
- BALANCE OF PAYMENTS.....................–$24m
- INFLATION 5.2%
- UNEMPLOYMENT 3%

STRENGTHS
High-tech fishing industry with exclusive access to prime fishing grounds. Low inflation and unemployment. Very cheap HEP and geothermal power, potential for use of hydrogen for fuel.

WEAKNESSES
Over half of export earnings from single source: the sea (fish and seafood). State-owned banking sector restricts flexibility.

EXPORTS

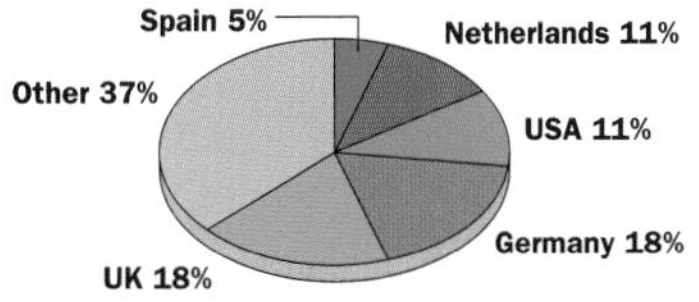
Spain 5%
Netherlands 11%
Other 37%
USA 11%
Germany 18%
UK 18%

IMPORTS

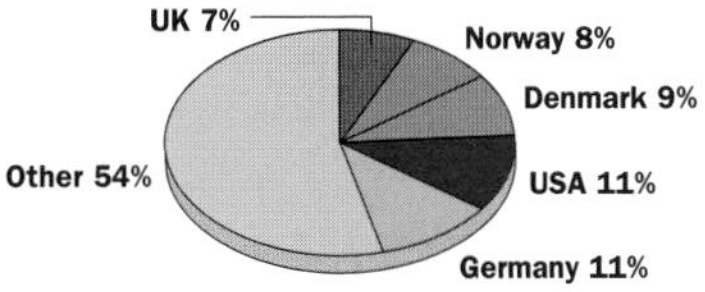
UK 7%
Norway 8%
Denmark 9%
Other 54%
USA 11%
Germany 11%

Lava towers, *near Lake Mývatn in northern Iceland – an area of grassy lowlands. Iceland's center consists of lava desert and glaciers.*

RESOURCES
Electric power 1.3m kW

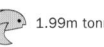

1.99m tonnes | Not an oil producer

470,000 sheep, 74,000 horses, 220,000 chickens | Diatomite

Iceland has virtually no minerals. All energy needs are met by geothermal and hydroelectric sources. A project coming onstream in 2007 will double aluminum-smelting capacity.

ENVIRONMENT
Sustainability rank: 8th

10% (8% partially protected) | 8.7 tonnes per capita

Iceland has no nuclear or coal-fired power plants. In 2006 it intends to resume commercial whaling, despite the possible impact on the tourist whale-watching industry, believing that minke whales are abundant and eat valuable cod stocks. Of concern is the planned aluminum-smelting plant in the east.

MEDIA
TV ownership high

Daily newspaper circulation 368 per 1000 people

PUBLISHING AND BROADCAST MEDIA

There are 4 daily newspapers, including *Dagbladid-Visir* and *Morgunbladid*, which has the largest circulation

11 services: 1 state-owned, 10 independent | 17 services: 1 state-owned, 16 independent

Iceland is renowned for having one of the highest per capita newspaper circulations in the world.

CRIME
No death penalty

107 prisoners | Crime rates are rising

Crime rates are comparatively low. Violent crime is rising, especially on weekends in Reykjavík.

EDUCATION
School leaving age: 16

99% | 13,884 students

Icelanders buy more books per capita than any other nation. Education is state-run; some 46% of school students go on to one of the country's four universities, or to a college abroad.

CHRONOLOGY

Settled by Norwegians in the 9th century, Iceland was ruled by Denmark from 1380 to 1944, becoming fully self-governing in 1918.

- **1940–1945** Occupied by UK and US.
- **1944** Independence as republic.
- **1949** Founder member of NATO.
- **1951** US air base built at Keflavík despite strong local opposition.
- **1972–1976** Extends fishing limits to 50 miles; two "cod wars" with UK.
- **1975** Sets 200-mile fishing limit.
- **1980** Vigdís Finnbogadóttir world's first elected woman head of state.
- **1985** Declares nuclear-free status.
- **1991** David Oddsson prime minister.
- **1995** Center-right coalition formed: reelected in 1999 and 2003.

HEALTH
Welfare state health benefits

1 per 286 people | Cancers, heart, cerebrovascular, and respiratory diseases

The state health system is free to all Icelanders. Iceland has one of the lowest infant mortality rates and one of the highest longevity rates in the world.

SPENDING
GDP/cap. increase

CONSUMPTION AND SPENDING

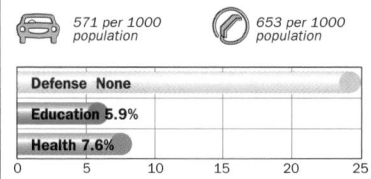

571 per 1000 population | *653 per 1000 population*

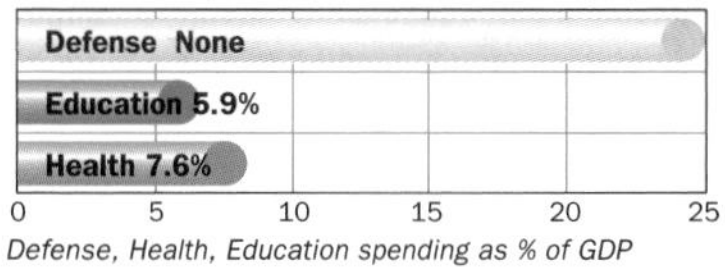
Defense None
Education 5.9%
Health 7.6%
0
5
10
15
20
25

Defense, Health, Education spending as % of GDP

The cost of living is high, but wealth distribution is fairly even, and there is ease of social mobility. Domestic heating, which comes from geothermal sources, is provided at very low cost.

WORLD RANKING

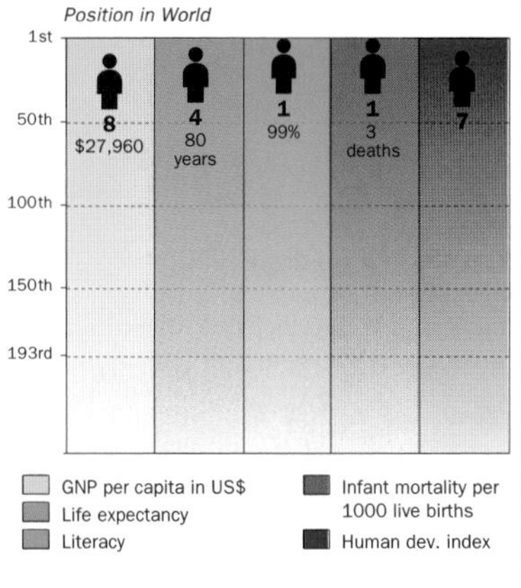
Position in World
1st
50th
100th
150th
193rd
8
$27,960
4
80
years
1
99%
1
3
deaths
7
GNP per capita in US$
Life expectancy
Literacy
Infant mortality per 1000 live births
Human dev. index

INDIA

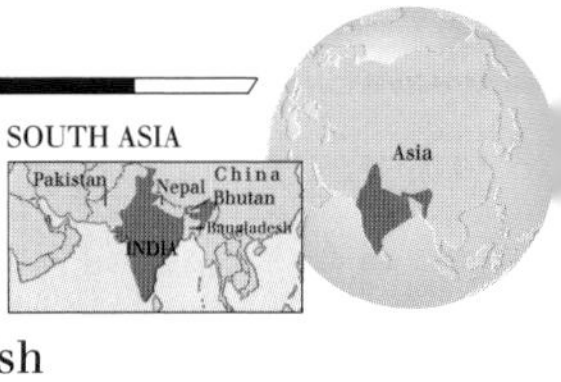
SOUTH ASIA
Pakistan
Nepal
China
Bhutan
Bangladesh
INDIA
Asia

OFFICIAL NAME: Republic of India **CAPITAL:** New Delhi
POPULATION: 1.07 billion **CURRENCY:** Indian rupee **OFFICIAL LANGUAGES:** Hindi and English

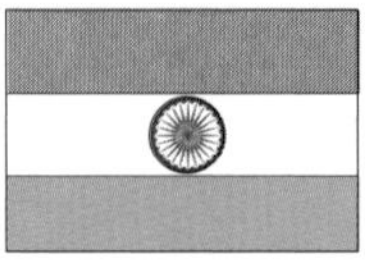

1947
1947
Jan 26
IND
+5.5
+91
.in

SEPARATED FROM the rest of Asia by the Himalaya mountain range, India forms the bulk of a subcontinent. As well as the Himalayas, there are two other main geographic regions, the Indo-Gangetic plain, which lies between the foothills of the Himalayas and the Vindhya Mountains, and the central–southern plateau. India is the world's largest democracy and second most populous country after China. The birthrate has recently been falling, but even at its current level India's population will probably overtake China's by 2030. After years of protectionism, India is opening up its economy to the outside world in the hope that the free market will go some way to alleviating one of the country's major problems – poverty.

CLIMATE

Tropical/subtropical/desert/mountain/monsoon

WEATHER CHART FOR NEW DELHI

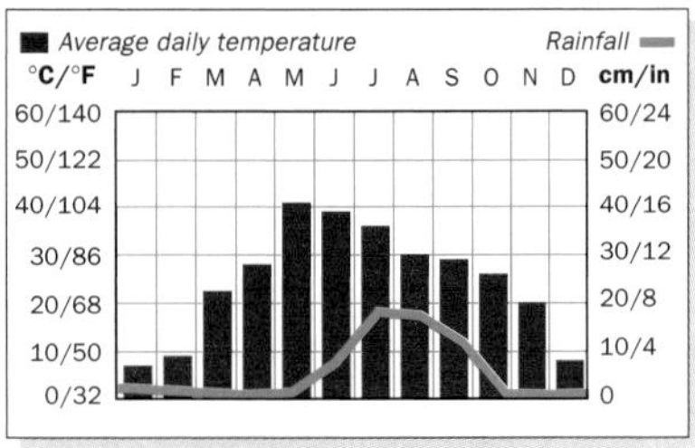
Average daily temperature
Rainfall
°C/°F
J F M A M J J A S O N D
cm/in
60/140
50/122
40/104
30/86
20/68
10/50
0/32
60/24
50/20
40/16
30/12
20/8
10/4
0

Temperatures in the north vary between 5°C (41°F) and 40°C (104°F). Heavy monsoon rains break in June, bringing severe flooding, and peter out by October. The south has a less variable climate. Chennai (Madras) is always hot: average temperatures range from 24°C (75°F) in January to 32°C (90°F) in May and June. Annual heatwaves in the southeast can be unbearable: over 1400 people died in 2003.

TRANSPORTATION

Drive on left

Mumbai
12.8m passengers

1010 ships
6.14m grt

THE TRANSPORTATION NETWORK

1.53m km (948,854 miles)

33,500 km (20,816 miles)

63,140 km (39,233 miles)

16,180 km (10,054 miles)

The state-owned railroad system, the largest in Asia, carries 14 million people a day and employs over 1.5 million. Strict controls on diesel emissions from cars and buses were enforced in 2001. Cycle and scooter rickshaws abound in urban centers. Kolkata (Calcutta), site of India's first metro system, still has rickshaws pulled by hand.

INDIA
Total Area : 3 287 590 sq. km
(1 269 338 sq. miles)
POPULATION
over 5 000 000
over 1 000 000
over 500 000
over 100 000
over 10 000
LAND HEIGHT
5000m/16 405ft
4000m/13 124ft
3000m/9843ft
2000m/6562ft
1000m/3281ft
500m/1640ft
200m/656ft
Sea Level
0
200 km
0
200 miles
N
Aksai Chin
Line of control
KARAKORAM RANGE
Indus
Srinagar
JAMMU & KASHMIR
Jammu
Amritsar
Jalandhar
Ludhiana
HIMACHAL PRADESH
Chandigarh
PUNJAB
Nanda Devi 7816m
HARYANA
Meerut
Delhi
NEW DELHI
Faridabad
Bareilly
Bikaner
THAR DESERT
PAKISTAN
CHINA
TIBET
NEPAL
Jaipur
Agra
Lucknow
Gorakhpur
RAJASTHAN
UTTAR PRADESH
Jodhpur
Gwalior
Kanpur
Yamuna
Patna
Allahabad
Ganges
Varanasi
Kota
Rann of Kachch
GUJARAT
Jabalpur
MADHYA PRADESH
Chota Nagpur Plateau
Gulf of Kachch
Jamnagar
Ahmadabad
Vindhya Range
Bhopal
Indore
Rajkot
Vadodara
Narmada
Bilaspur
Mahanadi
Satpura Range
Surat
Tapi
Nagpur
Raipur
Pimpri
Amravati
Diu
Gulf of Khambhat
Nashik
MAHARASHTRA
Nanded
Godavari
Thane
Kalyan
ARABIAN SEA
Mumbai (Bombay)
Pune
Nizamabad
DECCAN
Warangal
Visakhapatnam
Solapur
ANDHRA PRADESH
Hyderabad
Rajahmundry
KARNATAKA
Vijayawada
Kolhapur
Krishna
Guntur
Kurnool
Tungabhadra
Panaji
GOA
Hubli
Bellary
Western Ghats
Eastern Ghats
Cuddapah
Anantapur
Chennai (Madras)
Bangalore
Vellore
Mangalore
Mysore
Calicut
Salem
Pondicherry
Amindivi Is
KERALA
TAMIL NADU
Coimbatore
Tiruchchirappalli
LAKSHADWEEP (Laccadive Is)
Kavaratti I.
Kalpeni I.
Trichur
Dindigal
Cochin
Madurai
Palk Strait
Minicoy I.
Trivandrum
Tuticorin
SRI LANKA
Gulf of Mannar
Nagercoil
INDIAN OCEAN
North Andaman
Middle Andaman
South Andaman
Port Bl
Little Andaman
NICOBAR ISLANDS
Great Nicobar
(continuation on same

A religious festival. *Such festivals are a frequent occurrence and form an important part of Hindu culture.*

BHUTAN
ARUNACHAL PRADESH
Brahmaputra
Guwāhāti
ASSAM
Imphāl
ANGLADESH
BURMA (MYANMAR)
Kolkata (Calcutta)
Mouths of the Ganges
BAY OF
BENGAL

TOURISM

Visitors : Population 1:388

2.75m visitors

Up 15% in 2003

MAIN TOURIST ARRIVALS

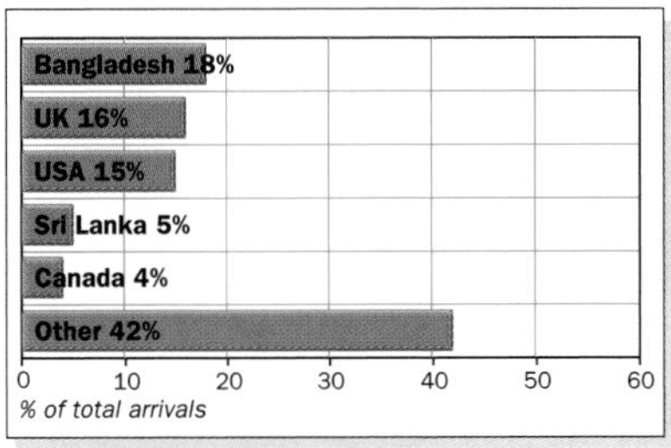
Bangladesh 18%
UK 16%
USA 15%
Sri Lanka 5%
Canada 4%
Other 42%
0 10 20 30 40 50 60
% of total arrivals

Tourism provides almost 8% of GDP. More luxury hotels are being built, and wildlife and adventure tourism are being promoted. India has only a small share of the world tourism market, however, and has suffered recently from security worries over the repercussions of the US-led "war on terrorism" and acute tensions with Pakistan, particularly over Kashmir.

PEOPLE

Pop. density high

Hindi, English, Urdu, Bengali, Marathi, Telugu, Tamil, Bihari, Gujarati,

358/km² (928/mi²)

THE URBAN/RURAL POPULATION SPLIT

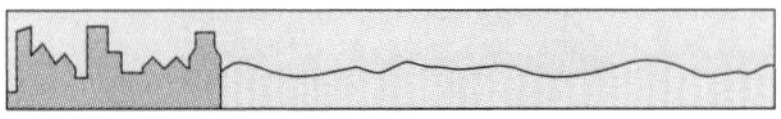
28%
72%

RELIGIOUS PERSUASION

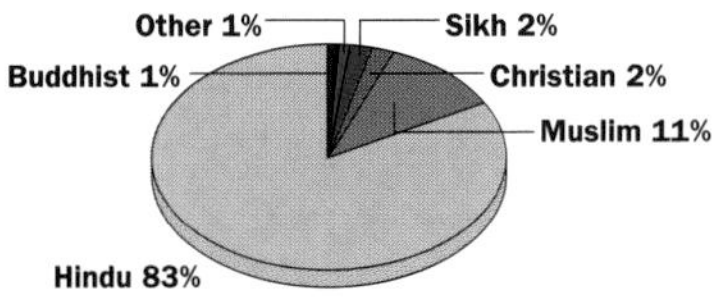
Other 1%
Sikh 2%
Buddhist 1%
Christian 2%
Muslim 11%
Hindu 83%

ETHNIC MAKEUP

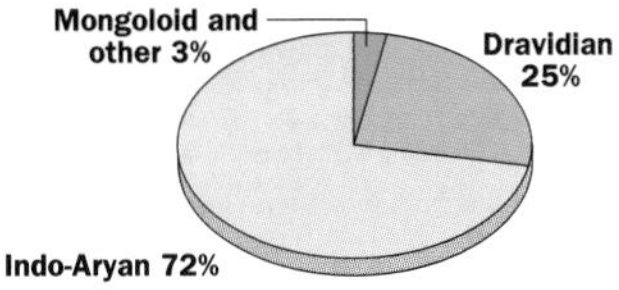
Mongoloid and other 3%
Dravidian 25%
Indo-Aryan 72%

India is the world's second most populous country after China, officially passing the one-billion mark in 2000. Despite a major birth control program, the decrease in population growth has been marginal. Nationwide awareness campaigns aim to promote the idea of smaller families. India's planners consider the rise in the population to be the most significant brake on development. Cultural and religious pressures encourage large families, however, and the extended family is seen as essential security for old age.

The fertile rice-growing areas of the Gangetic plain and delta are very densely populated. The northern state of Uttar Pradesh has the largest population, followed by the western state of Maharashtra and the eastern state of Bihar. Maharashtra is also the most urbanized state, with more than half of its people living in towns or cities. Elsewhere, most Indians live in rural areas, though poverty continues to drive many to the swelling cities.

The overwhelming majority of the population are Hindus, who belong to thousands of castes and subcastes, which largely determine status, occupation, and whom they marry. Tension between Hindus and Muslims has grown in recent years, and escalated sharply in 2002 during violent clashes in Gujarat.

POPULATION AGE BREAKDOWN

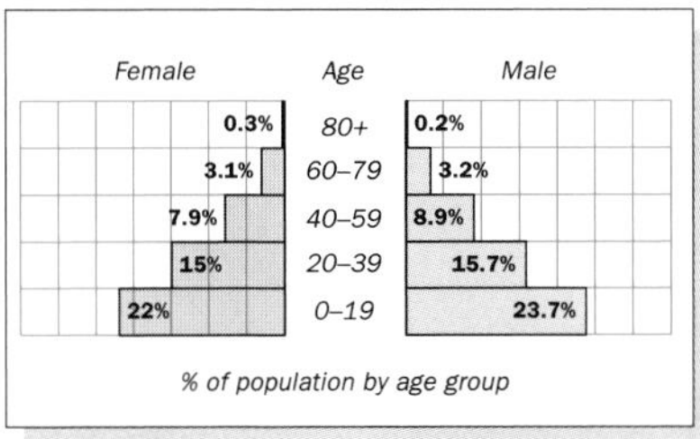
Female
Age
Male
0.3% 80+ 0.2%
3.1% 60–79 3.2%
7.9% 40–59 8.9%
15% 20–39 15.7%
22% 0–19 23.7%
% of population by age group

CHRONOLOGY

The origins of an Indus Valley civilization may be traced back to the third millennium BCE. By the 3rd century BCE, the Mauryan kingdom under Ashoka encompassed most of modern India. Following the Battle of Plassey in 1757, British rule – through the East India Company – was consolidated.

- **1885** Formation of Indian National Congress.
- **1919** Act of Parliament introduces "responsible government."
- **1920–1922** Mahatma Gandhi's first civil disobedience campaign.
- **1935** Government of India Act grants autonomy to provinces.
- **1936** First elections under new constitution.
- **1942–1943** "Quit India" movement.
- **1947** August, independence and partition into India and Pakistan. Jawarhalal Nehru becomes first prime minister.
- **1948** Assassination of Mahatma Gandhi. War with Pakistan over Kashmir. India becomes a republic.
- **1951–1952** First general election won by Congress party.
- **1957** Congress party reelected. First elected communist state government installed in Kerala.
- **1960** Bombay divided into states of Gujarat and Maharashtra.
- **1962** Congress party reelected. Border war with China.
- **1964** Death of Nehru. Lal Bahadur Shastri becomes prime minister.
- **1965** Second war with Pakistan over Kashmir.
- **1966** Shastri dies; Indira Gandhi (daughter of Jawarhalal Nehru) becomes prime minister.
- **1969** Congress party splits into two factions; larger faction led by Indira Gandhi.
- **1971** Indira Gandhi's Congress party wins elections. Third war with Pakistan, over creation of Bangladesh.
- **1972** Simla (peace) Agreement signed with Pakistan.
- **1974** Explosion of first nuclear device in underground test.
- **1975–1977** State of emergency: Gandhi guilty of electoral fraud.
- **1977** Congress loses general election. People's Party (JD) takes power at the center.
- **1978** New political group, Congress (Indira) – Congress (I) – formally established.
- **1980** Indira Gandhi's C(I) wins general election.
- **1984** Indian troops storm Sikh Golden Temple in Amritsar. Assassination of Indira Gandhi ⇨

I

CHRONOLOGY *continued*

by Sikh bodyguard; her son Rajiv becomes prime minister and C(I) leader. Gas explosion at US-owned Union Carbide Corporation plant in Bhopal kills 2000 people in India's worst industrial disaster.

- ❑ **1985** Peace accords with militant separatists in Assam and Punjab.
- ❑ **1987** Deployment of Indian peacekeeping force in Sri Lanka to combat Tamil Tigers.
- ❑ **1989** General election; National Front forms minority government with BJP support. C(I) implicated in Bofors scandal.
- ❑ **1990** Withdrawal of troops from Sri Lanka.
- ❑ **1991** Rajiv Gandhi assassinated. Narasimha Rao becomes prime minister of a C(I) minority government and initiates economic liberalization.
- ❑ **1992** Demolition of the Babri Masjid mosque at Ayodhya by Hindu extremists triggers widespread violence; 1200 people die.
- ❑ **1993** Resurgence of Hindu–Muslim riots. Bomb explosions in Bombay (Mumbai). Border troop agreement with China.
- ❑ **1994** Rupee made fully convertible. C(I) routed in key state elections amid increasing allegations of corruption in ruling party.
- ❑ **1995** Punjab chief minister assassinated by Sikh extremists.
- ❑ **1996** Corruption scandal triggers political crisis. C(I) suffers its worst electoral defeat. Leftist United Front coalition government takes office.
- ❑ **1997** Successive governments fall as C(I) withdraws support.
- ❑ **1998** General election; BJP led by Atal Bihari Vajpayee forms coalition government. Sonia Gandhi, widow of Rajiv Gandhi, becomes president of C(I). India and Pakistan test nuclear missiles.
- ❑ **1999** Vajpayee travels to Pakistan to inaugurate bus service between India and Pakistan. India and Pakistan engage in violent confrontation in Kashmir. BJP returned to power after elections triggered by vote of no confidence.
- ❑ **2001** Earthquake kills more than 25,000 in Gujarat. BJP government implicated in major bribery scandal.
- ❑ **2001–2002** Terrorist attacks by Kashmiri separatists precipitate crisis with Pakistan.
- ❑ **2002** More than 2000, mainly Muslims, killed in Gujarat following worst intercommunal riots since independence.
- ❑ **2003** Heatwave kills over 1400.
- ❑ **2004** C(I) wins elections; Manmohan Singh appointed prime minister.

POLITICS

Multiparty elections

L. House 2004/2009
U. House Varying

President A. P. J. Abdul Kalam

AT THE LAST ELECTION

House of the People (Lok Sabha) 545 seats

40% C(I)
34% NDA
11% LF
7% SP
8% Others

C(I) = Congress (I) and Allies
NDA = National Democratic Alliance (Bharatiya Janata Party–**BJP** and Allies)
LF = Left Front (Communist Party of India (Marxist)–**CPI(M)** and Allies) **SP** = Socialist Party **Nom** = Nominated

Others include independents and two appointed seats reserved for Anglo-Indians

Council of States (Rajya Sabha) 243 seats

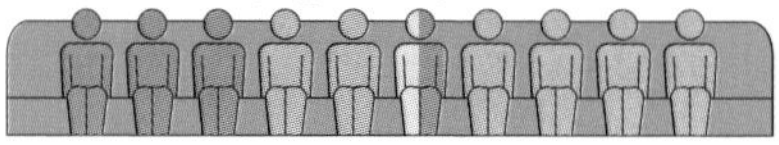
29% C(I)
20% BJP
6% CPI(M)
4% Nom
41% Others

234 members are elected to the Rajya Sabha by State Legislative Assemblies, and nine "distinguished citizens" are nominated by the head of state

India is a multiparty democracy. The Lok Sabha (lower house) is directly elected by universal adult suffrage, while the Rajya Sabha (upper house) is indirectly elected by the state assemblies. There are 28 self-governing states. Of the seven union territories, Delhi and Pondicherry have their own assemblies.

Profile

C(I) was founded in 1978 as the successor to the historic Congress party which led India to independence in 1947. Its bold program in the early 1990s of economic liberalization broke with the party's traditionally left-of-center policies. Allegations of corruption came to undermine it, resulting in heavy electoral defeats in 1996–1999.

The 1998 election established the Hindu nationalist BJP with a strong enough mandate to form a coalition government under A. B. Vajpayee, relegating C(I) to an unprecedented period of opposition at union level. Elections held in 1999 confirmed the BJP-led coalition in power with an overall majority.

Hopes for C(I)'s political revival rested on Sonia Gandhi, the Italian-born widow of the assassinated former prime minister Rajiv Gandhi. She restored the influence of the Nehru dynasty over the party, and led it to a surprise victory at the 2004 polls, but unexpectedly declined the post of prime minister and instead backed former finance minister Manmohan Singh.

Main Political Issues

Hindu militancy

The rise of the right-wing Hindu BJP, which emerged as a credible alternative to C(I) in the late 1990s and took office in 1998, raised fears about the future of India's secular constitution. Hindu nationalism was expressed in outbreaks of serious violence against Muslims and Christians. A campaign to rebuild a Hindu temple at Ayodhya on a sacred Muslim site symbolized this divisiveness. The BJP's failure to embrace the rural poor in its economic policies, however, led to its shock defeat in the 2004 elections.

Political corruption

Allegations of political corruption have dominated Indian politics for decades. In 1989, C(I) prime minister Rajiv Gandhi was accused of accepting bribes from Bofors, a Swedish arms company. In 1996, corruption forced the resignations of several C(I) government ministers and the leader of the opposition BJP. The issue resurfaced in 2001, when the BJP government was implicated in the "Tehelka scandal" over arms sales, which led to the resignation of the defense minister.

The free market

The introduction of economic reforms was controversial. Critics argued that free trade would undermine local production; the BJP-led coalition was generally opposed to competition from foreign firms. In the 1990s most governments increased spending on rural development programs in order to soften the impact of economic liberalization, though not enough to prevent a rural backlash in the 2004 election and the surprise victory of C(I), seen as less biased toward the urban elite. The appointment of Prime Minister Singh, referred to as the father of economic reform, offset investors' fears of the influence of leftist parties over the new government.

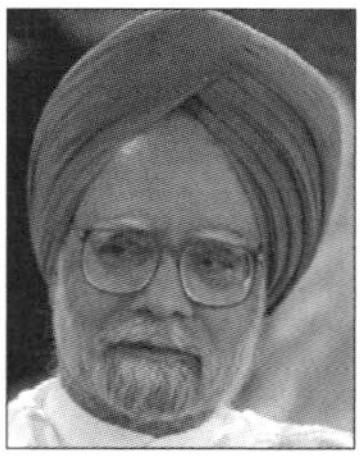

Manmohan Singh, *the first Sikh prime minister (from 2004).*

A. P. J. Abdul Kalam, *a Muslim nuclear scientist, elected president in 2002.*

Sonia Gandhi *led Congress (I) to electoral victory in 2004, but declined the premiership.*

WORLD AFFAIRS

Joined UN in 1945

Comm | G15 | G24 | NAM | SAARC

Even without its burgeoning economy and its 1.3 million men under arms, India's size, population, and strategic location would guarantee it a prominent voice in regional and world affairs. A traditional policy of nonalignment has allowed India to become a powerful and effective spokesman for developing countries within organizations such as the WTO. India wants a permanent seat on the UN Security Council, and is publicly supported in this ambition by the UK, the former colonial power.

Slow but steady talks on a long-running border dispute with China have averted a return to the dangerous tensions of the 1960s, and the main preoccupation of foreign policy has been the dispute with Pakistan over Kashmir. Pulling back from the brink of war in 2002, India and Pakistan have since opened high-level talks.

AID

Recipient

$1.46bn (receipts) — Down 15% in 2002

India does not depend on aid. The US suspended donations following nuclear tests in 1998, but restored payments in late 2001. The World Bank and Japan are the largest donors. International relief aid helped victims of the 2001 Gujarat earthquake.

DEFENSE

No compulsory military service

$13.1bn — Down 6% in 2002

INDIAN ARMED FORCES

3898 main battle tanks (700 T-55, 1900 T-72 M1, 1200 Vijayanta, 84 T-90S)	1.1m personnel
19 submarines, 1 carrier, 8 destroyers, 16 frigates, 4 corvettes, 45 patrol boats	55,000 personnel
744 combat aircraft (64 Jaguar S(I), 407 MiG-21/23/27/29, 40 Mirage 2000H/TH)	170,000 personnel
Capability undisclosed; weapons tested in 1998	

India considers a nuclear deterrent to be vital, and publicly tested weapons in 1998. It has the world's third-largest military, and produces its own hardware. In 2001 the Agni-II intermediate-range missile, which is able to carry a nuclear warhead anywhere in Pakistan, went into production, while the long-delayed Light Combat Aircraft began flight tests. Virtual nuclear tests became possible in 2003 with the construction of the Param Padma supercomputer. India aims to send its own probe to the Moon in 2008.

ECONOMICS

Inflation 7.6% p.a. (1990–2001)

$495bn

45.98 Indian rupees (46.47)

SCORE CARD

❑ World GNP Ranking	11th
❑ GNP per Capita	$470
❑ Balance of Payments	$4.66bn
❑ Inflation	4.4%
❑ Unemployment	9%

EXPORTS

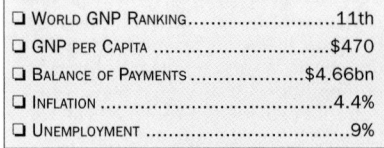

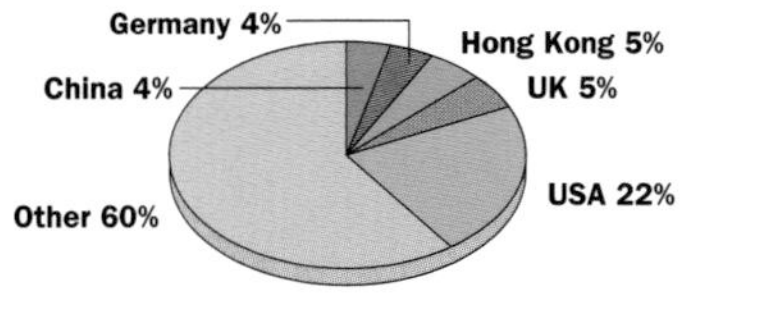
Germany 4%
China 4%
Hong Kong 5%
UK 5%
USA 22%
Other 60%

IMPORTS

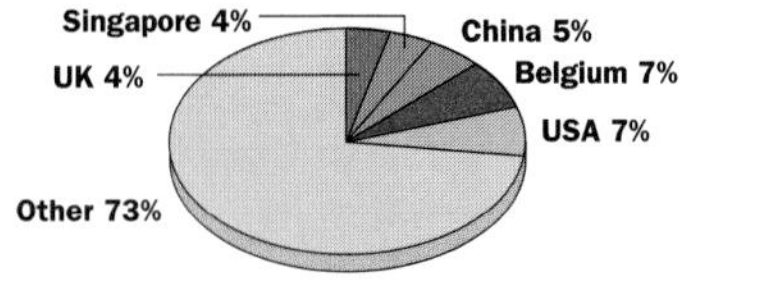
Singapore 4%
UK 4%
China 5%
Belgium 7%
USA 7%
Other 73%

STRENGTHS

Massive home market of over one billion people. Cheap labor. Call centers outsourced from Western countries. Pool of highly skilled workers, encouraging high-tech industries such as software programming. Bollywood film industry. Highly efficient textile sector and garment manufacturers. Growing competitiveness in world market, reflected in strong export growth. Competition encouraging improvement in manufacturing standards. Despite strong objections from opposition parties, India ratified the GATT world trade agreement in 1995.

Since the economy was opened up to foreign competition in 1991, foreign direct investment has risen massively. Much of this has gone into the power sector. Large multinationals, such as Coca-Cola and IBM, are expanding, despite some hostility while the BJP was in government to the growing presence of foreign businesses.

WEAKNESSES

A large budget deficit dogs the economy. Governments have found it politically difficult to move away from the old system of widespread subsidies. The value of the rupee has declined sharply. Poor communications systems and power shortages hinder growth. The prestige of Bollywood has been damaged by allegations of underworld connections.

PROFILE

India has the fastest-growing economy in Asia after China. From a highly protectionist mixed economy, which succeeded in building the basis of a modern industrial state, India has to a large extent converted to a free-market economy and is entering the global marketplace. Wide-ranging reforms, from lowering trade barriers to attracting foreign investment, have been put in place. The United Front and BJP-led governments in power from 1996 to 2004 did not undo these reforms, though they were criticized for not being wholehearted about driving them forward. Meanwhile, in the rural economy millions of people grapple with the problems of subsistence farming.

ECONOMIC PERFORMANCE INDICATOR

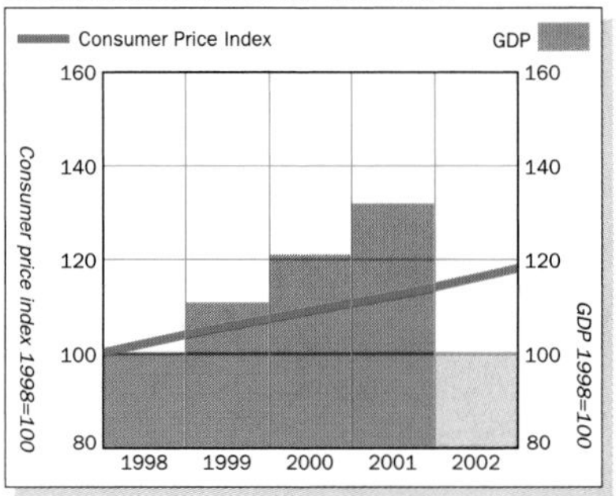
Consumer Price Index
GDP
160
140
120
100
80
Consumer price index 1998=100
GDP 1998=100
1998
1999
2000
2001
2002

INDIA : MAJOR BUSINESSES

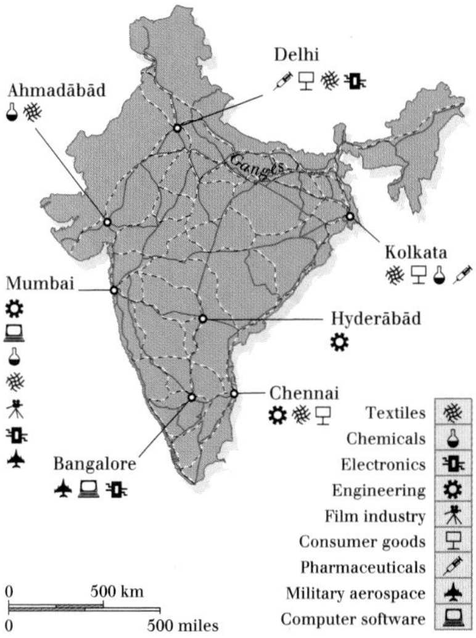
Delhi
Ahmadābād
Ganges
Kolkata
Mumbai
Hyderābād
Chennai
Bangalore
Textiles
Chemicals
Electronics
Engineering
Film industry
Consumer goods
Pharmaceuticals
Military aerospace
Computer software
0
500 km
0
500 miles

***Hillside monastery in Ladakh,** Kashmir, northern India. The Ladakhi Buddhists maintain their traditional farming existence and are known for their friendliness.*

I

RESOURCES

Electric power 115m kW

5.97m tonnes

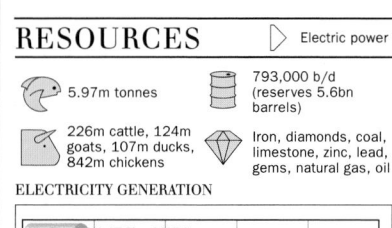

793,000 b/d (reserves 5.6bn barrels)

226m cattle, 124m goats, 107m ducks, 842m chickens

Iron, diamonds, coal, limestone, zinc, lead, gems, natural gas, oil

ELECTRICITY GENERATION

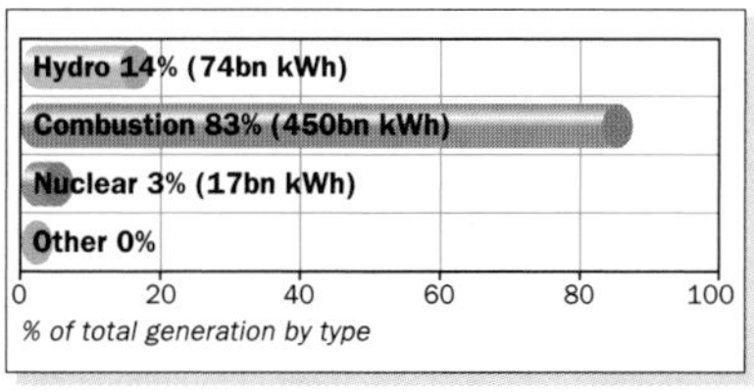

Hydro 14% (74bn kWh)
Combustion 83% (450bn kWh)
Nuclear 3% (17bn kWh)
Other 0%
0
20
40
60
80
100
% of total generation by type

Agriculture still dominates the economy, providing 25% of GDP and employing over 60% of the workforce. Tea, cotton, and rice are the principal cash crops, though agricultural products now only account for 12% of exports. Assam and Darjeeling are among India's most noted teas; cotton and jute provide the raw material for the strong textile industry.

Precious gems and jewelry, including cut diamonds, are the most valuable mineral exports, though iron ore is also important. In addition, there are large coal reserves: India is the world's third-largest coal producer. Despite this, and discoveries of new gas reserves, India is unable to meet its own domestic energy needs, and petroleum and coal dominate imports. Efforts to increase power production through a series of "mega projects" to construct large power plants have been hit by financial mismanagement and a lack of investor confidence. The government hopes to make over $1 billion from the part-privatization of the oil industry.

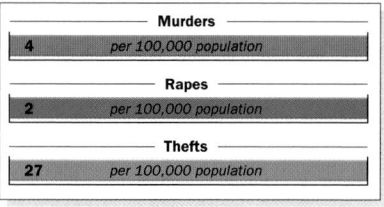

INDIA - LAND USE

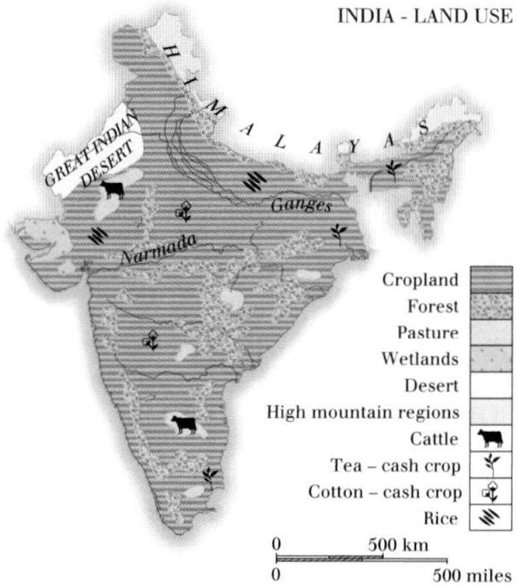

HIMALAYAS
GREAT INDIAN DESERT
Ganges
Narmada
Cropland
Forest
Pasture
Wetlands
Desert
High mountain regions
Cattle
Tea – cash crop
Cotton – cash crop
Rice
0
500 km
0
500 miles

ENVIRONMENT

Sustainability rank: 116th

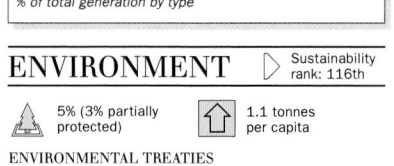

5% (3% partially protected)

1.1 tonnes per capita

ENVIRONMENTAL TREATIES

Yes

Yes

Yes

Yes

Yes

Yes

Deforestation is one of India's most pressing environmental problems. Industrial and agricultural pressures have felled almost 90% of original forest cover. This results in major soil erosion, the silting up of dams, and landslides. Unusually serious flooding in eastern states in 2000 was largely attributed to deforestation. On the other hand, dealing with water scarcities, such as the drought which affected much of the northwest in 2000, has become a major public policy issue.

MEDIA

TV ownership medium

Daily newspaper circulation 28 per 1000 people

PUBLISHING AND BROADCAST MEDIA

There are over 5000 daily newspapers. The *Times of India*, the *Statesman*, and the *India Express* publish nationally

1 state-owned service, several private stations

1 state-owned service, several music and educational stations

Audiences for the state-run Doordarshan TV channels have fallen since the arrival of satellite TV and private broadcasters. US news channel CNN pioneered India's cable TV industry in 1991, and there are now over 50 million connections. Indian films, largely produced at "Bollywood" (Mumbai), are now a major part of the economy, with millions of devotees worldwide. There are thousands of newspapers; the *Times of India* has over two million readers. Private radio stations cannot broadcast news, and some journalists suffer harassment.

CRIME

Death penalty in use

304,893 prisoners

Down 3% in 1999

CRIME RATES

Murders
4 *per 100,000 population*

Rapes
2 *per 100,000 population*

Thefts
27 *per 100,000 population*

Interreligious violence is sporadic but serious. Attacks on Christians draw particular attention, but were overshadowed by Hindu–Muslim violence in Gujarat in 2002. Security forces gained increased powers that year under the Prevention of Terrorism Ordinance, passed in response to Kashmiri separatist attacks in Delhi and other cities.

Violent crime is increasing, especially in the big cities. Gangs have made vast profits from smuggling, prostitution, narcotics, and protection and extortion rackets. Theft has risen as consumer spending increases. The first execution for 13 years was carried out in 2004.

Dacoits still operate in large areas of central India. Modeled on the *thugee* gangs of the 19th century, they are outlaws who live by highway robbery and terrorizing small rural communities.

EDUCATION

School leaving age: 12

61%

10.5m students

THE EDUCATION SYSTEM

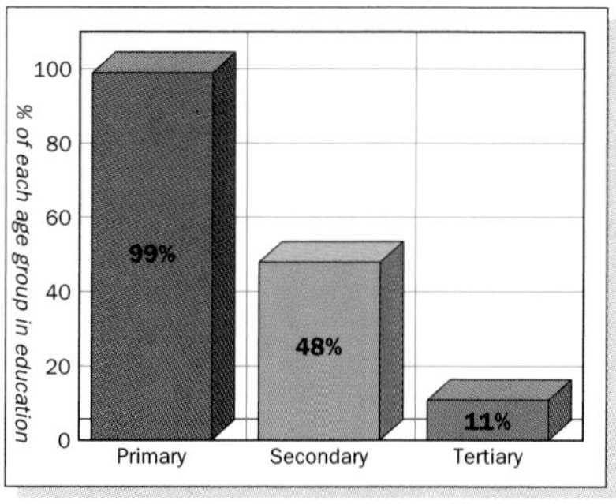

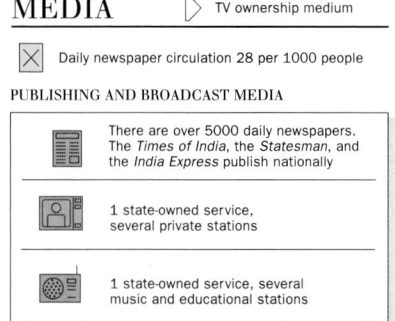

100
80
60
40
20
0
% of each age group in education
99%
48%
11%
Primary
Secondary
Tertiary

Education is primarily the responsibility of the individual state governments. There is now a primary school in every village across the subcontinent, but many children drop out of school to provide supplementary income for their families. There are more than 60 million students at secondary level, and an estimated 24 million graduates from more than 200 universities. Women make up around 40% of those enrolled in higher education, a good percentage for a low-income economy. Though the high level of illiteracy is a brake on development, India has one of the largest pools of science graduates anywhere in the world.

***Terraced fields** in central India. In addition to rice, wheat, sorghum, maize, millet, and barley are also important cereal crops.*

TERRORISM, SECURITY, AND NUCLEAR DETERRENCE

THE SEARCH FOR security in the face of terrorist threats is a sadly familiar problem for the world's largest democracy. Communal and separatist passions have bedeviled its politics since independence in 1947, and indeed lay at the heart of the partition of what had been British India to form the separate states of India and Pakistan.

HIGH-PROFILE ASSASSINATIONS

The ensuing years brought frequent reminders of the many varieties of violent extremism to which India was vulnerable. Notable were the murder of Mahatma Gandhi by a Hindu extremist in 1948, the death of Prime Minister Indira Gandhi at the hands of militant Sikhs in her own bodyguard in 1984, and the 1991 assassination of her son Rajiv Gandhi, himself an ex-prime minister, by Tamil separatists from neighboring Sri Lanka.

THE KASHMIR ISSUE

Throughout this period, India's troubled relationship with Pakistan never overcame their mutual hostility over Kashmir. India has regarded the state of Jammu and Kashmir as an integral part of its territory since the maharajah's decision to accede to the Union at the time of partition. Pakistan, however, points to the unfulfilled promise of a referendum on the matter among the state's majority Muslim population. Pakistan has occupied one-third of Kashmiri territory since 1948 (north of the de facto border, the Line of Control, where the fighting ended in the first India–Pakistan war that year). The two sides fought a second war over Kashmir in 1965 and sporadic bombardments across the Line of Control are a commonplace matter. More recently, Pakistan has sponsored a guerrilla war in Jammu and Kashmir that has claimed 60,000 lives. Serious fighting amounting to undeclared war broke out following a Pakistani cross-border incursion in 1999.

***Missile technology** and nuclear weapons raise the stakes of conflict.*

THE BRINK OF NUCLEAR WAR

The brink of all-out conflict was again reached in 2002, in the wake of terrorist attacks which reached into the heart of India, including a dramatic shooting at the parliament in New Delhi the preceding December. India mobilized its whole army, a million troops faced each other across the Line of Control, and the threat of nuclear war grabbed the world's attention.

India had carried out its first nuclear test in 1974, and ended any ambiguity about its nuclear weapons status with further underground test explosions in Rajasthan in May 1998. Its declared policy of "no first use" gave little reassurance to Pakistan, which was developing its own nuclear capability in direct response to the "Indian threat"; it went public with its own tests (linked to the development of its missile program) a few weeks later.

DEFUSING THE TENSION

The tension of 2002 has given way to a kind of rapprochement born out of fear, international pressure, and the crippling cost of escalating confrontation. In January 2004 the then Indian prime minister A. B. Vajpayee traveled to Pakistan for the first time in nearly five years to attend a south Asian regional summit. Travel and diplomatic links were restored, and a moratorium on further tests was confirmed by the two sides in June 2004 when a "hotline" was set up to defuse future tension. This agreement set the scene for a meeting of defense ministers in New Delhi in August, talks at foreign minister level in September, and even the prospect of a bilateral summit.

***Indian troops patrol** the Line of Control in Kashmir.*

HEALTH

Welfare state health benefits

1 per 1885 people

Respiratory, nutritional, and diarrheal diseases, malaria

Malnutrition is extremely common, increasing infant mortality, much of it due to preventable diseases. Air pollution from the domestic use of solid fuel kills half a million children every year. HIV infection rates are rising and 5.1 million adults were living with HIV/AIDS by 2004, the second-highest number in the world. State governments are responsible for most health programs, but various national projects include a huge polio eradication program. Plans to subsidize health insurance for the poorest of the poor were announced in 2000.

SPENDING

GDP/cap. increase

CONSUMPTION AND SPENDING

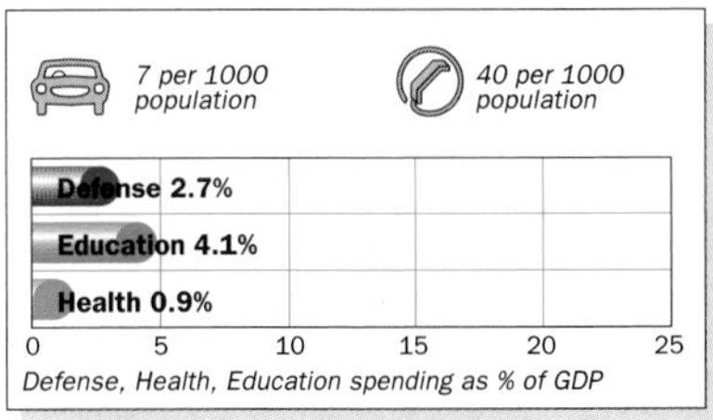
7 per 1000 population
40 per 1000 population
Defense 2.7%
Education 4.1%
Health 0.9%
0
5
10
15
20
25
Defense, Health, Education spending as % of GDP

India has become steadily more wealthy since independence, but distribution of this wealth has been far from even. Officially almost 300 million people – just under a third of the population – live in poverty. However, under the UN's $2-a-day guide the number is more like 800 million. Poverty is worse in the countryside, but more visible in the sprawling slums and on the crowded streets of the big cities.

Perched above the poverty line are the increasingly affluent middle classes, making up the bulk of the remaining population. With access to the new economy, the richest enjoy a standard of living comparable to that in the West, and have high expectations for their children.

WORLD RANKING

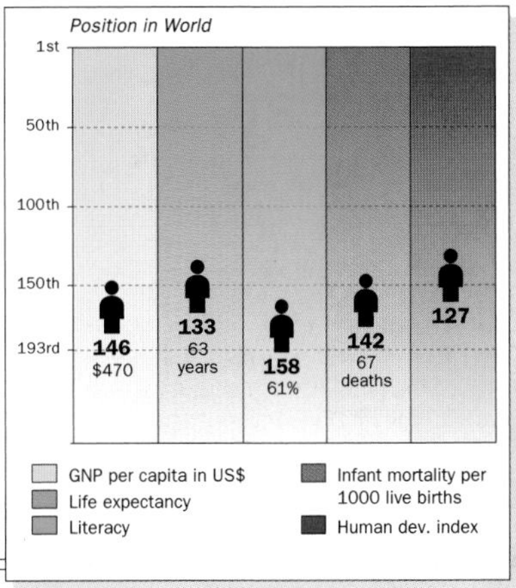
Position in World
1st
50th
100th
150th
193rd
146
$470
133
63 years
158
61%
142
67 deaths
127
GNP per capita in US$
Life expectancy
Literacy
Infant mortality per 1000 live births
Human dev. index

I

INDONESIA

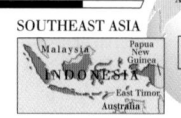

SOUTHEAST ASIA

OFFICIAL NAME: Republic of Indonesia **CAPITAL:** Jakarta
POPULATION: 220 million **CURRENCY:** Rupiah **OFFICIAL LANGUAGE:** Bahasa Indonesia

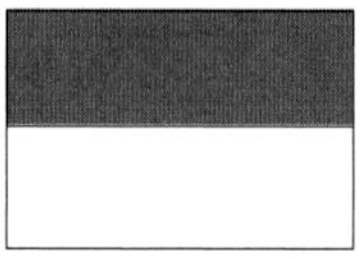

1949 | 1999 | Aug 17 | RI | +7 to +9 | +62 | .id

INDONESIA IS THE WORLD'S largest archipelago. Its 18,108 islands stretch 5000 km (3100 miles) from the Indian Ocean to New Guinea. Java, Kalimantan, Papua, Sulawesi, and Sumatra are mountainous, volcanic, and densely forested. Politics after independence was dominated by the military for over three decades, until the fall of the Suharto regime in 1998, when a partial "civilianization" began. In outlying regions, the forcibly suppressed demands for greater autonomy have flared up, bringing renewed violence. East Timor, which Indonesia invaded in 1975 and then annexed, voted for independence in 1999 and became a fully sovereign state in 2002.

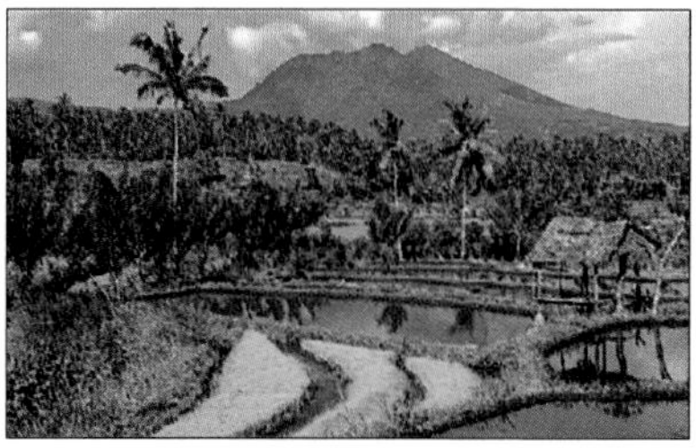

***Rice terraces on Bali,** one of Indonesia's many islands and its most popular tourist destination. Rice is the staple food crop.*

CLIMATE

Tropical equatorial/ monsoon

WEATHER CHART FOR JAKARTA

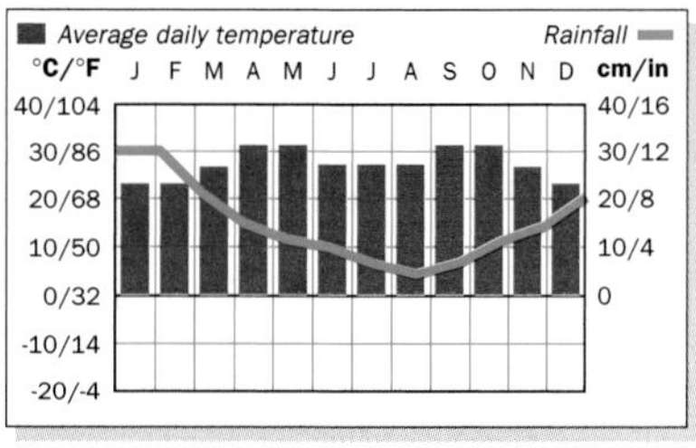

Average daily temperature
Rainfall
°C/°F J F M A M J J A S O N D cm/in
40/104
30/86
20/68
10/50
0/32
-10/14
-20/-4
40/16
30/12
20/8
10/4
0

Indonesia's climate is predominantly tropical. Variations relate mainly to differences in latitude, but hilly areas are cooler overall. Rain falls throughout the year, often in thunderstorms, but there is a relatively dry season from June to September. December to March is the wettest period, except in the Moluccas, which receive the bulk of their rain between June and September.

TRANSPORTATION

Drive on left

Sukarno–Hatta, Jakarta 19.7m passengers

2628 ships 3.72m grt

THE TRANSPORTATION NETWORK

203,200 km (126,262 miles)

200 km (124 miles)

6458 km (4013 miles)

21,579 km (13,409 miles)

For a multi-island state spread across three time zones, communications are an obvious government priority. Indonesia was an early entrant into satellite communications, providing an international satellite-based telephone system as early as 1976.

Conditions vary greatly, however, in the different provinces. Road surfaces in Java and Sumatra are excellent. Rail services are restricted to these two islands. In contrast, roads in Kalimantan and Papua are poor, and most travel is by air or river.

TOURISM

Visitors : Population 1:50

4.44m visitors

Down 12% in 2003

MAIN TOURIST ARRIVALS

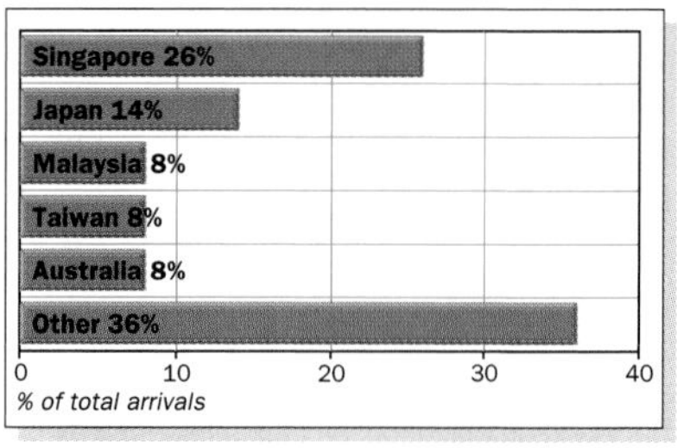

Singapore 26%
Japan 14%
Malaysia 8%
Taiwan 8%
Australia 8%
Other 36%
0
10
20
30
40
% of total arrivals

Tourism took off during the 1980s. The number of tourists now exceeds four million, though political unrest and the rise of Islamist militancy have discouraged many visitors. Expansion has been encouraged by major investment in hotels and the opening of Bali to airlines other than the national carrier, Garuda Indonesia. Tourism on Bali recovered quickly from the 2002 bombing.

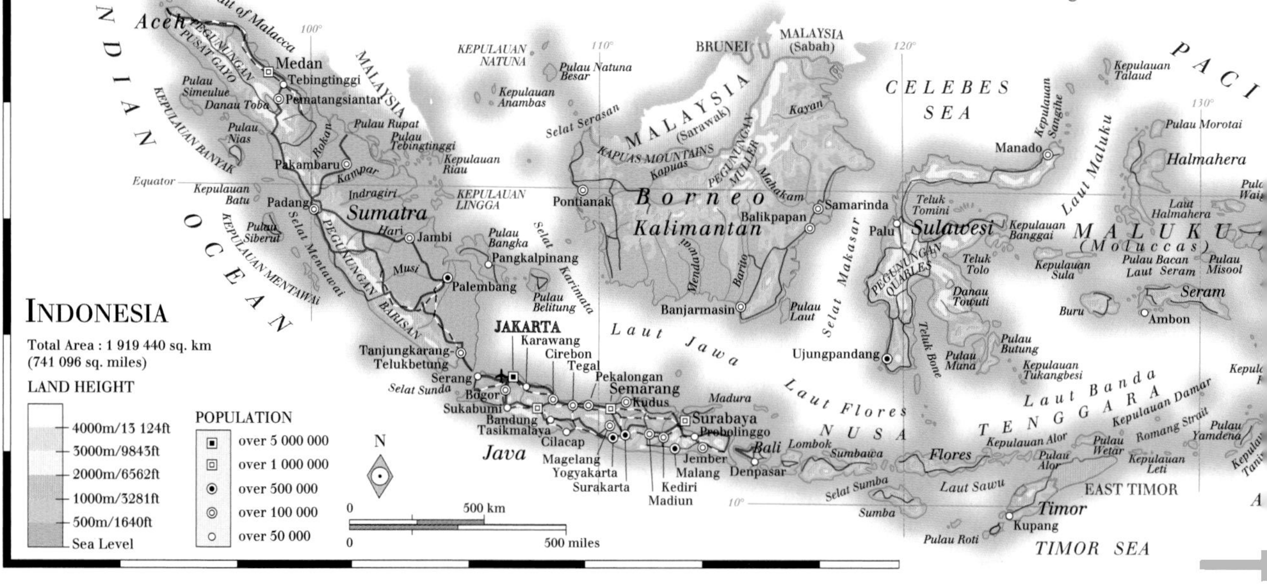

ANDAMAN SEA
INDIAN OCEAN
Strait of Malacca
Aceh
Medan
Tebingtinggi
Pematangsiantar
Pulau Simeulue
Danau Toba
Pulau Nias
KEPULAUAN BANYAK
Pakambaru
Kampar
Rokan
MALAYSIA
Pulau Rupat
Pulau Tebingtinggi
Kepulauan Riau
KEPULAUAN LINGGA
Equator
Kepulauan Batu
Padang
Indragiri
Sumatra
Hari
Jambi
Pulau Siberut
Selat Mentawai
KEPULAUAN MENTAWAI
Musi
Palembang
Pulau Bangka
Pangkalpinang
Selat Karimata
Pulau Belitung
Tanjungkarang-Telukbetung
Selat Sunda
JAKARTA
Karawang
Cirebon
Tegal
Pekalongan
Semarang
Kudus
Serang
Bogor
Sukabumi
Bandung
Tasikmalaya
Cilacap
Java
Magelang
Yogyakarta
Surakarta
Kediri
Madiun
Malang
Jember
Probolinggo
Surabaya
Madura
Bali
Denpasar
Lombok
Sumbawa
Flores
Selat Sumba
Sumba
Laut Sawu
Timor
Kupang
Pulau Roti
TIMOR SEA
EAST TIMOR
KEPULAUAN NATUNA
Pulau Natuna Besar
Kepulauan Anambas
Selat Serasan
BRUNEI
MALAYSIA (Sabah)
MALAYSIA (Sarawak)
KAPUAS MOUNTAINS
Kapuas
PEGUNUNGAN MULLER
Mahakam
Kayan
Pontianak
Borneo
Kalimantan
Balikpapan
Samarinda
Barito
Mendawai
Banjarmasin
Laut Jawa
Pulau Laut
Selat Makasar
Ujungpandang
Laut Flores
NUSA TENGGARA
CELEBES SEA
Kepulauan Sangihe
Manado
Teluk Tomini
Palu
Sulawesi
PEGUNUNGAN QUARLES
Teluk Tolo
Danau Towuti
Teluk Bone
Pulau Muna
Pulau Butung
Kepulauan Tukangbesi
Kepulauan Banggai
Kepulauan Sula
Laut Maluku
MALUKU (Moluccas)
Pulau Bacan
Pulau Morotai
Halmahera
Laut Halmahera
Kepulauan Talaud
Buru
Ambon
Seram
Laut Seram
Misool
Laut Banda
Kepulauan Alor
Pulau Alor
Pulau Wetar
Romang Strait
Kepulauan Damar
Kepulauan Leti
Pulau Yamdena
100°
110°
120°
130°
10°
INDONESIA
Total Area : 1 919 440 sq. km (741 096 sq. miles)
LAND HEIGHT
4000m/13 124ft
3000m/9843ft
2000m/6562ft
1000m/3281ft
500m/1640ft
Sea Level
POPULATION
over 5 000 000
over 1 000 000
over 500 000
over 100 000
over 50 000
N
0 500 km
0 500 miles

PEOPLE

Pop. density medium

Javanese, Sundanese, Madurese, Bahasa Indonesia, Dutch

122/km² (317/mi²)

THE URBAN/RURAL POPULATION SPLIT

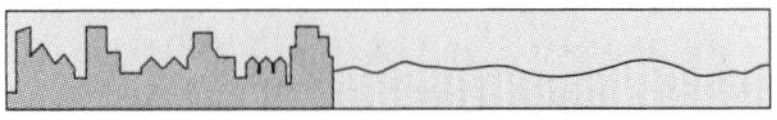
43%
57%

RELIGIOUS PERSUASION

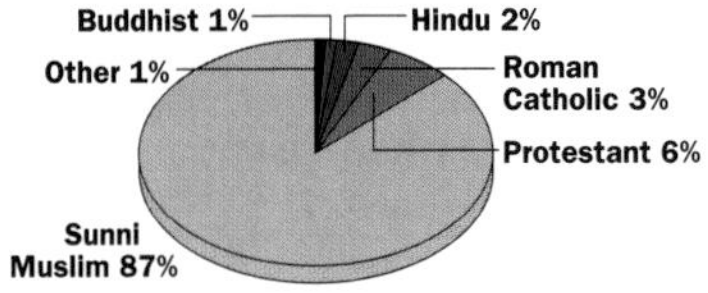
Buddhist 1%
Hindu 2%
Other 1%
Roman Catholic 3%
Protestant 6%
Sunni Muslim 87%

ETHNIC MAKEUP

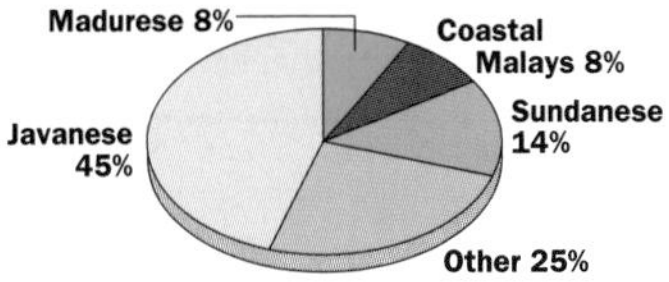
Madurese 8%
Coastal Malays 8%
Sundanese 14%
Javanese 45%
Other 25%

The basic Melanesian–Malay ethnic division disguises a diverse society. The national language, Bahasa Indonesia, coexists with at least 250 other spoken languages or dialects. Attempts by the Javanese political elite to suppress local cultures have been vigorously opposed, especially by the Aceh of northern Sumatra, and the Papuans of New Guinea.

Religious and interethnic hostility is increasing. Since 1998 there have been violent clashes between Muslims and Christians on Sulawesi, and in the Moluccas. Similar clashes occurred in Kalimantan in 1999 and 2001 between indigenous Dayaks and ethnic Madurese immigrants. Aceh introduced *sharia* (Islamic law) in 2000.

Discrimination against ethnic Chinese has encouraged vicious attacks on their businesses, as in Jakarta in 1998.

Gender equality is enshrined in law, and women are active in public life.

POPULATION AGE BREAKDOWN

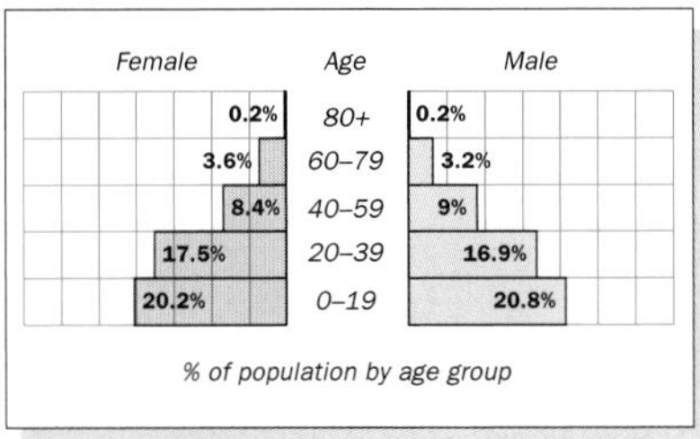
Female
Age
Male
0.2%
80+
0.2%
3.6%
60–79
3.2%
8.4%
40–59
9%
17.5%
20–39
16.9%
20.2%
0–19
20.8%
% of population by age group

WORLD AFFAIRS

Joined UN in 1950

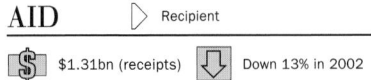

APEC ASEAN G15 OIC OPEC

Indonesia pursues a largely pro-Western foreign policy, though the government is under pressure to improve its human rights record, and it opposed the 2003 invasion of Iraq. The scale and nature of the East Timor massacres in 1999 severely damaged its standing. Internal security in the far-flung provinces tests regional relations.

China remains a concern, despite the restoration of diplomatic ties in 1990. Indonesia and Australia have cooperated on security since 1995, but the movement of illegal immigrants through Indonesia and recent Islamist terrorism have caused tensions.

AID

Recipient

$1.31bn (receipts)

Down 13% in 2002

Japan accounts for the bulk of bilateral aid. Multilateral aid comes above all from the World Bank, though it called for urgent reform in late 2001 before loaning more money. Aid has been notoriously subject to "leakage."

POLITICS

Multiparty elections

2004/2009

President Susilo Bambang Yudhoyono

AT THE LAST ELECTION

House of Representatives 550 seats

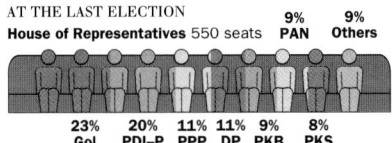

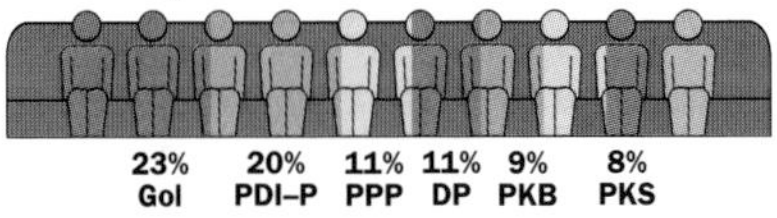
9% PAN
9% Others
23% Gol
20% PDI–P
11% PPP
11% DP
9% PKB
8% PKS

Gol = Golkar **PDI–P** = Indonesian Democratic Party of Struggle **PPP** = United Development Party **DP** = Democrat Party **PKB** = National Awakening Party **PAN** = National Mandate Party **PKS** = Prosperous Justice Party

38 seats are reserved for the army

Indonesia is a multiparty democracy.

PROFILE

In 1998 Gen. Suharto was forced to resign amid widespread protest over corruption, economic mismanagement, and denial of democratic rights. Elections were won by the mainly Muslim PDI–P, led by Megawati Sukarnoputri, daughter of the first president, but she was kept from presidential office until 2001. Her lackluster leadership in addressing economic problems alienated many voters, however, and in 2004 she lost the first direct presidential election to her former security minister, Gen. (retd.) Susilo Bambang Yudhoyono of the DP.

Jayapura
Papua
(Irian Jaya)
Puncak Jaya 5030 m
New Guinea
Digul
Pulau
Pulau Yos Sudarso
PAPUA NEW GUINEA

MAIN POLITICAL ISSUES

The army

Under Gen. Suharto (1966–1998), Golkar and the army were dominant, and the army remains heavily involved in politics. In early 2000, the influential Gen. Wiranto left the government, but the army refused to relinquish its 38-seat entitlement in the legislature before 2009. Golkar reclaimed its position as the largest party in the legislature at the 2004 election, but Wiranto came only third in the subsequent presidential poll.

Separatist and Islamist unrest

Separatism and religious violence threaten national unity. Though greater autonomy was granted to both Papua and Aceh in 2001, tensions persist. Since the late 1990s several groups have emerged which espoused radical Islamist agendas and were associated with violent incidents, most notably the Bali bombings of October 2002.

S. B. Yudhoyono, *won the presidential election in 2004.*

Megawati Sukarnoputri, *president 2001-2004.*

CHRONOLOGY

Hindu, Buddhist, and Islamic interest preceded 16th-century European rivalries over valuable spices. The Dutch had won control by the 17th century, when colonization began on Java. By 1910, the Dutch East Indies encompassed present-day Indonesia.

- **1920** Indonesian Communist Party (PKI) formed; leads revolt in West Java (1926) and Sumatra (1927).
- **1927** Indonesian National Party formed under Dr. Sukarno.
- **1930s** Dutch repress nationalists.
- **1942–1945** Japanese occupation. Autonomy within "Greater East Asia" state promised. Sukarno works with Japanese while promoting independence.
- **1945** Sukarno declares Indonesian independence. Dutch forces attempt to reassert control.
- **1945–1949** Nationalist guerrilla war.
- **1949** Dutch grant independence to federal-style United States of Indonesia under Sukarno as president.
- **1950** Union dissolved, Sukarno grows increasingly authoritarian.
- **1950s** Moluccas declare independence: unsuccessful separatist war.
- **1957–1959** Sukarno introduces authoritarian Guided Democracy.
- **1959** Sukarno extends

CHRONOLOGY *continued*

presidential powers. Civilian legislature replaced by military. Extreme nationalist and pro-Chinese policies.

- **1962** Dutch relinquish Western New Guinea.
- **1965** Communist PKI alliance with military ends. Army led by Gen. Suharto crushes abortive coup and acts to eliminate the now banned PKI; up to one million killed.
- **1966** Sukarno hands over power to Gen. Suharto temporarily; becomes permanent in 1967.
- **1968** Suharto becomes president: declares "New order"; introduces pro-Western liberal economic policies while transferring real power to small group of officers.
- **1971** First elections for 16 years. Government-sponsored Golkar wins landslide. Opposition parties now passive partners of government.
- **1975** Invasion of East Timor; its incorporation in 1976 as 27th province is not recognized by UN. Fretilin movement declares East Timor independent.
- **1984** Muslim protestors clash with troops in Jakarta. Start of resurgence of Islamic protest.
- **1989** Growing discontent with authoritarian government; student protests, unrest in Java and Sumbawa. Demands for Suharto to retire. Low-key official response.
- **1991** Indonesian troops massacre proindependence demonstrators in East Timor. Prodemocracy organizations allowed to form in response to growing demands for "openness."
- **1993** Suharto wins sixth term.
- **1996** Antigovernment demonstrations in Jakarta.
- **1997** Economic recession. Smog across region from forest fires.
- **1998** Suharto resigns amid unrest.
- **1999** Election victory for opposition led by Megawati Sukarnoputri. East Timor referendum backing independence triggers violent backlash. Abdurrahman Wahid of PKB elected president, Megawati named vice president.
- **2000** Aceh becomes first province to introduce *sharia*. Violence erupts again in Moluccas.
- **2001** Wahid removed, replaced by Megawati.
- **2002** January, autonomy officially granted to Papua. May, East Timor independent. October, terrorist attack in Bali kills over 200, mostly Western holidaymakers.
- **2003** Major offensive against Aceh separatists.
- **2004** Gen. Yudhoyono wins first direct presidential election.

DEFENSE

Compulsory military service

$6.25bn

Up 15% in 2002

INDONESIAN ARMED FORCES

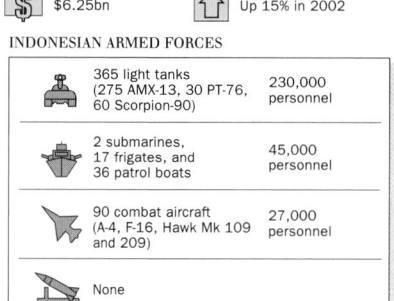

365 light tanks (275 AMX-13, 30 PT-76, 60 Scorpion-90)	230,000 personnel
2 submarines, 17 frigates, and 36 patrol boats	45,000 personnel
90 combat aircraft (A-4, F-16, Hawk Mk 109 and 209)	27,000 personnel
None	

Defense spending is rising, and the military has a high profile in public life; the constitution enshrines its political role. The civilianization of political parties, the bureaucracy, and state companies has reduced its presence in these areas, if not its influence.

The army is accused of human rights abuses and of involvement with militias, particularly in separatist regions. Seven special forces soldiers were convicted for the murder of a Papuan separatist leader in 2001 though their sentences were very short. No successful convictions have ensued from the violence in East Timor in 1999.

Western arms sales are increasingly dependent on the improvement of Indonesia's human rights record. There are tensions between the army and nonmilitary security forces.

ECONOMICS

Inflation 16% p.a. (1990–2001)

$150bn

9403 rupiahs (8250)

SCORE CARD

- World GNP Ranking 28th
- GNP per Capita $710
- Balance of Payments $7.45bn
- Inflation 11.5%
- Unemployment 6%

EXPORTS

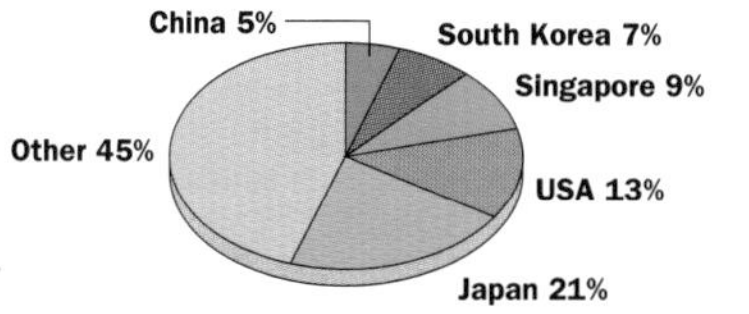
China 5%
South Korea 7%
Singapore 9%
Other 45%
USA 13%
Japan 21%

IMPORTS

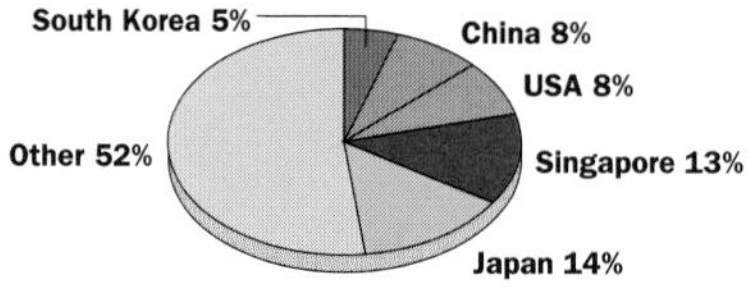
South Korea 5%
China 8%
USA 8%
Other 52%
Singapore 13%
Japan 14%

ECONOMIC PERFORMANCE INDICATOR

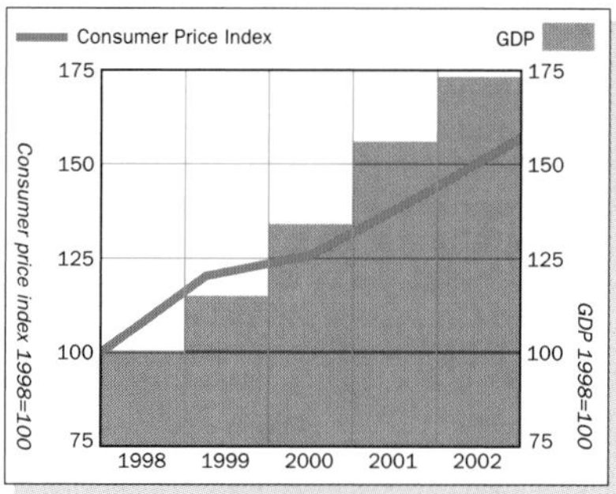
Consumer Price Index
GDP
Consumer price index 1998=100
GDP 1998=100
175
150
125
100
75
1998
1999
2000
2001
2002

Strengths

Varied resources, especially oil. Signs of recovery from Asian crisis. Debt successfully rescheduled. International credit rating improved.

Weaknesses

High level of bureaucracy. Endemic corruption. Huge wealth disparities. Regional insecurity deters investment. High underemployment. Piracy.

Profile

Under Suharto the economy grew rapidly, fueled largely by oil, until its collapse in the 1997–1998 Asian crisis. State-owned corporations, protected from foreign competition, had played a significant role in the expansion. Exports were diversified, but the debt burden used up a third of export earnings. Reform was delayed by conflict between "technologists" favoring industrialization over profit for state concerns and advocates of deregulation. Corruption remained rife, but by 2003 the country had achieved a measure of economic stability, consistent with developments in other emerging markets and the wider region. GDP and export growth lagged behind other Asian economies, however, reflecting weaknesses in taxation and regulation and comparative labor market inflexibility.

INDONESIA : MAJOR BUSINESSES

- Rubber
- Heavy engineering
- Gas
- Chemicals
- Timber industries
- Oil
- Oil refining
- Electronics
- Vehicle assembly
- Aerospace industry

* significant multinational ownership

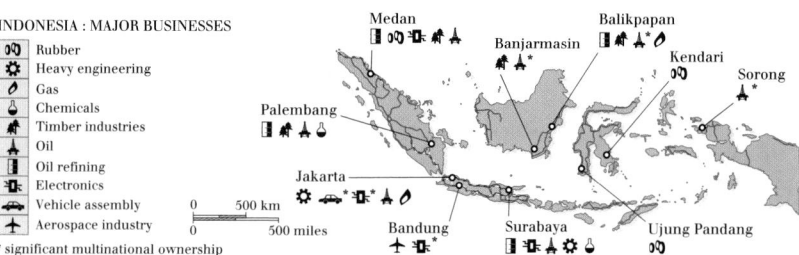

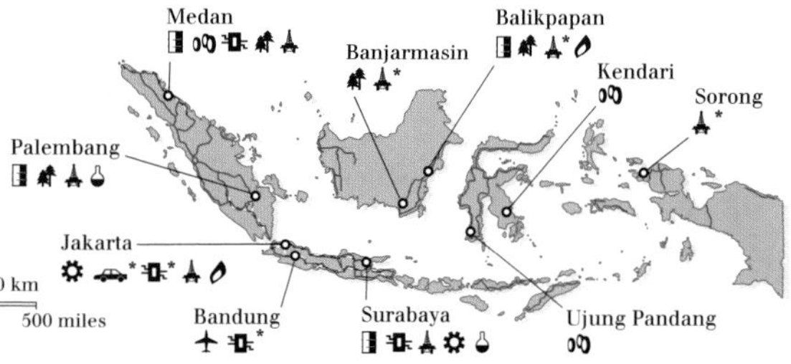
Medan
Balikpapan
Banjarmasin
Kendari
Sorong
Palembang
Jakarta
0 500 km
0 500 miles
Bandung
Surabaya
Ujung Pandang

RESOURCES

Electric power 25.4m kW

5.07m tonnes

1.18m b/d (reserves 4.4bn barrels)

48.1m ducks, 13.3m goats, 11.4m cattle, 1.29bn chickens

Oil, natural gas, coal, bauxite, nickel, copper, gold, tin

ELECTRICITY GENERATION

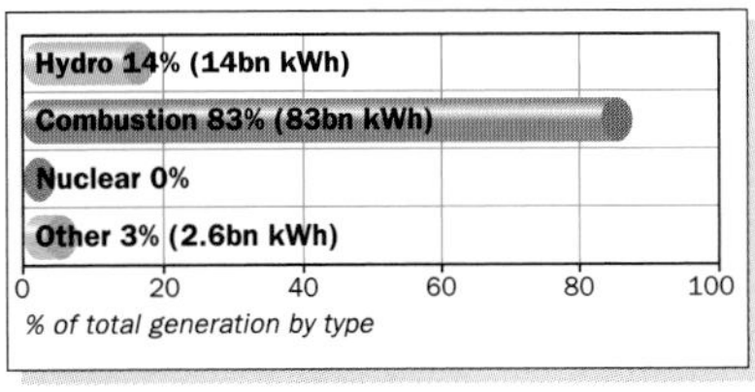
Hydro 14% (14bn kWh)
Combustion 83% (83bn kWh)
Nuclear 0%
Other 3% (2.6bn kWh)
0 20 40 60 80 100
% of total generation by type

INDONESIA : LAND USE

Cropland
Forest
Pasture
Wetlands
Rice
Nutmeg - cash crop
Cattle
0 500 km
0 500 miles
Sumatra
Kalimantan
Sulawesi
Moluku
PACIFIC OCEAN
Papua
Laut Jawa
Laut Banda
Java
Timor

Indonesia is rich in energy sources. The main export earners are liquefied natural gas (LNG), of which it is the world's largest exporter, and oil. However, oil output has been falling, and combined with rapid growth in domestic energy demand, this could turn Indonesia into an oil importer in the next decade. The government is therefore encouraging oil exploration in remote regions. It is also considering developing existing geothermal and hydroelectric energy sources. Indonesia's other main resources are coal, bauxite, and nickel, and agricultural products such as rubber and palm oil. Processed wood products are a significant export commodity; the rapid depletion of the rainforests has given rise to attempts to control timber exports.

ENVIRONMENT

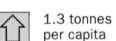

Sustainability rank: 100th

21% (10% partially protected)

1.3 tonnes per capita

ENVIRONMENTAL TREATIES

Yes	Yes	Yes
Yes	Yes	No

Environmental legislation is poorly enforced: the rich tropical forests suffer from excessive logging, and rare species, such as orangutans, are disappearing. The death penalty has been proposed to curb illegal logging. Smog from forest fires seriously contributes to global levels of greenhouse gases. The World Bank warned in 2003 of massive health problems from pollution, particularly in urban areas.

MEDIA

TV ownership medium

Daily newspaper circulation 23 per 1000 people

PUBLISHING AND BROADCAST MEDIA

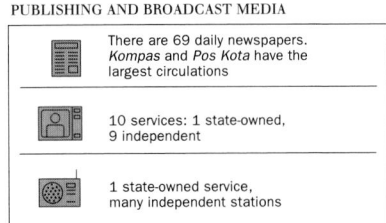

There are 69 daily newspapers. *Kompas* and *Pos Kota* have the largest circulations

10 services: 1 state-owned, 9 independent

1 state-owned service, many independent stations

The 1999 press law prohibits censorship, but journalists can still be fined for violating "religious and moral norms." Independent press and broadcasting have flourished since 1998.

CRIME

Death penalty in use

62,886 prisoners

Up 17% in 1999

CRIME RATES

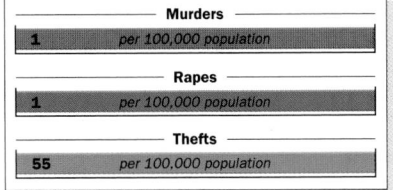

Murders	1 per 100,000 population
Rapes	1 per 100,000 population
Thefts	55 per 100,000 population

Suppression of secessionists is harsh. There is brutal ethnic and religious violence in the provinces. Piracy is rife.

EDUCATION

School leaving age: 15

88%

3.02m students

THE EDUCATION SYSTEM

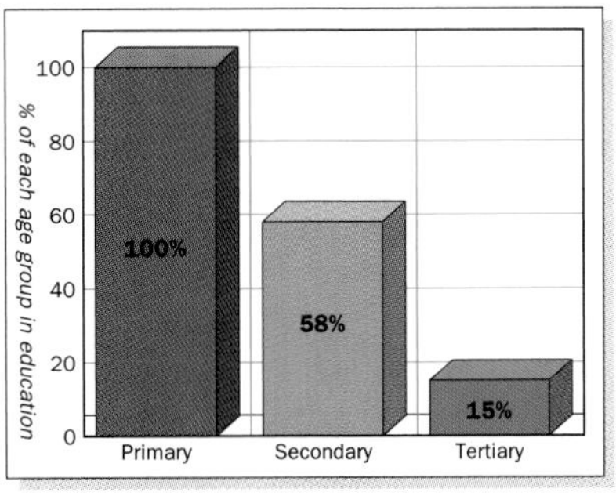
100
80
60
40
20
0
% of each age group in education
100%
58%
15%
Primary
Secondary
Tertiary

Primary education is subsidized by the state, compulsory, and often provided by Islamic schools. In contrast, good secondary education is hard to find in rural areas. University students come predominantly from the richer elites.

HEALTH

Welfare state health benefits

1 per 6564 people

Lower respiratory and diarrheal diseases

An extensive network of clinics, down to village level, means that access to health care is reasonable, and health indicators have improved significantly. The death rate declined from 2% in 1965 to 0.7% in 2000, thus helping to increase life expectancy, while infant mortality more than halved over this period. However, malnutrition and pollution-related health problems, which were estimated in 2003 to affect 30% of all children, remain a real problem. The World Bank has warned of massive poisoning from pollution. The rate of HIV infection among intravenous drug users, particularly in prisons, is rising.

SPENDING

GDP/cap. increase

CONSUMPTION AND SPENDING

15 per 1000 population

37 per 1000 population

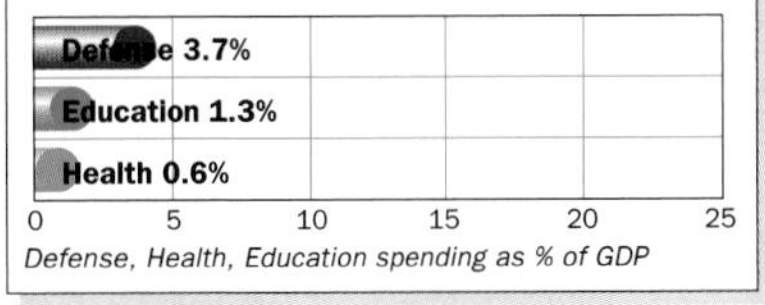
Defense 3.7%
Education 1.3%
Health 0.6%
0 5 10 15 20 25
Defense, Health, Education spending as % of GDP

Many Indonesians live in relative poverty and those on the peripheral islands in real poverty; large wealth disparities exist between the Javanese middle classes and the subsistence farmers and tribesmen of Papua and Kalimantan. This reflects both an accumulation of wealth in the hands of a limited number of key political and business figures, and a concentration of development and investment on the main islands, particularly Java. Since 1998 attempts have been made in the courts to tackle the issues of corruption and the concentration of wealth in the hands of close associates and relatives of former president Suharto and his political successors.

WORLD RANKING

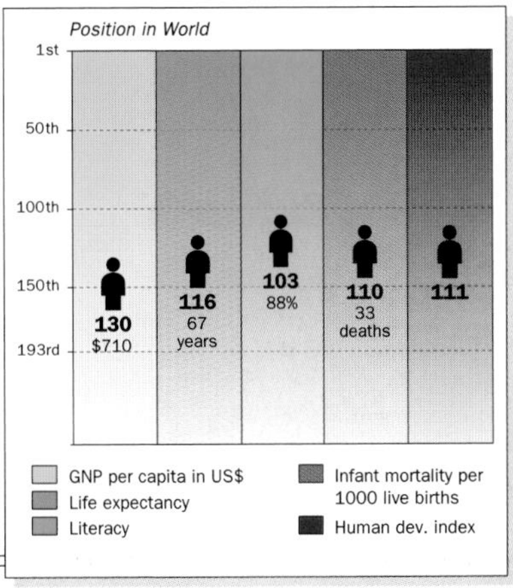
Position in World
1st
50th
100th
150th
193rd
130
$710
116
67
years
103
88%
110
33
deaths
111
GNP per capita in US$
Life expectancy
Literacy
Infant mortality per 1000 live births
Human dev. index

I

IRAN

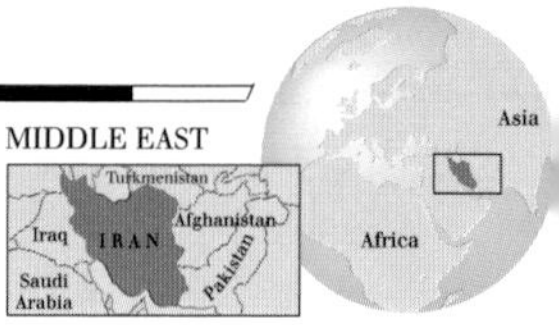
MIDDLE EAST
Turkmenistan
Iraq
IRAN
Afghanistan
Pakistan
Saudi Arabia
Asia
Africa

OFFICIAL NAME: Islamic Republic of Iran **CAPITAL:** Tehran
POPULATION: 68.9 million **CURRENCY:** Iranian rial **OFFICIAL LANGUAGE:** Farsi

1502 | 1990 | Feb 11 | IR | +3.5 | +98 | .ir

TURBULENT NEIGHBORS surround Iran; there are republics of the former Soviet Union to the north, Afghanistan and Pakistan to the east, and Iraq and Turkey to the west. The south faces the Persian Gulf and the Gulf of Oman. Since 1979, when a revolution led by Ayatollah Khomeini deposed the shah, Iran has become the world's largest theocracy and the leading center for militant Shi'a Islam. Iran's active support for Islamic fundamentalist movements has led to strained relations with central Asian, Middle Eastern, and north African states, as well as with the US and Europe.

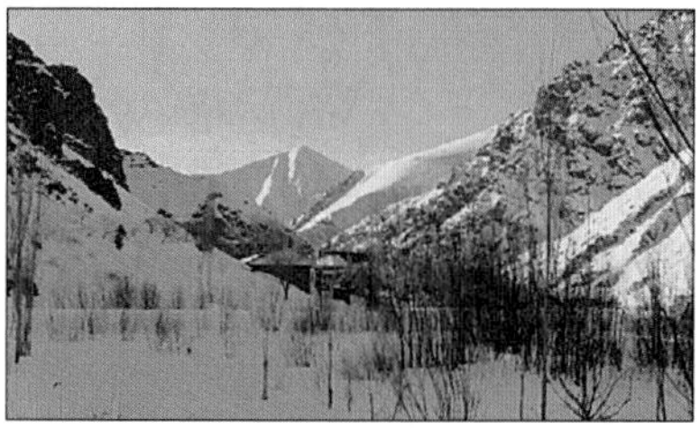

***The Reshteh-ye Kuhhā-ye Alborz** (Elburz Mountains). Their Caspian Sea slopes are rainy and forested; the southern slopes are dry.*

CLIMATE

Mountain/cold desert

WEATHER CHART FOR TEHRAN

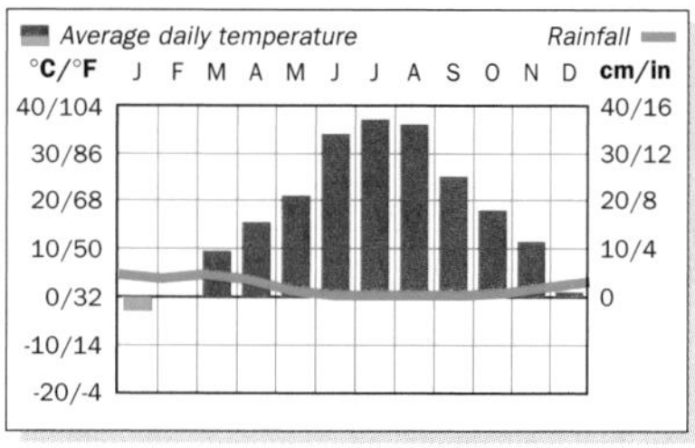
Average daily temperature
Rainfall
°C/°F
J F M A M J J A S O N D
cm/in
40/104
30/86
20/68
10/50
0/32
-10/14
-20/-4
40/16
30/12
20/8
10/4
0

The area bordering the Caspian Sea is Iran's most temperate region. Most of the country has a desert climate.

TRANSPORTATION

Drive on right

Mehrabad, Tehran 8.47m passengers

380 ships 4.13m grt

THE TRANSPORTATION NETWORK

93,608 km (58,165 miles)

890 km (553 miles)

6151 km (3822 miles)

904 km (562 miles)

Adequate roads link main towns, but rural areas are less well served. Most freight travels by rail. A ferry runs from Bandar-e Abbas to the UAE.

PEOPLE

Pop. density low

Farsi, Azeri, Luri, Gilaki, Mazanderani, Kurdish, Turkmen, Arabic, Baluchi

42/km² (109/mi²)

THE URBAN/RURAL POPULATION SPLIT

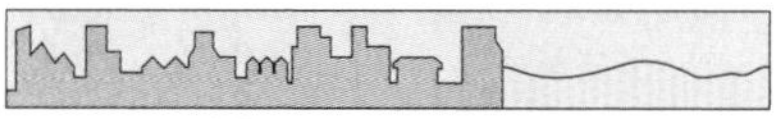
65%
35%

RELIGIOUS PERSUASION

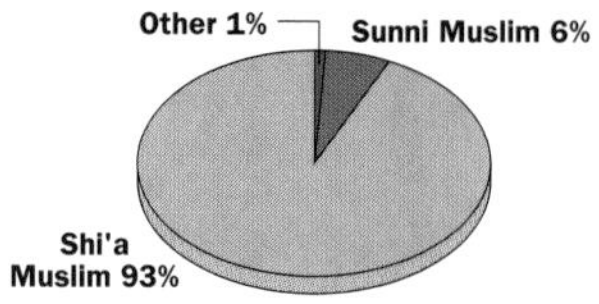
Other 1%
Sunni Muslim 6%
Shi'a Muslim 93%

ETHNIC MAKEUP

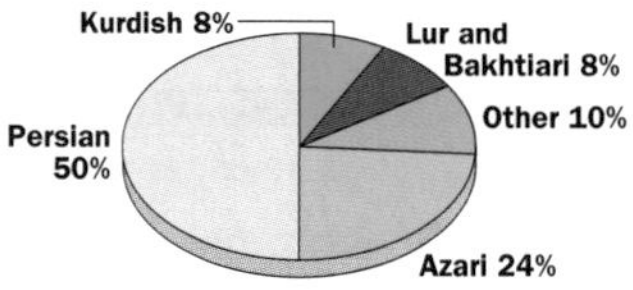
Kurdish 8%
Lur and Bakhtiari 8%
Other 10%
Persian 50%
Azari 24%

The people of the north and center of Iran – about half of all Iranians – speak Farsi (Persian), while about a quarter speak related languages, including Kurdish in the west and Baluchi in the southeast. Another quarter of the population speaks Turkic languages, primarily the Azaris and the Turkmen in the northwest. Smaller groups, such as the Circassians and Georgians, are found in the northern provinces.

Until the 16th century, much of Iran followed the Sunni interpretation of Islam, but since then the Shi'a sect has been dominant. Religious minorities, accounting for just 1% of the population, include followers of the Baha'i faith (who suffer discrimination), Zoroastrians, Christians, and Jews. The regime has a remarkably liberal attitude to refugees of the Muslim faith. Nearly three million Afghan refugees were received at the height of the Afghan civil war in the 1980s–1990s, though many have since returned. In 2003, Afghan refugee numbers had fallen to 830,000; Iraqi refugees numbered around 150,000, mostly housed in camps along Iran's western border. Many refugees are young, resulting in intense competition with Iranians for jobs and consequent ethnic tensions.

One of the main consequences of the 1979 Islamic revolution was to reverse the policy of female emancipation. The revolution restricted the public role of women and enforced a strict dress code, obliging women to cover themselves from head to foot in the chador (veil). More liberal attitudes have gradually emerged. Reform of the divorce laws, so that the wife could initiate proceedings, is backed by the reformist parliament, but strongly opposed by the conservative judiciary as un-Islamic.

POPULATION AGE BREAKDOWN

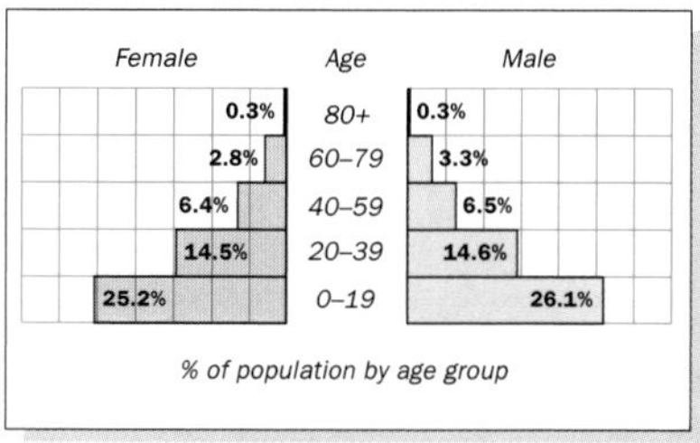
Female
Age
Male
0.3%
80+
0.3%
2.8%
60–79
3.3%
6.4%
40–59
6.5%
14.5%
20–39
14.6%
25.2%
0–19
26.1%
% of population by age group

TOURISM

Visitors : Population 1:43

1.58m visitors

Up 13% in 2002

MAIN TOURIST ARRIVALS

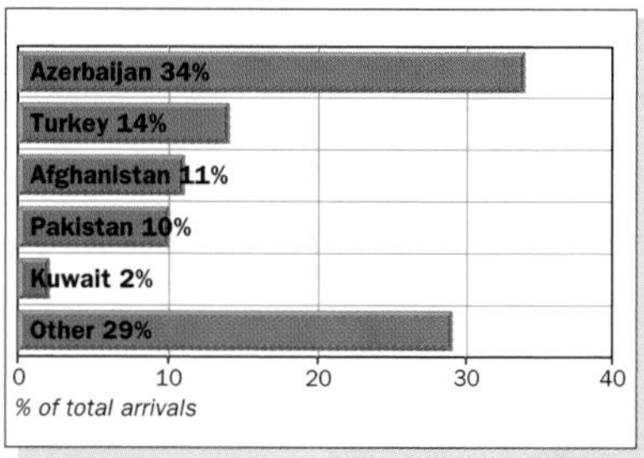
Azerbaijan 34%
Turkey 14%
Afghanistan 11%
Pakistan 10%
Kuwait 2%
Other 29%
0
10
20
30
40
% of total arrivals

Iran's historical heritage, mosques, and bazaars formerly attracted sizable numbers of tourists. This flow was cut off by the 1979 revolution, which deterred visitors, especially from the West. In the 1990s, however, there was a rise in the number of business people visiting Iran. Procedures at Tehran's Mehrabad airport have been simplified and the capital's hotels refurbished. In late 1998 President Khatami's more liberal regime welcomed a delegation of US tourists, despite opposition from conservative groups.

POLITICS

Multiparty elections

2004/2008

President Mohammad Khatami

AT THE LAST ELECTION

Consultative Council (Majlis al-Shoura) 290 seats

68%
C
17%
IIPF
14%
Ind
1%
Vacant

C = Coalition of Followers of the Line of Imam (conservatives)
IIPF = Islamic Iran Participation Front (reformists)
Ind = Independents

Iran has been an Islamist theocracy since 1979. Accordingly, the legislature, the executive, and the judiciary may, in theory, be overruled by the religious leadership.

PROFILE

The mullahs, in power since the religious revolution, have seen both their political standing and their moral authority eroded in recent years as the perception has spread that they can address neither economic problems nor social malaise. An opposition reformist movement developed, overturning the conservative majority in the Consultative Council in 1996. Leading reformist Mohammad Khatami, elected president in 1997, was reelected in 2001.

The clergy remains powerful, nonetheless, cracking down on reformist politicians and newspapers. Khatami has been left sandwiched between the powerful religious right and the popular desire to institute real political and economic reform. His position became even more uncomfortable after the conservative election victory in the 2004 poll. The reformists had called for a boycott after the clergy had banned thousands of reformist candidates from the poll, and then claimed electoral irregularities.

MAIN POLITICAL ISSUE

Mosque versus secular state

The power struggle between the clergy and the secular state is manifest in the ill-defined division of authority between the supreme religious leader and the secular, directly elected president. Since reformist President Khatami took office in 1997 the polarization has increased. He is opposed in his efforts to liberalize by the mullahs, for whom adherence to religious values is more important than material welfare. The mullahs wield power through the Council of Guardians which controls the judiciary and electoral procedures.

Ayatollah Khamenei, a former president, was appointed spiritual leader in 1989. Wary of Khatami's popularity, he has struggled to rein in the aggression of the mullahs and their militant supporters.

***Ayatollah Khamenei,** who became spiritual leader after the death of Ayatollah Khomeini.*

***Mohammad Khatami,** reformist president, in office since 1997.*

WORLD AFFAIRS

Joined UN in 1945

ECO | G24 | NAM | OIC | OPEC

After the 1979 revolution Iran assumed international significance as the voice of militant Shi'a Islam. It is accused of backing Muslim extremists and of fostering unrest throughout the region.

Under President Khatami, Iran has tried to convey a less confrontational image.

Improved relations with Saudi Arabia, troubled since Iran's seizure of the islands of Abu Musa and the Tunbs in 1970, resulted in the signing of a pact in 2001. Relations with the US remain tense. In 2002 US president George W. Bush cast Iran, with Iraq and North Korea, as an international "axis of evil." Though Iran was forced to open its nuclear installations to inspection by the IAEA, cooperation has since been slow. US aid sent in 2002 and 2003 in the aftermath of terrible earthquakes failed to signify a thaw in relations.

Iraq under the regime of Saddam Hussein had been Iran's main security preoccupation; following his removal in 2003, the resulting uncertainties thrown up by the US-led occupation are cause for continuing concern.

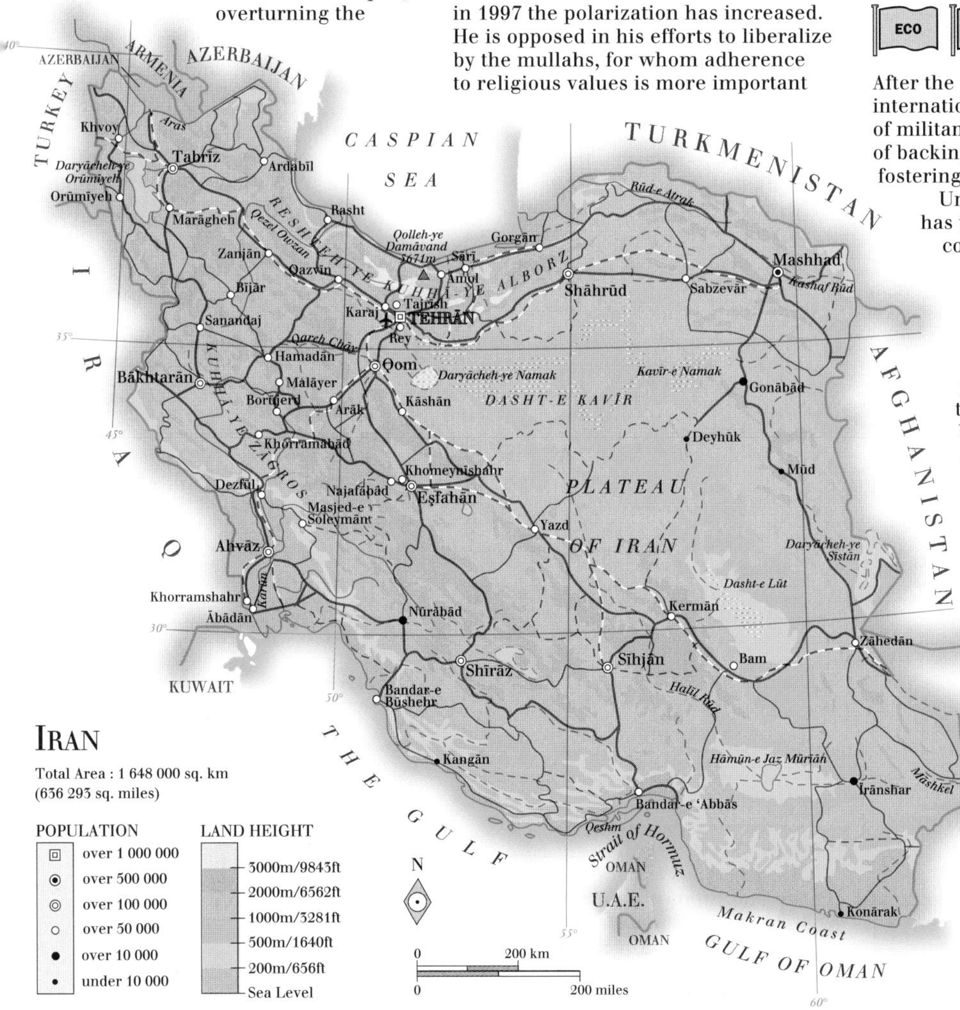
AZERBAIJAN
ARMENIA
AZERBAIJAN
TURKEY
CASPIAN SEA
TURKMENISTAN
AFGHANISTAN
PAKISTAN
IRAQ
KUWAIT
THE GULF
GULF OF OMAN
OMAN
U.A.E.
Tabrīz
Ardabīl
Khvoy
Orūmīyeh
Marāgheh
Rasht
Zanjān
Qazvīn
Bījār
Sanandaj
Karaj
TEHRĀN
Tajrīsh
Rey
Sārī
Āmol
Gorgān
Shāhrūd
Sabzevār
Mashhad
Hamadān
Bākhtarān
Malāyer
Borūjerd
Arāk
Qom
Kāshān
Khorramābād
Dezfūl
Najafābād
Khomeynīshahr
Eşfahān
Masjed-e Soleymān
Ahvāz
Khorramshahr
Ābādān
Yazd
Gonābād
Deyhūk
Mūd
Kermān
Bam
Zāhedān
Sīrjān
Shīrāz
Nūrābād
Bandar-e Būshehr
Kangān
Bandar-e 'Abbās
Īrānshahr
Konārak
Qeshm
Strait of Hormuz
Makran Coast
PLATEAU OF IRAN
DASHT-E KAVĪR
Dasht-e Lūt
Daryācheh-ye Namak
Kavīr-e Namak
Daryācheh-ye Sīstān
Daryācheh-ye Orūmīyeh
Qolleh-ye Damāvand 5671m
Ḩāmūn-e Jaz Mūrīān
IRAN
Total Area : 1 648 000 sq. km
(636 293 sq. miles)
POPULATION
over 1 000 000
over 500 000
over 100 000
over 50 000
over 10 000
under 10 000
LAND HEIGHT
3000m/9843ft
2000m/6562ft
1000m/3281ft
500m/1640ft
200m/656ft
Sea Level
0
200 km
200 miles

I

CHRONOLOGY

Persia was ruled by the shahs as an absolute monarchy until 1906, when the first constitution was approved. The Pahlavis took power in 1925 and changed the country's name to Iran in 1935.

- **1957** SAVAK, shah's secret police, established to control opposition.
- **1964** Ayatollah Khomeini is exiled for criticizing secular state.
- **1971** Shah celebrates 2500th anniversary of Persian monarchy.
- **1975** Agreement with Iraq over Shatt al Arab waterway.
- **1977** Anti-shah demonstrations.
- **1978** Riots and strikes.
- **1979** Shah goes into exile. Ayatollah Khomeini returns, declares an Islamic republic. Students seize 63 hostages at US embassy in Tehran.
- **1980** Shah dies in exile. Start of eight-year Iran–Iraq war.
- **1981** US hostages released. Hojatoleslam Ali Khamenei elected president.
- **1985** Khamenei reelected.
- **1987** Around 275 Iranian pilgrims killed in riots in Mecca.
- **1988** USS *Vincennes* shoots down Iranian airliner; 290 killed. End of Iran–Iraq war.
- **1989** Khomeini issues *fatwa* condemning UK author Salman Rushdie to death for blasphemy. Khomeini dies. President Ali Khamenei appointed Supreme Religious Leader. Hashemi Rafsanjani elected president.
- **1990** Earthquake in northern Iran kills 45,000 people.
- **1992** Majlis elections.
- **1993** Rafsanjani reelected president.
- **1995** Imposition of US sanctions.
- **1996** Majlis elections. Society for Combatant Clergy loses ground to more liberal Servants of Iran's Construction.
- **1997** Earthquake south of Mashhad kills 1500 people. Mohammad Khatami elected president.
- **1998** Khatami government dissociates itself from *fatwa* against Salman Rushdie.
- **1999** First nationwide local elections since 1979. President Khatami visits Italy: first Iranian leader to be welcomed by a Western government since 1979.
- **2000** Sweeping election victory for reformists. Crackdown on reformist newspapers.
- **2001** Khatami reelected, winning 77% of vote.
- **2003** Bam earthquake kills over 40,000.
- **2004** Conservatives win controversial election.

AID

Recipient

$116m (receipts) | Down 1% in 2002

As an oil exporter, Iran does not qualify for much aid, and hard-liners are opposed to money from the West. Iran receives some UN aid, however, for its thousands of refugees from Afghanistan and Iraq. Concern that Iran supports Islamist terrorism has affected aid programs. In 1994, the World Bank suspended loans. US sanctions imposed since 1995 have curtailed donations, but humanitarian assistance was provided after earthquakes in 2002 and 2003.

DEFENSE

Compulsory military service

$4.87bn | Up 56% in 2002

Iran has more than 500,000 men under arms, including the 125,000-strong Revolutionary Guard Corps (*Pasdaran Inqilab*), and is regarded by neighboring states as a serious military threat. The testing of medium-range cruise and ballistic missiles has heightened concern over Iran's possible military objectives: it can now theoretically strike as far as Israel. Iran has announced plans to launch its own satellite system by 2005.

Before the 1979 revolution Iran was part of a pro-Western alliance structure. The long war with Iraq in the 1980s diminished the military power of the revolutionary regime.

IRANIAN ARMED FORCES

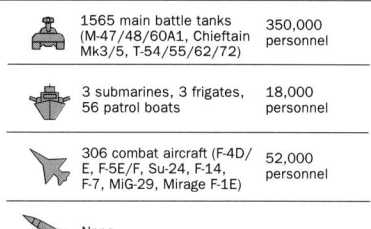

1565 main battle tanks (M-47/48/60A1, Chieftain Mk3/5, T-54/55/62/72)	350,000 personnel
3 submarines, 3 frigates, 56 patrol boats	18,000 personnel
306 combat aircraft (F-4D/E, F-5E/F, Su-24, F-14, F-7, MiG-29, Mirage F-1E)	52,000 personnel
None	

ECONOMICS

Inflation 26% p.a. (1990–2001)

$113bn | 8645 Iranian rials (8185)

SCORE CARD

- World GNP Ranking: 33rd
- GNP per capita: $1720
- Balance of Payments: $3.73bn
- Inflation: 14.3%
- Unemployment: 16%

EXPORTS

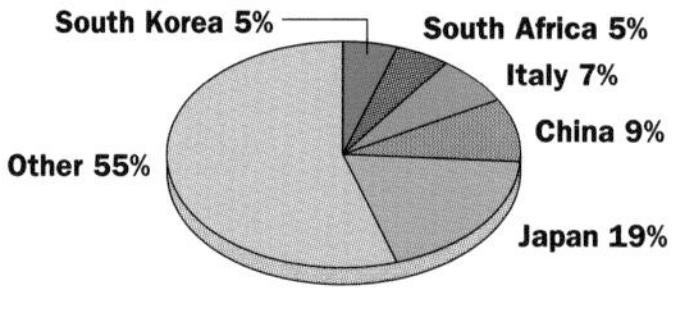
South Korea 5%
South Africa 5%
Italy 7%
China 9%
Japan 19%
Other 55%

IMPORTS

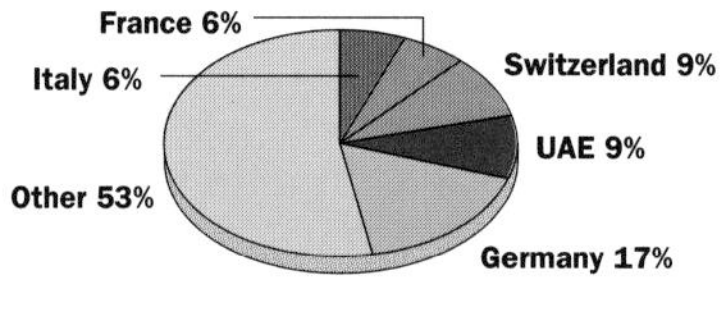
France 6%
Italy 6%
Switzerland 9%
UAE 9%
Germany 17%
Other 53%

STRENGTHS

OPEC's second-biggest oil producer. Second-largest natural gas reserves in the world. Potential for related industries and increased production of traditional exports: carpets, pistachio nuts, and caviar.

WEAKNESSES

Theocratic authorities restrict contact with West and access to technology. High unemployment and inflation. Infrastructure damaged by earthquakes. Excessive foreign debts.

ECONOMIC PERFORMANCE INDICATOR

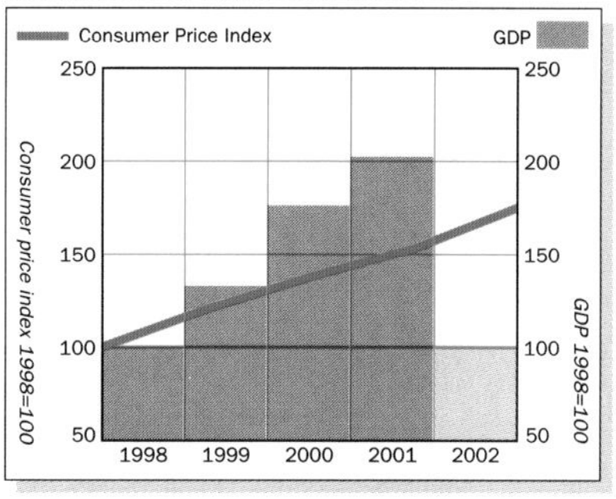
Consumer Price Index
GDP
250
200
150
100
50
Consumer price index 1998=100
GDP 1998=100
1998
1999
2000
2001
2002

PROFILE

With few industries other than oil, US sanctions and fluctuations in oil prices made foreign earnings volatile; higher prices in recent years have held out the prospect of investing in diversification.

IRAN : MAJOR BUSINESSES

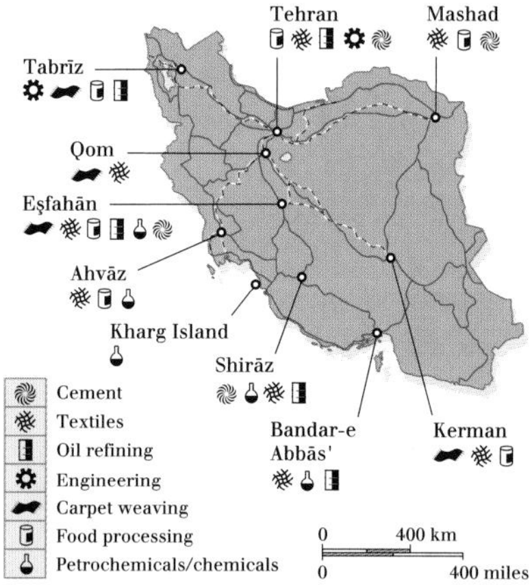
Tehran
Mashad
Tabrīz
Qom
Eşfahān
Ahvāz
Kharg Island
Shirāz
Bandar-e Abbās'
Kerman
Cement
Textiles
Oil refining
Engineering
Carpet weaving
Food processing
Petrochemicals/chemicals
0
400 km
0
400 miles

RESOURCES

Electric power 30.6m kW

399,000 tonnes

3.85m b/d (reserves 131bn barrels)

53.9m sheep, 26m goats, 9m cattle, 280m chickens

Iron, copper, lead, oil, natural gas, zinc, salt, chromite, manganese, coal, gypsum, uranium

ELECTRICITY GENERATION

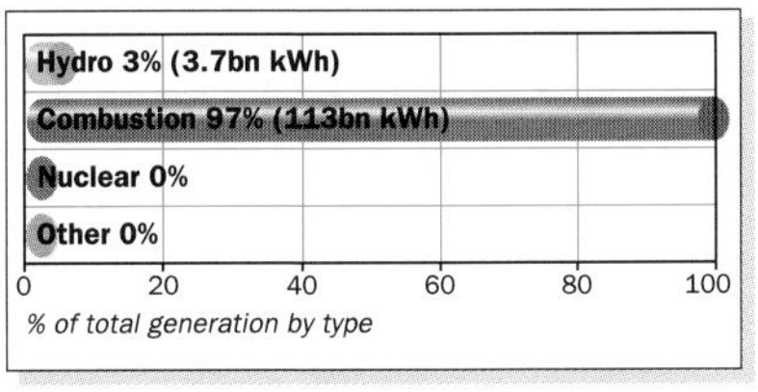
Hydro 3% (3.7bn kWh)
Combustion 97% (113bn kWh)
Nuclear 0%
Other 0%
0
20
40
60
80
100
% of total generation by type

Iran has substantial oil and natural gas reserves, plus relatively undeveloped deposits of metal ores, coal, and salt. A Russian-built nuclear power plant is set to open in 2005, powered by uranium mined in Iran. There is international concern over the government's aims.

The agricultural sector is a major part of the economy. Principal crops are fruit, wheat, barley, rice, sugar, and pistachio nuts. The Caspian Sea fisheries are controlled by the state, which sells caviar for export. Iran was once an opium exporter, but its cultivation and use have since been banned. The vodka industry has also been closed down.

IRAN : LAND USE

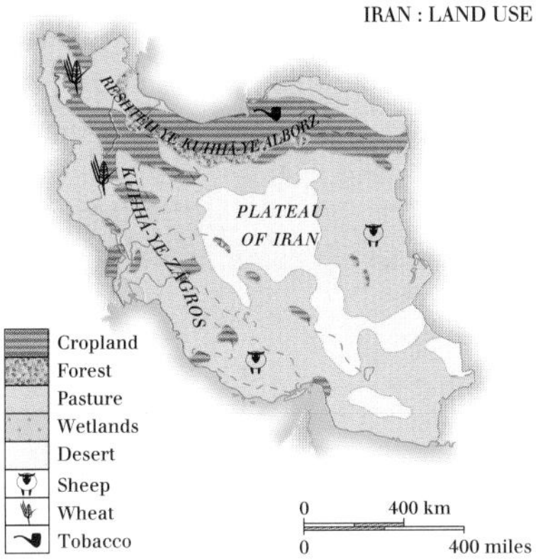
RESHTEH-YE KUHHA-YE ALBORZ
KUHHA-YE ZAGROS
PLATEAU OF IRAN
Cropland
Forest
Pasture
Wetlands
Desert
Sheep
Wheat
Tobacco
0
400 km
0
400 miles

ENVIRONMENT

Sustainability rank: 104th

5% (4% partially protected)

4.9 tonnes per capita

ENVIRONMENTAL TREATIES

Yes	Yes	Yes
Yes	Yes	No

Environmental issues have been seriously neglected. The growing population, an overreliance on old cars, and the abundance of cheap gasoline have combined to destroy urban air quality. Pollution from oil exploration in the Caspian Sea is of major concern.

MEDIA

TV ownership medium

Daily newspaper circulation 28 per 1000 people

PUBLISHING AND BROADCAST MEDIA

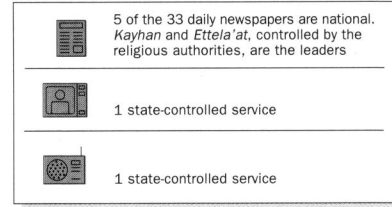

5 of the 33 daily newspapers are national. *Kayhan* and *Ettela'at*, controlled by the religious authorities, are the leaders

1 state-controlled service

1 state-controlled service

Radio and TV are state-controlled. Satellite dishes are banned. Closures of reformist newspapers by the conservative Council of Guardians, and prosecutions of their editors, continue.

CRIME

Death penalty in use

163,526 prisoners

Little change from year to year

CRIME RATES

Iran does not publish crime statistics. However, general crime rates are relatively low.

Revolutionary guards enforce order. More than 100 offenses carry the death sentence. Executions are common for political "crimes." Murderers can avoid the death penalty by paying a $19,000 "blood price" – or half if the victim was female. Narcotics addiction, prostitution, and the violent abuse of women are rife. Iran is accused by Western governments of supporting Islamist terrorism.

EDUCATION

School leaving age: 11

77%

1.68m students

THE EDUCATION SYSTEM

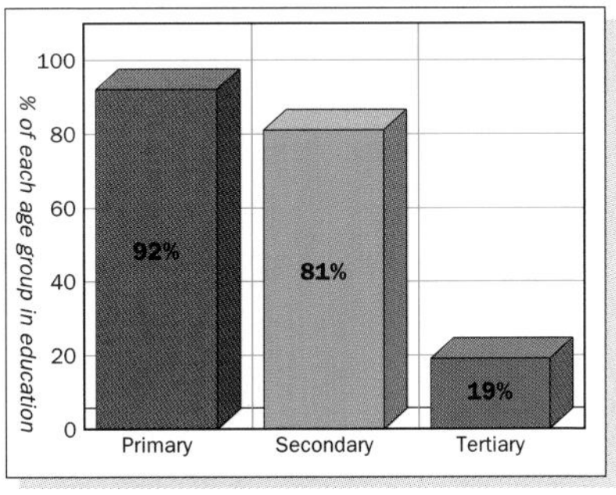
100
80
60
40
20
0
% of each age group in education
92%
81%
19%
Primary
Secondary
Tertiary

Primary education, which lasts for five years from the age of six, is free, as are universities. Most schools are single-sex. Since 2002, female students and staff in Tehran's classrooms have been permitted to lower their veils. There are 37 universities; their students are strong supporters of liberalization and reform.

HEALTH

Welfare state health benefits

1 per 2625 people

Heart and respiratory diseases, injuries, neonatal deaths

Though an adequate system of primary health care exists in the cities, conditions in rural areas are basic. Under Khomeini, having children became a political and religious duty, but the high birthrate has now forced the introduction of birth control programs, and sterilization and contraception are now officially promoted. Growing drug addiction has resulted in rehabilitation programs and antidrugs propaganda. AIDS is spreading; some 31,000 adults were estimated to be living with HIV/AIDS in 2003.

SPENDING

GDP/cap. increase

CONSUMPTION AND SPENDING

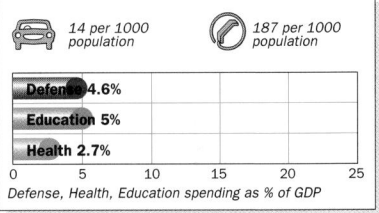

14 per 1000 population

187 per 1000 population

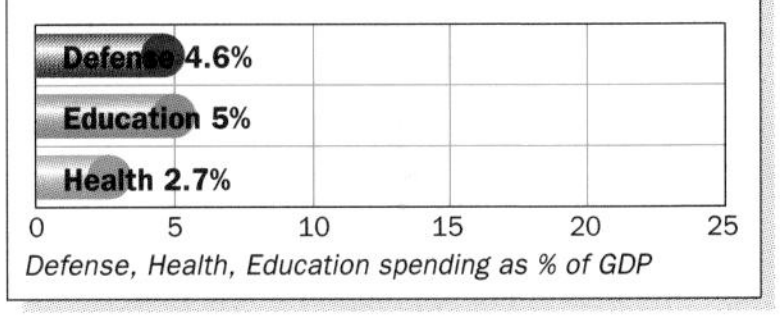
Defense 4.6%
Education 5%
Health 2.7%
0
5
10
15
20
25
Defense, Health, Education spending as % of GDP

After the 1979 revolution, living standards in Iran declined markedly. A shortage of foreign exchange has stifled imports of consumer goods. Rationing, brought in during the war with Iraq, is still partly in force, and smuggling from the Arab Gulf states is rife. Unemployment is high, and few Iranians are able to gain access to modern technology such as telephones. Official figures for income per capita do not relate to conditions on the ground. In reality, oil wealth fails to reach the economically deprived. Private businesses have gradually emerged in Iran since the launch in 1994 of the country's first private savings and loans associations.

WORLD RANKING

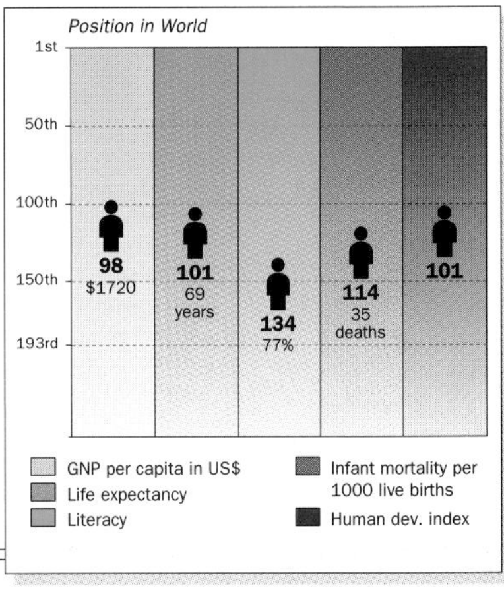
Position in World
1st
50th
100th
150th
193rd
98
$1720
101
69 years
134
77%
114
35 deaths
101
GNP per capita in US$
Life expectancy
Literacy
Infant mortality per 1000 live births
Human dev. index

I

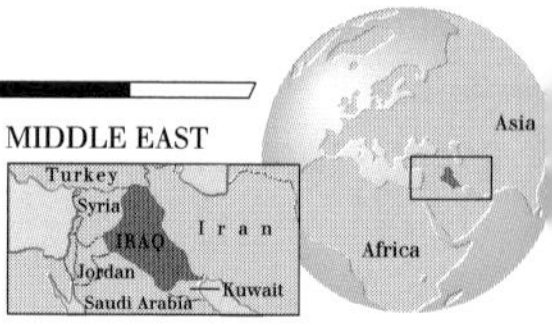
MIDDLE EAST
Turkey
Syria
IRAQ
Iran
Jordan
Kuwait
Saudi Arabia
Asia
Africa

IRAQ

OFFICIAL NAME: Republic of Iraq **CAPITAL:** Baghdad **POPULATION:** 25.2 million
CURRENCY: New Iraqi dinar **OFFICIAL LANGUAGES:** Arabic and Kurdish

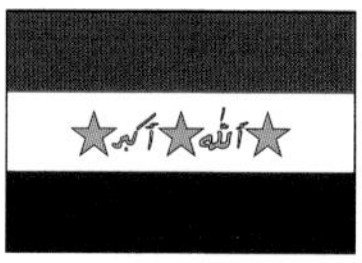

1932 | 1990 | None | IRQ | +3 | +964 | .iq

OIL-RICH IRAQ is divided by the Euphrates and Tigris Rivers. Mesopotamia, the region between them, saw the beginnings of writing and mathematics, and the invention of the wheel. While the river valleys are fertile, most of the country is inhospitable desert or mountains. The modern state encompasses Kurds in the north, Sunni Muslims largely in the center, and a Shi'a Muslim majority to the south. Saddam Hussein seized power in 1979 and maintained it through fear until his ouster in the rapid 2003 US-led invasion.

Golden Mosque at Sāmarrā' on the Tigris. Among the extensive remains of its ancient city are those of the Great Mosque built in 847 CE.

CLIMATE

Hot desert/steppe

WEATHER CHART FOR BAGHDAD

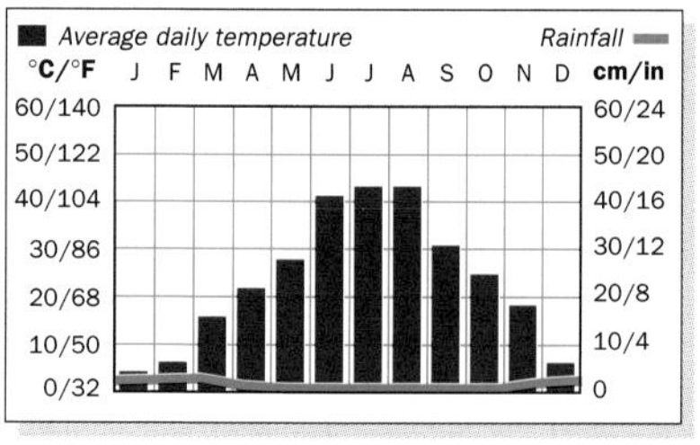
Average daily temperature
Rainfall
°C/°F
J F M A M J J A S O N D
cm/in
60/140
50/122
40/104
30/86
20/68
10/50
0/32
60/24
50/20
40/16
30/12
20/8
10/4
0

The weather is dry and rainfall is low and unreliable, except in the north. Iraq experiences a wide range of temperatures. The south has a desert climate, with hot, dry summers and mild winters. In mountainous Iranian and Turkish border regions winters can be harsh, with frost and heavy falls of snow. In the Mesopotamian plain huge dust storms are a regular feature of the summer.

TRANSPORTATION

Drive on right

Baghdad | 88 ships 188,200 grt

THE TRANSPORTATION NETWORK

38,262 km (23,775 miles)	1264 km (785 miles)
2339 km (1453 miles)	1015 km (631 miles)

Infrastructure was damaged during the 2003 invasion, though the rapid defeat of the Iraqi forces spared many key bridges and roads.

TOURISM

Visitors : Population 1:198

127,000 visitors | Up 63% in 2001

MAIN TOURIST ARRIVALS

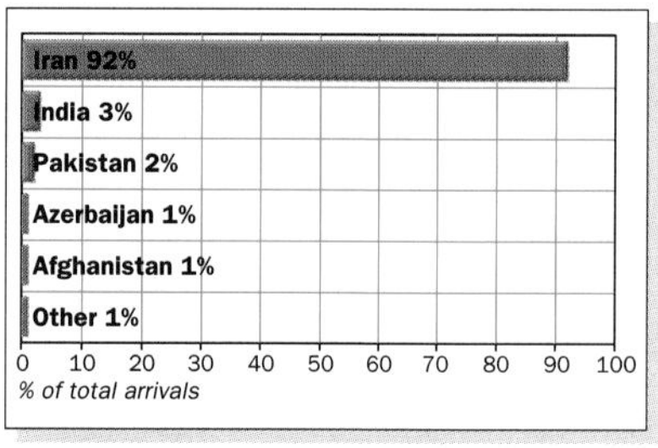
Iran 92%
India 3%
Pakistan 2%
Azerbaijan 1%
Afghanistan 1%
Other 1%
0 10 20 30 40 50 60 70 80 90 100
% of total arrivals

International isolation and war have prevented Iraq from making the most of its spectacular tourist potential. Visitors used to be attracted by Iraq's wealth of archaeological remains, in particular the ruins of Babylon and its fabled hanging gardens, near Al Hillah. Despite the security situation, Shi'a holy shrines attracted thousands of pilgrims once again after the overthrow of Saddam Hussein's regime. Western governments continue to warn their nationals against travel to Iraq.

IRAQ

Total Area : 437 072 sq. km (168 753 sq. miles)

POPULATION

- over 1 000 000
- over 500 000
- over 100 000
- over 50 000
- over 10 000

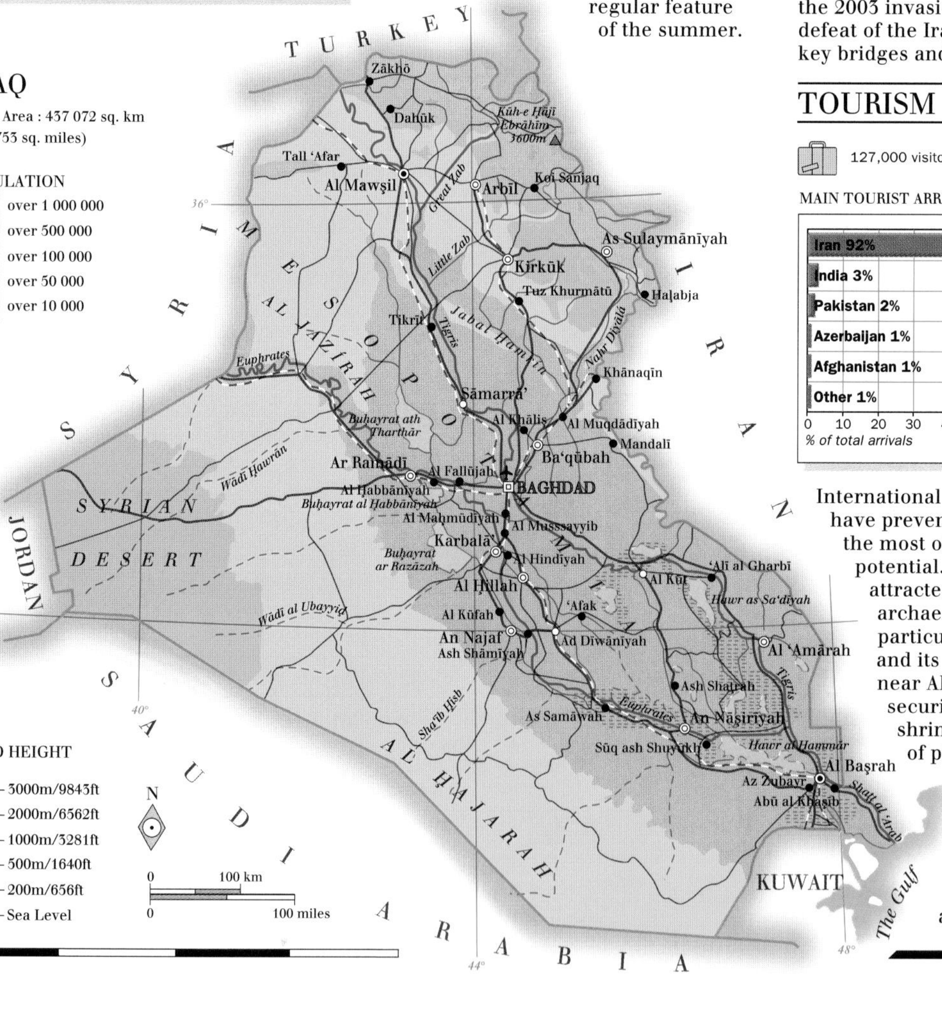
TURKEY
IRAN
SYRIA
JORDAN
SAUDI ARABIA
KUWAIT
The Gulf
MESOPOTAMIA
AL JAZIRAH
SYRIAN DESERT
AL HAJARAH
Zākhō
Dahūk
Kūh-e Hājī Ebrāhīm 3600m
Tall 'Afar
Al Mawşil
Arbīl
Koi Sanjaq
As Sulaymānīyah
Kirkūk
Tuz Khurmātū
Halabja
Tikrīt
Khānaqīn
Sāmarrā'
Al Khāliş
Al Muqdādīyah
Mandalī
Ba'qūbah
Ar Ramādī
Al Fallūjah
BAGHDAD
Al Habbānīyah
Buhayrat al Habbānīyah
Buhayrat ath Tharthār
Al Maḥmūdīyah
Al Musayyib
Karbalā'
Buhayrat ar Razāzah
Al Hindīyah
Al Hillah
Al Kūt
'Alī al Gharbī
Hawr as Sa'dīyah
'Afak
Al Kūfah
An Najaf
Ash Shāmīyah
Ad Dīwānīyah
Al 'Amārah
Ash Shaţrah
As Samāwah
An Nāşirīyah
Sūq ash Shuyūkh
Hawr al Hammār
Al Başrah
Az Zubayr
Abū al Khaşīb
Shaţţ al 'Arab
Euphrates
Tigris
Great Zab
Little Zab
Nahr Diyālā
Jabal Hamrīn
Wādī Hawrān
Wādī al Ubayyiḑ
Sha'īb Hisb
36°
32°
40°
44°
48°
N
0 100 km
0 100 miles

LAND HEIGHT

- 3000m/9843ft
- 2000m/6562ft
- 1000m/3281ft
- 500m/1640ft
- 200m/656ft
- Sea Level

PEOPLE

Pop. density medium

Arabic, Kurdish, Turkic languages, Armenian, Assyrian

58/km² (149/mi²)

THE URBAN/RURAL POPULATION SPLIT

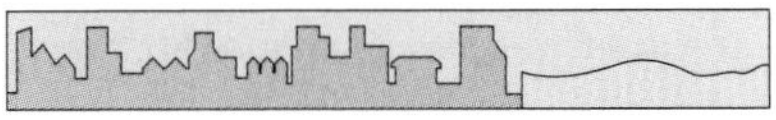
68%
32%

RELIGIOUS PERSUASION

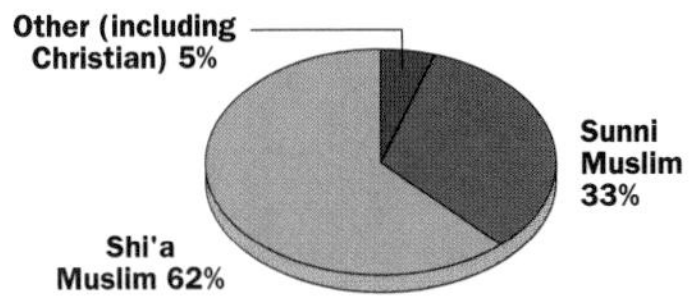
Other (including Christian) 5%
Sunni Muslim 33%
Shi'a Muslim 62%

ETHNIC MAKEUP

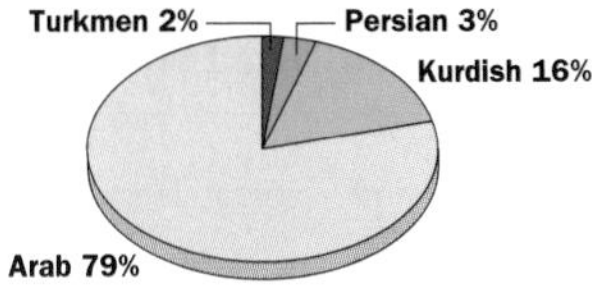
Turkmen 2%
Persian 3%
Kurdish 16%
Arab 79%

Carved out of remnants of the Ottoman Empire, Iraq is home to three distinct ethno-religious groups as well as smaller minorities, including Turkmen and Persians. There are several Christian sects, but all but a handful of Iraq's Jews have emigrated to Israel.

The Arab Muslims are divided between the Shi'a and Sunni sects; some of the holiest sites of Shi'a Islam are in Iraq. Religious tensions were violently suppressed by the Sunni-dominated regime of Saddam Hussein; the Shi'a Marsh Arabs were specifically targeted after an abortive uprising in 1991. The exploitation of religious feeling by extremists is undermining postwar Iraq.

The Kurdish community, based in the north, was granted de facto self-rule under the protection of the no-fly zones after 1991, but was riven by internal conflict. The new interim constitution in 2004 did not include the promised Kurdish veto over key national decisions, but did make Kurdish an official language.

POPULATION AGE BREAKDOWN

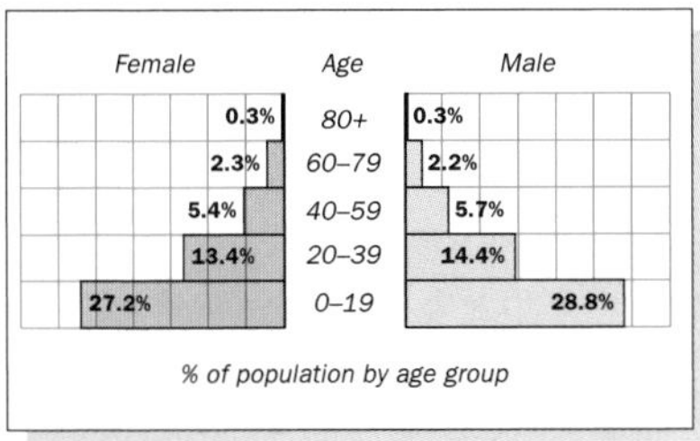
Female
Age
Male
0.3%
80+
0.3%
2.3%
60–79
2.2%
5.4%
40–59
5.7%
13.4%
20–39
14.4%
27.2%
0–19
28.8%
% of population by age group

WORLD AFFAIRS

Joined UN in 1945

AL | NAM | OAPEC | OIC | OPEC

Iraq's strategic importance rests on its vast oil reserves. During the 1980–1988 Iran–Iraq war, Saddam Hussein was armed by the West as an ally against Islamic fundamentalism. However, his invasion of Kuwait in 1990 was decried the world over. A US-led force, assisted by several Arab states, repelled Iraq in 1991. The US increased the pressure on Saddam Hussein after 2001, counting Iraq among the "axis of evil" states. France, Germany, and Russia were joined by most of Iraq's neighbors in opposing the war launched, without UN backing, by the US and allies in 2003. Hopes that military involvement could be short-lived soon proved illusory, Coalition troops remaining in Iraq after the political handover in 2004. The new government called on its neighbors to fulfill promises to prevent foreign insurgents from crossing its borders.

Iran and Syria, as well as Muslim extremists, are deeply suspicious of a potential US client state in their midst, while Turkey fears a resurgence of pan-Kurdish nationalism.

I

POLITICS

In transition

2000/2005

President Ghazi Mashal Ajil al-Yawer

AT THE LAST ELECTION

National Assembly (suspended) 250 seats

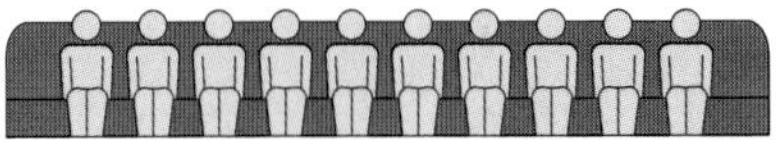

The National Assembly was suspended in 2003. A 100-member Interim National Council, with advisory powers, was chosen in 2004; a transitional National Assembly is due to be elected in 2005 and will draft a permanent constitution

Saddam Hussein held power through a brutal dictatorship after overthrowing his predecessor in 1979, until his dramatic removal by a US-led invasion in 2003.

Profile

Saddam Hussein's period in power was dominated by warfare and its consequences. The 1980–1988 war against Iran was followed by the 1990 invasion of Kuwait. A US-led alliance forced him to withdraw in 1991 and a harsh policy of international sanctions was imposed. Viciously crushing dissent, he retained his hold on power, and even drew support against the sanctions from previously hostile Arab neighbors. In March 2003, with UN weapons inspectors still failing to uncover his alleged arsenal of weapons of mass destruction (WMD), a US-led Coalition invaded Iraq and ousted Saddam Hussein within three weeks. While many welcomed his removal, few were happy at the prospect of a US-controlled regime; anti-Coalition guerrilla action intensified as the civilian death toll mounted and discontent within the Shi'a community grew. The US handed power to a transitional Iraqi government in June 2004. In advance, the US-appointed Iraqi Governing Council had elected its head, Sunni tribal leader Ghazi al-Yawer, as interim president and former exiled Shi'a opposition figure Iyad Allawi as prime minister. The interim government has the right to decide on the fate of the captured Saddam Hussein. A national conference was convened in August to elect an advisory Interim National Council, pending elections in 2005.

Main Political Issues

Postwar reconstruction

The standard of living had dropped dramatically under the UN sanctions in the 1990s, and this, coupled with the brutality of the Ba'athist regime, paved the way for the government's rapid fall in 2003. The fact that companies from Coalition countries have been favored for reconstruction contracts has prompted accusations of a new economic imperialism.

Ethnic and religious tensions

Though the Ba'athist regime began by asserting its secularity, in reality much power was concentrated in the hands of the Sunni Muslim Tikriti tribe

Ghazi al-Yawer, interim president from June 2004.

Saddam Hussein, Iraq's dictatorial leader in power from 1979 to 2003.

of Saddam Hussein. Domestic opposition was ruthlessly suppressed: chemical agents were used against the Kurds in the late 1980s and the habitat of the Shi'a Marsh Arabs was deliberately destroyed in the early 1990s. The 2003 invasion has reignited religious and ethnic tensions. An uprising in 2004 led by militant Shi'a cleric Muqtada al-Sadr in Najaf led to heavy fighting at some of Shi'a Islam's holiest sites.

AID

Recipient

$116m (receipts)

Down 5% in 2002

Regime change in Iraq has led to a reassessment of relations with donors and debtors. The US and its allies have pledged to reconstruct Iraq, while many countries are cutting debts and reinvesting; Russia canceled $5 billion of Iraqi debt in 2004.

CHRONOLOGY

Iraq became independent in 1932. In 1958, the Hashemite dynasty was overthrown when King Faisal died in a coup led by the military under Brig. Kassem. He was initially supported by the Iraqi Ba'ath Party.

- ❑ **1961** Start of Kurdish rebellion. Iraq claims sovereignty over Kuwait on the eve of Kuwait's independence.
- ❑ **1963** Kassem overthrown. Col. Abd as-Salem Muhammad Aref takes power. Kuwait's sovereignty recognized.
- ❑ **1964** Ayatollah Khomeini, future leader of Iran, takes refuge in Iraq.
- ❑ **1966** Aref is succeeded by his brother, Abd ar-Rahman.
- ❑ **1968** Ba'athists under Ahmad Hassan al-Bakr take power.
- ❑ **1970** Revolutionary Command Council agrees manifesto on Kurdish autonomy.
- ❑ **1972** Nationalization of Western-controlled Iraq Petroleum Company.
- ❑ **1978** Iraq and Syria form economic and political union.
- ❑ **1979** Saddam Hussein replaces al-Bakr as president.
- ❑ **1980** Outbreak of Iran–Iraq war.
- ❑ **1982** Shi'a leader Mohammed Baqir al-Hakim, exiled in Tehran, forms Supreme Council of the Islamic Revolution in Iraq.
- ❑ **1988** Iraq and Iran agree cease-fire. Iraqi chemical weapons attack on Kurdish village of Halabja.
- ❑ **1990** British journalist Farzad Bazoft hanged for spying. Iraq and Iran restore diplomatic relations. Iraq invades Kuwait. UN imposes trade sanctions.
- ❑ **1991** Gulf War. US-led military coalition defeats Iraq. Shi'a rebellion brutally suppressed. Northern no-fly zone enforced.
- ❑ **1992** Western powers proclaim air exclusion zone over south.
- ❑ **1994** Outbreak of Kurdish civil war. Iraq recognizes Kuwaiti sovereignty.
- ❑ **1995** Government minister Gen. Hussein Kamil defects to Jordan, and is murdered on his return to Iraq in January 1996.
- ❑ **1996** First legislative elections since 1989 won by ruling Ba'ath Party. UN supervises limited sales of Iraqi oil to purchase humanitarian supplies.
- ❑ **1998–1999** UN weapons inspection teams refused reentry into Iraq; US and UK mount punitive air strikes.
- ❑ **2002** Weapons inspectors return.
- ❑ **2003** Coalition forces invade. Saddam Hussein overthrown.
- ❑ **2004** Transitional constitution; handover to interim government.

I

DEFENSE

No compulsory military service

Not available — Not available

IRAQI ARMED FORCES

Army	To be recreated by 2006	No data
Navy	Disbanded	No data
Air force	Disbanded	No data
Missiles	None	

The military was intertwined with Saddam Hussein's regime. After the 1991 war Iraq's arsenal of weapons of mass destruction (WMD) were set to be destroyed under UN sanctions. The regime claimed to have complied but obstructed weapons inspectors, prompting the 2003 invasion. Iraqi troops melted away in the face of overwhelming force, but there is fierce resistance to occupying forces. No WMDs were found.

A UN resolution in 2004 handed control of Iraqi forces to the interim government and encouraged consultation on Coalition operations. The new army is planned to number 40,000; the air force will be primarily for reconnaissance. Following a request from Prime Minister Allawi, NATO has agreed to provide training.

ECONOMICS

Not available

$14.8bn

1456 new Iraqi dinars (0.311 old dinars)

SCORE CARD

❑ World GNP Ranking	76th
❑ GNP per Capita	$625
❑ Balance of Payments	Not available
❑ Inflation	70%
❑ Unemployment	Not available

EXPORTS

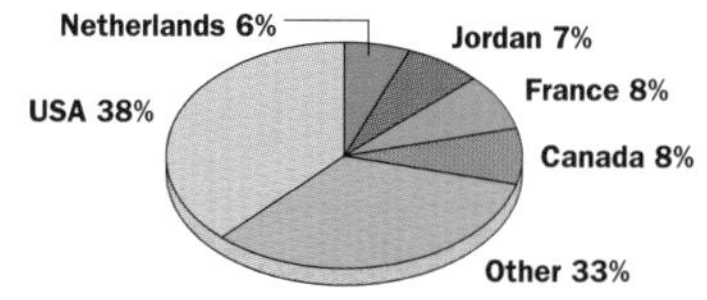
Netherlands 6%
Jordan 7%
France 8%
USA 38%
Canada 8%
Other 33%

IMPORTS

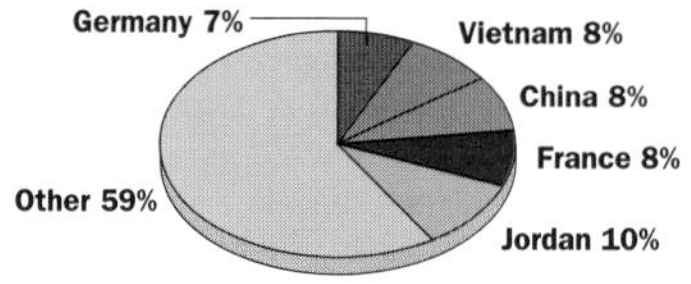
Germany 7%
Vietnam 8%
China 8%
France 8%
Other 59%
Jordan 10%

Strengths

Third-largest crude oil reserves in the world. Sizable natural gas reserves. US promises aid. Large labor force.

Weaknesses

Infrastructure devastated by war. Legacy of sanctions. War-ravaged agricultural sector.

Profile

Before 1990, Iraq was the world's third-largest oil supplier, but under sanctions oil was produced only for the domestic market. Limited exports under strict UN supervision were resumed in 1996, and in 2000 Iraq was permitted to buy parts and equipment for the oil industry.

The denial of Western assistance after the 1991 Gulf War stifled Iraq's economy. Agriculture, once thriving, was devastated. Manufacturing remains at a standstill. Harsh penalties, including the death sentence, failed to curb the black market or halt the sharp depreciation of the dinar. Efforts at recovery, such as the resumption of some informal economic links and the revision of UN sanctions in 2002, were undermined by the return of war in 2003. Hopes for the postwar economy will rest on the sale of oil and rebuilt infrastructure. New Saddam-less dinars came into circulation in October 2003.

ECONOMIC PERFORMANCE INDICATOR

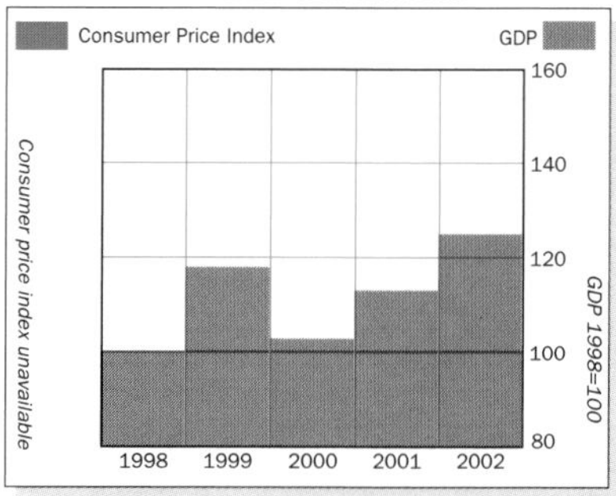
Consumer Price Index
GDP
Consumer price index unavailable
GDP 1998=100
160
140
120
100
80
1998
1999
2000
2001
2002

IRAQ : MAJOR BUSINESSES

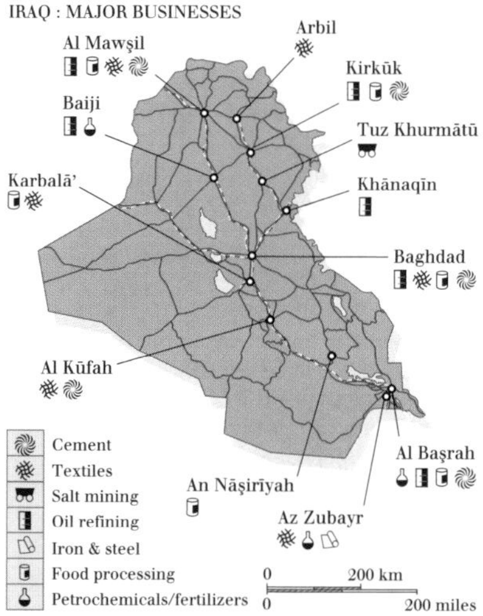
Al Mawşil
Arbil
Kirkūk
Baiji
Tuz Khurmātū
Karbalā'
Khānaqīn
Baghdad
Al Kūfah
Al Başrah
An Nāşirīyah
Az Zubayr
Cement
Textiles
Salt mining
Oil refining
Iron & steel
Food processing
Petrochemicals/fertilizers
0
200 km
0
200 miles

RESOURCES

Electric power 9.5m kW

22,800 tonnes

1.34m b/d (reserves 115bn barrels)

6.2m sheep, 1.65m goats, 1.4m cattle, 380,000 donkeys

Oil, natural gas, phosphates, sulfur, gypsum

ELECTRICITY GENERATION

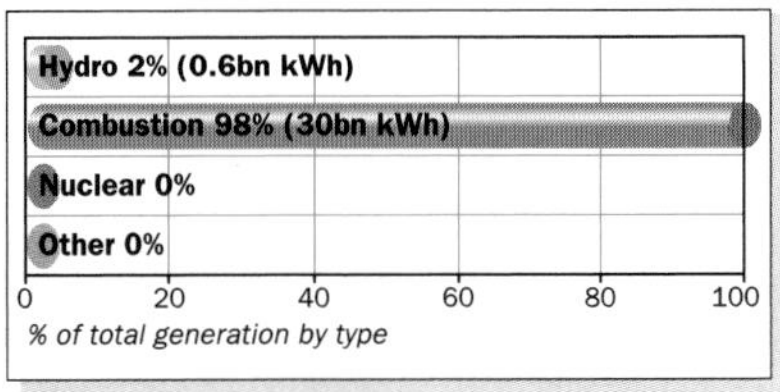
Hydro 2% (0.6bn kWh)
Combustion 98% (30bn kWh)
Nuclear 0%
Other 0%
0
20
40
60
80
100
% of total generation by type

Iraq has huge reserves of oil and natural gas (the third-largest in the world). Total gas reserves, many of which are associated with oil, are proven to be 3.11 trillion cu. m (110 trillion cu. ft), with estimates of a further 4.25 trillion cu. m (150 trillion cu. ft). The capture of oil fields was a key priority for the invading Coalition forces in 2003, ostensibly to provide a firm economic future for a postwar Iraq. US companies are likely to be at the forefront of reconstruction.

Before the 1990 invasion of Kuwait and the subsequent war, Iraq supplied 80% of the world's trade in dates. After the imposition of sanctions, food was produced simply for domestic consumption, and Iraq achieved a degree of self-sufficiency in such crops as wheat, rice, and sugarcane.

IRAQ : LAND USE

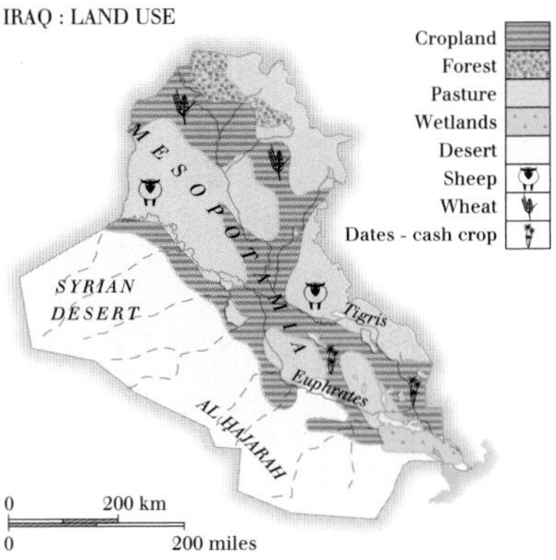
Cropland
Forest
Pasture
Wetlands
Desert
Sheep
Wheat
Dates - cash crop
MESOPOTAMIA
SYRIAN DESERT
Tigris
Euphrates
AL HAJARAH
0
200 km
0
200 miles

ENVIRONMENT

Sustainability rank: 139th

None

3.3 tonnes per capita

ENVIRONMENTAL TREATIES

No

No

No

No

No

No

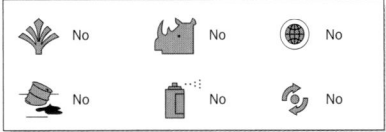

War has led to massive environmental damage. As a specific legacy of the first Gulf War, hundreds of thousands of landmines remain in the south, and there is concern about the long-term effects of the depleted uranium shells used by the US and its allies. The north has been affected by chemical weapons, used by Saddam Hussein's regime against the Kurds. In the southeast, an entire wetland ecosystem was largely destroyed by a politically motivated program to drain the marshes.

CRIME

Death penalty in use

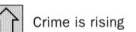

Iraq does not publish prison figures

Crime is rising

CRIME RATES

Murders

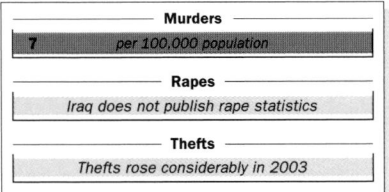

7 *per 100,000 population*

Rapes

Iraq does not publish rape statistics

Thefts

Thefts rose considerably in 2003

Looting was rife during the 2003 war. US troops were accused of serious abuses. Resistance to military occupation has given rise to widespread lawlessness and hostage-taking. The interim government has offered an amnesty to insurgents.

HEALTH

Welfare state health benefits

1 per 1667 people

Pneumonia, influenza, cancers, heart diseases

Deaths among children and the elderly had spiraled sharply before 2003, as UN sanctions led to shortages of medical supplies and equipment. Hospitals in major cities were damaged by looters in the aftermath of hostilities. Increases in birth defects since 1991 are attributed to the Allies' use of depleted uranium shells during the first Gulf War.

SPENDING

GDP/cap. decrease

CONSUMPTION AND SPENDING

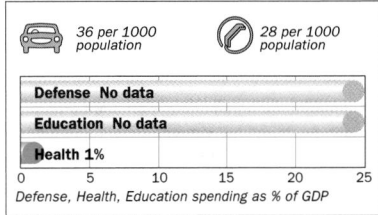

36 per 1000 population

28 per 1000 population

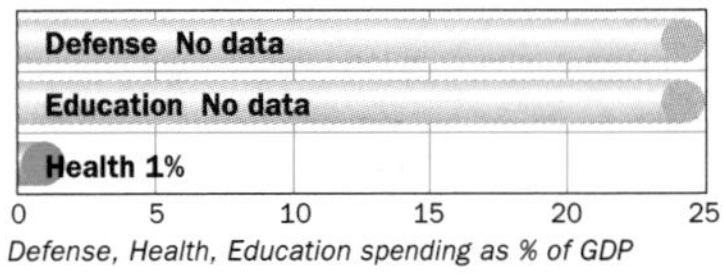
Defense No data
Education No data
Health 1%
0
5
10
15
20
25
Defense, Health, Education spending as % of GDP

The 2003 invasion has raised hopes among Iraqis of a more affluent future. The middle classes are likely to fare best, but all are currently affected by the appalling security situation.

I

MEDIA

TV ownership medium

Daily newspaper circulation 19 per 1000 people

PUBLISHING AND BROADCAST MEDIA

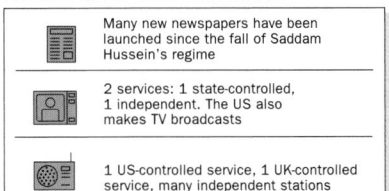

Many new newspapers have been launched since the fall of Saddam Hussein's regime

2 services: 1 state-controlled, 1 independent. The US also makes TV broadcasts

1 US-controlled service, 1 UK-controlled service, many independent stations

The media were strictly controlled under Saddam Hussein. During the 2003 war many journalists were "emedded" with invading troops. In the war's aftermath a flurry of new newspapers emerged, most controlled by aspiring political and social groups. The interim government closed the Baghdad office of influential pan-Arab broadcaster al-Jazeera in mid-2004 for "inciting violence."

EDUCATION

School leaving age: 11

40%

288,670 students

THE EDUCATION SYSTEM

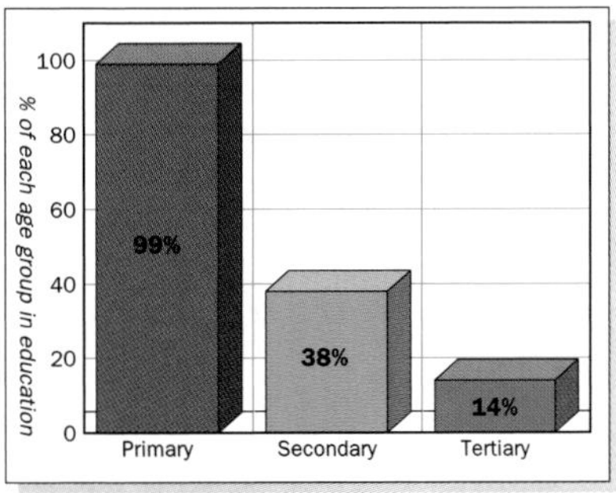
100
80
60
40
20
0
% of each age group in education
99%
38%
14%
Primary
Secondary
Tertiary

The Ba'athist regime controlled the education system, using it to instill loyalty. University scientists worked closely with the regime on weapons research programs. Many priceless museum artefacts were stolen by looters in 2003, and the Baghdad Library lies in ashes. In postwar Iraq the reconstruction of the education system was not immediately prioritized.

WORLD RANKING

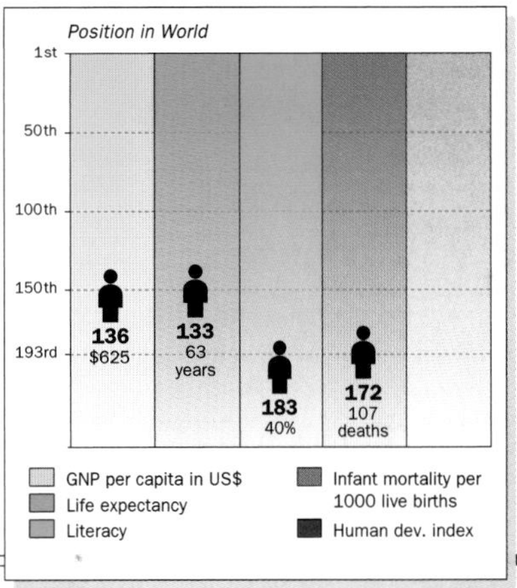
Position in World
1st
50th
100th
150th
193rd
136
$625
133
63
years
183
40%
172
107
deaths
GNP per capita in US$
Life expectancy
Literacy
Infant mortality per 1000 live births
Human dev. index

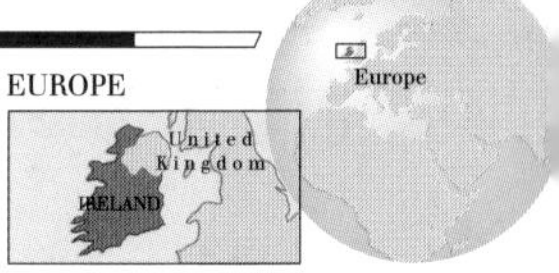
EUROPE
United Kingdom
IRELAND
Europe

IRELAND

OFFICIAL NAME: Ireland **CAPITAL:** Dublin
POPULATION: 4 million **CURRENCY:** Euro **OFFICIAL LANGUAGES:** Irish and English

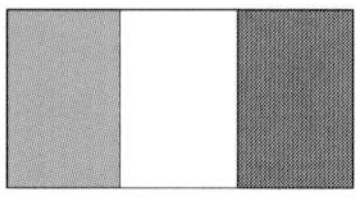

1922 | 1922 | March 17 | IRL | 0 | +353 | .ie

LYING IN THE Atlantic Ocean, off the west coast of Great Britain, the Irish republic occupies about 85% of the island of Ireland. Low coastal ranges surround a central basin with lakes, hills, and peat bogs. Centuries of struggle against English domination led in 1922 to the formation of the Irish Free State and in 1937 to full sovereignty. Efforts to resolve the Northern Ireland conflict center on the 1998 Good Friday accord, under which Ireland gave up its territorial claim.

CLIMATE

Maritime

WEATHER CHART FOR DUBLIN

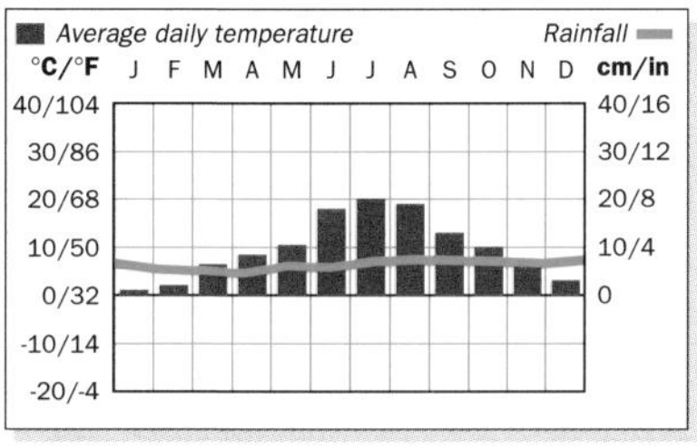
Average daily temperature
Rainfall
°C/°F
J F M A M J J A S O N D
cm/in
40/104
30/86
20/68
10/50
0/32
-10/14
-20/-4
40/16
30/12
20/8
10/4
0

Moderated by the Gulf Stream, the Irish climate is mild, equable, and wet. The mean annual temperature is 12°C (54°F).

TRANSPORTATION

Drive on left

Dublin 15.9m passengers

220 ships 279,560 grt

THE TRANSPORTATION NETWORK

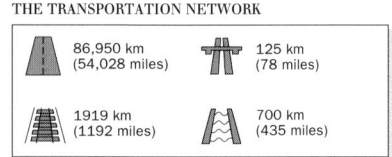

86,950 km (54,028 miles)

125 km (78 miles)

1919 km (1192 miles)

700 km (435 miles)

EU funds have improved road networks. A new tram system from 2004 is aimed at relieving Dublin's notorious congestion.

TOURISM

Visitors : Population 1.6:1

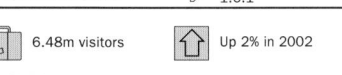

6.48m visitors

Up 2% in 2002

MAIN TOURIST ARRIVALS

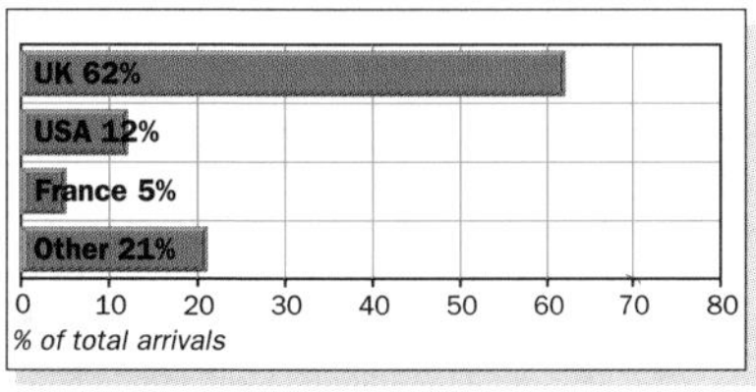
UK 62%
USA 12%
France 5%
Other 21%
0
10
20
30
40
50
60
70
80
% of total arrivals

Tourist numbers have increased steadily in recent years, exceeding six million a year. Vibrant Dublin attracts many on city breaks. Other draws are scenery, Ireland's "clean" environmental image, and the relaxed lifestyle.

PEOPLE

Pop. density medium

English, Irish Gaelic

58/km² (150/mi²)

THE URBAN/RURAL POPULATION SPLIT

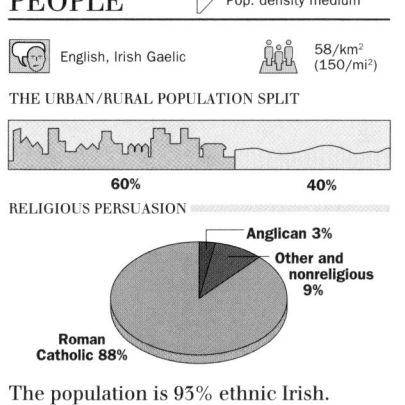

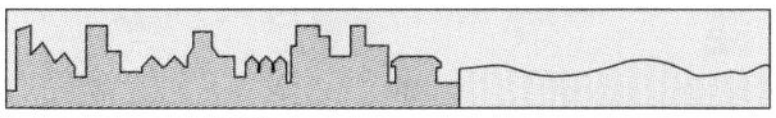
60%
40%

RELIGIOUS PERSUASION

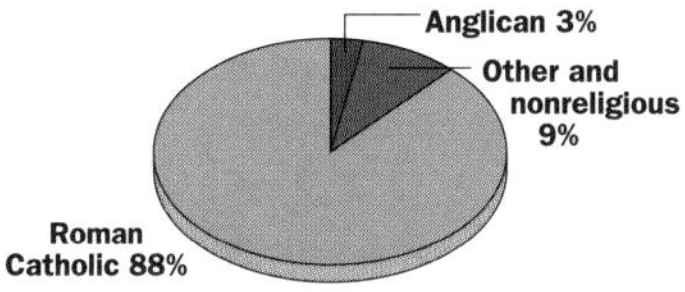
Anglican 3%
Other and nonreligious 9%
Roman Catholic 88%

The population is 93% ethnic Irish. The influence of the Roman Catholic Church is declining. Ireland is now a country of net immigration, against the trend of the past 150 years.

POLITICS

Multiparty elections

L. House 2002/2007
U. House 2002/2007

President Mary McAleese

AT THE LAST ELECTION

House of Representatives 166 seats

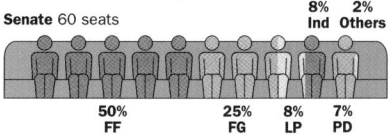

5% PD
3% SF
49% FF
19% FG
12% LP
4% GP
8% Others

FF = Fianna Fail **FG** = Fine Gael **LP** = Labour Party
PD = Progressive Democrats **GP** = Green Party
SF = Sinn Fein **Ind** = Independents

Senate 60 seats

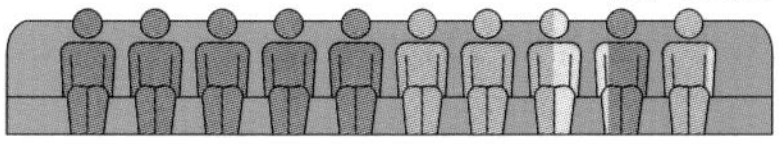
8% Ind
2% Others
50% FF
25% FG
8% LP
7% PD

Coalition governments have been the norm in recent decades, the *taoiseach* (prime minister) coming either from FG or FF. The latter, once seen as the traditional party of government, has dominated a coalition under Bertie Ahern since the 1997 elections. Though it improved its position in the April 2002 elections, Ahern's FF remains just short of an outright majority of seats in the legislature and so continues to depend on its junior partner, the PD.

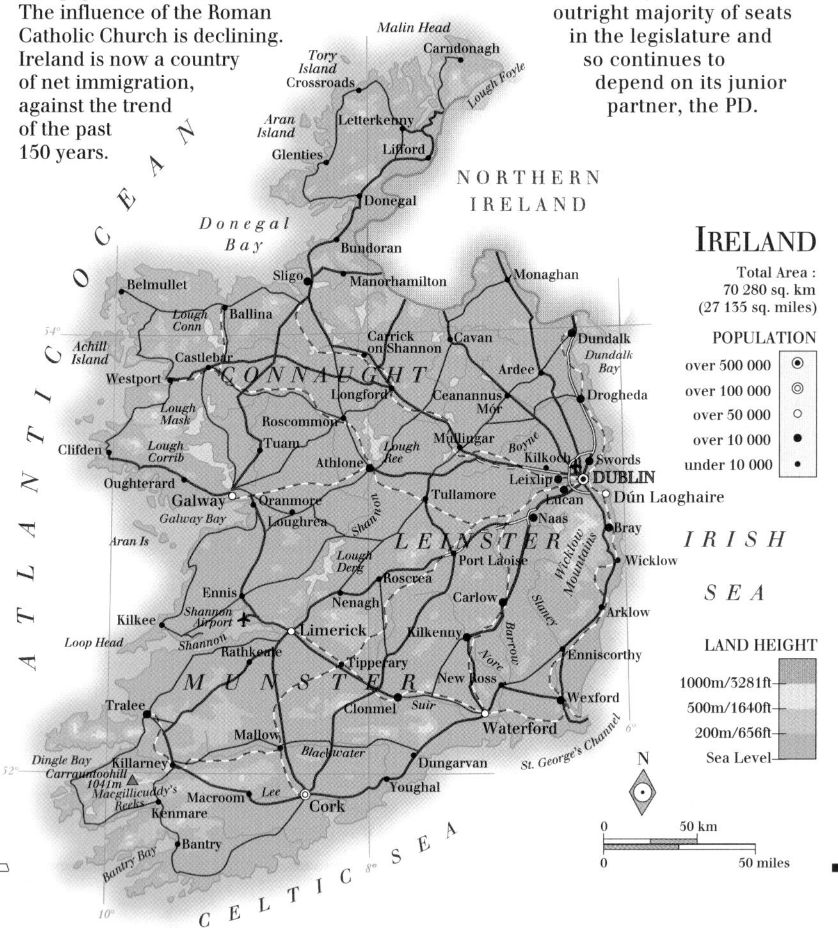
ATLANTIC OCEAN
CELTIC SEA
IRISH SEA
NORTHERN IRELAND
CONNAUGHT
LEINSTER
MUNSTER
Malin Head
Carndonagh
Tory Island
Crossroads
Lough Foyle
Aran Island
Letterkenny
Lifford
Glenties
Donegal
Donegal Bay
Bundoran
Belmullet
Sligo
Manorhamilton
Monaghan
Lough Conn
Ballina
Carrick on Shannon
Cavan
Dundalk
Dundalk Bay
Achill Island
Castlebar
Ardee
Westport
Longford
Ceanannus Mór
Drogheda
Lough Mask
Roscommon
Tuam
Mullingar
Boyne
Clifden
Lough Corrib
Athlone
Lough Ree
Kilkock
Swords
DUBLIN
Leixlip
Dún Laoghaire
Lucan
Oughterard
Galway
Galway Bay
Oranmore
Loughrea
Tullamore
Naas
Shannon
Bray
Aran Is
Lough Derg
Port Laoise
Wicklow Mountains
Wicklow
Roscrea
Ennis
Nenagh
Carlow
Slaney
Barrow
Shannon Airport
Limerick
Kilkenny
Arklow
Kilkee
Loop Head
Rathkeale
Nore
Enniscorthy
Tipperary
New Ross
Wexford
Clonmel
Suir
Tralee
Waterford
St. George's Channel
Mallow
Blackwater
Dingle Bay
Carrauntoohill 1041m
Killarney
Dungarvan
Macgillicuddy's Reeks
Macroom
Lee
Youghal
Cork
Kenmare
Bantry
Bantry Bay
IRELAND
Total Area : 70 280 sq. km (27 135 sq. miles)
POPULATION
over 500 000
over 100 000
over 50 000
over 10 000
under 10 000
LAND HEIGHT
1000m/3281ft
500m/1640ft
200m/656ft
Sea Level
N
0
50 km
0
50 miles

WORLD AFFAIRS

Joined UN in 1955

CE | ESA | EU | OECD | OSCE

Northern Ireland dominates relations with the UK. Ireland accepted the 2001 Treaty of Nice on EU enlargement only after a second referendum.

AID

Donor

$398m (donations) | Up 39% in 2002

Ireland has gone from benefiting from EU aid to being a net contributor.

DEFENSE

No compulsory military service

$718m | Up 11% in 2002

Ireland is determined to maintain its neutrality, despite EU moves to establish a common European defense policy. It has observer status at the WEU.

ECONOMICS

Inflation 3.7% p.a. (1990–2001)

$90.3bn | 0.822 euros (0.871)

SCORE CARD

- ❑ World GNP Ranking..........38th
- ❑ GNP per Capita..........$23,030
- ❑ Balance of Payments..........–$925m
- ❑ Inflation..........4.7%
- ❑ Unemployment..........4%

Strengths

Size of economy doubled during EU-backed "Celtic tiger" growth phase up to 2001, achieving trade surplus and full employment. Efficient agriculture and food processing. Foreign investment in high-tech sector: electronics account for 25% of exports. Highly educated workforce. Offshore gas and oil exploration.

Weaknesses

End of boom after 2001. Many key sectors owned by overseas multinationals. Housing shortages and strains on other infrastructure. Return of higher unemployment, and rising inflation.

EXPORTS

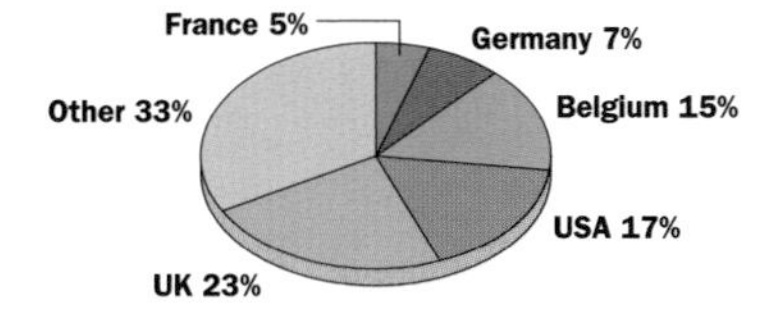
France 5%
Germany 7%
Other 33%
Belgium 15%
USA 17%
UK 23%

IMPORTS

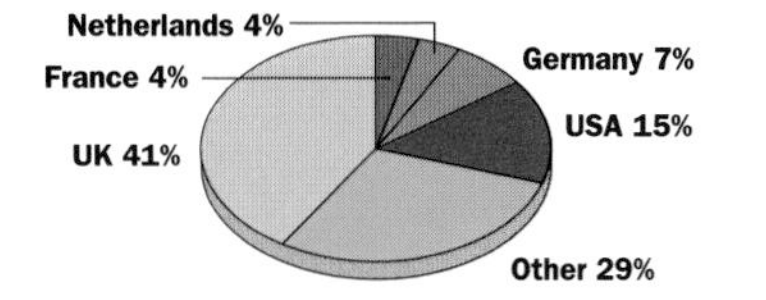
Netherlands 4%
France 4%
Germany 7%
USA 15%
UK 41%
Other 29%

RESOURCES

Electric power 4.7m kW

417,244 tonnes | Oil reserves not yet exploited

6.92m cattle, 4.83m sheep, 1.78m pigs, 11.3m chickens | Lead, zinc, natural gas, silver, coal, oil

Zinc and lead are the most important mineral resources and Ireland is one of the EU's major producers.

ENVIRONMENT

Sustainability rank: 37th

2% (0.3% partially protected) | 11.1 tonnes per capita

The main environmental concerns are overexploitation of the country's peat bogs for fuel and the recent expansion of conifer plantations, even though this increases forest cover. In 1994 stringent new laws increased pollution controls. Work began in 2003 on the world's largest offshore wind farm, off the coast of Arklow.

MEDIA

TV ownership high

Daily newspaper circulation 150 per 1000 people

PUBLISHING AND BROADCAST MEDIA

There are 6 daily newspapers. These include the *Irish Times* and the *Irish Independent*

2 services: 1 state-owned, 1 independent | 3 national services: 1 state-owned, 2 independent

The national Radio Telefis Éireann (RTE) dominates broadcasting. Radió na Gaeltachta and TG4 broadcast in Irish. Access to UK media is widespread.

CRIME

No death penalty

3366 prisoners | Up 41% in 2000–2001

Rural Ireland has one of the EU's lowest crime rates. Urban crime and narcotics are a problem in Dublin and Cork.

EDUCATION

School leaving age: 15

99% | 166,600 students

The Roman Catholic Church runs many schools. Increased education spending has resulted in a skilled workforce.

Clew Bay in County Mayo, *on the western coast of Connaught, viewed from the slopes of neighboring Croagh Patrick.*

CHRONOLOGY

English colonization, begun in 1167, was reinforced after 1558 by anti-Catholic legislation and settlement of Scottish Protestants in the north.

- ❑ **1845–1855** Famine. One million die, 1.5 million emigrate.
- ❑ **1919–1921** Anglo-Irish war after Sinn Fein proclaims independence.
- ❑ **1922** Irish Free State established.
- ❑ **1973** FG/LP alliance wins elections, ending FF's ascendancy since 1932.
- ❑ **1990** Mary Robinson elected first woman president.
- ❑ **1995** Referendum favors divorce.
- ❑ **1997** Bertie Ahern appointed *taioseach* (prime minister).
- ❑ **1998** Good Friday accord on Northern Ireland.
- ❑ **2002** Euro fully adopted.

I

HEALTH

Welfare state health benefits

1 per 417 people | Cancers, heart, cerebrovascular, and respiratory diseases

Care is means-tested; about two-thirds of people pay to see a doctor. There is a modest charge for hospital care. Smoking in enclosed public areas and workplaces was banned in 2004.

SPENDING

GDP/cap. increase

CONSUMPTION AND SPENDING

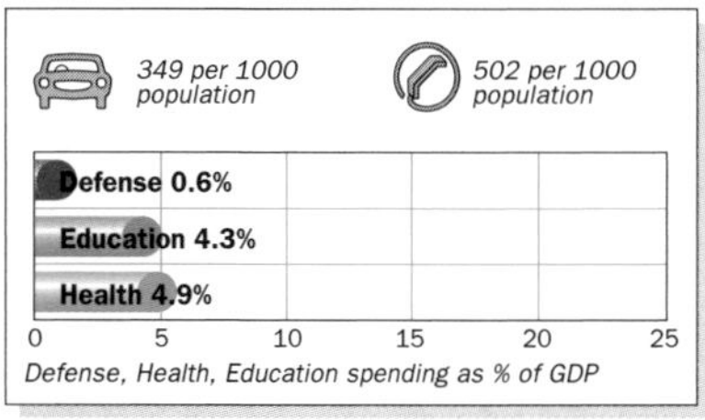
349 per 1000 population
502 per 1000 population
Defense 0.6%
Education 4.3%
Health 4.9%
0
5
10
15
20
25
Defense, Health, Education spending as % of GDP

Ireland has one of the highest levels of living standards in the EU, and welfare benefits are relatively generous.

WORLD RANKING

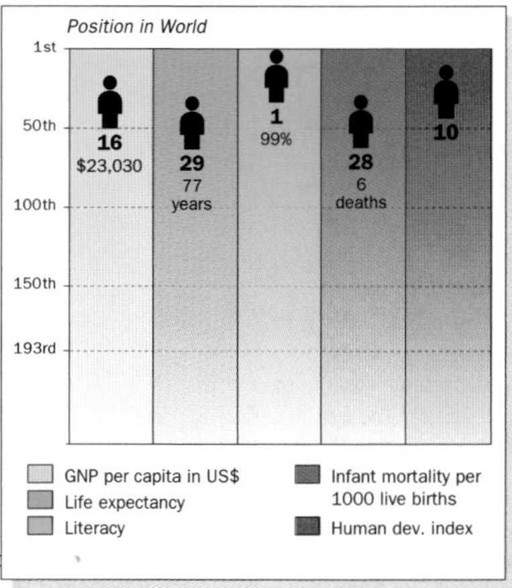
Position in World
1st
50th
100th
150th
193rd
16
$23,030
29
77
years
1
99%
28
6
deaths
10
GNP per capita in US$
Life expectancy
Literacy
Infant mortality per 1000 live births
Human dev. index

ISRAEL

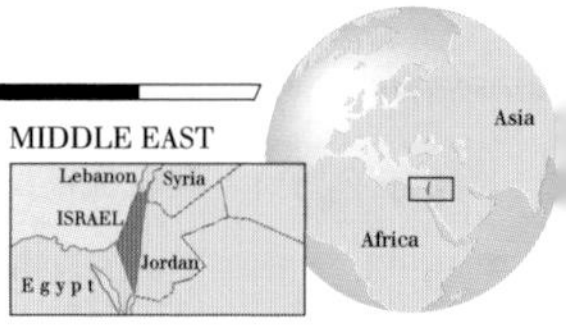
MIDDLE EAST
Lebanon
Syria
ISRAEL
Jordan
Egypt
Asia
Africa

OFFICIAL NAME: State of Israel **CAPITAL:** Jerusalem (not internationally recognized)
POPULATION: 6.4 million **CURRENCY:** Shekel **OFFICIAL LANGUAGES:** Hebrew and Arabic

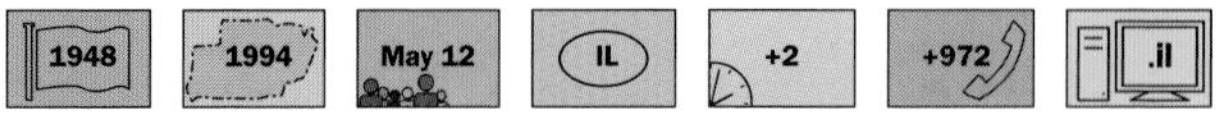
1948
1994
May 12
IL
+2
+972
.il

THE CREATION OF ISRAEL in 1948 in what was then British mandate of Palestine fulfilled the Zionist ambition for a Jewish state. Subsequent military victories over its Arab neighbors enabled Israel to annex or occupy additional territory, some of which it returned to Egypt under the 1978 Camp David agreement. Hopes in the 1990s for a "land for peace" deal to end the Israeli–Palestinian conflict became mired in a cycle of violence.

CLIMATE

Hot desert/ Mediterranean

WEATHER CHART FOR JERUSALEM

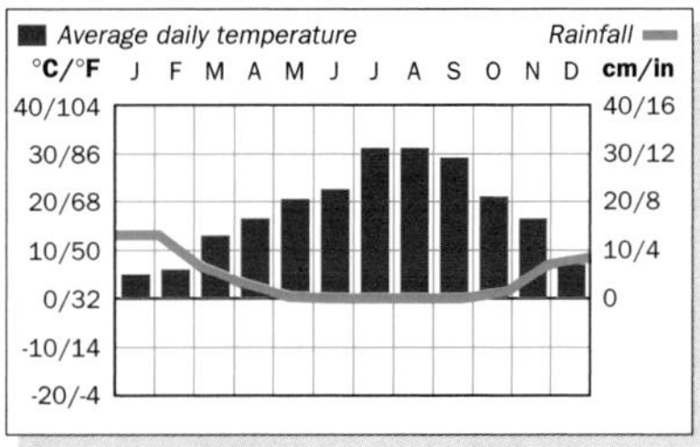
Average daily temperature
Rainfall
°C/°F J F M A M J J A S O N D cm/in
40/104
30/86
20/68
10/50
0/32
-10/14
-20/-4
40/16
30/12
20/8
10/4
0

Summers are hot and dry. The wet season is between November and March, when the weather is mild.

TRANSPORTATION

Drive on right

Ben-Gurion International, Tel Aviv
7.19m passengers

50 ships
765,300 grt

THE TRANSPORTATION NETWORK

16,521 km (10,266 miles)	56 km (35 miles)
676 km (420 miles)	None

Railroads are being extended. There are three commercial ports. Ben-Gurion international airport has been expanded.

TOURISM

Visitors : Population 1:7.4

862,300 visitors

Down 28% in 2002

MAIN TOURIST ARRIVALS

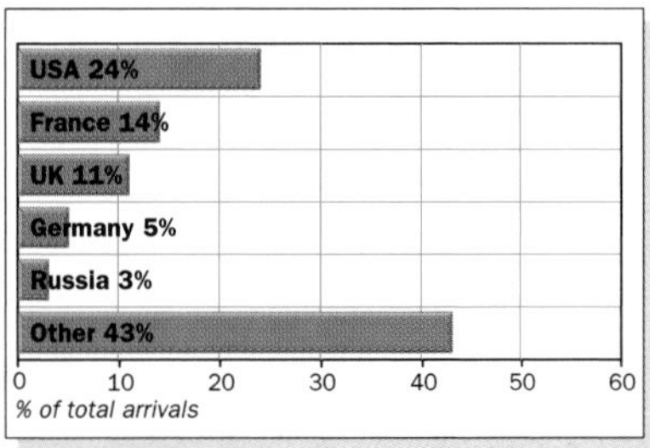
USA 24%
France 14%
UK 11%
Germany 5%
Russia 3%
Other 43%
0 10 20 30 40 50 60
% of total arrivals

Israel contains important sites for many faiths, but tourism has been damaged by the ongoing conflict.

PEOPLE

Pop. density high

Hebrew, Arabic, Yiddish, German, Russian, Polish, Romanian, Persian

315/km² (815/mi²)

THE URBAN/RURAL POPULATION SPLIT

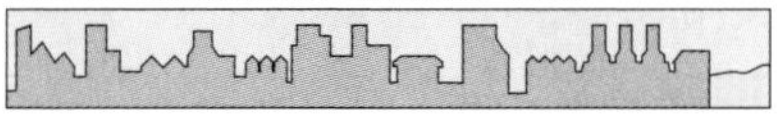
92%
8%

RELIGIOUS PERSUASION

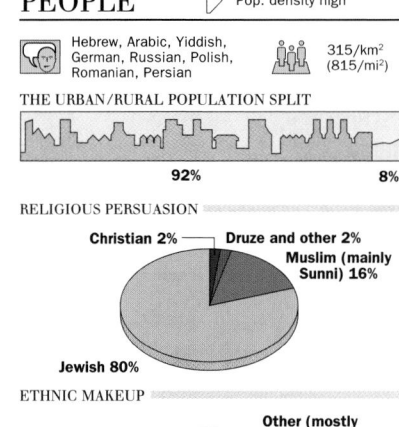

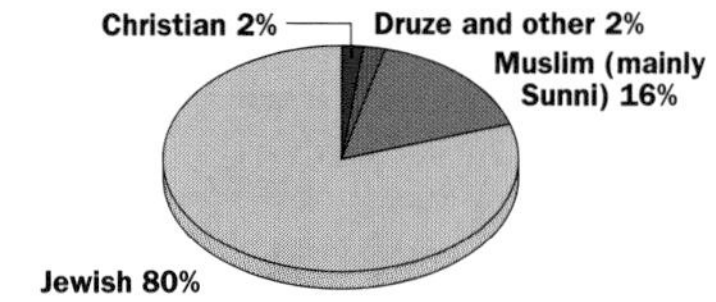
Christian 2%
Druze and other 2%
Muslim (mainly Sunni) 16%
Jewish 80%

ETHNIC MAKEUP

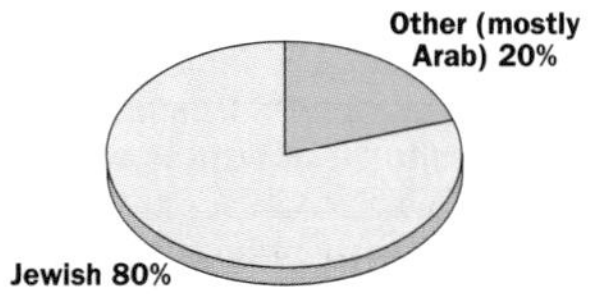
Other (mostly Arab) 20%
Jewish 80%

Large numbers of Jewish immigrants settled in Palestine before Israel was founded. Sephardi Jews from the Middle East and Mediterranean are now probably in the majority, but Ashkenazi Jews, most of central European origin, still dominate society. Hundreds of thousands of Russian Jews have arrived since 1989. Israel's non-Jewish minority population – mostly Arab and predominantly Muslim (with Christian and Druze minorities) – totals more than one million but remains largely sidelined in Israeli life. There are tensions between secular and Orthodox Jews, and between left and right over the pursuit of peace with the Palestinians.

POPULATION AGE BREAKDOWN

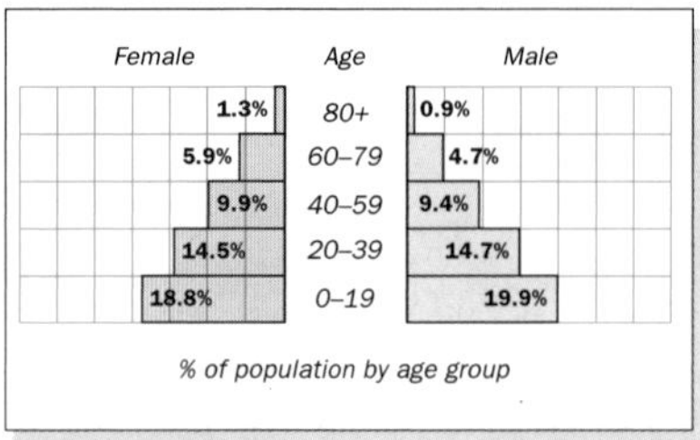
Female
Age
Male
1.3% 80+ 0.9%
5.9% 60–79 4.7%
9.9% 40–59 9.4%
14.5% 20–39 14.7%
18.8% 0–19 19.9%
% of population by age group

POLITICS

Multiparty elections

2003/2007

President Moshe Katzav

AT THE LAST ELECTION

Parliament (Knesset) 120 seats

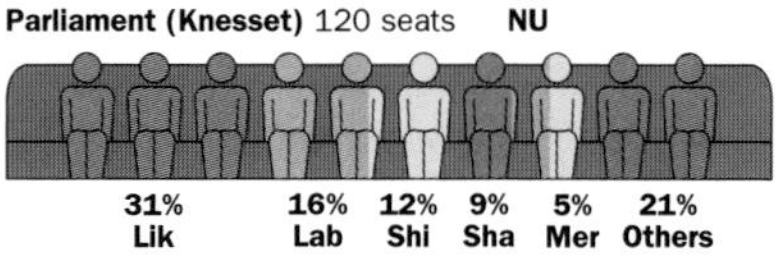
6% NU
31% Lik
16% Lab
12% Shi
9% Sha
5% Mer
21% Others

Lik = Likud **Lab** = Labor **Shi** = Shinui **Sha** = Shas **NU** = National Union **Mer** = Meretz

Israel is a multiparty democracy.

PROFILE

Governments alternate between right-wing Likud or left-of-center Labor leadership. Since neither can win an overall majority they must either join in a unity government, or bridge the religious–secular divide in fractious coalitions with smaller parties. Likud, under Prime Minister Ariel Sharon from 2001, doubled its presence in the Knesset in 2003. His right-wing coalition collapsed in 2004 over the proposed withdrawal from Gaza.

MAIN POLITICAL ISSUE
Peace with the Palestinians

The central question is whether Israel's security should be based solely on armed strength, or on agreements with Palestinians and neighboring countries. Small but influential religious parties support Jewish settlement of the occupied territories, which hampers any "land for peace" deal. Sharon has insisted on a change in the Palestinian leadership and an end to violence before talks could even begin. The renewed *intifada* (uprising), with Palestinian terror attacks and suicide bombings of civilians, reinforced skepticism about prospects for peace. An Israeli "security barrier" erected in the West Bank to block suicide bombers is criticized as illegal and irredentist.

Ariel Sharon, *Israel's hard-line prime minister elected in 2001.*

Yasser Arafat, *the militant-turned-moderate leader of the PLO.*

I

WORLD AFFAIRS

Joined UN in 1949

EBRD | IAEA | IBRD | IDB | WTO

Israel is technically at war with all Arab states except Egypt and Jordan. In 2000 it withdrew from southern Lebanon. Aside from ties with the US and Turkey, Israel's harsh response to Palestinian attacks leaves it increasingly isolated.

AID

Recipient

$754m (receipts) | Up 338% in 2002

Israel receives massive military and economic aid from the US. Large ad hoc donations are also received from Jewish NGOs.

ISRAEL

Total Area : 20 770 sq. km (8019 sq. miles)

POPULATION
over 100 000
over 50 000
over 10 000
LAND HEIGHT
1000m/3281ft
500m/1640ft
200m/656ft
Sea Level
-200m/-656ft
LEBANON
SYRIA
GOLAN HEIGHTS
MEDITERRANEAN SEA
WEST BANK
GAZA STRIP (under Palestinian administration)
EGYPT
JORDAN
HANEGEV
Qiryat Shemona
Haré Meron 1208m
Nahariyya
Mifraz Hefa
'Akko
Zefat
Qiryat Motzkin
Hefa
Karmi'él
Qiryat Ata
Shefar'am
Lake Tiberias
Teverya
Nazerat 'Illit
Nazerat
'Afula
Jenin
Hadera
Netanya
Tulkarm
Nablus
Ra'anana
Herzliyya
Kefar Sava
Tel Aviv-Yafo
Petah Tiqwa
Bat Yam
Ramat Gan
Holon
Rishon Le Ziyyon
Lod
Rehovot
Ramla
Ramallah
Jericho
Ashdod
JERUSALEM
Bet Shemesh
Bethlehem
Ashqelon
Gaza
Qiryat Gat
Hebron
Dead Sea
Khān Yūnis
Rafah
'Arad
Be'ér Sheva'
HOLOT HALUZA
Dimona
Wadi al 'Arabah
N
50 km
50 miles
Elat
Gulf of Aqaba

DEFENSE

Compulsory military service

$9.44bn | Down 4% in 2002

Israel, the only known nuclear-armed power in the Middle East, has a small regular defense force, which can be boosted by over 350,000 reservists. Equipped with some of the latest US technology, it is vastly superior to the forces of its Arab neighbors in firepower and training. To counter the Palestinian *intifada* (uprising) it uses punitive strikes and counterinsurgency methods, including targeted assassinations.

ISRAELI ARMED FORCES

3950 main battle tanks (Centurion, M-60A1/3, Magach 7, Merkava I–IV)	125,000 personnel
3 submarines and 53 patrol boats	7600 personnel
688 combat aircraft (50 F-4E-2000, 62 F-15, 203 F-16)	35,000 personnel
Unofficial arsenal of up to 100 warheads. Delivery via Jericho 1 and Jericho 2 missiles	

ECONOMICS

Inflation 9.3% p.a. (1990–2001)

$105bn | 4.501 sheqalim (4.324)

STRENGTHS

Modern infrastructure. Trade with EU. Sophisticated agriculture, high-tech industry, and manufacturing. Privatization initiatives. Educated population. Banking sector.

WEAKNESSES

Conflict. Large defense budget. Cost of settlement and integration of immigrants. Little trade with neighbors. Decline of tourism. Rising wealth disparities and unemployment; increasing labor unrest. Corruption.

PROFILE

The government seeks ways to reduce massive state spending. The state owns most of the land and controls over 20% of all industries and services. Public companies are being privatized and there are plans to end restrictive labor practices. Agriculture, highly specialized and profitable, has been eclipsed by high-tech industries. The state aims to boost the service sector.

Israel's economy expanded in the 1990s, benefiting from mass immigration of Jews from the former USSR. Though unemployment rose, new skills and contacts helped the economy toward sustained export-led growth. Pockets of poverty remain in "development towns."

ECONOMIC PERFORMANCE INDICATOR

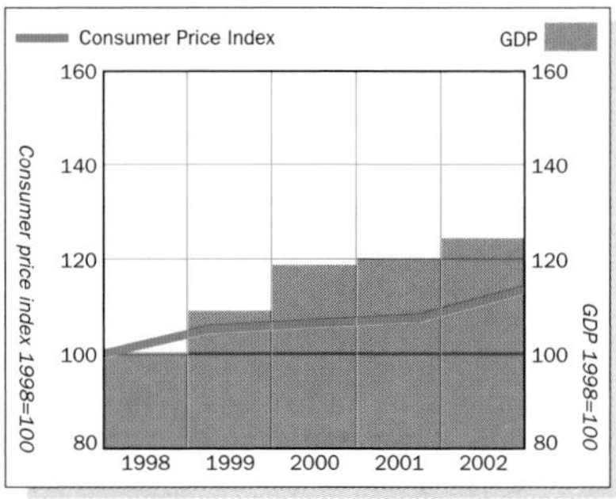
Consumer Price Index
GDP
160
140
120
100
80
Consumer price index 1998=100
GDP 1998=100
1998
1999
2000
2001
2002

SCORE CARD

❑ World GNP Ranking	35th
❑ GNP per capita	$16,020
❑ Balance of payments	–$2.14bn
❑ Inflation	5.6%
❑ Unemployment	10%

EXPORTS

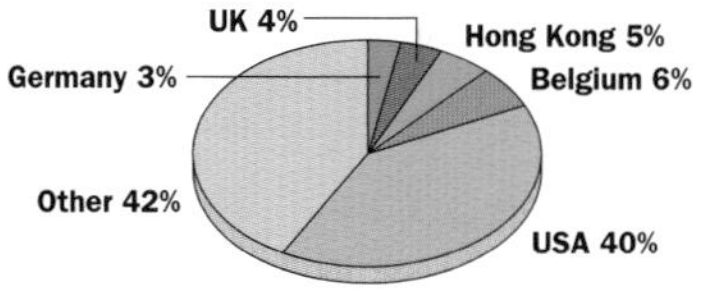
UK 4%
Hong Kong 5%
Germany 3%
Belgium 6%
Other 42%
USA 40%

IMPORTS

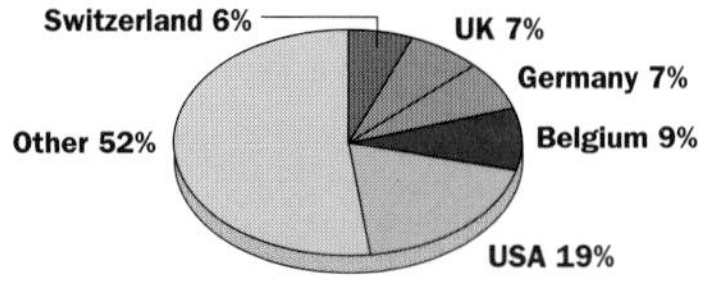
Switzerland 6%
UK 7%
Germany 7%
Other 52%
Belgium 9%
USA 19%

The Palestinian uprising since 2000 has led to recession and hit trade, tourism, and investment. Tough austerity measures have somewhat offset the trend. The military response has eaten into the Israeli budget and inflicted damage in the West Bank and Gaza Strip estimated at over $300 million.

ISRAEL : MAJOR BUSINESSES

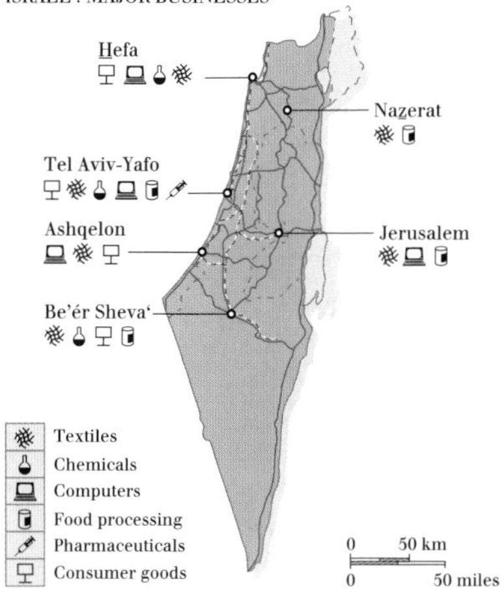
Hefa
Nazerat
Tel Aviv-Yafo
Ashqelon
Jerusalem
Be'ér Sheva'
Textiles
Chemicals
Computers
Food processing
Pharmaceuticals
Consumer goods
0
50 km
0
50 miles

I

I

ISRAEL AND THE PALESTINIANS

THE CONFLICT between Israel and the Palestinians is crucial to Middle East, and indeed global, politics. For Jews, the historic territory of Palestine is seen as the "promised land," with the holy city of Jerusalem at its center; Jerusalem, however, is not only the spiritual home of Judaism but a revered site for the other major Abrahamic religions – Christianity and Islam. For the Arab people living in Palestine the territory was simply their home until the creation of the state of Israel in 1948. Supported by the West as reparation for the Holocaust and centuries of persecution in Europe, this effectively turned almost one million Arabs into refugees overnight. Some 300,000 more left territories occupied by Israel in 1967. The Palestinian goal is now a separate and viable Palestinian state, to include at least the territories occupied in 1967 and especially East Jerusalem as its capital. Their struggle (*intifada*) has attracted international support, from Islamists in particular, while being met by an increasingly hard-line response from Israel.

The Palestinians

Palestinians in the occupied territories suffer from high unemployment and limited economic or educational opportunities. Two and a half million live as refugees in Jordan, Syria, and Lebanon. These conditions foster disillusionment and anger, leading a minority to adopt the tactics of *intifada*, from throwing stones at Israeli soldiers to suicide bombings. The 1993 accords granted the Palestinians internal self-rule in the West Bank (5900 sq. km – 2300 sq. miles) and Gaza (1000 sq. km – 400 sq. miles) – inhabited by two million Palestinians (and 300,000 Jewish settlers) – under the jurisdiction of the Palestinian National Authority (PNA). The PNA is governed by an 88-member Legislative Council, led by Palestine Liberation Organization (PLO) head Yasser Arafat, elected president in 1996. Secular groups such as Fatah (linked to the PLO) have now rejected violence against civilians, but others such as the religiously motivated Hamas and the al-Aqsa Martyrs' Brigade embrace death as a legitimate means to an end.

***Jerusalem,** a city divided by conflict.*

Gaza Strip

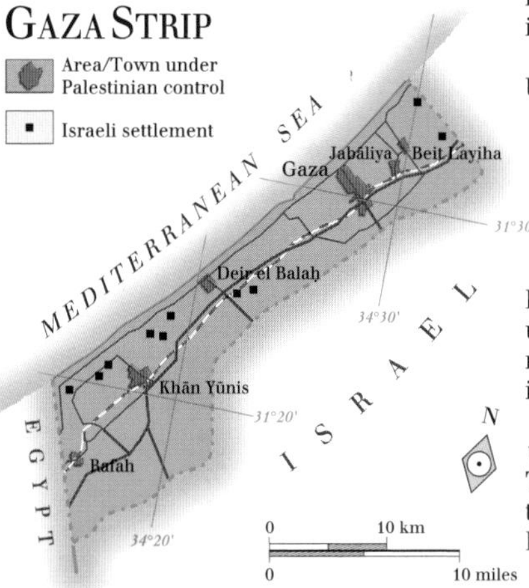
Area/Town under Palestinian control
Israeli settlement
MEDITERRANEAN SEA
Gaza
Jabāliya
Beit Lāyiha
Deir el Balah
Khān Yūnis
Rafah
EGYPT
ISRAEL
N
31°30'
31°20'
34°30'
34°20'
0
10 km
0
10 miles

Living in markedly superior conditions, Israelis see the existence of their country as an established fact and an inalienable right. Against the background of a Jewish history of persecution, the hostility of Palestinian militants and disaffected Muslims everywhere tends to harden Israeli resolve and the determination not to give way to "terrorism."

War and peace

In recent years Palestinian militants have adopted suicide bombing as the main weapon against the Israelis, as well as ambushes on Jewish settlers and sporadic low-level actions against Israeli troops. In response, Israel's tactics have ranged from closing borders, bulldozing the homes of suspected bombers, shooting individual stone-throwers, and, most recently, constructing a massive "security fence." Targeted assassination – the murder of senior militants by Israeli forces using precision missiles – is a strategy condemned by most of the international community, though importantly not by the US.

Under the 1993 Oslo Accords each side officially recognized the other, and accepted the concept of "land for peace" as a means of advancing toward "final status" talks. The slow progress of negotiations, however, and the heavy-handed response of Israel to low-level Palestinian violence, undid this apparent progress. Efforts to resurrect the peace process have involved various bold proposals by third-party mediators, the Israeli state, or unofficial Palestinian pressure groups. The 2003 US "roadmap" outlined a timetable for establishing a full Palestinian state and an end to the *intifada*. It was undermined within weeks as neither side complied with even the basic principles of dismantling settlements and ending suicide bombings. The right-wing Israeli government of Ariel Sharon has increasingly moved toward a unilateral approach; the "security fence," damned as illegal by the International Court of Justice in July 2004, is intended to act as a physical barrier around the West Bank to block suicide bombers. An agreement was reached within Sharon's party in 2004 to withdraw Jewish settlements from Gaza by 2006. For its part, the PNA has become increasingly unable to control radical militants and is facing serious internal divisions; open violence between rival factions broke out in Gaza in 2004.

West Bank

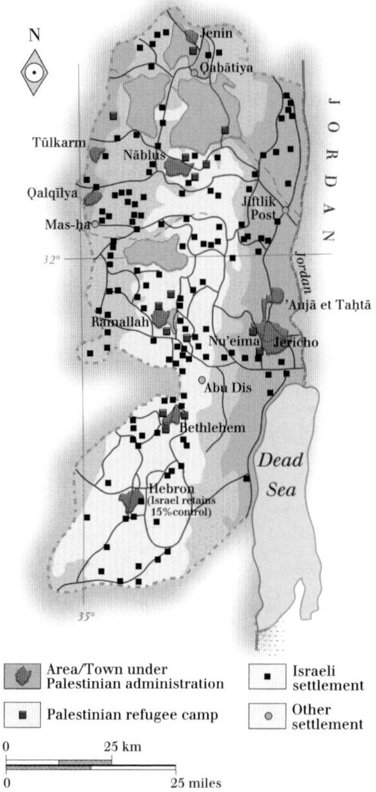
N
Jenin
Qabātiya
Tūlkarm
Nāblus
Qalqīlya
Mas-ha
Jiftlik Post
JORDAN
Jordan
32°
'Anjā et Taḥtā
Ramallah
Nu'eima
Jericho
Abu Dis
Bethlehem
Dead Sea
Hebron (Israel retains 15% control)
35°
Area/Town under Palestinian administration
Israeli settlement
Palestinian refugee camp
Other settlement
0
25 km
0
25 miles

***Palestinian supporters** display their opposition to the Israeli barrier.*

RESOURCES

Electric power 9.1m kW

25,100 tonnes

80 b/d (reserves 7.3m barrels)

4.8m turkeys, 1.4m geese, 395,000 sheep, 30m chickens

Natural gas, oil, salt, potash, copper, gold, magnesium, bromine

ELECTRICITY GENERATION

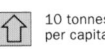

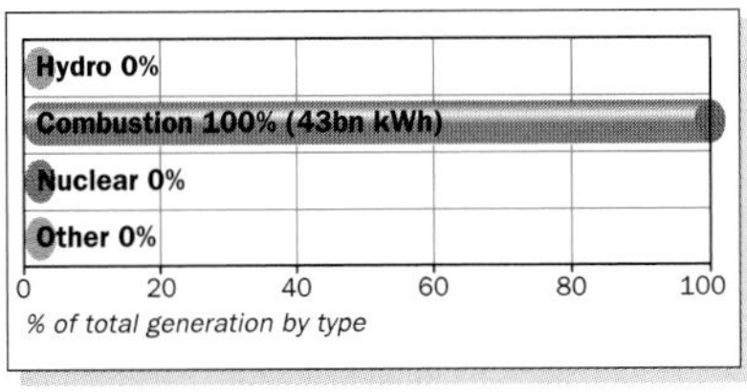
Hydro 0%
Combustion 100% (43bn kWh)
Nuclear 0%
Other 0%
0
20
40
60
80
100
% of total generation by type

Israel's most critical resource is water. The water of the River Jordan is shared by Jordan and Israel, and Israel also buys water from Turkey.

The country's most valuable mineral deposits are potash salts, bromine (of which Israel is the world's largest exporter), and other salts mined near the Dead Sea. Reserves of copper ore and gold were discovered in 1988. In the coastal plain, mixed farming, vineyards, and citrus groves are plentiful. Former desert areas now have extensive irrigation systems supporting specialized agriculture.

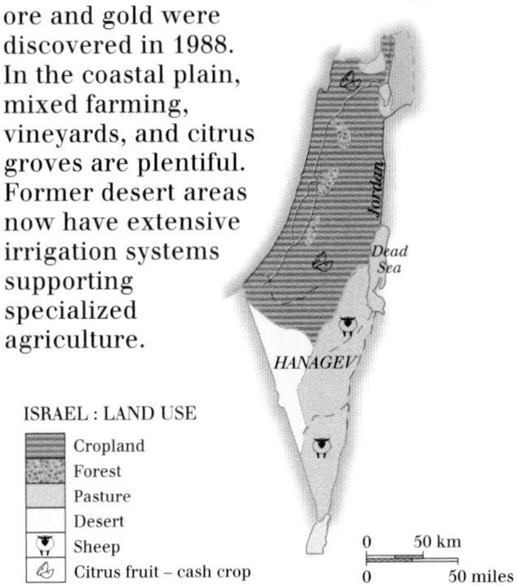
Jordan
Dead Sea
HANAGEV
ISRAEL : LAND USE
Cropland
Forest
Pasture
Desert
Sheep
Citrus fruit – cash crop
0
50 km
0
50 miles

ENVIRONMENT

Sustainability rank: 63rd

16% partially protected

10 tonnes per capita

Government environmental efforts focus on recycling and the cleanup of towns and rivers. In an effort to halt the depletion of the Dead Sea, water is to be piped from the Red Sea.

ENVIRONMENTAL TREATIES

Yes	Yes	Yes
Yes	Yes	Yes

MEDIA

TV ownership high

Daily newspaper circulation 290 per 1000 people

PUBLISHING AND BROADCAST MEDIA

There are 34 daily newspapers. The leading papers are the Hebrew *Ha'aretz*, and the English *Jerusalem Post*

3 services: 1 state-owned, 2 independent

2 state-owned services, many independent stations

The left-wing press favors the peace process. The number of private radio stations, many right-wing, is rising. Media freedom in Israel itself contrasts with severe restrictions in the occupied territories.

CRIME

Death penalty not used in practice

10,164 prisoners

Violent crime rose in 2000–2001

CRIME RATES

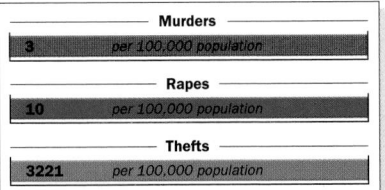

Murders
3 per 100,000 population

Rapes
10 per 100,000 population

Thefts
3221 per 100,000 population

The vast majority of violent attacks are due to the Israeli–Palestinian conflict. Car theft is a rising concern.

EDUCATION

School leaving age: 16

95%

270,979 students

THE EDUCATION SYSTEM

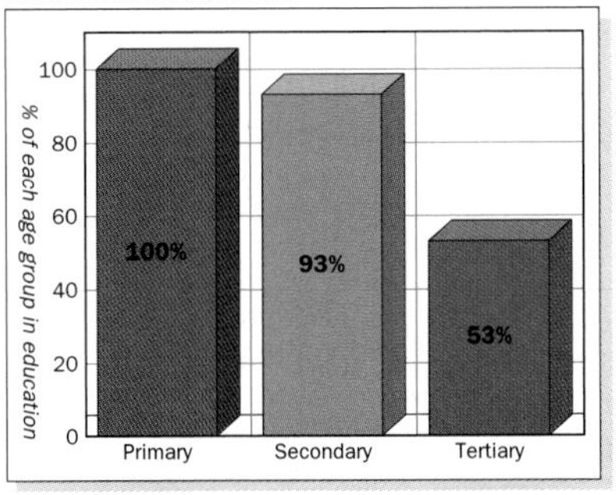
100
80
60
40
20
0
% of each age group in education
100%
93%
53%
Primary
Secondary
Tertiary

A highly educated population has been the engine of Israel's economic growth. State schools have religious (Jewish), secular, and Arab streams. Ultraorthodox and Sephardi Jews increasingly run their own private establishments.

HEALTH

Welfare state health benefits

1 per 270 people

Cancers, heart and cerebrovascular diseases

The ratio of doctors to the total population in Israel is one of the highest in the world. Primary health care reaches all Israeli communities. Its hospitals have pioneered many innovative treatments.

CHRONOLOGY

War with the neighboring Arab states followed immediately upon the creation of the state of Israel in 1948.

- **1967** Israeli victory in Six-Day War.
- **1973** Egypt and Syria attack Israel.
- **1978** Camp David accords with Egypt.
- **1979** Formal peace treaty, Sinai returned to Egypt.
- **1982** Israel invades Lebanon.
- **1987** Palestinians launch *intifada*.
- **1993** Oslo Accords.
- **1994** Palestinian autonomy begins in Gaza and Jericho.
- **1995** Prime Minister Yitzhak Rabin assassinated.
- **1996** Palestinian elections.
- **1998** Government stalls on US-backed plan to revive peace process.
- **1999** Ehud Barak (Labor) prime minister. Renewed peace process with Palestinians and Syria.
- **2000** Israel withdraws from Lebanon. *Intifada* relaunched.
- **2001** Ariel Sharon (Likud) prime minister; forms unity government.
- **2002** *Intifada* and reprisals intensify. Unity government collapses.
- **2003** Likud wins elections. US peace "roadmap" published.
- **2004** Gaza withdrawal agreed.

I

SPENDING

GDP/cap. increase

CONSUMPTION AND SPENDING

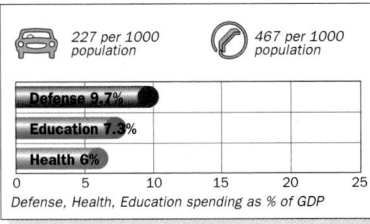

227 per 1000 population

467 per 1000 population

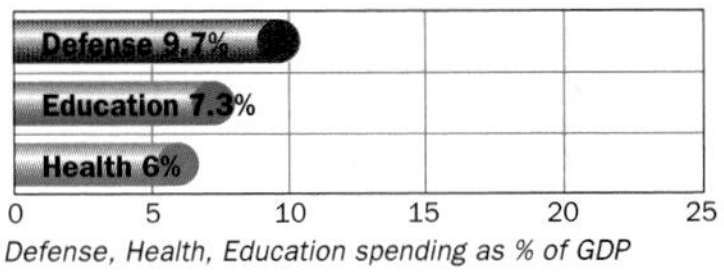
Defense 9.7%
Education 7.3%
Health 6%
0
5
10
15
20
25
Defense, Health, Education spending as % of GDP

Income per head is high, but taxation is heavy. In theory, those living in communes (*kibbutzim*) eschew personal material wealth.

WORLD RANKING

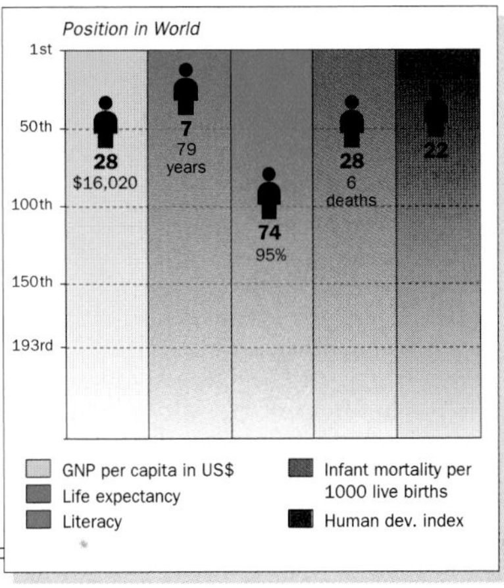
Position in World
1st
50th
100th
150th
193rd
28
$16,020
7
79
years
74
95%
28
6
deaths
22
GNP per capita in US$
Life expectancy
Literacy
Infant mortality per 1000 live births
Human dev. index

ITALY

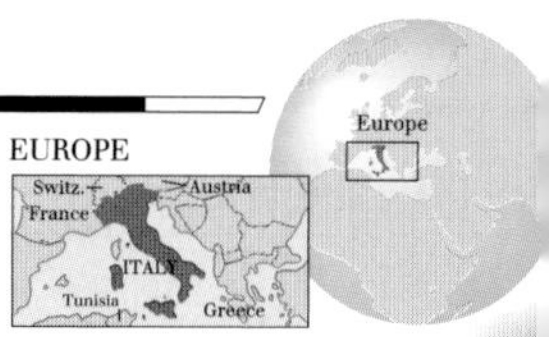

Europe
EUROPE
Switz.
Austria
France
ITALY
Tunisia
Greece

OFFICIAL NAME: Italian Republic **CAPITAL:** Rome
POPULATION: 57.4 million **CURRENCY:** Euro **OFFICIAL LANGUAGE:** Italian

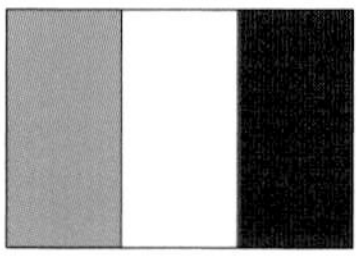

1861 | 1947 | June 2 | I | +1 | +39 | .it

THE BOOT-SHAPED Italian peninsula stretches 800 km (500 miles) southward into the Mediterranean, while the Alps form a natural boundary to the north. Italy also includes Sicily, Sardinia, and several smaller islands. The south is an area of seismic activity, with two famous volcanoes, Vesuvius and Etna. Rival city-states flourished in Renaissance Italy, a unified country only in Roman times and since 1861. Fascist rule under Mussolini from 1922 ended with Italy's defeat in World War II. The Christian Democrats (DC) then dominated Italy's notoriously short-lived governments for decades, until in the 1990s the established parties and patronage systems were shaken up by corruption investigations. New groupings emerged, power alternating between a right-wing coalition and a broad center-left Olive Tree alliance.

CLIMATE

Mediterranean/mountain

WEATHER CHART FOR ROME

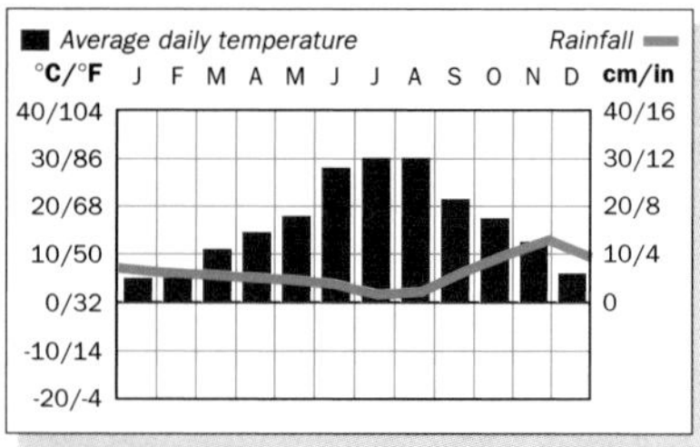

Average daily temperature
Rainfall
°C/°F J F M A M J J A S O N D cm/in
40/104 40/16
30/86 30/12
20/68 20/8
10/50 10/4
0/32 0
-10/14
-20/-4

A Mediterranean climate in the south contrasts with more temperate conditions in the north. Summers are hot and dry, especially in the south; Sardinia and Sicily have highs of more than 30°C (86°F). The Adriatic coast suffers from cold winds such as the *bora*. Southern winters are mild; northern ones are cooler and wetter, with heavy snow in the mountains.

TRANSPORTATION

Drive on right

Leonardo da Vinci (Fiumicino), Rome
26.3m passengers

1486 ships
9.6m grt

THE TRANSPORTATION NETWORK

479,688 km (298,064 miles)

6460 km (4014 miles)

16,307 km (10,133 miles)

2400 km (1491 miles)

Roads, which carry most of Italy's trade via Switzerland and Austria, are badly congested. The *autostrada* (expressway) network lacks key links, and serious bottlenecks affect the main north–south artery. Rail services are extensive and cheap. Luxurious Pendolino trains link Rome and Milan, but the high-speed TAV (*treno alta velocità*) project is behind schedule and over budget.

TOURISM

Visitors : Population 1:1.4

39.6m visitors

Down 1% in 2003

MAIN TOURIST ARRIVALS

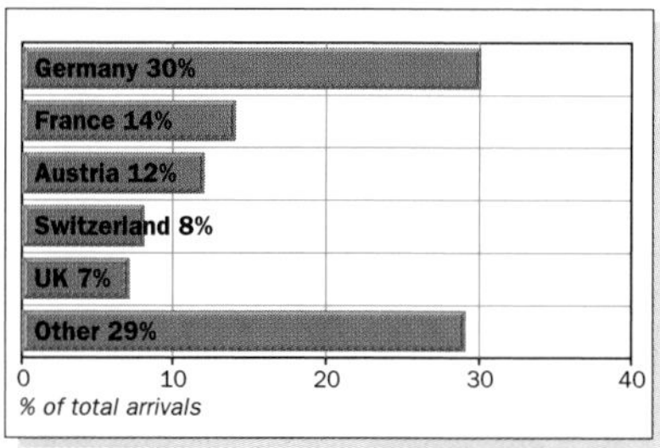

Germany 30%
France 14%
Austria 12%
Switzerland 8%
UK 7%
Other 29%
0 10 20 30 40
% of total arrivals

Italy has been a tourist destination since the 16th century. Roman popes consciously aimed to make their city the most beautiful in the world to attract travelers. In the 18th century, Italy was the focus of any Grand Tour. Today, its many unspoiled centers of Renaissance and ancient culture continue to make Italy one of the world's major tourism destinations. The industry accounts for 2.5% of Italy's GDP, and employs around a million people – 4% of the workforce.

Most visitors travel to the northern half of Italy, to cities such as Venice and Florence, and to Rome. Tourists are also drawn to the northern lakes, while beach resorts such as Rimini attract a large, youthful crowd in summer. Italy is also growing in popularity as a skiing destination. In the south the breathtaking ruins of Roman Pompeii are a particular magnet for visitors.

Fears have been expressed about the detrimental impact of tourism on Italy's environment. The millions of day-trippers who flood into Venice every year increase waste in the city, while high-speed pleasure boats erode and pollute the canals.

SWITZERLAND
FRANCE
Mont Blanc 4807m
Gran Paradiso 4061m
Lago Maggiore
Lago di Como
Aosta
Biella
Varese
Como
Lecco
Bergamo
Monza
Milano
Vercelli
Novara
Torino
Asti
Alessandria
Piacenza
Parma
Cueno
Appennino Ligure
Genova
Rapallo
Savona
Golfo di Genova
La Spezia
Carrara
Viareggio
Pisa
Livorno
MONACO
Imperia
San Remo
LIGURIAN SEA
Isola d'Elba
Arcipelago Toscano
Corsica (FRANCE)
Porto Torres
Sassari
Olbia
Alghero
Macomer
Nuoro
Sardegna (Sardinia)
Monti del Gennargentu
Oristano
Arbatax
Iglesias
Carbonia
Sant Antioco
Cagliari

***Tuscan landscape.** Chianti wine is produced in this region, where many northern Europeans own holiday homes.*

I

ITALY

Total Area : 301 230 sq. km (116 305 sq. miles)

POPULATION
over 1 000 000
over 500 000
over 100 000
over 50 000
over 10 000
LAND HEIGHT
3000m/9843ft
2000m/6562ft
1000m/3281ft
500m/1640ft
200m/656ft
Sea Level
SLOVENIA
Udine
Monfalcone
Trieste
Venezia
Golfo di Venezia
Ravenna
Rimini
Pesaro
Fano
SAN MARINO
Sengallia
Ancona
Fabriano
Perugia
Assisi
Ascoli Piceno
Teramo
Terni
Pescara
L'Aquila
Vasto
Avezzano
Tivoli
Rodi Garganico
San Severo
Manfredonia
Foggia
Campobasso
Latina
Teracina
Barletta
Benevento
Andria
Bari
Monopoli
Golfo di Gaeta
Vesuvio
Avellino
Napoli
Torre del Greco
Salerno
Potenza
La Murge
Brindisi
Isloe Ponziane
I. d'Ischia
Castellamare di Stabia
Isola di Capri
Taranto
Lecce
Golfo di Salerno
Penisola Salentina
Strait of Otranto
Golfo di Taranto
ADRIATIC SEA
Castrovillari
RHENIAN SEA
Rossano
Cosenza
Paola
La Sila
Crotone
Nicastro
Catanzaro
I. de Ustica
Isole Eolie
I. Lupari
Vulcano
Stretto di Messina
Messina
Locri
Reggio di Calabria
IONIAN SEA
Palermo
Barcellona
Alcamo
Taormina
Sicilia (Sicily)
Mt Etna 3323m
Corleone
Acireale
Enna
Caltanissetta
Catania
Sciacca
Caltagirone
Augusta
Agrigento
Siracusa
Licata
Gela
Ragusa
Vittoria

PEOPLE

Pop. density medium

Italian, German, French, Rhaeto-Romanic, Sardinian

195/km² (506/mi²)

THE URBAN/RURAL POPULATION SPLIT

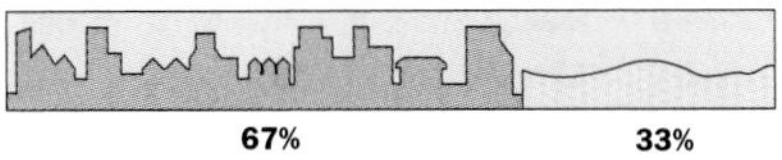
67%
33%

RELIGIOUS PERSUASION

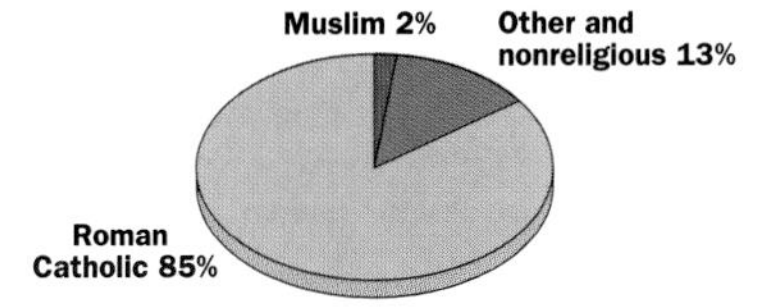
Muslim 2%
Other and nonreligious 13%
Roman Catholic 85%

ETHNIC MAKEUP

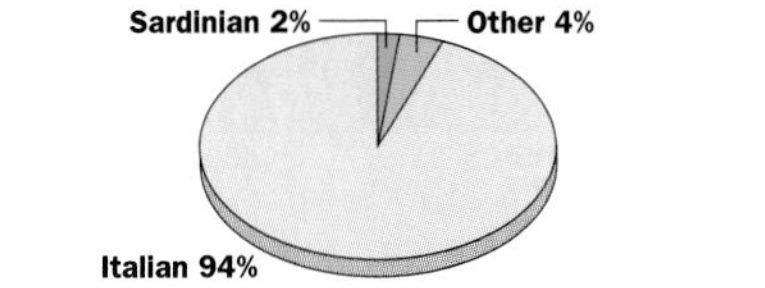
Sardinian 2%
Other 4%
Italian 94%

Italy is a remarkably homogeneous society. Most Italians are Roman Catholics and Italy has far fewer ethnic minorities, many of whom are Muslims, than its EU neighbors. Difficult economic conditions caused many Italians to emigrate in the 1950s and 1960s. There are now five million Italians living abroad. While many live in what are now other EU countries, a great number headed for the New World. The poorer south – the Mezzogiorno – has always been the source of most emigrants.

Within Italy, prejudice still exists in the north against southern Italians.

A sharp rise in illegal immigration in the 1980s and 1990s, from north and west Africa, Turkey, and Albania, became a major election issue and a factor in the rise of the federalist Northern League. Stringent measures were introduced in 1995 against illegal immigrants. Immigration is, nevertheless, vital for preserving the economy, as without it the country's population would be not only aging but decreasing in number.

International sporting occasions – especially soccer matches – have an unusual ability to bring out a strong sense of national identity among Italians. Otherwise, with state institutions viewed as inefficient and corrupt, most people feel a stronger allegiance to the region, or the community, and above all to the family. The extended family remains Italy's key social and economic support system. Most Italians live at home until marriage. Marriage rates are among the highest in Europe and divorce rates the lowest. Catholicism, however, has not stopped Italy having one of the lowest birthrates in the Western world.

Italians tend to dress well. Their preoccupation with style reflects the traditional importance of *bella figura* – image, cutting a dash – in Italian life as much as the high living standards which most now enjoy.

POPULATION AGE BREAKDOWN

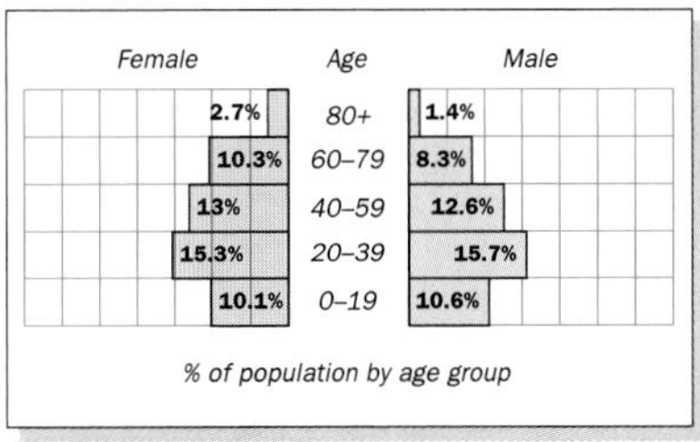
Female
Age
Male
2.7%
80+
1.4%
10.3%
60–79
8.3%
13%
40–59
12.6%
15.3%
20–39
15.7%
10.1%
0–19
10.6%
% of population by age group

CHRONOLOGY

Previously a collection of independent city-states, dukedoms, and monarchies, Italy became a unified state in 1861.

- **1922** Mussolini asked to form government by king.
- **1928** One-party rule by Fascists.
- **1929** Lateran Treaties with Vatican recognize sovereignty of Holy See.
- **1936–1937** Axis formed with Nazi Germany. Abyssinia (Ethiopia) conquered.
- **1939** Albania annexed.
- **1940** Italy enters World War II on German side.
- **1943** Invaded by Allies. Mussolini imprisoned by Victor Emmanuel III. Armistice with Allies. Italy declares war on Germany.

I

CHRONOLOGY *continued*

- **1945** Mussolini released; establishes puppet regime in north; executed by Italian partisans.
- **1946** Referendum votes in favor of Italy becoming a republic.
- **1947** Italy signs peace treaty, ceding border areas to France and Yugoslavia, Dodecanese to Greece, and giving up colonies.
- **1948** Elections: De Gaspieri of Christian Democrats (DC) heads coalition.
- **1949** Founder member of NATO.
- **1950** Agreement reached on US bases in Italy.
- **1951** Joins European Coal and Steel Community.
- **1957** Founder member of European Economic Community. Aided by funds from that organization and by Marshall Aid, industrial growth accelerates.
- **1964** DC government under Aldo Moro forms coalition with Socialist Party (PSI).
- **1969** Extreme left terrorist group, the Red Brigades, formed.
- **1972** Support for extreme right reaches postwar peak (9%). Rise in urban terrorism by both extreme left and right.
- **1976** Communist Party (PCI) support reaches a peak of 34% under Enrico Berlinguer's Eurocommunist philosophy.
- **1978** Aldo Moro abducted and murdered by Red Brigades.
- **1980** Extreme right bombing of Bologna station kills 84, wounds 200.
- **1983–1987** Center-left coalition formed under Bettino Craxi.
- **1990** LN attacks immigration policies and subsidies for the south.
- **1992** Corruption scandal, involving bribes for public contracts, uncovered in Milan. Government members accused.
- **1994** General election: DC support collapses; coalition government formed between Silvio Berlusconi's Forza Italia, LN, and "post-Fascists."
- **1995–1996** Technocrat government tackles budget, pensions, media, and regional issues.
- **1996** Center-left Olive Tree alliance wins general election; Romano Prodi prime minister.
- **1998** May, Italy qualifies to join euro currency from January 1999. October, Prodi government falls, Massimo D'Alema prime minister.
- **1999** Carlo Ciampi president.
- **2000** D'Alema replaced by Giuliano Amato.
- **2001** May, Berlusconi victory in general election.
- **2002** Euro fully adopted.
- **2004** Berlusconi government becomes longest serving since 1945.

POLITICS

Multiparty elections

L. House 2001/2006
U. House 2001/2006

President Carlo Azeglio Ciampi

AT THE LAST ELECTION

Chamber of Deputies 630 seats

1% U–SVP
58% PdL
38% U
2% PRC
1% Others

PdL = Freedom Alliance (includes Forza Italia, National Alliance – **AN**, and Northern League – **LN**)
U = Olive Tree alliance (includes Democrats of the Left – **DS** and Party of Italian Communists – **PdCI**)
PRC = Communist Refoundation Party
U–SVP = Olive Tree–South Tyrolese People's Party
Nom = Nominated

Senate of the Republic 324 seats

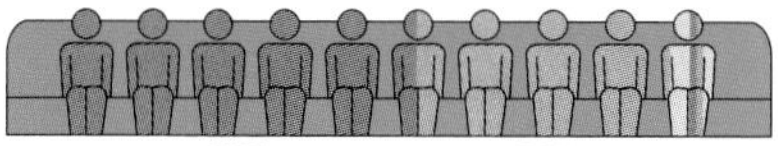
1% U–SVP
2% Others
55% PdL
38% U
3% Nom
1% PRC

The Senate of the Republic comprises 315 elected members and several life senators

Italy is a multiparty democracy.

Profile

Italian politics is rightly renowned for its instability; the role of prime minister changed hands 35 times between 1953 and 2001. Strong regionalism and a popular passion for politics mean that coalitions are essential, with broad left-wing, right-wing, or even technocratic groupings, frequently swapping the baton of power. The return in 2001 of the charismatic right-wing leader Silvio Berlusconi after six years in opposition highlighted the importance of personalities. His government replaced the left-wing Olive Tree alliance, which had successfully steered the country into the European single currency.

Berlusconi's administration proved remarkably durable, becoming in May 2004 the longest-lasting government since World War II. His coalition includes some uneasy bedfellows, however: his own Forza Italia, Gianfranco Fini's "post-Fascist" AN, and Umberto Bossi's xenophobic, northern-based LN, among others. Tensions within the government over corruption, constitutional reforms, ministerial representation, and spending cuts have led to a number of near splits. Friction was exacerbated in mid-2004 by the government's attempts to forge an emergency budget to bring Italy's deficit back below the EU's 3%-of-GDP maximum, and the simmering row over Berlusconi's commercial–political conflict of interests.

Carlo Azeglio Ciampi, elected president in 1999.

Umberto Bossi, leader of the controversial LN.

Silvio Berlusconi, conservative prime minister, elected for a second time in 2001.

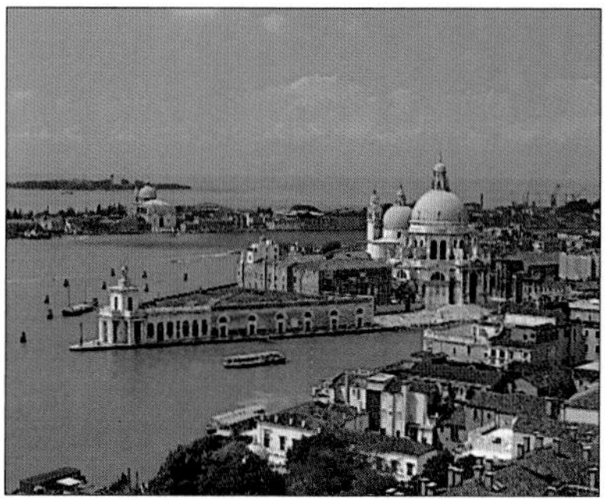
***The church of Santa Maria della Salute** marks the entrance to Venice. The city-state managed to retain its independence until Napoleon Bonaparte's invasion of Italy.*

Main Political Issues

Corruption

Berlusconi's return to power in 2001 brought the corruption issue back to the very heart of public life, as he pushed through reforms which gave him immunity as prime minister and meant that outstanding bribery-related charges against him could be quashed. Paradoxically, he himself had emerged as a leading figure in the country's new political makeup in the wake of the 1990s *mani pulite* (clean hands) investigations, which revealed a nationwide network of corruption and destroyed the old political order.

Institutional reform

The old proportional representation (PR) electoral system, blamed for a lack of strong government, was much modified in the early 1990s, but the process then lost impetus. Twice, in 1999 and in 2000, referenda failed to abolish the 25% of seats still elected by PR, not because voters opposed this, but merely due to inadequate turnout. Berlusconi favors a system with greater presidential powers, akin to that in France (and has made explicit his desire to go on to be head of state under such a system).

The LN is prominent in calling for greater regional autonomy, though it has long since abandoned its somewhat farcical call for the independence of northern Italy as "Padania."

WORLD AFFAIRS

Joined UN in 1955

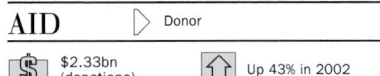

EU | G8 | NATO | OECD | OSCE

Italy was one of the founders of the EU, but the return of a right-wing government in 2001 encouraged the opponents of further integration. Tasteless remarks by Berlusconi in 2003 caused a rift with Germany just as Italy began its six-month term holding the EU presidency. The NATO South European Command is based in Naples. Despite a pro-Western orientation, Italy often contributes to mediation efforts in eastern Europe and the Middle East.

Major concerns in recent years have been upheaval in Albania, conflict in the former Yugoslavia, and involvement in the US-led "war on terrorism." NATO used Italian bases for air strikes against Yugoslavia in 1999, and Italy has backed the US-led occupation of Iraq.

AID

Donor

$2.33bn (donations)

Up 43% in 2002

A relatively small aid program makes major use of international organizations. In 2002, $4 billion of developing country debt was canceled. The countries of the former Yugoslavia and Albania have received funding to stave off a feared influx of economic migrants.

DEFENSE

Phasing out conscription

$24.2bn

Up 12% in 2002

ITALIAN ARMED FORCES

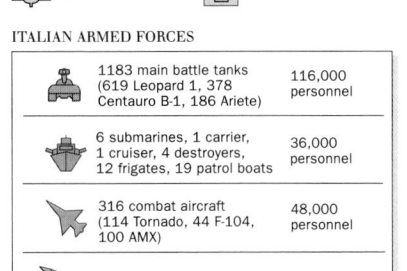

1183 main battle tanks (619 Leopard 1, 378 Centauro B-1, 186 Ariete)	116,000 personnel
6 submarines, 1 carrier, 1 cruiser, 4 destroyers, 12 frigates, 19 patrol boats	36,000 personnel
316 combat aircraft (114 Tornado, 44 F-104, 100 AMX)	48,000 personnel
None	

Since the ending of the Cold War, conflicts in former Yugoslavia have helped refocus defense priorities. A "New Model Defense" was announced in 1992, women soldiers have been allowed, and conscription will end by 2005. The envisaged professional army is to play a rapid-intervention role on NATO's southern flank, while the navy fulfills Mediterranean coastal functions rather than retaining ocean-going capabilities. Defense spending remains low, despite pressures to modernize weapons systems. In 2001, 2700 troops were sent to Afghanistan, while in 2003 another 3000 were deployed to Iraq.

ECONOMICS

Inflation 3.6% p.a. (1990–2001)

$1101bn

0.822 euros (0.871)

SCORE CARD

❑ WORLD GNP RANKING	7th
❑ GNP PER CAPITA	$19,080
❑ BALANCE OF PAYMENTS	–$6.74bn
❑ INFLATION	2.5%
❑ UNEMPLOYMENT	9%

EXPORTS

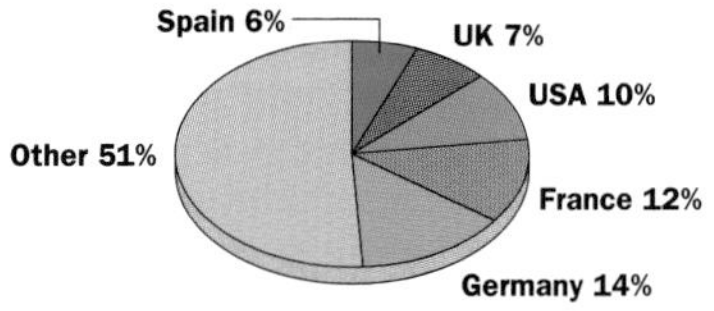
Spain 6%
UK 7%
USA 10%
France 12%
Germany 14%
Other 51%

IMPORTS

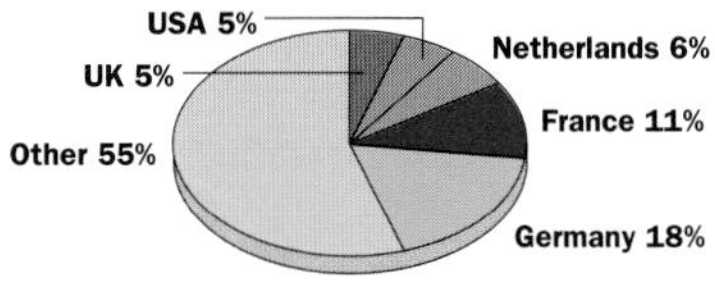
USA 5%
UK 5%
Netherlands 6%
France 11%
Germany 18%
Other 55%

STRENGTHS

Highly competitive, innovative small- to medium-size business sector. World leader in industrial and product design, textiles, and household appliances. Several highly innovative firms include Fiat (cars), Montedison (plastics), Olivetti (communications), and Benetton (clothes). Strong tourism and agriculture sectors, prestigious fashion houses.

WEAKNESSES

Public deficit and government debt remain high. Recession in 2003. Inefficient public sector undergoing major privatizations. Uneven wealth distribution: northern Italy far richer than the south, which suffers much more from unemployment. Poor record on tax collection, though now much improved. Relatively small companies facing foreign competition. Heavy dependence on imported energy.

PROFILE

Since World War II, Italy has developed from a mainly agricultural society into a world industrial power. The economy is characterized by a large state sector, a mass of family-owned businesses, relatively high levels of protectionism, and strong regional differences. Italy also has relatively few multinationals compared with other G7 economies.

The Institute for Industrial Reconstruction (IRI), a state-owned holding company dating from the Fascist era, progressively privatized its electronics, steel, engineering, shipbuilding, telecommunications, transportation, and aerospace companies, until closing down itself in

ECONOMIC PERFORMANCE INDICATOR

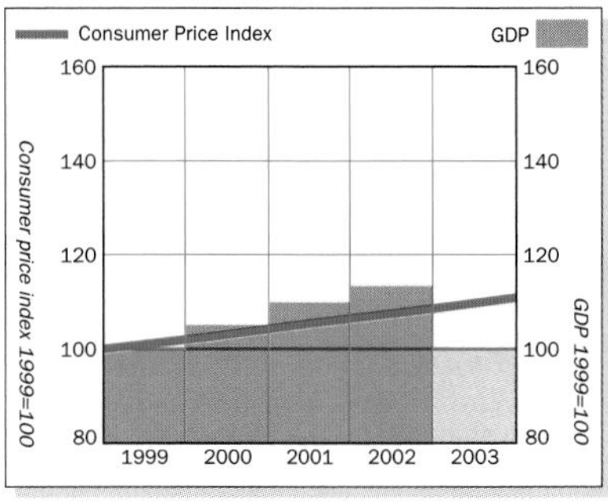
Consumer Price Index
GDP
160
140
120
100
80
1999
2000
2001
2002
2003
Consumer price index 1999=100
GDP 1999=100

2000. The National Hydrocarbons Group (ENI), one of the world's top players in the energy and chemicals sectors, has been privatized, as has Telecom Italia and the electricity corporation Enel. City and regional authorities own utilities, banks, and other businesses.

Family-owned businesses, which are the backbone of the private sector, include Fiat, whose interests cover aero engines, telecommunications, and bioengineering, as well as cars. Similar businesses tend to congregate, encouraging local competition which has translated into national success.

The Mezzogiorno remains an exception. State attempts to attract new investment have met with success in areas immediately south of Rome, but elsewhere organized crime has deterred investors and siphoned off state funds. Anger at the misuse of state funds in the south was a powerful factor in the growth of the LN, with its demands for autonomy; one-third of Italian tax revenue is generated in Italy's industrial heartland of Milan.

ITALY : MAJOR BUSINESSES

Milano
Torino
Venezia
Bologna
Firenze
Genova
Rome
Napoli
Palermo
Textiles
Chemicals
Garments
Electronics
Pharmaceuticals
Light engineering
Defence industries
Vehicle manufacture
Aerospace industries
0
200 km
0
200 miles

I

***Remains of the Greek theater** at Taormina, eastern Sicily. It was rebuilt by the Romans in the 2nd century CE. Today, the theater is the venue for an annual arts festival.*

RESOURCES

Electric power 85.1m kW

528,666 tonnes

107,000 b/d (reserves 700m barrels)

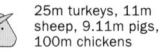

25m turkeys, 11m sheep, 9.11m pigs, 100m chickens

Coal, oil, lignite, pyrites, fluorite, barytes, bauxite, marble

ELECTRICITY GENERATION

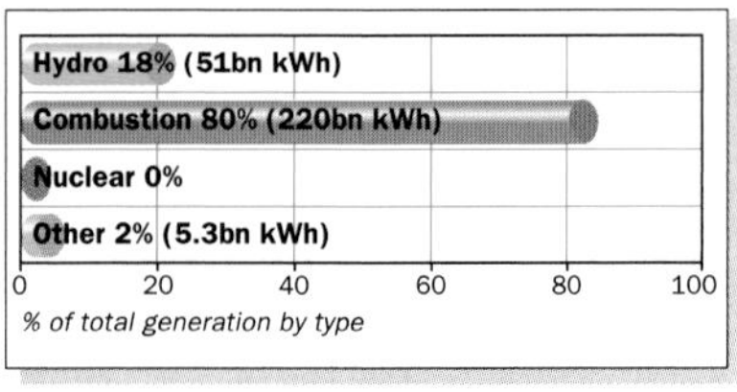
Hydro 18% (51bn kWh)
Combustion 80% (220bn kWh)
Nuclear 0%
Other 2% (5.3bn kWh)
0
20
40
60
80
100
% of total generation by type

Italy has very few natural resources. Its mineral assets are small and the sector contributes little to national wealth. Italy produces less than 10% of its oil needs and is highly vulnerable to both fluctuations in world prices and political instability in its traditional north African suppliers. Keen to diversify in areas of dependence, it has switched increasingly to natural gas in the last 30 years, cutting its reliance on oil from 71% of its energy needs to around 50%. Nuclear power was rejected in a 1987 referendum, though there are plans to invest in overseas plants.

ITALY : LAND USE

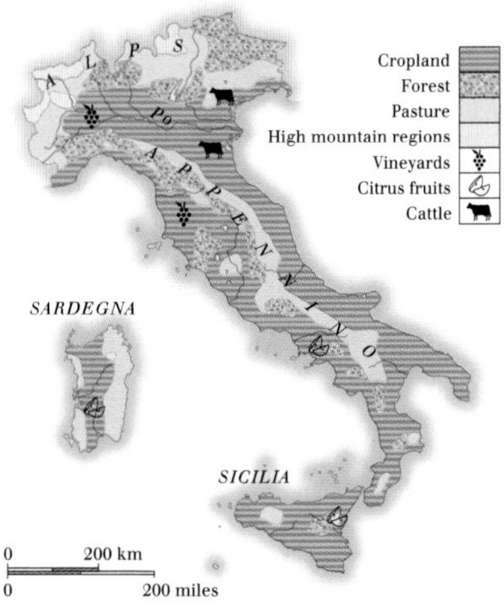
Cropland
Forest
Pasture
High mountain regions
Vineyards
Citrus fruits
Cattle
A L P S
Po
A P P E N N I N O
SARDEGNA
SICILIA
0 200 km
0 200 miles

ENVIRONMENT

Sustainability rank: 84th

8% (6% partially protected)

7.4 tonnes per capita

ENVIRONMENTAL TREATIES

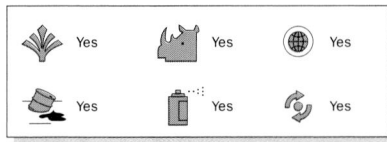

Yes Yes Yes

Yes Yes Yes

Italy has extensive environmental legislation, but has faced problems in enforcing directives. Wildlife successes include the return of the endangered lynx and brown bear, and growing numbers of wolves in the Appenines. The hunting of migrant birds, a popular sport in Italy, attracts international criticism. The use of drift nets, prone to catching dolphins and turtles as well as fish, has been made illegal under EU law. The right-wing government of the mid-1990s, returned to office in 2001, is suspicious of energy taxes and laws on waste recycling, not wanting to restrict business competitiveness. Green Party members in government in the Olive Tree alliance from 1996 to 2001 had insisted on a more active environmental stance.

Pollution in cities such as Naples and Rome is a major concern. Bans on traffic for up to seven hours during windless days are not uncommon. Acid rain has damaged forests and historic buildings.

MEDIA

TV ownership high

Daily newspaper circulation 104 per 1000 people

PUBLISHING AND BROADCAST MEDIA

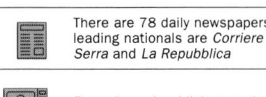

There are 78 daily newspapers. The leading nationals are *Corriere della Serra* and *La Repubblica*

5 services: 1 publicly owned, 4 independent

1 publicly owned service, over 2500 independent stations

Mediaset, owned by Prime Minister Silvio Berlusconi, is the main commercial operator. The state-operated Rai TV channels were traditionally highly politicized; until reforms in the 1990s, Rai Uno was apportioned to the Christian Democrats, Rai Due to the Socialists, and Rai Tre to the Communists. Now they cover general programming, entertainment, and education respectively. News Corporation bought out Vivendi in 2002 to gain a near-monopoly of pay-TV. All the media reflect the Italian love of sport, especially soccer: *La Gazzetta dello Sport* has one of the largest circulations of the national dailies. The press is highly regionalized.

CRIME

No death penalty

56,574 prisoners

Down 2% in 2001

CRIME RATES

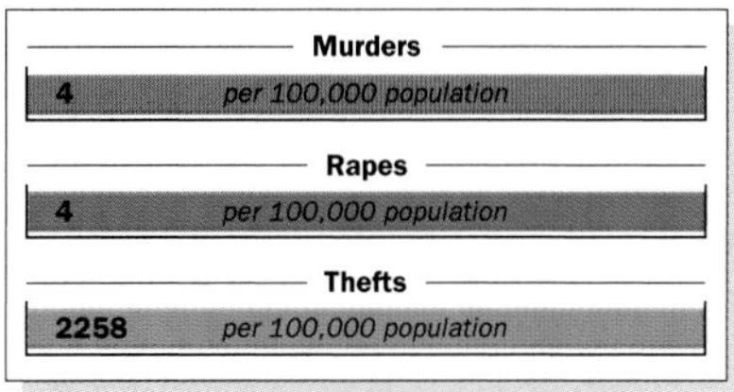
Murders
4 per 100,000 population
Rapes
4 per 100,000 population
Thefts
2258 per 100,000 population

Over 25% of prisoners are foreigners, many held for narcotics offenses. There is a huge backlog of cases. Organized crime has been weakened by the anticorruption drive and a cleaned-up bureaucracy. The Sicilian Mafia was hit hard by arrests and trials in which former members provided key evidence. The Mafia, however, and its counterparts in Naples, Calabria, and Apulia – Camorra, 'ndrangheta, and Sacra Corona Unita – still control wholesale agricultural markets and much of the narcotics trade, bleed businesses of protection money, and manipulate public works contracts.

EDUCATION

School leaving age: 16

99%

1.81m students

THE EDUCATION SYSTEM

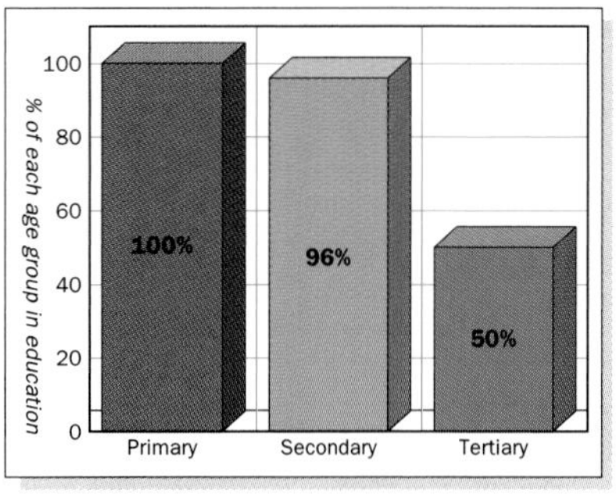
100
80
60
40
20
0
% of each age group in education
100%
96%
50%
Primary
Secondary
Tertiary

Schooling is state-run, apart from a few religious and elite private institutions. The pupil–teacher ratio in Italian schools is one of the best in Europe. In 1993, the minimum school leaving age was raised from 14 to 16 years, bringing Italy into line with most of Europe. An educational credit system aims to tackle shortcomings in information technology training.

Higher education is restricted to pupils who pass the *esamo di Stato*. There are almost 800 university-level institutions, including the University of Bologna – the oldest university in Europe, established in 1088. The government hopes to increase spending on research, which, at little more than 1% of GNP in recent years, has been less than half the European average.

ITALY, IMMIGRATION, AND FORTRESS EUROPE

THE IMMIGRATION ISSUE set the Italian media ablaze in the heat of summer 2004. A German-based human rights group, Cap Anamur, had rescued 37 African migrants off the Libyan coast and promptly headed straight for the EU to present them as needy asylum seekers. Already rejected by the Maltese authorities, the ship was kept away from Italian ports by a hostile government which had only just seen its tough immigration legislation battered by the High Court. The Italian authorities rejected the claim that the migrants were from the embattled Darfur region of Sudan, and though they proved to be correct on this score, they came under such heavy pressure from the UN and the Roman Catholic Church that they finally acquiesced in allowing the ship to dock. The crew were arrested, however, and the migrants refused asylum and put straight into the repatriation process.

HOSTILITY

With 7600 km (4750 miles) of coastline, some parts of which are barely 200 km (125 miles) from Africa and even closer to the Balkans, Italy has become a key point of entry for asylum seekers, genuine and otherwise, into Europe. As elsewhere, parts of Italian society treat immigrants, known as *clandestini*, with distrust and even hostility. The acceptance of inward migrants is not helped by a faltering economy, rising unemployment, and a climate of fear in a post-9/11 world. Neither is tolerance championed when the government includes such openly xenophobic parties as the Northern League, whose leader, Umberto Bossi, suggested firing on boats to deter would-be immigrants.

A EUROPE-WIDE ISSUE

Despite a recognized need for a common policy on immigration, the issue is too contentious for individual EU states to be seen to be giving up control of their borders. Consequently, different national governments battle

***Would-be immigrants** arrive by the boatload along Italy's extensive coast.*

***Italy's aging population** needs the rejuvenation that inward migration can bring.*

with their own public to put forward humane approaches which will not result in an "influx" of migrants, such as the UK's popular plan to remove the point of processing to the place of departure, establishing asylum centers in Africa and Asia rather than Europe.

Even for successful asylum seekers there has been a notable move away from the principle of multiculturalism in favor of open integration. Language lessons, civic tests, and allegiance pledges have been spoken of widely. Even the Netherlands has admitted that its celebrated open society has led to conservative foreign ghettos.

Hostility to the concept of immigration flies in the face of growing academic acceptance that only through opening its borders will Europe be spared economic decline. Italy is itself a prime example of the population problems identified starkly by the European Commission in 2003. Europe's population is not only aging, but will begin to contract in size as soon as 2010 unless there is substantial immigration. A net loss of 14 million people by 2030 could cost the pre-2004 EU countries a 7% drop in GDP. Economies would miss the contribution of adequate numbers of able workers, while tax revenues would fall just as they were most needed to foot the growing bill of coping with the estimated 50% of people by then over 50 and heading for retirement.

Nonetheless, a cultural tradition of intolerance of the "other," and a common concept of immigration as only some sort of temporary stopgap to help plug holes in the economy, present major problems in Italy, and western Europe in general. The case for accepting, and indeed welcoming, a sustained inflow of non-European migrants is now being cautiously put by sectors of national governments as they emphasize their tax contribution, the small burden they tend to put on public services, and their hardworking and entrepreneurial characteristics.

HEALTH

Welfare state health benefits

1 per 233 people

Cancers, heart, and respiratory diseases

Italy's health care system was rated by WHO in 2000 as the second most efficient in the world.

The state-run national health system was created in 1978, with authority based in the regions, and standards of care vary across the country. The system was further decentralized in 1999 in an effort to iron out irregularities. Charges are levied for some dental and prescription costs; patients also have to pay a daily hospital charge and a yearly health fee. AIDS patients are exempt.

SPENDING

GDP/cap. increase

CONSUMPTION AND SPENDING

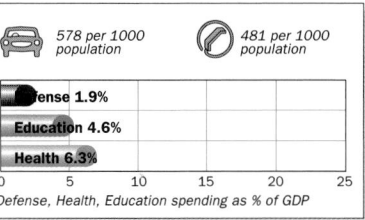

578 per 1000 population

481 per 1000 population

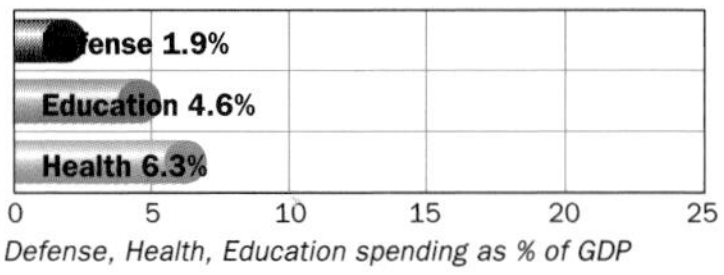
Defense 1.9%
Education 4.6%
Health 6.3%
0
5
10
15
20
25
Defense, Health, Education spending as % of GDP

Italians, particularly in the north, are today among the world's wealthiest people in terms of disposable income. This is a result not only of economic growth, but also of the structure of Italian society.

Many Italians (particularly in the south) have more than one job. The extended families in which most people still live often have access to more than one income. Few people have mortgages, and tax avoidance levels are high.

The main exceptions to general prosperity are confined to the south. Though inward investment has been attracted to the Bari area, many people still live in poverty in other places, such as Naples and the Calabria region, where investment has been lowest, unemployment is highest, and even tourism is underdeveloped.

WORLD RANKING

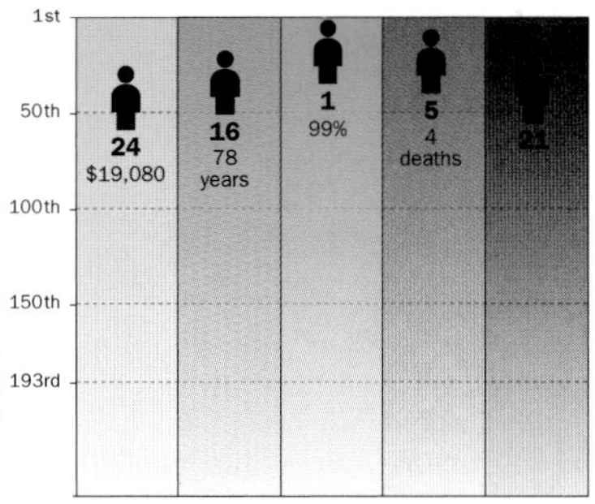
Position in World
1st
50th
100th
150th
193rd
24
$19,080
16
78
years
1
99%
5
4
deaths
21
GNP per capita in US$
Life expectancy
Literacy
Infant mortality per 1000 live births
Human dev. index

I

IVORY COAST

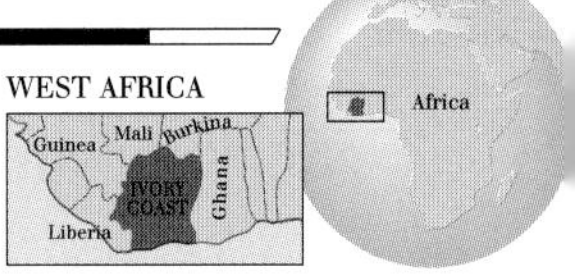
WEST AFRICA
Africa
Guinea
Mali
Burkina
IVORY COAST
Ghana
Liberia

OFFICIAL NAME: Republic of Côte d'Ivoire **CAPITAL:** Yamoussoukro
POPULATION: 16.6 million **CURRENCY:** CFA franc **OFFICIAL LANGUAGE:** French

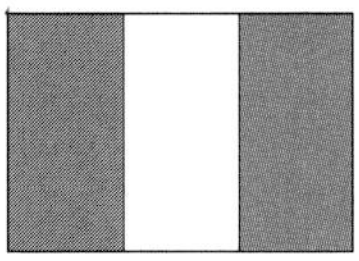

1960 | 1960 | Aug 7 | CI | 0 | +225 | .ci

ONE OF THE LARGER countries on the shores of west Africa, Ivory Coast – officially Côte d'Ivoire – is the world's biggest cocoa producer. Its reputation as an island of stability in a continent of chaos was largely due to the pro-Western and long-term president Félix Houphouët-Boigny (1960–1993). This image was shattered in 1999 by a military coup which was in turn followed by a popular uprising in 2000 and outright civil conflict in 2002–2003.

CLIMATE

Tropical wet and dry

WEATHER CHART FOR YAMOUSSOUKRO

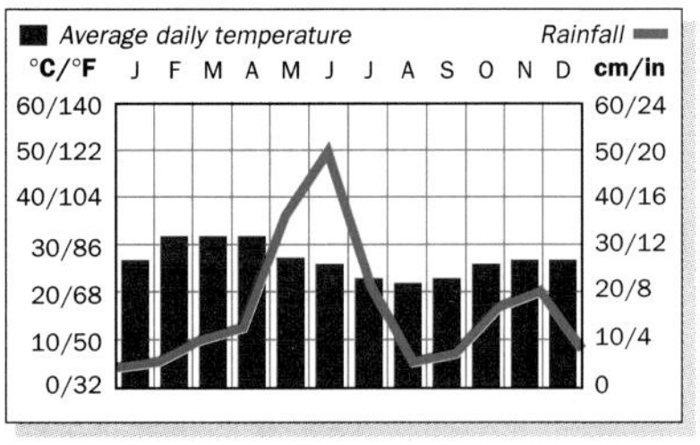
Average daily temperature
Rainfall
°C/°F
J F M A M J J A S O N D
cm/in
60/140
50/122
40/104
30/86
20/68
10/50
0/32
60/24
50/20
40/16
30/12
20/8
10/4
0

The south's four seasons – two rainy and two dry – merge in the north into a single wet season with lower rainfall.

TRANSPORTATION

Drive on right

Félix Houphouët-Boigny, Abidjan 759,940 passengers

33 ships 8900 grt

THE TRANSPORTATION NETWORK

5040 km (3132 miles)	None
639 km (397 miles)	980 km (609 miles)

The relatively good transportation system focuses on Abidjan, the premier port of francophone west Africa.

TOURISM

Visitors : Population 1:55

301,000 visitors

Up 10% in 1998

MAIN TOURIST ARRIVALS

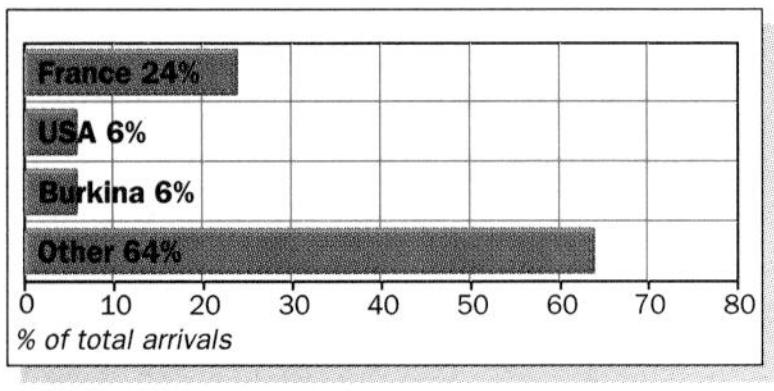
France 24%
USA 6%
Burkina 6%
Other 64%
0
10
20
30
40
50
60
70
80
% of total arrivals

Ambitious plans for an "African Riviera" east of Abidjan and the opening of a hotel by the French Club Méditerranée have been undermined by recent instability. The giant Roman Catholic basilica at Yamoussoukro is an attraction.

PEOPLE

Pop. density medium

Akan, French, Kru, Voltaic

52/km² (135/mi²)

THE URBAN/RURAL POPULATION SPLIT

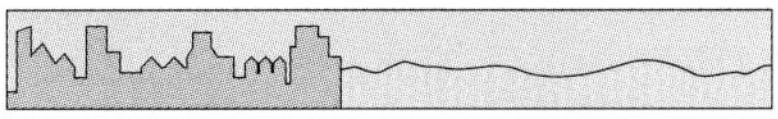
44%
56%

RELIGIOUS PERSUASION

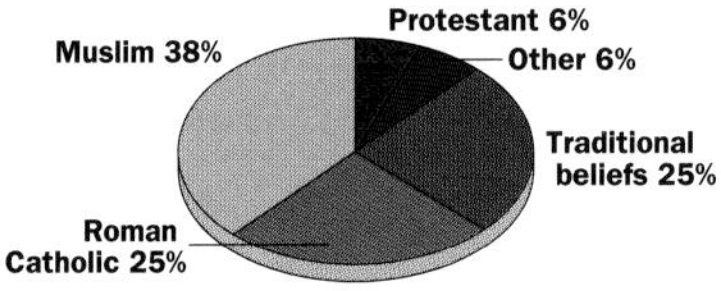
Muslim 38%
Protestant 6%
Other 6%
Traditional beliefs 25%
Roman Catholic 25%

There are more than 60 tribes in Ivory Coast, the key ones being the Baoulé in the center, the Agri in the east, the Senufo in the north, the Dioula in the northwest and west, the Bété in the center-west, and the Dan-Yacouba in the west.

Migrants from other west African countries, mainly Malians, Burkinabés, and mixed Ivorians, account for up to 40% of the population. Their presence has stirred conflict in recent years, leading to a growth in "identity politics" and a dangerous form of xenophobic ethno-nationalism. In addition, Christians in the south harbor resentment against non-Ivorian Muslims in the largely rebel-held north.

POLITICS

Multiparty elections

2000/2005

President Laurent Gbagbo

AT THE LAST ELECTION

National Assembly 225 seats

10% Ind
1% PIT
1% Vac
43% FPI
42% PDCI
2% RDR
1% Others

FPI = Ivorian Popular Front **PDCI** = Democratic Party of Ivory Coast **Ind** = Independents **RDR** = Rally of the Republicans **PIT** = Ivorian Labor Party **Vac** = Vacant

Since the death of President Houphouët-Boigny in 1993, Ivorian politics has become increasingly polarized. Attempts by his successor, Henri Konan Bédié, to ban the Muslim northerner and RDR leader Alassane Ouattara from the 1999 election prompted a coup by Gen. Robert Guei, who in turn barred Ouattara from the 2000 election. Guei's fraudulent attempt to claim victory in the vote led to an uprising which carried the poll's actual victor, Laurent Gbagbo of the socialist FPI, to power and was followed by violent political clashes. Again Ouattara became the focus of the opposition. An uprising in September 2002 by disgruntled soldiers quickly escalated into civil war, with Guei a prominent early casualty. The conflict tapped the country's latent ethnic tensions, with support divided between north and south, immigrants and Ivorians. A power-sharing government, formed in 2003 as part of peace initiatives, has proved unstable.

IVORY COAST

Total Area : 322 460 sq. km (124 502 sq. miles)

0 100 km
0 100 miles

POPULATION
- over 1 000 000
- over 100 000
- over 50 000
- over 10 000
- under 10 000

LAND HEIGHT
- 1000m/3281ft
- 500m/1640ft
- 200m/656ft
- Sea Level

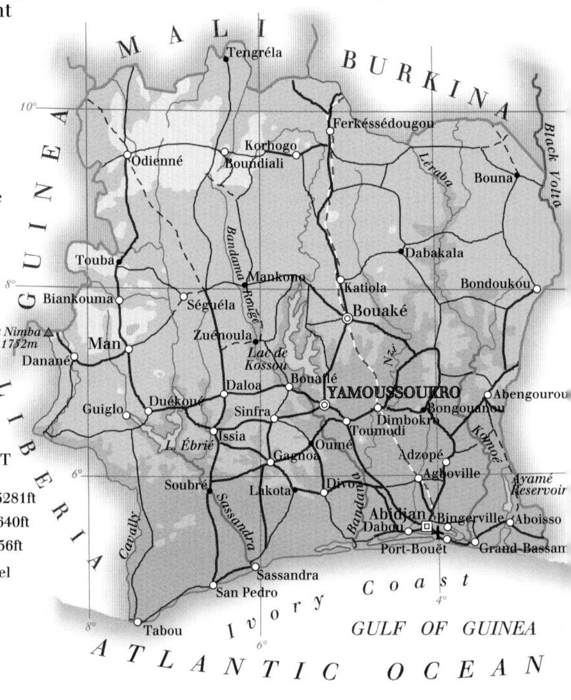
MALI
BURKINA
GUINEA
LIBERIA
Black Volta
Tengréla
Ferkéssédougou
Korhogo
Odienné
Boundiali
Bouna
Léraba
Touba
Dabakala
Biankouma
Mankono
Katiola
Bondoukou
Séguéla
Bouaké
Mount Nimba 1752m
Man
Zuénoula
Danané
Lac de Kossou
Bouaflé
YAMOUSSOUKRO
Abengourou
Guiglo
Duékoué
Daloa
Sinfra
Bongouanou
Dimbokro
Toumodi
Issia
Oumé
L. Ébrié
Gagnoa
Adzopé
Agboville
Ayamé Reservoir
Soubré
Lakota
Divo
Abidjan
Bingerville
Aboisso
Dabou
Port-Bouët
Grand-Bassam
Sassandra
San Pedro
Tabou
Bandama
Sassandra
Cavally
Komoé
Nzi
Ivory Coast
GULF OF GUINEA
ATLANTIC OCEAN
N

WORLD AFFAIRS

Joined UN in 1960

ECOWAS | FZ | G24 | OIC | AU

Good relations with donors will be vital for reconstruction. Regional violence has fueled tensions in Ivory Coast, enabling the movement of arms and troops across porous borders. ECOWAS and French troops mediated in the recent civil war; UN peacekeepers have replaced them. Ivory Coast has influence in international cocoa and coffee organizations.

AID

Recipient

$1.07bn (receipts)

Up 529% in 2002

France is by far the largest source of bilateral aid. Structural adjustment loans from the World Bank were particularly important in easing the acute burden of a debt accumulated on the strength of overinflated oil hopes.

DEFENSE

Compulsory military service

$136m

Up 11% in 2002

France trains officers for the Ivorian army and is the main supplier of equipment, though at the start of the 2002–2003 conflict the government purchased arms and equipment from Angola.

ECONOMICS

Inflation 8.4% p.a. (1990–2001)

$10.2bn

539.2 CFA francs (571.2)

SCORE CARD

- ❑ WORLD GNP RANKING 86th
- ❑ GNP PER CAPITA $620
- ❑ BALANCE OF PAYMENTS $767m
- ❑ INFLATION 3.1%
- ❑ UNEMPLOYMENT 13%

STRENGTHS

Well-developed agriculture: major cocoa, coffee, and timber producer. Relatively good infrastructure. Expanding oil and gas industries, largely unaffected by conflict.

WEAKNESSES

Instability. Failure to invest adequately in education and professional training. Overdependence on cocoa and coffee. Slave labor on plantations.

EXPORTS

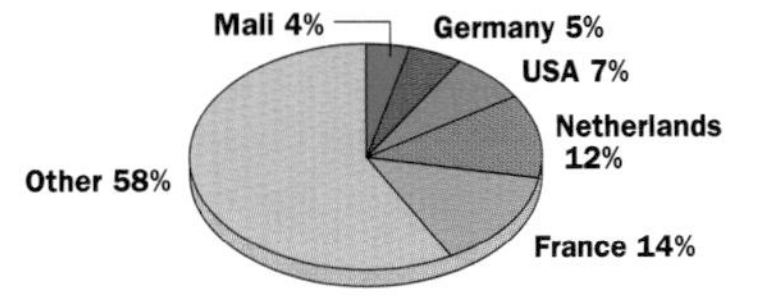
Mali 4%
Germany 5%
USA 7%
Netherlands 12%
Other 58%
France 14%

IMPORTS

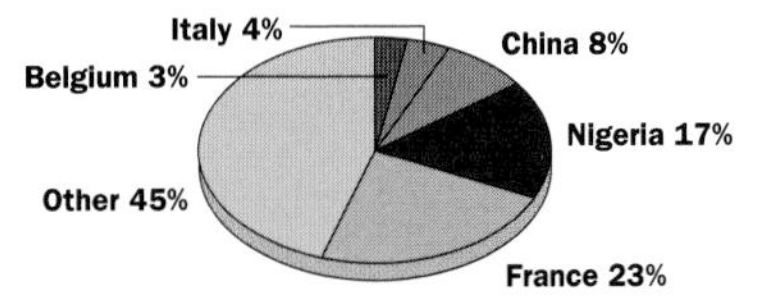
Italy 4%
Belgium 3%
China 8%
Nigeria 17%
Other 45%
France 23%

RESOURCES

Electric power 1.2m kW

74,581 tonnes

31,017 b/d (reserves 102m barrels)

1.52m sheep, 1.48m cattle, 1.19m goats, 33m chickens

Oil, gas, diamonds, cobalt, gold, iron, manganese, nickel

There are significant offshore oil and gas reserves. Most fuel is currently imported. Forest resources are badly depleted.

ENVIRONMENT

Sustainability rank: 108th

6% (0.3% partially protected)

0.7 tonnes per capita

Deforestation remains a problem in the Ivory Coast, despite a 1995 government ban on unprocessed timber exports.

MEDIA

TV ownership medium

Daily newspaper circulation 16 per 1000 people

PUBLISHING AND BROADCAST MEDIA

There are 16 daily newspapers, including *Fraternité Matin* and *Ivoir Soir*, both published by the government

1 state-owned service

1 state-owned service, around 30 independent stations

Media pressure has increased since the start of the 2002 conflict, and official harassment occurs. The UN launched a nationwide radio station in 2004.

EDUCATION

School leaving age: 15

50%

96,681 students

Baccalauréat pass rates are low. Cuts in spending have triggered student protests. Primary education fees ended in 2001.

CRIME

No death penalty

10,355 prisoners

Up sharply in 1997–2002

Foreign immigrants are often blamed for the widespread crime in Abidjan. Human rights abuses are common.

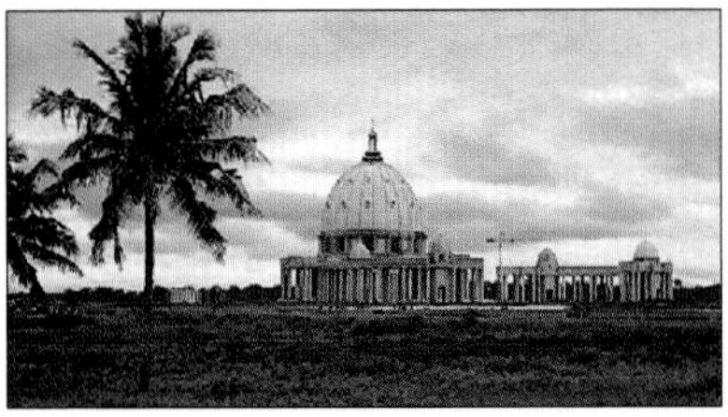

***The basilica, Yamoussoukro.** Built in the new capital, Houphouët-Boigny's birthplace, it is modeled on St. Peter's, Rome.*

CHRONOLOGY

One of the great trading emporia of west Africa, the Ivory Coast was made a French colony in 1893. By 1918, the French had defeated the Malinke empire and the forest peoples of the interior.

- ❑ **1903–1935** Plantations developed.
- ❑ **1960** Independence. Félix Houphouët-Boigny president.
- ❑ **1990** First contested polls: Houphouët-Boigny and PDCI win.
- ❑ **1993** Houphouët-Boigny dies.
- ❑ **1998** Power of president increased.
- ❑ **1999** Military coup by Gen. Guei.
- ❑ **2000** Guei ousted after false election victory claim. Gbagbo president.
- ❑ **2002–2003** Military uprising turns into major rebellion. Guei killed.
- ❑ **2003** Peace agreement signed.
- ❑ **2004** Power-sharing deal falters.

I

HEALTH

No welfare state health benefits

1 per 10,000 people

Malaria, communicable diseases, neonatal deaths, AIDS

The incidence of HIV/AIDS is high, affecting around 7% of adults. In 2001 drugs companies agreed to cut the prices of treatments by 80–90%.

SPENDING

GDP/cap. increase

CONSUMPTION AND SPENDING

7 per 1000 population

20 per 1000 population

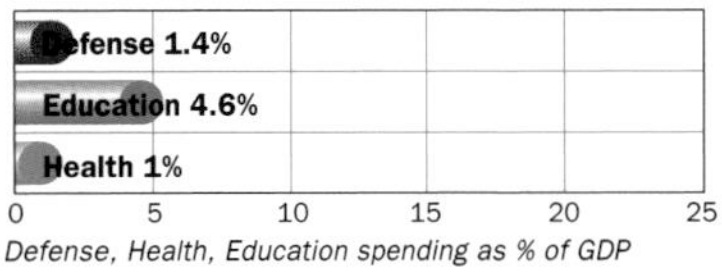
Defense 1.4%
Education 4.6%
Health 1%
0
5
10
15
20
25
Defense, Health, Education spending as % of GDP

A large bourgeoisie emerged after independence. Recent economic and security problems have eroded wealth generated through trade.

WORLD RANKING

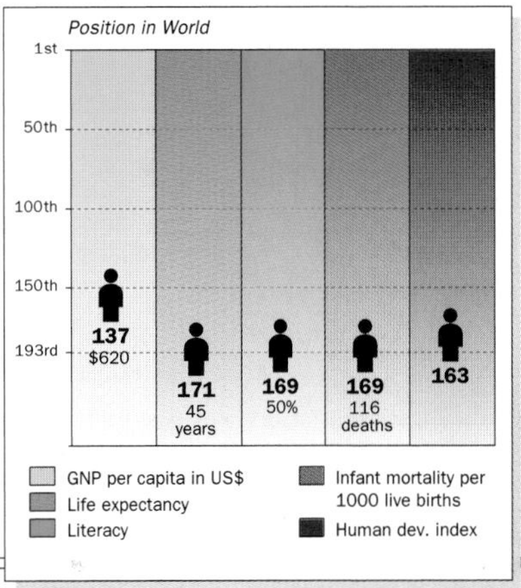
Position in World
1st
50th
100th
150th
193rd
137
$620
171
45 years
169
50%
169
116 deaths
163
GNP per capita in US$
Life expectancy
Literacy
Infant mortality per 1000 live births
Human dev. index

JAMAICA

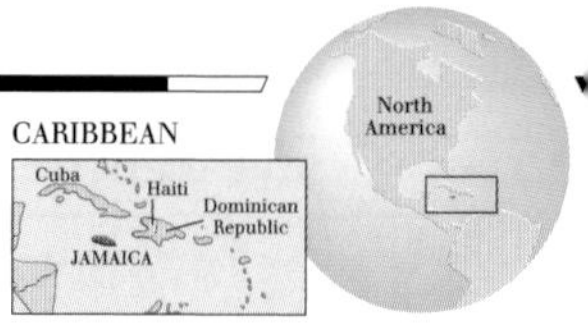
CARIBBEAN
Cuba
Haiti
Dominican Republic
JAMAICA
North America

OFFICIAL NAME: Jamaica **CAPITAL:** Kingston
POPULATION: 2.7 million **CURRENCY:** Jamaican dollar **OFFICIAL LANGUAGE:** English

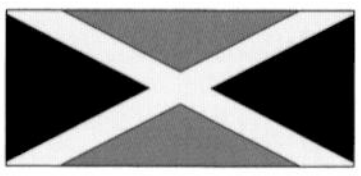

1962 | 1962 | Aug 5 | JA | -5 | +1876 | .jm

FIRST COLONIZED BY the Spanish and then, from 1655, by the English, Jamaica is located in the Caribbean, 145 km (90 miles) south of Cuba. It was the first of the Caribbean island countries to become independent in the postwar years, and remains an active force in regional politics. Jamaica is also influential on the world music scene: reggae, ska, and ragga (or dancehall) developed in the tough conditions of Kingston's poor districts.

CLIMATE

Tropical oceanic

WEATHER CHART FOR KINGSTON

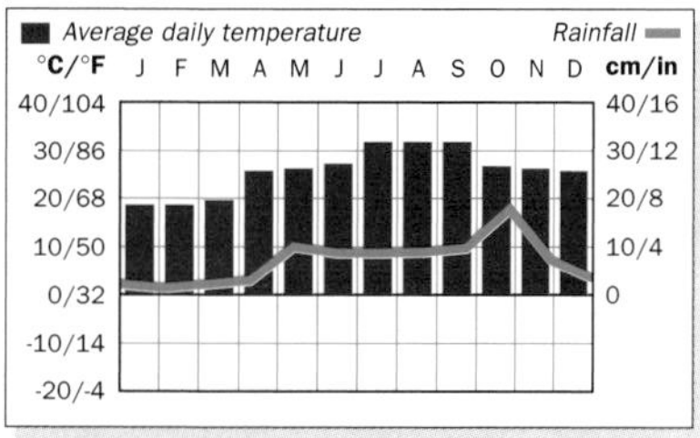
Average daily temperature
Rainfall
°C/°F J F M A M J J A S O N D cm/in
40/104
30/86
20/68
10/50
0/32
-10/14
-20/-4
40/16
30/12
20/8
10/4
0

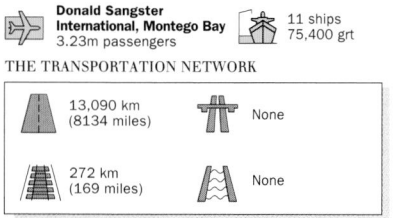

Tropical and humid conditions at sea level give way to temperate weather in mountain areas. Rainfall is seasonal, with marked regional variations.

TRANSPORTATION

Drive on left

Donald Sangster International, Montego Bay 3.23m passengers

11 ships 75,400 grt

THE TRANSPORTATION NETWORK

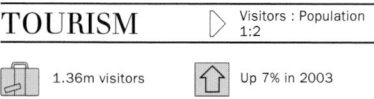

13,090 km (8134 miles)

None

272 km (169 miles)

None

Kingston's harbor has been expanded and its airport improved. The road network is extensive. Private buses provide public transportation.

TOURISM

Visitors : Population 1:2

1.36m visitors

Up 7% in 2003

MAIN TOURIST ARRIVALS

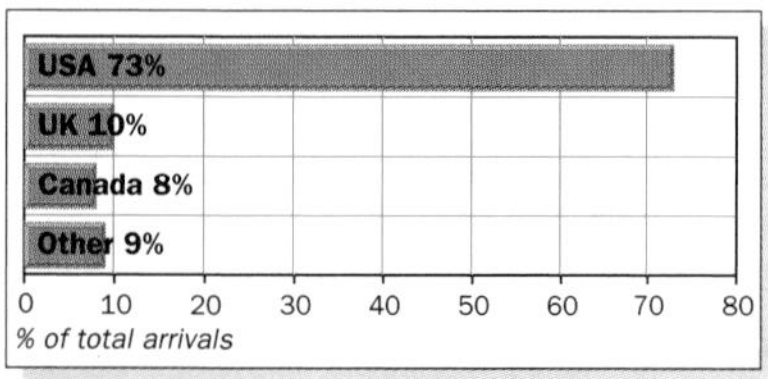
USA 73%
UK 10%
Canada 8%
Other 9%
0 10 20 30 40 50 60 70 80
% of total arrivals

Tourism is the major earner of foreign exchange. Most tourists stay in large, enclosed beach resorts; Jamaica originated the all-inclusive hotel.

PEOPLE

Pop. density high

English Creole, English

249/km² (646/mi²)

THE URBAN/RURAL POPULATION SPLIT

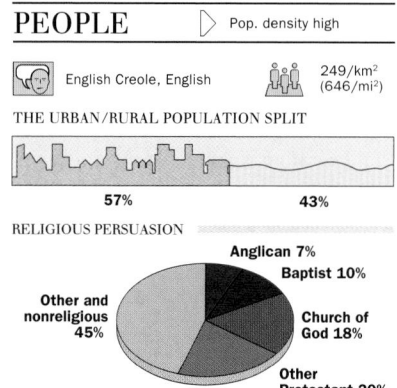

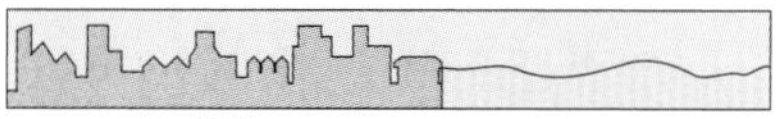
57%
43%

RELIGIOUS PERSUASION

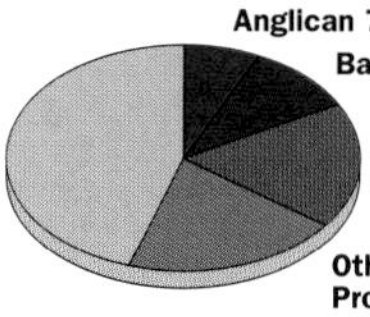
Anglican 7%
Baptist 10%
Church of God 18%
Other Protestant 20%
Other and nonreligious 45%

Most Jamaicans are the descendants of Africans brought to the island between the 16th and 19th centuries, but there are small minorities of Europeans, East Indians, Chinese, and Arabs.

Most social tension is the result of the marked disparities in wealth. Life in the ghettos of Kingston is often violent and based largely on gun law; the capital has one of the world's highest murder rates.

The Caribbean women's rights movement originated in Jamaica, and today many Jamaican women hold senior positions in economic and political life.

Jamaican music styles, including ska, ragga, and reggae, have become popular across the world. Reggae is particularly connected to Jamaica's Rastafarians, followers of the former Ethiopian emperor Haile Selassie.

Bauxite mine and terminal, *Runaway Bay. Bauxite – from which aluminum is extracted – is the main source of foreign income.*

POLITICS

Multiparty elections

L. House 2002/2007
U. House 2002/2007

H.M. Queen Elizabeth II

AT THE LAST ELECTION

House of Representatives 60 seats

57% PNP
43% JLP

PNP = People's National Party **JLP** = Jamaica Labour Party

Senate 21 seats

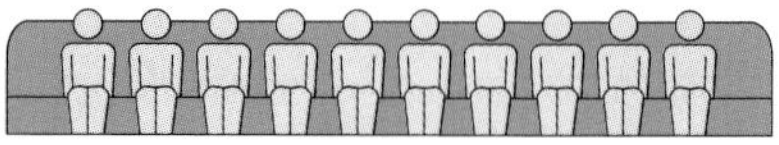

The members of the Senate are appointed. Thirteen members are chosen by the prime minister and eight by the leader of the opposition

In the late 1980s, the ideologies of the once socialist PNP and the conservative JLP converged toward a moderate free-market economic approach.

Violent disturbances in 1998 and 1999 were in response to the PNP government's attempts to deal with economic recession and a large fiscal deficit. The unrest, which led to several deaths, gave new life to the internally troubled JLP, as it then identified itself with opposition to fuel tax increases. Politically motivated gang warfare broke out in Kingston in 2001. The JLP increased its representation in the 2002 election, but failed to unseat the PNP, which began a historic fourth consecutive term in office.

WORLD AFFAIRS

Joined UN in 1962

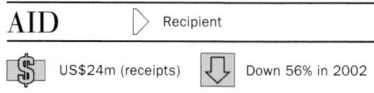

ACS | Caricom | Geplac | Comm | OAS

The main issue is Jamaica's position as a major transshipment point for narcotics heading for the US and the UK.

AID

Recipient

US$24m (receipts)

Down 56% in 2002

Most aid comes from the EU, the US, and Canada. It includes both project loans and balance-of-payments support.

DEFENSE

No compulsory military service

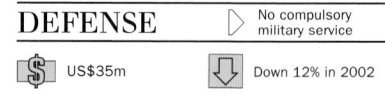

US$35m

Down 12% in 2002

Jamaica's defense force is trained with the assistance of Canada, the UK, and the US. Its main role is combating narcotics smuggling and assisting the police in breaking up unrest, as in 1999 and 2001.

J

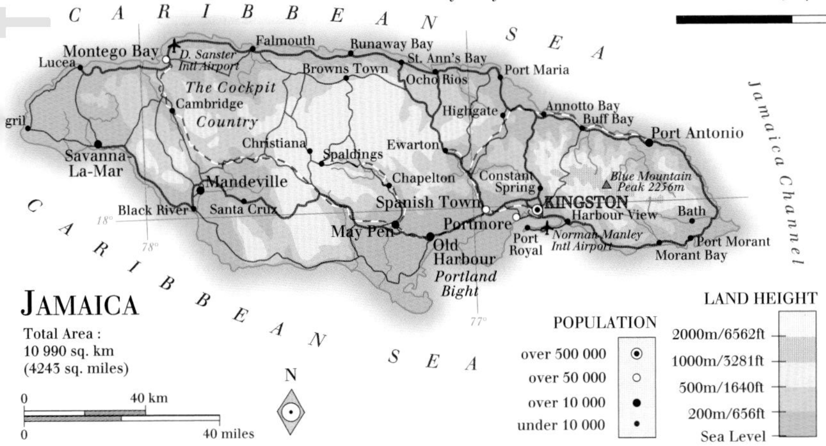
C A R I B B E A N S E A
Montego Bay
D. Sangster Intl Airport
Lucea
Falmouth
Runaway Bay
St. Ann's Bay
Port Maria
Browns Town
Ocho Rios
The Cockpit Country
Cambridge
Highgate
Annotto Bay
Buff Bay
Port Antonio
Jamaica Channel
Negril
Savanna-La-Mar
Christiana
Spaldings
Ewarton
Mandeville
Chapelton
Constant Spring
Blue Mountain Peak 2256m
Black River
Santa Cruz
Spanish Town
KINGSTON
Harbour View
Bath
May Pen
Portmore
Port Royal
Norman Manley Intl Airport
Port Morant
Morant Bay
Old Harbour
Portland Bight
18°
78°
77°
JAMAICA
Total Area : 10 990 sq. km (4243 sq. miles)
0 40 km
0 40 miles
N
POPULATION
over 500 000
over 50 000
over 10 000
under 10 000
LAND HEIGHT
2000m/6562ft
1000m/3281ft
500m/1640ft
200m/656ft
Sea Level

CHRONOLOGY

Spain occupied the island in 1510, wiping out the indigenous Arawak population. Britain seized it in 1655.

- **1958–1961** West Indies Federation.
- **1962** Independence under JLP.
- **1972** PNP elected. Reforms fail; street violence begins.
- **1980** Unpopular IMF austerity measures lead to JLP election win.
- **1989–2002** PNP wins elections and austerity continues.
- **1999** Violent protests over fuel tax increases.

ECONOMICS

Inflation 22% p.a. (1990–2001)

US$7.08bn

60.54 Jamaican dollars (58.7)

SCORE CARD

- WORLD GNP RANKING........................101st
- GNP PER CAPITA ....US$2690
- BALANCE OF PAYMENTS.............–US$1.12bn
- INFLATION 7.1%
- UNEMPLOYMENT.................................16%

STRENGTHS

Relatively diversified economy. Tourism. Mining and refining of bauxite for aluminum. Agriculture, including sugar, bananas, rum, and coffee. Light manufacturing.

WEAKNESSES

Banking and insurance sectors. Climbing debt burden, now around 150% of GDP, dominates budget. Financing of sugar production. Slow growth. High unemployment and crime.

EXPORTS

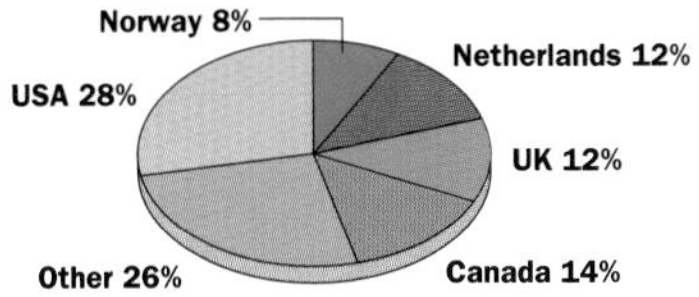
Norway 8%
Netherlands 12%
USA 28%
UK 12%
Other 26%
Canada 14%

IMPORTS

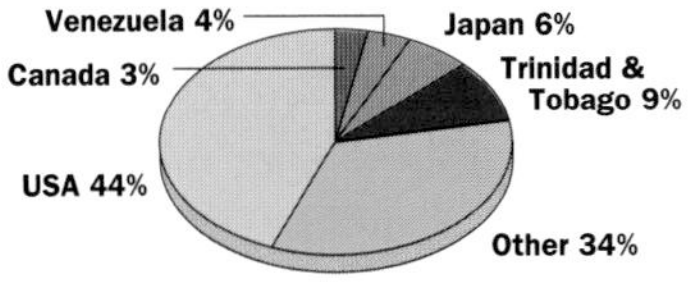
Venezuela 4%
Japan 6%
Canada 3%
Trinidad & Tobago 9%
USA 44%
Other 34%

RESOURCES

Electric power 1.4m kW

10,212 tonnes

Not an oil producer; refines 20,400 b/d

440,000 goats, 430,000 cattle, 11m chickens

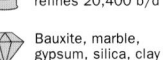

Bauxite, marble, gypsum, silica, clay

Jamaica is the world's fourth-largest producer of bauxite. Sugar and bananas are major exports.

ENVIRONMENT

Sustainability rank: 122nd

9% partially protected

4.2 tonnes per capita

Opencast bauxite mining has caused extensive deforestation. Jamaica set up 14 national parks in the 1990s, but has not provided funding to maintain them.

MEDIA

TV ownership high

Daily newspaper circulation 62 per 1000 people

PUBLISHING AND BROADCAST MEDIA

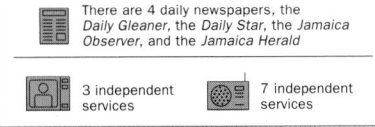

There are 4 daily newspapers, the *Daily Gleaner*, the *Daily Star*, the *Jamaica Observer*, and the *Jamaica Herald*

3 independent services

7 independent services

Television and radio services are diverse and predominantly commercial. The Jamaican press is one of the most influential in the Caribbean.

CRIME

Death penalty in use

4744 prisoners

Down 31% in 1999–2001

Much of the world crack trade is controlled from Jamaica. Large areas of Kingston are ruled by violent gang leaders, and many murders are the result of armed robberies linked to narcotics gangs competing for territory. The police are also frequently accused of the arbitrary shooting of suspects. Death sentences are still being imposed, but the UK-based Privy Council blocks executions; the last hangings were in 1988. The creation of a Caribbean Court of Justice could increase the likelihood of these sentences being carried out.

EDUCATION

School leaving age: 12

88%

33,200 students

Education is based on the former British 11-plus selection system. Jamaica hosts the largest of the three campuses of the University of the West Indies.

HEALTH

Welfare state health benefits

1 per 714 people

Cerebrovascular and heart diseases, cancers, diabetes

The once-efficient state health service is now seriously underfunded. Hospitals generally have a shortage of drugs and there is only rudimentary medical equipment. The incidence of HIV is small but growing fast.

SPENDING

GDP/cap. increase

CONSUMPTION AND SPENDING

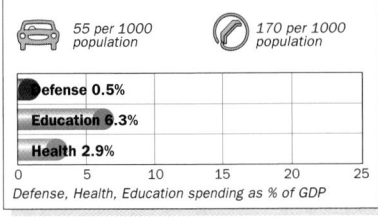

55 per 1000 population

170 per 1000 population

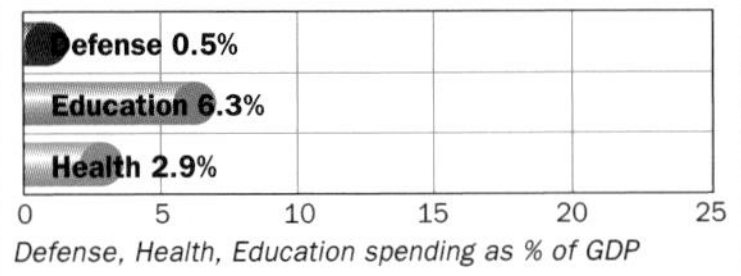
Defense 0.5%
Education 6.3%
Health 2.9%
0
5
10
15
20
25
Defense, Health, Education spending as % of GDP

Wealth disparities are very marked in Jamaica, though better education has seen an increase in the number of Afro-Jamaicans taking more lucrative, white-collar jobs. The poorest in Jamaica, mostly migrants from rural areas, live in the slums of Kingston.

WORLD RANKING

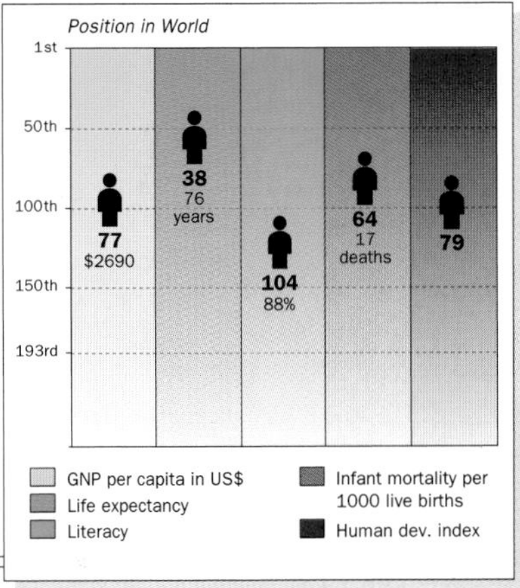
Position in World
1st
50th
100th
150th
193rd
77
$2690
38
76 years
104
88%
64
17 deaths
79
GNP per capita in US$
Life expectancy
Literacy
Infant mortality per 1000 live births
Human dev. index

J

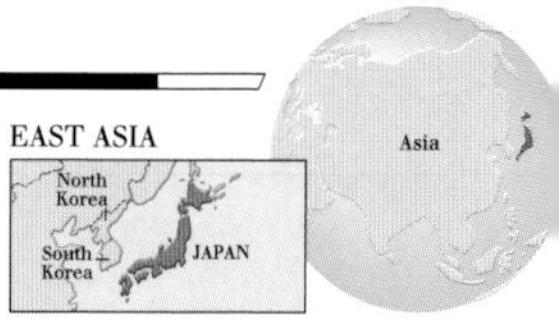
Asia
EAST ASIA
North Korea
South Korea
JAPAN

JAPAN

OFFICIAL NAME: Japan **CAPITAL:** Tokyo
POPULATION: 128 million **CURRENCY:** Yen **OFFICIAL LANGUAGE:** Japanese

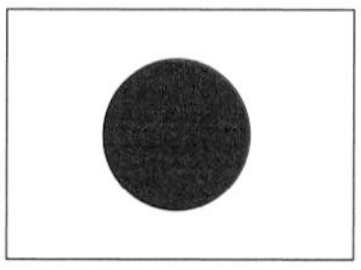

1590 | 1972 | Dec 23 | J | +9 | +81 | .jp

A CONSTITUTIONAL MONARCHY, with an emperor as ceremonial head of state, Japan is located off the east Asian coast in the north Pacific. It comprises four principal islands and more than 3000 smaller islands. Sovereignty over the most southerly and northerly islands is disputed with China and the Russian Federation respectively. The terrain is mostly mountainous, with fertile coastal plains; over two-thirds is woodland. The Pacific coast is vulnerable to tsunamis – tidal waves triggered by submarine earthquakes. Most cities are located by the sea; Tokyo, Kawasaki, and Yokohama together constitute the most populous and heavily industrialized area. Hokkaido is the most rural of the main islands. Japan's power in the global economy, with annual trade surpluses exceeding $100 billion and massive overseas investments, is recovering from a series of bad debt crises, bankruptcies in the financial sector, and two recessions since the early 1990s.

The Shinkansen bullet train *is the second-fastest train in the world. Its speed is matched by its punctuality.*

J

CLIMATE

Continental/subtropical

WEATHER CHART FOR TOKYO

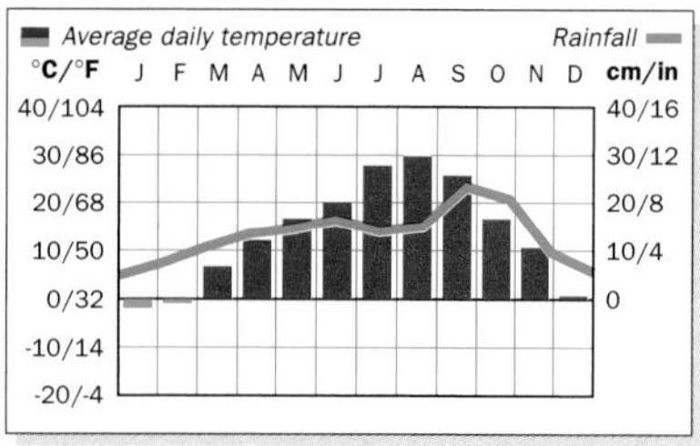
Average daily temperature
Rainfall
°C/°F
J F M A M J J A S O N D
cm/in
40/104
30/86
20/68
10/50
0/32
-10/14
-20/4
40/16
30/12
20/8
10/4
0

The Sea of Japan (East Sea) has a moderating influence on the climate. Winters are less cold than on the Asian mainland, and rainfall is much higher. Spring is perhaps the most pleasant season, with warm, sunny days without the sultry, oppressive heat and rainfall of the summer. Recent freak storms and heavy floods have raised concern over the implications of global climate change.

TRANSPORTATION

Drive on left

Haneda, Tokyo
63.2m passengers

7458 ships
13.9m grt

THE TRANSPORTATION NETWORK

898,082 km (558,041 miles)

6851 km (4257 miles)

20,096 km (12,487 miles)

1770 km (1100 miles)

Railroads are the most important means of transportation in Japan. The Shinkansen, known in the West as the bullet train, is the second-fastest in the world. It is renowned as much for its reliability – timed to the second – as for its speed. The Tokyo–Sapporo air route is said to be the busiest in the world.

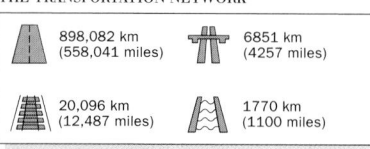

JAPAN
Total Area : 377 835 sq. km
(145 882 sq. miles)
POPULATION
over 5 000 000
over 1 000 000
over 500 000
over 100 000
over 50 000
over 10 000
LAND HEIGHT
1500m/4921ft
1000m/3281ft
500m/1640ft
Sea Level
0 100 km
0 100 miles
SEA OF JAPAN
PACIFIC
TOKYO
Kawasaki
Yokohama
Osaka
Kyōto
Kōbe
Nagoya
Hiroshima
Fukuoka
Kitakyūshū
Okayama
Kumamoto
Kagoshima
Nagasaki
Niigata
Sado
Oki
Tsushima
Tsushima Strait
Shimonoseki
SHIKOKU
KYŪSHŪ
HONSHU
Chūgoku-sanchi
Hida-sammyaku
Mikuni-sammyaku
Fuji-san 3776m
Kiju-san 1791m
Gotō-rettō
Amakusa-shotō
Ōsumi-shotō
Hachijō-jima
Sumisu-jima
TAIWAN
Senkaku-shotō
NANSEI-SHOTŌ
SAKISHIMA-SHOTŌ
Iriomote-jima
Ishigaki-jima
Miyako-jima
Okinawa-shotō
Naha
Amami-Ō-shima
Tokuno-shima
Amami-shotō
Satsunan-shotō
Ibusuki
PACIFIC OCEAN

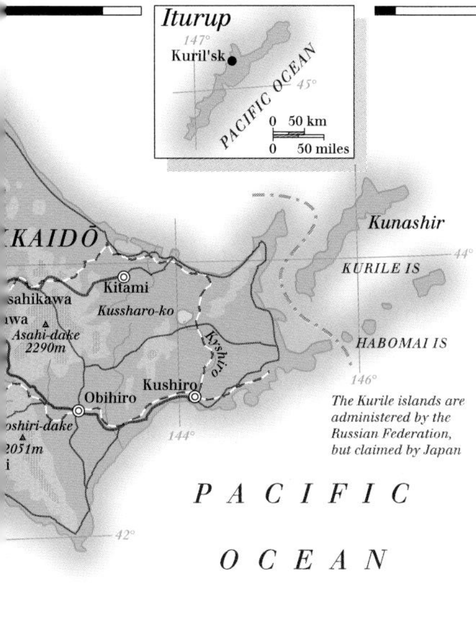
Iturup
Kuril'sk
PACIFIC OCEAN
0 50 km
0 50 miles
Kunashir
KAIDŌ
KURILE IS
HABOMAI IS
Kitami
Kussharo-ko
Asahikawa
Asahi-dake 2290m
Kushiro
Obihiro
The Kurile islands are administered by the Russian Federation, but claimed by Japan
P A C I F I C
O C E A N

TOURISM

Visitors : Population 1:24

5.24m visitors

Up 10% in 2002

MAIN TOURIST ARRIVALS

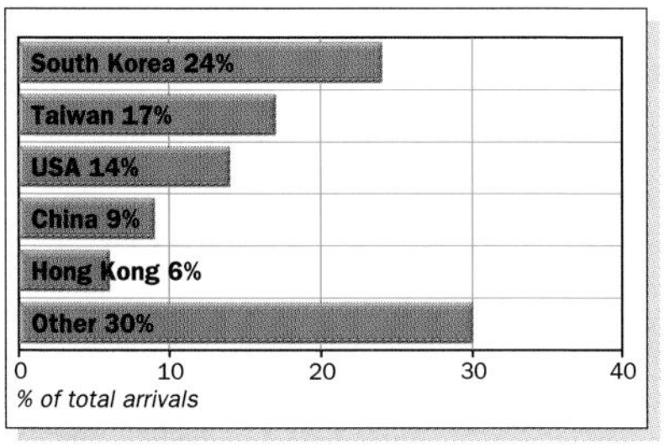
South Korea 24%
Taiwan 17%
USA 14%
China 9%
Hong Kong 6%
Other 30%
0
10
20
30
40
% of total arrivals

Japan is expensive for foreign tourists, despite reductions in the yen exchange rate. An increasing number of tourists are now coming from China. The ancient imperial capital, Kyoto, and the temples and gardens of Nara are popular tourist destinations. Other attractions include Mount Fuji and the extraordinary variety of energetic high-tech urban living in Tokyo and Osaka. Traditional agricultural life can be found in rural areas such as Tohoku in northern Honshu. Wilderness areas of Hokkaido attract mainly Japanese climbers and hikers.

High Street, Ginza District, Tokyo. *Japan's well-policed cities are among the safest in the world.*

PEOPLE

Pop. density high

Japanese, Korean, Chinese

339/km² (878/mi²)

THE URBAN/RURAL POPULATION SPLIT

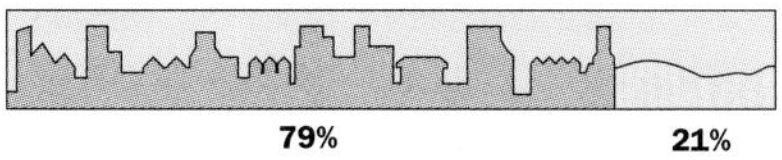
79%
21%

RELIGIOUS PERSUASION

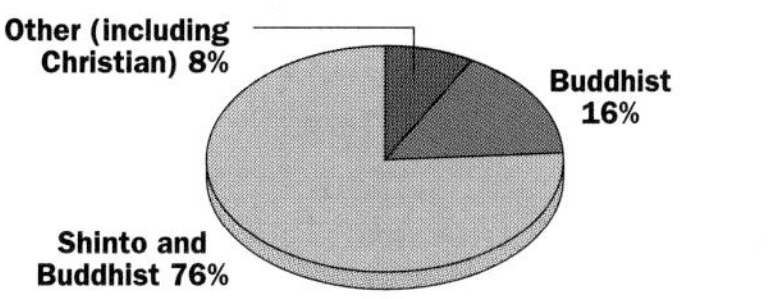
Other (including Christian) 8%
Buddhist 16%
Shinto and Buddhist 76%

ETHNIC MAKEUP

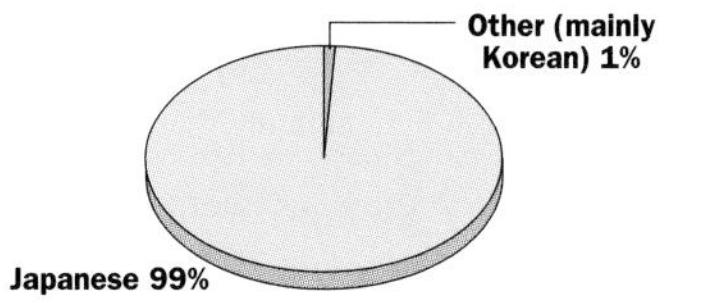
Other (mainly Korean) 1%
Japanese 99%

Japan is racially one of the most homogeneous societies in the world, its sense of order reflected in the tradition of the lifetime employer. Many Japanese men define themselves by the company they work for rather than their job. An employer's influence stretches into employees' social time, and even to encouraging and approving marriages.

Traditionally, women run the home and supervise the all-important education of their children. Many pursue careers until marriage, then continue to work part-time. However, some women are beginning to take on long-term careers, particularly in the medical and legal professions. Makiko Tanaka, the first-ever female foreign minister in 2001–2002, is still a very popular political figure.

Social form remains extremely important in Japanese society. Respect for elders and for social and business superiors is strongly ingrained. There is little tradition of generation rebellion, but the youth market is powerful and current fashions are geared toward teenagers. Many may still follow their parents' lifestyles, but established attitudes are being challenged. Working for the same company for life, and giving up evenings and weekends to entertain company clients, have become harder to justify amid economic turbulence.

POPULATION AGE BREAKDOWN

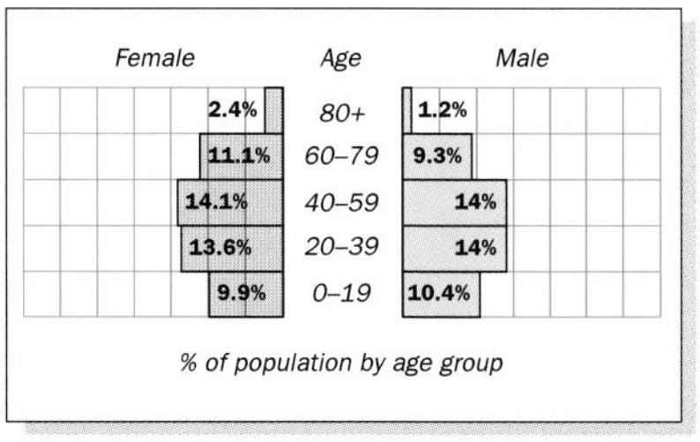
Female
Age
Male
2.4%
80+
1.2%
11.1%
60–79
9.3%
14.1%
40–59
14%
13.6%
20–39
14%
9.9%
0–19
10.4%
% of population by age group

CHRONOLOGY

Japan's tendency to limit its contacts with the outside world ended in 1853, when a US naval squadron forced trading concessions from the last of the Tokugawa shoguns.

- **1868** Meiji Restoration; overthrow of Tokugawa regime and restoration of imperial power.
- **1872** Modernization along Western lines. Japan's strong military tradition becomes state-directed.
- **1889** Constitution modeled on Bismarck's Germany adopted.
- **1894–1895** War with China, ending in Japanese victory.
- **1904–1905** War with Russia, ending in Japanese victory. Formosa (Taiwan) and Korea later annexed.
- **1914** Joins World War I on Allied side. Sees limited naval action.
- **1919** Versailles peace conference gives Japan limited territorial gains in the Pacific.
- **1923** Yokohama earthquake kills 140,000.
- **1927** Japan enters period of radical nationalism, and introduces the notion of a "coprosperity sphere" in southeast Asia under Japanese control. Interpreted in the US as a threat to its Pacific interests.
- **1931** Chinese Manchuria invaded and renamed Manchukuo.
- **1937** Japan launches full-scale invasion of China proper.
- **1938** All political parties placed under one common banner; Japan effectively ruled by militarists.
- **1939** Undeclared border war with Soviet Union; Japan defeated.
- **1940** Fall of France in Europe; Japan occupies French Indo-China.
- **1941** US imposes total trade embargo, including oil, on Japan thereby threatening to stifle its military machine. Japan responds in December by launching attack on US fleet at Pearl Harbor and invading US, British, and Dutch possessions in the Pacific.
- **1942** Japan loses decisive naval battle of Midway.
- **1945** Huge US bombing campaign culminates in atomic bombing of Hiroshima and Nagasaki: over 200,000 die. Soviet Union declares war on Japan. Emperor Hirohito surrenders, gives up divine status. Japan placed under US military government with Gen. MacArthur as supreme commander.
- **1947** New US-style constitution: retains emperor in ceremonial role.
- **1950** Korean War. US army contracts lead to quick expansion of Japanese economy.
- **1952** Treaty of San Francisco. Japan regains independence.

CHRONOLOGY *continued*

Industrial production recovers to 15% above 1936 levels.

- **1955** Formation of LDP, which governs for next 38 years.
- **1964** Tokyo Olympics. Bullet train (Shinkansen) inaugurated. Japan admitted to OECD.
- **1973** Oil crisis. Economic growth falls. Government-led economic reassessment decides to concentrate on high-tech industries.
- **1976** LDP shaken by Lockheed bribery scandal; in subsequent election it remains in power but loses outright majority for first time.
- **1979** Second oil crisis. Growth continues at 6% per year.
- **1980** LDP regains overall majority.
- **1982** Honda establishes first car factory in US.
- **1988** Japan becomes world's largest aid donor and overseas investor.
- **1989** Death of Emperor Hirohito. Accession of son, Akihito. Recruit–Cosmos bribery scandal leads to resignation of Prime Minister Noburo Takeshita; replaced by Sosuke Uno, in turn forced to resign over sex scandal.
- **1990** Tokyo stock market crash.
- **1991–1992** LDP torn by factional disputes, further financial scandals, and the issue of electoral reform.
- **1993** Reformists split from LDP and create new parties. Elections; LDP loses power. Morihiro Hosokawa becomes prime minister at head of seven-party coalition.
- **1994** Hosokawa resigns. Withdrawal of SDPJ causes collapse of coalition. New three-party coalition includes LDP and SDPJ. Opposition parties unified by creation of Shinshinto. Implementation of far-reaching political and electoral reforms designed to eradicate "money politics."
- **1995** Kobe earthquake kills more than 5000 people.
- **1996** Elections: LDP minority government. Copper trader Yasuo Yamanaka sentenced to eight years in prison for incurring losses of $2.6 billion while acting for the Sumitomo Corporation.
- **1997** Severe economic recession.
- **1998** Crisis over reform of banking and financial system.
- **2000** Prime Minister Keizo Obuchi falls into coma, replaced by Yoshiro Mori. LDP loses overall majority in general election.
- **2001** LDP turns to populist right-winger Junichiro Koizumi as prime minister; five women appointed to cabinet.
- **2002** Japan cohosts soccer World Cup.
- **2003** LDP reelected.

POLITICS

Multiparty elections

L. House 2003/2007
U. House 2004/2007

Emperor Tsegu no Miya Akihito

AT THE LAST ELECTION

House of Representatives 480 seats

2% **JCP** 3% **Others**

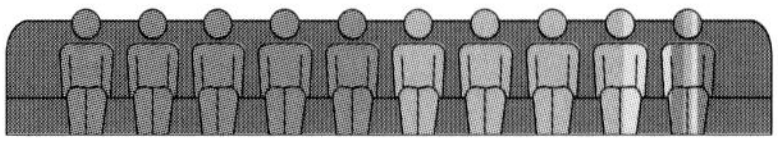

49% **LDP** 37% **DPJ** 7% **NK** 1% **SDPJ** 1% **NCP**

LDP = Liberal Democratic Party **DPJ** = Democratic Party of Japan **NK** = New Komeito **JCP** = Japan Communist Party **SDPJ** = Social Democratic Party of Japan **NCP** = New Conservative Party

House of Councillors 242 seats

10% **NK** 2% **SDPJ**

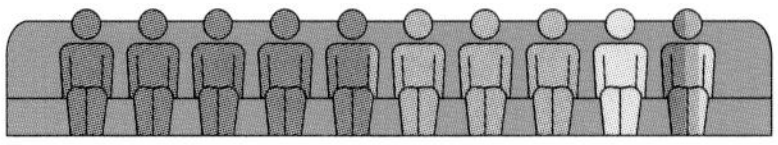

47% **LDP** 34% **DPJ** 4% **JCP** 3% **Others**

Japan is a multiparty democracy. The emperor has a purely ceremonial role.

Profile

The right-of-center LDP has dominated Japanese politics since its formation in 1955. For the first 21 years its parliamentary majority was untouched, but it has had to rely on occasionally shaky coalitions since 1976. In 1993 it lost power altogether, but recovered the following year and has remained in control ever since. The seven-party government which held power in 1993–1994 proved unworkable in the long run and the later Shinshinto coalition was unable to challenge the LDP despite the dire economic situation of the late 1990s.

Indeed, the LDP's position is threatened less by external opposition than by the machinations of its various internal factions. Prime Minister Yoshiro Mori led a lackluster campaign in a general election in 2000, from which the LDP emerged with a reduced representation but still as the largest party and the main force in government. Mori's unpopularity finally led to his replacement as LDP leader (and prime minister) in 2001 by charismatic newcomer Junichiro Koizumi.

With the economy stagnating, Koizumi took it upon himself to push a radical reformist agenda, making the most of his immense public popularity. However, though he promised much, he has delivered little in the way of significant change, especially in the political sphere. The inertia of the faction system and the fierce conservatism of the grass-roots LDP have forced him to scale down his visions and settle into the familiar routine of gentle persuasion and appeasement. His popularity has consequently suffered, and the DPJ made inroads into the LDP's majority in the 2003 elections.

Junichiro Koizumi, *populist premier who has promised economic reform.*

Katsuya Okada *has reinvigorated the opposition DPJ as leader from 2004.*

Emperor Akihito. *He acceded in 1989 on the death of his father, Hirohito.*

Traditional paddy field *in Hokkaido. Rice farming is among the most protected sectors of the Japanese economy.*

Main Political Issues

Economic reform

Efforts to restructure the way in which government money is spent have met stiff resistance. The achievements that Koizumi did make in 2001–2002 did little to offset the stagnation of the Japanese economy. He admitted in early 2003 that his reforms had been "derailed" and would take more time than had been anticipated. However, by 2004 export-led growth had begun to buoy up the domestic economy.

The emergence of two-party politics

The hegemony of the LDP, based on close links with big business and government bureaucracy, was first seriously challenged at the polls in 1993. Defeat prompted an overhaul of the electoral system, aimed at stamping out "money politics," and ensured that the party would rise again soon after, easily outmaneuvering the Shinshinto alliance. In 2003 the DPJ emerged as the main opposition, challenging the LDP on its unconvincing record of reform. Postelectoral opinion polls suggest support for a stronger opposition.

WORLD AFFAIRS

Joined UN in 1956

APEC | G8 | IAEA | WTO | OECD

Having spent decades since World War II limiting its international role, Japan has recently become more assertive on many global issues. Its eventual aim is a seat on the UN's Security Council, commensurate with its economic influence. In Asia, Japan remains burdened by the legacy of its wartime aggression, and has sometimes exacerbated the tension by moves such as revising its school history texts to downplay the crimes committed in its imperial expansion (especially in Korea) and in war. Relations with the West have been seriously strained over the issue of whaling, with Japan getting round an international moratorium by continuing to kill whales in the name of scientific monitoring.

AID

Donor

$9.28bn (donations) Down 6% in 2002

Japan's official aid donations are the second-largest of any single country (they were formerly the largest, until overtaken by the US in 2001). Most aid goes to Asia and the Pacific, especially China. In the Pacific, aid supports the fishing industry. In 2001, Japan admitted to "buying" support for whaling.

DEFENSE

No compulsory military service

$37.1bn Down 6% in 2002

JAPANESE ARMED FORCES

1020 main battle tanks (780 Type-74, 240 Type-90)	148,200 personnel
16 submarines, 45 destroyers, 9 frigates, 7 patrol boats	44,400 personnel
270 combat aircraft (F-1, F-2, F-4EJ, F-15J)	45,600 personnel
None	

The Japanese Self-Defense Forces (SDF) are among the best-funded in the world, but the constitution renounces war, and any military activity arouses fierce debate. Main concerns are North Korea and the threat of terrorism. Since 1999, force has been used to deter incursions by North Korean vessels. The construction of a missile defense system was agreed in 2003. The deployment in 2004 of an SDF contingent in Iraq in a humanitarian role, under legislation allowing noncombat assistance in the "war on terrorism," was the first time Japanese forces had entered an overseas combat zone since 1945.

ECONOMICS

Inflation –0.1% p.a. (1990–2001)

$4324bn 109.12 yen (120.08)

ECONOMIC PERFORMANCE INDICATOR

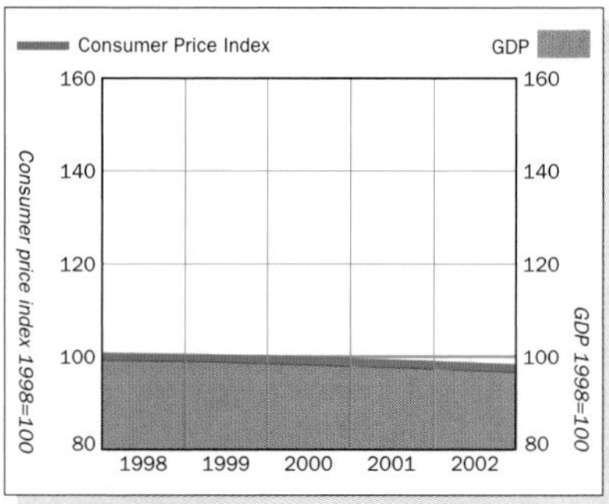

Consumer Price Index
GDP
Consumer price index 1998=100
GDP 1998=100
160
140
120
100
80
1998 1999 2000 2001 2002

STRENGTHS

Established market leader in high-tech products and cars. Commitment to long-term research. Talent for capitalizing on imported ideas. Manufacturing plants already established in the West. Domestic economy heavily protected from outside competition.

WEAKNESSES

Recent recession. Dependence on oil imports. Secretive and debt-ridden financial system. Falling industrial production, high-profile bankruptcies, and record unemployment levels. Lack of openness to foreign trade. Aging population and costly public pension scheme.

PROFILE

Once among the world's strongest performing economies, Japan's strengths have been overshadowed for a decade by growing weaknesses.

The 1990 crash of the Tokyo stock market marked the end of a period of remarkable growth. The government managed to spend its way out of disaster, effectively delaying the full impact of the downturn. Japan entered a brief recession for the second time in five years in 2001.

Bilateral trade has been promoted and Japan entered its first free trade agreement – with Singapore from April 2002. In an attempt to appease Western discontent over a huge trade surplus, the government encouraged a move away from a dependence on export revenues through stimulation of the domestic economy. However, the expanding economies of China and other Asian countries stimulated export-led growth again in 2004.

The financial sector remains in need of reform. The prominent corporate collapses of 1997 were repeated in 2001, with record losses reported across the high-tech industries in particular. Koizumi has promised radical change, rejecting the standard increase in government spending in favor of basic structural reform. Banks' bad loans have been cleared and the system of privileged "special public institutions" has been overhauled. Despite these measures, traditional economic power brokers have put a brake on the pace of reform and the overall economy continues to underachieve. In 2004 Koizumi renewed his pledge to stimulate the recovering economy by pushing ahead with structural reforms, and plans were approved to open the country's public road corporations to private investment.

SCORE CARD

- WORLD GNP RANKING 2nd
- GNP PER CAPITA $34,010
- BALANCE OF PAYMENTS $112bn
- INFLATION .... –0.9%
- UNEMPLOYMENT 5%

EXPORTS

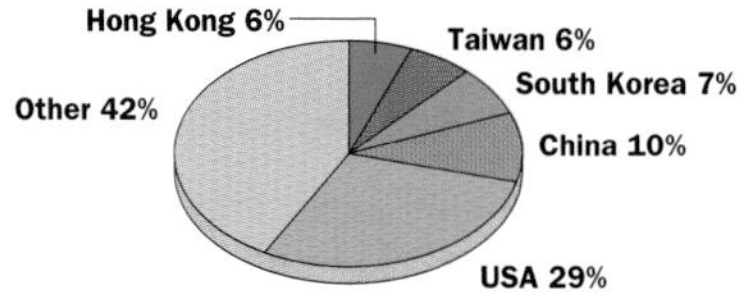

Hong Kong 6%
Taiwan 6%
South Korea 7%
China 10%
USA 29%
Other 42%

IMPORTS

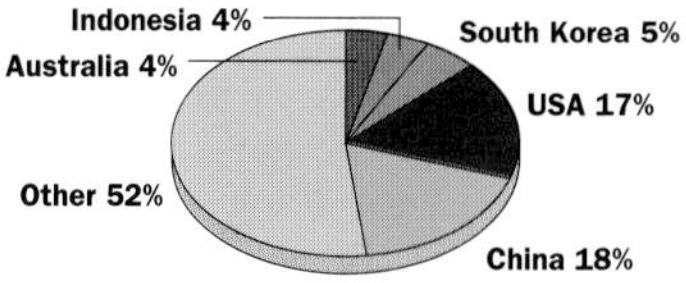

Indonesia 4%
Australia 4%
South Korea 5%
USA 17%
China 18%
Other 52%

JAPAN : MAJOR BUSINESSES

- Research & development
- Vehicle manufacture
- Heavy engineering
- Consumer goods
- Shipbuilding
- Iron & steel
- Electronics
- Chemicals
- Brewing
- Textiles
- Computers
- Banking & Finance

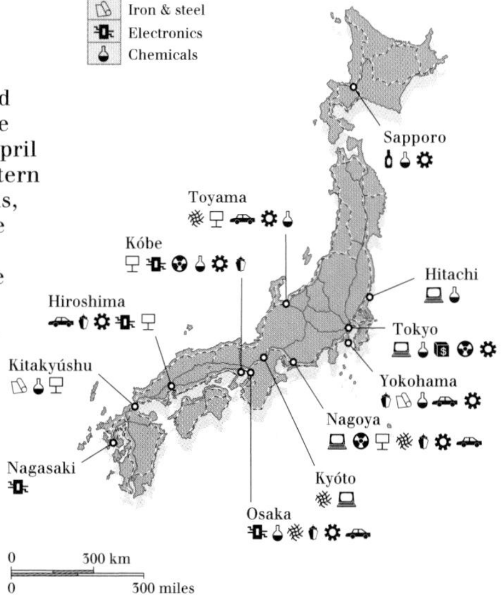

Sapporo
Toyama
Kóbe
Hitachi
Hiroshima
Tokyo
Kitakyúshu
Yokohama
Nagoya
Nagasaki
Kyóto
Osaka
0 300 km
0 300 miles

J

RESOURCES

Electric power 248m kW

5.52m tonnes

8040 b/d (reserves 52m barrels)

9.72m pigs, 4.52m cattle, 34,000 goats, 284m chickens

Limestone, sulfur, coal, oil

ELECTRICITY GENERATION

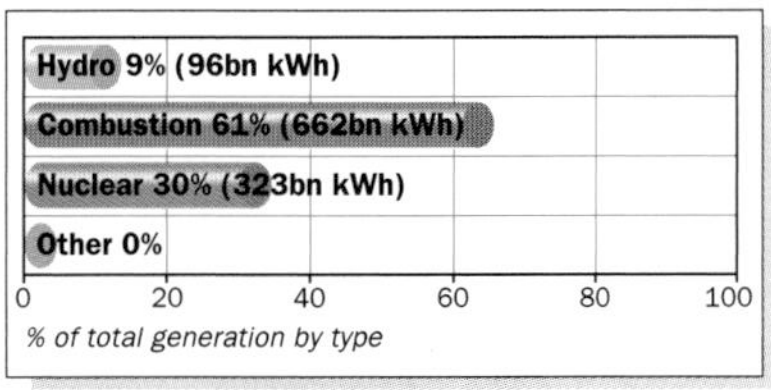
Hydro 9% (96bn kWh)
Combustion 61% (662bn kWh)
Nuclear 30% (323bn kWh)
Other 0%
0
20
40
60
80
100
% of total generation by type

Japan has few exploitable resources. The high cost of domestic coal extraction has made it the world's largest importer.

In an attempt to reduce dependence on imported fuels, Japan has developed alternative energy sources. It is now the world's third-biggest generator of nuclear power. Nuclear safety issues, highlighted following a radiation leak at Tokaimura in 1999, were again under the spotlight after a deadly (but nonradioactive) accident at the Mihama plant in 2004.

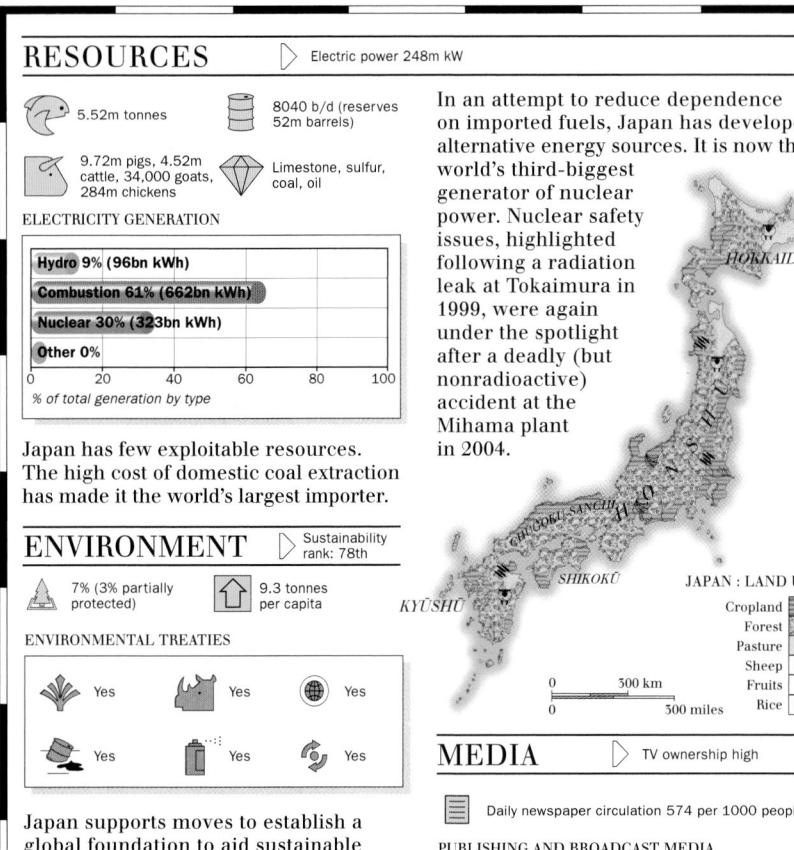

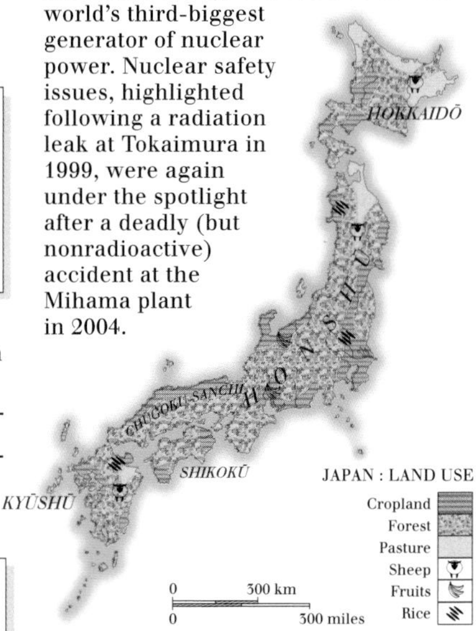
HOKKAIDŌ
HONSHU
CHUGOKU SANCHI
SHIKOKU
KYŪSHŪ
JAPAN : LAND USE
Cropland
Forest
Pasture
Sheep
Fruits
Rice
0 300 km
0 300 miles

ENVIRONMENT

Sustainability rank: 78th

7% (3% partially protected)

9.3 tonnes per capita

ENVIRONMENTAL TREATIES

Yes Yes Yes

Yes Yes Yes

Japan supports moves to establish a global foundation to aid sustainable development in the Third World. In 1997 it played host to the Kyoto climate conference, though it only agreed to a modest cut in its "greenhouse gas" emissions. It faces strong criticism for its consumption of tropical timber, overfishing, and continuing to catch whale species under the aegis of "scientific research."

Traditional Japanese respect for nature has spawned a vigorous grassroots ecological movement, which prevented a second runway at Tokyo's Narita airport, and opposes nuclear power expansion and waste processing. The most serious environmental disasters have been a nuclear accident at Tokaimura in 1999 and the breakup in early 1997 of a Russian oil tanker along Japan's western shoreline.

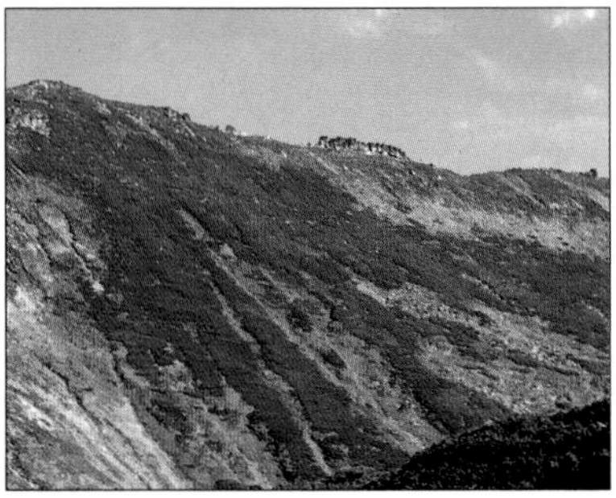

***Datsetsusan National Park**, Hokkaido. Japan's northerly island is the least populous of the main group.*

MEDIA

TV ownership high

Daily newspaper circulation 574 per 1000 people

PUBLISHING AND BROADCAST MEDIA

There are 122 daily newspapers. *Asahi Shimbun*, *Mainichi Shimbun*, and *Yomiuri Shimbun* are among the most popular

5 national services: 1 publicly owned, 4 commercial

100 services: 1 publicly owned, 99 commercial

The Japanese are among the world's most avid newspaper readers. Major papers are issued in simultaneous editions in the main urban centers. Most dailies are owned by large media groups who also have TV and cable interests. Weekly newspapers carry more tabloid journalism. *Manga*, Japanese comics, are massively popular, with their characteristic artwork influencing design and art across Japanese culture. They now account for 40% of all published material in Japan; the most popular title, *Shonen Jump*, sells over three million copies a week.

Japanese technology has defined the world's media. Along with the personal stereo, Japanese companies effectively created the huge international computer games market. Nintendo, a leading games company, is among the most profitable in Japan. Ironically, the Internet was slow to take off, though by 2001 Japan had the third-highest number of people "online." That year also saw Japan launch the world's first "third-generation" mobile phone service.

EDUCATION

School leaving age: 15

99%

3.11m students

THE EDUCATION SYSTEM

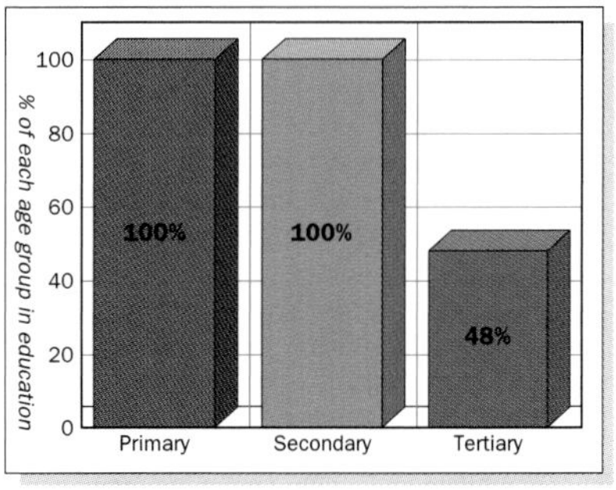
100
80
60
40
20
0
% of each age group in education
100%
100%
48%
Primary
Secondary
Tertiary

The Japanese education system is highly pressurized and competitive. One of the key dividing lines is between university graduates, who get the most coveted white-collar jobs, and nongraduates, who have difficulty reaching management level.

Competition for university places is intense, and starts with the choice of kindergarten, which the Japanese attend from the age of four. Academic pressure diminishes once at university. Graduates from Tokyo, Kyoto, Waseda, and Keio, which are the most prestigious universities, have access to top civil service and business jobs. The system succeeds in producing a uniformly well-educated workforce. However, it has also been criticized for not fostering individual responsibility, flexibility, or entrepreneurship.

CRIME

Death penalty in use

67,255 prisoners

Up 12% in 2001

CRIME RATE

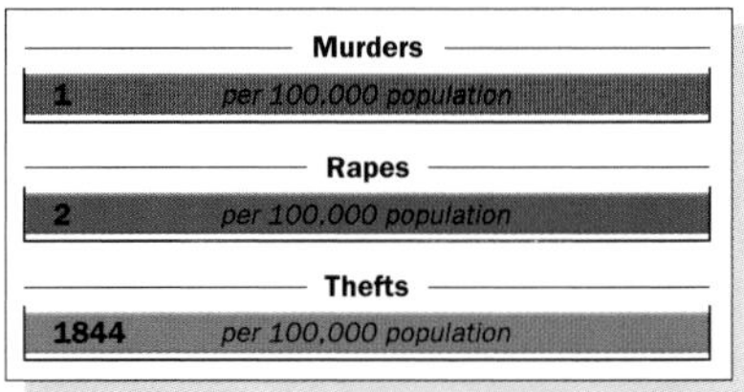
Murders
1 per 100,000 population
Rapes
2 per 100,000 population
Thefts
1844 per 100,000 population

Japan has one of the Western world's lowest crime rates, despite petty crime levels being at a 50-year high. Cities are safe, with police kiosks at frequent intervals on street corners. However, crime is involving more young people, and narcotics abuse is increasing.

Problems include fraud, human trafficking, and the activities of the *kumi*, organized Mafia-style syndicates. The authorities have been reluctant to challenge the *kumi*, seeking to contain rather than halt their activities. They are suspected of having connections with the political extreme right.

JAPAN AT WAR

JAPAN REPEATEDLY CHOSE isolationism over interaction for much of its history, with one striking exception. The Meiji Restoration of 1868 prompted a period of modernization and militarization, which culminated in the occupation of the Korean peninsula from 1910, growing imperial involvement in China (taking advantage of its internal chaos), and a rapid military advance across the Pacific Rim during World War II. Japan's 20th-century military ambitions proved short-lived, however, ending with defeat and surrender in 1945.

Members of the Self-Defense Forces *prepare themselves for peacekeeping duty.*

The atrocities carried out in east Asia in the name of the Japanese emperor have not been forgotten and continue to engender anger in Korea and China. To banish all prospect of a militarily strong Japan, pacifism was written directly into the postwar constitution, whose celebrated Article 9 stipulates that "the Japanese people forever renounce ... the threat or use of force as a means of settling international disputes." Instead of an army, navy, or air force, the constitution permitted the creation of Self-Defense Forces (SDF) to provide internal security. Politicians embraced Japan's new role as an international champion of peace, with successive mayors of Hiroshima campaigning against the international development and testing of nuclear weaponry in particular. As Japan's economic might grew, however, its nonmilitary status began to seem increasingly incongruous to some.

JAPAN IN THE WORLD

Japan lies close to four of the world's ten largest armies, those of China, North Korea, South Korea, and Russia. Perhaps the greatest argument for reexamining its pacifistic identity is the apparent threat from North Korea. Incursions into Japanese waters by North Korean "fishing vessels" and provocative missile tests frequently challenge Japan's neutrality. In 1998 North Korea test-fired a ballistic missile right across northern Japan, while since 1999 Japanese patrol boats have used force to repel intrusions, which in late 2001 included the sinking of a ship. Meanwhile Japan's SDF have grown to almost 250,000 personnel.

靖國神社國家奉護

Nationalists broadcast *their point of view from intimidating* gaisensha *(sound vans).*

NATIONALIST FEELING

Right-wing political agitation in Japan has grown. Shintaro Ishihara, the flamboyant governor of Tokyo since 1999, openly courts nationalist feelings and plays on the widespread fear of foreigners, particularly Koreans (the only sizable ethnic minority in Japan).

Prime Minister Junichiro Koizumi has also pushed against pacifism. Especially infuriating to many are his regular visits to the Yasakuni war shrine, which commemorates convicted war criminals among the more worthy. Insisting that his visits are personal, and do not represent tacit support for Japan's imperialist past, he continues, nonetheless, to sign the visitors' book as "Prime Minister Koizumi."

TROOPS IN IRAQ

New legislation has broken a further taboo, allowing 600 SDF troops to fly to Iraq in February 2004, in the first SDF involvement in a "combat zone."

SDF officers had first joined an international peacekeeping mission a decade earlier as electoral monitors and civilian policemen in Cambodia in 1993. For many this confirmed Japanese maturity, working within the bounds of the international state system. For others it was a highly symbolic and disturbing sign of a growing Japanese confidence.

The SDF troops in Iraq were stationed far from major flashpoints, with a strictly humanitarian brief. Their very presence, however, rang alarm bells, leaving many in east Asia to assume that the Japanese army was to be reborn in the 21st century.

HEALTH

Welfare state health benefits

1 per 496 people

Cancers, respiratory, cerebrovascular, and heart diseases

Japan's health care system, which has been ranked by WHO as the best in the world, delivers among the highest longevity and lowest infant mortality rates. The poorest in society receive free treatment; expensive high-tech hospital facilities can also offer the latest techniques. Contributory national health insurance is based on earnings-related premiums, and the cost of medical care for the elderly and the self-employed is subsidized, though the rapidly aging population presents a major future funding challenge.

SPENDING

GDP/cap. increase

CONSUMPTION AND SPENDING

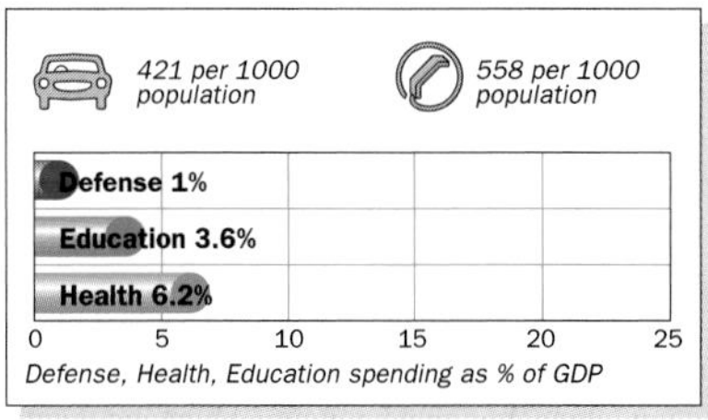
421 per 1000 population
558 per 1000 population
Defense 1%
Education 3.6%
Health 6.2%
0
5
10
15
20
25
Defense, Health, Education spending as % of GDP

Measured in consumer goods, the Japanese are wealthy; car ownership is only low because city parking is so restricted. Most households have substantial savings, enabling them to withstand economic recession.

The country's wealthiest men have seen their wealth decline markedly: the fortunes of the top ten averaged $4.5 billion in 2004, down from $7 billion in 2000. The richest, Nobutada Saji (and family), is worth $6.9 billion.

Tokyo's living costs are high, and most who work there live outside the city center, facing long, cramped commuter journeys to work and back.

Girls and young women still living in their parents' homes are one group with high disposable income.

WORLD RANKING

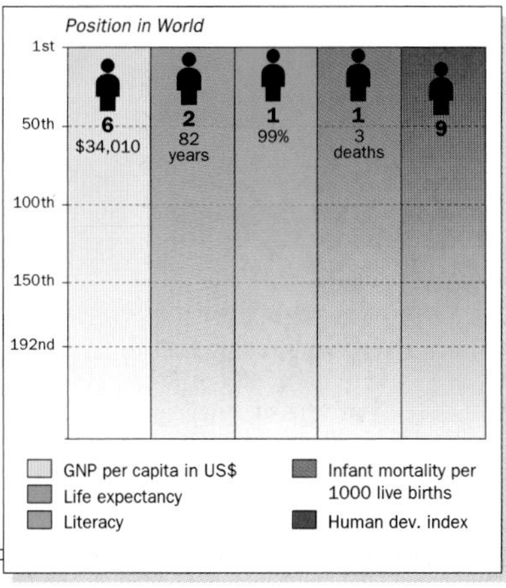
Position in World
1st
50th
100th
150th
192nd
6
$34,010
2
82 years
1
99%
1
3 deaths
9
GNP per capita in US$
Life expectancy
Literacy
Infant mortality per 1000 live births
Human dev. index

J

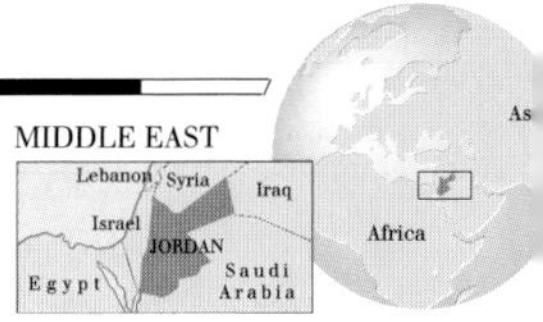
MIDDLE EAST
Lebanon
Syria
Iraq
Israel
JORDAN
Egypt
Saudi Arabia
Africa

JORDAN

OFFICIAL NAME: Hashemite Kingdom of Jordan **CAPITAL:** Amman
POPULATION: 5.5 million **CURRENCY:** Jordanian dinar **OFFICIAL LANGUAGE:** Arabic

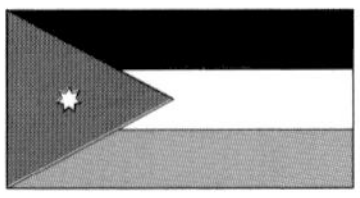

1946 | 1967 | May 25 | HKJ | +2 | +962 | .jo

SURROUNDED by the deserts of the Middle East, Jordan has just 26 km (16 miles) of maritime coastline on the Gulf of Aqaba. The vast majority of the population lives in the northwest, on the east bank of the River Jordan. Jordan ceded its claim to the West Bank of the river to the aspiring Palestinian state in 1988. Tourism, associated with important historical sites such as Petra, and phosphates are the mainstays of the economy.

CLIMATE

Hot desert/steppe/ Mediterranean

WEATHER CHART FOR AMMAN

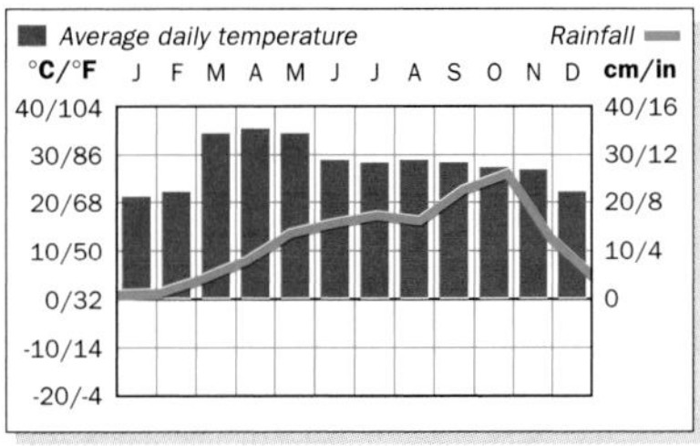
Average daily temperature
Rainfall
°C/°F
J F M A M J J A S O N D
cm/in
40/104
30/86
20/68
10/50
0/32
-10/14
-20/-4
40/16
30/12
20/8
10/4
0

Summers are hot and dry, winters cool. Areas below sea level are very hot in summer and warm in winter.

TRANSPORTATION

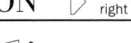

Drive on right

Queen Alia International, Amman
2.33m passengers

14 ships
68,700 grt

THE TRANSPORTATION NETWORK

7200 km (4474 miles)	None
292 km (181 miles)	None

Adequate roads link main cities. The only internal flights are between Amman and Aqaba. Rail services are limited.

TOURISM

Visitors : Population 1:3.5

1.57m visitors

Down 3% in 2003

MAIN TOURIST ARRIVALS

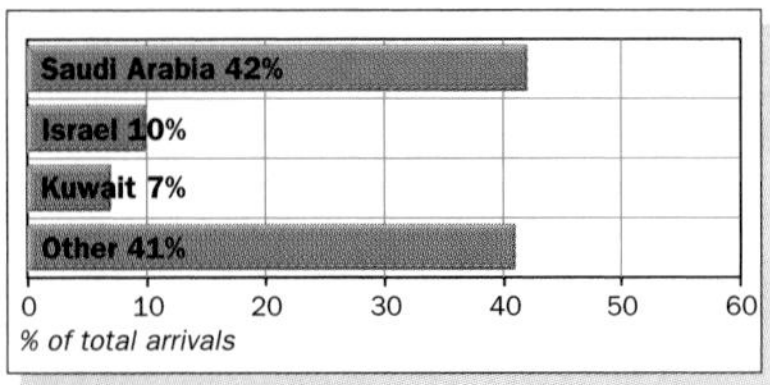
Saudi Arabia 42%
Israel 10%
Kuwait 7%
Other 41%
0
10
20
30
40
50
60
% of total arrivals

Tourists visit archaeological remains, such as the ancient city of Petra and the Roman city of Jerash, and resort facilities at Aqaba and the Dead Sea. Amman is developing as a center for Arab culture. Regional instability dents the industry.

PEOPLE

Pop. density medium

Arabic

62/km² (160/mi²)

THE URBAN/RURAL POPULATION SPLIT

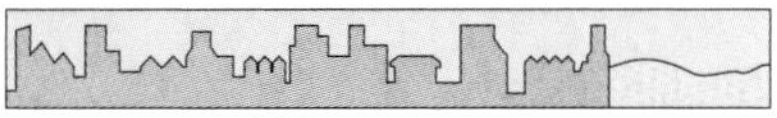
79%
21%

ETHNIC MAKEUP

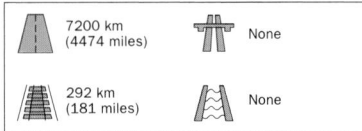

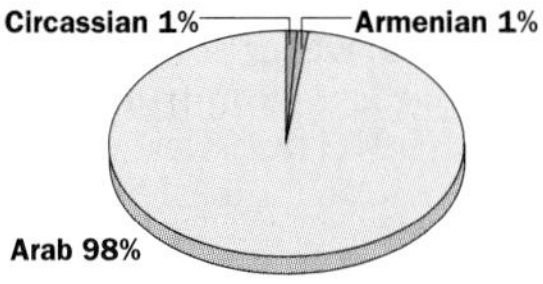
Circassian 1%
Armenian 1%
Arab 98%

Jordan is a predominantly Muslim country with Bedouin roots; there are Arab Christian and Muslim Circassian minorities. About half the population are Palestinian in origin. The monarchy's power base lies among the rural tribes, which provide the backbone of the military.

POLITICS

Multiparty elections

L. House 2003/2007
U. House 2003/2007

H.M. King Abdullah II

AT THE LAST ELECTION

House of Deputies 110 seats

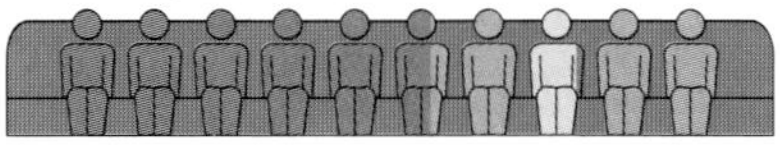
7%
Isl Ind
56%
Gov Ind
15%
IAF
3%
OP
19%
Others

Gov Ind = Progovernment independents
IAF = Islamic Action Front **Isl Ind** = Islamist independents
OP = Other parties
Nine seats are reserved for Christians, six for women, and three for Circassians

Senate 55 seats

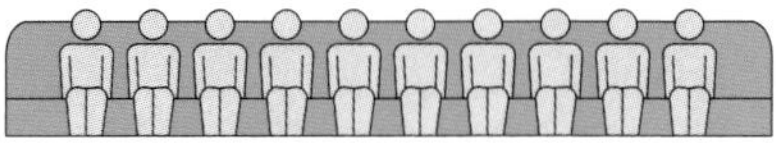

The members of the Senate are appointed by the king

King Abdullah II acceded in 1999. He enjoys the support of tribal leaders and the army. Multiparty elections in 1993 ended a period of martial law which had begun in 1967. Progovernment parties hold a majority, despite a strong Islamist opposition. Changes in prime minister in 2000 and 2003 marked a shift toward modernization. Clashes between police and Islamists in Ma'an in 2002 raised concern over the impact of regional tensions on the volatile populace.

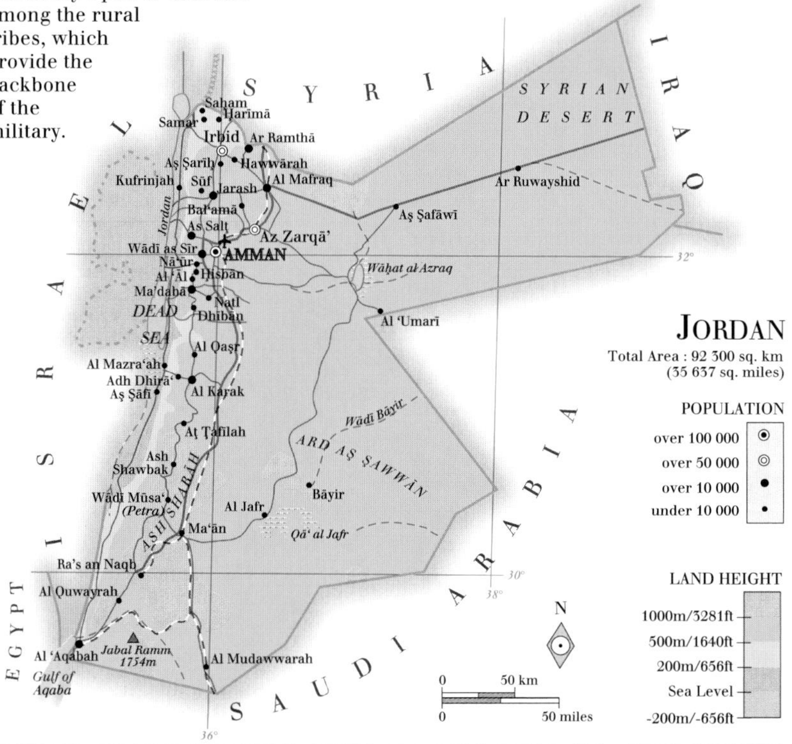
SYRIA
SYRIAN DESERT
IRAQ
ISRAEL
EGYPT
SAUDI ARABIA
Saham
Samar
Harīmā
Irbid
Ar Ramthā
Aş Şarīh
Ḩawwārah
Kufrinjah
Şūf
Jarash
Al Mafraq
Jordan
Bal'amā
As Salt
Az Zarqā'
Wādī as Sīr
AMMAN
Nā'ūr
Al 'Āl
Ḩisbān
Mādabā
Natl
Dhībān
DEAD SEA
Al Qaşr
Al Mazra'ah
Adh Dhirā'
Aş Şāfī
Al Karak
Aţ Ţafīlah
Ash Shawbak
Wādī Mūsá (Petra)
ASH SHARAH
Ma'ān
Al Jafr
Bāyir
Qā' al Jafr
ARD AS SAWWĀN
Wādī Bāyir
Ras an Naqb
Al Quwayrah
Al 'Aqabah
Gulf of Aqaba
Jabal Ramm 1754m
Al Mudawwarah
Ar Ruwayshid
Aş Şafāwī
Wāhat al Azraq
Al 'Umarī
32°
30°
36°
38°
N
0 50 km
0 50 miles
JORDAN
Total Area : 92 300 sq. km (35 637 sq. miles)
POPULATION
over 100 000
over 50 000
over 10 000
under 10 000
LAND HEIGHT
1000m/3281ft
500m/1640ft
200m/656ft
Sea Level
-200m/-656ft

WORLD AFFAIRS

Joined UN in 1955

AL | AMF | WTO | NAM | OIC

Jordan's position as a key player in Middle East politics is under question. It actively supports US peace moves, and is at peace with Israel. In 2004 it chided both Israeli and Palestinian leaders for the lack of progress toward peace. The US signed a ten-year free trade agreement with Jordan in 2000.

Jordan refused to join the anti-Iraq coalition formed by the Gulf states in 1991. Prior to the US invasion in 2003 it called for Iraq's rehabilitation, and went on to condemn the invasion.

AID

Recipient

$534m (receipts)

Up 23% in 2002

The US is by far the biggest single donor, reflected in the government's largely pro-US line in regional relations.

DEFENSE

No compulsory military service

$844m

Up 10% in 2002

The military is loyal to the monarchy. It has a reputation for thorough training and professionalism. The forces are dependent on Western support for credit for purchasing advanced arms and equipment, but Jordan, unlike many Arab neighbors, played no part in the 1991 Gulf War.

ECONOMICS

Inflation 2.9% p.a. (1990–2001)

$9.09bn

0.709 Jordanian dinars (0.709)

SCORE CARD

❑ WORLD GNP RANKING	91st
❑ GNP PER CAPITA	$1760
❑ BALANCE OF PAYMENTS	$468m
❑ INFLATION	1.8%
❑ UNEMPLOYMENT	13%

STRENGTHS

Major exporter of phosphates. Skilled workforce. US patronage. Port of Aqaba a special economic zone. Tourism.

WEAKNESSES

Lack of water. Unemployment. High foreign debt. Energy imported: loss of subsidized oil from Iraq. Poor export-to-import ratio. Tourism harmed by regional insecurity. Little arable land.

EXPORTS

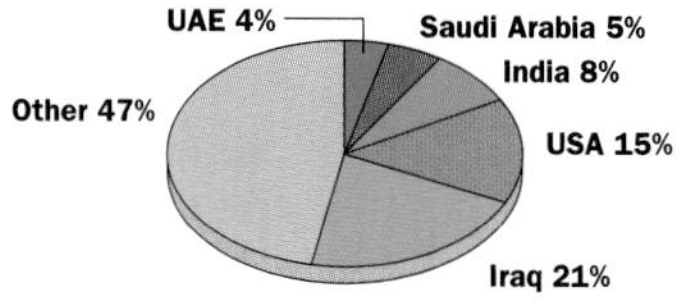
UAE 4%
Saudi Arabia 5%
India 8%
Other 47%
USA 15%
Iraq 21%

IMPORTS

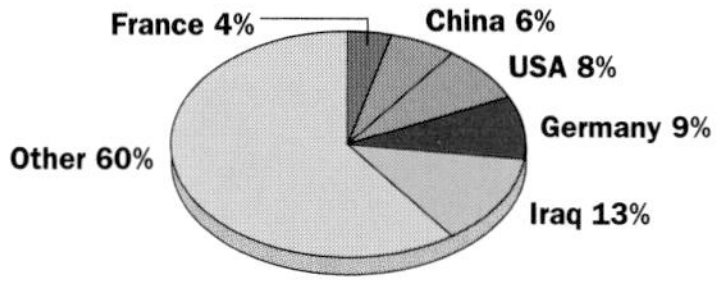
France 4%
China 6%
USA 8%
Germany 9%
Other 60%
Iraq 13%

RESOURCES

Electric power 1.7m kW

1060 tonnes

40 b/d (reserves 1m barrels)

1.48m sheep, 547,490 goats, 24m chickens

Phosphates, potash

Phosphates, livestock, and crops (wheat, tomatoes, olives) are the main resources. Rivers are drying up and groundwater is being pumped at unsustainable rates.

ENVIRONMENT

Sustainability rank: 53rd

3% partially protected

3.2 tonnes per capita

Conservation is a government priority. Rare animals are protected; the Arabian Oryx became extinct in the wild in the 1950s, but is being reintroduced into controlled environments.

MEDIA

TV ownership medium

Daily newspaper circulation 77 per 1000 people

PUBLISHING AND BROADCAST MEDIA

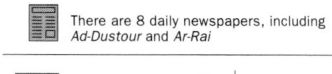

There are 8 daily newspapers, including *Ad-Dustour* and *Ar-Rai*

1 state-controlled service

2 state-controlled services

Press and publications laws were tightened in 2001. However, Internet access is extensive and unrestricted.

CRIME

Death penalty in use

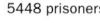

5448 prisoners

Up 7% in 1999

Jordan is largely peaceful. Crime levels are generally low, though theft in urban areas is rising.

EDUCATION

School leaving age: 15

91%

153,965 students

Women have equal access to education. Jordan has a large pool of graduates, who work all over the Middle East.

HEALTH

Welfare state health benefits

1 per 588 people

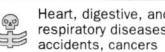

Heart, digestive, and respiratory diseases, accidents, cancers

Health care is subsidized by the government. Hospitals are well distributed throughout the country.

CHRONOLOGY

Jordan, previously the British-mandated territory of Transjordan, became independent in 1946.

- ❑ **1953** Hussein becomes king.
- ❑ **1967** Israel seizes West Bank territories.
- ❑ **1970** Massive crackdown on PLO – Palestine Liberation Organization.
- ❑ **1988** Jordan cedes claims to West Bank to PLO.
- ❑ **1994** Peace treaty with Israel.
- ❑ **1999** Death of King Hussein; succession of King Abdullah II.

***The King's Highway**, seen from the castle at Al Karak, a strategic fortress built by Crusader knights in the 12th century.*

SPENDING

GDP/cap. increase

CONSUMPTION AND SPENDING

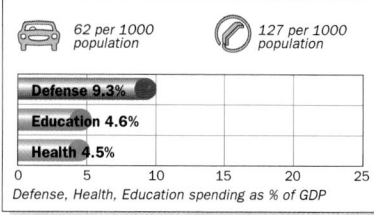

62 per 1000 population

127 per 1000 population

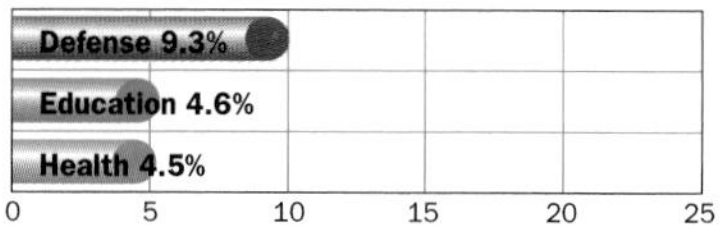
Defense 9.3%
Education 4.6%
Health 4.5%
0
5
10
15
20
25

Defense, Health, Education spending as % of GDP

Poverty is relatively rare among Jordanians, but widespread among refugees; Jordan has the world's highest proportion of refugees to population.

WORLD RANKING

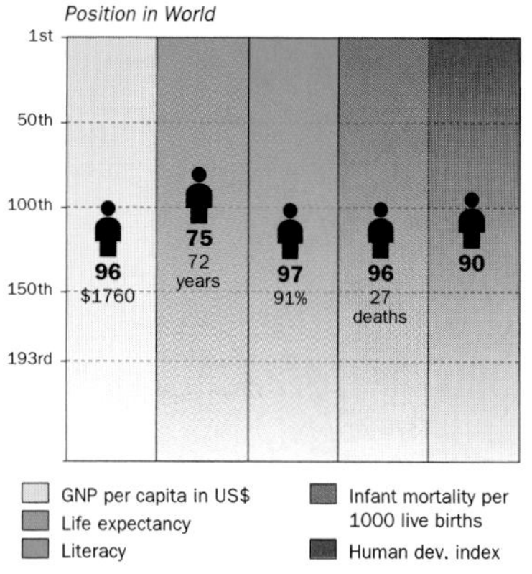
Position in World
1st
50th
100th
150th
193rd
96
$1760
75
72 years
97
91%
96
27 deaths
90
GNP per capita in US$
Life expectancy
Literacy
Infant mortality per 1000 live births
Human dev. index

J

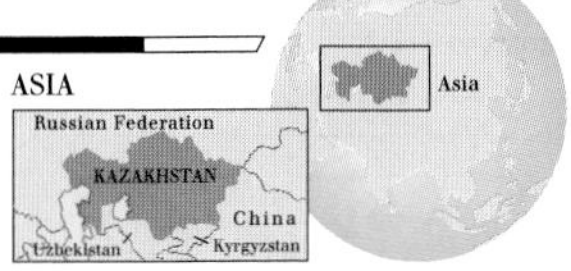
ASIA
Asia
Russian Federation
KAZAKHSTAN
China
Uzbekistan
Kyrgyzstan

KAZAKHSTAN

OFFICIAL NAME: Republic of Kazakhstan **CAPITAL:** Astana
POPULATION: 15.4 million **CURRENCY:** Tenge **OFFICIAL LANGUAGE:** Kazakh

1991 | 1991 | Oct 25 | KZ | +5 to +6 | +7 | .kz

THE SECOND-LARGEST of the former Soviet republics, Kazakhstan extends almost 3000 km (1900 miles) from the Caspian Sea in the west to the Altai Mountains in the east and 1600 km (1000 miles) north to south. It borders Russia to the north and China to the east. Kazakhstan was the last Soviet republic to declare its independence, in 1991. In 1999, elections confirmed the former communist Nursultan Nazarbayev and his supporters in power. Kazakhstan has considerable economic potential, and many Western companies seek to exploit its mineral resources.

***The Altai Mountains**, eastern Kazakhstan. Subject to harsh continental winters, the Altai range is a cold, inhospitable place. Rivers carry meltwater down onto the vast steppe.*

CLIMATE

Cold desert/steppe

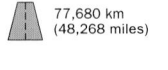

WEATHER CHART FOR ASTANA

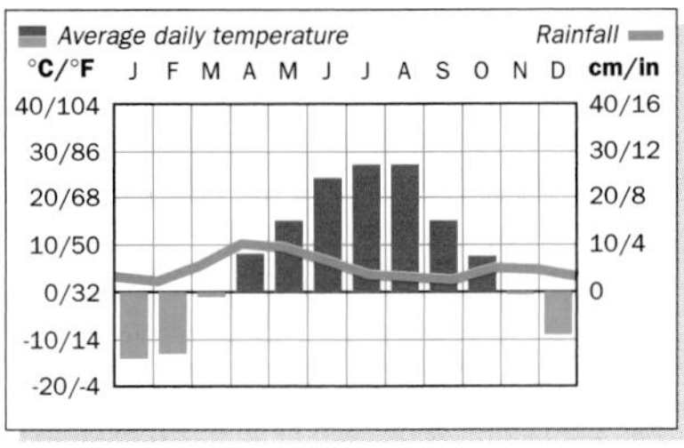
Average daily temperature
Rainfall
°C/°F
J F M A M J J A S O N D
cm/in
40/104
30/86
20/68
10/50
0/32
-10/14
-20/-4
40/16
30/12
20/8
10/4
0

Kazakhstan has a continental climate with large temperature variations: average January temperatures range from –18°C (0°F) on the northern Kazakh steppe to –3°C (27°F) in the deserts 1600 km (1000 miles) to the south; July temperatures average 19°C (66°F) and 30°C (86°F) respectively. The northern Caspian Sea freezes for up to three months in winter.

TRANSPORTATION

Drive on right

Astana 403,428 passengers

20 ships 11,845 grt

THE TRANSPORTATION NETWORK

77,680 km (48,268 miles)

None

13,597 km (8449 miles)

3900 km (2423 miles)

Transportation networks focus on the north and east as the key economic areas. Most of the roads in Kazakhstan are in urgent need of repair. Ambitious plans envisage a rail link to carry freight between China and Iran via the Caspian, rivaling Russia's trans-Siberian route. Helicopters are the main method of transportation for reaching remote destinations.

TOURISM

Visitors : Population 1:5.4

2.83m visitors

Up 53% in 2002

MAIN TOURIST ARRIVALS

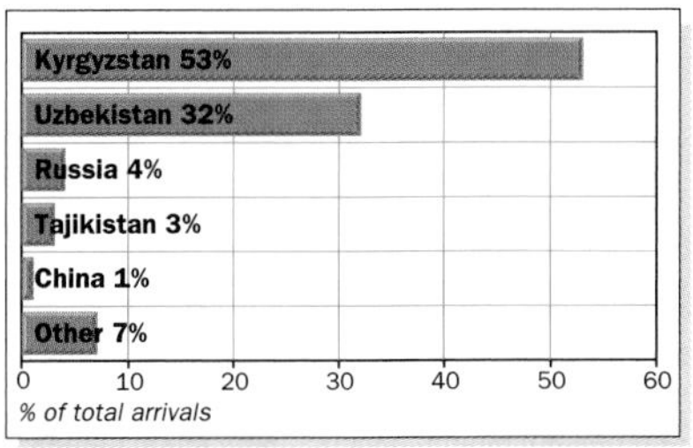
Kyrgyzstan 53%
Uzbekistan 32%
Russia 4%
Tajikistan 3%
China 1%
Other 7%
0
10
20
30
40
50
60
% of total arrivals

Most visitors are business travelers. The post-1991 influx of foreigners, seeking to exploit the country's rich natural resources, turned the former capital Almaty into central Asia's most cosmopolitan city. Tourists are few, but trekking in the Altai Mountains and spurs of the Tien Shan range in the southeast is becoming more popular.

KAZAKHSTAN

Total Area : 2 717 300 sq. km
(1 049 150 sq. miles)

RUSSIAN FEDERATION
Petropavlovsk
Kostanay
Kokshetau
Rudnyy
Shchuchinsk
Pavlodar
Irtysh
Kushmurun
Zhitikara
Yermak
Ishim
Ekibastuz
Atbasar
ASTANA
Semipalatinsk
Leninogorsk
Gora Belukha 4506m
Zyryanovsk
Ust'-Kamenogorsk
Shar
Ural'sk
Aksay
Aktobe
KIRGHIZ STEPPE
Ural
Alga
Uil
Temir
Emba
Ozero Tengiz
Arkalyk
Temirtau
Karaganda
Saran'
Shakhtinsk
Karkaralinsk
Ozero Zaysan
MELKOSOPOCHNIK
KAZAKHSKIY
Ayaguz
Turgay
Atyrau
Chelkar
Satpayev
Zhezkazgan
Balkhash
Ozero Balkhash
Ozero Alakol'
Aral'sk
Aral Sea
Ayteke Bi
Dzhusaly
Syr Darya
Taldykorgan
Tekeli
Ili
Caspian Sea
Fort-Shevchenko
Beyneu
Aktau
USTYURT PLATEAU
Zhanaozen
PESKI MOYYNKUM
Kzylorda
Panfilov
Shu
Almaty
Turkestan
Kentau
Karatau
Taraz
Arys'
Shymkent
Khan Tengri Pik 6398m
UZBEKISTAN
KYRGYZSTAN
CHINA
TURKMENISTAN
POPULATION
over 500 000
over 100 000
over 50 000
over 10 000
under 10 000
LAND HEIGHT
3000m/9843ft
2000m/6562ft
1000m/3281ft
500m/1640ft
200m/656ft
Sea Level
-200m/-656ft
N
0 200 km
0 200 miles

PEOPLE

Pop. density low

Kazakh, Russian, Ukrainian, Tatar, German, Uzbek, Uighur

6/km² (15/mi²)

THE URBAN/RURAL POPULATION SPLIT

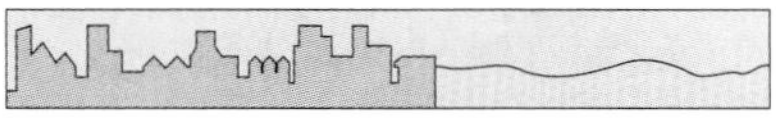
56%
44%

RELIGIOUS PERSUASION

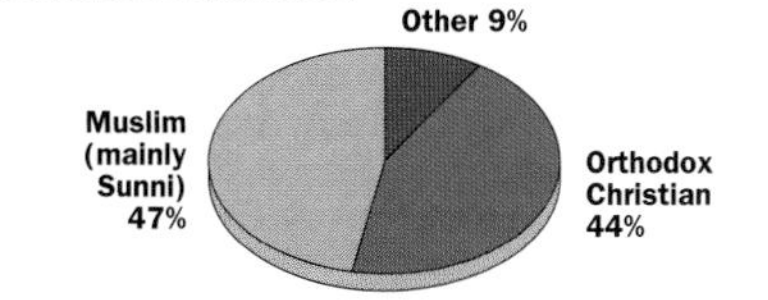
Other 9%
Muslim (mainly Sunni) 47%
Orthodox Christian 44%

ETHNIC MAKEUP

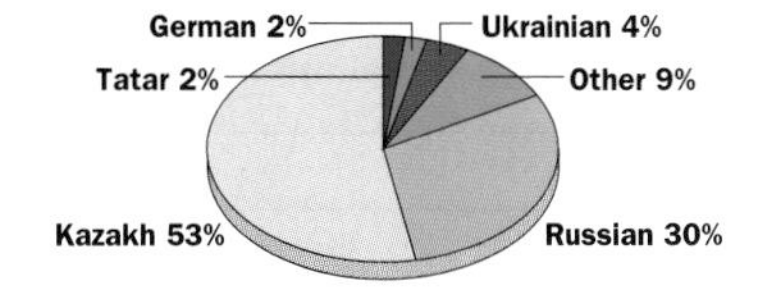
German 2%
Ukrainian 4%
Tatar 2%
Other 9%
Kazakh 53%
Russian 30%

POPULATION AGE BREAKDOWN

Female
Age
Male
0.8%
80+
0.3%
6%
60–79
3.7%
10.8%
40–59
9.6%
15.7%
20–39
15.8%
18.4%
0–19
18.9%
% of population by age group

Kazakhstan's ethnic diversity arose mainly from forced settlement of Tatars, Germans, and Russians during the Soviet era. By 1959, Kazakhs were outnumbered by ethnic Russians. This balance has been redressed by the immigration of ethnic Kazakhs from neighboring states and the departure in the 1990s of some 1.5 million ethnic Russians. In addition, most ethnic Germans have opted to live in Germany, though in 2000 the government began a campaign to try to lure some back.

In 1995, ethnic Russians criticized the country's new constitution for preventing dual citizenship with Russia and replacing Russian with Kazakh as the sole official language. Central control over ethnic Russians has been reinforced by shifting the capital to Astana (formerly Akmola) in the north, where most ethnic Russians reside.

Though few Kazakhs retain their traditional nomadic life, loyalty to the clan remains strong.

POLITICS

Multiparty elections

L. House 1999/2004
U. House 2002/2005

President Nursultan Nazarbayev

AT THE LAST ELECTION

Assembly 77 seats

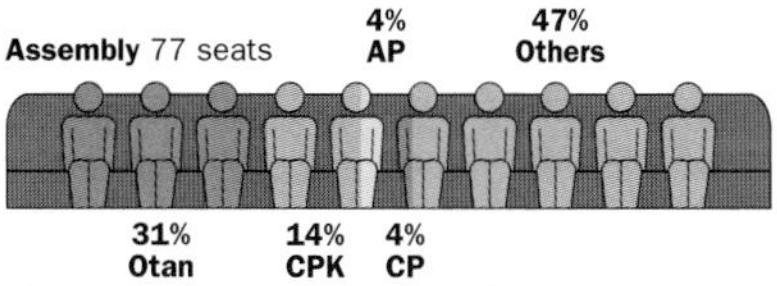
4% AP
47% Others
31% Otan
14% CPK
4% CP

Otan = Fatherland Republican Party of Kazakhstan
CPK = Civil Party of Kazakhstan **AP** = Agrarian Party
CP = Communist Party of Kazakhstan

Senate 39 seats

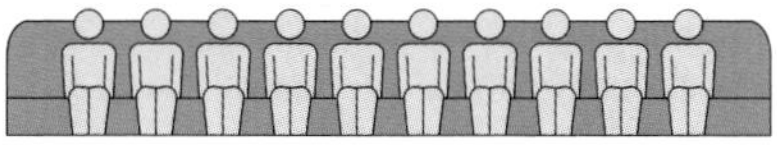

Two members are elected by each of 16 districts and seven are nominated by the president

Legislative authority is vested in the bicameral Parliament. The president has supreme executive power.

PROFILE

Despite a democratic government, the president enjoys political dominance, and the patronage of the Kazakh clans is still important. Since coming to power in 1989, President Nursultan Nazarbayev has concentrated on market reforms and increasing his own powers at the expense of any political opposition. In 2000 the Assembly granted him special powers to advise future presidents after his term expires in 2006, and opposition parties were effectively neutered in 2002 by reform of the party registration process. Opposition leaders are often the focus of corruption charges.

MAIN POLITICAL ISSUES

Presidential powers

Critics accuse Nazarbayev of developing a personality cult. The 1995 constitution strengthened his powers, conferring the right to veto Constitutional Council decisions, and resulting in his being able to ride out a number of controversies. His reelection in early elections in 1999 was tarnished by accusations of voting irregularities and in 2002 he was able to shrug off the revelation that he had moved $1 billion of state oil revenues into a secret overseas bank account, without parliament's knowledge.

The sale of farmland

Legislation allowing the sale of farmland, key to Nazarbayev's economic liberalization, met stiff opposition in 2003. After its ultimately successful struggle to get it passed, the government resigned, to be largely reappointed.

***President Nursultan Nazarbayev**, who steered Kazakhstan to independence.*

WORLD AFFAIRS

Joined UN in 1992

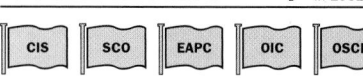

CIS | SCO | EAPC | OIC | OSCE

Relations with Russia are good but sometimes strained by concerns over Kazakhstan's ethnic Russians. However, Kazakhstan's earlier enthusiasm for greater integration of the former Soviet states has cooled.

The country's location, bridging Europe and Asia, has led to close relations with a variety of partners, and its rich mineral resources have attracted investors from Europe, the US, and Asia. Relations with China have improved, with agreements in 1998 and 1999 on border issues, and it joins China, Russia, and three other central Asian republics in the Shanghai Cooperation Organization. However, it competes with Uzbekistan to be the acknowledged central Asian regional power. Kazakhstan's southern borders were only officially delimited in 2003; its boundary with Russia remains disputed.

AID

Recipient

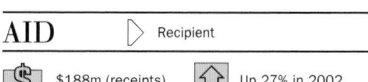

$188m (receipts)

Up 27% in 2002

Kazakhstan joined the IMF and the World Bank in 1992, and is also a member of the EBRD. Most multilateral and bilateral aid is aimed at supporting economic reform and improving health care, transportation, and communications.

CHRONOLOGY

Once part of the Mongol empire, Kazakhstan was absorbed by the Russian Empire in the 19th century. Ethnic Russians began to settle on land used by nomadic Kazakhs. Russian settlement intensified after the 1917 Revolution, and Kazakhstan was subjected to intensive industrial and agricultural development.

- **1916** Rebellion against Russian rule brutally suppressed.
- **1917** Russian Revolution inspires civil war in Kazakhstan between Bolsheviks, anti-Bolsheviks, and Kazakh nationalists.
- **1918** Kazakh nationalists set up autonomous republic.
- **1920** Bolsheviks take control. Kirghiz Autonomous Soviet Socialist Republic (ASSR) set up within Russian Soviet Federative Socialist Republic.
- **1925** Kirghiz ASSR renamed Kazakh ASSR.
- **1936** Kazakhstan becomes full union republic of the USSR as Kazakh SSR.

K

CHRONOLOGY *continued*

- **1930s** Stalin's collectivization program leads to increase in Russian settlement and deaths of an estimated one million Kazakhs. Large penal settlements established for victims of Stalinist purges.
- **1941–1945** Large-scale deportations from Russia of Germans, Jews, Crimean Tatars, and others to Kazakhstan.
- **1949–1989** Nuclear test site at Semipalatinsk carries out nearly 500 nuclear explosions.
- **1954–1960** Khrushchev's policy to plow "Virgin Lands" for grain most vigorously followed in Kazakhstan. Russian settlement reaches peak.
- **1986** Riots in Almaty after ethnic Russian Gennadi Kolbin appointed head of Kazakhstan Communist Party (CPK) to replace Kazakh Dinmukhamed Kunyev.
- **1989** Kolbin replaced by Nursultan Nazarbayev, ethnic Kazakh and chair of Council of Ministers. Reform of political and administrative system.
- **1990** CPK wins elections to Supreme Soviet by overwhelming majority. Nazarbayev appointed first president of Kazakhstan. Kazakhstan declares sovereignty.
- **1991** Kazakhstan votes to preserve USSR as union of sovereign states. USSR authorities hand over control of enterprises in Kazakhstan to Kazakh government. CPK ordered to cease activities in official bodies following abortive August coup in Moscow. CPK restructures itself as Socialist Party of Kazakhstan (SPK). Independence of Republic of Kazakhstan declared; joins CIS. Announcement of closure of Semipalatinsk nuclear test site.
- **1992** Opposition demonstrations against dominance of reformed communists in Supreme Soviet, now Supreme Kenges. Nationalist groups form Republican Party, Azat.
- **1993** Adoption of new constitution. Introduction of new currency, the tenge.
- **1994** Legislative elections annulled after proof of widespread voting irregularities.
- **1995** Adoption of new constitution broadening presidential powers; referendum extends Nazarbayev's term of office.
- **1998** Legislature approves constitutional amendments, including early presidential election.
- **1999** Nazarbayev reelected president for seven more years.
- **2003** Sale of farmland legalized.

DEFENSE

Phasing out conscription

$1.99bn

Up 8% in 2002

KAZAKH ARMED FORCES

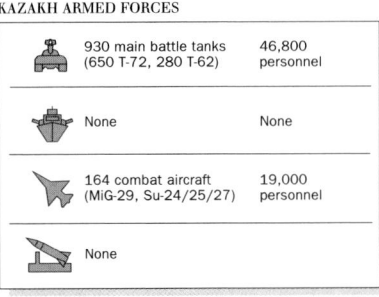

930 main battle tanks (650 T-72, 280 T-62)	46,800 personnel
None	None
164 combat aircraft (MiG-29, Su-24/25/27)	19,000 personnel
None	

Kazakhstan is a potential guarantor of peace and stability in the region. To comply with nonproliferation treaties, it had by 1995 destroyed all its remaining nuclear warheads or had transferred them to Russia. A four-year restructuring of the armed forces was launched in 2001, including moves to end conscription, already shortened.

Kazakhstan was the first central Asian state to offer military assistance in 2001 to the US as part of its "war on terrorism." Since then military ties have become much closer. The US has loaned helicopters and armored vehicles to the Kazakh army, while US warplanes have been granted access to Kazakh airfields. Kazakh engineers were active in the US-led Coalition in Iraq from mid-2003.

ECONOMICS

Inflation 169% p.a. (1990–2001)

$22.6bn

135.9 tenge (147.5)

SCORE CARD

- WORLD GNP RANKING....................60th
- GNP PER CAPITA....................$1520
- BALANCE OF PAYMENTS....................–$596m
- INFLATION....................5.8%
- UNEMPLOYMENT....................9%

EXPORTS

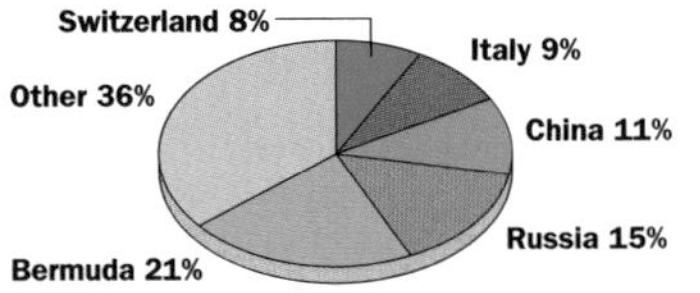
Switzerland 8%
Italy 9%
Other 36%
China 11%
Russia 15%
Bermuda 21%

IMPORTS

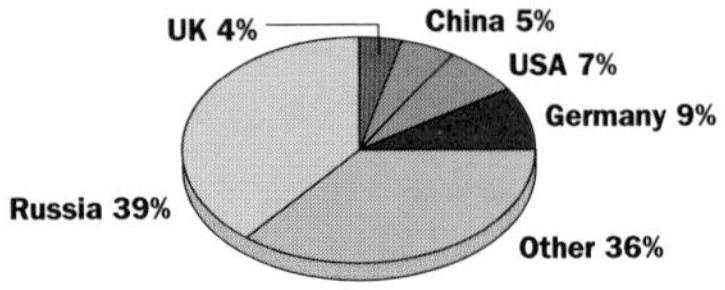
UK 4%
China 5%
USA 7%
Germany 9%
Russia 39%
Other 36%

ECONOMIC PERFORMANCE INDICATOR

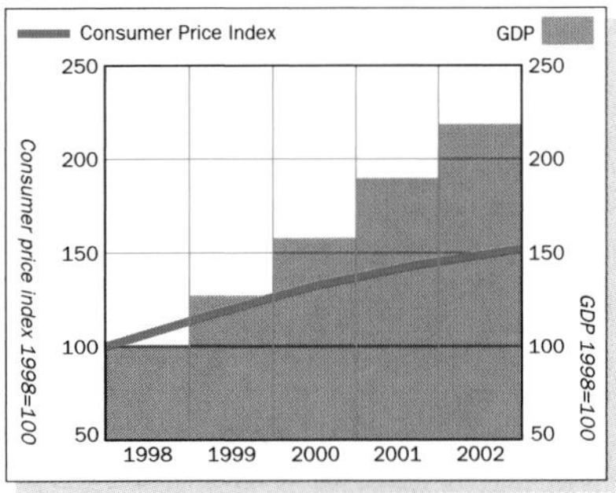
Consumer Price Index
GDP
250
200
150
100
50
1998
1999
2000
2001
2002
Consumer price index 1998=100
GDP 1998=100

STRENGTHS

Mineral resources: oil, gas, bismuth, uranium, and cadmium (used in the electronics industry). Joint oil and gas ventures with Western companies: pipeline from Tengiz oil field opened in 2001. Privatization and liberalization. Baikonur space center.

WEAKNESSES

Collapse of former Soviet economic and trading system. Reliance on imported consumer goods. Overdependence on oil sector. Inefficient industrial plants.

PROFILE

Kazakhstan has moved faster than other former Soviet republics to establish a market economy. Prices have been freed, foreign trade deregulated, and the tax system reformed. Oil revenues have been the main engine of growth, and inflation, at one time rising sharply, has now been brought under control.

Foreign direct investment focuses mainly on the energy sector. Outdated equipment and inadequate distribution networks mean that energy has to be imported, though Kazakhstan exports fossil fuel.

An oil price boom set the tone for the country's first "five-year plan" in 2000, part of President Nazarbayev's "Kazakhstan 2030" program. The sale of agricultural land and property was legalized in 2003.

KAZAKHSTAN : MAJOR BUSINESSES

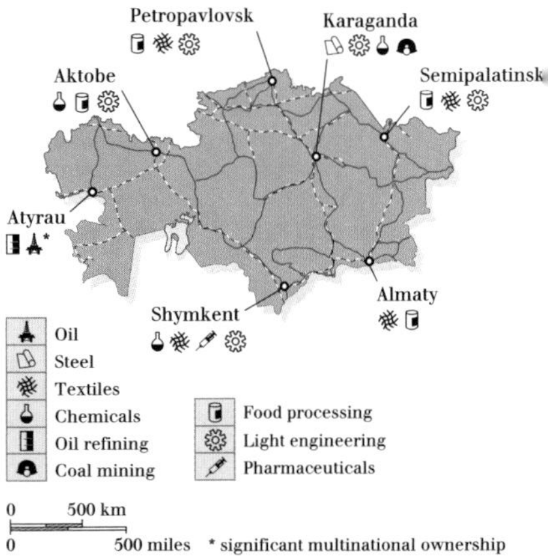
Petropavlovsk
Karaganda
Aktobe
Semipalatinsk
Atyrau
Almaty
Shymkent
Oil
Steel
Textiles
Chemicals
Oil refining
Coal mining
Food processing
Light engineering
Pharmaceuticals
0 500 km
0 500 miles
* significant multinational ownership

RESOURCES

Electric power 19m kW

31,071 tonnes

1.11m b/d (reserves 9bn barrels)

9.92m sheep, 4.56m cattle, 23.6m chickens

Oil, gas, uranium, gold, silver, coal, iron, tungsten, chromite, bismuth, cadmium

ELECTRICITY GENERATION

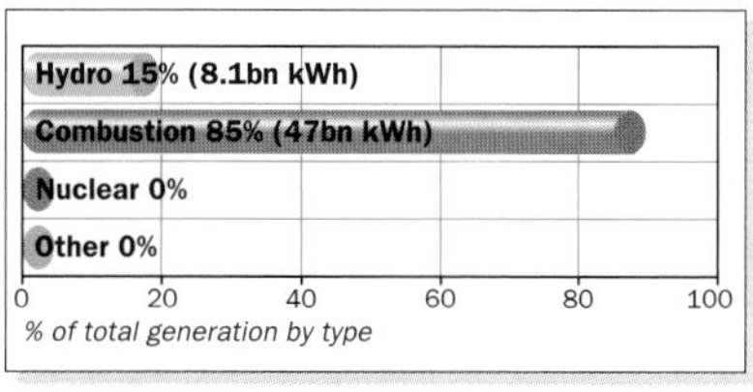
Hydro 15% (8.1bn kWh)
Combustion 85% (47bn kWh)
Nuclear 0%
Other 0%
0
20
40
60
80
100
% of total generation by type

Large oil and gas reserves were confirmed in the Caspian region in 2000, rewarding investments from overseas companies from the US, Russia, and Japan. A pipeline connecting the western Tengiz oil field to the Black Sea via Russia was opened in 2001. There are also vast iron ore and gold reserves and the world's second-largest uranium reserves after Canada.

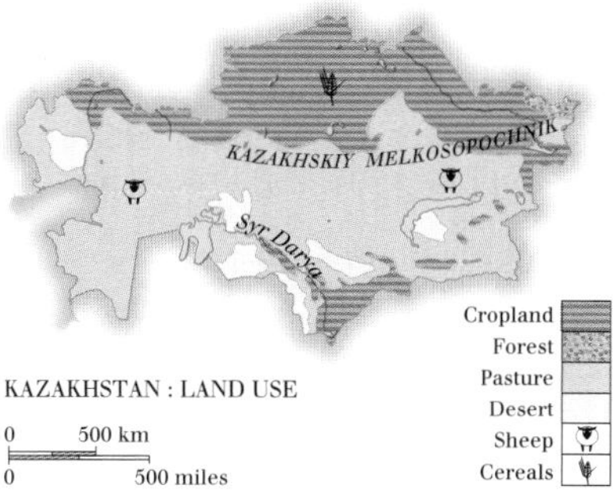
KAZAKHSKIY MELKOSOPOCHNIK
Syr Darya
Cropland
Forest
Pasture
Desert
Sheep
Cereals
0
500 km
0
500 miles

KAZAKHSTAN : LAND USE

ENVIRONMENT

Sustainability rank: 88th

3% (2% partially protected)

8.1 tonnes per capita

ENVIRONMENTAL TREATIES

No · Yes · Yes

Yes · No · No

Major environmental damage has been caused by intensive industrial and agricultural development. Eastern cities are heavily polluted and farmlands are being eroded. Half the country faces desertification. The northern Aral Sea is the focus for conservation efforts: the shallower southern sea will dry up completely by 2020. Environmental groups succeeded in ending nuclear testing at Semey (Semipalatinsk) and the green lobby is now pressing for tighter pollution controls.

MEDIA

TV ownership high

Daily newspaper circulation 30 per 1000 people

PUBLISHING AND BROADCAST MEDIA

There are 7 principal daily newspapers and over 900 other registered newspapers

2 state-owned services, several private services

1 state-owned service, several private stations

The state-owned media operate alongside independent publications and privately owned radio and television stations. Recent revisions to the Media Law have strengthened state control over broadcast outlets and Internet sites, and created more grounds for libel charges against editors and proprietors. Such state pressure has produced a drastic decline in the number of media outlets.

CRIME

Moratorium on death penalty

84,000 prisoners

Up 9% in 2000–2001

CRIME RATES

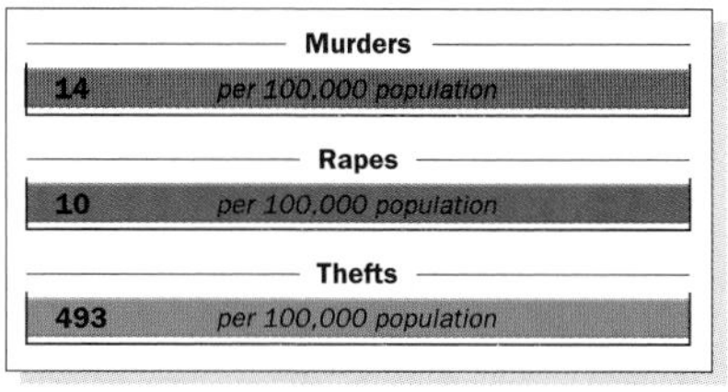
Murders
14 per 100,000 population
Rapes
10 per 100,000 population
Thefts
493 per 100,000 population

Narcotics smuggling is increasing. Corruption is rife. Political opponents are frequently jailed. Kazakhstan introduced life imprisonment as an alternative to the death penalty in 2004.

EDUCATION

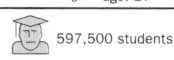

School leaving age: 17

99%

597,500 students

THE EDUCATION SYSTEM

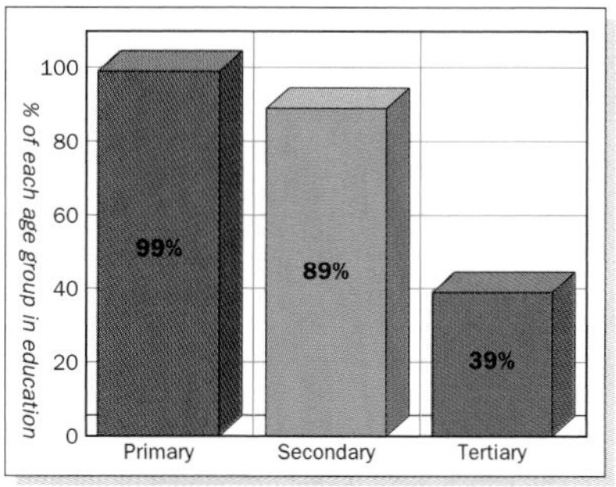
100
80
60
40
20
0
% of each age group in education
99%
89%
39%
Primary
Secondary
Tertiary

Education remains based on the Soviet model. Since its adoption as the state language in 1995, Kazakh is gradually replacing Russian as the main instruction medium in schools, but there is a shortage of Kazakh textbooks and Kazakh-speaking teachers. There are a large number of higher-education institutions and medical schools.

HEALTH

Welfare state health benefits

1 per 278 people

Cerebrovascular and heart diseases, cancers, accidents, violence

Kazakhstan's ill-equipped and poorly funded health system has produced the lowest average life expectancy in central Asia.

The health system is limited in terms of both facilities and coverage. Rural people have minimal access to clinics. The country's size means that extending coverage and improving the quality of care will be costly. Attempts are therefore being made to attract foreign investment into the health sector. Many doctors have emigrated to Russia.

SPENDING

GDP/cap. decrease

CONSUMPTION AND SPENDING

64 per 1000 population

130 per 1000 population

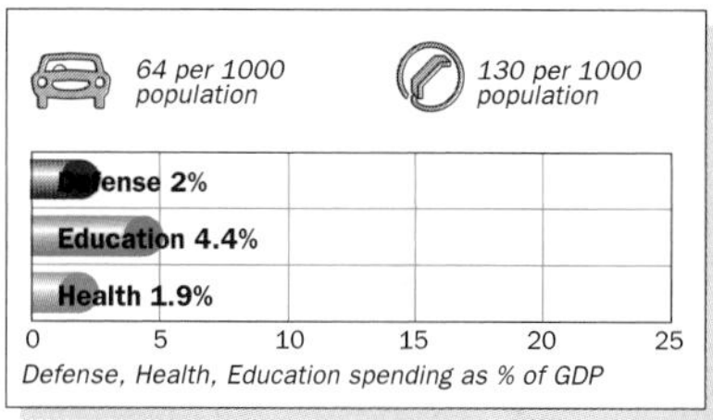
Defense 2%
Education 4.4%
Health 1.9%
0
5
10
15
20
25
Defense, Health, Education spending as % of GDP

Life for the majority of Kazakhs has always been hard, and has grown even more difficult since 1989. Unemployment rose and living standards deteriorated as a result of the market-oriented reforms within Kazakhstan in the 1990s. In addition, the liberalization of the economy has had the effect of fueling sharp price rises for essential commodities.

The rural population, the poorest group in Kazakhstan, has been badly affected. The small wealthy elite is made up mainly of former communist officials, many of whom have benefited from privatization or are members of President Nazarbayev's clan.

WORLD RANKING

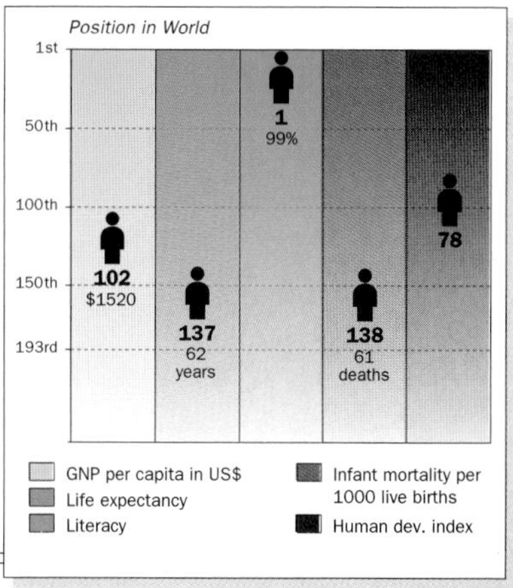
Position in World
1st
50th
100th
150th
193rd
102
$1520
137
62
years
1
99%
138
61
deaths
78
GNP per capita in US$
Life expectancy
Literacy
Infant mortality per 1000 live births
Human dev. index

K

KENYA

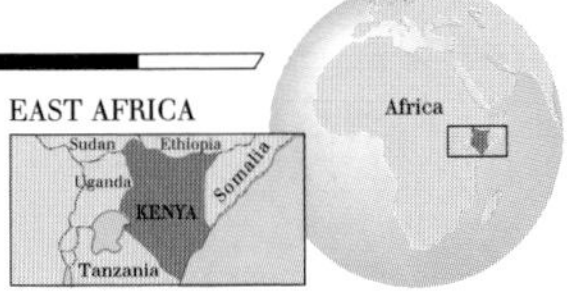
EAST AFRICA
Sudan
Ethiopia
Uganda
Somalia
KENYA
Tanzania
Africa

OFFICIAL NAME: Republic of Kenya **CAPITAL:** Nairobi
POPULATION: 32 million **CURRENCY:** Kenya shilling **OFFICIAL LANGUAGES:** Kiswahili and English

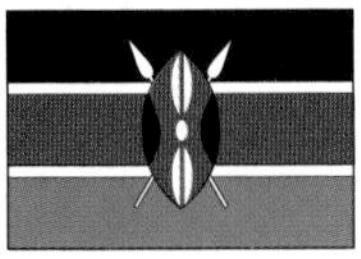

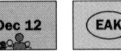

1963 | 1963 | Dec 12 | EAK | +3 | +254 | .ke

KENYA STRADDLES the equator on Africa's east coast. Its central plateau is bisected by the Great Rift Valley. The land to the north is desert, while to the east lies a fertile coastal belt. After independence from the UK in 1963, politics was dominated by Jomo Kenyatta. He was succeeded as president in 1978 by Daniel arap Moi, whose divide-and-rule policies drew accusations of favoritism and of fomenting ethnic hatreds. After 40 years in power, his KANU was finally defeated in 2002. Economic mainstays are tourism and agriculture.

__Kenyatta Conference Center,__ Nairobi. The modern skyline of the business center contrasts sharply with the slums on the city's outskirts.

CLIMATE

Steppe/mountain/tropical

WEATHER CHART FOR NAIROBI

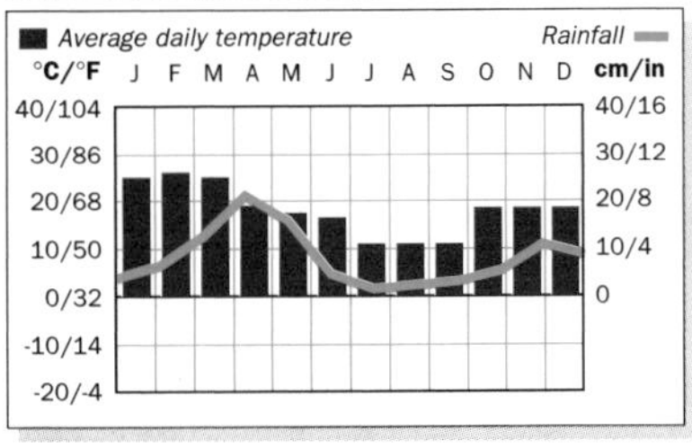
Average daily temperature
Rainfall
°C/°F
J F M A M J J A S O N D
cm/in
40/104
30/86
20/68
10/50
0/32
-10/14
-20/-4
40/16
30/12
20/8
10/4
0

The coast and Great Rift Valley are hot and humid, the plateau interior is temperate, and the northeastern desert hot and dry. Rain generally falls from April to May and October to November.

TRANSPORTATION

Drive on left

Jomo Kenyatta International, Nairobi 3.25m passengers

36 ships 19,100 grt

THE TRANSPORTATION NETWORK

7673 km (4768 miles)

None

2634 km (1637 miles)

Lake Victoria is navigable

Road conditions in Kenya vary greatly, though most are still unpaved. The main railroad connects Mombasa with the highland interior. There are over 200 airstrips across the country.

__Great Rift Valley,__ Kenya. This huge crack in the Earth's crust runs from Jordan right through Africa to the Zambezi River.

TOURISM

Visitors : Population 1:38

838,000 visitors

Little change in 2002

MAIN TOURIST ARRIVALS

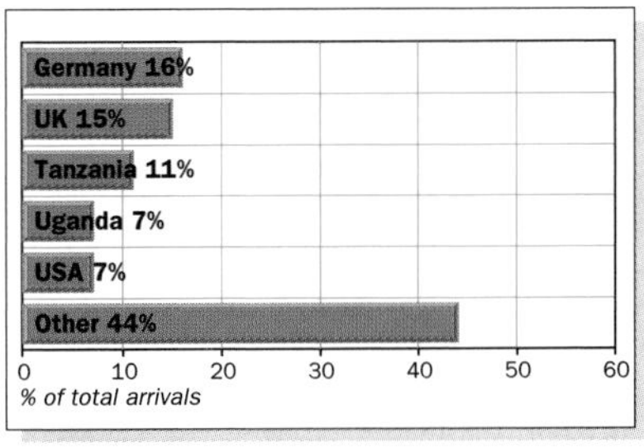
Germany 16%
UK 15%
Tanzania 11%
Uganda 7%
USA 7%
Other 44%
0
10
20
30
40
50
60
% of total arrivals

Tourism is vital to the economy and a key foreign exchange earner. After a boom in package safaris and beach vacations during the 1980s, Kenya has seen a general decline in visitor numbers since. World recession, reports of instability, the much-publicized murder of several tourists in the 1990s, and, more recently, a series of Islamist terrorist attacks have been to blame.

KENYA

Total Area : 582 650 sq. km (224 961 sq. miles)

POPULATION

- over 1 000 000
- over 500 000
- over 100 000
- over 50 000
- over 10 000
- under 10 000

LAND HEIGHT

- 3000m/9843ft
- 2000m/6562ft
- 1000m/3281ft
- 500m/1640ft
- 200m/656ft
- Sea Level

SUDAN
ETHIOPIA
SOMALIA
UGANDA
TANZANIA
ELEMI TRIANGLE
Lokitaung
Lake Turkana (Lake Rudolf)
Lodwar
CHALBI DESERT
Moyale
Marsabit
Wajir
BOKHOL PLAIN
GREAT RIFT VALLEY
Maralal
Kapenguria
Kitale
Eldoret
Bungoma
Kakamega
Busia
Kisumu
Winam Gulf
Kericho
Kisii
Homa Bay
Lake Victoria
Nakuru
Nyeri
Nanyuki
Isiolo
Meru
Kirinyaga 5199m
Embu
Thika
NAIROBI
Machakos
Kitui
Garissa
Narok
Magadi
Lake Magadi
Namanga
Oloitokitok
Taveta
Voi
Malindi
Kilifi
Mombasa
Kwale
Lamu
Garsen
Equator
INDIAN OCEAN
N
0 100 km
0 100 miles

PEOPLE

Pop. density medium

Kiswahili, English, Kikuyu, Luo, Kalenjin, Kamba

56/km² (146/mi²)

THE URBAN/RURAL POPULATION SPLIT

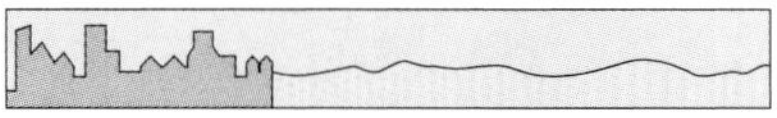
35%
65%

RELIGIOUS PERSUASION

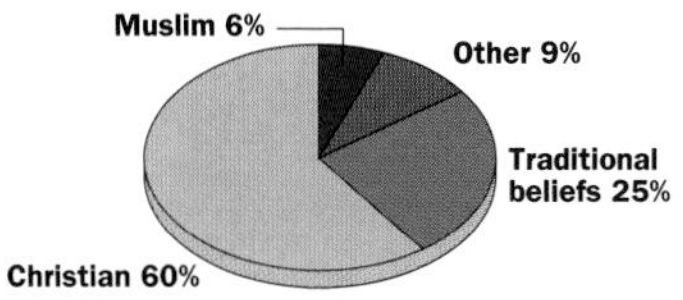
Muslim 6%
Other 9%
Traditional beliefs 25%
Christian 60%

ETHNIC MAKEUP

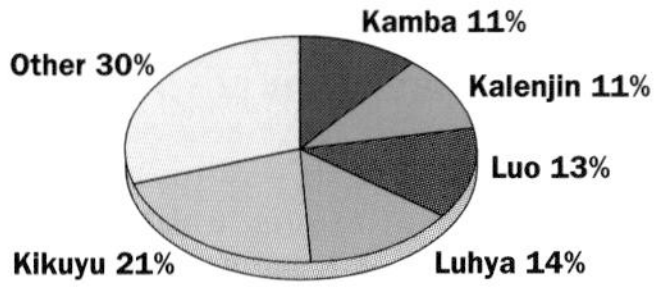
Kamba 11%
Other 30%
Kalenjin 11%
Luo 13%
Kikuyu 21%
Luhya 14%

Kenya's ethnic diversity, with about 70 different groups, reflects its past as a crossroads for population movements. Asians, Europeans, and Arabs form 1% of the population. The rural majority retains strong clan and extended family links, though these are being weakened by urban migration. Poverty, severe drought, and years of high population growth have created a land hunger which has fueled ethnic violence.

Though gender equality is written into law, social tradition means that women suffer from social, economic, and sexual repression. Violence and abuse are widespread, including female genital mutilation, criminalized only in 2001. The incidence of both AIDS and illiteracy is higher among women.

POPULATION AGE BREAKDOWN

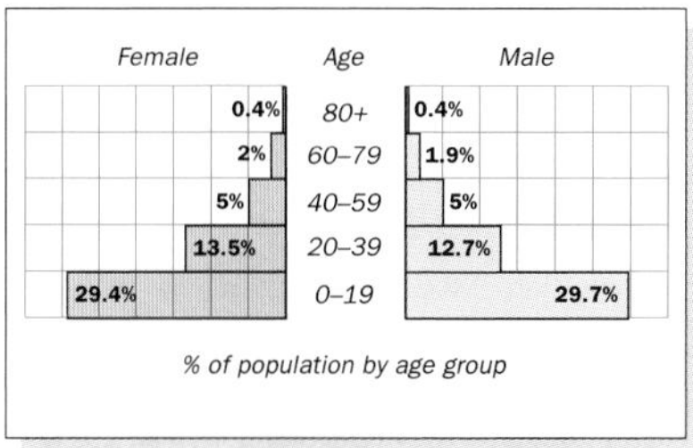
Female
Age
Male
0.4%
80+
0.4%
2%
60–79
1.9%
5%
40–59
5%
13.5%
20–39
12.7%
29.4%
0–19
29.7%
% of population by age group

POLITICS

Multiparty elections

2002/2007

President Mwai Kibaki

AT THE LAST ELECTION

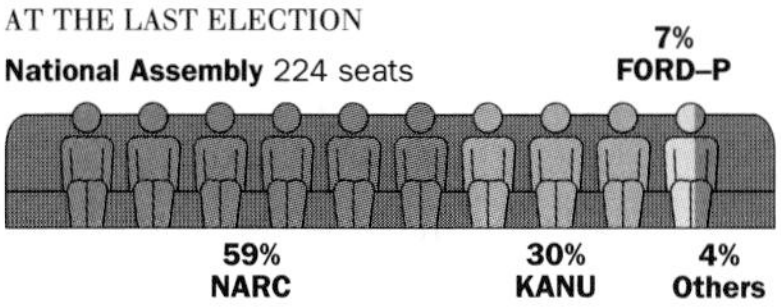
National Assembly 224 seats
7% FORD–P
59% NARC
30% KANU
4% Others

NARC = National Rainbow Coalition (including the Liberal Democratic Party–**LDP**, the Democratic Party–**DP**, and **FORD-Kenya**) **KANU** = Kenya African National Union **FORD–P** = Forum for the Restoration of Democracy–People Others include FORD–Asili, Sisi Kwa Sisi, Safina, Shirikisho, and two ex officio members.

The National Assembly comprises 210 elected members, 12 nominated by the president, and two ex officio members

KANU dominated Kenya for four decades, from independence in 1963 until its defeat in elections in 2002.

PROFILE

International criticism of human rights abuses, and internal unrest in response to President Daniel arap Moi's attempt to entrench KANU's power, forced the introduction of multipartyism in 1992. Despite increasing unpopularity, KANU and Moi remained in power in the face of a divided opposition and amid widespread allegations of electoral irregularities. Under Moi's presidency smaller ethnic groups had gained ascendancy in the ruling party and government, while the majority Kikuyu increasingly supported the opposition.

Moi's attempt to impose Uhuru, son of Jomo Kenyatta, Kenya's first president, as KANU candidate for the 2002 elections alienated many senior party members. NARC heavily defeated KANU in legislative elections, and Mwai Kibaki was elected president.

MAIN POLITICAL ISSUE

Government corruption

High-level corruption is entrenched in Kenyan politics and culture, and international donors pressed Moi to address the problem. In 2001 an anticorruption drive headed by former opposition figure Richard Leakey produced a "list of shame" which included senior government ministers. President Kibaki has promised to usher in a new corruption-free era, but will spare Moi himself from prosecution.

Daniel arap Moi, *dictatorial president 1978–2002.*

President Mwai Kibaki, *opposition figure elected in 2002.*

AID

Recipient

$393m (receipts)

Down 15% in 2002

Kenya has been a major recipient of aid from the World Bank, the US, the EU, Japan, and the UK. Little, however, has trickled down to the majority of the population. This is partly because of the high proportion of aid tied to contracts for firms from donor countries, and partly because of mismanagement and corruption. In 1996 aid disbursements were linked to improvements in human rights, and in 2001 the IMF and the World Bank withheld all aid pending anticorruption reforms. A budget deficit of almost $1 billion prompted a call in 2003 for financial aid.

CHRONOLOGY

From the 10th century, Arab coastal settlers mixed with indigenous peoples in the region. Britain's need for a route to landlocked Uganda led to the formation in 1895 of the British East African Protectorate in the coastal region.

- **1900–1918** White settlement.
- **1920** Interior becomes UK colony.
- **1930** Jomo Kenyatta goes to UK; stays 14 years.
- **1944** Kenyan African Union (KAU) formed; Kenyatta returns to lead it.
- **1952–1956** Mau Mau, Kikuyu-led violent campaign to restore African lands. State of emergency; 13,000 people killed.
- **1953** KAU banned. Kenyatta jailed.
- **1960** State of emergency ends. Tom Mboya and Oginga Odinga form KANU.
- **1961** Kenyatta freed; takes up presidency of KANU.
- **1963** KANU wins elections. Kenyatta prime minister. Full independence declared.
- **1964** Republic of Kenya formed with Kenyatta as president and Odinga as vice president.
- **1966** Odinga defects from KANU to form Kenya People's Union (KPU).

WORLD AFFAIRS

Joined UN in 1963

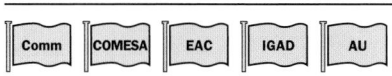

Comm | COMESA | EAC | IGAD | AU

Relations with neighboring states and with key Western donors are Kenya's priorities. In 1991, human rights issues were partly responsible for a two-year suspension of aid.

Kenya has become increasingly concerned about its apparent status as a "soft target" for terrorists seeking to attack the US and its allies. When the US embassy was destroyed by a car bomb in 1998, 254 people were killed and over 5000 injured, and in 2002, 15 died when a hotel was bombed in Mombasa in an attack aimed at Israelis.

Kenya is wary of the volatile security situations in neighboring states. It has recently sought to mediate in the many-sided conflict in Somalia, and hosted peace talks in 2002.

K

CHRONOLOGY *continued*

- **1969** KANU sole party to contest elections (also 1974). Tom Mboya of KANU assassinated. Unrest. KPU banned and Odinga arrested.
- **1978** Kenyatta dies. Vice President Daniel arap Moi succeeds him.
- **1982** Kenya declared a one-party state. Opposition to Moi. Abortive air force coup. Odinga rearrested.
- **1986** Open "queue-voting" replaces secret ballot in first stage of general elections. Other measures to extend Moi's powers stir up opposition.
- **1988** Moi wins third term and extends his control over judiciary.
- **1990** Government implicated in deaths of Foreign Minister Robert Ouko and Anglican archbishop. Riots. Odinga and others form FORD, outlawed by government.
- **1991** Arrest of FORD leaders, attempts to stop prodemocracy demonstrations. Donors suspend aid. Moi agrees to introduce multiparty system. Ethnic violence increases.
- **1992** FORD splits into factions. Opposition weakness helps Moi win elections.
- **1994** Odinga dies.
- **1997** Widely criticized elections.
- **1998** Bomb at US embassy kills 254.
- **1999** Moi appoints paleontologist Richard Leakey to lead government drive against corruption.
- **2000–2001** Worst drought since 1947 threatens millions with starvation.
- **2002** Thousands displaced by recurrence of major floods. Israeli tourists targeted in terrorist attacks. December, elections: KANU defeated by NARC and Mwai Kibaki elected president.

DEFENSE

No compulsory military service

$348m

Up 14% in 2002

KENYAN ARMED FORCES

78 main battle tanks (Vickers Mk 3)	20,000 personnel
4 patrol boats	1620 personnel
29 combat aircraft (9 F-5E/F)	2500 personnel
None	

The destabilization of the northeastern border by insecurity in Somalia is the main defense issue. The army has been deployed to suppress tribal fighting in the remote regions of the country. Military aid is provided by the UK and the US.

ECONOMICS

Inflation 13% p.a. (1990–2001)

$11.2bn

79.33 Kenya shillings (73.8)

SCORE CARD

- World GNP Ranking 85th
- GNP per Capita $360
- Balance of Payments $84m
- Inflation 2%
- Unemployment 40%

EXPORTS

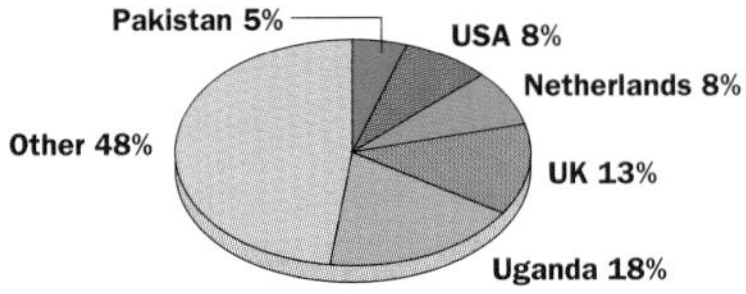

Pakistan 5%
USA 8%
Netherlands 8%
Other 48%
UK 13%
Uganda 18%

IMPORTS

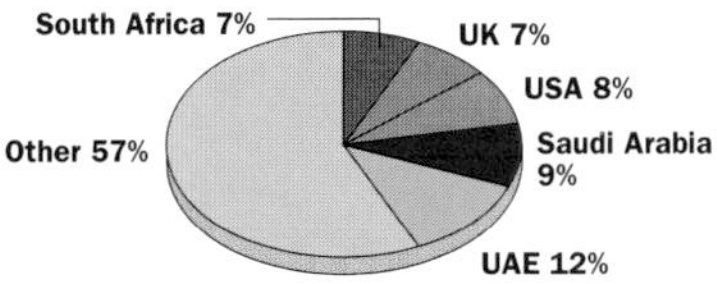

South Africa 7%
UK 7%
USA 8%
Other 57%
Saudi Arabia 9%
UAE 12%

Strengths

Tourism – largest foreign exchange earner. Broad agricultural base, especially cash crops such as coffee and tea. East Africa's largest, most diversified manufacturing sector.

Weaknesses

Fluctuating world prices for coffee and tea. Corruption. Poor recent GDP growth. High population growth in 1980s and 1990s. Land shortage means uneconomic small units. Country's image problem affects tourism.

Profile

Kenya has been hailed as an example to the rest of Africa of the benefits of a mainly free-market economy. Government involvement has been relatively limited, and recently further reduced by privatization. Foreign investment has been encouraged, with some success. Tourism has become the leading foreign exchange earner over the past 20 years, despite suffering serious setbacks since the 1990s. Manufacturing now accounts for 20% of GDP, and is the most diversified sector in east Africa, but needs to expand rapidly in order to create more jobs.

Economic growth was good by African standards during the 1980s, averaging over 4% a year. However, it was barely sufficient to compensate for one of the world's highest population growth rates, at its peak around 4.2%. For the majority of Kenyans, farming ever-smaller landholdings or earning a living in the informal sector, life has become harsher. The situation was exacerbated in 2001 by a ban on all trade with Somalia, which affected exports of the widely grown mild narcotic, qat. Severe drought from 2000 crippled the agricultural sector and put 20 million people at risk of starvation. By 2004, however, the population growth rate had almost halved.

The rise in poverty-linked violence and political unrest hit tourism; earnings fell by 15% in the early 1990s, and the industry had yet to recover fully when a global downturn caused further problems in 2001.

Other problems, including inflation, a heavy debt burden, and growing dependence on balance-of-payments support had come to a head in the early 1990s, when economic growth gave way to recession. Real GDP growth fell to 0.4% in 1992. The government responded with some economic liberalization measures, including floating the Kenyan shilling and raising interest rates. GDP growth, however, remained low, or even negative.

The Kibaki government has faced a formidable task, since taking office in 2002. Corruption has been met head on, allowing a slight boost in investor confidence; GDP growth even climbed, albeit to just 1.7%, in 2003.

ECONOMIC PERFORMANCE INDICATOR

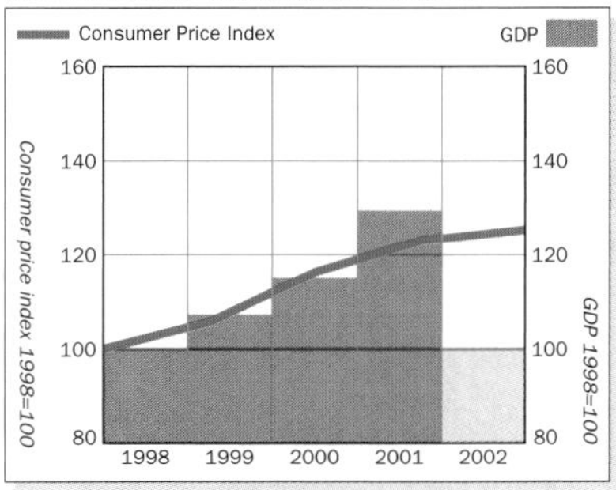

Consumer Price Index
GDP
160
140
120
100
80
1998
1999
2000
2001
2002
Consumer price index 1998=100
GDP 1998=100

KENYA : MAJOR BUSINESSES

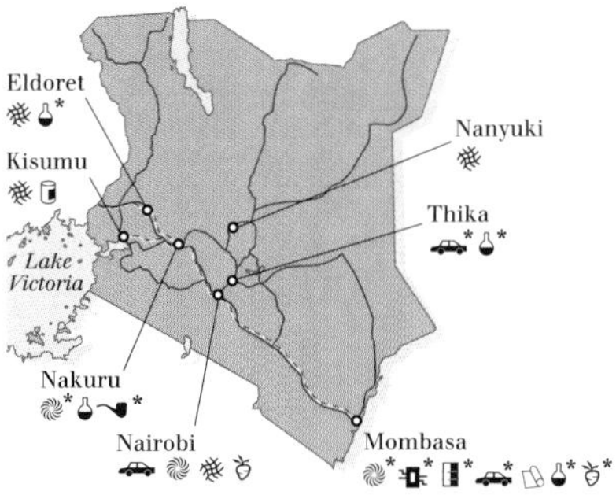

Eldoret
Kisumu
Lake Victoria
Nanyuki
Thika
Nakuru
Nairobi
Mombasa

- Cement
- Tobacco
- Oil refining
- Electronics
- Steel
- Textiles
- Vehicle assembly
- Food processing
- Agribusiness
- Chemicals

0 100 km
0 100 miles

* significant multinational ownership

RESOURCES

Electric power 1.1m kW

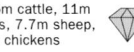

165,160 tonnes

Oil reserves not yet exploited; refines 41,400 b/d

11.5m cattle, 11m goats, 7.7m sheep, 28m chickens

Soda ash, fluorite, limestone, rubies, gold, vermiculite, oil, titaium

ELECTRICITY GENERATION

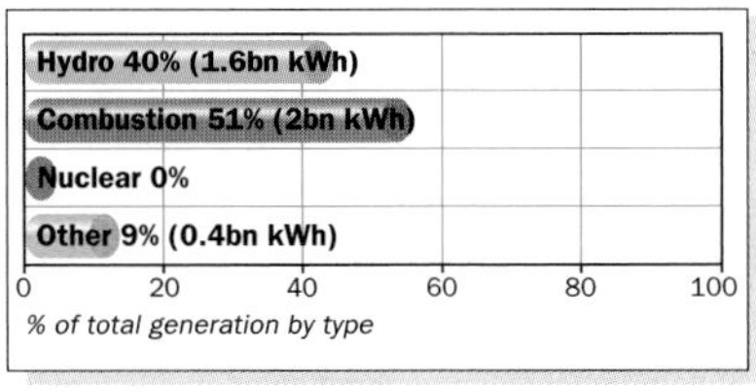
Hydro 40% (1.6bn kWh)
Combustion 51% (2bn kWh)
Nuclear 0%
Other 9% (0.4bn kWh)
0
20
40
60
80
100
% of total generation by type

Agriculture is still a key sector of the economy. Kenya's varied topography means that tropical, subtropical, and temperate crops may be grown. Coffee and tea, the main export crops, have been affected by falling world prices. Efforts to reduce dependence on these have led to the growth of a successful export-oriented horticultural industry.

A deal to mine titanium was signed with a Canadian firm in 2004. Oil exploration has revealed deposits in Turkana District. Hydropower provides two-fifths of electricity, and other sources are being developed to reduce the adverse effects of droughts; dry spells caused power shortages in 2000 and 2001, leading to the imposition of daily power cuts.

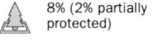

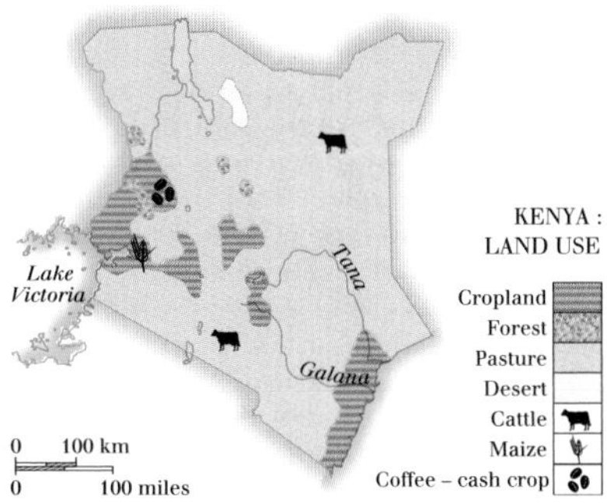
KENYA : LAND USE
Lake Victoria
Tana
Galana
Cropland
Forest
Pasture
Desert
Cattle
Maize
Coffee – cash crop
0 100 km
0 100 miles

ENVIRONMENT

Sustainability rank: 89th

8% (2% partially protected)

0.3 tonnes per capita

ENVIRONMENTAL TREATIES

Yes	Yes	Yes
Yes	Yes	No

The importance to tourism of wildlife conservation is recognized, and recent elephant protection schemes have been a success, but proposed national reserves compete with agriculture for land. Opposition to government plans to reallocate some national park land to squatters is growing.

MEDIA

TV ownership low

Daily newspaper circulation 8 per 1000 people

PUBLISHING AND BROADCAST MEDIA

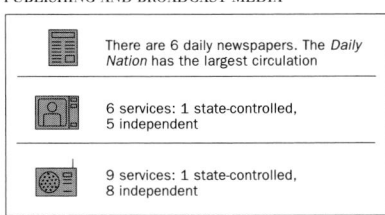

There are 6 daily newspapers. The *Daily Nation* has the largest circulation

6 services: 1 state-controlled, 5 independent

9 services: 1 state-controlled, 8 independent

Government intolerance of criticism is long-standing and includes plays and novels as well as the media. Ngugi wa Thiongo, Kenya's most famous novelist, was exiled for his criticism of KANU.

CRIME

Death penalty not used in practice

35,278 prisoners

Crime is rising

CRIME RATES

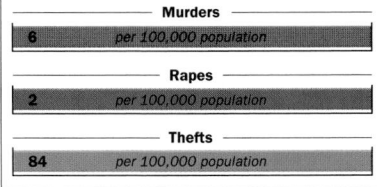

Murders
6 per 100,000 population

Rapes
2 per 100,000 population

Thefts
84 per 100,000 population

Nairobi's high crime levels are spreading countrywide as a result of worsening poverty, ethnic violence, and rising banditry in the northeast. An increase in the use of guns underlies the rapid increase in violent crime.

EDUCATION

School leaving age: 14

84%

98,583 students

THE EDUCATION SYSTEM

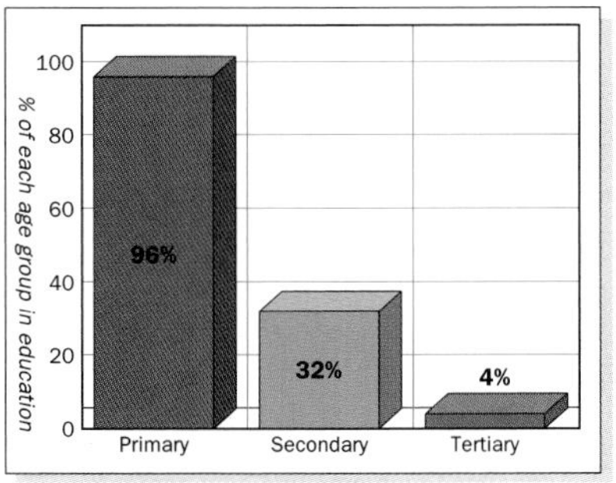
100
80
60
40
20
0
% of each age group in education
96%
32%
4%
Primary
Secondary
Tertiary

The education system is loosely based on the British model. Primary education, which lasts for eight years from the age of six, is free and compulsory. Attendance is over 90% of the age group, which contrasts sharply with the high drop-out rate in secondary schools. Many private higher education institutions are theological colleges.

HEALTH

Welfare state health benefits

1 per 10,000 people

Respiratory and diarrheal diseases, malaria, AIDS

The health system is a mixture of state and private facilities, the latter mainly run by charities and missions. Poverty-related illness, particularly among women and children, is increasing. In 2004 the government began to provide free basic health care to the poorest third of the population. HIV and AIDS reached epidemic proportions in some areas in the 1990s, and the UN calculated that by 2004 there were 650,000 AIDS orphans. Estimates of the national level of infection with HIV were revised downward, however, to around 7% of adults.

SPENDING

GDP/cap. increase

CONSUMPTION AND SPENDING

8 per 1000 population

10 per 1000 population

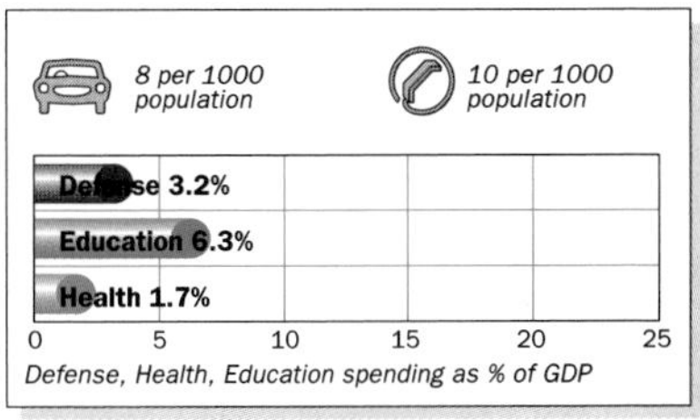
Defense 3.2%
Education 6.3%
Health 1.7%
0
5
10
15
20
25
Defense, Health, Education spending as % of GDP

Wealth disparities in Kenya are large and growing, exacerbated by land hunger and migration to the cities, where jobs are few and existence depends on the informal economy. More than half of all town dwellers live in slums, and the slum dwellers of Nairobi's Amarthi Valley are among Africa's poorest, worst-nourished people. Their lives contrast sharply with those of the country's elite – top government officials with access to patronage; white Kenyans, who derive their wealth largely from agricultural estates; and the largely Asian business community. Landless peasants have pushed for a redistribution of land similar to that in Zimbabwe.

WORLD RANKING

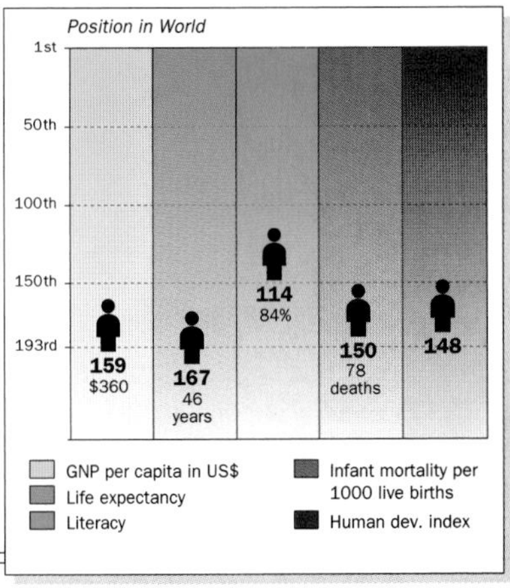
Position in World
1st
50th
100th
150th
193rd
159
$360
167
46
years
114
84%
150
78
deaths
148
GNP per capita in US$
Life expectancy
Literacy
Infant mortality per 1000 live births
Human dev. index

K

KIRIBATI

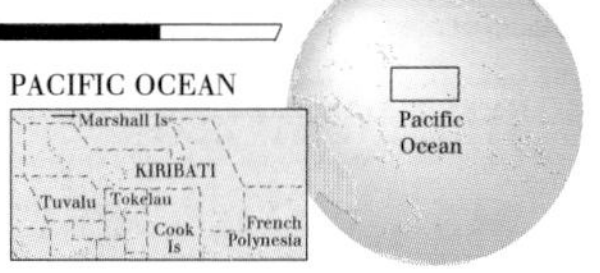
PACIFIC OCEAN
Pacific Ocean
Marshall Is
KIRIBATI
Tuvalu
Tokelau
Cook Is
French Polynesia

OFFICIAL NAME: Republic of Kiribati **CAPITAL:** Bairiki (Tarawa Atoll)
POPULATION: 98,549 **CURRENCY:** Australian dollar **OFFICIAL LANGUAGE:** English

1979 | 1979 | July 12 | KIR | +12 | +686 | .ki

FORMERLY PART OF THE colony of the Gilbert and Ellice Islands, the Gilberts became independent from Britain in 1979 and took the name Kiribati (pronounced "Keer-ee-bus"). British interest in the Gilbert Islands rested solely on the exploitation of the phosphate deposits on Banaba; these ran out in 1980. In 1981, Kiribati won damages (but not the costs of litigation) from the British for decades of phosphate exploitation.

***Banreaba Island, Tarawa Atoll.** None of the atolls are more than 8 m (26 ft) high except Banaba, once the source of phosphates.*

CLIMATE

Tropical oceanic

WEATHER CHART FOR BAIRIKI

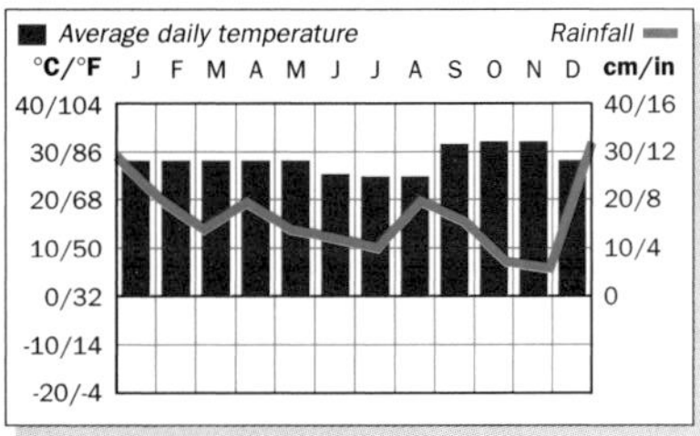
Average daily temperature
Rainfall
°C/°F
J F M A M J J A S O N D
cm/in
40/104
30/86
20/68
10/50
0/32
-10/14
-20/-4
40/16
30/12
20/8
10/4
0

Kiribati's small land area in the vast Pacific means that some atolls can often go for months without rain. In 1999, a nationwide drought emergency was declared.

TRANSPORTATION

Drive on right

Bonriki, Tarawa
51,000 passengers

8 ships
4198 grt

THE TRANSPORTATION NETWORK

483 km (300 miles) | None
None | 5 km (3 miles)

Air Kiribati links most outer islands to Tarawa. Passenger ferries run between the smaller islands. Only Tarawa and Kiritimati have all-weather roads.

TOURISM

Visitors : Population 1:23

4288 visitors

Down 11% in 2003

MAIN TOURIST ARRIVALS

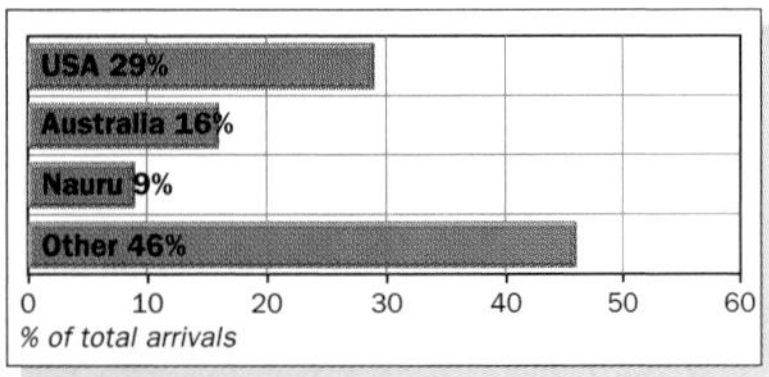
USA 29%
Australia 16%
Nauru 9%
Other 46%
0
10
20
30
40
50
60
% of total arrivals

Tourism is small-scale. The recently renamed Millennium Island is the first place on Earth to see in each new year.

PEOPLE

Pop. density medium

English, Kiribati

139/km² (360/mi²)

THE URBAN/RURAL POPULATION SPLIT

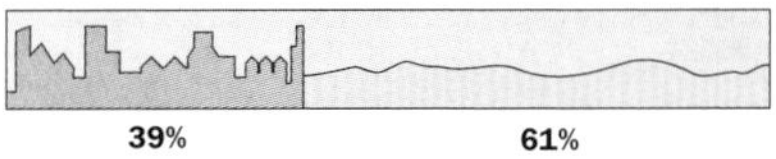
39%
61%

RELIGIOUS PERSUASION

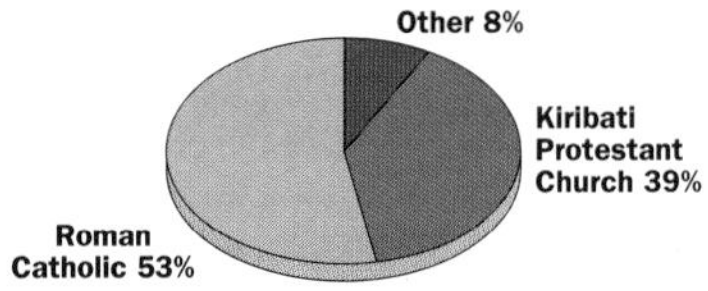
Other 8%
Kiribati Protestant Church 39%
Roman Catholic 53%

Almost all I-Kiribati (as the Gilbertese have been known since independence) are Micronesian, though the Banabans employed anthropologists to establish their racial distinctness. Tension with the Banabans is intense, though the majority now live on Rabi Island in Fiji; just 280 people remain on Banaba itself. Most I-Kiribati are poor, and many men leave the islands to work as merchant shipping crew. Those who stay at home go through a circular migration from the outlying islands to Tarawa, returning to see relatives. Women play a prominent role, especially on outlying islands, where they run most of the farms.

POLITICS

Nonparty elections

2003/2007

President Anote Tong

AT THE LAST ELECTION
House of Assembly 42 seats

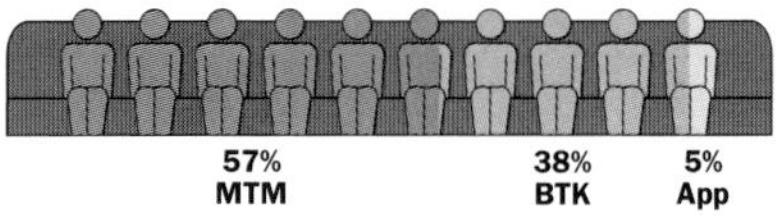
57% MTM
38% BTK
5% App

MTM = Protect the Maneaba **BTK** = Pillars of Truth
App = Appointed

The House of Assembly has one appointed member (for the Banaban community in Fiji) and one ex officio member

The traditional chiefs still effectively rule Kiribati. A period of political uncertainty followed the election victory of the opposition BTK in 2002. The party succeeded in ousting the incumbent president, and its candidate Anote Tong was elected president in 2003. In the meantime, however, the MTM had regained control of the House of Assembly in fresh elections. Overpopulation on Tarawa is a major issue, in part caused by the poverty and lack of opportunity on the outer islands; a resettlement program began in 1998. The economy's overdependence on coconut products is also of concern.

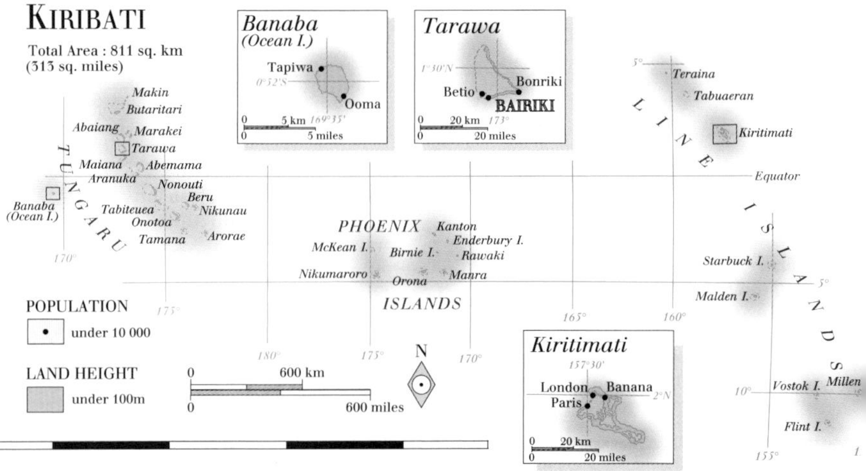
KIRIBATI
Total Area : 811 sq. km (313 sq. miles)
Banaba (Ocean I.)
Tapiwa
Ooma
5 km
5 miles
Tarawa
Betio
Bonriki
BAIRIKI
20 km
20 miles
Makin
Butaritari
Abaiang
Marakei
Tarawa
Maiana
Abemama
Aranuka
Nonouti
Beru
Nikunau
Tabiteuea
Onotoa
Tamana
Arorae
Banaba (Ocean I.)
TUNGARU
PHOENIX ISLANDS
Kanton
Enderbury I.
Rawaki
McKean I.
Birnie I.
Nikumaroro
Orona
Manra
Teraina
Tabuaeran
Kiritimati
LINE ISLANDS
Equator
Starbuck I.
Malden I.
Vostok I.
Millen
Flint I.
Kiritimati
London
Banana
Paris
20 km
20 miles
POPULATION
under 10 000
LAND HEIGHT
under 100m
600 km
600 miles
N

WORLD AFFAIRS

Joined UN in 1999

ACP | Comm | PC | PIF | ADB

Kiribati has little international significance because of its tiny size and remote location, but is able to make its voice heard regionally through the Pacific Islands Forum. In 1986, Kiribati was a signatory to a deal between the US and a number of Pacific Island states that resulted in the US paying US$60 million in return for access to Pacific fishing grounds. In the Cold War era Kiribati played the USSR off against the US, extracting a high price for fishing leases, which allowed boats to spy on US nuclear testing on the neighboring Kwajalein Atoll in the Marshall Islands.

AID

Recipient

US$21m (receipts) | Up 75% in 2002

Australia is the biggest donor. China withdrew funding from several projects in 2003 after Kiribati recognized Taiwan, which promptly made up the shortfall.

DEFENSE

No compulsory military service

Kiribati has no defense budget | Not applicable

Australia and New Zealand provide de facto protection, with regular antisubmarine patrols.

ECONOMICS

Inflation 3.3% p.a. (1990–2001)

US$91m | 1.44 Australian dollars (1.491)

SCORE CARD

- ❑ WORLD GNP RANKING........................189th
- ❑ GNP PER CAPITA..........................US$960
- ❑ BALANCE OF PAYMENTS....................US$2m
- ❑ INFLATION.......................................2.7%
- ❑ UNEMPLOYMENT..................................2%

STRENGTHS

Subsistence economy; only Tarawa imports food. Coconuts provide some export income, mostly from the EU. Fisheries have some potential. Upgraded port facilities at Betio.

WEAKNESSES

Lack of resources. High levels of poverty. Isolation, and large distances between islands. Heavy dependence on international aid. Almost no economic potential. Lack of rain.

EXPORTS

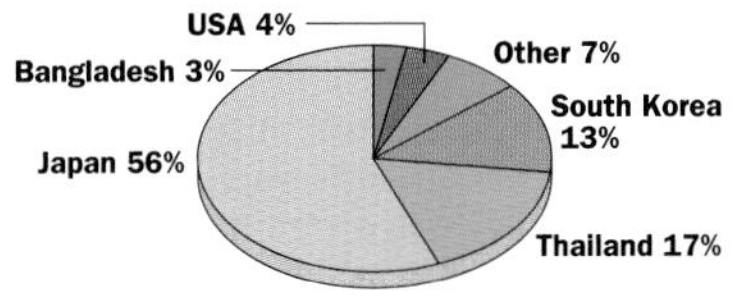
USA 4%
Bangladesh 3%
Other 7%
South Korea 13%
Japan 56%
Thailand 17%

IMPORTS

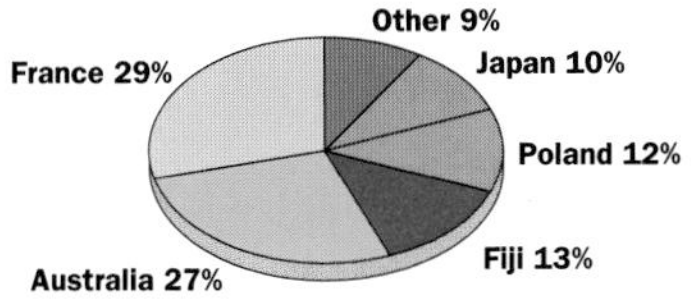
Other 9%
France 29%
Japan 10%
Poland 12%
Fiji 13%
Australia 27%

RESOURCES

Electric power 2000 kW

32,393 tonnes | Not an oil producer

12,000 pigs, 450,000 chickens | None

Phosphate deposits on Banaba ran out in 1980. All energy supplies have to be imported. A scheme to farm seaweed is under development.

ENVIRONMENT

Not available

39% (including marine and semi-protected areas) | 0.3 tonnes per capita

Rising sea levels cause coastal erosion and ultimately threaten Kiribati's existence. Global warming is a critical issue both for this reason and because of its damaging effects on the coral reef which protects Tarawa from the sea and holds important inshore fish stocks in the lagoon. The coral has also suffered from pollution by untreated effluent.

MEDIA

TV ownership low

There are no daily newspapers

PUBLISHING AND BROADCAST MEDIA

There are no daily newspapers. The weekly newspapers are *Butim'aea Manin te Euangkerio, Kiribati Newstar,* and *Te Uekera*

There is no domestic television | 1 state-owned service

The independent *Kiribati Newstar* competes with the state-owned *Te Uekera* and the Protestant Church's paper *Butim'aea Manin te Euangkerio*.

CRIME

No death penalty

64 prisoners | Crime is minimal

Crime, apart from brawls resulting from drunkenness, is minimal. The islands' judicial system is based on the British model.

EDUCATION

School leaving age: 15

99% | 568 students

Education is British-inspired and compulsory from six to 15. The best students go on to university in Fiji.

CHRONOLOGY

In 1892, the British established the phosphate-producing colony of the Gilbert and Ellice Islands.

- ❑ **1957** British nuclear tests take place near Kiritimati.
- ❑ **1979** Independence as two states, Kiribati and Tuvalu.
- ❑ **1981** Kiribati wins damages for phosphate mining from UK.
- ❑ **1986** Kiribati–US fishing deal.
- ❑ **1995** Dateline moved east to cover all atolls ahead of millennium.
- ❑ **1999** National drought emergency.
- ❑ **2003** Anote Tong of BTK president, despite MTM parliamentary majority.

HEALTH

Welfare state health benefits

1 per 3333 people | Heart diseases, diabetes

Alcoholism is common and some 80% of adults smoke. More worrying is the increasing HIV infection rate, a consequence of the large number of I-Kiribati who work as merchant seamen.

K

SPENDING

GDP/cap. increase

CONSUMPTION AND SPENDING

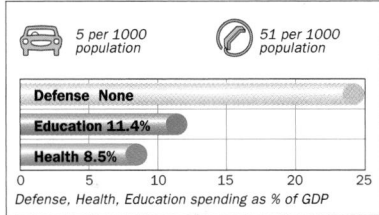

5 per 1000 population | *51 per 1000 population*

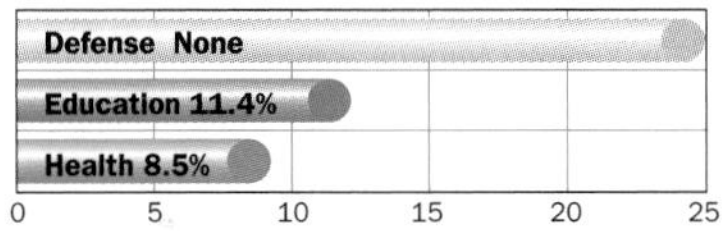
Defense None
Education 11.4%
Health 8.5%
0
5
10
15
20
25

Defense, Health, Education spending as % of GDP

Life in Kiribati is modest. Most I-Kiribati live by subsistence farming and fishing. Civil servants in Bairiki form the wealthiest group. The cost of living on Tarawa is higher than that on the outlying islands due to the need to import food, though fish is abundant and cheap everywhere.

WORLD RANKING

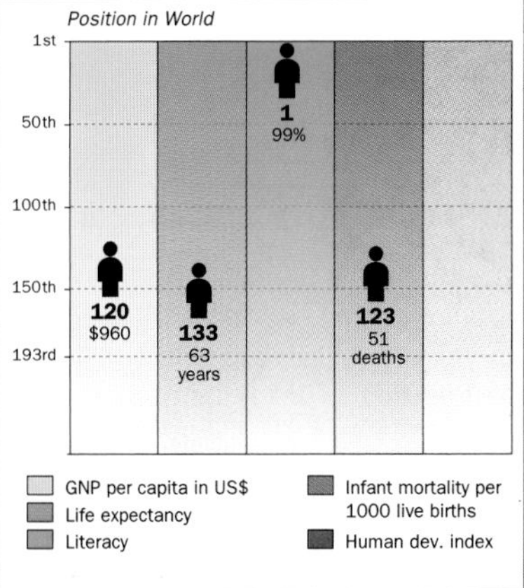
Position in World
1st
50th
100th
150th
193rd
120
$960
133
63 years
1
99%
123
51 deaths
GNP per capita in US$
Life expectancy
Literacy
Infant mortality per 1000 live births
Human dev. index

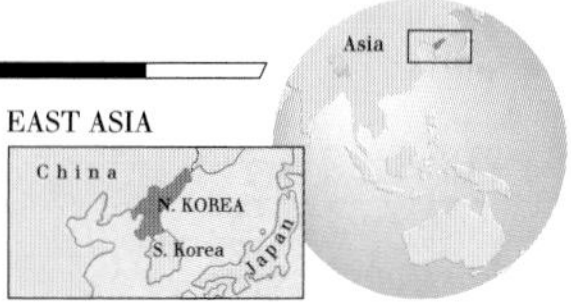
Asia
EAST ASIA
China
N. KOREA
S. Korea
Japan

NORTH KOREA

OFFICIAL NAME: Democratic People's Republic of Korea **CAPITAL:** Pyongyang
POPULATION: 22.7 million **CURRENCY:** North Korean won **OFFICIAL LANGUAGE:** Korean

1948 | 1953 | Sept 9 | DRK | +9 | +850 | .kp

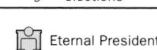

COMPRISING THE NORTHERN half of the Korean peninsula, North Korea is separated from the US-backed South by an armistice line straddling the 38th parallel. Much of the country is mountainous; the Chaeryong and Pyongyang plains in the southwest are the most fertile regions. An independent communist republic from 1948, it remains largely isolated. With its economy starved of capital, it now faces a food crisis requiring large-scale international assistance.

CLIMATE

Continental

WEATHER CHART FOR PYONGYANG

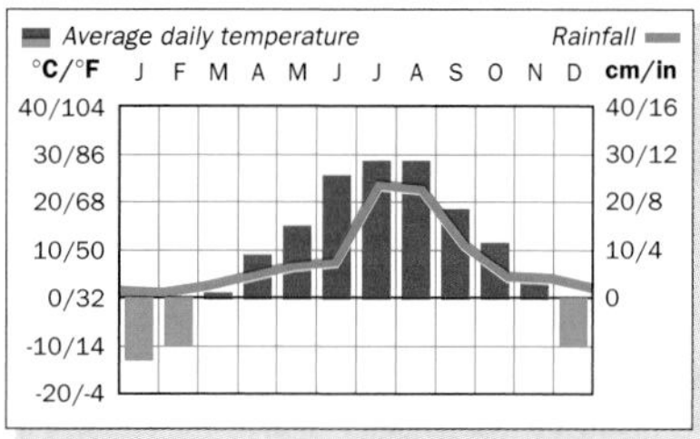
Average daily temperature
Rainfall
°C/°F
J F M A M J J A S O N D
cm/in
40/104
30/86
20/68
10/50
0/32
-10/14
-20/-4
40/16
30/12
20/8
10/4
0

North Korea has a continental climate, but with wet summers. Recent droughts and floods have led to serious famine.

TRANSPORTATION

Drive on right

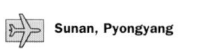

Sunan, Pyongyang

225 ships 870,500 grt

THE TRANSPORTATION NETWORK

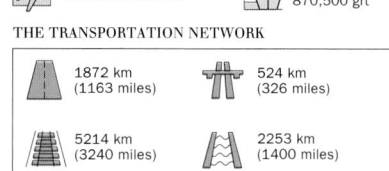

1872 km (1163 miles)

524 km (326 miles)

5214 km (3240 miles)

2253 km (1400 miles)

The heavily used railroads were built by the occupying Japanese after 1910. Highways are open only to very limited, officially approved traffic. Improving relations with South Korea in 2000 led to projects for cross-border links.

TOURISM

Visitors : Population 1:175

130,000 visitors

Up 2% in 1995–1998

MAIN TOURIST ARRIVALS

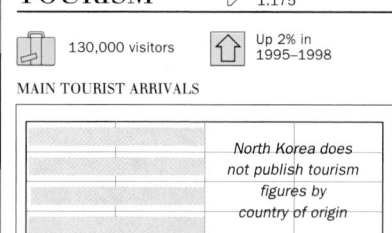

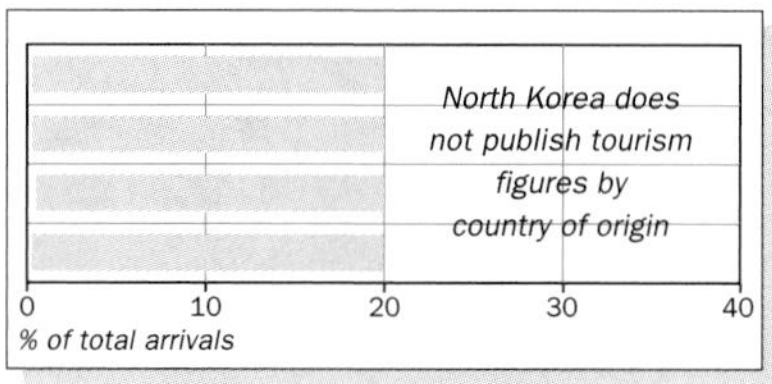
North Korea does not publish tourism figures by country of origin
0
10
20
30
40
% of total arrivals

Economic need has forced limited tourism. South Korean firms have developed resorts such as Mt. Kumgang.

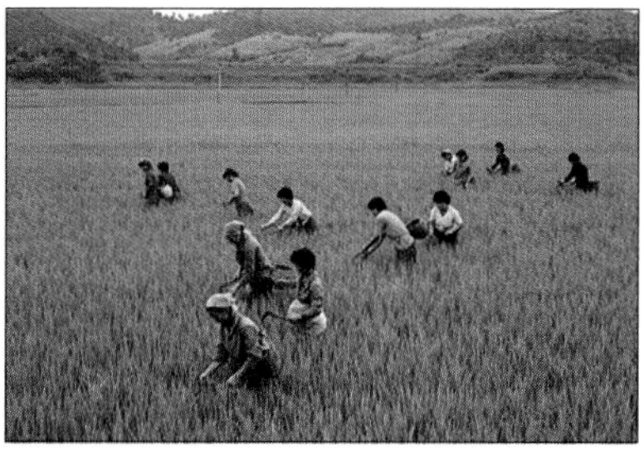

Paddy field. The hot, wet summers are ideal for rice growing. Most farms are run as cooperatives.

PEOPLE

Pop. density medium

Korean, Chinese

189/km² (488/mi²)

THE URBAN/RURAL POPULATION SPLIT

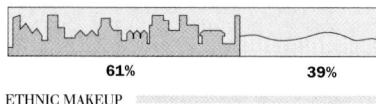

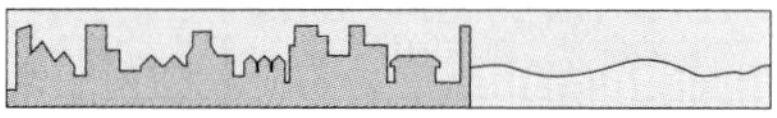
61%
39%

ETHNIC MAKEUP

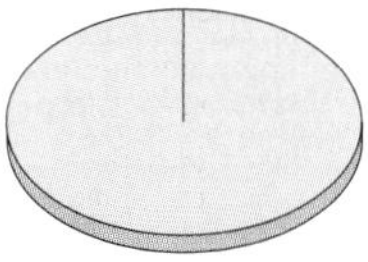
Korean 100%

The Korean peninsula is unusual in having been inhabited by a single ethnic group for the last 2000 years. Chinese and Japanese minorities amount to only 0.2% of the population.

Religions practiced under strict control are Buddhism, Christianity, and Chondogyo, a combination of Taoism, Confucianism, Buddhism, shamanism, and Christianity peculiar to the Koreas.

North Koreans live highly regulated lives. Divorce is nonexistent and extramarital sex frowned upon. Women form more than 50% of the workforce, but are also expected to run the home; it is not uncommon for them to work a 15-hour day. From an early age, children are looked after by an extensive system of state-run crèches. The privileged lifestyle of the political elite – some 200,000 in number – is rumored to be a source of popular resentment.

POLITICS

No multiparty elections

2003/2008

Eternal President Kim Il Sung

AT THE LAST ELECTION

Supreme People's Assembly 687 seats

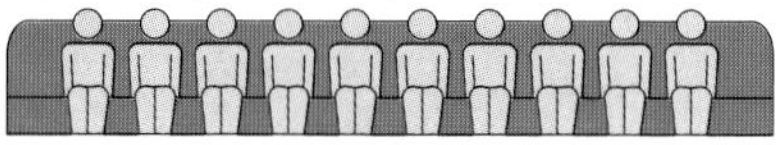
100%
KWP

KWP = Korean Workers' Party

The three million-strong KWP is the only legal party; membership is essential for individual advancement. State control is total.

After almost 50 years as leader Kim Il Sung, subject of a lavish personality cult, died in 1994. Kim Jong Il, his son and chosen successor, lacks his father's authority and has yet to seal the succession; in 1998 Kim Il Sung, by then four years dead, was declared "Eternal President." Nonetheless, Kim Jong Il is officially known as "Dear Leader" and is guaranteed 100% of the vote in elections.

WORLD AFFAIRS

Joined UN in 1991

NAM

China has been North Korea's closest ally since the collapse in 1991 of Soviet communism. The key relationship is with South Korea, with which the North is still notionally at war. A breakthrough in relations in 2000 has since been undermined by mutual suspicion. There has also been a growing antagonism with the US administration, particularly over North Korea's nuclear missile program. In 2002 the US designated North Korea part of an "axis of evil" and has intensified pressure ever since.

AID

Recipient

$267m (receipts)

Up 123% in 2002

Aid levels are insufficient to stave off starvation. Fuel aid was suspended from 2002 over the country's nuclear program. In 2004 a devastating train explosion in Ryongchon triggered emergency aid.

DEFENSE

Compulsory military service

$4.73bn

Up 8% in 2002

North Korea has continued its nuclear missile program despite the 1994 agreement to freeze its research. It develops and sells missiles.

NORTH KOREA

Total Area : 120 540 sq. km (46 540 sq. miles)

0 100 km
0 100 miles
N
CHINA
RUSSIAN FEDERATION
Onsŏng
Kyŏnghŭng
Hoeryŏng
Musan
Komusan
Najin
Tumen
Paektu-san 2744 m
Ch'ŏngjin
Hyesan
Yalu
Manp'o
Myŏngch'ŏn
Kilchu
Kanggye
Sup'ung-ho
HAMGYŎNG SANMAEK
Kimch'aek
Tanch'ŏn
Sakchu
Hŭich'ŏn
Pukch'ŏng
Iwŏn
EAST SEA (SEA OF JAPAN)
Kusŏng
Kujang
Oro
Sinp'o
Hongwŏn
Hamhŭng
Hŭngnam
Pakch'ŏn
Tŏkch'ŏn
Chŏngju
Anju
Kunu
Sunch'ŏn
Kowŏn
Yŏngnŭng
Munch'ŏn
Wŏnsan
Tongjosŏn-man
Sunan
PYONGYANG
Yangdŏk
Namp'o
Songnim
Kosan
Kuŭm
Kosŏng
Sariwŏn
Chaeryŏng
Changyŏn
Haeju
Kŭmch'ŏn
Kaesŏng
Ongjin
SOUTH KOREA
Kyŏnggi-man
YELLOW SEA
POPULATION
over 1 000 000
over 100 000
over 50 000
over 10 000
LAND HEIGHT
1500m/4920ft
1000m/3281ft
500m/1640ft
200m/656ft
Sea Level

CHRONOLOGY

Annexed by Japan in 1910, the peninsula was divided in 1945 at the 38th parallel; North Korea was made an independent state in 1948.

- ❑ **1950–1953** Korean War.
- ❑ **1994** Withdrawal from IAEA. Kim Il Sung dies; declared "Eternal President" four years later.
- ❑ **1997** Threat of famine worsens. Kim Jong Il becomes party leader.
- ❑ **2000** Historic North–South summit.

ECONOMICS

Not available

$18.2bn

900 North Korean won (2.2)

SCORE CARD

- ❑ World GNP Ranking..........................70th
- ❑ GNP per Capita $760
- ❑ Balance of Payments ....*Closed economy;*
- ❑ Inflation ....*does not publish*
- ❑ Unemployment ....*any figures*

Strengths

Few strengths except minerals. Some economic reforms launched in 2002.

Weaknesses

GNP has declined steadily since 1990. Isolation. Acute shortage of foreign capital and technology. Famine.

EXPORTS

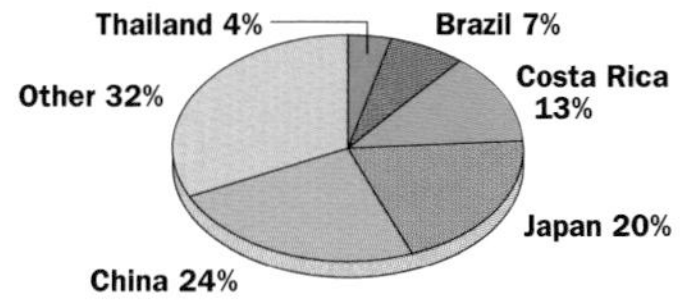
Thailand 4%
Brazil 7%
Other 32%
Costa Rica 13%
Japan 20%
China 24%

IMPORTS

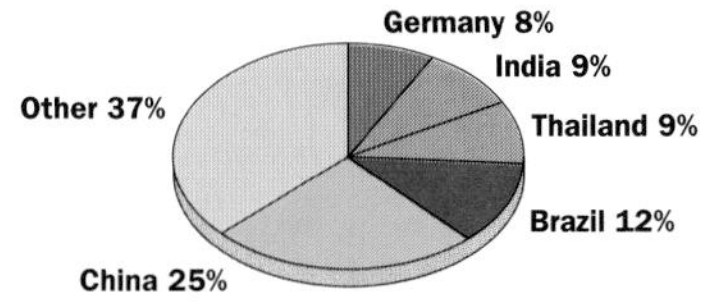
Germany 8%
India 9%
Other 37%
Thailand 9%
Brazil 12%
China 25%

RESOURCES

Electric power 9.5m kW

263,700 tonnes

Not an oil producer; refines 53,000 b/d

4.61m ducks, 3.18m pigs, 2.72m goats, 20m chickens

Coal, iron, lead, gold, copper, zinc, tungsten, silver, tin, uranium

North Korea is rich in minerals. Electricity supply remains a major problem, with frequent blackouts. US suspicion that nuclear power plants were being used to make weapons-grade material was borne out when in 2003 the government admitted to having a nuclear arsenal.

ENVIRONMENT

Sustainability rank: 140th

3% (1% partially protected)

8.5 tonnes per capita

Excessive use of fertilizers and unchecked pollution from heavy industry are the major problems.

MEDIA

TV ownership medium

Daily newspaper circulation 208 per 1000 people

PUBLISHING AND BROADCAST MEDIA

There are 5 daily newspapers, including the leading *Rodong Sinmun*, the party newspaper, and *Minju Choson*

1 state-controlled service

2 state-controlled services

TV consists mostly of musical shows praising Kim Il Sung and Kim Jong Il, and anti-American tirades directed against the Korean War.

CRIME

Death penalty in use

North Korea does not publish prison figures

Low level of violent street crime

At an individual level, crime is officially said hardly to exist. The criminal code is weighted to protect the state against "subversion," rather than the rights of the individual. North Korea has a very poor human rights record and there is a *gulag* of more than 100,000 "subversives," where whole families are sent along with those accused, and where torture is routine.

EDUCATION

School leaving age: 16

99%

390,000 students

Learning English is compulsory from age 14. Malnutrition has contributed to a decline in school attendance.

HEALTH

Welfare state health benefits

1 per 333 people

Heart disease, cancers, digestive diseases

Health care is free. Reasonable life expectancy is now threatened by malnutrition and outright starvation.

SPENDING

GDP/cap. decrease

CONSUMPTION AND SPENDING

11 per 1000 population

21 per 1000 population

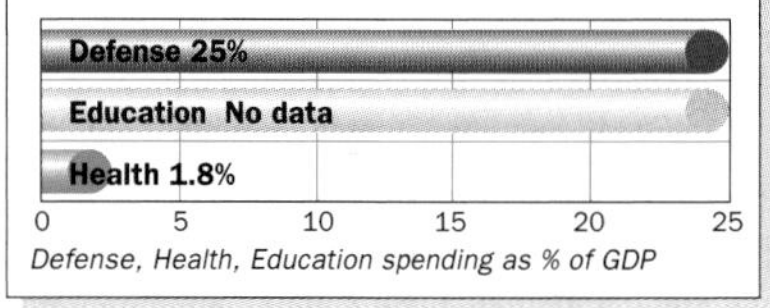
Defense 25%
Education No data
Health 1.8%
0
5
10
15
20
25
Defense, Health, Education spending as % of GDP

Most people live in poverty. An elite within the KWP lives well, with access to specialist shops and high-tech consumer goods. Personal ownership of telephones, private cars, and, in many areas, bicycles, is forbidden.

WORLD RANKING

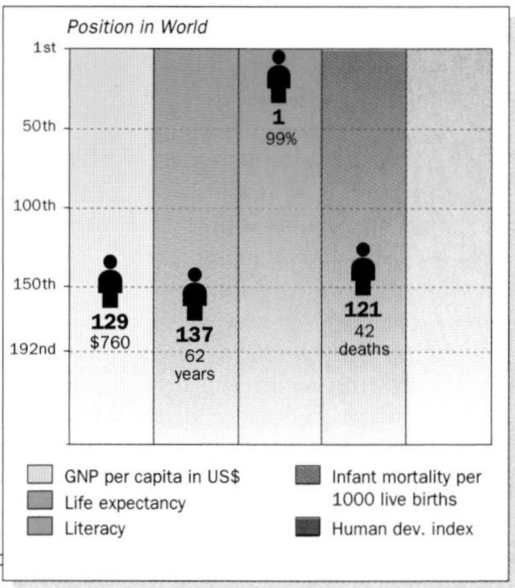
Position in World
1st
50th
100th
150th
192nd
129
$760
137
62 years
1
99%
121
42 deaths
GNP per capita in US$
Life expectancy
Literacy
Infant mortality per 1000 live births
Human dev. index

K

South Korea

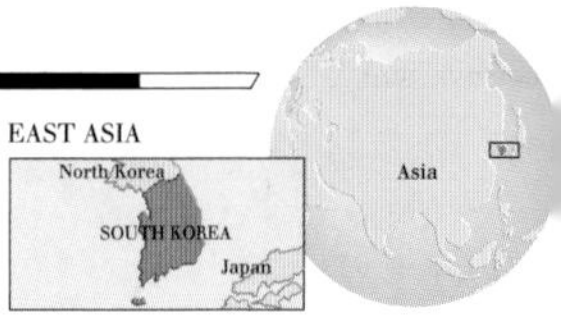
EAST ASIA
North Korea
SOUTH KOREA
Japan
Asia

Official Name: Republic of Korea **Capital:** Seoul
Population: 47.7 million **Currency:** South Korean won **Official Language:** Korean

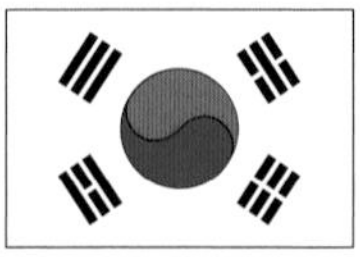

1948
1953
Aug 15
ROK
+9
+82
.kr

OCCUPYING THE SOUTHERN half of the Korean peninsula in east Asia, nearly 70% of South Korea is mountainous and two-thirds is forested. The whole peninsula was annexed by Japan from 1910 to 1945, and the split between South Korea and the communist North originated with the arrival of rival US and Soviet armies in 1945. Though the two states have discussed reunification, the legacy of hostility arising from the 1950–1953 Korean War remains a major obstacle. South Korea is the world's leading shipbuilder and a major force in high-tech industries.

TOURISM

Visitors : Population 1:10

4.75m visitors

Down 11% in 2003

MAIN TOURIST ARRIVALS

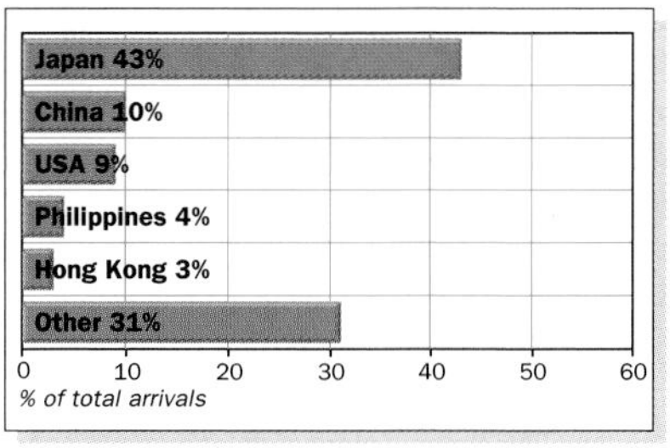
Japan 43%
China 10%
USA 9%
Philippines 4%
Hong Kong 3%
Other 31%
0
10
20
30
40
50
60
% of total arrivals

Overseas tourism to South Korea has increased tenfold since 1969. Most visitors are Japanese, who come for the golf and Seoul's nightlife; Jeju-do (Cheju-do) is a favored honeymoon destination. Whereas visiting relations of US army personnel once made up 13% of all tourists, today Los Angeles-based Korean-Americans make up the greatest proportion of US visitors. Despite the publicity generated by the 1988 Seoul Olympics and the 2002 soccer World Cup, South Korea is still not seen in the West as a prime tourist destination.

CLIMATE

Continental

WEATHER CHART FOR SEOUL

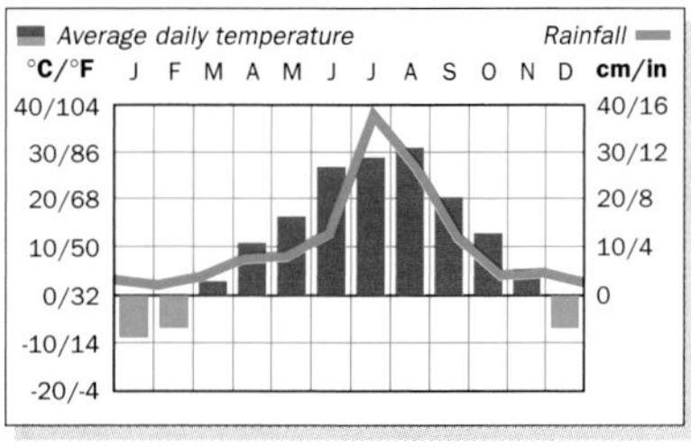
Average daily temperature
Rainfall
°C/°F
J F M A M J J A S O N D
cm/in
40/104
30/86
20/68
10/50
0/32
-10/14
-20/-4
40/16
30/12
20/8
10/4
0

South Korea has four distinct seasons. Winters are dry and can be bitterly cold. Summers are hot and humid, especially during July and August.

TRANSPORTATION

Drive on right

Incheon International, Seoul 19.9m passengers

2532 ships 7.05m grt

THE TRANSPORTATION NETWORK

70,146 km (43,587 miles)

3060 km (1901 miles)

3129 km (1944 miles)

1609 km (1000 miles)

The public transportation system is efficient and highly integrated. Buses, trains, boats, and airplanes are all included in one timetable, and have a reputation for punctuality. A toll-based nationwide expressway network links most major cities. Air travel has expanded rapidly as a convenient way to traverse the mountainous interior. A high-speed rail link will connect Seoul and Busan (Pusan) in 2010.

Improving relations with North Korea in 2000 led to projects for cross-border rail and road links and connecting flights. The first flights since 1953 took place in mid-2002, albeit limited to specific teams of construction workers in the nuclear industry, and the land border was opened for the first time in early 2003 for a South Korean tourist bus. Continuing political uncertainty has slowed the progress of other projects.

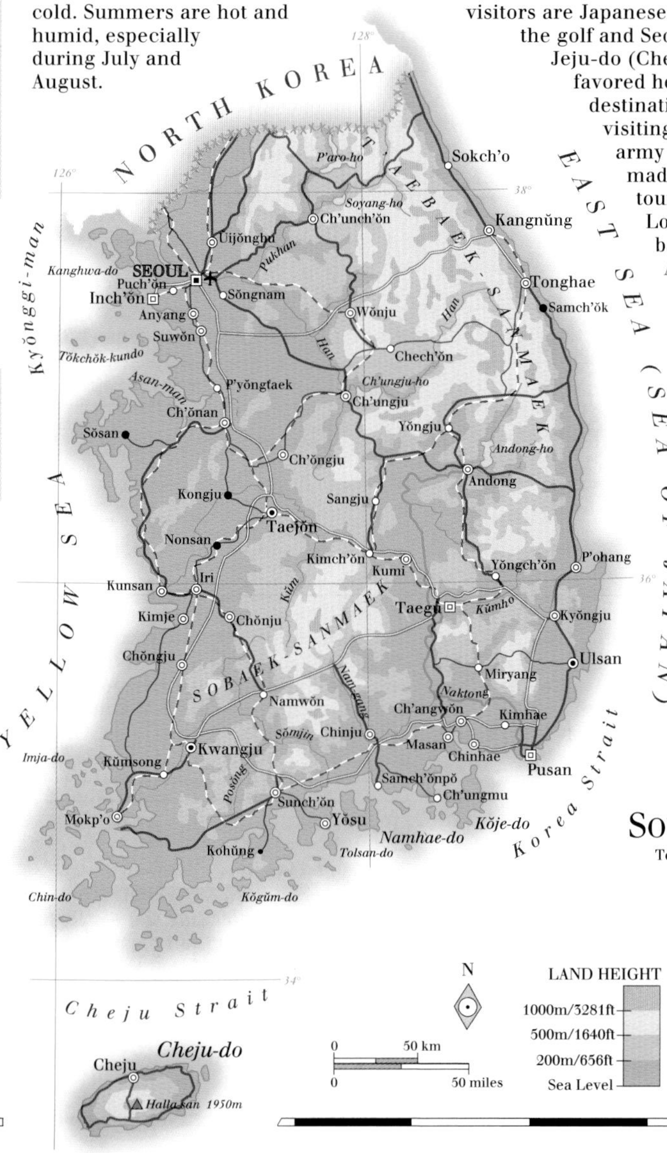
NORTH KOREA
EAST SEA (SEA OF JAPAN)
YELLOW SEA
Kyŏnggi-man
Asan-man
T'AEBAEK-SANMAEK
SOBAEK-SANMAEK
Korea Strait
Cheju Strait
SEOUL
Inch'ŏn
Puch'ŏn
Anyang
Suwŏn
Ŭijŏngbu
Sŏngnam
Kanghwa-do
Tŏkchŏk-kundo
P'yŏngtaek
Ch'ŏnan
Sŏsan
Ch'ŏngju
Kongju
Taejŏn
Nonsan
Kunsan
Iri
Kimje
Chŏnju
Chŏngju
Namwŏn
Kwangju
Kŭmsong
Mokp'o
Sunch'ŏn
Yŏsu
Kohŭng
Chinju
Masan
Chinhae
Pusan
Kimhae
Miryang
Ulsan
Kyŏngju
P'ohang
Yŏngch'ŏn
Taegu
Kumi
Kimch'ŏn
Sangju
Andong
Yŏngju
Ch'ungju
Chech'ŏn
Wŏnju
Ch'unch'ŏn
Sokch'o
Kangnŭng
Tonghae
Samch'ŏk
Ch'angwŏn
Samch'ŏnpŏ
Ch'ungmu
Kŏje-do
Namhae-do
Tolsan-do
Hŭksan-kundo
Chin-do
Imja-do
Kŏgŭm-do
Cheju
Cheju-do
Halla-san 1950m
Han
Pukhan
Kŭm
Naktong
Sŏmjin
Soyang-ho
P'aro-ho
Ch'ungju-ho
Andong-ho
Kŭmho
N
0
50 km
50 miles

South Korea

Total Area : 98 480 sq. km (38 023 sq. miles)

POPULATION
over 5 000 000
over 1 000 000
over 500 000
over 100 000
over 50 000
over 10 000
under 10 000

LAND HEIGHT
1000m/3281ft
500m/1640ft
200m/656ft
Sea Level

PEOPLE

Pop. density high

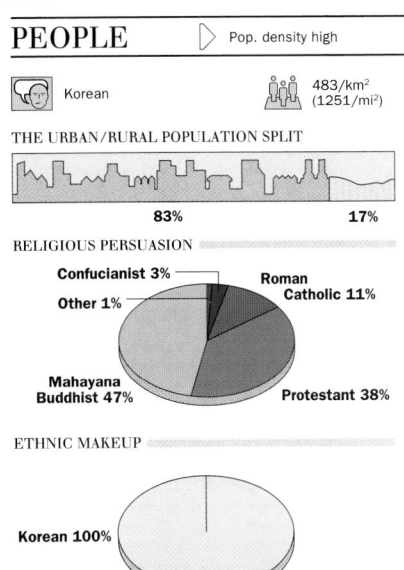

Korean

483/km² (1251/mi²)

THE URBAN/RURAL POPULATION SPLIT

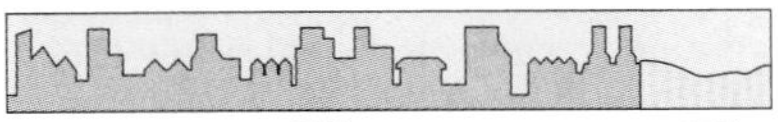
83%
17%

RELIGIOUS PERSUASION

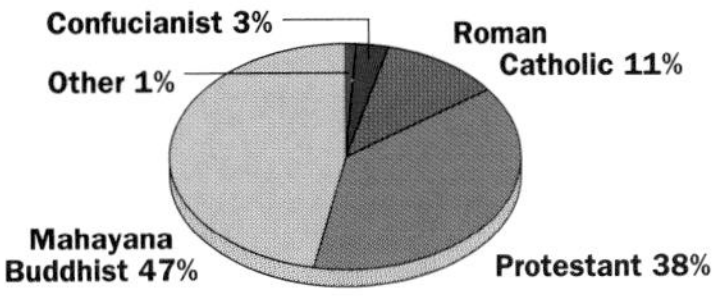
Confucianist 3%
Other 1%
Roman Catholic 11%
Mahayana Buddhist 47%
Protestant 38%

ETHNIC MAKEUP

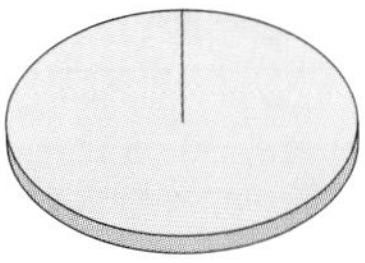
Korean 100%

Korean culture is strongly colored by its unusual racial homogeneity. Family life is a central and clearly defined part of society, though the nuclear family model is becoming the norm rather than the old-style household of the extended family. Most Koreans can trace their ancestry back thousands of years. Regional origin is important in determining blood heritage, since there are only 270 Korean surnames and half the population is named Kim, Lee, Park, or Choi.

Chondogyo, combining elements of Confucianism, Buddhism, shamanism, Taoism, and Christianity, is peculiar to the Koreas but has only a tiny following. Traditional values condition attitudes to women, and it is still not respectable for those who are married to have a job.

Economic growth has attracted illegal immigrants from the poorer Asian countries, who take menial jobs that South Koreans now refuse to do.

POPULATION AGE BREAKDOWN

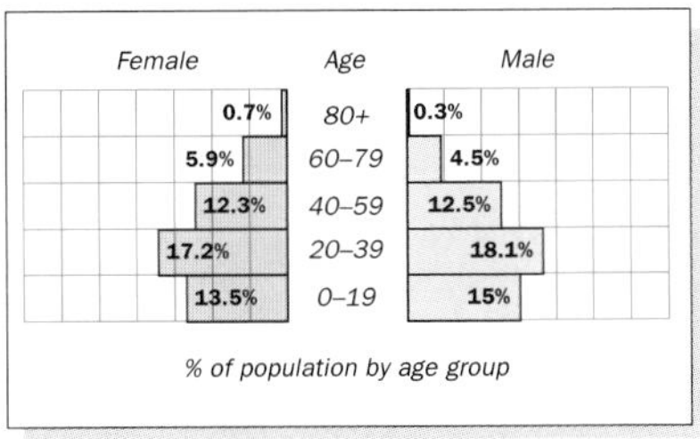
Female
Age
Male
0.7%
80+
0.3%
5.9%
60–79
4.5%
12.3%
40–59
12.5%
17.2%
20–39
18.1%
13.5%
0–19
15%
% of population by age group

WORLD AFFAIRS

Joined UN in 1991

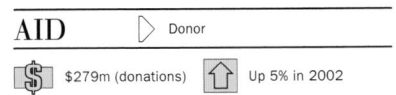

APEC | CP | IAEA | OECD | WTO

Since the division of Korea, relations with the North have dominated foreign policy. A historic summit meeting in 2000 in the North Korean capital, Pyongyang, opened a new phase, and cross-border diplomatic and economic cooperation briefly flourished. Reunification remains the ultimate goal of both Koreas, but with doubts about its social and economic costs. The border is still the most heavily defended in the world. Relations with China, the closest ally of North Korea, have improved. Japan is a major trading partner, though South Koreans continue to harbor resentment over the 1910–1945 Japanese annexation. Debate is fierce over South Korea's increasing involvement in Iraq.

AID

Donor

$279m (donations)

Up 5% in 2002

Once a massive recipient of US aid, and then of Japanese war reparations, South Korea emerged in the 1970s and 1980s as a major aid donor. The economic crisis in 1997–1998, however, forced it to seek international financial assistance to salvage key sectors of its threatened economy.

POLITICS

Multiparty elections

2004/2008

President Roh Moo Hyun

AT THE LAST ELECTION

National Assembly 299 seats

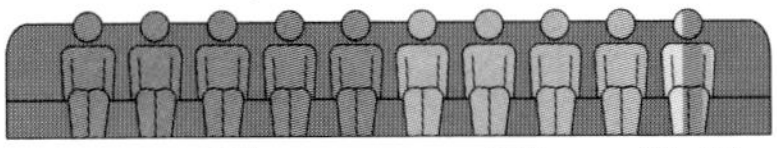
3% MDP
1% ULD
51% UP
41% GNP
3% DLP
1% Others

UP = Uri Party **GNP** = Grand National Party **DLP** = Democratic Labor Party **MDP** = Millennium Democratic Party **ULD** = United Liberal Democrats

Officially a democracy since its inception, South Korea was in practice ruled by military dictators until 1987, when direct presidential elections were introduced.

PROFILE

In 1993, Kim Young Sam became the first nonmilitary leader in 30 years. He launched a popular anticorruption campaign, targeting former presidents, but was brought down by a steel scandal in 1997. Veteran opposition leader, Kim Dae Jung, was elected president later that year in the first peaceful power transfer to the opposition. His supporters (subsequently renamed the MDP) did not hold a legislative majority, however, and instability continued.

Kim's final year in office was marred by corruption scandals, but his chosen successor Roh Moo Hyun was elected president in 2002. In March 2004 Roh was suspended briefly on charges of violating his political neutrality when he openly backed the UP, a splinter from the MDP. The UP performed well in the legislative elections the following month, becoming the first liberal party to win control of the National Assembly.

MAIN POLITICAL ISSUES

The economy

The Asian financial crisis of 1997–1998 was followed by global slowdown from 2001; efforts to recover in the intervening period by means of financial austerity and retrenchment were unsuccessful. Industrial action is frequent and effective.

Relations with North Korea

The sudden flowering of North–South relations in 2000 soon lost popularity. Expensive cross-border projects, and promises of aid, raised fears over rising costs, while erratic Northern diplomacy has done little to improve mutual trust.

***Kim Dae Jung**, president (1998–2003) and Nobel Peace Prize winner.*

***President Roh Moo Hyun** was chastized in 2004 for breaching presidential neutrality.*

CHRONOLOGY

The Yi dynasty, founded in Seoul in 1392, ruled the kingdom of Korea until 1910. Korea became a vassal state of China in 1644.

- **1860** Korea reacts to French and British occupation of Peking by preventing Western influence: becomes the "Hermit Kingdom."
- **1904–1905** Russo-Japanese War. Japan conquers Korea.
- **1910** Japan annexes Korea.
- **1919** Independence protests violently suppressed.
- **1945** US and Soviet armies arrive. Korea split at 38°N. South comes under de facto US rule.
- **1948** Republic of South Korea created; Syngman Rhee becomes president at head of an increasingly authoritarian regime.
- **1950** Hostilities between North and South, each aspiring to rule a united Korea. North invades, sparking Korean War. US, with UN backing, enters on South's side; China unofficially assists North. In 1951 fighting stabilizes near 38th parallel.
- **1953** Armistice; de facto border at cease-fire line, close to 38th parallel.

CHRONOLOGY *continued*

- ❑ **1960** Syngman Rhee resigns in face of popular revolt.
- ❑ **1961** Military coup leads to authoritarian junta led by Park Chung Hee.
- ❑ **1963** Pressure for civilian government. Park elected as president (reelected in 1967 and 1971). Strong manufacturing base and exports drive massive economic development program.
- ❑ **1965** Links restored with Japan.
- ❑ **1966** 45,000 troops engaged in South Vietnam.
- ❑ **1972** Martial law. New constitution with greater presidential powers.
- ❑ **1979** Park assassinated. Gen. Chun Doo Hwan, intelligence chief, leads coup. Kim Young Sam, opposition leader, expelled from parliament.
- ❑ **1980** Chun chosen as president. Kim Dae Jung and other opposition leaders arrested.
- ❑ **1986** Car exports start.
- ❑ **1987** Emergence of prodemocracy movement. Roh Tae Woo, Chun's chosen successor, elected president.
- ❑ **1988** Sixth Republic offers genuine multiparty democracy. Restrictions on foreign travel lifted.
- ❑ **1990** Government party and two opposition parties, including Kim Young Sam's, merge.
- ❑ **1991** South Korea joins UN.
- ❑ **1992** Diplomatic links with China established. Kim Young Sam elected president.
- ❑ **1996** Chun sentenced to death on charges of organizing 1979–1980 overthrow of government; Roh given a lengthy prison term. Both sentences were rescinded.
- ❑ **1997** Violent protests against new labor laws. Steel scandal brings down government. Economic crisis.
- ❑ **1998** Kim Dae Jung president.
- ❑ **2000** Historic North–South summit in Pyongyang.
- ❑ **2002** Roh Moo Hyun president.
- ❑ **2003** 182 die in subway arson attack.
- ❑ **2004** Roh suspended for two months. UP wins elections. Loudspeakers in DMZ cease propaganda broadcasts.

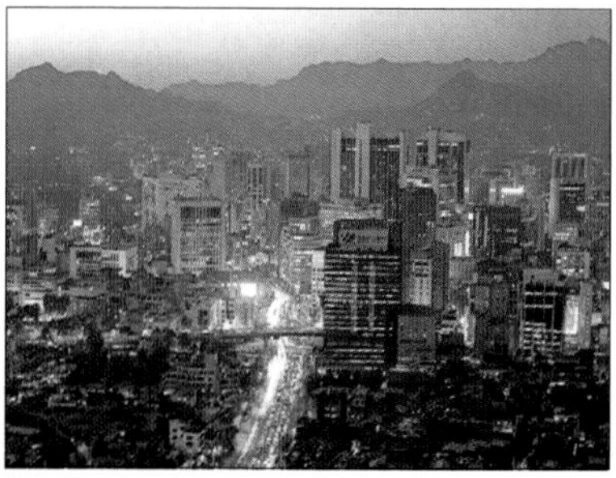

Seoul, meaning "capital," is overcrowded and dominates the country's economy. A new capital is to be built north of Taejon by 2030.

DEFENSE

Compulsory military service

$12.6bn

Up 14% in 2002

SOUTH KOREAN ARMED FORCES

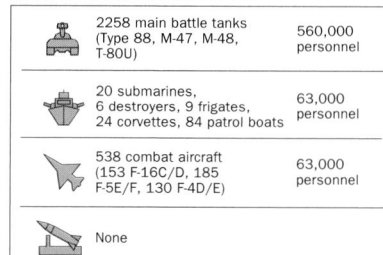

2258 main battle tanks (Type 88, M-47, M-48, T-80U)	560,000 personnel
20 submarines, 6 destroyers, 9 frigates, 24 corvettes, 84 patrol boats	63,000 personnel
538 combat aircraft (153 F-16C/D, 185 F-5E/F, 130 F-4D/E)	63,000 personnel
None	

The military has retreated from politics since a major corruption investigation in the mid-1990s. The main defense concern is North Korea. South Korea has fewer troops, tanks, artillery, and aircraft than the North, but claims parity through superior technology and the presence of thousands of US troops on its territory. The manufacture of missiles capable of striking any target in North Korea was legalized in 2001. Since the demilitarized zone (DMZ) is only 55 km (35 miles) from Seoul, however, the South's ability to resist invasion by the North is questionable. Stumbling efforts at improving cross-border relations led to a commitment in 2002 to clear landmines from the DMZ to allow construction of transportation links, and in 2004 to the first radio contact between the navies.

ECONOMICS

Inflation 4.5% p.a. (1990–2001)

$473bn

1156 South Korean won (1195)

SCORE CARD

- ❑ World GNP Ranking..........................13th
- ❑ GNP per Capita $9930
- ❑ Balance of Payments...................$6.09bn
- ❑ Inflation 2.8%
- ❑ Unemployment 3%

EXPORTS

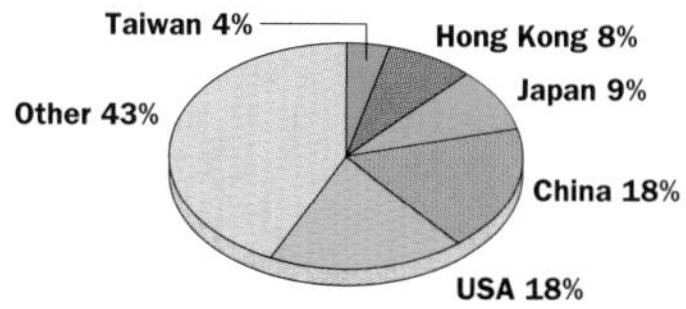

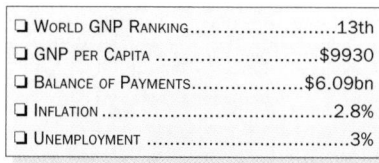

Taiwan 4%
Hong Kong 8%
Japan 9%
Other 43%
China 18%
USA 18%

IMPORTS

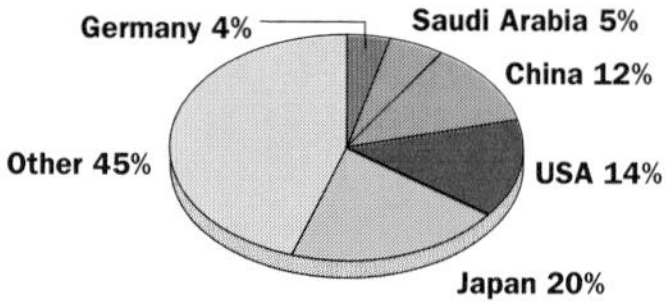

Germany 4%
Saudi Arabia 5%
China 12%
Other 45%
USA 14%
Japan 20%

Strengths

World's most successful shipbuilder, with bulk of the market. Demand from China, particularly for cars. Well-developed high-tech industry.

Weaknesses

High level of indebtedness and vulnerability to international capital movements. Increasingly militant workforce since 1997. State sector a burden on the economy. Strong competition from Japan.

Profile

South Korea's economic miracle began with centralized planning. Chaebol (conglomerates) such as Samsung achieved impressive growth rates in strategic industries such as car manufacturing, shipbuilding, and semiconductors. Cheap state credit and a well-educated workforce gave South Korea a competitive edge. The government then encouraged foreign investment and an emphasis on smaller industries to maintain growth. In 1997, however, a major financial crisis and the threat of a debt implosion forced the government to turn to the IMF for a huge credit agreement. The central bank forecast economic growth of over 5% for 2004, signaling confidence that the economy was recovering from a short recession in the first half of 2003.

ECONOMIC PERFORMANCE INDICATOR

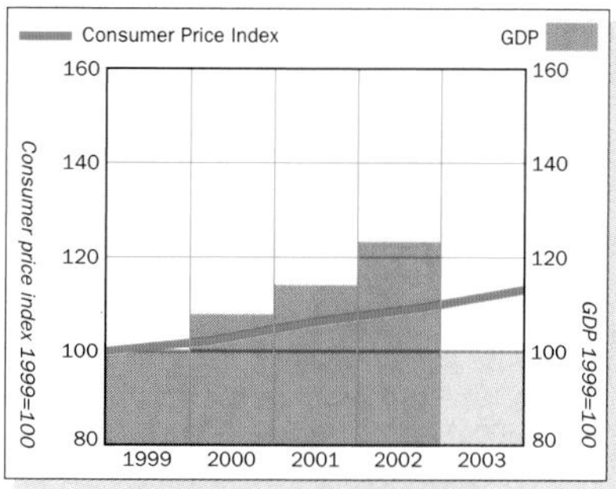

Consumer Price Index
GDP
Consumer price index 1999=100
GDP 1999=100
160
140
120
100
80
1999
2000
2001
2002
2003

SOUTH KOREA : MAJOR BUSINESSES

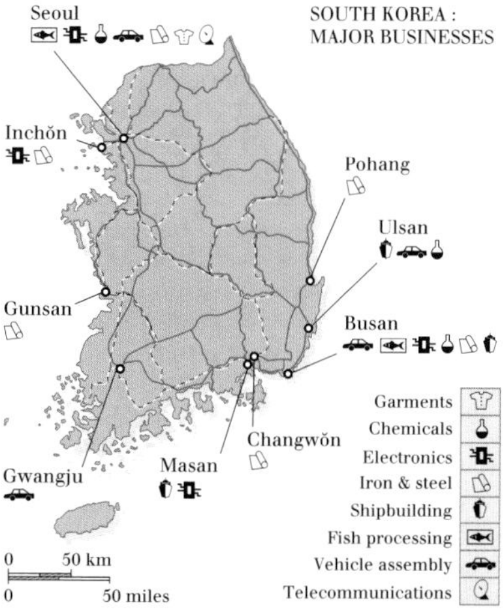

Seoul
Inchŏn
Pohang
Ulsan
Gunsan
Busan
Changwŏn
Masan
Gwangju
0 50 km
0 50 miles
Garments
Chemicals
Electronics
Iron & steel
Shipbuilding
Fish processing
Vehicle assembly
Telecommunications

RESOURCES

Electric power 53.7m kW

2.28m tonnes

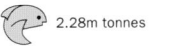

Not an oil producer; refines 2.4m b/d

8.91m pigs, 6m ducks, 98m chickens

Coal, iron, lead, zinc, tungsten, gold, graphite, fluorite

ELECTRICITY GENERATION

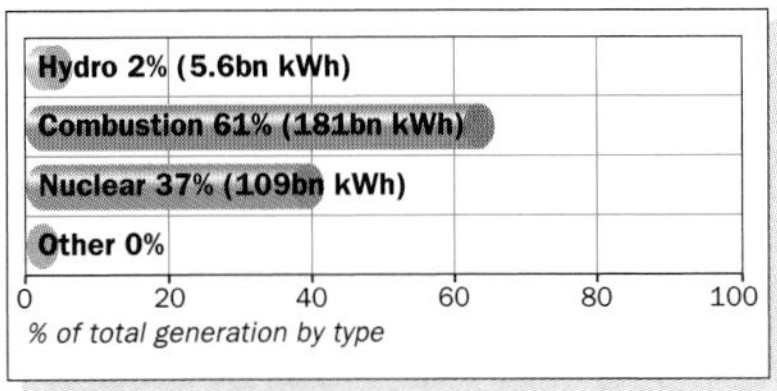

Hydro 2% (5.6bn kWh)
Combustion 61% (181bn kWh)
Nuclear 37% (109bn kWh)
Other 0%
0
20
40
60
80
100
% of total generation by type

South Korea has few natural resources. It has to import all of its oil and has built a series of nuclear reactors for generating electricity. Under the terms of the 1994 agreement between North Korea and the US, South Korea is constructing two reactors in the North which, in the event of reunification, would be added to the national grid.

Agriculture remains a highly protected sector of the economy. Plans to open up the rice market have in the past provoked massive demonstrations in Seoul.

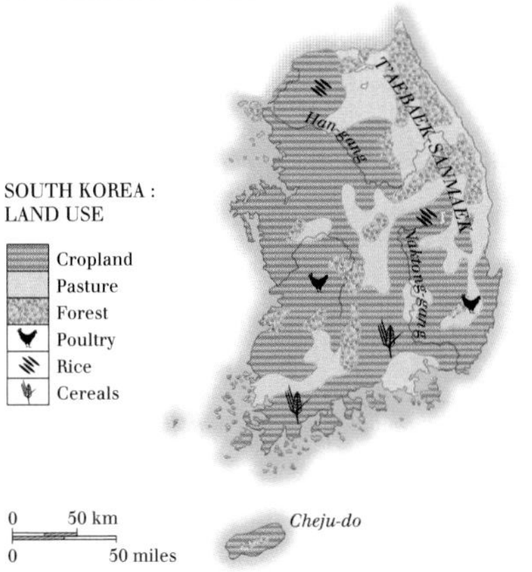

SOUTH KOREA : LAND USE
Cropland
Pasture
Forest
Poultry
Rice
Cereals
TAEBAEK-SANMAEK
Han-gang
Naktong-gang
0 50 km
0 50 miles
Cheju-do

ENVIRONMENT

Sustainability rank: 135th

7% partially protected

9.1 tonnes per capita

ENVIRONMENTAL TREATIES

Yes Yes Yes

Yes Yes Yes

Environmental groups remain hostile to South Korea's nuclear power program. Rapid industrialization has resulted in environmental problems, especially pollution. The government only ratified the Kyoto Protocol, which aims to reduce carbon dioxide emissions, as late as November 2002. Steps have recently been taken to address the severe problem of air pollution in urban areas, particularly in Seoul. Rivers in rural areas have been polluted by fertilizers and chemicals.

CRIME

Death penalty in use

60,721 prisoners

Down 52% in 2000–2001

CRIME RATES

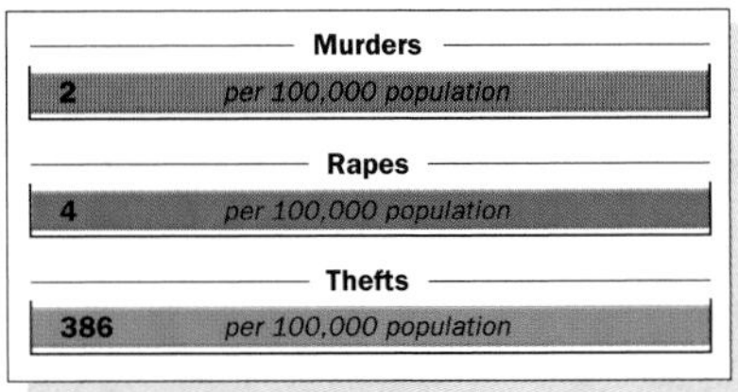

Murders
2 per 100,000 population
Rapes
4 per 100,000 population
Thefts
386 per 100,000 population

Violent crime is relatively uncommon in South Korea. Since 1987, the internal security forces' operations have been restricted, though left-wing activists are still harassed. Striking workers and student demonstrators encounter – and prepare for – confrontational and forceful crowd control. Police brutality was highlighted by the death of a detained suspect in 2002.

HEALTH

Welfare state health benefits

1 per 714 people

Cancers, cerebro-vascular disease, senility, accidents

The health service has improved in line with economic growth. Most hospitals are equipped with modern facilities, and many offer advanced treatments comparable with those in the US and western Europe. Health indicators such as infant mortality and longevity have likewise improved.

SPENDING

GDP/cap. increase

CONSUMPTION AND SPENDING

215 per 1000 population

489 per 1000 population

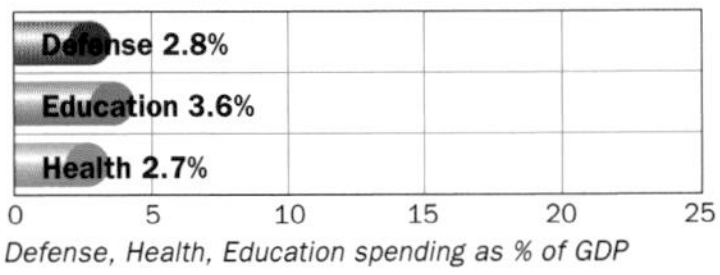

Defense 2.8%
Education 3.6%
Health 2.7%
0
5
10
15
20
25
Defense, Health, Education spending as % of GDP

An increase in credit-card spending had created massively bloated levels of private debt by 2002. Wealth is unevenly distributed; the Jolla (Cholla) region in the southwest remains the poorest.

MEDIA

TV ownership high

Daily newspaper circulation 393 per 1000 people

PUBLISHING AND BROADCAST MEDIA

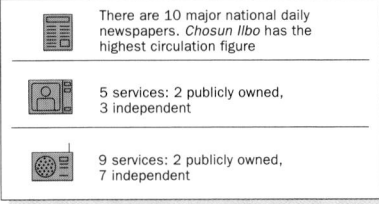

There are 10 major national daily newspapers. *Chosun Ilbo* has the highest circulation figure

5 services: 2 publicly owned, 3 independent

9 services: 2 publicly owned, 7 independent

South Korea's media have been freed of most restrictions since the advent of full democracy. Criticisms of the armed forces and their role in society are still frowned upon, however, and are generally avoided. Caution also has to be exercised in reporting facts about North Korea. In the past, South Korean journalists who made favorable mention of the North Korean regime suffered harassment. Plans to break into the satellite industry by 2015 were boosted by the successful launch in 2003 of the first domestically built rocket.

EDUCATION

School leaving age: 15

98%

3.02m students

THE EDUCATION SYSTEM

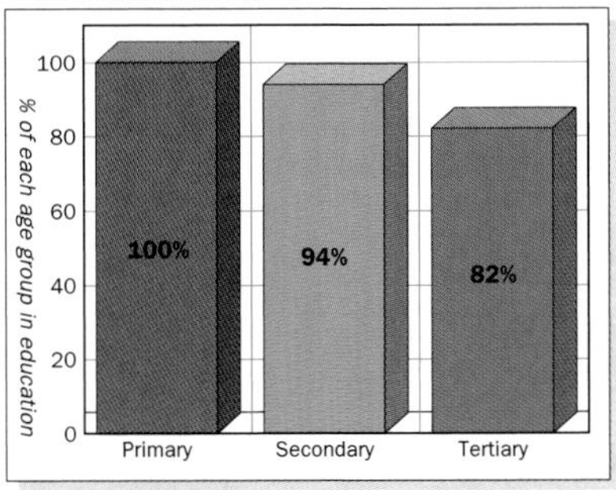

100
80
60
40
20
0
% of each age group in education
100%
94%
82%
Primary
Secondary
Tertiary

South Korea began a concentrated education program in the 1950s, and a well-educated workforce has been the foundation of impressive economic growth. Education is compulsory from age five to 15. The final three-year cycle of secondary school is voluntary but attendance is high. The rate of tertiary enrollment, at over 80%, is among the highest in the world.

WORLD RANKING

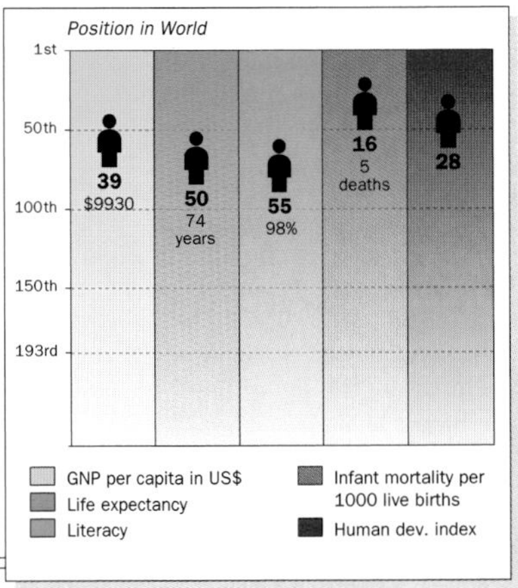

Position in World
1st
50th
100th
150th
193rd
39
$9930
50
74 years
55
98%
16
5 deaths
28
GNP per capita in US$
Life expectancy
Literacy
Infant mortality per 1000 live births
Human dev. index

K

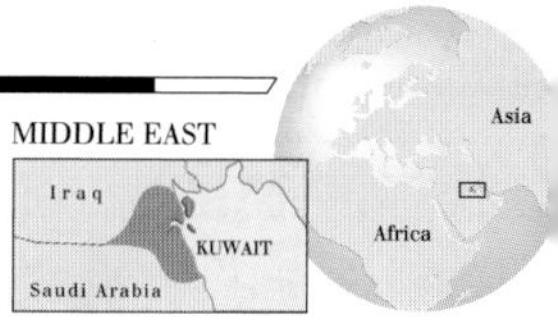
MIDDLE EAST
Iraq
KUWAIT
Saudi Arabia
Asia
Africa

KUWAIT

OFFICIAL NAME: State of Kuwait **CAPITAL:** Kuwait City
POPULATION: 2.5 million **CURRENCY:** Kuwaiti dinar **OFFICIAL LANGUAGE:** Arabic

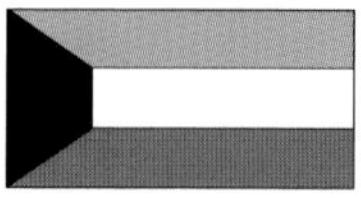

1961
1961
Feb 25
KWT
+3
+965
.kw

AT THE NORTHWEST EXTREME of the Gulf, Kuwait is dwarfed by its neighbors. The flat, almost featureless landscape conceals huge oil and gas reserves which put Kuwait among the world's first oil-rich states. In 1990 Iraq invaded, claiming it as its 19th province. A US-led alliance, under the aegis of the UN, expelled Iraqi forces following a short war in 1991 and restored the rule of the al-Sabah dynasty. Kuwait served as the launching point for the 2003 invasion of Iraq.

***Saffar Towers** in the business center of Kuwait City. Rebuilding Kuwait's postwar economy is estimated to have cost $25 billion.*

CLIMATE

Hot desert

WEATHER CHART FOR KUWAIT CITY

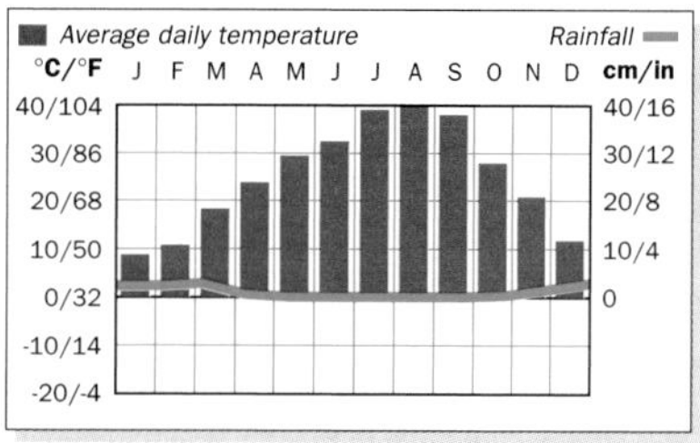
Average daily temperature
Rainfall
°C/°F
J F M A M J J A S O N D
cm/in
40/104
30/86
20/68
10/50
0/32
-10/14
-20/-4
40/16
30/12
20/8
10/4
0

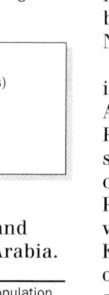

Summer temperatures can soar to over 40°C (104°F), but winters can be cold, with frost at night.

TRANSPORTATION

Drive on right

Kuwait International, Kuwait City
4.32m passengers

201 ships
2.26m grt

THE TRANSPORTATION NETWORK

3605 km (2240 miles)	280 km (174 miles)
None	None

Kuwait has a system of radial expressways around the capital and good connecting roads to Saudi Arabia.

TOURISM

Visitors : Population 1:34

73,000 visitors

Down 8% in 2001

MAIN TOURIST ARRIVALS

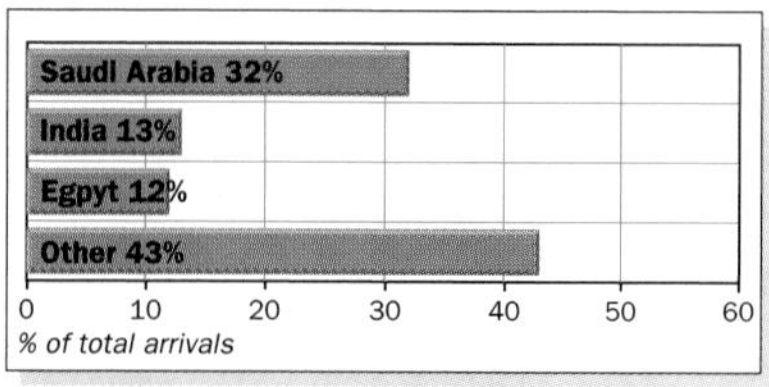
Saudi Arabia 32%
India 13%
Egypt 12%
Other 43%
0
10
20
30
40
50
60
% of total arrivals

Ongoing insecurity in Iraq has had a knock-on effect on tourism in Kuwait. Western visitors have been targeted by terrorists. Seeing the success of Dubai's expanded tourist sector, however, Kuwait is planning a major beach resort.

PEOPLE

Pop. density medium

Arabic, English

140/km² (363/mi²)

THE URBAN/RURAL POPULATION SPLIT

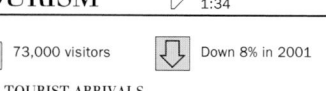

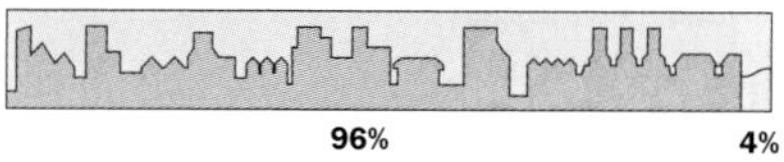
96%
4%

ETHNIC MAKEUP

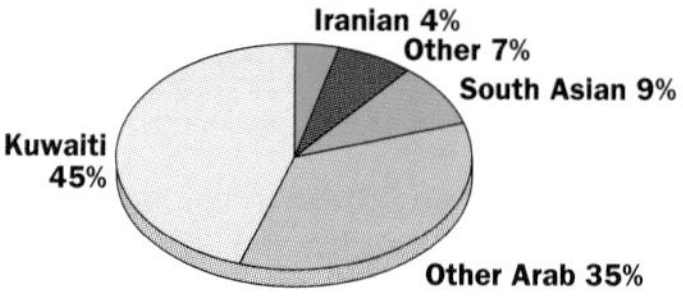
Iranian 4%
Other 7%
South Asian 9%
Kuwaiti 45%
Other Arab 35%

Kuwait is a conservative Sunni Muslim society (27% of the population is Shi'a). Women have considerable freedom, though the amir's decree providing for female enfranchisement has been repeatedly rejected by the National Assembly.

Kuwait's oil wealth has drawn in thousands of workers from other Arab countries and south Asia. The Palestine Liberation Organization's support for the 1990 Iraqi invasion of Kuwait led to most Palestinians, hitherto very numerous in Kuwait, being driven out. Native Kuwaitis are outnumbered by resident foreign nationals.

POLITICS

Nonparty elections

2003/2007

Amir Shaikh Jabir al-Ahmad al-Jabir al-Sabah

AT THE LAST ELECTION

National Assembly 50 seats

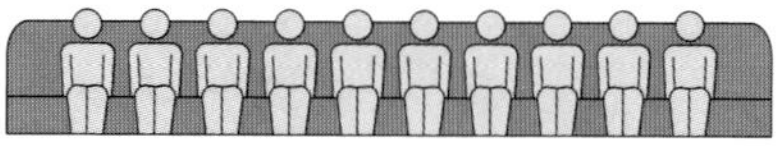

The electorate comprises civilian men over 21 years of age whose families have been resident in Kuwait since before 1921. Elections on July 5, 2003, were contested by independents: Islamists won just under half of the seats and government supporters won just over a quarter.

In 1992 Amir Shaikh Jabir restored the National Assembly. Since 1999 nonparty elections have strengthened the amir's Islamist opponents. Following elections in 2003, Crown Prince Shaikh Saad was replaced as prime minister after 25 years by the amir's half brother Shaikh Sabah in the first separation of the roles of crown prince and premier.

KUWAIT

Total Area :
17 820 sq. km
(6880 sq. miles)

POPULATION
- over 100 000
- over 50 000
- over 10 000
- under 10 000

LAND HEIGHT
- 200m/656ft
- Sea Level

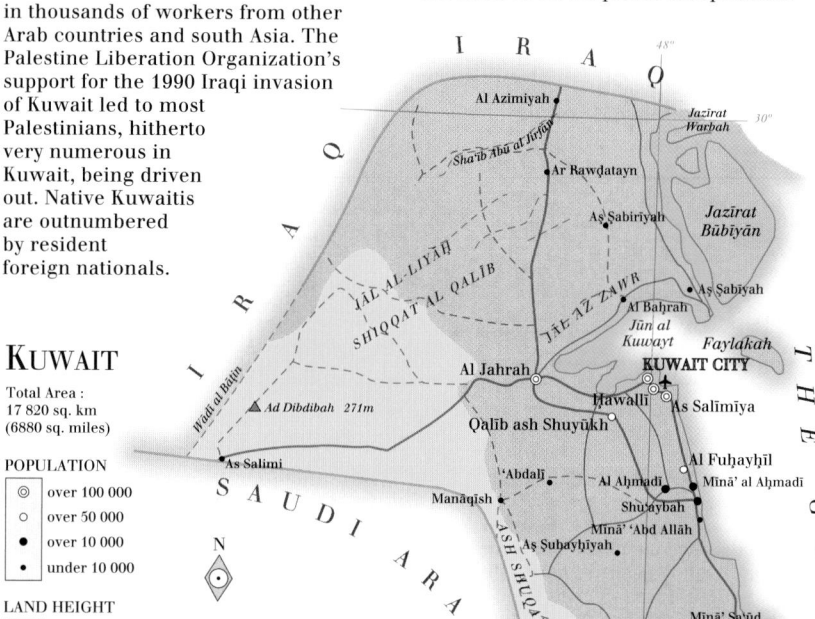

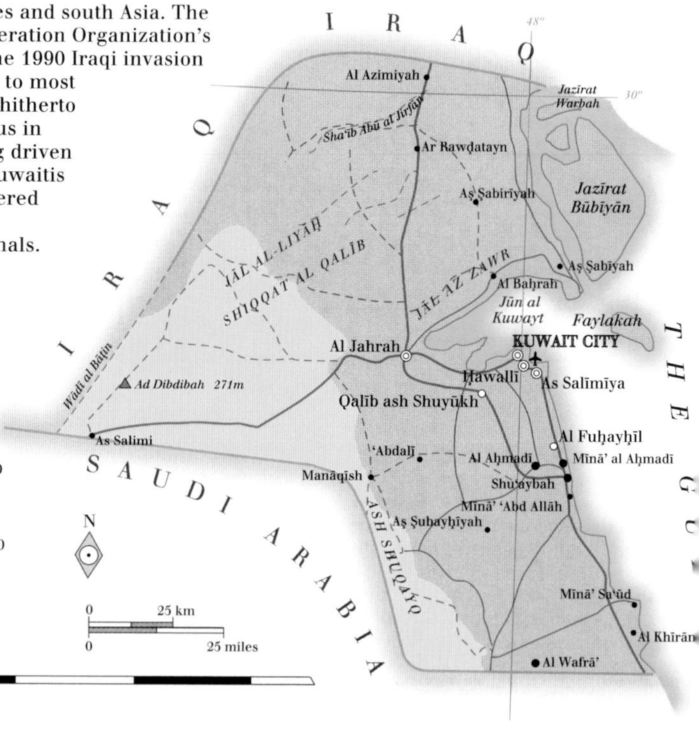
IRAQ
Al Azimiyah
Jazīrat Warbah
Sha'ib Abū al Jirfān
Ar Rawḑatayn
Aş Şabirīyah
Jazīrat Būbiyān
JAL AL-LIYĀH
SHIQQAT AL QALĪB
JAL AZ ZAWR
Aş Şabiyah
Al Bahrah
Jūn al Kuwayt
Faylakah
Al Jahrah
KUWAIT CITY
Wādī al Bāţin
Ad Dibdibah 271m
Hawallī
As Salīmīya
Qalīb ash Shuyūkh
As Salimi
SAUDI ARABIA
'Abdalī
Al Ahmadi
Al Fuhayhīl
Mīnā' al Ahmadī
Manāqish
Shu'aybah
Mīnā' 'Abd Allāh
Aş Şubayhīyah
ASH SHUQAYQ
Mīnā' Su'ūd
Al Khīrān
Al Wafrā'
THE GULF
N
0 25 km
0 25 miles

WORLD AFFAIRS

Joined UN in 1963

AL | Damasc | GCC | OIC | OPEC

Strategically important as a major exporter of crude oil and natural gas, Kuwait has close links with the West. These were strengthened by the 1991 war which secured Iraq's withdrawal from Kuwait after its invasion the previous year, and further bolstered in 2003 when Kuwait supported and facilitated the US advance into Iraq.

AID

Donor

$20m (donations)

Down 73% in 2002

The Kuwait Fund for Arab Economic Development continued to give aid even during the invasion crisis.

DEFENSE

Compulsory military service

$3.3bn

No change in 2002

In August 1990 Kuwait's 11,000-strong, partly volunteer army was easily overrun by vastly superior Iraqi forces. Kuwait rearmed fast after liberation, and defense pacts were signed with the US, the UK, France, and Russia. Kuwaiti forces did not participate in the 2003 US-led invasion of Iraq.

ECONOMICS

Inflation 1.9% p.a. (1990–2000)

$38bn

0.2948 Kuwaiti dinars (0.3003)

SCORE CARD

❑ World GNP Ranking	55th
❑ GNP per Capita	$16,340
❑ Balance of Payments	$4.19bn
❑ Inflation	1.4%
❑ Unemployment	1%

Strengths

Oil (fifth-largest reserves in world) and gas. Large overseas investments. Stable banking. Trade. Good communications.

Weaknesses

Overreliance on oil and gas. Adverse effects of 1990 Iraqi invasion, including debt to Western liberators. Strategic vulnerability deters investment. Reliance on imported skilled labor, food, and raw materials. Privatization package delayed.

EXPORTS

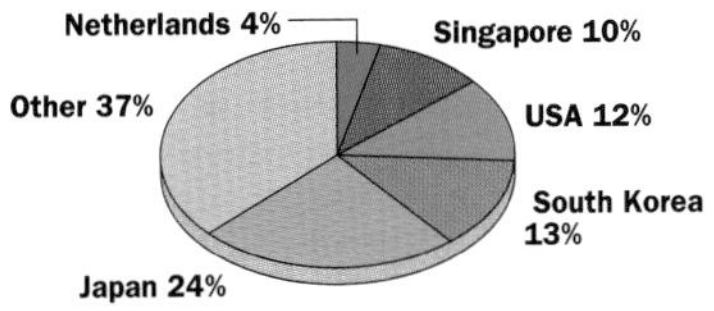
Netherlands 4%
Singapore 10%
Other 37%
USA 12%
South Korea 13%
Japan 24%

IMPORTS

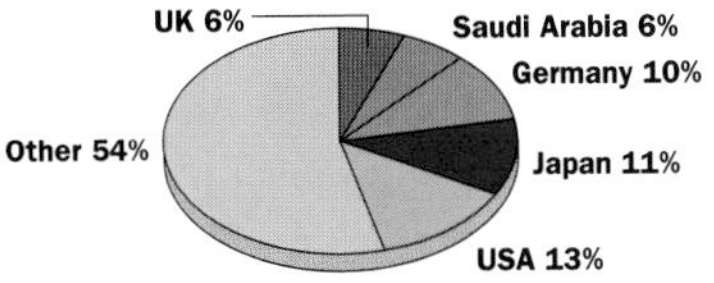
UK 6%
Saudi Arabia 6%
Germany 10%
Other 54%
Japan 11%
USA 13%

RESOURCES

Electric power 9.4m kW

6041 tonnes

2.24m b/d (reserves 96.5bn barrels)

850,000 sheep, 130,000 goats, 32.5m chickens

Oil, natural gas, salt

The oil industry is Kuwait's most profitable sector, accounting for around 90% of export earnings. Though badly hit by the Gulf War, when a number of wells were deliberately fired, it was quickly rehabilitated. Kuwait also possesses valuable reserves of natural gas. Other resources are dates, fish, ammonia, and chemicals.

ENVIRONMENT

Sustainability rank: 142nd

2% (1% partially protected)

21.9 tonnes per capita

The Iraqi invasion in 1990 and the subsequent war caused an ecological disaster. Though the effects of this did not prove as grave as some observers first feared, marine life was damaged and many thousands of hectares of cultivated land were obliterated. Millions of landmines were left strewn across border areas. Water is a scarce resource.

MEDIA

TV ownership high

Daily newspaper circulation 374 per 1000 people

PUBLISHING AND BROADCAST MEDIA

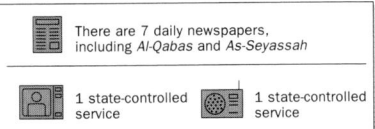

There are 7 daily newspapers, including *Al-Qabas* and *As-Seyassah*

1 state-controlled service

1 state-controlled service

Radio and TV are state-controlled, but satellite TV is freely available. The press can be aggressively critical.

CRIME

Death penalty in use

1735 prisoners

Up 8% in 1996–1998

Women can be physically and verbally harassed. There have been occasional terrorist attacks on Western targets.

EDUCATION

School leaving age: 14

83%

32,320 students

Kuwaiti citizens receive free education from nursery to university. Since the liberation, more emphasis has been placed on technology in the curriculum.

CHRONOLOGY

Kuwait traces its independence to 1710, but was under British rule from the late 18th century until 1961. The government denies any historical link with Iraq.

- ❑ **1961** Independence from UK. Iraq claims Kuwait.
- ❑ **1976** Amir suspends National Assembly.
- ❑ **1990** Iraqi invasion.
- ❑ **1991** Liberation following Gulf War.
- ❑ **1992** National Assembly elections.
- ❑ **1999, 2003** Elections: opposition Islamists win most seats.

HEALTH

Welfare state health benefits

1 per 526 people

Heart diseases, cancers, car accidents, diabetes

Despite theft of equipment during the Iraqi invasion, Kuwait has restored its Western-standard health care service. Nationals receive free treatment.

SPENDING

GDP/cap. increase

CONSUMPTION AND SPENDING

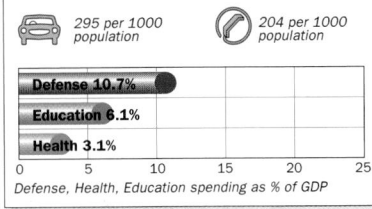

295 per 1000 population

204 per 1000 population

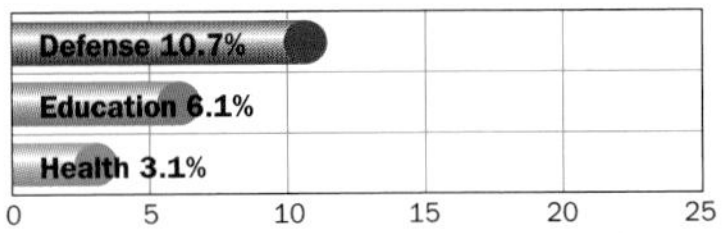
Defense 10.7%
Education 6.1%
Health 3.1%
0
5
10
15
20
25

Defense, Health, Education spending as % of GDP

Most Kuwaitis – not only the oil-rich elite – enjoy high incomes, and the government has repeatedly rescued citizens who have suffered stock market or other financial losses. School and university leavers are guaranteed jobs. Capital is easily transferred abroad and there are effectively no exchange controls.

WORLD RANKING

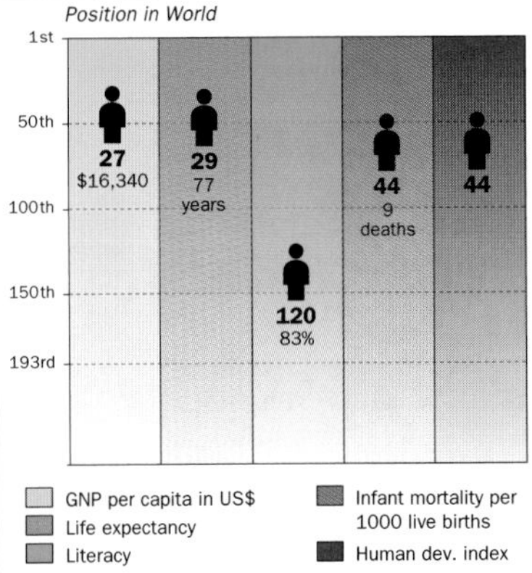
Position in World
1st
50th
100th
150th
193rd
27
$16,340
29
77
years
120
83%
44
9
deaths
44
GNP per capita in US$
Life expectancy
Literacy
Infant mortality per 1000 live births
Human dev. index

K

Kyrgyzstan

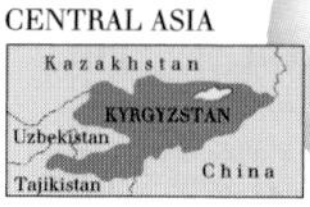
CENTRAL ASIA
Kazakhstan
KYRGYZSTAN
Uzbekistan
China
Tajikistan

Official Name: Kyrgyz Republic **Capital:** Bishkek
Population: 5.1 million **Currency:** Som **Official Languages:** Kyrgyz and Russian

1991 | 1991 | Aug 31 | KS | +6 | +996 | .kg

KYRGYZSTAN IS A SMALL and very mountainous state in central Asia. It is one of the least urbanized of the former Soviet republics (the rural population is growing faster than that in the towns) and was among the last to develop its own cultural nationalism. Its increasingly autocratic government tries to steer between Kyrgyz nationalist pressures and ensuring that the Russian minority is not alienated, since it tends to possess the skills necessary to run a market-based economy.

CLIMATE

Mountain

WEATHER CHART FOR BISHKEK

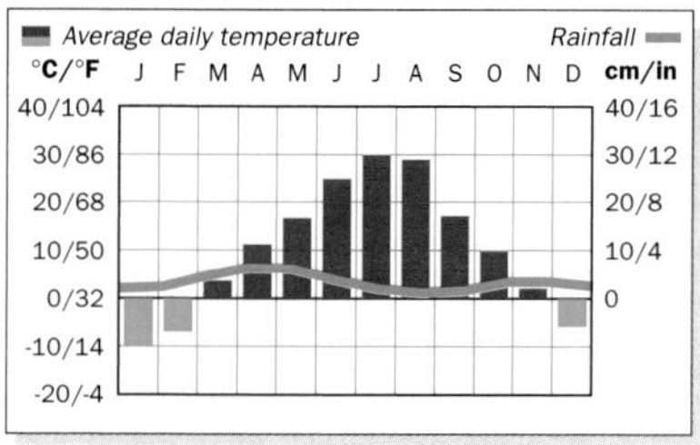
Average daily temperature
Rainfall
°C/°F
J F M A M J J A S O N D
cm/in
40/104
30/86
20/68
10/50
0/32
-10/14
-20/-4
40/16
30/12
20/8
10/4
0

Conditions vary from permanent snow and cold deserts at altitude to hot deserts in lower regions. Intermediate slopes and valleys receive some rain.

TRANSPORTATION

Drive on right

Bishkek Manas

Has no fleet

THE TRANSPORTATION NETWORK

16,835 km (10,461 miles)

140 km (87 miles)

417 km (259 miles)

600 km (373 miles)

Kyrgyzstan does not have the necessary finances to improve its poor mountain road network.

TOURISM

Visitors : Population 1:37

139,589 visitors

Up 102% in 2002

MAIN TOURIST ARRIVALS

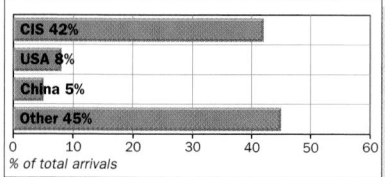

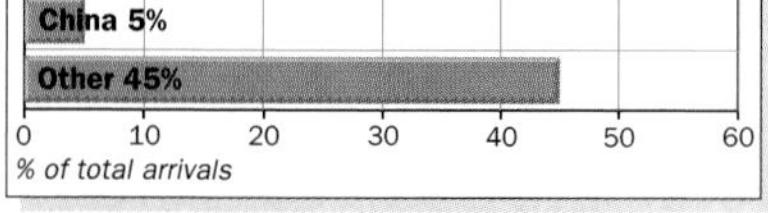
CIS 42%
USA 8%
China 5%
Other 45%
0 10 20 30 40 50 60
% of total arrivals

Tourism is undeveloped; most visitors are on business or aid workers. Tourism promotion centers on Kyrgyzstan's position on the Silk Road and on its mountain scenery.

PEOPLE

Pop. density low

Kyrgyz, Russian, Uzbek, Tatar, Ukrainian

26/km² (67/mi²)

THE URBAN/RURAL POPULATION SPLIT

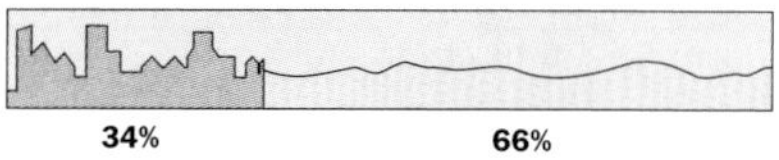
34%
66%

ETHNIC MAKEUP

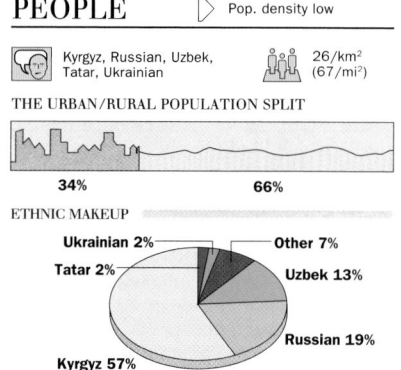

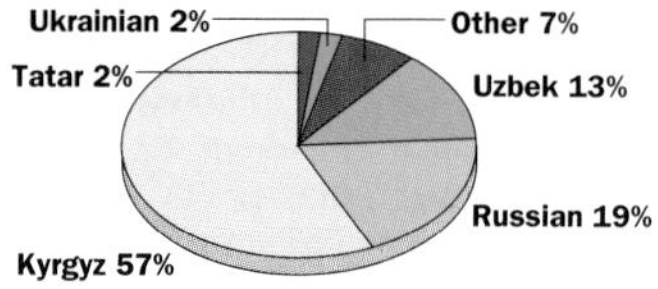
Ukrainian 2%
Other 7%
Tatar 2%
Uzbek 13%
Russian 19%
Kyrgyz 57%

The Kyrgyz are a Turkic-speaking people, closely related to the neighboring Kazakhs. They were forced to abandon their traditional nomadic way of life under Soviet rule, though many cultural practices linger, especially in rural areas.

Following the breakup of the Soviet Union, Kyrgyzstan witnessed a major exodus of its ethnic Russian population, with more than 200,000 leaving between 1989 and 1998, reconfirming the majority status of the Kyrgyz. The government has attempted to stem the tide by making Russian an official language, with full equal status with Kyrgyz from 2000. Kyrgyz relations with the substantial Uzbek minority are largely stable despite cases of severe ethnic unrest in the past, most notably in the city of Osh in 1990. The south of Kyrgyzstan, around the Fergana Valley, has witnessed growing Islamization and Muslim radicalism.

Loess landscape, Naryn valley. *Kyrgyzstan is dominated by the ice-capped Tien Shan mountains, but valleys are green and fertile.*

POLITICS

Multiparty elections

L. House 2000/2005
U. House 2000/2005

President Askar Akayev

AT THE LAST ELECTION

Legislative Assembly 60 seats

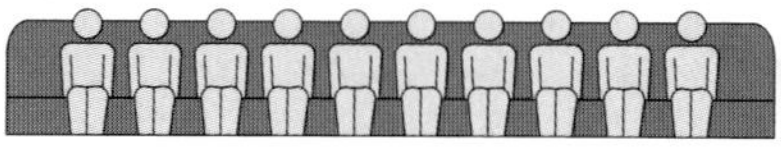

Election results by party were announced only for the 15 national list seats. The other 45 seats are elected on a constituency basis. The Party of Communists of Kyrgyzstan is the largest party and the Union of Democratic Forces the second-largest.

Assembly of People's Representatives 45 seats

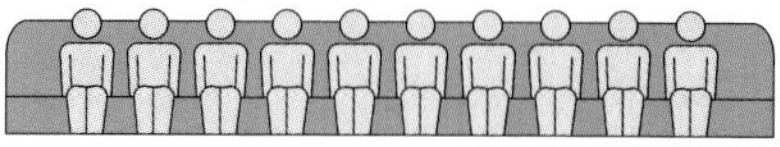

The members represent Kyrgyzstan's different regional and ethnic communities

President Akayev's administration has become increasingly autocratic, ending Kyrgyzstan's reputation as one of the region's most liberal societies. Already damaged democratic credentials were destroyed by accusations of fraud during the 2000 legislative and presidential elections. The main opposition leader, Felix Kulov, was imprisoned only weeks before the presidential poll (in which Akayev won his third term in office). In 2002, the death of protestors during demonstrations over the temporary imprisonment of Kulov's successor ultimately forced the entire cabinet to resign. In 2003 constitutional changes were approved by 75% of voters in a hastily called referendum. Among them were the scrapping of the upper house at the next elections and, as a rebuff to Akayev's opponents, a clause confirming that he should remain in power until the end of his current term.

WORLD AFFAIRS

Joined UN in 1992

CIS
SCO
OIC
OSCE
EAPC

Kyrgyzstan is working to reduce its dependence on Russia. Turkey is developing close links based on ethnic similarities and aimed at restraining Iranian influence. Relations with Uzbekistan, which allegedly supports some of the antigovernment forces in Kyrgyzstan, are tense, though in 2000 both countries joined with Tajikistan to combat Islamist militants in the region.

AID

Recipient

$186m (receipts)

Down 2% in 2002

The ADB, the US, and the World Bank are the main donors. Japan is also an important source of financial assistance.

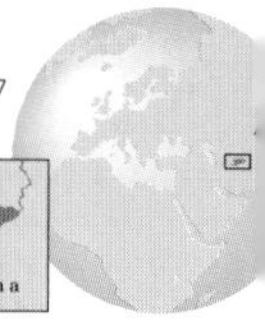

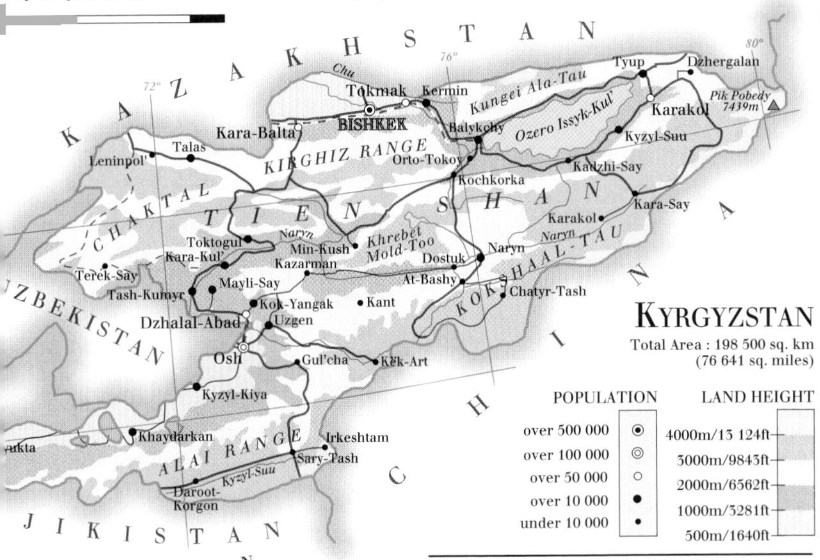
KAZAKHSTAN
UZBEKISTAN
TAJIKISTAN
CHINA
Chu
Tokmak
Kermin
BISHKEK
Kara-Balta
Talas
Leninpol'
KIRGHIZ RANGE
Kungei Ala-Tau
Tyup
Dzhergalan
Pik Pobedy 7439m
Karakol
Ozero Issyk-Kul'
Balykchy
Kyzyl-Suu
Orto-Tokoy
Kadzhi-Say
Kochkorka
TIEN SHAN
Kara-Say
CHATKAL
Toktogul
Kara-Kul'
Naryn
Min-Kush
Khrebet Mold-Too
Karakol
Naryn
Kazarman
Dostuk
Terek-Say
Mayli-Say
At-Bashy
KOKSHAAL-TAU
Tash-Kumyr
Kok-Yangak
Kant
Chatyr-Tash
Dzhalal-Abad
Uzgen
Osh
Gul'cha
Kök-Art
Kyzyl-Kiya
Khaydarkan
Irkeshtam
ALAI RANGE
Sary-Tash
Kyzyl-Suu
Daroot-Korgon
72°
76°
80°
0 100 km
0 100 miles
N

KYRGYZSTAN

Total Area : 198 500 sq. km (76 641 sq. miles)

POPULATION	
over 500 000	◉
over 100 000	◎
over 50 000	○
over 10 000	●
under 10 000	•

LAND HEIGHT
4000m/13 124ft
3000m/9843ft
2000m/6562ft
1000m/3281ft
500m/1640ft

CHRONOLOGY

The Kyrgyz first developed a recognizable ethnic consciousness in the late 18th century.

- ❑ **1860s** Expansion of Russian Empire into Kyrgyz lands.
- ❑ **1924–1991** Incorporated in USSR.
- ❑ **1995** New constitution adopted.
- ❑ **2000** Legislative and presidential elections; Askar Akayev reelected.
- ❑ **2002** Government resigns after police shoot demonstrators.

DEFENSE

▷ Phasing out conscription

$265m | Up 5% in 2002

In 2002 the US established an air base in Kyrgyzstan, and Russia has had one since 2003, manned by a new military alliance of six ex-Soviet states.

ECONOMICS

▷ Inflation 95% p.a. (1990–2001)

$1.44bn | 42.50 soms (41.18)

SCORE CARD

❑ World GNP Ranking	147th
❑ GNP per Capita	$290
❑ Balance of Payments	–$35m
❑ Inflation	2.1%
❑ Unemployment	9%

Strengths

Agricultural self-sufficiency. Private land ownership since 2000. Gold and mercury exports. Hydropower potential.

Weaknesses

Dominant state and collective farming mentality. Sharp economic decline since USSR's breakup. History of high inflation. Increasing political instability.

EXPORTS

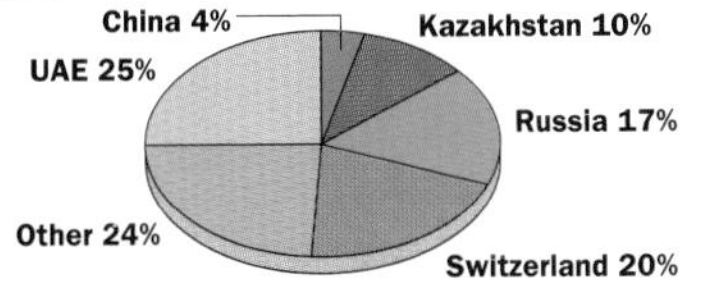
China 4%
Kazakhstan 10%
UAE 25%
Russia 17%
Other 24%
Switzerland 20%

IMPORTS

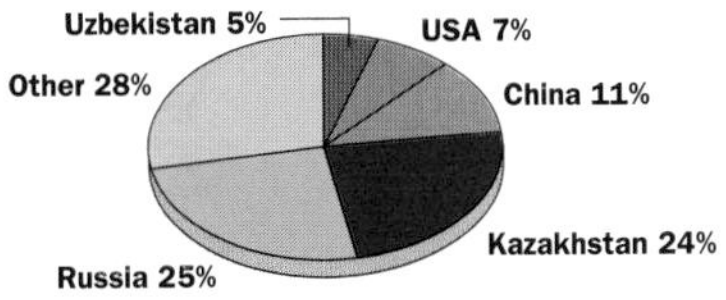
Uzbekistan 5%
USA 7%
Other 28%
China 11%
Kazakhstan 24%
Russia 25%

RESOURCES

▷ Electric power 3.7m kW

201 tonnes | 1544 b/d (reserves 37m barrels)

3.1m sheep, 988,016 cattle, 3.65m chickens | Coal, antimony, gas, oil, tin, mercury, iron, uranium, zinc, gold

Kyrgyzstan has large reserves of coal but lacks the investment needed to exploit them. It also has great hydroelectric power potential. Energy policy, which relies on Western aid and technology, is primarily aimed at developing these further in order to reduce dependence on supplies from Russia, and eventually to achieve self-sufficiency in energy.

ENVIRONMENT

▷ Sustainability rank: 56th

13% (2% partially protected) | 0.9 tonnes per capita

The major problem is the salination of the soil caused by excessive irrigation of cotton crops. Kyrgyzstan has a poor record in limiting industrial pollution.

MEDIA

▷ TV ownership low

Daily newspaper circulation 27 per 1000 people

PUBLISHING AND BROADCAST MEDIA

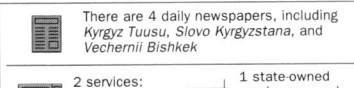

There are 4 daily newspapers, including *Kyrgyz Tuusu*, *Slovo Kyrgyzstana*, and *Vechernii Bishkek*

2 services: 1 state-owned, 1 independent | 1 state-owned service, several independent services

The Kyrgyz press is increasingly under pressure from the government's efforts to silence opposition.

CRIME

▷ Moratorium on death penalty

19,500 prisoners | Down 4% in 2000

Ethnic tension fuels violence. The narcotics trade flourishes. Nearly 800 prisoners were amnestied in 2003 to relieve severe overcrowding of jails.

EDUCATION

▷ School leaving age: 16

97% | 190,508 students

The role of the Russian language has been reappraised, and most schools in Bishkek now teach in both Russian and Kyrgyz. New private universities have opened, but vocational training is scarce.

HEALTH

▷ Welfare state health benefits

1 per 385 people | Cerebrovascular and heart diseases, cancers, accidents

Infant mortality is high. The health care system is slowly being restructured with international help.

SPENDING

▷ GDP/cap. decrease

CONSUMPTION AND SPENDING

38 per 1000 population | *77 per 1000 population*

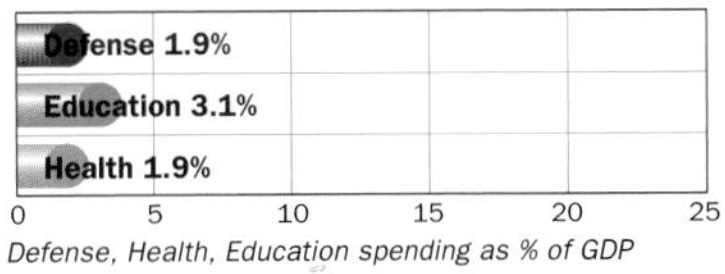
Defense 1.9%
Education 3.1%
Health 1.9%
0
5
10
15
20
25
Defense, Health, Education spending as % of GDP

Around one-third of the population of Kyrgyzstan live below the UN poverty level of $2 a day. Extreme poverty in the south has led to labor migration.

WORLD RANKING

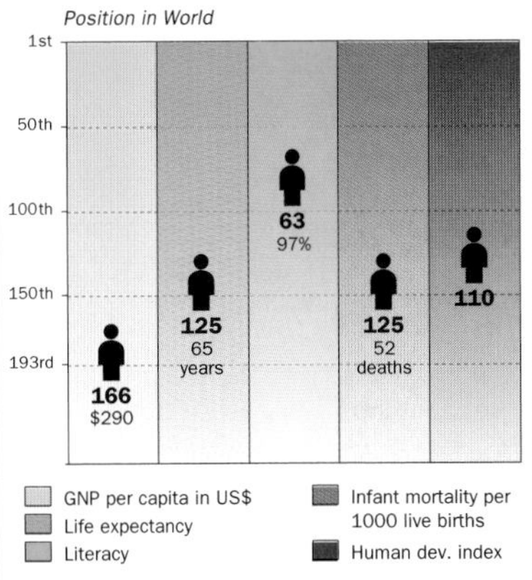
Position in World
1st
50th
100th
150th
193rd
166
$290
125
65 years
63
97%
125
52 deaths
110
GNP per capita in US$
Life expectancy
Literacy
Infant mortality per 1000 live births
Human dev. index

K

LAOS

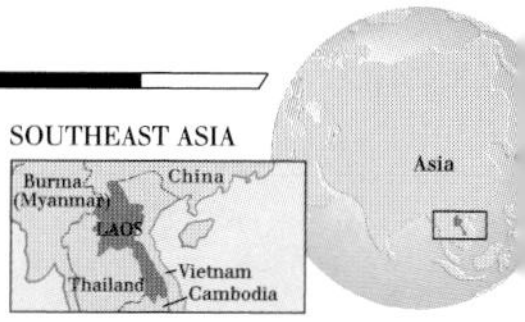
SOUTHEAST ASIA
Burma (Myanmar)
China
LAOS
Thailand
Vietnam
Cambodia
Asia

OFFICIAL NAME: Lao People's Democratic Republic **CAPITAL:** Vientiane
POPULATION: 5.7 million **CURRENCY:** New kip **OFFICIAL LANGUAGE:** Lao

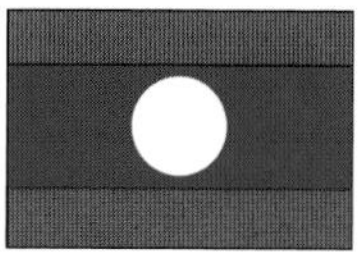

1953
1953
Dec 2
LAO
+7
+856
.la

THE MEKONG RIVER, Laos's main thoroughfare, feeds the fertile lowlands of the Mekong valley. Two decades of civil war followed independence from France in 1953, and Laos was bombed heavily during the Vietnam War. The communist Lao People's Revolutionary Party (LPRP) has held power since 1975. Market-oriented reforms began to be introduced in 1986, while power was handed to a younger generation within the LPRP in the 1990s.

CLIMATE

Tropical monsoon

WEATHER CHART FOR VIENTIANE

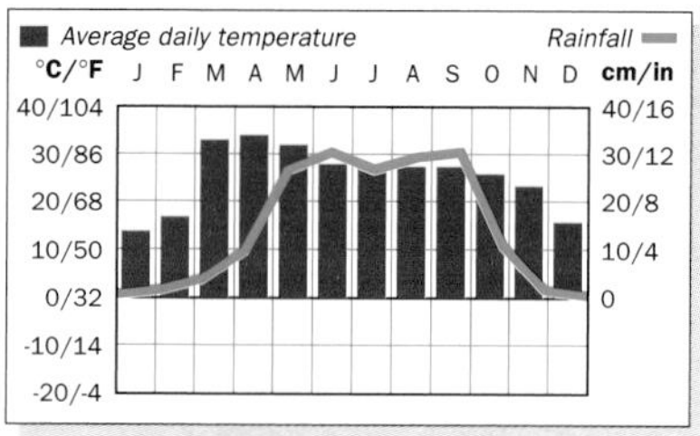
Average daily temperature
Rainfall
°C/°F
J F M A M J J A S O N D
cm/in
40/104
30/86
20/68
10/50
0/32
-10/14
-20/-4
40/16
30/12
20/8
10/4
0

The tropical southerly monsoon brings heavy rains from May to September.

TRANSPORTATION

Drive on right

Wattay, Vientiane 165,000 passengers

1 ship 2400 grt

THE TRANSPORTATION NETWORK

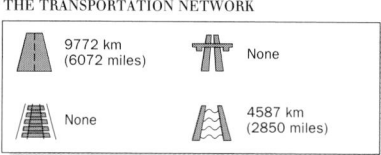

9772 km (6072 miles)

None

None

4587 km (2850 miles)

A major new Thailand–Vietnam road via Savannakhét is almost complete. Freight goes mainly by river, though roads have improved.

TOURISM

Visitors : Population 1:27

215,000 visitors

Up 24% in 2002

MAIN TOURIST ARRIVALS

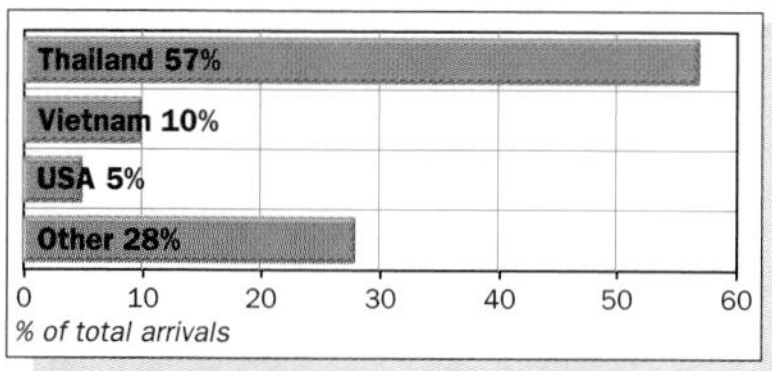
Thailand 57%
Vietnam 10%
USA 5%
Other 28%
0
10
20
30
40
50
60
% of total arrivals

Tourists were first allowed into Laos in 1989; numbers have risen rapidly since then. Mass tourism is discouraged and preference given to small package tours. Hotels are few, and travel outside Vientiane is difficult.

PEOPLE

Pop. density low

Lao, Mon-Khmer, Yao, Vietnamese, Chinese, French

25/km² (64/mi²)

THE URBAN/RURAL POPULATION SPLIT

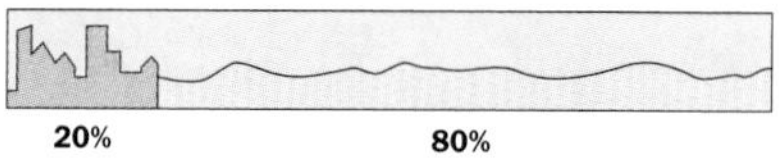
20%
80%

RELIGIOUS PERSUASION

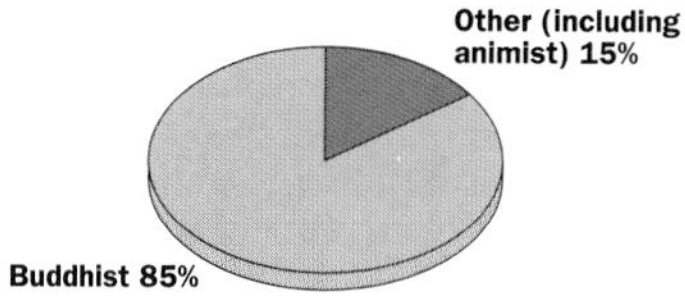
Other (including animist) 15%
Buddhist 85%

There are more than 60 ethnic groups in Laos and this considerable diversity has hindered national integration. Society is broadly divided by geography, but by altitude rather than by region. The lowland Laotians (*Lao Loum*) make up some 60% of the population. The upland Laotians (*Lao Theung*), who live in the hills above the valleys, account for 30%. The small minority of highland Laotians (*Lao Soung*), among whom are included the Hmong, Yao, and Man groups, have resisted government efforts to introduce substitutes for traditional cash crops such as opium. The government continues to face small pockets of Hmong resistance.

Two-thirds of Laotians speak Lao, and many tribal dialects are also spoken. Buddhism is the main religion, but there are some Christians and animists.

POLITICS

No multiparty elections

2002/2007

President Khamtay Siphandone

AT THE LAST ELECTION

National Assembly 109 seats

99% LPRP
1% Ind

LPRP = Lao People's Revolutionary Party (the sole legal political party) **Ind** = Independent

All candidates were approved by the LPRP

Though a new nomenklatura came to power in the 1990s, the established pillars of the military, the LPRP, and the executive branch remain closely intertwined. Party chairman Gen. Khamtay Siphandone became the country's president in February 1998. Despite limited moves toward political reform, the LPRP, which is modeled on the Communist Party of Vietnam, continues to dominate political life at every level. The long-standing problem of corruption, sometimes at high levels, has become a matter of concern as Laos has opened up to foreign investors. Economic reform has not been accompanied by political liberalization. Tensions continue to be felt between the government and the rural areas, where there is particular resistance to attempts to alter traditional farming methods.

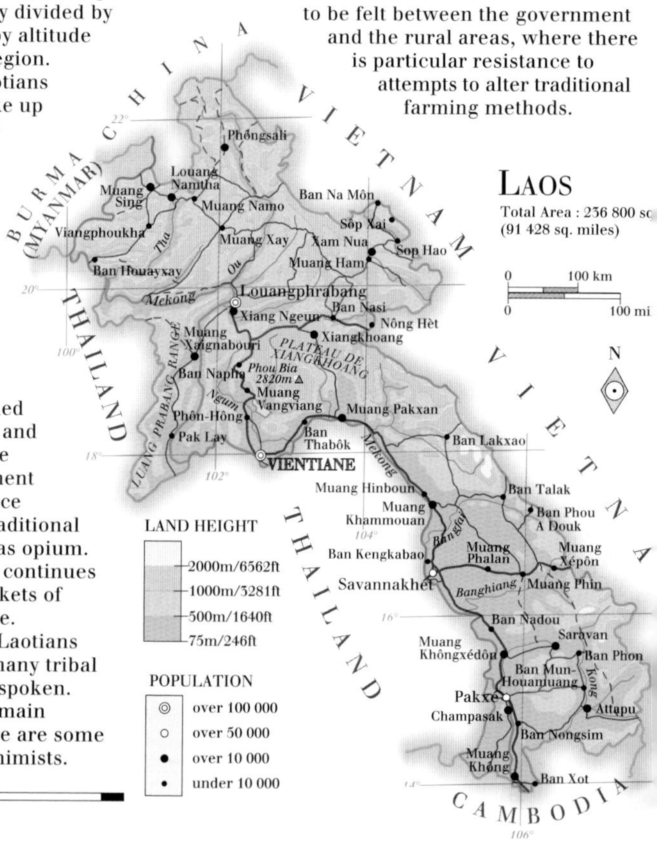
CHINA
VIETNAM
BURMA (MYANMAR)
THAILAND
CAMBODIA
LAOS
Total Area : 236 800 sq. km
(91 428 sq. miles)
0 100 km
0 100 mi
N
Phôngsali
Louang Namtha
Muang Sing
Muang Namo
Viangphoukha
Ban Houayxay
Muang Xay
Ban Na Môn
Sôp Xai
Xam Nua
Sop Hao
Muang Ham
Louangphrabang
Ban Nasi
Nông Hèt
Xiang Ngeun
Xiangkhoang
Muang Xaignabouri
PLATEAU DE XIANGKHOANG
Phou Bia 2820m
Ban Napha
Muang Vangviang
Muang Pakxan
Phôn-Hông
Pak Lay
Ban Thabôk
VIENTIANE
Ban Lakxao
Mekong
Muang Hinboun
Muang Khammouan
Ban Talak
Ban Phou A Douk
Ban Kengkabao
Muang Phalan
Muang Xépôn
Savannakhét
Banghiang
Muang Phin
Ban Nadou
Saravan
Muang Khôngxédôn
Ban Phon
Ban Mun-Houamuang
Kong
Pakxe
Champasak
Attapu
Ban Nongsim
Muang Không
Ban Xot
LUANG PRABANG RANGE
Tha
Ou
Ngum
LAND HEIGHT
2000m/6562ft
1000m/3281ft
500m/1640ft
75m/246ft
POPULATION
over 100 000
over 50 000
over 10 000
under 10 000

WORLD AFFAIRS

Joined UN in 1955

ASEAN | CP | OIF | Mekong River | NAM

Vietnam was Laos's most important ally from 1975 until the late 1980s, when the LPRP began to seek improved relations with Thailand and the West. The change was mainly due to the need for foreign aid. In 1992, Laos acceded to the Treaty of Amity and Concord of ASEAN, marking the beginning of a new relationship with former adversaries. Laos was admitted to full membership of ASEAN in 1997.

AID

Recipient

$278m (receipts)

Up 13% in 2002

Laos has one of the highest per capita aid inflows in south or east Asia, with Japan being the major donor.

DEFENSE

Compulsory military service

$14m

Down 12% in 2002

The armed forces are estimated by the West to number around 29,000 personnel. This total is further swelled by a paramilitary militia. A minimum of 18 months' military service is compulsory for all Laotian men.

ECONOMICS

Inflation 29% p.a. (1990–2001)

$1.71bn

7882 new kips (7600)

SCORE CARD

❑ World GNP Ranking	143rd
❑ GNP per Capita	$310
❑ Balance of Payments	–$82m
❑ Inflation	10.6%
❑ Unemployment	6%

EXPORTS

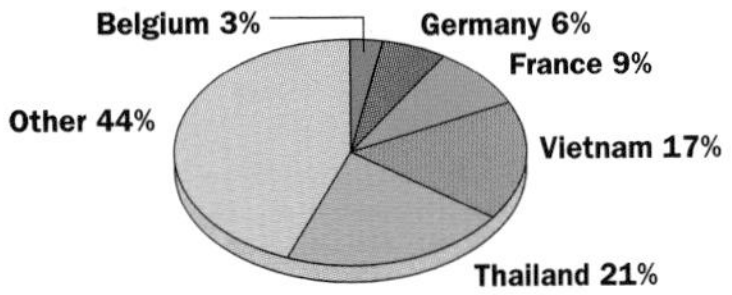
Belgium 3%
Germany 6%
France 9%
Other 44%
Vietnam 17%
Thailand 21%

IMPORTS

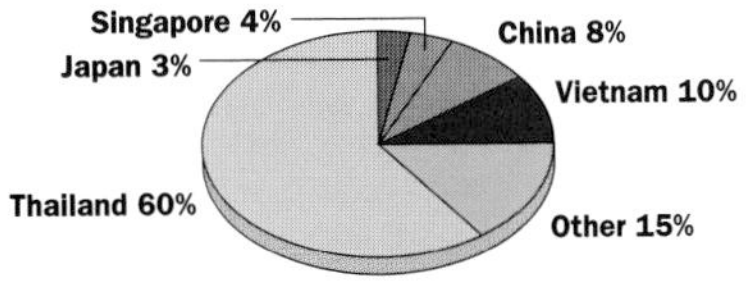
Singapore 4%
China 8%
Japan 3%
Vietnam 10%
Thailand 60%
Other 15%

Strengths

Rising levels of investment from overseas. Potential of garment manufacturing, timber plantations, mining, wood processing, tourism, banking, and aviation. Minerals and possible oil and gas deposits.

Weaknesses

One of the world's least developed countries. Subsistence agriculture accounts for half of GDP. Imbalance in sources of foreign investment – most is Thai. Primitive infrastructure.

RESOURCES

Electric power 256,000 kW

80,000 tonnes

Not an oil producer

3m ducks, 1.65m pigs, 1.2m cattle, 20m chickens

Tin, gypsum, iron, coal, copper, lead, antimony, gold, precious stones

Laos has significant hydroelectric power potential and exports electricity to Thailand. It also exports timber, coffee, gold, and precious stones.

ENVIRONMENT

Sustainability rank: 32nd

13% (12% partially protected)

0.1 tonnes per capita

Bombing and the use of defoliants in the Vietnam War did serious ecological damage. Slash and burn farming and illegal logging are destroying forests.

MEDIA

TV ownership medium

Daily newspaper circulation 4 per 1000 people

PUBLISHING AND BROADCAST MEDIA

There is 1 daily newspaper, the government-published *Vientiane Mai*

2 services: 1 fully state-owned, 1 30% state-owned

1 state-owned service

Newspapers are owned and controlled by the LPRP; one is published by the Lao People's Army. Revelations of corruption by state officials are not uncommon, but criticism of the party and its leaders remains taboo.

CRIME

Death penalty in use

Laos does not publish prison figures

Rising overall, particularly corruption

Laos is the world's third-largest opium producer. The US has provided funds to replace poppies with alternative cash crops in the northeast provinces.

Farm in northeastern Laos. *The only lowlands are along the Mekong River. Three-quarters of Laotians are subsistence farmers.*

CHRONOLOGY

In 1899, the three small Lao kingdoms were unified under the French.

- ❑ **1953** Independence.
- ❑ **1963** Left-wing armed struggle, overshadowed by Vietnam War.
- ❑ **1975** LPRP seizes power.
- ❑ **1986** Market-oriented reforms.
- ❑ **1997** Accession to ASEAN.
- ❑ **1999** Protests demanding greater political freedom.
- ❑ **2001** Prime minister resigns over economic mismanagement.

EDUCATION

School leaving age: 10

66%

16,621 students

Adult education is being expanded. Since 1990, private schools have been allowed, in order to help meet demand.

HEALTH

Welfare state health benefits

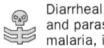

1 per 5000 people

Diarrheal, respiratory, and parasitic diseases, malaria, influenza

Since 1975, public health care has developed steadily. HIV infection rates are among the lowest in the region.

SPENDING

GDP/cap. increase

CONSUMPTION AND SPENDING

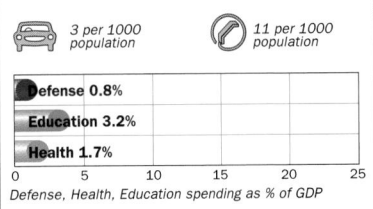

3 per 1000 population

11 per 1000 population

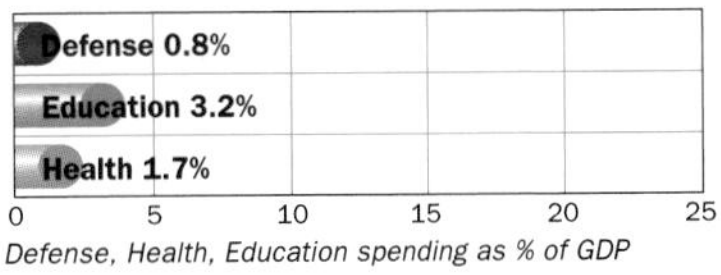
Defense 0.8%
Education 3.2%
Health 1.7%
0
5
10
15
20
25
Defense, Health, Education spending as % of GDP

While a rapidly expanding group of entrepreneurs profits from the gradual liberalization of the country's economy, many in highland and mountainous regions lead a subsistence existence.

WORLD RANKING

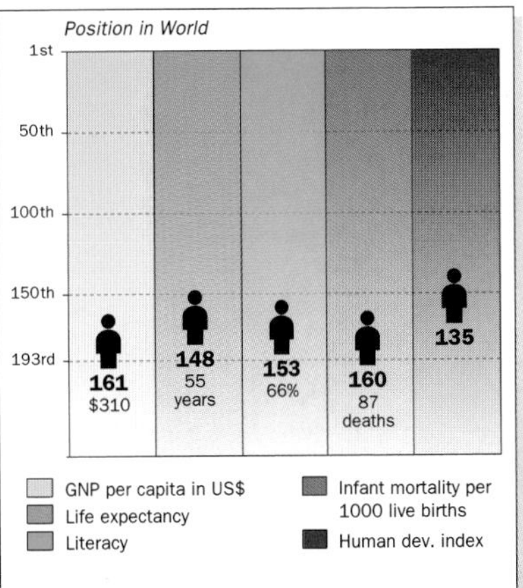
Position in World
1st
50th
100th
150th
193rd
161
$310
148
55 years
153
66%
160
87 deaths
135
GNP per capita in US$
Life expectancy
Literacy
Infant mortality per 1000 live births
Human dev. index

L

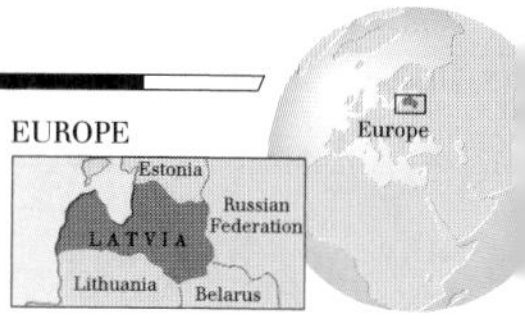
EUROPE
Europe
Estonia
Russian Federation
LATVIA
Lithuania
Belarus

LATVIA

OFFICIAL NAME: Republic of Latvia **CAPITAL:** Riga
POPULATION: 2.3 million **CURRENCY:** Lats **OFFICIAL LANGUAGE:** Latvian

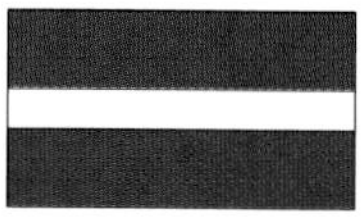

1991 | 1991 | Nov 18 | LV | +2 | +371 | .lv

LATVIA IS ONE of the three Baltic states (with Estonia to the north and Lithuania to the south) which regained independence from Soviet rule in 1991. It lies on a low plain, which nowhere rises above 300 m (975 ft). Almost one-third of the population lives in the capital, Riga. Defense-related industries and agriculture play an important role in the economy, though services now dominate. Only just over half of the population are ethnic Latvians.

CLIMATE

Continental

WEATHER CHART FOR RIGA

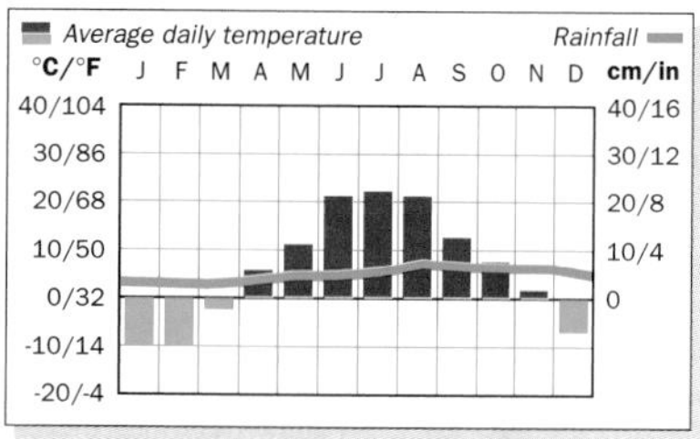
Average daily temperature
Rainfall
°C/°F
J F M A M J J A S O N D
cm/in
40/104
30/86
20/68
10/50
0/32
-10/14
-20/-4
40/16
30/12
20/8
10/4
0

Latvia's coastal position moderates its continental-type climate and summers are cool, but winters are cold.

TRANSPORTATION

Drive on right

Spilve, Riga
712,451 passengers

158 ships
88,700 grt

THE TRANSPORTATION NETWORK

28,559 km (17,746 miles)

None

2270 km (1411 miles)

300 km (186 miles)

Riga is well-served with trams, trolleys, and buses. The EU-backed Via Baltica highway, linking Poland and Finland, runs north–south through Latvia. An east–west link of a similar standard is a priority.

Riga, the Latvian capital. The Russian Orthodox cathedral in the foreground was used as a planetarium during the Soviet era.

TOURISM

Visitors : Population 1:2.7

848,000 visitors

Up 44% in 2002

MAIN TOURIST ARRIVALS

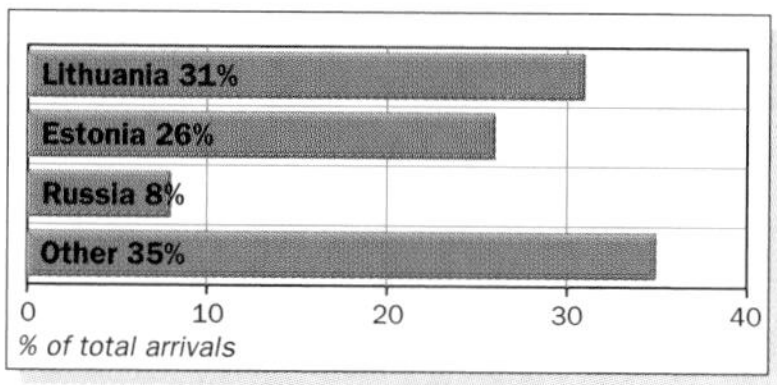
Lithuania 31%
Estonia 26%
Russia 8%
Other 35%
0
10
20
30
40
% of total arrivals

Riga is the main tourist destination, though the many medieval castles throughout the country also draw visitors.

PEOPLE

Pop. density low

Latvian, Russian

36/km² (92/mi²)

THE URBAN/RURAL POPULATION SPLIT

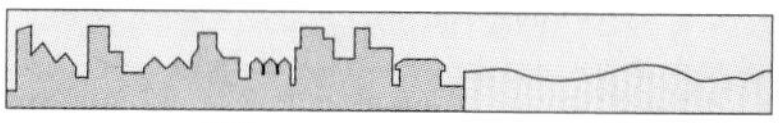
60%
40%

ETHNIC MAKEUP

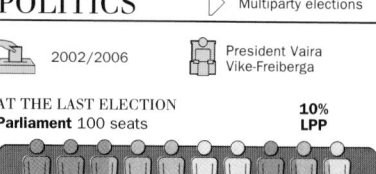

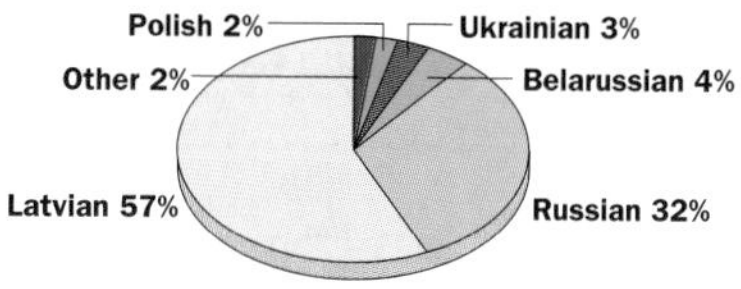
Polish 2%
Ukrainian 3%
Other 2%
Belarussian 4%
Latvian 57%
Russian 32%

Latvians (who form the minority in Riga and are mostly Lutheran) have since 1991 been effectively favored by the state over the Orthodox Russian minority (which was boosted by Soviet-era migrations). The naturalization process was simplified in 1998, but Latvian was proclaimed the only official language for state and private sectors in 2000 and will be used in all schools from 2004.

POLITICS

Multiparty elections

2002/2006

President Vaira Vike-Freiberga

AT THE LAST ELECTION
Parliament 100 seats

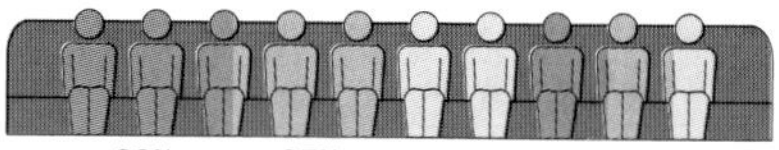
10% LPP
26% JL
25% PCTVL
20% TP
12% ZZS
7% TB/LNNK

JL = New Era **PCTVL** = For Human Rights in a United Latvia (including the National Harmony Party–**TSP**) **TP** = People's Party **ZZS** = Green and Farmers' Union **LPP** = Latvia's First Party **TB/LNNK** = Fatherland and Freedom

Recent elections have boosted center-right parties, all in favor of EU membership and continuing market reforms. Coalitions have been short-lived; there were four different governments between 1998 and 2002. Einars Repse, former state banker and leader of the recently formed JL, became prime minister at the head of a center-right coalition after the 2002 elections. Amid corruption allegations and criticisms of his authoritarian style, he was forced from power when the LPP withdrew in January 2004. He was replaced in March by Indulis Emsis, the world's first Green prime minister.

LATVIA

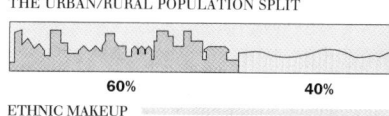

Total Area :
64 589 sq. km
(24 938 sq. miles)

POPULATION
over 500 000
over 100 000
over 50 000
over 10 000
under 10 000

LAND HEIGHT
200m/656ft
Sea Level

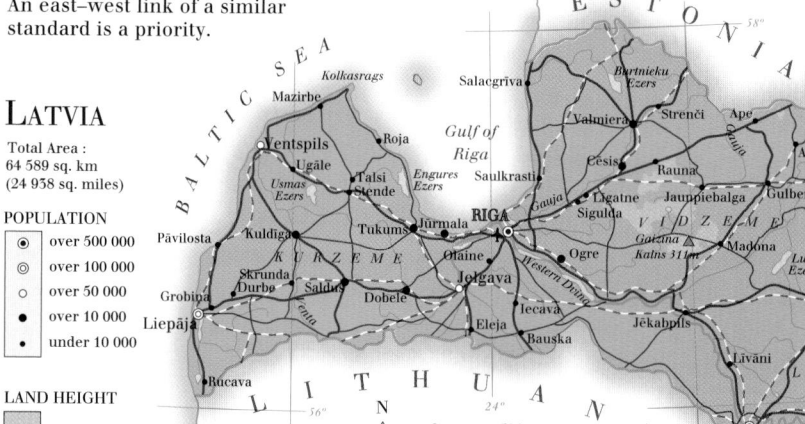

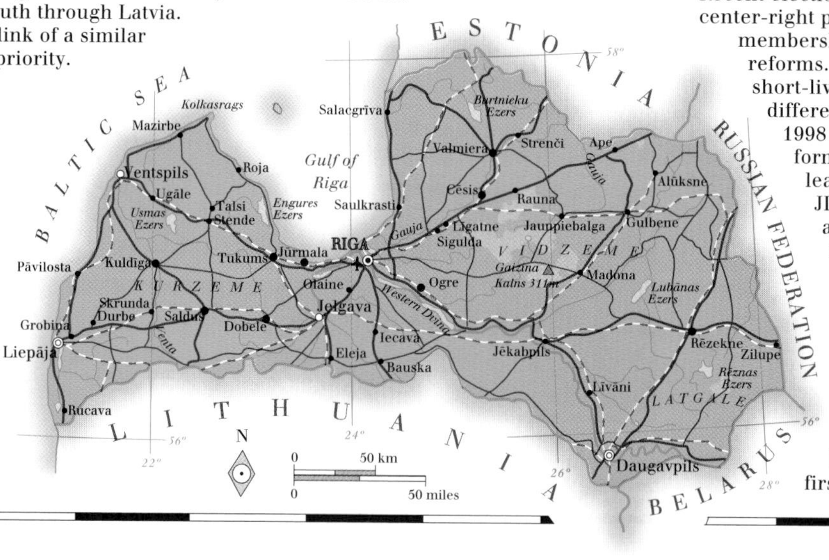
ESTONIA
RUSSIAN FEDERATION
BELARUS
LITHUANIA
BALTIC SEA
Gulf of Riga
Kolkasrags
Mazirbe
Ventspils
Ugāle
Roja
Talsi
Stende
Usmas Ezers
Engures Ezers
Salacgrīva
Saulkrasti
Pāvilosta
Kuldīga
KURZEME
Skrunda
Durbe
Saldus
Tukums
Jūrmala
RIGA
Dobele
Grobiņa
Liepāja
Rucava
Olaine
Jelgava
Eleja
Iecava
Bauska
Venta
Western Dvina
Ogre
Gauja
Sigulda
Līgatne
Cēsis
Valmiera
Burtnieku Ezers
Strenči
Ape
Rauna
Jaunpiebalga
Gulbene
Alūksne
VIDZEME
Gaizina Kalns 311m
Madona
Lubānas Ezers
Jēkabpils
Rēzekne
Zilupe
Rēznas Ezers
LATGALE
Līvāni
Daugavpils
N
0
50 km
50 miles
58°
56°
22°
24°
26°
28°

WORLD AFFAIRS

Joined UN in 1991

CE | CBSS | EU | NATO | OSCE

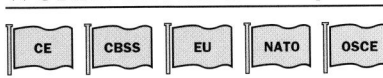

Latvia had strong US backing for its successful bid to join NATO in 2004. It was also one of ten countries that became full members of the EU in the same year. Discrimination against Russian-speakers, exemplified by laws passed in 2000 making Latvian the only official language, have strained relations with Russia.

AID

Recipient

$86m (receipts)

Down 19% in 2002

Latvia now receives direct EU funding and aid donations from other member states. Most is spent on improving the country's infrastructure.

DEFENSE

Compulsory military service

$141m

Up 68% in 2002

Building up the military is a priority. Full membership of NATO, achieved in 2004, was preceded by collaboration with the Partnership for Peace program. In February 2000, Russian forces finished dismantling their last military installation in Latvia, the Skrunda radar station.

ECONOMICS

Inflation 42% p.a. (1990–2001)

$8.13bn

0.5404 lats (0.5666)

SCORE CARD

- World GNP Ranking........95th
- GNP per Capita........$3480
- Balance of Payments........–$659m
- Inflation........2%
- Unemployment........16%

Strengths

Thriving service sector: now provides over 70% of GDP. Buoyant manufacturing industries. Low inflation. Foreign investment.

Weaknesses

Dependence on imports for energy. Lack of raw materials. Farming technically backward after dismantling of collective farms. Sizable current account deficit.

EXPORTS

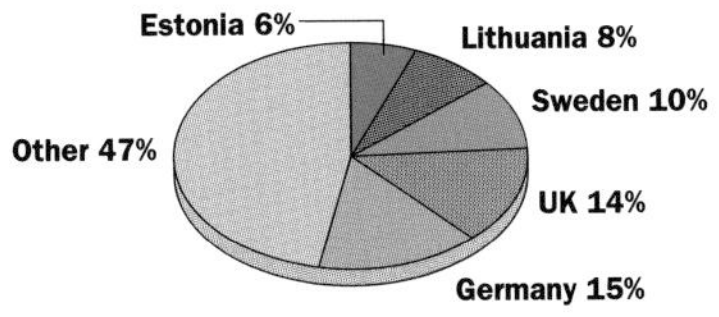
Estonia 6%
Lithuania 8%
Sweden 10%
Other 47%
UK 14%
Germany 15%

IMPORTS

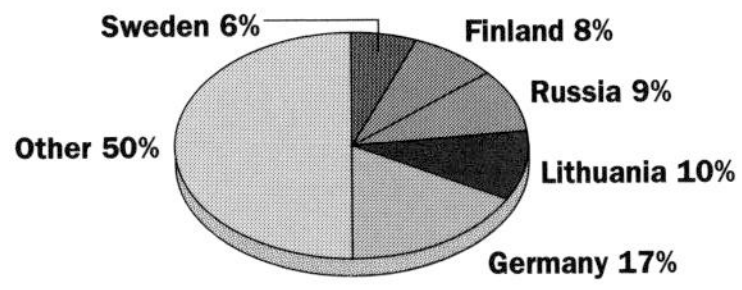
Sweden 6%
Finland 8%
Russia 9%
Other 50%
Lithuania 10%
Germany 17%

RESOURCES

Electric power 2.1m kW

125,896 tonnes

Not an oil producer

453,200 pigs, 450,000 turkeys, 3.88m chickens

Amber, dolomite, gravel, gypsum, limestone, peat, sand

Latvia has limited resources, and is dependent on imports to meet most of its energy needs. Electricity comes chiefly from hydroelectric power and regular imports from Lithuania and Estonia. The Baltic port of Ventspils has lost significant trade as a regional oil terminal since the completion of the Russian port of Primorsk in 2002.

ENVIRONMENT

Sustainability rank: 10th

13% (12% partially protected)

2.5 tonnes per capita

Peat extraction has damaged valuable bog habitat. Pollution of the Baltic Sea and air and water quality in industrial centers are also of concern.

In 2001 Latvia committed to full enforcement of EU environmental directives by 2010.

MEDIA

TV ownership high

Daily newspaper circulation 135 per 1000 people

PUBLISHING AND BROADCAST MEDIA

There are 5 daily newspapers, including *Diena* and *Neatkariga Rita Avize*

4 services: 1 state-owned, 3 independent

15 services: 1 state-owned, 14 independent

The press is now relatively free from state interference. Previously, the media were predominantly in Russian. Since 1991 the state, aiming to broaden the use of the official language, has actively promoted Latvian publications.

CRIME

Death penalty not used in practice

8156 prisoners

Up 2% in 2001

General crime levels are lower in Latvia than in Russia, but organized crime is a growing problem.

EDUCATION

School leaving age: 15

99%

118,944 students

Latvian became the main language of instruction in 2004, prompting anger from the Russian-speaking minority.

CHRONOLOGY

Governed in turn by Teutons, Poles, and Swedes, Latvia was conquered by Russia in 1795.

- **1917** Declares independence.
- **1918–1920** Latvia invaded.
- **1920** Gains independence.
- **1944** Incorporated into USSR.
- **1989** Popular Front wins elections; declares independence.
- **1991** Independence recognized.
- **1998** Naturalization procedure eased.
- **1998–2002** Four different premiers.
- **1999** Vaira Vike-Freiberga elected first woman president.
- **2002** JL wins elections.
- **2004** Indulis Emsis becomes world's first Green prime minister. Latvia joins NATO and EU.

HEALTH

Welfare state health benefits

1 per 345 people

Cerebrovascular and heart diseases, cancers, car accidents, suicide

The state-run system suffers shortages of medicines and equipment. Some improvements have been made, but it is still seriously underfunded.

SPENDING

GDP/cap. decrease

CONSUMPTION AND SPENDING

258 per 1000 population

301 per 1000 population

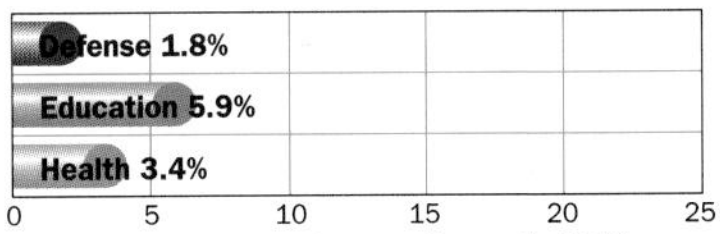
Defense 1.8%
Education 5.9%
Health 3.4%
0
5
10
15
20
25

Defense, Health, Education spending as % of GDP

The old bureaucracy has retained its privileged status and contacts, and remains the wealthiest group. Farmers are among the poorest.

WORLD RANKING

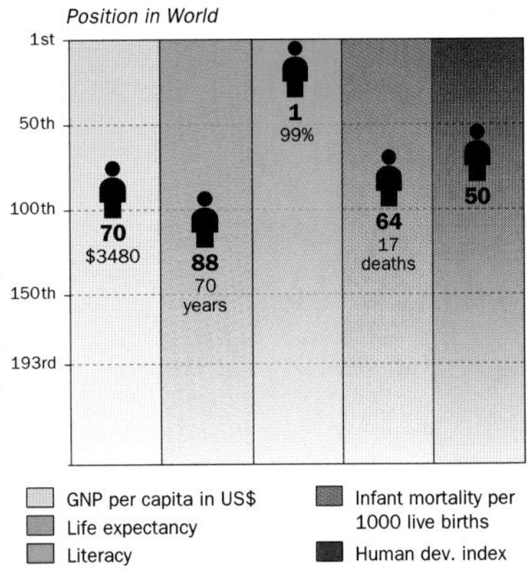
Position in World
1st
50th
100th
150th
193rd
70
$3480
88
70
years
1
99%
64
17
deaths
50
GNP per capita in US$
Life expectancy
Literacy
Infant mortality per 1000 live births
Human dev. index

L

LEBANON

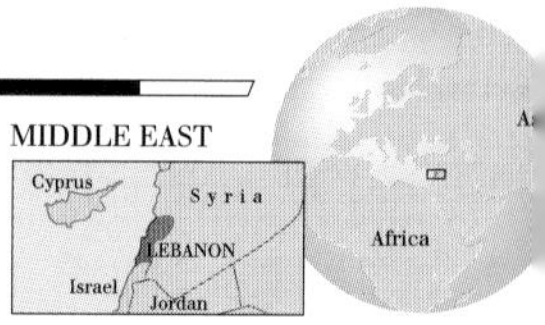
MIDDLE EAST
Cyprus
Syria
LEBANON
Israel
Jordan
Africa

OFFICIAL NAME: Republic of Lebanon **CAPITAL:** Beirut
POPULATION: 3.7 million **CURRENCY:** Lebanese pound **OFFICIAL LANGUAGE:** Arabic

1941 | 1941 | Nov 22 | RL | +2 | +961 | .lb

LEBANON LIVES in the shadow of its powerful neighbors, Syria and Israel. The coastal strip is fertile and the hinterland mountainous. The minority Maronite Christians have traditionally dominated the government. Civil war between Muslim and Christian factions from 1975, complicated by an Israeli invasion in 1982, threatened a breakup of the state, until Saudi Arabia brokered a peace deal in 1989. Greater political stability and reconstruction have ensued.

CLIMATE

Mediterranean/ mountain

WEATHER CHART FOR BEIRUT

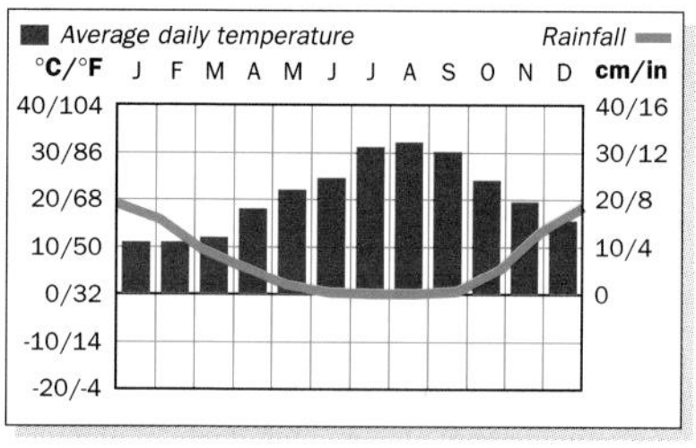
Average daily temperature
Rainfall
°C/°F J F M A M J J A S O N D cm/in
40/104
30/86
20/68
10/50
0/32
-10/14
-20/-4
40/16
30/12
20/8
10/4
0

Winters are mild and summers hot, with high humidity on the coast. Snow falls on high ground in the winter.

TRANSPORTATION

Drive on right

Beirut International, Khaldeh 2.84m passengers

89 ships 229,300 grt

THE TRANSPORTATION NETWORK

6205 km (3856 miles)

None

401 km (249 miles)

None

The redevelopment of Beirut could see it regain its position as one of the Middle East's major entrepôts.

TOURISM

Visitors : Population 1:3.6

1.02m visitors

Up 6% in 2003

MAIN TOURIST ARRIVALS

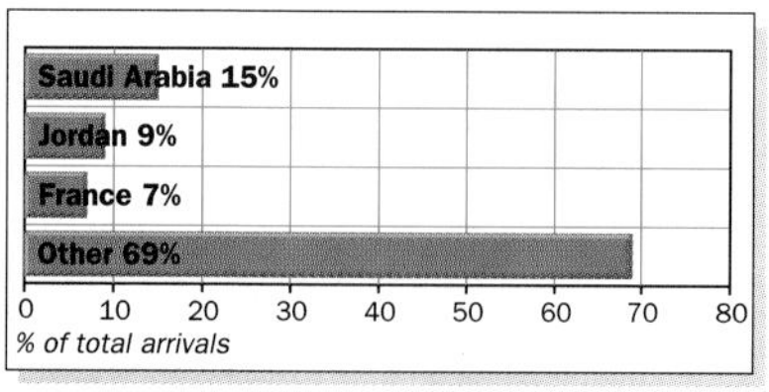
Saudi Arabia 15%
Jordan 9%
France 7%
Other 69%
0 10 20 30 40 50 60 70 80
% of total arrivals

Tourists have gradually returned since the devastation of the civil war. The main attractions are Beirut, Tripoli, Crusader castles, the Roman remains and the festival at Baalbek, and the Phoenician city of Gubla (Byblos).

PEOPLE

Pop. density high

Arabic, French, Armenian, Assyrian

362/km² (937/mi²)

THE URBAN/RURAL POPULATION SPLIT

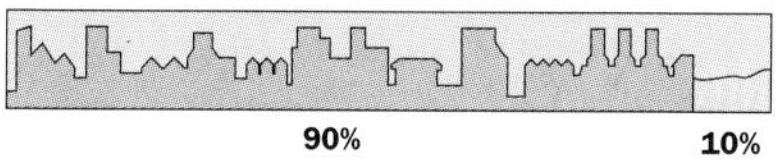
90%
10%

RELIGIOUS PERSUASION

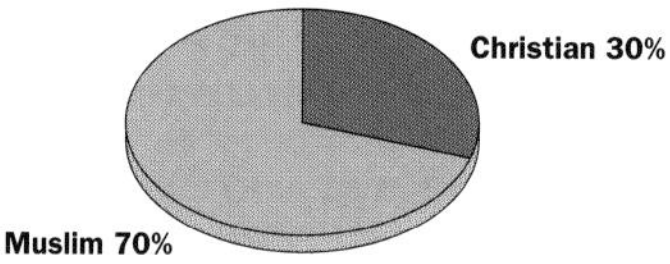
Christian 30%
Muslim 70%

The Lebanese are fragmented in religious terms into subsects of Christians and Muslims, but retain a strong sense of national identity. There has been a large Palestinian refugee population since 1948. Islamic fundamentalism is influential among poorer Shi'a Muslims, the largest single group. Many expatriate Syrians live and work in Lebanon.

POLITICS

Multiparty elections

2000/2005

President Emile Lahoud

AT THE LAST ELECTION

National Assembly 128 seats

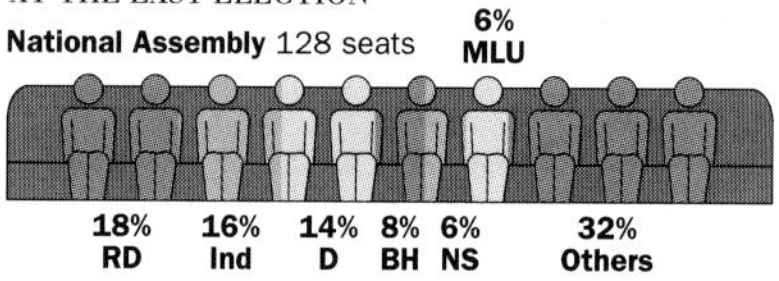
6% MLU
18% RD
16% Ind
14% D
8% BH
6% NS
32% Others

RD = Resistance and Development List **Ind** = Independents **D** = Dignity **BH** = Baalbek–Hermel List **NS** = National Struggle List **MLU** = Mount Lebanon Unity

The Arab-brokered 1989 Taif peace agreement ending the 14-year civil war redressed the constitutional balance between Christians and Muslims and formally guaranteed power-sharing. Syria remains the main power broker in Lebanon, especially following the withdrawal of Israeli troops in 2000. A once popular campaign for the removal of Syrian forces has abated. The first postwar legislative elections were held in 1992, and Rafiq al-Hariri, a Sunni Muslim, was appointed prime minister. He began a third term in 2000, after his supporters won three-quarters of the seats in the Assembly. However, an economic downturn led to clashes between Hariri and Gen. Emile Lahoud, president since 1998.

LEBANON

Total Area : 10 400 sq. km (4015 sq. miles)

0 20 km
0 20 miles

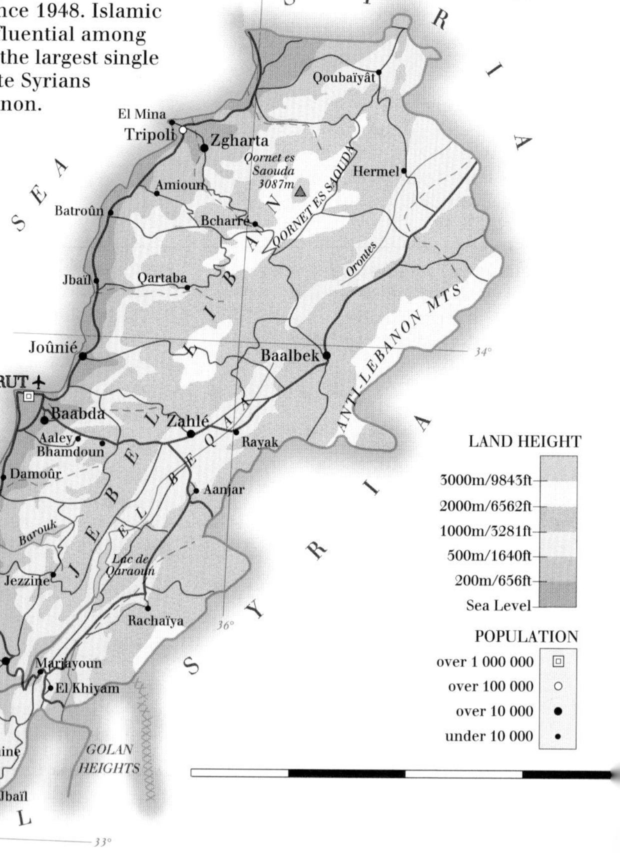
SYRIA
MEDITERRANEAN SEA
Qoubaïyât
El Mina
Tripoli
Zgharta
Qornet es Saouda 3087m
Amioun
Hermel
Batroûn
Bcharré
QORNET ES SAOUDA
Orontes
Jbaïl
Qartaba
ANTI-LEBANON MTS
Joûnié
Baalbek
BEIRUT
Baabda
Zahlé
Rayak
Aaley
Bhamdoun
Damoûr
Aanjar
Saïda
Barouk
Lac de Qaraoun
Jezzine
JEBEL LIBNAN
BEQAA
Rachaïya
Nabatîyé
Litani
Marjayoun
El Khiyam
Soûr
Tibnine
GOLAN HEIGHTS
En Nâqoûra
Bent Jbaïl
ISRAEL
LAND HEIGHT
3000m/9843ft
2000m/6562ft
1000m/3281ft
500m/1640ft
200m/656ft
Sea Level
POPULATION
over 1 000 000
over 100 000
over 10 000
under 10 000

WORLD AFFAIRS

Joined UN in 1945

AL | G24 | OIF | NAM | OIC

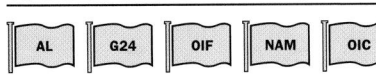

The 1989 Taif Agreement gave Syria vast influence in Lebanese politics; its forces remain in central and eastern Lebanon. Anti-Israeli rhetoric is the political lingua franca. Until Israel withdrew in 2000 the Hezbollah militia fought frequent skirmishes with the occupying forces (and their proxy militias). A UN force patrols the still-volatile border. In 2002 tensions rose after Israel accused Lebanon of diverting shared water sources.

AID

Recipient

$456m (receipts)

Up 89% in 2002

The World Bank has become an increasingly important source of loans for improving Lebanon's infrastructure.

DEFENSE

Compulsory military service

$509m

Down 11% in 2002

The army has over 70,000 troops. Hezbollah guerrillas rapidly regained control of southern Lebanon after the Israeli withdrawal in 2000. There is a UN peacekeeping force on the Israeli border. Syrian forces, whose dominant security role had been formalized in 1991, withdrew from Beirut in 2001.

ECONOMICS

Inflation 15% p.a. (1990–2001)

$17.7bn

1514 Lebanese pounds (1514)

SCORE CARD

- ❑ WORLD GNP RANKING 72nd
- ❑ GNP PER CAPITA $3990
- ❑ BALANCE OF PAYMENTS ....–$5.64bn
- ❑ INFLATION 2.5%
- ❑ UNEMPLOYMENT 9%

STRENGTHS

Financial services industry. Potential for wine and fruit production. Low inflation. Lifting of US financial restrictions.

WEAKNESSES

Dependent on imported oil and gas. Agriculture below prewar levels. High public debt. Alleged Syrian "dumping" of cheap produce. Narcotics and corruption undermine investor confidence. Delayed privatization.

EXPORTS

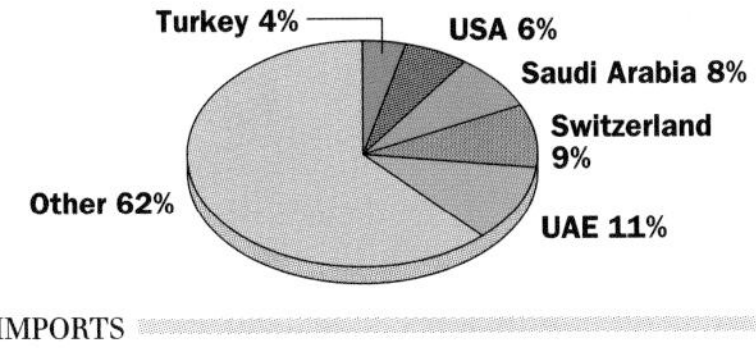
Turkey 4%
USA 6%
Saudi Arabia 8%
Switzerland 9%
UAE 11%
Other 62%

IMPORTS

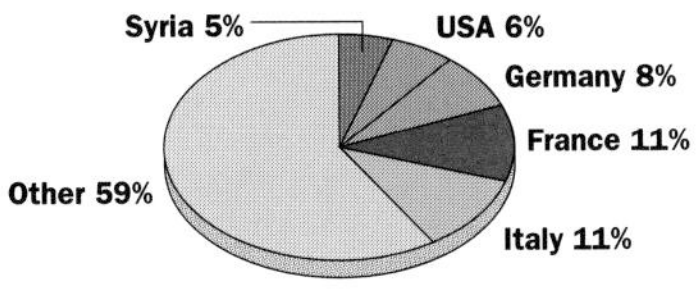
Syria 5%
USA 6%
Germany 8%
France 11%
Italy 11%
Other 59%

RESOURCES

Electric power 2.3m kW

3970 tonnes

Not an oil producer

382,000 goats, 350,000 sheep, 35m chickens

Lignite, iron ore

Wine, cotton, fruit, and vegetables are the main crops. Power plants are fueled by imported petroleum.

ENVIRONMENT

Sustainability rank: 106th

0.5%

3.5 tonnes per capita

Lack of central authority during the civil war allowed unregulated building, logging, and quarrying to flourish.

MEDIA

TV ownership high

Daily newspaper circulation 74 per 1000 people

PUBLISHING AND BROADCAST MEDIA

There are 41 daily newspapers, including *Al-Anwar*, *An-Nahar*, and its French companion, *L'Orient-Le Jour*

5 services: 1 state-controlled, 4 independent

1 state-owned service, several independent stations

Restrictions have been tightened on opposition media outlets. In 2003 the privately owned Murr TV was shut down.

CRIME

Death penalty in use

6382 prisoners

Down 1% in 2000

Politically motivated violence has largely declined since the end of the civil war, though the risk of urban terrorism remains. Rural areas, which were untouched by the conflict, have maintained low levels of crime.

Executions must be approved by the premier; they were restarted in 2004 after a six-year hiatus.

The Corniche, Beirut, *was rebuilt after the civil war by US consultant engineers and architects in a privately financed scheme.*

CHRONOLOGY

Under French mandate from 1920, Lebanon declared independence in 1941, achieving full autonomy in 1946.

- ❑ **1975** Civil war erupts.
- ❑ **1982** Israeli invasion.
- ❑ **1989** Taif Agreement ends civil war.
- ❑ **1992** First election in 20 years. Rafiq al-Hariri prime minister.
- ❑ **1996** Israeli attack kills over 100 civilians at UN base in Qana.
- ❑ **1998** Emile Lahoud president.
- ❑ **2000** Israeli forces withdraw. Hariri reelected by a landslide.

EDUCATION

School leaving age: 12

87%

134,018 students

Lebanon has one of the highest literacy rates in the Arab world. Education was severely disrupted by the war.

HEALTH

Welfare state health benefits

1 per 476 people

Heart disease, infectious and parasitic diseases

An adequate system of primary health care exists. Hospital staffing is returning to prewar levels.

SPENDING

GDP/cap. increase

CONSUMPTION AND SPENDING

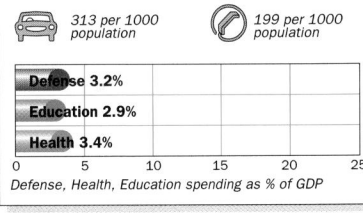

313 per 1000 population

199 per 1000 population

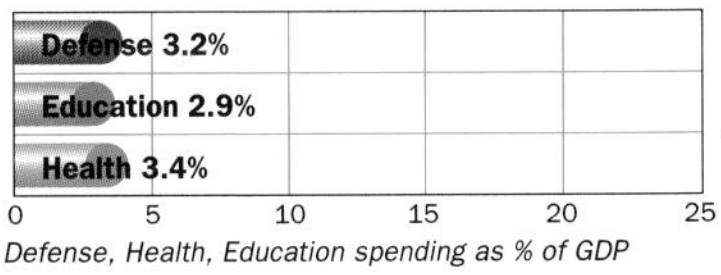
Defense 3.2%
Education 2.9%
Health 3.4%
0
5
10
15
20
25
Defense, Health, Education spending as % of GDP

Average income per capita statistics conceal the fact that a huge gulf exists between the poor and a small, massively rich elite.

WORLD RANKING

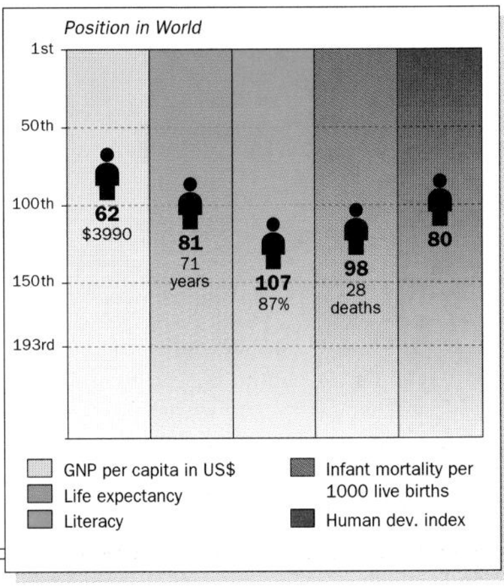
Position in World
1st
50th
100th
150th
193rd
62
$3990
81
71
years
107
87%
98
28
deaths
80
GNP per capita in US$
Life expectancy
Literacy
Infant mortality per 1000 live births
Human dev. index

L

LESOTHO

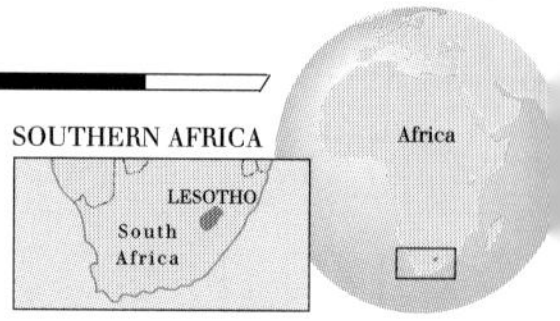
SOUTHERN AFRICA
Africa
LESOTHO
South
Africa

OFFICIAL NAME: Kingdom of Lesotho **CAPITAL:** Maseru
POPULATION: 1.8 million **CURRENCY:** Loti **OFFICIAL LANGUAGES:** English and Sesotho

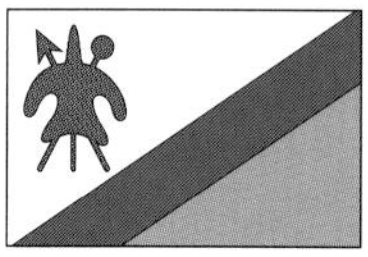

1966 | 1966 | Oct 4 | LS | +2 | +266 | .ls

A MOUNTAINOUS AND landlocked country entirely surrounded by South Africa, Lesotho is economically dependent on its larger neighbor. However, Lesotho is beginning to benefit from the export of energy from the recently completed megaproject, the Highlands Water Scheme (HWS). Elections in 1993 ended a period of military rule, but South Africa had to send in its troops when serious political unrest erupted in 1998.

CLIMATE

Mountain

WEATHER CHART FOR MASERU

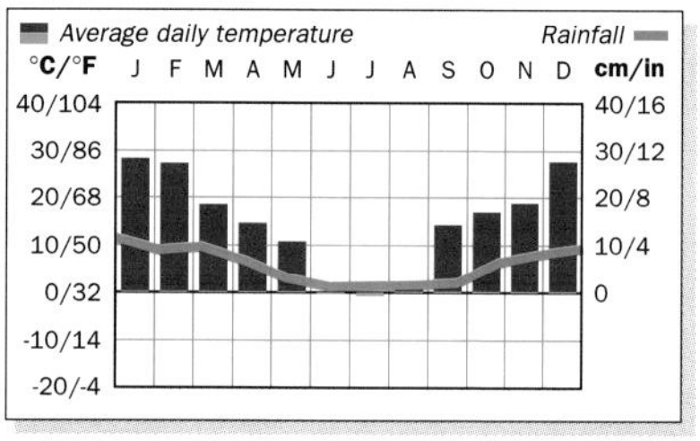
Average daily temperature
Rainfall
°C/°F
J F M A M J J A S O N D
cm/in
40/104
30/86
20/68
10/50
0/32
-10/14
-20/-4
40/16
30/12
20/8
10/4
0

Drought is often followed by torrential rain storms. Snow is frequent in winter in the mountains.

TRANSPORTATION

Drive on left

Moshoeshoe International, Maseru 43,000 passengers

Has no fleet

THE TRANSPORTATION NETWORK

1069 km (664 miles)	None
3 km (2 miles)	None

Lesotho has to rely on South African road and rail outlets. New roads have been constructed to service the Highlands Water Scheme.

TOURISM

Visitors : Population 1:15

123,571 visitors

Down 47% in 2001–2002

MAIN TOURIST ARRIVALS

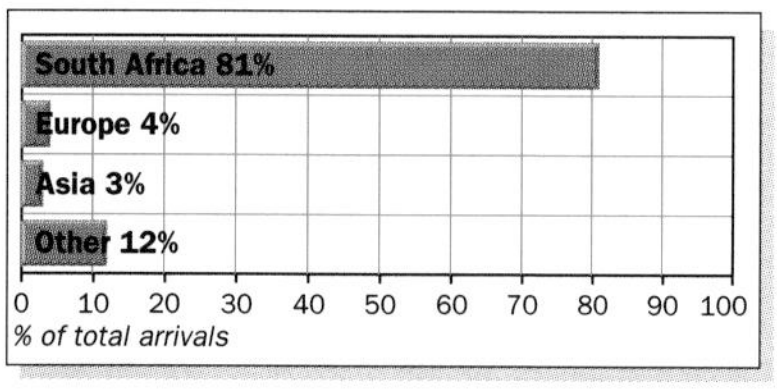
South Africa 81%
Europe 4%
Asia 3%
Other 12%
0 10 20 30 40 50 60 70 80 90 100
% of total arrivals

Tourists are attracted by the dramatic mountain scenery and watersports on artificially created lakes. Another draw is Thaba-Bosiu, King Moshoeshoe the Great's mountain stronghold.

PEOPLE

Pop. density medium

English, Sesotho, isiZulu

59/km² (154/mi²)

THE URBAN/RURAL POPULATION SPLIT

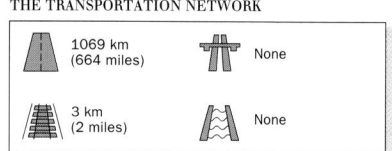

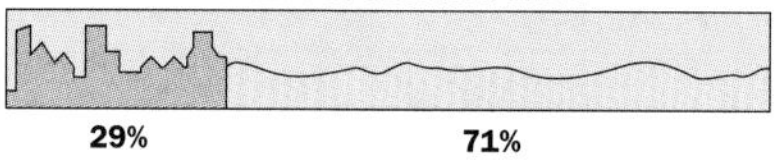
29%
71%

RELIGIOUS PERSUASION

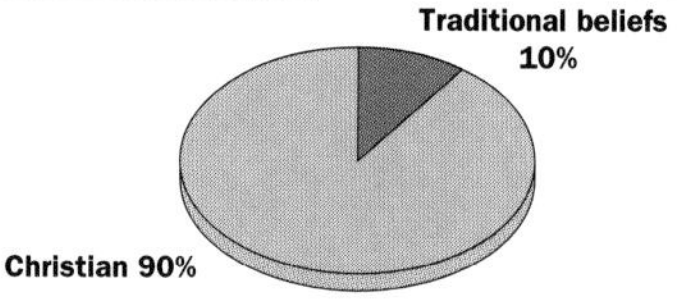
Traditional beliefs 10%
Christian 90%

The overwhelming majority of the population are Sotho, though there is a small community of European origin, as well as south Asian and Chinese minorities, which are active in the retail business. Ethnic homogeneity and a strong sense of national identity have tended to minimize ethnic tension.

The long-standing, though now declining, export of male contract labor to South African mines means that women head many households; they also run farming, regarded by men as "women's work."

POLITICS

Multiparty elections

L. House 2002/2007
U. House 2002/2007

H.M. King Letsie III

AT THE LAST ELECTION

National Assembly 120 seats

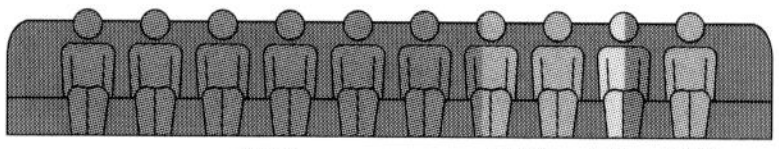
4% LPC
64% LCD
18% BNP
4% NIP
10% Others

LCD = Lesotho Congress for Democracy **BNP** = Basotho National Party **NIP** = National Independent Party **LPC** = Lesotho People's Congress

Senate 33 seats

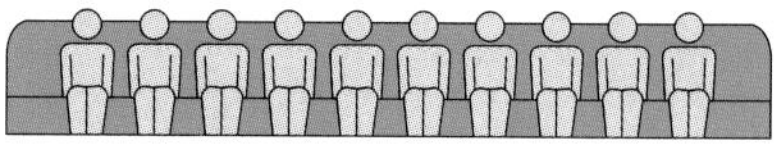

The Senate comprises 22 principal chiefs and 11 other members named by the king

The armed forces have played a key role in Lesotho since a bloodless coup in 1986. Direct military rule ended in 1993, and a free and peaceful general election resulted in a sweeping victory for the Basotho Congress Party (BCP), though the army maintained its powers over national security. Tensions escalated in 1994, when mutinous troops killed the deputy prime minister. King Moshoeshoe II was restored to the throne, and was succeeded by his son Letsie III in 1996.

Accusations of vote rigging and mass protests greeted a general election win in 1998 by the LCD (a splinter of the BCP). After an attempted coup in September, the South African military intervened to restore democracy, brokering an agreement between the king and Lesotho's 12 parties. When elections were finally held in 2002, the LCD, under Prime Minister Bethuel Mosisili, retained its majority.

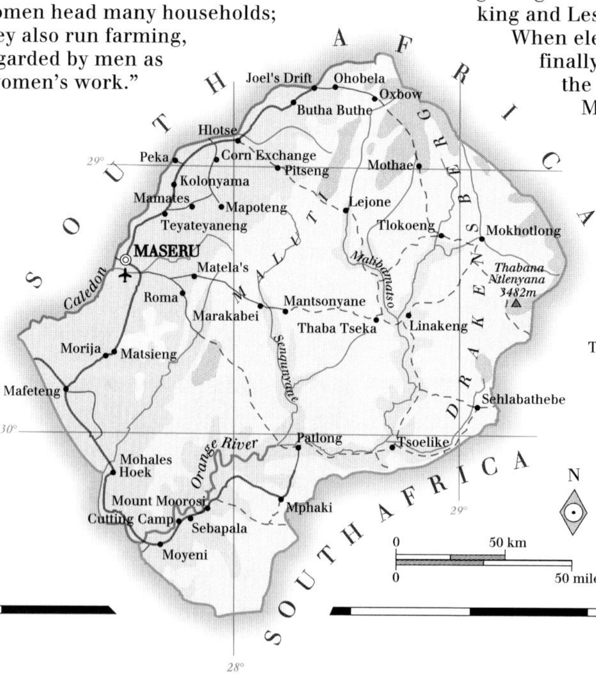
SOUTH AFRICA
Joel's Drift
Ohobela
Oxbow
Butha Buthe
Hlotse
Peka
Corn Exchange
Pitseng
Mothae
Kolonyama
Mamates
Mapoteng
Lejone
Teyateyaneng
Tlokoeng
Mokhotlong
MASERU
Matela's
MALUTI
Malibamatso
Thabana Ntlenyana 3482m
Caledon
Roma
Mantsonyane
Marakabei
Thaba Tseka
Linakeng
Senqunyane
DRAKENSBERG
Morija
Matsieng
Mafeteng
Sehlabathebe
Orange River
Qacha's Nek
Patlong
Tsoelike
Mohales Hoek
Mount Moorosi
Mphaki
Cutting Camp
Sebapala
Moyeni
29°
30°
28°
N
0 50 km
0 50 miles

LESOTHO

Total Area : 30 355 sq. km (11 720 sq. miles)

POPULATION

over 100 000
under 10 000

LAND HEIGHT

3000m/9843ft
2000m/6562ft
1000m/3281ft

WORLD AFFAIRS

Joined UN in 1966

Comm | ACP | NAM | AU | SADC

Foreign policy is dominated by the nature of Lesotho's relationship with South Africa. Lesotho currently has duty-free access to the EU for most manufactured goods, and also has preferential access to US and Scandinavian markets.

AID

Recipient

$76m (receipts) — Up 36% in 2002

Aid has become less important as a proportion of GNP, and mostly comes from the EU and the World Bank. A national famine was formally declared in 2002 to encourage donations of emergency assistance.

DEFENSE

No compulsory military service

$21m — Down 12% in 2002

Lesotho's 2000-strong army relied on South African assistance to quell political violence in 1998.

ECONOMICS

Inflation 9.5% p.a. (1990–2001)

$973m — 6.21 maloti (7.51)

SCORE CARD

❑ WORLD GNP RANKING	154th
❑ GNP PER CAPITA	$550
❑ BALANCE OF PAYMENTS	–$119m
❑ INFLATION	33.8%
❑ UNEMPLOYMENT	45%

STRENGTHS

Textiles and other manufacturing. Educated workforce. Water: exports and HEP sales. SACU membership.

WEAKNESSES

Dependence on South Africa. Loss of workforce to South African mines. Weak agricultural sector. Sporadic disturbances in retail sector. Severe drought in 2003–2004. Spread of AIDS.

EXPORTS

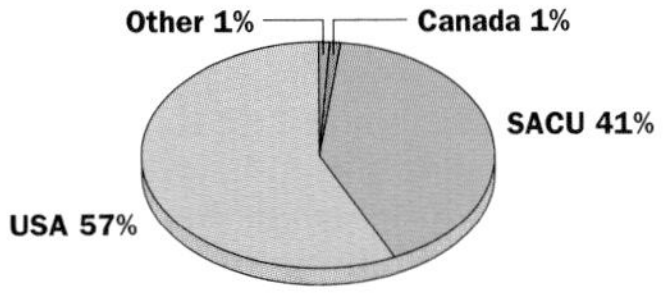
Other 1%
Canada 1%
SACU 41%
USA 57%

IMPORTS

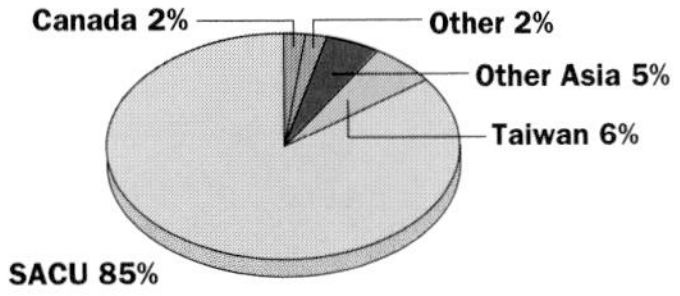
Canada 2%
Other 2%
Other Asia 5%
Taiwan 6%
SACU 85%

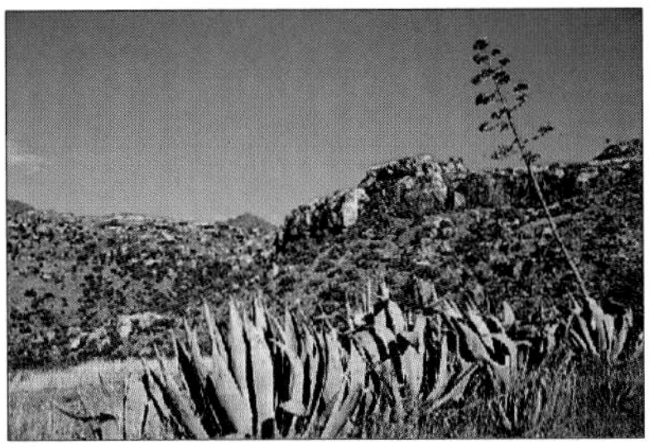

***Landscape near Mohales Hoek** in Lesotho's lowest lands – over 1300 m (4260 ft) above sea level.*

RESOURCES

Electric power: Included in South African total

32 tonnes — Not an oil producer

850,000 sheep, 650,000 goats, 1.8m chickens — Diamonds

The Highlands Water hydroelectric scheme has the capacity to supply all of Lesotho's energy requirements, as well as 62 cu. m (2200 cu. ft) of water per second for South African use. Diamonds are mined in the northeast.

ENVIRONMENT

Not available

0.2% partially protected — Negligible emissions per capita

Climate and overgrazing have seriously eroded the land. The Highlands Water Scheme has flooded acres of peasant farmland. Supporters of this massive dam project stress encouragement for wildlife in reservoirs and on bird-friendly pylons.

MEDIA

TV ownership low

Daily newspaper circulation 8 per 1000 people

PUBLISHING AND BROADCAST MEDIA

There are no daily newspapers. *Leselinyana la Lesotho* is a popular religious periodical

1 state-owned service — 1 state-owned service, several independent stations

In 1998 state-controlled media were used for political ends. The six independent weeklies often carry opposition views.

CRIME

Death penalty in use

3000 prisoners — Up sharply in 1998–1999

The return from South Africa of many unemployed miners has contributed to an increase in crime levels.

EDUCATION

School leaving age: 13

81% — 5005 students

Schools have very high enrollment levels, and Lesotho has one of the highest literacy rates in Africa.

CHRONOLOGY

As Basutoland, Lesotho became a British Crown colony in 1884.

- ❑ **1966** Independent kingdom.
- ❑ **1986** Military coup.
- ❑ **1990** King Moshoeshoe II exiled. Son installed as Letsie III.
- ❑ **1993** Free elections.
- ❑ **1994** Return of Moshoeshoe II.
- ❑ **1996** Letsie III succeeds to throne.
- ❑ **1998** New LCD wins polls. South Africa intervenes after coup attempt.
- ❑ **2002** Food emergency follows successive poor harvests. LCD wins long-postponed elections.
- ❑ **2004** First stage of HWS inaugurated.

HEALTH

Welfare state health benefits

1 per 10,000 people — AIDS, tuberculosis, parasitic diseases, nutritional disorders

Private health organizations and NGOs account for half of all health services. A government-operated flying doctor service covers the highlands. An estimated 2% of adults are HIV positive and life expectancy is falling. Food shortages in 2002 exacerbated the country's health problems.

L

SPENDING

GDP/cap. increase

CONSUMPTION AND SPENDING

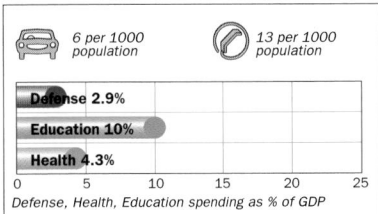

6 per 1000 population — *13 per 1000 population*

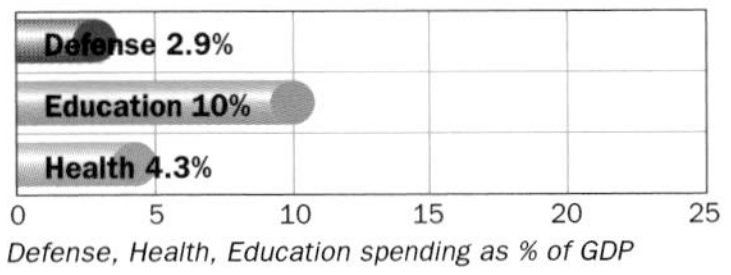
Defense 2.9%
Education 10%
Health 4.3%
0
5
10
15
20
25
Defense, Health, Education spending as % of GDP

Social mobility is limited in Lesotho; the ruling elite keeps a tight hold on power and wealth. Around 66% of the population live below the UN poverty line and many are migrant laborers.

WORLD RANKING

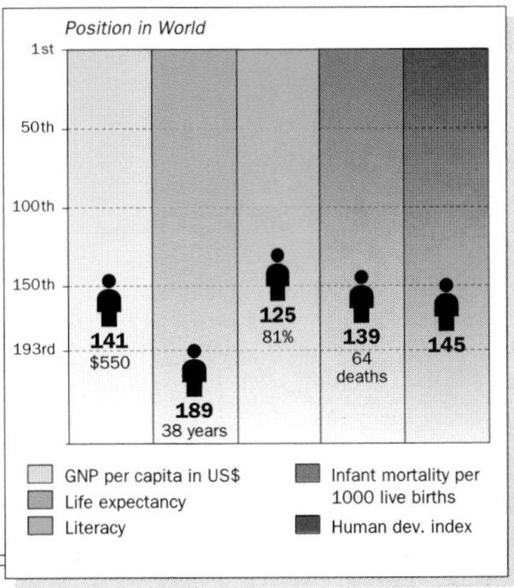
Position in World
1st
50th
100th
150th
193rd
141
$550
189
38 years
125
81%
139
64
deaths
145
GNP per capita in US$
Life expectancy
Literacy
Infant mortality per 1000 live births
Human dev. index

LIBERIA

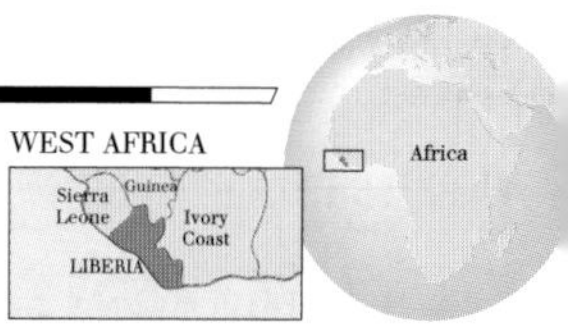
WEST AFRICA
Sierra Leone
Guinea
Ivory Coast
LIBERIA
Africa

OFFICIAL NAME: Republic of Liberia **CAPITAL:** Monrovia
POPULATION: 3.4 million **CURRENCY:** Liberian dollar **OFFICIAL LANGUAGE:** English

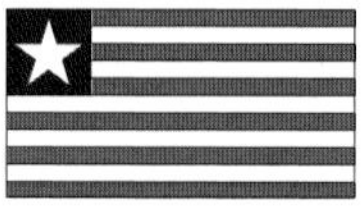

1847
1847
July 26
LB
0
+231
.lr

FACING THE ATLANTIC in equatorial west Africa, most of Liberia's coastline is characterized by lagoons and mangrove swamps. Inland, a grassland plateau supports limited agriculture. Founded in 1847 by freed US slaves, Liberia today has largely been reduced to anarchy after renewed offensives by rebel factions opposed to the government of former coup leader Charles Taylor. Hundreds of civilians were killed in 2003 alone as fighting reached Monrovia.

CLIMATE

Tropical equatorial

WEATHER CHART FOR MONROVIA

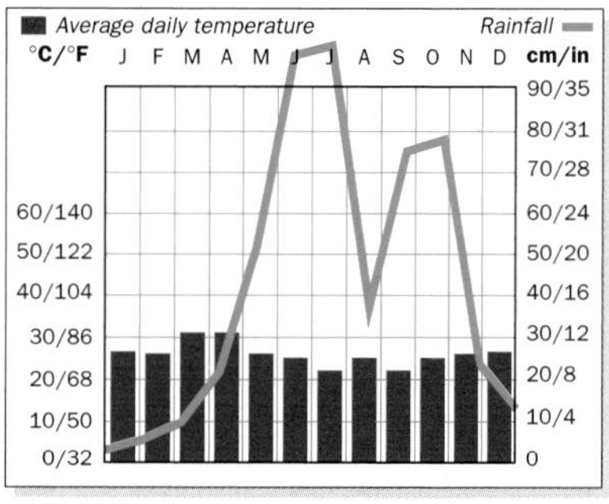
Average daily temperature
Rainfall
°C/°F
J F M A M J J A S O N D
cm/in
90/35
80/31
70/28
60/24
50/20
40/16
30/12
20/8
10/4
0
60/140
50/122
40/104
30/86
20/68
10/50
0/32

There is one long rainy season from May to October, with a brief interlude in most of the country of about two weeks in August.

Temperatures are consistently high. During the dry season, when the dust-laden *harmattan* wind blows, they rise even higher inland.

TRANSPORTATION

Drive on right

Roberts International, Monrovia 44,444 passengers

1535 ships 50.4m grt

THE TRANSPORTATION NETWORK

636 km (395 miles)

None

490 km (304 miles)

None

Most roads are unpaved. The railroad was built to transport iron ore, but large parts have been dismantled and sold as scrap. Roberts airport was built by the US during World War II.

TOURISM

Not available

Tourists deterred by civil war

Little change from year to year

MAIN TOURIST ARRIVALS

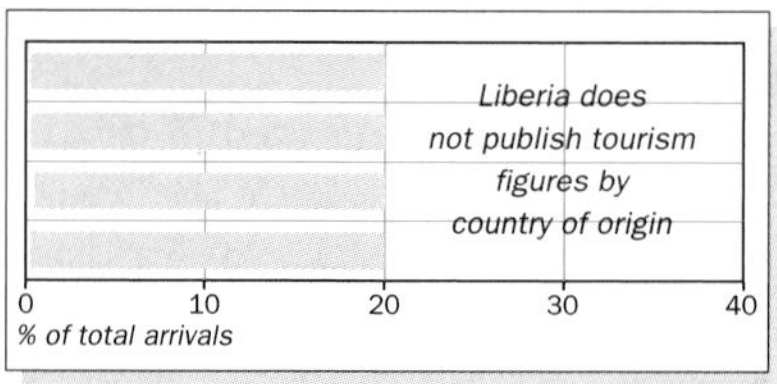
Liberia does not publish tourism figures by country of origin
0
10
20
30
40
% of total arrivals

As a result of the continuing complete breakdown in public order, tourism, never significant in Liberia, is now nonexistent.

PEOPLE

Pop. density low

Kpelle, Vai, Bassa, Kru, Grebo, Kissi, Gola, Loma, English

35/km² (91/mi²)

THE URBAN/RURAL POPULATION SPLIT

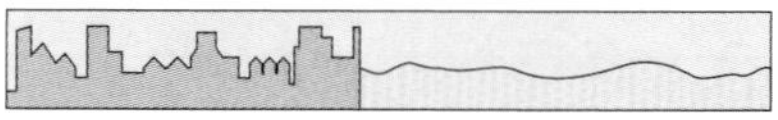
46%
54%

ETHNIC MAKEUP

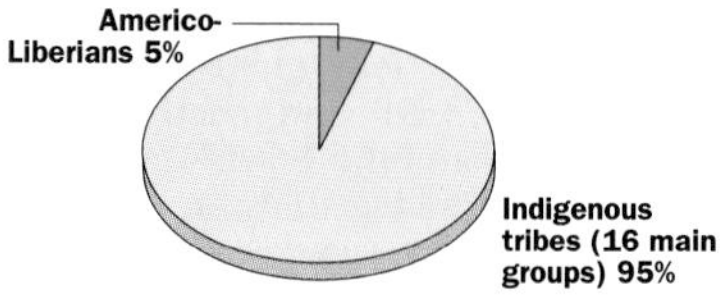
Americo-Liberians 5%
Indigenous tribes (16 main groups) 95%

A key distinction has been between Americo-Liberians, the descendants of those freed from slavery (known as "civilized persons"), and the majority indigenous "tribals." The latter were long held in contempt by the Americos, but intermarriage and political assimilation since 1944 have softened attitudes. Intertribal tension is now a far more serious problem for Liberia.

Christianity and Islam are practiced alongside traditional beliefs.

POLITICS

In transition

1997/2005

National Transitional Government Chairman Gyude Bryant

LEGISLATIVE OR ADVISORY BODIES

National Transitional Legislative Assembly 76 seats

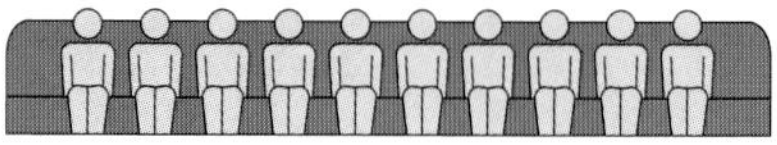

An appointed National Transitional Legislative Assembly was convened in October 2003, including representatives of the government, LURD, Model, political parties, civil society, and interest groups. It replaced the suspended bicameral legislature elected in 1997.

A chaotic, bloody, and many-sided conflict erupted in 1990 and continued despite elections in 1997 (won by warlord Charles Taylor and his NPP – National Patriotic Party). The rebel Liberians United for Reconciliation and Democracy (LURD) and its splinter Movement for Democracy in Liberia (Model) took control of much of the country and had entered Monrovia when a peace deal was signed in August 2003 and Taylor stepped down. An interim authority took office in October, headed by businessman Gyude Bryant, but lives circumscribed by poverty and widespread availability of drugs have created a volatile climate where youths have a heightened sense of power and looting is the norm. Clashes between armed unemployed youths frequently escalate into bloody ethnic battles.

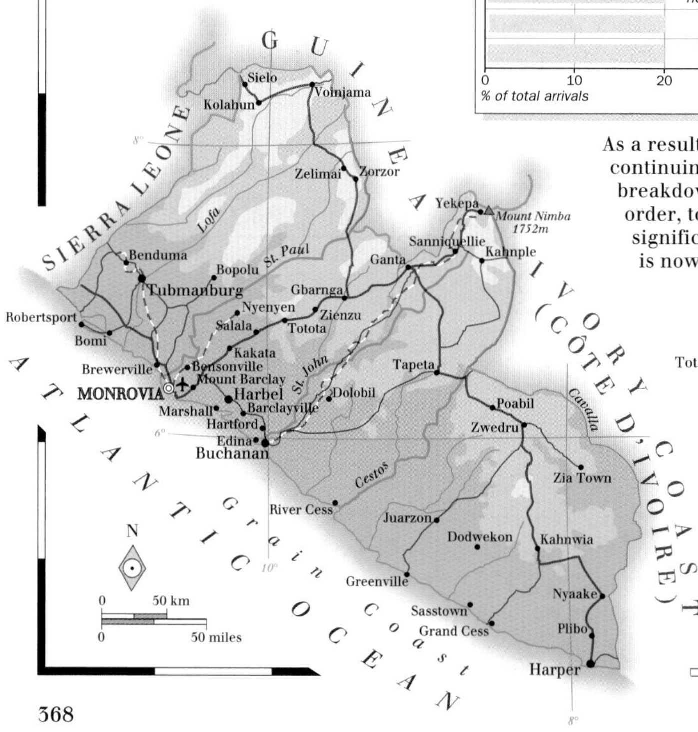
GUINEA
SIERRA LEONE
IVORY COAST (CÔTE D'IVOIRE)
ATLANTIC OCEAN
Grain Coast
Sielo
Kolahun
Voinjama
Zelimai
Zorzor
Yekepa
Mount Nimba 1752m
Sanniquellie
Kahnple
Ganta
Lofa
St. Paul
Benduma
Bopolu
Tubmanburg
Gbarnga
Robertsport
Nyenyen
Zienzu
Salala
Totota
Bomi
Kakata
Brewerville
Bensonville
Mount Barclay
St. John
Tapeta
MONROVIA
Harbel
Dolobil
Marshall
Barclayville
Poabil
Hartford
Cavalla
Edina
Zwedru
Buchanan
Cestos
Zia Town
River Cess
Juarzon
Dodwekon
Kahnwia
Greenville
Nyaake
Sasstown
Grand Cess
Plibo
Harper
N
0 50 km
0 50 miles

LIBERIA

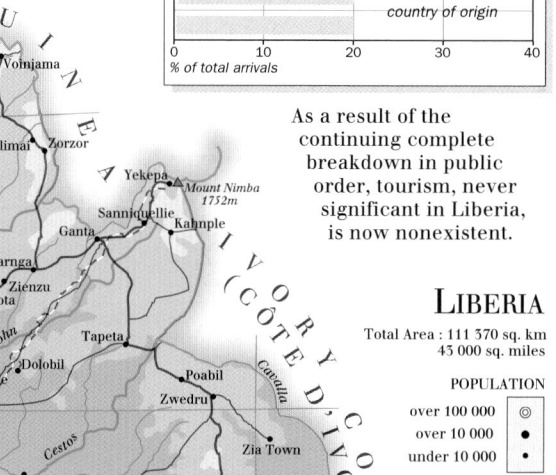

Total Area : 111 370 sq. km
43 000 sq. miles

POPULATION

over 100 000
over 10 000
under 10 000

LAND HEIGHT

1000m/3281ft
500m/1640ft
200m/656ft
Sea Level

WORLD AFFAIRS

Joined UN in 1945

ACP | ECOWAS | IAEA | NAM | AU

The UN imposed sanctions in 2001, accusing Liberia of fomenting war in west Africa. Relations with neighboring states have been badly affected by these conflicts, and Liberian fighters have been directly implicated in hostilities in Sierra Leone and Ivory Coast. In 2003 international peacekeepers from the US, the UN, and ECOWAS were brought in to calm Liberia's own civil war.

AID

Recipient

US$52m (receipts) — Up 33% in 2002

Regional and civil war have seriously disrupted aid flows. In 2004 international donors pledged US$500 million for reconstruction.

DEFENSE

No compulsory military service

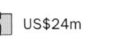

US$24m — No change in 2002

The government admitted in 2003 that it had contravened a UN weapons embargo in order to boost its defenses against the rebel LURD.

ECONOMICS

Inflation 53% p.a. (1990–2001)

US$476m — 56 Liberian dollars (1)

SCORE CARD

- World GNP Ranking 172nd
- GNP per Capita .... US$140
- Balance of Payments .... –US$52m
- Inflation 31.5%
- Unemployment 85%

Strengths

Timber. Potential for reviving rubber and iron ore industries. Registration fees from flag-of-convenience fleet.

Weaknesses

Severe instability. Internal population displacement. Little commercial activity and low business confidence. Diamond trade interrupted by conflict.

EXPORTS

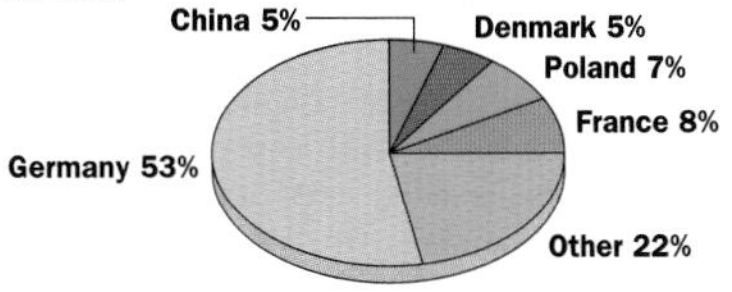
China 5%
Denmark 5%
Poland 7%
France 8%
Germany 53%
Other 22%

IMPORTS

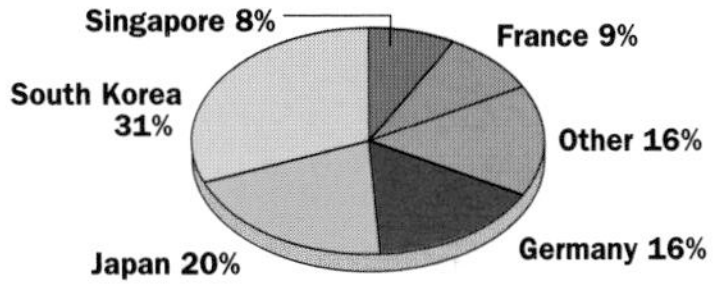
Singapore 8%
France 9%
South Korea 31%
Other 16%
Japan 20%
Germany 16%

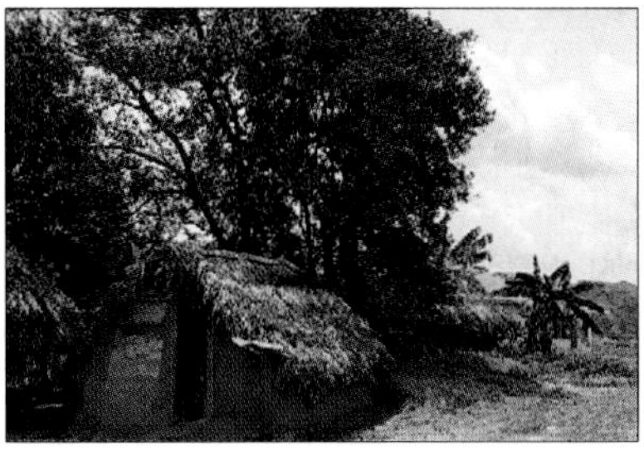

Village near Gbarnga. *The Kpelle, the largest of Liberia's 16 indigenous ethnic groups, are concentrated in this part of Liberia.*

RESOURCES

Electric power 334,000 kW

- 11,300 tonnes
- Not an oil producer
- 220,000 goats, 210,000 sheep, 6m chickens
- Iron ore, diamonds, gold, barytes, kyanite, columbite, manganese

There are an estimated billion tonnes of iron ore reserves, but production is at a standstill. Spanish company Repsol was allowed to explore for oil from 2004.

ENVIRONMENT

Sustainability rank: 130th

2% — 0.1 tonnes per capita

Illegal logging has damaged forest cover and ecosystems. Electricity shortages mean that trees are also felled for fuel.

MEDIA

TV ownership low

Daily newspaper circulation 12 per 1000 people

PUBLISHING AND BROADCAST MEDIA

There are 4 daily newspapers, including the independents *The Analyst, The Inquirer*, and *News*

No domestic television service — 1 state-owned service, several independent stations

Print media have grown since Taylor's resignation, but TV and radio stations have been slower to recover from the depredations of years of war.

CRIME

Death penalty in use

Liberia does not publish prison figures — Crime is rampant. There are no enforcing agencies

The peace accord provides for a truth and reconciliation commission, but the transitional government, which includes former combatants and leaders of disarming rebel factions, has been in no hurry to set it up. Looting and rape occur in areas without UN peacekeepers.

EDUCATION

School leaving age: 16

56% — 20,804 students

Originally based on the US model, the education system effectively collapsed during the civil war.

CHRONOLOGY

Between 1816 and 1892, 22,000 liberated slaves, most from the US, settled in Liberia, established as a republic in 1847.

- **1980** Coup. President assassinated by Samuel Doe.
- **1990** Outbreak of civil war.
- **1991** Doe assassinated.
- **1996** Second peace agreement.
- **1997** Charles Taylor president.
- **2001** Conflict with rebels escalates.
- **2002** State of emergency declared.
- **2003** Rebels reach Monrovia. Taylor ousted. Transitional government.

HEALTH

No welfare state health benefits

1 per 20,000 people — Communicable, diarrheal, parasitic, and heart diseases

A large increase in the number of internally displaced persons (IDPs) within Liberia has had a detrimental effect on already low health standards.

SPENDING

GDP/cap. increase

CONSUMPTION AND SPENDING

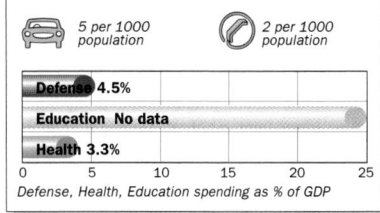

5 per 1000 population — *2 per 1000 population*

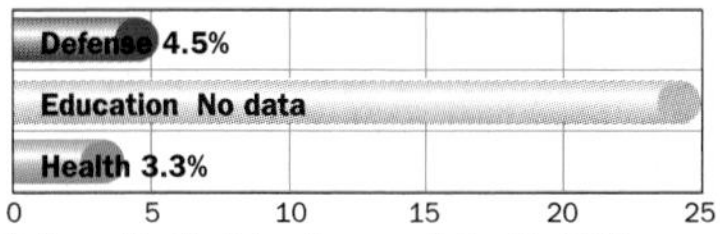
Defense 4.5%
Education No data
Health 3.3%
0
5
10
15
20
25

Defense, Health, Education spending as % of GDP

By 1996, real GDP was as low as one-tenth of its prewar level. Real income per capita remains at about one-third of prewar levels. Any increase will depend on the government carrying out major reforms of Liberia's war-ravaged economy, including the encouragement of foreign investment. Most ordinary Liberians continue to live in rural poverty.

WORLD RANKING

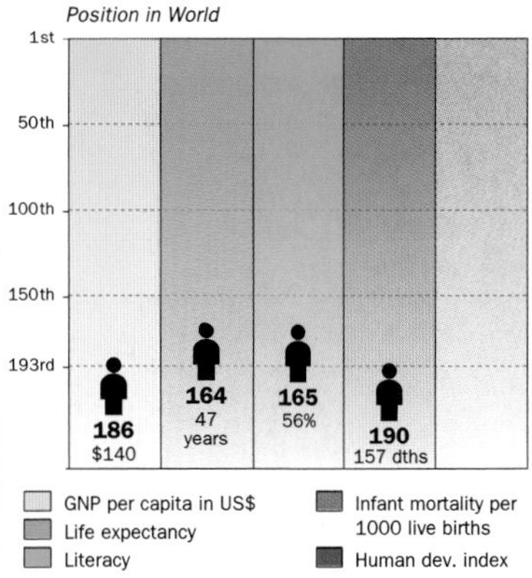
Position in World
1st
50th
100th
150th
193rd
186
$140
164
47 years
165
56%
190
157 dths
GNP per capita in US$
Life expectancy
Literacy
Infant mortality per 1000 live births
Human dev. index

L

LIBYA

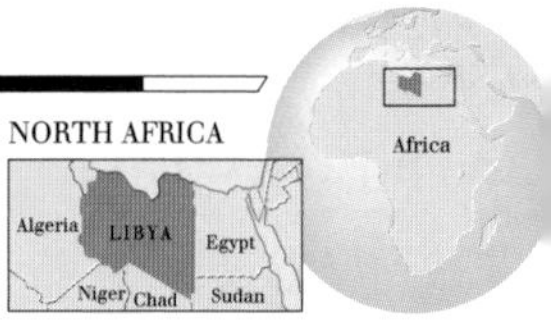
NORTH AFRICA
Africa
Algeria
LIBYA
Egypt
Niger
Chad
Sudan

OFFICIAL NAME: Great Socialist People's Libyan Arab Jamahiriyah
CAPITAL: Tripoli **POPULATION:** 5.6 million **CURRENCY:** Libyan dinar **OFFICIAL LANGUAGE:** Arabic

1951
1951
Sept 1
LAR
+1
+218
.ly

LIBYA IS SITUATED in north Africa between Egypt and Algeria, with the Mediterranean to the north and Chad and Niger on its southern borders. Apart from the coastal strip and the mountains in the south, it is desert or semidesert. Libya's strategic position in north Africa and its abundant oil and gas resources made it an important trading partner for European states. It has for many years been politically marginalized by the West for its links with terrorist groups, but UN sanctions were lifted in 2003, when it agreed to pay compensation for terrorist bombings in the 1980s.

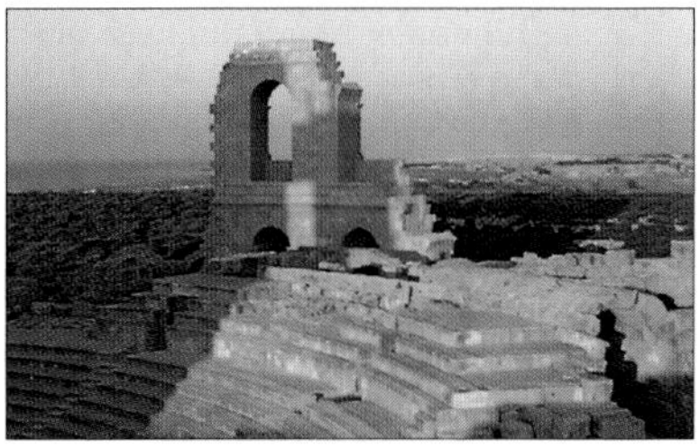

Roman theater, Sabrata. *Libya's impressive classical heritage testifies to its importance in ancient times.*

CLIMATE

Hot desert

WEATHER CHART FOR TRIPOLI

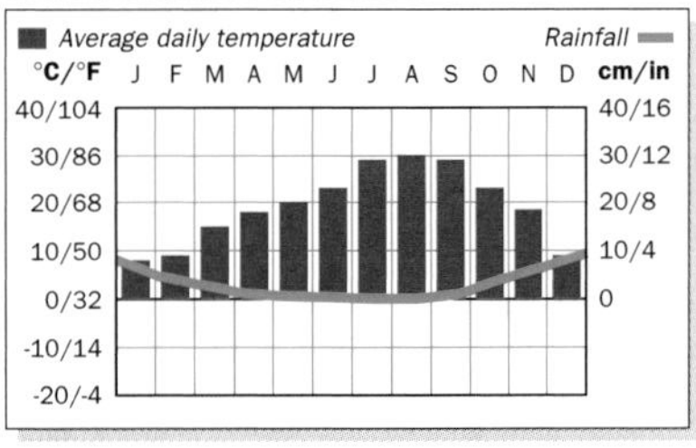
Average daily temperature
Rainfall
°C/°F
J F M A M J J A S O N D
cm/in
40/104
30/86
20/68
10/50
0/32
-10/14
-20/-4
40/16
30/12
20/8
10/4
0

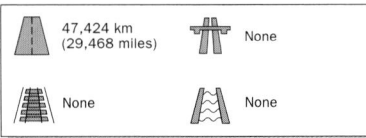

The coastal region has a warm, temperate climate, with mild, wet winters and hot, dry summers.

TRANSPORTATION

Drive on right

Tripoli International

140 ships
164,900 grt

THE TRANSPORTATION NETWORK

47,424 km (29,468 miles)

None

None

None

The National Coast Road runs 1825 km (1135 miles) between the Tunisian and Egyptian borders, linking the principal urban centers. There are no railroads, but some are planned. Since sanctions were suspended in 1999, international airlines have resumed flights to Libya.

Al Kufrah Oasis. *As 90% of Libya is arid rock and sand, oases provide essential agricultural land, besides being tourist attractions.*

TOURISM

Visitors : Population 1:6.5

857,952 visitors

Up 393% in 2001–2002

Libya possesses a rich Roman and Greek heritage, centered on the ancient Roman coastal towns of Labdah (Leptis Magna) and Sabrata near Tripoli, and Shahhat (Cyrene) further east. There are fine beaches at Tripoli. The government is keen to invest in attracting tourists, in 2000 launching a $2–3 billion program. Western tourists have begun to return since sanctions were eased in 1999.

MAIN TOURIST ARRIVALS

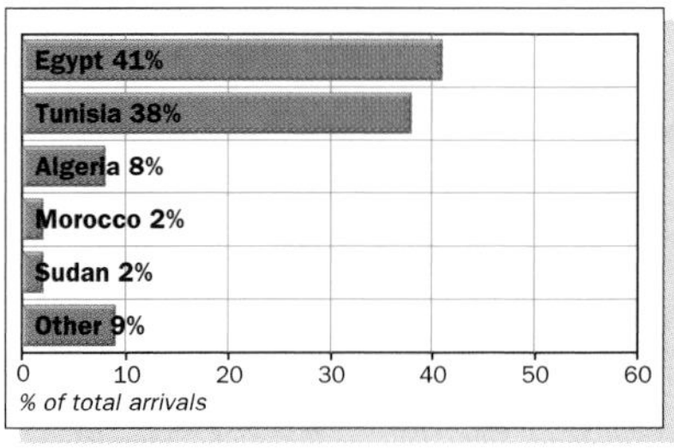
Egypt 41%
Tunisia 38%
Algeria 8%
Morocco 2%
Sudan 2%
Other 9%
0 10 20 30 40 50 60
% of total arrivals

PEOPLE

Pop. density low

Arabic, Tuareg

3/km² (8/mi²)

THE URBAN/RURAL POPULATION SPLIT

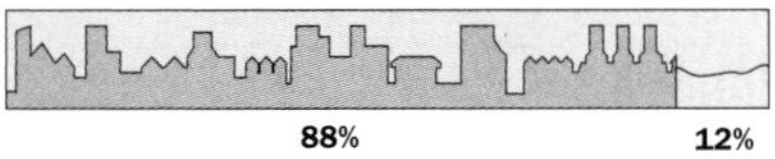
88%
12%

RELIGIOUS PERSUASION

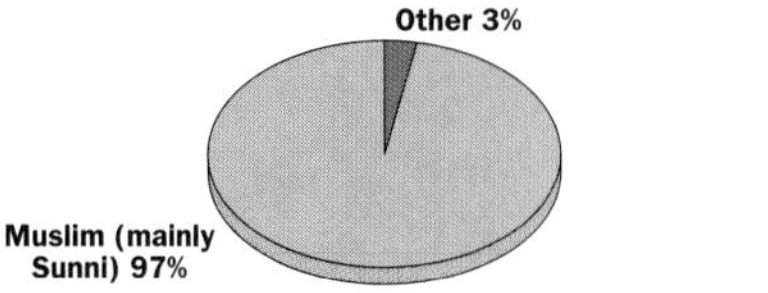
Other 3%
Muslim (mainly Sunni) 97%

ETHNIC MAKEUP

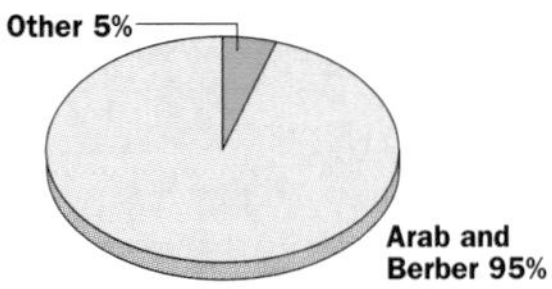
Other 5%
Arab and Berber 95%

Arabs and Berbers, split into many tribal groupings, form 95% of the population. They were artificially brought together when Libya was created in 1951 by the unification of three historic Ottoman provinces. The newly established pro-Western monarchy then perpetuated the dominance of Cyrenaican tribes and the Sanusi religious order.

The 1969 revolution brought to the fore Arab nationalist Col. Muammar al-Gaddafi, who embodied the character

POPULATION AGE BREAKDOWN

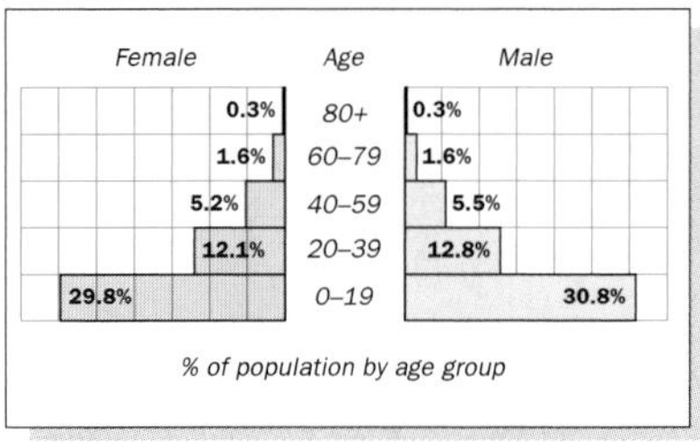
Female
Age
Male
0.3%
80+
0.3%
1.6%
60–79
1.6%
5.2%
40–59
5.5%
12.1%
20–39
12.8%
29.8%
0–19
30.8%
% of population by age group

and aspirations of the rural Sirtica tribes from Fazzan: fierce independence, deep Islamic convictions, belief in a communal lifestyle, and hatred for the urban rich. His revolution wiped out private enterprise and the middle class, banished European settlers and Jews, undermined the religious Muslim establishment, and imposed a form of popular democracy through the *jamahiriyah* (state of the masses). However, resentment of the regime grew as it became clear that power now lay mainly with the Sirtica tribes, especially Gaddafi's own clan, the Qadhadhfa.

Since the revolution, Libya has become a society where most are city dwellers. Jews have been invited to return as investors, and immigrants from sub-Saharan Africa have been drawn in to provide low-cost labor. However, clashes in 2000, in which 100 died, highlighted unresolved social issues.

L

POLITICS

No multiparty elections

Not applicable

Leader of the Revolution Col. Muammar al-Gaddafi

LEGISLATIVE OR ADVISORY BODIES

General People's Congress 750 seats

The constitution makes no provision for direct elections. Last renewal May 2003

Executive power is theoretically exercised by the General People's Committee while the General People's Congress (GPC) elects the head of state. In reality Libya is run as a military dictatorship.

Profile

Political power is concentrated in the hands of revolutionary leader Col. Muammar al-Gaddafi, the de facto head of state; he holds no official title but is known as the leader, or guide, of the revolution. Gaddafi's unique political system is based on his own *Green Book* which draws on the ideology of Islam, socialism, and Bedouin tradition. In theory direct rule is practiced through 2000 People's Congresses intended to involve all citizens in policy making. The highest congress, the GPC, is theoretically responsible for introducing and passing laws.

Gaddafi's blatantly autocratic style of leadership has alienated many, even within his inner circle. He now relies on members of his own clan, particularly his five sons. The much-touted concept of African unity has proved unpopular with the wider populace.

Main Political Issues

Repression

Political dissidents, including Islamist militants, have been violently suppressed. Libyan dissidents have been murdered abroad, allegedly by government agents. Political parties were banned in 1971, but opposition groups are active in Egypt and Sudan.

The regime's public image

In the past few years, the regime has made an effort to improve its image. Measures have included freeing political prisoners, welcoming back exiles, accepting legal responsibility for past acts of terrorism, and renouncing weapons of mass destruction.

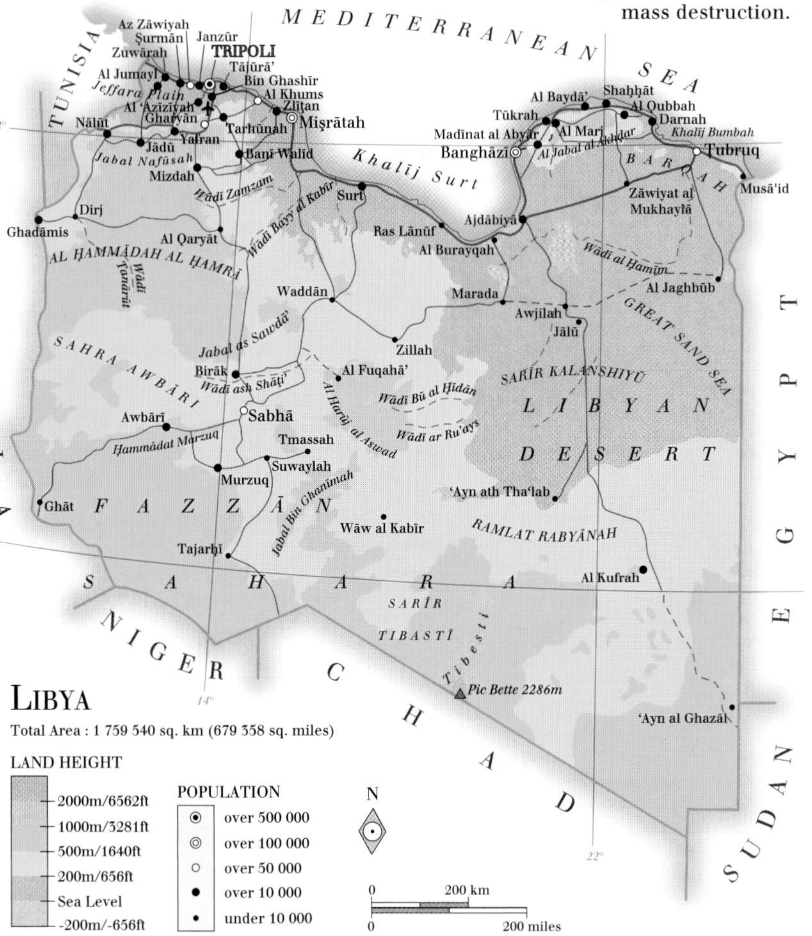
MEDITERRANEAN SEA
TRIPOLI
Az Zāwiyah
Şurmān
Janzūr
Zuwārah
Tājūrā'
Al Jumayl
Bin Ghashīr
Jeffara Plain
Al Khums
Al 'Azīzīyah
Zlītan
Gharyān
Mişrātah
Nālūt
Jādū
Yafran
Tarhūnah
Banī Walīd
Jabal Nafūsah
Mizdah
Khalīj Surt
Sirt
Dirj
Ghadāmis
Al Qaryāt
AL ḤAMMĀDAH AL ḤAMRĀ'
Waddān
Banghāzī
Madīnat al Abyār
Al Marj
Al Bayḑā'
Shaḩḩāt
Al Qubbah
Darnah
Ţūkrah
Khalīj Bumbah
Ţubruq
Mūsā'id
Zāwiyat al Mukhaylā
Ajdābiyā
Ras Lānūf
Al Burayqah
Marada
Awjilah
Jālū
Al Jaghbūb
Zillah
Al Fuqahā'
Birāk
Sabhā
Awbārī
Tmassah
Suwaylah
Murzuq
Ghāt
FAZZĀN
Wāw al Kabīr
'Ayn ath Tha'lab
RAMLAT RABYĀNAH
Al Kufrah
Tajarhī
SAHARA
SARĪR TIBASTĪ
Pic Bette 2286m
'Ayn al Ghazāl
LIBYAN DESERT
GREAT SAND SEA
SARĪR KALANSHIYU
TUNISIA
ALGERIA
NIGER
CHAD
SUDAN
EGYPT
LIBYA
Total Area : 1 759 540 sq. km (679 358 sq. miles)
LAND HEIGHT
2000m/6562ft
1000m/3281ft
500m/1640ft
200m/656ft
Sea Level
-200m/-656ft
POPULATION
over 500 000
over 100 000
over 50 000
over 10 000
under 10 000
N
0 200 km
0 200 miles

Col. Gaddafi, Libya's leader since 1969, shies from official titles.

Ex-king Idris was deposed by Col. Gaddafi in 1969.

WORLD AFFAIRS

Joined UN in 1955

AL AU NAM OIC OPEC

Gaddafi has attempted to style himself the champion of African integration and regional stability. He was a chief architect of the AU, and has hosted various peace talks in the trans-Saharan area. This transformation has also involved a less confrontational stance toward the West, dropping key policies which had left Libya isolated in the past – support for various terrorist groups and strong opposition to Israel – and rooting out internal corruption. UN sanctions imposed in 1992 have been lifted, and relations with the UK were resumed in 1999. Gaddafi's boldest move was his commitment in December 2003 to end his illegal weapons program; this was rewarded in 2004 by the resumption of relations with the US.

CHRONOLOGY

Italy occupied Libya and expelled the Turks in 1911. Britain and France agreed to a UN plan for an independent monarchy in 1951.

- **1969** King Idris deposed in coup led by Col. Gaddafi. Revolution Command Council established. Tripoli Charter sets up revolutionary alliance with Egypt and Sudan.
- **1970** UK and US military ordered out. Property belonging to Italians and Jews confiscated. Western oil company assets nationalized, a process completed in 1973.
- **1973** Libya forms abortive union with Egypt. Libya occupies Aozou Strip in Chad.
- **1974** Libya proposes union of Libya and Tunisia.
- **1977** Official name changed to Great Socialist People's Libyan Arab Jamahiriyah. Revolution Command Council dissolved. Gaddafi elected Leader of the Revolution. Council of Ministers replaced by General People's Committee.

L

CHRONOLOGY *continued*

- **1981** US shoots down two Libyan aircraft over Gulf of Sirte.
- **1984** Gunman at Libyan embassy in UK kills British policewoman; UK severs diplomatic relations (until 1999). Oudja Accord signed with Morocco for Arab Africa Federation.
- **1985** 30,000 foreign workers expelled. Tunisia severs links.
- **1986** US aircraft bomb Libya, killing 101 people and destroying Gaddafi's residence.
- **1988** Pan-Am airliner explodes over Lockerbie, Scotland; allegations of Libyan complicity.
- **1989** Arab Maghreb Union established with Algeria, Morocco, Mauritania, and Tunisia. Cease-fire in Aozou Strip.
- **1990** Libya expels Palestinian splinter group led by Abu Abbas.
- **1991** Opening of first branch of Great Man-Made River project.
- **1992–1993** UN sanctions imposed as Libya fails to hand over Lockerbie suspects; sanctions made stricter.
- **1994** Religious leaders obtain right to issue religious decrees (*fatwas*) for first time since 1969. Return of Aozou Strip to Chad.
- **1996** US legislation imposes penalties on foreign companies investing in Libya's energy sector.
- **1999** Lockerbie suspects handed over for trial in the Netherlands under Scottish law; UN sanctions suspended.
- **2001** Lockerbie trial verdict: one suspect convicted.
- **2002** US–Libya talks, but Libya added to "axis of evil."
- **2003** Compensation agreed for 1980s terrorism; UN sanctions lifted. Weapons program ended.
- **2004** Relations restored with US.

AID

Recipient

$10m (receipts)

Little change in 2002

As an oil-exporting state, Libya fails to qualify for much international aid, despite being a developing country. During the 1970s, Col. Gaddafi aided several African liberation movements, notably the ANC in South Africa. He has backed factions during civil conflicts in neighboring countries, including Chad and the Central African Republic, and helped dissidents by training them in his Pan-African legion. He has also financed or supplied arms to the Palestine Liberation Organization in the Middle East, Irish republicans in Northern Ireland, the Moros in the southern Philippines, and Basques, Corsicans, and other separatist groups in Europe.

DEFENSE

Compulsory military service

$531m

Down 45% in 2002

LIBYAN ARMED FORCES

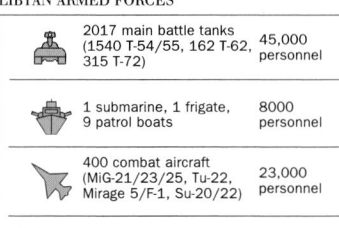

2017 main battle tanks (1540 T-54/55, 162 T-62, 315 T-72)	45,000 personnel
1 submarine, 1 frigate, 9 patrol boats	8000 personnel
400 combat aircraft (MiG-21/23/25, Tu-22, Mirage 5/F-1, Su-20/22)	23,000 personnel
None	

The armed forces suffered a blow in 1987 with the loss of thousands of men and equipment worth $1.4 billion when Libya became embroiled in the Chad civil war; in 1994 it agreed to hand back to Chad the Aozou Strip, which it had first occupied in 1973. In 1988–1989 the armed forces were replaced by "the Armed People." Conscription is selective, and can last up to two years. Reserves form a 40,000-strong People's Militia.

Attempts to depoliticize the army received a setback following confirmation of an abortive military coup in 1993. UN sanctions resulted in military hardware becoming outdated. Despite the removal of sanctions in 2003, fresh arms contracts would still be too controversial for most potential suppliers.

ECONOMICS

Not available

$31bn

1.315 Libyan dinars (1.206)

SCORE CARD

- World GNP Ranking..........59th
- GNP per Capita..........$5540
- Balance of Payments..........$2.14bn
- Inflation..........1%
- Unemployment..........30%

EXPORTS

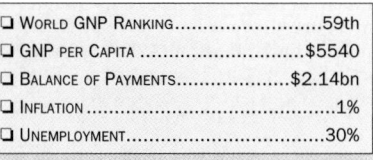

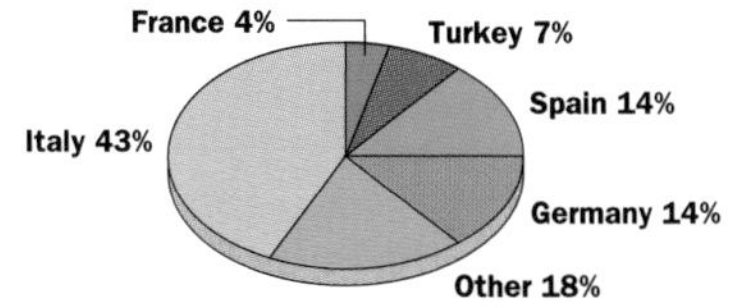
France 4%
Turkey 7%
Spain 14%
Italy 43%
Germany 14%
Other 18%

IMPORTS

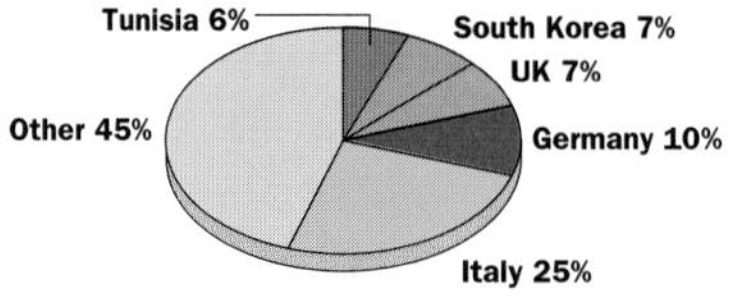
Tunisia 6%
South Korea 7%
UK 7%
Other 45%
Germany 10%
Italy 25%

Strengths

Oil and gas production. High levels of investment in downstream industries: petrochemicals, refineries, fertilizers, and aluminum smelting.

Weaknesses

Single-resource economy: subject to oil-market fluctuations. Most food imported. Reliance on foreign labor. Lack of water for agriculture. History of international unreliability.

Profile

An ambitious industrialization program was launched in the 1970s. Gaddafi's most controversial economic project has been the Great Man-Made River. Started in 1984, it was designed to bring water from under the Sahara to the coast, but the pipes are already corroding, with water leaking into the sand.

ECONOMIC PERFORMANCE INDICATOR

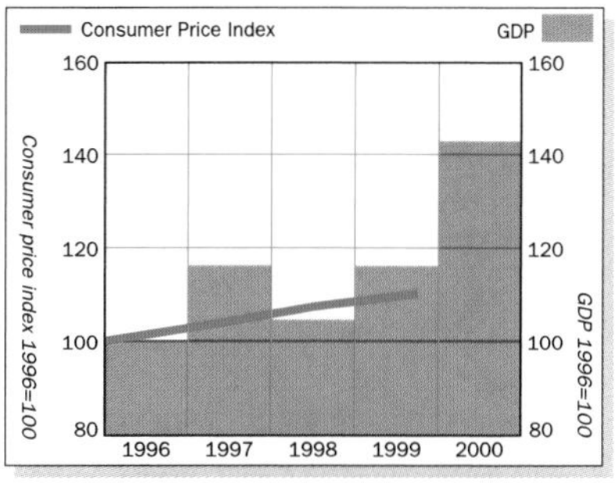
Consumer Price Index
GDP
160
140
120
100
80
1996
1997
1998
1999
2000
Consumer price index 1996=100
GDP 1996=100

Western oil companies had close business ties with Libya until the imposition in 1992 of UN sanctions over the Lockerbie affair. Gaddafi's 2003 offer of compensation for 1980s terrorist acts enabled UN sanctions to be lifted ; US sanctions were eased the following year, allowing oil companies, in particular, to reestablish links. WTO membership talks began in 2004.

LIBYA : MAJOR BUSINESSES

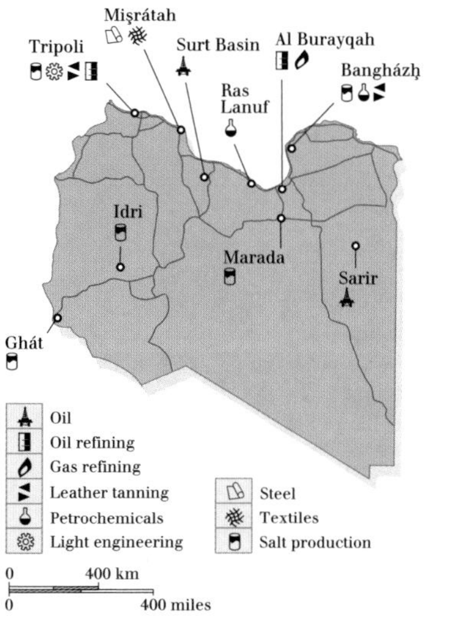
Mişrátah
Tripoli
Surt Basin
Al Burayqah
Banghāzḩ
Ras Lanuf
Idri
Marada
Sarir
Ghāt
Oil
Oil refining
Gas refining
Leather tanning
Petrochemicals
Light engineering
Steel
Textiles
Salt production
0
400 km
0
400 miles

RESOURCES

Electric power 4.6m kW

33,339 tonnes

1.49m b/d (reserves 36bn barrels)

4.13m sheep, 1.26m goats, 25m chickens

Oil, natural gas, iron, potassium, sulfur, magnesium, gypsum

ELECTRICITY GENERATION

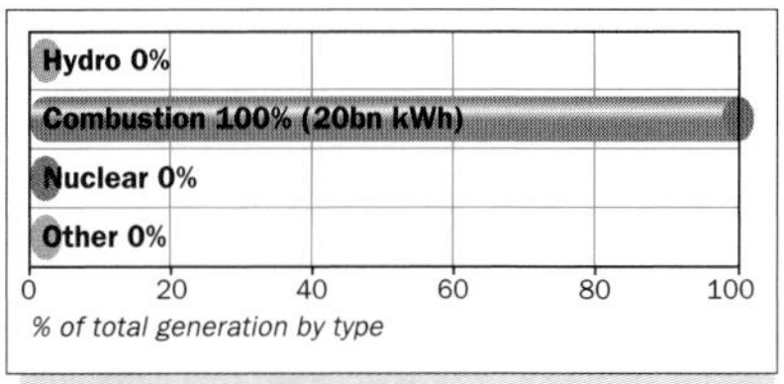
Hydro 0%
Combustion 100% (20bn kWh)
Nuclear 0%
Other 0%
0
20
40
60
80
100
% of total generation by type

Libya's economy depends almost entirely on its oil and natural gas resources. It has considerable crude oil reserves and is likely to remain an oil-exporting country for many decades. Natural gas potential is more limited but, provided links are developed with other north African states, the future is assured. Libya also has reserves of iron ore, potassium, sulfur, magnesium, and gypsum, though these contribute little to the overall economy and most minerals are imported.

The aging Great Man-Made River project means that the area of irrigated land has grown, but 90% of Libya is desert. Animal husbandry, particularly of sheep, is the basis of farming, but some cereal crops are grown, as well as tomatoes, watermelons, and olives.

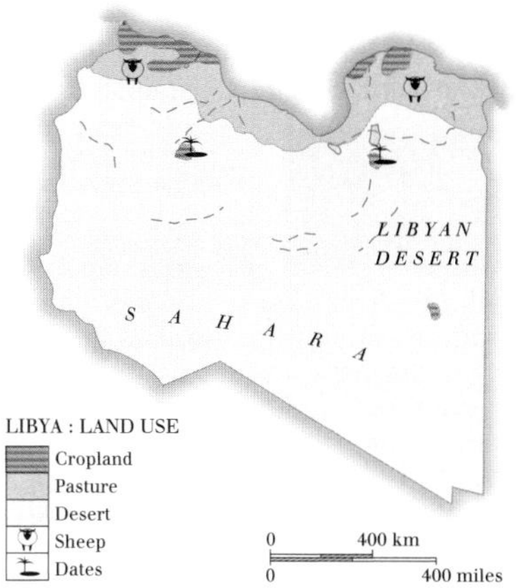
LIBYAN DESERT
S A H A R A
LIBYA : LAND USE
Cropland
Pasture
Desert
Sheep
Dates
0
400 km
0
400 miles

ENVIRONMENT

Sustainability rank: 124th

0.1% partially protected

10.9 tonnes per capita

ENVIRONMENTAL TREATIES

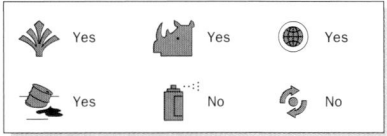

Yes	Yes	Yes
Yes	No	No

The UN Development Program has described Libya as more than 90% "wasteland." Both nature and man have conspired against the environment. Apart from two coastal strips – the Jeffara Plain and the Jabal al Akhdar in Cyrenaica – together with the Fazzan Oasis, most of Libya is desert. Much of the irrigated area is saline because of unwise use of naturally occurring water from artesian wells. Near Tripoli, seawater has penetrated the water table as far as 20 km (12 miles) inland.

MEDIA

TV ownership medium

Daily newspaper circulation 15 per 1000 people

PUBLISHING AND BROADCAST MEDIA

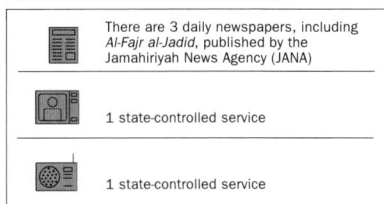

There are 3 daily newspapers, including *Al-Fajr al-Jadid*, published by the Jamahiriyah News Agency (JANA)

1 state-controlled service

1 state-controlled service

Libya's press and TV are a mouthpiece for the leadership. Satellite TV and the Internet are widely available, but heavily censored. The main daily newspaper is published in Arabic and has a circulation of 40,000 readers. The TV station broadcasts mostly in Arabic. Plans to start radio broadcasts in Kiswahili, Hausa, Fulani, and Amharic have been shelved.

CRIME

Death penalty in use

6750 prisoners

Up 10% in 1999

CRIME RATES

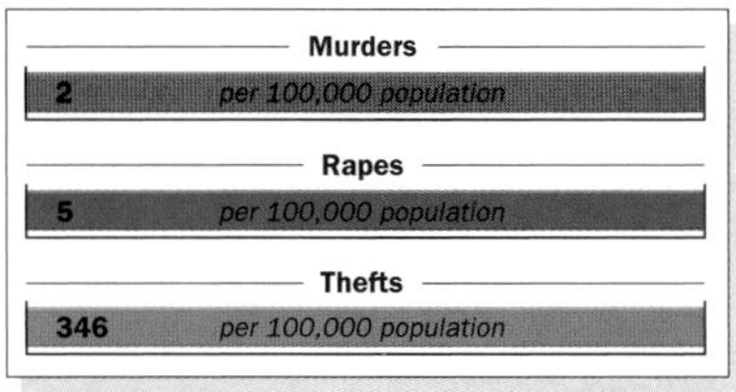
Murders
2
per 100,000 population
Rapes
5
per 100,000 population
Thefts
346
per 100,000 population

As part of rapprochement with the West, Gaddafi has pledged to crack down on torture and to open up the judicial system. His regime had been heavily criticized for human rights abuses.

EDUCATION

School leaving age: 15

82%

287,172 students

THE EDUCATION SYSTEM

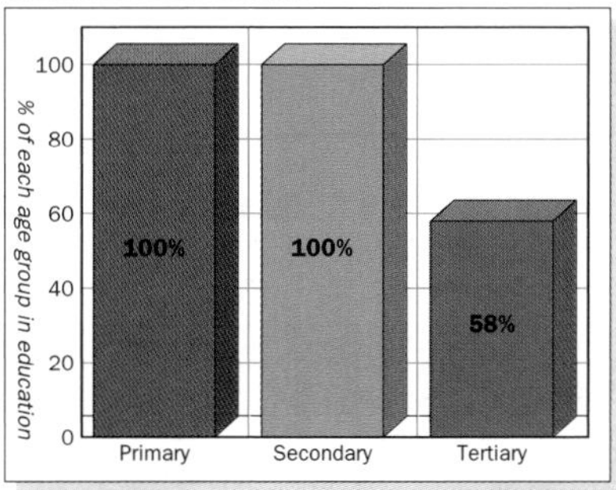
100
80
60
40
20
0
% of each age group in education
100%
100%
58%
Primary
Secondary
Tertiary

Some 1.8 million Libyans are in formal education. It is compulsory for nine years from the age of six and rates of attendance are very high, but it varies in quality and can be rudimentary in rural areas. Secondary education, from the age of 15, lasts for three years. There are 13 universities, and several institutes for vocational training. The literacy rate has more than doubled from a level of 39% in 1970.

HEALTH

Welfare state health benefits

1 per 769 people

Pneumonia, diarrheal diseases, accidents, cancers

An adequate system of free primary health care exists except in remote areas, and there are two big hospitals, in Benghazi and Tripoli. Sanctions have led to a lack of equipment and a shortage of medical supplies.

SPENDING

GDP/cap. decrease

CONSUMPTION AND SPENDING

159 per 1000 population

111 per 1000 population

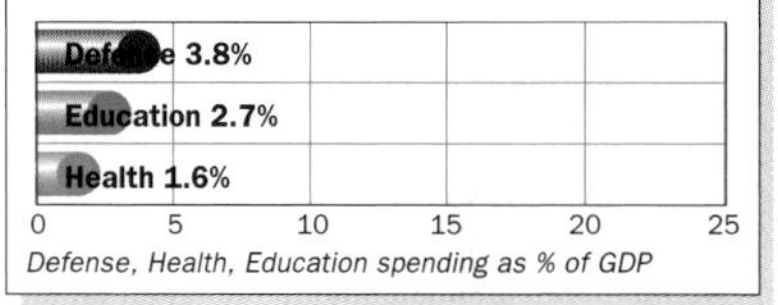
Defense 3.8%
Education 2.7%
Health 1.6%
0
5
10
15
20
25
Defense, Health, Education spending as % of GDP

There is widespread poverty after years of import constraints; UN sanctions worsened the situation. Gaddafi refuses to use oil revenues for basic expenses, such as salaries: wage levels have been frozen since the 1980s.

WORLD RANKING

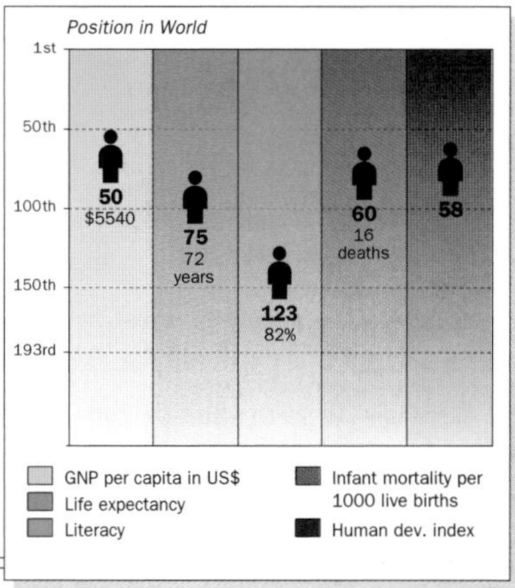
Position in World
1st
50th
100th
150th
193rd
50
$5540
75
72 years
123
82%
60
16 deaths
58
GNP per capita in US$
Life expectancy
Literacy
Infant mortality per 1000 live births
Human dev. index

L

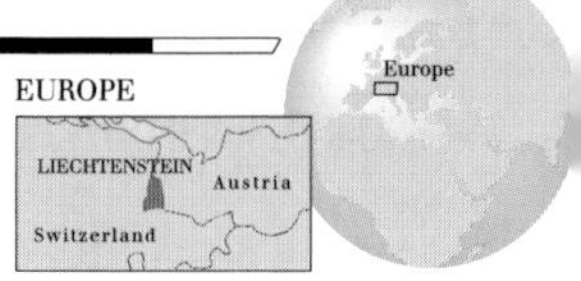
EUROPE
Europe
LIECHTENSTEIN
Austria
Switzerland

LIECHTENSTEIN

OFFICIAL NAME: Principality of Liechtenstein **CAPITAL:** Vaduz
POPULATION: 33,145 **CURRENCY:** Swiss franc **OFFICIAL LANGUAGE:** German

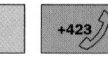

1719 | 1719 | Aug 15 | FL | +1 | +423 | .li

PERCHED IN THE ALPS, Liechtenstein is rare among small states in having both a thriving banking sector and a well-diversified manufacturing economy. It is closely allied to Switzerland, which handles its foreign relations and defense. Life in Liechtenstein is stable and conservative. The traditional secrecy surrounding the country's financial industry, and low taxes, mean that many overseas trusts, banks, and investment companies are located there.

CLIMATE

Mountain

WEATHER CHART FOR VADUZ

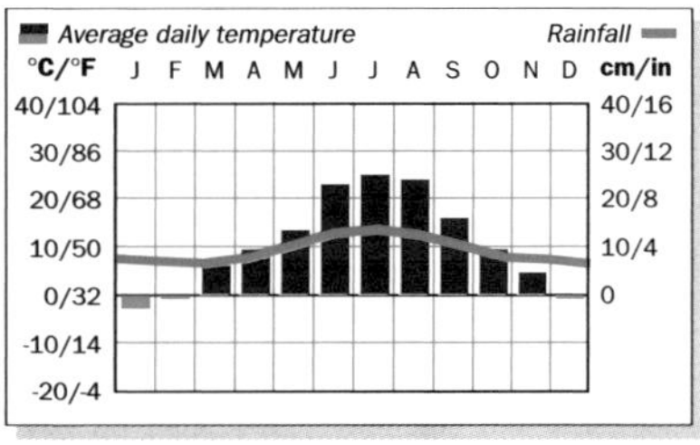
Average daily temperature
Rainfall
°C/°F J F M A M J J A S O N D cm/in
40/104 40/16
30/86 30/12
20/68 20/8
10/50 10/4
0/32 0
-10/14
-20/-4

Climate varies with altitude. Excellent skiing conditions are the result of heavy settling snow from December to March. Summers are warm and wet.

TRANSPORTATION

Drive on right

None | Has no fleet

THE TRANSPORTATION NETWORK

250 km (155 miles)	None
19 km (12 miles)	26 km (16 miles)

Public transportation in Liechtenstein is mostly by the postal bus network. The single-track railroad has few stops. Zürich, a two-hour drive away in Switzerland, is the nearest airport.

TOURISM

Visitors : Population 1.5:1

48,727 visitors | Down 13% in 2002

MAIN TOURIST ARRIVALS

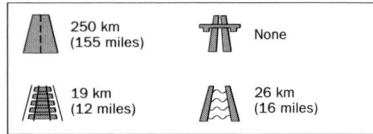

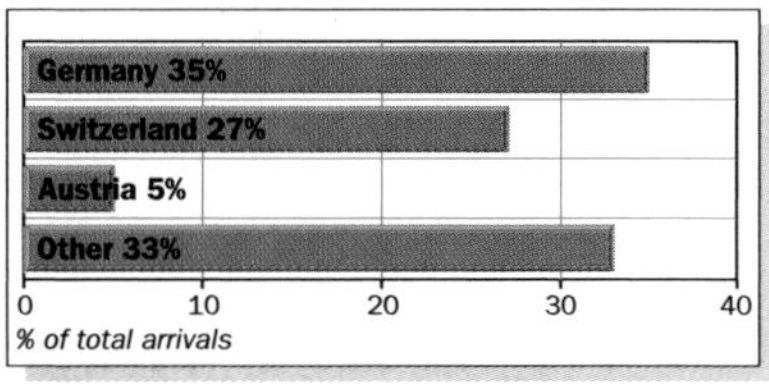
Germany 35%
Switzerland 27%
Austria 5%
Other 33%
0 10 20 30 40
% of total arrivals

Alpine scenery attracts skiers and walkers. The whole country was made available to rent for conferences in 2003.

PEOPLE

Pop. density high

German, Alemannish dialect, Italian | 207/km² (535/mi²)

THE URBAN/RURAL POPULATION SPLIT

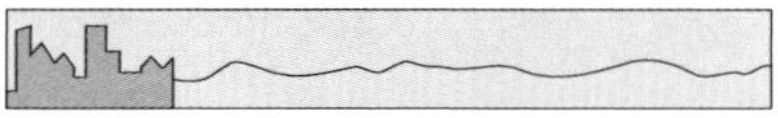
22%
78%

RELIGIOUS PERSUASION

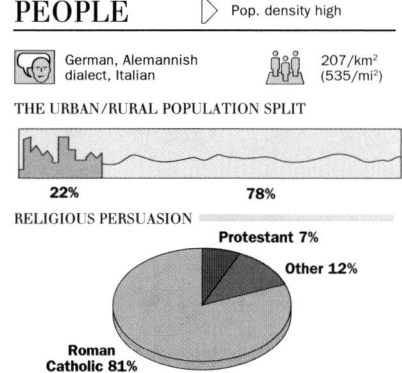

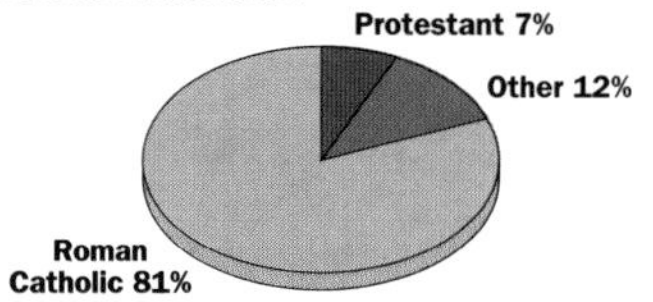
Protestant 7%
Other 12%
Roman Catholic 81%

Liechtenstein's role as a financial center accounts for the many foreign residents (over 35% of the population), of whom half are Swiss and the rest mostly German. Family life is highly traditional; women received the vote only in 1984, after much controversy. A proposal to enshrine equal rights for women in the constitution was rejected in a referendum in 1985 by a large majority and only finally passed in 1992. Abortion laws are restrictive but rarely enforced in practice.

POLITICS

Multiparty elections

2001/2005 | Prince Hans-Adam II von und zu Liechtenstein

AT THE LAST ELECTION
Parliament 25 seats

52% FBP
44% VU
4% FL

FBP = Progressive Citizens' Party **VU** = Fatherland Union
FL = Free List

From 1938 to 1997 the VU and the FBP alternated as coalition leaders. Mario Frick formed a VU-only government in 1997, ending the partnership. In elections in 2001 the FBP under Otmar Hasler overtook the VU. In 2003 Prince Hans-Adam II threatened to emigrate if he did not gain greater political powers; in 2004 he handed control to his son Alois while remaining head of state.

WORLD AFFAIRS

Joined UN in 1990

CE | EFTA | IAEA | OSCE | WTO

Liechtenstein effectively gave up control of its external relations in 1924 when it signed a Customs Union Treaty with Switzerland. This agreement requires Swiss approval for any treaty arrangements between Liechtenstein and a third state. Liechtenstein became a member of the UN only in 1990. It joined EFTA and the EBRD in 1991, and has been a participant in the EEA since 1995. However, Swiss rejection of EU membership in 1992 effectively ended any prospect of Liechtenstein joining the EU in the foreseeable future.

AID

Donor

Donor, but does not publish figures | Not available

Though overseas aid donations are small and aid issues have little political importance, Liechtenstein has helped to fund shelter and reconstruction projects in the former Yugoslavia and local development projects in Bulgaria.

LIECHTENSTEIN

Total Area : 160 sq. km (62 sq. miles)

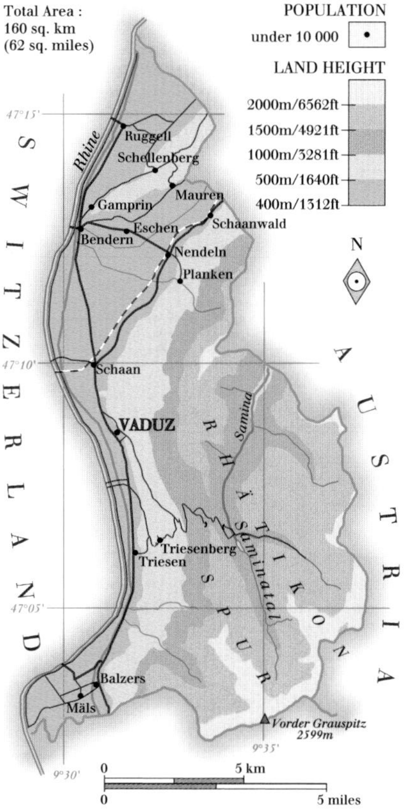
POPULATION
under 10 000
LAND HEIGHT
2000m/6562ft
1500m/4921ft
1000m/3281ft
500m/1640ft
400m/1312ft
SWITZERLAND
AUSTRIA
Rhine
Ruggell
Schellenberg
Gamprin
Mauren
Schaanwald
Eschen
Bendern
Nendeln
Planken
Schaan
VADUZ
Samina
RHÄTIKON
Saminatal
Triesenberg
Triesen
Balzers
Mäls
Vorder Grauspitz 2599m
N
0 5 km
0 5 miles

Alpine scenery near Vaduz. *The state budget includes 2% allocated to restoring mountain vegetation and coordinating land use.*

DEFENSE

No compulsory military service

No defense force | Not applicable

There has been no standing army since 1868, and there is only a small police force. De facto protection is provided by Switzerland. In theory, any male under 60 is liable for military service during a national emergency, though this law has never been invoked.

ECONOMICS

Inflation 2.9% p.a. (1985–1996)

$1.6bn | 1.252 Swiss francs (1.355)

SCORE CARD

- ❏ WORLD GNP RANKING........................146th
- ❏ GNP PER CAPITA $50,000
- ❏ BALANCE OF PAYMENTS.....Included in Swiss total
- ❏ INFLATION 1%
- ❏ UNEMPLOYMENT 1%

STRENGTHS

Stability and customs union with Switzerland make Liechtenstein a favored tax haven; its lack of EU membership makes the banking sector less vulnerable to future changes in EU banking laws. The economy is well diversified: chemicals, furniture, coatings for the electro-optical industry, construction services, and precision instruments are all thriving sectors.

WEAKNESSES

Lack of resources. Need to balance integration with other countries with safeguarding economic independence.

EXPORTS

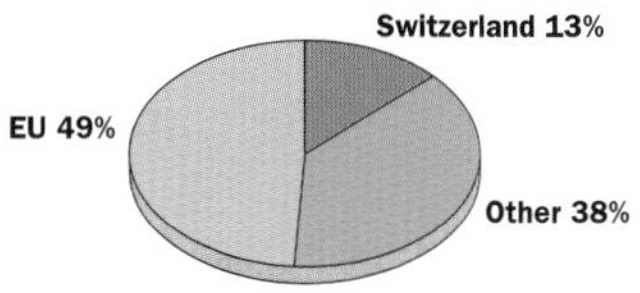
Switzerland 13%
EU 49%
Other 38%

IMPORTS

With a limited domestic market, Liechtenstein's industry is export-oriented. Liechtenstein has a customs union with Switzerland and does not publish separate import figures.

RESOURCES

Electric power: Included in Swiss total

None | Not an oil producer

6000 cattle, 3000 pigs, 2900 sheep, 280 goats | None

Liechtenstein has to import most of its energy. Almost all of its electricity comes from German power plants.

ENVIRONMENT

Not available

38% partially protected | 6.1 tonnes per capita

Protection of Liechtenstein's alpine scenery is high enough on the political agenda for one of the five councillors, or ministers, to have responsibility for the environment. As in Switzerland, the greatest worry is the effect of high rates of car use and of through traffic. However, a 1988 trial in providing free public bus transportation proved a failure, as Liechtensteiners remained firmly wedded to their automobiles.

MEDIA

TV ownership high

Daily newspaper circulation 602 per 1000 people

PUBLISHING AND BROADCAST MEDIA

There are 2 daily newspapers, *Liechtensteiner Vaterland* and *Liechtensteiner Volksblatt*

No domestic TV service | 1 radio service

The two daily newspapers, though free of formal state control, are both run by political parties: the *Vaterland*, with the larger circulation (over 10,000), by the VU, the *Volksblatt* by the FBP.

CRIME

No death penalty

17 prisoners | Crime does not pose any great problems

Crime is a minor problem, a result of the relatively even distribution of wealth and high average living standard. Liechtenstein has also taken great care to protect its tax-haven status by careful regulation of its financial sector. It has avoided major scandals, and took steps in 2000 to tighten precautions against the growing problem of money laundering.

EDUCATION

School leaving age: 16

99% | Not available

Education, modeled on the German system, includes two types of school at secondary level – the more academic *Gymnasium* and the *Realschule*. Liechtenstein has no university; students go on to colleges in Austria, Switzerland, or Germany, or to business schools in the US.

CHRONOLOGY

In 1719 Liechtenstein became an independent principality of the Holy Roman Empire.

- ❏ **1924** Customs union with Switzerland.
- ❏ **1992** Women given equal rights.
- ❏ **1997** VU government ends VU–FBP coalition dominant since 1938.
- ❏ **2001** FBP wins majority in elections; Otmar Hasler premier.
- ❏ **2003** Prince wins greater powers.
- ❏ **2004** Prince hands control to son.

HEALTH

Welfare state health benefits

1 per 763 people | Heart and respiratory diseases, cancers

Though clinics and hospitals are few, the health system provides advanced care. Many Liechtensteiners have private health insurance arrangements, so that they have access to Swiss medical expertise and facilities as well as their own.

SPENDING

GDP/cap. increase

CONSUMPTION AND SPENDING

710 per 1000 population | *583 per 1000 population*

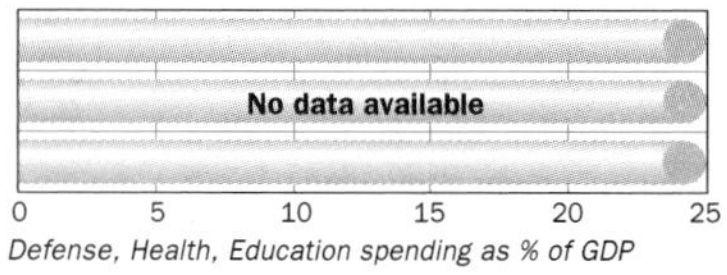
No data available
0
5
10
15
20
25
Defense, Health, Education spending as % of GDP

Unlike other tax havens, Liechtenstein displays a more conservative prosperity. Private deposit accounts are not a key part of its banking business, but an increase in money-laundering activities and the country's appearance on a blacklist of financial centers led to a ban on anonymous accounts in mid-2000.

WORLD RANKING

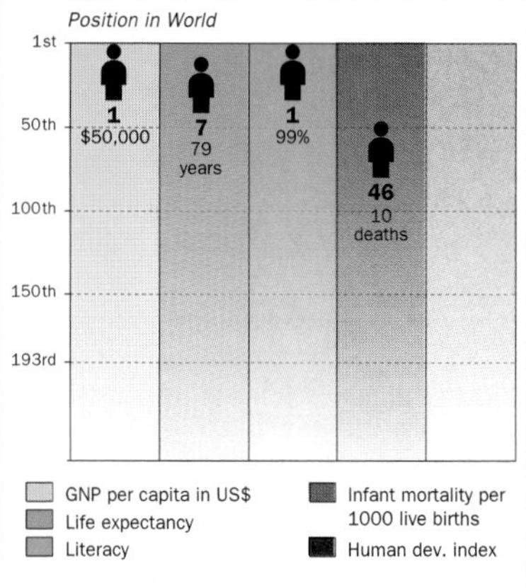
Position in World
1st
50th
100th
150th
193rd
1
$50,000
7
79 years
1
99%
46
10 deaths
GNP per capita in US$
Life expectancy
Literacy
Infant mortality per 1000 live births
Human dev. index

L

LITHUANIA

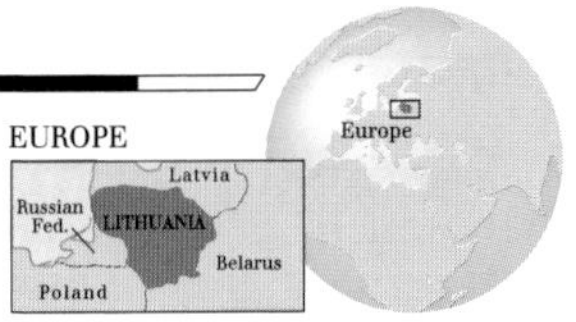
EUROPE
Europe
Latvia
Russian Fed.
LITHUANIA
Belarus
Poland

OFFICIAL NAME: Republic of Lithuania **CAPITAL:** Vilnius **POPULATION:** 3.4 million
CURRENCY: Litas (euro is also legal tender) **OFFICIAL LANGUAGE:** Lithuanian

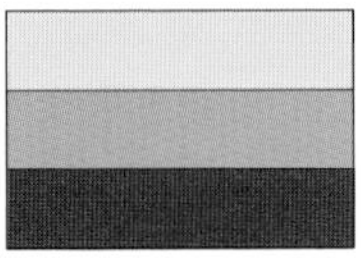

1991 | 1991 | Feb 16 | LT | +2 | +370 | .lt

LYING ON THE EASTERN COAST of the Baltic Sea, Lithuania was the last European country formally to embrace Christianity, in about 1400. Its terrain is mostly flat, with many lakes, moors, and bogs. Now a multiparty democracy, Lithuania regained independence from the former USSR in 1991. Industrial production and agriculture are the mainstays of the economy. Russia finally withdrew all its troops from Lithuania in 1993.

CLIMATE

Continental

WEATHER CHART FOR VILNIUS

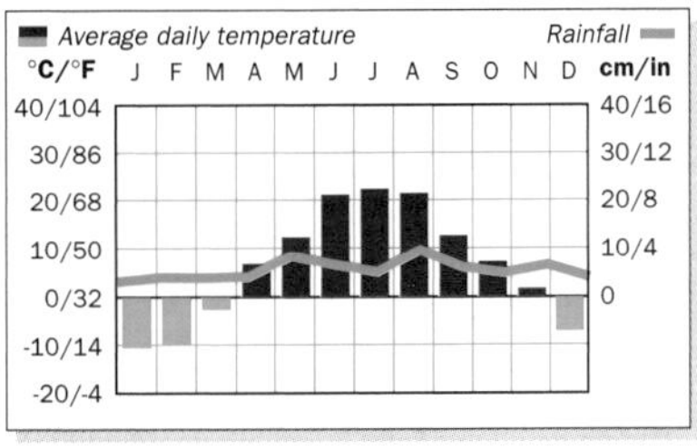
Average daily temperature
Rainfall
°C/°F
J F M A M J J A S O N D
cm/in
40/104
30/86
20/68
10/50
0/32
-10/14
-20/-4
40/16
30/12
20/8
10/4
0

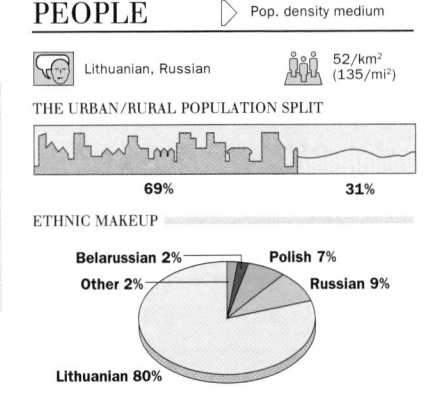

Lithuania's coastal position moderates an otherwise continental-type climate. Summers are cool.

TRANSPORTATION

Drive on right

Vilnius 719,850 passengers

184 ships 435,300 grt

THE TRANSPORTATION NETWORK

69,681 km (43,298 miles)

417 km (259 miles)

1775 km (1103 miles)

600 km (373 miles)

Lithuania is crossed by international rail routes, and Klaipeda provides extensive connections to other Baltic ports.

TOURISM

Visitors : Population 1:2.4

1.43m visitors

Up 12% in 2002

MAIN TOURIST ARRIVALS

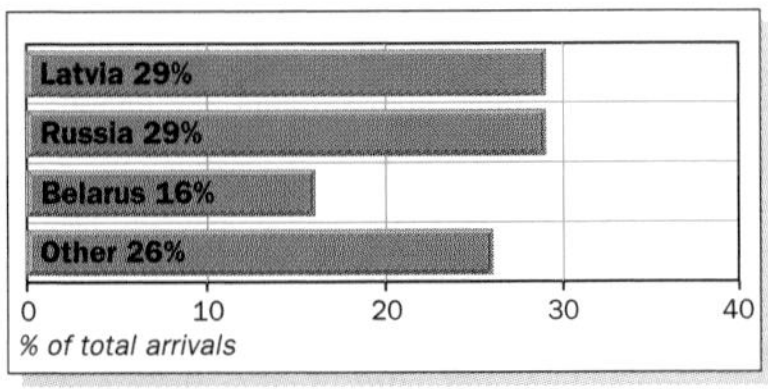
Latvia 29%
Russia 29%
Belarus 16%
Other 26%
0
10
20
30
40
% of total arrivals

The tourist industry boomed after independence. Vilnius is well preserved; its historic center survived German and Russian occupation. Trakai, the capital of the Grand Duchy in the 16th century, is also popular with visitors.

PEOPLE

Pop. density medium

Lithuanian, Russian

52/km² (135/mi²)

THE URBAN/RURAL POPULATION SPLIT

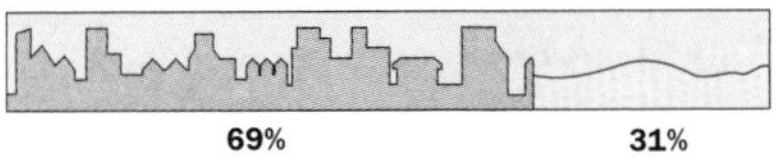
69%
31%

ETHNIC MAKEUP

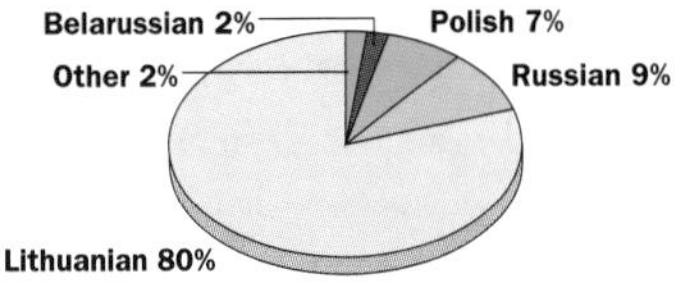
Belarussian 2%
Polish 7%
Other 2%
Russian 9%
Lithuanian 80%

With a mainly Catholic population, Lithuania has strong historical links with Poland, with which it was once united, though there is tension between ethnic Lithuanians and Poles. Relations with the Jewish minority are strained. More than 90% of nonethnic Lithuanians have been granted citizenship. Of all the Baltic states, Lithuania has the best relations with ethnic Russians, but they form a smaller minority there than in Estonia or Latvia.

POLITICS

Multiparty elections

2000/2004

President Valdas Adamkus

AT THE LAST ELECTION

Parliament 141 seats

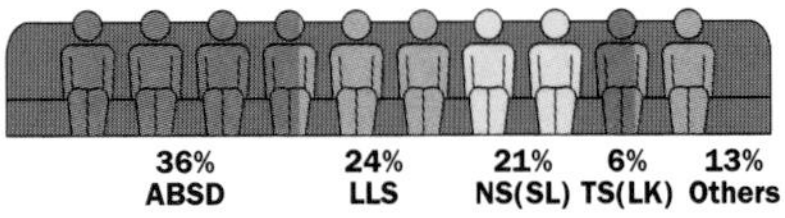
36% ABSD
24% LLS
21% NS(SL)
6% TS(LK)
13% Others

ABSD = A. Brazauskas Social Democratic Coalition
LLS = Lithuanian Liberal Union
NS(SL) = New Union (Social Liberals)
TS(LK) = Homeland Union (Lithuanian Conservatives)

Though governments have proved somewhat shortlived in recent years and personalities dominate politics, Lithuania's overall drive since independence in 1991 toward market reform and integration with the West has been unhindered. Former communist and conservative parties have led coalitions, with increasing levels of fractiousness – there were four different governments between 1999 and 2001. On the collapse in 2001 of a promarket coalition headed by Rolandas Paksas of the LLS, a new government was formed by Parliament's largest bloc, the ABSD, headed by former president and reformed communist Algirdas Brazauskas. He promised to maintain the country's economic reforms while pursuing more socially oriented policies. Paksas unexpectedly won presidential elections in 2003, but was removed from office in April 2004 because of his links with organized crime. Fresh elections were won by former president Valdas Adamkus.

LITHUANIA

Total Land Area : 65 200 sq. km (25 174 sq. miles)

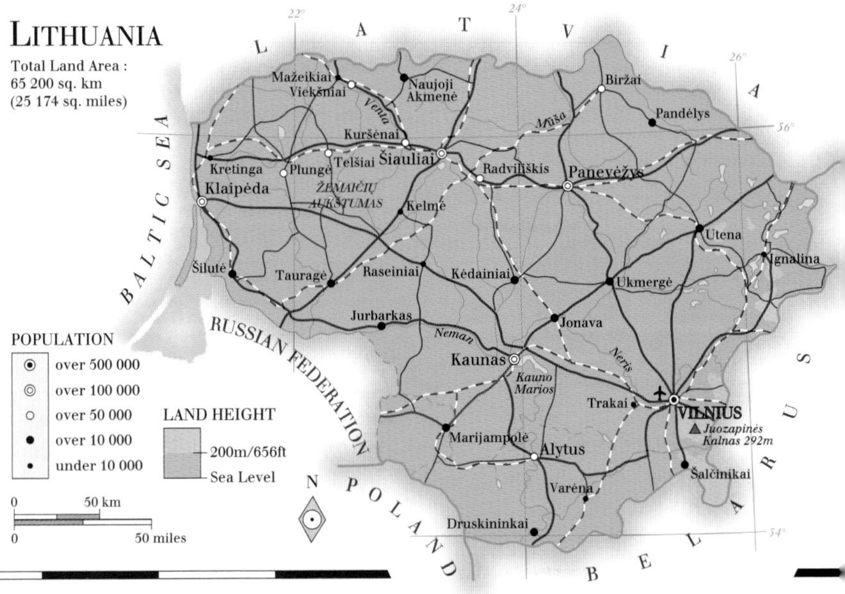
LATVIA
BALTIC SEA
RUSSIAN FEDERATION
POLAND
BELARUS
Mažeikiai
Viekšniai
Venta
Naujoji Akmenė
Biržai
Pandėlys
Mūša
Kuršėnai
Kretinga
Plungė
Telšiai
Šiauliai
Radviliškis
Panevėžys
Klaipėda
ŽEMAIČIŲ AUKŠTUMAS
Kelmė
Utena
Ignalina
Šilutė
Tauragė
Raseiniai
Kėdainiai
Ukmergė
Jurbarkas
Jonava
Neman
Neris
Kaunas
Kauno Marios
Trakai
VILNIUS
Juozapinės Kalnas 292m
Marijampolė
Alytus
Šalčininkai
Varėna
Druskininkai
POPULATION
over 500 000
over 100 000
over 50 000
over 10 000
under 10 000
LAND HEIGHT
200m/656ft
Sea Level
0 50 km
0 50 miles

WORLD AFFAIRS

Joined UN in 1991

CE | CBSS | EU | NATO | OSCE

Lithuania currently has the best relations with Russia of all the Baltic states. This is balanced with close ties to the West; in 2004 it joined NATO and the EU, in March and May respectively.

AID

Recipient

$147m (receipts) | Up 13% in 2002

Aid donations and, since 2004, direct EU funding promote infrastructure projects and private enterprise.

DEFENSE

Compulsory military service

$233m | Up 11% in 2002

A large National Guard patrols the country's frontiers. Legislation was passed in 2003 to cut active troop numbers by 5000 within five years through a reduction in both the length of military service (from one year) and the size of the active reserve force.

ECONOMICS

Inflation 63% p.a. (1990–2001)

$12.7bn | 2.838 litai (3.007)

SCORE CARD

❏ World GNP Ranking	81st
❏ GNP per Capita	$3670
❏ Balance of Payments	–$721m
❏ Inflation	0.3%
❏ Unemployment	14%

Strengths

Successful transition to stable market economy. Increase in foreign investment. Low inflation. Litas pegged to euro (legal tender from 2002).

Weaknesses

Agriculture slow to recover from decollectivization. Exports dependent on health of Russian economy. Poor raw materials base. Widening external current account deficit.

EXPORTS

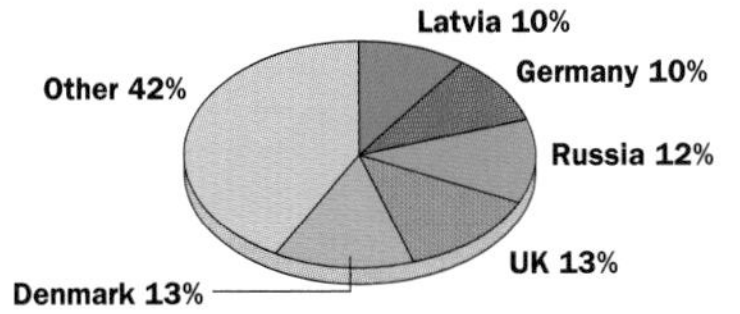
Latvia 10%
Germany 10%
Other 42%
Russia 12%
UK 13%
Denmark 13%

IMPORTS

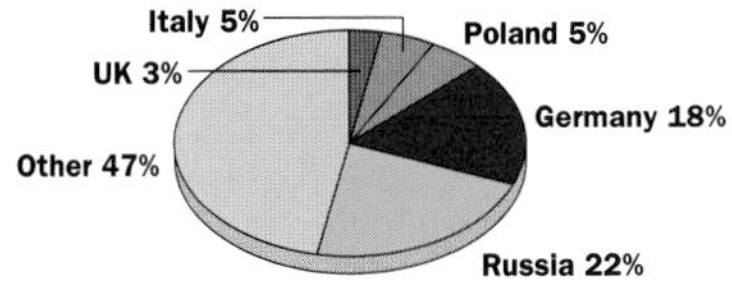
Italy 5%
Poland 5%
UK 3%
Germany 18%
Other 47%
Russia 22%

One of Lithuania's 3000 lakes. The entire country is low-lying. Its coast, fringed by dunes and pine forests, is famous for amber.

RESOURCES

Electric power 6.6m kW

153,932 tonnes | 6336 b/d (reserves 14m barrels)

1.06m pigs, 779,100 cattle, 6.85m chickens | Sand, gravel, clay, limestone, gypsum, oil, amber

Lithuania has significant reserves of peat and of materials used in the construction industry. The Ignalina nuclear plant provides more than 75% of the country's electricity. Oil is mostly imported from Russia.

ENVIRONMENT

Sustainability rank: 27th

10% (7% partially protected) | 3.4 tonnes per capita

Radioactive leaks and the risk of accident at the giant Chernobyl-type nuclear plant at Ignalina cause much concern. In 2002 the government agreed to decommission it by 2009, after pressure from the EU, which will share the $2.6 billion cost.

MEDIA

TV ownership high

Daily newspaper circulation 29 per 1000 people

PUBLISHING AND BROADCAST MEDIA

There are 9 daily newspapers, including *Lietuvos Rytas* and *Respublika*

10 services: 1 state-owned, 9 independent | 26 services: 1 state-owned, 25 independent

Mainstream media are mainly printed and broadcast in Lithuanian, having been in Russian under communism.

CRIME

No death penalty

9217 prisoners | Down 4% in 2001

Carjackings are increasingly common. Racially motivated attacks against foreigners have been reported.

EDUCATION

School leaving age: 15

99% | 168,200 students

Teaching at all levels is in Lithuanian, making access to higher education harder for minorities. Half of all students go on to university.

CHRONOLOGY

The commonwealth of Lithuania and Poland formed the largest state in Europe until Lithuania was annexed by Russia in 1795.

- ❏ **1915** Occupied by German troops.
- ❏ **1918** Independence declared.
- ❏ **1926** Military coup; one-party rule.
- ❏ **1940** Annexed by Soviet Union.
- ❏ **1941–1944** Nazi occupation.
- ❏ **1945** Incorporated into USSR.
- ❏ **1991** Achieves full independence.
- ❏ **1992** First multiparty elections.
- ❏ **1993** Russian troops withdraw.
- ❏ **1996** General election follows banking scandal; TS(LK) wins.
- ❏ **2000** Brief center-left coalition.
- ❏ **2001** Ex-president Brazauskas becomes prime minister.
- ❏ **2004** Joins NATO. President Paksas impeached. Joins EU.

HEALTH

Welfare state health benefits

1 per 250 people | Heart diseases, cancers, cerebrovascular diseases, accidents

The reorganization of the health service, begun in 1997, has replaced state funding with finance from insurance funds.

SPENDING

GDP/cap. decrease

CONSUMPTION AND SPENDING

319 per 1000 population | *270 per 1000 population*

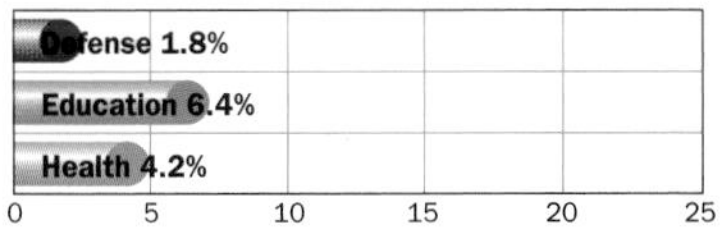
Defense 1.8%
Education 6.4%
Health 4.2%
0
5
10
15
20
25

Defense, Health, Education spending as % of GDP

High unemployment and weak consumption have held back growth. Since 1991 a large gap has opened between the incomes of rich and poor.

WORLD RANKING

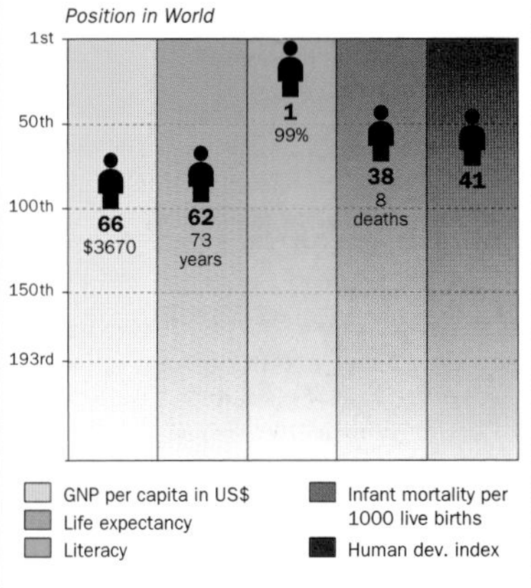
Position in World
1st
50th
100th
150th
193rd
66
$3670
62
73 years
1
99%
38
8 deaths
41
GNP per capita in US$
Life expectancy
Literacy
Infant mortality per 1000 live births
Human dev. index

L

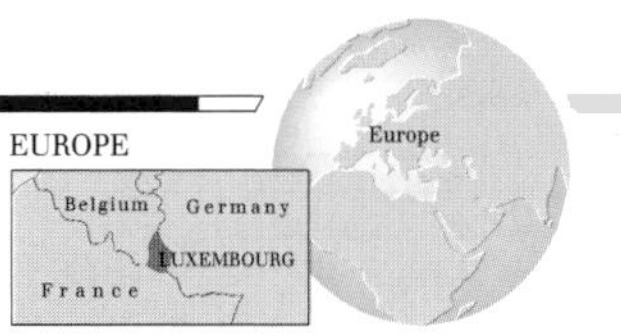
EUROPE
Europe
Belgium
Germany
LUXEMBOURG
France

LUXEMBOURG

OFFICIAL NAME: Grand Duchy of Luxembourg **CAPITAL:** Luxembourg-Ville
POPULATION: 453,000 **CURRENCY:** Euro **OFFICIAL LANGUAGES:** French, German, and Luxembourgish

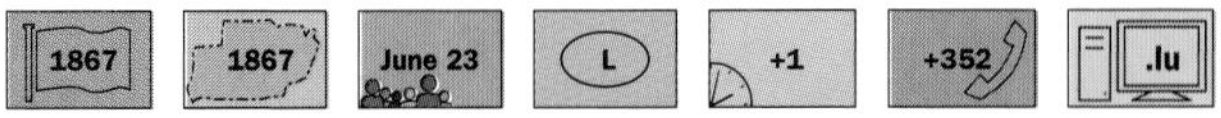
1867
1867
June 23
L
+1
+352
.lu

LUXEMBOURG SHARES BORDERS with the industrial regions of Germany, France, and Belgium, and has the highest per capita income in the EU. The northern Ösling region is part of the plateau of the Ardennes, and is undulating and forested. Luxembourg's prosperity was once based on steel; before World War II it produced more per capita than the US. Today, it is known as the headquarters of key EU institutions and as a banking center.

CLIMATE

Maritime

WEATHER CHART FOR LUXEMBOURG-VILLE

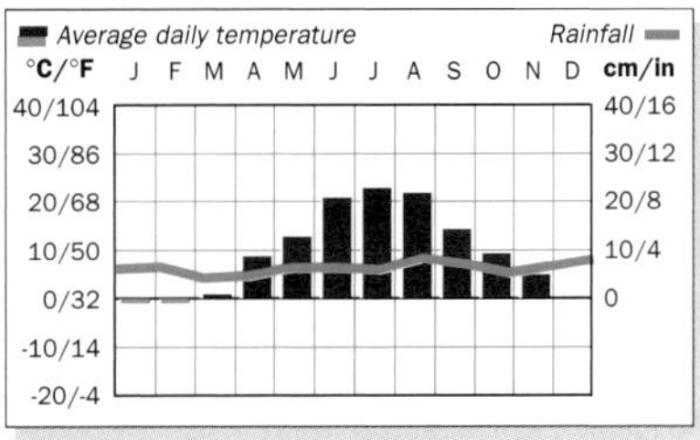
Average daily temperature
Rainfall
°C/°F
J F M A M J J A S O N D
cm/in
40/104
30/86
20/68
10/50
0/32
-10/14
-20/-4
40/16
30/12
20/8
10/4
0

The south, where vines grow, is the warmest area. Winter is cold and snowy, especially in the Ardennes.

TRANSPORTATION

Drive on right

Findel, Luxembourg-Ville
1.46m passengers

Has no fleet

THE TRANSPORTATION NETWORK

5189 km (3224 miles)	126 km (78 miles)
274 km (170 miles)	37 km (23 miles)

There is an excellent road network, though congestion is a problem. Rail and bus services are integrated.

TOURISM

Visitors : Population 1.9:1

876,000 visitors

Up 6% in 2002

MAIN TOURIST ARRIVALS

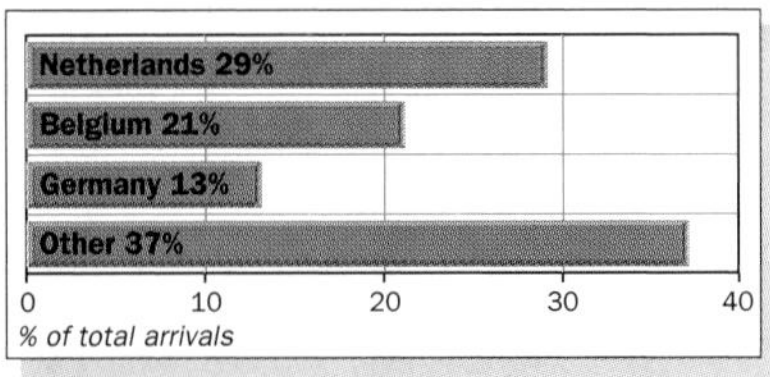
Netherlands 29%
Belgium 21%
Germany 13%
Other 37%
0
10
20
30
40
% of total arrivals

Key attractions are the hills and forests, 76 castles, and the Benedictine abbey at Echternach. Under a government initiative, foreign hotel workers learn about the history, language, and culture of the duchy.

PEOPLE

Pop. density medium

Luxembourgish, German, French

175/km² (454/mi²)

THE URBAN/RURAL POPULATION SPLIT

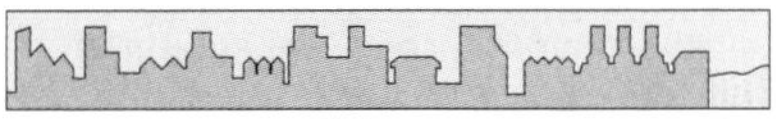
92%
8%

RELIGIOUS PERSUASION

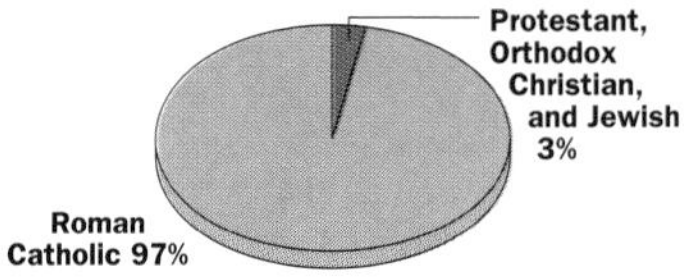
Protestant, Orthodox Christian, and Jewish 3%
Roman Catholic 97%

Nearly a third of its residents and half of Luxembourg's workers are foreigners. Integration has been straightforward; most are fellow western Europeans and Roman Catholics, mainly from Italy and Portugal. Life in Luxembourg is comfortable. Salaries are high, unemployment very low, and social tensions few.

POLITICS

Multiparty elections

L. House 2004/2009

Grand Duke Henri

AT THE LAST ELECTION

Chamber of Deputies 60 seats

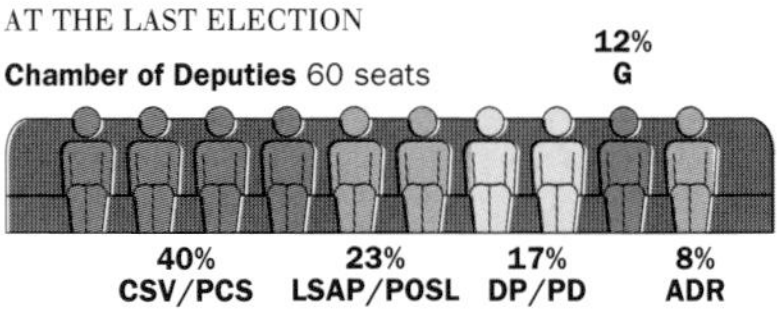
12%
G
40%
CSV/PCS
23%
LSAP/POSL
17%
DP/PD
8%
ADR

CSV/PCS = Christian Social People's Party
LSAP/POSL = Luxembourg Socialist Workers' Party
DP/PD = Democratic Party **G** = Greens
ADR = Action Committee for Democracy and Justice

Council of State 21 seats

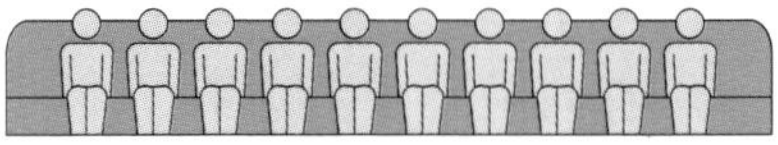

The members of the Council of State are appointed for life by the grand duke

There is remarkable political consensus, and governments are characterized by coalitions and long-serving prime ministers; the grand duke's role is mostly ceremonial. Main issues relate to European integration.

WORLD AFFAIRS

Joined UN in 1945

Benelux | EU | NATO | OECD | OSCE

Luxembourg has long supported integration within the EU. During its EU presidency the Maastricht agreement for closer European union was brokered, and Luxembourg was not only the first member state to meet all the economic, financial, and legal requirements of union under Maastricht, but did so a year early. It is a firm advocate of a strong EU common foreign and security policy and is critical of the proposed European constitution's failure to scrap the right to veto in this field. This commitment to the EU reflects the tremendous benefits Luxembourg has gained from membership. It is home to both the Secretariat of the European Parliament and the Court of Justice.

Buurgplaatz 559m
BELGIUM
GERMANY
FRANCE
ÖSLING
ARDENNES
GUTLAND
Our
Clervaux
Wiltz
Lac de la Haute Sûre
Vianden
Diekirch
Sûre
Ettelbrück
Echternach
Redange
Mersch
Wasserbillig
Grevenmacher
Walferdange
Capellen
Mamer
Findel Airport
LUXEMBOURG
Moselle
Pétange
Hesperange
Sanem
Remich
Differdange
Schifflange
Bettembourg
Esch-sur-Alzette
Kayl
Dudelange
50°
49°30'
6°
6°30'

LUXEMBOURG

Total Area : 2586 sq. km (998 sq. miles)

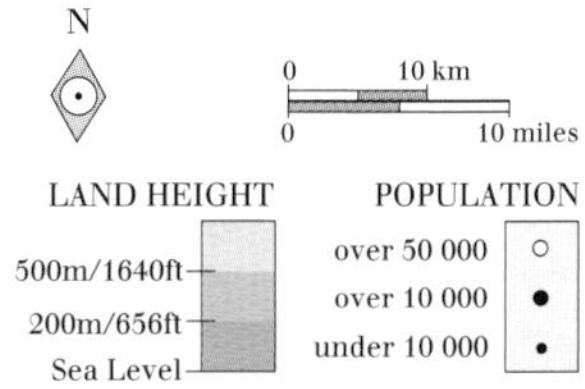
N
0 10 km
0 10 miles
LAND HEIGHT
500m/1640ft
200m/656ft
Sea Level
POPULATION
over 50 000
over 10 000
under 10 000

***Charlotte Bridge, Luxembourg.** The modern road system provides excellent links with the rest of Europe.*

AID

Donor

$147m (donations) — Up 6% in 2002

Aid equaled 0.77% of GNP in 2002; it is given to least developed countries or as specific economic aid.

DEFENSE

No compulsory military service

$193m — Up 24% in 2002

A few members of the 900-strong army assist in international peacekeeping missions. There is no navy or air force.

ECONOMICS

Inflation 2.2% p.a. (1990–2001)

$17.5bn — 0.822 euros (0.871)

SCORE CARD

❑ WORLD GNP RANKING	73rd
❑ GNP PER CAPITA	$39,470
❑ BALANCE OF PAYMENTS	$1.64bn
❑ INFLATION	2.1%
❑ UNEMPLOYMENT	3%

STRENGTHS

Location for some EU institutions. Banking secrecy and expertise make the capital home to around 1000 investment funds and over 200 banks – more than in any other city in the world.

WEAKNESSES

International service industries account for 65% of GDP, making Luxembourg vulnerable to changing conditions overseas. Downturn in steel market.

EXPORTS

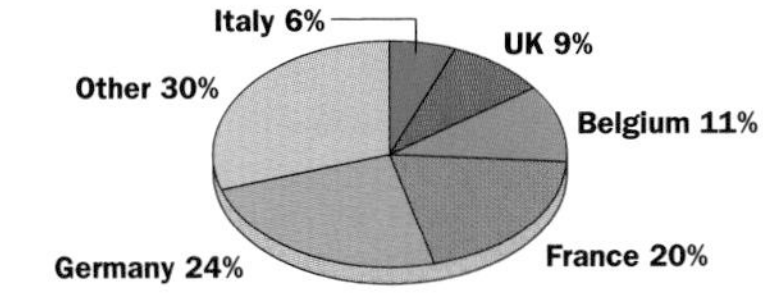

Italy 6%
UK 9%
Other 30%
Belgium 11%
Germany 24%
France 20%

IMPORTS

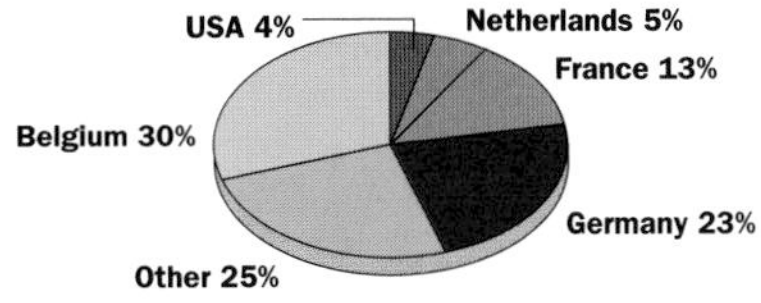

USA 4%
Netherlands 5%
France 13%
Belgium 30%
Germany 23%
Other 25%

RESOURCES

Electric power 1.2m kW

None — Not an oil producer

197,257 cattle, 79,665 pigs, 9104 sheep — Iron

Luxembourg is a key processor of steel; the Arbed company was a founder in 2002 of the multinational Arcelor Group, the world's largest steel company.

ENVIRONMENT

Not available

14% partially protected — 19.1 tonnes per capita

Acid rain from European industry has affected 20% of Luxembourg's trees and, in the worst cases, 30% of trees in mature stands. Luxembourg is a member of an international committee on reducing pollution of the Rhine.

MEDIA

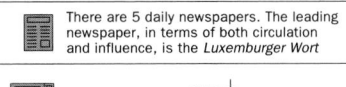

TV ownership high

Daily newspaper circulation 325 per 1000 people

PUBLISHING AND BROADCAST MEDIA

There are 5 daily newspapers. The leading newspaper, in terms of both circulation and influence, is the *Luxemburger Wort*

2 independent services — 11 independent services

Broadcasting is dominated by RTL (Radio–Television Luxembourg), one of the largest media groups in Europe, which exports its programs in a variety of languages.

CRIME

No death penalty

380 prisoners — Down 7% in 2000–2002

Luxembourg's banking secrecy rules have provoked international criticism, as they can provide a cover for both tax evasion and fraud. Violent crime remains uncommon.

EDUCATION

School leaving age: 15

99% — 2533 students

Teaching is mainly in German at primary and French at secondary level. Higher education is limited and many students go to universities in other European countries. Training given by Luxembourg banks is reputed to be the best in Europe.

HEALTH

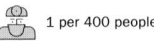

Welfare state health benefits

1 per 400 people — Cancers, heart and cerebrovascular diseases, accidents

There are no private commercial hospitals in Luxembourg; they are run either by the state or by nuns. Patients' fees are refunded from the state sickness fund.

CHRONOLOGY

Until 1867, Luxembourg was ruled by a succession of neighboring European powers.

- ❑ **1890** Link with Dutch throne ends.
- ❑ **1921** Economic union with Belgium. End of German ties.
- ❑ **1940–1944** German occupation.
- ❑ **1948** Benelux treaty (1944) creating a customs union comes into effect.
- ❑ **1957** One of six signatories of Treaty of Rome, the principal foundation of what develops into the EU.
- ❑ **1995** Premier Jacques Santer is president of European Commission.
- ❑ **1999** Santer resigns amid corruption allegations. Socialist election losses.
- ❑ **2000** Grand Duke Jean abdicates in favor of his son, Henri.
- ❑ **2002** Euro fully adopted.

SPENDING

GDP/cap. increase

CONSUMPTION AND SPENDING

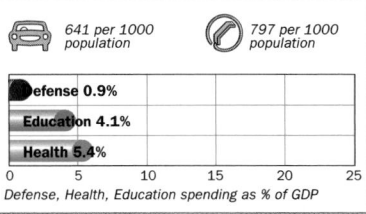

641 per 1000 population — *797 per 1000 population*

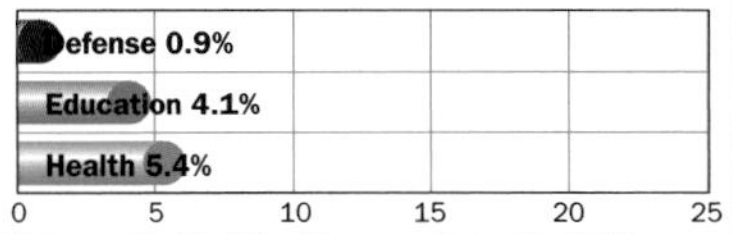

Defense 0.9%
Education 4.1%
Health 5.4%
0
5
10
15
20
25

Defense, Health, Education spending as % of GDP

With the world's second-highest per capita income, Luxembourgers enjoy a comfortable lifestyle. Recent strong economic performance has allowed them to benefit both from lower taxes and increased social security spending. Low unemployment has led to the recruitment of foreign workers, mainly from neighboring countries or from other EU countries such as Portugal and Italy, to take less well-paid jobs. As elsewhere in western Europe, financing care of the aging population is likely to be a burden in the future.

WORLD RANKING

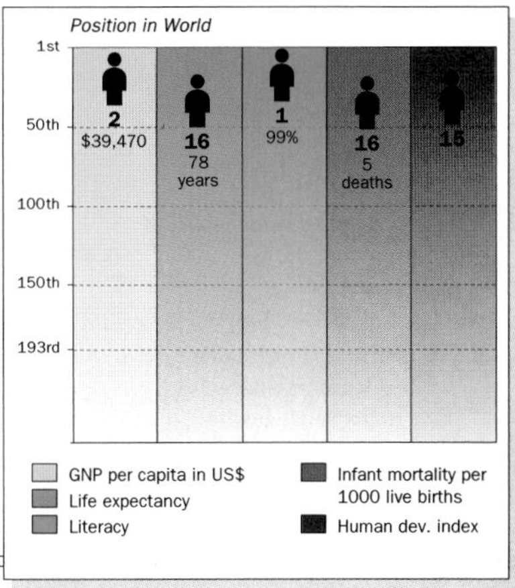

Position in World
1st
50th
100th
150th
193rd
2
$39,470
16
78 years
1
99%
16
5 deaths
15
GNP per capita in US$
Life expectancy
Literacy
Infant mortality per 1000 live births
Human dev. index

L

MACEDONIA

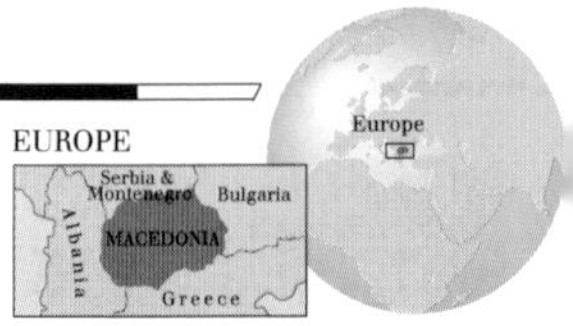
EUROPE
Europe
Serbia & Montenegro
Bulgaria
Albania
MACEDONIA
Greece

OFFICIAL NAME: Republic of Macedonia **CAPITAL:** Skopje
POPULATION: 2.02 million **CURRENCY:** Macedonian denar **OFFICIAL LANGUAGES:** Macedonian and Albanian

1991 | 1991 | Aug 2 | MK | +1 | +389 | .mk

THE FORMER YUGOSLAV REPUBLIC of Macedonia (FYRM) is landlocked in southeastern Europe. Despite the signing of an accord in 1995, Greece remains suspicious that it harbors ambitions about absorbing northern Greece – also called Macedonia – into a "Greater Macedonia." A militant movement among ethnic Albanians erupted into violent conflict in March–September 2001, but a peace agreement was reached after the involvement of a NATO force.

A fisherman's hut on Lake Dojran. The lake lies on the border with Greece in southeastern Macedonia and is shared by the two countries.

CLIMATE

Continental

WEATHER CHART FOR SKOPJE

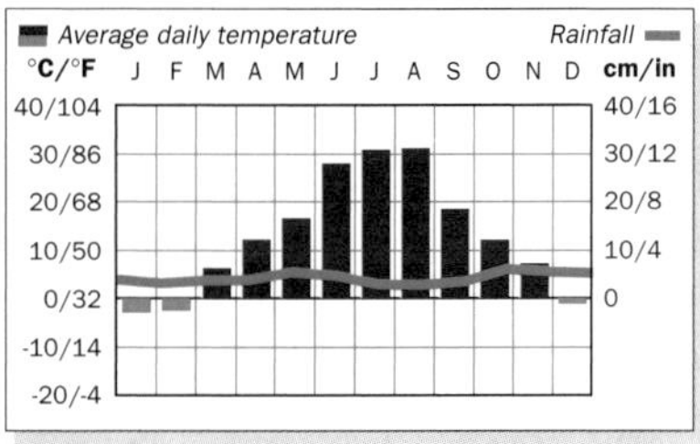
Average daily temperature
Rainfall
°C/°F
J F M A M J J A S O N D
cm/in
40/104
30/86
20/68
10/50
0/32
-10/14
-20/-4
40/16
30/12
20/8
10/4
0

Macedonia has a continental climate. Winter snow supports skiing.

TRANSPORTATION

Drive on right

Skopje 500,012 passengers

Has no fleet

THE TRANSPORTATION NETWORK

5558 km (3454 miles)

133 km (83 miles)

699 km (434 miles)

Only lakes navigable

An east–west road and rail route from Tirana in Albania through Macedonia to Sofia in Bulgaria is planned, to reduce reliance on routes through Serbia.

PEOPLE

Pop. density medium

Macedonian, Albanian, Serbo-Croat

79/km² (204/mi²)

THE URBAN/RURAL POPULATION SPLIT

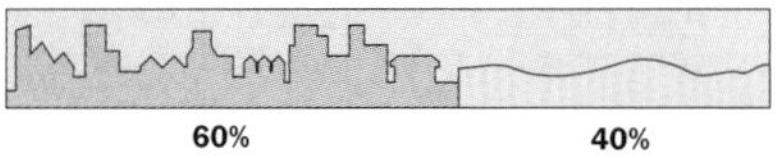
60%
40%

ETHNIC MAKEUP

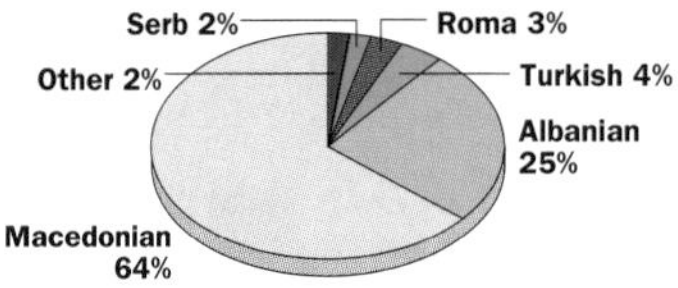
Serb 2%
Roma 3%
Other 2%
Turkish 4%
Albanian 25%
Macedonian 64%

Slav Macedonians, speaking a language akin to Bulgarian, are in the majority. The Albanian minority, claiming to amount to over one-third of the population, maintains strong links with Albanians in neighboring states. Violent conflict erupted in 2001 as ethnic Albanian insurgents sought greater autonomy and equal rights.

Macedonians are mostly Orthodox Christians, but there are a substantial number of Slavic Muslims (Pomaks), whose ancestors converted during the Ottoman occupation. Ethnic Albanians are mostly Muslim.

WORLD AFFAIRS

Joined UN in 1993

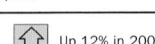

CE | WTO | EAPC | PfP | OSCE

Macedonia hosted NATO troops in the 1999 Kosovo conflict, placing it firmly in the Western fold. NATO intervened in the 2001 conflict; the EU took charge of the force in 2003, leaving in December.

AID

Recipient

$277m (receipts)

Up 12% in 2002

The EU, the US, and other Western countries are the main channels for economic development assistance. The EU and the US pledged $515 million for reconstruction in 2002. Regional security fears limit foreign investment.

DEFENSE

Compulsory military service

$96m

Up 33% in 2002

The army relies heavily on officer training in NATO countries. A major overhaul has been announced, with the aim being to tackle weaknesses revealed by the 2001 conflict.

TOURISM

Visitors : Population 1:16

123,000 visitors

Up 24% in 2002

MAIN TOURIST ARRIVALS

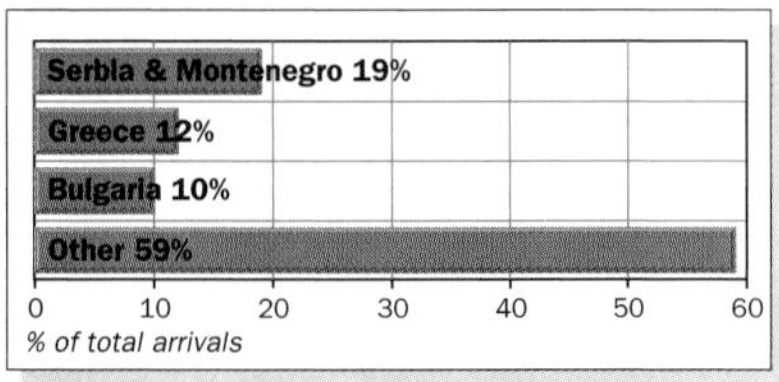
Serbia & Montenegro 19%
Greece 12%
Bulgaria 10%
Other 59%
0 10 20 30 40 50 60
% of total arrivals

The major attraction is the ecclesiastical center of Ohrid, situated on Europe's deepest lake, with Roman and Byzantine ruins. Other lake resorts and skiing in the Sara mountains in the northwest have potential once stability is secured.

POLITICS

Multiparty elections

2002/2006

President Branko Crvenkovski

AT THE LAST ELECTION

Assembly 120 seats

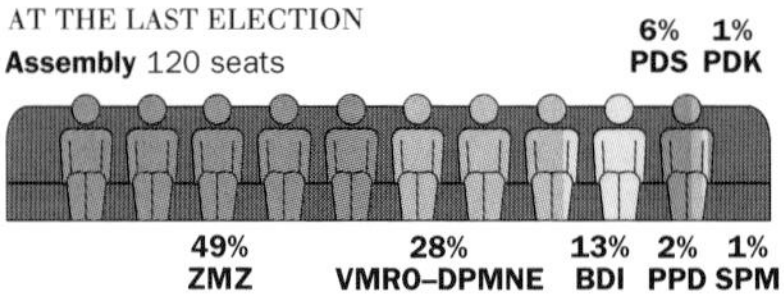
6% PDS
1% PDK
49% ZMZ
28% VMRO–DPMNE
13% BDI
2% PPD
1% SPM

ZMZ = Together for Macedonia, headed by the Social Democratic Alliance of Macedonia (**SDSM**) **VMRO–DPMNE** = Internal Macedonian Revolutionary Organization–Democratic Party for Macedonian National Unity **BDI** = Democratic Union for Integration **PDS** = Democratic Party of Albanians **PPD** = Party for Democratic Prosperity **PDK** = National Democratic Party **SPM** = Socialist Party of Macedonia

Political parties follow ethnic lines. The Social Democrats and the right-wing VMRO–DPMNE are predominantly Slav, while Albanians vote mainly for the BDI, the PDS, and the smaller PPD.

A fragile "national unity" government led by the VMRO–DPMNE signed a peace deal in 2001 to end an armed insurrection by the Albanian rebel National Liberation Army (UCK), ushering in a new constitution and guarantees on minority rights. The "unity" government subsequently fractured. At the 2002 polls the Social Democrat-led ZMZ alliance fell just short of a majority, and formed a coalition with the BDI. Pro-Western prime minister Branko Crvenkovski stepped up to the presidency in 2004, and Interior Minister Hari Kostov was appointed prime minister.

ECONOMICS

Inflation 66% p.a. (1990–2001)

$3.49bn

50.38 Macedonian denari (53.69)

SCORE CARD

- World GNP Ranking........................128th
- GNP per Capita $1710
- Balance of Payments....................–$325m
- Inflation 0.1%
- Unemployment...............................32%

EXPORTS

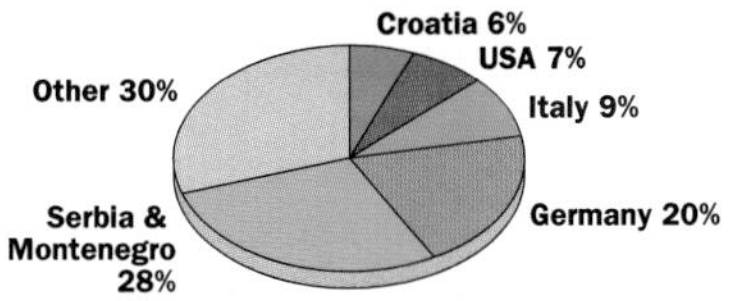
Croatia 6%
USA 7%
Italy 9%
Germany 20%
Serbia & Montenegro 28%
Other 30%

IMPORTS

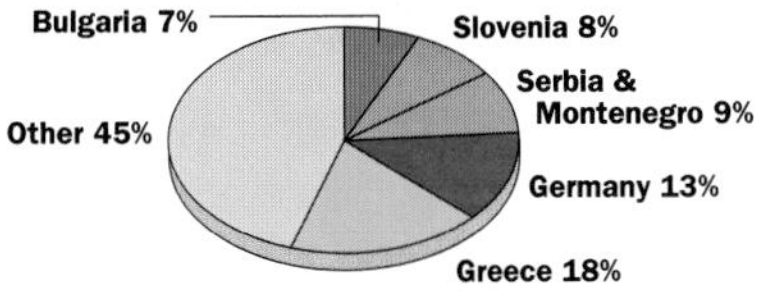
Bulgaria 7%
Slovenia 8%
Serbia & Montenegro 9%
Germany 13%
Greece 18%
Other 45%

STRENGTHS

Growth in private sector and foreign investment. Mineral resources.

WEAKNESSES

Among poorest of former Yugoslav republics. Trade hit in mid-1990s by sanctions on Yugoslavia and Greek embargo. Dependence on oil, gas, and machinery imports. Investors wary of ethnic unrest. High unemployment.

RESOURCES

Electric power 1.5m kW

1181 tonnes

Not an oil producer; refines 19,000 b/d

1.2m sheep, 265,000 cattle, 3.35m chickens

Coal, copper, bauxite, iron, antimony, chromium, lead, zinc

Minerals remain underexploited. South-facing fertile plains produce early fruit and vegetables for EU markets.

ENVIRONMENT

Sustainability rank: 83rd

7% (0.7% partially protected)

5.5 tonnes per capita

Industrial pollution affects water quality. The Titov Veles lead and zinc smelter is the worst culprit for toxic waste.

MEDIA

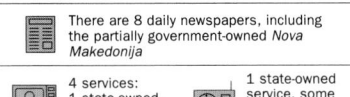

TV ownership medium

Daily newspaper circulation 53 per 1000 people

PUBLISHING AND BROADCAST MEDIA

There are 8 daily newspapers, including the partially government-owned *Nova Makedonija*

4 services: 1 state-owned, 3 independent

1 state-owned service, some independent stations

Newspaper sales have expanded rapidly. In 2001, two independent newspapers "voluntarily" ceased publication.

CRIME

No death penalty

1248 prisoners

Down 18% in 1999–2002

Cigarette smuggling is dominated by criminal gangs also involved in the illegal arms trade and heroin trafficking.

EDUCATION

School leaving age: 14

94%

45,624 students

A new university at Tetovo, teaching in Albanian as well as Macedonian, became a state institution in 2004.

CHRONOLOGY

The end of Ottoman rule saw historic Macedonia divided between Serbia, Bulgaria, and Greece in 1912–1913. Modern Macedonia was incorporated into Serbia.

- **1944** Yugoslav leader Tito establishes Macedonian republic.
- **1989–1990** Multiparty elections.
- **1991** Independence declared.
- **1998–1999** Right-wing VMRO-DPMNE coalition wins elections.
- **1999** Upheaval over Kosovo conflict.
- **2001** Conflict with ethnic Albanian militants. NATO intervenes. New, more egalitarian constitution.
- **2002** Left-of-center ZMZ alliance wins elections.
- **2004** Prime Minister Branko Crvenkovski elected president.

HEALTH

Welfare state health benefits

1 per 455 people

Pulmonary, cerebro-vascular, and heart diseases, cancers

In theory, the state guarantees universal health care, but effective and speedy treatment is increasingly only available in the private sector.

SPENDING

GDP/cap. decrease

CONSUMPTION AND SPENDING

146 per 1000 population

271 per 1000 population

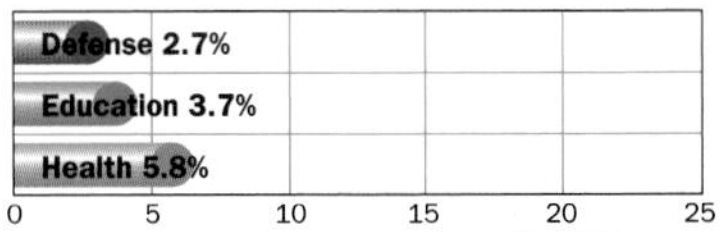
Defense 2.7%
Education 3.7%
Health 5.8%
0
5
10
15
20
25

Defense, Health, Education spending as % of GDP

Incomes have fallen by more than two-thirds since 1990, though smuggling and organized crime have made a few people conspicuously wealthy.

WORLD RANKING

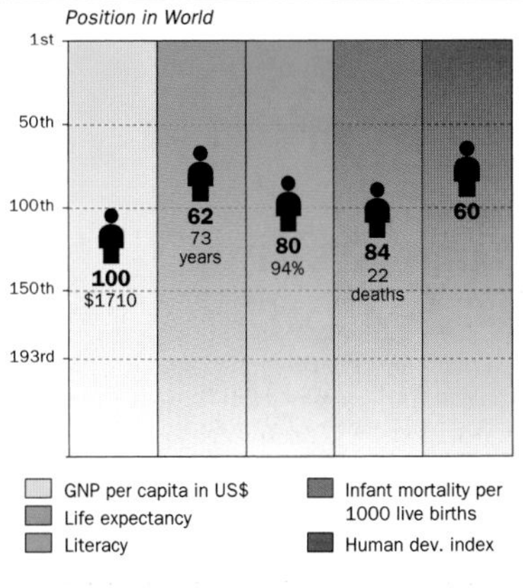
Position in World
1st
50th
100th
150th
193rd
100
$1710
62
73 years
80
94%
84
22 deaths
60
GNP per capita in US$
Life expectancy
Literacy
Infant mortality per 1000 live births
Human dev. index

M

FORMER YUGOSLAV REPUBLIC OF MACEDONIA

Total Area : 25 333 sq. km (9781 sq. miles)

POPULATION

- over 500 000
- over 100 000
- over 50 000
- over 10 000
- under 10 000

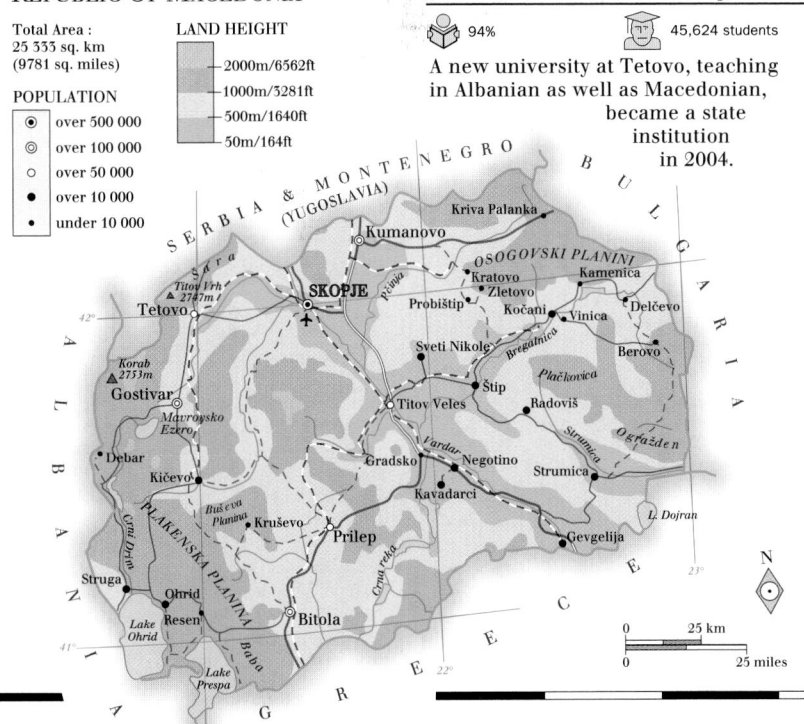

LAND HEIGHT

- 2000m/6562ft
- 1000m/3281ft
- 500m/1640ft
- 50m/164ft

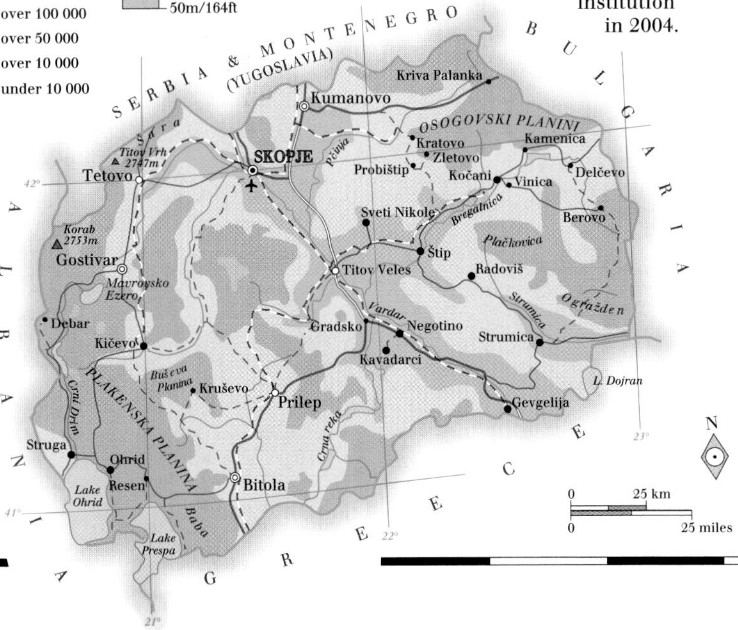
SERBIA & MONTENEGRO (YUGOSLAVIA)
BULGARIA
ALBANIA
GREECE
Kumanovo
Kriva Palanka
OSOGOVSKI PLANINI
Kratovo
Kamenica
Zletovo
Probištip
Kočani
Vinica
Delčevo
Berovo
SKOPJE
Tetovo
Šara
Titov Vrh 2747m
Korab 2753m
Gostivar
Mavrovsko Ezero
Debar
Kičevo
Sveti Nikole
Bregalnica
Pčinja
Štip
Plačkovica
Titov Veles
Radoviš
Strumica
Ogražden
Vardar
Gradsko
Negotino
Kavadarci
Buševa Planina
Kruševo
Prilep
Crni Drim
PLAKENSKA PLANINA
Crna reka
Gevgelija
L. Dojran
Struga
Ohrid
Resen
Lake Ohrid
Lake Prespa
Baba
Bitola
42°
41°
21°
22°
23°
N
0
25 km
25 miles

MADAGASCAR

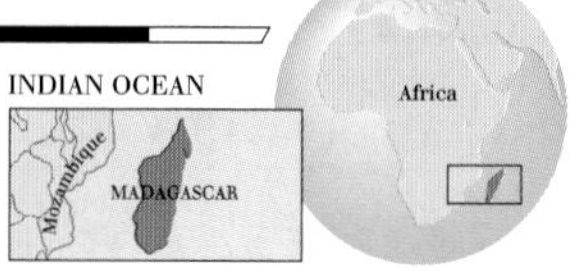
INDIAN OCEAN
Africa
MADAGASCAR

OFFICIAL NAME: Republic of Madagascar **CAPITAL:** Antananarivo
POPULATION: 17.4 million **CURRENCY:** Ariary **OFFICIAL LANGUAGES:** French and Malagasy

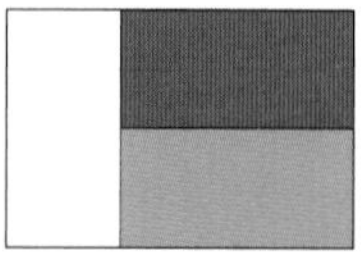

1960
1960
June 26
RM
+3
+261
.mg

LYING IN THE INDIAN Ocean, Madagascar is the world's fourth-largest island. Its isolation means that there is a host of unique wildlife and plants. To the east, the large central plateau drops precipitously through forested cliffs to the coast; in the west, gentler gradients give way to fertile plains. After 18 years of radical socialism, it became a multiparty democracy in 1993. Internal conflict over disputed elections in 2002 seriously damaged the economy.

CLIMATE

Tropical

WEATHER CHART FOR ANTANANARIVO

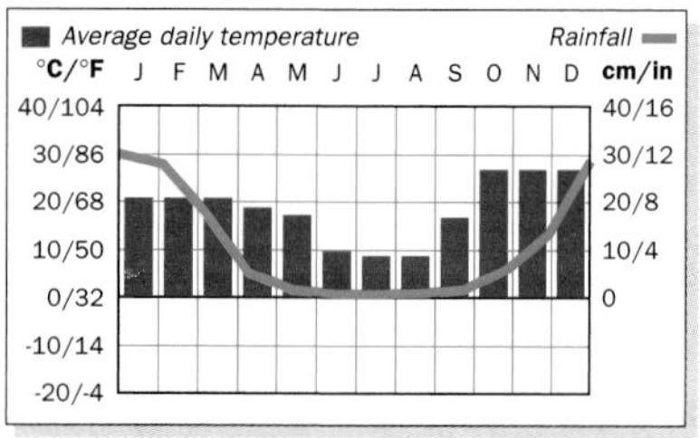
Average daily temperature
Rainfall
°C/°F J F M A M J J A S O N D cm/in
40/104
30/86
20/68
10/50
0/32
-10/14
-20/-4
40/16
30/12
20/8
10/4
0

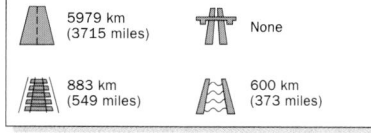

Tropical Madagascar often has cyclones. The coastal lowlands are humid, while the central plateau is cooler.

TRANSPORTATION

Drive on right

Antananarivo 561,320 passengers

103 ships 34,800 grt

THE TRANSPORTATION NETWORK

5979 km (3715 miles)	None
883 km (549 miles)	600 km (373 miles)

An extensive domestic air network – due for privatization – compensates for a very limited rail network and roads that are impassable during the rains.

TOURISM

Visitors : Population 1:282

61,674 visitors

Down 64% in 2002

MAIN TOURIST ARRIVALS

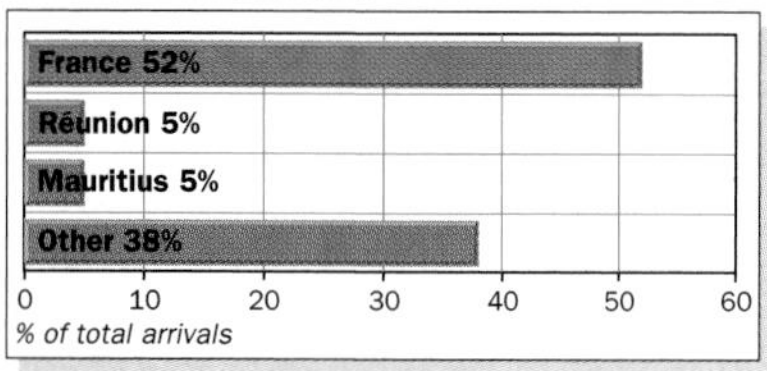
France 52%
Réunion 5%
Mauritius 5%
Other 38%
0 10 20 30 40 50 60
% of total arrivals

Extensive tropical beaches and unique flora and fauna offer great tourism potential. Political stability after 1993 led to a marked increase in arrivals which was threatened by the chaos in 2002.

PEOPLE

Pop. density low

Malagasy, French

30/km² (77/mi²)

THE URBAN/RURAL POPULATION SPLIT

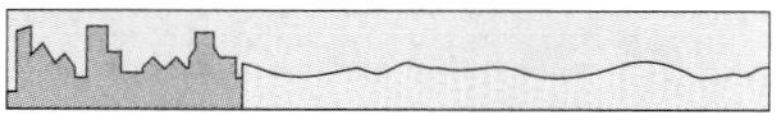
31%
69%

RELIGIOUS PERSUASION

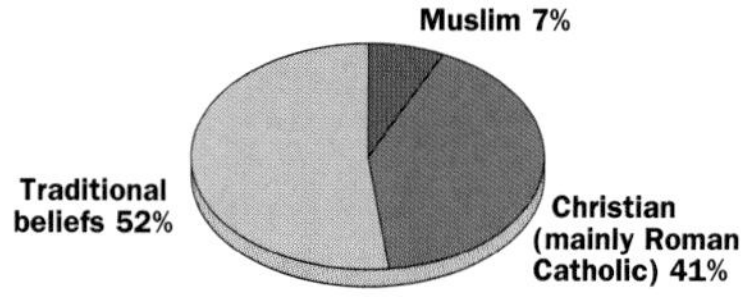
Muslim 7%
Traditional beliefs 52%
Christian (mainly Roman Catholic) 41%

Madagascans are largely Malay–Indonesian in origin. Their ancestors migrated across the Indian Ocean from the 1st century CE. Later migrants from the African mainland intermixed. Arab traders added another ingredient to the racial blend. The main ethnic division is between the central plateau and *côtier* peoples. Of more pronounced Malay extraction, the plateau Merina were Madagascar's historic rulers. They remain the social elite – to the resentment of the poorer *côtiers*, who were championed by former president Ratsiraka. The extended family remains the focus of social life for the rural majority.

POLITICS

Multiparty elections

L. House 2002/2007
U. House 2001/2007

President Marc Ravalomanana

AT THE LAST ELECTION

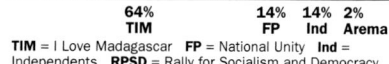

National Assembly 160 seats

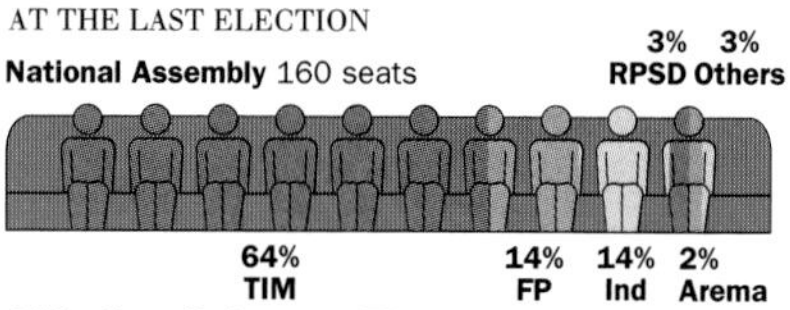
3% 3%
RPSD Others
64% TIM
14% FP
14% Ind
2% Arema

TIM = I Love Madagascar **FP** = National Unity **Ind** = Independents **RPSD** = Rally for Socialism and Democracy **Arema** = Association for the rebirth of Madagascar

Senate 90 seats

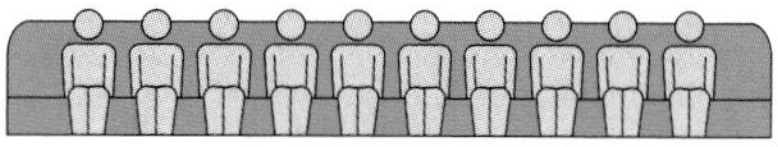

Two-thirds of Senate members are elected by regional governments; the remainder are nominated by the president

From 1975 until 2002 politics was dominated by radical socialist Didier Ratsiraka. He refused to accept the election victory of business tycoon Marc Ravalomanana in 2001 and the resulting power struggle violently divided the island. Eventually support for Ravalomanana proved overwhelming and he was internationally recognized as president in June 2002. His TIM party decisively won legislative elections later that year, but he now faces growing opposition from former paramilitary supporters. An ineffectual military coup was foiled in 2003.

A key issue is decentralization of power.

MADAGASCAR

Total Area : 587 040 sq. km (226 656 sq. miles)

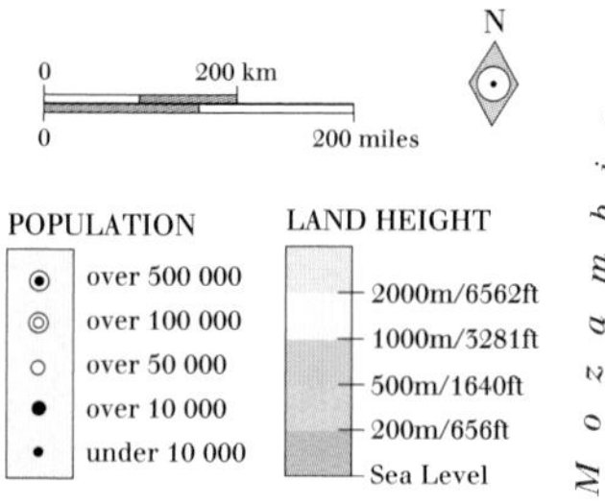
0 200 km
0 200 miles
N
POPULATION
over 500 000
over 100 000
over 50 000
over 10 000
under 10 000
LAND HEIGHT
2000m/6562ft
1000m/3281ft
500m/1640ft
200m/656ft
Sea Level

Antsirañana
Nosy Be
Andoany
Ambanja
Ambilobe
Maromokotro 2876m
Sambava
Andapa
Antalaha
Analalava
Antsohihy
Maroantsetra
Sofia
Mahajanga
Marovoay
Analamaitso
Besalampy
Nosy Sainte Marie
Fenoarivo Atsinanana
Ambatondrazaka
Maintirano
Ambohidratrimo
Toamasina
Tsiroanomandidy
ANTANANARIVO
Moramanga
Belo Tsiribihina
Antsirabe
Mahanoro
Fandriana
Morondava
Ambositra
Itremo
Mananjary
Fianarantsoa
Morombe
Ambalavao
Manakara
Ihosy
Manombo Atsimo
Farafangana
Toliara
Vangaindrano
Tôlañaro (Fort Dauphin)
Amboasary
Mozambique Channel
INDIAN OCEAN

M

WORLD AFFAIRS

Joined UN in 1960

COMESA | OIF | IAEA | COI | AU

Once-close ties with Moscow and North Korea waned as Madagascar cemented relations with its main Western trading partners, especially France and the US. Since 1997 cooperation with the IMF has also improved. In 2003 the AU gave belated recognition to Ravalomanana's government. Traditional links with francophone Africa remain strong.

AID

Recipient

$373m (receipts)

Up 2% in 2002

International donors pledged $2.3 billion in July 2002 in a four-year emergency aid package to support the new government and fund reconstruction.

DEFENSE

Compulsory military service

$45m

Down 4% in 2002

The army was briefly divided during the 2002 turmoil and was implicated in an abortive coup in 2003.

ECONOMICS

Inflation 18% p.a. (1990–2001)

$3.84bn

9305 ariary (5880 Malagasy francs)

SCORE CARD

- ❑ World GNP Ranking....................121st
- ❑ GNP per Capita.............................$230
- ❑ Balance of Payments...................–$270m
- ❑ Inflation...15.9%
- ❑ Unemployment..................................6%

Strengths

Agricultural exports: vanilla, coffee, and cloves. Offshore oil and gas. Prawns. Literate workforce. Chromium. Fabrics.

Weaknesses

Disruption caused by instability in 2002. Undercut by cheaper vanilla exporters. Vulnerability to drought and cyclones; storm damage in 2004. Not self-sufficient in rice, the food staple.

EXPORTS

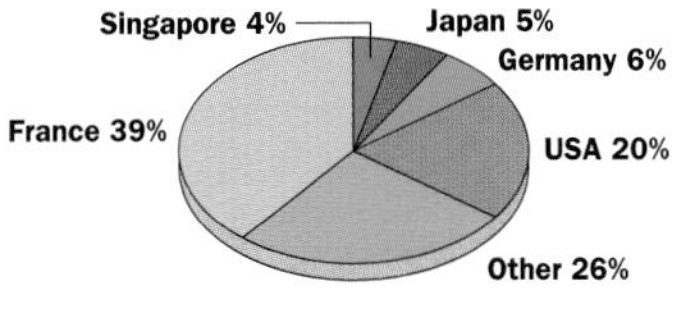
Singapore 4%
Japan 5%
Germany 6%
France 39%
USA 20%
Other 26%

IMPORTS

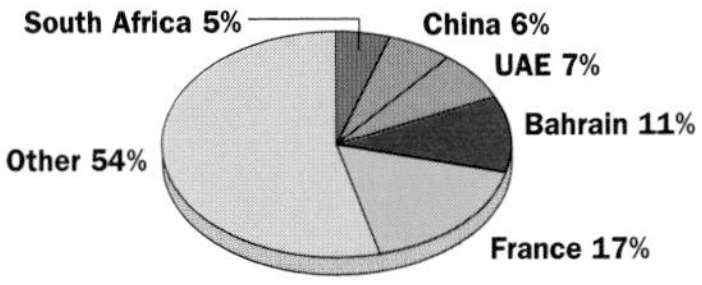
South Africa 5%
China 6%
UAE 7%
Bahrain 11%
Other 54%
France 17%

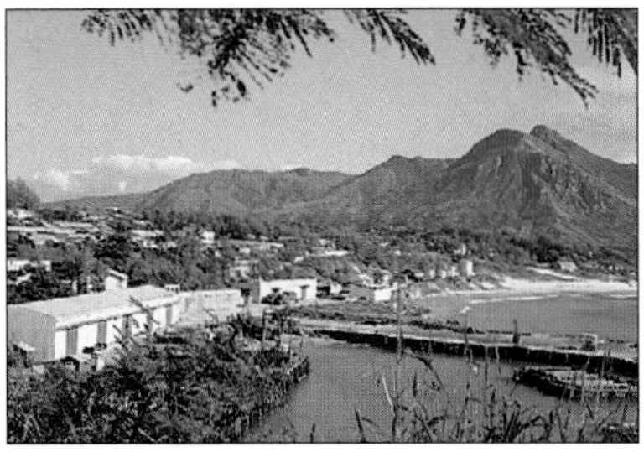

***Tôlañaro** (also known as Fort Dauphin), a port on the southeast coast. This was the area first settled by the French in the 16th century.*

RESOURCES

Electric power 228,000 kW

143,332 tonnes

Oil reserves not yet exploited; refines 6400 b/d

10.5m cattle, 3.8m ducks, 3m geese, 24m chickens

Chromite, graphite, oil, mica, iron, bitumen, gemstones, marble, gas

Electricity is produced by waterpower. There are underexploited mineral reserves and offshore oil and gas. High-quality sapphires were found in 1998.

ENVIRONMENT

Sustainability rank: 128th

4% (1% partially protected)

0.1 tonnes per capita

Madagascar's environment is a unique resource; 80% of its plant species and many animal species, such as the lemur, are found nowhere else. Aid helps to combat deforestation and soil erosion.

MEDIA

TV ownership low

Daily newspaper circulation 5 per 1000 people

PUBLISHING AND BROADCAST MEDIA

There are 6 daily newspapers, including the *Madagascar Tribune* and *Midi Madagasikara*

4 services: 1 state-owned, 3 privately owned

1 state-owned service, many independent stations

Even before the return of multiparty democracy in 1993, there was a flourishing opposition press. There are over 80 local radio stations.

CRIME

Death penalty not used in practice

20,109 prisoners

Crime is rising

Urban crime levels are rising in Madagascar, with theft becoming a particular concern. Police broke up an illegal adoption ring in 2004.

EDUCATION

School leaving age: 14

67%

31,386 students

Primary education will soon be based on French, not Malagasy. Attendance at secondary level is rising, as is the number of teachers; the government has increased spending in recent years.

CHRONOLOGY

Increasing European contacts after the 16th century culminated in the 1895 French invasion. Madagascar became a French colony and the Merina monarchy was abolished.

- ❑ **1947–1948** French troops kill thousands in nationalist uprisings.
- ❑ **1960** Independence.
- ❑ **1975** Radical socialist Didier Ratsiraka takes power.
- ❑ **1991** Forces Vives (CFV) coalition set up, led by Albert Zafy. Mass strikes.
- ❑ **1992** Civilian rule restored.
- ❑ **1993** Zafy's CFV defeats Ratsiraka's coalition in free elections.
- ❑ **1996** Zafy impeached.
- ❑ **1997** Ratsiraka reelected president.
- ❑ **2002** Country divided after opposition leader Marc Ravalomanana claims victory in 2001 presidential election.

HEALTH

Welfare state health benefits

1 per 11,111 people

Malaria, enteric and respiratory diseases

Private health care was legalized in 1993. State care is free but inadequate. Malaria is at epidemic levels. There are outbreaks of bubonic plague.

SPENDING

GDP/cap. increase

CONSUMPTION AND SPENDING

4 per 1000 population (cars)

4 per 1000 population (telephones)

Defense 1%
Education 2.5%
Health 1.2%
0
5
10
15
20
25

Defense, Health, Education spending as % of GDP

Most of Madagascar's people are terribly poor, though those who live on the central plateau are richer than the *côtier* farmers and fishermen.

WORLD RANKING

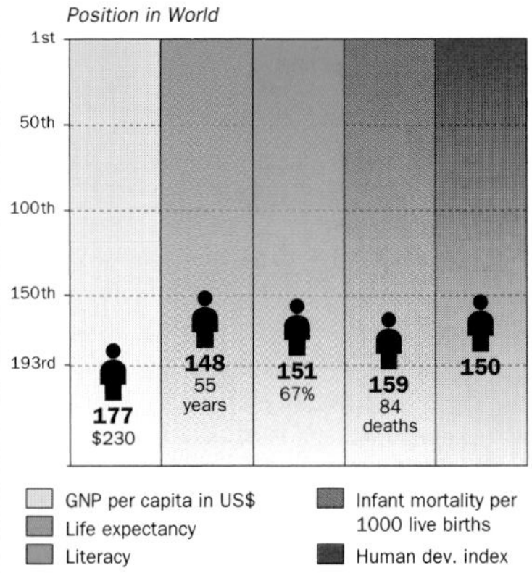
Position in World
1st
50th
100th
150th
193rd
177
$230
148
55 years
151
67%
159
84 deaths
150
GNP per capita in US$
Life expectancy
Literacy
Infant mortality per 1000 live births
Human dev. index

M

MALAWI

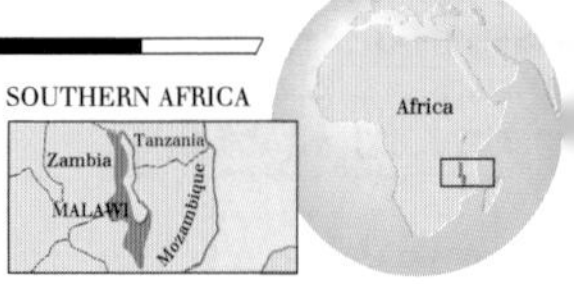
SOUTHERN AFRICA
Africa
Tanzania
Zambia
MALAWI
Mozambique

OFFICIAL NAME: Republic of Malawi **CAPITAL:** Lilongwe
POPULATION: 12.1 million **CURRENCY:** Malawi kwacha **OFFICIAL LANGUAGE:** English

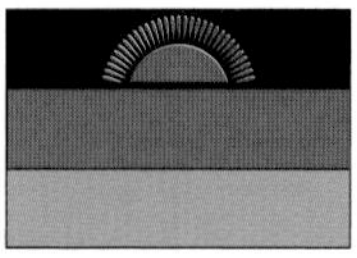

1964 | 1964 | July 6 | MW | +2 | +265 | .mw

LANDLOCKED IN SOUTHEAST Africa, Malawi lies on the Great Rift Valley and is dominated by Lake Malawi (Nyasa), Africa's third-largest lake. In the 1980s Malawi hosted large numbers of Mozambican refugees, at some cost to its fragile economy; food shortages are a recurrent and serious threat. Three decades of one-party rule under Hastings Banda followed independence from the UK. Democracy was established in 1994.

CLIMATE

Tropical wet and dry

WEATHER CHART FOR LILONGWE

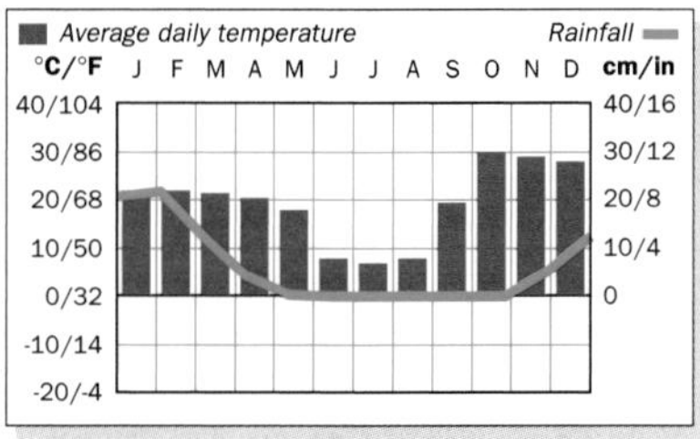
Average daily temperature
Rainfall
°C/°F J F M A M J J A S O N D cm/in
40/104
30/86
20/68
10/50
0/32
-10/14
-20/-4
40/16
30/12
20/8
10/4
0

The south is hot and humid. The rest of Malawi is warm and very sunny in the dry season, but cooler in the highlands.

TRANSPORTATION

Drive on left

Lilongwe International 176,848 passengers

Has no fleet

THE TRANSPORTATION NETWORK

5396 km (3353 miles)

None

797 km (495 miles)

144 km (89 miles)

The Kamuzu Highway has been upgraded, and the Nacala Rail Corridor, a vital link to the distant sea, has attracted private investment.

TOURISM

Visitors : Population 1:42

285,000 visitors

Up 25% in 2001–2002

MAIN TOURIST ARRIVALS

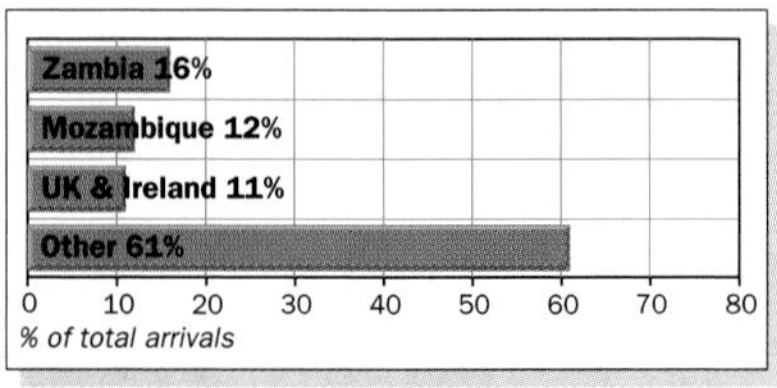
Zambia 16%
Mozambique 12%
UK & Ireland 11%
Other 61%
0 10 20 30 40 50 60 70 80
% of total arrivals

The national parks and Lake Malawi's fishing and water sports are the main tourist attractions. The opening of international airports at Blantyre and Lilongwe has increased accessibility.

PEOPLE

Pop. density medium

Chewa, Lomwe, Yao, Ngoni, English

129/km² (333/mi²)

THE URBAN/RURAL POPULATION SPLIT

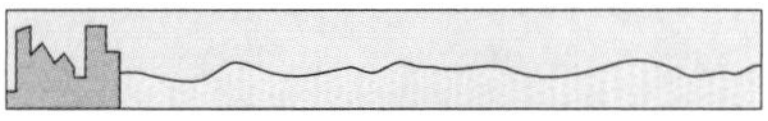
15%
85%

RELIGIOUS PERSUASION

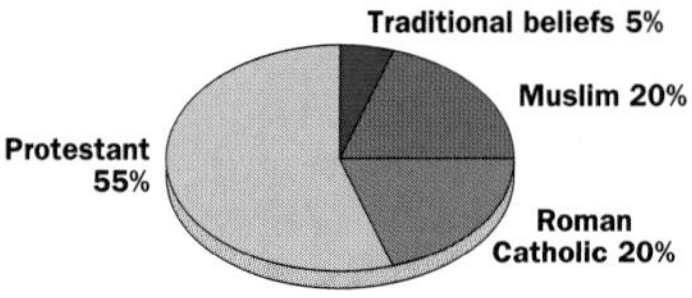
Traditional beliefs 5%
Muslim 20%
Protestant 55%
Roman Catholic 20%

Ethnicity has not been exploited for political ends in Malawi as has been the case in neighboring states. Most Malawians share a common Bantu origin. Of the various groups, the Chewa are dominant in the central region, Nyanja in the south, Tumbuka in the north, the mostly Muslim Yao in the southeast, and the Ngoni, a Zulu offshoot, in the lowlands. Other groups include the Chieoka and Tonga. Northerners felt ignored by Banda and his MCP, but the UDF government has largely succeeded in reducing tensions.

The election as president in 1994 of Bakili Muluzi, a member of Malawi's Muslim minority, arguably signaled the failure of Banda's plan to enforce Protestant domination in Malawi. Many Muslim Asians work in the retail sector.

Society is strongly patriarchal. Women form the majority of farmers.

***Fruit and vegetable sellers** offering their wares on the border with Mozambique. The south of Malawi is intensively cultivated.*

POLITICS

Multiparty elections

2004/2009

President Bingu wa Mutharika

AT THE LAST ELECTION

National Assembly 193 seats

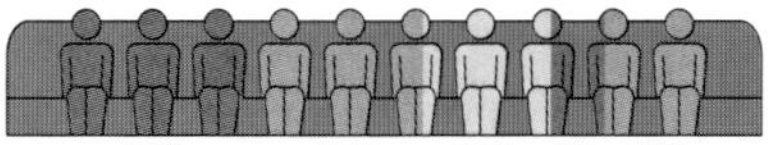
31% MCP
25% UDF
20% Ind
8% RP
16% Others

MCP = Malawi Congress Party **UDF** = United Democratic Front **Ind** = Independents **RP** = Republican Party

For 30 years from independence in 1964 Malawi was ruled by the autocratic Hastings Banda. His single-party regime outlawed dissent; torture and imprisonment without trial were common. A referendum forced Banda to introduce multiparty politics in 1994, when the mainly southern-based UDF scored a dramatic victory. Its leader Bakili Muluzi won the presidency and shrewdly recruited several prominent MCP politicians to his team. He vowed to restore personal freedoms and to revive and liberalize the shattered economy.

Muluzi was narrowly reelected in 1999, but the MCP contested the results, and violence against Muslims and UDF supporters erupted in the north. Muluzi failed to push through changes allowing himself a third term from 2004, but his chosen successor Bingu wa Mutharika won the hotly disputed presidential election. The MCP won the concurrent legislative polls, but independents joined the UDF to give Mutharika a majority.

WORLD AFFAIRS

Joined UN in 1964

Comm | COMESA | NAM | AU | SADC

Relations with potential aid donors are key. The West backs the government's reformist policies, but accuses it of mismanagement. Malawi also wants to preserve its close ties with South Africa. One in ten Mozambicans fled to Malawi as refugees in the 1980s. A 2002 ban on "foreign" ownership of land concerns investors and the Asian minority.

AID

Recipient

$377m (receipts)

Down 7% in 2002

Nonhumanitarian aid resumed with the advent of democracy. However, the EU, the US, and the UK suspended aid in late 2001 in response to corruption and economic mismanagement. Emergency food aid was granted in May 2002.

DEFENSE

No compulsory military service

$12m

No change in 2002

In the last days of Banda's rule, the military lost confidence in the ruling MCP, forcing the pace of democratization. Since then, women have been inducted into the defense force, and Malawian forces have taken part in peacekeeping missions.

ECONOMICS

Inflation 33% p.a. (1990–2001)

$1.7bn

108.6 Malawi kwacha (89.5)

SCORE CARD

❑ WORLD GNP RANKING	144th
❑ GNP PER CAPITA	$160
❑ BALANCE OF PAYMENTS	–$201m
❑ INFLATION	14.7%
❑ UNEMPLOYMENT	1%

STRENGTHS

Tobacco. Tea and sugar production. Growing contribution of industry to GDP. Unexploited bauxite, asbestos, and coal reserves. Much tourism potential, especially around Lake Malawi.

WEAKNESSES

Agriculture vulnerable to drought and price fluctuations: severe famine in 2002. Small domestic market, few skilled workers.

EXPORTS

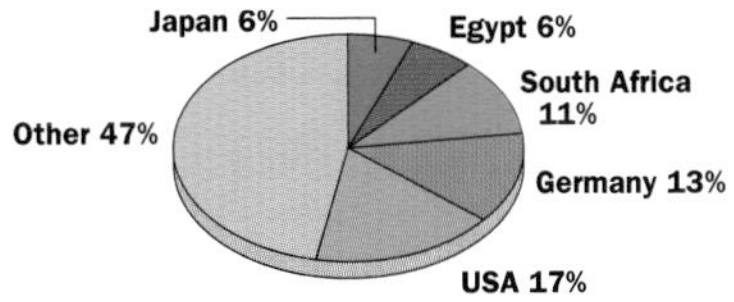
Japan 6%
Egypt 6%
South Africa 11%
Other 47%
Germany 13%
USA 17%

IMPORTS

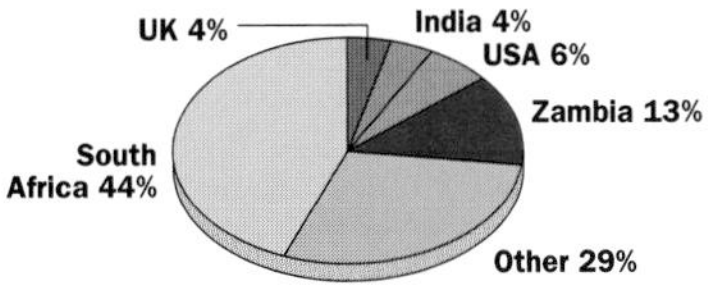
UK 4%
India 4%
USA 6%
Zambia 13%
South Africa 44%
Other 29%

RESOURCES

Electric power 196,000 kW

41,187 tonnes

Not an oil producer

1.7m goats, 750,000 cattle, 15.2m chickens

Coal, limestone, gemstones, bauxite, graphite, uranium

Hydropower plants on the Shire River account for nearly 85% of generating capacity, but only 3% of total energy use. Most people rely on fuelwood for their energy needs. Malawi now encourages privatization, crop diversification, improved irrigation, and regional economic integration via the SADC to exploit its naturally limited resources. A deep-seam coal mine is currently being worked at Rumphi.

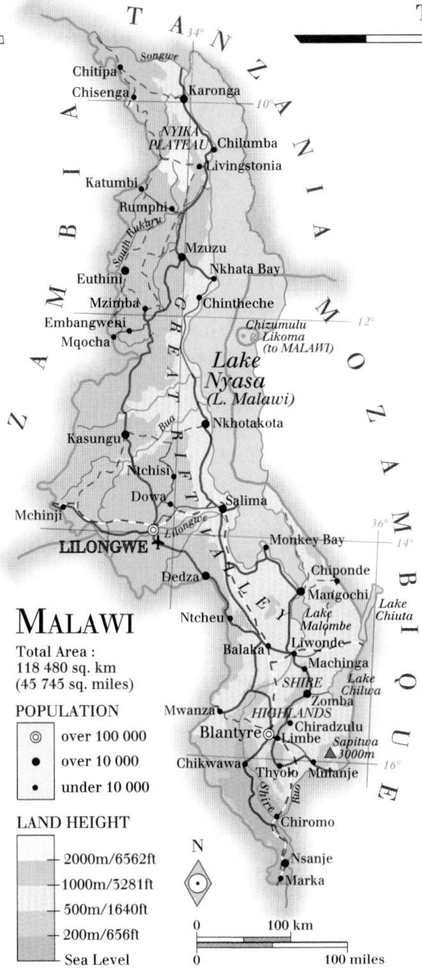
TANZANIA
ZAMBIA
MOZAMBIQUE
Chitipa
Chisenga
Karonga
NYIKA PLATEAU
Chilumba
Livingstonia
Katumbi
Rumphi
Mzuzu
Nkhata Bay
Euthini
Mzimba
Chintheche
Embangweni
Mqocha
GREAT RIFT VALLEY
Chizumulu
Likoma
(to MALAWI)
Lake Nyasa
(L. Malawi)
Nkhotakota
Kasungu
Ntchisi
Dowa
Salima
Mchinji
LILONGWE
Monkey Bay
Dedza
Chiponde
Mangochi
Lake Malombe
Lake Chiuta
Ntcheu
Balaka
Liwonde
Machinga
SHIRE HIGHLANDS
Lake Chilwa
Zomba
Mwanza
Chiradzulu
Blantyre
Limbe
Sapitwa 3000m
Chikwawa
Thyolo
Mulanje
Shire
Chiromo
Nsanje
Marka
POPULATION
over 100 000
over 10 000
under 10 000
LAND HEIGHT
2000m/6562ft
1000m/3281ft
500m/1640ft
200m/656ft
Sea Level
0
100 km
100 miles

MALAWI

Total Area : 118 480 sq. km (45 745 sq. miles)

ENVIRONMENT

Sustainability rank: 82nd

11% (4% partially protected)

0.1 tonnes per capita

Drought, with its devastating effects on agriculture, eclipses all other problems. Ecological husbandry attracts tourism.

MEDIA

TV ownership low

Daily newspaper circulation 3 per 1000 people

PUBLISHING AND BROADCAST MEDIA

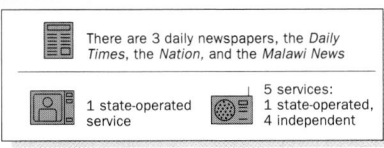

There are 3 daily newspapers, the *Daily Times*, the *Nation*, and the *Malawi News*

1 state-operated service

5 services: 1 state-operated, 4 independent

Journalists on private newspapers have been threatened and physically attacked. Television was introduced in 1999.

CRIME

Death penalty in use

8566 prisoners

Crime is rising

Urban crime is on the increase. The proliferation of weapons, particularly guns, is contributing to a rise in cases of armed robbery.

CHRONOLOGY

After strong Scottish missionary activity, Malawi came under British rule as Nyasaland in 1891.

- ❑ **1964** Independence under Hastings Banda.
- ❑ **1966** One-party state.
- ❑ **1992** Antigovernment riots. Illegal prodemocracy groups unite.
- ❑ **1993** Referendum for multipartyism.
- ❑ **1994** UDF wins multiparty polls.
- ❑ **2002** Severe cholera epidemic, exacerbated by food shortages.

EDUCATION

School leaving age: 14

62%

3179 students

Primary-level education is widespread, with 69% of boys and 73% of girls attending school regularly.

HEALTH

Welfare state health benefits

1 per 20,000 people

Infectious, parasitic, and respiratory diseases, AIDS

A cholera epidemic, exacerbated by malnutrition, killed 1000 people in 2002.

SPENDING

GDP/cap. increase

CONSUMPTION AND SPENDING

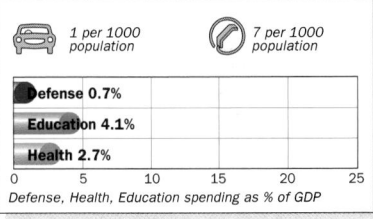

1 per 1000 population

7 per 1000 population

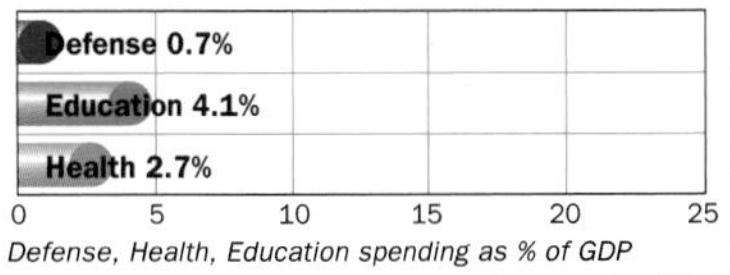
Defense 0.7%
Education 4.1%
Health 2.7%
0
5
10
15
20
25
Defense, Health, Education spending as % of GDP

The ousted MCP elite grew wealthy, allegedly through embezzlement. However, 80% of Malawians remain mired in poverty, and are forced to survive on less than $2 a day.

WORLD RANKING

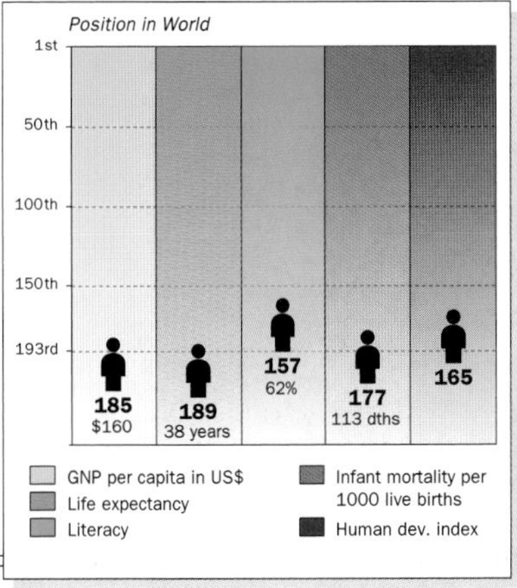
Position in World
1st
50th
100th
150th
193rd
185
$160
189
38 years
157
62%
177
113 dths
165
GNP per capita in US$
Life expectancy
Literacy
Infant mortality per 1000 live births
Human dev. index

M

MALAYSIA

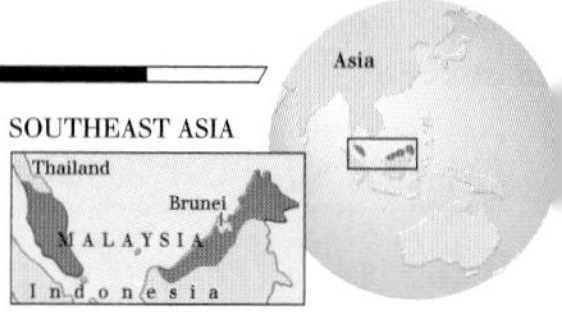
Asia
SOUTHEAST ASIA
Thailand
Brunei
MALAYSIA
Indonesia

OFFICIAL NAME: Federation of Malaysia **POPULATION:** 24.4 million **CURRENCY:** Ringgit
CAPITALS: Kuala Lumpur; Putrajaya (administrative) **OFFICIAL LANGUAGE:** Bahasa Malaysia

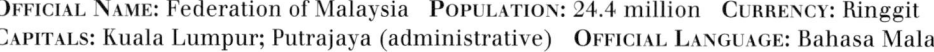

1963
1965
Aug 31
MAL
+8
+60
.my

MALAYSIA COMPRISES the three territories of Peninsular Malaysia, Sarawak, and Sabah, stretching over 2000 km (1240 miles) from the edge of the Indian Ocean to the northeastern end of the island of Borneo. A central mountain chain separates the coastal lowlands of Peninsular Malaysia; Sarawak and Sabah have swampy coastal plains rising to mountains on the border with Indonesia. Putrajaya, just south of Kuala Lumpur, is a high-tech new development intended as the home of government. The United Malays National Organization (UMNO) has dominated politics since independence.

CLIMATE

Tropical equatorial

WEATHER CHART FOR KUALA LUMPUR

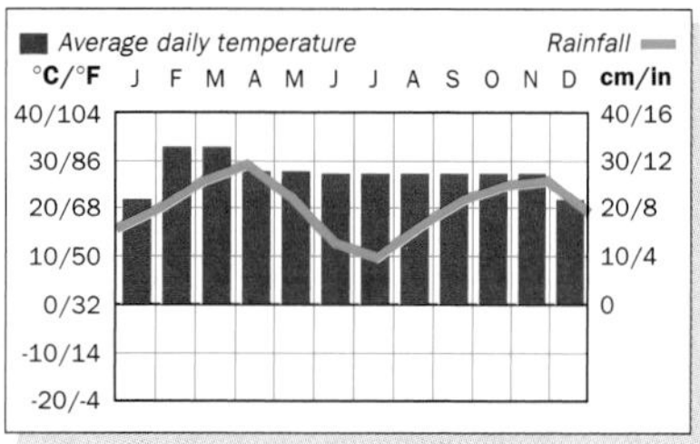
Average daily temperature
Rainfall
°C/°F
J F M A M J J A S O N D
cm/in
40/104
30/86
20/68
10/50
0/32
-10/14
-20/-4
40/16
30/12
20/8
10/4
0

The whole of Malaysia has an equatorial climate: very hot and very humid all year round. While there are two distinct rainy seasons, from March to May and from September to November, it is generally wet throughout the year: almost everywhere experiences some rain on between 150 and 200 days a year. Coastal areas are also subject to monsoon winds, which alternate in direction between the southwest and northeast.

Tea plantations and colonial-style houses and gardens make Cameron Highlands, in Peninsular Malaysia, one of Asia's most popular mountain resorts.

TRANSPORTATION

Drive on left

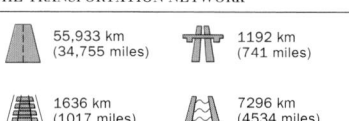

Kuala Lumpur International, Sepang
17.5m passengers

915 ships
5.39m grt

THE TRANSPORTATION NETWORK

55,933 km (34,755 miles)	1192 km (741 miles)
1636 km (1017 miles)	7296 km (4534 miles)

Transportation in Peninsular Malaysia is well developed. A major north–south highway connects the urban centers of the west coast. Roads in Sabah are also good, with an efficient bus network linking the towns. Travel in Sarawak, on the other hand, is hindered by poorly maintained roads and a lack of public transportation. East Malaysia is most effectively traversed by air.

TOURISM

Visitors : Population 1:2.3

10.6m visitors

Down 20% in 2003

MAIN TOURIST ARRIVALS

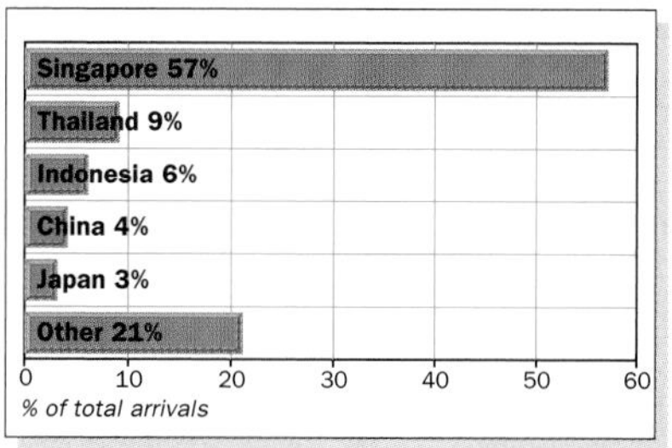
Singapore 57%
Thailand 9%
Indonesia 6%
China 4%
Japan 3%
Other 21%
0
10
20
30
40
50
60
% of total arrivals

Malaysia is southeast Asia's major tourist destination. Most tourists come for the excellent tropical beaches on the peninsula's east coast, to hike in the Cameron Highlands region, or to trek in the world's oldest rainforests in Borneo. There has recently been an increase in the international business convention trade, and hotel capacity has been growing at 10% a year.

By 1990, when the government ran the Visit Malaysia Year campaign, tourism had become Malaysia's third-biggest foreign exchange earner. Two other such campaigns were launched in 1994 and 1998. However, the resurgence since 1999 of pro-Islamic parties, which favor stricter dress codes for women and a ban on alcohol, has deterred some Western tourists. In 2000 Malaysia backed an integrated tourism package with Thailand, Indonesia, and Singapore to enable tourists to visit the four countries under a common program.

MALAYSIA

Total Area : 329 750 sq. km (127 316 sq. miles)

POPULATION	LAND HEIGHT
over 500 000	2000m/6562ft
over 100 000	1000m/3281ft
over 50 000	500m/1640ft
over 10 000	200m/656ft
under 10 000	Sea Level

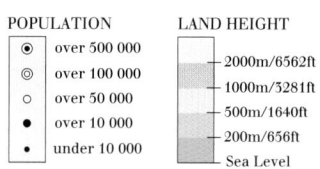

THAILAND
Kangar
Pulau Langkawi
Alor Setar
Sungai Petani
Pulau Pinang
George Town
Butterworth
Kulim
Perai
Bukit Mertajam
Taiping
Kuala Kangsar
Sungai Siput
Ipoh
Cameron Highlands
Batu Gajah
Kampar
Teluk Intan
PENINSULAR MALAYSIA
Tumpat
Pasir Mas
Kota Bharu
Peringat
Kuala Terengganu
Tasek Kenyir
Kuala Dungun
Chukai
Kuantan
Raub
Bentong
Mentakap
Temerluh
Petaling Jaya
Shah Alam
Klang
KUALA LUMPUR
Kajang
PUTRAJAYA
Kuala Pilah
Seremban
Port Dickson
Segamat
Melaka
Tangkak
Muar
Ayer Hitam
Keluang
Kulai
Batu Pahat
Pontian Kechil
Johor Bahru
SINGAPORE
Singapore Strait
Pulau Tioman
Mersing
MALAY PENINSULA

Kepulauan Anambas (INDONESIA)
Kepulauan Natuna (INDONESIA)
SOUTH CHINA SEA
Kepulauan Tambelan (INDONESIA)
Selat Serasan
Teluk Datu
Pulau Beruit
SARAWAK
Sibu
Bintulu
Kuching
Bandar Sri Aman
EAST
Rajang
Pegunungan Boven Kapuas
Kapuas
INDON

PEOPLE

Pop. density medium

Bahasa Malaysia, Malay, Chinese, Tamil, English

74/km² (192/mi²)

THE URBAN/RURAL POPULATION SPLIT

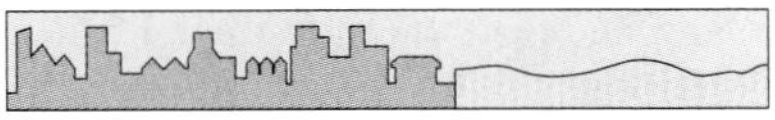
59%
41%

RELIGIOUS PERSUASION

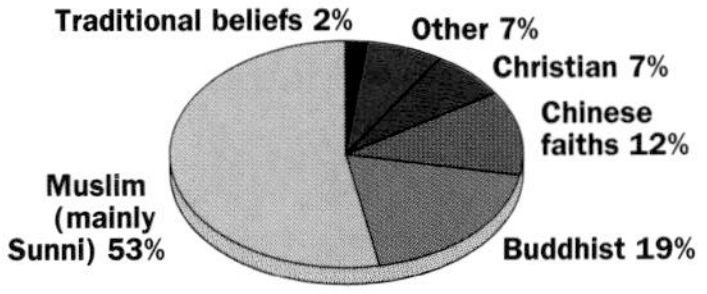
Traditional beliefs 2%
Other 7%
Christian 7%
Chinese faiths 12%
Muslim (mainly Sunni) 53%
Buddhist 19%

ETHNIC MAKEUP

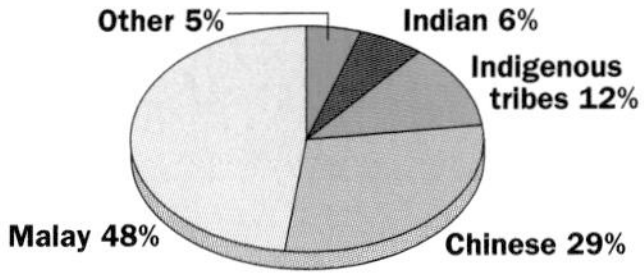
Other 5%
Indian 6%
Indigenous tribes 12%
Malay 48%
Chinese 29%

POPULATION AGE BREAKDOWN

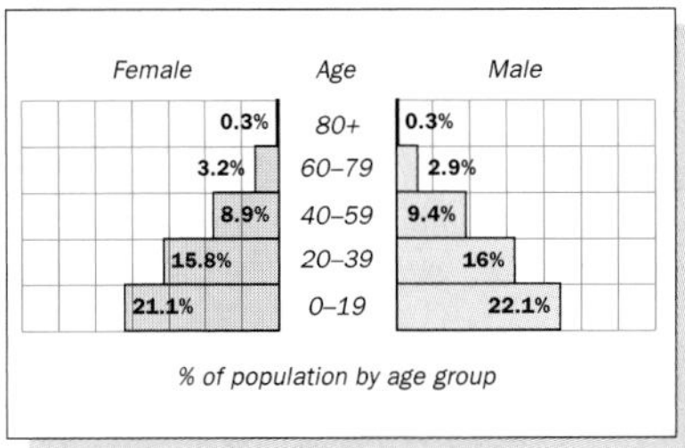
Female
Age
Male
0.3%
80+
0.3%
3.2%
60–79
2.9%
8.9%
40–59
9.4%
15.8%
20–39
16%
21.1%
0–19
22.1%
% of population by age group

The key distinction in Malaysian society is between the indigenous Malays, termed the Bumiputras ("sons of the soil"), and the Chinese. The Malays form the largest group, accounting for just under half of the population. However, the Chinese have traditionally controlled most business activity. The New Economic Policy (NEP), introduced in the 1970s, was designed to address this imbalance by offering positive opportunities to the Malays through the education system and by making jobs available to them in both the state and private sectors. There are estimated to be more than one million Indonesian and Filipino immigrants in Malaysia, a dearth of employment in their own countries complementing Malaysia's demand for labor. In addition, nearly 255,000 Vietnamese refugees were offered temporary refuge in Malaysia between 1975 and 1997; most have now been resettled in third countries, but several thousand remain. Gender discrimination was only outlawed in 2001. Muslim women are encouraged to wear a veil.

POLITICS

Multiparty elections

L. House 2004/2009
U. House Varying

Raja Tuanku Syed Sirajuddin ibni al-Marhum Syed Putra Jamalullail

AT THE LAST ELECTION

House of Representatives 219 seats

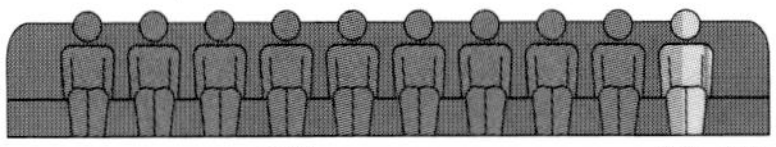
5% DAP
1% PKR
90% BN
3% PAS
1% Ind

BN = National Front (dominated by the United Malays National Organization – **UMNO**) **DAP** = Democratic Action Party **PAS** = Pan-Malaysian Islamic Party **PKR** = People's Justice Party (Keadilan) **Ind** = Independent

Senate 70 seats

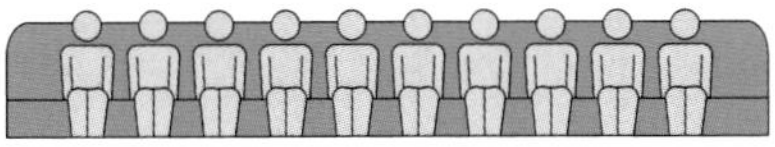

The Senate comprises 26 members indirectly elected by the State Legislative Assemblies, and 44 appointed by the head of state

Balabac Strait
Pulau Banggi
Kudat
SULU SEA
Gunung Kinabalu 4094m
Telukan Labuk
Kota Kinabalu
Labuk
Sandakan
Sibutu Passage
Kinabatangan
Banjaran Witti
CROCKER
SABAH
Banjaran Brassey
Telukan Lahad Datu
Tawau
Banjaran Pemabo
CELEBES SEA
116°
118°
4°
N
0
100 km
0
100 miles

Supreme power rests in theory with the monarch, acting on the advice of parliament. In practice, the prime minister wields executive authority. Opposition parties, while legal, are under tight control.

Profile

Malaysia has been dominated by UMNO, part of the ruling BN coalition, since Malay independence in 1957. It controls a huge network of patronage. In 2002, Prime Minister Mahathir Mohamed tearfully announced that he would retire in 2003, after 22 years at the helm. He had appeared unassailable, though his authority had been shaken by the economic crisis of 1997–1998 and dissent within the ruling coalition. He was succeeded by his deputy Abdullah Badawi. The 2004 election was seen as a referendum on Badawi's rule: the BN won a landslide victory, with the Islamic PAS dropping to third place.

Main Political Issues

Malay dominance of government

Mahathir's administration moved to end positive discrimination in favor of Malays, but the Chinese community accuses the government of corruption and uncompetitive practices, declaring that Malays are still favored for government contracts. The Chinese are further alienated by the more restrictive nature of Islamic society.

Prime Minister Abdullah Badawi, appointed in 2003.

Mahathir Mohamed, prime minister from 1981 to 2003.

The prosecution of Anwar Ibrahim

In 1998, Anwar Ibrahim, deputy prime minister and once Mahathir's chosen successor, was dismissed after calling for political reform. Convicted in 1999 of corruption, his sentence was extended after his conviction for sodomy. The initial verdict sparked riots and gained support for the new opposition Keadilan (Justice) party headed by Anwar's wife, Wan Azizah. His sodomy conviction was overturned in 2004 and he was released.

WORLD AFFAIRS

Joined UN in 1957

APEC | ASEAN | Comm | G15 | OIC

Mahathir styled himself as one of the developing world's leading voices. He maintained a strongly anti-US line in his public speeches and chastised the West for singling out Islamic countries in its campaign against international terrorism. Mahathir's pro-Malay policies caused tensions with Singapore, exacerbated by the latter's dependence on Malaysia for water.

AID

Recipient

$86m (receipts)

Up 219% in 2002

Most Western aid to Malaysia was used until recently to finance large infrastructure projects. The economic crisis which affected southeast Asia in 1997–1998 forced Malaysia to seek foreign assistance to support an economic recovery program.

M

M

CHRONOLOGY

The former British protectorate of Malaya gained independence in 1957. The federation of Malaysia, incorporating Singapore, Sarawak, and Sabah, was founded in 1963.

- **1965** Singapore leaves federation, reducing Malaysian states to 13.
- **1970** Malay–Chinese ethnic tension forces resignation of Prime Minister Tunku Abdul Rahman. New prime minister, Tun Abdul Razak, creates the BN coalition.
- **1976** Death of Tun Abdul Razak.
- **1976–1978** Guerrilla attacks by banned Communist Party of Malaya (CPM), based in southern Thailand.
- **1977** Unrest in Kelantan following expulsion of its chief minister from PAS. National emergency declared. PAS expelled from BN.
- **1978** Elections consolidate BN power. PAS marginalized. Government rejects plans for Chinese university.
- **1978–1989** Unrestricted asylum given to Vietnamese refugees.
- **1981** Mahathir Mohamed becomes prime minister.
- **1982** General election returns BN with increased majority.
- **1985** BN defeated by the Sabah United Party (PBS) in Sabah state elections.
- **1986** PBS joins BN coalition. Dispute between Mahathir and his deputy, Dakuk Musa, triggers general election, won by BN.
- **1987** Detention without trial of 106 politicians from all parties suspected of Chinese sympathies. Media censored.
- **1989** Disaffected UMNO members join PAS. Screening of Vietnamese refugees introduced. CPM signs peace agreement with Malaysian and Thai governments.
- **1990** General election. BN returned to power with reduced majority.
- **1993** Sultans lose powers, including legal immunity.
- **1995** BN wins landslide victory.
- **1997** Major financial crisis ends decade of spectacular economic growth.
- **1998–1999** Deputy Prime Minister Anwar Ibrahim dismissed from office; launches Reformasi (Reform) movement; found guilty of corruption, later convicted of sodomy. His wife, Wan Azizah, forms Keadilan (renamed as PKR).
- **1999** UMNO loses ground in general election.
- **2002** Chinese university opened.
- **2003** Mahathir steps down after 22 years: Abdullah Badawi succeeds.
- **2004** BN wins landslide victory. Anwar Ibrahim released.

DEFENSE

No compulsory military service

$3.26bn

Up 1% in 2002

MALAYSIAN ARMED FORCES

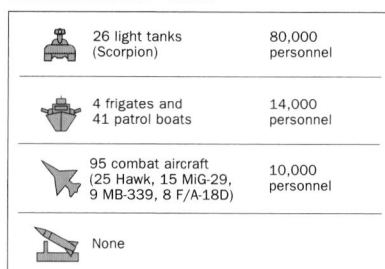

26 light tanks (Scorpion)	80,000 personnel
4 frigates and 41 patrol boats	14,000 personnel
95 combat aircraft (25 Hawk, 15 MiG-29, 9 MB-339, 8 F/A-18D)	10,000 personnel
None	

Malaysia's armed forces are predominantly composed of Malays. Main defense concerns are Singapore, with its large and highly mechanized army, and more recently, though to a lesser extent, Indonesia. Also important to Malaysia is the growing Chinese influence in the South China Sea. Patrolling east and west Malaysia is a key function of the navy.

Malaysia is an important market for international arms suppliers and has purchased equipment from all over the world, including over 200 armored vehicles bought from Turkey in 2000.

ECONOMICS

Inflation 3.6% p.a. (1990–2001)

$86.1bn

3.8 ringgits (3.8)

SCORE CARD

- WORLD GNP RANKING........................40th
- GNP PER CAPITA $3540
- BALANCE OF PAYMENTS...................$7.19bn
- INFLATION 1.8%
- UNEMPLOYMENT 3%

EXPORTS

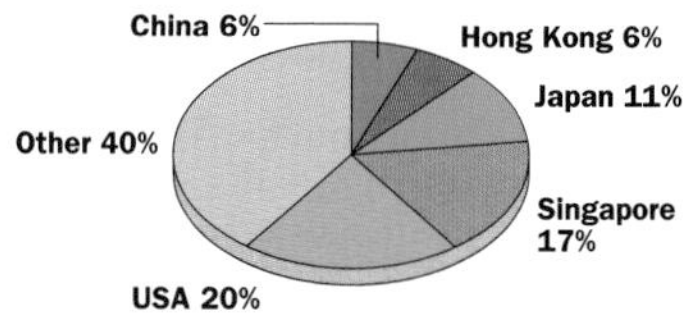
China 6%
Hong Kong 6%
Japan 11%
Singapore 17%
USA 20%
Other 40%

IMPORTS

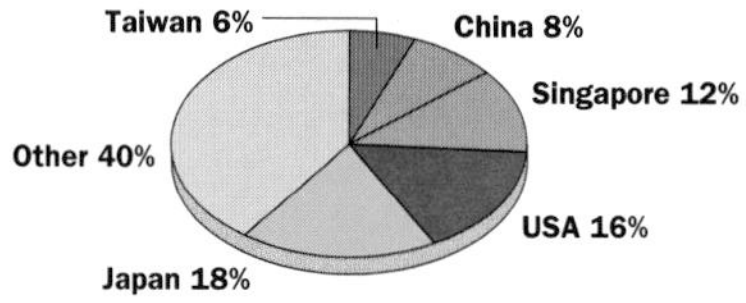
Taiwan 6%
China 8%
Singapore 12%
USA 16%
Japan 18%
Other 40%

STRENGTHS

Electronics, computer hardware, and electrical appliances. Tourism. Heavy industries such as steel. Palm oil. Latex, rubber, chemical products. Success of "national car," the Proton. Ringgit pegged to US dollar.

ECONOMIC PERFORMANCE INDICATOR

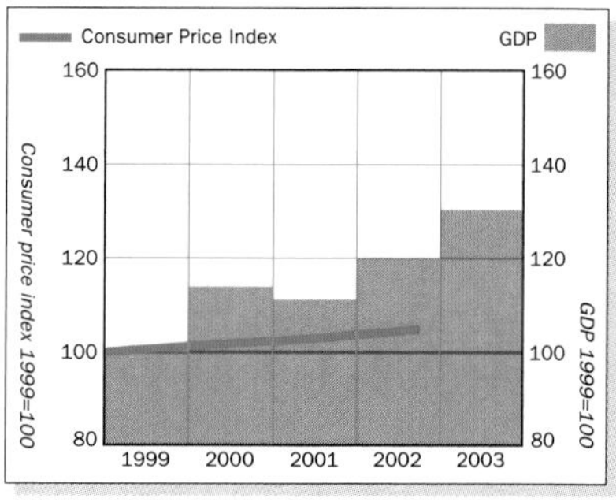
Consumer Price Index
GDP
160
140
120
100
80
1999
2000
2001
2002
2003
Consumer price index 1999=100
GDP 1999=100

WEAKNESSES

High level of debt. Shortage of skilled labor. Corruption. High government budget spending. Rising regional competition. Low foreign investment.

PROFILE

From 1987, for almost a decade, Malaysia expanded faster than any other southeast Asian nation, at an average yearly rate of 8%, with much of the growth state-directed. However, plans for full industrialization, named "Vision 2020," were revised after the 1997 financial crisis. The construction of Putrajaya provided a renewed stimulus to growth at the end of the 1990s. A project for a Multimedia Super Corridor (MSC), located south of Kuala Lumpur, had already attracted over 1000 companies, including 60 multinationals, by mid-2004.

MALAYSIA : MAJOR BUSINESSES

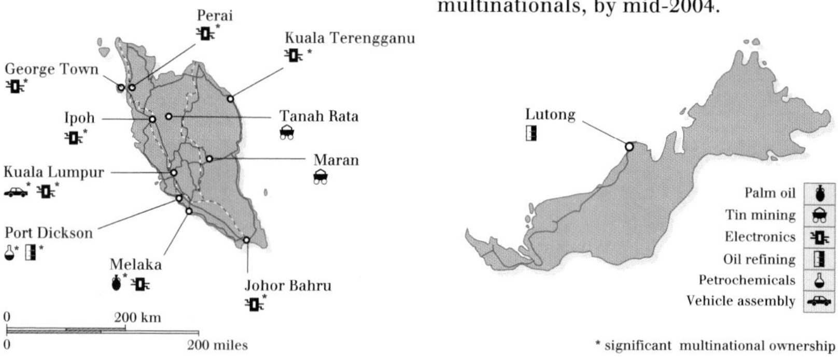
Perai
Kuala Terengganu
George Town
Ipoh
Tanah Rata
Maran
Kuala Lumpur
Port Dickson
Melaka
Johor Bahru
Lutong
0
200 km
0
200 miles
Palm oil
Tin mining
Electronics
Oil refining
Petrochemicals
Vehicle assembly

* significant multinational ownership

RESOURCES

Electric power 13.8m kW

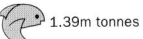

1.39m tonnes

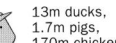

875,000 b/d (reserves 4bn barrels)

13m ducks, 1.7m pigs, 170m chickens

Natural gas, oil, tin, bauxite, copper, iron, coal

ELECTRICITY GENERATION

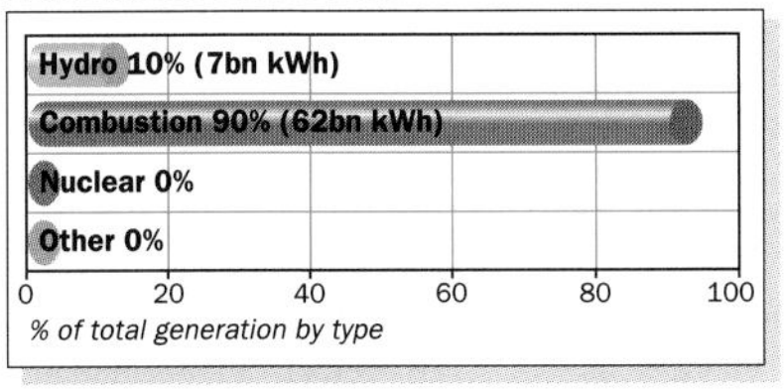
Hydro 10% (7bn kWh)
Combustion 90% (62bn kWh)
Nuclear 0%
Other 0%
0
20
40
60
80
100
% of total generation by type

Palm oil, of which Malaysia is the world's largest producer, and petroleum are the key resources. Chemical products from both are now the major resource-based exports. Gas and petroleum reserves lie offshore from Sabah and Sarawak. The petroleum is high grade; most is exported, while crude imports are refined. Malaysia has the world's second-largest proven tin reserves, but low world prices hold back production. Timber, mostly from Sarawak, accounts for nearly half of world exports.

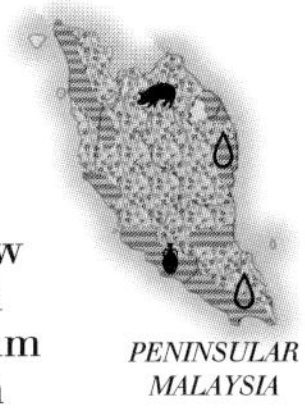
PENINSULAR MALAYSIA

MALAYSIA : LAND USE

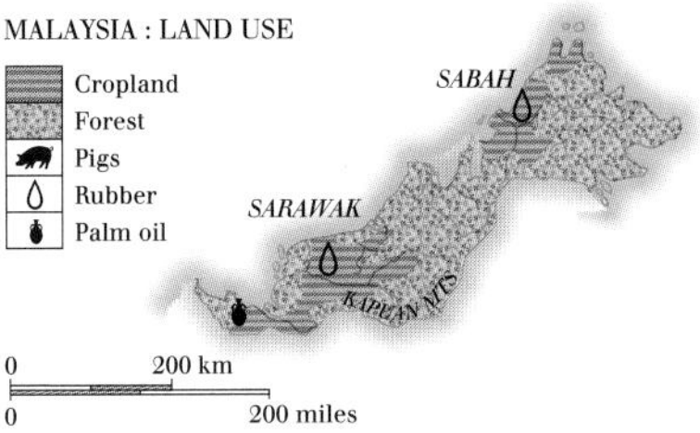
Cropland
Forest
Pigs
Rubber
Palm oil
SABAH
SARAWAK
KAPUAS MTS
0
200 km
0
200 miles

ENVIRONMENT

Sustainability rank: 68th

6% (2% partially protected)

6.2 tonnes per capita

ENVIRONMENTAL TREATIES

Yes · Yes · Yes

Yes · Yes · Yes

Logging is the overwhelming concern. Some species of tree are near extinction, and indigenous forest communities are being destroyed. The government launched a program in 1997 to plant 20 million trees by 2020. 100,000 were planted simultaneously to draw attention to the scheme in 2000.

Periodic forest fires in the region produce dramatic smog clouds covering whole countries. As well as damaging woodland, the smog poses very serious health problems.

Traditional lifestyles are threatened by grandiose modernization schemes. The Bakun Dam project, shelved in 1997 due to a lack of investment confidence, was restarted in 2000.

MEDIA

TV ownership medium

Daily newspaper circulation 112 per 1000 people

PUBLISHING AND BROADCAST MEDIA

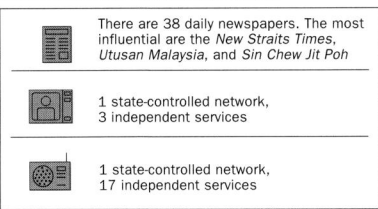

There are 38 daily newspapers. The most influential are the *New Straits Times*, *Utusan Malaysia*, and *Sin Chew Jit Poh*

1 state-controlled network, 3 independent services

1 state-controlled network, 17 independent services

Almost all newspapers, TV stations, and radio broadcasts are strictly controlled by the state and UMNO, which claim a need to protect the country from un-Islamic influences. A series of laws passed in the 1980s regulate content. The Internet provides a medium for free reporting. One of the leading websites is Malaysiakini.

CRIME

Death penalty in use

28,804 prisoners

Up 21% in 1999–2002

CRIME RATES

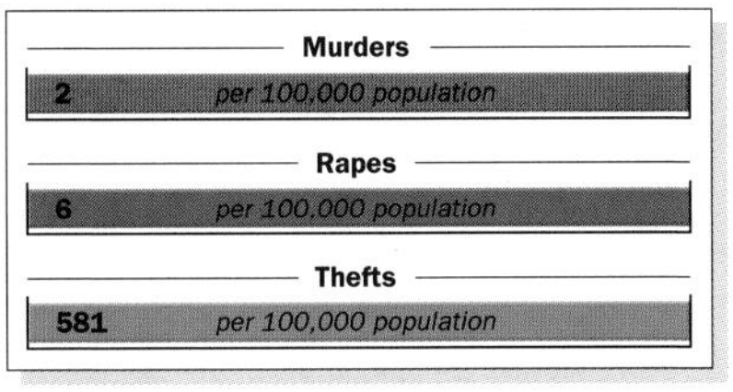
Murders
2
per 100,000 population
Rapes
6
per 100,000 population
Thefts
581
per 100,000 population

Migrants are blamed for rising crime. Those found working illegally can now be imprisoned or whipped. The death sentence for possession of narcotics is mandatory. The Internal Security Act allows arbitrary detention without trial. The police are accused of corruption.

EDUCATION

School leaving age: 15

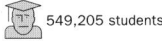

89%

549,205 students

THE EDUCATION SYSTEM

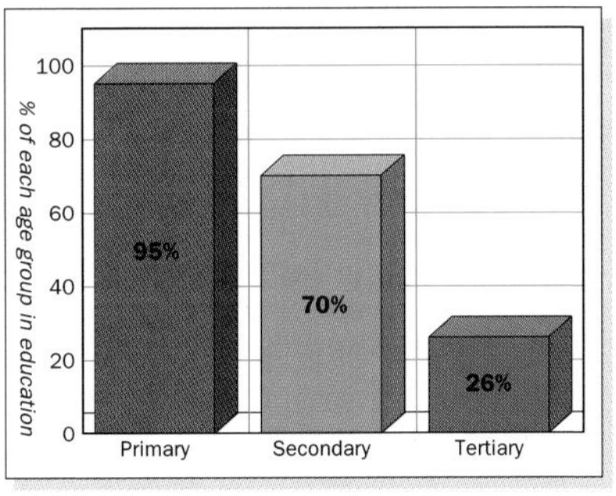
100
80
60
40
20
0
% of each age group in education
95%
70%
26%
Primary
Secondary
Tertiary

Racial integration in multiethnic schools is encouraged, but teaching is to remain in separate languages.

At tertiary level a quota system gives Malays preference for places. The Chinese community has its own schools, and much-delayed plans for a private Chinese university were finally realized in 2002. Many students, particularly the Chinese, complete their studies in the UK or the US. Since 2002, university students and staff have had to swear allegiance to the state.

HEALTH

Welfare state health benefits

1 per 1474 people

Heart diseases, cancers

There is growing disparity between the modern facilities available in cities and the traditional medicine practiced in rural and outlying areas. Traditional practices such as acupuncture and herbal medicine continue to be used by the Chinese community.

SPENDING

GDP/cap. increase

CONSUMPTION AND SPENDING

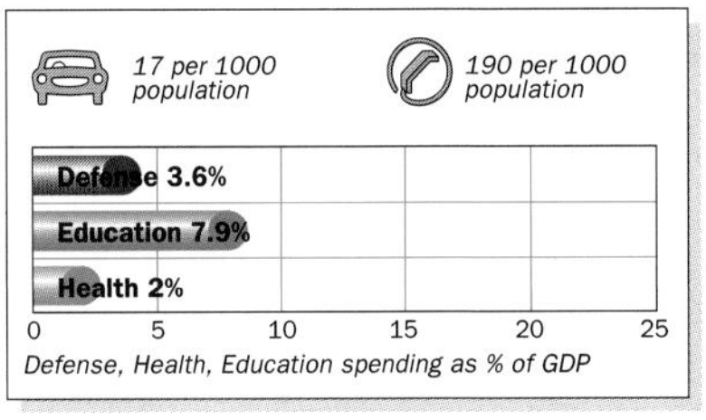
17 per 1000 population
190 per 1000 population
Defense 3.6%
Education 7.9%
Health 2%
0
5
10
15
20
25
Defense, Health, Education spending as % of GDP

The Chinese remain the wealthiest community in Malaysia. Following riots in 1970, however, the UMNO government embarked on a deliberate program of achieving 30% Malay ownership of the corporate sector. The "extremely rich" were barred from government service in 2001 in an effort to stamp out "money politics."

WORLD RANKING

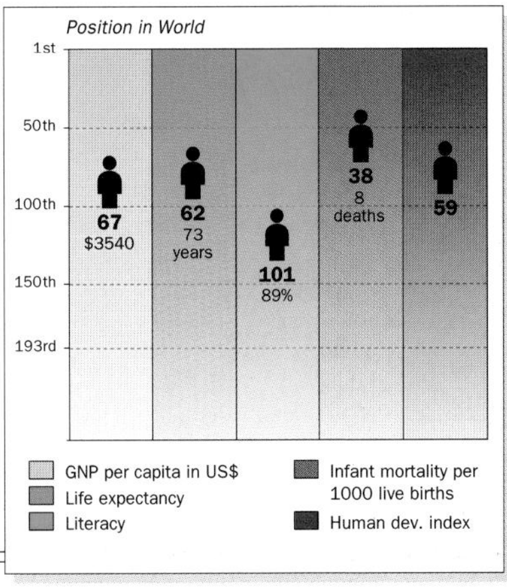
Position in World
1st
50th
100th
150th
193rd
67
$3540
62
73 years
101
89%
38
8 deaths
59
GNP per capita in US$
Life expectancy
Literacy
Infant mortality per 1000 live births
Human dev. index

M

MALDIVES

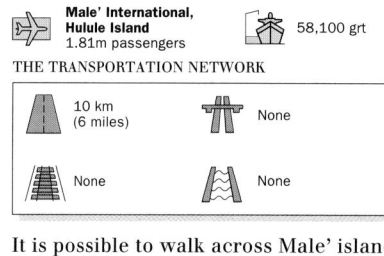

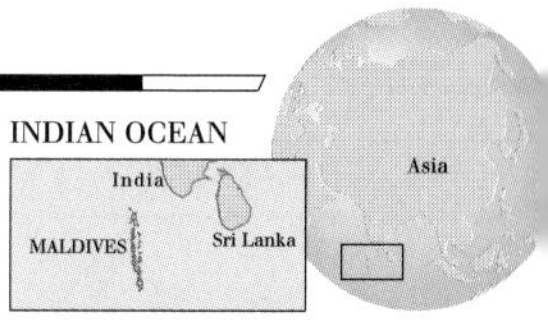
INDIAN OCEAN
India
MALDIVES
Sri Lanka
Asia

OFFICIAL NAME: Republic of Maldives **CAPITAL:** Male'
POPULATION: 318,000 **CURRENCY:** Rufiyaa **OFFICIAL LANGUAGE:** Dhivehi

1965
1965
July 26
MV
+5
+960
.mv

AN ISLAMIC SULTANATE until 1968, the Maldives is an archipelago of 1190 small coral islands or atolls (a word derived from the local Dhivehi language), set in the Indian Ocean southwest of India. The islands, most of which do not rise more than 1.5 m (5 ft) above sea level, are protected by encircling reefs or faros. Only 200 are inhabited. Tourism has grown in recent years, though vacation islands are separate from settled islands.

Traditional Maldivian trading yacht. *The 1190 coral islands are grouped in atolls, a word derived from the Dhivehi "atolu."*

CLIMATE

Tropical oceanic

WEATHER CHART FOR MALE'

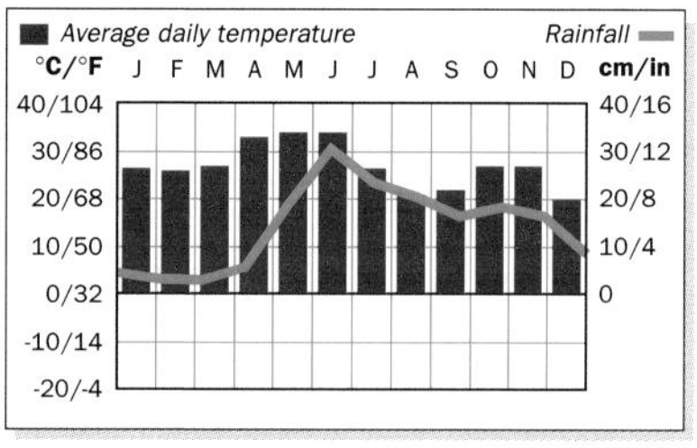
Average daily temperature
Rainfall
°C/°F
J F M A M J J A S O N D
cm/in
40/104
30/86
20/68
10/50
0/32
-10/14
-20/-4
40/16
30/12
20/8
10/4
0

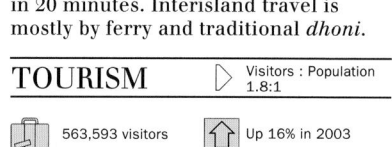

The Maldives has a tropical climate, with abundant rainfall and high temperatures throughout the year. The northern islands are occasionally affected by violent storms caused by tropical cyclones. Most rain falls in the southern islands.

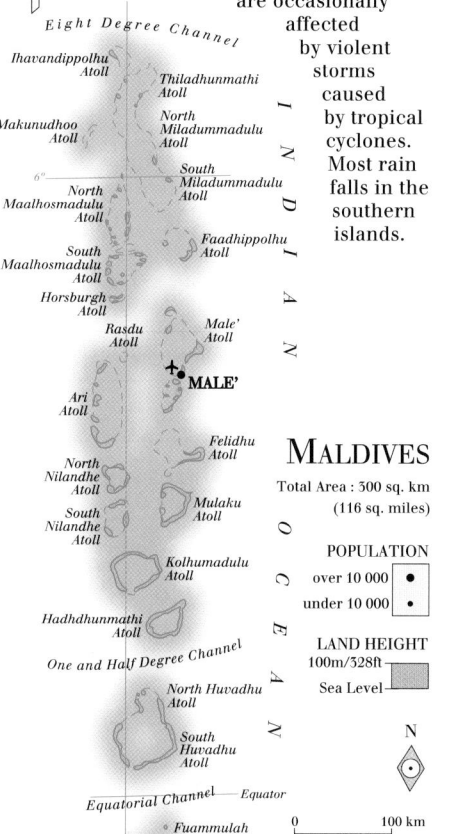

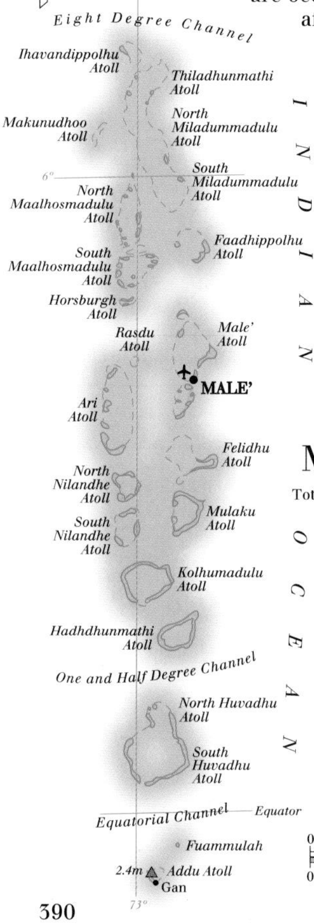
Eight Degree Channel
Ihavandippolhu Atoll
Thiladhunmathi Atoll
Makunudhoo Atoll
North Miladummadulu Atoll
South Miladummadulu Atoll
North Maalhosmadulu Atoll
Faadhippolhu Atoll
South Maalhosmadulu Atoll
Horsburgh Atoll
Rasdu Atoll
Male' Atoll
MALE'
Ari Atoll
Felidhu Atoll
North Nilandhe Atoll
Mulaku Atoll
South Nilandhe Atoll
Kolhumadulu Atoll
Hadhdhunmathi Atoll
One and Half Degree Channel
North Huvadhu Atoll
South Huvadhu Atoll
Equatorial Channel
Equator
Fuammulah
2.4m
Addu Atoll
Gan
INDIAN OCEAN
MALDIVES
Total Area : 300 sq. km (116 sq. miles)
POPULATION
over 10 000
under 10 000
LAND HEIGHT
100m/328ft
Sea Level
N
0
100 km
0
100 miles

TRANSPORTATION

Drive on left

Male' International, Hulule Island
1.81m passengers

58,100 grt

THE TRANSPORTATION NETWORK

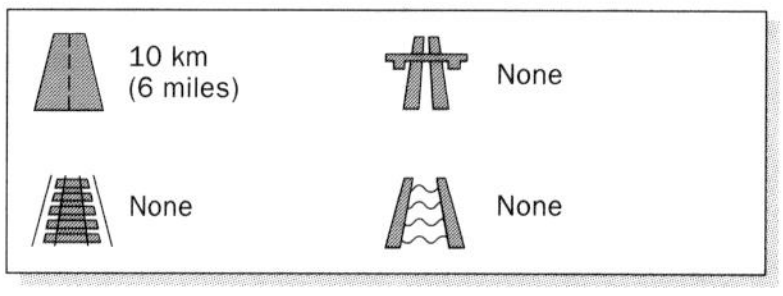
10 km (6 miles)
None
None
None

It is possible to walk across Male' island in 20 minutes. Interisland travel is mostly by ferry and traditional *dhoni*.

TOURISM

Visitors : Population 1.8:1

563,593 visitors

Up 16% in 2003

MAIN TOURIST ARRIVALS

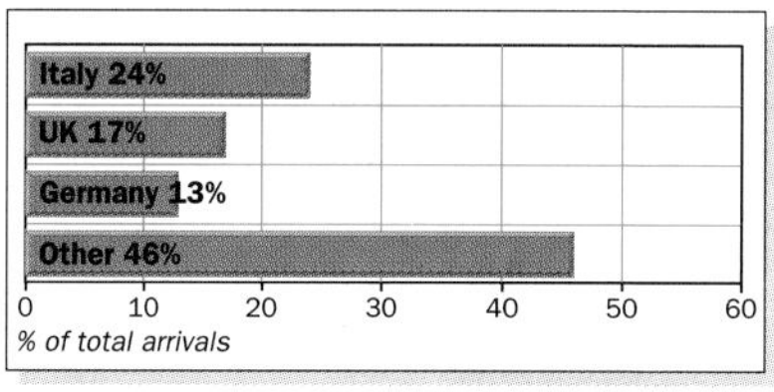
Italy 24%
UK 17%
Germany 13%
Other 46%
0
10
20
30
40
50
60
% of total arrivals

Tourism is the largest source of foreign exchange, accounting for almost 20% of GDP. The first resort was opened in 1972, and hotels financed by local and foreign capital have since been built on the uninhabited islands. From 2004, more islands are to be developed for tourism.

POLITICS

Nonparty elections

1999/2004

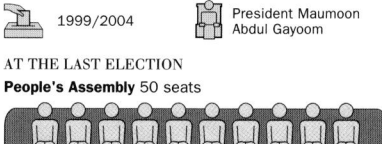

President Maumoon Abdul Gayoom

AT THE LAST ELECTION

People's Assembly 50 seats

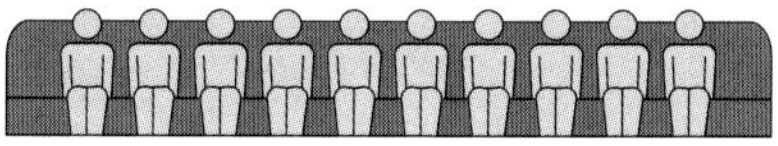

There are no political parties. 42 members of the Majlis (Assembly) are elected, and eight appointed by the president

Politics is the preserve of a small group of families. Most were already dominant under the sultanate. Formal parties with ideological objectives are virtually nonexistent, politics being organized around family and clan loyalties.

Former president Ibrahim Nasir abolished the premiership in 1975 and strengthened the presidency. Maumoon Abdul Gayoom has been president since 1978. His brother-in-law, Ilyas Ibrahim, is regarded as his main rival.

A young Westernized elite has increased the pressure for political reform. Under a constitution effective since 1998, rival candidates may seek to be parliament's presidential nominee, though only one name goes forward to a referendum. A further constitutional review began in 2004, but a state of emergency was imposed following a crackdown on prodemocracy protestors.

PEOPLE

Pop. density high

Dhivehi (Maldivian), Sinhala, Tamil, Arabic

1060/km² (2741/mi²)

THE URBAN/RURAL POPULATION SPLIT

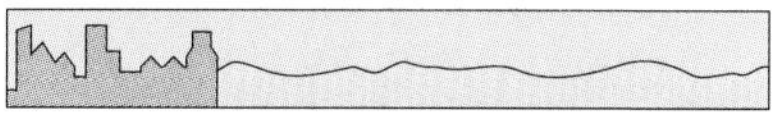
28%
72%

RELIGIOUS PERSUASION

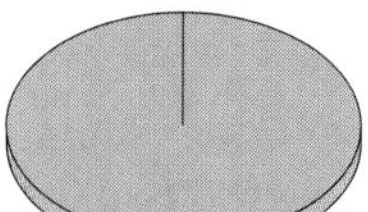
Sunni Muslim 100%

It is believed that the islands were inhabited as early as 1500 BCE. Aryan immigrants arrived around 500 BCE. The islands were then discovered by Arab traders. The people, who are all Sunni Muslims, live on only 200 of the 1190 islands. About 25% of the total population live on the island capital of Male'. It is estimated that 12,000 guest workers from neighboring Sri Lanka and India work in the Maldives. The country's newfound prosperity has seen the emergence of a commercial elite.

M

WORLD AFFAIRS

Joined UN in 1965

Comm | NAM | OIC | SAARC | WTO

The Maldives is a long-standing member of the Non-Aligned Movement. A strong Islamic lobby close to President Gayoom favors closer ties with other Muslim countries, particularly in the Middle East. The Maldives' international standing was enhanced in 1990, when it hosted the fifth SAARC summit meeting, held in Male'.

AID

Recipient

$27m (receipts)

Up 8% in 2002

Aid has helped to finance the development of port and airport facilities. Japan is the most important bilateral aid donor. The Maldives is classed by the UN as a Least Developed Country, granting it access to special financial programs, though it is preparing to graduate from this listing.

DEFENSE

No compulsory military service

$36m

Up 6% in 2002

Security is provided by the small National Security Service, created in 1970 from an elite royal militia. It is armed with mostly US weaponry. The Maldives has relied on Indian military assistance in times of political strife, most recently during a coup in 1988.

ECONOMICS

Inflation 1.8% p.a. (1990–2000)

$622m

12.8 rufiyaa (12.8)

SCORE CARD

❑ World GNP Ranking	165th
❑ GNP per Capita	$2170
❑ Balance of Payments	–$44m
❑ Inflation	0.9%
❑ Unemployment	2%

Strengths

Boom in tourism. Thriving fishing industry, especially tuna. Shipping. Clothing. Coconut production. Economic reforms since 1989 have eased import restrictions and encouraged foreign investment.

Weaknesses

Too dependent on fluctuating tourist industry. Growing trade deficit. Skilled labor shortage. Small manufacturing base. Cottage industries employ 25% of workforce; little scope for expansion.

EXPORTS

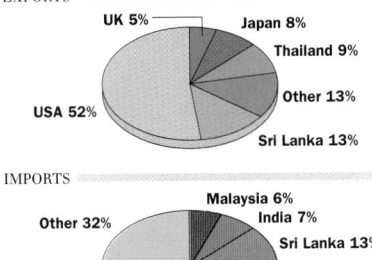

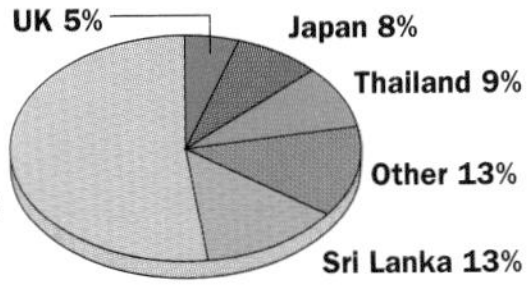
UK 5%
Japan 8%
Thailand 9%
Other 13%
USA 52%
Sri Lanka 13%

IMPORTS

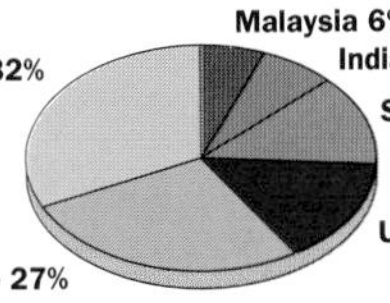
Malaysia 6%
India 7%
Other 32%
Sri Lanka 13%
UAE 15%
Singapore 27%

RESOURCES

Electric power 36,000 kW

125,814 tonnes

Not an oil producer

31,000 cattle, 20,000 goats, 11,000 sheep

None

Natural resources include abundant stocks of fish, particularly tuna. Fishing, still carried out by the traditional pole and line method to help conserve stocks, employs over 10% of the working population. Coconut production is also important. All oil products and virtually all staple foods are imported.

ENVIRONMENT

Not available

None

1.7 tonnes per capita

Rising sea levels due to global warming and climate change threaten the islands, which have an average height of just 1.5 m (5 ft). A sea wall has been built around the capital island.

Other environmental concerns are sewerage, waste disposal, and the mining of coral for building.

MEDIA

TV ownership medium

Daily newspaper circulation 20 per 1000 people

PUBLISHING AND BROADCAST MEDIA

There are 3 daily newspapers, including *Haveeru Daily* and *Aafathis Daily News*, published in Dhivehi and English

1 state-owned service

2 state-owned services

There is a marked degree of press self-censorship; in the past, journalists have been imprisoned. An Internet café opened in Male' in 1998.

CRIME

Death penalty not used in practice

6 prisoners

Up 34% in 1997

The Maldives is a strict Islamic society. Narcotics crimes are heavily punished. Political prisoners are banished to outer islands. The country was dropped from the OECD's tax haven list in 2002.

CHRONOLOGY

The Maldives was a British protectorate from 1887 and gained its independence in 1965.

- ❑ **1932** First written constitution.
- ❑ **1968** Sultanate abolished. Declared a republic. Ibrahim Nasir elected as first president.
- ❑ **1978** Gayoom becomes president.
- ❑ **1994** Nonparty legislative elections.
- ❑ **1998** New constitution.
- ❑ **2003** Gayoom wins sixth term.

EDUCATION

School leaving age: 12

97%

Not available

Primary education has been improved. Secondary education is less developed in the outer islands; the first school outside Male' was opened in 1992.

HEALTH

Welfare state health benefits

1 per 1049 people

Infectious and parasitic diseases, tuberculosis, perinatal deaths

There is a lack of general equipment and facilities. Health care is less developed on the outlying islands.

SPENDING

GDP/cap. increase

CONSUMPTION AND SPENDING

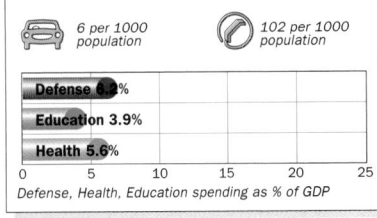

6 per 1000 population

102 per 1000 population

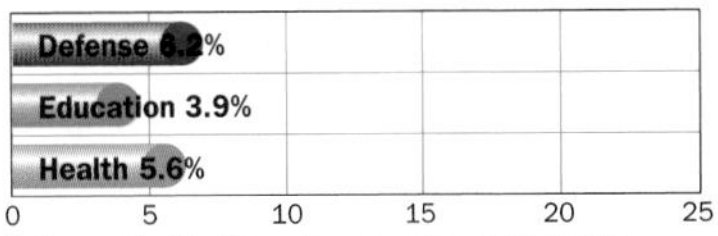
Defense 6.2%
Education 3.9%
Health 5.6%
0
5
10
15
20
25

Defense, Health, Education spending as % of GDP

Great disparities of wealth exist between the people who live in Male' and those who live on the more distant outer islands.

WORLD RANKING

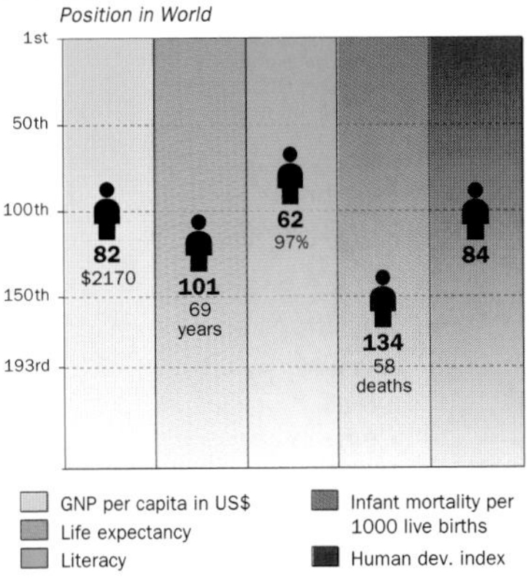
Position in World
1st
50th
100th
150th
193rd
82
$2170
101
69
years
62
97%
134
58
deaths
84
GNP per capita in US$
Life expectancy
Literacy
Infant mortality per 1000 live births
Human dev. index

M

MALI

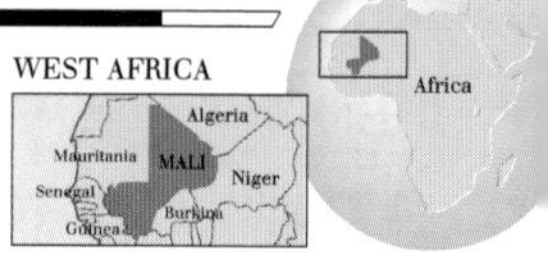
WEST AFRICA
Algeria
Mauritania
MALI
Niger
Senegal
Burkina
Guinea
Africa

OFFICIAL NAME: Republic of Mali **CAPITAL:** Bamako
POPULATION: 13 million **CURRENCY:** CFA franc **OFFICIAL LANGUAGE:** French

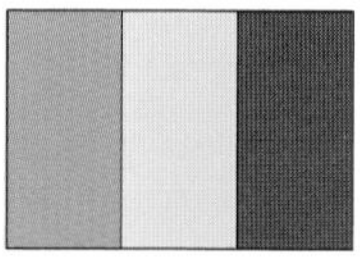

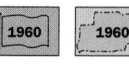

1960 | 1960 | Sept 22 | RMM | 0 | +223 | .ml

MALI IS LANDLOCKED in the heart of west Africa. Its mostly flat terrain comprises virtually uninhabited Saharan plains in the north and more fertile savanna land in the south, where most of the population live. The Niger River irrigates the central and southwestern regions. Mali achieved independence from France in 1960. Multiparty democratic elections under a new constitution, in 1992 and then in 1997, provoked accusations of severe irregularities.

CLIMATE

Hot desert/steppe

WEATHER CHART FOR BAMAKO

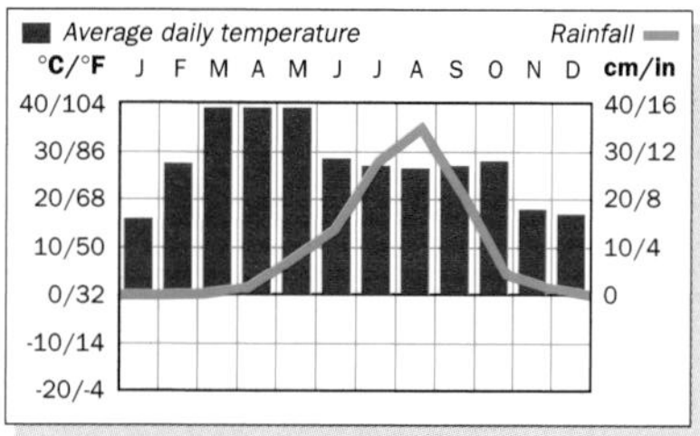
Average daily temperature
Rainfall
°C/°F J F M A M J J A S O N D cm/in
40/104
30/86
20/68
10/50
0/32
-10/14
-20/-4
40/16
30/12
20/8
10/4
0

In the south, intensely hot, dry weather precedes the westerly rains. Mali's northern half is almost rainless.

TRANSPORTATION

Drive on right

Bamako 423,460 passengers

Has no fleet

THE TRANSPORTATION NETWORK

1812 km (1126 miles)	None
733 km (455 miles)	1815 km (1128 miles)

Mali is linked by rail with the port of Dakar in Senegal, and by good roads to the port of Abidjan in Ivory Coast.

TOURISM

Visitors : Population 1:135

96,000 visitors

Up 8% in 2002

MAIN TOURIST ARRIVALS

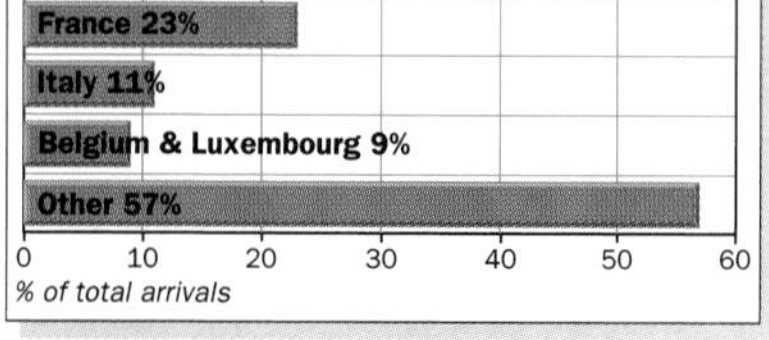
France 23%
Italy 11%
Belgium & Luxembourg 9%
Other 57%
0 10 20 30 40 50 60
% of total arrivals

Tourism is largely safari-oriented, though the historic cities of Djénné, Gao, and Mopti, lying on the banks of the Niger River, also attract visitors. A national domestic airline began operating in 1990.

PEOPLE

Pop. density low

Bambara, Fulani, Senufo, Soninke, French

$11/km^2$ $(28/mi^2)$

THE URBAN/RURAL POPULATION SPLIT

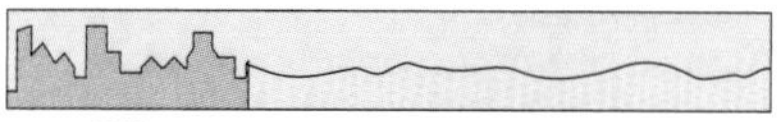
32%
68%

RELIGIOUS PERSUASION

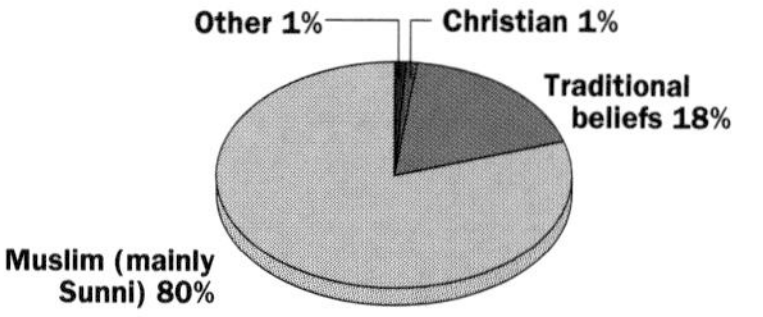
Other 1%
Christian 1%
Traditional beliefs 18%
Muslim (mainly Sunni) 80%

Mali's most significant ethnic group, the Bambara, is also politically dominant. The Bambara speak the lingua franca of the Niger River; other groups using it include the Malinke. The relationship between the Bambara–Malinke majority and the Tuareg nomads of the Saharan north is tense and sometimes violent. The extended family is a vital social security system and link between the urban and rural poor. Though there are a few powerful women in Mali, in general women have little status.

POLITICS

Multiparty elections

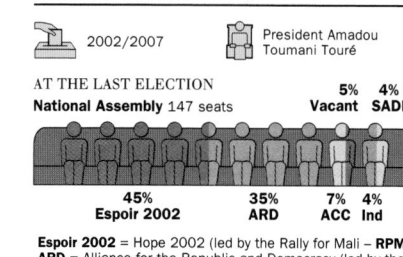

2002/2007

President Amadou Toumani Touré

AT THE LAST ELECTION

National Assembly 147 seats

Party	Share
Espoir 2002	45%
ARD	35%
ACC	7%
Ind	4%
Vacant	5%
SADI	4%

Espoir 2002 = Hope 2002 (led by the Rally for Mali – **RPM**)
ARD = Alliance for the Republic and Democracy (led by the Alliance for Democracy in Mali – **ADEMA**)
ACC = Convergence for Rotation and Change
Ind = Independents **SADI** = Party for African Solidarity, Democracy, and Integration

The successful transition to multiparty politics in 1992 followed the overthrow the previous year of Moussa Traoré, Mali's dictator for 23 years. The army's role was crucial in leading the coup, while Col. Amadou Toumani Touré, who acted as interim president, was responsible for the swift return to civilian rule in less than a year. For a decade the ADEMA government of President Alpha Oumar Konaré attempted to alleviate poverty while placating the opposition. However, its economic austerity measures eventually proved unpopular, and Touré was returned to power in the 2002 presidential elections. He was supported by all the main opposition parties, and in the legislative polls ADEMA saw its majority disappear.

Maintaining good relations with the Tuareg remains a key issue.

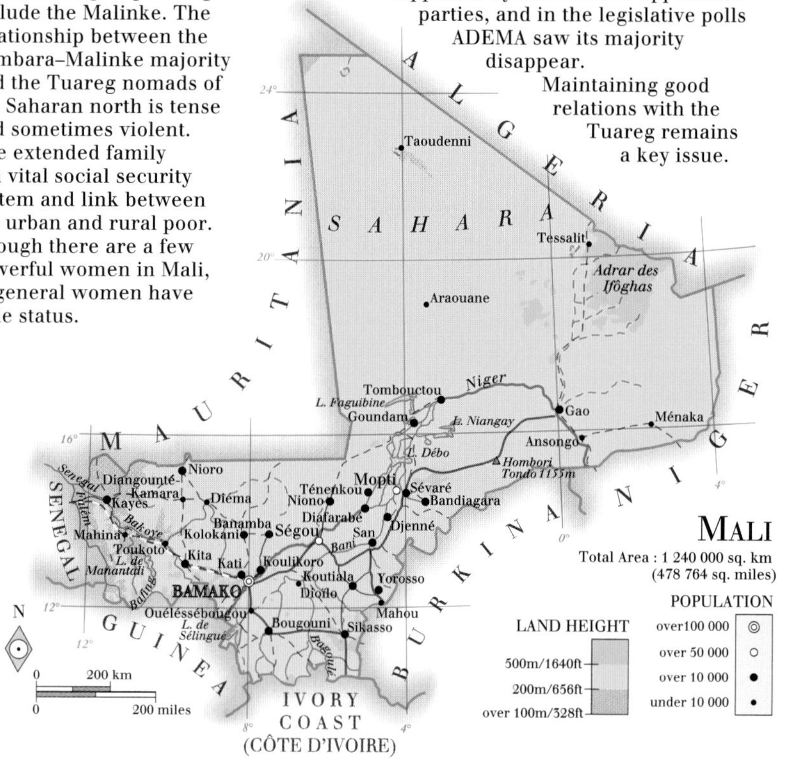
ALGERIA
MAURITANIA
SAHARA
Taoudenni
Tessalit
Adrar des Ifôghas
Araouane
NIGER
Tombouctou
Niger
L. Faguibine
Goundam
L. Niangay
Gao
Ménaka
Ansongo
L. Débo
Hombori Tondo 1155m
Nioro
Diangounté-Kamara
Kayes
Diéma
Ténenkou
Niono
Mopti
Sévaré
Bandiagara
Diafarabé
Djenné
Banamba
Mahina
Kolokani
Ségou
San
Bani
Toukoto
L. de Manantali
Kita
Kati
Koulikoro
Koutiala
BAMAKO
Yorosso
Dioïla
Ouéléssébougou
L. de Sélingué
Bougouni
Mahou
Sikasso
SENEGAL
GUINEA
BURKINA
IVORY COAST (CÔTE D'IVOIRE)
0 200 km
0 200 miles
N
MALI
Total Area : 1 240 000 sq. km (478 764 sq. miles)
POPULATION
over 100 000
over 50 000
over 10 000
under 10 000
LAND HEIGHT
500m/1640ft
200m/656ft
over 100m/328ft

WORLD AFFAIRS

Joined UN in 1960

ECOWAS | FZ | AU | OIC | OIF

Apart from a brief war with Burkina in 1985, Mali has been on relatively peaceful terms with its neighbors. It concentrates on maintaining good relations with ECOWAS and northern neighbors such as Algeria. Relations with Libya, which is suspected of fomenting Tuareg revolt, are tense.

AID

Recipient

$472m (receipts) | Up 33% in 2002

Mali is highly dependent on foreign aid, which principally comes from the World Bank, France, the US, Germany, the Netherlands, Japan, and the EU.

DEFENSE

Compulsory military service

$68m | Up 10% in 2002

Mali's 7350-strong armed forces have stayed out of politics since the overthrow of President Traoré in 1991.

ECONOMICS

Inflation 6.9% p.a. (1990–2001)

$2.72bn | 539.2 CFA francs (571.2)

SCORE CARD

❑ World GNP Ranking	134th
❑ GNP per Capita	$240
❑ Balance of Payments	–$310m
❑ Inflation	5%
❑ Unemployment	15%

Strengths

Producer of high-quality cotton. Irrigation potential from the Niger and Senegal Rivers. Expansion of gold production. Tourism.

Weaknesses

Serious poverty and underdevelopment. Overdependence on cotton: falling world prices. Communications difficulties of vast landlocked country. Drought-prone climate.

EXPORTS

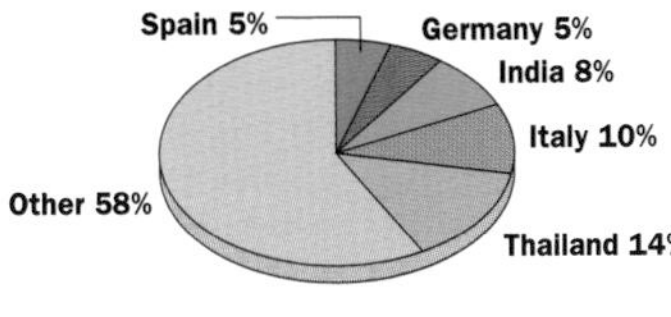
Spain 5%
Germany 5%
India 8%
Italy 10%
Thailand 14%
Other 58%

IMPORTS

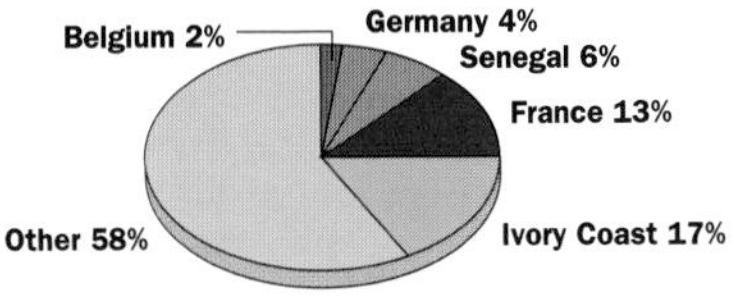
Belgium 2%
Germany 4%
Senegal 6%
France 13%
Ivory Coast 17%
Other 58%

Village near Bandiagara. The low, broken hills typical of the east and southeast of Mali are the homeland of the Dogon people.

RESOURCES

Electric power 114,000 kW

100,035 tonnes | Oil reserves not yet exploited

11.5m goats, 7.97m sheep, 7.31m cattle, 29m chickens | Gold, salt, marble, phosphates, tungsten, diamonds, oil

Gold deposits are now being mined, and prospecting is under way for tungsten, diamonds, and oil. Exploitation of natural resources is hampered by Mali's poor infrastructure and landlocked situation. Electric power comes from the Selingue Dam on the Niger and the Manantali Dam on the Senegal. The latter produced its first electricity in 2001 – 13 years after it was completed.

ENVIRONMENT

Sustainability rank: 85th

4% (3% partially protected) | 0.1 tonnes per capita

Frequent droughts destroy herds and accelerate desertification. Tree-felling was banned in 2004 in an attempt to slow deforestation. The Selingue Dam seriously affects the level of the Niger.

MEDIA

TV ownership low

Daily newspaper circulation 1 per 1000 people

PUBLISHING AND BROADCAST MEDIA

There are 5 daily newspapers, including the progovernment *L'Essor – La Voix du Peuple*

3 services: 1 state-owned, 2 independent | 1 state-owned service, about 100 private stations

Even before the 1991 coup, previously rigid controls were being relaxed. The 1992 constitution guarantees the freedom of the press, and Mali's broadcast and print media are now among the freest in Africa.

CRIME

Death penalty not used in practice

4040 prisoners | Crime is rising slowly

Crime is not particularly prevalent compared with some other countries in the region, owing at least in part to the relative lack of urbanization. In towns, robbery, juvenile delinquency, and smuggling are problems.

CHRONOLOGY

Mali was a major trans-Saharan trading empire. The French colonized the area between 1881 and 1895.

- ❑ **1960** Independence.
- ❑ **1968** Coup by Gen. Moussa Traoré.
- ❑ **1990** Prodemocracy demonstrations.
- ❑ **1991** Traoré arrested.
- ❑ **1992** Free multiparty elections.
- ❑ **1997** President Konaré and ADEMA party reelected in disputed polls.
- ❑ **2002** Elections: Col. Touré president; ADEMA loses majority.

EDUCATION

School leaving age: 15

26% | 37,635 students

Just over half of children go to primary school and only 15% to secondary school. A ten-year program to raise education levels for girls was launched in 2001.

HEALTH

No welfare state health benefits

1 per 10,000 people | Malaria, pneumonia, parasitic and diarrheal diseases

The government committed itself in late 2003 to tackling the widespread practice of female genital mutilation.

SPENDING

GDP/cap. increase

CONSUMPTION AND SPENDING

2 per 1000 population | 5 per 1000 population

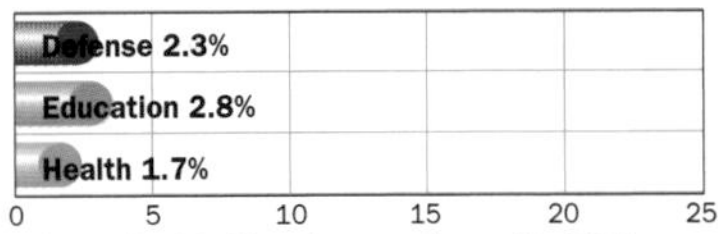
Defense 2.3%
Education 2.8%
Health 1.7%
0
5
10
15
20
25

Defense, Health, Education spending as % of GDP

Poverty is widespread, and wealth is limited to a very small group. Malians disapprove of flaunted wealth and public ostentation is rare.

WORLD RANKING

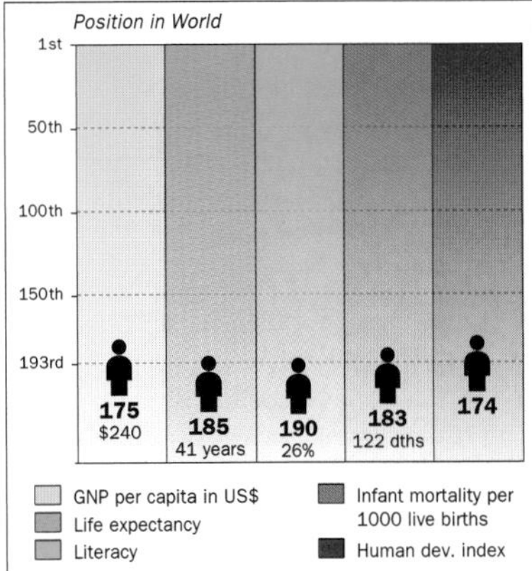
Position in World
1st
50th
100th
150th
193rd
175
$240
185
41 years
190
26%
183
122 dths
174
GNP per capita in US$
Life expectancy
Literacy
Infant mortality per 1000 live births
Human dev. index

MALTA

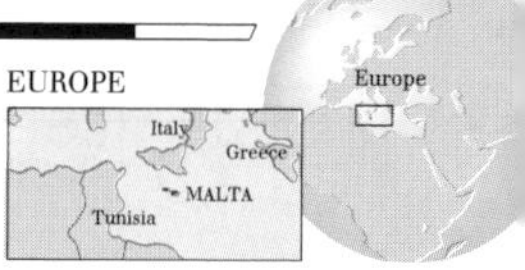
EUROPE
Italy
Greece
MALTA
Tunisia
Europe

OFFICIAL NAME: Republic of Malta **CAPITAL:** Valletta
POPULATION: 394,000 **CURRENCY:** Maltese lira **OFFICIAL LANGUAGES:** Maltese and English

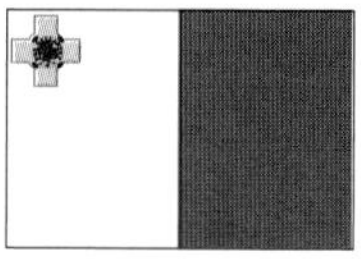

1964 | 1964 | Sept 21 | M | +1 | +356 | .mt

THE MALTESE ISLAND group is strategically located, lying between Europe and north Africa. Controlled throughout its history by successive colonial powers, Malta finally gained independence from the UK in 1964. The islands are mainly low-lying, with rocky coastlines; only Malta, Gozo (Ghawdex), and Kemmuna are inhabited. Tourism is Malta's chief source of income, with an influx of tourists each year of three times the islands' population.

CLIMATE

Mediterranean

WEATHER CHART FOR VALLETTA

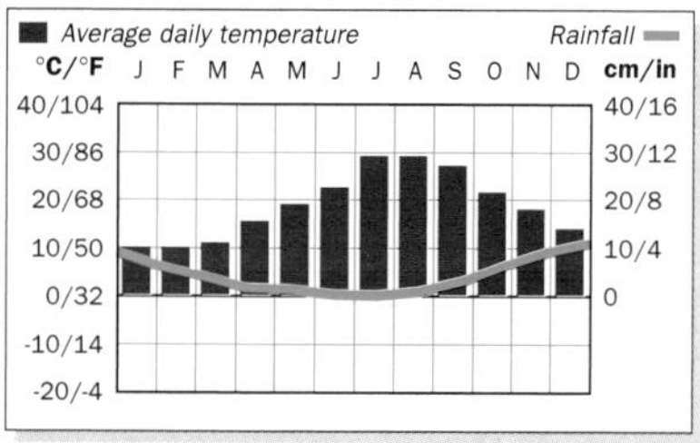
Average daily temperature
Rainfall
°C/°F J F M A M J J A S O N D cm/in
40/104
30/86
20/68
10/50
0/32
-10/14
-20/-4
40/16
30/12
20/8
10/4
0

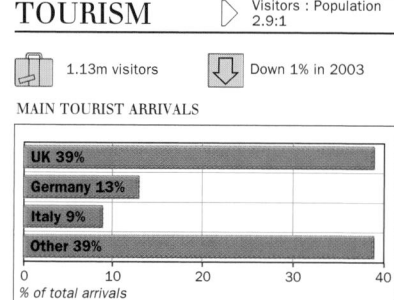

The climate is typical of the southern Mediterranean – with at least six hours of sunshine a day, even in winter.

TRANSPORTATION

Drive on left

Luqa International, Valletta 2.67m passengers

1350 ships 26.3m grt

THE TRANSPORTATION NETWORK

2186 km (1358 miles)	None
None	None

Malta Freeport at Birzebbuga exploits Malta's strategic shipping location in the Mediterranean. In summer, a five-minute helicopter flight from the international airport links the islands of Malta and Gozo. There is a well-developed public transportation system, with ferry and hovercraft services and buses on both islands.

Traditionally painted **luzzus** *in St. Julian's harbor. The fish caught are now only for domestic and tourist consumption.*

TOURISM

Visitors : Population 2.9:1

1.13m visitors

Down 1% in 2003

MAIN TOURIST ARRIVALS

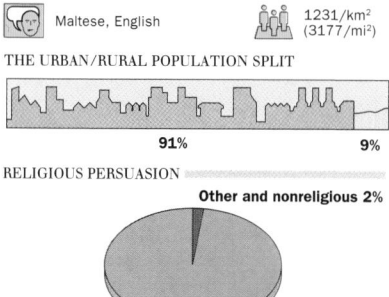

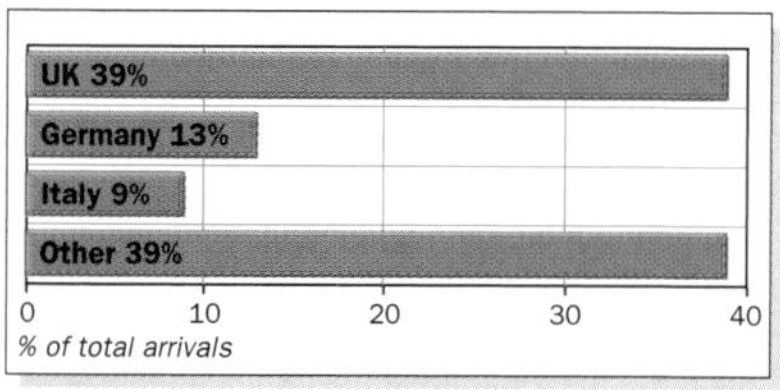
UK 39%
Germany 13%
Italy 9%
Other 39%
0
10
20
30
40
% of total arrivals

Tourism is vital to the economy and accounts for more than 30% of GDP, even though most visitors are budget vacationers. In addition to beaches and scenery, there are the historical attractions of Mdina and Valletta. Development on the quieter island of Gozo is limited to luxury-grade hotels.

PEOPLE

Pop. density high

Maltese, English

1231/km² (3177/mi²)

THE URBAN/RURAL POPULATION SPLIT

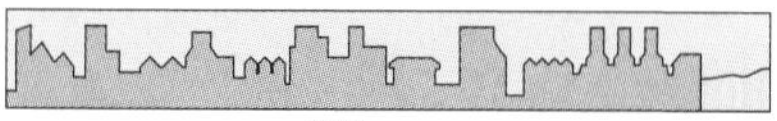
91%
9%

RELIGIOUS PERSUASION

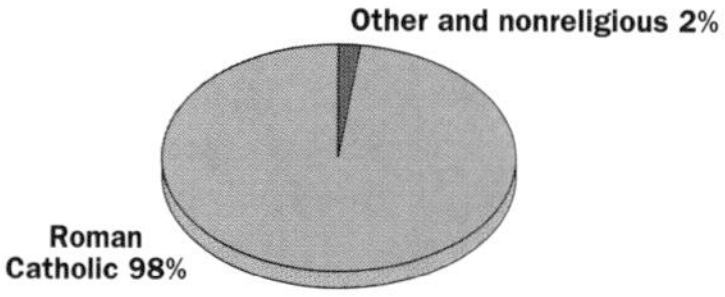
Other and nonreligious 2%
Roman Catholic 98%

Malta's population has been subject over the centuries to diverse Arab, Sicilian, Norman, Spanish, British, and Italian influences. Today, much of the younger Maltese population goes abroad to find work, especially to the US or Australia; opportunities for them on the islands are few.

The Maltese are staunch Roman Catholics, on a percentage basis more so than virtually any other nation. The remainder are mainly Anglicans, who are included within the diocese of Gibraltar. Divorce is not allowed.

POLITICS

Multiparty elections

2003/2008

President Edward Fenech Adami

AT THE LAST ELECTION

House of Representatives 65 seats

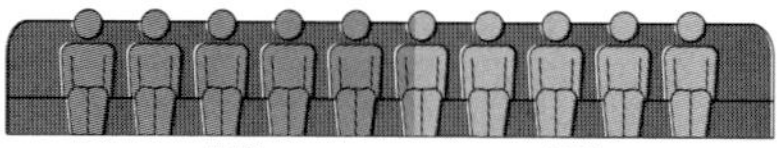
54% NP
46% MLP

NP = Nationalist Party **MLP** = Malta Labour Party

Politics is strongly adversarial and split evenly between the right-wing NP and the left-wing MLP. The latter was in power in the 1970s and most of the 1980s, ensuring state control of industry and pursuing a nonaligned foreign policy.

The late 1980s and 1990s saw a switch to the NP. Prime Minister Edward Fenech Adami's government moved toward ever closer ties with Europe, and favored a free-market approach to the economy. A modernized MLP ended the NP's nine-year reign in 1996. Under Alfred Sant, it weakened traditional links with the unions and stalled Malta's EU application. However, the MLP's small parliamentary majority undermined the government, and the NP won early elections in 1998. Fenech Adami went on to secure Malta's membership of the EU (from May 2004), and his party was reelected in 2003. He handed over the premiership to Lawrence Gonzi in March 2004, and was elected to the more ceremonial post of president.

WORLD AFFAIRS

Joined UN in 1964

CE | Comm | EU | NAM | OSCE

Malta has played on its location on the fringe of Europe, with a staunchly nonaligned foreign policy for many years. Ties are traditionally strong with the Arab world and north Africa, and relations with Libya remain good. There are also close commercial links with Russia and China.

It is Malta's relationship with Europe, however, that has dominated recent policy. The country's formal application for EU membership, made in 1990, was derailed by the anti-EU MLP government in 1996. With the application frozen, Malta was initially denied a place in the "first wave" of potential EU members. However, the return to power of the pro-EU NP in 1998 restarted the bid, and Malta's accession to the union took place in 2004.

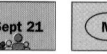

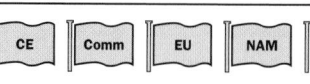

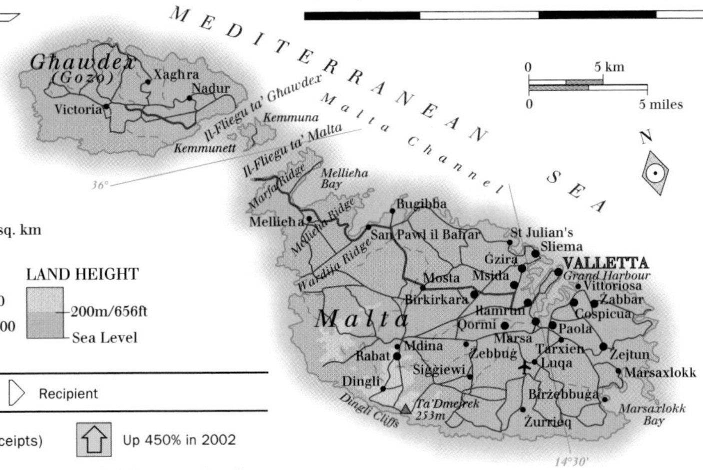
MEDITERRANEAN SEA
Ghawdex (Gozo)
Xaghra
Nadur
Victoria
Il-Fliegu ta' Ghawdex
Kemmuna
Kemmunett
Malta Channel
Il-Fliegu ta' Malta
Mellieha Bay
Marfa Ridge
Mellieha
Mellieha Ridge
Bugibba
San Pawl il Bahar
St Julian's
Sliema
Gzira
VALLETTA
Grand Harbour
Vittoriosa
Zabbar
Cospicua
Mosta
Msida
Birkirkara
Wardija Ridge
Malta
Hamrun
Qormi
Paola
Marsa
Tarxien
Zejtun
Mdina
Rabat
Zebbug
Luqa
Marsaxlokk
Siggiewi
Dingli
Dingli Cliffs
Ta' Dmejrek 253m
Birzebbuga
Marsaxlokk Bay
Zurrieq
0 5 km
0 5 miles
N
36°
14°30'

MALTA

Total Area : 316 sq. km (122 sq. miles)

POPULATION
- over 10 000
- under 10 000

LAND HEIGHT
- 200m/656ft
- Sea Level

AID

Recipient

$11m (receipts)

Up 450% in 2002

Prior to EU accession, Malta received assistance under a special agreement. Italy was its main source of bilateral aid.

DEFENSE

No compulsory military service

$25m

No change in 2002

The Maltese army, advised by the Libyans in the 1980s, now receives training and equipment from Italy, Germany, and the UK.

ECONOMICS

Inflation 2.8% p.a. (1990–2001)

$3.68bn

0.350 Maltese liri (0.372)

SCORE CARD

- ❑ WORLD GNP RANKING........................124th
- ❑ GNP PER CAPITA $9260
- ❑ BALANCE OF PAYMENTS....................–$180m
- ❑ INFLATION 2.2%
- ❑ UNEMPLOYMENT 8%

STRENGTHS

Tourism and naval dockyards. Schemes to attract foreign high-tech industry. Malta Freeport container distribution center. Offshore banking. Strategic position between Europe and Africa, on main Mediterranean shipping lines.

WEAKNESSES

Cut-rate competition from Africa and Asia in traditional textile industry. Almost all material needs imported.

EXPORTS

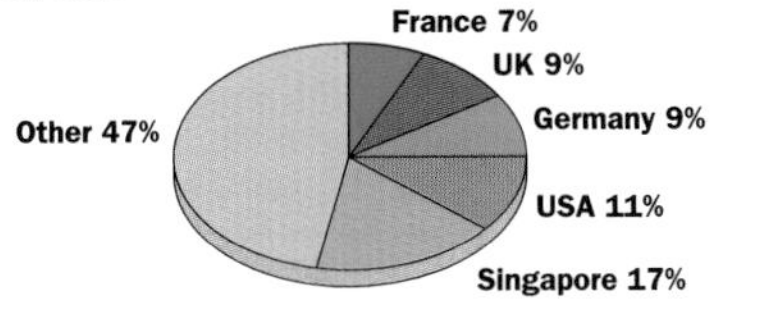
France 7%
UK 9%
Germany 9%
USA 11%
Singapore 17%
Other 47%

IMPORTS

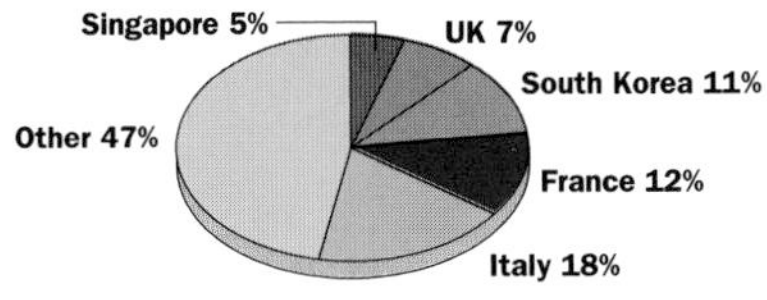
Singapore 5%
UK 7%
South Korea 11%
France 12%
Italy 18%
Other 47%

RESOURCES

Electric power 570,000 kW

2117 tonnes

Reserves under exploration

73,067 pigs, 17,940 cattle, 958,000 chickens

Stone, sand, oil

Malta is dependent on desalination plants for most of its water supply. All oil has to be imported, mostly from Libya. However, there are petroleum reserves currently under exploration in Maltese waters.

ENVIRONMENT

Not available

0.6% partially protected

7.1 tonnes per capita

The main environmental concern is linked to the tourist industry. A lack of planning controls in the 1970s was responsible for unsightly beach developments. These are now tightly controlled, particularly on Gozo.

MEDIA

TV ownership high

Daily newspaper circulation 126 per 1000 people

PUBLISHING AND BROADCAST MEDIA

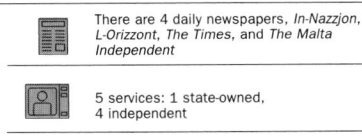

There are 4 daily newspapers, *In-Nazzjon*, *L-Orizzont*, *The Times*, and *The Malta Independent*

5 services: 1 state-owned, 4 independent

12 services: 1 state-owned, 11 independent

The Maltese press is largely party politically oriented. Two of the three main press groups are affiliated to the NP or MLP; one is independent.

CRIME

No death penalty

283 prisoners

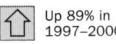

Up 89% in 1997–2000

Crime rates are low compared with those on the European mainland. There has been an increase in narcotics transshipment and associated crimes.

CHRONOLOGY

Malta has been dominated by a host of rulers: Phoenicians, Greeks, Romans, Arabs, Norman Sicily, Spain, France, and, finally, the UK.

- ❑ **1964** Full independence from UK.
- ❑ **1971–1987** Dom Mintoff and MLP government push nonaligned status.
- ❑ **1987–1996** Ruling NP in EU talks.
- ❑ **1998** NP and Prime Minister Edward Fenech Adami reelected after brief MLP interlude.
- ❑ **2004** Lawrence Gonzi takes over as prime minister. Malta joins EU.

EDUCATION

School leaving age: 16

93%

7422 students

One-third of pupils attend non-state schools, including heavily subsidized church-run institutions. There is a state university in Valletta.

HEALTH

Welfare state health benefits

1 per 345 people

Heart diseases, cancers, cerebrovascular and pulmonary diseases

Malta has five state-run and a couple of private hospitals. Diabetes is prevalent, as on other Mediterranean islands.

SPENDING

GDP/cap. increase

CONSUMPTION AND SPENDING

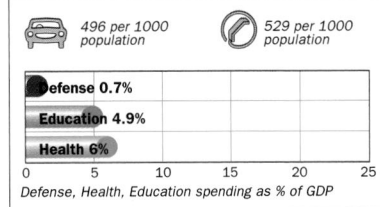

496 per 1000 population

529 per 1000 population

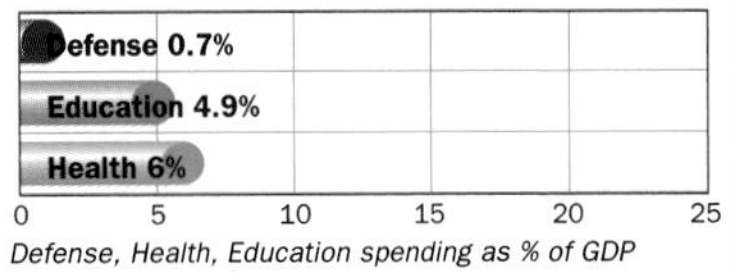
Defense 0.7%
Education 4.9%
Health 6%
0
5
10
15
20
25
Defense, Health, Education spending as % of GDP

Remittances from Maltese working abroad are an important source of income for many island families.

WORLD RANKING

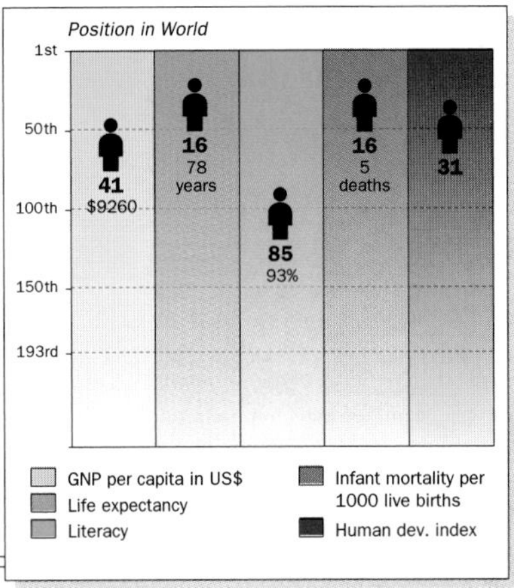
Position in World
1st
50th
100th
150th
193rd
41
$9260
16
78 years
85
93%
16
5 deaths
31
GNP per capita in US$
Life expectancy
Literacy
Infant mortality per 1000 live births
Human dev. index

M

Marshall Islands

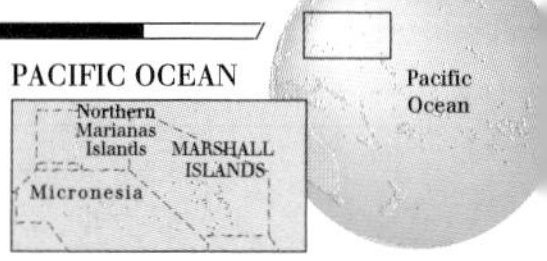
PACIFIC OCEAN
Northern Marianas Islands
MARSHALL ISLANDS
Micronesia
Pacific Ocean

Official Name: Republic of the Marshall Islands **Capital:** Majuro
Population: 56,429 **Currency:** US dollar **Official Languages:** English and Marshallese

1986
1986
May 1
MH
+12
+692
.mh

THE MARSHALL ISLANDS comprises a group of 34 widely scattered atolls in the central Pacific Ocean, formerly under US rule as part of the UN Trust Territory of the Pacific Islands. An agreement which granted internal sovereignty in free association with the US became operational in 1986, and the Trust was formally dissolved in 1990. The economy is almost entirely dependent on US aid and rent for the US missile base on Kwajalein Atoll.

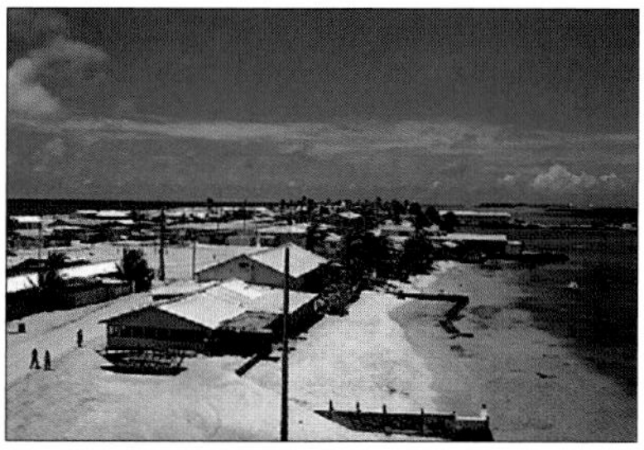

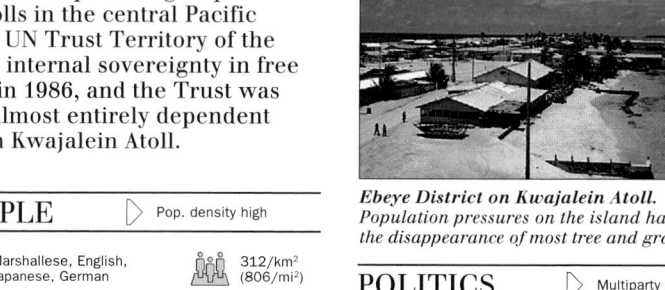

Ebeye District on Kwajalein Atoll. *Population pressures on the island have led to the disappearance of most tree and grass cover.*

CLIMATE

Tropical oceanic

WEATHER CHART FOR MAJURO

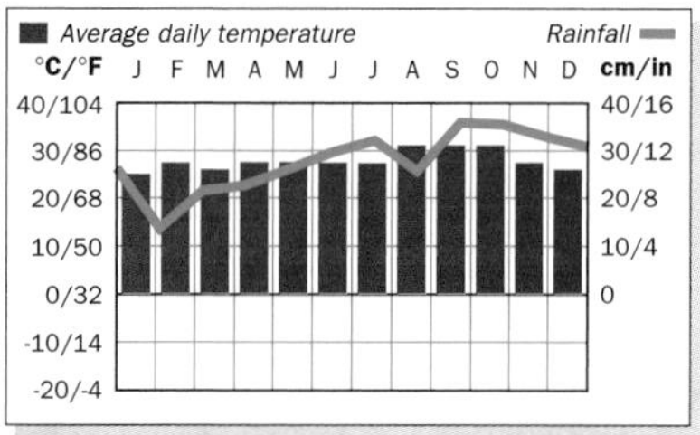
Average daily temperature
Rainfall
°C/°F
J F M A M J J A S O N D
cm/in
40/104
30/86
20/68
10/50
0/32
-10/14
-20/-4
40/16
30/12
20/8
10/4
0

The climate is tropical oceanic with little seasonal variation; temperatures average just under 30°C (86°F).

TRANSPORTATION

Drive on right

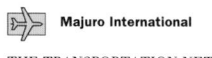

Majuro International

428 ships 14.7m grt

THE TRANSPORTATION NETWORK

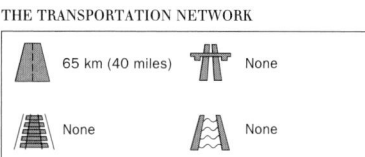

65 km (40 miles)	None
None	None

The transportation system is limited, though there is some interisland shipping. State carrier Air Marshalls has experienced economic difficulties.

TOURISM

Visitors : Population 1:9.4

6000 visitors

Up 20% in 2002

MAIN TOURIST ARRIVALS

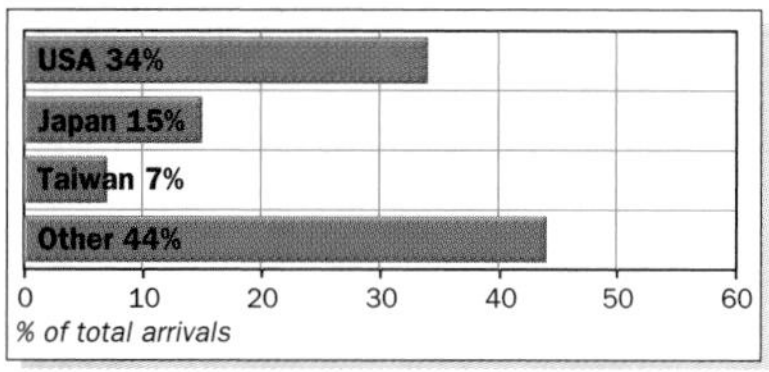
USA 34%
Japan 15%
Taiwan 7%
Other 44%
0 10 20 30 40 50 60
% of total arrivals

In the late 1990s major resort complexes were established on Majuro and on Mili Atoll. Attractions include diving, game fishing, and exploring the sites and relics of World War II battles.

PEOPLE

Pop. density high

Marshallese, English, Japanese, German

312/km² (806/mi²)

THE URBAN/RURAL POPULATION SPLIT

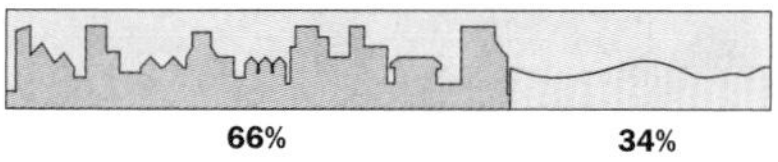
66%
34%

ETHNIC MAKEUP

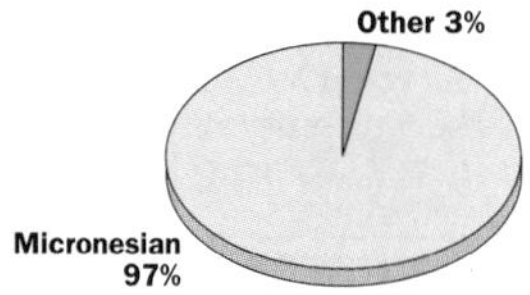
Other 3%
Micronesian 97%

Of the 34 atolls making up the Marshall Islands, 24 are inhabited. Majuro, the capital and commercial center, is home to almost half of the population, many of whom live in its overcrowded slums. The other main center of population is Ebeye Island in the Kwajalein Atoll, where tensions are high due to poor living conditions. Most of Kwajalein Atoll's inhabitants were forcibly relocated to Ebeye from 1947 to make way for US missile tests; many still travel daily to work at the base. Life on the outlying islands is still centered on subsistence agriculture and fishing. Society is traditionally matrilineal.

POLITICS

Multiparty elections

L. House 2003/2007

President Kessai Note

AT THE LAST ELECTION

Parliament 33 seats

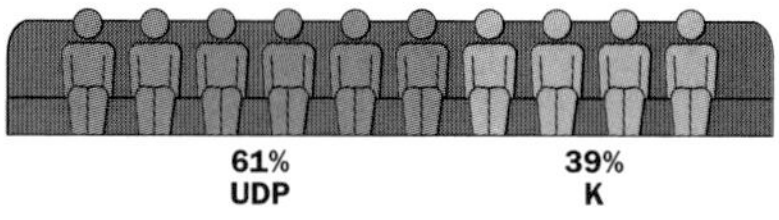
61% UDP
39% K

UDP = United Democratic Party **K** = Pro-Kabua Grouping

Council of Chiefs 12 seats

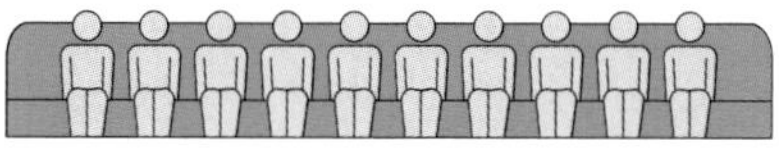

All 12 members are high chiefs

Politics is traditionally dominated by chiefs and groupings of their supporters. Amata Kabua, the islands' high chief and first president until his death in 1996, was succeeded in early 1997 by his cousin Imata Kabua. The UDP has won elections since 1999, and its presidential candidate, commoner and former parliamentary speaker Kessai Note, was elected in 2000. Just over a year later Imata Kabua instigated an unsuccessful vote of no confidence in Note's administration – only the second in the islands' history. The vote was motivated by criticism of the government's approach to the crucial renegotiation of the Compact of Free Association with the US. The original treaty, which provided most of the islands' revenue and defense, expired in 2001; a new 20-year treaty was signed in 2003, and Note was reelected the following January.

Marshall Islands

Total Area : 181 sq. km (70 sq. miles)

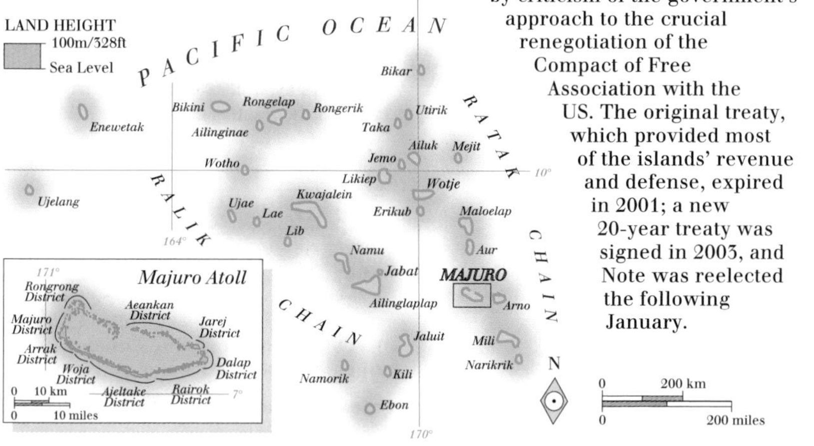
LAND HEIGHT
100m/328ft
Sea Level
PACIFIC OCEAN
RALIK CHAIN
RATAK CHAIN
Bokak
Bikar
Bikini
Rongelap
Rongerik
Utirik
Enewetak
Ailinginae
Taka
Ailuk
Mejit
Wotho
Jemo
Likiep
Wotje
Ujelang
Ujae
Lae
Kwajalein
Erikub
Maloelap
Lib
Namu
Aur
Jabat
MAJURO
Ailinglaplap
Arno
Jaluit
Mili
Narikrik
Namorik
Kili
Ebon
164°
170°
10°
N
0 200 km
0 200 miles
Majuro Atoll
171°
Rongrong District
Majuro District
Aeankan District
Jarej District
Arrak District
Woja District
Dalap District
Ajeltake District
Rairok District
7°
0 10 km
0 10 miles

WORLD AFFAIRS

Joined UN in 1991

IAEA | PIF | ACP | PC | ADB

The Compact of Free Association has made ties to the US of central importance. From 1986 the US has provided $1 billion for its continuing use of Kwajalein Atoll as a missile testing site and has determined the islands' foreign and defense policies. A new Compact was signed in 2003. Taiwan has become a source of funding for development, provoking controversy over the issue of diplomatic recognition.

AID

Recipient

$62m (receipts) — Down 16% in 2002

US aid accounts for 60% of revenue. A trust fund was created under the 2003 Compact to provide aid after 2023.

DEFENSE

No compulsory military service

US is responsible for defense — Not applicable

There is no defense force; all defense is provided by the US under the Compact of Free Association. The US does not have offensive weapons sited in the Marshalls, but its navy patrols regularly.

ECONOMICS

Inflation 5.3% p.a. (1990–2001)

$126m — Currency is US dollar

SCORE CARD

❑ WORLD GNP RANKING	188th
❑ GNP PER CAPITA	$2380
❑ BALANCE OF PAYMENTS	$14m
❑ INFLATION	1.9%
❑ UNEMPLOYMENT	30%

STRENGTHS

US guarantee against economic collapse to preserve strategic influence. Aid from the US. Huge tourism potential.

WEAKNESSES

High unemployment. Dependence on aid and imports (nine times as large as exports). All fuel imported. Large state sector. Drop in world copra trade.

EXPORTS

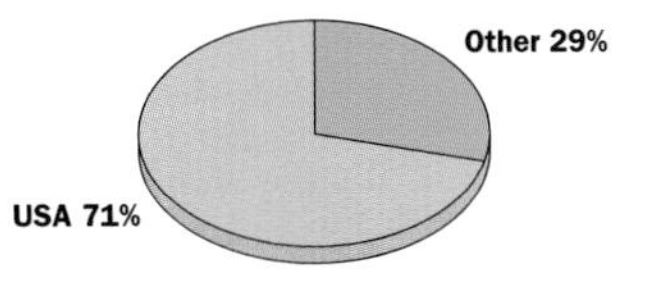
Other 29%
USA 71%

IMPORTS

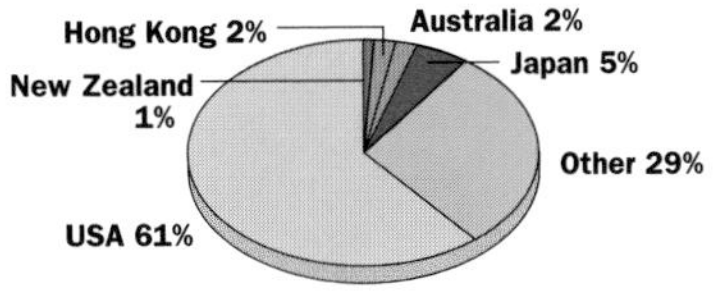
Hong Kong 2%
Australia 2%
Japan 5%
New Zealand 1%
Other 29%
USA 61%

RESOURCES

Not available

37,098 tonnes — Not an oil producer

Not available — Phosphates

There are few known strategic resources. Exploratory tests have revealed some high-grade phosphate deposits, but not in economically viable quantities. Small diesel generators are used for electricity production.

ENVIRONMENT

Not available

None — Not available

Between 1946 and 1958, Bikini, Enewetak, and neighboring atolls were rendered uninhabitable by a series of US nuclear military tests. Enewetak residents were allowed to return in 1980, and Rongelap was declared habitable in 2001. A 1999 tribunal adopted stringent standards for further decontamination. The US has now paid out over $101 million to victims of nuclear testing. Nuclear waste imports were banned in 1999. The effects of rising sea levels are a major concern. Erosion affects beaches and soil is being lost and also contaminated by brackish water.

MEDIA

TV ownership low

There are no daily newspapers

PUBLISHING AND BROADCAST MEDIA

There are no daily newspapers. The one weekly newspaper, the *Marshall Islands Journal*, is privately owned

2 services: 1 state-owned, 1 independent — 4 services: 1 state-owned, 3 independent

Radio is the major source of information in the Marshalls. The main TV service is subscription-only. The US personnel stationed on Kwajalein have their own TV and radio stations.

CRIME

No death penalty

23 prisoners — Crime levels are rising slightly

Crime levels are generally low; however, the rate is up in Ebeye. Outlying islands are crime-free.

EDUCATION

School leaving age: 14

91% — 251 students

Education, compulsory between the ages of six and 14 years, is based on the US model. The number of secondary school graduates exceeds the availability of suitable employment in the Marshall Islands. Many go on to university in the US.

CHRONOLOGY

After a period under Spanish rule, the Marshall Islands became a German protectorate in 1885; Japan took possession at the start of World War I. The islands were transferred to US control in 1945.

- ❑ **1946** US nuclear testing begins.
- ❑ **1947** UN Trust Territory of the Pacific Islands established.
- ❑ **1961** Kwajalein developed as US army missile range.
- ❑ **1979** Constitution approved in referendum. Government set up.
- ❑ **1986** Compact of Free Association with US operational.
- ❑ **1990** Trust terminated by UN.
- ❑ **1997** President Amata Kabua dies: succeeded by his cousin, Imata.
- ❑ **2000** Kessai Note president after opposition election victory.
- ❑ **2003** New Compact agreed.

HEALTH

No welfare state health benefits

1 per 2500 people — Respiratory, heart, and diarrheal diseases

There are two oversubscribed hospitals in the urban centers of Majuro and Ebeye. Radiation fallout has left a legacy of cancers and birth defects.

SPENDING

Not available

CONSUMPTION AND SPENDING

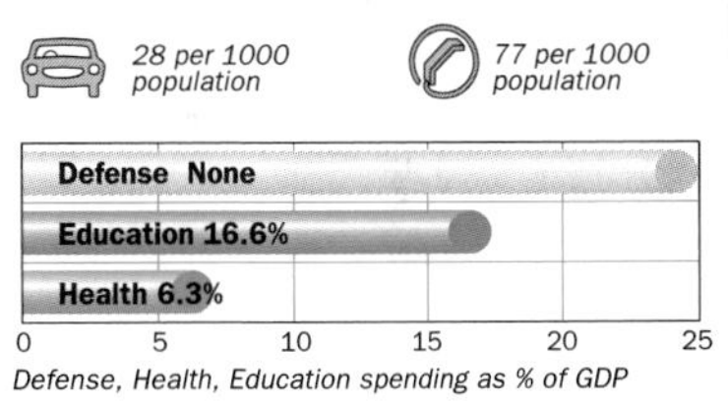
28 per 1000 population
77 per 1000 population
Defense None
Education 16.6%
Health 6.3%
0
5
10
15
20
25
Defense, Health, Education spending as % of GDP

Wealth disparities are small. Very few citizens can afford luxuries such as air-conditioning and cars.

WORLD RANKING

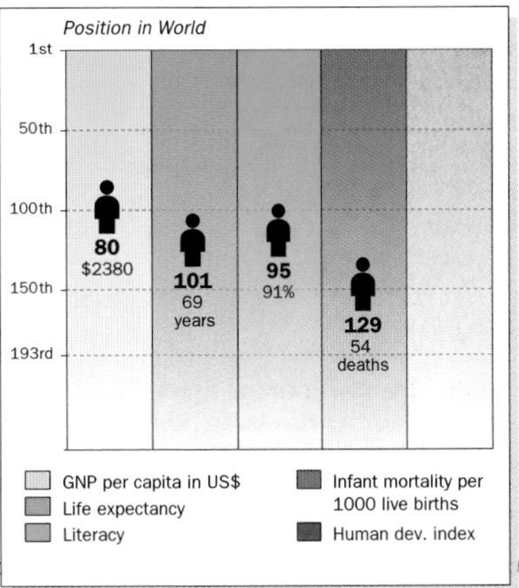
Position in World
1st
50th
100th
150th
193rd
80
$2380
101
69 years
95
91%
129
54 deaths
GNP per capita in US$
Life expectancy
Literacy
Infant mortality per 1000 live births
Human dev. index

M

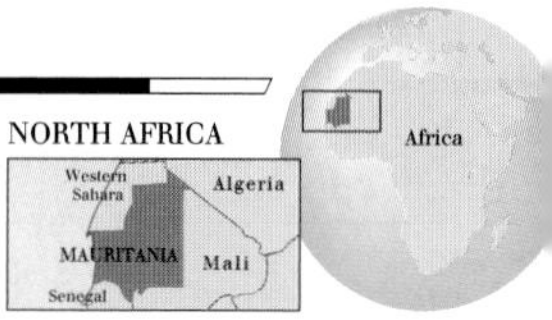
NORTH AFRICA
Africa
Western Sahara
Algeria
MAURITANIA
Mali
Senegal

Mauritania

Official Name: Islamic Republic of Mauritania **Capital:** Nouakchott
Population: 2.9 million **Currency:** Ouguiya **Official Language:** Arabic

1960
1960
Nov 28
RIM
0
+222
.mr

Located in northwest Africa, Mauritania is a member of both the AU and the Arab League. Formerly a French colony, the country has taken a strongly Arab direction since 1964; today, it is the Maures who control political life and dominate the minority black population. The Sahara extends across two-thirds of Mauritania's territory; the only productive land is that drained by the Senegal River in the south and southwest.

Climate

Hot desert

WEATHER CHART FOR NOUAKCHOTT

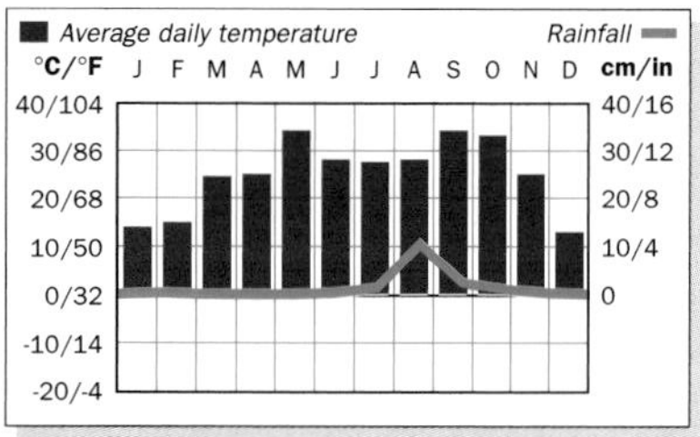
Average daily temperature
Rainfall
°C/°F
J F M A M J J A S O N D
cm/in
40/104
30/86
20/68
10/50
0/32
-10/14
-20/-4
40/16
30/12
20/8
10/4
0

The dusty Saharan *harmattan* wind often aggravates the very hot, dry conditions. Some rain falls in the south.

Transportation

Drive on right

Nouakchott 226,096 passengers

142 ships 47,600 grt

THE TRANSPORTATION NETWORK

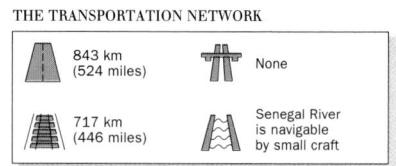

843 km (524 miles)

None

717 km (446 miles)

Senegal River is navigable by small craft

The transportation system is limited and unevenly developed. There are two major roads, but shifting sands mean that they require constant maintenance.

Tourism

Visitors : Population 1:97

30,000 visitors

Up 25% in 2000

MAIN TOURIST ARRIVALS

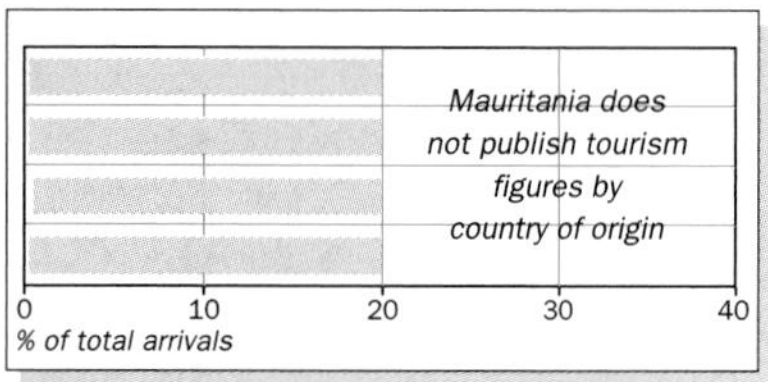
Mauritania does not publish tourism figures by country of origin
0
10
20
30
40
% of total arrivals

There are few tourists apart from desert safari enthusiasts. The more mountainous areas are especially dramatic, but access is difficult. Nouakchott has some hotels.

People

Pop. density low

Hassaniyah Arabic, Wolof, French

3/km² (7/mi²)

THE URBAN/RURAL POPULATION SPLIT

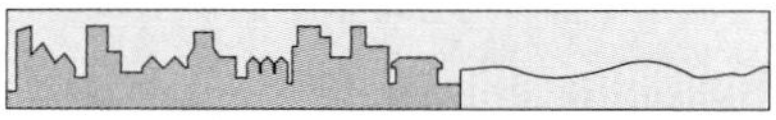
60%
40%

RELIGIOUS PERSUASION

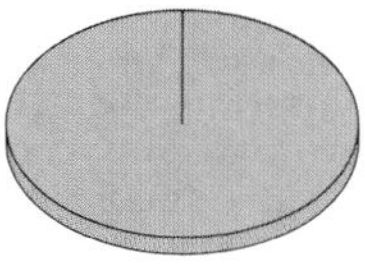
Sunni Muslim 100%

The Maure majority is politically dominant. Ethnic tension centers on its oppression of the black minority, which comprises the Havalin, the Senegalese, and the Peulh, Tukolor, and Wolof groups. The old black bourgeoisie has now been superseded by a Maurish class; tens of thousands of blacks are estimated to be in slavery. The arrival of 200,000 Maures from Senegal in 1989 caused ethnic tension to come to a head: there were attacks on Senegalese in Mauritania and many fled or were deported to refugee camps along the Senegal River.

Family solidarity among nomads is particularly strong.

Politics

Multiparty elections

L. House 2001/2006
U. House 2004/2006

President Maaouya ould Sid Ahmed Taya

AT THE LAST ELECTION

National Assembly 81 seats

79% PRDS
5% AC
16% Others

PRDS = Democratic and Social Republican Party **AC** = Action for Change **Rep** = Representatives of Mauritanians living abroad **Ind** = Independents

Senate 56 seats

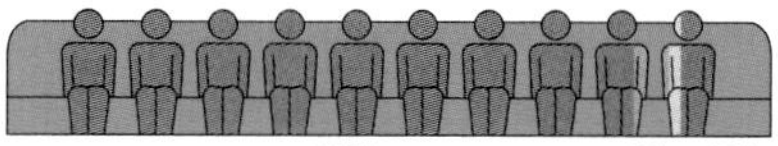
2% Ind
88% PRDS
5% Rep
5% Others

The Senate is indirectly elected

Mauritania adopted multiparty democracy in 1991, but elections since then have simply returned to power the incumbent military ruler, President Maaouya ould Sid Ahmed Taya. Amid accusations of electoral fraud, the opposition initially boycotted legislative polls, but increased their representation in 2001; the AC was subsequently banned. Taya's Islamist opponent in the 2003 presidential poll, Mohamed Khouna ould Haidalla, was arrested in connection with an earlier coup plot and has been imprisoned.

The blacks of the south support exiled parties, such as the Senegal-based African Liberation Forces of Mauritania (FLAM).

Mauritania

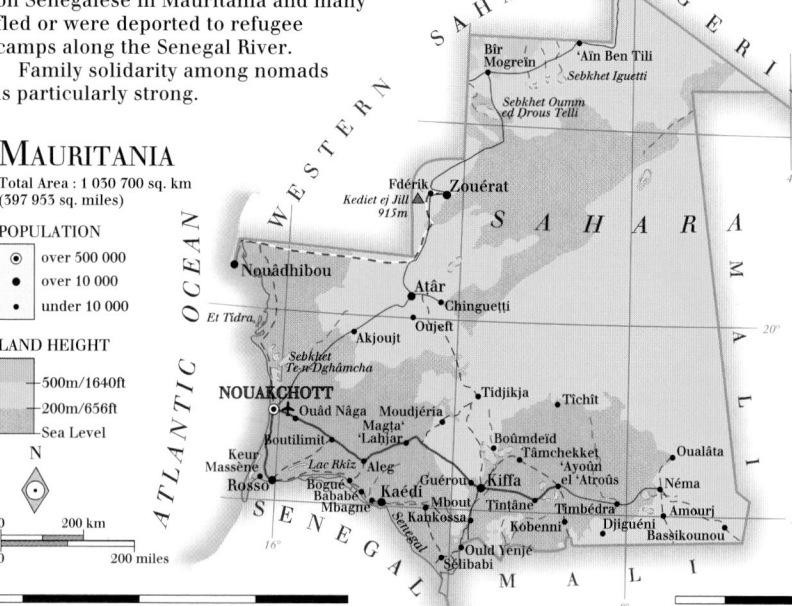

Total Area : 1 030 700 sq. km (397 953 sq. miles)

POPULATION
- over 500 000
- over 10 000
- under 10 000

LAND HEIGHT
- 500m/1640ft
- 200m/656ft
- Sea Level

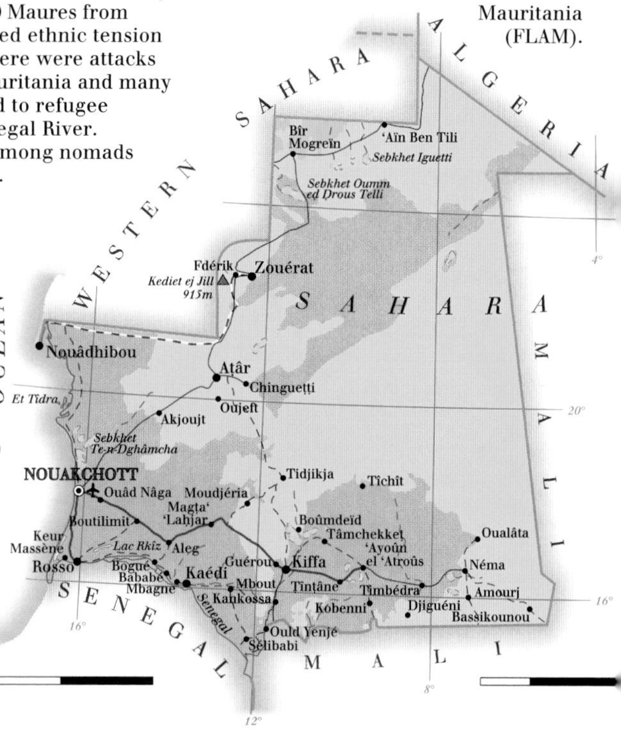
N
0 200 km
0 200 miles
WESTERN SAHARA
ALGERIA
SAHARA
MALI
SENEGAL
ATLANTIC OCEAN
Bîr Mogreïn
'Aïn Ben Tili
Sebkhet Iguetti
Sebkhet Oumm ed Drous Telli
Fdérik
Zouérat
Kediet ej Jill 915m
Nouâdhibou
Atâr
Chinguetti
Oujeft
Et Tidra
Akjoujt
Sebkhet Te-n-Dghâmcha
NOUAKCHOTT
Ouâd Nâga
Moudjéria
Tidjikja
Tîchît
Magta' Lahjar
Boutilimit
Boûmdeïd
Tâmchekket
'Ayoûn el 'Atroûs
Oualâta
Néma
Keur Massène
Lac Rkiz
Aleg
Rosso
Bogué
Bababé
Mbagne
Kaédi
Guérou
Kiffa
Mbout
Tintâne
Kankossa
Kobenni
Timbédra
Djiguéni
Amourj
Bassikounou
Ould Yenjé
Sélibabi
Senegal
4°
8°
12°
16°
20°

WORLD AFFAIRS

Joined UN in 1961

AL | CILSS | AU | OIF | OIC

Mauritania seeks to maintain a balance between sub-Saharan Africa and the Arab world, but has had tense relations with all its neighbors. The border with Mali is notorious for smuggling and banditry. Mauritania maintains good relations with Israel and the West.

AID

Recipient

$355m (receipts) | Up 32% in 2002

The EU, the World Bank, and Japan are the main donors. Most aid is used for development projects, such as the EU-funded Trans-Mauritanian Highway.

DEFENSE

Compulsory military service

$16m | Down 6% in 2002

The 15,000-strong army is a strain on Mauritania's budget. Troops are used increasingly in public works projects. France is the main arms supplier.

ECONOMICS

Inflation 6.2% p.a. (1990–2001)

$791m | 267.5 ouguiyas (266.7)

SCORE CARD

❑ WORLD GNP RANKING	159th
❑ GNP PER CAPITA	$280
❑ BALANCE OF PAYMENTS	–$51m
❑ INFLATION	3.8%
❑ UNEMPLOYMENT	21%

STRENGTHS

Iron from the Cominor mine at Zouérat. Gypsum. Exports of oil, gold, and silver set to increase from 2005. Offshore fishing among the best in west Africa. Significant debt cancellations in 2002.

WEAKNESSES

Poor land. Drought, locust attacks. Fluctuating commodity prices. Very hot, dry desert climate.

EXPORTS

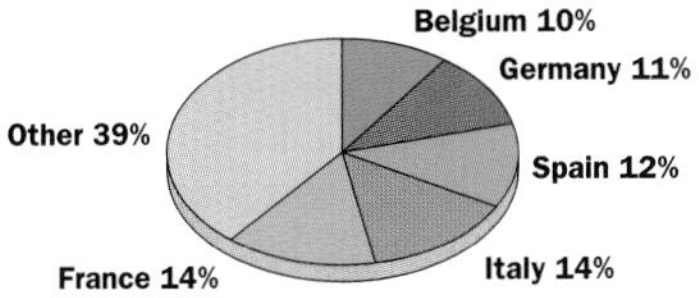
Belgium 10%
Germany 11%
Spain 12%
Italy 14%
France 14%
Other 39%

IMPORTS

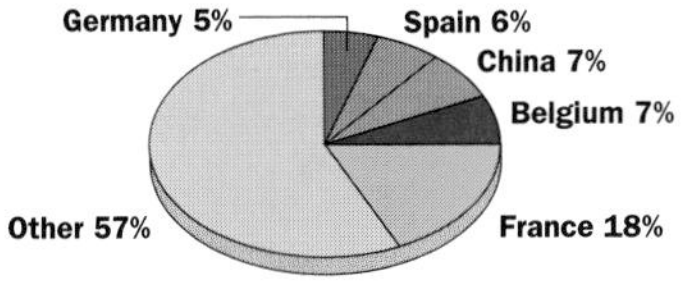
Germany 5%
Spain 6%
China 7%
Belgium 7%
France 18%
Other 57%

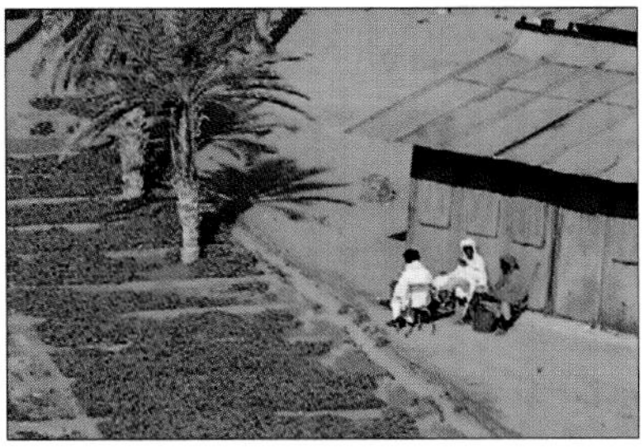

***Mauritania's extreme aridity** means that only 1% of the land is arable. Two-thirds of the country are part of the Sahara Desert; sparse vegetation over the rest supports some livestock.*

RESOURCES

Electric power 115,000 kW

83,596 tonnes | Oil reserves not yet exploited (reserves 65m barrels)

8.7m sheep, 5.5m goats, 1.5m cattle, 4.2m chickens | Iron, gypsum, copper, gold, diamonds, oil, phosphates, silver

Mauritania has the world's largest gypsum deposits. An upturn in iron ore prices has given new impetus to the industry. A new mine in the western desert will increase gold and silver production. Offshore oil is to come onstream in 2005. The national electricity company put the exploration of alternative energy sources on hold until after its privatization in 2004.

ENVIRONMENT

Sustainability rank: 126th

2% (0.2% partially protected) | 1.2 tonnes per capita

The chief environmental problem in Mauritania is that of the encroaching Sahara Desert, a situation worsened by the droughts of 1973 and 1983, which caused widespread loss of grazing land. The consequent exodus of people away from the land and into the towns has raised Nouakchott's population from 20,000 in 1960 to over 600,000 today.

MEDIA

TV ownership medium

Daily newspaper circulation 0.5 per 1000 people

PUBLISHING AND BROADCAST MEDIA

There is one daily newspaper, *Chaab*, published by the government

1 state-owned service | 1 state-owned service

The press is heavily censored, and the broadcast media are state-owned. *Chaab*, the government newspaper, is also published in French (*Horizons*).

CRIME

Death penalty not used in practice

1354 prisoners | Down 45% in 1997–1999

Smuggling and robbery are rife in border areas. A growing number of children are abandoned in the cities.

CHRONOLOGY

Once part of the Islamic Almoravid state, Mauritania became a French colony in 1814.

❑ **1960** Independence; one-party state.
❑ **1972** Peace with Polisario in war waged over Western Sahara.
❑ **1984** Col. Maaouya Taya takes power in bloodless coup.
❑ **1992** First multiparty elections.
❑ **2003** Apparent coup fails.

EDUCATION

School leaving age: 14

41% | 9033 students

Though over half the population is still illiterate, primary school enrollment rates have increased from 49% in 1987 to 86% in 2002.

HEALTH

No welfare state health benefits

1 per 10,000 people | Diarrheal and respiratory diseases, influenza, tuberculosis

Historic regional inequalities persist and the best facilities are in the capital. The overall level of care is on a par with neighboring states.

SPENDING

GDP/cap. increase

CONSUMPTION AND SPENDING

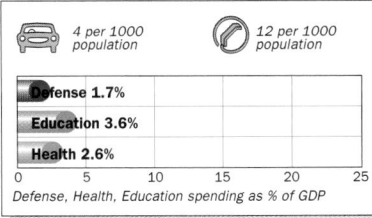

4 per 1000 population | *12 per 1000 population*

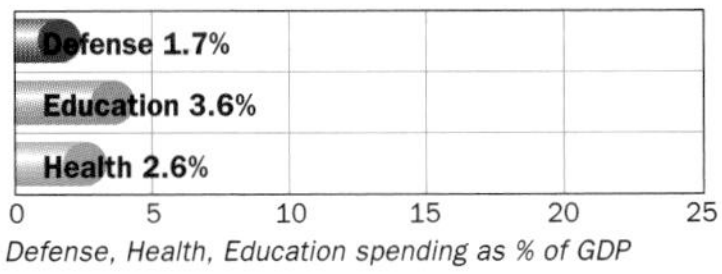
Defense 1.7%
Education 3.6%
Health 2.6%
0
5
10
15
20
25
Defense, Health, Education spending as % of GDP

The small ruling Maurish elite forms the richest sector. Wealthy Maures travel to Mecca, Saudi Arabia, to perform the *haj* (Muslim pilgrimage).

WORLD RANKING

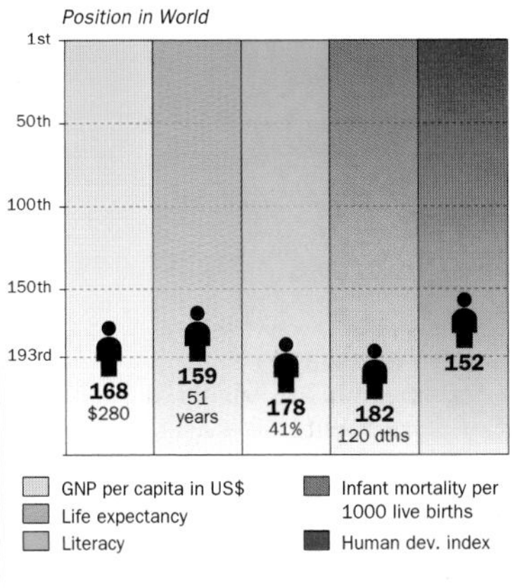
Position in World
1st
50th
100th
150th
193rd
168
$280
159
51 years
178
41%
182
120 dths
152
GNP per capita in US$
Life expectancy
Literacy
Infant mortality per 1000 live births
Human dev. index

M

MAURITIUS

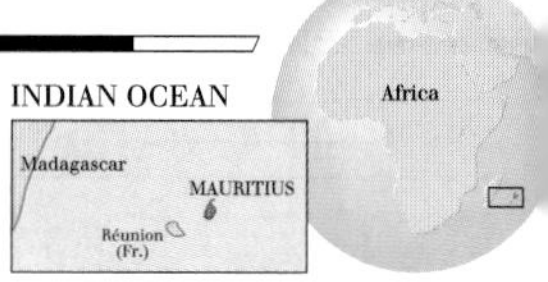
INDIAN OCEAN
Africa
Madagascar
MAURITIUS
Réunion (Fr.)

OFFICIAL NAME: Republic of Mauritius **CAPITAL:** Port Louis
POPULATION: 1.2 million **CURRENCY:** Mauritian rupee **OFFICIAL LANGUAGE:** English

1968 | 1968 | March 12 | MS | +4 | +230 | .mu

THE ISLANDS THAT MAKE UP Mauritius lie in the Indian Ocean east of Madagascar. The main island, from which the country takes its name, is of volcanic origin and surrounded by coral reefs. Along with Rodrigues to the east, the country includes the Agalega Islands and the Cargados Carajos Shoals, 500 km (300 miles) to the north. Mauritius has enjoyed considerable economic success following recent industrial diversification and the expansion of tourism.

CLIMATE

Tropical oceanic

WEATHER CHART FOR PORT LOUIS

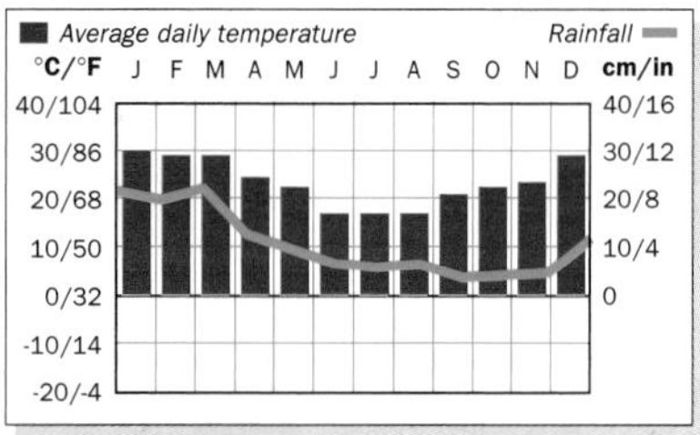
Average daily temperature
Rainfall
°C/°F J F M A M J J A S O N D cm/in
40/104
30/86
20/68
10/50
0/32
-10/14
-20/-4
40/16
30/12
20/8
10/4
0

The climate is subtropical and humid. December to March are the hottest and wettest months. Tropical cyclones are an occasional threat during this time.

TRANSPORTATION

Drive on left

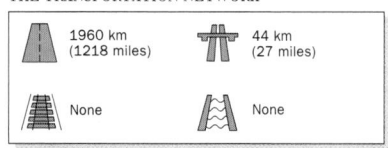

Sir Seewoosagur Ramgoolam International 1.98m passengers

45 ships 62,700 grt

THE TRANSPORTATION NETWORK

1960 km (1218 miles)

44 km (27 miles)

None

None

Roads are extensive, but often congested. Plans exist for a monorail link between Port Louis and Curepipe.

TOURISM

Visitors : Population 1:1.7

702,000 visitors

Up 3% in 2003

MAIN TOURIST ARRIVALS

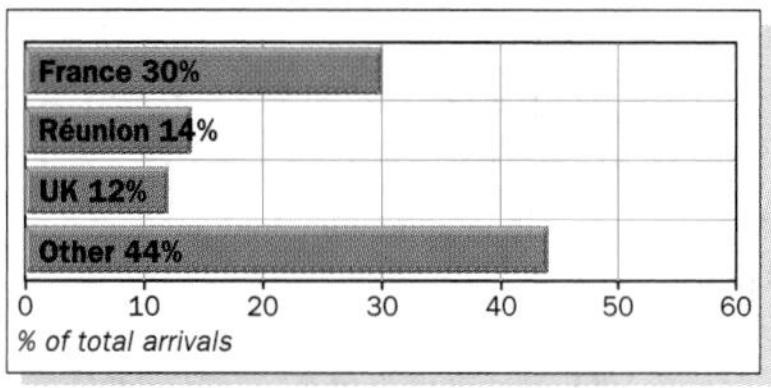
France 30%
Réunion 14%
UK 12%
Other 44%
0 10 20 30 40 50 60
% of total arrivals

Tourism expanded rapidly in the 1990s. Spectacular beaches, water sports, and big game fishing are major attractions. Around 30% of visitors each year come from France.

PEOPLE

Pop. density high

French Creole, Hindi, Urdu, Tamil, Chinese, English, French

645/km² (1671/mi²)

THE URBAN/RURAL POPULATION SPLIT

42%
58%

RELIGIOUS PERSUASION

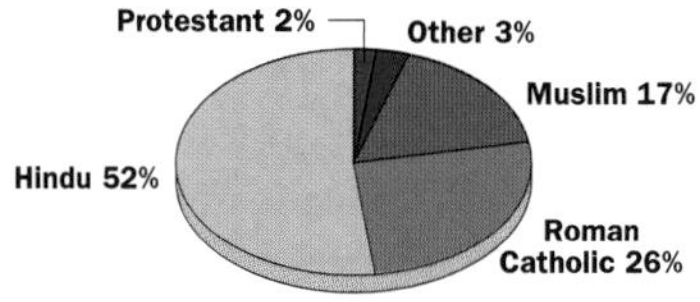
Protestant 2%
Other 3%
Muslim 17%
Hindu 52%
Roman Catholic 26%

Mauritius is one of the world's most densely populated countries. Most Mauritians are descended from indentured laborers brought from India. Creoles, the descendants of African slaves, make up a third of the population. There is also a small Chinese minority. Clashes between the main ethnic groups no longer occur, though Creoles complain of discrimination.

POLITICS

Multiparty elections

2000/2005

President Sir Anerood Jugnauth

AT THE LAST ELECTION
National Assembly 70 seats

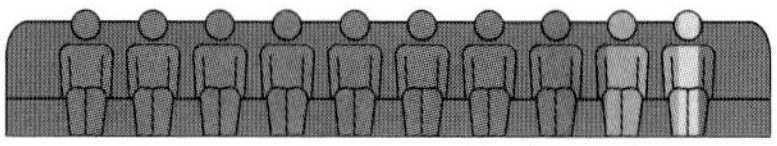
11% PTr–PMXD
3% MR
83% MSM–MMM
3% OPR

MSM–MMM = Mauritian Socialist Movement–Mauritian Militant Movement **PTr–PMXD** = Labour Party–Mauritian Social Democratic Party of Xavier Duval **OPR** = Organization of the People of Rodrigues **MR** = Mouvement Rodriguais

Rodrigues has its own legislature which exercises local power

Mauritius became a republic in 1992. Sir Anerood Jugnauth of the MSM had been prime minister for 13 years before losing elections in 1995 to the PTr. He was returned to power when corruption scandals led to early elections in 2000; under the coalition deal that he made with the MMM, Jugnauth stepped aside in favor of MMM leader Paul Bérenger in October 2003, and was then appointed president.

WORLD AFFAIRS

Joined UN in 1968

Comm | COMESA | COI | AU | SADC

Mauritius hosted a francophone nations summit in 1995, and the first OAU human rights conference in 1999. Links with South Africa and India are important. Disputes persist over UK-administered Diego Garcia and the French-ruled island of Tromelin.

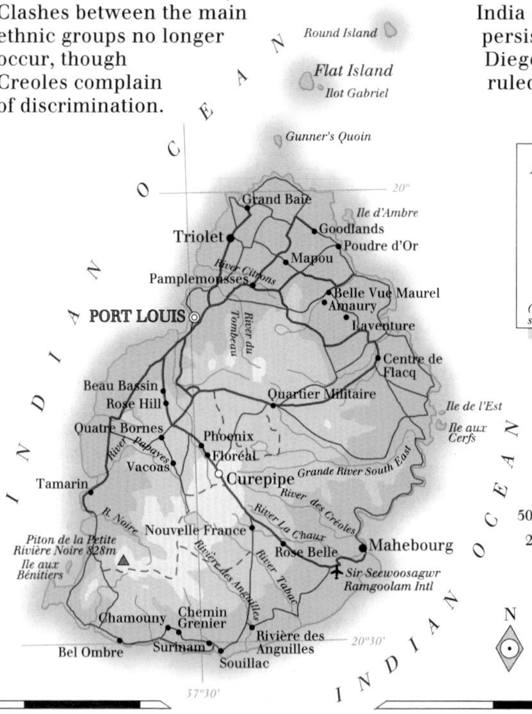
INDIAN OCEAN
Round Island
Flat Island
Ilot Gabriel
Gunner's Quoin
Grand Baie
Ile d'Ambre
Triolet
Goodlands
Poudre d'Or
Mapou
Pamplemousses
River Citrons
Belle Vue Maurel
Amaury
PORT LOUIS
River du Tombeau
Laventure
Centre de Flacq
Beau Bassin
Rose Hill
Quartier Militaire
Ile de l'Est
Ile aux Cerfs
Quatre Bornes
Phoenix
Vacoas
Floréal
Tamarin
Curepipe
Grande River South East
River des Créoles
Nouvelle France
River La Chaux
Piton de la Petite Rivière Noire 828m
Ile aux Bénitiers
Rose Belle
Mahebourg
Sir Seewoosagur Ramgoolam Intl
Chamouny
Chemin Grenier
Surinam
Bel Ombre
Souillac
Rivière des Anguilles
20°
20°30'
57°30'
N

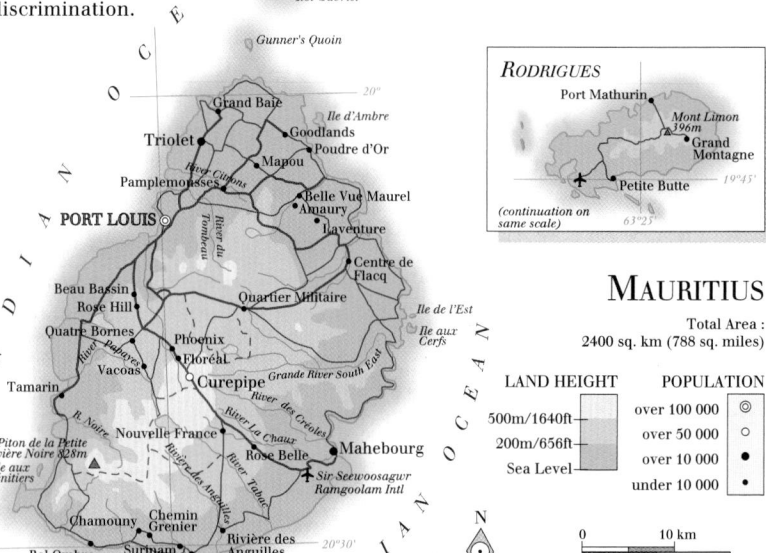

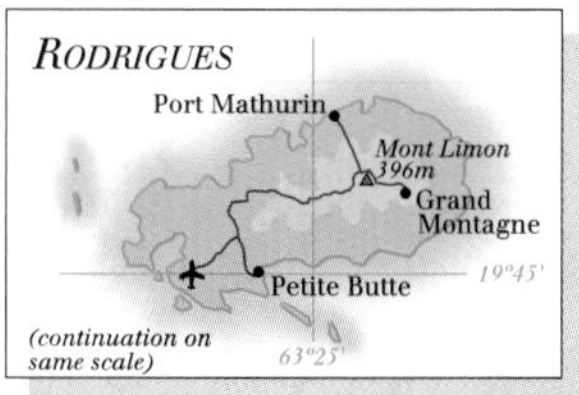
RODRIGUES
Port Mathurin
Mont Limon 396m
Grand Montagne
Petite Butte
19°45'
63°25'
(continuation on same scale)

MAURITIUS

Total Area : 2400 sq. km (788 sq. miles)

LAND HEIGHT	POPULATION
500m/1640ft	over 100 000
200m/656ft	over 50 000
Sea Level	over 10 000
	under 10 000

0 10 km
0 10 miles

AID

Recipient

$24m (receipts) — Up 9% in 2002

Aid is predominantly bilateral, with the EU and France as the main donors. Mauritius also receives aid from Arab aid agencies and Japan, and from the UN and other international organizations. Aid levels are fairly low due to the strength of the Mauritian economy. The World Bank is helping to develop sewerage facilities to mitigate the effect of tourism on the environment.

DEFENSE

No compulsory military service

$7m — Down 22% in 2002

Mauritius has no standing defense forces. There is, however, a 1500-strong special police mobile unit to ensure internal security. There is also a coast guard numbering 500.

ECONOMICS

Inflation 6.2% p.a. (1990–2001)

$4.68bn — 28.22 Mauritian rupees (29.15)

SCORE CARD

- ❑ WORLD GNP RANKING........................116th
- ❑ GNP PER CAPITA $3860
- ❑ BALANCE OF PAYMENTS $259m
- ❑ INFLATION.......................................6.7%
- ❑ UNEMPLOYMENT.................................10%

STRENGTHS

Strong economic growth. Export processing zone (EPZ), especially for clothing manufacture. Sugar industry. Tourism. Highly educated workforce. Offshore financial services. Ranked by World Economic Forum in 2003 as third most competitive economy in Africa.

WEAKNESSES

Vulnerability to droughts. Most food has to be imported: few crops other than sugar can be grown. Banking scandals have dented investor confidence. Enduring pockets of poverty. Lack of strategic resources. Remoteness.

EXPORTS

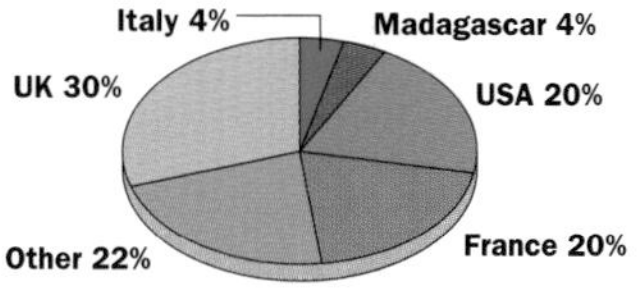
Italy 4%
Madagascar 4%
UK 30%
USA 20%
Other 22%
France 20%

IMPORTS

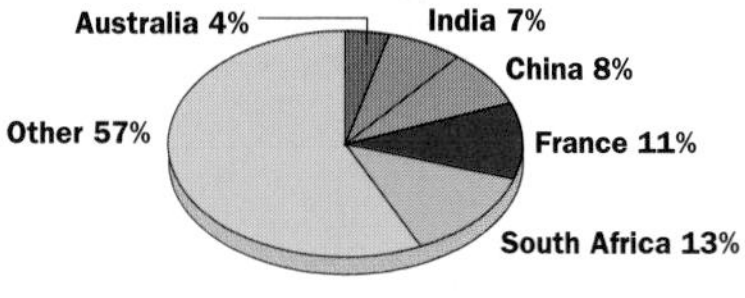
Australia 4%
India 7%
China 8%
Other 57%
France 11%
South Africa 13%

Villagers at a water source in the center of Mauritius Island. Mauritius's main rivers are used for hydropower generation.

RESOURCES

Electric power 661,000 kW

10,753 tonnes — Not an oil producer

93,000 goats, 28,000 cattle, 9.8m chickens — None

Mauritius has to import oil, so the government has invested heavily in alternative indigenous energy schemes, including HEP generation and power plants fueled by bagasse (a by-product of the sugar industry). An $800,000 solar energy project was launched in 2000 for street and government office lighting.

ENVIRONMENT

Not available

8% (5% partially protected) — 2.4 tonnes per capita

Rapid industrialization as well as unchecked hotel building have caused environmental problems. Coral reefs are under threat from both coral sand mining and the discharging of untreated sewage into the sea.

MEDIA

TV ownership medium

Daily newspaper circulation 119 per 1000 people

PUBLISHING AND BROADCAST MEDIA

There are 10 daily newspapers. *Le Quotidien*, *L'Express*, and *Le Mauricien* have the largest circulations

1 independent service — 4 services: 1 state-owned, 3 independent

Mauritius has an active press, which is subject to few regulations and has a wide readership. Newspapers are published in English, French, Creole, Hindi, Chinese, and Tamil. The creation of several "cybercities" is planned, with high-tech Internet and telecommunications facilities.

CRIME

No death penalty

2565 prisoners — Up 23% in 2000–2001

Crime rates on the main island are fairly low. There has been a small increase in thefts and narcotics smuggling. Outlying islands are virtually crime-free.

CHRONOLOGY

Mauritius was colonized and ruled by the Dutch in the 17th century, the French (1710–1810), and the British.

- ❑ **1968** Independence. Riots between Creoles and Muslims.
- ❑ **1982–1995** Sir Anerood Jugnauth prime minister; forms MSM.
- ❑ **2000** Elections won by MSM–MMM. Return of Jugnauth.
- ❑ **2003** Paul Bérenger of MMM takes over as prime minister.

EDUCATION

School leaving age: 12

84% — 12,481 students

Educational provision is good, and over 90% of Mauritians under the age of 30 are literate. The University of Mauritius has about 4000 students.

HEALTH

Welfare state health benefits

1 per 1111 people — Cerebrovascular and heart diseases, cancers

In Mauritius free health care is universally available. There are 14 state hospitals and eight private clinics.

SPENDING

GDP/cap. increase

CONSUMPTION AND SPENDING

85 per 1000 population — *270 per 1000 population*

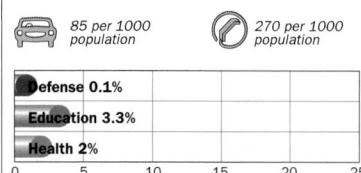

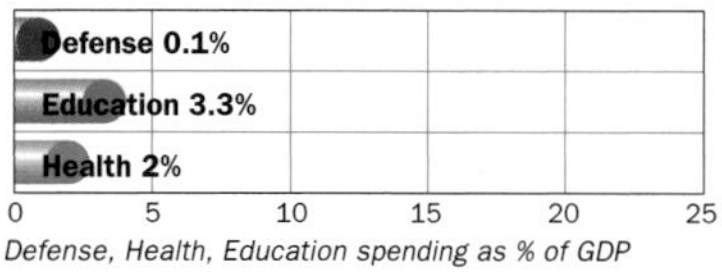
Defense 0.1%
Education 3.3%
Health 2%
0
5
10
15
20
25
Defense, Health, Education spending as % of GDP

French-descended hotel and plantation owners are the country's wealthiest social group. Mauritius has one of the highest incomes per capita in Africa.

WORLD RANKING

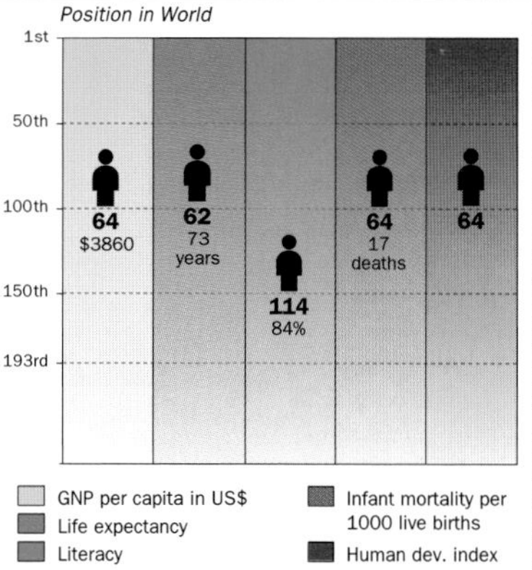
Position in World
1st
50th
100th
150th
193rd
64
$3860
62
73 years
114
84%
64
17 deaths
64
GNP per capita in US$
Life expectancy
Literacy
Infant mortality per 1000 live births
Human dev. index

M

MEXICO

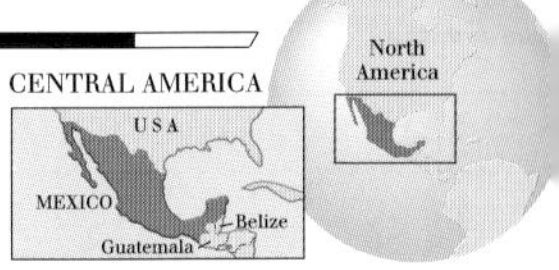
CENTRAL AMERICA
North America
USA
MEXICO
Belize
Guatemala

OFFICIAL NAME: United Mexican States **CAPITAL:** Mexico City
POPULATION: 104 million **CURRENCY:** Mexican peso **OFFICIAL LANGUAGE:** Spanish

1836
1848
Sept 16
MEX
-6
+52
.mx

The cathedral of Santa Prisca at Taxco near Cuernavaca. It was built in Spanish Churriguera style between 1748 and 1758.

INCREASINGLY CONSIDERED a part of North rather than Central America, Mexico separates the US from the rest of Latin America. Coastal plains along its Pacific and Caribbean seaboards rise into an arid central plateau, which includes the world's second-biggest conurbation, Mexico City, built on the site of the Aztec capital, Tenochtitlán. Colonized by the Spanish for its silver mines, Mexico achieved independence in 1836. In the "Epic Revolution" of 1910–1920, in which 250,000 died, much of modern Mexico's structure was established. In 1994, Mexico signed the North American Free Trade Agreement (NAFTA).

CLIMATE

Tropical/mountain/desert

WEATHER CHART FOR MEXICO CITY

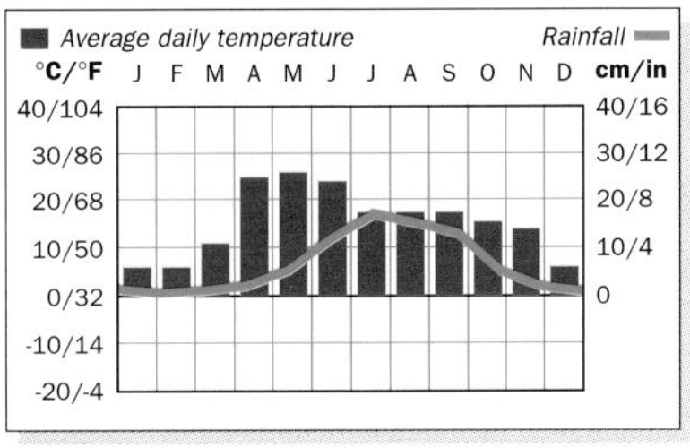
Average daily temperature
Rainfall
°C/°F
J F M A M J J A S O N D
cm/in
40/104
30/86
20/68
10/50
0/32
-10/14
-20/-4
40/16
30/12
20/8
10/4
0

The plateau and high mountains are warm for much of the year. The Pacific coast has a tropical climate.

TRANSPORTATION

Drive on right

Benito Juárez, Mexico City 21.7m passengers

658 ships 937,200 grt

THE TRANSPORTATION NETWORK

108,746 km (67,572 miles)

6429 km (3995 miles)

26,656 km (16,563 miles)

2900 km (1802 miles)

A privately financed $14 billion road network – some 6000 km (3730 miles) of toll roads – is seriously underused and a commercial failure. Regional travel is mainly by bus; the unreliable railroad is largely for freight. Plans to construct a new international airport serving Mexico City were abandoned in 2002 as local farmers staged violent protests against the implied acquisition of their lands.

TOURISM

Visitors : Population 1:5.5

18.7m visitors

Down 5% in 2003

MAIN TOURIST ARRIVALS

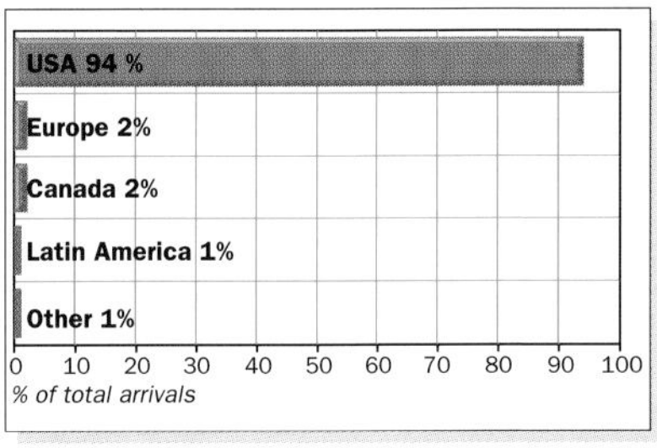
USA 94 %
Europe 2%
Canada 2%
Latin America 1%
Other 1%
0 10 20 30 40 50 60 70 80 90 100
% of total arrivals

Tourism employs around 5% of the workforce and is a major source of foreign exchange. Attractions include excellent beach resorts such as Acapulco on the Pacific coast, and the new resorts of the Peninsula de Yucatán on the Caribbean coast. Impressive coastal scenery, volcanoes, the Sierra Madre, and archaeological remains of Aztec and Mayan civilizations, designated as World Heritage sites, are major draws, as are the many Spanish colonial cities, such as Morelia and Guadalajara, which have remained virtually intact since their construction after the conquest.

UNITED STATES OF AMERICA
Tijuana
Mexicali
Ensenada
Ciudad Juárez
Isla Ángel de la Guarda
Isla del Tiburón
Hermosillo
Isla Cedros
Bahía Sebastián Vizcaíno
BAJA CALIFORNIA
Golfo de California
Chihuahua
BOLSÓN DE MAPIMÍ
ALTIPLANICIE
SIERRA MADRE OCCIDENTAL
SIERRA MADRE ORIENTAL
Ciudad Obregón
Nuevo Laredo
Monclova
Reynosa
Matamoros
Monterrey
Saltillo
Gómez Palacio
Torreón
Guasave
Los Mochis
Culiacán
La Paz
Durango
Ciudad Victoria
Mazatlán
Zacatecas
Tampico
San Luis Potosí
Aguascalientes
Tepic
Islas Marías
León
Guanajuato
Irapuato
Querétaro
Guadalajara
Puerto Vallarta
Lago de Chapala
Salamanca
Celaya
Pachuca
Poza Rica
Jalapa
MEXICO CITY
Morelia
Uruapan
Toluca
Cuernavaca
Puebla
Veracruz
Volcán Pico de Orizaba 5700m
Coatzacoalcos
Minatitlán
Villahermosa
ISTMO DE TEHUANTEPEC
Tuxtla Gutiérrez
Oaxaca
Acapulco
SIERRA MADRE DEL SUR
Golfo de Tehuantepec
Tapachula
GULF OF MEXICO
Bahía de Campeche
Campeche
Mérida
Cancún
Isla de Cozumel
Yucatan Channel
PENÍNSULA DE YUCATÁN
BELIZE
GUATEMALA
CARIBBEAN SEA
PACIFIC OCEAN
MEXICO
Total Area : 1 972 550 sq. km (761 602 sq. miles)
LAND HEIGHT
3000m/9843ft
2000m/6562ft
1000m/3281ft
500m/1640ft
200m/656ft
Sea Level
POPULATION
over 5 000 000
over 1 000 000
over 500 000
over 100 000
over 50 000
N
0 200 km
0 200 miles

M

PEOPLE

Pop. density medium

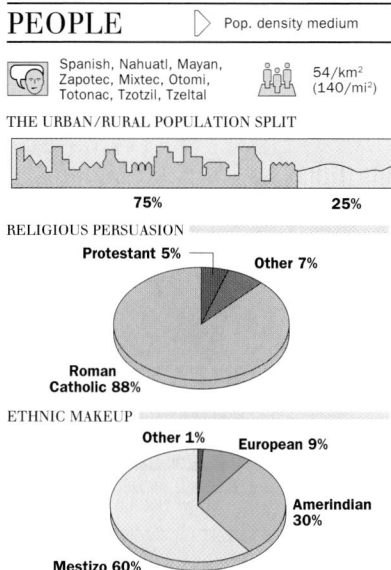

Spanish, Nahuatl, Mayan, Zapotec, Mixtec, Otomi, Totonac, Tzotzil, Tzeltal

54/km² (140/mi²)

THE URBAN/RURAL POPULATION SPLIT

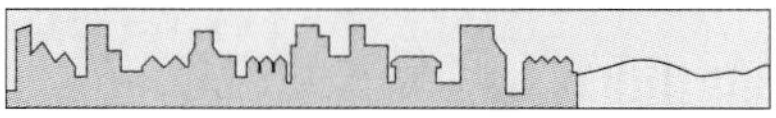
75%
25%

RELIGIOUS PERSUASION

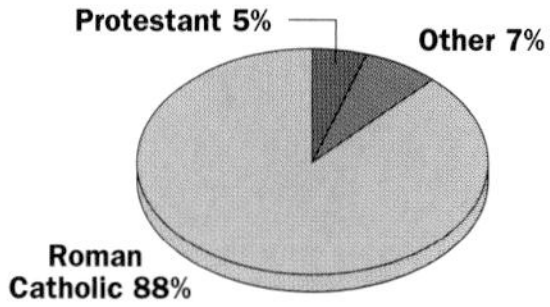
Protestant 5%
Other 7%
Roman Catholic 88%

ETHNIC MAKEUP

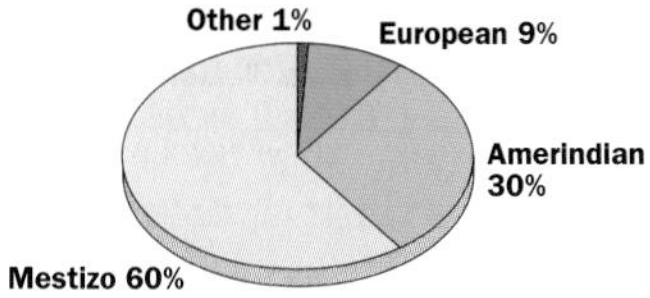
Other 1%
European 9%
Amerindian 30%
Mestizo 60%

While most Mexicans are *mestizo* (mixed race), it is Mexico's Amerindian culture which is promoted by the state. This obscures the fact that rural Amerindians are largely segregated from Hispanic society, a situation that dates back to the Spanish colonial period and which has only recently been seriously challenged. The 1994 Zapatista National Liberation Army (EZLN) guerrilla uprising in Chiapas was on behalf of Amerindian rights, and in protest against the poverty of landless Amerindians. President Vicente Fox promised to act, but the Indigenous Rights and Culture Bill, watered down by a hostile Congress and enacted in 2001, was rejected by the EZLN and all the main indigenous groups.

The small black community, which is concentrated along the eastern coast, is well integrated.

As in much of Latin America, men retain their dominance in both the commercial and political spheres.

POPULATION AGE BREAKDOWN

Female
Age
Male
0.5%
80+
0.4%
2.9%
60–79
2.7%
7.4%
40–59
7.1%
16.7%
20–39
15.5%
23.2%
0–19
23.6%

% of population by age group

WORLD AFFAIRS

Joined UN in 1945

G15 NAFTA OECD OAS RG

NAFTA has bonded the economies of Mexico and the US. Progress on economic migrants remains stalled, but long-running disputes with the US on tuna and trucking are all but resolved. Unable to compete against heavily subsidized US farmers, far poorer Mexican producers have staged border protests and demanded protection, especially since the lifting of most trade tariffs on agricultural products in 2003. The Mexican government has promised renegotiation, but the US and Canada remain strongly opposed. Tariffs on Mexican beans and corn are to be removed in 2008.

Under Fox, traditional support for Cuba has diminished in favor of the US. Mexico has free trade agreements with 32 countries, as well as with the EU and EFTA, and competes with Brazil to play a leading negotiating role for Latin America in the formation of a Free Trade Area of the Americas (FTAA) due to be signed in 2005.

AID

Recipient

$136m (receipts) Up 81% in 2002

In 2002 the IDB made its biggest loan – $1 billion – to support a six-year antipoverty project in Mexico. European and US NGOs provide assistance.

POLITICS

Multiparty elections

L. House 2003/2006
U. House 2000/2006

President Vicente Fox

AT THE LAST ELECTION

Chamber of Deputies 500 seats

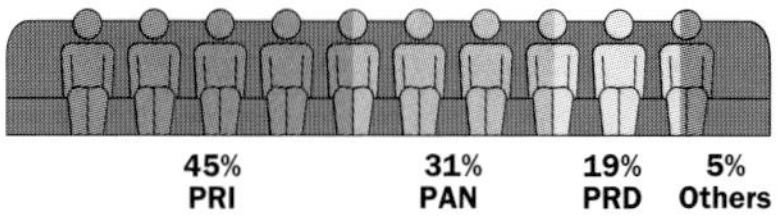
45% PRI
31% PAN
19% PRD
5% Others

PRI = Institutional Revolutionary Party **PAN** = National Action Party **PRD** = Party of the Democratic Revolution **PAN–PVEM** = Alliance for Change (PAN and Green Party) **PRD–PT** = Alliance for Mexico (PRD and Labor Party)

Senate of the Republic 128 seats

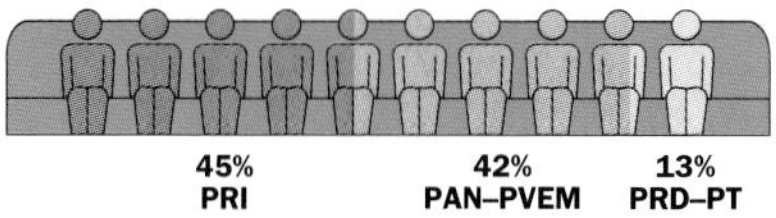
45% PRI
42% PAN–PVEM
13% PRD–PT

Mexico was a multiparty democracy in name only until 1997; reforms culminated in a PAN presidency in 2000.

PROFILE

The PRI dominated Mexico from 1929. The strength of opposition parties grew during the 1990s, and, after grudging electoral reform, the PRI lost its monopoly on power in 1997. After the 2000 elections the PAN was the largest party in the Chamber of Deputies, but it lacked an overall majority and was overtaken once more by the PRI in the 2003 midterm poll.

MAIN POLITICAL ISSUES

President Fox's administration

The first half of President Fox's six-year term (2000–2006) was uneven. His failure to consult and to build consensus, coupled with PRI opposition in Congress, resulted in key policy failures, notably in the areas of electricity, telecommunications, and fiscal reform. Promises on job creation went unmet but government accountability and transparency improved. An economic downturn was also seen off without the specter of hyperinflation. Fox's position was made all the more difficult when the PRI emerged as the victors in the July 2003 congressional midterm elections.

Future of the PRI

Election defeats in the late 1990s left the PRI rudderless and faction-ridden. It turned to hard-liner Roberto Madrazo, party leader from 2002, to translate public disillusionment with the PAN into popular support for the PRI.

***Vicente Fox**, elected president in 2000, ending 70 years of PRI dominance.*

***Subcomandante Marcos**, Zapatista National Liberation Army (EZLN) leader.*

CHRONOLOGY

The Aztec kingdom of Montezuma II was defeated in war by the Spaniard, Hernán Cortés, in 1521. By 1546, the Spaniards had discovered large silver mines at Zacatecas. Mexico, then known as New Spain, became a key part of the Spanish colonial empire.

- **1810** Fr. Miguel Hidalgo leads abortive rising against Spanish.
- **1821** Spanish viceroy forced to leave by Agustín de Iturbide.
- **1822** Federal Republic established.
- **1823** Texas opened to US immigration.
- **1829** Spanish military expedition fails to regain control.
- **1836** US is first country to recognize Mexico's independence. Spain follows suit. Texas declares its independence from Mexico.
- **1846** War breaks out with US.
- **1848** Loses modern-day New Mexico, Arizona, Nevada, Utah, California, and part of Colorado.
- **1858–1861** War of Reform won by anticlerical Liberals.
- **1862** France, Britain, and Spain launch military expedition.

M

CHRONOLOGY *continued*

- **1863** French troops capture Mexico City. Maximilian of Austria established as Mexican emperor.
- **1867** Mexico recaptured by Benito Juárez. Maximilian shot.
- **1876** Porfirio Díaz president. Economic growth; rail system built.
- **1901** First year of oil production.
- **1910–1920** Epic Revolution provoked by excessive exploitation by foreign companies and desire for land reform. 250,000 killed.
- **1911** Díaz overthrown by Francisco Madero. Guerrilla war breaks out in north. Emilio Zapata leads peasant revolt in the south.
- **1913** Madero murdered.
- **1917** New constitution limits power of Roman Catholic Church. Minerals and subsoil rights reserved for the nation.
- **1926–1929** Cristero rebellion led by militant Catholic priests.
- **1929** National Revolutionary Party (later PRI) formed.
- **1934** Gen. Cárdenas president. Land reform accelerated, cooperative farms established, railroads nationalized, and US and UK oil companies expelled.
- **1940s** US war effort helps Mexican economy to grow.
- **1970** Accelerating population growth reaches 3% a year.
- **1982** Mexico declares it cannot repay its foreign debt of over $800 billion. IMF insists on economic reforms to reschedule the debt.
- **1984** Government contravenes constitution by relaxing laws on foreign investment.
- **1985** Earthquake in Mexico City. Official death toll 7000. Economic cost estimated at $425 million.
- **1988** Carlos Salinas de Gortari, minister of planning during the earthquake, elected president.
- **1990** Privatization program begins.
- **1994–1995** Guerrilla rebellion in southern Chiapas state brutally suppressed by army: 100 dead. Mexico joins NAFTA. Luis Colosio, PRI presidential candidate, murdered. Ernesto Zedillo replaces him and is elected. Economic crisis.
- **1997–1999** PRI's monopoly on power in Congress ended. Banks bailed out.
- **2000** July, PAN wins presidency and elections, ending 70 years of PRI rule. December, President Vicente Fox takes office.
- **2001** EZLN guerrillas and supporters make 16-day motorcade from Chiapas to Mexico City to push for indigenous rights law.
- **2002** Hard-liner Roberto Madrazo elected PRI leader.
- **2003** PRI gain in midterm elections.

M

DEFENSE

Compulsory military service

$5.32bn

Down 6% in 2002

The military has, on the whole, avoided direct interference in politics and has no ambitions beyond Mexico's borders. The army mainly defends internal security; border control is handled by the police. The military is now closely involved in antinarcotics efforts. Most arms procurement is from the US.

The Zapatista rebellion in Chiapas in 1994 elicited a brutal response from the army, acting on PRI orders. The increasing militarization of the small state over the next six years hindered the peace process and led to a proliferation of paramilitaries, with the tacit blessing of the local PRI, who were blamed by human rights groups for the massacre of Amerindians. The PAN government has withdrawn some forces from key areas.

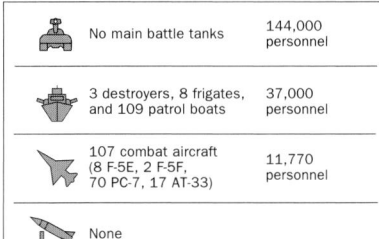

MEXICAN ARMED FORCES

No main battle tanks	144,000 personnel
3 destroyers, 8 frigates, and 109 patrol boats	37,000 personnel
107 combat aircraft (8 F-5E, 2 F-5F, 70 PC-7, 17 AT-33)	11,770 personnel
None	

ECONOMICS

Inflation 18% p.a. (1990–2001)

$597bn

11.53 Mexican pesos (10.42)

SCORE CARD

World GNP Ranking	9th
GNP per Capita	$5920
Balance of Payments	–$14.1bn
Inflation	5%
Unemployment	2%

EXPORTS

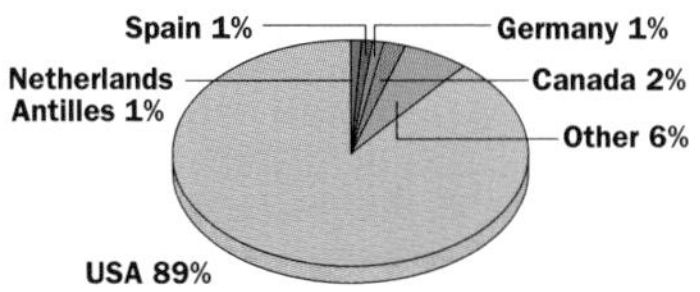
Spain 1%
Germany 1%
Netherlands Antilles 1%
Canada 2%
Other 6%
USA 89%

IMPORTS

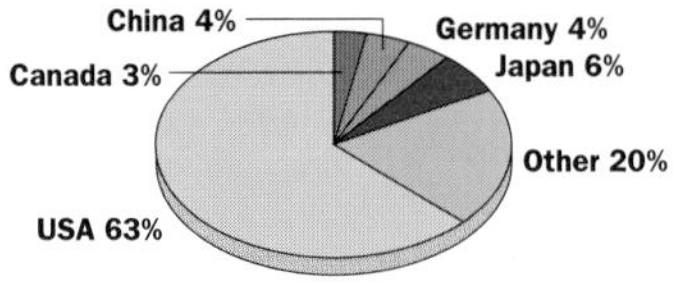
China 4%
Germany 4%
Canada 3%
Japan 6%
Other 20%
USA 63%

Strengths

Global oil producer, with substantial reserves. Extensive mineral resources. Strong foreign direct investment. Diversification of exports. NAFTA membership. Low overheads.

Weaknesses

Debt burden. Vulnerable currency. Corruption. Affected by US slowdown. Oil price fluctuations. Weak tax system.

Profile

While in power, the PRI effectively ran the economy. The debt crisis of the 1980s, however, forced privatizations. The 1994 peso crisis needed a US-led $20 billion international bailout and resulted in a severe slump. The Zedillo government launched tough reforms, but a global loss of confidence in emerging markets affected growth. Tighter fiscal management was rewarded by 2000, when investor confidence improved. The Fox government's tight fiscal and monetary stance won approval from the IMF and major credit agencies. Social relief pledges, however, went unfulfilled as the export-led economy echoed the slowdown in the US from 2001. Proposals to extend sales tax to medicines and food, and talk of encouraging investment in the energy sector met stiff public opposition in 2003.

ECONOMIC PERFORMANCE INDICATOR

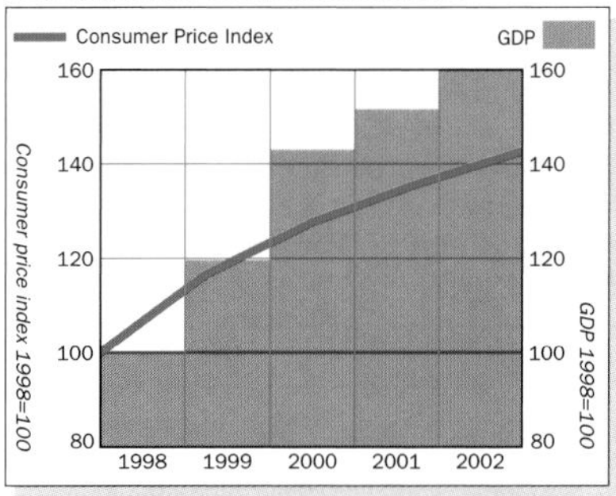
Consumer Price Index
GDP
160
140
120
100
80
Consumer price index 1998=100
GDP 1998=100
1998
1999
2000
2001
2002

MEXICO : MAJOR BUSINESSES

Food processing
Vehicle assembly
Petrochemicals
Oil refining
Computers
Silver mining
Electronics
Brewing
Textiles
Tijuana
Ciudad Juárez
Monterrey
Reynosa
Tampico
Minatitlán
Durango
Guadalajara
Salamanca
Mexico City
0 400 km
0 400 miles
* significant multinational ownership

RESOURCES

Electric power 45.7m kW

1.47m tonnes

3.79m b/d (reserves 16bn barrels)

30.8m cattle, 18.1m pigs, 9.5m goats, 540m chickens

Oil, gas, gold, silver, copper, coal, fluorite, mercury, antimony

ELECTRICITY GENERATION

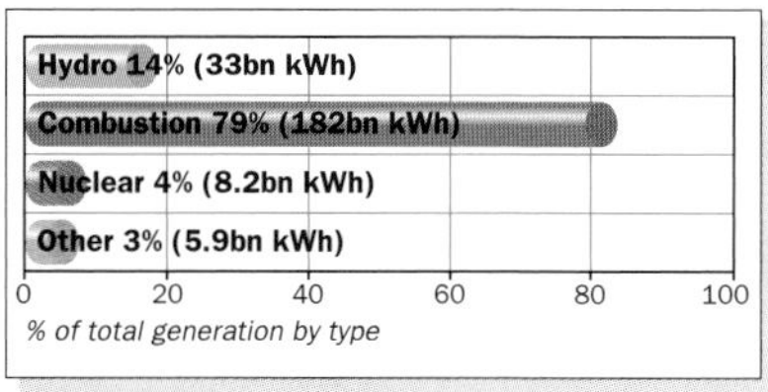

Hydro 14% (33bn kWh)
Combustion 79% (182bn kWh)
Nuclear 4% (8.2bn kWh)
Other 3% (5.9bn kWh)
0
20
40
60
80
100
% of total generation by type

MEXICO : LAND USE

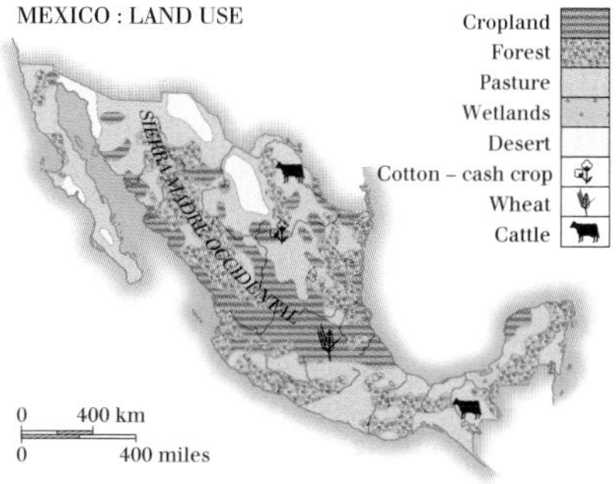

Cropland
Forest
Pasture
Wetlands
Desert
Cotton – cash crop
Wheat
Cattle
SIERRA MADRE OCCIDENTAL
0 400 km
0 400 miles

Mexico is one of the largest oil exporters outside OPEC. Most oil production comes from offshore drilling platforms in the Gulf of Mexico. The industry is state-owned and state-run by PEMEX, the world's fifth-largest oil company, employing 120,000 people. Plans to privatize PEMEX have provoked serious social unrest, and proposed sell-offs and deregulation remain politically highly sensitive. Despite its oil reserves, Mexico has embarked on a nuclear power program and projects to modernize the national electricity grid and boost natural gas production to overcome an energy crisis.

ENVIRONMENT

Sustainability rank: 92nd

10% (7% partially protected)

4.3 tonnes per capita

ENVIRONMENTAL TREATIES

Yes Yes Yes
Yes Yes Yes

Mexico City, largely unplanned, struggles to accommodate around 20 million inhabitants as the absence of environmental controls contributes to perhaps the world's worst air quality and waste problems. PEMEX (the state petroleum company) stands accused of massive pollution. *Maquiladoras* – assembly plants on the Mexico–US border – have no effective environmental controls and are usually surrounded by slums. Environmentalists oppose the intense development of tourism along the coast and are concerned about high rates of deforestation.

MEDIA

TV ownership medium

Daily newspaper circulation 94 per 1000 people

PUBLISHING AND BROADCAST MEDIA

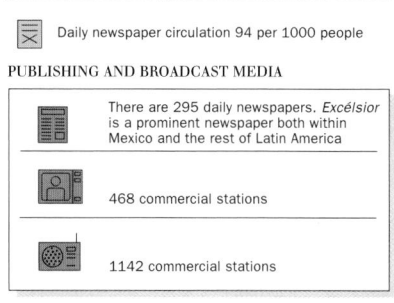

There are 295 daily newspapers. *Excélsior* is a prominent newspaper both within Mexico and the rest of Latin America

468 commercial stations

1142 commercial stations

There has been greater media freedom since 2000. The Televisa broadcasting empire faces growing competition.

CRIME

Death penalty not used in practice

154,765 prisoners

Crime is rising

CRIME RATES

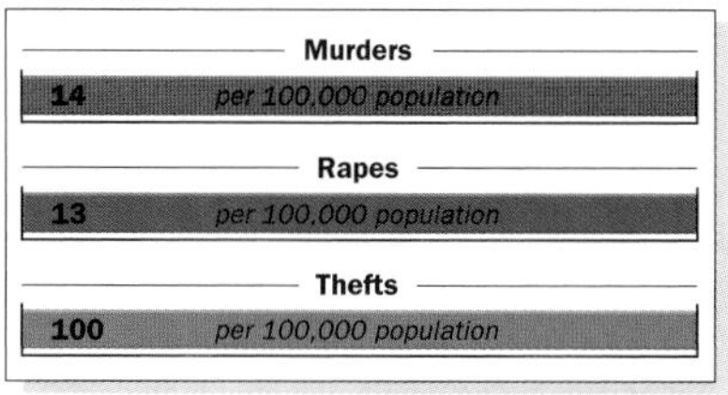

Murders
14 per 100,000 population
Rapes
13 per 100,000 population
Thefts
100 per 100,000 population

Northern Mexico is a major center for narcotics shipments to the US. Antidrugs police are specifically accused of collusion by the US; police corruption is a perennial issue. Guns are rife.

EDUCATION

School leaving age: 14

91%

2.15m students

THE EDUCATION SYSTEM

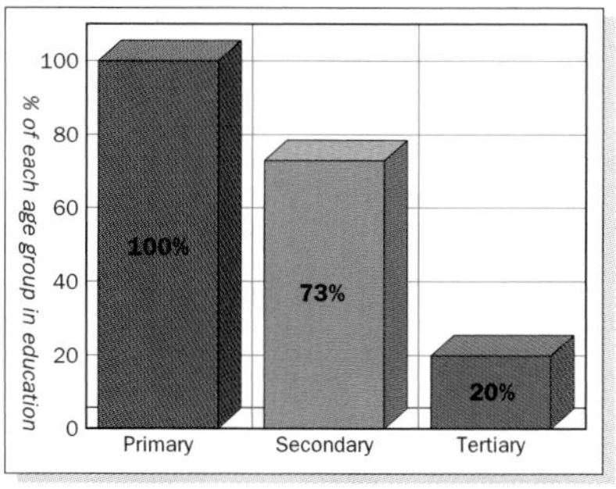

% of each age group in education
100
80
60
40
20
0
100%
73%
20%
Primary
Secondary
Tertiary

Public education, officially compulsory for the first six years, is underfunded and rural provision is poor. The system is a mixture of the French and US models. There is a well-developed public university system.

HEALTH

Welfare state health benefits

1 per 667 people

Cancers, diabetes, heart and respiratory diseases, accidents

The national health care system is basic and badly underfunded. A five-year reform program launched in 1995 focused more on management infrastructure and less on provision. Mexico has a good reputation for surgery and dentistry, but this is mostly in the private sector, which is itself fragmented. The rich also go to the US for treatment.

SPENDING

GDP/cap. increase

CONSUMPTION AND SPENDING

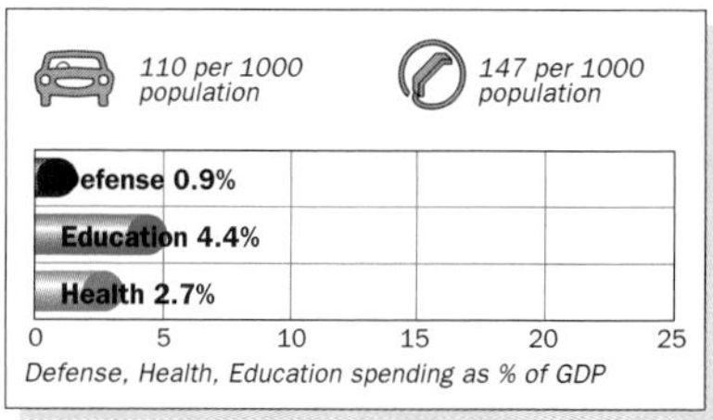

110 per 1000 population
147 per 1000 population
Defense 0.9%
Education 4.4%
Health 2.7%
0
5
10
15
20
25
Defense, Health, Education spending as % of GDP

Mexico has enormous wealth disparities. The World Bank estimates that 45 million Mexicans live in poverty, surviving on less than $2 a day, and a quarter of them struggle in extreme poverty, coping on half that amount. There is little social mobility; the old Spanish families retain their hold on institutions. In the past, the wealthy did not generally pay taxes and often benefited from the large state machine. Tax evasion remains a serious problem.

Rural Amerindians are probably the most disadvantaged group. In the last decade, poverty has forced them into city slums to work in factories or *maquiladoras*, where conditions and pay are poor. The 1994 Chiapas rebellion was fed by demands for more land and more assistance in farming it. The flow of poor rural migrants to the US stems largely from the need to subsidize families back home.

WORLD RANKING

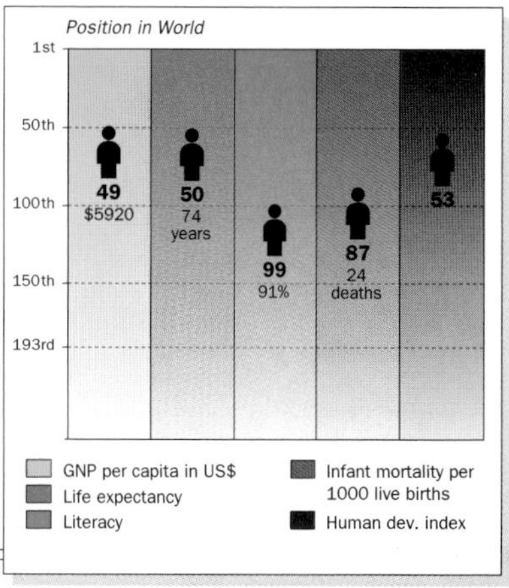

Position in World
1st
50th
100th
150th
193rd
49
$5920
50
74
years
99
91%
87
24
deaths
53
GNP per capita in US$
Life expectancy
Literacy
Infant mortality per 1000 live births
Human dev. index

M

MICRONESIA

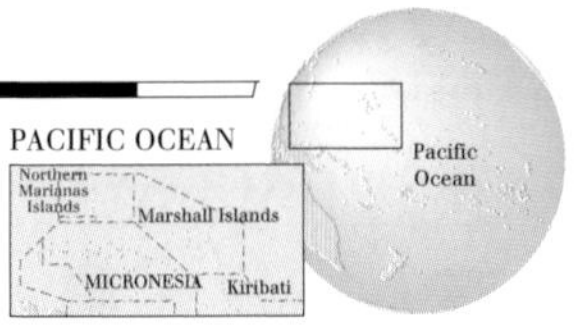
PACIFIC OCEAN
Northern Marianas Islands
Marshall Islands
MICRONESIA
Kiribati
Pacific Ocean

OFFICIAL NAME: Federated States of Micronesia **CAPITAL:** Palikir (Pohnpei Island)
POPULATION: 108,143 **CURRENCY:** US dollar **OFFICIAL LANGUAGE:** English

1986 | 1986 | May 10 | FSM | +10 to +11 | +691 | .fm

SITUATED IN THE PACIFIC OCEAN, the Federated States of Micronesia (FSM) encompasses all the Caroline Islands except Palau. It is composed of four island cluster states: Pohnpei, Kosrae, Chuuk, and Yap. The FSM was formerly under US rule as part of the UN Trust Territory of the Pacific Islands. An agreement which granted internal sovereignty in free association with the US became operational in 1986, and the Trust was formally dissolved in 1990. The islands continue to receive considerable aid from the US.

CLIMATE

Tropical oceanic

WEATHER CHART FOR PALIKIR

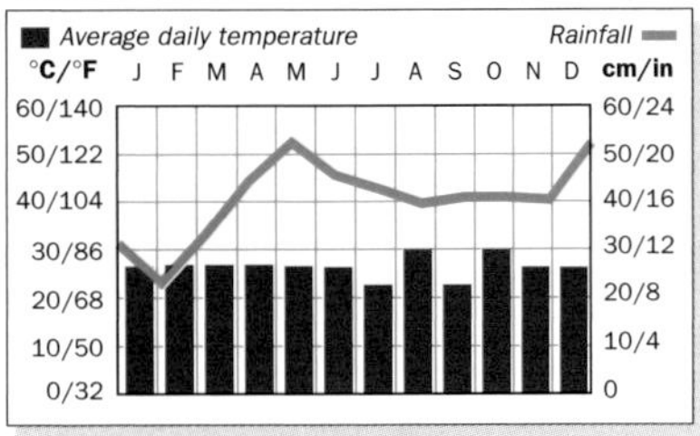
Average daily temperature
Rainfall
°C/°F J F M A M J J A S O N D cm/in
60/140
50/122
40/104
30/86
20/68
10/50
0/32
60/24
50/20
40/16
30/12
20/8
10/4
0

The islands are humid and fairly hot all year round, and the daily temperature range is small. Rainfall is abundant.

TRANSPORTATION

Drive on right

Pohnpei, Kolonia 58,029 passengers

19 ships 13,400 grt

THE TRANSPORTATION NETWORK

43 km (27 miles)	None
None	None

The inauguration in 2000 of flights by a Boeing 737 opened the way for greater air traffic between the islands. Shipping is mainly used for bulk cargoes and copra. Some island roads are surfaced with coral.

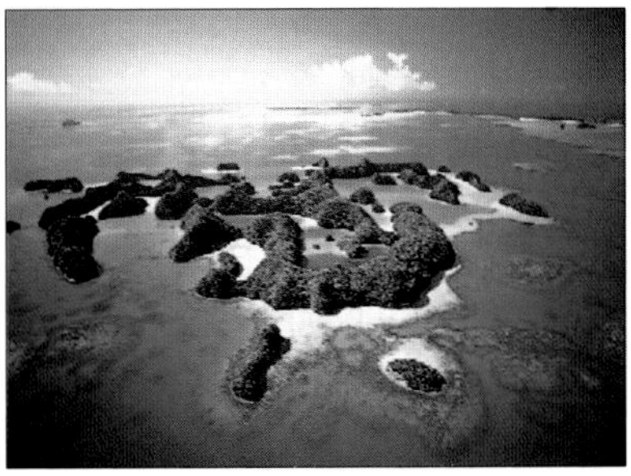

Micronesia, aerial view of rock islands. *Like many Pacific states, Micronesia fears rising sea levels as a result of global warming.*

TOURISM

Visitors : Population 1:5.7

19,000 visitors

Up 27% in 2002

MAIN TOURIST ARRIVALS

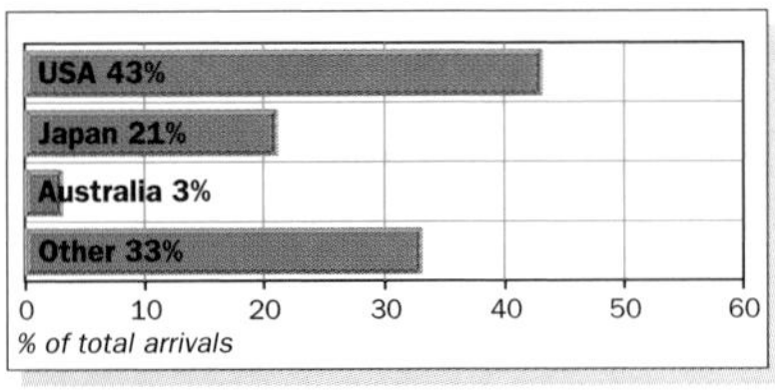
USA 43%
Japan 21%
Australia 3%
Other 33%
0
10
20
30
40
50
60
% of total arrivals

Outlying islands remain untouched and unspoiled. Chuuk's underwater war wreckage and Kosrae's beaches attract visitors. Lack of infrastructure is hindering the growth of tourism.

PEOPLE

Pop. density medium

Trukese, Pohnpeian, Mortlockese, Kosraean, English

154/km² (399/mi²)

THE URBAN/RURAL POPULATION SPLIT

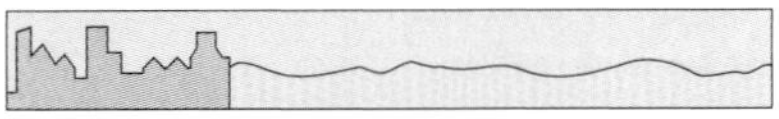
29%
71%

RELIGIOUS PERSUASION

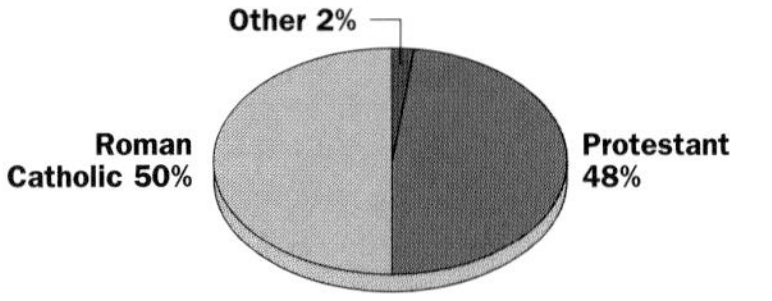
Other 2%
Roman Catholic 50%
Protestant 48%

The Micronesians are physically, linguistically, and culturally diverse. Melanesians live on Yap, and Polynesians occupy southwestern atolls in Pohnpei state. Most islanders live without electricity or running water, and many are effectively recipients of US welfare. Society is traditionally matrilineal.

POLITICS

Nonparty elections

2003/2005

President Joseph J. Urusemal

AT THE LAST ELECTION

Congress 14 seats

There are no political parties. Ten senators are directly elected for a two-year term and four "at-large" senators (one from each state) are elected for a four-year term

The executive is drawn from the "at-large" senators, but the power of the traditional chiefs remains very strong. The country's relationship with the US is vital and the negotiation of the new Compact of Free Association – which was agreed in 2003 – dominated recent politics. The Faichuk islands, in the western corner of the Chuuk Lagoon, have pressed for the status of a full state, or even independence, complaining of long-term economic neglect.

MICRONESIA

Total Area : 702 sq. km (271 sq. miles)

POPULATION

• under 10 000

LAND HEIGHT

100m/328ft

Sea Level

0 200 km

0 200 miles

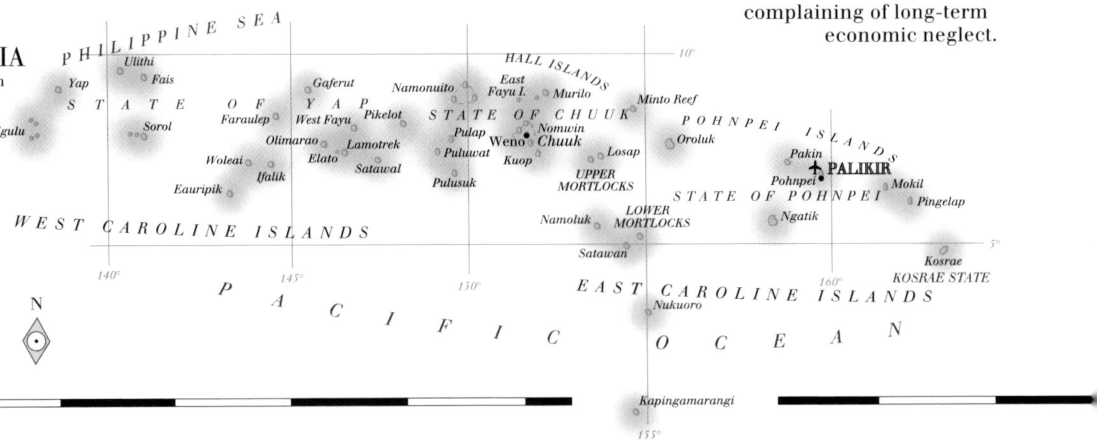
PHILIPPINE SEA
Ulithi
Fais
Yap
STATE OF YAP
Ngulu
Sorol
Gaferut
Faraulep
West Fayu
Pikelot
Olimarao
Lamotrek
Elato
Satawal
Woleai
Ifalik
Eauripik
Namonuito
HALL ISLANDS
East Fayu I.
Murilo
STATE OF CHUUK
Minto Reef
Pulap
Nomwin
Weno
Chuuk
Puluwat
Kuop
Losap
Pulusuk
UPPER MORTLOCKS
LOWER MORTLOCKS
Namoluk
Satawan
POHNPEI ISLANDS
Oroluk
Pakin
PALIKIR
Pohnpei
Mokil
Pingelap
Ngatik
STATE OF POHNPEI
Kosrae
KOSRAE STATE
WEST CAROLINE ISLANDS
EAST CAROLINE ISLANDS
Nukuoro
PACIFIC OCEAN
Kapingamarangi
140°
145°
150°
155°
160°
10°
5°
N

WORLD AFFAIRS

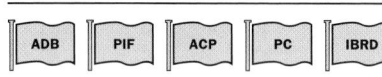

Joined UN in 1991

ADB | PIF | ACP | PC | IBRD

Micronesia's most important relationship is with the US, which administered the islands from 1947 as part of the UN Trust Territory of the Pacific Islands. Under the Compact of Free Association, the US has control over the FSM's foreign and defense policies. Alternative financial assistance is an increasing priority as the new 20-year Compact, which was agreed in May 2003, will not be renewed. Japan is also important, the Tokyo government providing aid, and the FSM has recently cultivated strong links with China.

AID

Recipient

$112m (receipts)

Down 19% in 2002

The US is by far the biggest donor. In 2004 it approved federal disaster aid when Yap was devastated by a typhoon.

DEFENSE

No compulsory military service

US is responsible for defense

Not applicable

Defense is entirely in the hands of the US. Airstrips in the FSM were used by the US in the Vietnam War.

ECONOMICS

Inflation 3% p.a. (1990–2001)

$240m

Currency is US dollar

SCORE CARD

❑ World GNP Ranking	181st
❑ GNP Per Capita	$1970
❑ Balance of Payments	$9m
❑ Inflation	–1.1%
❑ Unemployment	3%

Strengths

Access to US economy, especially for garment manufacture, through preferential trading rights. Large construction industry. Tourism, fishing, and copra production. US strategic interest in Micronesia, and US budget subsidies.

Weaknesses

Lack of resources. Dependence on US for imports, especially for fuel. Heavy indebtedness. Acute shortage of water limits development potential. High levels of underemployment.

EXPORTS

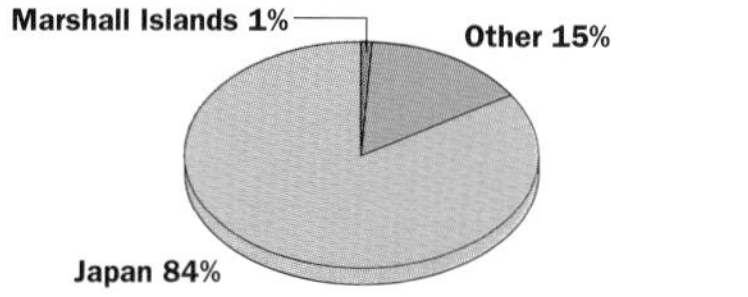
Marshall Islands 1%
Other 15%
Japan 84%

IMPORTS

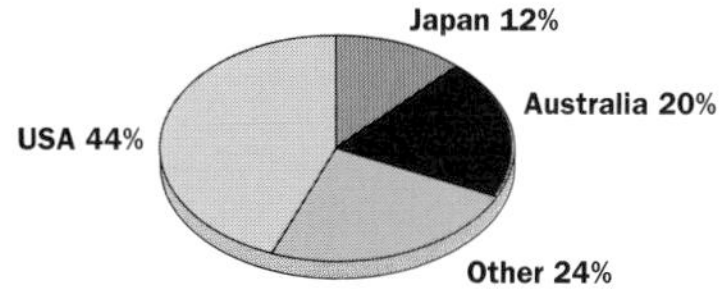
Japan 12%
Australia 20%
USA 44%
Other 24%

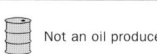

RESOURCES

Not available

18,062 tonnes

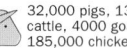

Not an oil producer

32,000 pigs, 13,900 cattle, 4000 goats, 185,000 chickens

None

The FSM is entirely dependent on external sources for its energy supply. Almost all electricity is produced by small diesel generators. The main resources are copra and valuable fish stocks, especially tuna.

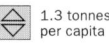

ENVIRONMENT

Not available

None

1.3 tonnes per capita

The FSM does not face pollution on the scale of that in the neighboring Marshall Islands. However, an oil leak in 2001 from a World War II wreck endangered wildlife on Yap. Chuuk suffers serious droughts. The growth of marine-based tourism is monitored by the South Pacific Environment Program, which aims to promote sustainable development.

MEDIA

TV ownership low

There are no daily newspapers

PUBLISHING AND BROADCAST MEDIA

There are no daily newspapers. *The National Union* is a popular biweekly

4 services: 1 state-owned, 3 independent

3 services: 1 state-owned, 2 independent

Press freedoms have not been infringed since the strongly criticized expulsion of a Canadian journalist in 1997.

CRIME

No death penalty

39 prisoners

Little change from year to year

Crime is rare and the outlying islands are crime-free. Some alcohol-related assault occurs on Chuuk.

EDUCATION

School leaving age: 13

81%

1510 students

Education is compulsory (for seven years) from the age of six. Most university students are supported by US grants and a large number attend US colleges.

CHRONOLOGY

The Caroline Islands were first colonized by the Spanish. Sold to Germany in 1899, the islands were occupied by Japan from 1914 and served as an important base in World War II. US control of the islands began in 1945.

- ❑ **1947** UN Trust Territory of the Pacific Islands established.
- ❑ **1986** Independence. Compact of Free Association with US operational.
- ❑ **1990** Official termination of trusteeship agreement.
- ❑ **1991** Joins UN.
- ❑ **2001** Submerged remains of USS *Mississinewa* causes oil leak in Yap.
- ❑ **2003** Joseph Urusemal elected president. New Compact agreed.

HEALTH

Welfare state health benefits

1 per 1667 people

Cerebrovascular, heart, and intestinal diseases

Basic health care is accessible to all. WHO has warned of an obesity epidemic; in 2004, 80% of adults were overweight, and one in eight had diabetes.

SPENDING

GDP/cap. decrease

CONSUMPTION AND SPENDING

No data

87 per 1000 population

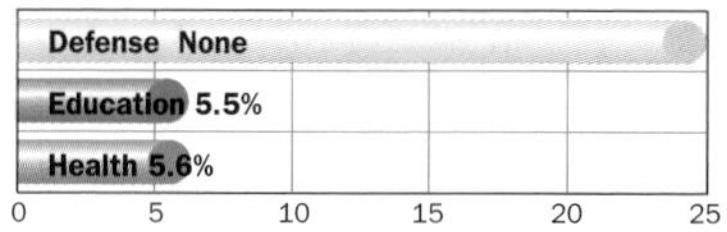
Defense None
Education 5.5%
Health 5.6%
0
5
10
15
20
25

Defense, Health, Education spending as % of GDP

The gap between rich and poor is increasing as Micronesia's businessmen and local officials exploit US aid donations.

WORLD RANKING

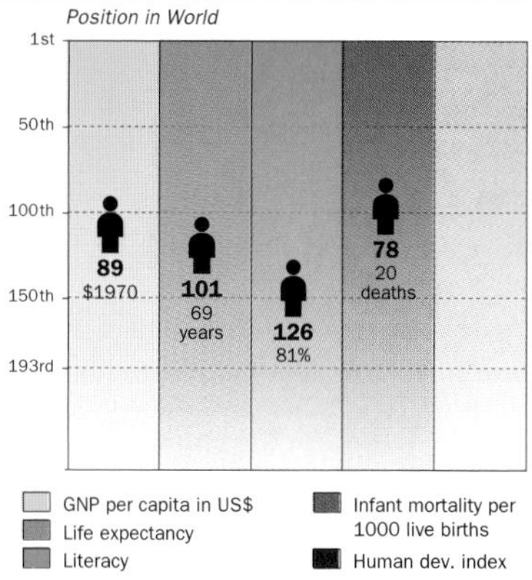
Position in World
1st
50th
100th
150th
193rd
89
$1970
101
69 years
126
81%
78
20 deaths
GNP per capita in US$
Life expectancy
Literacy
Infant mortality per 1000 live births
Human dev. index

M

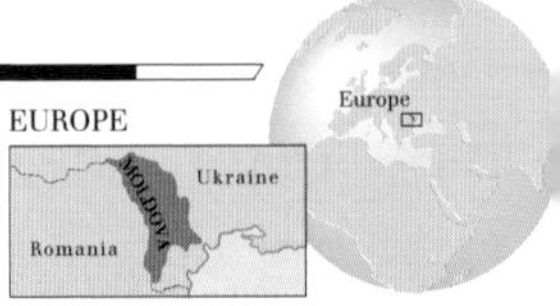
Europe
EUROPE
Ukraine
MOLDOVA
Romania

MOLDOVA

OFFICIAL NAME: Republic of Moldova **CAPITAL:** Chisinau
POPULATION: 4.3 million **CURRENCY:** Moldovan leu **OFFICIAL LANGUAGE:** Moldovan

1991 | 1991 | Aug 27 | MD | +2 | +373 | .md

MOSTLY UNDULATING steppe country, Moldova is the most densely populated of the former Soviet republics. Once a part of Romania, it was incorporated into the Soviet Union in 1940. Independence in 1991 brought with it the expectation that Moldova would be reunited with Romania. In a 1994 plebiscite, however, Moldovans voted against the proposal. Most of Moldova's population is engaged in intensive agriculture.

Agricultural landscape. *Warm summers and even rainfall are ideal for cereal and fruit farming. Moldova is famous for its wine.*

CLIMATE

Continental

WEATHER CHART FOR CHISINAU

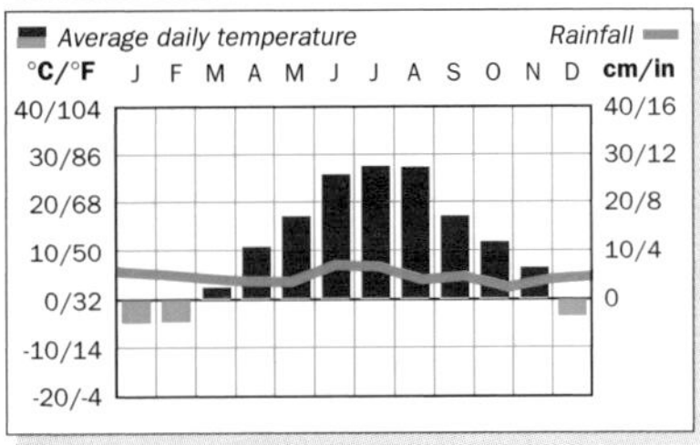
Average daily temperature
Rainfall
°C/°F
J F M A M J J A S O N D
cm/in
40/104
30/86
20/68
10/50
0/32
-10/14
-20/-4
40/16
30/12
20/8
10/4
0

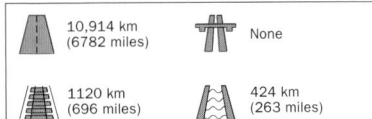

Warm summers, mild winters, and moderate rainfall give Moldova an ideal climate for cultivation.

TRANSPORTATION

Drive on right

Chisinau International 339,485 passengers

Small Black Sea fleet

THE TRANSPORTATION NETWORK

10,914 km (6782 miles)

None

1120 km (696 miles)

424 km (263 miles)

The transportation infrastructure is to be part of a planned "Transport Corridor Europe–Caucasus–Asia" (TRACECA).

TOURISM

Visitors : Population 1:182

23,598 visitors

Up 17% in 2003

MAIN TOURIST ARRIVALS

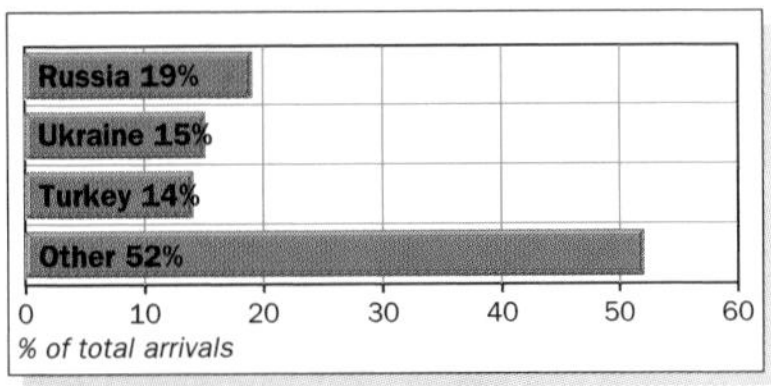
Russia 19%
Ukraine 15%
Turkey 14%
Other 52%
0
10
20
30
40
50
60
% of total arrivals

Few tourists go to Moldova, though some visitors to Romania do combine the two. Hopes for the expansion of tourism focus on vineyards and underground wine vault "streets" as the main attractions.

PEOPLE

Pop. density medium

Moldovan, Ukrainian, Russian

128/km² (330/mi²)

THE URBAN/RURAL POPULATION SPLIT

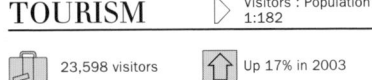

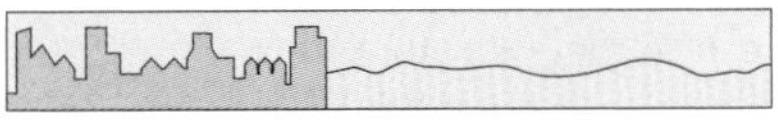
42%
58%

ETHNIC MAKEUP

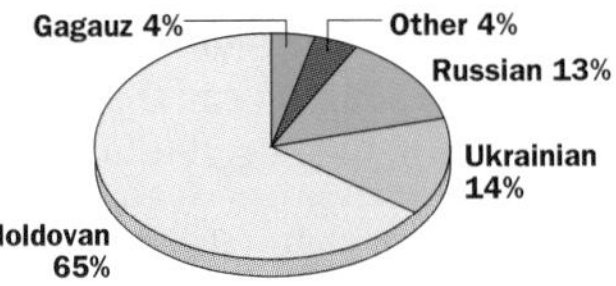
Gagauz 4%
Other 4%
Russian 13%
Ukrainian 14%
Moldovan 65%

Moldovans are ethnically identical to Romanians. There are 153,000 Gagauz (Orthodox Christian Turks) in the south, and a population of mixed Russian–Moldovan–Ukrainian parentage on the eastern bank of the Dniester.

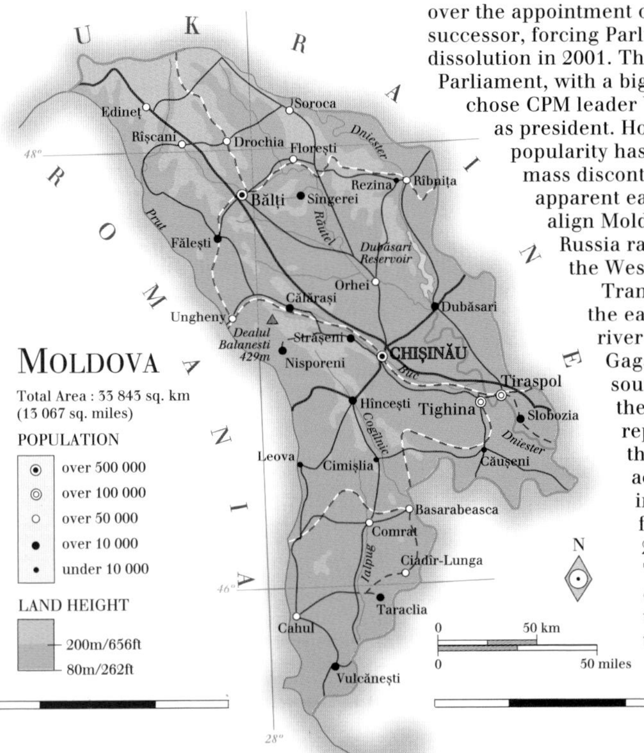
UKRAINE
ROMANIA
Edineț
Soroca
Rîșcani
Drochia
Florești
Rezina
Ribnița
Bălți
Sîngerei
Prut
Răutel
Dubăsari Reservoir
Fălești
Orhei
Călărași
Dubăsari
Ungheny
Dealul Balanesti 429m
Strășeni
Nisporeni
CHIȘINĂU
Bîc
Tiraspol
Hîncești
Tighina
Slobozia
Cogîlnic
Dniester
Leova
Cimișlia
Căușeni
Basarabeasca
Comrat
Ialpug
Ciadir-Lunga
Taraclia
Cahul
Vulcănești
48°
46°
28°
N
0 50 km
0 50 miles
MOLDOVA
Total Area : 33 843 sq. km (13 067 sq. miles)
POPULATION
over 500 000
over 100 000
over 50 000
over 10 000
under 10 000
LAND HEIGHT
200m/656ft
80m/262ft

POLITICS

Multiparty elections

2001/2005

President Vladimir Voronin

AT THE LAST ELECTION

Parliament 101 seats

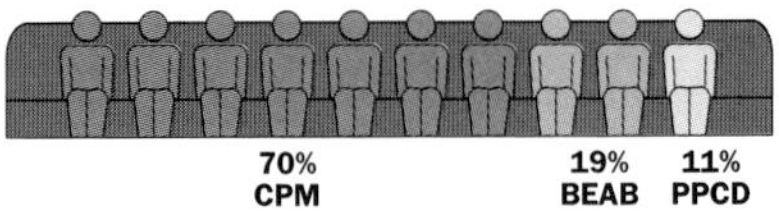
70% CPM
19% BEAB
11% PPCD

CPM = Communist Party of Moldova
BEAB = Electoral Bloc Braghis Alliance
PPCD = Christian-Democratic People's Party

Moldova declared its independence in 1991. Reformist Petru Lucinschi was elected president in 1996 but faced stiff opposition from the increasingly powerful left: the revived CPM won most seats in the 1998 elections. Parliament ended direct presidential elections in 2000, but deadlock ensued over the appointment of Lucinschi's successor, forcing Parliament's dissolution in 2001. The new Parliament, with a big CPM majority, chose CPM leader Vladimir Voronin as president. However, the left's popularity has faltered, with mass discontent over its apparent eagerness to align Moldova with Russia rather than the West.

Transdniestria (on the eastern bank of the river Dniester) and Gagauzia (in the south) declared themselves to be republics in 1990, though Gagauzia accepted autonomy in 1994. Tensions flared in 2004 when Transdniestria closed schools that were using the Latin script.

M

WORLD AFFAIRS

Joined UN in 1992

BSEC CE CIS EAPC OSCE

Moldova has joined NATO's Partnership for Peace program but retains close links to Russia. Ties with countries in the Black Sea Economic Zone are being developed. The creation of a free economic zone near the mouth of the Danube is under discussion. The EU has imposed travel restrictions on Transdniestrian separatists.

AID

Recipient

$142m (receipts) — Up 16% in 2002

The World Bank resumed lending in 2002, granting $30 million. The US, EU member states, and the IMF are also important sources of aid.

DEFENSE

Compulsory military service

$151m — Up 3% in 2002

In 1999 plans were announced to cut army personnel by 30%; military service has been reduced. In 2003 the Transdniestrian authorities finally permitted the full withdrawal of Russian forces.

ECONOMICS

Inflation 103% p.a. (1990–2001)

$1.68bn — 11.9 Moldovan lei (14.1)

SCORE CARD

- ❑ WORLD GNP RANKING........................145th
- ❑ GNP PER CAPITA..............................$460
- ❑ BALANCE OF PAYMENTS.....................–$109m
- ❑ INFLATION..5.1%
- ❑ UNEMPLOYMENT..................................8%

STRENGTHS

Agriculture (wine, tobacco, and cotton) and food processing. Signs of economic improvement. Remittances from overseas Moldovans.

WEAKNESSES

One of Europe's poorest countries. Instability over Transdniestria deters investment. Dependent on Russia for raw materials and fuel, and as market for exports. Isolated; weak transportation network. Slow pace of reform. Strong black economy. Massive foreign debt eats into export earnings.

EXPORTS

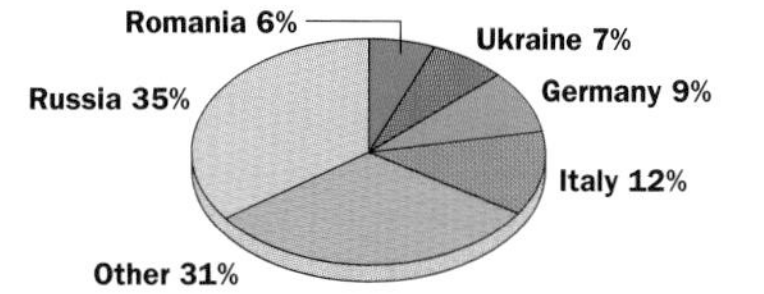
Romania 6%
Ukraine 7%
Russia 35%
Germany 9%
Italy 12%
Other 31%

IMPORTS

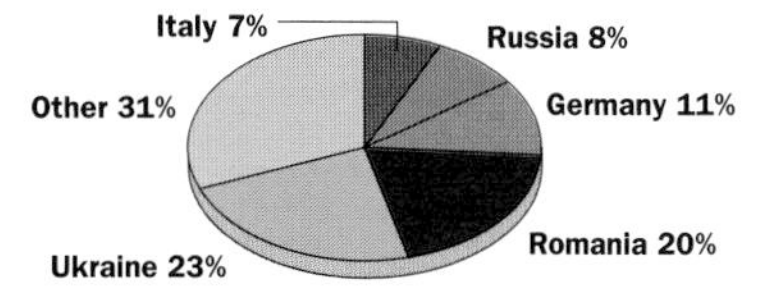
Italy 7%
Russia 8%
Other 31%
Germany 11%
Ukraine 23%
Romania 20%

RESOURCES

Electric power 1m kW

1576 tonnes

Oil and gas reserves not yet exploited

829,725 sheep, 508,345 pigs, 14.9m chickens

Lignite, phosphates, gypsum, oil, natural gas

Gas supplies, imported mostly from Russia, are vulnerable as pipelines are routed through separatist Transdniestria.

ENVIRONMENT

Sustainability rank: 39th

1.4% (0.9% partially protected) — 1.5 tonnes per capita

Overuse of agricultural chemicals and pesticides on tobacco farms is a problem, as is soil erosion. There is little spending on environmental improvement.

MEDIA

TV ownership medium

Daily newspaper circulation 153 per 1000 people

PUBLISHING AND BROADCAST MEDIA

There are 4 leading daily newspapers. *Komsomol'skaya Pravda* has the highest circulation

33 services: 1 state-controlled, 32 independent

25 services: 1 state-controlled, 24 independent

There are several television stations, though many broadcast repeats of Romanian or Russian schedules.

CRIME

No death penalty

10,903 prisoners — Up 9% in 1999–2001

Economic decline has caused crime to increase. The unstable situation in Transdniestria has encouraged smuggling, particularly of Russian arms. The Council of Europe has accused the police of routinely using torture.

EDUCATION

School leaving age: 16

99% — 114,939 students

Education has followed a Romanian (French-inspired) system since 1991. Mass protests met plans in 2002 to make Russian compulsory in schools.

HEALTH

Welfare state health benefits

1 per 370 people

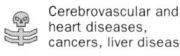

Cerebrovascular and heart diseases, cancers, liver disease

The centralized health service is poor by regional standards. There are serious shortages of medical supplies.

CHRONOLOGY

Modern Moldova corresponds roughly to the eastern part of the Romanian principality of Moldavia, which existed for 500 years from 1359. Most of it was annexed by Russia in 1812 as Bessarabia.

- ❑ **1918** Bessarabia joins Romania.
- ❑ **1924** Moldovan Autonomous Soviet Republic formed within USSR.
- ❑ **1940** Romania cedes Bessarabia to Ukrainian and Moldovan SSRs.
- ❑ **1941–1945** Bessarabia again under Romanian control.
- ❑ **1945** Returns to Soviet control.
- ❑ **1990** Declares sovereignty.
- ❑ **1991** Independence.
- ❑ **1993–1994** Prounification parties' election defeat; referendum rejects Romanian unification. Rejoins CIS.
- ❑ **1998** Elections: communist revival.
- ❑ **2001** CPM wins big majority. Vladimir Voronin becomes president.
- ❑ **2002** Mass protests over education plans.

SPENDING

GDP/cap. decrease

CONSUMPTION AND SPENDING

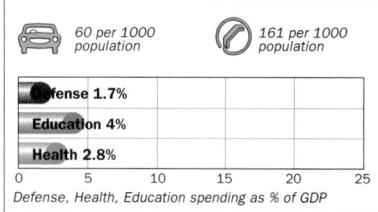

60 per 1000 population — *161 per 1000 population*

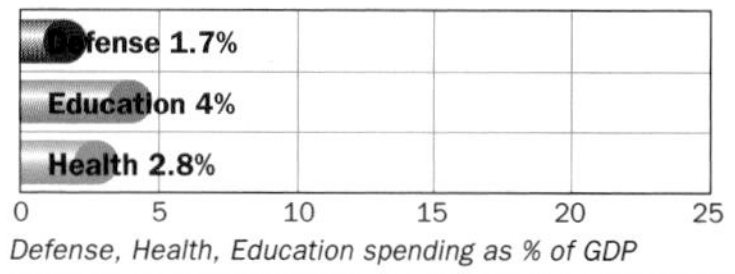
Defense 1.7%
Education 4%
Health 2.8%
0
5
10
15
20
25
Defense, Health, Education spending as % of GDP

Former communist officials have been well placed to benefit from the sale of state-owned businesses. Car ownership is low but rising. However, pensions and wages are often months in arrears. In 1998 the benefits for low-income families and veterans were scrapped. Ethnic Gagauz (Orthodox Christian Turks) are the poorest group.

WORLD RANKING

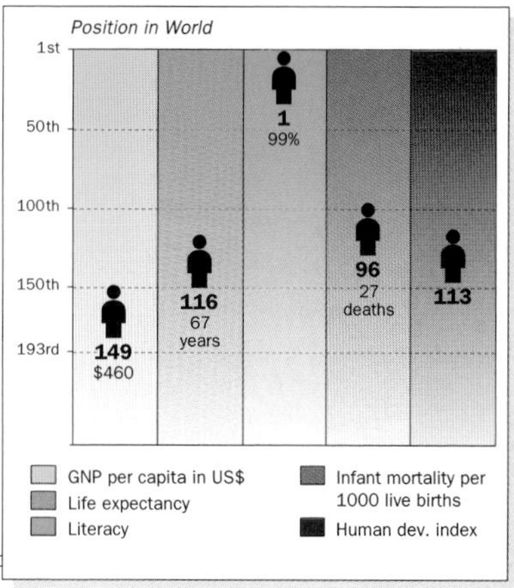
Position in World
1st
50th
100th
150th
193rd
149
$460
116
67
years
1
99%
96
27
deaths
113
GNP per capita in US$
Life expectancy
Literacy
Infant mortality per 1000 live births
Human dev. index

M

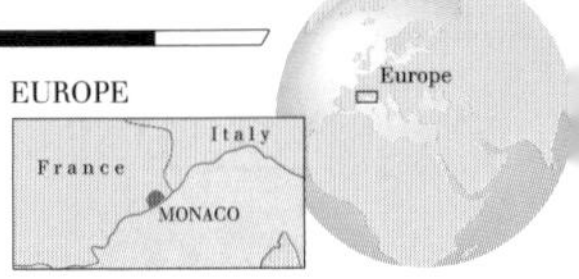
EUROPE
Europe
France
Italy
MONACO

MONACO

OFFICIAL NAME: Principality of Monaco **CAPITAL:** Monaco-Ville
POPULATION: 32,130 **CURRENCY:** Euro **OFFICIAL LANGUAGE:** French

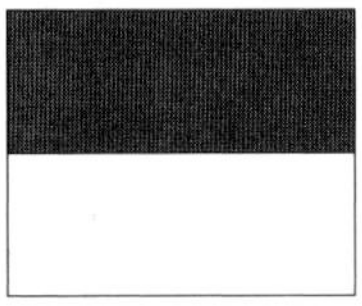

1861 | 1861 | Nov 19 | MC | +1 | +377 | .mc

MONACO IS A TINY ENCLAVE on the French Côte d'Azur. Its destiny changed radically in 1863, when Prince Charles III, after whom Monte Carlo is named, opened the casino there. Today, Monaco is a lucrative banking and services center, as well as a tourist destination. Prince Rainier's marriage to film star Grace Kelly, and some astute management of the economy, successfully transformed Monaco into a center for the international jet set. In 1962, the prince's absolute authority was abolished by a new, democratic constitution.

CLIMATE

Mediterranean

WEATHER CHART FOR MONACO-VILLE

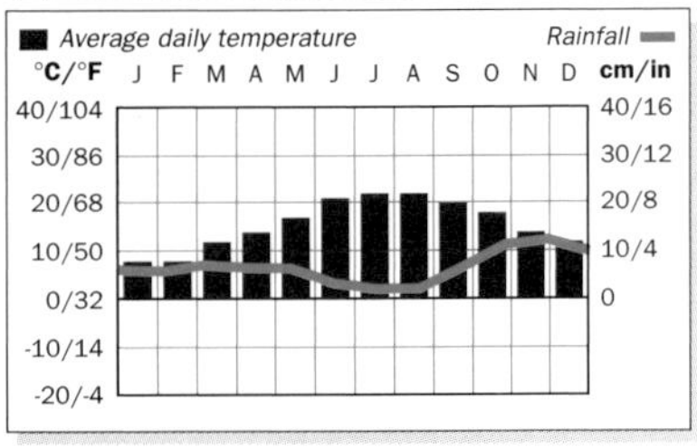
Average daily temperature
Rainfall
°C/°F
J F M A M J J A S O N D
cm/in
40/104
30/86
20/68
10/50
0/32
-10/14
-20/-4
40/16
30/12
20/8
10/4
0

Summers are hot and dry; days with 12 hours of sunshine are not uncommon. Winters are mild and sunny.

TRANSPORTATION

Drive on right

Héliport de Monaco, Fontvieille 120,151 passengers

8 ships

THE TRANSPORTATION NETWORK

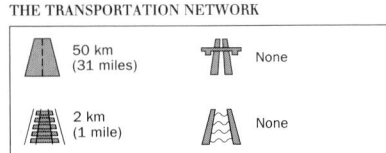

50 km (31 miles)

None

2 km (1 mile)

None

An underground railroad system opened in 1999, with the consequence that 2% of Monaco's area could be reused. Part of the network of roads and tunnels is used for the Grand Prix each year. Air Monaco provides helicopter flights from Nice airport.

TOURISM

Visitors : Population 8.2:1

263,000 visitors

Down 3% in 2002

MAIN TOURIST ARRIVALS

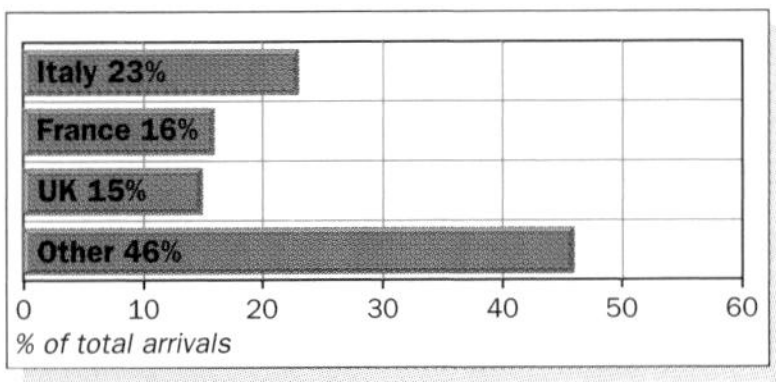
Italy 23%
France 16%
UK 15%
Other 46%
0
10
20
30
40
50
60
% of total arrivals

Huge numbers of tourists, greatly outnumbering the inhabitants, are attracted to Monaco, most coming from Italy and France. Almost all are day-trippers drawn by the casinos and Monaco's conspicuous high society. Around 75% of hotel rooms are classed as "four-star deluxe," and the principality is a particular favorite of wealthy Italians. The Grimaldi Forum conference center, which opened in 2000, hopes to attract more business travelers.

A number of social and sporting events attract particularly large crowds each spring, including the Rose Ball (March), the Tennis Open (April), and the Grand Prix (May).

PEOPLE

Pop. density high

French, Italian, Monégasque, English

16,477/km² (42,840/mi²)

THE URBAN/RURAL POPULATION SPLIT

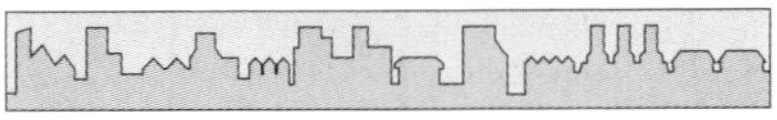
100%

RELIGIOUS PERSUASION

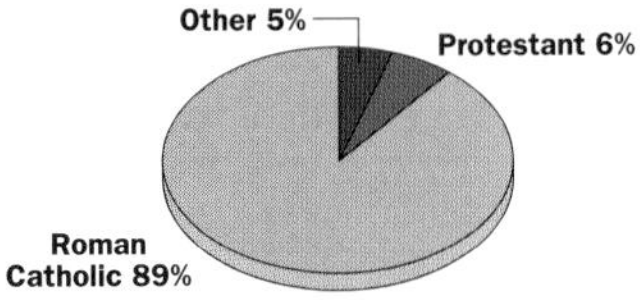
Other 5%
Protestant 6%
Roman Catholic 89%

Fewer than a fifth of Monaco's residents are Monégasque. Around half are French, the rest Italian, American, British, and Belgian. Monégasques enjoy considerable privileges, including housing subsidies to protect them from Monaco's high property prices, and the right of first refusal before a job can be offered to a foreigner. Women have equal status, but only acquired the vote in the constitutional changes of 1962.

POLITICS

Multiparty elections

2003/2008

H.S.H. Prince Rainier III

AT THE LAST ELECTION

National Council 24 seats

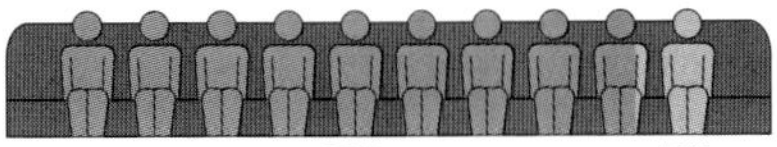
88%
UPM
12%
UND

UPM = Union for Monaco group
UND = National and Democratic Union group
There are no formal political parties

Prince Rainier III retains considerable power, appointing the government head from a list of French diplomats. The 2003 election, ending 40 years of UND rule, was seen as a vote of no confidence in UND leader Jean-Louis Campora, who was also president of the financially troubled AS Monaco soccer team, which plays in the French league.

WORLD AFFAIRS

Joined UN in 1993

IWC | IAEA | OSCE | OIF

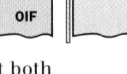

A key concern is to protect both banking secrecy and the liberal tax regime from EU regulation, though the principality has adopted the euro. France is particularly critical, and Monaco has banned French citizens from banking there since 1962.

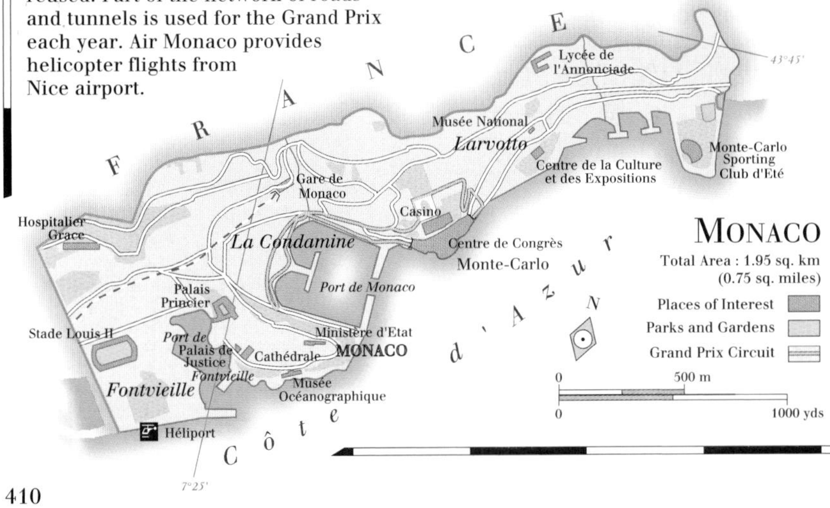
FRANCE
Côte d'Azur
Lycée de l'Annonciade
43°45'
Musée National
Larvotto
Monte-Carlo Sporting Club d'Eté
Centre de la Culture et des Expositions
Gare de Monaco
Casino
Hospitalier Grace
La Condamine
Centre de Congrès Monte-Carlo
Port de Monaco
Palais Princier
Stade Louis II
Port de Fontvieille
Palais de Justice
Ministère d'Etat
MONACO
Cathédrale
Musée Océanographique
Fontvieille
Héliport
7°25'
N
MONACO
Total Area : 1.95 sq. km (0.75 sq. miles)
Places of Interest
Parks and Gardens
Grand Prix Circuit
0
500 m
0
1000 yds

M

***Monte Carlo** with its luxury hotels and yacht harbor. The only space for new development is on land reclaimed from the sea.*

AID

Not applicable

Monaco has no aid receipts or donations

Not applicable

Monaco neither receives nor gives aid, and the issue is not of concern to Monégasques.

DEFENSE

No compulsory military service

France responsible for defense

Not applicable

Monaco has no armed forces and no defense budget. France, as the protecting power, bears responsibility for the defense of the principality.

ECONOMICS

Inflation 2.6% p.a. (1985–1996)

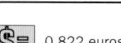

$870m

0.822 euros (0.871)

SCORE CARD

- ❑ World GNP Ranking........................156th
- ❑ GNP per Capita $27,500
- ❑ Balance of Payments.....Included in French total
- ❑ Inflation ....Included in French total
- ❑ Unemployment 3%

Strengths

Strong tourism sector. Strict banking confidentiality and low taxes attract billions of dollars of overseas deposits. Assets managed by Monaco banks increased by 18% a year in the late 1990s. Very low unemployment. No formal debt and reserves of over €2.5 billion. Main port expanded in 2002.

Weaknesses

Continuing vulnerability to money laundering despite the 1994 accord with France obliging banks to furnish details of suspicious accounts. Subject to fluctuations of French and Italian economies. Dependence on VAT for bulk of revenues. Pressure from EU states to end privileged banking and tax laws. Lack of natural resources means total dependence on imports.

EXPORTS/IMPORTS

Monaco has a full customs union with France

RESOURCES

Electric power: Included within French total

3 tonnes

Not an oil producer

None

None

Monaco has no strategic resources and imports all its energy from France. It has no agricultural land.

ENVIRONMENT

Not available

None

4.1 tonnes per capita

Monaco has built the most extensive underground car parking facilities in the world to tackle congestion. The quality of the built environment around the harbor occasionally arouses local passions. Important populations of red coral are under threat from land reclamation and pollution.

MEDIA

TV ownership high

Daily newspaper circulation 251 per 1000 people

PUBLISHING AND BROADCAST MEDIA

There is 1 daily newspaper. *Nice-Matin*, a regional French newspaper, publishes a Monaco edition

2 services

4 services: 1 part-owned by French state, 3 independent

In addition to its domestic radio and TV, Monaco receives all the mainstream French and Italian channels.

CRIME

No death penalty

13 prisoners

Up 35% in 2000–2001

Monaco was censured in 2002 by the OECD as one of seven "uncooperative tax havens" failing to respond to a campaign for greater financial transparency.

EDUCATION

School leaving age: 15

99%

Not available

The education system is essentially the same as that of France, with students studying for the *baccalauréat* exam. Most go on to university in France, but then return to claim good jobs in Monaco. The Catholic Church exerts considerable influence and is still responsible for primary schooling.

HEALTH

Welfare state health benefits

1 per 152 people

Cerebrovascular and heart diseases, cancers

Most medical care is provided by private health insurance. Doctors train in France. The Princess Grace Hospital can serve 60,000 people, also catering for patients from outside Monaco.

CHRONOLOGY

In 1297, the Grimaldis first seized control of the territory of which they became hereditary rulers.

- ❑ **1861** Independent under French protection.
- ❑ **1863** Monte Carlo casino opens.
- ❑ **1949** Rainier III accedes to throne.
- ❑ **1962** Constitution rewritten: end of absolute authority of the prince.
- ❑ **1963** Democratic legislative elections held for first time.
- ❑ **1982** Princess Grace dies following car accident.
- ❑ **2002** Euro introduced.

SPENDING

GDP/cap. increase

CONSUMPTION AND SPENDING

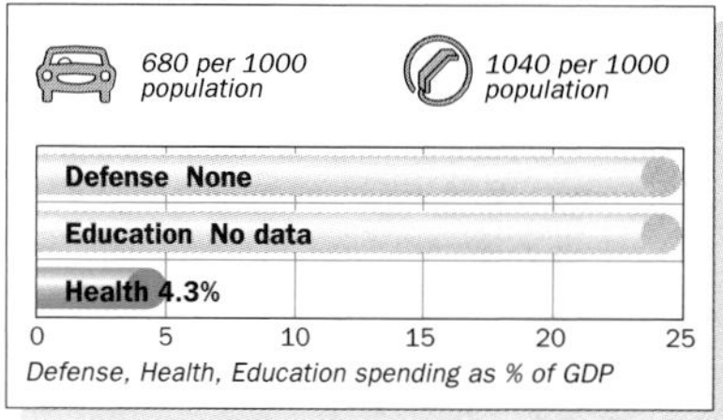
680 per 1000 population
1040 per 1000 population
Defense None
Education No data
Health 4.3%
0
5
10
15
20
25
Defense, Health, Education spending as % of GDP

Monaco's image abroad has changed dramatically since Prince Rainier acceded in 1949. From being considered simply as a gambling spot, it is now ranked as one of the world's most glamorous international jet-set destinations. In part, this was the result of Prince Rainier's marriage to Grace Kelly, then a leading Hollywood star, which brought Monaco to the attention of US high society. More important was the prince's work in turning Monaco into a major tax haven and an upmarket resort, by making the most of its Mediterranean coastal location. Many celebrities are residents, among them Luciano Pavarotti, Ringo Starr, and racing drivers David Coulthard and Jenson Button.

WORLD RANKING

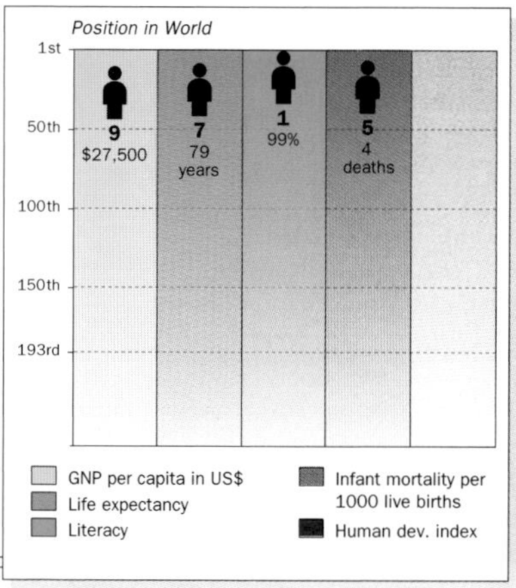
Position in World
1st
50th
100th
150th
193rd
9
$27,500
7
79 years
1
99%
5
4 deaths
GNP per capita in US$
Life expectancy
Literacy
Infant mortality per 1000 live births
Human dev. index

M

MONGOLIA

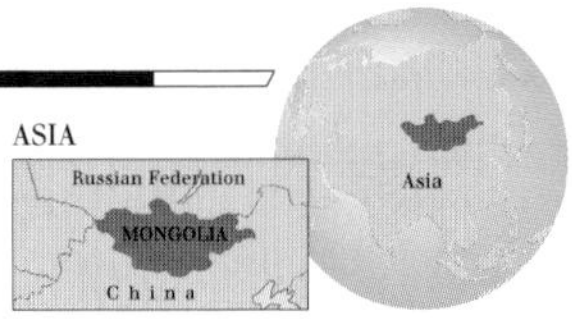
ASIA
Russian Federation
MONGOLIA
China
Asia

OFFICIAL NAME: Mongolia **CAPITAL:** Ulan Bator **POPULATION:** 2.6 million
CURRENCY: Tugrik (tögrög) **OFFICIAL LANGUAGE:** Khalkha Mongolian

1924 | 1924 | July 11 | MGL | +8 | +976 | .mn

LANDLOCKED BETWEEN Siberia and China's Mongolian provinces, Mongolia rises from the semiarid Gobi Desert to mountainous steppe. The traditionally nomadic Mongols were first unified by Genghis Khan in 1206. "Outer" Mongolia achieved independence from China as a communist state in 1924 and was officially aligned with the USSR from 1936. In 1990, it abandoned communist rule; widespread poverty ensued. Extremely harsh winters in 1999–2001 devastated the rural economy.

CLIMATE

Mountain/cold desert/steppe

WEATHER CHART FOR ULAN BATOR

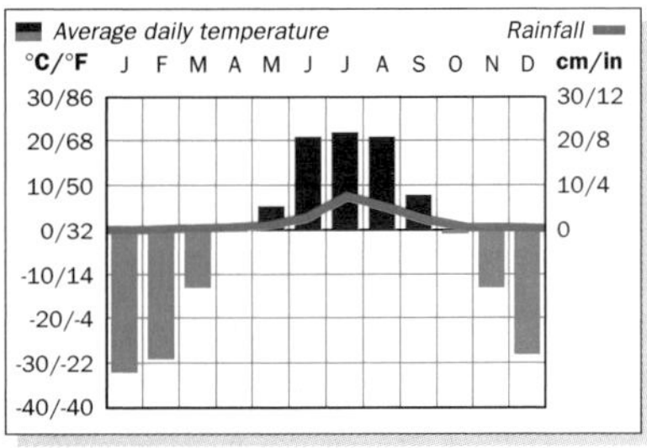
Average daily temperature
Rainfall
°C/°F J F M A M J J A S O N D cm/in
30/86 20/68 10/50 0/32 -10/14 -20/-4 -30/-22 -40/-40
30/12 20/8 10/4 0

Temperature variations are extreme. Dry summers combine with severe winters, known as *zud*, to devastate livestock, as happened in 1999 and 2000.

TRANSPORTATION

Drive on right

Buyant Ukhaa, Ulan Bator Has no fleet

THE TRANSPORTATION NETWORK

1970 km (1224 miles)	None
1810 km (1125 miles)	400 km (249 miles)

Lack of investment has left Mongolia's infrastructure to decay, increasing transportation and distribution costs. Links to China and the Pacific are priorities. Gasoline shortages have meant a large increase in the use of animals for transportation.

Traditional gers in the Gobi Desert. *Many Mongolians still choose to pursue a nomadic lifestyle, living in felt tents or gers.*

TOURISM

Visitors : Population 1:13

198,000 visitors Up 3% in 2002

MAIN TOURIST ARRIVALS

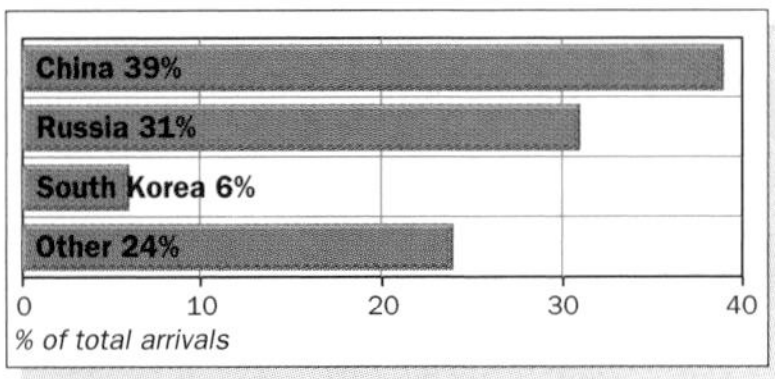
China 39%
Russia 31%
South Korea 6%
Other 24%
0 10 20 30 40
% of total arrivals

Tourism has expanded since the easing of visa restrictions in 1991. Under communism, all travel was arranged through the state agency, Zhuuichin, but private companies have now entered the market.

PEOPLE

Pop. density low

Khalkha Mongolian, Kazakh, Chinese, Russian

2/km² (4/mi²)

THE URBAN/RURAL POPULATION SPLIT

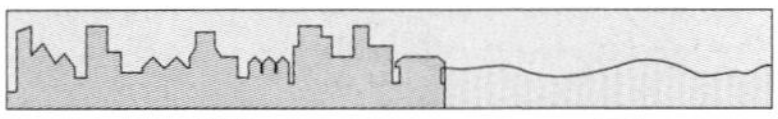
57%
43%

ETHNIC MAKEUP

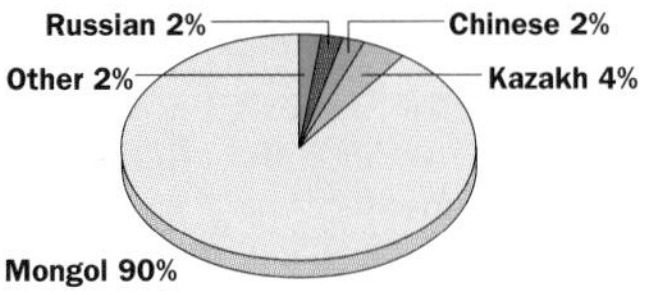
Russian 2%
Chinese 2%
Other 2%
Kazakh 4%
Mongol 90%

Most Mongolians remain nomadic, but one-third live in Ulan Bator. Khalkh Mongols, who adhere to Tibetan Buddhism, are the main ethnic group. Turkic Kazakhs in the west form the largest minority, but many have emigrated since 1990. Family or clan names, banned under the communists, have been relegalized; Genghis Khan's name, Borjigin, is immensely popular.

POLITICS

Multiparty elections

2004/2008 President Natsagyn Bagabandi

AT THE LAST ELECTION

State Great Hural 76 seats

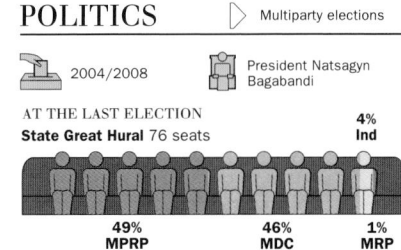

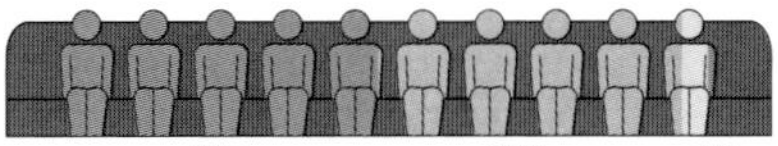
4% Ind
49% MPRP
46% MDC
1% MRP

MPRP = Mongolian People's Revolutionary Party
MDC = Motherland–Democratic Coalition
Ind = Independents **MRP** = Mongolian Republican Party

The end of communism in 1990 revolutionized Mongolian politics. The shock of economic reform led many Mongolians to regret the lost certainties of the communist era. The failure of the former communist MPRP to revive the economy led to the victory of a democratic coalition in 1996, though from 1997 this was faced with cohabitation with MPRP President Natsagyn Bagabandi. 2000 saw a sweeping MPRP victory, reducing the democrats to a single seat, but the election four years later was neck and neck between the two parties, who after much wrangling agreed to share power.

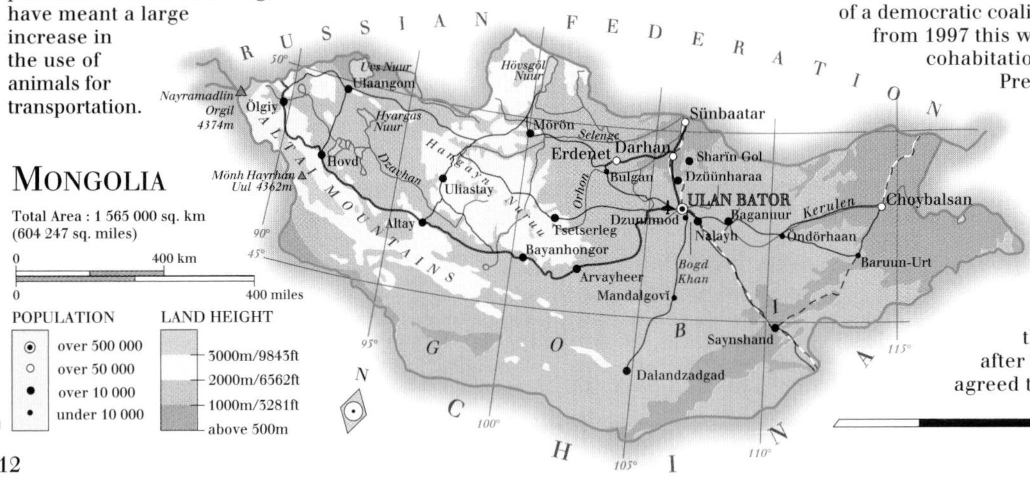
MONGOLIA
Total Area : 1 565 000 sq. km (604 247 sq. miles)
0 400 km
0 400 miles
POPULATION
over 500 000
over 50 000
over 10 000
under 10 000
LAND HEIGHT
3000m/9843ft
2000m/6562ft
1000m/3281ft
above 500m
RUSSIAN FEDERATION
CHINA
GOBI
ALTAI MOUNTAINS
Hangayn Nuruu
Nayramadlin Orgil 4374m
Mönh Hayrhan Uul 4362m
Üves Nuur
Ulaangom
Ölgiy
Hovd
Hyargas Nuur
Dzavhan
Uliastay
Altay
Hövsgöl Nuur
Mörön
Selenge
Erdenet
Darhan
Bulgan
Orhon
Tsetserleg
Bayanhongor
Arvayheer
Mandalgovi
Dzuunmod
ULAN BATOR
Sühbaatar
Sharin Gol
Dzüünharaa
Baganuur
Nalayh
Bogd Khan
Kerulen
Öndörhaan
Choybalsan
Baruun-Urt
Saynshand
Dalandzadgad
50° 45° 90° 95° 100° 105° 110° 115°

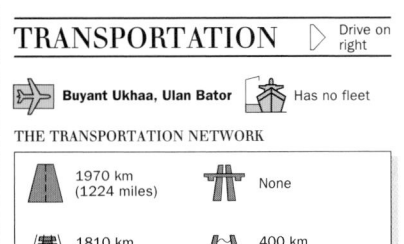

M

WORLD AFFAIRS

Joined UN in 1961

IAEA IBRD NAM ADB WTO

Closer relations with Japan and other east Asian states have failed to weaken Mongolia's ties with Russia and China. There are residual tensions with China, since the majority of ethnic Mongols actually reside in the adjoining Chinese province of Inner Mongolia, but there is no longer a fear of Chinese designs on Mongolian sovereignty.

AID

Recipient

$208m (receipts) — Down 2% in 2002

A balance-of-payments deficit and severe weather make aid vital. The main donors are Japan and the ADB.

DEFENSE

Compulsory military service

$23m — Down 4% in 2002

The last Soviet forces left in 1992. However, ties are still strong, and under agreements reached in 2000 and 2001, Russia is helping to reform the greatly reduced and poorly equipped Mongolian forces.

ECONOMICS

Inflation 51% p.a. (1990–2001)

$1.06bn — 1174 tugriks (1126)

SCORE CARD

❑ WORLD GNP RANKING	153rd
❑ GNP PER CAPITA	$430
❑ BALANCE OF PAYMENTS	–$105m
❑ INFLATION	21.1%
❑ UNEMPLOYMENT	3%

STRENGTHS

Copper and cashmere. Largely untapped coal and oil reserves. Traditional and efficient rural economy.

WEAKNESSES

Harsh winters ravaged livestock between 1999 and 2001. Decaying infrastructure. Rising poverty.

EXPORTS

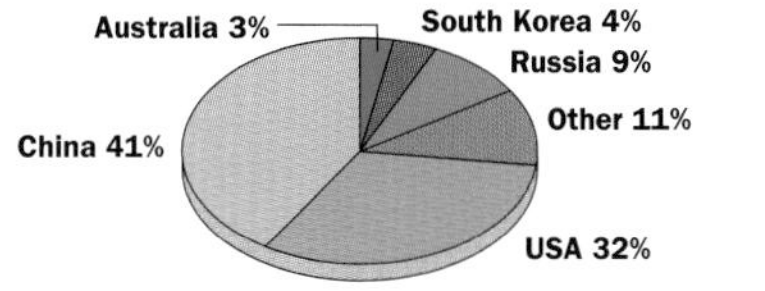
Australia 3%
South Korea 4%
Russia 9%
Other 11%
China 41%
USA 32%

IMPORTS

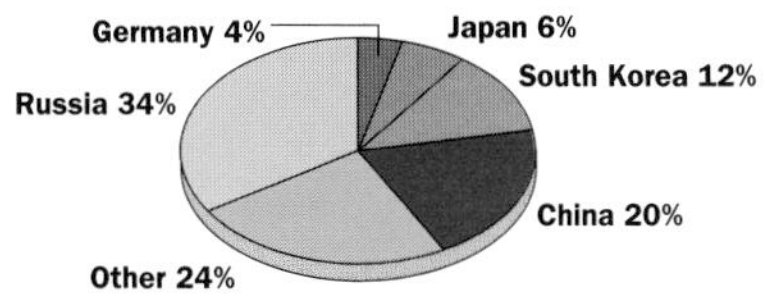
Germany 4%
Japan 6%
South Korea 12%
Russia 34%
China 20%
Other 24%

RESOURCES

Electric power 901,000 kW

117 tonnes — 200 b/d (reserves 1.5bn barrels)

11.8m sheep, 8.86m goats, 2.2m horses — Oil, coal, copper, lead, fluorite, tungsten, tin, gold, uranium

Under communism, Mongolia's vast mineral resources were barely exploited. Mining and minerals-related industries are now rapidly growing sectors of the economy. A uranium-mining joint venture with Russia has been established. Mongolia's oil reserves are sufficient to meet future domestic needs; in 1999 an oil extraction agreement was signed with China.

ENVIRONMENT

Sustainability rank: 42nd

12% — 3.1 tonnes per capita

The air in Ulan Bator is heavily polluted as a result of burning soft coal in power plants and the nonenforcement of environmental laws. In 2001 efforts were renewed to preserve the Bogd Khan, the world's oldest protected area, from air pollution, hunting, and illegal logging.

MEDIA

TV ownership medium

Daily newspaper circulation 17 per 1000 people

PUBLISHING AND BROADCAST MEDIA

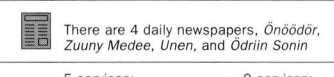

There are 4 daily newspapers, *Önöödör, Zuuny Medee, Unen,* and *Ödriin Sonin*

5 services: 1 state-owned, 4 independent — 9 services: 1 state-owned, 8 independent

Slander and libel laws were abolished in 1990, and legislation enacted in 1999 eased curbs on the media. However, paper and fuel shortages have restricted the number of publications and their distribution. Several independent radio and TV stations compete with the state-owned service.

CRIME

Death penalty in use

7256 prisoners — Down 1% in 2000–2001

Crime rose rapidly in the early 1990s, particularly organized crime and muggings by knife gangs. Ulan Bator is the most dangerous area, especially for foreigners; Russians, Chinese, and dollar-carrying US tourists are the main targets.

EDUCATION

School leaving age: 15

98% — 98,400 students

Education is modeled on the former Soviet system. Most teachers are women on low salaries. Private universities and higher education institutions outnumber state-run facilities.

CHRONOLOGY

In the 17th century, the Manchus took control of Mongolia. It stayed in Chinese hands until 1911.

- ❑ **1919** China reoccupies Mongolia.
- ❑ **1924** Independent communist state.
- ❑ **1989–1990** Prodemocracy protests; first multiparty elections.
- ❑ **1992** New constitution.
- ❑ **1996** Democratic Union coalition wins general election.
- ❑ **1997** MPRP wins presidency.
- ❑ **1999–2001** Severe winters.
- ❑ **2000** Landslide victory for MPRP.
- ❑ **2004** Election leaves both MPRP and MDC just short of a majority.

HEALTH

Welfare state health benefits

1 per 366 people — Heart, parasitic, and respiratory diseases

Shortages of drugs and equipment have renewed interest in traditional Mongolian herbal medicine. As well as the state-run system, some Buddhist monasteries provide health care.

SPENDING

GDP/cap. increase

CONSUMPTION AND SPENDING

18 per 1000 population — *53 per 1000 population*

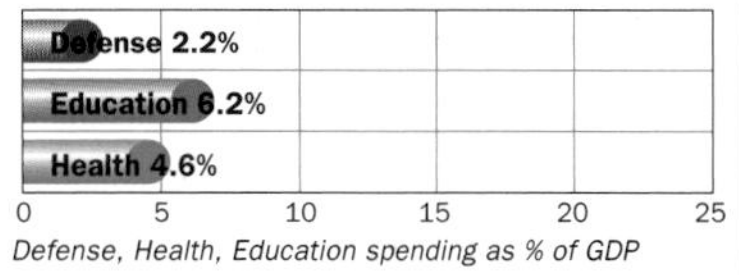
Defense 2.2%
Education 6.2%
Health 4.6%
0
5
10
15
20
25
Defense, Health, Education spending as % of GDP

Economic liberalization has fueled great disparities in wealth. An estimated 50% of the population live below the poverty line; the poorest cannot even afford to buy bread. Starvation threatened after the severe winters of 1999–2001.

WORLD RANKING

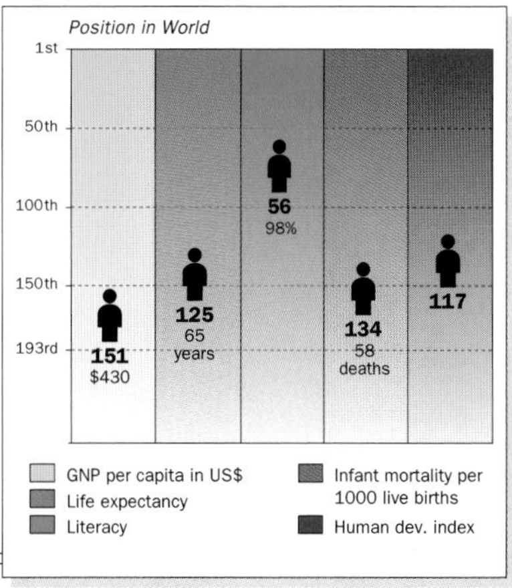
Position in World
1st
50th
100th
150th
193rd
151
$430
125
65 years
56
98%
134
58 deaths
117
GNP per capita in US$
Life expectancy
Literacy
Infant mortality per 1000 live births
Human dev. index

M

Morocco

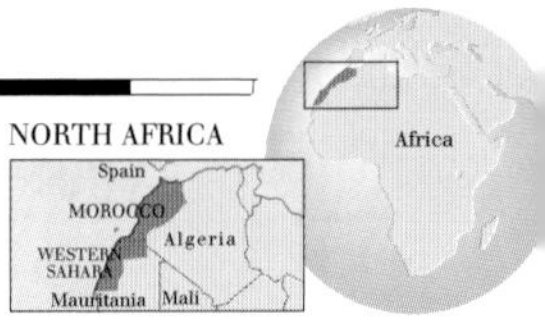
NORTH AFRICA
Africa
Spain
MOROCCO
Algeria
WESTERN SAHARA
Mauritania
Mali

Official Name: Kingdom of Morocco **Capital:** Rabat
Population: 30.6 million **Currency:** Moroccan dirham **Official Language:** Arabic

1956
1969
July 30
MA
0
+212
.ma

MOROCCO IS SITUATED in north Africa, but at its northernmost point lies only 12 km (8 miles) from mainland Europe, across the Strait of Gibraltar. The northern regions have a Mediterranean climate, while the south comprises semiarid desert. The late King Hassan's international prestige gave Morocco status out of proportion to its wealth. The main issues facing the country are the internal threat of Islamist militancy and the stalled political process in Western Sahara, the former Spanish colony occupied by Morocco since 1975. Key economic strengths are tourism, phosphates, and agriculture.

CLIMATE

Hot desert/mountain/ Mediterranean

WEATHER CHART FOR RABAT

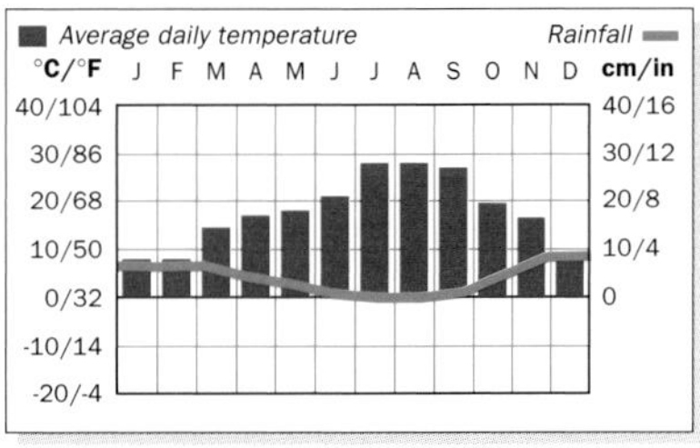
Average daily temperature
Rainfall
°C/°F J F M A M J J A S O N D cm/in
40/104
30/86
20/68
10/50
0/32
-10/14
-20/-4
40/16
30/12
20/8
10/4
0

The climate ranges from warm and temperate in the north to semiarid in the south, but temperatures are cooler in the mountains, especially in the High (Haut) Atlas. During the summer, the effects of the *sirocco* and *chergui*, hot winds from the Sahara, are felt.

TRANSPORTATION

Drive on right

Mohammed V, Casablanca
3.4m passengers

483 ships
501,700 grt

THE TRANSPORTATION NETWORK

32,311 km (20,077 miles)

481 km (299 miles)

1907 km (1185 miles)

None

The public transportation network is good. A highway links Rabat and Casablanca, and plans for a new trans-Sahara highway from Tanger to Lagos, Nigeria, were announced in 2000. In rural areas, however, roads tend to peter out.

TOURISM

Visitors : Population 1:7.3

4.19m visitors

Down 1% in 2002

MAIN TOURIST ARRIVALS

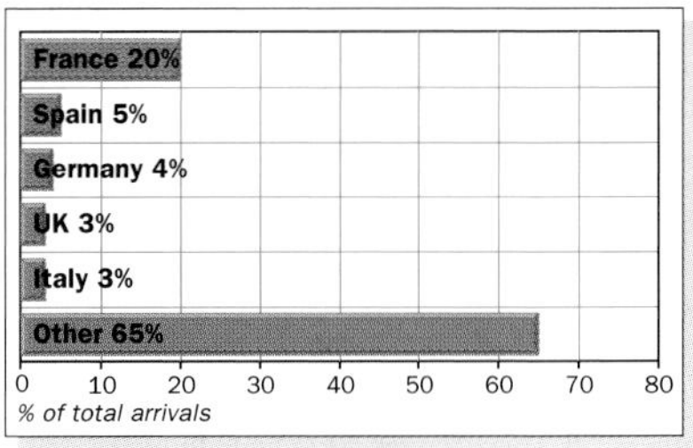
France 20%
Spain 5%
Germany 4%
UK 3%
Italy 3%
Other 65%
0 10 20 30 40 50 60 70 80
% of total arrivals

Tourism is vital to the Moroccan economy. Good beaches abound; Agadir has 300 days of sunshine a year. Fès and Marrakech offer remarkable architecture and bustling markets, while the Atlas Mountains attract walkers and skiers. Desert safaris are offered in the Sahara. The threat of Islamist terrorist activity has deterred some Western visitors.

M

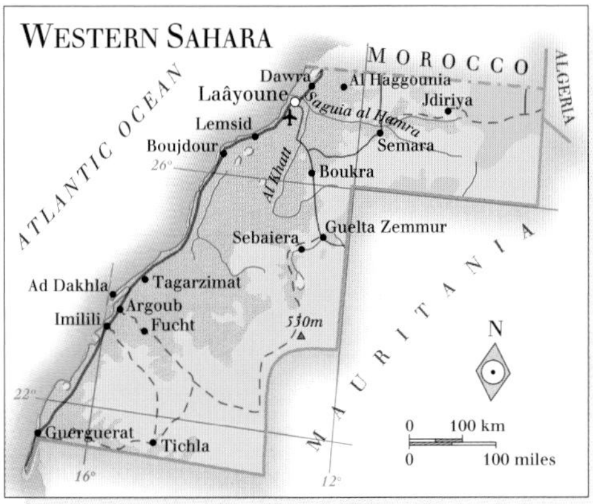
WESTERN SAHARA
MOROCCO
ALGERIA
ATLANTIC OCEAN
MAURITANIA
Dawra
Al Haggounia
Laâyoune
Saguia al Hamra
Jdiriya
Lemsid
Semara
Boujdour
Boukra
Al Khatt
Sebaiera
Guelta Zemmur
Ad Dakhla
Tagarzimat
Argoub
Imilili
Fucht
530m
Guerguerat
Tichla
N
0 100 km
0 100 miles

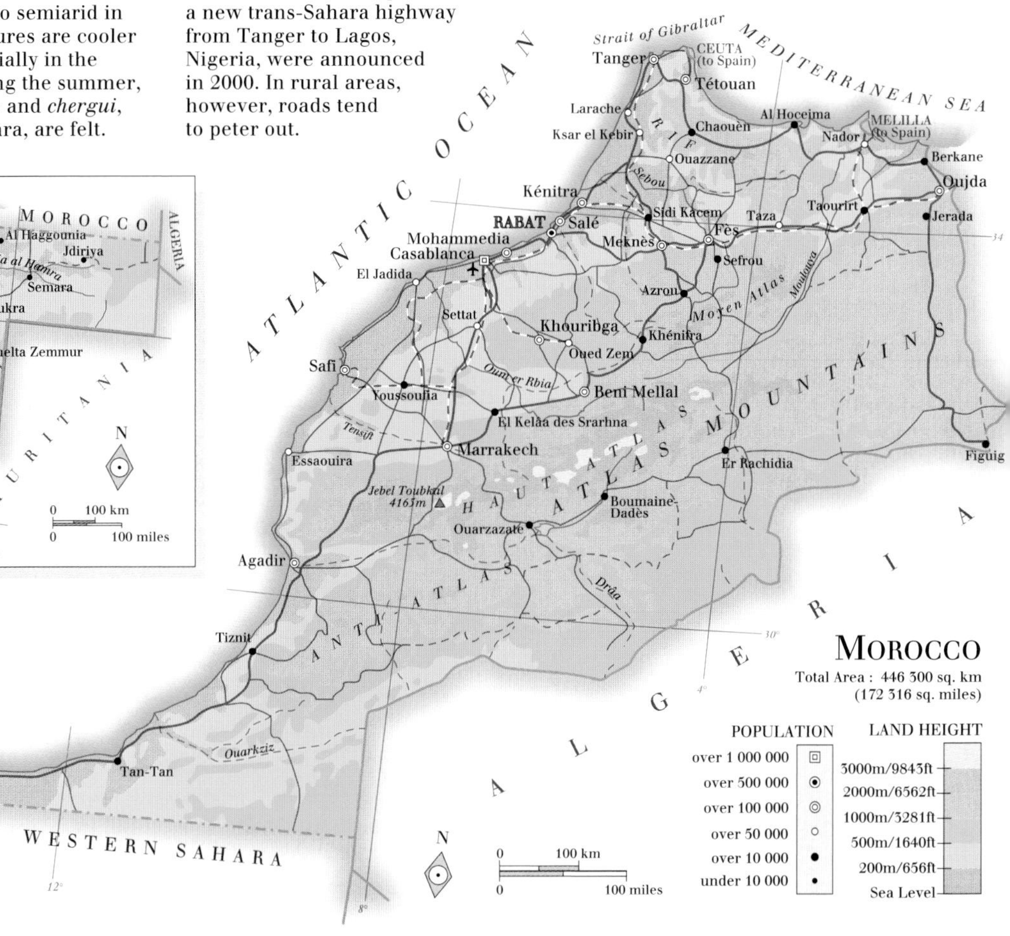
Strait of Gibraltar
MEDITERRANEAN SEA
ATLANTIC OCEAN
Tanger
CEUTA (to Spain)
Tétouan
Larache
Ksar el Kebir
Chaouèn
Al Hoceïma
MELILLA (to Spain)
Nador
Berkane
Oujda
Ouazzane
Kénitra
RABAT
Salé
Sidi Kacem
Taza
Taourirt
Jerada
Mohammedia
Casablanca
Meknès
Fès
Sefrou
El Jadida
Azrou
Settat
Khouribga
Khénifra
Oued Zem
Safi
Youssoufia
Beni Mellal
El Kelâa des Srarhna
Marrakech
Essaouira
Jebel Toubkal 4165m
HAUT ATLAS
ATLAS MOUNTAINS
Er Rachidia
Figuig
Boumaine-Dadès
Ouarzazate
Agadir
ANTI ATLAS
Drâa
Tiznit
Tan-Tan
WESTERN SAHARA
ALGERIA
MOROCCO
Total Area : 446 300 sq. km (172 316 sq. miles)
POPULATION
over 1 000 000
over 500 000
over 100 000
over 50 000
over 10 000
under 10 000
LAND HEIGHT
3000m/9843ft
2000m/6562ft
1000m/3281ft
500m/1640ft
200m/656ft
Sea Level
0 100 km
0 100 miles

PEOPLE

Pop. density medium

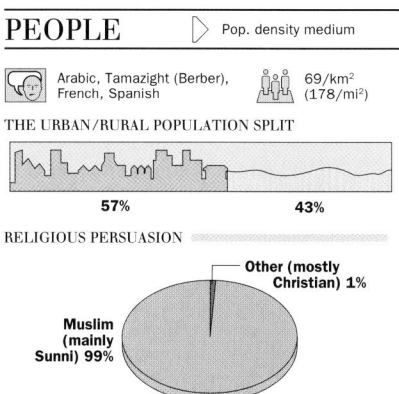

Arabic, Tamazight (Berber), French, Spanish

69/km² (178/mi²)

THE URBAN/RURAL POPULATION SPLIT

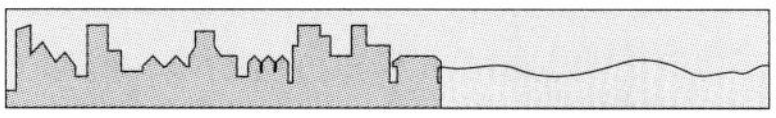
57%
43%

RELIGIOUS PERSUASION

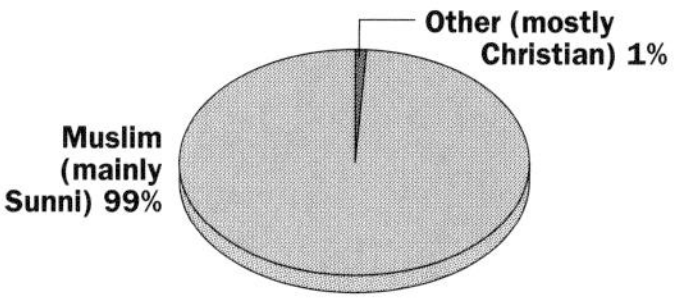
Other (mostly Christian) 1%
Muslim (mainly Sunni) 99%

ETHNIC MAKEUP

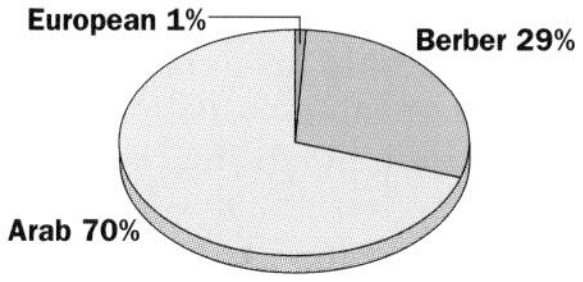
European 1%
Berber 29%
Arab 70%

Morocco, the westernmost of the Maghreb states, is the main refuge for descendants of the original Berber inhabitants of northwest Africa. About 35% of Moroccans speak Berber languages, mainly Tamazight. They live mainly in mountain villages, while the Arab majority inhabit the lowlands. Before independence from France, 450,000 Europeans lived in Morocco; numbers have since greatly diminished. Some 6000 Jews enjoy religious freedom and full civil rights – a position in society unique among Arab countries. Most people speak Arabic, and French is also spoken in urban areas.

Sunni Islam is the religion of almost all of the population. The king is the spiritual leader through his position as Commander of the Faithful.

Female emancipation was boosted by reforms in 2004, giving women equal responsibility in family matters and greatly restricting polygamy.

POPULATION AGE BREAKDOWN

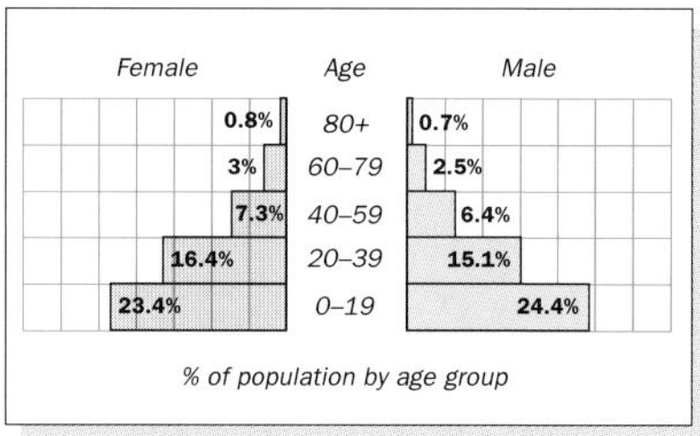
Female
Age
Male
0.8%
80+
0.7%
3%
60–79
2.5%
7.3%
40–59
6.4%
16.4%
20–39
15.1%
23.4%
0–19
24.4%
% of population by age group

POLITICS

Multiparty elections

L. House 2002/2007
U. House 2003/2006

H.M. King Mohammed VI

AT THE LAST ELECTION

House of Representatives 325 seats

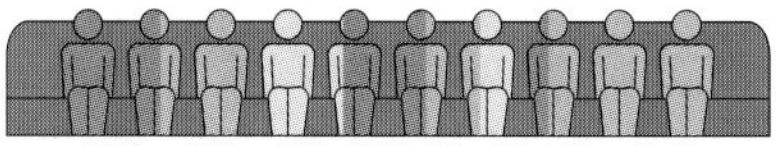

15%	15%	13%	13%	8%	6%	5%	25%
USFP	I	PJD	RNI	MP	MNP	UC	Others

USFP = Socialist Union of Popular Forces **I** = Istiqlal (Independence) **PJD** = Justice and Development Party **RNI** = National Rally of Independents **MP** = Popular Movement **MNP** = National Popular Movement **UC** = Constitutional Union

House of Councillors 270 seats

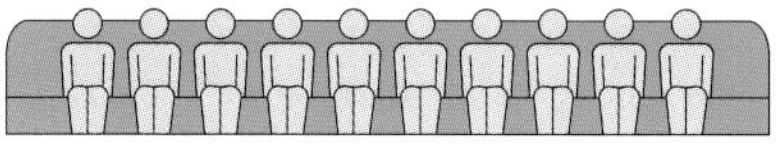

An indirectly elected House of Councillors was formed in 1997

Morocco is a constitutional monarchy with a bicameral legislature. The king appoints (and may dismiss) the prime minister and, on the prime minister's recommendation, other members of the cabinet.

PROFILE

The formation of a socialist-led government after the elections in 1997 was seen as a breakthrough in terms of indicating the growing role of the party system. The ruling parties maintained their strength in the 2002 elections, with the USFP and Istiqlal gaining most seats, but support for Islamists (the PJD) rose dramatically. Independent Driss Jettou was appointed prime minister.

MAIN POLITICAL ISSUES

The post-Hassan monarchy

King Mohammed VI is seen as a less dominating figure than his father, Hassan II, and his accession in 1999 raised hopes for change. His marriage in 2002 to computer engineer Salma Bennani was presented as evidence of a more modern and open outlook. Mohammed has proved cautious, however, in his approach to reform.

Islamist militancy

There is now a more tolerant stance toward Islamist politics. In 2000, Abdessalam Yassine, spiritual leader of the banned Justice and Good Deeds movement, was released after ten years in prison without trial. Pro-Islamic rallies have far outnumbered those by supporters of greater rights for women. In 2003, suicide bombings in Casablanca were linked to al-Qaida, suggesting a widening of Islamic extremist activities.

***Prime Minister Driss Jettou**, appointed in 2002.*

***King Mohammed VI**, who succeeded his father, Hassan II.*

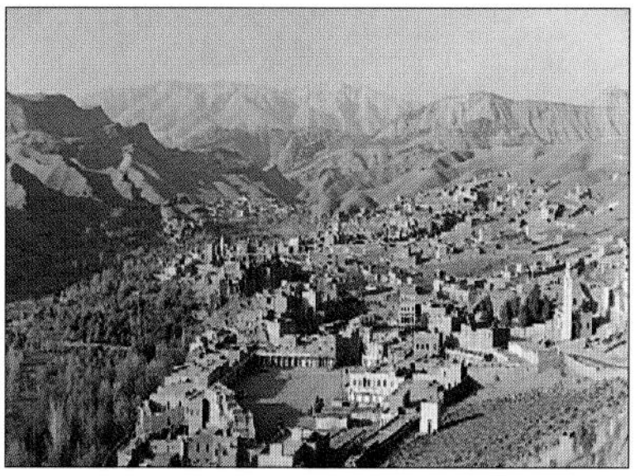

***The town of Boumaine-Dadès** lies in the southern foothills of the Atlas Mountains. The region's outstanding scenery makes it one of Morocco's major tourist attractions.*

WORLD AFFAIRS

Joined UN in 1956

AL AMU NAM OIC OIF

King Hassan II held an ambiguous position in global politics as both a supporter of the West and a leading figure in the Islamic community. A defender of Jewish minority rights, he was viewed by successive Israeli leaders in particular as an Arab moderate. In contrast, his son Mohammed VI has so far failed to make his mark in international Islamic politics or the Arab–Israeli conflict to any comparable extent.

International concern has focused on Morocco's occupation since 1975 of the former Spanish colony of Western Sahara. Resistance by Polisario Front guerrillas, who are fighting for an independent Western Sahara, began in 1983 and has continued, despite a 1991 UN-brokered peace plan. Since then, UN proposals have included a referendum on self-determination and autonomy for Western Sahara under Moroccan sovereignty. The process remains stalled, with the UN repeatedly extending its mandate.

Relations with the EU are complicated by the production of cannabis in Morocco. Nonetheless, moves toward closer ties were advanced by the signing of an association agreement in late 1995, envisaging free trade in industrial goods within 12 years. In recognition of its role in the "war on terrorism" the US named Morocco a major non-NATO ally in 2004.

Sovereignty disputes with Spain over rocky islets in the Mediterranean were at the heart of a high-profile confrontation in 2002.

AID

Recipient

$636m (receipts)

Up 23% in 2002

The main donors of aid to Morocco are the EU, France, and other Arab countries. Many countries provided assistance after the 2004 earthquake.

CHRONOLOGY

Independence from France in 1956 ended colonial rule over the oldest monarchy in the Arab world. The present Alaoui dynasty has ruled Morocco since 1666.

- **1956** France recognizes Moroccan independence under Sultan Mohammed ibn Yousif. Morocco joins UN. Spain renounces control over most of its territories.
- **1957** Sultan Mohammed king.
- **1961** Hassan succeeds his father.
- **1967** Morocco backs Arab cause in Six-Day War with Israel.
- **1969** Spain returns Ifni to Morocco.
- **1972** King Hassan survives assassination attempt.
- **1975** International Court of Justice grants right of self-determination to Western Saharan people. Moroccan forces seize Saharan capital.
- **1976** Morocco and Mauritania partition Western Sahara.
- **1979** Mauritania renounces claim to part of Western Sahara, which is added to Morocco's territory.
- **1984** King Hassan signs Oujda Treaty with Col. Gaddafi of Libya as first step toward Maghreb union. Morocco leaves OAU after criticism of its role in Western Sahara.
- **1986** Morocco abrogates Oujda Treaty.
- **1987** Defensive wall built around Western Sahara.
- **1989** Arab Maghreb Union (AMU) creates tariff-free zone between Morocco, Algeria, Tunisia, Libya, and Mauritania.
- **1990** Morocco condemns Iraq's invasion of Kuwait.
- **1991** Morocco accepts UN plan for referendum in Western Sahara.
- **1992** New constitution grants majority party in parliament right to choose government.
- **1993** First general election for nine years. After major parties refuse his invitation, king appoints nonparty government.
- **1994** King Hassan replaces veteran prime minister Karim Lamrani with Abdellatif Filali.
- **1995** Islamist opposition leader Mohamed Basri returns after 28 years of exile. Severe drought.
- **1998** Socialists enter government under Abderrahmane el Youssoufi.
- **1999** Death of King Hassan. Mohammed VI enthroned. Liberalization program announced.
- **2002** Islamists gain in elections.
- **2003** Polisario accepts UN plan to grant Western Sahara autonomy within Morocco, though Moroccan government rejects it.
- **2004** Over 500 killed in earthquake.

M

DEFENSE

Compulsory military service

$1.31bn

Down 3% in 2002

MOROCCAN ARMED FORCES

744 main battle tanks (224 M-48A5, 420 M-60, 100 T-72)	175,000 personnel
2 frigates and 27 patrol boats	7800 personnel
95 combat aircraft (39 F-5, 29 Mirage F-1, 4 0V-10, 23 Alpha Jet)	13,500 personnel
None	

Morocco's long struggle in Western Sahara against Polisario Front guerrillas earned its forces a formidable reputation. Moroccans have also fought as mercenaries in the Gulf. In the 1980s, sappers constructed a 2500-km (1550-mile) defensive wall to cordon off Western Sahara in an attempt to prevent incursions from Polisario guerrillas based in Algeria. Polisario forces themselves number some 3000–6000.

Morocco's pro-Western stance has allowed its forces access to sophisticated weapons and training from the West, particularly the US, which in 2004 named Morocco a major non-NATO ally.

The air force was formed in 1956 and flies US and European aircraft, notably Mirage interceptors. The navy uses Western-supplied ships, but is insignificant in regional terms. In addition, there are 50,000 paramilitaries.

Spending on defense as a percentage of gross national product is relatively high for a developing country.

Conscription lasts for 18 months. In practice most enlisted personnel are volunteers.

ECONOMICS

Inflation 2.7% p.a. (1990–2001)

$34.7bn

9.024 Moroccan dirhams (9.455)

SCORE CARD

- World GNP Ranking..........58th
- GNP per Capita..........$1170
- Balance of Payments..........$1.49bn
- Inflation..........2.8%
- Unemployment..........19%

EXPORTS

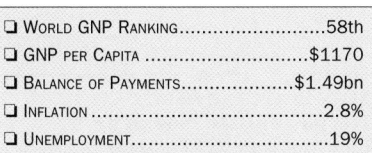

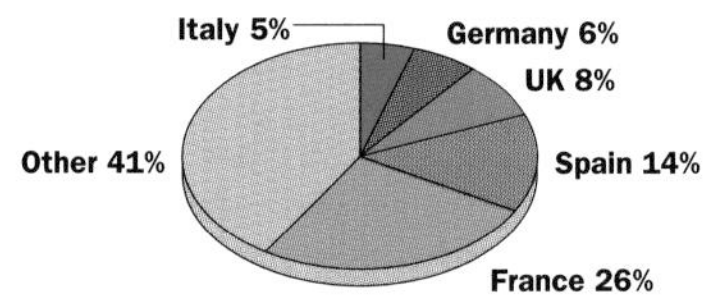
Italy 5%
Germany 6%
UK 8%
Spain 14%
France 26%
Other 41%

IMPORTS

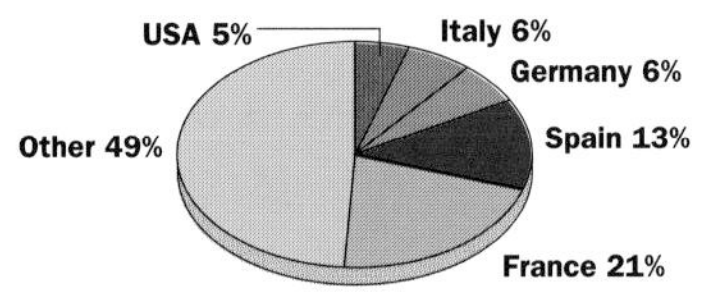
USA 5%
Italy 6%
Germany 6%
Spain 13%
France 21%
Other 49%

ECONOMIC PERFORMANCE INDICATOR

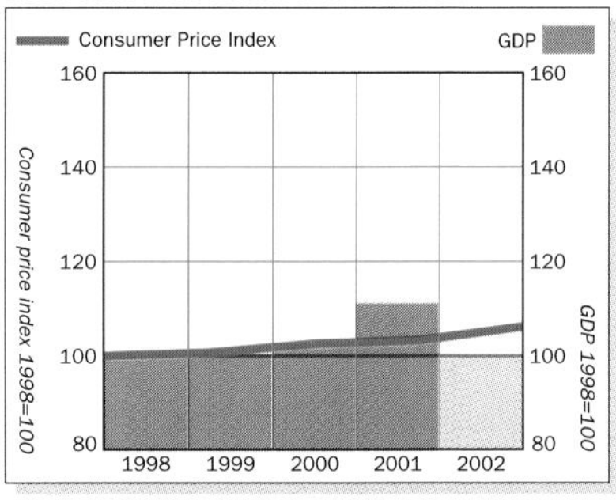
Consumer Price Index
GDP
160
140
120
100
80
Consumer price index 1998=100
GDP 1998=100
1998
1999
2000
2001
2002

Severe drought in 1995 made austerity measures necessary. Socialist-led governments have given social policy a higher priority. Expected revenue from oil reserves will be channeled into the development of rural areas. A free trade deal was signed with the US in 2004 – its first with an African country.

Strengths

Probusiness policies and abundant labor attract foreign investment. Key sectors are tourism, mining (particularly phosphates), agriculture, textiles, and leather. Discovery of oil and gas.

Weaknesses

High unemployment and population growth. Overdependence on drought-prone agriculture. External debt restrains modernization.

Profile

The privatization program, begun in 1992, was designed to attract investment, from Europe in particular.

MOROCCO : MAJOR BUSINESSES

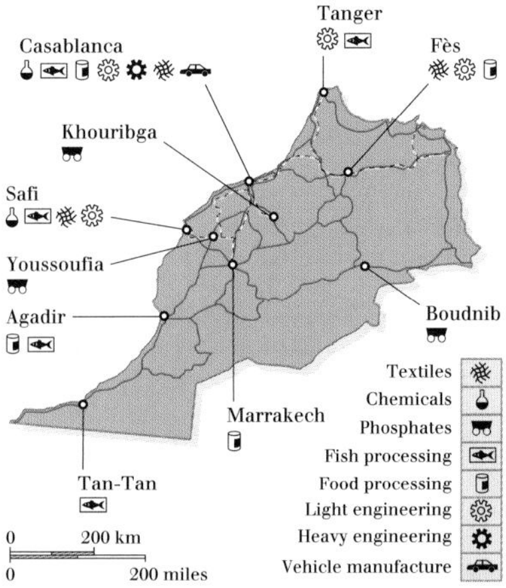
Tanger
Casablanca
Fès
Khouribga
Safi
Youssoufia
Agadir
Boudnib
Marrakech
Tan-Tan
0 200 km
0 200 miles
Textiles
Chemicals
Phosphates
Fish processing
Food processing
Light engineering
Heavy engineering
Vehicle manufacture

RESOURCES

Electric power 4m kW

1.08m tonnes

261 b/d (reserves 659m barrels)

16.7m sheep, 5.21m goats, 137m chickens

Phosphates, oil, gas, coal, iron, barytes, lead, copper, zinc

ELECTRICITY GENERATION

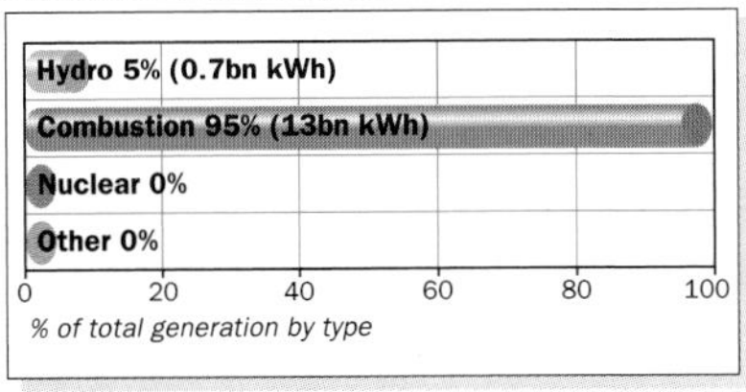
Hydro 5% (0.7bn kWh)
Combustion 95% (13bn kWh)
Nuclear 0%
Other 0%
0
20
40
60
80
100
% of total generation by type

Morocco possesses around a third of the world's phosphate reserves. The discovery of large oil and gas deposits in the northeastern desert in mid-2000 could yield an annual revenue of $400 million.

MOROCCO : LAND USE

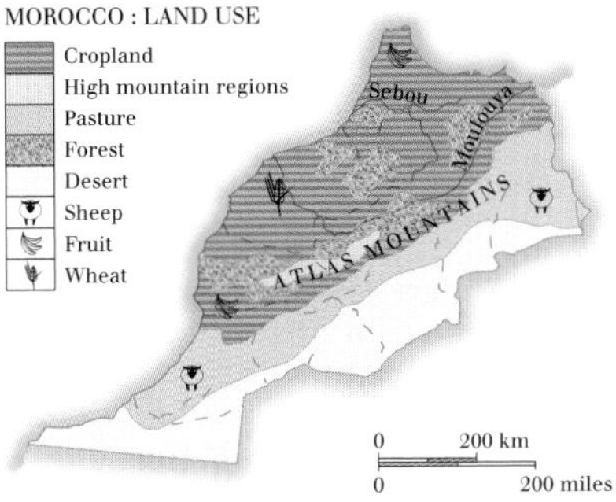
Cropland
High mountain regions
Pasture
Forest
Desert
Sheep
Fruit
Wheat
Sebou
Moulouya
ATLAS MOUNTAINS
0
200 km
0
200 miles

ENVIRONMENT

Sustainability rank: 73rd

0.7% partially protected

1.3 tonnes per capita

ENVIRONMENTAL TREATIES

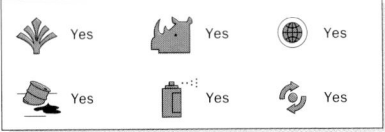

Yes · Yes · Yes

Yes · Yes · Yes

Morocco's wealth of plant and animal life has suffered severely from long periods of drought, most recently in the early 1980s and early 1990s. The unplanned development of tourist resorts is posing a threat to fragile coastal ecosystems.

MEDIA

TV ownership medium

Daily newspaper circulation 28 per 1000 people

PUBLISHING AND BROADCAST MEDIA

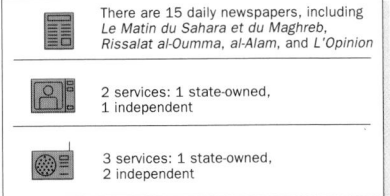

There are 15 daily newspapers, including *Le Matin du Sahara et du Maghreb*, *Rissalat al-Oumma*, *al-Alam*, and *L'Opinion*

2 services: 1 state-owned, 1 independent

3 services: 1 state-owned, 2 independent

The succession of Mohammed VI fueled hopes of a more liberal climate, but the media remain effectively controlled by pressure from the state. Self-censorship is commonplace, particularly over reporting of the Western Sahara issue and royal stories. In 2000, the outspoken French-language weekly *Demain* was banned. The sports pages, especially the soccer reports, are the most dynamic sections of the press. Radio broadcasts are in Arabic, Berber, French, Spanish, and English. International broadcasts are readily available to those who can afford satellite television.

CRIME

Death penalty in use

54,207 prisoners

Crime has risen sharply

CRIME RATES

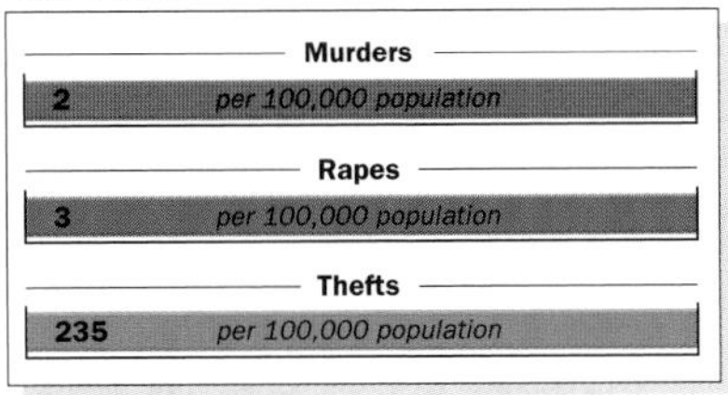
Murders
2
per 100,000 population
Rapes
3
per 100,000 population
Thefts
235
per 100,000 population

Urban crime is increasing; tourists offer a soft target. Prisons are overcrowded, and conditions are poor. Civil occasions are used to pardon thousands of prisoners at a time.

EDUCATION

School leaving age: 14

51%

276,018 students

THE EDUCATION SYSTEM

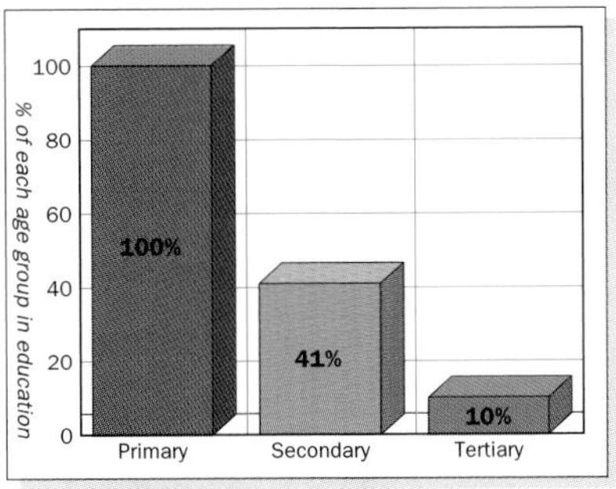
% of each age group in education
100
80
60
40
20
0
100%
41%
10%
Primary
Secondary
Tertiary

Literacy and elementary school net enrollment rates compare unfavorably with neighboring north African states; the widespread use of child labor is a cause for international concern.

The Berber language Tamazight was used in primary schools for the first time in 2003 as part of a ten-year pledge to introduce it at all levels of education.

Al-Qarawiyin University in Fès was reputedly founded in the 9th century.

HEALTH

Welfare state health benefits

1 per 2000 people

Neonatal causes, cerebrovascular and heart diseases

There is one hospital bed for every 1000 people. Despite recent progress, child mortality and nutritional standards for the poorest Moroccans remain substantially below the average. Outside the cities, access to primary health care is poor, with the result that people depend on traditional remedies for illnesses. All employees are required to contribute to a social welfare fund, which operates a system of benefits in the event of illness and occupational accidents, and during old age.

SPENDING

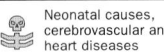

GDP/cap. increase

CONSUMPTION AND SPENDING

42 per 1000 population

38 per 1000 population

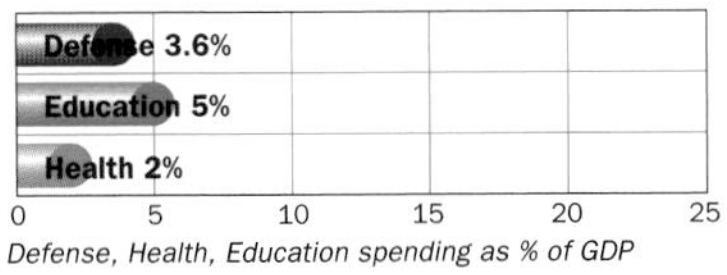
Defense 3.6%
Education 5%
Health 2%
0
5
10
15
20
25
Defense, Health, Education spending as % of GDP

Average income per head is much lower than in the neighboring countries of Algeria and Tunisia. Over 14% of Moroccans live below the UN poverty line of $2 a day, and the rural–urban gap in wealth is considerable; just under half of the population live in rural areas. A period of drought in the 1990s encouraged urban drift.

Unrest has largely been avoided owing to the fact that Morocco has a thriving informal sector. This provides jobs in food processing, clothes manufacturing, goods transportation, and the hotel and building trades. In addition, there is work to be found in the illegal hashish trade and the smuggling of alcohol and Western goods.

WORLD RANKING

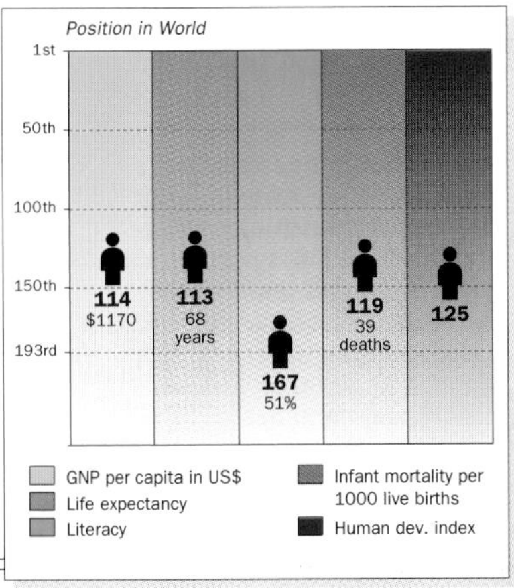
Position in World
1st
50th
100th
150th
193rd
114
$1170
113
68
years
167
51%
119
39
deaths
125
GNP per capita in US$
Life expectancy
Literacy
Infant mortality per 1000 live births
Human dev. index

M

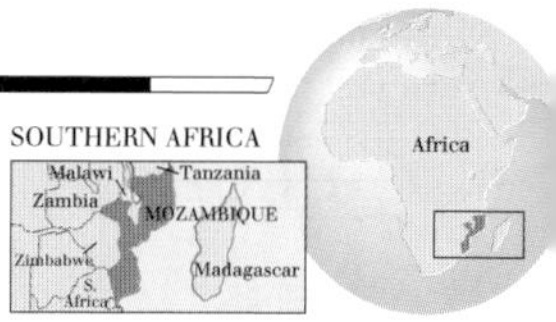
SOUTHERN AFRICA
Malawi
Tanzania
Zambia
MOZAMBIQUE
Zimbabwe
Madagascar
S. Africa
Africa

MOZAMBIQUE

OFFICIAL NAME: Republic of Mozambique **CAPITAL:** Maputo
POPULATION: 18.9 million **CURRENCY:** Metical **OFFICIAL LANGUAGE:** Portuguese

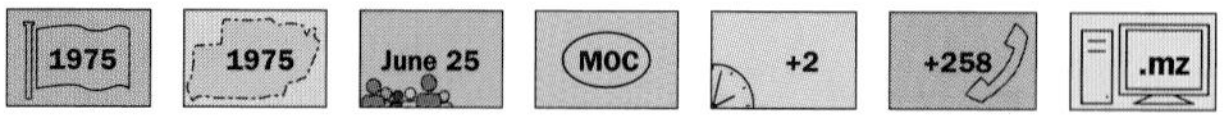
1975
1975
June 25
MOC
+2
+258
.mz

SITUATED ON THE SOUTHEAST African coast, Mozambique is bisected by the Zambezi River. South of the Zambezi lies a semiarid savanna lowland. The more fertile north-central delta provinces around Tete are home to most of Mozambique's ethnically diverse population. Following independence from Portugal in 1975, Mozambique was torn apart by civil war between the (then Marxist) Frelimo government and the South African-backed Mozambique National Resistance (Renamo). The conflict finally ended in 1992 after UN arbitration. Multiparty elections in 1994 returned Frelimo to power. Hit by devastating floods in 2000 and 2001, Mozambique is now one of Africa's top attractors of foreign investment.

CLIMATE

Tropical wet and dry

WEATHER CHART FOR MAPUTO

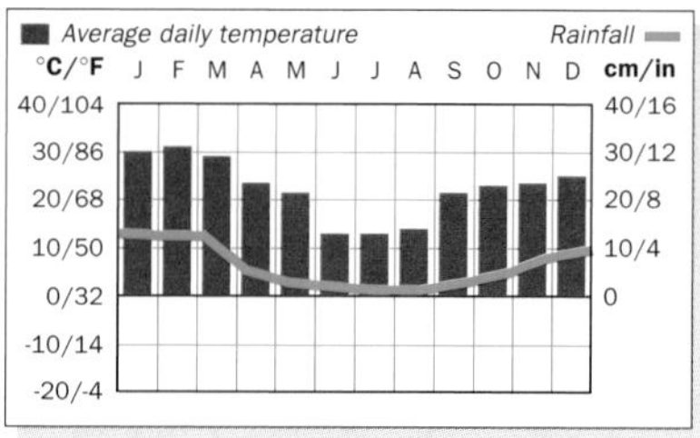
Average daily temperature
Rainfall
°C/°F J F M A M J J A S O N D cm/in
40/104
30/86
20/68
10/50
0/32
-10/14
-20/-4
40/16
30/12
20/8
10/4
0

Generally, Mozambique has a rainy season and a dry season; the coast at Beira and at Quelimane and the highlands west of Nampula are the wettest areas; the Zambezi valley is the hottest region. The country is prone, however, to weather extremes. In the 1980s, frequent failure of the rains contributed to two disastrous famines, while devastating floods occurred in 2000 and 2001, and drought returned in 2002.

TRANSPORTATION

Drive on left

Maputo International 445,383 passengers

131 ships 37,200 grt

THE TRANSPORTATION NETWORK

5776 km (3589 miles)	None
2072 km (1287 miles)	3750 km (2330 miles)

The billion-dollar Maputo Corridor connects South African industrial centers with the Mozambican coast, and has facilitated port modernization since its completion in 1995. CFM, the state-owned railroad company, is cooperating with other neighboring states. The national airline is no longer state-owned and has faced difficulty in recent years. Landmines still hamper access, particularly in rural areas. Remote communities remain isolated.

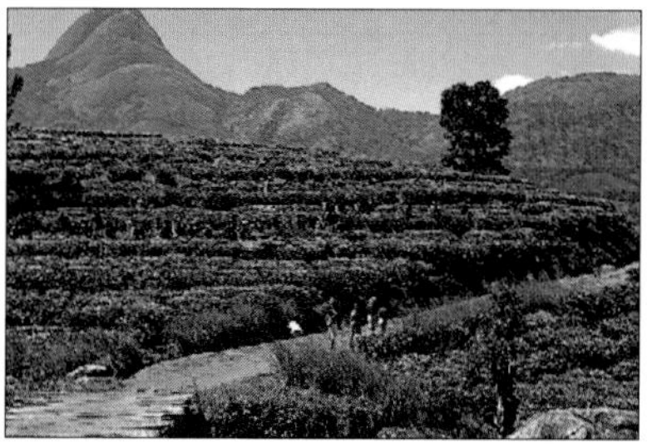

Tea picking. *Other important cash crops are cashew nuts, cotton, sugar, copra, and citrus fruits. Agriculture employs 85% of workers.*

TOURISM

Visitors : Population 1:20

942,885 visitors

Up 95% in 2002

MAIN TOURIST ARRIVALS

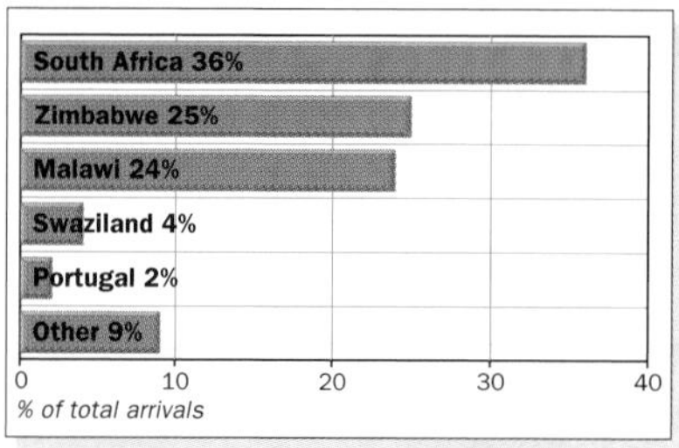
South Africa 36%
Zimbabwe 25%
Malawi 24%
Swaziland 4%
Portugal 2%
Other 9%
0
10
20
30
40
% of total arrivals

Mozambique used to attract around 300,000 South Africans and Rhodesians a year in the 1970s. The tourist industry was destroyed by the civil war and is still being rebuilt. Landmines still render travel outside the capital hazardous, while food shortages, poor infrastructure, and costly international flights are added obstacles. The floods in 2000 and 2001 were the cause of further setbacks.

Given political stability, though, Mozambique could yet exploit its excellent beaches and game reserves, which include the Gorongosa National Park. Some hotel groups are once more targeting Maputo as a luxury tourist and conference venue.

PEOPLE

Pop. density low

Makua, Xitsonga, Sena, Lomwe, Portuguese

24/km² (62/mi²)

THE URBAN/RURAL POPULATION SPLIT

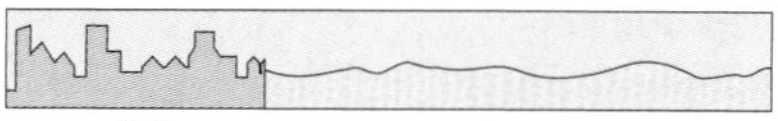
34%
66%

RELIGIOUS PERSUASION

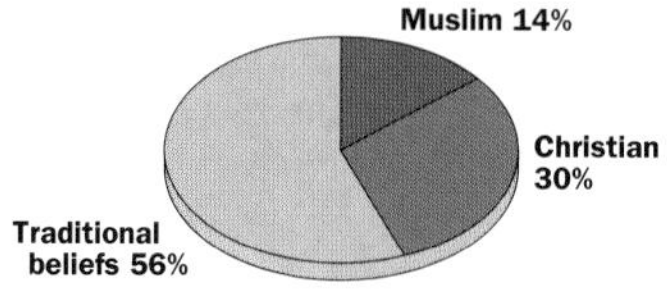
Muslim 14%
Christian 30%
Traditional beliefs 56%

ETHNIC MAKEUP

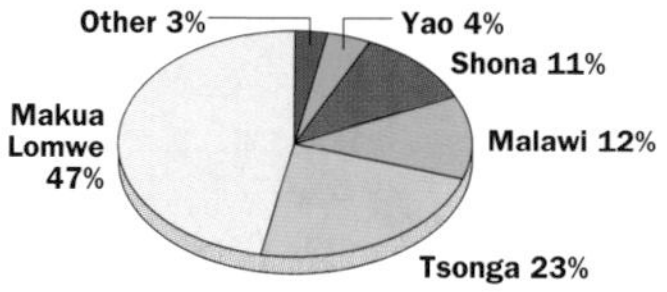
Other 3%
Yao 4%
Shona 11%
Malawi 12%
Tsonga 23%
Makua Lomwe 47%

The very large black African majority is divided into numerous groups. There are tiny minorities of whites, mixed-race groups, and Asians. However, the predominant social tensions are regional: Renamo, strong in the north and the center, accuses the Frelimo government of consistently favoring the south. Antiwhite feelings are growing too, as "Africanists" claim that whites enjoy disproportionate political and economic influence.

Society centers on the extended family. In some northern provinces this is matriarchal. Polygamy is fairly widespread among men who can support second wives. Frelimo emphasizes women's rights. Many women served in Frelimo armies, and are now protected by divorce, child-custody, and husband-desertion laws. The Mozambican Women's Organization encourages political participation.

The death of almost a million people during 17 years of civil war has seriously affected the economy and society. The sheer loss of manpower is exacerbated by the parallel increase in the number of orphans, widows, and amputees.

POPULATION AGE BREAKDOWN

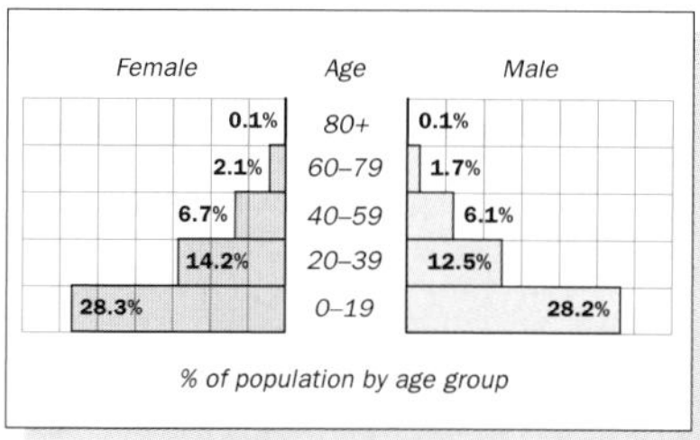
Female
Age
Male
0.1%
80+
0.1%
2.1%
60–79
1.7%
6.7%
40–59
6.1%
14.2%
20–39
12.5%
28.3%
0–19
28.2%
% of population by age group

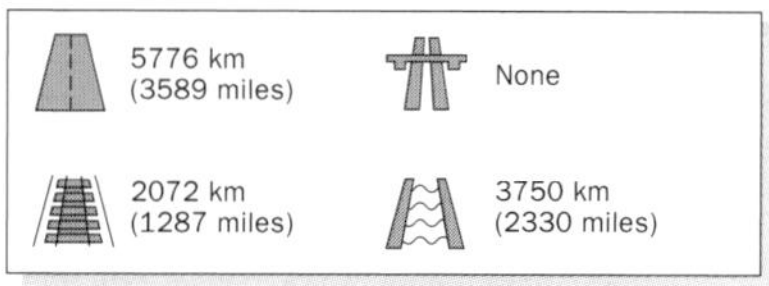

M

POLITICS

Multiparty elections

1999/2004

President Joaquim Alberto Chissano

AT THE LAST ELECTION

Assembly of the Republic 250 seats

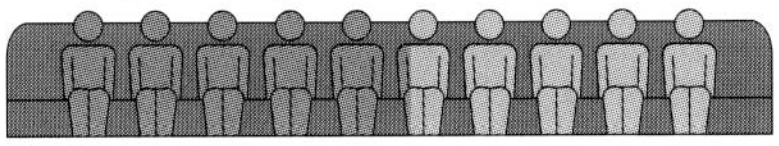
53%
Frelimo
47%
Renamo

Frelimo = Front for the Liberation of Mozambique
Renamo = Mozambique National Resistance

Mozambique held its first multiparty elections in 1994.

PROFILE

Changing international realities in 1990 at the end of the Cold War persuaded the previously Soviet-backed Frelimo government to adopt a democratic constitution. Its civil-war rival Renamo lost the support of South Africa after the fall of apartheid there in the same year, and today little distinguishes the two parties ideologically. Though Frelimo is the larger party in the Assembly, Renamo is clearly popular, and demands recognition for its 15 years of struggle. New groups, such as the antiwhite Palmo, Coinmo, and Unamo, have recently emerged; Frelimo is pushing ahead with plans to decentralize power. Fears for the future of Mozambican democracy have been rekindled since 1999 amid worsening disputes between Renamo and Frelimo. Contentious issues include provincial representation, the murder of a prominent journalist in 2000, and parliamentary defections between parties. There has been occasional violent rioting.

Joaquim Chissano, president since 1986, has pushed toward political pluralism.

Afonso Dhlakama, Renamo leader, has turned from militarism to politics.

MAIN POLITICAL ISSUES

The move to democracy

The country's first democratic elections were held in 1994 and returned Frelimo to power. However, support for Renamo was stronger than had been expected. Their leader Afonso Dhlakama polled strongly in the presidential elections in both 1994 and 1999, contesting Joaquim Chissano's claim of victory. In 2002 Frelimo chose Armando Guebeza as its candidate for the 2004 presidential elections to replace incumbent Chissano.

Reconstruction

The government is slowly rebuilding a country where devastating floods in 2000 and 2001, and severe drought in 2002, have simply added to the ravages of civil war. The fighting had left 900,000 dead, one million refugees, and an estimated 80% of the remaining population living below the national poverty line.

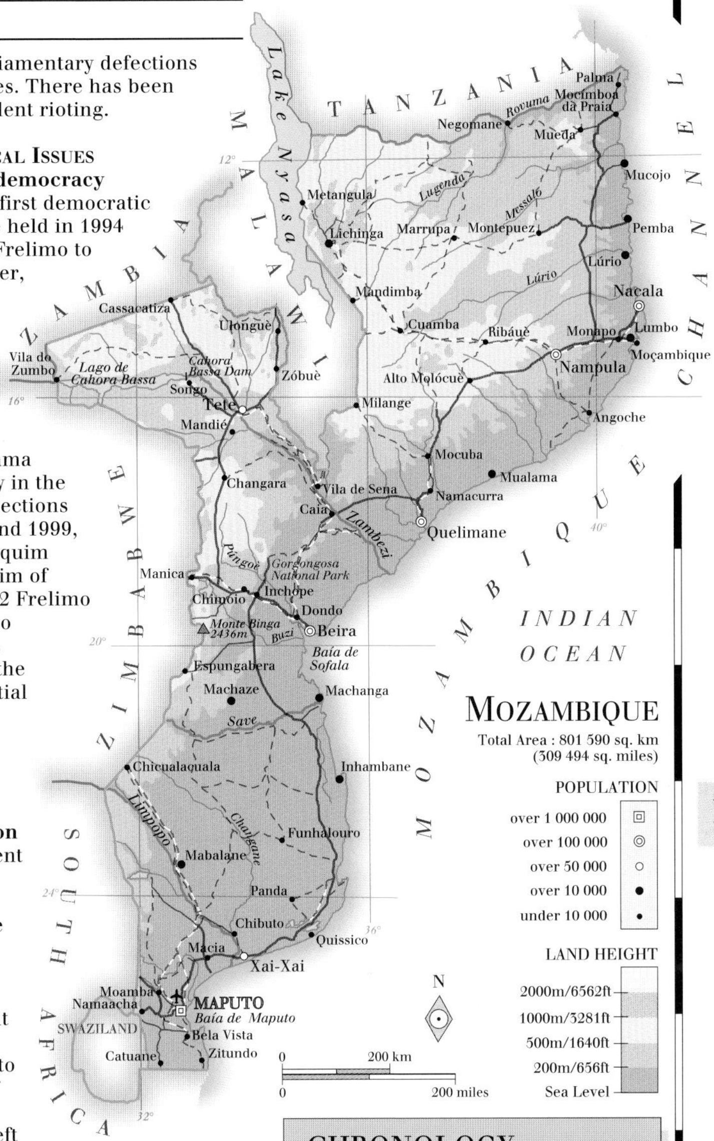
TANZANIA
MALAWI
ZAMBIA
ZIMBABWE
SOUTH AFRICA
SWAZILAND
MOZAMBIQUE CHANNEL
INDIAN OCEAN
Lake Nyasa
Palma
Mocímboa da Praia
Negomane
Rovuma
Mueda
Mucojo
Pemba
Metangula
Lugenda
Messalo
Lichinga
Marrupa
Montepuez
Lúrio
Mandimba
Nacala
Cuamba
Ribáuè
Monapo
Lumbo
Moçambique
Nampula
Alto Molócuè
Cassacatiza
Ulongue
Vila do Zumbo
Lago de Cahora Bassa
Cahora Bassa Dam
Songo
Tete
Zóbuè
Milange
Mandié
Angoche
Mocuba
Mualama
Changara
Vila de Sena
Namacurra
Caia
Zambezi
Quelimane
Pungoè
Gorongosa National Park
Manica
Inchope
Chimoio
Dondo
Monte Binga 2436m
Buzi
Beira
Baía de Sofala
Espungabera
Machaze
Machanga
Save
Chicualacuala
Inhambane
Limpopo
Changane
Funhalouro
Mabalane
Panda
Chibuto
Quissico
Macia
Xai-Xai
Moamba
Namaacha
MAPUTO
Baía de Maputo
Bela Vista
Catuane
Zitundo
N
0
200 km
0
200 miles
MOZAMBIQUE
Total Area : 801 590 sq. km (309 494 sq. miles)
POPULATION
over 1 000 000
over 100 000
over 50 000
over 10 000
under 10 000
LAND HEIGHT
2000m/6562ft
1000m/3281ft
500m/1640ft
200m/656ft
Sea Level

CHRONOLOGY

The Portuguese tapped the local trade in slaves, gold, and ivory in the 16th century and made Mozambique a colony in 1752. Large areas were run by private companies until 1929.

- **1964** Frelimo starts war of liberation.
- **1975** Independence. Frelimo leader Samora Machel is president.
- **1976** Rhodesians set up Renamo resistance movement inside Mozambique.
- **1976–1980** Mozambique closes Rhodesian border and supports Zimbabwean freedom fighters. Reprisals by Renamo.
- **1977** Frelimo constitutes itself as Marxist-Leninist party.
- **1980** South Africa takes over backing of Renamo.

WORLD AFFAIRS

Joined UN in 1975

Comm | CPLP | AU | OIC | SADC

Mozambique was a key Cold War battleground between Soviet-backed Marxism and capitalism sponsored by the US and South Africa. The resulting civil war devastated the country until peace in 1992.

In the early 1980s, however, the Frelimo government's position began to shift as Soviet aid became erratic. Responding to President Samora Machel's overtures, the US lifted its ban on economic assistance in 1984. Britain agreed to train Frelimo's forces in 1987. South Africa continued tacitly to support Renamo until at least 1990. Zimbabwean troops helped Mozambique guard the strategically important Beira and Limpopo corridors, but left in 1993.

In 1995, the UN withdrew its peacekeepers and a democratic Mozambique joined the Commonwealth, despite having no formal links with the old British Empire. President Chissano became deputy head of the SADC, but regional tensions persisted, with Mozambique accusing South Africans of gun-running, and Swaziland claiming Maputo Province as its own.

CHRONOLOGY *continued*

- **1982** Zimbabwean troops arrive to guard Mutare–Beira corridor.
- **1984** Nkomati Accord: South Africa agrees to stop support for Renamo, and Mozambique for ANC, but fighting continues.
- **1986** Renamo declares war on Zimbabwe. Tanzanian troops reinforce Frelimo. Machel dies in mysterious air crash in South Africa. Joaquim Chissano replaces him.
- **1988** Nkomati Accord reactivated. Mozambicans allowed back to work in South African mines.
- **1989** War and malnutrition said to claim one million lives. Frelimo drops Marxism-Leninism.
- **1990** Multipartyism and free-market economy in new constitution. Renamo breaches cease-fire.
- **1992** Chissano signs peace agreement with Renamo.
- **1994** Democratic elections return Frelimo to power.
- **1995** Joins Commonwealth. Economic reforms begun.
- **1999** G7 chooses Mozambique as flagship for international debt relief initiative. Renamo disputes results of December elections.
- **2000–2001** Thousands displaced by devastating floods.

AID

Recipient

$2.06bn (receipts) — Up 121% in 2002

Mozambique is one of the most aid-dependent countries in the world; aid accounted for over half of GNP in 2002. In 1999, however, it became one of only four countries to benefit from the G7 debt-relief scheme for HIPCs, which is worth nearly $3 billion. Debt servicing still accounted for almost 50% of aid in 2001–2002, but recent cancellations under the HIPC scheme have slashed hundreds of millions of dollars from the debt total. The main donor states are France, Italy, Germany, the US, and the UK.

DEFENSE

Compulsory military service

$76m — Down 12% in 2002

Since the civil war ended in 1992 the military's once dominant role in society has greatly diminished. Military figures have been largely stripped of political influence and defense spending has been cut dramatically. Internal security is now a police issue.

Mozambique's new postwar, British-trained permanent army was formally inaugurated in 1994. Truly national in character, and only around 8000 strong, it contains both former government and Renamo troops. While there are some military aircraft, they are mostly nonoperational.

One by-product of reorganization, however, was the demobilization of some 75,000 battle-hardened soldiers. Their severance pay ended in 1996, and it has not been easy to retrain them, or reintegrate them into civilian life. Some have turned to banditry.

The end of the civil war saw the departure of external forces, such as UN peacekeepers and also the Zimbabwean troops who once guarded strategic railroads against Renamo attack.

MOZAMBICAN ARMED FORCES

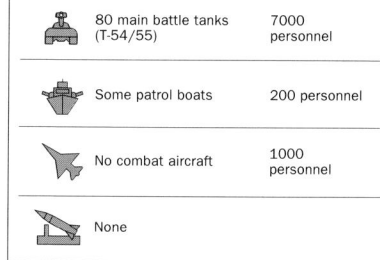

80 main battle tanks (T-54/55)	7000 personnel
Some patrol boats	200 personnel
No combat aircraft	1000 personnel
None	

M

ECONOMICS

Inflation 30% p.a. (1990–2001)

$3.64bn — 22,852 meticais (23,345)

SCORE CARD

World GNP Ranking	125th
GNP per Capita	$200
Balance of Payments	–$421m
Inflation	16.8%
Unemployment	21%

EXPORTS

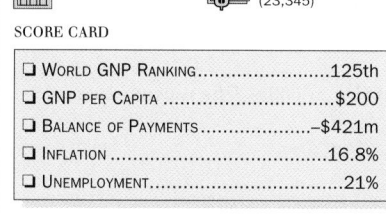

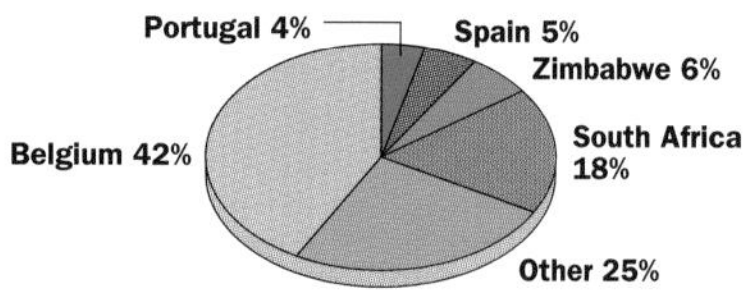
Portugal 4%
Spain 5%
Zimbabwe 6%
South Africa 18%
Belgium 42%
Other 25%

IMPORTS

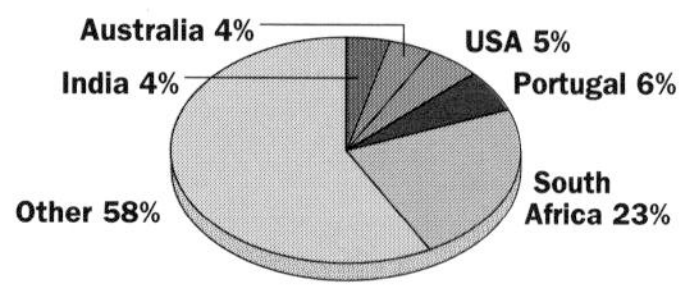
Australia 4%
USA 5%
India 4%
Portugal 6%
Other 58%
South Africa 23%

ECONOMIC PERFORMANCE INDICATOR

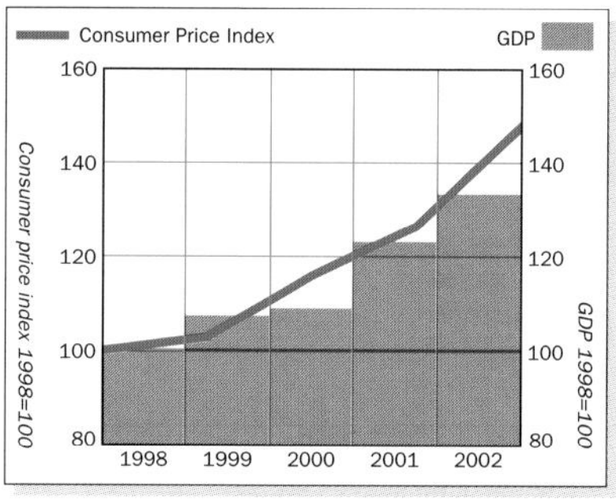
Consumer Price Index
GDP
160
140
120
100
80
1998
1999
2000
2001
2002
Consumer price index 1998=100
GDP 1998=100

Strengths

IMF-sponsored program of privatization, exchange-rate reforms, and trade liberalization have helped attract aid and investment and increase exports. Relative political stability. Massive rural development programs target agriculture, which employs 85% of the workforce. Fisheries industry has great potential. Improved transportation links with Maputo, Africa's second-largest harbor, will help to service southern Africa's landlocked regions.

Weaknesses

Overseas aid is essential to prevent at least half the population starving. Overdependence on foreign donors and companies is another long-term concern. The country is susceptible to drought, floods, and cyclones. Skilled workers often choose to work in other countries, impeding Mozambique's return to normal economic activity. Increase in corruption.

Profile

Though Mozambique has enormous economic problems, the Chissano government in 1995 produced an optimistic plan, based on World Bank recommendations, to eradicate poverty and raise annual GDP growth to 8–9% by 2000. Despite the devastation resulting from the floods of 2000 and 2001, GDP growth soon recovered, averaging 9% in 2003–2004. The go-ahead for a new port at Dobela, in the south, was given in 2002.

MOZAMBIQUE : MAJOR BUSINESSES

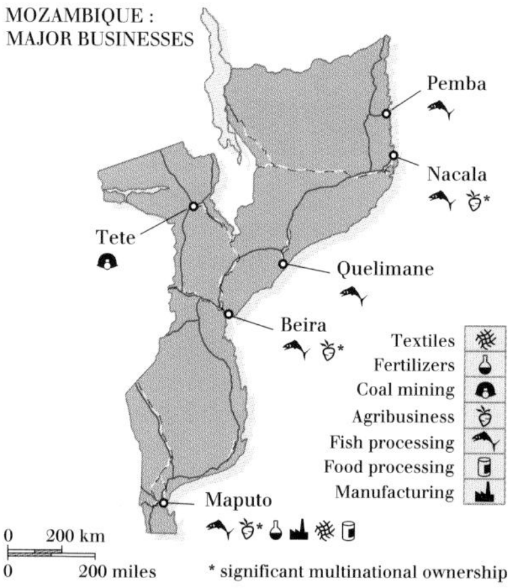
Pemba
Nacala
Tete
Quelimane
Beira
Maputo
Textiles
Fertilizers
Coal mining
Agribusiness
Fish processing
Food processing
Manufacturing
0 200 km
0 200 miles
* significant multinational ownership

RESOURCES

Electric power 2.1m kW

32,512 tonnes

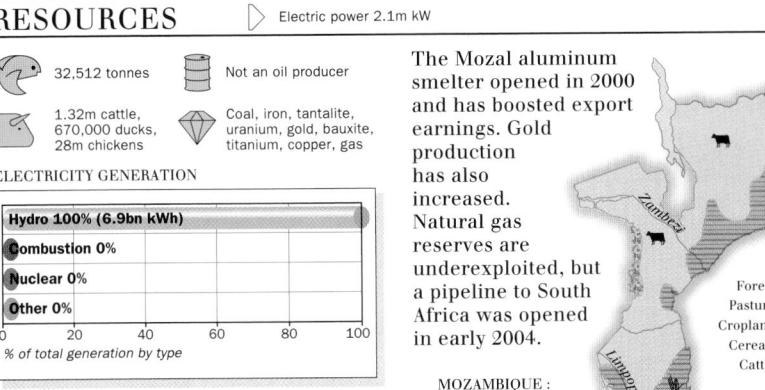

Not an oil producer

1.32m cattle, 670,000 ducks, 28m chickens

Coal, iron, tantalite, uranium, gold, bauxite, titanium, copper, gas

ELECTRICITY GENERATION

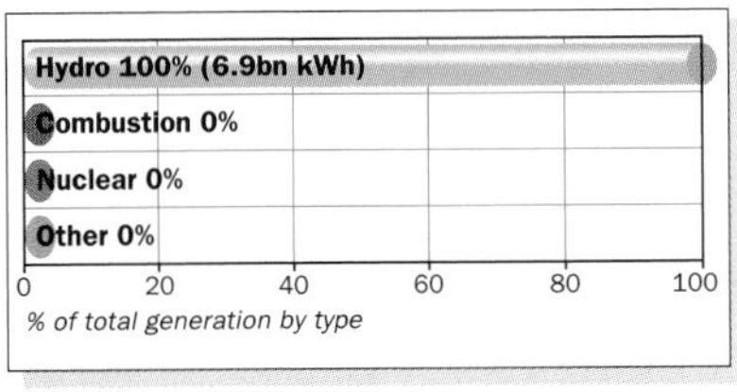
Hydro 100% (6.9bn kWh)
Combustion 0%
Nuclear 0%
Other 0%
0
20
40
60
80
100
% of total generation by type

Shrimp and prawns are farmed and exported. On dry land, cotton vies with cashew nuts as the chief crop.

The Mozal aluminum smelter opened in 2000 and has boosted export earnings. Gold production has also increased. Natural gas reserves are underexploited, but a pipeline to South Africa was opened in early 2004.

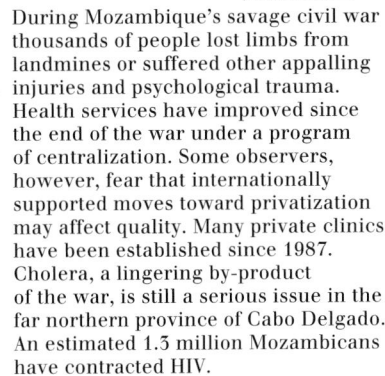

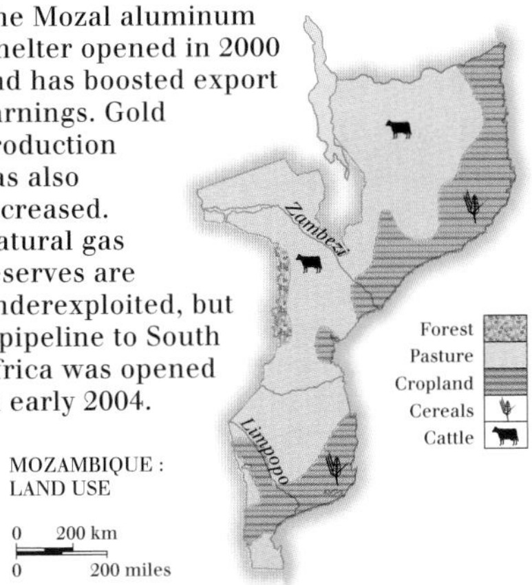
Zambezi
Limpopo
Forest
Pasture
Cropland
Cereals
Cattle
MOZAMBIQUE : LAND USE
0 200 km
0 200 miles

ENVIRONMENT

Sustainability rank: 59th

8% (6% partially protected)

0.1 tonnes per capita

ENVIRONMENTAL TREATIES

No	Yes	Yes
Yes	Yes	No

Floods followed by droughts are often devastating. Floods in 2000 and 2001, resulting from a combination of cyclones and torrential rain, affected around one million people. Civil war had pushed people toward the cities and coasts, causing overcrowding, disease, pollution, and desertification of abandoned farms. The Great Limpopo Transfrontier Park opened in 2002. Straddling the border with South Africa and Zimbabwe and covering 35,000 sq. km (13,500 sq. miles), it is Africa's largest reserve. Ecological concerns, however, are still low on the national agenda.

MEDIA

TV ownership low

Daily newspaper circulation 2 per 1000 people

PUBLISHING AND BROADCAST MEDIA

There are 5 daily newspapers, including *Notícias* and *Diário de Moçambique*

2 services: 1 state-owned, 1 independent

5 services: 2 state-owned, 3 independent

The press, hitherto a Frelimo publicity machine, has enjoyed greater freedom in the 1990s. The killing in 2000 of a popular and outspoken editor, Carlos Cardoso, shocked the country. TV sets are still a rarity. The state-owned radio station broadcasts in Portuguese, English, and vernacular languages.

CRIME

No death penalty

8812 prisoners

Little change from year to year

CRIME RATES

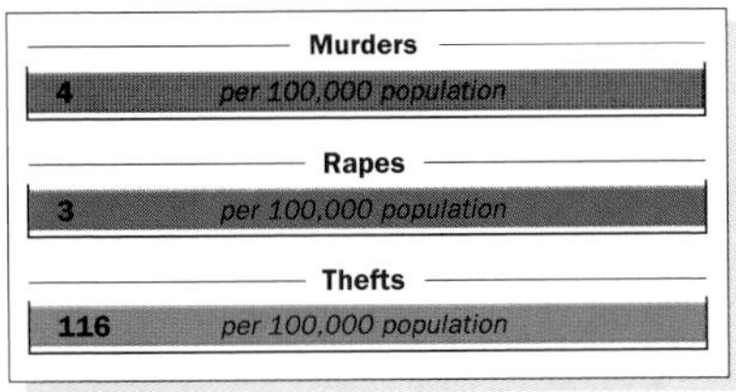
Murders
4 per 100,000 population
Rapes
3 per 100,000 population
Thefts
116 per 100,000 population

Weapons are easily obtainable. In rural areas there are many bandits, often former soldiers; road travel is unsafe. Senior officials stand accused of misappropriating food aid money.

EDUCATION

School leaving age: 12

47%

9774 students

THE EDUCATION SYSTEM

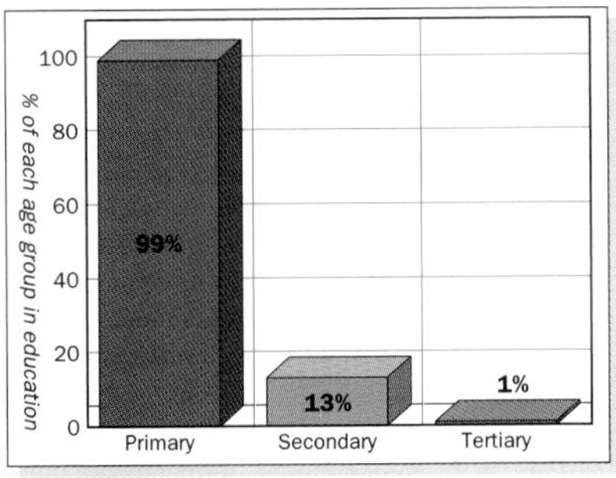
100
80
60
40
20
0
% of each age group in education
99%
13%
1%
Primary
Secondary
Tertiary

At independence, between 85% and 95% of the adult population were illiterate, while school closures during the civil war created a lost generation of uneducated people. In 2001, around two-thirds of youths (15–24) could read, thanks to a concerted literacy campaign. The government used World Bank/IMF debt relief to strengthen the education budget in 2001.

HEALTH

Welfare state health benefits

1 per 50,000 people

Tuberculosis, gastroenteric infections, pneumonia, AIDS

During Mozambique's savage civil war thousands of people lost limbs from landmines or suffered other appalling injuries and psychological trauma. Health services have improved since the end of the war under a program of centralization. Some observers, however, fear that internationally supported moves toward privatization may affect quality. Many private clinics have been established since 1987. Cholera, a lingering by-product of the war, is still a serious issue in the far northern province of Cabo Delgado. An estimated 1.3 million Mozambicans have contracted HIV.

SPENDING

GDP/cap. increase

CONSUMPTION AND SPENDING

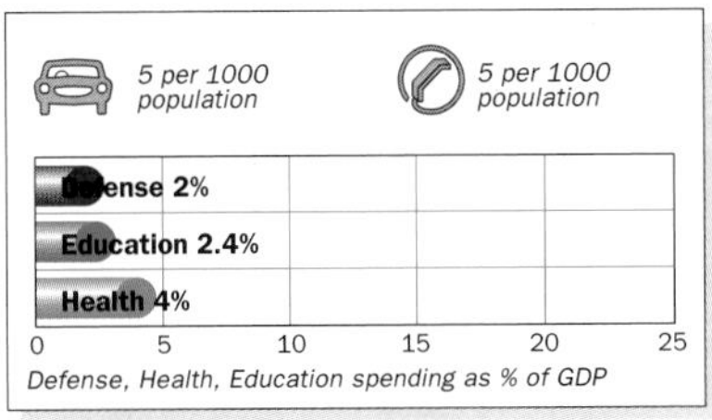
5 per 1000 population
5 per 1000 population
Defense 2%
Education 2.4%
Health 4%
0
5
10
15
20
25
Defense, Health, Education spending as % of GDP

Mozambique is one of the world's poorest countries, with around 80% of the people living below the national poverty line even before the floods of 2000 and 2001, which left thousands homeless. Measures adopted in the 1990s to attract Western aid made conditions tougher, raising the price of rice by 600%. The recent export boom has generally bypassed the traditional subsistence farmer. Only the higher echelons of Frelimo, Renamo, and other political parties have cars, air-conditioning, and brick-built apartments. Free-market reforms, however, are gradually increasing access to consumer goods.

WORLD RANKING

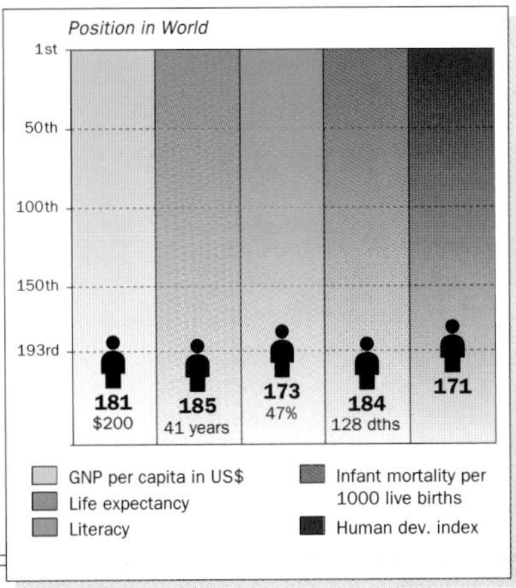
Position in World
1st
50th
100th
150th
193rd
181
$200
185
41 years
173
47%
184
128 dths
171
GNP per capita in US$
Life expectancy
Literacy
Infant mortality per 1000 live births
Human dev. index

M

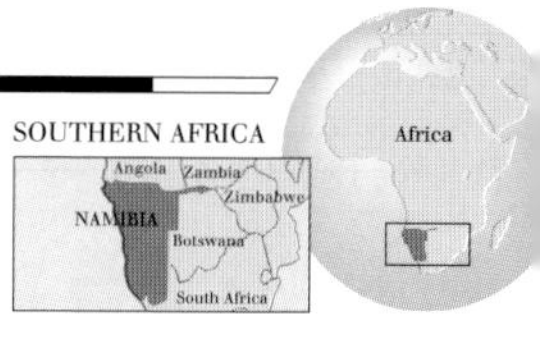
SOUTHERN AFRICA
Africa
Angola
Zambia
Zimbabwe
NAMIBIA
Botswana
South Africa

NAMIBIA

OFFICIAL NAME: Republic of Namibia **CAPITAL:** Windhoek
POPULATION: 2 million **CURRENCY:** Namibian dollar **OFFICIAL LANGUAGE:** English

1990 | 1994 | March 21 | NAM | +2 | +264 | .na

NAMIBIA LIES IN SOUTHWEST Africa, the ecologically unique Namib Desert extending the length of its long coastline. After many years of guerrilla warfare, Namibia won independence from South Africa in 1990. Despite the move away from apartheid, Namibia's economy remains reliant on the expertise of the small white population, a legacy of the previously poor education for blacks. Namibia is one of Africa's leading mineral producers.

CLIMATE

Hot desert/steppe

WEATHER CHART FOR WINDHOEK

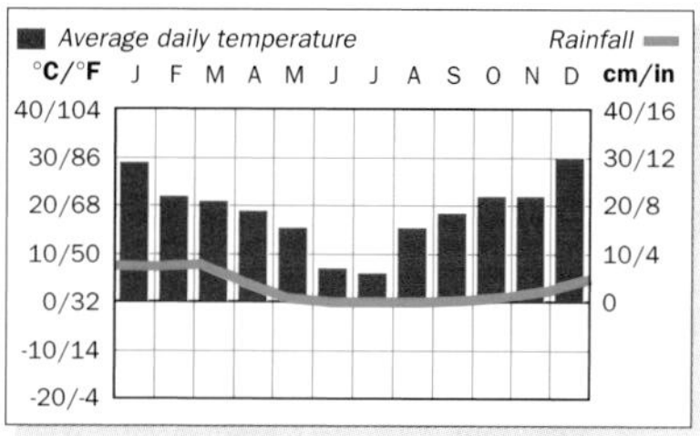
Average daily temperature
Rainfall
°C/°F J F M A M J J A S O N D cm/in
40/104
30/86
20/68
10/50
0/32
-10/14
-20/-4
40/16
30/12
20/8
10/4
0

Namibia is almost rainless. The coast is usually shrouded in thick, cold fog unless the hot, very dry *berg* blows.

TRANSPORTATION

Drive on left

Windhoek International
506,077 passengers

126 ships
69,488 grt

THE TRANSPORTATION NETWORK

8091 km (5028 miles) | None
2382 km (1480 miles) | None

Large-scale industry is well served by road and rail. Plans exist to build a new harbor at Walvis Bay.

TOURISM

Visitors : Population 1:2.3

861,000 visitors

Up 40% in 1999–2001

MAIN TOURIST ARRIVALS

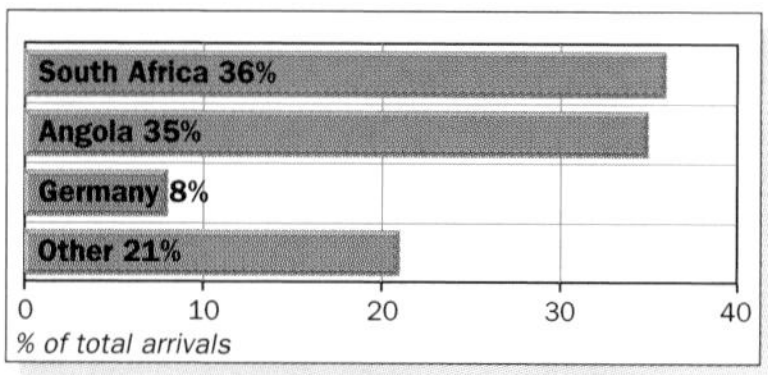
South Africa 36%
Angola 35%
Germany 8%
Other 21%
0
10
20
30
40
% of total arrivals

Tourists, mainly from neighboring countries and Germany, the former colonial power, make a very limited contribution to GDP. There are plans to limit tourists to 300,000 a year to preserve the fragile desert ecology.

Spitzkoppe, west of Karibib. *Unique scenery such as this is attracting increasing numbers of tourists to Namibia.*

PEOPLE

Pop. density low

Ovambo, Kavango, English, Bergdama, German, Afrikaans

2/km² (6/mi²)

THE URBAN/RURAL POPULATION SPLIT

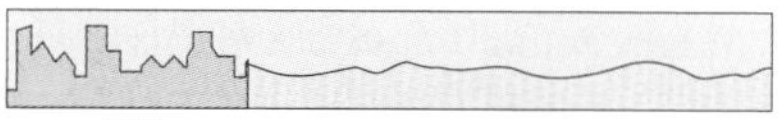
32%
68%

ETHNIC MAKEUP

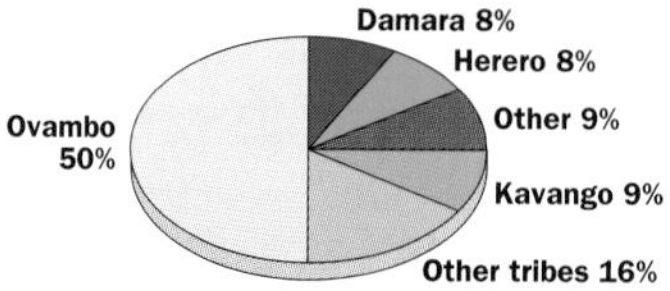
Damara 8%
Herero 8%
Other 9%
Kavango 9%
Other tribes 16%
Ovambo 50%

The largest ethnic group, the Ovambo, tend to live in the sparsely populated north. Smaller groups, such as the Herero and the Afrikaans-speaking Basters, are politically vocal. Whites – most of whom speak Afrikaans – are concentrated in Windhoek. The capital is also home to a wealthy century-old German community. Namibia's original inhabitants, the San and Khoi (once called Bushmen) now constitute a tiny, marginalized minority. The ethnic strife predicted in 1990 has not materialized.

Black Namibians are predominantly subsistence farmers. Many black women have six or more children. The constitution supports gender equality and discriminates in favor of women; few, however, have official jobs or own property. Homosexuality is not tolerated.

POLITICS

Multiparty elections

L. House 1999/2004
U. House 1998/2004

President Sam Nujoma

AT THE LAST ELECTION

National Assembly 72 seats

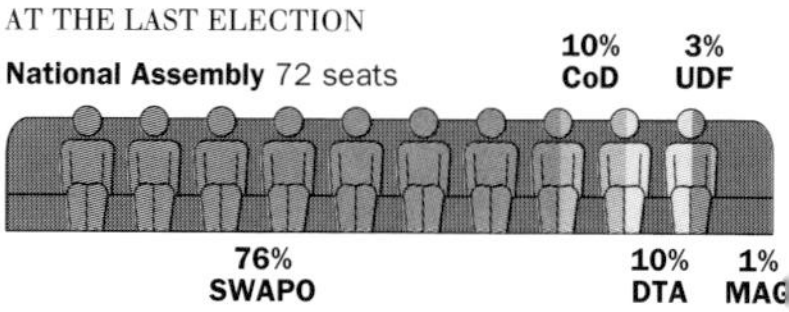
10% CoD
3% UDF
76% SWAPO
10% DTA
1% MAG

SWAPO = South West Africa People's Organization **CoD** = Congress of Democrats **DTA** = Democratic Turnhalle Alliance **UDF** = United Democratic Front **MAG** = Monitor Action Group
Six additional nonvoting members may be appointed to the National Assembly by the president

National Council 26 seats

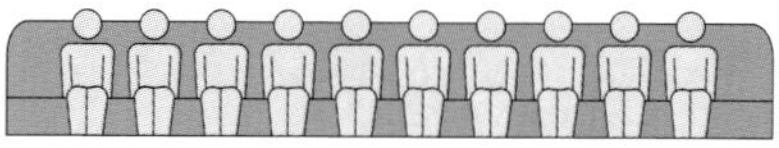

Two members are elected by each of the 13 Regional Councils to the National Council

Namibia became a multiparty democracy at independence in 1990. The center-left SWAPO, the former guerrilla force, has dominated politics ever since. A 1998 constitutional amendment allowed President Sam Nujoma a third term in 1999, despite violence among separatists in the Caprivi Strip. Theo-Ben Gurirab, prime minister since 2002, has made redistribution of land a priority. SWAPO backed Lands Minister Hifikepunye Pohamba in the 2004 presidential election.

WORLD AFFAIRS

Joined UN in 1990

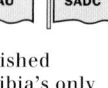

Comm | COMESA | NAM | AU | SADC

In 1994 South Africa relinquished control of Walvis Bay – Namibia's only deepwater port. South Africa has also written off Namibia's earlier debts. Remaining border disputes were settled in the late 1990s. Namibian troops withdrew from the war-torn Democratic Republic of the Congo in 2001.

AID

Recipient

US$135m (receipts)

Up 23% in 2002

The EU provides most aid; Germany is the main unilateral donor. Around 30% of aid is spent on education.

DEFENSE

No compulsory military service

US$79m

Down 5% in 2002

Fishing grounds are patrolled to prevent raids by foreign trawlers. In 2003, Namibian soldiers performed a peacekeeping role in Liberia.

N

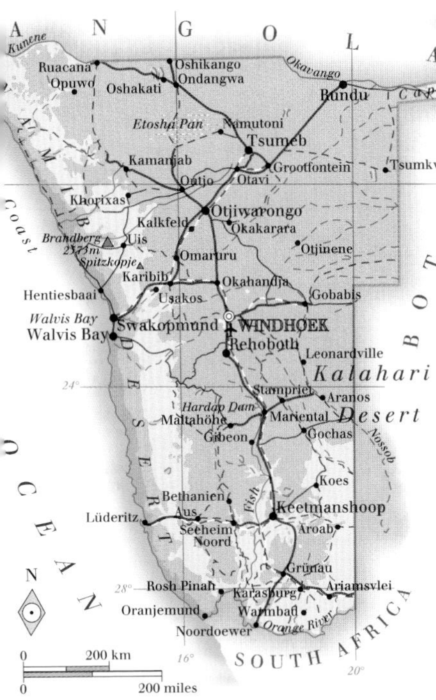
ANGOLA
Kunene
Ruacana
Opuwo
Oshakati
Oshikango
Ondangwa
Okavango
Rundu
Caprivi Strip
Etosha Pan
Namutoni
Tsumeb
Grootfontein
Tsumkwe
Kamanjab
Outjo
Otavi
Khorixas
Kalkfeld
Otjiwarongo
Okakarara
Otjinene
Brandberg 2573m
Uis
Spitzkopje
Omaruru
Karibib
Okahandja
Gobabis
Hentiesbaai
Usakos
Walvis Bay
Swakopmund
WINDHOEK
Rehoboth
Leonardville
Kalahari Desert
Stampriet
Aranos
Hardap Dam
Maltahöhe
Mariental
Gibeon
Gochas
Nossob
Koes
Bethanien
Fish
Keetmanshoop
Lüderitz
Aus
Seeheim
Noord
Aroab
Grünau
Rosh Pinah
Karasburg
Ariamsvlei
Oranjemund
Warmbad
Noordoewer
Orange River
SOUTH AFRICA
BOTSWANA
ATLANTIC OCEAN
Namib Desert
Skeleton Coast
200 km
200 miles

ZAMBIA

Zambezi

Katima Mulilo

ZIMBABWE

LAND HEIGHT

2000m/6562ft
1000m/3281ft
500m/1640ft
200m/656ft
Sea Level

NAMIBIA

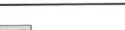

Total Area :
825 418 sq. km
(318 694 sq. miles)

POPULATION

over 100 000
over 10 000
under 10 000

CHRONOLOGY

In 1915, South Africa took over the former German colony known as South West Africa.

- ❑ **1966** Apartheid laws imposed. SWAPO begins armed struggle.
- ❑ **1968** Renamed Namibia.
- ❑ **1973** UN recognizes SWAPO.
- ❑ **1990** Independence.
- ❑ **1994** South Africa relinquishes Walvis Bay.
- ❑ **1999** President Sam Nujoma wins third term, agrees not to stand again.

ECONOMICS

Inflation 8.5% p.a. (1990–2001)

US$3.55bn

6.21 Namibian dollars (7.51)

SCORE CARD

❑ World GNP Ranking	127th
❑ GNP per Capita	US$1790
❑ Balance of Payments	US$130m
❑ Inflation	11.3%
❑ Unemployment	34%

Strengths

Varied mineral resources. Rich fishing grounds. Potential of Walvis Bay as conduit for landlocked neighbors. Low external debt. Foreign investment.

Weaknesses

Most goods imported. Fluctuations in mineral prices. Lack of skilled labor; high unemployment. Potential for disruption from land redistribution, favoring smaller farms over large white-owned estates. AIDS epidemic.

EXPORTS

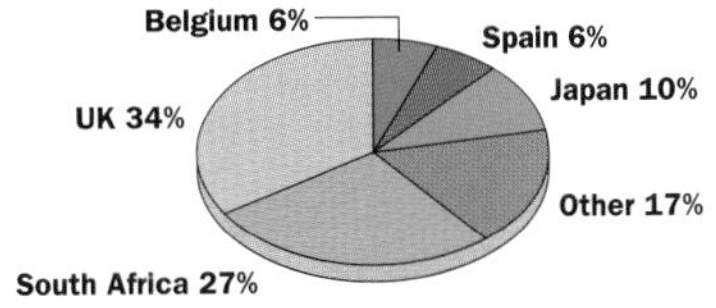
Belgium 6%
Spain 6%
Japan 10%
UK 34%
Other 17%
South Africa 27%

IMPORTS

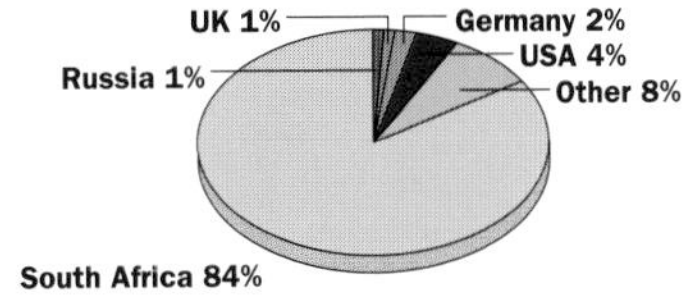
UK 1%
Germany 2%
USA 4%
Russia 1%
Other 8%
South Africa 84%

RESOURCES

Electric power: Included in South African total

547,542 tonnes

Included in South African total

2.51m cattle, 2.37m sheep, 1.78m goats, 2.6m chickens

Uranium, lead, gold, cadmium, oil, copper, diamonds, zinc, silver,

Namibia has abundant uranium, lead, and cadmium resources. Large oil deposits were discovered in 2000. Hydroelectric power and offshore diamond mining have huge potential. The Okavango river system carries more water than all South Africa's rivers combined.

ENVIRONMENT

Sustainability rank: 26th

14% (2% partially protected)

1 tonne per capita

Illegal poaching and the presence of anthrax threaten the unique Namibian desert-adapted elephant (fewer than 50 remain) and the black rhino. Vast expanses of the fragile, unspoiled Namib and Kalahari Desert ecosystems are protected. The government is generally sensitive to environmental issues (the annual seal cull to protect fish stocks is an exception) and wishes to attract "eco-tourists" rather than invest in mass-market developments.

MEDIA

TV ownership medium

Daily newspaper circulation 19 per 1000 people

PUBLISHING AND BROADCAST MEDIA

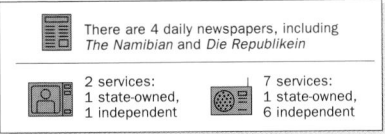

There are 4 daily newspapers, including *The Namibian* and *Die Republikein*

2 services: 1 state-owned, 1 independent

7 services: 1 state-owned, 6 independent

An active press targets corrupt politicians, but foreign TV programs are banned. State radio transmits in 11 languages.

CRIME

No death penalty

4814 prisoners

Down 51% in 1999

Burglary and theft are rising, particularly in urban areas. Ostrich smuggling to the US has been a problem.

EDUCATION

School leaving age: 16

83%

9561 students

Most children attend primary school, but illiteracy among black adults remains a legacy of apartheid.

HEALTH

Welfare state health benefits

1 per 3333 people

AIDS, respiratory, heart, and intestinal diseases

Preventive care and rural health care have top priority. Many areas lack safe water. AIDS is the leading cause of death.

SPENDING

GDP/cap. increase

CONSUMPTION AND SPENDING

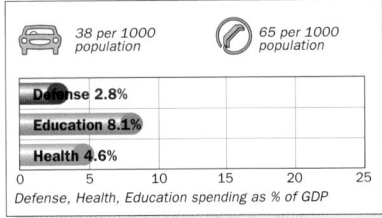

38 per 1000 population

65 per 1000 population

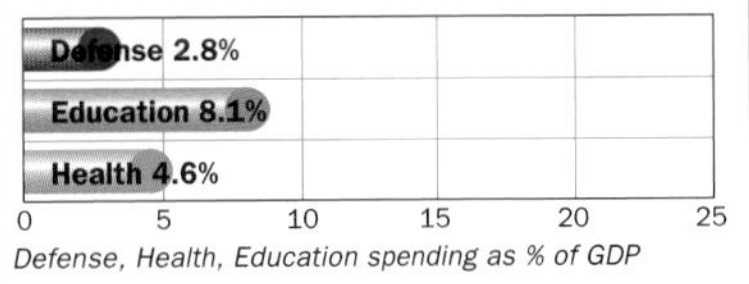
Defense 2.8%
Education 8.1%
Health 4.6%
0
5
10
15
20
25
Defense, Health, Education spending as % of GDP

Gross disparities in wealth persist throughout Namibia: the top 0.5% of households consumes as much as the poorest 57%.

WORLD RANKING

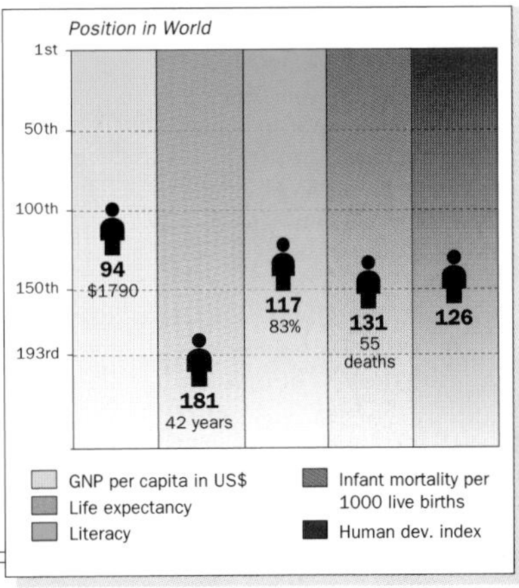
Position in World
1st
50th
100th
150th
193rd
94
$1790
181
42 years
117
83%
131
55 deaths
126
GNP per capita in US$
Life expectancy
Literacy
Infant mortality per 1000 live births
Human dev. index

N

NAURU

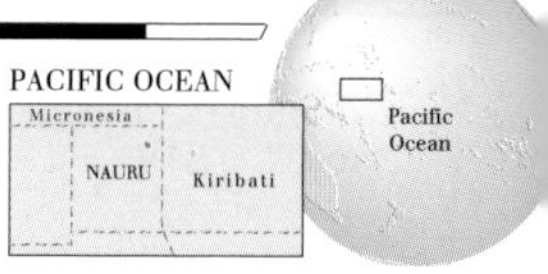
PACIFIC OCEAN
Micronesia
NAURU
Kiribati
Pacific Ocean

OFFICIAL NAME: Republic of Nauru **CAPITAL:** None
POPULATION: 12,570 **CURRENCY:** Australian dollar **OFFICIAL LANGUAGE:** Nauruan

1968 | 1968 | Jan 31 | NAU | +12 | +674 | .nr

THE WORLD'S SMALLEST REPUBLIC, Nauru lies in the Pacific Ocean, 4000 km (2480 miles) northeast of Australia. Once a British colony exploited for its phosphates by the UK, Australia, and New Zealand, it became independent in 1968. The phosphates industry made Nauruans among the wealthiest people in the world, but the imminent end of phosphate reserves, economic mismanagement, and bad investment decisions have left Nauru facing financial ruin.

CLIMATE

Tropical oceanic

WEATHER CHART FOR NAURU

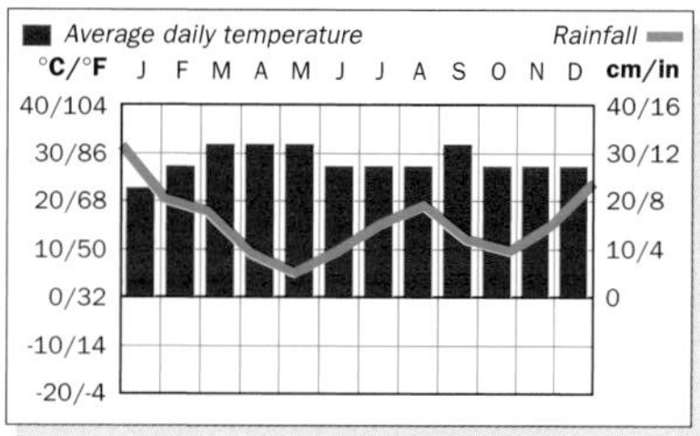
Average daily temperature
Rainfall
°C/°F J F M A M J J A S O N D cm/in
40/104
30/86
20/68
10/50
0/32
-10/14
-20/-4
40/16
30/12
20/8
10/4
0

Nauru's tiny size means that rain clouds often miss the island; years can pass without rain.

TRANSPORTATION

Drive on left

Nauru International

3 ships 1000 grt

THE TRANSPORTATION NETWORK

24 km (15 miles)

None

5 km (3 miles)

None

Nauru's own airline has been cut to a single Boeing 737 flown by Australian pilots which is frequently grounded by the Australian aviation authorities due to safety concerns. All external travel is very expensive. Nauru has no harbor: to load cargoes of phosphates, ships had to dock, engines still running, with huge concrete caissons floating out at sea. The circular ring road is often littered with abandoned cars, since it has been much cheaper for Nauruans to import new vehicles than to attempt to repair existing ones. The number of car accident fatalities is one of the highest in the South Pacific.

TOURISM

Not available

Minimal tourist arrivals

Little variation from year to year

MAIN TOURIST ARRIVALS

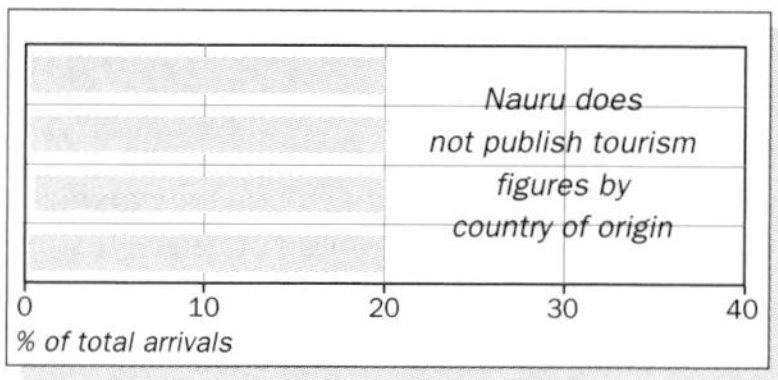
Nauru does not publish tourism figures by country of origin
0 10 20 30 40
% of total arrivals

Even if Nauru had any conventional tourist attractions, the enormous cost of getting there would dissuade most people from making the journey. The main feature of interest is the bizarre lunar landscape created by over 90 years of phosphate extraction. Diving and fishing are potential activities. There are few beaches and only two hotels.

NAURU

Total Area : 21 sq. km (8.1 sq. miles)

LAND HEIGHT

200m/565ft

Sea Level

Urban area

Phosphate mineworks

0 1 km

0 1 mile

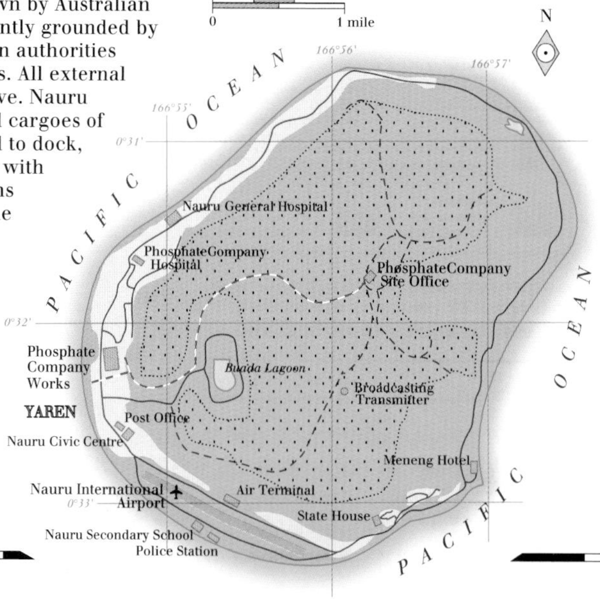
N
166°55'
166°56'
166°57'
0°31'
0°32'
0°33'
PACIFIC OCEAN
Nauru General Hospital
Phosphate Company Hospital
Phosphate Company Site Office
Phosphate Company Works
Buada Lagoon
Broadcasting Transmitter
YAREN
Post Office
Nauru Civic Centre
Meneng Hotel
Nauru International Airport
Air Terminal
State House
Nauru Secondary School
Police Station

PEOPLE

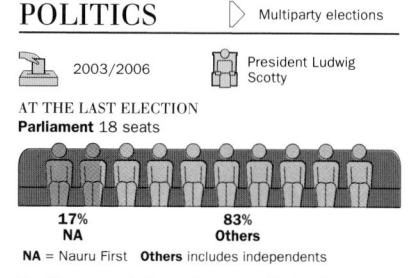

Pop. density high

Nauruan, Kiribati, Chinese, Tuvaluan, English

599/km² (1552/mi²)

THE URBAN/RURAL POPULATION SPLIT

Nauru is 100% semiurban

ETHNIC MAKEUP

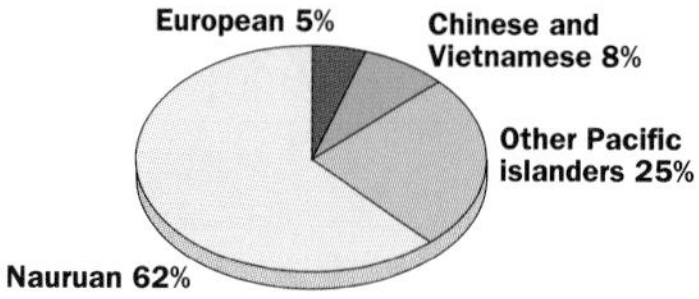
European 5%
Chinese and Vietnamese 8%
Other Pacific islanders 25%
Nauruan 62%

Indigenous Nauruans are a homogeneous blend of Melanesian, Micronesian, and Polynesian strands. They have traditionally held posts in government service, while a large imported workforce – mainly from Kiribati – mined the phosphates.

A society of just over 12,000 people, Nauru is mostly self-regulating. There is some tension between younger Nauruans, who go to Australia to study but have little incentive to do well, and their parents, who fought hard for independence. As the phosphates run out, an increasing feeling of futility is gripping the young. Many see their future in Australia or New Zealand, but fear a drop in living standards and the loss of the luxury of sovereignty. These fears led Nauruans to reject the offer of resettlement on an island off the Queensland coast of Australia.

POLITICS

Multiparty elections

2003/2006

President Ludwig Scotty

AT THE LAST ELECTION
Parliament 18 seats

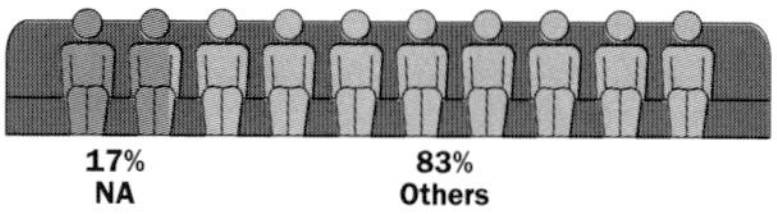
17% NA
83% Others

NA = Nauru First **Others** includes independents

Parliament is based on the British model, but traditional leaders are the dominant figures. Politics revolves around personalities rather than ideologies, leading to conflict between the president and the legislature and a high turnover at the top. There have been 25 changes of president since independence in 1968 (though only ten different presidents), while two men – Bernard Dowiyogo and Rene Harris – alternated as president six times between 1999 and 2003. Harris was removed in 2004 in favor of Ludwig Scotty.

N

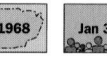

WORLD AFFAIRS

Joined UN in 1999

Comm | PC | PIF | ADB | ACP

The case for compensation for phosphate exploitation brought by Nauru against the UK government was rejected in 1992, after the longest suit in British legal history. However, an Australian settlement that year brought payments eventually totaling US$79 million. Nauru played a central role from 2001 in Australia's "Pacific solution," accepting asylum seekers in return for aid. Poor overseas investments have endangered the trust fund meant to support Nauruans when phosphate income runs out.

AID

Recipient

US$12m (receipts)

Up 71% in 2002

Nauru depends on Australian aid, partly in return for handling asylum seekers.

DEFENSE

No compulsory military service

Australia responsible for defense

Not applicable

Nauru has no defense force. Australia, under a de facto arrangement, is responsible for the island's security.

ECONOMICS

Not available

US$42m

1.44 Australian dollars (1.491)

SCORE CARD

- World GNP Ranking.......................191st
- GNP per Capita.........................US$3540
- Balance of Payments...............Not available
- Inflation.......................................–3.6%
- Unemployment...........Minimal unemployment

Strengths

Very few. Strong Australian dollar.

Weaknesses

Remaining phosphate reserves are economically unviable. Trust funds for post-phosphate era damaged by bad overseas investment decisions. High cost of rehabilitating land. Loss of offshore banking industry.

EXPORTS

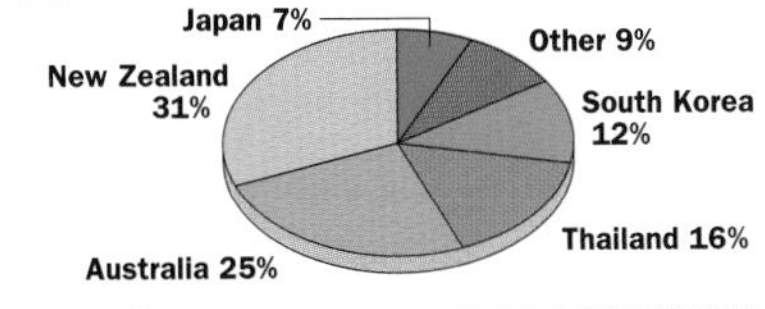
Japan 7%
Other 9%
New Zealand 31%
South Korea 12%
Thailand 16%
Australia 25%

IMPORTS

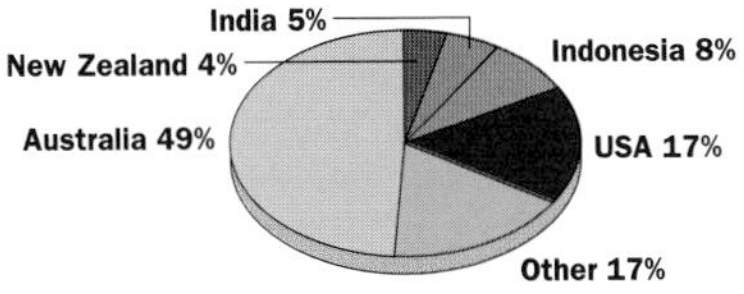
India 5%
New Zealand 4%
Indonesia 8%
Australia 49%
USA 17%
Other 17%

RESOURCES

Electric power 10,000 kW

400 tonnes

Not an oil producer

2800 pigs, 5000 chickens

Guano (phosphates)

Nauru has been exploited for its valuable phosphate reserves by Germans, the British, Australians, and New Zealanders since 1906, and recently by Nauruans themselves. Extraction has destroyed four-fifths of the island, and the deposits are almost exhausted. Nauru has no other mineral resources.

The island is entirely dependent on outside energy supplies, and the cost of oil is 50% higher than the Pacific average, since Nauru does not lie on any shipping routes. Most electricity is produced by small diesel generators.

ENVIRONMENT

Not available

None

11.4 tonnes per capita

Nauru is an environmental disaster area. Mining has destroyed 80% of its ecosystem and, like other Pacific islands, it faces the increasing threat of rising sea levels. Also of concern is contamination from the nearby former French nuclear test sites in the Pacific.

MEDIA

TV ownership low

There are no daily newspapers

PUBLISHING AND BROADCAST MEDIA

There are no daily newspapers. The *Nasero Bulletin* is published biweekly

1 state-owned service

1 state-owned service

Nauru has one national TV broadcasting service and one radio station. Both are state-run.

CRIME

Death penalty not used in practice

Nauru does not publish prison figures

Crime levels are rising slightly

Theft is almost nonexistent. Assaults and dangerous driving as a result of drunkenness are the major problems.

Nauru is almost circular, *with a 16-km (10-mile) ring road. The overcrowded coastal strip is the sole habitable land.*

CHRONOLOGY

Colonized by Germany in 1888, from 1919 the island was administered by the UK, Australia, and New Zealand.

- **1968** Independence.
- **1970** Gains phosphate control.
- **1992** Australia agrees compensation for phosphate extraction.
- **1998–2003** Rene Harris and Bernard Dowiyogo alternate presidency.

EDUCATION

School leaving age: 16

95%

Not available

Many Nauruans attend boarding school in Australia from a young age. Few go on to university.

HEALTH

Welfare state health benefits

1 per 637 people

Tuberculosis, vitamin deficiencies, diabetes

A diet largely of processed imported foods has led to widespread health problems. Over one-third of people are diabetic, while 77% of adults are obese – the highest rate in the world.

SPENDING

GDP/cap. increase

CONSUMPTION AND SPENDING

No data

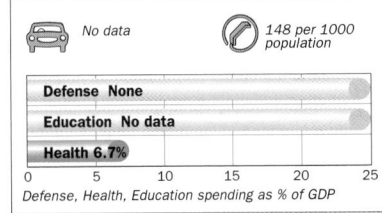

148 per 1000 population

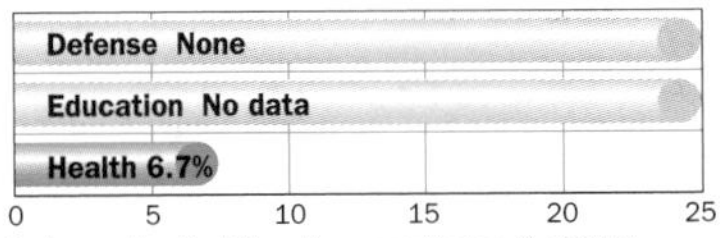
Defense None
Education No data
Health 6.7%
0
5
10
15
20
25

Defense, Health, Education spending as % of GDP

A major economic adjustment program, funded by the ADB, is intended to allow Nauru to adjust to the loss of phosphate income as reserves run out. However, the country was brought to the brink of bankruptcy in 2004.

WORLD RANKING

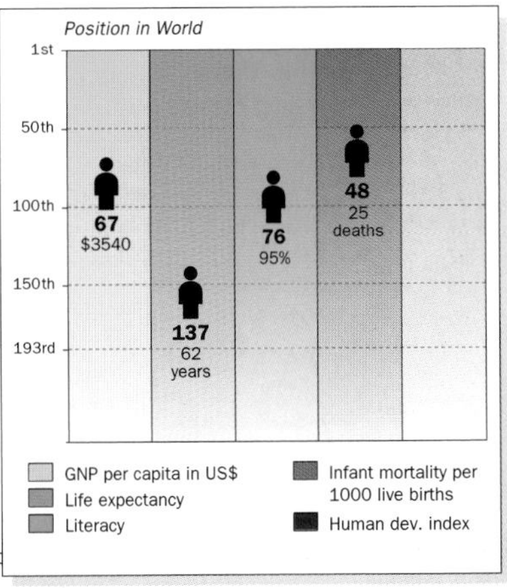
Position in World
1st
50th
100th
150th
193rd
67
$3540
137
62
years
76
95%
48
25
deaths
GNP per capita in US$
Life expectancy
Literacy
Infant mortality per 1000 live births
Human dev. index

N

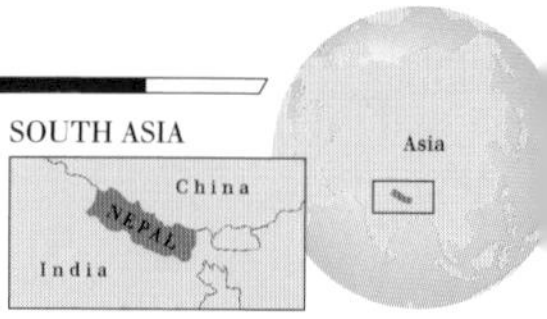
SOUTH ASIA
Asia
China
NEPAL
India

NEPAL

OFFICIAL NAME: Kingdom of Nepal **CAPITAL:** Kathmandu
POPULATION: 25.2 million **CURRENCY:** Nepalese rupee **OFFICIAL LANGUAGE:** Nepali

1769 | 1769 | Dec 28 | NEP | +5.75 | +977 | .np

LYING ALONG the southern Himalayas, Nepal was an absolute monarchy until 1990, since when politics has become increasingly turbulent. The mainly agricultural economy depends heavily on the prompt arrival of the monsoon. Hopes for development have been invested in hydropower, despite the adverse impact of large dams. A Maoist insurgency, begun in 1999, threw the country into chaos in 2001.

CLIMATE

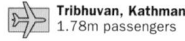

Mountain/subtropical

WEATHER CHART FOR KATHMANDU

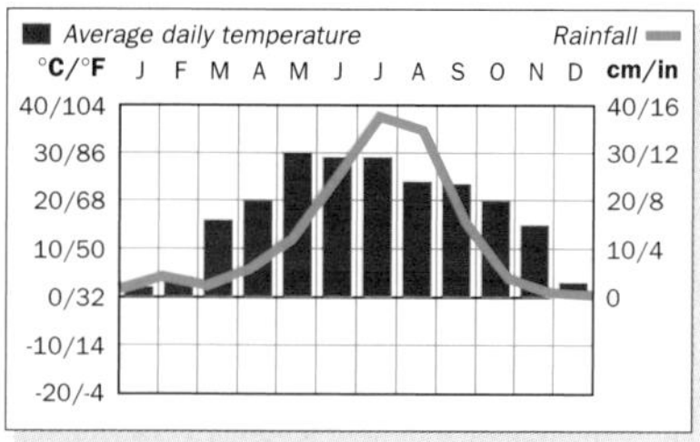
Average daily temperature
Rainfall
°C/°F J F M A M J J A S O N D cm/in
40/104 40/16
30/86 30/12
20/68 20/8
10/50 10/4
0/32 0
-10/14
-20/-4

The warm July to October monsoon affects the whole country, causing flooding in the hot Terai plain, but generally decreases northward and westward. The rest of the year is dry, sunny, and mild, except in the Himalayas, where valley temperatures in winter may average –10°C (14°F).

TRANSPORTATION

Drive on left

Tribhuvan, Kathmandu 1.78m passengers

Has no fleet

THE TRANSPORTATION NETWORK

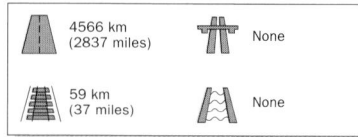

4566 km (2837 miles)	None
59 km (37 miles)	None

Domestic flights link the main towns. There are paved roads in the south and in the Kathmandu valley; only one runs north to China. Two short stretches of railroad cross into India.

Himalayan harvest. Steep mountainsides and easily eroded soils mean that most fields are terraced. A majority of Nepalese are farmers.

TOURISM

Visitors : Population 1:92

275,000 visitors

Down 24% in 2002

MAIN TOURIST ARRIVALS

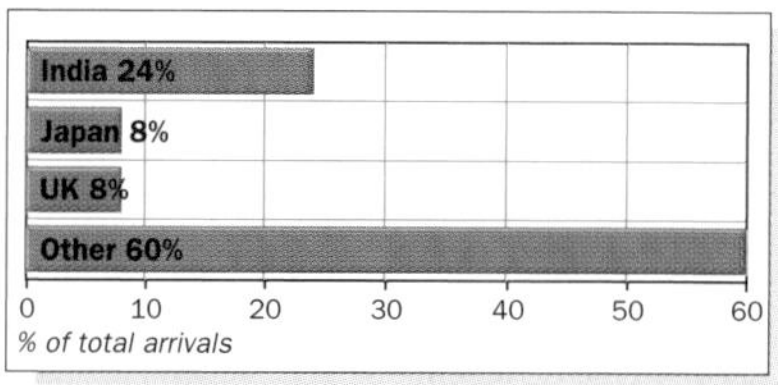
India 24%
Japan 8%
UK 8%
Other 60%
0 10 20 30 40 50 60
% of total arrivals

The Maoist insurgency has devastated the country's important and previously healthy tourism industry. A steady stream of backpackers from the West has dried up, though tourist numbers from neighboring India have actually increased.

The wish to preserve the environment conflicts with the desire for tourist revenue. Child labor was banned in the tourism industry from 2000.

PEOPLE

Pop. density medium

Nepali, Maithili, Bhojpuri

184/km² (477/mi²)

THE URBAN/RURAL POPULATION SPLIT

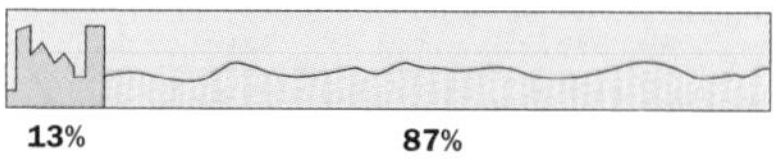
13%
87%

RELIGIOUS PERSUASION

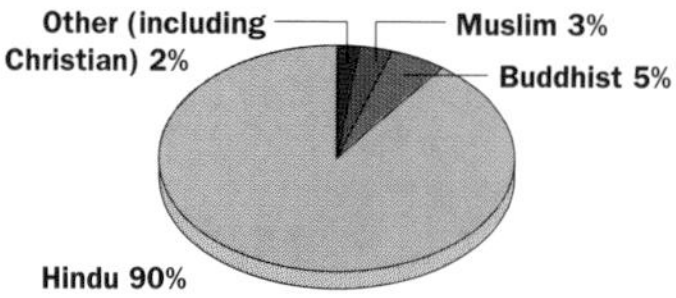
Other (including Christian) 2%
Muslim 3%
Buddhist 5%
Hindu 90%

Tensions are few among the diverse ethnic groups such as the Sherpas in the north, "Hill Hindu" Brahmins and Chhettris, Newars, and others in the Kathmandu valley, and Terai in the south. The Sherpa and other Buddhist women are less restricted than Hindus. Polygamy is practiced in the hills. Since 1990 many ethnic Nepali refugees from Bhutan have settled in Nepal.

POLITICS

Multiparty elections

L. House 1999/2002
U. House 2001/2003
(both postponed)

H.M. King Gyanendra Bir Bikram Shah Dev

AT THE LAST ELECTION

House of Representatives (dissolved) 205 seats

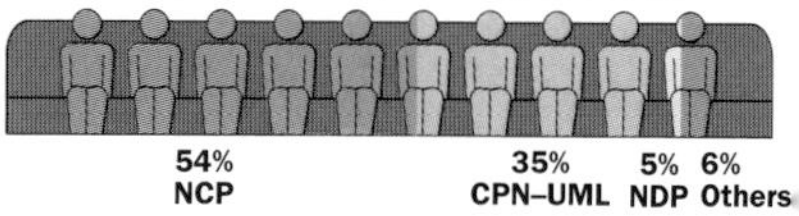
54% NCP
35% CPN–UML
5% NDP
6% Others

NCP = Nepali Congress Party **CPN–UML** = Communist Party of Nepal–United Marxist-Leninist **NDP** = National Democratic Party **App** = Appointed by the king

The House of Representatives was dissolved prior to early elections in 2002, which have been repeatedly postponed

National Council 60 seats

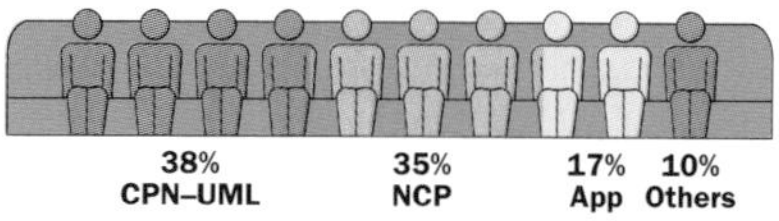
38% CPN–UML
35% NCP
17% App
10% Others

Multipartyism, reinstated in 1990, produced a short-lived communist government in 1994, then unstable coalitions until the NCP won elections in 1999. In 2001 the royal family was murdered, and the Maoist rebel uprising intensified; a state of emergency was imposed. In 2002 unpopular new king Gyanendra dismissed the elected NCP government of Sher Bahadur Deuba and appointed an NDP administration. The prime minister resigned in 2004, prompting Deuba's reinstatement.

WORLD AFFAIRS

Joined UN in 1955

ADB | CP | NAM | SAARC | WTO

The NCP government revived relations with India, but there are tensions over India's alleged links with Maoist rebels, some said to operate from over the border. Agreement has been reached with Bhutan over the issue of ethnic Nepali Bhutanese refugees in Nepal.

AID

Recipient

$365m (receipts)

Down 7% in 2002

Nepal's strategic position has made it a focus for powerful donors. Insecurity caused aid agencies to withdraw from the west of the country in 2004.

DEFENSE

No compulsory military service

$99m

Up 12% in 2002

The 63,000-strong army has no tanks or combat aircraft. Nepalese Gurkhas serve in the UK army. US military aid assists the war against Maoist insurgents.

N

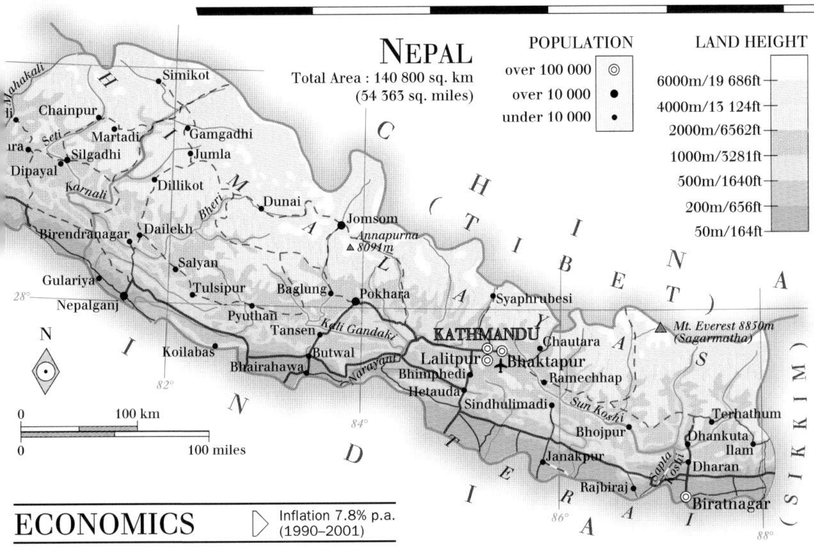
NEPAL
Total Area : 140 800 sq. km
(54 363 sq. miles)
POPULATION
over 100 000
over 10 000
under 10 000
LAND HEIGHT
6000m/19 686ft
4000m/13 124ft
2000m/6562ft
1000m/3281ft
500m/1640ft
200m/656ft
50m/164ft
CHINA (TIBET)
INDIA
SIKKIM
KATHMANDU
Simikot
Chainpur
Martadi
Silgadhi
Dipayal
Gamgadhi
Jumla
Dillikot
Dunai
Jomsom
Annapurna 8091m
Birendranagar
Dailekh
Salyan
Gulariya
Nepalganj
Tulsipur
Baglung
Pokhara
Pyuthan
Tansen
Kali Gandaki
Syaphrubesi
Mt. Everest 8850m (Sagarmatha)
Chautara
Lalitpur
Bhaktapur
Bhimphedi
Hetauda
Ramechhap
Koilabas
Butwal
Bhairahawa
Sindhulimadi
Sun Koshi
Terhathum
Bhojpur
Dhankuta
Ilam
Janakpur
Dharan
Rajbiraj
Biratnagar
Karnali
Bheri
Seti
Narayani
N
0 100 km
0 100 miles

ECONOMICS

Inflation 7.8% p.a. (1990–2001)

$5.54bn

73.56 Nepalese rupees (75.65)

SCORE CARD

❏ WORLD GNP RANKING	111th
❏ GNP PER CAPITA	$230
❏ BALANCE OF PAYMENTS	–$165m
❏ INFLATION	2.8%
❏ UNEMPLOYMENT	47%

STRENGTHS

Self-sufficiency in grain most years. Economic liberalization under NCP government. Potential for hydroelectric power generation. Low debt level.

WEAKNESSES

Instability. Agricultural dependency: only 10% of GDP from manufacturing. Landlocked. Low savings rate. Absence of active entrepreneurial class.

EXPORTS

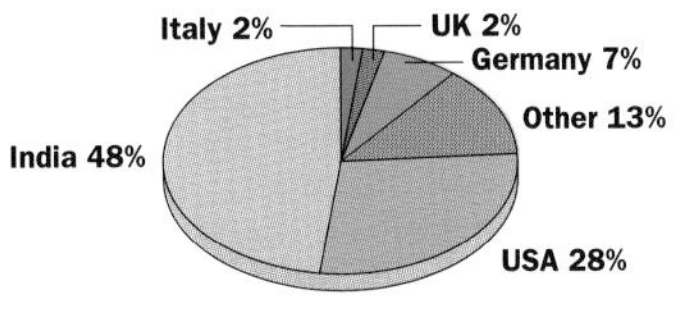
Italy 2%
UK 2%
Germany 7%
Other 13%
India 48%
USA 28%

IMPORTS

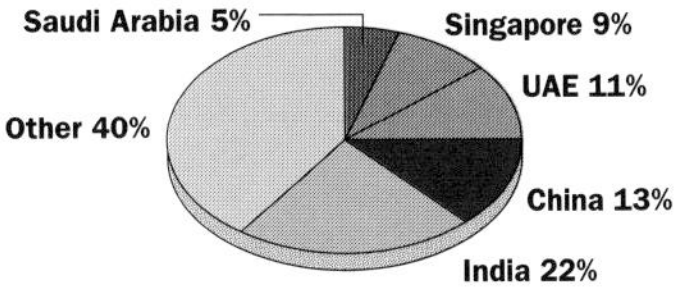
Saudi Arabia 5%
Singapore 9%
UAE 11%
Other 40%
China 13%
India 22%

RESOURCES

Electric power 458,000 kW

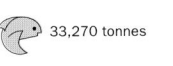

33,270 tonnes

Not an oil producer

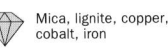

7m cattle, 6.65m goats, 4m buffaloes, 21.5m chickens

Mica, lignite, copper, cobalt, iron

The first privately owned power plant, situated near Ramechhap, opened in mid-2000. HEP is being developed.

ENVIRONMENT

Sustainability rank: 99th

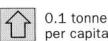

9% (2% partially protected)

0.1 tonnes per capita

Kathmandu has chronic traffic and pollution problems. Deforestation and soil erosion are serious. The native tiger is fast disappearing. Approval of the controversial Arun III hydroelectric project was granted in mid-2000.

MEDIA

TV ownership low

Daily newspaper circulation 12 per 1000 people

PUBLISHING AND BROADCAST MEDIA

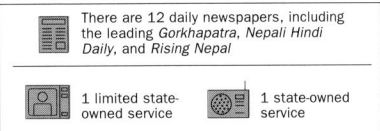

There are 12 daily newspapers, including the leading *Gorkhapatra*, *Nepali Hindi Daily*, and *Rising Nepal*

1 limited state-owned service

1 state-owned service

The Nepal TV service began in 1986; under 25% of the population receives it. The press is mainly Kathmandu-based with low circulations. Press watchdogs warned of censorship under the state of emergency imposed in 2001.

CRIME

No death penalty

7132 prisoners

Up slightly in 2000

Petty theft and smuggling are the main problems. The legal provision for detention without trial is used, and police suppression of demonstrations is often brutal.

EDUCATION

School leaving age: 10

44%

103,290 students

Around 70% of boys attend school in Nepal, but enrollment for girls is still barely half. Nepal's literacy rate is among the lowest in the world.

CHRONOLOGY

The foundations of the Nepalese state were laid in 1769, when King Prithvi Narayan Shah conquered the region.

- ❏ **1816–1923** Quasi-British protectorate.
- ❏ **1959** First multiparty constitution.
- ❏ **1960** Constitution suspended.
- ❏ **1962–1990** *Panchayat* nonparty system.
- ❏ **1991** NCP victory in elections.
- ❏ **1994–1995** Communist government.
- ❏ **1999** NCP election victory. Maoist insurgency in rural areas.
- ❏ **2001** King and family shot by crown prince; Gyanendra crowned amid unrest. Upsurge in Maoist violence; state of emergency declared.
- ❏ **2002** Gyanendra dismisses Sher Bahadur Deuba's government.
- ❏ **2004** Deuba reinstated.

HEALTH

Welfare state health benefits

1 per 12,500 people

Respiratory and diarrheal diseases, maternal deaths

There are about 100 *dharmi-jhankri* (faith healers) for every health worker. Maternal mortality is high, the result of harmful traditional birth practices; a reeducation program for midwives has been established.

SPENDING

GDP/cap. increase

CONSUMPTION AND SPENDING

2 per 1000 population

14 per 1000 population

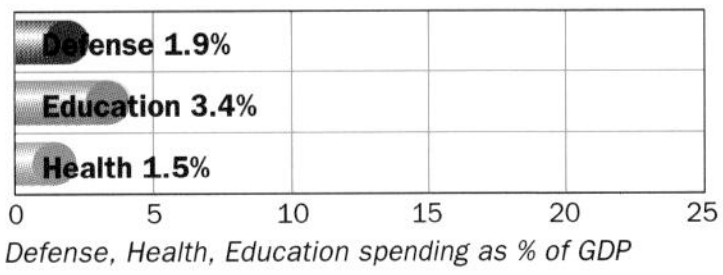
Defense 1.9%
Education 3.4%
Health 1.5%
0
5
10
15
20
25
Defense, Health, Education spending as % of GDP

Nepal is one of the poorest countries in the world. Bonded labor was abolished in mid-2000, releasing 36,000 people.

WORLD RANKING

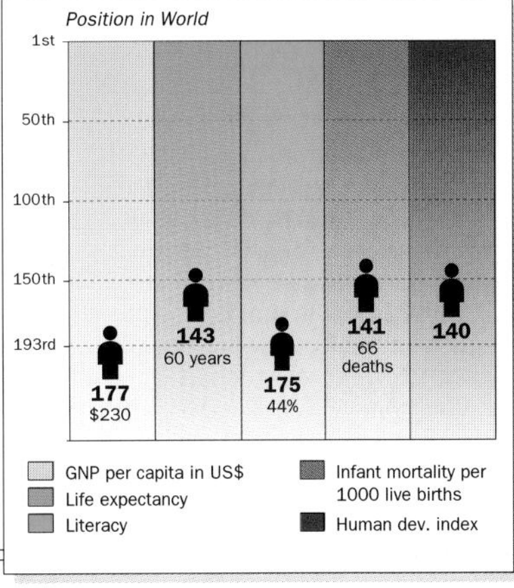
Position in World
1st
50th
100th
150th
193rd
177
$230
143
60 years
175
44%
141
66
deaths
140
GNP per capita in US$
Life expectancy
Literacy
Infant mortality per 1000 live births
Human dev. index

N

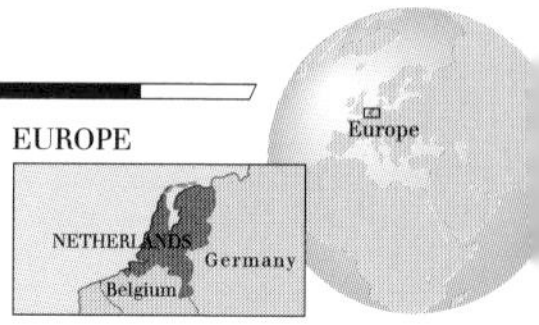
EUROPE
Europe
NETHERLANDS
Germany
Belgium

NETHERLANDS

OFFICIAL NAME: Kingdom of the Netherlands **POPULATION:** 16.1 million
CAPITALS: Amsterdam; The Hague (administrative) **CURRENCY:** Euro **OFFICIAL LANGUAGE:** Dutch

1648 | 1839 | April 30 | NL | +1 | +31 | .nl

THE NETHERLANDS IS LOCATED at the delta of four major rivers in northwest Europe. The few hills in the eastern and southern part of the country descend to a flat coastal area, bordered by the North Sea to the north and west. This is protected by a giant infrastructure of dunes, dikes, and canals, since 27% of the coast is below sea level. The Netherlands became one of the world's first confederative republics after Spain recognized its independence in 1648. Its highly successful economy has a long trading tradition, and Rotterdam is the world's largest port.

CLIMATE

Maritime

WEATHER CHART FOR AMSTERDAM

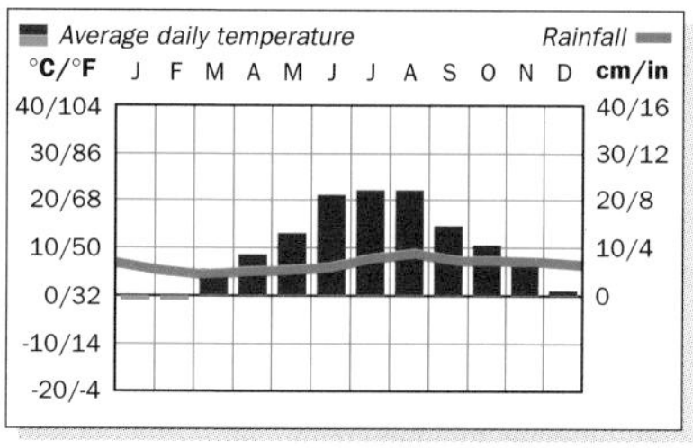
Average daily temperature
Rainfall
°C/°F
J F M A M J J A S O N D
cm/in
40/104
30/86
20/68
10/50
0/32
-10/14
-20/-4
40/16
30/12
20/8
10/4
0

The Netherlands has a temperate climate, with mild winters which rarely fall much below freezing, and cool summers with a mean temperature of 20°C (68°F). The country's coastal areas have the mildest climate, though northerly gales are fairly frequent, particularly in autumn and winter.

TRANSPORTATION

Drive on right

Schiphol, Amsterdam 40m passengers

1316 ships 5.66m grt

THE TRANSPORTATION NETWORK

104,850 km (65,151 miles)

2274 km (1413 miles)

2806 km (1744 miles)

5046 km (3135 miles)

Rotterdam, the key transshipment port for northern Europe, is also the world's busiest. Schiphol airport is one of the air transportation hubs of Europe.

A high-speed passenger rail line is due to link Amsterdam and Rotterdam with Brussels (Belgium) and Paris (France) in 2005, and a high-speed freight line from Rotterdam to Germany should be completed in 2006.

TOURISM

Visitors : Population 1:1.7

9.6m visitors

Up 1% in 2002

MAIN TOURIST ARRIVALS

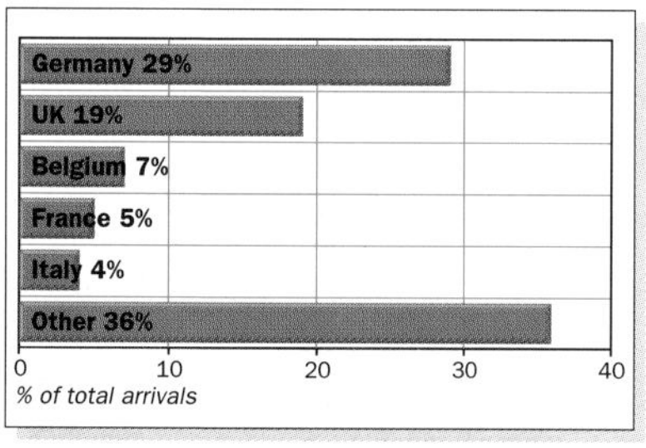
Germany 29%
UK 19%
Belgium 7%
France 5%
Italy 4%
Other 36%
0
10
20
30
40
% of total arrivals

Tourism is a major business in the Netherlands. Visitors go mainly to Amsterdam, though cities such as Groningen and Maastricht are growing in popularity. Amsterdam caters for a diverse tourism market. Its world-famous museums include the Rijksmuseum, with its collection of Vermeers and Rembrandts, while its network of canals is popular. Amsterdam is also renowned for its liberal attitude to sex; its red-light district attracts millions every year. In the past decade, the city has become a center for the European gay community, with celebrations on April 30 (Queen's Day – the monarch's official birthday) and in August (Amsterdam Pride). A thriving club scene and liberal drug laws draw enthusiasts from neighboring countries. In spring and summer, the tulip fields and North Sea beaches attract large numbers of visitors.

Windmill at Baambrugge, *near Amsterdam. A century ago there were 10,000 in the country compared with today's 1000. A protective ring of 900 mills kept Amsterdam from flooding.*

PEOPLE

Pop. density high

Dutch, Frisian

475/km² (1229/mi²)

THE URBAN/RURAL POPULATION SPLIT

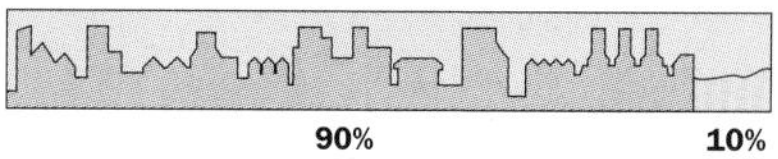
90%
10%

RELIGIOUS PERSUASION

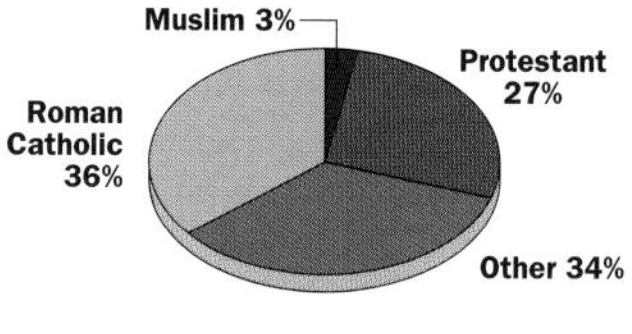
Muslim 3%
Protestant 27%
Roman Catholic 36%
Other 34%

ETHNIC MAKEUP

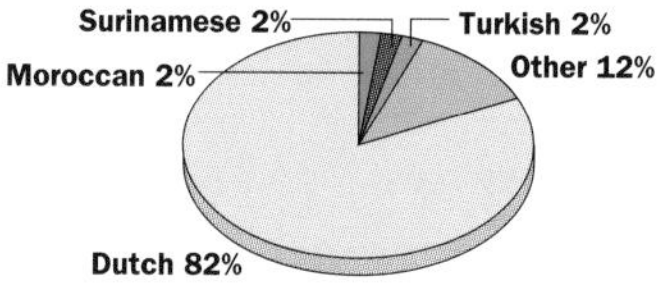
Surinamese 2%
Turkish 2%
Moroccan 2%
Other 12%
Dutch 82%

The Netherlands has a long history of welcoming those seeking religious and political asylum. Immigrants from former colonies settled during the 20th century, coming first from Indonesia, then from the Netherlands Antilles and Suriname. In the 1960s and 1970s Moroccan and Turkish "guestworkers" arrived. There is now concern at the apparent lack of integration among immigrant communities, especially Muslims.

A tradition of tolerance is reflected in liberal attitudes to sexuality. In 2001, same-sex marriages were legalized, giving gay couples full equality, including the right of adoption (after three years of marriage).

The state does not try to impose a particular morality on its citizens. The consumption of soft drugs is seen as a matter of personal choice. In 2001 the Netherlands became the first country in the world to legalize euthanasia, albeit under strict conditions.

Women enjoy equal rights and hold 37% of seats in the Second Chamber of the States-General, but are not well represented in boardrooms.

POPULATION AGE BREAKDOWN

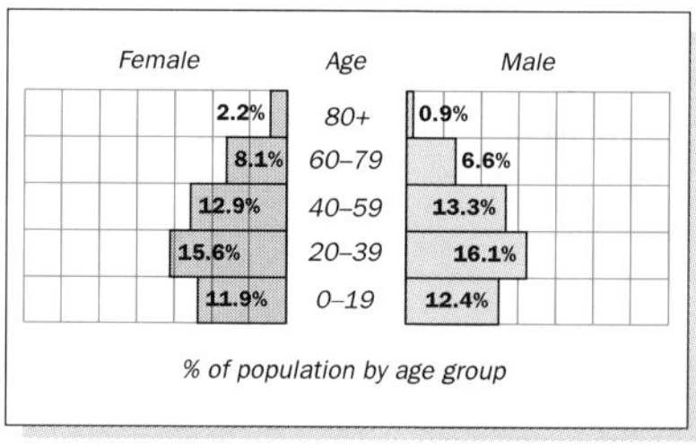
Female
Age
Male
2.2%
80+
0.9%
8.1%
60–79
6.6%
12.9%
40–59
13.3%
15.6%
20–39
16.1%
11.9%
0–19
12.4%
% of population by age group

N

POLITICS

Multiparty elections

L. House 2003/2007
U. House 2003/2007

H.M. Queen Beatrix

AT THE LAST ELECTION

Second Chamber of the States-General 150 seats

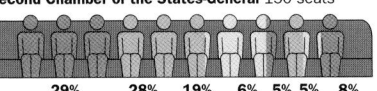

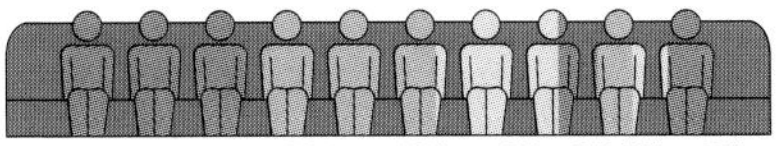

29% **CDA** **28%** **PvdA** **19%** **VVD** **6%** **SP** **5%** **GL** **5%** **LPF** **8%** **Others**

CDA = Christian Democratic Appeal **PvdA** = Labor Party
VVD = People's Party for Freedom and Democracy
SP = Socialist Party **GL** = Green Left
LPF = Pim Fortuyn List **D66** = Democrats 66

First Chamber of the States-General 75 seats

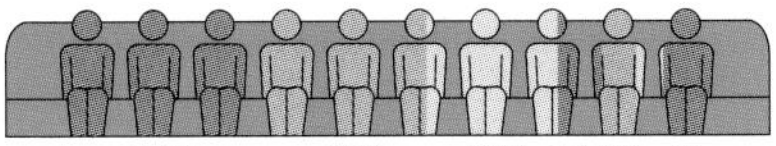

31% **CDA** **25%** **PvdA** **20%** **VVD** **7%** **GL** **5%** **SP** **4%** **D66** **8%** **Others**

The First Chamber of the States-General is indirectly elected

The Netherlands is a constitutional monarchy. Legislative power is vested in parliament, and the monarch has only nominal power.

PROFILE

Dutch politics shows a high degree of consensus. Since the early 1980s, governments have employed the "polder model," which focuses on a social compact, pay moderation, job creation, economic deregulation, and generous social protection.

The CDA has traditionally led a two-party governing coalition, joining with either the left-of-center PvdA or the right-wing VVD. However, after the 1994 election the CDA was out of government for eight years, and the PvdA under Wim Kok ruled in coalition with the VVD and the left-liberal D66.

The 2002 elections produced a shock. The populist LPF leader Pim Fortuyn was assassinated a few days before the poll and, coming from nowhere, the party finished second, playing on the themes of a failing asylum system and fears of immigrant crime and Islamic fundamentalism. Just as astonishing was the reemergence of the CDA as the country's leading party. However, the resulting CDA–LPF–VVD coalition soon collapsed as a result of the LPF's political inexperience. Fresh elections in 2003 were a neck-and-neck race between the CDA and a reborn PvdA. Punished by the electorate, the LPF was substituted in the new CDA-led coalition by the small D66.

Queen Beatrix, who acceded in 1980 and rebuilt support for the Dutch monarchy.

CDA leader Jan Peter Balkenende was appointed prime minister in 2002.

MAIN POLITICAL ISSUES

The future of social welfare

Despite cutbacks in the 1980s, the Dutch still have one of Europe's most generous welfare systems. Most parties accepted that levels of welfare could not be maintained indefinitely. The debate thus centers on how much and in which areas cuts should be made.

Refugees and asylum seekers

Asylum laws have been tightened since 1994 as the number of immigrants has risen. First- and second-generation immigrants made up 18% of the national population in 2002, but 40% (30% non-European) in Rotterdam, where support for the LPF was greatest. Concern focuses on asylum policies and the role of Islam in Dutch society.

NETHERLANDS

Total Area : 41 526 sq. km (16 033 sq. miles)

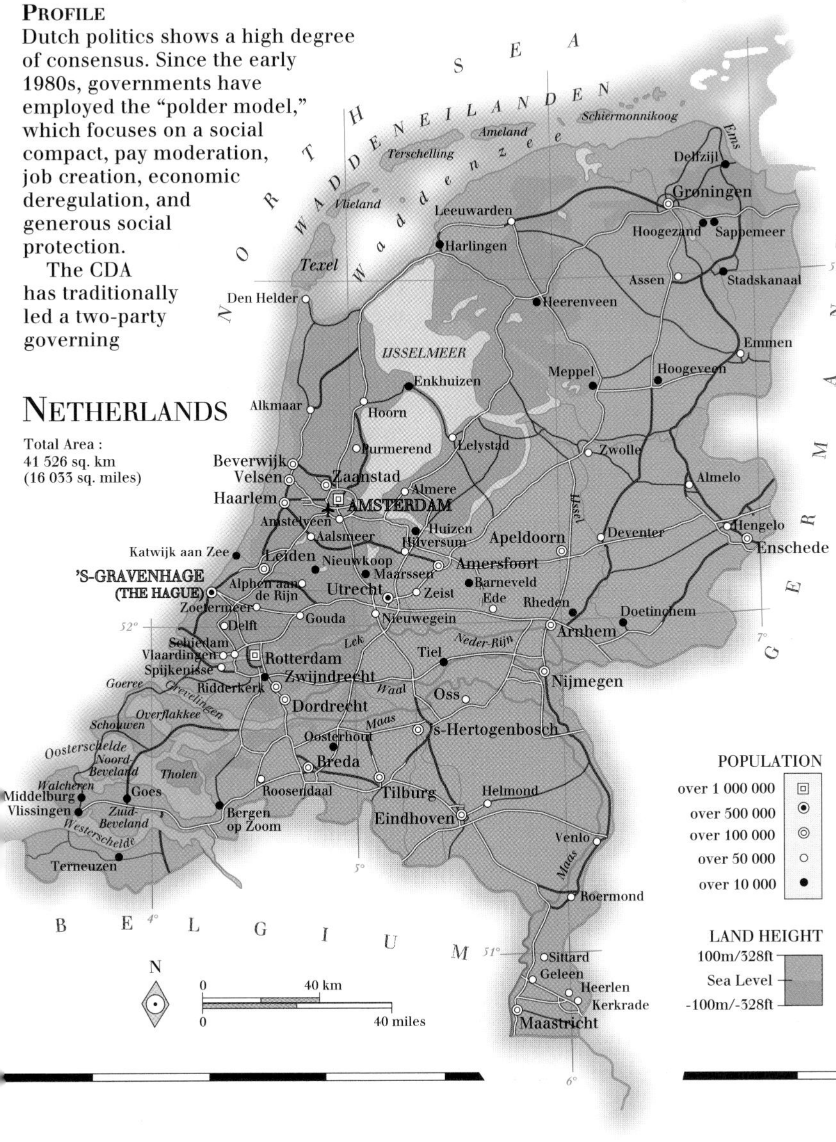
NORTH SEA
WADDENEILANDEN
WADDENZEE
Schiermonnikoog
Ameland
Terschelling
Vlieland
Texel
Delfzijl
Groningen
Leeuwarden
Harlingen
Hoogezand
Sappemeer
Assen
Stadskanaal
Den Helder
Heerenveen
Emmen
IJSSELMEER
Enkhuizen
Meppel
Hoogeveen
Alkmaar
Hoorn
Purmerend
Lelystad
Zwolle
Beverwijk
Velsen
Zaanstad
Almere
Almelo
Haarlem
AMSTERDAM
Amstelveen
Aalsmeer
Huizen
Hilversum
Apeldoorn
Deventer
Hengelo
Enschede
Katwijk aan Zee
Leiden
Nieuwkoop
Maarssen
Amersfoort
Barneveld
'S-GRAVENHAGE (THE HAGUE)
Alphen aan de Rijn
Utrecht
Zeist
Ede
Rheden
Zoetermeer
Delft
Gouda
Nieuwegein
Doetinchem
Arnhem
Schiedam
Vlaardingen
Spijkenisse
Rotterdam
Zwijndrecht
Neder-Rijn
Lek
Tiel
Nijmegen
Goeree
Ridderkerk
Waal
Oss
Dordrecht
Grevelingen
Overflakkee
Schouwen
Maas
Oosterhout
's-Hertogenbosch
Oosterschelde
Noord-Beveland
Tholen
Breda
Walcheren
Middelburg
Vlissingen
Goes
Roosendaal
Tilburg
Helmond
Zuid-Beveland
Westerschelde
Bergen op Zoom
Eindhoven
Venlo
Terneuzen
Roermond
IJssel
Ems
GERMANY
BELGIUM
Sittard
Geleen
Heerlen
Kerkrade
Maastricht
53°
52°
51°
4°
5°
6°
7°
N
0 40 km
0 40 miles
POPULATION
over 1 000 000
over 500 000
over 100 000
over 50 000
over 10 000
LAND HEIGHT
100m/328ft
Sea Level
-100m/-328ft

WORLD AFFAIRS

Joined UN in 1945

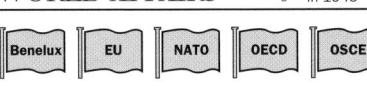

Benelux | EU | NATO | OECD | OSCE

The Dutch strongly support political and monetary integration within the EU; the euro was fully adopted in 2002. Traditionally, the Netherlands has favored EU enlargement, but recent CDA-led governments have expressed reservations. The Netherlands is also strongly Atlanticist; the CDA's Jaap de Hoop Scheffer became NATO secretary-general in 2004.

The International Court of Justice, the International Criminal Tribunal for the former Yugoslavia, and the International Criminal Court sit in The Hague.

AID

Donor

$3.34bn (donations)

Up 5% in 2002

The Netherlands continues to be one of the few countries which exceeds the UN target of devoting 0.7% of GNP to development aid. The government actively pursues a policy of linking foreign aid and human rights. It also gives priority to projects which link longer-term development goals with efforts to manage and reduce intergroup conflict.

N

CHRONOLOGY

Suppression of Protestantism by the ruling Spanish Habsburgs led to the revolt of the Netherlands and the declaration of independence of the northern provinces as a republic in 1581, recognized by Spain in 1648.

- ❑ **1813** Dutch oust French after 18 years of French rule and choose to become a constitutional monarchy.
- ❑ **1815** United Kingdom of Netherlands formed to include Belgium and Luxembourg.
- ❑ **1839** Recognition of 1830 secession of Catholic southern provinces as Belgium.
- ❑ **1848** New constitution – ministers to be accountable to parliament.
- ❑ **1897–1901** Wide-ranging social legislation enacted. Development of strong trade unions.
- ❑ **1898** Wilhelmina succeeds to throne, ending Luxembourg union, where male hereditary Salic Law is in force.
- ❑ **1914–1918** Dutch neutrality respected in World War I.
- ❑ **1922** Women fully enfranchised.
- ❑ **1940** Dutch assert neutrality in World War II, but Germany invades.
- ❑ **1942** Japan invades Dutch East Indies.
- ❑ **1944–1945** "Winter of starvation" in German-occupied western provinces.
- ❑ **1945** Liberation. International Court of Justice set up in The Hague.
- ❑ **1946–1958** PvdA leads coalitions.
- ❑ **1948** Juliana becomes queen.
- ❑ **1949** Joins NATO. Most of East Indies colonies gain independence as Indonesia.
- ❑ **1957** Founder member of European Economic Community.
- ❑ **1960** Economic union with Belgium and Luxembourg comes into effect.
- ❑ **1973** PvdA wins power after 15 years spent mainly in opposition. Center-left coalition until 1977.
- ❑ **1980** CDA alliance of the "confessional" parties forms a single party. Beatrix becomes queen.
- ❑ **1982–1994** CDA-led coalitions under Ruud Lubbers.
- ❑ **1990** 20-year National Environment Policy (NEP) introduced.
- ❑ **1992** Licensed brothels legalized.
- ❑ **1994** Elections: Wim Kok of PvdA heads coalition with VVD and D66.
- ❑ **2001** Euthanasia and gay marriage legalized.
- ❑ **2002** January, euro fully adopted. April, government resigns after report blames Dutch military in Bosnia for failing to prevent Srebrenica massacre in 1995. May, populist politician Pim Fortuyn assassinated. Elections. October, CDA-led coalition collapses.
- ❑ **2003** CDA reelected; forms coalition with VVD and D66.

N

DEFENSE

No compulsory military service

$7.33bn

Up 20% in 2002

DUTCH ARMED FORCES

283 main battle tanks (Leopard 1 and 2)	23,150 personnel
4 submarines, 6 destroyers, and 9 frigates	12,130 personnel
137 combat aircraft (F-16A/B)	11,050 personnel
None	

The Dutch military has undergone major restructuring since the end of the Cold War with the aim of making it a rapidly deployable, more flexible military force as befits a NATO member state. Compulsory military service was abolished in 1996 and personnel cut by 44%, with the number of army divisions reduced from three to two. In 1995, a joint Dutch–German, 28,000-strong army corps was inaugurated. The Dutch army was criticized for failing to prevent the massacre at Srebrenica, Bosnia, in 1995, but it has continued to play a role in other international peacekeeping efforts since.

The Netherlands also has a large defense industry, which specializes in submarines, weapons systems, and aircraft.

ECONOMICS

Inflation 2.1% p.a. (1990–2001)

$378bn

0.822 euros (0.871)

SCORE CARD

❑ World GNP Ranking	15th
❑ GNP per Capita	$23,390
❑ Balance of Payments	$9.87bn
❑ Inflation	3.5%
❑ Unemployment	3%

EXPORTS

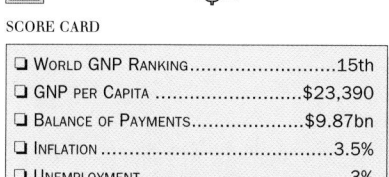

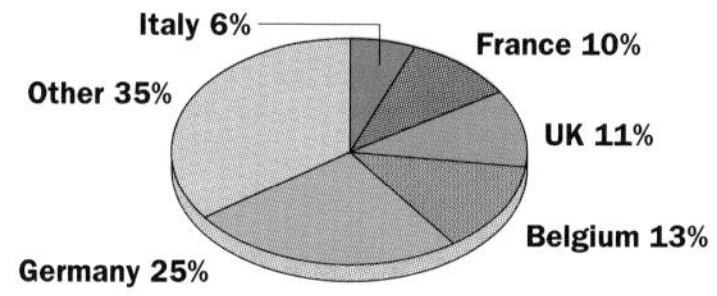
Italy 6%
France 10%
Other 35%
UK 11%
Belgium 13%
Germany 25%

IMPORTS

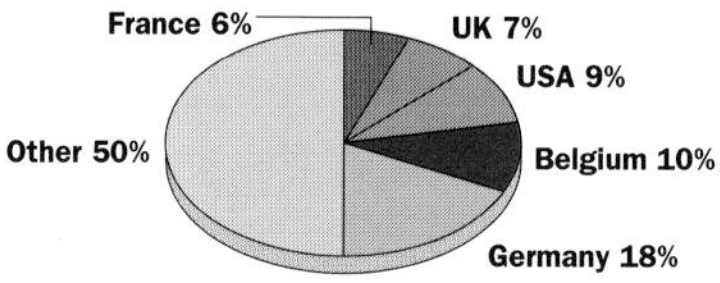
France 6%
UK 7%
USA 9%
Other 50%
Belgium 10%
Germany 18%

STRENGTHS

Highly skilled, educated, multilingual workforce. Sophisticated infrastructure. Many blue-chip multinationals, including Philips and Shell. Harmony between employers and employees. Low inflation and unemployment. Tradition of high-tech innovation, including development of music cassette and CD.

WEAKNESSES

Costly welfare system, resulting in high taxes and social insurance premiums; one-third of national income spent on social security. Aging population. High labor costs.

PROFILE

Historically, trade has been central to the success of the economy of the Netherlands. Most goods travel through Rotterdam, the world's biggest port. As well as high-tech industries such as electronics, telecommunications, and chemicals, there is a successful and intensive agricultural sector. Dependence on trade makes the economy vulnerable to world economic fluctuations; high growth rates in 1997–2000 have been followed by a marked downturn and budgetary problems since 2001.

ECONOMIC PERFORMANCE INDICATOR

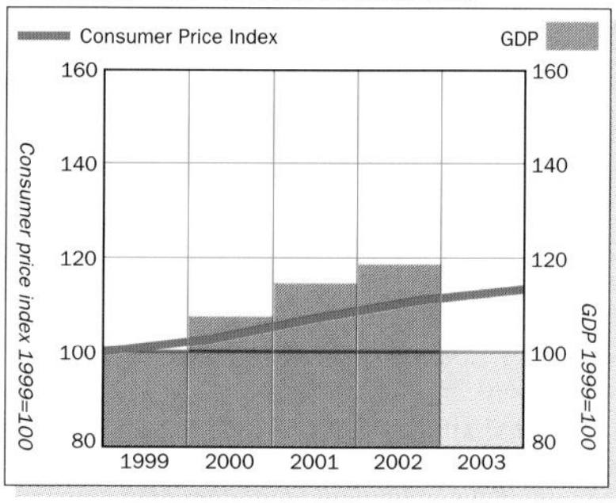
Consumer Price Index
GDP
160
140
120
100
80
Consumer price index 1999=100
GDP 1999=100
1999
2000
2001
2002
2003

NETHERLANDS : MAJOR BUSINESSES

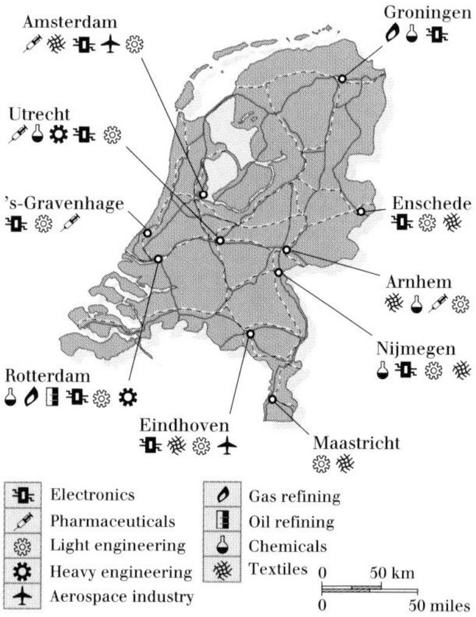
Amsterdam
Groningen
Utrecht
's-Gravenhage
Enschede
Arnhem
Nijmegen
Rotterdam
Eindhoven
Maastricht
Electronics
Pharmaceuticals
Light engineering
Heavy engineering
Aerospace industry
Gas refining
Oil refining
Chemicals
Textiles
0 50 km
0 50 miles

RESOURCES

Electric power 21m kW

570,226 tonnes

28,932 b/d (reserves 106m barrels)

11.2m pigs, 3.78m cattle, 98m chickens

Natural gas, oil

ELECTRICITY GENERATION

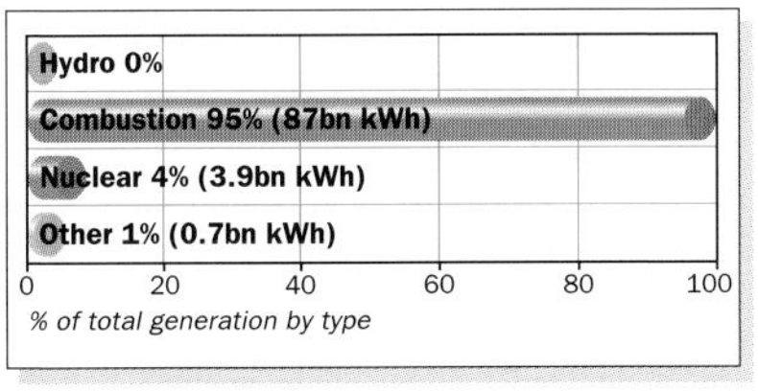
Hydro 0%
Combustion 95% (87bn kWh)
Nuclear 4% (3.9bn kWh)
Other 1% (0.7bn kWh)
0
20
40
60
80
100
% of total generation by type

There are large natural gas reserves in the north. A 22.5 MW wind power station near Rotterdam began operation in 2002.

ENVIRONMENT

Sustainability rank: 34th

14% (10% partially protected)

8.7 tonnes per capita

ENVIRONMENTAL TREATIES

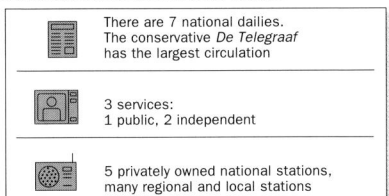

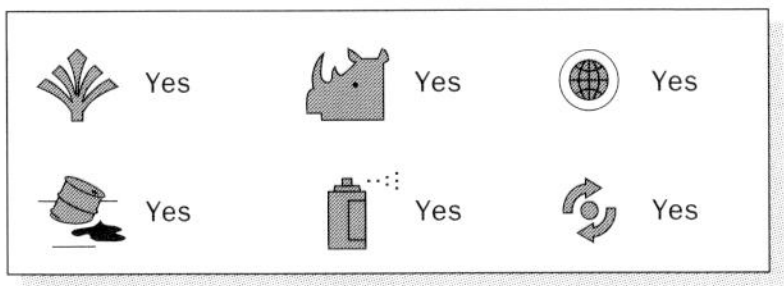
Yes
Yes
Yes
Yes
Yes
Yes

There is a strong environmental tradition, a legacy in part of living in one of the most densely populated states in the world. NGOs such as Greenpeace are well supported and the Green Left party is represented in parliament.

The Dutch recycle domestic trash, have a good record on energy efficiency, and have developed innovative projects in housing and local transportation. An eco-tax on energy users was introduced in 1996 – the first of its kind in the West – though big businesses are exempt.

Serious flooding of the rivers Maas and Waal (an arm of the Rhine) in 1993 and 1995 raised concern about the state of the country's flood defenses and the use of floodplains for development.

MEDIA

TV ownership high

Daily newspaper circulation 306 per 1000 people

PUBLISHING AND BROADCAST MEDIA

There are 7 national dailies. The conservative *De Telegraaf* has the largest circulation

3 services: 1 public, 2 independent

5 privately owned national stations, many regional and local stations

Newspaper circulation is high. While editorially independent, broadcasting is strongly regulated. Dutch law does not recognize a right of reply or a right to protect information sources.

NETHERLANDS : LAND USE

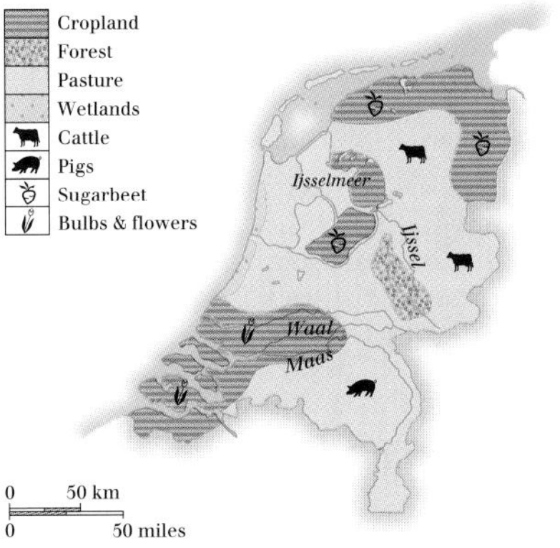
Cropland
Forest
Pasture
Wetlands
Cattle
Pigs
Sugarbeet
Bulbs & flowers
IJsselmeer
IJssel
Waal
Maas
0
50 km
0
50 miles

CRIME

No death penalty

16,239 prisoners

Up 4% in 2001

CRIME RATES

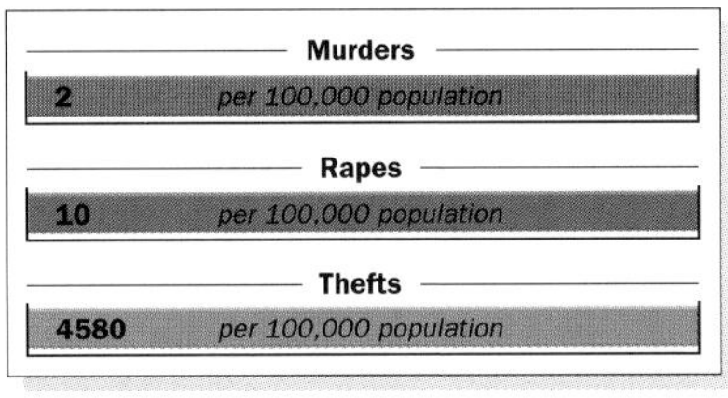
Murders
2
per 100,000 population
Rapes
10
per 100,000 population
Thefts
4580
per 100,000 population

The Netherlands treats the use of hard drugs more as a medical and social issue than a criminal one. Other member states of Europe's Schengen Convention, particularly France, fear that this makes Dutch ports a soft point of entry for narcotics. Possessing cannabis for personal use has been decriminalized – stopping short of actual legalization.

EDUCATION

School leaving age: 18

97%

504,042 students

THE EDUCATION SYSTEM

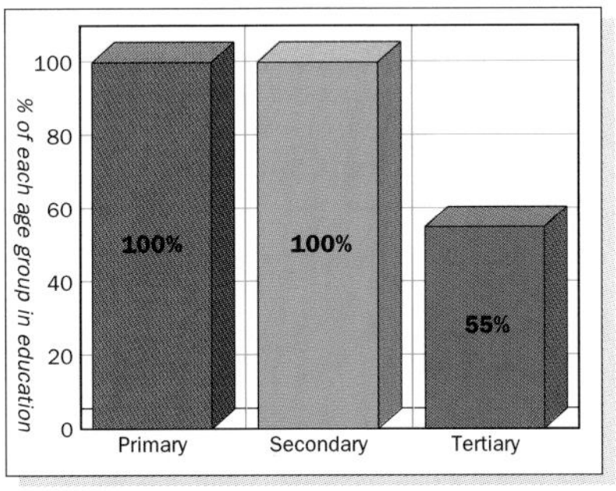
100
80
60
40
20
0
% of each age group in education
100%
100%
55%
Primary
Secondary
Tertiary

Private schools take 65% of students; most of them are run by the various religious denominations. Both public and private institutions are state-funded.

There are 13 universities in the Netherlands. Corporate funding plays an important part in research.

HEALTH

Welfare state health benefits

1 per 303 people

Cancers, heart, cerebrovascular, and respiratory diseases

The quality of health care, largely state-funded and currently among the best in the world, is threatened by a rapidly aging population. The Netherlands was the first country to legalize abortion; it has one of the lowest rates of terminations in the world, but numbers are increasing steadily. Major health problems are similar to those in the rest of western Europe. Smoking was banned in most public places from January 2004 in a bid to reduce the prevalence of the habit among the Dutch.

SPENDING

GDP/cap. increase

CONSUMPTION AND SPENDING

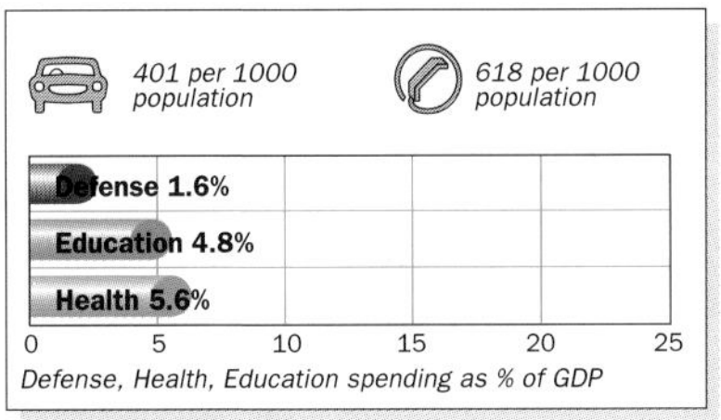
401 per 1000 population
618 per 1000 population
Defense 1.6%
Education 4.8%
Health 5.6%
0
5
10
15
20
25
Defense, Health, Education spending as % of GDP

The Netherlands is, per capita, one of the richest countries in the world. Oil executives, stock market traders, and businessmen are among the wealthiest sector of the population. A progressive taxation system and extensive social welfare mean that wealth is reasonably evenly distributed. A small elite have considerable inherited wealth, but extravagant displays of affluence are rare.

Class does not play a big part in Dutch society. Most citizens would consider themselves middle class. Immigrant communities are the exception; they often live on the edges of towns in deprived areas. The poorest group of all are the illegal immigrants.

WORLD RANKING

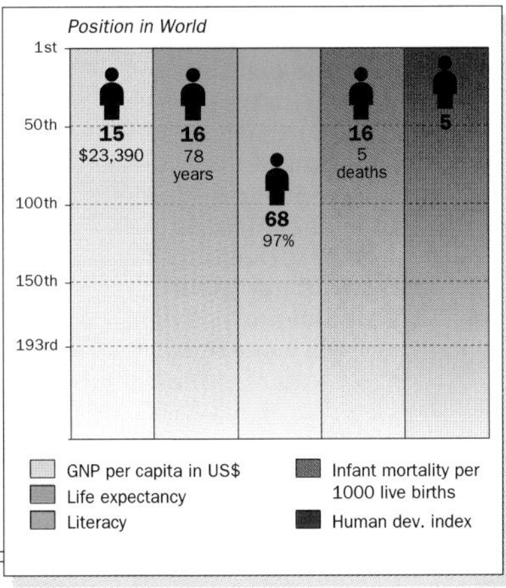
Position in World
1st
50th
100th
150th
193rd
15
$23,390
16
78 years
68
97%
16
5 deaths
5
GNP per capita in US$
Life expectancy
Literacy
Infant mortality per 1000 live births
Human dev. index

N

NEW ZEALAND

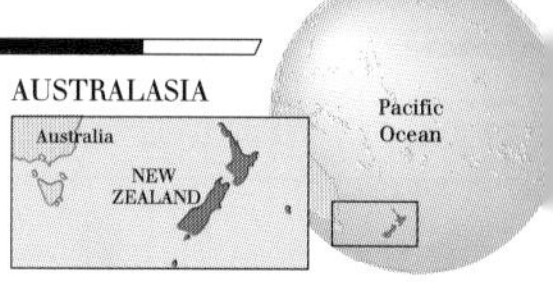
AUSTRALASIA
Australia
NEW ZEALAND
Pacific Ocean

OFFICIAL NAME: New Zealand **CAPITAL:** Wellington **POPULATION:** 3.9 million
CURRENCY: New Zealand dollar **OFFICIAL LANGUAGES:** English and Maori

1947
1947
Feb 6
NZ
+12
+64
.nz

LYING IN THE SOUTH PACIFIC, 1600 km (992 miles) southeast of Australia, New Zealand comprises the main North and South Islands, separated by the Cook Strait, and a number of smaller islands. South Island is the more mountainous; North Island contains hot springs and geysers, and the bulk of the population. The political tradition is liberal and egalitarian, and has been dominated by the National and Labour parties. Radical, and often unpopular, reforms since 1984 have restored economic growth, speeded up economic diversification, and strengthened New Zealand's position within the Pacific Rim countries.

CLIMATE

Maritime/subtropical

WEATHER CHART FOR WELLINGTON

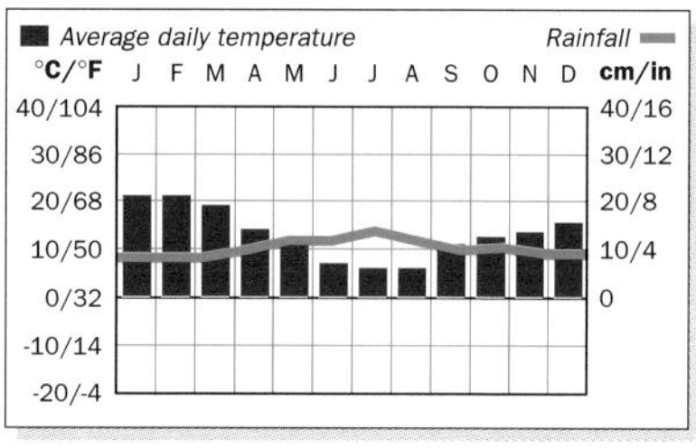
Average daily temperature
Rainfall
°C/°F
J F M A M J J A S O N D
cm/in
40/104
30/86
20/68
10/50
0/32
-10/14
-20/-4
40/16
30/12
20/8
10/4
0

New Zealand's climate is generally temperate and damp, with an average temperature of 12°C (54°F). There are differences between the islands, which extend north–south nearly 2000 km (1240 miles). The extreme north is almost subtropical; southern winters are cold. It is windy: Wellington, in particular, is known for bouts of blustery weather and occasional violent storms.

TRANSPORTATION

Drive on left

Auckland International 9.83m passengers

173 ships 180,435 grt

THE TRANSPORTATION NETWORK

58,090 km (36,095 miles)

169 km (105 miles)

3898 km (2422 miles)

1609 km (1000 miles)

Though both the main islands are well provided with transportation services, the more populous North Island's road and rail network is more extensive than the South's. Air and ferry services complement the land networks and provide links between the North and South Islands, as well as with the numerous smaller islands. Cargo ferry services are particularly important for Antarctic bases in the Ross Dependency. Links with New Zealand's other associated territories – the Cook Islands, Niue, and the atolls of Tokelau – are underdeveloped.

TOURISM

Visitors : Population 1:1.9

2.1m visitors

Up 3% in 2003

MAIN TOURIST ARRIVALS

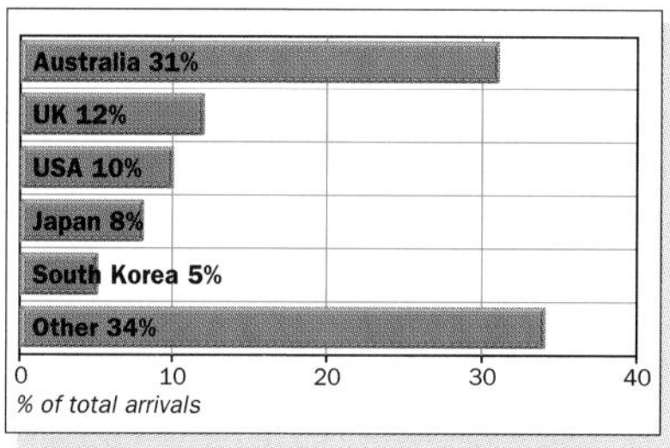
Australia 31%
UK 12%
USA 10%
Japan 8%
South Korea 5%
Other 34%
0
10
20
30
40
% of total arrivals

New Zealand's prime attraction is its scenery. Unspoiled and, relative to the country's size, the most varied in the world, it offers mountains, fiords and lakes, glaciers, rainforests, beaches, boiling mud pools, and geysers. Other attractions are the Maori culture and outdoor activities such as river rafting, fishing, skiing, whale watching, and bungee jumping – a local invention.

Tourism is the largest single foreign-exchange earner and it continues to grow, though the 1997–1998 Asian economic crisis saw the number of Asian tourists drop by 10%. An increase in visitor numbers has followed the huge global success of the three *Lord of the Rings* films: the whole series was shot in various locations across New Zealand.

***Mount Egmont,** an extinct volcano, is one of the numerous popular natural attractions of New Zealand's North Island.*

PEOPLE

Pop. density low

English, Maori

15/km² (38/mi²)

THE URBAN/RURAL POPULATION SPLIT

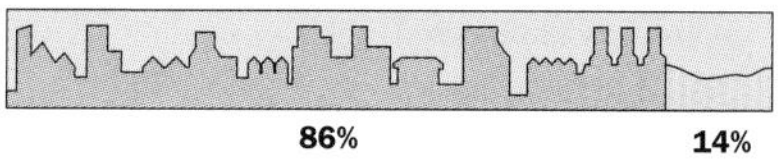
86%
14%

RELIGIOUS PERSUASION

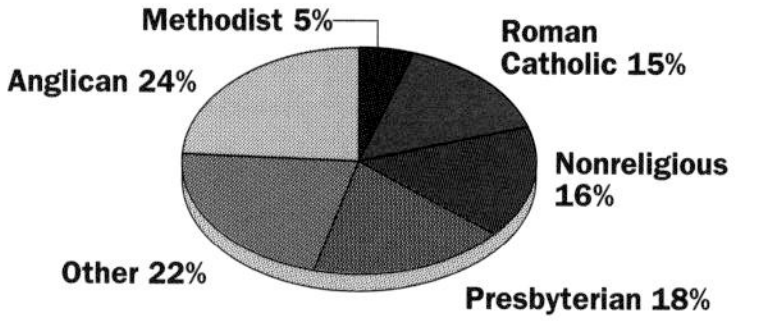
Methodist 5%
Roman Catholic 15%
Anglican 24%
Nonreligious 16%
Other 22%
Presbyterian 18%

ETHNIC MAKEUP

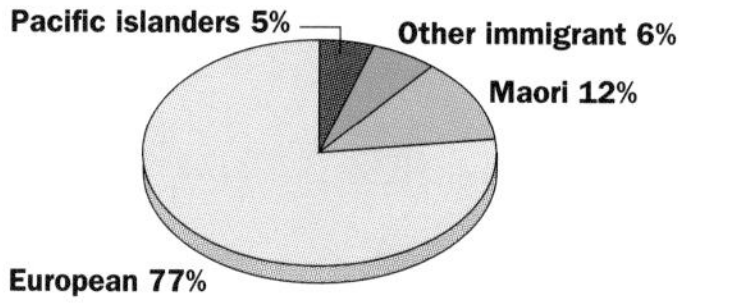
Pacific islanders 5%
Other immigrant 6%
Maori 12%
European 77%

New Zealand is a country of migrants. The first settlers, the Maoris, migrated from Polynesia about 1200 years ago. Today's majority European population is mainly descended from British migrants who settled after 1840. Newer migrants include Asians from Hong Kong and Malaysia, and Polynesians. The government is keen to attract skilled South Americans, Russians, Chinese, and Africans to revitalize the economy.

The living standards and unemployment rates of the Maoris compare adversely with those of the European-descended majority, and relations can be tense. The Waikato Raupatu Claims Settlement Act was signed in 1995 and an official apology to the Maoris was made. In 1998 the Waitangi Tribunal ordered the return of confiscated land.

New Zealand became the first country in the world to give women the vote – in 1893. In 2001, the posts of prime minister, leader of the opposition, and governor-general were all held by women.

POPULATION AGE BREAKDOWN

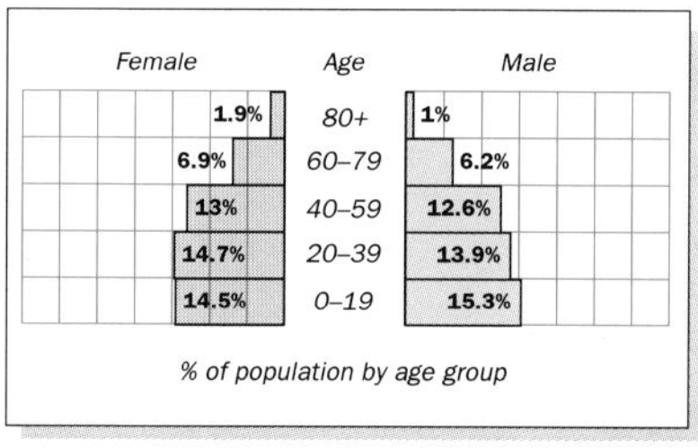
Female
Age
Male
1.9%
80+
1%
6.9%
60–79
6.2%
13%
40–59
12.6%
14.7%
20–39
13.9%
14.5%
0–19
15.3%
% of population by age group

POLITICS

Multiparty elections

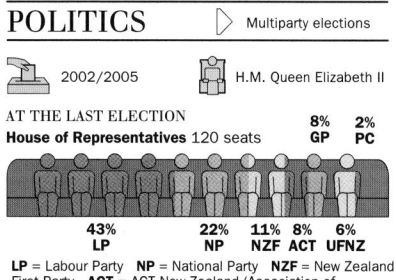

2002/2005 H.M. Queen Elizabeth II

AT THE LAST ELECTION

House of Representatives 120 seats

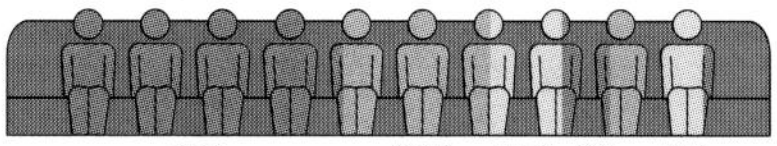

43% LP
22% NP
11% NZF
8% ACT
6% UFNZ
8% GP
2% PC

LP = Labour Party **NP** = National Party **NZF** = New Zealand First Party **ACT** = ACT New Zealand (Association of Consumers and Taxpayers) **GP** = Green Party **UFNZ** = United Future **PC** = Progressive Coalition

Helen Clark, *LP leader and prime minister since 1999.*

Jenny Shipley, *the first woman prime minister (NP, 1997–1999).*

New Zealand is a parliamentary democracy. The Cook Islands and Niue are self-governing territories.

PROFILE

Since 1984 the economy has undergone massive reforms; cuts to the welfare system and privatization of public assets have been unpopular. The NP and the LP dominated politics until 1996 and the first use of proportional representation (PR), a reform endorsed by referendum in 1993. Jenny Shipley of the NP became the country's first woman prime minister in 1997 at the head of a coalition with the small NZF, and from 1998 led a minority administration when the NZF withdrew. A new minority coalition of the LP and the Alliance assumed power under LP leader Helen Clark in 1999. The LP remained in power after the 2002 elections, forming a minority coalition with the PC (renamed the Progress Party in 2003).

MAIN POLITICAL ISSUE

Electoral reform

New Zealand shifted from a first-past-the-post electoral system to PR for the 1996 general election. The new German-style system strengthened the role of smaller parties. As predicted, the first election to use the system in 1996 produced a coalition government, led by the NP. Forced into opposition in 1998, the NP has, unsuccessfully, called for a review of PR.

WORLD AFFAIRS

Joined UN in 1945

Comm APEC OECD PIF PC

Many New Zealanders are strongly committed to the British monarchy and the Commonwealth, but the UK's EU involvement has forced New Zealand to reorient its trade and foreign policy toward its Pacific Rim neighbors, especially Australia, now New Zealand's largest single trading partner. Their 1983 Closer Economic Relationship (CER) treaty was strengthened in 1996 by the signing of a mutual recognition agreement.

Relations with Asia are growing in importance. The 1997–1998 Asian economic crisis significantly affected trade, particularly tourism.

Relations with the US are improving after a low point when New Zealand's antinuclear stance led to its exclusion from the ANZUS pact. Official ties with France, cut in 1985 after French agents bombed Greenpeace's *Rainbow Warrior* in Auckland harbor, were restored in 1997.

AID

Donor

US$122m (donations) Up 9% in 2002

Around 75% of New Zealand's overseas aid is bilateral. Particular areas of focus are the Pacific states and Pacific-wide organizations. New Zealand is a major supporter of the Pacific Islands Forum, the University of the South Pacific, and the Pacific Environment Program. It also offers scholarships to overseas students for study or training in New Zealand.

NORTH ISLAND
SOUTH ISLAND
TASMAN SEA
SOUTH PACIFIC OCEAN
Great Exhibition Bay
Kaitaia
Whangarei
Dargaville
Little Barrier I.
Great Barrier I.
Colville Channel
Kaipara Harbour
Hauraki Gulf
Waiheke I.
Great Mercury I.
Takapuna
Auckland
Coromandel Peninsula
Papatoetoe
Manurewa
Manukau Harbour
Papakura
Pukekohe
Bay of Plenty
Mount Maunganui
White I.
Hamilton
Cambridge
Tauranga
Whakatane
Ruatoria
L. Rotorua
Rotorua
Tokoroa
Taupo
L. Taupo
Murupara
Gisborne
L. Waikaremoana
Taumarunui
New Plymouth
Mt Taranaki (Mt Egmont) 2518m
Mt Ruapehu 2797m
Cape Egmont
Hawera
Wairoa
Hawke Bay
Mahia Peninsula
Napier
Hastings
North Taranaki Bight
South Taranaki Bight
Wanganui
Feilding
Palmerston North
Levin
Kapiti I.
Paraparaumu
Masterton
Porirua
Upper Hutt
L. Wairarapa
Lower Hutt
WELLINGTON
Cook Strait
Golden Bay
D'Urville Island
Tasman Bay
Nelson
Blenheim
Karamea Bight
Westport
Buller
Reefton
Clarence
Kaikoura
Greymouth
Hokitika
Hurunui
Waimakariri
Rangiora
Pegasus Bay
Christchurch
Banks Peninsula
Aoraki (Mount Cook) 3744m
SOUTHERN ALPS
CANTERBURY PLAINS
L. Tekapo
Rangitata
Ashburton
L. Pukaki
L. Ohau
Twizel
Timaru
Canterbury Bight
L. Hawea
L. Wanaka
Wanaka
Waitaki
L. Wakatipu
Queenstown
Oamaru
L. Te Anau
Alexandra
Te Anau
Clutha
Taieri
Resolution I.
Waiau
Oreti
Mataura
Mosgiel
Otago Peninsula
Dunedin
Gore
Balclutha
Invercargill
Foveaux Strait
Stewart Island
Halfmoon Bay
Chatham Is
Petre Bay
Chatham I.
Waitangi
Pitt Strait
Pitt I.
(continuation on same scale)
NEW ZEALAND
Total Area : 268 680 sq. km (103 737 sq. miles)
LAND HEIGHT
2000m/6562ft
1000m/3281ft
500m/1640ft
200m/656ft
Sea Level
POPULATION
over 500 000
over 100 000
over 50 000
over 10 000
under 10 000
100 km
100 miles

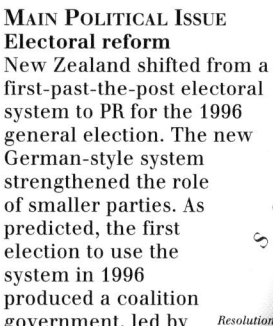

CHRONOLOGY

A former British colony, New Zealand became a dominion in 1907, self-governing from 1926, and fully independent in 1947.

- ❑ **1962** Western Samoa (now Samoa) gains independence.
- ❑ **1965** Cook Islands gain autonomy.
- ❑ **1975** Conservative NP wins elections. Economic austerity program introduced.
- ❑ **1976** Immigration cut by over 80%.
- ❑ **1984** LP elected; David Lange prime minister. Auckland harbor headland restored to Maoris.
- ❑ **1985** New Zealand prohibits nuclear vessels from ports and waters. French agents sink Greenpeace ship *Rainbow Warrior* in Auckland harbor.
- ❑ **1986** US suspends military obligations under ANZUS Treaty.
- ❑ **1987** LP wins elections. Introduction of controversial privatization plan. Nuclear ban enshrined in legislation.
- ❑ **1990** LP defeated by NP in elections. James Bolger prime minister.
- ❑ **1991** Widespread protests at spending cuts.
- ❑ **1992** Maoris win South Island fishing rights. Majority vote for electoral reform in referendum.
- ❑ **1993** Docking of first French naval ship for eight years. NP returned with single-seat majority in election. Proportional representation introduced by referendum.
- ❑ **1994** Senior-level US contacts restored; agrees not to send nuclear-armed ships to New Zealand ports. Maoris reject government ten-year land claims settlement of US$660 million.
- ❑ **1995** Waitangi Day celebrations abandoned after Maori protests. Crown apologizes to Maoris and signs Waikato Raupatu Claims Act. UK warship visits resume.
- ❑ **1996** NP forms coalition to preserve overall legislative majority. First general election under new proportional representation system.
- ❑ **1997** NP forms coalition with New Zealand First (NZF) party. Bolger resigns. Jenny Shipley becomes first woman prime minister.
- ❑ **1998** Shipley sacks NZF leader Winston Peters as deputy prime minister. Waitangi Tribunal orders government to return to Maoris US$3.3 million of confiscated land.
- ❑ **1999** LP led by Helen Clark wins general election.
- ❑ **2001** Air New Zealand renationalized.
- ❑ **2002** Combat wing of air force taken out of service. July, elections: LP reelected.

N

DEFENSE

No compulsory military service

US$630m

Down 4% in 2002

Military cuts announced in 2001 emphasized the aim to refocus defense policy on small-scale peacekeeping, protection against low-level economic threats, and terrorism. As part of cutbacks the combat wing of the air force was taken out of active service in 2002. The move put renewed stress on the historic security pact with Australia and the US (ANZUS).

The 1984 decision to refuse access to nuclear warships (effective from 1985) damaged defense cooperation with the US and other Western powers for a decade, forcing New Zealand to seek closer links with Australia. Senior-level contacts were resumed in 1994. Since then, the US and the UK have resumed naval visits, though not with nuclear-armed vessels.

NEW ZEALAND ARMED FORCES

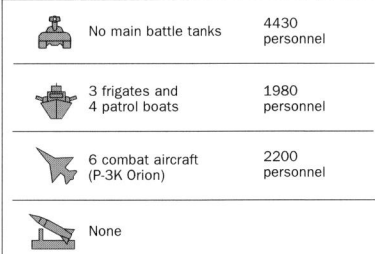

No main battle tanks	4430 personnel
3 frigates and 4 patrol boats	1980 personnel
6 combat aircraft (P-3K Orion)	2200 personnel
None	

ECONOMICS

Inflation 1.6% p.a. (1990–2001)

US$52.2bn

1.575 New Zealand dollars (1.708)

SCORE CARD

❑ World GNP Ranking	49th
❑ GNP per Capita	US$13,260
❑ Balance of Payments	–US$1.95bn
❑ Inflation	2.7%
❑ Unemployment	5%

EXPORTS

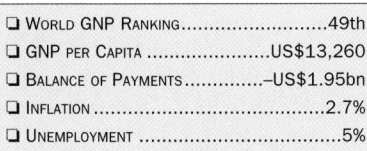

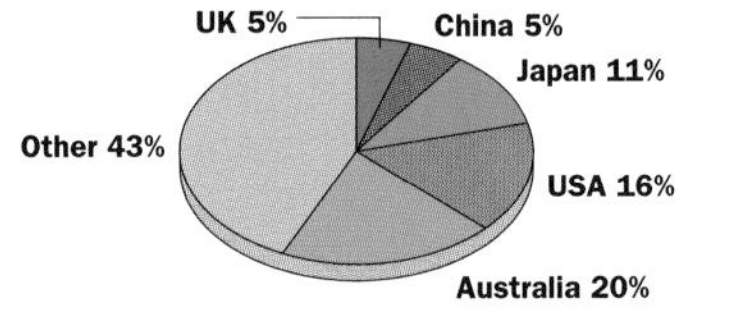
UK 5%
China 5%
Japan 11%
USA 16%
Australia 20%
Other 43%

IMPORTS

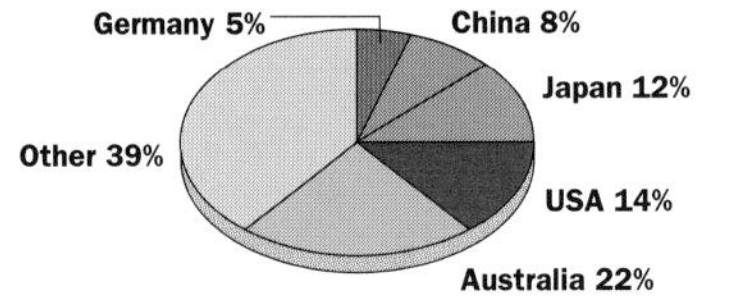
Germany 5%
China 8%
Japan 12%
USA 14%
Australia 22%
Other 39%

ECONOMIC PERFORMANCE INDICATOR

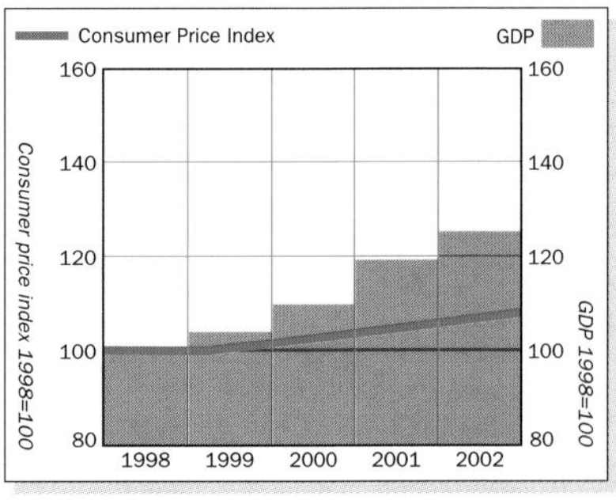
Consumer Price Index
GDP
160
140
120
100
80
1998
1999
2000
2001
2002
Consumer price index 1998=100
GDP 1998=100

Strengths

Modern agricultural sector; one of the five biggest exporters of dairy products. Rapidly expanding tourist sector. Manufacturing, with emphasis on high-tech. One of world's most open economies. Strong trade links within Pacific Rim.

Weaknesses

One of the highest levels of public debt outside developing world. Continuing reliance on imported manufactured goods and foreign investment.

Profile

Since 1984, New Zealand has changed from being one of the most regulated to one of the most open economies in the world. Radical reforms and drastic cuts in social security and related government spending helped to restore growth and cut inflation to a minimum. Diversification into new markets and products recovered after the 1997–1998 Asian economic crisis. Prime Minister Clark dropped objections in 2001 to the idea of a unified Australia–New Zealand dollar. High public debt and poor levels of private investment remain a problem.

NEW ZEALAND : MAJOR BUSINESSES

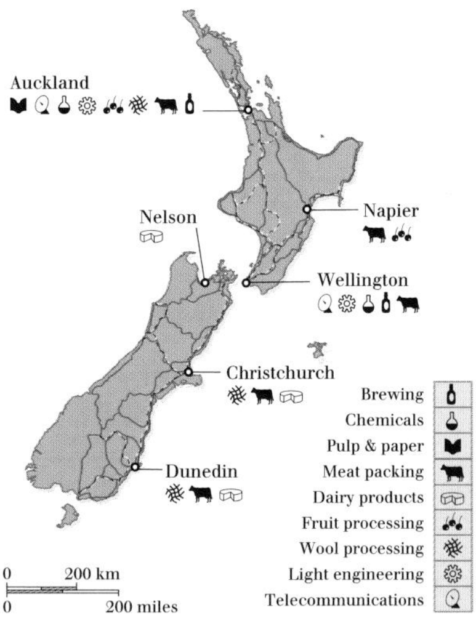
Auckland
Nelson
Napier
Wellington
Christchurch
Dunedin
Brewing
Chemicals
Pulp & paper
Meat packing
Dairy products
Fruit processing
Wool processing
Light engineering
Telecommunications
0 200 km
0 200 miles

RESOURCES

Electric power 8.5m kW

637,134 tonnes

23,318 b/d (reserves 106m barrels)

39.3m sheep, 9.66m cattle, 18m chickens

Coal, oil, natural gas, iron, gold, silica sand

ELECTRICITY GENERATION

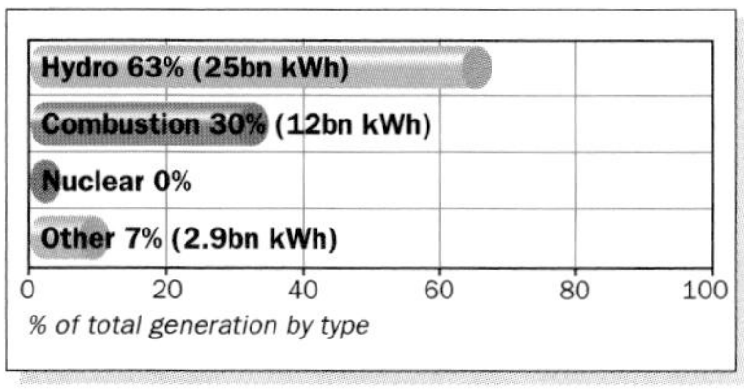
Hydro 63% (25bn kWh)
Combustion 30% (12bn kWh)
Nuclear 0%
Other 7% (2.9bn kWh)
0
20
40
60
80
100
% of total generation by type

New Zealand's rich pastures, a result of even rainfall throughout the year, have traditionally been its key resource. The sheep, wool, and dairy products on which the country's wealth was built are still important. Newer export industries include products such as fruit, vegetables, fish, cork, wood, wine, and textile fibers.

New Zealand is well endowed with energy resources. It has coal, oil, and natural gas reserves, but most energy is generated by hydroelectric plants.

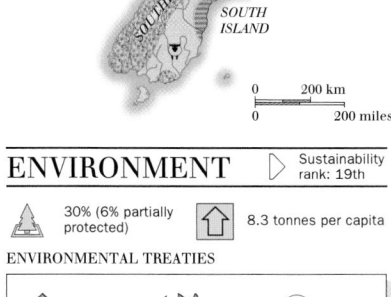

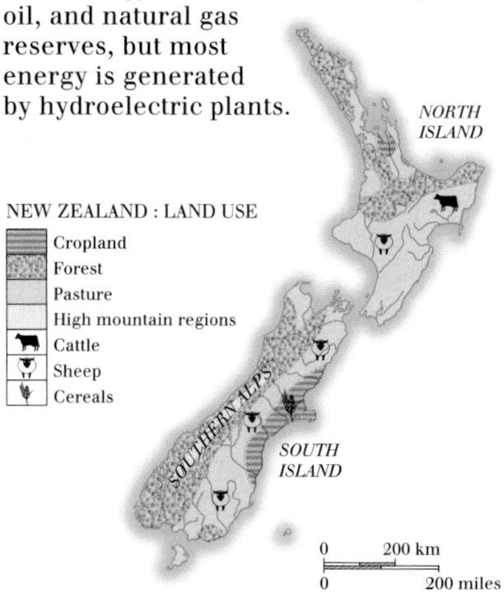
NORTH ISLAND
NEW ZEALAND : LAND USE
Cropland
Forest
Pasture
High mountain regions
Cattle
Sheep
Cereals
SOUTHERN ALPS
SOUTH ISLAND
0
200 km
0
200 miles

ENVIRONMENT

Sustainability rank: 19th

30% (6% partially protected)

8.3 tonnes per capita

ENVIRONMENTAL TREATIES

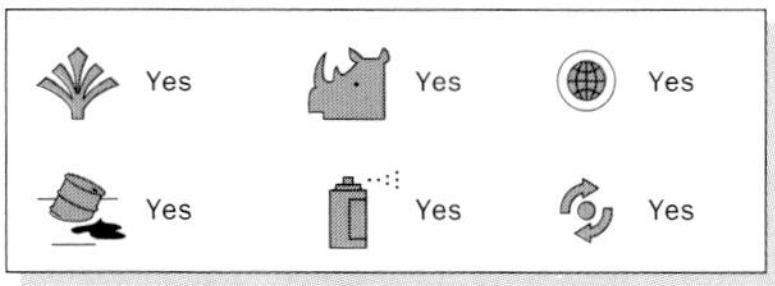
Yes
Yes
Yes
Yes
Yes
Yes

New Zealand's isolation, small population, and limited industry have helped to keep it one of the world's most pollution-free countries. It was a leading opponent of French nuclear testing in the Pacific and has banned nuclear vessels from its ports. Ozone depletion over Antarctica, deforestation, and protection of native flora and fauna are major issues.

MEDIA

TV ownership high

Daily newspaper circulation 362 per 1000 people

PUBLISHING AND BROADCAST MEDIA

There are 29 regional daily newspapers. The leading newspaper is the *New Zealand Herald*

4 services: 1 state-owned, 3 independent

2 state-owned services, over 200 independent stations

Deregulated in 1988, New Zealand television is one of the most liberal in the world. Maori-language radio broadcasts began in 1996, and a television channel followed in 2004.

CRIME

No death penalty

5881 prisoners

Little change in 2001

CRIME RATES

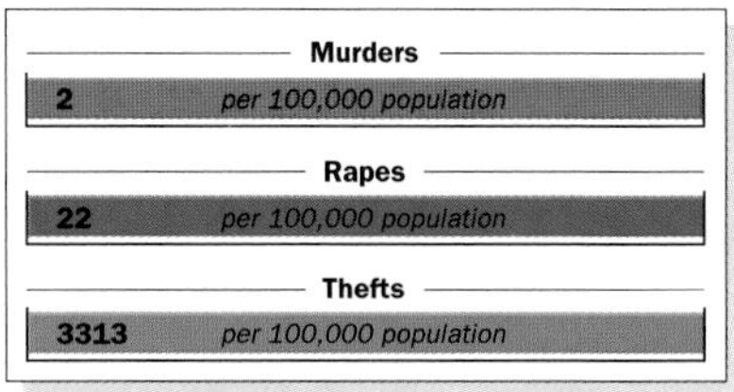
Murders
2 per 100,000 population
Rapes
22 per 100,000 population
Thefts
3313 per 100,000 population

Crime rates in New Zealand's urban areas have increased in recent years. Overall, however, the country remains one of the world's safest and most peaceful places in which to live.

EDUCATION

School leaving age: 16

99%

266,501 students

THE EDUCATION SYSTEM

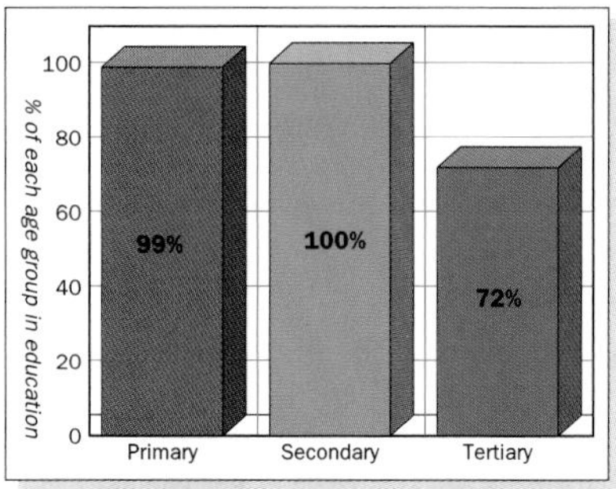
100
80
60
40
20
0
% of each age group in education
99%
100%
72%
Primary
Secondary
Tertiary

Education is free, and compulsory between six and 16. A number of schools are composite, providing both primary and secondary education. New Zealand has one of the highest proportions of the population with tertiary qualifications in the OECD. Nearly all adults are literate, but the standard of literacy is not always very high: a government initiative, More than Words, was launched in 2000.

HEALTH

Welfare state health benefits

1 per 225 people

Cancers, respiratory, cerebrovascular, and heart diseases

In 1936, New Zealand became the first country to introduce a full welfare state. Government efforts since 1991 to impose UK-style market systems on the health service have been very unpopular. While life expectancy continues to improve, the nation's OECD health ranking has fallen. In comparison with other OECD countries, New Zealand has high mortality rates for heart diseases, respiratory disease, breast and bowel cancer, motor vehicle accidents, and suicide.

SPENDING

GDP/cap. increase

CONSUMPTION AND SPENDING

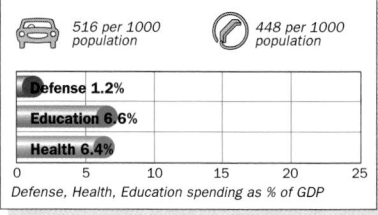

516 per 1000 population

448 per 1000 population

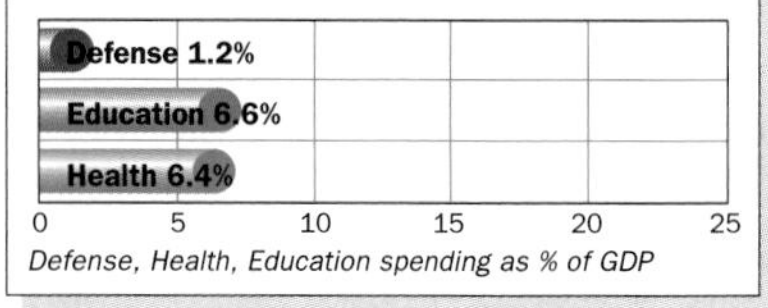
Defense 1.2%
Education 6.6%
Health 6.4%
0
5
10
15
20
25
Defense, Health, Education spending as % of GDP

The years since 1984 have been very difficult for New Zealanders, who are used to affluence within a generous welfare state. A rash of economic and social reforms has held back wages, raised unemployment, and cut welfare benefits. Even so, average living standards are still high, and a strong egalitarian tradition means that wealth remains relatively evenly distributed.

The quality of life in New Zealand is among the best in the world, in terms of access to basic necessities, and a pure, healthy, urban and rural environment. Social mobility is fairly high. Wealthier people tend to spend their money on houses close to the water. Yachts are a common status symbol.

WORLD RANKING

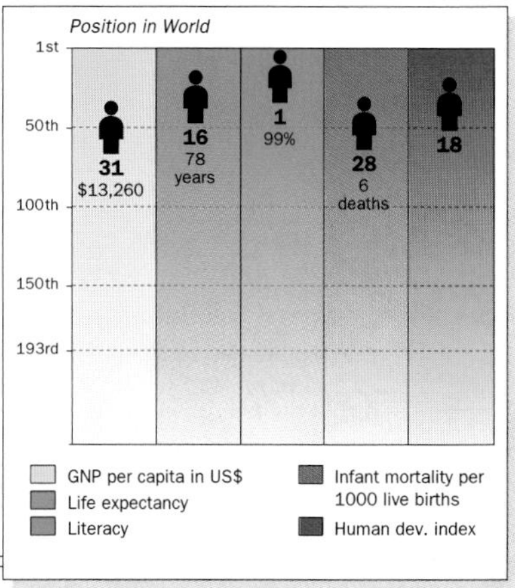
Position in World
1st
50th
100th
150th
193rd
31
$13,260
16
78
years
1
99%
28
6
deaths
18
GNP per capita in US$
Life expectancy
Literacy
Infant mortality per 1000 live births
Human dev. index

N

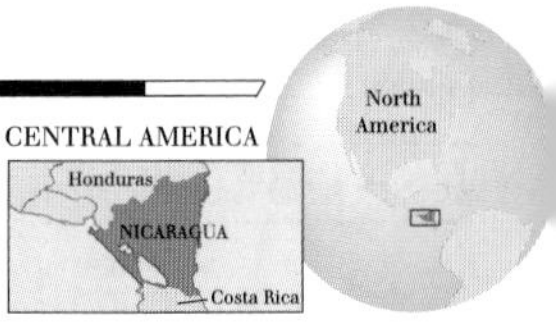
North America
CENTRAL AMERICA
Honduras
NICARAGUA
Costa Rica

NICARAGUA

OFFICIAL NAME: Republic of Nicaragua **CAPITAL:** Managua
POPULATION: 5.5 million **CURRENCY:** Córdoba oro **OFFICIAL LANGUAGE:** Spanish

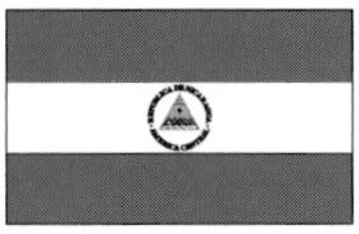

1838 | 1838 | Sept 15 | NIC | -6 | +505 | .ni

BOUNDED BY the Pacific Ocean to the west and the Caribbean Sea to the east, Nicaragua lies at the heart of Central America. After more than 40 years of dictatorship, the Sandinista revolution in 1978 led to social reforms, but also to a decade of civil war, which almost destroyed the economy. Right-wing parties have held power since the Sandinistas unexpectedly lost the 1990 elections. Despite the devastation of Hurricane Mitch in 1998, the economy is slowly strengthening.

*Oil refinery at **Bluefields**, on the Caribbean coast. Under the Sandinistas, most crude oil came from the Soviet Union, via Cuba.*

CLIMATE

Tropical equatorial/wet and dry

WEATHER CHART FOR MANAGUA

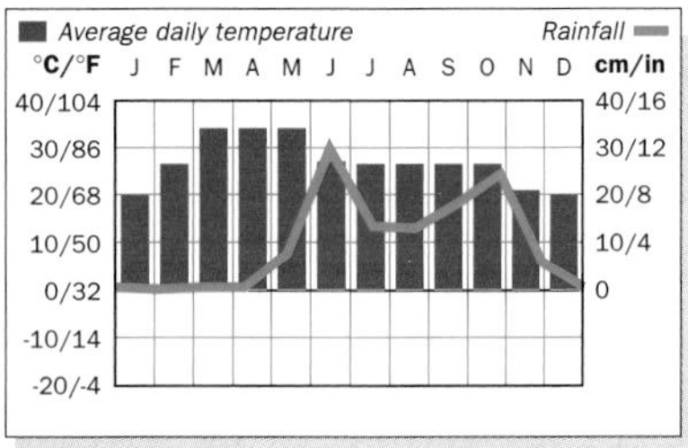
Average daily temperature
Rainfall
°C/°F
J F M A M J J A S O N D
cm/in
40/104
30/86
20/68
10/50
0/32
-10/14
-20/-4
40/16
30/12
20/8
10/4
0

The climate is tropical and often violent, as evidenced by seasonal hurricanes, such as Hurricane Mitch in 1998.

TRANSPORTATION

Drive on right

Augusto C. Sandino, Managua
913,534 passengers

26 ships
3600 grt

THE TRANSPORTATION NETWORK

2094 km (1301 miles)

Pan-American Highway: 384 km (239 miles)

6 km (4 miles)

2220 km (1379 miles)

Nicaragua lacks a Caribbean deepwater port. There are three domestic airlines. Some areas are only accessible by boat.

TOURISM

Visitors : Population 1:11

518,250 visitors

Up 10% in 2003

MAIN TOURIST ARRIVALS

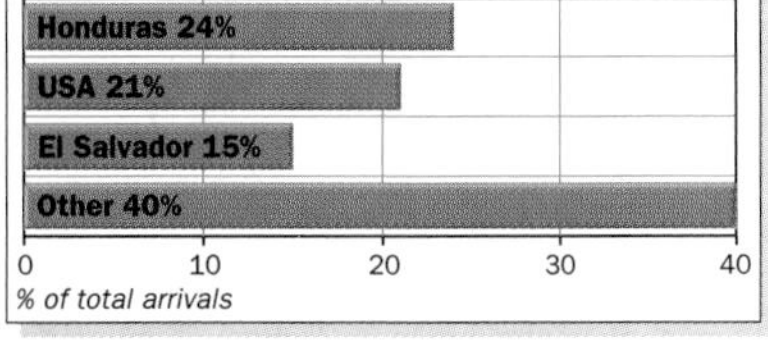
Honduras 24%
USA 21%
El Salvador 15%
Other 40%
0
10
20
30
40
% of total arrivals

The civil war caused the near-collapse of the tourist industry, and its recovery was interrupted by the devastation caused by Hurricane Mitch in 1998. The 1999 "incentive law" encourages investment in tourist infrastructure.

PEOPLE

Pop. density low

Spanish, English Creole, Miskito

46/km² (120/mi²)

THE URBAN/RURAL POPULATION SPLIT

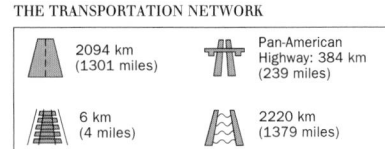

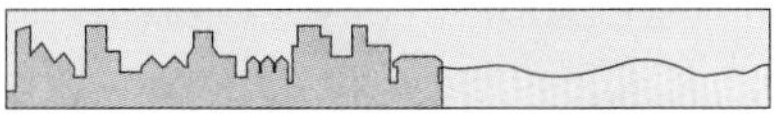
57%
43%

ETHNIC MAKEUP

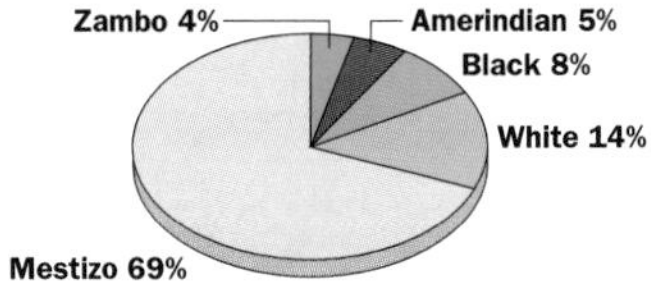
Zambo 4%
Amerindian 5%
Black 8%
White 14%
Mestizo 69%

The Caribbean regions, which in 1987 achieved limited autonomy, are isolated from the more populous Pacific regions. The indigenous Miskito tribes and the descendants of Africans, brought over by Spanish colonists in the 18th century to work the plantations, are concentrated along the Caribbean coast, where English Creole is widely spoken. The Sandinista revolution improved the status of women through changes in the legal system and the incorporation of women into economic and political life. However, poverty and lack of permanent employment have since forced many women into prostitution.

POLITICS

Multiparty elections

2001/2006

President Enrique Bolaños

AT THE LAST ELECTION
National Assembly 92 seats

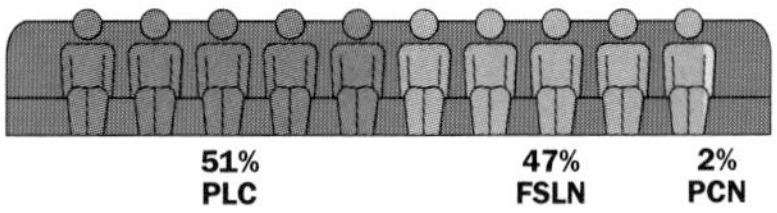
51% PLC
47% FSLN
2% PCN

PLC = Liberal Constitutionalist Party
FSLN = Sandinista National Liberation Front
PCN = Conservative Party of Nicaragua

Right-wing coalitions have held power since 1990. The PLC took office in 1997, promising to unite the country, but quickly became unpopular due to austerity measures and allegations of corruption. Recent two-party domination of politics, shared between the PLC and the FSLN, has strained democracy. Charges of corruption, backed by President Enrique Bolaños and leveled against former PLC president and party leader Arnoldo Alemán, polarized Congress and the party in 2003.

NICARAGUA

Total Area : 129 494 sq. km (49 998 sq. miles)

POPULATION
- over 500 000
- over 100 000
- over 50 000
- over 10 000
- under 10 000

LAND HEIGHT
- 1000m/3281ft
- 500m/1640ft
- 200m/656ft
- Sea Level

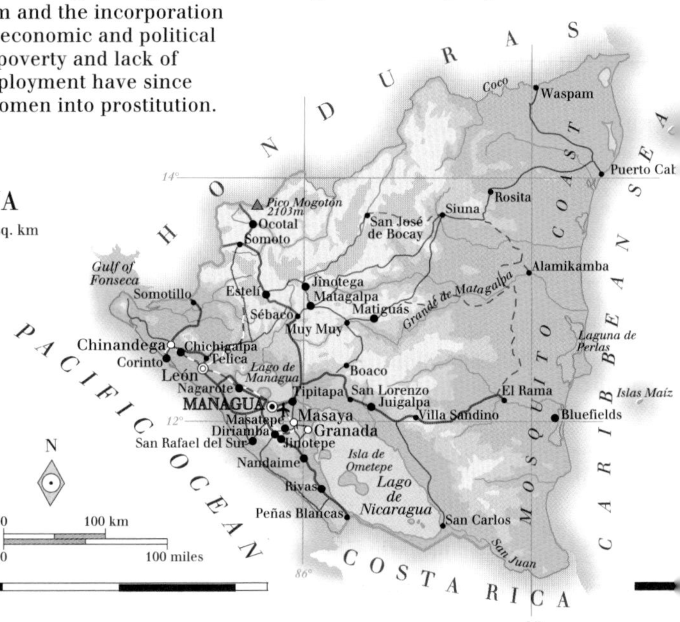
HONDURAS
Coco
Waspam
MOSQUITO COAST
Puerto Cabezas
Pico Mogotón 2103m
Ocotal
Somoto
San José de Bocay
Siuna
Rosita
Gulf of Fonseca
Somotillo
Estelí
Jinotega
Matagalpa
Sébaco
Matiguás
Grande de Matagalpa
Alamikamba
CARIBBEAN SEA
Chinandega
Chichigalpa
Telica
Corinto
León
Muy Muy
Lago de Managua
Boaco
Laguna de Perlas
Islas Maíz
PACIFIC OCEAN
Nagarote
MANAGUA
Tipitapa
San Lorenzo
Juigalpa
El Rama
Masaya
Villa Sandino
Bluefields
Masatepe
Diriamba
Granada
Jinotepe
San Rafael del Sur
Nandaime
Isla de Ometepe
Lago de Nicaragua
Rivas
Peñas Blancas
San Carlos
San Juan
COSTA RICA
14°
12°
86°
84°
N
0
100 km
0
100 miles

WORLD AFFAIRS

Joined UN in 1945

ACS | Geplac | NAM | OAS | San José

Main issues are debt relief in the wake of Hurricane Mitch, cooperation with neighboring countries for increased US trade access, and the treatment of over 300,000 Nicaraguan immigrants in Costa Rica. A free trade agreement with Mexico is important. A dispute over the common border with Costa Rica was resolved in 2000. Ongoing border and navigation rights disputes exist with Honduras and Colombia.

AID

Recipient

$517m (receipts)

Down 44% in 2002

Hurricane Mitch damage elicited new World Bank and IDB loans. Cuba, France, Finland, and Spain pardoned all or part of Nicaragua's debt. Nicaragua was included in the Highly Indebted Poor Countries initiative, and the World Bank and the IMF canceled over 80% of outstanding debt in 2004.

DEFENSE

No compulsory military service

$31m

Up 15% in 2002

FSLN forces once formed the basis of the army, which was cut from a civil war peak of 134,000 to 10,000 by 1995. Senior Sandinistas were among officers retired in 1998. The army is to be involved in more community-based roles focused on the defense of natural resources and mine clearance. Russia agreed in 2001 to help upgrade the military.

ECONOMICS

Inflation 45% p.a. (1990–2000)

$3.82bn

15.82 córdobas oro (15)

SCORE CARD

- World GNP Ranking 122nd
- GNP per Capita $710
- Balance of Payments .... –$888m
- Inflation 4%
- Unemployment 12%

Strengths

Coffee, sugar, and grain exports. Foreign aid and public and private reconstruction work after Hurricane Mitch will benefit tourism, energy, services, and construction. Large foreign debt cancellations.

Weaknesses

Main exports subject to price fluctuations. High unemployment. Poor energy supply and infrastructure. Lack of investment and diversification. Weak banks. Delays in privatization. Skewed land ownership and protracted property disputes. Corruption. Frequent natural disasters.

EXPORTS

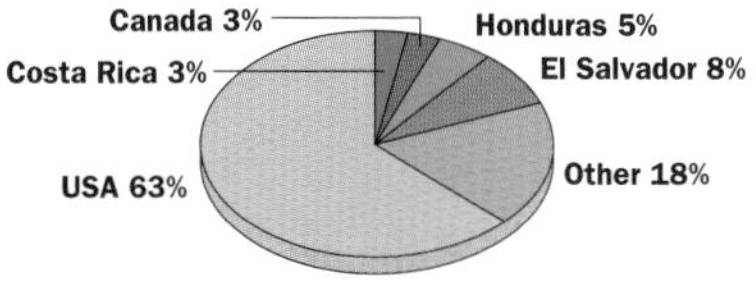
Canada 3%
Honduras 5%
Costa Rica 3%
El Salvador 8%
USA 63%
Other 18%

IMPORTS

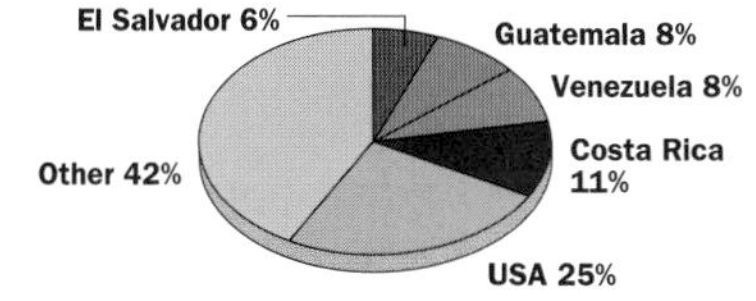
El Salvador 6%
Guatemala 8%
Venezuela 8%
Other 42%
Costa Rica 11%
USA 25%

RESOURCES

Electric power 641,000 kW

28,520 tonnes

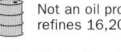

Not an oil producer; refines 16,200 b/d

3.5m cattle, 440,000 pigs, 16.2m chickens

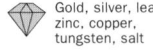

Gold, silver, lead, zinc, copper, tungsten, salt

Nicaragua has small quantities of gold and silver. New thermal generation projects are planned to overcome energy deficits. There is possible offshore oil.

ENVIRONMENT

Sustainability rank: 52nd

18% (8% partially protected)

0.7 tonnes per capita

Deforestation over large areas and the widespread use of pesticides are serious environmental concerns.

MEDIA

TV ownership medium

Daily newspaper circulation 30 per 1000 people

PUBLISHING AND BROADCAST MEDIA

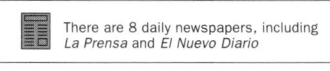

There are 8 daily newspapers, including *La Prensa* and *El Nuevo Diario*

7 services: 1 state-owned, 6 independent

62 stations: 1 state-owned, 61 independent

Since the civil war, radio, TV, and newspapers have tended to ally themselves with the government or the opposition; there is little room for political neutrality.

CRIME

No death penalty

7198 prisoners

Up 23% in 1997–1998

Former combatants have menaced parts of central and northern regions. Violent crime is rising, as is drug trafficking.

CHRONOLOGY

Nicaragua became an independent state in 1838. Guerrilla forces, led by Gen. Sandino, opposed the US marine presence in the early 1930s.

- 1978 FSLN, formed in 1961, ends 44-year Somoza dictatorship; ensuing conflict between FSLN and Contras.
- 1984 Daniel Ortega, FSLN leader, elected president.
- 1990 End of civil war. Center-right National Opposition Union (UNO) unexpectedly wins elections.
- 1998 Hurricane Mitch causes havoc.
- 2002 Bolaños becomes president.

EDUCATION

School leaving age: 12

77%

89,438 students

Nicaragua's adult literacy rate is one of the lowest in Latin America; few students complete fifth grade.

HEALTH

Welfare state health benefits

1 per 1111 people

Cancers, heart diseases, perinatal causes, accidents

Nicaragua has 27 public hospitals. The government is in the process of reforming the health service.

SPENDING

GDP/cap. increase

CONSUMPTION AND SPENDING

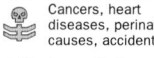

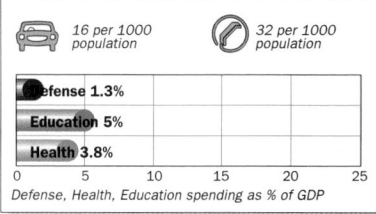

16 per 1000 population

32 per 1000 population

Defense 1.3%
Education 5%
Health 3.8%
0
5
10
15
20
25

Defense, Health, Education spending as % of GDP

Just under half of Nicaragua's population live below the national poverty line, rising to 69% in rural areas.

WORLD RANKING

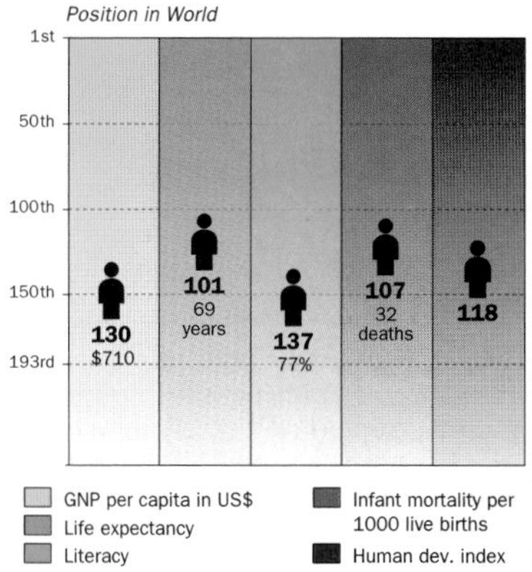
Position in World
1st
50th
100th
150th
193rd
130
$710
101
69
years
137
77%
107
32
deaths
118
GNP per capita in US$
Life expectancy
Literacy
Infant mortality per 1000 live births
Human dev. index

N

NIGER

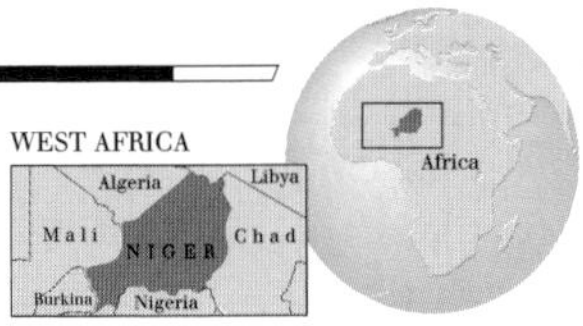
WEST AFRICA
Algeria
Libya
Mali
NIGER
Chad
Burkina
Nigeria
Africa

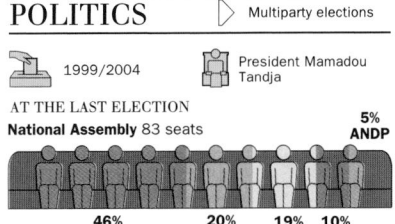

OFFICIAL NAME: Republic of Niger **CAPITAL:** Niamey
POPULATION: 12 million **CURRENCY:** CFA franc **OFFICIAL LANGUAGE:** French

1960 | 1960 | Dec 18 | RN | +1 | +227 | .ne

LANDLOCKED IN THE WEST of Africa, Niger is linked to the sea by the Niger River. Saharan conditions prevail in the northern regions, in the area around the Aïr Mountains, and, particularly, in the vast uninhabited northeast. Niger was ruled by one-party or military regimes until multiparty elections in 1993. A much-troubled democratic process was then disrupted by military coups in 1996 and 1999. Niger is one of the poorest countries in Africa.

CLIMATE

Hot desert/steppe

WEATHER CHART FOR NIAMEY

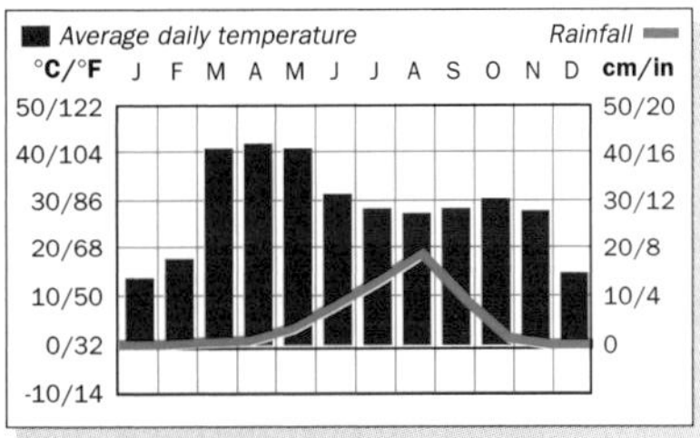
Average daily temperature
Rainfall
°C/°F J F M A M J J A S O N D cm/in
50/122
40/104
30/86
20/68
10/50
0/32
-10/14
50/20
40/16
30/12
20/8
10/4
0

The Saharan north is virtually rainless. The south, in the Sahel belt, has an unreliable rainy season, preceded by a period of extreme daytime heat.

TRANSPORTATION

Drive on right

Niamey International 79,789 passengers

Has no fleet

THE TRANSPORTATION NETWORK

808 km (502 miles)

Trans-Sahara Highway: 428 km (266 miles)

None, but shares administration of Benin's railroad

300 km (186 miles)

A very small proportion of Niger's road network is paved. There are international airports at Niamey and Agadez. There is no railroad.

TOURISM

Visitors : Population 1:308

39,000 visitors

Down 25% in 2002

MAIN TOURIST ARRIVALS

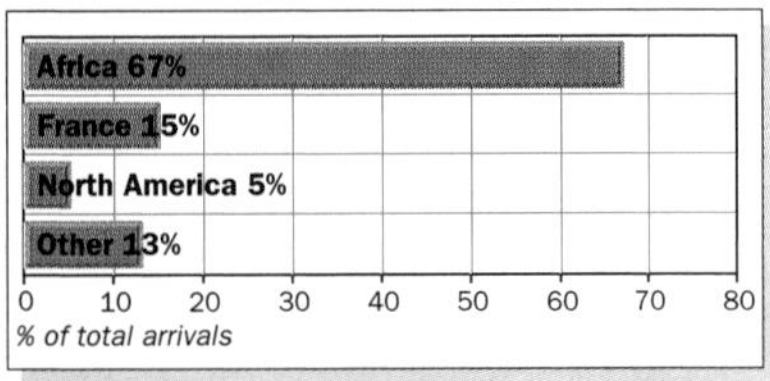
Africa 67%
France 15%
North America 5%
Other 13%
0 10 20 30 40 50 60 70 80
% of total arrivals

The Aïr Mountains, southern Hausa cities, and Saharan Tuareg culture attract some tourists in spite of Niger's limited infrastructure and its instability.

PEOPLE

Pop. density low

Hausa, Djerma, Fulani, Tuareg, Teda, French

9/km² (25/mi²)

THE URBAN/RURAL POPULATION SPLIT

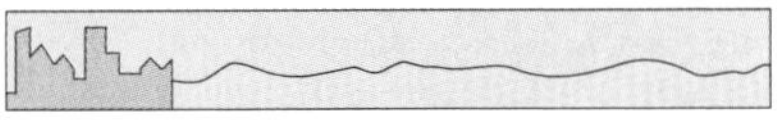
22%
78%

ETHNIC MAKEUP

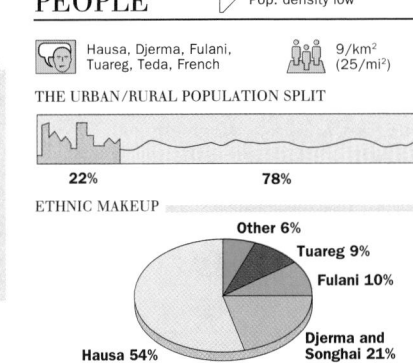

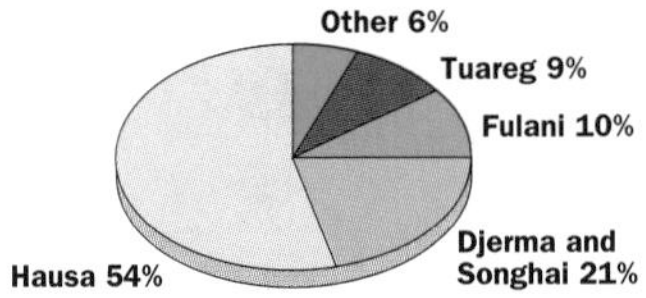
Other 6%
Tuareg 9%
Fulani 10%
Djerma and Songhai 21%
Hausa 54%

Considerable tensions exist between the Tuareg in the north and the southern groups. The Tuareg's sense of alienation from mainstream Nigerien politics has increased since the 1973 and 1984 droughts, which disrupted their nomadic way of life. A five-year rebellion ended in 1995 with a peace agreement. In eastern Niger, Toubou and Arab groups have also been in revolt.

A more subtle antagonism exists between the Djerma and Hausa groups. The Djerma elite from the southwest dominated politics for many years until 1993, when control passed to the Hausa majority.

Niger is an overwhelmingly Islamic society. Women have only limited rights and restricted access to education. The implementation of *sharia* (Islamic law) is fiercely resisted by President Tandja.

***Testing boating poles in the market** at Ayorou on the Niger River, the country's only major permanent watercourse.*

POLITICS

Multiparty elections

1999/2004

President Mamadou Tandja

AT THE LAST ELECTION

National Assembly 83 seats

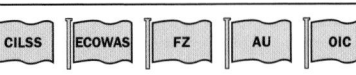

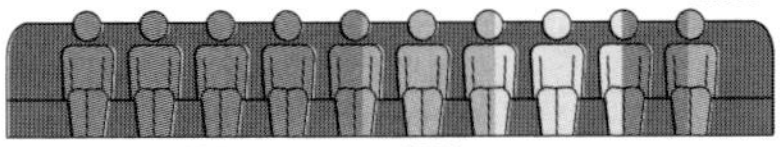
5% ANDP
46% MNSD
20% CDS
19% PNDS
10% RDP

MNSD = National Movement for the Development of Society **CDS** = Democratic and Social Convention **PNDS** = Niger Party for Democracy and Socialism **RDP** = Rally for Democracy and Progress **ANDP** = Niger Alliance for Democracy and Progress

Multiparty elections were held in 1993 after six years of demonstrations following the death of the military dictator Seyni Kountché. An ensuing power struggle between President Mahamane Ousmane and his political opponents led to a military coup in 1996. Gen. Ibrahim Barre Mainassara issued a new constitution and won an election condemned as fraudulent by the opposition. Mainassara was assassinated by his presidential guard in early 1999. Mamadou Tandja won the presidential poll later that year. His MNSD is allied to Ousmane's CDS and the two dominate the National Assembly. The sacking as tourism minister and subsequent arrest of former Tuareg rebel leader Rhissa ag Boula in 2004 heightened tensions.

WORLD AFFAIRS

Joined UN in 1960

CILSS | ECOWAS | FZ | AU | OIC

Relations with Libya and Algeria have improved since the end of the Tuareg rebellion in 1995. ECOWAS members and the OAU condemned the 1999 coup, as did all key donors, led by France.

AID

Recipient

$298m (receipts)

Up 16% in 2002

The World Bank is the principal donor, followed by France and the EU. Most aid was frozen immediately following the 1999 coup, but in late 2000 the IMF approved a three-year loan under its Poverty Reduction and Growth Facility.

DEFENSE

Compulsory military service

$33m

Up 14% in 2002

Niger's armed forces and paramilitary elements total 10,700. A brief army mutiny was quelled in August 2002.

N

NIGER

Total Area : 1 267 000 sq. km
(489 188 sq. miles)

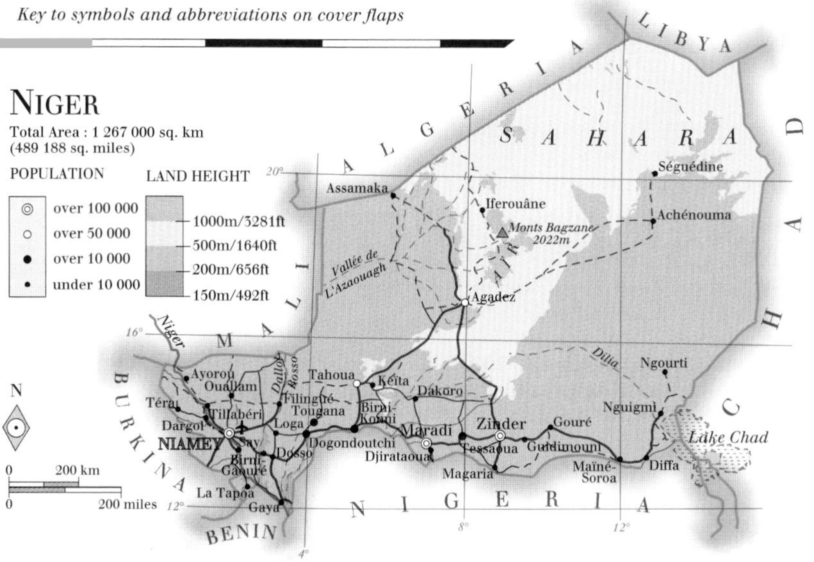
POPULATION
over 100 000
over 50 000
over 10 000
under 10 000
LAND HEIGHT
1000m/3281ft
500m/1640ft
200m/656ft
150m/492ft
N
0 200 km
0 200 miles
LIBYA
ALGERIA
SAHARA
CHAD
MALI
BURKINA
NIGERIA
BENIN
Assamaka
Iferouâne
Monts Bagzane 2022m
Séguédine
Achénouma
Vallée de L'Azaouagh
Agadez
Niger
Ayorou
Ouallam
Téra
Tillabéri
Dargol
NIAMEY
Say
Birni-Gaouré
La Tapoa
Gaya
Dosso
Loga
Filingué
Tougana
Tahoua
Birni-Konni
Kéita
Dakoro
Dogondoutchi
Djirataoua
Maradi
Zinder
Tessaoua
Gouré
Guidimouni
Magaria
Maïné-Soroa
Diffa
Nguigmi
Ngourti
Dilia
Lake Chad
20°
16°
12°
4°
8°
12°

CHRONOLOGY

The powerful Islamic Sokoto empire dissolved as the French took over Niger between 1883 and 1901.

- ❑ **1960** Independence.
- ❑ **1968** French open uranium mines.
- ❑ **1973** Drought; 60% of livestock die.
- ❑ **1974** Military coup. Gen. Seyni Kountché bans political parties.
- ❑ **1984** New drought; Niger River dries up. Uranium boom ends.
- ❑ **1987** Kountché dies. Gen. Ali Saibou begins transition to democracy.
- ❑ **1990–1995** Tuareg rebellion.
- ❑ **1992** Multiparty constitution.
- ❑ **1993** Democratic elections.
- ❑ **1996** Military coup. Staged elections.
- ❑ **1999** Gen. Mainassara assassinated. New constitution. Multiparty elections won by Mamadou Tandja.
- ❑ **2001** Hunting banned in effort to save wildlife.

ECONOMICS

Inflation 5.8% p.a. (1990–2001)

$2.01bn

539.2 CFA francs (571.2)

SCORE CARD

❑ WORLD GNP RANKING	139th
❑ GNP PER CAPITA	$180
❑ BALANCE OF PAYMENTS	–$170m
❑ INFLATION	2.6%
❑ UNEMPLOYMENT	3%

STRENGTHS

Vast uranium deposits. Gold and oil discoveries in late 1990s revived hopes for economic viability.

WEAKNESSES

Aid-dependent. Collapse of uranium prices in 1980s created large debt burden. Only 3% of land cultivable. Weak infrastructure. Frequent droughts. Political instability. Banditry.

EXPORTS

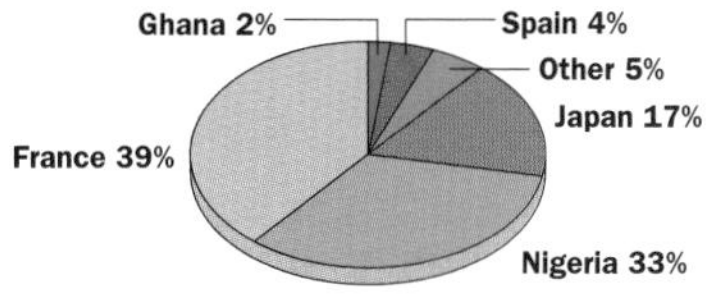
Ghana 2%
Spain 4%
Other 5%
Japan 17%
France 39%
Nigeria 33%

IMPORTS

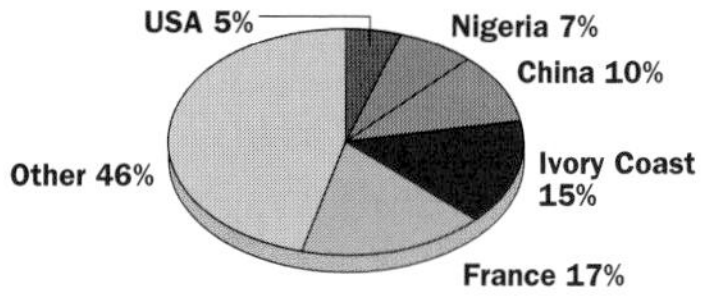
USA 5%
Nigeria 7%
China 10%
Ivory Coast 15%
Other 46%
France 17%

ENVIRONMENT

Sustainability rank: 123rd

8% (7% partially protected)

0.1 tonnes per capita

Serious droughts intensify desertification. Hunting was banned in 2001, in an effort to preserve wildlife numbers.

MEDIA

TV ownership low

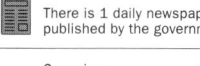

Daily newspaper circulation 0.2 per 1000 people

PUBLISHING AND BROADCAST MEDIA

There is 1 daily newspaper, *Le Sahel*, published by the government

2 services: 1 state-owned, 1 independent

1 state-owned service, several independent local stations

The world's lowest literacy levels mean that radio is the most important medium. The government controls most broadcasting.

CRIME

Death penalty not used in practice

6000 prisoners

Down 36% in 1996–1998

Crime is at critical levels in urban areas, with carjackings, theft, and robbery rife. Rural banditry is common, and smuggling is a way of life in border areas.

EDUCATION

School leaving age: 12

17%

13,400 students

Local languages receive greater emphasis than in most francophone states. Only one-third of children attend primary school.

HEALTH

No welfare state health benefits

1 per 25,000 people

Malaria, tuberculosis, meningitis, measles, malnutrition

Rural health care has improved, but progress in immunization, malaria control, and child nutrition is limited.

SPENDING

GDP/cap. increase

CONSUMPTION AND SPENDING

3 per 1000 population

2 per 1000 population

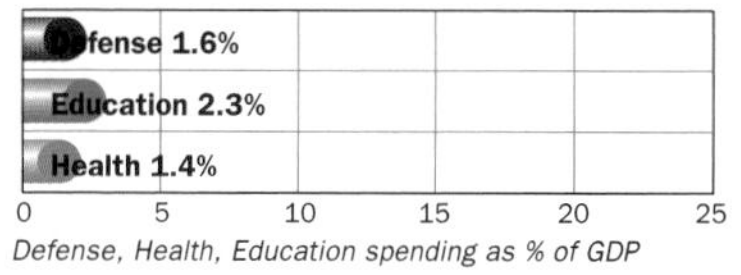
Defense 1.6%
Education 2.3%
Health 1.4%
0
5
10
15
20
25
Defense, Health, Education spending as % of GDP

A small circle of secretive trading families controls much of Niger's wealth and tends to evade taxation. Over 870,000 people live in slavery.

WORLD RANKING

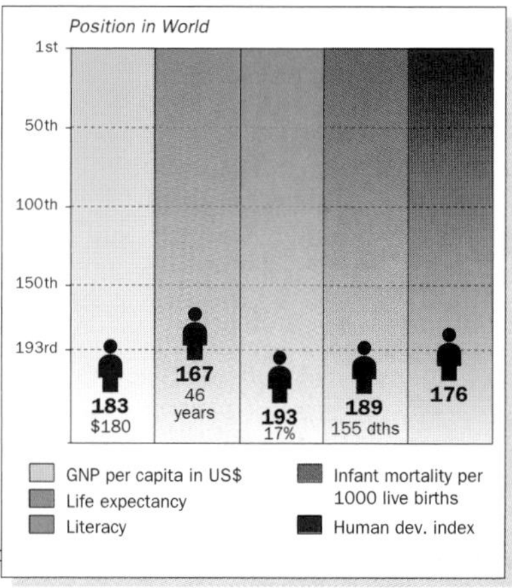
Position in World
1st
50th
100th
150th
193rd
183
$180
167
46 years
193
17%
189
155 dths
176
GNP per capita in US$
Life expectancy
Literacy
Infant mortality per 1000 live births
Human dev. index

RESOURCES

Electric power 105,000 kW

20,821 tonnes

Oil reserves not yet exploited

6.9m goats, 4.5m sheep, 2.26m cattle, 25m chickens

Uranium, tin, gypsum, coal, salt, tungsten, oil, iron, phosphates, gold

During the 1970s, Niger's uranium mines boomed, but output collapsed in the 1980s when world prices slumped. Other mining is small-scale and oil reserves, discovered in the Lake Chad area, are not yet commercially viable. Salt has been mined and traded for centuries. Doum and palmyra palms are often used to make household products.

N

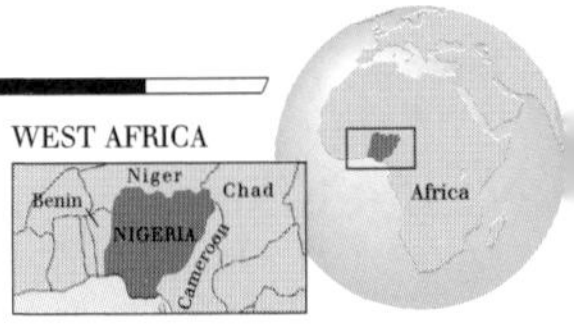
WEST AFRICA
Niger
Benin
Chad
NIGERIA
Cameroon
Africa

NIGERIA

OFFICIAL NAME: Federal Republic of Nigeria **CAPITAL:** Abuja
POPULATION: 124 million **CURRENCY:** Naira **OFFICIAL LANGUAGE:** English

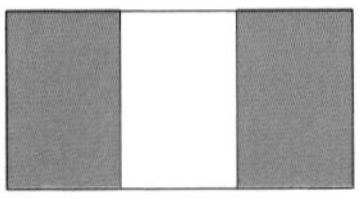

1960 | 1961 | Oct 1 | NGR | +1 | +234 | .ng

AFRICA'S MOST POPULOUS state, Nigeria gained its independence from the UK in 1960. Bordered by Benin, Niger, Chad, and Cameroon, its terrain varies from tropical rainforest and swamps in the south to savanna in the north. Nigeria has been dominated by military governments since 1966. After many delays, a promised return to civilian rule came about in 1999, with the election as president of Olusegun Obasanjo, a former general who had been head of state from 1976 to 1979. Nigeria is a major OPEC oil producer, but it experienced a fall in living standards after the end of the 1970s oil boom.

***Village beneath Tengele Peak** in Bauchi State. A large proportion of Nigerians live by subsistence agriculture.*

CLIMATE

Tropical/steppe

WEATHER CHART FOR ABUJA

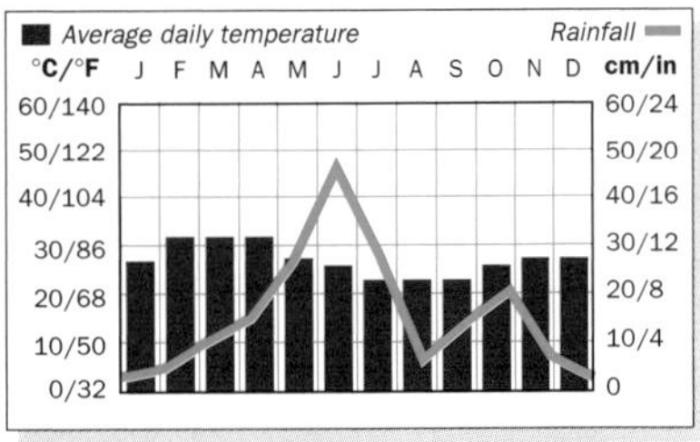
Average daily temperature
Rainfall
°C/°F
J F M A M J J A S O N D
cm/in
60/140
50/122
40/104
30/86
20/68
10/50
0/32
60/24
50/20
40/16
30/12
20/8
10/4
0

The south is hot, rainy, and humid for most of the year. The arid north experiences only one, uncomfortably humid, rainy season from May to September. Its very hot dry season is marked by the *harmattan* wind. The Jos Plateau and the eastern highlands are cooler than the rest of Nigeria. Forcados, in the Niger Delta, gets most rain, with 380 cm (150 in) a year.

TRANSPORTATION

Drive on right

Murtala Muhammad, Lagos 3.26m passengers

303 ships 410,600 grt

THE TRANSPORTATION NETWORK

60,262 km (37,445 miles)	1194 km (742 miles)
3505 km (2178 miles)	8575 km (5328 miles)

Nigeria relies almost entirely on road transportation. During the oil-boom years of the 1970s, new long-distance roads and stretches of freeway were built. The road network is now badly maintained and in urgent need of repair. The road accident rate is among the world's highest and there is chronic traffic congestion in Lagos. In 2000, plans for a new trans-Sahara highway from Lagos to Tanger, Morocco, were announced. Work started in 2001 on a $40 million ports project to boost the development of the five southeastern states.

TOURISM

Visitors : Population 1:61

2.04m visitors

Up 114% in 2002

Nigeria is gradually developing its tourist industry. Year-round tropical humidity and poor infrastructure have limited its growth. The major deterrent to visitors, however, is crime. Travel can be hazardous, and Lagos has one of the world's highest crime rates.

MAIN TOURIST ARRIVALS

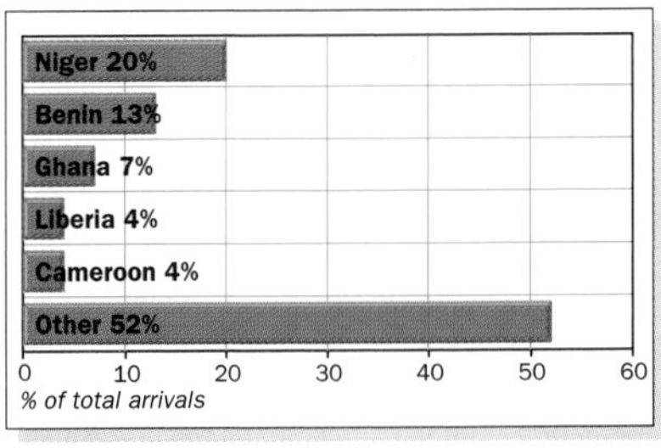
Niger 20%
Benin 13%
Ghana 7%
Liberia 4%
Cameroon 4%
Other 52%
0
10
20
30
40
50
60
% of total arrivals

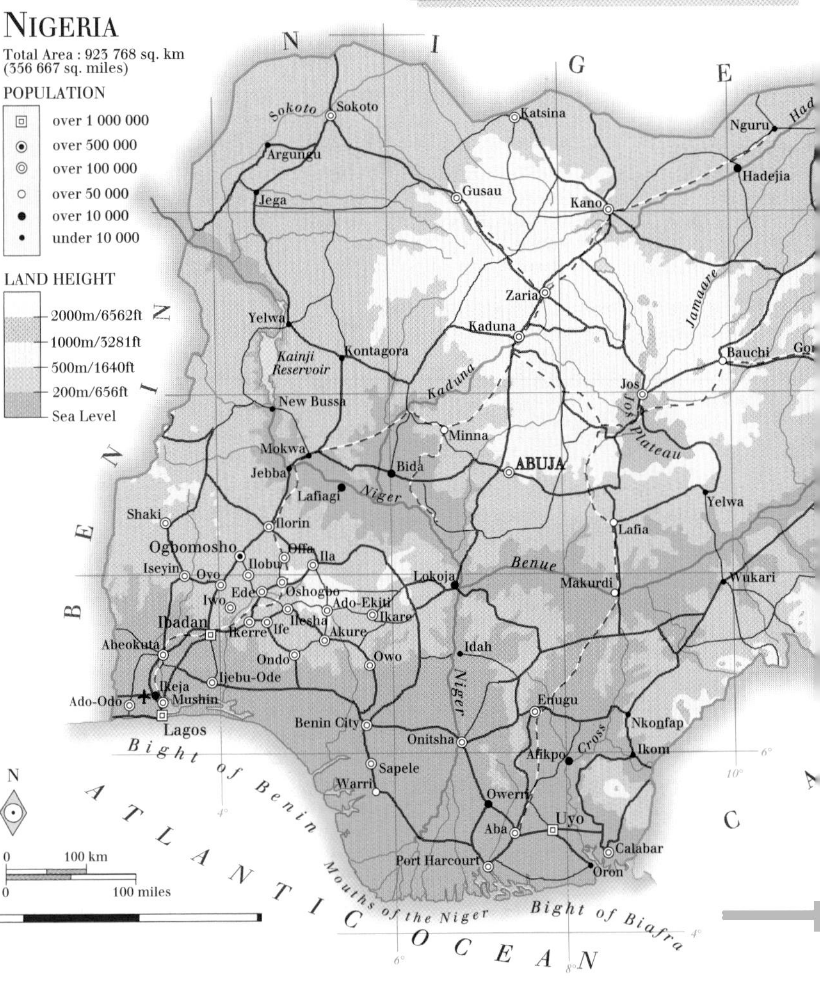
NIGERIA
Total Area : 923 768 sq. km (356 667 sq. miles)
POPULATION
over 1 000 000
over 500 000
over 100 000
over 50 000
over 10 000
under 10 000
LAND HEIGHT
2000m/6562ft
1000m/3281ft
500m/1640ft
200m/656ft
Sea Level
0
100 km
100 miles
N I G E R
B E N I N
C
Sokoto
Argungu
Jega
Gusau
Katsina
Kano
Nguru
Hadejia
Zaria
Kaduna
Yelwa
Kainji Reservoir
Kontagora
New Bussa
Minna
Jos
Jos Plateau
Bauchi
Mokwa
Jebba
Lafiagi
Bida
ABUJA
Niger
Benue
Lafia
Yelwa
Shaki
Ilorin
Ogbomosho
Offa
Ila
Iseyin
Oyo
Ilobu
Iwo
Ede
Oshogbo
Ado-Ekiti
Ikare
Ibadan
Ikerre
Ife
Ilesha
Akure
Lokoja
Makurdi
Wukari
Abeokuta
Ondo
Owo
Idah
Ijebu-Ode
Ikeja
Mushin
Ado-Odo
Lagos
Benin City
Onitsha
Enugu
Nkonfap
Ikom
Afikpo
Cross
Sapele
Warri
Owerri
Aba
Uyo
Calabar
Oron
Port Harcourt
Bight of Benin
Mouths of the Niger
Bight of Biafra
ATLANTIC OCEAN

PEOPLE

Pop. density medium

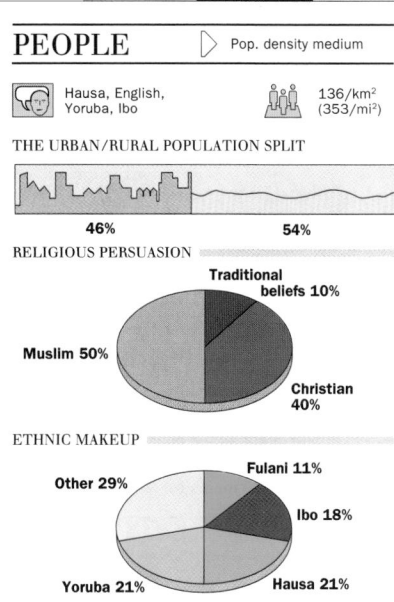

Hausa, English, Yoruba, Ibo

136/km² (353/mi²)

THE URBAN/RURAL POPULATION SPLIT

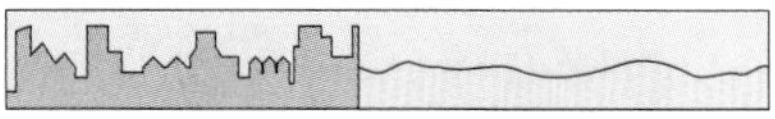
46%
54%

RELIGIOUS PERSUASION

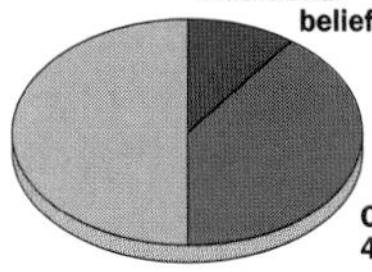
Traditional beliefs 10%
Muslim 50%
Christian 40%

ETHNIC MAKEUP

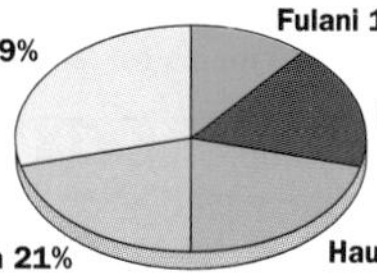
Other 29%
Fulani 11%
Ibo 18%
Yoruba 21%
Hausa 21%

Nigeria had been fairly successful in containing tensions caused by ethnic and religious diversity until fighting erupted between Hausas and Yorubas in the southwest in 1999. There is also rivalry between these two and the third main ethnic group, the Ibo. There are 245 smaller groups. Allegations of state repression on behalf of multinational interests cause unrest in the oil-rich Niger Delta.

The northern state of Zamfara was, in 1999, the first state to adopt *sharia* (Islamic law), and its introduction in other northern states has exacerbated religious tensions. Rioting by both Christians and Muslims has caused hundreds of deaths and thousands of people to be displaced from their homes.

Traditionally women have had independent economic status, especially in southern urban areas. Recent *sharia* rulings have exposed the severity of restrictions in the more conservative Islamic north.

POPULATION AGE BREAKDOWN

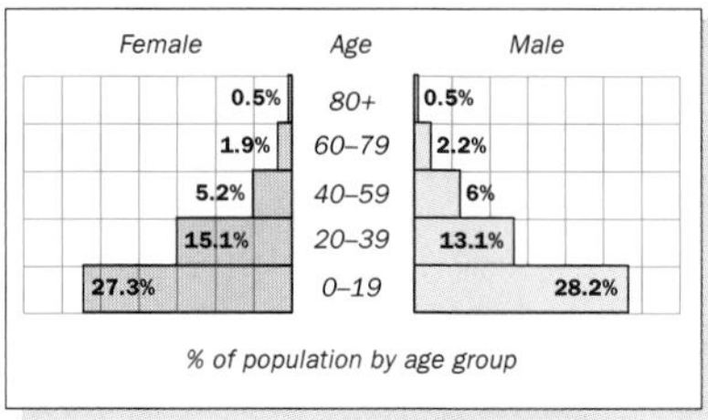
Female
Age
Male
0.5% 80+ 0.5%
1.9% 60–79 2.2%
5.2% 40–59 6%
15.1% 20–39 13.1%
27.3% 0–19 28.2%
% of population by age group

POLITICS

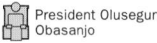

Multiparty elections

L. House 2003/2007
U. House 2003/2007

President Olusegun Obasanjo

AT THE LAST ELECTION

House of Representatives 360 seats

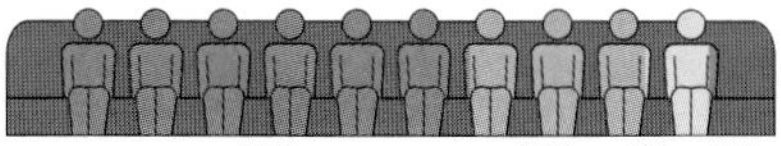
62% PDP
27% ANPP
9% AD
2% Others

PDP = People's Democratic Party **ANPP** = All Nigeria People's Party **AD** = Alliance for Democracy

Senate 109 seats

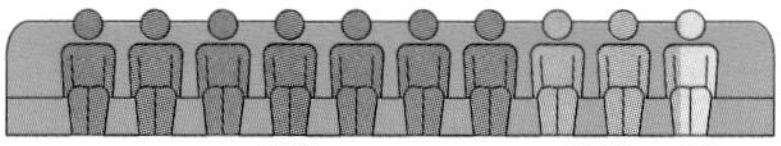
70% PDP
25% ANPP
5% AD

Since May 1999 Nigeria has had a civilian constitution, after 16 years of military dictatorships. President Olusegun Obasanjo and his PDP promise national reconciliation.

PROFILE

The sudden death of military ruler Sani Abacha in 1998, followed by that of the imprisoned Chief Moshood Abiola, the presumed winner of the annulled 1993 presidential elections, left Gen. Abdulsalam Aboubakar to usher in civilian rule. Olusegun Obasanjo, a popular general who was head of state in 1976–1979, won elections held in 1999 and 2003. His PDP won a contested majority in legislative elections in April 2003.

MAIN POLITICAL ISSUES

Corruption

Corruption is a major cause of Nigeria's debt levels. Accusations at all levels of government peaked in 2000 with the impeachment of the Senate president.

Ethnic and religious tensions

The Obasanjo regime faces difficulties in stemming rivalries between the Hausa, Yoruba, and Ibo, and between Christians and Muslims. The introduction of often brutal *sharia* punishments has heightened international concern over human rights, which had previously focused on the apparent repression of the local population in the southern delta region. Religious violence flares sporadically in the central and northern states.

Olusegun Obasanjo, *elected president in 1999.*

Gen. Sani Abacha, *head of state from 1993 until 1998.*

CHRONOLOGY

Before formal colonization by the British, begun only in 1861, Nigeria was a collection of African states owing their considerable wealth to trans-Saharan and transatlantic trade. During the 18th century the principal commodity was slaves: over 15,000 people a year were exported from the Bight of Benin and another 15,000 from the Bight of Biafra.

- **1885** Royal Niger Company given official responsibility for British sphere of influence along Niger and Benue Rivers. British armed forces coerce local rulers into accepting British rule.
- **1897** West Africa Frontier Force (WAFF) established; subjugation of the north begins.
- **1900** British Protectorate of Northern Nigeria established.
- **1906** Lagos incorporated into the Protectorate of Southern Nigeria.
- **1914** Protectorates of Northern and Southern Nigeria joined to form colony of Nigeria.
- **1960** Independence. Nigeria established as a federation.
- **1961** Northern part of UK-administered UN Trust Territory of the Cameroons incorporated as part of Nigeria's Northern Region.
- **1966** January, first coup, led by Maj. Gen. Ironsi. July, countercoup. Thousands of Ibo in Northern Region massacred. Gen. Gowon in control of north and west.
- **1967–1970** Civil war. Lt. Col. Ojukwu calls for secession of oil-rich east under the new name Biafra. Over one million Nigerians die before secessionists defeated by federal forces.
- **1970** Gen. Gowon in power.
- **1975** Gowon toppled in bloodless coup. Brig. Mohammed takes power.
- **1976** Mohammed murdered in abortive coup. Succeeded by Gen. Olusegun Obasanjo.
- **1978** Political parties legalized, on condition they represent national, not tribal, interests.
- **1979** Elections won by Alhaji Shehu Shagari and the National Party of Nigeria (NPN), marking return to civilian government.
- **1983** Military coup. Maj. Gen. Mohammed Buhari heads Supreme Military Council.
- **1985** Maj. Gen. Ibrahim Babangida heads bloodless coup, promising a return to democracy.
- **1993** August, elections annulled; Babangida resigns; military sets up Interim National Government (ING). November, ING dissolved. Military, headed by Gen. Sani Abacha, takes over.

N

CHRONOLOGY *continued*

- **1994** Moshood Abiola arrested, opposition harassed.
- **1995** Ban on parties lifted. Obasanjo and 39 others convicted of plotting coup. Execution of Ken Saro-Wiwa and eight other Ogoni activists: EU sanctions, suspension of Commonwealth membership.
- **1998** Abacha dies; Abiola dies; return to civilian rule timetabled.
- **1999** Elections: presidency won by Obasanjo. Sanctions lifted, Commonwealth membership restored. Zamfara becomes first state to introduce *sharia*.
- **2000** Ethnic violence escalates, threatens national unity.
- **2001** 700 killed in clashes between Muslims and Christians in Jos.
- **2002** 1000 killed in Lagos munitions dump explosion and ensuing chaos.
- **2003** PDP majority and Obasanjo reelected in disputed elections.
- **2004** 57,000 flee religious violence in Kano and Plateau State. Shell admits that its activities fueled corruption and poverty.

WORLD AFFAIRS

Joined UN in 1960

Comm | ECOWAS | AU | OIC | OPEC

Nigeria sees itself as one of Africa's leading voices alongside South Africa – a role commensurate with its large population. A strong supporter of the AU and ECOWAS, it has been the main contributor to regional peacekeeping forces, though it also granted asylum to Liberia's Charles Taylor. It has played a key role in attempting to mediate in Zimbabwe. Marine oil reserves have been the cause of border tensions with Cameroon; a similar dispute with Equatorial Guinea was settled in 2001.

Human rights abuses under the military regime (most notoriously the murder of human rights campaigner Ken Saro-Wiwa in 1995) led to Nigeria's suspension from the Commonwealth. It rejoined after civilian rule was restored in 1999, but concerns remain.

AID

Recipient

$314m (receipts) | Up 70% in 2002

The 1981 drop in world oil prices turned Nigeria from an aid donor into a major receiver of World Bank assistance. Aid flows were interrupted in late 1995, but were resumed in 2000. Aid agreed at the G8 summit in 2002 was welcomed by President Obasanjo, one of the architects of the New Partnership for Africa's Development (Nepad) plan.

DEFENSE

No compulsory military service

$546m | Up 4% in 2002

Nigeria has contributed a significant number of forces to international peacekeeping missions under ECOWAS and UN coordination. Nigerian forces served in Liberia (for which the ECOWAS force ECOMOG was first created) in 1990–1999 and in 2003, and in Sierra Leone in 1993–2000 and from 2002.

Since 2001 the armed forces have also been deployed to restore internal control after outbreaks of religious unrest in northern and central states, in which hundreds of civilians have been killed. Government troops themselves, however, were reported to have massacred some 200 villagers in the eastern state of Benue in 2001, in retaliation for the abduction of 19 members of the armed forces who had been deployed to quell unrest.

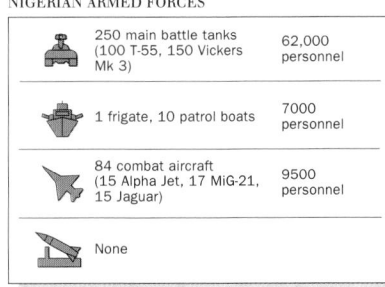

NIGERIAN ARMED FORCES

250 main battle tanks (100 T-55, 150 Vickers Mk 3)	62,000 personnel
1 frigate, 10 patrol boats	7000 personnel
84 combat aircraft (15 Alpha Jet, 17 MiG-21, 15 Jaguar)	9500 personnel
None	

ECONOMICS

Inflation 27% p.a. (1990–2001)

$39.5bn | 133.1 naira (130.1)

SCORE CARD

World GNP Ranking	54th
GNP per Capita	$300
Balance of Payments	$1bn
Inflation	12.9%
Unemployment	3%

EXPORTS

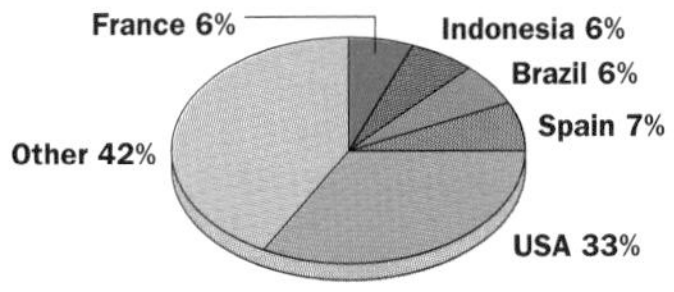
France 6%
Indonesia 6%
Brazil 6%
Spain 7%
Other 42%
USA 33%

IMPORTS

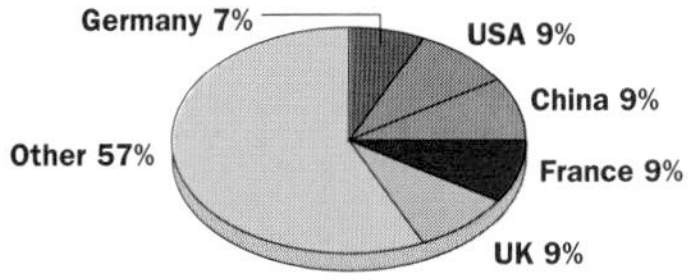
Germany 7%
USA 9%
China 9%
Other 57%
France 9%
UK 9%

Strengths

One of world's top oil producers. Vast reserves of natural gas, still only partly exploited. Soaring world oil prices from 2000 onward. Almost self-sufficient in food. Strong entrepreneurial class. Large population, provides workforce and domestic market.

Weaknesses

Overdependence on oil since the 1970s encourages massive state inefficiency. Ongoing conflict in the Delta disrupts production. Advantages of a large domestic market mitigated by low per capita purchasing power and high unit transportation costs. Entrepreneurs focus on trade rather than production. Of Nigeria's traditional agricultural exports only cocoa remains. Endemic corruption and instability undermine investors' confidence.

ECONOMIC PERFORMANCE INDICATOR

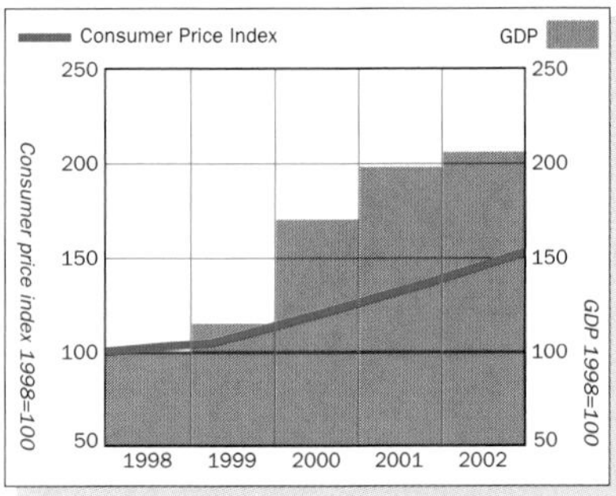
Consumer Price Index
GDP
Consumer price index 1998=100
GDP 1998=100
250
200
150
100
50
1998
1999
2000
2001
2002

Profile

Massive government spending ran up huge debts which could not be serviced after the 1981 oil price fall. Led by the IMF, creditors want major cuts in subsidies and spending – especially on loss-making public-sector companies. Gasoline subsidies alone are estimated to have cost $2.4 billion a year, but tampering with the price of fuel in particular is politically fraught, leading to strikes in 2003–2004. Economic policy is likely to focus on building on recent limited gains.

NIGERIA : MAJOR BUSINESSES

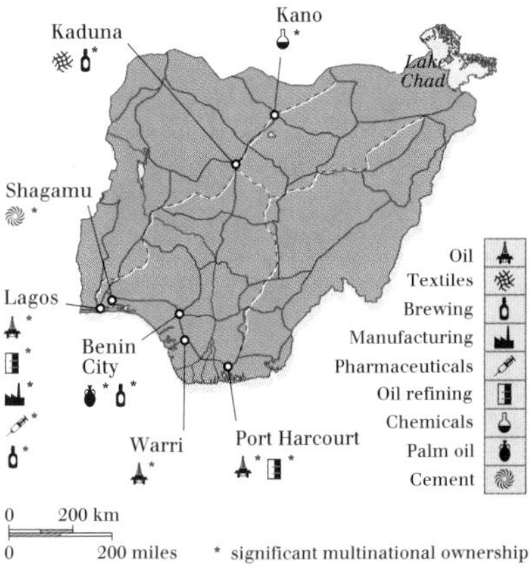
Kaduna
Kano
Lake Chad
Shagamu
Lagos
Benin City
Warri
Port Harcourt
Oil
Textiles
Brewing
Manufacturing
Pharmaceuticals
Oil refining
Chemicals
Palm oil
Cement
0 200 km
0 200 miles
* significant multinational ownership

RESOURCES

Electric power 5.9m kW

476,544 tonnes

2.18m b/d (reserves 34.3bn barrels)

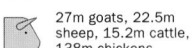

27m goats, 22.5m sheep, 15.2m cattle, 138m chickens

Oil, natural gas, coal, tin, iron, bauxite, columbite, lead

ELECTRICITY GENERATION

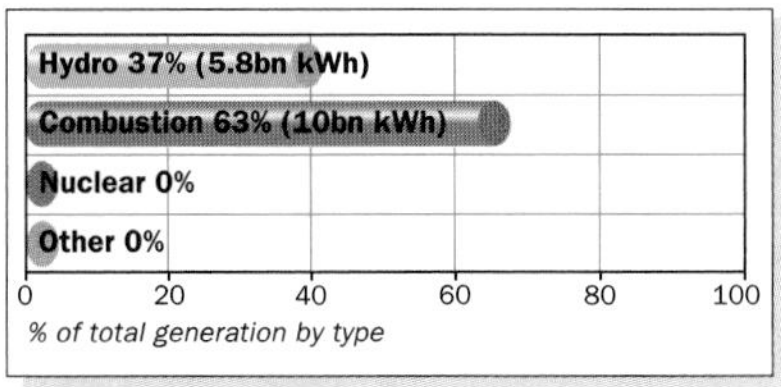

Hydro 37% (5.8bn kWh)
Combustion 63% (10bn kWh)
Nuclear 0%
Other 0%
0
20
40
60
80
100
% of total generation by type

Oil has been the main resource since the 1970s, and Nigeria is one of Africa's largest producers. The state retains 60% control of the industry. Shell is the main foreign shareholder, but most oil multinationals are represented. Production is frequently interrupted by regional unrest. As much as 100,000 b/d is smuggled to neighboring countries. Nigeria's vast gas deposits are still underexploited.

Nigeria has sizable iron ore deposits. These are only slowly being utilized in the state-run steel industry; traditionally, imported ore is used instead. Bauxite deposits are beginning to be exploited by the fledgling aluminum industry. Nigeria also has deposits of coal and tin.

NIGERIA : LAND USE

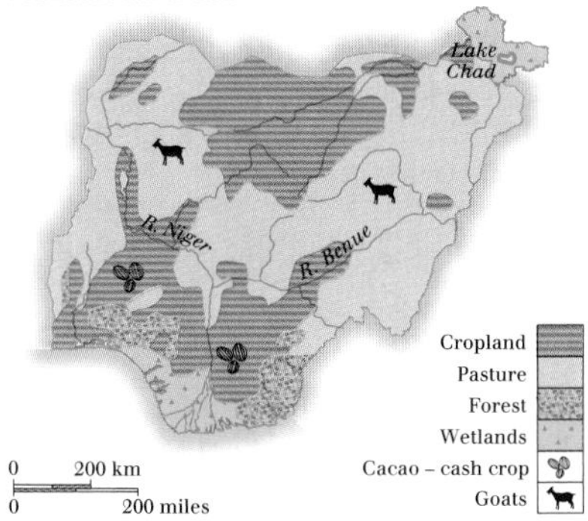

Lake Chad
R. Niger
R. Benue
Cropland
Pasture
Forest
Wetlands
Cacao – cash crop
Goats
0 200 km
0 200 miles

ENVIRONMENT

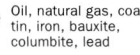

Sustainability rank: 133rd

3% (1% partially protected)

0.3 tonnes per capita

ENVIRONMENTAL TREATIES

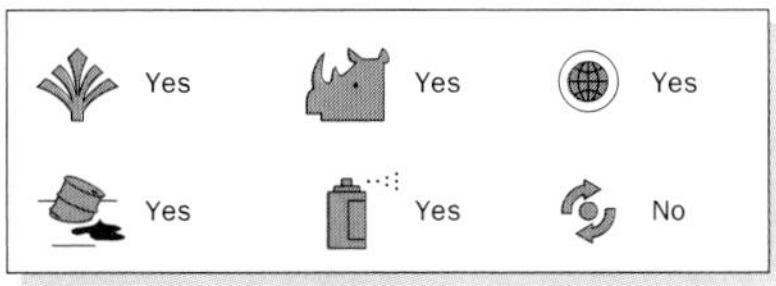

Yes
Yes
Yes
Yes
Yes
No

Oil industry pollution in the Niger Delta, a major local concern, came to international attention in 1995; Shell has been particularly condemned. Before the discovery of a highly toxic cargo in 1988, Nigeria was a dumping ground for European chemical waste.

MEDIA

TV ownership medium

Daily newspaper circulation 24 per 1000 people

The Nigerian press is traditionally one of Africa's liveliest. Media freedom has improved since the return to civilian government. There are over 100 TV stations; the state-owned Nigerian Television Authority runs 67, having introduced digital channels in 2003.

CRIME

Death penalty in use

39,368 prisoners

Crime is rising

CRIME RATES

Murders

94 per 100,000 population

Rapes

Nigeria does not publish rape statistics

Thefts

Nigeria does not publish theft statistics

Nigeria has one of the highest crime rates in the world. Murder often accompanies even minor burglaries. Rich Nigerians live in high-security compounds. Police in some states are empowered to "shoot on sight" violent criminals. Brutal *sharia* punishments are claimed to have reduced crime in northern states. Vigilante gangs are used to fight crime in the southeastern states.

EDUCATION

School leaving age: 12

67%

207,982 students

THE EDUCATION SYSTEM

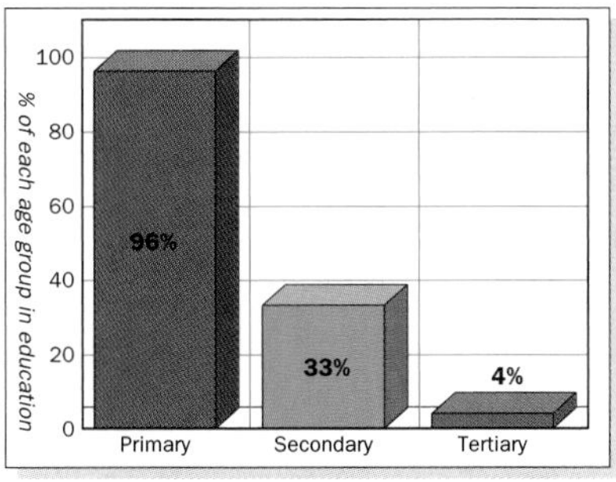

100
80
60
40
20
0
% of each age group in education
96%
33%
4%
Primary
Secondary
Tertiary

Responsibility for education is shared between the federal and the state governments. Education has suffered from the government's massive debt repayment burden. During the oil-boom years, Nigeria concentrated on creating 31 universities with prestigious medical and scientific schools. Primary education did not receive the same level of investment and standards have fallen. In 2003 it was revealed that around six million children do not attend school at all, while another eight million work part-time to help fund their education.

PUBLISHING AND BROADCAST MEDIA

There are 22 daily newspapers. The *Daily Times*, published by the government, has the highest circulation

1 state-controlled service, many private stations

2 state-controlled services, many independent stations

HEALTH

Welfare state health benefits

1 per 3704 people

Yellow fever, malaria, trachoma, yaws

The health service functions mainly in urban areas and has suffered from the crisis in government revenues. Around 3.6 million Nigerians were living with HIV/AIDS as at end-2003. Free generic versions of AIDS treatments became available in 2001 and the government supports a successful AIDS awareness strategy. An 11-month suspension in polio vaccinations in Kano from 2003 threatened to cause a regional epidemic.

SPENDING

GDP/cap. increase

CONSUMPTION AND SPENDING

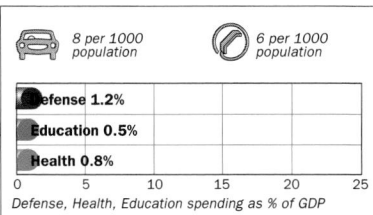

8 per 1000 population

6 per 1000 population

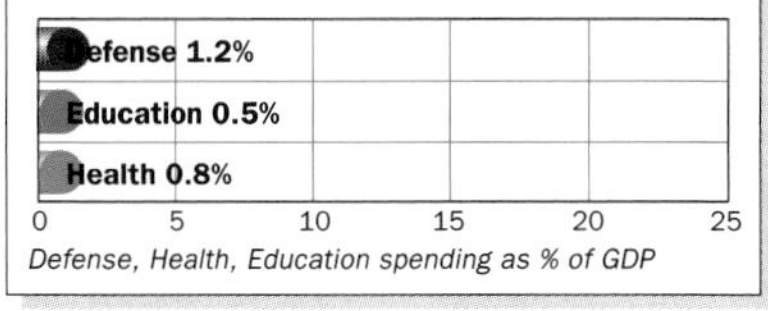

Defense 1.2%
Education 0.5%
Health 0.8%
0
5
10
15
20
25
Defense, Health, Education spending as % of GDP

Nigerians with access to the rich pickings of political office spent on a massive scale during the country's 1970s oil boom. Government loans financed much of it. Habits did not change with the fall in oil revenues: borrowing simply grew. Poverty levels rose in 1999–2003 as intercommunal violence displaced around 800,000.

WORLD RANKING

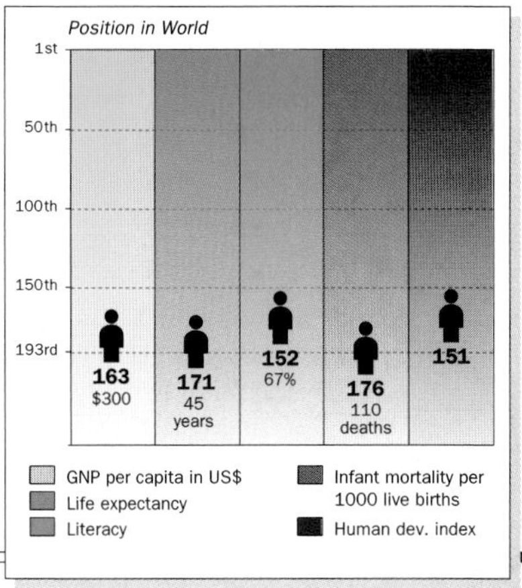

Position in World
1st
50th
100th
150th
193rd
163
$300
171
45
years
152
67%
176
110
deaths
151
GNP per capita in US$
Life expectancy
Literacy
Infant mortality per 1000 live births
Human dev. index

N

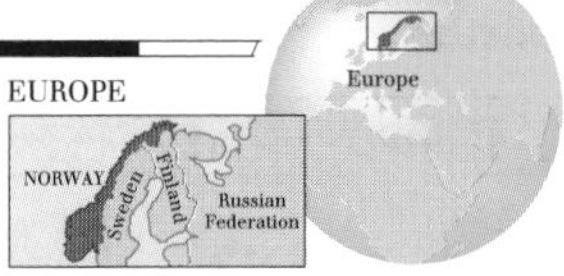
EUROPE
NORWAY
Sweden
Finland
Russian Federation
Europe

Norway

Official Name: Kingdom of Norway **Capital:** Oslo
Population: 4.5 million **Currency:** Norwegian krone **Official Language:** Norwegian

1905
1905
May 17
N
+1
+47
.no

Occupying the western part of Scandinavia, Norway's western coastline is characterized by numerous fjords and islands. Large oil and gas revenues have brought prosperity. Gro Harlem Brundtland, Norway's first woman prime minister, went on to take top UN posts. Despite the Europe-wide recession in the early 1990s, Norway was able to contain rising unemployment, which peaked at 6% in 1993. A constitutional requirement is that government creates conditions that enable every person to find work.

***The village of Reine** on Moskenesøya, deep inside the Arctic Circle in the Lofoten Islands. It is a popular destination for summer visitors.*

CLIMATE

Maritime/subarctic

WEATHER CHART FOR OSLO

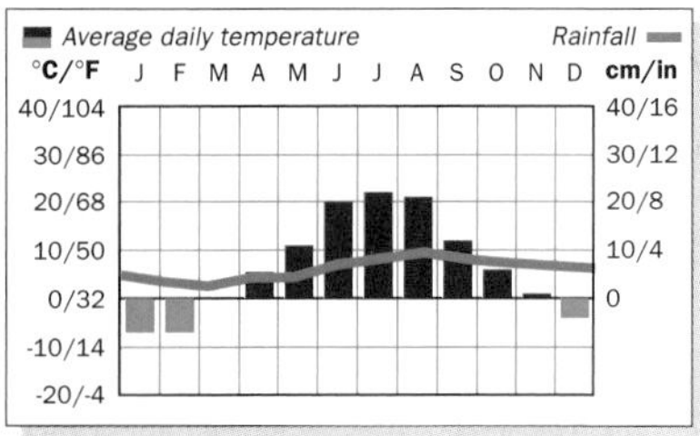
Average daily temperature
Rainfall
°C/°F
J F M A M J J A S O N D
cm/in
40/104
30/86
20/68
10/50
0/32
-10/14
-20/-4
40/16
30/12
20/8
10/4
0

The whole of Norway's west coast is kept ice-free by the warm Gulf Stream. It receives much more precipitation than the rest of the country; Bergen has a yearly average of 225 cm (89 in). Norway enjoys the highest mean temperatures in Scandinavia, but in winter the temperature in Oslo can fall as low as –25°C (–13°F).

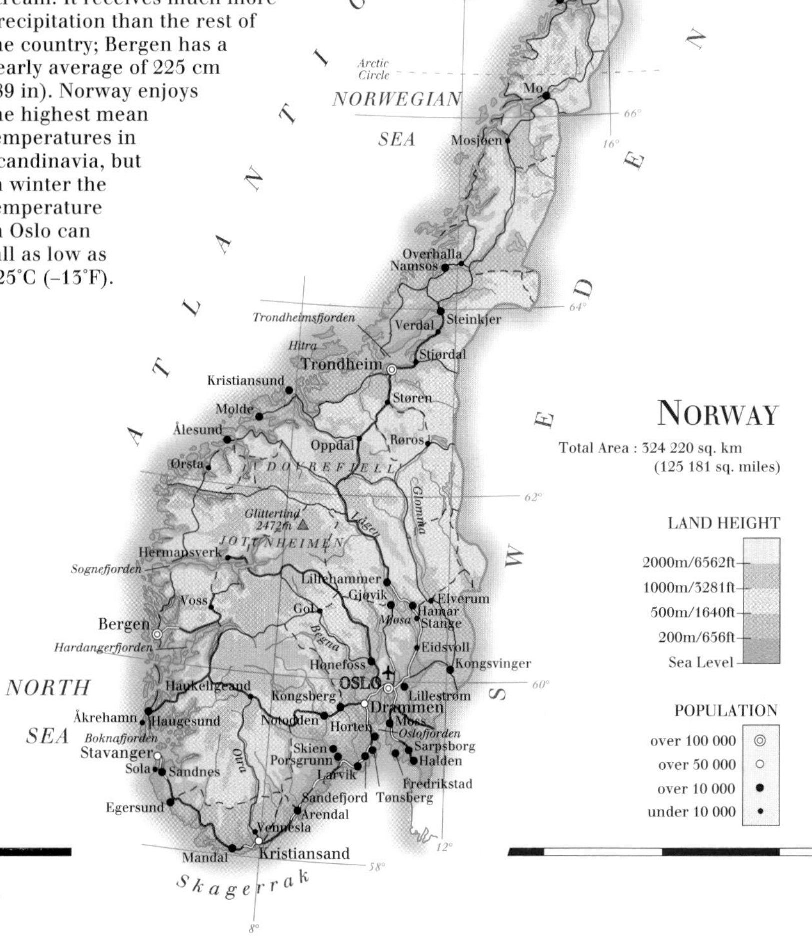
ARCTIC OCEAN
BARENTS SEA
Magerøya
Hammerfest
Sørøya
Porsangen
Tana
Tana Bru
Varangerfjorden
Kirkenes
Ringvassøya
Alta
Kvaløya
Tromsø
Karasjok
RUSSIAN FEDERATION
Senja
FINNMARKSVIDDA
Vesterålen
Andfjorden
Harstad
LAPLAND
FINLAND
Narvik
Stamsund
Lofoten
Vestfjorden
ATLANTIC OCEAN
Bodø
0 100 km
0 100 miles
Arctic Circle
NORWEGIAN SEA
Mo
Mosjøen
SWEDEN
Overhalla
Namsos
Trondheimsfjorden
Verdal
Steinkjer
Hitra
Trondheim
Stjørdal
Kristiansund
Molde
Støren
Ålesund
Oppdal
Røros
Ørsta
DOVREFJELL
Glomma
Glittertind 2472m
Lågen
JOTUNHEIMEN
Hermansverk
Sognefjorden
Lillehammer
Elverum
Gjøvik
Hamar
Voss
Gol
Mjøsa
Stange
Bergen
Begna
Hardangerfjorden
Eidsvoll
Hønefoss
Kongsvinger
NORTH SEA
OSLO
Haukeligrend
Kongsberg
Lillestrøm
Drammen
Åkrehamn
Haugesund
Notodden
Horten
Moss
Boknafjorden
Oslofjorden
Stavanger
Skien
Sarpsborg
Porsgrunn
Halden
Sola
Sandnes
Otra
Larvik
Fredrikstad
Sandefjord
Tønsberg
Egersund
Arendal
Vennesla
Mandal
Kristiansand
Skagerrak
NORWAY
Total Area : 324 220 sq. km (125 181 sq. miles)
LAND HEIGHT
2000m/6562ft
1000m/3281ft
500m/1640ft
200m/656ft
Sea Level
POPULATION
over 100 000
over 50 000
over 10 000
under 10 000

TRANSPORTATION

Drive on right

Oslo International (Gardermoen) 13.6m passengers

2299 ships 22.2m grt

THE TRANSPORTATION NETWORK

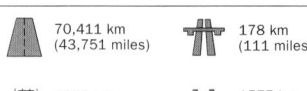

70,411 km (43,751 miles)	178 km (111 miles)
4077 km (2533 miles)	1577 km (980 miles)

It has been impossible to extend rail links further north than Bodø, inside the Arctic Circle. To reach the Lofotens or Narvik and beyond, the most common form of transportation is air. Norwegian merchant ships account for 10% of the world's fleet, making Norway one of the world's largest shipping nations.

***The royal palace, Oslo.** This is situated near the national theater, at one end of the Karl Johanisgate, the city's main thoroughfare.*

N

TOURISM

Visitors : Population 1:1.4

3.11m visitors

Up 1% in 2002

MAIN TOURIST ARRIVALS

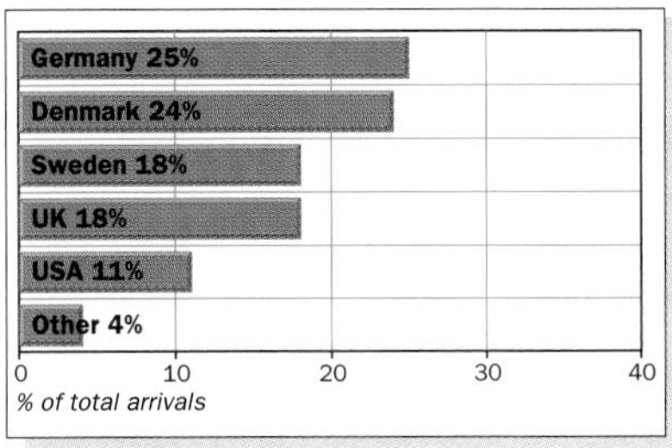
Germany 25%
Denmark 24%
Sweden 18%
UK 18%
USA 11%
Other 4%
0
10
20
30
40
% of total arrivals

Norway's biggest attraction, to its mostly north European visitors, is its natural beauty. Many people venture beyond the Arctic Circle in search of the midnight sun in summer and Arctic wildlife all year round. The dramatic, and world famous, fjords of the west coast attract cruise ships. Oslo has a reputation for good classical music and jazz, while other, smaller cities, have a distinct Scandinavian charm. Skiing in the mountains is also very popular. The strength of the krone, however, and the high cost of living can deter budget travelers.

PEOPLE

Pop. density low

Norwegian (*Bokmål* "book language" and *Nynorsk* "new Norsk"), Sámi

15/km² (38/mi²)

THE URBAN/RURAL POPULATION SPLIT

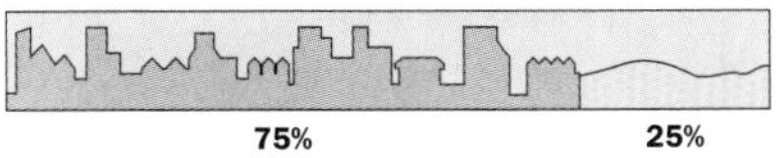
75%
25%

RELIGIOUS PERSUASION

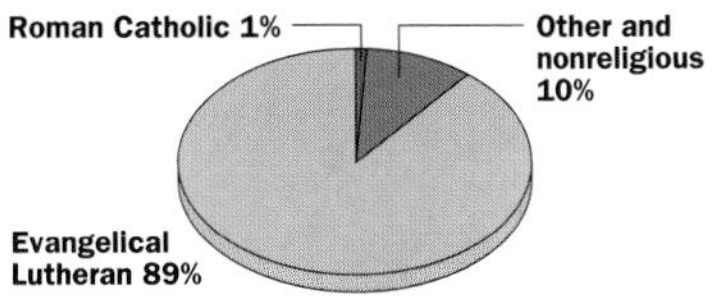
Roman Catholic 1%
Other and nonreligious 10%
Evangelical Lutheran 89%

ETHNIC MAKEUP

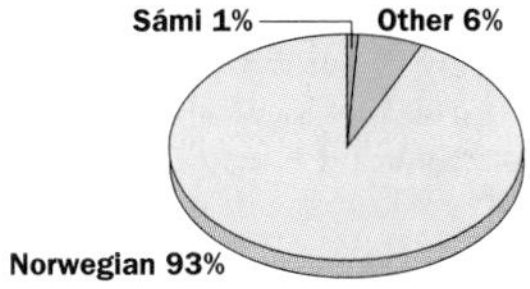
Sámi 1%
Other 6%
Norwegian 93%

Norway's largest minority is formed by the 45,000 Sámi, traditionally nomadic reindeer hunters, who are concentrated in the far north of the country – the largest community in Scandinavia; the Nordic Sámi Council was founded in Norway in 1956. Norway also has a small but growing immigrant community, forming 5.6% of the population in 2001. Some refugees have been attacked by right-wing groups.

The family is traditionally close and nuclear. Men are expected to help raise children. Women enjoy considerable power and freedom, and comprise over 40% of government ministers. More than half of marriages end in divorce.

POPULATION AGE BREAKDOWN

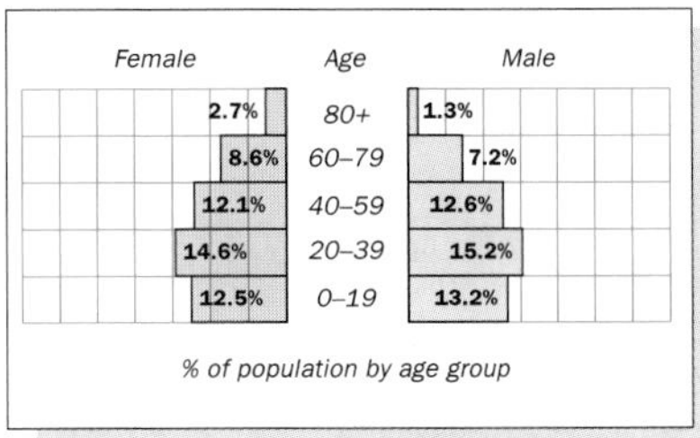
Female
Age
Male
2.7%
80+
1.3%
8.6%
60–79
7.2%
12.1%
40–59
12.6%
14.6%
20–39
15.2%
12.5%
0–19
13.2%
% of population by age group

POLITICS

Multiparty elections

2001/2005

H.M. King Harald V

AT THE LAST ELECTION

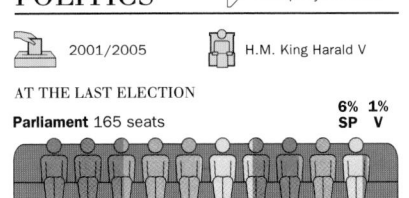

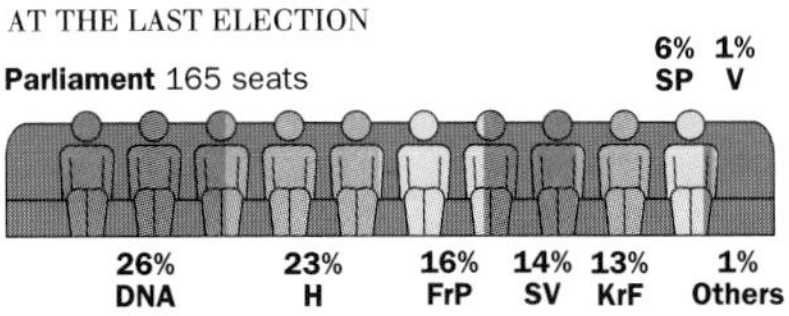
Parliament 165 seats
6% SP
1% V
26% DNA
23% H
16% FrP
14% SV
13% KrF
1% Others

DNA = Norwegian Labor Party **H** = Hoeyre (Conservative Party) **FrP** = Progress Party **SV** = Socialist Left Party **KrF** = Christian Democratic Party **SP** = Center Party **V** = Venstre (Liberal Party)

The Parliament (Storting) is elected as one body but divides itself for most legislative purposes into an upper chamber (Lagting, with 42 members) and a lower chamber (Odelsting, with 123 members)

Norway is a constitutional monarchy, with a king as head of state and an elected parliament.

PROFILE

Political decisions are based on consensus building between the government, parliament, and the strong trade unions. In 1993, opposition to EU membership boosted support for the SP, but the DNA remained the largest party.

In 1997 the DNA lost ground to the center right, which formed a coalition led by Kjell Magne Bondevik of the KrF. Returned to office in 2000, the DNA suffered heavy losses in the 2001 polls, and Bondevik, who had campaigned for using oil revenues to fund tax cuts and public service improvements, was reappointed prime minister. He heads a minority government, in coalition with the Conservatives and the Liberals.

MAIN POLITICAL ISSUE

The rise of the far right

The anti-immigration FrP, originally formed in 1973, grew in popularity during the 1990s as the number of asylum seekers rose. It emerged as the third-largest party in the 2001 election, and is now a significant force in parliamentary politics. The minority government was forced to rely on its support to pass the 2003 budget, promising further tax cuts in return for FrP backing.

WORLD AFFAIRS

Joined UN in 1945

CE NATO OECD OSCE EFTA

A founder member of NATO, Norway continues to offer it strong support. The 1994 referendum rejecting EU membership means that the European Economic Area (EEA) offers Norway its main access to the European single market. As a Nordic Council member it is associated with the Schengen Convention on passport-free borders. In 2002 Prime Minister Bondevik stated that there would be no referendum on joining the EU, despite increased popular support for the idea, but an opinion poll in 2004 suggested that only a minority now favored membership.

Norway has played peacemaker on a number of occasions, notably in attempting to mediate in the Israeli–Palestinian conflict during the mid-1990s, and in Sri Lanka since 2002.

The government has been unable to control the ecological effects of acid rain, which is destroying its forests. Representatives of 25 European countries and Canada met in Oslo in 1994 and signed a UN protocol on reducing sulfur emissions.

King Harald V, who succeeded his father King Olav V in 1991.

Prime Minister Kjell Magne Bondevik, *reelected in 2001.*

CHRONOLOGY

Norway gained independence from the Swedish crown in 1905 and elected its own king, Håkon VII.

- **1935** DNA forms government.
- **1940–1945** Nazi occupation. Puppet regime led by Vidkun Quisling.
- **1945** DNA resumes power.
- **1949** Founder member of NATO.
- **1957** King Håkon dies. Succeeded by son, Olav V.
- **1960** Becomes member of EFTA.
- **1962** Unsuccessfully applies to join European Communities (EC).
- **1965** DNA electoral defeat by SP coalition led by Per Borten.
- **1967** Second bid for EC membership.
- **1971** Borten resigns following disclosure of secret negotiations to join EC; DNA government, led by Trygve Bratteli.

N

CHRONOLOGY *continued*

- **1972** EC membership rejected in popular referendum by 3% majority. Bratteli resigns. Center coalition government takes power. Lars Korvald prime minister.
- **1973** Elections. Bratteli returns to power as prime minister.
- **1976** Bratteli succeeded by Odvar Nordli.
- **1981** Nordli resigns owing to ill health. Gro Harlem Brundtland becomes first woman prime minister. Elections bring to power Conservative Party (H) government for first time in 53 years. Kare Willoch prime minister.
- **1983** Conservatives form coalition with SP and KrF.
- **1985** Election. Willoch's H–SP–KrF coalition returned. Norway agrees to suspend commercial whaling.
- **1986** 100,000 demonstrate for better working conditions. Brundtland forms minority DNA government. Currency devalued by 12%.
- **1989** Brundtland resigns. H–KrF coalition in power. USSR agrees exchange of information after fires break out on Soviet nuclear submarines off Norwegian coast.
- **1990** H–KrF coalition breaks up over closer ties with EU (formerly EC). Brundtland and DNA in power.
- **1991** Olav V dies; succeeded by son, Harald V.
- **1994** EEA comes into effect. Referendum rejects EU membership.
- **1996** Brundtland resigns; replaced by Thorbjørn Jagland (also DNA).
- **1997** Kjell Magne Bondevik forms center-right coalition.
- **2000** Jens Stoltenberg (DNA) heads three-party coalition.
- **2001** Right-wing victory in elections. Bondevik heads coalition government.

AID

Donor

$1.7bn (donations) | Up 26% in 2002

Norway has granted more than the UN target of 0.7% of GNP in development aid every year since 1975. Though Norway's ratio of aid to GNP has declined, to 0.89% in 2002, it remains one of the highest in the world. The vast majority of Norway's bilateral aid goes to the least developed countries of sub-Saharan Africa, south and central Asia, and eastern Europe. In 2002 the largest single recipient of Norwegian aid was Afghanistan. The government also allocates funds to various multilateral assistance programs. The 1999 budget included a debt-relief program to help reduce developing country indebtedness.

DEFENSE

Compulsory military service

$3.43bn | Up 19% in 2002

Plans have been announced to almost halve Norway's conscript army, which traditionally has absorbed most of the defense budget. Norway joined NATO in 1949. The overriding defense issue is the stability of Russia and the security of their common border. Five Russian diplomats were expelled in 1998 after a double agent revealed that Russia had extensive information on Norway's defenses and its oil industry.

NORWEGIAN ARMED FORCES

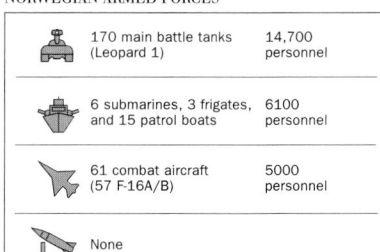

170 main battle tanks (Leopard 1)	14,700 personnel
6 submarines, 3 frigates, and 15 patrol boats	6100 personnel
61 combat aircraft (57 F-16A/B)	5000 personnel
None	

ECONOMICS

Inflation 3.2% p.a. (1990–2001)

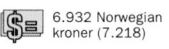

$176bn | 6.932 Norwegian kroner (7.218)

SCORE CARD

- WORLD GNP RANKING........................24th
- GNP PER CAPITA..........................$38,730
- BALANCE OF PAYMENTS....................$25.1bn
- INFLATION..1.3%
- UNEMPLOYMENT...................................5%

EXPORTS

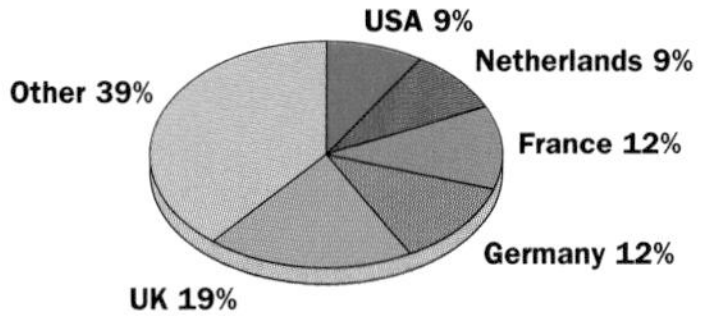

USA 9%
Netherlands 9%
France 12%
Germany 12%
UK 19%
Other 39%

IMPORTS

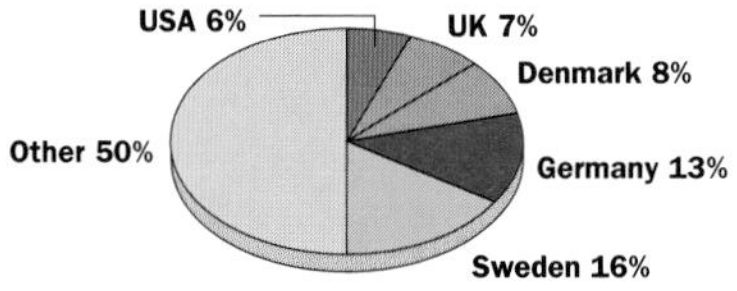

USA 6%
UK 7%
Denmark 8%
Germany 13%
Sweden 16%
Other 50%

STRENGTHS

Western Europe's biggest producer and exporter of oil and natural gas. Mineral reserves. Hydroelectric power satisfies much of country's energy demands, allowing most oil to be exported. Petroleum fund to ensure current profits provide for future generations. Large merchant shipping fleet. Low inflation and unemployment compared with rest of Europe.

WEAKNESSES

Overdependence on oil revenue. Small home market and relatively remote location. Shortage of skilled labor. Harsh climate limits agriculture.

PROFILE

The state is interventionist by nature. In 1991, it stepped in to rescue most of the main commercial banks, which had been hit by bad loans. It began returning them to the private sector in 1994. The state also manages the distribution of offshore oil and gas licenses, and owns 45% of the Norsk Hydro conglomerate. In 2000 the state sold a 20% share in its oil and telecommunications companies.

Norway's immediate future prosperity is guaranteed by its offshore oil sector. There is a shortage of skilled labor, which has partly been eased by the arrival of workers from other Scandinavian countries, but has created upward pressure on wages. Continuing the strong regional policy of redirecting resources from the more prosperous south to the isolated north is likely to remain a priority, both for social and strategic reasons.

ECONOMIC PERFORMANCE INDICATOR

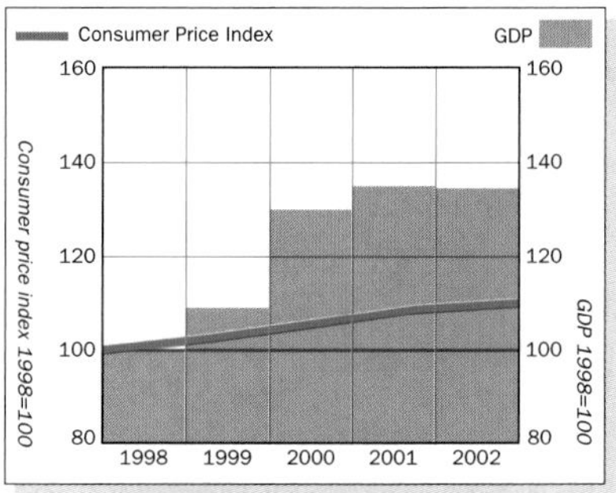

Consumer Price Index
GDP
160
140
120
100
80
Consumer price index 1998=100
GDP 1998=100
1998
1999
2000
2001
2002

NORWAY : MAJOR BUSINESSES

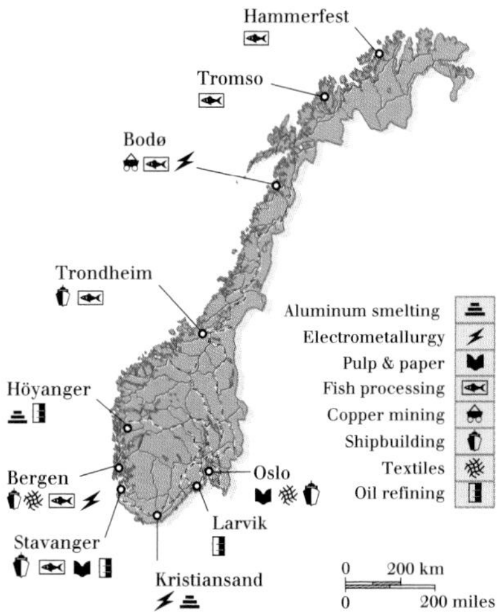

Hammerfest
Tromso
Bodø
Trondheim
Höyanger
Bergen
Stavanger
Kristiansand
Larvik
Oslo
Aluminum smelting
Electrometallurgy
Pulp & paper
Fish processing
Copper mining
Shipbuilding
Textiles
Oil refining
0 200 km
0 200 miles

RESOURCES

Electric power 30m kW

3.2m tonnes

3.26m b/d (reserves 10.1bn barrels)

1.08m sheep, 922,500 cattle, 3.33m chickens

Oil, natural gas, iron, coal, copper, lead, zinc

ELECTRICITY GENERATION

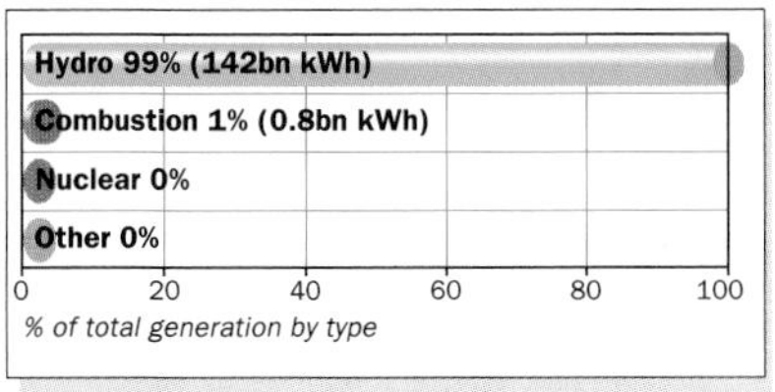
Hydro 99% (142bn kWh)
Combustion 1% (0.8bn kWh)
Nuclear 0%
Other 0%
0 20 40 60 80 100
% of total generation by type

Though Norway is Europe's largest oil producer and has sizable gas reserves, almost all of its electricity is produced by hydropower. In summer, the HEP surplus is exported. Fish and forestry are traditionally significant sectors – salmon farming, managed with particular efficiency, has grown rapidly – though together with agriculture they account for only 2% of GDP and 4% of the workforce.

A 2002 report warned that cod stocks in the North Sea were under threat from the waste products of oil-drilling.

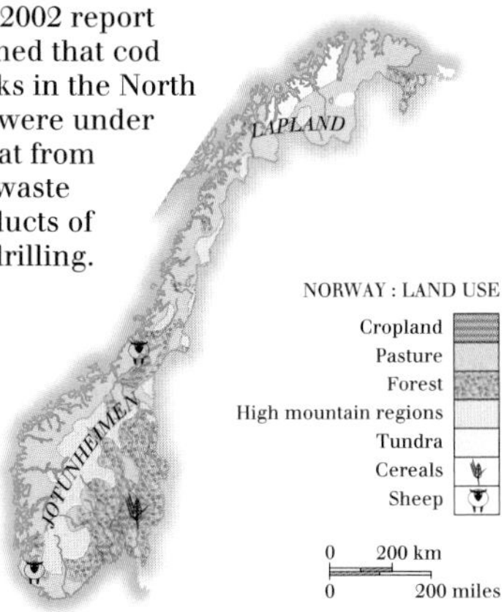
LAPLAND
JOTUNHEIMEN
NORWAY : LAND USE
Cropland
Pasture
Forest
High mountain regions
Tundra
Cereals
Sheep
0 200 km
0 200 miles

ENVIRONMENT

Sustainability rank: 2nd

7% (2% partially protected)

11.1 tonnes per capita

ENVIRONMENTAL TREATIES

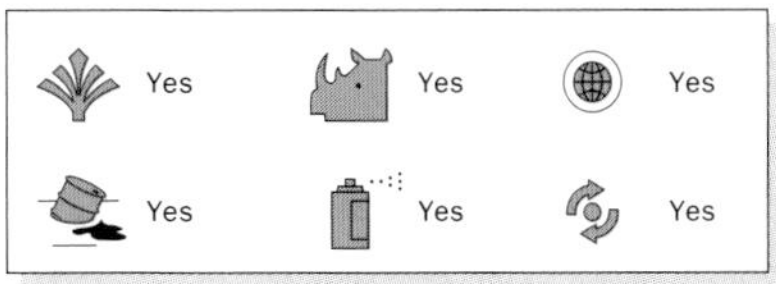
Yes
Yes
Yes
Yes
Yes
Yes

In 1986 northern Norway suffered radioactive contamination after the Chernobyl nuclear disaster. Norway has a tax on carbon dioxide emissions and was instrumental in securing agreement on the 1997 Kyoto Protocol on greenhouse gas emissions. In 1993, it lifted a ban on fishing minke whales, and in 2001 it allowed the export of whale products. It was also criticized in 2001 for a cull of (endangered) gray wolves and for plans to develop a coalfield on Svalbard.

MEDIA

TV ownership high

Daily newspaper circulation 569 per 1000 people

PUBLISHING AND BROADCAST MEDIA

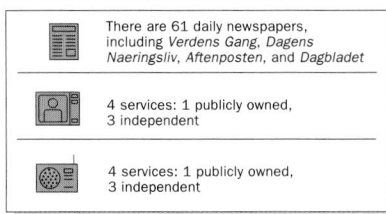

There are 61 daily newspapers, including *Verdens Gang, Dagens Naeringsliv, Aftenposten*, and *Dagbladet*

4 services: 1 publicly owned, 3 independent

4 services: 1 publicly owned, 3 independent

The state broadcaster NRK enjoys comparatively generous funding and attracts around a third of viewers. Norwegians are often rated as the most avid newspaper readers in the world.

CRIME

No death penalty

2662 prisoners

Down 2% in 2001

CRIME RATES

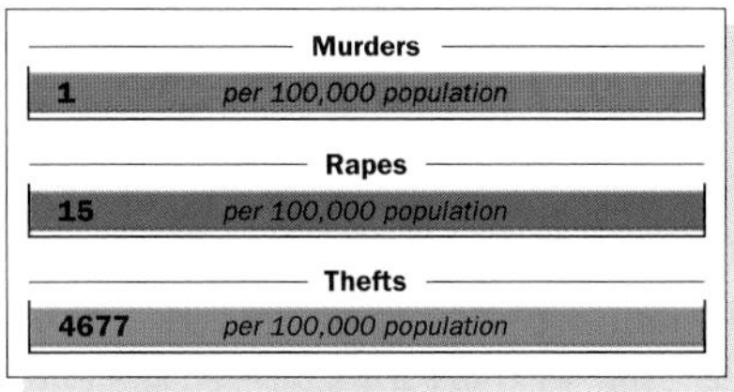
Murders
1 per 100,000 population
Rapes
15 per 100,000 population
Thefts
4677 per 100,000 population

Crime rates in Norway are very low. The increasing use of weapons in robberies is a worrying trend. Norway is a popular destination for asylum seekers; the Norwegian government is working to tackle people smuggling.

EDUCATION

School leaving age: 16

99%

197,614 students

THE EDUCATION SYSTEM

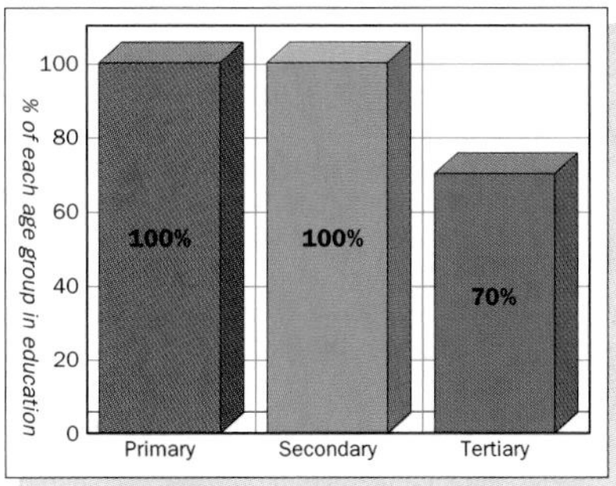
100
80
60
40
20
0
% of each age group in education
100%
100%
70%
Primary
Secondary
Tertiary

Compulsory schooling starts at six years of age and lasts for ten years. Most schools are run by municipalities. There are four universities; the University of Oslo, founded in 1811, is the largest and oldest. Specialized colleges include the Nordic College of Fisheries. Promotion of continuing education kept youth unemployment down during the early 1990s recession.

HEALTH

Welfare state health benefits

1 per 333 people

Cancers, heart and respiratory diseases, accidental falls

The health system is ranked by WHO as the best in Scandinavia and 11th in the world. Infant mortality is among the world's lowest, and life expectancy at birth is one of the highest. Health-care spending is among the highest of OECD states. A new health plan announced in 2002 will place the high-spending hospitals under central control. Smoking in bars and restaurants was banned from 2004.

Telemedicine (online remote audio and image diagnosis) allows remote northern hospitals to obtain specialist consultations without having to send patients to the regional hospital.

SPENDING

GDP/cap. increase

CONSUMPTION AND SPENDING

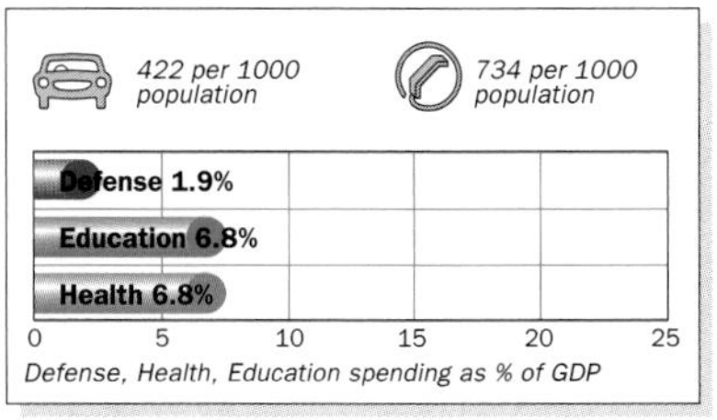
422 per 1000 population
734 per 1000 population
Defense 1.9%
Education 6.8%
Health 6.8%
0 5 10 15 20 25
Defense, Health, Education spending as % of GDP

In terms of income distribution, the Scandinavian countries are among the most egalitarian in the world, and the richest 10% of Norway's population owns much less of the country's wealth than in other developed countries. The cost of living is high; Oslo is one of the world's most expensive cities. Refugees from the 1990s Bosnian conflict are the most disadvantaged.

The discrepancy between pay for men and women is greater than elsewhere in Scandinavia, though still much smaller than the European average. Social provision has been maintained even through economic recession. Benefits are generous.

WORLD RANKING

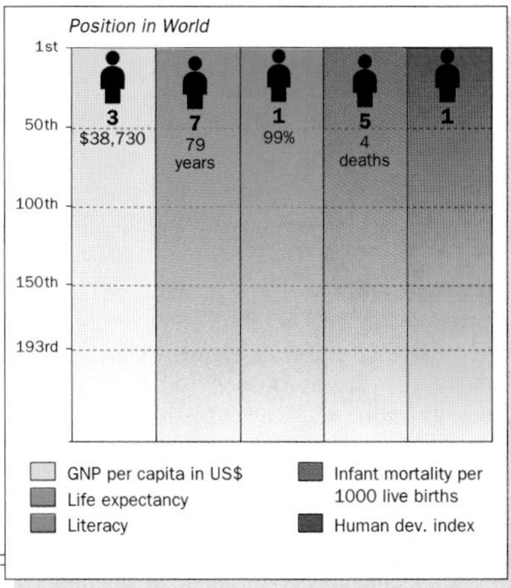
Position in World
1st
50th
100th
150th
193rd
3
$38,730
7
79 years
1
99%
5
4 deaths
1
GNP per capita in US$
Life expectancy
Literacy
Infant mortality per 1000 live births
Human dev. index

N

OMAN

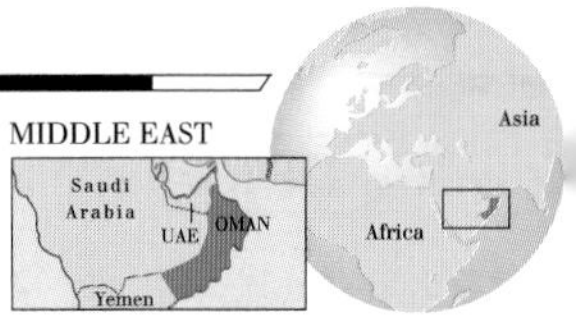
MIDDLE EAST
Saudi Arabia
UAE
OMAN
Yemen
Asia
Africa

OFFICIAL NAME: Sultanate of Oman **CAPITAL:** Muscat
POPULATION: 2.9 million **CURRENCY:** Omani rial **OFFICIAL LANGUAGE:** Arabic

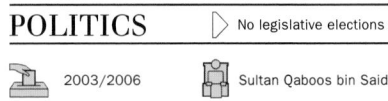

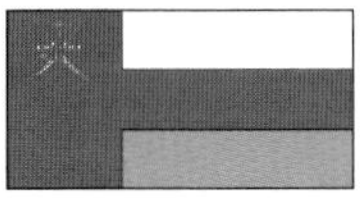

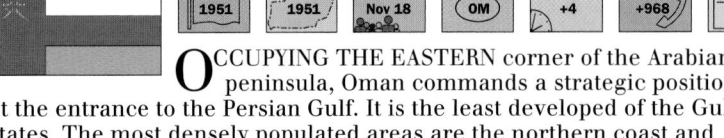

1951 | 1951 | Nov 18 | OM | +4 | +968 | .om

OCCUPYING THE EASTERN corner of the Arabian peninsula, Oman commands a strategic position at the entrance to the Persian Gulf. It is the least developed of the Gulf states. The most densely populated areas are the northern coast and the southern Salalah plain. Oil exports have given Oman modest prosperity under a paternalistic sultan. A Marxist-led insurgency supported by southern Dhofaris was defeated in the 1970s.

CLIMATE

Hot desert/monsoon

WEATHER CHART FOR MUSCAT

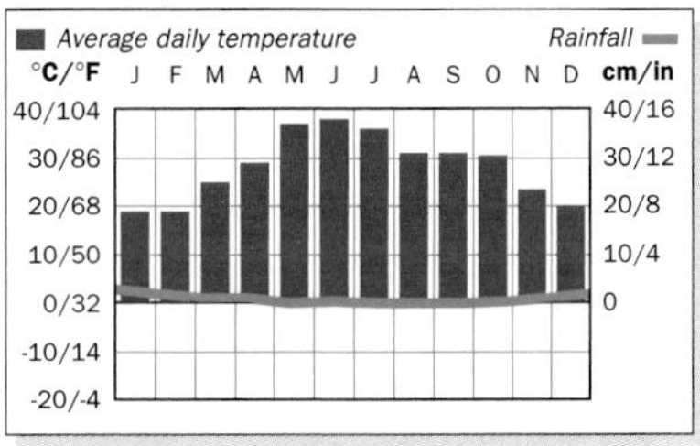
Average daily temperature
Rainfall
°C/°F J F M A M J J A S O N D cm/in
40/104
30/86
20/68
10/50
0/32
-10/14
-20/4
40/16
30/12
20/8
10/4
0

In the north temperatures often climb above 45°C (113°F) in summer. The south has a monsoon climate.

TRANSPORTATION

Drive on right

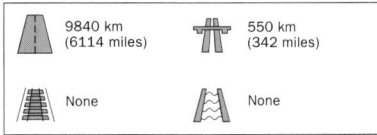

Seeb International, Muscat 2.8m passengers

26 ships 19,200 grt

THE TRANSPORTATION NETWORK

9840 km (6114 miles)

550 km (342 miles)

None

None

Northern cities are well served by good roads, but some places, in the south particularly, are best reached by air.

TOURISM

Visitors : Population 1:4.8

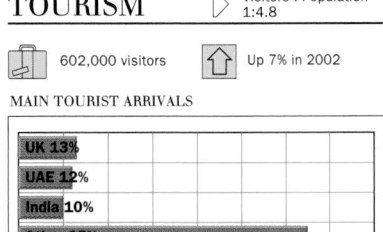

602,000 visitors

Up 7% in 2002

MAIN TOURIST ARRIVALS

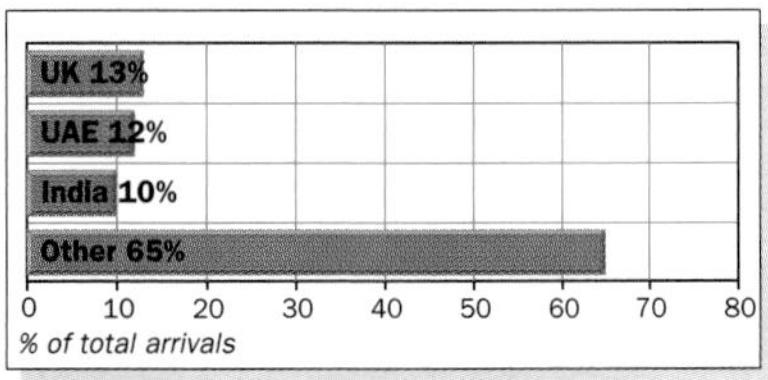
UK 13%
UAE 12%
India 10%
Other 65%
0 10 20 30 40 50 60 70 80
% of total arrivals

Until the late 1980s, Oman was closed to all but business or official visitors. The number of visitors to the sultanate's rich cultural heritage, fine beaches, and luxury hotels was badly affected by the 2003 war on Iraq.

PEOPLE

Pop. density low

Arabic, Baluchi, Farsi, Hindi, Punjabi

14/km² (35/mi²)

THE URBAN/RURAL POPULATION SPLIT

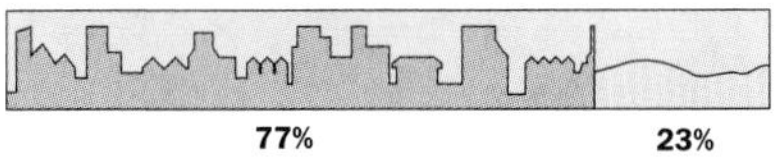
77%
23%

RELIGIOUS PERSUASION

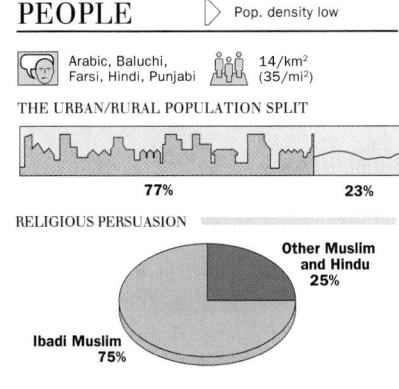

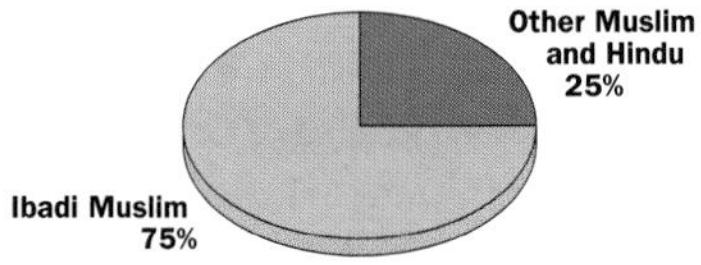
Other Muslim and Hindu 25%
Ibadi Muslim 75%

Native Omanis, who include Arab refugees who fled Zanzibar in the 1960s, make up three-quarters of the mostly young population. Baluchi, from Pakistan, are the largest foreign grouping among large numbers of foreign workers employed in the building and service industries on two-year contracts. A process of urban drift means that most Omanis now live in cities. Oman has a number of distinct minorities: the most numerous are the Jebalis in Dhofar – nomadic herdsmen who speak a language resembling Amharic. Many Dhofaris supported the Marxist-led insurgents in the 1970s, but they are now considered to be loyal.

Most Omanis are Ibadi Muslims who follow an appointed leader, known as the imam. Ibadism does not oppose freedom for women, and a few enjoy positions of authority; suffrage was extended to women in 2002.

POLITICS

No legislative elections

2003/2006

Sultan Qaboos bin Said

LEGISLATIVE OR ADVISORY BODIES

Consultative Council 83 seats

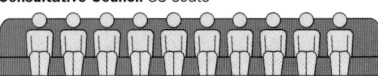

There are no political parties. The members of the Consultative Council (Majlis al-Shoura) were directly elected for the first time in 2000, and by universal suffrage from 2003.

Sultan Qaboos, ruler since 1970, is an authoritarian but paternalistic monarch. He is head of state, prime minister, and minister for foreign affairs, defense, and finance. Family members hold other key positions. Civil rights were enshrined in the 1996 constitution. The regime faces no serious challenge, though Qaboos keeps a careful eye on the religious right wing. Qaboos has no immediate heirs, raising concern for the succession.

The Consultative Council was created in 1991, giving a semblance of democracy. Universal suffrage was introduced in 2003. Major political issues include the planned privatization of medium-sized government projects, and improving Oman's self-defense capability.

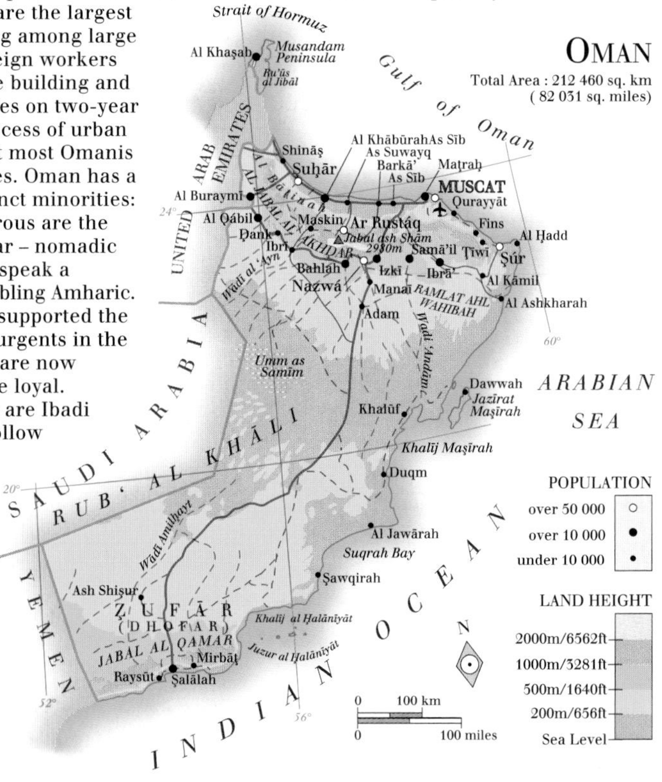
OMAN
Total Area : 212 460 sq. km (82 031 sq. miles)
Strait of Hormuz
Al Khaşab
Musandam Peninsula
Gulf of Oman
UNITED ARAB EMIRATES
Shināş
Şuḩār
Al Khābūrah
As Sīb
As Suwayq
Barkā'
Maţraḩ
MUSCAT
Qurayyāt
Al Buraymī
Al Qābil
Ar Rustāq
Fins
Al Ḩadd
Şūr
Al Kāmil
Al Ashkharah
Ibrī
Bahlāh
Nazwá
Izkī
Ibrā'
Manah
Adam
Jabal ash Shām 2980m
RAMLAT AHL WAHIBAH
SAUDI ARABIA
RUB' AL KHĀLĪ
Umm as Samīm
Dawwah
Jazīrat Maşīrah
ARABIAN SEA
Khalūf
Khalīj Maşīrah
Duqm
Al Jawārah
Suqrah Bay
Şawqirah
Ash Shişur
ZUFĀR (DHOFAR)
JABAL AL QAMAR
Mirbāţ
Raysūt
Şalālah
Khalīj al Ḩalānīyāt
Juzur al Ḩalānīyāt
YEMEN
INDIAN OCEAN
0 100 km
0 100 miles
POPULATION
over 50 000
over 10 000
under 10 000
LAND HEIGHT
2000m/6562ft
1000m/3281ft
500m/1640ft
200m/656ft
Sea Level

O

WORLD AFFAIRS

Joined UN in 1971

AL | AMF | Damasc | GCC | OIC

Border disputes with the UAE were finally resolved in 2003. Relations with Israel were cut off after the outbreak of the Palestinian *intifada* in 2000. Oman has ties with Iran and called for easing sanctions against Iraq, but supported the US-led military actions in 1991 and 2003.

***A watchtower above an oasis.** Much of Oman is gravelly desert. The only large area of cultivation is the 20-km-wide Al Batinah plain.*

AID

Recipient

$41m (receipts)

Up sharply in 2002

Aid used to come mainly from the US, but Japanese aid is now of greater significance. The UN is also a contributor. Oman makes occasional donations of its own to Arab and Muslim causes.

DEFENSE

No compulsory military service

$2.57bn

Down 9% in 2002

The UK is the main equipment supplier. Oman has provided communications and services to US and UK forces in their campaigns against Iraq. The government increased social spending at the expense of the defense budget in 2002, aware of the possible domestic repercussions of its support for the US.

ECONOMICS

Inflation 1.8% p.a. (1990–2000)

$19.9bn

0.385 Omani rials (0.385)

SCORE CARD

❑ WORLD GNP RANKING	66th
❑ GNP PER CAPITA	$7830
❑ BALANCE OF PAYMENTS	$2.32bn
❑ INFLATION	–0.7%
❑ UNEMPLOYMENT	5%

STRENGTHS

Oil industry, led by Royal Dutch/Shell: has benefited from staying out of OPEC and selling oil at spot prices without quotas. Exports from new pipeline and terminal. Stable agriculture. Potential for sizable fishing industry. Trend toward privatization, free markets.

WEAKNESSES

Overdependence on oil (90% of GNP), with fewer than 20 years' known reserves. Services sector could be better developed. Foreign workers needed in all economic sectors.

EXPORTS

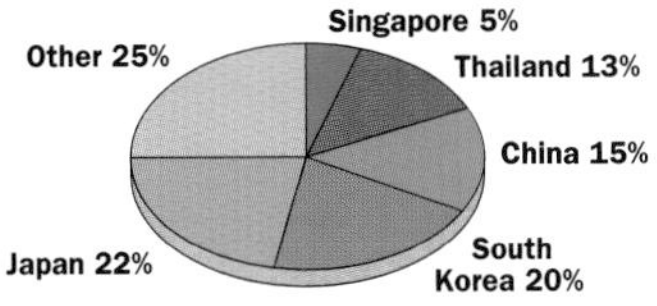
Singapore 5%
Other 25%
Thailand 13%
China 15%
Japan 22%
South Korea 20%

IMPORTS

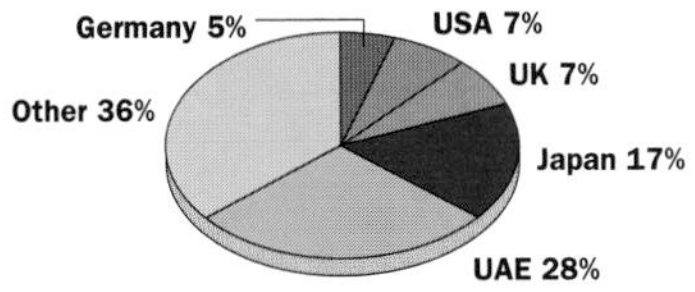
Germany 5%
USA 7%
UK 7%
Other 36%
Japan 17%
UAE 28%

RESOURCES

Electric power 2.4m kW

128,544 tonnes

823,000 b/d (reserves 5.6bn barrels)

1m goats, 355,000 sheep, 3.4m chickens

Oil, natural gas, copper, chromite, marble, gypsum

The government invested $3 billion in 2003 in a number of projects to encourage diversification and cut down dependence on oil revenues.

ENVIRONMENT

Sustainability rank: 120th

14%

8.2 tonnes per capita

Overpumping of groundwater causes seawater to seep into traditional irrigation areas. Nature reserves and antihunting laws protect rich wildlife.

MEDIA

TV ownership high

Daily newspaper circulation 29 per 1000 people

PUBLISHING AND BROADCAST MEDIA

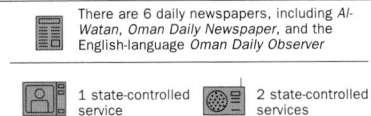

There are 6 daily newspapers, including *Al-Watan, Oman Daily Newspaper*, and the English-language *Oman Daily Observer*

1 state-controlled service

2 state-controlled services

Nothing critical of the government may be published in Oman, despite a 1984 law allowing for "freedom of opinion."

CRIME

Death penalty in use

2020 prisoners

Up 25% in 2000

Reckless driving by young Omani males is a problem. A "flying court" serves remote communities.

CHRONOLOGY

The present Albusaidi dynasty has ruled in Oman since 1749.

- ❑ **1932** Sultan bin Taimur in power.
- ❑ **1951** Sovereignty recognized by UK.
- ❑ **1970** Sultan Qaboos bin Said seizes power from his father.
- ❑ **1975** Suppression of Dhofar revolt.
- ❑ **1991** Consultative Council set up.
- ❑ **2003** Universal suffrage introduced for Consultative Council elections.

EDUCATION

Schooling is not compulsory

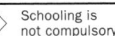

74%

19,297 students

Education has improved, but rural illiteracy is still high. Between 1996 and 2000, over 200 new schools were built.

HEALTH

Welfare state health benefits

1 per 769 people

Cerebrovascular and heart diseases, accidents

There is a policy of replacing expatriate medical staff with Omani nationals. Rural areas are served by clinics.

SPENDING

GDP/cap. increase

CONSUMPTION AND SPENDING

134 per 1000 population

84 per 1000 population

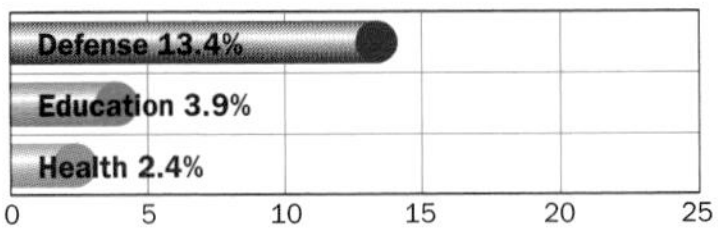
Defense 13.4%
Education 3.9%
Health 2.4%
0
5
10
15
20
25

Defense, Health, Education spending as % of GDP

Omanis in urban areas enjoy the same high living standards that are to be found in other Gulf states. Hunting trips to Pakistan are popular among the rich Omani elite, and a *khanjar*, a curved dagger, is seen as a status symbol.

WORLD RANKING

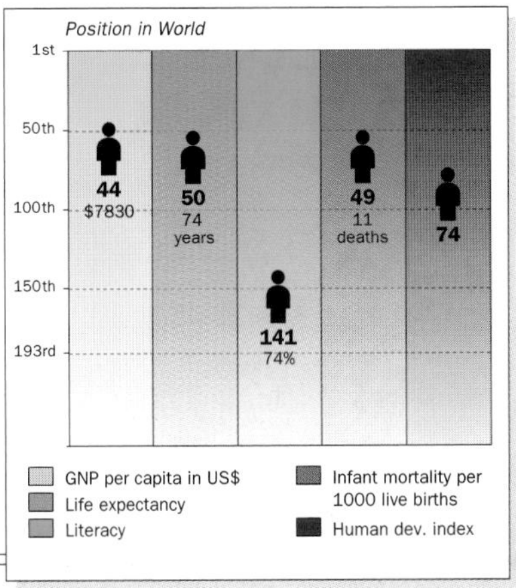
Position in World
1st
50th
100th
150th
193rd
44
$7830
50
74 years
141
74%
49
11 deaths
74
GNP per capita in US$
Life expectancy
Literacy
Infant mortality per 1000 live births
Human dev. index

O

PAKISTAN

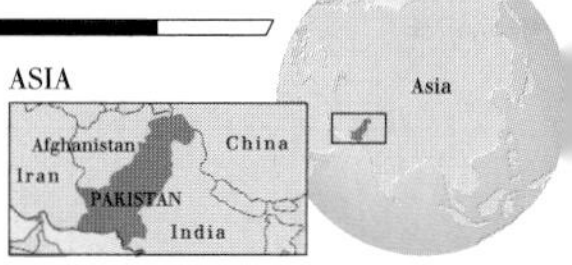
ASIA
Asia
Afghanistan
Iran
China
PAKISTAN
India

OFFICIAL NAME: Islamic Republic of Pakistan **CAPITAL:** Islamabad
POPULATION: 154 million **CURRENCY:** Pakistani rupee **OFFICIAL LANGUAGE:** Urdu

1947
1971
March 23
PK
+5
+92
.pk

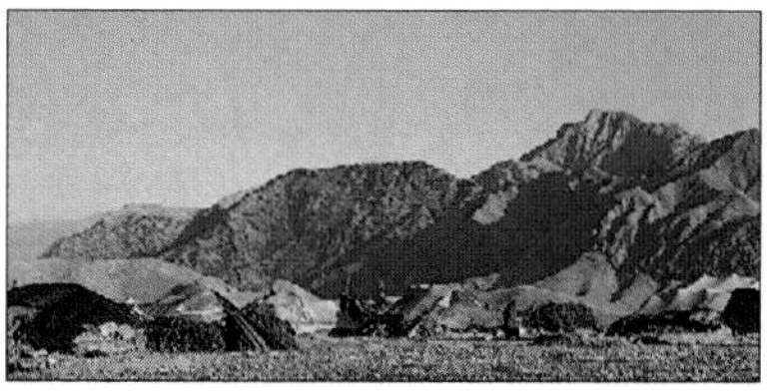

Barren landscape in Kachhi, Baluchistan. *This area of Pakistan has some of the highest May–September temperatures in the world.*

ONCE A PART OF BRITISH INDIA, Pakistan was created in 1947 in response to the demand for an independent and predominantly Muslim Indian state. Initially the new nation included East Pakistan, present-day Bangladesh, which seceded from Pakistan in 1971. Eastern and southern Pakistan, the floodplain of the Indus River, is highly fertile and produces cotton, the basis of the large textile industry.

CLIMATE

Mountain/steppe/ hot desert

WEATHER CHART FOR ISLAMABAD

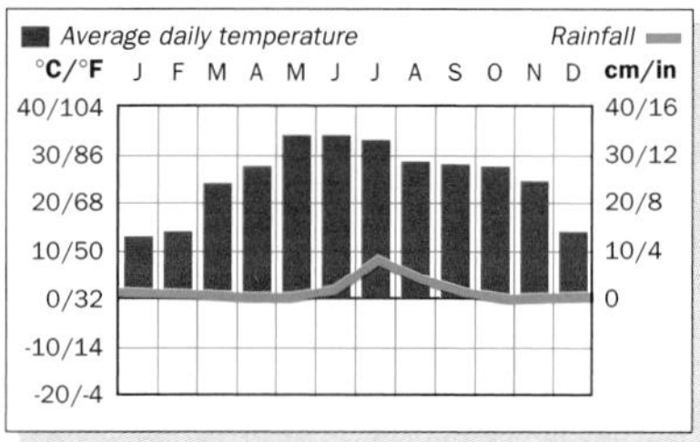
Average daily temperature
Rainfall
°C/°F J F M A M J J A S O N D cm/in
40/104
30/86
20/68
10/50
0/32
-10/14
-20/-4
40/16
30/12
20/8
10/4
0

Temperatures can soar to 50°C (122°F) in Sindh and Baluchistan and fall to –20°C (–4°F) in the northern mountains.

TRANSPORTATION

Drive on left

Quaid-e-Azam, Karachi 4.15m passengers

49 ships 247,400 grt

THE TRANSPORTATION NETWORK

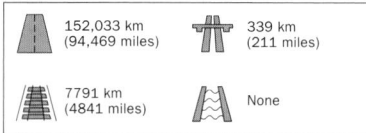

152,033 km (94,469 miles)

339 km (211 miles)

7791 km (4841 miles)

None

Buses are the most effective way of traveling across Pakistan; routes are comprehensive but poorly organized.

TOURISM

Visitors : Population 1:308

498,000 visitors

Little change in 2002

MAIN TOURIST ARRIVALS

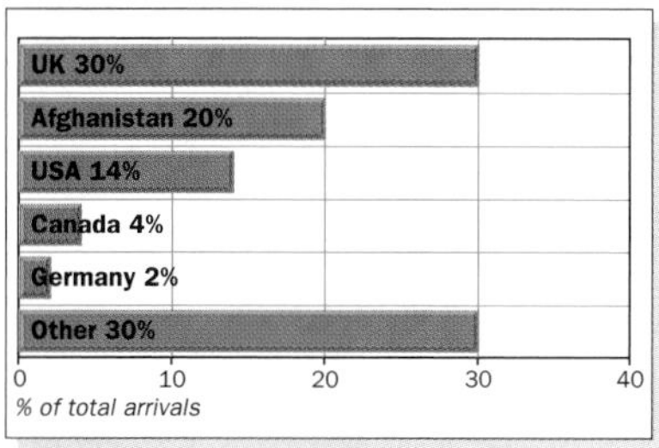
UK 30%
Afghanistan 20%
USA 14%
Canada 4%
Germany 2%
Other 30%
0
10
20
30
40
% of total arrivals

Relatively few tourists visit Pakistan, despite its rich cultural heritage and unspoiled natural beauty.

PEOPLE

Pop. density medium

Punjabi, Sindhi, Pashtu, Urdu, Baluchi, Brahui

199/km² (516/mi²)

THE URBAN/RURAL POPULATION SPLIT

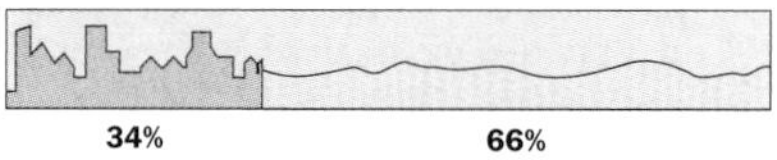
34%
66%

RELIGIOUS PERSUASION

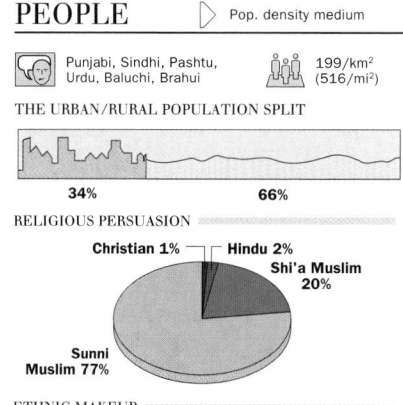

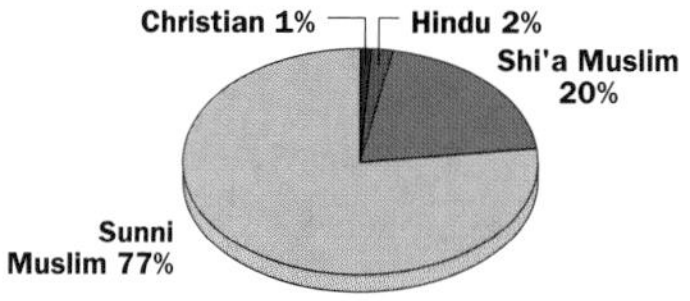
Christian 1%
Hindu 2%
Shi'a Muslim 20%
Sunni Muslim 77%

ETHNIC MAKEUP

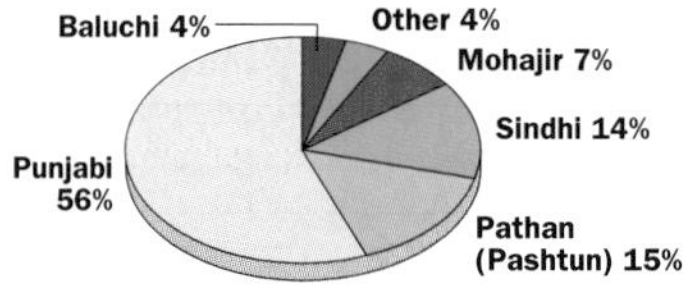
Baluchi 4%
Other 4%
Mohajir 7%
Sindhi 14%
Punjabi 56%
Pathan (Pashtun) 15%

POPULATION AGE BREAKDOWN

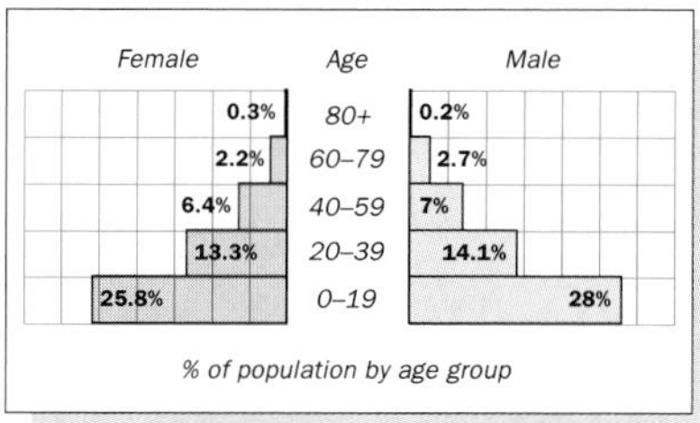
Female
Age
Male
0.3%
80+
0.2%
2.2%
60–79
2.7%
6.4%
40–59
7%
13.3%
20–39
14.1%
25.8%
0–19
28%
% of population by age group

Punjabis account for over 50% of the population; Sindhis, Pathans (Pashtuns), and Baluchi make up most of the rest. *Mohajirs* – Urdu-speaking immigrants from prepartition India – predominate in Karachi and Hyderabad. Punjabi political and military dominance of the centralized state has spawned many separatist and autonomy movements. Pathans have frequently threatened to establish a homeland with ethnic kin in Afghanistan. Tensions between the Baluchi and Pashtun refugees from Afghanistan sporadically erupt into violence, as do those between native Sindhis and immigrant *mohajirs*.

The gap between rich and poor, for example between the feudal landowning class and their serfs, is considerable. There is an expanding middle class of small-scale traders and manufacturers.

Recent years have witnessed a marked increase in Islamist militancy, accompanied by sectarian conflict between Sunnis and Shi'as and by growing discrimination against religious minorities. After the 1999 coup, the Musharraf regime trod a fine line in trying to avoid conflict with Islamist militants, both over issues such as the strict application of *sharia* (Islamic law) and over foreign policy.

The extended family is an enduring institution, and ties between family members are strong, reflected in the dynastic and nepotistic nature of the political system. Though some women hold prominent positions, and Benazir Bhutto has twice been prime minister, relatively few are allowed to work by their religiously conservative menfolk. Pakistan has one of the world's lowest ratios of females to males, implying widespread neglect and some female infanticide. Amnesty International has criticized Pakistan for its failure to give women's rights sufficient protection. Women's rights groups are mainly based in cities, and have made little headway nationally.

I R A N
CHĀGAI HI
Hāmūn-i Mās
Turbat
Dasht Kaur
Gwādar
CENTRA
A R A B I

P

POLITICS

Multiparty elections

L. House 2002/2007
U. House 2003/2006

President Pervez Musharraf

AT THE LAST ELECTION

National Assembly 342 seats

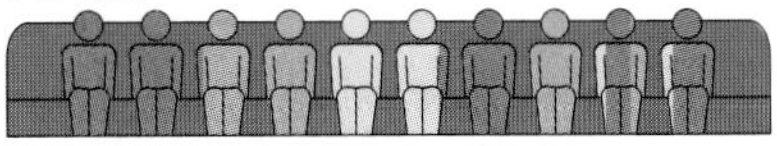
4% PML(N)
3% N-M
7% Others
22% PML(Q)
18% PPP
18% W
13% MMA
8% Ind
4% NA
3% MQM

PML(Q) = Pakistan Muslim League (Quaid-e-Azam)
PPP = Pakistan People's Party (Parliamentarians)
W = Women **MMA** = Muttahida Majlis-e-Amal
Ind = Independents **PML(N)** = Pakistan Muslim League (Nawaz) **NA** = National Alliance **N-M** = Non-Muslim minorities **MQM** = Muttahida Qaumi Movement

Senate 100 seats

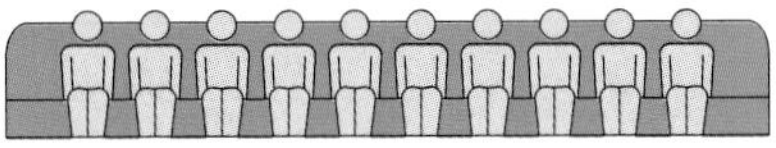

The Senate is indirectly elected. Seventeen seats are reserved for women

Multiparty democracy was suspended from 1999 to 2002. The military-dominated National Security Council advises the president.

PROFILE

In the 1990s fragile coalitions had to rule in cooperation with the president and the army. Popular support for the 1999 coup, which removed PML Prime Minister Nawaz Sharif, indicated the loss of respect for the country's much-abused democratic institutions. In 2001, coup leader Gen. Musharraf appointed himself president.

The 2002 elections were won by the pro-Musharraf PML(Q), which outmaneuvered the PPP and the Islamist MMA to secure the appointment of their candidate as prime minister. Controversial constitutional changes enlarging Musharraf's powers were eventually passed in late 2003, after he had pledged to relinquish control of the army within a year. Tensions were reignited in 2004 by the peremptory manner of his installation of technocrat Shaukat Aziz as prime minister.

MAIN POLITICAL ISSUE
Militant Islam

Pressure to curb the ambitions of Islamists in Kashmir is balanced by the popularity in domestic politics of militant Islam, which has a powerful grip on the poor. In 2002 the MMA became the third-largest party in parliament, and in 2003 its North West Frontier Province government imposed *sharia* (Islamic law).

***Benazir Bhutto**, PPP leader and former prime minister.*

***Pervez Musharraf**, self-appointed president.*

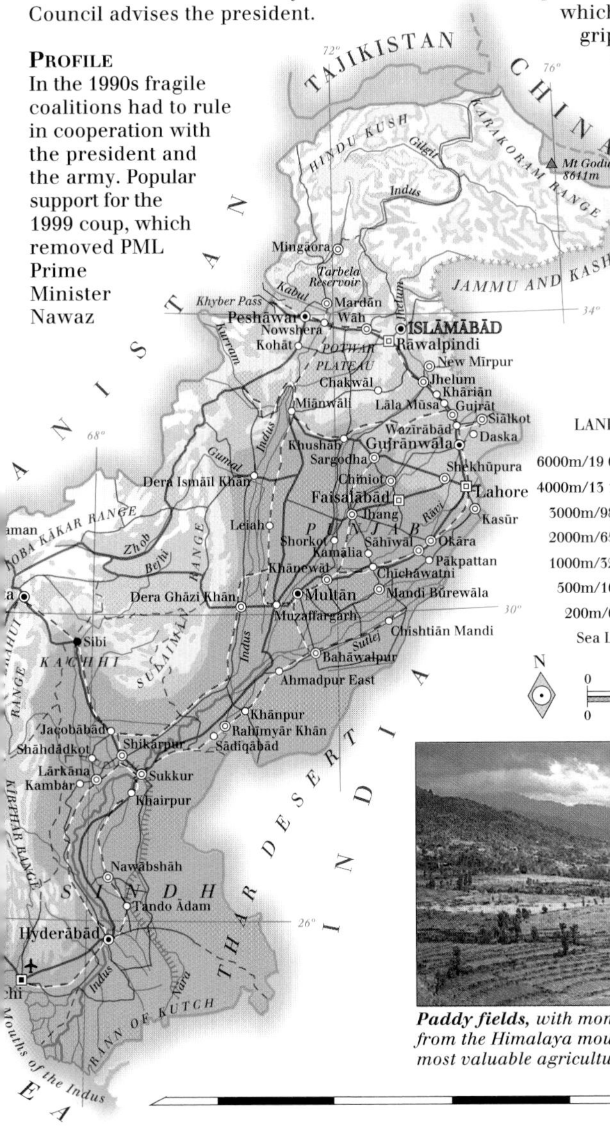
PAKISTAN
Total Area : 803 940 sq. km (310 401 sq. miles)
LAND HEIGHT
6000m/19 686ft
4000m/13 124ft
3000m/9843ft
2000m/6562ft
1000m/3281ft
500m/1640ft
200m/656ft
Sea Level
POPULATION
over 5 000 000
over 1 000 000
over 500 000
over 100 000
over 50 000
over 10 000
0 200 km
0 200 miles
TAJIKISTAN
CHINA
HINDU KUSH
KARAKORAM RANGE
Mt Godwen Austen (K2) 8611m
Gilgit
Indus
JAMMU AND KASHMIR
Mingāora
Tarbela Reservoir
Kabul
Khyber Pass
Mardān
Peshāwar
Wah
Nowshera
ISLĀMĀBĀD
Kohāt
Rāwalpindi
POTWAR PLATEAU
New Mīrpur
Chakwāl
Jhelum
Khāriān
Miānwāli
Lāla Mūsa
Gujrāt
Siālkot
Wazīrābād
Daska
Khushāb
Gujrānwāla
Sargodha
Shekhūpura
Chiniot
Dera Ismāīl Khān
Lahore
Faisalābād
Jhang
Kasūr
Leiah
Shorkot
Sāhīwāl
Okāra
Kamālia
Pākpattan
Khānewāl
Chichāwatni
Dera Ghāzi Khān
Multān
Mandi Būrewāla
Muzaffargarh
Chishtiān Mandi
Sibi
Bahāwalpur
Ahmadpur East
Khānpur
Rahīmyār Khān
Sādiqābād
Jacobābād
Shāhdādkot
Shikārpur
Lārkāna
Sukkur
Kambar
Khairpur
Nawābshāh
SINDH
Tando Ādam
Hyderābād
THAR DESERT
INDIA
RANN OF KUTCH
Mouths of the Indus
Zhob
Beji
SULAIMAN RANGE
KACHHI
KIRTHAR RANGE
PUNJAB
Ravi
Sutlej
Jhelum
Kurram
Gumal
Nara
AFGHANISTAN
N

***Paddy fields,** with monsoon rains threatening from the Himalaya mountains. Rice is the second most valuable agricultural export after cotton.*

WORLD AFFAIRS

Joined UN in 1947

Comm | ECO | NAM | OIC | SAARC

The last of three wars with India was more than three decades ago, but their dispute over Kashmir has repeatedly stoked tensions. In 1998, Pakistan carried out a series of nuclear tests in response to Indian tests, provoking international condemnation and a tightening of US sanctions (to 2001).

In 2004 Pakistan faced international condemnation over its role in nuclear proliferation, following the arrest and subsequent pardon of Abdul Qadeer Khan, the "father of the bomb," for selling classified information abroad.

Since the fall of the *taliban* in Afghanistan, Pakistan has courted the US-installed interim regime. A major army offensive in 2004 against Islamist militants in the north coincided with the US naming Pakistan as a key non-NATO ally. It was also readmitted to the Commonwealth in 2004, having been suspended following the 1999 coup.

P

CHRONOLOGY

From the 8th to the 16th centuries, Islamic rule extended to northwest and northeast India. Punjab and Sindh, annexed by the British East India Company in the 1850s, were ceded to the British Raj in 1857.

- **1906** Muslim League founded as organ of Indian Muslim separatism.
- **1947** Partition of India. Pakistan divided by 1600 km (1000 miles) of Indian territory into East and West Pakistan. Millions displaced by large-scale migration. Muhammad Ali Jinnah first governor-general.
- **1948** First India–Pakistan war over Kashmir.
- **1949** New Awami League (AL) demands East Pakistan's autonomy.
- **1956** Constitution establishes Pakistan as an Islamic republic.
- **1958** Martial law. Gen. Muhammad Ayub Khan takes over; elected president two years later.

CHRONOLOGY *continued*

- **1965** Second India–Pakistan war over Kashmir.
- **1970** Ayub Khan resigns. Gen. Agha Yahya Khan takes over. First direct elections won by AL; West Pakistani parties reject results. War with India over East Pakistan.
- **1971** East Pakistan secedes as Bangladesh. PPP leader Zulfikar Ali Bhutto president.
- **1972** Simla (peace) Agreement with India.
- **1973** Bhutto, now prime minister, initiates Islamic socialism.
- **1977** General election. Riots over allegations of vote rigging. Gen. Zia ul-Haq stages military coup.
- **1979** Bhutto executed.
- **1986** Bhutto's daughter Benazir returns from exile to lead PPP.
- **1988** Zia killed in air crash. PPP wins general election.
- **1990** Ethnic violence in Sindh. President dismisses Benazir Bhutto. Nawaz Sharif of PML premier.
- **1991** Islamic *sharia* incorporated in legal code.
- **1992** Violence between Sindhis and *mohajirs* escalates in Sindh.
- **1993** President Khan and Prime Minister Sharif resign. Elections; Bhutto returns to power.
- **1996** President dismisses Bhutto.
- **1997** PML wins landslide election victory; Sharif prime minister.
- **1998** Nuclear tests.
- **1999–2000** Military coup. Sharif found guilty of treason.
- **2001** Parliament suspended, Gen. Musharraf appoints himself president. Pakistan key ally in US-led "war on terrorism."
- **2002** US and French nationals killed in terrorist attacks. Threat of war with India over Kashmir. October, PML(Q) wins elections.
- **2004** Musharraf chooses Shaukat Aziz to become prime minister.

AID

Recipient

$2.14bn (receipts) | Up 10% in 2002

Pakistan is heavily dependent on aid, though the government has a long history of misdirecting aid payments. Aid intended for major projects has regularly been used to fund the current-account deficit. In 1998 the IMF agreed to help Pakistan meet its international debt obligations after the US and other Western aid donors cut off aid in protest against Pakistan's nuclear tests. The US subsequently agreed to resume aid, and boosted its support in late 2001 to reward the regime for supporting the "war on terrorism." Japan and the World Bank are among other main bilateral donors.

DEFENSE

No compulsory military service

$2.54bn | Up 5% in 2002

Pakistan is an important regional arms trader and established itself as a nuclear power with successful nuclear tests in 1998; leading scientists in the program were later accused of selling secrets to Iran, Libya, and North Korea. Defense spending accounts for about a quarter of government expenditure; troop numbers were cut for the first time in 2004. The US, once a key arms supplier, imposed sanctions in 1990–2001 and most military hardware is now produced domestically; the Shaheen surface-to-surface missile was tested in 2004.

The army has been heavily involved in politics, even at times when a military regime was not actually in power. The National Security Council assures it a formal role in civilian decision-making.

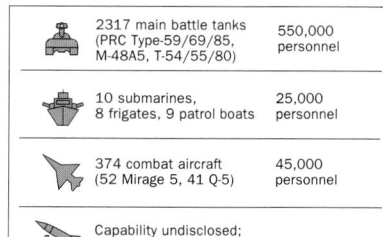

PAKISTANI ARMED FORCES

2317 main battle tanks (PRC Type-59/69/85, M-48A5, T-54/55/80)	550,000 personnel
10 submarines, 8 frigates, 9 patrol boats	25,000 personnel
374 combat aircraft (52 Mirage 5, 41 Q-5)	45,000 personnel
Capability undisclosed; weapons tested in 1998	

ECONOMICS

Inflation 9.6% p.a. (1990–2001)

$60.9bn | 58.14 Pakistani rupees (57.86)

SCORE CARD

World GNP Ranking	44th
GNP per Capita	$420
Balance of Payments	$3.87bn
Inflation	3.3%
Unemployment	8%

EXPORTS

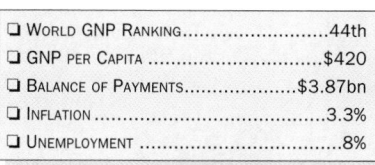

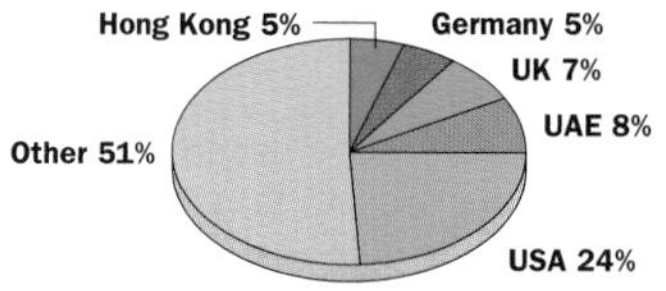
Hong Kong 5%
Germany 5%
UK 7%
UAE 8%
USA 24%
Other 51%

IMPORTS

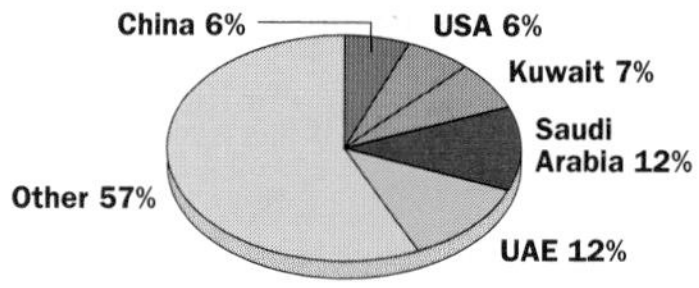
China 6%
USA 6%
Kuwait 7%
Saudi Arabia 12%
UAE 12%
Other 57%

ECONOMIC PERFORMANCE INDICATOR

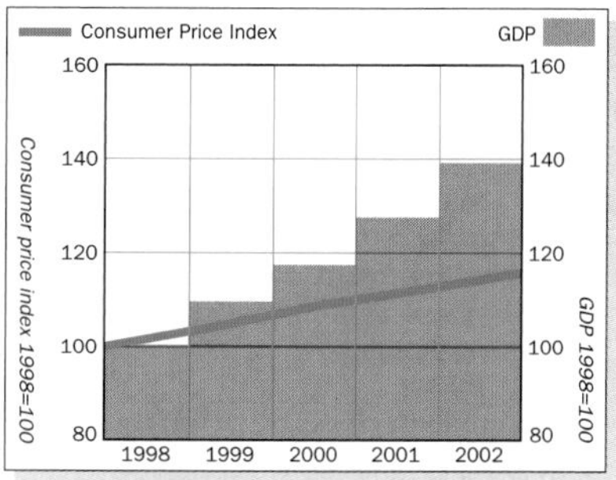
Consumer Price Index
GDP
160
140
120
100
80
Consumer price index 1998=100
GDP 1998=100
1998
1999
2000
2001
2002

Strengths
Gas, water, coal, oil. Substantial untapped natural resources. Low labor costs. Potentially huge market. One of the world's leading producers of cotton and a major exporter of rice.

Weaknesses
Production of cotton and rice vulnerable to weather conditions. Weak and overstretched infrastructure. History of inefficient and haphazard government economic policies. Terrorism threat inhibits foreign investment.

Profile
Pakistan has yet to show progress in tackling its considerable economic problems. Though successive governments have reversed the nationalization policies instituted in the 1970s, private enterprise has been stifled by the rules of a massive bureaucracy. There is some foreign investment in previously state-only sectors such as water, other utilities, and banking. Efforts by the military government to tackle endemic corruption and widespread poverty were praised by the World Bank in 2001. Pakistan has benefited from its role as a frontline state in the "war on terrorism" through international aid and the rescheduling of debt. Defense spending remains high.

PAKISTAN : MAJOR BUSINESSES

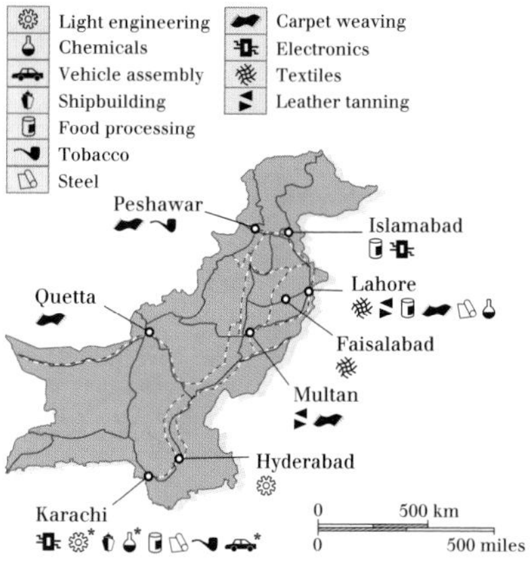
Light engineering
Chemicals
Vehicle assembly
Shipbuilding
Food processing
Tobacco
Steel
Carpet weaving
Electronics
Textiles
Leather tanning
Peshawar
Islamabad
Lahore
Quetta
Faisalabad
Multan
Hyderabad
Karachi
0
500 km
0
500 miles

* significant multinational ownership

P

RESOURCES

Electric power 17.4m kW

623,425 tonnes

56,701 b/d (reserves 220m barrels)

52.8m goats, 24.8m buffaloes, 155m chickens

Oil, natural gas, coal, limestone, salt, gypsum, silica sand

ELECTRICITY GENERATION

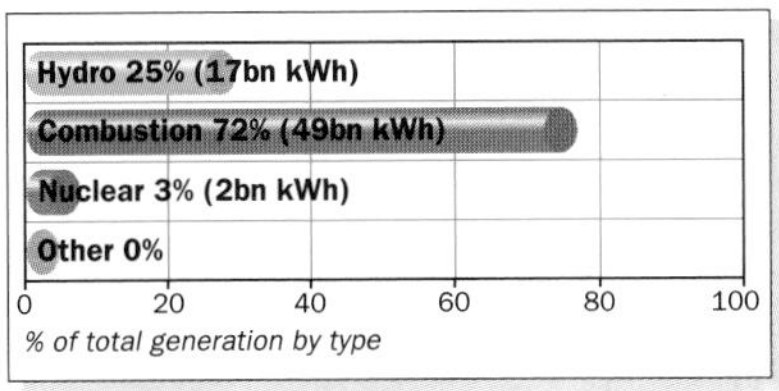

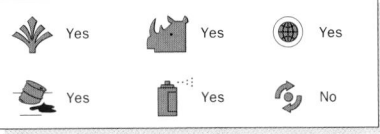

Hydro 25% (17bn kWh)
Combustion 72% (49bn kWh)
Nuclear 3% (2bn kWh)
Other 0%
0
20
40
60
80
100
% of total generation by type

Apart from cotton and rice, Pakistan's major resources are oil, coal, gas, and water. Oil-refining capacity is well below present demand. The French firm Total was awarded a $3 billion contract in 2003 to explore for offshore oil and gas.

Power theft is a problem, constituting a sizable proportion of the overall 30% power loss rate, and army units were assigned to investigate illegal connections in 1999. China agreed in 2003 to help build a second nuclear reactor at the existing Chashma plant.

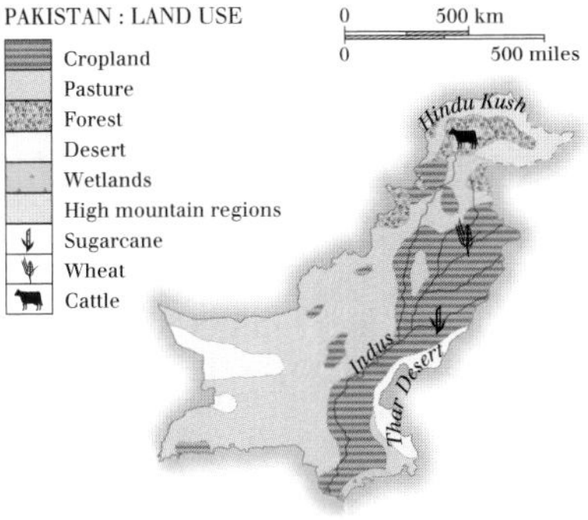

PAKISTAN : LAND USE
Cropland
Pasture
Forest
Desert
Wetlands
High mountain regions
Sugarcane
Wheat
Cattle
0
500 km
0
500 miles
Hindu Kush
Indus
Thar Desert

ENVIRONMENT

Sustainability rank: 112th

5% (4% partially protected)

0.8 tonnes per capita

ENVIRONMENTAL TREATIES

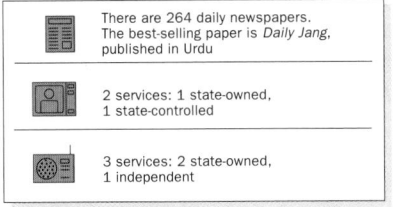

Yes | Yes | Yes

Yes | Yes | No

Illegal logging and urban pollution are major problems. The stranding of the *Tasman Spirit* oil tanker in 2003 caused widespread devastation near Karachi.

EDUCATION

Schooling is not compulsory

44%

1.11m students

THE EDUCATION SYSTEM

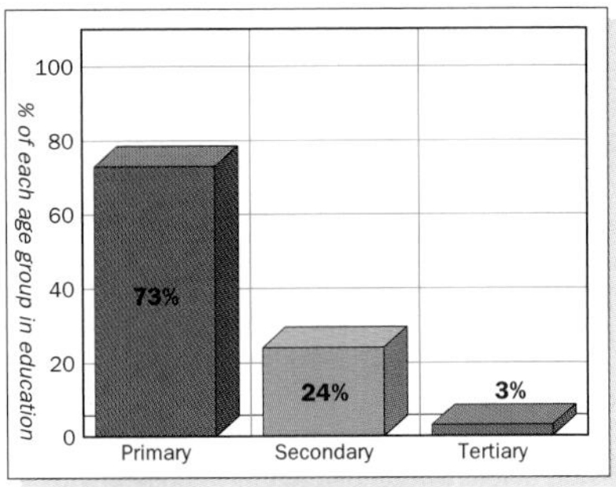

100
80
60
40
20
0
% of each age group in education
73%
24%
3%
Primary
Secondary
Tertiary

Though universal free primary education is a constitutional right, it is not compulsory. Literacy rates are among the lowest in the world. The education system is heavily Islamized, and weighted toward educating males: a large majority of children enrolled in primary schools are boys.

There are 26 universities, 853 arts and sciences colleges, and 308 professional colleges, all of which have a heavy preponderance of arts students. Wealthy parents frequently choose to send their children abroad for higher education, mainly to colleges in the UK or the US.

HEALTH

No welfare state health benefits

1 per 1436 people

Malaria, tuberculosis, diarrheal diseases

Availability of doctors and hospital beds is low, and there is a shortage of equipment and medicines. Uncontrolled counterfeit drugs are common. A specialized cancer hospital in Lahore, opened in 1995, offers modern facilities and advanced treatment. Pakistan has a high incidence of heroin addicts, due largely to its proximity to Afghanistan.

SPENDING

GDP/cap. increase

CONSUMPTION AND SPENDING

6 per 1000 population

25 per 1000 population

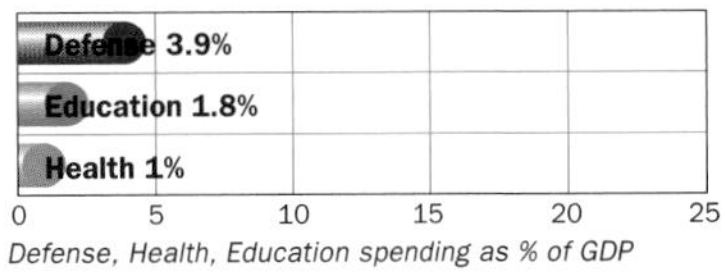

Defense 3.9%
Education 1.8%
Health 1%
0
5
10
15
20
25
Defense, Health, Education spending as % of GDP

Members of the bureaucratic and political elite tend to be extremely rich, as are some of the top military. Despite Pakistan's considerable economic potential, two-thirds of the population live below the poverty line.

MEDIA

TV ownership medium

Daily newspaper circulation 40 per 1000 people

PUBLISHING AND BROADCAST MEDIA

There are 264 daily newspapers. The best-selling paper is *Daily Jang*, published in Urdu

2 services: 1 state-owned, 1 state-controlled

3 services: 2 state-owned, 1 independent

Private broadcasts were licensed in 2003. Journalists who challenge official views are systematically harassed.

CRIME

Death penalty in use

87,000 prisoners

Down 27% in 2000

CRIME RATES

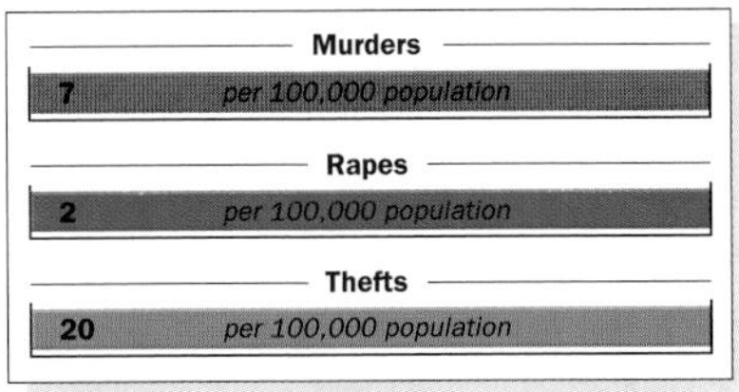

Murders
7
per 100,000 population
Rapes
2
per 100,000 population
Thefts
20
per 100,000 population

Compared with similar Islamic states, rates of murder, kidnapping, narcotics trafficking, and rape are high, though offical reporting of crime is low.

Corruption and the abuse of women are major causes for concern; reports of deaths or death threats for refusing to accept arranged marriages are rising. Torture and rape of prisoners and deaths in custody are frequent. The most dangerous area is Sindh: Karachi is terrorized by severe factional violence. Militant sectarian groups are also blamed for a recent rise in crime in Punjab. Special part-military courts were established in 2002 to combat terrorism and other "serious" crimes. The MMA provincial government of North West Frontier Province fulfilled its electoral promise to impose *sharia* (Islamic law) in 2003.

WORLD RANKING

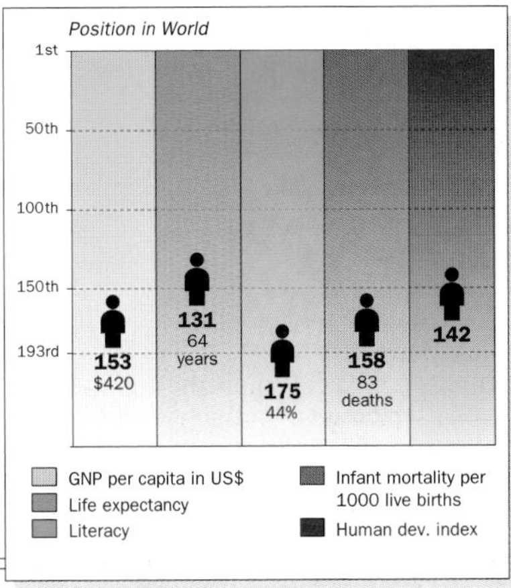

Position in World
1st
50th
100th
150th
193rd
153
$420
131
64
years
175
44%
158
83
deaths
142
GNP per capita in US$
Life expectancy
Literacy
Infant mortality per 1000 live births
Human dev. index

P

PALAU

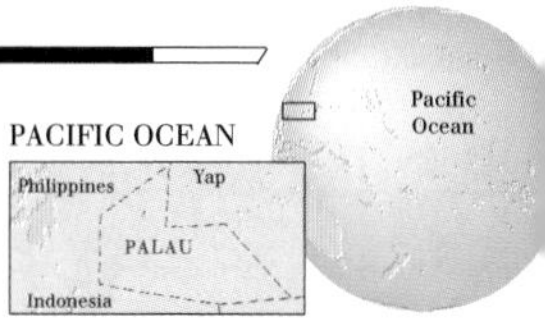
PACIFIC OCEAN
Pacific Ocean
Philippines
Yap
PALAU
Indonesia

OFFICIAL NAME: Republic of Palau **CAPITAL:** Koror
POPULATION: 19,717 **CURRENCY:** US dollar **OFFICIAL LANGUAGES:** Palauan and English

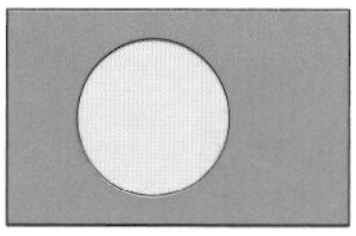

1994 | 1994 | Oct 1 | PAL | +9 | +680 | .pw

THE REPUBLIC OF PALAU (locally known as Belau) is situated in the western Pacific and comprises more than 300 islands in the Caroline Islands archipelago, only nine of which are inhabited. Formerly a part of the US-administered Trust Territory of the Pacific Islands, Palau became independent in association with the US in 1994, but remains economically and militarily dependent.

CLIMATE

Tropical oceanic

WEATHER CHART FOR KOROR

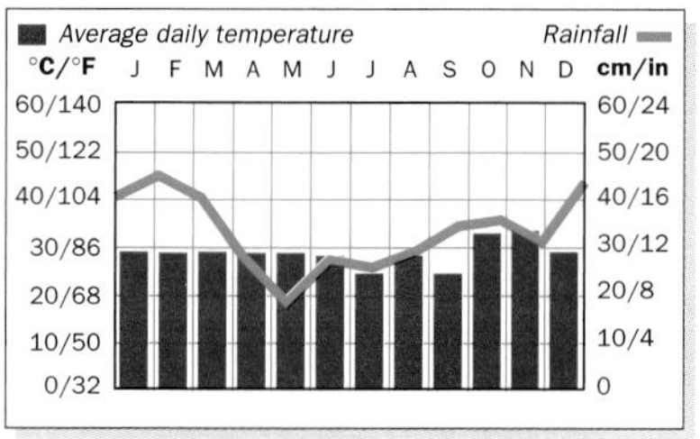
Average daily temperature
Rainfall
°C/°F
J F M A M J J A S O N D
cm/in
60/140
50/122
40/104
30/86
20/68
10/50
0/32
60/24
50/20
40/16
30/12
20/8
10/4
0

The islands are humid, with fairly constant temperatures and heavy rainfall all year round. The mean temperature is 27°C (81°F).

TRANSPORTATION

Drive on right

Koror Babelthuap

Has no fleet

THE TRANSPORTATION NETWORK

36 km (22 miles)

None

None

None

The locally owned Palau Micronesia Air was launched in 2004. A circular highway is being constructed around Babelthuap.

TOURISM

Visitors : Population 3:1

59,000 visitors

Up 9% in 2002

MAIN TOURIST ARRIVALS

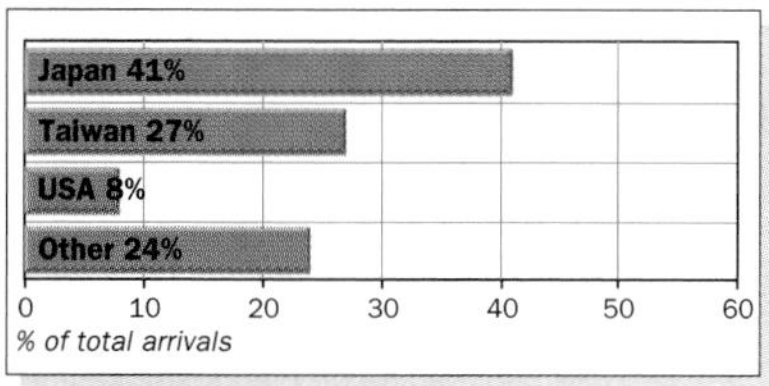
Japan 41%
Taiwan 27%
USA 8%
Other 24%
0
10
20
30
40
50
60
% of total arrivals

Tourism is very important, though there are concerns about its impact on traditional culture. A golf course is being built, and some islands have battle sites from the Pacific War.

PEOPLE

Pop. density low

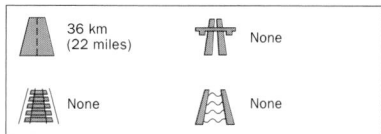

Palauan, English, Japanese, Angaur, Tobi, Sonsorolese

39/km² (101/mi²)

THE URBAN/RURAL POPULATION SPLIT

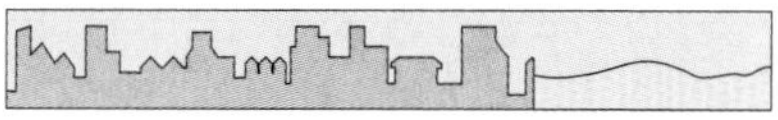
69%
31%

RELIGIOUS PERSUASION

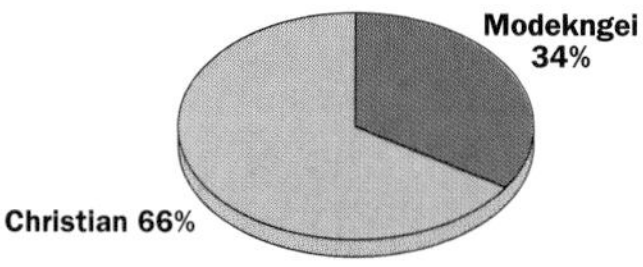
Modekngei 34%
Christian 66%

Palau was first colonized by southeast Asian peoples some 3000 years ago. There has also been mixing with other Melanesian and Polynesian peoples. The recent influx of migrants from Asia has raised tensions. Low-skilled Filipinos now make up over 16% of the population. Immigration from south Asia was explicitly banned in 2001.

Around 70% of Palauans live on the island city of Koror (a new capital is being constructed on neighboring Babelthuap). The thinly scattered remaining population are linguistically diverse, with distinct languages in the south. Cultural influence from the US and Japan has been strong, though traditional culture has been maintained on the more remote islands. Society remains largely matrilineal. The indigenous Modekngei religion is a blend of traditional beliefs and Christianity.

Palau's islands have many idyllic beaches, but a lack of resources means that tourism remains underdeveloped.

POLITICS

Nonparty elections

L. House 2000/2004
U. House 2000/2004

President Tommy Remengesau

AT THE LAST ELECTION

House of Delegates 16 seats

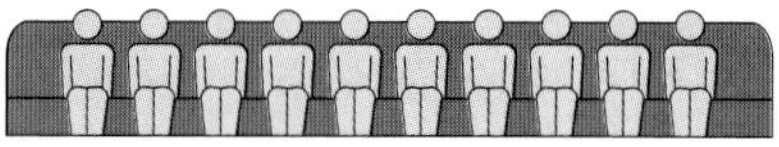

One member is elected to the House of Delegates to represent each of the 16 states

Senate 14 seats

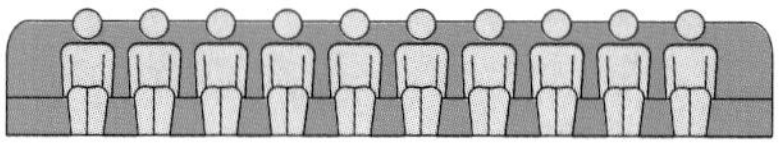

The 14 senators represent geographical districts, according to population

Palau's independence was delayed until 1994, after a 1993 referendum had finally accepted the transit and storage of US nuclear materials as stipulated under the Compact of Free Association with the US. Vice President Tommy Remengesau was elected president in 2000. He has clashed with the legislature over control of the budget. Overcrowding in Koror and immigration are main issues.

WORLD AFFAIRS

Joined UN in 1994

ACP | ADB | IWC | PC | PIF

The US has exclusive control over Palau's foreign affairs and defense policies under the conditions of the 1994 Compact of Free Association. Cordial relations with the Pacific Islands Forum were restored in 1999 after tensions caused by Palau's bid to give Japan the right to veto the establishment of a whale sanctuary in the South Pacific.

AID

Recipient

$31m (receipts)

Down 9% in 2002

Palau is heavily dependent on aid, which accounts for around 30% of GDP. Under the 15-year Compact of Free Association with the US, effective from 1994, Palau is set to receive up to $700 million in return for the use of military facilities. Japan is also a key donor, and funded the new Babelthuap–Koror bridge which opened in 2002.

DEFENSE

No compulsory military service

There are no armed forces

Not applicable

Under the 1994 Compact of Free Association, the US is responsible for Palau's defense.

P

ECONOMICS

Inflation 2.8% p.a. (1994–2001)

$136m

Currency is US dollar

SCORE CARD

- WORLD GNP RANKING......187th
- GNP PER CAPITA......$6820
- BALANCE OF PAYMENTS......–$16m
- INFLATION......3%
- UNEMPLOYMENT......2%

EXPORTS

Palau does not publish export figures by country

IMPORTS

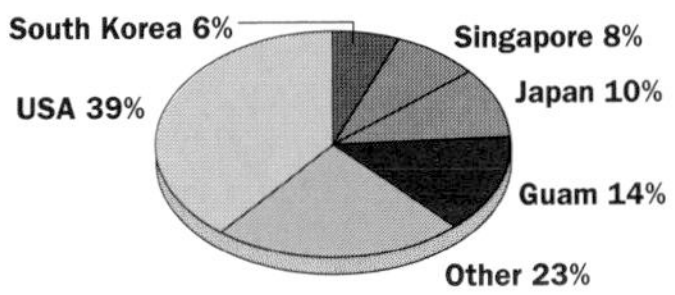
South Korea 6%
Singapore 8%
USA 39%
Japan 10%
Guam 14%
Other 23%

STRENGTHS

Relationship with aid donors – US and Japan – provides economic stability and access to lucrative markets. Tourism industry growing. Transportation infrastructure improving. Fishing and copra production important. Increasing regional trade. Trust funds established from Compact money.

WEAKNESSES

Heavy dependence on aid. Remote location. Underemployment. Poor transportation links between islands and to other countries. Few resources.

CHRONOLOGY

The Caroline Islands were colonized in turn by Spain, Germany, and Japan, coming under US control in 1945.

- **1947** UN Trust Territory of the Pacific Islands established.
- **1982** Compact of Free Association with US provisionally signed.
- **1993** Compact finally approved.
- **1994** Independence in free association with US.
- **2001** Tommy Remengesau takes office as president.

HEALTH

Welfare state health benefits

1 per 909 people

Cerebrovascular, heart, and intestinal diseases

Palau has three private clinics and a newly built public hospital. The government spends more on health than most Pacific island nations; immunization programs are the priority. An epidemic of mosquito-borne dengue fever hit Palau in 2000.

RESOURCES

Electric power 62,000 kW

2002 tonnes

Not an oil producer

Not available

Gold

On some islands the soil is highly fertile, though the terrain of the larger islands makes farming difficult. Some islands are densely forested. Palau has copra and some gold deposits. There is also the possibility of exploitation of reserves of minerals on the seabed. Palau has a small fishing industry with the potential for development.

ENVIRONMENT

Not available

8% (6% partially protected)

12.1 tonnes per capita

Palau suffers from inadequate facilities for the disposal of solid waste. Sand and coral dredging, and illegal fishing practices, pose a significant threat to the marine ecosystem. Palau and its surrounding waters are Micronesia's richest habitat; in 2004 Palau moved to protect the diversity of fish in its waters by culling thousands of the voracious tilapia. Typhoons sometimes cause severe damage to infrastructure.

SPENDING

Not available

CONSUMPTION AND SPENDING

No data

19 per 1000 population

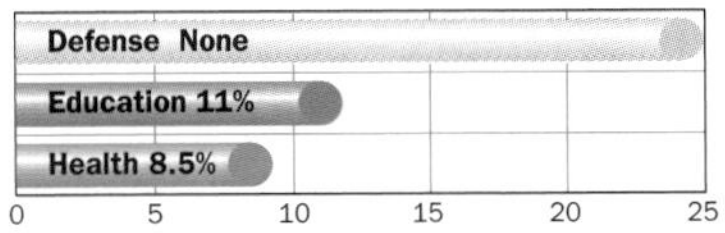
Defense None
Education 11%
Health 8.5%
0
5
10
15
20
25

Defense, Health, Education spending as % of GDP

The gap between rich and poor is growing steadily, as entrepreneurs and government officials exploit aid and develop the tourist industry. In 2001, a program providing cheap rental housing for low-income families received a US grant of $200,000.

PALAU

Total Area : 458 sq. km (177 sq. miles)

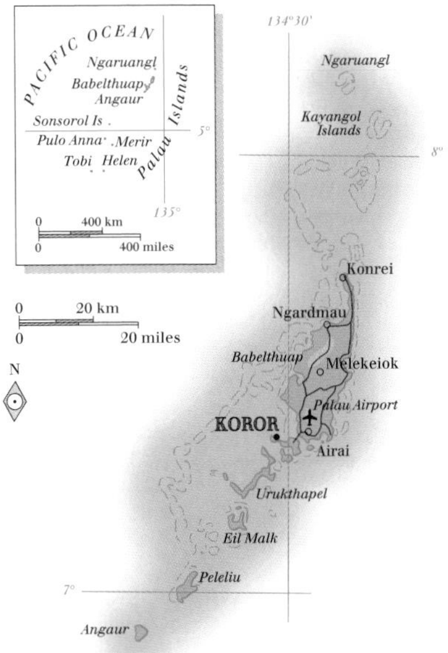
PACIFIC OCEAN
Ngaruangl
Babelthuap
Angaur
Sonsorol Is.
Pulo Anna
Merir
Tobi
Helen
Palau Islands
400 km
400 miles
134°30'
Ngaruangl
Kayangol Islands
Konrei
Ngardmau
Babelthuap
Melekeiok
KOROR
Palau Airport
Airai
Urukthapel
Eil Malk
Peleliu
Angaur
20 km
20 miles
N

MEDIA

TV ownership high

There are no daily newspapers

PUBLISHING AND BROADCAST MEDIA

There are no daily newspapers. *Tia Belau* is published biweekly in English and Palauan

No terrestrial broadcaster

4 stations: 1 government-owned, 3 private

The country's TV and radio stations tend to broadcast material which is largely derived from the US.

CRIME

No death penalty

Palau does not publish prison figures

Little change from year to year

There is a little alcohol-related crime, but most of the country, particularly the outlying islands, is crime-free.

EDUCATION

School leaving age: 14

98%

480 students

Elementary education is compulsory between the ages of six and 14. The Micronesian Occupational College, based in Palau, provides two-year training programs.

WORLD RANKING

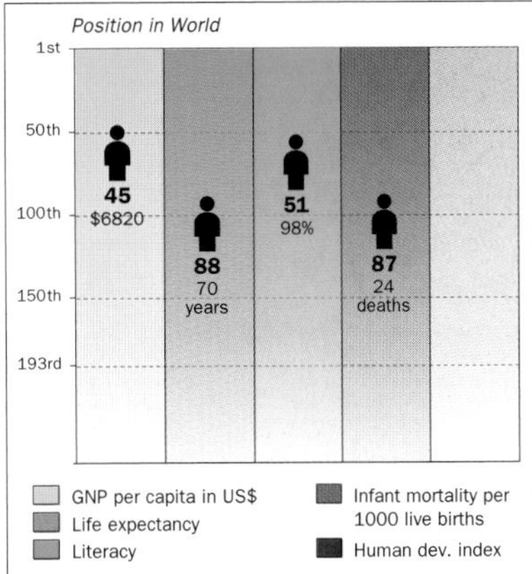
Position in World
1st
50th
100th
150th
193rd
45
$6820
88
70 years
51
98%
87
24 deaths
GNP per capita in US$
Life expectancy
Literacy
Infant mortality per 1000 live births
Human dev. index

P

Panama

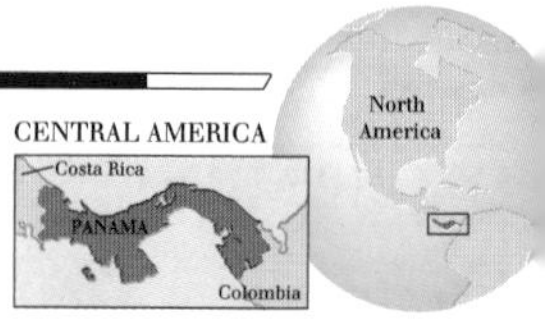
CENTRAL AMERICA
North America
Costa Rica
PANAMA
Colombia

Official Name: Republic of Panama **Capital:** Panama City
Population: 3.1 million **Currency:** Balboa **Official Language:** Spanish

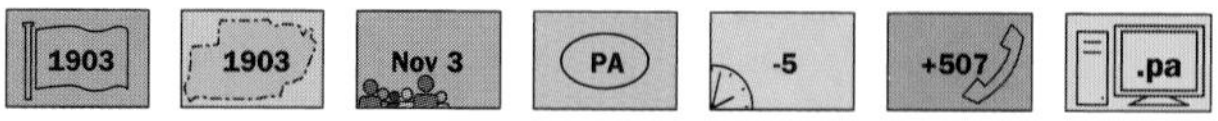
1903
1903
Nov 3
PA
-5
+507
.pa

PANAMA IS THE SOUTHERNMOST of the seven countries occupying the isthmus that joins North and South America. The rainforests of the southeastern Darien region are some of the most pristine left in the Americas. Elected governments have held power since the US invasion of 1989. Panama's traditional economic strength is its banking sector. The US returned control of the Panama Canal Zone to Panama on December 31, 1999.

Cruise liner on the Panama Canal. The Canal shortens the sea route between the east coast of the US and Japan by 4800 km (3000 miles).

CLIMATE

Tropical wet and dry

WEATHER CHART FOR PANAMA CITY

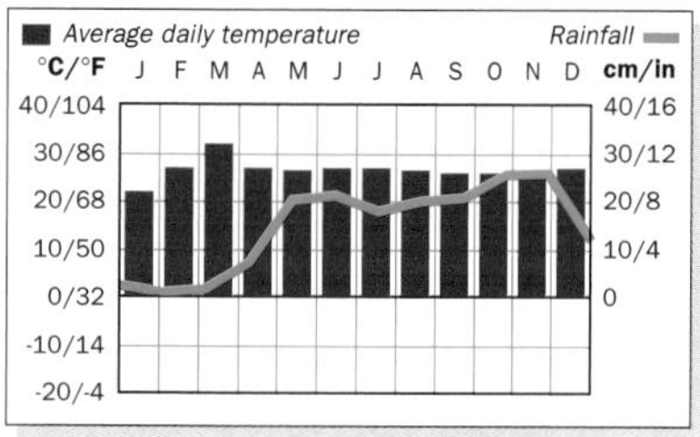
Average daily temperature
Rainfall
°C/°F J F M A M J J A S O N D cm/in
40/104
30/86
20/68
10/50
0/32
-10/14
-20/-4
40/16
30/12
20/8
10/4
0

Panama has a humid tropical climate; rainfall is twice as heavy on the Caribbean coast as on the Pacific coast.

TRANSPORTATION

Drive on right

Tocumen, Panama City 898,000 passengers

6247 ships 125m grt

THE TRANSPORTATION NETWORK

3990 km (2479 miles)

Pan-American Highway: 30 km (19 miles)

355 km (221 miles)

882 km (548 miles)

The 80-km (50-mile) Panama Canal cuts around two weeks off the voyage between the Atlantic and Pacific Oceans. Boats form the most convenient means of transportation for the coastal regions. Many roads are in disrepair.

TOURISM

Visitors : Population 1:5.8

534,000 visitors

Up 3% in 2002

MAIN TOURIST ARRIVALS

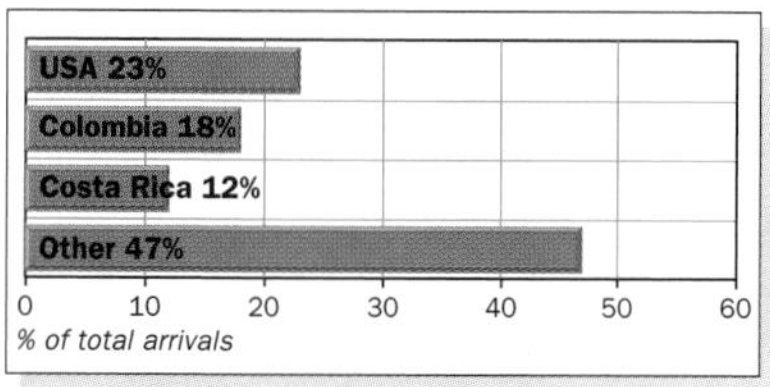
USA 23%
Colombia 18%
Costa Rica 12%
Other 47%
0 10 20 30 40 50 60
% of total arrivals

Portobelo and Panama City have old Spanish colonial buildings. In 2000, new cruise-ship facilities opened in Colón.

PEOPLE

Pop. density low

English Creole, Spanish, Amerindian languages, Chibchan languages

41/km² (106/mi²)

THE URBAN/RURAL POPULATION SPLIT

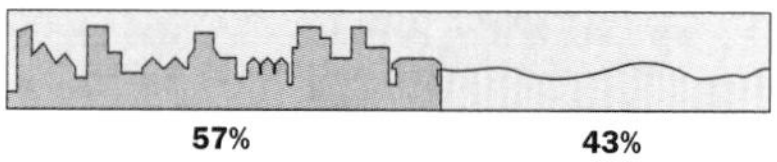
57%
43%

ETHNIC MAKEUP

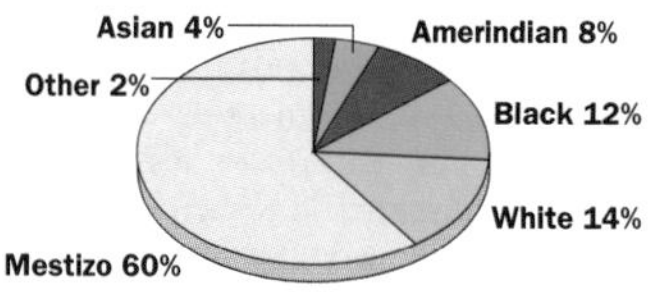
Asian 4%
Amerindian 8%
Other 2%
Black 12%
White 14%
Mestizo 60%

The northwest coast has a large black community, mostly descended from African immigrants who worked the plantations. The majority speak English Creole rather than Spanish. About 8% of the population are Amerindians mainly from the Guaymies, Chocoes, Kunas, and Ngobe-Buglé tribes. Roman Catholicism and the extended family remain strong, though the Canal and the former US military bases have given society a cosmopolitan outlook.

POLITICS

Multiparty elections

2004/2009

President Martin Torrijos

AT THE LAST ELECTION

Legislative Assembly 78 seats

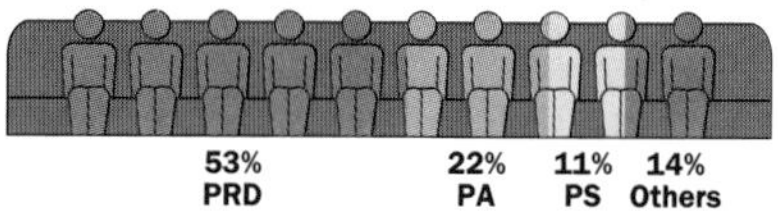
53% PRD
22% PA
11% PS
14% Others

PRD = Democratic Revolutionary Party **PA** = Arnulfist Party
PS = Solidarity Party

In 1989, the US invaded Panama and arrested its ruler, Gen. Manuel Noriega, for narcotics smuggling. US forces installed the compliant Endara government, criticized for corruption. The 1994 presidential and legislative elections were won by the PRD, Noriega's old party, but the new government was largely pro-US and its economic reforms attracted widespread discontent. In May 1999 Mireya Moscoso of the PA was elected Panama's first woman president. Lacking a congressional majority until mid-2002, she struggled to address economic problems and meet promises to help the poor.
In May 2004 the PRD regained the ascendancy with the election of Martin Torrijos, son of the country's former military leader, as president.

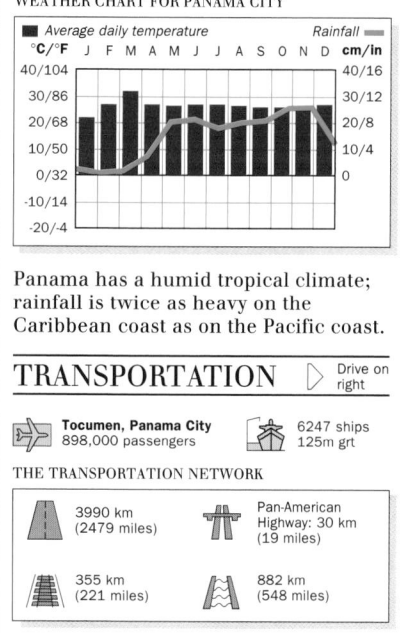

Panama

Total Area : 78 200 sq. km (30 193 sq. miles)

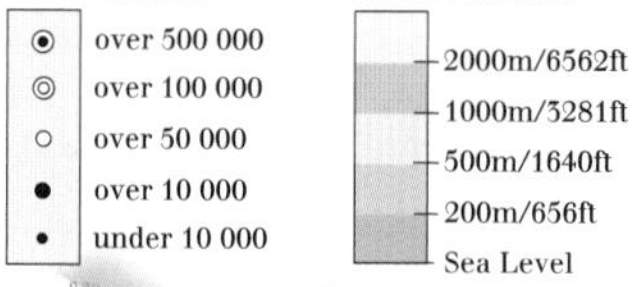
POPULATION
over 500 000
over 100 000
over 50 000
over 10 000
under 10 000
LAND HEIGHT
2000m/6562ft
1000m/3281ft
500m/1640ft
200m/656ft
Sea Level

CARIBBEAN SEA
PACIFIC OCEAN
COSTA RICA
COLOMBIA
Changuinola
Bocas del Toro
Almirante
Laguna de Chiriquí
Golfo de los Mosquitos
Volcán Barú 3475m
Chiriquí Grande
Río Sereno
Volcán
Boquete
La Concepción
David
Pedregal
Puerto Armuelles
Guabalá
Golfo de Chiriquí
Isla de Coiba
Isla Cébaco
Sona
El Tigre de San Lorenzo
Serranía de Tabasará
Santa Fé
Santiago
Divisa
Aguadulce
Bahía de Parita
Penonomé
El Copé
Monagrillo
Chitré
Las Tablas
Pocrí
Península de Azuero
Tonosí
Arenas
Portobelo
Colón
Cristóbal
Lago Gatún
Panama Canal
Alcalde Díaz
Arraiján
La Chorrera
Guadalupe
San Miguelito
Tocumen
PANAMA CITY
Balboa
Bahía de Panamá
Punta Chame
Chepo
El Porvenir
Narganá
Ailigandí
Cordillera de San Blas
Lago Bayano
Archipiélago de las Perlas
Isla del Rey
San Miguel
La Palma
Golfo de San Miguel
Yaviza
Tuira
Serranía del Darién
Golfo de Panamá
Istmo de Panamá
0 50 km
0 50 miles

P

WORLD AFFAIRS

Joined UN in 1945

RG | Geplac | NAM | OAS | San José

The Canal Zone reverted to Panama on December 31, 1999, and US forces vacated their 14 military bases there.

Spillover from the Colombian civil war is a major concern. Border incidents have increased since 1999, and Panama is accused of involvement in arms and narcotics smuggling, and forced repatriations of Colombian refugees.

AID

Recipient

$35m (receipts)

Up 25% in 2002

The IDB pledged $3.3 million in 2000 to rehabilitate a former US base; Japan has loaned $1 million for the project.

DEFENSE

No compulsory military service

$131m

No change in 2002

The National Guard and defense forces were disbanded in 1990 following the 1989 US invasion. They were replaced by the Panamanian Public Force, numbering some 11,800 and comprising the National Police, the National Air Service, and the National Maritime Service.

ECONOMICS

Inflation 1.9% p.a. (1990–2001)

$11.8bn

1 Balboa (1)

SCORE CARD

- World GNP Ranking.........83rd
- GNP per Capita.........$4020
- Balance of Payments.........–$154m
- Inflation.........1%
- Unemployment.........13%

Strengths

Colón Free Trade Zone: second-largest free port in the world. Income from Canal. Financial services. Banana, shrimp exports. Merchant shipping payments for sailing under the Panamanian flag. Tourism potential.

Weaknesses

History of political instability and corruption. Large foreign debt. High unemployment, underemployment. Poor infrastructure.

EXPORTS

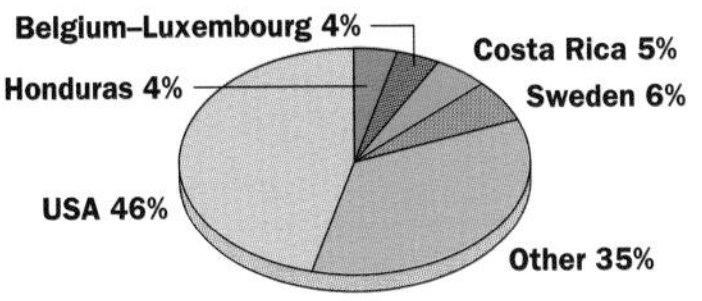
Belgium–Luxembourg 4%
Costa Rica 5%
Honduras 4%
Sweden 6%
USA 46%
Other 35%

IMPORTS

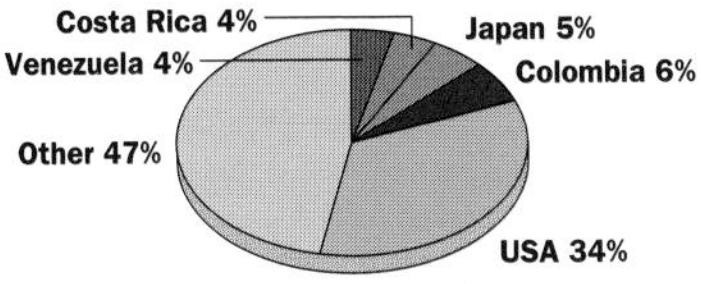
Costa Rica 4%
Japan 5%
Venezuela 4%
Colombia 6%
Other 47%
USA 34%

RESOURCES

Electric power 1.3m kW

237,394 tonnes

Not an oil producer; refines 41,600 b/d

1.55m cattle, 305,000 pigs, 14m chickens

Copper, coal, gold, silver, manganese, salt, clay

The Petaquilla area, west of the Canal, has great copper and gold potential. To reduce the country's dependence on oil imports, the government has stepped up hydroelectric production; four state energy plants were privatized in 1999. Tropical hardwoods are being cut down at an alarming rate.

ENVIRONMENT

Sustainability rank: 17th

22% (2% partially protected)

2.2 tonnes per capita

The destruction of rainforests is proceeding at an increasingly rapid rate, resulting in widespread soil erosion. Large numbers of rare bird and animal species are threatened. Sewage from Panama City and Colón is discharged directly into coastal waters, canals, and ditches. Stretches of mangrove swamps are cut down for urban development, shrimp farms, and resorts.

MEDIA

TV ownership medium

Daily newspaper circulation 62 per 1000 people

PUBLISHING AND BROADCAST MEDIA

There are 8 daily newspapers, including *La Prensa* and *La Estrella de Panamá*

7 independent services

1 state-owned service, over 200 independent stations

A more independent press has flourished since Noriega's overthrow. Radio reaches the greatest number.

CRIME

No death penalty

10,630 prisoners

Crime is rising

Panama City and Colón have high crime levels. Money laundering, narcotics trafficking, and corruption are rife.

EDUCATION

School leaving age: 11

92%

89,352 students

Schooling is based on the US model; the system is free. The first of the four universities was founded in 1935.

CHRONOLOGY

On independence from Spain in 1821, Panama was incorporated into Gran Colombia. Panama gained independence from Colombia with US support in 1903.

- **1903** US buys Canal concession.
- **1914–1939** Canal opens to traffic. US protectorate status ended.
- **1968–1981** Rule of Col. Torrijos Herrera.
- **1989** Indicted narcotics trafficker Gen. Noriega annuls elections to retain power. US invasion.
- **1994** PRD wins presidency and is largest party in parliament.
- **1999** PA's Mireya Moscoso elected first woman president. Canal Zone reverts to Panama.
- **2004** Martin Torrijos of the PRD elected president.

HEALTH

Welfare state health benefits

1 per 588 people

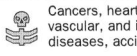

Cancers, heart, cerebro-vascular, and infectious diseases, accidents

The US provides about 80% of medical equipment. In 1998 the government embarked on a project to reform health care with the help of World Bank funds.

SPENDING

GDP/cap. increase

CONSUMPTION AND SPENDING

108 per 1000 population

122 per 1000 population

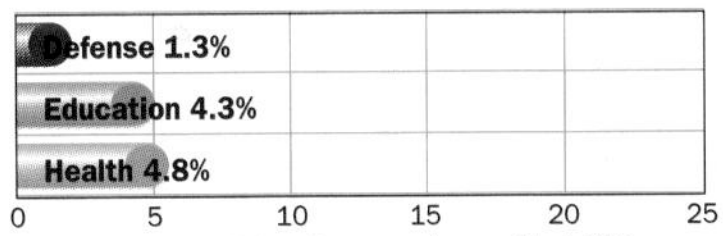
Defense 1.3%
Education 4.3%
Health 4.8%
0
5
10
15
20
25

Defense, Health, Education spending as % of GDP

Wealth disparities are large. Almost 30% of the population are estimated to live below the poverty line – clustered in the cities rather than in rural areas.

WORLD RANKING

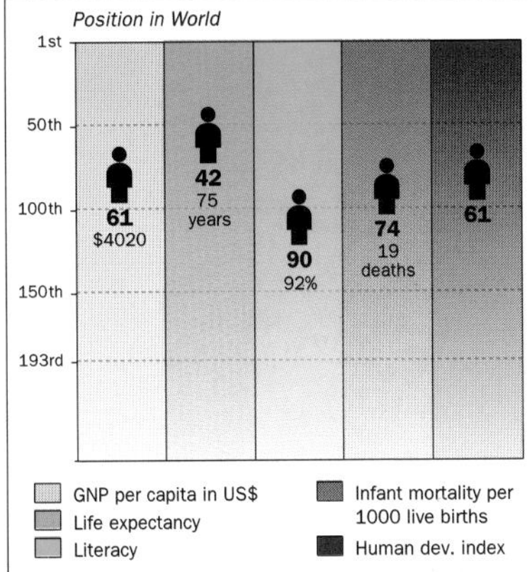
Position in World
1st
50th
100th
150th
193rd
61
$4020
42
75 years
90
92%
74
19 deaths
61
GNP per capita in US$
Life expectancy
Literacy
Infant mortality per 1000 live births
Human dev. index

P

PAPUA NEW GUINEA

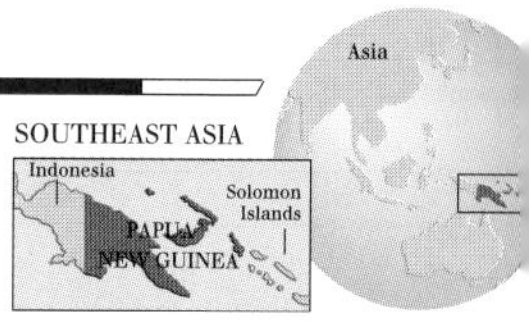

Asia
SOUTHEAST ASIA
Indonesia
Solomon Islands
PAPUA NEW GUINEA

OFFICIAL NAME: Independent State of Papua New Guinea **CAPITAL:** Port Moresby
POPULATION: 5.7 million **CURRENCY:** Kina **OFFICIAL LANGUAGE:** English

1975 | 1975 | Sept 16 | PNG | +10 | +675 | .pg

THE MOST LINGUISTICALLY diverse country in the world, with approximately 750 languages, Papua New Guinea (PNG) achieved independence from Australia in 1975. It occupies the eastern end of New Guinea, the world's third-largest island, and several other groups of islands. Much of the country is still isolated, and in rural areas living conditions are often basic. Bougainville has been promised autonomy.

CLIMATE

Tropical equatorial/monsoon

WEATHER CHART FOR PORT MORESBY

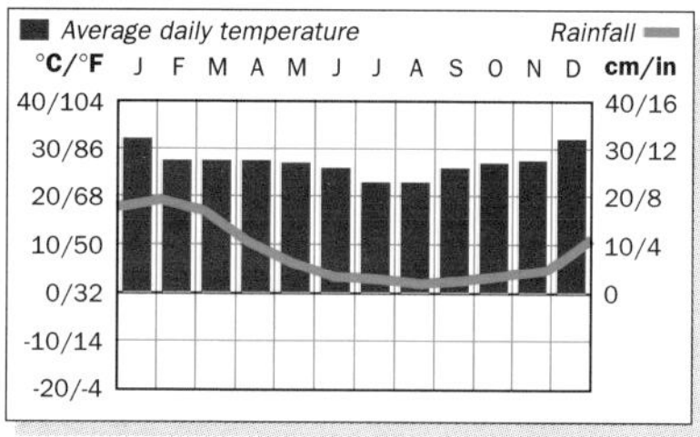

Average daily temperature
Rainfall
°C/°F J F M A M J J A S O N D cm/in
40/104 40/16
30/86 30/12
20/68 20/8
10/50 10/4
0/32 0
-10/14
-20/-4

Unvaryingly hot lowlands contrast with snow on Mount Victoria. Severe weather followed El Niño of 1997–1998.

TRANSPORTATION

Drive on left

Jacksons, Port Moresby 745,000 passengers

111 ships 72,400 grt

THE TRANSPORTATION NETWORK

784 km (487 miles)	Highlands Highway
None	10,940 km (6798 miles)

Flood damage in 2004 to the poorly maintained Highlands Highway cut off fuel deliveries to several regions.

Papua New Guinea's 600 or so outer islands are mainly mountainous and volcanic, with lush vegetation and fringing coral reefs.

TOURISM

Visitors : Population 1:106

54,000 visitors

Little change in 2002

MAIN TOURIST ARRIVALS

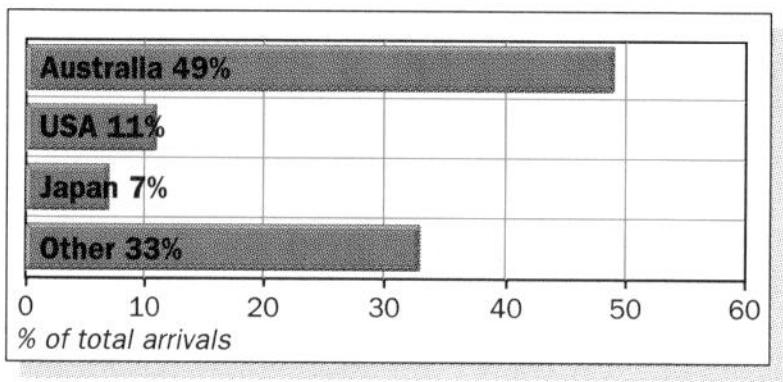

Australia 49%
USA 11%
Japan 7%
Other 33%
0 10 20 30 40 50 60
% of total arrivals

Tourism has great potential, but is hampered by lack of infrastructure and high rates of poverty-related violent crime, particularly in urban centers.

PEOPLE

Pop. density low

Pidgin English, Papuan, English, Motu, 750 (est.) native languages

13/km² (33/mi²)

THE URBAN/RURAL POPULATION SPLIT

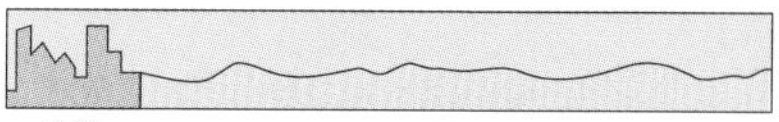

18%
82%

RELIGIOUS PERSUASION

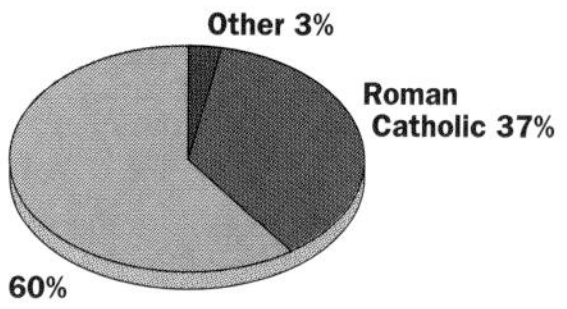

Other 3%
Roman Catholic 37%
Protestant 60%

PNG has an extraordinary diversity of peoples, with around 750 different languages and even more tribes. The key distinction is between lowlanders, who have frequent contact with the outside world, and the very isolated highlanders. Highland tribes see all strangers as potentially hostile. Vendettas can last for generations and tribal battles are not infrequent. A majority of people are nominally Christian, but indigenous beliefs and practices are widespread.

POLITICS

Multiparty elections

2002/2007

H.M. Queen Elizabeth II

AT THE LAST ELECTION

National Parliament 109 seats

5% PAP
17% NAP
16% Ind
11% PDM
7% PPP
6% V
6% PP
32% Others

NAP = National Alliance Party **Ind** = Independents
PDM = People's Democratic Movement
PPP = People's Progress Party **V** = Vacant
PP = Pangu Pati **PAP** = People's Action Party

The many parties lack clear ideological foundations, creating long-term political instability. The patronage required to maintain coalitions breeds corruption. A PDM-led government worked to overhaul the system, and claimed the first simple majority in 2001. However, the party was overshadowed in the 2002 elections by the NAP. Veteran NAP leader Sir Michael Somare returned as prime minister.

A ten-year insurgency by separatists on Bougainville ended with a 1998 cease-fire. Autonomy has been promised, along with a future referendum on independence. Elsewhere, strong local traditions and communications problems have made centralization difficult.

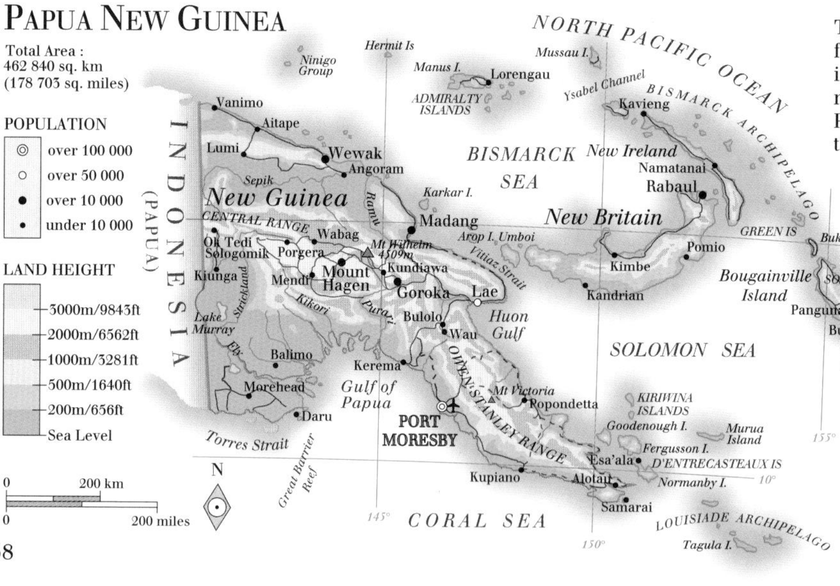

PAPUA NEW GUINEA
Total Area : 462 840 sq. km (178 703 sq. miles)
POPULATION
over 100 000
over 50 000
over 10 000
under 10 000
LAND HEIGHT
3000m/9843ft
2000m/6562ft
1000m/3281ft
500m/1640ft
200m/656ft
Sea Level
0 200 km
0 200 miles
N
NORTH PACIFIC OCEAN
BISMARCK ARCHIPELAGO
BISMARCK SEA
INDONESIA (PAPUA)
New Guinea
New Britain
New Ireland
Bougainville Island
SOLOMON SEA
CORAL SEA
Gulf of Papua
Huon Gulf
Torres Strait
Great Barrier Reef
Ninigo Group
Hermit Is
Manus I.
Mussau I.
Lorengau
ADMIRALTY ISLANDS
Ysabel Channel
Kavieng
Namatanai
Rabaul
Vanimo
Aitape
Lumi
Wewak
Angoram
Sepik
Ramu
Karkar I.
Madang
CENTRAL RANGE
Ok Tedi
Sologomik
Porgera
Wabag
Mt Wilhelm 4509m
Arop I.
Umboi
Vitiaz Strait
Mount Hagen
Kundiawa
Kiunga
Mendi
Goroka
Lae
Kimbe
Kandrian
Pomio
GREEN IS
Buka I.
SOLOMON IS
Arawa
Kieta
Panguna
Buin
Lake Murray
Strickland
Kikori
Purari
Bulolo
Wau
Fly
Balimo
Kerema
Morehead
Daru
Mt Victoria
Popondetta
OWEN STANLEY RANGE
PORT MORESBY
KIRIWINA ISLANDS
Goodenough I.
Murua Island
Fergusson I.
D'ENTRECASTEAUX IS
Esa'ala
Normanby I.
Alotau
Samarai
Kupiano
LOUISIADE ARCHIPELAGO
Tagula I.
145°
150°
155°
5°
10°

WORLD AFFAIRS

Joined UN in 1975

APEC | Comm | NAM | PC | PIF

Australia provides help to fight crime and corruption in PNG, a focus of its regional economic and security interests. Allegations of PNG support for separatists in Papua, the neighboring Indonesian province, have strained relations.

AID

Recipient

$203m (receipts) | Little change in 2002

Australia is the major aid donor. The World Bank has suspended several projects over allegations of corruption.

DEFENSE

No compulsory military service

$13m | Down 50% in 2002

The army has expressed its doubts over political and economic reforms, most recently in a mutiny in March 2001.

ECONOMICS

Inflation 7.3% p.a. (1990–2001)

$2.84bn | 3.170 kina (3.497)

SCORE CARD

❑ WORLD GNP RANKING	133rd
❑ GNP PER CAPITA	$530
BALANCE OF PAYMENTS	$286m
❑ INFLATION	11.8%
❑ UNEMPLOYMENT	8%

STRENGTHS
Significant copper, gold, nickel, cobalt, oil, and natural gas reserves. Proposed gas pipeline between highlands and Australia expected to net $219 million a year. Agriculture sustains population.

WEAKNESSES
Agricultural production and mining prone to disruption from occasional drought. High spending: government close to bankruptcy in 2002.
Poor transportation and banking infrastructures. Political instability. Foreign exploitation of resources.

EXPORTS

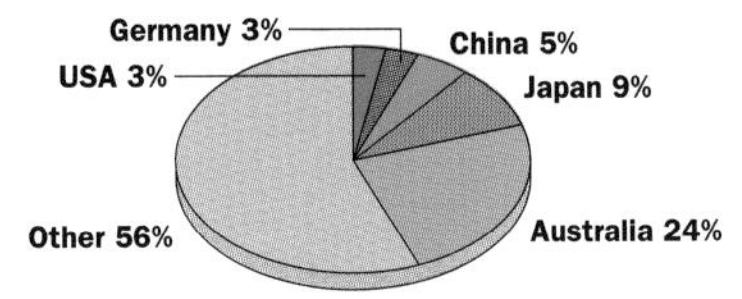
Germany 3%
China 5%
USA 3%
Japan 9%
Other 56%
Australia 24%

IMPORTS

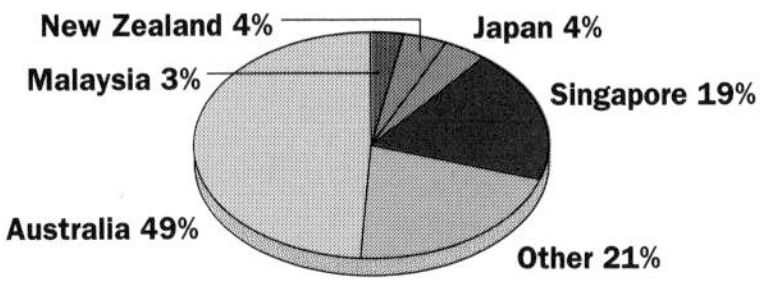
New Zealand 4%
Japan 4%
Malaysia 3%
Singapore 19%
Australia 49%
Other 21%

RESOURCES

Electric power 543,000 kW

122,434 tonnes | 49,000 b/d (reserves 400m barrels)

1.8m pigs, 90,000 cattle, 3.9m chickens | Copper, gold, silver, natural gas, nickel, chromite, cobalt, oil

PNG is rich in minerals. The Ok Tedi gold/copper mine in the Star Mountains is the most productive in the country; the Porgera gold mine is one of the world's largest, though tensions over land ownership could endanger its future. Prospecting has revealed extensive oil and natural gas reserves.

ENVIRONMENT

Sustainability rank: 51st

2% partially protected | 0.5 tonnes per capita

Deforestation and heavy-metal pollution are major issues. Cyanide poisoning from an Australian-owned mine in 2000 caused serious water pollution. Subduction of continental plates has forced the relocation of thousands of people from the more low-lying islands.

MEDIA

TV ownership low

Daily newspaper circulation 14 per 1000 people

PUBLISHING AND BROADCAST MEDIA

There are 2 daily newspapers, the *National* and the *Papua New Guinea Post-Courier*

1 independent service | 3 services: 2 state- or partly state-owned, 1 independent

In 2003, the government shelved a bill that would have led to restrictions on the freedom of journalists to criticize the government.

CRIME

Death penalty not used in practice

3302 prisoners | Down 6% in 2000

Violent crime by gangs of "Rascals" is very common. A cultural tradition of vendettas persists in rural communities.

EDUCATION

Schooling is not compulsory

65% | 9859 students

Education is not compulsory. Equipment charges and fees have been introduced. Universities are suffering funding cuts.

HEALTH

Welfare state health benefits

1 per 10,000 people | Malaria, pneumonia, diarrheal diseases, tuberculosis

The health system has suffered from recent cuts. HIV and tuberculosis co-infections are at crisis level. Life expectancy rates are among the lowest in the Pacific. Access to clean water and sanitation are major issues.

CHRONOLOGY

The British annexed the southeast and the Germans the northeast of the island of New Guinea in 1884.

- ❑ **1904** Australia takes over British sector; renamed Papua in 1906.
- ❑ **1914** German sector occupied by Australia.
- ❑ **1942–1945** Japanese occupation.
- ❑ **1964** National Parliament created.
- ❑ **1971** Renamed Papua New Guinea.
- ❑ **1975** Independence under Michael Somare, leader since 1972.
- ❑ **1988** Bougainville Revolutionary Army begins guerrilla campaign.
- ❑ **1997** El Niño causes severe drought and tsunamis. Prime Minister Julius Chan resigns over use of Western-led mercenaries in Bougainville.
- ❑ **2000** Loloata Understanding promises autonomy for Bougainville.
- ❑ **2001** PDM claims parliamentary majority. Final peace accord with Bougainville ratified after three-year cease-fire.
- ❑ **2002** NAP wins elections. Somare returns as prime minister.

SPENDING

GDP/cap. increase

CONSUMPTION AND SPENDING

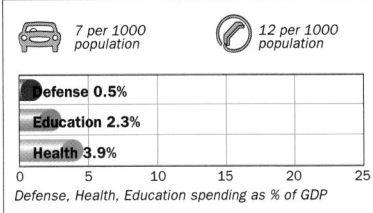

7 per 1000 population | *12 per 1000 population*

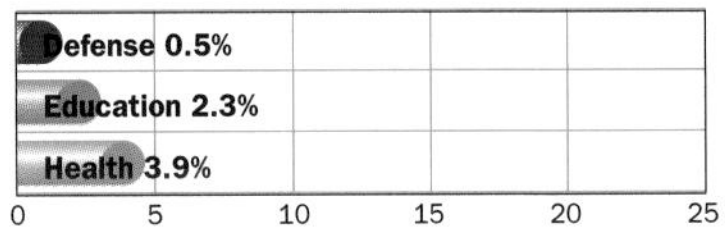
Defense 0.5%
Education 2.3%
Health 3.9%
0
5
10
15
20
25

Defense, Health, Education spending as % of GDP

There is a growing gap between rich and poor, particularly in urban areas. Spending on education and health was cut in 1998, when the kina dropped in value, but it was increased again in 2000, and the 2002 budget proposed the reintroduction of free schooling.

WORLD RANKING

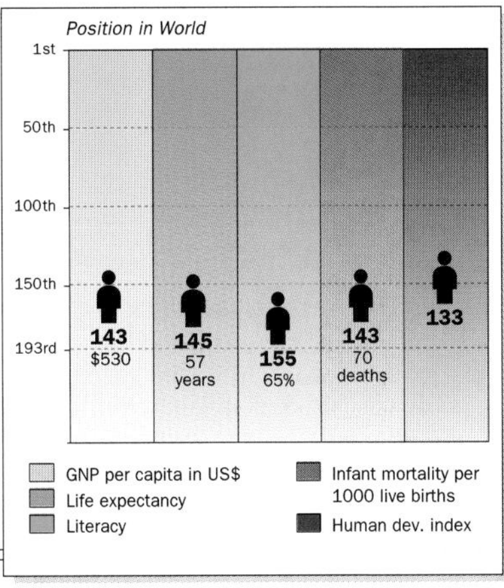
Position in World
1st
50th
100th
150th
193rd
143
$530
145
57 years
155
65%
143
70 deaths
133
GNP per capita in US$
Life expectancy
Literacy
Infant mortality per 1000 live births
Human dev. index

P

PARAGUAY

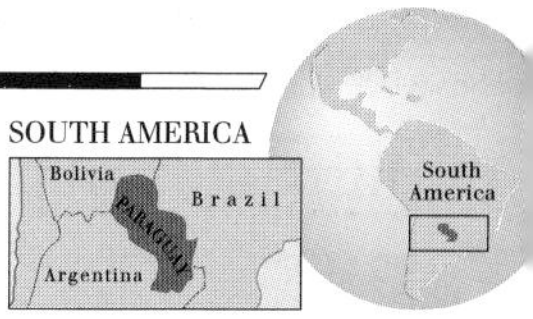
SOUTH AMERICA
Bolivia
Brazil
Argentina
PARAGUAY
South America

OFFICIAL NAME: Republic of Paraguay **CAPITAL:** Asunción
POPULATION: 5.9 million **CURRENCY:** Guaraní **OFFICIAL LANGUAGE:** Spanish

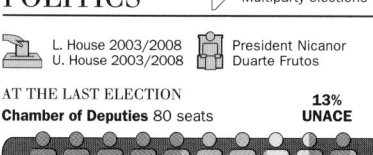

1811 | 1938 | May 14 | PY | -4 | +595 | .py

LANDLOCKED IN SOUTH America and a Spanish possession until 1811, Paraguay gained large tracts of land from Bolivia in 1938. The Paraguay River divides the eastern hills and fertile plains, where 90% of people live, from the almost uninhabited Chaco in the west. Paraguay's economy is largely agricultural. Periods of anarchy and military rule followed until the overthrow in 1989 of Gen. Alfredo Stroessner, South America's longest-ruling dictator.

CLIMATE

Tropical/subtropical

WEATHER CHART FOR ASUNCIÓN

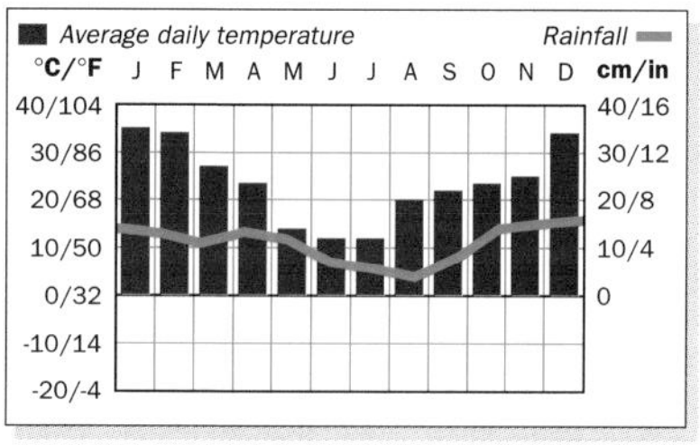
Average daily temperature
Rainfall
°C/°F J F M A M J J A S O N D cm/in
40/104
30/86
20/68
10/50
0/32
-10/14
-20/-4
40/16
30/12
20/8
10/4
0

Paraguay is subtropical, with all parts experiencing floods and droughts, but the Chaco is generally drier and hotter.

TRANSPORTATION

Drive on right

Silvio Pettirossi, Asunción 465,664 passengers

46 ships 47,500 grt

THE TRANSPORTATION NETWORK

15,045 km (9349 miles)

Pan-American Highway: 700 km (435 miles)

441 km (274 miles)

3100 km (1926 miles)

Roads serving the main cities are in good condition. Rail services are largely provided by elderly steam trains.

TOURISM

Visitors : Population 1:22

267,750 visitors

Up 7% in 2003

MAIN TOURIST ARRIVALS

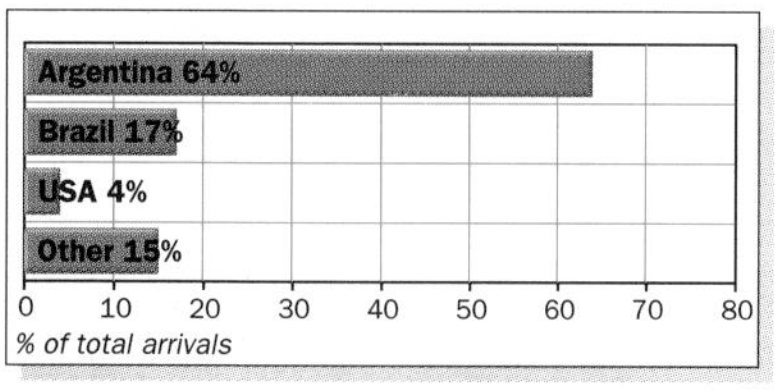
Argentina 64%
Brazil 17%
USA 4%
Other 15%
0 10 20 30 40 50 60 70 80
% of total arrivals

Tourist numbers are small. Most visitors are cross-border day-trippers from Brazil and Argentina, who flock to Ciudad del Este to buy cheap, mainly Far Eastern, electrical goods. The Chaco attracts tourists for safaris.

PEOPLE

Pop. density low

Guaraní, Spanish, German

15/km² (38/mi²)

THE URBAN/RURAL POPULATION SPLIT

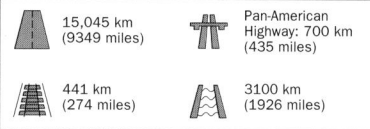

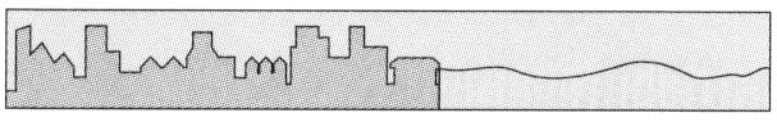
57%
43%

ETHNIC MAKEUP

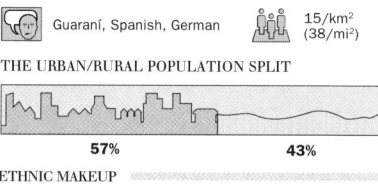

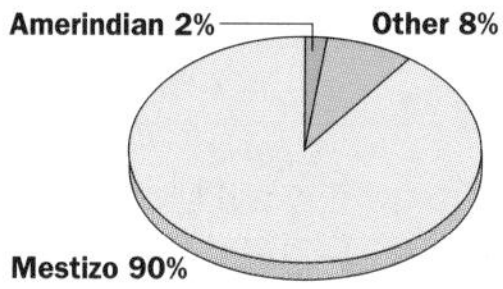
Amerindian 2%
Other 8%
Mestizo 90%

Most Paraguayans are of combined Spanish and native Guaraní origin. The majority are bilingual, though outside the large cities Guaraní is spoken almost exclusively. Rural Guaraní, deprived of ancestral lands, have been forced into marginal labor and prostitution. While most immigrants historically have been European, recent arrivals have also come from Japan, Korea, and South Africa.

POLITICS

Multiparty elections

L. House 2003/2008
U. House 2003/2008

President Nicanor Duarte Frutos

AT THE LAST ELECTION

Chamber of Deputies 80 seats

13% UNACE
46% ANR–PC
26% PLRA
13% MPQ
2% PPS

ANR–PC = National Republican Association–Colorado Party **PLRA** = Authentic Radical Liberal Party **MPQ** = Beloved Fatherland Movement **UNACE** = National Union of Ethical Citizens **PPS** = Party of a United Country **PEN** = National Encounter Party

Senate 45 seats

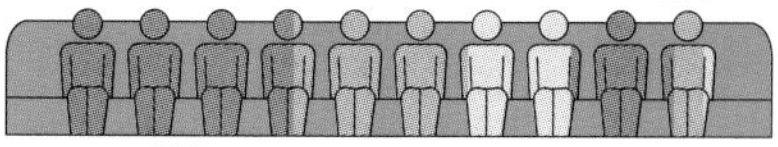
4% PPS
36% ANR–PC
26% PLRA
16% MPQ
16% UNACE
2% PEN

Gen. Stroessner, dictator since 1954, was overthrown in a 1989 coup. In 1993, his PC won the first free elections in 60 years, but with continued reliance on the military. Former army chief Gen. Lino Oviedo was pivotal to the country's instability, leading three failed coups between 1993 and 2000. He went into exile in 1999 after the assassination of his main opponent in the PC, Vice President Luis Argaña. President Luis Gonzalez Macchi's personal unpopularity failed to undermine the PC, whose candidate Nicanor Duarte Frutos won the presidency in 2003. Oviedo returned to Paraguay in 2004, intending to clear his name in order to stand in the 2008 presidential election, and was arrested on arrival.

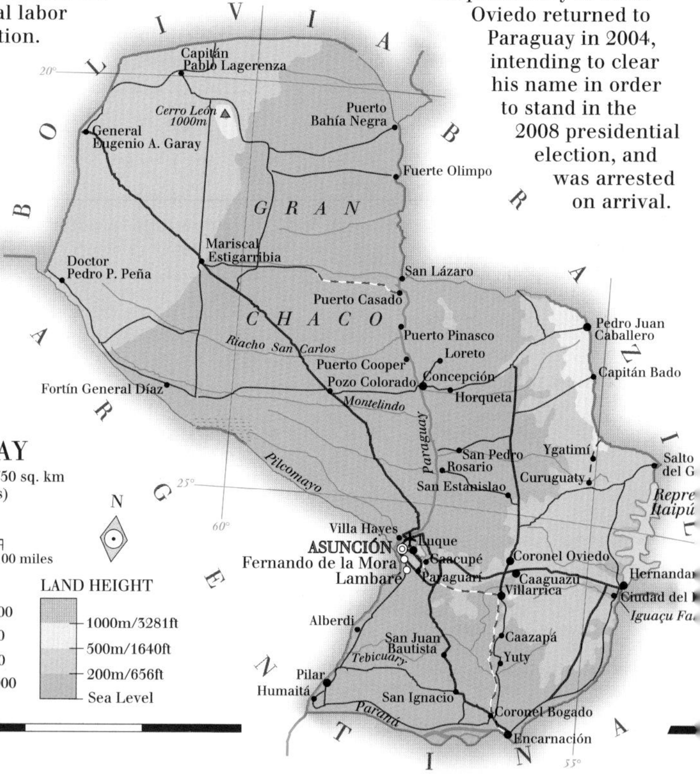
BOLIVIA
BRAZIL
ARGENTINA
GRAN CHACO
Capitán Pablo Lagerenza
Cerro León 1000m
General Eugenio A. Garay
Puerto Bahía Negra
Fuerte Olimpo
Mariscal Estigarribia
Doctor Pedro P. Peña
San Lázaro
Puerto Casado
Puerto Pinasco
Loreto
Riacho San Carlos
Puerto Cooper
Pozo Colorado
Concepción
Horqueta
Fortín General Díaz
Montelindo
Pilcomayo
Paraguay
Pedro Juan Caballero
Capitán Bado
San Pedro
Rosario
San Estanislao
Ygatimí
Curuguaty
Salto del G
Repre Itaipú
Villa Hayes
ASUNCIÓN
Luque
Fernando de la Mora
Lambaré
Capiatá
Areguá
Paraguarí
Coronel Oviedo
Caaguazú
Villarrica
Hernandar
Ciudad del
Iguaçu Fa
Alberdi
San Juan Bautista
Tebicuary
Caazapá
Yuty
Pilar
Humaitá
San Ignacio
Paraná
Coronel Bogado
Encarnación
20°
25°
60°
55°
N

PARAGUAY
Total Area : 406 750 sq. km (157 046 sq. miles)

0 100 km
0 100 miles

POPULATION
- over 100 000
- over 50 000
- over 10 000
- under 10 000

LAND HEIGHT
- 1000m/3281ft
- 500m/1640ft
- 200m/656ft
- Sea Level

P

WORLD AFFAIRS

Joined UN in 1945

IBRD | IAEA | Geplac | Mercosr | RG

The main aims are fairer integration in the Mercosur common market and good relations with the US.

AID

Recipient

$57m (receipts)

Down 7% in 2002

Japan offers most development aid; the IMF provides conditional loans. NGOs run small programs in rural areas.

DEFENSE

Compulsory military service

$54m

Down 29% in 2002

Under Stroessner, the military controlled political and economic life. In 1994–1995, Congress tried to limit its powers, but President Juan Carlos Wasmosy endorsed its political and institutional role. The pact between the military and the PC, in power since 1947, has been weakened by factionalism.

ECONOMICS

Inflation 12% p.a. (1990–2001)

$6.43bn

5920 guaraníes (6200)

SCORE CARD

❑ WORLD GNP RANKING	103rd
❑ GNP PER CAPITA	$1170
❑ BALANCE OF PAYMENTS	$294m
❑ INFLATION	10.5%
❑ UNEMPLOYMENT	16%

STRENGTHS

Electricity exporter – earnings obtain foreign exchange. Self-sufficiency in wheat and other staple foodstuffs. Oilseeds, notably soybeans, and cotton.

WEAKNESSES

Overreliance on agriculture and shaky Brazilian and Argentinian markets. No hydrocarbons produced. Weak banking and financial sectors. High unemployment. Political instability deters foreign investment.

EXPORTS

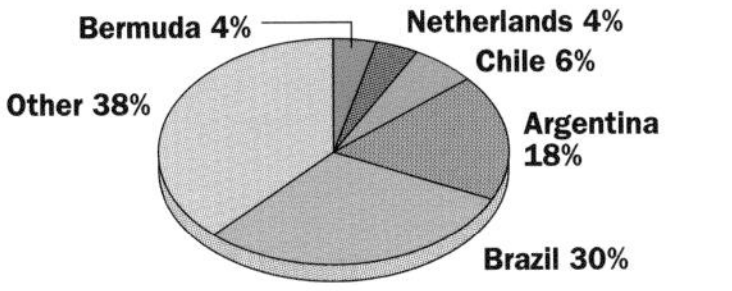
Bermuda 4%
Netherlands 4%
Chile 6%
Other 38%
Argentina 18%
Brazil 30%

IMPORTS

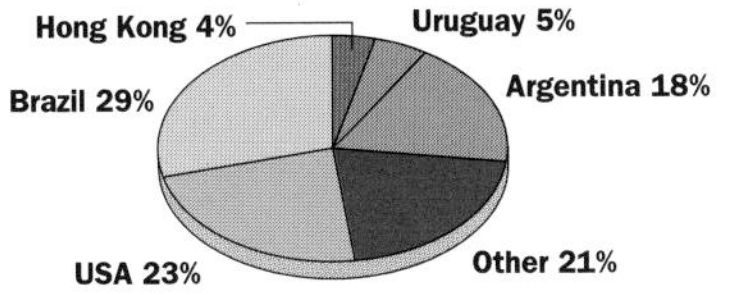
Hong Kong 4%
Uruguay 5%
Brazil 29%
Argentina 18%
USA 23%
Other 21%

The Iguaçu Falls, on the border with Brazil and Argentina, comprise over 20 cataracts, separated by rocks and tree-covered islands.

RESOURCES

Electric power 8.1m kW

25,110 tonnes

Not an oil producer; refines 2000 b/d

8.81m cattle, 3.25m pigs, 725,000 ducks, 15.6m chickens

Gypsum, marble, clay, kaolin, iron, manganese, uranium

The joint Paraguay–Brazil Itaipú hydroelectric dam is the world's second-largest. The massive Yacyretá Dam is operated with Argentina.

ENVIRONMENT

Sustainability rank: 25th

4% (0.1% partially protected)

0.7 tonnes per capita

Apart from the destruction of forests for farming and for dams, a major ecological worry is the smuggling abroad of endangered species.

MEDIA

TV ownership medium

Daily newspaper circulation 43 per 1000 people

PUBLISHING AND BROADCAST MEDIA

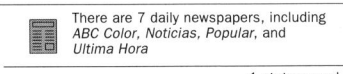

There are 7 daily newspapers, including *ABC Color*, *Noticias*, *Popular*, and *Ultima Hora*

4 independent services

1 state-owned service, many independent stations

The media, historically sponsored by political parties, flourished after the fall of Stroessner, publishing details of corruption and abuses of human rights. The constitution in theory protects the rights of columnists to air their views.

CRIME

No death penalty

3373 prisoners

Up 10% in 2000–2001

Paraguay is the contraband capital of Latin America, with trade in everything from cars to cocaine. Jungle airstrips near Brazil provide a route for narcotics.

EDUCATION

School leaving age: 15

92%

83,041 students

The state-run National University of Asunción has 25,000 students; there are many private universities. Since 1994, teaching Guaraní has been mandatory.

CHRONOLOGY

Paraguay was controlled by Spain from 1536 until 1811.

- ❑ **1864–1870** War of Triple Alliance against Argentina, Uruguay, and Brazil kills over half the population.
- ❑ **1928–1935** Two Chaco Wars against Bolivia over disputed territory.
- ❑ **1938** Boundary with Bolivia fixed; Paraguay awarded large tracts.
- ❑ **1954–1989** Rule of Gen. Stroessner: repressive military regime.
- ❑ **1993** First democratic elections.
- ❑ **1993–2000** Three coup attempts by Gen. Lino Oviedo.
- ❑ **1998–1999** Raúl Cubas elected president; resigns after assassination of vice president; Cubas and Oviedo leave country.
- ❑ **2003** Nicanor Duarte Frutos of PC wins presidency.

HEALTH

Welfare state health benefits

1 per 909 people

Cerebrovascular and heart diseases, cancers, infectious diseases

The current government has pledged to address health care provision, which is fragmented and often expensive.

SPENDING

GDP/cap. increase

CONSUMPTION AND SPENDING

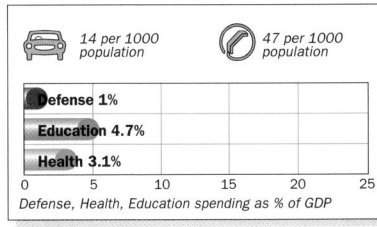

14 per 1000 population

47 per 1000 population

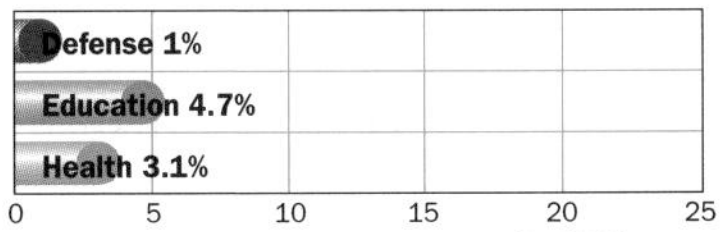
Defense 1%
Education 4.7%
Health 3.1%
0
5
10
15
20
25

Defense, Health, Education spending as % of GDP

Income inequality is great and rural poverty serious. Senior military officers, business leaders, and the country's landed elite control wealth.

WORLD RANKING

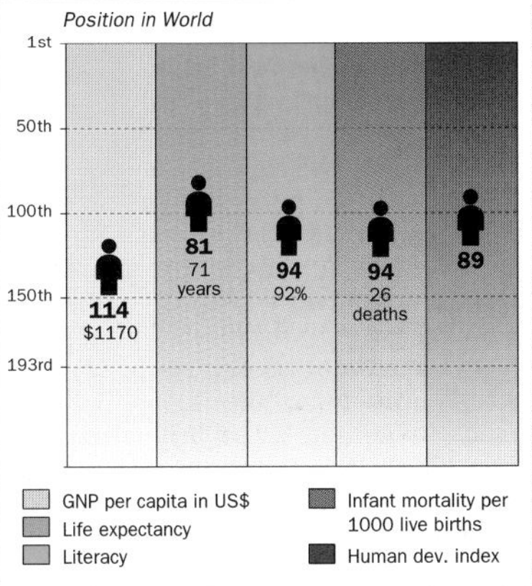
Position in World
1st
50th
100th
150th
193rd
114
$1170
81
71 years
94
92%
94
26 deaths
89
GNP per capita in US$
Life expectancy
Literacy
Infant mortality per 1000 live births
Human dev. index

P

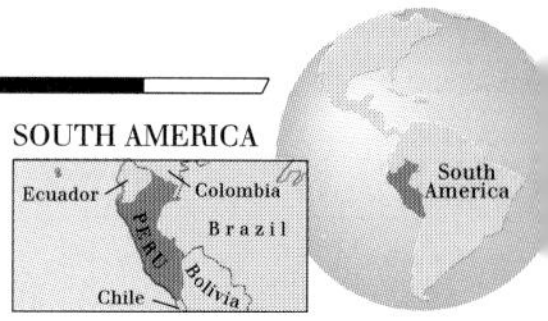
SOUTH AMERICA
Ecuador
Colombia
Brazil
PERU
Bolivia
Chile
South America

PERU

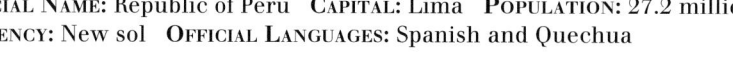

OFFICIAL NAME: Republic of Peru **CAPITAL:** Lima **POPULATION:** 27.2 million
CURRENCY: New sol **OFFICIAL LANGUAGES:** Spanish and Quechua

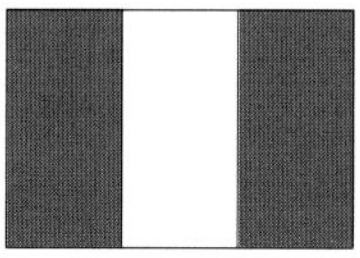

1824
1941
July 28
PE
-5
+51
.pe

LYING JUST SOUTH of the equator, on the Pacific coast of South America, Peru became independent of Spain in 1824. It rises from an arid coastal strip to the Andes, dominated in the south by volcanoes, then descending into the Amazon Basin. About half of Peru's population live in mountain regions. Peru's border with Bolivia to the south runs through Lake Titicaca, the highest navigable lake in the world. Alejandro Toledo became the first Amerindian president in 2001, but his popularity fell rapidly.

CLIMATE

Tropical/mountain/desert

WEATHER CHART FOR LIMA

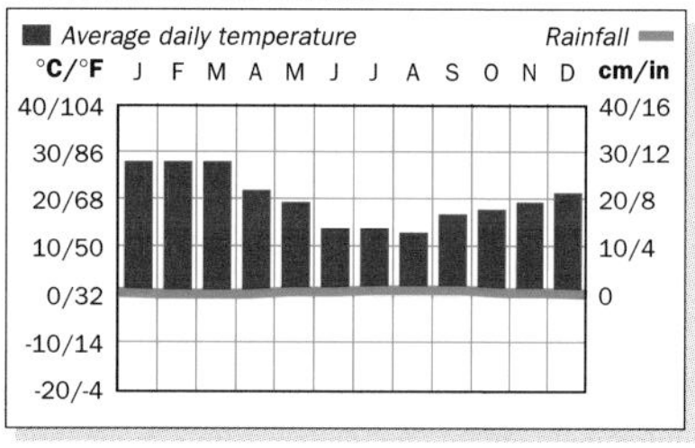
Average daily temperature
Rainfall
°C/°F J F M A M J J A S O N D cm/in
40/104
30/86
20/68
10/50
0/32
-10/14
-20/-4
40/16
30/12
20/8
10/4
0

Peru has several distinct climatic regions. The arid or desert coastal region experiences the *garúa*, persistent low cloud and fog, giving Lima cool winters even though it is close to the equator. The temperate slopes of the Andes have large daily temperature ranges and a rainy season in December–March, while parts of the Amazon Basin receive rain all year.

TRANSPORTATION

Drive on right

Jorge Chávez International, Lima
4.54m passengers

719 ships
240,300 grt

THE TRANSPORTATION NETWORK

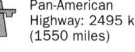

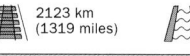

- 9477 km (5889 miles)
- Pan-American Highway: 2495 km (1550 miles)
- 2123 km (1319 miles)
- 8808 km (5473 miles)

Most roads remain unpaved. Work on a transcontinental highway from Ilo, a Pacific free port, via Puerto Suárez in Bolivia, to the port of Portos in Brazil is ongoing. The two rail networks, the Central and Southern, are as yet unconnected. The La Oroya–Huancayo line is the world's highest standard-gauge track. River transportation is important in Amazonia. Jorge Chávez airport is a major regional hub. There are also more than 200 small airstrips across the country. The largest airline, Aero Continente, was briefly grounded in 2004 after its owners were linked to the narcotics trade.

Spanish colonial church *near the Urubamba River. This area was known to the Incas as the Sacred Valley.*

TOURISM

Visitors : Population 1:29

933,550 visitors

Up 8% in 2003

MAIN TOURIST ARRIVALS

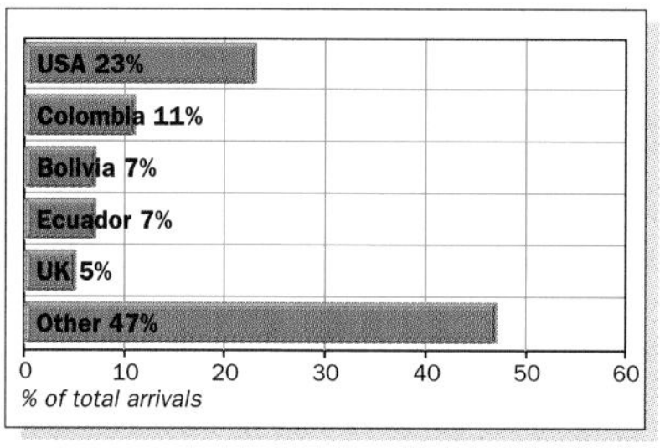
USA 23%
Colombia 11%
Bolivia 7%
Ecuador 7%
UK 5%
Other 47%
0 10 20 30 40 50 60
% of total arrivals

Tourism is gradually recovering after being plunged into crisis in the early 1990s by guerrilla activity, high crime rates, and outbreaks of cholera. The heavily indebted industry has been unable to take full advantage of new investment opportunities, but privatization programs have seen the sale of state hotels. Visitors come to see incomparable sites such as the Inca ruins at Machu Picchu in the Andes. The Nazca lines, patterns and drawings in the desert made by the Nazca people (200 BCE to 700 CE), are also a major attraction. Tourism to the Amazon is growing, but environmentalists are concerned about the impact on indigenous peoples. The Spanish colonial architecture of Lima and the floating Uros Islands, made of reed, on Lake Titicaca are other draws.

PEOPLE

Pop. density low

Spanish, Quechua, Aymara

21/km² (55/mi²)

THE URBAN/RURAL POPULATION SPLIT

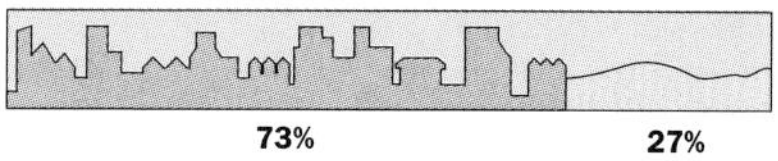
73%
27%

RELIGIOUS PERSUASION

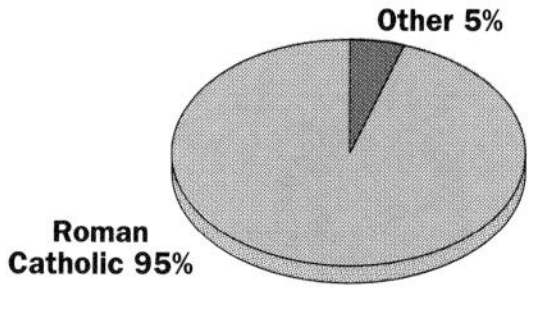
Other 5%
Roman Catholic 95%

ETHNIC MAKEUP

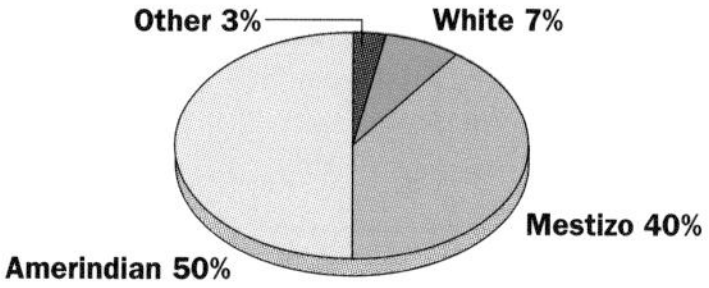
Other 3%
White 7%
Mestizo 40%
Amerindian 50%

Most Peruvians are Amerindian or *mestizo* (mixed race). A small elite of European descent retains a strong hold on the economy, power, and social standing. A few Chinese and Japanese live in the northern cities.

Previously remote Andean Amerindians are increasingly informed of events in Lima and the coastal strip by radio and by relatives in cities. This has compensated for problems associated with the marginalization of their native Quechua and Aymara languages in a Spanish-speaking culture. A further 250,000 Amazonian Amerindians live in the eastern lowlands. Together with the small community of Africans (descendants of plantation workers), they tend to suffer the worst discrimination in towns.

The extended family, part of traditional native Amerindian culture, remains strong; its role as a social bond is reinforced by Roman Catholicism. In recent years, economic difficulties have raised its profile as the key social support system for most Peruvians.

POPULATION AGE BREAKDOWN

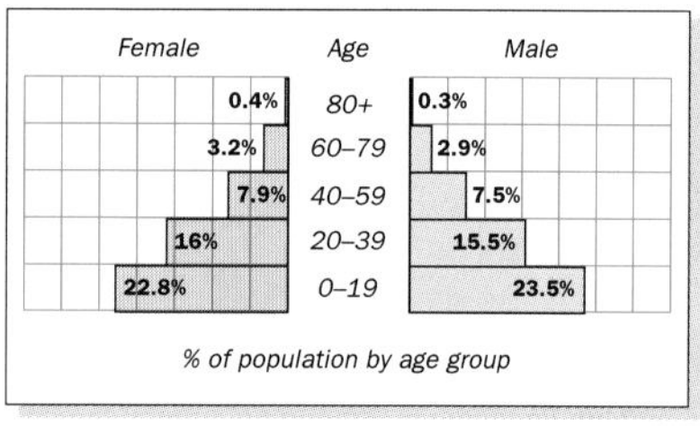
Female
Age
Male
0.4% 80+ 0.3%
3.2% 60–79 2.9%
7.9% 40–59 7.5%
16% 20–39 15.5%
22.8% 0–19 23.5%
% of population by age group

P

POLITICS

Multiparty elections

2001/2006

President Alejandro Toledo

Alberto Fujimori, president 1990–2000, ran an increasingly autocratic regime.

***President Alejandro Toledo,** Peru's first Amerindian head of state, elected in 2001.*

AT THE LAST ELECTION

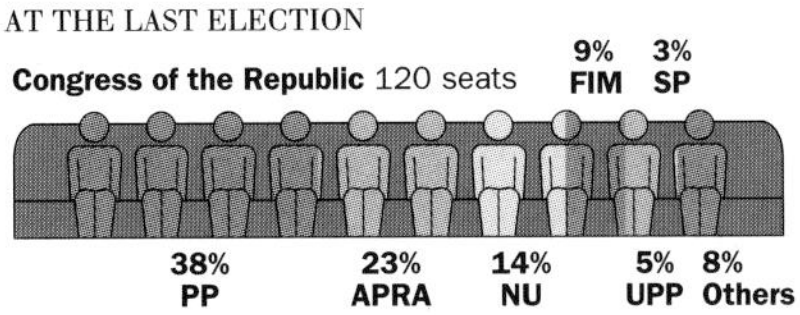
Congress of the Republic 120 seats
9% FIM
3% SP
38% PP
23% APRA
14% NU
5% UPP
8% Others

PP = Peru Posible **APRA** = American Popular Revolutionary Alliance **NU** = National Unity **FIM** = Independent Moralizing Front **UPP** = Union for Peru **SP** = Somos Peru

Peru is a multiparty democracy in which the president holds executive power.

PROFILE

The long tradition of large parties dominating politics ended with Alberto Fujimori's election as president in 1990. His "self-coup" created a compliant legislature and judiciary, and approval of a new constitution permitted his reelection in 1995. His popularity was greatly boosted by successes against hyperinflation and the Sendero Luminoso (Shining Path) guerrillas. It faded in the late 1990s as he tightened his personal control of the government, and appeared increasingly reliant on the army. Few checks on the executive remained, and Fujimori was able to obtain his third term in 2000. However, blatant electoral fraud and abuse of power were exposed when his security service chief Vladimiro Montesinos was videoed bribing opposition legislators. Fujimori's position was irrevocably damaged, and he resigned in November, having fled to Japan. Fresh elections in April 2001 were won by populist Alejandro Toledo and his Peru Posible (PP) party.

MAIN POLITICAL ISSUES

Disenchantment with Toledo

President Toledo promised reforms, but his low ratings in opinion polls suggested public impatience. Respondents expressed disappointment that he had failed to fulfill election promises, especially on job creation, as the government committed itself to IMF goals on structural reform and fiscal restraint. Toledo's popularity keeps falling, in spite of positive macroeconomic indicators, due to his perceived inadequate handling of domestic issues, though he is given credit for more direct speaking and his perceived tough stance on corruption and terrorism. Newly created regional governments threaten to increase pressure on his still weak government, with a possible negative impact on fiscal stability.

The resurgence of APRA

APRA won 12 of the new regional presidencies in 2002, compared with 11 won by independents and one each by PP and SP. APRA leader Alan García, who had presided over a bankrupt country in the 1980s, used the result to increase pressure on Toledo for more budgetary clout for regional government, but did not press for a PP–APRA coalition. Distancing himself from a potentially unpopular government will improve his chances in the 2006 presidential elections.

COLOMBIA
ECUADOR
BRAZIL
BOLIVIA
CHILE
PACIFIC OCEAN
Equator
Putumayo
Napo
Arica
Tigre
Amazon
Iquitos
Pastaza
Marañón
Sullana
Chulucanas
Catacaos
Bernal
Moyobamba
Tarapoto
Chachapoyas
Chiclayo
Saña
Cajamarca
San Pedro de Lloc
Ucayali
Huallaga
Pucallpa
Trujillo
Chimbote
Nevado Huascarán 6768m
Huaraz
Huánuco
Cerro de Pasco
las Piedras
Urubamba
Madre de Dios
Puerto Maldonado
Huacho
La Oroya
Tarma
Huancayo
Huaral
Comas
Callao
Chaclacayo
LIMA
Huancavelica
Apurímac
Urubamba
Machu Picchu
Chincha Alta
Ayacucho
Abancay
Cusco
Pisco
Ica
Nazca
San Juán
Juliaca
Puno
Lake Titicaca
Socabaya
Arequipa
Matarani
Moquegua
Ilo
Tacna
Cordillera Oriental
Cordillera Occidental
PERU
Total Area : 1 285 200 sq. km (496 223 sq. miles)
POPULATION
over 1 000 000
over 500 000
over 100 000
over 50 000
under 50 000
LAND HEIGHT
4000m/13124ft
2000m/6562ft
500m/1640ft
Sea Level
N
0 200 km
0 200 miles

CHRONOLOGY

Francisco Pízarro's arrival in 1532 during a war of succession between two Inca rulers marked the start of the Spanish colonization of Peru and the end of the Inca empire.

- ❑ **1821** Independence proclaimed in Lima after its capture by Argentine liberator, José de San Martín, who had just freed Chile.
- ❑ **1824** Spain defeated at battles of Junín and Ayacucho by Simón Bolívar and Gen. Sucre, liberators of Venezuela and Colombia.
- ❑ **1836–1839** Peru and Bolivia joined in short-lived confederation.
- ❑ **1866** Peruvian–Spanish War.
- ❑ **1879–1884** War of the Pacific. Chile defeats Peru and Bolivia. Peru loses territory in south.
- ❑ **1908** Augusto Leguía y Salcedo's dictatorial rule begins.
- ❑ **1924** Dr. Víctor Raúl Haya de la Torre founds nationalist APRA in exile in Mexico.
- ❑ **1930** Leguía ousted. APRA moves to Peru as first political party.
- ❑ **1931–1945** APRA banned.
- ❑ **1939–1945** Moderate, pro-US civilian government.
- ❑ **1948** Gen. Manuel Odría takes power. APRA banned again.
- ❑ **1956** Civilian government restored.
- ❑ **1962–1963** Two military coups.
- ❑ **1963** Election of Fernando Belaúnde Terry. Land reform, but military used to suppress communist-inspired insurgency.
- ❑ **1968** Military junta takes over.

P

CHRONOLOGY *continued*

Attempts to alleviate poverty. Large-scale nationalizations.

- **1975–1978** New right-wing junta.
- **1980** Belaúnde reelected. Maoist Sendero Luminoso (Shining Path) begins armed struggle.
- **1982** Deaths and "disappearances" start to escalate as army cracks down on guerrillas and narcotics.
- **1985** Electoral win for left-wing APRA under Alan García Pérez.
- **1987** Peru bankrupt. Plans to nationalize banks blocked by new Libertad movement led by writer Mario Vargas Llosa.
- **1990** Over 3000 political murders. Alberto Fujimori, an independent, elected president on anticorruption platform. Severe austerity program.
- **1992–95** Fujimori "self-coup." New constitution. Fujimori reelected.
- **1995–1998** Final border war with Ecuador over access to the Amazon; the key Cordillera del Cóndor had been awarded to Peru in 1942 leading to a series of clashes.
- **1996–1997** Left-wing Tupac Amarú guerrillas seize hundreds of hostages at Japanese ambassador's residence in four-month siege.
- **2000** November, Fujimori seeks refuge in Japan and resigns amid corruption scandal despite having won controversial third term in May.
- **2001** Fresh presidential elections: Alejandro Toledo defeats García.
- **2003** Beatriz Merino appointed first female prime minister.

P

WORLD AFFAIRS

Joined UN in 1945

AP | AmCC | NAM | OAS | RG

Cooperation with the US, which is the main source of aid, extends to the war on cocaine, though Peru remains one of the world's largest coca producers. Security along the Colombian border is a key issue; there have been reported incursions by paramilitaries and narcotics traffickers. Peru signed a deal in 2004 to process and export Bolivian natural gas, even though the route is longer than the Chilean alternative.

AID

Recipient

$491m (receipts) — Up 8% in 2002

Aid from the US is mostly directed at antinarcotics activity. Loans worth some $1.3 billion in recent years from the IDB, the World Bank, and Japan were conditional on Peru's meeting specific health and educational targets and on making progress on privatizations.

DEFENSE

Compulsory military service

$865m — Down 3% in 2002

The military, in power from 1968 to 1980, supported President Fujimori's 1992 "self-coup." A quarter of national territory remained under states of emergency until early 2000, despite the apparent defeat of the Sendero Luminoso guerrillas. Fujimori's control over promotions and the National Intelligence Service (SIN) guaranteed the loyalty of senior military officers. After his resignation and the dissolution of the SIN in 2000, the new government cut back military influence. Guerrillas were widely blamed for bomb attacks in Lima in 2002 prior to the visit of US president Bush, but a theory studied by the interior ministry was that elements in the military, intelligence, or police still sympathetic to ousted security service chief Montesinos were responsible.

PERUVIAN ARMED FORCES

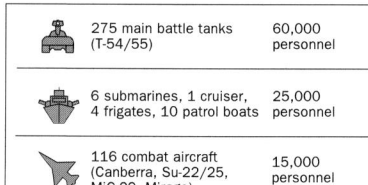

275 main battle tanks (T-54/55)	60,000 personnel
6 submarines, 1 cruiser, 4 frigates, 10 patrol boats	25,000 personnel
116 combat aircraft (Canberra, Su-22/25, MiG-29, Mirage)	15,000 personnel
None	

ECONOMICS

Inflation 23% p.a. (1990–2001)

$54bn — 3.473 new soles (3.472)

SCORE CARD

- World GNP Ranking 46th
- GNP per Capita $2020
- Balance of Payments .... –$1.21bn
- Inflation 0.2%
- Unemployment 9%

EXPORTS

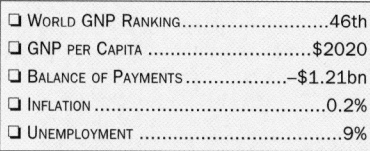

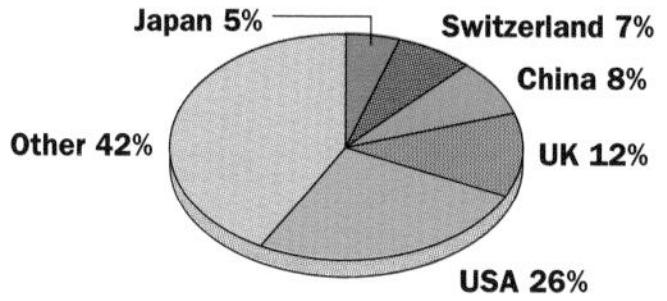
Japan 5%
Switzerland 7%
China 8%
UK 12%
USA 26%
Other 42%

IMPORTS

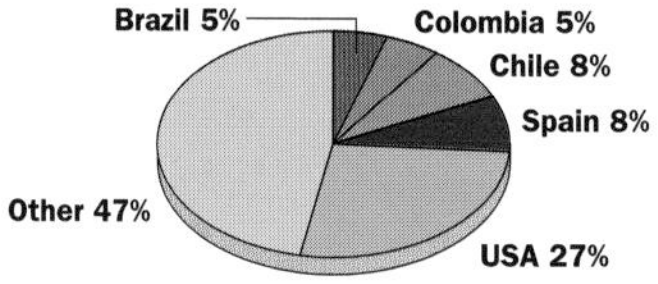
Brazil 5%
Colombia 5%
Chile 8%
Spain 8%
USA 27%
Other 47%

Strengths
Abundant mineral resources, including natural gas. Rich fish stocks. Climatic variation allows diverse and productive agriculture, especially cotton and coffee. Well-developed textile industry.

Weaknesses
Overdependence on metals and commodities whose fluctuating prices undermine trade and investment. Stalled privatization. Corruption and poor infrastructure deterring investment. Social instability.

Profile
Wealth and economic activity are largely confined to the cities of the coastal plain. The inhabitants of the Andean uplands are subsistence farmers or coca producers. Peru's strict fiscal and monetary policy continued under Fujimori. Growth was hit hard in 1998 by the disruption of fishing by El Niño-generated storms, the Asian economic crises, turmoil in emerging markets following Russia's economic troubles, and depressed world commodity prices. In 1999 the IMF granted a three-year loan package, extended in 2002, to support comprehensive structural reform and fiscal restraint. Strong growth in 2002, led by mining, construction, and manufacturing, aided recovery.

ECONOMIC PERFORMANCE INDICATOR

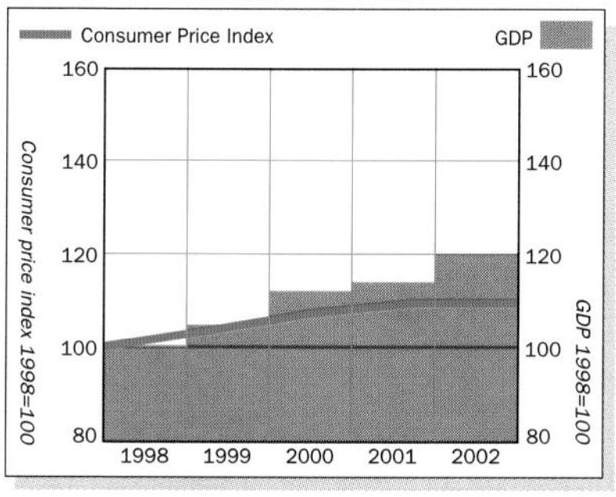
Consumer Price Index
GDP
Consumer price index 1998=100
GDP 1998=100
160
140
120
100
80
1998
1999
2000
2001
2002

PERU : MAJOR BUSINESSES

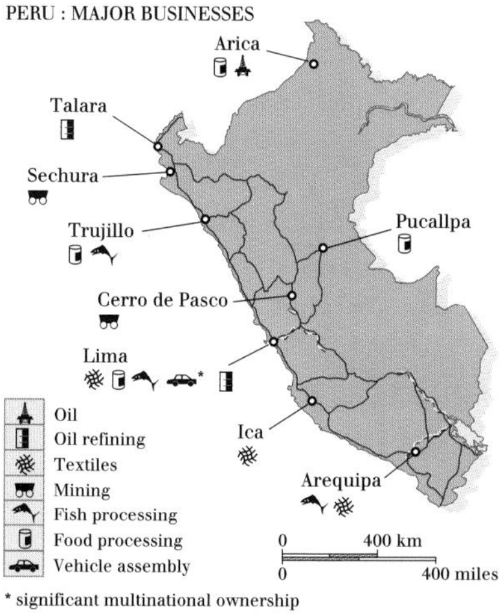
Arica
Talara
Sechura
Trujillo
Pucallpa
Cerro de Pasco
Lima
Ica
Arequipa
Oil
Oil refining
Textiles
Mining
Fish processing
Food processing
Vehicle assembly
0
400 km
0
400 miles
* significant multinational ownership

RESOURCES

Electric power 6.1m kW

8m tonnes

92,000 b/d (reserves 1bn barrels)

14.1m sheep, 4.99m cattle, 2.86m pigs, 95m chickens

Oil, natural gas, coal, lead, zinc, silver, iron, gold, copper

ELECTRICITY GENERATION

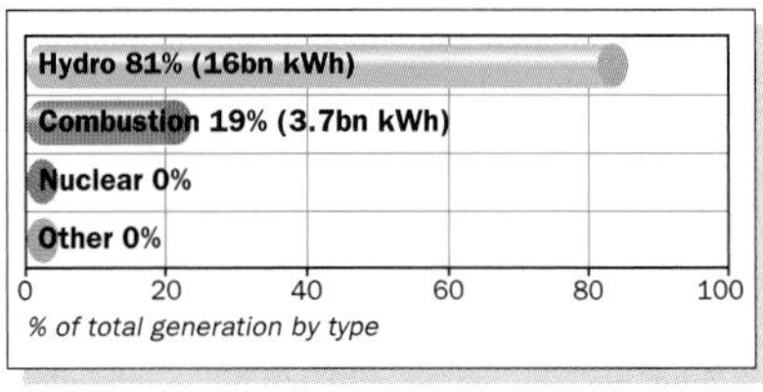
Hydro 81% (16bn kWh)
Combustion 19% (3.7bn kWh)
Nuclear 0%
Other 0%
0
20
40
60
80
100
% of total generation by type

Peru is a key exporter of copper and lead. The huge Antamina copper, zinc, and silver deposit began production in 2001. Peru is attempting to reduce its dependence on hydroelectric power because inconsistent rainfall patterns cause output to fluctuate. The new Camisea gas project will make Peru a net energy exporter by 2007.

PERU : LAND USE

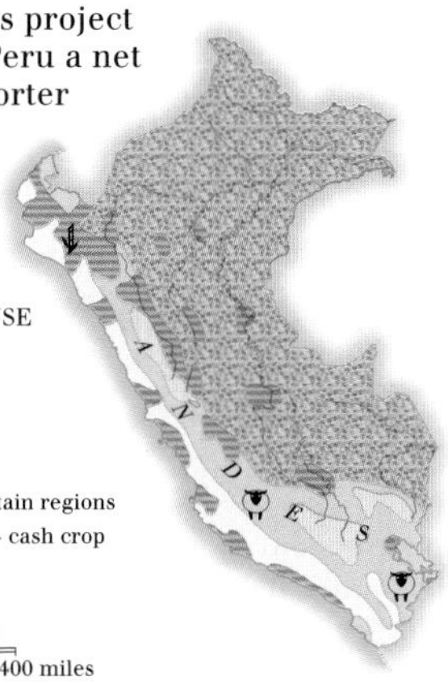
ANDES

Cropland
Pasture
Forest
Desert
High mountain regions
Sugarcane - cash crop
Sheep

0 400 km
0 400 miles

ENVIRONMENT

Sustainability rank: 29th

6% (3% partially protected)

1.1 tonnes per capita

ENVIRONMENTAL TREATIES

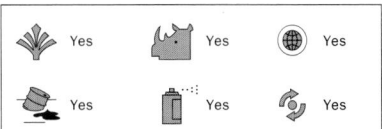

Yes	Yes	Yes
Yes	Yes	Yes

Environmentalists have long been concerned about coastal industrial pollution and the activities of the fishing industry. Overfishing of anchovies almost resulted in their extinction in the 1970s. Today, attention has switched to the rising number of dolphins being caught in drift nets. Unchecked urban and industrial pollution, especially in Lima, is a serious concern.

Environmentalists fear that the policy of using powerful air-sprayed herbicides to destroy coca crops is adding to river pollution in the Andes, where mining also causes severe environmental problems.

MEDIA

TV ownership medium

Daily newspaper circulation 4 per 1000 people

PUBLISHING AND BROADCAST MEDIA

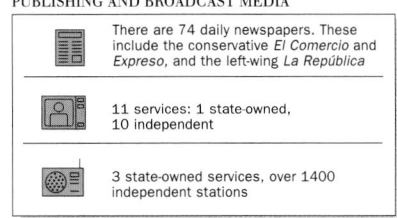

There are 74 daily newspapers. These include the conservative *El Comercio* and *Expreso*, and the left-wing *La República*

11 services: 1 state-owned, 10 independent

3 state-owned services, over 1400 independent stations

Main cities have their own newspapers; Lima's papers cater to diverse political readerships. State TV is not popular.

CRIME

Death penalty not used in practice

27,493 prisoners

Urban crime levels are high

CRIME RATES

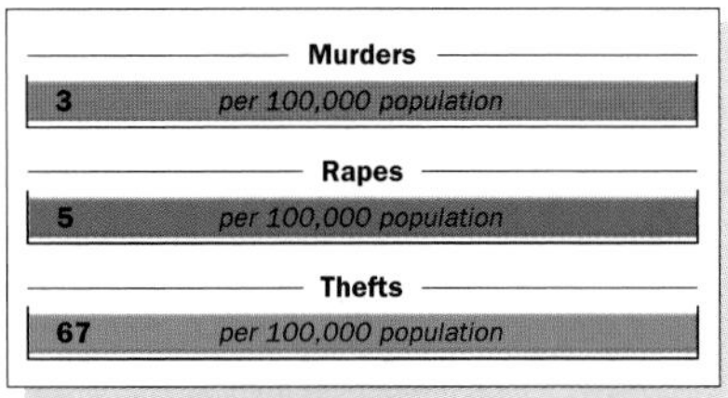
Murders
3 per 100,000 population
Rapes
5 per 100,000 population
Thefts
67 per 100,000 population

Kidnappings, murders, armed robberies, and narcotics-related crime remain serious problems, especially in Lima. Corruption is deep-seated in the police and security forces, and was a major political issue throughout the 1990s. Despite the near-destruction of the Sendero Luminoso and Tupac Amarú guerrilla groups, main cities frequently have curfews. There is international pressure to halt coca production, but chewing coca is traditional in the Andes for its medicinal properties.

EDUCATION

School leaving age: 16

85%

1.5m students

THE EDUCATION SYSTEM

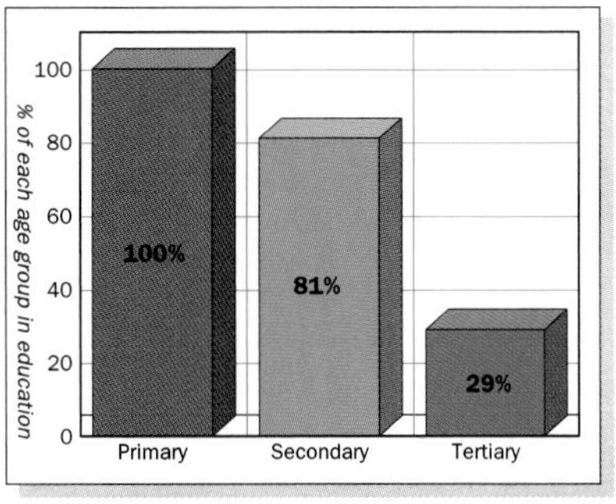
100
80
60
40
20
0
% of each age group in education
100%
81%
29%
Primary
Secondary
Tertiary

Education is based on the US system; spending has declined. The provision of state education, especially for the poor, remains a serious challenge.

HEALTH

Welfare state health benefits

1 per 1111 people

Cancers, pneumonia, accidents, infectious diseases

The poor public health system almost collapsed in the 1980s. In many areas primary care is nonexistent. Advanced treatment is available only to private patients in city clinics. Goiter, a thyroid abnormality, is widespread, especially in mountain areas. Infant mortality is high in remote areas due to social deprivation, diarrheal diseases, and tuberculosis. Cholera reached epidemic proportions in 1994, and malaria is again widespread. Thousands of poor women were forcibly sterilized in the late 1990s as part of a government program to lower the birthrate. Social welfare is compulsory, and benefits cover sickness, disability, and old age.

SPENDING

GDP/cap. increase

CONSUMPTION AND SPENDING

28 per 1000 population

66 per 1000 population

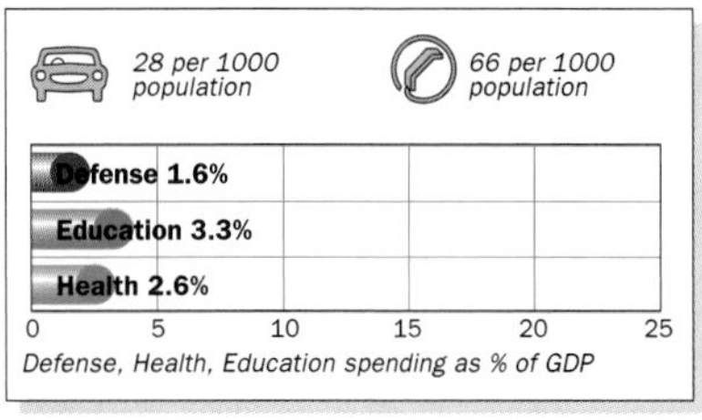
Defense 1.6%
Education 3.3%
Health 2.6%
0
5
10
15
20
25
Defense, Health, Education spending as % of GDP

Most wealth and power in Peru is still retained by old Spanish families. Indigenous peoples remain excluded from both. The rich live in a state of siege; the number of armed guards and security cameras protecting family property has become a status symbol. Overpopulation and rural migration accentuate poverty in Lima, where some 2.7 million people live in shanty towns, many of them lacking such basic utilities as running water and electricity. The UN estimates that around 40% of the population live below the poverty line.

WORLD RANKING

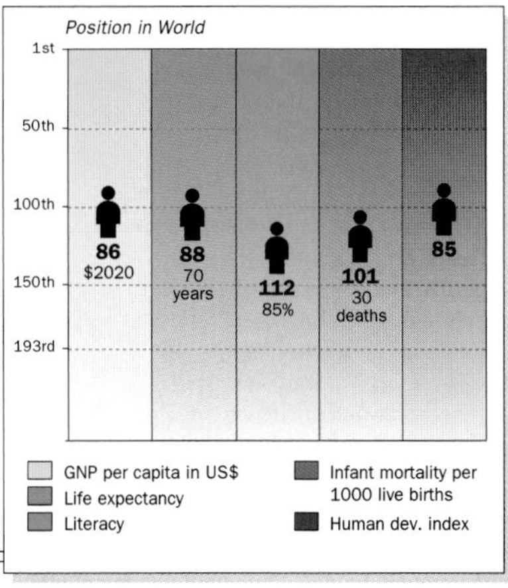
Position in World
1st
50th
100th
150th
193rd
86
$2020
88
70
years
112
85%
101
30
deaths
85
GNP per capita in US$
Life expectancy
Literacy
Infant mortality per 1000 live births
Human dev. index

P

SOUTHEAST ASIA
China
Taiwan
PHILIPPINES
Malaysia
Asia

PHILIPPINES

OFFICIAL NAME: Republic of the Philippines **CAPITAL:** Manila
POPULATION: 80 million **CURRENCY:** Philippine peso **OFFICIAL LANGUAGES:** English and Filipino

1946 | 1946 | June 12 | RP | +8 | +63 | .ph

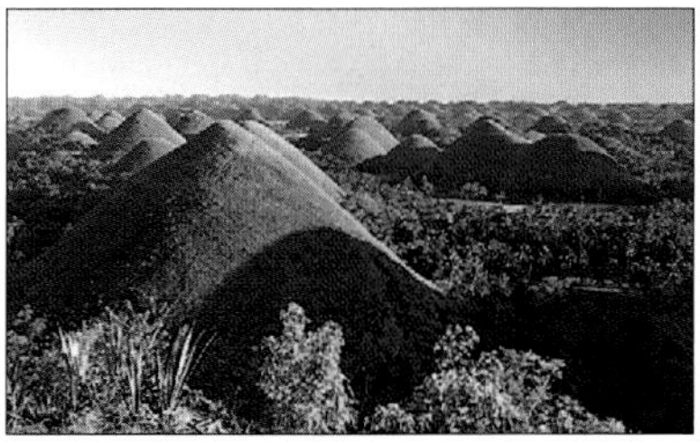
Bohol Island *has over 1000 of these famous mounds, known as "the chocolate hills."*

LYING ON THE WESTERN RIM of the Pacific Ocean, the Philippines is the world's second-largest archipelago-state. Of its 7107 islands, 4600 are named and 1000 inhabited. There are three main island groupings: Luzon, Visayan, and the Mindanao and Sulu islands. Located on the Pacific "ring of fire," it is subject to frequent earthquakes and volcanic activity. Economic growth outstripped population increase in the 1990s, until the 1997–1998 Asian crisis, but efforts to build a stable democracy have been compromised by high-level corruption, leading to the ouster of President Estrada in 2001.

CLIMATE

Tropical monsoon/equatorial

WEATHER CHART FOR MANILA

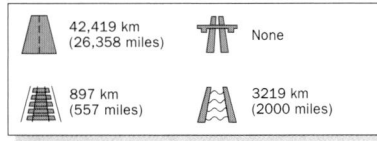

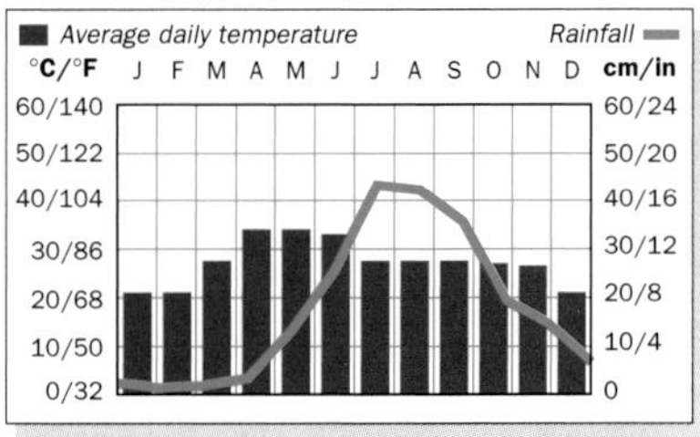
Average daily temperature
Rainfall
°C/°F
J F M A M J J A S O N D
cm/in
60/140
50/122
40/104
30/86
20/68
10/50
0/32
60/24
50/20
40/16
30/12
20/8
10/4
0

The Philippines is warm and humid all year. The rainy season lasts from June to October. Humidity falls from 85% in September to 71% in March.

TRANSPORTATION

Drive on right

Ninoy Aquino, Manila 12.9m passengers

1686 ships 5.32m grt

THE TRANSPORTATION NETWORK

42,419 km (26,358 miles)	None
897 km (557 miles)	3219 km (2000 miles)

Basic infrastructure lacks investment and many main roads are in desperate need of repair. Chronic traffic congestion in Manila holds back economic growth.

Air travel is the only means of getting around the islands quickly. Philippines Airlines, privatized in 1992, has invested heavily in new aircraft and in expanding its regional route network. Work on a new 28-gate terminal at Ninoy Aquino international airport ran into financial difficulties in 2002.

Subic Bay, a massive US naval base until 1992, is now being exploited as a commercial asset, thanks to its prime location. Opening on to the South China Sea, its deep natural harbor has been developed as a free port and enterprise zone. The Taiwanese are the biggest investors in this project.

TOURISM

Visitors : Population 1:41

1.93m visitors

Up 8% in 2002

MAIN TOURIST ARRIVALS

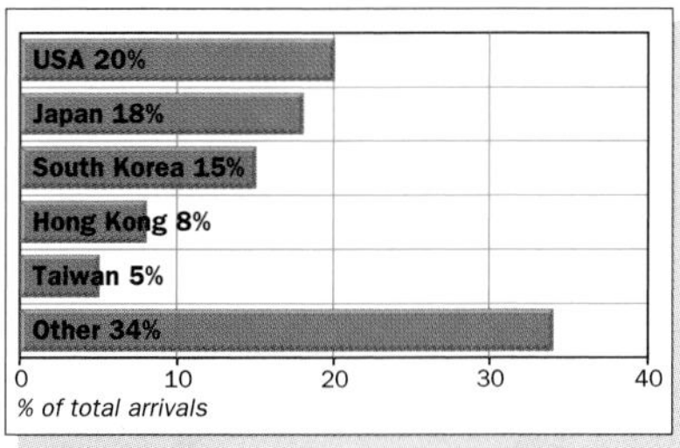
USA 20%
Japan 18%
South Korea 15%
Hong Kong 8%
Taiwan 5%
Other 34%
0
10
20
30
40
% of total arrivals

There is less tourism in the Philippines than in other regional NICs. Dubious images conveyed by sex tourism have become a liability. International pressure to end this abuse has intensified. Muslim secessionists have seized tourists on nearby Malaysian islands as hostages. The tiny island of Boracay, off Panay, is a popular resort, and Palawan retains most of its tropical rainforest and coral lagoons, though coral reefs elsewhere are badly damaged. The rice terraces of northern Luzon are another attraction.

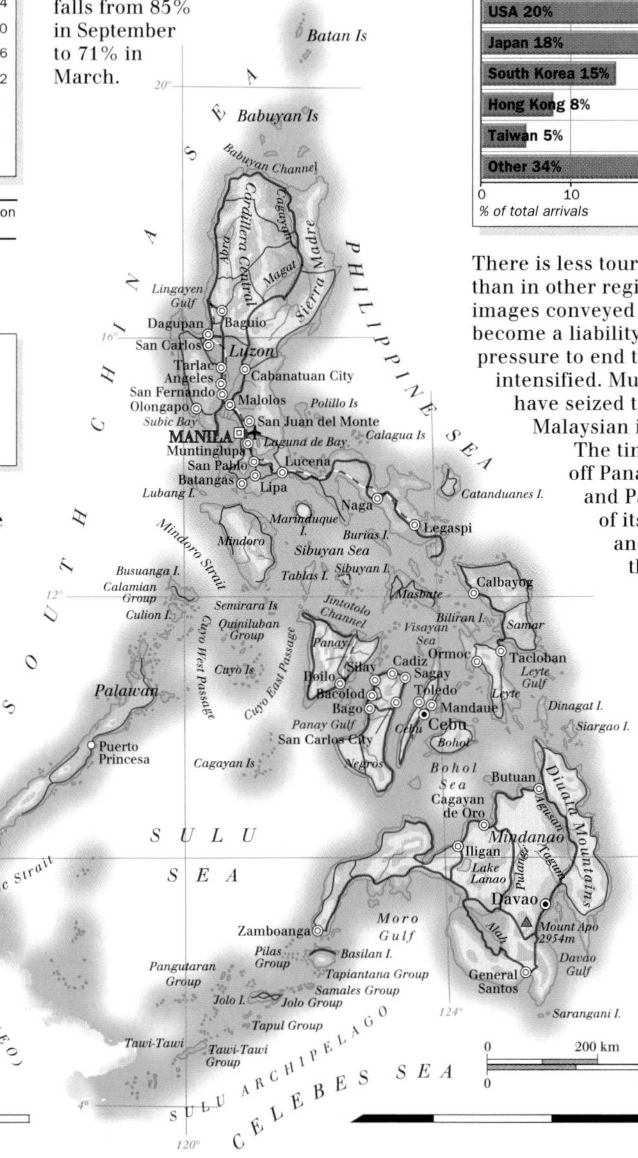
Batan Is
Babuyan Is
Babuyan Channel
Cordillera Central
Cagayan
Sierra Madre
Magat
Abra
SOUTH CHINA SEA
PHILIPPINE SEA
Lingayen Gulf
Dagupan
Baguio
San Carlos
Luzon
Tarlac
Angeles
San Fernando
Olongapo
Subic Bay
Cabanatuan City
Malolos
Polillo Is
San Juan del Monte
MANILA
Muntinlupa
Laguna de Bay
Calagua Is
San Pablo
Batangas
Lucena
Lipa
Lubang I.
Naga
Catanduanes I.
Marinduque I.
Burias I.
Legaspi
Mindoro
Mindoro Strait
Sibuyan Sea
Tablas I.
Sibuyan I.
Busuanga I.
Calamian Group
Culion I.
Semirara Is
Quiniluban Group
Jintotolo Channel
Masbate
Calbayog
Biliran I.
Samar
Visayan Sea
Panay
Cuyo Is
Cuyo West Passage
Cuyo East Passage
Silay
Cadiz
Sagay
Ormoc
Tacloban
Leyte Gulf
Leyte
Iloilo
Bacolod
Bago
Toledo
Mandaue
Cebu
Dinagat I.
Siargao I.
Palawan
Puerto Princesa
Panay Gulf
San Carlos City
Negros
Bohol
Cagayan Is
Bohol Sea
Butuan
Cagayan de Oro
Diuata Mountains
Agusan
Mindanao
Iligan
Lake Lanao
Pulangi
Tagum
SULU SEA
Balabac I.
Balabac Strait
Davao
Mount Apo 2954m
Zamboanga
Moro Gulf
Pilas Group
Basilan I.
Tapiantana Group
Samales Group
Pangutaran Group
Jolo I.
Jolo Group
Tapul Group
General Santos
Davao Gulf
Sarangani I.
(BORNEO)
Tawi-Tawi
Tawi-Tawi Group
SULU ARCHIPELAGO
CELEBES SEA
20°
16°
12°
8°
4°
116°
120°
124°
N
0
200 km
200 miles
PHILIPPINES
Total Area : 300 000 sq. km (115 830 sq. miles)
POPULATION
over 1 000 000
over 500 000
over 100 000
over 50 000
LAND HEIGHT
2000m/6562ft
1000m/3281ft
500m/1640ft
200m/656ft
Sea Level

PEOPLE

Pop. density high

Filipino, English, Tagalog, Cebuano, Ilocano, Hiligaynon, many other local languages

268/km² (695/mi²)

THE URBAN/RURAL POPULATION SPLIT

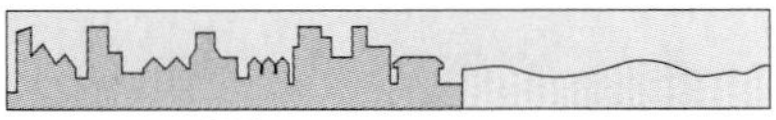
60%
40%

RELIGIOUS PERSUASION

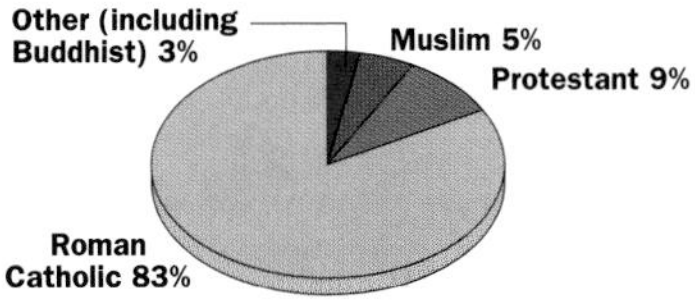
Other (including Buddhist) 3%
Muslim 5%
Protestant 9%
Roman Catholic 83%

ETHNIC MAKEUP

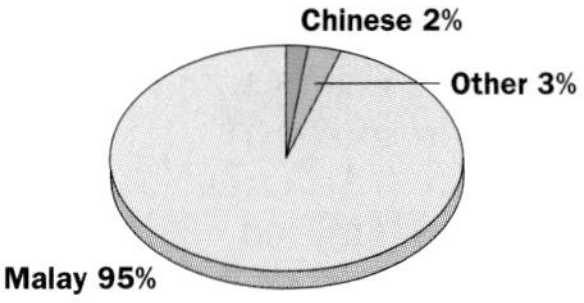
Chinese 2%
Other 3%
Malay 95%

POPULATION AGE BREAKDOWN

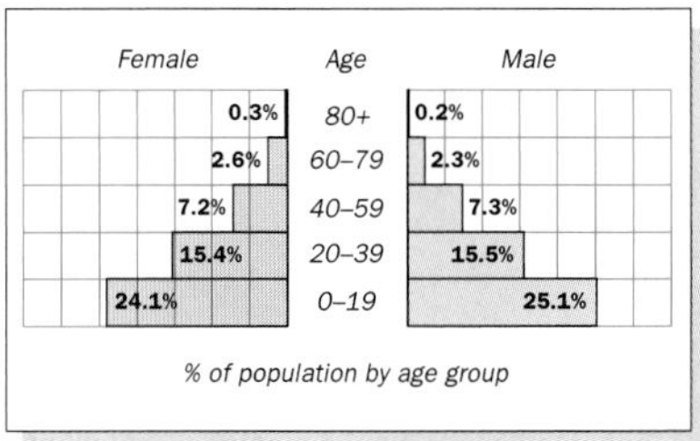
Female
Age
Male
0.3%
80+
0.2%
2.6%
60–79
2.3%
7.2%
40–59
7.3%
15.4%
20–39
15.5%
24.1%
0–19
25.1%
% of population by age group

The Philippines encompasses more than 100 distinct ethnic groups, many of Malay origin. The national language, Filipino, is based on Tagalog, spoken by the largest of the various groups. Other groups include Cebuano, Ilocan, Longgo, Bicolano, Waray, Pampangan, and Pangasinan. They are concentrated on the main island, Luzon, and are also a majority on Mindanao. Most Muslims live on Mindanao, but many are also found in the Sulu archipelago. The Chinese minority, which was well established by 1603, has remained significant in business and trade. More than 120 Chinese schools have ensured that it has retained a distinct identity.

There are also a number of cultural minorities who practice animist religions. They include the Ifugaos, Bontocks, Kalingas, and Ibalois on Luzon, the Manobo and Bukidnon on Mindanao, and the Mangyans on Palawan. Many of these groups speak Malayo-Polynesian dialects. Limited intermarriage with other peoples has meant that groups in the more remote regions have managed to retain their traditional ways of life.

The Philippines is one of only two Christian states in Asia. Over 80% of Filipinos are Roman Catholics, and the Church is the dominant cultural force. It opposes state-sponsored preventive family planning programs aimed at curbing accelerating population growth. Abortion is illegal but widespread.

Women have traditionally played a prominent part in Philippine public and professional life. Inheritance laws give them equal rights to men. Many go into politics, banking, and business, and in several professional sectors they form a majority.

POLITICS

Multiparty elections

L. House 2004/2007
U. House 2004/2007

President Gloria Macapagal Arroyo

AT THE LAST ELECTION

House of Representatives 236 seats

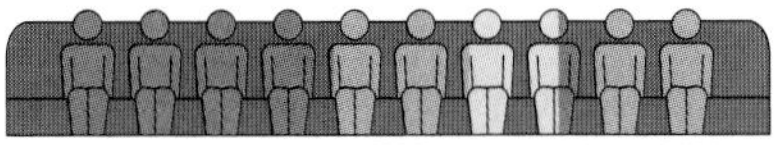
42% Lakas–CMD
21% NPC
13% LP
4% LDP
20% Others

Lakas–CMD = Lakas – Christian Muslim Democrats **NPC** = Nationalist People's Coalition **LP** = Liberal Party **LDP** = Fight of Democratic Filipinos **K4** = K4 coalition (led by Lakas and including the NPC and the LP) **KNP** = Coalition of United Filipinos (led by the LDP) **Ind** = Independent

Senate 24 seats

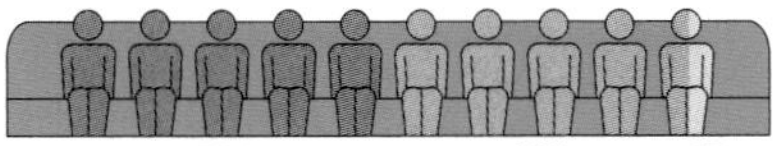
50% K4
46% KNP
4% Ind

The Philippines is a multiparty democracy.

Profile

By 1986, the 21-year dictatorship of Ferdinand Marcos had no popular backing. A massive "people power" movement supported his opponent Corazon Aquino, declared the true winner of the presidential elections. Losing US support, Marcos was forced into exile.

Former film star Joseph Estrada was elected president in 1998. Accusations that he was involved in a gambling syndicate led to impeachment proceedings and he relinquished power in 2001. Vice President Gloria Macapagal Arroyo of opposition party Lakas, who had led the united political challenge to Estrada, was appointed to replace him. The May 2004 presidential election was a tight race, Arroyo just beating movie star Fernando Poe Jr. after a lengthy count.

Main Political Issues

Political stability

After the downfall of the Marcos regime, the subsequent two presidents passed on power smoothly to an elected successor, but Estrada was quickly mired in corruption scandals. Moves for his impeachment were overtaken by mass rallies in Manila. Out of office he retains widespread support among the rural poor, who question the legitimacy of Arroyo's appointment. She has since faced popular discontent, a failed military rebellion in July 2003, and a serious electoral challenge in May 2004.

Insurgency and separatism

Communists and Muslim separatists have been fighting government forces for over 30 years, with more than 10,000 armed confrontations with rebels recorded by the army. Support for secession has been fueled by government failure to alleviate poverty.

The communist New People's Army (NPA), once regarded as a heroic army of the oppressed and as an alternative to traditional politics, has declined in significance, but launched new offensives in 2000. Of greater importance is the Muslim insurrection on Mindanao and other southern islands. The Moro National Liberation Front (MNLF) signed a peace agreement in 1996.

Joseph Estrada, film-star-turned-president, ousted in 2001.

Gloria Arroyo, president after a popular uprising.

The splinter Muslim Islamic Liberation Front (MILF) continued fighting, but joined the peace process in mid-2001. Nonetheless, the government launched a major offensive against MILF headquarters in 2003. The smaller, but internationally backed, Abu Sayyaf continues low-level fighting in the Sulu region.

Alleged links with Islamist terrorists have brought full military assistance from the US in its "war on terrorism." The presence of US troops on Philippine soil has provoked controversy.

WORLD AFFAIRS

Joined UN in 1945

APEC ASEAN G24 NAM WTO

Regionally, there are sporadic frictions with Malaysia, while sovereignty of the Spratly Islands is hotly contested by China. President Arroyo quickly pledged support for the US-led "war on terrorism" in 2001. The 50 soldiers sent to Iraq were withdrawn after militants kidnapped a Filipino civilian in 2004.

CHRONOLOGY

Ceded to the US by Spain in 1898, the Philippines became self-governing in 1935, and an independent republic in 1946.

- ❑ **1965** Ferdinand Marcos president.
- ❑ **1972** Marcos declares martial law. Opposition leaders arrested, parliament suspended, press censored.
- ❑ **1977** Ex-Liberal Party leader Benigno Aquino sentenced to death. Criticism forces Marcos to delay execution.
- ❑ **1978** Elections won by Marcos's New Society (KBL). He is named president and prime minister.
- ❑ **1980** Aquino allowed to travel to US for medical treatment.
- ❑ **1981** Martial law ends. Marcos reelected president by referendum.
- ❑ **1983** Aquino shot dead on return from US. Inquiry blames military conspiracy.
- ❑ **1986** US compels presidential election. Result disputed. Army rebels led by Gen. Fidel Ramos, and public demonstrations, bring Aquino's widow, Corazon, to power. Marcos exiled to US.
- ❑ **1987** New constitution. Aquino-led coalition wins Congress elections.
- ❑ **1988** Marcos and wife Imelda indicted for massive racketeering.
- ❑ **1989** Marcos dies in US.
- ❑ **1990** Imelda Marcos acquitted of fraud charges in US. Earthquake in Baguio city leaves 1600 dead.
- ❑ **1991** Mt. Pinatubo erupts. US leaves Clark Air Base.
- ❑ **1992** Ramos wins presidency. US withdraws from Subic Bay base.
- ❑ **1996** Peace agreement with Muslim MNLF secessionists.
- ❑ **1998** Joseph Estrada president.
- ❑ **1999** First execution in 22 years.
- ❑ **2000** Tourists kidnapped by Islamic extremists.
- ❑ **2001** Estrada overthrown by popular protest. Gloria Macapagal Arroyo assumes presidency. August, Muslim MILF joins peace process.
- ❑ **2002** Local elections, described as "peaceful" despite 86 deaths.
- ❑ **2004** Arroyo reelected.

AID

Recipient

$560m (receipts) | Down 3% in 2002

The Philippines' main bilateral aid donors are Japan and, to a lesser extent, the US. Many NGOs operate in the outlying islands. Large remittances are sent home by Filipinos working overseas: funds received from these hundreds of thousands of emigrant workers exceeded $7 billion in 2003.

DEFENSE

No compulsory military service

$1.51bn | Up 35% in 2002

The military retains political influence. An abortive army mutiny called for President Arroyo's resignation in 2003.

The historic tie to the US has been translated in modern times into a close strategic relationship; US forces were deployed to help the government combat Muslim rebels in the south from 2001. Modernization of the armed forces is being undertaken with US assistance.

PHILIPPINE ARMED FORCES

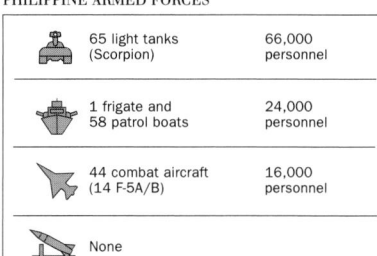

65 light tanks (Scorpion)	66,000 personnel
1 frigate and 58 patrol boats	24,000 personnel
44 combat aircraft (14 F-5A/B)	16,000 personnel
None	

ECONOMICS

Inflation 8.2% p.a. (1990–2001)

$82.4bn | 56.16 Philippine pesos (53.45)

SCORE CARD

❑ World GNP Ranking	41st
❑ GNP per capita	$1030
❑ Balance of Payments	$4.2bn
❑ Inflation	3.1%
❑ Unemployment	11%

EXPORTS

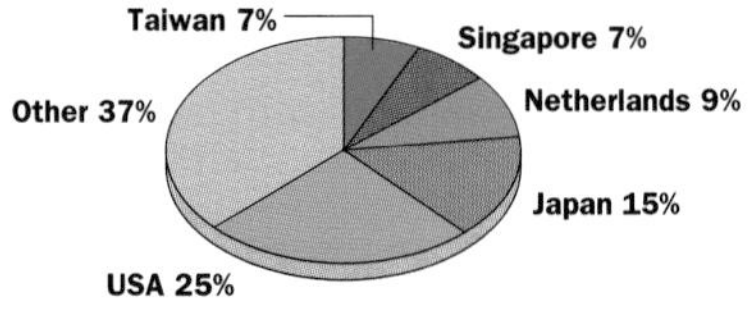
Taiwan 7%
Singapore 7%
Netherlands 9%
Other 37%
Japan 15%
USA 25%

IMPORTS

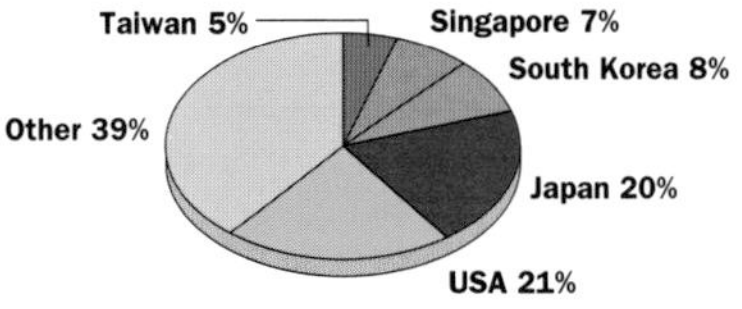
Taiwan 5%
Singapore 7%
South Korea 8%
Other 39%
Japan 20%
USA 21%

STRENGTHS

Now fully open to outside investment. Agricultural productivity rising. Strong pineapple and banana export industries. Remittances from Filipinos overseas.

WEAKNESSES

Power failures limit scope for expansion. Rudimentary infrastructure. Large disparities in income, ownership of assets, and geographical concentration of activity.

PROFILE

Once one of Asia's strongest economies, the Philippines has now fallen behind previously much poorer countries such as Thailand, Malaysia, and South Korea. Around half of the population live below the UN poverty line, on less than $2 a day, fueling many of the secessionist movements that have undermined the stability of successive governments.

The financial successes of the early 1990s – opening up to foreign investment, cutting back private monopolies – were

ECONOMIC PERFORMANCE INDICATOR

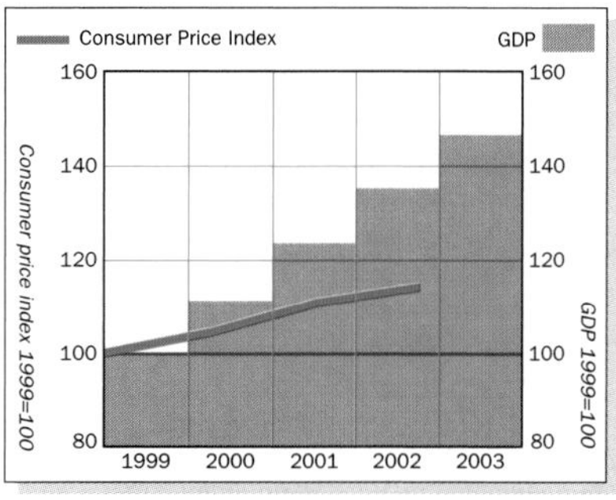
Consumer Price Index
GDP
160
140
120
100
80
1999
2000
2001
2002
2003
Consumer price index 1999=100
GDP 1999=100

effectively nullified by the crippling 1997–1998 Asian economic and financial crises. The government of Joseph Estrada failed to shore up the economy and ran up a crippling budget deficit, and investor confidence vanished amid political scandals. His successor, President Arroyo, has done much to regain the approval of the IMF and the international community, mainly through further deregulation and privatization. Growth is back on track, thanks mainly to increased agricultural production, but many public works projects have simply been put on hold.

PHILIPPINES : MAJOR BUSINESSES

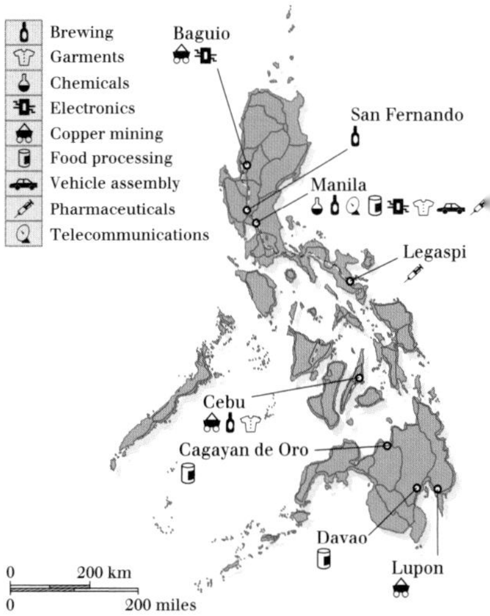
Brewing
Garments
Chemicals
Electronics
Copper mining
Food processing
Vehicle assembly
Pharmaceuticals
Telecommunications
Baguio
San Fernando
Manila
Legaspi
Cebu
Cagayan de Oro
Davao
Lupon
0
200 km
0
200 miles

RESOURCES

Electric power 12.3m kW

2.38m tonnes

1103 b/d (reserves 205m barrels)

12.6m ducks, 12.4m pigs, 6.3m goats, 128m chickens

Coal, copper, nickel, chromium, silver, gas, manganese, gold, oil

ELECTRICITY GENERATION

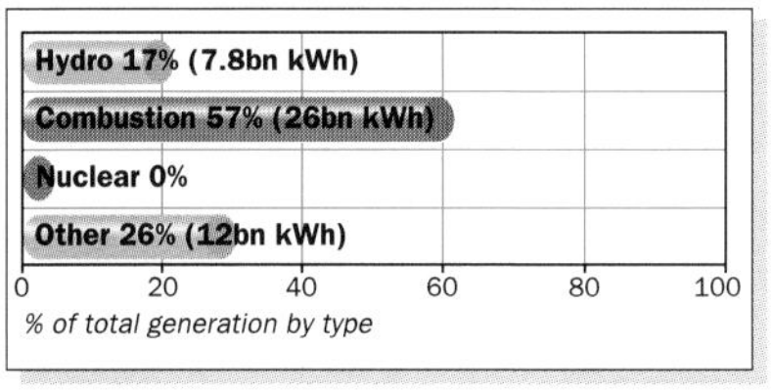
Hydro 17% (7.8bn kWh)
Combustion 57% (26bn kWh)
Nuclear 0%
Other 26% (12bn kWh)
0
20
40
60
80
100
% of total generation by type

The Philippines is the world's biggest supplier of refractory chrome. Copper is also a significant export. Substantial gold reserves have been mined since 1996. Falling global prices for minerals have seen a rapid decline in the Philippine mining industry. Oil production off Palawan began in 1979. A major natural gas discovery in the Malampaya field, officially inaugurated in 2001, could prove to have a significant impact. Though timber exports were halted in 1989, illegal logging continues to cause deforestation.

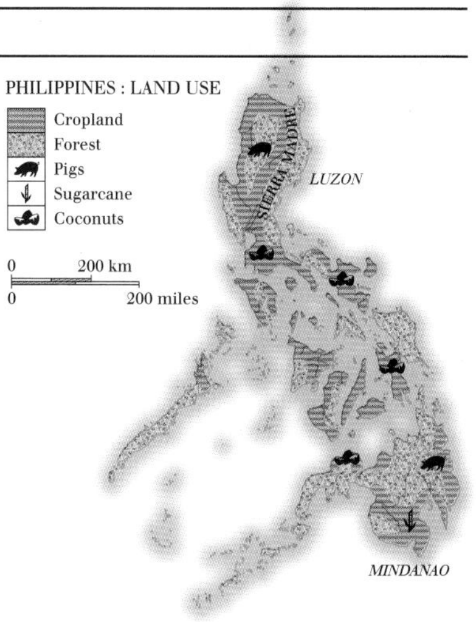
PHILIPPINES : LAND USE
Cropland
Forest
Pigs
Sugarcane
Coconuts
0
200 km
0
200 miles
SIERRA MADRE
LUZON
MINDANAO

ENVIRONMENT

Sustainability rank: 117th

6% (3% partially protected)

1 tonne per capita

ENVIRONMENTAL TREATIES

Yes	Yes	Yes
Yes	Yes	Yes

The environment has become a major issue. Most of the tropical rainforest has been destroyed, except for pockets such as the island of Palawan. Unique coral habitats have been dynamited, and fishermen continue to use cyanide and *muro-ami* (reef-hunting) techniques to increase the size of their catches.

The government recognizes the costs of environmental damage, as soil run-off silts rivers and reduces the power generated by hydroelectric dams, and fast-depleting coral habitats reduce the attraction of the Philippines for tourists.

Enforcement of a ban on logging is difficult; many loggers have their own private armies. In addition, continued use of slash-and-burn farming has contributed to deforestation.

MEDIA

TV ownership medium

Daily newspaper circulation 63 per 1000 people

PUBLISHING AND BROADCAST MEDIA

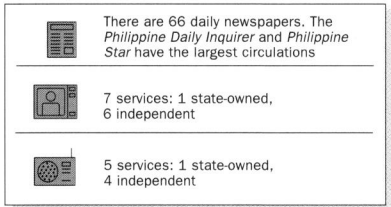

There are 66 daily newspapers. The *Philippine Daily Inquirer* and *Philippine Star* have the largest circulations

7 services: 1 state-owned, 6 independent

5 services: 1 state-owned, 4 independent

Censorship was lifted under the 1987 constitution, but harassment of journalists still occurs. As well as the lively national press, there are more than 250 regional newspapers in local dialects. State TV and radio broadcast in English and Filipino. Powerful families control many independent outlets.

CRIME

Death penalty in use

24,400 prisoners

Down 5% in 2000

CRIME RATES

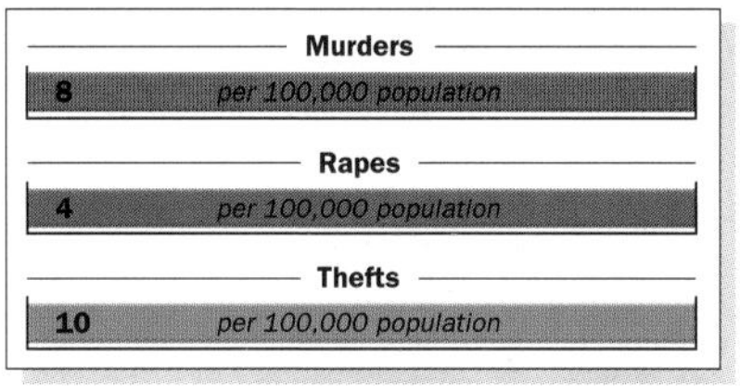
Murders
8
per 100,000 population
Rapes
4
per 100,000 population
Thefts
10
per 100,000 population

President Arroyo has been forced to take a hard line against a series of high-profile kidnappings, ending in 2004 a five-year moratorium on executions.

EDUCATION

School leaving age: 12

93%

2.43m students

THE EDUCATION SYSTEM

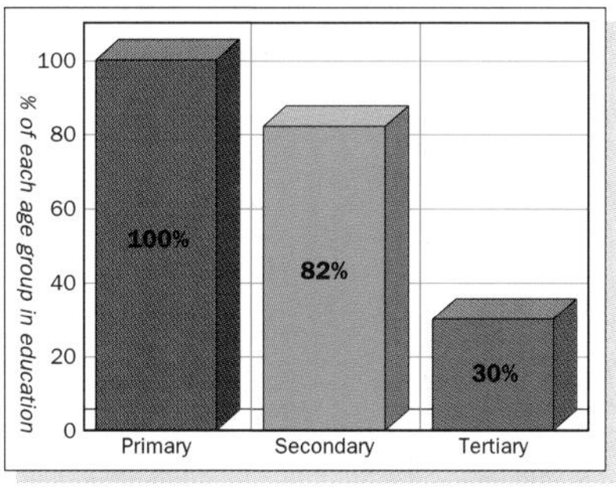
100
80
60
40
20
0
% of each age group in education
100%
82%
30%
Primary
Secondary
Tertiary

The Philippines has a relatively high literacy rate for a developing country. The education system is based on the US model, but with a higher proportion of private schools. The main teaching languages are English and Filipino/Tagalog.

Though there is a national curriculum up to age 15, sectarianism is common; the Chinese community has its own schools. Most colleges and universities are also run privately. The universities of San Carlos in Cebu and Santo Tomas in Manila are Spanish colonial foundations, dating from 1595 and 1611 respectively.

HEALTH

No welfare state health benefits

1 per 2599 people

Pneumonia, tuberculosis, violence, accidents, typhoid

Most general hospitals are privately run. Malaria, which was once a major problem, has been eradicated in all but remote areas. Poor sanitation and disease are common in the sprawling slums around Manila.

SPENDING

GDP/cap. increase

CONSUMPTION AND SPENDING

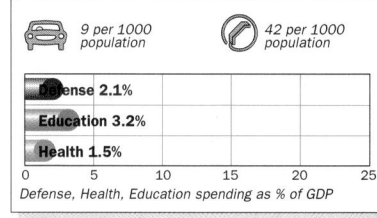

9 per 1000 population

42 per 1000 population

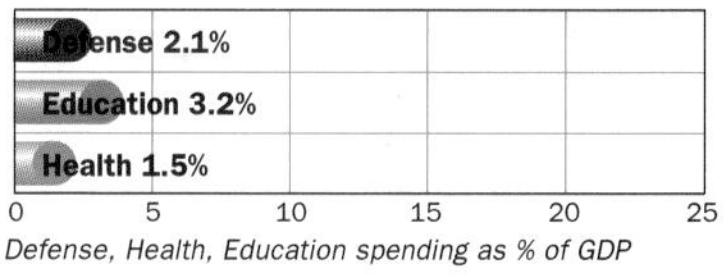
Defense 2.1%
Education 3.2%
Health 1.5%
0
5
10
15
20
25
Defense, Health, Education spending as % of GDP

The contrast between extremes of wealth and poverty is particularly marked. Wealth remains highly concentrated in a few select business families which are based in Manila.

WORLD RANKING

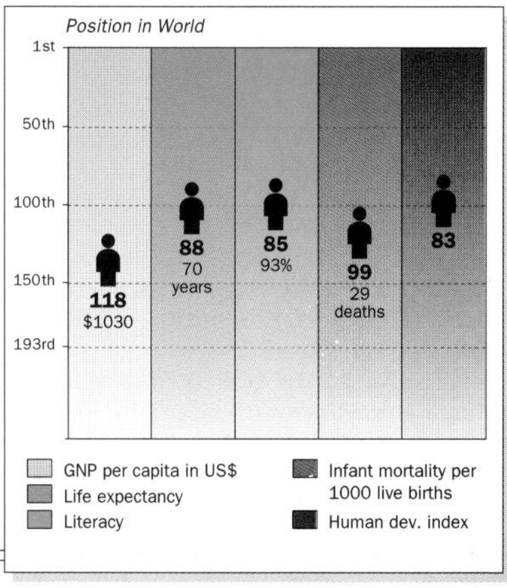
Position in World
1st
50th
100th
150th
193rd
118
$1030
88
70
years
85
93%
99
29
deaths
83
GNP per capita in US$
Life expectancy
Literacy
Infant mortality per 1000 live births
Human dev. index

P

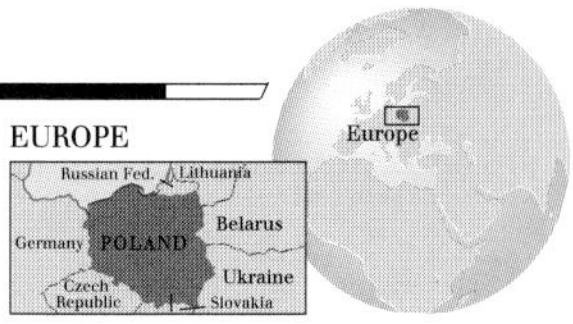
EUROPE
Russian Fed.
Lithuania
Germany
POLAND
Belarus
Czech Republic
Ukraine
Slovakia
Europe

POLAND

OFFICIAL NAME: Republic of Poland **CAPITAL:** Warsaw
POPULATION: 38.6 million **CURRENCY:** Zloty **OFFICIAL LANGUAGE:** Polish

1918 | 1945 | May 3 | PL | +1 | +48 | .pl

LOCATED IN THE HEART of Europe, Poland's low-lying plains extend from the Baltic shore in the north to the Tatra Mountains on its southern border with Slovakia. Since the collapse of communism, Poland has undergone massive social, economic, and political change. Opting for a radical form of economic "shock therapy" in the early 1990s to kick-start the switch to a market economy, it experienced rapid growth. One of the ten countries that joined the EU in the 2004 enlargement, Poland had already been accepted as a member of NATO five years earlier.

CLIMATE

Continental

WEATHER CHART FOR WARSAW

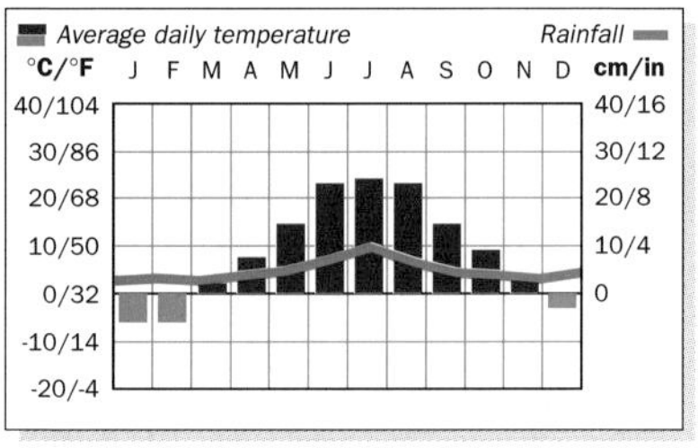
Average daily temperature
Rainfall
°C/°F
J F M A M J J A S O N D
cm/in
40/104
30/86
20/68
10/50
0/32
-10/14
-20/4
40/16
30/12
20/8
10/4
0

Most of the country has the same climate. Summers are hot, with heavy rainfall often accompanied by thunder. Winters are severe, with snow covering the ground on the southern mountains, for as much as 60–70 days in the east.

TRANSPORTATION

Drive on right

Okecie, Warsaw
5.17m passengers

383 ships
585,600 grt

THE TRANSPORTATION NETWORK

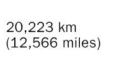

247,994 km (154,096 miles)

405 km (252 miles)

20,223 km (12,566 miles)

3812 km (2369 miles)

The national airline LOT has increased its charter business as more middle-class Poles vacation abroad. Russian aircraft have all been replaced with Western models. A 15-year roads expansion program was begun in 1997. "Fast tram" systems for cities and long-distance high-speed rail links need major investment. The government backs the streamlining of the rail workforce and the commercialization and part-privatization of the Polish State Railways (PKP).

The advent of mobile phones has affected telecommunications, as has the privatization of Telekomunikacja Polska and the end of its monopoly on long-distance calls.

***The medieval administrative center of Lublin** lies in Poland's southeastern agricultural heartland.*

TOURISM

Visitors : Population 1:2.8

14m visitors

Down 7% in 2002

MAIN TOURIST ARRIVALS

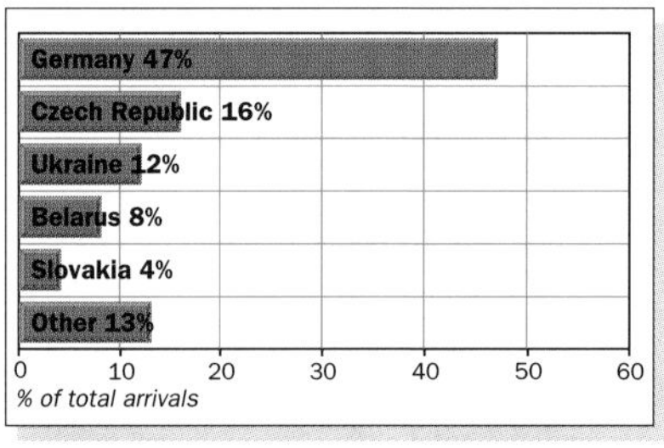
Germany 47%
Czech Republic 16%
Ukraine 12%
Belarus 8%
Slovakia 4%
Other 13%
0
10
20
30
40
50
60
% of total arrivals

Despite environmental problems, Poland is renowned for its skiing and hiking, especially in the Tatra Mountains. Kraków's medieval core has been preserved, while Toruń has restored its historic German Hanseatic buildings.

Warsaw's historic center has been reconstructed following the destruction of 80% of it by the German army in 1944. More hotels and restaurants are being opened.

Poznań has exploited its location between Warsaw and Berlin to create an international exhibition and business convention industry.

Airlines have increased their flights from the West to take advantage of the country's tourist potential.

PEOPLE

Pop. density medium

Polish

127/km² (328/mi²)

THE URBAN/RURAL POPULATION SPLIT

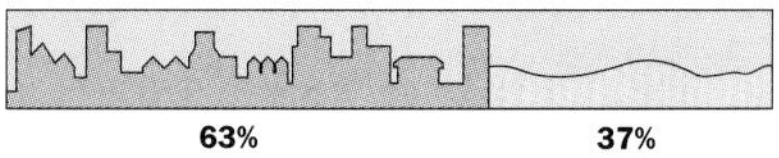
63%
37%

RELIGIOUS PERSUASION

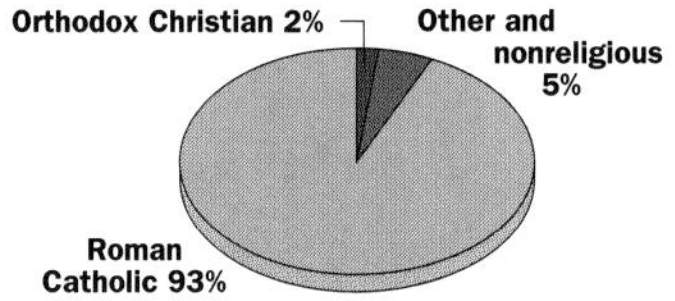
Orthodox Christian 2%
Other and nonreligious 5%
Roman Catholic 93%

ETHNIC MAKEUP

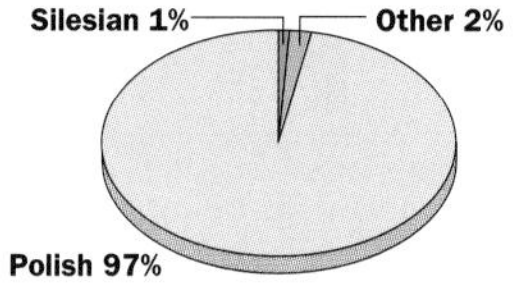
Silesian 1%
Other 2%
Polish 97%

Poland has a strongly Roman Catholic population, and in addition there is little ethnic diversity. The Church believes that stronger links with the West, especially through joining the EU, will weaken its influence. Abortion is still a major issue, and attempts to liberalize the law in 1996 were overturned by the Constitutional Tribunal.

Some small ethnic groups have opened schools and cultural and religious centers. Others, particularly ethnic Germans and German-dialect speakers in Silesia, are becoming more assertive. Jews are still resentful of past discrimination, and there is some evidence of residual antisemitism at a high level. Disputes over the special significance of the site of the Auschwitz concentration camp, near Kraków, have caused conflict between Jews and Catholics.

Wealth disparities are small, though the growing wealth of the entrepreneurial class is causing tension. The major political parties on left and right agree on continuing economic reform.

POPULATION AGE BREAKDOWN

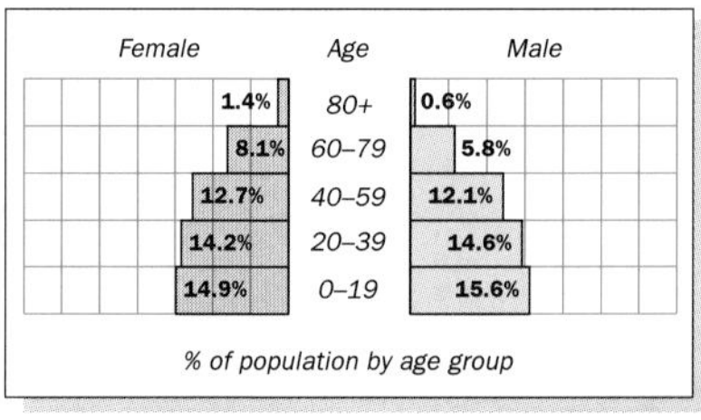
Female
Age
Male
1.4%
80+
0.6%
8.1%
60–79
5.8%
12.7%
40–59
12.1%
14.2%
20–39
14.6%
14.9%
0–19
15.6%
% of population by age group

POLITICS

Multiparty elections

L. House 2001/2005
U. House 2001/2005

President Aleksander Kwasniewski

AT THE LAST ELECTION

Diet 460 seats

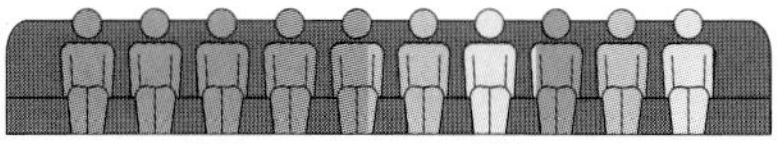
10% PiS
8% LPR
47% SLD–UP
14% PO
11% S
9% PSL
1% GM

SLD–UP = Democratic Left Alliance–Labor Union **PO** = Civic Platform **S** = Self-defense **PiS** = Law and Justice **PSL** = Polish Peasant Party **LPR** = League of Polish Families **GM** = German Minority of Lower Silesia **Bloc** = Senate 2001 Bloc **Ind** = Independents

Senate 100 seats

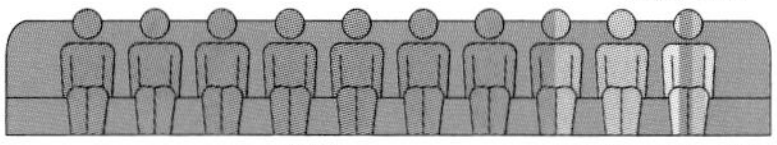
4% PSL
2% Ind
75% SLD–UP
15% Bloc
2% LPR
2% S

Since 1989, Poland has been a multiparty parliamentary democracy.

PROFILE

The reformed communists of the SLD and the PSL pursued a policy of market reforms in successive governments from 1993 until 1997. Aleksander Kwasniewski of the SLD was elected president in 1995, and reelected in 2000. More right-wing groups held sway for the 1997–2001 parliamentary term, with Jerzy Buzek as prime minister. His Solidarity Electoral Action (AWS) alliance, a right-wing grouping with vocal Catholic and nationalist elements, formed a coalition with the liberal Freedom Union (UW), but remained in office as a minority government after the UW withdrew in 2000.

In 2001 the Solidarity trade union wing voted to withdraw from politics, and the AWS lost all its seats in the elections that September. A new left-of-center coalition was brought together under former communist Leszek Miller of the SLD. After dismissing the PSL from his coalition in March 2003, Miller also headed a minority government. He resigned on May 2, 2004, the day after Poland joined the EU; he was succeeded by his chosen replacement, Finance Minister Marek Belka.

MAIN POLITICAL ISSUES

Minority rule

A superfluity of political parties has meant that fractious coalitions are the norm. Both Buzek and Miller were forced to lead minority governments after the loss of quarrelsome partners, leaving them reliant on parliamentary maneuvering to ensure the day-to-day survival of their governments.

Marek Belka *succeeded Leszek Miller as prime minister in 2004.*

President Aleksander Kwasniewski *of the SLD, elected in 1995.*

Church–state relations

A heated dialogue over the proper role of the Church has been fueled by the Church's outspoken views in debates over abortion, worship in schools, and values in the media, and against membership of the EU – despite Pope John Paul II's open backing of Poland's accession. However, the eclipse of Solidarity and the AWS has left the Church without its voice in parliament.

WORLD AFFAIRS

Joined UN in 1945

CE | EU | NATO | OECD | OSCE

Poland is keen to integrate with the West, though eastern ties remain important. It was admitted to NATO in 1999 and joined the EU in 2004. Membership of the latter rested on negotiating restrictions on the sale of Polish land to foreigners and the migration of Poles westward. Poland was an active partner in the US-led invasion of Iraq in 2003 and was given control over one of the military commands established there.

CHRONOLOGY

Poland was the second country in Europe to have a written constitution. In 1795, it was partitioned between Austria-Hungary, Prussia, and Russia.

- **1918** Polish state recreated.
- **1921** Democratic constitution.
- **1926–1935** Marshal Jozef Pilsudski heads military coup. Nine years of authoritarian rule.
- **1939** Germany invades and divides Poland with Russia.
- **1941** First concentration camps built on Polish soil.
- **1944** Warsaw Uprising.
- **1945** Potsdam and Yalta Conferences set present borders and determine political allegiance to Soviet Union.
- **1947** Communists manipulate elections to gain power.

POLAND

Total Area : 312 685 sq. km (120 728 sq. miles)

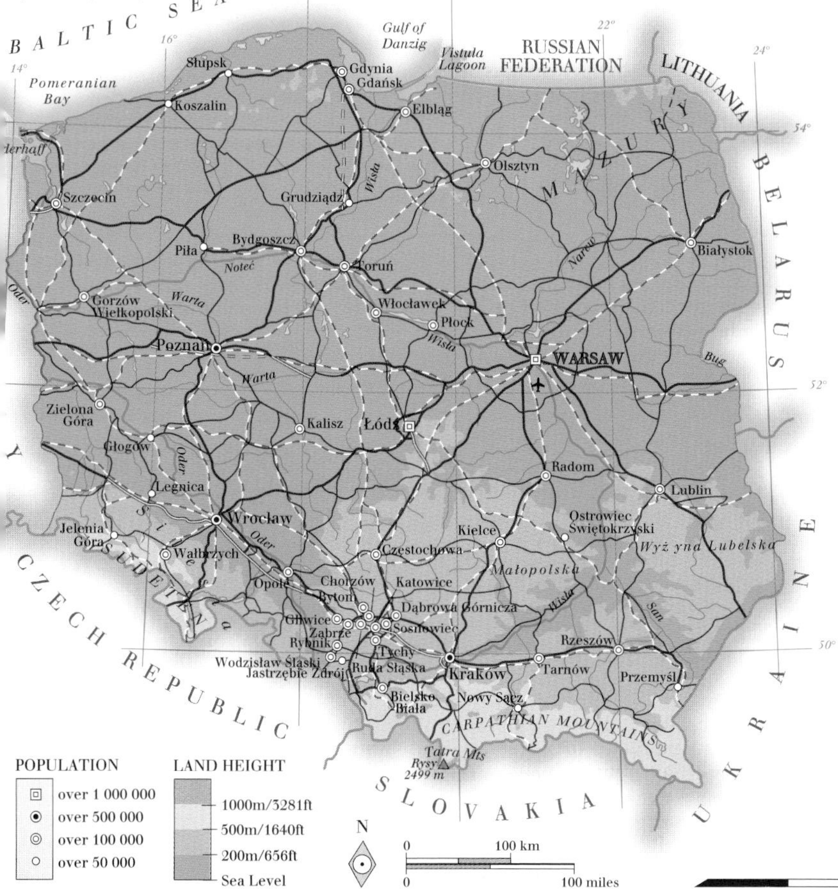
BALTIC SEA
Pomeranian Bay
Gulf of Danzig
Vistula Lagoon
RUSSIAN FEDERATION
LITHUANIA
BELARUS
UKRAINE
SLOVAKIA
CZECH REPUBLIC
MAZURY
SUDETEN
CARPATHIAN MOUNTAINS
Tatra Mts
Rysy 2499 m
Słupsk
Gdynia
Gdańsk
Koszalin
Elbląg
Olsztyn
Szczecin
Grudziądz
Bydgoszcz
Piła
Toruń
Białystok
Gorzów Wielkopolski
Włocławek
Płock
Poznań
WARSAW
Zielona Góra
Kalisz
Łódź
Głogów
Radom
Legnica
Lublin
Wrocław
Jelenia Góra
Wałbrzych
Kielce
Ostrowiec Świętokrzyski
Częstochowa
Wyżyna Lubelska
Małopolska
Opole
Chorzów
Bytom
Katowice
Dąbrowa Górnicza
Gliwice
Zabrze
Sosnowiec
Rybnik
Tychy
Wodzisław Śląski
Jastrzębie Zdrój
Ruda Śląska
Kraków
Tarnów
Rzeszów
Przemyśl
Bielsko Biała
Nowy Sącz
Wisła
Noteć
Warta
Oder
Narew
Bug
San
POPULATION
over 1 000 000
over 500 000
over 100 000
over 50 000
LAND HEIGHT
1000m/3281ft
500m/1640ft
200m/656ft
Sea Level
N
0 100 km
0 100 miles

P

CHRONOLOGY *continued*

- **1956** More than 50 killed in rioting in Poznań.
- **1970** Food price increases lead to strikes and riots in the Baltic port cities. Hundreds are killed.
- **1979** Cardinal Karol Wojtyla of Kraków is elected pope (John Paul II).
- **1980** Strikes force government to negotiate with Solidarity union. Resulting Gdańsk Accords grant right to strike and to form free trade unions.
- **1981** Gen. Wojciech Jaruzelski becomes prime minister.
- **1981–1983** Martial law. Solidarity forced into underground existence. Many of its leaders, including Lech Walesa, interned.
- **1983** Walesa awarded Nobel Peace Prize.
- **1986** Amnesty for political prisoners.
- **1987** Referendum rejects government austerity program.
- **1988** Renewed industrial unrest.
- **1989** Ruling party holds talks with Solidarity, which is relegalized. Partially free elections held. First postwar noncommunist government formed.
- **1990** Launch of market reforms. Walesa elected president.
- **1991** Free elections lead to fragmented parliament.
- **1992** Last Russian troops leave.
- **1993** Elections: new coalition headed by reformed communists.
- **1994** Launch of mass privatization.
- **1995** Aleksander Kwasniewski, leader of reformed communists, elected president.
- **1996** Historic Gdańsk shipyard declared bankrupt and closed down.
- **1997** Parliament finally adopts new postcommunist constitution. Legislative elections end former communist majority with big swing to right-wing AWS coalition.
- **1999** Joins NATO.
- **2001** Elections: AWS routed, left-of-center coalition formed under Leszek Miller.
- **2004** Joins EU. Miller resigns. Marek Belka appointed prime minister.

AID

Recipient

$1.16bn (receipts) — Up 20% in 2002

Large-scale aid for economic transformation was a phenomenon of the early 1990s. The IMF, the EBRD, and the EU all supported Poland's stabilization and reform program. EU funding now focuses on debt-servicing and helping Poland to reach the environmental standards required of it as an EU member.

DEFENSE

Compulsory military service

$3.4bn — Down 1% in 2002

Poland joined NATO in 1999. Its standing army is among the largest in Europe, and additional paramilitary units include over 14,000 border guards. A 15-year program to modernize the armed forces was introduced in 1997. A civilian alternative to military service was first offered in 1998, and military service, already cut from 18 months to a year in 1999, is being gradually reduced to nine months by 2006.

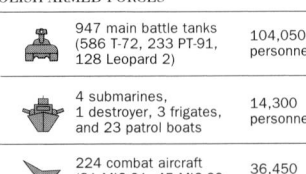

POLISH ARMED FORCES

947 main battle tanks (586 T-72, 233 PT-91, 128 Leopard 2)	104,050 personnel
4 submarines, 1 destroyer, 3 frigates, and 23 patrol boats	14,300 personnel
224 combat aircraft (81 MiG-21, 45 MiG-29, 98 Su-22)	36,450 personnel
None	

ECONOMICS

Inflation 21% p.a. (1990–2001)

$177bn — 3.697 zlotys (3.904)

SCORE CARD

World GNP Ranking	23rd
GNP per Capita	$4570
Balance of Payments	–$5.01bn
Inflation	1.9%
Unemployment	20%

EXPORTS

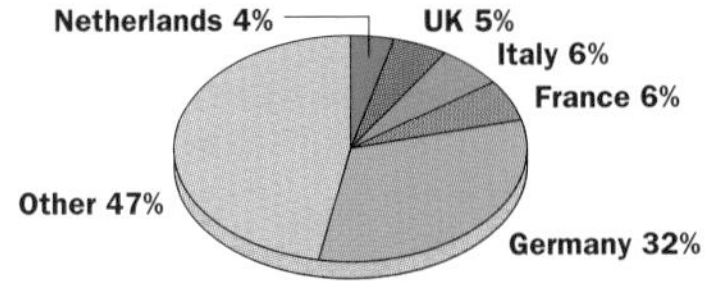
Netherlands 4%
UK 5%
Italy 6%
France 6%
Other 47%
Germany 32%

IMPORTS

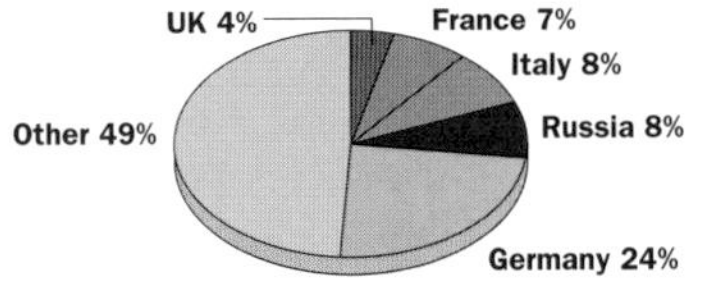
UK 4%
France 7%
Italy 8%
Russia 8%
Other 49%
Germany 24%

Strengths

Restructuring of coal industry, electricity supply, and oil refining. Successful privatizations accelerated again in late 1990s. High rates of foreign investment reflect status as largest market in central Europe. Booming construction industry.

Weaknesses

High and rising unemployment. Agriculture suffers from overmanning, tiny farms, and lack of investment. Compensation for communist-era property expropriations unresolved. Heavy industries not competitive.

Profile

After a decade of economic crisis, the postcommunist government in 1990 drove through the most determined plan in the whole region to make the transition to a market economy. Most prices were freed, trade was opened, and the zloty was made convertible. Foreign investment and economic growth soared, especially after Western creditors agreed to cancel half of the country's foreign debt in 1994. Poland now attracts the most foreign capital in central and eastern Europe.

There are still large-scale heavy industrial plants left over from the communist era, but some have been converted or reorganized successfully. Many state farms have been liquidated, but agricultural efficiency is improving only slowly. Some 24% of the workforce is employed in farming. Economic growth slowed at the end of the 1990s, but was back to 4% in 2000. Inflation has fallen since the 1990s, but unemployment has hit a postcommunist record level, exceeding 20% in 2003.

ECONOMIC PERFORMANCE INDICATOR

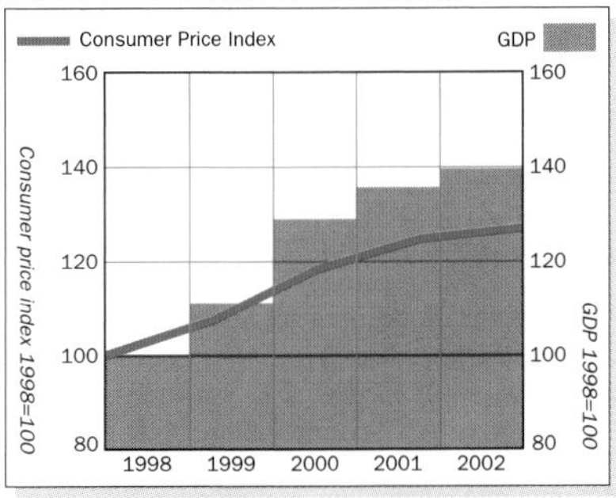
Consumer Price Index
GDP
160
140
120
100
80
Consumer price index 1998=100
GDP 1998=100
1998
1999
2000
2001
2002

POLAND : MAJOR BUSINESSES

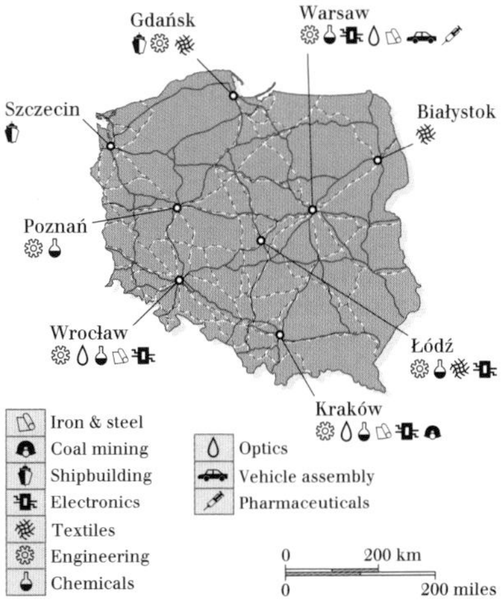
Gdańsk
Warsaw
Szczecin
Białystok
Poznań
Wrocław
Łódź
Kraków
Iron & steel
Coal mining
Shipbuilding
Electronics
Textiles
Engineering
Chemicals
Optics
Vehicle assembly
Pharmaceuticals
0
200 km
0
200 miles

P

RESOURCES

Electric power 30.6m kW

261,376 tonnes

13,093 b/d (reserves 38m barrels)

18.6m pigs, 5.49m cattle, 3.59m ducks, 48.4m chickens

Coal, copper, silver, sulfur, natural gas, lead, salt, iron, oil

ELECTRICITY GENERATION

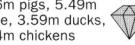

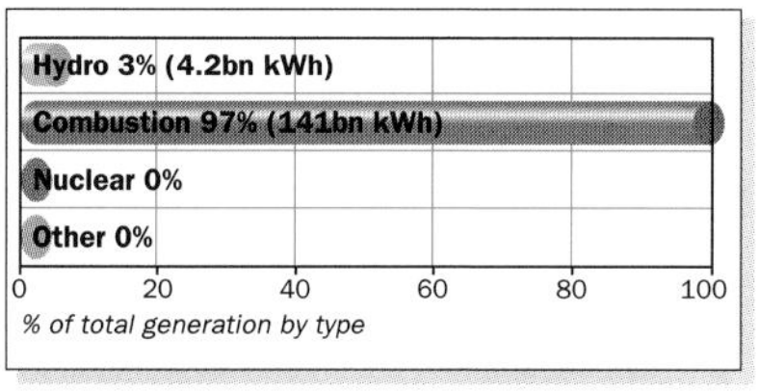
Hydro 3% (4.2bn kWh)
Combustion 97% (141bn kWh)
Nuclear 0%
Other 0%
0
20
40
60
80
100
% of total generation by type

Poland has significant quantities of coal, copper, silver, sulfur, natural gas, lead, and salt. The government's aim is to achieve self-sufficiency in energy resources and eventually to be able to export them; plans are in place to privatize the fuel and energy industries. The government also intends to reduce dependence on coal and to generate more electricity from natural gas.

POLAND : LAND USE

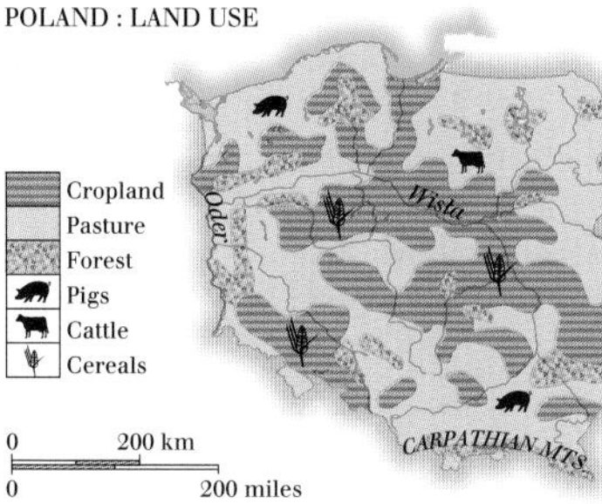
Cropland
Pasture
Forest
Pigs
Cattle
Cereals
Oder
Wisła
CARPATHIAN MTS
0
200 km
0
200 miles

ENVIRONMENT

Sustainability rank: 87th

12% (9% partially protected)

7.8 tonnes per capita

ENVIRONMENTAL TREATIES

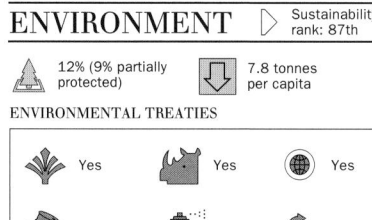

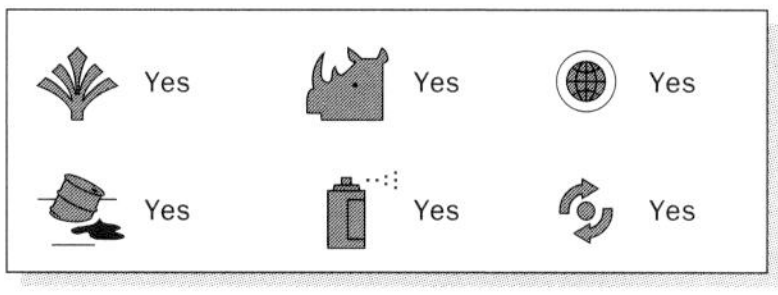
Yes
Yes
Yes
Yes
Yes
Yes

Pollution problems are serious, but lessening. Upper Silesia and the Kraków area are still badly affected, but industry there only emits a third of the pollutants it emitted in 1990. Now that much heavy industry has been cleaned up or closed down, there is more concern about small factories, domestic coal fires, and the increased use of private cars.

Water pollution, mainly from untreated sewage and industrial discharges, is a major problem. Rivers flowing into the Baltic are badly affected by nitrates and phosphates used in farming. Polish standards, themselves widely disregarded, need to be raised to meet EU minimum requirements.

MEDIA

TV ownership high

Daily newspaper circulation 102 per 1000 people

The constitution guarantees media freedom. *Gazeta Wyborcza*, set up by Solidarity in 1989, is still the leading daily, and its owners are expanding into other media. In 2003 the government ordered the bugging of all telecommunications, including e-mail, citing security concerns.

CRIME

No death penalty

83,113 prisoners

Up 10% in 2001

CRIME RATES

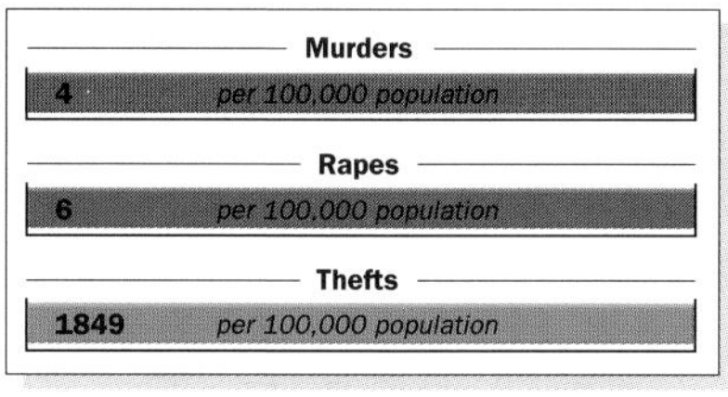
Murders
4
per 100,000 population
Rapes
6
per 100,000 population
Thefts
1849
per 100,000 population

Smuggling is the most significant problem, and Warsaw is a main center for this. Narcotics are transferred westward to Germany and expensive cars eastward to Russia. A National Remembrance Institute was set up in 2000 to investigate and prosecute the Nazi- and communist-era crimes of 1939–1989.

EDUCATION

School leaving age: 16

99%

1.8m students

THE EDUCATION SYSTEM

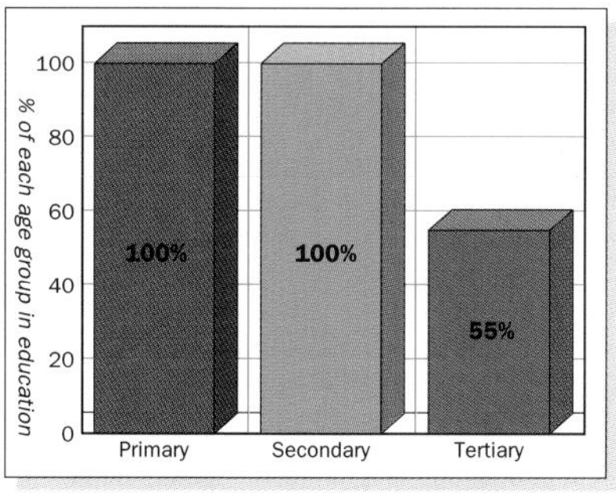
100
80
60
40
20
0
% of each age group in education
100%
100%
55%
Primary
Secondary
Tertiary

Primary education lasts from the age of seven to 13; lower secondary level follows until 16. At upper secondary level, exam-based selection separates the academic, technical, and vocational schools. A standard curriculum is followed in all schools. Despite the high official literacy figures, a relatively large proportion of school-leavers still lack basic skills. Public spending on education fell in real terms in the 1990s. Since 1989 the Roman Catholic Church has been allowed to operate schools. Most of the higher education institutions offer business-related courses.

PUBLISHING AND BROADCAST MEDIA

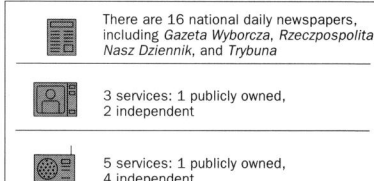

There are 16 national daily newspapers, including *Gazeta Wyborcza*, *Rzeczpospolita*, *Nasz Dziennik*, and *Trybuna*

3 services: 1 publicly owned, 2 independent

5 services: 1 publicly owned, 4 independent

HEALTH

Welfare state health benefits

1 per 455 people

Cancers, heart and cerebrovascular diseases

Fundamental reforms introduced in 1999 created a "market" health system, giving patients the right to choose where to go for treatment. Intended to be decentralized and less bureaucratic, the new system was confusing for some patients, with hospitals and doctors competing for business. Medical care is free for most people, but there are now a number of private health clinics.

SPENDING

GDP/cap. increase

CONSUMPTION AND SPENDING

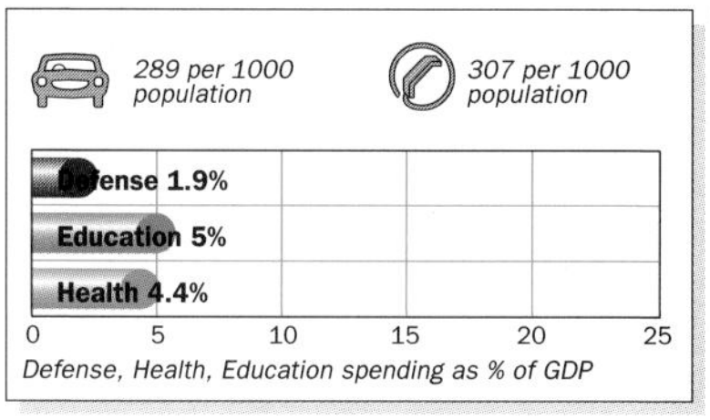
289 per 1000 population
307 per 1000 population
Defense 1.9%
Education 5%
Health 4.4%
0
5
10
15
20
25
Defense, Health, Education spending as % of GDP

Market reforms have led to some structural unemployment, and the inevitable hardship that this represents. More restructuring of heavy industry is planned. Pensioners have enjoyed benefits amounting to a higher percentage of GDP than in most countries, but state cutbacks are making private pensions more necessary.

WORLD RANKING

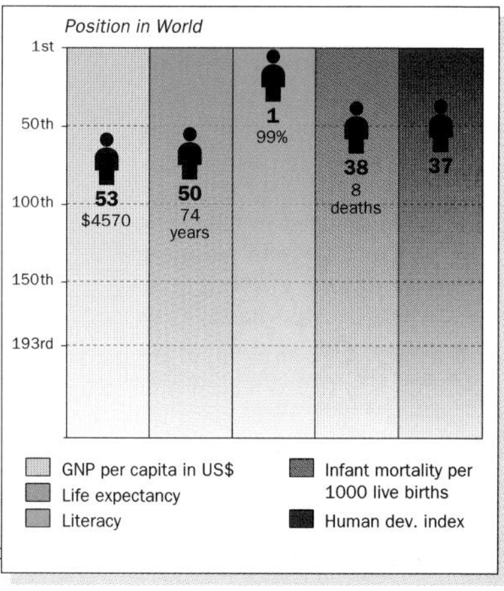
Position in World
1st
50th
100th
150th
193rd
53
$4570
50
74
years
1
99%
38
8
deaths
37
GNP per capita in US$
Life expectancy
Literacy
Infant mortality per 1000 live births
Human dev. index

P

PORTUGAL

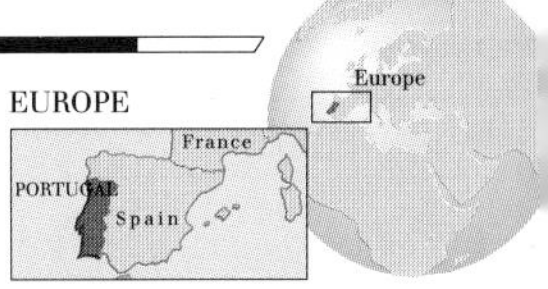

EUROPE
Europe
France
PORTUGAL
Spain

OFFICIAL NAME: Republic of Portugal **CAPITAL:** Lisbon
POPULATION: 10.1 million **CURRENCY:** Euro **OFFICIAL LANGUAGE:** Portuguese

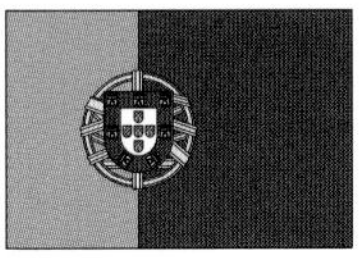

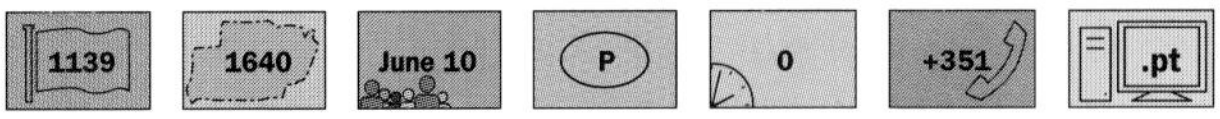

1139
1640
June 10
P
0
+351
.pt

PORTUGAL, WITH ITS long Atlantic coast, lies on the western side of the Iberian peninsula. The River Tagus divides the more mountainous north from the lower, undulating terrain to the south. In 1974, a bloodless military coup overthrew a long-standing conservative dictatorship. A constituent assembly was elected in 1975 and the armed forces withdrew from politics thereafter. Portugal then began a substantial program of economic modernization and accompanying social change. Membership of the EU has helped underpin this process.

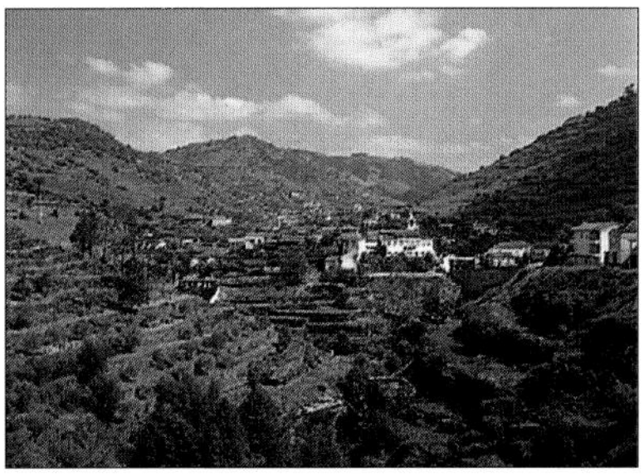

Santa Marta de Penaguiao, *a small village in the heart of Portugal's wine-producing region, which is centered on the Douro valley.*

CLIMATE

Mediterranean/ maritime

WEATHER CHART FOR LISBON

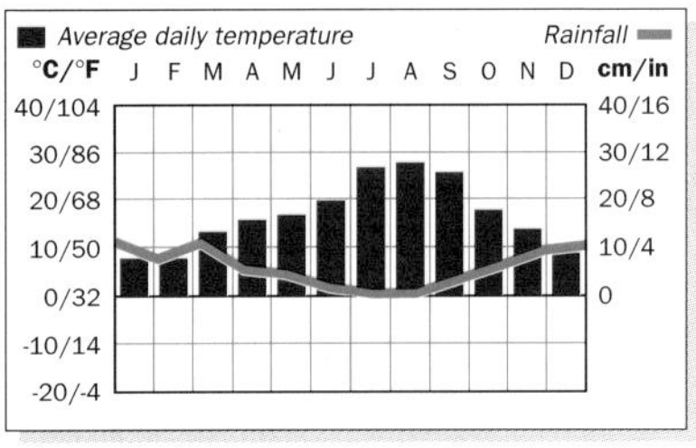

Average daily temperature
Rainfall
°C/°F
J F M A M J J A S O N D
cm/in
40/104
30/86
20/68
10/50
0/32
-10/14
-20/-4
40/16
30/12
20/8
10/4
0

Portugal has a mild, Mediterranean climate, which is moderated by the influence of the Atlantic. Summers can be hot and sultry, while winters are relatively mild. Inland areas have more variable weather than coastal regions. Rainfall is generally higher in the mountainous north, while the central areas are more temperate. The southern Algarve region is predominantly dry and sunny.

TRANSPORTATION

Drive on right

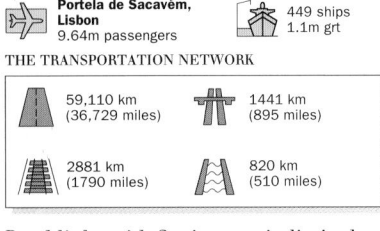

Portela de Sacavém, Lisbon
9.64m passengers

449 ships
1.1m grt

THE TRANSPORTATION NETWORK

59,110 km (36,729 miles)

1441 km (895 miles)

2881 km (1790 miles)

820 km (510 miles)

Road links with Spain remain limited, despite modernization schemes and the new southern Guadiana bridge. The Lisbon–Madrid expressway was finally completed in 1999, the year after the 17-km Vasco da Gama bridge in Lisbon opened. Poor road construction, heavy traffic, and dangerous driving mean that Portugal has one of Europe's highest rates of road deaths. Lisbon's small, efficient metro complements its trams, but Porto's metro remains unfinished. A high-speed rail link with Spain is due for completion in 2008.

TOURISM

Visitors : Population 1.2:1

11.6m visitors

Down 4% in 2002

MAIN TOURIST ARRIVALS

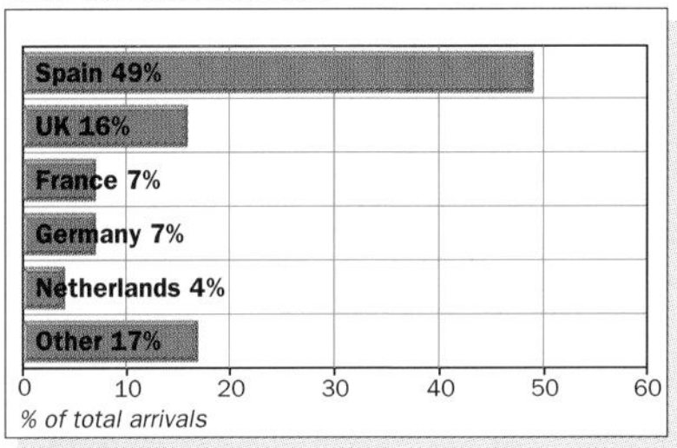

Spain 49%
UK 16%
France 7%
Germany 7%
Netherlands 4%
Other 17%
0 10 20 30 40 50 60
% of total arrivals

From the 1960s, Portugal's popularity as a tourist destination has been linked in part to qualities which reflected its relatively poor economic development, such as low prices and little crime. Thus some of the consequences of its substantial economic growth may have eroded part of Portugal's appeal, but since it now has a healthy number of visitors each year, tourism remains a major income-earner. The most popular destination is the Algarve, the southernmost province, followed by the western resorts of Figueira da Foz and the Tróia Peninsula. Visitors are also attracted by Portugal's architecture, notably that dating from the Manueline period (1490–1520), by its wine and port, and by its handicrafts, such as ceramics, lace, and tapestries. In addition, Portugal is noted for being the location of some of Europe's finest golf courses.

PORTUGAL

Total Area : 92 391 sq. km (35 672 sq. miles)

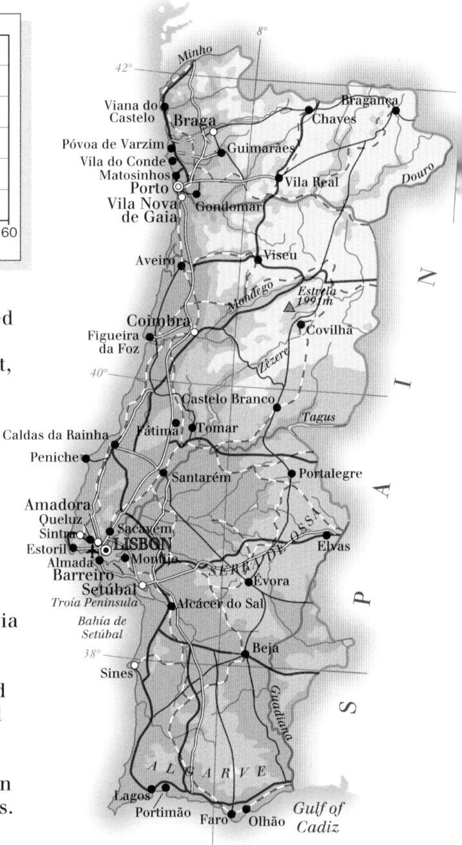

Minho
Viana do Castelo
Braga
Bragança
Chaves
Póvoa de Varzim
Vila do Conde
Matosinhos
Porto
Vila Nova de Gaia
Guimarães
Vila Real
Douro
Gondomar
Aveiro
Viseu
Mondego
Estrela 1991m
Coimbra
Figueira da Foz
Covilhã
Zêzere
Castelo Branco
Tagus
Caldas da Rainha
Fátima
Tomar
Peniche
Santarém
Portalegre
Amadora
Queluz
Sintra
Estoril
Almada
Barreiro
LISBON
Sacavém
Montijo
Setúbal
Tróia Peninsula
Bahía de Setúbal
Évora
Elvas
Alcácer do Sal
Beja
Sines
Guadiana
ALGARVE
Lagos
Portimão
Faro
Olhão
Gulf of Cadiz
SPAIN

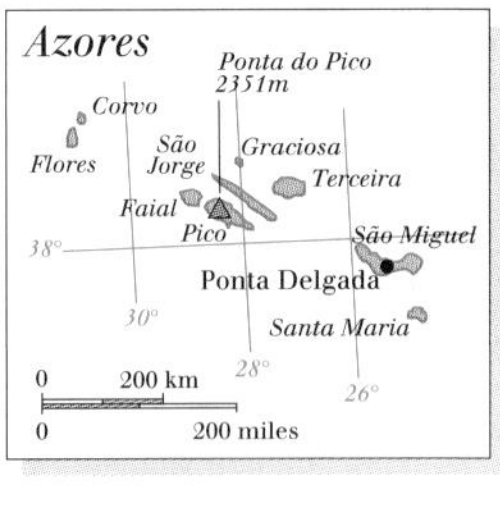

Azores
Ponta do Pico 2351m
Corvo
Flores
São Jorge
Graciosa
Terceira
Faial
Pico
São Miguel
Ponta Delgada
Santa Maria
200 km
200 miles

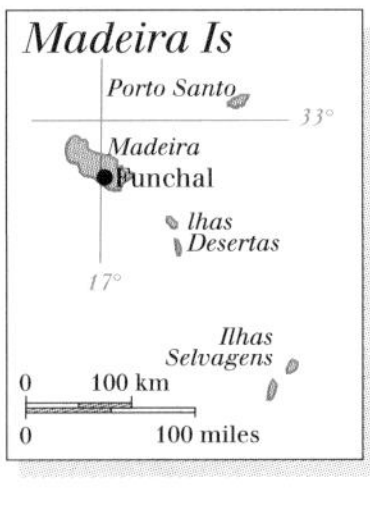

Madeira Is
Porto Santo
Madeira
Funchal
Ilhas Desertas
Ilhas Selvagens
100 km
100 miles

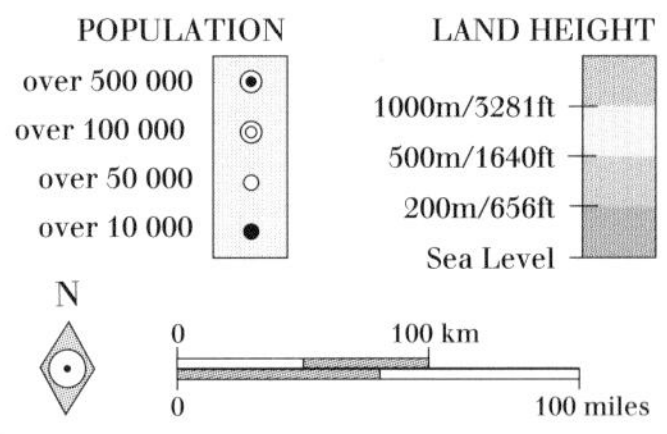

POPULATION
over 500 000
over 100 000
over 50 000
over 10 000
LAND HEIGHT
1000m/3281ft
500m/1640ft
200m/656ft
Sea Level
N
100 km
100 miles

P

PEOPLE

Pop. density medium

Portuguese

110/km² (284/mi²)

THE URBAN/RURAL POPULATION SPLIT

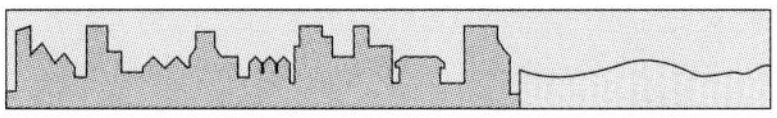
67%
33%

RELIGIOUS PERSUASION

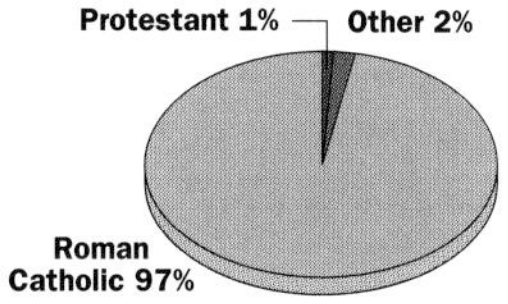
Protestant 1%
Other 2%
Roman Catholic 97%

ETHNIC MAKEUP

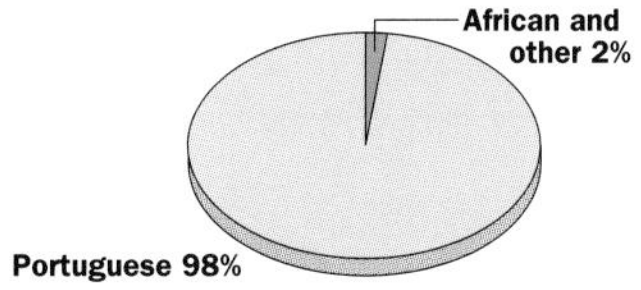
African and other 2%
Portuguese 98%

Portuguese society, once regarded as rather inward-looking, has become much more egalitarian since the 1974 revolution. It is increasingly integrated into the rest of western Europe.

The Roman Catholic Church has lost some of its social influence, as shown by falling birthrates and more liberal attitudes to abortion, divorce, and unmarried mothers (almost one in five children are born outside marriage). Apart from urban areas, the north is still devoutly Catholic. Family ties remain all-important.

Ethnic and religious tensions are limited. Immigration increased after 1974, and foreigners now constitute 2% of the population. Early arrivals came from the former African colonies, but recently there has been an influx of east European workers.

Women got the vote only in 1976; now 60% of university students are women, and 63% of women of working age have jobs.

POPULATION AGE BREAKDOWN

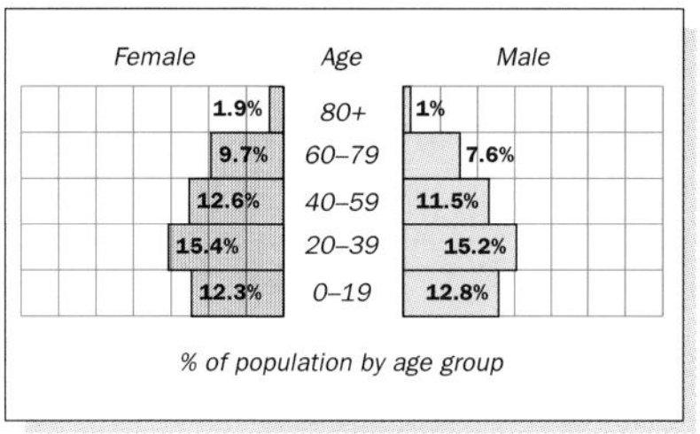
Female
Age
Male
1.9%
80+
1%
9.7%
60–79
7.6%
12.6%
40–59
11.5%
15.4%
20–39
15.2%
12.3%
0–19
12.8%
% of population by age group

WORLD AFFAIRS

Joined UN in 1955

EU | CE | NATO | OECD | OSCE

Foreign relations are now based on Portugal's membership of the EU and NATO. Government support for the US-led invasion of Iraq in 2003 continues Portugal's traditional cooperation with the US on Middle East affairs.

Support for East Timor's struggle for independence, the smooth return of Macao to China in 1999, and bilateral ties with Brazil and a number of African countries are reminders of Portugal's past position as the first preeminent colonial power.

AID

Donor

$323m (donations)

Up 21% in 2002

Portugal is a major beneficiary of EU aid from the so-called structural funds. It currently earmarks around 0.27% of its GNP for aid to developing countries. More than 50% goes to former colonies in Africa, especially Mozambique, where Portuguese funding helped rebuild the massive war-damaged Cahora Bassa Dam and power plant.

POLITICS

Multiparty elections

2002/2006

President Jorge Sampãio

AT THE LAST ELECTION

Assembly of the Republic 230 seats

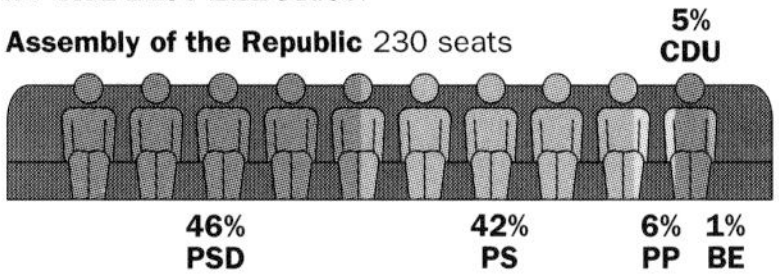
5% CDU
46% PSD
42% PS
6% PP
1% BE

PSD = Social Democratic Party
PS = Socialist Party **PP** = People's Party
CDU = United Democratic Coalition **BE** = Left Bloc

Portugal is a multiparty democracy.

Profile

A decade of center-right government ended in the 1995 elections, when the PSD lost to the PS, under António Guterres. His government gave priority to fiscal control. Despite a privatization program, however, the size of the public sector actually increased in 1995–1999. The PS was reelected in 1999, but soon lost popularity, and was ousted by the PSD in early elections in 2002. Lacking an overall majority, the PSD allied with the right-wing PP. The new government pledged to cut public spending and speed privatization. Prime Minister José Manuel Durão Barroso resigned in July 2004 to head the European Commission, and Pedro Santana Lopes replaced him.

Main Political Issues

Presidency and parliament

For ten years up to 1995, the presidency and the government were controlled by opposing parties, a situation which encouraged conflict and obstruction. A succession of PS presidents and minority governments then followed. Former PS leader Jorge Sampãio, who succeeded Mário Soares as president in 1996, was reelected comfortably in early 2001, but was to see a PSD government take office a year later, returning the executive to an uneasy "cohabitation."

Portugal and Spain

Since both Portugal and Spain joined the EU in 1986, Portugal's global position has been undermined by its larger neighbor. Multinational companies sometimes view Portugal just as a province of Spain and a division of Spanish operations. Events such as Expo '98 and the 2004 European Cup soccer competition have been used to promote Portugal's cultural identity and economic potential.

***President Jorge Sampãio**, socialist president since 1996.*

***Pedro Santana Lopes**, PSD prime minister since 2004.*

CHRONOLOGY

Portugal has existed as a nation state since 1139, though it was frequently challenged by Spain. It reached its zenith in the 16th century, before being annexed by Spain in 1580.

- **1640** Independence from Spain.
- **1755** Earthquake destroys Lisbon.
- **1793** Joins coalition against revolutionary France.
- **1807** France invades; royal family flees to Brazil.
- **1808** British troops arrive under Wellington. Start of Peninsular War.
- **1810** French leave Portugal.
- **1820** Liberal revolution.
- **1822** King João VI returns and accepts first Portuguese constitution. His son Dom Pedro declares independence of Brazil.
- **1834** Dom Pedro returns to Portugal to end civil war and installs his daughter as Queen Maria II.
- **1875–1876** Republican and Socialist parties founded.
- **1891** Republican uprising in Porto.
- **1908** Assassination of King Carlos I and heir to the throne.
- **1910** Abdication of Manuel II and proclamation of the Republic. Church and state separated.
- **1916** Portugal joins Allies in World War I.
- **1917–1918** New Republic led by Sidónio Pais.

P

CHRONOLOGY *continued*

- **1926** Army overturns republic.
- **1928** António Salazar joins government as finance minister. Economy improves significantly.
- **1932** Salazar prime minister.
- **1933** Promulgation of the constitution of the "New State," instituting right-wing dictatorship.
- **1936–1939** Salazar assists Franco in Spanish Civil War.
- **1939–1945** Portugal neutral during World War II, but lets UK use air bases in Azores.
- **1949** Founder member of NATO.
- **1958** Américo Thómas appointed president, following fraudulent defeat of Gen. Humberto Delgado.
- **1961** India annexes Goa. Guerrilla warfare breaks out in Angola, Mozambique, and Guinea.
- **1970** Death of Salazar, incapacitated since 1968; succeeded by Marcelo Caetano.
- **1971** Caetano attempts liberalization.
- **1974** "Carnation Revolution" – left-wing Armed Forces Movement overthrows Caetano.
- **1974–1975** African possessions attain independence. Some 750,000 expatriates return to Portugal.
- **1975** Communist takeover foiled by moderates and Mário Soares's PS. Indonesia seizes former Portuguese East Timor unopposed.
- **1976** Gen. António Eanes elected president. New constitution. Soares appointed prime minister.
- **1978** Period of nonparty technocratic government instituted.
- **1980** Center-right wins elections. Gen. Eanes reelected.
- **1982** Full civilian government formally restored.
- **1983** Soares caretaker prime minister, PS majority party.
- **1985** Anibal Cavaco Silva prime minister, minority PSD government.
- **1986** Soares elected president. Portugal joins EU, which funds major infrastructure and construction projects.
- **1987** Cavaco Silva wins absolute majority in parliament.
- **1991** Soares reelected president.
- **1995** PS wins elections; António Guterres prime minister.
- **1996** Former PS leader Jorge Sampãio elected president.
- **1999** PS strengthens its position in general election. December, Macao returned to China.
- **2001** Sampãio reelected.
- **2002** Euro fully adopted. PSD wins early elections, forms coalition with PP. José Manuel Durão Barroso prime minister.
- **2004** Hosts Euro 2004 soccer cup. Durão Barroso resigns to head European Commission.

DEFENSE

No compulsory military service

$2.95bn

Up 29% in 2002

Portugal has been a member of NATO since 1949. It has a small but relatively modern navy, while army and air force equipment is less up-to-date. Compulsory military service (with a civilian alternative) was substantially cut to just four months – the shortest in the world – before being abolished completely in 2004. The US, which is the major arms supplier, has a strategic air base in the Azores.

PORTUGUESE ARMED FORCES

187 main battle tanks (86 M-48A5, 101 M-60)	26,700 personnel
2 submarines, 6 frigates, and 28 patrol boats	10,950 personnel
50 combat aircraft (25 Alpha Jet, 6 P-3P, 19 F-16A/B)	7250 personnel
None	

ECONOMICS

Inflation 5.1% p.a. (1990–2001)

$109bn

0.822 euros (0.871)

SCORE CARD

World GNP Ranking	34th
GNP per capita	$10,720
Balance of Payments	–$9.12bn
Inflation	3.5%
Unemployment	5%

EXPORTS

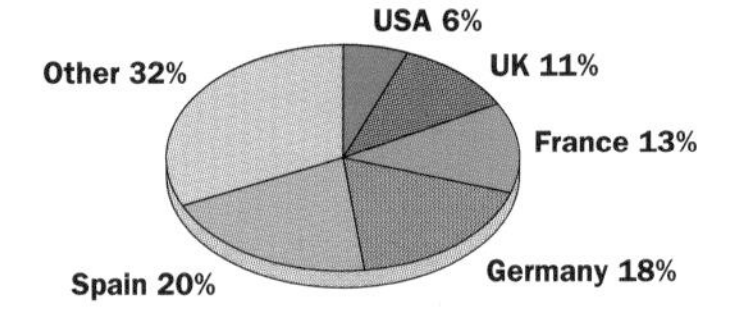
USA 6%
UK 11%
France 13%
Germany 18%
Spain 20%
Other 32%

IMPORTS

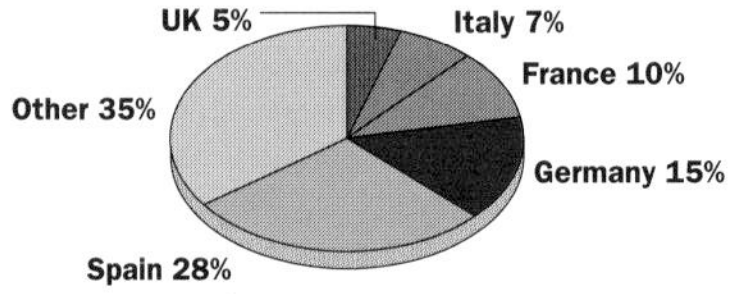
UK 5%
Italy 7%
France 10%
Germany 15%
Spain 28%
Other 35%

Strengths

Flexible labor market. High domestic and direct foreign investment. Strong banking sector. Tourism, now earning 6% of GDP – highest percentage in EU. Clothing and shoe manufacturing now joined by cars (notably Volkswagens) and machinery as major exports. Fast-track improvement of transportation infrastructure. Good deepwater port at Lisbon. Wine, especially port. Tomatoes, citrus fruit, cork, sardines.

Weaknesses

High dependence on imported oil. Few natural resources. Public sector remains overstaffed, underproductive, and a drain on resources. Large agricultural sector (4% of GDP, 13% of workforce) is inefficient; product prices undercut by Spain. Concern over Spanish control of industries, banking in particular. Rising labor costs: manufacturers moving to eastern Europe. EU sanctions in 2002 when budget deficit passed 3%-of-GDP limit.

ECONOMIC PERFORMANCE INDICATOR

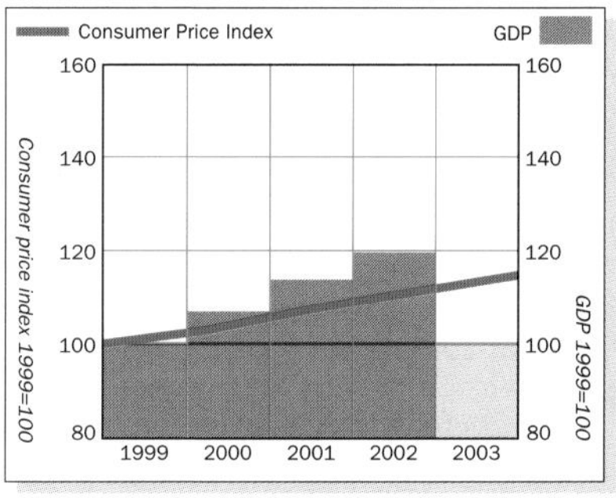
Consumer Price Index
GDP
160
140
120
100
80
1999
2000
2001
2002
2003
Consumer price index 1999=100
GDP 1999=100

Profile

Since entering the EU in 1986, Portugal has experienced significant foreign investment and economic growth. Early economic priorities were modernizing agriculture and industry, and the creation of an effective anti-inflationary policy in the face of growing wages. Though unemployment is among the lowest in the EU, meeting the criteria for entry into the eurozone proved a major challenge. Since full adoption of the euro in 2002, Portugal has had difficulty keeping its budget deficit under the permitted limit of 3% of GDP. New measures to streamline the public sector were introduced by the PSD-led government in 2003.

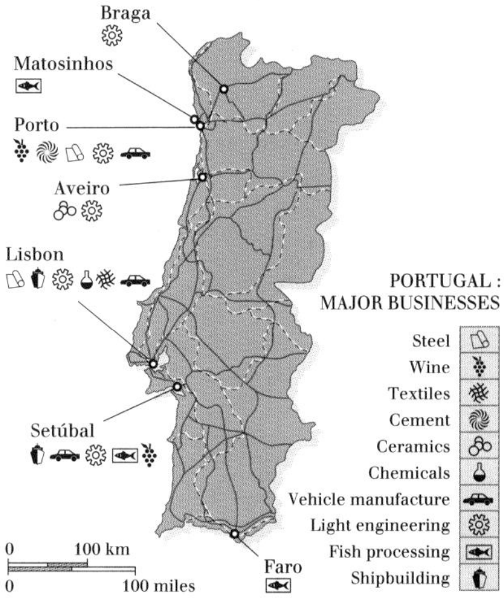
Braga
Matosinhos
Porto
Aveiro
Lisbon
Setúbal
Faro
0
100 km
0
100 miles
PORTUGAL : MAJOR BUSINESSES
Steel
Wine
Textiles
Cement
Ceramics
Chemicals
Vehicle manufacture
Light engineering
Fish processing
Shipbuilding

P

RESOURCES

Electric power 10.9m kW

199,038 tonnes

Not an oil producer; refines 247,000 b/d

7m turkeys, 5.5m sheep, 2.34m pigs, 35m chickens

Coal, limestone, granite, marble, tin, copper, tungsten

ELECTRICITY GENERATION

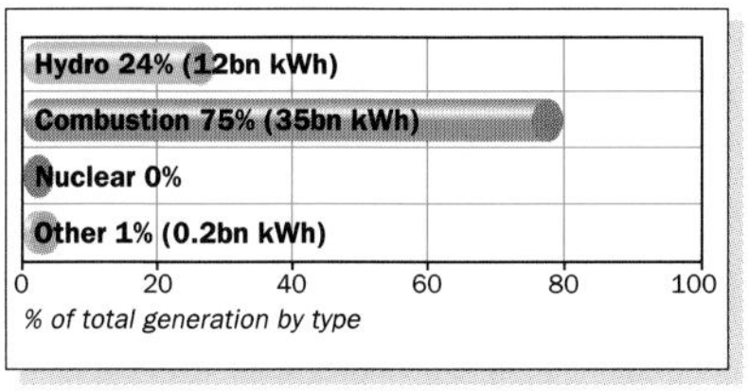

Hydro 24% (12bn kWh)
Combustion 75% (35bn kWh)
Nuclear 0%
Other 1% (0.2bn kWh)
0
20
40
60
80
100
% of total generation by type

Portugal is disadvantaged by a lack of natural resources, including water. Mining has historically been important, notably for tungsten, copper, and tin. The last coal mine closed in the mid-1990s. The fish catch, once central to the economy, has been declining in recent years.

PORTUGAL : LAND USE

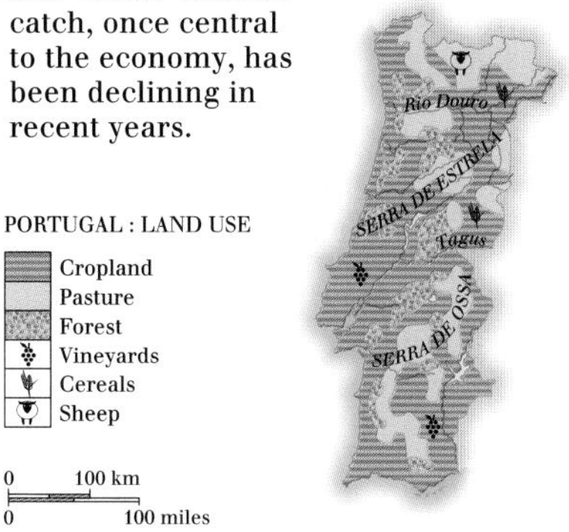

Cropland
Pasture
Forest
Vineyards
Cereals
Sheep
0
100 km
0
100 miles
Rio Douro
SERRA DE ESTRELA
Tagus
SERRA DE OSSA

ENVIRONMENT

Sustainability rank: 28th

7% (6% partially protected)

5.9 tonnes per capita

ENVIRONMENTAL TREATIES

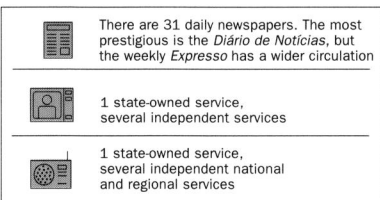

Yes Yes Yes

Yes Yes Yes

The unrestricted development of tourist resorts in the Algarve and major infrastructure projects are having a detrimental effect on natural habitats. EU membership has led to efforts to raise environmental standards, though EU agricultural grants for projects such as draining meadows, and monoculture afforestation, notably of eucalyptus and pine, are degrading biodiversity. Concerns include air pollution caused by industrial and vehicle emissions, and water pollution in coastal areas.

MEDIA

TV ownership high

Daily newspaper circulation 73 per 1000 people

PUBLISHING AND BROADCAST MEDIA

There are 31 daily newspapers. The most prestigious is the *Diário de Notícias*, but the weekly *Expresso* has a wider circulation

1 state-owned service, several independent services

1 state-owned service, several independent national and regional services

Most newspapers have only regional distribution. TV is the dominant medium. The Roman Catholic TVI was sold in 1998 to Media Capital, one of four groups that control most of the press and broadcasting. In 2002, the government strengthened its control over the state-owned RTP, raising fears for its political independence.

CRIME

No death penalty

14,300 prisoners

Up sharply in 2000–2002

CRIME RATES

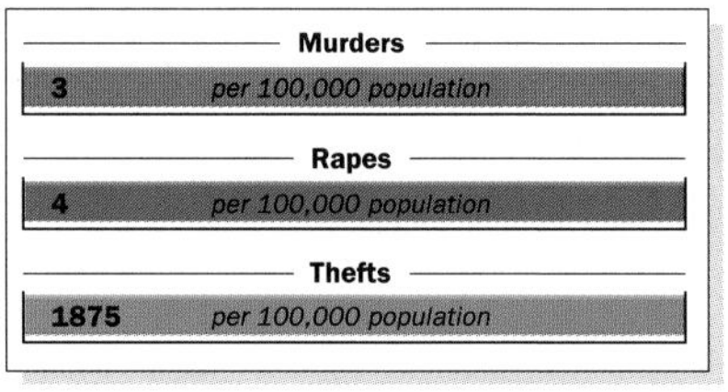

Murders
3 per 100,000 population
Rapes
4 per 100,000 population
Thefts
1875 per 100,000 population

Thefts have increased in recent years, raising the low crime rate. Possession and consumption of small quantities of narcotics were decriminalized in 2000 and legalized a year later.

EDUCATION

School leaving age: 15

93%

387,703 students

THE EDUCATION SYSTEM

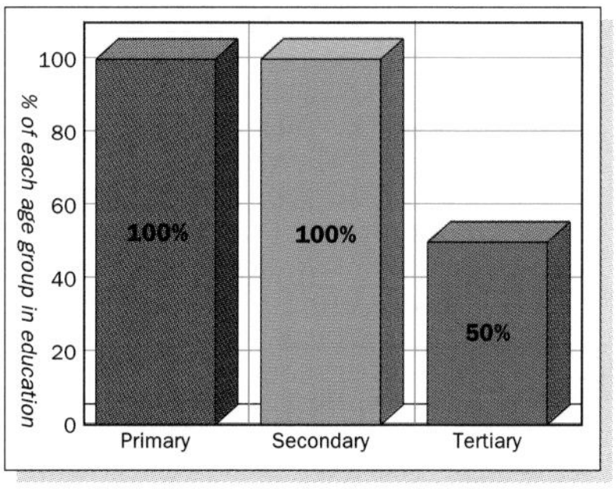

100
80
60
40
20
0
% of each age group in education
100%
100%
50%
Primary
Secondary
Tertiary

Portuguese is the sixth most widely spoken language in the world.

Free state education is available to all pupils between the ages of three and 15. Nursery provision has been greatly expanded, though the preschool stage is not compulsory. Middle-class parents rely heavily on the private sector. State universities have been expanded to ease the pressure on places. There are several prestigious private universities.

HEALTH

Welfare state health benefits

1 per 312 people

Cancers, cerebro-vascular, respiratory, and heart diseases

Of total government expenditure nearly 10% is spent on health.

Portugal has had a publicly funded, free national health service since 1979. Spending on health has increased markedly in recent years, but care remains below the EU average. There are strong regional differences in facilities. Larger urban hospitals are modern and well equipped. Private health care schemes, which are allowed to coexist, are both affordable and good value for money; a large proportion of the population use the private system.

SPENDING

GDP/cap. increase

CONSUMPTION AND SPENDING

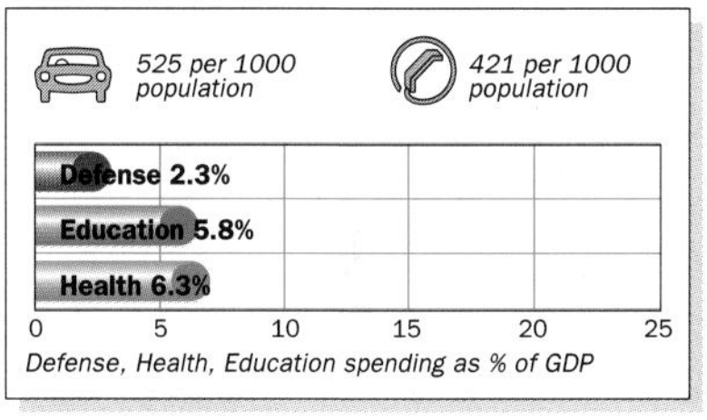

525 per 1000 population
421 per 1000 population
Defense 2.3%
Education 5.8%
Health 6.3%
0
5
10
15
20
25
Defense, Health, Education spending as % of GDP

Wealth differentials in Portugal are smaller than in most west European countries. The 1976 constitution committed Portugal to making the transition to socialism, and since then governments have introduced limited wealth redistribution measures.

Internal investment is directed chiefly through the property market, and there was a surge of purchases in the late 1990s. External investment goes to the EU and Brazil. In 2000, 14.5% of the population held shares directly. Average incomes have risen significantly since the mid-1980s, coming closer in the early 2000s to the levels of its European neighbors. Portugal pioneered prepayment systems for mobile phones, which are widely owned.

WORLD RANKING

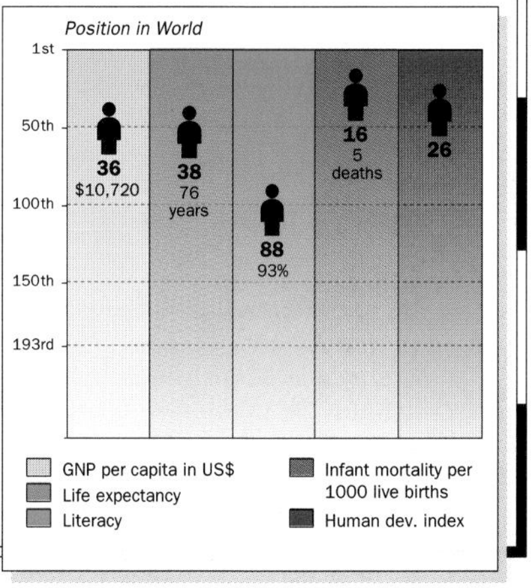

Position in World
1st
50th
100th
150th
193rd
36
$10,720
38
76
years
88
93%
16
5
deaths
26
GNP per capita in US$
Life expectancy
Literacy
Infant mortality per 1000 live births
Human dev. index

P

QATAR

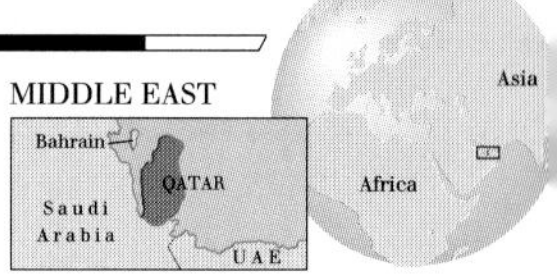
MIDDLE EAST
Bahrain
QATAR
Saudi Arabia
UAE
Asia
Africa

OFFICIAL NAME: State of Qatar **CAPITAL:** Doha
POPULATION: 610,000 **CURRENCY:** Qatar riyal **OFFICIAL LANGUAGE:** Arabic

1971 | 1971 | Sept 3 | Q | +3 | +974 | .qa

PROJECTING NORTH FROM the Arabian peninsula into the Gulf, Qatar is mostly flat, semiarid desert. Oil production began in the late 1940s and quickly transformed Qatar from an impoverished pearl producer into a prosperous shaikhdom and a founder member of OPEC. Plentiful oil and gas reserves have made it one of the wealthiest states in the region. Politics is being democratized gradually under the ruling al-Thani clan.

CLIMATE

Hot desert

WEATHER CHART FOR DOHA

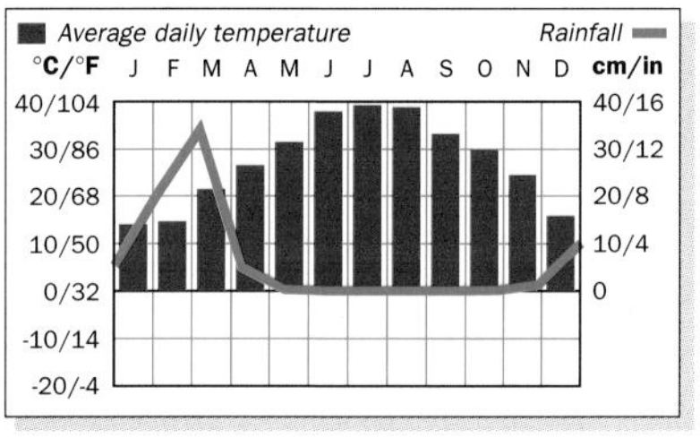
Average daily temperature
Rainfall
°C/°F J F M A M J J A S O N D cm/in
40/104
30/86
20/68
10/50
0/32
-10/14
-20/-4
40/16
30/12
20/8
10/4
0

The climate is hot and sultry, with midsummer temperatures reaching 44°C (111°F). Rainfall is infrequent.

TRANSPORTATION

Drive on right

Doha International 3.41m passengers

67 ships 622,893 grt

THE TRANSPORTATION NETWORK

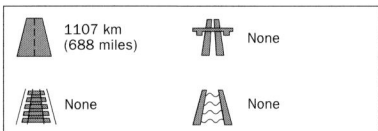

1107 km (688 miles)

None

None

None

A 45-km "Friendship Bridge," the world's longest fixed link, is planned to connect Qatar to Bahrain.

TOURISM

Visitors : Population 1:8.1

75,760 visitors

Down 83% in 1999–2001

MAIN TOURIST ARRIVALS

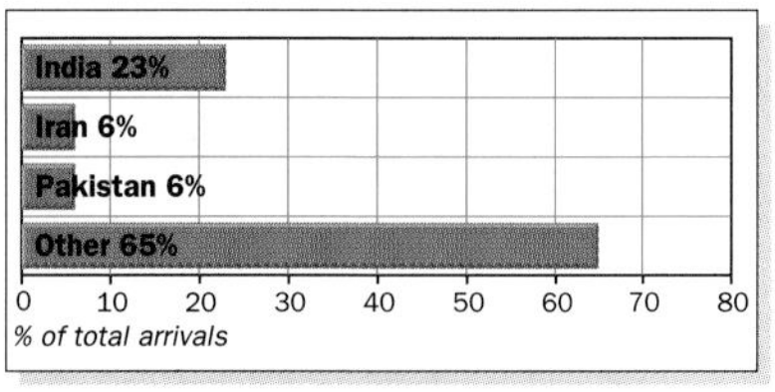
India 23%
Iran 6%
Pakistan 6%
Other 65%
0 10 20 30 40 50 60 70 80
% of total arrivals

A government drive to improve Qatar's image as a tourist destination aims to net more than 1.5 million tourists a year by 2010. Attractions include unspoiled beaches, duty-free shopping, and modern hotels.

PEOPLE

Pop. density medium

Arabic

55/km² (144/mi²)

THE URBAN/RURAL POPULATION SPLIT

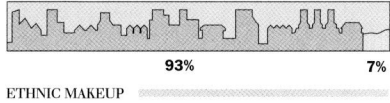

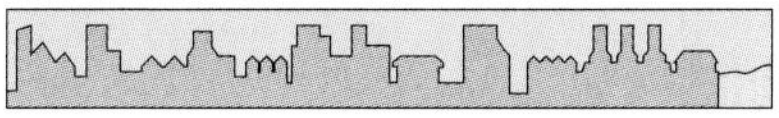
93%
7%

ETHNIC MAKEUP

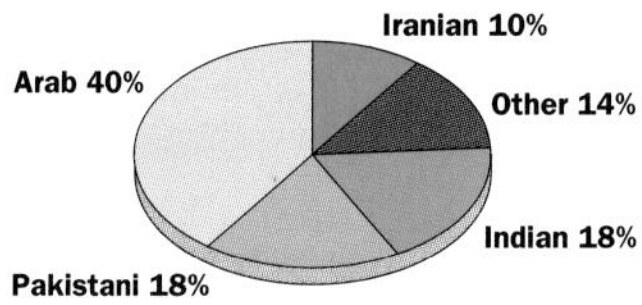
Iranian 10%
Arab 40%
Other 14%
Indian 18%
Pakistani 18%

Only one in five inhabitants is native-born. Most are guest workers from the Indian subcontinent, Iran, and north African countries. Western expatriates enjoy a high standard of living and take no part in politics.

Most Qataris follow the Wahhabi interpretation of Sunni Islam and espouse conservative religious views. However, women are not obliged to wear a veil and can hold a driving license. Expatriate Christians may worship freely but may not promote Christianity.

Since the advent of oil wealth, the Qataris, who were formerly nomadic Bedouin, have become a nation of city dwellers who enjoy high life expectancy and literacy. Almost 90% of the population now inhabit the capital Doha and its suburbs. As a result, northern Qatar is dotted with depopulated and abandoned villages.

Doha, the capital. *Though desert covers the whole country, Qatar now grows most of its own vegetables by tapping groundwater.*

POLITICS

In transition

Not applicable/ 2005

Amir Shaikh Hamad bin Khalifa al-Thani

LEGISLATIVE OR ADVISORY BODIES

Advisory Council 35 seats

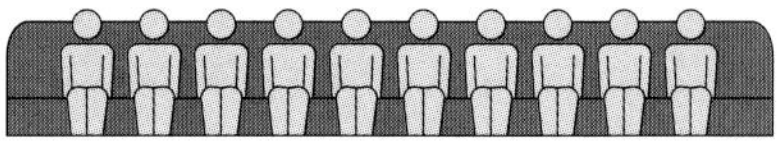

Qatar is an absolute monarchy. The amir rules with the assistance of the Council of Ministers and the Advisory Council. A partially elected 45-member parliament is to be created, with elections expected by 2005.

Qatar is a traditional emirate. The government and religious establishment are dominated by the amir, Shaikh Hamad, who ousted his father, Shaikh Khalifa, in 1995. A failed coup against Hamad in early 1996 suggested efforts by Khalifa to regain power. The prodemocracy movement has called for reform of the 35-member Advisory Council. Shaikh Hamad responded by authorizing Qatar's first elections, to a new 29-member municipal council for Doha, in 1999. All adults were able to vote and stand as candidates. The creation of a partially elected 45-seat legislature was approved overwhelmingly in a 2003 referendum.

WORLD AFFAIRS

Joined UN in 1971

AL | OIC | GCC | OAPEC | OPEC

Though Qatar was a founder member of the GCC, Shaikh Hamad has adopted a lukewarm stance toward it. However, Qatar entered into the region's first mutual defense pact, under the aegis of the GCC, in 2000. In 2001 Qatar reached an agreement on the border with Saudi Arabia, but lost its claim to the Hawar Islands when the International Court of Justice ruled in Bahrain's favor.

Qatar supplied liquefied natural gas (LNG) to Israel in the late 1990s, but relations, previously the most cordial of the Gulf states, have suffered greatly since the new Palestinian *intifada* in 2000. The amir had criticized previous US and UK air strikes on Iraq, but allowed the country to be used as a base for the US Central Command during the 2003 invasion.

AID

Recipient

$2m (receipts)

Up 100% in 2002

Qatar was an aid donor in the 1970s and early 1980s. Now it receives small amounts of aid, mainly from France; around 70% is allocated to education.

Q

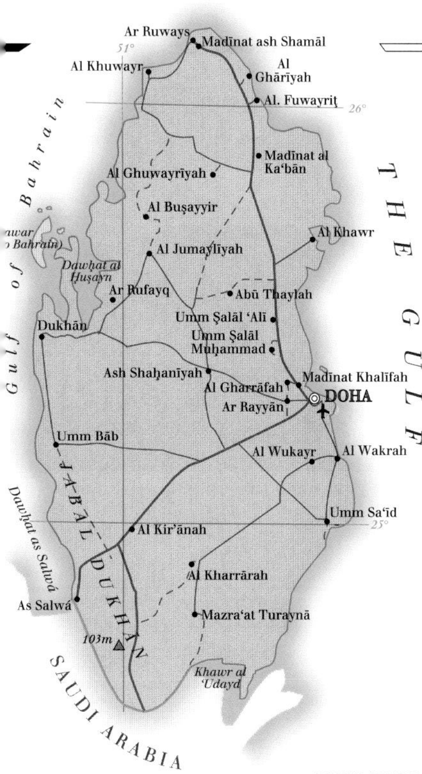
Ar Ruways
Madīnat ash Shamāl
Al Khuwayr
Al Ghārīyah
Al. Fuwayrit
26°
51°
Madīnat al Ka'bān
Al Ghuwayrīyah
Al Buşayyir
Al Khawr
Al Jumaylīyah
Gulf of Bahrain
Dawḩat al Ḩuşayn
Ar Rufayq
Abū Thaylah
Umm Şalāl 'Alī
Umm Şalāl Muḩammad
Dukhān
Ash Shaḩanīyah
Al Gharrāfah
Madīnat Khalīfah
DOHA
Ar Rayyān
THE GULF
Umm Bāb
Al Wukayr
Al Wakrah
JABAL DUKHĀN
Umm Sa'īd
25°
Al Kir'ānah
Dawḩat as Salwá
Al Kharrārah
As Salwá
Mazra'at Turaynā
103m
Khawr al 'Udayd
SAUDI ARABIA

QATAR

Total Area : 11 437 sq. km (4416 sq. miles)

POPULATION
over 100 000
under 10 000

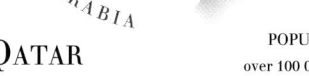

LAND HEIGHT
200m/1640ft
Sea Level

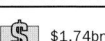

0 20 km
0 20 miles

DEFENSE

No compulsory military service

$1.74bn

Up 7% in 2002

The armed forces are too small – at an estimated 12,400 – to play a significant role in Qatari affairs, even in the event of political turmoil. A defense agreement with the US, extended in 2002, provides for joint exercises, stockpiling of US equipment, and US access to bases.

RESOURCES

Electric power 1.9m kW

8607 tonnes

917,000 b/d (reserves 15.2bn barrels)

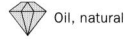

200,000 sheep, 180,000 goats, 4m chickens

Oil, natural gas

Qatar has the third-smallest reserves of crude oil within OPEC but abundant reserves of gas (the third-largest in the world), including the world's largest field of gas unassociated with oil.

ENVIRONMENT

Not available

0.1% partially protected

66.7 tonnes per capita

The desert hinterland supports little plant or animal life, though Qatar is an important staging point for migrating birds. Oil pollution has damaged marine life. There are salt flats in the south.

MEDIA

TV ownership high

Daily newspaper circulation 175 per 1000 people

PUBLISHING AND BROADCAST MEDIA

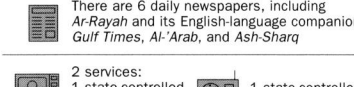

There are 6 daily newspapers, including *Ar-Rayah* and its English-language companion *Gulf Times*, *Al-'Arab*, and *Ash-Sharq*

2 services: 1 state-controlled, 1 independent

1 state-controlled service

Al-Jazeera TV offers the leading Arab perspective internationally, especially since the events of 2001, though it is careful not to criticize Qatar itself.

CRIME

Death penalty in use

570 prisoners

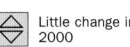

Little change in 2000

Traditional Islamic punishments have deterred crime. However, narcotics trafficking is on the increase. The incidence of street crime is low.

CHRONOLOGY

The al-Thanis, related to the Khalifa family of Bahrain, took control of the Qatar peninsula in the 18th century.

- **1971** Sovereignty recognized by UK.
- **1972** Accession of Amir Khalifa.
- **1995** Shaikh Hamad takes power.
- **1999** First ever (municipal) polls.
- **2003** Referendum approves creation of partially elected legislature.

EDUCATION

School leaving age: 11

82%

9915 students

Education is free from primary to university level. The government finances students to study overseas.

HEALTH

Welfare state health benefits

1 per 769 people

Heart, circulatory, and infectious diseases, cancers

Primary health care is free to Qataris. Hospitals operate to Western standards of care and the government also funds treatment abroad.

SPENDING

GDP/cap. increase

CONSUMPTION AND SPENDING

343 per 1000 population

289 per 1000 population

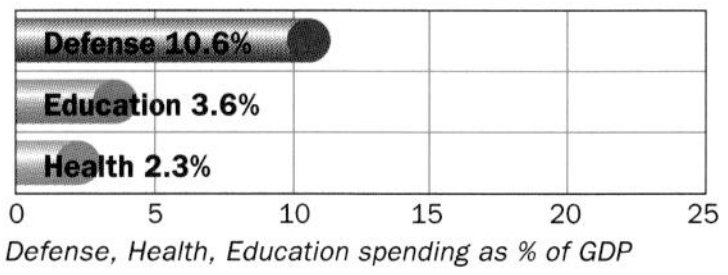
Defense 10.6%
Education 3.6%
Health 2.3%
0
5
10
15
20
25
Defense, Health, Education spending as % of GDP

Qataris have a high per capita income. There is no income tax, public services are free, and the government guarantees jobs for school-leavers. There are no exchange controls.

ECONOMICS

Inflation 2.5% p.a. (1990–2000)

$8.4bn

3.640 Qatar riyals (3.639)

SCORE CARD

World GNP Ranking	94th
GNP per Capita	$12,000
Balance of Payments	$4.38bn
Inflation	1%
Unemployment	3%

STRENGTHS

Steady supply of crude oil and increased exploitation of gas reserves, plus related industries. Modern infrastructure. Budget surplus.

WEAKNESSES

Dependence on foreign workforce. Oil price fluctuations. All other raw materials imported. Virtually all water has to be desalinated. Large foreign reserves, but new industries depend on cementing agreements with foreign partners. Regional security threats deter investment.

EXPORTS

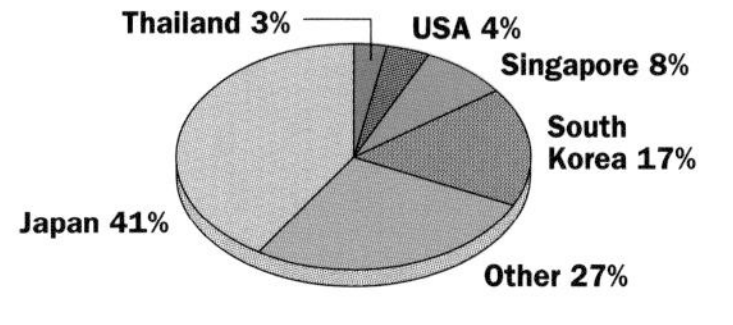
Thailand 3%
USA 4%
Singapore 8%
South Korea 17%
Japan 41%
Other 27%

IMPORTS

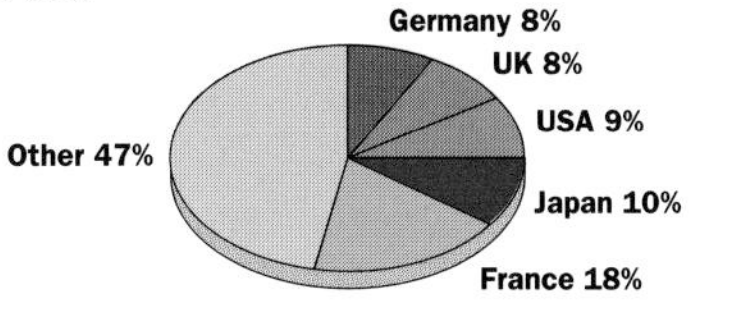
Germany 8%
UK 8%
USA 9%
Other 47%
Japan 10%
France 18%

WORLD RANKING

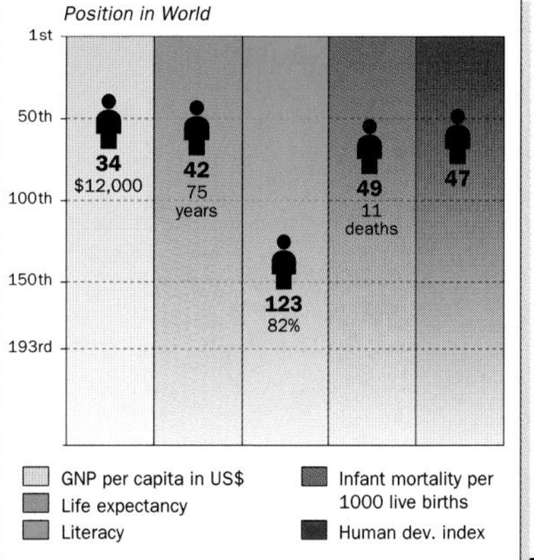
Position in World
1st
50th
100th
150th
193rd
34
$12,000
42
75 years
123
82%
49
11 deaths
47
GNP per capita in US$
Life expectancy
Literacy
Infant mortality per 1000 live births
Human dev. index

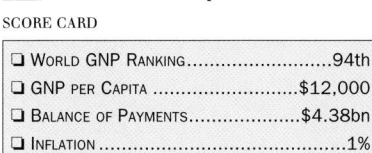

Q

ROMANIA

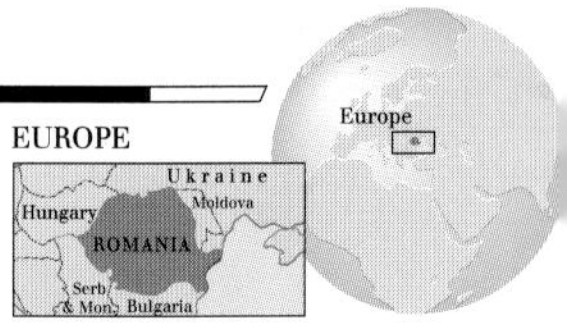

Europe
EUROPE
Ukraine
Moldova
Hungary
ROMANIA
Serb & Mon.
Bulgaria

OFFICIAL NAME: Romania **CAPITAL:** Bucharest
POPULATION: 22.3 million **CURRENCY:** Romanian leu **OFFICIAL LANGUAGE:** Romanian

1878 | 1947 | Dec 1 | RO | +2 | +40 | .ro

Village in northeastern Romania, in the foothills of the Carpathian Mountains, close to the border with Ukraine. Corn and wheat are Romania's main crops.

ROMANIA LIES ON THE Black Sea coast, with the Danube as its southern border. The Carpathian Mountains form an arc across the country, curving around the upland basin of Transylvania. Long dominated by Poles, Hungarians, and Ottomans, Romania became an independent monarchy in 1878. After World War II, this was supplanted by a communist People's Republic, headed from 1965 by Nicolae Ceauşescu. A coup in 1989 resulted in his execution and a limited democracy under Ion Iliescu. Defeated in elections in 1996, Iliescu was returned to office in 2000.

CLIMATE

Continental

WEATHER CHART FOR BUCHAREST

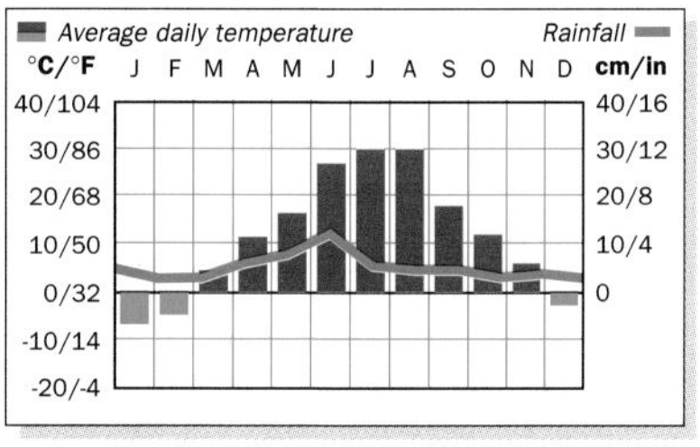

Average daily temperature
Rainfall
°C/°F
J F M A M J J A S O N D
cm/in
40/104
30/86
20/68
10/50
0/32
-10/14
-20/-4
40/16
30/12
20/8
10/4
0

Romania has a continental climate. Rainfall is generally moderate, with most rain falling in spring and early summer. Very heavy spring rains occasionally destroy new crops. Snow is frequent in the bitterly cold winters, and can linger on higher ground until May.

TRANSPORTATION

Drive on right

Otopeni, Bucharest 2.35m passengers

237 ships 622,000 grt

THE TRANSPORTATION NETWORK

99,302 km (61,703 miles)	113 km (70 miles)
11,364 km (7061 miles)	1724 km (1071 miles)

The road network is inadequate, and traffic levels are rising. EBRD, EU, World Bank, and Japanese funding has focused on the expressway from Bucharest to Hungary, and on improving major roads. Modernization of the port of Constanţa to include a container port and new barge terminal is also under way.

TOURISM

Visitors : Population 1:7

3.2m visitors

Down 3% in 2002

MAIN TOURIST ARRIVALS

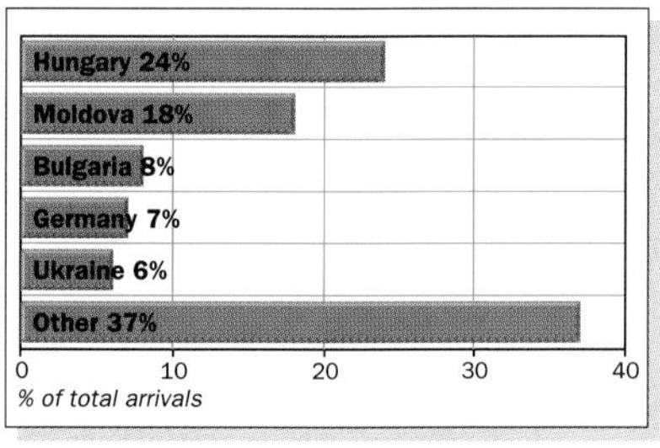

Hungary 24%
Moldova 18%
Bulgaria 8%
Germany 7%
Ukraine 6%
Other 37%
0
10
20
30
40
% of total arrivals

The Black Sea and the Carpathian Mountains are the primary natural attractions, while Transylvania has a rich historical heritage. A proposal to build a theme park to exploit the Dracula legend was shelved in 2002 after an international outcry over its proposed location in a historic town. Under Ceauşescu, the need for foreign currency meant that tourist facilities were prioritized over housing. Today, privatization of property and an acute housing shortage have reduced the accommodation available to visitors.

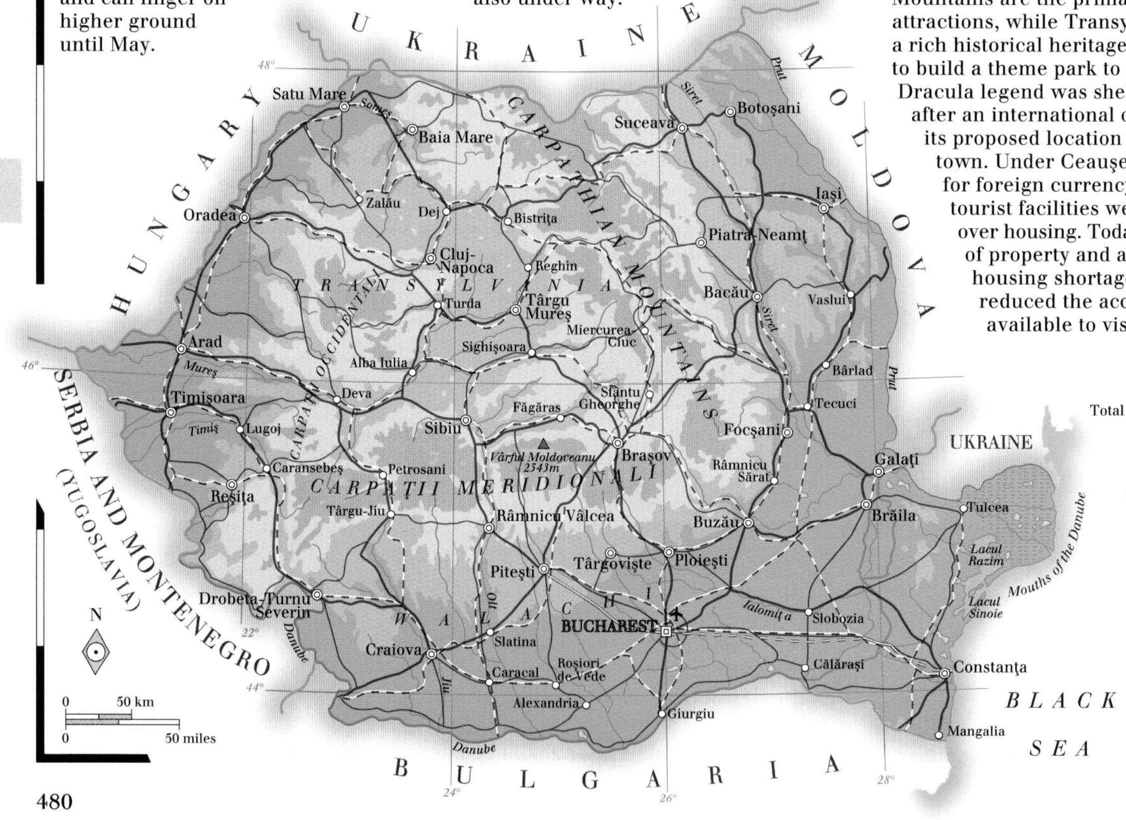

UKRAINE
MOLDOVA
HUNGARY
SERBIA AND MONTENEGRO (YUGOSLAVIA)
BULGARIA
BLACK SEA
CARPATHIAN MOUNTAINS
TRANSYLVANIA
CARPATII MERIDIONALI
CARPAŢII OCCIDENTALI
WALACHIA
Satu Mare
Baia Mare
Suceava
Botoşani
Oradea
Zalău
Dej
Bistriţa
Iaşi
Piatra-Neamţ
Cluj-Napoca
Reghin
Turda
Târgu Mureş
Bacău
Vaslui
Miercurea-Ciuc
Arad
Sighişoara
Alba Iulia
Bârlad
Timişoara
Deva
Sfântu Gheorghe
Tecuci
Lugoj
Făgăras
Focşani
Sibiu
Braşov
Vârful Moldoveanu 2543m
Caransebeş
Petrosani
Râmnicu Sărat
Galaţi
Reşiţa
Târgu-Jiu
Râmnicu Vâlcea
Brăila
Tulcea
Buzău
Piteşti
Târgovişte
Ploieşti
Lacul Razim
Lacul Sinoie
Mouths of the Danube
Drobeta-Turnu Severin
BUCHAREST
Slobozia
Slatina
Craiova
Roşiori de Vede
Călăraşi
Constanţa
Caracal
Alexandria
Giurgiu
Mangalia
Danube
Mureş
Timiş
Someş
Siret
Prut
Olt
Jiu
Ialomiţa
0 50 km
0 50 miles
N
48°
46°
44°
22°
24°
26°
28°
UKRAINE

ROMANIA

Total Area: 237 500 sq. km (91 699 sq. miles)

POPULATION

over 1 000 000

over 100 000

over 50 000

LAND HEIGHT

2000m/6562ft

1000m/3281ft

500m/1640ft

200m/656ft

Sea Level

PEOPLE

Pop. density medium

Romanian, Hungarian (Magyar), Romani, German

97/km² (251/mi²)

THE URBAN/RURAL POPULATION SPLIT

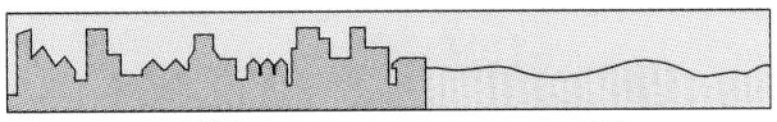
55%
45%

RELIGIOUS PERSUASION

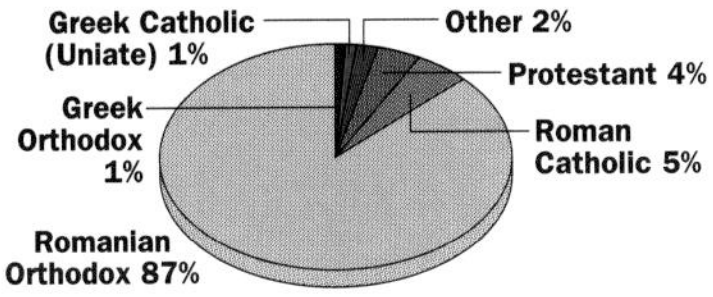
Greek Catholic (Uniate) 1%
Other 2%
Protestant 4%
Greek Orthodox 1%
Roman Catholic 5%
Romanian Orthodox 87%

ETHNIC MAKEUP

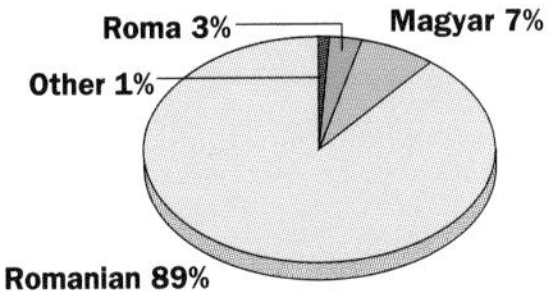
Roma 3%
Magyar 7%
Other 1%
Romanian 89%

Since 1989, Romanian nationalism has increased, aggravated by economic austerity measures. The incidence of ethnic violence has also risen, toward Roma and Hungarians in particular. Ethnic Hungarians, or Magyar, who form the largest minority group, are partly protected by the influence of Hungary, whereas the Roma do not have any similar support and tend to suffer greater discrimination.

The population is currently shrinking, due to rising emigration since 1989, mainly for economic reasons, and to a falling birthrate since the early 1990s. The latter trend is in sharp contrast to the 1980s, when the Ceauşescu regime enforced a "pronatalist" policy, banning abortion and contraception; the birthrate rose, but the population as a whole did not grow significantly due to an increase in the mortality rate. Abortion was legalized in 1989 and maternal death rates have since declined. Adoptions by foreigners, spurred partly by shocking conditions in orphanages, were in 2001 suspended amid concerns over a "trade in children," and banned in 2004. The last country in Europe to lift its ban on homosexuality, the law was repealed only in 2001; public prejudice against homosexuals remains high.

POPULATION AGE BREAKDOWN

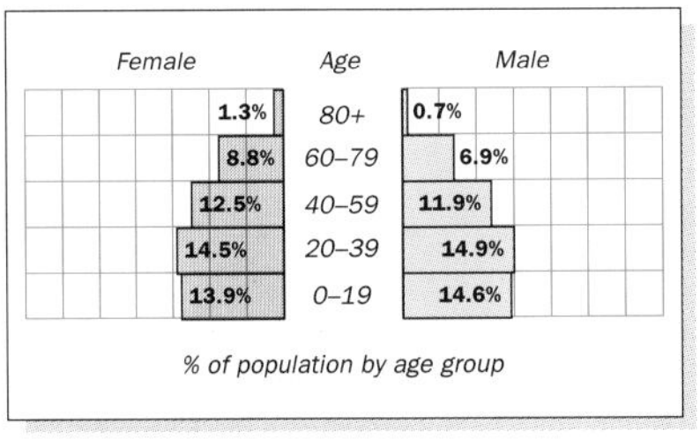
Female
Age
Male
1.3%
80+
0.7%
8.8%
60–79
6.9%
12.5%
40–59
11.9%
14.5%
20–39
14.9%
13.9%
0–19
14.6%
% of population by age group

WORLD AFFAIRS

Joined UN in 1955

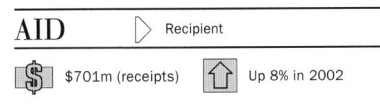

BSEC | CE | CEFTA | NATO | OSCE

Romania's priority is building closer links with western Europe. In 1993, it signed an association agreement with the EU, and in 1995 formally applied for membership; this is expected in 2007. Romania is also a member of the Stability Pact for South East Europe, created after the 1999 Kosovo conflict.

Relations with Hungary remain tense over the treatment of the Magyar minority in Transylvania. Romania's relations with ethnically related Moldova are important and Russia's influence there is eyed with mistrust.

Improving ties with Ukraine are hampered by a lingering territorial dispute over Serpents' Island in the Black Sea, which has potentially rich offshore oil deposits.

AID

Recipient

$701m (receipts)

Up 8% in 2002

Western aid declined after the mid-1990s, reflecting uncertainty about the implementation of reform. In October 2001 the World Bank announced that it would loan $1 billion between 2002 and 2004 for a series of social and environmental projects.

POLITICS

Multiparty elections

L. House 2000/2004
U. House 2000/2004

President Ion Iliescu

AT THE LAST ELECTION

House of Deputies 345 seats

9% PNL
5% Min
45% PDSR
24% PRM
9% PD
8% UDMR

PDSR = Social Democratic Pole of Romania (led by the Social Democracy Party of Romania) **PRM** = Greater Romania Party
PD = Democratic Party **PNL** = National Liberal Party
UDMR = Hungarian Democratic Union of Romania
Min = Minority representatives: 18 seats in the House of Deputies are reserved for national minorities

Senate 140 seats

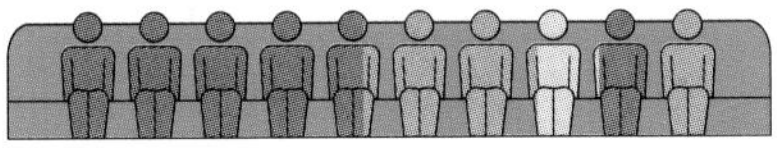
46% PDSR
27% PRM
9% PD
9% PNL
9% UDMR

Romania is a multiparty democracy led by a directly elected president.

PROFILE

The 1989 "revolution" left an old communist elite in power, under President Ion Iliescu, with no group ready to introduce reform. Only the center-right victory in 1996 brought more far-reaching change and a democrat as president. In 2000 these parties came a poor third, however, behind Iliescu's PDSR and the extreme nationalist PRM; Iliescu, now a declared social democrat, won the presidential vote, retaining the support of such conservative groups as miners and rural workers. In mid-2001 the PDSR electoral coalition was formalized in a merger of its two main constituent parties to form the Social Democrat Party (PSD), which is headed by Prime Minister Adrian Nastase. A new opposition grouping, formed by the consolidation of the PD and the PNL, is gaining in popularity.

MAIN POLITICAL ISSUES

The pace of liberalization

The success of the left in 2000 was based on a commitment to promote social concerns alongside economic reform. However, amid pressure from the IMF and other lending bodies, the government has been forced to maintain and even increase the pace of economic liberalization, creating serious tensions within government.

Ethnic tensions

The economic difficulties of the 1990s saw far-right political gains and increased nationalism. Roma have been victims of violent, racially motivated attacks. Benefits given to ethnic Magyars by the Hungarian government have provoked an outcry in Romania.

***Ion Iliescu**, Romania's first postcommunist president, reelected in 2000.*

***Adrian Nastase**, prime minister since December 2000.*

R

CHRONOLOGY

Dominated by Hungary and the Ottoman Empire for centuries, the Romanian provinces of Wallachia and Moldavia were united for the first time in 1859, forming the basis of the modern Romanian state.

- **1878** Independence, but at cost of losing eastern Moldavia to Russia.
- **1916–1918** Enters World War I on Allied side. At end of war gains substantial territory, including Transylvania from Hungary.
- **1924** Communists banned in unstable political arena. Rise

CHRONOLOGY *continued*

of fascist "Iron Guard."
- ❑ **1938** King Carol sets up autocracy.
- ❑ **1940** Territory forcibly ceded to Soviet Union, Bulgaria, and Hungary. Coup by Iron Guard. King Carol abdicates in favor of son, Michael. Tripartite Pact with Germany.
- ❑ **1941** Enters war on Axis side, hoping to recover Moldavian lands.
- ❑ **1944** Romania switches sides as Soviet troops reach border.
- ❑ **1945** Soviet-backed regime installed. Romanian Communist Party plays an increasing role.
- ❑ **1946–1947** Romania regains Transylvania. Eastern Moldavia reverts to USSR, which also demands huge reparations. Communist-led National Democratic Front wins majority in disputed elections.
- ❑ **1947** Michael forced to abdicate.
- ❑ **1948–1953** Centrally planned economy put in place.
- ❑ **1953** Leaders of Jewish community prosecuted for Zionism.
- ❑ **1958** Soviet troops withdraw.
- ❑ **1964** Prime Minister Gheorghiu-Dej declares national sovereignty. Proposes joint planning by all communist countries to lessen Soviet economic control.
- ❑ **1965** Ceauşescu party secretary after death of Gheorghiu-Dej.
- ❑ **1968–1980** Condemns Soviet invasion of Czechoslovakia; courts US and European Communities.
- ❑ **1982** Ceauşescu vows to pay off foreign debt.
- ❑ **1989** Demonstrations; many killed by military. Armed forces join with opposition in National Salvation Front (NSF) to form government. Ion Iliescu declared president. Ceauşescu summarily tried and shot.
- ❑ **1990** NSF election victory. Political prisoners freed.
- ❑ **1991** New constitution, providing for market reform, approved.
- ❑ **1992** Second free elections. NSF splits. Nicolae Vacaroiu forms minority government.
- ❑ **1994** General strike demands faster economic reform. Referendum in Moldova rejects reunification with Romania.
- ❑ **1996** Reconciliation treaty with Hungary. Center right wins elections, breaking with communist past; Emil Constantinescu president.
- ❑ **2000** Ion Iliescu and social democrats win elections. Adrian Nastase prime minister.
- ❑ **2001** Repeal of Article 200: Romania becomes last country in Europe to decriminalize homosexuality.
- ❑ **2004** Joins NATO.

R

DEFENSE

Phasing out conscription

$999m

Up 4% in 2002

The military received limited funding under the Ceauşescu regime, and troops were routinely deployed as cheap labor. Romania was the first country to join NATO's Partnership for Peace program in 1994, and was among the seven eastern European and former Soviet-bloc countries to gain full NATO membership in 2004. Romanian troops were deployed in the US-led "war on terrorism" in Afghanistan from 2002.

ROMANIAN ARMED FORCES

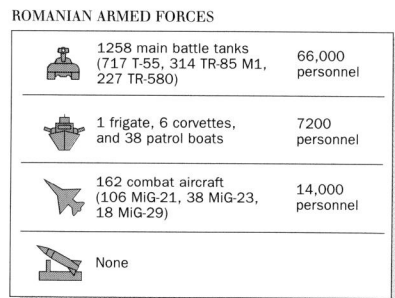

1258 main battle tanks (717 T-55, 314 TR-85 M1, 227 TR-580)	66,000 personnel
1 frigate, 6 corvettes, and 38 patrol boats	7200 personnel
162 combat aircraft (106 MiG-21, 38 MiG-23, 18 MiG-29)	14,000 personnel
None	

ECONOMICS

Inflation 91% p.a. (1990–2001)

$41.7bn

33,407 Romanian lei (32,788)

SCORE CARD

❑ World GNP Ranking	53rd
❑ GNP per Capita	$1870
❑ Balance of Payments	–$1.57bn
❑ Inflation	22.5%
❑ Unemployment	8%

EXPORTS

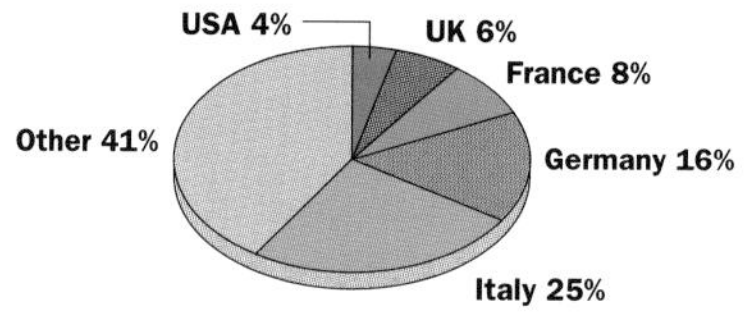
USA 4%
UK 6%
France 8%
Other 41%
Germany 16%
Italy 25%

IMPORTS

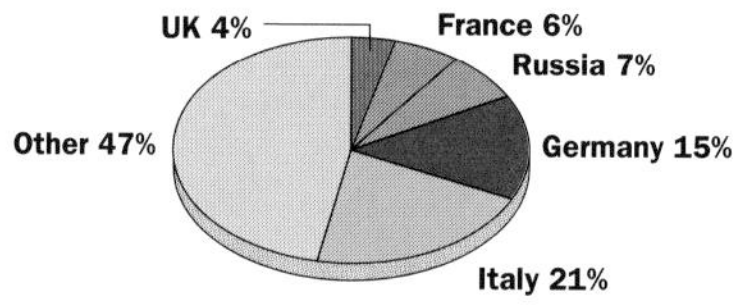
UK 4%
France 6%
Russia 7%
Other 47%
Germany 15%
Italy 21%

Strengths

Oil reserves. Tourism potential. Export-led recovery from 2000. Progress with privatization.

Weaknesses

High inflation. Growing trade deficit. Slow transition to market economy. Delays in economic reform. Low foreign investment confidence.

Profile

Despite being the first east European country to allow foreign investment, Romania was relatively slow to launch economic reforms, and suffered severe recession for most of the 1990s. Priority industries for structural overhaul and liberalization are food, petrochemicals, chemicals, metals, and transportation. Efforts from 1996 to curb inflation and the budget deficit had little impact. Output fell sharply, and trade was disrupted by the 1999 Kosovo conflict. From 1990, 100% foreign ownership of ventures was permitted. Joint ventures, while now numerous, are small in scale; larger investors are put off by bureaucracy and doubts about stability. Privatization, a priority for government since 1996, was delayed by problems in the sale of larger companies, but by 2000 the private sector accounted for over 60% of GDP and a renewed drive to privatize was begun in 2001. 2000 saw an export-led recovery after three straight years of recession, though since then consumer spending has fueled a growth in the trade deficit.

Most farmland has been restored to private hands. Agriculture, highly undermechanized, still employs over 40% of the workforce. The worst drought for 50 years severely affected production in 2000.

ECONOMIC PERFORMANCE INDICATOR

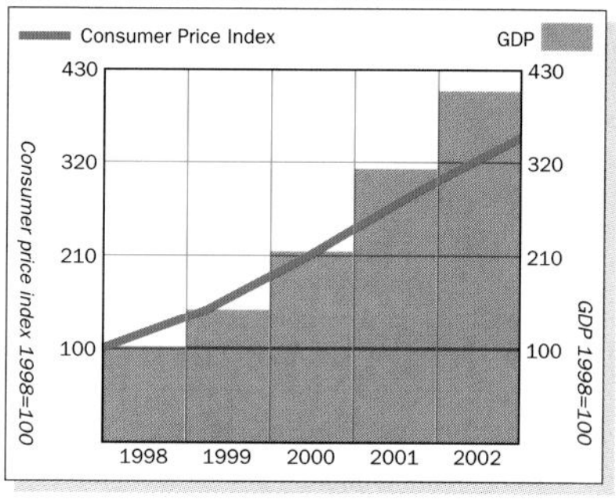
Consumer Price Index
GDP
430
320
210
100
Consumer price index 1998=100
GDP 1998=100
1998
1999
2000
2001
2002

ROMANIA : MAJOR BUSINESSES

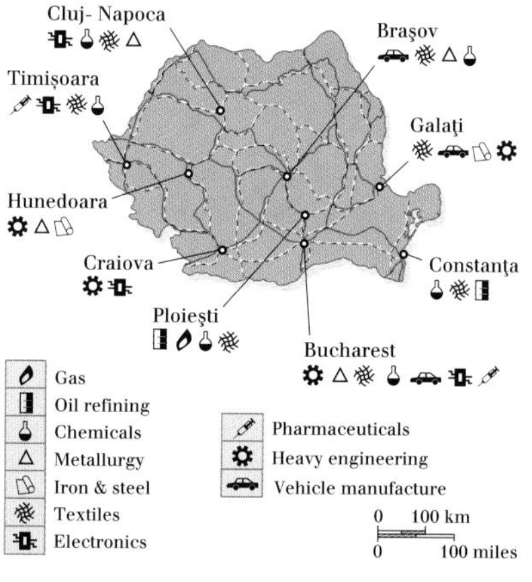
Cluj- Napoca
Braşov
Timişoara
Galaţi
Hunedoara
Craiova
Constanţa
Ploieşti
Bucharest
Gas
Oil refining
Chemicals
Metallurgy
Iron & steel
Textiles
Electronics
Pharmaceuticals
Heavy engineering
Vehicle manufacture
0 100 km
0 100 miles

RESOURCES

Electric power 21.9m kW

18,455 tonnes

123,000 b/d (reserves 900m barrels)

7.45m sheep, 5.15m pigs, 4m geese, 76.6m chickens

Oil, coal, salt, natural gas, methane, bauxite, iron, copper, lead, zinc

ELECTRICITY GENERATION

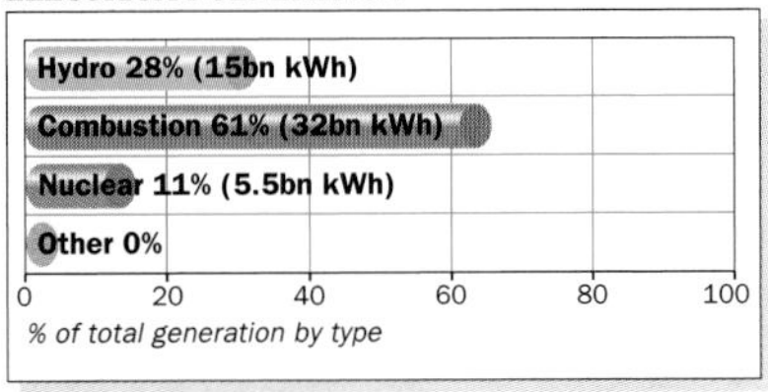
Hydro 28% (15bn kWh)
Combustion 61% (32bn kWh)
Nuclear 11% (5.5bn kWh)
Other 0%
0 20 40 60 80 100
% of total generation by type

Romania has large reserves of oil, but there is little left of proven gas reserves. Oil and gas production from onshore fields has fallen since 1976, and the country is a net oil importer. Since the mid-1990s efforts have been focused on developing offshore reserves in the Black Sea, opening up exploration and processing to foreign investors. Deposits of other minerals are small and contribute little to export earnings. Many coal mines have been shut down.

The electricity industry is outdated but does produce a surplus for export. An agreement in 2000 connected the national grid with that of Bulgaria. A series of blackouts prompted the government to commit in 2003 to expanding nuclear and hydroelectric power production and also to improving infrastructure.

ROMANIA : LAND USE

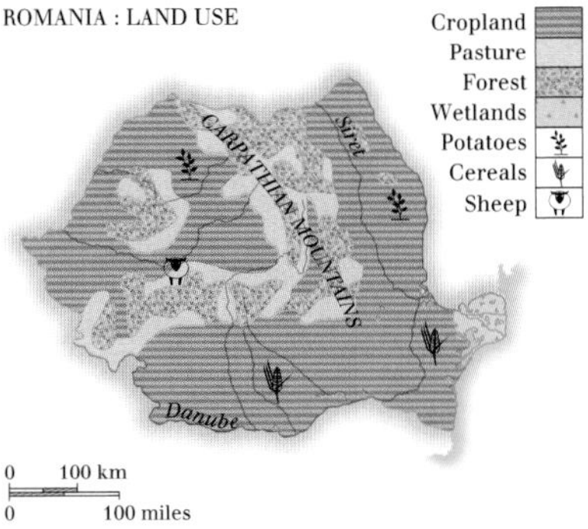
Cropland
Pasture
Forest
Wetlands
Potatoes
Cereals
Sheep
CARPATHIAN MOUNTAINS
Siret
Danube
0 100 km
0 100 miles

ENVIRONMENT

Sustainability rank: 66th

5% (0.2% partially protected)

3.8 tonnes per capita

ENVIRONMENTAL TREATIES

Yes Yes Yes

Yes Yes Yes

Saddled with the disastrous legacy of its communist-era industry, Romania needs help with a major cleanup. Air pollution, mainly from emissions from cement and power plants but also from exhaust fumes and low-quality coal, is most serious in the south. Cyanide and heavy metal leaked from a gold mine in Baia Mare in 2000, creating a transborder pollution catastrophe in the Tisza River in Hungary. The Danube delta, despite serious pollution, was designated a UNESCO biosphere reserve in 1998.

MEDIA

TV ownership high

Daily newspaper circulation 300 per 1000 people

PUBLISHING AND BROADCAST MEDIA

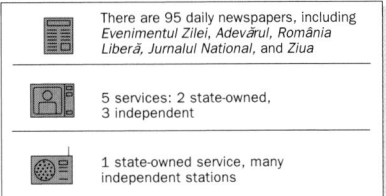

There are 95 daily newspapers, including *Evenimentul Zilei, Adevărul, România Liberă, Jurnalul National,* and *Ziua*

5 services: 2 state-owned, 3 independent

1 state-owned service, many independent stations

Newspapers proliferated after 1989, but have since struggled to retain readers. The government-controlled national TV service faces a strong challenge from commercial channels Pro TV and Antena Independenta. Pro TV dominates urban viewing, and cable TV is common in the capital. The first exclusively Hungarian-language radio station began broadcasting in 1999.

CRIME

No death penalty

43,489 prisoners

Down 4% in 2001

CRIME RATES

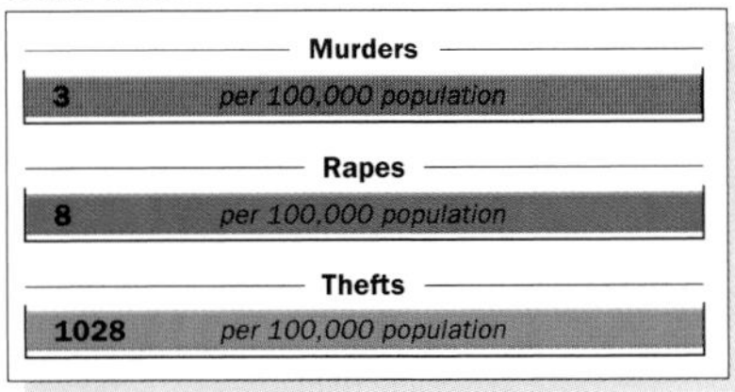
Murders
3 per 100,000 population
Rapes
8 per 100,000 population
Thefts
1028 per 100,000 population

The black economy is the main source of income for a third of the population. Levels of tax evasion are extremely high. Romania is a source and transit country for people trafficking.

EDUCATION

School leaving age: 14

97%

582,221 students

THE EDUCATION SYSTEM

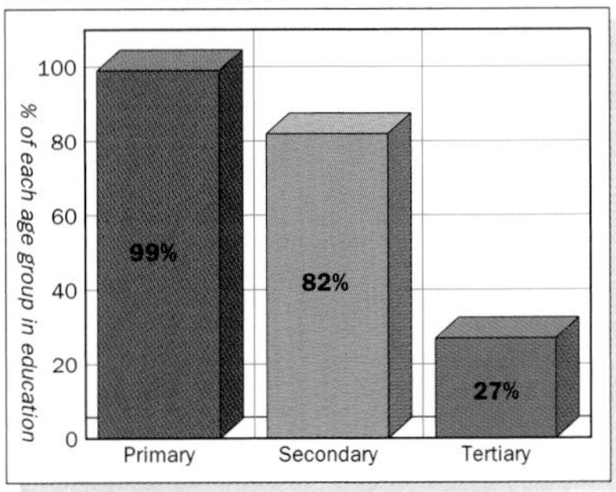
100
80
60
40
20
0
% of each age group in education
99%
82%
27%
Primary
Secondary
Tertiary

Attendance at secondary schools is below the European average. As university enrollment is no longer restricted, the number of tertiary students has risen rapidly. The government increased education expenditure in early 2000, pledging further increases in future years and going some way to meet criticisms over the chronic underfunding of the school system.

HEALTH

Welfare state health benefits

1 per 526 people

Heart, respiratory, and cerebrovascular diseases, cancers

Average life expectancy is among the lowest in Europe; in the worst-polluted parts of Transylvania it is as low as 61 years. The incidence of tuberculosis is the highest in Europe. After years of chronic state underfunding, there was a shift in 1999–2001 toward an insurance-based system.

SPENDING

GDP/cap. decrease

CONSUMPTION AND SPENDING

144 per 1000 population

194 per 1000 population

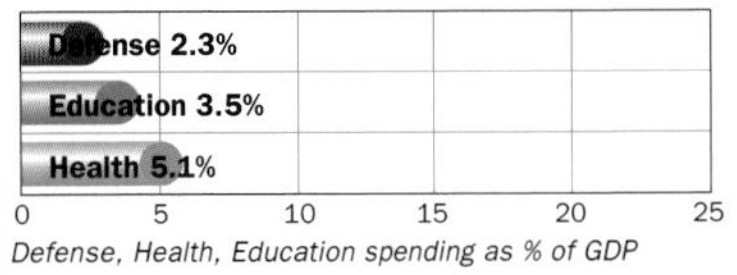
Defense 2.3%
Education 3.5%
Health 5.1%
0 5 10 15 20 25
Defense, Health, Education spending as % of GDP

Real income was hit hard by a decade of economic decline: 20% of people live below the UN poverty line (less than $2 a day). Most families own their own homes (often overcrowded); many have small plots of land. Few rural homes have running water or sewerage.

WORLD RANKING

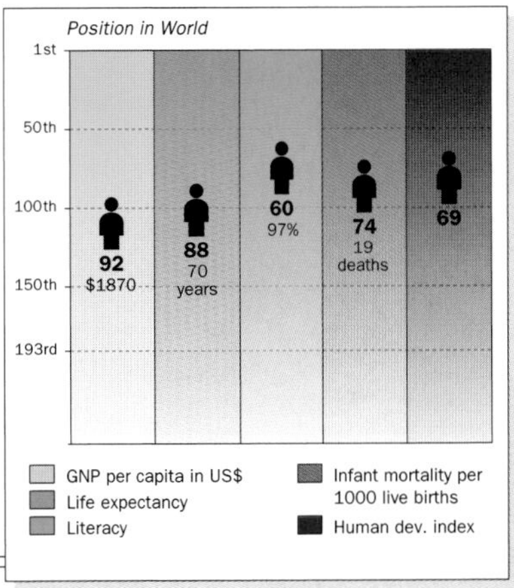
Position in World
1st
50th
100th
150th
193rd
92
$1870
88
70
years
60
97%
74
19
deaths
69
GNP per capita in US$
Life expectancy
Literacy
Infant mortality per 1000 live births
Human dev. index

R

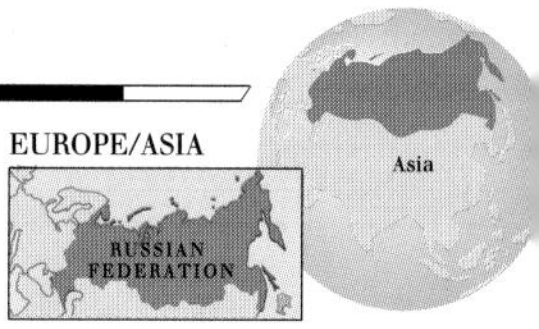
EUROPE/ASIA
RUSSIAN FEDERATION
Asia

Russian Federation

Official Name: Russian Federation **Capital:** Moscow
Population: 143 million **Currency:** Russian rouble **Official Language:** Russian

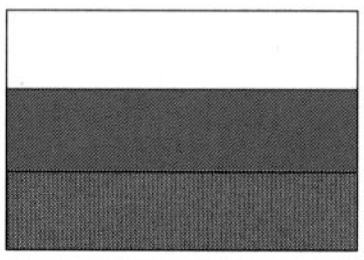

1480 | 1991 | June 12 | RUS | +1 to +11 | +7 | .ru

Tundra in Russia's far east. *Russia has some of the largest uninhabited tracts of land in the world.*

Bounded by the Arctic and Pacific Oceans to the north and east, Russia extends over 17 million sq. km (6.6 million sq. miles). By far the world's largest state, it is almost twice as big as either the US or China. With the modern borders of the Russian federative state established in 1954, the sovereign status of the Russian Federation itself dates from 1991 – the dissolution of the USSR. Within the CIS it maintains a traditionally dominant role in central Asia and the Caucasus. Ethnic Russians make up 82% of the population, but there are around 150 smaller ethnic groups, many with their own national territories within Russia's borders. Regionalism and separatism are major political issues. The situation is complicated by the fact that many of these territories are rich in key resources such as oil, gas, gold, and diamonds.

CLIMATE

Subarctic/continental/mountain/steppe

WEATHER CHART FOR MOSCOW

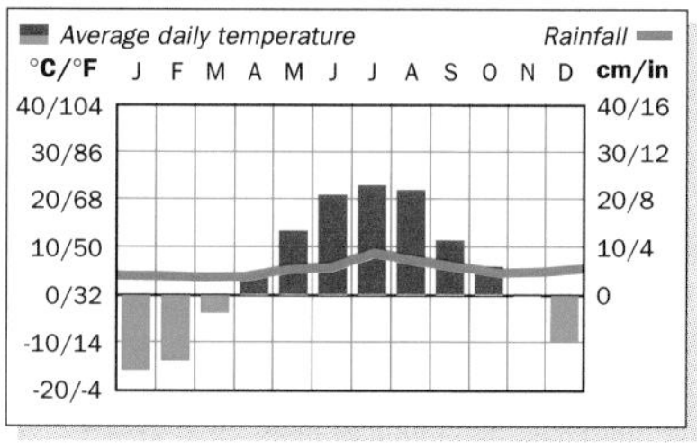
Average daily temperature
Rainfall
°C/°F
J F M A M J J A S O N D
cm/in
40/104
30/86
20/68
10/50
0/32
-10/14
-20/-4
40/16
30/12
20/8
10/4
0

Russia has a cold continental climate, characterized by two widely divergent main seasons. Spring and autumn are very brief periods of transition between warm summers and freezing winters. The country is open to the influences of the Arctic and Atlantic to the north and west. Mountains to the south and east, however, prevent any warming effects from the Indian and Pacific Oceans filtering across. Severe winters affect most regions. Winter temperatures vary surprisingly little from north to south, but fall sharply in eastern regions. The January temperature of –70°C (–94°F) recorded at Verkhoyansk in Siberia is the world record low outside Antarctica.

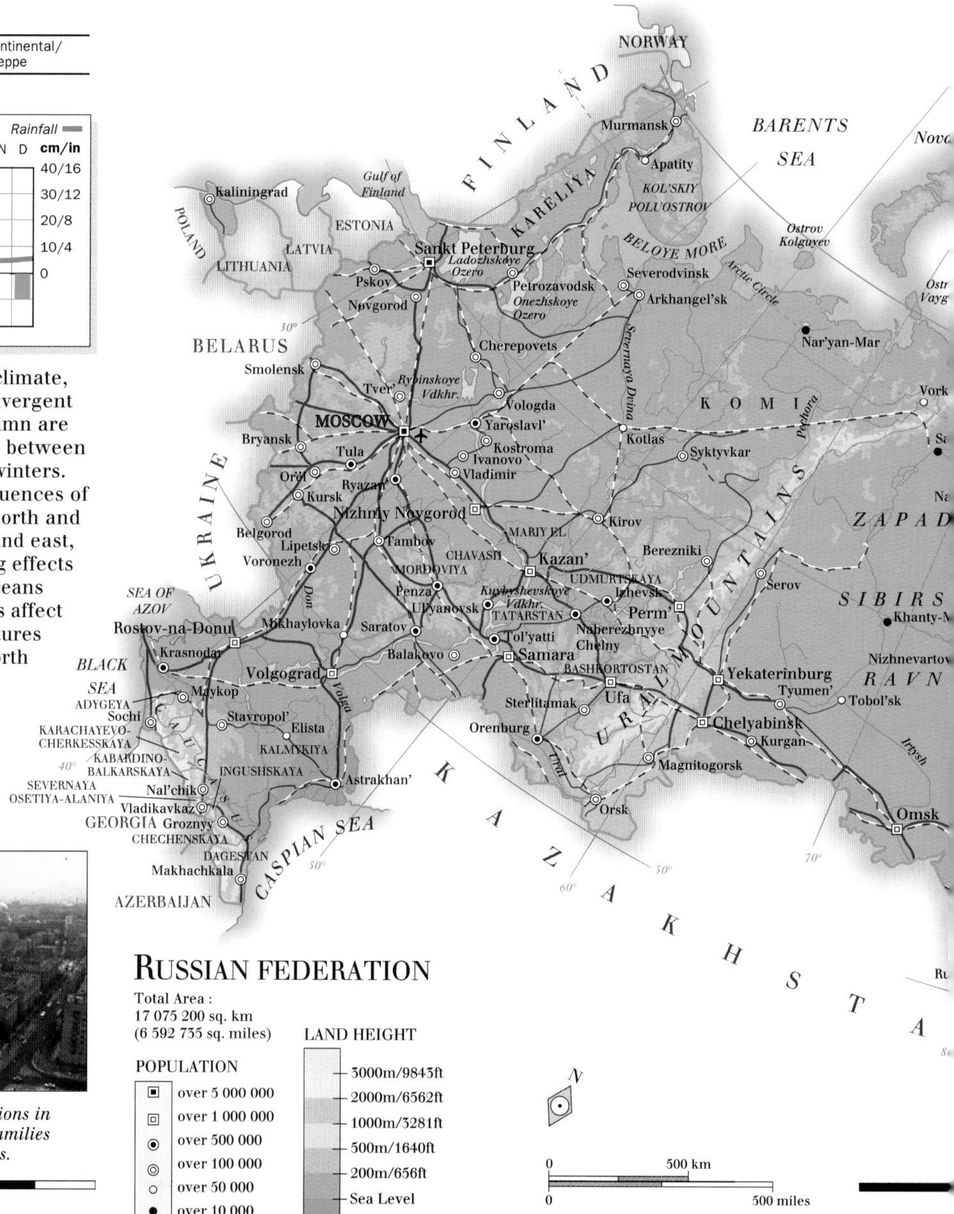
NORWAY
FINLAND
BARENTS SEA
Murmansk
Apatity
KOL'SKIY POLUOSTROV
Ostrov Kolguyev
BELOYE MORE
Arctic Circle
Kaliningrad
POLAND
LITHUANIA
LATVIA
ESTONIA
Gulf of Finland
KARELIYA
Sankt Peterburg
Ladozhskoye Ozero
Petrozavodsk
Onezhskoye Ozero
Severodvinsk
Arkhangel'sk
Pskov
Novgorod
Nar'yan-Mar
BELARUS
Smolensk
Cherepovets
Severnaya Dvina
Rybinskoye Vdkhr.
Tver'
Vologda
KOMI
MOSCOW
Yaroslavl'
Kotlas
Bryansk
Tula
Kostroma
Ivanovo
Vladimir
Syktyvkar
UKRAINE
Orël
Kursk
Ryazan'
Nizhniy Novgorod
Kirov
Belgorod
Lipetsk
Tambov
MARIY EL
Voronezh
CHAVASH
Kazan'
Bereznikí
MORDOVIYA
UDMURTSKAYA
Penza
Ul'yanovsk
Izhevsk
Kuybyshevskoye Vdkhr.
TATARSTAN
Perm'
SEA OF AZOV
Don
Rostov-na-Donu
Mikhaylovka
Saratov
Naberezhnyye Chelny
Tol'yatti
Samara
Krasnodar
Balakovo
BASHKORTOSTAN
BLACK SEA
Volgograd
Volga
Ufa
Yekaterinburg
URAL MOUNTAINS
Serov
SIBIRS
Tyumen'
Tobol'sk
ADYGEYA
Maykop
Sochi
Stavropol'
Sterlitamak
Chelyabinsk
Kurgan
KARACHAYEVO-CHERKESSKAYA
Elista
Orenburg
KABARDINO-BALKARSKAYA
KALMYKIYA
Magnitogorsk
Ural
INGUSHSKAYA
Astrakhan'
SEVERNAYA OSETIYA-ALANIYA
Nal'chik
Vladikavkaz
Orsk
GEORGIA
Groznyy
CHECHENSKAYA
CASPIAN SEA
DAGESTAN
Makhachkala
AZERBAIJAN
KAZAKHSTAN
Omsk
Irtysh
Pechora
Khanty-Mansiysk
Nizhnevartovsk
ZAPAD
RAVN
Vorkuta
30°
40°
50°
60°
70°
N
0 500 km
0 500 miles

Russian Federation

Total Area :
17 075 200 sq. km
(6 592 735 sq. miles)

POPULATION
- over 5 000 000
- over 1 000 000
- over 500 000
- over 100 000
- over 50 000
- over 10 000

LAND HEIGHT
- 3000m/9843ft
- 2000m/6562ft
- 1000m/3281ft
- 500m/1640ft
- 200m/656ft
- Sea Level
- -200m/-656ft

Housing in Moscow. *Living conditions in major cities can be cramped, with families often sharing their small apartments.*

R

TRANSPORTATION

Drive on right

Sheremetyevo, Moscow
11.5m passengers

4943 ships
10.4m grt

THE TRANSPORTATION NETWORK

351,976 km (218,707 miles)	Not available
85,542 km (53,153 miles)	95,900 km (59,589 miles)

Russia has a comprehensive transportation network, though since 1991 all systems have seen some decline due to lack of funding. Cities are still served by good trolley and bus systems and Moscow has one of the most impressive subway systems in the world. In rural areas, car ownership is low and the population relies on an extensive bus service.

About 20% of the railroad track should be renewed annually owing to frost and other damage. Shortage of funds means that this is no longer done. The railroads are heavily used but seriously overburdened and liable to accidents and delays. New track has been laid for the Sokol (Falcon) high-speed rail link between Moscow and St. Petersburg; the first trains to use it in 2000 cut over an hour off the previous minimum journey time and further dramatic reductions are expected.

Roads in major cities are deteriorating, as are interurban highways. Crime is a problem on railroads – notably the Trans-Siberian – and roads.

The former Aeroflot monopoly of air transportation has been broken up. Aeroflot now competes as Aeroflot Russian Airlines, but hundreds of regional "babyflot" airlines run mainly domestic routes, some with alarming accident records.

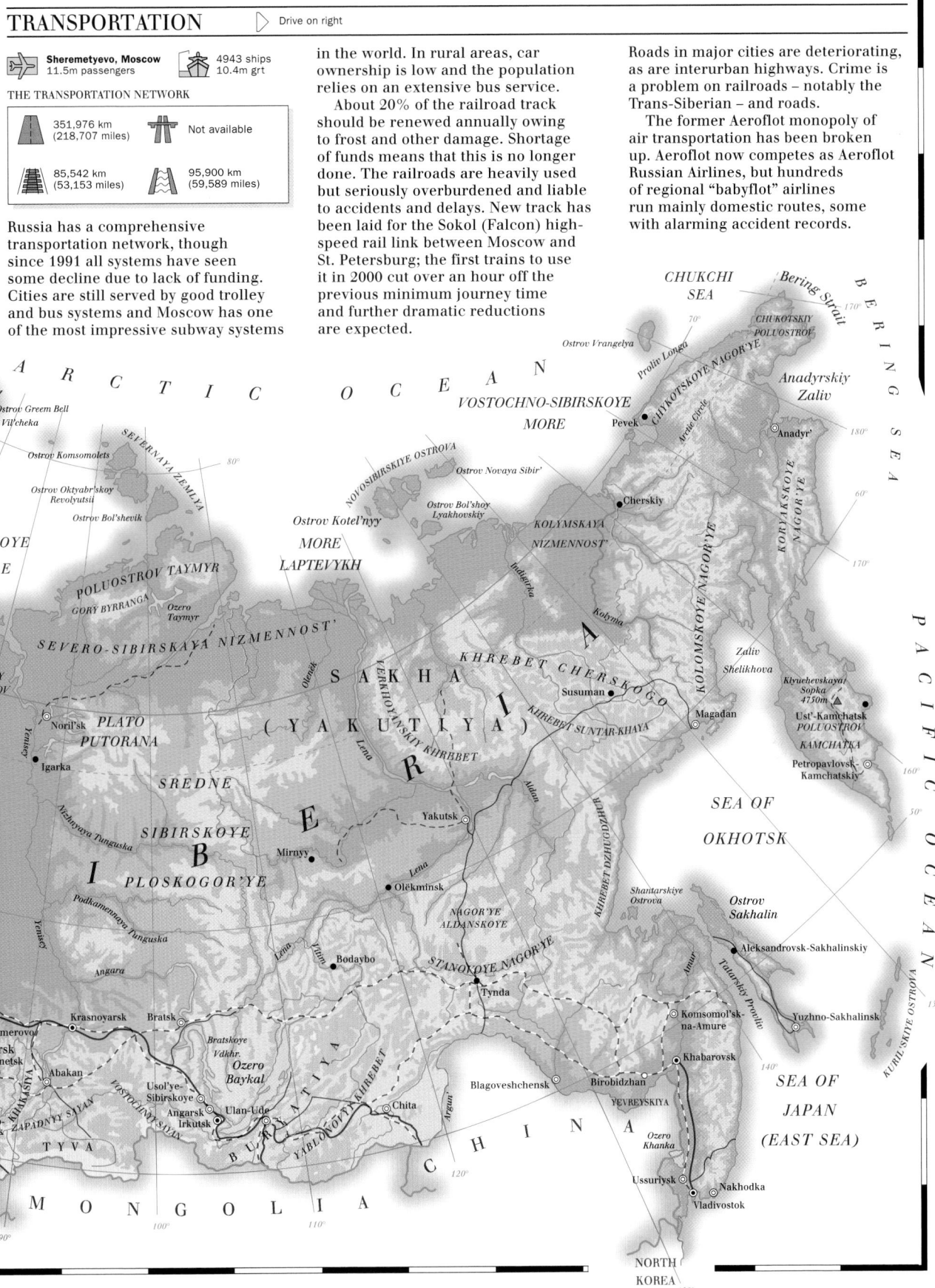

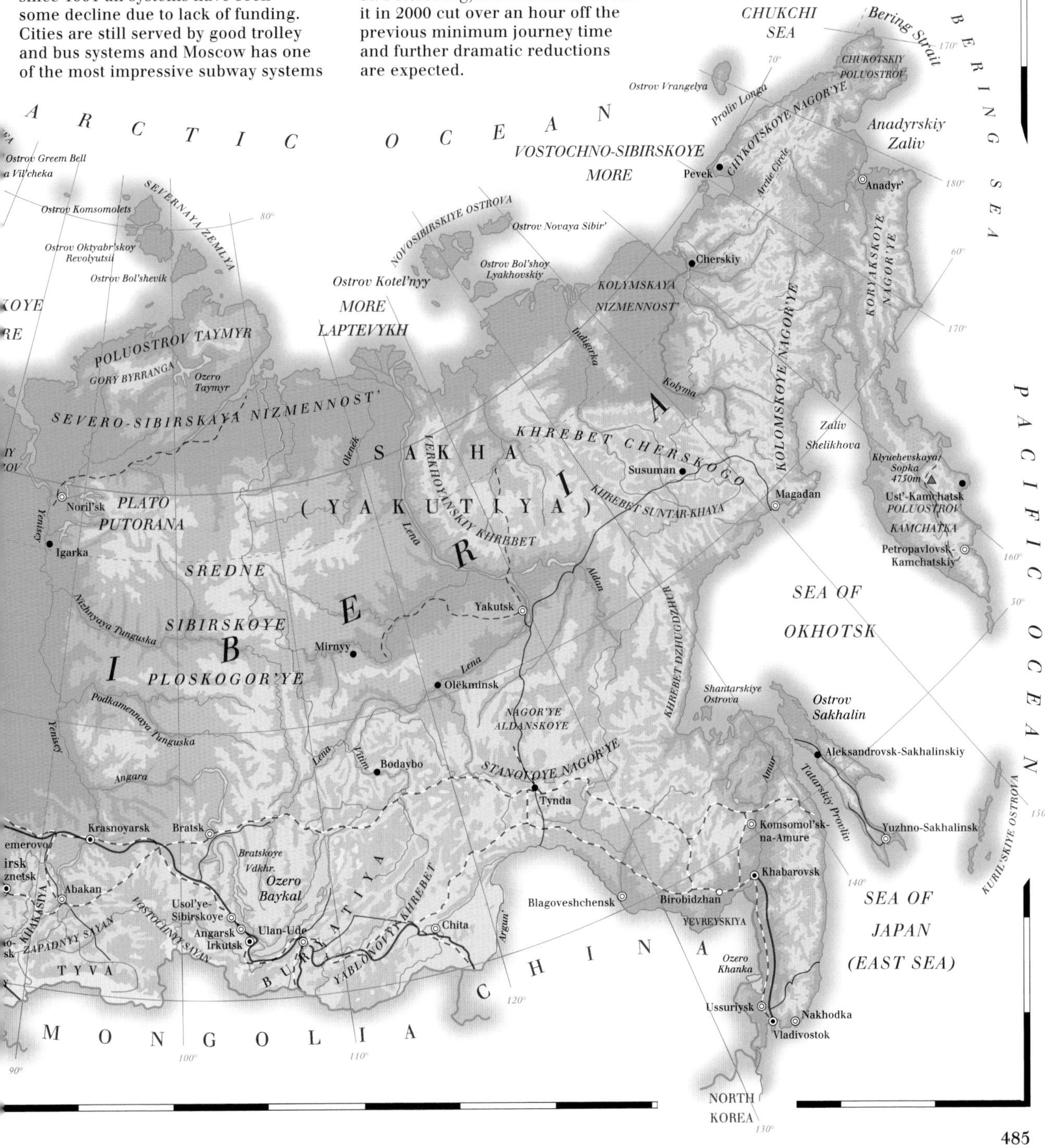
CHUKCHI SEA
Bering Strait
BERING SEA
CHUKOTSKIY POLUOSTROV
Ostrov Vrangelya
Proliv Longa
CHYKOTSKOYE NAGOR'YE
Anadyrskiy Zaliv
ARCTIC OCEAN
VOSTOCHNO-SIBIRSKOYE MORE
Pevek
Arctic Circle
Anadyr'
Ostrov Greem Bell
Ostrov Komsomolets
SEVERNAYA ZEMLYA
NOVOSIBIRSKIYE OSTROVA
Ostrov Novaya Sibir'
Ostrov Oktyabr'skoy Revolyutsii
Ostrov Bol'shoy Lyakhovskiy
Cherskiy
KORYAKSKOYE NAGOR'YE
Ostrov Bol'shevik
Ostrov Kotel'nyy
MORE LAPTEVYKH
KOLYMSKAYA NIZMENNOST'
POLUOSTROV TAYMYR
GORY BYRRANGA
Ozero Taymyr
Indigirka
Kolyma
KOLOMSKOYE NAGOR'YE
PACIFIC OCEAN
SEVERO-SIBIRSKAYA NIZMENNOST'
SAKHA (YAKUTIYA)
KHREBET CHERSKOGO
Zaliv Shelikhova
Klyuchevskaya Sopka 4750m
Susuman
Olenëk
VERKHOYANSKIY KHREBET
KHREBET SUNTAR-KHAYA
Magadan
Ust'-Kamchatsk
POLUOSTROV KAMCHATKA
Noril'sk
PLATO PUTORANA
Lena
Petropavlovsk-Kamchatskiy
Igarka
SIBERIA
Aldan
SEA OF OKHOTSK
SREDNE SIBIRSKOYE PLOSKOGOR'YE
Yakutsk
Nizhnyaya Tunguska
KHREBET DZHUGDZHUR
Mirnyy
Olëkminsk
Shantarskiye Ostrova
Ostrov Sakhalin
Podkamennaya Tunguska
NAGOR'YE ALDANSKOYE
Aleksandrovsk-Sakhalinskiy
Vitim
Bodaybo
STANOVOYE NAGOR'YE
Tatarskiy Proliv
Amur
Angara
Tynda
KURIL'SKIYE OSTROVA
Krasnoyarsk
Bratsk
Komsomol'sk-na-Amure
Yuzhno-Sakhalinsk
Bratskoye Vdkhr.
Ozero Baykal
Khabarovsk
SEA OF JAPAN (EAST SEA)
Abakan
Usol'ye-Sibirskoye
Angarsk
Irkutsk
Ulan-Ude
BURYATIYA
YABLONOVYY KHREBET
Chita
Argun'
Blagoveshchensk
Birobidzhan
YEVREYSKIYA
KHAKASIYA
ZAPADNYY SAYAN
VOSTOCHNYY SAYAN
TYVA
CHINA
Ozero Khanka
Ussuriysk
Nakhodka
Vladivostok
MONGOLIA
NORTH KOREA

TOURISM

Visitors : Population 1:18

7.94m visitors

Down 62% in 2001–2002

MAIN TOURIST ARRIVALS

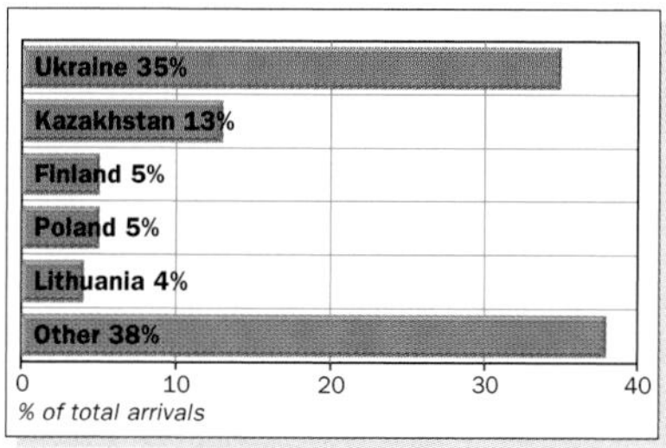
Ukraine 35%
Kazakhstan 13%
Finland 5%
Poland 5%
Lithuania 4%
Other 38%
0
10
20
30
40
% of total arrivals

The breakup of the previous monopoly tourist agency, Intourist, has led to a vast expansion of tourism opportunities: each region is keen to earn hard currency and to attract rich visitors. Russia now ranks seventh in the world as a tourist destination.

Moscow and St. Petersburg remain favorite destinations, where hotels tend either to be for the well-off or of a basic standard. Near St. Petersburg, Novgorod has many fine churches, and the Pskov area is celebrated as the setting for many of Pushkin's works, including *Eugene Onegin* and *Boris Godunov*.

At the luxury end of the market, trips from St. Petersburg to Tashkent on former president Brezhnev's official train are now available. River trips down the Volga and visits to medieval monasteries are increasingly popular. Tourists can also explore forests or fish for salmon in the Kola Peninsula. The defense sector has opened up to tourism and now offers flights in MiG jets, or rides in Russian T-80 tanks. Even the space industry has begun to court tourists.

Many parts of Russia remain inaccessible to most travelers. The Communist-era ban on foreigners visiting the Urals has been lifted, but the area still has very few facilities. Resorts such as the subtropical Sochi on the Black Sea, where powerful Russians have *dachas* (country houses), have experienced a building boom.

PEOPLE

Pop. density low

Russian, Tatar, Ukrainian, Chavash, various other national languages

8/km² (22/mi²)

THE URBAN/RURAL POPULATION SPLIT

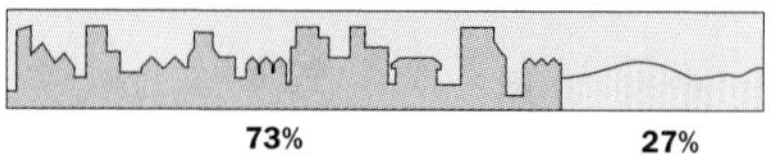
73%
27%

RELIGIOUS PERSUASION

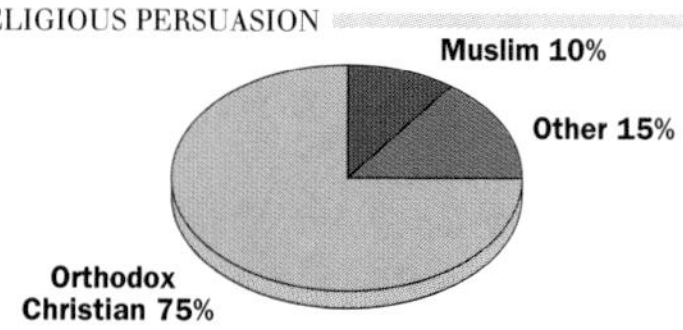
Muslim 10%
Other 15%
Orthodox Christian 75%

ETHNIC MAKEUP

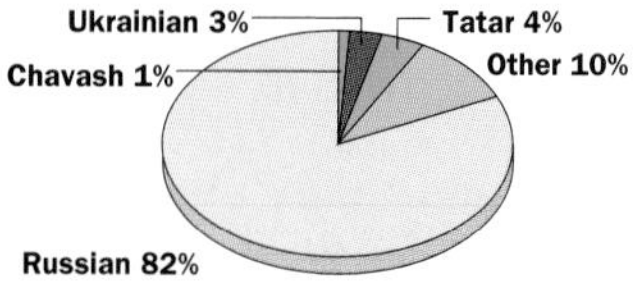
Ukrainian 3%
Tatar 4%
Chavash 1%
Other 10%
Russian 82%

Within the Russian Federation there are 57 "nationalities" with their own republic or territory, and a further 95 (who make up just 6% of the population) without a territory. The boundaries of the republics, and Soviet-era persecution, ensure that ethnic Russians are dominant almost everywhere. The minorities include Turkic speakers, Finno-Ugrians, Muslims, Buddhists, indigenous Arctic peoples, and the various peoples of the Caucasus. Russians form by far the largest single group, and the dominance of Russian culture and Orthodox Christianity is supported by the federal state. The forced use of Cyrillic script is one of a number of points of conflict between the republics and Moscow. Since the breakup of the Soviet Union, Russia's quest for a renewed national identity has led to a rise in right-wing extremist groups. Violence has been targeted at people from the north Caucasus, central Asia, and the dark-skinned in general. Antisemitism is also increasing.

The collapse of the Soviet Union has also been followed by a marked increase in materialism and a greater expression of sexuality and of politics and Russian Orthodoxy. The expensive rebuilding of Moscow's Church of Christ the Savior symbolized this change. The strong revival of Orthodox Christianity is boosted by legal recognition of its "special role" in Russia's history. Many small minority faiths have been unable to meet strict new registration requirements.

Though the fall of communism has brought more opportunities in business and politics for some women, for others it has meant resorting to very badly paid menial work. Domestic abuse has increased. Most Russians have very modest living standards and were further impoverished by the economic turmoil of the 1990s.

POPULATION AGE BREAKDOWN

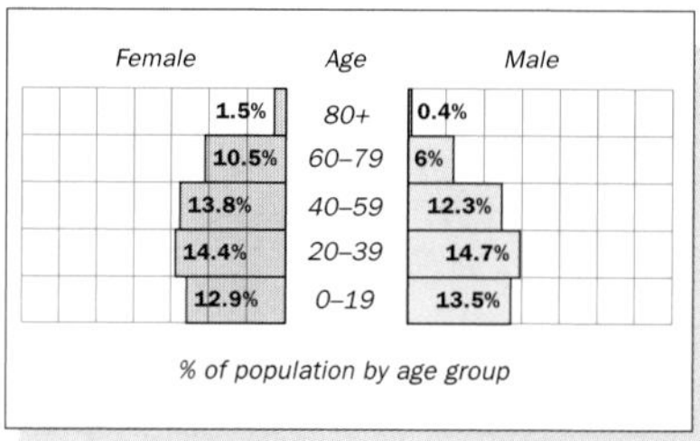
Female
Age
Male
1.5%
80+
0.4%
10.5%
60–79
6%
13.8%
40–59
12.3%
14.4%
20–39
14.7%
12.9%
0–19
13.5%
% of population by age group

POLITICS

Multiparty elections

L. House 2003/2007
U. House Varying

President Vladimir Putin

AT THE LAST ELECTION

State Duma 450 seats

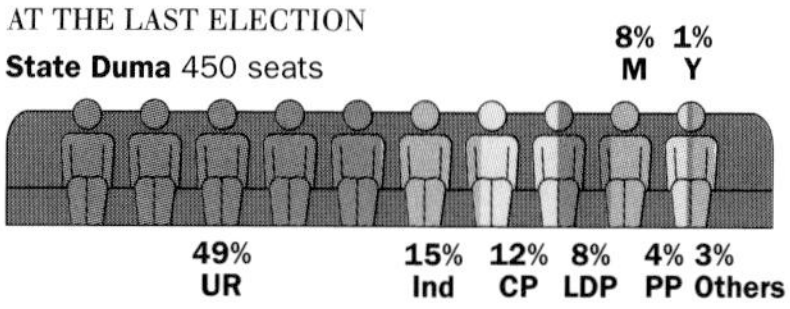
8% 1%
M Y
49%
UR
15%
Ind
12%
CP
8%
LDP
4%
PP
3%
Others

U = United Russia **Ind** = Independents **CP** = Communist Party **LDP** = Liberal Democratic Party **M** = Motherland **PP** = People's Party **Y** = Yabloko

Council of the Federation 178 seats

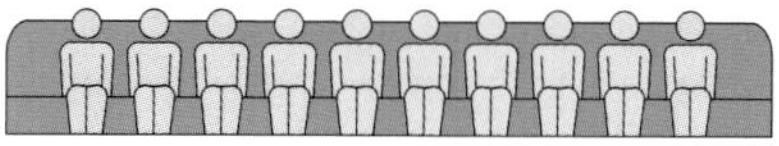

Each of 89 regions is represented in the Council of the Federation (Soviet Federatsii) by two members chosen by the regional legislature

The government is responsible to the Duma, but executive power lies firmly with the president.

PROFILE

President Boris Yeltsin's second term (from 1996) was overshadowed by his health problems, economic crisis, and corruption. Under his rule a number of so-called "oligarchs" gained considerable power, snapping up control of the liberalizing economy. Dramatic changes of government personnel were another characteristic of this period, as Yeltsin confronted the Duma in both 1998 and 1999 over his choice of prime minister.

Vladimir Putin, a little-known former head of the Federal Security Service (FSB), was unexpectedly nominated prime minister in 1999 and was made heir apparent to Yeltsin. He took over in an acting capacity on New Year's Eve 1999 and was resoundingly elected as president a few months later.

He has greatly consolidated his position since, tackling the power of the business "oligarchs," and of Russia's 89 regional governors, with his program of centralization. The conflict in Chechnya, though internationally damaging to Putin's image, has by contrast been a key element in his domestic appeal as a strong leader. His popularity was shaken by criticism of his handling of the *Kursk* submarine disaster in 2000, in which 118 sailors

Former president Boris Yeltsin, *renowned for his erratic behavior, stepped down in 1999.*

Mikhail Gorbachev, *whose restructuring ultimately led to the breakup of the Soviet Union.*

R

POLITICS *continued*

died. However, the marked improvement in the economy during his first year in office stood greatly to his credit in popular opinion, as it also did to that of Putin's first prime minister, Mikhail Kasyanov (2000–2004).

Putin's support within the Duma was consolidated by the sweeping election victory in 2003 of the UR party, which pushed the once mighty Communists into a distant second place not far ahead of the ultranationalist LDP. Many pro-market center-right parties failed even to break the minimum 5% support barrier for representation in the Duma. Observers in the West were wary of the blatant bias in the all-powerful state-run media in favor of UR. Similar criticisms were made of the presidential poll in 2004, in which Putin won over 70% of the vote. Two weeks before the election he appointed civil servant Mikhail Fradkov as prime minister.

MAIN POLITICAL ISSUES

Centralization versus regionalism

Nation-based separatism is brutally suppressed. Nowhere has this been made clearer than by the ferocious military campaign in Chechnya. Begun under Yeltsin in 1994, the conflict there has dragged on despite declarations of an end to the war in 2000 and 2002. The installation of a pro-federal government and constitution in Chechnya in 2003 has transformed the battle into a civil conflict.

The Turkic republic of Tatarstan has theoretically buried its own secessionist desires, signing a new federation treaty in 1994. Nonetheless, regional autonomy remains a powerful issue, and many of the 21 republics continue to have laws which are out of synch with the central Russian constitution.

Influence accumulated under Yeltsin by Russia's 89 regional governors was reversed by Putin's efforts to concentrate power in the presidency. Control of police and taxation has been centralized in seven huge federal districts, and the governors have been stripped of their seats in the upper house. Separatist terrorism has encouraged further sweeping centralist reforms.

Vladimir Putin *was handed power by Yeltsin in 1999, and was elected president in 2000.*

Mikhail Fradkov, *relatively unknown diplomat appointed prime minister in 2004.*

Crime and corruption

Crime levels rose alarmingly under the post-Soviet regime. Widespread bureaucratic corruption was countered by the power acquired by business tycoons, the so-called "oligarchs," who snapped up privatized industries at bargain prices. Putin launched a crusade against them, highlighted by the arrest and imprisonment of oil magnate Mikhail Khodorkovsky in 2003 and the punitive tax demands against his oil conglomerate Yukos in 2004.

Political violence

A number of high-profile murders of Duma members and regional administrators has rocked Russian politics in recent years. Always blamed immediately on contract killings, the assassinations attest to the apparent links between organized crime and the political mainstream.

WORLD AFFAIRS

Joined UN in 1945

CE | CIS | IAEA | G8 | OSCE

The September 11, 2001, terrorist attacks on the US laid the foundations for a massive change in Russia's relations with the US and the wider international community. President Putin pledged immediate support to the US-led "war on terrorism," securing in return unqualified backing for the Chechnya campaign which was recast as a legitimate battle against "terrorism." Russia and NATO also appeared to bury their grievances; in 2002 a new NATO–Russia Council was established. Russia is uneasy, however, over the growth of US influence in central Asia and the Caucasus, particularly in the form of military bases. A key point of contention is US activity in Georgia where a new pro-Western president has cosied up to the US administration, while volubly protesting Russia's involvement in the breakaway regions of Abkhazia and South Ossetia.

Many of the other successor states of the USSR, the "near abroad," retain close links with Russia and are still viewed, at least domestically, as Russia's sphere of influence. A "joint economic space" comprising Russia, Belarus, Kazakhstan, and Ukraine was announced in 2003. Belarus has pushed for full reunification, but plans for monetary and political union have stalled in recent years. Relations with the Baltic states are the least cordial, but are improving after tension over discrimination against ethnic Russians there. Special transit passes for the people of Kaliningrad came into force when the EU expanded up to Russia's border in 2004.

The Rodina (Motherland) statue, Volgograd, *stands 52 m (171 ft) high. Russia is littered with enormous Communist-era monuments.*

AID

Recipient

$1.3bn (receipts) — Up 17% in 2002

Russia has received billions of dollars in aid from Western countries on several occasions to stave off government debt and to promote economic restructuring. Large-scale IMF credits were obtained during the economic crises of the mid- and late 1990s.

DEFENSE

Phasing out conscription

$48bn — Up 7% in 2002

RUSSIAN ARMED FORCES

21,870 main battle tanks (T-34, T-55, T-62, T-64, T-72, T-80, T-90)	321,000 personnel
53 submarines, 1 carrier, 14 destroyers, 7 cruisers, 10 frigates, 88 patrol boats	155,000 personnel
2434 combat aircraft (MiG-25/29/31, Su-24/25/27, Tu-22)	184,600 personnel
735 ICBM, 13 SSBN, 100 ABM	

The loss of the 118-man Kursk nuclear submarine in 2000 symbolized the long-term decline in Russia's military might. Maintaining and using the enormous former-communist war machine has proved too expensive. Reforms aimed to cut troop numbers by hundreds of thousands by 2004, while the proportion of professional units is rising. Public anger at conditions has led to pay increases.

Spending on nuclear forces is limited to the physical protection of warheads. In 2002, Russia agreed to cut its nuclear arsenal further, slashing the number of warheads by 60%. It also dropped previous objections to the proposed US national missile defense system.

The Northern and Pacific navy fleets are inactive and deteriorating fast. A major naval exercise attended by President Putin in the run-up to the 2004 presidential election was marred when missiles failed to fire.

RUSSIA IN THE POST-9/11 WORLD

RUSSIAN FEDERATION
ESTONIA
LATVIA
LITHUANIA
RUSS. FED.
EAST GERMANY
POLAND
BELORUSSIA
CZECHOSLOVAKIA
HUNGARY
UKRAINE
ROMANIA
ALBANIA
BULGARIA
MOLDAVIA
GEORGIA
ARMENIA
AZERBAIJAN
KAZAKHSTAN
UZBEKISTAN
TURKMENISTAN
KYRGYSZTAN
TAJIKISTAN
Russian Federation
Ex-Soviet countries
Former Warsaw Pact countries

As the world's largest country, Russia inevitably has a significant geopolitical role. Its massive resource base, coupled with a modernized culture, have made it a key economic power. The nearly 700,000-strong military machine is equipped with high-tech weaponry that gave it superpower status. As the first Communist state it was a political inspiration to the world.

Between 1991 and 2001 the Western world was consciously dealing with a crippled Russia which had only just shrugged off more than seven decades of Communist rule, revealing the deep wounds beneath the red banner. Relations had begun to change with the ascendancy of Vladimir Putin in 2000. A program of reform and centralization saw a resurgence of Russia's place in the global political system. Tensions once again increased over Russia's relations with the ex-Soviet states and the Arab–Muslim world, over its nuclear inheritance, and particularly over the Muslim insurgency in Chechnya.

The Islamist terrorist attacks on the US on September 11, 2001, served as a catalyst in the sweeping away of the old perceptions of the West's rivalry with Russia, but at the same time encouraged other tensions to develop.

Russia and the US

From 1945 to 1991 the world had been divided between two superpowers. The US and its allies stood on one side, Soviet Russia and its allies on the other. The Cold War informed the political situation in every sovereign state, with the superpowers taking an active role in internal conflicts across the globe. For Russia, a state of constant readiness for a third world war against the West prompted the creation of a mighty armory (the cost of which ultimately proved crippling), and a military-based economy embracing self-sufficiency as far as possible. Its sphere of influence consisted of bordering countries and those African, Asian, and Latin American countries which embraced some form of socialist government. After 1991, though the obvious antagonism of the Cold War vanished, some of the structures of the Cold War persisted, most notably the Western military alliance NATO.

September 11, 2001, provided the impetus for the overhaul of the framework of Russian–Western relations. President Putin took the opportunity to give his backing to the US "war on terrorism," and the US responded by agreeing to reform the NATO–Russia system. In May 2002 the NATO–Russia Council (NRC) was established, nominally bringing Russia into the NATO decision-making process as an equal partner and formalizing the relationship propounded by NATO's 1997 Founding Act on Mutual Relations, Cooperation, and Security.

***President Vladimir Putin** and the then secretary-general of NATO, Lord Robertson, at the first NATO–Russia summit in 2002.*

The new reality, however, of a "single ultrapower" world in which the US dominates global relations and expands its sphere of influence at will, has left a bitter taste in Russian mouths. In 2004 Russia had no choice but to accept the extension of the NATO alliance right up to its borders.

Meanwhile, on the disarmament front, Putin tacitly accepted US president George W. Bush's decision to withdraw from the 1972 Antiballistic Missile (ABM) treaty as part of his plans to establish a National Missile Defense system (NMD). Putin also agreed to the Strategic Offensive Reductions Treaty (SORT). Though this SORT agreement went further in terms of cutting warhead deployment than the now abandoned "START III" treaty, many observers regarded it as strategically more favorable to the US in that it spoke of nondeployment rather than decommissioning of nuclear missiles, leaving the US with a larger arsenal.

War on terrorism

Russian support for the US concept of a "war on terrorism" has been put to the test since it was declared in 2001.

The first act in the "war" was the defeat of the *taliban* in Afghanistan in October–December 2001. US military bases established in the central Asian states to the north of Afghanistan have since been made an integral part of the US strategy against Islamists, bringing US troops onto the very territory of the former Soviet Union. While Russia approved of the Afghan offensive, it has been deeply irritated by the retention of this central Asian foothold.

As with the attack on Afghanistan, so with the US-led invasion of Iraq, the "war on terrorism" has in practice seen the extension of US sway in regions where Russia once held great influence. As the rival of the US, Russia had always maintained close ties with those Middle Eastern states opposed to the West, promoting the Arab socialist movement in Syria and notably in Iraq, as well as being highly critical of Israel.

R

In the buildup to the US-led invasion of Iraq in 2003, it was thus not surprising that Russia supported an emphasis on UN weapons inspections rather than military intervention. In the scramble for oil and reconstruction contracts which followed the formal ending of hostilities in Iraq, Russia has been keenly aware of the US advantage being forged.

The most obvious trade-off for Putin from Russia's closer relations with the West has been tolerance of military and security force action against Islamist separatists in Chechnya. Heightened security measures adopted elsewhere to protect against would-be Islamist bombers have been implemented in Russia with the specific intention of cracking down on Chechen activists; for Russia the "war on terrorism" was already being fought from 1994 around the Chechen capital Grozny. Hostage crises – at a Moscow theater in 2002, killing over 100, and a school in Beslan in 2004, causing the deaths of hundreds of children – have further stifled criticism of Russia's heavyhanded approach to the breakaway republic.

***In September 2004, Chechen separatists** took over a school in Beslan, in neighboring North Ossetia. Video footage was shot by the terrorists during the 3-day siege, which ended in carnage with some 300 dead, mainly children.*

RUSSIA AND EUROPE

One notable feature of the international alignment over the US-led invasion of Iraq is that Russia found itself standing alongside Germany and France, or what the US chose to call "old Europe." Throughout its history, the Russian state has seen repeated shifts of emphasis between a European identity and a more eastward-facing orientation. The current more European emphasis is identified with Putin's leadership. It would be ironic if its continuation should coincide with Russia becoming an increasingly isolated exception to the trend toward increasing EU membership, possibly extending to former Soviet states like Georgia and Ukraine. On the other hand the pendulum could swing east again should Russia's economy strengthen.

ECONOMICS

Inflation 140% p.a. (1990–2001)

$307bn

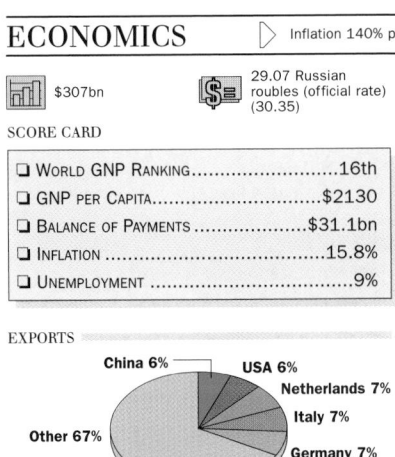

29.07 Russian roubles (official rate) (30.35)

SCORE CARD

❑ WORLD GNP RANKING	16th
❑ GNP PER CAPITA	$2130
❑ BALANCE OF PAYMENTS	$31.1bn
❑ INFLATION	15.8%
❑ UNEMPLOYMENT	9%

EXPORTS

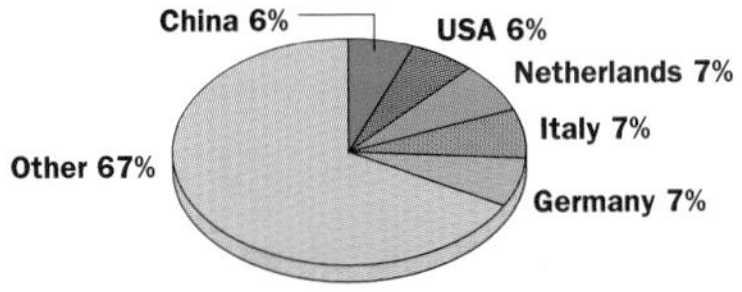
China 6%
USA 6%
Netherlands 7%
Italy 7%
Germany 7%
Other 67%

IMPORTS

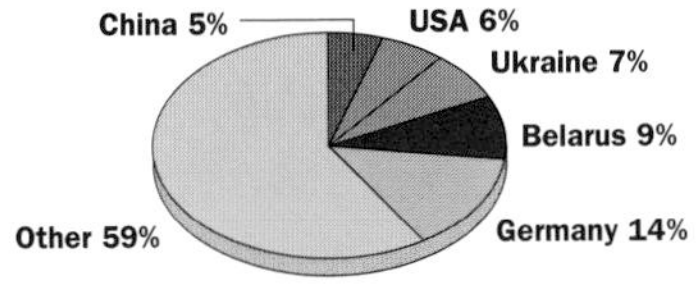
China 5%
USA 6%
Ukraine 7%
Belarus 9%
Germany 14%
Other 59%

STRENGTHS

Huge natural resources, in particular hydrocarbons, precious metals, fuel, timber. Potential from future international oil pipelines. Enormous engineering and scientific base. Massive arms export industry: world's largest in 2002. Government revenue increased by tax reforms. Lucrative privatizations. Recognized as a market economy in 2002, encouraging foreign investment.

WEAKNESSES

Crumbling infrastructure. Attempts by government to exert control over commercial sector, particularly oil. Privatized companies asset-stripped by former managers. Organized crime controls huge areas of the economy. Regional investment hindered by uneven implementation of federal laws. Tax evasion and corruption remain widespread. Oil giant Yukos in crisis. Rising wages and strengthening rouble have promoted boom in imports, narrowing trade gap, harming local production, and stifling small enterprises.

ECONOMIC PERFORMANCE INDICATOR

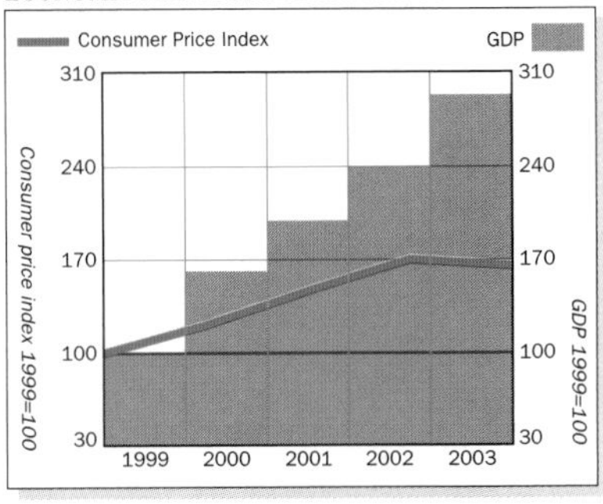
Consumer Price Index
GDP
310
240
170
100
30
1999
2000
2001
2002
2003
Consumer price index 1999=100
GDP 1999=100

PROFILE

The few gains made in the early postcommunist era were swept aside in the 1998 economic crisis. Powerful financial "oligarchs" emerged, and organized crime moved into most areas of the economy. However, the devaluation of the rouble ironically served to promote a miniboom in the last years of the 20th century. Real wages fell, encouraging small enterprises to expand, while the devaluation made imports too expensive for the average consumer – promoting local production. Industrial production increased and GDP grew by 7.6% in 2000. Putin has moved to dismantle the power of the economic elites. The private sale of land was permitted from 2001, and a new 13% flat rate of income tax promised to help reduce widespread tax evasion. However, while the economy weathered the 2001 global slowdown, the rise in real wages and the strengthening of the rouble have begun to offset the previous years' gains. Some 50% of the economy is conducted on the black market.

RUSSIAN FEDERATION : MAJOR BUSINESSES

Nizhniy Novgorod
West Siberian Plain
Sankt Peterburg
Kazan'
Krasnoyarsk
Moscow
Rostov-na-Donu
Volgograd
Samara
Novosibirsk
Perm'
Yekaterinburg
Vladivostok
Ufa
Chelyabinsk
Irkutsk
Ob'
Yenisey
Lena
Textiles
Chemicals
Metallurgy
Computers
Electronics
Engineering
Vehicle assembly
Defense industry
Oil refining
Oil & gas
0
1000 km
0
1000 miles

R

CHRONOLOGY

The first Russian state (Rus) was in present-day Ukraine. Occupation by the Tatars (1240–1480) marked the Russian language and character. From the 17th century, the Romanovs ruled an expanding empire.

- **1904–1905** Russian war against Japan; ends in defeat for Russia.
- **1905** "Bloody Sunday" revolution.
- **1909–1914** Rapid economic expansion.
- **1914** Enters World War I against Germany.
- **1917** February Revolution; abdication of Nicholas II. October Revolution; Bolsheviks take over with Lenin as leader.
- **1918** Nicholas II and family shot.
- **1918–1920** Civil war.
- **1921** New Economic Policy; retreat from socialism.
- **1922** USSR established.
- **1924** Lenin dies. Leadership struggle eventually won by Stalin.
- **1928** First Five-Year Plan: forced industrialization and collectivization.
- **1936–1938** Show trials and campaigns against actual and suspected members of opposition. Millions sent to gulags in Siberia and elsewhere. Purges widespread.
- **1939** Hitler–Stalin pact gives USSR Baltic states, eastern Poland, and Bessarabia (Moldova).
- **1941** Germany attacks USSR.
- **1943** February, tide of war turns with lifting of siege of Stalingrad.
- **1944–1945** Soviet offensive penetrates Balkans.
- **1945** Germany defeated. Under Yalta and Potsdam agreements eastern and southeastern Europe are Soviet zone of influence.
- **1947** Cold War begins; Stalin on defensive and fears penetration of Western capitalist values.
- **1953** Stalin dies.
- **1956** Hungarian uprising crushed. Krushchev's "secret speech" attacking Stalin at party congress.
- **1957** Krushchev consolidates power. *Sputnik* launched.
- **1961** Yuri Gagarin first man in space.
- **1962** Cuban missile crisis.
- **1964** Krushchev ousted in coup, replaced by Leonid Brezhnev.
- **1975** Helsinki Final Act; confirms European frontiers as at end of World War II. Soviets agree human rights are concern of international community.
- **1979** Soviets invade Afghanistan. New intensification of Cold War.
- **1982** Brezhnev dies.
- **1985** Gorbachev in power. Start of *perestroika*, "restructuring." First of three US–USSR summits, resulting in arms

RESOURCES

Electric power 213m kW

3.72m tonnes

8.54m b/d (reserves 69.1bn barrels)

26.5m cattle, 17.3m pigs, 13.7m sheep, 337m chickens

Coal, oil, gas, gold, diamonds, iron, aluminum, manganese

ELECTRICITY GENERATION

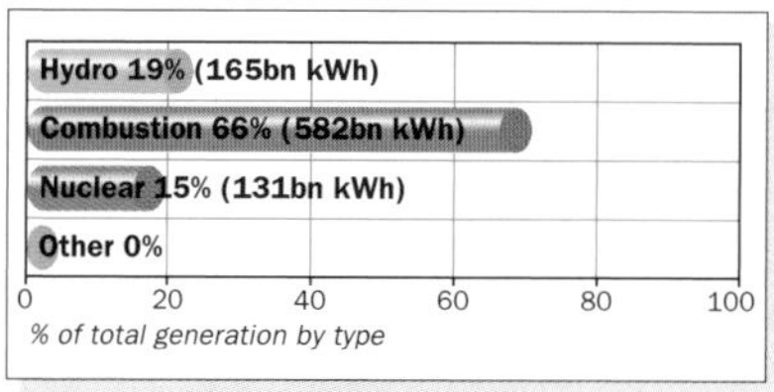
Hydro 19% (165bn kWh)
Combustion 66% (582bn kWh)
Nuclear 15% (131bn kWh)
Other 0%
0
20
40
60
80
100
% of total generation by type

Russia is a major producer of oil, natural gas, and electricity, among other resources. Confirmed reserves make Russia the world's leading country in terms of hydrocarbons, gold, other precious metals, diamonds, and timber.

Russia has been slow to open up its mineral sector to foreign concerns, but is starting to realize the potential of its vast resources. In 2003 foreign firms invested in a mammoth $10 billion liquefied natural gas plant in Sakhalin – set to be the world's largest integrated oil and gas project.

However, geographic remoteness has held back exploitation, while the fact that some of the richest deposits are located in national territories such as Tatarstan and Sakha (Yakutia) in Siberia has turned the ownership of these resources into a delicate political issue.

RUSSIAN FEDERATION : LAND USE

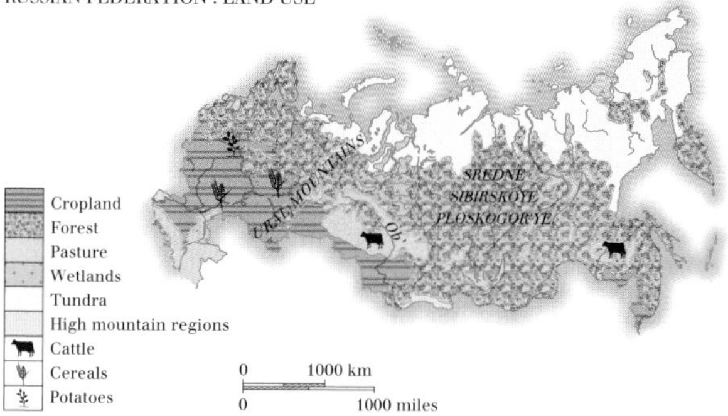
Cropland
Forest
Pasture
Wetlands
Tundra
High mountain regions
Cattle
Cereals
Potatoes
URAL MOUNTAINS
Ob
SREDNE SIBIRSKOYE PLOSKOGOR'YE
0
1000 km
0
1000 miles

ENVIRONMENT

Sustainability rank: 72nd

8% (0.8% partially protected)

9.9 tonnes per capita

ENVIRONMENTAL TREATIES

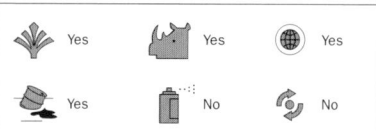

Yes	Yes	Yes
Yes	No	No

Though awareness of environmental problems has risen sharply, resources, political will, and know-how to tackle them are still lacking. In 2004 the government agreed to ratify the Kyoto Protocol on greenhouse gas emissions, but an active green movement has yet to win significant electoral support.

Each region has its own particular problems. The northwest risks contamination from the neglected Soviet-era nuclear submarine fleet and from nuclear waste containers dumped in the Barents Sea. Thousands of tonnes of chemical weapons have been dumped in the Baltic, though their exact location has not been revealed. In the Urals and the cities of European Russia, many chemical and heavy industrial plants do not treat their effluents at all. Several fish species are now extinct in the Volga River in central Russia. In 2001 parliament approved a bill to allow the atomic energy ministry Minatom to earn $2 billion a year from storing and reprocessing foreign nuclear waste.

MEDIA

TV ownership high

Daily newspaper circulation 105 per 1000 people

PUBLISHING AND BROADCAST MEDIA

There are 285 daily newspapers, including *Izvestiya*, *Komsomolskaya Pravda*, and *Trud*

2 main national and regional services, partly state-owned, several localized independent channels

1 main state-run service, broadcasting 2 channels, 1 foreign broadcasting service, several independent stations

There is growing concern over state control of the media. Bias in TV reporting, rife under Yeltsin, continues under Putin. Reporting on Chechnya is subject to particular pressure. The NTV network, flagship of exiled magnate Vladimir Gusinsky, was taken over in 2001 by the state-run gas company Gazprom, while the remaining independent national broadcaster, TVS, was shut down due to poor finances in 2003. Critical editorial staff have been dismissed from the daily *Sevodnya* and weekly *Itogi*. Many Russians have satellite dishes and tune in to CNN and other Western channels.

Argumenty i Fakty is the best-selling weekly paper, with a circulation of nearly three million. *Trud* is the biggest-selling daily. The Soviet state organ *Izvestiya* is now independent.

Overall, 9% of the population have access to the Internet, but use is concentrated among Muscovites.

R

CHRONOLOGY *continued*

reduction treaties. Nationality conflicts surface.

- **1988** Law of State Enterprises gives more power to enterprises; inflation and dislocation of economy.
- **1990** Gorbachev becomes Soviet president. First partly freely elected parliament (Supreme Soviet) meets.
- **1991** Boris Yeltsin elected president of Russia. Yeltsin and Muscovites resist hard-line communist coup. Gorbachev sidelined. CIS established; demise of USSR.
- **1992** Economic shock therapy.
- **1993** Yeltsin decrees dissolution of Supreme Soviet and uses force to disband parliament. Elections return conservative State Duma.
- **1994** First Russian military offensive against Chechnya.
- **1995** Communists win elections.
- **1996** Yeltsin reelected despite strong Communist challenge. Peace accord in Chechnya.
- **1998** Economic turmoil forces devaluation of rouble. Severe recession, rampant inflation.
- **1998–1999** Yeltsin repeatedly changes prime minister in successive political crises.
- **1999** Yeltsin resigns; Prime Minister Putin is acting president.
- **1999–2000** Terrorist violence blamed on Islamic separatists in Dagestan and Chechnya. Military offensive against Chechnya; fall of Grozny.
- **2000** Putin elected president. Attack on "oligarchs" in big business. Improvement in economy. *Kursk* nuclear submarine disaster.
- **2001** Party mergers: Putin's Unity party largest grouping in parliament. Russian–Chinese friendship treaty.
- **2002** May, Cam Ranh Bay base in Vietnam, last Russian outpost beyond former USSR, closed. October, Moscow theater hostage crisis: Chechen separatists and 128 hostages killed during rescue.
- **2003** Pro-Putin UR wins elections.
- **2004** Putin reelected. Militants seize hostages in Beslan school; hundreds killed, mainly children.

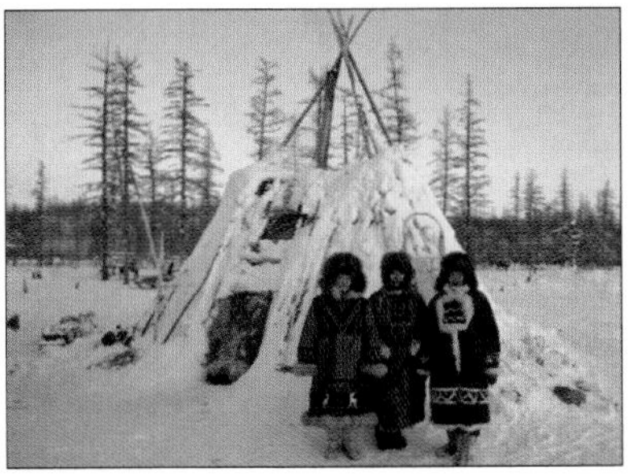

A golomo (winter dwelling) of the Evenk people from Yakutia, northeastern Siberia. Russia is home to 152 different nationalities.

CRIME

Death penalty not used in practice

864,590 prisoners

Down 14% in 2000–2002

CRIME RATES

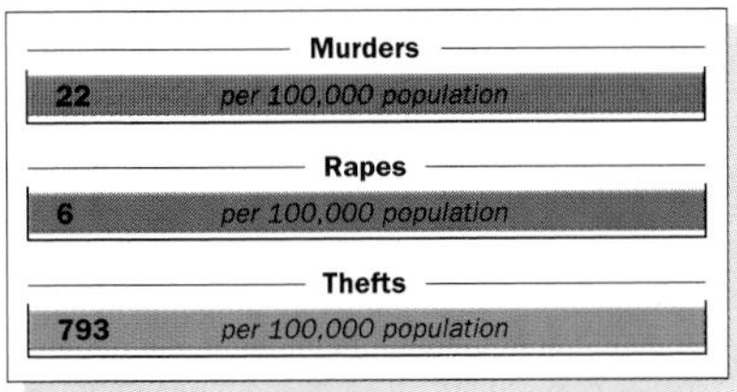
Murders
22 per 100,000 population
Rapes
6 per 100,000 population
Thefts
793 per 100,000 population

Policing cannot keep pace with the formidable levels of crime in Russia.

Intergang violence accounts for a recent rise in the murder rate. Street crime has also increased in the larger cities. Corruption is rife, particularly in the regions. The Russian mafia profits from protection rackets, prostitution, smuggling operations, and narcotics, and is also active in western Europe.

Public fear resulting from the level of crime and high-profile attacks by separatists has contributed to a rise in popularity for authoritarian political platforms.

Overcrowding, poor conditions, and disease are major problems in prisons.

EDUCATION

School leaving age: 15

99%

5.43m students

THE EDUCATION SYSTEM

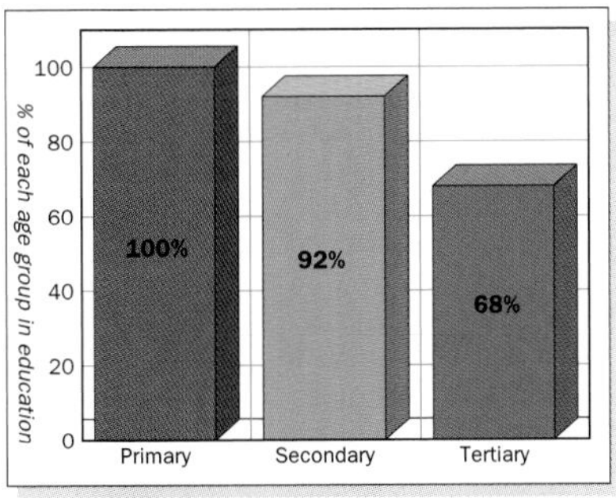
100
80
60
40
20
0
% of each age group in education
100%
92%
68%
Primary
Secondary
Tertiary

Schooling is free, and is compulsory for nine years up to age 15.

Attempts to change the Soviet-based curriculum, still widely in use, are hampered by lack of funds. Hundreds of private lycées, such as those run by the Orthodox Church, offer courses in west European languages. German in particular has made a comeback as a key language for international commerce. The state-subsidized higher education system is seriously underfunded, and some institutions have begun charging students. Prestigious institutions such as the Academy of Sciences have been forced to cut staff and research. Most academics have to rely on extramural earnings.

HEALTH

Limited welfare state health benefits

1 per 238 people

Cerebrovascular and heart diseases, accidents, cancers

The health care system is in crisis and medicines are often in short supply. Nearly two-thirds of children are deemed "unhealthy."

Until 1991, state enterprises provided considerable health care for employees. Employers should now make payments through the Medical Insurance Fund, but many privatized concerns seek to cut costs. Bribing medical staff to obtain treatment is commonplace, and there is a lack of pharmaceutical products and drugs. Alcoholism is increasing as a cause of death.

SPENDING

GDP/cap. decrease

CONSUMPTION AND SPENDING

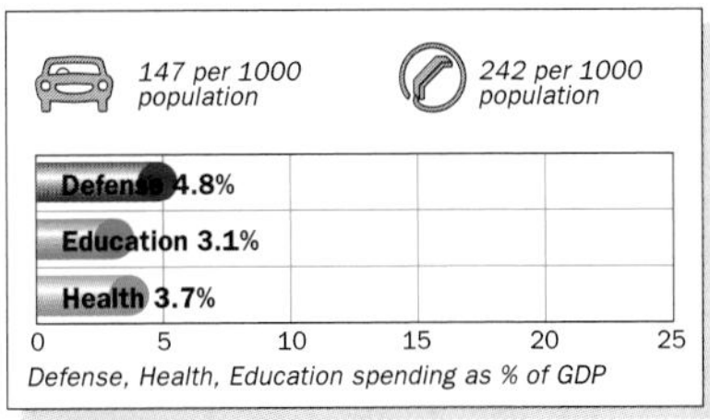
147 per 1000 population
242 per 1000 population
Defense 4.8%
Education 3.1%
Health 3.7%
0
5
10
15
20
25
Defense, Health, Education spending as % of GDP

Wealth disparities have increased sharply. A small minority made huge profits from the dismantling of the old Soviet command economy, while 20% of the population live below the government's "subsistence minimum." The replacement of benefits, such as free health care and transportation, by cash payments is likely to impoverish veterans and pensioners further.

A growing number of dollar millionaires flaunt their wealth, especially in Moscow. Organized crime bosses are Russian society's wealthiest group. Russia is now the biggest buyer of Rolls Royces. There are thousands of Russian offshore bank accounts; the Turkish Republic of Northern Cyprus has been a favorite location.

WORLD RANKING

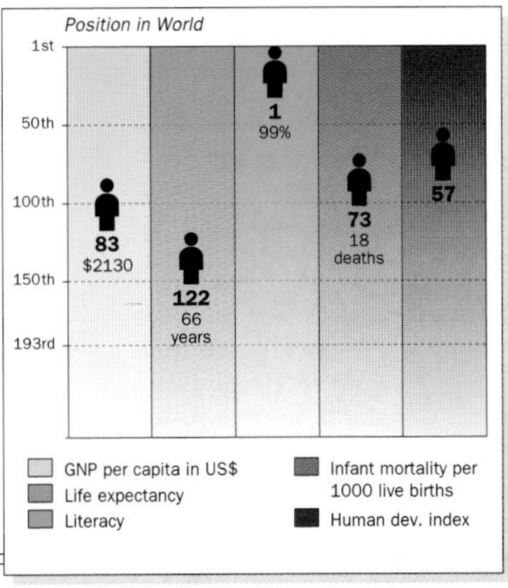
Position in World
1st
50th
100th
150th
193rd
83
$2130
122
66 years
1
99%
73
18 deaths
57
GNP per capita in US$
Life expectancy
Literacy
Infant mortality per 1000 live births
Human dev. index

R

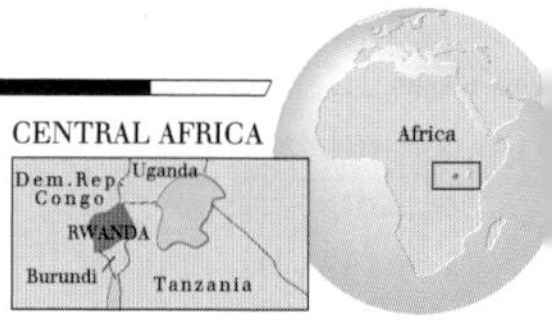
CENTRAL AFRICA
Africa
Dem.Rep. Congo
Uganda
RWANDA
Burundi
Tanzania

RWANDA

OFFICIAL NAME: Republic of Rwanda **CAPITAL:** Kigali **POPULATION:** 8.4 million
CURRENCY: Rwanda franc **OFFICIAL LANGUAGES:** French, English, and Kinyarwanda

1962 | 1962 | July 1 | RWA | +2 | +250 | .rw

LANDLOCKED RWANDA lies just south of the equator in east central Africa. Since independence in 1962, ethnic tensions have dominated politics. In 1994, the violent death of the president led to appalling political and ethnic violence. Over half of the surviving population were displaced. The perpetrators of the genocide held sway in desperately overcrowded refugee camps in adjacent countries, greatly complicating the process of eventual repatriation and reintegration.

CLIMATE

Tropical wet and dry

WEATHER CHART FOR KIGALI

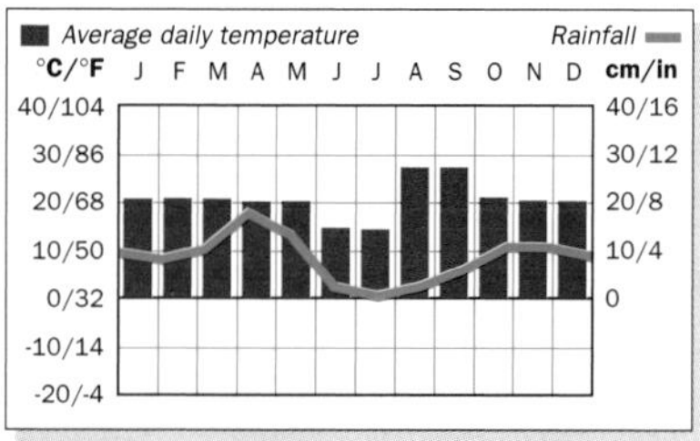
Average daily temperature
Rainfall
°C/°F
J F M A M J J A S O N D
cm/in
40/104
30/86
20/68
10/50
0/32
-10/14
-20/-4
40/16
30/12
20/8
10/4
0

Rwanda's climate is tropical, tempered by altitude. Two wet seasons allow for two harvests each year.

TRANSPORTATION

Drive on right

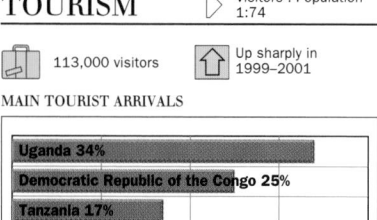

Kigali International 113,375 passengers

Has no fleet

THE TRANSPORTATION NETWORK

960 km (597 miles)

None

None

Lake Kivu navigable by small craft

The road network is well developed, and Rwanda has access by road to the Tanzanian railroad system.

TOURISM

Visitors : Population 1:74

113,000 visitors

Up sharply in 1999–2001

MAIN TOURIST ARRIVALS

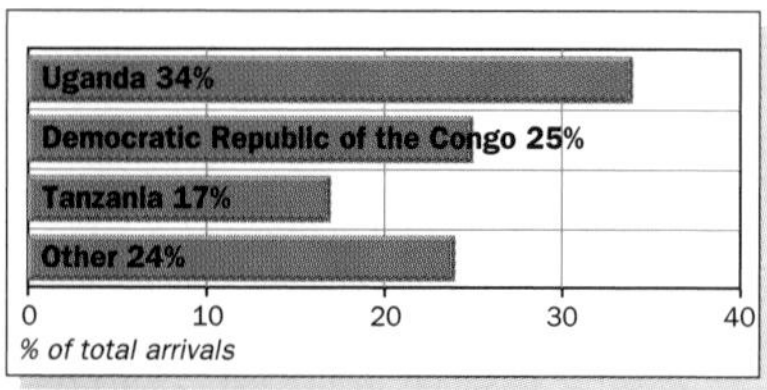
Uganda 34%
Democratic Republic of the Congo 25%
Tanzania 17%
Other 24%
0
10
20
30
40
% of total arrivals

Tourism effectively ceased as a result of civil war. Wealthy wildlife enthusiasts are a potential market. The presence of international NGO staff has raised prices for hotels and food, making it comparatively expensive for tourists.

PEOPLE

Pop. density high

Kinyarwanda, French, Kiswahili, English

337/km² (872/mi²)

THE URBAN/RURAL POPULATION SPLIT

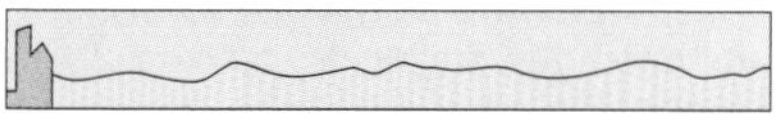
6%
94%

ETHNIC MAKEUP

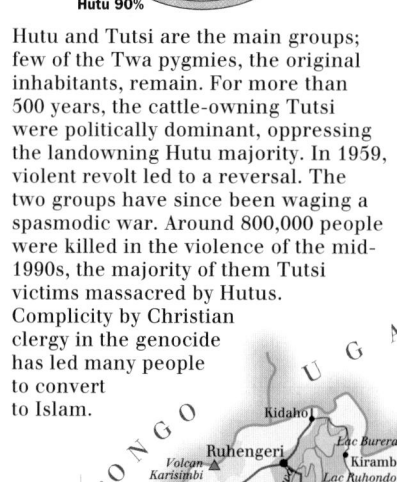

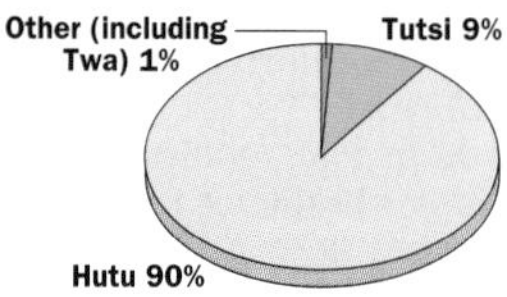
Other (including Twa) 1%
Tutsi 9%
Hutu 90%

Hutu and Tutsi are the main groups; few of the Twa pygmies, the original inhabitants, remain. For more than 500 years, the cattle-owning Tutsi were politically dominant, oppressing the landowning Hutu majority. In 1959, violent revolt led to a reversal. The two groups have since been waging a spasmodic war. Around 800,000 people were killed in the violence of the mid-1990s, the majority of them Tutsi victims massacred by Hutus. Complicity by Christian clergy in the genocide has led many people to convert to Islam.

POLITICS

Multiparty elections

L. House 2003/2008
U. House 2003/2011

President Paul Kagame

AT THE LAST ELECTION

Chamber of Deputies 80 seats

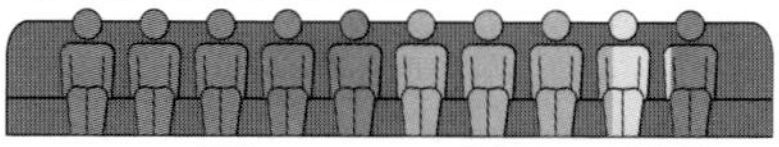
50% FPR
34% Reserved
9% PSD
7% PL

FPR = Rwandan Patriotic Front and allies
Reserved = 24 for women, elected by provinces, two youth representatives, and one representative of the disabled
PSD = Social Democratic Party **PL** = Liberal Party

Senate 26 seats

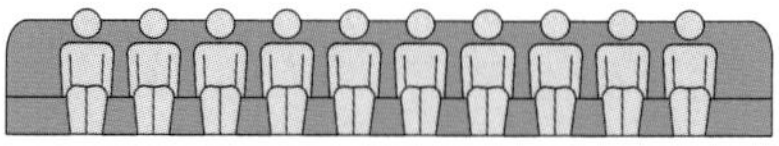

The Senate comprises representatives from provinces, historically marginalized communities, the political parties' forum, and universities. Ex-presidents can also request seats

A peace accord in 1993 ended a three-year rebellion by the Tutsi-dominated Rwandan Patriotic Front (FPR). In 1994, however, the predominantly Hutu supporters of the old regime massacred almost a million of their mainly, but not exclusively, Tutsi opponents. The FPR eventually gained control in the conflict and offered Hutu key posts in a new government. The 2003 constitution includes safeguards against ethnic hatred and one-party dominance, but allows the curtailment of free speech. Paul Kagame, a Tutsi who had succeeded as president in 2000, was convincingly reelected in August 2003 while his FPR won legislative polls.

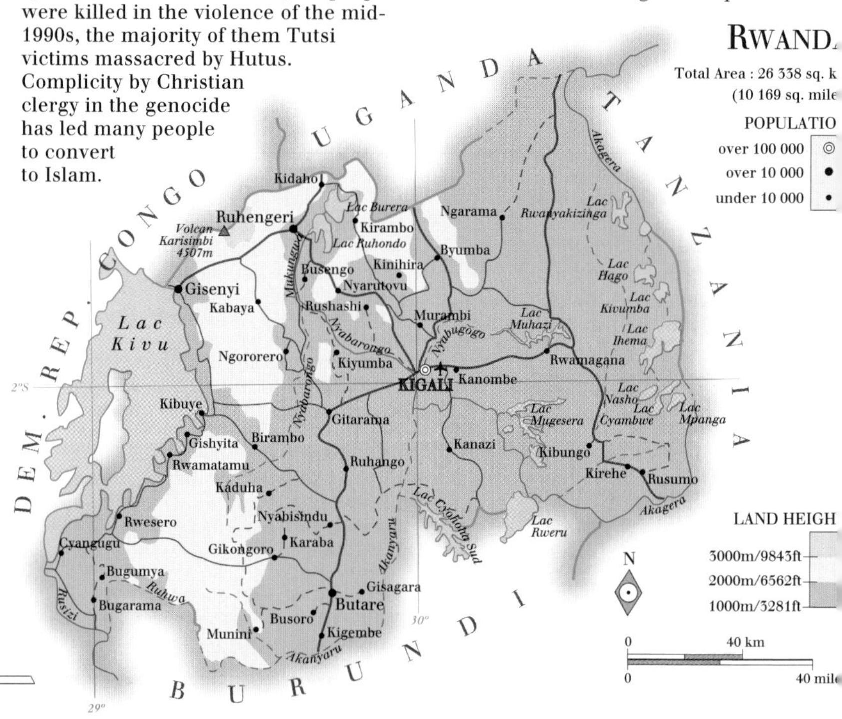
RWAND
Total Area : 26 338 sq. k
(10 169 sq. mile
POPULATIO
over 100 000
over 10 000
under 10 000
LAND HEIGH
3000m/9843ft
2000m/6562ft
1000m/3281ft
0
40 km
0
40 mil
UGANDA
TANZANIA
DEM. REP. CONGO
BURUNDI
Lac Kivu
KIGALI
Kidaho
Ruhengeri
Volcan Karisimbi 4507m
Gisenyi
Kabaya
Ngororero
Kibuye
Gishyita
Rwamatamu
Birambo
Kaduha
Rwesero
Cyangugu
Bugumya
Bugarama
Gikongoro
Nyabisindu
Karaba
Butare
Gisagara
Busoro
Kigembe
Munini
Gitarama
Ruhango
Kiyumba
Rushashi
Busengo
Nyarutovu
Kinihira
Kirambo
Lac Burera
Lac Ruhondo
Byumba
Ngarama
Murambi
Kanombe
Kanazi
Kibungo
Kirehe
Rusumo
Rwamagana
Lac Rwanyakizinga
Lac Hago
Lac Kivumba
Lac Ihema
Lac Muhazi
Lac Nasho
Lac Cyambwe
Lac Mpanga
Lac Mugesera
Lac Rweru
Lac Cyohoha Sud
Akagera
Nyabarongo
Mukungwa
Nyabugogo
Akanyaru
Rusizi
Ruhwa
2°S
29°
30°
N

WORLD AFFAIRS

Joined UN in 1962

COMESA | CEPGL | OIF | NAM | AU

Rwanda is accused of supporting rebel groups in the east of the DRC; relations are tense. Elements involved in the 1994 genocide operate near the borders and continue to threaten stability, as does ethnic strife in neighboring Burundi.

AID

Recipient

$356m (receipts) | Up 19% in 2002

The country continues to be heavily dependent on foreign aid. Donors have been able to use this as a lever to curb the government's activities in neighboring conflict zones. The UK is the biggest bilateral donor.

DEFENSE

No compulsory military service

$68m | Up 3% in 2002

The Rwandan Defense Force takes a disproportionate share of the national budget. In 2002, plans were announced for a smaller, more professional force.

ECONOMICS

Inflation 13% p.a. (1990–2001)

$1.85bn | 562.8 Rwanda francs (525.1)

SCORE CARD

- World GNP Ranking........................140th
- GNP per Capita..............................$230
- Balance of Payments....................–$126m
- Inflation...2.5%
- Unemployment.........Few have formal employment

Strengths

Currently few. With stability, Rwanda can produce tea (the main export) and coffee. Possible oil and gas reserves. Tourism potential. Mining.

Weaknesses

Economic activity completely disrupted by 1994 violence. Distance to nearest ports raises transportation costs. Few resources. Border instability. Refugees.

EXPORTS

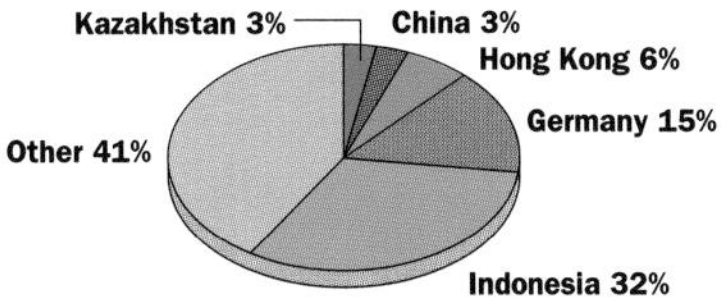
Kazakhstan 3%
China 3%
Hong Kong 6%
Germany 15%
Other 41%
Indonesia 32%

IMPORTS

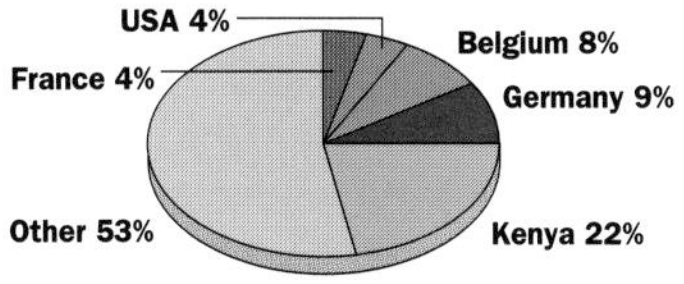
USA 4%
Belgium 8%
France 4%
Germany 9%
Other 53%
Kenya 22%

Terraced hillside. *Before the war, Rwanda was the most densely populated country in Africa and its land was intensively cultivated.*

RESOURCES

Electric power 43,000 kW

7263 tonnes | Not an oil producer

815,000 cattle, 760,000 goats, 1.2m chickens | Tin, tungsten, gold, columbo-tantalite, methane gas

There are plans to extract natural gas from Lake Kivu: the reserves could potentially supply Rwanda's current electricity needs for 400 years.

ENVIRONMENT

Sustainability rank: 119th

6% (5% partially protected) | 0.1 tonnes per capita

Apart from the effects of war, soil erosion and forest loss are the major environmental problems. The tourist industry underpinned the preservation of the mountain gorilla.

MEDIA

TV ownership low

Daily newspaper circulation 0.1 per 1000 people

PUBLISHING AND BROADCAST MEDIA

There is 1 daily newspaper. The monthly *Inkingi* and *La Relève* are published in Kinyarwanda and French respectively

1 state-controlled service | 1 state-owned service, several independent services

Radio broadcasts initiated and fueled the genocide in 1994. The first new private station since then went on air in 2004.

CRIME

Death penalty in use

112,000 prisoners | Crime is rising

Rehabilitation centers have opened for those who have admitted to taking part in the genocide and who are being released from prison, reeducated, and sent back to their communities.

EDUCATION

School leaving age: 12

69% | 12,802 students

The state and Christian missions run schools. Primary schooling is compulsory; almost all children were enrolled in 2002, up from 66% a decade earlier. Just 12% go on to secondary school.

CHRONOLOGY

The Hutu majority began to arrive in the 14th century, the warrior Tutsi in the 15th. From 1890, German and then Belgian colonizers acted to reinforce Tutsi dominance.

- **1962** Independence. Hutu-led government.
- **1960s** Tutsi revolt; massacres by Hutu; thousands of Tutsis in exile.
- **1973** Coup by Gen. Habyarimana.
- **1994** Habyarimana dies in plane crash. Genocidal violence unleashed by Hutu extremist regime, ousted by Tutsi-led FPR. Hutu refugee exodus.
- **1995** Start of war crimes tribunal.
- **1997** Refugees forcibly repatriated.
- **2000** Prominent Hutus leave office.
- **2003** New constitution. Paul Kagame and FPR reelected.

HEALTH

Welfare state health benefits

1 per 20,000 people | Malaria, measles, diarrheal diseases, violence

Rwanda has a network of 34 hospitals and 300 health centers. At the end of 2003 over 5% of the adult population was estimated to be HIV-positive.

SPENDING

GDP/cap. increase

CONSUMPTION AND SPENDING

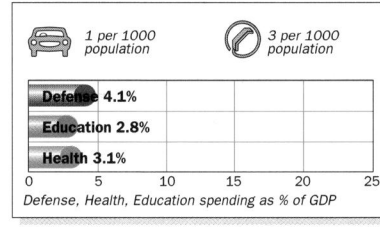

1 per 1000 population | *3 per 1000 population*

Defense 4.1%
Education 2.8%
Health 3.1%
0
5
10
15
20
25

Defense, Health, Education spending as % of GDP

Wealth is limited to the country's political elite and representatives of international NGOs. Most Rwandans are poor farmers.

WORLD RANKING

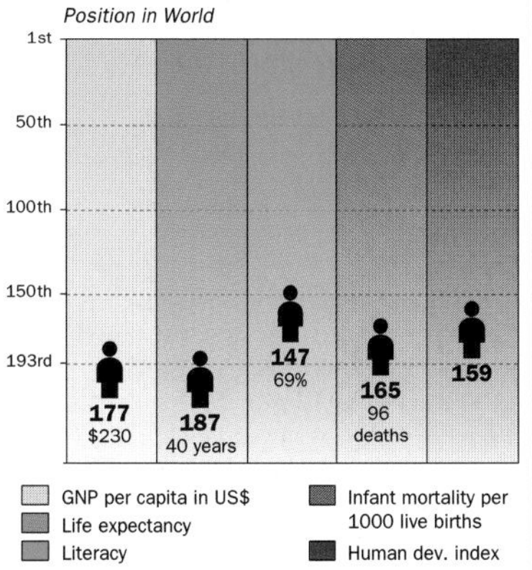
Position in World
1st
50th
100th
150th
193rd
177
$230
187
40 years
147
69%
165
96
deaths
159
GNP per capita in US$
Life expectancy
Literacy
Infant mortality per 1000 live births
Human dev. index

R

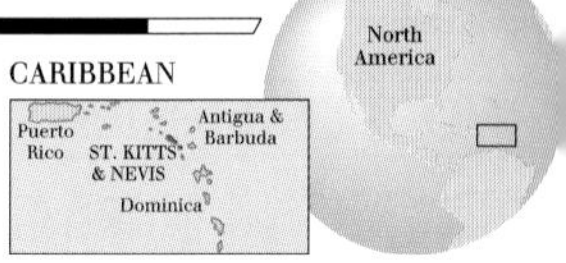
North America
CARIBBEAN
Puerto Rico
ST. KITTS & NEVIS
Antigua & Barbuda
Dominica

ST. KITTS & NEVIS

OFFICIAL NAME: Federation of Saint Christopher and Nevis **CAPITAL:** Basseterre
POPULATION: 38,763 **CURRENCY:** Eastern Caribbean dollar **OFFICIAL LANGUAGE:** English

1983 | 1983 | Sept 19 | KN | -4 | +1869 | .kn

ONE OF THE CARIBBEAN'S most popular tourist destinations, St. Kitts and Nevis, a former British colony, lies at the northern end of the Leeward Islands chain. St. Kitts is of volcanic origin; Mount Liamuiga, a dormant volcano with a crater 227 m (745 ft) deep, is the highest point on the island. Nevis, separated from St. Kitts by a channel 3 km (2 miles) wide, is the lusher but less developed of the two islands. In the 18th century, its famed hot and cold springs gained Nevis the title "the Spa of the Caribbean."

CLIMATE

Tropical oceanic

WEATHER CHART FOR BASSETERRE

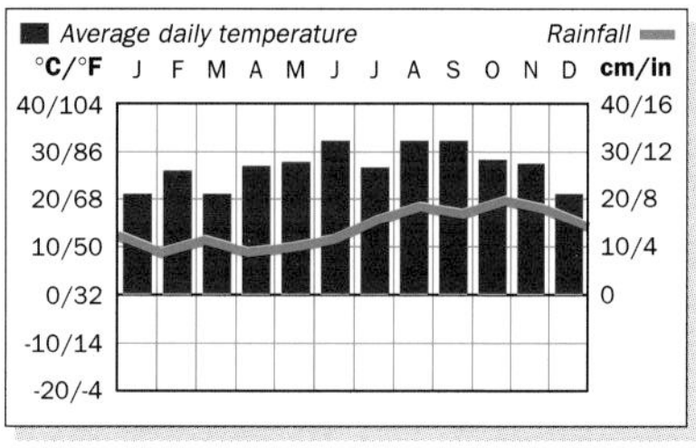
Average daily temperature
Rainfall
°C/°F J F M A M J J A S O N D cm/in
40/104
30/86
20/68
10/50
0/32
-10/14
-20/-4
40/16
30/12
20/8
10/4
0

A combination of high temperatures, trade breezes, and moderate rainfall in summer constitute St. Kitts's typically Caribbean climate.

TRANSPORTATION

Drive on left

Robert Llewellyn Bradshaw, Basseterre

1 ship
600 dwt

THE TRANSPORTATION NETWORK

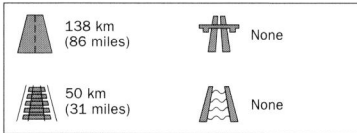

138 km (86 miles)	None
50 km (31 miles)	None

Most roads on the islands follow the coast; a few cross the interior. Access to the remote southeastern peninsula of St. Kitts has been improved. The airport on St. Kitts takes large jets; the runway at Nevis airport has been extended so that larger planes can land. Regular ferries connect the islands.

The southeastern peninsula of St. Kitts, looking across to Nevis in the background, on a typical December evening.

TOURISM

Visitors : Population 1.8:1

68,000 visitors

Down 4% in 2002

MAIN TOURIST ARRIVALS

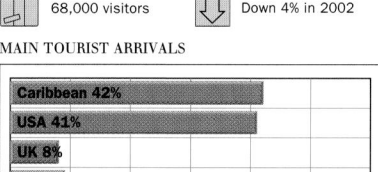

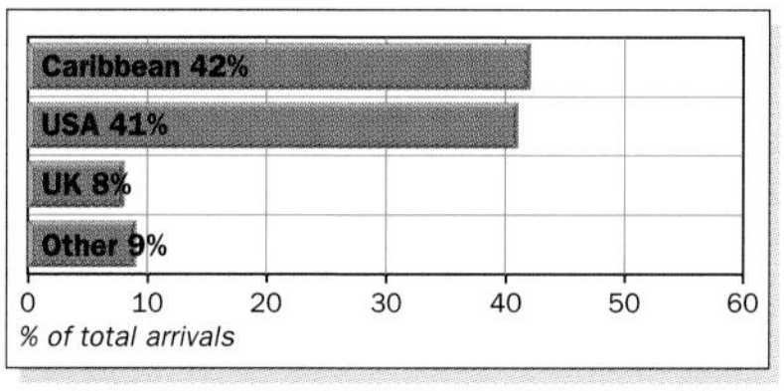
Caribbean 42%
USA 41%
UK 8%
Other 9%
0
10
20
30
40
50
60
% of total arrivals

St. Kitts has long targeted the mass US tourist market. Improvements to boost tourism include the opening up of the St. Kitts southern peninsula to large-scale tourist developments, and the expansion of the main port to accommodate two cruise ships simultaneously. Most visitors come for sand, sun, and the Caribbean mood, though in recent years safaris inland to see local wildlife and mineral springs have become more popular. On St. Kitts, the old Brimstone Hill fortress has been converted into a museum, as has the Nevis birthplace of Alexander Hamilton, one of the architects of the US constitution.

PEOPLE

Pop. density medium

English, English Creole

108/km² (279/mi²)

THE URBAN/RURAL POPULATION SPLIT

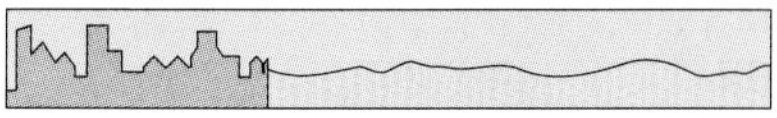
34%
66%

RELIGIOUS PERSUASION

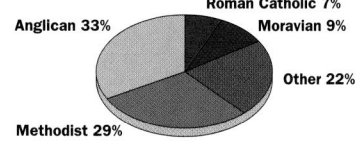

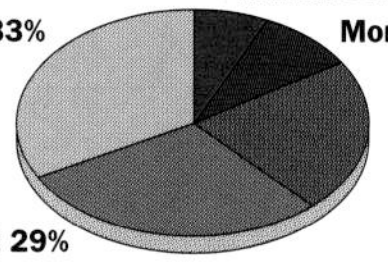
Roman Catholic 7%
Anglican 33%
Moravian 9%
Other 22%
Methodist 29%

Most of the population is descended from Africans brought over as slaves in the 17th century. There are small numbers of Europeans and south Asians, and a community of Lebanese. Levels of emigration are high; remittances from abroad provide an important source of revenue.

POLITICS

Multiparty elections

2000/2005

H.M. Queen Elizabeth II

AT THE LAST ELECTION

National Assembly 15 seats

53% SKLP
13% CCM
7% NRP
27% App

SKLP = St. Kitts Labour Party **CCM** = Concerned Citizens' Movement **NRP** = Nevis Reformation Party **App** = Appointed

Nevis has its own executive and legislature, the Nevis Island Assembly, which exercise local power

Fifteen years of rule by the People's Action Movement ended in 1995 amid concerns over narcotics trafficking. The center-left SKLP has held power since, and in the 2000 election won all the seats contested on St. Kitts itself. The secessionist movement on Nevis is energetic.

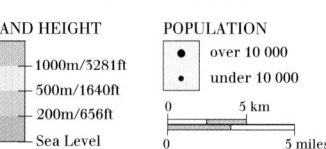

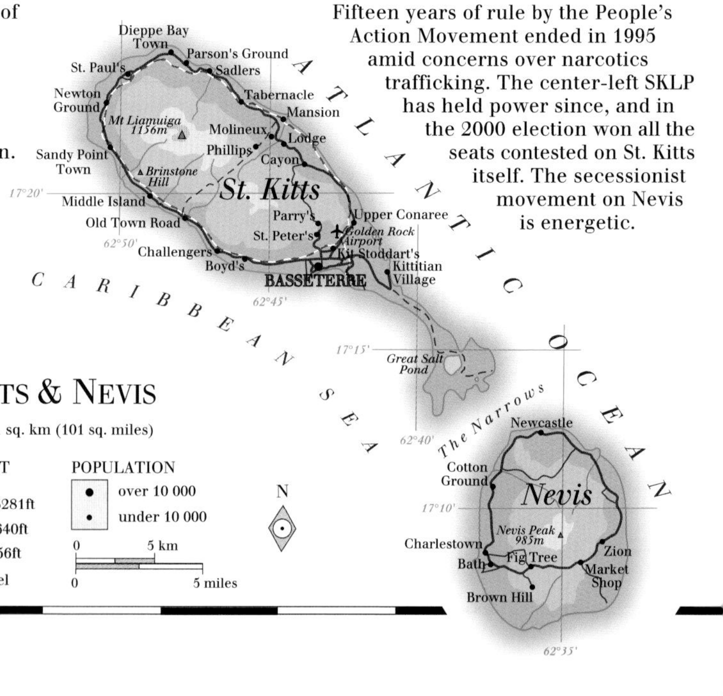
Dieppe Bay Town
Parson's Ground
Sadlers
St. Paul's
Newton Ground
Tabernacle
Mansion
Mt Liamuiga 1156m
Molineux
Lodge
Phillips
Cayon
Sandy Point Town
Brimstone Hill
St. Kitts
Middle Island
Old Town Road
Parry's
St. Peter's
Upper Conaree
Golden Rock Airport
Challengers
Boyd's
Kit Stoddart's
BASSETERRE
Kittitian Village
ATLANTIC OCEAN
CARIBBEAN SEA
Great Salt Pond
The Narrows
Newcastle
Cotton Ground
Nevis
Nevis Peak 985m
Charlestown
Bath
Fig Tree
Zion
Market Shop
Brown Hill
17°20'
62°50'
62°45'
17°15'
62°40'
17°10'
62°35'
ST. KITTS & NEVIS
Total Area : 261 sq. km (101 sq. miles)
LAND HEIGHT
1000m/3281ft
500m/1640ft
200m/656ft
Sea Level
POPULATION
over 10 000
under 10 000
0
5 km
0
5 miles
N

WORLD AFFAIRS

Joined UN in 1983

ACS | Comm | Caricom | OAS | OECS

St. Kitts' financial system was rebuked by G7 in 2000 for enabling money laundering. It is an active member of the OECS, and Basseterre hosts the Eastern Caribbean Central Bank.

AID

Recipient

US$29m (receipts)

Up 164% in 2002

International aid in 1999 supported an economic recovery and relief program, following hurricanes Georges and Lenny, which significantly damaged buildings and infrastructure. About 50% of aid is through the CDB.

DEFENSE

No compulsory military service

Not available

Little change from year to year

An army existed for six years before it was disbanded to cut government spending in 1981. In 1997 the National Assembly approved the reestablishment of a full-time defense force; it has around 200 personnel, plus reserves.

ECONOMICS

Inflation 3% p.a. (1990–2001)

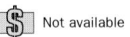

US$301m

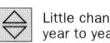

2.7 Eastern Caribbean dollars (2.67)

SCORE CARD

- ❑ WORLD GNP RANKING........................178th
- ❑ GNP PER CAPITA ....US$6540
- ❑ BALANCE OF PAYMENTS................–US$116m
- ❑ INFLATION 3.7%
- ❑ UNEMPLOYMENT 5%

STRENGTHS

Tourism industry. Growth in light manufacturing and financial services.

WEAKNESSES

Tourism sector vulnerable to downturns in key US market. Islands prone to hurricane damage. Sugar industry in steep decline, may soon be phased out entirely.

EXPORTS

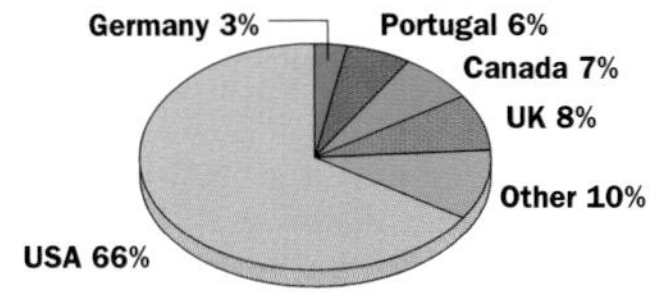
Germany 3%
Portugal 6%
Canada 7%
UK 8%
Other 10%
USA 66%

IMPORTS

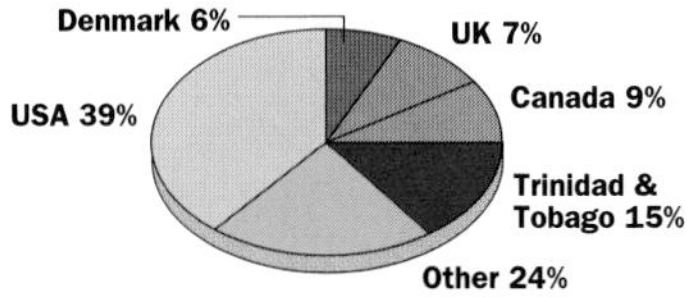
Denmark 6%
UK 7%
USA 39%
Canada 9%
Trinidad & Tobago 15%
Other 24%

RESOURCES

Electric power 20,000 kW

596 tonnes

Not an oil producer

14,400 goats, 14,000 sheep, 60,000 chickens

None

St. Kitts has no strategic resources. Almost all energy has to be imported (mainly oil from Venezuela and Mexico). The government is attempting to close down the loss-making sugar industry, retrain the workforce, and diversify, including growing Sea Island cotton.

ENVIRONMENT

Not available

10%

2.4 tonnes per capita

Hurricanes are the greatest environmental threat. Hurricane Georges alone caused damage in 1998 estimated at US$400 million. It was followed in 1999 by Hurricane Lenny. As in the rest of the Caribbean, benefits from encouraging tourism must be set against potential ecological damage. The government has shown sensitivity, with strict preservation orders on the remaining rainforest and on indigenous monkeys.

MEDIA

TV ownership medium

There are no daily newspapers

PUBLISHING AND BROADCAST MEDIA

There are no daily newspapers. The two main newspapers are the weekly *The Democrat* and the twice-weekly *Labour Spokesman*

1 state-owned service

8 services: 1 state-owned, 7 independent

Opposition parties have difficulty broadcasting their views on state-owned TV and radio. However, dissent is expressed in the printed press. The two main papers are run by political parties.

CRIME

Death penalty in use

135 prisoners

Down 31% in 1999

The judicial system is based on British common law. Hanging was resumed in 1998, and plans agreed in 2001 to replace the role of the UK Privy Council with a Caribbean Court of Justice raised fears of more executions being carried out. Money laundering and narcotics-related crime are increasing.

EDUCATION

School leaving age: 17

98%

1235 students

Education is free, and the government is keen to promote information technology subjects. Students attend the regional University of the West Indies, or go on to colleges in the US and the UK.

CHRONOLOGY

A British colony since 1783, the islands were a part of the Leeward Islands Federation until 1956.

- ❑ **1932** Proindependence St. Kitts–Nevis–Anguilla Labour Party set up.
- ❑ **1967** Internal self-government.
- ❑ **1980** Anguilla formally separates from St. Kitts and Nevis.
- ❑ **1983** Independence.
- ❑ **1995** Opposition SKLP wins election.
- ❑ **1998** Nevis referendum narrowly rejects secession.
- ❑ **2000** Prime Minister Denzil Douglas and SKLP reelected. Blacklisted by G7 for financial dealings.

HEALTH

Welfare state health benefits

1 per 833 people

Heart and respiratory diseases, cancers

The government-run health service now provides rudimentary care on both St. Kitts and Nevis. The EU and France provided EC$8 million in 1998 for repairs to the main hospital at Basseterre, which was badly damaged by Hurricane Georges.

SPENDING

GDP/cap. increase

CONSUMPTION AND SPENDING

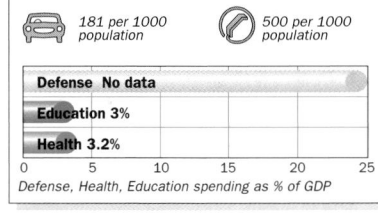

181 per 1000 population

500 per 1000 population

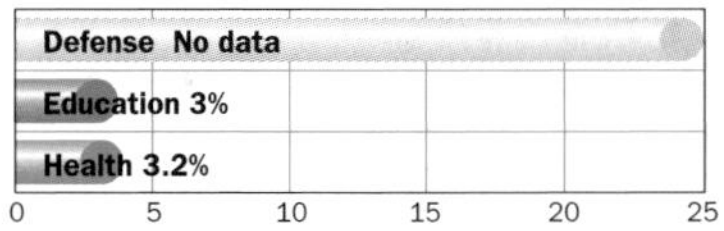
Defense No data
Education 3%
Health 3.2%
0
5
10
15
20
25

Defense, Health, Education spending as % of GDP

Native professionals and civil servants have replaced expatriates over the years since independence. They are now the best-paid group, but there are no great extremes of income.

WORLD RANKING

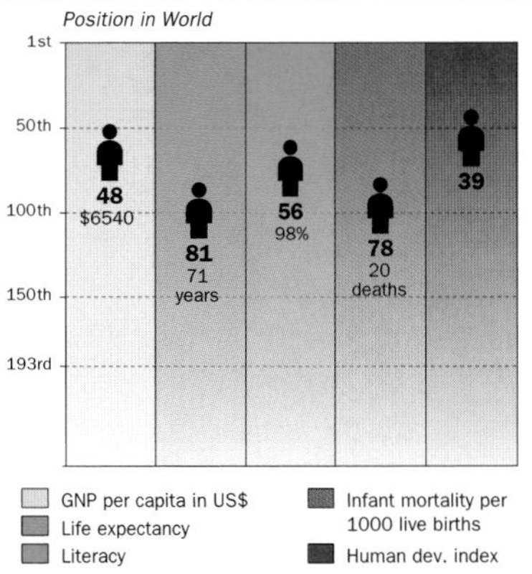
Position in World
1st
50th
100th
150th
193rd
48
$6540
81
71
years
56
98%
78
20
deaths
39
GNP per capita in US$
Life expectancy
Literacy
Infant mortality per 1000 live births
Human dev. index

S

ST. LUCIA

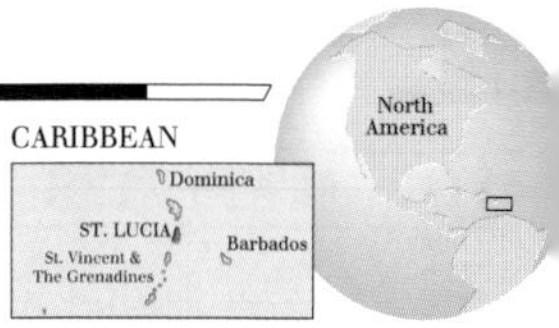
CARIBBEAN
Dominica
ST. LUCIA
Barbados
St. Vincent & The Grenadines
North America

OFFICIAL NAME: Saint Lucia **CAPITAL:** Castries **POPULATION:** 162,157
CURRENCY: Eastern Caribbean dollar **OFFICIAL LANGUAGE:** English

1979 | 1979 | Feb 22 | WL | -4 | +1758 | .lc

ST. LUCIA IS ONE OF THE MOST beautiful islands of the Windward group of the Antilles. The twin Pitons, south of Soufrière, are among the most striking natural features in the Caribbean. Ruled by the French and the British at different times in its past, St. Lucia retains the character of both. A multiparty democracy, it has an economy based on bananas and tourism, with enticing beaches and a rich variety of wildlife in the rainforest.

CLIMATE

Tropical oceanic

WEATHER CHART FOR CASTRIES

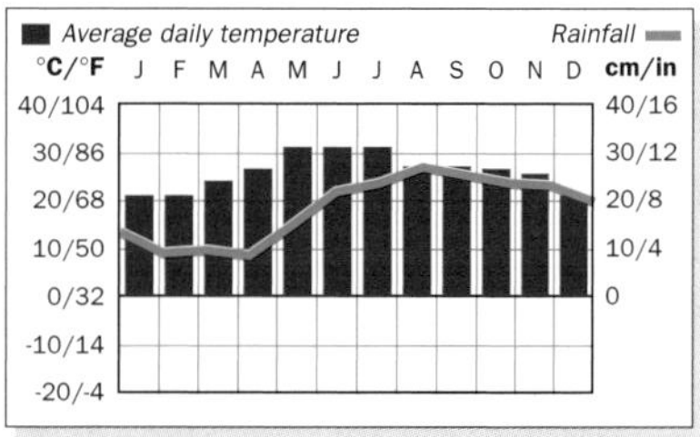
Average daily temperature
Rainfall
°C/°F
J F M A M J J A S O N D
cm/in
40/104
30/86
20/68
10/50
0/32
-10/14
-20/-4
40/16
30/12
20/8
10/4
0

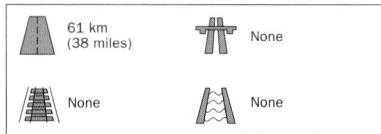

The dry season, from January to April, brings intense heat to sheltered parts of St. Lucia. During the rainy season, short warm showers can be expected daily. Rainfall is highest in the mountains.

TRANSPORTATION

Drive on left

George F. L. Charles, Castries
488,693 passengers

3 ships
911 grt

THE TRANSPORTATION NETWORK

61 km (38 miles)

None

None

None

Roads are confined to the west and southeast coasts; only half are paved. Flights arrive from major European and North American cities, and other Caribbean locations. Direct passage to South America is largely by sea.

One of the twin Pitons south of Soufrière, marking the entrance to the Jalousie Plantation harbor.

TOURISM

Visitors : Population 1.7:1

276,530 visitors

Up 9% in 2003

MAIN TOURIST ARRIVALS

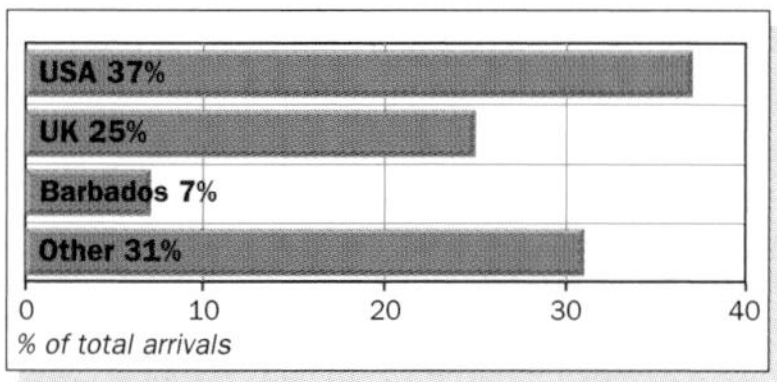
USA 37%
UK 25%
Barbados 7%
Other 31%
0
10
20
30
40
% of total arrivals

Tropical beaches and typical Caribbean towns make St. Lucia a favorite destination for cruise ships and stay-over tourists. The number of hotel rooms continues to rise. The pristine rainforest has become the focus of nature tourism, with tours often organized by the National Trust.

PEOPLE

Pop. density high

English, French Creole

266/km² (687/mi²)

THE URBAN/RURAL POPULATION SPLIT

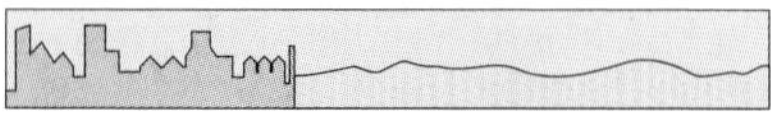

38% 62%

RELIGIOUS PERSUASION

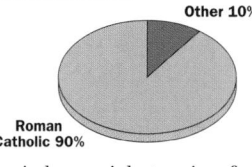

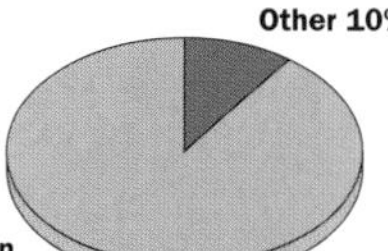
Other 10%
Roman Catholic 90%

St. Lucia has a rich, tension-free racial mix of descendants of Africans, Caribs, and European settlers. Despite relaxed attitudes, family life is central to most St. Lucians, many of whom are practicing Roman Catholics. As in much of the Caribbean, absentee fathers are fairly common in rural districts, where women run many of the farms. In recent years, women have had greater access to higher education and have moved into professions. A bill to permit the occasional use of Creole in parliament was passed in 1998.

POLITICS

Multiparty elections

L. House 2001/2006
U. House 2001/2006

H.M. Queen Elizabeth II

AT THE LAST ELECTION

House of Assembly 18 seats

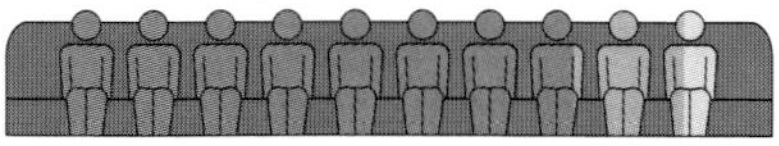

78% SLP **17% UWP** **5% App**

SLP = St. Lucia Labour Party **UWP** = United Workers' Party
App = Appointed

Senate 11 seats

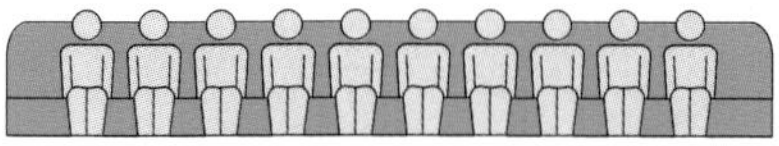

Six Senate members are nominated by the government, three by the opposition, and two by the governor-general on a nonparty basis

St. Lucian politics was long dominated by personalities, particularly John Compton of the conservative UWP. The election victory in 1997 of the SLP, led by Kenny Anthony, ending 15 years of UWP government, saw a shift in the political climate. Divided and factionalized, the UWP was unable to prevent the SLP's reelection in 2001.

WORLD AFFAIRS

Joined UN in 1979

ACS | Comm | Caricom | OECS | OAS

St. Lucia took a leading role in 1999 in the unsuccessful campaign to preserve preferential access to the EU market for bananas from the Windward Islands. Good relations with the UK and EU remain central, but it is feared that from 2006 the Caribbean will be unable to compete with cheaper fruit from US-owned growers in Latin America. St. Lucia is active in the OECS and hosts the regional secretariat. Prime Minister Kenny Anthony has emerged as an important spokesman for regional affairs.

AID

Recipient

US$34m (receipts)

Up 113% in 2002

The EU, Japan, and the CDB are the main donors. China has also given aid and grant loans in recent years.

DEFENSE

No compulsory military service

US$5m

Little change from year to year

The police force is supported by a small paramilitary unit. Training is provided by the US and the UK.

S

ST. LUCIA

Total Area : 620 sq. km (239 sq. miles)

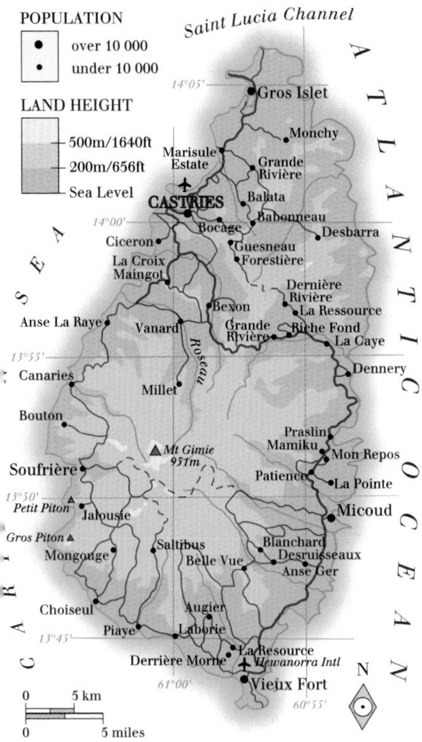
POPULATION
over 10 000
under 10 000
LAND HEIGHT
500m/1640ft
200m/656ft
Sea Level
Saint Lucia Channel
ATLANTIC OCEAN
CARIBBEAN SEA
Gros Islet
Monchy
Marisule Estate
Grande Rivière
CASTRIES
Balata
Babonneau
Bocage
Desbarra
Ciceron
La Croix Maingot
Guesneau
Forestière
Dernière Rivière
La Ressource
Bexon
Anse La Raye
Vanard
Grande Rivière
Riche Fond
La Caye
Roseau
Canaries
Millet
Dennery
Bouton
Mt Gimie 951m
Praslin
Mamiku
Mon Repos
Soufrière
Patience
La Pointe
Petit Piton
Jalousie
Micoud
Gros Piton
Saltibus
Blanchard
Mongouge
Belle Vue
Desruisseaux
Anse Ger
Choiseul
Augier
Piaye
Laborie
Derrière Morne
La Ressource
Hewanorra Intl
Vieux Fort
14°05'
14°00'
13°55'
13°50'
13°45'
61°00'
60°55'
N
0 5 km
0 5 miles

ECONOMICS

Inflation 2.7% p.a. (1990–2001)

US$600m

2.7 Eastern Caribbean dollars (2.67)

SCORE CARD

❑ WORLD GNP RANKING	166th
❑ GNP PER CAPITA	US$3750
❑ BALANCE OF PAYMENTS	–US$56m
❑ INFLATION	1.6%
❑ UNEMPLOYMENT	17%

STRENGTHS

Banana industry (privatized in 1998). Tourism and services.

WEAKNESSES

Preferential banana trade with EU to be phased out. Global slumps affect tourism.

EXPORTS

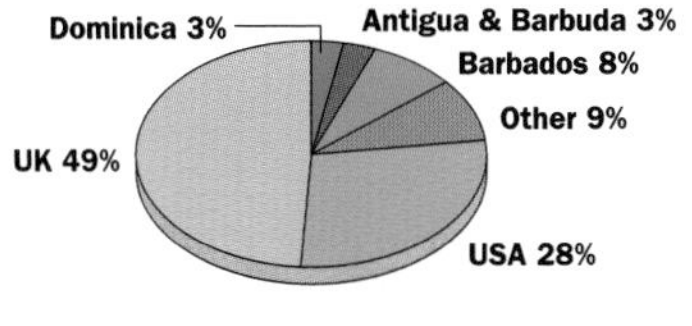
Dominica 3%
Antigua & Barbuda 3%
Barbados 8%
Other 9%
UK 49%
USA 28%

IMPORTS

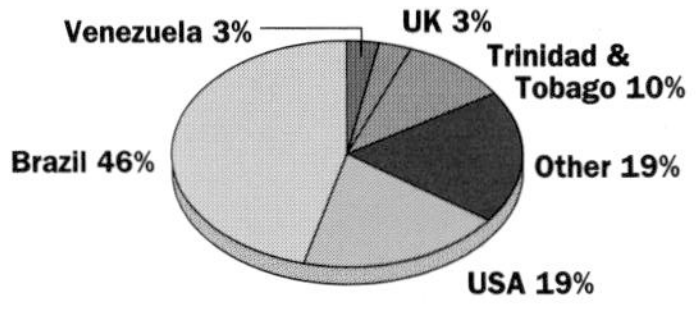
Venezuela 3%
UK 3%
Trinidad & Tobago 10%
Brazil 46%
Other 19%
USA 19%

RESOURCES

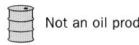

Electric power 66,000 kW

1984 tonnes

Not an oil producer

14,950 pigs, 12,500 sheep, 240,000 chickens

None

St. Lucia has no mineral resources and imports most of its energy. Plans exist to develop geothermal energy from the hot springs in the volcanic interior.

ENVIRONMENT

Not available

16% partially protected

2.2 tonnes per capita

St. Lucians are proud of their island, and environmental questions arouse fierce debate. In recent years the greatest controversy surrounded the decision to allow a luxury hotel development on the ecologically important Jalousie Plantation, which encompasses the extraordinary twin Pitons and includes an important Amerindian archaeological site. The issue illustrates a key problem in St. Lucia, where business pressures to develop tourism can outweigh vital environmental concerns. One notable conservation success has been the St. Lucia parrot. In 1978, there were 150 birds; strict laws against the trade in parrots ensured that by 2000 numbers had risen to 500.

MEDIA

TV ownership medium

There are no daily newspapers

PUBLISHING AND BROADCAST MEDIA

There are no daily newspapers. *The Star* and *The Mirror* are published weekly

5 independent services

5 services: 1 state-owned, 4 independent

The privately owned press is free from government intervention. It is possible to receive TV programs from US, Mexican, and some Caribbean stations.

CRIME

Death penalty in use

365 prisoners

Crime is rising

Murder is rare, but narcotics-related deaths are increasing, as is violence in schools. The government has strengthened the police force to combat rising urban crime.

EDUCATION

School leaving age: 16

95%

3881 students

Education is based on the British system. Nobel prizewinners Sir Arthur Lewis (economics) and Derek Walcott (literature) give St. Lucia the world's highest per capita ratio of laureates.

CHRONOLOGY

An excellent naval raiding base in the Caribbean in the 17th and 18th centuries, St. Lucia was fought over by France and Britain. Ownership alternated before it was finally ceded to Britain in 1814. French influence survives in St. Lucian patois and the local cuisine.

- ❑ **1958** Joins West Indies Federation.
- ❑ **1964** Sugar growing ceases.
- ❑ **1979** Gains independence and joins Commonwealth.
- ❑ **1990** Establishes body with Dominica, Grenada, and St. Vincent to discuss forming a Windward Islands Federation.
- ❑ **1997** Hitherto ruling UWP reduced to one seat in general election.
- ❑ **2000** Blacklisted by OECD as international tax haven.

HEALTH

Welfare state health benefits

1 per 2000 people

Heart and respiratory diseases, cancers

The National Insurance Scheme provides free medical cover for all. Work on a new general hospital began in 2001.

SPENDING

GDP/cap. increase

CONSUMPTION AND SPENDING

142 per 1000 population

320 per 1000 population

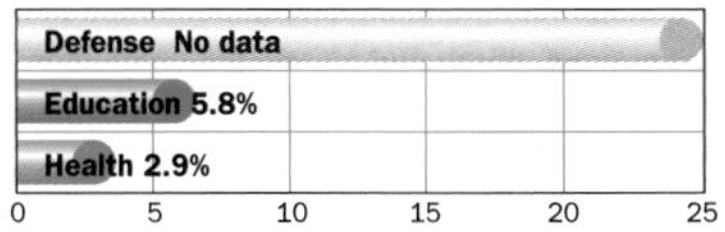
Defense No data
Education 5.8%
Health 2.9%
0
5
10
15
20
25

Defense, Health, Education spending as % of GDP

The island's large-scale banana growers and hotel owners form the richest section of society. Nearly one-fifth of households are considered to be poor.

WORLD RANKING

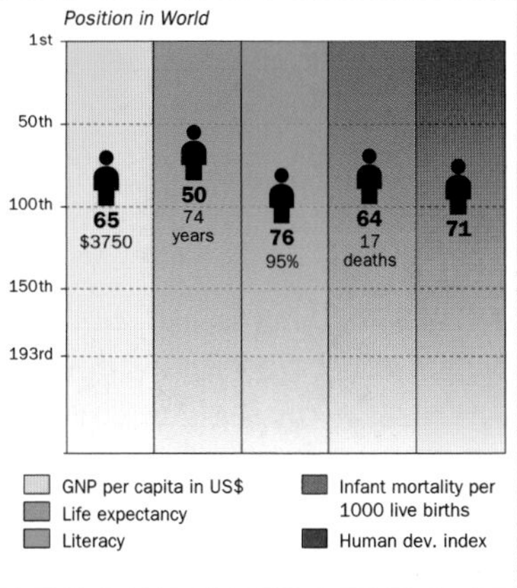
Position in World
1st
50th
100th
150th
193rd
65
$3750
50
74 years
76
95%
64
17 deaths
71
GNP per capita in US$
Life expectancy
Literacy
Infant mortality per 1000 live births
Human dev. index

S

ST. VINCENT & THE GRENADINES

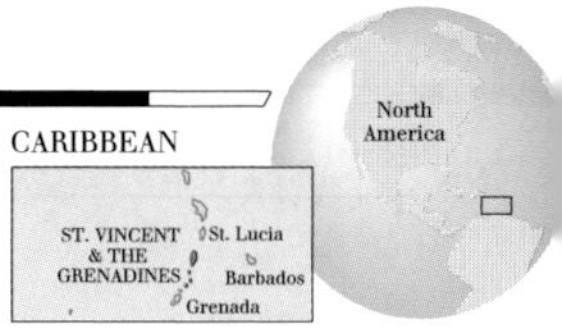
North America
CARIBBEAN
ST. VINCENT & THE GRENADINES
St. Lucia
Barbados
Grenada

OFFICIAL NAME: Saint Vincent and the Grenadines **CAPITAL:** Kingstown
POPULATION: 116,812 **CURRENCY:** Eastern Caribbean dollar **OFFICIAL LANGUAGE:** English

1979 | 1979 | Oct 27 | WV | -4 | +1784 | .vc

PART OF THE WINDWARD ISLANDS group, and bounded by submerged coral reefs, St. Vincent and the Grenadines is the Caribbean playground of the international celebrity circuit. Tourism and bananas are the economic mainstays; St. Vincent is also the world's largest arrowroot producer. It is mostly volcanic; the one remaining active volcano, La Soufrière, last erupted in 1979. The Grenadines are flat, mainly bare, coral islands.

CLIMATE

Tropical oceanic

WEATHER CHART FOR KINGSTOWN

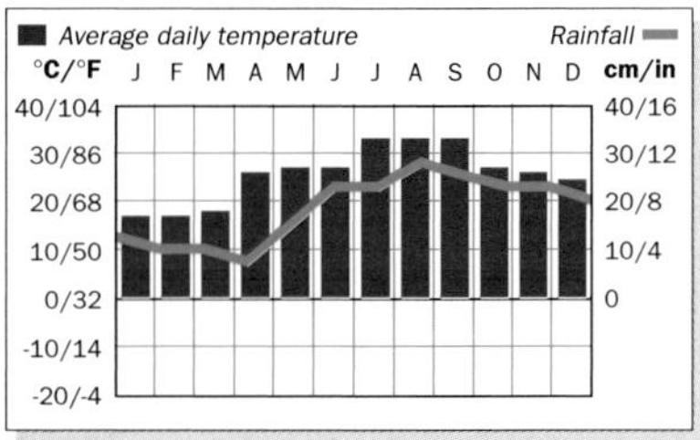
Average daily temperature
Rainfall
°C/°F J F M A M J J A S O N D cm/in
40/104
30/86
20/68
10/50
0/32
-10/14
-20/-4
40/16
30/12
20/8
10/4
0

Constant trade winds moderate St. Vincent's tropical climate. Rainfall is heaviest during the summer months. Deep depressions and hurricanes are likely between June and November.

TRANSPORTATION

Drive on left

E. T. Joshua, Kingstown | 1304 ships 6.58m grt

THE TRANSPORTATION NETWORK

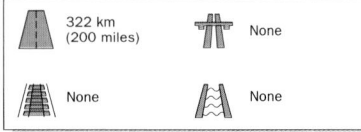

322 km (200 miles)	None
None	None

Access by air is via neighboring islands. Only one-third of roads are paved; there are few roads in the interior. Port improvements have been completed in recent years. A proposed runway extension for Arnos Vale airport on St. Vincent was put on hold in 2000.

Aerial view of Union Island in the Grenadines chain. The government is developing the island as a major yachting center.

TOURISM

Visitors : Population 1:1.5

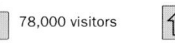

78,000 visitors | Up 9% in 2002

MAIN TOURIST ARRIVALS

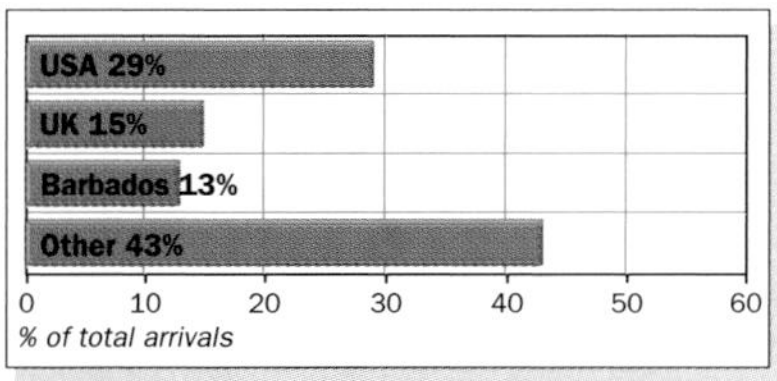
USA 29%
UK 15%
Barbados 13%
Other 43%
0 10 20 30 40 50 60
% of total arrivals

Tourism is targeted at celebrities and cruise ships rather than the mass market, and is concentrated on the Grenadines. Mustique, long associated with the UK's Princess Margaret, has a rock music clientele. Union Island draws the yachting rich, and luxury villas, apartments, a golf course, and a casino have been built on Canouan. Layou, on St. Vincent, is the site of pre-Columbian Amerindian petroglyphs.

PEOPLE

Pop. density high

English, English Creole | 344/km² (892/mi²)

THE URBAN/RURAL POPULATION SPLIT

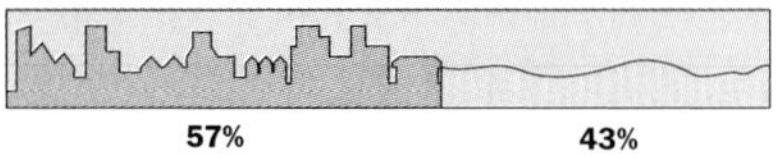
57%
43%

RELIGIOUS PERSUASION

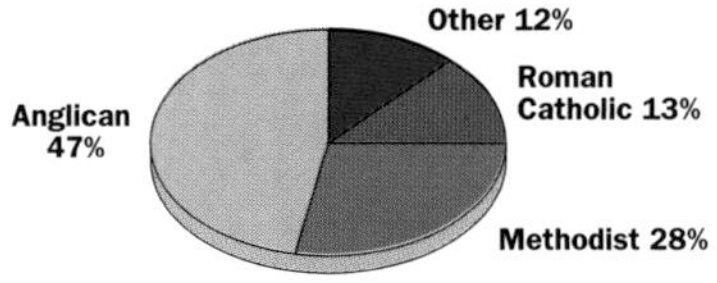
Other 12%
Roman Catholic 13%
Anglican 47%
Methodist 28%

The majority of people are descendants of Africans brought over in the 18th century. Racial tensions are few, and intermarriage has meant that the original communities of descendants of African slaves, Europeans, and the few indigenous Caribs can no longer be distinguished. St. Vincent has a high rate of emigration, partly due to the level of unemployment; population growth is very low.

POLITICS

Multiparty elections

2001/2006 | H.M. Queen Elizabeth II

AT THE LAST ELECTION
House of Assembly 21 seats

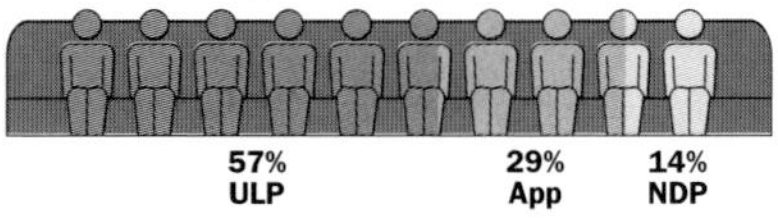
57% ULP
29% App
14% NDP

ULP = Unity Labour Party **App** = Appointed
NDP = New Democratic Party
Six senators are appointed to the House of Assembly by the governor-general

In 2001, 17 years of NDP rule ended with a crushing electoral defeat. The leader of the long-term opposition ULP, Ralph Gonsalves, became prime minister. He has launched initiatives to modernize the government and economy and restructure the banana industry, and strongly advocates closer integration among east Caribbean states.

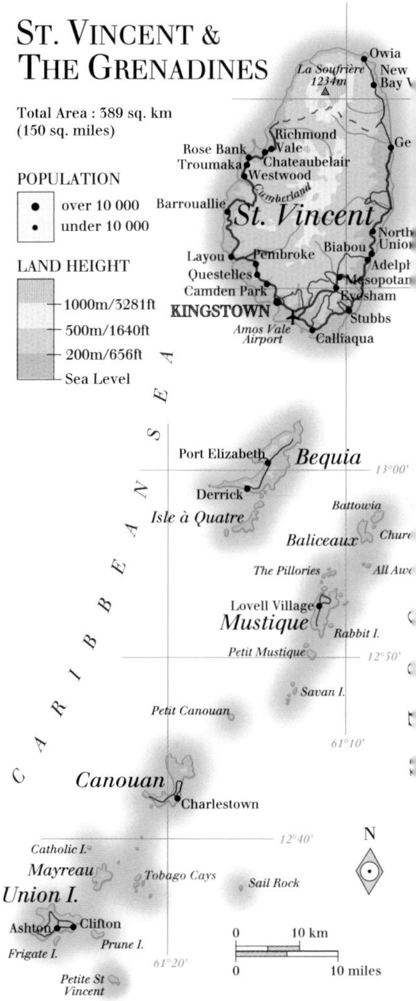
ST. VINCENT & THE GRENADINES
Total Area : 389 sq. km (150 sq. miles)
POPULATION
over 10 000
under 10 000
LAND HEIGHT
1000m/3281ft
500m/1640ft
200m/656ft
Sea Level
La Soufrière 1234m
Owia
New Bay
Richmond
Rose Bank
Vale
Troumaka
Chateaubelair
Westwood
Barrouallie
Cumberland
St. Vincent
Layou
Pembroke
Biabou
Questelles
Camden Park
Mesopotamia
Evesham
KINGSTOWN
Stubbs
Amos Vale Airport
Calliaqua
CARIBBEAN SEA
Port Elizabeth
Bequia
Derrick
Isle à Quatre
Battowia
Baliceaux
The Pillories
Lovell Village
Mustique
Rabbit I.
Petit Mustique
Savan I.
Petit Canouan
Canouan
Charlestown
Catholic I.
Mayreau
Tobago Cays
Sail Rock
Union I.
Ashton
Clifton
Prune I.
Frigate I.
Petite St Vincent
13°00'
12°50'
12°40'
61°10'
61°20'
N
0 10 km
0 10 miles

WORLD AFFAIRS

Joined UN in 1980

ACS | Comm | Caricom | OAS | OECS

The most important links are with the EU and the UK. The government promotes regional integration and has played a leading role in Caribbean affairs. The successful US bid to end EU preferential treatment of Caribbean banana imports has strained relations.

AID

Recipient

US$5m (receipts)

Down 44% in 2002

The Caribbean Development Bank and the EU are the major sources of development aid. Significant funds also come from Japan and France.

DEFENSE

No compulsory military service

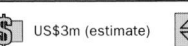

US$3m (estimate)

No significant change from year to year

St. Vincent has no army. Its small police force, trained by the US and the UK, is part of the Windward and Leeward Islands' Regional Security System.

ECONOMICS

Inflation 2.1% p.a. (1990–2001)

US$330m

2.7 Eastern Caribbean dollars (2.67)

SCORE CARD

❑ World GNP Ranking	176th
❑ GNP per Capita	US$2820
❑ Balance of Payments	–US$43m
❑ Inflation	0.8%
❑ Unemployment	22%

Strengths

Bananas, but preferential access to EU markets will end in 2006. Top producer of arrowroot starch. Tourist potential. Improving infrastructure.

Weaknesses

Little diversification. Development of financial services hit by OECD blacklisting for money laundering. Vulnerable to hurricane damage.

EXPORTS

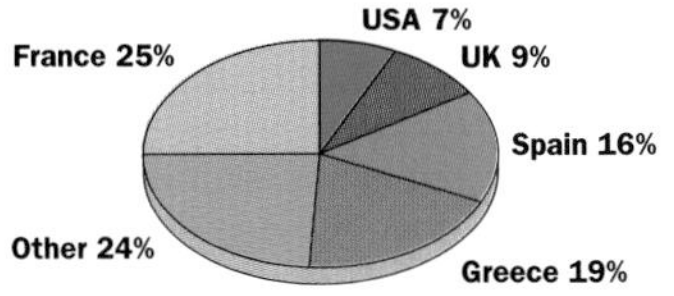
USA 7%
France 25%
UK 9%
Spain 16%
Other 24%
Greece 19%

IMPORTS

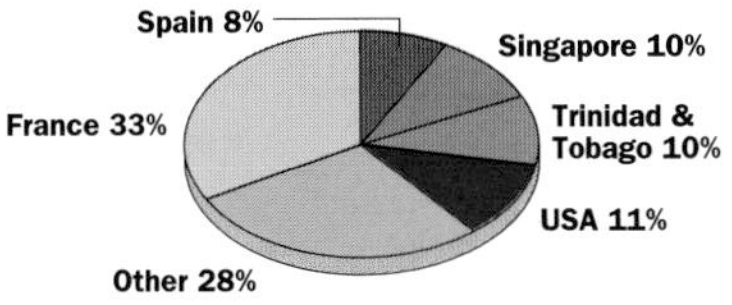
Spain 8%
Singapore 10%
France 33%
Trinidad & Tobago 10%
USA 11%
Other 28%

RESOURCES

Electric power 16,000 kW

45,778 tonnes

Not an oil producer

12,000 sheep, 9150 pigs, 125,000 chickens

None

There is a hydroelectric plant on the Cumberland River. Virtually all other energy requirements have to be imported. Some of the Grenadines have no fresh water sources.

ENVIRONMENT

Not available

21% partially protected

1.4 tonnes per capita

Hurricanes are the main environmental threat, sometimes destroying as much as 70% of the banana crop. The former inaccessibility of St. Vincent and the Grenadines meant that tourism was a minor environmental threat, and the untouched, idyllic landscape of islands such as Mustique was their attraction. Mustique is reasonably well protected – building has been restricted and further development is limited since fresh water has to be shipped in. On Bequia, the new airport and consequent increase in visitors are seen as a mixed blessing. Some development schemes on Canouan have been opposed by locals.

MEDIA

TV ownership medium

Daily newspaper circulation 0.5 per 1000 people

PUBLISHING AND BROADCAST MEDIA

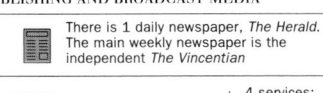

There is 1 daily newspaper, *The Herald*. The main weekly newspaper is the independent *The Vincentian*

1 state-owned service

4 services: 2 state-owned, 2 independent

Of the many periodicals, three are published by the political parties; the rest are independent. Freedom of the press is written into the constitution.

CRIME

Death penalty in use

302 prisoners

Little change from year to year

The incidence of rape and robbery causes most concern, though on the outlying islands both crimes are very rare. St. Vincent is used for narcotics transshipment to the US.

EDUCATION

School leaving age: 15

83%

904 students

The school curriculum has been modified in recent years; pupils now study Caribbean literature and history, and more vocational training is offered. The University of the West Indies in Jamaica is popular, though increasing numbers are studying in the US and the UK.

CHRONOLOGY

In 1795, the local Carib population staged a revolt against the British, who deported them, leaving a largely black African population.

- ❑ **1951** Universal suffrage.
- ❑ **1969** Internal self-government.
- ❑ **1972** James Mitchell premier; holds balance of power between People's Political Party (PPP) and St. Vincent Labour Party (SVLP).
- ❑ **1974** PPP–SVLP coalition.
- ❑ **1979** Full independence under Milton Cato of SVLP. La Soufrière volcano erupts.
- ❑ **1984** NDP, founded by Mitchell in 1975, wins first of four terms.
- ❑ **2000** Mitchell resigns premiership.
- ❑ **2001** ULP wins landslide victory. Ralph Gonsalves prime minister.

HEALTH

Welfare state health benefits

1 per 1111 people

Heart and respiratory diseases, cancers

Doctors train at the University of the West Indies. The system is a mixture of state and private hospitals and clinics; facilities are scarcer on the Grenadines.

SPENDING

GDP/cap. increase

CONSUMPTION AND SPENDING

84 per 1000 population

234 per 1000 population

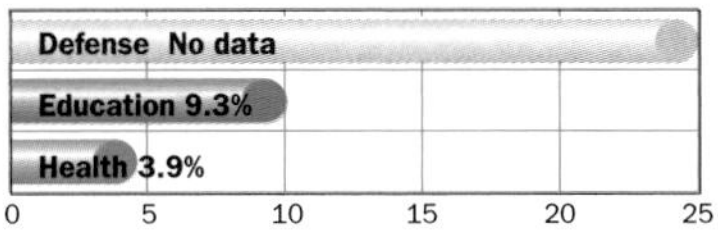
Defense No data
Education 9.3%
Health 3.9%
0
5
10
15
20
25

Defense, Health, Education spending as % of GDP

Jet-set wealth in the islands coexists with the low wages paid to most local workers. Union Island and Mustique in particular attract the wealthy, with their motor yachts and jeeps.

WORLD RANKING

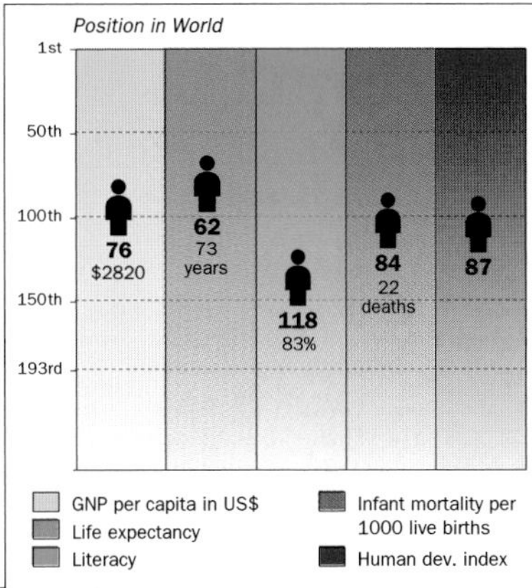
Position in World
1st
50th
100th
150th
193rd
76
$2820
62
73
years
118
83%
84
22
deaths
87
GNP per capita in US$
Life expectancy
Literacy
Infant mortality per 1000 live births
Human dev. index

S

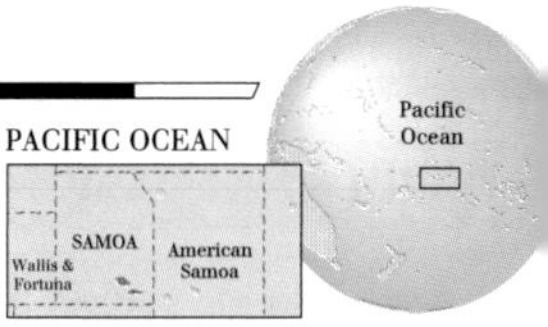
PACIFIC OCEAN
Pacific Ocean
SAMOA
Wallis & Fortuna
American Samoa

SAMOA

OFFICIAL NAME: Independent State of Samoa **CAPITAL:** Apia
POPULATION: 178,000 **CURRENCY:** Tala **OFFICIAL LANGUAGES:** Samoan and English

1962 | 1962 | June 1 | WS | -11 | +685 | .ws

SAMOA, LYING IN THE HEART of the South Pacific, 2400 km (1500 miles) north of New Zealand, comprises nine volcanic islands. Four are inhabited – Apolima, Manono, Savai'i, and Upolu (where 72% of the population live). Rainforests cloak the mountains; vegetable gardens and coconut plantations thrive around the coasts. A relative boom in the economy in recent years has not lifted Samoa from the ranks of the UN's Least Developed Countries.

CLIMATE

Tropical oceanic

WEATHER CHART FOR APIA

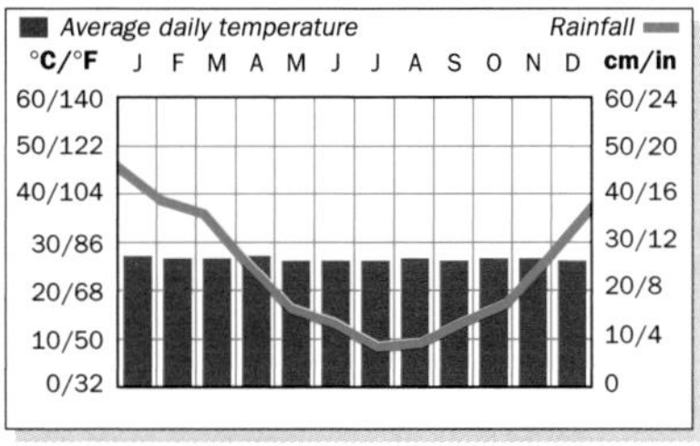
Average daily temperature
Rainfall
°C/°F
J F M A M J J A S O N D
cm/in
60/140
50/122
40/104
30/86
20/68
10/50
0/32
60/24
50/20
40/16
30/12
20/8
10/4
0

The climate is humid and temperatures rarely drop below 25°C (77°F). December to March is the hurricane season.

TRANSPORTATION

Drive on right

Faleolo, Apia 176,831 passengers

8 ships 10,000 grt

THE TRANSPORTATION NETWORK

332 km (206 miles)

None

None

None

Apia port has been improved with Japanese aid. International links are mainly by air. Ferries provide interisland connections.

TOURISM

Visitors : Population 1:1.9

92,300 visitors

Up 4% in 2003

MAIN TOURIST ARRIVALS

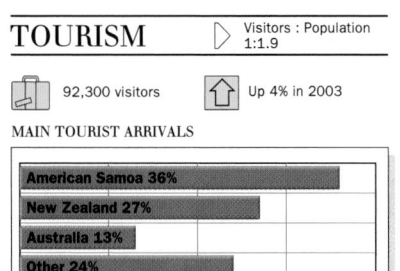

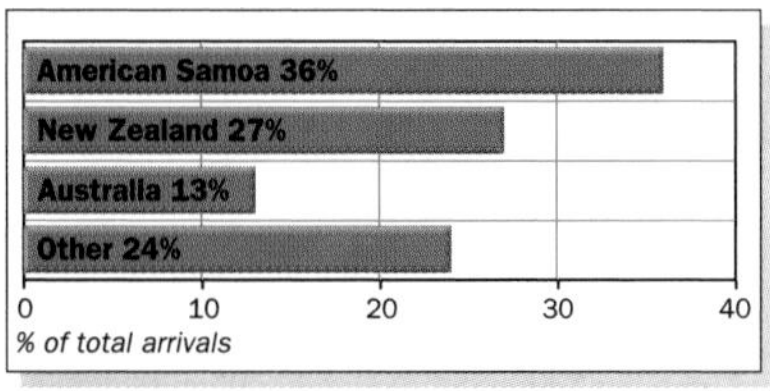
American Samoa 36%
New Zealand 27%
Australia 13%
Other 24%
0
10
20
30
40
% of total arrivals

Tourism is a rapidly growing industry. Small-scale village-based tourism is encouraged. Tourists are attracted by the climate and the easygoing *fa'a Samoa* (Samoan way of life).

PEOPLE

Pop. density medium

Samoan, English

63/km² (163/mi²)

THE URBAN/RURAL POPULATION SPLIT

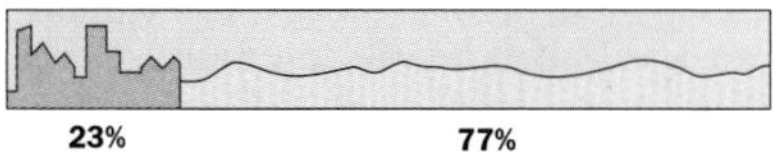
23%
77%

ETHNIC MAKEUP

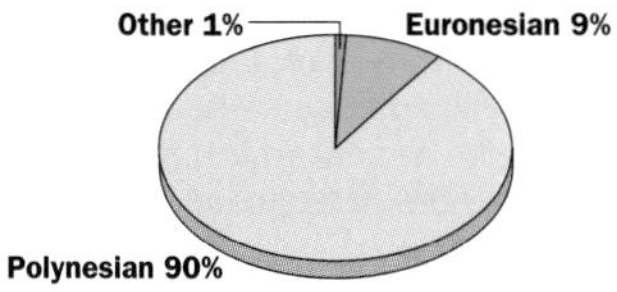
Other 1%
Euronesian 9%
Polynesian 90%

Ethnic Samoans form the world's second-largest Polynesian group. Euronesians, making up 9% of the population, are those of mixed European/Polynesian descent. The *fa'a Samoa* – Samoan way of life – is communal and conservative. Extended family groups, in which most people live, own 80% of the land and cannot sell it. Each is headed by a *matai*, or elected chief, who looks after its social and political interests. Conflict between the *fa'a Samoa* and modern life is strongest among the young, who have a high suicide rate.

Almost 100% of Samoans are nominally Christian.

SAMOA

Total Area : 2944 sq. km (1137 sq. miles)

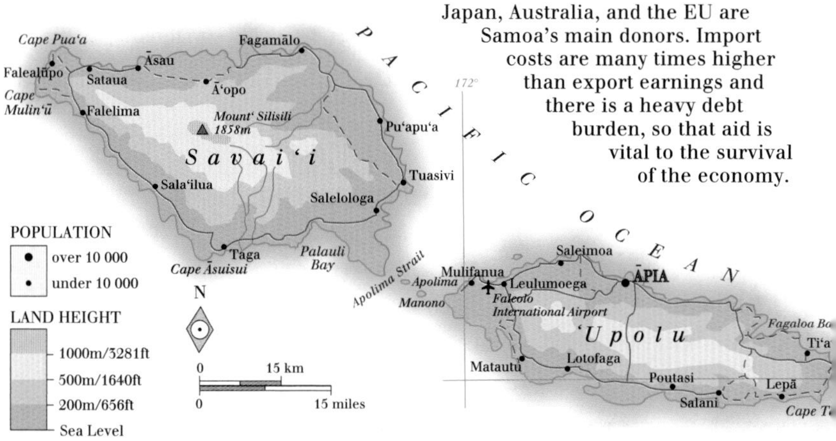
Cape Pua'a
Fagamālo
Falealupo
Āsau
Sataua
Ā'opo
Cape Mulin'ū
Falelima
Mount Silisili 1858m
Savai'i
Pu'apu'a
Tuasivi
Sala'ilua
Salelologa
PACIFIC OCEAN
172°
POPULATION
over 10 000
under 10 000
LAND HEIGHT
1000m/3281ft
500m/1640ft
200m/656ft
Sea Level
N
0
15 km
0
15 miles
Taga
Cape Āsuisui
Palauli Bay
Apolima Strait
Apolima
Manono
Mulifanua
Leulumoega
Faleolo International Airport
Saleimoa
APIA
'Upolu
Mataautu
Lotofaga
Poutasi
Salani
Lepā
Fagaloa Ba
Ti'a
Cape T

POLITICS

Multiparty elections

2001/2006

H.H. Susuga Malietoa Tanumafili II

AT THE LAST ELECTION

Legislative Assembly 49 seats

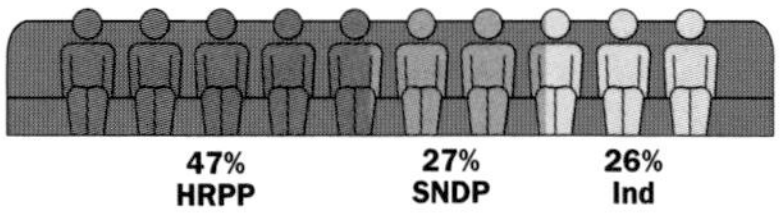
47% HRPP
27% SNDP
26% Ind

HRPP = Human Rights Protection Party **SNDP** = Samoan National Development Party **Ind** = Independents

The conservatism of the *fa'a Samoa* and the Church underpins Samoa's political stability. Allegiance to the two main parties is quite fluid. Until 1990, only the 1800 elected chiefs, or *matai*, could vote for the 47 ethnic Samoan seats in the Assembly; the other two seats are elected by non-Samoans. Universal suffrage was introduced at the 1991 elections. Tofilau Eti Alesana of the HRPP, prime minister twice since 1988, resigned in 1998 amid widespread protest against the government's autocratic style. His successor, Tuilaepa Sailele Malielegaoi, also of the HRPP, was reappointed in 2001.

WORLD AFFAIRS

Joined UN in 1976

ACP | Comm | IBRD | PC | PIF

Australia is Samoa's main trading partner. The US, New Zealand, Fiji, Indonesia, Japan, and American Samoa are also important. Relations with China are well established. Samoa has trade links with the Cook Islands, and supports a Polynesian free trade agreement.

AID

Recipient

$38m (receipts)

Down 12% in 2002

Japan, Australia, and the EU are Samoa's main donors. Import costs are many times higher than export earnings and there is a heavy debt burden, so that aid is vital to the survival of the economy.

S

DEFENSE

No compulsory military service

Samoa has no army and few police — Not applicable

New Zealand looks after defense under a 1962 treaty. Internal order is mostly maintained by the *matai* (chiefs).

ECONOMICS

Inflation 3.8% p.a. (1990–2001)

$251m — 2.845 tala (2.892)

SCORE CARD

❏ World GNP Ranking	180th
❏ GNP per Capita	$1430
❏ Balance of Payments	$9m
❏ Inflation	8.1%
❏ Unemployment	Widespread underemployment

Strengths
Light manufacturing expanding, attracting foreign, especially Japanese, firms. Tourism growing rapidly with improved infrastructure. Services expanding rapidly since 1989 launch of offshore banking. Tropical agriculture: taro, coconut products (cream, oil, copra) main exports. Large fishing potential.

Weaknesses
Development adversely affected by cyclones. Fluctuating international markets for coconut products. Dependence on aid and expatriate remittances.

EXPORTS

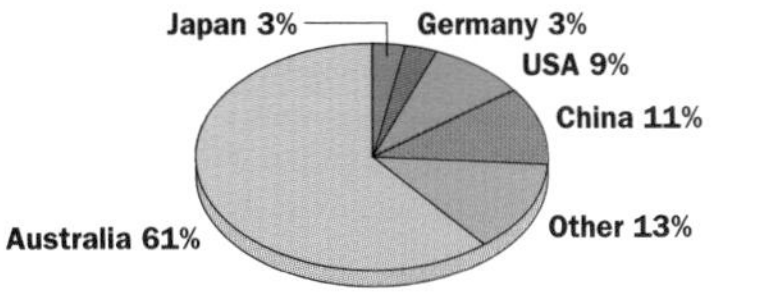
Japan 3%
Germany 3%
USA 9%
China 11%
Other 13%
Australia 61%

IMPORTS

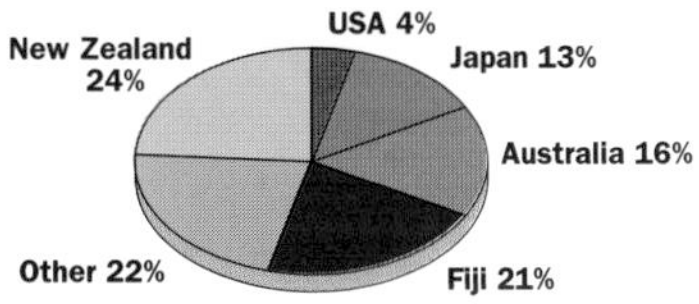
USA 4%
New Zealand 24%
Japan 13%
Australia 16%
Fiji 21%
Other 22%

RESOURCES

Electric power 20,000 kW

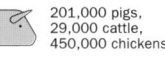

12,966 tonnes — Not an oil producer

201,000 pigs, 29,000 cattle, 450,000 chickens — None

With no minerals, Samoa's main resources are its forests and tropical agriculture. The rainforests in lower-lying areas are increasingly exploited for timber. Mahogany and teak plantations are being developed. The volcanic soils, particularly on Upolu, support a wide range of staple and export crops. Two-thirds of the population work in agriculture.

***Apia, the capital**, on Upolu, Samoa's second-largest island. It has a central volcanic range of mountains and many rivers.*

ENVIRONMENT

Not available

4% (3% partially protected) — 0.8 tonnes per capita

Strict logging regulations have been introduced to halt irreparable damage to the environment; over 80% of forests have been replaced by plantations. Overhunting and loss of habitat have endangered rare species of fruit bat and pigeon. Samoa is concerned about its marine resources and has taken a firm stance against driftnet fishing.

MEDIA

TV ownership medium

Daily newspaper circulation figures are not available

PUBLISHING AND BROADCAST MEDIA

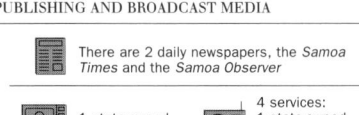

There are 2 daily newspapers, the *Samoa Times* and the *Samoa Observer*

1 state-owned service — 4 services: 1 state-owned, 3 independent

The independent media generally report the news freely, though there has been government harassment.

CRIME

No death penalty

281 prisoners — Crime is rising slowly

Crime levels are low, though alcohol-related violence is a problem at weekends and theft is increasing in towns. The death penalty was abolished in 2004.

EDUCATION

School leaving age: 14

99% — 1874 students

Education is based on the New Zealand system. School attendance is universal. A university was established in Samoa in 1988. There is widespread use of corporal punishment.

HEALTH

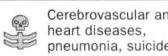

No welfare state health benefits

1 per 3333 people — Cerebrovascular and heart diseases, pneumonia, suicide

The Samoan preference for being big went well with traditional diets. Diabetes and heart disease are rising as people change to Western-style foods.

CHRONOLOGY

Polynesians settled Samoa in about 1000 BCE. Western rivalry after 1830 led to the 1899 division of the islands into German Western and American Eastern Samoa.

- ❏ **1914** New Zealand occupies Western Samoa.
- ❏ **1962** Becomes first independent Polynesian nation.
- ❏ **1990** Cyclone Ofa leaves 10,000 people homeless.
- ❏ **1991** HRPP retains power in first election under universal adult suffrage.
- ❏ **1996, 2001** HRPP returned to power in elections.
- ❏ **1997** Country's name changed from Western Samoa to Samoa.

SPENDING

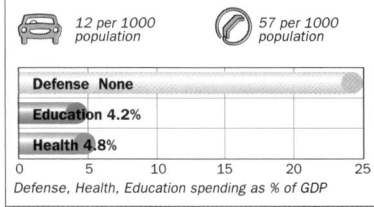

GDP/cap. increase

CONSUMPTION AND SPENDING

12 per 1000 population — *57 per 1000 population*

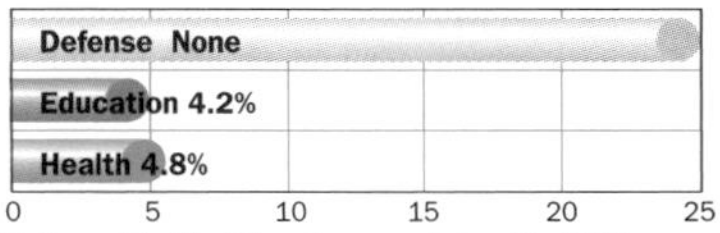
Defense None
Education 4.2%
Health 4.8%
0
5
10
15
20
25

Defense, Health, Education spending as % of GDP

Most of the population depend on subsistence farming and the remittances of relatives for their livelihood. Samoa is classified by the UN as a Least Developed Country. Two-thirds of those with a permanent job work for the government. The prospect of earning higher wages by working in other, wealthier countries in the Pacific region, notably in the tuna canneries of American Samoa, the neighboring US dependency, leads thousands of young Samoans to emigrate every year.

S

WORLD RANKING

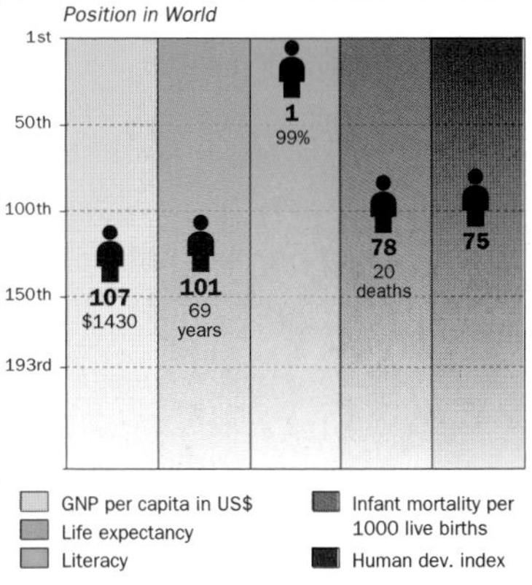
Position in World
1st
50th
100th
150th
193rd
107
$1430
101
69 years
1
99%
78
20 deaths
75
GNP per capita in US$
Life expectancy
Literacy
Infant mortality per 1000 live births
Human dev. index

SAN MARINO

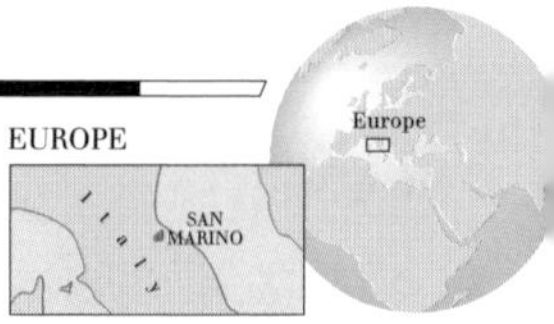
EUROPE
SAN MARINO
Europe

OFFICIAL NAME: Republic of San Marino **CAPITAL:** San Marino
POPULATION: 28,119 **CURRENCY:** Euro **OFFICIAL LANGUAGE:** Italian

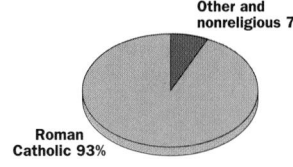

1631 | 1631 | Sept 3 | RSM | +1 | +378 | .sm

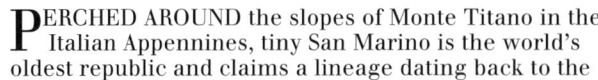

PERCHED AROUND the slopes of Monte Titano in the Italian Appennines, tiny San Marino is the world's oldest republic and claims a lineage dating back to the 4th century. The territory is divided into nine castles, or districts. One-third of Sammarinesi live in the northern town of Serravalle. Today San Marino makes its living through agriculture, tourism, philately, and limited industry. Italy effectively controls most of its affairs.

***San Marino's** second fortress, la Cesta, built in the 13th century, dominates the republic from its pinnacle, 755 m (2477 ft) above sea level.*

CLIMATE

Mediterranean

WEATHER CHART FOR SAN MARINO

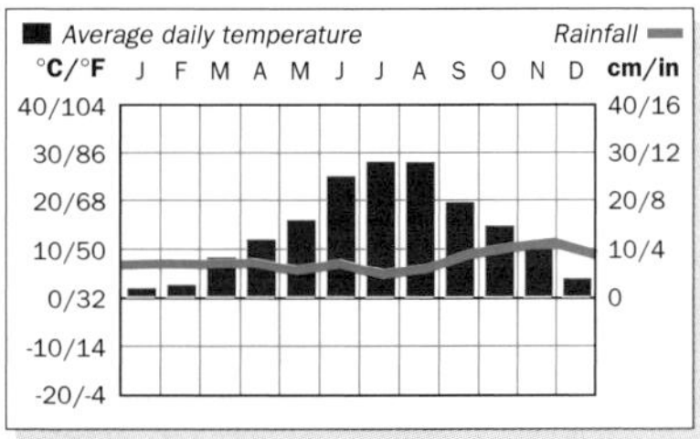
Average daily temperature
Rainfall
°C/°F
J F M A M J J A S O N D
cm/in
40/104
30/86
20/68
10/50
0/32
-10/14
-20/-4
40/16
30/12
20/8
10/4
0

San Marino's Mediterranean climate is moderated by cool sea breezes and its height above sea level. In summer, temperatures can reach 27°C (81°F), while in winter they fall to 2°C (35°F). There is rarely any snow.

TRANSPORTATION

Drive on right

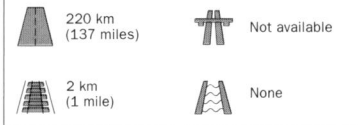

None | Has no fleet

THE TRANSPORTATION NETWORK

220 km (137 miles)	Not available
2 km (1 mile)	None

The 24-km (15-mile) highway to Rimini, which has the nearest airport, is San Marino's most important link. Congestion is a major problem, especially during the annual Mille Miglia car rally. A funicular railroad climbs the east side of Monte Titano. The railroad to Rimini has been closed since World War II.

PEOPLE

Pop. density high

Italian | 461/km² (1172/mi²)

THE URBAN/RURAL POPULATION SPLIT

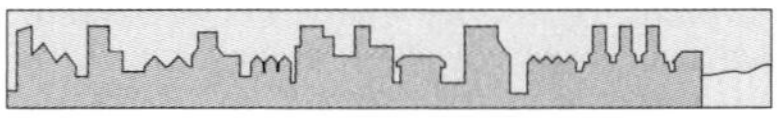
91%
9%

RELIGIOUS PERSUASION

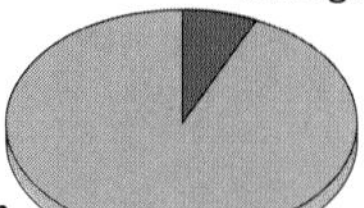
Other and nonreligious 7%
Roman Catholic 93%

Citizenship requires 30 years' residence; it is no longer transmissible by marriage. Women gained the vote in 1960, but could not stand for public office until 1973. Some Sammarinesi speak a distinct regional dialect. Around 20,000 live abroad, mainly in Italy.

TOURISM

Visitors : Population 1.6:1

45,000 visitors | Down 8% in 2002

MAIN TOURIST ARRIVALS

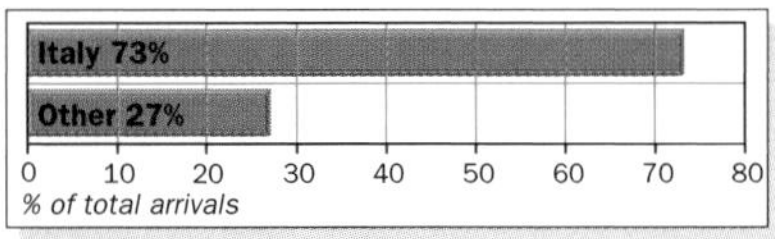
Italy 73%
Other 27%
0 10 20 30 40 50 60 70 80
% of total arrivals

Tourism is the mainstay of San Marino's economy, contributing about 60% of government revenue and employment for almost 20% of the workforce. Earnings from tourism are the largest share of GDP. Every year around three million visitors pass through San Marino, though most do not stay overnight. They are drawn by its mild climate and contrasting scenery, and come to sample its folklore and museums. The fortresses of Monte Titano – la Rocca, la Cesta, and Montale – built during the Middle Ages, command superb views and are the main attractions, along with the medieval city of San Marino itself. Many visitors to San Marino are day-trippers from Italy, though tourism is also boosted by the close proximity of the international airport at Rimini.

The San Marino tourist bureau also attracts thousands of sports enthusiasts to the republic by hosting a series of top international sporting events. In March, both the Rimini–San Marino marathon and the Mille Miglia veteran car meeting are held. May heralds the San Marino Grand Prix, when thousands of Formula 1 fans descend on the country. June, meanwhile, attracts more motor-racing fans for the World Motocross Championships. A renowned crossbow competition is held to mark San Marino's national day, September 3.

Efforts have been made to attract business meetings and conferences by means of extensive publicity in the Italian media.

***Religious procession.** The official state religion of San Marino is Roman Catholicism, in contrast to Italy, which has no state religion.*

SAN MARINO

Total Area : 61 sq. km (23.6 sq. miles)

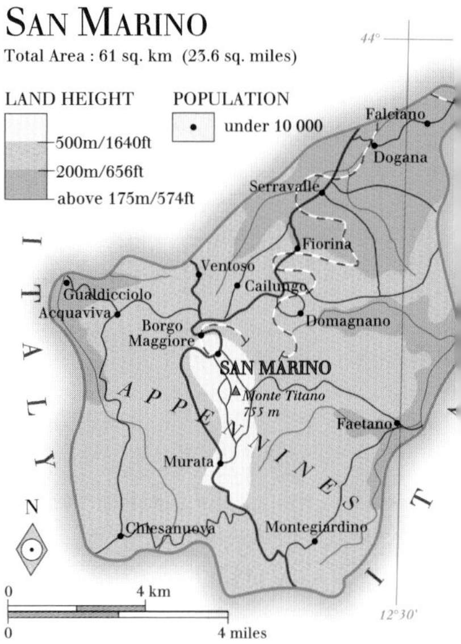
LAND HEIGHT
500m/1640ft
200m/656ft
above 175m/574ft
POPULATION
under 10 000
Falciano
Dogana
Serravalle
Fiorina
Ventoso
Gualdicciolo
Acquaviva
Cailungo
Domagnano
Borgo Maggiore
SAN MARINO
Monte Titano 755 m
Faetano
Murata
Chiesanuova
Montegiardino
ITALY
APPENNINES
N
0 4 km
0 4 miles
44°
12°30'

POLITICS

Multiparty elections

2001/2006

Captains-Regent Paolo Bollini and Marino Riccardi

AT THE LAST ELECTION

Great and General Council 60 seats

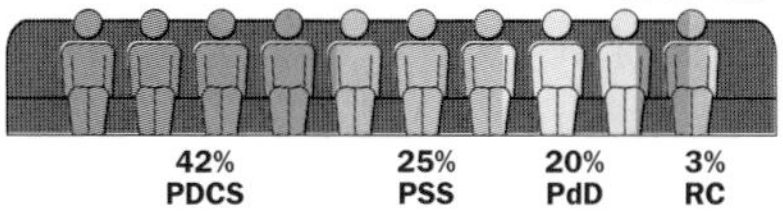
8% APDS
2% AN
42% PDCS
25% PSS
20% PdD
3% RC

PDCS = San Marino Christian Democratic Party **PSS** = Socialist Party of San Marino **PdD** = Party of Democrats **APDS** = Popular Democratic Alliance **RC** = Communist Refoundation **AN** = National Alliance

San Marino is a parliamentary democracy headed by two captains-regent elected every six months. Though the PDCS is the largest single party, it is not guaranteed a place in the ever-shifting ruling coalition. Plans have been discussed to restructure the system to strengthen coalitions.

WORLD AFFAIRS

Joined UN in 1992

CE | OSCE | IBRD | IMF | IWC

Foreign affairs are effectively decided by Italy, on which San Marino is entirely dependent. In 1992, San Marino acquired a seat at the UN.

AID

Neither

Neither an aid donor nor receiver

Not applicable

San Marino does not receive aid. However, annual subsidies from Italy and free access to the Italian market are essential to the economy.

DEFENSE

No compulsory military service

$1m

Little change from year to year

San Marino has a small territorial army and fortification guards. There is no compulsory military service, but males aged 16–55 may be called up in a national emergency.

ECONOMICS

Inflation 5.9% p.a. (1985–1996)

$520m

0.822 euros (0.871)

SCORE CARD

- ❑ World GNP Ranking........................170th
- ❑ GNP per Capita..........................$19,000
- ❑ Balance of Payments......................$11m
- ❑ Inflation..3.3%
- ❑ Unemployment.................................3%

Strengths

Tourism, providing over 50% of GDP. Light industry, notably mechanical engineering and clothing, with emphasis on sportswear and high-quality prestige lines. Philately.

Weaknesses

All raw materials need to be imported.

EXPORTS/IMPORTS

San Marino does not publish independent trade statistics; trade movements are included in the Italian totals.

RESOURCES

Electric power: Included in Italian total

None

Not an oil producer

Not available

None

San Marino has to import all its energy from Italy. It has no exploitable mineral resources now that the stone quarry on Monte Titano has been exhausted.

ENVIRONMENT

Not available

None

Not available

Monte Titano is a unique limestone outcrop in the surrounding Italian plain. It thus has a very localized ecosystem.

MEDIA

TV ownership high

Daily newspaper circulation 70 per 1000 people

PUBLISHING AND BROADCAST MEDIA

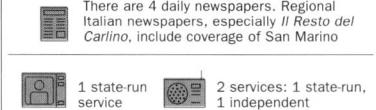

There are 4 daily newspapers. Regional Italian newspapers, especially *Il Resto del Carlino*, include coverage of San Marino

1 state-run service

2 services: 1 state-run, 1 independent

In 1993, a local TV station, San Marino RTV, began broadcasting. Sammarinesi can also receive Italian TV.

CRIME

No death penalty

Prisoners are held in Italy

Little change from year to year

San Marino has a low crime rate. Justice is mainly administered in Italy. Until mid-1997 homosexuality was illegal.

EDUCATION

School leaving age: 14

99%

950 students

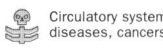

All teachers are trained abroad, mostly in Italy. Secondary school pupils can go on to Italian universities.

HEALTH

Welfare state health benefits

1 per 397 people

Circulatory system diseases, cancers

Health care is free and available to all. There is a hospital, but those requiring difficult operations normally go to Rimini for treatment.

CHRONOLOGY

Traditionally held to have been founded in the 4th century, the Republic of San Marino, one of many medieval Italian city-states, was recognized by the papacy in 1631.

- ❑ **1797** San Marino rejects expansion offered by Napoléon I.
- ❑ **1861** Refuses to join unified Italy.
- ❑ **1914–1918** Fights for Italy in World War I.
- ❑ **1940** Supports Axis powers and declares war on Allies.
- ❑ **1943** Declares neutrality shortly before Italy surrenders.
- ❑ **1960** Women obtain vote.
- ❑ **1978** Coalition of San Marino Communist Party (PCS) and PSS: sole communist-led government in Western Europe.
- ❑ **1986** Financial scandals lead to new PDCS–PCS government.
- ❑ **1988** Joins Council of Europe.
- ❑ **1992** Joins UN. Collapse of communism in Europe: reformed PCS ousted from ruling coalition.
- ❑ **2001** Reformed communists form new party: PdD.
- ❑ **2002** Adoption of euro.

SPENDING

GDP/cap. increase

CONSUMPTION AND SPENDING

No data

763 per 1000 population

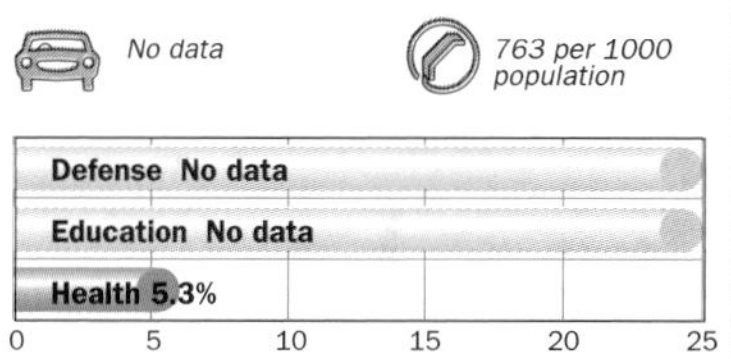
Defense No data
Education No data
Health 5.3%
0
5
10
15
20
25

Defense, Health, Education spending as % of GDP

Living standards are similar to those of northern Italy, while the unemployment rate is well below the Italian average.

WORLD RANKING

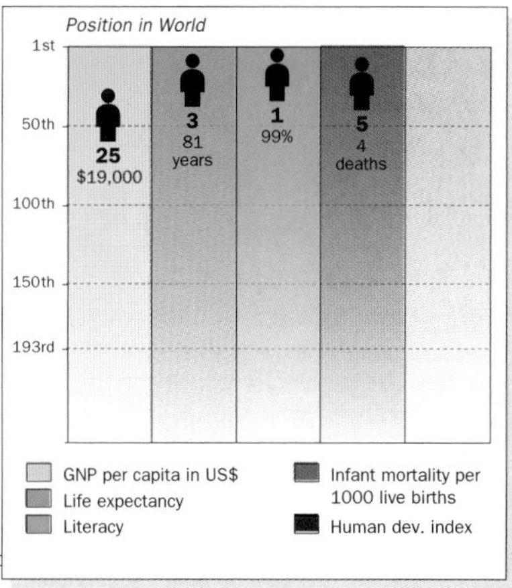
Position in World
1st
50th
100th
150th
193rd
25
$19,000
3
81 years
1
99%
5
4 deaths
GNP per capita in US$
Life expectancy
Literacy
Infant mortality per 1000 live births
Human dev. index

S

São Tomé & Príncipe

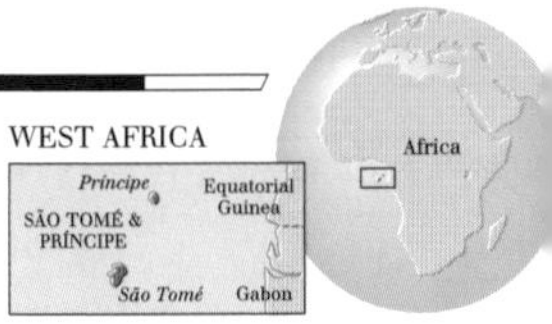
WEST AFRICA
Príncipe
Equatorial Guinea
SÃO TOMÉ & PRÍNCIPE
São Tomé
Gabon
Africa

Official Name: Democratic Republic of São Tomé and Príncipe **Capital:** São Tomé
Population: 175,883 **Currency:** Dobra **Official Language:** Portuguese

1975 | 1975 | July 12 | STP | 0 | +239 | .st

Composed of two main islands and their surrounding islets, São Tomé and Príncipe is situated off the west coast of Africa. In 1975, a classic Marxist single-party regime was established following independence from Portugal, but a referendum in 1990 resulted in a 72% vote in favor of democracy. São Tomé's main concerns are relations with Portugal and seeking closer ties with the EU and the US.

CLIMATE

Tropical equatorial

WEATHER CHART FOR SÃO TOMÉ

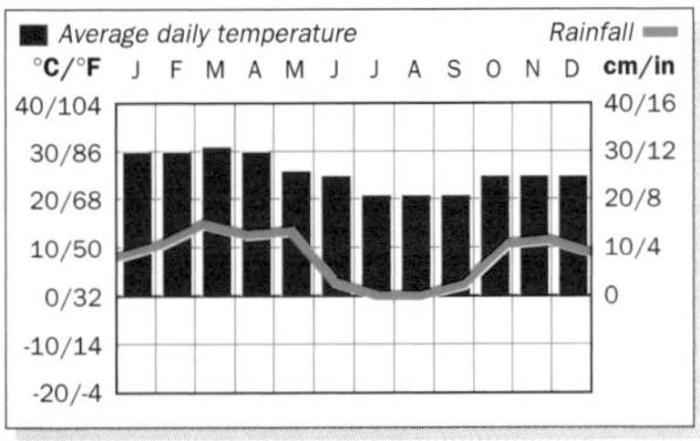
Average daily temperature
Rainfall
°C/°F
J F M A M J J A S O N D
cm/in
40/104
30/86
20/68
10/50
0/32
-10/14
-20/-4
40/16
30/12
20/8
10/4
0

The humid islands straddle the equator. The southwest of São Tomé is much wetter than the northern lowlands.

TRANSPORTATION

Drive on right

São Tomé International
23,000 passengers

49 ships
86,116 grt

THE TRANSPORTATION NETWORK

218 km (135 miles)

None

None

None

Public transportation is woefully underdeveloped. On Príncipe it consists of a solitary minibus.

TOURISM

Visitors : Population 1:23

7569 visitors

Up 51% in 1999–2001

MAIN TOURIST ARRIVALS

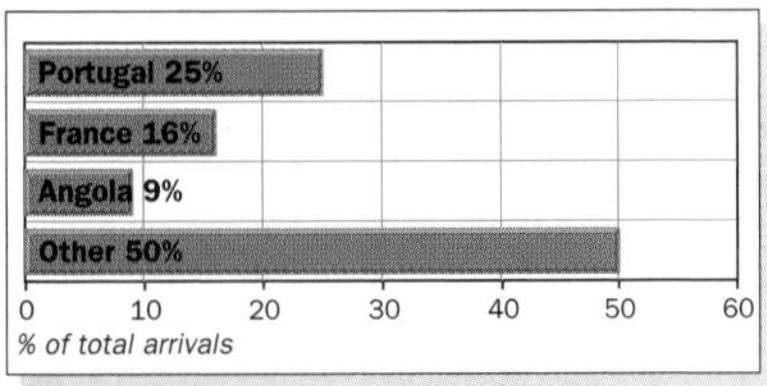
Portugal 25%
France 16%
Angola 9%
Other 50%
0
10
20
30
40
50
60
% of total arrivals

Despite recent foreign investment, the islands attract relatively few tourists annually, mainly wealthy Africans and Europeans. Attractions include snorkeling, scenery, and wildlife. The first modern hotel opened in 1986.

PEOPLE

Pop. density medium

Portuguese Creole, Portuguese

183/km² (474/mi²)

THE URBAN/RURAL POPULATION SPLIT

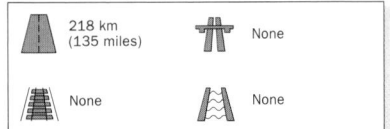

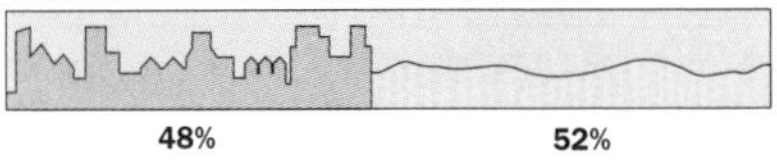
48%
52%

ETHNIC MAKEUP

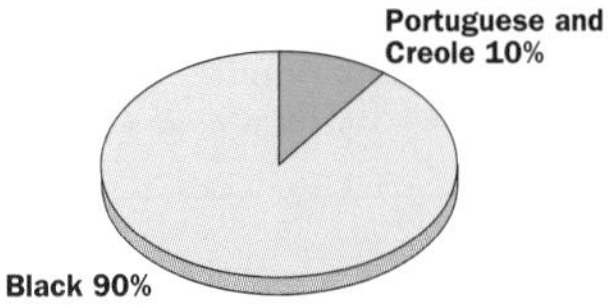
Portuguese and Creole 10%
Black 90%

The population is entirely descended from immigrants, since the islands were uninhabited when the Portuguese arrived in 1470. As the Portuguese settled, they imported Africans as slaves to work the sugar and cocoa plantations. The abolition of slavery in the 19th century, and the departure of 4000 Portuguese at independence, has resulted in a population which is 10% Portuguese and Creole and 90% black African, though Portuguese culture predominates. Blacks run the political parties. Society is well integrated and free of racial tensions. The main conflicts relate to class or differing ideologies. The extended family still offers the best, if not the only, form of social security. Women have a higher status than in most other African states; in 2002, Maria das Neves de Souza became the first female prime minister.

Lush vegetation on São Tomé. *The tropical climate is slightly moderated by the cool Benguela current.*

POLITICS

Multiparty elections

2002/2006

President Fradique de Menezes

AT THE LAST ELECTION

National Assembly 55 seats

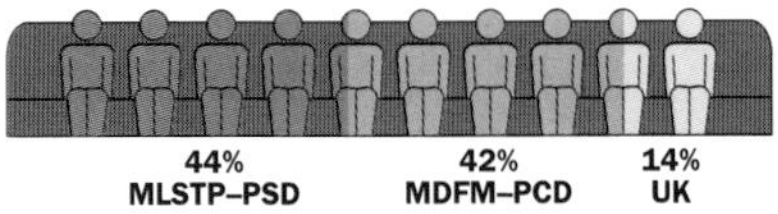
44% MLSTP–PSD
42% MDFM–PCD
14% UK

MLSTP–PSD = São Tomé and Príncipe Liberation Movement –Social Democratic Party **MDFM–PCD** = Force for Change Democratic Movement–Democratic Convergence Party **UK** = Ue Kedadji coalition

In 1990, a new multiparty constitution was introduced, ending the Marxist single-party state that had existed since independence in 1975. The opposition PCD was swept to victory in 1991, and later that year Miguel Trovoada returned from 11 years' exile to be elected as an independent to the presidency. Early elections in 1994 saw the return to power of the MLSTP as the renamed MLSTP–PSD. In the 2001 presidential elections, businessman Fradique de Menezes defeated former Marxist president Manuel Pinto da Costa. However, de Menezes was forced to negotiate the formation of a coalition government with the MLSTP–PSD after the party won elections in 2002. Conflict with the legislature developed over the president's power to control policy, especially in relation to the undersea oil reserves. A brief army takeover in 2003 forced de Menezes to promise greater cooperation with parliament.

WORLD AFFAIRS

Joined UN in 1975

CPLP | ACP | OIF | NAM | AU

São Tomé has achieved rapprochement with Portugal and seeks to maintain links with other former Portuguese colonies, notably Angola. It has always had close ties with Gabon and, while not dropping its ex-communist links, seeks closer relations with other central African states, France, and the US.

AID

Recipient

$26m (receipts)

Down 32% in 2002

São Tomé has one of the highest aid-to-population ratios in Africa. The government was granted $200 million in debt relief in 2001 by the World Bank Group's International Development Fund and the International Monetary Fund under the Initiative for Heavily Indebted Poor Countries program.

S

DEFENSE

No compulsory military service

$400,000

Little change

Since independence, the armed forces have figured prominently in national life. There have been a number of attempted coups, notably in 1978 (after which 2000 Angolan troops plus Soviet and Cuban advisers were invited in), 1988, and 1995. The most recent, in 2003, saw the brief establishment of a military junta. The national armed forces are believed to number 2000. With the collapse of the Eastern bloc, São Tomé now receives military assistance from the West.

RESOURCES

Electric power 6000 kW

3500 tonnes

Oil reserves not yet exploited

30,000 ducks, 4850 goats, 350,000 chickens

Oil

An offshore oil exploration agreement with Nigeria was signed in 2001: deposits are expected to come onstream by 2007. There are no other mineral resources. São Tomé is very fertile; cocoa estates are finally back to pre-1975 productivity, and diversification of crops is now a priority. Príncipe has better ports, but its wild scenery makes it more suitable for tourism than farming.

CHRONOLOGY

The entire preindependence history of the islands was as a Portuguese colony exploited by plantation owners.

- **1972–1973** Strikes by plantation workers.
- **1975** Independence as Marxist state. Plantations nationalized.
- **1990** New democratic constitution.
- **1991–2000** Miguel Trovoada president for two terms.
- **1995** Príncipe granted autonomy.
- **2001** De Menezes wins presidency.
- **2003** Brief military takeover.

ECONOMICS

Inflation 47% p.a. (1990–2001)

$46m

8700 dobras (8700)

SCORE CARD

World GNP Ranking	190th
GNP per Capita	$300
Balance of Payments	–$23m
Inflation	6.8%
Unemployment	50%

EXPORTS

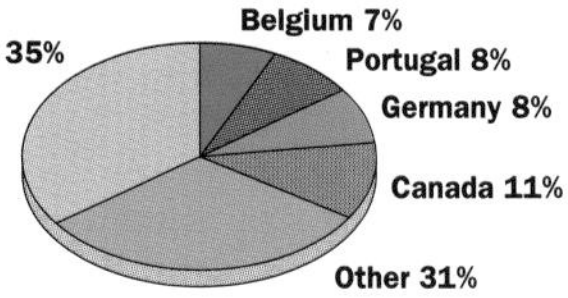

Netherlands 35%
Belgium 7%
Portugal 8%
Germany 8%
Canada 11%
Other 31%

IMPORTS

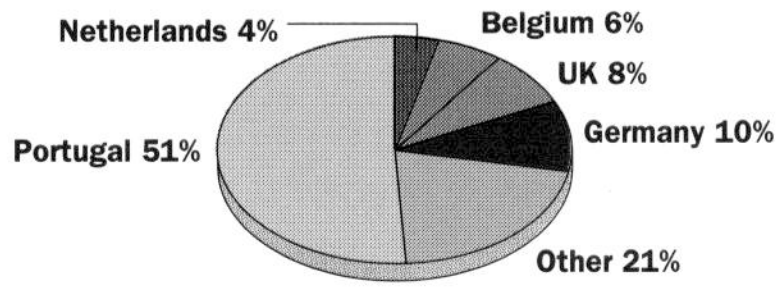

Netherlands 4%
Belgium 6%
UK 8%
Germany 10%
Portugal 51%
Other 21%

Strengths

Legacy of Portuguese-built infrastructure. Potential for development of fisheries, agriculture, tourism, and oil. Able to attract substantial aid.

Weaknesses

Cocoa accounts for 90% of export earnings. Skillful diplomacy has attracted high levels of aid, but mismanagement of these funds has resulted in severe debt. Weak currency.

EDUCATION

School leaving age: 14

83%

181 students

Education is officially compulsory only for a four-year period between the ages of six and 14.

HEALTH

No welfare state health benefits

1 per 2000 people

Malaria, other parasitic diseases, respiratory and diarrheal diseases

Health care is not free, but São Tomé has a better system of basic care than other African countries.

SPENDING

GDP/cap. decrease

CONSUMPTION AND SPENDING

31 per 1000 population

41 per 1000 population

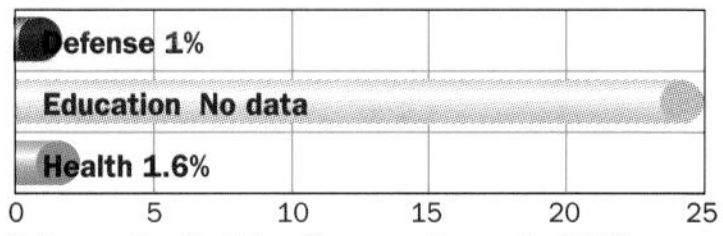

Defense 1%
Education No data
Health 1.6%
0
5
10
15
20
25

Defense, Health, Education spending as % of GDP

Wealth disparities are not conspicuous, though there is a growing business class. Cocoa plantation workers form the country's poorest group.

São Tomé & Príncipe

Total Area : 1001 sq. km (386 sq. miles)

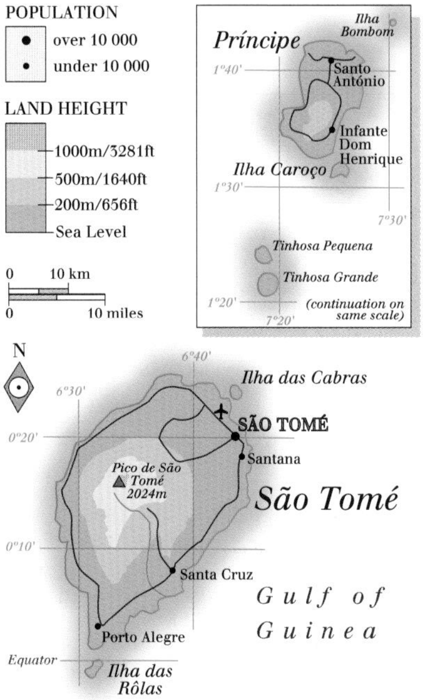

POPULATION
over 10 000
under 10 000
LAND HEIGHT
1000m/3281ft
500m/1640ft
200m/656ft
Sea Level
0
10 km
0
10 miles
N
Príncipe
Ilha Bombom
Santo António
Infante Dom Henrique
Ilha Caroço
1°40'
1°30'
1°20'
7°30'
7°20'
Tinhosa Pequena
Tinhosa Grande
(continuation on same scale)
Ilha das Cabras
SÃO TOMÉ
Santana
Pico de São Tomé 2024m
São Tomé
Santa Cruz
Porto Alegre
Gulf of Guinea
Equator
Ilha das Rôlas
6°40'
6°30'
0°20'
0°10'

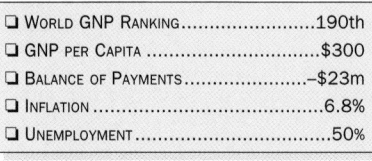

ENVIRONMENT

Not available

None

0.6 tonnes per capita

Fish conservation, deforestation for fuelwood, and potential tourism expansion are the major issues.

MEDIA

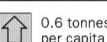

TV ownership medium

Daily newspaper circulation not available

PUBLISHING AND BROADCAST MEDIA

There is 1 daily newspaper, the indedependent *Téla Nón Diário de São Tomé e Príncipe*

1 state-controlled service

1 state-controlled service

Freedom of expression is respected. The state controls radio and TV stations. Radio ownership is high for Africa.

CRIME

No death penalty

130 prisoners

Little change in 1999

Crime levels are fairly low owing to the tight-knit nature of communities. Robbery is a problem in urban areas.

WORLD RANKING

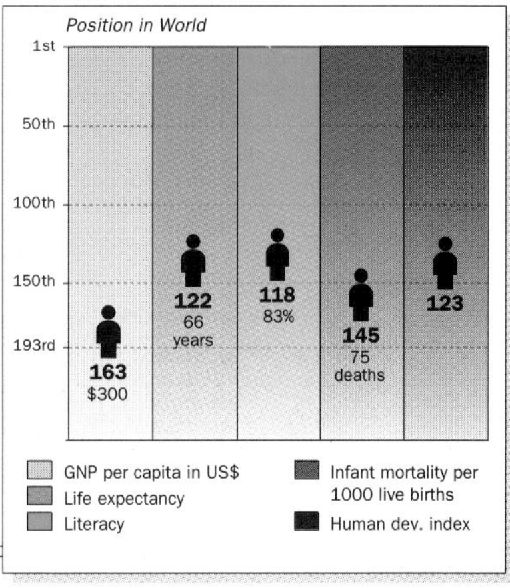

Position in World
1st
50th
100th
150th
193rd
163
$300
122
66 years
118
83%
145
75 deaths
123
GNP per capita in US$
Life expectancy
Literacy
Infant mortality per 1000 live births
Human dev. index

S

SAUDI ARABIA

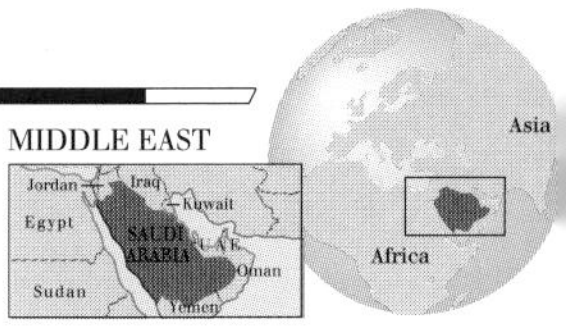
MIDDLE EAST
Jordan
Iraq
Kuwait
Egypt
SAUDI ARABIA
Oman
Sudan
Yemen
Asia
Africa

OFFICIAL NAME: Kingdom of Saudi Arabia **CAPITAL:** Riyadh; Jiddah (administrative)
POPULATION: 24.2 million **CURRENCY:** Saudi riyal **OFFICIAL LANGUAGE:** Arabic

1932 | 1932 | Sept 23 | SA | +3 | +966 | .sa

OCCUPYING MOST OF THE Arabian peninsula, Saudi Arabia covers an area as large as western Europe. Over 95% of its land is desert, with the most arid part, known as the Empty Quarter or Rub al Khali, being in the southeast. Saudi Arabia has the world's largest oil reserves. It includes Islam's holiest cities, Medina and Mecca, visited each year by two million Muslims performing the pilgrimage known as the *haj*. The al-Sa'ud family have been Saudi Arabia's absolutist rulers since 1932. In theory, Islamic *sharia* underpins the constitution.

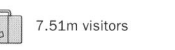

CLIMATE

Hot desert

WEATHER CHART FOR RIYADH

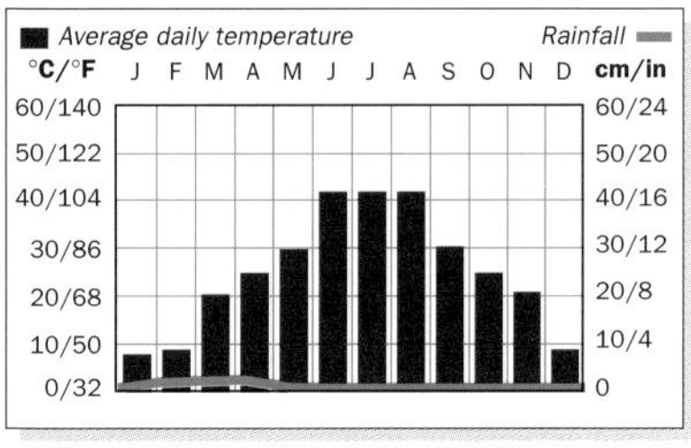
Average daily temperature
Rainfall
°C/°F
J F M A M J J A S O N D
cm/in
60/140
50/122
40/104
30/86
20/68
10/50
0/32
60/24
50/20
40/16
30/12
20/8
10/4
0

The kingdom's only reliable rainfall is in the southern Asir province, making agriculture viable there. The central plateau requires deep artesian wells to water crops. Inland, summer temperatures often soar above 48°C (118°F), but in winter, especially in the northwest, they may fall to freezing point.

TRANSPORTATION

Drive on right

King Abd al-Aziz International, Jiddah
11.4m passengers

280 ships
1.47m grt

THE TRANSPORTATION NETWORK

45,613 km (28,343 miles)

Trans-Arabian Highway

1078 km (670 miles)

None

A modern transportation infrastructure links the main population centers to the Gulf states and Jordan. Saudi Arabia has the only rail system in the Arabian peninsula.

TOURISM

Visitors : Population 1:3.2

7.51m visitors

Up 19% in 2001–2002

MAIN TOURIST ARRIVALS

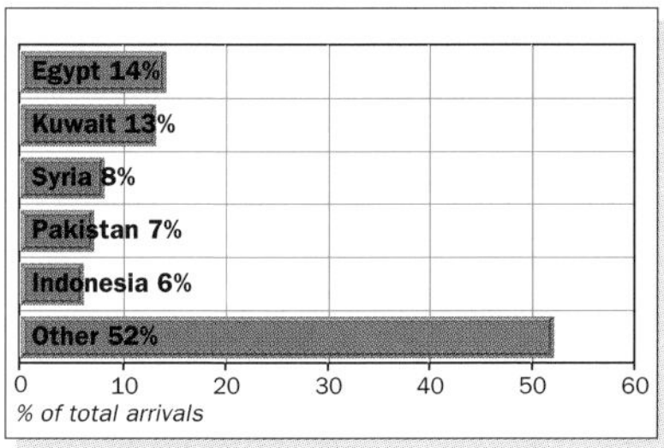
Egypt 14%
Kuwait 13%
Syria 8%
Pakistan 7%
Indonesia 6%
Other 52%
0
10
20
30
40
50
60
% of total arrivals

Foreign tourism is discouraged. Until a limited relaxation in 2000, only Muslim pilgrims, business people, and foreign workers were permitted entry. Non-Muslims are banned from the holy cities of Mecca and Medina. Though strict quotas have been imposed to avoid overcrowding, stampedes of *haj* pilgrims in 1990, 1997, and 2001 killed or injured thousands. Also popular is the *umra*, or little pilgrimage, since it can be made at any time of year. An estimated $2.5 billion has been spent on improving *haj* facilities in recent years.

Jizan on the Red Sea offers superb scuba diving. The Hejaz railroad and the Nabatean ruins at Medain Salih are of historical interest. To escape the summer heat, the government relocates to mountainous Taif, used as a resort by the Saudis.

SAUDI ARABIA

Total Area : 1 960 582 sq. km (756 981 sq. miles)

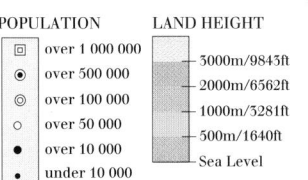

POPULATION
- over 1 000 000
- over 500 000
- over 100 000
- over 50 000
- over 10 000
- under 10 000

LAND HEIGHT
- 3000m/9843ft
- 2000m/6562ft
- 1000m/3281ft
- 500m/1640ft
- Sea Level

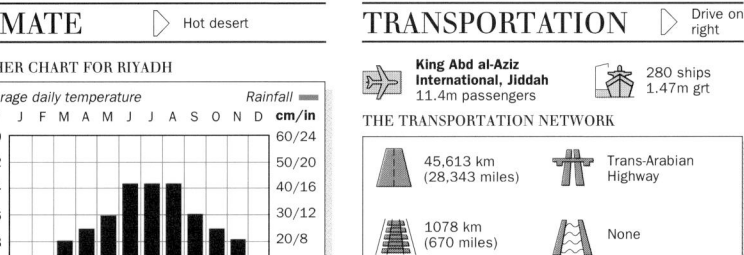

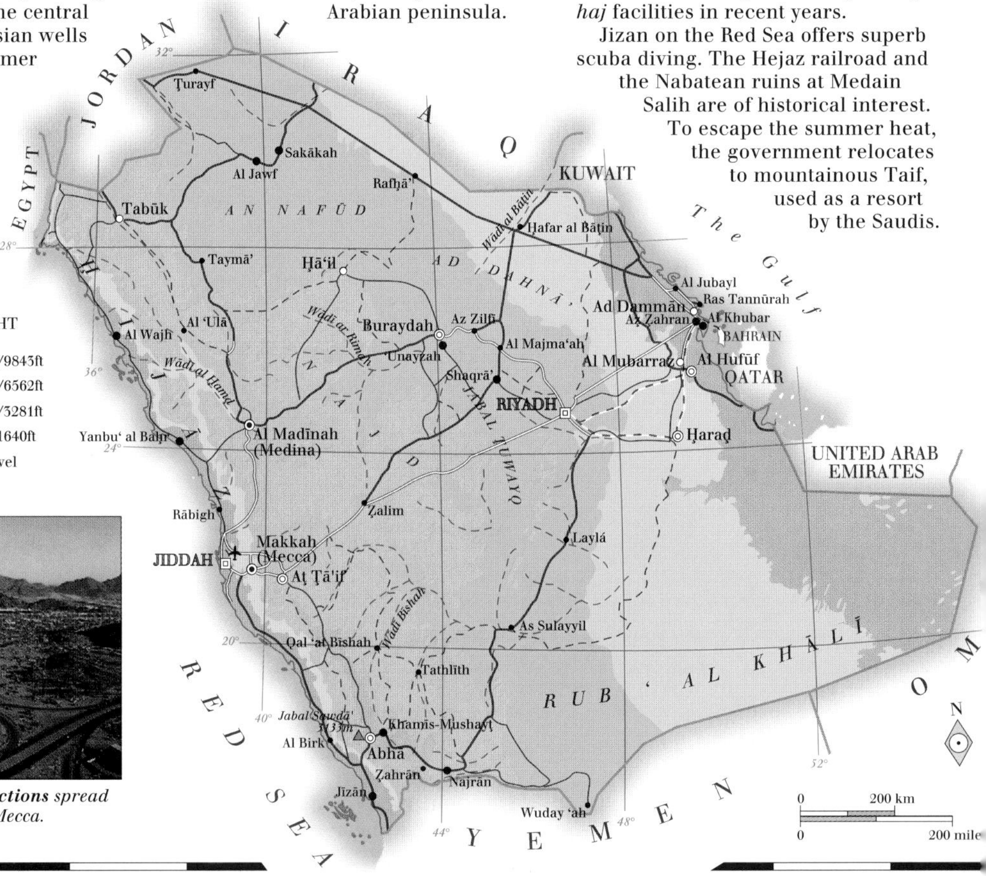
JORDAN
IRAQ
KUWAIT
EGYPT
The Gulf
BAHRAIN
QATAR
UNITED ARAB EMIRATES
OMAN
YEMEN
RED SEA
Ţurayf
Sakākah
Al Jawf
Rafḩā'
AN NAFŪD
Tabūk
Taymā'
Ḩā'il
Ḩafar al Bāţin
Wādī al Bāţin
AD DAHNĀ'
Al Jubayl
Ras Tannūrah
Ad Dammām
Az Zahran
Al Khubar
Al Wajh
Al 'Ulā
Wādī al Ḩamḑ
Wādī ar Rimah
Buraydah
'Unayzah
Az Zilfī
Al Majma'ah
Shaqrā'
Al Mubarraz
Al Hufūf
RIYADH
NAJD
JABAL ŢUWAYQ
Ḩaraḑ
Yanbu' al Baḩr
Al Madīnah (Medina)
Rābigh
Ẓalim
Laylá
JIDDAH
Makkah (Mecca)
Aţ Ţā'if
Wādī Bīshah
As Sulayyil
Qal 'at Bīshah
Tathlīth
RUB ' AL KHĀLĪ
Jabal Sawdā' 3133m
Al Birk
Khamīs-Mushayţ
Abhā
Ẓahrān
Najrān
Jīzān
Wuday 'ah
N
0 200 km
0 200 miles

***Network of modern road junctions** spread out across the landscape near Mecca.*

PEOPLE

Pop. density low

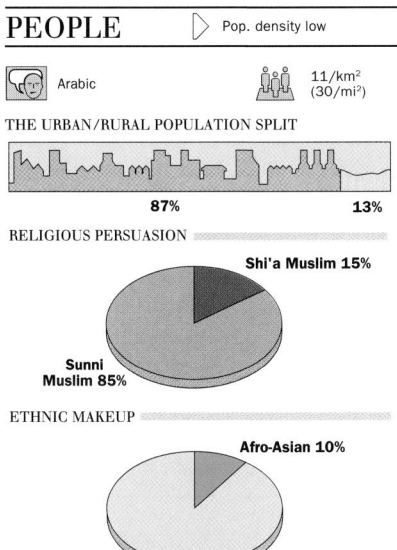

Arabic

11/km² (30/mi²)

THE URBAN/RURAL POPULATION SPLIT

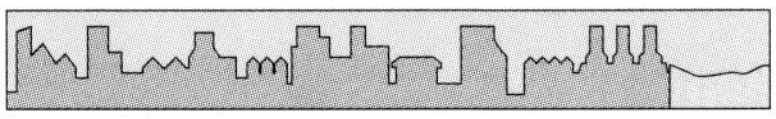
87%
13%

RELIGIOUS PERSUASION

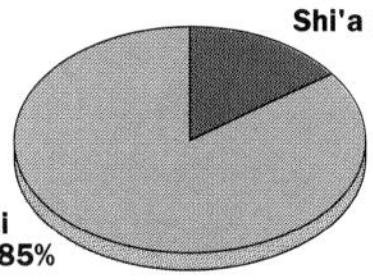
Shi'a Muslim 15%
Sunni Muslim 85%

ETHNIC MAKEUP

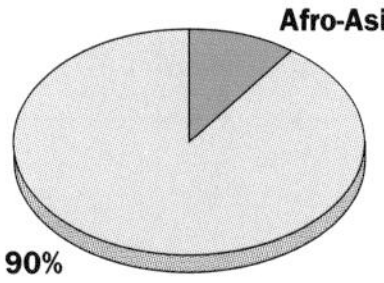
Afro-Asian 10%
Arab 90%

The Saudis, who take their name from the ruling al-Sa'ud family, were united by conquest between 1902 and 1932 by King Abd al-Aziz al-Sa'ud. The vast majority are Sunni Muslims who follow a puritanical Wahhabi interpretation of Islam and embrace *sharia* (Islamic law). The politically dominant Nejdi tribes from the central plateau around Riyadh are Bedouin in origin. The more cosmopolitan, mercantile Hejazi tribes, from the south and west, take little part in politics. In the eastern oil fields of Al-Hasa province there is a Shi'a minority of some 500,000. Women wear the veil, cannot hold a driving license, play little part in public life, and are effectively barred from work except as teachers and nurses. In 2000, however, Saudi Arabia signed the UN convention on women's rights – provided it did not contradict *sharia* – and in 2004 there were moves toward giving women the vote. The population is young and literate, though expatriates do much of the work.

POPULATION AGE BREAKDOWN

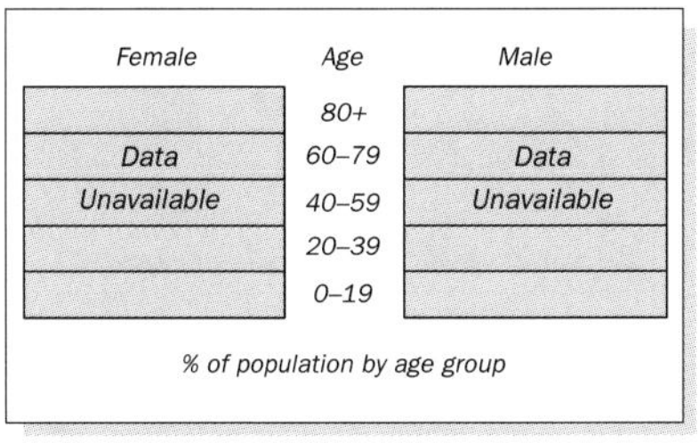
Female
Age
Male
80+
60–79
40–59
20–39
0–19
Data Unavailable
Data Unavailable
% of population by age group

POLITICS

No legislative elections

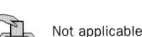

Not applicable

H.M. King Fahd ibn Abd al-Aziz

LEGISLATIVE OR ADVISORY BODIES

Consultative Council 120 seats

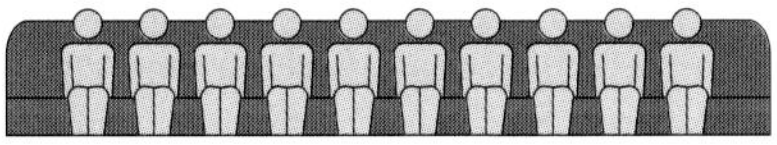

Saudi Arabia is an absolute monarchy. The king rules with the assistance of an appointed Council of Ministers and the Consultative Council

Saudi Arabia is an absolute monarchy. Since 1993 the king has appointed a Consultative Council (Majlis al-Shoura). The Majlis gained powers to initiate legislation in 2003.

PROFILE

The royal family, the House of Sa'ud, rules by manipulating appointments in all sectors of government. Frequent changes of personnel within the armed forces ensure that officers do not build personal followings. All influential cabinet portfolios, apart from those of oil and religious affairs, are held by members of the royal family.

Absolutist rule means that domestic politics is virtually nonexistent. The regime retains feudal elements: at weekly *majalis*, or councils, citizens can present petitions or grievances to leading royals. The first nationwide local elections are to be held in 2005.

The legitimacy of the regime is built on its adherence to Islamic values, and the backing of the *ulema* (scholars). Emphasis on Islam strongly colors Saudi life. The 5000-strong *mutawa* (religious police) enforce the five-times-a-day call to prayer, when businesses must close. During Ramadan the *mutawa* are especially active.

MAIN POLITICAL ISSUES

Questioning the ruling family

Following the 1991 Gulf War, a civil rights campaign challenged the authority of the ruling family, demanding closer adherence to Islamic values. Dissidents objected to the presence of US troops on Saudi territory and the consequent exposure to "corrupt" Western culture. The al-Sa'uds quashed the protest but exiled opponents have continued their activities using faxes and e-mail. The most vociferous denunciations of the royal family come from terrorist mastermind Osama bin Laden, who was formerly a member of the inner circle, operating from bases abroad. Unprecedented public protest in 2003 led to mass arrests.

The succession issue

The question of succession and the possibility of a future power struggle, rooted in rivalries endemic to the House of Sa'ud, emerged in 1996, when King Fahd suffered a stroke. The management of day-to-day affairs passed briefly to his half-brother, Crown Prince Abdullah, who remains in effective control.

WORLD AFFAIRS

Joined UN in 1945

AL | Damasc | GCC | OIC | OPEC

Saudi Arabia's strategic importance is derived from its oil reserves and the presence of the holy sites of Mecca and Medina. Relations with the US, though close, have been frayed by the recent US-led campaigns in Afghanistan and Iraq. After Iraq's invasion of Kuwait in 1990, the kingdom helped to lead the Arab coalition against Iraq, sheltering the Kuwaiti royal family, providing military bases to the Western allies, and supplying more troops than any other Arab state. The continued presence of US training personnel angers Saudi Islamist militants. Most of those who carried out the September 11, 2001, attacks on the US were Saudi, as is al-Qaida leader Osama bin Laden. The US pledged to withdraw troops after the invasion of Iraq, but attacks continued, with suicide bombings of Westerners in Riyadh in 2003 and further attacks in 2004.

A pact signed with Yemen in 2000 ended a simmering border dispute. In 2002 Crown Prince Abdullah's peace plan for Israel/Palestine won praise from Arabs and the West – and hinted at a major change in Saudi policy.

AID

Donor

$2.48bn (donations)

Up 406% in 2002

Generous loans and grants from the Saudi Fund for Development are made to other Arab and developing countries, mainly for infrastructure projects. Saudi Arabia promotes Islam through charitable foundations, especially in Africa, Asia, and the former Soviet Union. The royal purse also supports scientific and medical research. Since the liberation of Kuwait in 1991, Saudi Arabia has given large sums to countries that supported the US-led alliance, notably Egypt, Syria, Morocco, and Turkey. In addition, the Saudi government substantially reimbursed the US and the UK for the cost of their expeditionary forces, as well as favoring companies from the allied countries for reconstruction contracts.

King Fahd ibn Abd al-Aziz *acceded to the Saudi throne in 1982.*

Crown Prince Abdullah, *effectively in control of the country.*

S

CHRONOLOGY

The unification of Saudi Arabia under King Abd al-Aziz (ibn Sa'ud) was achieved in 1932. The kingdom remains the only country in the world which is named after its royal family.

- ❑ **1937** Oil reserves discovered near Riyadh.
- ❑ **1939** Ceremonial start of oil production at Az Zahran.
- ❑ **1953** King Sa'ud succeeds on the death of his father Abd al-Aziz.
- ❑ **1964** King Sa'ud abdicates in favor of his brother Faisal.
- ❑ **1973** Saudi Arabia imposes oil embargo on Western supporters of Israel.
- ❑ **1975** King Faisal assassinated by a deranged nephew; succeeded by his brother Khalid.
- ❑ **1979** Muslim fundamentalists led by Juhaiman ibn Seif al-Otaibi seize Grand Mosque in Mecca, proclaim a *mahdi* (savior) on first day of Islamic year 1400.
- ❑ **1981** Formation of GCC, with its secretariat in Riyadh.
- ❑ **1982** King Fahd succeeds on the death of his brother King Khalid. Promises to create consultative assembly.
- ❑ **1986** Opening of King Fahd Causeway to Bahrain. Shaikh Yamani sacked as oil minister.
- ❑ **1987** Diplomatic relations with Iran deteriorate after 402 people die in riots involving Islamic fundamentalists at Mecca during the *haj* (pilgrimage).
- ❑ **1989** Saudi Arabia signs nonaggression pact with Iraq. Saudi Arabia brokers political settlement to Lebanese civil war.
- ❑ **1990** Kuwaiti royal family seeks sanctuary in Taif after Iraqi invasion. Many allegedly pro-Iraqi Jordanians and Yemenis expelled.
- ❑ **1990–1991** US, UK, French, Egyptian, and Syrian forces assemble in Saudi Arabia for Operation Desert Storm. Public executions are halted.
- ❑ **1991** Iraqis seize border town of Al Khafji, but are repulsed by Saudi, US, and Qatari forces.
- ❑ **1993** King Fahd appoints Consultative Council (Majlis al-Shoura).
- ❑ **1996** King Fahd briefly relinquishes control to Crown Prince Abdullah. Bomb attack at US military complex in Az Zahran kills 19 US citizens.
- ❑ **1997, 2001** Consultative Council expanded, first to 90 then to 120 members.
- ❑ **2002** Crown Prince Abdullah unveils Middle East peace plan; endorsed by AL summit in Beirut.

DEFENSE

No compulsory military service

$21bn

Down 13% in 2002

Saudi Arabia's substantial military contribution to the 1991 Gulf War, at a cost of $55 billion, enhanced its image as a major regional power. Military equipment is purchased mostly from the US, the UK, France, and Canada. Weapons systems are advanced and include Patriot missiles and AWACS early warning radar. US personnel provide training, but the thousands of US combat troops once stationed in Saudi Arabia were deployed elsewhere in mid-2003.

The air force is the elite branch of the military. It had one brief period of politicization in 1969 when officers attempted a coup. The paramilitary National Guard is drawn from tribal supporters of the al-Sa'ud regime. Its commander-in-chief is the crown prince rather than the defense minister.

SAUDI ARABIAN ARMED FORCES

1055 main battle tanks (315 M-1A2 Abrams, 290 AMX-30, 450 M60A3)	75,000 personnel
4 frigates, 4 corvettes, and 26 patrol boats	15,500 personnel
294 combat aircraft (29 F-5, 158 F-15, 85 Tornado IDS, 22 Tornado ADV)	16,000 personnel
None	

ECONOMICS

Inflation 3.7% p.a. (1990–2001)

$187bn

3.7503 Saudi riyals (3.7502)

SCORE CARD

- ❑ World GNP Ranking 22nd
- ❑ GNP per Capita $8530
- ❑ Balance of Payments...................$11.7bn
- ❑ Inflation ....–0.5%
- ❑ Unemployment................................25%

EXPORTS

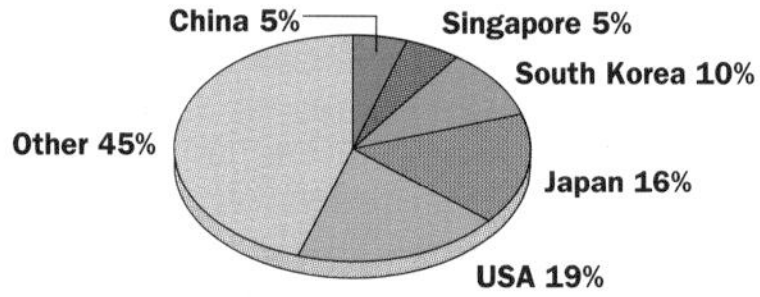
China 5%
Singapore 5%
South Korea 10%
Other 45%
Japan 16%
USA 19%

IMPORTS

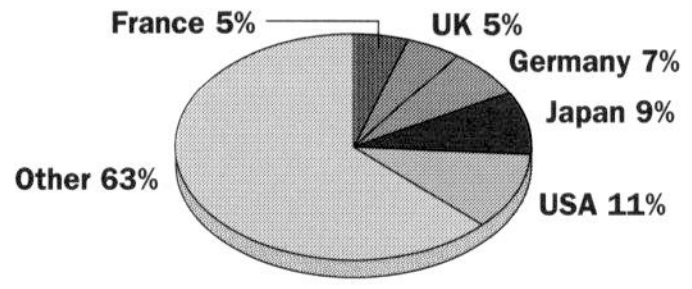
France 5%
UK 5%
Germany 7%
Japan 9%
Other 63%
USA 11%

Strengths

Vast oil and gas reserves. World-class associated industries. Accumulated surpluses and steady current income. Large earnings from pilgrims to Mecca. Influence in Muslim world.

Weaknesses

Heavily subsidized food production. Most consumer items and industrial raw materials imported. High youth unemployment. Large national debt. National wealth concentrated within royal family. Dependence on foreign workers, who fear terror attacks.

Profile

Great efforts have been made to reduce dependence on oil exports and to provide employment for young Saudis as opposed to foreign workers, with limited success so far. Saudi Arabia aims to control oil prices through OPEC in an effort to buoy up industrialized countries while dampening demand for alternative energy. In 2004 it boosted production in an attempt to lower global oil prices. Approved foreigners have been allowed complete ownership of Saudi businesses and rights to property since 2000. Large sums have been spent on creating an infrastructure for a manufacturing economy. A drive for privatization was announced in 2002.

ECONOMIC PERFORMANCE INDICATOR

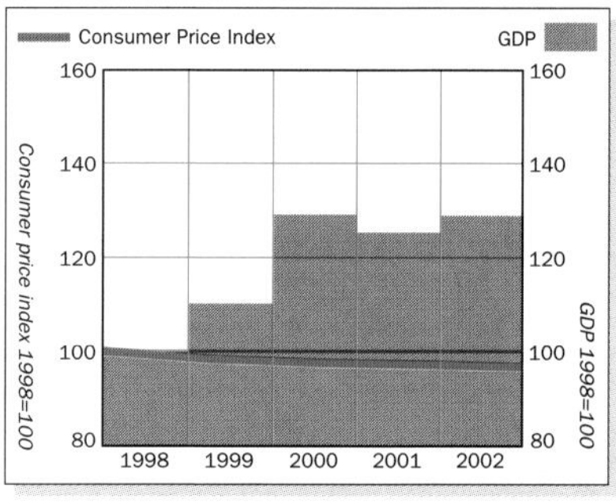
Consumer Price Index
GDP
Consumer price index 1998=100
GDP 1998=100
160
140
120
100
80
1998
1999
2000
2001
2002

SAUDI ARABIA : MAJOR BUSINESSES

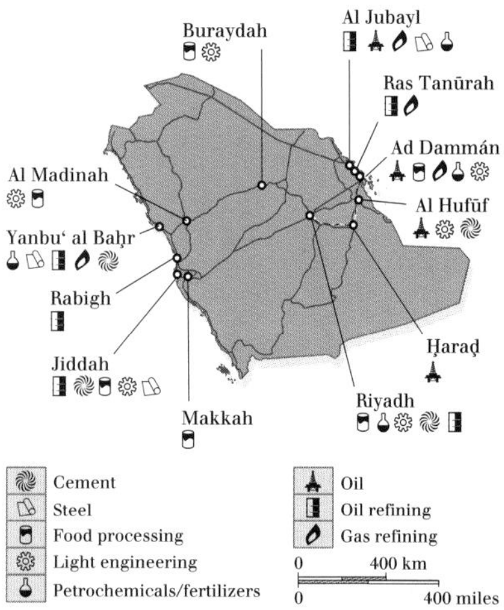
Buraydah
Al Jubayl
Ras Tanūrah
Ad Dammān
Al Madinah
Al Hufūf
Yanbu' al Baḩr
Rabigh
Jiddah
Ḩaraḑ
Riyadh
Makkah
Cement
Steel
Food processing
Light engineering
Petrochemicals/fertilizers
Oil
Oil refining
Gas refining
0
400 km
0
400 miles

RESOURCES

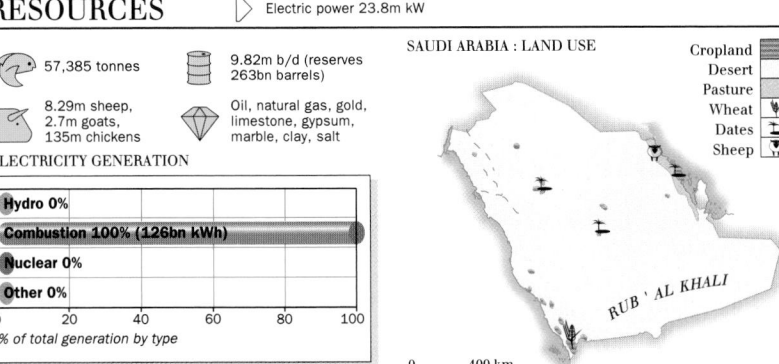

Electric power 23.8m kW

57,385 tonnes

9.82m b/d (reserves 263bn barrels)

8.29m sheep, 2.7m goats, 135m chickens

Oil, natural gas, gold, limestone, gypsum, marble, clay, salt

ELECTRICITY GENERATION

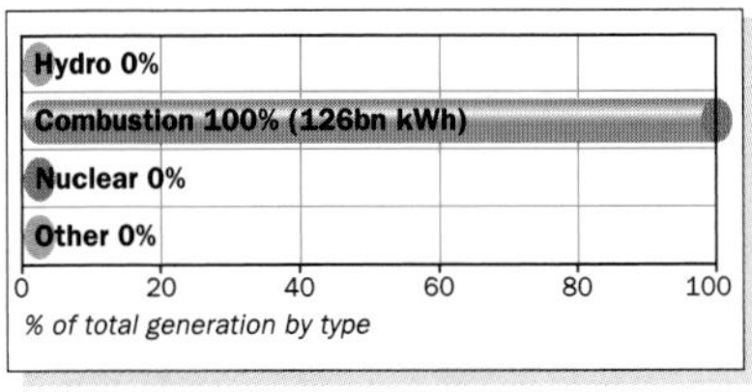
Hydro 0%
Combustion 100% (126bn kWh)
Nuclear 0%
Other 0%
0
20
40
60
80
100
% of total generation by type

SAUDI ARABIA : LAND USE

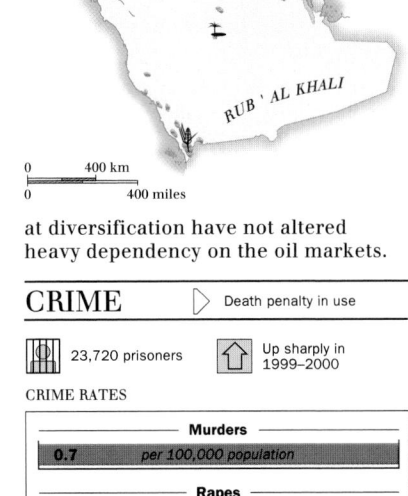

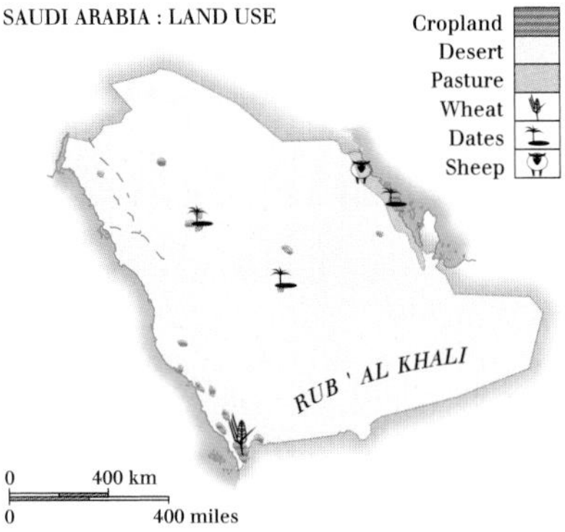
Cropland
Desert
Pasture
Wheat
Dates
Sheep
RUB ' AL KHALI
0
400 km
0
400 miles

With the world's biggest oil reserves and sizable gas deposits, Saudi Arabia has a key role in the global economy. Attempts at diversification have not altered heavy dependency on the oil markets.

HEALTH

Welfare state health benefits

1 per 588 people

Diarrheal, respiratory, heart, metabolic, and parasitic diseases

Infant mortality has dropped and endemic disease has been nearly eradicted. Health care outside major centers such as Riyadh and Jiddah still remains relatively undeveloped, given Saudi Arabia's huge economic resources. However, large sums have been spent on employing Western expertise. Many Saudis are still sent overseas by the government for treatment, especially for transplant operations, which pose some ethical problems for religious leaders. The private sector has also been encouraged.

ENVIRONMENT

Sustainability rank: 138th

38% (33% partially protected)

18.1 tonnes per capita

ENVIRONMENTAL TREATIES

No	Yes	Yes
Yes	Yes	No

Pollution in the Gulf and Red Sea has threatened some wildlife and their habitats, as have hunters using high-velocity rifles and off-road vehicles. The government has taken steps to confine manufacturing to industrial estates. Environmental legislation is, nevertheless, poorly developed, though planning controls apply in the major cities.

CRIME

Death penalty in use

23,720 prisoners

Up sharply in 1999–2000

CRIME RATES

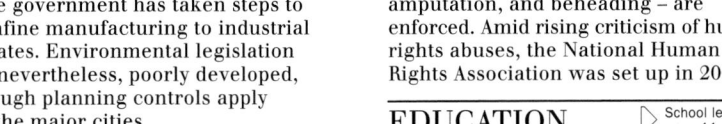

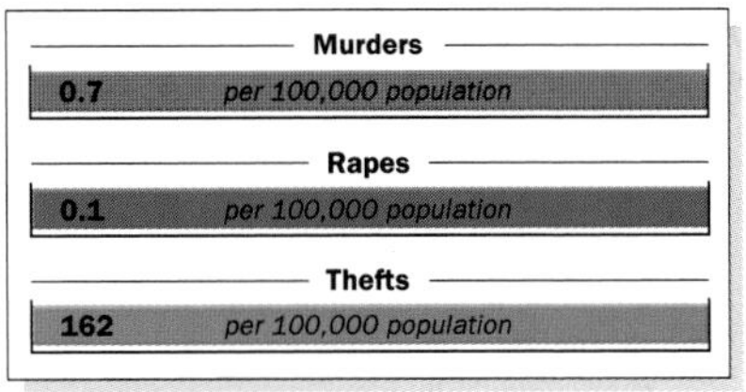
Murders
0.7
per 100,000 population
Rapes
0.1
per 100,000 population
Thefts
162
per 100,000 population

Strict Islamic punishments – stoning, amputation, and beheading – are enforced. Amid rising criticism of human rights abuses, the National Human Rights Association was set up in 2004.

SPENDING

GDP/cap. increase

CONSUMPTION AND SPENDING

339 per 1000 population

144 per 1000 population

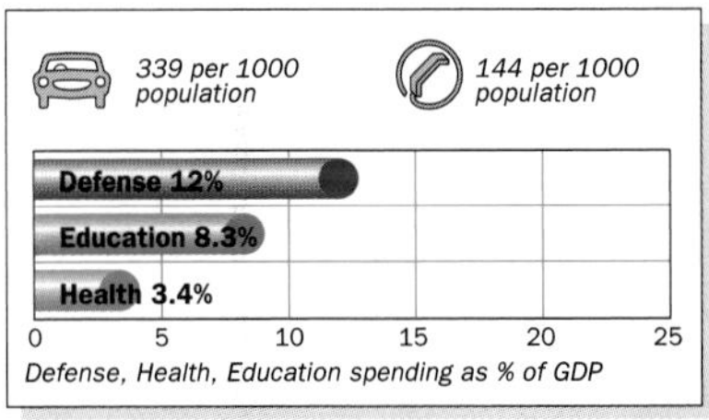
Defense 12%
Education 8.3%
Health 3.4%
0
5
10
15
20
25
Defense, Health, Education spending as % of GDP

Members of the Saudi elite are among the most wealthy people in the world. Non-Saudi citizens, especially guest workers from the Indian subcontinent and the Philippines, are much poorer. The al-Sa'uds have used their wealth to create a cradle-to-grave welfare system. Ownership of telephones, TVs, VCRs, and other consumer goods is high. The distribution of wealth is carefully controlled by the royal family through the *majlis* system. There is no stock market, though shares in public companies are traded privately. Many Saudis refuse for religious reasons to accept interest on deposits with banks, but Islamic banks offer profit-sharing investment schemes as an alternative.

MEDIA

TV ownership medium

Daily newspaper circulation 326 per 1000 people

PUBLISHING AND BROADCAST MEDIA

There are 10 daily newspapers, in Arabic and English. The leading papers are *Ar-Riyadh*, *Al-Watan*, and *Arab News*

2 state-owned services

2 services: 1 state-owned, 1 owned by a private oil company

The government imposes total press censorship and insists on strict morality. In 1994, private citizens were banned from owning satellite dishes, but the authorities turn a blind eye to their use. No allowance is made for Arab satellite broadcasts, which have been criticized for covering anti-Islamic views. The international *Asharq Al-Awsat* is a leading Arabic daily. In 2001 the government announced strict rules regarding references to the state and religion on the Internet.

EDUCATION

School leaving age: 11

78%

404,094 students

THE EDUCATION SYSTEM

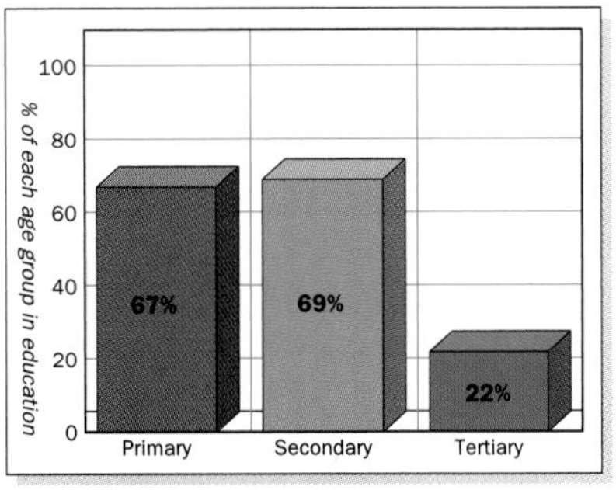
100
80
60
40
20
0
% of each age group in education
67%
69%
22%
Primary
Secondary
Tertiary

The growing number of Western-educated Saudis has intensified pressure for social and political change. In the 1950s, the religious establishment was persuaded to give women equal opportunities in education. Analysts have criticized universities for turning out many graduates in Islamic theology, but not enough engineers and technocrats; a high percentage of graduates struggle to find work.

WORLD RANKING

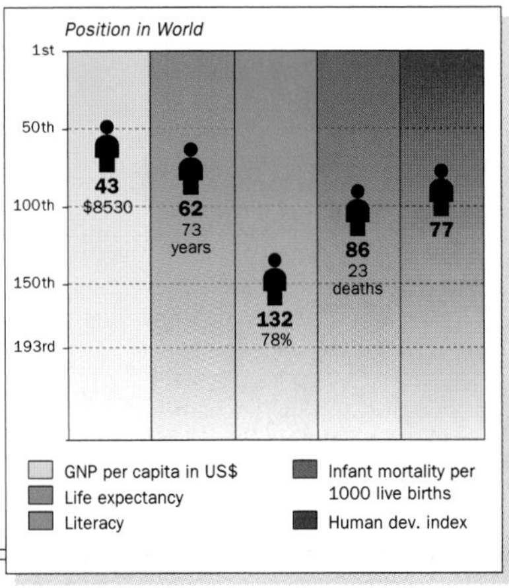
Position in World
1st
50th
100th
150th
193rd
43
$8530
62
73 years
132
78%
86
23 deaths
77
GNP per capita in US$
Life expectancy
Literacy
Infant mortality per 1000 live births
Human dev. index

S

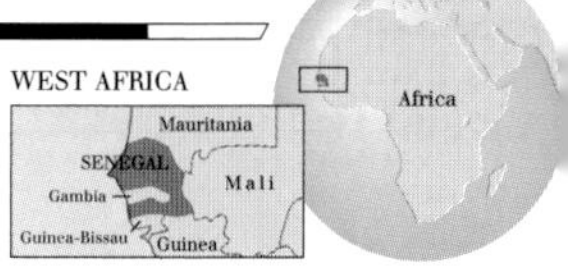

WEST AFRICA
Africa
Mauritania
SENEGAL
Mali
Gambia
Guinea-Bissau
Guinea

SENEGAL

OFFICIAL NAME: Republic of Senegal **CAPITAL:** Dakar
POPULATION: 10.1 million **CURRENCY:** CFA franc **OFFICIAL LANGUAGE:** French

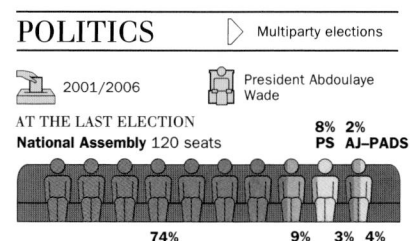

1960 | 1960 | April 4 | SN | 0 | +221 | .sn

SENEGAL'S CAPITAL, Dakar, lies on the westernmost cape of Africa. The country is mostly low-lying, with open savanna and semidesert in the north and thicker savanna in the south. After independence from France in 1960, Senegal was ruled until 1981 by President Léopold Senghor. He was succeeded by his prime minister, Abdou Diouf, who held power for almost 20 years until his election defeat in 2000.

CLIMATE

Steppe/tropical

WEATHER CHART FOR DAKAR

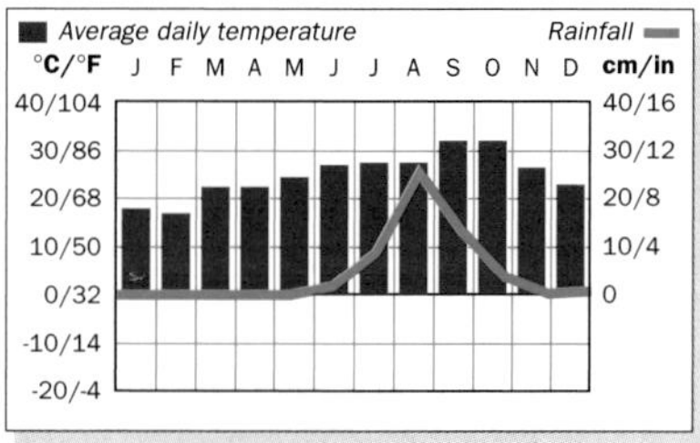

Average daily temperature
Rainfall
°C/°F J F M A M J J A S O N D cm/in
40/104
30/86
20/68
10/50
0/32
-10/14
-20/-4
40/16
30/12
20/8
10/4
0

The coastal regions, which project into the path of the northern trade winds, are remarkably cool given their latitude.

TRANSPORTATION

Drive on right

Leopold Sedar Senghor, Dakar
1.26m passengers

190 ships
46,600 grt

THE TRANSPORTATION NETWORK

4227 km (2627 miles)
7 km (4 miles)
906 km (563 miles)
897 km (557 miles)

Dakar is a major west African port. The rail link to Mali was built in the 1920s. The 2002 *Joola* ferry disaster highlighted the overloading of the navy-run service between Ziguinchor and Dakar.

TOURISM

Visitors : Population 1:24

427,000 visitors

Up 10% in 2001–2002

MAIN TOURIST ARRIVALS

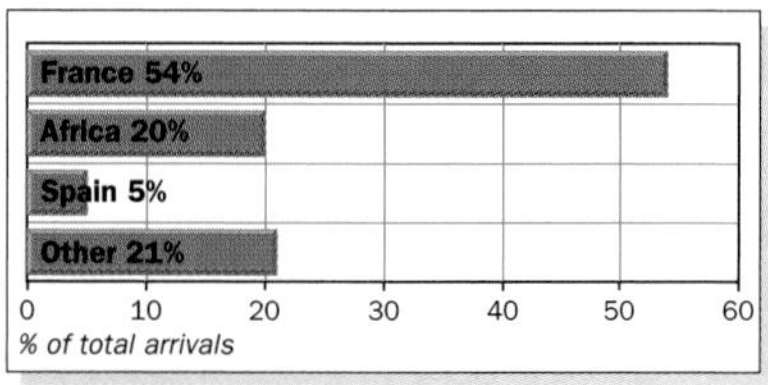

France 54%
Africa 20%
Spain 5%
Other 21%
0 10 20 30 40 50 60
% of total arrivals

In addition to French package tours to coastal resorts, tours for African-Americans to Gorée, a former slave island, are increasingly popular.

PEOPLE

Pop. density medium

Wolof, Pulaar, Serer, Diola, Mandinka, Malinke, Soninke, French

52/km² (136/mi²)

THE URBAN/RURAL POPULATION SPLIT

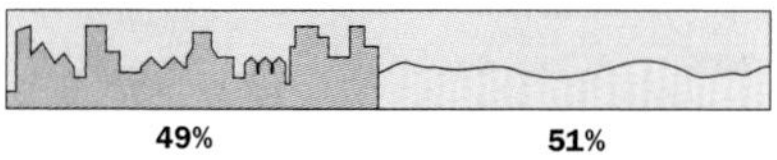

49%
51%

RELIGIOUS PERSUASION

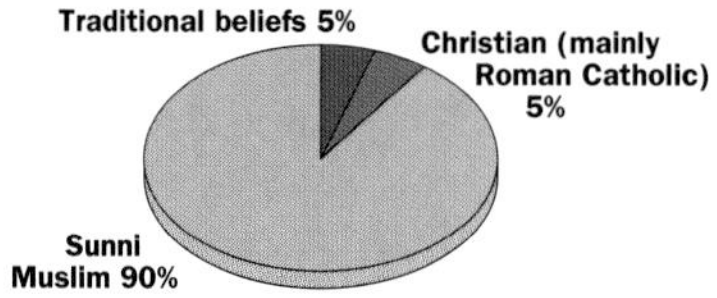

Traditional beliefs 5%
Christian (mainly Roman Catholic) 5%
Sunni Muslim 90%

National identity is fairly well developed, and intermarriage has reduced ethnic tensions. Groups can still be identified regionally, however. Dakar is a Wolof area, the Senegal River is dominated by the Toucouleur, the Malinke mostly live in the east, and the Diola (Jola) in Casamance, where the feeling of the Diola that they are excluded from politics has led to a long-running rebellion. A large Senegalese diaspora has increased global awareness of the country's culture, particularly its music. The 2001 constitution gave women property rights for the first time.

POLITICS

Multiparty elections

2001/2006

President Abdoulaye Wade

AT THE LAST ELECTION

National Assembly 120 seats

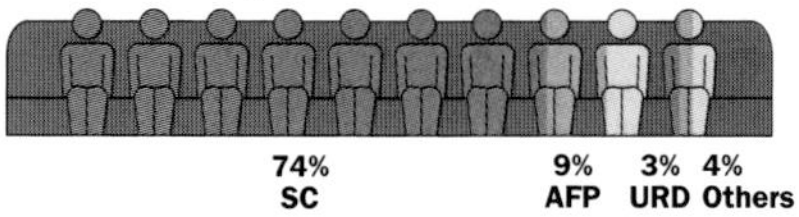

8% PS
2% AJ–PADS
74% SC
9% AFP
3% URD
4% Others

SC = Sopi (Change) coalition (led by the Senegalese Democratic Party – **PDS**) **AFP** = Alliance of Progressive Forces **PS** = Senegalese Socialist Party **URD** = Union for Democratic Renewal **AJ–PADS** = And Jëf – African Party for Democracy and Socialism

Senegal has been a multiparty democracy since 1981, when, under the then new president Abdou Diouf, the constitution was amended to allow more than four political parties. However, the PS held power from the 1950s until 2000, and its influence has been pervasive. Presidential elections in 2000 marked a political watershed. Diouf was defeated by Abdoulaye Wade of the liberal democratic PDS, the dominant party in the "Sopi" (Change) coalition which went on to win a landslide victory in the 2001 legislative elections.

A new constitution, approved in 2001 by referendum, abolished the Senate and restricts the president to two terms.

WORLD AFFAIRS

Joined UN in 1960

CILSS | ECOWAS | FZ | OIC | OMVG

Preserving good relations with France, Senegal's main ally and aid donor, is the most important foreign affairs concern. Senegal maintains cordial relations with neighbors including Gambia and Guinea-Bissau, and hosts some 20,000 mostly integrated Mauritanian refugees.

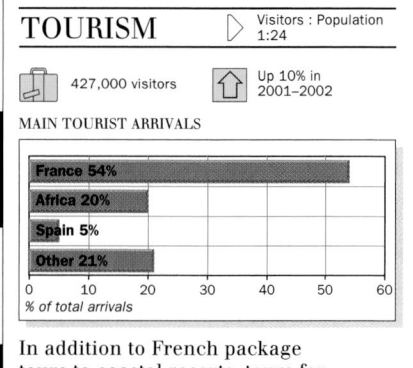

S

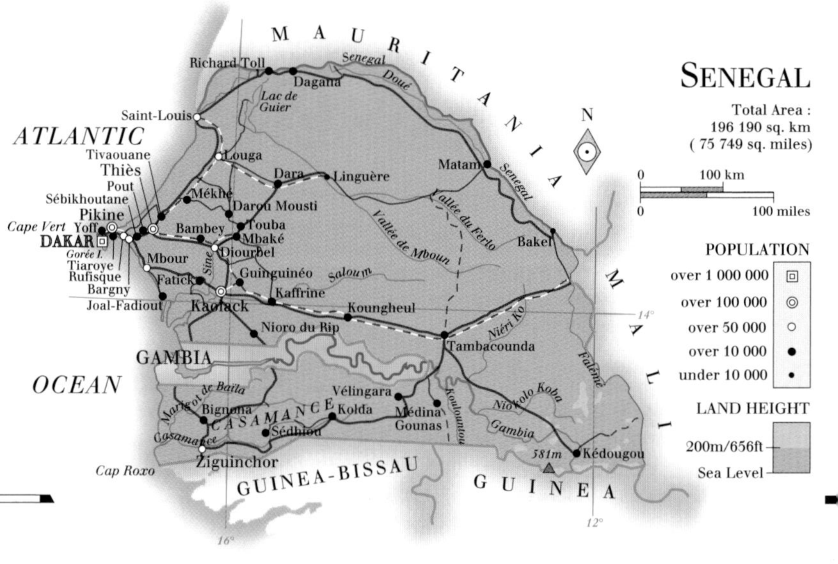

MAURITANIA
MALI
GUINEA
GUINEA-BISSAU
GAMBIA
ATLANTIC
OCEAN
CASAMANCE
Richard Toll
Dagana
Senegal
Doué
Lac de Guier
Saint-Louis
Louga
Tivaouane
Thiès
Pout
Sébikhoutane
Pikine
Cape Vert
Yoff
DAKAR
Gorée I.
Tiaroye
Rufisque
Bargny
Joal-Fadiout
Mékhé
Dara
Linguère
Darou Mousti
Bambey
Touba
Mbaké
Diourbel
Mbour
Fatick
Sine
Guinguinéo
Saloum
Kaffrine
Kaolack
Koungheul
Nioro du Rip
Vallée de Mboun
Vallée du Ferlo
Matam
Bakel
Tambacounda
Niéri Ko
Falémé
Koulountou
Niokolo Koba
Gambia
Vélingara
Kolda
Médina Gounas
Sédhiou
Bignona
Marigot de Baïla
Ziguinchor
Cap Roxo
581m
Kédougou
14°
12°
16°
N
SENEGAL
Total Area : 196 190 sq. km (75 749 sq. miles)
0 100 km
0 100 miles
POPULATION
over 1 000 000
over 100 000
over 50 000
over 10 000
under 10 000
LAND HEIGHT
200m/656ft
Sea Level

AID

Recipient

$449m (receipts) — Up 9% in 2002

Senegal is one of the highest recipients of aid per capita in Africa, mostly from France, the World Bank, and Japan. Aid is used to import 400,000 tonnes of rice annually, but also helps finance a sizable civil service, now being cut back. The IMF approved a three-year, $33 million poverty reduction and growth facility program in April 2003 to support economic reform.

***The mosque in Touba**, religious capital of the Muslim Mouride sect, which was founded in 1887 in Senegal's groundnut-growing district.*

CHRONOLOGY

Senegal, a major entrepôt from the 15th century, was colonized by France in 1890. Dakar was the capital of French West Africa.

- ❑ **1885** Gambia split off from Senegal.
- ❑ **1960** Independence under Senghor.
- ❑ **1966–1976** One-party state.
- ❑ **1981** Full multipartyism restored.
- ❑ **2000** Presidency won by Abdoulaye Wade in first ever defeat for PS.
- ❑ **2001** New constitution.
- ❑ **2002** 1800 die in ferry disaster.

DEFENSE

Compulsory military service

$65m — Down 6% in 2002

France maintains an important naval base at Dakar. The armed forces total 13,620, plus a paramilitary force of 5000, but the military has never intervened in politics. Senegalese troops took part in Operation Desert Storm in 1991, and intervened in conflicts in Liberia, Rwanda, and the Central African Republic. They also helped to quell revolts in Gambia and Guinea-Bissau.

ECONOMICS

Inflation 4.2% p.a. (1990–2001)

$4.6bn — 539.2 CFA francs (571.2)

SCORE CARD

- ❑ WORLD GNP RANKING........................117th
- ❑ GNP PER CAPITA $470
- ❑ BALANCE OF PAYMENTS....................–$478m
- ❑ INFLATION 2.2%
- ❑ UNEMPLOYMENT.................................48%

STRENGTHS

Good infrastructure. Relatively strong industrial sector. Agricultural boom. Revenue from sale of fishing rights. Dakar port an important west African entrepôt. Tourism potential.

WEAKNESSES

Many natural resources underexploited.

EXPORTS

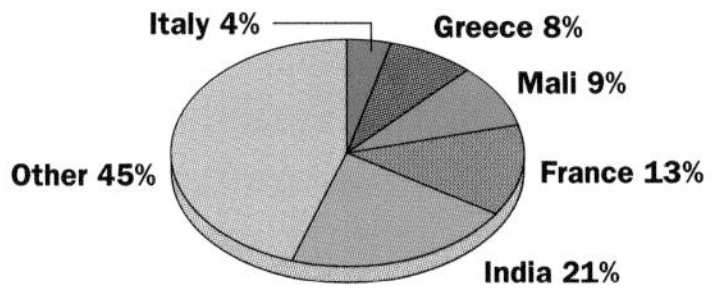
Italy 4%
Greece 8%
Mali 9%
France 13%
India 21%
Other 45%

IMPORTS

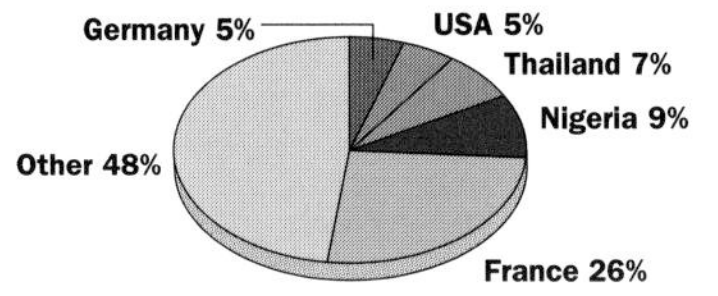
Germany 5%
USA 5%
Thailand 7%
Nigeria 9%
France 26%
Other 48%

Access to oil potential of Casamance region hampered by rebellion and poor transportation links.

EDUCATION

School leaving age: 12

39% — 29,303 students

Illiteracy is Senegal's major educational challenge. There are universities at Dakar and St.-Louis.

HEALTH

No welfare state health benefits

1 per 10,000 people — Malaria, diarrheal diseases

The state health system is rudimentary. A successful education campaign helps to contain the incidence of HIV/AIDS.

SPENDING

GDP/cap. increase

CONSUMPTION AND SPENDING

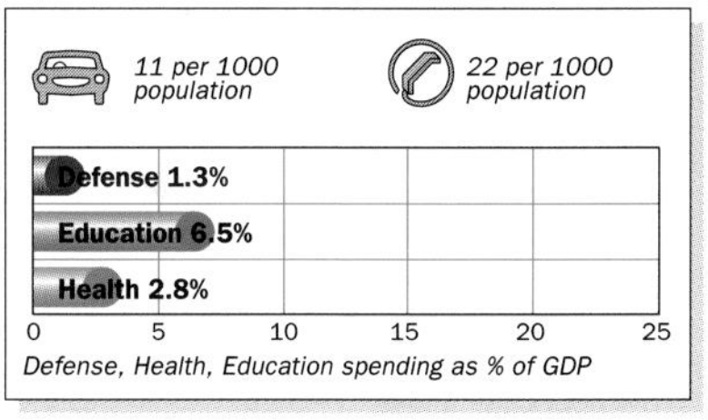
11 per 1000 population
22 per 1000 population
Defense 1.3%
Education 6.5%
Health 2.8%
0
5
10
15
20
25
Defense, Health, Education spending as % of GDP

Wealth disparities are considerable in Senegal, and poverty is widespread. Members of the former ruling PS are the wealthiest group.

RESOURCES

Electric power 237,000 kW

405,560 tonnes — Oil reserves not yet exploited; refines 19,900 b/d

4.61m sheep, 3.97m goats, 45m chickens — Phosphates, bauxite, salt, natural gas, oil, marble, iron, copper

Senegal's electricity capacity is largely dependent on imported fuel; cheaper supplies are expected to become available soon from the Manantali Dam in Mali. Initial explorations suggest that oil reserves may exist off Casamance.

ENVIRONMENT

Sustainability rank: 81st

12% (6% partially protected) — 0.4 tonnes per capita

Senegal, under pressure from neighboring Mauritania, abandoned plans to build a controversial dam on the Senegal River in 2000. The scheme caused concern that traditional farming practices, which rely on seasonal floods, might be disrupted.

MEDIA

TV ownership medium

Daily newspaper circulation 5 per 1000 people

PUBLISHING AND BROADCAST MEDIA

There are 16 daily newspapers, including *Le Soleil, Wal Fadjiri,* and *Sud Quotidien*

3 services: 1 state-owned, 2 independent — 8 services: 1 state-owned, 7 independent

The independent media flourished with multipartyism. Senegal had the first satirical journal in Africa with the founding of *Le Politicien* in 1978.

CRIME

Death penalty not used in practice

5360 prisoners — Up 21% in 2000–2001

Crime rates are low in rural areas of Senegal, but Dakar and its surrounding shanty towns have become notorious for gang-related crime.

WORLD RANKING

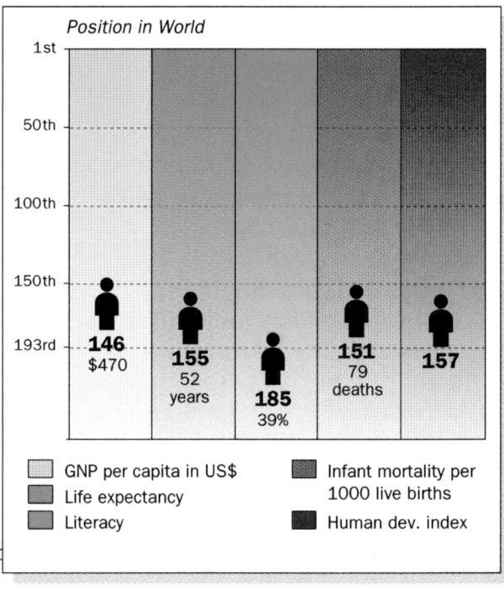
Position in World
1st
50th
100th
150th
193rd
146
$470
155
52 years
185
39%
151
79 deaths
157
GNP per capita in US$
Life expectancy
Literacy
Infant mortality per 1000 live births
Human dev. index

S

SERBIA & MONTENEGRO

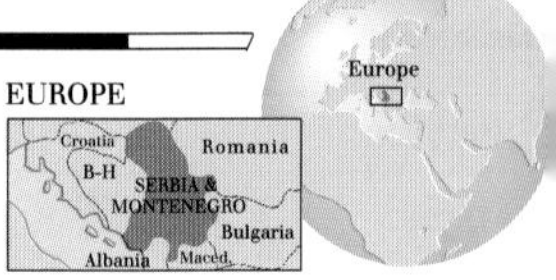
EUROPE
Europe
Croatia
B-H
Romania
SERBIA & MONTENEGRO
Bulgaria
Albania
Maced.

OFFICIAL NAME: Serbia and Montenegro **CAPITAL:** Belgrade **POPULATION:** 10.5 million
CURRENCY: Dinar (Serbia); euro (Montenegro) **OFFICIAL LANGUAGE:** Serbo-Croat

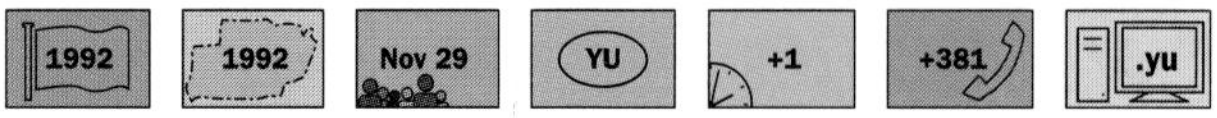
1992
1992
Nov 29
YU
+1
+381
.yu

ADOPTING A NEW CONSTITUTION in 2003, Serbia and Montenegro redefined their relationship after their emergence from the wreckage of Yugoslavia. Aid is vital to the recovery of the economy after years of isolation. Serbia, forming the bulk of the country, has a troubled history as a would-be regional power. The machinations of former leader Slobodan Milosevic hastened the end of the former Yugoslavia and precipitated bloody conflicts in 1991–1995 and 1999. Montenegro, the "black mountain" republic, has few resources save for its access to the Adriatic, but is keen to pursue its dream of independence.

CLIMATE

Continental

WEATHER CHART FOR BELGRADE

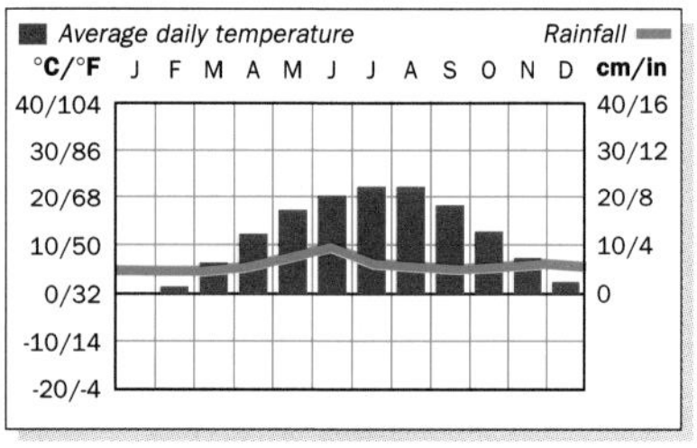
Average daily temperature
Rainfall
°C/°F
J F M A M J J A S O N D
cm/in
40/104
30/86
20/68
10/50
0/32
-10/14
-20/-4
40/16
30/12
20/8
10/4
0

There are three climate zones. The northern plains are characteristically continental: rainy springs, warm summers, and cold winters. While the southern highlands have colder winters with heavy snowfalls, the Adriatic coast boasts hot summers and milder winters.

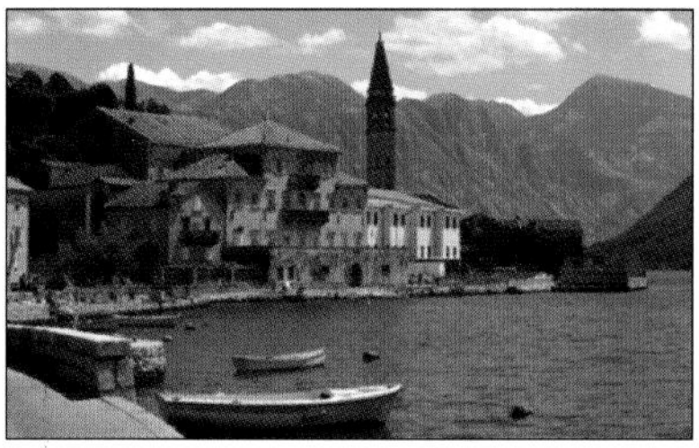

Montenegro's stunning scenery *is a potential draw for tourists.*

TOURISM

Visitors : Population 1:23

448,000 visitors

Up 28% in 2002

MAIN TOURIST ARRIVALS

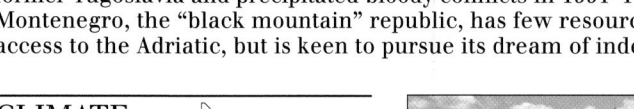

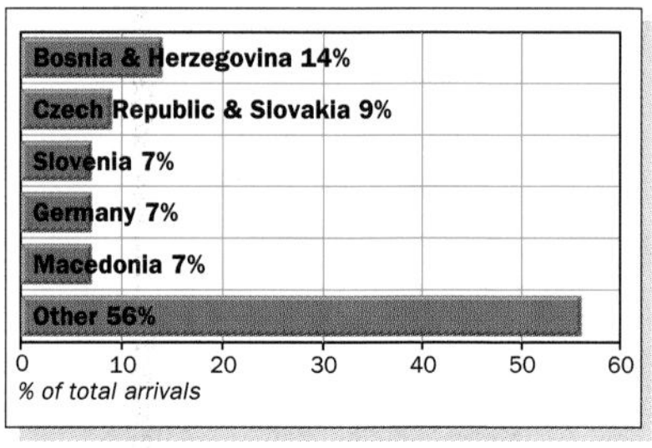
Bosnia & Herzegovina 14%
Czech Republic & Slovakia 9%
Slovenia 7%
Germany 7%
Macedonia 7%
Other 56%
0
10
20
30
40
50
60
% of total arrivals

Instability, the impact of UN sanctions, and the Kosovo conflict meant that foreign tourism ceased in the 1990s. Serbia has never been a center for tourism, whereas the Montenegrin coast has renowned beaches. In the 1990s they were monopolized by Serbians, particularly by political and criminal elements of the Serbian elite. Hyperinflation and recession kept the average vacationer away.

TRANSPORTATION

Drive on right

Surcin, Belgrade 1.86m passengers

6 ships 4800 grt

THE TRANSPORTATION NETWORK

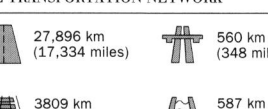

27,896 km (17,334 miles)

560 km (348 miles)

3809 km (2367 miles)

587 km (365 miles)

About one-third of railroads are electrified. The rail link to Greece via Macedonia is one of Serbia's main trading routes, and lines through Serbia remain the best link between Budapest and Sofia. For internal travel, trains are cheaper, but slower, than buses. Several daily flights link Belgrade with the airports in Montenegro.

Bridges and railroads were specifically targeted during the NATO bombing in 1999. The bombing of bridges over the Danube at Novi Sad closed the river as a major regional trading artery; with much international assistance it was finally cleared of debris in 2003, but traffic is unlikely to return to former levels.

SERBIA & MONTENEGRO (YUGOSLAVIA)

Total Area : 102 350 sq. km (39 517 sq. miles)

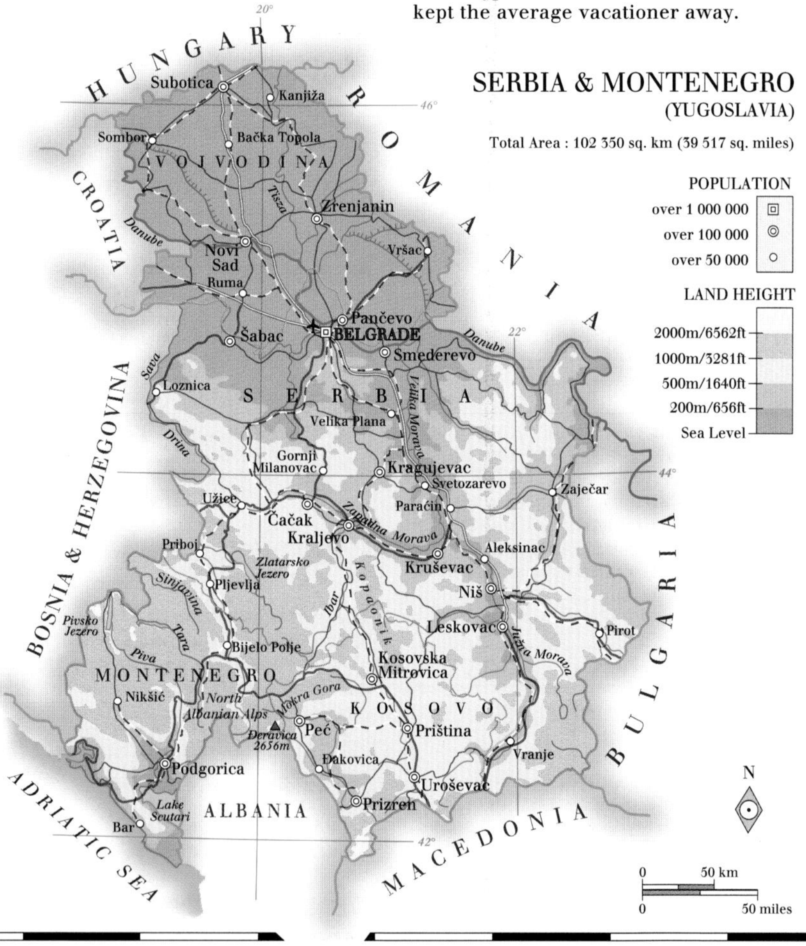
POPULATION
over 1 000 000
over 100 000
over 50 000
LAND HEIGHT
2000m/6562ft
1000m/3281ft
500m/1640ft
200m/656ft
Sea Level
HUNGARY
ROMANIA
CROATIA
BOSNIA & HERZEGOVINA
BULGARIA
MACEDONIA
ALBANIA
ADRIATIC SEA
VOJVODINA
SERBIA
MONTENEGRO
KOSOVO
Subotica
Kanjiža
Sombor
Bačka Topola
Zrenjanin
Novi Sad
Ruma
Vršac
Pančevo
BELGRADE
Šabac
Smederevo
Loznica
Velika Plana
Gornji Milanovac
Kragujevac
Svetozarevo
Zaječar
Užice
Čačak
Kraljevo
Paraćin
Priboj
Aleksinac
Kruševac
Pljevlja
Niš
Leskovac
Pirot
Bijelo Polje
Kosovska Mitrovica
Nikšić
Peć
Priština
Đakovica
Podgorica
Vranje
Uroševac
Prizren
Bar
Danube
Tisza
Sava
Drina
Velika Morava
Zapadna Morava
Južna Morava
Ibar
Tara
Piva
Sinjajevina
Zlatarsko Jezero
Pivsko Jezero
Kopaonik
North Albanian Alps
Mokra Gora
Deravica 2656m
Lake Scutari
20°
22°
46°
44°
42°
N
0 50 km
0 50 miles

PEOPLE

Pop. density medium

Serbo-Croat, Albanian, Hungarian (Magyar)

103/km² (266/mi²)

THE URBAN/RURAL POPULATION SPLIT

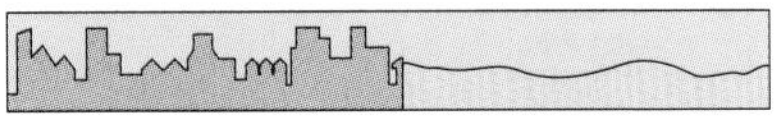
52%
48%

RELIGIOUS PERSUASION

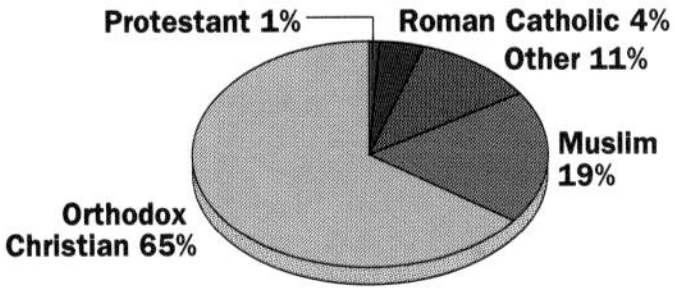
Protestant 1%
Roman Catholic 4%
Other 11%
Muslim 19%
Orthodox Christian 65%

ETHNIC MAKEUP

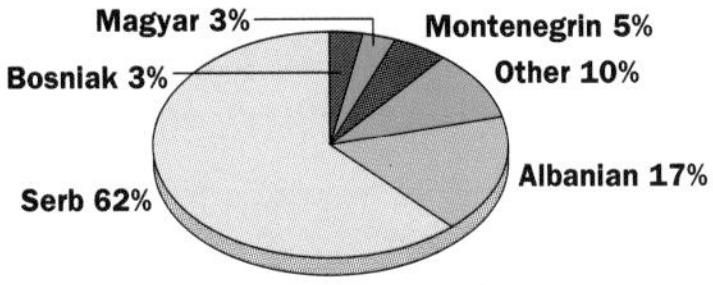
Magyar 3%
Montenegrin 5%
Bosniak 3%
Other 10%
Albanian 17%
Serb 62%

Society was severely shaken in the 1990s by the conflict following the collapse of Socialist Yugoslavia. The wars were fueled by ethnic divisions: while Serbs and Montenegrins share a language and a common religion (Orthodox Christianity), the mostly Muslim Kosovan Albanians have a different culture and heritage. Attempts by Milosevic to suppress Kosovan calls for autonomy directly prompted the 1999 NATO bombing; large migrations of refugees occurred. Albanian nationalism there has alienated the province's dwindling minority Serb population. The Magyar (Hungarian) minority, mainly Roman Catholic, is concentrated in the relatively prosperous northern province of Vojvodina. Limited autonomy was restored in 2002, after economically motivated pressure from within the region. The Muslim Bosniak population has renewed calls for autonomy for their communities in the Sandzak region (shared by Serbia and Montenegro).

POPULATION AGE BREAKDOWN

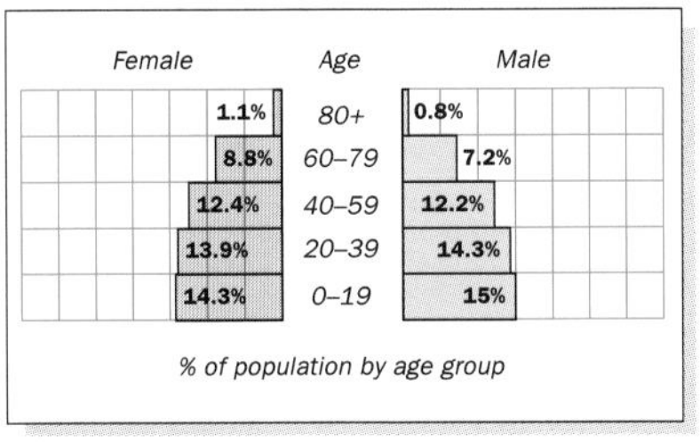
Female
Age
Male
1.1%
80+
0.8%
8.8%
60–79
7.2%
12.4%
40–59
12.2%
13.9%
20–39
14.3%
14.3%
0–19
15%
% of population by age group

POLITICS

Multiparty elections

2003/2005

President Svetozar Marovic

AT THE LAST ELECTION

Assembly of Serbia and Montenegro 126 seats

6%
SPO–NS
24% SRS
16% DSS
15% DLECG
11% ZZP
10% DS
10% G17+
6% SPS
2% Others

SRS = Serbian Radical Party **DSS** = Democratic Party of Serbia **DLECG** = Democratic List for European Montenegro (led by the Democratic Party of Socialists–**DPS**) **ZZP** = Together for Changes (led by the Socialist People's Party–**SNP**) **DS** = Democratic Party **G17+** = G 17 Plus **SPS** = Socialist Party of Serbia **SPO–NS** = Serbian Renewal Movement – New Serbia

Serbia and Montenegro agreed to a new confederal union in 2003. The separate republican governments maintain real power with control over domestic policy, while a small confederal authority governs overall foreign affairs and defense. Both republics will have the option for independence in 2006.

PROFILE

The overthrow in 2000 of Serbian nationalist Slobodan Milosevic marked the transition to full democracy. The Democratic Opposition headed by Zoran Djindjic was swept to power in Serbia and Vojislav Kostunica was elected federal president, but relations between the two soon soured. The Montenegrin government, headed by Milo Djukanovic of the DPS, meanwhile distanced itself from Serbia as much as possible. The public remains disillusioned by high-level corruption and the nonappearance of the promised economic recovery.

In Serbia, the assassination of Djindjic in 2003 prompted a crackdown on corruption and organized crime. By year's end, however, the public had seen few real results: electoral victory went to nationalists. Kostunica returned to power as Serbian prime minister in 2004.

MAIN POLITICAL ISSUE
Kosovo

The withdrawal from Kosovo of the Yugoslav (effectively Serbian) army ended the NATO bombing of Serbia in 1999, and the region came under UN administration. A separate Kosovo assembly was elected in 2001. The ethnic Albanian majority awaits a promised referendum on its future, but local Serbs are wary of Albanian calls for independence. Unresolved tensions flared into violent clashes in 2004.

Milo Djukanovic *hopes to lead Montenegro to independence.*

Vojislav Kostunica, *the last president of Yugoslavia and Serb premier from 2004.*

WORLD AFFAIRS

Joined UN in 1945

CE | CEI | IAEA | IBRD | OSCE

In 1995, mutual recognition among the countries which had constituted the Socialist Federal Republic of Yugoslavia paved the way for the normalization of relations.

The pariah status of the Milosevic regime in the late 1990s was underlined by his indictment by the International Criminal Tribunal for the former Yugoslavia (ICTY) in 1999 and the military action by NATO forces over "ethnic cleansing" in Kosovo. Russia, long an ally of Serbia, shares its Orthodox Christianity and its Slavic ethnicity, and strongly opposed the NATO military action, but backed the settlement proposals required to end it. The inauguration of the new democratic government was welcomed enthusiastically by the West and Russia, and the new regime was quickly invited to take the vacant seat in the UN. The electoral victory three years later of the far right in Serbia, however, spells trouble for future relations.

AID

Recipient

$1.93bn (receipts)

Up 48% in 2002

Milosevic's removal was an explicit condition of large-scale Western aid, urgently needed to rebuild the damaged economy. The country rejoined the World Bank in May 2001 and received pledges of $1.3 billion in aid immediately on the extradition of Milosevic.

CHRONOLOGY

The Serbs were defeated by the Turks at the Battle of Kosovo in 1389. Parts of the region were later ruled by the Austro-Hungarian Empire.

- **1878** Independence gained by Serbia and Montenegro at Congress of Berlin.
- **1918** Joint Kingdom of Serbs, Croats, and Slovenes created.
- **1929** King Alexander of Serbia assumes absolute powers over state, which changes name to Yugoslavia.
- **1941** Germans launch surprise attack. Rival resistance groups: Chetniks (Serb royalist) and Partisans (communist, under Tito).
- **1945** Federal People's Republic of Yugoslavia founded with Tito as prime minister (and president from 1953).
- **1948** Tito breaks with Stalin.
- **1951** Farmers permitted to sell produce on free market.
- **1955** Yugoslav–Soviet détente.

S

CHRONOLOGY *continued*

- **1963** Third postwar constitution adopts name Socialist Federal Republic of Yugoslavia (SFRY).
- **1973** Economic cooperation agreement with West Germany. Noninterference accord with USSR.
- **1974** New constitution decentralizes government. Vojvodina and Kosovo given greater autonomy.
- **1980** Tito dies. Collective presidency.
- **1981** Unrest among Kosovo Albanians; state of emergency.
- **1985** Serbian intellectuals publish memorandum listing Serb grievances within Yugoslavia.
- **1986** Slobodan Milosevic becomes leader of Communist (later Socialist) Party of Serbia.
- **1987** Wage freeze to combat inflation. Banking system crisis.
- **1988** Belgrade protests against economic austerity. Government brought down over budget failure.
- **1989** 600th anniversary of Battle of Kosovo. Kosovo Albanians protest against Serb police unit; crackdown ends Kosovo's autonomy. Milosevic elected president of Serbia.
- **1990** SPS wins elections in Serbia. Communists win presidency and dominate Montenegro elections.
- **1992** EU recognizes breakaway republics of Croatia, Slovenia, and Bosnia and Herzegovina. Bosnian war begins. UN sanctions imposed. Ibrahim Rugova elected president of self-declared republic of Kosovo. Milosevic reelected president of Serbia, but SPS loses majority.
- **1995** Bosnian peace accord.
- **1996** UN sanctions formally lifted.
- **1997** Milosevic becomes federal president.
- **1998** Conflict in Kosovo escalates.
- **1999** March, "ethnic cleansing" in Kosovo precipitates mass exodus. NATO aerial bombing. June, withdrawal of Serbian forces and police from Kosovo, and entry of international force, KFOR.
- **2000** Milosevic refuses to accept defeat in presidential election. Opposition candidate Vojislav Kostunica swept to power. Democratic Opposition of Serbia dominates elections in Serbia.
- **2001** Arrest of Milosevic, who is subsequently extradited to face war crimes tribunal in The Hague.
- **2002–2003** Low turnouts invalidate republican presidential elections.
- **2003** February, new state of Serbia and Montenegro. March, Serbian Prime Minister Zoran Djindjic shot dead. December, far-right SRS wins polls in Serbia.
- **2004** Kostunica becomes Serbian prime minister. Resurgence of ethnic violence in Kosovo.

DEFENSE

Compulsory military service

$706m

Up 17% in 2002

SERBIA & MONTENEGRO ARMED FORCES

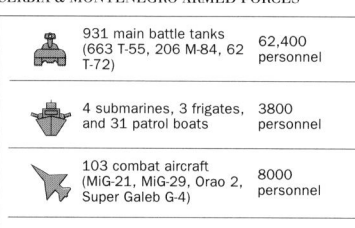

931 main battle tanks (663 T-55, 206 M-84, 62 T-72)	62,400 personnel
4 submarines, 3 frigates, and 31 patrol boats	3800 personnel
103 combat aircraft (MiG-21, MiG-29, Orao 2, Super Galeb G-4)	8000 personnel
None	

Military capability was specifically targeted for "degrading" by the NATO air strikes in 1999. However, the impact on antiaircraft defenses, heavy weaponry, logistics capacity, and infrastructure was less severe than had first been claimed.

The Serbian military had played a major role in the conflicts in the former Yugoslavia in the early 1990s. Traditionally the center of Yugoslav armaments manufacture, Serbia was able to arm itself – though the need to create money to pay for domestically produced weapons was a major factor in the crippling hyperinflation of that era.

In 2002 the country made its first (modest) contribution to a UN peacekeeping force, in East Timor.

ECONOMICS

Not available

$11.6bn

53.50 dinars (56.48); 0.822 euros (0.871)

SCORE CARD

World GNP Ranking	84th
GNP per Capita	$1400
Balance of Payments	–$1.38bn
Inflation	25.5%
Unemployment	30%

ECONOMIC PERFORMANCE INDICATOR

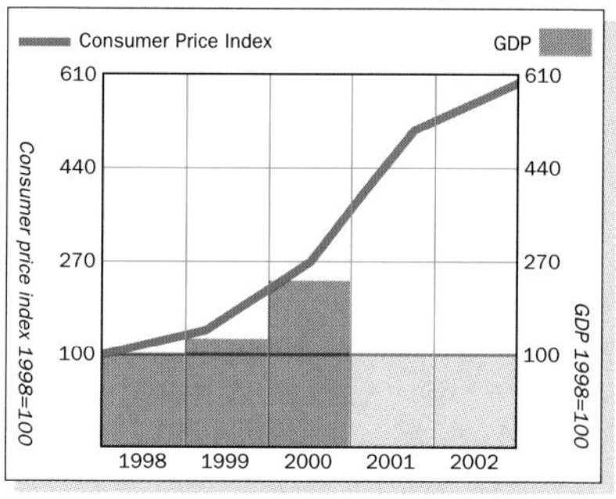
Consumer Price Index
GDP
610
440
270
100
Consumer price index 1998=100
GDP 1998=100
1998
1999
2000
2001
2002

EXPORTS

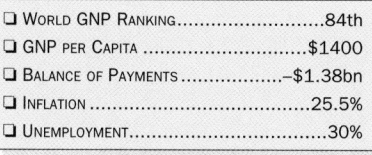

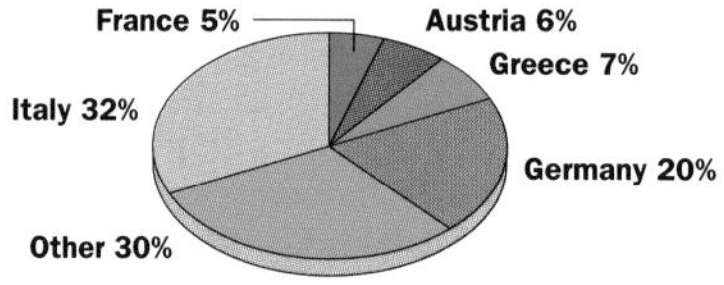
France 5%
Austria 6%
Greece 7%
Italy 32%
Germany 20%
Other 30%

IMPORTS

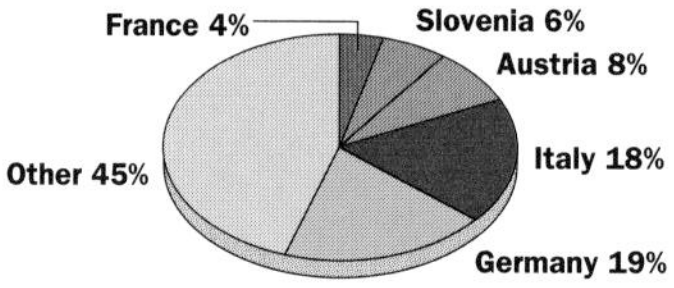
France 4%
Slovenia 6%
Austria 8%
Other 45%
Italy 18%
Germany 19%

Strengths

Return of international aid and investment in 2000–2001. Economic potential of Danube.

Weaknesses

Severe damage caused by sanctions and 1999 bombings. Low hard-currency reserves. Outflow of skilled professionals. High unemployment.

Profile

Yugoslavia's living standards were among the highest of the socialist countries. The 1990s conflicts effectively stalled much-needed economic reform. Sanctions, maintained until 1996 and reimposed more fully in 1999, stifled trade and decimated both the emerging private and the state sectors. Hyperinflation had already pushed the economy to virtual collapse. Now, as much as 50% of all economic activity goes on within the resilient informal sector. NATO bombing in 1999 caused extensive infrastructure damage; the EBRD estimated reconstruction costs at $20 billion over three years. Sanctions were lifted shortly after Milosevic's downfall in 2000, and investment prospects were boosted by his extradition and initial cooperation with the ICTY.

SERBIA & MONTENEGRO : MAJOR BUSINESSES

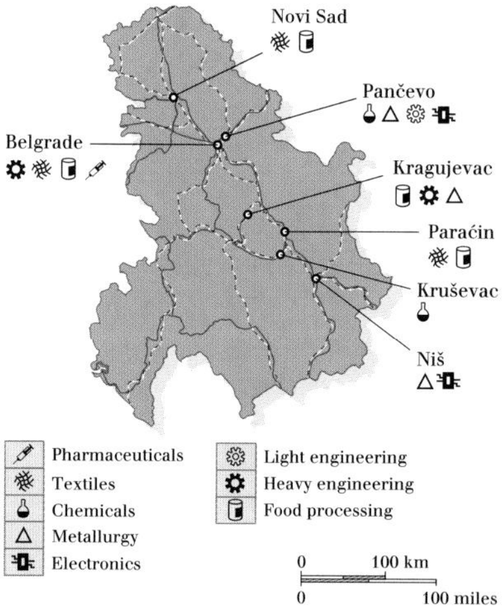
Novi Sad
Pančevo
Belgrade
Kragujevac
Paraćin
Kruševac
Niš
Pharmaceuticals
Textiles
Chemicals
Metallurgy
Electronics
Light engineering
Heavy engineering
Food processing
0
100 km
0
100 miles

S

RESOURCES

Electric power 11.8m kW

3557 tonnes

16,341 b/d (reserves 78m barrels)

3.66m pigs, 1.76m sheep, 1.34m cattle, 21.1m chickens

Coal, bauxite, iron, lead, copper, zinc, oil

ELECTRICITY GENERATION

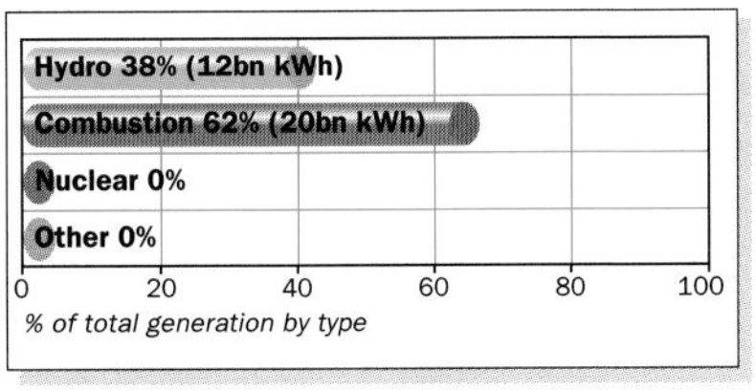
Hydro 38% (12bn kWh)
Combustion 62% (20bn kWh)
Nuclear 0%
Other 0%
0
20
40
60
80
100
% of total generation by type

Coal production has fallen, prompting imports of natural gas. Vojvodina's oil industry could cater for one-third of total demand, but was badly hit by NATO bombing in March–June 1999.

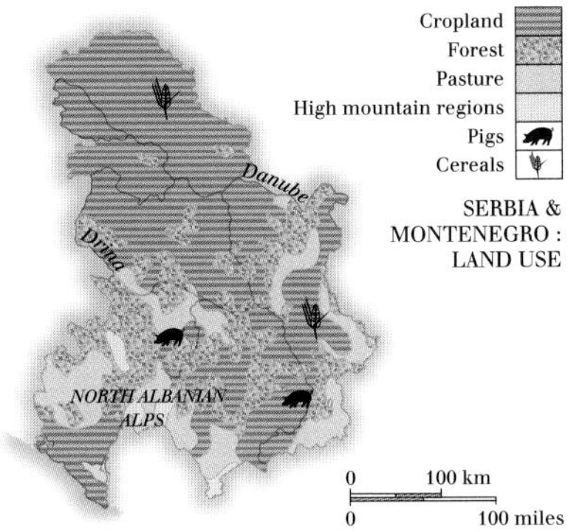
Cropland
Forest
Pasture
High mountain regions
Pigs
Cereals
SERBIA & MONTENEGRO : LAND USE
Danube
Drina
NORTH ALBANIAN ALPS
0
100 km
0
100 miles

ENVIRONMENT

Not available

3% (2% partially protected)

3.7 tonnes per capita

ENVIRONMENTAL TREATIES

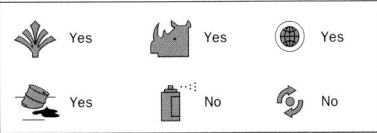

Yes | Yes | Yes

Yes | No | No

Ecological awareness peaked in the late 1980s, when the Ecological Forum was active. NATO bombing of Serbia in 1999 caused extensive pollution of the Danube and raised fears of contamination from dioxins. Depleted uranium from NATO munitions has also aroused serious concerns both in Kosovo and Serbia proper.

CRIME

No death penalty

7241 prisoners

High crime levels

CRIME RATES

Serbia & Montenegro does not publish statistics for murder, rape, and theft

Organized crime was rife under Milosevic and continues to be a problem and a cause for public concern. The elite "red beret" police were implicated in the assassination of Serbian Prime Minister Zoran Djindjic in 2003. Domestic war crimes trials had begun in Serbia in 2002, but in 2004 full cooperation with the ICTY faltered.

MEDIA

TV ownership medium

Daily newspaper circulation 107 per 1000 people

PUBLISHING AND BROADCAST MEDIA

There are 18 daily newspapers. *Vecernje Novosti* and *Blic* have the largest circulation.

2 state-controlled services, several independent services

3 state-controlled services, several independent services

Strict censorship and government control vanished with the ouster of Milosevic in 2000. In Montenegro, broadcasters and the press had already begun to express independent viewpoints, and their Serbian counterparts quickly followed suit; self-censorship is now the norm. The B92 radio station had been a beacon of independent reporting and remains confrontational. In Kosovo, however, intimidation by criminal gangs and paramilitaries has hampered the appearance of a free press.

EDUCATION

School leaving age: 14

98%

208,689 students

THE EDUCATION SYSTEM

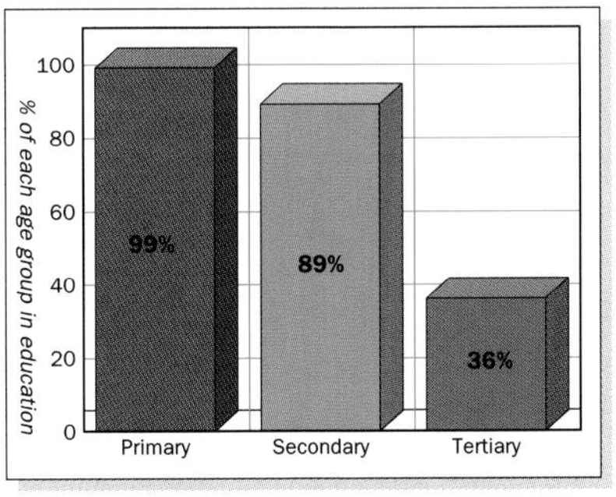
100
80
60
40
20
0
% of each age group in education
99%
89%
36%
Primary
Secondary
Tertiary

Schooling was totally disrupted by the Kosovo conflict in 1999, leaving the education system in crisis; the wealthy go abroad for their education. Literacy rates in Kosovo, where ethnic Albanian schools were closed in 1990, were low even before the conflict. Rebuilding the basic education system is key to reconstruction and reconciliation.

HEALTH

Welfare state health benefits

1 per 476 people

Heart diseases, cancers, cerebrovascular and respiratory diseases

Isolation in the 1990s affected the health service, despite the exemption of medicines and medical supplies from sanctions. Death rates among infants and the elderly have risen dramatically. Health problems can be aggravated by bitingly cold winters. Social insurance is obligatory for those in employment, but medicines are scarce and costly. Montenegro unexpectedly banned public smoking in 2004.

SPENDING

GDP/cap. increase

CONSUMPTION AND SPENDING

150 per 1000 population

233 per 1000 population

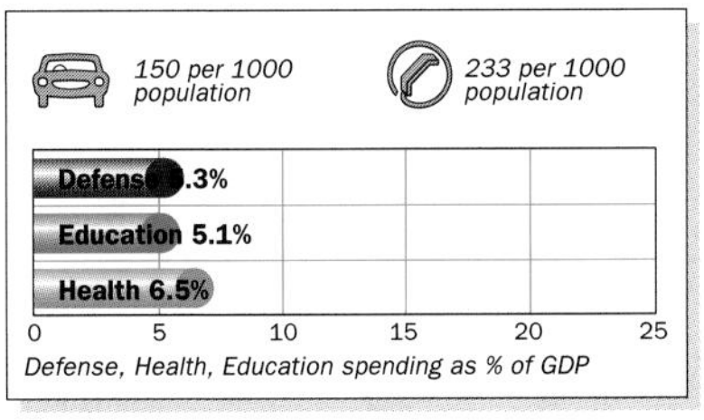
Defense 4.3%
Education 5.1%
Health 6.5%
0
5
10
15
20
25
Defense, Health, Education spending as % of GDP

Living standards in the rump state of Yugoslavia were badly affected by years of sanctions and the 1999 NATO bombing. Even before 1999, two-thirds of the population were living below subsistence levels. Bank collapses and hyperinflation had effectively wiped out domestic savings. Only those involved in illegal sanctions-busting imports made any gains in this period.

Moving toward democracy opened up channels of aid and investment which have helped boost the standard of living across the country, though troubled relations with the West threaten these gains. The illegal economy still thrives, and those in power or with the right connections remain the wealthiest members of society. Apart from the desperate situation of refugees and internally displaced families, unsupported pensioners fare worst.

WORLD RANKING

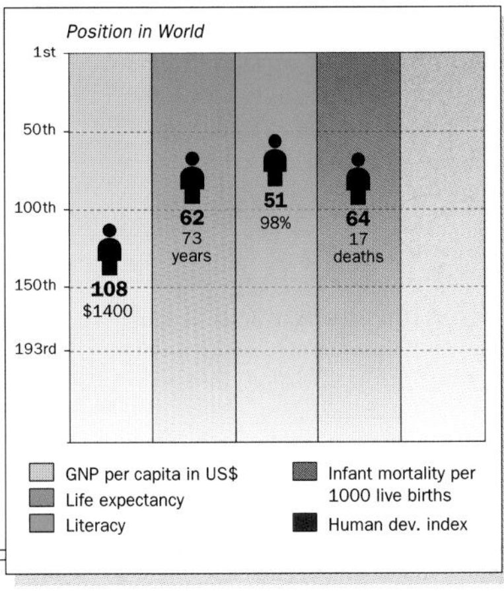
Position in World
1st
50th
100th
150th
193rd
108
$1400
62
73
years
51
98%
64
17
deaths
GNP per capita in US$
Life expectancy
Literacy
Infant mortality per 1000 live births
Human dev. index

S

SEYCHELLES

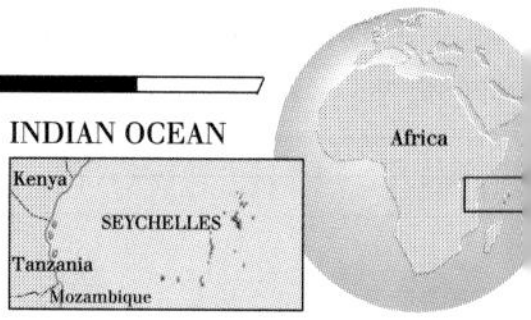
INDIAN OCEAN
Africa
Kenya
SEYCHELLES
Tanzania
Mozambique

OFFICIAL NAME: Republic of Seychelles **CAPITAL:** Victoria **POPULATION:** 80,469
CURRENCY: Seychelles rupee **OFFICIAL LANGUAGES:** French Creole, English, and French

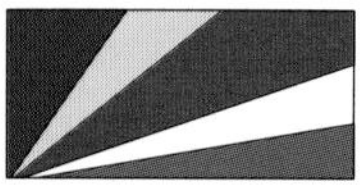

1976
1976
June 18
SY
+4
+248
.sc

THE 115 ISLANDS of the Seychelles, lying in the Indian Ocean, support unique flora and fauna, including the giant tortoise and the world's largest seed, the *coco-de-mer*. Formerly a UK colony and then under one-party rule for 14 years, the Seychelles became a multiparty democracy in 1993. The economy relies on tourism.

CLIMATE

Tropical oceanic

WEATHER CHART FOR VICTORIA

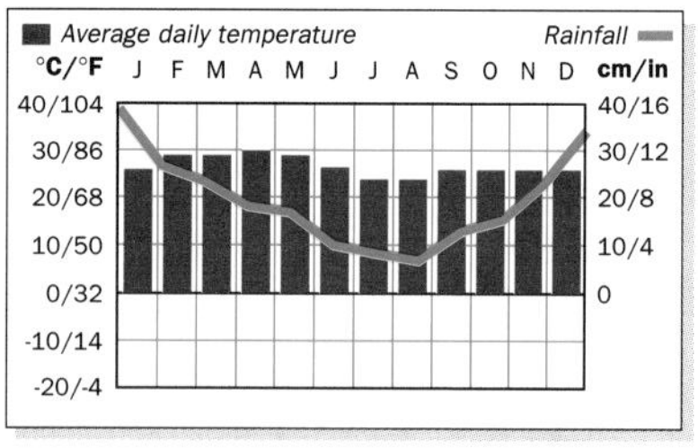
Average daily temperature
Rainfall
°C/°F J F M A M J J A S O N D cm/in
40/104
30/86
20/68
10/50
0/32
-10/14
-20/-4
40/16
30/12
20/8
10/4
0

The islands have a tropical oceanic climate, with only small temperature variations throughout the year.

TRANSPORTATION

Drive on left

Seychelles International, Mahé 155,000 passengers

31 ships 64,673 grt

THE TRANSPORTATION NETWORK

317 km (197 miles)	None
None	None

There are airstrips on the larger islands. Buses and roads are being renewed. Victoria's deep-sea harbor is one of the best run in the region.

TOURISM

Visitors : Population 1.6:1

132,000 visitors

Up 2% in 2002

MAIN TOURIST ARRIVALS

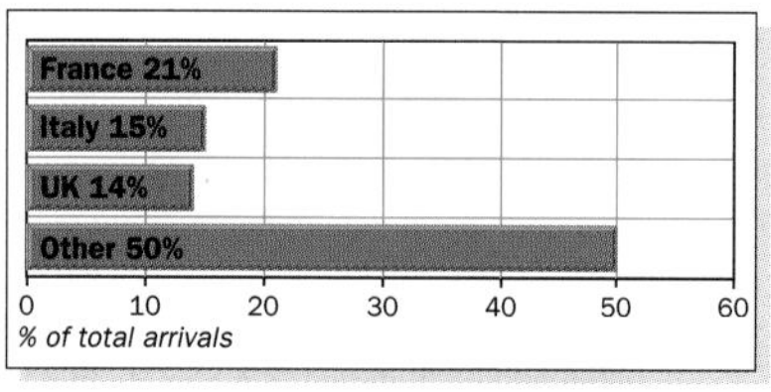
France 21%
Italy 15%
UK 14%
Other 50%
0 10 20 30 40 50 60
% of total arrivals

Since the international airport was opened at Mahé in 1971, tourism has become the mainstay of the economy, and employs 20% of the workforce. New hotels must comply with laws to protect the islands' beauty and unique wildlife. There is substantial foreign investment.

PEOPLE

Pop. density high

French Creole, English, French

298/km² (774/mi²)

THE URBAN/RURAL POPULATION SPLIT

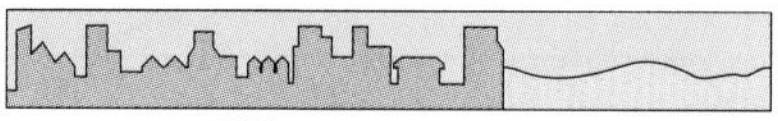
65%
35%

RELIGIOUS PERSUASION

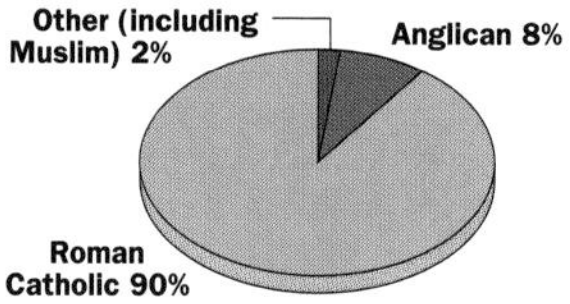
Other (including Muslim) 2%
Anglican 8%
Roman Catholic 90%

The Seychelles islands were uninhabited before French settlers arrived in the 1770s. Today, the population is markedly homogeneous as a result of intermarriage between different ethnic groups. The Creoles are descendants of French settlers and Africans who were settled on the islands by British administrators. There are small Chinese and Indian minorities.

Almost 90% of Seychellois live on Mahé. Population growth has been very low, as about 1000 people emigrate every year. It is conceivable that the transition to democracy could reverse this trend.

POLITICS

Multiparty elections

2002/2007

President James Michel

AT THE LAST ELECTION

National Assembly 34 seats

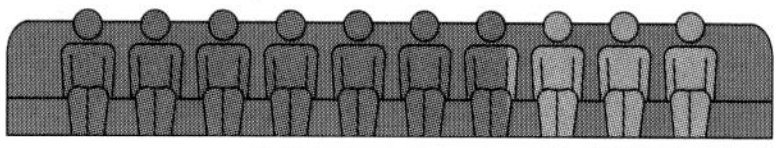
68%
SPPF
32%
SNP

SPPF = Seychelles People's Progressive Front
SNP = Seychelles National Party

France Albert René seized power soon after independence. Multiparty elections were held in 1993 after 14 years of one-party socialist rule; opposition divisions allowed him to retain the presidency. His SPPF kept its majority in the 1998 poll, abandoned its leftist ideology, and adopted a plan to develop the Seychelles as an International Trading Zone, with free-port facilities and new industry. René faced a stiff electoral challenge in 2001, while the opposition SNP gained in legislative polls in 2002. He retired in 2004, handing over power to his deputy, James Michel.

WORLD AFFAIRS

Joined UN in 1976

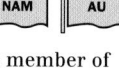

OIF Comm COI NAM AU

The Seychelles is an active member of the Alliance of Small Island States and also of the Commonwealth. It disputes ownership of the UK-ruled Chagos Islands. It has trade accords with Indian Ocean states.

SEYCHELLES

Total Area : 455 sq. km (176 sq. miles)

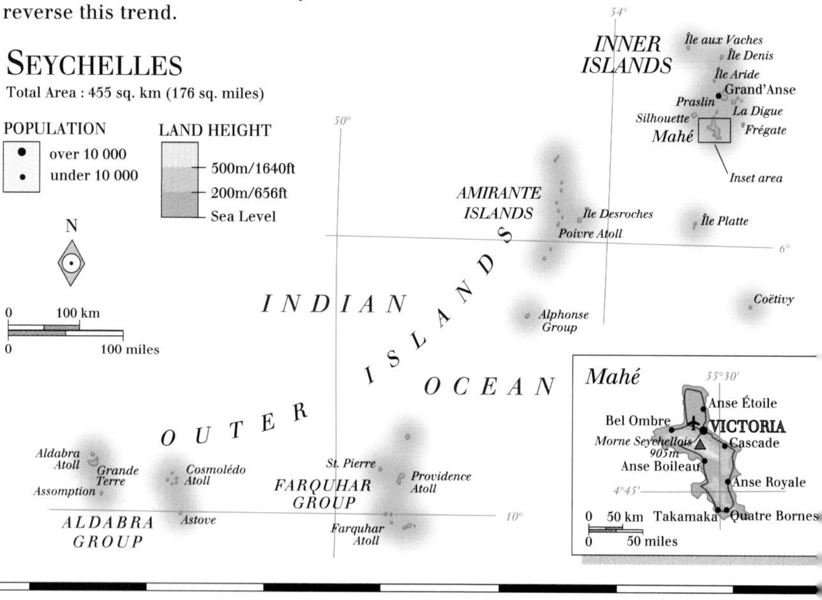
POPULATION
over 10 000
under 10 000
LAND HEIGHT
500m/1640ft
200m/656ft
Sea Level
N
0 100 km
0 100 miles
INNER ISLANDS
Île aux Vaches
Île Denis
Île Aride
Grand'Anse
Praslin
La Digue
Silhouette
Frégate
Mahé
Inset area
AMIRANTE ISLANDS
Île Desroches
Poivre Atoll
Île Platte
INDIAN OCEAN
Alphonse Group
Coëtivy
OUTER ISLANDS
Aldabra Atoll
Grande Terre
Assomption
Cosmolédo Atoll
Astove
ALDABRA GROUP
St. Pierre
FARQUHAR GROUP
Farquhar Atoll
Providence Atoll
Mahé
Anse Étoile
Bel Ombre
VICTORIA
Morne Seychellois 905m
Cascade
Anse Boileau
Anse Royale
Takamaka
Quatre Bornes
0 50 km
0 50 miles

S

AID

Recipient

$8m (receipts)

Down 43% in 2002

Multilateral agencies, notably the EU and the Arab Development Fund, support a range of development projects. Recent aid has focused on protecting the environment, transportation links, and refurbishing Victoria Market, on Mahé. Bilateral aid comes from Japan, France, and other Western donors.

DEFENSE

No compulsory military service

$11m

No change in 2002

The Seychelles has a 200-strong army, and a paramilitary guard. The latter includes the coast guard, which is made up of air and sea forces. The army, set up in 1977, was initially trained by Tanzania, and Tanzanian troops were brought in for three years after a coup attempt in 1981. North Korea provided advisers until 1989.

ECONOMICS

Inflation 3.9% p.a. (1990–2001)

$569m

5.521 Seychelles rupees (5.618)

SCORE CARD

- World GNP Ranking 169th
- GNP per capita $6780
- Balance of Payments .... –$124m
- Inflation 0.2%
- Unemployment 9%

Strengths

Tourism. Fish exports, especially shrimp and tuna. Profitable reexport trade. International Trading Zone attracting foreign industrial interest. Copra, cinnamon, tea.

Weaknesses

High debt-servicing costs. Need for food imports, especially for tourist industry. Copra production declining. Reliance on expatriate labor. Foreign exchange shortage. Corruption. Growing deficits in early 1990s, caused by drop in tourism, spending on hosting 1993 Indian Ocean Games, and cost of four elections.

EXPORTS

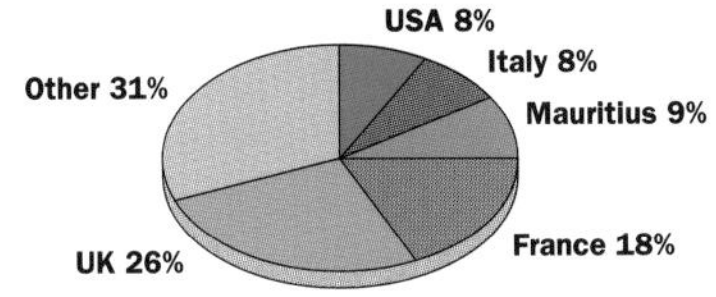
USA 8%
Italy 8%
Mauritius 9%
France 18%
UK 26%
Other 31%

IMPORTS

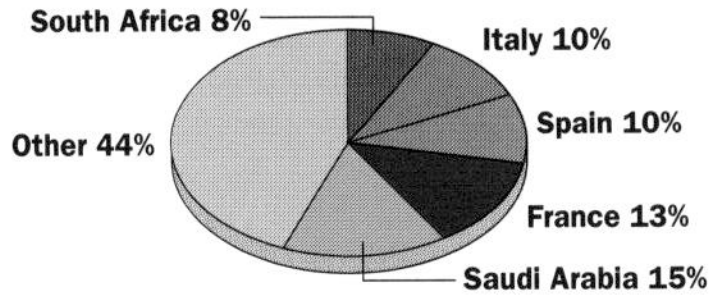
South Africa 8%
Italy 10%
Spain 10%
France 13%
Saudi Arabia 15%
Other 44%

***One of the Inner Islands,** which are home to most of the population. Unlike any other mid-ocean islands, all but two are granitic.*

RESOURCES

Electric power 28,000 kW

47,832 tonnes

Not an oil producer

18,500 pigs, 5150 goats, 520,000 chickens

Phosphates (guano), salt, granite, natural gas

Mineral resources are very limited. All fuel is imported; only three islands have electricity. Offshore discoveries of natural gas have spurred a search for oil. Natural habitat and the free trade environment are great assets.

ENVIRONMENT

Not available

111% partially protected (including marine areas)

2.7 tonnes per capita

The Seychelles has been praised for its commitment to conservation. It has two natural World Heritage sites, and helped promote the idea of whale sanctuaries.

MEDIA

TV ownership medium

Daily newspaper circulation 39 per 1000 people

PUBLISHING AND BROADCAST MEDIA

There is 1 daily newspaper, the state-run *Seychelles Nation*

2 state-owned services

3 state-owned services

Broadcasting services are state-owned, as private licenses are too costly. The government has sued the opposition weekly *Regar* ten times in six years.

CRIME

No death penalty

157 prisoners

Up slightly in 2000–2002

Violent crime is rare in the Seychelles. The main concern is the increasing rate of petty theft.

EDUCATION

School leaving age: 15

92%

1652 students

The 1995–2008 Educational and Training Plan places special emphasis on increasing levels of female enrollment. National Youth Service is mandatory for entry to higher education.

CHRONOLOGY

The French claimed the islands in 1756. Franco-British rivalry for control ended when France ceded them to Britain in 1815.

- **1952** Political parties formed, led by F. A. René (proindependence) and James Mancham (pro-UK rule).
- **1965** UK returns Desroches, Aldabra, and Farquhar islands, which are leased to US until 1976.
- **1976** Independence. Coalition: Mancham president, René premier.
- **1977** René takes over in coup.
- **1979** One-party socialist state.
- **1979–1987** Several coup attempts.
- **1993** Democratic elections.
- **2002** Opposition gain in elections.
- **2004** René retires; succeeded by Vice President James Michel.

HEALTH

Welfare state health benefits

1 per 769 people

Heart and cerebrovascular diseases, cancers

State health care is free, and the system is one of the best in the region. Private medicine has been allowed under new social legislation.

SPENDING

GDP/cap. increase

CONSUMPTION AND SPENDING

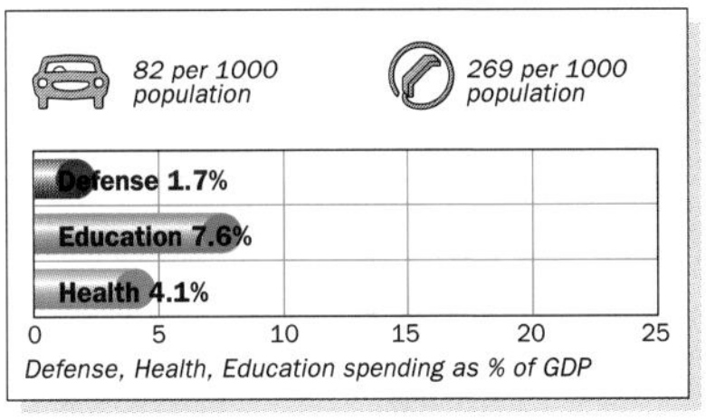
82 per 1000 population
269 per 1000 population
Defense 1.7%
Education 7.6%
Health 4.1%
0
5
10
15
20
25
Defense, Health, Education spending as % of GDP

Living standards are the highest among AU states. There are no slums in the Seychelles, and the state welfare system caters for all.

WORLD RANKING

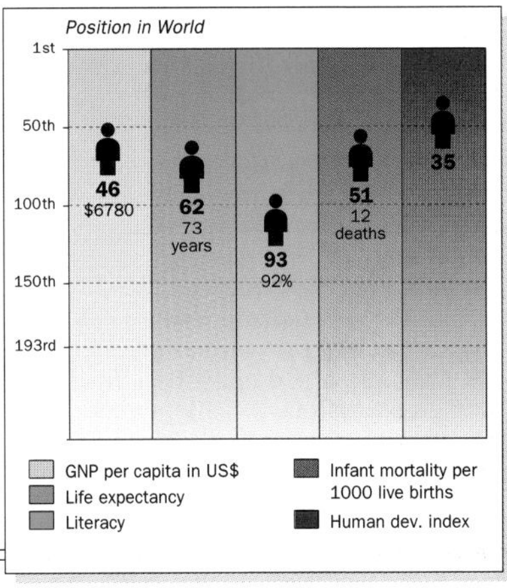
Position in World
1st
50th
100th
150th
193rd
46
$6780
62
73 years
93
92%
51
12 deaths
35
GNP per capita in US$
Life expectancy
Literacy
Infant mortality per 1000 live births
Human dev. index

S

SIERRA LEONE

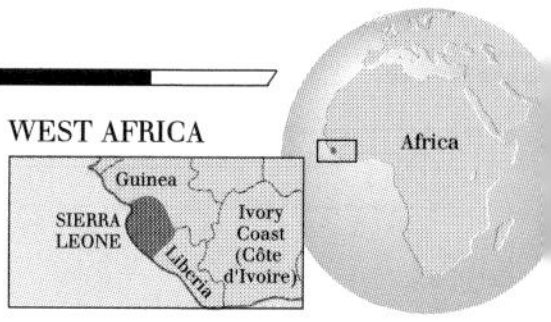
WEST AFRICA
Guinea
SIERRA LEONE
Liberia
Ivory Coast (Côte d'Ivoire)
Africa

OFFICIAL NAME: Republic of Sierra Leone **CAPITAL:** Freetown
POPULATION: 5 million **CURRENCY:** Leone **OFFICIAL LANGUAGE:** English

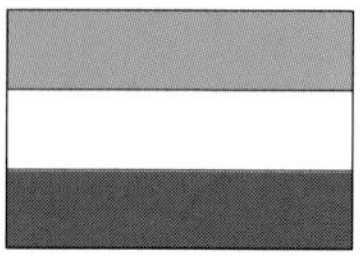

1961
1961
April 27
WAL
0
+232
.sl

THE WEST AFRICAN state of Sierra Leone was founded by the British in 1787 for Africans freed from slavery. The terrain rises from coastal lowlands to mountains in the northeast. A democratic government took office in 1996 against a background of bloody rebellion. Sierra Leone soon plunged back into a savage civil war. Though a 1999 peace agreement was short-lived, an ECOWAS-brokered accord signed in late 2000 seems to be holding.

CLIMATE

Tropical equatorial/ monsoon

WEATHER CHART FOR FREETOWN

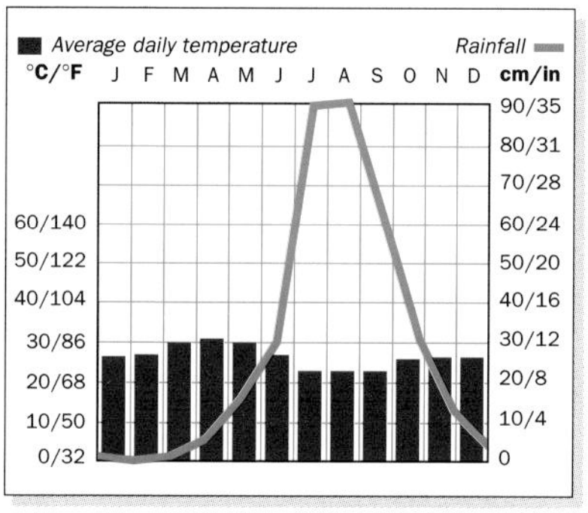
Average daily temperature
Rainfall
°C/°F
J F M A M J J A S O N D
cm/in
90/35
80/31
70/28
60/24
50/20
40/16
30/12
20/8
10/4
0
60/140
50/122
40/104
30/86
20/68
10/50
0/32

Coastal rainfall can be as high as 500 cm (197 in) a year, making Sierra Leone one of the wettest places in coastal west Africa. Humidity is consistently high – about 80% – during the rainy season. The dusty, northeasterly *harmattan* wind often blows during the hotter dry season from November to April. The northeastern savannas are drier, with 190–250 cm (75–98 in) of rain, and are one of the hottest areas.

TRANSPORTATION

Drive on right

Lungi, Freetown 84,547 passengers

43 ships 22,733 grt

THE TRANSPORTATION NETWORK

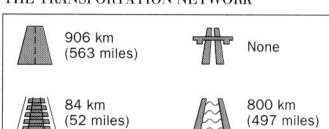

906 km (563 miles)	None
84 km (52 miles)	800 km (497 miles)

A major road resurfacing project is under way in Freetown. The 300-km (190-mile) narrow-gauge railroad was abandoned in 1971 as uneconomic, though 84 km (52 miles) of track still run to the closed iron ore mines at Marampa. Sierra National Airlines does not provide domestic flights, but private planes may be chartered. There are catamaran and helicopter links between Freetown and the airport at Lungi, as well as taxis and buses.

TOURISM

Visitors : Population 1:179

28,000 visitors

Up 17% in 2002

MAIN TOURIST ARRIVALS

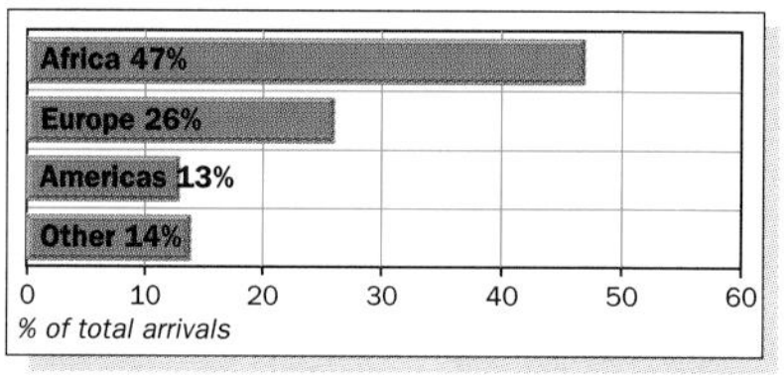
Africa 47%
Europe 26%
Americas 13%
Other 14%
0
10
20
30
40
50
60
% of total arrivals

Sierra Leone has never attracted much tourism, and years of civil war have prevented its development. Among the chief potential attractions are the beaches along the Freetown peninsula, at present virtually undeveloped. China is investing $270 million in hotel infrastructure.

SIERRA LEONE

Total Area : 71 740 sq. km (27 698 sq. miles)

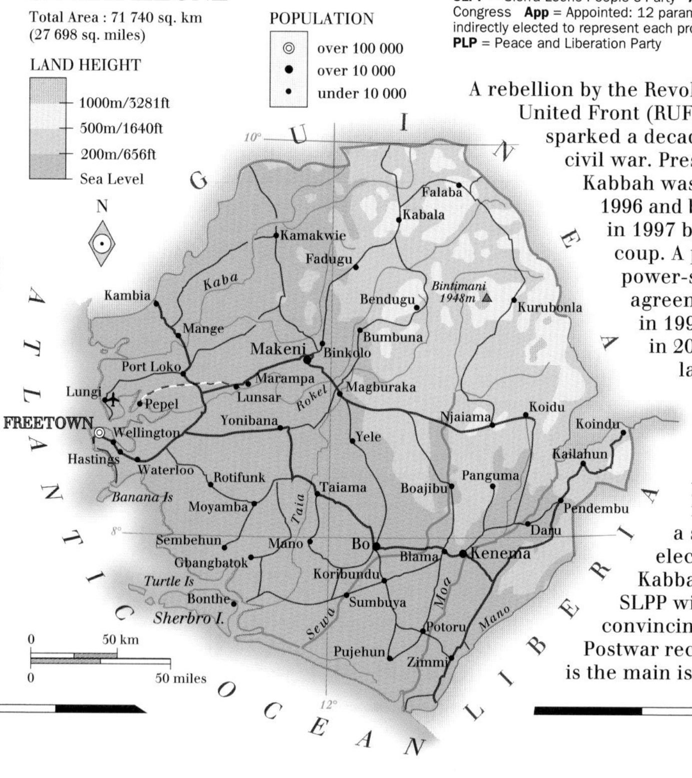
POPULATION
over 100 000
over 10 000
under 10 000
LAND HEIGHT
1000m/3281ft
500m/1640ft
200m/656ft
Sea Level
N
GUINEA
ATLANTIC OCEAN
LIBERIA
Falaba
Kabala
Kamakwie
Fadugu
Kambia
Kaba
Bintimani 1948m
Bendugu
Kurubonla
Mange
Bumbuna
Makeni
Binkolo
Port Loko
Marampa
Lunsar
Magburaka
Lungi
Pepel
Rokel
FREETOWN
Wellington
Yonibana
Njaiama
Koidu
Koindu
Yele
Hastings
Kailahun
Waterloo
Rotifunk
Taiama
Boajibu
Panguma
Banana Is
Moyamba
Taia
Pendembu
Sembehun
Mano
Bo
Daru
Gbangbatok
Blama
Kenema
Turtle Is
Koribundu
Moa
Bonthe
Sumbuya
Sherbro I.
Sewa
Potoru
Mano
Pujehun
Zimmi
0 50 km
0 50 miles

PEOPLE

Pop. density medium

Mende, Temne, Krio, English

70/km² (181/mi²)

THE URBAN/RURAL POPULATION SPLIT

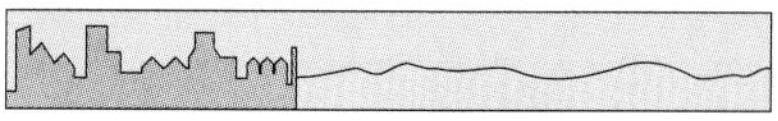
38%
62%

ETHNIC MAKEUP

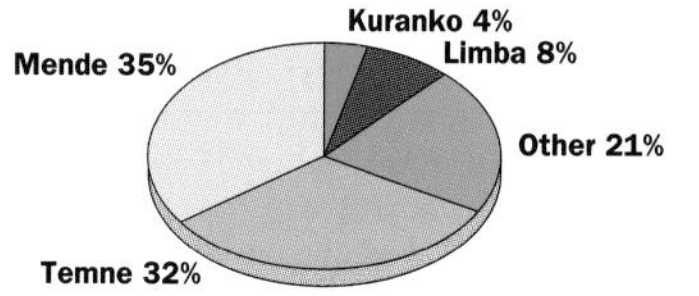
Kuranko 4%
Mende 35%
Limba 8%
Other 21%
Temne 32%

Freetown was founded as a settlement for people freed from slavery. There is a strongly Anglicized Creole culture in the capital compared with the underdeveloped and rural interior. An estimated two million people were displaced by the civil war.

POLITICS

Multiparty elections

2002/2007

President Ahmad Tejan Kabbah

AT THE LAST ELECTION

Parliament 124 seats

67% SLPP
22% APC
10% App
1% PLP

SLPP = Sierra Leone People's Party **APC** = All People's Congress **App** = Appointed: 12 paramount chiefs are indirectly elected to represent each province
PLP = Peace and Liberation Party

A rebellion by the Revolutionary United Front (RUF) in 1991 sparked a decade of savage civil war. President Ahmad Kabbah was elected in 1996 and briefly ousted in 1997 by a military coup. A peace and power-sharing agreement, signed in 1999, collapsed in 2000, but a large UN and British force secured a new cease-fire later that year. The RUF failed to gain a single seat in elections in 2002, Kabbah and his SLPP winning a convincing victory. Postwar reconstruction is the main issue.

S

WORLD AFFAIRS

Joined UN in 1961

Comm | ECOWAS | MRU | AU | OIC

UN peacekeepers and British forces turned the tide in the civil war. There are ongoing border tensions.

AID

Recipient

$353m (receipts)

Up 2% in 2002

The IMF and the World Bank agreed in 2002 to drop 80% of Sierra Leone's debt in return for key reforms.
Aid funds efforts to cope with the humanitarian needs of refugees from Liberia, internal migrants displaced by the civil war, and the near-collapse of public services.

DEFENSE

No compulsory military service

$17m

Up 42% in 2002

The UK has been retraining the army since 2000 and has established a new police force. Both sides in the civil war exploited child fighters.

ECONOMICS

Inflation 29% p.a. (1990–2001)

$723m

2455 leones (2370)

SCORE CARD

❑ World GNP Ranking	161st
❑ GNP per Capita	$140
❑ Balance of Payments	–$79m
❑ Inflation	–3.3%
❑ Unemployment	70%

Strengths

Diamonds, though much of the output smuggled. Freetown port. Some bauxite and rutile production. Palm products.

Weaknesses

Legacy of war: disruption to diamond trade, agriculture, and mining sector. Traumatized and untrained youth population. High unemployment. Institutional corruption. Refugees and internally displaced population.

EXPORTS

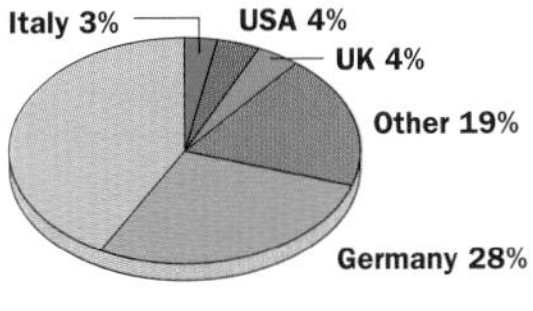
Italy 3%
USA 4%
UK 4%
Belgium 42%
Other 19%
Germany 28%

IMPORTS

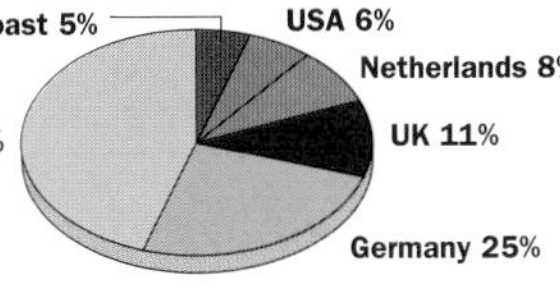
Ivory Coast 5%
USA 6%
Netherlands 8%
Other 45%
UK 11%
Germany 25%

RESOURCES

Electric power 130,000 kW

75,240 tonnes

Not an oil producer; refines 4450 b/d

400,000 cattle, 375,000 sheep, 7.5m chickens

Diamonds, rutile, bauxite, gold, titanium

Exploiting the large diamond deposits needs fresh investment as areas currently being mined become exhausted. The southeast is the most fertile region.

ENVIRONMENT

Sustainability rank: 134th

2% partially protected

0.1 tonnes per capita

Population pressures and the neglect resulting from years of civil war have depleted the land's productivity.

MEDIA

TV ownership low

Daily newspaper circulation 4 per 1000 people

PUBLISHING AND BROADCAST MEDIA

Many local daily newspapers, especially in Freetown

1 state-controlled service

1 state-controlled service, many independent stations

A broad range of periodicals is available. Press freedom has improved since the end of the civil war, though there is still some censorship.

CRIME

Death penalty in use

Sierra Leone does not publish prison figures

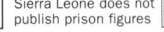

Crime is rising

Savage atrocities and mass looting of resources occurred during the civil war. As a consequence, the UN initiated the setting up of a war crimes tribunal; the first trials began in 2004. International restrictions were imposed on trade in diamonds from war-torn areas, but illegal diamond mining and smuggling remain lucrative crimes.

EDUCATION

Schooling is not compulsory

36%

8795 students

Freetown has a long tradition of education, and its university, Fourahbay College, became affiliated with Durham University in the UK in 1876. In recent times, its students have often been active in political dissent. Educational provision has inevitably deteriorated over the past decade.

HEALTH

No welfare state health benefits

1 per 10,000 people

Communicable diseases, malaria, malnutrition

Foreign aid agencies have set up clinics and hospitals outside the capital. WHO has ranked Sierra Leone's health indicators as the worst in the world.

***The main street, Kabala.** Sierra Leone is consistently at the bottom of the UN's human development index.*

CHRONOLOGY

Freetown was founded in 1787 and became a British colony in 1808; the interior was annexed in 1896.

- ❑ **1961** Independence.
- ❑ **1978** Single-party republic.
- ❑ **1991** RUF rebellion starts.
- ❑ **1996** Civilian rule restored after 1992 army coup; Kabbah president.
- ❑ **1997** Coup ousts Kabbah for a year.
- ❑ **1999–2000** Power-sharing attempt.
- ❑ **2001** RUF ends insurgency.
- ❑ **2002** Government and UN agree to set up war crimes court. Kabbah and SLPP reelected.

SPENDING

GDP/cap. decrease

CONSUMPTION AND SPENDING

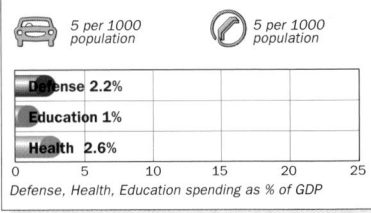

5 per 1000 population

5 per 1000 population

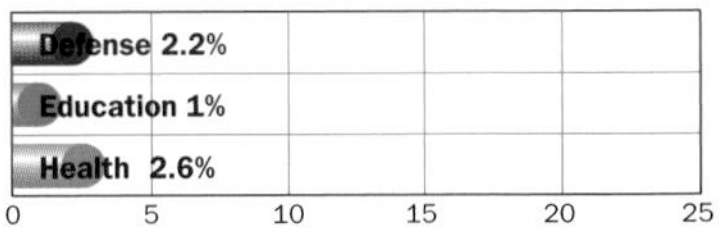
Defense 2.2%
Education 1%
Health 2.6%
0
5
10
15
20
25

Defense, Health, Education spending as % of GDP

In terms of quality of life, the UN has repeatedly ranked Sierra Leoneans as the world's poorest people. Any wealth is associated with political power.

WORLD RANKING

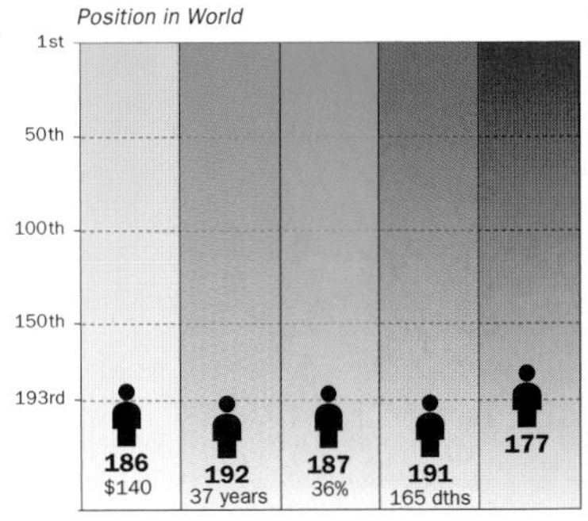
Position in World
1st
50th
100th
150th
193rd
186
$140
192
37 years
187
36%
191
165 dths
177
GNP per capita in US$
Life expectancy
Literacy
Infant mortality per 1000 live births
Human dev. index

S

SINGAPORE

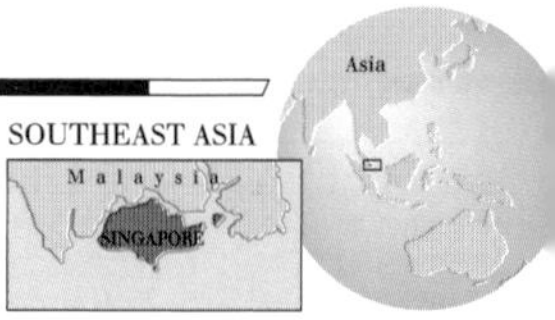
SOUTHEAST ASIA
Asia
Malaysia
SINGAPORE

OFFICIAL NAME: Republic of Singapore **CAPITAL:** Singapore **POPULATION:** 4.3 million
CURRENCY: Singapore dollar **OFFICIAL LANGUAGES:** Malay, English, Mandarin, and Tamil

1965 | 1965 | Aug 9 | SGP | +8 | +65 | .sg

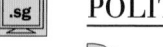

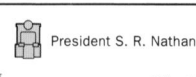

AN ISLAND STATE now linked to the southernmost tip of the Malay Peninsula by a causeway, Singapore ("lion city") was largely uninhabited until the 19th century. In 1819, an official of the British East India Company, Sir Stamford Raffles, recognized the island's strategic position on key trade routes, and established a trading settlement. Today, Singapore remains one of the most important entrepôts in Asia.

CLIMATE

Tropical equatorial

WEATHER CHART FOR SINGAPORE

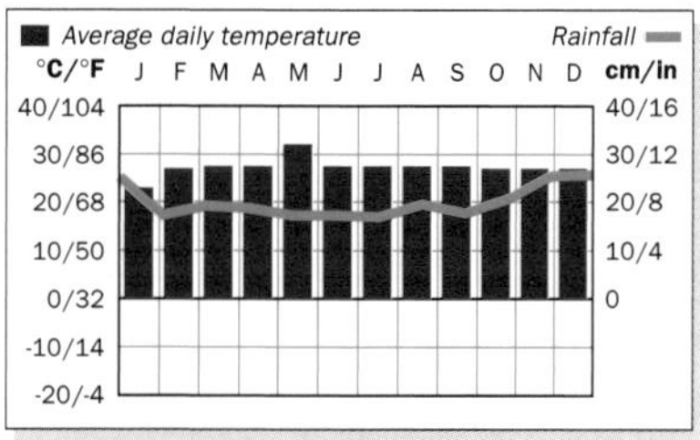
Average daily temperature
Rainfall
°C/°F
J F M A M J J A S O N D
cm/in
40/104
30/86
20/68
10/50
0/32
-10/14
-20/-4
40/16
30/12
20/8
10/4
0

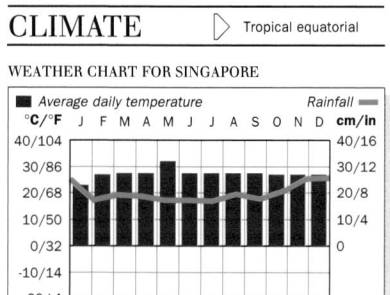

The only variations in the hot, wet, and humid climate are the airless months of September and March, when the trade winds change direction.

TRANSPORTATION

Drive on left

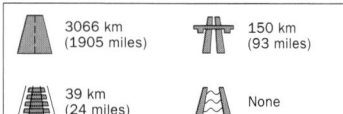

Changi 24.7m passengers

1768 ships 21.1m grt

THE TRANSPORTATION NETWORK

3066 km (1905 miles)

150 km (93 miles)

39 km (24 miles)

None

The Mass Rapid Transit System (subway), completed in 1991, is among the world's most efficient. Space for new roads has run out and monthly auctions are held to sell certificates entitling people to buy from a quota of new cars. The massive port at Pasir Panjang is being expanded on reclaimed land.

The financial center. *More than a quarter of Singapore's GDP is generated by financial and business services.*

TOURISM

Visitors : Population 1.4:1

6.13m visitors

Down 12% in 2003

MAIN TOURIST ARRIVALS

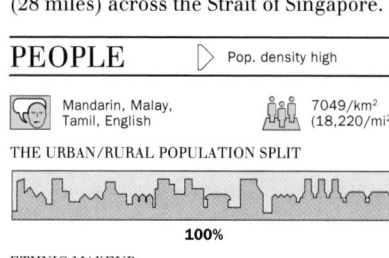

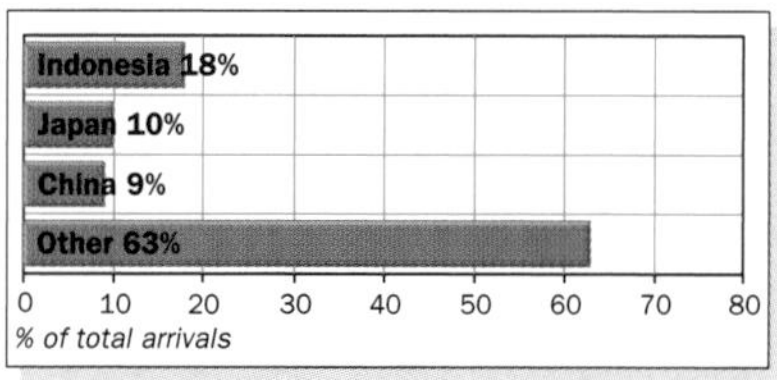
Indonesia 18%
Japan 10%
China 9%
Other 63%
0 10 20 30 40 50 60 70 80
% of total arrivals

The buildings of Chinatown, recognized as a picturesque tourist asset, are being restored. A Singaporean consortium was involved in developing a resort on Indonesia's Bintan island, some 45 km (28 miles) across the Strait of Singapore.

PEOPLE

Pop. density high

Mandarin, Malay, Tamil, English

7049/km² (18,220/mi²)

THE URBAN/RURAL POPULATION SPLIT

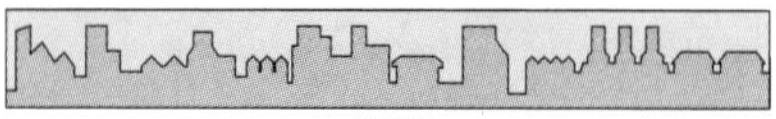
100%

ETHNIC MAKEUP

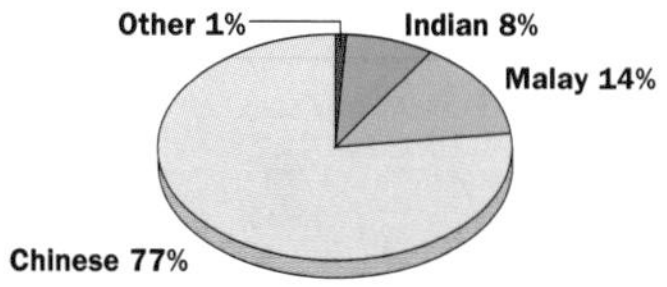
Other 1%
Indian 8%
Malay 14%
Chinese 77%

Singapore is dominated by the Chinese – the old-established English-speaking Straits Chinese and newer Mandarin speakers – who make up almost 80% of the community. Indigenous Malays are generally the poorest group, but today there is little overt ethnic tension. There is also a significant foreign workforce in Singapore.

Long-term plans to stabilize the population structure include cash bonuses for families with more than one child and extensions to maternity leave. Society is highly regulated and government campaigns to improve public behavior are frequent.

POLITICS

Multiparty elections

2001/2006

President S. R. Nathan

AT THE LAST ELECTION
Parliament 94 seats

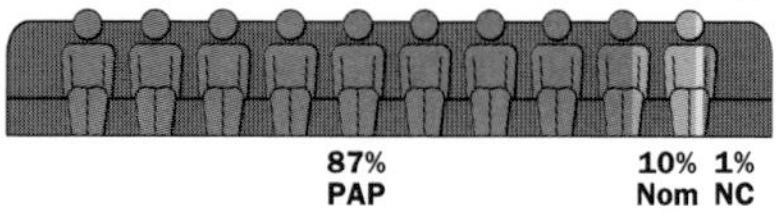
1% SPP
1% WP
87% PAP
10% Nom
1% NC

PAP = People's Action Party **Nom** = Nominated
SPP = Singapore People's Party **NC** = Nonconstituency member **WP** = Workers' Party

In addition to the 84 elected members, up to six "nonconstituency" members may be nominated from the losers with the most votes and nine members may be nominated to ensure a wider representation in Parliament

Singapore is a multiparty democracy, though the ruling PAP effectively controls all parts of the political process and much of the economy. There are plans to create a national ideology ("shared values") based on Confucian traditions. Lee Kuan Yew, prime minister for more than 30 years until 1990, still exercises great influence. Lee's successor, Goh Chok Tong, failed to fully stamp his authority on politics. He stepped down in 2004 in favor of Lee's son, Lee Hsien Loong, part of the upcoming "third generation."

The PAP retains its grip on power, having given Singapore one of the highest living standards in the world, based on a free-market economy. The first antigovernment rally was permitted in 2001, but the PAP was sure of reelection in November even before the ballot, since fewer than half of the seats were contested.

WORLD AFFAIRS

Joined UN in 1965

APEC | ASEAN | Comm | NAM | WTO

Singapore has established diplomatic relations with China, while continuing to maintain close economic ties with Taiwan. It became the beneficiary in 2001 of Japan's first free trade agreement.

AID

Recipient

US$7m (receipts)

Up 600% in 2002

Aid is not an important issue in Singapore. France and Japan are the most significant bilateral donors.

DEFENSE

Compulsory military service

US$4.33bn

Up 2% in 2002

Despite Singapore's small size, its armed forces have a total strength of over 70,000.

S

ECONOMICS

Inflation 0.9% p.a. (1990–2001)

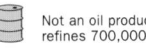

US$86.2bn

1.722 Singapore dollars (1.761)

SCORE CARD

- ❑ WORLD GNP RANKING 39th
- ❑ GNP PER CAPITA .... US$20,690
- ❑ BALANCE OF PAYMENTS .... US$18.7bn
- ❑ INFLATION .... –0.4%
- ❑ UNEMPLOYMENT 5%

EXPORTS

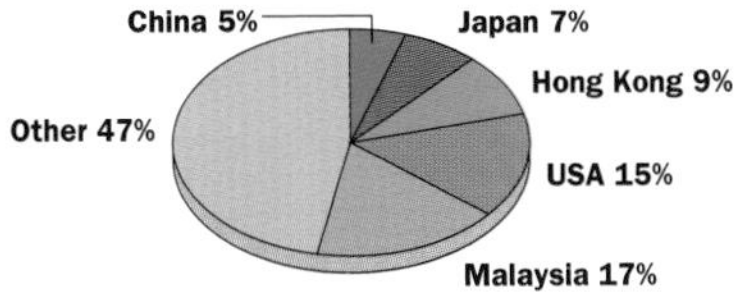
China 5%
Japan 7%
Hong Kong 9%
Other 47%
USA 15%
Malaysia 17%

IMPORTS

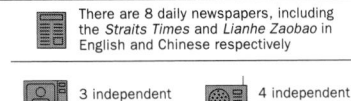

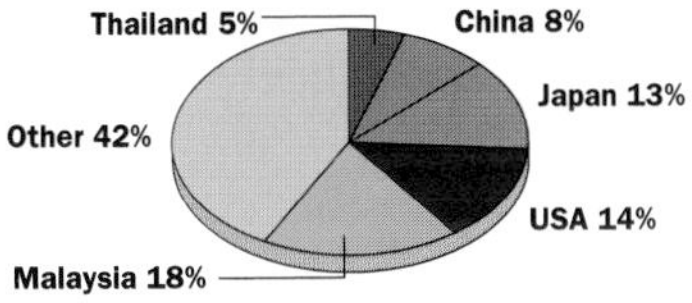
Thailand 5%
China 8%
Japan 13%
Other 42%
USA 14%
Malaysia 18%

STRENGTHS

Massive accumulated wealth derived from success as entrepôt and as center of high-tech industries. Major producer of computer disk drives. Huge state enterprises, such as TAMESEK, with over 450 companies, highly flexible in responding to market conditions. World leader in new biotechnologies.

WEAKNESSES

Dependent on Malaysia for water. Rigid education system stifles entrepreneurial system. Specialization in electronics makes economy highly sensitive to world market fluctuations. Lack of land.

RESOURCES

Electric power 5.7m kW

8704 tonnes

Not an oil producer; refines 700,000 b/d

600,000 ducks, 250,000 pigs, 300 goats, 2m chickens

None

Singapore has no strategic resources and has to import almost all the energy and food it needs. Its main resources, on which its wealth as a center of commerce has been built, are its strategic position and its people.

ENVIRONMENT

Not available

5% partially protected

14.7 tonnes per capita

There is a small green belt around the causeway. The streets are largely litter-free – due to instant heavy fines. Chewing gum is now available on prescription after a ten-year outright ban was lifted in 2002.

MEDIA

TV ownership high

Daily newspaper circulation 298 per 1000 people

PUBLISHING AND BROADCAST MEDIA

There are 8 daily newspapers, including the *Straits Times* and *Lianhe Zaobao* in English and Chinese respectively

3 independent services

4 independent services

The government is very sensitive to any criticism. Nevertheless, the media sector was partially liberalized in 2000, though new entrants found it difficult to make a profit. Foreigners may not own newspapers or broadcasting stations.

CRIME

Death penalty in use

16,310 prisoners

Down 10% in 2000–2001

Crime levels are low and punishment can be severe, but incidents of violent crime are rising. The main concern is intellectual piracy.

CHRONOLOGY

In 1819, Sir Stamford Raffles set up a trading post in the village of Singapore; by 1826 it was Britain's colonial center in southeast Asia.

- ❑ **1959** First elections: won by PAP.
- ❑ **1963** Included in Malay federation.
- ❑ **1965** Independence.
- ❑ **1990** Lee Kuan Yew resigns.
- ❑ **1993** Ong Teng Cheong first directly elected president.
- ❑ **2004** Lee's son Lee Hsien Loong becomes prime minister.

EDUCATION

Schooling is not compulsory

93%

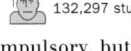

132,297 students

Schooling is not compulsory, but attendance is high. Education is seen as the key to a good salary, especially among the Chinese community.

HEALTH

Welfare state health benefits

1 per 698 people

Cancers, respiratory, heart, and cerebro-vascular diseases

Singapore has an efficient modern health system. There are incentives to ensure the continuation of the extended family, so that the elderly are cared for at home.

SPENDING

GDP/cap. increase

CONSUMPTION AND SPENDING

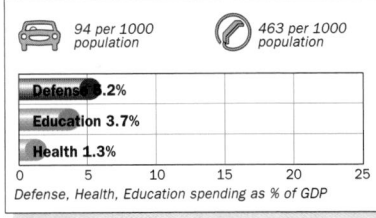

94 per 1000 population

463 per 1000 population

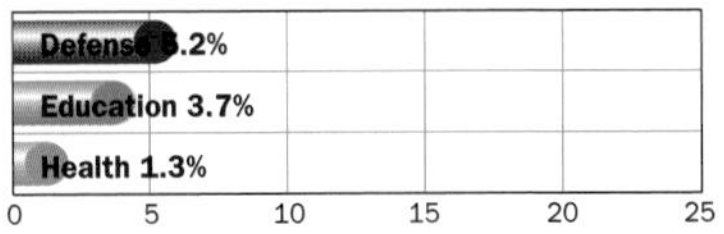
Defense 6.2%
Education 3.7%
Health 1.3%
0
5
10
15
20
25

Defense, Health, Education spending as % of GDP

The 2001 "Singapore Share" scheme promises to give Singaporeans a stake in the country's economy.

WORLD RANKING

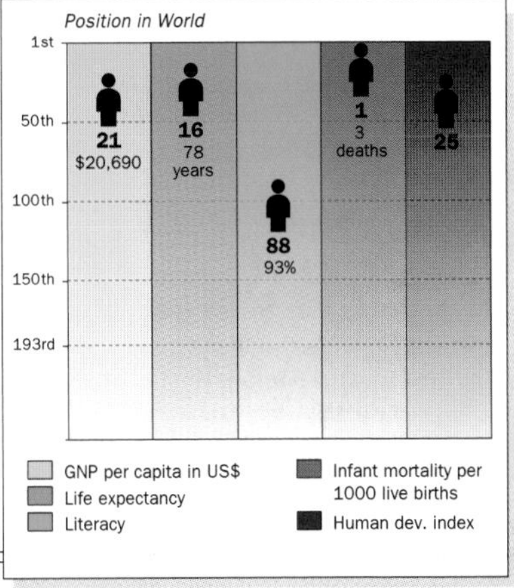
Position in World
1st
50th
100th
150th
193rd
21
$20,690
16
78 years
88
93%
1
3 deaths
25
GNP per capita in US$
Life expectancy
Literacy
Infant mortality per 1000 live births
Human dev. index

SINGAPORE

Total Area : 693 sq. km (267 sq. miles)

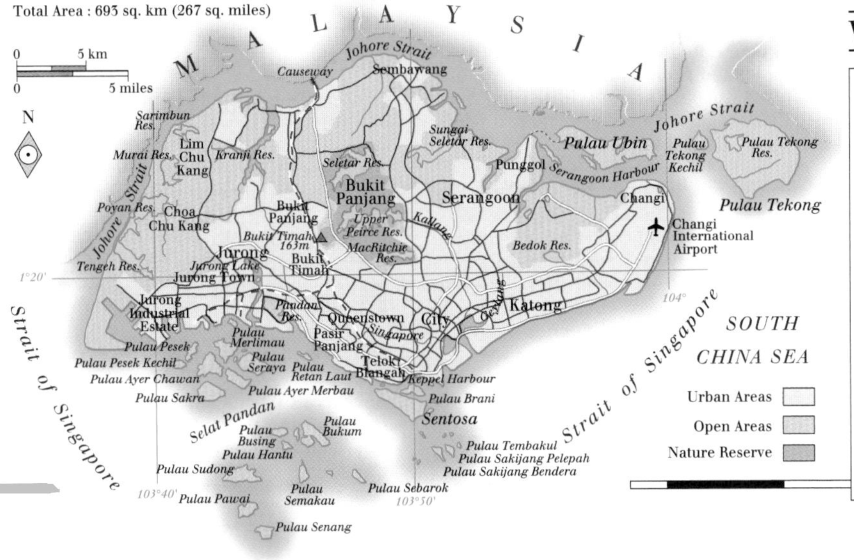
M A L A Y S I A
0
5 km
0
5 miles
N
Johore Strait
Causeway
Sembawang
Sarimbun Res.
Murai Res.
Lim Chu Kang
Kranji Res.
Poyan Res.
Choa Chu Kang
Johore Strait
Tengeh Res.
Seletar Res.
Sungei Seletar Res.
Bukit Panjang
Bukit Panjang
Bukit Timah 163m
Upper Peirce Res.
MacRitchie Res.
Jurong
Jurong Lake
Jurong Town
Bukit Timah
Jurong Industrial Estate
Pandan Res.
Pulau Ubin
Pulau Tekong Kechil
Pulau Tekong Res.
Pulau Tekong
Punggol
Serangoon Harbour
Serangoon
Kallang
Changi
Changi International Airport
Bedok Res.
Geylang
Katong
City
Queenstown
Singapore
Pasir Panjang
Telok Blangah
Keppel Harbour
Pulau Pesek
Pulau Pesek Kechil
Pulau Ayer Chawan
Pulau Sakra
Pulau Merlimau
Pulau Seraya
Pulau Retan Laut
Pulau Ayer Merbau
Selat Pandan
Pulau Busing
Pulau Bukum
Pulau Hantu
Pulau Sudong
Pulau Brani
Sentosa
Pulau Tembakul
Pulau Sakijang Pelepah
Pulau Sakijang Bendera
Pulau Semakau
Pulau Sebarok
Pulau Pawai
Pulau Senang
1°20'
103°40'
103°50'
104°
Strait of Singapore
Strait of Singapore
SOUTH CHINA SEA
Urban Areas
Open Areas
Nature Reserve

S

SLOVAKIA

EUROPE
Europe
Czech Republic
Poland
SLOVAKIA
Austria
Ukraine
Hungary

OFFICAL NAME: Slovak Republic **CAPITAL:** Bratislava
POPULATION: 5.4 million **CURRENCY:** Slovak koruna **OFFICAL LANGUAGE:** Slovak

1993 | 1993 | Oct 1 | SK | +1 | +421 | .sk

DOMINATED FOR 900 YEARS by neighboring Hungary, Slovakia spent much of the 20th century as the less developed half of communist Czechoslovakia. An independent democracy since 1993, Slovakia has struggled to create a modern market-led economy, but was among the ten countries which joined the EU in its major eastward expansion in 2004.

Levoča, in northeastern Slovakia, dates from the 13th century and still retains its medieval street plan and town walls.

CLIMATE

Continental

WEATHER CHART FOR BRATISLAVA

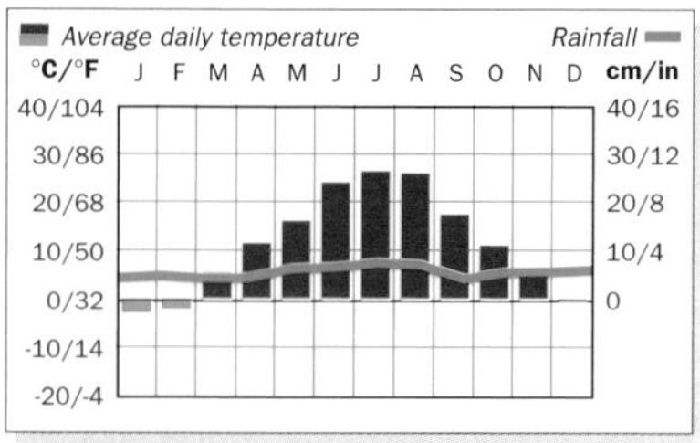

Average daily temperature
Rainfall
°C/°F J F M A M J J A S O N D cm/in
40/104 30/86 20/68 10/50 0/32 -10/14 -20/-4
40/16 30/12 20/8 10/4 0

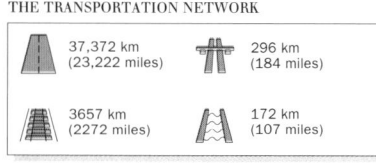

Slovakia has a continental climate. Snowfalls are heavy in winter, while summers are moderately warm.

TRANSPORTATION

Drive on right

Milan Rastislav Stefánik, Bratislava 366,907 passengers

Has no fleet

THE TRANSPORTATION NETWORK

37,372 km (23,222 miles)

296 km (184 miles)

3657 km (2272 miles)

172 km (107 miles)

The River Danube is a vital artery. Trains are cheap and efficient. Buses and trams are the mainstay of urban transportation.

TOURISM

Visitors : Population 1:3.9

1.4m visitors

Up 15% in 2002

MAIN TOURIST ARRIVALS

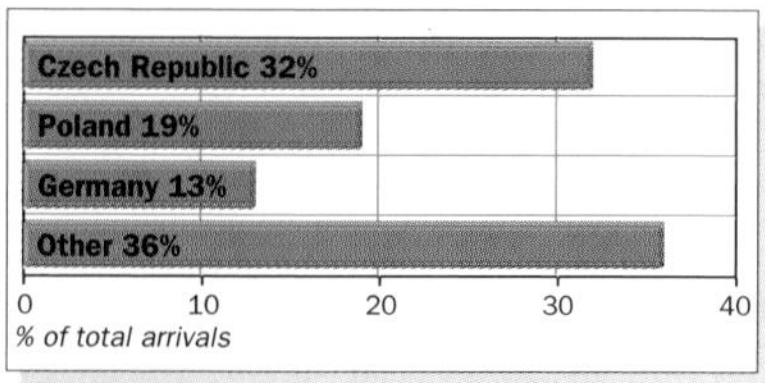

Czech Republic 32%
Poland 19%
Germany 13%
Other 36%
0 10 20 30 40
% of total arrivals

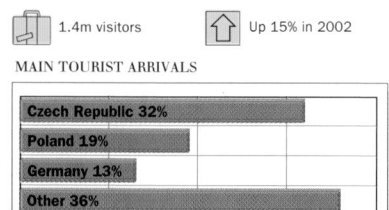

The High Tatras, one of the smallest high-mountain ranges in the world, and the Vrátna valley in the Little Tatras draw hikers and skiers. Tourists also visit Bratislava's castle and old city, and the many thermal-spring health spas.

PEOPLE

Pop. density medium

Slovak, Hungarian (Magyar), Czech

110/km² (285/mi²)

THE URBAN/RURAL POPULATION SPLIT

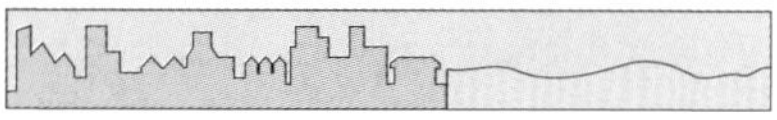

58%
42%

RELIGIOUS PERSUASION

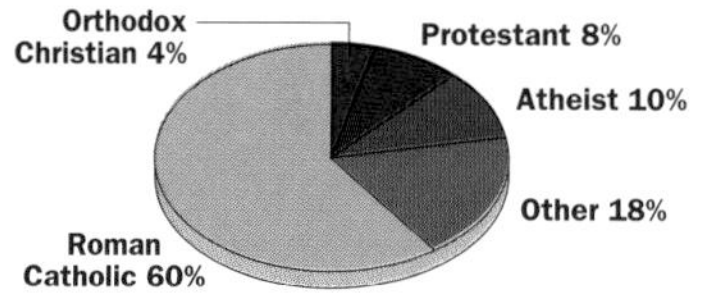

Orthodox Christian 4%
Protestant 8%
Atheist 10%
Other 18%
Roman Catholic 60%

Slovaks dominate society, but 11% of the population is Magyar, and there is a significant Roma minority which faces discrimination. The Magyar community, backed by Hungary, seeks protection for its language and culture. Tensions lessened in 1998 when its main political voice, the Hungarian Coalition Party, joined the government. There were 300,000 Slovaks living in Czech lands in 1993. Dual citizenship is now permitted.

POLITICS

Multiparty elections

2002/2006

President Ivan Gasparovic

AT THE LAST ELECTION

National Council of the Slovak Republic 150 seats

24% HZDS	19% SDKU	17% Smer	13% SMK	10% KDH	10% ANO	7% KSS

HZDS = Movement for a Democratic Slovakia
SDKU = Slovak Democratic and Christian Union
Smer = Direction **SMK** = Hungarian Coalition Party
KDH = Christian Democratic Movement **ANO** = New Civic Alliance **KSS** = Slovak Communist Party

The political ambitions of Slovak leader Vladimir Meciar were a major factor in the separation of Czechoslovakia in 1993. The populist Meciar was prime minister and dominated Slovak politics until 1998, but clashed repeatedly with President Michal Kovac, both of the HZDS.

The HZDS remained the largest party in the National Council after the 1998 elections, but was unable to form a government. Instead Mikulas Dzurinda of the Democratic Coalition (now the SDKU) led a broad center-right coalition. The SDKU formed a new four-party coalition after the 2002 election, despite a strong showing again by the HZDS and by the new populist Smer party.

Direct presidential elections were introduced in 1999; Meciar, by then out of office, lost that year to the pro-Western Rudolf Schuster, and in 2004 to former ally Ivan Gasparovic.

WORLD AFFAIRS

Joined UN in 1993

CE | EU | NATO | OECD | OSCE

Slovakia adopted a distinctly pro-Russian stance under Meciar. Since his defeat in 1998 it has turned increasingly to the West. It joined the OECD in 2000, NATO in March 2004, and the EU in May of the same year.

AID

Recipient

$189m (receipts)

Up 15% in 2002

Foreign aid fell after the mid-1990s, but EU programs helped the country to prepare for membership in 2004.

DEFENSE

Phasing out conscription

$439m

Up 15% in 2002

Conscription has been cut from nine months to six from January 2004 and is to be phased out by 2006. Prime Minister Dzurinda, in office since 1998, reversed Meciar's pro-Russian defense policies.

RESOURCES

Electric power 8.2m kW

2530 tonnes

1183 b/d (reserves 7.3m barrels)

5.8m turkeys, 1.6m ducks, 1.44m pigs, 5.6m chickens

Coal, lignite, gas, oil, antimony, copper, iron, mercury, zinc

Slovakia's two nuclear plants, Mochovce and Jaslovske Bohunice, generated almost 60% of electricity in 2001.

S

SLOVAKIA

Total Area : 48 845 sq. km
(18 859 sq. miles)

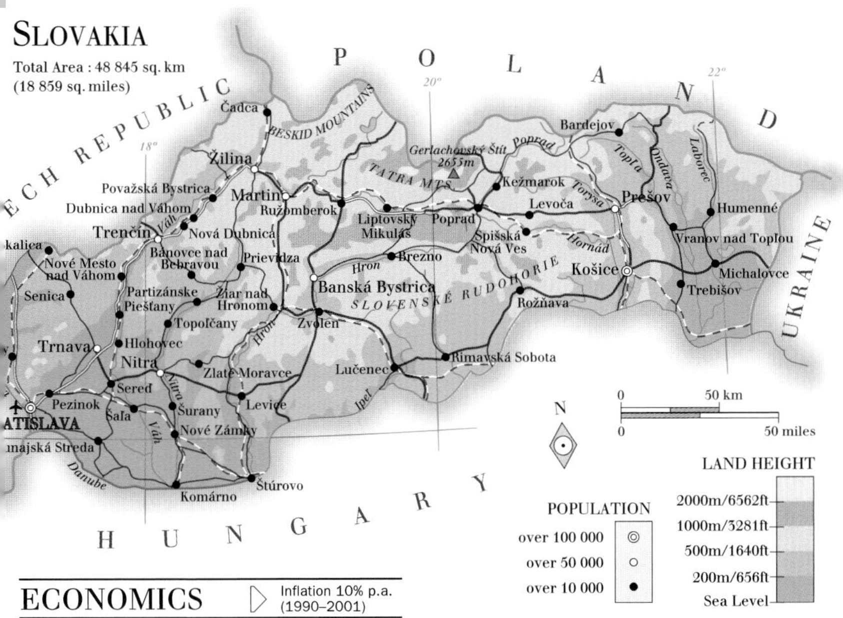
POLAND
CZECH REPUBLIC
HUNGARY
UKRAINE
BESKID MOUNTAINS
TATRA MTS
Gerlachovský Štít 2655m
SLOVENSKÉ RUDOHORIE
Čadca
Žilina
Považská Bystrica
Dubnica nad Váhom
Martin
Ružomberok
Trenčín
Nová Dubnica
Bánovce nad Bebravou
Prievidza
Liptovský Mikuláš
Poprad
Kežmarok
Levoča
Spišská Nová Ves
Bardejov
Prešov
Humenné
Vranov nad Toplou
Košice
Michalovce
Trebišov
Rožňava
Brezno
Banská Bystrica
Nové Mesto nad Váhom
Senica
Partizánske
Piešťany
Žiar nad Hronom
Topoľčany
Zvolen
Trnava
Hlohovec
Nitra
Zlaté Moravce
Lučenec
Rimavská Sobota
Sereď
Pezinok
Šaľa
Šurany
Levice
Nové Zámky
Dunajská Streda
Komárno
Štúrovo
Danube
Váh
Hron
Nitra
Ipeľ
Hornád
Poprad
Topľa
Ondava
Laborec
Torysa
N
0
50 km
50 miles
LAND HEIGHT
2000m/6562ft
1000m/3281ft
500m/1640ft
200m/656ft
Sea Level
POPULATION
over 100 000
over 50 000
over 10 000

CHRONOLOGY

Once part of the Austro-Hungarian Empire, Slovakia and the Czech Lands formed the Republic of Czechoslovakia in 1918.

- ❑ **1939–1945** Separate Slovak state under pro-Nazi Jozef Tiso.
- ❑ **1945** Czechoslovak state restored.
- ❑ **1947** Communists seize power.
- ❑ **1968** "Prague Spring" ended by Warsaw pact invasion.
- ❑ **1989** "Velvet Revolution."
- ❑ **1993** January 1, separate Slovak and Czech states established.
- ❑ **1994** HZDS election victory.
- ❑ **1998** Broad-based coalition under Dzurinda wins general election.
- ❑ **2002** Dzurinda coalition reelected.
- ❑ **2004** Slovakia joins NATO and EU. June, Ivan Gasparovic sworn in as president.

ECONOMICS

▷ Inflation 10% p.a. (1990–2001)

$21.3bn

32.75 Slovak koruny (36.21)

SCORE CARD

❑ WORLD GNP RANKING	61st
❑ GNP PER CAPITA	$3970
❑ BALANCE OF PAYMENTS	–$1.94bn
❑ INFLATION	3.3%
❑ UNEMPLOYMENT	19%

STRENGTHS

Expansion of manufacturing, especially in Bratislava and surrounding area. Increase in foreign investment and relative success of privatization program. Growth in exports to EU and promise of stability through membership. Potential for tourism, particularly skiing in the Tatra Mountains.

WEAKNESSES

High foreign indebtedness. High unemployment. Dependence on foreign trade makes the economy vulnerable to global recession. Heavy industry struggles with poor productivity. Much poorer eastern region. Collapse of "pyramid" investor schemes in 2002.

EXPORTS

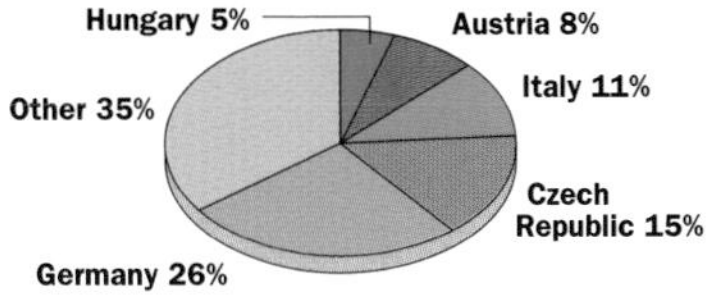
Hungary 5%
Austria 8%
Italy 11%
Czech Republic 15%
Germany 26%
Other 35%

IMPORTS

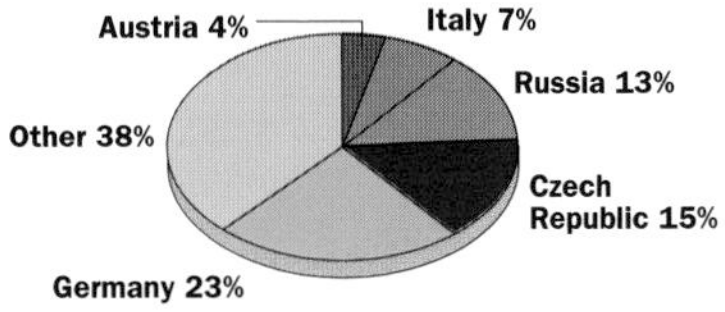
Austria 4%
Italy 7%
Russia 13%
Czech Republic 15%
Germany 23%
Other 38%

ENVIRONMENT

▷ Sustainability rank: 14th

23%

6.6 tonnes per capita

The Gabcikovo Dam and the Bohunice nuclear reactors, now scheduled for partial closure, have provoked criticism.

MEDIA

▷ TV ownership high

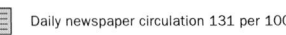

Daily newspaper circulation 131 per 1000 people

PUBLISHING AND BROADCAST MEDIA

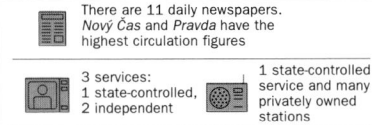

There are 11 daily newspapers. *Nový Čas* and *Pravda* have the highest circulation figures

3 services: 1 state-controlled, 2 independent

1 state-controlled service and many privately owned stations

The state news agency TASR, accused of lacking objectivity and depending on government funding, resisted the emergence of independent rival SITA.

CRIME

▷ No death penalty

8829 prisoners

Up 5% in 2001

Organized crime has increased rapidly in recent years, as has "white collar crime" such as business fraud. A new law to control money laundering took effect in 2001. A former economics minister accused of embezzlement was murdered in 1999.

EDUCATION

▷ School leaving age: 15

99%

139,036 students

Schooling now draws on pre-1939 Slovak traditions but it is not adequately resourced, especially in rural areas. There is a modern university in Bratislava.

HEALTH

▷ Welfare state health benefits

1 per 278 people

Heart diseases, cancers, cerebro-vascular disease

Rising demand and costs are straining the health service severely. Restoring viability is now a government priority.

SPENDING

▷ GDP/cap. increase

CONSUMPTION AND SPENDING

246 per 1000 population

268 per 1000 population

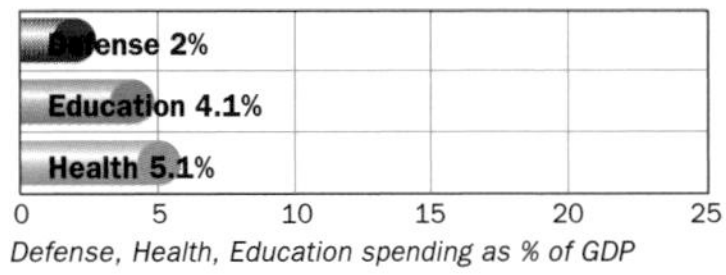
Defense 2%
Education 4.1%
Health 5.1%
0
5
10
15
20
25
Defense, Health, Education spending as % of GDP

A new elite is increasing demand for Western goods. Rural workers, Roma, and those living in the east are the poorest.

WORLD RANKING

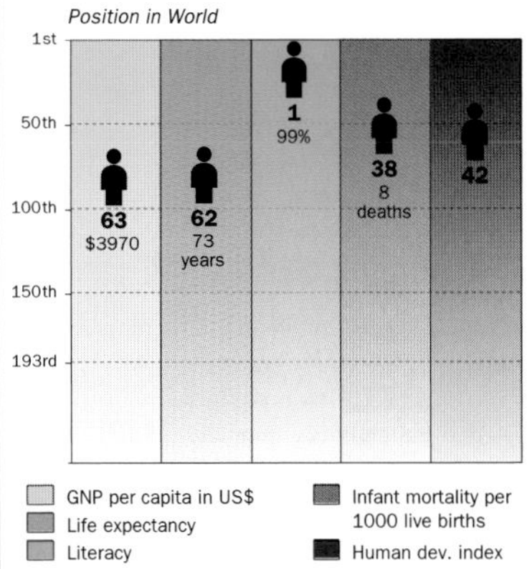
Position in World
1st
50th
100th
150th
193rd
63
$3970
62
73 years
1
99%
38
8 deaths
42
GNP per capita in US$
Life expectancy
Literacy
Infant mortality per 1000 live births
Human dev. index

S

SLOVENIA

EUROPE
Europe
Austria
Hungary
Italy
SLOVENIA
Croatia

OFFICIAL NAME: Republic of Slovenia **CAPITAL:** Ljubljana
POPULATION: 2 million **CURRENCY:** Tolar **OFFICIAL LANGUAGE:** Slovene

1991 | 1991 | June 25 | SLO | +1 | +386 | .si

OF ALL THE FORMER Yugoslav republics, Slovenia has the closest links with western Europe. Located at the northeastern end of the Adriatic Sea, this small, Alpine country controls some of Europe's major transit routes. Slovenia's transition to independence in 1991 avoided the violence of the breakup of Yugoslavia. The most prosperous of the former communist European states, it was the only former Yugoslav republic to join the EU and NATO in 2004.

CLIMATE

Continental/ Mediterranean

WEATHER CHART FOR LJUBLJANA

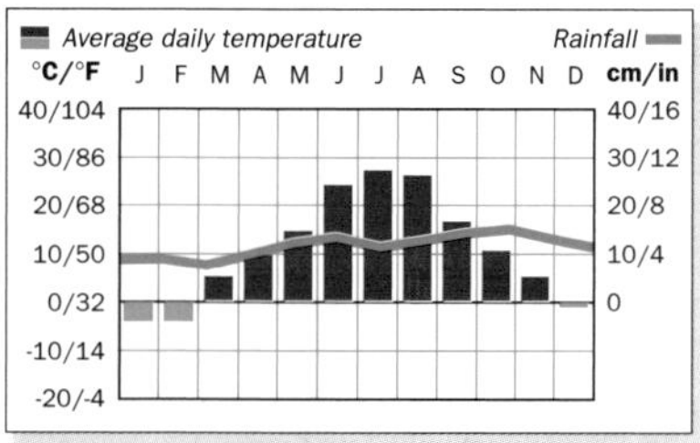
Average daily temperature
Rainfall
°C/°F
J F M A M J J A S O N D
cm/in
40/104
30/86
20/68
10/50
0/32
-10/14
-20/-4
40/16
30/12
20/8
10/4
0

Slovenia's interior has a continental climate. Its small coastal region has a mild Mediterranean climate.

TRANSPORTATION

Drive on right

Brnik, Ljubljana 921,335 passengers

11 ships 2251 grt

THE TRANSPORTATION NETWORK

20,236 km (12,574 miles)

456 km (283 miles)

1229 km (764 miles)

None

Slovenia is strategically situated at some of Europe's major crossroads. In addition, its Adriatic ports provide Austria with its main maritime outlet.

TOURISM

Visitors : Population 1:1.5

1.37m visitors

Up 5% in 2003

MAIN TOURIST ARRIVALS

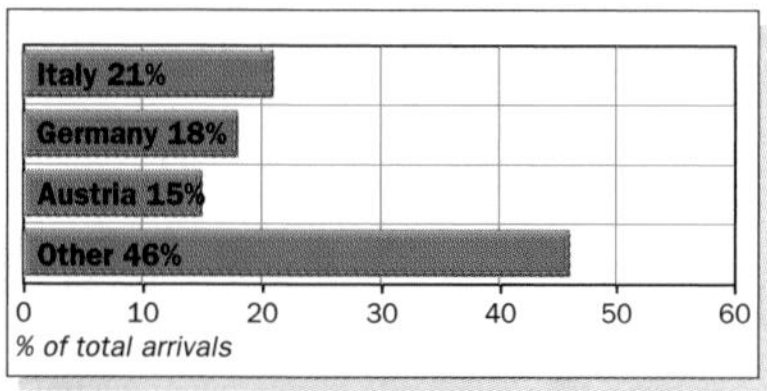
Italy 21%
Germany 18%
Austria 15%
Other 46%
0
10
20
30
40
50
60
% of total arrivals

A revival in tourism has been helped by Slovenia's political stability. Particular attractions include skiing in the Julian Alps, picturesque Ljubljana, and the wine-growing region around Ptuj.

PEOPLE

Pop. density medium

Slovene, Serbo-Croat

99/km² (256/mi²)

THE URBAN/RURAL POPULATION SPLIT

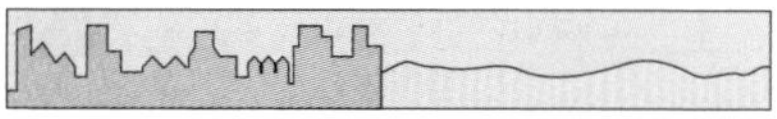
49%
51%

ETHNIC MAKEUP

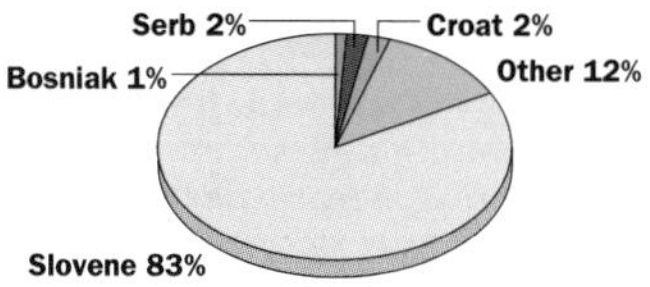
Serb 2%
Croat 2%
Bosniak 1%
Other 12%
Slovene 83%

Slovenes are ethnically very similar to the neighboring Croats and, like them, are predominantly Roman Catholic. However, Slovenia's long historical association with western Europe, and particularly with Austria, created a distinct Slovene identity, enabling a smooth transition to independence in 1991. The major non-Slavic minorities are small communities of Hungarians in the east and Italians in the southwestern Istrian region; tensions are few.

Women are not particularly disadvantaged in Slovenian society.

POLITICS

Multiparty elections

L. House 2004/2008
U. House 2002/2007

President Janez Drnovsek

AT THE LAST ELECTION

National Assembly 90 seats

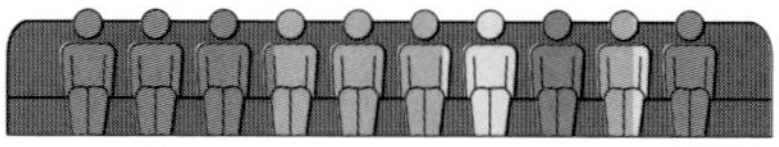
11% ZLSD
8% SLS/SKD
32% SDS
26% LDS
10% NSi
2% MR
11% Others

SDS = Social Democratic Party of Slovenia
LDS = Liberal Democracy of Slovenia
ZLSD = United List of Social Democrats
NSi = New Slovenia – Christian People's Party
SLS/SKD = Slovene People's Party/Christian Democrats of Slovenia **MR** = Two seats are reserved for Italian and Hungarian minority representatives

National Council 40 seats

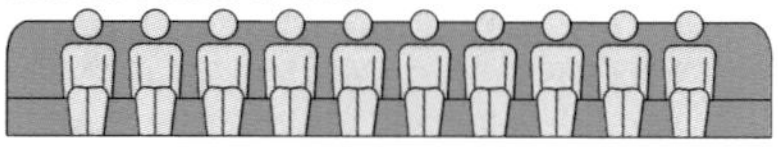

22 members of the National Council, which has an advisory role, are indirectly elected, and 18 are chosen by an electoral college to represent various interests

Slovenia has been strikingly stable since independence, but fragmented party politics makes coalition governments essential. Milan Kucan was elected president in 1990 and 1997, and Janez Drnovsek, leader of the center-left LDS, was prime minister almost continuously from 1992 until he was elected to replace Kucan in December 2002, with Finance Minister Anton Rop appointed prime minister in his stead. In 2004 the center-right SDS won a surprise election victory on the back of a general desire for change rather than major policy differences.

A smooth integration into the Western international community is the main political issue, while reform of the pension system and controlling inflation are also of concern.

SLOVENIA

Total Area : 20 253 sq. km (7820 sq. miles)

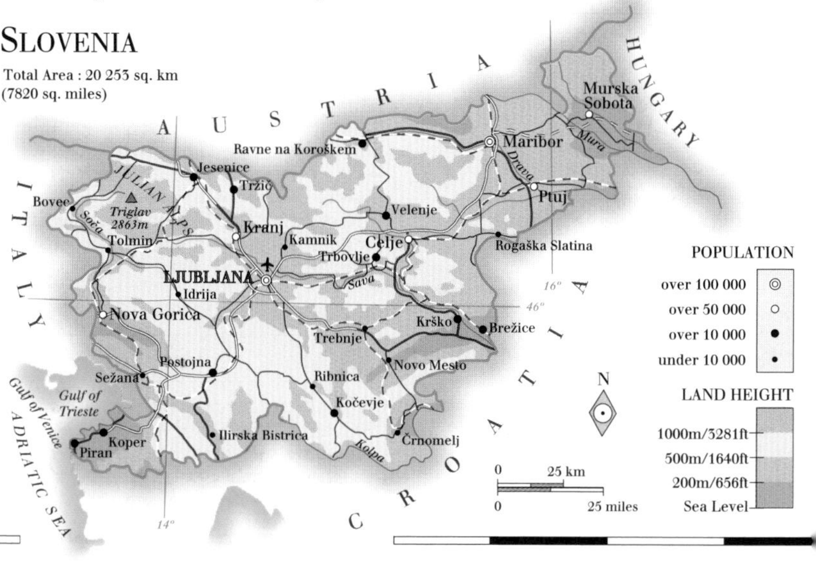
AUSTRIA
HUNGARY
ITALY
CROATIA
Murska Sobota
Mura
Maribor
Drava
Ptuj
Ravne na Koroškem
Jesenice
Tržič
Bovec
JULIAN ALPS
Triglav 2863m
Soča
Tolmin
Kranj
Kamnik
Velenje
Celje
Trbovlje
Sava
Rogaška Slatina
LJUBLJANA
Idrija
Nova Gorica
Krško
Brežice
Trebnje
Postojna
Novo Mesto
Sežana
Ribnica
Kočevje
Gulf of Trieste
Gulf of Venice
ADRIATIC SEA
Koper
Piran
Ilirska Bistrica
Kolpa
Črnomelj
14°
16°
46°
N
0 25 km
0 25 miles
POPULATION
over 100 000
over 50 000
over 10 000
under 10 000
LAND HEIGHT
1000m/3281ft
500m/1640ft
200m/656ft
Sea Level

S

WORLD AFFAIRS

Joined UN in 1992

CE | CEFTA | EU | NATO | OSCE

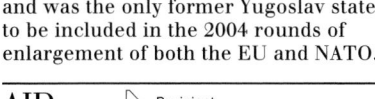

Slovenia has close ties to the West and was the only former Yugoslav state to be included in the 2004 rounds of enlargement of both the EU and NATO.

AID

Recipient

$171m (receipts) — Up 36% in 2002

Post-1991 aid came overwhelmingly from the EU, increasing markedly in preparation for membership in 2004. A key focus is on improving education.

DEFENSE

No compulsory military service

$311m — Up 13% in 2002

Troops staved off Yugoslav forces after secession in 1991. Compulsory military service was phased out in 2003 and replaced by a voluntary option.

ECONOMICS

Inflation 18% p.a. (1993–2001)

$20.4bn — 197.2 tolars (203.7)

SCORE CARD

❑ WORLD GNP RANKING	63rd
❑ GNP PER CAPITA	$10,370
❑ BALANCE OF PAYMENTS	$375m
❑ INFLATION	7.5%
❑ UNEMPLOYMENT	6%

EXPORTS

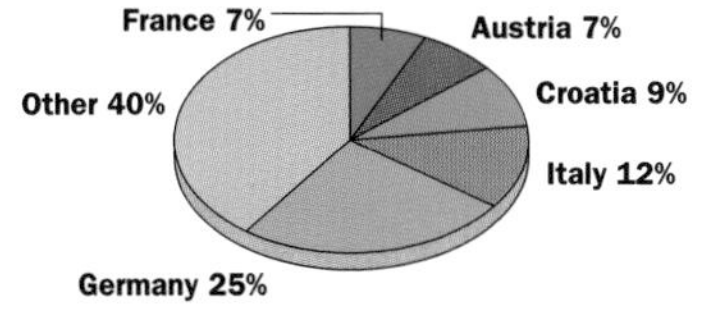
France 7%
Austria 7%
Other 40%
Croatia 9%
Italy 12%
Germany 25%

IMPORTS

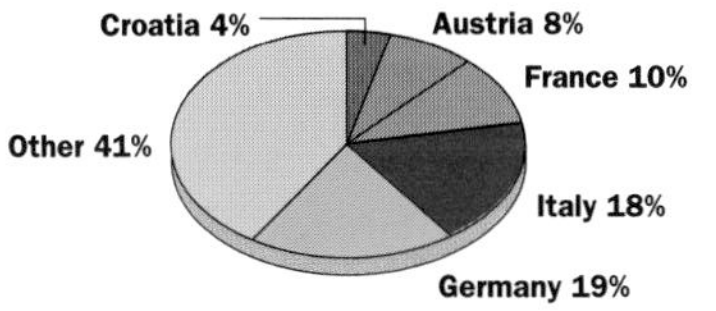
Croatia 4%
Austria 8%
France 10%
Other 41%
Italy 18%
Germany 19%

STRENGTHS

Stability. Competitive manufacturing industry. Healthy exports. Prospects of increased trade from EU membership. Revoz car plant: produces Renault Clios. Competitive port at Koper. Free trade pact with Bosnia from 2001. Least indebted of central and eastern European states.

WEAKNESSES

Foreign investment slow to take off despite market reforms. Sluggish privatization, particularly of banking sector. Inflation high, but falling.

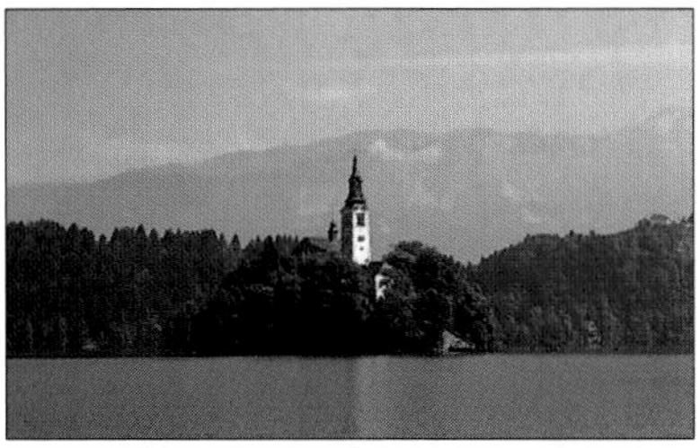

Lake Bled in the Julian Alps, *which lie astride the Slovenian–Italian border. The lake is a popular tourist destination.*

RESOURCES

Electric power 2.5m kW

3089 tonnes — 20 b/d

655,665 pigs, 473,242 cattle, 4.98m chickens — Coal, lignite, lead, zinc, uranium, silver, mercury, oil

Slovenia has come under pressure from Austria to close the nuclear plant at Krško, which provides one-third of Slovenia's power. There are deposits of brown coal and lignite, but they are difficult to extract and of poor quality.

ENVIRONMENT

Sustainability rank: 23rd

6% (2% partially protected) — 7.3 tonnes per capita

Protecting the country's alpine ecology is a priority. Pollution comes mainly from smelting, the chemicals industry, and burning brown coal and lignite.

MEDIA

TV ownership high

Daily newspaper circulation 169 per 1000 people

PUBLISHING AND BROADCAST MEDIA

There are 6 daily newspapers. *The Delo* has the largest circulation

4 services: 1 state-controlled, 3 independent — 4 services and many regional stations

A free and critical press has developed. State broadcasters have a new ethical code, protecting journalists' sources. POP TV is a commercial success.

CRIME

No death penalty

1120 prisoners — Up 11% in 2001

Slovenia's prison population is proportionately among the lowest in Europe. Smuggling people into western Europe is overtaking narcotics smuggling as the focus of organized crime.

EDUCATION

School leaving age: 14

99% — 91,494 students

Primary schooling now begins at the age of six, lowered from seven. Preschooling is available. Ljubljana and Maribor have universities.

CHRONOLOGY

Slovenia was part of the Austro-Hungarian Empire until 1918, when it joined the Kingdom of Serbs, Croats, and Slovenes (Yugoslavia).

- ❑ **1948** Tito's break with Moscow.
- ❑ **1989** Parliament confirms right to secede. Calls multiparty elections.
- ❑ **1990** Control over army asserted, referendum approves secession.
- ❑ **1991** Independence declared; first republic to secede. Yugoslav federal army repelled.
- ❑ **1992** First multiparty elections. Milan Kucan president, Janez Drnovsek prime minister.
- ❑ **1993** Joins IMF and World Bank.
- ❑ **2002** Drnovsek elected president; Anton Rop prime minister.
- ❑ **2004** Joins NATO and EU. SDS wins elections.

HEALTH

Welfare state health benefits

1 per 455 people — Cancers, heart, cerebrovascular, and respiratory diseases

National health care in Slovenia uses health centers and outpatient clinics to increase accessibility for patients.

SPENDING

GDP/cap. increase

CONSUMPTION AND SPENDING

445 per 1000 population — 506 per 1000 population

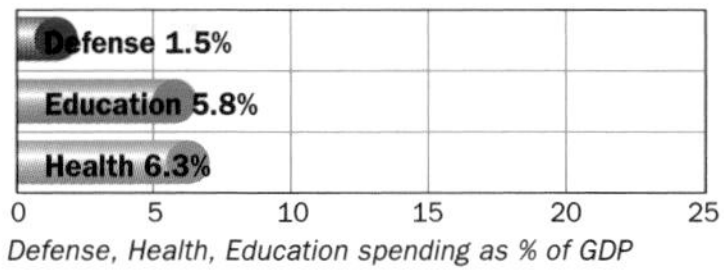
Defense 1.5%
Education 5.8%
Health 6.3%
0
5
10
15
20
25

Defense, Health, Education spending as % of GDP

Slovenia has the highest standard of living of all the central and eastern European states of the former Soviet bloc.

WORLD RANKING

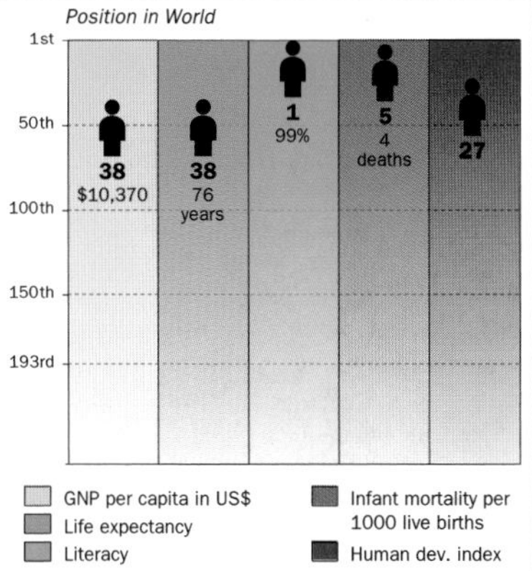
Position in World
1st
50th
100th
150th
193rd
38
$10,370
38
76 years
1
99%
5
4 deaths
27
GNP per capita in US$
Life expectancy
Literacy
Infant mortality per 1000 live births
Human dev. index

S

SOLOMON ISLANDS

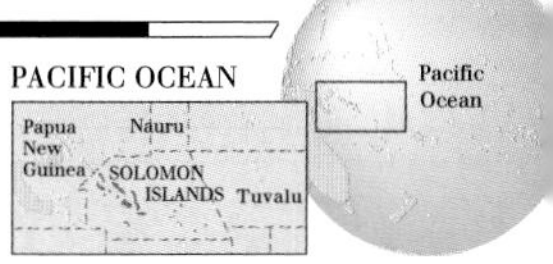
PACIFIC OCEAN
Papua New Guinea
Nauru
SOLOMON ISLANDS
Tuvalu
Pacific Ocean

OFFICIAL NAME: Solomon Islands **CAPITAL:** Honiara
POPULATION: 477,000 **CURRENCY:** Solomon Islands dollar **OFFICIAL LANGUAGE:** English

1978 | 1978 | July 7 | SLB | +11 | +677 | .sb

SCATTERED OVER 645,000 sq. km (250,000 sq. miles), the Solomons archipelago has several hundred islands, but most people live on the six largest – Guadalcanal, Malaita, New Georgia, Makira, Santa Isabel, and Choiseul. The Solomons have been settled since at least 1000 BCE; the Spanish arrived in 1568. Since 1998 ethnic conflict between rival islanders has destabilized the country. Most of the Solomons are coral reefs. Just 1% of the land area is cultivable.

CLIMATE

Tropical equatorial

WEATHER CHART FOR HONIARA

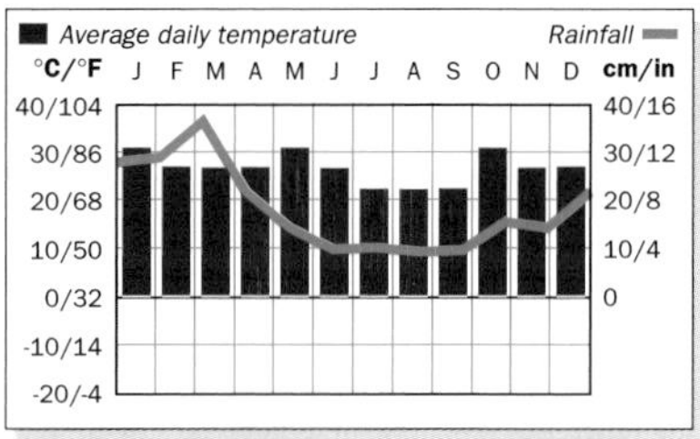
Average daily temperature
Rainfall
°C/°F
J F M A M J J A S O N D
cm/in
40/104
30/86
20/68
10/50
0/32
-10/14
-20/-4
40/16
30/12
20/8
10/4
0

There is little temperature variation in the humid climate, but ferocious cyclones can occur in the rainy season.

TRANSPORTATION

Drive on left

Henderson Field, Honiara 22,000 passengers

28 ships 8400 grt

THE TRANSPORTATION NETWORK

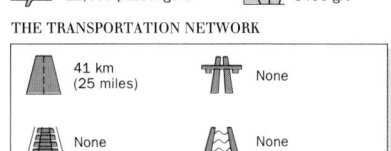

41 km (25 miles)	None
None	None

International flights from the principal airport, 13 km (8 miles) outside Honiara, were resumed in late 2000 after the ending of open hostilities.

***Unloading seed coconuts** near Munda on New Georgia in the Solomons' northern chain of islands. Coconuts are by far the largest and most commercially important crop.*

TOURISM

Visitors : Population 1:23

21,000 visitors

Down in 2000

MAIN TOURIST ARRIVALS

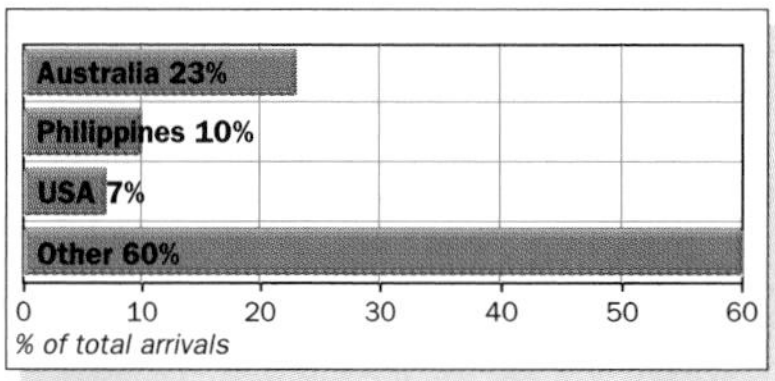
Australia 23%
Philippines 10%
USA 7%
Other 60%
0
10
20
30
40
50
60
% of total arrivals

The importance of Guadalcanal during World War II and the tranquility of the outer islands used to attract tourists. However, ethnic conflict all but destroyed tourism in 1998 and again when fighting intensified in 2000. Lack of funding hampers recovery.

PEOPLE

Pop. density low

English, Pidgin English, Melanesian Pidgin

17/km² (44/mi²)

THE URBAN/RURAL POPULATION SPLIT

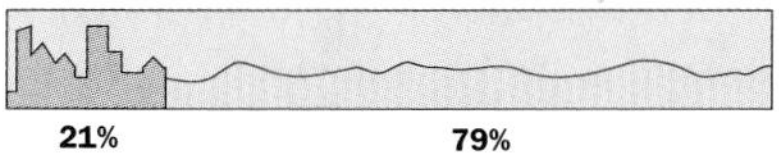
21%
79%

RELIGIOUS PERSUASION

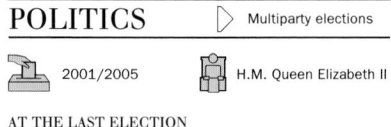

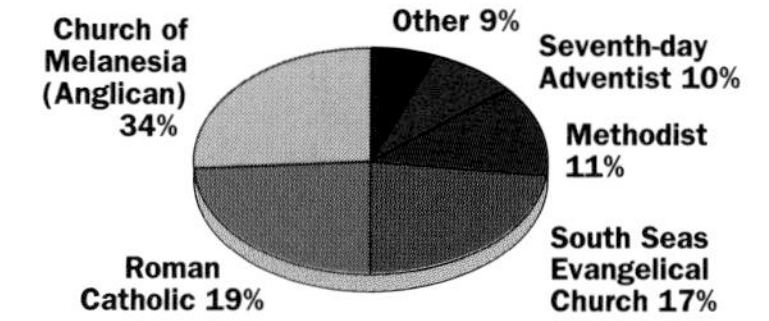
Church of Melanesia (Anglican) 34%
Other 9%
Seventh-day Adventist 10%
Methodist 11%
South Seas Evangelical Church 17%
Roman Catholic 19%

Almost all Solomon Islanders are Melanesian; relations between islands are tense. During the 1998–2000 conflict, 20,000 Malaitans were forced from their homes on Guadalcanal by native (Isatabu) militias. Authorities in outlying islands have pressed for greater autonomy. There are small communities of Micronesians who are descended from I-Kiribati temporarily relocated in 1957. More than 50 dialects are spoken. Though the islanders are nominally Christian, animist beliefs are widespread.

POLITICS

Multiparty elections

2001/2005

H.M. Queen Elizabeth II

AT THE LAST ELECTION

National Parliament 50 seats

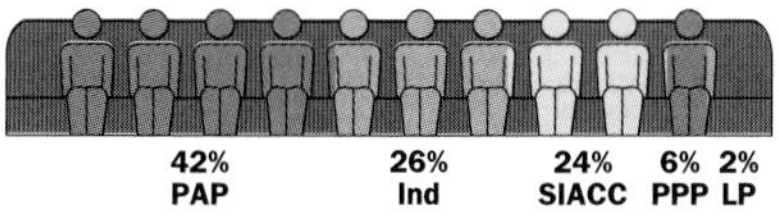
42% PAP
26% Ind
24% SIACC
6% PPP
2% LP

PAP = People's Alliance Party **Ind** = Independents
SIACC = Solomon Islands Alliance for Change Coalition
PPP = People's Progressive Party **LP** = Labour Party

The government was briefly ousted during civil conflict on Guadalcanal in 2000. Though a new devolved "state system" provided a semblance of stability, with greater regional autonomy, militias maintained effective control. "Compensation" claims from the conflict quickly outstripped aid funds, and the government is frequently close to bankruptcy. Prime Minister Allan Kamakeza and his PAP government (elected in 2001) called for the intervention of an Australian-led Regional Assistance Mission which arrived in 2003 to restore order and reform the country's finances.

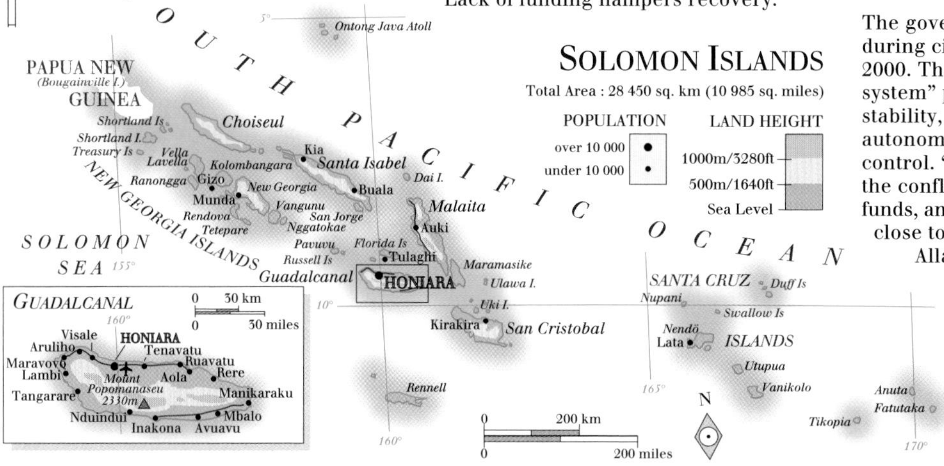
SOLOMON ISLANDS
Total Area : 28 450 sq. km (10 985 sq. miles)
POPULATION
over 10 000
under 10 000
LAND HEIGHT
1000m/3280ft
500m/1640ft
Sea Level
SOUTH PACIFIC OCEAN
SOLOMON SEA
PAPUA NEW GUINEA
(Bougainville I.)
Ontong Java Atoll
Shortland Is
Shortland I.
Treasury Is
Choiseul
Vella Lavella
Kolombangara
Ranongga
Gizo
Munda
New Georgia
Rendova
Tetepare
NEW GEORGIA ISLANDS
Vangunu
San Jorge
Nggatokae
Kia
Santa Isabel
Buala
Dai I.
Malaita
Auki
Pavuvu
Russell Is
Florida Is
Tulagi
HONIARA
Guadalcanal
Maramasike
Ulawa I.
Uki I.
Kirakira
San Cristobal
Rennell
SANTA CRUZ ISLANDS
Duff Is
Nupani
Swallow Is
Nendö
Lata
Utupua
Vanikolo
Anuta
Fatutaka
Tikopia
0 200 km
0 200 miles
N
GUADALCANAL
0 30 km
0 30 miles
Visale
HONIARA
Aruliho
Tenavatu
Maravovo
Ruavatu
Lambi
Mount Popomanaseu 2330m
Aola
Rere
Tangarare
Manikaraku
Nduindui
Inakona
Avuavu
Mbalo

WORLD AFFAIRS

Joined UN in 1978

ACP | Comm | IBRD | PC | PIF

The intensification of violence in 2000 caused great concern around the Pacific, and heightened international mediation efforts, in which Australia in particular was involved. The Solomons government was increasingly eager to secure direct intervention in order to restore law and order. In 2003, Australia agreed to lead a regional peacekeeping force.

AID

Recipient

US$26m (receipts)

Down 56% in 2002

Aid has focused very specifically on restoring stability and rebuilding infrastructure after years of brutal conflict. Regional powers Australia, New Zealand, and Taiwan are key in aiding recovery. Australia has taken on most responsibility in the reconstruction efforts through its commanding role in the Regional Assistance Mission.

DEFENSE

No compulsory military service

Australia responsible for defense

Not applicable

The Australian-led Regional Assistance Mission to Solomon Islands (RAMSI) was invited by the Solomons government in 2003 amid continuing insecurity. RAMSI brought a robust military presence, and the militias' control over outlying islands was quickly broken. A gun amnesty netted nearly 4000 weapons.

ECONOMICS

Inflation 8.2% p.a. (1990–2001)

US$256m

7.435 Solomon Islands dollars (7.521)

SCORE CARD

- WORLD GNP RANKING........................179th
- GNP PER CAPITA ....US$580
- BALANCE OF PAYMENTS ....US$21m
- INFLATION 9.4%
- UNEMPLOYMENT...........Some underemployment

EXPORTS

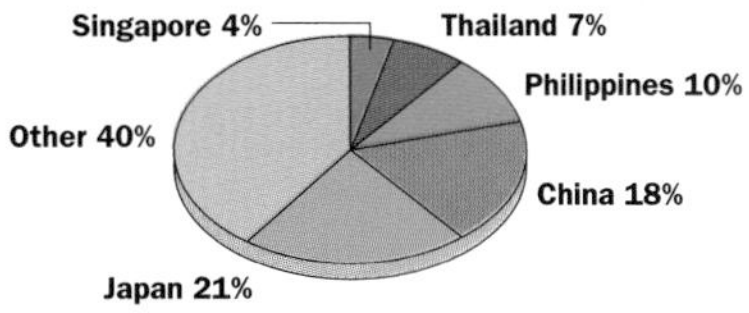
Singapore 4%
Thailand 7%
Philippines 10%
China 18%
Japan 21%
Other 40%

IMPORTS

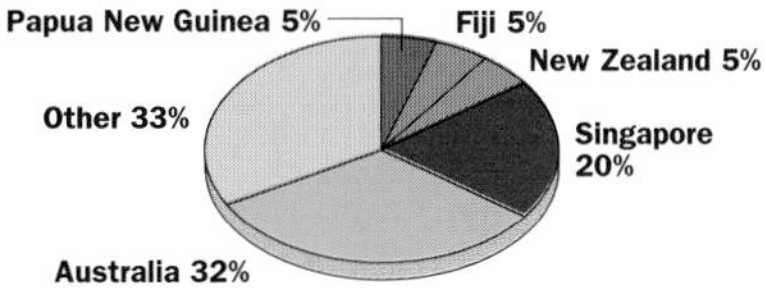
Papua New Guinea 5%
Fiji 5%
New Zealand 5%
Singapore 20%
Australia 32%
Other 33%

STRENGTHS

Good mineral and agricultural resources. Influx of international aid.

WEAKNESSES

Economy near collapse after ethnic conflict. Destruction of infrastructure. Key gold mine shut by militias. Grossly inflated compensation claims from conflict. Revenue from copra, gold, fish, and palm oil dried up. Lack of social stability deters investment.

RESOURCES

Electric power 12,000 kW

30,090 tonnes

Not an oil producer

68,000 pigs, 13,000 cattle, 220,000 chickens

Gold, copper, bauxite, lead, zinc, silver, cobalt, phosphates

Bauxite deposits have been discovered on Rennell Island, and there are traces of gold and copper on Guadalcanal.

Electricity was rationed in Honiara in 2004, since there was only enough fuel to run one generator.

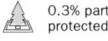

ENVIRONMENT

Not available

0.3% partially protected

0.4 tonnes per capita

The environmental movement is strong. Depletion of forest and marine resources are a major concern. In 1998 a sustainable forest-harvesting policy was introduced, but the need to restore the economy puts pressure on environmentally sensitive areas.

MEDIA

TV ownership low

Daily newspaper circulation 16 per 1000 people

PUBLISHING AND BROADCAST MEDIA

There is 1 daily newspaper, *The Solomon Star*

No terrestrial service

2 services: 1 state-owned, 1 independent

Australia has donated technical equipment to the national broadcaster and has sponsored peace programs.

CRIME

No death penalty

134 prisoners

Crime is rising

The Australian-led peacekeeping force is providing security while the criminal justice system is completely overhauled.

CHRONOLOGY

Settled since before 1000 BCE by Melanesian peoples, the Solomons became a British colony in 1893.

- **1942–1943** Japanese occupation.
- **1978** Independence from UK.
- **1983** Diplomatic relations with Taiwan established.
- **1998–2000** Civil conflict between Guadalcanal and Malaita islanders.
- **2003** International peacekeeping force arrives.

EDUCATION

School leaving age: 14

77%

Not available

Education is modeled on the British system. Tertiary students go to the University of the South Pacific in Fiji.

HEALTH

Welfare state health benefits

1 per 10,000 people

Not available

There is one hospital in Honiara; during the recent crisis, smaller clinics were damaged and staff fled. The return of security has allowed services to recover.

SPENDING

GDP/cap. decrease

CONSUMPTION AND SPENDING

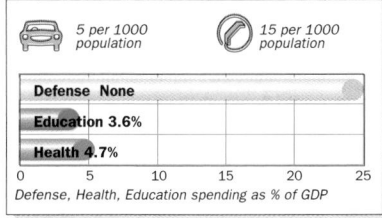

5 per 1000 population

15 per 1000 population

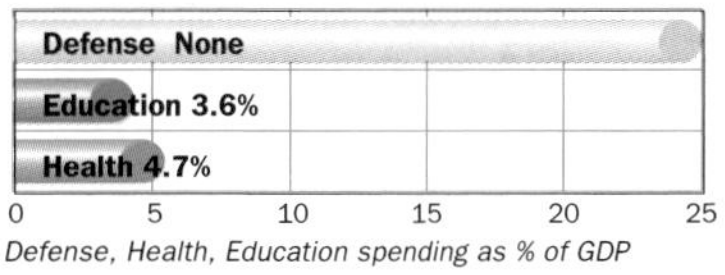
Defense None
Education 3.6%
Health 4.7%
0
5
10
15
20
25
Defense, Health, Education spending as % of GDP

Solomon Islanders in government jobs are the wealthiest group. Inhabitants of the outlying islands are extremely poor.

WORLD RANKING

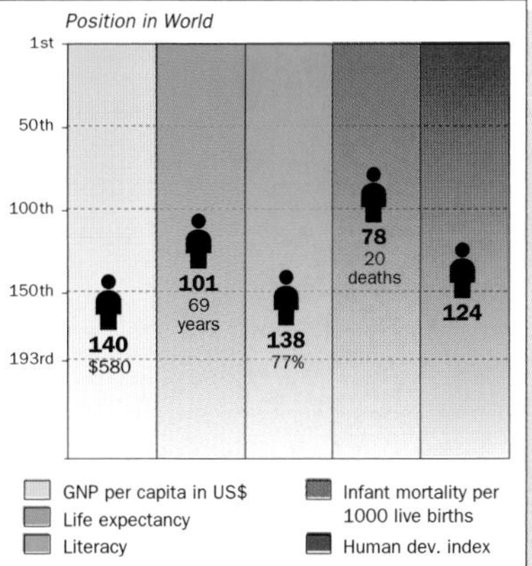
Position in World
1st
50th
100th
150th
193rd
140
$580
101
69
years
138
77%
78
20
deaths
124
GNP per capita in US$
Life expectancy
Literacy
Infant mortality per 1000 live births
Human dev. index

S

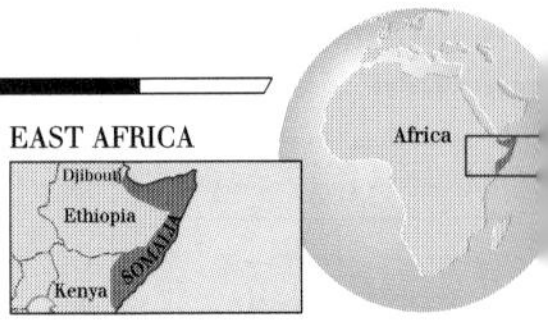
EAST AFRICA
Djibouti
Ethiopia
Kenya
SOMALIA
Africa

SOMALIA

OFFICIAL NAME: Somalia **CAPITAL:** Mogadishu **POPULATION:** 9.9 million
CURRENCY: Somali shilling **OFFICIAL LANGUAGES:** Somali and Arabic

1960 | 1960 | Oct 21 | SO | +3 | +252 | .so

OCCUPYING THE HORN of Africa, Italian Somaliland and British Somaliland joined in 1960 to form an independent Somalia. Except in the more fertile south, the land is semiarid. Years of clan-based civil war have resulted in the collapse of central government, the frustration of US and UN intervention initiatives aimed at easing a huge refugee crisis, and mass starvation.

CLIMATE

Hot desert/steppe

WEATHER CHART FOR MOGADISHU

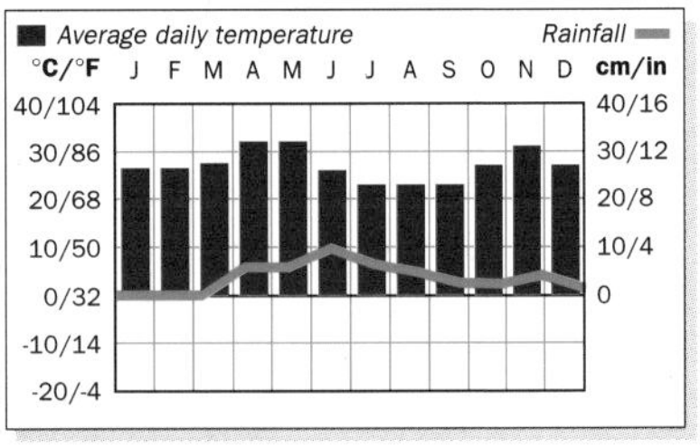
Average daily temperature
Rainfall
°C/°F J F M A M J J A S O N D cm/in
40/104
30/86
20/68
10/50
0/32
-10/14
-20/-4
40/16
30/12
20/8
10/4
0

Somalia is very dry. The northern coast is very hot and humid, the eastern less so. The interior has some of the world's highest mean yearly temperatures.

TRANSPORTATION

Drive on left

Mogadishu

17 ships
6300 grt

THE TRANSPORTATION NETWORK

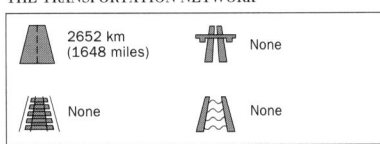

2652 km (1648 miles)

None

None

None

About 50% of Somalis are nomads for whom the donkey is the principal means of transportation. In 1990, the IDA agreed to repair the road network, but work on the seven-year project has not yet begun.

TOURISM

Visitors : Population 1:990

10,000 visitors

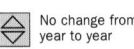

No change from year to year

MAIN TOURIST ARRIVALS

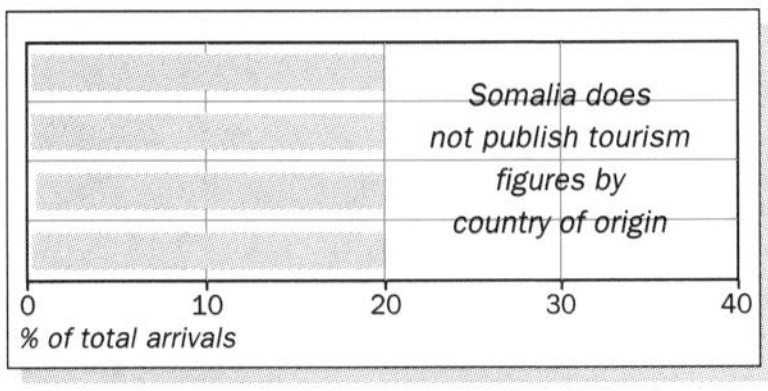
Somalia does not publish tourism figures by country of origin
0
10
20
30
40
% of total arrivals

Aid workers and foreign journalists are the only visitors. Landmines are a widespread hazard.

Baydhabo market. *Subsistence farming supports most people, despite chaos created by the fighting.*

PEOPLE

Pop. density low

Somali, Arabic, English, Italian

16/km² (41/mi²)

THE URBAN/RURAL POPULATION SPLIT

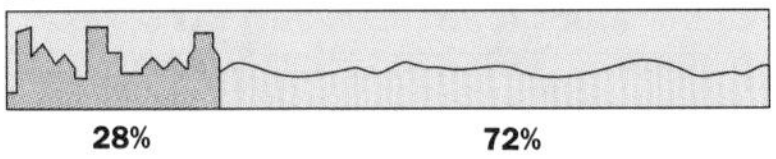
28%
72%

RELIGIOUS PERSUASION

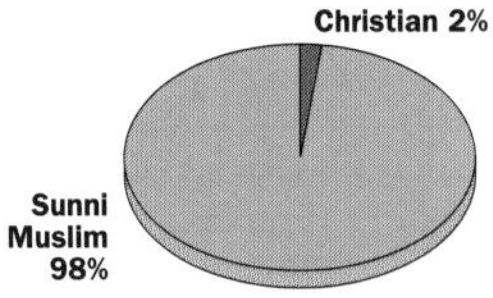
Christian 2%
Sunni Muslim 98%

The clan system is fundamental. Shifting allegiances characterize its structure – a tendency stifled by Siad Barre's dictatorship but revived after his fall in 1991. Barre's undermining of the elders – the traditional brokers of justice – contributed to the power vacuum that resulted in civil war. His persecution of the Issaqs led to Somaliland's declaration of secession in 1991. However, most people are ethnic Somali, and national identity remains strong, with both Somaliland and Puntland recognizing reintegration as an acceptable end to peace talks.

POLITICS

No legislative elections

1984/Uncertain

Interim President Ahmed Abdullahi Yusuf

AT THE LAST ELECTION

National Assembly (suspended)

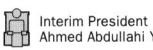

There has been no prospect of organizing new elections since the overthrow of Siad Barre. A transitional assembly was formed in 2004 on a nonparty basis.

Somalia has remained in anarchy since former dictator Siad Barre fled in 1991. The unified state dissolved amid conflict in the south and separatism in the north. Throughout the 1990s rival warlords, including the powerful Gen. Aideed, vied for control, undermining a US-led peacekeeping force in 1992.

After many false starts at reinstating a political system, a conference of businessmen, clan leaders, and power brokers met in Kenya in 2004 and established an interim assembly with a broad base of support. This time around the peace process was backed by all Somalia's neighbors and donors, and the 275 members of the assembly included, crucially, most of the regional warlords and the leaders of the semi-autonomous region of Puntland. In October a speaker was chosen, and Col. Ahmed Abdullahi Yusuf, military ruler of Puntland, was elected as interim federal president of Somalia.

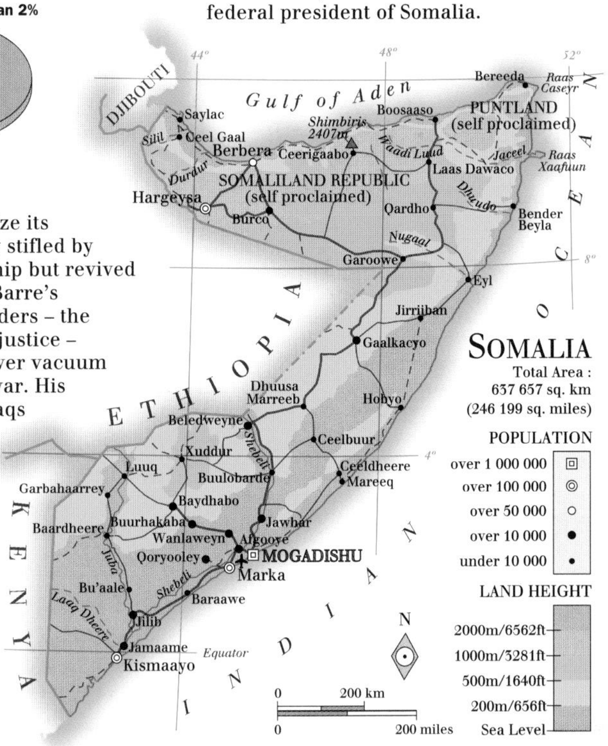
DJIBOUTI
Gulf of Aden
Saylac
Ceel Gaal
Berbera
Shimbiris 2407m
Ceerigaabo
Boosaaso
Bereeda
Raas Caseyr
PUNTLAND (self proclaimed)
Laas Dawaco
Raas Xaafuun
SOMALILAND REPUBLIC (self proclaimed)
Hargeysa
Burco
Qardho
Bender Beyla
Nugaal
Garoowe
Eyl
ETHIOPIA
Jirriiban
Gaalkacyo
Dhuusa Marreeb
Hobyo
Beledweyne
Ceelbuur
Xuddur
Luuq
Ceeldheere
Mareeq
Garbahaarrey
Buulobarde
Baydhabo
Baardheere
Buurhakaba
Jawhar
Wanlaweyn
Afgooye
Qoryooley
MOGADISHU
Marka
Bu'aale
Baraawe
Jilib
Jamaame
Kismaayo
Equator
KENYA
INDIAN OCEAN
SOMALIA
Total Area : 637 657 sq. km (246 199 sq. miles)
POPULATION
over 1 000 000
over 100 000
over 50 000
over 10 000
under 10 000
LAND HEIGHT
2000m/6562ft
1000m/3281ft
500m/1640ft
200m/656ft
Sea Level
0 200 km
0 200 miles

WORLD AFFAIRS

Joined UN in 1960

AL · IGAD · NAM · AU · OIC

After a UN force withdrew in 1995, the international community appeared to have abandoned Somalia until it gave support to the transitional assembly in 2000. Somalia accuses Ethiopia of sending troops to assist opposition warlords. The US belief in the existence of terrorist training camps in Somalia has eroded relations since September 11, 2001. Kenya and the UAE stopped issuing visas to Somalis in 2004.

AID

Recipient

$194m (receipts)

Up 29% in 2002

Mass starvation among the Somali population in 1991 finally prompted the UN to launch a large-scale humanitarian aid effort which was fairly effective. The UNDP and the World Bank returned to Somalia in 2002, having withdrawn due to internal insecurity.

DEFENSE

No compulsory military service

$38m

Down 3% in 2002

The demobilization of thousands of militia is key to ensuring stability; there has so far been little progress.

ECONOMICS

Not available

$1.21bn

2620 Somali shillings (2620)

SCORE CARD

- WORLD GNP RANKING........151st
- GNP PER CAPITA........$120
- BALANCE OF PAYMENTS........–$157m
- INFLATION........Over 100%
- UNEMPLOYMENT........Widespread underemployment

STRENGTHS

Very few. Export of livestock to Arabian peninsula resumed in the north. Inflow of money from Somalis abroad. Coca-Cola bottling plant opened in 2004.

WEAKNESSES

Every commodity, except arms, in extremely short supply. Little economic potential in the south. Livestock destroyed by drought. Banditry, extortion, and kidnapping hamper aid agencies.

EXPORTS

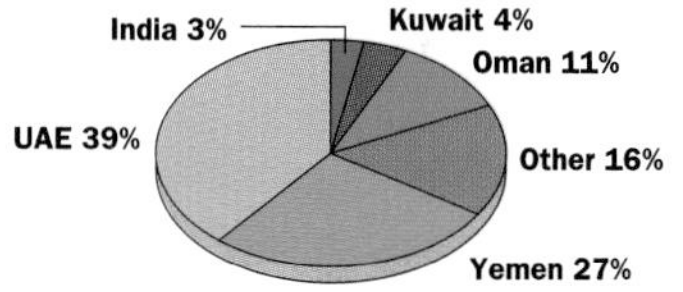
India 3%
Kuwait 4%
Oman 11%
UAE 39%
Other 16%
Yemen 27%

IMPORTS

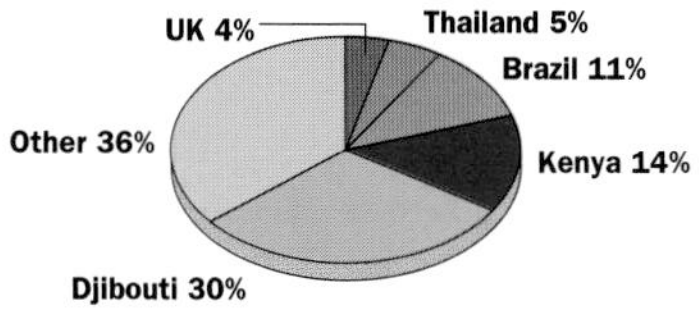
UK 4%
Thailand 5%
Brazil 11%
Other 36%
Kenya 14%
Djibouti 30%

RESOURCES

Electric power 80,000 kW

20,200 tonnes

Not an oil producer

13.2m sheep, 12.5m goats, 6.2m camels

Salt, tin, zinc, copper, gypsum, manganese, uranium, iron

Commercially exploitable minerals remain untapped. An oil exploration agreement was signed with a French oil group in 2001.

ENVIRONMENT

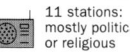

Sustainability rank: 132nd

0.8% partially protected

0.003 tonnes per capita

Human deprivation and starvation caused by the effects of drought and war on land and livestock outweigh all ecological considerations.

MEDIA

TV ownership low

Daily newspaper circulation 1 per 1000 people

PUBLISHING AND BROADCAST MEDIA

8 daily newspapers serve Mogadishu and the breakaway republics. *Xog-ogaal* has the highest circulation in Mogadishu

2 services: limited to the Mogadishu area

11 stations: mostly political or religious

Mogadishu has a number of faction-run radio stations. Somali Television Network, an independent multichannel, multilingual service, began broadcasting in 1999. Independent newspapers also serve the self-proclaimed areas.

CRIME

Death penalty in use

Somalia does not publish prison figures

Widespread breakdown of law and order since 1991

Armed clan factions (some, in remoter regions, engaged in family feuds rather than civil war) and bandits rule large areas. In Mogadishu a "national" police force has been established, and possession of firearms outlawed. *Sharia* (Islamic law), now the de facto system, is run in a makeshift fashion by elders.

EDUCATION

School leaving age: 14

24%

10,400 students

The education system has collapsed. Primary school enrollment is still below the prewar level of just 17%. Somali has been a written language only since 1972.

CHRONOLOGY

The lands of the Somalis became British and Italian colonies in the 1880s. Most were unified as Somalia at independence in 1960.

- **1964–1987** Conflict with Ethiopia over Somali-inhabited Ogaden.
- **1969** Gen. Siad Barre takes power.
- **1991** Siad Barre ousted. Civil war and clan chaos. Mass starvation. Somaliland declares secession.
- **1992** Abortive US intervention.
- **1995** UN force withdrawn.
- **1997** Accord signed by 26 clans.
- **2000** National reconciliation conference appoints government; warlords dispute its authority.
- **2001** Somali Reconciliation and Restoration Council set up in south.
- **2004** New transitional assembly sworn in.

HEALTH

No welfare state health benefits

1 per 20,000 people

Diarrheal, communicable, and parasitic diseases

The state-run system has collapsed. Mogadishu's main hospital reopened in 2004, funded by wealthy Somalis.

SPENDING

GDP/cap. decrease

CONSUMPTION AND SPENDING

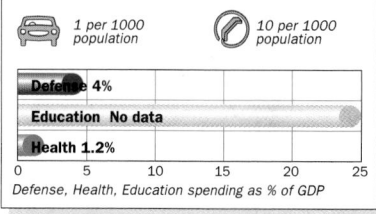

1 per 1000 population

10 per 1000 population

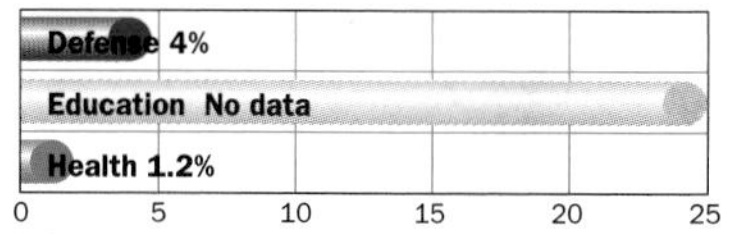
Defense 4%
Education No data
Health 1.2%
0
5
10
15
20
25

Defense, Health, Education spending as % of GDP

Bandits and warlords have gained rich pickings. Money sent by relatives living overseas is the main income for some people.

WORLD RANKING

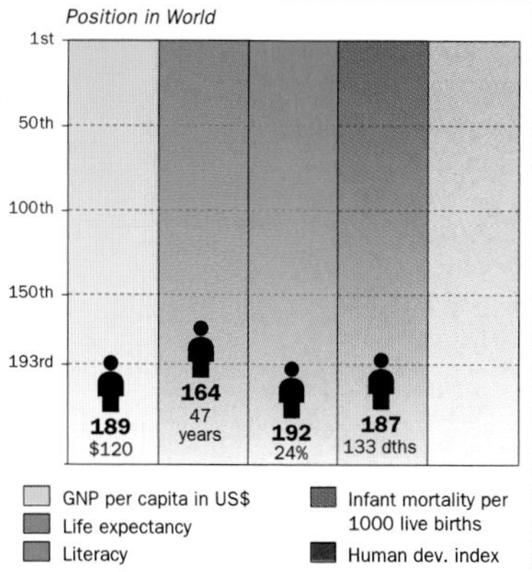
Position in World
1st
50th
100th
150th
193rd
189
$120
164
47 years
192
24%
187
133 dths
GNP per capita in US$
Life expectancy
Literacy
Infant mortality per 1000 live births
Human dev. index

S

SOUTH AFRICA

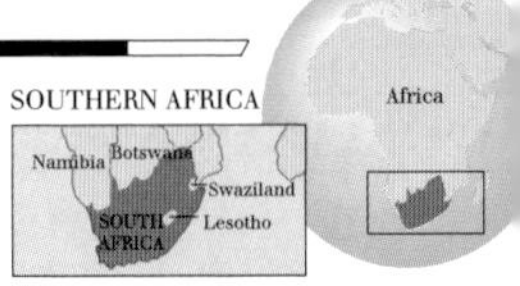
SOUTHERN AFRICA
Africa
Namibia
Botswana
Swaziland
SOUTH AFRICA
Lesotho

OFFICIAL NAME: Republic of South Africa **CAPITALS:** Pretoria; Cape Town; Bloemfontein
POPULATION: 45 million **CURRENCY:** Rand **OFFICIAL LANGUAGES:** Afrikaans, English, and 9 African languages

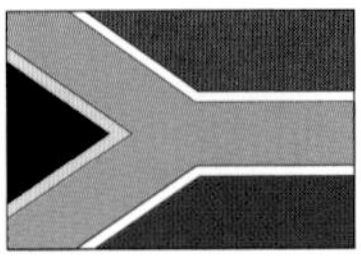

1934 | 1994 | April 27 | ZA | +2 | +27 | .za

RICH IN NATURAL RESOURCES, South Africa comprises a central plateau, or *veld*, bordered to the south and east by the Drakensberg Mountains. After eight decades of white minority rule, with racial segregation under the apartheid policy since 1948, South Africa from 1990 underwent a social and political revolution. The first multiracial elections were held in 1994 and the African National Congress (ANC), under Nelson Mandela and his successor Thabo Mbeki, has been the leading political movement ever since. Poverty and the spread of crime and HIV/AIDS are major problems.

Nelson Mandela, *who became president of South Africa in April 1994.*

Thabo Mbeki, *elected president in 1999 to succeed Mandela.*

CLIMATE

Desert/subtropical/ Mediterranean

WEATHER CHART FOR PRETORIA

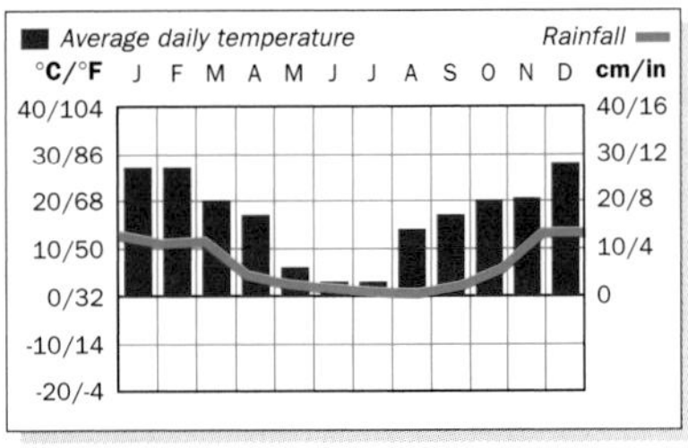
Average daily temperature
Rainfall
°C/°F J F M A M J J A S O N D cm/in
40/104
30/86
20/68
10/50
0/32
-10/14
-20/-4
40/16
30/12
20/8
10/4
0

Despite the moderating effects of oceans on three sides, the warm temperate climate is dry; 65% of the country has less than 50 cm (20 in) of rain a year. Drought is a periodic hazard.

TRANSPORTATION

Drive on left

Johannesburg International 13.5m passengers

196 ships 144,500 grt

THE TRANSPORTATION NETWORK

72,420 km (45,000 miles)

2032 km (1263 miles)

20,041 km (12,453 miles)

None

Priorities include expanding port capacity and cross-border rail networks. Public transportation is limited and expensive, but there is an extensive informal network of minibuses and taxis.

Cape Town, *set on a peninsula ending at the Cape of Good Hope, where the Indian and Atlantic Oceans meet.*

TOURISM

Visitors : Population 1:6.9

6.55m visitors

Up 11% in 2002

MAIN TOURIST ARRIVALS

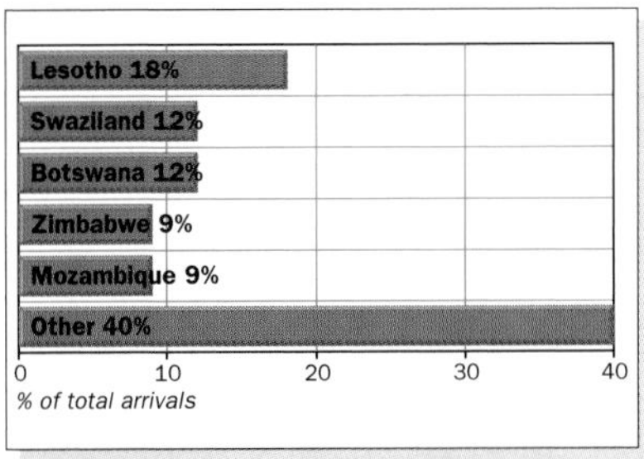
Lesotho 18%
Swaziland 12%
Botswana 12%
Zimbabwe 9%
Mozambique 9%
Other 40%
0
10
20
30
40
% of total arrivals

South Africa has huge tourist potential, with attractions ranging from beaches to mountains, and from prizewinning vineyards to world-renowned wildlife reserves. The enormous Kruger National Park boasts 137 mammal species and 450 bird species. Visitor numbers increased throughout the 1990s, but tourism was slow to recover from the country's isolation during the apartheid era. Today, the key constraint on growth is rising crime. Studies suggest that by 2005 tourism could create an additional 450,000 jobs and contribute 10% toward GDP (compared with 4% in 1995).

PEOPLE

Pop. density low

English, isiZulu, isiXhosa, Afrikaans, Sepedi, Setswana, Sesotho, Xitsonga, siSwati, Tshivenda, isiNdebele

37/km² (95/mi²)

THE URBAN/RURAL POPULATION SPLIT

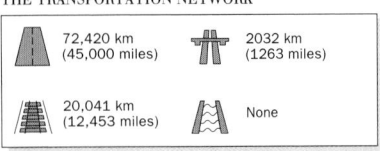

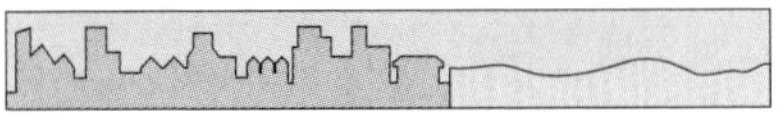
58%
42%

RELIGIOUS PERSUASION

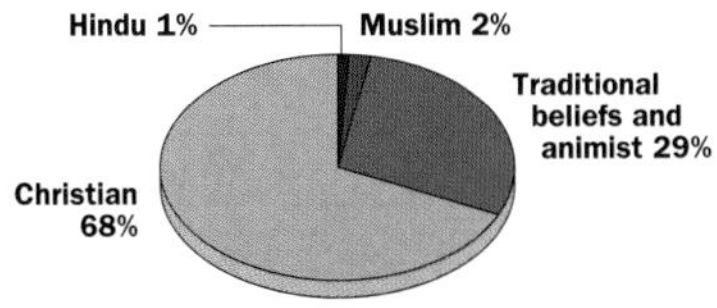
Hindu 1%
Muslim 2%
Traditional beliefs and animist 29%
Christian 68%

ETHNIC MAKEUP

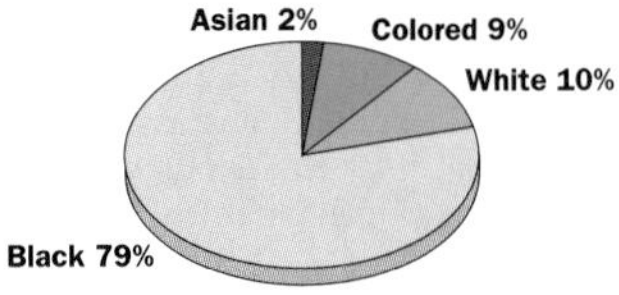
Asian 2%
Colored 9%
White 10%
Black 79%

Under apartheid, people were divided into racial categories: Whites (Afrikaners and English speakers), with the most privileges, and three black groups – Coloreds (people whose descent was deemed mixed), Asians (mainly Indians), and Africans, by far the largest single group. While blacks now dominate politics, whites still control the economy.

The traditional African extended family has been undermined by the need for men to migrate to towns for work. Once enforced by the state, this remains as an economic necessity. A small black middle class has developed, but most blacks are underemployed. There is considerable resentment over wealth disparities in the many townships.

The expected postapartheid ethnic conflict failed to materialize. Race-based movements such as Inkatha have not made a national impact. An area of the Kalahari Desert was returned to a Khomani San tribe in 1999.

The constitution enshrines equality of the sexes; many women are now prominent in public life. South Africa has led the way in Africa in providing homosexuals with legal rights.

POPULATION AGE BREAKDOWN

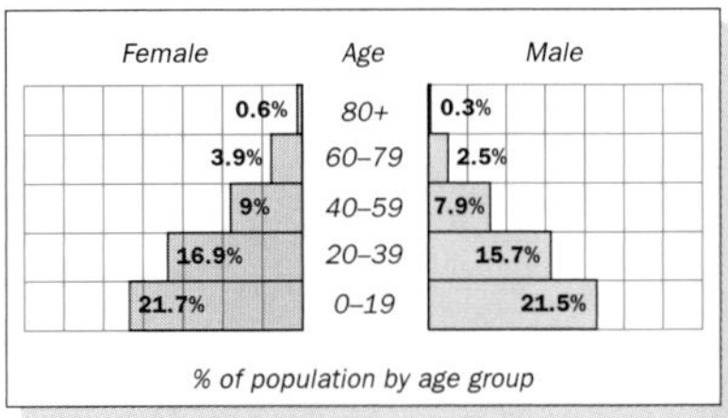
Female
Age
Male
0.6%
80+
0.3%
3.9%
60–79
2.5%
9%
40–59
7.9%
16.9%
20–39
15.7%
21.7%
0–19
21.5%
% of population by age group

S

POLITICS

Multiparty elections

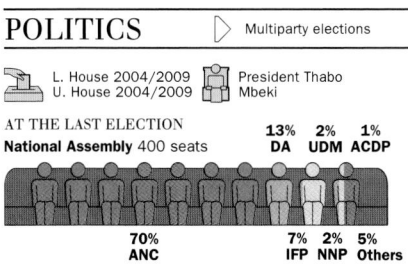

L. House 2004/2009
U. House 2004/2009

President Thabo Mbeki

AT THE LAST ELECTION

National Assembly 400 seats

13% DA
2% UDM
1% ACDP
70% ANC
7% IFP
2% NNP
5% Others

ANC = African National Congress **DA** = Democratic Alliance **IFP** = Inkatha Freedom Party **UDM** = United Democratic Movement **NNP** = New National Party **ACDP** = African Christian Democratic Party

National Council of Provinces 90 seats

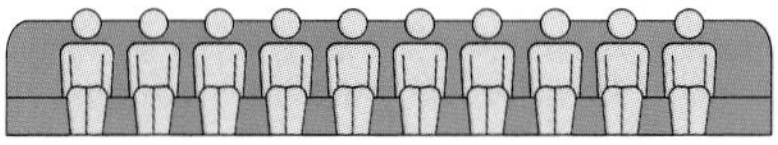

10 members are elected to the National Council of Provinces by each of the nine provincial legislatures

South Africa became a multiracial democracy following elections in 1994.

PROFILE

The 1994 elections ended 45 years of apartheid and saw political power transferred to the ANC, with veteran ANC activist Nelson Mandela as president. In 1999 the party increased its majority, while Thabo Mbeki succeeded as president. Its dominance has enabled the introduction of reform but has stifled debate. Parliamentary defections gave the ANC a two-thirds majority, which it retained in the 2004 elections. The former white-rule NNP disbanded in 2004, many of its members joining the ANC.

MAIN POLITICAL ISSUES

Truth and reconciliation

The creation of the Truth and Reconciliation Commission (TRC) in 1996 to investigate and air the horrors of apartheid was a truly innovative step and one since replicated in other countries emerging from conflict. Two years of painful and often controversial hearings culminated in a final report in 1998. Initial praise has been modified by allegations of corruption. In 2003 the government agreed to pay $3800 to each victim of apartheid – a figure derided by many as too little.

Coping with AIDS

South Africa is home to more than five million of the world's 40 million AIDS sufferers. The cost to the economy of health care, as well as coping with losses in the workforce, is debilitating and set to rise. The provision of treatments has been held up by controversy over international patents for drugs and even by President Mbeki's unorthodox stance on the nature of the infection itself. Public ignorance permeates national attitudes.

WORLD AFFAIRS

Joined UN in 1945

Comm | WTO | G24 | AU | SADC

After several decades of political isolation and economic sanctions, South Africa has been welcomed back into the international fold, rejoining the UN and Commonwealth. It is a key member of the SADC and also leads continental opinion on regional issues; it was in Durban that the AU was founded in 2002. Former president Mandela often intervened to help resolve foreign conflicts, and passed the role of main mediator in Burundi to Mbeki's deputy Jacob Zuma in 2000. Mandela prompted some criticism from the West for his relations with apartheid-era supporters Libya and Cuba. Mbeki has pushed for peace in the Democratic Republic of the Congo, but has been criticized internationally for tacitly supporting Robert Mugabe's regime in neighboring Zimbabwe, and for his controversial opinions about HIV/AIDS.

SOUTH AFRICA

Total Area : 1 219 912 sq. km (471 008 sq. miles)

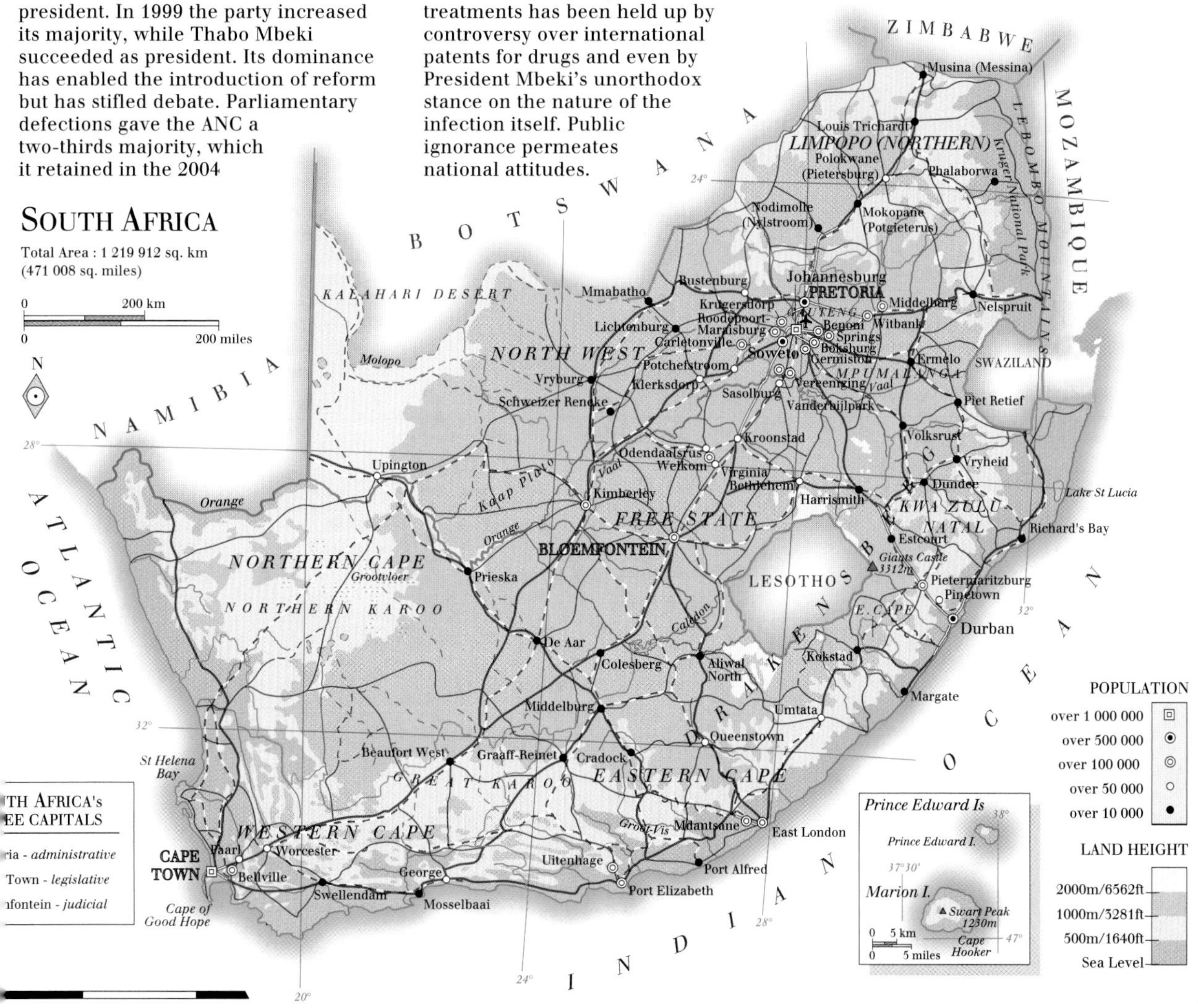
0 200 km
0 200 miles
N
ZIMBABWE
BOTSWANA
NAMIBIA
MOZAMBIQUE
SWAZILAND
LESOTHO
ATLANTIC OCEAN
INDIAN OCEAN
KALAHARI DESERT
LIMPOPO (NORTHERN)
NORTH WEST
GAUTENG
MPUMALANGA
FREE STATE
KWA ZULU NATAL
NORTHERN CAPE
NORTHERN KAROO
EASTERN CAPE
WESTERN CAPE
GREAT KAROO
DRAKENSBERG
LEBOMBO MOUNTAINS
Kruger National Park
Musina (Messina)
Louis Trichardt
Polokwane (Pietersburg)
Phalaborwa
Modimolle (Nylstroom)
Mokopane (Potgieterus)
Rustenburg
Johannesburg
PRETORIA
Middelburg
Nelspruit
Mmabatho
Krugersdorp
Roodepoort
Lichtenburg
Marisburg
Carletonville
Soweto
Benoni
Witbank
Springs
Boksburg
Germiston
Ermelo
Potchefstroom
Vryburg
Klerksdorp
Sasolburg
Vereeniging
Vanderbijlpark
Schweizer Reneke
Piet Retief
Kroonstad
Volksrust
Upington
Odendaalsrus
Welkom
Virginia
Bethlehem
Harrismith
Vryheid
Dundee
Kimberley
BLOEMFONTEIN
Estcourt
Richard's Bay
Lake St Lucia
Giants Castle 3312m
Prieska
Pietermaritzburg
Pinetown
Durban
De Aar
Colesberg
Aliwal North
Kokstad
Margate
Middelburg
Umtata
Queenstown
Beaufort West
Graaff-Reinet
Cradock
St Helena Bay
Mdantsane
East London
Paarl
Worcester
CAPE TOWN
Bellville
Swellendam
George
Mosselbaai
Uitenhage
Port Alfred
Port Elizabeth
Cape of Good Hope
Orange
Molopo
Vaal
Caledon
Kaap Plato
Grootvloer
Groot-Vis
SOUTH AFRICA'S THREE CAPITALS
Pretoria - administrative
Cape Town - legislative
Bloemfontein - judicial
Prince Edward Is
Prince Edward I.
Marion I.
Swart Peak 1230m
Cape Hooker
0 5 km
0 5 miles
POPULATION
over 1 000 000
over 500 000
over 100 000
over 50 000
over 10 000
LAND HEIGHT
2000m/6562ft
1000m/3281ft
500m/1640ft
Sea Level

AID

Recipient

$657m (receipts) — Up 54% in 2002

Apartheid-era South Africa was denied aid, particularly from the World Bank and the IMF. It now seeks financial assistance for massive reconstruction programs. As part of Nepad – Africa's "Marshall Plan" launched in 2002 – President Mbeki stressed the importance of ending reliance on foreign aid.

CHRONOLOGY

Until 1652, what is now South Africa was peopled by Bantu-speaking groups and San nomads. Then Dutch settlers arrived. British colonizers followed in the 18th century.

- **1910** Union of South Africa set up as British dominion; white monopoly of power formalized.
- **1912** ANC formed.
- **1934** Independence.
- **1948** National Party takes power; apartheid segregationist policy introduced.
- **1958–1966** Hendrik Verwoerd prime minister. "Grand Apartheid" policy implemented.
- **1959** Pan-Africanist Congress (PAC) formed.
- **1960** Sharpeville massacre. ANC, PAC banned.
- **1961** South Africa becomes republic; leaves Commonwealth.
- **1964** Senior ANC leader Nelson Mandela jailed.
- **1976** Soweto uprisings by black students; hundreds killed.
- **1978** P. W. Botha in office.
- **1984** New constitution: Indians and Coloreds get some representation. Growing black opposition.
- **1985** State of emergency. Sanctions.
- **1989** F. W. De Klerk replaces Botha as president.
- **1990** De Klerk legalizes ANC and PAC; frees Nelson Mandela.
- **1990–1993** International sanctions gradually withdrawn.
- **1991** Convention for a Democratic South Africa (CODESA) starts work.
- **1993** Mandela and De Klerk win Nobel Peace Prize.
- **1994** Multiracial elections won by ANC; Mandela president.
- **1996** TRC begins work.
- **1997** New constitution takes effect.
- **1998** TRC report condemns both apartheid crimes and ANC excesses.
- **1999** ANC election victory; Thabo Mbeki succeeds Mandela.
- **2001–2002** Rand goes from record low to record high.
- **2002** World summit on sustainable development held in Johannesburg.
- **2004** Elections: ANC wins over two-thirds of vote.

DEFENSE

No compulsory military service

$1.7bn — Down 6% in 2002

SOUTH AFRICAN ARMED FORCES

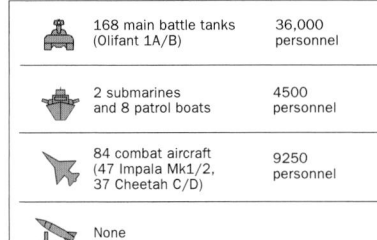

168 main battle tanks (Olifant 1A/B)	36,000 personnel
2 submarines and 8 patrol boats	4500 personnel
84 combat aircraft (47 Impala Mk1/2, 37 Cheetah C/D)	9250 personnel
None	

The creation by postapartheid South Africa of a truly national defense force seems almost miraculous, as it fuses together once bitter enemies: soldiers from the old white-run army, and guerrillas from the liberation groups.

However, doubts have been raised over the army's ability to operate effectively. A recruitment freeze since 1994 has raised the average age and created a glut of higher-ranking officers, while the incidence of AIDS increases. A large arms procurement program has failed to overcome the effects of previous swingeing cuts in spending. Few tanks are operational and the air force tends to run out of fuel toward the end of each financial year. A full strategic defense review was announced in 2004.

A major arms industry is the legacy of years of sanctions.

ECONOMICS

Inflation 9.3% p.a. (1990–2001)

$113bn — 6.212 rand (7.51)

SCORE CARD

World GNP Ranking	32nd
GNP per Capita	$2500
Balance of Payments	$290m
Inflation	8.9%
Unemployment	28%

EXPORTS

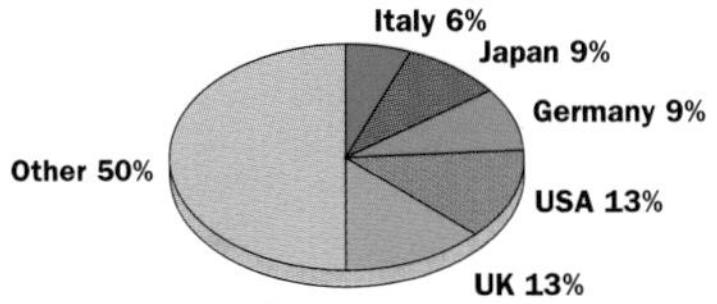

Italy 6%
Japan 9%
Germany 9%
USA 13%
UK 13%
Other 50%

IMPORTS

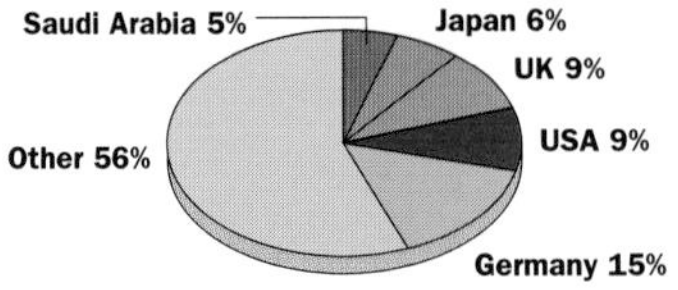

Saudi Arabia 5%
Japan 6%
UK 9%
USA 9%
Germany 15%
Other 56%

Strengths
Africa's largest and most developed economy; highly diversified with modern infrastructure. Strong financial sector for mobilizing investment. Growing manufacturing sector. Varied resource base.

Weaknesses
Security fears deter investment. Growth too low to overcome deprivation among blacks; black unemployment growing by 2.5% a year. Cost of AIDS treatments. Population boom. Fluctuations in rand and gold prices undermine many sectors. Emigration of skilled workers.

Profile
South Africa has a large and diverse private sector, much of it controlled by multinationals. Privatizations have gone some way to reverse the strong state-control necessitated by apartheid-era sanctions. The ANC cooperates with big business in an effort to revivify the economy and develop the townships, but a report in 2003 showed that wealth disparities between the wealthy white elite and the majority black community are widening.

ECONOMIC PERFORMANCE INDICATOR

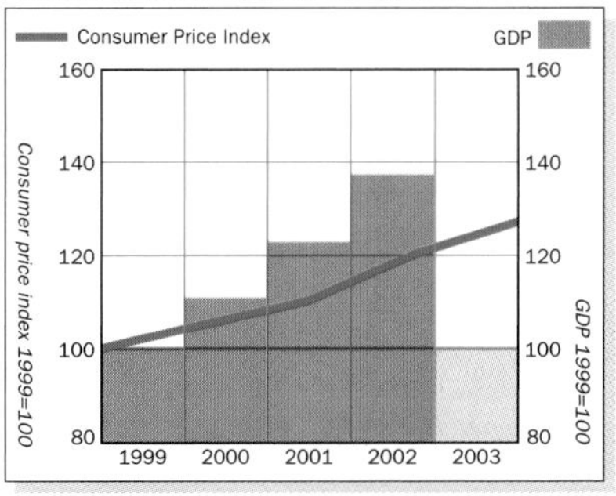

Consumer Price Index
GDP
Consumer price index 1999=100
GDP 1999=100
160
140
120
100
80
1999
2000
2001
2002
2003

SOUTH AFRICA : MAJOR BUSINESSES

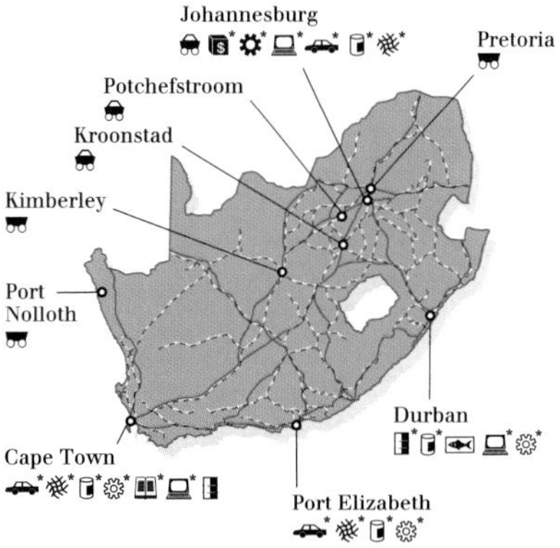

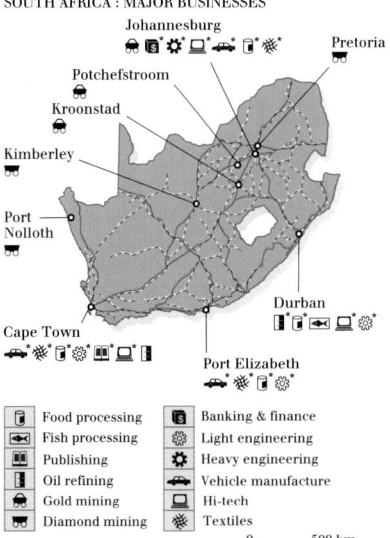

Johannesburg
Pretoria
Potchefstroom
Kroonstad
Kimberley
Port Nolloth
Durban
Cape Town
Port Elizabeth
0
500 km
500 miles

Food processing	Banking & finance	Fish processing	Light engineering
Publishing	Heavy engineering	Oil refining	Vehicle manufacture
Gold mining	Hi-tech	Diamond mining	Textiles

* significant multinational ownership

S

RESOURCES

Electric power 39.6m kW

759,522 tonnes

164,871 b/d (reserves 60m barrels)

29.1m sheep, 13.6m cattle, 120m chickens

Gold, coal, vanadium, vermiciline, diamonds, chromium, uranium, manganese, nickel, oil

ELECTRICITY GENERATION

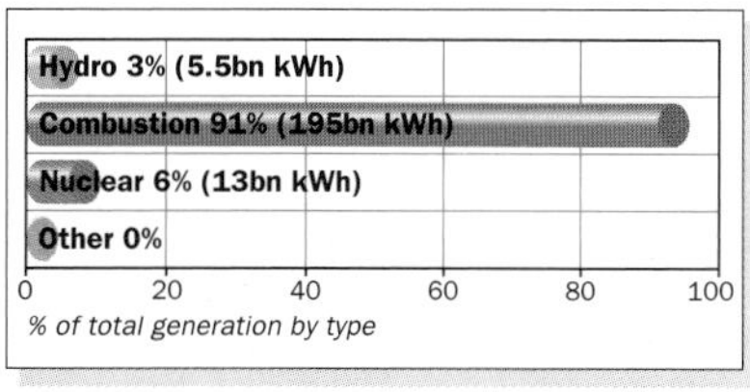
Hydro 3% (5.5bn kWh)
Combustion 91% (195bn kWh)
Nuclear 6% (13bn kWh)
Other 0%
0
20
40
60
80
100
% of total generation by type

South Africa has some of the continent's richest natural resources, in particular minerals. Its dominance of the world market in gold and diamonds helped it survive sanctions during apartheid. The falling price of gold in 2000 meant that for the first time sales of platinum group metals outstripped those of gold. South Africa is the largest single producer of manganese, chrome ore, and vermiciline. It also produces uranium, vanadium, and nickel.

With little oil, South Africa pioneered the transformation of coal into oil, and otherwise uses its huge coal reserves to generate electricity. Almost 15 million black South Africans are without electricity, and nongrid options are being considered, including developing solar energy.

SOUTH AFRICA : LAND USE

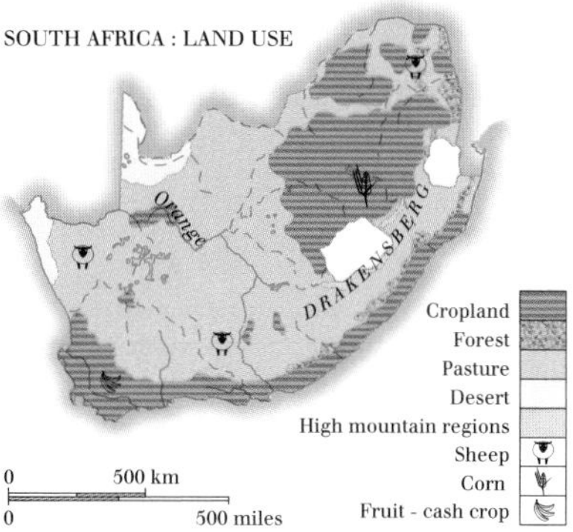
Orange
DRAKENSBERG
Cropland
Forest
Pasture
Desert
High mountain regions
Sheep
Corn
Fruit - cash crop
0
500 km
0
500 miles

ENVIRONMENT

Sustainability rank: 77th

6% (2% partially protected)

7.4 tonnes per capita

ENVIRONMENTAL TREATIES

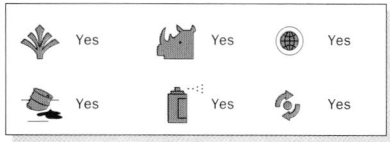

Yes	Yes	Yes
Yes	Yes	Yes

Floods and drought are familiar hazards. The world's largest game park, straddling the borders with Zimbabwe and Mozambique, was opened in 2002. The littering of flimsy plastic bags was so severe that they were banned in 2003.

MEDIA

TV ownership medium

Daily newspaper circulation 29 per 1000 people

PUBLISHING AND BROADCAST MEDIA

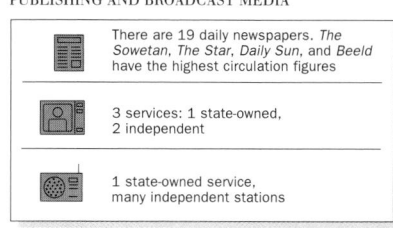

There are 19 daily newspapers. *The Sowetan, The Star, Daily Sun,* and *Beeld* have the highest circulation figures

3 services: 1 state-owned, 2 independent

1 state-owned service, many independent stations

A drive to combat racial stereotyping in the media was launched following a report on the subject to the Human Rights Commission in early 2000.

CRIME

No death penalty

180,952 prisoners

Up 14% in 2000–2001

CRIME RATES

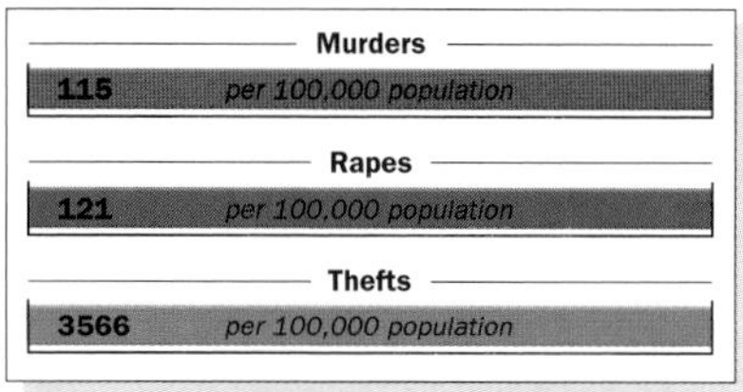
Murders
115 per 100,000 population
Rapes
121 per 100,000 population
Thefts
3566 per 100,000 population

South Africa is a dangerous country, and crime rates are rising: murders occur with extreme frequency, and rape, armed robberies, and muggings are rife. Vigilantism is a huge problem in the Cape. The death penalty was abolished in 1997. New gun control laws came into force in 2004.

EDUCATION

School leaving age: 15

86%

644,763 students

THE EDUCATION SYSTEM

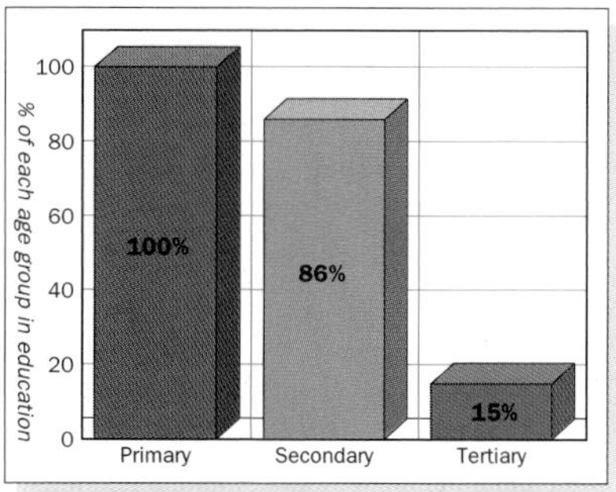
100
80
60
40
20
0
% of each age group in education
100%
86%
15%
Primary
Secondary
Tertiary

Education reform is a central task of the postapartheid government. Progress has been made in improving national literacy, and access to education has been widened through the Tirisano (working together) education program, launched in 2000. Long-established universities continue to be white-dominated.

HEALTH

Welfare state health benefits

1 per 1667 people

AIDS, accidents, violence, infectious and respiratory diseases

Health services were desegregated formally in 1990, but equal access to care is still a distant goal. Statistics on medical provision hide a strong bias toward whites and urban areas, where the vast majority of doctors work; infant mortality rates are increasing sharply among the poorly provisioned rural communities, most of whom are black. South Africa has over five million HIV sufferers, more than any other country. The government has won the right to buy cheaper generic drugs for HIV/AIDS sufferers and has increased spending – with a fourfold rise in the AIDS budget for 2004.

SPENDING

GDP/cap. increase

CONSUMPTION AND SPENDING

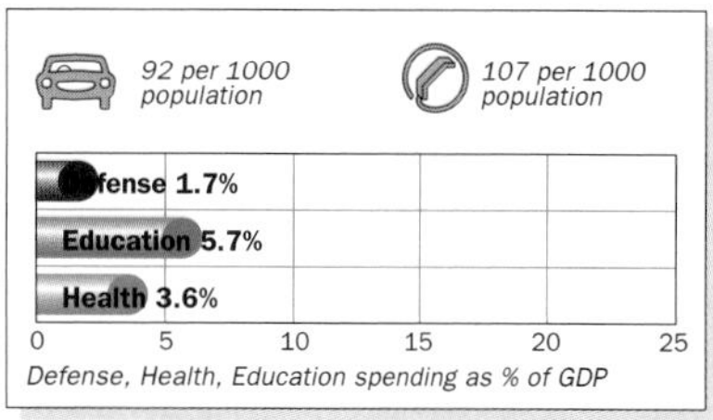
92 per 1000 population
107 per 1000 population
Defense 1.7%
Education 5.7%
Health 3.6%
0
5
10
15
20
25
Defense, Health, Education spending as % of GDP

Wealth disparities are marked and widening. At the top, the white elite enjoys living standards similar to those of Californians. In contrast, living conditions for the poorest group, the majority black community, are among Africa's lowest; more than 40% of black adults are unemployed. In between are the mixed-race and Asian communities, who enjoyed more privileges under apartheid's strict racial hierarchy. However, a small black middle class is growing slowly, with some black-owned firms doing well on the stock market. In 2003, the government offered $3800 each to victims of apartheid.

S

WORLD RANKING

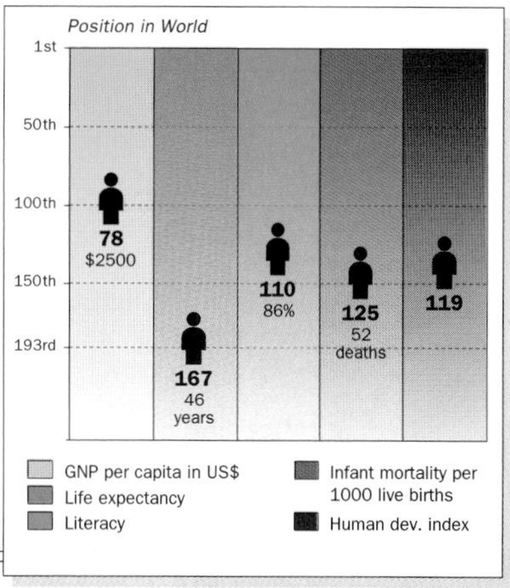
Position in World
1st
50th
100th
150th
193rd
78
$2500
167
46 years
110
86%
125
52 deaths
119
GNP per capita in US$
Life expectancy
Literacy
Infant mortality per 1000 live births
Human dev. index

SPAIN

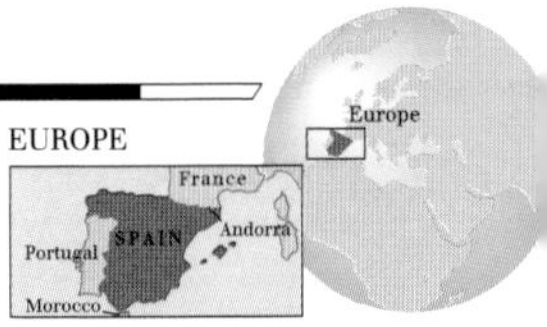
EUROPE
Europe
France
Portugal
SPAIN
Andorra
Morocco

OFFICIAL NAME: Kingdom of Spain **CAPITAL:** Madrid **POPULATION:** 41.1 million
CURRENCY: Euro **OFFICIAL LANGUAGES:** Spanish, Galician, Basque, and Catalan

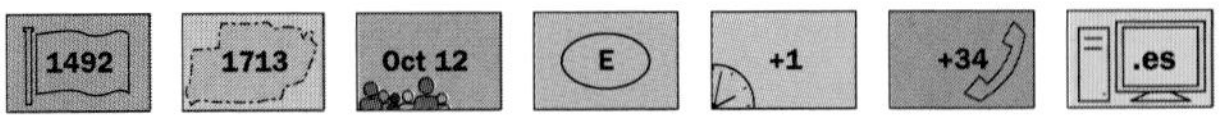
1492
1713
Oct 12
E
+1
+34
.es

THE MAJOR PART of the Iberian peninsula in southwest Europe, Spain has both an Atlantic and a Mediterranean coast, and is dominated by a central plateau. After the death of Gen. Franco in 1975, the country managed a rapid and relatively peaceful transition to democracy under the supervision of King Juan Carlos I. Since EU membership in 1986, there has been an increasing devolution of power to the regions. The socialists were returned to power in 2004 when the public turned against the two-term center-right regime following the Madrid train bombings.

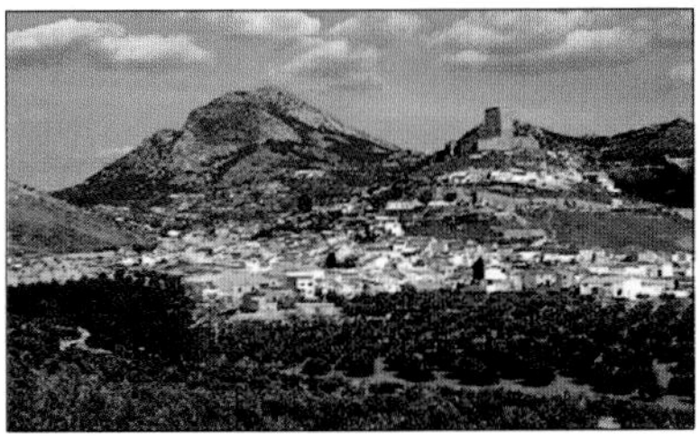

Alcaudete, Jaén Province, *in the Andalusian mountains between the Guadalquivir River and Granada. The ruined castle is Moorish.*

CLIMATE

Mediterranean/ maritime/mountain

WEATHER CHART FOR MADRID

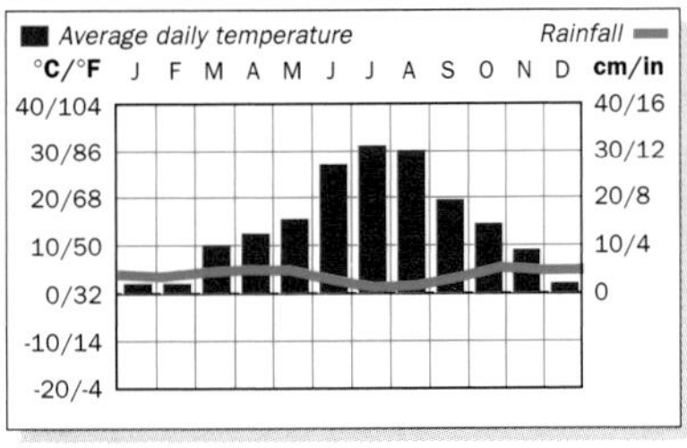
Average daily temperature
Rainfall
°C/°F
J F M A M J J A S O N D
cm/in
40/104
30/86
20/68
10/50
0/32
-10/14
-20/-4
40/16
30/12
20/8
10/4
0

The central plateau, or *meseta*, endures an extreme climate. Coastal areas are milder, and are wetter in the north than in the south.

TRANSPORTATION

Drive on right

Barajas, Madrid 35.7m passengers

1568 ships 2.37m grt

THE TRANSPORTATION NETWORK

657,157 km (408,338 miles)

10,317 km (6411 miles)

13,856 km (8610 miles)

1045 km (649 miles)

The AVE high-speed train links Madrid and Seville; more routes are planned. The state-run rail company RENFE is to be privatized gradually.

PEOPLE

Pop. density medium

Spanish, Catalan, Galician, Basque

82/km² (213/mi²)

THE URBAN/RURAL POPULATION SPLIT

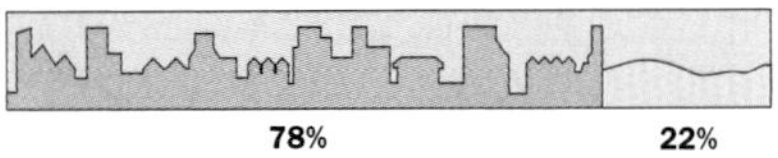
78%
22%

RELIGIOUS PERSUASION

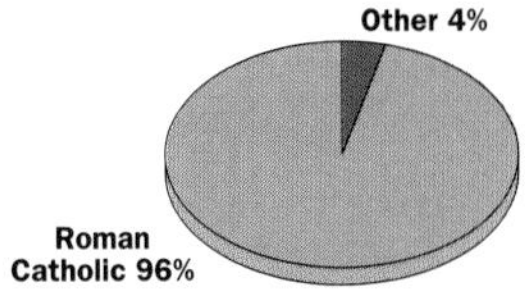
Other 4%
Roman Catholic 96%

ETHNIC MAKEUP

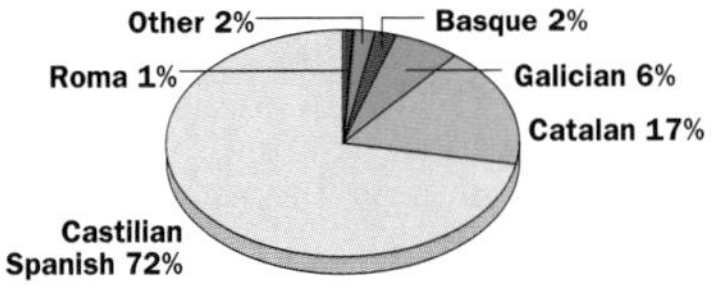
Other 2%
Basque 2%
Roma 1%
Galician 6%
Catalan 17%
Castilian Spanish 72%

Spain under Franco was isolated and socially conservative. It was dominated by the army, the Roman Catholic Church, and the fascist party. Since the 1970s, Spanish society, at least in urban areas, has become increasingly socially liberal and culturally sophisticated, symbolized by the success of the Guggenheim Museum, Bilbao, which turned an industrial wasteland into a place of cultural pilgrimage.

POPULATION AGE BREAKDOWN

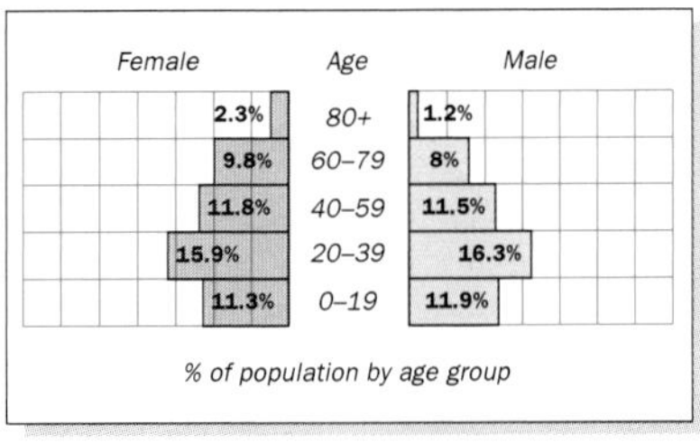
Female
Age
Male
2.3%
80+
1.2%
9.8%
60–79
8%
11.8%
40–59
11.5%
15.9%
20–39
16.3%
11.3%
0–19
11.9%
% of population by age group

Divorce rates remain low and close family ties are still important, but the influence of the Church on personal behavior and attitudes to sexual issues has lessened among younger generations. Spanish women are increasingly emancipated and influential in public life, constituting almost a third of members of parliament and heading around the same proportion of businesses.

A vigorous regionalism, suppressed under Franco, now flourishes. In the Basque region, the ETA separatists' campaign of terror remains a national concern. Migration from rural regions to the coast since the 1970s has been associated with the arrival of immigrants from Latin America and north Africa. A rise in racial tensions and racism has resulted.

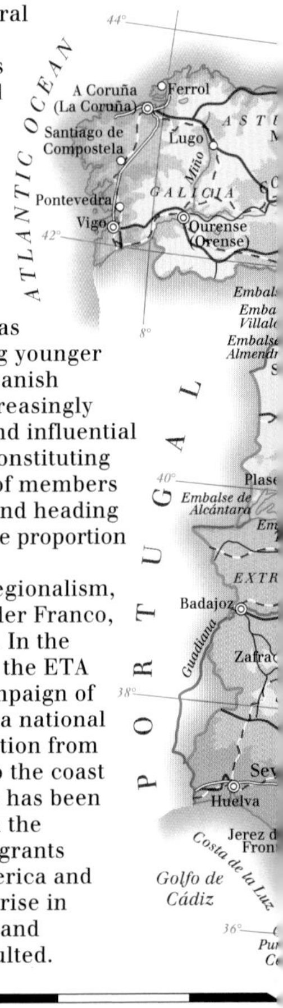
ATLANTIC OCEAN
A Coruña (La Coruña)
Ferrol
Santiago de Compostela
Lugo
Pontevedra
GALICIA
Vigo
Ourense (Orense)
PORTUGAL
Badajoz
Zafra
Huelva
Golfo de Cádiz
Costa de la Luz
Guadiana
Miño

TOURISM

Visitors : Population 1.3:1

52.5m visitors

Little change in 2003

MAIN TOURIST ARRIVALS

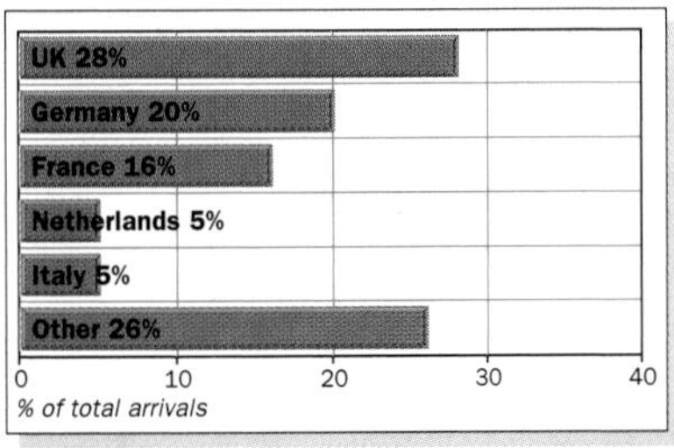
UK 28%
Germany 20%
France 16%
Netherlands 5%
Italy 5%
Other 26%
0
10
20
30
40
% of total arrivals

Tourism earnings in 2003 topped $41 billion. Long dominant in the vacation-package sector, Spain has recently adopted marketing strategies to boost additional cultural, historical, and environmental tourism. Several areas began levying an environmental tax on tourist arrivals in 2001. The cut-price package industry benefited from political turbulence in competitor countries in the Mediterranean but is facing long-term decline. The four Balearic Islands attract large numbers of visitors.

POLITICS

Multiparty elections

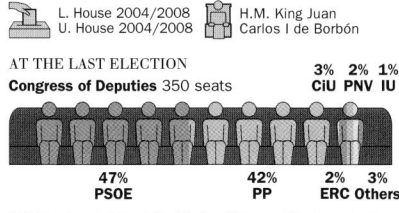

L. House 2004/2008
U. House 2004/2008

H.M. King Juan Carlos I de Borbón

AT THE LAST ELECTION

Congress of Deputies 350 seats

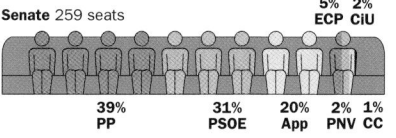

3% CiU
2% PNV
1% IU
47% PSOE
42% PP
2% ERC
3% Others

PSOE = Spanish Socialist Workers' Party **PP** = Popular Party **CiU** = Convergence and Union **ERC** = Republican Left of Catalonia **PNV** = Basque Nationalist Party **IU** = United Left **App** = Appointed **ECP** = Alliance of Catalonian Parties **CC** = Canarian Coalition

Senate 259 seats

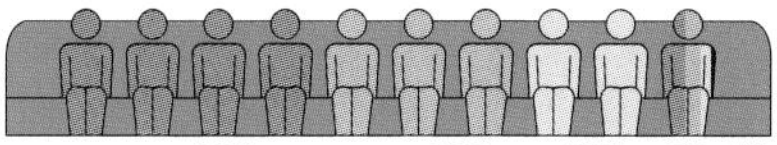
5% ECP
2% CiU
39% PP
31% PSOE
20% App
2% PNV
1% CC

208 members are directly elected to the Senate, and 51 appointed by autonomous communities

Since 1978, Spain has been a semifederal multiparty parliamentary monarchy. Each region has a legislative assembly.

PROFILE

During the PSOE's long period in power (1982–1996), voters were increasingly alienated by high levels of corruption and the failure of the Cortes (parliament) to check executive power. The PP government of 1996–2004, led by José María Aznar, was credited with good management of the economy and taking an unequivocal stance agains the Basque separatists ETA. Aznar's support for the 2003 US invasion of Iraq, however, was deeply unpopular. Promising to withdraw troops from the quagmire, the PSOE under José Luis Rodríguez Zapatero won the 2004 election with the support of smaller parties.

MAIN POLITICAL ISSUES

Increasing regionalism

Spain's 17 autonomous regions all vie for greater funds or independence from Madrid. Many have bypassed central government to borrow funds on international money markets. In 1996 the PP government approved a fresh model of financing for the regions which gave them new powers for raising tax revenue. The Basque country, Catalonia, and Galicia each use their own language alongside Castilian Spanish. Spain has championed regionalism inside the EU and has supported the establishment of an EU Committee of the Regions.

Terrorism

The Basque separatist movement ETA has, with intermittent cease-fire announcements, waged a protracted violent struggle for independence, prompting large-scale demonstrations against violence. Its political wing, Batasuna, was banned in 2003. ETA was initially blamed for the devastating Madrid train bombings in March 2004, but evidence quickly pointed to a revenge attack by al-Qaida for Spain's involvement in the occupation of Iraq.

King Juan Carlos, *who became head of state on the death of Franco in 1975.*

José Luis Rodríguez Zapatero, *the surprise victor in elections in 2004.*

WORLD AFFAIRS

Joined UN in 1955

CE | NATO | OECD | OSCE | EU

Inside the EU, Spain has tried to play a leading role in the evolving Common Security and Foreign Policy. Support for the 2003 Iraq war was partly motivated by a desire to increase Spain's status as a European power, but ran contrary to public opinion. Regionally, Spain has played a key role in the Barcelona Process which promotes Mediterranean–EU relations. There are tensions with Morocco over illegal immigrants, sovereignty over rocky islets, and the exclaves of Ceuta and Melilla. There is also a long-standing dispute with the UK over Gibraltar; intergovernmental negotiations continue, but the colony itself resists a change of status.

SPAIN
Total Area : 504 782 sq. km
(194 896 sq. miles)
POPULATION
over 1 000 000
over 500 000
over 100 000
over 50 000
over 10 000
LAND HEIGHT
3000m/9843ft
2000m/6562ft
1000m/3281ft
500m/1640ft
Sea Level
N
0 100 km
0 100 miles
FRANCE
ANDORRA
MEDITERRANEAN SEA
Golfo de Valencia
Islas Baleares
Menorca
Mallorca
Palma
Eivissa
Formentera
Bilbao
Irún
Donostia-San Sebastian
Pamplona (Iruña)
Vitoria
Miranda de Ebro
Logroño
Huesca
Figueres
Girona (Gerona)
Soria
Zaragoza
Lleida
Terrassa
Sabadell
Mataró
Badalona
Barcelona
Tarragona
Reus
Tortosa
Teruel
Alcalá de Henares
Getafe
Cuenca
Castellón de la Plana
Paterna
Valencia
Albacete
Gandia
Elda
Benidorm
Alicante
Cieza
Elche
Murcia
Linares
Jaén
Lorca
Cartagena
Almería
Motril
Costa del Sol
Costa Brava
Costa Daurada
Costa del Azahar
Costa Blanca
Costa Calida
Melilla (SPAIN)
Cerro de Mulhacén 3481m
Islas Canarias
La Palma
La Laguna
Santa Cruz de Tenerife
Lanzarote
Gomera
Tenerife
Las Palmas
Fuerteventura
Hierro
Gran Canaria
0 100 km
0 100 miles

CHRONOLOGY

United under Ferdinand and Isabella in 1492, Spain became a dominant force. A long period of economic and political decline followed, however, and by the mid-19th century, Spain lagged behind many other European countries in stability and prosperity.

- **1874** Constitutional monarchy restored under Alfonso XII.
- **1879** PSOE founded.
- **1881** Trade unions legalized.
- **1885** Death of Alfonso XII.
- **1898** Defeat in war with US results in loss of Cuba, Puerto Rico, and the Philippines.
- **1914–1918** Spain neutral in World War I.
- **1921** Spanish army routed by Berbers in Spanish Morocco.
- **1923** Coup by Gen. Primo de Rivera accepted by King Alfonso XIII. Military dictatorship.
- **1930** Primo de Rivera dismissed by monarchy.
- **1931** Second Republic proclaimed. Alfonso XIII flees Spain.
- **1933** Center-right coalition wins general election.

S

CHRONOLOGY *continued*

- **1934** Asturias uprising quashed by army. Failure of attempt to form Catalan state.
- **1936–1939** Popular Front wins elections. Gen. Francisco Franco becomes leader of right-wing military uprising. Ensuing civil war, won by Nationalists under Franco, claims 300,000 lives.
- **1940** Franco meets Hitler, but does not enter World War II.
- **1946** UN condemns Franco regime.
- **1948** Spain excluded from the Marshall Plan.
- **1950** UN lifts veto.
- **1953** Concordat with Vatican. Spain grants US military bases.
- **1959** Stabilization Plan is basis for 1960s rapid economic growth.
- **1962** Franco government applies for eventual membership of EEC.
- **1969** Franco names Juan Carlos, grandson of Alfonso XIII, his successor.
- **1973** Basque separatists assassinate Prime Minister Luis Carrero Blanco; replaced by Carlos Arias Navarro.
- **1975** Death of Franco. Proclamation of King Juan Carlos I.
- **1976** King appoints Adolfo Suárez as prime minister.
- **1977** First democratic elections since 1936 won by Suárez's Democratic Center Union.
- **1978** New constitution declares Spain a parliamentary monarchy.
- **1981** Leopoldo Calvo Sotelo replaces Suárez. King foils military coup. Calvo takes Spain into NATO.
- **1982** Felipe González wins landslide victory for PSOE.
- **1986** Joins European Communities. González wins referendum on keeping Spain in NATO.
- **1992** Olympic Games held in Barcelona, Expo '92 in Seville.
- **1996** PSOE loses election; José María Aznar of PP prime minister.
- **1998** Former PSOE minister found guilty of involvement in Basque kidnappings. September, ETA cease-fire; holds until December 1999.
- **2002** Euro fully adopted. Sunken oil tanker *Prestige* pollutes Galicia.
- **2004** March 11, Madrid train bombings kill 201 people. PSOE wins election; José Luis Rodríguez Zapatero becomes prime minister.

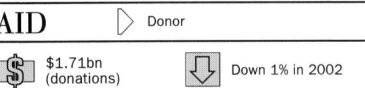

AID

Donor

$1.71bn (donations)

Down 1% in 2002

Spain has taken steps to increase grant aid after criticism that Spanish aid was of poor quality and tied to the acquisition of goods and services. Aid in 2002 represented 0.26% of GNP.

DEFENSE

No compulsory military service

$8.25bn

Up 18% in 2002

A substantial, largely state-owned, and commercially nonviable defense industry is subsidized for strategic reasons. Full integration of NATO military structures was approved in 1997. A trend of falling defense spending was halted in 2002. National service has been abolished. Spanish troops assisted in the US-led invasion of Iraq in 2003, but the new government in 2004 fulfilled its election pledge to withdraw them.

SPANISH ARMED FORCES

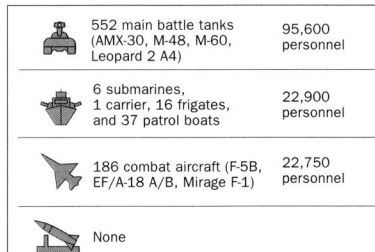

552 main battle tanks (AMX-30, M-48, M-60, Leopard 2 A4)	95,600 personnel
6 submarines, 1 carrier, 16 frigates, and 37 patrol boats	22,900 personnel
186 combat aircraft (F-5B, EF/A-18 A/B, Mirage F-1)	22,750 personnel
None	

ECONOMICS

Inflation 3.9% p.a. (1990–2001)

$596bn

0.822 euros (0.871)

SCORE CARD

- World GNP Ranking..........10th
- GNP per Capita..........$14,580
- Balance of Payments..........–$15.9bn
- Inflation..........3.1%
- Unemployment..........11%

EXPORTS

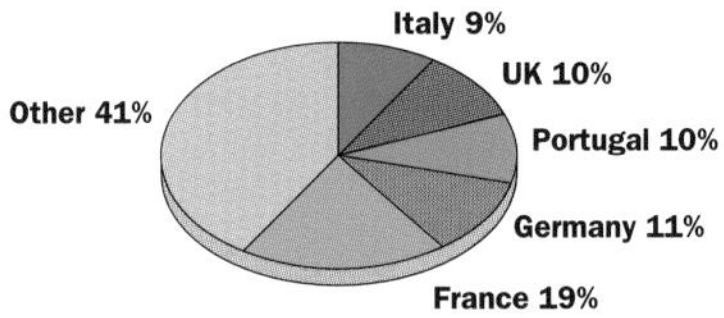
Italy 9%
UK 10%
Portugal 10%
Germany 11%
France 19%
Other 41%

IMPORTS

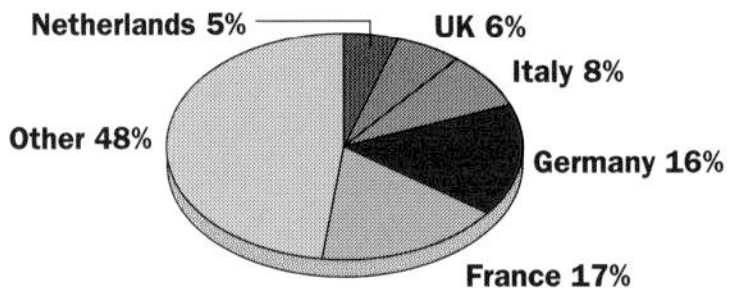
Netherlands 5%
UK 6%
Italy 8%
Germany 16%
France 17%
Other 48%

Strengths

One of the fastest-growing OECD economies. Well-qualified labor force with relatively low labor costs. Privatization has introduced greater competition into gas, oil-refining, electricity, and telecommunications sectors.

Weaknesses

Foreign ownership of companies, amounting to 50% of production: few homegrown multinationals. Low investment in research and development, concentration in declining industries, and low productivity – notably in agriculture. Persistent high unemployment. Recent major investments in Latin American market undermined by Argentine crisis.

Profile

Real convergence with the major European economies first became a realistic objective in the late 1980s, as Spain posted the highest investment-led output growth in the OECD.

ECONOMIC PERFORMANCE INDICATOR

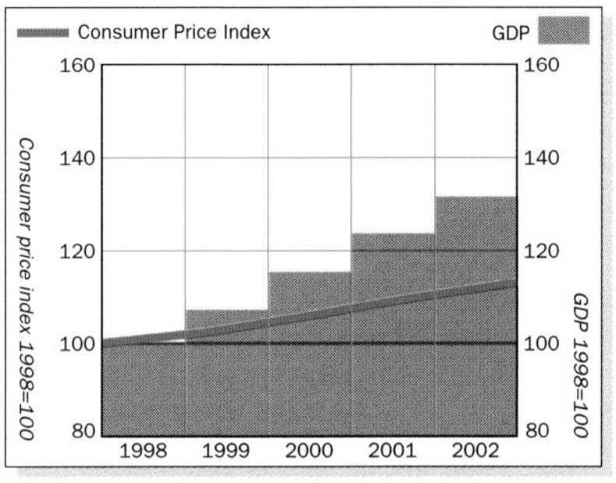
Consumer Price Index
GDP
Consumer price index 1998=100
GDP 1998=100
160
140
120
100
80
1998
1999
2000
2001
2002

By 1991, GDP per capita stood at almost 80% of the EU average. Recession in the early 1990s was turned around in mid-decade, and growth averaged 4% over 1997–2000, with public debt brought below 60% of GDP by 2001. The economy slowed markedly through 2001, and the annualized growth rate dropped to around 2%.

Spain succeeded in meeting the economic convergence criteria necessary for European economic and monetary union and was among the 12 EU countries to adopt the euro fully in January 2002.

SPAIN : MAJOR BUSINESSES

La Coruña
Bilbao
Zaragoza
Barcelona
Vigo
Madrid
Huelva
Valencia
Sevilla
Málaga
Cartagena
Textiles
Agribusiness
Chemicals
Shipbuilding
Vehicle manufacture
Heavy engineering
Light engineering
Fish processing
0
200 km
0
200 miles
* significant multinational ownership

S

RESOURCES

Electric power 52.9m kW

1.4m tonnes

4551 b/d (reserves 6.6m barrels)

23.8m sheep, 23.5m pigs, 128m chickens

Coal, oil, iron, uranium, mercury, fluorite, gypsum

ELECTRICITY GENERATION

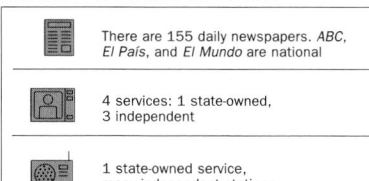

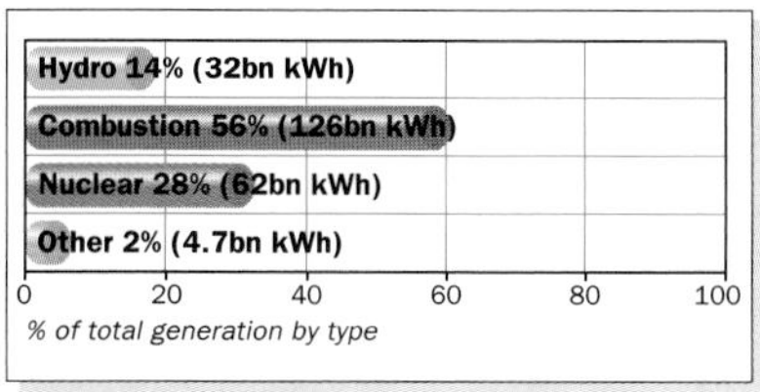
Hydro 14% (32bn kWh)
Combustion 56% (126bn kWh)
Nuclear 28% (62bn kWh)
Other 2% (4.7bn kWh)
0 20 40 60 80 100
% of total generation by type

Spain lacks natural resources, especially water, and is heavily dependent on imported oil and gas. Coal, mined mainly to generate industry, is a declining but still subsidized sector, concentrated in the Asturias region. Spain has one of the world's largest fishing fleets, but EU restrictions have forced cuts in catches since the 1990s.

SPAIN : LAND USE

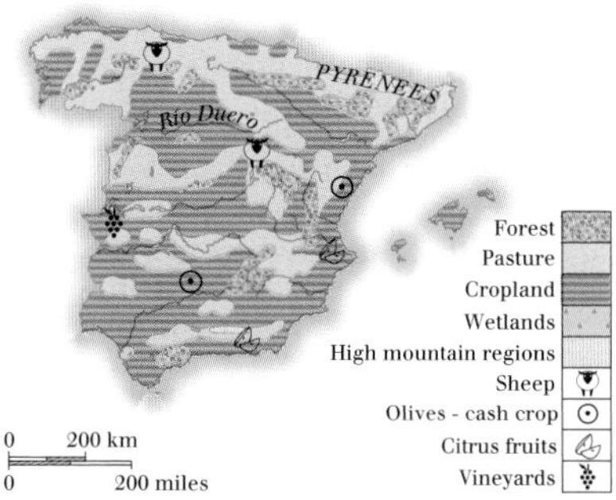
PYRENEES
Río Duero
Forest
Pasture
Cropland
Wetlands
High mountain regions
Sheep
Olives - cash crop
Citrus fruits
Vineyards
0 200 km
0 200 miles

ENVIRONMENT

Sustainability rank: 44th

9% (8% partially protected)

7 tonnes per capita

ENVIRONMENTAL TREATIES

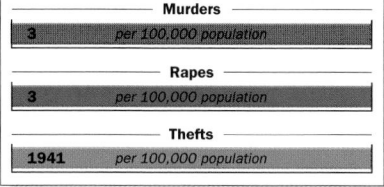

Yes	Yes	Yes
Yes	Yes	Yes

Public awareness of environmental matters is increasing. Renewable energy, though still tiny in extent, is becoming more visible, particularly with the growth of wind farms. The benefits of a national tree-planting scheme to reduce soil erosion have been offset by increasingly frequent intentional forest fires. More land has national park status than in any other country in Europe. A project to bring water from the Ebro River to counter desertification in the south was canceled in 2004 by the new government, though the alternatives of dams, canals, and desalinization plants are also unpopular. Oil from the *Prestige* oil tanker which sank off Galicia in 2002 caused extensive pollution.

MEDIA

TV ownership high

Daily newspaper circulation 100 per 1000 people

PUBLISHING AND BROADCAST MEDIA

There are 155 daily newspapers. *ABC*, *El País*, and *El Mundo* are national

4 services: 1 state-owned, 3 independent

1 state-owned service, many independent stations

Despite the large number of daily newspapers, readership is among the lowest in Europe. Both public and private TV services are popular. Radio is of a generally high standard.

CRIME

No death penalty

56,140 prisoners

Up 10% in 2001

CRIME RATES

Murders	3	per 100,000 population
Rapes	3	per 100,000 population
Thefts	1941	per 100,000 population

Spain is a major crossroads in the world narcotics trade, and drugs-related crime is rising. Illegal immigration has soared, with authorities in the south unable to cope with the influx.

EDUCATION

School leaving age: 16

98%

1.57m students

THE EDUCATION SYSTEM

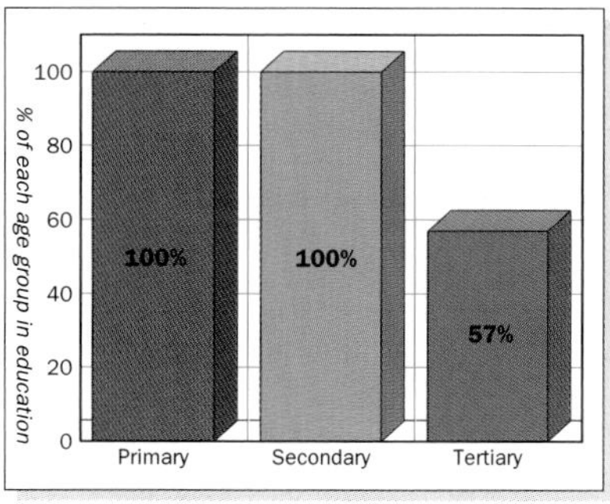
100
80
60
40
20
0
% of each age group in education
100%
100%
57%
Primary
Secondary
Tertiary

The school leaving age has risen since 1990 from 14 to 16. The latest secondary education reforms, announced in 2000, offer a number of additional subjects, improvements in mathematics, philosophy, and languages, and greater attention to information technology. Autonomous regions regulate by decree the teaching of languages other than Castilian Spanish, such as Basque or Catalan.

HEALTH

Welfare state health benefits

1 per 303 people

Cancers, heart, cerebrovascular, and respiratory diseases

Public health care is of high quality and readily available. Public hospitals, though widely considered to be superior, are outnumbered by private ones. In spite of very high tobacco and alcohol consumption, Spain has a healthy population, possibly due to its Mediterranean diet. The incidence of AIDS has risen alarmingly, however, to become one of the highest in western Europe.

SPENDING

GDP/cap. increase

CONSUMPTION AND SPENDING

444 per 1000 population

506 per 1000 population

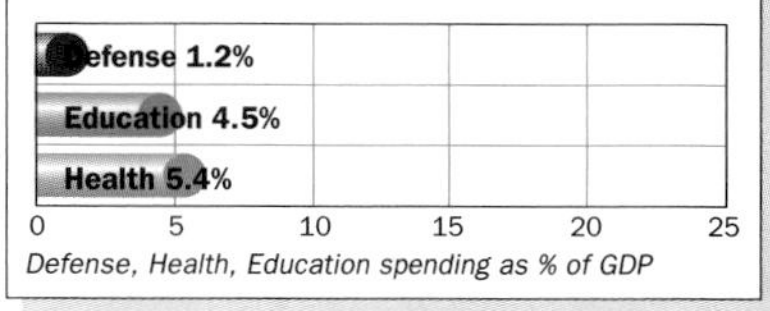
Defense 1.2%
Education 4.5%
Health 5.4%
0 5 10 15 20 25
Defense, Health, Education spending as % of GDP

In the late 1980s, it became fashionable in Spain to compete openly, make money, and acquire consumer goods. Rapid economic growth at this time greatly enriched the professional and managerial classes. The latter became the best-paid, in real terms, in Europe, and Spain quickly became an important market for luxury cars and yachts. In the early 1990s this ostentatious affluence waned in the face of recession and an unemployment rate which soared to become one of the highest in Europe. The boom of 1997–2000 boosted the number of jobs, but also gave rise to anxiety over inflation. By 2001 this boom too had subsided, and there was less financial security, with about one-third of employees on only temporary contracts.

WORLD RANKING

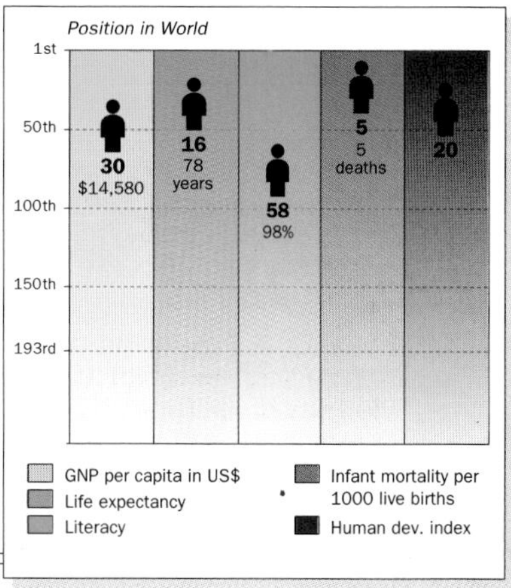
Position in World
1st
50th
100th
150th
193rd
30
$14,580
16
78
years
58
98%
5
5
deaths
20
GNP per capita in US$
Life expectancy
Literacy
Infant mortality per 1000 live births
Human dev. index

S

SRI LANKA

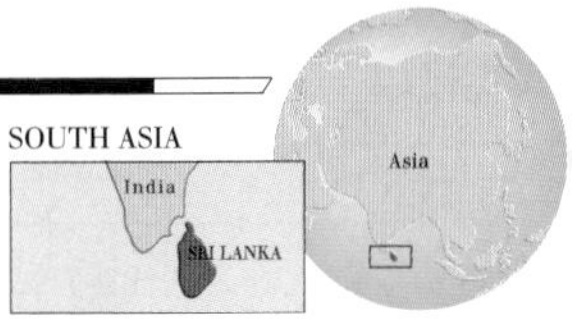
SOUTH ASIA
India
SRI LANKA
Asia

OFFICIAL NAME: Democratic Socialist Republic of Sri Lanka **CAPITAL:** Colombo
POPULATION: 19.1 million **CURRENCY:** Sri Lanka rupee **OFFICIAL LANGUAGES:** Sinhala and Tamil

1948 | 1948 | Feb 4 | CL | +5.5 | +94 | .lk

THE TEARDROP-SHAPED island of Sri Lanka is separated from India by the Palk Strait. Rugged central uplands give way to fertile plains in the north. The majority Sinhalese, an Indo-Aryan people originating in northern India, have a Buddhism-based identity. Independent since 1948, Sri Lanka suffered from 1983 from a protracted civil war involving the attempted secession of the minority (and mainly Hindu) Tamils in the north and east.

CLIMATE

Tropical monsoon/ equatorial

WEATHER CHART FOR COLOMBO

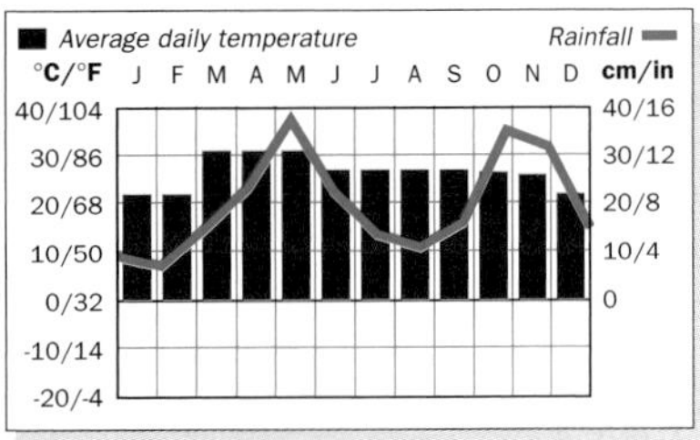
Average daily temperature
Rainfall
°C/°F J F M A M J J A S O N D cm/in
40/104
30/86
20/68
10/50
0/32
-10/14
-20/4
40/16
30/12
20/8
10/4
0

The climate is tropical, with afternoon breezes on the coast and cooler air in the highlands. The northeast is driest.

TRANSPORTATION

Drive on left

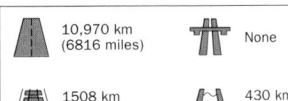

Bandaranaike, Katunayake 3.23m passengers

66 ships 80,900 grt

THE TRANSPORTATION NETWORK

10,970 km (6816 miles)	None
1508 km (937 miles)	430 km (267 miles)

Main roads are crowded and slow. Routes to the Tamil-dominated north and east have been reopened.

TOURISM

Visitors : Population 1:38

500,642 visitors

Up 27% in 2003

MAIN TOURIST ARRIVALS

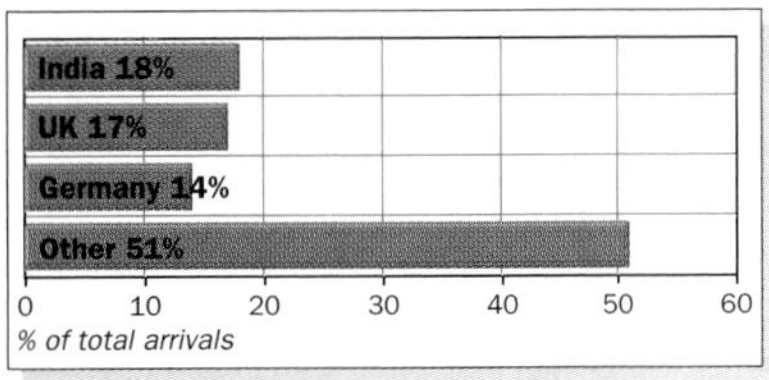
India 18%
UK 17%
Germany 14%
Other 51%
0 10 20 30 40 50 60
% of total arrivals

Stunning scenery and the Buddhist cultural heritage have made Sri Lanka a popular destination, despite years of civil war. High-profile attacks in Colombo did affect tourism, but peace has paved the way for a recovery.

PEOPLE

Pop. density high

Sinhala, Tamil, Sinhala-Tamil, English

295/km² (764/mi²)

THE URBAN/RURAL POPULATION SPLIT

23%
77%

ETHNIC MAKEUP

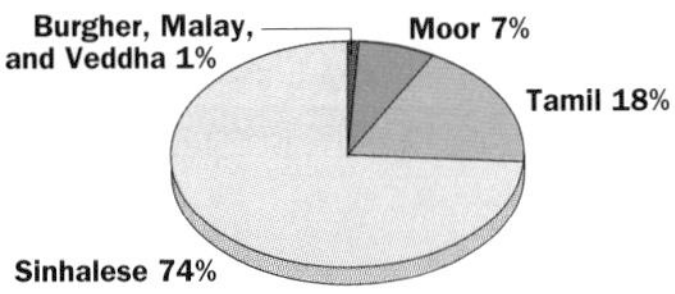
Burgher, Malay, and Veddha 1%
Moor 7%
Tamil 18%
Sinhalese 74%

Ethnic tensions focus on the 19-year conflict between the minority, Hindu, Tamils and majority, Buddhist, Sinhalese. Favored by the British administration, the Tamils were subject to attempts by the Sinhalese to redress the balance after independence. The Tamil Tigers seek a homeland in the north. A tentative peace was reached in 2002 and talks have continued since.

The Moors are the Muslim descendants of Arab traders. A few indigenous forest-dwelling Veddhas survive in the remote east of the island.

POLITICS

Multiparty elections

2004/2010

President Chandrika Bandaranaike Kumaratunga

AT THE LAST ELECTION

Parliament 225 seats

4% JHU
2% SLMC
47% UPFA
36% UNP
10% ITAK
1% Others

UPFA = United People's Freedom Alliance, dominated by the Sri Lanka Freedom Party – **SLFP** **UNP** = United National Party **ITAK** = Tamil State of Lanka Party **JHU** = National Sinhala Heritage **SLMC** = Sri Lanka Muslim Congress

Politics has been indelibly colored by the 19-year civil war, which claimed more than 50,000 lives. Breakthrough came in 2001 when the left-wing SLFP-led government was soundly beaten in legislative elections by the right-of-center UNP, which sought to bring a swift end to the conflict. A permanent cease-fire was agreed in 2002, and the separatist Liberation Tigers of Tamil Eelam (LTTE or Tamil Tigers) have since agreed in principle to settle for autonomy. The negotiations caused serious divisions between President Kumaratunga, of the UPFA, and the UNP prime minister. Kumaratunga called snap legislative elections for April 2004, won by her UPFA.

INDIA
Palk Strait
Bay of Bengal
Gulf of Mannar
INDIAN OCEAN
Kankesanturai
Jaffna
Mannar I.
Kayts
Punkudutivu
Delft
Pooneryn
Jaffna Lagoon
Kilinochchi
Nanthi Kadal Lagoon
Mullaittivu
Karaitivu
Adam's Bridge
Mannar
Talladi
Mankulam
Vavuniya
Horowupotana
Trincomalee
Koddiyar Bay
Medawachchiya
Anuradhapura
Yan
Upaar Lagoon
Puttalam Lagoon
Puttalam
Habarana
Polonnaruwa
Dambulla
Mundal Lagoon
Chenkaladi
Batticaloa
Dedura
Mahaweli Ganga
Chilaw
Matale
Kurunegala
Mahiyangana
Ampara
Negombo
Kegalla
Kandy
Senanayake Samudra
Akkaraipattu
Pidurutalagala 2524m
Gampaha
Badulla
COLOMBO
Dehiwala-Mount Lavinia
Moratuwa
Talawakele
Sri Jayawardenapura
Nuwara Eliya
Namunukula
Monaragala
Pottuvil
Panadura
Kalu
Beragala
Ratnapura
Wellawaya
Kalutara
Pelmadulla
Elpitiya
Ambalangoda
Hambantota
Galle
Weligama
Matara
10°
8°
6°
80°
82°

SRI LANKA

Total Area : 65 610 sq. km (25 332 sq. miles)

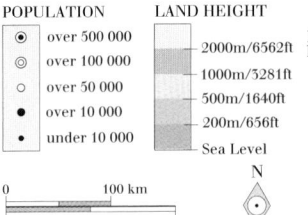

POPULATION
- over 500 000
- over 100 000
- over 50 000
- over 10 000
- under 10 000

LAND HEIGHT
- 2000m/6562ft
- 1000m/3281ft
- 500m/1640ft
- 200m/656ft
- Sea Level

0 100 km
0 100 miles

N

WORLD AFFAIRS

Joined UN in 1955

Comm | G24 | NAM | SAARC | WTO

Relations with India are paramount. However, India's role as peacemaker under the 1987 Indo-Sri Lankan accords was fiercely resisted by the Tamil Tigers, and India was forced to withdraw its peacekeeping troops. In recent years Norway has taken on the role of mediator in the conflict.

AID

Recipient

$344m (receipts)

Up 10% in 2002

International donors offered a four-year $4.5 billion aid package in 2003 in return for progress in the peace process.

DEFENSE

No compulsory military service

$504m

Down 35% in 2002

Recent drives to recruit 5000 more soldiers have shown a marked shift in policy, from simply enlarging the army to modernizing it.

ECONOMICS

Inflation 9.1% p.a. (1990–2001)

$16.1bn

102.4 Sri Lanka rupees (97.16)

SCORE CARD

- ❑ WORLD GNP RANKING........................74th
- ❑ GNP PER CAPITA.............................$850
- ❑ BALANCE OF PAYMENTS...................–$264m
- ❑ INFLATION.......................................9.6%
- ❑ UNEMPLOYMENT.................................9%

STRENGTHS

World's largest tea exporter. Foreign investment attracted by privatization, despite left-wing stance of President Kumaratunga.

WEAKNESSES

Civil war has severely drained government funds, and lingering tensions continue to deter investors and many tourists. High unemployment.

EXPORTS

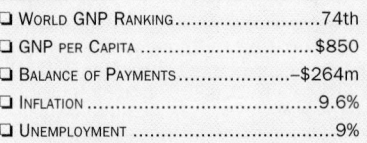

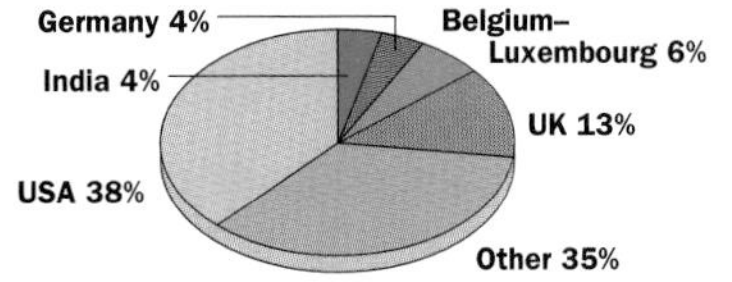
Germany 4%
Belgium–Luxembourg 6%
India 4%
UK 13%
USA 38%
Other 35%

IMPORTS

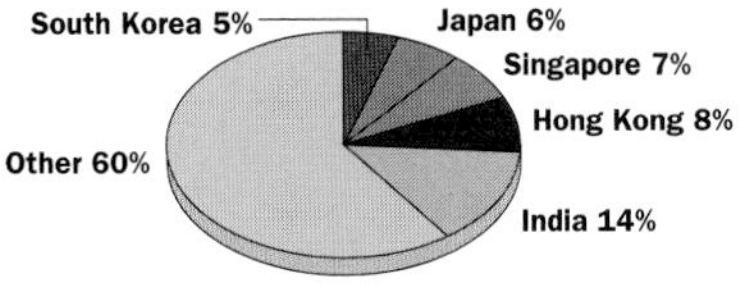
South Korea 5%
Japan 6%
Singapore 7%
Hong Kong 8%
Other 60%
India 14%

***Adam's Peak** in mountainous central Sri Lanka is a famous religious site with a Buddhist shrine at the summit.*

RESOURCES

Electric power 2.1m kW

288,010 tonnes

Not an oil producer; refines 47,000 b/d

1.14m cattle, 635,000 buffaloes, 9.77m chickens

Gemstones, graphite, iron, monazite, clay, uranium, ilmenite

Sri Lanka has to import all its oil. Hydropower is the main source of electricity; droughts are frequent and supplies can be erratic. Sri Lanka is keen to diversify power sources and is turning to coal-powered generation.

ENVIRONMENT

Sustainability rank: 55th

14% (5% partially protected)

0.6 tonnes per capita

Sri Lanka has successfully promoted national parks. Their development is opposed by the Veddha people, who have traditionally occupied such land.

MEDIA

TV ownership medium

Daily newspaper circulation 29 per 1000 people

PUBLISHING AND BROADCAST MEDIA

There are 9 daily newspapers, including the *Daily News, Evening Observer,* and *Dinamina*

8 services: 2 state-run, 6 independent

7 services: 1 state-owned, 6 independent

In 2002, the government permitted Tamil Tigers openly to broadcast from their previously clandestine Voice of Tigers radio station in the north.

CRIME

Death penalty not used in practice

17,485 prisoners

Crime is rising

Extrajudicial killings and other human rights abuses increased the toll of deaths and disappearances during the civil war. New laws have been introduced to combat sex tourism.

EDUCATION

School leaving age: 13

92%

48,667 students

The ADB approved a $50 million loan in 2000 to modernize and expand the secondary education system.

CHRONOLOGY

Tamils and Sinhalese have inhabited Sri Lanka since before the 6th century. Named Ceylon by the British, it became independent in 1948.

- ❑ **1956** SLFP wins election.
- ❑ **1960** Sirimavo Bandaranaike becomes world's first woman prime minister.
- ❑ **1972** Renamed Sri Lanka.
- ❑ **1983** Tamil Tigers begin civil war.
- ❑ **1993** President Premadasa killed.
- ❑ **1994** Left-wing alliance takes power; Chandrika Kumaratunga president.
- ❑ **1995–1996** Collapse of peace talks.
- ❑ **1999** Kumaratunga reelected.
- ❑ **2001** Opposition UNP wins election.
- ❑ **2002** Comprehensive cease-fire.
- ❑ **2003** Over 200 die in worst flooding for 50 years.
- ❑ **2004** UPFA wins election.

HEALTH

Welfare state health benefits

1 per 2319 people

Heart attacks, cancers, pneumonia, strokes

Years of high spending on health have resulted in an accessible, fee-free system. Ayurvedic medicine is popular.

SPENDING

GDP/cap. increase

CONSUMPTION AND SPENDING

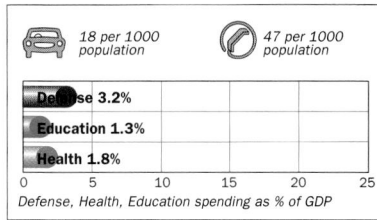

18 per 1000 population

47 per 1000 population

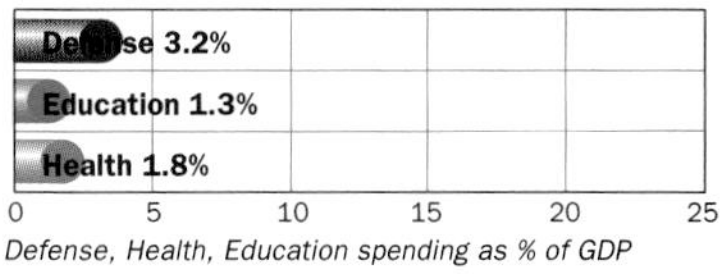
Defense 3.2%
Education 1.3%
Health 1.8%
0
5
10
15
20
25
Defense, Health, Education spending as % of GDP

Economic growth has created a new class of wealthy Sinhalese. Tamil tea workers are the poorest group.

WORLD RANKING

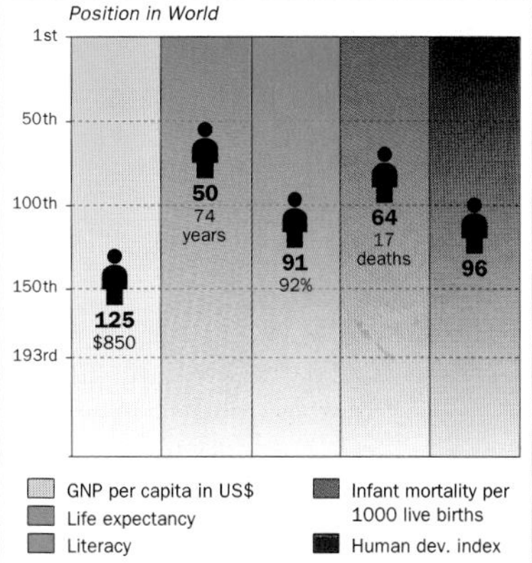
Position in World
1st
50th
100th
150th
193rd
125
$850
50
74
years
91
92%
64
17
deaths
96
GNP per capita in US$
Life expectancy
Literacy
Infant mortality per 1000 live births
Human dev. index

S

SUDAN

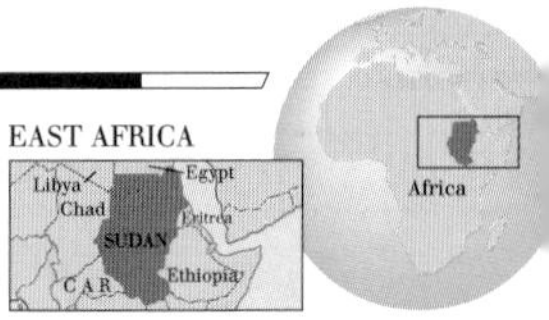
EAST AFRICA
Libya
Egypt
Chad
Eritrea
SUDAN
C.A.R.
Ethiopia
Africa

OFFICIAL NAME: Republic of the Sudan **CAPITAL:** Khartoum **POPULATION:** 33.6 million
CURRENCY: Sudanese pound or dinar **OFFICIAL LANGUAGE:** Arabic

1956
1956
Jan 1
SUD
+2
+249
.sd

BORDERED ON THE EAST by the Red Sea, Sudan is the largest country in Africa. Its landscape changes from desert in the north to lush tropical in the south, with grassy plains and swamps in the center. Since independence from British and Egyptian rule in 1956, tensions between the Arab north and African south have led to two civil wars. In 1989, an army coup installed a military Islamic fundamentalist regime headed by Gen. Omar al-Bashir.

Camel caravan in the dry north. *Periodic drought coupled with war disruption mean that Sudan requires large amounts of food aid.*

CLIMATE

Hot desert/steppe/tropical

WEATHER CHART FOR KHARTOUM

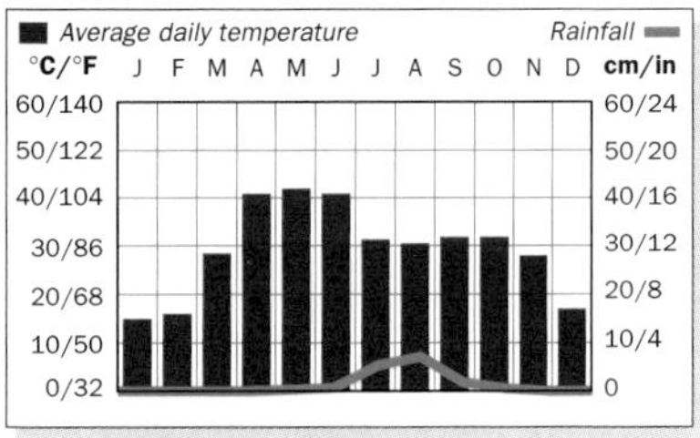
Average daily temperature
Rainfall
°C/°F J F M A M J J A S O N D cm/in
60/140
50/122
40/104
30/86
20/68
10/50
0/32
60/24
50/20
40/16
30/12
20/8
10/4
0

Sudan's northern half is hot arid desert with constant dry winds. The rest has a rainy season varying from two months in the center to eight in the south.

TRANSPORTATION

Drive on right

Khartoum

17 ships 33,287 grt

THE TRANSPORTATION NETWORK

4284 km (2662 miles)	None
4578 km (2845 miles)	5310 km (3299 miles)

The Port Sudan–Khartoum railroad and road are Sudan's most important links. There are few other roads, but Iran is financing a north–south highway. Civil war has interrupted all Nile shipping.

TOURISM

Visitors : Population 1:646

52,000 visitors

Up 4% in 2002

MAIN TOURIST ARRIVALS

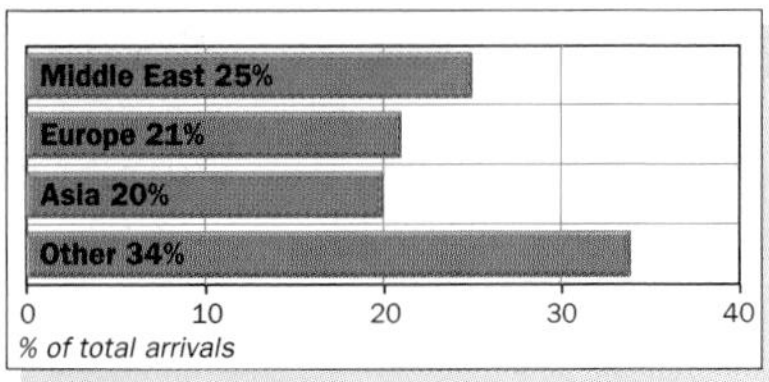
Middle East 25%
Europe 21%
Asia 20%
Other 34%
0
10
20
30
40
% of total arrivals

Ongoing violence means that Sudan has very few tourists. Visitors are mostly aid workers or on business.

PEOPLE

Pop. density low

Arabic, Dinka, Nuer, Nubian, Beja, Zande, Bari, Fur, Shilluk, Lotuko

13/km² (35/mi²)

THE URBAN/RURAL POPULATION SPLIT

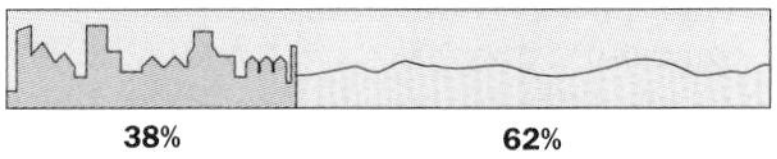
38%
62%

RELIGIOUS PERSUASION

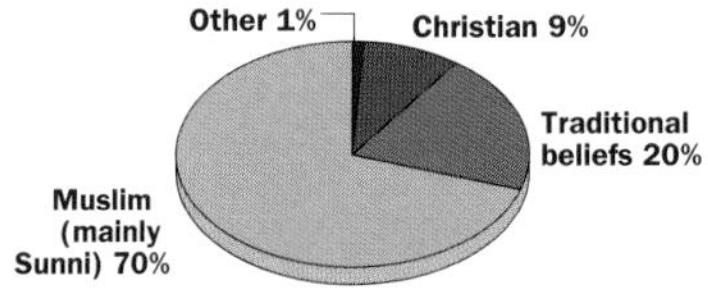
Other 1%
Christian 9%
Traditional beliefs 20%
Muslim (mainly Sunni) 70%

Sudan has a large number of ethnic and linguistic groups. About two million Sudanese are nomads. The major social division, however, is between the Arabized Muslims in the north and the mostly African, largely animist or Christian population in the south. Attempts to impose Arab and Islamic values throughout Sudan have been the root cause of the civil war that has ravaged the south since 1983. Women not wearing Islamic dress can suffer harassment or even public flogging. There are some non-Arab groups in the north and in the densely populated Darfur region. The Janjaweed Arab militia targeted black Africans in Darfur for "ethnic cleansing" in 2004.

POLITICS

Multiparty elections

2000/2004

President Omar Hassan Ahmad al-Bashir

AT THE LAST ELECTION

National Assembly 400 seats

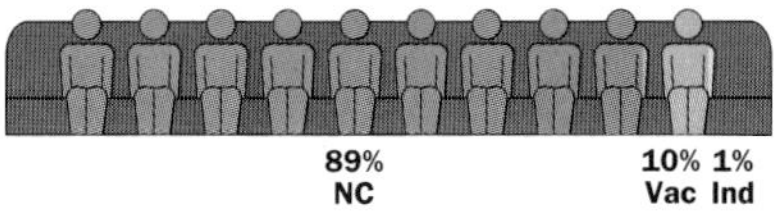
89% NC
10% Vac
1% Ind

NC = National Congress supporters **Vac** = Vacant
Ind = Independents

Elections in 2000, boycotted by the opposition, returned Gen. Omar al-Bashir and his NC bloc to power. "Political associations" have been allowed since 1999, and in 2002 pre-1989 parties were unbanned. An end may be in sight to two decades of war between Muslim north and Christian south, after provisional peace accords were signed in 2004 with the southern Sudan People's Liberation Army (SPLA). The government is accused of backing Arab militias committing atrocities in the Darfur region from late 2003, causing thousands to flee and an acute humanitarian crisis.

SUDAN

Total Area : 2 505 810 sq. km (967 493 sq. miles)

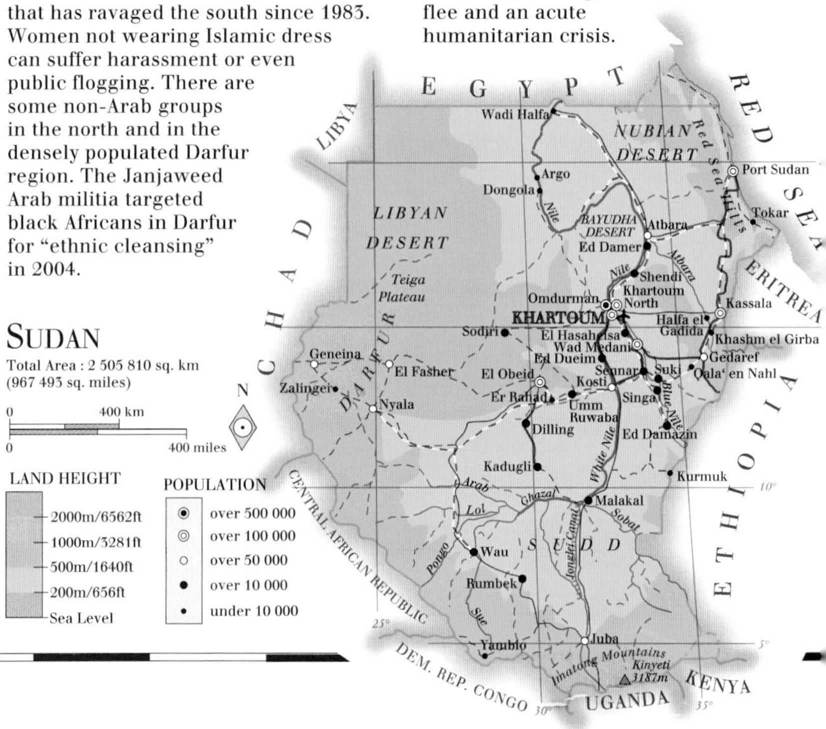
0
400 km
0
400 miles
LAND HEIGHT
2000m/6562ft
1000m/3281ft
500m/1640ft
200m/656ft
Sea Level
POPULATION
over 500 000
over 100 000
over 50 000
over 10 000
under 10 000
N
EGYPT
LIBYA
RED SEA
ERITREA
ETHIOPIA
KENYA
UGANDA
DEM. REP. CONGO
CENTRAL AFRICAN REPUBLIC
CHAD
Wadi Halfa
NUBIAN DESERT
Port Sudan
Tokar
Argo
Dongola
LIBYAN DESERT
BAYUDHA DESERT
Atbara
Ed Damer
Teiga Plateau
Shendi
Khartoum North
Omdurman
KHARTOUM
Kassala
Halfa el Gadida
Khashm el Girba
Gedaref
Qala'en Nahl
Sodiri
El Hasaheisa
Wad Medani
Ed Dueim
Geneina
El Fasher
El Obeid
Kosti
Sennar
Suki
Singa
Zalingei
DARFUR
Nyala
Er Rahad
Umm Ruwaba
Dilling
Ed Damazin
Kadugli
Kurmuk
Malakal
SUDD
Wau
Rumbek
Juba
Yambio
Imatong Mountains
Kinyeti 3187m
Nile
Blue Nile
White Nile
Atbara
Red Sea Hills
Sobat
Jonglei Canal
Arab
Ghazal
Lol
Pongo
Sue
10°
5°
25°
30°
35°

WORLD AFFAIRS

Joined UN in 1956

AL | OIC | COMESA | IGAD | AU

Only Iran, Yemen, and Libya maintain friendly ties, though relations with Uganda have recently improved. In mid-2004 the UN threatened sanctions if the Arab millitias in the western region of Darfur were not reined in.

AID

Recipient

$351m (receipts)

Up 90% in 2002

The US is the largest bilateral aid donor, followed by the Netherlands. Most aid is spent on emergency food supplies.

DEFENSE

Compulsory military service

$629m

Up 11% in 2002

The NC controls the military and police and has its own paramilitary militia. Sudan's 100,000-strong army was for many years engaged in fighting the two southern factions – the SPLA and the Sudan People's Democratic Front.

ECONOMICS

Inflation 58% p.a. (1990–2001)

$12.2bn

259.5 Sudanese dinars (258.7)

SCORE CARD

- World GNP Ranking 82nd
- GNP per Capita $370
- Balance of Payments .... –$960m
- Inflation 0.9%
- Unemployment 19%

STRENGTHS

Oil, gas, cotton, gum arabic, sesame, sugar. Some gold mining.

WEAKNESSES

Low industrialization. Lack of foreign exchange for importing energy and spare parts for industry. Drought. Little transportation infrastructure. Huge distances between towns. Civil war delayed exploitation of oil reserves. Alienation of Arab donors and investors.

EXPORTS

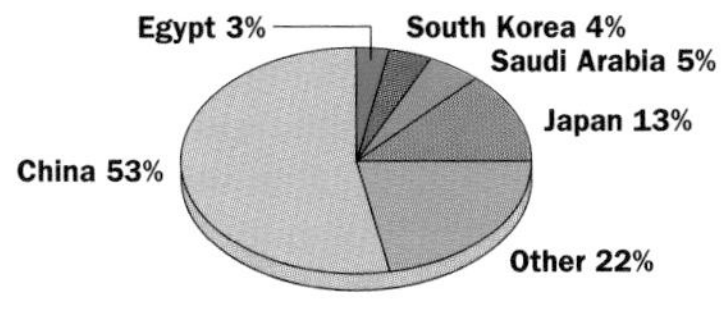

Egypt 3%
South Korea 4%
Saudi Arabia 5%
Japan 13%
China 53%
Other 22%

IMPORTS

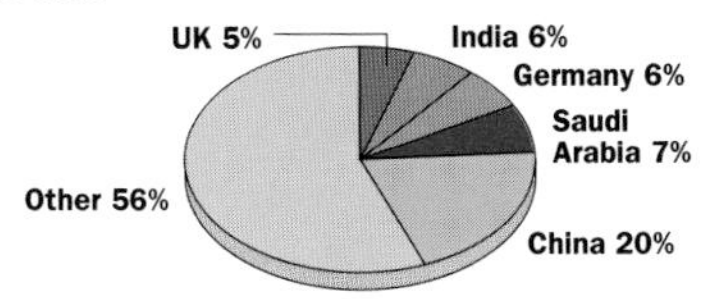

UK 5%
India 6%
Germany 6%
Saudi Arabia 7%
Other 56%
China 20%

RESOURCES

Electric power 757,000 kW

59,000 tonnes

255,000 b/d (reserves 700m barrels)

47m sheep, 40m goats, 38.3m cattle, 38.5m chickens

Oil, gas, gold, copper, gypsum, marble, mica, silver, chromium, zinc

Large oil and gas reserves were found in the south in the 1980s; oil exports started in 1999. The half-thermal, half-hydroelectric generating capacity is insufficient, and weeklong power cuts are frequent. Gold mining has the potential for expansion.

ENVIRONMENT

Sustainability rank: 102nd

5% (2% partially protected)

0.2 tonnes per capita

The Jonglei canal project, halted by rebel attacks when only 70% complete, could still devastate the Sudd, the world's largest swamp and a rich wetland habitat, fed by the White Nile.

MEDIA

TV ownership high

Daily newspaper circulation 26 per 1000 people

PUBLISHING AND BROADCAST MEDIA

There are 8 daily newspapers, including *Al-Anbaa*, *Ar-Rai al-Amm*, and *Al-Nasr*

1 state-controlled service

2 services: 1 state-controlled, 1 rebel-controlled

President Bashir promised in 2003 to lift restrictions on the media as part of peace negotiations.

CRIME

Death penalty in use

12,000 prisoners

Crime is rising

Antigovernment dissent is often suppressed by violence, and torture by the security forces is widespread. The UN has condemned Sudan's poor human rights record.

EDUCATION

School leaving age: 14

60%

200,538 students

In 1991, measures were introduced to Islamize education. Primary school children must have two years of Islamic religious instruction, and men wishing to enter university must first serve for a year in the People's Militia.

HEALTH

Welfare state health benefits

1 per 10,000 people

Infectious and parasitic diseases, malnutrition

Health service standards in rural areas are basic. Civil war has led to an increase in communicable diseases and malnutrition. The parasitic infection leishmaniasis is prevalent.

CHRONOLOGY

Northern Sudan was taken by Egypt in 1821, the south by Britain in 1877.

- **1882** British invade Egypt.
- **1883–1898** Muslim revolt led by Muhammad Ahmed, the Mahdi.
- **1954** Becomes self-governing.
- **1955** Rebellion in south starts 17 years of civil war.
- **1956** Independence as republic.
- **1958–1964** Military rule.
- **1965** Civilian revolution, elections.
- **1969** Coup led by Col. Jaafar Nimeiri.
- **1972** South gets limited autonomy.
- **1973** Socialist Union sole party.
- **1983** Southern rebellion resumes. *Sharia* (Islamic law) imposed.
- **1984** Devastating drought.
- **1986** Army coup.
- **1989** Gen. Bashir takes over.
- **1991** *Sharia* penal code instituted. Pro-Iraq stance in Gulf War.
- **2000** Bashir ousts fundamentalist Turabi from leadership of NC.
- **2002** SPLA signs cease-fire. Fighting increases between rival factions over southern oil reserves.
- **2004** Ethnic violence in Darfur escalates into humanitarian crisis.

SPENDING

GDP/cap. increase

CONSUMPTION AND SPENDING

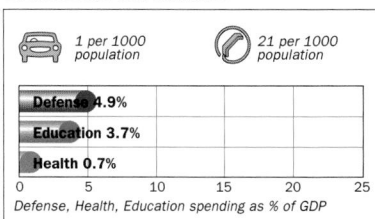

1 per 1000 population

21 per 1000 population

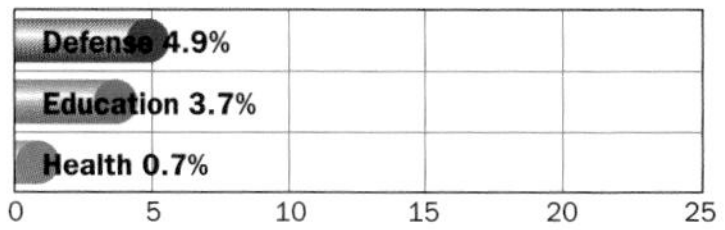

Defense 4.9%
Education 3.7%
Health 0.7%
0
5
10
15
20
25

Defense, Health, Education spending as % of GDP

There are large disparities between rich and poor. Wealth is limited to the NC and southern rebel elites. Most of the population struggles to survive.

S

WORLD RANKING

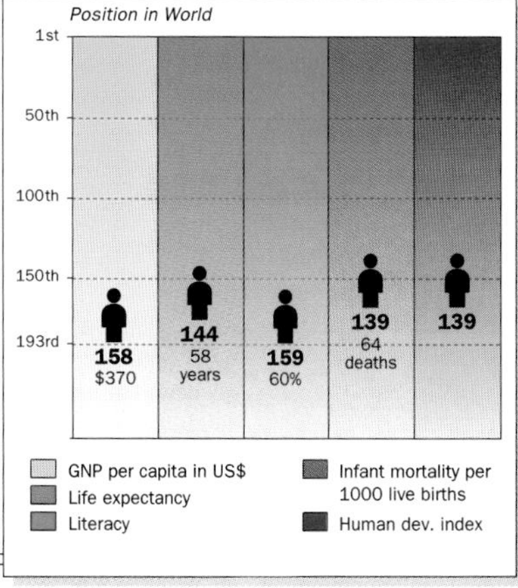

Position in World
1st
50th
100th
150th
193rd
158
$370
144
58 years
159
60%
139
64 deaths
139
GNP per capita in US$
Life expectancy
Literacy
Infant mortality per 1000 live births
Human dev. index

SURINAME

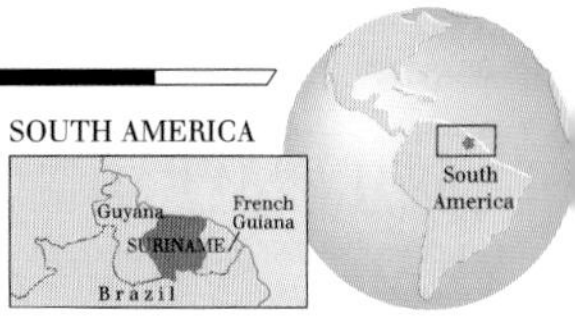
SOUTH AMERICA
Guyana
French Guiana
SURINAME
Brazil
South America

OFFICIAL NAME: Republic of Suriname **CAPITAL:** Paramaribo **POPULATION:** 436,000
CURRENCY: Suriname dollar (guilder until 2004) **OFFICIAL LANGUAGE:** Dutch

1975 | 1975 | Nov 25 | SME | -3 | +597 | .sr

BOUNDED EAST AND WEST by rivers, Suriname sits on the north coast of South America in the center of the "Guyana Plateau." The interior is rainforested highlands; most people live near the coast. In 1975, after over 300 years of Dutch rule, Suriname became independent. The Netherlands is still its main aid supplier, and is home to one-third of Surinamese. Multiparty democracy was restored in 1991, after almost 11 years of military rule.

***Congested street in Paramaribo.** It boasts 18th- and 19th-century Dutch architecture. The large mosque is next to a Jewish synagogue.*

CLIMATE

Tropical equatorial

WEATHER CHART FOR PARAMARIBO

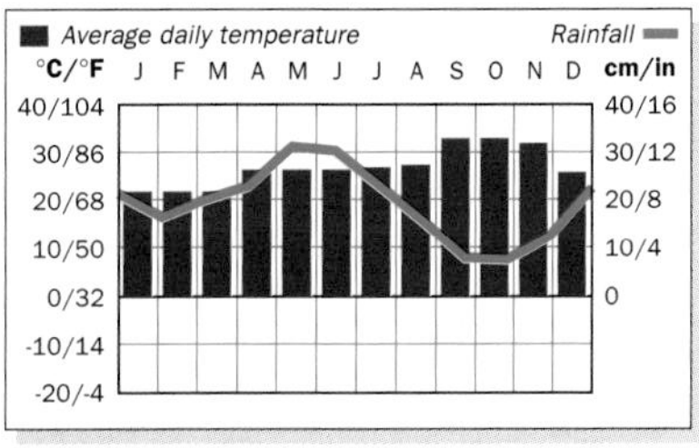
Average daily temperature
Rainfall
°C/°F
J F M A M J J A S O N D
cm/in
40/104
30/86
20/68
10/50
0/32
-10/14
-20/-4
40/16
30/12
20/8
10/4
0

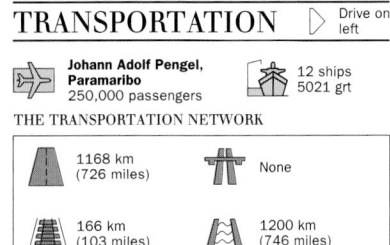

Suriname's tropical climate is cooled by the trade winds. Annual rainfall varies from 150 to 300 cm (60 to 120 in) between coast and interior.

TRANSPORTATION

Drive on left

Johann Adolf Pengel, Paramaribo
250,000 passengers

12 ships
5021 grt

THE TRANSPORTATION NETWORK

1168 km (726 miles)	None
166 km (103 miles)	1200 km (746 miles)

Rivers provide the main north–south links, and the interior relies on water or air transportation. The road network runs east–west and focuses on the coast and its immediate hinterland.

TOURISM

Visitors : Population 1:7.5

58,000 visitors

Down 8% in 2000

MAIN TOURIST ARRIVALS

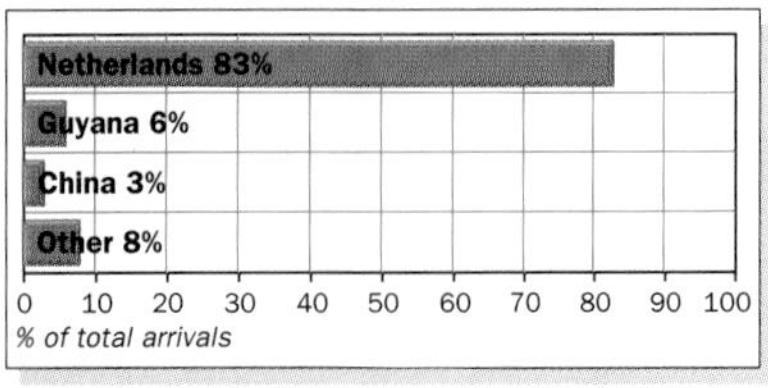
Netherlands 83%
Guyana 6%
China 3%
Other 8%
0 10 20 30 40 50 60 70 80 90 100
% of total arrivals

Tourism is undeveloped. Travelers outside Paramaribo are advised to carry their own hammock and food.

PEOPLE

Pop. density low

Sranan (Creole), Dutch, Javanese, Sarnami Hindi, Saramaccan, Chinese, Carib

3/km² (7/mi²)

THE URBAN/RURAL POPULATION SPLIT

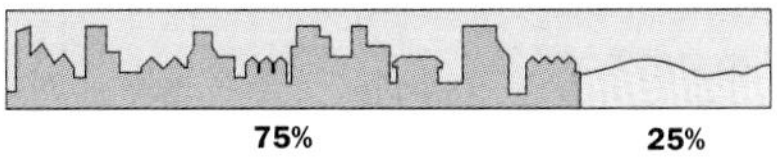
75%
25%

ETHNIC MAKEUP

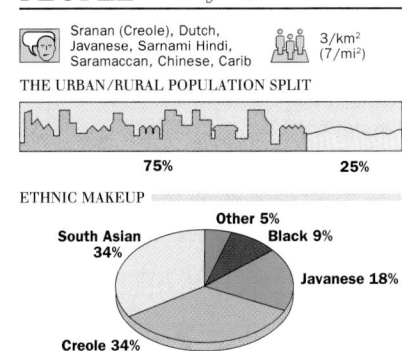

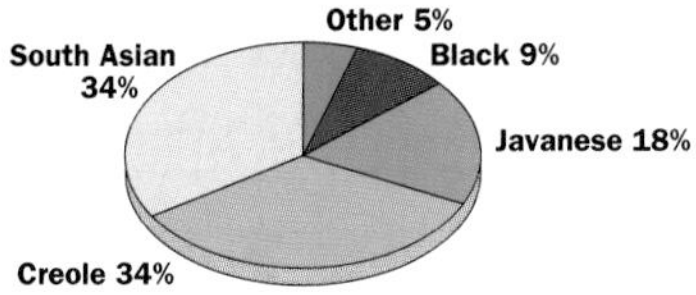
Other 5%
Black 9%
South Asian 34%
Javanese 18%
Creole 34%

Suriname comprises people with origins in Africa, India, Indonesia, and Europe, and also native Amerindians. Christianity, Hinduism, and Islam are the dominant religions. About 250,000 Surinamese have emigrated since 1975. Of those who remain, 90% live near the coast, while the rest live in scattered rainforest communities. *Bosnegers* are the descendants of runaway slaves, long established in the rainforest as a tribalized society of four clans.

POLITICS

Multiparty elections

2000/2005

President Ronald Venetiaan

AT THE LAST ELECTION
National Assembly 51 seats

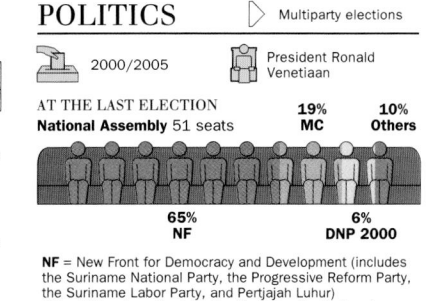

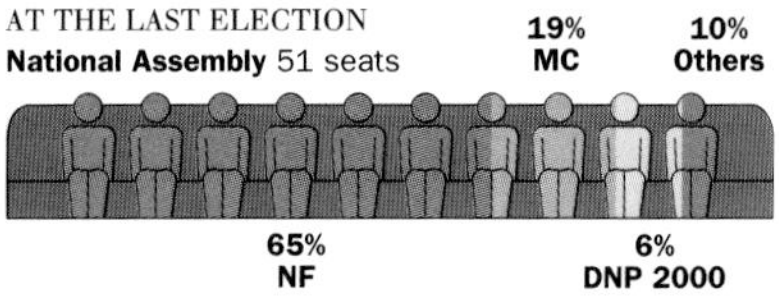
19% MC
10% Others
65% NF
6% DNP 2000

NF = New Front for Democracy and Development (includes the Suriname National Party, the Progressive Reform Party, the Suriname Labor Party, and Pertjajah Luhur)
MC = Millennium Combination (includes the National Democratic Party (**NDP**), the Democratic Alternative, and the Party for Unity and Harmony)
DNP 2000 = Democratic National Platform 2000

A coalition government representing Creoles, south Asians, and Javanese took power under Ronald Venetiaan in 1991. Five years later it was defeated by the NDP, controlled by Desi Bouterse, the military dictator from 1980 to 1988, and behind the 1990 coup which ended Suriname's first attempt at a return to democracy. Between 1996 and 2000 President Jules Wijdenbosch of the NDP withstood the efforts of opponents in the National Assembly to replace him. In the 2000 legislative elections, however, the NDP was massively defeated by the opposition NF. The new Assembly went on to reelect NF leader Venetiaan as president.

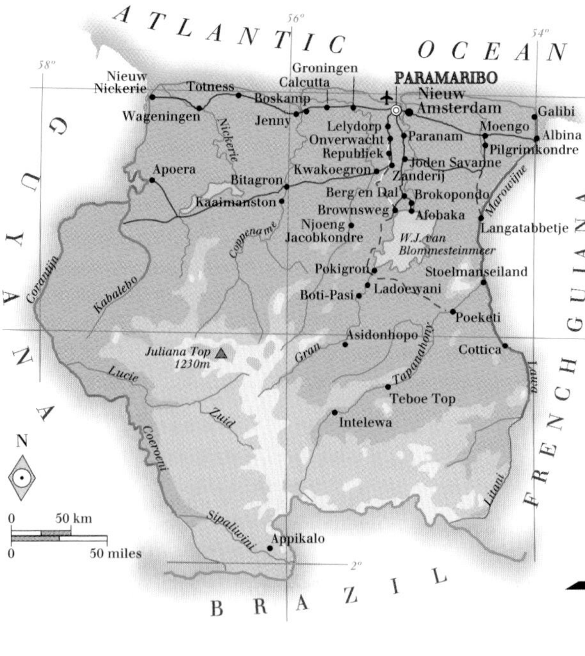
ATLANTIC OCEAN
GUYANA
FRENCH GUIANA
BRAZIL
PARAMARIBO
Nieuw Nickerie
Totness
Groningen
Calcutta
Boskamp
Wageningen
Jenny
Nieuw Amsterdam
Galibi
Lelydorp
Onverwacht
Republiek
Paranam
Moengo
Albina
Pilgrimkondre
Joden Savanne
Zanderij
Kwakoegron
Apoera
Bitagron
Kaaimanston
Berg en Dal
Brokopondo
Brownsweg
Afobaka
Njoeng Jacobkondre
W.J. van Blommesteinmeer
Langatabbetje
Pokigron
Stoelmanseiland
Boti-Pasi
Ladoewani
Poeketi
Asidonhopo
Cottica
Juliana Top 1230m
Teboe Top
Intelewa
Appikalo
Nickerie
Coppename
Corantijn
Kabalebo
Marowijne
Lucie
Zuid
Coeroeni
Gran
Tapanahony
Sipaliwini
Litani
Lawa
N
0 50 km
0 50 miles

SURINAME

Total Area : 163 270 sq. km (63 039 sq. miles)

LAND HEIGHT
1000m/3281ft
500m/1640ft
200m/1640ft
Sea Level

POPULATIC
over 1
over 1
under

S

WORLD AFFAIRS

Joined UN in 1975

ACS | AmCC | Caricom | OAS | OIC

Relations with the Netherlands and the US, the key aid and trading partners, have been weakened over charges of official connivance in narcotics trafficking. Suriname claims the southeastern corner of Guyana in a border dispute. Relations were damaged further when Suriname took action against oil prospectors in 2000.

AID

Recipient

US$12m (receipts) | Down 48% in 2002

The Netherlands is the largest donor, but it has on occasion suspended aid amid deteriorating relations. The IDB and European Investment Bank have granted loans for agricultural and industrial development.

DEFENSE

No compulsory military service

US$8m | Down 11% in 2002

The army was politically dominant in the 1980s under Lt. Col. Desi Bouterse. A six-year war with *Bosneger* rebels ended in 1992. Aid and training have been provided in recent years by both the US and China.

ECONOMICS

Inflation 83% p.a. (1990–2001)

US$841m | 2.74 Suriname dollars (2515 guilders)

SCORE CARD

❑ World GNP Ranking	157th
❑ GNP per Capita	US$1940
❑ Balance of Payments	–US$131m
❑ Inflation	24.1%
❑ Unemployment	14%

STRENGTHS

Bauxite. Gold. Timber potential. Oil. Food exports: rice, bananas, citrus fruits, shrimp. Surinamese dollar replaced weak guilder in 2004.

WEAKNESSES

Chronic economic mismanagement, leading to low, or negative, growth and difficulty in utilizing Dutch aid. High inflation. High-cost, inefficient public sector. Net food importer.

EXPORTS

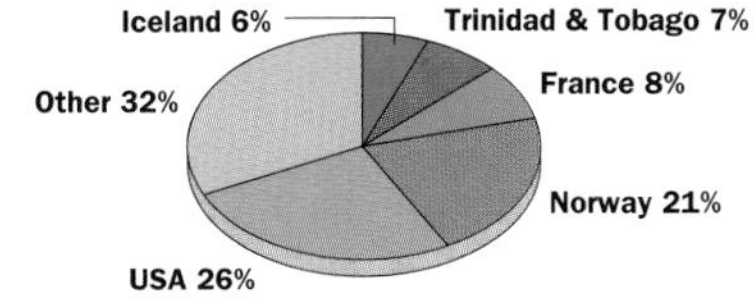
Iceland 6%
Trinidad & Tobago 7%
France 8%
Other 32%
Norway 21%
USA 26%

IMPORTS

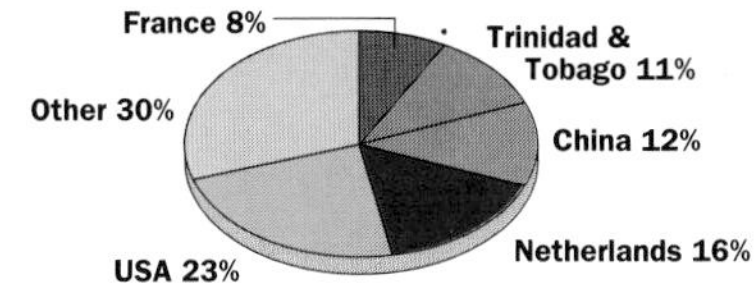
France 8%
Trinidad & Tobago 11%
Other 30%
China 12%
USA 23%
Netherlands 16%

RESOURCES

Electric power 425,000 kW

19,337 tonnes | 12,070 b/d (reserves 88m barrels)

137,000 cattle, 66,000 ducks, 3.8m chickens | Bauxite, iron, gold, manganese, copper, nickel, platinum, oil

The bauxite deposits are among the richest in the world, and Suriname is a major exporter of aluminum. Cheap hydroelectric power is a big advantage. Gold mining is largely unregulated, though international corporations have begun to move in. More oil production may also be possible. Rice and fruit are Suriname's key agricultural products.

ENVIRONMENT

Not available

10% partially protected | 1.9 tonnes per capita

In 1998 the government declared some 16,000 sq. km (6150 sq. miles) of rainforest – almost 10% of the country – to be a natural reserve barred to logging, but its exploitation for economic gain is still of real concern to environmentalists.

MEDIA

TV ownership medium

Daily newspaper circulation 68 per 1000 people

PUBLISHING AND BROADCAST MEDIA

There are 2 daily newspapers, *De Ware Tijd* and *De West*

2 state-owned services | 10 services: 1 state-owned, 9 independent

There are radio broadcasts in a number of languages. Dutch is used by the daily newspapers and for most TV programs.

CRIME

Death penalty not used in practice

786 prisoners | Relatively high crime levels

Human rights abuses associated with the former military regime have largely ended. Rival armed factions remain in some regions in the interior. Narcotics trafficking and money laundering are a problem, as is urban street crime.

EDUCATION

School leaving age: 12

94% | 4400 students

Education is free and includes adult literacy programs. There is a long tradition of higher education, but most graduates now live in the Netherlands.

CHRONOLOGY

Dutch rule began in 1667, after an Anglo-Dutch treaty whose terms included Britain ceding its colony in Suriname to the Dutch but gaining Nieuw Amsterdam (New York).

- ❑ **1975** Independence.
- ❑ **1980** Coup. Rule by Lt. Col. Desi Bouterse.
- ❑ **1982** Opponents executed. Dutch suspend aid for six years.
- ❑ **1986–1992** War with *Bosneger* rebels.
- ❑ **1988–1991** Elections, coup, and new elections. Ronald Venetiaan elected president.
- ❑ **1992** Bouterse quits as army head.
- ❑ **1996** Pro-Bouterse NDP wins polls.
- ❑ **2000** NF defeats NDP. Venetiaan again elected president.

HEALTH

Welfare state health benefits

1 per 3333 people | Heart attacks, cancers, malaria, malnutrition, tuberculosis

Urban medical facilities in Suriname are relatively good; Paramaribo has several hospitals. However, provision in the interior is basic.

SPENDING

GDP/cap. increase

CONSUMPTION AND SPENDING

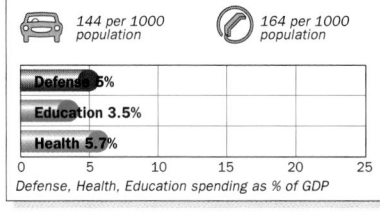

144 per 1000 population | *164 per 1000 population*

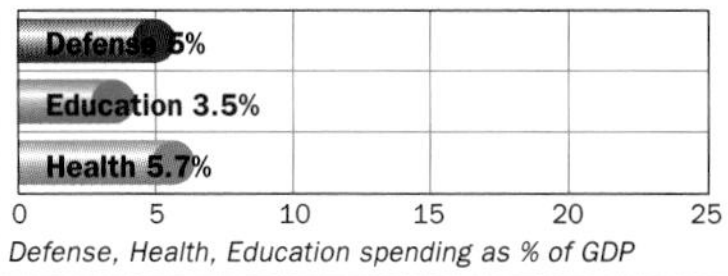
Defense 5%
Education 3.5%
Health 5.7%
0
5
10
15
20
25
Defense, Health, Education spending as % of GDP

Living standards have fallen since 1982, due to the effects of civil war and to aid and loan suspension. Urban Creoles dominate the rich elite. Amerindians and *Bosnegers* are the poorest groups.

WORLD RANKING

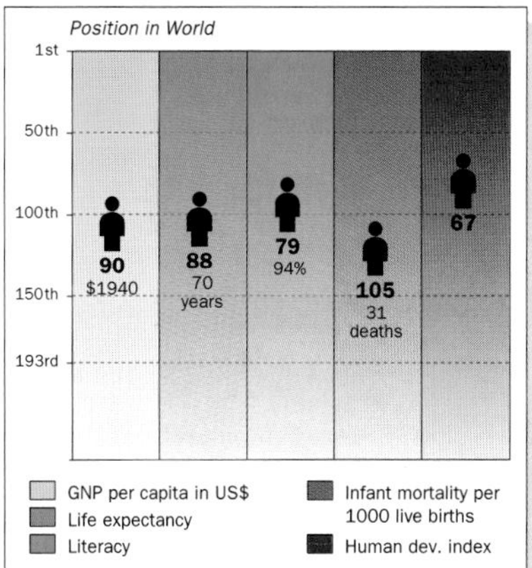
Position in World
1st
50th
100th
150th
193rd
90
$1940
88
70 years
79
94%
105
31 deaths
67
GNP per capita in US$
Life expectancy
Literacy
Infant mortality per 1000 live births
Human dev. index

S

SWAZILAND

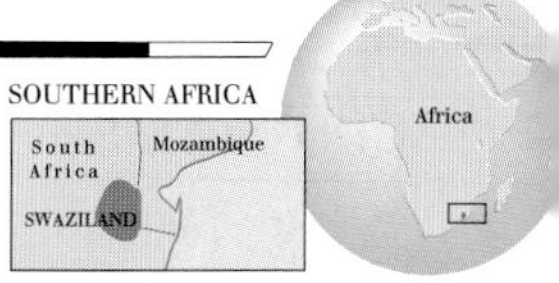
SOUTHERN AFRICA
South Africa
Mozambique
SWAZILAND
Africa

OFFICIAL NAME: Kingdom of Swaziland **CAPITAL:** Mbabane
POPULATION: 1.1 million **CURRENCY:** Lilangeni **OFFICIAL LANGUAGES:** English and siSwati

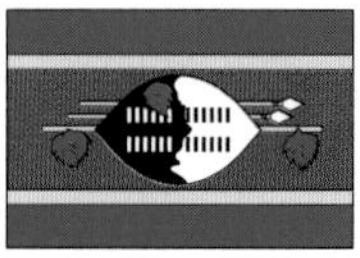

1968 | 1968 | Sept 6 | SD | +2 | +268 | .sz

THE LANDLOCKED southern African kingdom of Swaziland, bordered on three sides by South Africa and to the east by Mozambique, comprises mainly upland plateaus and mountains. Governed by a strong hereditary monarchy, Swaziland is a country in which tradition is being challenged by demands for modern multiparty government. King Mswati III, crowned in 1986, has overhauled the electoral process but is unwilling to legalize party politics.

CLIMATE

Subtropical

WEATHER CHART FOR MBABANE

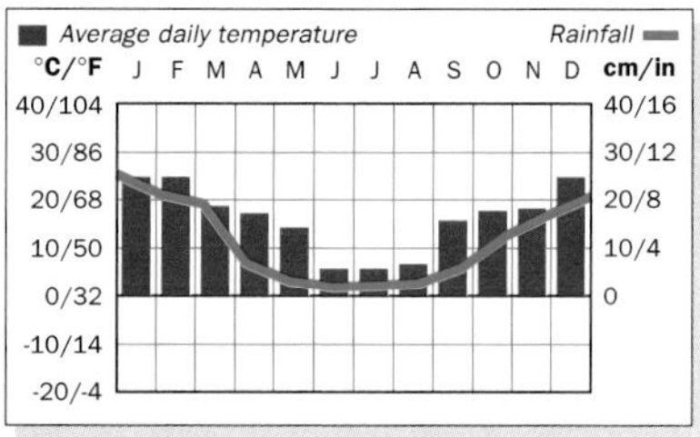
Average daily temperature
Rainfall
°C/°F J F M A M J J A S O N D cm/in
40/104 30/86 20/68 10/50 0/32 -10/14 -20/-4
40/16 30/12 20/8 10/4 0

Swaziland is temperate. Temperatures rise and rainfall declines as the land descends eastward, from high to low *veld*. The low *veld* is prone to drought.

TRANSPORTATION

Drive on left

Matsapha, Manzini
93,000 passengers

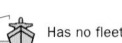

Has no fleet

THE TRANSPORTATION NETWORK

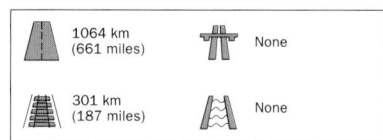

1064 km (661 miles)	None
301 km (187 miles)	None

The road system is largely well maintained, except out in the bush. The railroad, running to Mozambique and South Africa, mainly carries freight.

TOURISM

Visitors : Population 1:4.3

256,000 visitors

Down 9% in 2001–2002

MAIN TOURIST ARRIVALS

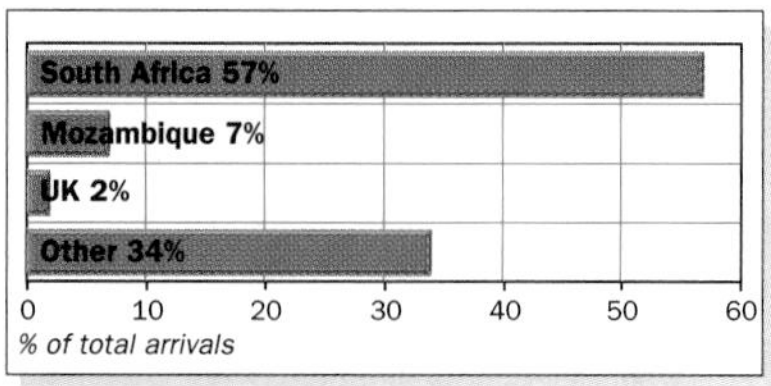
South Africa 57%
Mozambique 7%
UK 2%
Other 34%
0 10 20 30 40 50 60
% of total arrivals

Swaziland's attractions are its game reserves, mountain scenery, and, particularly for the numerous South African tourists, its casinos.

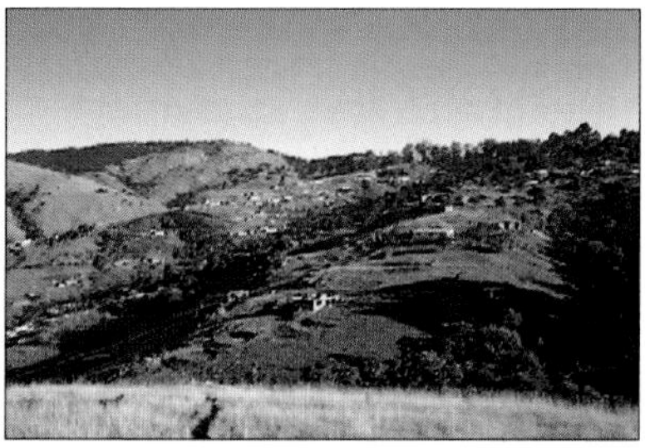

***The outskirts of Mbabane.** It lies on the high veld, where traditional cattle farming has become more difficult owing to overgrazing.*

PEOPLE

Pop. density medium

English, siSwati, isiZulu, Xitsonga

64/km² (166/mi²)

THE URBAN/RURAL POPULATION SPLIT

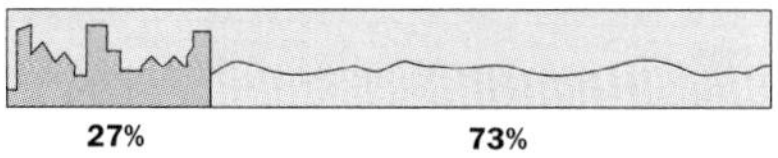
27%
73%

RELIGIOUS PERSUASION

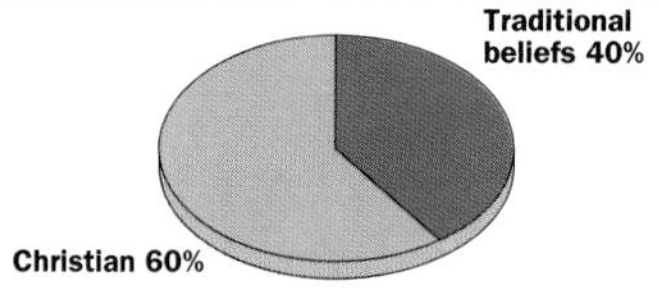
Traditional beliefs 40%
Christian 60%

Over 95% of the population belong to the Swazi ethnic group, making Swaziland one of Africa's most homogeneous states. It is also very conservative, but is now facing pressure from urban-based modernizers. The powerful monarchy dominates politics. Ancient traditions, such as *incwala*, the rainy season's annual movable feast, remain popular. Society is patriarchal and focused around the clan. Chiefs own much "national land," and wield authority through local consultations, or *tindkhundla*. Polygamy is tolerated. Women are openly discriminated against, even though the Queen Mother, the "Great She Elephant," ruled as regent during the mid-1980s. In an effort to combat the spread of AIDS, the king encourages chastity.

POLITICS

Nonparty elections

L. House 2003/2008
U. House 2003/2008

H.M. King Mswati III

AT THE LAST ELECTION

House of Assembly 65 seats

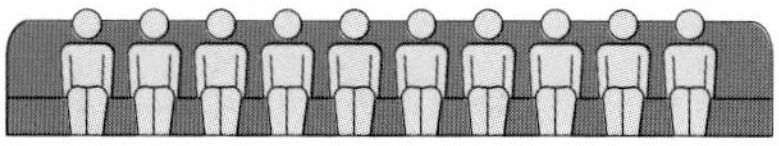

There are no political parties. Ten members of the House of Assembly are appointed by the king

Senate 30 seats

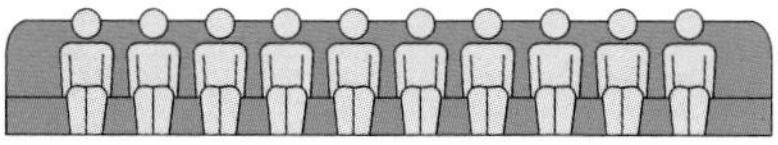

Twenty members of the Senate are appointed by the king and ten elected by the House of Assembly

King Mswati III, one of the world's last absolute monarchs, dominates politics. Political parties are banned, but opposition, led by the trade union movement, is vocal. Particular points of contention are the suppression of parties, nepotism favoring the ruling Dlamini clan, and even the king's personal life. After mounting pressure from 2000, a new constitution was issued in 2003 guaranteeing human rights but maintaining the ban on parties.

SWAZILAND

Total Area : 17 363 sq. km (6704 sq. miles)

POPULATION
over 50 000
over 10 000
under 10 000
LAND HEIGHT
1000m/3281ft
500m/1640ft
200m/656ft
Sea Level
N
0 25 km
0 25 miles
Emlembe 1862m
Bulembu
Rocklands
Kuthuleni
Piggs Peak
Komati
Bordergate
Lomahasha
Tshaneni
Mhlume
Madlangampisi
Mbuluzi
Mnjoli Dam
Simunye
Mhlumeni
Motjane
MBABANE
Ezulwini
Mhlambanyatsi
Nkanini
Lonhlupheko
Ngogolo
Siteki
Nkundla
Bhunya
Manzini
Matsapha
Lusutfu
Sidvokodvo
Siphofaneni
Mankayane
Ngwempisi
Mkhondvo
Mayaluka
Big Bend
Sicunusa
Sitobela
Gege
Salem
Hlathikulu
Maloma
Nsoko
Mbulungwane
Lukhalweni
Mahamba
Nhlangano
Ngwavuma
Mhlosheni
Salitje
Lavumisa
Jozini Dam
INKANGALA
LEBOMBO MOUNTAINS
MOZAMBIQUE
SOUTH AFRICA
31°
32°
27°

S

WORLD AFFAIRS

Joined UN in 1968

ACP | Comm | NAM | AU | SADC

Swaziland's membership of the SACU reinforces its traditional dependence on its giant neighbor, South Africa. Having welcomed the election of an ANC-led government there, King Mswati has objected to its support for Swazi prodemocracy campaigners. Peace in Mozambique has meant the return there of 134,000 refugees.

AID

Recipient

$25m (receipts) | Down 14% in 2002

Aid helps the balance of payments, and has funded the development of roads, the Matsapha industrial estate, and social projects. Aid has recently focused on mitigating the effects of HIV/ AIDS, including food insecurity and a growing number of orphans. Donors include the EU, Japan, the UK, and the AfDB.

DEFENSE

No compulsory military service

$23m | Up 15% in 2000

The Swaziland Defense Force numbers just 3000 troops. Though it does not play an overt political role, its loyalty is to the monarch and the status quo.

ECONOMICS

Inflation 12% p.a. (1990–2001)

$1.35bn | 6.21 emalangeni (7.51)

SCORE CARD

❑ World GNP Ranking	148th
❑ GNP per Capita	$1240
❑ Balance of Payments	–$46m
❑ Inflation	12%
❑ Unemployment	34%

Strengths

Economy quite diversified and buoyant. Manufacturing. Investment rules attractive. Sugar. Wood pulp. Debt service low. Renewed regional stability has reduced risk to exports.

Weaknesses

Severe drought. Sugar vulnerable to price fluctuations. Dependence on South Africa for jobs, revenue, investment, electricity, and imported goods. Small plots of land and lack of land title hinder farm modernization. High population growth: increase in dependent children. AIDS: loss of workforce, cost of medical care.

EXPORTS

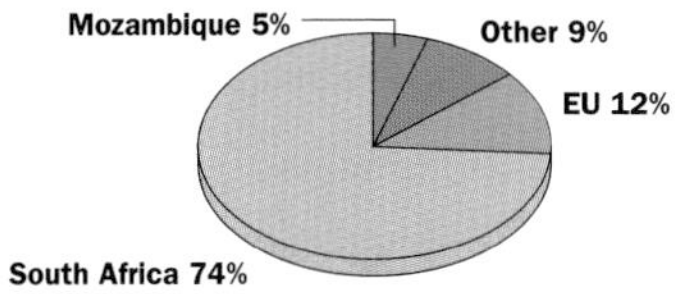

Mozambique 5%
Other 9%
EU 12%
South Africa 74%

IMPORTS

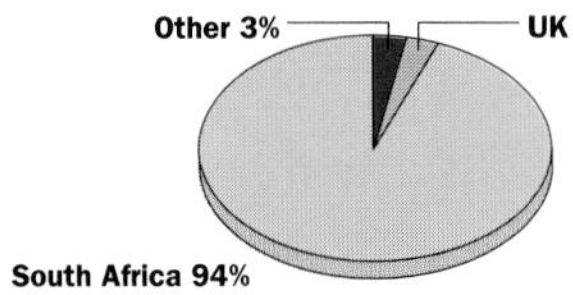

Other 3%
UK 3%
South Africa 94%

RESOURCES

Electric power: Included in South African total

142 tonnes | Not an oil producer

580,000 cattle, 422,000 goats, 3.2m chickens | Coal, diamonds, gold, asbestos, cassiterite, iron, tin

Swaziland's main exports are sugarcane, wood pulp, and coal. Asbestos mining ceased in 2000. The development of hydroelectric power plants has cut energy imports from South Africa.

ENVIRONMENT

Not available

4% partially protected | 0.4 tonnes per capita

Swaziland's natural resources are well managed, and after a 70-year absence rhinos have been reintroduced. Factories have been closed for polluting rivers.

MEDIA

TV ownership low

Daily newspaper circulation 26 per 1000 people

PUBLISHING AND BROADCAST MEDIA

The Times and the state-owned *Swazi Observer* are dailies

1 state-owned service | 2 services: 1 state-owned, 1 independent

Laws on press freedoms have come under pressure, notably over the state-owned *Swazi Observer*, which was banned for a period in 2001.

CRIME

Death penalty in use

3400 prisoners | Up 28% in 2000

The crime rate is generally low. Serial killer David Mhlanga was charged in 2001 with 34 murders.

EDUCATION

School leaving age: 12

81% | 4198 students

Primary enrollment is almost 100% despite fees paid for all except orphans and "vulnerable children." Drop-out rates at secondary level are high.

CHRONOLOGY

Swaziland became a British protectorate in 1903.

- ❑ **1968** Independence.
- ❑ **1973** King bans political activity, repeals constitution.
- ❑ **1978** New constitution confirms king's executive, legislative control.
- ❑ **1982** King Sobhuza dies. Queen Mother becomes regent for Prince Makhosetive. Power struggle between modernists and traditionalists in royal Dlamini clan.
- ❑ **1986** Makhosetive crowned King Mswati III at the age of 18.
- ❑ **1992** Limited electoral reforms; parties still banned.
- ❑ **1993** Elections under new system.
- ❑ **2000** Mass prodemocracy protests.
- ❑ **2003** New constitution offers human rights but parties still banned.

HEALTH

No welfare state health benefits

1 per 5000 people | AIDS, diarrheal and respiratory diseases

Health facilities are rudimentary. Nearly 40% of adults are HIV-positive, the highest infection rate in the world.

SPENDING

GDP/cap. increase

CONSUMPTION AND SPENDING

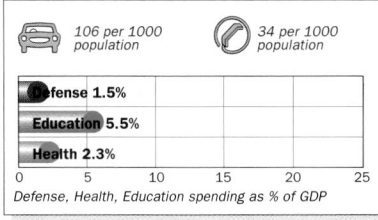

106 per 1000 population | *34 per 1000 population*

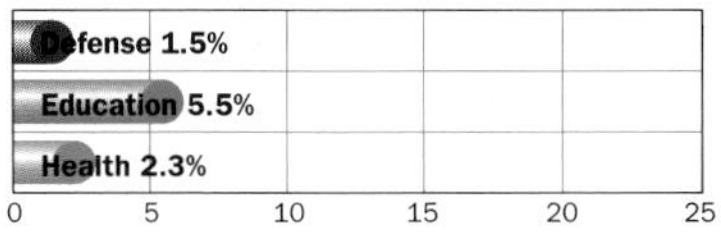

Defense 1.5%
Education 5.5%
Health 2.3%
0
5
10
15
20
25

Defense, Health, Education spending as % of GDP

About two-thirds of Swazis live below the poverty line. The royal Dlamini clan enjoys Western luxuries and travel.

WORLD RANKING

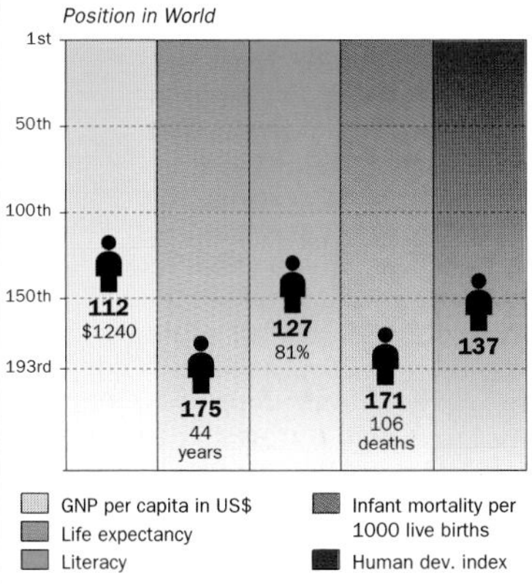

Position in World
1st
50th
100th
150th
193rd
112
$1240
175
44 years
127
81%
171
106 deaths
137
GNP per capita in US$
Life expectancy
Literacy
Infant mortality per 1000 live births
Human dev. index

S

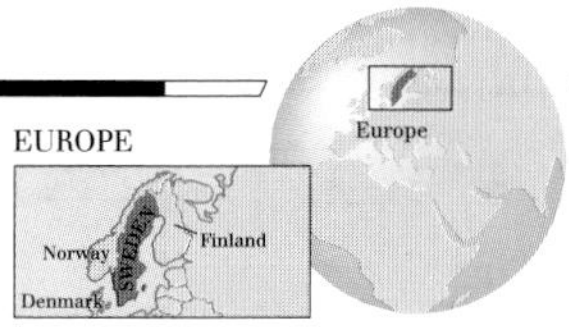
EUROPE
Europe
Norway
Finland
Denmark
SWEDEN

SWEDEN

OFFICIAL NAME: Kingdom of Sweden **CAPITAL:** Stockholm
POPULATION: 8.9 million **CURRENCY:** Swedish krona **OFFICIAL LANGUAGE:** Swedish

1523
1921
June 6
S
+1
+46
.se

SITUATED ON THE SCANDINAVIAN peninsula with Norway to its west, Sweden is a densely forested country with numerous lakes. The north of Sweden falls within the Arctic Circle; much of the south is fertile and widely cultivated. Sweden has one of the most extensive welfare systems in the world, and is among the world's leading proponents of equal rights for women. It is home to global companies including high-tech firm Ericsson and notable car manufacturers Volvo and Saab. Unlike neighboring Norway, it is an EU member, having joined in 1995.

CLIMATE

Subarctic/continental

WEATHER CHART FOR STOCKHOLM

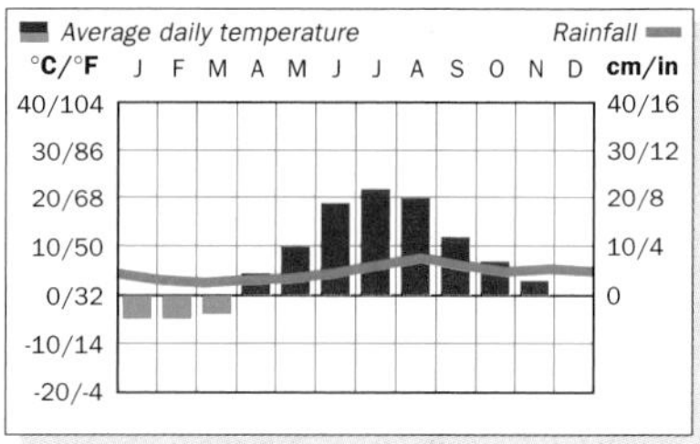
Average daily temperature
Rainfall
°C/°F
J F M A M J J A S O N D
cm/in
40/104
30/86
20/68
10/50
0/32
-10/14
-20/-4
40/16
30/12
20/8
10/4
0

Sweden has a largely continental climate. The Baltic Sea often freezes in winter, making the east coast much colder than western regions. Summers are mild everywhere, with temperatures varying surprisingly little between northern and southern regions.

TRANSPORTATION

Drive on right

Arlanda, Stockholm
15.2m passengers

571 ships
3.18m grt

THE TRANSPORTATION NETWORK

168,239 km (104,539 miles)

1507 km (936 miles)

9857 km (6125 miles)

2052 km (1275 miles)

Transportation links are of prime concern in what is Europe's fifth-largest country. Swedish governments have traditionally spent large sums on maintaining and improving infrastructure, as a way of boosting the economy as a whole.

A high-speed rail link between Arlanda airport and Stockholm opened in 1999. The 16-km (10-mile) Øresund road and rail link by bridge and tunnel connecting Malmö with Copenhagen opened in 2000, providing Sweden with better communications with Denmark and the rest of Europe. By law, cars must travel with their headlights on at all times, and there are very strict laws against drink-driving.

TOURISM

Visitors : Population 1:1.2

7.38m visitors

Down 1% in 2003

MAIN TOURIST ARRIVALS

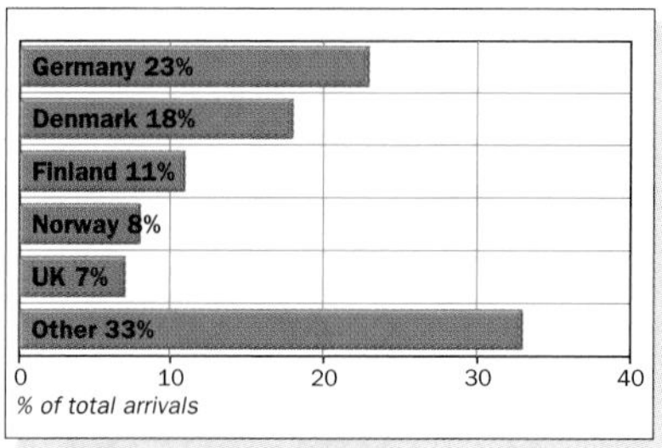
Germany 23%
Denmark 18%
Finland 11%
Norway 8%
UK 7%
Other 33%
0
10
20
30
40
% of total arrivals

Sweden expanded rapidly as a tourist destination in the 1970s and 1980s. Stockholm is renowned for the beauty of its setting, its Old Town, and the *Vasa*, a magnificent 17th-century warship raised from the harbor bed in the 1960s.

Sweden has fewer lakes than Finland, and lacks Norway's dramatic scenery, but it has many natural attractions. The mountains of the midnight sun lie north of the Arctic Circle, while the southern coast has many white sandy beaches. The vast tracts of deserted landscape and the simple country communal living also attract visitors, but the cost of travel to Sweden and living expenses mean that affluent north Europeans top the list of visitors.

***A crofter's holding in Dalarna,** central Sweden, an area which is still mainly forested. The timber and paper industries play a major role in Sweden's economy.*

PEOPLE

Pop. density low

Swedish, Finnish, Sámi

22/km² (56/mi²)

THE URBAN/RURAL POPULATION SPLIT

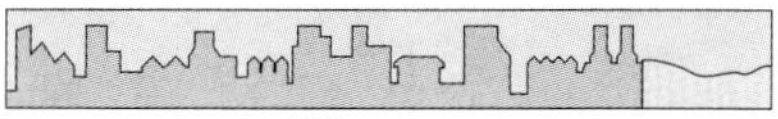
83%
17%

RELIGIOUS PERSUASION

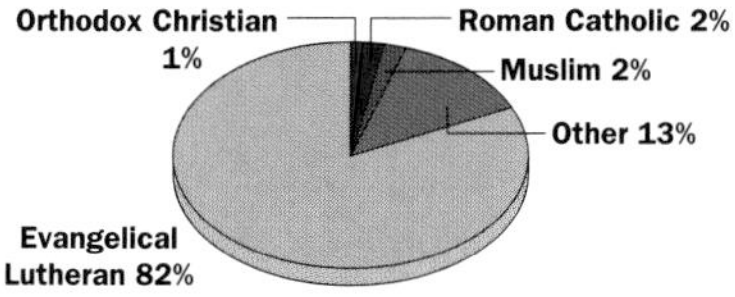
Orthodox Christian 1%
Roman Catholic 2%
Muslim 2%
Other 13%
Evangelical Lutheran 82%

ETHNIC MAKEUP

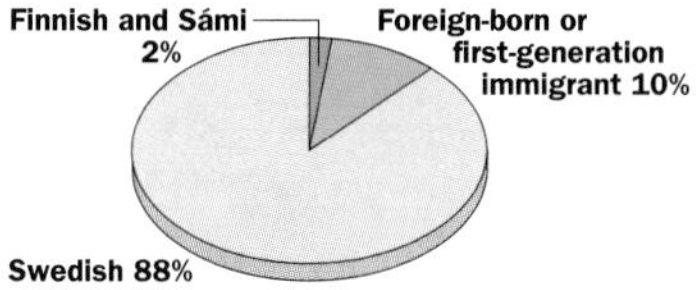
Finnish and Sámi 2%
Foreign-born or first-generation immigrant 10%
Swedish 88%

The nuclear family forms the basis of society. The birthrate is low with, on average, fewer than two children per family. Cohabitation is common, and the marriage rate is declining.

Swedish society has an egalitarian tradition. The role of the state is seen as providing conditions allowing each person to gain economic independence through employment. The welfare system is one of the most extensive in the world. However, in the early 1990s, recession reduced benefits; mothers in particular face problems with the closure of child-care facilities. Women make up nearly half the workforce. Over 45% of MPs are women, the highest percentage in the world. In 1999 the Swedish cabinet became the first in the world to have a majority of women ministers.

A 15,000-strong minority of Sámi live in the north, their traditional way of life protected. Sweden's generous asylum laws cause popular concern, but parliament rejected moves to prevent immigration from the expanded EU.

The Evangelical Lutheran Church was disestablished in 2000.

POPULATION AGE BREAKDOWN

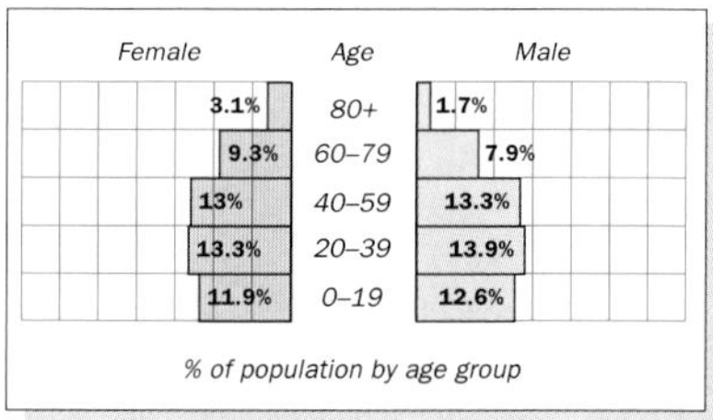
Female
Age
Male
3.1%
80+
1.7%
9.3%
60–79
7.9%
13%
40–59
13.3%
13.3%
20–39
13.9%
11.9%
0–19
12.6%
% of population by age group

S

POLITICS

Multiparty elections

2002/2006

H.M. King Carl XVI Gustaf

AT THE LAST ELECTION

Parliament (Riksdag) 349 seats

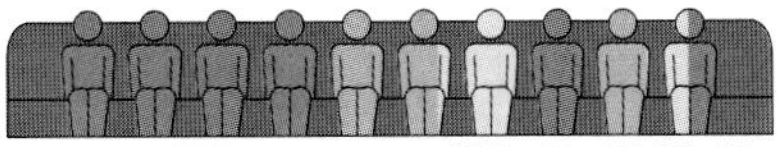

41% SAP	16% M	14% FP	9% Kd	9% VP	6% CP	5% MpG

SAP = Social Democratic Labor Party **M** = Moderate Party
FP = Liberal Party **Kd** = Christian Democratic Party
VP = Left Party **CP** = Center Party **MpG** = Green Party

Sweden is a constitutional monarchy with an elected parliament under the leadership of the prime minister.

PROFILE

Politics has traditionally been split between the SAP and trade unions on the left, and a host of moderate center and right-wing parties. Since the 1930s, the SAP has governed every term, except in 1976–1982 and 1991–1994. A shift to the right in 1991 was reversed in the 1994 elections. Ingvar Carlsson, SAP leader, formed a minority government but resigned in 1996 and was replaced by Göran Persson. The SAP lost ground in elections in 1998, increasing its dependence on Left Party and Green support. A further shift in the 2002 elections left the Greens holding the balance of power.

MAIN POLITICAL ISSUES

EU membership

Sweden joined the EU in 1995. Like the UK and Denmark it opted out of introducing the euro, the idea again being rejected in a referendum in September 2003. It supports expansion of the EU.

The high cost of the welfare state

The cost of the welfare system contributed to enormous budget deficits in the late 1980s and early 1990s. While this has been brought under control, and unemployment has been reduced, the growing number of pensioners means that social security pressures remain.

Carl XVI Gustaf, ascended the throne in 1973. His role is purely ceremonial.

Göran Persson of the SAP became prime minister in 1996.

SWEDEN

Total Area : 449 964 sq. km (173 731 sq. miles)

POPULATION

- over 1 000 000
- over 100 000
- over 50 000
- over 10 000

LAND HEIGHT

- 1000m/3281ft
- 500m/1640ft
- 200m/656ft
- Sea Level

N

0 100 km
0 100 miles

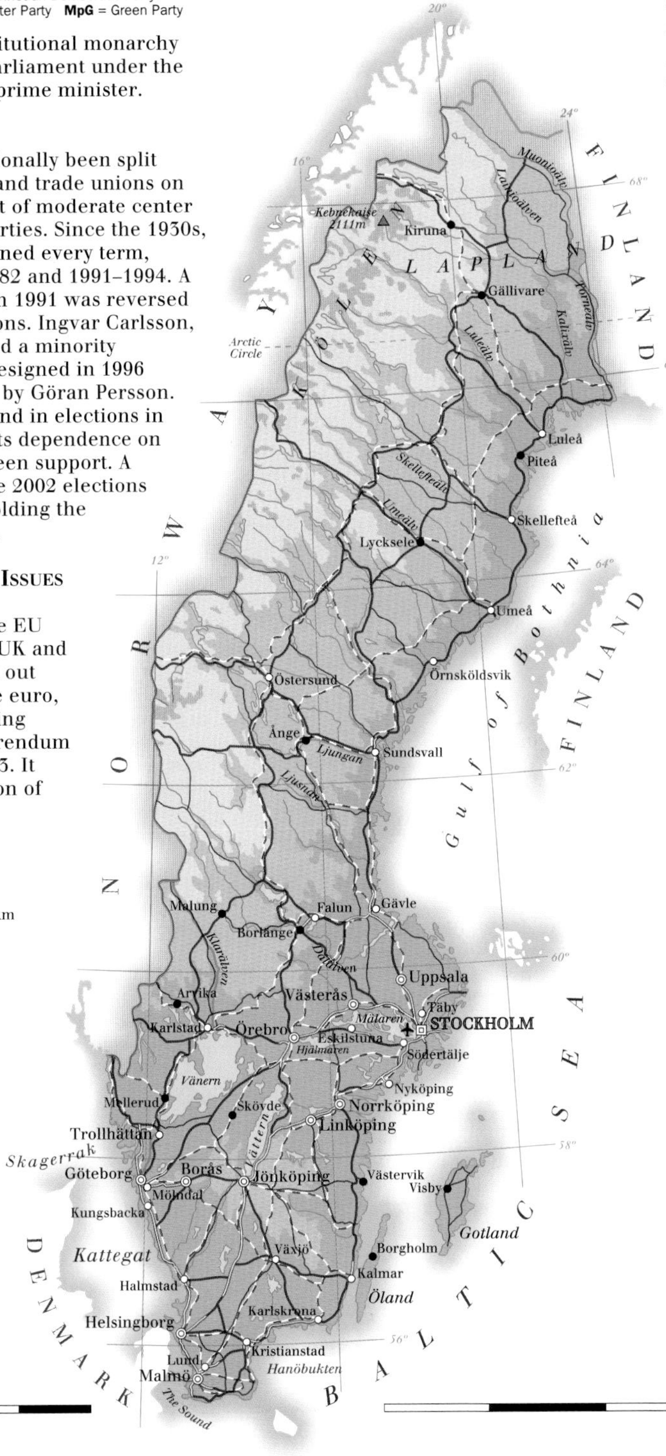

NORWAY
FINLAND
LAPLAND
Gulf of Bothnia
BALTIC SEA
DENMARK
Skagerrak
Kattegat
The Sound
Arctic Circle
Kebnekaise 2111m
Kiruna
Gällivare
Luleå
Piteå
Skellefteå
Lycksele
Umeå
Örnsköldsvik
Östersund
Ånge
Sundsvall
Malung
Falun
Gävle
Borlänge
Uppsala
Arvika
Västerås
Täby
STOCKHOLM
Karlstad
Örebro
Eskilstuna
Mälaren
Hjälmaren
Södertälje
Vänern
Nyköping
Mellerud
Skövde
Norrköping
Trollhättan
Linköping
Vättern
Göteborg
Borås
Mölndal
Jönköping
Västervik
Visby
Gotland
Kungsbacka
Växjö
Borgholm
Kalmar
Öland
Halmstad
Karlskrona
Helsingborg
Kristianstad
Hanöbukten
Lund
Malmö
Muonioälven
Lainioälven
Torneälv
Kalixälv
Luleälv
Skellefteälv
Umeälv
Ljungan
Ljusnan
Klarälven
Dalälven

WORLD AFFAIRS

Joined UN in 1946

EU | CE | NC | OECD | OSCE

Sweden's main recent foreign policy concern has been its adjustment to membership of the EU, which it joined in 1995. In 1998 it voted to join the Schengen passport-free zone, but has not adopted the euro. In the 1980s, Sweden was a vociferous critic of the antagonistic policy pursued by the US toward the USSR. Since the collapse of the Soviet Union, and more recently the September 11, 2001, attack on the US, it has altered its traditionally neutral stance. Sweden has WEU observer status, and participates in NATO exercises and several UN peacekeeping operations.

AID

Donor

$1.99bn (donations)

Up 20% in 2002

Sweden is one of the few countries to exceed the UN target of 0.7% of GNP in development aid, donating 0.83% in 2002 to a variety of recipients.

CHRONOLOGY

Sweden's history has been closely linked to the control of the Baltic Sea and its highly profitable trade routes. Under the house of Vasa, Sweden became a major power, controlling much of the Baltic region. By the 18th century, however, Sweden's position had been eroded by its regional rivals, particularly Russia.

- **1814–1815** Congress of Vienna. Sweden cedes territory to Russia and Denmark. Prolonged period of peace begins.
- **1865–1866** Riksdag (parliament) reformed into a bicameral structure.
- **1905** Norway gains independence from Sweden.
- **1911** First Liberal government comes to power.
- **1914** Government resigns over defense policy.

S

CHRONOLOGY *continued*

- ❑ **1914–1917** Neutral during World War I, but supplies Germany. Allied blockade.
- ❑ **1917** Food shortages. Conservative government falls. Nils Edén forms a Liberal government: limits exports contributing to German war effort.
- ❑ **1919** Universal adult suffrage.
- ❑ **1921** Finland gains Åland Islands as retribution for Sweden's war role.
- ❑ **1932** Severe recession. Social Democrat government under Per Albin Hansson elected.
- ❑ **1939–1945** Sweden neutral. Grants transit rights to German forces.
- ❑ **1945–1976** Continuing Social Democratic rule under Tage Erlander establishes Sweden as world's most advanced welfare state, and one of the most affluent.
- ❑ **1950** Gustav VI Adolf becomes king.
- ❑ **1953** Joins Nordic Council.
- ❑ **1959** Founder member of EFTA.
- ❑ **1969** Erlander succeeded by Olof Palme as prime minister.
- ❑ **1973** Carl XVI Gustaf on throne.
- ❑ **1975** Major constitutional reform. Riksdag (parliament) becomes unicameral. Role of monarchy greatly reduced.
- ❑ **1976** Nonsocialist coalition led by Thorbjörn Fälldin replaces SAP government.
- ❑ **1978** Fälldin resigns over issue of nuclear power. Ola Ullsten prime minister.
- ❑ **1979** Fälldin prime minister again.
- ❑ **1982** Elections. SAP forms minority government. Palme returns as prime minister.
- ❑ **1986** Palme shot dead. His deputy, Ingvar Carlsson, succeeds him. Police fail to find killer.
- ❑ **1990** Carlsson introduces moderate austerity package, cuts government spending, raises indirect taxes.
- ❑ **1991** Sweden applies to join EU. SAP wins election but is unable to form government; Carlsson resigns. Moderate Party leader Carl Bildt forms coalition of nonsocialist parties amid serious recession.
- ❑ **1992** Austerity measures succeed in reducing inflation but SAP refuses to support further spending cuts.
- ❑ **1994** EU membership terms agreed. Elections: SAP returns to power.
- ❑ **1995** Joins EU.
- ❑ **1996** Carlsson resigns; replaced by Göran Persson.
- ❑ **1998** Persson remains in office, despite SAP losses in elections; dependent on Left and Greens.
- ❑ **2001** Defense reform program.
- ❑ **2002** Elections: SAP still largest party but lacking majority.
- ❑ **2003** Foreign Minister Anna Lindh stabbed to death. Euro rejected in referendum.

DEFENSE

▷ Compulsory military service

$3.95bn

Up 2% in 2002

SWEDISH ARMED FORCES

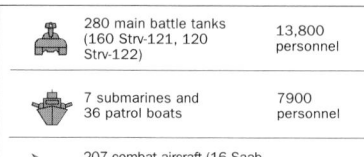

280 main battle tanks (160 Strv-121, 120 Strv-122)	13,800 personnel
7 submarines and 36 patrol boats	7900 personnel
207 combat aircraft (16 Saab AJSH-37/AJSF-37, 135 Saab JAS-39, 47 Saab JA-37)	5900 personnel
None	

Sweden's sophisticated and powerful military force is supplied with weaponry manufactured by its advanced home defense industry, including Saab fighter jets and Bofors antiaircraft guns. However, with the ending of the Cold War, strategic priorities have changed. Sweden feels less bound to maintain its neutral stance: it has participated in NATO's Partnership for Peace program since 1994 and has WEU observer status. In 1999 spending cuts were announced, foreshadowing halving the size of the armed forces, because of the reduced military threat in the Scandinavian and Baltic region. A ten-year reform program began in 2001, offering personnel regular office hours and canceling large-scale exercises.

ECONOMICS

▷ Inflation 2% p.a. (1990–2001)

$232bn

7.533 Swedish kronor (8.005)

SCORE CARD

❑ World GNP Ranking	20th
❑ GNP per Capita	$25,970
❑ Balance of Payments	$10.6bn
❑ Inflation	2.2%
❑ Unemployment	5%

EXPORTS

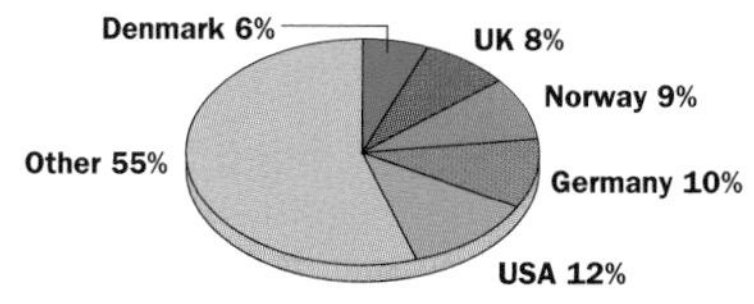
Denmark 6%
UK 8%
Norway 9%
Germany 10%
USA 12%
Other 55%

IMPORTS

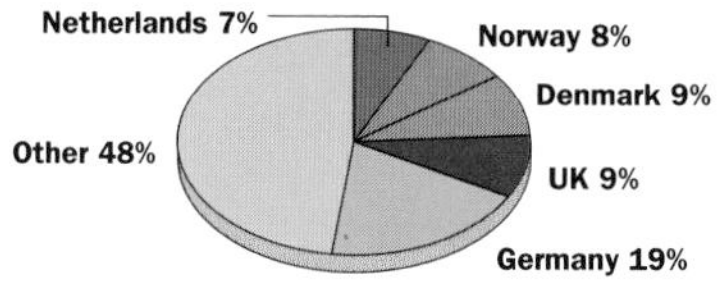
Netherlands 7%
Norway 8%
Denmark 9%
UK 9%
Germany 19%
Other 48%

Strengths

Companies of global importance, including Saab, Volvo, Electrolux, and SKF, the world's biggest roller bearing manufacturer. Highly developed and constantly updated infrastructure. Sophisticated technology. Skilled labor force virtually bilingual in English.

Weaknesses

Labor costs remain uncompetitive. One of the highest rates of taxation in the OECD, accounting for almost 35% of GDP. Peripheral location, raising costs for producers and exporters. Major losses by Ericsson, giant telecoms company.

Profile

The state plays a significant role in the economy, particularly the services sector and infrastructure. Sweden's industrial giants have mostly been private-sector companies. Though the early 1990s saw a shift in economic policy to favor business, greater growth did not follow, and unemployment and welfare costs drove up the budget deficit to one of the OECD's highest in 1994. Growth has now been resumed, unemployment halved, and the deficit cut back, but inflation has started to rise. The world downturn in 2001 brought the krona under pressure. Sweden opted not to adopt the euro from 1999; the ruling SAP took a pro-euro stance in 2000, but a national referendum in 2003 again rejected joining the eurozone.

ECONOMIC PERFORMANCE INDICATOR

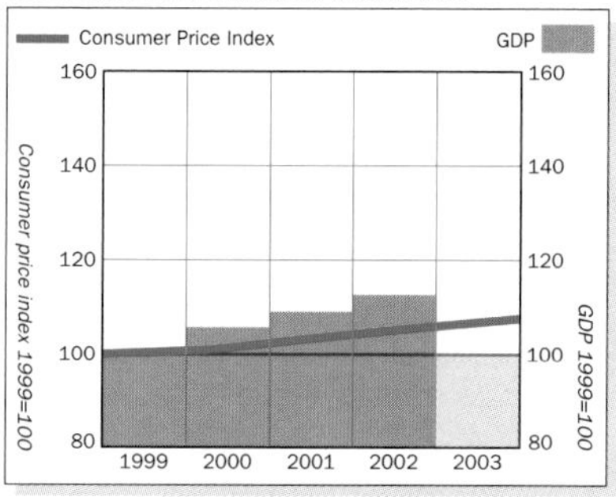
Consumer Price Index
GDP
Consumer price index 1999=100
GDP 1999=100
160
140
120
100
80
1999
2000
2001
2002
2003

SWEDEN : MAJOR BUSINESSES

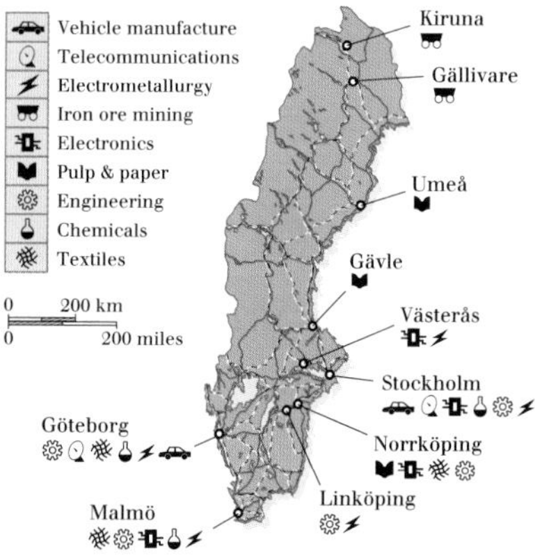
Vehicle manufacture
Telecommunications
Electrometallurgy
Iron ore mining
Electronics
Pulp & paper
Engineering
Chemicals
Textiles
0 200 km
0 200 miles
Kiruna
Gällivare
Umeå
Gävle
Västerås
Stockholm
Norrköping
Linköping
Göteborg
Malmö

S

RESOURCES

Electric power 32.8m kW

318,589 tonnes

Low levels of oil production; refines 432,000 b/d

1.9m pigs, 1.61m cattle, 5.75m chickens

Iron, uranium, copper, lead, zinc, silver

ELECTRICITY GENERATION

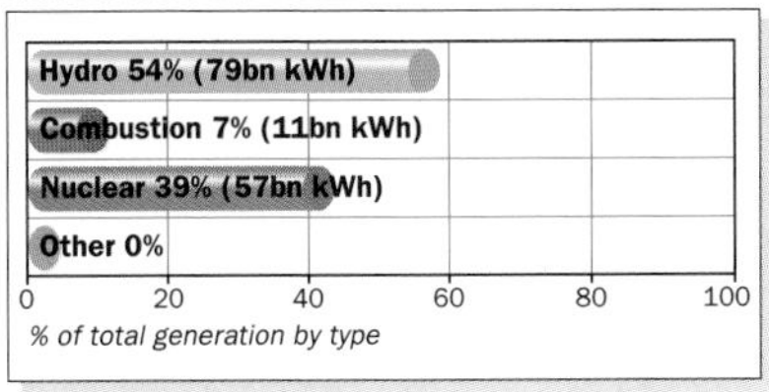
Hydro 54% (79bn kWh)
Combustion 7% (11bn kWh)
Nuclear 39% (57bn kWh)
Other 0%
0
20
40
60
80
100
% of total generation by type

Sweden is rich in minerals including iron, copper, and silver. While mining and quarrying account for only 0.2% of GDP, they underpin other industrial sectors. In a referendum in 1980 Sweden decided, on environmental grounds, to abandon nuclear power by 2010. However, problems in securing sufficient new energy supplies and in cutting consumption meant that, by mid-2004, only one of the 12 nuclear reactors had been closed down and nuclear power still accounted for nearly half of electricity generation.

SWEDEN : LAND USE

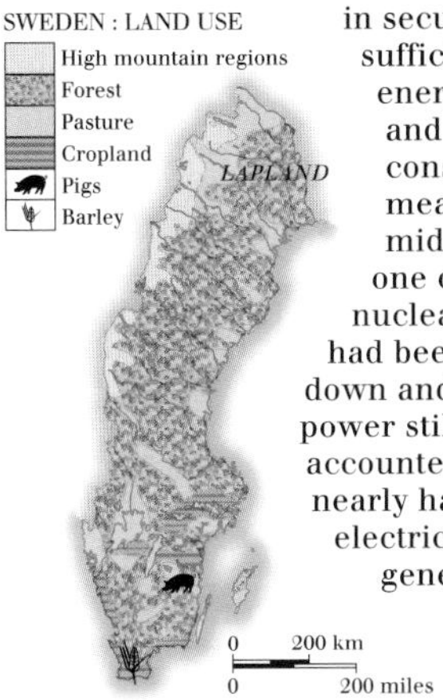
High mountain regions
Forest
Pasture
Cropland
Pigs
Barley
LAPLAND
0
200 km
0
200 miles

ENVIRONMENT

Sustainability rank: 3rd

9% (4% partially protected)

5.3 tonnes per capita

ENVIRONMENTAL TREATIES

Yes · Yes · Yes

Yes · Yes · Yes

Since Sweden's pioneering Environment Protection Act in 1969, it has invested heavily in environmental protection measures. It blames acid rain damage to forests and lakes on airborne sulfur dioxide from factories in western Europe. Swedish nuclear reactors are said to be very safe, with filtered venting systems designed to retain 90% of all radioactivity released if there were a core meltdown. Nonetheless, all reactors are due to be phased out.

MEDIA

TV ownership high

Daily newspaper circulation 410 per 1000 people

PUBLISHING AND BROADCAST MEDIA

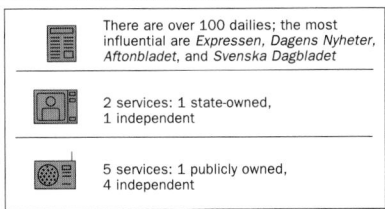

There are over 100 dailies; the most influential are *Expressen, Dagens Nyheter, Aftonbladet*, and *Svenska Dagbladet*

2 services: 1 state-owned, 1 independent

5 services: 1 publicly owned, 4 independent

Press freedom is entrenched, though radical views are rarely expressed. The influence of the major daily newspapers is largely confined to Stockholm: the provinces have their own strong press. Six companies control most of Sweden's magazines. Two-thirds of the population have cable or satellite TV.

CRIME

No death penalty

6506 prisoners

Down 2% in 2001

CRIME RATES

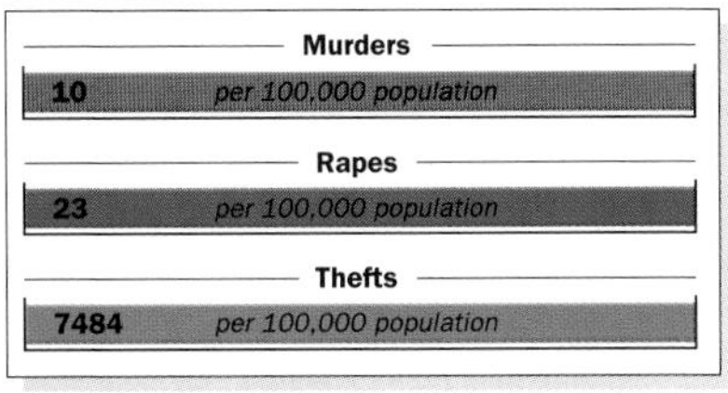
Murders
10 per 100,000 population
Rapes
23 per 100,000 population
Thefts
7484 per 100,000 population

Crime rates are much higher than in Norway or Denmark, and the high reporting rate puts them above the European average. Violent crime is increasing, especially in the cities.

EDUCATION

School leaving age: 16

99%

358,020 students

THE EDUCATION SYSTEM

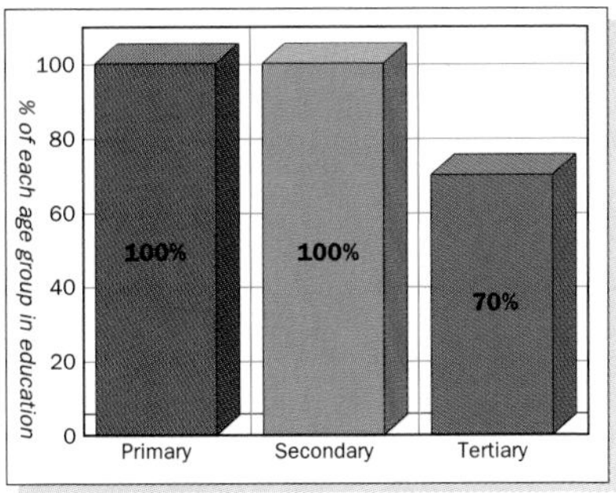
100
80
60
40
20
0
% of each age group in education
100%
100%
70%
Primary
Secondary
Tertiary

Education spending (public and private) is among the OECD's highest as a percentage of GDP.

Coeducational comprehensive schools are the norm. The higher education system is freely available to most of the population, and many adults return to college to do further courses.

HEALTH

Welfare state health benefits

1 per 333 people

Cancers, heart, cerebrovascular, and pulmonary diseases

Sweden's health care system is comprehensive and of a universally high standard. Spending fell by an average of 2% in real terms in the 1990s, but the trend has since reversed. Savings have been made by increasing outpatient care, reducing the number of hospital beds, and cutting jobs. Since 1994 individuals have had the right to choose their own doctor. In 1999 the government agreed to compensate more than 60,000 people subjected to enforced sterilization in 1935–1975. Smoking was banned in public places from 2004.

SPENDING

GDP/cap. increase

CONSUMPTION AND SPENDING

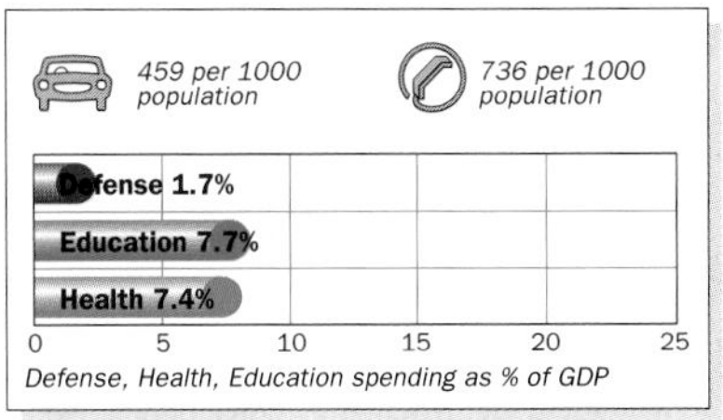
459 per 1000 population
736 per 1000 population
Defense 1.7%
Education 7.7%
Health 7.4%
0
5
10
15
20
25
Defense, Health, Education spending as % of GDP

Sweden has small income differentials, and Swedish executives are paid less than some of their European counterparts. Compared with other European states or the US, social competition and a sense of hierarchy are limited. Despite some cuts in services, the welfare system still rates highly in Europe.

Swedes are keen overseas property buyers, particularly of villas in Italy and France. Net overseas per capita investment remains among the highest in the world and about two-thirds of households own shares. PC ownership is high, and over 50% of Swedes have access to the Internet.

WORLD RANKING

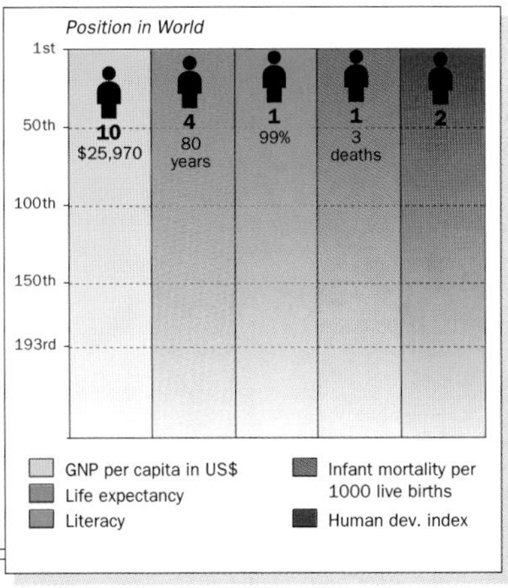
Position in World
1st
50th
100th
150th
193rd
10
$25,970
4
80 years
1
99%
1
3 deaths
2
GNP per capita in US$
Life expectancy
Literacy
Infant mortality per 1000 live births
Human dev. index

S

SWITZERLAND

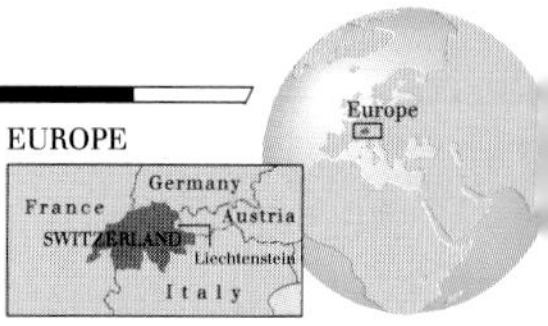
Europe
EUROPE
Germany
France
SWITZERLAND
Austria
Liechtenstein
Italy

OFFICIAL NAME: Swiss Confederation **CAPITAL:** Bern
POPULATION: 7.2 million **CURRENCY:** Swiss franc **OFFICIAL LANGUAGES:** French, German, and Italian

1291 | 1857 | Aug 1 | CH | +1 | +41 | .ch

SWITZERLAND LIES at the center of western Europe geographically, but outside it politically. Sometimes called Europe's water tower, it is the source of all four of the region's major river systems: the Po, the Rhône, the Rhine, and the Inn–Danube. Switzerland has built one of the world's most prosperous economies, aided by the fact that it has retained its neutral status through every major European conflict since 1815. The process of European integration has been the latest and strongest challenge to Swiss neutralism, but it remains outside the EU.

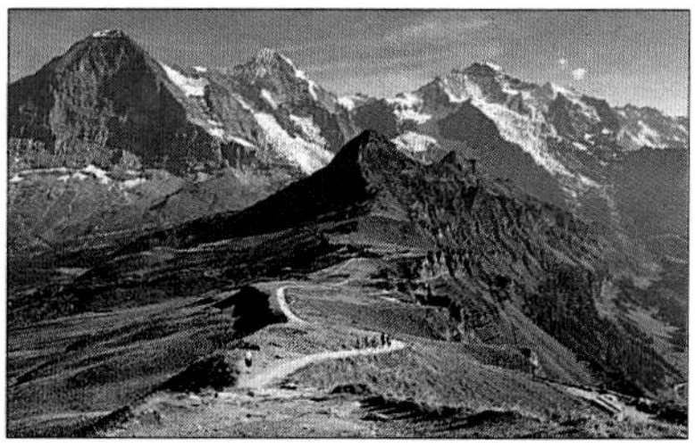

The Eiger in the Berner Oberland. *In 1994, a referendum voted to ban all truck transit traffic from the Swiss Alps from 2004.*

CLIMATE

Mountain/continental

WEATHER CHART FOR BERN

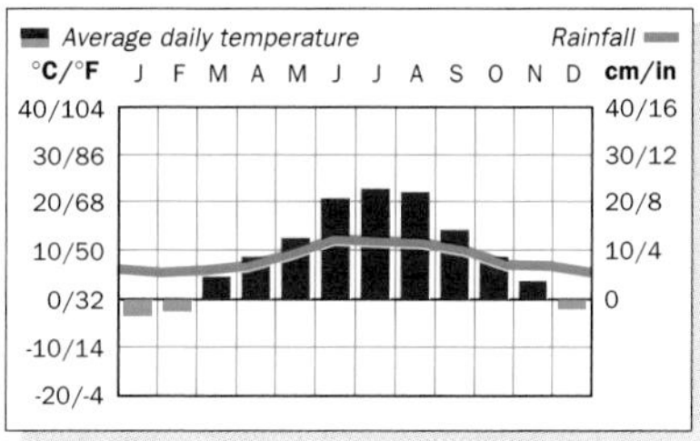
Average daily temperature
Rainfall
°C/°F
J F M A M J J A S O N D
cm/in
40/104
30/86
20/68
10/50
0/32
-10/14
-20/-4
40/16
30/12
20/8
10/4
0

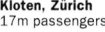

Temperature and weather fluctuate enormously, not only seasonally but because of the huge variations in altitude and the country's location in central Europe. On the plateau north of the Alps, where most of the population lives, summers are warm and winters dry, cool, and often foggy. South of the Alps, it is warmer and sunnier. Strong southerly winds, or *föhn*, can bring summerlike weather even in winter. Avalanches have been a problem in recent years.

TRANSPORTATION

Drive on right

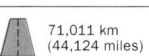

Kloten, Zürich
17m passengers

24 ships
559,100 grt

THE TRANSPORTATION NETWORK

71,011 km (44,124 miles)	1305 km (811 miles)
3222 km (2002 miles)	1214 km (754 miles)

Switzerland is a major freight transit route. Pollution and safety are major concerns: 11 people died in a fire in 2001 in the Gotthard road tunnel. High-speed trains operated by Cisalpino connect Basel, Geneva, and Zürich with Stuttgart, Milan, Florence, and Venice. Swissair, bankrupted in 2001, has been replaced by a new airline, named simply "Swiss."

TOURISM

Visitors : Population 1.4:1

10m visitors

Down 7% in 2002

MAIN TOURIST ARRIVALS

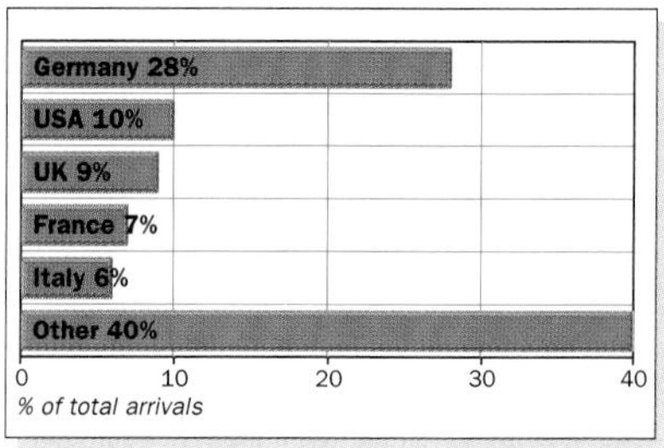
Germany 28%
USA 10%
UK 9%
France 7%
Italy 6%
Other 40%
0
10
20
30
40
% of total arrivals

Tourism is Switzerland's third-largest foreign exchange earner. It accounts for around 3% of GDP, though receipts have fallen in recent years. The Alps are the main attraction, drawing winter and summer tourists from around the world, and Chillon Castle on Lake Geneva continues to be the country's most popular tourist site. In recent years, warmer winters have shortened the skiing season. "Suicide tourism," as a recent development has been termed, has seen terminally ill people taking advantage of less stringent Swiss laws on euthanasia.

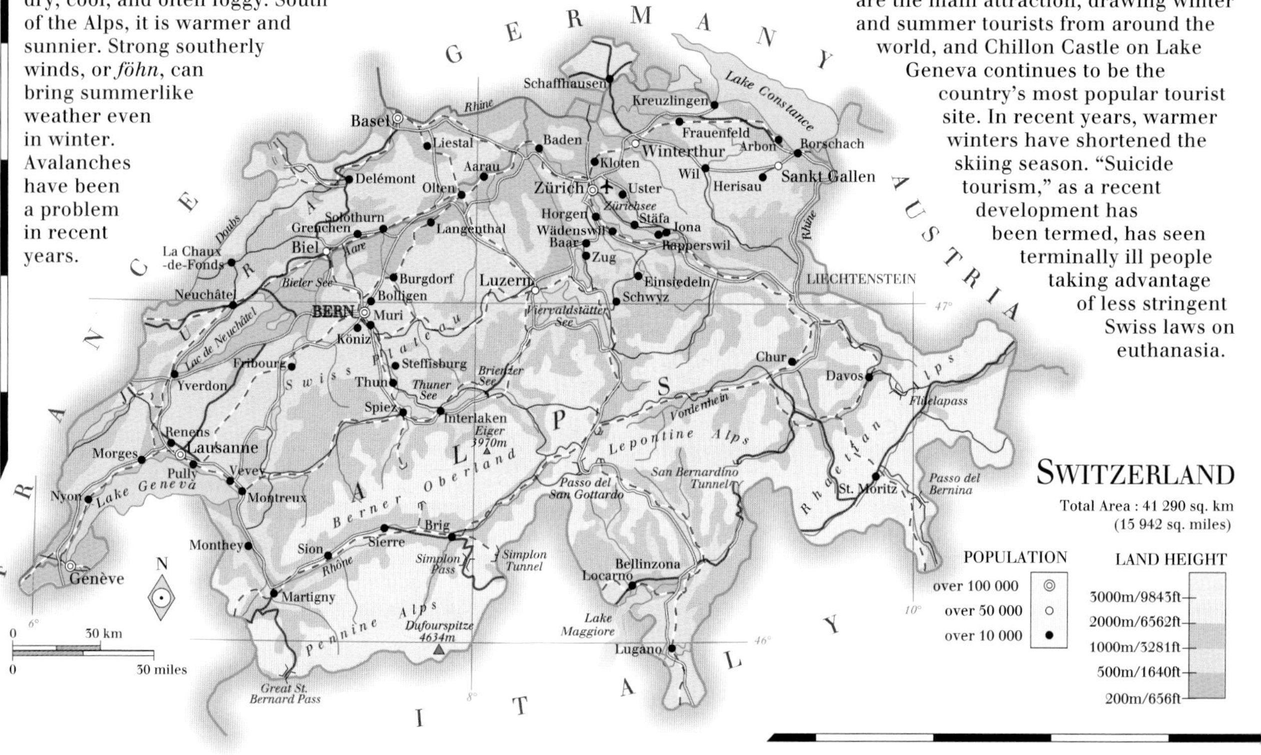
GERMANY
FRANCE
AUSTRIA
ITALY
LIECHTENSTEIN
Basel
Schaffhausen
Kreuzlingen
Lake Constance
Rhine
Frauenfeld
Winterthur
Arbon
Rorschach
Sankt Gallen
Herisau
Wil
Liestal
Baden
Kloten
Aarau
Delémont
Olten
Zürich
Uster
Zürichsee
Horgen
Stäfa
Wädenswil
Jona
Baar
Rapperswil
Zug
Solothurn
Grenchen
Langenthal
Biel
Aare
La Chaux-de-Fonds
Doubs
JURA
Burgdorf
Bieler See
Luzern
Einsiedeln
Bolligen
Schwyz
Neuchâtel
BERN
Muri
Vierwaldstätter See
Köniz
Lac de Neuchâtel
Swiss Plateau
Fribourg
Steffisburg
Chur
Davos
Yverdon
Thun
Thuner See
Brienzer See
Flüelapass
Spiez
Interlaken
Eiger 3970m
Vorderrhein
ALPS
Lepontine Alps
Renens
Lausanne
Morges
Pully
Vevey
Passo del San Gottardo
San Bernardino Tunnel
Rhaetian Alps
St. Moritz
Passo del Bernina
Nyon
Lake Geneva
Montreux
Berner Oberland
Brig
Monthey
Sion
Sierre
Rhône
Simplon Pass
Simplon Tunnel
Bellinzona
Genève
Locarno
Martigny
Pennine Alps
Dufourspitze 4634m
Lake Maggiore
Lugano
Great St. Bernard Pass
47°
46°
6°
8°
10°
0
30 km
30 miles
SWITZERLAND
Total Area : 41 290 sq. km (15 942 sq. miles)
POPULATION
over 100 000
over 50 000
over 10 000
LAND HEIGHT
3000m/9843ft
2000m/6562ft
1000m/3281ft
500m/1640ft
200m/656ft

PEOPLE

Pop. density medium

German, Swiss-German, French, Italian, Romansch

181/km² (469/mi²)

THE URBAN/RURAL POPULATION SPLIT

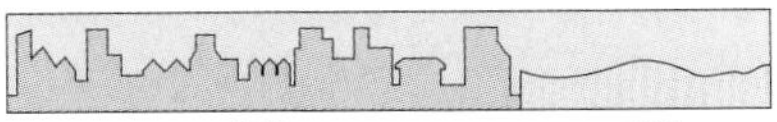
67%
33%

RELIGIOUS PERSUASION

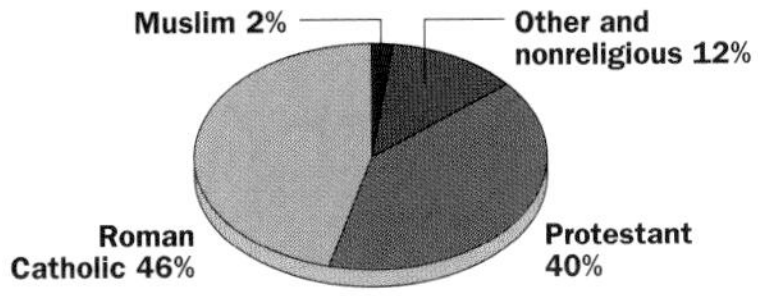
Muslim 2%
Other and nonreligious 12%
Roman Catholic 46%
Protestant 40%

ETHNIC MAKEUP

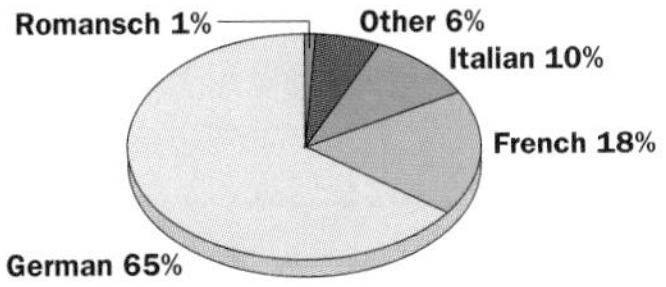
Romansch 1%
Other 6%
Italian 10%
French 18%
German 65%

The Swiss comprise distinct German-Swiss, French-Swiss, and Italian-Swiss linguistic groups. About 40,000 people in the eastern canton of Grisons speak Romansch. The German-Swiss, in the majority, are a tightly knit community, with a dialect that is impenetrable to most outsiders. In recent years, the three groups have grown further apart. The French-Swiss, in favor of joining the EU, are opposed by the German-Swiss. In Italian-speaking Ticino, a political party has emerged to champion Italian-Swiss interests. Despite tensions between Swiss and immigrant workers, referenda proposing strict limits on numbers of foreigners and the restriction of asylum were heavily defeated in 2000 and 2002 respectively.

Society retains strong conservative elements. Two half-cantons granted women the vote at regional level only in 1989 and 1990. The marriage rate is high and the divorce rate lower than the European average.

POPULATION AGE BREAKDOWN

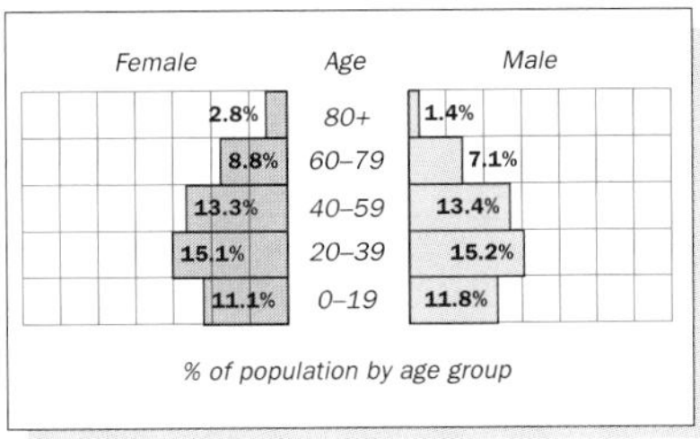
Female
Age
Male
2.8%
80+
1.4%
8.8%
60–79
7.1%
13.3%
40–59
13.4%
15.1%
20–39
15.2%
11.1%
0–19
11.8%
% of population by age group

WORLD AFFAIRS

Joined UN in 2002

CE | G10 | EFTA | OSCE | PfP

The basis of Swiss foreign policy remains its neutrality. Geneva is a center for many international organizations, including the ICRC and the European headquarters of the UN (though Switzerland only voted to join the UN in 2002). The city has often hosted diplomatic negotiations: those for the START nuclear arms reduction treaties and peace talks for the former Yugoslavia took place there.

A member of EFTA, Switzerland has so far not joined the process of closer European integration. In 1992 voters rejected EEA membership, widely seen as a precursor of EU membership. Many advocates of joining the EU believe the economy will suffer without closer integration. Others argue Switzerland's isolation will enhance its role as a tax haven. In 2001 a proposal in favor of EU membership was overwhelmingly rejected. A series of bilateral cooperation agreements with the EU entered into force in 2002; a second set of accords are under negotiation.

Joseph Deiss of the CVP/PDC, who held the one-year presidency in 2004.

Samuel Schmid of the far-right SVP/UDC, vice president in 2004.

POLITICS

Multiparty elections

L. House 2003/2007
U. House 2003/2007

President Joseph Deiss

AT THE LAST ELECTION

National Council 200 seats

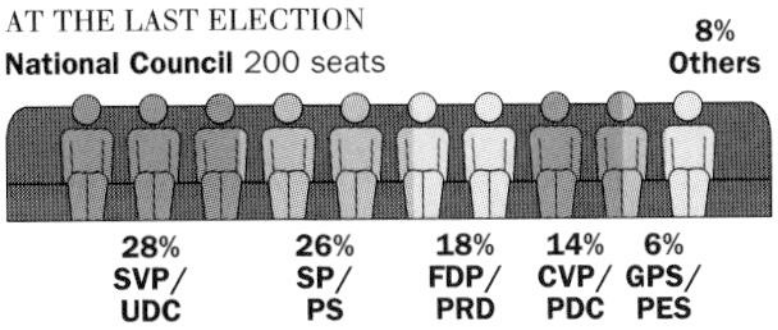
8%
Others
28%
SVP/
UDC
26%
SP/
PS
18%
FDP/
PRD
14%
CVP/
PDC
6%
GPS/
PES

SVP/UDC = Swiss People's Party **SP/PS** = Social Democratic Party **FDP/PRD** = Radical Democratic Party **CVP/PDC** = Christian Democratic People's Party **GPS/PES** = Green Party of Switzerland

Council of States 46 seats

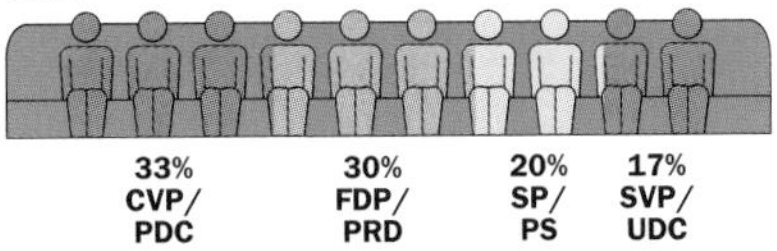
33%
CVP/
PDC
30%
FDP/
PRD
20%
SP/
PS
17%
SVP/
UDC

Switzerland is a federal democratic republic with 26 autonomous cantons. The presidency rotates every year.

PROFILE

The same four-party coalition has been in power in Switzerland since 1959. Domestic and foreign policies have changed little. Politics has recently become more contentious, however, with voting patterns becoming more polarized. Divisive issues are those of narcotics and of membership of the EU. The right-wing SVP/UDC in particular capitalized on growing hostility to immigration to perform strongly in the 1999 and 2003 elections. It was rewarded with an extra seat in the cabinet in December 2003, upsetting the 44-year-old "magic formula."

Switzerland's political system is unique in Europe, in that important decisions depend on the results of referenda. A petition of more than 100,000 signatures can force a referendum on any issue.

MAIN POLITICAL ISSUES

European integration

Almost all politicians and business leaders favor joining the EU, or at least the EEA, but voters remain sharply divided. Decisions taken in Brussels nevertheless affect Swiss economic policy and the government is negotiating further bilateral accords with the EU. Many Swiss fear that their decentralized style of government would be lost within the EU.

Switzerland and World War II

In 2002 the Bergier report criticized Swiss refusal to admit many Jewish refugees during World War II, but found that the banking system was not built on the assets of Holocaust victims. In 1998 the two largest Swiss banks had agreed to pay $1.25 billion to 31,500 victims and their families in return for agreement that there would be no future claims against Swiss banks or the government. A government Fund for Needy Holocaust Victims was wound up in 2002 after paying $179 million to 309,000 survivors.

CHRONOLOGY

The autonomy of the Swiss cantons was curtailed by the Habsburgs in the 11th century. In 1291, the three cantons of Unterwalden, Schwyz, and Uri set up the Perpetual League to pursue Swiss liberty. Joined by other cantons, they succeeded in 1499 in gaining virtual independence. The Habsburgs retained a titular role.

- **1648** Peace of Westphalia recognizes full Swiss independence.
- **1798** Invaded by French.
- **1815** Congress of Vienna after Napoléon's defeat confirms Swiss independence and establishes its neutrality. Geneva and Valais join Swiss Confederation.
- **1848** New constitution after brief civil war (1847) – central

CHRONOLOGY *continued*

government given more powers, but cantons' powers guaranteed.

- **1857** Neuchâtel joins confederation.
- **1863** Henri Dunant founds ICRC in Geneva.
- **1874** Referendum established as important decision-making tool.
- **1914–1918** Plays humanitarian role in World War I.
- **1919** Proportional representation ensures future political stability.
- **1920** Joins League of Nations.
- **1939–1945** Neutral in World War II.
- **1945** Refuses to join UN.
- **1959** Founder member of EFTA. Present four-party coalition comes to power, taking over FDP/PRD dominance of government.
- **1967** Right-wing groups make electoral gains, campaigning to restrict entry of foreign workers.
- **1971** Most women granted right to vote in federal elections.
- **1984** Parliament approves application for UN membership. Elisabeth Kopp is first woman minister (justice portfolio).
- **1986** Referendum opposes joining UN. Immigrant numbers restricted.
- **1988** Kopp resigns over allegedly violating secrecy of information laws.
- **1990** Kopp acquitted. Case revealed public prosecutor's office held secret files on 200,000 people. Violent protests. State security laws amended.
- **1991** Large increase in attacks on asylum seekers' hostels.
- **1992** Joins IMF and World Bank. Referendum vetoes joining EEA.
- **1994** Referendum approves new antiracism law and tighter laws against narcotics traffickers and illegal immigrants.
- **1998** $1.25 billion compensation for Holocaust victims whose funds were deposited in Swiss banks.
- **1999** Ruth Dreifuss first woman president.
- **2002** Third referendum on joining UN gives approval. Legalization of abortions as currently carried out also approved by referendum.
- **2003** SVP/UDC becomes largest party.

AID

Donor

$939m (donations) — Up 3% in 2002

With total disbursements amounting to 0.32% of GNP in 2002, Switzerland ranks above the (OECD) average of 0.23% as an aid donor, though the level of assistance remains below its target of 0.4% of GNP, set in 1994. The focus of aid has in recent years moved to central Asia.

DEFENSE

Compulsory military service

$2.85bn — Up 1% in 2002

SWISS ARMED FORCES

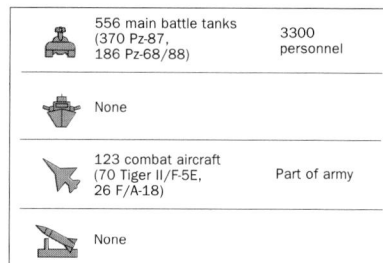

556 main battle tanks (370 Pz-87, 186 Pz-68/88)	3300 personnel
None	
123 combat aircraft (70 Tiger II/F-5E, 26 F/A-18)	Part of army
None	

The army is, in one sense, among the largest in Europe as it is organized so that almost 400,000 conscripts can be called up and armed in a few hours; it still uses skis and horses to protect the Alps. Bridges and tunnels are mined in accordance with a defense strategy drafted in the early 1900s. Military service and further training at intervals are compulsory for males up to the age of 42. An air wing is included as part of the army.

Force numbers are being cut in response to the end of the Cold War. In 1995, legislation allowing civilian service in place of military service was passed. Voters approved in 2001 a referendum proposal allowing Swiss soldiers to bear arms when on international peacekeeping operations.

ECONOMICS

Inflation 1.2% p.a. (1990–2001)

$264bn — 1.252 Swiss francs (1.355)

SCORE CARD

World GNP Ranking	18th
GNP per Capita	$36,170
Balance of Payments	$26bn
Inflation	0.6%
Unemployment	3%

EXPORTS

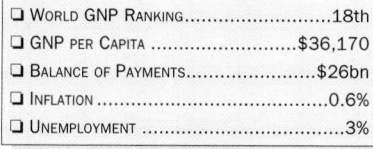

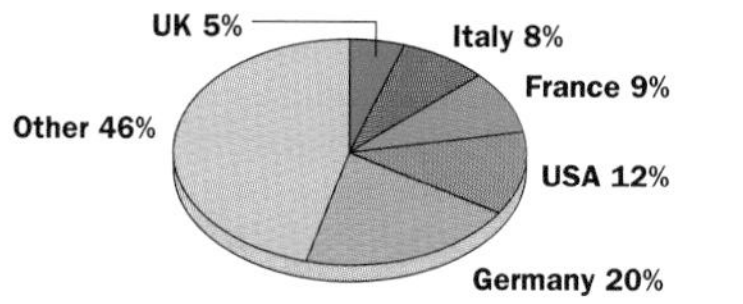
UK 5%
Italy 8%
France 9%
USA 12%
Germany 20%
Other 46%

IMPORTS

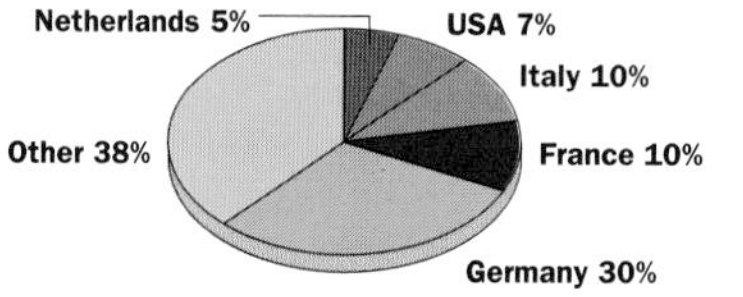
Netherlands 5%
USA 7%
Italy 10%
France 10%
Germany 30%
Other 38%

Strengths

Highly skilled workforce. Reliable service provider. Major machine tool and precision engineering industries. Powerful chemical, pharmaceutical, and banking multinationals. Banking secrecy laws attract foreign capital; banking sector contributes 9% of GNP. Ability to innovate to capture mass markets, typified by Swatch watch and Swatch-designed Smart car.

Weaknesses

Protected cartels result in many overpriced goods. Highly subsidized agricultural sector.

Profile

The economy is widely diversified. There are several large multinational enterprises and a large banking sector managing around one-third of the world's offshore private wealth. There was limited growth during the 1990s, and an economic downturn since 2001 has resulted in job losses in such sectors as banking and civil aviation. There is pressure to cater for the needs of an aging population, and in 2003 plans were announced to raise the retirement age from 65 to 67.

ECONOMIC PERFORMANCE INDICATOR

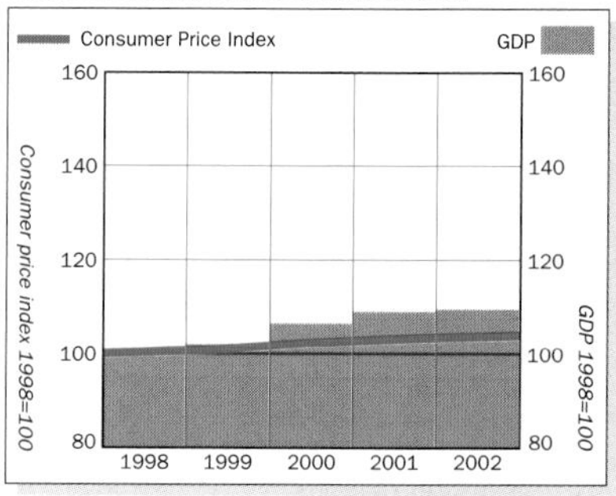
Consumer Price Index
GDP
160
140
120
100
80
1998
1999
2000
2001
2002
Consumer price index 1998=100
GDP 1998=100

SWITZERLAND : MAJOR BUSINESSES

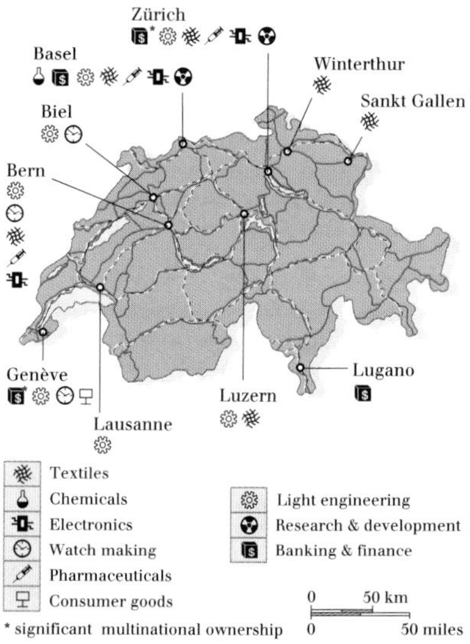
Zürich
Basel
Winterthur
Sankt Gallen
Biel
Bern
Genève
Lausanne
Luzern
Lugano
Textiles
Chemicals
Electronics
Watch making
Pharmaceuticals
Consumer goods
Light engineering
Research & development
Banking & finance
* significant multinational ownership
0 50 km
0 50 miles

RESOURCES

Electric power 18m kW

2850 tonnes

Not an oil producer; refines 93,000 b/d

1.56m cattle, 1.53m pigs, 7.44m chickens

Rock salt, marble, gypsum

ELECTRICITY GENERATION

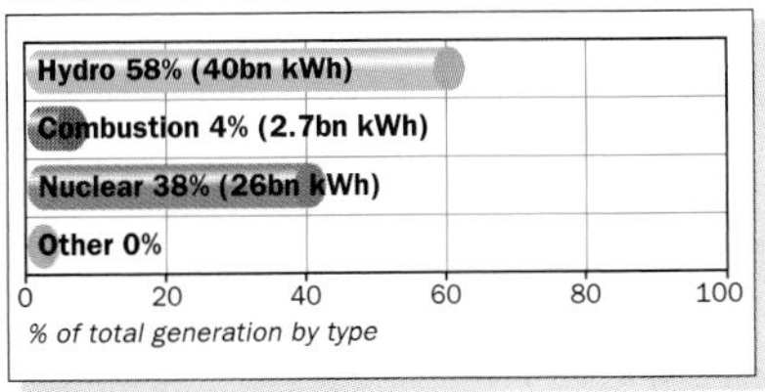
Hydro 58% (40bn kWh)
Combustion 4% (2.7bn kWh)
Nuclear 38% (26bn kWh)
Other 0%
0
20
40
60
80
100
% of total generation by type

Switzerland is poor in natural resources, having no valuable minerals in commercially exploitable quantities. Over half of its electricity comes from hydropower, while five nuclear plants supply most of the rest, so that spending on imported oil and coal is kept to a minimum – they account for less than 5% of the total import bill. Large-scale antinuclear power demonstrations in the 1980s led to the cancellation of plans for a new nuclear power plant, but a referendum approved continued use of existing plants.

SWITZERLAND : LAND USE

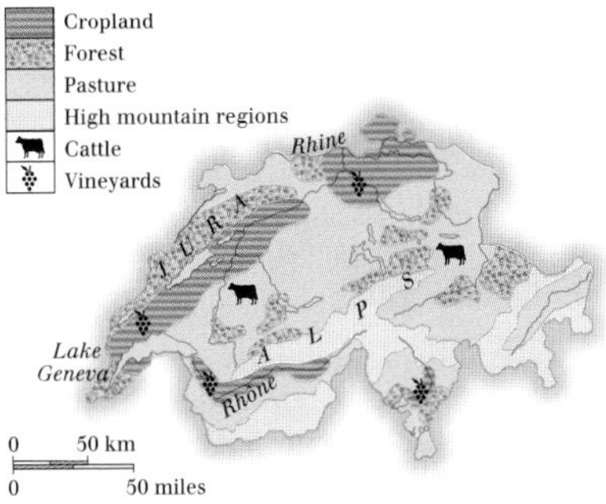
Cropland
Forest
Pasture
High mountain regions
Cattle
Vineyards
Rhine
JURA
ALPS
Lake Geneva
Rhone
0
50 km
0
50 miles

ENVIRONMENT

Sustainability rank: 5th

30% (18% partially protected)

5.4 tonnes per capita

ENVIRONMENTAL TREATIES

Yes Yes Yes

Yes Yes Yes

The Swiss are among the most environmentally conscious people in the world and are willing to back their convictions with money. The Basel–Milan link, designed to carry trucks by rail through a tunnel instead of having them cross the Alps by road, was approved by referendum, despite the estimated $13.3bn cost. The ultimate aim is a total ban on carrying freight by road through Switzerland; this ban may not be necessary if major time savings make the tunnel sufficiently attractive. The Swiss are keen recyclers and taxation is used to encourage this.

CRIME

No death penalty

4987 prisoners

Up 2% in 2001

CRIME RATES

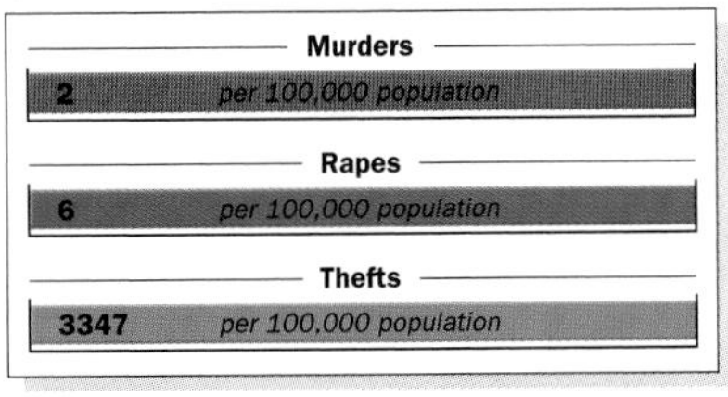
Murders
2 per 100,000 population
Rapes
6 per 100,000 population
Thefts
3347 per 100,000 population

Crime rates are low by international standards. Muggings and burglaries are on the increase and are often related to narcotics. More cases of banking secrecy laws attracting laundered funds are coming to light.

HEALTH

Welfare state health benefits

1 per 286 people

Heart diseases, cancers, cerebrovascular and respiratory diseases

The health system is among the most efficient and pioneering in the world, and is ranked by WHO second, after Japan, for attainment. High treatment costs are covered by compulsory insurance schemes.

SPENDING

GDP/cap. increase

CONSUMPTION AND SPENDING

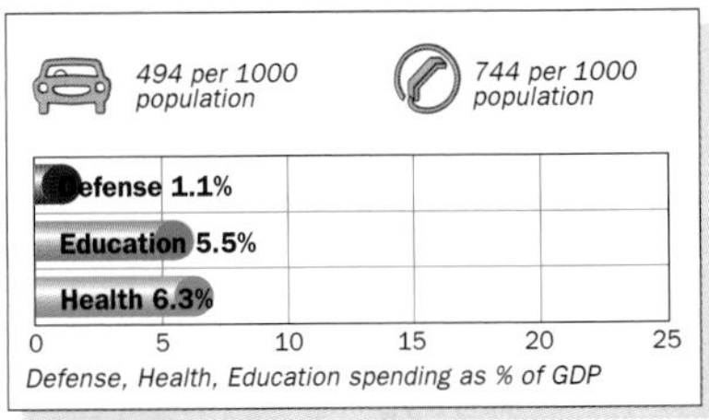
494 per 1000 population
744 per 1000 population
Defense 1.1%
Education 5.5%
Health 6.3%
0
5
10
15
20
25
Defense, Health, Education spending as % of GDP

Immigrant workers do most low-paid and menial jobs. Wages in office jobs are relatively high, though the cost of living is also well above the European average. Many workers choose to live in France and commute across the border. The property market is highly regulated.

EDUCATION

School leaving age: 16

99%

163,373 students

THE EDUCATION SYSTEM

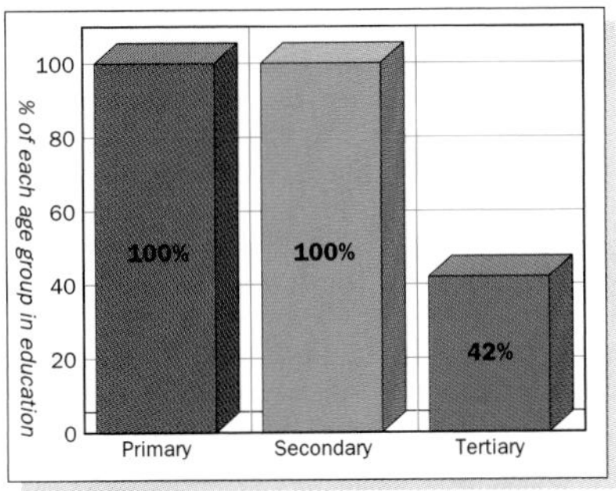
100
80
60
40
20
0
% of each age group in education
100%
100%
42%
Primary
Secondary
Tertiary

State spending on education is high. Primary and secondary education are controlled by the cantons, so that there are 26 different systems in operation. In some German-speaking cantons, including Zürich, children begin learning English before French or Italian.

Revelations of poor literacy levels among Swiss schoolchildren prompted an action plan, unveiled in mid-2003, which proposed lowering the school entry age from seven to five and providing extra help to foreign children.

MEDIA

TV ownership high

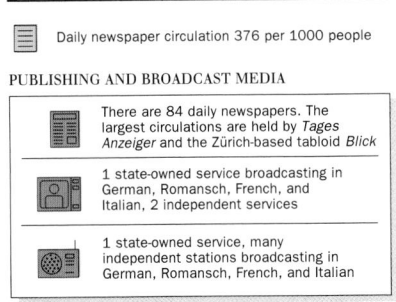

Daily newspaper circulation 376 per 1000 people

PUBLISHING AND BROADCAST MEDIA

There are 84 daily newspapers. The largest circulations are held by *Tages Anzeiger* and the Zürich-based tabloid *Blick*

1 state-owned service broadcasting in German, Romansch, French, and Italian, 2 independent services

1 state-owned service, many independent stations broadcasting in German, Romansch, French, and Italian

The Swiss media are organized broadly along regional lines, and reflect the country's linguistic divisions. The German-, Romansch-, French-, and Italian-language TV and radio stations tend to focus on the interests of their specific communities. German, Italian, and French satellite TV is widely available. Almost no Swiss newspapers are distributed throughout the country. Papers from France and Italy are widely read.

WORLD RANKING

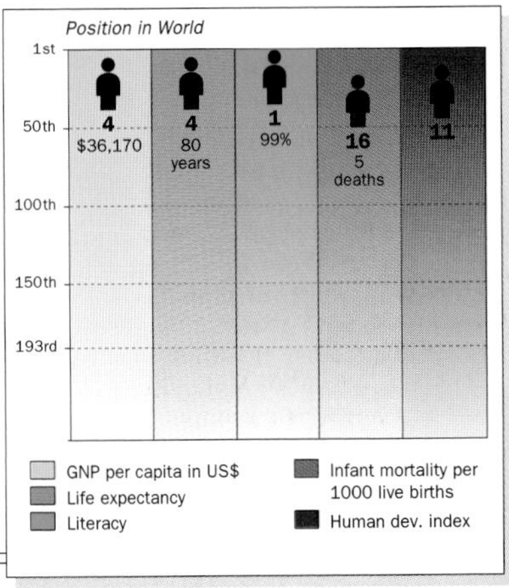
Position in World
1st
50th
100th
150th
193rd
4
$36,170
4
80
years
1
99%
16
5
deaths
11
GNP per capita in US$
Life expectancy
Literacy
Infant mortality per 1000 live births
Human dev. index

S

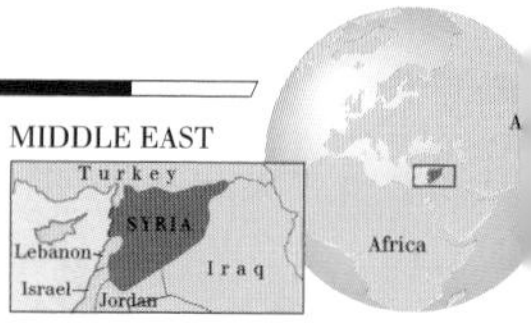
MIDDLE EAST
Turkey
SYRIA
Lebanon
Israel
Jordan
Iraq
Africa

SYRIA

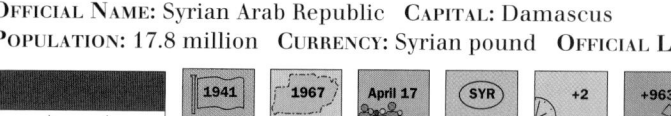

OFFICIAL NAME: Syrian Arab Republic **CAPITAL:** Damascus
POPULATION: 17.8 million **CURRENCY:** Syrian pound **OFFICIAL LANGUAGE:** Arabic

1941 | 1967 | April 17 | SYR | +2 | +963 | .sy

SYRIA IS REGARDED by many of its people as an artificial creation left over from the era of French-mandated rule (1920–1941). They identify instead with a Greater Syria, successor to the medieval Ummayad caliphate encompassing Lebanon, Jordan, and Palestine. Since independence, Syria's foreign relations have been turbulent, but the authoritarian Ba'athist regime under the Assads has brought a measure of internal stability.

CLIMATE

Steppe/hot desert/ Mediterranean

WEATHER CHART FOR DAMASCUS

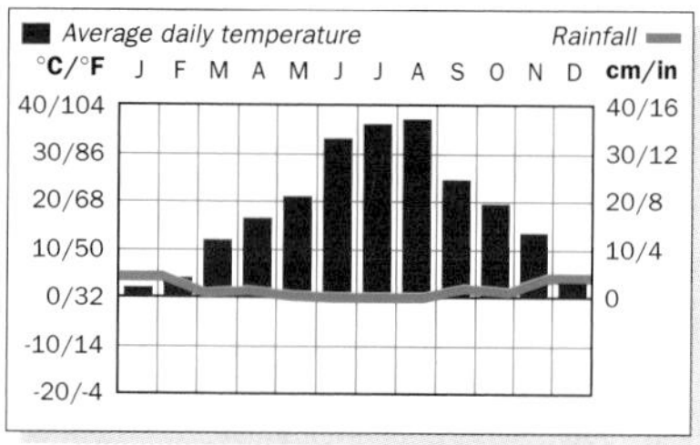
Average daily temperature
Rainfall
°C/°F
J F M A M J J A S O N D
cm/in
40/104
30/86
20/68
10/50
0/32
-10/14
-20/-4
40/16
30/12
20/8
10/4
0

The coastal climate is Mediterranean, with mild, wet winters and dry, hot summers. Most of the country gets fewer than 25 cm (10 in) of rainfall a year. Away from the coast, rainfall is very unpredictable and the country becomes increasingly arid, with some desert areas. In the mountains, snow is common in winter.

TRANSPORTATION

Drive on right

Damascus 1.5m passengers

190 ships 472,100 grt

THE TRANSPORTATION NETWORK

9361 km (5817 miles)

877 km (545 miles)

2450 km (1522 miles)

870 km (541 miles)

The road network is unreliable in rural areas, especially during the winter after rain. Bus services operate to most towns from Damascus and Aleppo. Roads are integrated with the railroads, which carry over four million passengers a year and are vital to freight transportation. The rail link from Aleppo to Mosul, in Iraq, reopened in mid-2000. Damascus is the main international airport and Latakia the main port.

TOURISM

Visitors : Population 1:11

1.66m visitors

Up 26% in 2002

MAIN TOURIST ARRIVALS

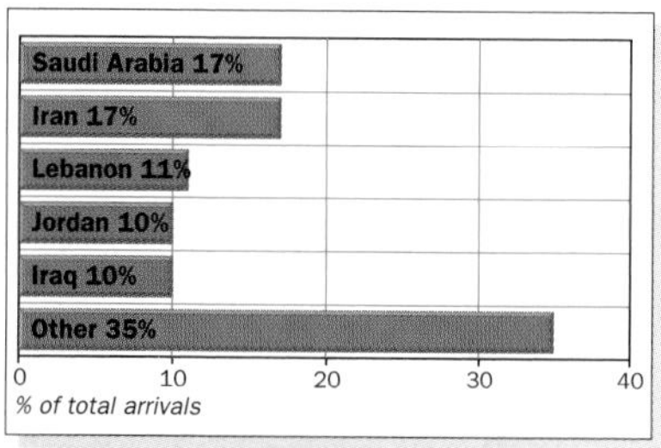
Saudi Arabia 17%
Iran 17%
Lebanon 11%
Jordan 10%
Iraq 10%
Other 35%
0
10
20
30
40
% of total arrivals

Years of political turbulence, allegations of human rights abuses committed under Hafez al-Assad's regime, and strict, complex travel regulations retarded the development of tourism. However, just before the 1991 Gulf War, Syria began to compete with other Middle Eastern states as a tourist destination. Modern hotels were built in most cities and facilities improved to cater for growing numbers of Western visitors. Tourist numbers have slumped following the al-Qaida attacks on the US in 2001 and the 2003 invasion of Iraq. Syria's main attractions are its antiquities, such as the ruined desert city of Palmyra; and historic cities, with their souks, baths, and mosques – Damascus, said to be the oldest inhabited city in the world, and Aleppo, with its citadel. Syria has a wealth of castles dating back to the Crusades and sites associated with the advent of Islam. In addition, there are as many as 3500 as yet unexcavated archaeological sites. Syria's coastline on the Mediterranean has fine beaches, and there are mountain resorts near Latakia.

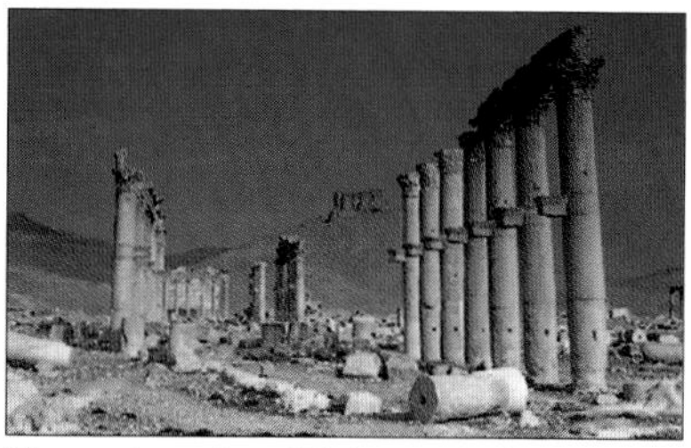

***The ancient city of Palmyra,** in Syria's central region, was once the capital of the kingdom of Queen Zenobia.*

PEOPLE

Pop. density medium

Arabic, French, Kurdish, Armenian, Circassian, Turkic languages, Assyrian, Aramaic

97/km² (250/mi²)

THE URBAN/RURAL POPULATION SPLIT

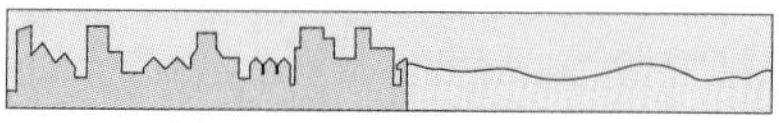
52%
48%

RELIGIOUS PERSUASION

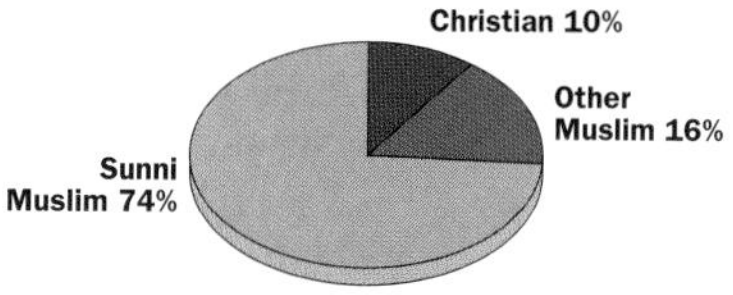
Christian 10%
Other Muslim 16%
Sunni Muslim 74%

ETHNIC MAKEUP

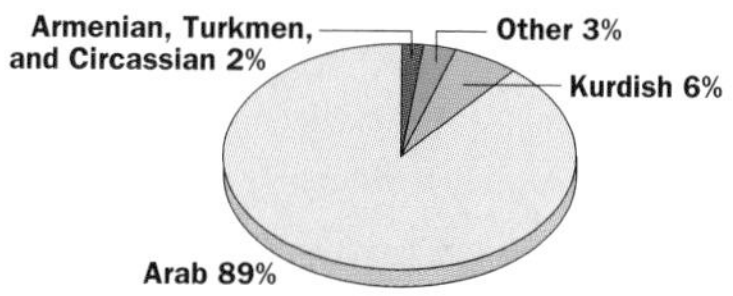
Armenian, Turkmen, and Circassian 2%
Other 3%
Kurdish 6%
Arab 89%

Most Syrians live in the west, where the largest cities are sited. About 90% are Muslim. They include the politically dominant Alawis, a heterodox offshoot of Shi'a, comprising 12% of the population, based in Latakia and Tartous provinces. There is also a sizable Christian minority; there are three villages where Aramaic is spoken. In the west and north a mosaic of groups includes Kurds, Turkic speakers, and urban-based Armenians. In addition, some 300,000 Palestinian refugees have settled in Syria. Violent demonstrations by Kurds in the northeast testify to unresolved ethnic tensions. Minorities were initially attracted to the ruling Ba'ath Party because of its emphasis on the state over sectarian interests. However, disputes between factions led to the Alawis taking control, creating resentment among the Sunni Muslim majority.

The emancipation of women, promoted initially in the late 1960s, was carried forward under President Hafez al-Assad, whose first woman cabinet minister was appointed in 1976.

POPULATION AGE BREAKDOWN

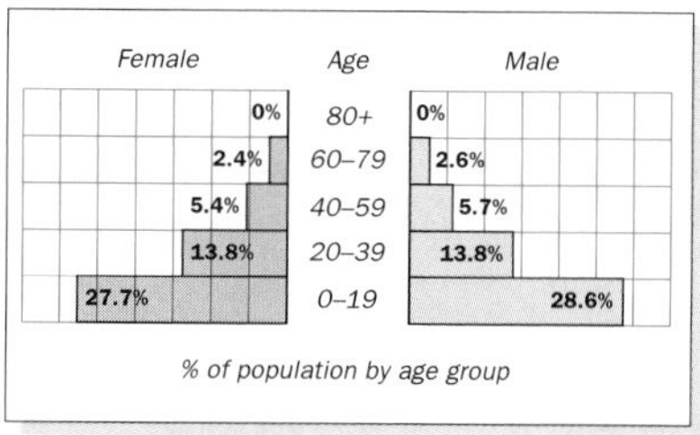
Female
Age
Male
0%
80+
0%
2.4%
60–79
2.6%
5.4%
40–59
5.7%
13.8%
20–39
13.8%
27.7%
0–19
28.6%
% of population by age group

S

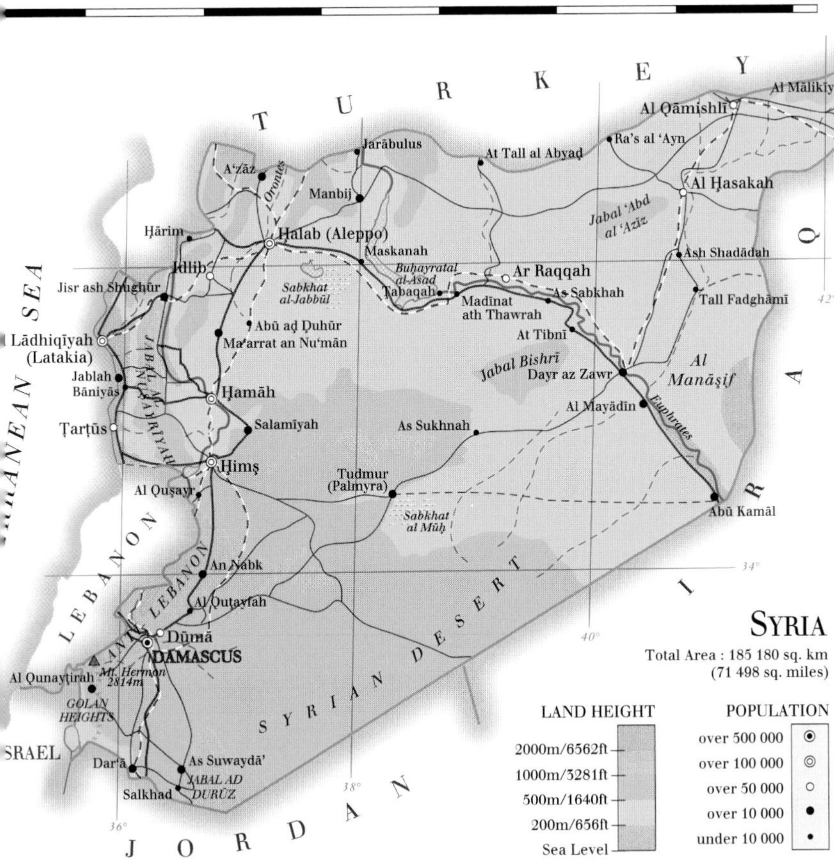
TURKEY
IRAQ
JORDAN
LEBANON
ISRAEL
SYRIAN DESERT
Al Mālikīyah
Al Qāmishlī
Ra's al 'Ayn
At Tall al Abyaḍ
Jarābulus
A'zāz
Manbij
Ḥārim
Ḥalab (Aleppo)
Maskanah
Idlib
Jisr ash Shughūr
Sabkhat al-Jabbūl
Buḥayrat al-Asad
Ṭabaqah
Ar Raqqah
As Sabkhah
Madīnat ath Thawrah
At Tibnī
Al Ḥasakah
Ash Shadādah
Tall Fadghāmī
Jabal 'Abd al 'Azīz
Abū aḍ Ḍuhūr
Ma'arrat an Nu'mān
Lādhiqīyah (Latakia)
Jablah
Bāniyās
Ṭarṭūs
Ḥamāh
Salamīyah
Ḥimṣ
Al Quṣayr
Jabal Bishrī
Dayr az Zawr
Al Mayādīn
Al Manāṣif
Euphrates
Orontes
As Sukhnah
Tudmur (Palmyra)
Sabkhat al Mūḥ
Abū Kamāl
An Nabk
Al Quṭayfah
Dūmā
DAMASCUS
Al Qunayṭirah
Mt. Hermon 2814m
GOLAN HEIGHTS
Dar'ā
As Suwaydā'
JABAL AD DURŪZ
Salkhad
N
0 100 km
0 100 miles
SYRIA
Total Area : 185 180 sq. km (71 498 sq. miles)
LAND HEIGHT
2000m/6562ft
1000m/3281ft
500m/1640ft
200m/656ft
Sea Level
POPULATION
over 500 000
over 100 000
over 50 000
over 10 000
under 10 000

WORLD AFFAIRS

Joined UN in 1945

AL | Damasc | G24 | NAM | OIC

Syria sees itself as the major barrier to Israel's perceived dominance. It has considerable control over Lebanon, hosts radical Palestinian factions, and has forged alliances with north African states. Pressure in Lebanon for the removal of Syrian troops, especially after the Israeli withdrawal in 2000, has recently abated. The biggest issue with Israel remains the strategically vital Golan Heights, seized by Israel during the Six-Day War in 1967. Peace negotiations foundered when Ariel Sharon came to power in Israel in 2001.

President Bashar al-Assad has worked to end traditional enmity with Turkey over attitudes to Israel and to Turkish Kurdish guerrillas, access to water, and Syria's former coastal Alexandretta Province. In 2004 he made the first state visit to Turkey.

Syria, alone among Arab states, backed Iran in the 1980s Iran–Iraq War. Hafez al-Assad joined the US-led allies in the 1991 Gulf War, legitimizing the action in Arab eyes. In 2000, however, Syria openly defied UN sanctions against Iraq. The US has since accused it of aiding resistance there, and of pursuing the development of weapons of mass destruction, in 2004 imposing economic sanctions. Traditionally, Syria has better ties with Europe than with the US.

AID

Recipient

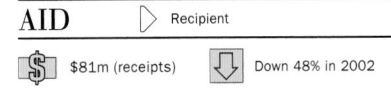

$81m (receipts) — Down 48% in 2002

Syria has historically received little aid, owing partly to its human rights record and partly to its self-sufficiency in oil. In 1997, the Syrian government settled its debt of $526 million to the World Bank. Arab countries and Germany are the main aid donors; assistance also comes from Japan, the UN, and France.

Hafez al-Assad ruled for three decades until his death in 2000.

Bashar al-Assad succeeded his father as president.

POLITICS

No multiparty elections

2003/2007 — President Bashar al-Assad

AT THE LAST ELECTION

People's Assembly 250 seats

67% Ba'ath Party — **33% Other Ba'ath**

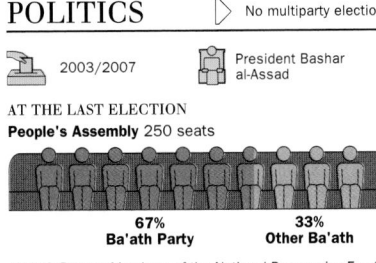

Ba'ath Party = Members of the National Progressive Front (allies of the Ba'ath Party) **Other Ba'ath** = Parties allied to the Ba'ath Party

Syria is in effect a single-party state. Its leader from 1970 to 2000 was Hafez al-Assad, a lifelong Ba'ath Party militant. His personal dominance ensured the succession of his son Bashar after his death in June 2000.

PROFILE

The Ba'athist military swept to power in 1963 with a vision of uniting all Arab nations under a single Syrian-dominated socialist system. To this end, Assad consolidated the Ba'ath Party as the major political force in Syria and focused on foreign affairs, bidding to make Syria a major power; plans to unite with fellow Ba'athist Iraq ended in 1981, however, amid mutual recriminations.

The transition of power to Bashar al-Assad in 2000 raised hopes of political reform. Initial tentative changes – such as the spread of "discussion clubs" and the release of some jailed dissidents – were later curtailed and crackdowns have occurred once again. The destruction of Saddam Hussein's Ba'athist regime in Iraq in 2003 has led to fears for the durability of the Syrian regime.

MAIN POLITICAL ISSUES

Human rights

Martial law has not been rescinded since 1963, but the regime has improved its human rights record in recent years. Political prisoners are released under occasional amnesties, and in 1994 all Jews were granted visas to travel abroad.

Political pluralism

Hafez al-Assad dominated politics for 30 years. His military-backed regime, drawn mainly from his Alawi minority, kept a tight hold on power, though in his last decade Sunnis gained high political posts. Despite international pressure Assad never permitted genuine multipartyism. The modernizing Mohammed Miro was made prime minister in early 2000, and Bashar was hastily appointed party leader soon after his father's death, but there has been little real progress in political liberalization.

S

CHRONOLOGY

Under French mandate from 1920, Syria declared independence in 1941, and achieved full autonomy in 1946. From 1958 to 1961 Syria merged with Egypt to form the United Arab Republic.

- ❑ **1963** Ba'athist military junta seizes power. Maj. Gen. Amin al-Hafez president.
- ❑ **1966** Hafez ousted by military coup supported by radical Ba'ath Party members.
- ❑ **1967** Israel overruns Syrian positions above Lake Tiberias, seizes Golan Heights, and occupies Quneitra. Syria boycotts Arab summit and rejects compromise with Israel.
- ❑ **1970** Hafez al-Assad seizes power in "corrective coup."
- ❑ **1971–1999** Assad elected president; reelected four times.
- ❑ **1973** New constitution confirms dominance of Ba'ath Party. War launched with Egypt against Israel to regain territory lost in 1967. More territory temporarily lost to Israel.
- ❑ **1976** With peacekeeping mandate from Arab League, Syria intervenes to quell fighting in Lebanon.
- ❑ **1977** Relations broken off with Egypt after Egyptian president Sadat's visit to Jerusalem.
- ❑ **1978** National charter signed with Iraq for union.
- ❑ **1980** Membership of Muslim Brotherhood made capital offense. Treaty of Friendship with USSR.
- ❑ **1981** Israel formally annexes Golan Heights. Charter with Iraq collapses.
- ❑ **1982** Islamic extremist uprising in Hamah crushed. Israel invades Lebanon; Syrian missiles in Bekaa Valley destroyed.
- ❑ **1985** US claims Syrian links to Rome and Vienna airport bombings.
- ❑ **1986** Alleged Syrian complicity in planting of bomb on Israeli airliner in London. EU states, except Greece, impose sanctions and arms embargo.
- ❑ **1989** Diplomatic relations reestablished with Egypt.
- ❑ **1990–1991** Syrian forces crush renegade Gen. Aoun in Beirut. Steers Taif Accords over Lebanon.
- ❑ **1991** Troops take part in Operation Desert Storm. Damascus Declaration aid and defense pact signed with Egypt, Saudi Arabia, Kuwait, UAE, Qatar, Bahrain, and Oman.
- ❑ **1995** Inconclusive talks with Israel.
- ❑ **2000** Forced resignation after 13 years and subsequent suicide of prime minister, Mahmoud az-Zoubi. Death of Hafez al-Assad; succession of son Bashar.
- ❑ **2003** Israel bombs "terrorist camps" in Syria.

DEFENSE

Compulsory military service

$1.82bn

Down 3% in 2002

Syria sees its extensive military capability as a significant deterrent to Israel's territorial expansion. It has fought four wars against Israel since 1948, and is the Arab world's strongest military power after Egypt. Most of its military equipment was obtained from the former Soviet Union. Its defense spending as a percentage of GDP is among the highest in the world.

Throughout 2000, increasing numbers of Lebanese protested against the continuing presence of Syrian troops on their soil – in apparent contravention of the 1989 Taif Accords – and in 2001, Syrian troops were withdrawn from Beirut. In May 2002 a US State Department official accused Syria of harboring weapons of mass destruction.

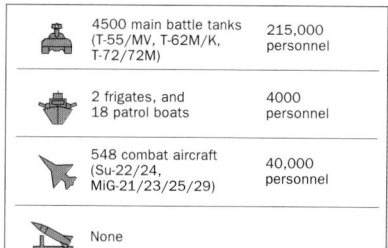

SYRIAN ARMED FORCES

4500 main battle tanks (T-55/MV, T-62M/K, T-72/72M)	215,000 personnel
2 frigates, and 18 patrol boats	4000 personnel
548 combat aircraft (Su-22/24, MiG-21/23/25/29)	40,000 personnel
None	

ECONOMICS

Inflation 7.4% p.a. (1990–2001)

$19.1bn

48.57 Syrian pounds (46)

SCORE CARD

- ❑ World GNP Ranking..........68th
- ❑ GNP per Capita..........$1130
- ❑ Balance of Payments..........$1.08bn
- ❑ Inflation..........2.5%
- ❑ Unemployment..........12%

EXPORTS

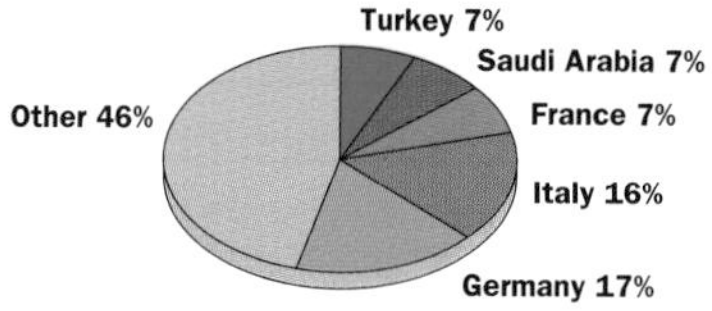
Turkey 7%
Saudi Arabia 7%
France 7%
Italy 16%
Germany 17%
Other 46%

IMPORTS

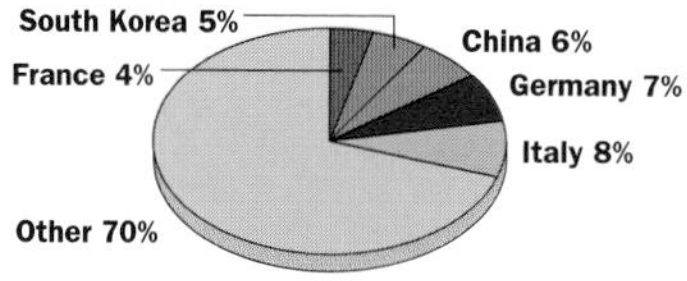
South Korea 5%
France 4%
China 6%
Germany 7%
Italy 8%
Other 70%

Strengths

Crude oil exports – production increasing. Manufacturing base has grown. Thriving agricultural sector. Low inflation. Private banks recently opened.

Weaknesses

High defense spending. Corruption. Domination of inefficient state-run companies. Lack of foreign investment. High population growth, unemployment. Vulnerable water supply. Demise of cross-border trade with Iraq, and US sanctions from 2004.

Profile

Billions of dollars flowed into the economy from the West and the Gulf states after the 1991 Gulf War. Along with increased oil revenue, this led to rapid growth. Diversion of water from the Euphrates toward fertile plains, rather than poorer land, boosted agricultural output. Yet long-term economic prospects remain uncertain. The public sector employs 20% of the workforce, and state controls inhibit private enterprise and investment, and have created a booming black market. Businessmen often channel funds through the freer Lebanese economy. An economic reform package in 2000 created a stock exchange and permitted private banks. Holding foreign currency has been allowed since late 2002.

ECONOMIC PERFORMANCE INDICATOR

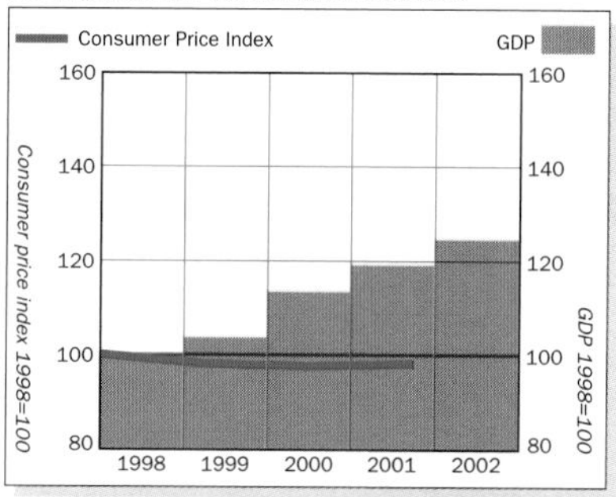
Consumer Price Index
GDP
160
140
120
100
80
Consumer price index 1998=100
GDP 1998=100
1998
1999
2000
2001
2002

SYRIA : MAJOR BUSINESSES

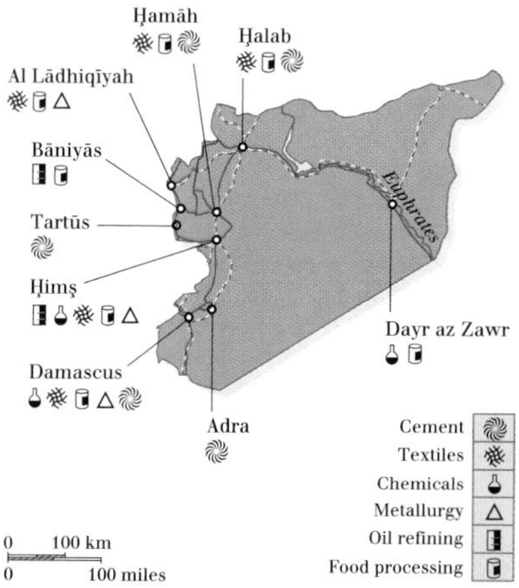
Ḩamāh
Ḩalab
Al Lādhiqīyah
Bāniyās
Ţarţūs
Ḩimş
Damascus
Adra
Dayr az Zawr
Euphrates
Cement
Textiles
Chemicals
Metallurgy
Oil refining
Food processing
0 100 km
0 100 miles

RESOURCES

Electric power 6m kW

14,171 tonnes

594,000 b/d (reserves 2.3bn barrels)

13.5m sheep, 1m goats, 30m chickens

Phosphates, oil, natural gas, iron

ELECTRICITY GENERATION

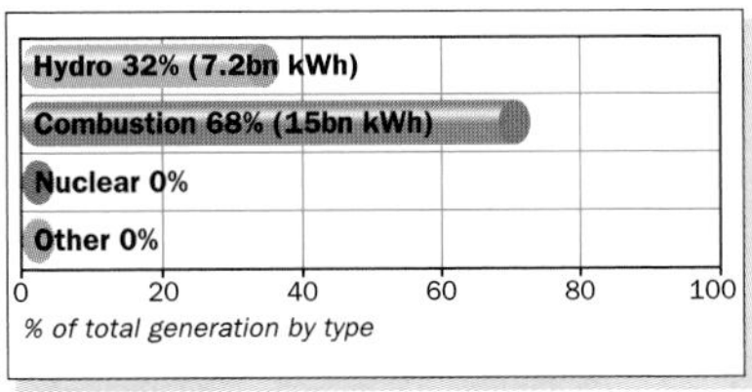
Hydro 32% (7.2bn kWh)
Combustion 68% (15bn kWh)
Nuclear 0%
Other 0%
0
20
40
60
80
100
% of total generation by type

Syria has reversed a trend of declining oil production in the late 1990s through intensifying oil and natural gas exploration efforts, and effecting a switch from oil- to natural-gas-fired electric power plants. Hydroelectric power is providing a growing share of electricity-generating capacity; known exploitable potential hydroelectric energy is 4500 MW. Manufacturing is largely limited to oil-derived industries, textiles, and food products. Cotton is the main cash crop; fruit and vegetables are also grown. Livestock, especially sheep and goats, support the rural economy.

SYRIA : LAND USE

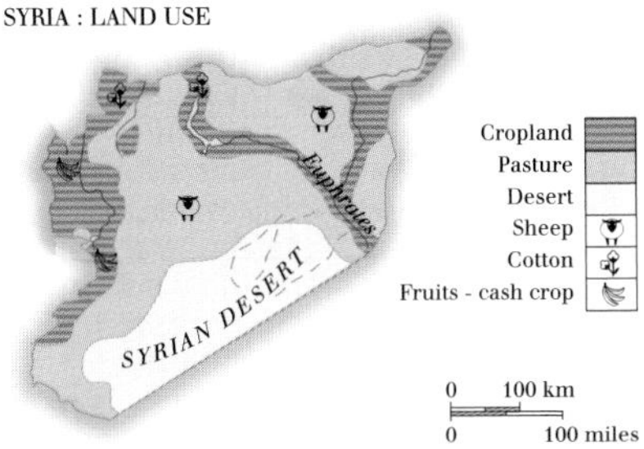
Euphrates
SYRIAN DESERT
Cropland
Pasture
Desert
Sheep
Cotton
Fruits - cash crop
0
100 km
0
100 miles

ENVIRONMENT

Sustainability rank: 107th

None

3.3 tonnes per capita

ENVIRONMENTAL TREATIES

Yes | Yes | Yes

Yes | Yes | No

The Assad regime's most expensive and controversial environmental project has been the Euphrates Dam, power plant, and irrigation network at Tabaqah. The dam's vast man-made reservoir, Buhayrat al-Assad, engulfed some 300 villages and destroyed 25,000 hectares (62,000 acres) of fertile farmland. A giant cement factory at Tartus, built by former East Germany in the mid-1970s, has increased pollution along a stretch of Syria's Mediterranean coastline. However, the interior of the country remains relatively unspoiled.

MEDIA

TV ownership medium

Daily newspaper circulation 20 per 1000 people

Information became freer after Jordanian papers were again allowed into Syria in 1999, and with the advent of satellite TV. Bashar al-Assad encourages Internet use, albeit highly regulated, and in 2001 he allowed independent publications, including *Ad-domari*, the first satirical journal in 38 years.

PUBLISHING AND BROADCAST MEDIA

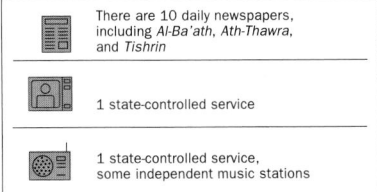

There are 10 daily newspapers, including *Al-Ba'ath*, *Ath-Thawra*, and *Tishrin*

1 state-controlled service

1 state-controlled service, some independent music stations

CRIME

Death penalty in use

14,000 prisoners

Up sharply in 1995–1999

CRIME RATES

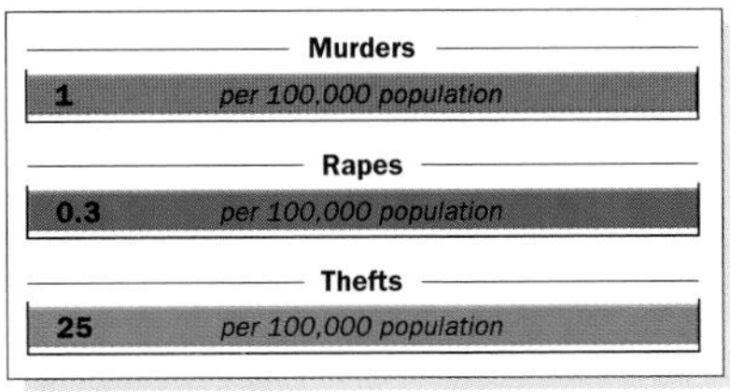
Murders
1 per 100,000 population
Rapes
0.3 per 100,000 population
Thefts
25 per 100,000 population

Most politicians imprisoned by President Hafez al-Assad in the 1970s have been released. In 1997 Syria was removed from the US government's list of major narcotics-distributing countries, following a joint eradication program with Lebanon. There are continued reports of torture in custody.

EDUCATION

School leaving age: 11

83%

94,110 students

THE EDUCATION SYSTEM

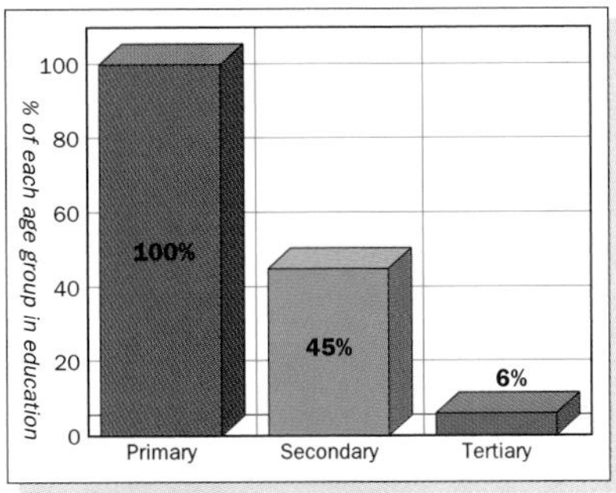
100
80
60
40
20
0
% of each age group in education
100%
45%
6%
Primary
Secondary
Tertiary

A modern and universally accessible system of education remains an important objective. Free and compulsory primary education for all was a priority of the Ba'ath Party when it came to power. Coeducation began in the cities and spread to rural areas under the Assad regime. There are seven state universities, notably at Damascus, Aleppo, Tishrin, and Homs (Hims). Private universities were allowed from 2001. Education ranks second in government expenditure, though is far behind defense. UK and US politicians protest at incitement to racism in Syrian school textbooks.

HEALTH

Welfare state health benefits

1 per 769 people

Heart, respiratory, digestive, infectious, and parasitic diseases

An adequate system of primary health care has been set up since the Ba'ath Party came to power. Treatment is free for those unable to pay. However, hospitals often lack modern equipment and medical services are in need of further investment. Rural areas in particular need assistance to combat the spread of heart, respiratory, and infectious diseases.

SPENDING

GDP/cap. increase

CONSUMPTION AND SPENDING

11 per 1000 population

123 per 1000 population

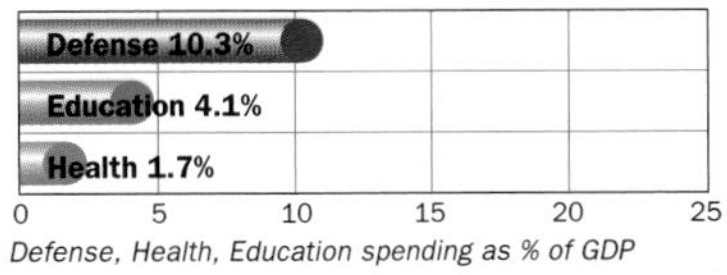
Defense 10.3%
Education 4.1%
Health 1.7%
0
5
10
15
20
25
Defense, Health, Education spending as % of GDP

Syria is far from the equitable society that early Ba'ath Party thinkers envisioned. The gulf between Syria's rich and poor is widening. The political elite, many of whom live in the West Malki suburb of Damascus, is more numerous and richer than ever before. Palestinian refugees and the urban unemployed make up the poorest groups.

WORLD RANKING

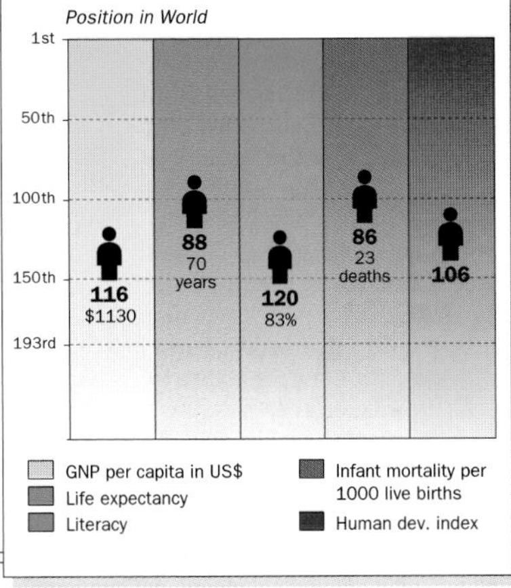
Position in World
1st
50th
100th
150th
193rd
116
$1130
88
70 years
120
83%
86
23 deaths
106
GNP per capita in US$
Life expectancy
Literacy
Infant mortality per 1000 live births
Human dev. index

S

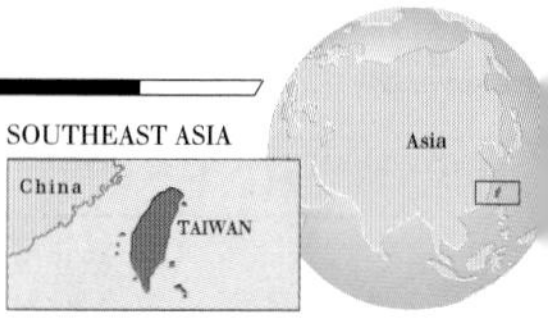

SOUTHEAST ASIA
China
TAIWAN
Asia

TAIWAN

OFFICIAL NAME: Republic of China (ROC) **CAPITAL:** Taipei
POPULATION: 22.6 million **CURRENCY:** Taiwan dollar **OFFICIAL LANGUAGE:** Mandarin Chinese

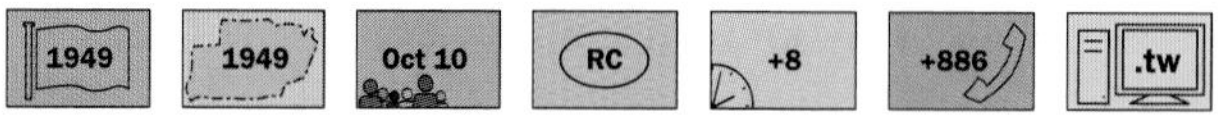

1949
1949
Oct 10
RC
+8
+886
.tw

THE ISLAND OF TAIWAN, formerly known as Formosa, lies off the southeast coast of mainland China. Mountains running north to south cover two-thirds of the island. The lowlands are highly fertile, planted mostly with rice, and densely populated. In 1949, when the Chinese Communists ousted Chiang Kai-shek's nationalist Kuomintang (KMT) from power on the mainland, he established the Republic of China government on the island. De facto military rule has been democratized progressively since 1986. Mainland China still considers Taiwan to be a renegade province, and only a few countries now give official recognition to the regime on the island.

Wen Wu Temple, on the shores of Sun Moon Lake in the mountains of central Taiwan – a region famous for its many temples. Nearly the whole population is Buddhist.

CLIMATE

Tropical monsoon

WEATHER CHART FOR TAIPEI

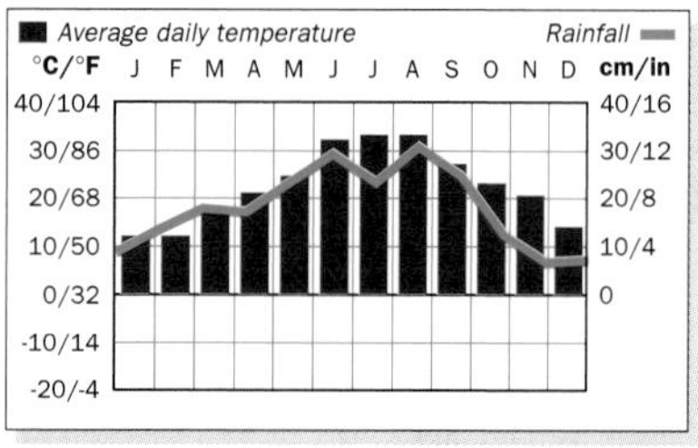

Average daily temperature
Rainfall
°C/°F
J F M A M J J A S O N D
cm/in
40/104
30/86
20/68
10/50
0/32
-10/14
-20/-4
40/16
30/12
20/8
10/4
0

Taiwan has a tropical monsoon climate similar to that of the southern Chinese mainland. Typhoons from the South China Sea bring the heaviest rains between June and September.

TRANSPORTATION

Drive on right

Chiang Kai-shek International, T'aoyüan
15.5m passengers

649 ships
4.29m grt

THE TRANSPORTATION NETWORK

31,583 km (19,625 miles)

Sun Yat-sen Highway; 608 km (378 miles)

1097 km (682 miles)

None

A railroad encircles the island, and a US$16 billion high-speed rail link along the west coast, linking Taipei to Kaohsiung, is under construction with the help of the Japanese Shinkansen Corporation; it is due for completion in 2005. Car ownership has risen dramatically in the last 30 years. The bicycle is not as popular as in mainland China, and exports of Taiwanese cycles, mostly to Europe and the US, have declined in recent years.

Access to mainland China has increased as relations slowly improve. By boat, passengers have to travel from the tiny offshore islands of Matsu and Quemoy. The number of visitors is limited both ways by yearly quotas.

TOURISM

Visitors : Population 1:10

2.25m visitors

Down 25% in 2003

MAIN TOURIST ARRIVALS

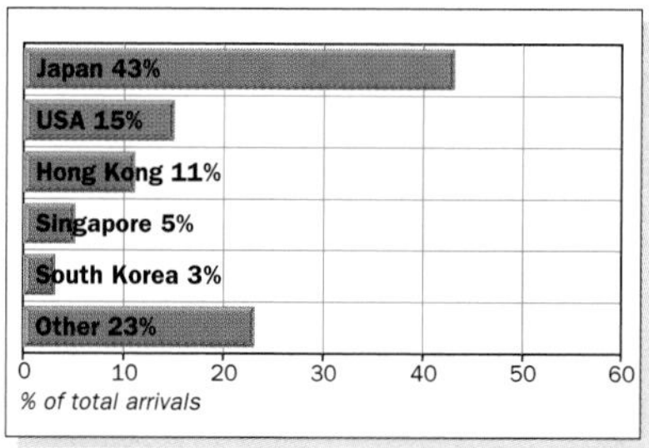

Japan 43%
USA 15%
Hong Kong 11%
Singapore 5%
South Korea 3%
Other 23%
0
10
20
30
40
50
60
% of total arrivals

Taiwan is not a major tourist destination, but it has successfully targeted vacationers from the US and Japan in recent years. Restrictions on Chinese tourists are being eased. Successive Six-Year Plans focus on upgrading hotels and improving tourist facilities at international airports. The major attraction is the Palace Museum in Taipei, which includes the massive treasure looted by the nationalists from Beijing. Only 2% can be shown at any one time. Sex tourism is an important business in Taipei. Sex establishments often masquerade as barbershops.

PEOPLE

Pop. density high

Amoy Chinese, Mandarin Chinese, Hakka Chinese

701/km² (1815/mi²)

THE URBAN/RURAL POPULATION SPLIT

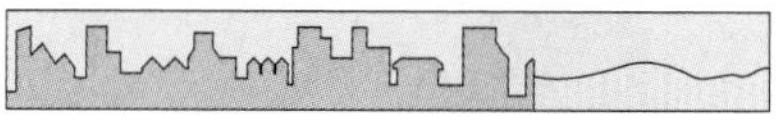

69% 31%

RELIGIOUS PERSUASION

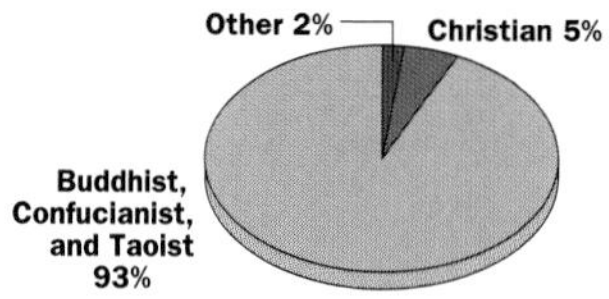

Other 2%
Christian 5%
Buddhist, Confucianist, and Taoist 93%

ETHNIC MAKEUP

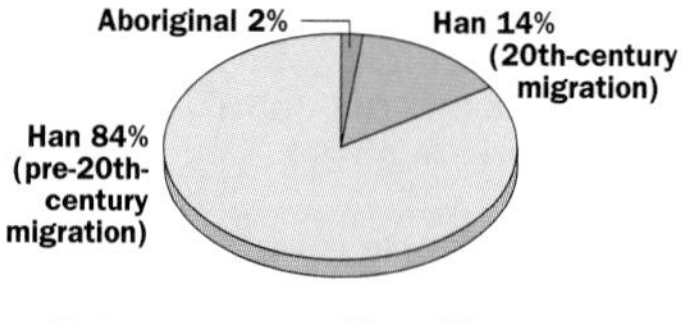

Aboriginal 2%
Han 14% (20th-century migration)
Han 84% (pre-20th-century migration)

Most Taiwanese are Han Chinese, descendants of the 1644 migration of the Ming dynasty from mainland China. The 100,000 nationalists who arrived in 1949 established themselves as a ruling class and monopolized the most prestigious jobs in the civil service.

This caused resentment among the local inhabitants, but as the generation elected on the mainland in 1947 passed on, local Taiwanese entered the political process. Indigenous minorities who live in the eastern hills suffer considerable discrimination.

Housing shortages are a major issue. The trend is toward European-style nuclear families, though the extended family is still important and provides a social security net for the elderly. Cultural Westernization challenges traditional values; in 2004 a law ordered that official documents be written only from left to right. Women are less well represented in politics than in business and the civil service.

POPULATION AGE BREAKDOWN

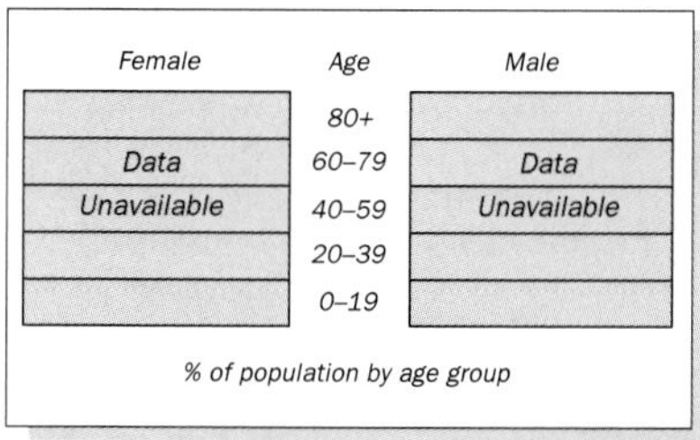

Female
Age
Male
80+
60–79
40–59
20–39
0–19
Data Unavailable
Data Unavailable
% of population by age group

T

POLITICS

Multiparty elections

2001/2004

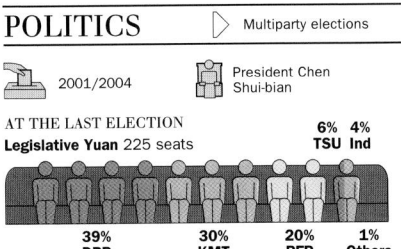

President Chen Shui-bian

AT THE LAST ELECTION

Legislative Yuan 225 seats

6% TSU
4% Ind
39% DPP
30% KMT
20% PFP
1% Others

DPP = Democratic Progressive Party **KMT** = National Party of China (Kuomintang) **PFP** = People First Party **TSU** = Taiwan Solidarity Union **Ind** = Independents

Taiwan has been a multiparty democracy since 1986, though electoral domination by the KMT only ended in 2000. The government is headed by the president, who is answerable to the National Assembly, a body which is convened only when matters of constitutional significance arise.

PROFILE

For nearly four decades from the establishment of the Republic of China government on Taiwan in 1949, Chiang Kai-shek's KMT monopolized political power and ruled by strict martial law. Gen. Chiang Ching-kuo, Chiang Kai-shek's son and successor, held the first free multiparty elections in 1986. Ten years later, Lee Teng-hui became the country's first directly elected president.

Though the KMT retained power in the 1998 legislative elections, winning an absolute majority of seats, its 50-year political monopoly came to an end with the 2000 presidential elections. The KMT candidate came a poor third, and Chen Shui-bian of the proindependence DPP took office. The KMT went on to lose support in the 2001 legislative elections, when the DPP became the largest party in the Yuan, though it did not achieve a majority.

Chen was shot and wounded during the 2004 presidential election campaign. In the disputed poll two days later, he won by less than 1% from KMT candidate Lien Chan, prompting a lengthy recount.

Chiang Kai-shek, who established the ROC in Taiwan in 1949.

Chen Shui-bian, the first non-KMT president since 1949.

TAIWAN

Total Area : 35 980 sq. km (13 892 sq. miles)

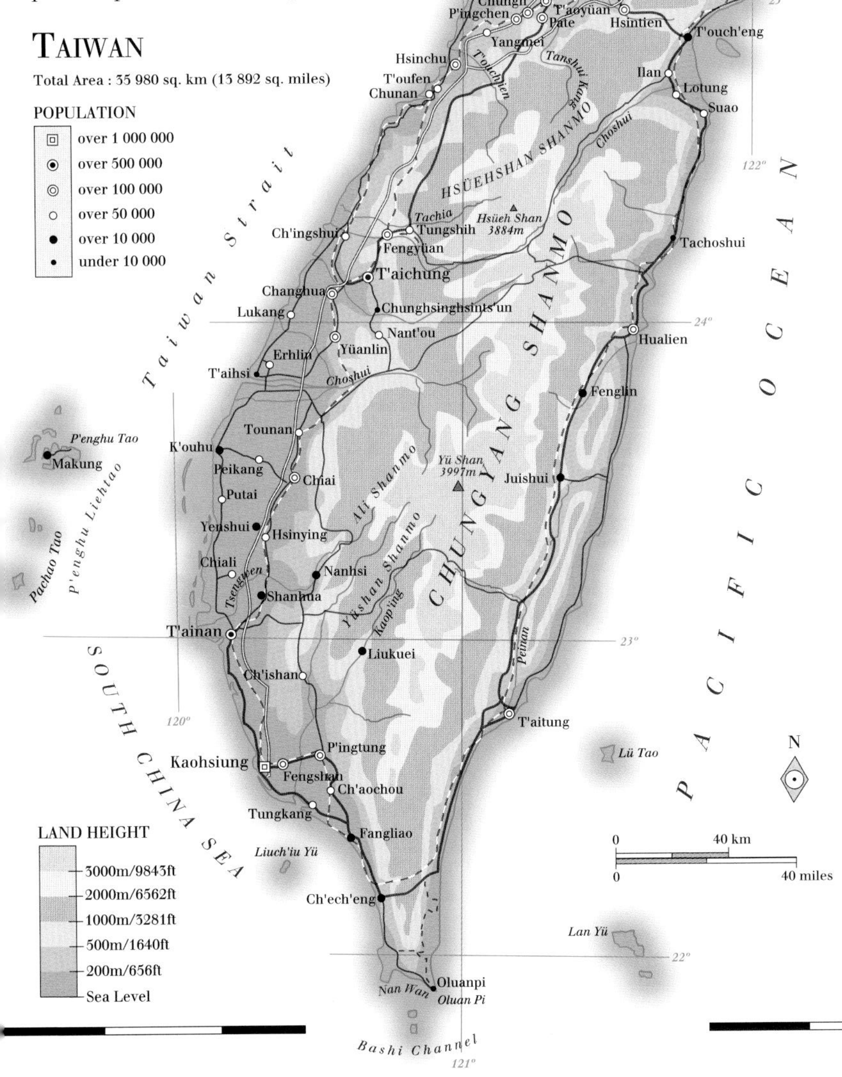

POPULATION
over 1 000 000
over 500 000
over 100 000
over 50 000
over 10 000
under 10 000
LAND HEIGHT
3000m/9843ft
2000m/6562ft
1000m/3281ft
500m/1640ft
200m/656ft
Sea Level
EAST CHINA SEA
Taiwan Strait
SOUTH CHINA SEA
PACIFIC OCEAN
Bashi Channel
T'AIPEI
Tanshui
Chilung
Sanch'ung
Hsinchuang
Chiang Kai Shek Intl
Chungho
Chungli
T'aoyüan
P'ingchen
Pate
Hsintien
T'ouch'eng
Yangmei
Hsinchu
T'oufen
Chunan
Ilan
Lotung
Suao
HSÜEHSHAN SHANMO
Hsüeh Shan 3884m
Tachia
Tungshih
Fengyüan
Ch'ingshui
T'aichung
Tachoshui
Changhua
Lukang
Chunghsinghsints'un
Nant'ou
Yüanlin
Erhlin
T'aihsi
Choshui
Hualien
Fenglin
P'enghu Tao
Makung
P'enghu Liehtao
Pachao Tao
Tounan
K'ouhu
Peikang
Chiai
Putai
Yü Shan 3997m
Juishui
Alishan Shanmo
Yenshui
Hsinying
Chiali
Nanhsi
Yüshan Shanmo
Shanhua
CHUNGYANG SHANMO
T'ainan
Liukuei
Ch'ishan
T'aitung
Kaohsiung
P'ingtung
Fengshan
Ch'aochou
Lü Tao
Tungkang
Fangliao
Liuch'iu Yü
Ch'ech'eng
Lan Yü
Oluanpi
Oluan Pi
Nan Wan
0 40 km
0 40 miles
N
25°
24°
23°
22°
120°
121°
122°

MAIN POLITICAL ISSUES

Relations with China

The DPP has advocated independence from China, despite Chinese threats of military action. Adopting a more prudent stance after his election victory, President Chen promised to make no independence declaration during his term of office. The KMT, officially committed to eventual reunification with China, now favors a more flexible arrangement that presupposes the recognition of a separate Taiwanese national identity.

Political stability

The eclipse of the KMT in elections in 2000 ended over 50 years of enforced stability. Taiwanese politics has had to come to terms with the idea of consensus politics, since the victory of Chen and the DPP was based as much on the divisions of the right as on the strength of their own popularity.

WORLD AFFAIRS

Not a UN member

APEC ADB WTO

Relations with China dominate. Reunification has long been the ultimate goal, though the idea of pursuing de facto independence has gained strength among younger Taiwanese; China insists on the "one country, two systems" approach pioneered in Hong Kong. Mention of Taiwanese statehood provokes a fierce reaction from Beijing, and military posturing on both sides is common. Both countries are acutely aware of their economic interdependence; Taiwan is a major foreign investor in China. Physical and economic links have been developed in recent years despite the rhetoric.

Taiwan lost its place at the UN to China in 1971. It is forced to conduct overseas relations via trade delegations. Aid plays a vital role in securing smaller states' support. There are strong bilateral ties with the US and Japan, and the US unofficially guarantees Taiwan's security.

AID

Donor

US$500m (donations) — Up in 2001

Taiwan has a large aid fund devoted to those states which have granted it diplomatic recognition. These include Pacific islands and countries in Africa, the Caribbean, and Central America. In return, aid recipients promote Taiwan's interests in the UN. Taiwan also receives a small amount of aid from Germany and France, and is granted international assistance in the aftermath of natural disasters.

DEFENSE

Compulsory military service

US$7.48bn — Down 5% in 2002

China remains the main defense threat, given the recurring tensions over the issue of independence or reunification. Taiwan has the tenth-largest navy in the world and a sizable army, in order to face a possible Chinese invasion: there are over 1.6 million reservists, but military service was reduced to 20 months from January 2004. The US is by far the largest supplier of arms and military hardware.

TAIWANESE ARMED FORCES

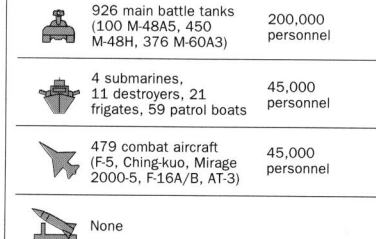

926 main battle tanks (100 M-48A5, 450 M-48H, 376 M-60A3)	200,000 personnel
4 submarines, 11 destroyers, 21 frigates, 59 patrol boats	45,000 personnel
479 combat aircraft (F-5, Ching-kuo, Mirage 2000-5, F-16A/B, AT-3)	45,000 personnel
None	

CHRONOLOGY

Following the 1949 communist revolution in China, Gen. Chiang Kai-shek's nationalist KMT party sought refuge in the island province of Taiwan. The KMT saw the revolution as illegal and itself as the sole rightful Chinese government.

- **1971** People's Republic of China replaces Taiwan at UN, including on UN Security Council.
- **1973** Taipei's KMT regime rejects Beijing's offer of secret talks on reunification of China.
- **1975** President Chiang Kai-shek dies. His son Gen. Chiang Ching-kuo becomes KMT leader. Yen Chia-kan succeeds as president.
- **1978** Chiang Ching-kuo elected president.
- **1979** US severs relations with Taiwan and formally recognizes People's Republic of China.
- **1984** President Chiang reelected.
- **1986** Political reforms: KMT allows multiparty democracy, ends martial law, and permits visits to Chinese mainland for "humanitarian" purposes for first time in 38 years. From 1988, mainland Chinese can visit Taiwan on same basis.
- **1988** Lee Teng-hui president.
- **1990** KMT formally ends state of war with People's Republic of China.
- **1991** DPP draft constitution for an independent Taiwan opposed by ruling KMT and Beijing. KMT reelected with large majority.
- **1995–1996** Legislative elections. KMT majority reduced.
- **1996** Lee Teng-hui wins first direct presidential elections.
- **1998** KMT secures absolute majority in elections to Legislative Yuan.
- **1999** Chinese threats over reference to "separate states" status. Thousands die in earthquake.
- **2000** Chen Shui-bian of DPP wins presidency; ends KMT dominance.
- **2001** Elections: DPP largest single party. Taiwan admitted to WTO.
- **2004** Chen narrowly reelected.

ECONOMICS

Inflation 5% p.a. (1985–1996)

US$287bn — 33.64 Taiwan dollars (34.61)

SCORE CARD

World GNP Ranking	17th
GNP per Capita	US$12,920
Balance of Payments	US$25.7bn
Inflation	–0.2%
Unemployment	5%

EXPORTS

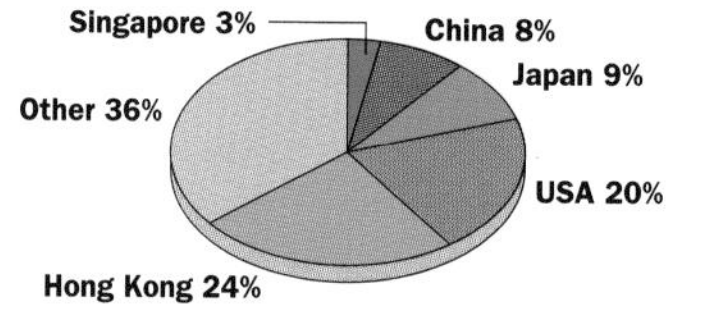

Singapore 3%
China 8%
Japan 9%
Other 36%
USA 20%
Hong Kong 24%

IMPORTS

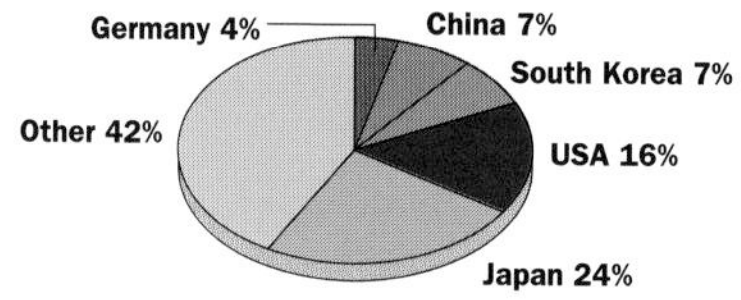

Germany 4%
China 7%
South Korea 7%
Other 42%
USA 16%
Japan 24%

ECONOMIC PERFORMANCE INDICATOR

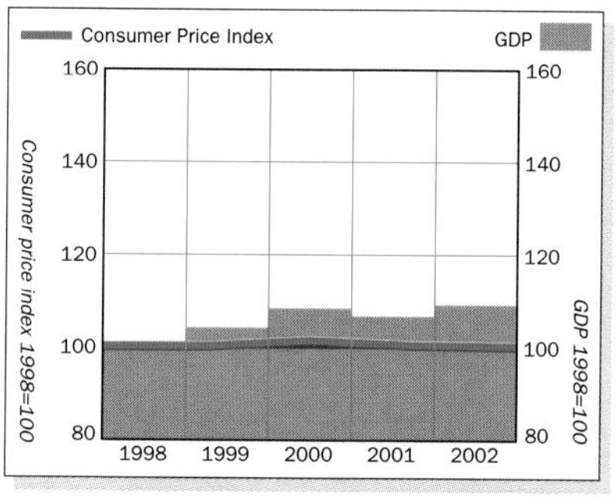

Consumer Price Index
GDP
160
140
120
100
80
Consumer price index 1998=100
GDP 1998=100
1998
1999
2000
2001
2002

Strengths
Highly educated and ambitious workforce, many US-trained and educated, with an inside knowledge of the US market. Manufacturing economy based on small companies which have proved extremely adaptable to changing market conditions. Track record of capturing major markets. Successively the world's biggest TV, watch, PC, and track shoe manufacturer. Economy in strong surplus, allowing it to invest in other Asian economies.

Weaknesses
Small economic units lack the muscle of Western multinationals, and are unable to follow predatory pricing policies. Weak research and development: economy has no tradition of generating new products or creating new markets. Unresponsive banking system.

Profile
Taiwan's economy has proved resilient. Double-digit growth ended with the Asian financial crisis of 1997–1998, but Taiwan emerged relatively unscathed, and global downturn caused only a brief recession in 2001. Competition from underdeveloped countries with low production costs is dictating a difficult transition toward service industries. This will entail moving from labor-intensive to capital- and technology-intensive industries. Comprehensive Six-Year Plans reflect a strong element of state direction. Heavy investment abroad includes over 60% of inward investment into China since 1990. Taiwan was admitted to the WTO, along with China, in 2001.

TAIWAN : MAJOR BUSINESSES

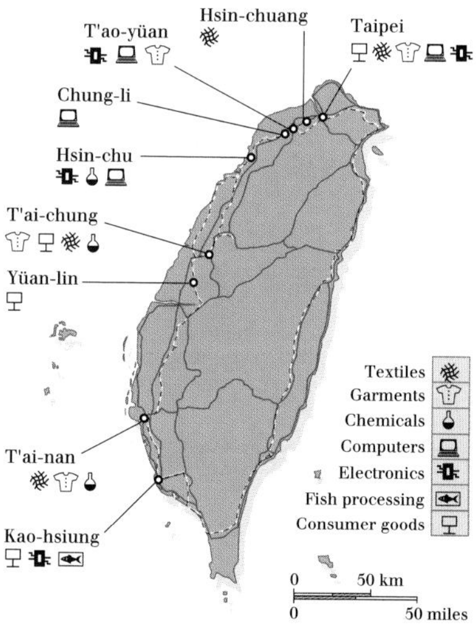

Hsin-chuang
T'ao-yüan
Taipei
Chung-li
Hsin-chu
T'ai-chung
Yüan-lin
T'ai-nan
Kao-hsiung
Textiles
Garments
Chemicals
Computers
Electronics
Fish processing
Consumer goods
0
50 km
0
50 miles

RESOURCES

Not available

1.29m tonnes

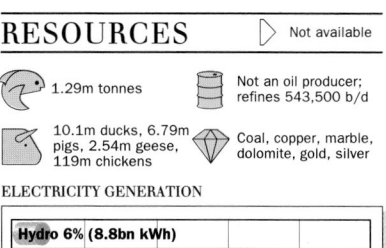

Not an oil producer; refines 543,500 b/d

10.1m ducks, 6.79m pigs, 2.54m geese, 119m chickens

Coal, copper, marble, dolomite, gold, silver

ELECTRICITY GENERATION

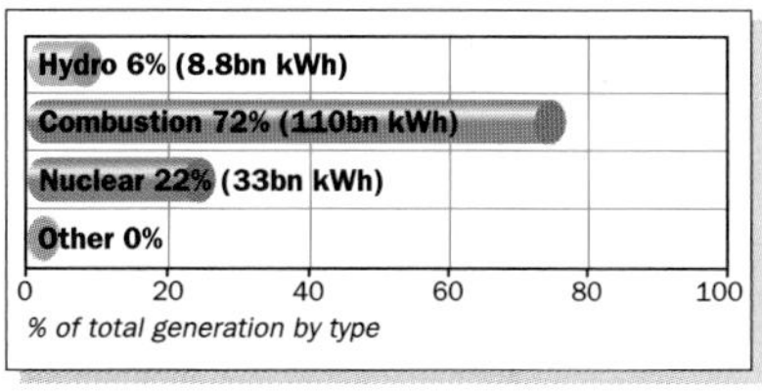
Hydro 6% (8.8bn kWh)
Combustion 72% (110bn kWh)
Nuclear 22% (33bn kWh)
Other 0%
0
20
40
60
80
100
% of total generation by type

Taiwan has few strategic resources and its minerals industry is not a major foreign exchange earner. Oil is imported. Taiwan is a major buyer of South African uranium, but proposals to increase reliance on nuclear power have met strong opposition on safety and waste disposal grounds. Combustion, however, is a controversial option, and hydroelectric power has already been largely exploited.

Fishing is an extremely successful sector of the economy, and Taiwan is a major supplier to the huge Japanese market. The fleet is often accused of plundering Atlantic stocks.

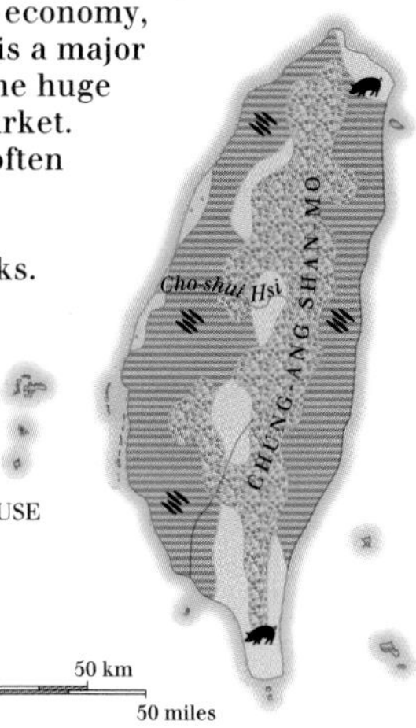
Cho-shui Hsi
CHUNG-YANG SHAN-MO
0
50 km
0
50 miles

TAIWAN : LAND USE

- Cropland
- Forest
- Pasture
- Wetlands
- Pigs
- Rice

ENVIRONMENT

Not available

11%

9.8 tonnes per capita

ENVIRONMENTAL TREATIES

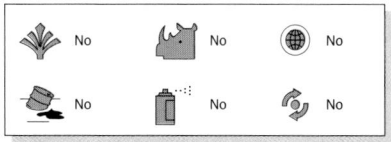

No · No · No
No · No · No

The dash for growth meant the absence of city planning or pollution laws. There is growing opposition to a fourth nuclear power plant, set for completion in 2006, and concern over coal-fired thermal power. Taiwan's fishing industry has been criticized for using longline techniques which trap dolphins, and for plundering other countries' fishing grounds without regard to stock levels.

MEDIA

TV ownership high

Daily newspaper circulation figures not available

PUBLISHING AND BROADCAST MEDIA

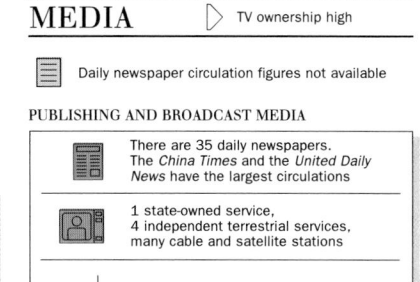

There are 35 daily newspapers. The *China Times* and the *United Daily News* have the largest circulations

1 state-owned service, 4 independent terrestrial services, many cable and satellite stations

1 state-owned service, many independent stations

The rigid state control which used to exist over the media has been relaxed. Opposition parties now have access to the state media. Before the 1990s, print with simplified Chinese characters was banned, thus excluding all publications from the mainland. Taiwan has a large domestic TV and film industry.

CRIME

Death penalty in use

56,225 prisoners

Little change from year to year

CRIME RATES

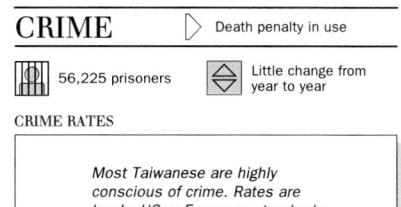

Most Taiwanese are highly conscious of crime. Rates are low by US or European standards.

Since the end of martial law in 1986, most political prisoners have been released. Taiwan does not suffer from organized crime to the extent found in Hong Kong or Japan. Multimedia pirating is a seroius problem.

EDUCATION

School leaving age: 15

96%

1.24m students

THE EDUCATION SYSTEM

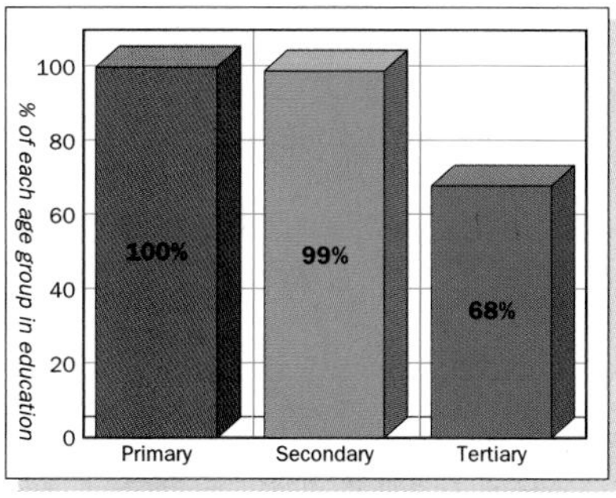
100
80
60
40
20
0
% of each age group in education
100%
99%
68%
Primary
Secondary
Tertiary

Since 2000, government funding has given less priority to higher education and more to reforming and improving the antiquated school system, which is rigid and heavily exam-oriented. Free schooling is available from the age of six to 15 and there are also a number of private schools.

Enrollment levels at tertiary and vocational institutions are among the highest in the world.

HEALTH

No welfare state health benefits

1 per 714 people

Cerebrovascular and heart diseases, hypertension

Most health provision in Taiwan is in the private sector. Taiwanese take out elaborate health insurance schemes and it is essential to prove cover before treatment is provided. Health facilities are on a par with the best in the world, and the Taiwanese enjoy a high life expectancy, similar to that in the US. The incidence of AIDS is low, but the rate of new infections is increasing. The 2003 outbreak of acute pneumonia (SARS) affected over 350 Taiwanese, killing more than 50 people.

SPENDING

GDP/cap. increase

CONSUMPTION AND SPENDING

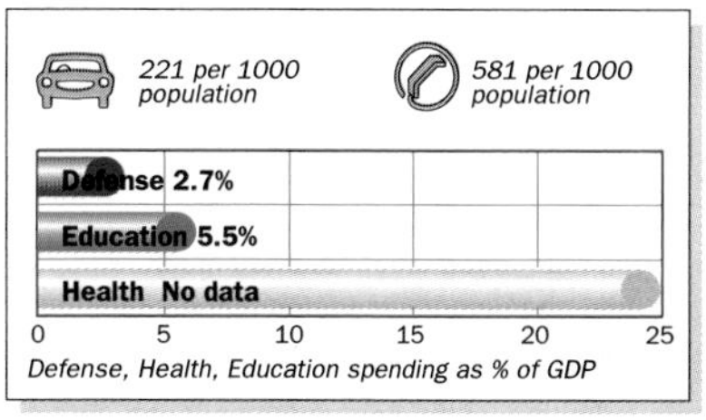
221 per 1000 population
581 per 1000 population
Defense 2.7%
Education 5.5%
Health No data
0
5
10
15
20
25
Defense, Health, Education spending as % of GDP

Export-led growth over a long period enabled Taiwan to build up large cash reserves. The Taiwanese people share much of the benefit of this success, and average living standards are among the highest in Asia. Inequalities of income distribution are comparatively small, and a high degree of social cohesion has been achieved. In part, this is the result of the land reforms of the 1950s, which gave agricultural workers control of the land while compensating landowners and encouraging them to set up in business in the cities. Today, the great majority of Taiwanese would describe themselves as middle class. Consumer goods are widely available, and conspicuous consumption is celebrated.

WORLD RANKING

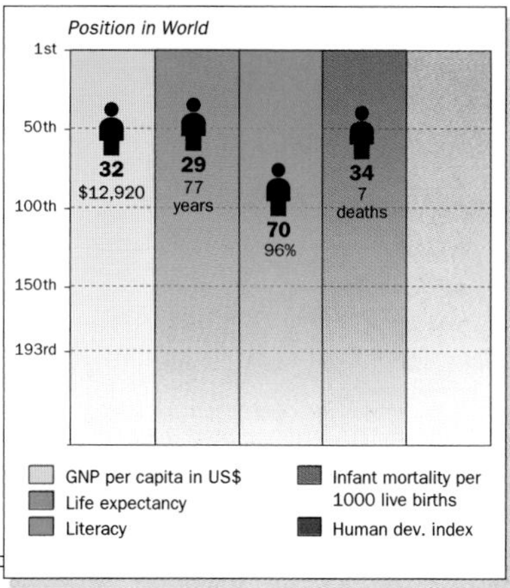
Position in World
1st
50th
100th
150th
193rd
32
$12,920
29
77
years
70
96%
34
7
deaths
GNP per capita in US$
Life expectancy
Literacy
Infant mortality per 1000 live births
Human dev. index

T

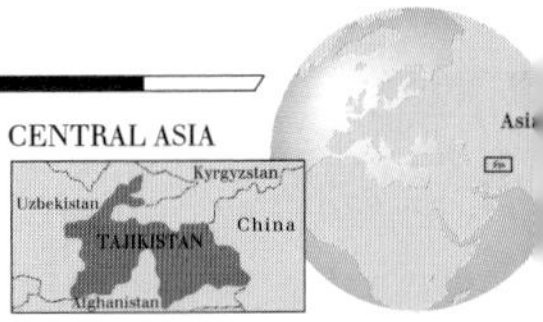

CENTRAL ASIA
Kyrgyzstan
Uzbekistan
TAJIKISTAN
China
Afghanistan
Asia

TAJIKISTAN

OFFICIAL NAME: Republic of Tajikistan **CAPITAL:** Dushanbe
POPULATION: 6.2 million **CURRENCY:** Somoni **OFFICIAL LANGUAGE:** Tajik

1991 | 1991 | Sept 9 | TJ | +5 | +992 | .tj

TAJIKISTAN LIES ON the western slopes of the Pamirs in central Asia. Language and traditions are similar to those of Iran rather than those of its northern Turkic neighbors. Tajikistan decided on independence only when neighboring Soviet republics declared theirs in late 1991. Fighting between communist government forces and Islamist rebels, which erupted shortly afterward, has been contained since 1997 by a fragile peace agreement.

A herd of goats in the Varzob Gorge, north of Dushanbe. Livestock drives the rural economy.

CLIMATE

Mountain

WEATHER CHART FOR DUSHANBE

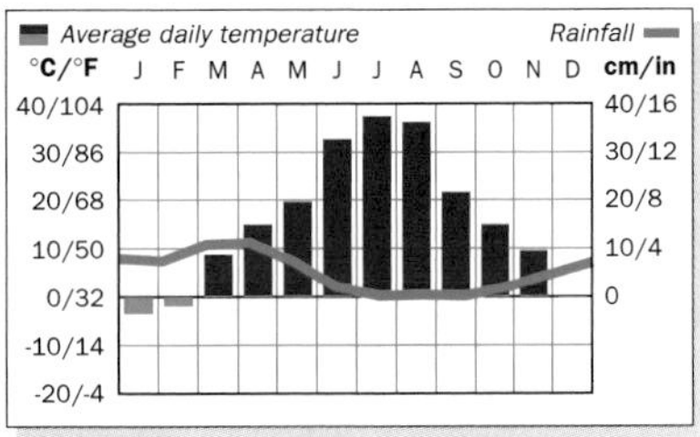

Average daily temperature
Rainfall
°C/°F
J F M A M J J A S O N D
cm/in
40/104
30/86
20/68
10/50
0/32
-10/14
-20/-4
40/16
30/12
20/8
10/4
0

Rainfall is low in the valleys. Winter temperatures can fall below –45°C (–49°F) in mountainous areas.

TRANSPORTATION

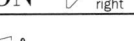

Drive on right

Dushanbe | Has no fleet

THE TRANSPORTATION NETWORK

11,288 km (7014 miles)	None
617 km (383 miles)	200 km (124 miles)

Tajikistan has good cross-border roads and well-maintained airfields, the result of its use by Soviet and US forces during conflicts in neighboring Afghanistan. The best way to reach the mountainous interior is by air.

TOURISM

Visitors : Population 1:1550

4000 visitors | Down 99% in 1999–2001

MAIN TOURIST ARRIVALS

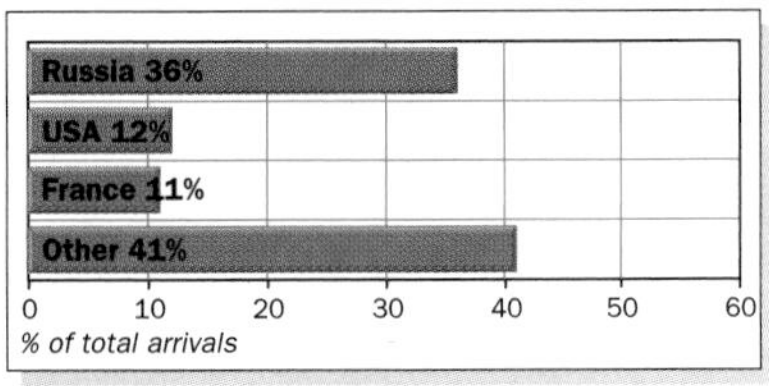

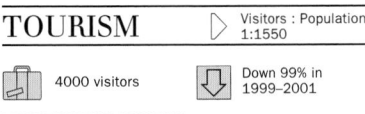

Russia 36%
USA 12%
France 11%
Other 41%
0
10
20
30
40
50
60
% of total arrivals

Tourism is virtually nonexistent, and poverty and a history of instability make it unlikely to be developed soon.

PEOPLE

Pop. density low

Tajik, Uzbek, Russian | 43/km² (112/mi²)

THE URBAN/RURAL POPULATION SPLIT

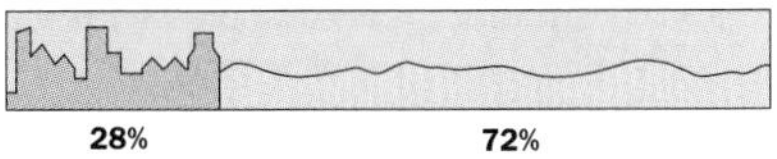

28%
72%

RELIGIOUS PERSUASION

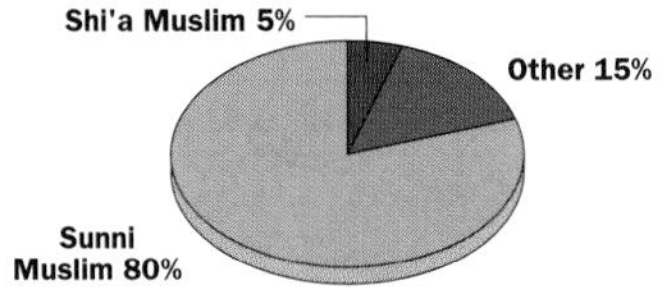

Shi'a Muslim 5%
Other 15%
Sunni Muslim 80%

Unlike the other former Soviet -stans, Tajikistan is dominated by a people of Persian (Iranian), rather than Turkic, origin; ethnic Tajiks make up around 65% of the population. Uzbeks constitute the second-largest group – around 25%. Tajikistan's brutal, clan-based civil war (1992–1997) had a devastating effect on the country's demographics. In addition to claiming approximately 60,000 lives, the war displaced more than half a million Tajiks, and prompted two-thirds of the 600,000 ethnic Russians to leave the country. Another 60,000 Tajiks fled to neighboring Afghanistan.

POLITICS

Multiparty elections

L. House 2000/2005
U. House 2000/2005

President Imomali Rakhmanov

AT THE LAST ELECTION

Assembly of Representatives 63 seats

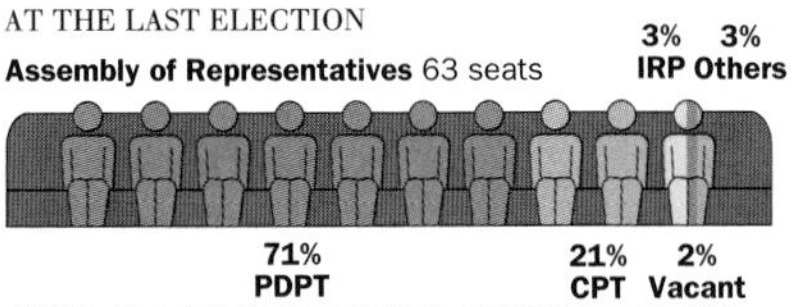

3% IRP
3% Others
71% PDPT
21% CPT
2% Vacant

PDPT = People's Democratic Party of Tajikistan and allies
CPT = Communist Party of Tajikistan
IRP = Islamic Revival Party

National Assembly 33 seats

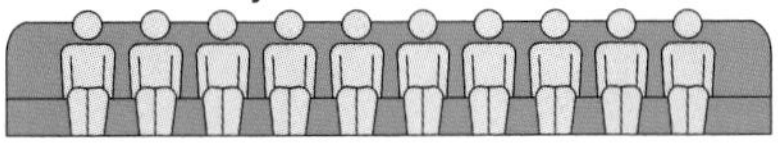

Five deputies are elected by each regional assembly, and a further eight deputies are appointed by the president

Peace has consolidated the regime of former communists led by President Rakhmanov. Under the 1997 peace accord the Islamist United Tajik Opposition (UTO) joined the government in 1998. The pro-Rakhmanov PDPT headed polls in 2000, claiming some support from former UTO members. Rakhmanov has been accused by human rights groups of using the international "war on terrorism" to crack down on political opponents. In 2003 a referendum endorsed two possible further terms for him.

TAJIKISTAN

Total Area : 143 100 sq. km (55 251 sq. miles)

POPULATION

- over 500 000
- over 100 000
- over 50 000
- over 10 000
- under 10 000

LAND HEIGHT

- 4000m/13 124ft
- 3000m/9843ft
- 2000m/6562ft
- 1000m/3281ft
- 500m/1640ft
- 200m/656ft

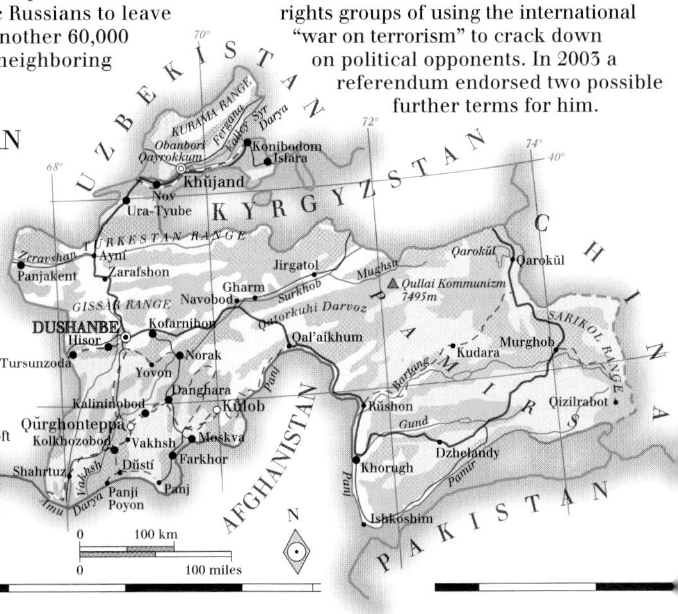

UZBEKISTAN
KYRGYZSTAN
CHINA
AFGHANISTAN
PAKISTAN
KURAMA RANGE
Fergana Valley
Syr Darya
Obanbori Qayrokkum
Konibodom
Isfara
Khŭjand
Nov
Ura-Tyube
TURKESTAN RANGE
Zeravshan
Ayni
Panjakent
Zarafshon
Jirgatol
Qarokŭl
Qarokŭl
Mughsu
Qullai Kommunizm 7495m
Surkhob
GISSAR RANGE
Navobod
Gharm
Qatorkuhi Darvoz
DUSHANBE
Hisor
Kofarnihon
Qal'aikhum
Tursunzoda
Norak
Yovon
Danghara
Kŭlob
Kalininobod
Qŭrghonteppa
Kolkhozobod
Vakhsh
Moskva
Farkhor
Shahrtuz
Dŭsti
Panji Poyon
Panj
Amu Darya
Bartang
PAMIRS
Kudara
Murghob
SARIKOL RANGE
Rŭshon
Qizilrabot
Gund
Khorugh
Dzhelandy
Pamir
Ishkoshim
Panj
0 100 km
0 100 miles
N
68°
70°
72°
74°
40°

WORLD AFFAIRS

Joined UN in 1992

CIS | SCO | PfP | OIC | OSCE

The introduction in 1995 of its own currency enabled Tajikistan to wrest economic control from Russia, though it remains heavily dependent on its former master, particularly for economic and military assistance. A joint operation with Uzbekistan and Kyrgyzstan was launched in 2000 to combat the Islamic Movement of Uzbekistan, based in northern Tajikistan. Tajik airfields were crucial during the US-led action in Afghanistan in 2001, and in 2002 Tajikistan became the last of the former Soviet Union countries to join NATO's Partnership for Peace program.

AID

Recipient

$168m (receipts) — Down 1% in 2002

The US, the World Bank, and the EU are the main donors. Aid worth $900 million over three years was pledged in 2003.

DEFENSE

Compulsory military service

$123m — Down 2% in 2002

The army numbers only about 6000. Around 12,000 Russian border guards patrol the Afghan border, while a further 7800 Russian soldiers are stationed in Tajikistan. The civil war left almost 20,000 landmines across the country.

ECONOMICS

Inflation 202% p.a. (1990–2001)

$1.12bn — 3.01 somoni (2.7804)

SCORE CARD

- World GNP Ranking 152nd
- GNP per Capita $180
- Balance of Payments ....–$66m
- Inflation 21.6%
- Unemployment 40%

Strengths

Few. Uranium. Overseas remittances. Hydroelectric potential. Carpet making. International donors' favorable attitude.

Weaknesses

Formal economy precarious; dependence on barter economy. No central planning. Little diversification in agriculture; only 6% of land is arable. Exodus of skilled Russians. High levels of inflation and poverty. Production in all sectors in decline.

EXPORTS

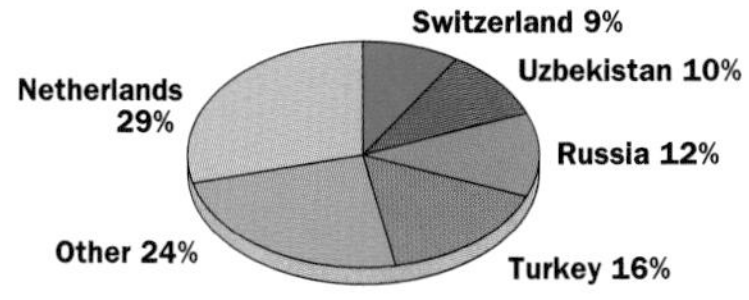
Switzerland 9%
Uzbekistan 10%
Netherlands 29%
Russia 12%
Other 24%
Turkey 16%

IMPORTS

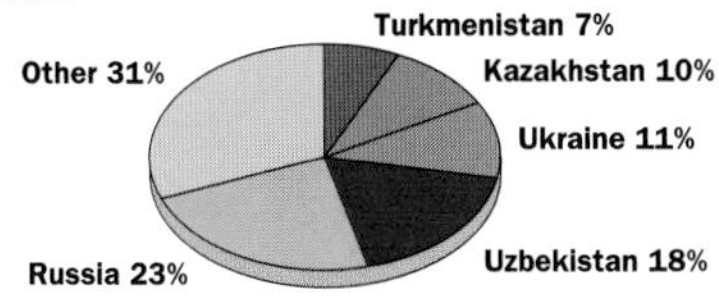
Turkmenistan 7%
Other 31%
Kazakhstan 10%
Ukraine 11%
Uzbekistan 18%
Russia 23%

RESOURCES

Electric power 4.4m kW

236 tonnes — 361 b/d (reserves 15m barrels)

1.59m sheep, 1.14m cattle, 1.54m chickens — Uranium, gold, iron, coal, lead, mercury, tin, oil

Tajikistan has one key resource – uranium – which accounted for 30% of the USSR's total production before 1990. The end of the nuclear arms race has reduced its value, however. Most of Tajikistan is bare mountain, and just 6% of the land can be used for agriculture. Industry is concentrated in the Fergana Valley, close to the Uzbek border.

ENVIRONMENT

Sustainability rank: 110th

4% (3.5% partially protected) — 0.6 tonnes per capita

Landslides, particularly on the lower slopes of the Pamirs, are a serious problem. They are caused as much by the natural geography and by earthquakes as by human activity.

MEDIA

TV ownership high

Daily newspaper circulation 20 per 1000 people

PUBLISHING AND BROADCAST MEDIA

Weekly newspapers dominate. *Kurer Tajikistana* and the Russian-language *Biznes i Politika* have the highest circulations

5 services: 2 state-controlled, 3 independent — 3 state-controlled services

The underdeveloped media are prone to self-censorship and progovernment reporting. Foreign broadcasts may not be retransmitted.

CRIME

Moratorium on death penalty

10,000 prisoners — Down 3% in 1997

Only remote areas escape the violence perpetrated by armed gangs. Narcotics smuggling along the border with Afghanistan is a key international issue.

EDUCATION

School leaving age: 16

99% — 84,400 students

Russian was made compulsory in schools again from 2003. English lessons are also compulsory.

CHRONOLOGY

In the 19th century, Tajikistan was a collection of semi-independent principalities, some under Russian control, others under the influence of the Emirate of Bukhara.

- **1925** Soviets take over Tajikistan.
- **1940** Cyrillic script introduced.
- **1989** Tajik becomes official language.
- **1991** Independence from Moscow.
- **1992** Islamists capture Dushanbe. Imomali Rakhmanov president.
- **1995** Tajik rouble introduced; replaced by somoni in 2000.
- **1997–1998** Peace accord with rebels; UTO joins government.
- **2000** Pro-Rakhmanov PDPT wins legislative elections.

HEALTH

Welfare state health benefits

1 per 476 people — Heart, respiratory, and infectious diseases, atherosclerosis

For years, medical services have had to be paid for, and in 2003 the nominal free health care system was finally abolished amid a package of reforms.

SPENDING

GDP/cap. decrease

CONSUMPTION AND SPENDING

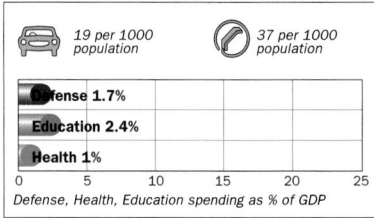

19 per 1000 population — *37 per 1000 population*

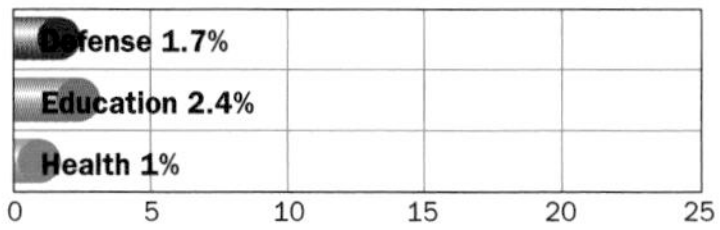
Defense 1.7%
Education 2.4%
Health 1%
0
5
10
15
20
25

Defense, Health, Education spending as % of GDP

Over half of the population of Tajikistan lives below the UN poverty line; the war against the Islamist rebels worsened conditions. The former communist bureaucrats continue to be the wealthiest group.

WORLD RANKING

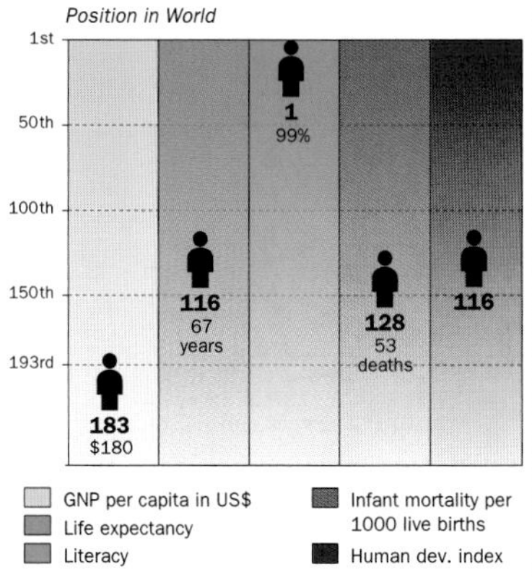
Position in World
1st
50th
100th
150th
193rd
183
$180
116
67
years
1
99%
128
53
deaths
116
GNP per capita in US$
Life expectancy
Literacy
Infant mortality per 1000 live births
Human dev. index

T

TANZANIA

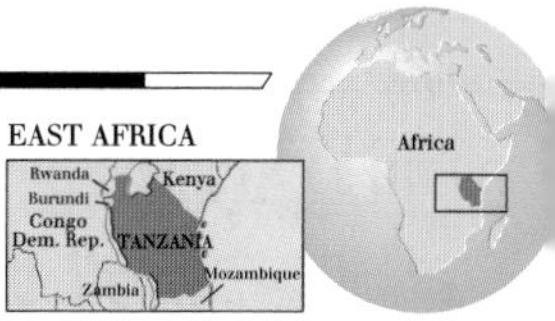

EAST AFRICA
Africa
Rwanda
Burundi
Kenya
Congo
Dem. Rep.
TANZANIA
Zambia
Mozambique

OFFICIAL NAME: United Republic of Tanzania **CAPITAL:** Dodoma
POPULATION: 37 million **CURRENCY:** Tanzanian shilling **OFFICIAL LANGUAGES:** English and Kiswahili

1964 | 1964 | April 26 | EAT | +3 | +255 | .tz

TANZANIA LIES BETWEEN Kenya and Mozambique on the east African coast. Formed by the union of Tanganyika and the Zanzibar islands, Tanzania comprises a coastal lowland, volcanic highlands, and the Great Rift Valley. It includes Mount Kilimanjaro, Africa's highest peak. Tanzania was led by the socialist Julius Nyerere from 1962 until 1985. His Revolutionary Party of Tanzania (CCM) has won multiparty elections held in 1995 and 2000.

Arusha National Park. *Lying within the Ngurdoto volcanic crater, the park has herds of buffalo, rhino, elephant, and giraffe.*

CLIMATE

Tropical/mountain

WEATHER CHART FOR DODOMA

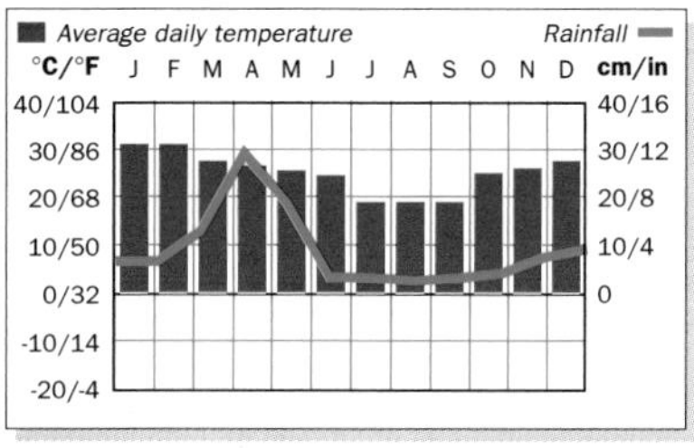

Average daily temperature
Rainfall
°C/°F
J F M A M J J A S O N D
cm/in
40/104
30/86
20/68
10/50
0/32
-10/14
-20/-4
40/16
30/12
20/8
10/4
0

The coast and Zanzibar are tropical. The central plateau is semiarid and the highlands are semitemperate.

TRANSPORTATION

Drive on left

Dar es Salaam International 816,263 passengers

58 ships 47,100 grt

THE TRANSPORTATION NETWORK

3528 km (2192 miles)

None

4460 km (2771 miles)

Lakes Tanganyika, Victoria, and Nyasa are navigable

The port of Dar es Salaam handles 75% of Tanzania's trade and has good road and rail links. A fourth international airport is being built at Mwanza.

TOURISM

Visitors : Population 1:67

552,120 visitors

Up 3% in 2003

MAIN TOURIST ARRIVALS

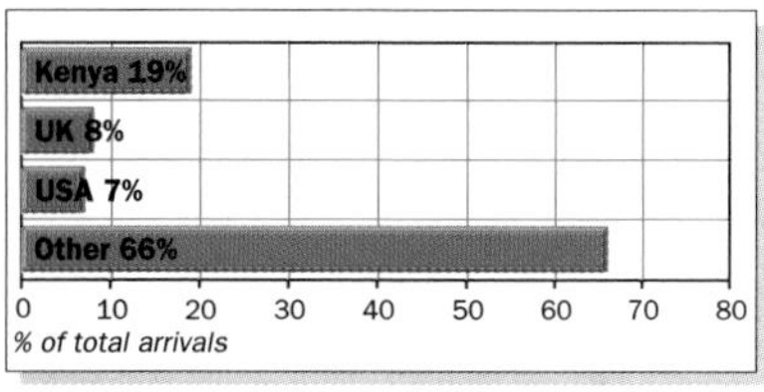

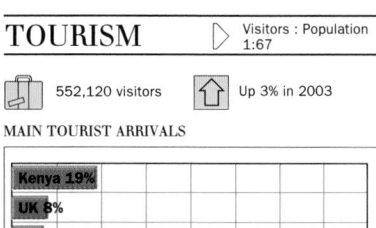

Kenya 19%
UK 8%
USA 7%
Other 66%
0
10
20
30
40
50
60
70
80
% of total arrivals

One-third of Tanzania is national park or game reserve. The Ngorongoro Crater and the Serengeti Plain are top attractions. Tourist numbers increased dramatically in the 1990s.

PEOPLE

Pop. density low

Kiswahili, Sukuma, Chagga, Nyamwezi, Hehe, Makonde, Yao, Sandawe, English

42/km² (108/mi²)

THE URBAN/RURAL POPULATION SPLIT

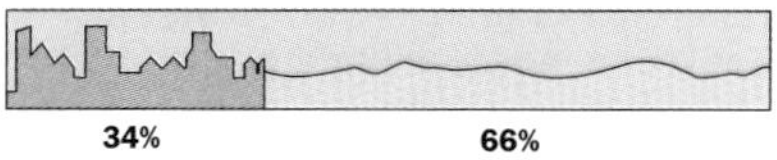

34%
66%

RELIGIOUS PERSUASION

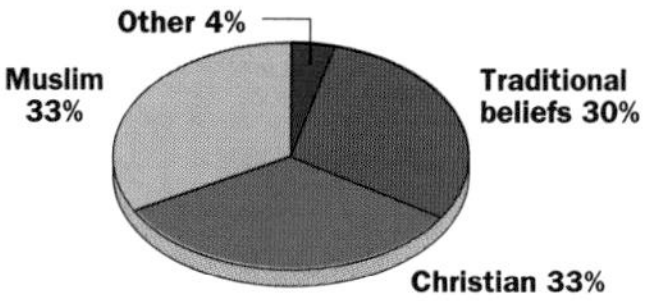

Other 4%
Muslim 33%
Traditional beliefs 30%
Christian 33%

For many Tanzanians the family is the focus of traditional rural life. About 99% belong to one of 120 small ethnic Bantu groups. The remainder comprise Arab, Asian, and European minorities. The use of Kiswahili as a *lingua franca* has helped make ethnic rivalries almost nonexistent.

POLITICS

Multiparty elections

2000/2005

President Benjamin Mkapa

AT THE LAST ELECTION

National Assembly 296 seats

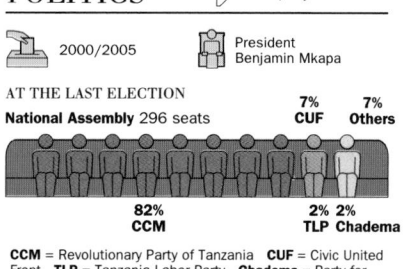

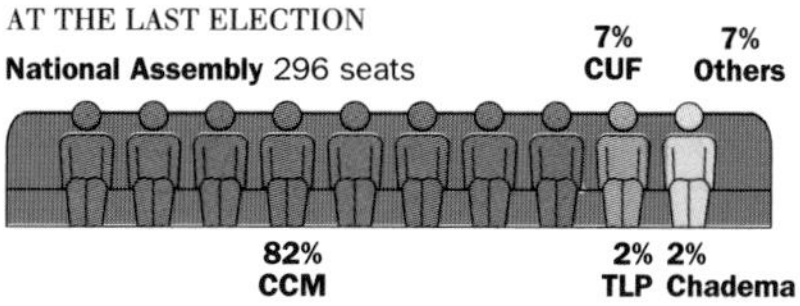

7% CUF
7% Others
82% CCM
2% 2% TLP Chadema

CCM = Revolutionary Party of Tanzania **CUF** = Civic United Front **TLP** = Tanzania Labor Party **Chadema** = Party for Democracy and Progress
Others include five members chosen by the Zanzibar House of Representatives, ten appointed by the president, and the attorney general who has a seat ex officio

Julius Nyerere was the dominant force in Tanzanian politics for over two decades. He founded the ruling party, the CCM, and his philosophy of African socialism guided Tanzania's development. Ali Hassan Mwinyi succeeded Nyerere as president in 1985, introducing a transition to multiparty democracy. Mwinyi stood down in 1995, and Benjamin Mkapa was elected president. Separatism in Zanzibar is a key issue; there were violent protests in 2001, and disaffection remains.

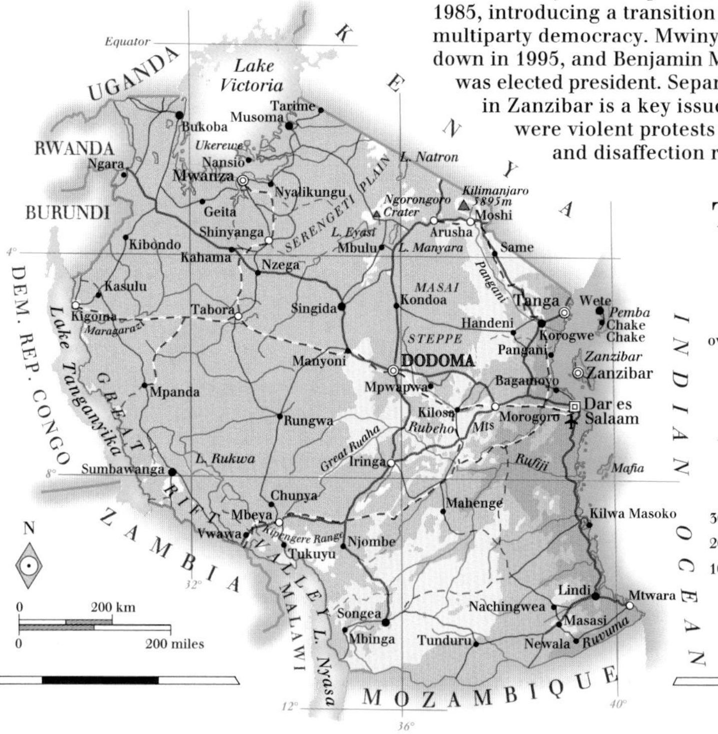

Equator
UGANDA
Lake Victoria
KENYA
RWANDA
BURUNDI
DEM. REP. CONGO
Lake Tanganyika
GREAT RIFT VALLEY
ZAMBIA
MALAWI
L. Nyasa
MOZAMBIQUE
INDIAN OCEAN
Bukoba
Musoma
Tarime
Ukerewe
Nansio
Ngara
Mwanza
Nyalikungu
SERENGETI PLAIN
L. Natron
Ngorongoro Crater
Kilimanjaro 5895m
Moshi
Arusha
Geita
Shinyanga
L. Eyasi
Mbulu
L. Manyara
Same
Kibondo
Kahama
Nzega
Pangani
Kasulu
MASAI STEPPE
Kondoa
Tanga
Wete
Pemba
Chake Chake
Kigoma
Maragarazi
Tabora
Singida
Handeni
Korogwe
Pangani
Zanzibar
Manyoni
DODOMA
Mpwapwa
Bagamoyo
Mpanda
Kilosa
Rubeho Mts
Morogoro
Dar es Salaam
Rungwa
Great Ruaha
Iringa
Rufiji
Mafia
L. Rukwa
Sumbawanga
Chunya
Mahenge
Kilwa Masoko
Mbeya
Vwawa
Kipengere Range
Tukuyu
Njombe
Lindi
Mtwara
Nachingwea
Songea
Masasi
Mbinga
Tunduru
Newala
Ruvuma
N
0 200 km
0 200 miles

TANZANIA
Total Area: 945 087 sq. km (364 898 sq. miles)

POPULATION
over 1 000 000
over 100 000
over 50 000
over 10 000
under 10 000

LAND HEIGHT
3000m/9843ft
2000m/6562ft
1000m/3281ft
500m/1640ft
200m/656ft
Sea Level

T

WORLD AFFAIRS

Joined UN in 1961

Comm ACP EAC AU SADC

The instability of Tanzania's central African neighbors is a concern. Over half a million Rwandan and Burundian refugees arrived in the 1990s. By 2001, official numbers were almost unchanged; unofficial estimates added at least 300,000. Improved relations with Uganda and Kenya led to the rebirth in 2001 of the East African Community.

AID

Recipient

$1.23bn (receipts) Down 3% in 2002

Tanzania is heavily dependent on aid to help offset a severe balance-of-payments deficit. The UK is the largest donor; 75% of its contribution goes directly into the government budget. Most aid is now linked to an IMF-backed economic reform program.

DEFENSE

Compulsory military service

$127m Down 9% in 2002

The Tanzanian armed forces, which number 27,000, are closely linked with the ruling CCM. There is an 80,000-strong citizens' reserve force.

ECONOMICS

Inflation 20% p.a. (1990–2001)

$9.67bn 1109 Tanzanian shillings (1039)

SCORE CARD

- ❑ World GNP Ranking 87th
- ❑ GNP per capita $290
- ❑ Balance of payments .... –$251m
- ❑ Inflation 4.6%
- ❑ Unemployment .... Not available

Strengths

Coffee, cotton, sisal, tea, cashew nuts. Zanzibar a major producer of cloves. Diamonds, gold. State commitment to effective reforms. Expansion in nontraditional exports. Rise in inward investment. Return to positive growth.

Weaknesses

Growth still too low to increase per capita income. Shortage of foreign exchange. Poor credit and equipment limit agricultural development.

EXPORTS

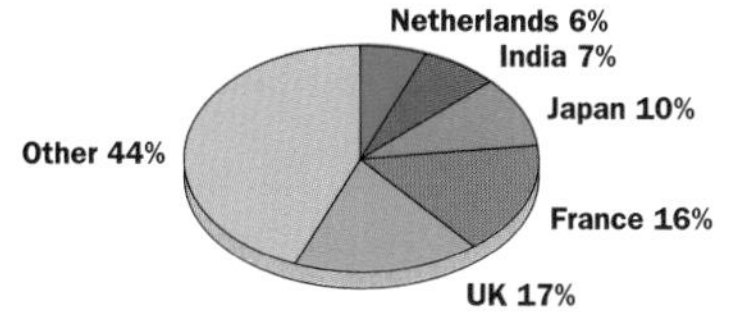

Netherlands 6%
India 7%
Japan 10%
Other 44%
France 16%
UK 17%

IMPORTS

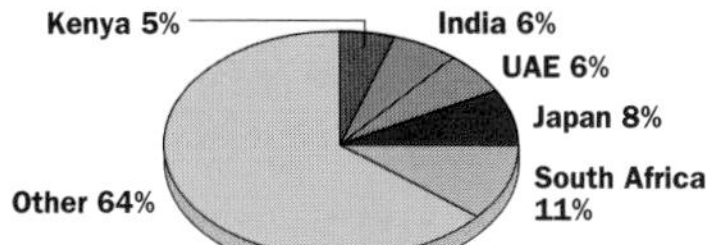

Kenya 5%
India 6%
UAE 6%
Japan 8%
Other 64%
South Africa 11%

RESOURCES

Electric power 543,000 kW

336,200 tonnes

Oil reserves not yet exploited; refines 9600 b/d

17.7m cattle, 12.6m goats, 3.52m sheep, 30m chickens

Natural gas, oil, iron, diamonds, gold, salt, phosphates, coal

Agriculture accounts for almost half of GDP and 80% of employment. Forests cover 50% of Tanzania; wood and charcoal meet over 90% of fuel demand. Hydropower provides 84% of electricity, but droughts have led to blackouts. Oil imports take 40% of export earnings, but offshore gas is being exploited; oil has been found off Pemba Island. The opening of a gold mine near Mwanza makes Tanzania Africa's fourth-largest gold producer.

ENVIRONMENT

Sustainability rank: 80th

30% (24% partially protected) 0.1 tonnes per capita

The demand for fuelwood is a threat to forests. Tourism's demands have to be carefully balanced with those of fragile wildlife environments such as the Ngorongoro Crater and the Serengeti.

MEDIA

TV ownership low

Daily newspaper circulation 4 per 1000 people

PUBLISHING AND BROADCAST MEDIA

There are 12 daily newspapers, including the *Daily News*, *Uhuru*, and *Kipanga*

5 services: 2 state-owned, 3 independent

3 state-owned services, many independent stations

The media have grown rapidly since the launch of the first TV station in 1994. Zanzibar is less liberal.

CRIME

Death penalty in use

44,063 prisoners Down 4% in 2000

Crime levels are low, though theft in Dar es Salaam has risen. Tanzania's human rights record is good.

EDUCATION

School leaving age: 14

77% 21,960 students

Primary education, which begins at seven and lasts for seven years, is free; secondary students pay fees. Enrollment is 63% at primary level, but only 6% for secondary education.

CHRONOLOGY

The mainland became the German colony of Tanganyika in 1884. The Sultanate of Zanzibar became a British protectorate in 1890.

- ❑ **1918** Tanganyika under British mandate after World War I.
- ❑ **1961** Tanganyika independent.
- ❑ **1962** Nyerere becomes president.
- ❑ **1963** Zanzibar independent.
- ❑ **1964** Zanzibar signs union with Tanganyika to form Tanzania.
- ❑ **1985** President Mwinyi begins relaxation of socialist policies.
- ❑ **1992** Political parties allowed.
- ❑ **1995** Multiparty elections. Benjamin Mkapa becomes president.
- ❑ **1999** Death of Nyerere.
- ❑ **2000** Mkapa reelected.
- ❑ **2001** Increasing unrest among Zanzibari separatists.

HEALTH

Welfare state health benefits

1 per 25,000 people

Diarrheal and respiratory diseases, malaria, AIDS

An immunization program for under-twos was introduced in 2001. There is a national campaign against HIV/AIDS, which affects 8.8% of adults.

SPENDING

GDP/cap. increase

CONSUMPTION AND SPENDING

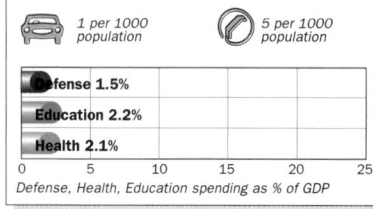

1 per 1000 population *5 per 1000 population*

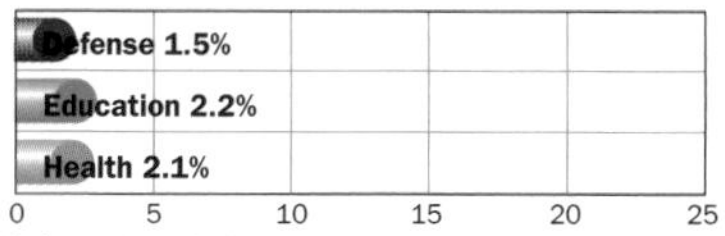

Defense 1.5%
Education 2.2%
Health 2.1%
0 5 10 15 20 25

Defense, Health, Education spending as % of GDP

The majority of Tanzanians are subsistence farmers. The small wealthy elite is composed mainly of Asian and Arab business families.

WORLD RANKING

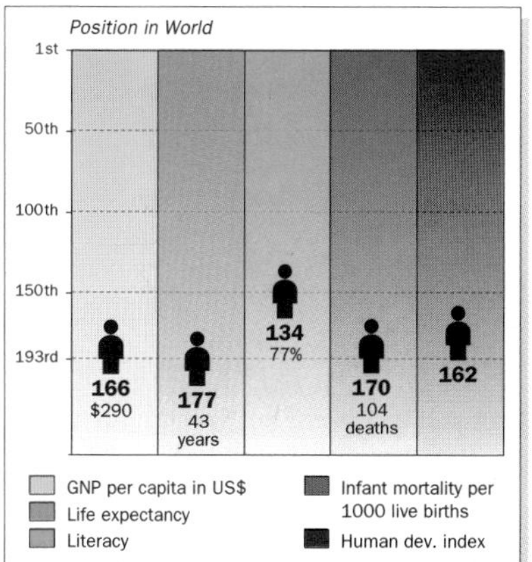

Position in World
1st
50th
100th
150th
193rd
166
$290
177
43 years
134
77%
170
104 deaths
162
GNP per capita in US$
Life expectancy
Literacy
Infant mortality per 1000 live births
Human dev. index

T

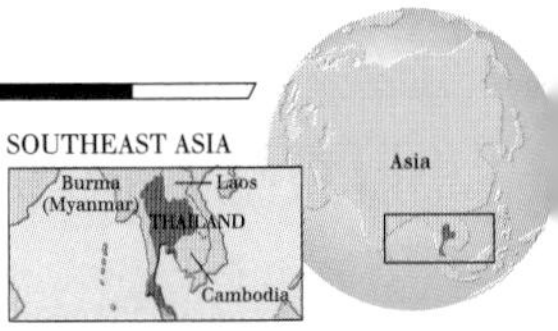
SOUTHEAST ASIA
Burma (Myanmar)
Laos
THAILAND
Cambodia
Asia

THAILAND

OFFICIAL NAME: Kingdom of Thailand **CAPITAL:** Bangkok
POPULATION: 62.8 million **CURRENCY:** Baht **OFFICIAL LANGUAGE:** Thai

1238 | 1907 | Dec 5 | T | +7 | +66 | .th

THAILAND LIES IN THE HEART of southeast Asia. The north, the border with Burma, and the long Isthmus of Kra between the Andaman Sea and the Gulf of Thailand are mountainous. The central plain is the most fertile and densely populated area, while the low northeastern plateau is the poorest region. Thailand, formerly Siam, has been an independent kingdom for most of its history, and since 1932 a constitutional monarchy, though with frequent periods of military government. Continuing rapid industrialization results in congestion in Bangkok and depletion of natural resources.

CLIMATE

Tropical equatorial/ monsoon

WEATHER CHART FOR BANGKOK

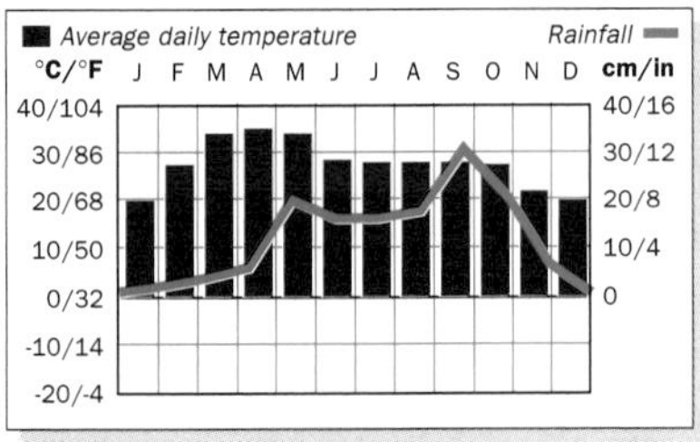
Average daily temperature
Rainfall
°C/°F J F M A M J J A S O N D cm/in
40/104
30/86
20/68
10/50
0/32
-10/14
-20/-4
40/16
30/12
20/8
10/4
0

Thailand's tropical monsoon climate has three seasons – a hot sultry period, rains from May to October, and a dry, cooler season from November to March.

TRANSPORTATION

Drive on left

Don Muang, Bangkok 30.2m passengers

629 ships 1.88m grt

THE TRANSPORTATION NETWORK

52,652 km (32,716 miles)

None

4071 km (2530 miles)

4000 km (2485 miles)

Bangkok has huge traffic jams. Its first mass transit system became operational in 1999, including the elevated Sky Train, and the first phase of the subway opened in 2004. A road corridor through Laos into Vietnam was agreed in 2001.

Island in the Andaman Sea. *Overdevelopment at Thailand's best-known resorts is pushing tourism into new, remoter locations.*

TOURISM

Visitors : Population 1:5.8

10.9m visitors

Up 7% in 2002

MAIN TOURIST ARRIVALS

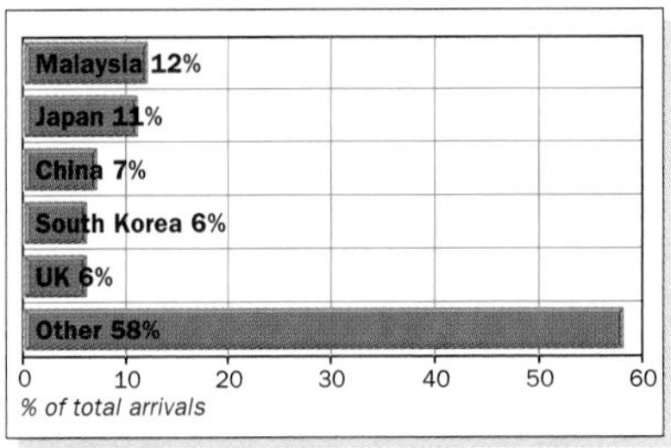
Malaysia 12%
Japan 11%
China 7%
South Korea 6%
UK 6%
Other 58%
0 10 20 30 40 50 60
% of total arrivals

Tourism is an important contributor to the Thai economy. Tourist numbers fell in the early 1990s as a result of both the worldwide recession and local overdevelopment during the 1980s boom. Though the number of arrivals has since recovered, visitors are tending to seek the less developed resorts. Bangkok's hotel occupancy rates continue to fall as yet more hotels are built. Pattaya beach resort, opposite Phetchaburi, has seen such uncontrolled development that sea pollution is now a serious problem, while opposition to the intrusion of large numbers of tourists is growing among northern hill tribes.

Though prostitution is illegal, Bangkok and Pattaya are centers for sex tourism, which thrives despite the state's embarrassment at its effect on Thailand's image. Japanese and German men are among the main clients, while Burmese girls are increasingly recruited as prostitutes. The child sex trade is a serious social problem.

There has been a boom in golf tourism, especially among the Japanese. The large number of new golf courses have made Thailand one of the best golf destinations in Asia. The vast amounts of water needed to maintain the courses is aggravating Thailand's serious water shortage.

PEOPLE

Pop. density medium

Thai, Chinese, Malay, Khmer, Mon, Karen, Miao

123/km² (318/mi²)

THE URBAN/RURAL POPULATION SPLIT

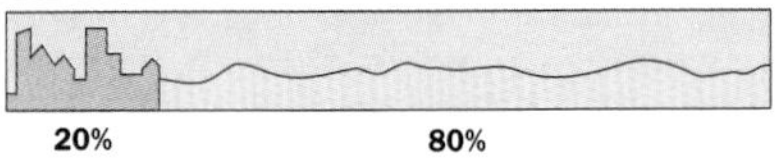
20%
80%

RELIGIOUS PERSUASION

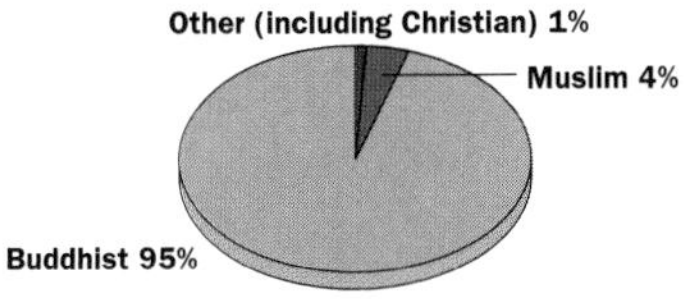
Other (including Christian) 1%
Muslim 4%
Buddhist 95%

ETHNIC MAKEUP

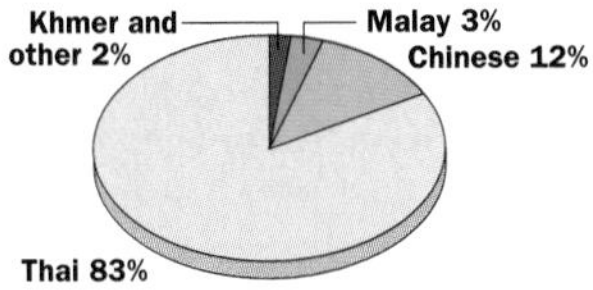
Khmer and other 2%
Malay 3%
Chinese 12%
Thai 83%

There is little ethnic tension in Thailand, and Buddhism is a great binding force. The majority of Thais follow Theravada Buddhism, though the reformist Asoke Santi Buddhist sect, which advocates a new moral austerity, is gaining influence. Its principles have been championed by political parties in a bid to clean up politics.

The far north and northeast hills are home to about 600,000 tribespeople with their own languages. Up to 300,000 Hmong fled to Thailand from Laos in 1975; most have been integrated, 14,000 are being resettled in the US.

The large Chinese community is the most assimilated in southeast Asia. Sino-Thais are particularly dominant in agricultural marketing. Most of the one million Muslim Malays live in southern Thailand, close to Malaysia. They feel stronger affinity with Muslims in Malaysia than with Thai culture, and this has given rise to a secessionist movement and a sharp increase in violence in the south in 2004.

Women are important in business, but have limited involvement in politics.

POPULATION AGE BREAKDOWN

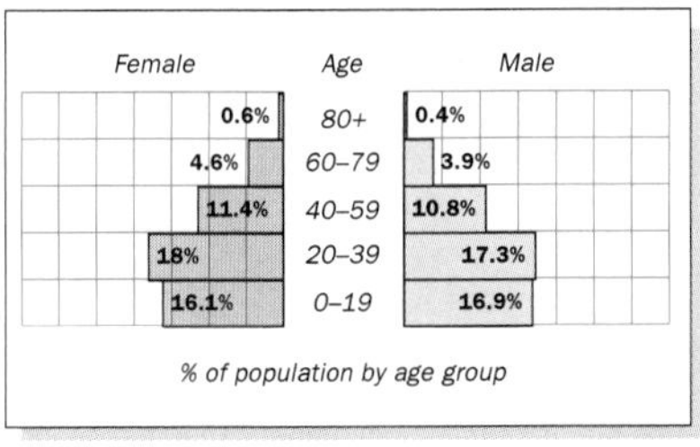
Female
Age
Male
0.6% 80+ 0.4%
4.6% 60–79 3.9%
11.4% 40–59 10.8%
18% 20–39 17.3%
16.1% 0–19 16.9%
% of population by age group

T

POLITICS

Multiparty elections

L. House 2001/2005
U. House 2000/2006

H.M. King Bhumibol Adulyadej (Rama IX)

AT THE LAST ELECTION

House of Representatives 500 seats

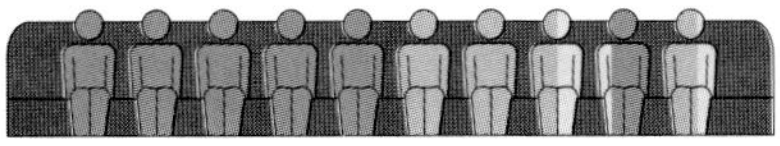
8% CT
6% CP
49% TRT
26% DP
7% NAP
4% Others

TRT = Thais Love Thais **DP** = Democrat Party
CT = Thai Nation **NAP** = New Aspiration Party
CP = National Development

Senate 200 seats

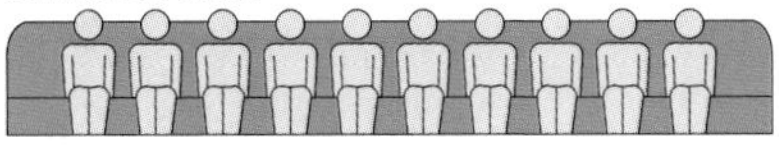

Under the 1997 constitution, the members of the Senate are directly elected on a nonparty basis.

LAOS
BURMA (MYANMAR)
CAMBODIA
MALAYSIA
Gulf of Thailand
BANGKOK
Chiang Mai
Nakhon Ratchasima
Udon Thani
Ubon Ratchathani
Khon Kaen
Nakhon Sawan
Phitsanulok
Hat Yai
Songkhla
Surat Thani
Nakhon Si Thammarat
Phuket
Chumphon
Isthmus of Kra
MALAY PENINSULA
KORAT PLATEAU
Doi Inthanon 2594m
200 km
200 miles

Thailand is a multiparty parliamentary democracy. Despite his position as a constitutional monarch, the king has immense personal prestige, and criticism of the monarchy is not tolerated.

Profile

The Thai political process, which was dominated by the military for decades until the 1990s, is highly personalized. Parties seldom have strong ideologies. Coalitions are often unstable, while the lack of coordination between coalition partners has been a recurring problem. The NAP was the largest party in the parliament elected in 1996, but its leader Chaovalit Yongchaiyuth was prime minister for only a year. His government, which was blamed for mismanaging an economic crisis, was then ousted in favor of another coalition under the DP, which, despite the volatility of coalition politics, succeeded in staying in office for four years. However, in the 2001 elections the new populist TRT triumphed, winning just short of a majority of seats. TRT leader Thaksin Shinawatra, the country's richest man and a former deputy prime minister, formed a three-party government. The NAP and TRT merged in 2002. Thaksin has pledged to tackle poverty and fight the narcotics trade.

Main Political Issues

Congestion in Bangkok

The concentration of industry and commerce in the Bangkok area causes problems. Uncontrolled development has left the city with traffic congestion which is not only among the world's worst but is also a serious hindrance to economic activity. A mass transit system is under construction, with a subway and an elevated railroad now in use. Since 1993, the government has offered incentives for relocating industry to the provinces. This is also intended to help distribute wealth more evenly – up to 60% of GDP is generated in the Bangkok area.

King Bhumibol. On the throne since 1946, he is the world's longest-serving ruler.

Thaksin Shinawatra, a controversial billionaire, elected premier in 2001.

Narcotics smuggling

The flow of narcotics through Thailand is of serious concern. It badly damages international relations, takes money out of the legitimate economy, and has led to a rise in violent crime. In the south of the country narcotics smugglers have even targeted the police directly.

Prime Minister Thaksin launched a concerted campaign against narcotics in February 2003, noting that some 700 government officials were in some way connected to the trade. By the end of March over 1300 people had been killed during police raids, 42,000 had been arrested, and $12 million worth of assets had been seized.

THAILAND

Total Area : 514 000 sq. km (198 455 sq. miles)

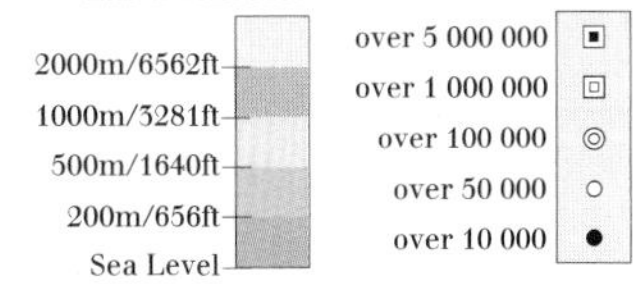
LAND HEIGHT
2000m/6562ft
1000m/3281ft
500m/1640ft
200m/656ft
Sea Level
POPULATION
over 5 000 000
over 1 000 000
over 100 000
over 50 000
over 10 000

WORLD AFFAIRS

Joined UN in 1946

APEC
ASEAN
Mekong River
NAM
WTO

Thailand has friendly relations with China. However, relations with neighboring Burma have been strained over Burma's alleged support for Thai ethnic guerrillas operating along the Thai–Burmese border. Many Thai logging companies, often run by the military, have been active in Burma since Thailand's 1988 logging ban at home. Relations with Vietnam are now cordial, though Thailand had been opposed to the Vietnamese regime in Cambodia in the 1980s.

Thailand, Indonesia, and Malaysia have liberalized trade to promote development in each country in regions which are distant from their respective capitals.

Thailand maintains close relations with the US, despite some tension over intellectual property rights and minor trade issues, but no longer has any US military bases on its territory.

T

AID

Recipient

$296m (receipts)

Up 5% in 2002

Japan is by far the largest single aid donor. Thailand has imposed a ceiling on foreign borrowing to try to slow the growth of debt.

CHRONOLOGY

Thailand emerged as a kingdom in the 13th century, and by the late 17th century its then capital, Ayutthya, was the largest city in southeast Asia. In 1782, the present Chakri dynasty and a new capital, Bangkok, were founded.

- **1855** King Mongut signs Bowring trade treaty with British – Thailand never colonized by Europeans.
- **1868–1910** King Chulalongkorn westernizes Thailand.
- **1907** Thailand cedes western Khmer (Cambodia) to France.
- **1925** King Prajadhipok begins absolute rule.
- **1932** Bloodless military–civilian coup. Constitutional monarchy.
- **1933** Military takes control.
- **1941** Japanese invade. Government collaborates.
- **1944** Pro-Japanese prime minister and prewar military dictator Phibun voted out of office.
- **1945** Exiled King Ananda returns.
- **1946** Ananda assassinated. King Bhumibol accedes.
- **1947** Military coup. Phibun back.
- **1957** Military coup. Constitution abolished.
- **1965** Thailand allows US to use Thai bases in Vietnam War.
- **1969** New constitution endorses elected parliament.
- **1971** Army suspends constitution.
- **1973–1976** Student riots lead to interlude of democracy.
- **1976** Military takeover.
- **1980–1988** Gen. Prem Tinsulanond prime minister. Partial democracy.
- **1988** Elections. Gen. Chatichai Choonhaven, right-wing CT leader, named prime minister.
- **1991** Military coup. Civilian Anand Panyarachun caretaker premier.
- **1992** Elections. Gen. Suchinda named premier. Demonstrations. King forces Suchinda to step down and reinstalls Anand. Moderates win new elections.
- **1995** CT wins general election.
- **1996** Early elections; Chaovalit Yongchaiyuth of NAP becomes prime minister.
- **1997** Financial and economic crisis; Chaovalit government falls; DP's Chuan Leekpai prime minister.
- **2001** TRT, led by Thaksin Shinawatra, wins elections.

DEFENSE

Compulsory military service

$1.73bn

Down 7% in 2002

THAI ARMED FORCES

333 main battle tanks (50 PRC Type-69, 105 M-48A5, 178 M-60)	190,000 personnel
1 carrier, 12 frigates, and 115 patrol boats	79,200 personnel
194 combat aircraft (13 F-5A/B, 50 F-16A/B, 36 F-5E/F, 34 L-39ZA/MP)	45,000 personnel
None	

The military either ruled Thailand, or played a prominent role in politics, for over half a century from 1932. In 1996, its role in the appointed Senate – hitherto a military stronghold – was reduced. Retired military figures are, however, prominent in the major political parties.

Since 1986, defense spending has tended to focus on the navy and the air force. The US is the principal supplier of hardware, while naval vessels have also been bought from Italy, and aircraft from Germany and Israel.

Thailand's main defense concerns are border disputes with Cambodia, Burma, and Laos; the Muslim secessionist movement in the south; and piracy and fishing disputes in the South China Sea.

ECONOMICS

Inflation 3.9% p.a. (1990–2001)

$123bn

40.89 baht (42.04)

SCORE CARD

World GNP Ranking	31st
GNP per Capita	$2000
Balance of Payments	$7.65bn
Inflation	0.6%
Unemployment	2%

EXPORTS

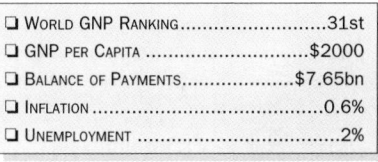

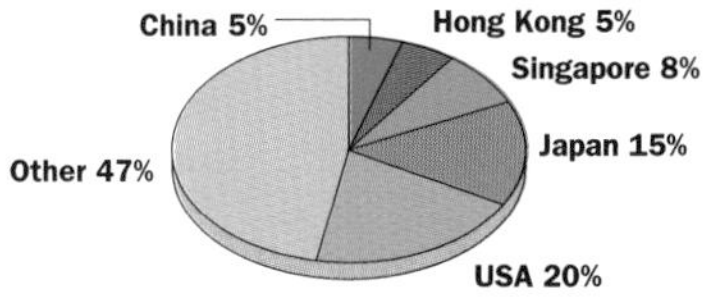
China 5%
Hong Kong 5%
Singapore 8%
Japan 15%
Other 47%
USA 20%

IMPORTS

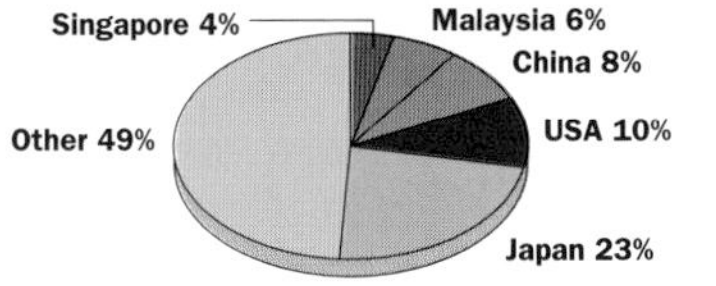
Singapore 4%
Malaysia 6%
China 8%
USA 10%
Other 49%
Japan 23%

Strengths

Success of export-based and import-substituting manufacturing. Rapid economic growth. Natural gas. Tourism. Major world exporter of rice and rubber.

Weaknesses

Concentration of economic activity in congested Bangkok area. Inadequate water storage facilities. Rapid growth of foreign debt. Low-profit farming.

Profile

Until the late 1990s, the economy grew at over 9% a year for a decade, driven by a rise in manufacturing and huge overseas investments, especially from Japan. However, as domestic wages rose, Thailand faced stiff competition from China and Vietnam. Thailand also lacked a skilled labor force to develop high-tech production, though it is a big producer of electronics goods.

In 1997 mounting foreign debt and the sharp depreciation of the baht made necessary an IMF-led rescue package. Retrenchment and stringent austerity measures followed. By 2000 the IMF had ended its direct involvement and in 2003 Thailand repaid the last of its debt for the 1997 bailout. GDP grew by 6.7% in 2003 and was expected to improve on the back of strong exports.

ECONOMIC PERFORMANCE INDICATOR

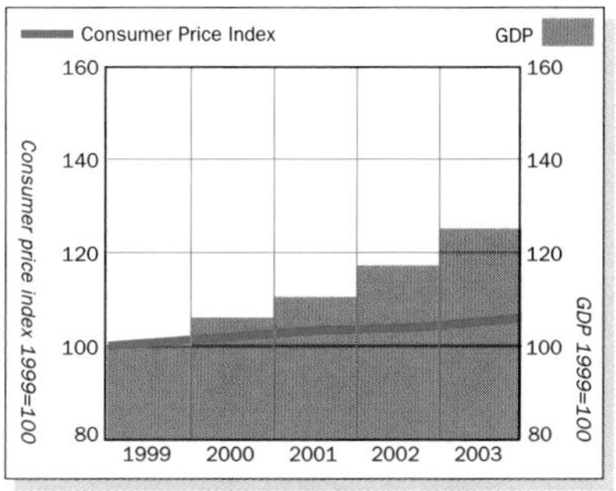
Consumer Price Index
GDP
160
140
120
100
80
Consumer price index 1999=100
GDP 1999=100
1999
2000
2001
2002
2003

THAILAND : MAJOR BUSINESSES

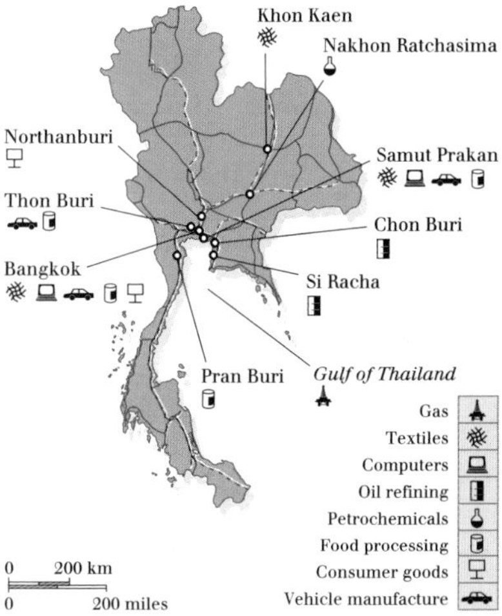
Khon Kaen
Nakhon Ratchasima
Northanburi
Samut Prakan
Thon Buri
Chon Buri
Bangkok
Si Racha
Pran Buri
Gulf of Thailand
Gas
Textiles
Computers
Oil refining
Petrochemicals
Food processing
Consumer goods
Vehicle manufacture
0 200 km
0 200 miles

RESOURCES

Electric power 27.6m kW

3.61m tonnes

217,000 b/d (reserves 700m barrels)

20m ducks, 7.06m pigs, 5.05m cattle, 177m chickens

Tin, lignite, gas, gems, oil, tungsten, lead, zinc, antimony, gold, copper

ELECTRICITY GENERATION

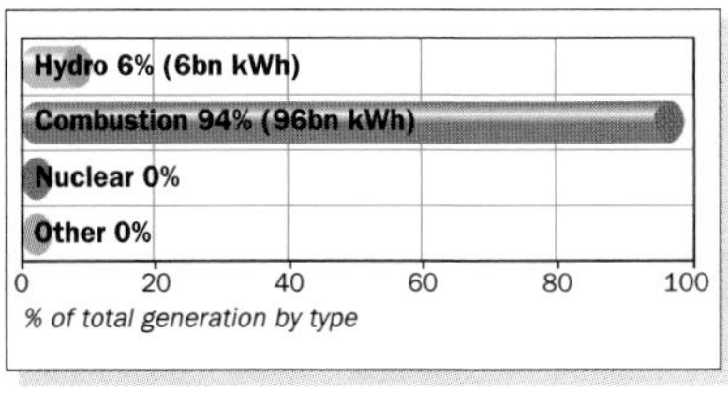
Hydro 6% (6bn kWh)
Combustion 94% (96bn kWh)
Nuclear 0%
Other 0%
0
20
40
60
80
100
% of total generation by type

Thailand has minimal crude oil and has rejected the nuclear option in favor of speeding up development of its large natural gas fields. It also has significant lignite deposits for power generation. World demand for its tin has declined, but recent gold and copper finds offer new potential. Thailand has valuable gemstone deposits. It is the world's fourth-largest producer of prawns and shrimp.

THAILAND : LAND USE

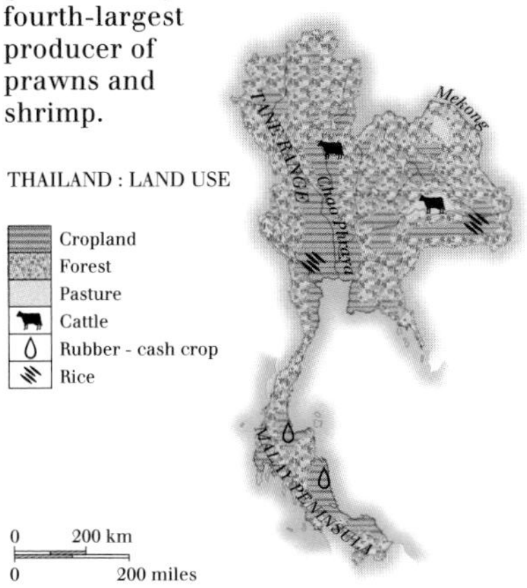
Cropland
Forest
Pasture
Cattle
Rubber - cash crop
Rice
Mekong
Chao Phraya
TANEN RANGE
MALAY PENINSULA
0 200 km
0 200 miles

ENVIRONMENT

Sustainability rank: 54th

14% (5% partially protected)

3.3 tonnes per capita

ENVIRONMENTAL TREATIES

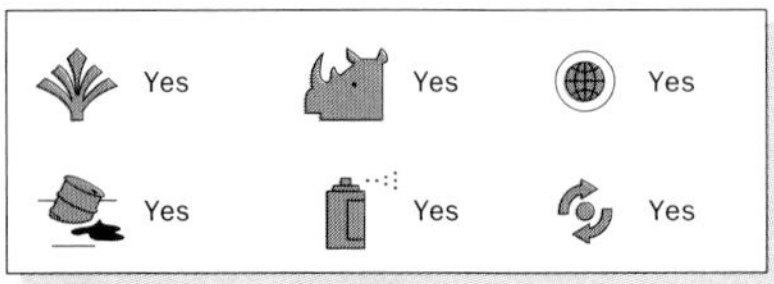
Yes
Yes
Yes
Yes
Yes
Yes

Deforestation, especially of the watersheds in the north, has led to the increasing severity of both floods and droughts. Particularly serious flooding in the south resulted in a total logging ban in 1988. Illegal logging continues, however. Reafforestation projects are often criticized for using quick-growing species. Intensive inland prawn farming leaves a legacy of salination. Mass tourism has brought pollution problems to resorts, while backpackers lead the way in exposing remoter locations.

MEDIA

TV ownership medium

Daily newspaper circulation 64 per 1000 people

PUBLISHING AND BROADCAST MEDIA

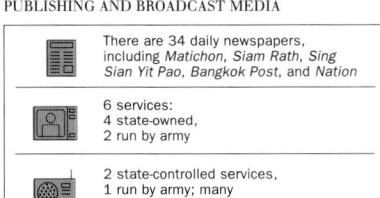

There are 34 daily newspapers, including *Matichon*, *Siam Rath*, *Sing Sian Yit Pao*, *Bangkok Post*, and *Nation*

6 services: 4 state-owned, 2 run by army

2 state-controlled services, 1 run by army; many independent stations

The media enjoy free political reporting but may be censored on military, royal, and other sensitive matters. Two TV services are run by the military. Most radio stations are in or near Bangkok.

CRIME

Death penalty in use

258,076 prisoners

Down 12% in 1996–2000

CRIME RATES

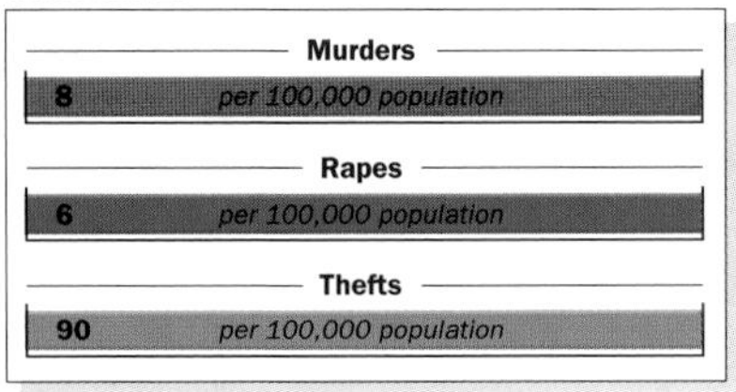
Murders
8 per 100,000 population
Rapes
6 per 100,000 population
Thefts
90 per 100,000 population

Political imprisonment is now extremely rare. There have been reports of some police abuse, including extrajudicial killings and ill-treatment of prisoners in detention. The king has encouraged an opium-substitution crop program. In the south, drug addiction is a major problem and crime is rising. Almost 2000 people were killed during a crackdown on narcotics in 2003.

EDUCATION

School leaving age: 14

93%

2.1m students

THE EDUCATION SYSTEM

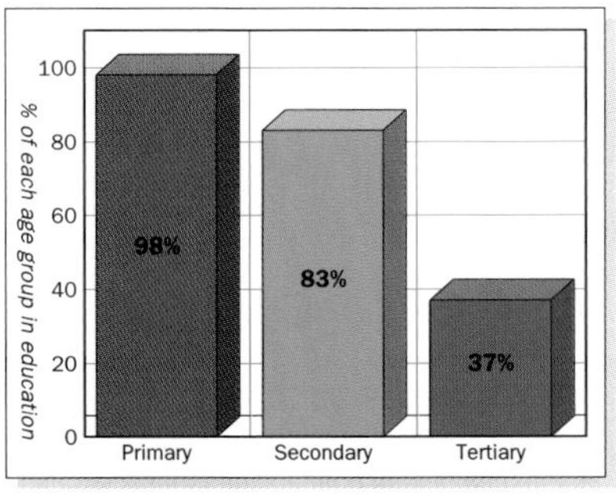
100
80
60
40
20
0
% of each age group in education
98%
83%
37%
Primary
Secondary
Tertiary

A poorly developed education system has led to a shortage of skills needed for the expansion of high-tech industries. Efforts to improve adult literacy are ongoing. Over half of the 20 state universities are in Bangkok.

HEALTH

Welfare state health benefits

1 per 3427 people

Heart diseases, gastroenteritis

High-quality health care is heavily concentrated in Bangkok. Most of the rural population has access to primary health care, and a new scheme to provide care for the poor for just $1 per person was launched in 2001. Trained personnel are aided by village health volunteers, monks, teachers, and traditional healers.

However, estimates suggest that only 30% of users can afford to pay. The poorest people can apply annually for a certificate entitling them to free health care.

High-profile family planning programs are slowing population growth. An effective AIDS prevention campaign has helped reduce the number of new infections, though the government has been in conflict with international drug companies over the production of cheaper generic drugs for AIDS sufferers. Prostitutes have benefited from an extensive sex education program.

SPENDING

GDP/cap. increase

CONSUMPTION AND SPENDING

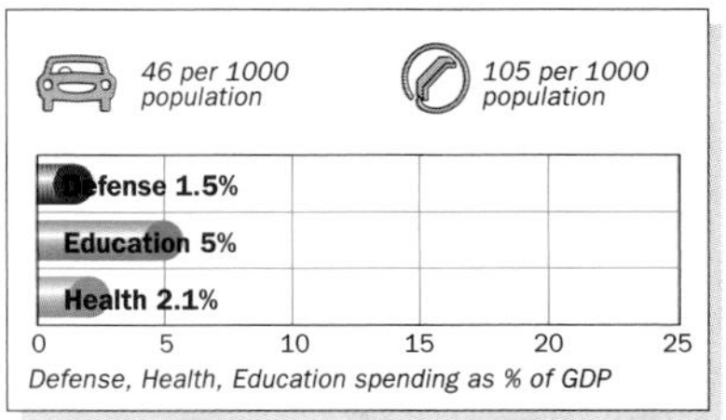
46 per 1000 population
105 per 1000 population
Defense 1.5%
Education 5%
Health 2.1%
0
5
10
15
20
25
Defense, Health, Education spending as % of GDP

The government is trying to disperse to the provinces some of the people and wealth currently concentrated to a very great extent in the capital, Bangkok. The northeast in particular is very poor. Housing initiatives saw the rate of home ownership rise significantly during the 1990s.

WORLD RANKING

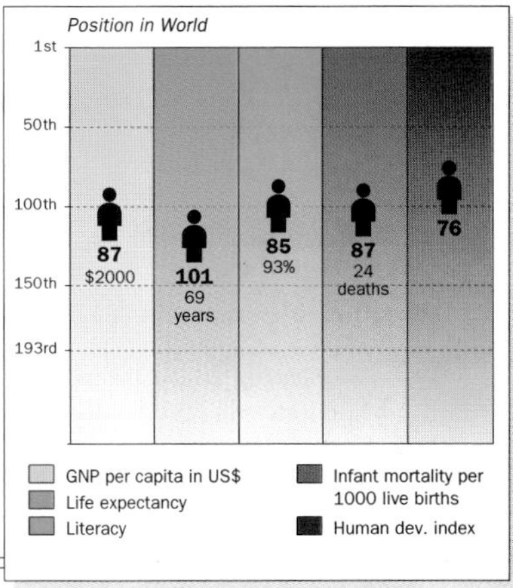
Position in World
1st
50th
100th
150th
193rd
87
$2000
101
69
years
85
93%
87
24
deaths
76
GNP per capita in US$
Life expectancy
Literacy
Infant mortality per 1000 live births
Human dev. index

T

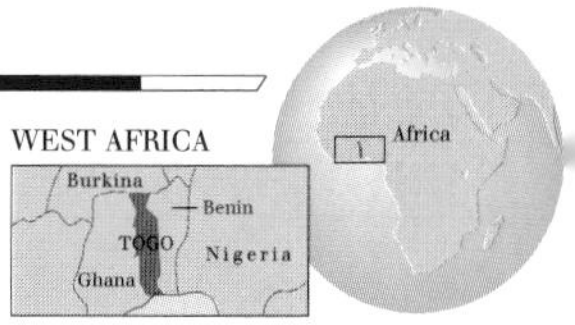
WEST AFRICA
Burkina
Benin
TOGO
Nigeria
Ghana
Africa

Togo

Official Name: Republic of Togo **Capital:** Lomé **Population:** 4.9 million
Currency: CFA franc **Official Language:** French

1960 | 1960 | April 27 | TG | 0 | +228 | .tg

TOGO IS SANDWICHED between Ghana and Benin in west Africa. A central forested region is bounded by savanna lands to the north and south. The port of Lomé is an important entrepôt for west African trade. Togo's president, Gen. Gnassingbé Eyadéma, has been in power since 1967.

CLIMATE

Tropical equatorial/ wet and dry

WEATHER CHART FOR LOMÉ

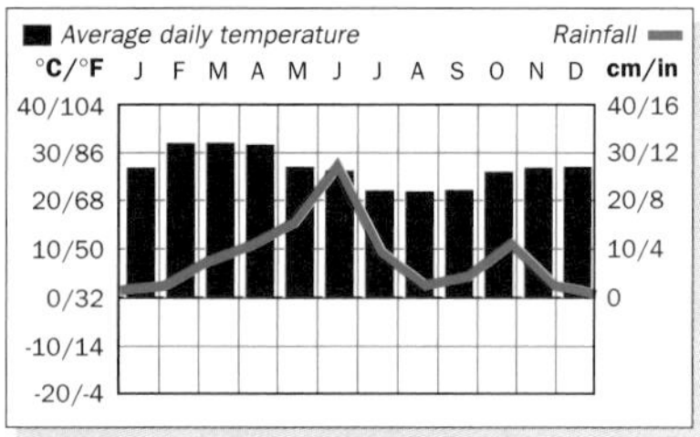
Average daily temperature
Rainfall
°C/°F
J F M A M J J A S O N D
cm/in
40/104
30/86
20/68
10/50
0/32
-10/14
-20/-4
40/16
30/12
20/8
10/4
0

Togo has a typical Gulf of Guinea climate – very hot and humid on the coast, and drier inland.

TRANSPORTATION

Drive on right

Lomé 215,663 passengers

17 ships 13,300 grt

THE TRANSPORTATION NETWORK

2406 km (1495 miles)

None

525 km (326 miles)

50 km (31 miles)

Improving the already good road network and Lomé's port facilities are priorities, given Togo's role as an entrepôt. Air and rail links to the interior, however, are limited.

TOURISM

Visitors : Population 1:85

57,539 visitors

Up 1% in 2002

MAIN TOURIST ARRIVALS

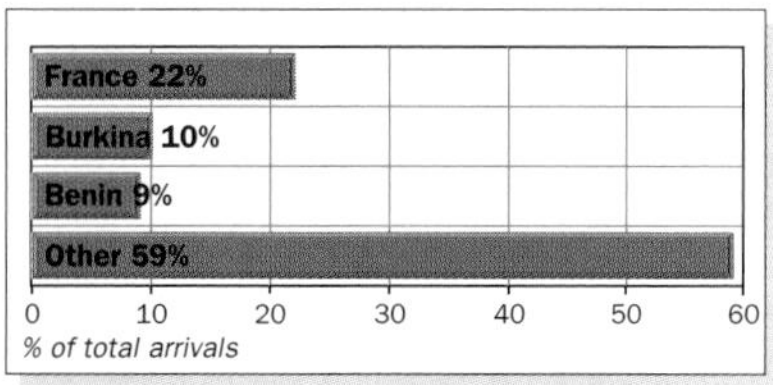
France 22%
Burkina 10%
Benin 9%
Other 59%
0
10
20
30
40
50
60
% of total arrivals

With sandy beaches and lively nightlife, Togo was one of west Africa's most popular destinations until the political uncertainty of the early 1990s. The hotels remain, but tourist numbers are only slowly recovering.

PEOPLE

Pop. density medium

Ewe, Kabye, Gurma, French

90/km² (233/mi²)

THE URBAN/RURAL POPULATION SPLIT

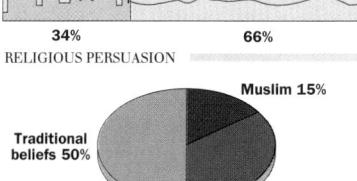

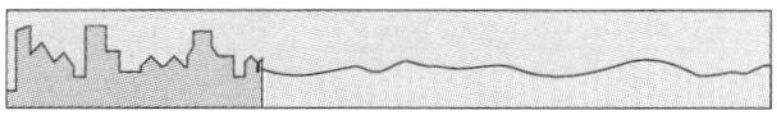
34%
66%

RELIGIOUS PERSUASION

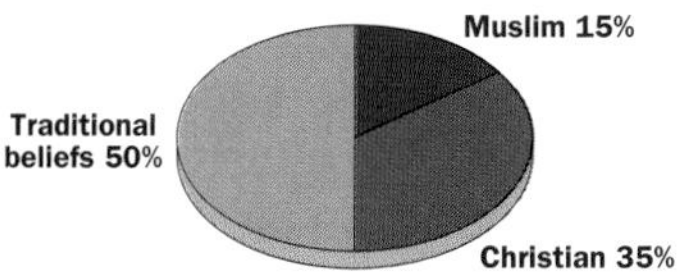
Muslim 15%
Traditional beliefs 50%
Christian 35%

A bitter divide has existed between north and south since before independence. Most southern resentment is directed toward a northern minority, the Kabye people from the Kabye plateau, because of their domination of the military. The Kabye and other northerners in turn resent their own underdevelopment in contrast to the high development, especially educational, of southerners. The dominant southern group is the Ewe, who make up more than 40% of the total population.

As elsewhere in Africa, the extended family is important and tribalism and nepotism are key factors in everyday life. Some Togolese ethnic groups, such as the Mina, have matriarchal societies. The "Nana Benz," the market-women of Lomé, control the retail trade and have considerable private money. Politics, however, remains a male preserve.

***Kabye cultivation near Kara,** in northern Togo. The main food crops grown are cassava, yams, and maize.*

POLITICS

Multiparty elections

2002/2007

President Gnassingbé Eyadéma

AT THE LAST ELECTION

National Assembly 81 seats

4%
RSDD
89%
RPT
7%
Others

RPT = Rally of the Togolese People
RSDD = Rally for Democracy and Development

Politics is dominated by Africa's longest-serving leader, Gen. Gnassingbé Eyadéma, in power since 1967.

A democracy movement has been gathering momentum since 1990. Multiparty presidential elections held in 1993 were won by Eyadéma, some opposition candidates boycotting the poll. Eyadéma claimed victory again in presidential elections in 1998, amid accusations of malpractice and of the killing of hundreds of opposition supporters immediately afterward in the run-up to the 1999 Assembly election. (Serious human rights violations were later confirmed in a UN/OAU report.) The opposition accepted the election results in subsequent negotiations. Eyadéma's RPT retained its huge majority in 2002 after the repeatedly postponed poll was boycotted by the main opposition parties. The constitution was then amended, paving the way for Eyadéma's third-term victory in June 2003; exiled opposition leader Gilchrist Olympio was barred from contesting the election. The EU has made the resumption of financial aid dependent on talks with opposition groups.

WORLD AFFAIRS

Joined UN in 1960

OIC | ECOWAS | FZ | AU | UEMOA

Togo places priority on maintaining traditional links, especially with France. While President Eyadéma was chair of ECOWAS in 1989–1999, he acted as mediator in the Guinea-Bissau conflict and hosted talks on Sierra Leone. Regional relations are very good.

AID

Recipient

$51m (receipts)

Up 16% in 2002

Development projects and the health of the economy overall have suffered as a result of aid suspensions in the 1990s by donors including the US and the EU.

T

TOGO

Total Area : 56 785 sq. km (21 924 sq. miles)

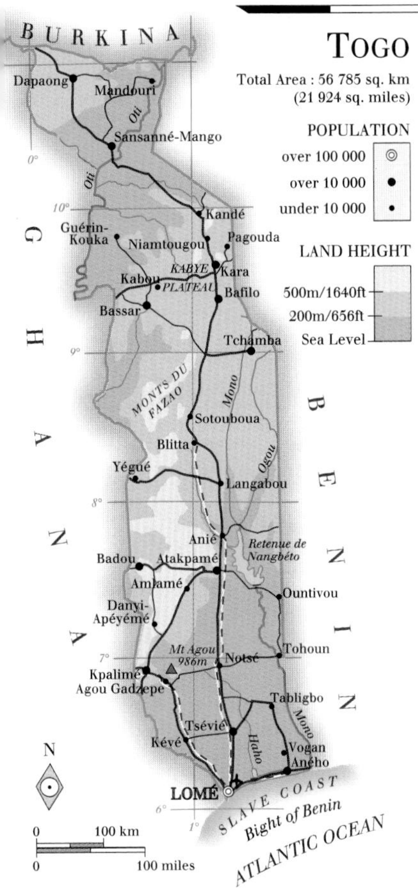
POPULATION
over 100 000
over 10 000
under 10 000
LAND HEIGHT
500m/1640ft
200m/656ft
Sea Level
BURKINA
GHANA
BENIN
Dapaong
Mandouri
Sansanné-Mango
Oti
Guérin-Kouka
Niamtougou
Kandé
Pagouda
KABYE PLATEAU
Kara
Kabou
Bafilo
Bassar
Tchamba
MONTS DU FAZAO
Mono
Sotouboua
Blitta
Ogou
Yégué
Langabou
Anié
Retenue de Nangbéto
Badou
Atakpamé
Amlamé
Ountivou
Danyi-Apéyémé
Mt Agou 986m
Notsé
Tohoun
Kpalimé
Agou Gadzepe
Tabligbo
Tsévié
Haho
Kévé
Vogan
Aného
LOMÉ
SLAVE COAST
Bight of Benin
ATLANTIC OCEAN
N
100 km
100 miles

DEFENSE

Compulsory military service

$23m | Up 10% in 2002

The military has an important role in Togo, and spending on defense is quite high. The army's senior ranks are dominated by loyalists from President Eyadéma's northern Kabye tribe. France guarantees Togo's security through a defense accord, and supplies most military equipment and training.

RESOURCES

Electric power 38,000 kW

23,283 tonnes | Oil reserves not yet exploited

1.8m sheep, 1.47m goats, 310,000 pigs, 8.5m chickens | Phosphates, iron, oil, marble, chromite, gas, bauxite, dolomite

Phosphates are Togo's most important resource. Offshore oil and gas deposits were found in 1999. The Nangbeto Dam, opened in 1988, has reduced dependence on Ghana for energy. Coffee, cocoa, and cotton are important cash crops.

ENVIRONMENT

Sustainability rank: 105th

8% (1% partially protected) | 0.4 tonnes per capita

Ecologists have been critical of the transformation of nature reserves into hunting grounds for the military elite. Other problems include coastal erosion around Aneho and desertification.

MEDIA

TV ownership medium

Daily newspaper circulation 2 per 1000 people

PUBLISHING AND BROADCAST MEDIA

There is one daily newspaper, *Togo Presse*, published by the government

1 state-owned service | 1 state-owned service, 11 private stations

Press freedom is improving, but newspapers are regularly confiscated and reporters harassed and arrested.

CRIME

Death penalty not used in practice

2043 prisoners | Crime is rising

Togo is normally relatively peaceable, but urban crime generally increased during the 1990s, particularly during periods of political unrest in the capital.

CHRONOLOGY

After colonization by Germany in 1894, Togoland was divided between France and the UK in 1922.

- **1960** French sector independent as Togo (UK part joined to Ghana).
- **1967** Eyadéma takes power.
- **1991–1992** General strike; repression.
- **1993** Eyadéma elected president.
- **1998, 1999** Disputed elections.
- **2002, 2003** RPT, Eyadéma reelected.

EDUCATION

School leaving age: 15

60% | 15,171 students

Schooling is based on the French model. Unpaid grants provoked unrest at the University of Lomé in 2001.

HEALTH

No welfare state health benefits

1 per 10,000 people | Malaria, diarrheal, infectious, and parasitic diseases

Health care suffers from a lack of resources and funding. Around 4% of adults were HIV positive by 2003.

SPENDING

GDP/cap. increase

CONSUMPTION AND SPENDING

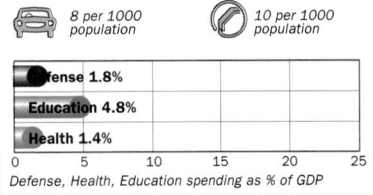

8 per 1000 population | *10 per 1000 population*

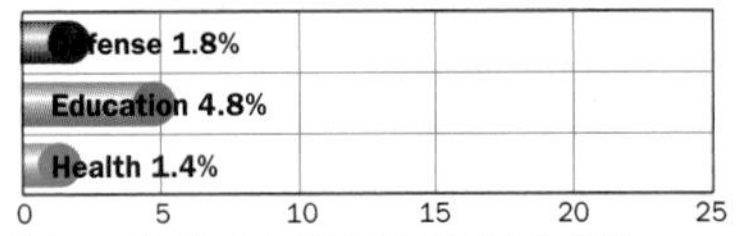
Defense 1.8%
Education 4.8%
Health 1.4%
0
5
10
15
20
25

Defense, Health, Education spending as % of GDP

Considerable wealth disparities exist between those who work the land and the country's political and business classes. However, the urban class was hit by an economic downturn in the late 1990s.

ECONOMICS

Inflation 6.6% p.a. (1990–2001)

$1.28bn | 539.2 CFA francs (571.2)

SCORE CARD

- WORLD GNP RANKING........149th
- GNP PER CAPITA........$270
- BALANCE OF PAYMENTS........–$169m
- INFLATION........3.1%
- UNEMPLOYMENT........Not available

STRENGTHS

Efficient civil service. Ideal location for role as entrepôt, based on Lomé port. Resourceful entrepreneurs, notably market-women. Proceeds of widespread smuggling. Phosphate deposits have the world's highest mineral content. Self-sufficient in basic foodstuffs.

EXPORTS

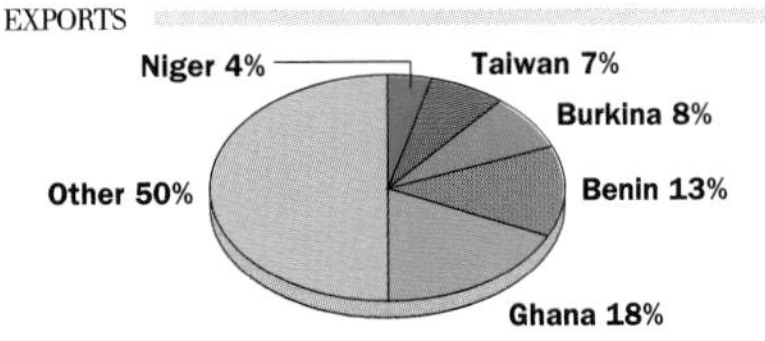
Niger 4%
Taiwan 7%
Burkina 8%
Benin 13%
Ghana 18%
Other 50%

IMPORTS

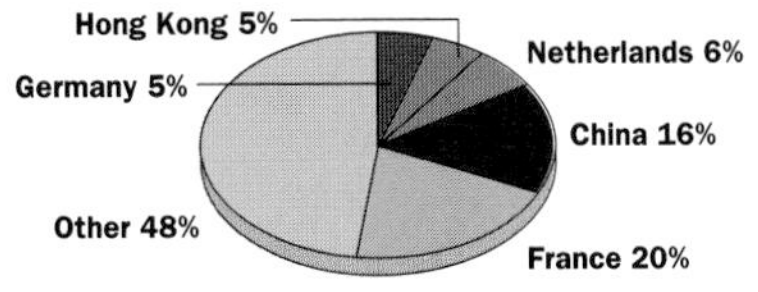
Hong Kong 5%
Netherlands 6%
Germany 5%
China 16%
France 20%
Other 48%

WEAKNESSES

Political pariah status led to aid reductions in the 1990s. Low world prices for phosphates. Hydropower generation is vulnerable to drought.

WORLD RANKING

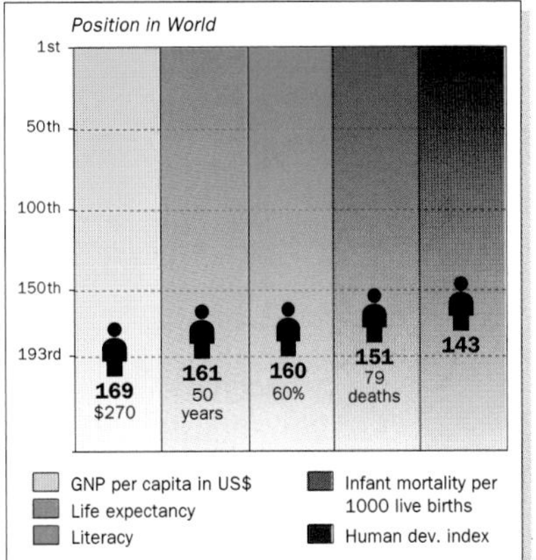
Position in World
1st
50th
100th
150th
193rd
169
$270
161
50 years
160
60%
151
79 deaths
143
GNP per capita in US$
Life expectancy
Literacy
Infant mortality per 1000 live births
Human dev. index

T

TONGA

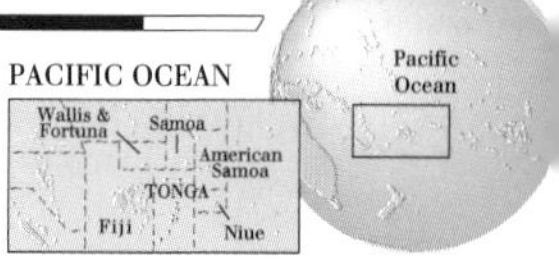
PACIFIC OCEAN
Wallis & Futuna
Samoa
American Samoa
TONGA
Fiji
Niue
Pacific Ocean

OFFICIAL NAME: Kingdom of Tonga **CAPITAL:** Nuku'alofa **POPULATION:** 108,141
CURRENCY: Pa'anga (Tongan dollar) **OFFICIAL LANGUAGES:** English and Tongan

1970
1970
June 4
TO
+12
+676
.to

LOCATED IN THE SOUTH PACIFIC 1600 km (1000 miles) northeast of New Zealand, Tonga is an archipelago of 170 islands. These are divided into three main groups, Vava'u, Ha'apai, and Tongatapu. Tonga's easterly islands are generally low and fertile. Those in the west are higher and volcanic in origin. Tonga's economy is based on agriculture, especially coconut, cassava, and passion fruit production. Politics is effectively controlled by the king.

CLIMATE

Tropical oceanic

WEATHER CHART FOR NUKU'ALOFA

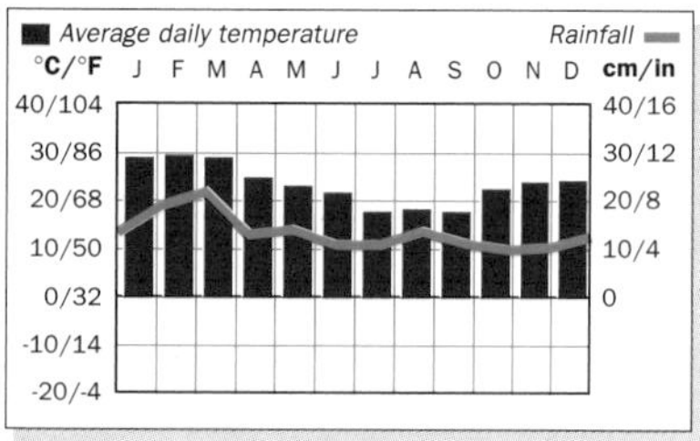
Average daily temperature
Rainfall
°C/°F
J F M A M J J A S O N D
cm/in
40/104
30/86
20/68
10/50
0/32
-10/14
-20/-4
40/16
30/12
20/8
10/4
0

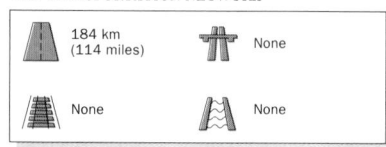

Tonga has a tropical oceanic climate, with year-round temperatures ranging between 17°C (63°F) and 30°C (86°F).

TRANSPORTATION

Drive on left

Fua'amotu International, Tongatabu
67,000 passengers

151 ships
290,500 grt

THE TRANSPORTATION NETWORK

184 km (114 miles)

None

None

None

Royal Tongan Airlines stranded 1800 passengers when its only international aircraft was repossessed in 2004.

TOURISM

Visitors : Population 1:2.9

37,000 visitors

Up 14% in 2002

MAIN TOURIST ARRIVALS

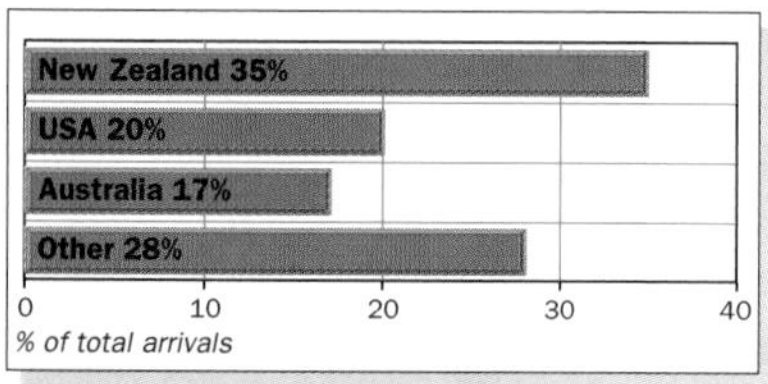
New Zealand 35%
USA 20%
Australia 17%
Other 28%
0
10
20
30
40
% of total arrivals

Tonga's main attractions are its tropical beaches. Flagging tourism has been boosted by political insecurity in the Solomon Islands and Fiji. Fears have been expressed that too many visitors may erode traditional Tongan culture.

***Mountainous scenery** typical of the westerly islands. Tonga's 170 islands are scattered over a wide expanse of the South Pacific. Only 45 are inhabited.*

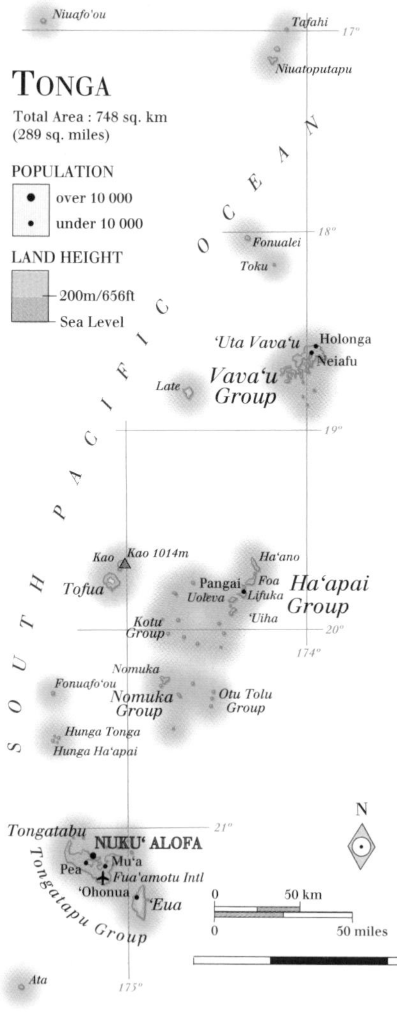
Niuafo'ou
Tafahi
Niuatoputapu
TONGA
Total Area : 748 sq. km (289 sq. miles)
POPULATION
over 10 000
under 10 000
LAND HEIGHT
200m/656ft
Sea Level
SOUTH PACIFIC OCEAN
Fonualei
Toku
'Uta Vava'u
Holonga
Neiafu
Late
Vava'u Group
Kao
Kao 1014m
Tofua
Ha'ano
Pangai
Foa
Uoleva
Lifuka
Ha'apai Group
'Uiha
Kotu Group
Nomuka
Fonuafo'ou
Nomuka Group
Otu Tolu Group
Hunga Tonga
Hunga Ha'apai
Tongatabu
NUKU' ALOFA
Mu'a
Pea
Fua'amotu Intl
'Ohonua
'Eua
Tongatapu Group
Ata
N
0
50 km
50 miles
17°
18°
19°
20°
21°
174°
175°

PEOPLE

Pop. density medium

English, Tongan

150/km² (389/mi²)

THE URBAN/RURAL POPULATION SPLIT

33%
67%

RELIGIOUS PERSUASION

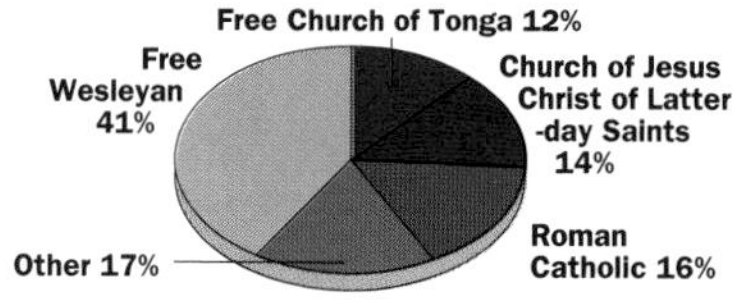
Free Church of Tonga 12%
Free Wesleyan 41%
Church of Jesus Christ of Latter-day Saints 14%
Roman Catholic 16%
Other 17%

Tonga has strong ethnic ties with eastern Fiji, and there has traditionally been considerable movement between the two states. Tongans see themselves as unique among Pacific islanders, retaining their monarchy and never having been fully colonized. Respect for traditional institutions and values remains high. Tongans are strong churchgoers; churches often fund education. A new generation of Western-educated Tongans queries some traditional attitudes. Apparent ethnic tensions and a drive to improve native employment prompted the government to ban unskilled immigrants in 2001.

POLITICS

Nonparty elections

2002/2005

H.M. King Taufa'ahau Tupou IV

AT THE LAST ELECTION

Legislative Assembly 30 seats

The Legislative Assembly comprises the king, the 11 members of the Privy Council, nine members indirectly elected by nobles, and nine directly elected members. There are no political parties: of those elected in 2002, seven were part of the Human Rights and Democracy Movement.

The main power brokers in Tongan politics are the king, the noble establishment, and the landowners. King Taufa'ahau, on the throne since 1965, frequently exercises kingly powers. His resistance to growing calls for democracy was typified in 2000 by his appointing his conservative third son, Prince Ulukalala Lavaka Ata, as premier for life, overlooking his reformist eldest son. There is an increasingly vocal opposition which was roused to anger in 2003 when the king, in an effort to silence permanently the independent *Taimi 'o Tonga* newspaper, demanded a revision of the constitution to prevent the courts from questioning his decrees.

T

WORLD AFFAIRS
Joined UN in 1999

ACP | Comm | PC | PIF | ADB

In 1998 Tonga broke off ties with Taiwan and instead forged links with China. The discovery of arms bound for Palestine aboard a Tongan-registered vessel in 2002 raised international concern over the security of its flag-of-convenience registration system.

AID
Recipient

$22m (receipts) — Up 10% in 2002

Aid finances major infrastructure projects; Japan, Australia, and New Zealand are primary donors. Japan mainly funds projects involving fisheries and the environment, while Australia concentrates on security.

DEFENSE
No compulsory military service

$2m (estimate) — No significant change

Tonga has a small defense force, which includes both regulars and reserves. Tongan police assisted in security efforts in the Solomon Islands in 2000.

ECONOMICS
Inflation 2.2% p.a. (1990–2001)

$146m — 2.001 pa'anga (1.491)

SCORE CARD

❑ WORLD GNP RANKING	186th
❑ GNP PER CAPITA	$1440
❑ BALANCE OF PAYMENTS	$10m
❑ INFLATION	10.4%
❑ UNEMPLOYMENT	13%

STRENGTHS
Agriculture: contributes largest percentage of GDP. Tourism main source of hard currency earnings.

WEAKNESSES
Off main shipping routes. Aid-dependent. Importer of food. High youth unemployment. Corruption scandal in royal court in 2001.

EXPORTS

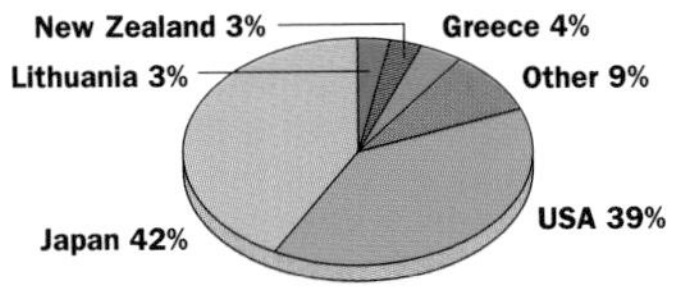
New Zealand 3%
Greece 4%
Lithuania 3%
Other 9%
USA 39%
Japan 42%

IMPORTS

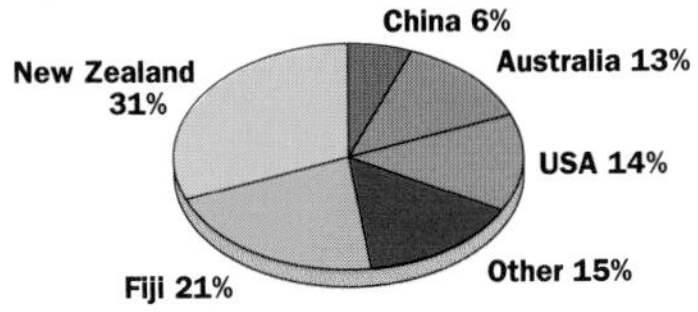
China 6%
New Zealand 31%
Australia 13%
USA 14%
Other 15%
Fiji 21%

RESOURCES
Electric power 8000 kW

4673 tonnes — Not an oil producer

81,000 pigs, 12,500 goats, 300,000 chickens — None

Tonga has no strategic or mineral resources. Electricity is generated entirely from imported fuel. Recent exploration has failed to identify any oil reserves. Tongan waters contain large numbers of tuna.

ENVIRONMENT
Not available

5% (4.6% partially protected) — 1.2 tonnes per capita

Many beaches in populated areas are affected by sand quarrying, and giant clams are under threat. Coral reefs are often poisoned and damaged in the search for fish. An increase in tourism could further disrupt the ecosystem.

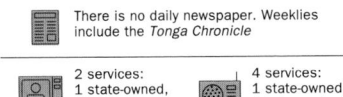

MEDIA
TV ownership medium

Daily newspaper circulation 72 per 1000 people

PUBLISHING AND BROADCAST MEDIA

There is no daily newspaper. Weeklies include the *Tonga Chronicle*

2 services: 1 state-owned, 1 independent — 4 services: 1 state-owned, 3 independent

In 2004, the king took over control of media licensing, raising concerns over freedom of speech. The independent *Taimi 'o Tonga* has been banned.

CRIME
Death penalty not used in practice

110 prisoners — Crime is risng

Offenses such as breaking and entering have increased among young Tongans, along with unemployment. The practice of stranding young offenders on an uninhabited island has been questioned in parliament.

EDUCATION
School leaving age: 14

99% — 364 students

Plans for a new national university were approved in 2000 following violence in Fiji, where Tongan students attend the University of the South Pacific. Scholarship schemes enable students to go abroad for higher education.

HEALTH
No welfare state health benefits

1 per 2273 people — Cerebrovascular, heart, and diarrheal diseases

Tonga has some modern health care facilities. However, patients have to be flown out to Australia or New Zealand for sophisticated surgery.

CHRONOLOGY

Originally discovered by the Polynesians, Tonga was visited by the Dutch in the 17th century and Capt. Cook in the 18th century. In the latter half of the 19th century, during the reign of King George Tupou I, the islands became a unified state after a period of civil war.

- ❑ **1875** First constitution established.
- ❑ **1900** Concern over German ambitions in region; Treaty of Friendship and Protection with UK.
- ❑ **1918–1965** Reign of Queen Salote Tupou III.
- ❑ **1958** Greater autonomy from UK enshrined in Friendship Treaty.
- ❑ **1965** King Taufa'ahau Tupou IV accedes on his mother's death.
- ❑ **1970** Full independence within British Commonwealth.
- ❑ **1988** Treaty allows US nuclear warships right of transit.
- ❑ **2000** King appoints third son as prime minister for life.
- ❑ **2001** Court jester steals US$20 million of state funds.
- ❑ **2002** Election sees strong showing by prodemocracy candidates, as in 1996 and 1999.

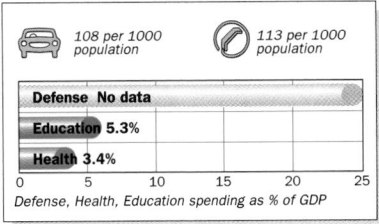

SPENDING
GDP/cap. increase

CONSUMPTION AND SPENDING

108 per 1000 population — *113 per 1000 population*

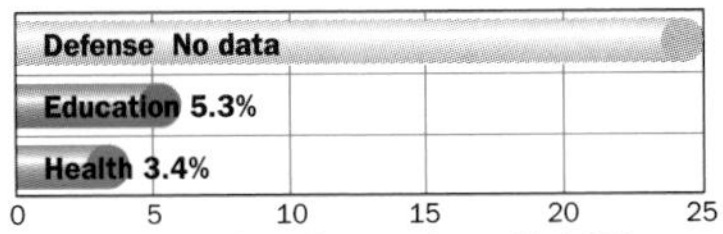
Defense No data
Education 5.3%
Health 3.4%
0
5
10
15
20
25

Defense, Health, Education spending as % of GDP

Tongans indulge in few ostentatious displays of wealth. The well-off provide financial support for relatives.

WORLD RANKING

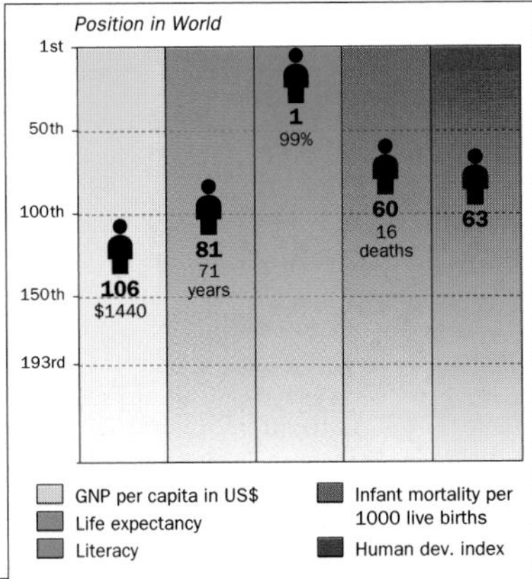
Position in World
1st
50th
100th
150th
193rd
106
$1440
81
71 years
1
99%
60
16 deaths
63
GNP per capita in US$
Life expectancy
Literacy
Infant mortality per 1000 live births
Human dev. index

T

TRINIDAD & TOBAGO

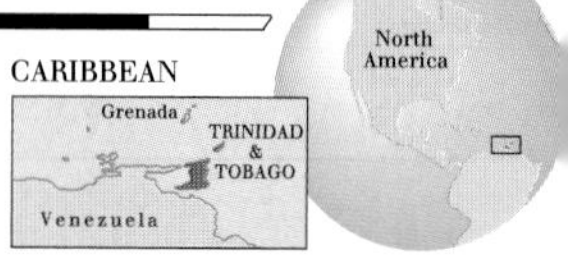
CARIBBEAN
Grenada
TRINIDAD & TOBAGO
Venezuela
North America

OFFICIAL NAME: Republic of Trinidad and Tobago **CAPITAL:** Port-of-Spain
POPULATION: 1.3 million **CURRENCY:** Trinidad and Tobago dollar **OFFICIAL LANGUAGE:** English

1962 | 1962 | Aug 31 | TT | -4 | +1868 | .tt

THE TWO ISLANDS OF Trinidad and Tobago are the most southerly of the Caribbean Windward Islands and lie just 15 km (9 miles) off the Venezuelan coast. They gained joint independence from Britain in 1962, and Tobago was given internal autonomy in 1987. The spectacular mountain ranges and large swamps are rich in tropical flora and fauna. Pitch Lake in Trinidad is the world's largest natural reservoir of asphalt.

CLIMATE

Tropical oceanic

WEATHER CHART FOR PORT-OF-SPAIN

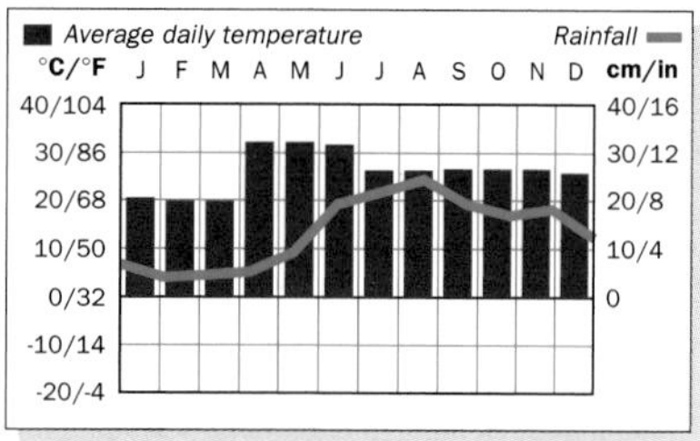
Average daily temperature
Rainfall
°C/°F
J F M A M J J A S O N D
cm/in
40/104
30/86
20/68
10/50
0/32
-10/14
-20/4
40/16
30/12
20/8
10/4
0

The islands are a little warmer than others in the Caribbean and escape the hurricanes, which pass by to the north.

TRANSPORTATION

Drive on left

Piarco International, Port-of-Spain 2.16m passengers

69 ships 26,800 grt

THE TRANSPORTATION NETWORK

4243 km (2636 miles) | None
Small sections | None

The road network is well developed; there are taxis or minibuses for set routes. National carrier BWIA and Air Caribbean operate Trinidad–Tobago flights. BWIA also flies to the US.

TOURISM

Visitors : Population 1:3.4

384,000 visitors

Little change in 2002

MAIN TOURIST ARRIVALS

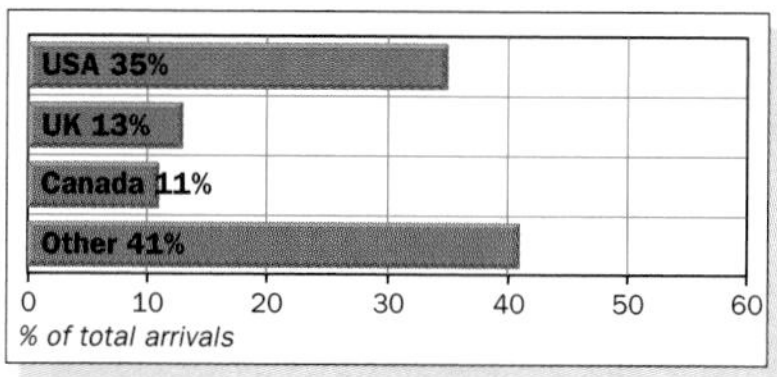
USA 35%
UK 13%
Canada 11%
Other 41%
0 10 20 30 40 50 60
% of total arrivals

Oil revenue meant that Trinidad was one of the last Caribbean states to develop tourism. Most is centered on Tobago (said to be the model for the island in *Robinson Crusoe*), famous for its huge variety of South American wildlife, including 210 species of tropical bird.

TRINIDAD & TOBAGO

Total Area : 5128 sq. km (1980 sq. miles)

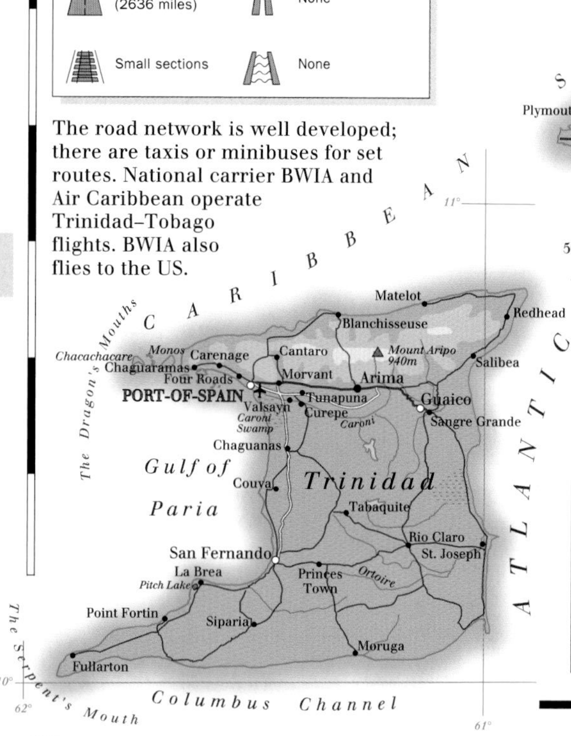
SEA
St. Giles Is
Charlotteville
Little Tobago
Tobago
Roxborough
Plymouth
Scarborough
OCEAN
N
LAND HEIGHT
500m/1640ft
200m/656ft
Sea Level
POPULATION
over 50 000
over 10 000
under 10 000
0 30 km
0 30 miles
CARIBBEAN
ATLANTIC
11°
10°
62°
61°
The Dragon's Mouths
Chacachacare
Monos
Chaguaramas
Carenage
Four Roads
PORT-OF-SPAIN
Matelot
Blanchisseuse
Redhead
Cantaro
Mount Aripo 940m
Salibea
Morvant
Arima
Valsayn
Tunapuna
Guaico
Caroni Swamp
Curepe
Caroni
Sangre Grande
Chaguanas
Gulf of Paria
Couva
Trinidad
Tabaquite
Rio Claro
St. Joseph
San Fernando
La Brea
Pitch Lake
Princes Town
Ortoire
Point Fortin
Siparia
Moruga
Fullarton
The Serpent's Mouth
Columbus Channel

PEOPLE

Pop. density high

English Creole, English, Hindi, French, Spanish

253/km² (656/mi²)

THE URBAN/RURAL POPULATION SPLIT

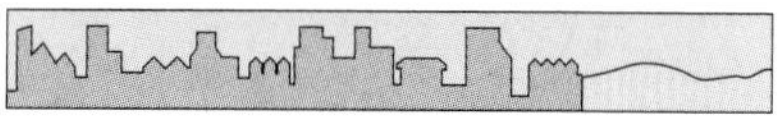
75%
25%

ETHNIC MAKEUP

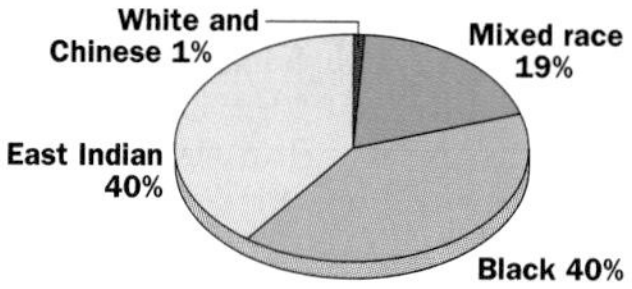
White and Chinese 1%
Mixed race 19%
East Indian 40%
Black 40%

Trinidad's south Asian community is the largest in the Caribbean and holds on to its Muslim and Hindu inheritance. Ethnic tensions with the predominantly Christian black Trinidadians continue to exist but are muted. Blacks form the majority on Tobago.

POLITICS

Multiparty elections

L. House 2002/2007
U. House 2002/2007

President Maxwell Richards

AT THE LAST ELECTION

House of Representatives 36 seats

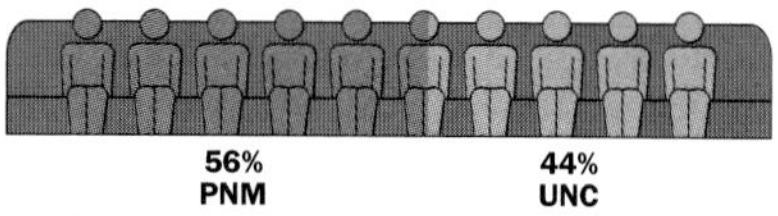
56% PNM
44% UNC

PNM = People's National Movement
UNC = United National Congress

Senate 31 seats

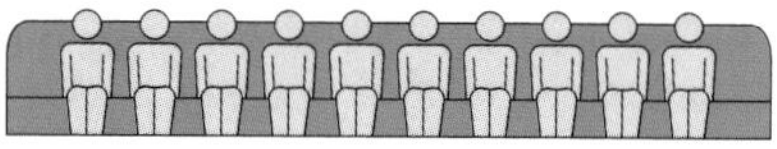

Senators are appointed by the president, including 16 nominated by the prime minister and six by the leader of the opposition

Politics is mainly polarized by race. The largely black-based PNM dominated politics from independence in 1962 to the 1990s, leading to political fragmentation. In 1990 an attempted coup was mounted by Muslim extremists. The UNC's Basdeo Panday, the first ethnic Asian prime minister, was elected in 1995. In elections six years later, the UNC's outright majority was reduced to a tie with the PNM. The political stalemate led to new elections being called in 2002, which were decisively won by the PNM, with Patrick Manning remaining in office as prime minister.

Tobago's white sand beaches, *verdant landscape, and natural anchorages have enabled it to develop a thriving tourist industry.*

T

WORLD AFFAIRS

Joined UN in 1962

ACS | Caricom | Comm | NAM | OAS

Foreign policy aims for maximum advantage from the booming oil and gas industry and rapidly growing industrial and financial sectors. There are close economic ties with the US and good relations with the EU. Trinidad strongly favors regional integration. Marine territory disputes with Venezuela and Barbados relate to fishing and oil rights.

AID

Recipient

No net receipts

Loan repayments exceeded aid received in 2002

Aid is modest. Japan controversially offers fisheries aid in return for support on whaling issues.

DEFENSE

No compulsory military service

US$64m

Down 4% in 2002

Defense forces comprise a land army and a coast guard (with air wing), used to patrol fishing grounds.

ECONOMICS

Inflation 5.4% p.a. (1990–2001)

US$8.8bn

6.15 Trinidad and Tobago dollars (6.14)

SCORE CARD

❑ World GNP Ranking	92nd
❑ GNP per Capita	US$6750
❑ Balance of Payments	US$416m
❑ Inflation	4.2%
❑ Unemployment	11%

Strengths
Oil, which accounts for 70% of export earnings. Gas increasingly exploited to support new industries. Methanol, ammonia, iron, and steel exports. Tourism, especially on Tobago. Strong commercial and financial sectors.

Weaknesses
High dependence on oil and gas. Failing sugar industry. High kidnapping and murder rates discourage investment.

EXPORTS

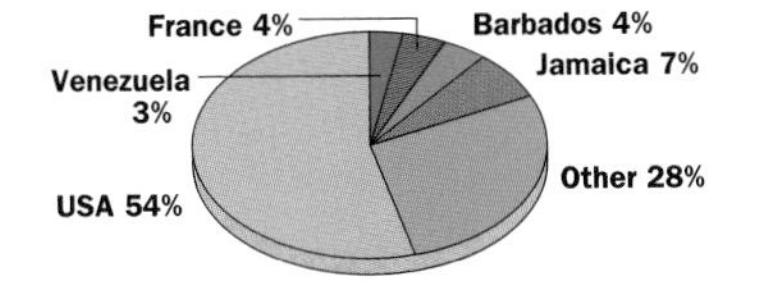
France 4%
Barbados 4%
Jamaica 7%
Venezuela 3%
Other 28%
USA 54%

IMPORTS

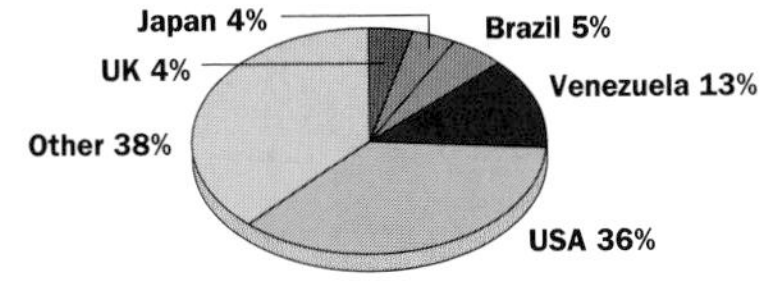
Japan 4%
Brazil 5%
UK 4%
Venezuela 13%
Other 38%
USA 36%

RESOURCES

Electric power 1.5m kW

11,415 tonnes

163,000 b/d (reserves 1.9bn barrels)

75,686 pigs, 28,980 cattle, 27.5m chickens

Oil, natural gas, asphalt, iron

Oil and gas are major resources. The country is the world's fifth-largest exporter of liquefied natural gas, and supplies over 65% of US imports.

ENVIRONMENT

Sustainability rank: 121st

6% (4% partially protected)

20.5 tonnes per capita

Spillages from oil tankers threaten coastal conservation areas such as the Caroni Swamp, with its many species of butterflies. Forest fires due to periodic drought, and traffic-related pollution and congestion are serious concerns.

MEDIA

TV ownership high

Daily newspaper circulation 123 per 1000 people

PUBLISHING AND BROADCAST MEDIA

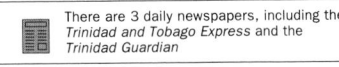

There are 3 daily newspapers, including the *Trinidad and Tobago Express* and the *Trinidad Guardian*

2 services: 1 state-owned, 1 independent

8 services: 1 state-owned, 7 independent

The government generally respects press freedom and the media are lively. Television schedules are dominated by US programs, particularly soap operas.

CRIME

Death penalty in use

4794 prisoners

Up 3% in 1999–2001

Narcotics-related crime increases the murder rate. The country was party to the decision taken in 2001 to replace the authority of the UK's Privy Council with a Caribbean Court of Justice.

EDUCATION

School leaving age: 11

99%

8614 students

Education is based on the former British system. Most students go on to the University of the West Indies; Trinidad hosts the St. Augustine campus. Wealthy Trinidadians, however, go to universities in the US.

HEALTH

Welfare state health benefits

1 per 1250 people

Heart disease, cancers, diabetes, accidents, violence

Oil wealth has given Trinidad a better public health service than most Caribbean states and more private clinics, mainly serving the expatriate community. However, treatment delays are a problem. The spread of HIV/AIDS is of particular concern on Tobago.

CHRONOLOGY

Britain seized Trinidad from Spain in 1797 and Tobago from France in 1802. They were unified in 1888.

- ❑ **1956** Eric Williams founds PNM and wins general election, mainly with support from blacks.
- ❑ **1958–1961** Member of West Indian Federation.
- ❑ **1962** Independence.
- ❑ **1970** Black Power demonstrations.
- ❑ **1980** Tobago gets own House of Assembly; internal autonomy 1987.
- ❑ **1990–1991** Premier taken hostage in failed fundamentalist coup. PNM returned to power.
- ❑ **1995** UNC's Basdeo Panday is first ethnic Asian prime minister.
- ❑ **1998–1999** Trinidad withdraws from international human rights bodies over death sentences.
- ❑ **2001** Elections result in tie.
- ❑ **2002** PNM wins fresh elections.

SPENDING

GDP/cap. increase

CONSUMPTION AND SPENDING

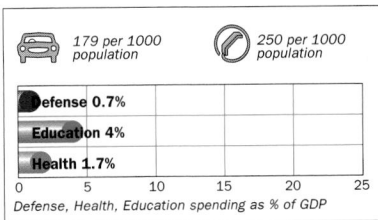

179 per 1000 population

250 per 1000 population

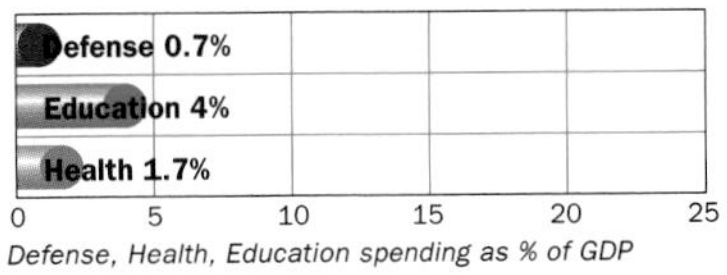
Defense 0.7%
Education 4%
Health 1.7%
0
5
10
15
20
25
Defense, Health, Education spending as % of GDP

Rural poverty in the interior of Trinidad, particularly among south Asian Trinidadian farmers, is a serious problem. Wealth disparities are particularly marked between them and the affluent oil-rich business elite, many of whom are expatriate. Service workers in Tobago's high-value tourism sector are poorly paid.

WORLD RANKING

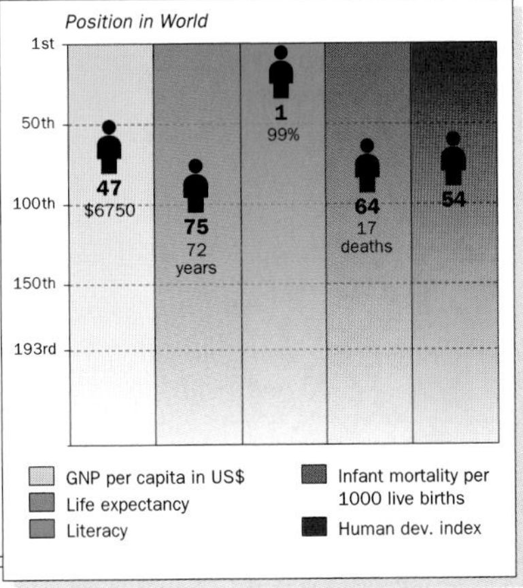
Position in World
1st
50th
100th
150th
193rd
47
$6750
75
72
years
1
99%
64
17
deaths
54
GNP per capita in US$
Life expectancy
Literacy
Infant mortality per 1000 live births
Human dev. index

T

TUNISIA

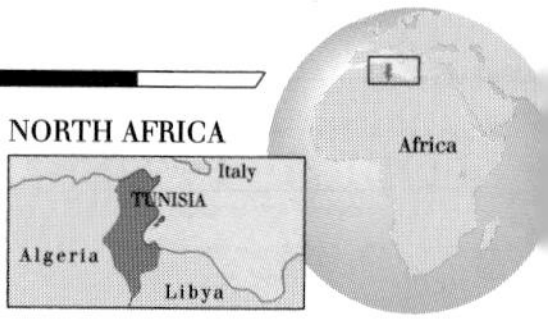
NORTH AFRICA
Italy
TUNISIA
Algeria
Libya
Africa

OFFICIAL NAME: Republic of Tunisia **CAPITAL:** Tunis
POPULATION: 9.8 million **CURRENCY:** Tunisian dinar **OFFICIAL LANGUAGE:** Arabic

1956
1956
March 20
TN
+1
+216
.tn

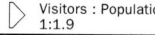

NORTH AFRICA'S SMALLEST country, Tunisia lies sandwiched between Libya and Algeria. The populous north is mountainous and fertile in places and has a long Mediterranean coastline. The south is largely desert. Habib Bourguiba ruled the country from independence in 1956 until a bloodless coup in 1987. Under President Ben Ali, the government has slowly moved toward multiparty democracy, but is challenged by Islamic fundamentalism. Ties with the EU, whose members include Tunisia's main trading partners, were strengthened through the first Euro-Mediterranean conference held in 1995. Manufacturing and tourism are expanding.

CLIMATE

Mediterranean/ hot desert

WEATHER CHART FOR TUNIS

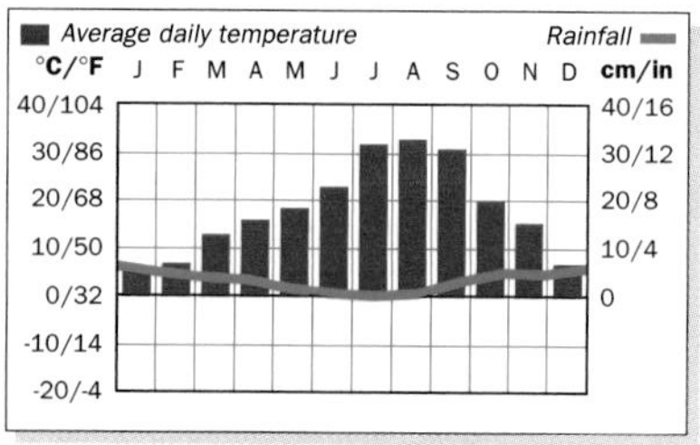
Average daily temperature
Rainfall
°C/°F
J F M A M J J A S O N D
cm/in
40/104
30/86
20/68
10/50
0/32
-10/14
-20/-4
40/16
30/12
20/8
10/4
0

Tunisia is hot in summer. The north can be wet and windy in winter. The far south is arid. The spring brings the dry, dusty *chili* wind from the Sahara.

TRANSPORTATION

Drive on right

Skanes, Monastir 3.06 passengers

75 ships 185,500 grt

THE TRANSPORTATION NETWORK

12,348 km (7673 miles)	142 km (88 miles)
1909 km (1186 miles)	None

Tunisia has six international airports. The transportation network is modern, efficient, and extensive. Tunis has both a modern light metro system and a suburban railroad line. The mostly uninhabited south has few roads.

TOURISM

Visitors : Population 1:1.9

5.16m visitors

Up 2% in 2003

MAIN TOURIST ARRIVALS

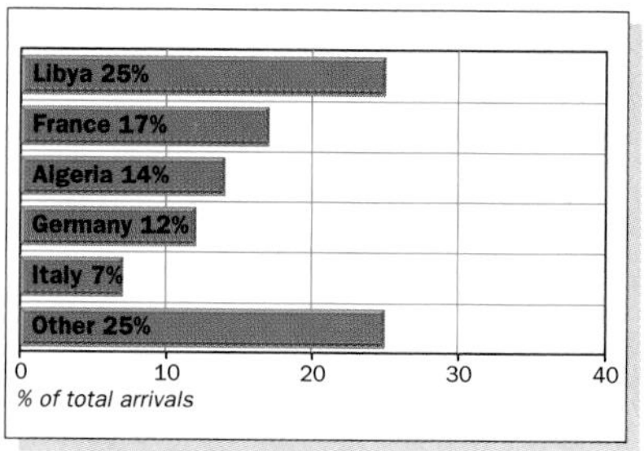
Libya 25%
France 17%
Algeria 14%
Germany 12%
Italy 7%
Other 25%
0
10
20
30
40
% of total arrivals

Tourists have flocked to Tunisia since the 1960s, attracted by its winter sunshine, beaches, desert, and archaeological remains. One of the Mediterranean's cheapest package destinations, Tunisia attracts almost three million European visitors a year, though some tourists are deterred by the fear of attacks by Islamists. In 2002, 14 German tourists were killed by a suicide bombing on the island of Jerba.

Tourism employs more than 200,000 people and is a focus of investment. However, concern about its environmental impact is growing.

PEOPLE

Pop. density medium

Arabic, French

63/km² (163/mi²)

THE URBAN/RURAL POPULATION SPLIT

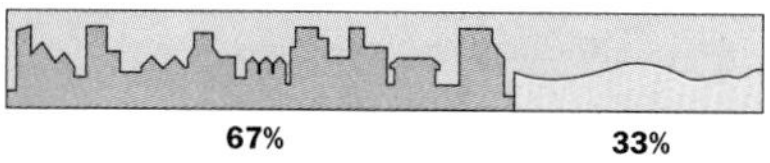
67%
33%

RELIGIOUS PERSUASION

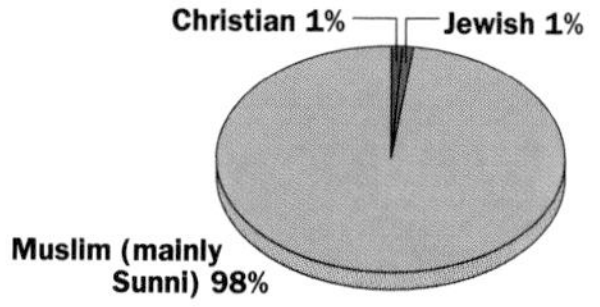
Christian 1%
Jewish 1%
Muslim (mainly Sunni) 98%

ETHNIC MAKEUP

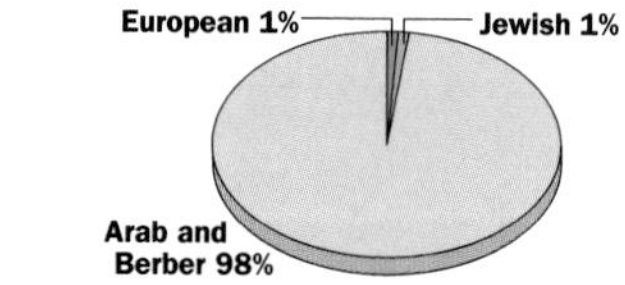
European 1%
Jewish 1%
Arab and Berber 98%

The population is almost entirely Muslim, of Arab and Berber descent, though there are Jewish and Christian minorities. Many Tunisians still live in extended family groups, in which three or four generations are represented.

Socially at least, Tunisia is one of the most liberal Arab states. The 1956 Personal Statutes Code gave women fuller rights than in any other Arab country. Contraception and family planning were made freely available in the 1960s. Since the 1980s a wide-ranging social modernization program has promoted education and women's rights while legislation has given women the right to custody of children in divorce cases, made domestic violence punishable by law, and helped divorced women to get alimony. Women make up 31% of the total workforce and 35% of the industrial workforce. Female literacy, however, is still 20% lower than male, and politics remains a mostly male preserve.

These freedoms are threatened by the growth in recent years of Islamic fundamentalism, which also worries the mainly French-speaking political and business elite who wish to strengthen links with Europe.

The Ben Ali regime has been criticized for its actions against Islamist activists. Despite continuing condemnation of its human rights record, the government's efforts to foster democracy were praised in 2002 when it received the "Mediterranean Award," given by European human rights leagues.

POPULATION AGE BREAKDOWN

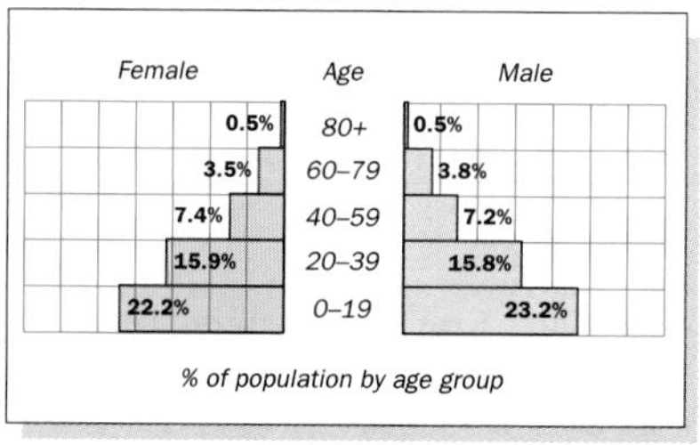
Female
Age
Male
0.5%
80+
0.5%
3.5%
60–79
3.8%
7.4%
40–59
7.2%
15.9%
20–39
15.8%
22.2%
0–19
23.2%
% of population by age group

***Roman remains** in the western Tozeur region. Diverse archaeological remains can be found throughout Tunisia.*

T

POLITICS

Multiparty elections

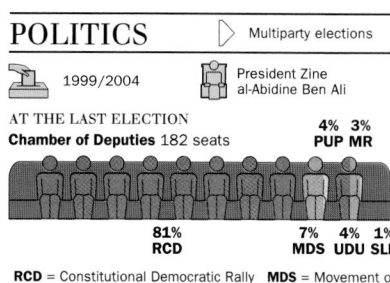

1999/2004

President Zine al-Abidine Ben Ali

AT THE LAST ELECTION

Chamber of Deputies 182 seats

4% PUP
3% MR
81% RCD
7% MDS
4% UDU
1% SLP

RCD = Constitutional Democratic Rally **MDS** = Movement of Social Democrats **PUP** = Popular Unity Party **UDU** = Unionist Democratic Union **MR** = Movement for Renewal **SLP** = Social Liberal Party

President Ben Ali *became head of state in 1987.*

Mohammed Ghannouchi, *prime minister since 1999.*

Formally a multiparty democracy since 1988, Tunisia is effectively dominated by the RCD and President Zine al-Abidine Ben Ali.

PROFILE

Taking over from the 31-year presidency of Habib Bourguiba in 1987, President Ben Ali inherited a modernizing and robust economy. Though he has turned his attention to a program of social development and education, Ben Ali has done little to liberalize the political system. The RCD won overwhelmingly in the 1994 and 1999 elections and the abolishment of the life presidency was undermined in 2002 when a constitutional referendum gave Ben Ali a mandate to stand for a further two terms.

MAIN POLITICAL ISSUES

Fundamentalism

With the failure of political dialogue, Ben Ali has attempted instead to neutralize any Islamic fundamentalist opposition; the al-Nahda (Renewal Party) has been outlawed. An attack in 2002 on a synagogue in Jerba was claimed by the Islamic Army for the Liberation of Holy Places, the same group responsible for attacks in Kenya and Tanzania in 1998.

Human rights

The RCD has been under increasing attack over its human rights record, despite its commitment to women's rights. The activities of the Tunisia League of Human Rights were suspended in 2001, while journalists practice heavy self-censorship.

TUNISIA

Total Area : 163 610 sq. km (63 169 sq. miles)

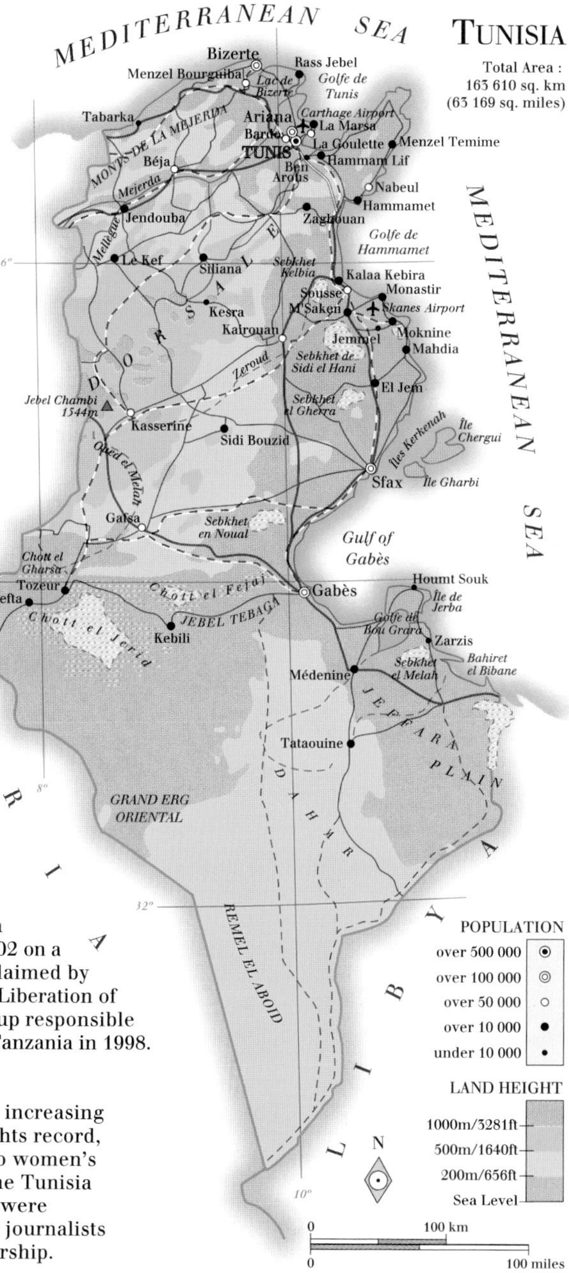
MEDITERRANEAN SEA
Bizerte
Rass Jebel
Menzel Bourguiba
Lac de Bizerte
Golfe de Tunis
Tabarka
Ariana
Carthage Airport
La Marsa
Bardo
TUNIS
La Goulette
Menzel Temime
Hammam Lif
Béja
Ben Arous
Nabeul
Hammamet
Golfe de Hammamet
Jendouba
Zaghouan
Le Kef
Siliana
Sebkhet Kelbia
Kalaa Kebira
Monastir
Sousse
Skanes Airport
M'Saken
Kesra
Kairouan
Jemmel
Moknine
Mahdia
Sebkhet de Sidi el Hani
El Jem
Jebel Chambi 1544m
Kasserine
Sidi Bouzid
Sebkhet el Gherra
Île Chergui
Îles Kerkenah
Sfax
Île Gharbi
Gafsa
Sebkhet en Noual
Gulf of Gabès
Chott el Gharsa
Tozeur
Nefta
Chott el Fejaj
Gabès
Houmt Souk
Île de Jerba
Chott el Jerid
JEBEL TEBAGA
Kebili
Golfe de Bou Grara
Zarzis
Médenine
Sebkhet el Melah
Bahiret el Bibane
JEFFARA PLAIN
Tataouine
GRAND ERG ORIENTAL
DAHAR
REMEL EL ABOID
ALGERIA
LIBYA
MONTS DE LA MEJERDA
DORSALE
MEDITERRANEAN SEA
POPULATION
over 500 000
over 100 000
over 50 000
over 10 000
under 10 000
LAND HEIGHT
1000m/3281ft
500m/1640ft
200m/656ft
Sea Level
N
0
100 km
0
100 miles

WORLD AFFAIRS

Joined UN in 1956

AL | AMU | OIF | NAM | OIC

Economic and political relations with the EU are the top priority, though for many years Tunisia pursued a foreign policy which alienated it from the West. From the early 1980s until 1994, Tunis was host to the Palestine Liberation Organization (PLO), President Ben Ali supported Iraq in the 1991 Gulf War, and the Tunisian government turned a blind eye to "sanctions-busters" supplying Libya. While these policies have been rendered meaningless by world events, concern remains over the government's human rights record.

Liberal economic and social policies, however, have done much to counteract questionable diplomacy in Western eyes. In particular, the government's effective struggle against Islamic extremists has enamored it to the US, which now sees Tunisia as a close military and intelligence ally in the "war on terrorism."

CHRONOLOGY

Tunisia has been home to the Zenata Berbers since earliest times and its history is linked to the rise and fall of the Mediterranean-centered empires. Carthage (near present-day Tunis), founded by the Phoenicians in the 9th century BCE, became the hub of the 1000-year Carthaginian empire which linked European and African trading networks. Tunisia was then ruled by the Romans, Byzantines, Egyptians, Ottomans, and, finally, the French.

- **1883** La Marsa Treaty makes Tunisia a French protectorate, ending its semi-independence. Bey of Tunis remains monarch.
- **1900** Influx of French and Italians.
- **1920** Destour (Constitution) Party formed; calls for self-government.
- **1935** Habib Bourguiba forms Neo-Destour (New Constitution) Party.
- **1943** Defeat of Axis powers by British troops restores French rule.
- **1955** Internal autonomy. Bourguiba returns from exile.
- **1956** Independence. Bourguiba elected prime minister. Personal Statutes Code gives rights to women. Family planning introduced.
- **1957** Bey is deposed. Tunisia becomes republic with Bourguiba as first president.
- **1964** Neo-Destour made sole legal party; renamed Destour Socialist Party (PSD). Moderate socialist economic program is introduced.
- **1969** Agricultural collectivization program, begun 1964, abandoned.

T

CHRONOLOGY *continued*

- **1974** Bourguiba elected president-for-life by National Assembly.
- **1974–1976** Hundreds imprisoned for belonging to "illegal organizations."
- **1978** Trade union movement, UGTT, holds 24-hour general strike; more than 50 killed in clashes. UGTT leadership replaced with PSD loyalists.
- **1980** New prime minister Muhammed Mazli ushers in greater political tolerance.
- **1981** Elections. Opposition groups allege electoral malpractice.
- **1984** Widespread riots after food price increases.
- **1986** Gen. Zine al-Abidine Ben Ali becomes interior minister. Four Islamic fundamentalists sentenced to death.
- **1987** Fundamentalist leader Rachid Ghannouchi arrested. Ben Ali becomes prime minister; takes over presidency after doctors certify Bourguiba senile. PSD renamed RCD.
- **1988** Most political prisoners released. Constitutional reforms introduce multiparty system and abolish life presidency. Two opposition parties legalized.
- **1989** Elections: RCD wins all seats, Ben Ali president. Fundamentalists take 13% of vote.
- **1990** Tunisia backs Iraq over invasion of Kuwait. Clampdown on fundamentalists intensifies.
- **1991** Abortive coup blamed on al-Nahda; over 500 arrests.
- **1993** Multiparty agreement on electoral reform.
- **1994** Presidential and legislative elections. Ben Ali, sole candidate, is reelected.
- **1996** MDS leader Mohammed Moada imprisoned.
- **1999** Ben Ali and RCD win elections.
- **2002** Referendum allows Ben Ali to stand for office after 2004. Suicide bomb attack in Jerba kills 14 German tourists.

T

AID

Recipient

$475m (receipts) | Up 26% in 2002

The EU and France are the two major international donors, providing over half of all bilateral aid. Japan, Germany, Arab countries, and Italy are other important sources of assistance. As a result of strong economic growth, the ratios of external debt to GNP and of debt service to exports receipts have improved markedly since the early 1990s; Tunisia's total external debt is now estimated to be around two-thirds of GNP.

DEFENSE

Compulsory military service

$383m | Up 22% in 2002

Despite the military's small size – 35,000 troops, of which around two-thirds are conscripts – it is a major political force. Its weaponry comes mainly from the US, and officer training is carried out in the US and France, as well as in Tunisia. Border security with Algeria was tightened in 1995 after Algerian Islamists attacked Tunisian border guards in protest against Tunisian support for Algerian security forces.

TUNISIAN ARMED FORCES

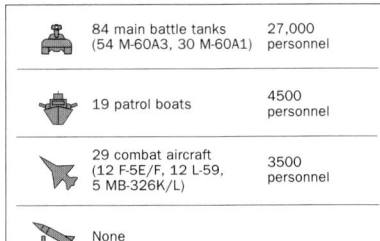

84 main battle tanks (54 M-60A3, 30 M-60A1)	27,000 personnel
19 patrol boats	4500 personnel
29 combat aircraft (12 F-5E/F, 12 L-59, 5 MB-326K/L)	3500 personnel
None	

ECONOMICS

Inflation 4.3% p.a. (1990–2001)

$19.5bn | 1.261 Tunisian dinars (1.275)

SCORE CARD

World GNP Ranking	67th
GNP per Capita	$1990
Balance of Payments	–$746m
Inflation	2.7%
Unemployment	14%

EXPORTS

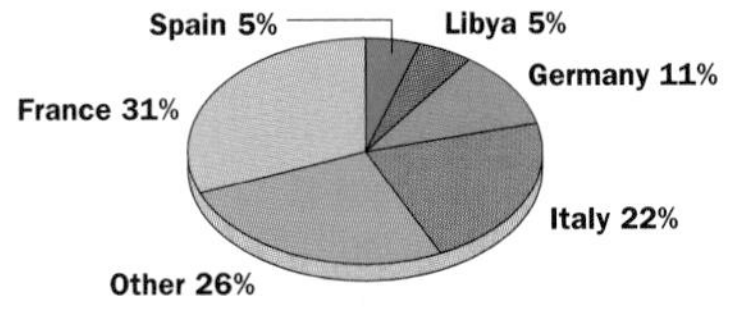
Spain 5%
Libya 5%
Germany 11%
France 31%
Italy 22%
Other 26%

IMPORTS

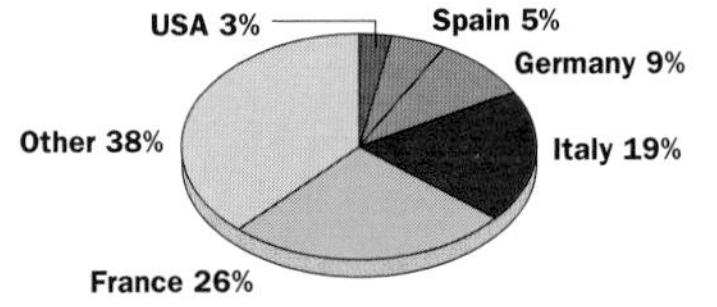
USA 3%
Spain 5%
Germany 9%
Other 38%
Italy 19%
France 26%

Strengths

Well-diversified economy, despite limited resources. Tourism. Oil and gas exports, also traditional agricultural exports: olive oil, olives, citrus fruit, dates. Manufacturing sectors strong. Key products are textiles, construction materials, machinery, chemicals. European investment. Ranked as most competitive economy in Africa in World Economic Forum's 2000–2001 report.

Weaknesses

Agricultural sector largely unproductive and prone to drought. Growing domestic energy demand on oil and gas resources: net energy importer. Regional instability negatively affects tourism and investment. High unemployment and trade deficit.

Profile

Since it began a process of structural adjustment in 1988, supported by the IMF and the World Bank, Tunisia's economy has become increasingly open and market-oriented. Real GDP growth has averaged 5% since 1987. Prices have been freed, some state companies privatized, and import barriers reduced. There have been numerous attempts to modernize the agricultural sector.

The balance of payments relies on fluctuating tourism receipts to offset a trade deficit. The government must also balance growth with better social provisions. Tunisia has committed itself to a free trade area with the EU by 2010; there is concern that the potential influx of European imports will harm local producers.

ECONOMIC PERFORMANCE INDICATOR

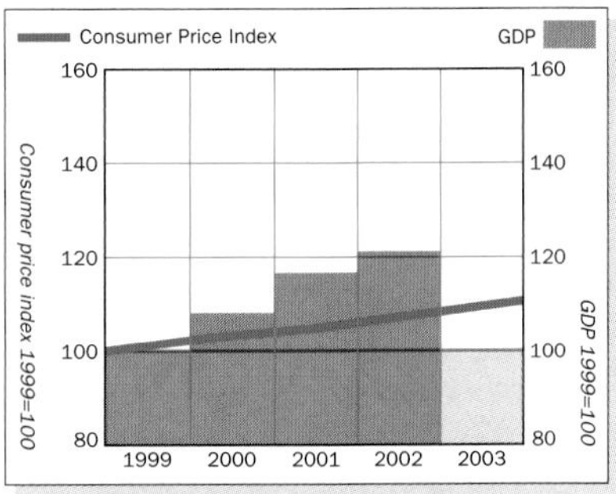
Consumer Price Index
GDP
160
140
120
100
80
Consumer price index 1999=100
GDP 1999=100
1999
2000
2001
2002
2003

TUNISIA : MAJOR BUSINESSES

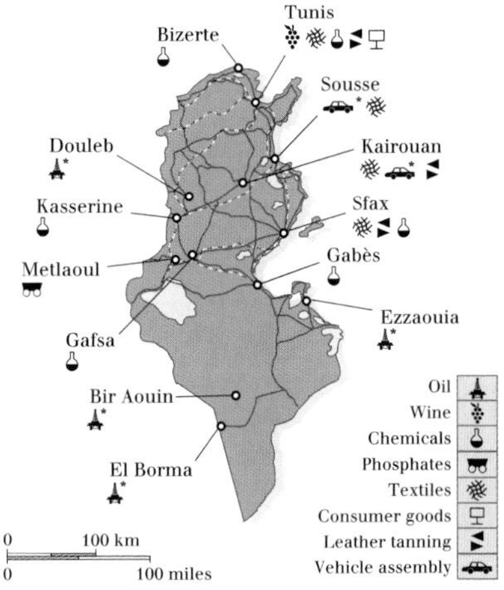
Tunis
Bizerte
Sousse
Douleb
Kairouan
Kasserine
Sfax
Gabès
Metlaoui
Ezzaouia
Gafsa
Bir Aouin
El Borma
Oil
Wine
Chemicals
Phosphates
Textiles
Consumer goods
Leather tanning
Vehicle assembly
0
100 km
0
100 miles

* significant multinational ownership

RESOURCES

Electric power 2.3m kW

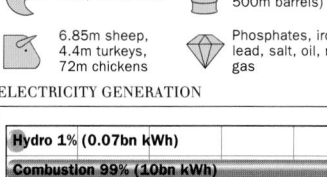

100,350 tonnes

66,000 b/d (reserves 500m barrels)

6.85m sheep, 4.4m turkeys, 72m chickens

Phosphates, iron, zinc, lead, salt, oil, natural gas

ELECTRICITY GENERATION

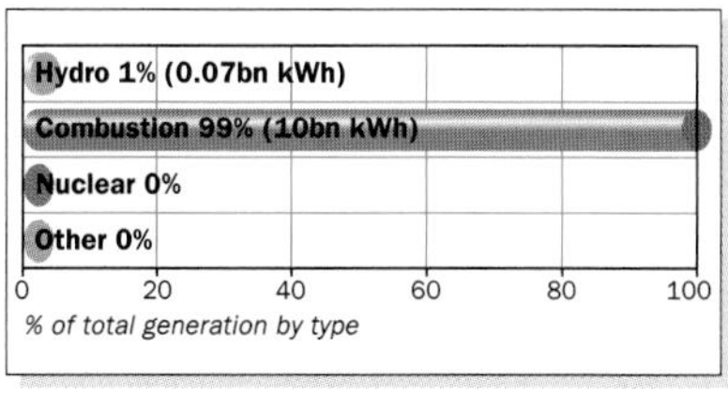

Hydro 1% (0.07bn kWh)
Combustion 99% (10bn kWh)
Nuclear 0%
Other 0%
0
20
40
60
80
100
% of total generation by type

TUNISIA : LAND USE

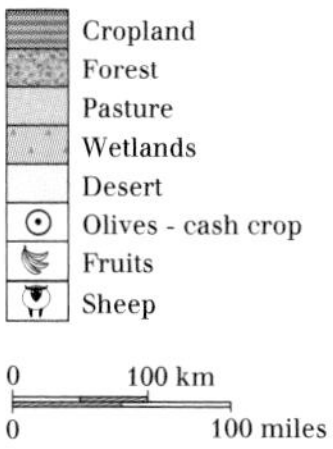

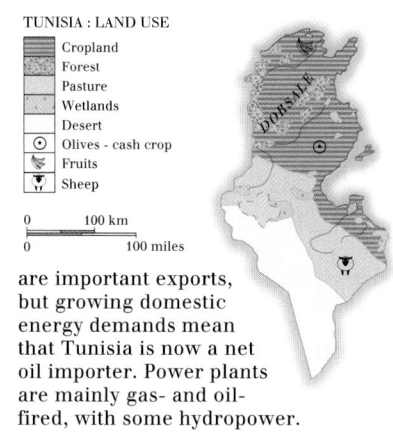

Cropland
Forest
Pasture
Wetlands
Desert
Olives - cash crop
Fruits
Sheep
0
100 km
0
100 miles

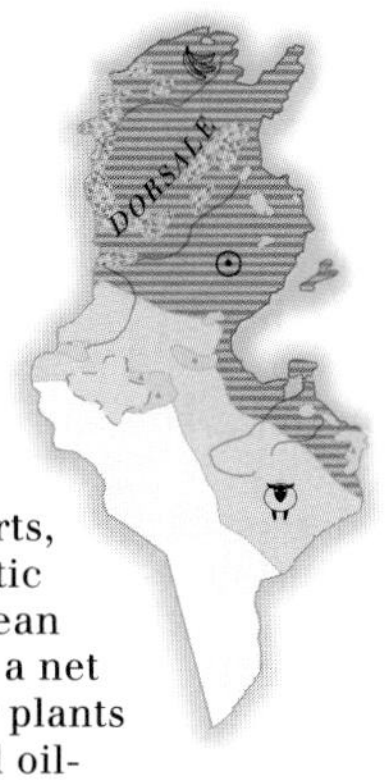

DORSALE

Tunisia is a leading producer of phosphates for fertilizers, mainly from mines near Gafsa. Oil and gas are important exports, but growing domestic energy demands mean that Tunisia is now a net oil importer. Power plants are mainly gas- and oil-fired, with some hydropower.

HEALTH

Welfare state health benefits

1 per 1429 people

Heart and cerebrovascular diseases

Well-developed family-planning facilities have almost halved Tunisia's birthrate over the past 30 years. The population growth rate has dropped from 3.2% to around 1% – the lowest in the region. The mortality rate has been reduced, to six per 1000 people, reflecting the extension of free medical services to over 70% of the population. While services lack sophistication, an umbrella of primary care facilities covers all but the most isolated rural communities. Regional committees organize care for the old, the needy, and the orphaned.

ENVIRONMENT

Sustainability rank: 61st

0.3%

1.9 tonnes per capita

ENVIRONMENTAL TREATIES

Yes Yes Yes

Yes Yes Yes

Desertification is a serious problem in the largely arid central and southern regions. However, the dominant environmental issue is the rapid expansion of tourism since the 1980s. Large, insensitively designed hotel and resort developments, which do not fit in with the local architecture, are spoiling coastal areas such as the island of Jerba and Hammamet (though building height restrictions are applied here). Tourism is also making an impact on the fragile desert ecology of the south.

CRIME

Death penalty not used in practice

23,165 prisoners

Down 8% in 2000–2002

CRIME RATES

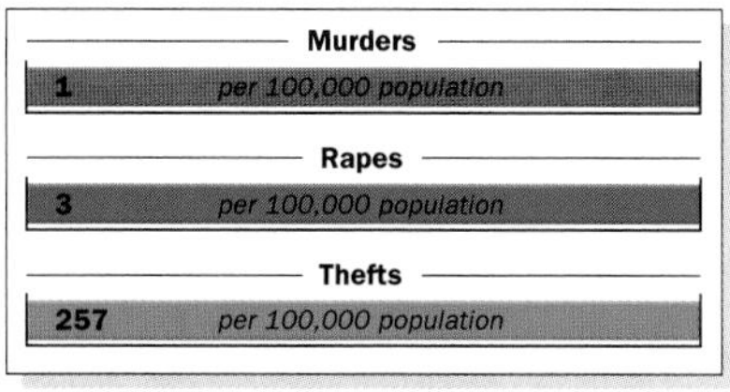

Murders
1
per 100,000 population
Rapes
3
per 100,000 population
Thefts
257
per 100,000 population

Street crime is unusual. However, Tunisia's poor human rights record has prompted criticism of its maltreatment of political and other detainees. Arbitrary arrests and torture while in police custody, especially of suspected Islamist activists, are routine.

SPENDING

GDP/cap. increase

CONSUMPTION AND SPENDING

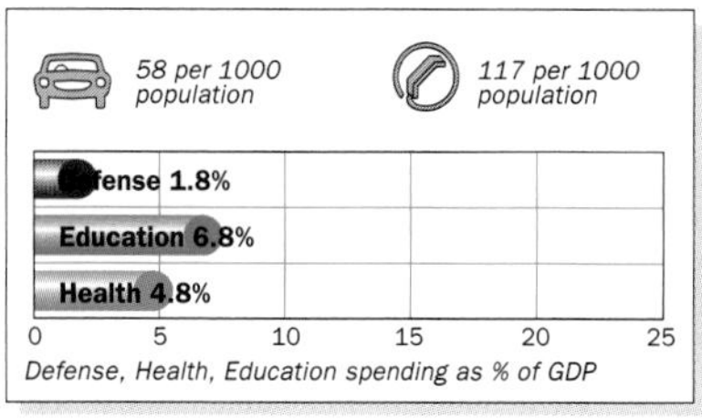

58 per 1000 population
117 per 1000 population
Defense 1.8%
Education 6.8%
Health 4.8%
0
5
10
15
20
25
Defense, Health, Education spending as % of GDP

Around 10% of Tunisians are estimated to live below the UN poverty line. The poorest in the community tend to live in the urban shanty towns, or *bidonvilles*. The Western-oriented elite has links with government or business.

Unemployment benefits from the National Social Security Fund are limited to nonagricultural workers and are only provided for three months. The government is concerned that the lack of jobs is encouraging the spread of Islamic fundamentalism; economic growth is its medium-term solution to the problem. Special projects are being set up in the most deprived urban areas to offset the worst effects of poverty.

MEDIA

TV ownership medium

Daily newspaper circulation 23 per 1000 people

PUBLISHING AND BROADCAST MEDIA

There are 8 daily newspapers, including *al-Amal*, *La Presse de Tunisie*, and *As-Sabah*

2 state-owned services

2 services: 1 state-owned, 1 independent

Reforms since the late 1980s have in theory increased press freedom in Tunisia, traditionally considered a source of liberal ideas in the Arab world. In practice, government restrictions remain. The foreign press is also occasionally banned. Only the arrival of satellite TV from Europe has enabled people to receive a wide range of programs. The Internet is heavily censored.

EDUCATION

School leaving age: 16

73%

262,502 students

THE EDUCATION SYSTEM

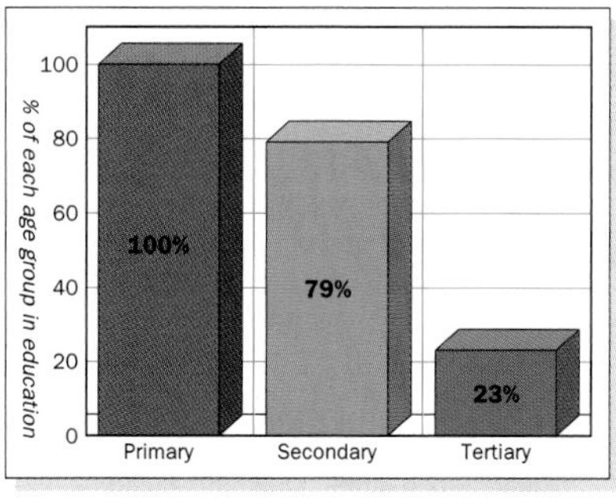

% of each age group in education
100
80
60
40
20
0
100%
79%
23%
Primary
Secondary
Tertiary

Education is compulsory in Tunisia from the age of six, with secondary education beginning at 12. Arabic is the first language in schools, but French is also taught and is used almost exclusively in higher education. There are eight universities (one is private); student enrollment has doubled since 1995.

WORLD RANKING

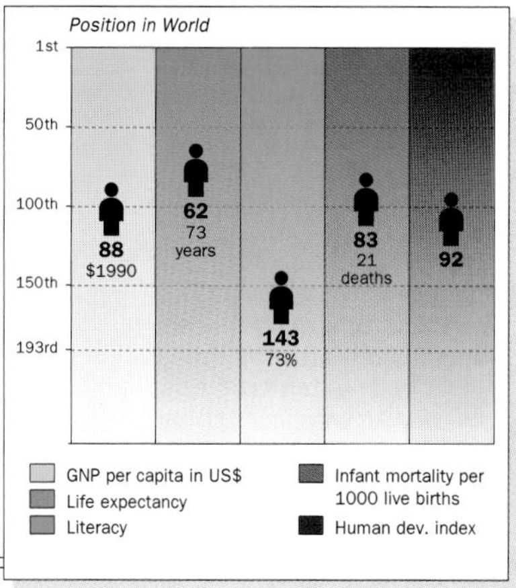

Position in World
1st
50th
100th
150th
193rd
88
$1990
62
73 years
143
73%
83
21 deaths
92
GNP per capita in US$
Life expectancy
Literacy
Infant mortality per 1000 live births
Human dev. index

T

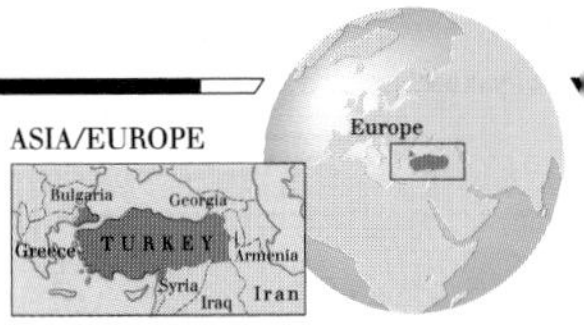
ASIA/EUROPE
Europe
Bulgaria
Georgia
Greece
TURKEY
Armenia
Syria
Iraq
Iran

TURKEY

OFFICIAL NAME: Republic of Turkey **CAPITAL:** Ankara
POPULATION: 71.3 million **CURRENCY:** Turkish lira **OFFICIAL LANGUAGE:** Turkish

1923
1939
Oct 29
TR
+2
+90
.tr

THOUGH ITS TERRITORY lies mainly in western Asia, Turkey also includes the region of Eastern Thrace in Europe. It thus controls the entrance to the Black Sea, which is straddled by Turkey's largest city, Istanbul. Most Turks live in the western half of the country. The eastern and southeastern reaches of the Anatolia Plateau are Kurdish regions. Turkey's location gives it great strategic influence in the Black Sea, the Mediterranean, and the Middle East. Turkey lies on a major earthquake fault line, so that many towns are vulnerable to earthquakes such as that which devastated Izmit in 1999.

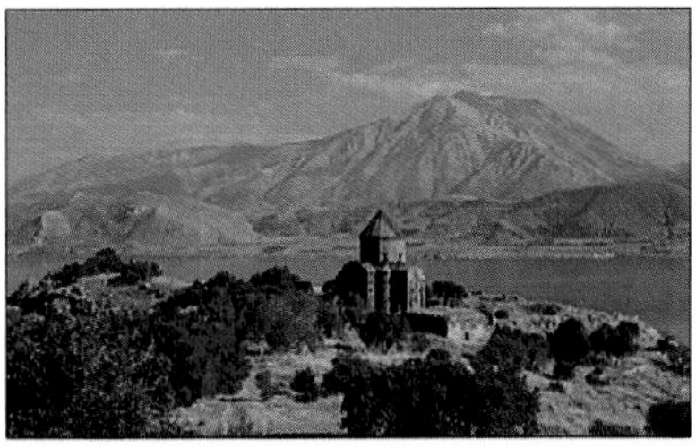

The Church of the Holy Cross, on Akdamar Island in Lake Van, was built in the 10th century when Christianity was dominant in the region.

CLIMATE

Mountain/ Mediterranean

WEATHER CHART FOR ANKARA

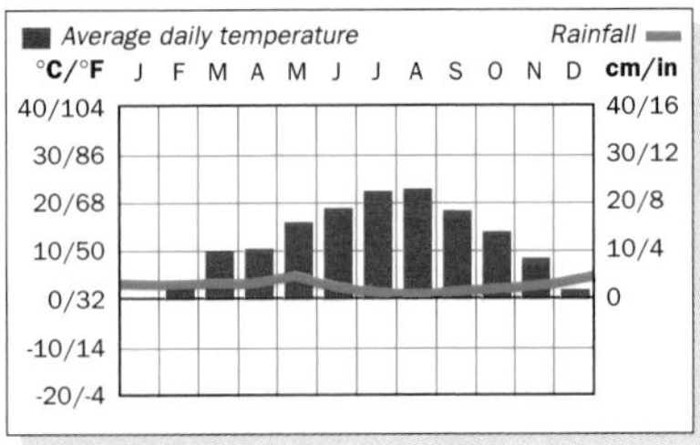
Average daily temperature
Rainfall
°C/°F
J F M A M J J A S O N D
cm/in
40/104
30/86
20/68
10/50
0/32
-10/14
-20/-4
40/16
30/12
20/8
10/4
0

Coastal regions have a Mediterranean climate. The interior has cold, snowy winters and hot, dry summers.

TRANSPORTATION

Drive on right

Atatürk International, Istanbul
14m passengers

1147 ships
5.66m grt

THE TRANSPORTATION NETWORK

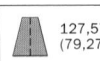

127,574 km (79,271 miles)

1773 km (1102 miles)

8671 km (5388 miles)

1200 km (746 miles)

Recent rail projects include a high-speed link between Istanbul and Ankara, a light rail system in Istanbul, and a tunnel beneath the Bosphorus Straits. An extensive network of ports and harbors includes Istanbul and Izmir.

PEOPLE

Pop. density medium

Turkish, Kurdish, Arabic, Circassian, Armenian, Greek, Georgian, Ladino

93/km² (240/mi²)

THE URBAN/RURAL POPULATION SPLIT

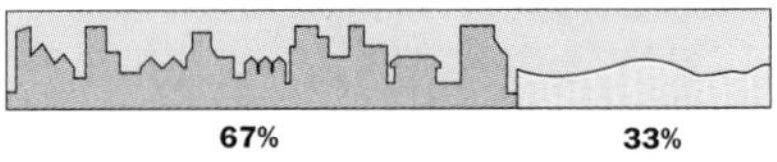
67%
33%

RELIGIOUS PERSUASION

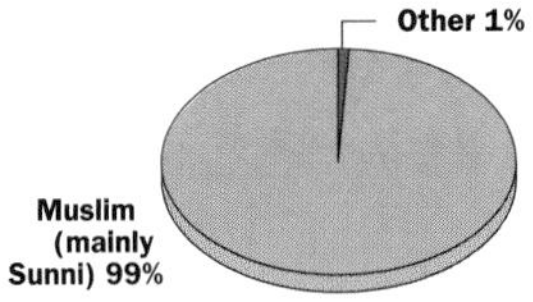
Other 1%
Muslim (mainly Sunni) 99%

ETHNIC MAKEUP

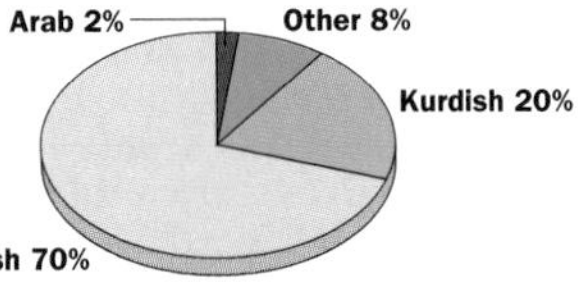
Arab 2%
Other 8%
Kurdish 20%
Turkish 70%

The Turks are racially diverse. Many are the descendants of refugees, often from the Balkans, but a strong sense of national identity is rooted in a shared language and religion. Most are Sunni Muslim, though a Shi'a community, including the heterodox Alawite sect, is growing fast. The largest minority are the Kurds, and there are some 500,000 Arabic speakers. While women have equal rights in law, men dominate political and even family life. In 2002 women gained the right to an equal portion in the case of divorce.

With population growth at 2%, Turkey is projected to have a larger population than any EU country by 2020.

POPULATION AGE BREAKDOWN

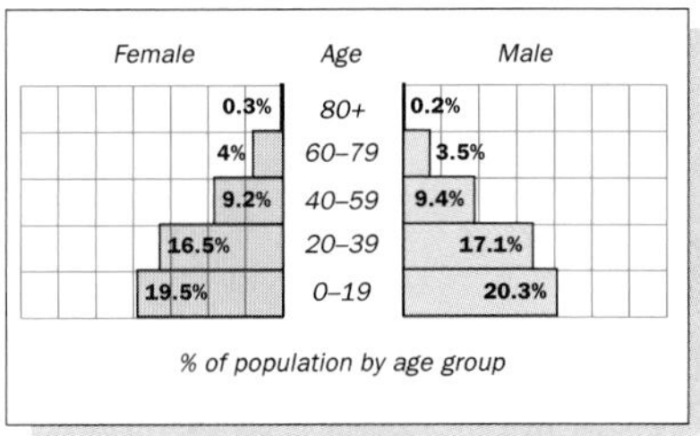
Female
Age
Male
0.3%
80+
0.2%
4%
60–79
3.5%
9.2%
40–59
9.4%
16.5%
20–39
17.1%
19.5%
0–19
20.3%
% of population by age group

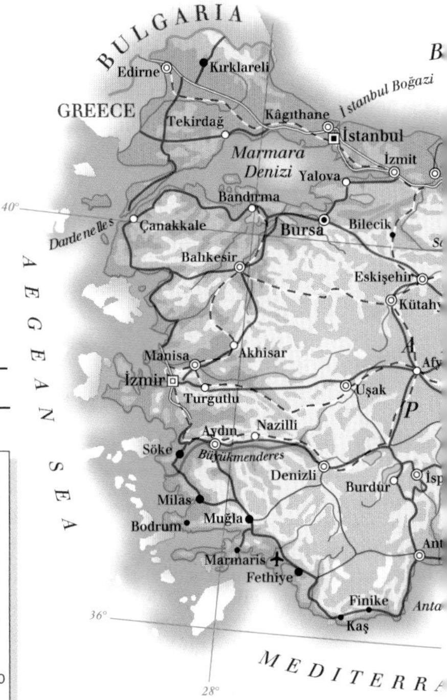
BULGARIA
GREECE
Edirne
Kırklareli
Tekirdağ
Kâğıthane
İstanbul Boğazi
İstanbul
İzmit
Marmara Denizi
Yalova
Bandırma
Dardeneles
Çanakkale
Bursa
Bilecik
Balıkesir
Eskişehir
Kütahya
AEGEAN SEA
Manisa
Akhisar
İzmir
Turgutlu
Uşak
Aydın
Nazilli
Söke
Büyükmenderes
Denizli
Burdur
Milas
Muğla
Bodrum
Marmaris
Fethiye
Finike
Kaş
MEDITERRA
40°
36°
28°

TOURISM

Visitors : Population 1:5.4

13.3m visitors

Up 4% in 2003

Visitors are attracted by fine beaches, classical sites such as Ephesus and Troy, and archaeological remains from the prehistoric to the Ottoman periods. Attacks on foreigners by Kurdish militants in 1994 hit the tourist trade, but business then recovered, and in 2001 tourists spent $8 billion. Visitor numbers dropped after the September 2001 attacks on the US, but bounced back in 2002.

MAIN TOURIST ARRIVALS

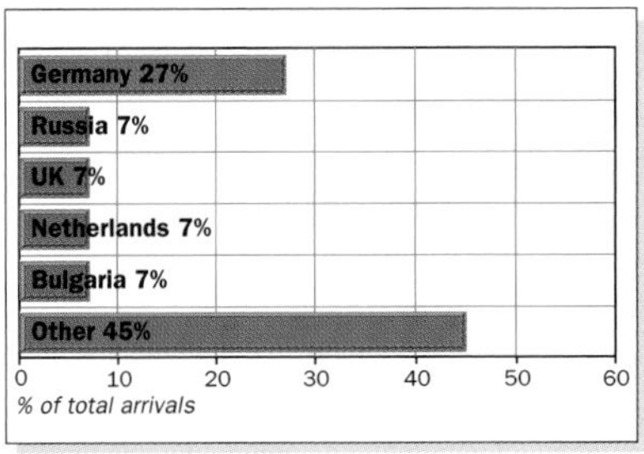
Germany 27%
Russia 7%
UK 7%
Netherlands 7%
Bulgaria 7%
Other 45%
0
10
20
30
40
50
60
% of total arrivals

T

POLITICS

Multiparty elections

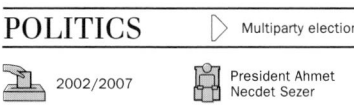

2002/2007

President Ahmet Necdet Sezer

AT THE LAST ELECTION

Turkish Grand National Assembly 550 seats

66% AK
32% CHP
2% Ind

AK = Justice and Development Party
CHP = Republican People's Party **Ind** = Independents

Turkey is a multiparty republic. The president, who serves a seven-year term, appoints the prime minister.

PROFILE

The main ideological division in politics is Islamic–secular. In 2002 the powers of the National Security Council were restricted and its membership altered to give civilian dominance.

From 2000 on, the coalition government of Bulent Ecevit clashed with independent president Ahmet Necdet Sezer. Fresh elections in 2002 produced a stunning victory for the Islamist-dominated AK, while Ecevit's party, and many others, failed to gain any seats in the legislature. AK leader Recep Tayyip Erdogan, banned from the 2002 election for previous militant remarks, succeeded his deputy as prime minister in March 2003.

MAIN POLITICAL ISSUES

Islamist advances

The popularity of Islamist parties has challenged Turkey's cherished identity as a secular state. In 1995 the Welfare Party (RP) became the largest party, forming the government in 1996. Ousted by the army in mid-1997, it was banned in 1998. Many of its members took refuge in its successor, the Virtue Party, which in turn was banned in 2001. The succeeding AK scored a comprehensive victory in 2002. It has asserted that it does not wish to impose a theocracy, but the army remains wary.

Kurdish separatism

From 1984 a bitter civil war was fought in southeast Turkey, killing thousands of people over the next two decades. In 1999 Abdullah Ocalan, leader of the secessionist Kurdistan Workers' Party (PKK),was sentenced to death, his sentence commuted in 2002 to life imprisonment. Meanwhile, the PKK disbanded and regrouped as a political organization committed to seeking equal rights for Kurds within Turkey, under Ocalan's leadership. Turkey's treatment of the Kurds has been widely criticized internationally, and pressure from the EU in particular has led to constitutional amendments lifting the harsh ban on broadcasting and education in Kurdish.

European aspirations

Turkey's human rights record has long frustrated its European ambitions, but recent reforms have sought to meet EU standards. Civil liberties have been improved, and the government agreed in 2004 to abolish executions entirely. In September it pushed through a revised penal code, and days later the European Commission finally recommended that Turkey begin EU accession talks.

Recep Tayyip Erdogan, *AK leader and prime minister since 2003.*

Ahmet Necdet Sezer, *an independent, elected president in 2000.*

TURKEY

Total Area : 780 580 sq. km (301 382 sq. miles)

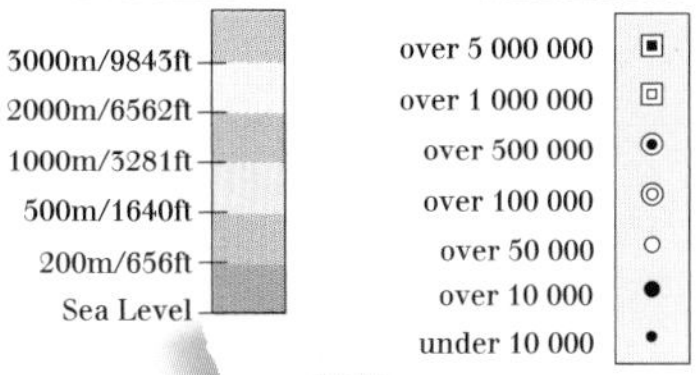
LAND HEIGHT
3000m/9843ft
2000m/6562ft
1000m/3281ft
500m/1640ft
200m/656ft
Sea Level
POPULATION
over 5 000 000
over 1 000 000
over 500 000
over 100 000
over 50 000
over 10 000
under 10 000

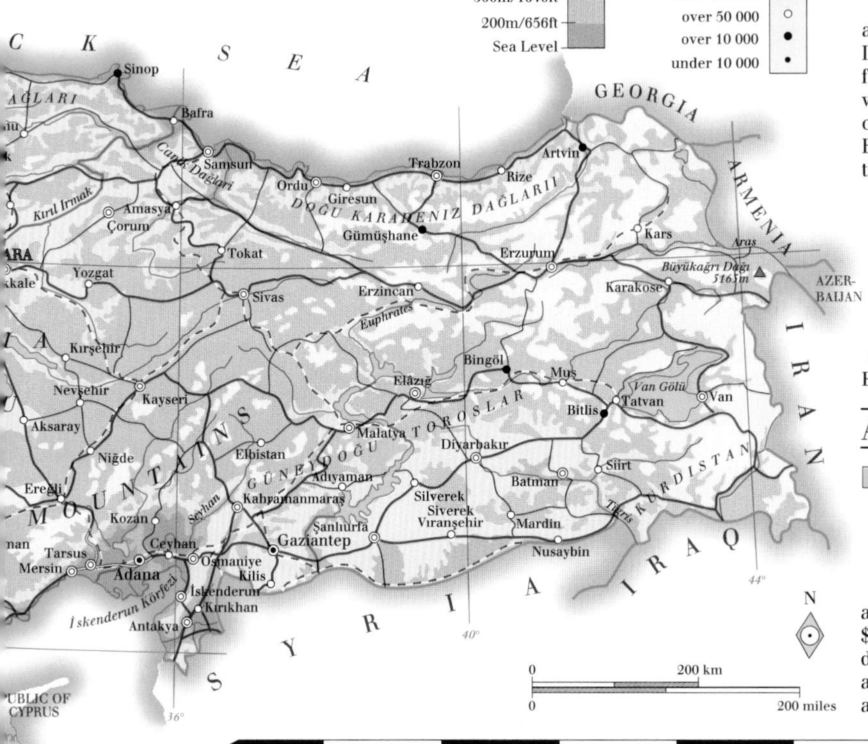
SEA
GEORGIA
ARMENIA
AZER-BAIJAN
IRAN
IRAQ
SYRIA
KURDISTAN
CYPRUS
Sinop
Bafra
Samsun
Trabzon
Artvin
Rize
Ordu
Giresun
DOĞU KARADENIZ DAĞLARI
Amasya
Çorum
Gümüşhane
Kars
Tokat
Erzurum
Büyükağrı Dağı 5165m
Yozgat
Karakose
Sivas
Erzincan
Euphrates
Kırşehir
Bingöl
Muş
Elazığ
Nevşehir
Van Gölü
Van
Kayseri
Tatvan
Bitlis
Aksaray
Malatya
TOROSLAR
Diyarbakır
Niğde
Elbistan
GÜNEYDOĞU
Adıyaman
Siirt
Batman
Ereğli
Kahramanmaraş
Silverek
Siverek
Viranşehir
Kozan
Şanlıurfa
Mardin
Ceyhan
Gaziantep
Nusaybin
Tarsus
Osmaniye
Mersin
Adana
Kilis
İskenderun
Kırıkhan
İskenderun Körfezi
Antakya
Tigris
Seyhan
Kızıl Irmak
40°
44°
36°
N
0 200 km
0 200 miles

WORLD AFFAIRS

Joined UN in 1945

CE NATO OECD OIC OSCE

Turkey has strategic significance as the only Muslim member of NATO. Its support for the US in the 1991 Gulf War was maintained in 2003, but less strongly: it refused passage to US troops for the invasion of Iraq. The presence in north Iraq of an autonomous Kurdish region is of great concern.

Turkey retains close ties to Israel and the more moderate Muslim states. It has developed links with many former communist states, especially with the Turkic-speaking central Asian countries, and is a member of the BSEC. In 2002 it held the leadership of the peacekeeping force in Afghanistan.

The quest to join the EU, aided by improving relations with Greece, has been impeded by EU concerns over human rights abuses. Turkey's presence in northern Cyprus is also problematic, though its 2004 backing of a UN settlement plan for the island (rejected by Greek Cypriots) raised its European and international standing.

AID

Recipient

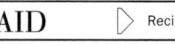

$636m (receipts) Up 281% in 2002

Turkey's diplomatic support for the Coalition in the 2003 war on Iraq boosted aid levels. The US, which had suspended aid in 1994 in protest at the treatment of Kurds, pledged $8.5 billion in 2003 in compensation for damage to the Turkish economy. Greece, a traditional enemy, offered humanitarian aid after the 1999 Izmit earthquake.

T

CHRONOLOGY

Following the collapse of the Ottoman Empire and Turkey's defeat in World War I, nationalist Mustafa Kemal Atatürk deposed the ruling sultan in 1922, declaring Turkey a republic in 1923.

- ❑ **1924** Religious courts abolished.
- ❑ **1928** Islam no longer state religion.
- ❑ **1934** Women given the vote.
- ❑ **1938** President Atatürk dies. Succeeded by Ismet Inönü.
- ❑ **1945** Turkey declares war on Germany. Joins UN.
- ❑ **1952** Joins CE and NATO.
- ❑ **1960** Military coup; National Assembly suspended.
- ❑ **1961** New constitution.
- ❑ **1963** Association agreement with European Economic Community.
- ❑ **1974** Invades northern Cyprus.
- ❑ **1980** Military coup; martial law.
- ❑ **1982** New constitution.
- ❑ **1983** Election won by Turgut Özal's Motherland Party (ANAP).
- ❑ **1984** Turkey recognizes "Turkish Republic of Northern Cyprus." Kurdish separatist PKK launches guerrilla war in southeast Turkey.
- ❑ **1991** US-led coalition launches air strikes on Iraq from Turkish bases. True Path Party (DYP) wins polls. Süleyman Demirel premier.
- ❑ **1992** Joins Black Sea alliance.
- ❑ **1993** Demirel elected president. Tansu Çiller DYP leader, heads coalition.
- ❑ **1995** Major anti-Kurdish offensive. Voting age lowered to 18. Çiller coalition collapses. Pro-Islamic RP wins election, but center-right DYP–ANAP coalition takes office. Customs union with EU.
- ❑ **1996–1997** RP leader Necmettin Erbakan heads first pro-Islamic government since 1923.
- ❑ **1997** Mesut Yilmaz reappointed to head minority ANAP government.
- ❑ **1998** RP banned. Yilmaz resigns, replaced by Bulent Ecevit of Democratic Left Party.
- ❑ **1999** Ecevit heads coalition after elections. Kurdish leader Abdullah Ocalan sentenced to death. Izmit earthquake kills 14,000.
- ❑ **2000** Demirel denied second term: Ahmet Necdet Sezer president.
- ❑ **2001** Acute financial crisis. Hunger strikes in high-security prisons. Virtue Party banned.
- ❑ **2002** Constitutional prodemocracy and human rights amendments, with goal of EU membership. April, PKK renounces violence and disbands. November, early elections won by Islamist AK.
- ❑ **2003** Recep Tayyip Erdogan becomes prime minister after by-election. Spate of bombings in Istanbul.

DEFENSE

▷ Compulsory military service

$8.73bn — Up 24% in 2002

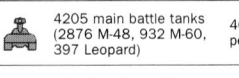

TURKISH ARMED FORCES

4205 main battle tanks (2876 M-48, 932 M-60, 397 Leopard)	402,000 personnel
13 submarines, 19 frigates, 21 missile craft, and 28 patrol boats	52,750 personnel
483 combat aircraft (224 F-16C/D, 87 F/NF-5A/B, 172 F-4E)	60,100 personnel
None	

Turkey's armed forces are the second-largest in NATO, which it joined in 1952. Turkey is a sizable military power, and it spends a higher percentage of GDP on defense than any other NATO country. NATO membership gives Turkey easy access to Western arms suppliers, though sales to Turkey are opposed on human rights grounds. Israel is an important source of arms. Campaigning against Kurdish separatists in southeast Turkey and Iraq has been scaled back in light of Turkey's bid for EU membership and the fall of Saddam Hussein in Iraq in 2003.

The great majority of Turkey's armed forces are conscripts, though military service has been cut from 18 months to 15 months, with university graduates only serving for a year.

ECONOMICS

▷ Inflation 74% p.a. (1990–2001)

$173bn — 1.484m Turkish lira (1.418m)

SCORE CARD

- ❑ World GNP Ranking......................25th
- ❑ GNP per Capita.........................$2490
- ❑ Balance of Payments.................–$1.79bn
- ❑ Inflation.....................................45%
- ❑ Unemployment..............................11%

EXPORTS

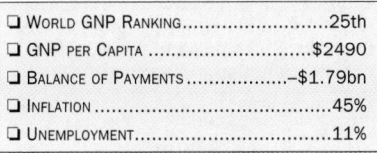

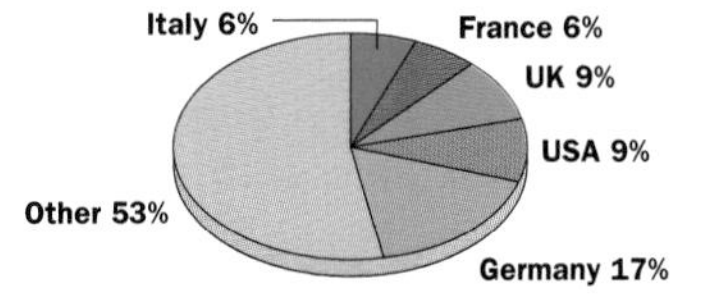
Italy 6%
France 6%
UK 9%
USA 9%
Other 53%
Germany 17%

IMPORTS

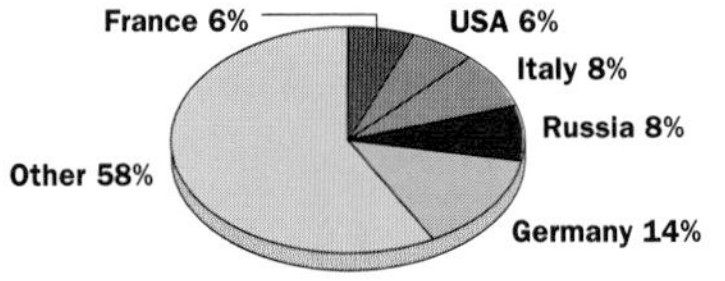
France 6%
USA 6%
Italy 8%
Russia 8%
Other 58%
Germany 14%

Strengths

Liberalized economy: strong growth since 2002. Near self-sufficiency in agriculture. Textiles, manufacturing, and construction sectors competitive in world markets. Tourism industry. Dynamic private sector economy. Skilled labor force. Customs union with EU.

Weaknesses

Persistently high inflation. Unsound public finances. Large government bureaucracy. Uneven privatization program. Ailing banking sector. Influence of organized crime. High cost of military action against Kurds.

Profile

Turkey has one of the oldest and most advanced of the emerging market economies. In the 1990s it grew strongly, but continued to suffer from high inflation. Despite structural reforms the economy reached crisis point in early 2001, with a collapse of the banking system and the loss of over 500,000 jobs. This was compounded by the global effect of the 2001 attack on the US. Three IMF rescue packages were agreed in the course of the year in return for the privatization of debt-laden state companies and banking reform, and growth returned in 2002.

ECONOMIC PERFORMANCE INDICATOR

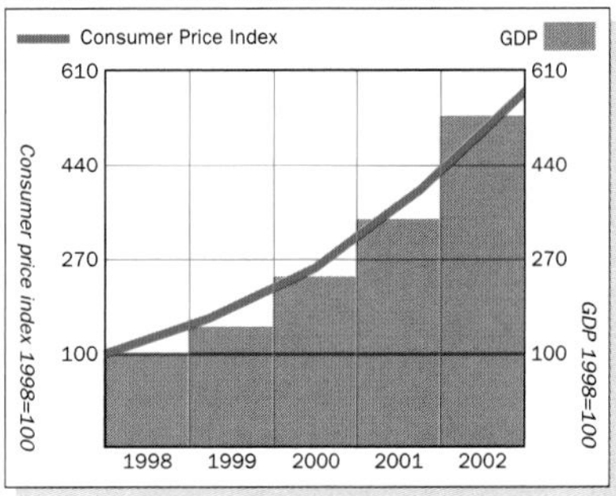
Consumer Price Index
GDP
610
440
270
100
Consumer price index 1998=100
GDP 1998=100
1998
1999
2000
2001
2002

TURKEY : MAJOR BUSINESSES

Istanbul
Ankara
Bursa
İzmit
Kırıkkale
Erzurum
Sivas
Isparta
Adana
Diyarbakır
İzmir
Mersin
Cement
Textiles
Chemicals
Electronics
Oil refining
Iron & steel
Food processing
Vehicle manufacture
0 200 km
0 200 miles
* significant multinational ownership

RESOURCES

Electric power 27.3m kW

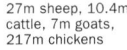

594,971 tonnes

51,148 b/d (reserves 243m barrels)

27m sheep, 10.4m cattle, 7m goats, 217m chickens

Chromium, oil, copper, borax, coal, gas, bauxite, iron

ELECTRICITY GENERATION

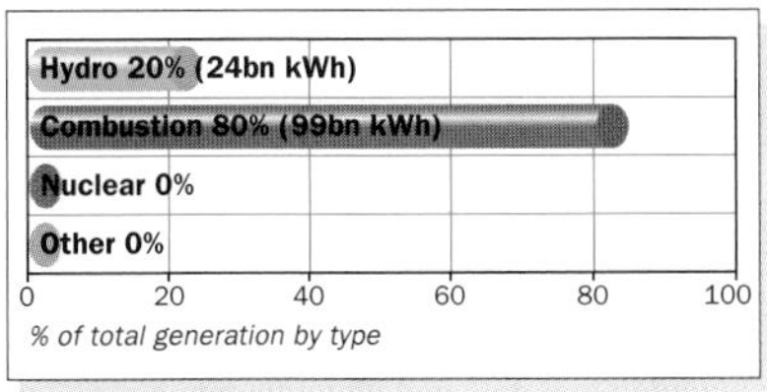
Hydro 20% (24bn kWh)
Combustion 80% (99bn kWh)
Nuclear 0%
Other 0%
0 20 40 60 80 100
% of total generation by type

Under the controversial Southeastern Anatolian Project (GAP) launched in the mid-1980s, Turkey is building 22 dams on the Tigris and Euphrates rivers. In 1999 controversy focused on the Ilisu Dam on the Tigris, which would flood a large number of towns and villages, and in 2001 on the Birecik Dam on the Euphrates, which has engulfed the ancient Roman town of Zeugma. Turkey produces oil around Raman, on the Tigris. Eastern provinces are rich in minerals, such as chromium, of which Turkey is a leading producer.

TURKEY : LAND USE

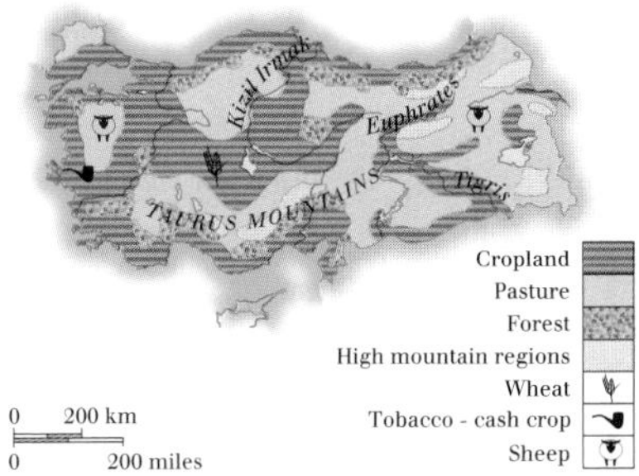
Kizil Irmak
Euphrates
Tigris
TAURUS MOUNTAINS
Cropland
Pasture
Forest
High mountain regions
Wheat
Tobacco - cash crop
Sheep
0 200 km
0 200 miles

ENVIRONMENT

Sustainability rank: 62nd

2% (1% partially protected)

3.3 tonnes per capita

ENVIRONMENTAL TREATIES

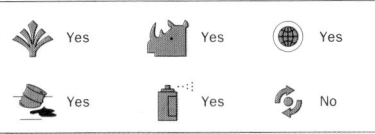

Yes	Yes	Yes
Yes	Yes	No

Turkey's program of dam-building on the Tigris and Euphrates has met with condemnation, particularly from Syria and Iraq, whose rivers will suffer reduced flow rates. Plans for the Ilisu Dam were shelved in 2001. Concern has also been expressed at proposals to build a nuclear power plant. There has been uncontrolled tourist development along the western coast.

CRIME

Death penalty not used in practice

64,051 prisoners

Up 4% in 2000–2002

CRIME RATES

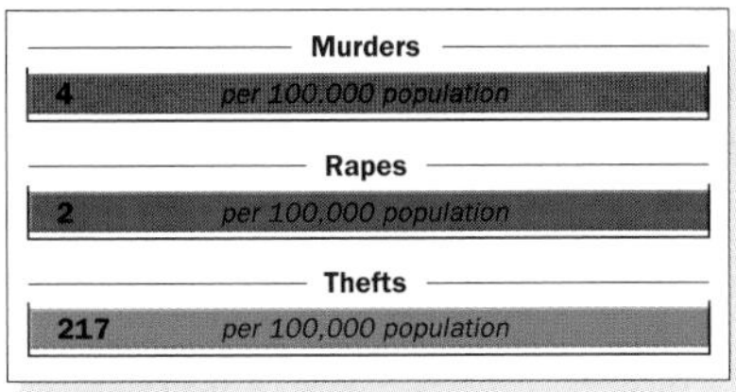
Murders
4 per 100,000 population
Rapes
2 per 100,000 population
Thefts
217 per 100,000 population

The routine use of torture and rape by the police and the deaths of prisoners in custody cause widespread concern among human rights groups. The death penalty was in 2002 limited to "times of war" and terrorism; the government agreed in 2004 to phase it out entirely.

HEALTH

Welfare state health benefits

1 per 769 people

Cerebrovascular, heart, respiratory, and digestive diseases

Turkey possesses an adequate national system of primary health care, though by Western standards hospitals are underequipped. There are fewer doctors per head than in Albania, which has the worst level in Europe.

SPENDING

GDP/cap. increase

CONSUMPTION AND SPENDING

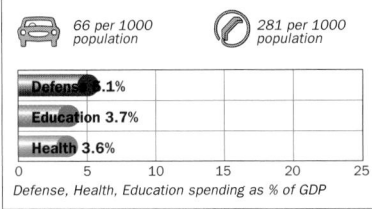

66 per 1000 population

281 per 1000 population

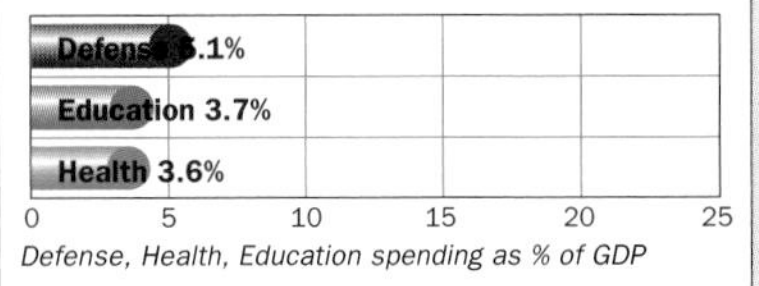
Defense 5.1%
Education 3.7%
Health 3.6%
0 5 10 15 20 25
Defense, Health, Education spending as % of GDP

The economic expansion of the 1980s created a new class of wealthy entrepreneurs. Urban/rural differences remain pronounced. High inflation in the 1990s eroded earnings of those on fixed incomes, and income inequality has grown. Many Turks take jobs as *Gastarbeiter* (guest workers) in Germany and the Netherlands.

MEDIA

TV ownership high

Daily newspaper circulation 64 per 1000 people

PUBLISHING AND BROADCAST MEDIA

There are 35 daily newspapers. The leaders are *Sabah* and the sensationalist *Hürriyet*

1 state-controlled service with 5 national channels, 300 private stations

1 state-controlled national service and over 1000 local stations

The Turkish press is diverse, vigorous, and largely privately owned. Almost all Istanbul newspapers are also printed in Ankara and Izmir on the same day.

Foreign satellite or cable broadcasts are available, as well as the five national channels of the state Turkish Radio and Television Corporation. Censorship laws have been amended to ease restrictions on non-Turkish-language broadcasting, and, after pressure from the EU, 30 minutes a day of Kurdish programming was allowed from 2002.

A particularly high number of journalists are imprisoned, and state control over Internet content was even increased in 2002.

EDUCATION

School leaving age: 14

87%

1.61m students

THE EDUCATION SYSTEM

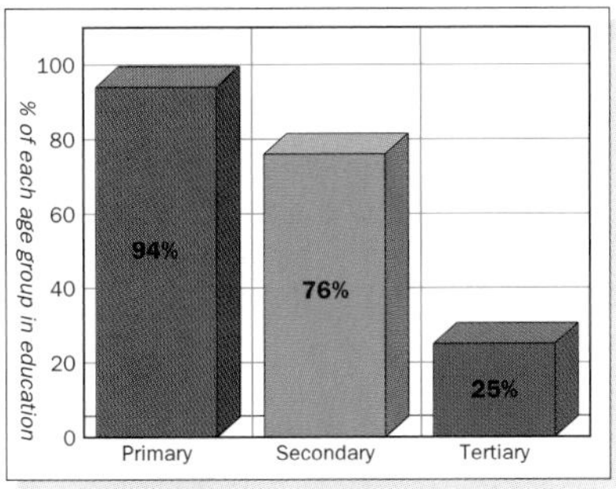
100
80
60
40
20
0
% of each age group in education
94%
76%
25%
Primary
Secondary
Tertiary

State schools are coeducational and free. Engineering is usually the strongest faculty in Turkey's many universities. In 1997, compulsory education was extended from five to eight years, raising the age for entry into Islamic schools from 11 to 14, in a move seen as designed to reduce attendance at such schools. Educational reforms by the Islamist AK government in 2004 plan to widen university access for pupils of Islamic schools.

WORLD RANKING

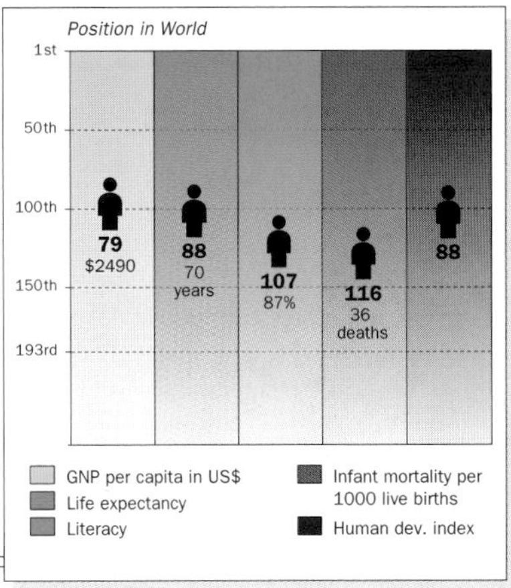
Position in World
1st
50th
100th
150th
193rd
79
$2490
88
70
years
107
87%
116
36
deaths
88
GNP per capita in US$
Life expectancy
Literacy
Infant mortality per 1000 live births
Human dev. index

T

TURKMENISTAN

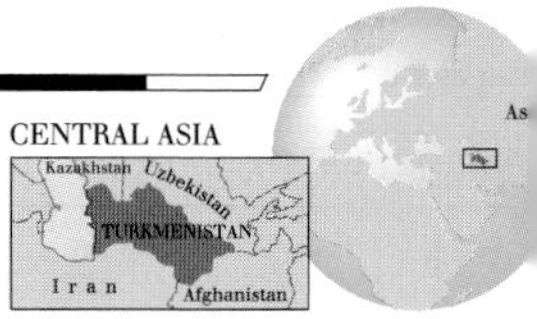
CENTRAL ASIA
Kazakhstan
Uzbekistan
TURKMENISTAN
Iran
Afghanistan
Asia

OFFICIAL NAME: Turkmenistan **CAPITAL:** Ashgabat
POPULATION: 4.9 million **CURRENCY:** Manat **OFFICIAL LANGUAGE:** Turkmen

1991 | 1991 | Oct 27 | TM | +5 | +993 | .tm

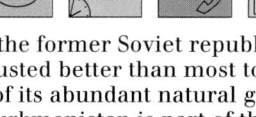

ONCE THE POOREST of the former Soviet republics, Turkmenistan has adjusted better than most to independence, exploiting the market value of its abundant natural gas supplies. A largely Sunni Muslim country, Turkmenistan is part of the former Turkestan, the last expanse of central Asia incorporated into czarist Russia. Much of life is still based on tribal relationships. Turkmenistan is isolated – telephones are relatively rare and other communications limited.

CLIMATE

Desert/steppe

WEATHER CHART FOR ASHGABAT

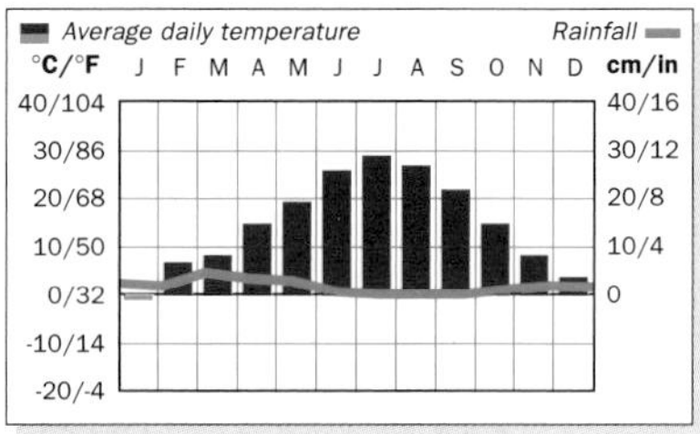
Average daily temperature
Rainfall
°C/°F
J F M A M J J A S O N D
cm/in
40/104
30/86
20/68
10/50
0/32
-10/14
-20/-4
40/16
30/12
20/8
10/4
0

Most of Turkmenistan is arid desert, so that only 2% of the total land area is suitable for agriculture.

TRANSPORTATION

Drive on right

Turkmenistan International, Ashgabat

41 ships
45,700 grt

THE TRANSPORTATION NETWORK

19,440 km (12,079 miles)

None

2523 km (1568 miles)

Amu-Darya River

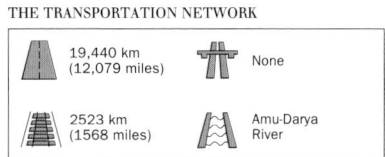

Trains are cramped and chaotic, and buses unreliable. The border with Iran is officially closed to "foreigners."

TOURISM

Visitors : Population 1:16

300,000 visitors

Up 26% in 1998

MAIN TOURIST ARRIVALS

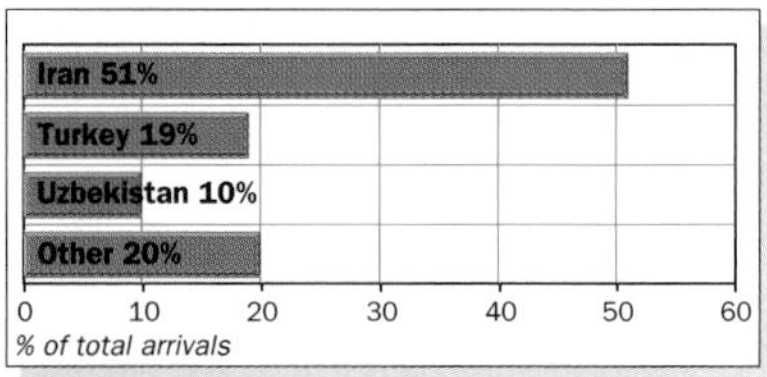
Iran 51%
Turkey 19%
Uzbekistan 10%
Other 20%
0
10
20
30
40
50
60
% of total arrivals

Most visitors are businessmen attracted by Turkmenistan's stability under President Niyazov. Turkmenistan may become a popular tourist destination in future; traditional Turkmen Muslim monuments are slowly being restored.

Karakum Canal zone: *salt flats and the Kopetdag Mountains. The Karakumy Desert forms a large part of Turkmenistan's interior.*

PEOPLE

Pop. density low

Turkmen, Uzbek, Russian, Kazakh, Tatar

10/km² (26/mi²)

THE URBAN/RURAL POPULATION SPLIT

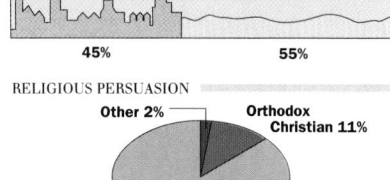

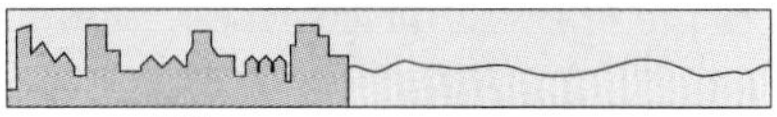
45%
55%

RELIGIOUS PERSUASION

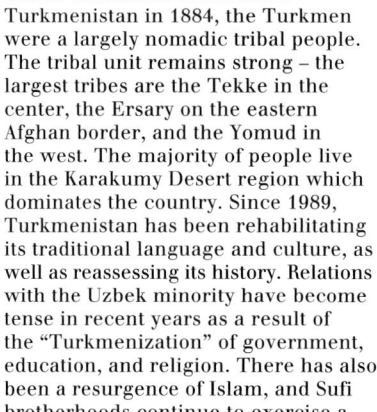

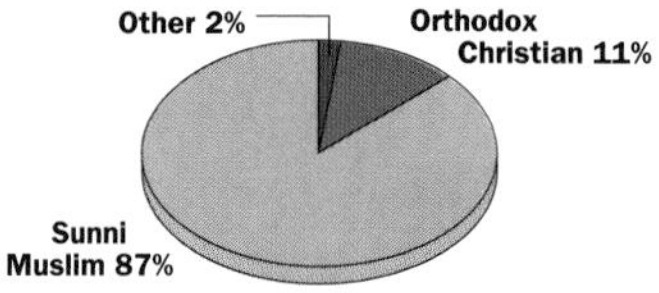
Other 2%
Orthodox Christian 11%
Sunni Muslim 87%

Before czarist Russia annexed Turkmenistan in 1884, the Turkmen were a largely nomadic tribal people. The tribal unit remains strong – the largest tribes are the Tekke in the center, the Ersary on the eastern Afghan border, and the Yomud in the west. The majority of people live in the Karakumy Desert region which dominates the country. Since 1989, Turkmenistan has been rehabilitating its traditional language and culture, as well as reassessing its history. Relations with the Uzbek minority have become tense in recent years as a result of the "Turkmenization" of government, education, and religion. There has also been a resurgence of Islam, and Sufi brotherhoods continue to exercise a powerful influence over the Turkmen. Russian is widely spoken and remains an important language in urban areas.

POLITICS

No multiparty elections

L. House 1999/2004
U. House 2003/2008

President Saparmurad Niyazov

AT THE LAST ELECTION

Parliament 50 seats

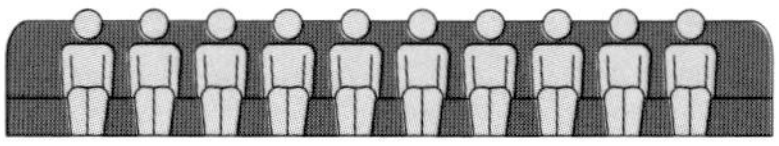

In elections to the Parliament in 1999 all of the seats were won by supporters of the ruling Democratic Party of Turkmenistan (**DPT**) – the only registered party

People's Council 2507 seats

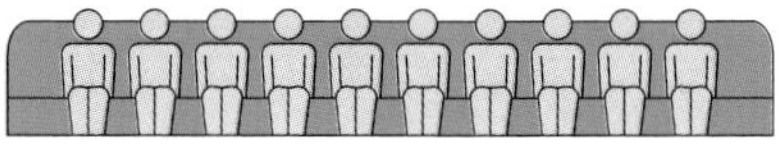

The People's Council includes the president, Council of Ministers, members of Parliament, and regional and ethnic representatives

Officially, Turkmenistan became a multiparty democracy at independence, but President Saparmurad Niyazov has banned the formation of new parties. As in some other ex-Soviet states, former communists (regrouped here as the DPT) still dominate the political process, harboring the traditional communist suspicion of Islamic fundamentalism. A main political concern is to prevent the social and nationalistic conflicts that have blighted other former Soviet republics.

President Niyazov has encouraged an elaborate personality cult, adopting the title of Turkmenbashi (father of all Turkmen), and there are golden statues of him throughout Ashgabat. His spiritual guide to living, *Ruhnama*, has been adopted as a national code, and the days of the week and months have been officially changed to reflect key national symbols; January is now Turkmenbashi, and September, Ruhnama.

WORLD AFFAIRS

Joined UN in 1992

CIS | ECO | EAPC | OIC | OSCE

Turkmenistan's key relations are with Iran and Turkey. It needs investment from both, but is wary of Islamic fundamentalism. President Niyazov opposes economic union with the CIS and political union among Turkic-speaking states. Relations with Russia were soured in 2003 by the ending of dual citizenship for ethnic Russians.

AID

Recipient

$41m (receipts)

Down 43% in 2002

The World Bank has halted new loans in the light of Turkmenistan's failure to report its external debt.

T

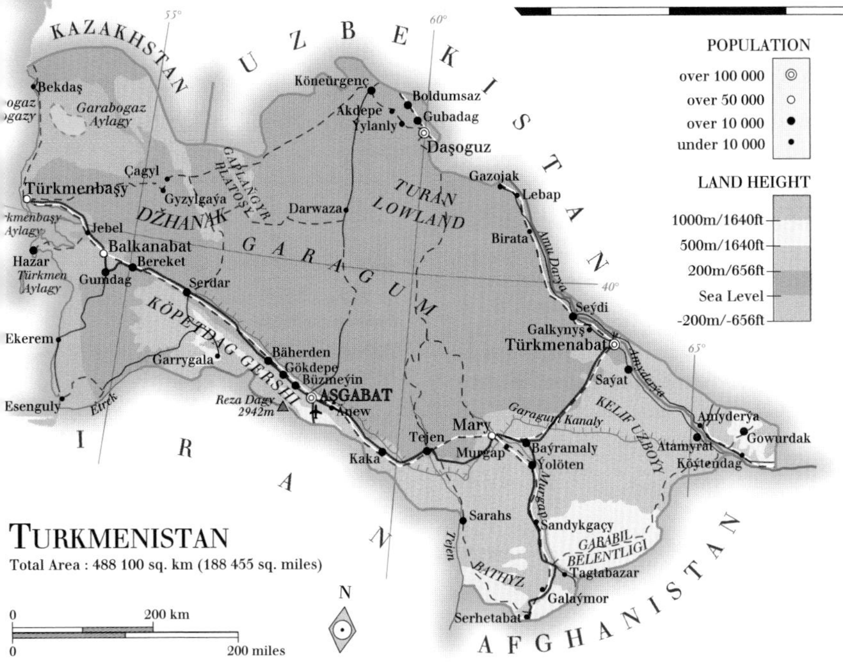
KAZAKHSTAN
UZBEKISTAN
IRAN
AFGHANISTAN
POPULATION
over 100 000
over 50 000
over 10 000
under 10 000
LAND HEIGHT
1000m/1640ft
500m/1640ft
200m/656ft
Sea Level
-200m/-656ft
Bekdaş
Garabogaz Aylagy
Köneürgenç
Boldumsaz
Akdepe
Gubadag
Ylanly
Daşoguz
Çagyl
Türkmenbaşy
Gyzylgaýa
DZHANAK
Darwaza
TURAN LOWLAND
Gazojak
Lebap
Birata
Amu Darya
Jebel
Balkanabat
Bereket
GARAGUM
Hazar
Türkmen Aylagy
Gumdag
Serdar
KÖPETDAG GERSHI
Seýdi
Galkynyş
Türkmenabat
Ekerem
Bäherden
Gökdepe
Büzmeýin
Garrygala
Saýat
Reza Dagy 2942m
AŞGABAT
Änew
Esenguly
Etrek
Garagum Kanaly
KELIF UZBOY
Amyderýa
Gowurdak
Mary
Tejen
Murgap
Baýramaly
Ýolöten
Atamyrat
Köýtendag
Kaka
Sarahs
Sandykgaçy
GARABIL BELENTLIGI
BATHYZ
Tagtabazar
Galaýmor
Serhetabat
N
0
200 km
200 miles

TURKMENISTAN

Total Area : 488 100 sq. km (188 455 sq. miles)

CHRONOLOGY

The nomadic peoples of western Turkestan came under Russian imperial control from the 1850s.

- **1924** Creation of Turkmenistan.
- **1991** Independence from USSR. Niyazov retains power, becoming president.
- **1994** Former communists win first elections.
- **1999** Niyazov's term extended indefinitely by parliament.

DEFENSE

Compulsory military sevice

$284m

Down 3% in 2002

Russia provides security; Pakistan trains pilots. A navy was formed in 2003.

ECONOMICS

Inflation 328% p.a. (1990–2001)

$5.88bn

5200 manats (5200.7)

SCORE CARD

- World GNP Ranking......................107th
- GNP per Capita..........................$1200
- Balance of Payments....................–$74m
- Inflation...12%
- Unemployment..................................3%

Strengths

Cotton and gas. Decision to abolish collective farms gradually encouraging private initiative and enterprise.

Weaknesses

Cotton monoculture has forced rising food imports. Thriving black market threatens value of manat.

EXPORTS

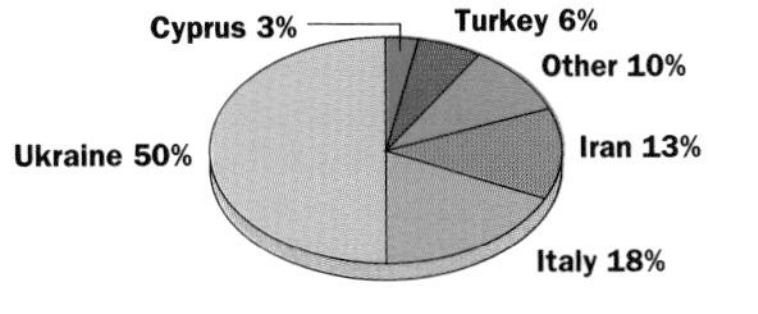
Cyprus 3%
Turkey 6%
Other 10%
Ukraine 50%
Iran 13%
Italy 18%

IMPORTS

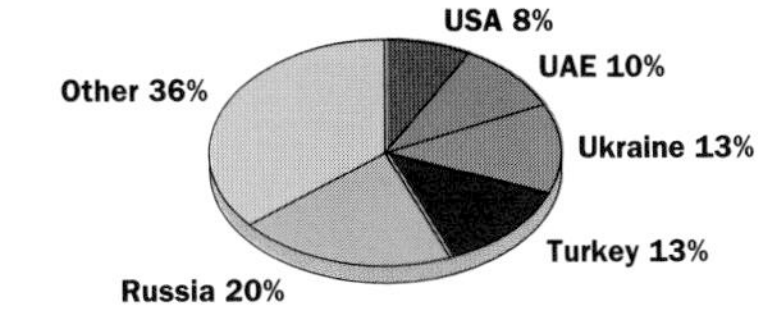
USA 8%
UAE 10%
Other 36%
Ukraine 13%
Turkey 13%
Russia 20%

RESOURCES

Electric power 3.9m kW

12,792 tonnes

210,000 b/d (reserves 500m barrels)

6m sheep, 860,000 cattle, 4.8m chickens

Oil, natural gas, potassium, sulfur, sodium sulfate

Under a ten-year program, Turkmenistan aims to raise its oil production to nearly one million barrels per day by 2010.

ENVIRONMENT

Sustainability rank: 131st

4% (2% partially protected)

7.5 tonnes per capita

The building of the Karakum Canal has reduced the flow of water to the Aral Sea by 33%. Plans were announced in 2000 for the construction of a large artificial lake in the Karakumy Desert.

MEDIA

TV ownership medium

Daily newspaper circulation 7 per 1000 people

PUBLISHING AND BROADCAST MEDIA

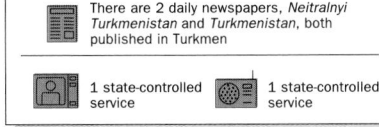

There are 2 daily newspapers, *Neitralnyi Turkmenistan* and *Turkmenistan*, both published in Turkmen

1 state-controlled service

1 state-controlled service

Iranian and Afghan radio stations, beaming in Islamic programs, are popular. TV is only available in cities.

CRIME

No death penalty

22,000 prisoners

Increasing levels of theft

Levels of crime are generally low. The death penalty was finally abolished in December 1999.

EDUCATION

School leaving age: 17

98%

76,000 students

University students must know the life and works of President Niyazov. They now have to work for two years after their first two years of study.

HEALTH

Welfare state health benefits

1 per 382 people

Heart, respiratory, pulmonary, and infectious diseases

In 2004, military conscripts replaced regular health workers. Health indicators are among the worst in the region.

SPENDING

GDP/cap. decrease

CONSUMPTION AND SPENDING

No data

77 per 1000 population

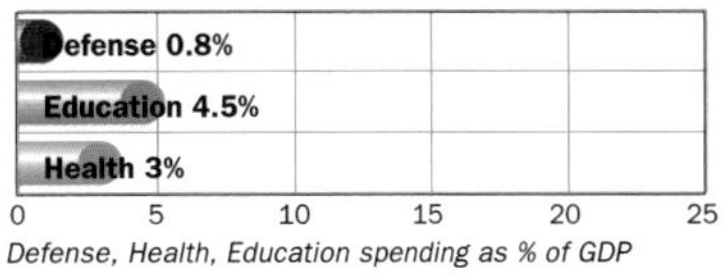
Defense 0.8%
Education 4.5%
Health 3%
0
5
10
15
20
25
Defense, Health, Education spending as % of GDP

The wealthiest group is connected to the government. Transition to a liberal economy has attracted high spending.

WORLD RANKING

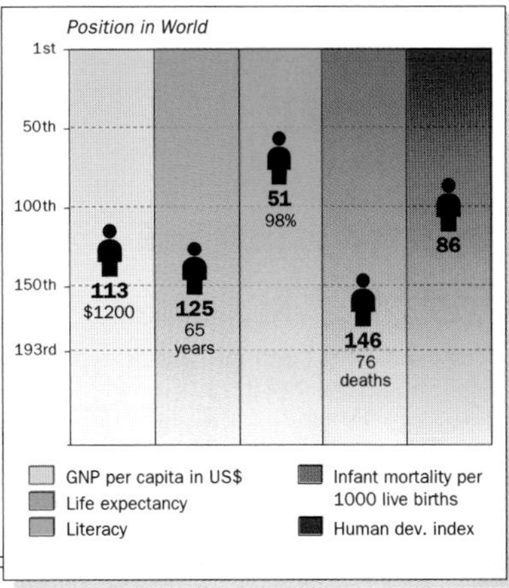
Position in World
1st
50th
100th
150th
193rd
113
$1200
125
65 years
51
98%
146
76 deaths
86
GNP per capita in US$
Life expectancy
Literacy
Infant mortality per 1000 live births
Human dev. index

T

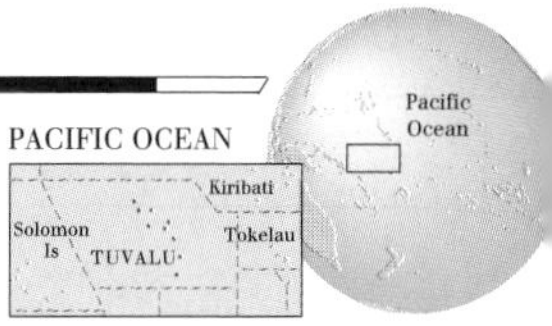

PACIFIC OCEAN
Kiribati
Solomon Is
Tokelau
TUVALU
Pacific Ocean

TUVALU

OFFICIAL NAME: Tuvalu **CAPITAL:** Fongafale, on Funafuti Atoll **POPULATION:** 11,305
CURRENCIES: Australian dollar and Tuvaluan dollar **OFFICIAL LANGUAGE:** English

1978 | 1978 | Oct 1 | TUV | +12 | +688 | .tv

ONE OF THE WORLD'S smallest, most isolated states, Tuvalu lies around 2000 km (1250 miles) north of Fiji in the Pacific. A chain of nine coral atolls, it has a land area of just 26 sq. km (10 sq. miles). As the Ellice Islands, it was linked to the Gilbert Islands (now Kiribati) as a British colony until independence in 1978. Politically and socially conservative, Tuvaluans live by subsistence farming and fishing.

CLIMATE

Tropical oceanic

WEATHER CHART FOR FONGAFALE

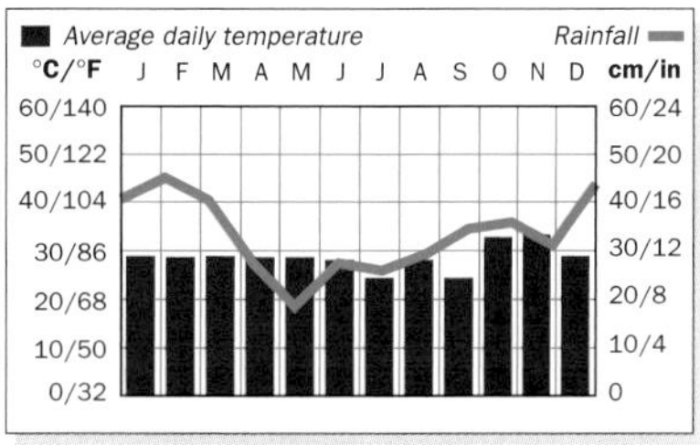

Average daily temperature
Rainfall
°C/°F
J F M A M J J A S O N D
cm/in
60/140
50/122
40/104
30/86
20/68
10/50
0/32
60/24
50/20
40/16
30/12
20/8
10/4
0

The climate is pleasantly warm, though average humidity exceeds 90%. The October–March hurricane season brings many violent storms. High "king" tides can swamp the atolls.

TRANSPORTATION

Drive on right

There is an airstrip on Funafuti Atoll

9 ships 38,200 grt

THE TRANSPORTATION NETWORK

None

None

None

None

A ferry links the atolls. There are air links with Kiribati and Fiji. Funafuti and Nukufetau have deepwater berths.

TOURISM

Visitors : Population 1:8.6

1313 visitors

Down 53% in 2002

MAIN TOURIST ARRIVALS

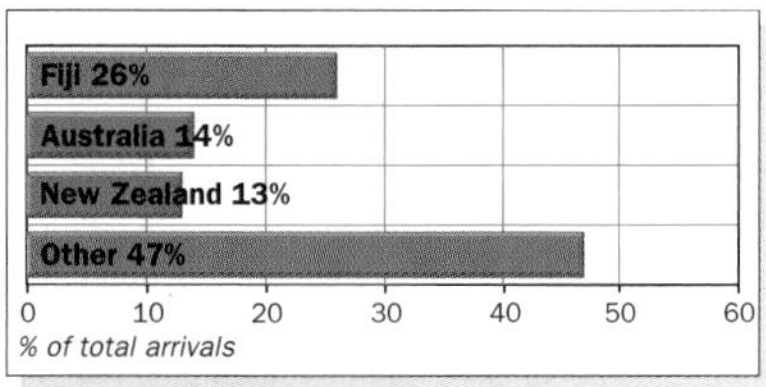

Fiji 26%
Australia 14%
New Zealand 13%
Other 47%
0 10 20 30 40 50 60
% of total arrivals

Unspoiled and lapped by some of the world's warmest waters, the remote islands of Tuvalu have surprisingly few visitors. The islands' only paved airstrip and sole hotel are to be found on Funafuti.

PEOPLE

Pop. density high

Tuvaluan, Kiribati, English

435/km² (1130/mi²)

THE URBAN/RURAL POPULATION SPLIT

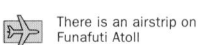

45%
55%

RELIGIOUS PERSUASION

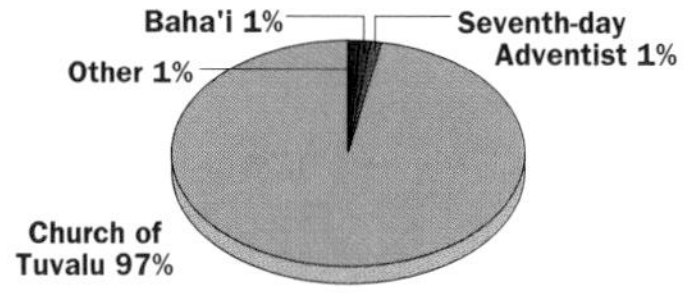

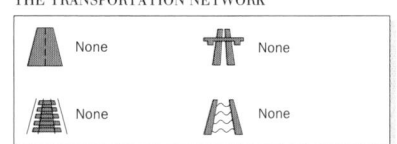

Baha'i 1%
Seventh-day Adventist 1%
Other 1%
Church of Tuvalu 97%

Around 95% of Tuvaluans are ethnically Polynesian. Their ancestors came from Tonga and Samoa 2000 years ago. Nui Atoll has Micronesian influences. There is an I-Kiribati community on Funafuti; many Tuvaluans who worked in Kiribati took local wives. Over 40% of the population now live on Funafuti, pushing its population density to almost 1600 per sq. km (4100 per sq. mile). Life is still communal, traditional, and hard. Droughts are common and fresh water is precious. Around two-thirds of people depend on subsistence farming, digging special pits out of the coral to grow most of the islands' limited range of crops. Fishing is also important, and Tuvaluans have a reputation as excellent sailors; many work as merchant seamen. Nauru's 2004 economic collapse stranded some 300 Tuvaluan phosphate miners without pay.

***Tuvalu's soil** is porous, but sufficiently fertile to support coconut palms, pandanus, and salt-tolerant plants. Freshwater supply is limited.*

POLITICS

Nonparty elections

2002/2006

H.M. Queen Elizabeth II

AT THE LAST ELECTION

Parliament of Tuvalu 15 seats

There are no political parties. All members are independent candidates

The 15 MPs, elected every four years, are independents who form loose political associations. The prime minister, an MP elected by parliament, works with a cabinet of up to four other MPs. Day-to-day administration lies in the hands of an elected council on each of Tuvalu's islands. From independence until 1998 politics was dominated by Tomasi Puapua and Bikenibeu Paeniu. Parliamentary defections are common, and brought down the government of Prime Minister Faimalaga Luka (now governor-general) in 2001, and in 2004 that of Saufatu Sopoanga, appointed prime minister after elections in 2002.

WORLD AFFAIRS

Joined UN in 2000

ACP | Comm | PC | PIF | ADB

Tuvalu was admitted as a full member of both the UN and the Commonwealth in 2000 in recognition of its regional importance. Agreements exist with Taiwan, South Korea, and the US, whose vessels may exploit Tuvalu's fish-rich territorial waters. Calls for cutting constitutional ties to the British monarchy have been revived by Prime Minister Saufatu Sopoanga.

AID

Recipient

US$12m (receipts)

Up 20% in 2002

Tuvalu has a visible trade deficit, and aid is crucial. Most importantly, in 1987 a trust fund was set up, with US$29 million in grants from Australia, New Zealand, and the UK. While support from the UK has shrunk, aid from Taiwan and Japan grows. Tuvalu plans to reduce its reliance on aid through public-sector reform and privatization.

DEFENSE

No compulsory military service

There are no armed forces

Not applicable

Tuvalu has no military. Internal security is the responsibility of the small police force.

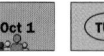

ECONOMICS

Not available

US$21m

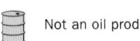

1.436 Australian dollars (1.491)

SCORE CARD

❑ WORLD GNP RANKING	192nd
❑ GNP PER CAPITA	US$1930
❑ BALANCE OF PAYMENTS	Not available
❑ INFLATION	5%
❑ UNEMPLOYMENT	Low

STRENGTHS

Sustainable subsistence economy. EEZ: source of jobs and income. Revenue from trust fund and multimillion-dollar Internet deal for use of ".tv" suffix.

WEAKNESSES

World's smallest sovereign economy. Physical isolation. Few exports: copra, stamps, garments. Dependence on imports and aid. Poor soil. Remittances from overseas workers falling as Nauru's phosphate reserves run out.

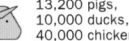

EXPORTS

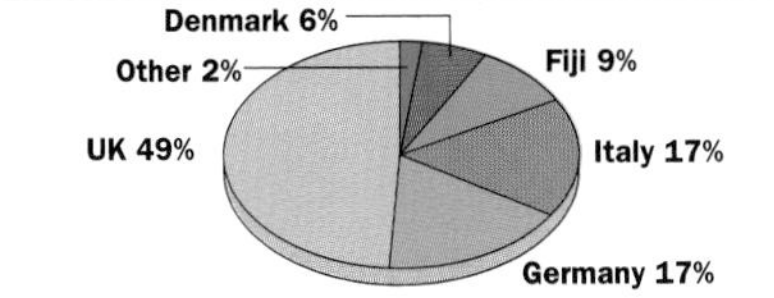
Denmark 6%
Other 2%
Fiji 9%
UK 49%
Italy 17%
Germany 17%

IMPORTS

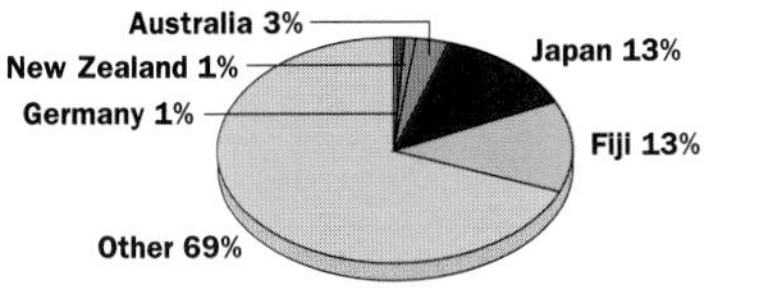
Australia 3%
New Zealand 1%
Germany 1%
Japan 13%
Fiji 13%
Other 69%

RESOURCES

Not available

500 tonnes

Not an oil producer

13,200 pigs, 10,000 ducks, 40,000 chickens

None

Tuvalu's resource potential lies in the waters of its 8.3 million sq. km (3.2 million sq. mile) EEZ. Its rich fish stocks are exploited mainly by foreign boats in return for licensing fees. The salination of soil is increasing, leaving less and less cultivable land. Solar energy is reducing dependence on gasoline for power generation. Fuel accounts for about 14% of import costs. Tuvalu has leased its ".tv" Internet suffix to a Californian media company for US$50 million over 12 years, plus 20% of profits.

TUVALU

Total Area : 26 sq. km (10 sq. miles)

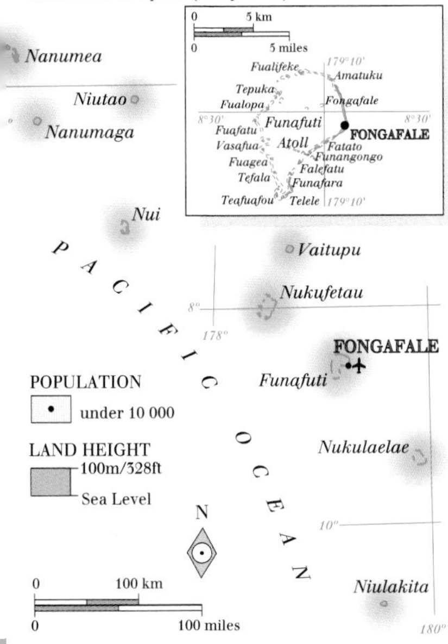
0 5 km
0 5 miles
Fualifeke
Amatuku
Tepuka
Fualopa
Fongafale
Fuafatu
Funafuti
Atoll
FONGAFALE
Vasafua
Fatato
Funangongo
Fuagea
Falefatu
Tefala
Funafara
Teafuafou
Telele
Nanumea
Niutao
Nanumaga
Nui
PACIFIC OCEAN
Vaitupu
Nukufetau
FONGAFALE
Funafuti
Nukulaelae
Niulakita
POPULATION
under 10 000
LAND HEIGHT
100m/328ft
Sea Level
N
0 100 km
0 100 miles

ENVIRONMENT

Not available

132% partially protected (including marine areas)

0.5 tonnes per capita

Efforts to protect the environmentally fragile atolls include reafforestation and solar energy projects. On Funafuti, population pressure is leading to overfishing in the atoll lagoon. The "greenhouse effect" is a major concern, since climate changes attributed to it are blamed for a steep rise in cyclone frequency. Any rise in sea levels induced by global warming would quickly submerge the low-lying atolls.

MEDIA

TV ownership low

There are no daily newspapers

PUBLISHING AND BROADCAST MEDIA

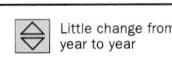

There are no daily newspapers. The English-language *Tuvalu Echoes* is published biweekly

No TV service

1 state-owned service

Tuvalu Echoes and its Tuvaluan version, *Sikuleo o Tuvalu*, are published by the government.

CRIME

No death penalty

6 prisoners

Little change from year to year

Crime is minimal and the result mainly of alcohol-related violence, particularly at the weekend.

EDUCATION

School leaving age: 14

98%

Not available

Each island has a primary school. A secondary school and a marine training school are based on Funafuti. Students who attend the University of the South Pacific in Fiji are state-funded.

CHRONOLOGY

The former Ellice Islands, together with the Gilbert Islands, were annexed by the UK in 1892.

- ❑ **1974** Ellice Islanders vote to separate from Gilbertese.
- ❑ **1978** Independence as Tuvalu.
- ❑ **1987** Tuvalu Trust Fund set up.
- ❑ **1998** Internet deal for ".tv" suffix.
- ❑ **2000** Joins UN as 189th member. Full member of Commonwealth.
- ❑ **2002** Saufatu Sopoanga appointed prime minister.

HEALTH

No welfare state health benefits

1 per 3333 people

Malaria, diarrheal, infectious, and parasitic diseases

Concerted efforts since independence to improve health care facilities and programs have cut the incidence of communicable diseases. Serious cases of illness or injury are referred to better-equipped hospitals in Australia or New Zealand.

SPENDING

GDP/cap. increase

CONSUMPTION AND SPENDING

No data

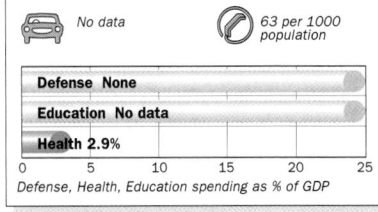

63 per 1000 population

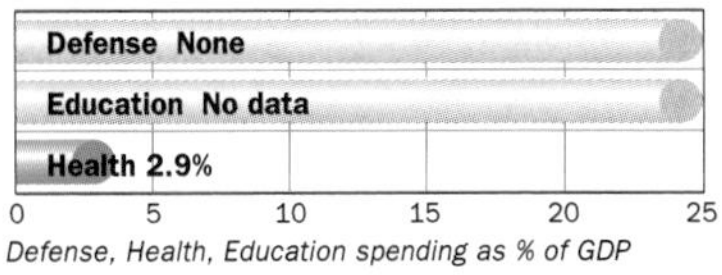
Defense None
Education No data
Health 2.9%
0
5
10
15
20
25
Defense, Health, Education spending as % of GDP

Though living standards are very low, traditional social support systems mean that extreme poverty is rare. Most people rely on subsistence agriculture and fishing, supplemented by remittances from expatriate Tuvaluans.

WORLD RANKING

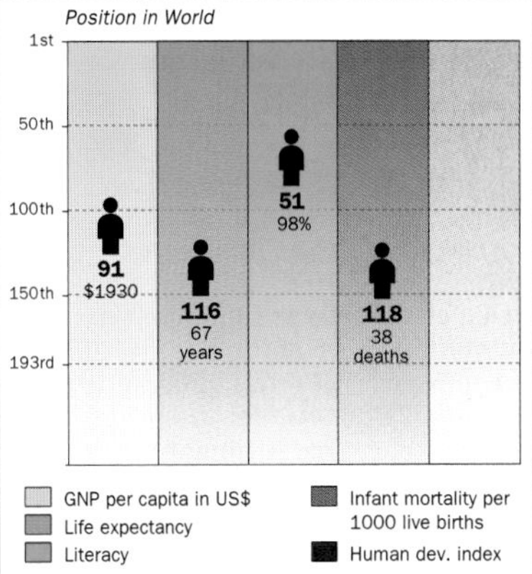
Position in World
1st
50th
100th
150th
193rd
91
$1930
116
67 years
51
98%
118
38 deaths
GNP per capita in US$
Life expectancy
Literacy
Infant mortality per 1000 live births
Human dev. index

T

UGANDA

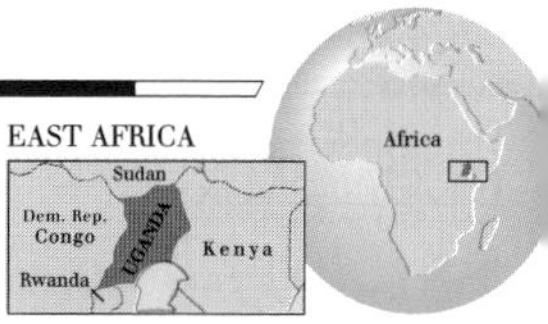
EAST AFRICA
Sudan
Dem. Rep. Congo
Rwanda
UGANDA
Kenya
Africa

OFFICIAL NAME: Republic of Uganda **CAPITAL:** Kampala **POPULATION:** 25.8 million
CURRENCY: New Uganda shilling **OFFICIAL LANGUAGE:** English

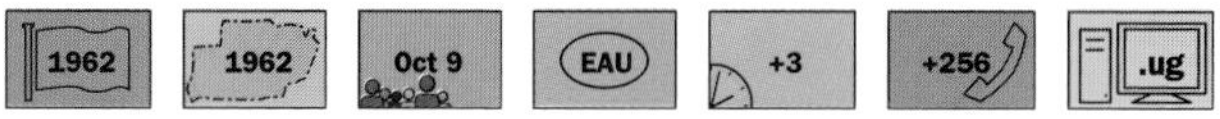
1962
1962
Oct 9
EAU
+3
+256
.ug

AN EAST AFRICAN COUNTRY of fertile upland plateaus and mountains, Uganda has outlets to the sea through Kenya and Tanzania. Its history from independence in 1962 until 1986 was one of ethnic strife. Since 1986, under President Museveni, peace has been restored and steps have been taken to rebuild the economy and democracy.

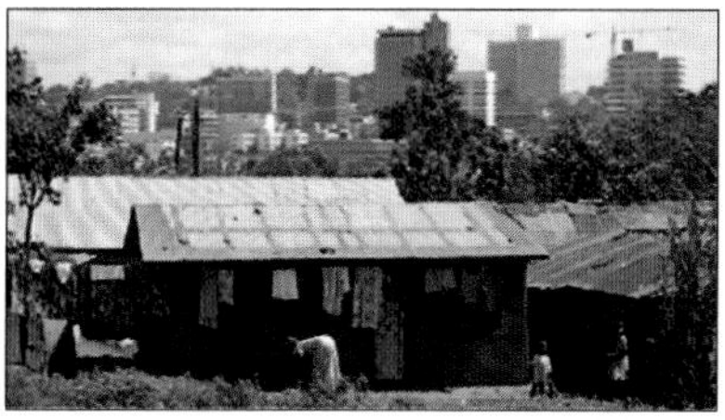

Kampala, Uganda's capital. *Only a tiny proportion of the city's households are supplied with running water.*

CLIMATE

Tropical wet and dry

WEATHER CHART FOR KAMPALA

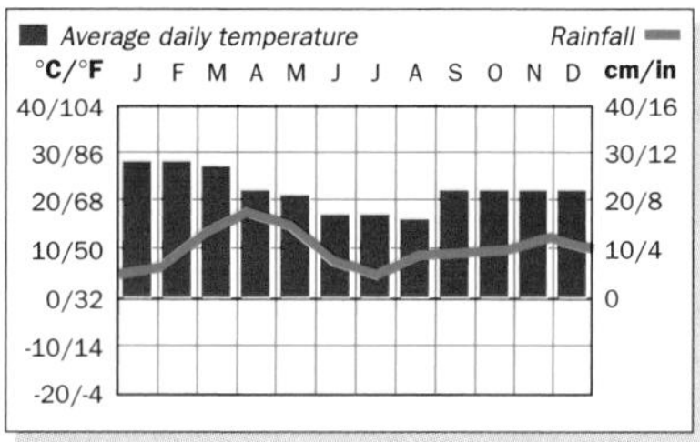
Average daily temperature
Rainfall
°C/°F J F M A M J J A S O N D cm/in
40/104
30/86
20/68
10/50
0/32
-10/14
-20/-4
40/16
30/12
20/8
10/4
0

Altitude and the influence of Lake Victoria moderate Uganda's climate. March–May is the wettest period.

TRANSPORTATION

Drive on left

Entebbe International 493,976 passengers

2 ships 5900 dwt

THE TRANSPORTATION NETWORK

1890 km (1174 miles)

None

259 km (161 miles)

Lake Victoria and other lakes are navigable

The government is rebuilding the transportation infrastructure with the help of international aid.

TOURISM

Visitors : Population 1:102

254,000 visitors

Up 24% in 2002

MAIN TOURIST ARRIVALS

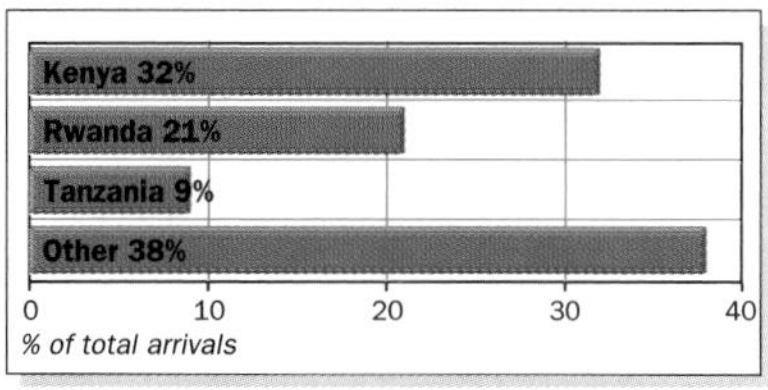
Kenya 32%
Rwanda 21%
Tanzania 9%
Other 38%
0
10
20
30
40
% of total arrivals

Major attractions are Uganda's lakes and mountains, notably the rugged Ruwenzori range – the Mountains of the Moon. The brutal murder of eight foreign tourists by Rwandan fighters at the Bwindi national park in 1999 was a severe setback for Uganda's recovery as a tourist destination.

PEOPLE

Pop. density medium

Luganda, Nkole, Chiga, Lango, Acholi, Teso, Lugbara, English

129/km² (335/mi²)

THE URBAN/RURAL POPULATION SPLIT

15%
85%

RELIGIOUS PERSUASION

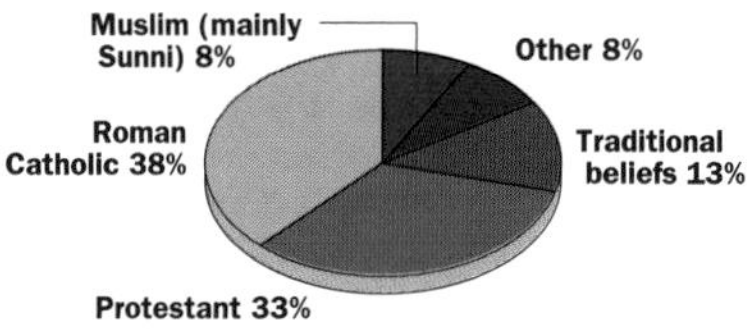
Muslim (mainly Sunni) 8%
Other 8%
Roman Catholic 38%
Traditional beliefs 13%
Protestant 33%

The predominantly rural population comprises 13 main ethnic groups; traditional animosities were manipulated by ex-rulers Amin and Obote. Since 1986 President Museveni has worked hard for reconciliation, with a visible improvement in the country's human rights record, but a noticeable north–south divide persists, with development focused on the south.

POLITICS

Nonparty elections

2001/2006

President Yoweri Kaguta Museveni

AT THE LAST ELECTION

Parliament 276 members

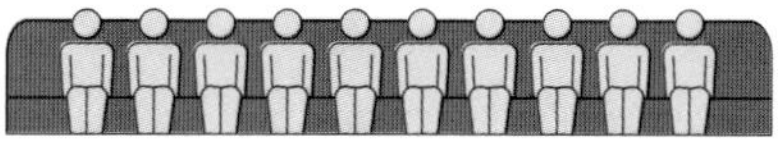

Elections to the Parliament took place on a "no-party" basis in June 2001

Since 1986, President Museveni has run a "no-party democracy," with political parties represented in a broadly based government, but banned from campaigning. Continuing to overcome ethnic tension is the main issue after its catastrophic effects in the 1970s and 1980s, when rebel insurgencies in the north and west led to the deaths, kidnapping, and displacement of tens of thousands of people, and destroyed the economy. In 2001, Museveni won another term in office with 69% of the vote, and in legislative elections his supporters retained a clear majority. Despite the endorsement of the "no-party" system in a referendum in 2000, Museveni has made a commitment to multipartyism and promised a new referendum in 2005.

UGANDA

Total Area : 236 040 sq. km (91 135 sq. miles)

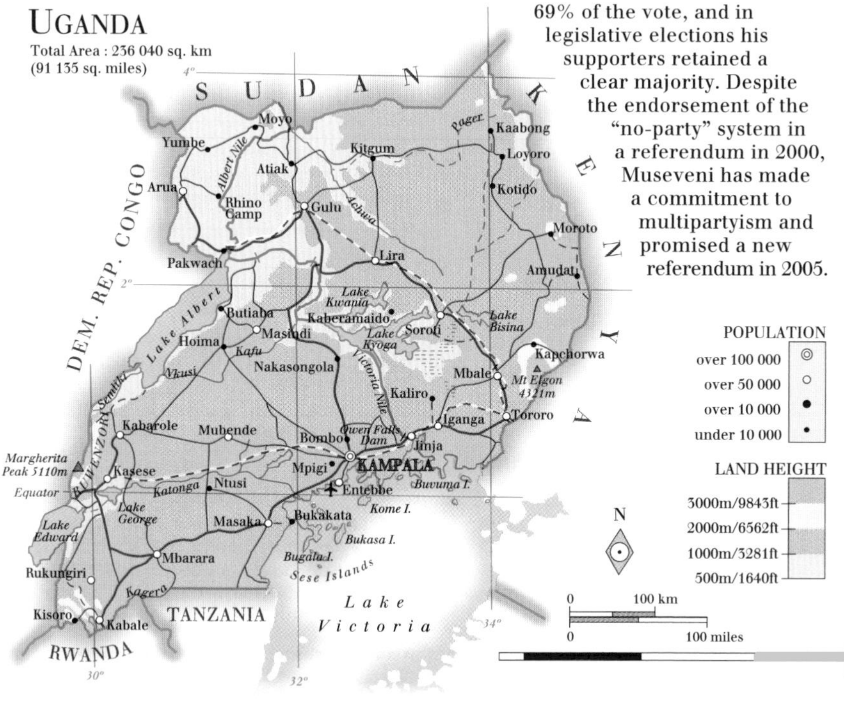
SUDAN
KENYA
DEM. REP. CONGO
TANZANIA
RWANDA
Moyo
Yumbe
Albert Nile
Atiak
Kitgum
Pager
Kaabong
Loyoro
Kotido
Arua
Rhino Camp
Gulu
Achwa
Moroto
Pakwach
Lira
Amudat
Lake Kwania
Kaberamaido
Lake Bisina
Butiaba
Lake Albert
Masindi
Lake Kyoga
Soroti
Hoima
Kafu
Nakasongola
Victoria Nile
Kapchorwa
Mbale
Mt Elgon 4321m
Vkusi
Semliki
Kaliro
Tororo
Ruwenzori
Kabarole
Mubende
Owen Falls Dam
Iganga
Bombo
Jinja
Margherita Peak 5110m
Kasese
Mpigi
KAMPALA
Buvuma I.
Equator
Katonga
Ntusi
Entebbe
Lake George
Kome I.
Lake Edward
Masaka
Bukakata
Bukasa I.
Mbarara
Bugala I.
Sese Islands
Rukungiri
Kagera
Lake Victoria
Kisoro
Kabale
30°
32°
34°
4°
2°
POPULATION
over 100 000
over 50 000
over 10 000
under 10 000
LAND HEIGHT
3000m/9843ft
2000m/6562ft
1000m/3281ft
500m/1640ft
N
0 100 km
0 100 miles

U

WORLD AFFAIRS

Joined UN in 1962

Comm | COMESA | IGAD | EAC | OIC

Conflicts in Sudan, the DRC (where Uganda was one of the protagonists), and Rwanda have caused a large influx of refugees into Uganda. Relations with Sudan have improved since 1999: each has dropped support for cross-border rebels and Sudan has allowed Ugandan forces to pursue Lord's Resistance Army (LRA) fighters into its territory.

AID

Recipient

$638m (receipts)

Down 20% in 2002

Aid, mainly from the World Bank and the UK, has risen, its donors encouraged by Uganda's adoption of economic liberalization and private-sector investment policies. Aid has focused on balance-of-payments support, the rehabilitation of the key transportation sector, and the fight against AIDS.

DEFENSE

No compulsory military service

$158m

Down 19% in 2002

The pre-1986 army was responsible for many atrocities under Amin's rule. In the 1990s, Uganda was preoccupied with conflicts in neighboring countries, particularly the DRC, where it supported antigovernment rebels. The army has also been deployed to suppress internal rebellions, notably that of the Lord's Resistance Army.

ECONOMICS

Inflation 11% p.a. (1990–2001)

$5.93bn

1785 new Uganda shillings (2001)

SCORE CARD

❏ WORLD GNP RANKING	106th
❏ GNP PER CAPITA	$240
❏ BALANCE OF PAYMENTS	–$353m
❏ INFLATION	–0.3%
❏ UNEMPLOYMENT	7%

STRENGTHS

Agriculture. Coffee brings in most of export earnings. Potential for more export crops. Road system is being repaired. Proinvestment policies.

WEAKNESSES

Lack of skilled workforce. Regional instability affects confidence. Unsustainable foreign debt. World coffee price fluctuations.

EXPORTS

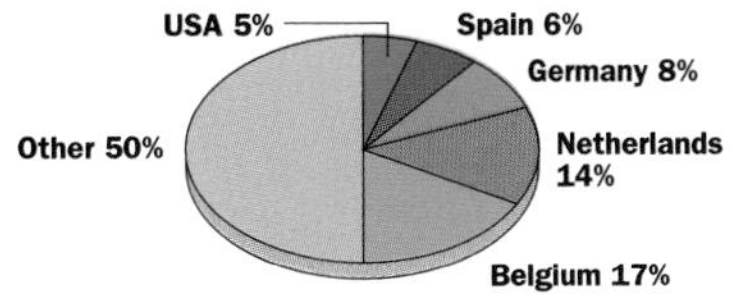
USA 5%
Spain 6%
Germany 8%
Netherlands 14%
Belgium 17%
Other 50%

IMPORTS

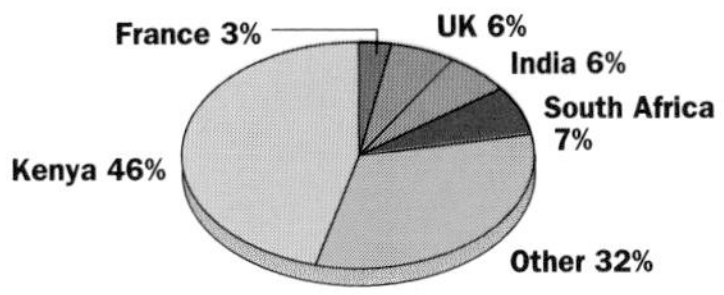
France 3%
UK 6%
India 6%
South Africa 7%
Other 32%
Kenya 46%

RESOURCES

Electric power 264,000 kW

223,086 tonnes

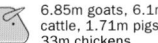

Not an oil producer

6.85m goats, 6.1m cattle, 1.71m pigs, 33m chickens

Copper, cobalt, tin, apatite, magnetite, tungsten, gold

Mineral resources are varied but barely exploited. Uganda has sizable copper deposits; the mines, closed under Obote, are now being reopened. Gold and cobalt mining are also due to resume and oil exploration is under way. Hydroelectric output is being expanded, notably at Owen Falls, with the aim of replacing 50% of oil imports.

ENVIRONMENT

Sustainability rank: 76th

25% (17% partially protected)

0.1 tonnes per capita

Uganda's priority is economic reconstruction, but ecological issues are not ignored. The construction of a huge hydroelectric power plant at the Kabalega (Murchison) Falls, above Lake Albert, was canceled following widespread environmental objections.

MEDIA

TV ownership low

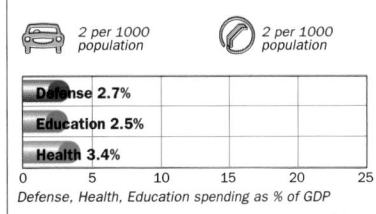

Daily newspaper circulation 2 per 1000 people

PUBLISHING AND BROADCAST MEDIA

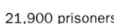

There are 6 daily newspapers, including *New Vision, The Star,* and *The Monitor*

3 services: 1 state-controlled, 2 independent

1 state-controlled service, many independent stations

The 13 daily and weekly papers cover the political and religious spectrum; eight are published in English. Only *New Vision* is government-controlled.

CRIME

Death penalty in use

21,900 prisoners

Down 41% in 2000–2002

Torture is allegedly used to deter political opposition. Theft is rising in Kampala. In 2000, the bodies of 780 followers of the cult of the Restoration of the Ten Commandments of God were found.

CHRONOLOGY

Uganda's ancient kingdoms were ruled under a British protectorate from 1893 until independence in 1962.

- ❏ **1962–1971** Milton Obote in power.
- ❏ **1971–1986** Ethnic strife, economic collapse under Idi Amin and, from 1980, under Obote once more.
- ❏ **1986** President Museveni in power, establishes the "no-party" system.
- ❏ **1996** Museveni wins first presidential elections.
- ❏ **2004** Commitment to multipartyism.

EDUCATION

Schooling is not compulsory

69%

63,165 students

All schools charge fees. Only 12% of pupils go on to secondary school and just 3% to tertiary education.

HEALTH

Welfare state health benefits

1 per 20,000 people

Malaria, respiratory, and diarrheal diseases, measles

A successful education and prevention campaign has reduced the prevalence of HIV/AIDS to about 4% of adults, from a peak of 14% in the early 1990s.

SPENDING

GDP/cap. increase

CONSUMPTION AND SPENDING

2 per 1000 population

2 per 1000 population

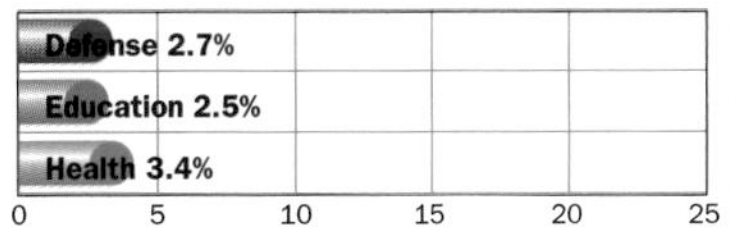
Defense 2.7%
Education 2.5%
Health 3.4%
0
5
10
15
20
25

Defense, Health, Education spending as % of GDP

Uganda has a small but growing middle class. Those close to the government form the wealthiest group. 96% of the population live below the poverty line.

WORLD RANKING

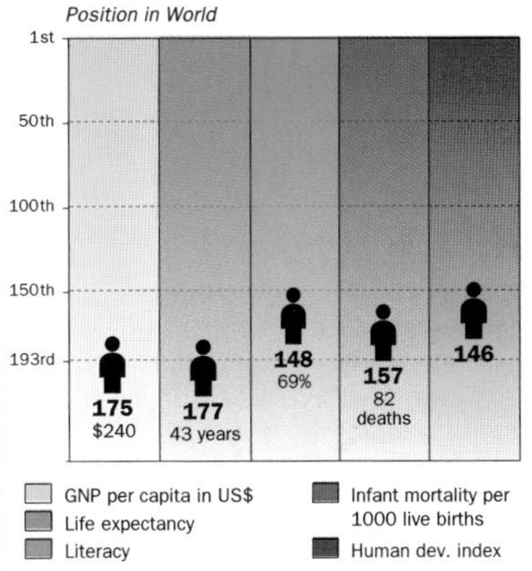
Position in World
1st
50th
100th
150th
193rd
175
$240
177
43 years
148
69%
157
82
deaths
146
GNP per capita in US$
Life expectancy
Literacy
Infant mortality per 1000 live births
Human dev. index

U

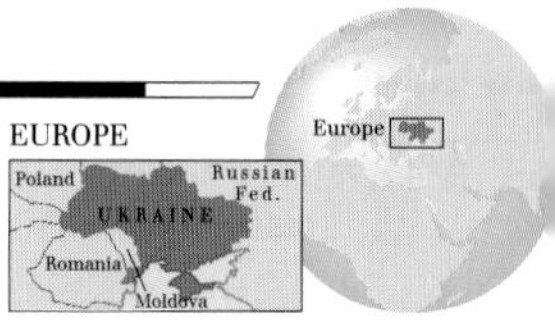

Europe
EUROPE
Poland
Russian Fed.
UKRAINE
Romania
Moldova

UKRAINE

OFFICIAL NAME: Ukraine **CAPITAL:** Kiev
POPULATION: 47.7 million **CURRENCY:** Hryvna **OFFICIAL LANGUAGE:** Ukrainian

1991 | 1991 | Aug 24 | UA | +2 | +380 | .ua

ITS NAME TRANSLATED literally as "on the border," Ukraine was long considered merely to be the edge of the Russian Empire. It is now the second-largest country in Europe, after Russia. An independent Ukrainian state was established in 1918, but was overrun the following year by Russian forces from the east and Polish forces from the west. In 1991, Ukraine again became independent. The country is divided between the nationally conscious and Ukrainian-speaking west (including areas which were part of Poland until World War II) and the east, which has a large ethnic Russian population.

View toward the Cathedral of the Assumption in Kharkiv. Many Ukrainian cities are equipped with elaborate trolley networks.

CLIMATE

Continental/steppe/Mediterranean

WEATHER CHART FOR KIEV

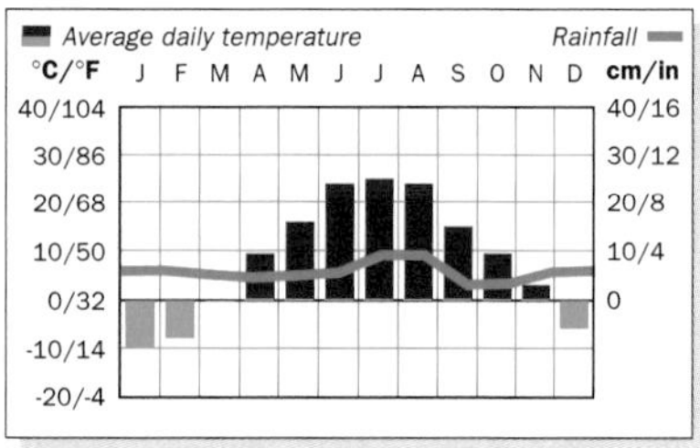

Average daily temperature
Rainfall
°C/°F
J F M A M J J A S O N D
cm/in
40/104
30/86
20/68
10/50
0/32
-10/14
-20/-4
40/16
30/12
20/8
10/4
0

Ukraine has a continental climate, with the exception of the southern coast of Crimea, which has a Mediterranean climate. There are four distinct seasons.

TRANSPORTATION

Drive on right

Boryspil International, Kiev 2.36m passengers

828 ships 1.35m grt

THE TRANSPORTATION NETWORK

164,541 km (102,241 miles)

1770 km (1100 miles)

22,079 km (13,719 miles)

4499 km (2796 miles)

There are Soviet-style subways and trolley networks in the major cities. The rail network connects most towns. Road conditions across the country are poor. Part of a former submarine port at Sevastopol has been opened to commercial shipping.

TOURISM

Visitors : Population 1:7.5

6.33m visitors

Up 9% in 2002

MAIN TOURIST ARRIVALS

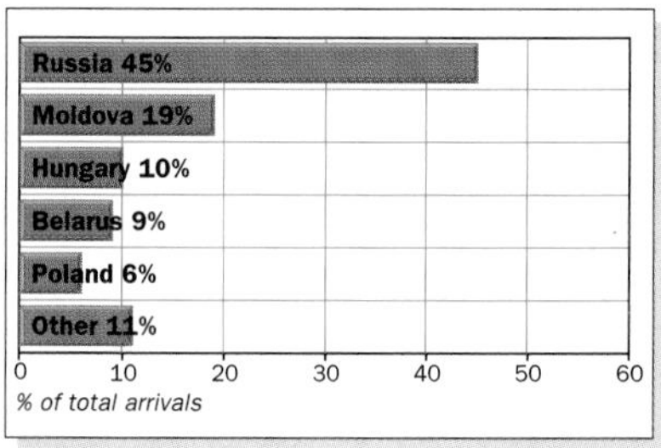

Russia 45%
Moldova 19%
Hungary 10%
Belarus 9%
Poland 6%
Other 11%
0
10
20
30
40
50
60
% of total arrivals

Among potential tourist attractions are the resorts along the warm south coast, notably in Crimea, and the Carpathian Mountains. A highly regulated system of managing tourism has been maintained, and bureaucratic hurdles have held up the development of Western-style hotels.

BELARUS
POLAND
RUSSIAN FEDERATION
ROMANIA
MOLDOVA
SLOVAKIA
HUNGARY
BLACK SEA
Sea of Azov
Gulf of Taganrog
PRIPET MARSHES
Kovel'
Luts'k
Rivne
Chornobyl'
Korosten'
Chernihiv
Shostka
Konotop
Nezhyn
Sumy
KIEV
Fastiv
Zhytomyr
L'viv
Ternopil'
Bila Tserkva
Khmel'nyts'kyy
Ivano-Frankivs'k
Vinnytsya
Uzhhorod
Mukacheve
Kam"yanets'-Podil's'kyy
Chernivtsi
Hoverla 2061m
CARPATHIAN MOUNTAINS
PRYDNIPROVS'KA VYSOCHYNA
PODIL'S'KA VYSOCHYNA
PRYDNIPROVS'KA NYZOVYNA
PRYCHORNOMORS'KA NYZOVYNA
PRYAZOVS'KA VYSOCHYNA
Kharkiv
Kup"yans'k
Lubny
Poltava
Cherkasy
Smila
Kremenchuk
Kremenchuts'ke Vdskh.
Kanivs'ke Vdskh.
Kyyivs'ke Vdskh.
Dniprodzerzhyns'ke Vdskh.
Kakhovs'ke Vdskh.
Uman'
Kirovohrad
Oleksandriya
Dniprodzerzhyns'k
Dnipropetrovs'k
Pavlohrad
Slov"yans'k
Luhans'k
Alchevs'k
Yenakiyeve
Horlivka
Krasnyy Luch
Makiyivka
Donets'k
Kryvyy Rih
Nikopol'
Zaporizhzhya
Mariupol'
Berdyans'k
Melitopol'
Mykolayiv
Kherson
Nova Kakhovka
Odesa
Dnistrovs'kyy Lyman
Ozero Yalpuh
Karkinits'ka Zatoka
Zatoka Syvash
KRYM (CRIMEA)
Yevpatoriya
Simferopol'
Kerch
Yalta
Sevastopol'
Dnieper
Dniester
Desna
Bug
Prut
Danube
Donets
Vorskla
Pivdennyy Bug
52°
48°
24°
28°
32°
36°
40°
N
UKRAINE
Total Area : 603 700 sq. km (223 089 sq. miles)
POPULATION
over 1 000 000
over 500 000
over 100 000
over 50 000
over 10 000
LAND HEIGHT
2000m/6562ft
1000m/3281ft
500m/1640ft
200m/656ft
Sea Level
0 100 km
0 100 miles

U

PEOPLE

Pop. density medium

Ukrainian, Russian, Tatar

79/km² (205/mi²)

THE URBAN/RURAL POPULATION SPLIT

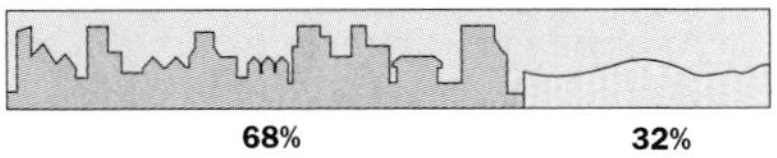
68%
32%

RELIGIOUS PERSUASION

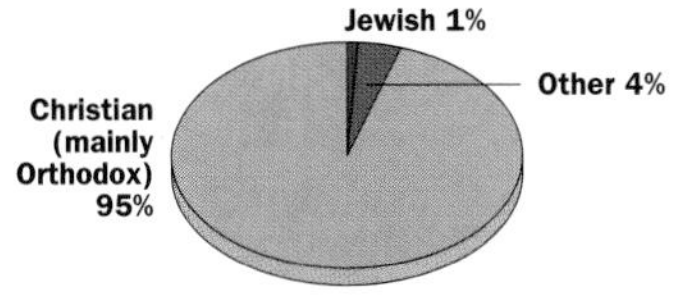
Jewish 1%
Other 4%
Christian (mainly Orthodox) 95%

ETHNIC MAKEUP

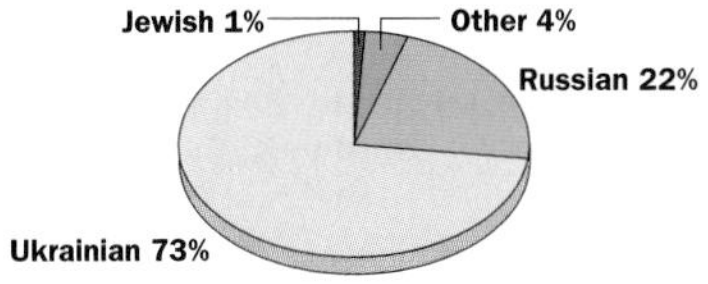
Jewish 1%
Other 4%
Russian 22%
Ukrainian 73%

In the cities and countryside of western Ukraine, Ukrainians make up the vast majority of the population. However, in several of the large cities of the east and south, ethnic Russians form a majority and Russian is spoken by 60% of Ukrainians – a legacy of 19th-century industrialization and of more recent migration in the Soviet era. At independence in 1991, most Russians accepted Ukrainian sovereignty, though tensions remain.

The central government is wary of separatist tendencies in Crimea, however, where Russians make up two-thirds of the population. The Crimea's other main minority, besides ethnic Ukrainians, is the Turkic-speaking Tatar people. Deported en masse to the eastern USSR in 1944 under Stalin, the Tatars have been returning to Crimea since 1990 and now make up 12% of its population. There is a Romanian-speaking minority in the southern Odessa region.

POPULATION AGE BREAKDOWN

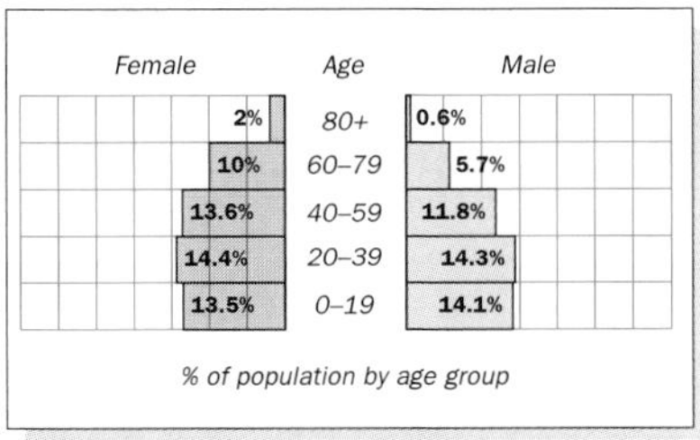
Female
Age
Male
2%
80+
0.6%
10%
60–79
5.7%
13.6%
40–59
11.8%
14.4%
20–39
14.3%
13.5%
0–19
14.1%
% of population by age group

Leonid Kuchma, who became president in 1994.

Viktor Yanukovych, close ally of Kuchma, appointed prime minister in 2002.

WORLD AFFAIRS

Joined UN in 1945

BSEC | CE | CIS | IAEA | OSCE

The unqualified backing given by the West to Ukraine at its independence from the Soviet Union has been eroded by the West's improving relations with Russia and by distrust of President Kuchma. Conversely, Ukraine's ties with Russia, initially seen as a potential aggressor, have been strengthened under Kuchma. In 1995, Ukraine signed a trade agreement with the EU and was admitted to the Council of Europe, but it has since been censured for the slow pace of reform and for authoritarianism.

Despite an ongoing territorial dispute with Romania over the potentially oil-rich Serpents' Island, a friendship treaty was signed in 1997.

Ukraine participates actively in global affairs, sending troops to support the invasion of Iraq in 2003 and to bolster peacekeeping efforts in Liberia in 2004. It has been criticized, however, for dealing with "rogue" states, including military deals with pre-invasion Iraq.

POLITICS

Multiparty elections

2002/2006

President Leonid Kuchma

AT THE LAST ELECTION

Supreme Council 450 seats

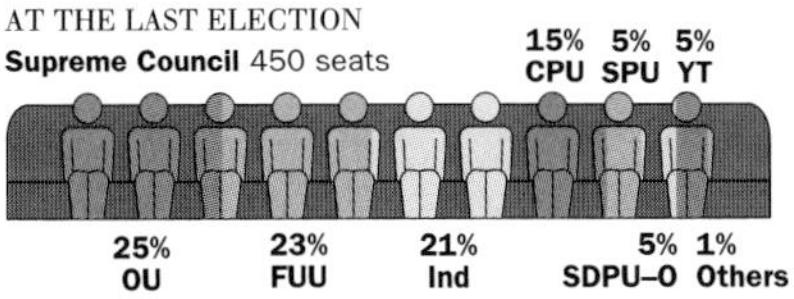
15% CPU
5% SPU
5% YT
25% OU
23% FUU
21% Ind
5% SDPU–O
1% Others

OU = Our Ukraine (Viktor Yushchenko bloc)
FUU = For United Ukraine **Ind** = Independents
CPU = Communist Party **SPU** = Socialist Party of Ukraine
SDPU–O = United Social-Democratic Party of Ukraine
YT = Yulia Timoshenko Election Bloc

Ukraine introduced a multiparty system in 1991.

PROFILE

Ex-premier Leonid Kuchma, who had defeated Ukrainian nationalist Leonid Kravchuk in the 1994 presidential elections, then gained increased powers under constitutional changes in 1996. Multiparty legislative elections were first held in 1994, and the strong position of the communists and allied pro-Kuchma groups was confirmed four years later. Kuchma's own reelection in 1999 was fiercely contested, his opponents claiming fraud and violent confrontations taking place in parliament and on the streets. The boost which Kuchma gained in early 2000 from a referendum backing electoral changes, and Western enthusiasm for his new proreform government, was dissipated by a scandal linking him with the murder of a journalist later that year, and the uncovering of massive financial frauds. The ranks of his opponents included growing numbers of discarded former ministers, and the pro-Kuchma For United Ukraine was pushed into second place by the opposition Our Ukraine bloc in legislative elections in 2002.

MAIN POLITICAL ISSUE

Presidential integrity

Thousands of protestors gather regularly across Ukraine calling for President Kuchma's resignation, offering a litany of complaints.

The principal accusation is that he personally authorized the murder of outspoken Internet journalist Georgy Gongadze in 2000. Though the case was officially "solved" in 2001, the prosecutor-general announced in 2003 that it had been a politically motivated killing, and many believe that responsibility lies at least as high as the interior ministry.

Kuchma is also heavily criticized for the sale in 2000 of a Kolchuga early warning system to Iraq, in breach of international sanctions then in place, and for corruption in general.

He has failed notably to appease his opponents, despite offering in 2003 to water down the constitutional powers of the presidency, which he had himself increased and had approved by a dubious referendum in 2000.

CHRONOLOGY

In 1240, Kiev was conquered by the Mongols. The Ukrainian Cossacks later came under the domination of Lithuania, Poland, and Russia.

- **1918** Independent Ukrainian state after collapse of Russian and Austro-Hungarian empires.
- **1920** After two years of civil war, Ukrainian Soviet Socialist Republic (SSR) established.
- **1921** Treaty of Riga ends Soviet–Polish war: western Ukraine lost.
- **1922** USSR formed, Ukrainian SSR a founding member.
- **1922–1930** Cultural revival under Lenin's "Ukrainianization" policy to pacify national sentiment.
- **1932–1933** "Ukrainianization" policy reversed. Stalin uses famine to eliminate Ukraine as source of opposition; seven million die.

U

CHRONOLOGY *continued*

- **1939** Soviet Union invades Poland and incorporates its ethnic Ukrainian territories into the Ukrainian SSR.
- **1941** Germany invades USSR; 7.5 million Ukrainians die by 1945.
- **1942** Nationalists form Ukrainian Insurgent Army which wages war against both Germans and Soviets.
- **1954** Crimea ceded to Ukrainian SSR.
- **1972** Widespread arrests of intellectuals and dissidents by Soviet state. Vladimir Shcherbitsky, a Brezhnevite, replaces moderate reformer Petr Shelest as head of Communist Party of Ukraine (CPU).
- **1986** World's worst nuclear disaster at Chernobyl power plant.
- **1989** First major coalminers' strike in Donbass. Pro-Gorbachev Volodymyr Ivashko heads CPU.
- **1990** Ukrainian parliament declares Ukrainian SSR a sovereign state. Leonid Kravchuk replaces Ivashko.
- **1991** Full independence declared, conditional on approval by referendum, supported by 90% of voters. CPU banned. Crimea becomes an autonomous republic within Ukrainian SSR.
- **1993** Major strike in Donbass results in costly settlement, which exacerbates budget deficit and stimulates hyperinflation. CPU reestablished at Donetsk congress.
- **1994** Crimea elects Yuri Meshkov as its first president. Leonid Kuchma defeats Kravchuk to become first democratically elected president of Ukraine.
- **1996** Hryvna replaces karbovanets as national currency. New constitution comes into force.
- **1997** Friendship treaty signed with Russia. Accord on Black Sea fleet.
- **1998** Ten-year cooperation agreement with Russia. CPU wins largest number of seats in election.
- **1999** Reelection of Kuchma. Opposition claims of fraud. Kuchma appoints proreform government.
- **2000** Chernobyl site closed.
- **2001** Kuchma linked with murder of journalist. Reformist government replaced after parliamentary defeat.
- **2002** Opposition parties make large gains in legislative elections.

AID

Recipient

$484m (receipts) — Down 7% in 2002

In the 1990s US assistance was the world's fourth-largest aid program, and EU assistance totaled $3.5 billion. Some US aid was held up in 2002 over Ukraine's alleged dealings with Iraq.

DEFENSE

Phasing out conscription

$4.73bn — Down 3% in 2002

UKRAINIAN ARMED FORCES

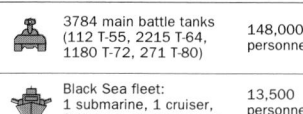

3784 main battle tanks (112 T-55, 2215 T-64, 1180 T-72, 271 T-80)	148,000 personnel
Black Sea fleet: 1 submarine, 1 cruiser, 2 frigates, 8 patrol boats	13,500 personnel
499 combat aircraft (Tu-22M, MiG-29, Su-24/25/27)	49,100 personnel
None	

Ukraine was a center for arms manufacture under the old Soviet system, and now has a major weapons export trade. A member of the CIS, Ukraine finally resolved in 1997 its long-smoldering dispute with Russia over control of the Black Sea fleet, with agreement on its division and a 20-year Russian lease on port facilities in Sevastopol. Meanwhile, the Ukrainian parliament had ratified the START-I nuclear disarmament treaty, and Ukraine's nuclear warheads were transferred to Russia under a trilateral weapons dismantling accord also involving substantial US aid.

In 2000 it was decided that compulsory military service, which lasts a minimum of 18 months, should be ended by 2015. The armed forces have been slimmed down, with further cuts planned to result in a total strength of 100,000 (including paramilitary forces) by 2015.

Ukraine joined NATO's Partnership for Peace program in 1995, signed a security pact with the alliance in 1997, and announced in 2002 its intention to apply for full NATO membership.

ECONOMICS

Inflation 221% p.a. (1990–2001)

$37.9bn — 5.318 hryvnas (5.333)

SCORE CARD

- WORLD GNP RANKING........56th
- GNP PER CAPITA........$780
- BALANCE OF PAYMENTS........$3.17bn
- INFLATION........3.4%
- UNEMPLOYMENT........11%

EXPORTS

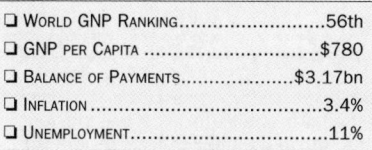

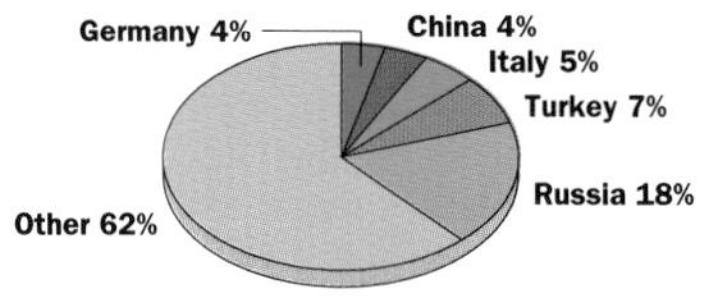
Germany 4%
China 4%
Italy 5%
Turkey 7%
Russia 18%
Other 62%

IMPORTS

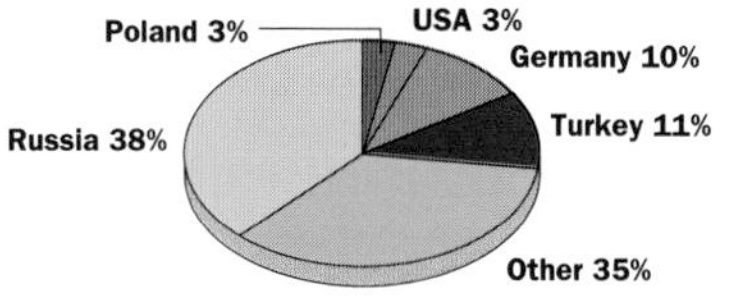
Poland 3%
USA 3%
Germany 10%
Turkey 11%
Russia 38%
Other 35%

ECONOMIC PERFORMANCE INDICATOR

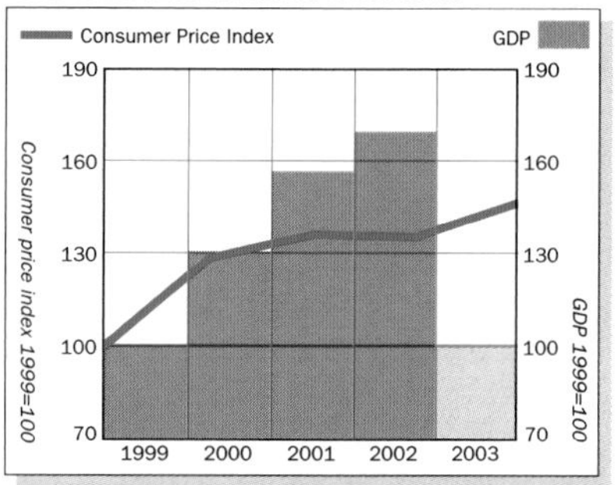
Consumer Price Index
GDP
190
160
130
100
70
Consumer price index 1999=100
GDP 1999=100
1999
2000
2001
2002
2003

STRENGTHS

Well-educated workforce. Potential for grain and food export. Mineral reserves. Strategic position bordering the EU. Technological potential, especially in aerospace and computers.

WEAKNESSES

Failure to reform centrally planned economy. Low foreign investment. Weak currency. Huge debt. Antireform political elites. Inefficient, subsidized manufacturing industries. Corruption.

PROFILE

Real growth was recorded at last in 2000, the economy having contracted by over half over ten years. Privatization of large enterprises has barely begun, and bureaucracy stifles private enterprise and investment. Lack of land reform holds back agriculture in the "bread basket" of Europe. Controversial legislation passed in 2001 paved the way for the sale of farmland after 2004.

UKRAINE : MAJOR BUSINESSES

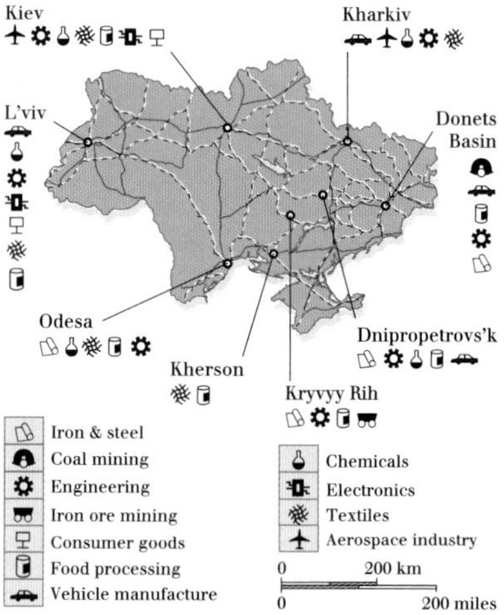
Kiev
Kharkiv
L'viv
Donets Basin
Odesa
Kherson
Kryvyy Rih
Dnipropetrovs'k
Iron & steel
Coal mining
Engineering
Iron ore mining
Consumer goods
Food processing
Vehicle manufacture
Chemicals
Electronics
Textiles
Aerospace industry
0 200 km
0 200 miles

RESOURCES

Electric power 53.9m kW

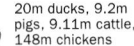

382,297 tonnes

76,070 b/d (reserves 1.6bn barrels)

20m ducks, 9.2m pigs, 9.11m cattle, 148m chickens

Coal, iron, titanium, oil, gas, manganese, lignite, peat, mercury, uranium, nickel, gold

ELECTRICITY GENERATION

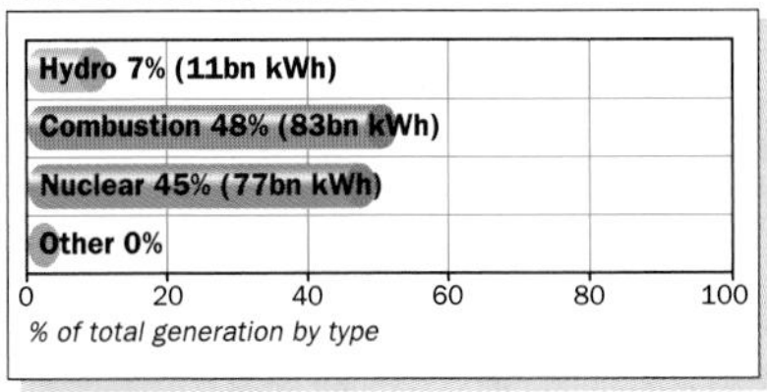
Hydro 7% (11bn kWh)
Combustion 48% (83bn kWh)
Nuclear 45% (77bn kWh)
Other 0%
0
20
40
60
80
100
% of total generation by type

Ukraine imports 75% of its oil and 70% of its gas, mostly from Russia. Some gas is in lieu of transit fees for pipelines carrying Russian gas, but it often misses payments for imports. Yet Ukraine has oil and gas reserves of its own. Coal is mined, in poor safety conditions, in the Donbass–Donetsk region. Just under half of electricity is nuclear-generated.

Ukraine has 5% of global mineral reserves, including the largest titanium reserves, the third-largest deposits of iron ore, and 30% of global manganese ore. There are also deposits of mercury, uranium, nickel, and some gold. In 2000, Ukraine exported $6 billion-worth of metal products, which accounted for 40% of export earnings. The steel industry has begun to grow again after several years of decline.

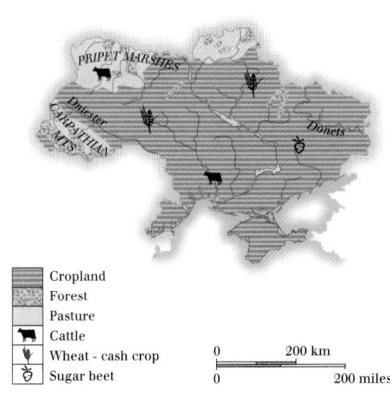

UKRAINE : LAND USE

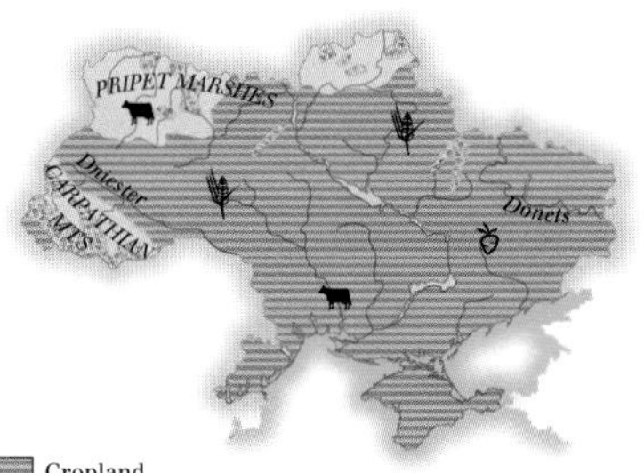
PRIPET MARSHES
Dnester
CARPATHIAN MTS
Donets

Cropland
Forest
Pasture
Cattle
Wheat - cash crop
Sugar beet

0 200 km
0 200 miles

ENVIRONMENT

Sustainability rank: 136th

4% (0.3% partially protected)

6.9 tonnes per capita

ENVIRONMENTAL TREATIES

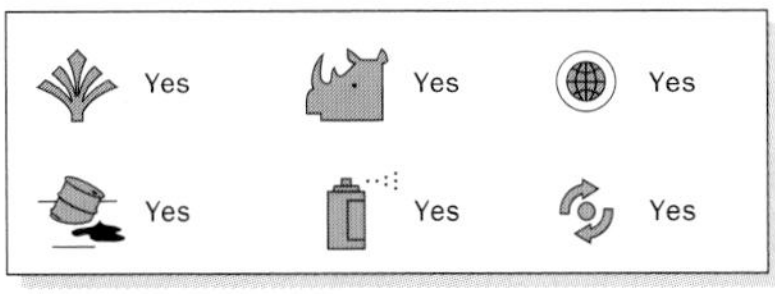
Yes
Yes
Yes
Yes
Yes
Yes

As a result of the Chernobyl nuclear disaster in 1986 – the world's worst nuclear accident – over three million Ukrainians live in dangerously radioactive areas and 12% of arable land is contaminated. The last working reactor at Chernobyl closed at the end of 2000, under agreements in which Western countries provided large-scale financial assistance. However, nuclear production continues elsewhere because of the cost of Russian oil and gas imports. Coal-fired power plants are old-fashioned, highly polluting, and inefficient. Industrial pollution is widespread, especially from steel and chemical works in the Donbass region, contributing to the acute problem of low air quality in eight major cities.

MEDIA

TV ownership high

Daily newspaper circulation 175 per 1000 people

PUBLISHING AND BROADCAST MEDIA

There are 44 daily newspapers, including *Holos Ukrainy*, which has the highest circulation figures

6 services: 1 state-controlled, 5 independent

3 services: 2 state-controlled, 1 independent

Mass-circulation newspapers are mainly in Russian. TV stations reflect regional differences. Journalists fear repression and extrajudicial violence.

CRIME

No death penalty

198,858 prisoners

Down 16% in 2000–2002

CRIME RATES

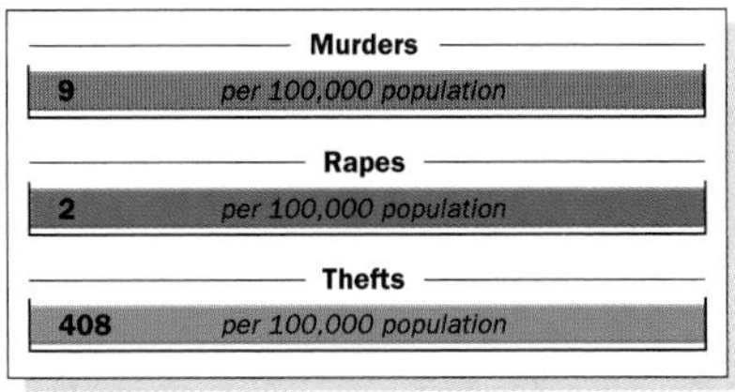
Murders
9 per 100,000 population
Rapes
2 per 100,000 population
Thefts
408 per 100,000 population

Street crime, robberies, violence, and carjackings have increased sharply. Ukraine is a major source of people-trafficking to the West. Corruption is rampant across the economy. Political killings make headlines, as did the murder in 2000 of journalist Georgy Gongadze. The death penalty was abolished in 2000.

EDUCATION

School leaving age: 15

99%

2.27m students

THE EDUCATION SYSTEM

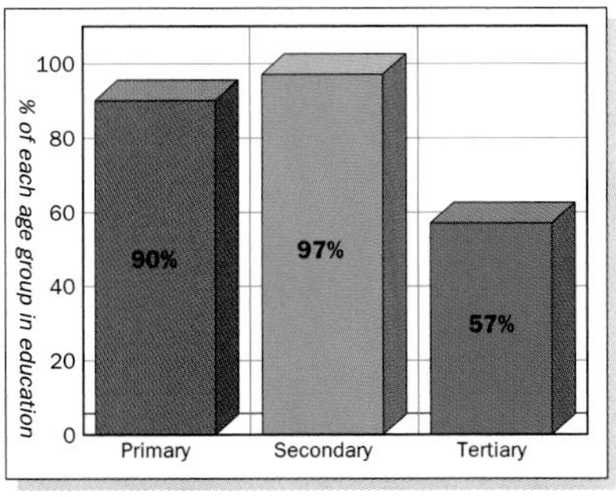
100
80
60
40
20
0
% of each age group in education
90%
97%
57%
Primary
Secondary
Tertiary

Using Ukrainian in schools is the main element in the drive to promote the once-banned language. Some schools in the west no longer teach Russian. Most university teaching is in Russian in eastern regions, and in Ukrainian in those in the west.

HEALTH

Welfare state health benefits

1 per 333 people

Cerebrovascular and heart diseases, cancers, accidents

Health care, supposedly free to all, has declined significantly in the post-Soviet period. A $2 million UN program provides treatment and preventive care for people affected by the Chernobyl disaster. By 2004, 1.4% of the population was HIV positive.

SPENDING

GDP/cap. decrease

CONSUMPTION AND SPENDING

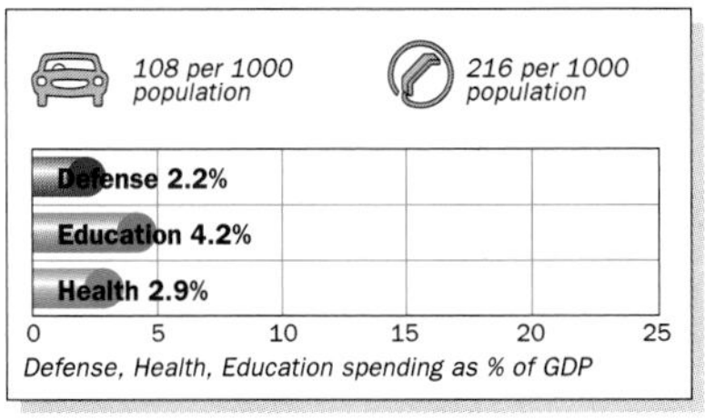
108 per 1000 population
216 per 1000 population
Defense 2.2%
Education 4.2%
Health 2.9%
0
5
10
15
20
25
Defense, Health, Education spending as % of GDP

Just under half the population live below the UN poverty line. Wage arrears – and massive hidden unemployment – are major problems.

WORLD RANKING

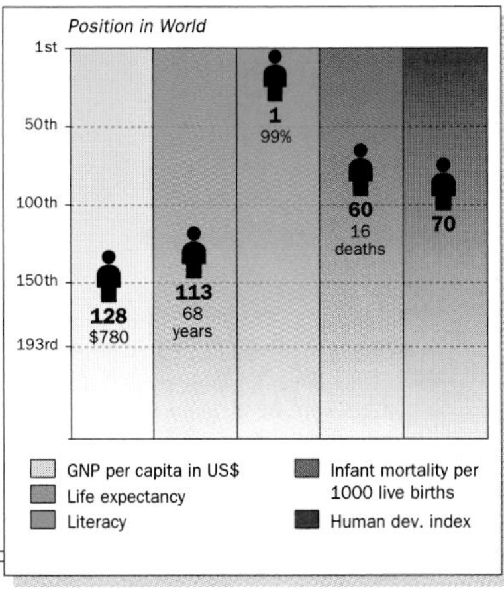
Position in World
1st
50th
100th
150th
193rd
128
$780
113
68
years
1
99%
60
16
deaths
70
GNP per capita in US$
Life expectancy
Literacy
Infant mortality per 1000 live births
Human dev. index

U

UNITED ARAB EMIRATES

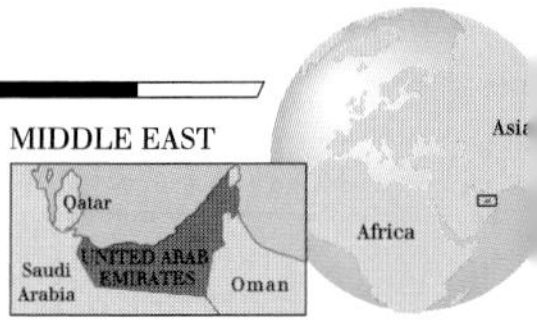
MIDDLE EAST
Qatar
UNITED ARAB EMIRATES
Saudi Arabia
Oman
Africa
Asia

OFFICIAL NAME: United Arab Emirates **CAPITAL:** Abu Dhabi
POPULATION: 3 million **CURRENCY:** UAE dirham **OFFICIAL LANGUAGE:** Arabic

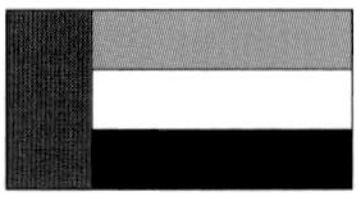

1971 | 1972 | Dec 2 | UAE | +4 | +971 | .ae

THE UNITED ARAB EMIRATES (UAE), created in 1971, is the Arab world's only working federation. Six of its seven emirates cluster around the northeastern corner of the country, while Abu Dhabi has a larger hinterland of semiarid desert relieved by occasional oases. The cities, watered by extensive irrigation systems, have lavish greenery. Prosperity once relied on pearls, but the UAE is now a sizable gas and oil exporter, and has a growing services sector.

CLIMATE

Hot desert

WEATHER CHART FOR ABU DHABI

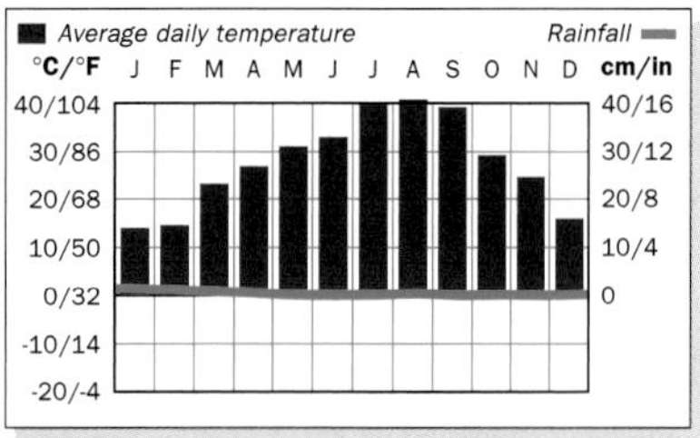
Average daily temperature
Rainfall
°C/°F
J F M A M J J A S O N D
cm/in
40/104
30/86
20/68
10/50
0/32
-10/14
-20/-4
40/16
30/12
20/8
10/4
0

Though rainfall is minimal, summers are humid. Sand-laden *shamal* winds often blow in winter and spring.

TRANSPORTATION

Drive on right

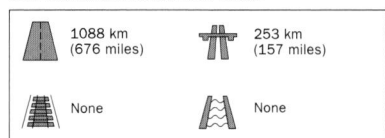

Dubai International 18.1m passengers

356 ships 703,300 grt

THE TRANSPORTATION NETWORK

1088 km (676 miles)

253 km (157 miles)

None

None

The roads are good. Five of the seven emirates have international airports, of which the busiest is Dubai International.

TOURISM

Visitors : Population 1.8:1

5.44m visitors

Up 39% in 2001–2002

MAIN TOURIST ARRIVALS

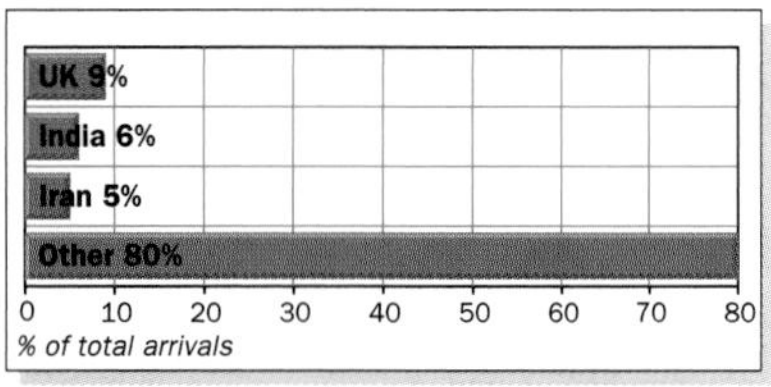
UK 9%
India 6%
Iran 5%
Other 80%
0 10 20 30 40 50 60 70 80
% of total arrivals

Tourism was minimal until the mid-1980s. Since then, Dubai in particular has redefined itself as a tourist haven of sun, sand, safari, sailing, and shopping; attractions include an underwater hotel and an indoor ski center.

PEOPLE

Pop. density low

Arabic, Farsi, Indian and Pakistani languages, English

36/km² (93/mi²)

THE URBAN/RURAL POPULATION SPLIT

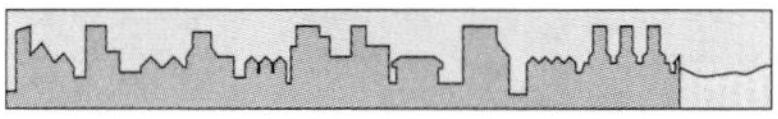
88%
12%

ETHNIC MAKEUP

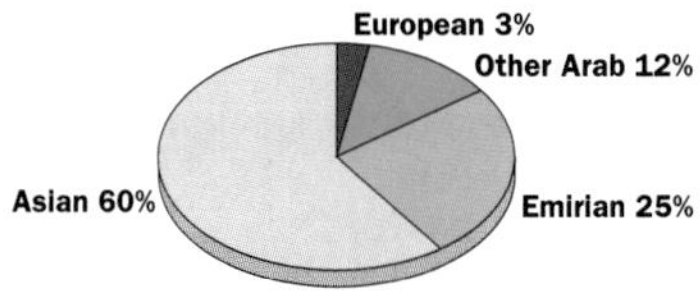
European 3%
Other Arab 12%
Asian 60%
Emirian 25%

UAE nationals are largely city dwellers, with Abu Dhabi and Dubai the main centers. They are greatly outnumbered by expatriates who arrived in the 1970s during the oil boom, and the Western expatriate community is permitted a virtually unrestricted lifestyle. Most UAE nationals are conservative Sunni Muslims of Bedouin descent, though there is a Shi'a community in Dubai with links to Iran. Islamic fundamentalism is a growing force among the young.

Poverty is rare in the UAE, where the government remains the biggest employer. Women in theory enjoy equal rights with men. A Presidential Marriage Fund discourages UAE men from taking foreign wives.

POLITICS

No legislative elections

Not applicable

President Shaikh Zayed bin Sultan al-Nahyan

LEGISLATIVE OR ADVISORY BODIES

Federal National Council 40 seats

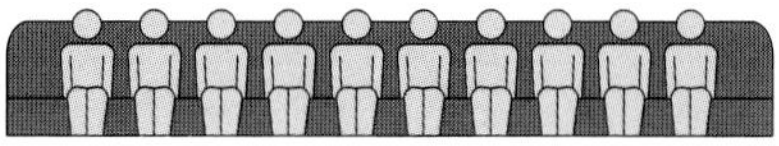

There are no political parties. The method of appointment of members of the Federal National Council is determined individually by each of the seven members of the federation.

The UAE's seven emirates – Abu Dhabi, Dubai, Sharjah, Ras al Khaimah, Ajman, Umm al Qaiwain, and Fujairah – are dominated by their ruling families. The main personalities are the ruler of Abu Dhabi, Shaikh Zayed, who holds the UAE presidency, and the four al-Maktoum brothers who control Dubai. The eldest, Shaikh Maktoum al-Maktoum, is ruler of Dubai as well as vice president and prime minister of the UAE.

President Zayed has relaunched the advisory Federal National Council in response to criticism of the lack of democracy, but parties remain banned. The growth of Islamic fundamentalism is a concern. The freedoms granted to Westerners have aroused some anger but, for economic reasons, they are unlikely to be withdrawn.

UNITED ARAB EMIRATES

Total Area : 82 880 sq. km (32 000 sq. miles)

POPULATION

◎ over 100 000

• under 10 000

LAND HEIGHT

1000m/3281ft

500m/1640ft

Sea Level

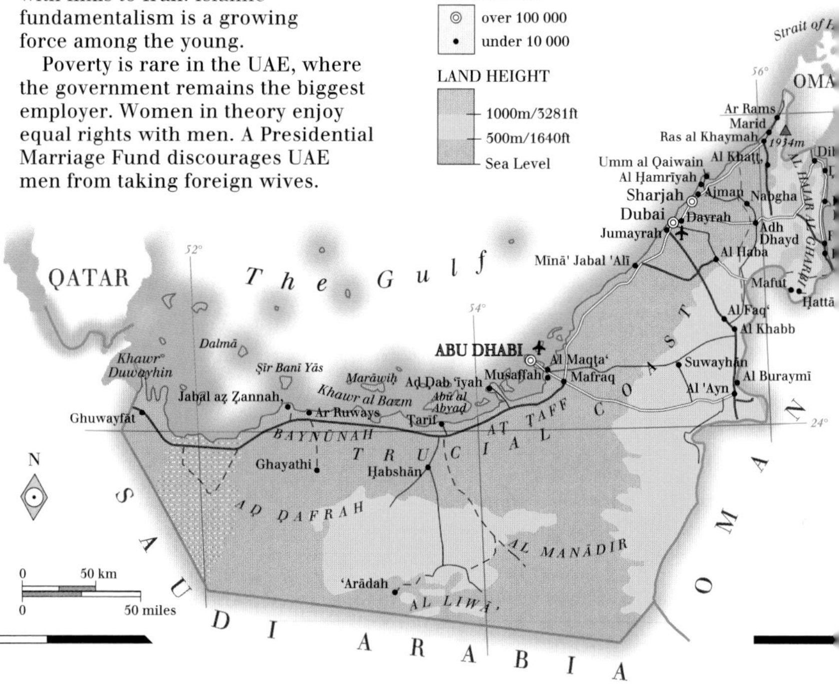
Strait of H
OMAN
Ar Rams
Marid
Ras al Khaymah
1934m
Umm al Qaiwain
Al Khatt
Al Hamriyah
Sharjah
Ajman
Nabgha
Dubai
Dayrah
Jumayrah
Adh Dhayd
Al Haba
Mina' Jabal 'Ali
Mafut
Hatta
QATAR
The Gulf
Al Faq'
Al Khabb
Dalma
ABU DHABI
Al Maqta'
Suwayhan
Khawr Duwayhin
Sir Bani Yas
Marawih
Ad Dab 'iyah
Musaffah
Mafraq
Al Buraymi
Khawr al Bazm
Abu al Abyad
Al 'Ayn
Jabal az Zannah
Ar Ruways
Tarif
Ghuwayfat
BAYNUNAH
TRUCIAL COAST
Ghayathi
Habshan
N
SAUDI ARABIA
AD DAFRAH
AL MANADIR
OMAN
0 50 km
0 50 miles
'Aradah
AL LIWA
52°
54°
56°
24°

U

WORLD AFFAIRS

Joined UN in 1971

AL | OIC | GCC | OAPEC | OPEC

The West sees the UAE as a moderate Arab state. It maintains especially close links with the UK and the US. In 1992, conflict flared when Iran seized three disputed islands: negotiations continue. The UAE signed a crucial boundary agreement with Oman in 2003. Also in that year, it urged Iraqi president Saddam Hussein to resign to avoid war.

AID

Donor

$156m (donations) — Up 23% in 2002

The UAE gives substantial humanitarian and development assistance, largely to Arab and Muslim countries.

DEFENSE

No compulsory military sevice

$2.71bn — Down 3% in 2002

The training of UAE forces is limited, and personnel are mainly drawn from other Arab states and the Indian subcontinent. US air bases in the UAE supply refueling craft and have been used consistently in regional conflicts, including the 2001 war in Afghanistan and the 2003 invasion of Iraq. The countries of the GCC signed their first defense pact in 2000.

ECONOMICS

Inflation 2.3% p.a. (1990–1999)

$49.2bn — 3.673 UAE dirhams (3.673)

SCORE CARD

- ❑ World GNP Ranking 51st
- ❑ GNP per Capita $18,060
- ❑ Balance of Payments $10.8bn
- ❑ Inflation 2.8%
- ❑ Unemployment 2%

Strengths

Oil and gas reserves. Development of service industries and manufacturing sector. Improving education system. Regional tax-free base for e-commerce.

Weaknesses

Lack of skilled labor. Most raw materials and food imported. Water scarce, concentrated in Abu Dhabi. Fears for stability after Shaikh Zayed dies.

EXPORTS

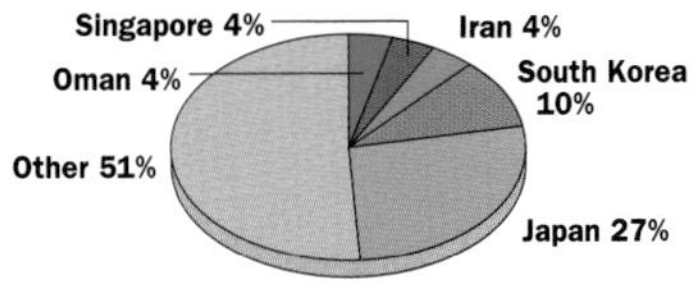
Singapore 4%
Iran 4%
Oman 4%
South Korea 10%
Other 51%
Japan 27%

IMPORTS

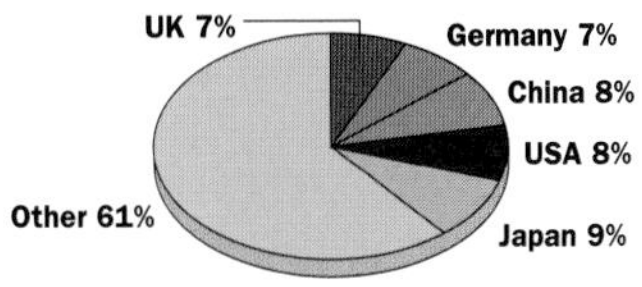
UK 7%
Germany 7%
China 8%
USA 8%
Other 61%
Japan 9%

RESOURCES

Electric power 5.8m kW

110,000 tonnes — 2.52m b/d (reserves 97.8bn barrels)

1.45m goats, 560,000 sheep, 12.7m chickens — Oil, natural gas

The UAE is a major exporter of crude oil and natural gas; oil production accounts for a great part of export revenue. More than 200 factories operate at Mina Jabal Ali in Dubai, the world's largest man-made port. The Dubai International Finance Center aims to challenge Bahrain as the region's financial hub.

ENVIRONMENT

Sustainability rank: 141st

None — 21 tonnes per capita

Despite the harsh desert climate, there is a rich variety of plants and animals. Shaikh Zayed champions conservation parks to avert the threat from hunting.

MEDIA

TV ownership medium

Daily newspaper circulation 156 per 1000 people

PUBLISHING AND BROADCAST MEDIA

There are 7 daily newspapers. The leading Arabic newspaper is *Al-Khaleej*. *Gulf News* is its English-language counterpart

2 state-owned, several independent services — 1 state-owned service, many independent stations

Satellite TV is unrestricted. Dubai Media City, opened in 2001, promotes greater press freedom.

CRIME

Death penalty in use

6000 prisoners — Up 2% in 2000

Street crime and muggings are rare. Dubai is reputed to be a transit point for the smuggling of narcotics and caviar.

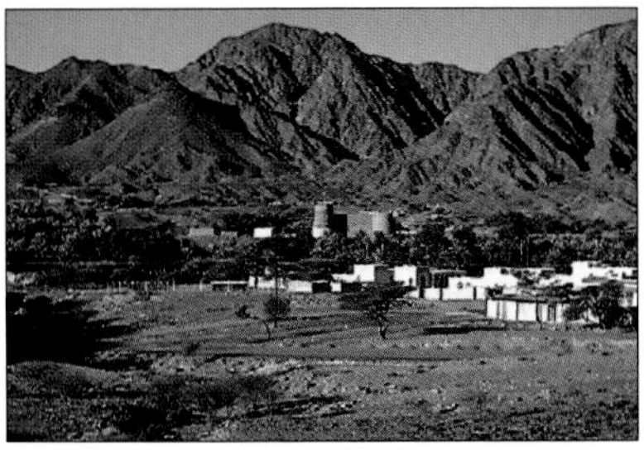

An oasis village, *inland from Fujairah, now accessible by means of a well-developed network of new roads.*

CHRONOLOGY

The UAE was influenced by the Portuguese and the Ottomans, but the British became dominant in the 19th century.

- ❑ **1971** The UK withdraws as protecting power and UAE federation is formed.
- ❑ **1991** UAE offers bases to Western forces after Kuwait is invaded.
- ❑ **2000** GCC defense pact signed.

EDUCATION

School leaving age: 11

77% — 56,401 students

UAE citizens enjoy completely free education. Zayed University was set up in three emirates in 1998.

HEALTH

Welfare state health benefits

1 per 556 people — Circulatory and respiratory diseases, cancers

A high-quality system of primary health care is in place for all UAE citizens, with hospitals able to carry out most operations.

SPENDING

GDP/cap. increase

CONSUMPTION AND SPENDING

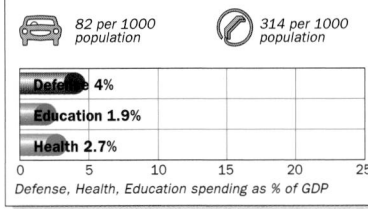

82 per 1000 population — *314 per 1000 population*

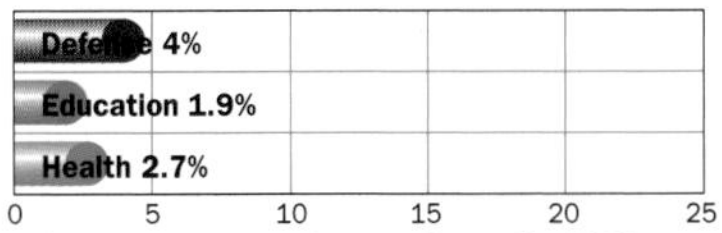
Defense 4%
Education 1.9%
Health 2.7%
0
5
10
15
20
25

Defense, Health, Education spending as % of GDP

UAE nationals enjoy one of the highest per capita incomes in the Arab world. There is no income tax, and oil revenues subsidize public services. Entrepreneurship is encouraged.

WORLD RANKING

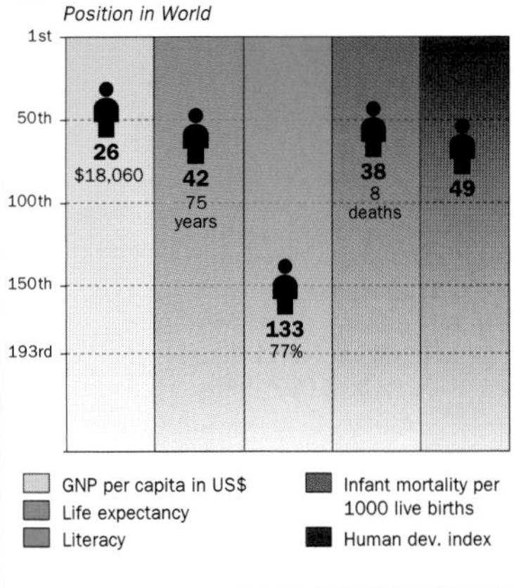
Position in World
1st
50th
100th
150th
193rd
26
$18,060
42
75
years
133
77%
38
8
deaths
49
GNP per capita in US$
Life expectancy
Literacy
Infant mortality per 1000 live births
Human dev. index

U

UNITED KINGDOM

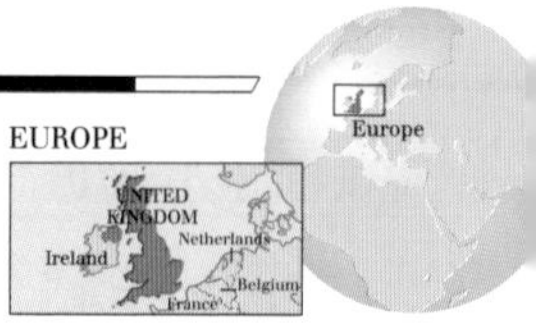
Europe
EUROPE
UNITED KINGDOM
Ireland
Netherlands
Belgium
France

OFFICIAL NAME: United Kingdom of Great Britain and Northern Ireland **CAPITAL:** London
POPULATION: 59.3 million **CURRENCY:** Pound sterling **OFFICIAL LANGUAGES:** English, Welsh (in Wales)

1707 | 1922 | None | GB | 0 | +44 | .uk

LYING IN NORTHWESTERN Europe, the United Kingdom (UK) occupies the major portion of the British Isles. It includes the countries of England, Scotland, and Wales, the constitutionally distinct region of Northern Ireland, and several outlying islands. Its only land border is with the Irish republic. The UK is separated from the European mainland by the English Channel and the North Sea. To the west lies the Atlantic Ocean. The most densely populated region is the southeast, while Scotland is the wildest region, with the Highlands less populated today than in the 18th century. The UK joined the European Communities (EC – later the EU) in 1973, and most of its trade is now with its European partners. Leadership of the Commonwealth and permanent membership of the UN Security Council give the UK a prominent role in international politics.

CLIMATE

Maritime

WEATHER CHART FOR LONDON

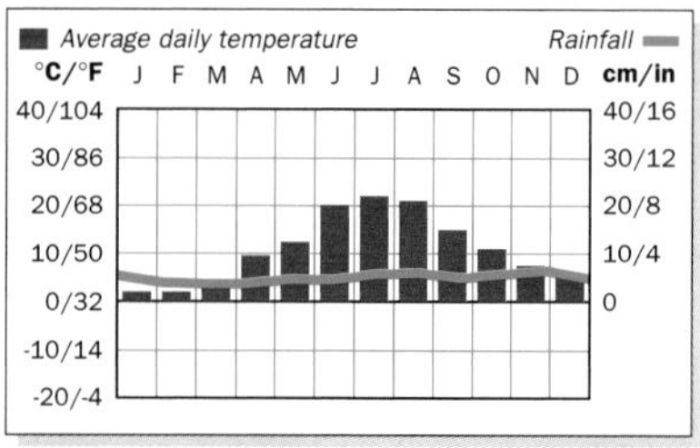
Average daily temperature
Rainfall
°C/°F J F M A M J J A S O N D cm/in
40/104
30/86
20/68
10/50
0/32
-10/14
-20/-4
40/16
30/12
20/8
10/4
0

The UK has a generally mild, temperate, and highly changeable climate. Rain, regarded as synonymous with Britain's weather, is fairly well distributed throughout the year, but recently unusually long dry or wet spells have caused water shortages in some areas, and flooding in others. The west is generally wetter than the east, and the south warmer than the north.

TRANSPORTATION

Drive on left

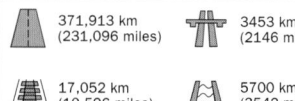

Heathrow, London 63.5m passengers

1525 ships 8.05m grt

THE TRANSPORTATION NETWORK

371,913 km (231,096 miles)

3453 km (2146 miles)

17,052 km (10,596 miles)

5700 km (3542 miles)

The government has not fulfilled its 1997 campaign promise of a more integrated policy, faced with congestion, pollution, and motorists' resentment of high fuel taxes. The rail system, after the rushed privatization of the 1990s, suffers from underinvestment, maintenance problems, and fragmented services. In 2003, central London introduced a "congestion charge" for road use.

TOURISM

Visitors : Population 1:2.4

24.8m visitors

Up 3% in 2003

MAIN TOURIST ARRIVALS

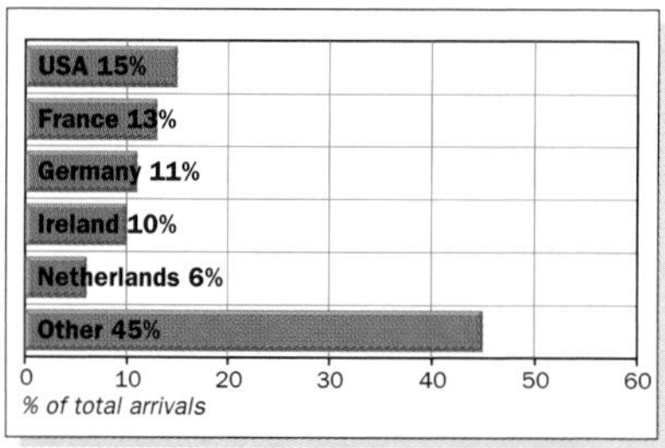
USA 15%
France 13%
Germany 11%
Ireland 10%
Netherlands 6%
Other 45%
0 10 20 30 40 50 60
% of total arrivals

The UK ranks sixth in the world as a tourist destination. Tourism is among its most important industries and is a growing source of employment. Heritage is the principal selling point, North Americans, French, and Germans are the main visitors, and London, with its art galleries, theaters, and historic buildings, remains the major destination. Visitors also head for Stonehenge, the Roman splendors of Bath, the medieval buildings of Oxford, Cambridge, and York, Shakespeare's Stratford-upon-Avon, and Scotland, where the Highlands are a particular attraction.

***Oxford,** home to the oldest university in the UK. Teaching began in 1096; the first college was founded in 1249. One of the city's finest buildings is the 17th-century semi-oval Sheldonian Theatre.*

PEOPLE

Pop. density high

English, Welsh, Scottish Gaelic, Irish Gaelic

245/km² (636/mi²)

THE URBAN/RURAL POPULATION SPLIT

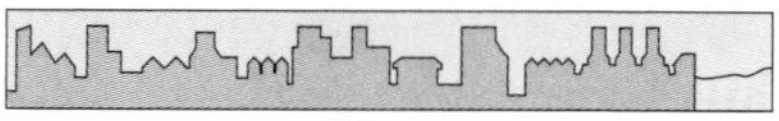
90%
10%

RELIGIOUS PERSUASION

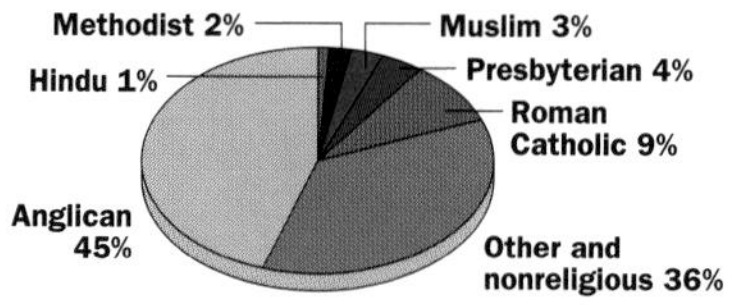
Methodist 2%
Muslim 3%
Hindu 1%
Presbyterian 4%
Roman Catholic 9%
Anglican 45%
Other and nonreligious 36%

ETHNIC MAKEUP

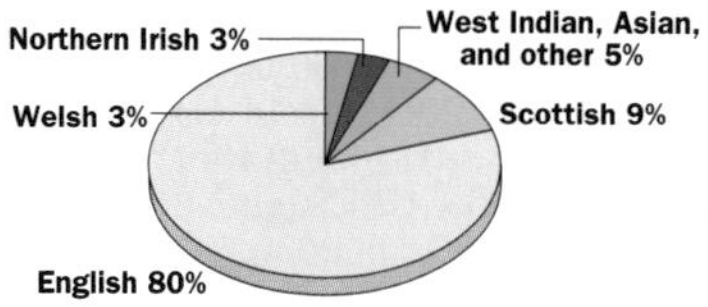
Northern Irish 3%
West Indian, Asian, and other 5%
Welsh 3%
Scottish 9%
English 80%

The Scottish and Welsh nations remain recognizably distinct, despite forming part of a unified state. Scotland retains its own legal and educational systems, and recent steps in devolution have given both countries greater autonomy.

Britain's ethnic minorities account for 5% of the total population; over 50% of their members were born in Britain. Ethnic minority communities are generally concentrated in the inner cities, where they face problems of deprivation and social stress, and may also suffer from isolation, particularly women. Though there is not much support for overtly racist politics, multiethnic recruitment has made little progress in key areas such as policing, and prejudices persist. The level of institutionalized racism was criticized by the UN in 2000.

Two-fifths of all births occur outside marriage, compared with 12% in 1980, but most of these are to cohabiting couples. Single-parent households account for one-fifth of all families with children under 18.

POPULATION AGE BREAKDOWN

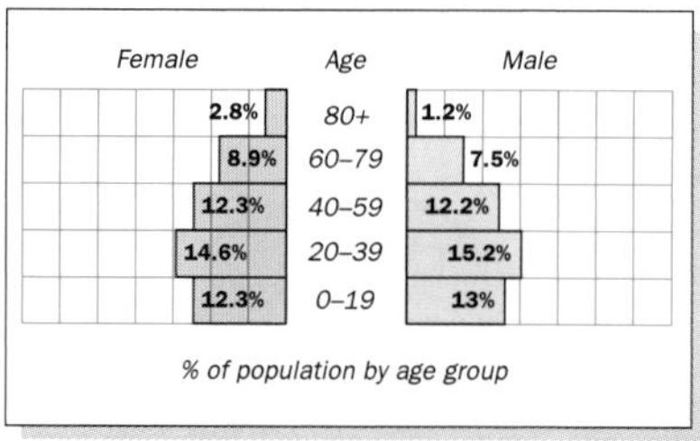
Female
Age
Male
2.8% 80+ 1.2%
8.9% 60–79 7.5%
12.3% 40–59 12.2%
14.6% 20–39 15.2%
12.3% 0–19 13%
% of population by age group

U

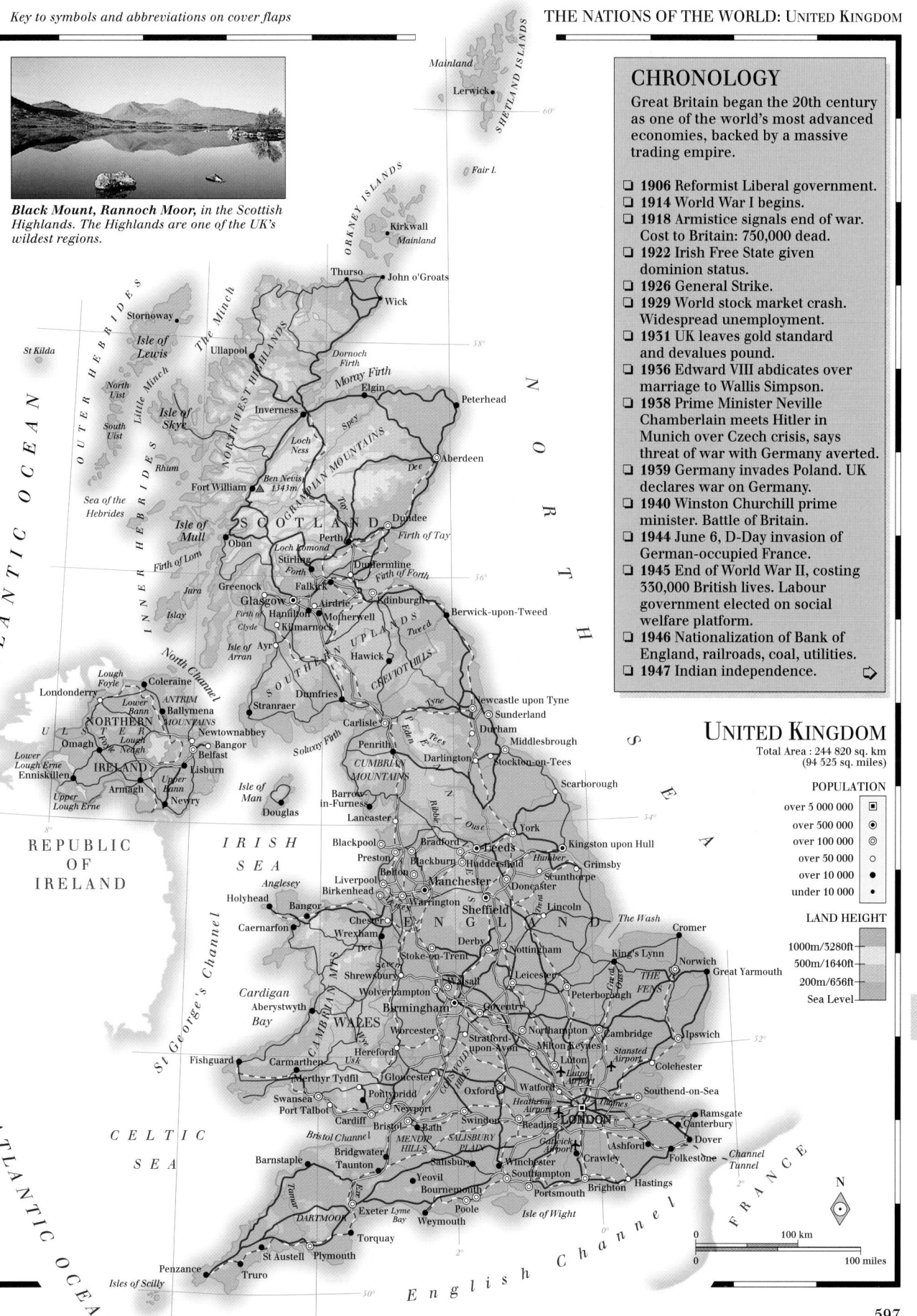

Black Mount, Rannoch Moor, *in the Scottish Highlands. The Highlands are one of the UK's wildest regions.*

CHRONOLOGY

Great Britain began the 20th century as one of the world's most advanced economies, backed by a massive trading empire.

- ❑ **1906** Reformist Liberal government.
- ❑ **1914** World War I begins.
- ❑ **1918** Armistice signals end of war. Cost to Britain: 750,000 dead.
- ❑ **1922** Irish Free State given dominion status.
- ❑ **1926** General Strike.
- ❑ **1929** World stock market crash. Widespread unemployment.
- ❑ **1931** UK leaves gold standard and devalues pound.
- ❑ **1936** Edward VIII abdicates over marriage to Wallis Simpson.
- ❑ **1938** Prime Minister Neville Chamberlain meets Hitler in Munich over Czech crisis, says threat of war with Germany averted.
- ❑ **1939** Germany invades Poland. UK declares war on Germany.
- ❑ **1940** Winston Churchill prime minister. Battle of Britain.
- ❑ **1944** June 6, D-Day invasion of German-occupied France.
- ❑ **1945** End of World War II, costing 330,000 British lives. Labour government elected on social welfare platform.
- ❑ **1946** Nationalization of Bank of England, railroads, coal, utilities.
- ❑ **1947** Indian independence. ⇨

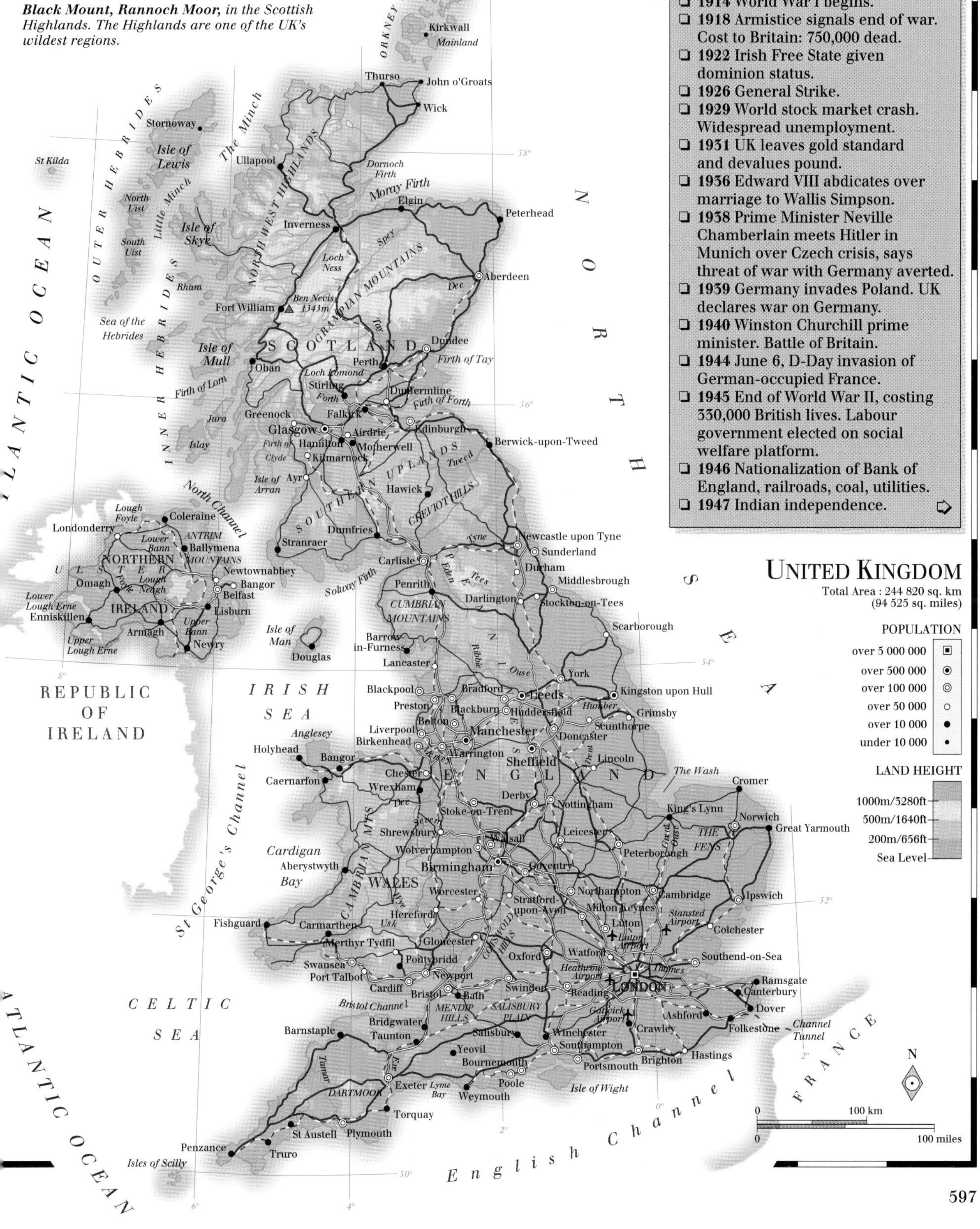
UNITED KINGDOM
Total Area : 244 820 sq. km
(94 525 sq. miles)
POPULATION
over 5 000 000
over 500 000
over 100 000
over 50 000
over 10 000
under 10 000
LAND HEIGHT
1000m/3280ft
500m/1640ft
200m/656ft
Sea Level
0 100 km
0 100 miles
N
SHETLAND ISLANDS
Mainland
Lerwick
Fair I.
ORKNEY ISLANDS
Kirkwall
Mainland
Thurso
John o'Groats
Wick
OUTER HEBRIDES
Stornoway
Isle of Lewis
The Minch
St Kilda
Ullapool
North Uist
Little Minch
South Uist
Isle of Skye
NORTH WEST HIGHLANDS
Dornoch Firth
Moray Firth
Elgin
Peterhead
Inverness
Loch Ness
Spey
GRAMPIAN MOUNTAINS
Aberdeen
Dee
Rhum
INNER HEBRIDES
Fort William
Ben Nevis 1343m
Sea of the Hebrides
Tay
SCOTLAND
Dundee
Firth of Tay
Isle of Mull
Oban
Perth
Loch Lomond
Stirling
Forth
Firth of Lorn
Dunfermline
Firth of Forth
Falkirk
Jura
Greenock
Glasgow
Airdrie
Edinburgh
Berwick-upon-Tweed
Islay
Firth of Clyde
Hamilton
Motherwell
Kilmarnock
Tweed
SOUTHERN UPLANDS
Isle of Arran
Ayr
Hawick
CHEVIOT HILLS
North Channel
Dumfries
Stranraer
Lough Foyle
Coleraine
Londonderry
ANTRIM MOUNTAINS
Ballymena
Lower Bann
NORTHERN IRELAND
ULSTER
Newtownabbey
Bangor
Belfast
Omagh
Lough Neagh
Foyle
Lower Lough Erne
Enniskillen
Lisburn
Upper Bann
Armagh
Newry
Upper Lough Erne
Solway Firth
Carlisle
Eden
Tyne
Newcastle upon Tyne
Sunderland
Durham
Middlesbrough
Stockton-on-Tees
Tees
Penrith
Darlington
PENNINES
CUMBRIAN MOUNTAINS
Isle of Man
Douglas
Barrow-in-Furness
Scarborough
Lancaster
Ribble
Ouse
York
REPUBLIC OF IRELAND
IRISH SEA
Blackpool
Preston
Bradford
Leeds
Kingston upon Hull
Blackburn
Huddersfield
Humber
Grimsby
Bolton
Scunthorpe
Anglesey
Liverpool
Birkenhead
Manchester
Doncaster
Holyhead
Bangor
Mersey
Warrington
Sheffield
Trent
Lincoln
Caernarfon
Chester
ENGLAND
The Wash
Cromer
Wrexham
Dee
Derby
Nottingham
King's Lynn
Norwich
Stoke-on-Trent
Great Yarmouth
Severn
THE FENS
Great Ouse
Shrewsbury
Walsall
Leicester
Peterborough
Cardigan Bay
Wolverhampton
Aberystwyth
Birmingham
Coventry
CAMBRIAN MTS
WALES
Worcester
Northampton
Cambridge
Ipswich
Wye
Stratford-upon-Avon
Milton Keynes
Hereford
COTSWOLD HILLS
Stansted Airport
Fishguard
Carmarthen
Usk
Luton
Luton Airport
Colchester
Merthyr Tydfil
Gloucester
Watford
Southend-on-Sea
Swansea
Pontypridd
Oxford
Heathrow Airport
Thames
Port Talbot
Newport
LONDON
Ramsgate
Cardiff
Swindon
Reading
Canterbury
Bristol
Bath
Bristol Channel
MENDIP HILLS
SALISBURY PLAIN
Gatwick Airport
Dover
Ashford
Bridgwater
Crawley
Folkestone
Channel Tunnel
CELTIC SEA
Barnstaple
Taunton
Salisbury
Winchester
Southampton
Yeovil
Tamar
Exe
Bournemouth
Portsmouth
Brighton
Hastings
Poole
Isle of Wight
DARTMOOR
Exeter
Lyme Bay
Weymouth
Torquay
Plymouth
St Austell
Penzance
Truro
Isles of Scilly
English Channel
FRANCE
ATLANTIC OCEAN
NORTH SEA
St George's Channel

U

CHRONOLOGY *continued*

- **1948** NHS established.
- **1949** Founder member of NATO.
- **1956** Suez crisis: UK intervenes in Canal Zone, withdraws under US pressure.
- **1957** US nuclear missiles accepted on UK soil.
- **1961** UK application to join the EEC rejected by French president Charles de Gaulle.
- **1968** Abortion and homosexuality are legalized.
- **1969** British troops sent into Northern Ireland.
- **1973** Joins EEC under Conservative Edward Heath. Oil crisis. Industry on three-day week following strikes by power workers and miners.
- **1974** Labour government, under Harold Wilson, concedes miners' demands. High inflation.
- **1975** Referendum ratifies EC membership. First North Sea oil pipeline in operation.
- **1979–1997** Conservative rule, until 1990 under Margaret Thatcher.
- **1980** Anti-US Cruise missile protests. Rising unemployment. Inner-city riots.
- **1981** Privatization program begun.
- **1982** Argentina invades Falklands. Islands retaken by UK task force.
- **1983** Tax-cutting policies.
- **1986** Financial services market deregularized ("Big Bang").
- **1990** John Major replaces Thatcher.
- **1991** UK in Gulf War.
- **1992** Conservatives win fourth term.
- **1996** Dunblane primary school massacre; tightening of gun control laws. Health crisis linking "mad cow" disease (BSE) with fatal variant Creutzfeldt-Jakob disease (vCJD).
- **1997** Landslide election victory for Labour under Tony Blair. Diana, Princess of Wales, killed in car crash in Paris. Scottish and Welsh referenda approve creation of own assemblies.
- **1998–1999** Good Friday agreement on political settlement in Northern Ireland, endorsed by referendum but held up by disputes over decommissioning weapons.
- **1999** Involvement in NATO air war with Yugoslavia over Kosovo crisis. Scottish Parliament and Welsh Assembly elected, inaugurated. Devolution to power-sharing executive in Northern Ireland.
- **2001** Foot-and-mouth epidemic and mass livestock culling. June, Labour reelected by huge majority. October, military participation in US-led "war on terrorism" in Afghanistan.
- **2002** 50th anniversary of accession to throne of Queen Elizabeth II.
- **2003** UK troops invade Iraq alongside US forces.

U

POLITICS

Multiparty elections

L. House 2001/2006

H.M. Queen Elizabeth II

AT THE LAST ELECTION

House of Commons 659 seats

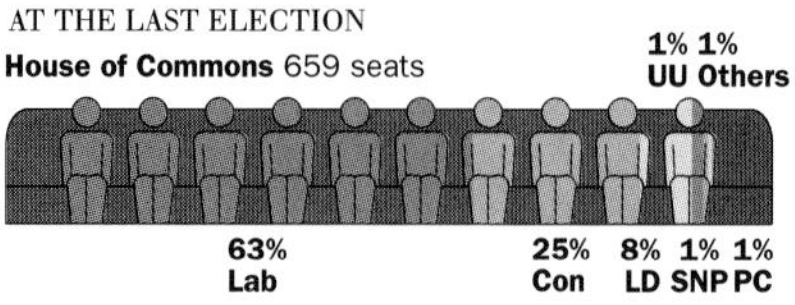
1% 1%
UU Others
63%
Lab
25%
Con
8% 1% 1%
LD SNP PC

Lab = Labour Party **Con** = Conservative and Unionist Party **LD** = Liberal Democrats **UU** = Ulster Unionist parties – (official) Ulster Unionist Party, Democratic Unionist Party, UK Unionist **SNP** = Scottish National Party **PC** = Plaid Cymru

House of Lords 679 seats

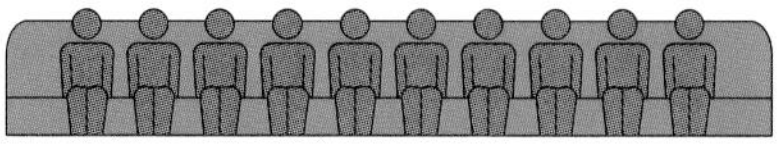

The House of Lords is an unelected body of just under 100 hereditary peers, 26 spiritual peers (bishops), and over 500 life peers (including lords of appeal – judges), appointed by the monarch

The UK is a multiparty democracy. The monarch's power is largely ceremonial.

Profile

Tony Blair's "New Labour" government, occupying the political center, won power in 1997 after almost 18 years of Conservative rule, and retained a massive majority in the 2001 election. In opposition, the Conservatives have struggled to build a credible challenge.

Main Political Issues

Europe

The government ruled in 2003 that the UK was not yet ready to join the eurozone. It has agreed, reluctantly, to hold an eventual referendum on new EU constitutional proposals; opinion polls show little public support. The Conservatives have become increasingly "eurosceptic," believing that EU membership erodes national sovereignty.

Constitutional change

Major changes were made to the UK's system of government in the late 1990s. A Scottish Parliament, with substantial devolved powers, was elected in 1999, as was a Welsh Assembly. The House of Lords was considerably changed by the abolition of voting rights for nearly all hereditary peers, pending its complete overhaul. London gained greater autonomy in 2000 with the election of its own assembly and mayor.

In Northern Ireland, the 1998 Good Friday agreement brought unionists and Irish republicans into a power-sharing government. Internal disagreements and distrust, however, have caused the joint executive formed in 1999 to be suspended on occasion and direct rule reimposed.

The economy

Fundamental alternatives on running the economy are no longer argued within mainstream politics. "New Labour" is wary of increasing taxes. Far from seeking to reverse the privatization of industry, it now advocates using private finance and management within publicly owned services too. This has alienated some traditional Labour supporters. Elite "foundation hospitals," with substantial financial independence from the National Health Service (NHS), and variable university tuition fees are especially controversial.

The war on Iraq

Blair committed the UK to war in Iraq in 2003 without an explicit UN mandate, based on "evidence" of an arsenal of weapons of mass destruction (WMD). The war aroused strong public opposition and huge demonstrations. Though an inquiry cleared Blair of deliberate deception, the failure to find any WMD hurt his credibility. However, with a general election looming in 2005, voters' attention turned from Iraq to focus on domestic issues.

Queen Elizabeth II, *head of state since 1952 and head of the Commonwealth.*

Tony Blair, *prime minister since 1997, and leader of the Labour Party.*

Chancellor of the Exchequer Gordon Brown, *known as the "Iron Chancellor."*

Baroness Thatcher, *the country's only female prime minister (1979–1990).*

London's City Hall, *designed by the world famous architect Sir Norman Foster. It has been home to the London Assembly since 2002.*

WORLD AFFAIRS

Joined UN in 1945

Comm | EU | G8 | NATO | OECD

In 2002 Prime Minister Blair claimed that the UK, if no longer a "great power," could still play a "pivotal role" in world affairs. It holds a permanent seat on the UN Security Council, and being the head of the Commonwealth offers a means of maintaining diplomatic and economic links with the UK's former possessions.

The UK joined the EEC late, and resists the concept of full European integration. Lately, it has been seeking to establish a new coalition in Europe as a counterweight to the Franco-German axis.

Cherishing the UK–US "special relationship," the New Labour government strongly backed the US-led invasion of Iraq in 2003.

AID

Donor

$4.92bn (donations)

Up 8% in 2002

UK foreign aid fell between 1980 and 1997 to below the European average, and well below the nominal target of 0.7% of GNP for industrialized states. After 1997 the government moved to end the decline, though the figure in 2002 was only 0.31% of GNP. More significant was its concentration on the poorest countries and on partnership with NGOs, building on a change of emphasis already introduced in 1996: over half of bilateral aid goes to the poorest states of sub-Saharan Africa and south Asia. The "trade for aid" provision, tying much of the aid budget to contracts for British firms, has been abolished. The aid program's aims include encouraging good government, widening opportunities for women, and protecting the environment.

DEFENSE

No compulsory military service

$35.2bn

Up 4% in 2002

UK ARMED FORCES

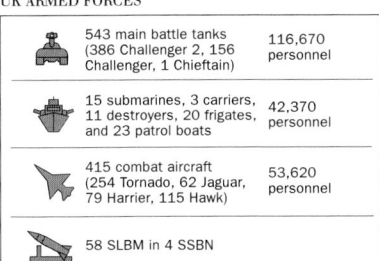

543 main battle tanks (386 Challenger 2, 156 Challenger, 1 Chieftain)	116,670 personnel
15 submarines, 3 carriers, 11 destroyers, 20 frigates, and 23 patrol boats	42,370 personnel
415 combat aircraft (254 Tornado, 62 Jaguar, 79 Harrier, 115 Hawk)	53,620 personnel
58 SLBM in 4 SSBN	

Despite significant post-Cold War cuts in army and navy personnel and equipment orders, defense spending is high and has risen in recent years, focusing on developing rapid reaction capabilities. The UK's independent nuclear deterrent has been scaled down. UK forces were prominent in peacekeeping in the Balkans and Sierra Leone and have been engaged in full conflicts over Kosovo in 1999 and in Iraq in 2003. Troops remain stationed in Northern Ireland; it was revealed in 2003 that army agents had colluded in terrorist activity while gathering intelligence there.

The UK is a leading arms exporter. Major buyers include Middle Eastern and southeast Asian countries.

ECONOMICS

Inflation 2.8% p.a. (1990–2001)

$1511bn

0.551 pounds sterling (0.606)

SCORE CARD

❑ WORLD GNP RANKING	4th
❑ GNP PER CAPITA	$25,510
❑ BALANCE OF PAYMENTS	–$14.4bn
❑ INFLATION	1.6%
❑ UNEMPLOYMENT	5%

EXPORTS

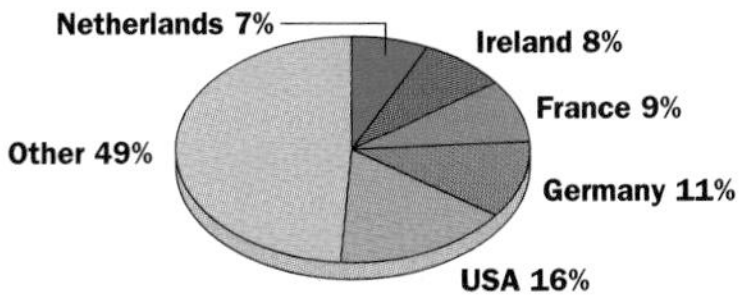
Netherlands 7%
Ireland 8%
France 9%
Germany 11%
USA 16%
Other 49%

IMPORTS

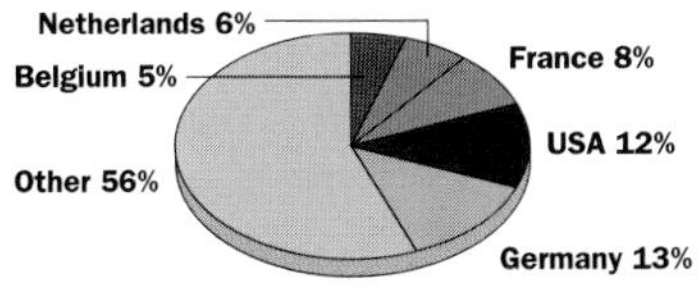
Netherlands 6%
Belgium 5%
France 8%
USA 12%
Germany 13%
Other 56%

STRENGTHS

World leader in financial services. Important pharmaceutical and defense industries. Strong multinationals. Precision engineering and high-tech industries, including telecommunications and biotechnology. Innovative in computer software development. Flexible working practices. Success in controlling inflationary tendencies. Low unemployment.

WEAKNESSES

Decline of manufacturing sector since 1970s. Need to plan for eventual end of North Sea oil and gas. Quick-return mentality behind many investment decisions. Nonparticipation in euro threatens former status as EU's largest recipient of inward investment; has prompted closure of UK factories.

PROFILE

Manufacturing has been in long-term decline, while sectors such as financial services have expanded rapidly. After sharp recession in 1991, revival was sluggish, but by the late 1990s growth in the UK was faster than that of its European competitors. The rural economy was hit hard by a foot-and-mouth epidemic in 2001, while the wider economy suffered in 2001–2002 after the US economic downturn and the collapse of the Internet "dotcom" boom. Interest rates were cut to try to boost domestic spending, while the government in 2002 massively increased its own spending on education, health, and defense. Economic growth at 2.3% exceeded forecasts in 2003, and in 2004 unemployment reached a 29-year low. Mortgage borrowing continues to grow, raising fears of a house price "bubble."

ECONOMIC PERFORMANCE INDICATOR

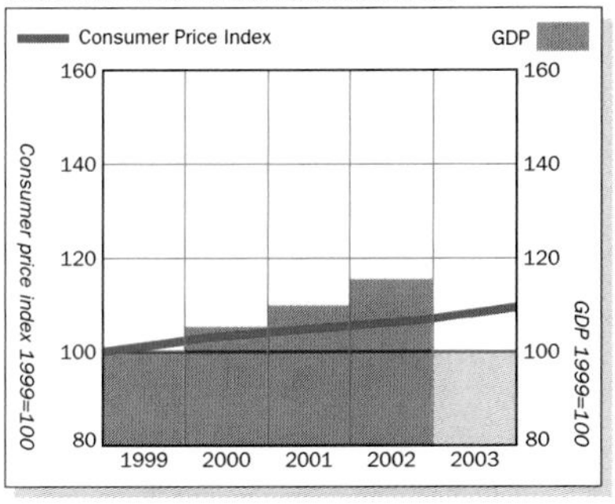
Consumer Price Index
GDP
Consumer price index 1999=100
GDP 1999=100
160
140
120
100
80
1999
2000
2001
2002
2003

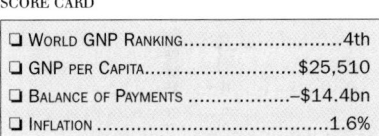

UNITED KINGDOM : MAJOR BUSINESSES

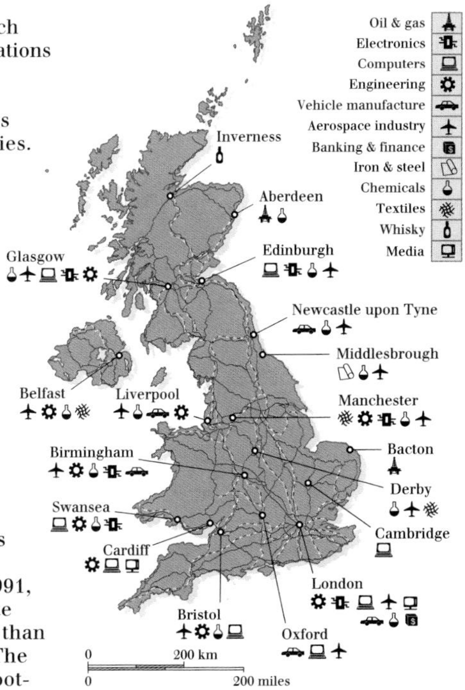
Oil & gas
Electronics
Computers
Engineering
Vehicle manufacture
Aerospace industry
Banking & finance
Iron & steel
Chemicals
Textiles
Whisky
Media
Inverness
Aberdeen
Edinburgh
Glasgow
Newcastle upon Tyne
Middlesbrough
Belfast
Liverpool
Manchester
Birmingham
Bacton
Derby
Swansea
Cambridge
Cardiff
London
Bristol
Oxford
0
200 km
200 miles

U

RESOURCES

Electric power 79.5m kW

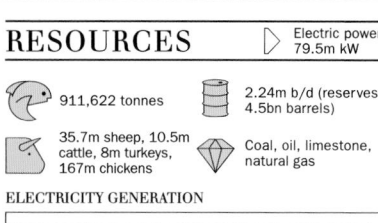

911,622 tonnes

2.24m b/d (reserves 4.5bn barrels)

35.7m sheep, 10.5m cattle, 8m turkeys, 167m chickens

Coal, oil, limestone, natural gas

ELECTRICITY GENERATION

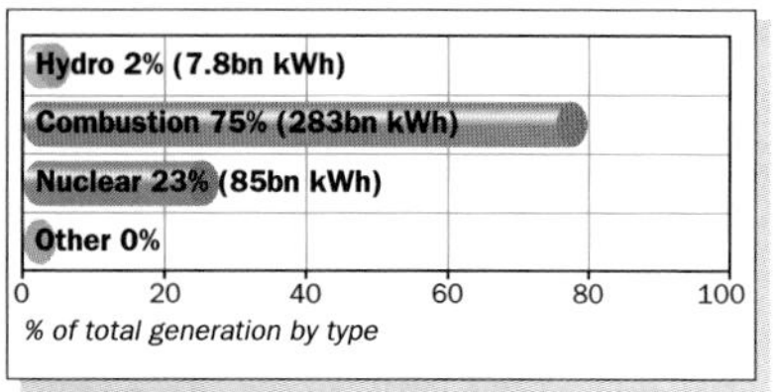

Hydro 2% (7.8bn kWh)
Combustion 75% (283bn kWh)
Nuclear 23% (85bn kWh)
Other 0%
0
20
40
60
80
100
% of total generation by type

The UK has the largest energy resources of any EU state, with substantial oil and gas reserves offshore on the continental shelf in the North Sea, and fresh fields in the north Atlantic. Drilled under difficult conditions, North Sea oil is of a high grade. Revenues from taxes on oil companies have been a major contributor to government finances, averaging around $12 billion a year.

Sizable coal reserves are economically unexploitable. Privatization of the electricity industry, and pressure to cut pollution, encouraged the switch from coal- to gas-fired power plants, prompting efforts to boost the role of "cleaner coal" technology. The UK is also developing wind power and other renewable energy sources.

The UK produces few other minerals in significant quantities. Cornwall's last tin mines teeter between closure and rescue. Some very small-scale gold mining survives in Wales and Scotland.

UNITED KINGDOM : LAND USE

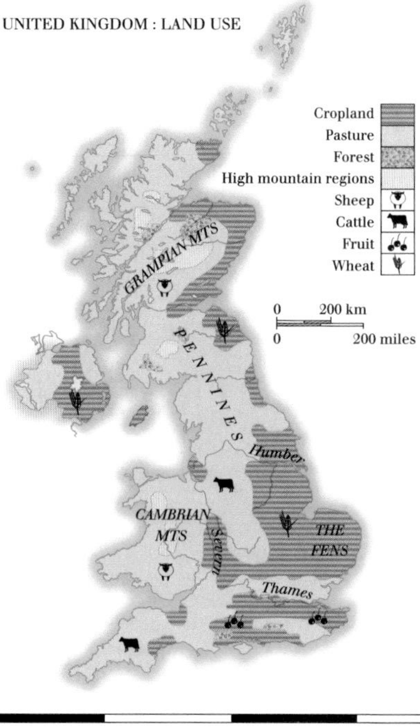

Cropland
Pasture
Forest
High mountain regions
Sheep
Cattle
Fruit
Wheat
0 200 km
0 200 miles
GRAMPIAN MTS
PENNINES
Humber
CAMBRIAN MTS
Severn
THE FENS
Thames

ENVIRONMENT

Sustainability rank: 91st

21% (20% partially protected)

9.6 tonnes per capita

ENVIRONMENTAL TREATIES

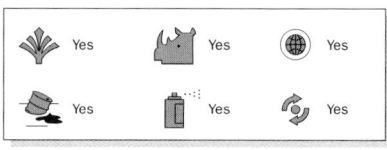

Yes Yes Yes

Yes Yes Yes

Concerns range from the level of greenhouse gas emissions to the adverse effects on rural environments of road building and the need for large-scale house-building programs. Other main issues are health-related, and urban air pollution caused by traffic is a key subject, as are aspects of nuclear safety. Opposition to genetically modified (GM) foods is widespread and GM crop trials have been disrupted; however, in 2004 the government approved the first commercial planting of GM maize.

MEDIA

TV ownership high

Daily newspaper circulation 329 per 1000 people

PUBLISHING AND BROADCAST MEDIA

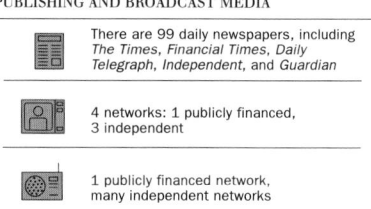

There are 99 daily newspapers, including *The Times, Financial Times, Daily Telegraph, Independent,* and *Guardian*

4 networks: 1 publicly financed, 3 independent

1 publicly financed network, many independent networks

Newspapers are owned mostly by large media corporations. Many publish Internet editions. Criticized for invasions of privacy, the press presents self-regulation as preferable to legislation. Publications deemed contrary to "national interests" may be banned. Satellite TV and digital terrestrial broadcasting have increased competition with the BBC. The BBC's World Service, despite cutbacks, remains an influential news source internationally.

***The Welsh coal industry** has virtually disappeared. Wales now has the highest percentage of small business start-ups, relative to the population, of any part of the UK.*

CRIME

No death penalty

82,241prisoners

Down 4% in 1999–2001

CRIME RATES

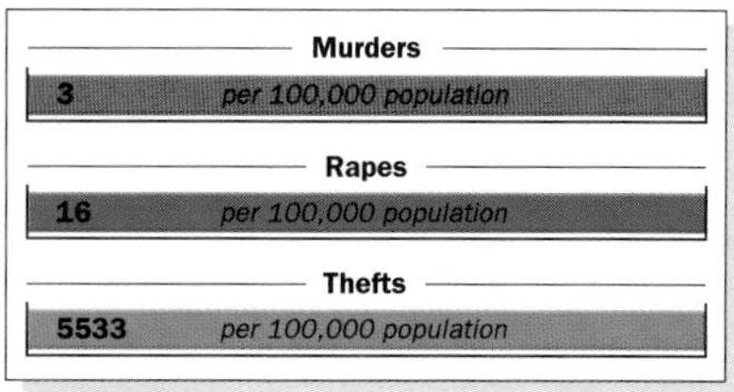

Murders
3 per 100,000 population
Rapes
16 per 100,000 population
Thefts
5533 per 100,000 population

Violent crime and domestic abuse are growing problems. Inner-city violence is partly fueled by narcotics dependency and trafficking. The government has maintained a "tough on crime" stance, but sentencing policies place the penal system under serious strain. Cannabis is increasingly tolerated in order to focus on "harder" narcotics. In 2001 "antiterrorism" laws gave police extra powers. Public fear of pedophilia fueled a reform of outdated sex laws in 2002.

EDUCATION

School leaving age: 16

99%

2.29m students

THE EDUCATION SYSTEM

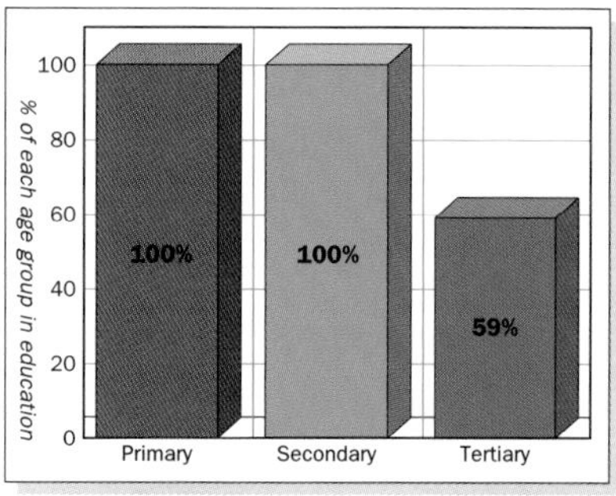

100
80
60
40
20
0
% of each age group in education
100%
100%
59%
Primary
Secondary
Tertiary

The state system is used by 94% of children. Fee-paying private schools include the traditional elite institutions confusingly known as public schools. There is now a new enthusiasm in government for "faith-based" schools.

From the 1960s onward, a two-tier state school system based on academic selection at age 11 was to a great extent replaced by mixed ability comprehensive schools. The 1988 education reforms introduced a national curriculum and weakened the role of local education authorities. The Labour government has focused on testing, assessing teaching standards, and tackling "failing" schools. Public spending targets in 2002 promised significantly increased education expenditure within four years, to 5.6% of GDP.

More colleges were given university status in the 1990s, but established centers, particularly Oxford and Cambridge, continue to be the most prestigious and best resourced.

U

FACING UP TO CLIMATE CHANGE

MORE THAN A decade after the 1992 UN Convention on Climate Change, the UK is slowly waking up to the urgent need for action. Prime Minister Tony Blair proclaimed in 2004 that the world faces no greater threat; chief scientific adviser Sir David King pointedly called it a greater danger than international terrorism. On this the UK government disagrees with the skeptical US administration, which remains hostile to having to modify its economic and oil-based energy policies.

IMPLEMENTING KYOTO

The 1997 Kyoto agreement, of which the UK was a leading advocate, seeks to control the output of "greenhouse gases" – principally carbon dioxide, given off by burning fossil fuels like coal, oil, and gas. Scientific consensus (now overwhelming) is that a "greenhouse effect" – the slowing of the dissipation of heat from the sun, aggravates a cycle of global warming; that the impact on world climate is already significant; and that worldwide catastrophe this century is possible.

Kyoto sets greenhouse gas emissions limits for industrialized countries in an initial period (by 2010–2012), the EU's target being an 8% overall reduction compared with a 1990 baseline; more far-reaching cuts will then be crucial. While the US has refused to sign up, the Blair government has adopted somewhat more ambitious UK targets – though it has backed away from politically sensitive fuel tax increases. It still expects to achieve a 10% cut in carbon dioxide output by 2010, despite real problems restricting motor vehicle emissions. Its longer-term goal is to cut emissions by 60% by 2050.

CHANGING THE ENERGY MIX

Attempts to integrate this into a sustainable development policy are most evident in efforts to cut energy wastage (for example by raising insulation standards in buildings) and promote zero-emission renewable energy technologies. Wind power is the most developed of these (others

***Extreme weather events** appear to be occurring more frequently.*

***Britain's largest offshore wind farm** at North Hoyle, in north Wales.*

include solar, wave, and tidal power and biomass conversion). Land-based turbines can meet opposition as visually intrusive; offshore wind farms, though more expensive, raise fewer planning and consent issues. UK energy policy envisages generating 10% of all electricity from renewables by 2010 and 20% by 2020. The nuclear industry, currently limited by a moratorium on all new development, seeks to revive its claim to be the best option for generating zero-carbon power, while hopes for the future include the possibility of an energy economy based on hydrogen fuel cell technology.

ATTITUDES AND REALITY

Some still lightheartedly see "global warming" as bringing welcome improvements to British weather, evoking notions of Mediterranean lifestyles and urban café culture. "Extreme weather events," notably the widespread flooding of October–November 2000, periodically disrupt such complacency, while scientists warn that global warming could cause a "big chill" in the UK's moderate maritime climate by disrupting the Gulf Stream – the Atlantic's ocean current conveyor system carrying warm water to its shores.

Even the recent warmer, drier summers have had negative impacts, with record highs – the hottest day ever registered was part of the August 2003 heatwave – causing discomfort to many and health damage to some. Suburban gardens, so dear to "middle Britain," wilt depressingly during unpopular summertime bans on hosepipes and sprinklers. More seriously, periods of drought hurt agricultural productivity and the natural environment, and increase subsidence damage to buildings. With the growing risk and cost of flood damage at other times of year, this has brought dire warnings from the Association of British Insurers about householders' building insurance premiums.

HEALTH

Welfare state health benefits

1 per 500 people

Cancers, heart, cerebrovascular, and respiratory diseases

The National Health Service (NHS) offers universal free health care, but financial pressures have led to shortages, hospital closures, and charges in some sectors. In response, the government in 2002 announced record levels of investment over a five-year period, aiming to match the European average (8% of GDP) by 2004. Recent crises have focused on food safety, from *E. coli* outbreaks to fatal brain disease attributed to eating beef from cattle with "mad cow" disease. Asthma affects over 25% of people.

SPENDING

GDP/cap. increase

CONSUMPTION AND SPENDING

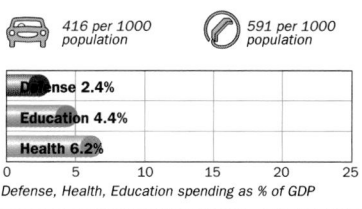

416 per 1000 population

591 per 1000 population

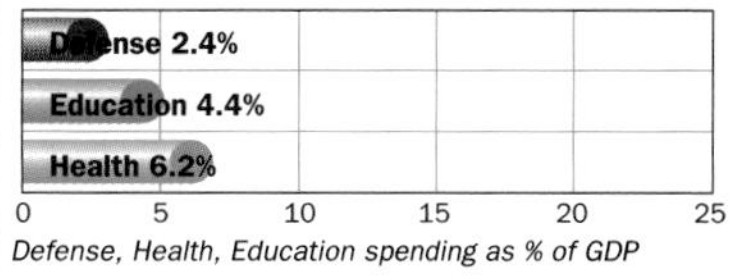

Defense 2.4%
Education 4.4%
Health 6.2%
0
5
10
15
20
25
Defense, Health, Education spending as % of GDP

Income inequality is greater than in 1884, when records began. In 2002, the income of 13.4% of the population was half the average or less, with poverty rates higher among some ethnic minorities. Average wages for manufacturing workers in 2001 were $29,000 a year, only 4% of the average received by chief executives in large companies. Under Conservative governments in the 1980s and early 1990s, taxation for higher earners was cut, whereas the value of state benefits and pensions fell. Since the mid-1990s, economic growth has helped to bring unemployment down. Labour's 1997 election promises precluded raising income tax. This limited the scope for redistributive action, leaving antipoverty strategies dependent on better targeting of welfare benefits.

WORLD RANKING

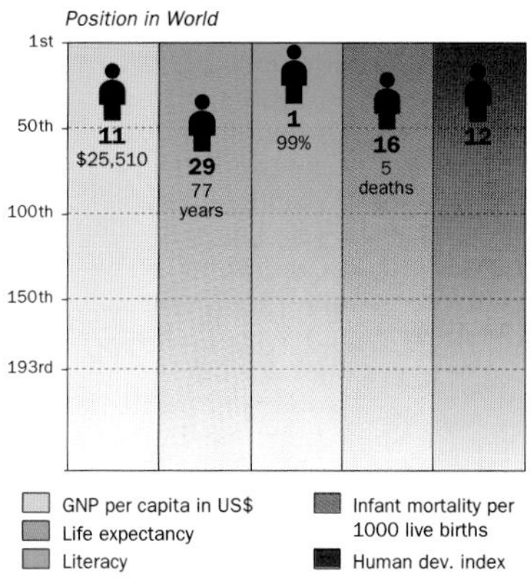

Position in World
1st
50th
100th
150th
193rd
11
$25,510
29
77
years
1
99%
16
5
deaths
12
GNP per capita in US$
Life expectancy
Literacy
Infant mortality per 1000 live births
Human dev. index

U

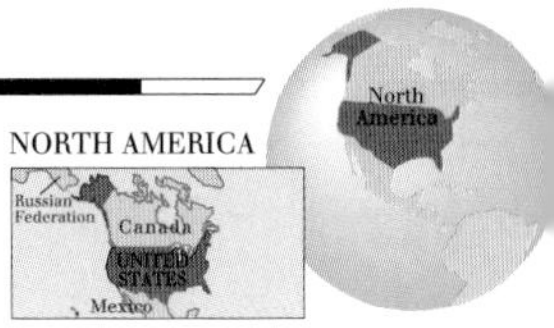
NORTH AMERICA
North America
Russian Federation
Canada
UNITED STATES
Mexico

UNITED STATES

OFFICIAL NAME: United States of America **CAPITAL:** Washington D.C.
POPULATION: 294 million **CURRENCY:** US dollar **OFFICIAL LANGUAGE:** English

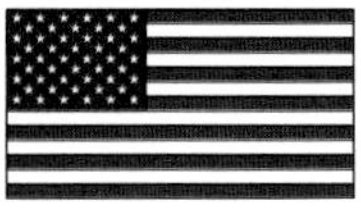

1776
1959
July 4
USA
-5 to -11
+1
n/a

THE WORLD'S THIRD-LARGEST country, the United States is neither overpopulated (like China) nor in the main subject to extremes of climate (like much of Russia and Canada). Its main landmass, bounded by Canada and Mexico, contains 48 of its 50 states. The two others, Alaska at the northwest tip of the Americas and Hawaii in the Pacific, became states in 1959. The US was not built on ethnic identity but on a concept of nationhood intimately bound up with the 18th-century founding fathers' ideas of democracy and liberty – still powerful touchstones in both a political and an economic sense. Since the breakup of the Soviet Union, the US holds a unique position – but arouses extreme hatreds – as the sole global superpower.

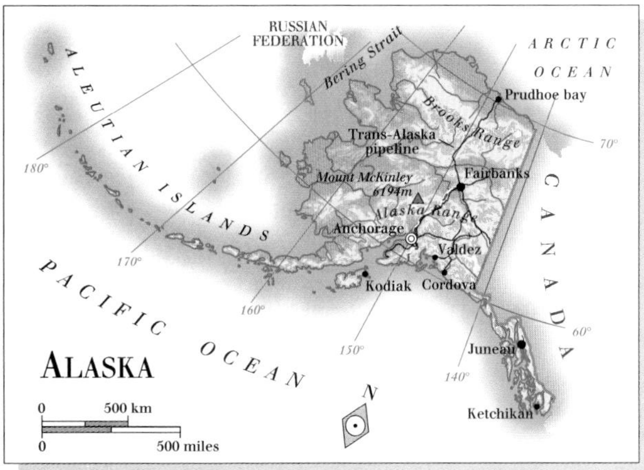
RUSSIAN FEDERATION
Bering Strait
ARCTIC OCEAN
Prudhoe bay
ALEUTIAN ISLANDS
Brooks Range
Trans-Alaska pipeline
Mount McKinley 6194m
Fairbanks
Alaska Range
Anchorage
Valdez
Kodiak
Cordova
CANADA
PACIFIC OCEAN
Juneau
Ketchikan
ALASKA
0 500 km
0 500 miles
180°
170°
160°
150°
140°
70°
60°
N

CLIMATE

Continental/subtropical/mountain/desert/maritime

WEATHER CHART FOR WASHINGTON D.C.

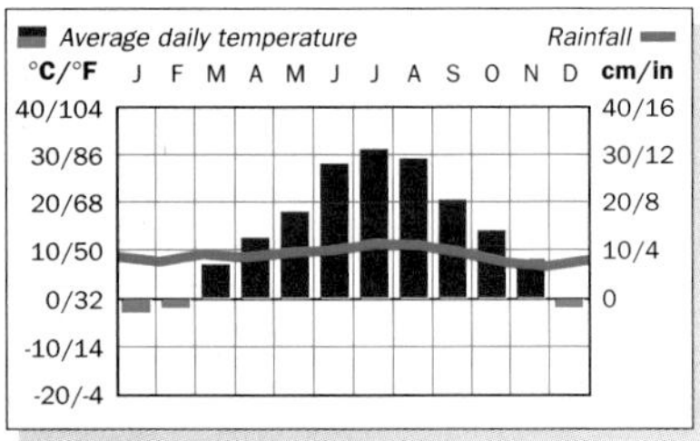
Average daily temperature
Rainfall
°C/°F
J F M A M J J A S O N D
cm/in
40/104
30/86
20/68
10/50
0/32
-10/14
-20/4
40/16
30/12
20/8
10/4
0

Spanning a continent and extending far into the Pacific Ocean, the US displays a wide range of climatic conditions. Mean annual temperatures range from 29°C (84°F) in Florida to -13°C (9°F) in Alaska. Except for New England, Alaska, and the Pacific northwest, summer temperatures are higher than in Europe. Southern summers are humid; in the southwest they are dry. Winters are particularly severe in the western mountains and plains and in the Midwest – where the Great Lakes can freeze. The northeast can have heavy snow from November to April. The weather is frequently dramatic, with tornadoes, cyclones, thunderstorms, hurricanes, floods, and droughts. Since 1990, weather-related damage has risen, a trend linked with global climate change.

The Chippendale Block, New York, a notable example of postmodern architecture by the influential US architect Philip Johnson.

PACIFIC OCEAN
C
Seattle
Tacoma
Olympia
WASHINGTON
Spokane
Portland
Salem
Corvallis
Columbia
Lewiston
Missoula
Great
Helena
Eugene
OREGON
IDAHO
Snake
Medford
Nampa
Boise
Idaho Falls
Pocatello
Twin Falls
COAST RANGES
CASCADE RANGE
ROCKY MOUNTAINS
Great Salt Lake
Ogden
Reno
Carson City
GREAT BASIN
Salt Lake City
Orem
Provo
Sacramento
Oakland
San Francisco
NEVADA
SIERRA NEVADA
UTAH
Mount Whitney 4418m
COAST RANGES
Lake Powell
Las Vegas
CALIFORNIA
Lake Mead
Grand Canyon
Los Angeles
Colorado
San Diego
ARIZONA
Phoenix
Albuquer
Tucson
Las Cru
El P
MEX
120°
110°

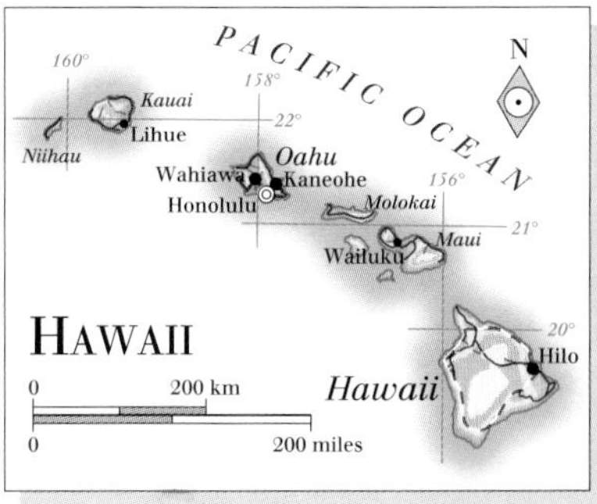
PACIFIC OCEAN
Kauai
Lihue
Niihau
Oahu
Wahiawa
Kaneohe
Honolulu
Molokai
Maui
Wailuku
Hawaii
Hilo
HAWAII
0 200 km
0 200 miles
160°
158°
156°
22°
21°
20°
N

U

TRANSPORTATION

Drive on right

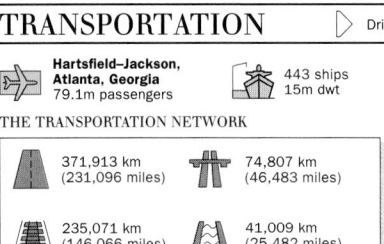

Hartsfield–Jackson, Atlanta, Georgia
79.1m passengers

443 ships
15m dwt

THE TRANSPORTATION NETWORK

371,913 km (231,096 miles)	74,807 km (46,483 miles)
235,071 km (146,066 miles)	41,009 km (25,482 miles)

Arterial river systems provided the first transportation networks in the US. Today, the US has the world's cheapest, most extensive internal air network and a good system of interstate highways. Railroads, comparatively neglected for years, mainly carry freight, though modern high-speed trains are starting to attract passengers back. Americans have been wedded to the car since Henry Ford began mass production in 1908. By 1919 there were nine million cars in the US. Today the total tops 210 million, including pickups and the ubiquitous "sports utes" (SUVs). Americans make more than half of the world's car journeys. Cheap gasoline underpinned the rise of the car; despite problems of congestion and pollution, and the environmental costs of ever more oil production, its centrality in society is rarely questioned.

***Malls, a typical feature** of the suburban landscape, are losing popularity to speedier online shopping.*

N
A
D
A
Lake Superior
Lake Huron
L. Ontario
L. Erie
Lake Michigan
St Lawrence
MAINE
NORTH DAKOTA
SOUTH DAKOTA
MINNESOTA
WISCONSIN
MICHIGAN
IOWA
NEBRASKA
KANSAS
MISSOURI
ILLINOIS
INDIANA
OHIO
KENTUCKY
TENNESSEE
ARKANSAS
OKLAHOMA
TEXAS
LOUISIANA
MISSISSIPPI
ALABAMA
GEORGIA
FLORIDA
SOUTH CAROLINA
NORTH CAROLINA
VIRGINIA
WEST VIRGINIA
PENNSYLVANIA
NEW YORK
NEW JERSEY
MARYLAND
DEL.
CONN.
RHODE I.
MASS.
VERM.
NEW HAMP.
APPALACHIAN
WASHINGTON DC
ATLANTIC OCEAN
GULF OF MEXICO
BAHAMAS
Minot
Grand Forks
Bismarck
Fargo
Duluth
Aberdeen
Pierre
Minneapolis
St Paul
Rochester
Sioux Falls
Sioux City
Des Moines
Cedar Rapids
Omaha
Lincoln
Grand Island
Topeka
Kansas City
Jefferson City
St Louis
Wichita
Springfield
Tulsa
Oklahoma City
Norman
Lawton
Fort Smith
Fayetteville
Little Rock
Hot Springs
Pine Bluff
Memphis
Fort Worth
Dallas
Shreveport
Austin
San Antonio
Houston
Baton Rouge
New Orleans
Biloxi
Mobile
Jackson
Hattiesburg
Meridian
Montgomery
Tuscaloosa
Birmingham
Huntsville
Nashville
Knoxville
Chattanooga
Atlanta
Columbus
Macon
Savannah
Jacksonville
Tallahassee
Tampa
St Petersburg
L. Okeechobee
Fort Lauderdale
Miami
Charleston
Columbia
Greenville
Spartanburg
Charlotte
Winston-Salem
Greensboro
Raleigh
Richmond
Newport News
Norfolk
Lexington
Frankfort
Louisville
Evansville
Huntington
Charleston
Cincinnati
Dayton
Columbus
Indianapolis
Springfield
Peoria
Davenport
Rockford
Madison
Milwaukee
Green Bay
Racine
Chicago
Gary
South Bend
Fort Wayne
Grand Rapids
Lansing
Flint
Detroit
Ann Arbor
Toledo
Cleveland
Akron
Erie
Buffalo
Rochester
Syracuse
Albany
Pittsburgh
Harrisburg
Allentown
Trenton
Philadelphia
Wilmington
Dover
Baltimore
Annapolis
New York
JFK
New Haven
Hartford
Springfield
Worcester
Providence
Boston
Lowell
Manchester
Concord
Portland
Lewiston
Augusta
Bangor
Burlington
Montpelier
Hudson
Missouri
Mississippi
Arkansas
Red
Ohio
Colorado
Rio Grande
Platte
GREAT PLAINS
50°
40°
30°
70°
80°
90°
100°
0
400 km
400 miles
UNITED STATES
Total Area : 9 626 091 sq. km
(3 717 792 sq. miles)
POPULATION
over 5 000 000
over 1 000 000
over 500 000
over 100 000
over 50 000
over 10 000
under 10 000
LAND HEIGHT
3000m/9843ft
2000m/6562ft
1000m/3281ft
500m/1640ft
200m/656ft
Sea Level

U

TOURISM

Visitors : Population 1:7.3

40.4m visitors

Down 4% in 2003

MAIN TOURIST ARRIVALS

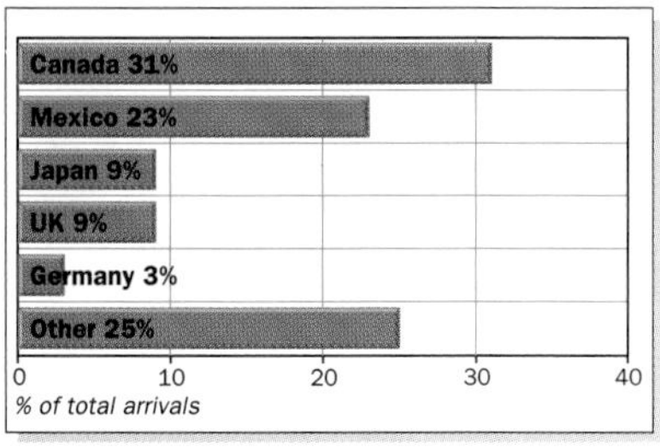
Canada 31%
Mexico 23%
Japan 9%
UK 9%
Germany 3%
Other 25%
0
10
20
30
40
% of total arrivals

The US as a destination for international tourism benefited greatly from the deregulation of air fares. Domestic tourism expanded just as rapidly, along with the rise in real incomes. The impact of the 2001 terrorist attacks was complex. While confidence in air travel took time to be rebuilt, the fact that US tourists put safety first meant that over 80% vacationed within the US in 2002.

All the states have their attractions, and most court tourists. Top tourist destinations include Florida's Disney World and Disneyland in California, Niagara Falls, Las Vegas, New York, San Francisco, Los Angeles and Hollywood, the Grand Canyon, Death Valley, New Orleans, Atlantic City, and Washington D.C.

Tourism's rapid expansion has also brought some problems. The parks and sites run by the National Parks Service (NPS) have been particular casualties; visitor numbers rocketed in the three decades after 1970. To try to reduce pressure on the most popular areas, there has been a significant expansion in the area of protected land under NPS management since the mid-1970s. Even so, Yellowstone Park has a continuing traffic management crisis, bumper-to-bumper cars plague other high-profile attractions, and those wanting to take a raft ride down the Grand Canyon are likely to spend many months on a waiting list.

PEOPLE

Pop. density low

English, Spanish, Chinese, French, German, Tagalog, Vietnamese, Italian, Korean, Russian, Polish

32/km² (83/mi²)

THE URBAN/RURAL POPULATION SPLIT

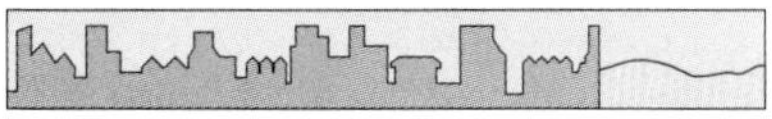
78%
22%

RELIGIOUS PERSUASION

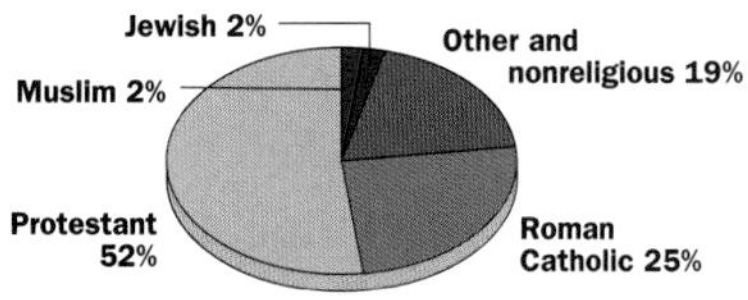
Jewish 2%
Muslim 2%
Other and nonreligious 19%
Protestant 52%
Roman Catholic 25%

ETHNIC MAKEUP

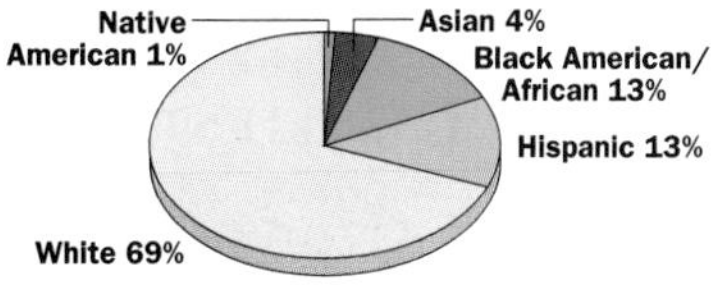
Native American 1%
Asian 4%
Black American/ African 13%
Hispanic 13%
White 69%

The demographic, economic, and cultural dominance of the white community is firmly entrenched after almost 400 years of settlement. However, the balance of ethnicity is rapidly shifting. An immigration boom peaked in the early 1990s, with many new arrivals from Latin America and Asia. The birthrate is particularly high in the Hispanic community, now the largest single minority in the US. The Census Bureau projects that in the year 2050 almost 25% of the population will be Hispanic, 14% black, and 9% Asians and Pacific islanders.

More than two-thirds of the Hispanic, or Latino, population originated in Mexico, and thousands of Mexicans risk their lives crossing the border every year. Despite its growing size, the Hispanic community still struggles to compete politically and economically with the better established, and more politically sensitive, black population.

Within the black community, their ancestors infamously brought to the New World as slaves, an African-American business leadership class has grown up, but only two black people – media moguls Oprah Winfrey and Robert L. Johnson – make the list of the 400 richest Americans.

The country's original inhabitants, the Native Americans, or Amerindians, were dispossessed in the 19th century and now make up little more than 1% of the population. Some of the worst poverty and deprivation in the US can be found in their reservations.

The separation of state and religion is guaranteed by the constitution, but Christian values dominate. Many evangelical churches, particularly well established in the south, forcefully oppose abortion, the teaching of evolution, and the social acceptance of homosexuality.

POPULATION AGE BREAKDOWN

Female
Age
Male
2.1%
80+
1.1%
7.4%
60–79
6%
12.7%
40–59
12.2%
14.8%
20–39
15%
14%
0–19
14.7%
% of population by age group

POLITICS

Multiparty elections

L. House 2004/2006
U. House 2004/2006

President George W. Bush

AT THE LAST ELECTION

House of Representatives 435 seats

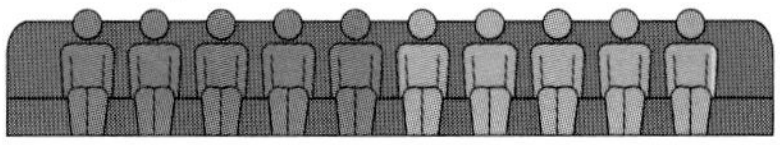
53% Rep
46% Dem
1% Ind

Rep = Republican Party **Dem** = Democratic Party
Ind = Independents

Senate 100 seats

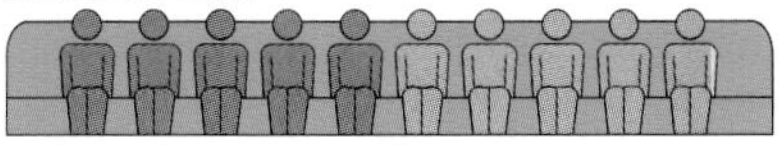
55% Rep
44% Dem
1% Ind

Presidential elections take place every four years, House elections every two years. One-third of the senators are elected every two years for six-year terms.

The US is a democracy with a federal system of government. Many issues are dealt with by the 50 individual states. Each state sends two senators and a number of representatives, according to population size, to Congress.

Profile

US politics is dominated by two main parties. With few major differences between them, the right-wing Republicans and the right-of-center Democrats regularly trade position in control of the White House and Congress. Presidential elections are based largely on personalities, with televised debates, inaugurated in the 1960s, playing a significant role. Election campaigns are lengthy and increasingly expensive affairs; Republican candidates are traditionally better funded.

Republican George W. Bush won the presidency in 2000. His predecessors, whether Democrat or Republican, had struggled to get major initiatives enacted by a hostile Congress, but in midterm elections in 2002 Republicans gained firm control of the House and the Senate, giving Bush a complete congressional majority, which he retained in 2004.

Main Political Issues

The prestige of the presidency

George W. Bush faced questions of legitimacy even before he took the

George W. Bush, took office in 2001 after a controversial presidential election.

Gen. Colin Powell, who became the first African-American Secretary of State.

U

POLITICS *continued*

oath of office in January 2001. The contentious manner of his election (with fewer popular votes than his rival Al Gore), concern over voting procedures in Florida, his "big business" affiliation, and controversial policies (notably on energy), were added to a string of verbal gaffes and an embarrassing lack of current affairs knowledge to divide popular opinion. He gained overwhelming support, however, when a wave of patriotic emotion generated by the al-Qaida attacks on New York and Washington D.C. on September 11 rallied the nation behind him and his declaration of a "war on terrorism."

By the end of his four-year term, Bush's popularity had been battered again, this time by the quagmire of Iraqi occupation, the debate over the reliability of the intelligence that had suggested the existence of weapons of mass destruction in Iraq, and revelations of controversial personal ties to the Enron financial scandal. His administration was struggling with a record deficit, which peaked at $300 billion in 2003. The most potentially damaging moment in 2004 was the publication of the 9/11 Commission's report, which cast doubt on the government's assertion of a link between al-Qaida and Iraq, discrediting the invasion's justification; some left-wing critics were openly calling Bush corrupt.

Nonetheless, with security dominating the agenda of heartland America, Bush capitalized on his war-president image to beat off a serious challenge from Democrat John Kerry to win the 2004 presidential election.

The limits of government

The US has a strong tradition of resisting the extension of government powers. The vigorous defense of constitutional liberties and the rights of citizens, such as freedom of speech or the right to bear arms, is sometimes taken to lengths which appear extreme to other societies. States resist the arrogation of powers by the federal authorities. In areas such as health care and education, conservatives oppose as interference what others see as the proper concern of government with social welfare. "Big government" is also denounced in the economic sphere. Opponents of environmental controls portray them as obstructing free enterprise and wealth creation. Under Bush, social issues such as homosexual unions have taken on a particularly high-profile role in the battle between federal and state control.

Hillary Clinton, *senator for New York and wife of former president Bill Clinton.*

Senator John Kerry, *Democrat challenger against President Bush in 2004.*

Energy and the environment

Bush advocated some controversial energy policies in 2001, amid a pressing crisis over electricity shortages in California. Conservation activists were appalled by plans to allow further oil exploration in Alaska, and the Senate excised funding for the search from the 2004 budget. The expansion of nuclear power was also revived under the energy plan, while the US chose to repudiate the international Kyoto agreement on cutting carbon dioxide emissions, suggesting it could harm the economy. To offset criticism, Bush has earmarked $1.2 billion for research into hydrogen fuel cells.

The Mittens, Monument Valley, Arizona. *These striking natural rock formations are created by erosion of red sandstone. The valley is in the Navajo National Monument.*

Welfare

State support for the unemployed, poor families, college students, and the elderly provides a rare ideological divide between the main parties. The Republican Party favors cuts and the intervention of private groups, while Democrats call for a repeal of recent tax cuts in order to bankroll a broader funding program. Reform of the system, held back by strong state control, remains a key political issue.

WORLD AFFAIRS

Joined UN in 1945

G8 | NATO | NAFTA | OAS | OECD

Isolated by two great oceans, the US has been able for much of its history to choose the extent of its participation in world affairs. Only reluctantly drawn into the two world wars, after 1945 it swapped isolationism for involvement. The US took its seat on the Security Council of the new UN, founded in San Francisco and now based in New York, and helped to set up NATO. For the US the Cold War was most immediate – and costly – in the Korean and Vietnam wars. The death toll and shock of defeat in Vietnam in the 1970s kept the US out of direct military involvement overseas for over a decade. Instead, it focused on diplomacy, and on supporting the opponents of left-wing regimes in developing countries including Nicaragua, Cuba, and Angola.

Since the collapse of the Eastern bloc after 1989 the US has had to redetermine the scope of its foreign responsibilities as the only remaining superpower. Until 2001 policy remained cautious. It had led the intervention in the 1991 Gulf War, but a fiasco in Somalia and a lack of clear objectives in Bosnia & Herzegovina and Haiti showed its uncertainty about a role as world policeman. The September 11, 2001, terrorist attacks provoked the Bush regime into reclaiming the international initiative. Bush is inspired in part by the right-wing doctrine of the "new American century," which advocates making use of unrivaled US power to shape world affairs to the country's benefit.

The first act to follow the adoption of this new approach was the declaration of a "war on terrorism," which seeks to build a global, US-led consensus in the fight against nonstate combatants. The "successful" war in Afghanistan in late 2001 raised concerns in the Islamic world that Muslims were being unfairly targeted, while global tensions increased in 2002 when Bush declared Iran, Iraq, and North Korea to be an "axis of evil" states which sponsored terrorists.

Threats against Iraq culminated in the 2003 invasion. Many people, particularly in "old" Europe, saw the war as an attempt to settle old scores and seize the riches of Iraq's vast oil reserves, and were concerned when the US did not allow international relations, and specifically the diplomatic wrangling of the UN, to stand in the way of realizing its foreign policy aims.

As a result, global opinion toward the US has grown increasingly negative, potentially fueling the ranks of anti-US terrorist groups: an opposition backed by a popular grassroots movement in the developed world which identifies US military and economic hegemony, as well as its dominant culture, with the perceived evils of globalization.

THE "WAR ON TERRORISM"

By launching the coordinated attacks on September 11, 2001, which destroyed the World Trade Center in New York, seriously damaged the US Pentagon military headquarters in Washington D.C., and killed almost 3000 people, the Islamist al-Qaida terrorist network provided the *casus belli* for a US administration eager to reshape the world and confront its enemies. Within three weeks President George W. Bush unveiled his strategy for responding to the 9/11 attacks. In the "Bush doctrine," the countries of the world were either "with us ... or with the terrorists." His promised "war on terrorism" began with the overthrow of Afghanistan's Islamist *taliban* regime, known to be sheltering al-Qaida leader Osama bin Laden. Its focus then shifted to Iraq.

***The "Tribute in Light"** marked the site of the fallen World Trade Center in 2002.*

Afghanistan and Iraq

US forces provided air support to the opposition Northern Alliance in Afghanistan from October 2001, allowing them to push their offensive against the *taliban*; they reached the capital Kabul in November. A new pro-US government was installed while US troops arrived to flush out al-Qaida and *taliban* remnants; those taken prisoner while fighting against the US now await trial, held at the US base in Cuba, at Guantánamo Bay. By classifying them as "illegal combatants," the US has avoided the application of Geneva Convention III on the treatment of prisoners of war.

The Afghan conflict was widely accepted as morally sound, with the *taliban*'s treatment of women and destruction of culturally significant monuments raising anger across the world. Even the legally ambiguous incarcerations at Guantánamo have been largely left alone by governments, apart from concern for their own nationals held there. Negative opinion was much more openly expressed, however, over the 2003 invasion of Iraq.

***Responses to the destruction** of the World Trade Center have varied from vociferous patriotism to a fervent desire for peace.*

Citing ill-defined links between al-Qaida and the Ba'ath Arab socialist regime of Saddam Hussein, and the fear that Iraq had not destroyed its arsenal of weapons of mass destruction (WMD), US forces opened hostilities in March 2003. The Iraqi regime was toppled by early April. International concern over the motives for the war and the subsequent lengthy and bloody process of reconstructing Iraq in the face of significant local hostility have prompted growing criticism from within the US. Of particular concern was the intelligence used to justify the attacks in the first place. In July 2004 a congressional commission concluded that there had been no link whatsoever between al-Qaida and Iraq.

Homeland security

The commission did praise the Bush administration for increasing security through the war on Afghanistan and the reform of "homeland security" institutions. In the immediate aftermath of the 2001 attacks, a new cabinet-level position was announced to cover homeland security. A full department, created the following year with Tom Ridge as its first secretary, combines 22 previously disparate agencies in an effort to coordinate the response to future attacks. It has the assistance of a reformed Central Intelligence Agency (CIA), which has been reoriented to pay special attention to international terrorism, with a new post of national intelligence director created in August 2004. While the commission criticized the CIA for failing to act on available information which might have prevented the 9/11 attacks, of all those involved in the intelligence community and in preparing the case for war against Iraq, CIA director George Tenet is the only high-profile person to have resigned, albeit for "personal reasons."

Human rights campaigners have expressed concern over some of the security measures adopted, in particular the increased scrutiny of visitors to the US arriving from Muslim countries. Men arriving from Iran, Iraq, Libya, Pakistan, Saudi Arabia, Sudan, Syria, or Yemen are now officially registered, photographed, and fingerprinted. There has also been a crackdown on immigrants from the Middle East and north Africa, hundreds having been detained after complying with new rules under antiterrorist legislation demanding registration.

Culturally, there has been an increase in public patriotism, as well as acts of protest and defiance: public figures have been vilified for expressing disapproval of the government. Campaigns by celebrities and opposition politicians against the "war" have been muted, and bounded by caveats asserting patriotism alongside a desire for the respect of human rights. The filmmaker Michael Moore was a noticeable exception with his polemical *Fahrenheit 9/11* (2004).

Winning the war

Immediately the "war" began it was pointed out that little was being done to address the motivation of the 9/11 attackers – whose actions, as proclaimed by bin Laden, were directed at US cultural hegemony and in particular its historic support for Israel in the conflict with the Palestinians. US efforts in the Middle East have fallen by the wayside, while the Bush administration has remained almost unequivocally supportive of the Israeli government. Anti-US sentiment has noticeably grown across the Muslim world, as well as among the public in former allied states. A chaotic Iraq has emerged from the invasion, where US soldiers and foreign civilians have been murdered with impunity by Islamist groups, and where al-Qaida can now more easily operate and recruit. The chances of a swift end to the "war on terrorism" now seem very unlikely.

***Suspected terrorists and** taliban **fighters** held in the Camp Delta facility of the US base at Guantánamo Bay in Cuba.*

AID

Donor

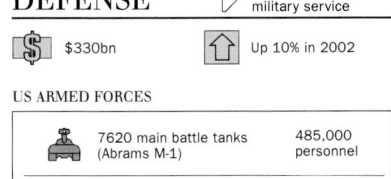

$13.3bn (donations)

Up 16% in 2002

The US gives only 0.13% of GNP in foreign aid, and aid allocations are often stalled in Congress. Egypt, Russia, and Israel are the major recipients. The US is keen to further its strategic aims with some high-profile pledges, including a $15 billion AIDS campaign and $5 billion to tackle poverty.

DEFENSE

No compulsory military service

$330bn

Up 10% in 2002

US ARMED FORCES

7620 main battle tanks (Abrams M-1)	485,000 personnel
70 submarines, 12 carriers, 27 cruisers, 49 destroyers, 30 frigates, 21 patrol boats	400,000 personnel
3716 combat aircraft (B-52H, B-1B, F-4, F-15, F-16, F-111, F-117, OA-10A)	367,600 personnel
432 SLBM in 18 SSBN, 550 ICBM	

Even before the 9/11 attacks, emphasis in defense policy had been shifting away from strategic nuclear deterrence and large warships to "smart" missile systems and long-range power projection, with rapid intervention capabilities built around air power. Despite setbacks in early tests, the first "interceptor" missiles of the national missile defense "shield" system were scheduled for deployment in late 2004.

The enormous US military–industrial complex dates only from the close of World War II. In the 1990s, the end of the Cold War and the need to cut the budget deficit combined to slash defense funds to their lowest level in real terms since 1945. Nuclear weapons tests were superseded by computerized "virtual" tests after the creation of the powerful ASCI White computer.

However, the Bush administration has steadily increased defense spending. The 2004 budget saw a return to Cold War levels, passing $400 billion – amounting to more than the combined defense budgets of the world's next 12 largest military spenders. The Bush government also hinted that it was considering developing small and "precision" nuclear weapons as part of its expanding arsenal.

Fearing that its troops could be prosecuted for political reasons, the US opposed the establishment of the International Criminal Court. This stance threatens to undermine overseas peacekeeping missions, and has led to cuts in military aid to countries which have not agreed to protect US soldiers from prosecution.

ECONOMICS

Inflation 2% p.a. (1990–2001)

$10,207bn

Currency is US dollar

SCORE CARD

❑ WORLD GNP RANKING	1st
❑ GNP PER CAPITA	$35,400
❑ BALANCE OF PAYMENTS	–$481bn
❑ INFLATION	1.6%
❑ UNEMPLOYMENT	6%

EXPORTS

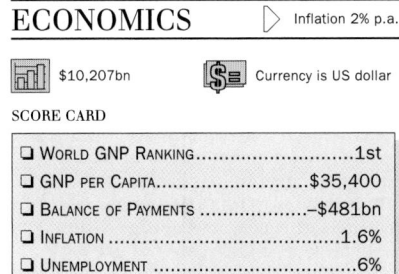

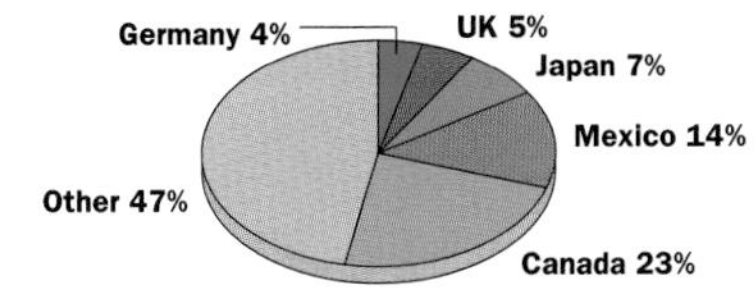
Germany 4%
UK 5%
Japan 7%
Mexico 14%
Other 47%
Canada 23%

IMPORTS

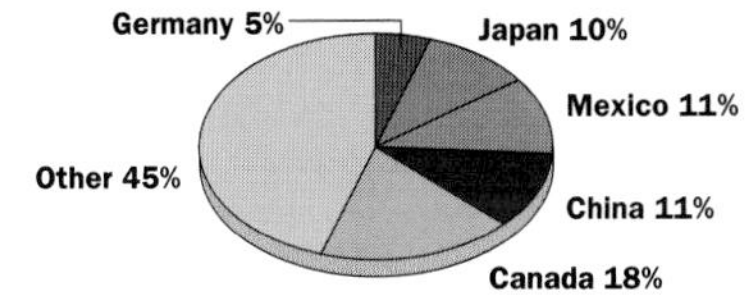
Germany 5%
Japan 10%
Mexico 11%
Other 45%
China 11%
Canada 18%

STRENGTHS

World's largest economy. Wealth of natural resources: energy, raw materials, and food. Strong high-tech base; world-leading research and development. Global leader in computer software. World-class multinationals. Sophisticated service sector; advanced and competitive manufacturing industry. Entrepreneurial business ethic. High-quality postgraduate education, especially in high-tech business. Global dominance of US culture major boost to US manufacturers. Subsidized crops and favorable tariffs for domestic industries.

UNITED STATES : MAJOR BUSINESSES

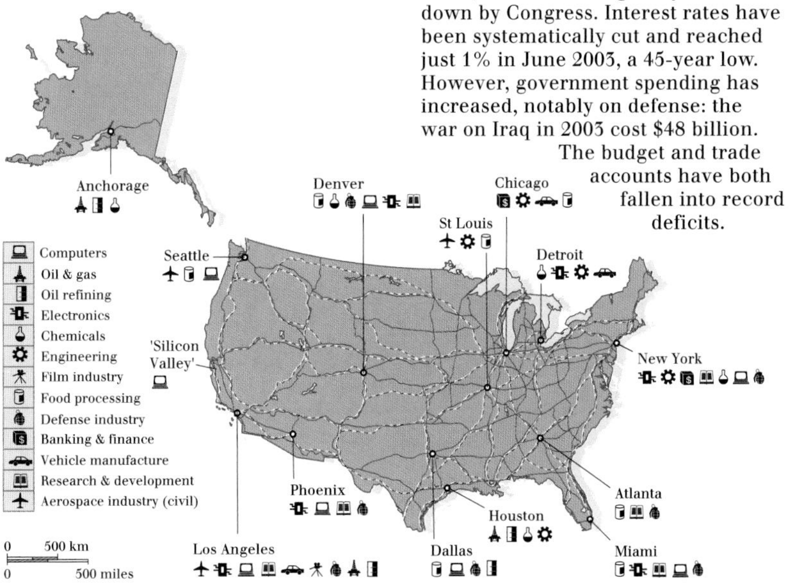
Anchorage
Denver
Chicago
St Louis
Seattle
Detroit
'Silicon Valley'
New York
Phoenix
Atlanta
Houston
Los Angeles
Dallas
Miami
Computers
Oil & gas
Oil refining
Electronics
Chemicals
Engineering
Film industry
Food processing
Defense industry
Banking & finance
Vehicle manufacture
Research & development
Aerospace industry (civil)
0 500 km
0 500 miles

ECONOMIC PERFORMANCE INDICATOR

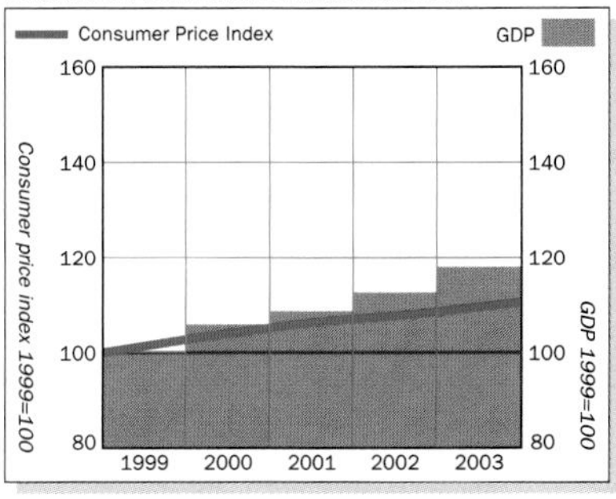
Consumer Price Index
GDP
160
140
120
100
80
1999
2000
2001
2002
2003
Consumer price index 1999=100
GDP 1999=100

WEAKNESSES

Dramatic fall in manufacturing employment as jobs lost to lower-wage economies. Competition from Asia and EU in leading-edge technologies. Volatile market values driven by speculation. Accusations of short-termism. Recent major corporate collapses. Increase in imports despite relatively weak dollar: competition from euro as global currency. Major budget deficit.

PROFILE

In 2001 a record nine-year boom came to an end. The downturn greatly affected big business. The collapse of WorldCom in 2002, the largest ever bankruptcy, threatened confidence in business values, while media-giant AOL Time Warner posted historic losses of $98.7 billion for 2002. Unemployment has increased as companies tighten their budgets, reaching a nine-year high of 6.4% in June 2003.

Recovery efforts have focused on promoting consumer spending, and President Bush touted a $2000 billion package of tax cuts – though, in the event, the cuts were greatly watered down by Congress. Interest rates have been systematically cut and reached just 1% in June 2003, a 45-year low. However, government spending has increased, notably on defense: the war on Iraq in 2003 cost $48 billion.

The budget and trade accounts have both fallen into record deficits.

RESOURCES

Electric power 799m kW

5.41m tonnes

7.45m b/d (reserves 30.7bn barrels)

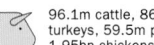

96.1m cattle, 86.5m turkeys, 59.5m pigs, 1.95bn chickens

Phosphates, gypsum, oil, coal, sulfur, lead, zinc, copper, gold

ELECTRICITY GENERATION

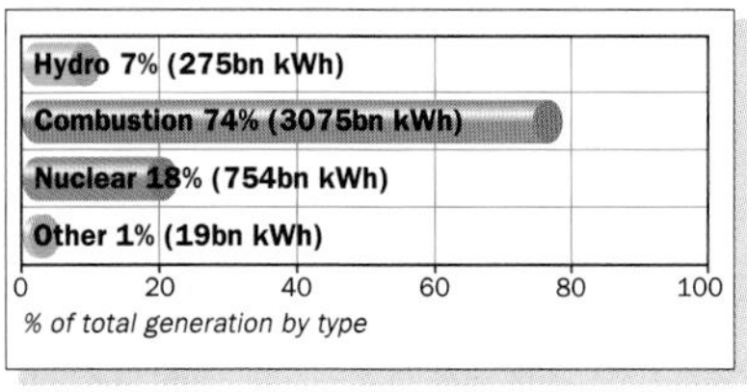
Hydro 7% (275bn kWh)
Combustion 74% (3075bn kWh)
Nuclear 18% (754bn kWh)
Other 1% (19bn kWh)
0
20
40
60
80
100
% of total generation by type

BROOKS RANGE
ALASKA RANGE

The US has an abundance of natural resources, including oil. The 2001 energy plan aimed to step up oil exploration and output, reducing the need for imports. There are massive deposits of coal in the western states – where almost all mining is opencast – and substantial mineral deposits in the mountains and intramontane basins.

Nuclear power is becoming increasingly important as an energy source with 28% of it generated from just three states: Illinois, Pennsylvania, and South Carolina. The timber industry, forced to retreat by conservationists in the Pacific northwest, especially Washington State, has moved to the south, where great stands of pine are harvested as if they were fields of wheat. Hydropower dominates the domestic sources of renewable energy. Other sources are small-scale but growing.

In comparison with western Europe, the US is not intensively farmed. The huge size of farms in the Midwest and west has allowed both arable and livestock farming to be based on a low-input for low-output model.

UNITED STATES : LAND USE

- Cropland
- Pasture
- Forest
- High mountain regions
- Wetland
- Desert/tundra
- Cattle
- Cotton
- Cereals
- Tobacco
- Citrus fruits

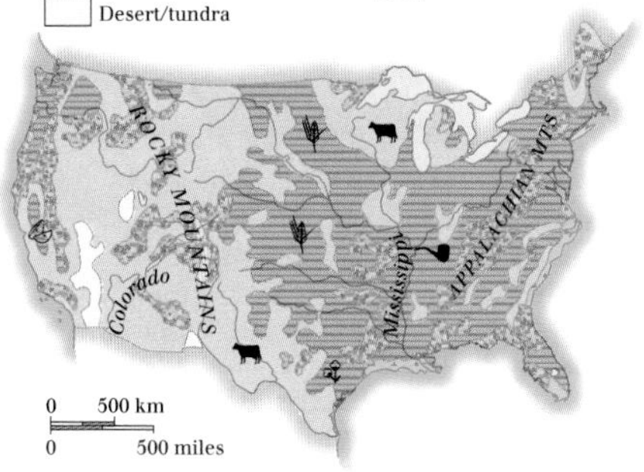
ROCKY MOUNTAINS
APPALACHIAN MTS
Colorado
Mississippi
0 500 km
0 500 miles

ENVIRONMENT

Sustainability rank: 45th

26% (14% partially protected)

19.8 tonnes per capita

ENVIRONMENTAL TREATIES

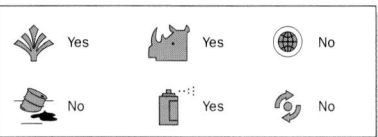

Yes	Yes	No
No	Yes	No

The US lags far behind other Western countries on environmental issues. The international commitment made at the 1997 Kyoto conference on cutting carbon dioxide emissions was scrapped by President Bush in 2001. The Rockies are a battleground between those who want to maintain their beauty, and those who advocate "wise use" – in practice this often means giving ranchers and miners free rein. In 2002, Congress approved plans to dump nuclear waste in Mt. Yucca, Nevada. Similar issues surround the arguments over extending oil drilling in the Alaskan wilderness. The US is leading the field in genetically modified (GM) food. Huge acreages have been planted with GM cereals, and by 2004 over 80% of soybean production was GM. A consumer backlash, especially in Europe, has worried many farmers.

MEDIA

TV ownership high

Daily newspaper circulation 201 per 1000 people

PUBLISHING AND BROADCAST MEDIA

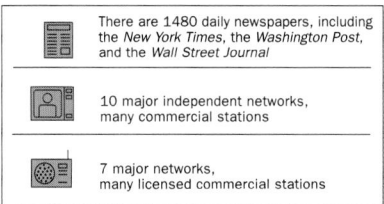

There are 1480 daily newspapers, including the *New York Times*, the *Washington Post*, and the *Wall Street Journal*

10 major independent networks, many commercial stations

7 major networks, many licensed commercial stations

Mass media as a phenomenon was born in the US. No other society has ever had anything quite like US network TV, or moved so easily into the world of multichannel TV; homes with 50 or more channels are commonplace. The Internet, the most recent in the series of nationwide communication revolutions, is now used regularly by the majority of the population. Newspapers, mostly local rather than national, tend to have very low cover prices, and gain most of their revenue from advertising. They are under increasing threat from cable TV and other outlets. Radio broadcasts remain popular, with outspoken disc jockeys, often expressing views firmly on the firm right-wing end of the political spectrum.

CHRONOLOGY

The original 13 colonies, first established by British settlers on the eastern seaboard in the 17th century, joined to wage a war for independence (1775–1781), which Britain recognized in 1783. The 1776 Declaration of Independence was followed by the writing of the world's first constitution. A century of westward expansion began. Following the victory of the northern states in the 1861–1865 Civil War, slavery was ended throughout the US, but Native Americans were dispossessed of their land in a series of conflicts.

- **1917** US enters World War I.
- **1929** New York stock market collapse; economic depression.
- **1941** Japanese attack on Pearl Harbor; US enters World War II.
- **1950–1953** Korean War.
- **1950–1954** Senator Joe McCarthy investigates supposed communist sympathizers in witch hunt.
- **1954** Supreme Court rules racial segregation in schools to be unconstitutional. Blacks, seeking constitutional rights, start campaign of civil disobedience.
- **1959** Alaska, Hawaii become states.
- **1961** John F. Kennedy president. Promises aid to South Vietnam. US-backed invasion of Cuba defeated at Bay of Pigs.
- **1962** Soviet missile bases found on Cuba; resulting threat of nuclear war narrowly averted.
- **1963** Kennedy assassinated. Lyndon Baines Johnson president.
- **1964** US involvement in Vietnam stepped up. Civil Rights Act gives blacks constitutional equality.
- **1968** Civil rights leader Martin Luther King is assassinated.
- **1969** Republican Richard Nixon takes office as president. Growing public opposition to Vietnam War.
- **1972** Nixon reelected. Makes historic visit to China.
- **1973** Withdrawal of US troops from Vietnam; 58,000 US troops dead by end of war.
- **1974** August, Nixon resigns following Watergate scandal over break-in to Democrat headquarters. Gerald Ford president.
- **1976** Democrat Jimmy Carter elected president.
- **1979** Seizure of US hostages in Iran.
- **1980** Ronald Reagan wins elections for Republicans. Adopts tough anticommunist foreign policy.
- **1983** Military invasion of Grenada.
- **1985** Air strikes against Libyan cities. Relations with USSR improve; first of three summits held.
- **1986** Iran–Contra affair revealed.

CHRONOLOGY *continued*

- **1987** Intermediate Nuclear Forces Treaty signed by US and USSR.
- **1988** Republican George Bush Sr. wins presidency.
- **1989** US overthrows Panama's Gen. Noriega, then arrests him on narcotics charges.
- **1991** January–February, Gulf War against Iraq. US and USSR sign START arms reduction treaty.
- **1992** Black youths riot in Los Angeles and other cities. Bush–Yeltsin summit agrees further arms reductions. Democrat Bill Clinton defeats Bush in presidential election.
- **1994** Midterm elections: Republican majorities in both houses of Congress.
- **1995** Oklahoma bombing by Timothy McVeigh: over 160 die.
- **1998** Scandal over Clinton's affair with White House intern leads to impeachment proceedings. August, bombing of US embassies in Kenya and Tanzania; revenge air strikes on Sudan and Afghanistan. December, air strikes against Iraq.
- **1999** February, Clinton acquitted in Senate impeachment trial. April, Columbine High School shootings. March–June, NATO intervenes in Kosovo conflict, bombardment of Yugoslavia.
- **2000** Democrat Al Gore concedes tightest presidential election ever to Republican George W. Bush.
- **2001** January, President Bush takes office. September 11, world's worst terrorist attack kills thousands as hijacked planes destroy World Trade Center, damage Pentagon. October, US-led military action in "war on terrorism" begins with intensive aerial bombing campaign in Afghanistan.
- **2002** July, WorldCom bankruptcy is biggest ever corporate collapse.
- **2003** Bush launches war on Iraq, despite lack of UN backing.
- **2004** Bush defeats Democrat John Kerry in presidential election.

Bison in Yellowstone National Park. *The park's ecosystem is under severe strain due to the number of visitors it attracts.*

CRIME

Death penalty in use

2.08m prisoners

Up 2% in 2001

CRIME RATES

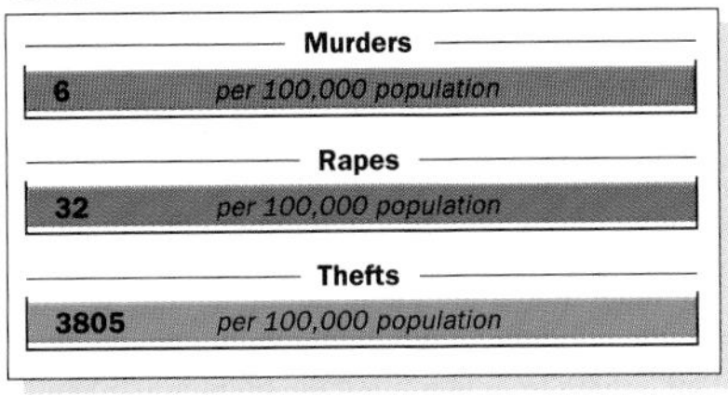
Murders
6 per 100,000 population
Rapes
32 per 100,000 population
Thefts
3805 per 100,000 population

Violent crime – especially murder – is much more common than in other developed countries, even in relatively well-off areas. However, the murder rate has fallen, and by 2001 was at its lowest for over 30 years. Mass shootings have made gun control a major issue, but a powerful lobby opposes restrictions, basing its arguments on the constitution and the defense of individual liberties.

Imprisonment for narcotics crimes in the US is much more widespread than in most Western countries. Capital punishment has increased since the 1980s, especially in the south. Texas carries out most executions. There are around two million people in prison in the US, almost a quarter of the world total.

EDUCATION

School leaving age: 17

99%

15.3m students

THE EDUCATION SYSTEM

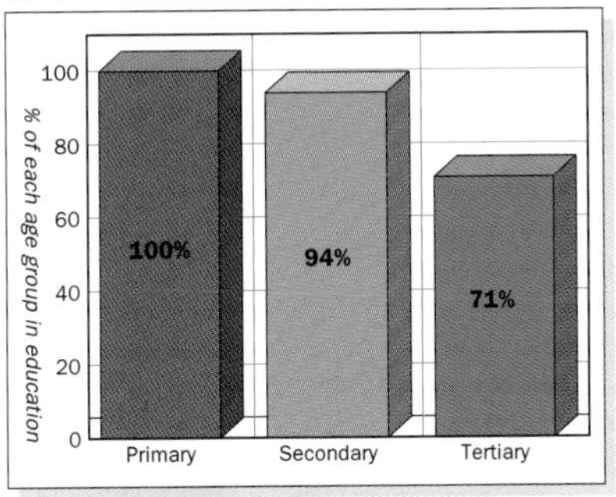
100
80
60
40
20
0
% of each age group in education
100%
94%
71%
Primary
Secondary
Tertiary

Education in the US is primarily the responsibility of the state governments.

Reports critical of standards in US public high schools cite problems of discipline, a devaluation in the worth of leaving diplomas, and a lack of resources in many areas. Private education at secondary level continues to develop rapidly, catering for 9% of high-school students. While the number of Roman Catholic private schools has shrunk, more nondenominational fee-paying schools have been founded.

Three-quarters of students now go on to some form of tertiary college. The leading US universities are internationally recognized as being world-class.

HEALTH

Limited welfare state health benefits

1 per 370 people

Cancers, heart, cerebrovascular, and respiratory diseases

US researchers lead in pioneering new treatments. Sophisticated techniques are available to those with insurance (which they typically receive, at least in part, from their employer); the Texas Medical Center has a budget equivalent to that of some small countries. On the other hand, costs have skyrocketed, and state medical care facilities are woefully underfunded. Infant mortality rates in some areas are at levels more commonly found in developing countries. Notable health campaigns have focused on smoking, which is now banned in public places in many major cities. Around 30% of the population is clinically obese; obesity kills nearly as many people as smoking. Abortion is a highly sensitive issue; unborn fetuses were covered as separate individuals under new legislation in 2004.

SPENDING

GDP/cap. increase

CONSUMPTION AND SPENDING

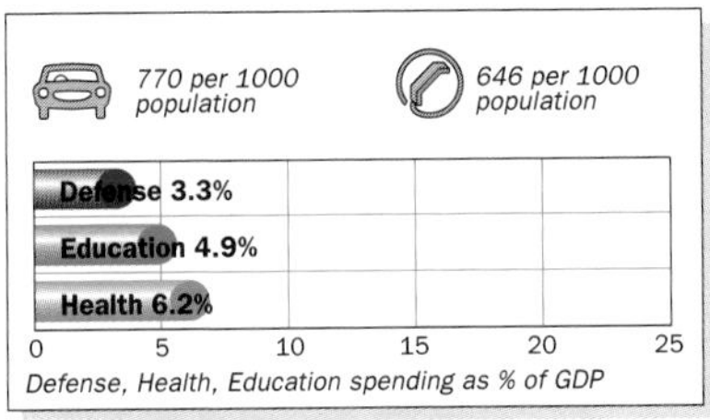
770 per 1000 population
646 per 1000 population
Defense 3.3%
Education 4.9%
Health 6.2%
0
5
10
15
20
25
Defense, Health, Education spending as % of GDP

Between 1945 and 1973, most Americans got richer. Since then, however, living standards have gone on rising only among those who finish high school. This "education effect" has led to noticeable class divisions, despite the long economic boom of the 1990s. The top 20% had average household incomes of $137,500 by 2000, whereas the incomes of the poorest 20% averaged only $13,000 – and were lower in real terms than in 1980.

WORLD RANKING

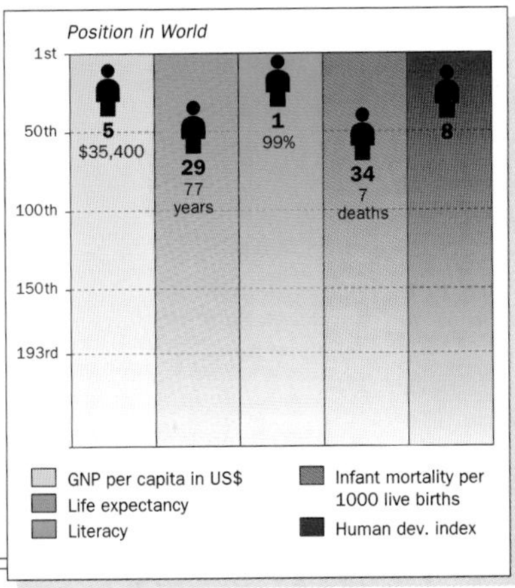
Position in World
1st
50th
100th
150th
193rd
5
$35,400
29
77 years
1
99%
34
7 deaths
8
GNP per capita in US$
Life expectancy
Literacy
Infant mortality per 1000 live births
Human dev. index

U

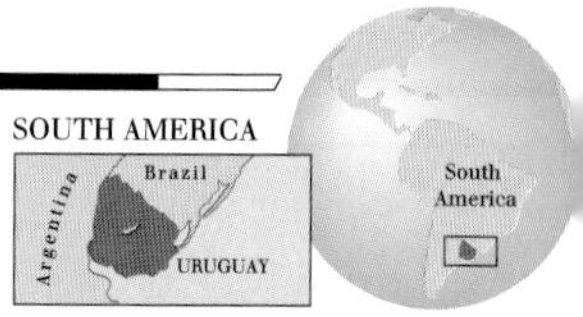
SOUTH AMERICA
Brazil
Argentina
URUGUAY
South America

URUGUAY

OFFICIAL NAME: Eastern Republic of Uruguay **CAPITAL:** Montevideo
POPULATION: 3.4 million **CURRENCY:** Uruguayan peso **OFFICIAL LANGUAGE:** Spanish

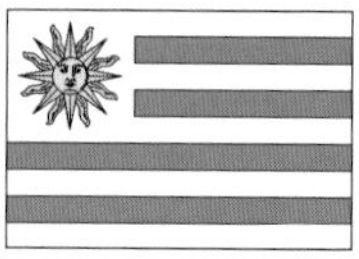

1828
1828
Aug 25
ROU
-3
+598
.uy

URUGUAY IS SITUATED IN the southeast of South America, sandwiched between its larger neighbors Brazil and Argentina. Its capital, Montevideo, is an Atlantic port on the River Plate, lying on the opposite bank to the Argentine capital Buenos Aires. Uruguay became independent in 1828, after nearly 150 years of Spanish and Portuguese control. Decades of liberal government ended in 1973 with a military coup that was to result in 12 years of dictatorship, during which 400,000 people emigrated. Most have since returned. Almost the entire low-lying landscape is devoted to the rearing of livestock, especially cattle and sheep. Uruguay is a leading wool exporter, but in recent years modern service industries have become increasingly important.

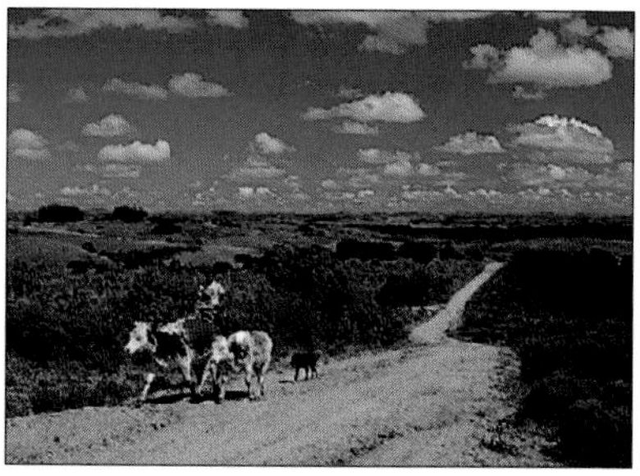

Uruguayan grasslands. *Rich pasture covers three-quarters of the country, ideal for cattle and sheep. Animals and animal products account for over a third of export earnings.*

CLIMATE

Subtropical

WEATHER CHART FOR MONTEVIDEO

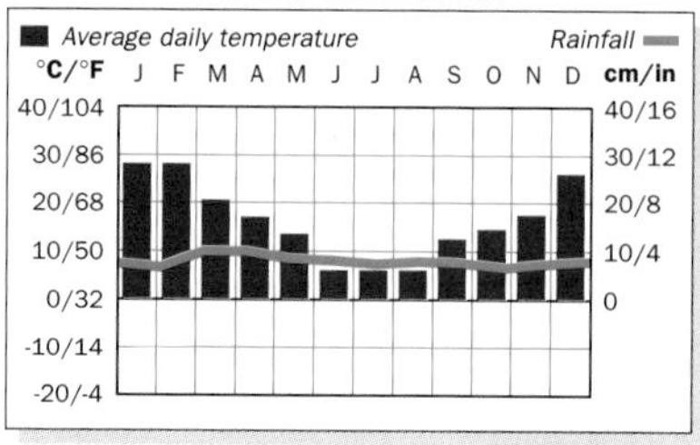
Average daily temperature
Rainfall
°C/°F
J F M A M J J A S O N D
cm/in
40/104
30/86
20/68
10/50
0/32
-10/14
-20/-4
40/16
30/12
20/8
10/4
0

Uruguay has one of the most benign climates in the world. It is uniformly temperate over the whole country. Winters are mild, frost is rare, and it never snows. Summers are generally cool for these latitudes and rarely tropically hot. The moderate rainfall tends to fall in heavy showers, leaving most days sunny.

TRANSPORTATION

Drive on right

Carrasco, Montevideo
1.17m passengers

90 ships
74,700 grt

THE TRANSPORTATION NETWORK

40,000 km (24,855 miles)

8983 km (5582 miles)

2993 km (1860 miles)

1600 km (994 miles)

There are extensive internal and international coach and bus services. The government has sold off its share in the national bus industry and has closed down all passenger railroad services. A multimillion-dollar project to build a 45-km (30-mile) road bridge across the River Plate from Colonia to Buenos Aires is still under review. The bridge is to be privately financed, recouping costs with a toll.

TOURISM

Visitors : Population 1:2.4

1.42m visitors

Up 13% in 2003

MAIN TOURIST ARRIVALS

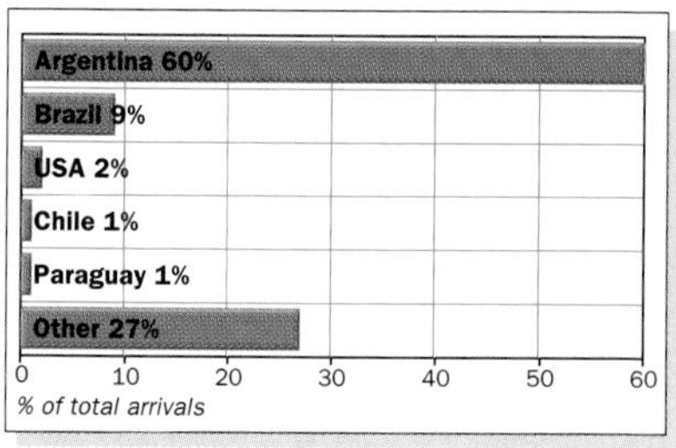
Argentina 60%
Brazil 9%
USA 2%
Chile 1%
Paraguay 1%
Other 27%
0
10
20
30
40
50
60
% of total arrivals

Sandy beaches near the River Plate estuary are a major attraction; Punta del Este is the main beach resort. The old Spanish fortifications of Montevideo have been destroyed, but the city retains a colonial atmosphere.

PEOPLE

Pop. density low

Spanish

19/km² (50/mi²)

THE URBAN/RURAL POPULATION SPLIT

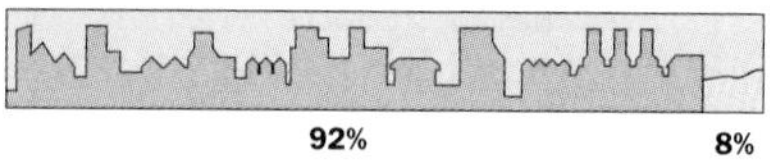
92%
8%

RELIGIOUS PERSUASION

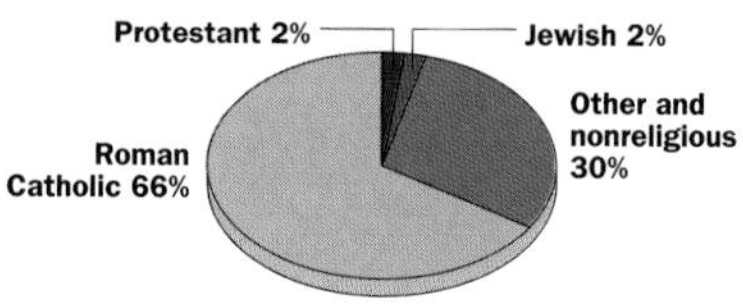
Protestant 2%
Jewish 2%
Other and nonreligious 30%
Roman Catholic 66%

ETHNIC MAKEUP

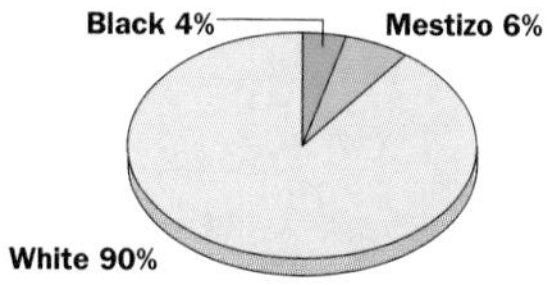
Black 4%
Mestizo 6%
White 90%

Most Uruguayans are second- or third-generation European, mainly of Spanish or Italian descent. There are also some mixed European–Amerindian mestizos (a group which had absorbed all indigenous Amerindians by the mid-19th century) and a small minority of people descended from Africans or immigrants from Brazil, who live near the Brazilian border or in and around Montevideo. More recent immigrants include Jews, Armenians, and Lebanese. Historically, ethnic tensions have been few. The birthrate is low for Latin America.

The considerable prosperity derived from cattle ranching allowed Uruguay to become a welfare state long before any other Latin American country. In spite of Uruguay's serious economic decline since the end of the 1950s, there is still a sizable, if less prosperous, middle class. A clear sign of the country's economic and social deterioration during the years of military dictatorship was the unprecedented growth of shanty towns around Montevideo.

Uruguay is largely a Roman Catholic country, but it is liberal in its attitude to religion, and all forms are tolerated. Divorce is legal. Women, who gained the vote in 1932, are regarded as equal to men.

POPULATION AGE BREAKDOWN

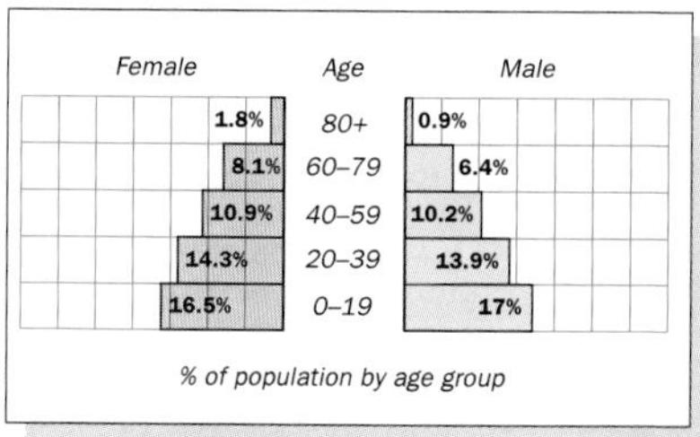
Female
Age
Male
1.8%
80+
0.9%
8.1%
60–79
6.4%
10.9%
40–59
10.2%
14.3%
20–39
13.9%
16.5%
0–19
17%
% of population by age group

U

POLITICS

Multiparty elections

L. House 1999/2004
U. House 1999/2004

President Jorge Batlle Ibáñez

AT THE LAST ELECTION

Chamber of Representatives 99 seats

41% EPFA	33% PC	22% PN	4% NE

EPFA = Progressive Broad Front **PC** = Colorado Party (Colorados) **PN** = National Party (Blancos) **NE** = New Space **Res** = Reserved for the vice president

Chamber of Senators 31 seats

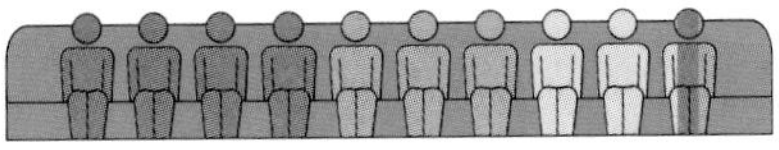

39% EPFA	32% PC	23% PN	3% NE	3% Res

Uruguay is a presidential multiparty democracy.

PROFILE

The elections of 1984 heralded a return to democracy. Since then the main Colorado (PC) and Blanco (PN) parties have monopolized power, either alone or in coalitions, despite being traditional opponents. The left-wing EPFA has been the effective opposition, frequently in alliance with trade unions fighting austerity measures and reform of the social security system. Despite the crowded electoral calendar in 1999, and infighting among Blanco factions, there was broad consensus on the need for continuing economic reform. In the 1999 elections, Colorado candidate Jorge Batlle won the presidency in the face of an unusually strong left-wing challenge.

MAIN POLITICAL ISSUES

Government credibility

Batlle was seriously weakened by the early departure of junior coalition Blancos from his cabinet in 2002. With elections due in 2004, the Blancos were seen to be distancing themselves from Batlle's harsh austerity program, already affecting the Colorados' popularity.

Economic malaise

The economy entered its fifth year of recession in 2003. Government forecasts of a 2% contraction for the year were far below what independent economists predicted.

Luis Alberto Lacalle Herrera, *president in 1990–1995.*

Jorge Batlle Ibáñez, *who took office for a four-year term as president in 2000.*

URUGUAY

Total Area : 176 220 sq. km (68 039 sq. miles)

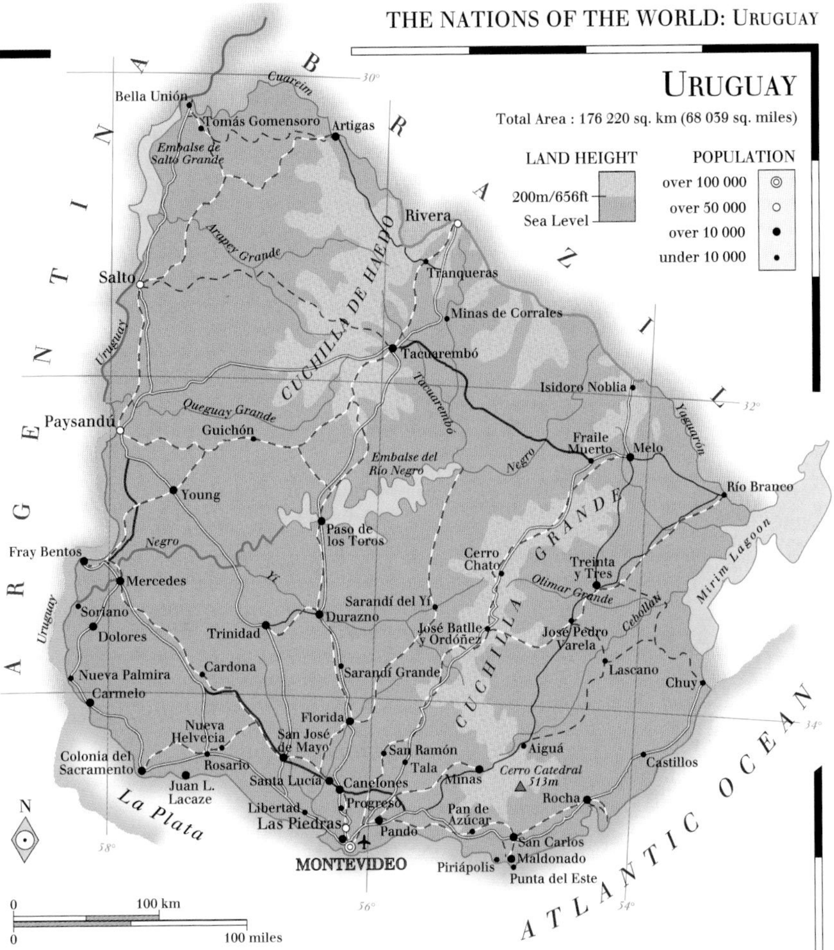
LAND HEIGHT
200m/656ft
Sea Level
POPULATION
over 100 000
over 50 000
over 10 000
under 10 000
BRAZIL
ARGENTINA
ATLANTIC OCEAN
La Plata
Bella Unión
Tomás Gomensoro
Artigas
Embalse de Salto Grande
Rivera
Tranqueras
Salto
Minas de Corrales
Tacuarembó
CUCHILLA DE HAEDO
Isidoro Noblia
Paysandú
Guichón
Embalse del Río Negro
Fraile Muerto
Melo
Río Branco
Young
Paso de los Toros
Fray Bentos
Mercedes
Cerro Chato
Treinta y Tres
Mirim Lagoon
Soriano
Dolores
Sarandí del Yí
Durazno
Trinidad
José Batlle y Ordóñez
José Pedro Varela
CUCHILLA GRANDE
Nueva Palmira
Carmelo
Cardona
Sarandí Grande
Lascano
Chuy
Florida
Nueva Helvecia
San José de Mayo
Colonia del Sacramento
Rosario
San Ramón
Tala
Aiguá
Juan L. Lacaze
Santa Lucía
Canelones
Minas
Cerro Catedral 513m
Castillos
Rocha
Libertad
Las Piedras
Progreso
Pando
Pan de Azúcar
MONTEVIDEO
Piriápolis
San Carlos
Maldonado
Punta del Este
0 100 km
0 100 miles

WORLD AFFAIRS

Joined UN in 1945

Geplac | Mercsr | IBRD | OAS | RG

Regional integration is a major focus, but President Batlle's determination to clinch a bilateral trade deal with the US caused a row with the Brazilian government, which said that it contravened the official policy of Mercosur to negotiate trade agreements as a bloc. Argentina also took exception to plans to impose protective tariffs to cushion Uruguayan industry from the effects of Argentine devaluation. Such difficulties complicated diplomatic moves to strengthen Mercosur as a negotiating bloc in upcoming talks to establish a Free Trade Area of the Americas (FTAA).

Uruguay and the US have agreed a legal assistance treaty to allow easier access to bank accounts of those suspected of laundering the proceeds from narcotics trafficking.

AID

Recipient

$13m (receipts) — Down 13% in 2002

Uruguay received an IMF standby loan of $1.5 billion for 2002–2003, but aid remains otherwise modest.

CHRONOLOGY

The Spaniards were the first to colonize the area north of the River Plate. In 1680, the Portuguese also founded a colony there, at Colonia del Sacramento, so starting 150 years of rivalry between the colonial powers for control of the territory.

- **1726** Spaniards found Montevideo. By 1800, whole country is divided into large cattle ranches.
- **1808** Montevideo declares independence from Buenos Aires.
- **1811** Patriotic rancher and local caudillo, José Gervasio Artigas, fends off Brazilian attack.
- **1812–1820** Uruguayans, known as Orientales ("Easterners," from the eastern side of the River Plate), fight wars against Argentinian and Brazilian invaders. Brazil finally takes Montevideo.
- **1827** Gen. Lavalleja defeats Brazilians with Argentine help.
- **1828** Seeing trade benefits that an independent Uruguay would bring as a buffer state between Argentina and Brazil, Britain mediates and secures Uruguayan independence.
- **1836** Start of large-scale European immigration.

⇨

U

CHRONOLOGY *continued*

- **1838–1865** La Guerra Grande civil war between Blancos (Whites, future conservative party) and Colorados (Reds, future liberals).
- **1865–1870** President Venancio Flores of Colorados takes Uruguay into War of Triple Alliance against Paraguay.
- **1872** Peace under military rule. Blancos strong in country, Colorados in cities.
- **1890s** Violent strikes by immigrant trade unionists against landed elite enriched by massive European investment in ranching.
- **1903–1907** Reformist Colorado, José Batlle y Ordóñez, president.
- **1911–1915** Batlle serves second term in office. Batllismo creates the only welfare state in Latin America with pensions, social security, and free education and health service; also nationalizations, disestablishment of Church, abolition of death penalty.
- **1933** Military coup. Opposition groups excluded from politics.
- **1939–1945** Neutral in World War II.
- **1942** President Alfredo Baldomir dismisses government and tries to bring back proper representation.
- **1951** New constitution replaces president with nine-member council. Decade of great prosperity follows until world agricultural prices plummet. Sharp drop in foreign investment.
- **1958** Blancos win elections for first time in 93 years.
- **1962–1973** Tupamaros urban guerrillas battle government.
- **1966** Presidency reinstated. Colorados back in power.
- **1967** Jorge Pacheco president. Tries to stifle opposition to tough anti-inflation policies.
- **1973** Military coup. Promises to encourage foreign investment counteracted by denial of political freedom and brutal repression of the left; 400,000 emigrate.
- **1984** Free presidential elections won by Julio Sanguinetti (Colorado).
- **1985** Military step down, Sanguinetti inaugurated.
- **1986** Those guilty of human rights abuse granted amnesty.
- **1989** Referendum endorses amnesty in interests of stability. Elections won by Luis Alberto Lacalle Herrera and Blancos.
- **1994–1995** Sanguinetti reelected, forms coalition government. Mercosur membership.
- **1999** October, presidential election won by Colorado Jorge Batlle.
- **2002** Uruguay loses investment grade status due to impact of Argentine crisis.

DEFENSE

No compulsory military service

$212m

Down 39% in 2002

The military withdrew from power in 1985 and has since respected civilian rule. "Lodges" operate within the army to promote officers' interests and have displayed opposition to the government's replacements and promotions within the military hierarchy. A 1986 law virtually blocked investigations into killings, torture, and "disappearances" during the dictatorship, but there is still pressure to bring guilty officers to justice. A presidential decree in 1997 granted amnesty to officers punished for political offenses under military rule.

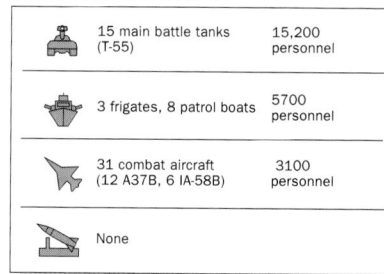

URUGUAYAN ARMED FORCES

15 main battle tanks (T-55)	15,200 personnel
3 frigates, 8 patrol boats	5700 personnel
31 combat aircraft (12 A37B, 6 IA-58B)	3100 personnel
None	

The defense budget is modest; recent purchases have come from Israel and the Czech Republic.

ECONOMICS

Inflation 28% p.a. (1990–2001)

$14.6bn

29.73 Uruguayan pesos (26.82)

SCORE CARD

World GNP Ranking	77th
GNP per capita	$4340
Balance of payments	$262m
Inflation	14%
Unemployment	17%

EXPORTS

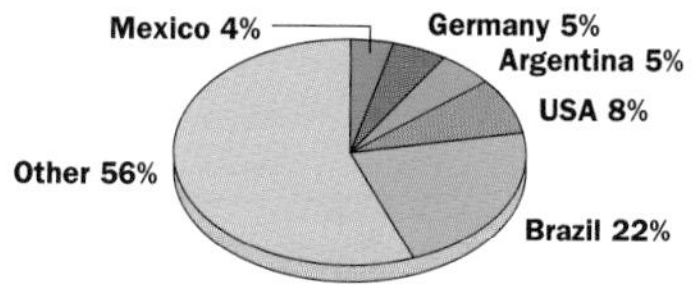
Mexico 4%
Germany 5%
Argentina 5%
USA 8%
Other 56%
Brazil 22%

IMPORTS

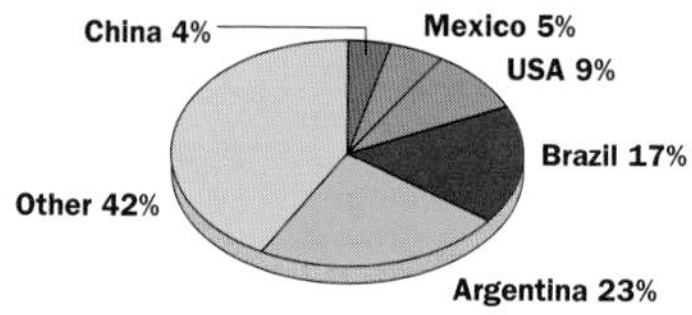
China 4%
Mexico 5%
USA 9%
Brazil 17%
Other 42%
Argentina 23%

Strengths

Fertile grasslands. Major wool exporter. Beef-meat products. Fishing. Competitive exchange rate.

Weaknesses

Few natural resources. Dependence on Brazilian and Argentine markets. Modest industry. Large public sector deficit. Prolonged economic recession. Troubled banking sector.

Profile

Uruguay's economy is traditionally agricultural. Three-quarters of the land is rich pasture, supporting livestock; much of the rest is given over to crops. Farming, which formerly brought great wealth, has given way to services as a major employer. Manufacturing now accounts for some 16% of GDP yet remains tied to the land with farm-based goods accounting for half of

ECONOMIC PERFORMANCE INDICATOR

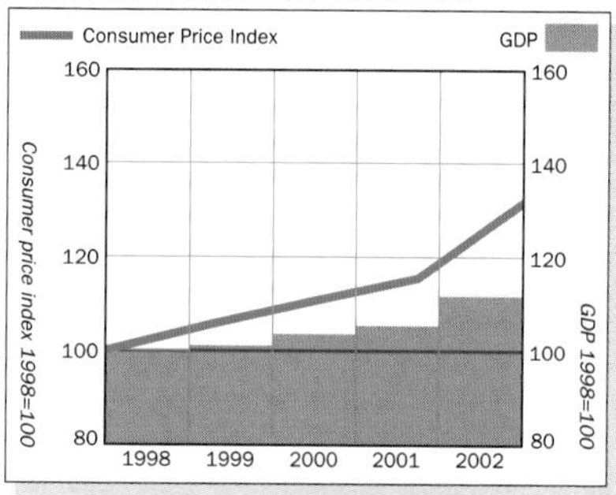
Consumer Price Index
GDP
160
140
120
100
80
Consumer price index 1998=100
GDP 1998=100
1998
1999
2000
2001
2002

production; livestock and animal products, especially meat and wool, bring in over one-third of export earnings. Tourism is increasingly important. Most economic activity – and half the population – is concentrated in Montevideo. A shrinking economy has made it difficult to achieve GDP and fiscal targets agreed with the IMF. Unions resist spending cuts and, with public opinion hostile to major privatizations, there has been little progress in necessary structural reforms.

URUGUAY : MAJOR BUSINESSES

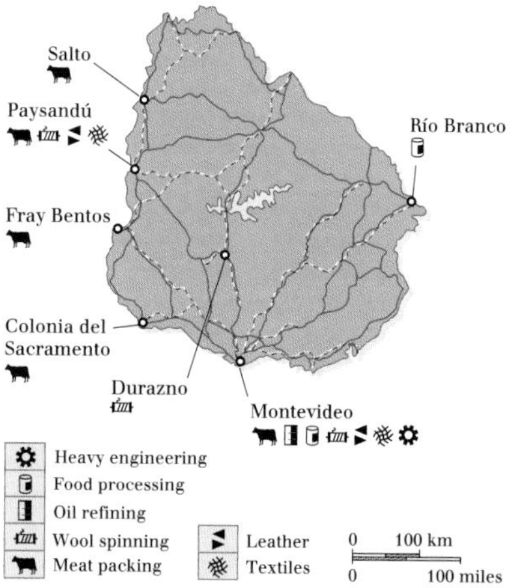
Salto
Paysandú
Río Branco
Fray Bentos
Colonia del Sacramento
Durazno
Montevideo
Heavy engineering
Food processing
Oil refining
Wool spinning
Meat packing
Leather
Textiles
0
100 km
0
100 miles

U

RESOURCES

Electric power 2.2m kW

105,051 tonnes

Not an oil producer; refines 38,400 b/d

11.7m cattle, 9.78m sheep, 13.3m chickens

Gold, iron, gemstones, copper, zinc, lead, manganese

ELECTRICITY GENERATION

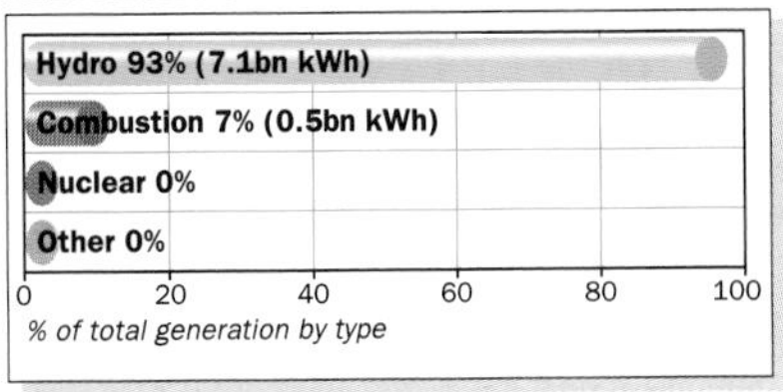

Hydro 93% (7.1bn kWh)
Combustion 7% (0.5bn kWh)
Nuclear 0%
Other 0%
0
20
40
60
80
100
% of total generation by type

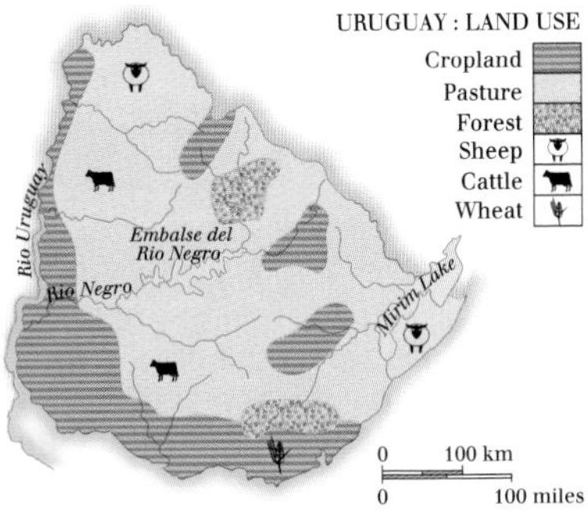

URUGUAY : LAND USE
Cropland
Pasture
Forest
Sheep
Cattle
Wheat
Rio Uruguay
Embalse del Rio Negro
Rio Negro
Mirim Lake
0
100 km
0
100 miles

Most of Uruguay is farmland, much of it given over to cattle and sheep. Rice is the country's only other significant export. There are no known oil or natural gas resources; most electricity is imported. Considerable potential is believed to exist for the mining sector, but only small quantities of building materials and jewelry-quality agate and amethysts are so far extracted. The mining of gold deposits is currently being developed and exploration continues.

ENVIRONMENT

Sustainability rank: 6th

0.3% (0.2% partially protected)

1.6 tonnes per capita

ENVIRONMENTAL TREATIES

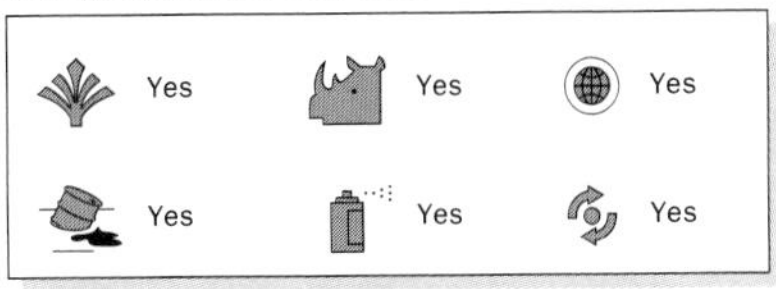

Yes
Yes
Yes
Yes
Yes
Yes

Pollution of the main Uruguay and Plate Rivers is a concern, as is traffic density in Montevideo.

MEDIA

TV ownership high

Daily newspaper circulation 293 per 1000 people

PUBLISHING AND BROADCAST MEDIA

There are 16 daily newspapers, including *El País*, *El Diario*, and *La Mañana*

4 services: 1 state-owned, 3 independent

1 state-owned service, 100 independent stations

The press is relatively free. *El País* supports the Blancos (PN), while *La Mañana* backs the Colorados (PC).

CRIME

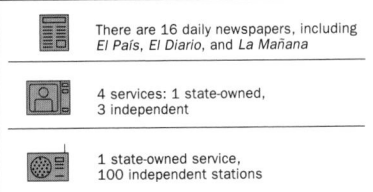

No death penalty

7100 prisoners

Up 15% in 2000

CRIME RATES

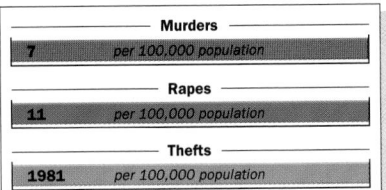

Murders
7 per 100,000 population

Rapes
11 per 100,000 population

Thefts
1981 per 100,000 population

Levels of violent crime are generally low in comparison with neighboring Brazil and Argentina. However, rises in street violence and organized crime are of growing concern.

EDUCATION

School leaving age: 15

98%

97,541 students

THE EDUCATION SYSTEM

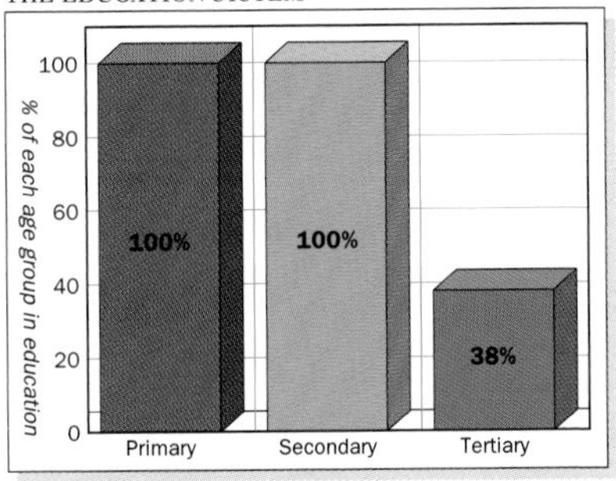

100
80
60
40
20
0
% of each age group in education
100%
100%
38%
Primary
Secondary
Tertiary

Education, inspired by the French *lycée* system, is state-funded for 12 years up to secondary level and is compulsory for all children for nine years from the age of six. Both state and private schools follow the same curriculum; private schools are monitored by the government. Facilities are rudimentary in rural areas. Uruguay has two state-funded universities. The children of wealthy Uruguayans tend to complete their studies in the US. Resistance to tax increases and pressure to reduce the fiscal deficit have both placed serious constraints on education spending. Secondary school students continue to stage protests against the resulting effects on the system.

HEALTH

Welfare state health benefits

1 per 270 people

Cancers, heart and cerebrovascular diseases

Most Uruguayans have easy access to health services. Average life expectancy is high. The health system faces a challenge, however, with a large number of people unable to afford health insurance. Despite opposition, the government has privatized some of the state medical establishments.

Health spending has in recent years been a victim of the budget cuts and social welfare reforms aimed at controlling the fiscal deficit.

SPENDING

GDP/cap. increase

CONSUMPTION AND SPENDING

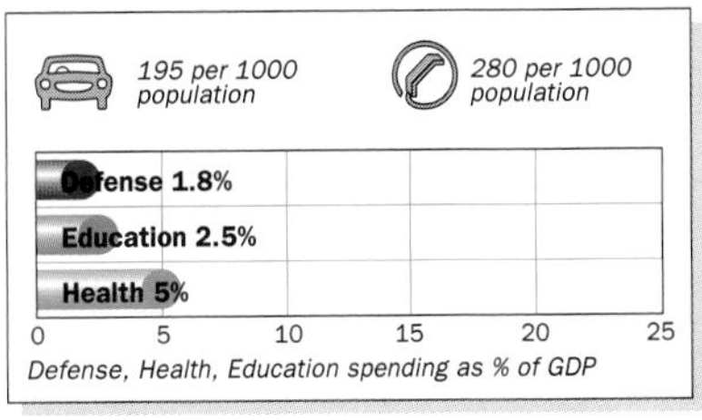

195 per 1000 population
280 per 1000 population
Defense 1.8%
Education 2.5%
Health 5%
0
5
10
15
20
25
Defense, Health, Education spending as % of GDP

Uruguay possesses the social mobility which is typical of countries created through decades of large-scale immigration, and many professionals come from modest backgrounds. A 1999 report by the IDB exempted Uruguay from the regional trend of serious income inequality.

The wealthy members of society either tend to be landowners or are employed in the financial sector. They have traditionally looked toward Europe, rather than the US, for luxury goods.

The most deprived sections of Uruguayan society are the urban poor of Montevideo, a large proportion of whom are of mixed African and European descent, and the rural poor, who own little or no land.

WORLD RANKING

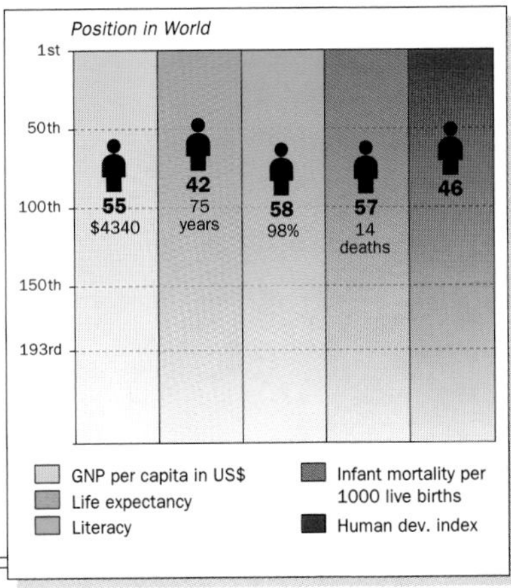

Position in World
1st
50th
100th
150th
193rd
55
$4340
42
75 years
58
98%
57
14 deaths
46
GNP per capita in US$
Life expectancy
Literacy
Infant mortality per 1000 live births
Human dev. index

U

Uzbekistan

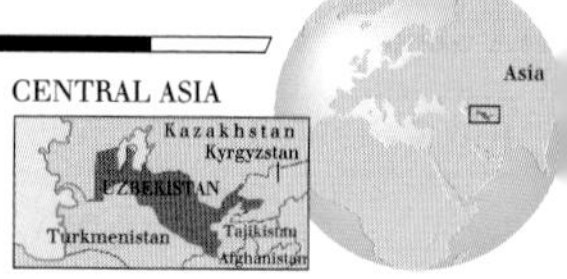
CENTRAL ASIA
Asia
Kazakhstan
Kyrgyzstan
UZBEKISTAN
Turkmenistan
Tajikistan
Afghanistan

Official Name: Republic of Uzbekistan **Capital:** Tashkent
Population: 26.1 million **Currency:** Som **Official Language:** Uzbek

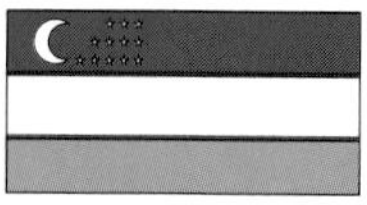

1991
1991
Sept 1
UZ
+5 to +6
+998
.uz

SHARING WHAT IS LEFT of the Aral Sea with Kazakhstan, its northern neighbor, Uzbekistan contains the ancient cities of Samarqand, Bukhara (Buxoro), Khiva, and Tashkent. It is the most populous central Asian republic and has considerable natural resources. The dictatorship of President Karimov has prevented the spread of Islamic fundamentalism.

CLIMATE

Desert/mountain

WEATHER CHART FOR TASHKENT

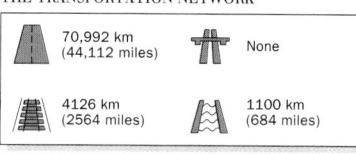

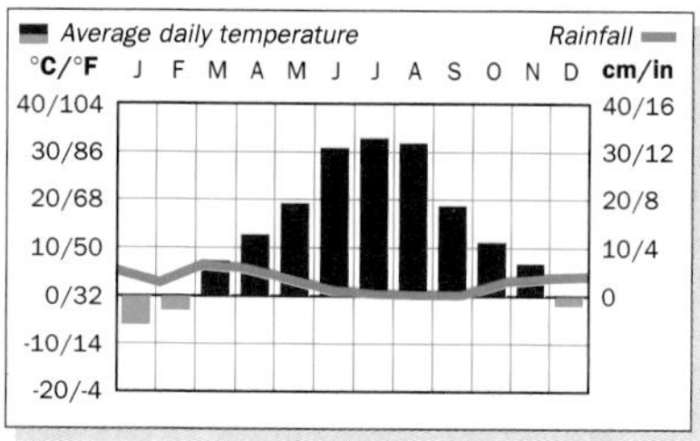
Average daily temperature
Rainfall
°C/°F
J F M A M J J A S O N D
cm/in
40/104
30/86
20/68
10/50
0/32
-10/14
-20/-4
40/16
30/12
20/8
10/4
0

Uzbekistan has a harsh continental climate. Summers can be extremely hot and dry. Large areas of the country are desert.

TRANSPORTATION

Drive on right

Tashkent International 1.52m passengers

Has no fleet

THE TRANSPORTATION NETWORK

70,992 km (44,112 miles)	None
4126 km (2564 miles)	1100 km (684 miles)

Uzbekistan has a well-developed transportation system. An extensive network of buses serves country areas, while good Soviet-style systems of trolley buses and trams operate in the major cities. Tashkent's subway system was the first in central Asia. Road and rail networks have deteriorated since 1991, however, and are concentrated in the south and east.

TOURISM

Visitors : Population 1:79

332,000 visitors

Up 22% in 1999–2002

MAIN TOURIST ARRIVALS

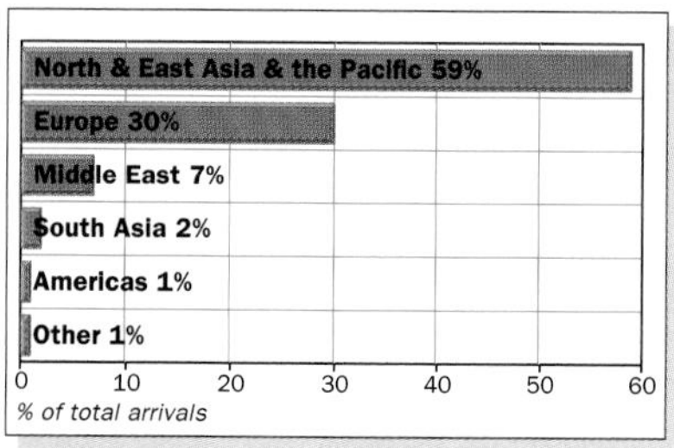
North & East Asia & the Pacific 59%
Europe 30%
Middle East 7%
South Asia 2%
Americas 1%
Other 1%
0
10
20
30
40
50
60
% of total arrivals

Uzbekistan has considerable tourist potential. Bukhara, once a trading center on the silk route, is famous worldwide for its architecture and carpet-making. It has great religious significance for Muslims, who are encouraged to make at least one pilgrimage to its holy shrines. Bukhara's Kalyan Mosque is famous for its minaret built of unbaked bricks. The city of Samarqand was expanded in the 14th century by Timur, and contains the monumental gateway of the Shir Dar Madrasa, one of the most beautiful buildings in the Islamic world.

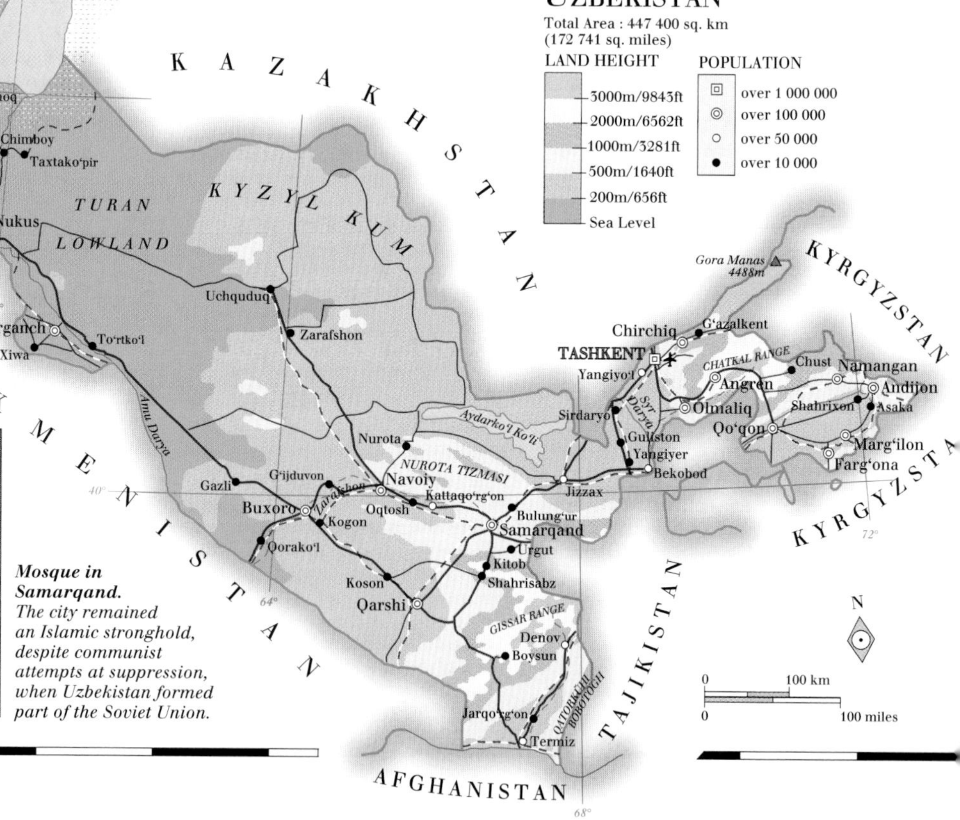
UZBEKISTAN
Total Area : 447 400 sq. km
(172 741 sq. miles)
LAND HEIGHT
3000m/9843ft
2000m/6562ft
1000m/3281ft
500m/1640ft
200m/656ft
Sea Level
POPULATION
over 1 000 000
over 100 000
over 50 000
over 10 000
KAZAKHSTAN
KAZAKHSTAN
TURKMENISTAN
KYRGYZSTAN
KYRGYZSTAN
TAJIKISTAN
AFGHANISTAN
ARAL SEA
USTYURT PLATEAU
TURAN LOWLAND
KYZYL KUM
Mo'ynoq
Chimboy
Taxtako'pir
Qo'ng'irot
Amu Darya
Nukus
Xo'jayli
Taxiatosh
Uchquduq
Zarafshon
Urganch
Xiwa
To'rtko'l
Gora Manas 4488m
Chirchiq
G'azalkent
TASHKENT
Yangiyo'l
CHATKAL RANGE
Chust
Namangan
Angren
Andijon
Olmaliq
Shahrixon
Asaka
Qo'qon
Marg'ilon
Farg'ona
Sirdaryo
Syr Darya
Guliston
Yangiyer
Bekobod
Aydarko'l Ko'li
Nurota
NUROTA TIZMASI
Navoiy
Kattaqo'rg'on
Jizzax
G'ijduvon
Gazli
Buxoro
Zarafshon
Kogon
Oqtosh
Bulung'ur
Samarqand
Urgut
Qorako'l
Kitob
Shahrisabz
Koson
Qarshi
GISSAR RANGE
Denov
Boysun
Jarqo'rg'on
Termiz
N
0
100 km
0
100 miles

Mosque in Samarqand. *The city remained an Islamic stronghold, despite communist attempts at suppression, when Uzbekistan formed part of the Soviet Union.*

PEOPLE

Pop. density medium

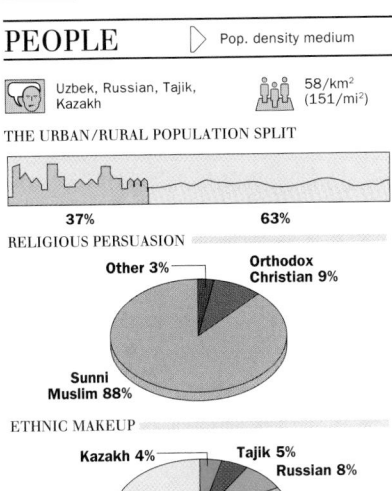

Uzbek, Russian, Tajik, Kazakh

58/km² (151/mi²)

THE URBAN/RURAL POPULATION SPLIT

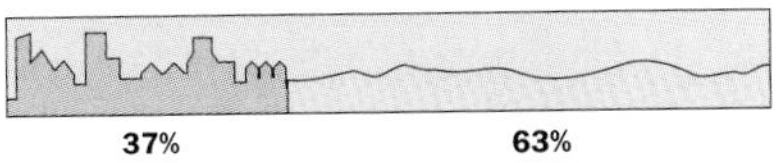
37%
63%

RELIGIOUS PERSUASION

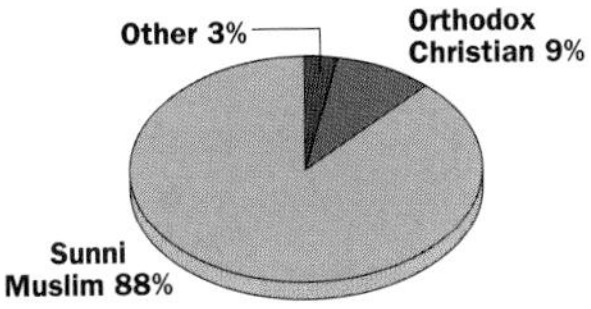
Other 3%
Orthodox Christian 9%
Sunni Muslim 88%

ETHNIC MAKEUP

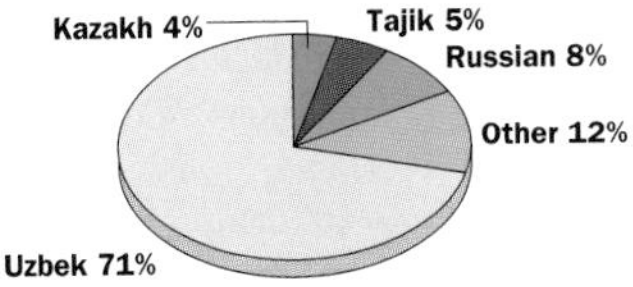
Kazakh 4%
Tajik 5%
Russian 8%
Other 12%
Uzbek 71%

Among the former Soviet republics, Uzbekistan has a relatively complex ethnic makeup. In addition to the Uzbeks, Russians, Tajiks, and Kazakhs, there are small minorities of Tatars and Karakalpaks. The proportion of Russians has been declining since the 1970s, when net emigration of Russians began. The authoritarian nature of the Karimov leadership has prevented potential antagonism between the country's ethnic groups from becoming violent; incidents such as the 1989 and 1990 clashes between Meskhetians and Uzbeks are rare. The removal of the dominance of the Communist Party has meant that Uzbek society has reverted to traditional social patterns based on family, religion, clan, neighborhood (*mahalla*), and region, rather than on membership of the party. Independence has done little to alter the peripheral role of women in politics. Arranged marriages are still the custom in the countryside.

POPULATION AGE BREAKDOWN

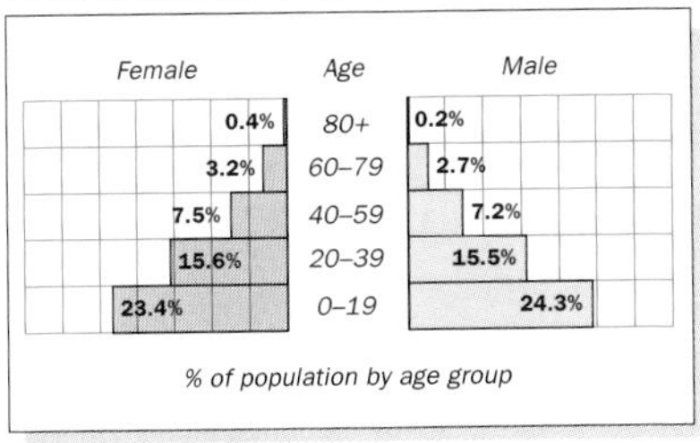
Female
Age
Male
0.4%
80+
0.2%
3.2%
60–79
2.7%
7.5%
40–59
7.2%
15.6%
20–39
15.5%
23.4%
0–19
24.3%
% of population by age group

POLITICS

Multiparty elections

1999/2004

President Islam Karimov

AT THE LAST ELECTION

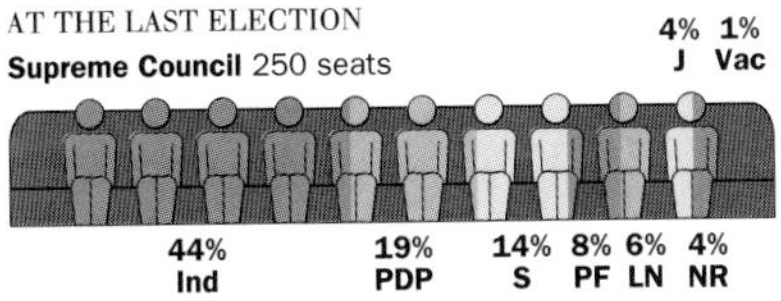
Supreme Council 250 seats
4% J
1% Vac
44% Ind
19% PDP
14% S
8% PF
6% LN
4% NR

Ind = Independents **PDP** = People's Democratic Party **S** = Self-sacrifice (Fidorkorlar) **PF** = Progress of the Fatherland **LN** = Local nominees **J** = Justice (Adolat) **NR** = National Renaissance **Vac** = Vacant

Uzbekistan is effectively run by a presidential dictatorship. In 2002 a referendum approved the creation of a second legislative chamber and lengthened the presidential term.

PROFILE

President Islam Karimov's former communist PDP has not been willing to devolve or share power. The 1992 constitution appeared to endorse multipartyism, but Karimov took advantage of his enhanced powers to ban several opposition parties, including the nationalist Birlik (Unity) and the Islamic Renaissance Party. Erk (Will), the only legal opposition party, was proscribed in 1993, and in 1995, a group of its activists received stiff sentences for political subversion. Real opposition is now entirely underground. The intimidation and arbitrary imprisonment of dissidents are common, and have increased since bomb attacks in Tashkent in 1999. Karimov has kept the support of the Russian minority by avoiding nationalist rhetoric.

MAIN POLITICAL ISSUES

Islamic fundamentalism

Civil war in Tajikistan and the rise of the *taliban* in Afghanistan raised fears of Islamic fundamentalism. A joint operation with Kyrgyzstan and Tajikistan against the pan-regional Islamic Movement of Uzbekistan (IMU) took place in 2000, as cross-border attacks rose. IMU leader Juma Namangani was reported killed alongside *taliban* fighters in Afghanistan in late 2001. A clampdown against the Hizb-ut Tahrir group continues.

Regionalism

The high birthrate puts pressure on limited agricultural resources. Migration from poorer areas has led to calls for secession from some regions. In the densely populated eastern Fergana Valley there have been a number of violent incidents.

Islam Karimov, *first elected president in 1990 and Uzbekistan's sole leader since independence.*

WORLD AFFAIRS

Joined UN in 1992

CIS | SCO | OIC | NAM | OSCE

Unlike neighboring Turkmenistan, Kyrgyzstan, and Tajikistan, Uzbekistan has the resources to allow it to follow a relatively independent foreign policy. The Karimov leadership has used this to promote Uzbekistan as the leading central Asian state, a role for which it vies with Kazakhstan. It is a member of the Georgia–Ukraine–Uzbekistan–Azerbaijan–Moldova (GUUAM) group of ex-Soviet states, signifying a wish to maintain a certain distance in relations with Russia, though it suspended its membership for a year in 2002. It has border disputes with its immediate neighbors, in particular over the laying of landmines on its borders with Tajikistan and Kyrgyzstan to prevent terrorist incursions.

Ties with the US were strengthened when Uzbekistan hosted US forces during the war in Afghanistan in 2001. The US offered support after a wave of terrorist attacks in early 2004. Relations with Turkey are also developing. While Western companies have difficulty in sealing contracts in Uzbekistan, Turkish companies have been commissioned to build vital installations such as those for telecommunications.

CHRONOLOGY

Once part of the great Mongol Empire, present-day Uzbekistan was incorporated into the Russian Empire between 1865 and 1876. Russification of the area was superficial, and it was not until Soviet rule that significant Russian immigration occurred. A further influx of Russians occurred during Stalin's program of forced collectivization.

- **1917** Soviet power established in Tashkent.
- **1918** Turkestan Autonomous Soviet Socialist Republic (ASSR), incorporating present-day Uzbekistan, proclaimed.
- **1923–1941** Alphabet changes, from Arabic to Latin to Iranized Tashkent, finally to Cyrillic.
- **1924** Basmachi rebels who resisted Soviet rule crushed. Uzbek SSR founded (which, until 1929, included the Tajik ASSR).
- **1925** Anti-Islamic campaign bans schools and closes mosques.
- **1936** Karakalpak ASSR (formerly part of the Russian Soviet Federative Socialist Republic) incorporated into the Uzbek SSR.
- **1937** Uzbek communist leadership is purged by Stalin.

U

CHRONOLOGY *continued*

- **1941–1945** Industrial boom.
- **1959** Sharaf Rashidov becomes first secretary of Communist Party of Uzbekistan (CPUz). Retains position until 1983.
- **1966** Tashkent razed by earthquake. Rebuilding brings in large number of Russian and other non-Uzbek migrants.
- **1982–1983** Yuri Andropov becomes leader in Moscow. His anticorruption purge results in emergence of a new generation of central Asian officials.
- **1989** First noncommunist political movement, Birlik (Unity), formed but not officially registered. June, clashes erupt between Meskhetians and indigenous Uzbek population of Fergana Valley, resulting in more than 100 deaths. October, Birlik campaign leads to Uzbek being declared official language.
- **1990** Islam Karimov becomes executive president of the new Uzbek Supreme Soviet. Further interethnic fighting in Fergana Valley; 320 killed.
- **1991** August, independence is proclaimed and Republic of Uzbekistan is adopted as official name. October, Uzbekistan signs treaty establishing economic community with seven other former Soviet republics. November, CPUz restructured as the People's Democratic Party of Uzbekistan (PDP); Karimov remains its leader. December, Karimov confirmed in post of president. Uzbekistan joins the CIS.
- **1992** Price liberalization provokes student riots in Tashkent. New post-Soviet constitution adopted along Western democratic lines. All religious parties banned. September, Uzbekistan sends troops to Tajikistan to suppress violence and strengthen border controls.
- **1993** Growing harassment of opposition political parties, Erk (Will) and Birlik.
- **1994** Introduction of som.
- **1995** January, Karimov's PDP wins legislative elections. March, referendum extends Karimov's presidential term until 2000.
- **1999** Bomb attacks by Islamist terrorists lead to crackdown and arrests of hundreds of opposition activists. Legislative elections.
- **2000** Karimov reelected.
- **2002** Referendum extends president's term to seven years.
- **2003** Utkur Sultanov replaced as prime minister by Shavkat Mirziyayev after eight-year term.

AID

Recipient

$189m (receipts)

Up 24% in 2002

Uzbekistan's lack of commitment to economic stabilization and its record of rights violations have generally deterred bilateral aid donors. US aid linked to the "war on terrorism" had become the largest single source, overtaking inflows from Japan, but was slashed in 2004 due to continuing human rights abuses.

DEFENSE

Phasing out conscription

$1.8bn

Up 3% in 2002

Uzbekistan has a standing army of around 40,000 personnel, mainly conscripts, as well as over 17,000 internal security troops and a 1000-strong National Guard. The military is being restructured, with a view to full professionalization of the armed forces.

A policy of mining the land borders with Kyrgyzstan and Uzbekistan to thwart incursions by Islamist militants has drawn international criticism.

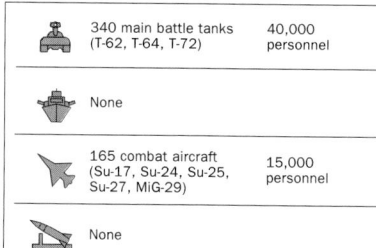

UZBEK ARMED FORCES

340 main battle tanks (T-62, T-64, T-72)	40,000 personnel
None	
165 combat aircraft (Su-17, Su-24, Su-25, Su-27, MiG-29)	15,000 personnel
None	

ECONOMICS

Inflation 211% p.a. (1990–2001)

$7.85bn

1020 som (974)

SCORE CARD

World GNP Ranking	98th
GNP per Capita	$310
Balance of Payments	$239m
Inflation	45.5%
Unemployment	10%

EXPORTS

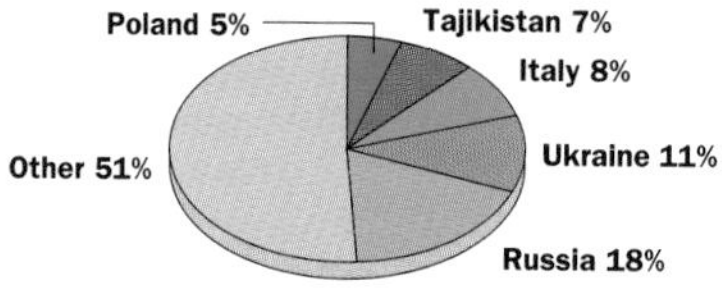
Poland 5%
Tajikistan 7%
Italy 8%
Ukraine 11%
Russia 18%
Other 51%

IMPORTS

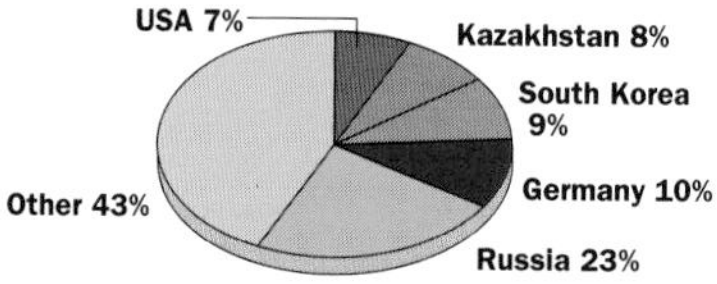
USA 7%
Kazakhstan 8%
South Korea 9%
Germany 10%
Russia 23%
Other 43%

ECONOMIC PERFORMANCE INDICATOR

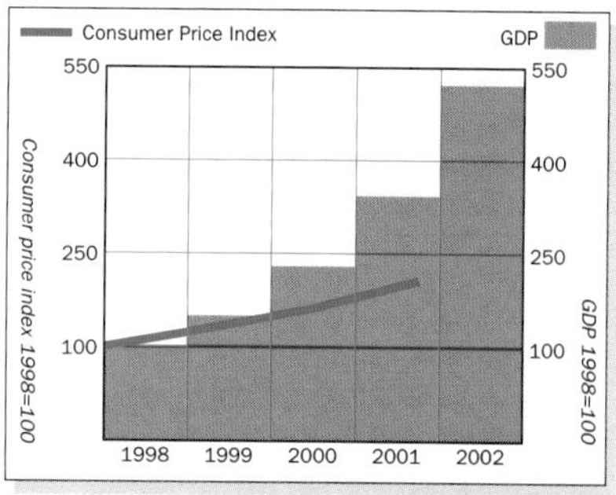
Consumer Price Index
GDP
550
400
250
100
Consumer price index 1998=100
GDP 1998=100
1998
1999
2000
2001
2002

Strengths

Gold. Well-developed cotton market. Considerable unexploited deposits of oil and natural gas. Current production of natural gas makes significant contribution to electricity generation. Manufacturing tradition includes agricultural machinery and central Asia's first aviation factory.

Weaknesses

Dependent on grain imports, as domestic production meets only 25% of needs. Very limited economic reform. High inflation. Environmentally damaging irrigation scheme for cotton production.

Profile

With the exception of Tashkent, which became an industrial area during World War II, Uzbekistan's economy is predominantly agricultural. Promarket reforms have been slow, despite fresh assistance from the World Bank to increase the efficiency of privatized companies. The gold sector has attracted investment from US companies. Energy resources are still to be fully exploited. The som was devalued by 50% in 2001.

UZBEKISTAN : MAJOR BUSINESSES

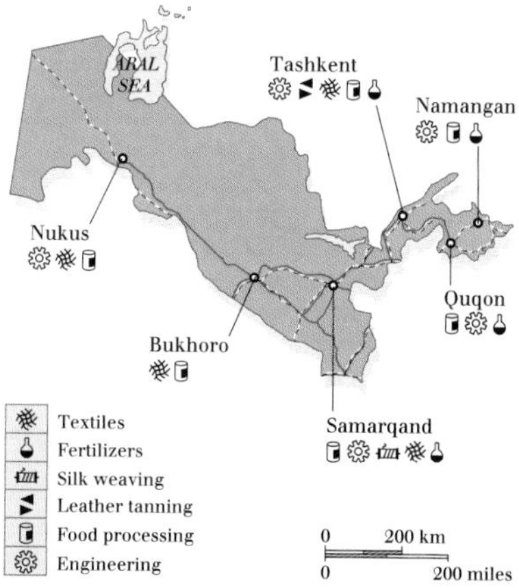
ARAL SEA
Tashkent
Namangan
Nukus
Quqon
Bukhoro
Samarqand
Textiles
Fertilizers
Silk weaving
Leather tanning
Food processing
Engineering
0 200 km
0 200 miles

U

RESOURCES

Electric power 11.7m kW

8152 tonnes

166,000 b/d (reserves 600m barrels)

8.2m sheep, 5.4m cattle, 14.5m chickens

Natural gas, coal, oil, gold, uranium, copper, tungsten, aluminum

ELECTRICITY GENERATION

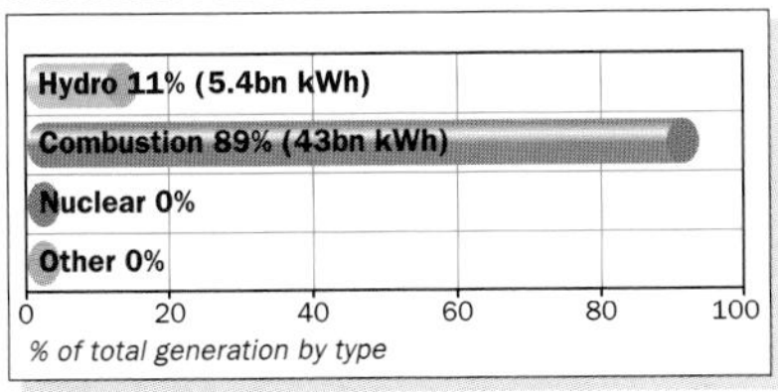

Hydro 11% (5.4bn kWh)
Combustion 89% (43bn kWh)
Nuclear 0%
Other 0%
0
20
40
60
80
100
% of total generation by type

UZBEKISTAN : LAND USE
ARAL SEA
KYZYL KUM
Amu Darya
Cropland
Pasture
Forest
High mountain regions
Desert
Wetlands
Sheep
Cotton - cash crop
0
200 km
0
200 miles

Uzbekistan has one of the world's largest gold mines, at Murantau in the Kyzyl Kum desert, and also large deposits of natural gas, oil, coal, and uranium. An important oil field was discovered in 1992 in the Namangan region and production will rise with further investment. Most gas produced is currently used domestically, but it could also become a strong export.

Cotton is the main focus of agriculture: Uzbekistan is the world's fifth-largest producer. A decision after independence to diversify was reversed when the value of cotton as a commodity on the world market became clear. Fruit, silk cocoons, and vegetables for Russian markets are also of rising importance.

ENVIRONMENT

Sustainability rank: 118th

2%

4.8 tonnes per capita

ENVIRONMENTAL TREATIES

Yes	Yes	Yes
Yes	Yes	Yes

The irrigation schemes required to sustain the cotton industry have wreaked considerable environmental damage. Soil salination is now a major problem. The Aral Sea has also been seriously depleted. It has shrunk in size by more than half in the last 30 years and is now divided in two. In 2004 the World Bank backed a $75 million project to save the Aral Sea region; the southern section is to be left to dry up completely. The indiscriminate use of fertilizers and pesticides to increase production has polluted many rivers.

MEDIA

TV ownership medium

Daily newspaper circulation 3 per 1000 people

PUBLISHING AND BROADCAST MEDIA

There are 3 daily newspapers, including the Uzbek *Khalk suzi* and the Russian *Pravda Vostoka*

2 state-controlled services, 35 private stations

2 state-controlled services, over 15 private stations

Uzbekistan's restrictions on independent publications are designed to encourage the promotion of the personality cult and policies of Karimov, and manifest themselves both in overt censorship and self-censorship by media outlets. Independent journalists face harassment. The expression of Islamist and nationalist opinion is forbidden.

CRIME

Death penalty in use

48,000 prisoners

Down 2% in 2000–2002

CRIME RATES

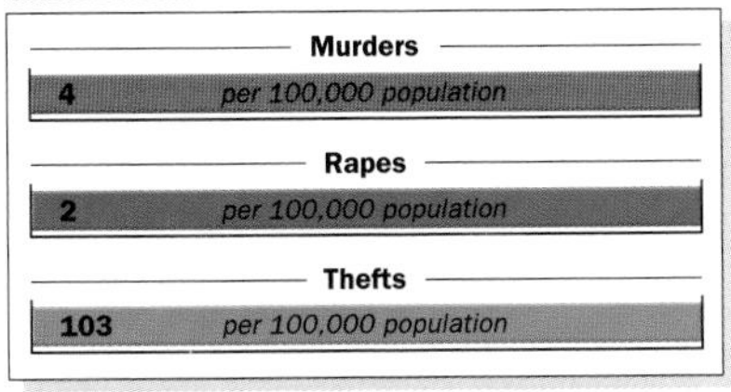

Murders
4
per 100,000 population
Rapes
2
per 100,000 population
Thefts
103
per 100,000 population

Crime rose in the 1990s as living standards declined. In 2001 the number of crimes carrying the death penalty was reduced to four. Unofficial Islamic courts in the Fergana Valley are a sign of opposition to the government.

EDUCATION

School leaving age: 18

99%

183,600 students

THE EDUCATION SYSTEM

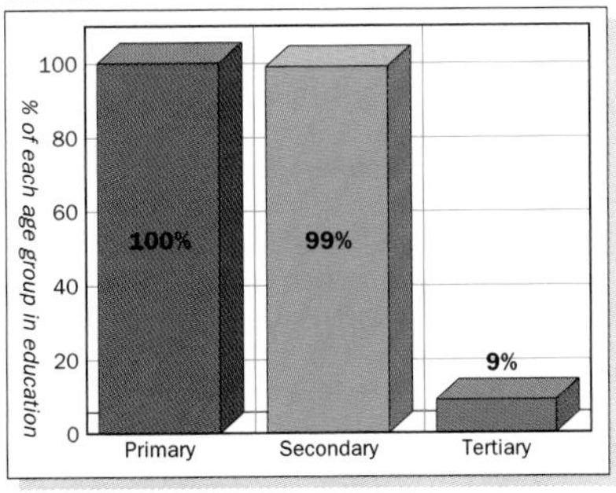

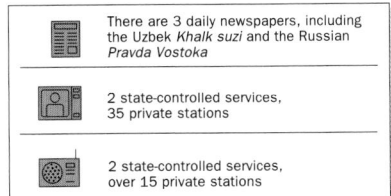

100
80
60
40
20
0
% of each age group in education
100%
99%
9%
Primary
Secondary
Tertiary

The state system still follows the Soviet model, though some instruction is in Uzbek. In the late 1980s, there were a few ethnic Tajik schools and a university in Samarqand. These were closed down in 1992 as relations deteriorated between Uzbekistan and Tajikistan. The rise in Islamic consciousness has led to a growing number of *madaris* – schools attached to mosques. In 1999 the establishment of Tashkent Islamic University was agreed.

HEALTH

Welfare state health benefits

1 per 345 people

Heart, respiratory, and cerebrovascular diseases, cancers

The health service has been in decline since the dissolution of the USSR. Some rural areas are not served at all. In 1998 a $69.7 million project to improve health services was announced, with the World Bank providing a loan of some $30 million. Serious respiratory diseases among cotton growers are increasing.

SPENDING

GDP/cap. increase

CONSUMPTION AND SPENDING

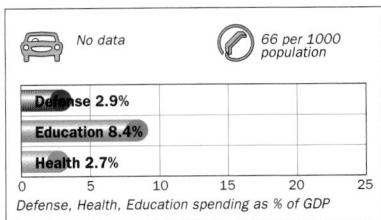

No data

66 per 1000 population

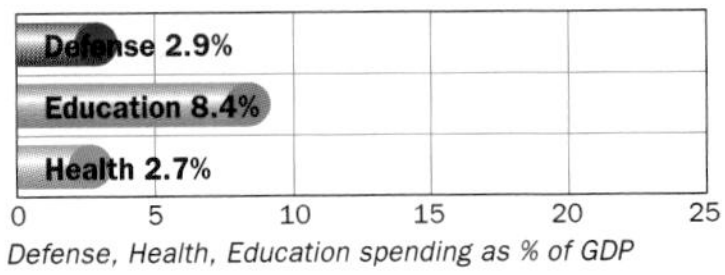

Defense 2.9%
Education 8.4%
Health 2.7%
0
5
10
15
20
25
Defense, Health, Education spending as % of GDP

Former communists are still the wealthiest group, since they retain control of the economy. Many rural poor live below the poverty line.

WORLD RANKING

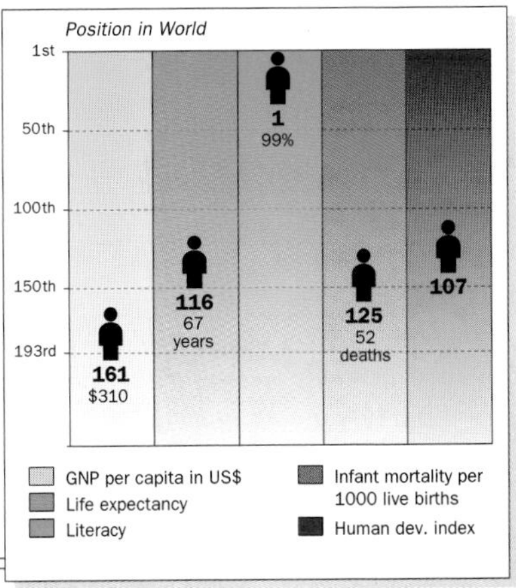

Position in World
1st
50th
100th
150th
193rd
161
$310
116
67
years
1
99%
125
52
deaths
107
GNP per capita in US$
Life expectancy
Literacy
Infant mortality per 1000 live births
Human dev. index

U

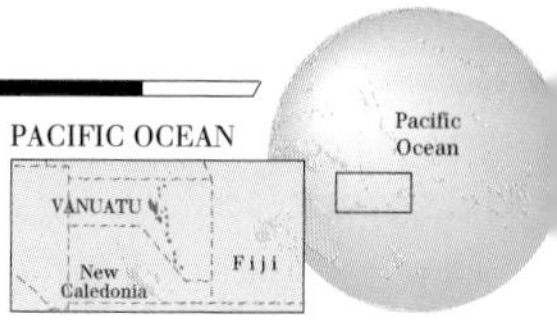

PACIFIC OCEAN
VANUATU
New Caledonia
Fiji
Pacific Ocean

VANUATU

OFFICIAL NAME: Republic of Vanuatu **CAPITAL:** Port Vila
POPULATION: 212,000 **CURRENCY:** Vatu **OFFICIAL LANGUAGES:** Bislama, English, and French

1980 | 1980 | July 30 | VU | +11 | +678 | .vu

THE ARCHIPELAGO OF Vanuatu stretches over 1300 km (800 miles) in the South Pacific. Mountainous and volcanic in origin, only 12 of the 82 islands are a significant size – Espiritu Santo and Malekula are the largest. Formerly known as the New Hebrides – ruled jointly by France and Britain from 1906 – Vanuatu became independent in 1980. Politics since then has been democratic but volatile.

CLIMATE
Tropical oceanic

WEATHER CHART FOR PORT VILA

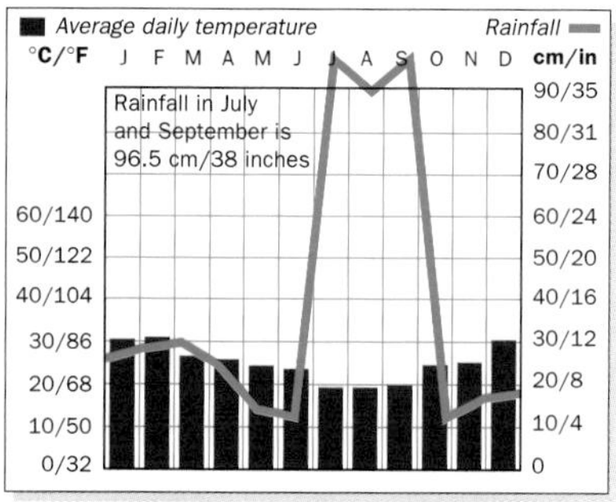

Average daily temperature
Rainfall
°C/°F
J F M A M J J A S O N D
cm/in
Rainfall in July and September is 96.5 cm/38 inches
90/35
80/31
70/28
60/24
50/20
40/16
30/12
20/8
10/4
0
60/140
50/122
40/104
30/86
20/68
10/50
0/32

The climate is tropical and hot. Rainfall and temperatures decrease north to south. Cyclones occur November–April.

TRANSPORTATION
Drive on right

Bauerfield, Port Vila

321 ships 1.38m grt

THE TRANSPORTATION NETWORK

257 km (160 miles)	None
None	None

Road quality is generally poor, with routes on some remote islands impassable in the wet season.

TOURISM
Visitors : Population 1:4.2

50,400 visitors

Up 29% in 2003

MAIN TOURIST ARRIVALS

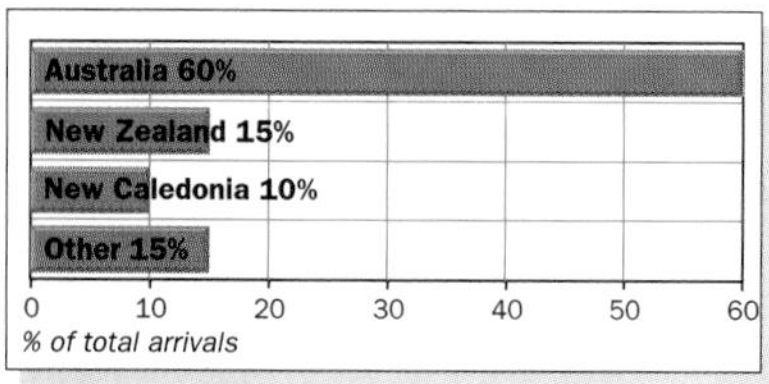

Australia 60%
New Zealand 15%
New Caledonia 10%
Other 15%
0
10
20
30
40
50
60
% of total arrivals

Tourism in Vanuatu is facing stiff competition from cheaper regional rivals. Organized tours include sea fishing, sailing, kayaking, and diving.

PEOPLE
Pop. density low

Bislama (Melanesian pidgin), English, French, other indigenous languages

17/km² (45/mi²)

THE URBAN/RURAL POPULATION SPLIT

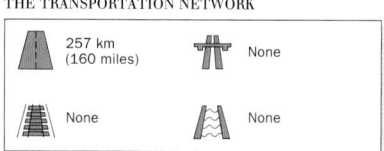

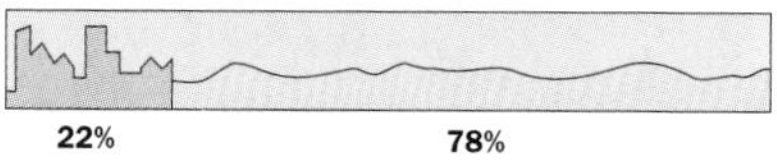

22%
78%

RELIGIOUS PERSUASION

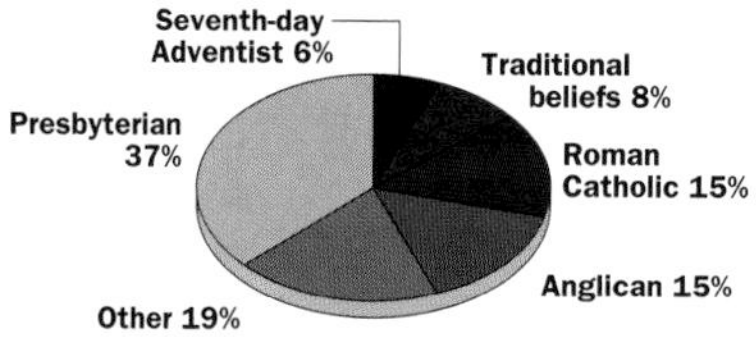

Seventh-day Adventist 6%
Traditional beliefs 8%
Presbyterian 37%
Roman Catholic 15%
Anglican 15%
Other 19%

Indigenous Melanesians – ni-Vanuatu – comprise 94% of the population. Of Vanuatu's 82 islands, 67 are inhabited, but 80% of people live on 12 main islands. The population is becoming more urbanized and one in eight ni-Vanuatu now lives in Port Vila. However, 60% of the population still live by subsistence agriculture.

Vanuatu is home to some of the Pacific's most traditional peoples, and local social and religious customs are strong. With 105 indigenous languages, Vanuatu boasts the world's highest per capita density of languages. Bislama pidgin is the lingua franca.

Women have lower social status than men, and bride price is still commonly paid. Many educated women refuse to marry because of loss of property rights. To boost equality, primary schools are encouraged to take girls.

***Vanuatu's unspoiled beaches** are one of the reasons for the upsurge in the tourist industry.*

POLITICS
Multiparty elections

2004/2006

President Kalkot Mataskelekele

AT THE LAST ELECTION

Parliament 52 seats

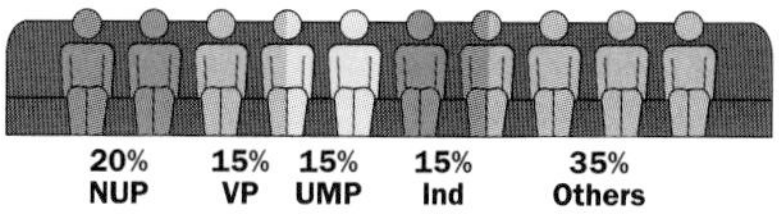

20% NUP
15% VP
15% UMP
15% Ind
35% Others

NUP = National United Party **VP** = Vanua'aku Pati
UMP = Union of Moderate Parties **Ind** = Independents

Ni-Vanuatu politics is best described as anarchic. Political allegiances are swiftly changed and governments frequently toppled. Independence leader Fr. Walter Lini remained a powerful political figure despite being ousted as VP leader and premier in 1991. He went on to lead the NUP until his death in 1999.

Power has shifted between shaky coalitions headed by either the VP (1980–1991) or the UMP (1991–2001). A grand coalition between the two parties, forged in 2001 under Edward Natapei of the VP, came undone amid infighting in late 2003. Natapei's next coalition was brought down by a series of defections. Fresh elections in 2004 again left no faction with enough seats to form a government. A shaky coalition led by Serge Vohor of the UMP was shored up by the addition of the 10-seat NUP.

WORLD AFFAIRS
Joined UN in 1981

OIF | Comm | NAM | PC | PIF

Political instability prompted France to recognize independence only reluctantly in 1980. The UK, on the other hand, did not share its partner's hesitation. The anti-French VP government of the day accused France of supporting an abortive bid for independence by Espiritu Santo that year. Vanuatu was the first South Pacific state to gain full membership of the Non-Aligned Movement. In 2002–2003 it was forced by the OECD to improve financial transparency.

AID
Recipient

$28m (receipts)

Down 13% in 2002

Vanuatu is heavily dependent on aid. Leading donors include Australia, France, the ADB, the EU, Japan, and New Zealand. Vanuatu is classed by the UN as a Least Developed Country (LDC), and as such receives guaranteed aid support.

V

DEFENSE

No compulsory military service

There is no army | Not applicable

There is no army. A small paramilitary force receives training from the US. Papua New Guinean troops helped to end the 1980 secessionist movement on Espiritu Santo.

ECONOMICS

Inflation 2.9% p.a. (1990–2001)

$221m | 116.3 vatu (120.5)

SCORE CARD

- ❑ WORLD GNP RANKING........................183rd
- ❑ GNP PER CAPITA $1070
- ❑ BALANCE OF PAYMENTS.......................–$15m
- ❑ INFLATION 2.1%
- ❑ UNEMPLOYMENT ....Low

STRENGTHS

Expanding services sector, including tourism. Major economic reforms instituted, including introduction of value-added tax and resizing public service in return for assistance from ADB. Large fishing potential.

WEAKNESSES

Large trade and budget deficits. Rate of growth stagnating: contracted in 1999 and 2001. Offshore banking stopped after international pressure. Dependence on agricultural sector, vulnerable to adverse weather and fluctuating market prices.

EXPORTS

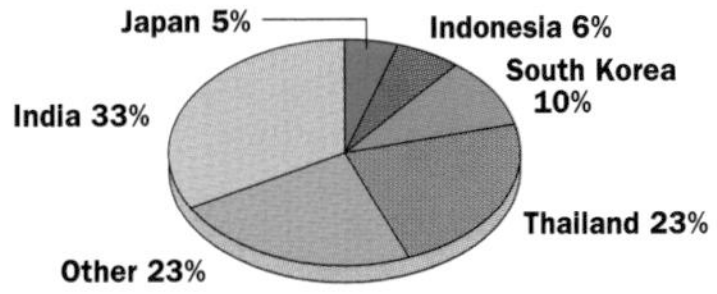
Japan 5%
Indonesia 6%
South Korea 10%
India 33%
Thailand 23%
Other 23%

IMPORTS

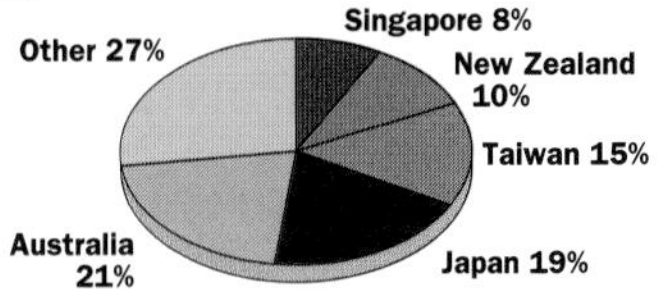
Singapore 8%
Other 27%
New Zealand 10%
Taiwan 15%
Australia 21%
Japan 19%

RESOURCES

Electric power 12,000 kW

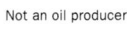

26,690 tonnes | Not an oil producer

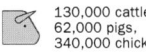

130,000 cattle, 62,000 pigs, 340,000 chickens | None

Vanuatu's main resources are its arable land – only partly utilized – and its forests and waters. These could be exploited by the tourist, timber, and fishing industries. New export crops are being explored to offset declining copra and cocoa exports. Beef is of growing importance. Nuclear power development was banned under 1983 legislation.

VANUATU

Total Area : 12 200 sq. km (4710 sq. miles)

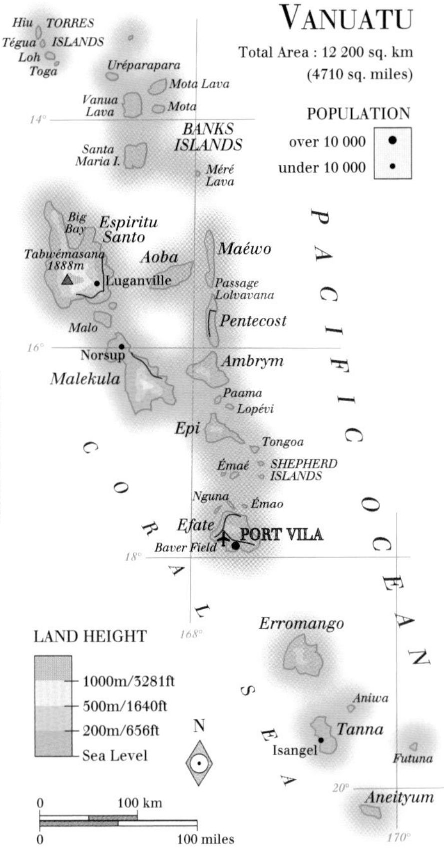
POPULATION
over 10 000
under 10 000
Hiu
TORRES ISLANDS
Tégua
Loh
Toga
Uréparapara
Mota Lava
Vanua Lava
Mota
BANKS ISLANDS
Santa Maria I.
Méré Lava
Big Bay
Espiritu Santo
Tabwémasana 1888m
Luganville
Aoba
Maéwo
Passage Lolvavana
Pentecost
Malo
Norsup
Malekula
Ambrym
Paama
Lopévi
Epi
Tongoa
Émaé
SHEPHERD ISLANDS
Nguna
Émao
Efate
PORT VILA
Bauer Field
PACIFIC OCEAN
CORAL SEA
Erromango
Aniwa
Tanna
Isangel
Futuna
Aneityum
LAND HEIGHT
1000m/3281ft
500m/1640ft
200m/656ft
Sea Level
N
0 100 km
0 100 miles

ENVIRONMENT

Not available

0.2% partially protected | 0.4 tonnes per capita

Logging is increasing, but most of the rainforest remains intact, and roundwood exports are banned.

Population growth is high, at nearly 3% a year, but is falling. A majority of the population does not have access to a potable and reliable water supply.

MEDIA

TV ownership low

Daily newspaper circulation is very low

PUBLISHING AND BROADCAST MEDIA

There is 1 daily newspaper, the *Vanuatu Daily Post*. A number of weeklies are published in Bislama, English, and French

1 state-owned limited service | 1 state-owned service

The *Vanuatu Weekly* appears in each official language. Television Blong Vanuatu broadcasts four hours a day.

CRIME

No death penalty

96 prisoners | Little change from year to year

The Australian aid agency AusAID is funding a $1.4 million reform program for the Vanuatu police service.

CHRONOLOGY

In 1906, Britain and France set up the New Hebrides under joint rule.

- ❑ **1980** Independence; Walter Lini prime minister (until 1991). Secession bid by Espiritu Santo.
- ❑ **1999** Tidal wave. Death of Lini.
- ❑ **2002** Vanuatu's first ever hailstorm hits Tanna.
- ❑ **2003** Reforms take Vanuatu off blacklist of tax havens.
- ❑ **2004** Serge Vohor prime minister.

EDUCATION

Schooling is not compulsory

34% | 52 students

The abolition of fees has helped to boost primary enrollment. Illiteracy is a major concern.

HEALTH

Welfare state health benefits

1 per 10,000 people | Heart diseases, cancers, malaria

A network of rural clinics and village health workers has helped to improve health levels. Nominal fees are charged.

SPENDING

GDP/cap. decrease

CONSUMPTION AND SPENDING

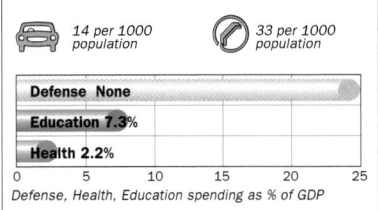

14 per 1000 population | *33 per 1000 population*

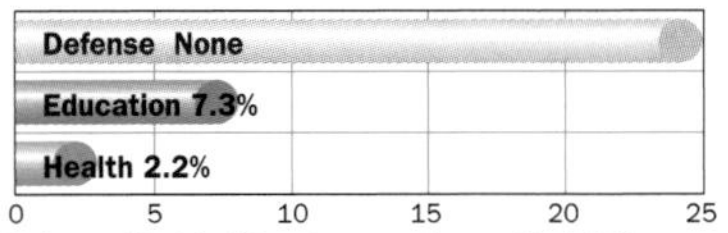
Defense None
Education 7.3%
Health 2.2%
0
5
10
15
20
25

Defense, Health, Education spending as % of GDP

The dominance of subsistence farming and small-scale cash cropping has helped to prevent extreme poverty. Most of the rich are not ni-Vanuatu.

WORLD RANKING

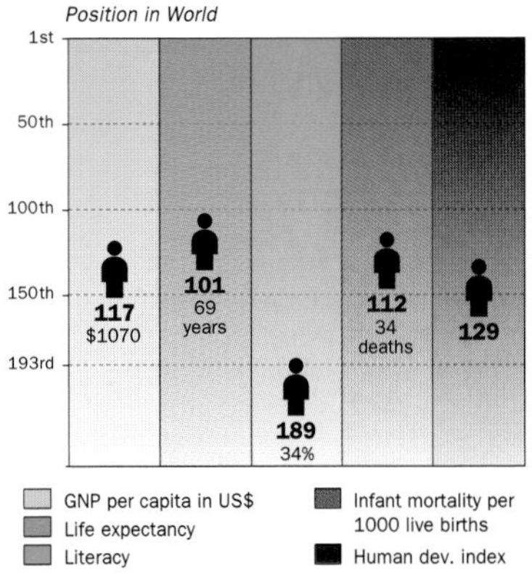
Position in World
1st
50th
100th
150th
193rd
117
$1070
101
69 years
189
34%
112
34 deaths
129
GNP per capita in US$
Life expectancy
Literacy
Infant mortality per 1000 live births
Human dev. index

V

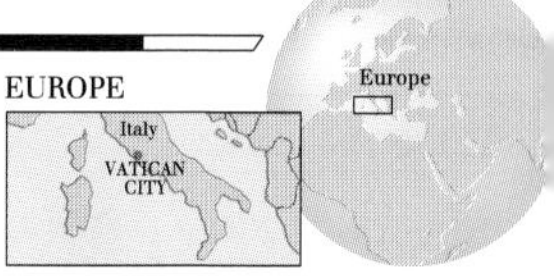
EUROPE
Europe
Italy
VATICAN CITY

VATICAN CITY

OFFICIAL NAME: State of the Vatican City **CAPITAL:** Vatican City
POPULATION: 911 **CURRENCY:** Euro **OFFICIAL LANGUAGES:** Italian and Latin

THE VATICAN CITY, which lies in central Rome, is the world's smallest independent state. It includes ten other buildings in Rome and also the pope's summer residence at Castel Gandolfo. As the Holy See it is the seat of the Roman Catholic Church, deriving its income from investments and voluntary contributions known as Peter's Pence.

***The buildings and gardens** of the Vatican City. St. Peter's Basilica was built from 1506–1626 on the traditional site of St. Peter's tomb.*

CLIMATE

Mediterranean

WEATHER CHART FOR THE VATICAN CITY

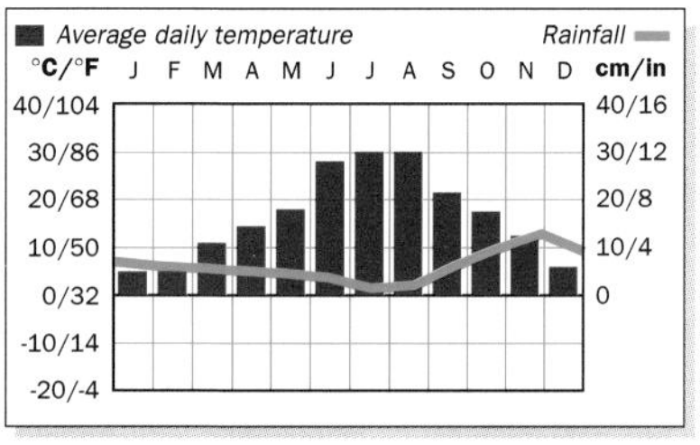
Average daily temperature
Rainfall
°C/°F
J F M A M J J A S O N D
cm/in
40/104
30/86
20/68
10/50
0/32
-10/14
-20/-4
40/16
30/12
20/8
10/4
0

Summers are hot; winters are mild. November is particularly rainy.

TRANSPORTATION

Drive on right

Heliport for official visitors

Has no fleet

THE TRANSPORTATION NETWORK

None	None
1 km (0.6 miles)	None

The railroad is used only for carrying freight. Official visitors are transferred from Rome airport by helicopter.

TOURISM

Not available

The Vatican museums can accommodate 20,000 visitors daily

Little change from year to year

MAIN TOURIST ARRIVALS

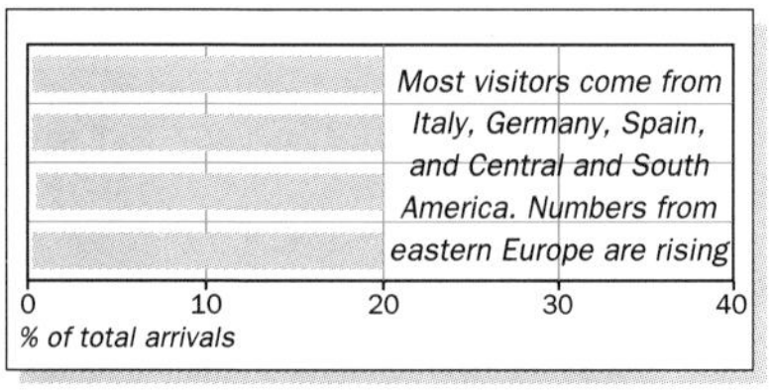
Most visitors come from Italy, Germany, Spain, and Central and South America. Numbers from eastern Europe are rising
0
10
20
30
40
% of total arrivals

Almost all tourists who visit Rome go to the Vatican, while others come as pilgrims. Up to 100,000 hear the pope's annual Easter Message in St. Peter's Square. The Vatican's art collections are among the greatest in the world. Years of restoration work on the Sistine Chapel frescoes were completed in 1999.

PEOPLE

Pop. density high

Italian, Latin

2070/km² (5359/mi²)

THE URBAN/RURAL POPULATION SPLIT

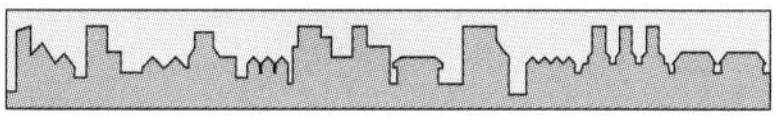

100%

RELIGIOUS PERSUASION

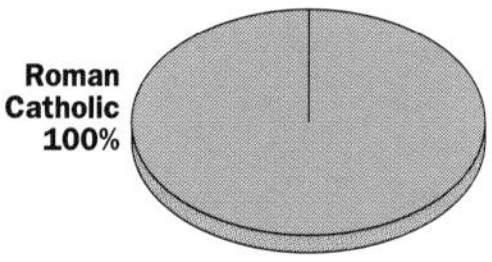
Roman Catholic 100%

The Vatican has more than 900 citizens, including over 100 lay persons. Several hundred more lay staff are employed in the city-state. Citizenship can be acquired through stable residence and holding an office or job within the City. A citizen's family can gain residence only by authorization.

The pope is the spiritual leader of around 17% of the world's population. The countries with the largest number of Roman Catholics are Brazil, Mexico, Italy, the US, and the Philippines.

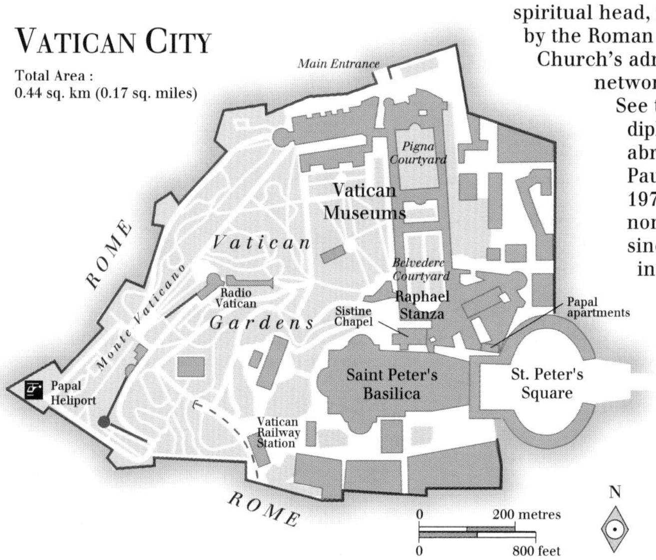
VATICAN CITY
Total Area :
0.44 sq. km (0.17 sq. miles)
Main Entrance
Pigna Courtyard
Vatican Museums
Vatican
Gardens
ROME
Monte Vaticano
Radio Vatican
Belvedere Courtyard
Raphael Stanza
Sistine Chapel
Papal apartments
Saint Peter's Basilica
St. Peter's Square
Papal Heliport
Vatican Railway Station
ROME
0
200 metres
0
800 feet
N

POLITICS

No legislative elections

On death of reigning pope

His Holiness Pope John Paul II

LEGISLATIVE OR ADVISORY BODIES

Sacred College of Cardinals 120 seats

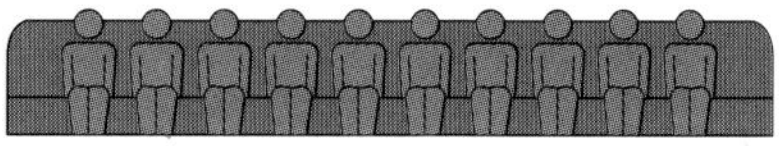

Cardinals under the age of 80 are eligible to elect a new pope. There are no political parties.

The Vatican City operates in the manner of an elected monarchy, as the reigning pope has supreme executive, legislative, and judicial powers, and holds office for life. He is elected by the College of Cardinals, who vote until one candidate for the position of Supreme Pontiff achieves a two-thirds majority.

The administration of the Vatican City State, of which the pope is temporal head, is conducted by the Pontifical Commission. The Holy See, which is the governing body of the Roman Catholic Church worldwide and of which the pope is spiritual head, is governed by the Roman Curia, the Church's administrative network. It is the Holy See that maintains diplomatic relations abroad. Pope John Paul II, elected in 1978, was the first non-Italian pope since 1523. Now in his 80s, he continues to fulfill his duties despite visibly suffering from Parkinson's disease and arthritis.

V

WORLD AFFAIRS

Not a UN member

OSCE | IAEA

The Vatican is neutral, with observer status in many international organizations, but papal opinion greatly influences the world's one billion Catholics. In 2003 John Paul II was vital in building support in his native Poland for its membership of the EU. He has traveled more extensively than any other pope, completing his 100th foreign visit (to Croatia) in 2003. Trips are used to promote political as well as religious dialogue. In 2000 the pope made an unprecedented apology for 2000 years of anti-Judaism and in 2001 he became the first pope to enter (and pray in) a mosque and the first to visit Orthodox Christian Greece.

AID

Donor

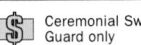

Undisclosed | Undisclosed

Aid is donated through the pope's charities (such as the Holy Childhood Association, which distributes around $15 million a year to children's causes), through funds donated for use at the pope's discretion, and through religious orders acting under papal charter.

DEFENSE

No compulsory military service

Ceremonial Swiss Guard only | Not applicable

The Vatican is strictly neutral territory. Under the 1954 Hague Convention, it is recognized as "a moral, artistic, and cultural patrimony worthy of being respected as a treasure for all mankind."

ECONOMICS

Not applicable

Not applicable | 0.822 euros (0.871)

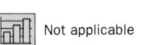

SCORE CARD

- WORLD GNP RANKING ....*The Vatican*
- GNP PER CAPITA ....*does not have*
- BALANCE OF PAYMENTS ....*a national*
- INFLATION ....*economy in the*
- UNEMPLOYMENT ....*usual sense*

STRENGTHS

Istituto per le Opere di Religione has assets of $3–4 billion. Interest on investments. Voluntary contributions from Catholics worldwide (Peter's Pence). Gold reserves in Fort Knox, US. Stamp and coin issues. Receipts from tourists.

WEAKNESSES

Losses incurred by Radio Vaticana and *L'Osservatore Romano*. Cost of foreign papal visits, buildings maintenance, and diplomatic missions. Total lack of natural resources of any kind.

EXPORTS/IMPORTS

The Vatican produces no goods for export. All commodities are imported, mainly from Italy.

RESOURCES

Electric power: None

None | Not an oil producer

None | None

The Vatican imports all its energy. It has no farmland; its area is restricted to buildings and their formal gardens.

ENVIRONMENT

Not available

None | Not available

The Vatican is increasingly concerned about the need to balance development and conservation. In 1993, the pope urged a gathering of scientists to press colleagues worldwide to inform people on the need to protect the environment.

MEDIA

TV ownership high

Daily newspaper circulation figures not available

PUBLISHING AND BROADCAST MEDIA

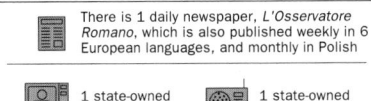

There is 1 daily newspaper, *L'Osservatore Romano*, which is also published weekly in 6 European languages, and monthly in Polish

1 state-owned service | 1 state-owned service

Radio Vaticana's longwave broadcasts are continuing after a brief suspension caused by concern over radiation.

CRIME

No death penalty

Prisoners are held in Italy | Minimal crime levels

The reputation of the 105-strong Swiss Guard was shaken in 1998, when a young guard shot dead his commandant and the latter's wife and then committed suicide. Three Vatican Bank officials were earlier alleged to have been involved in the Banco Ambrosiano affair.

EDUCATION

Not applicable

99% | 9389 students

The university, founded by Gregory XIII, is renowned for its theological and philosophical learning. There are more than 110,000 primary and secondary Catholic schools around the world.

CHRONOLOGY

The Vatican is located in Rome because tradition held that St. Peter was buried on the site of the Church of Constantine, which was pulled down in the Renaissance to make way for the building of St. Peter's Basilica. The Vatican has been the pope's usual residence since 1417, when the pontiffs returned from Avignon in France at the end of the 39 years of Great Schism.

- **1870** Italy annexes Papal States.
- **1929** Lateran Treaty – Fascist Italy accepts Vatican City as independent state.
- **1978** Cardinal Karol Wojtyla pope.
- **1981–1982** Attempts on pope's life.
- **1984** Catholicism disestablished as Italian state religion.
- **1985** Catholic Catechism revised for first time since 1566.
- **1994–1995** Opposition to abortion and contraception reiterated at UN conferences in Cairo and Beijing.
- **1998** Statement repenting Catholic passivity during Nazi Holocaust.
- **2000** Jubilee Year. Papal apology for Catholic violence and oppression over two millennia.
- **2001** John Paul II becomes first pope to enter a mosque.

HEALTH

Welfare state health benefits

Pope's own doctor is in permanent residence at Vatican | Heart and cardiovascular diseases, cancers

Pope John Paul II's strong opposition to abortion and contraception has prompted criticism from around the world, and from within the Church.

SPENDING

Not applicable

CONSUMPTION AND SPENDING

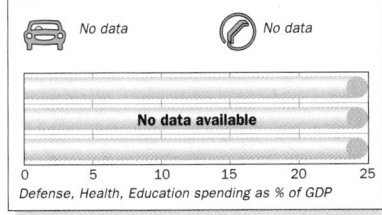

No data | *No data*

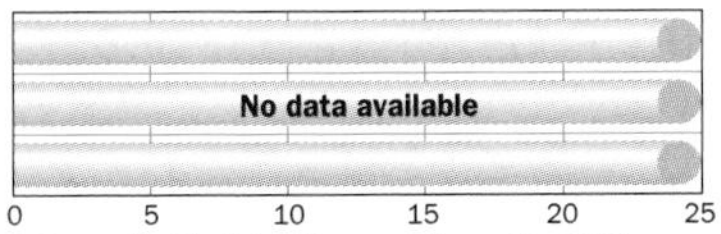
No data available
0
5
10
15
20
25
Defense, Health, Education spending as % of GDP

The wealth of the Vatican is primarily that of the Catholic Church. Its art treasures may not be sold. It is not known how much personal wealth its citizens have.

WORLD RANKING

The pope and his Vatican staff enjoy one of the highest standards of living in the world

V

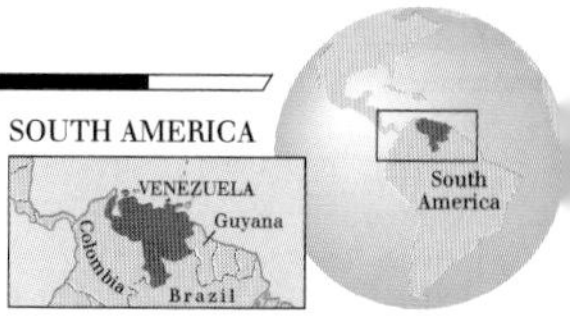
SOUTH AMERICA
VENEZUELA
Guyana
Colombia
Brazil
South America

VENEZUELA

OFFICIAL NAME: Bolivarian Republic of Venezuela **CAPITAL:** Caracas
POPULATION: 25.7 million **CURRENCY:** Bolívar **OFFICIAL LANGUAGE:** Spanish

1830
1830
July 5
YV
-4
+58
.ve

LOCATED IN THE NORTH of South America, with a long Caribbean coastline, Venezuela has a vast central plain (the Llanos) drained by the Orinoco, while the Guiana Highlands dominate the southwest of the country. A Spanish colony until 1811, Venezuela was lauded as Latin America's most stable democracy until its recent political upheavals. Though the country has some of the largest known oil deposits outside the Middle East, much of Venezuela's population still lives in shanty-town squalor.

President Hugo Chávez *changed the name of the country as part of his Bolivarian Revolution.*

CLIMATE

Tropical wet and dry/ equatorial

WEATHER CHART FOR CARACAS

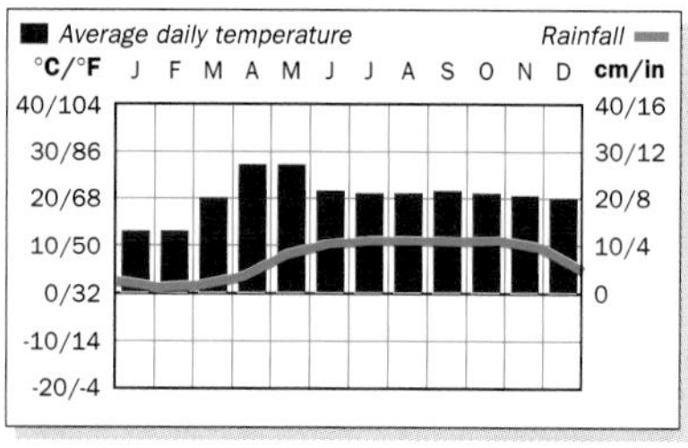
Average daily temperature
Rainfall
°C/°F J F M A M J J A S O N D cm/in
40/104
30/86
20/68
10/50
0/32
-10/14
-20/-4
40/16
30/12
20/8
10/4
0

The hot Maracaibo coast is surprisingly dry; the Orinoco Llanos are alternately parched or flooded. Uplands are cold.

TRANSPORTATION

Drive on right

Simón Bolívar International, Caracas 5.13m passengers

274 ships 865,400 grt

THE TRANSPORTATION NETWORK

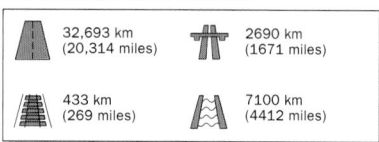

32,693 km (20,314 miles)

2690 km (1671 miles)

433 km (269 miles)

7100 km (4412 miles)

Massive road-building programs from the 1960s onward have benefited the oil and aluminum industries. Because of the limited railroad system, buses are the main form of transportation throughout most of the country. The French-designed subway in Caracas was completed in 1995.

The Orinoco. *The huge Llanos ("plains") are grazed by five million cattle, which are herded close to the river in the dry season.*

TOURISM

Visitors : Population 1:59

432,000 visitors

Down 8% in 2001–2002

MAIN TOURIST ARRIVALS

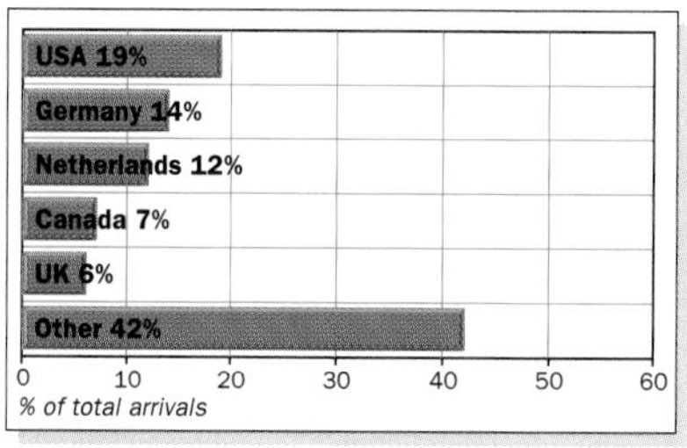
USA 19%
Germany 14%
Netherlands 12%
Canada 7%
UK 6%
Other 42%
0 10 20 30 40 50 60
% of total arrivals

Tourism is still a relatively minor industry in Venezuela, but one with enormous potential. Venezuela has many beaches that are the equal of any Caribbean island's, and a fascinating jungle interior which is a target for more adventurous tourists. For many years, the high value of the bolívar made Venezuela an expensive destination, but, after recent devaluations, it has become one of the cheapest in the Caribbean. Privatizing state-run hotels was part of a drive to attract foreign investment.

PEOPLE

Pop. density low

Spanish, Amerindian languages

29/km² (75/mi²)

THE URBAN/RURAL POPULATION SPLIT

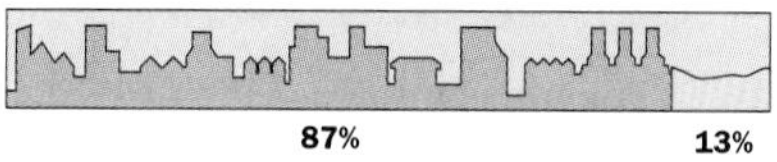
87%
13%

RELIGIOUS PERSUASION

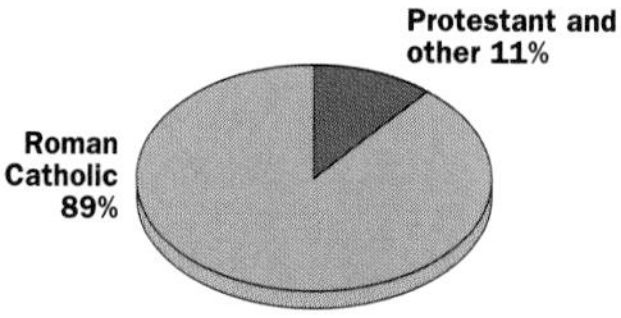
Protestant and other 11%
Roman Catholic 89%

ETHNIC MAKEUP

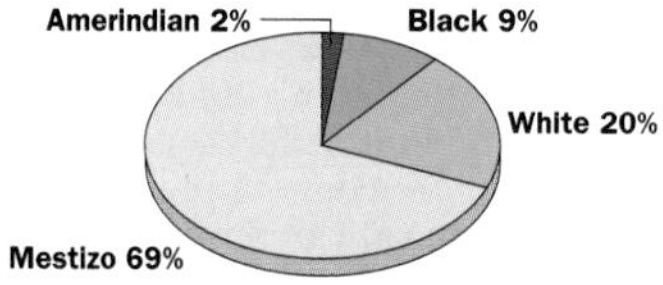
Amerindian 2%
Black 9%
White 20%
Mestizo 69%

Venezuela is one of the most highly urbanized societies in Latin America, with most of its population living in cities, mainly in the north. A historic "melting pot," it has experienced large-scale immigration from Italy, Portugal, Spain, and all over Latin America. There remains little of the white Hispanic aristocracy that survives in Colombia and Ecuador. The small number of native Amerindians, such as the Yanomami and Pemón, live in remote regions now threatened by illegal settlers. Most of the black population, who are descended from Africans brought over to work in the cacao industry in the 19th century, live along the Caribbean coast.

Oil wealth has brought comparative prosperity, but life in the *barrios* (shanty towns) which sprawl over the hillsides around Caracas is one of extreme poverty. Discontent peaked in the food riots of 1989 and 1991, leaving hundreds dead, along with the country's reputation for being a model democracy. The oil boom accelerated change for women, who today are to be found in all the professions. Politics, however, remains a largely masculine preserve. Oil wealth has also brought a measure of Americanization – boxing and baseball are among the most popular sports.

POPULATION AGE BREAKDOWN

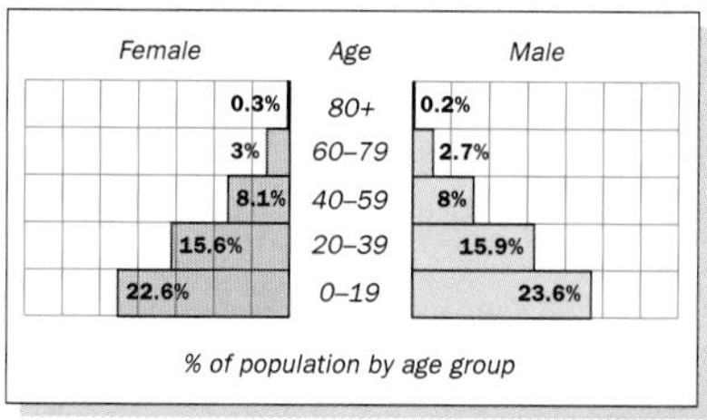
Female
Age
Male
0.3% 80+ 0.2%
3% 60–79 2.7%
8.1% 40–59 8%
15.6% 20–39 15.9%
22.6% 0–19 23.6%
% of population by age group

V

Key to symbols and abbreviations on cover flaps

VENEZUELA

Total Area : 912 050 sq. km (352 143 sq. miles)

POPULATION

- over 1 000 000
- over 500 000
- over 100 000
- over 50 000
- over 10 000

LAND HEIGHT

- 3000m/9843ft
- 2000m/6562ft
- 1000m/3281ft
- 500m/1640ft
- Sea Level

Projected Railway

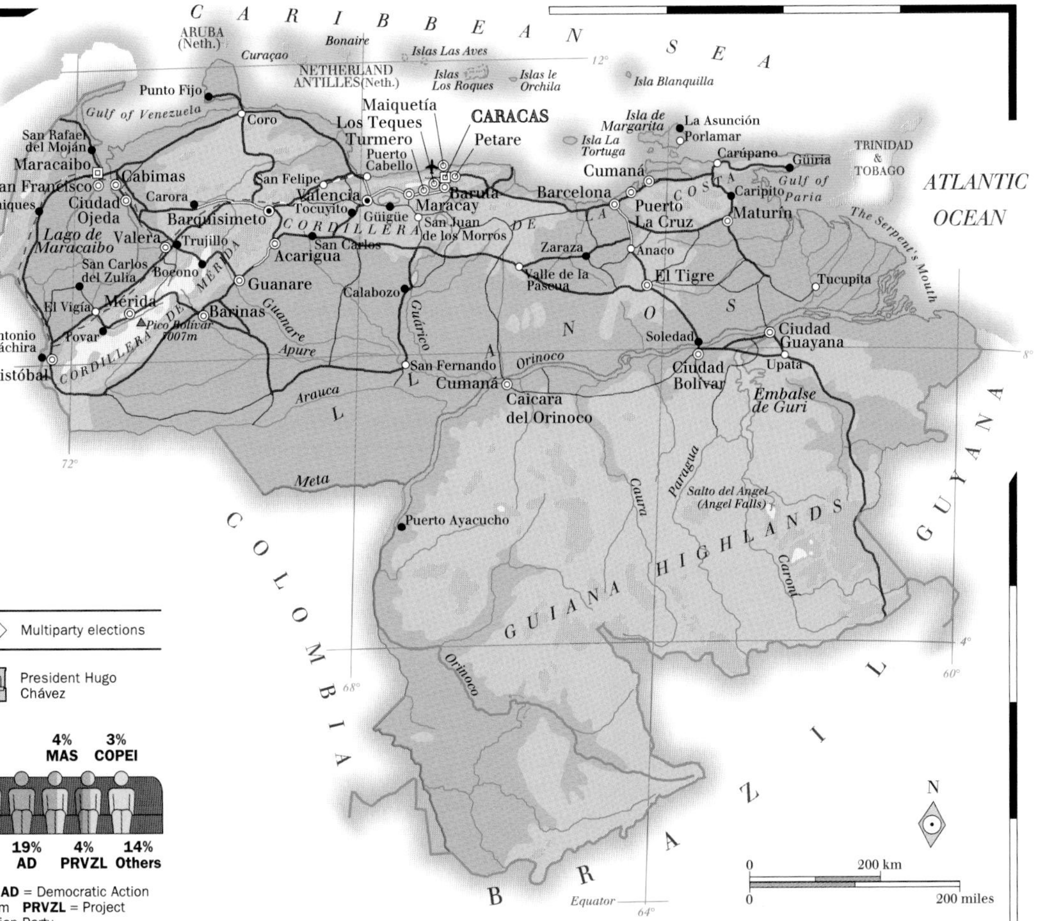

C A R I B B E A N S E A
ARUBA (Neth.)
Bonaire
Curaçao
Islas Las Aves
NETHERLAND ANTILLES(Neth.)
Islas Los Roques
Islas le Orchila
Isla Blanquilla
Punto Fijo
Gulf of Venezuela
Coro
Maiquetía
Los Teques
Turmero
Puerto Cabello
CARACAS
Petare
Isla de Margarita
La Asunción
Porlamar
Isla La Tortuga
Carúpano
Güiria
TRINIDAD & TOBAGO
ATLANTIC OCEAN
San Rafael del Moján
Maracaibo
Cabimas
San Francisco
Machiques
Ciudad Ojeda
Carora
San Felipe
Valencia
Tocuyito
Maracay
Baruta
Barcelona
Cumaná
Caripito
Gulf of Paria
Maturín
Puerto La Cruz
Barquisimeto
Güigüe
San Juan de los Morros
Lago de Maracaibo
Valera
Trujillo
San Carlos
Acarigua
Zaraza
Anaco
The Serpent's Mouth
San Carlos del Zulia
Boconó
Guanare
Calabozo
Valle de la Pascua
El Tigre
Tucupita
El Vigía
Mérida
Barinas
Pico Bolívar 5007m
San Antonio del Táchira
Tovar
San Cristóbal
Apure
Arauca
Guárico
San Fernando
Cumaná
Orinoco
Soledad
Ciudad Bolívar
Ciudad Guayana
Upata
Caicara del Orinoco
Embalse de Guri
Meta
Puerto Ayacucho
Caura
Paragua
Salto del Angel (Angel Falls)
Caroní
GUIANA HIGHLANDS
C O L O M B I A
G U Y A N A
B R A Z I L
Equator
N
0 200 km
0 200 miles

POLITICS

Multiparty elections

2000/2005

President Hugo Chávez

AT THE LAST ELECTION

National Assembly 165 seats

4% MAS
3% COPEI
56% MVR
19% AD
4% PRVZL
14% Others

MVR = Fifth Republic Movement **AD** = Democratic Action **MAS** = Movement toward Socialism **PRVZL** = Project Venezuela **COPEI** = Social Christian Party
The Patriotic Front (**PP**) comprises the MVR, the MAS, and some smaller parties

Venezuela is a multiparty democracy.

Profile

Hugo Chávez led a coup attempt in 1992, against a backdrop of corruption, poverty, austerity, and riots in Caracas. His election as president in 1998 broke the traditional parties' stranglehold on power and raised expectations among the poor.

He embarked on root and branch reform of the political and judicial systems, and enacted a new "Bolivarian" constitution. With his mandate renewed in 2000, his command-style running of the country fomented political opposition and deterred investment. A one-day military coup in April 2002 failed when officers changed tack following mass protests and the largely unfavorable international response. Restored to office, Chávez mollified rather than punished opponents, but was unable to prevent protests from spiraling later that year into a prolonged general strike which paralyzed the country.

Main Political Issues

Political stability

The general strike petered out in early 2003, but the opposition managed to force a referendum on Chávez's rule, in August 2004. Dissatisfaction continued despite a clear vote of support for the president.

Oil policy

Support of oil prices and quotas within OPEC remain central, despite Chávez's desire to use oil revenue to build a broader economy. The nine-week 2002–2003 general strike crippled the industry to the tune of billions of US dollars and forced the import of oil from Brazil.

WORLD AFFAIRS

Joined UN in 1945

ACS AP OAS OPEC RG

A traditionally pro-US orientation was challenged by Chávez, with his personal friendship with Cuba's Fidel Castro, visits to Libya and Iraq, and opposition to "Plan Colombia." The Bush administration acknowledged the new interim government during the April 2002 military coup, but denied helping to install it, though the main coup participants had made very public visits to the US State Department in preceding months. The OAS announced opposition to the coup, as did all of Venezuela's neighbors. Better regional economic integration with the Caribbean and Central and South America are important.

CHRONOLOGY

Venezuela was the first of the Spanish imperial colonies to repudiate Madrid's authority under the guidance of the revolutionary, Simón Bolívar, in 1811.

- **1821** Battle of Carabobo finally overthrows Spanish rule and leads to consolidation of independence within Gran Colombia (Venezuela, Colombia, and Ecuador).
- **1830** Gran Colombia collapses. José Antonio Páez rules Venezuela; coffee planters effectively in control.
- **1870** Guzmán Blanco in power. Rail system constructed.
- **1908** Gen. Juan Vicente Gómez dictator; oil industry developed.
- **1935** Gómez falls from power. Increasing mass participation in political process.
- **1945** Military coup. Rómulo Betancourt of AD takes power as leader of a civilian–military junta.
- **1948** AD wins elections, with novelist Rómulo Gallegos as presidential candidate. Military coup. Marcos Pérez Jiménez forms government, with US and military backing.

CHRONOLOGY *continued*

- **1958** General strike. Adm. Larrázabal leads military coup. Free elections. Betancourt, newly returned from exile, wins presidency election for AD. Anticommunist campaign mounted. A few state welfare programs introduced.
- **1960** Movement of the Revolutionary Left (MIR) splits from AD, begins antigovernment activities.
- **1961** Founder member of OPEC.
- **1962** Communist-backed guerrilla warfare attempts repetition of Cuban revolution in Venezuela; fails to gain popular support.
- **1963** Raúl Leoni (AD) elected president – first democratic transference of power. Antiguerrilla campaign continues.
- **1966** Unsuccessful coup attempt by supporters of former president, Pérez Jiménez.
- **1969** Rafael Caldera Rodríguez of COPEI becomes president. Continues Leoni policies.
- **1973** Oil and steel industries nationalized. World oil crisis. Currency peaks against US dollar.
- **1978** Elections won by COPEI's Luis Herrera Campíns. Disastrous economic programs.
- **1983** AD election victory under Jaime Lusinchi. Fall in world oil prices leads to unrest and cuts in state welfare.
- **1988** Carlos Andrés Pérez of AD wins presidency.
- **1989** Caracas food riots; 1500 dead.
- **1992** Attempted coup, led by Col. Hugo Chávez.
- **1993–1995** Andrés Pérez ousted for corruption; Caldera Rodríguez reelected. More social unrest.
- **1998–2000** Chávez and PP defeat COPEI-led coalition in elections; embark on radical political reform. New controversial Constituent Assembly approves new constitution, later endorsed by referendum. Chávez reelected. New unicameral National Assembly.
- **2002** April, Chávez ousted in military coup. Reinstalled a day later, after foreign and domestic protests. December, mass strike cripples economy (ends early 2003).
- **2004** Chávez wins approval in referendum called by opposition.

AID

Recipient

$57m (receipts) — Up 27% in 2002

The IDB provided loans totaling $52.5 million in 2002 for the promotion of child care and agricultural technology.

DEFENSE

Compulsory military service

$1.08bn — Down 43% in 2002

Chávez had led officers opposed to austerity and corruption in a 1992 coup attempt. Military leaders claimed in April 2002 that civil unrest forced them to oust him, and they backed interim president Pedro Carmona, who dissolved the National Assembly and Supreme Court by decree. After widespread protests middle-ranking officers got cold feet and rapidly reinstalled Chávez.

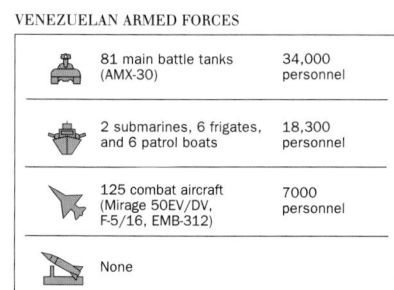

VENEZUELAN ARMED FORCES

81 main battle tanks (AMX-30)	34,000 personnel
2 submarines, 6 frigates, and 6 patrol boats	18,300 personnel
125 combat aircraft (Mirage 50EV/DV, F-5/16, EMB-312)	7000 personnel
None	

ECONOMICS

Inflation 43% p.a. (1990–2001)

$102bn — 2601 bolívares (1598)

SCORE CARD

World GNP Ranking	36th
GNP per Capita	$4080
Balance of Payments	$7.71bn
Inflation	22.4%
Unemployment	16%

EXPORTS

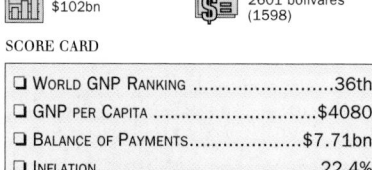

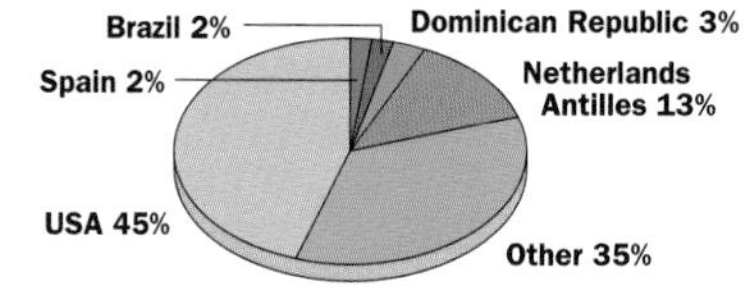
Brazil 2%
Dominican Republic 3%
Spain 2%
Netherlands Antilles 13%
USA 45%
Other 35%

IMPORTS

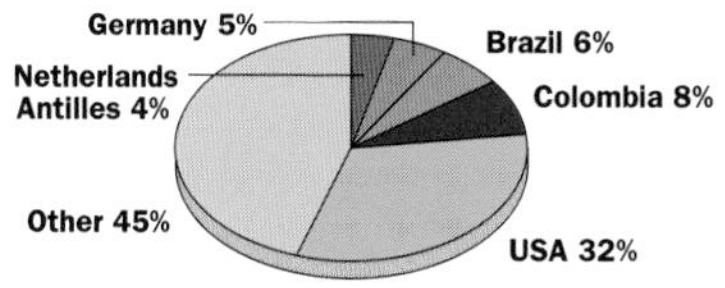
Germany 5%
Brazil 6%
Netherlands Antilles 4%
Colombia 8%
Other 45%
USA 32%

Strengths

Large proven oil deposits. Massive reserves of coal, bauxite, iron, and gold; successful development of new bitumen fuel which has attracted considerable foreign investment. Telecommunications, banking, iron, and steel also attract foreign capital. Producer of high-grade aluminum. Labor market becoming more flexible.

Weaknesses

Political instability. Huge, cumbersome state sector; despite some privatization, large areas still overmanned, inefficient, and subject to widespread corruption. Poor public services which, despite Venezuela's wealth during the oil-boom years, have been badly maintained. Fluctuations in world oil prices. Major infrastructure renewal is now long overdue. Widespread tax evasion.

Profile

Government finances have habitually been in crisis as a result of a culture of nonaccountability and patronage in state-owned industries and government bureaucracies. Privatizations and government cuts have failed to solve the problem. Promises by President Chávez to deal with excesses and diversify the economy, by promoting domestic processing industries over crude oil exports, have received a mixed response from investors, who favor more market-oriented reforms. A general strike in late 2002–early 2003 crippled the economy, especially the oil industry. The bolívar has been pegged to the US dollar on favorable terms since 2003. Its devaluation in 2004 increased the value of oil revenue, while rising world prices magnified the effect.

ECONOMIC PERFORMANCE INDICATOR

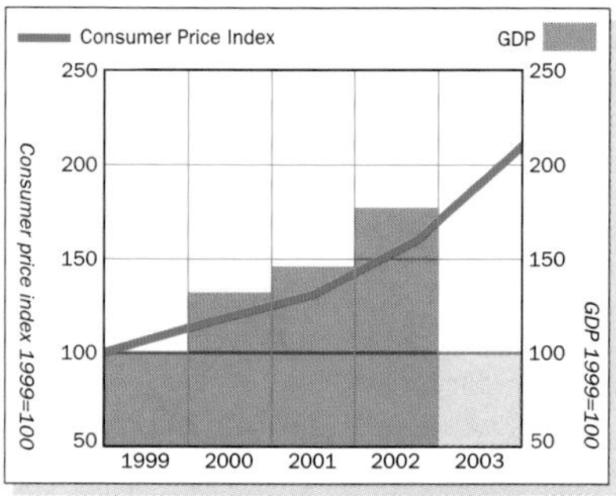
Consumer Price Index
GDP
250
200
150
100
50
Consumer price index 1999=100
GDP 1999=100
1999
2000
2001
2002
2003

VENEZUELA : MAJOR BUSINESSES

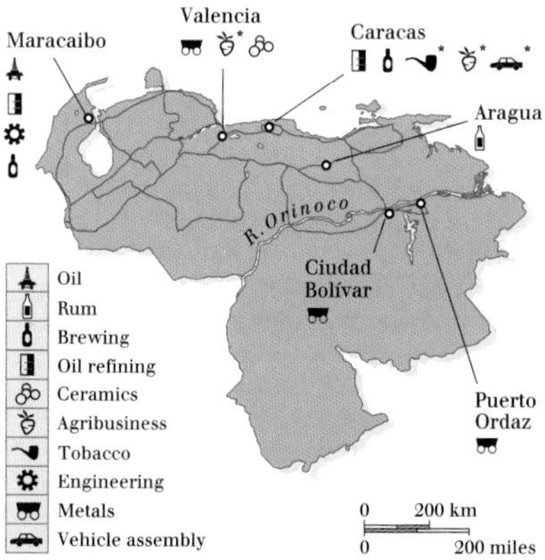
Maracaibo
Valencia
Caracas
Aragua
R. Orinoco
Ciudad Bolívar
Puerto Ordaz
Oil
Rum
Brewing
Oil refining
Ceramics
Agribusiness
Tobacco
Engineering
Metals
Vehicle assembly
0 200 km
0 200 miles

* significant multinational ownership

V

RESOURCES

Electric power 21.3m kW

434,569 tonnes

2.99m b/d (reserves 78bn barrels)

16.1m cattle, 2.92m pigs, 2.7m goats, 110m chickens

Oil, bauxite, iron, natural gas, coal, gold, diamonds, aluminum

ELECTRICITY GENERATION

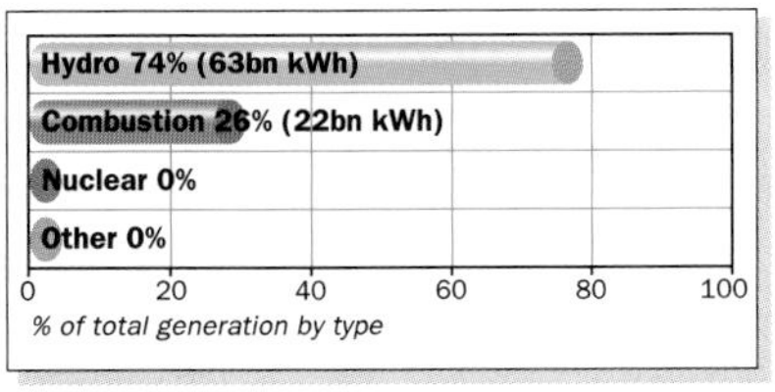
Hydro 74% (63bn kWh)
Combustion 26% (22bn kWh)
Nuclear 0%
Other 0%
0
20
40
60
80
100
% of total generation by type

Venezuela has a remarkable diversity of resources. It has the world's sixth-largest proven oil reserves, vast quantities of coal, iron ore, bauxite, and gold, and cheap hydroelectric power. Huge investment programs are currently under way to raise production in all these sectors as well as in oil-refining capacity. However, the Chávez government wants to cut the investment budget of the state oil company, PDVSA, reduce its output, and increase its contributions to the exchequer. Such uncertainty has deterred private investors. Venezuela has begun exploitation of Orimulsion, a new bitumen-based fuel from the Orinoco; commercially exploitable reserves are estimated at 270 billion barrels. Venezuela's aim to be the world's largest aluminum producer is threatened after difficulties associated with privatizing the sector.

VENEZUELA : LAND USE

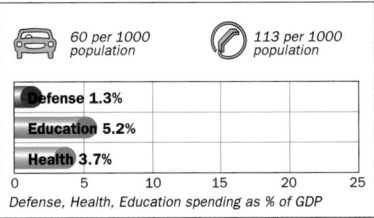

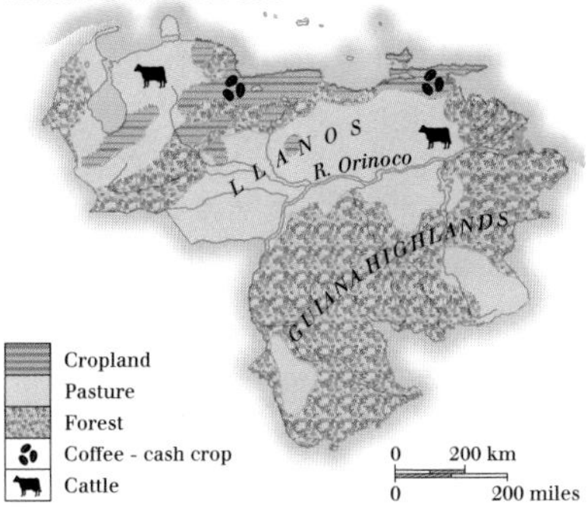
LLANOS
R. Orinoco
GUIANA HIGHLANDS
Cropland
Pasture
Forest
Coffee - cash crop
Cattle
0
200 km
0
200 miles

ENVIRONMENT

Sustainability rank: 48th

64% (40% partially protected)

6.5 tonnes per capita

ENVIRONMENTAL TREATIES

Yes Yes Yes

Yes Yes No

Flooding and mudflows, exacerbated by overdevelopment of the coastal strip, caused thousands of deaths in late 1999.

MEDIA

TV ownership medium

Daily newspaper circulation 206 per 1000 people

PUBLISHING AND BROADCAST MEDIA

There are 86 daily newspapers. *El Universal* and *El Nacional* are the most prominent

8 services: 1 state-owned, 7 private

1 state-owned service, 500 independent stations

In 2003 President Chávez threatened to revoke private TV broadcasters' licenses, accusing stations of supporting the crippling two-month general strike.

EDUCATION

School leaving age: 12

93%

681,174 students

THE EDUCATION SYSTEM

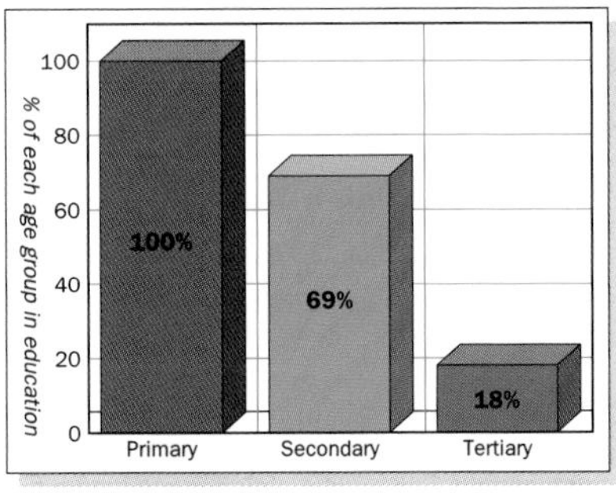
100
80
60
40
20
0
% of each age group in education
100%
69%
18%
Primary
Secondary
Tertiary

An extra $1 billion in social spending approved in 2000 includes raising entitlement in the state sector. Education is characterized by teacher shortages and a high drop-out rate; the quality of education at state universities is low. The private sector is growing.

SPENDING

GDP/cap. increase

CONSUMPTION AND SPENDING

60 per 1000 population

113 per 1000 population

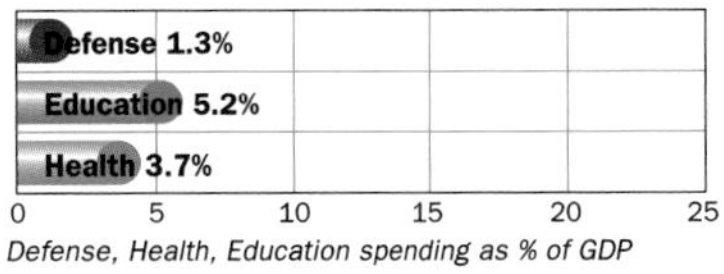
Defense 1.3%
Education 5.2%
Health 3.7%
0
5
10
15
20
25
Defense, Health, Education spending as % of GDP

The oil boom years of the 1970s largely benefited those already rich, and middle-income consumers did well out of state-sponsored improvements in health and education and subsidized goods, largely at the expense of the poor.

The collapse of world oil prices, economic austerity measures, high inflation, and the devaluation of the bolívar in the 1980s and 1990s squeezed the middle class and in addition seriously eroded the living standards of working-class households. In 2001, more than 20% of people were living in extreme poverty, according to official figures. An estimated 16% of the labor force were unemployed in 2002, and many of those who were working were in the informal sector.

CRIME

No death penalty

19,554 prisoners

Down 20% in 1997–2000

CRIME RATES

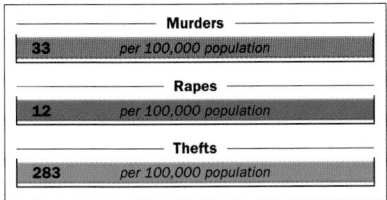

Murders: 33 *per 100,000 population*

Rapes: 12 *per 100,000 population*

Thefts: 283 *per 100,000 population*

Urban robberies and violence involving young delinquents are major problems, as is narcotics-related crime. Cattle smuggling to Colombia is rife.

HEALTH

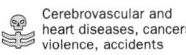

Welfare state health benefits

1 per 417 people

Cerebrovascular and heart diseases, cancers, violence, accidents

The health service suffered along with other public services from poor management in the 1970s and severe cuts in the 1980s and 1990s. Most health care is concentrated in the towns, and people from indigenous communities often have to travel long distances to receive treatment. Medicines, which have to be paid for, are expensive, and preventable diseases are recurring. Hospitals need modernization.

An additional $1 billion in social spending approved in 2000 includes spending on health.

WORLD RANKING

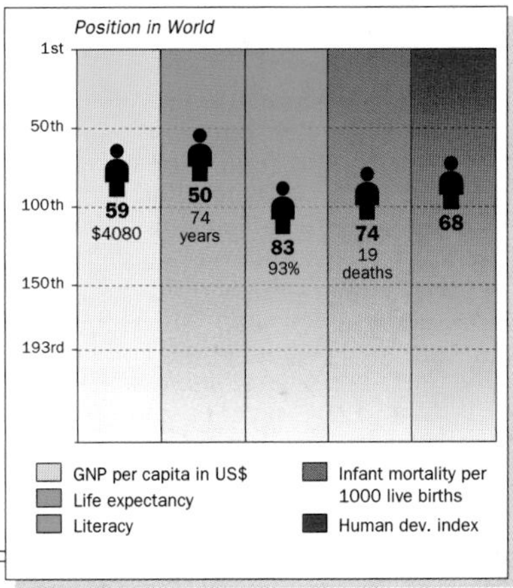
Position in World
1st
50th
100th
150th
193rd
59
$4080
50
74
years
83
93%
74
19
deaths
68
GNP per capita in US$
Life expectancy
Literacy
Infant mortality per 1000 live births
Human dev. index

V

VIETNAM

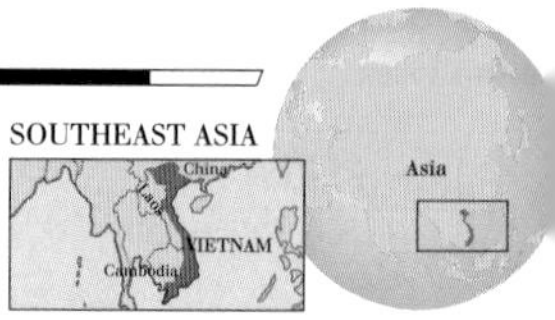
SOUTHEAST ASIA
Asia
China
Laos
VIETNAM
Cambodia

OFFICIAL NAME: Socialist Republic of Vietnam **CAPITAL:** Hanoi
POPULATION: 81.4 million **CURRENCY:** Dông **OFFICIAL LANGUAGE:** Vietnamese

1976
1976
Sept 2
VN
+7
+84
.vn

VIETNAM LIES ON the eastern side of the Indochinese peninsula. Over half the country is dominated by the heavily forested mountain range, the Chaîne Annamitique. The most populated areas, which are also the most intensively cultivated, are along the Red and Mekong Rivers. Partitioned in 1954 after a war against France, Vietnam was not reunited until 1976, a few months after the communist north finally defeated the southern regime and its US allies in the Vietnam War. Vietnam is now a single-party state ruled by the Communist Party. Since 1986, the regime has pursued a liberal economic policy known as *doi moi* (renovation).

CLIMATE

Tropical monsoon

WEATHER CHART FOR HANOI

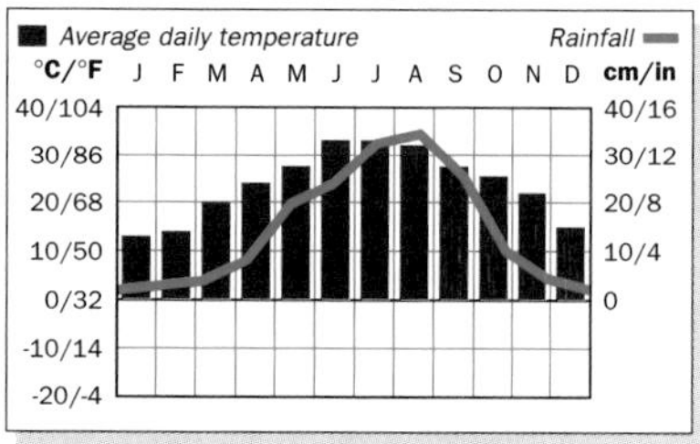
Average daily temperature
Rainfall
°C/°F
J F M A M J J A S O N D
cm/in
40/104
30/86
20/68
10/50
0/32
-10/14
-20/-4
40/16
30/12
20/8
10/4
0

Vietnam's geography means that there are sharp local contrasts in the climate. The north has cool winters, while the south is tropical, with even temperatures all year round. The central provinces are affected by typhoons. The northern Red River delta is subject to drought, while the Mekong delta in the south suffers heavy flooding.

TRANSPORTATION

Drive on right

Tan Son Naht Intl, Ho Chi Minh City
5.06m passengers

721 ships
1.13m grt

THE TRANSPORTATION NETWORK

23,325 km (14,493 miles)

430 km (267 miles)

2545 km (1581 miles)

17,702 km (10,999 miles)

Rebuilding infrastructure is still a priority. The flagship project, the four-lane Ho Chi Minh Highway linking Hanoi and the south, has had its target completion date put back until after 2005. A major port development plan is under way. Trains travel slowly, with an average speed of around 15 km/h (9 mph), and Hanoi to Ho Chi Minh City takes three days. The bus network is extensive but journeys are also time-consuming. Taxis and cycles provide cheap local transportation. Hanoi has plans for an elevated metro line.

TOURISM

Visitors : Population 1:34

2.43m visitors

Up 52% in 2003

MAIN TOURIST ARRIVALS

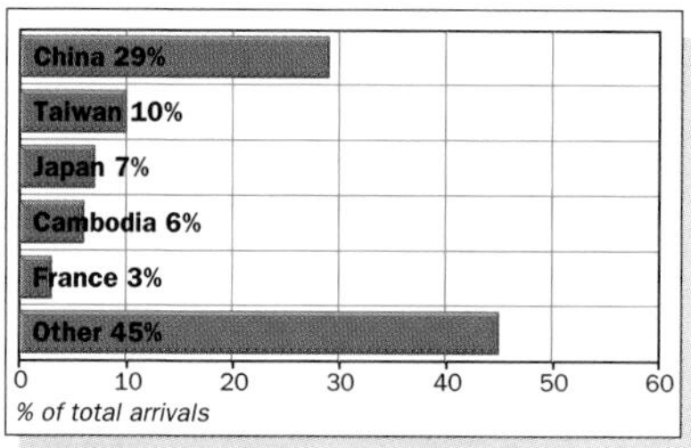
China 29%
Taiwan 10%
Japan 7%
Cambodia 6%
France 3%
Other 45%
0
10
20
30
40
50
60
% of total arrivals

Until the government opened the way to large-scale tourism in the 1990s, Russians, eastern Europeans, and backpackers from the West made up the bulk of visitors. Other travelers were either on business, or overseas Vietnamese, *Viet Kie*, who were visiting relatives.

Under a "master plan" adopted in 1995, massive investment was channeled into hotels, with an official target of three million tourists a year by 2000. This was not met but arrivals did increase. Poor transportation infrastructure remains a problem. Vietnam's appeal lies in its unspoiled Asian way of life and in the areas of spectacular natural beauty such as Ha Long Bay on the Red River delta.

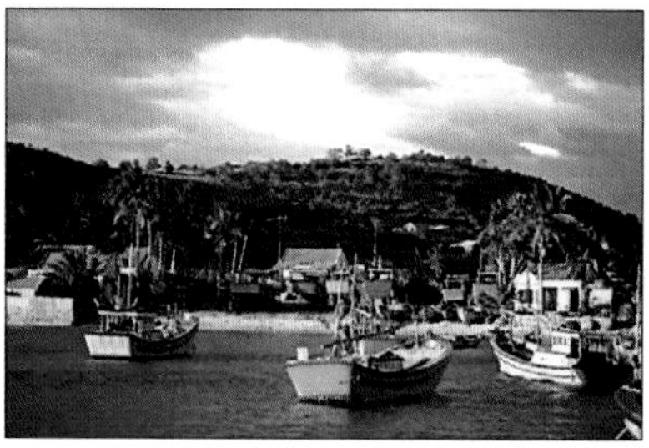

Boats moored near Nha Trang. *With 3444 km (2140 miles) of coastline, use of the sea, for transportation and fishing, is vital to Vietnam.*

PEOPLE

Pop. density high

Vietnamese, Chinese, Thai, Khmer, Muong, Nung, Miao, Yao, Jarai

250/km² (648/mi²)

THE URBAN/RURAL POPULATION SPLIT

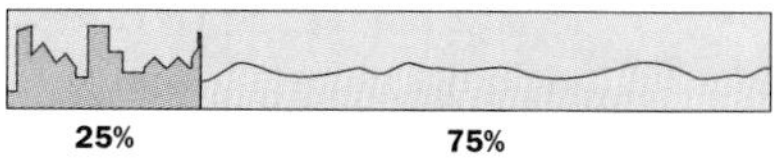
25%
75%

RELIGIOUS PERSUASION

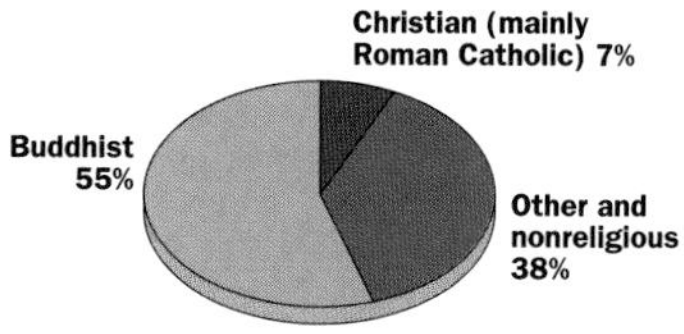
Christian (mainly Roman Catholic) 7%
Buddhist 55%
Other and nonreligious 38%

ETHNIC MAKEUP

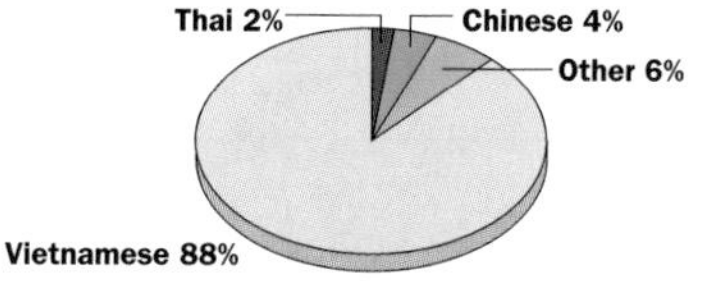
Thai 2%
Chinese 4%
Other 6%
Vietnamese 88%

Family life is strong and is based on kinship groups within village clans. A pronounced north–south cultural split remains evident in the cities. Chinese are the largest minority group. When the victorious communists reunited north and south Vietnam in 1976, they viewed the Saigon Chinese (in what was renamed Ho Chi Minh City), with their Taiwanese links, as a corrupt bourgeoisie. The northern Mountain Chinese were also suspect as a possible fifth column for China's ambitions in Vietnam. Various other mountain minorities (*montagnards*), with a history of collaboration with the French and Americans, were also sidelined by the regime in Hanoi. *Montagnard* resentment over the resettling of lowlanders in mountain regions sparked violent protests in early 2001.

War deaths cause older generations of women to outnumber men. Women form a high proportion of the labor force, and are starting to gain greater political prominence, most notably Vice President Nguyen Thi Binh. Female conscription was reinstated in 2001.

POPULATION AGE BREAKDOWN

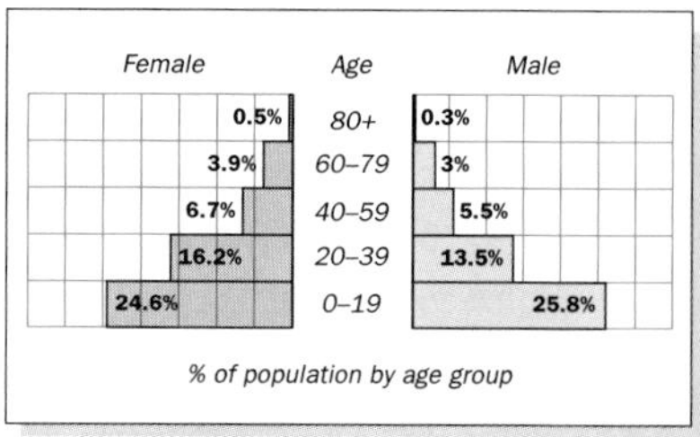
Female
Age
Male
0.5%
80+
0.3%
3.9%
60–79
3%
6.7%
40–59
5.5%
16.2%
20–39
13.5%
24.6%
0–19
25.8%
% of population by age group

Tran Duc Luong, *elected president in 1997.*

Nong Duc Manh, *powerful general secretary of the CPV.*

POLITICS

No multiparty elections

2002/2007

President Tran Duc Luong

AT THE LAST ELECTION

National Assembly 500 seats

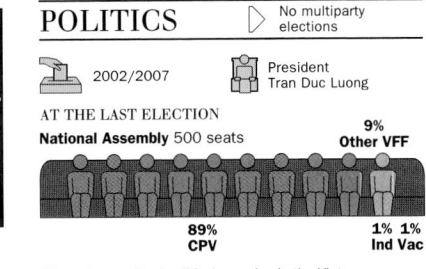

9%
Other VFF
89%
CPV
1% 1%
Ind Vac

The sole permitted political grouping is the Vietnamese Fatherland Front (**VFF**), which is dominated by the Communist Party of Vietnam (**CPV**)
Ind = Independents **Vac** = Vacant

Vietnam is effectively a single-party communist state.

PROFILE

A traditional communist system is still in place, with a powerful politburo elected by the party central committee. The CPV general secretary wields much power, alongside the prime minister and president. Changes in senior posts in 1997 left reformers such as new prime minister Phan Van Khai still outnumbered by conservatives. The 2001 party congress balanced the theme of greater democracy with a renewed commitment to socialism.

MAIN POLITICAL ISSUES

Economic reform

Vietnam is attempting to move to a market economy without political liberalization. Economic reformer Nong Duc Manh became party leader in 2001, but real concern remains that "individualism" will be encouraged, stability undermined, and the party's monopoly of power weakened by the opening to competition of collective farming and state enterprises.

Corruption

An investigation into crime boss Nam Cam (sentenced to death in 2003) revealed worrying levels of official collusion with organized crime.

WORLD AFFAIRS

Joined UN in 1977

ASEAN | CP | OIF | Mekong River | NAM

Economic liberalization has improved relations with the US, with lifting of the aid and trade embargo in 1992–1994, full diplomatic relations in 1995, and a landmark bilateral trade agreement in 2000, ahead of a visit by US president Bill Clinton that November.

Vietnam joined ASEAN in 1995, in the wake of the settlement of the Cambodia issue. Trade and economic cooperation links with Japan have been strengthened. Tension with China was reduced by an agreement in 1999 over their mutual land border, though competing claims to the Spratly Islands remain a source of friction.

AID

Recipient

$1.28bn (receipts)

Down 12% in 2002

Vietnam's invasion of Cambodia in 1978 halted all aid from China, Japan, and the West (except for Scandinavian countries), leaving it mostly dependent on the USSR. Western donors resumed assistance in the early 1990s. Their aid rapidly became the main source of capital for improving infrastructure, though foreign investment fell away significantly in the late 1990s.

CHRONOLOGY

From 1825, the brutal persecution of the Catholic community, originally converted by French priests in the 17th century, gave France the excuse to colonize Cochin-China, Annam, and Tonkin, and then merge them with Laos and Cambodia.

- **1920** *Quoc ngu* (Roman script) replaces Chinese script.
- **1930** Ho Chi Minh founds Indo-China Communist Party.
- **1940** Japanese invasion.
- **1941** Viet Minh resistance founded in exile in China.
- **1945** Viet Minh take Saigon and Hanoi. Emperor abdicates. Republic proclaimed with Ho Chi Minh as president.
- **1946** French reenter. First Indochina war.
- **1954** French defeated at Dien Bien Phu. Vietnam divided at 17°N. USSR supports North; US arms South.
- **1960** Groups opposed to southern regime unite as Viet Cong.
- **1964** US Congress approves war.
- **1965** Gen. Nguyen Van Thieu takes over military government of South. First US combat troops arrive.
- **1965–1968** Operation Rolling Thunder – intense bombing

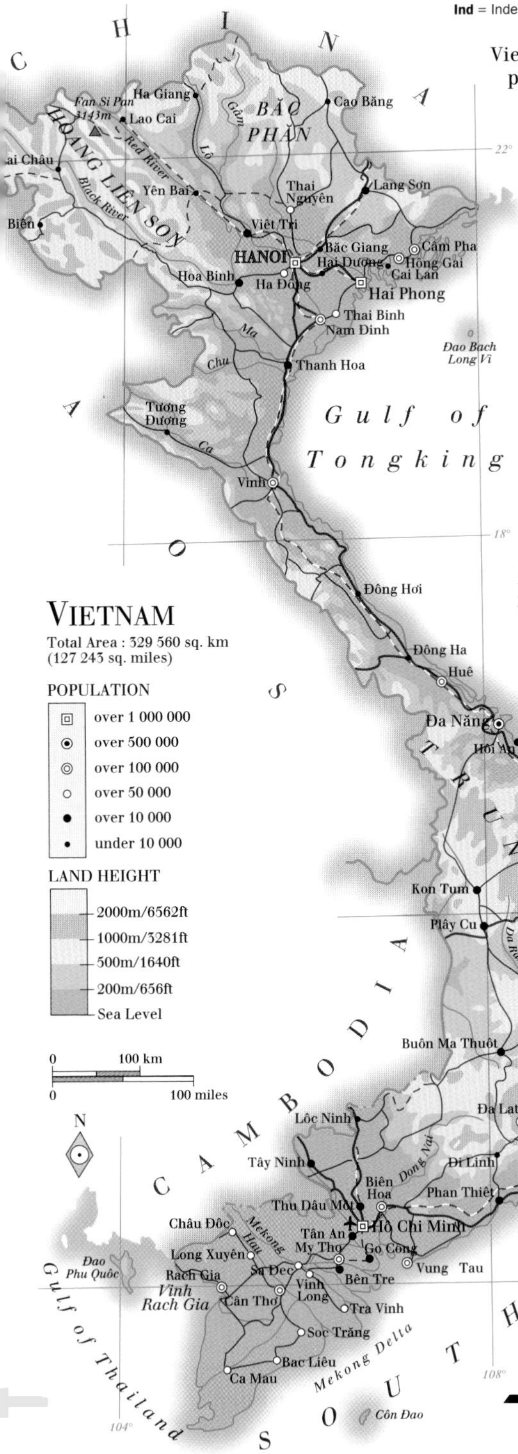
CHINA
Fan Si Pan 3143m
Ha Giang
Lao Cai
Cao Băng
BĂC PHẦN
Lang Sơn
Yên Bai
Thai Nguyên
Việt Tri
HANOI
Bǎc Giang
Câm Pha
Hai Dương
Hông Gai
Cai Lan
Hai Phong
Hoa Binh
Ha Đông
Thai Binh
Nam Đinh
HOANG LIEN SON
Red River
Black River
Đao Bach Long Vi
Thanh Hoa
Tương Đương
Gulf of Tongking
Vinh
LAOS
VIETNAM
Total Area : 329 560 sq. km (127 243 sq. miles)
POPULATION
over 1 000 000
over 500 000
over 100 000
over 50 000
over 10 000
under 10 000
LAND HEIGHT
2000m/6562ft
1000m/3281ft
500m/1640ft
200m/656ft
Sea Level
100 km
100 miles
N
Đông Hơi
Đông Ha
Huê
Đa Năng
Hoi An
Tam Ky
Quang Ngai
TRUNG PHẦN
Kon Tum
Plây Cu
Qui Nhơn
Tuy Hoa
Buôn Ma Thuôt
Nha Trang
Đa Lat
Cam Ranh
Phan Rang-Thap Cham
Lôc Ninh
Tây Ninh
Di Linh
Biên Hoa
Phan Thiêt
Thu Dâu Môt
Hô Chi Minh
Châu Đôc
Tân An
My Tho
Go Công
Vung Tau
Long Xuyên
Đao Phu Quôc
Rach Gia
Sa Đec
Vinh Long
Bên Tre
Cân Thơ
Tra Vinh
Soc Trăng
Bac Liêu
Ca Mau
Mekong Delta
Côn Đao
Gulf of Thailand
CAMBODIA
SOUTH CHINA SEA

CHRONOLOGY *continued*

of North by South and US.

- **1967** Antiwar protests start in US and elsewhere.
- **1968** Tet (New Year) Offensive – 105 towns attacked simultaneously in South with infiltrated arms. Viet Cong suffer serious losses. Peace talks begin. US eases bombing and starts withdrawing troops.
- **1969** Ho Chi Minh dies. Succeeded by Le Duan. War intensifies in spite of talks.
- **1972** 11-day Christmas Campaign is heaviest US bombing of war.
- **1973** Paris Peace Agreements signed, but fighting continues.
- **1975** Fall of Saigon to combined forces of North and Provisional Revolutionary (Viet Cong) Government of South. One million flee after end of war.
- **1976** Vietnam united as Socialist Republic of Vietnam. Saigon renamed Ho Chi Minh City.
- **1978** Invasion of Cambodia to oust Pol Pot regime (by January 1979).
- **1979** Nine-Day War with China. Chinese troops pushed back after destroying everything for 40 km (25 miles) inside Vietnam. "Boat people" crisis. At UN conference, Vietnam agrees to allow legal emigration, but exodus continues.
- **1986** Death of Le Duan. Nguyen Van Linh, new Communist Party general secretary, initiates liberal economic policy of *doi moi* (renovation).
- **1987** Fighting in Thailand as Vietnam pursues Kampuchean resistance fighters across border.
- **1989** Troops leave Cambodia.
- **1991** Open anticommunist dissent made a criminal offense.
- **1992** Revised constitution allows foreign investment, but essential role of Communist Party is unchanged.
- **1994** Having already lifted sanctions, US drops 30-year trade embargo.
- **1995** US–Vietnamese relations normalized. Vietnam joins ASEAN.
- **1997** Tran Duc Luong elected president, Phan Van Khai prime minister, by National Assembly.
- **1998** Asian financial crisis dampens economic boom.
- **1999** Signing of border treaty with China.
- **2000** Worst flooding along Mekong for 40 years. November, Bill Clinton becomes first US president to visit Vietnam since the war.
- **2001** March, visit by Russian president Vladimir Putin. April, ninth party congress. Nong Duc Manh becomes general secretary.
- **2003** An outbreak of acute pnuemonia (SARS) is contained.

DEFENSE

Compulsory military service

$2.29bn

Down 1% in 2002

Vietnam has large and well-equipped armed forces, notably the world's seventh-largest army. Military service is compulsory, and conscripts serve a two- or three-year term. The army's role in preserving both stability and socialism was reaffirmed in 2001. Increased defense spending on the navy reflects tensions in the South China Sea, where there are disputed claims to the Spratly and Paracel Islands.

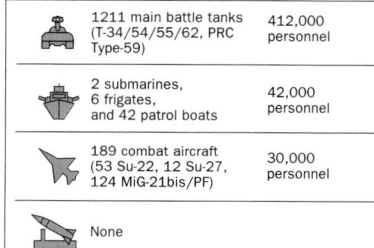

VIETNAMESE ARMED FORCES

1211 main battle tanks (T-34/54/55/62, PRC Type-59)	412,000 personnel
2 submarines, 6 frigates, and 42 patrol boats	42,000 personnel
189 combat aircraft (53 Su-22, 12 Su-27, 124 MiG-21bis/PF)	30,000 personnel
None	

ECONOMICS

Inflation 14% p.a. (1990–2001)

$34.8bn

15,722 dông (15,497)

SCORE CARD

World GNP Ranking	57th
GNP per capita	$430
Balance of payments	–$604m
Inflation	3.8%
Unemployment	25%

EXPORTS

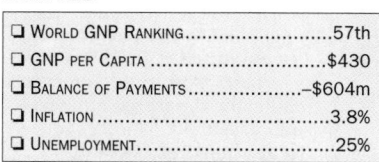

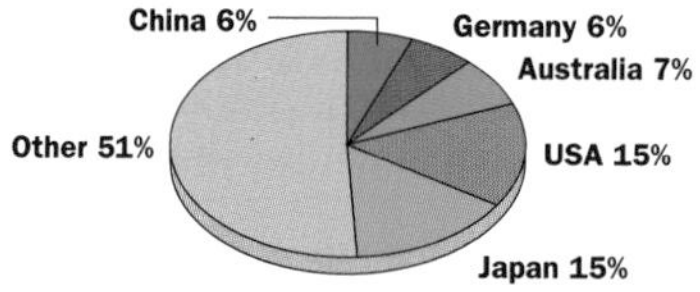
China 6%
Germany 6%
Australia 7%
USA 15%
Japan 15%
Other 51%

IMPORTS

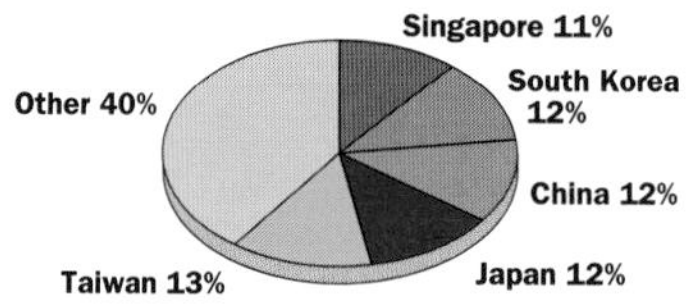
Singapore 11%
South Korea 12%
China 12%
Japan 12%
Taiwan 13%
Other 40%

Strengths

Diverse resources; oil and unexploited gas reserves. Young, literate, low-cost labor force. Strong light industrial and handicraft export industries.

Weaknesses

Weak economic institutions. Weight of bureaucracy. Heavy dependence on aid for reconstruction. Enduring suspicion of entrepreneurial southern attitudes and "individualism." Corruption.

Profile

The encouragement of private enterprise began in 1988. Touted in the mid-1990s as the next Asian "tiger," Vietnam has aimed at more moderate growth since the crisis of 1997–1998, achieving an impressive annual average GDP growth rate of over 6% for 1990–2003. Inflation, once a huge problem, was held down in the 1990s, and is now under firm control. Increased rice production has boosted incomes, and domestic demand helped the post-1998 upswing. The government has

ECONOMIC PERFORMANCE INDICATOR

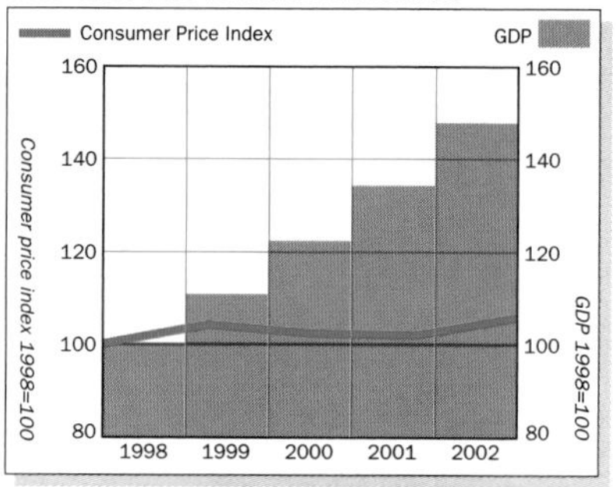
Consumer Price Index
GDP
Consumer price index 1998=100
GDP 1998=100
160
140
120
100
80
1998
1999
2000
2001
2002

promised massive investment in agriculture, but plans to cut back coffee production as world prices have fallen.

Attracting foreign investment through reform is essential; government policies regarding state-owned enterprises promise more scope for joint ventures, and new laws on trade-licensing and investment were passed in 2000. Also that year the country's first stock exchange opened. The government has set a target of doubling GDP in the next decade. The potential certainly exists, based on an educated and highly motivated young labor force and on mineral resources, located mostly in the north.

VIETNAM : MAJOR BUSINESSES

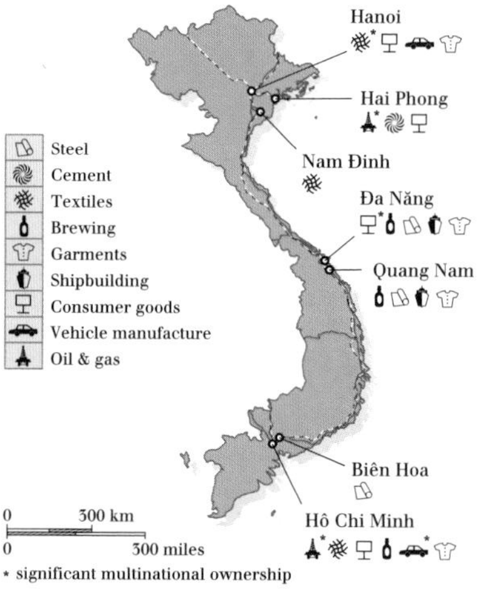
Hanoi
Hai Phong
Nam Đinh
Đa Năng
Quang Nam
Biên Hoa
Hô Chi Minh
Steel
Cement
Textiles
Brewing
Garments
Shipbuilding
Consumer goods
Vehicle manufacture
Oil & gas
0 300 km
0 300 miles
* significant multinational ownership

RESOURCES

Electric power 5m kW

2.01m tonnes

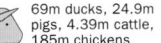

372,000 b/d (reserves 2.5bn barrels)

69m ducks, 24.9m pigs, 4.39m cattle, 185m chickens

Coal, oil, tin, zinc, iron, antimony, gas, apatite, salt, bauxite

ELECTRICITY GENERATION

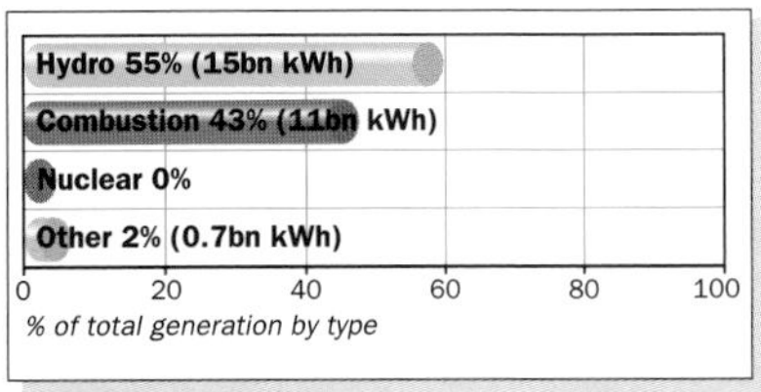
Hydro 55% (15bn kWh)
Combustion 43% (11bn kWh)
Nuclear 0%
Other 2% (0.7bn kWh)
0
20
40
60
80
100
% of total generation by type

Vietnam is now the world's third-largest coffee producer and is the third-largest exporter of rice – to the detriment of domestic stocks.

Oil production, small by world standards, is sufficient to make it Vietnam's biggest export earner. The Oil and Gas Corporation of Vietnam (PetroVietnam) is involved in joint ventures with international oil firms. Vietnam has unexploited gas reserves in the South China Sea; gas from the only producing field has to be flared off.

Timber exports have been banned since 1997 to preserve forests. Northern Vietnam has a surplus of electricity, mainly from hydroelectric schemes.

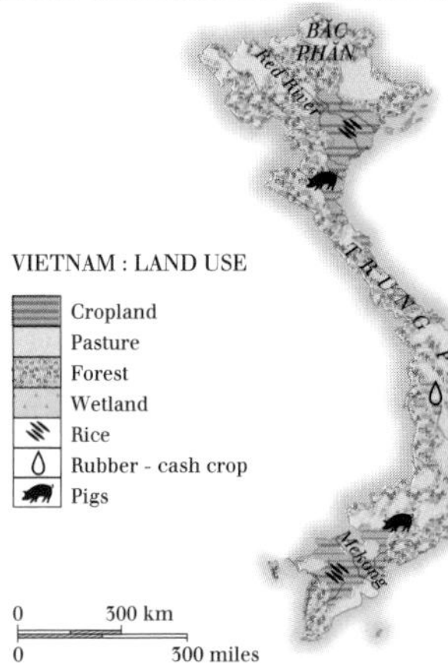
BAC PHAN
Red River
TRUNG PHAN
Mekong
VIETNAM : LAND USE
Cropland
Pasture
Forest
Wetland
Rice
Rubber - cash crop
Pigs
0
300 km
0
300 miles

ENVIRONMENT

Sustainability rank: 94th

4% (2% partially protected)

0.7 tonnes per capita

ENVIRONMENTAL TREATIES

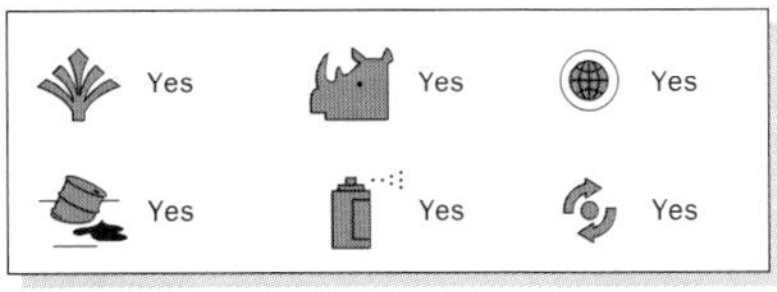
Yes
Yes
Yes
Yes
Yes
Yes

In the Vietnam War, seven million tonnes of bombs were dropped, and the defoliant chemical Agent Orange was sprayed over vast areas; a "census" of the continuing health impact was announced in 1999. Half of Vietnam's forests were seriously damaged and some 5% destroyed. Deforestation continued into the 1990s due to logging and expansion of coffee-growing, causing soil erosion and flooding. Floods along the Mekong in 2000 were the worst for 40 years.

CRIME

Death penalty in use

55,000 prisoners

Up 13% in 2000

CRIME RATES

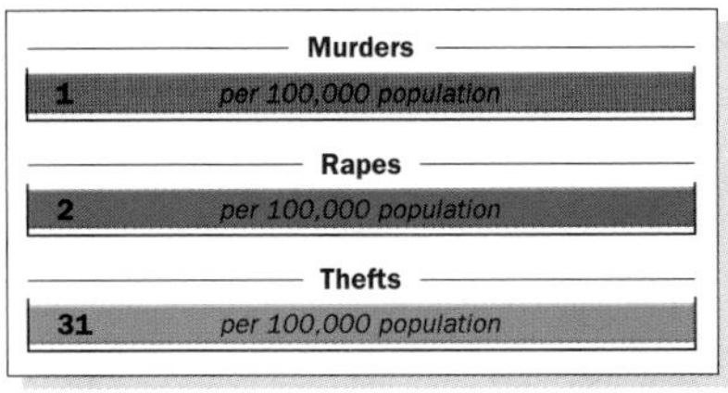
Murders
1 per 100,000 population
Rapes
2 per 100,000 population
Thefts
31 per 100,000 population

The judicial system is based on the Soviet model. The education camps established after liberation have now closed, but religious and political dissidents are still held without trial.

Corruption has risen sharply since economic liberalization, as has the illegal drift of young people to urban areas, where they are blamed for increasing petty crime and "social evils" such as begging, prostitution, and drug-taking. In major cities theft from foreigners is a problem .

HEALTH

Welfare state health benefits

1 per 1919 people

Heart disease, cancers, malaria

Vietnam's medical achievements include developing a vaccine for hepatitis B, and extracting an antimalarial drug, artemisinin, from the indigenous thanh hao tree. An extensive campaign is under way to combat the spread of AIDS.

SPENDING

GDP/cap. increase

CONSUMPTION AND SPENDING

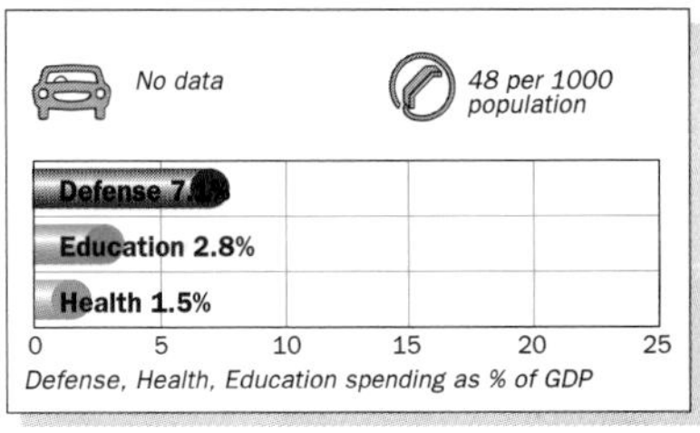
No data
48 per 1000 population
Defense 7.1%
Education 2.8%
Health 1.5%
0
5
10
15
20
25
Defense, Health, Education spending as % of GDP

Ostentatious consumerism is rising despite official disapproval, but is beyond most people's reach. Wealth disparities are growing, with rural areas falling deep into poverty.

MEDIA

TV ownership medium

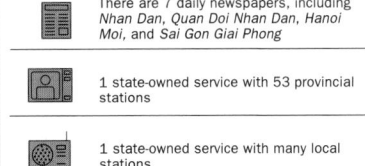

Daily newspaper circulation 4 per 1000 people

PUBLISHING AND BROADCAST MEDIA

There are 7 daily newspapers, including *Nhan Dan, Quan Doi Nhan Dan, Hanoi Moi,* and *Sai Gon Giai Phong*

1 state-owned service with 53 provincial stations

1 state-owned service with many local stations

The media are tightly regulated. TV is the dominant medium. All editors have to be Party members, but criticism of the authorities is still possible. Even *Nhan Dan*, the CPV newspaper, has been known to expose laxity in the system, especially in the judiciary. However, in 2002 the authorities sought out and destroyed books by proscribed authors.

EDUCATION

School leaving age: 10

93%

873,000 students

THE EDUCATION SYSTEM

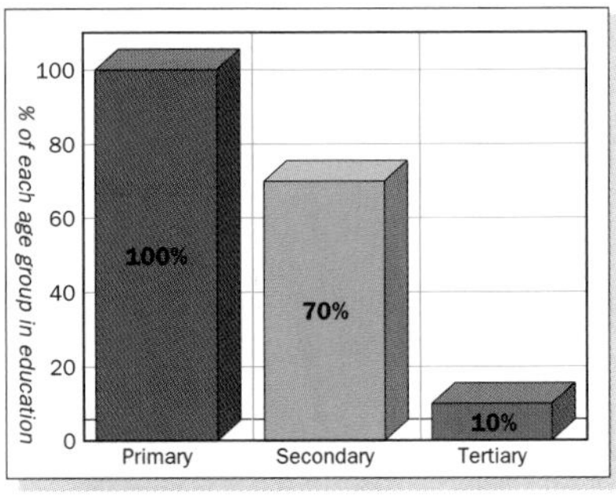
100
80
60
40
20
0
% of each age group in education
100%
70%
10%
Primary
Secondary
Tertiary

Private sponsorship helps fund education. Vietnamese universities have a strong liberal arts tradition. Social pressure to obtain a degree leads to high levels of cheating among university applicants.

WORLD RANKING

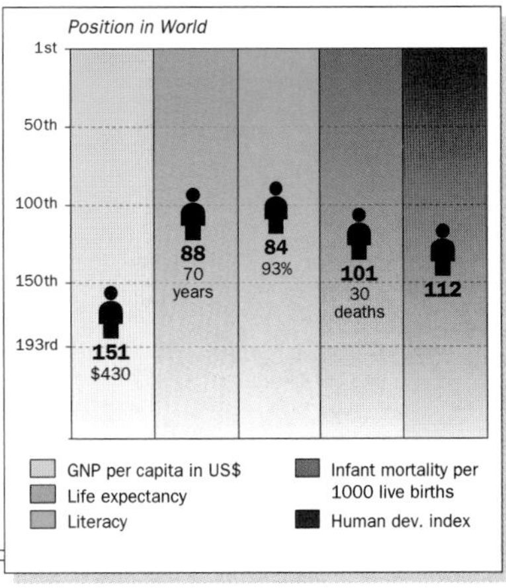
Position in World
1st
50th
100th
150th
193rd
151
$430
88
70 years
84
93%
101
30 deaths
112
GNP per capita in US$
Life expectancy
Literacy
Infant mortality per 1000 live births
Human dev. index

V

YEMEN

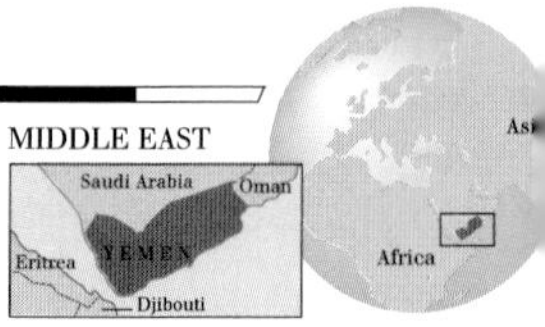
MIDDLE EAST
Saudi Arabia
Oman
Eritrea
YEMEN
Djibouti
Africa
Asia

OFFICIAL NAME: Republic of Yemen **CAPITAL:** Sana
POPULATION: 20 million **CURRENCY:** Yemeni rial **OFFICIAL LANGUAGE:** Arabic

1990 | 1990 | May 22 | ADN | +3 | +967 | .ye

YEMEN IS LOCATED in southern Arabia. The west is mountainous, with a fertile strip along the Red Sea. The center and south are largely arid mountains and desert. Until 1990 Yemen was two countries, the Yemen Arab Republic (YAR) in the west and the People's Democratic Republic of Yemen (PDRY) in the south. The YAR was run by successive military regimes; the poorer PDRY was the Arab world's only Marxist state. Postunification conflict between the two ruling hierarchies, nominally in coalition, led to a two-month civil war in 1994, the ousting of the former Marxists, and a new constitution.

CLIMATE

Hot desert/mountain

WEATHER CHART FOR SANA

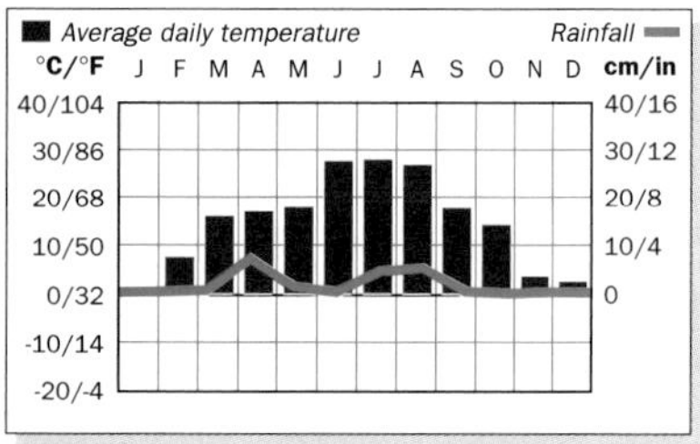
Average daily temperature
Rainfall
°C/°F J F M A M J J A S O N D cm/in
40/104
30/86
20/68
10/50
0/32
-10/14
-20/-4
40/16
30/12
20/8
10/4
0

The desert climate is modified by altitude, which affects temperatures by as much as 12°C (22°F). Rainfall increases in northwest and central Yemen.

TRANSPORTATION

Drive on right

El Rahaba, Sana
998,743 passengers

47 ships
78,000 grt

THE TRANSPORTATION NETWORK

8040 km (4996 miles)

None

None

None

Aden's history as a port stretches back 3000 years. Adequate roads link the main cities, but many rural areas are inaccessible. International airlines, including the modern fleet of Yemenia, serve Sana and Aden.

***Hilltop village** in northern Yemen, showing traditionally decorated, multistory houses built from unbaked mud bricks.*

TOURISM

Visitors : Population 1:263

76,000 visitors

Up 4% in 2001

MAIN TOURIST ARRIVALS

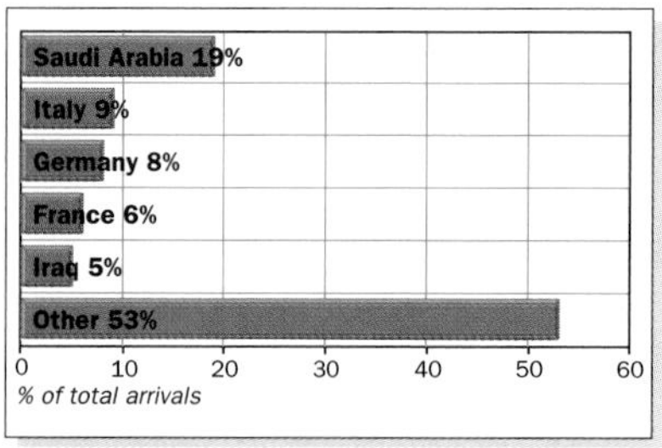
Saudi Arabia 19%
Italy 9%
Germany 8%
France 6%
Iraq 5%
Other 53%
0 10 20 30 40 50 60
% of total arrivals

The home of the legendary Queen of Sheba, Yemen attracts tourists interested in Arab society, architecture, archaeology, and historical remains. The Romans called Yemen *Arabia Felix* because of its fertile farmlands and dominance in the frankincense trade. Yemen was the second country, after Saudi Arabia, to convert to Islam.

Sana, a walled medieval city, is the most interesting center for tourists. It has impressive architecture, particularly tall stone and mud-brick Arab houses, and the palaces of the former imamate. Over 100 km (60 miles) from the capital, the Marib Dam, built in ancient times, is another major attraction. Southern Yemen has been open to Western visitors only since 1990. Its run-down infrastructure and lack of hotels, especially on the coast, have hindered tourism.

German and French tourists were the first to travel to northwest Yemen during the 1980s. Hopes of a major rise in tourism following the end of the 1994 civil war were dashed in 1998 after tribesmen kidnapped and killed four tourists. Fears of further attacks deterred Westerners.

Tourists are subject to a ban on the consumption of alcohol, except in five-star hotels. Whiskey and beer are available on the black market, which operates out of Djibouti.

PEOPLE

Pop. density low

Arabic

36/km² (92/mi²)

THE URBAN/RURAL POPULATION SPLIT

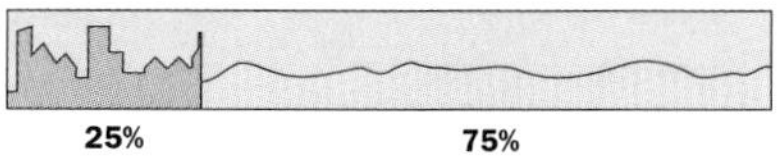
25%
75%

RELIGIOUS PERSUASION

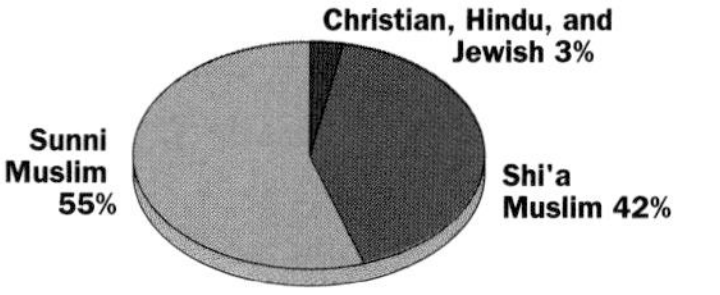
Christian, Hindu, and Jewish 3%
Sunni Muslim 55%
Shi'a Muslim 42%

ETHNIC MAKEUP

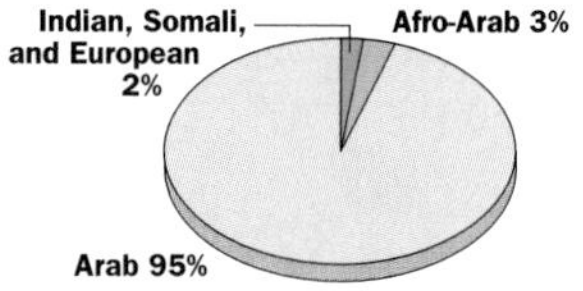
Indian, Somali, and European 2%
Afro-Arab 3%
Arab 95%

Yemenis are almost entirely of Arab and Bedouin descent, though there are people of mixed African and Arab descent along the south coast and a small, dwindling, Jewish minority. The majority are Sunni Muslims, of the Shafi sect. However, Zaydi Shi'a are strong in the north, where many people have close family in Saudi Arabia. Many Yemenis consider Saudi Arabia's Asir province to be part of Yemen.

Over a million Yemenis went to work in neighboring states during the 1970s oil boom, but most were forced to return in 1990 due to Yemen's support for Iraq's invasion of Kuwait.

Tensions, which in 1994 led to civil war, continue to exist between the south, led by cosmopolitan Aden, and the more conservative west.

In rural areas and in the western highlands, semifeudal tribal chiefs hold sway, Islamic orthodoxy is strong, and most women wear the veil. In the south, however, women still claim the educational, professional, and social freedoms they had under the Marxist regime, especially in urban areas.

POPULATION AGE BREAKDOWN

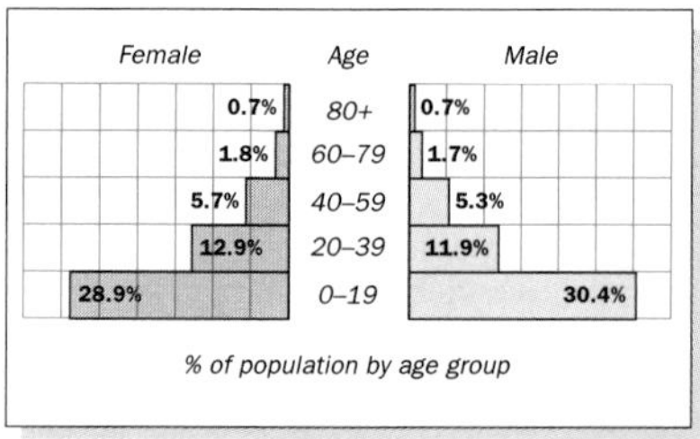
Female
Age
Male
0.7% 80+ 0.7%
1.8% 60–79 1.7%
5.7% 40–59 5.3%
12.9% 20–39 11.9%
28.9% 0–19 30.4%
% of population by age group

YEMEN

Total Area : 527 970 sq. km
(203 849 sq. miles)

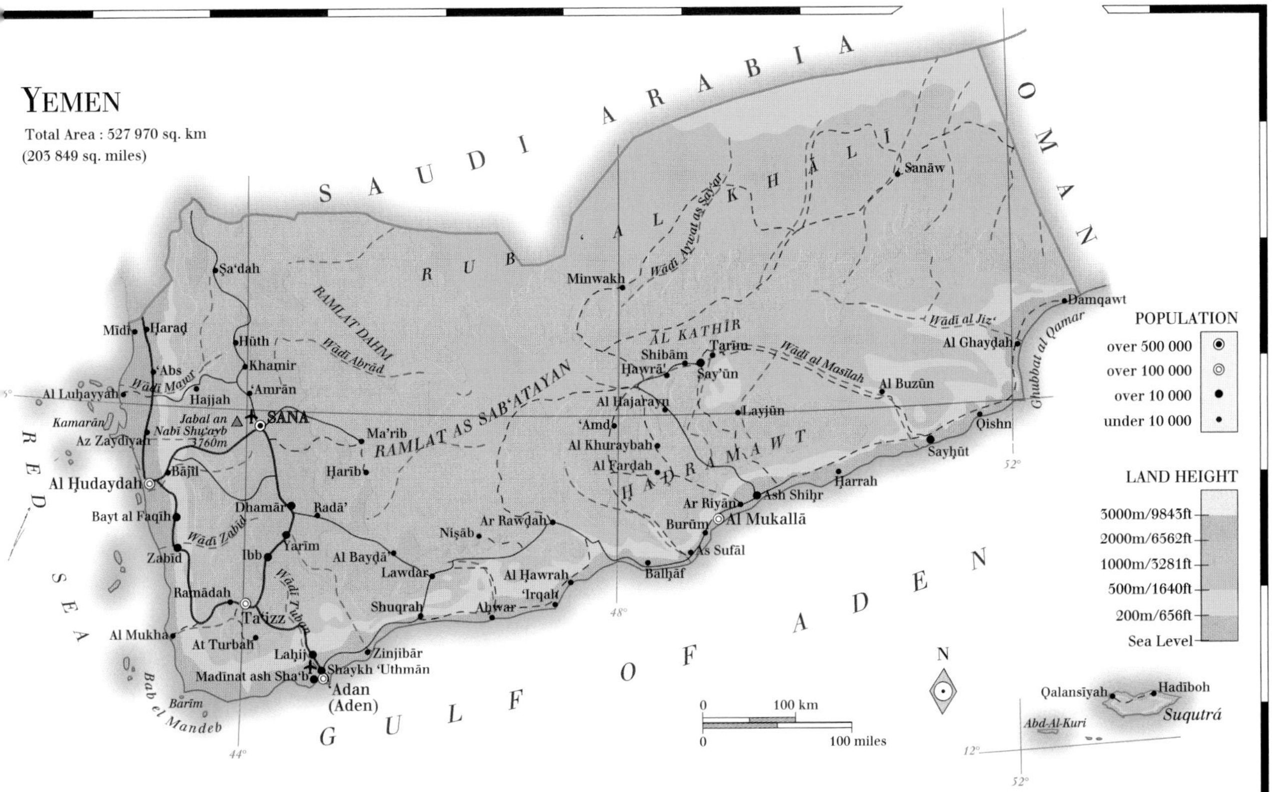
SAUDI ARABIA
OMAN
RUB AL KHALI
RAMLAT DAHM
RAMLAT AS SAB'ATAYN
AL KATHIR
HADRAMAWT
RED SEA
GULF OF ADEN
Bab el Mandeb
Şa'dah
Midi
Harad
'Abs
Hūth
Khamir
'Amrān
Hajjah
Al Luhayyah
Kamarān
Az Zaydiyah
Jabal an Nabī Shu'ayb 3760m
SANA
Ma'rib
Hārib
Bājil
Al Hudaydah
Bayt al Faqih
Dhamār
Radā'
Zabīd
Ibb
Yarīm
Al Baydā'
Ta'izz
Al Mukha
At Turbah
Lahij
Madīnat ash Sha'b
Shaykh 'Uthmān
'Adan (Aden)
Zinjibār
Shuqrah
Lawdar
Nişāb
Ar Rawdah
Al Hawrah
'Irqah
Ahwar
Balhāf
Minwakh
Shibām
Hawrā'
Tarīm
Say'ūn
Al Hajarayn
'Amd
Al Khuraybah
Al Fardah
Layjūn
Ar Riyān
Burūm
Al Mukallā
Ash Shihr
As Sufāl
Harrah
Sayhūt
Qishn
Al Buzūn
Al Ghaydah
Damqawt
Sanāw
Wādī al Masīlah
Wādī al Jiz'
Ghubbat al Qamar
Qalansīyah
Hadiboh
Suqutrá
Abd-Al-Kuri
Barīm
POPULATION
over 500 000
over 100 000
over 10 000
under 10 000
LAND HEIGHT
3000m/9843ft
2000m/6562ft
1000m/3281ft
500m/1640ft
200m/656ft
Sea Level
0 100 km
0 100 miles

POLITICS

Multiparty elections

2003/2009

President Ali Abdullah Saleh

AT THE LAST ELECTION

House of Representatives 301 seats

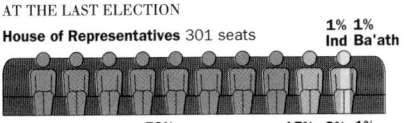

1% Ind
1% Ba'ath
79% GPC
15% al-Islah
3% YSP
1% NUPO

GPC = General People's Congress **al-Islah** = Yemeni Alliance for Reform **YSP** = Yemen Socialist Party **Ind** = Independents **NUPO** = Nasserite Unionist Popular Organization **Ba'ath** = Arab Socialist Ba'ath Party

Yemen is a multiparty, presidential democracy.

PROFILE

The merger of the YAR and the PDRY in 1990 united Yemenis for the first time since 1735; free elections were held in 1993. While President Ali Saleh initially maintained unity, a bloody civil war in 1994 fueled a southern secessionist movement, soon crushed. In 1999 Saleh won the region's first democratic presidential election, later extending his term to seven years. His GPC increased its majority in 2003, despite the participation in the poll of the former southern-ruling YSP (who had boycotted the 1997 election). The government still faces anger at the levels of poverty in an oil-rich country, and relies on familial ties to the army to retain power. The Islamist al-Islah, formerly a junior partner of the GPC, is now the chief opposition, having eclipsed the jaded YSP.

MAIN POLITICAL ISSUES

Relations with Saudi Arabia

Tensions persist over oil exploration rights, Yemeni claims on Asir, and accusations that Riyadh funds insurgent tribesmen and, until recently, al-Islah. The two sides clashed violently over 1600 km (1000 miles) of disputed border in 1998, despite a 1995 memorandum of understanding. In early 2001, both sides withdrew border troops under a pact reached in 2000.

Instability

For a decade Yemen has suffered from tribal insurgency and popular discontent with Saleh's government. Since 1992, tribesmen have kidnapped more than 100 foreigners, including diplomats and tourists. Leaders of four smaller opposition parties were arrested in 2003 following clashes at demonstrations.

Ali Abdullah Saleh, *former YAR president, now leader of the unified Yemen.*

Shaikh Abdullah al-Ahmar, *leader of the opposition al-Islah.*

CHRONOLOGY

From the 9th century, the Zaydi dynasty ruled Yemen until their defeat by the Ottoman Turks in 1517. The Turks were expelled by the Zaydi imams in 1636.

- **1839** Britain occupies Aden.
- **1918** Western Yemen independent.
- **1937** Aden made a crown colony, hinterland a protectorate.
- **1962** Army coup in west. Imam deposed, Yemen Arab Republic (YAR) declared. Civil war.
- **1963** Aden and protectorate united to form Federation of South Arabia.
- **1967** South Arabia independent as People's Republic of South Yemen. British troops leave Aden.
- **1970** South Yemen renamed People's Democratic Republic of Yemen (PDRY). Republican victory in YAR civil war.
- **1972** War between YAR and PDRY ends in peace settlement.
- **1974** Army coup in YAR.
- **1978** Lt. Col. Ali Saleh YAR president. Coup in PDRY: radical Abdalfattah Ismail in power.
- **1979** PDRY signs 20-year treaty with USSR.
- **1980** Ismail replaced by moderate Ali Muhammed.
- **1982** PDRY peace treaty with Oman. Major earthquake kills 3000.
- **1984** YAR signs 20-year cooperation treaty with USSR.

CHRONOLOGY *continued*

- **1986** Coup attempt in PDRY leads to civil war. Rebels take control of Aden. New PDRY president meets YAR counterpart.
- **1987** Oil production starts in YAR.
- **1988** YAR holds elections for consultative council; Muslim Brotherhood gains influence.
- **1989** Speeding-up of unification process. PDRY publishes a program of free-market reforms. YAR and PDRY sign unification agreement. Constitution of unified Yemen published.
- **1990** Restrictions on travel between YAR and PDRY lifted. Ali Saleh becomes president of Republic of Yemen. May, formal unification. Pro-Islamic groups oppose secular constitution.
- **1991** Yemeni guest workers expelled by Saudi Arabia in retaliation for Yemen's position over Iraqi invasion of Kuwait. Arab states boycott independence celebrations.
- **1992** Assassinations, food riots, and unrest delay elections until 1993.
- **1994** Southern secessionists defeated in civil war. Amended constitution adopted.
- **1997** Saleh's GPC wins absolute majority: poll boycotted by YSP.
- **1998–1999** Violent border dispute with Saudi Arabia. Kidnapping of tourists, four killed; three members of Islamic Army of Aden (IAA) sentenced to death.
- **1999** Saleh reelected.
- **2000** Yemen agrees border with Saudi Arabia after 66-year dispute. October, terror attacks on US naval vessel and UK embassy.
- **2001** Referendum approves extension of presidential term to seven years.
- **2002** Government targets suspected al-Qaida allies in tribal areas, expels 100 foreign "scholars."

WORLD AFFAIRS

Joined UN in 1947/1967

AL | AMF | IBRD | NAM | OIC

Isolated after its support for Iraq during the 1991 Gulf War, Yemen now actively supports the US; US agents operate on its soil in an attempt to tackle heavily armed Islamist terrorists believed to have strong links to al-Qaida.

AID

Recipient

$584m (receipts) | Up 27% in 2002

International donors pledged $2.3 billion in 2002 to fund the government's antipoverty programs. Arab countries are the largest source of aid.

DEFENSE

Compulsory military service

$486m | Down 7% in 2002

Following unification in 1990, mutual suspicion hampered the integration of the two separate defense forces. Sporadic, bitter clashes have taken place.

The main domestic security concern is insurgent tribesmen and, internationally, anti-Western terrorist activity such as the sinking of USS *Cole* off Aden in late 2000. US military aid has increased accordingly.

YEMENI ARMED FORCES

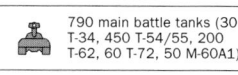

790 main battle tanks (30 T-34, 450 T-54/55, 200 T-62, 60 T-72, 50 M-60A1)	60,000 personnel
11 patrol boats	1700 personnel
116 combat aircraft (F-5E, Su-20/22, MiG-21, MiG-29)	5000 personnel
None	

ECONOMICS

Inflation 21% p.a. (1990–2001)

$9.15bn | 184.7 Yemeni rials (178)

SCORE CARD

- World GNP Ranking..........90th
- GNP per capita..........$490
- Balance of payments..........$342m
- Inflation..........15.9%
- Unemployment..........35%

EXPORTS

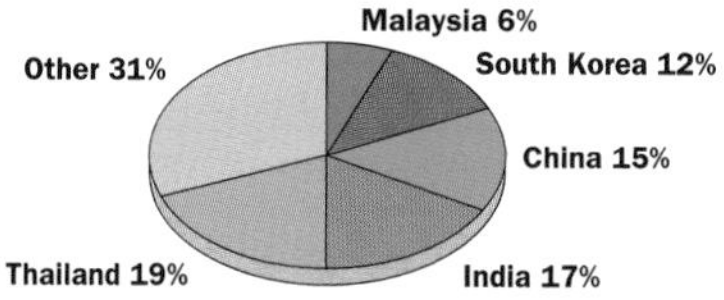
Malaysia 6%
South Korea 12%
Other 31%
China 15%
Thailand 19%
India 17%

IMPORTS

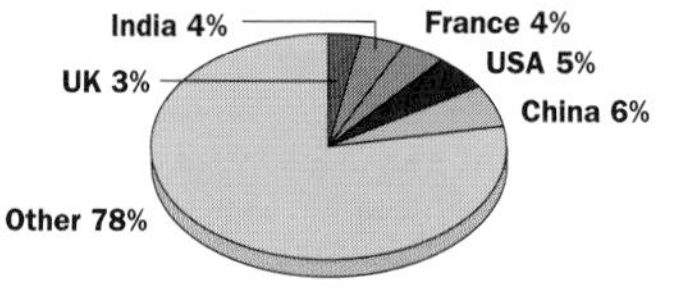
India 4%
France 4%
USA 5%
UK 3%
China 6%
Other 78%

Strengths

Rising oil production. Deposits of copper, gold, lead, molybdenum, and zinc. Industries: oil refining, chemicals, salt, foodstuffs, cement, leather. Aden "free zone." Improving private sector. Rural development program.

Weaknesses

Political instability deters investment. Civil war damage. Well-organized black market undermines tax base. Subsistence agriculture. High population growth, unemployment. Lack of central control, poor integration, and patronage politics hamper economic revival.

Profile

Unification in 1990 aimed to transform the economy, particularly through the exploitation of large oil and gas reserves, discovered in 1984; exports of oil began in 1987. Industrial investment around Aden was planned. These policies were severely affected by the 1991 Gulf War. In addition, the expulsion of over one million Yemeni guest workers from Saudi Arabia imposed a huge burden on the economy, boosting unemployment and ending the flow of workers' remittances.

The 1994 civil war seriously damaged oil refineries, water systems, and communications centers. Economic crisis forced the government to reduce expenditure and subsidies on certain staple foods. This provoked widespread civil unrest – there were particularly violent demonstrations in 1998 and 2003. Many farmers switched from food crops, such as wheat, to growing the more profitable narcotic plant qat, forcing Yemen to import food supplies. Strong oil prices in recent years and IMF-backed "streamlining" have encouraged substantial foreign debt relief and funded new dams and roads.

ECONOMIC PERFORMANCE INDICATOR

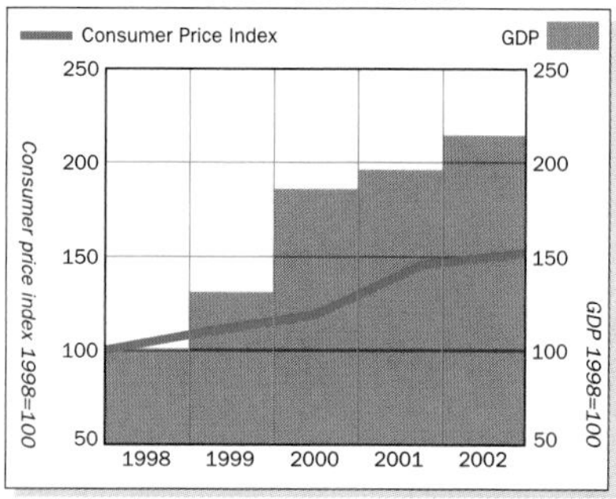
Consumer Price Index
GDP
Consumer price index 1998=100
GDP 1998=100
250
200
150
100
50
1998
1999
2000
2001
2002

YEMEN : MAJOR BUSINESSES

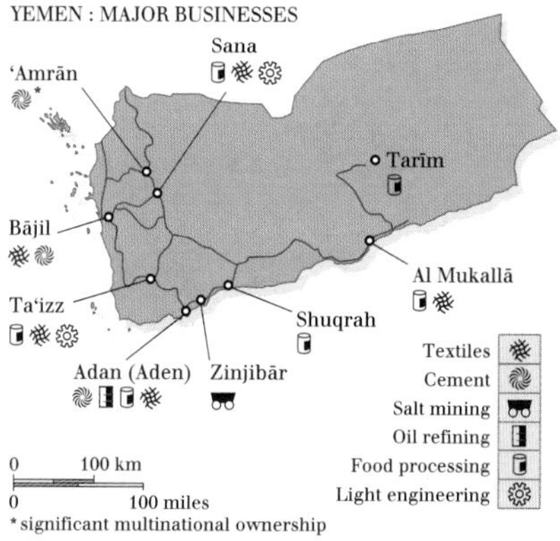
Sana
'Amrān
Tarīm
Bājil
Al Mukallā
Ta'izz
Shuqrah
Adan (Aden)
Zinjibār
Textiles
Cement
Salt mining
Oil refining
Food processing
Light engineering
0 100 km
0 100 miles
*significant multinational ownership

RESOURCES

Electric power 810,000 kW

142,198 tonnes

454,000 b/d (reserves 4bn barrels)

7.25m goats, 6.5m sheep, 34.8m chickens

Oil, natural gas, salt, copper, gold, lead, zinc, molybdenum

ELECTRICITY GENERATION

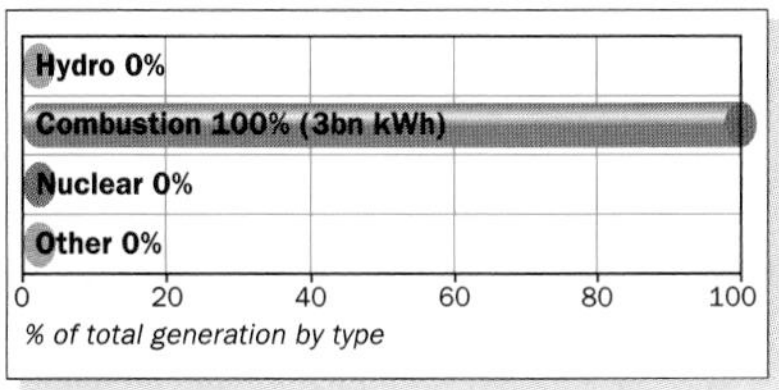
Hydro 0%
Combustion 100% (3bn kWh)
Nuclear 0%
Other 0%
0 20 40 60 80 100
% of total generation by type

Oil reserves are considerable, though initial estimates were exaggerated. The 2000 border agreement with Saudi Arabia promises better Yemeni access to oil fields. Salt is the only other mineral to be commercially exploited, and its production continues to grow steadily.

The agricultural sector employs just under half the working population. Cotton is a cash crop. Livestock and livestock products, including dairy produce and hides, are mainstays of the north. Yemen's rich fishing grounds in the Arabian Sea now provide a major source of earnings, despite poor equipment, though the "Aden free zone" project has encouraged investment in the port.

Yemen's population growth, averaging around 4% a year and among the highest in the world, is putting severe strain on the country's natural resources, especially water.

YEMEN : LAND USE

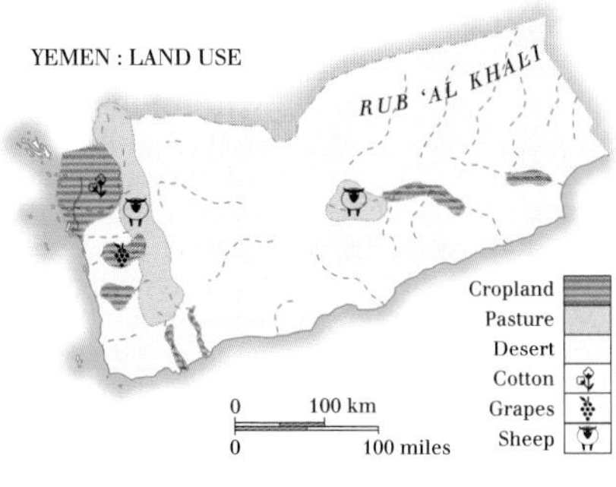
RUB 'AL KHALI
Cropland
Pasture
Desert
Cotton
Grapes
Sheep
0 100 km
0 100 miles

ENVIRONMENT

Not available

None

0.5 tonnes per capita

ENVIRONMENTAL TREATIES

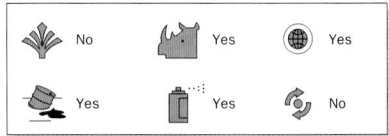

No	Yes	Yes
Yes	Yes	No

Large areas remain untouched by development, preserving habitats for rare birds. Problems include water scarcity, overgrazing, and soil erosion.

MEDIA

TV ownership high

Daily newspaper circulation 15 per 1000 people

PUBLISHING AND BROADCAST MEDIA

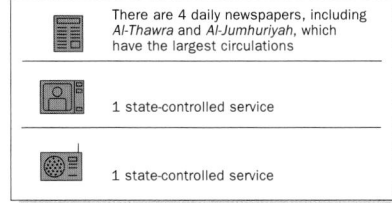

There are 4 daily newspapers, including *Al-Thawra* and *Al-Jumhuriyah*, which have the largest circulations

1 state-controlled service

1 state-controlled service

CRIME

Death penalty in use

14,000 prisoners

Up 42% in 2000

CRIME RATES

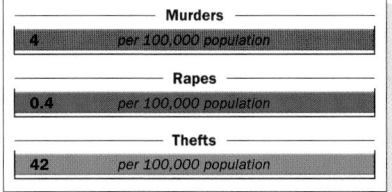

Murders
4 per 100,000 population

Rapes
0.4 per 100,000 population

Thefts
42 per 100,000 population

Political assassinations continue to threaten stability. There is little formal law enforcement outside the main cities; foreign companies risk kidnappings and theft by Bedouin raiders. There is a proliferation of illicit weapons: the number of firearms has been estimated at 60 million – three times the population size. Some blame lawlessness on the narcotic, qat.

EDUCATION

School leaving age: 14

49%

184,072 students

THE EDUCATION SYSTEM

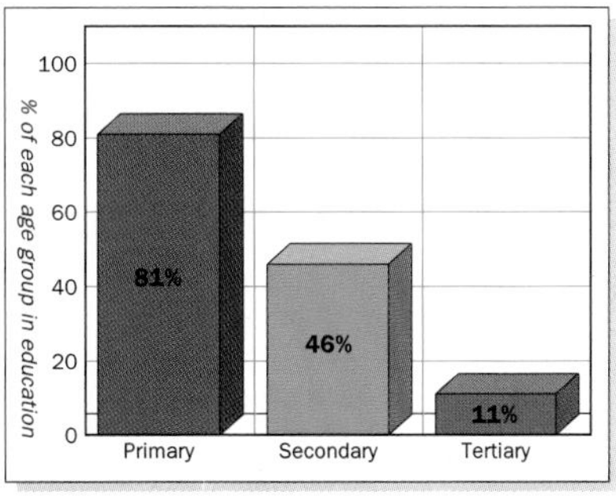
100
80
60
40
20
0
% of each age group in education
81%
46%
11%
Primary
Secondary
Tertiary

Some 80% of the population have had no formal classroom education; schooling barely extends beyond urban areas. Some 73% of women cannot read or write. In 2004 unregistered religious schools were ordered to be closed. There are two universities – Sana and Aden – as well as another five higher education institutions. The government's unpopular economic policies have encouraged student activism.

Yemen has a distinguished tradition of intellectual debate, and legislation embodies freedom of the press, but in practice this remains poorly developed. The government keeps tight control of the media and vets the entry of foreign journalists. TV and radio are state-controlled and have a limited range around the principal cities. Satellite TV is not generally available. Television and radio are particularly important media as illiteracy rates are very high.

HEALTH

No welfare state health benefits

1 per 5000 people

Diarrheal diseases, tuberculosis, malaria, bilharzia

The major cities have an adequate primary health care system. A new 300-bed hospital in Sana was due to be completed in 2004. Rural areas are less well served. In 2002 the World Bank approved a $27 million credit for a Health Reform Support Project to increase health provisions in poor communities. Health services are under threat from tribal gangs.

SPENDING

GDP/cap. increase

CONSUMPTION AND SPENDING

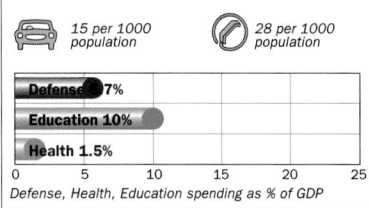

15 per 1000 population

28 per 1000 population

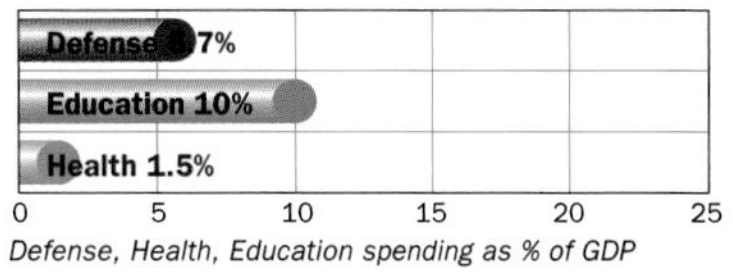
Defense 7%
Education 10%
Health 1.5%
0 5 10 15 20 25
Defense, Health, Education spending as % of GDP

Most Yemenis suffered a fall in living standards after Saudi Arabia expelled its Yemeni workers. A lack of jobs in other Gulf states has fueled unemployment, estimated at around 30%. Except for a small elite, the ownership of consumer goods is low.

WORLD RANKING

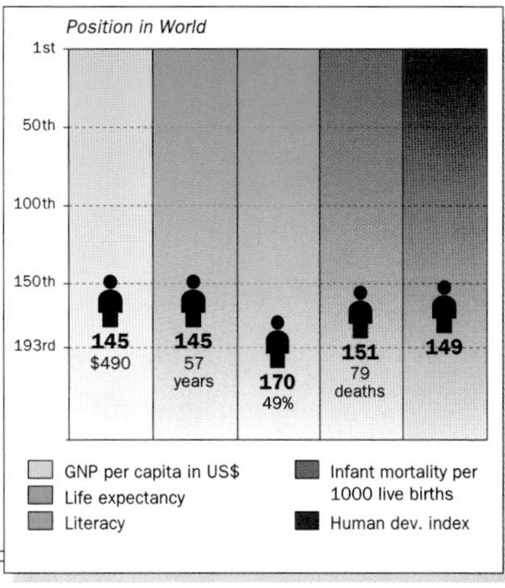
Position in World
1st
50th
100th
150th
193rd
145
$490
145
57 years
170
49%
151
79 deaths
149
GNP per capita in US$
Life expectancy
Literacy
Infant mortality per 1000 live births
Human dev. index

Y

ZAMBIA

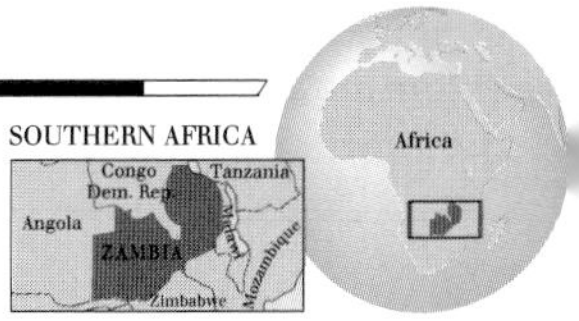
SOUTHERN AFRICA
Congo
Dem. Rep.
Tanzania
Angola
ZAMBIA
Zimbabwe
Mozambique
Africa

OFFICIAL NAME: Republic of Zambia **CAPITAL:** Lusaka
POPULATION: 10.8 million **CURRENCY:** Zambian kwacha **OFFICIAL LANGUAGE:** English

1964 | 1964 | Oct 24 | Z | +2 | +260 | .zm

LYING IN THE HEART of southern Africa, landlocked Zambia is a country of upland plateaus, bordered to the south by the Zambezi River. Its economic fortunes are tied to the copper industry: falling copper prices in the late 1970s, and then the growing inaccessibility of remaining reserves, have led to a severe decline in the economy. In 1991, Zambia achieved a peaceful transition from single-party rule to multiparty democracy.

CLIMATE

Tropical wet and dry

WEATHER CHART FOR LUSAKA

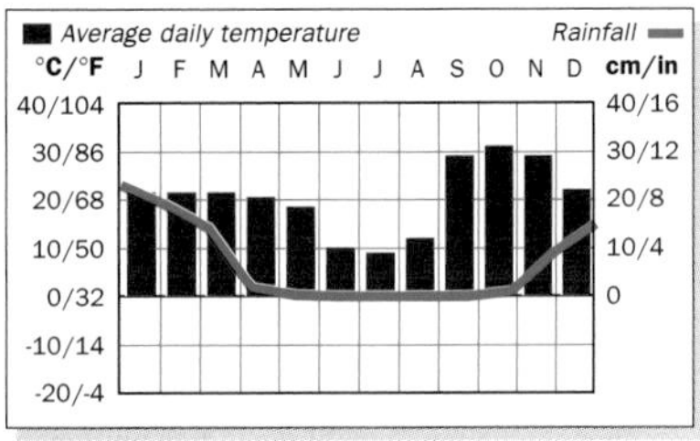
Average daily temperature
Rainfall
°C/°F
J F M A M J J A S O N D
cm/in
40/104
30/86
20/68
10/50
0/32
-10/14
-20/-4
40/16
30/12
20/8
10/4
0

Zambia has a tropical climate, with rains from November to April. The southwest is prone to drought.

TRANSPORTATION

Drive on left

Lusaka
390,406 passengers

Has no fleet

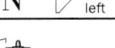

THE TRANSPORTATION NETWORK

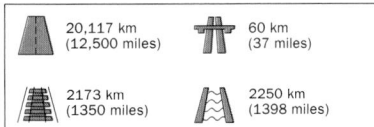

20,117 km (12,500 miles)

60 km (37 miles)

2173 km (1350 miles)

2250 km (1398 miles)

Road surfaces are often poor; railroads are being rehabilitated, especially those serving the copper mines. Zambian Airways was liquidated in 1994; private airlines are now in operation.

TOURISM

Visitors : Population 1:19

565,000 visitors

Down 2% in 2001–2002

MAIN TOURIST ARRIVALS

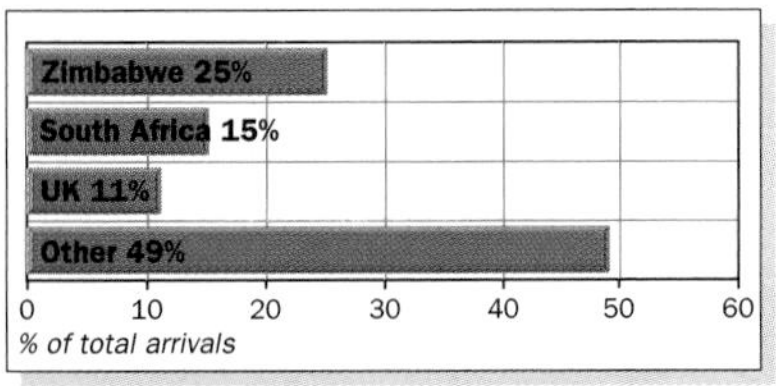
Zimbabwe 25%
South Africa 15%
UK 11%
Other 49%
0
10
20
30
40
50
60
% of total arrivals

The Victoria Falls, the country's most spectacular natural feature, draws many visitors. Wildlife and white-water rafting are other attractions.

PEOPLE

Pop. density low

Bemba, Tonga, Nyanja, Lozi, Lala-Bisa, Nsenga, English

15/km² (38/mi²)

THE URBAN/RURAL POPULATION SPLIT

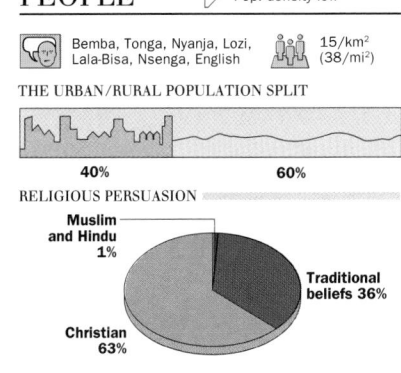

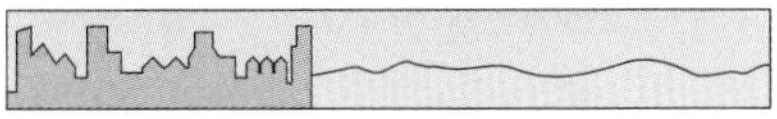
40%
60%

RELIGIOUS PERSUASION

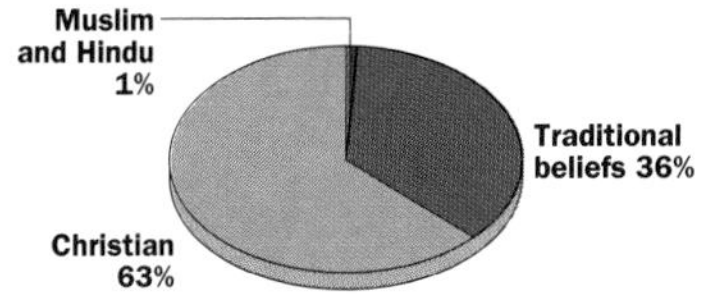
Muslim and Hindu 1%
Traditional beliefs 36%
Christian 63%

Though ethnically heterogeneous, with more than 70 different groups, Zambia has been less affected by ethnic tension than many African states. The largest group, about 34% of the population, is the Bemba, who live in the northeast and also predominate in the central Copperbelt. Other major groups are the southern Tonga, the eastern Nyanja, and the Lozi in the west. There are also thousands of refugees, from Angola and latterly from Zimbabwe and the DRC.

Zambia's main urban area is the Copperbelt, where many third- and fourth-generation town dwellers live. Some half a million children are employed there in hazardous conditions. The rural population lives mainly by subsistence farming.

A National Gender Policy was issued in October 2000 to redress inequalities between the sexes.

Musi-o-Tunya (The Smoke That Thunders), known in English as Victoria Falls. Spray from the falls can be seen 30 km (20 miles) away.

POLITICS

Multiparty elections

2001/2006

President Levy Mwanawasa

AT THE LAST ELECTION

National Assembly 158 seats

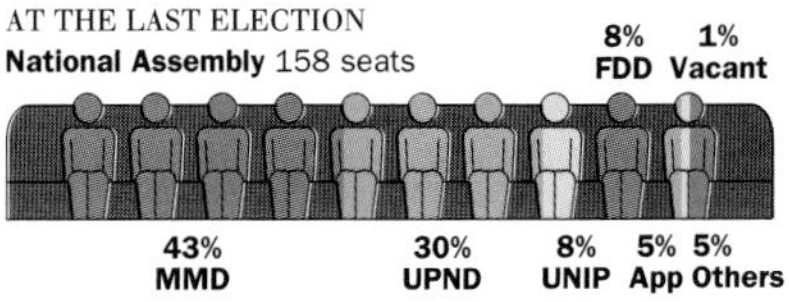
8% FDD
1% Vacant
43% MMD
30% UPND
8% UNIP
5% App
5% Others

MMD = Movement for Multiparty Democracy **UPND** = United Party for National Development **UNIP** = United National Independence Party **FDD** = Forum for Democracy and Development **App** = Appointed

Up to eight members are appointed by the president, and the speaker is also a member

Frederick Chiluba and the MMD defeated long-term president Kenneth Kaunda and the UNIP in 1991. Despite painful reforms Chiluba was eventually accused of the same failings as Kaunda: a struggling economy and authoritarian rule. In 2001 he purged the MMD of critics, prompting the formation of new opposition parties, and in 2002 his chosen successor, Levy Mwanawasa, won disputed elections. Mwanawasa condemned Chiluba's corruption, but he too soon faced the usual criticisms. He angered opposition parties by creating without their official consent a cross-party "national unity" government in 2003. He has questioned privatization policies, jeopardizing aid flows.

WORLD AFFAIRS

Joined UN in 1964

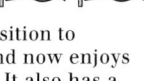

Comm | ACP | NAM | AU | SADC

Zambia led Africa's opposition to apartheid South Africa and now enjoys close links with Pretoria. It also has a significant role as a mediator in neighboring conflicts.

AID

Recipient

$641m (receipts)

Up 84% in 2002

Regional drought in 2002 dramatically increased the need for aid. Donors pledged $1.3 billion, returning aid to the yearly levels seen before a freeze in 1997 prompted by state corruption. By 2004 domestic food production had dramatically increased.

DEFENSE

No compulsory military service

$25m

Down 7% in 2002

Despite the relatively small budget, the 28,100-strong Zambian Defense Force is well equipped. Soldiers have been badly hit by HIV/AIDS.

ECONOMICS

Inflation 48% p.a. (1990–2001)

$3.46bn

4750 Zambian kwacha (4768)

SCORE CARD

❑ WORLD GNP RANKING	129th
❑ GNP PER CAPITA	$340
❑ BALANCE OF PAYMENTS	–$584m
❑ INFLATION	22.2%
❑ UNEMPLOYMENT	50%

STRENGTHS

Food produced for export. Boom in new export crops such as cotton and flowers. Minerals, notably copper, cobalt, and coal. Market-oriented reforms and privatization attracting foreign private investors. Copper industry finally privatized in 2003. Strategic location. Reduced customs duties.

WEAKNESSES

Overreliance on copper, which still accounts for around half of export earnings. Domestic reserves declining. Shortage of finance for restructuring. High inflation, negative growth, serious droughts. Arable land underused. Delays in privatization programs.

EXPORTS

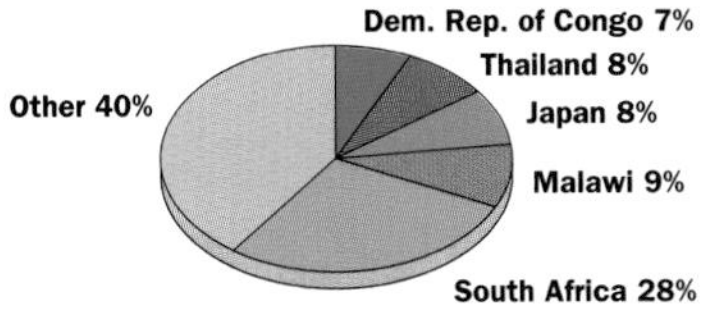
Dem. Rep. of Congo 7%
Thailand 8%
Japan 8%
Malawi 9%
South Africa 28%
Other 40%

IMPORTS

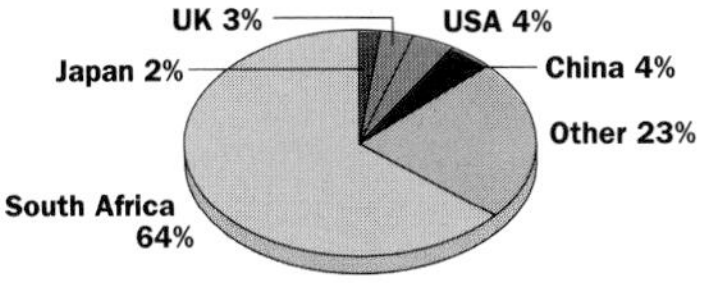
UK 3%
USA 4%
Japan 2%
China 4%
Other 23%
South Africa 64%

RESOURCES

Electric power 2.3m kW

69,200 tonnes

Not an oil producer

2.6m cattle, 1.27m goats, 340,000 pigs, 30m chickens

Copper, cobalt, coal, zinc, lead, gold, emeralds, amethysts

Copper production is rising after years of low world prices, and is expected soon to match the output of the 1970s. Zambia has rich hydropower potential.

ENVIRONMENT

Sustainability rank: 69th

32% (22% partially protected)

0.2 tonnes per capita

Drought is a recurrent hazard. Rhinos are almost extinct as a result of poaching. Revenues from legal hunting are being channeled into villages to encourage support for conservation.

MEDIA

TV ownership medium

Daily newspaper circulation 12 per 1000 people

PUBLISHING AND BROADCAST MEDIA

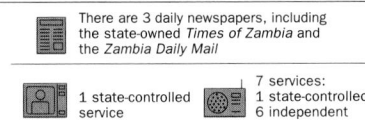

There are 3 daily newspapers, including the state-owned *Times of Zambia* and the *Zambia Daily Mail*

1 state-controlled service

7 services: 1 state-controlled, 6 independent

Broadcasting is dominated by the government. Opposition journalists have been accused of treason.

CRIME

Moratorium on death penalty

13,173 prisoners

Down 14% in 2000

Cases of violent crime and burglary are rising rapidly. President Mwanawasa pledged not to sign execution orders during his term of office.

CHRONOLOGY

Northern Rhodesia was developed by Britain solely for its copper. The UNIP, led by Kenneth Kaunda, took power at Zambian independence in 1964.

- ❑ **1972** UNIP one-party government.
- ❑ **1982–1991** Austerity measures and corruption: pressure for democracy.
- ❑ **1991** MMD government elected; Frederick Chiluba defeats Kaunda.
- ❑ **1996** Controversial elections.
- ❑ **2002** Levy Mwanawasa president.

EDUCATION

School leaving age: 13

80%

24,553 students

Schools are understaffed. Fees for secondary students have affected the already very low attendance rate.

HEALTH

Welfare state health benefits

1 per 10,000 people

Respiratory infections, diarrheal diseases, AIDS, malaria

HIV prevention programs are reducing infection rates in Lusaka. However, over 25% of town dwellers are HIV-positive.

SPENDING

GDP/cap. increase

CONSUMPTION AND SPENDING

17 per 1000 population

8 per 1000 population

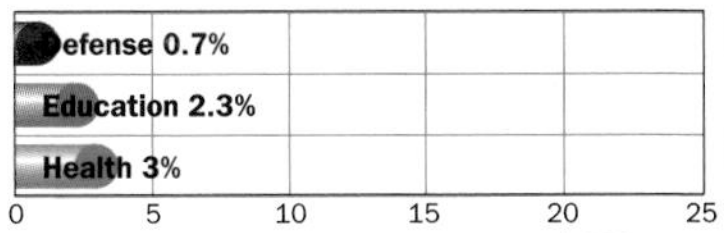
Defense 0.7%
Education 2.3%
Health 3%
0
5
10
15
20
25

Defense, Health, Education spending as % of GDP

Standards of living for most Zambians are now lower in real terms than at independence in 1964. Some people lack basic nutrition.

WORLD RANKING

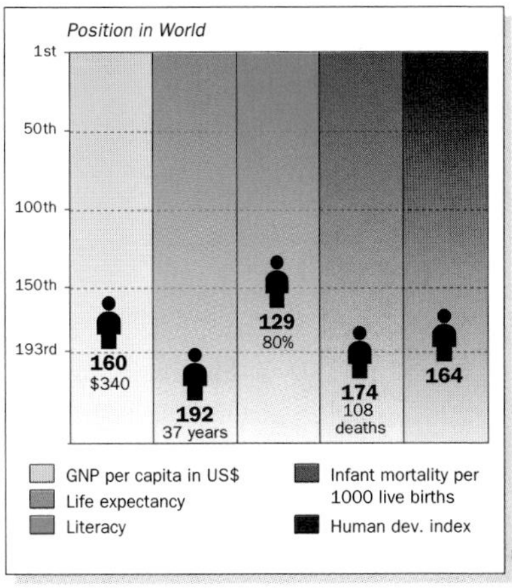
Position in World
1st
50th
100th
150th
193rd
160
$340
192
37 years
129
80%
174
108 deaths
164
GNP per capita in US$
Life expectancy
Literacy
Infant mortality per 1000 live births
Human dev. index

ZAMBIA

Total Area : 752 614 sq. km (290 584 sq. miles)

POPULATION

- ◉ over 500 000
- ◎ over 100 000
- ○ over 50 000
- ● over 10 000
- • under 10 000

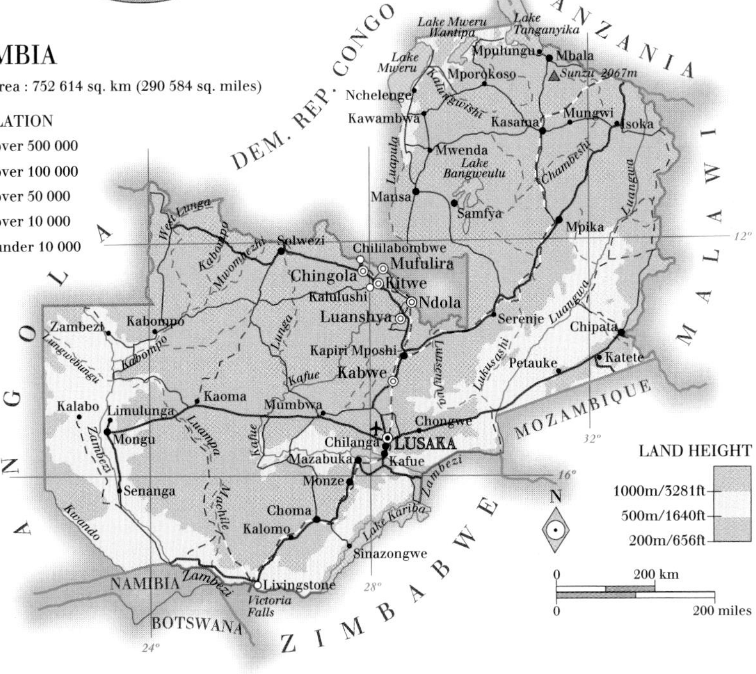
TANZANIA
DEM. REP. CONGO
ANGOLA
MALAWI
MOZAMBIQUE
ZIMBABWE
NAMIBIA
BOTSWANA
Lake Mweru Wantipa
Lake Tanganyika
Lake Mweru
Mpulungu
Mbala
Mporokoso
Sunzu 2067m
Nchelenge
Kawambwa
Kasama
Mungwi
Isoka
Mwenda
Lake Bangweulu
Mansa
Samfya
Mpika
Solwezi
Chililabombwe
Chingola
Mufulira
Kitwe
Kalulushi
Ndola
Luanshya
Serenje
Chipata
Zambezi
Kabompo
Kapiri Mposhi
Kabwe
Petauke
Katete
Kaoma
Kalabo
Limulunga
Mumbwa
Mongu
Chongwe
Chilanga
LUSAKA
Mazabuka
Kafue
Senanga
Monze
Choma
Kalomo
Sinazongwe
Livingstone
Victoria Falls
Lake Kariba
LAND HEIGHT
1000m/3281ft
500m/1640ft
200m/656ft
0
200 km
200 miles

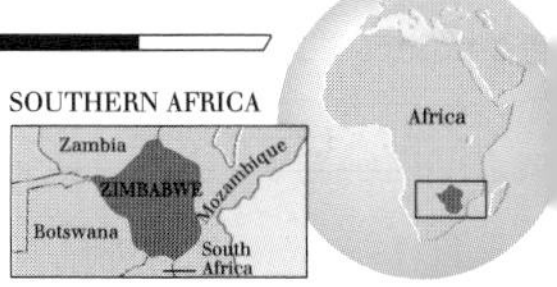
SOUTHERN AFRICA
Africa
Zambia
ZIMBABWE
Mozambique
Botswana
South Africa

ZIMBABWE

OFFICIAL NAME: Republic of Zimbabwe **CAPITAL:** Harare
POPULATION: 12.9 million **CURRENCY:** Zimbabwe dollar **OFFICIAL LANGUAGE:** English

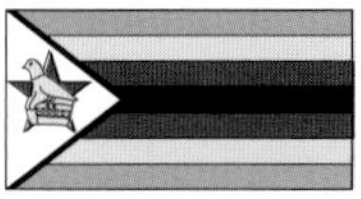

1980
1980
April 18
ZW
+2
+263
.zw

The Kariba Dam, which has created the vast Lake Kariba on the Zambezi River, lies on Zimbabwe's northwest border with Zambia.

ZIMBABWE IS SITUATED in southern Africa. Its upland center is crisscrossed by rivers flowing into Lake Kariba and the Zambezi River, on which lies the region's most spectacular natural feature, the Victoria Falls (Musi-o-Tunya). Attempts to preserve white rule in the former British colony led to a long guerrilla war before independence in 1980. Robert Mugabe, the country's leader since then and its president since 1987, has become increasingly authoritarian and divisive. Violent seizure of white-owned farmland and severe drought have contributed to virtual economic collapse.

CLIMATE

Tropical wet and dry/steppe

WEATHER CHART FOR HARARE

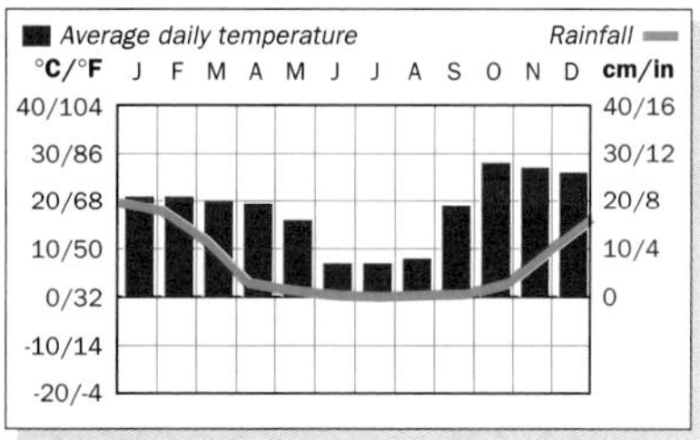
Average daily temperature
Rainfall
°C/°F
J F M A M J J A S O N D
cm/in
40/104
30/86
20/68
10/50
0/32
-10/14
-20/-4
40/16
30/12
20/8
10/4
0

Because of its altitude, Zimbabwe is comparatively temperate for a country in the tropics; humidity is also low. The rainy season occurs between November and March but, with the exception of the eastern highlands, rainfall is erratic and drought is common. Annual rainfall ranges from 140 cm (55 in) in the eastern highlands to 40 cm (16 in) in the Limpopo valley.

TRANSPORTATION

Drive on left

Harare 639,628 passengers

Has no fleet

THE TRANSPORTATION NETWORK

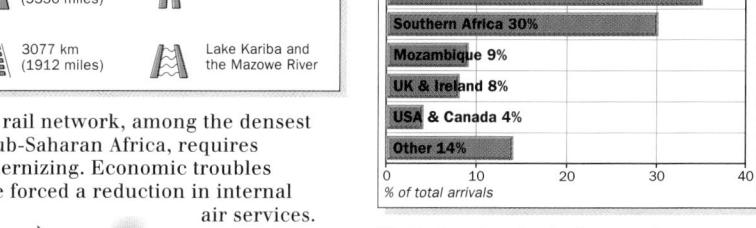

8619 km (5356 miles)

None

3077 km (1912 miles)

Lake Kariba and the Mazowe River

The rail network, among the densest in sub-Saharan Africa, requires modernizing. Economic troubles have forced a reduction in internal air services.

TOURISM

Visitors : Population 1:6.2

2.07m visitors

Up 11% in 2001

MAIN TOURIST ARRIVALS

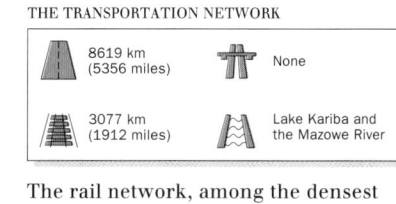

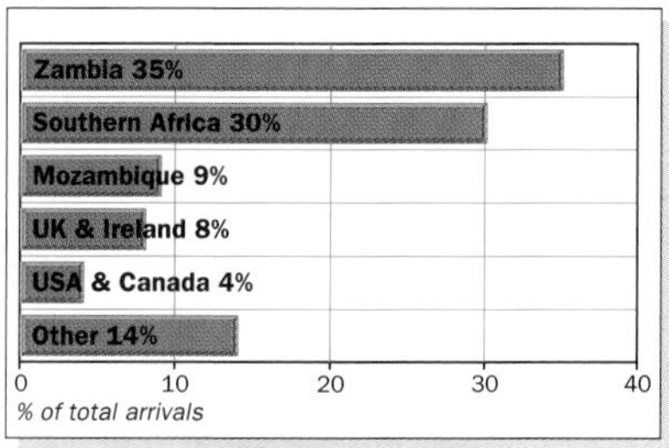
Zambia 35%
Southern Africa 30%
Mozambique 9%
UK & Ireland 8%
USA & Canada 4%
Other 14%
0
10
20
30
40
% of total arrivals

Zimbabwe's principal attractions are the Victoria Falls, the Kariba Dam, numerous national parks, the Great Zimbabwe ruins near Masvingo, and World's View in the Matopo Hills. Invasions of large commercial farms led by "war veterans", the violence in the run-up to the parliamentary elections in 2000, and the ensuing violent suppression of domestic political opposition have put Zimbabwe on the list of unsafe destinations for many visitors. Fuel and foreign currency shortages have further undermined the tourism sector.

In addition to these factors, Zimbabwe is wary that mass-market tourism might seriously damage the environment. However, the lure of foreign exchange has encouraged the development of conference facilities in Harare and vacation complexes, such as Elephant Hills, around Victoria Falls. State law requires there to be 30% local ownership of tourist ventures.

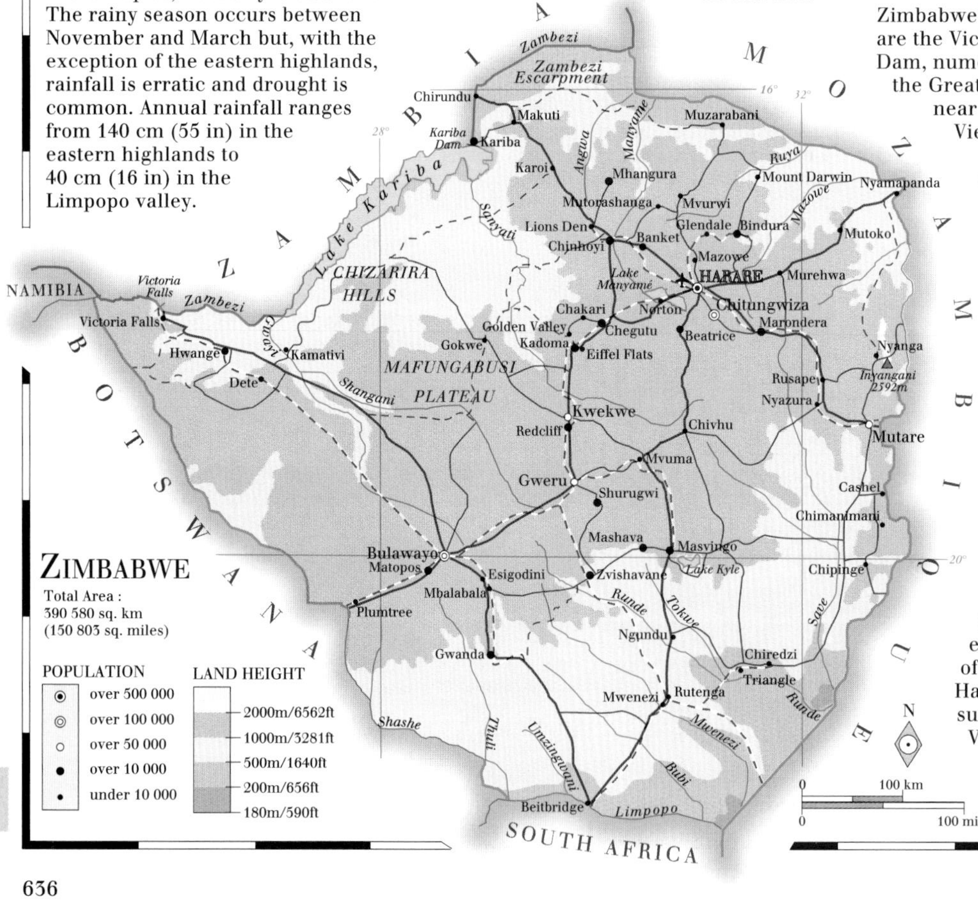
ZAMBIA
MOZAMBIQUE
BOTSWANA
NAMIBIA
SOUTH AFRICA
Zambezi
Zambezi Escarpment
Chirundu
Makuti
Kariba Dam
Kariba
Lake Kariba
Muzarabani
Karoi
Mhangura
Mount Darwin
Nyamapanda
Mutorashanga
Mvurwi
Lions Den
Glendale
Bindura
Mutoko
Chinhoyi
Banket
Mazowe
HARARE
Murehwa
Lake Manyame
Norton
Chitungwiza
Marondera
Chakari
Chegutu
Golden Valley
Kadoma
Eiffel Flats
Beatrice
Victoria Falls
Hwange
Kamativi
Dete
CHIZARIRA HILLS
Gokwe
MAFUNGABUSI PLATEAU
Shangani
Nyanga
Inyangani 2592m
Rusape
Nyazura
Kwekwe
Redcliff
Chivhu
Mutare
Mvuma
Gweru
Shurugwi
Cashel
Chimanimani
Mashava
Masvingo
Lake Kyle
Bulawayo
Matopos
Esigodini
Zvishavane
Chipinge
Mbalabala
Plumtree
Ngundu
Gwanda
Chiredzi
Triangle
Mwenezi
Rutenga
Shashe
Thuli
Umzingwani
Bubi
Runde
Tokwe
Save
Mwenezi
Beitbridge
Limpopo
Sanyati
Angwa
Manyame
Ruya
Mazowe
Gwai
16°
28°
32°
20°
ZIMBABWE
Total Area :
390 580 sq. km
(150 803 sq. miles)
POPULATION
over 500 000
over 100 000
over 50 000
over 10 000
under 10 000
LAND HEIGHT
2000m/6562ft
1000m/3281ft
500m/1640ft
200m/656ft
180m/590ft
N
0
100 km
100 miles

Z

PEOPLE

Pop. density low

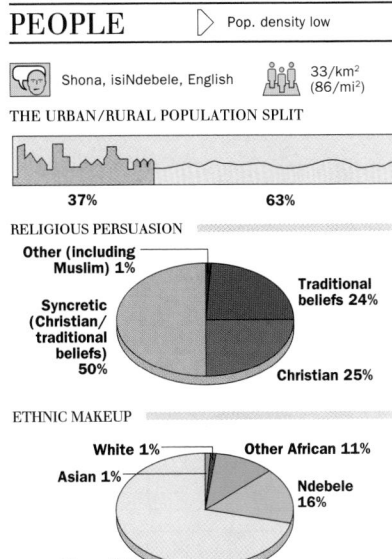

Shona, isiNdebele, English

33/km² (86/mi²)

THE URBAN/RURAL POPULATION SPLIT

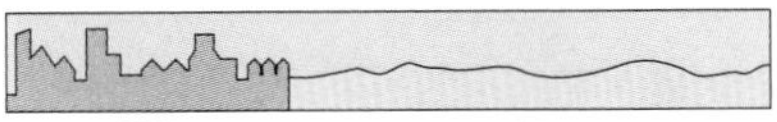
37%
63%

RELIGIOUS PERSUASION

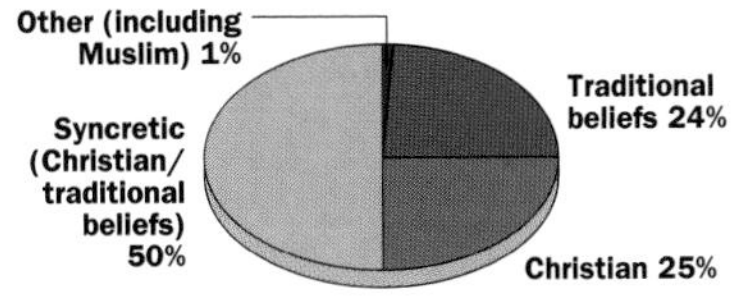
Other (including Muslim) 1%
Traditional beliefs 24%
Syncretic (Christian/ traditional beliefs) 50%
Christian 25%

ETHNIC MAKEUP

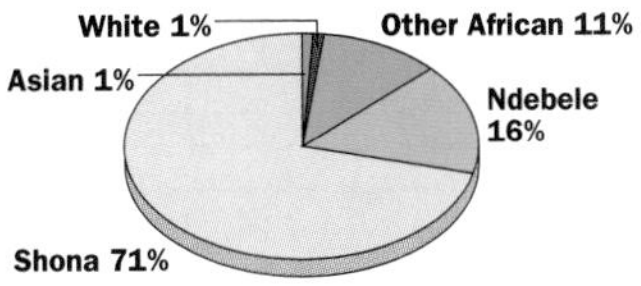
White 1%
Other African 11%
Asian 1%
Ndebele 16%
Shona 71%

There are two main ethnic groups, the majority Shona in the north and the Ndebele in the south. The European and Asian communities are declining.

Ethnic tensions plagued the 1980s. In 1983 alone 1500 Ndebele were massacred by the army as the ruling, Shona-dominated, ZANU–PF attempted to suppress the predominantly Ndebele Zimbabwe African People's Union (PF–ZAPU). A Unity Accord in 1987 eased the conflict, and ZAPU leader Joshua Nkomo was appointed vice president in 1990.

As a legacy of colonial rule, whites remain generally far more affluent than blacks, an imbalance partly redressed by policies to improve black education and increase employment. Redistribution of land, previously slow and dogged by accusations of corruption, was stepped up in 2000. A movement to seize white-owned farms was backed by the government and discrimination against whites officially endorsed. Tensions have increased massively.

POPULATION AGE BREAKDOWN

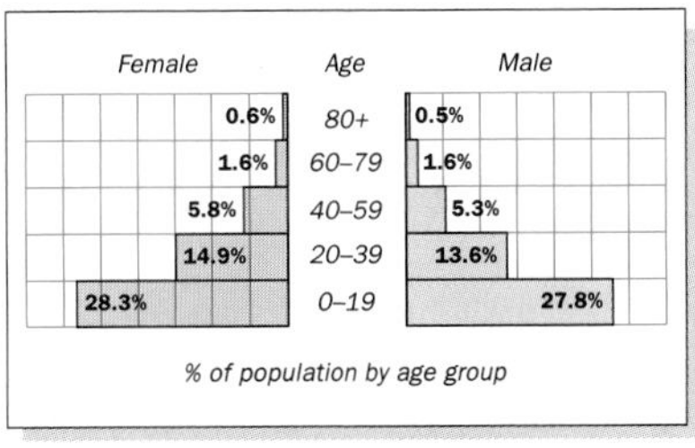
Female
Age
Male
0.6%
80+
0.5%
1.6%
60–79
1.6%
5.8%
40–59
5.3%
14.9%
20–39
13.6%
28.3%
0–19
27.8%
% of population by age group

Families are large, and almost half the population is under 15. Zimbabwean society is traditionally patriarchal. In 1999 a Supreme Court ruling provoked protest by according only "junior male" status to black women, especially those marrying under traditional law.

POLITICS

Multiparty elections

2000/2005

President Robert Gabriel Mugabe

AT THE LAST ELECTION

Parliament 150 seats

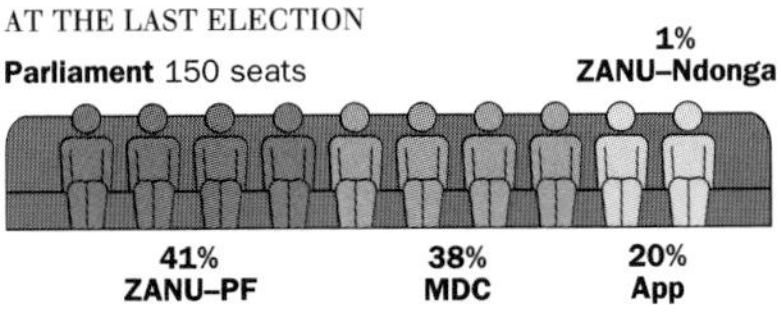
1%
ZANU–Ndonga
41%
ZANU–PF
38%
MDC
20%
App

ZANU–PF = Zimbabwe African National Union–Patriotic Front
MDC = Movement for Democratic Change **App** = Appointed
ZANU–Ndonga = Zimbabwe African National Union–Ndonga

30 seats are set aside for presidential appointments and traditional chiefs

80% of MPs are elected. The president is directly elected every six years.

PROFILE

After leading Zimbabwe to independence as a democracy and winning an internal dispute with the Zimbabwe African People's Union (ZAPU), Robert Mugabe's ZANU–PF has since dominated politics. However, its status has been questioned as support for the opposition MDC has grown since its formation in 1999. Despite widespread preelection intimidation, the MDC won a convincing share of votes in 2000, particularly in Harare and Bulawayo, and its members have since been victimized by government thugs. MDC leader Morgan Tsvangirai was charged with treason in 2002 and has been repeatedly arrested for organizing strikes. In 2004 the MDC vowed to boycott elections until Mugabe introduced genuine political reform.

MAIN POLITICAL ISSUES

The rule of President Mugabe

Mugabe, hitherto prime minister, was elected president unopposed in 1987. He dropped attempts to create a one-party socialist state in 1991. His position has become increasingly precarious as ZANU–PF has lost support in the face of economic collapse and a reinvigorated opposition led by the MDC. He has resorted to authoritarian and violent policies to stay in power. His reelection in 2002 drew widespread criticism, and in 2004 he banned human rights NGOs.

Land redistribution

Though most agree that the distribution of farmland unfairly favored the white minority, the speed and method of belated land redistribution has provoked protest. White-owned farms have been confiscated without compensation and violently occupied by self-styled "war veterans" who have government blessing. The policy has led to a huge drop in grain production.

Robert Mugabe, *elected prime minister in 1980 and president in 1987.*

Morgan Tsvangirai, *leader of the opposition MDC.*

AID

Recipient

US$201m (receipts)

Up 23% in 2002

Political violence since 2000 has prompted most international aid donors to suspend financial support. Struggling under massive food shortages, Zimbabwe agreed in 2002 to accept genetically modified food aid. However, in 2004 the World Food Program withdrew its teams after they were not allowed to survey food stocks; agencies were told that food aid was not needed, as Zimbabwe will be self-sufficient by the next harvest. The opposition has requested supplies to continue, fearing that scarce food supplies will be used as a political tool.

WORLD AFFAIRS

Joined UN in 1980

COMESA G15 NAM AU SADC

Zimbabwe is an active member of the SADC and COMESA. Relations with postapartheid South Africa are particularly good. Zimbabwean troops were active in the DRC from 1998 to 2002. This strong involvement in African affairs and Mugabe's own role as an anticolonial champion have led to regional support for the confrontational policy against white commercial farmers. His increasingly antidemocratic stance, however, has brought near-total isolation from the wider international community. The EU, the US, and the UK have been loud in their condemnation of Mugabe's regime, and sanctions and aid suspensions have contributed to the perilous state of the economy. Despite agreeing to Zimbabwe's suspension from the Commonwealth in 2002, southern African leaders were bitterly disappointed by its extension, which prompted Mugabe to withdraw Zimbabwe completely in late 2003.

CHRONOLOGY

In 1953, the British colony of Southern Rhodesia became part of the Federation of Rhodesia and Nyasaland with Northern Rhodesia (now Zambia) and Nyasaland (now Malawi).

- **1961** Joshua Nkomo forms ZAPU.
- **1962** ZAPU banned. Segregationist Rhodesian Front (RF) wins polls.
- **1963** African nationalists in Northern Rhodesia and Nyasaland demand dissolution of Federation. ZANU, offshoot of ZAPU, formed by Rev. Sithole and Robert Mugabe.
- **1964** New RF prime minister Ian Smith rejects British demands for majority rule. ZANU banned.
- **1965** May, RF reelected. November, state of emergency declared (renewed until 1990). Smith's unilateral declaration of independence. UK imposes economic sanctions. ANC, ZANU, and ZAPU begin guerrilla war.
- **1974** RF regime agrees cease-fire terms with African nationalists.
- **1976** ZANU and ZAPU unite as Patriotic Front (PF).
- **1977** PF backed by "frontline" African states: Mozambique, Tanzania, Botswana, and Zambia.
- **1979** Lancaster House talks produce agreement on constitution.
- **1980** Independence as Zimbabwe. Following violent election campaign, Mugabe becomes prime minister of ZANU–PF/ PF–ZAPU coalition. Relations severed with South Africa.
- **1983–1984** Unrest in Matabeleland, PF–ZAPU's power base.
- **1985** Elections return ZANU–PF, with manifesto to create one-party state. Many PF–ZAPU members arrested.
- **1987** Provision for white seats in parliament abolished. ZANU–PF and PF–ZAPU sign unity agreement (merge in 1989). Mugabe elected president.
- **1990** Elections won by ZANU–PF. Mugabe reelected president.
- **1991** Mugabe abandons plan for one-party state. Severe drought.
- **1999** Death of Vice President Nkomo. Opposition forms MDC.
- **2000** Government loses referendum on new constitution. Expropriations of white-owned farmland by squatters. Strong MDC performance in polls. ZANU–PF accused of using intimidation to retain majority.
- **2002** Mugabe reelected in flawed poll. Commonwealth membership suspended. Threat of mass starvation and economic collapse.
- **2003** Zimbabwe leaves Commonwealth.

Z

DEFENSE

No compulsory military service

US$637m

Up 122% in 2002

Nationalist guerrillas were the heroes of independence in 1980. By the late 1990s, however, resentment grew when ex-combatants demanded enormous pensions.

Though formally nonaligned, Zimbabwe supported the Mozambican regime against Renamo guerrillas and backed the US-led operation in Somalia in 1992–1995. The withdrawal of troops from the Democratic Republic of the Congo (DRC), dispatched there in 1998 to help President Laurent Kabila fight rebels, began in April 2001, following the Lusaka peace accord. Troops remained in the DRC for many months after the withdrawal was officially completed in 2002.

Despite economic crisis, US$200 million was spent on jet fighters and military vehicles from China in 2004.

ZIMBABWEAN ARMED FORCES

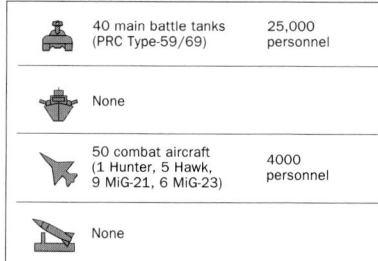

Army	40 main battle tanks (PRC Type-59/69)	25,000 personnel
Navy	None	
Air force	50 combat aircraft (1 Hunter, 5 Hawk, 9 MiG-21, 6 MiG-23)	4000 personnel
Missiles	None	

ECONOMICS

Inflation 28% p.a. (1990–2001)

US$6.16bn

5348 Zimbabwe dollars (824)

SCORE CARD

World GNP Ranking	105th
GNP per Capita	US$470
Balance of Payments	–US$467m
Inflation	140%
Unemployment	70%

EXPORTS

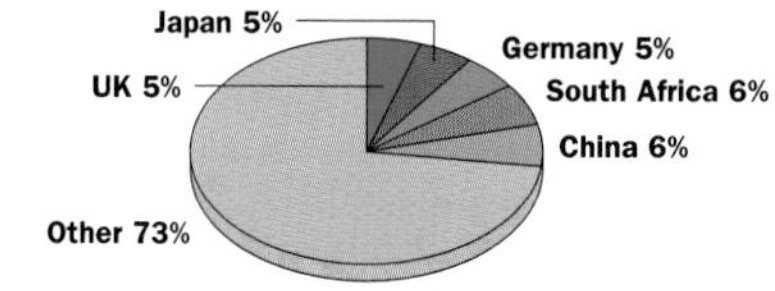

Japan 5%
UK 5%
Germany 5%
South Africa 6%
China 6%
Other 73%

IMPORTS

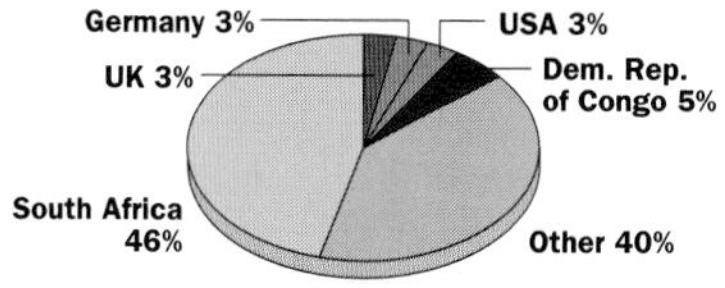

Germany 3%
UK 3%
USA 3%
Dem. Rep. of Congo 5%
South Africa 46%
Other 40%

ECONOMIC PERFORMANCE INDICATOR

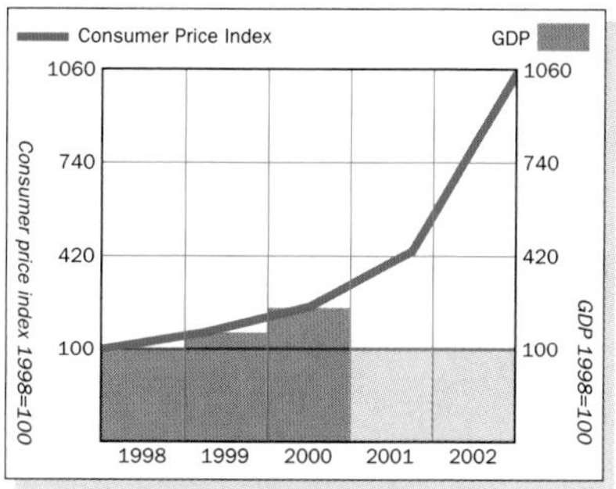

Consumer Price Index
GDP
1060
740
420
100
Consumer price index 1998=100
GDP 1998=100
1998
1999
2000
2001
2002

Strengths

Sound infrastructure. Broad-based economy. Virtual self-sufficiency in energy. Gold, coal, horticulture, cotton. Tourist potential. Good education system.

Weaknesses

Political violence since 2000: foreign investors deterred. Massive food shortages; risk of famine. Shortages of fuel and cash. Agriculture and hydroelectric output affected by drought. Mass emigration. Large budget deficits, unemployment, and inflation. Labor unrest, bank collapses, food price riots. Cheap imports damage local industries.

Profile

In 1991 a market-oriented economy superseded the socialist policies of the 1980s, increasing unemployment and inflation. Prospects for the mining industry appear particularly bleak: collapsing mineral prices have forced the closure of diamond, gold, platinum, and chromium mines. The cost of living and inflation have soared amid economic chaos; prices for basic provisions were fixed in 2001. The black market is now more important than the formal economy, while there is greater reliance on remittances from economic emigrants.

ZIMBABWE : MAJOR BUSINESSES

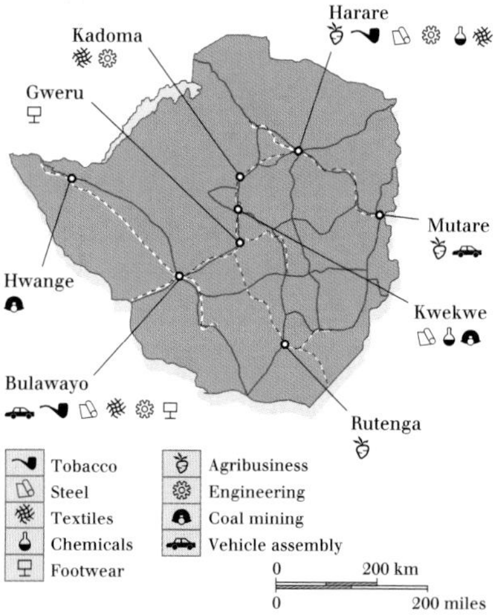

Harare
Kadoma
Gweru
Mutare
Hwange
Kwekwe
Bulawayo
Rutenga
Tobacco
Steel
Textiles
Chemicals
Footwear
Agribusiness
Engineering
Coal mining
Vehicle assembly
0
200 km
0
200 miles

RESOURCES

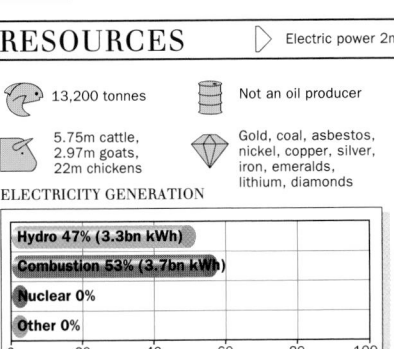

Electric power 2m kW

13,200 tonnes

Not an oil producer

5.75m cattle, 2.97m goats, 22m chickens

Gold, coal, asbestos, nickel, copper, silver, iron, emeralds, lithium, diamonds

ELECTRICITY GENERATION

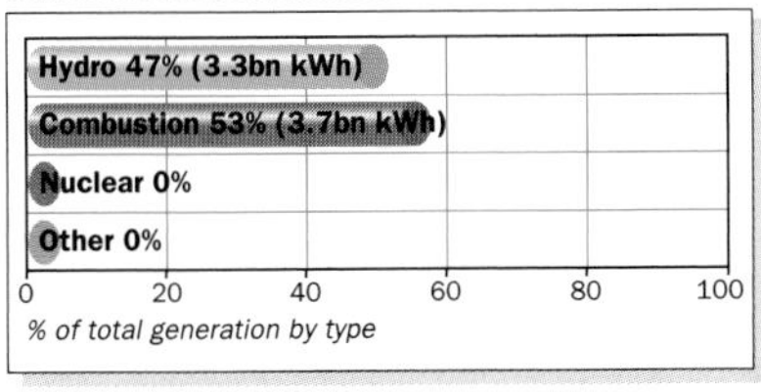
Hydro 47% (3.3bn kWh)
Combustion 53% (3.7bn kWh)
Nuclear 0%
Other 0%
0
20
40
60
80
100
% of total generation by type

Over 45% of electricity needs are met by hydropower; the Kariba Dam provides the bulk of this energy. The plant is run by the Central African Power Company and is jointly owned with Zambia. There are plans to privatize the Zimbabwean power company ZESA. Plans to build new hydroelectric dams in the region have been shelved as the Zimbabwean economy stagnates. Coal production declined by 17% at Hwange in 2000, but Malaysian investments there are set to exploit large deposits. Zimbabwe is a net energy importer.

ZIMBABWE : LAND USE

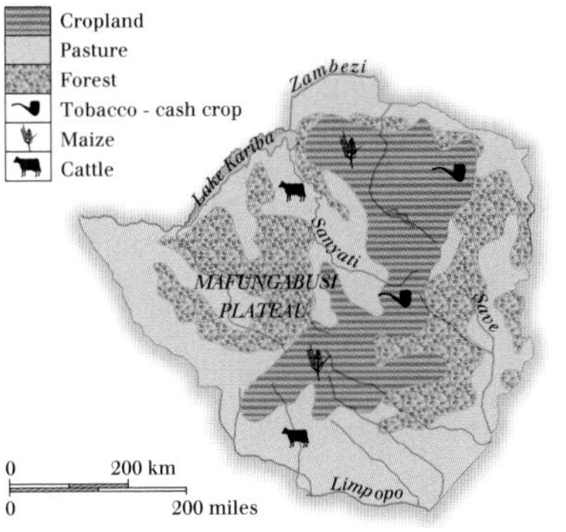
Cropland
Pasture
Forest
Tobacco - cash crop
Maize
Cattle
Zambezi
Lake Kariba
Sanyati
MAFUNGABUSI PLATEAU
Save
Limpopo
0
200 km
0
200 miles

ENVIRONMENT

Sustainability rank: 46th

12% (6% partially protected)

1.2 tonnes per capita

ENVIRONMENTAL TREATIES

No	Yes	Yes
No	Yes	No

In communal areas, the land is suffering from overpopulation and overstocking. Deforestation, soil erosion, and deterioration of wildlife and water resources are widespread. There are concerns over future plans to build more hydroelectric dams.

Measures have been taken to protect the black rhinoceros, including moving them to safer areas and combating poaching: patrols have killed some 200 poachers since 1984 when a shoot-to-kill policy was first introduced. The government also supports a scheme for dehorning – the horn is the poachers' main target. In 1997 Zimbabwe led the move at the Convention on International Trade in Endangered Species to allow a limited resumption of international trade in ivory. An increase in ivory poaching since 1999 has led to calls for more protection for elephants.

CRIME

Death penalty in use

21,000 prisoners

Up 17% in 2000–2001

CRIME RATES

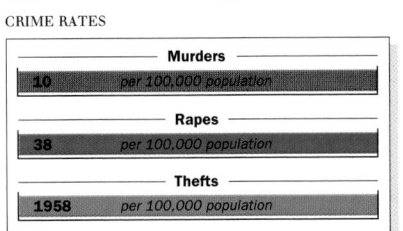

Murders	10 per 100,000 population
Rapes	38 per 100,000 population
Thefts	1958 per 100,000 population

Murder and narcotics-related offenses are rife in urban areas. The illegal occupation of white-owned farms, supported by the government, and electoral violence have led to many deaths. The secret service and the army have been criticized for human rights abuses.

HEALTH

Welfare state health benefits

1 per 10,000 people

AIDS, tuberculosis, accidents, malaria, heart disease, cancers

The largest threat to health is AIDS. It has dramatically reduced average life expectancy, created around a million orphans, and kills 3000 people a week. A belated AIDS program, offering generic drugs, is now in place. Malaria and tuberculosis account for many other deaths. The beleaguered health system is free for the poor.

SPENDING

GDP/cap. increase

CONSUMPTION AND SPENDING

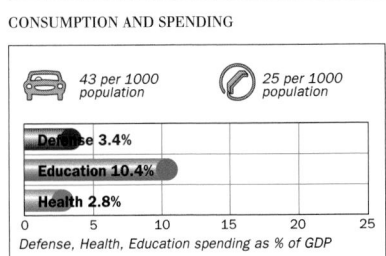

43 per 1000 population

25 per 1000 population

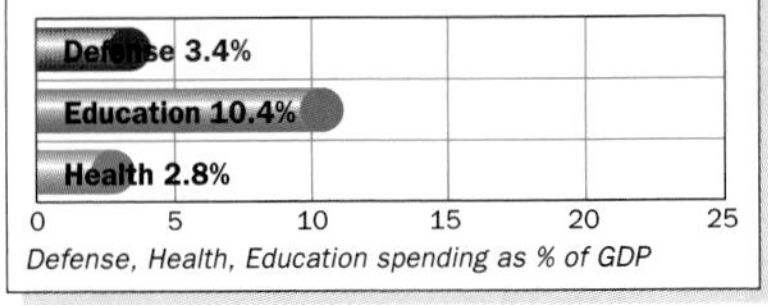
Defense 3.4%
Education 10.4%
Health 2.8%
0
5
10
15
20
25
Defense, Health, Education spending as % of GDP

Socialist policies in the 1980s lessened the gap between blacks and whites. But currency depreciation and inflation have since greatly reduced real wages.

MEDIA

TV ownership medium

Daily newspaper circulation 18 per 1000 people

PUBLISHING AND BROADCAST MEDIA

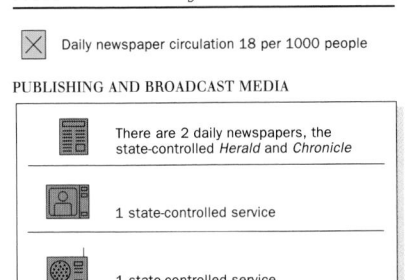

There are 2 daily newspapers, the state-controlled *Herald* and *Chronicle*

1 state-controlled service

1 state-controlled service

Persecution of journalists has increased since a 2002 press law. The independent *Daily News* has faced severe government harassment, and has been closed intermittently under the legislation.

EDUCATION

School leaving age: 12

90%

48,894 students

THE EDUCATION SYSTEM

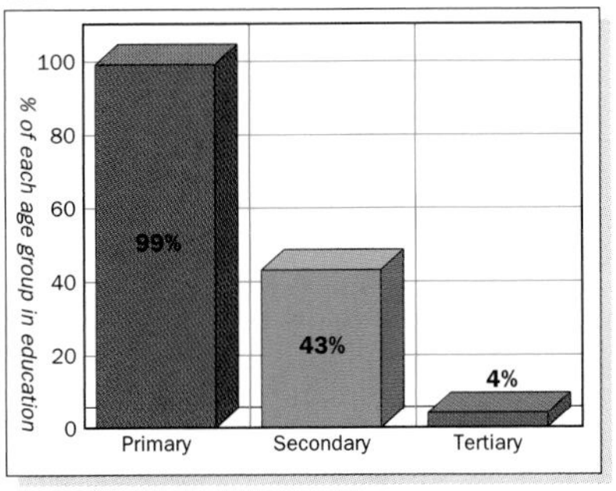
100
80
60
40
20
0
% of each age group in education
99%
43%
4%
Primary
Secondary
Tertiary

Improving education, and trebling attendance at primary school, were signal successes in the postindependence period. Education is compulsory and instruction is in English. The introduction of fees in 1992 raised fears that many parents would be forced to pull at least some of their children out of school, particularly girls. In 2004, when private schools hiked fees, the authorities closed 45 of them, accusing them of seeking to deter black pupils.

WORLD RANKING

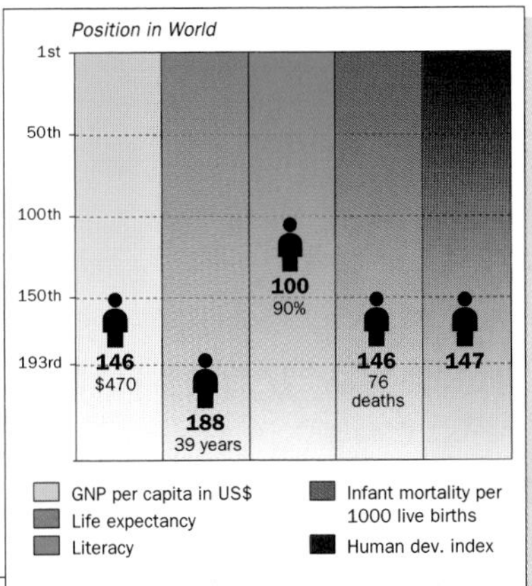
Position in World
1st
50th
100th
150th
193rd
146
$470
188
39 years
100
90%
146
76
deaths
147
GNP per capita in US$
Life expectancy
Literacy
Infant mortality per 1000 live births
Human dev. index

Z

Overseas Territories & Dependencie

DESPITE THE RAPID process of decolonization since 1945 (pages 52–55), roughly seven million people around the world still live in nonsovereign territories under the protection of the UK, the US, France, Netherlands, Denmark, Norway, Australia, or New Zealand. These remnants of former colonial empires may have persisted for economic, strategic, or political reasons. Hong Kong and Macao reverted to Chinese control in the late 1990s. Others await political developments, such as referenda, which will determine their future status. Finally, there is a large group of territories that are considered too small, remote, or weak to be able to survive as independent states.

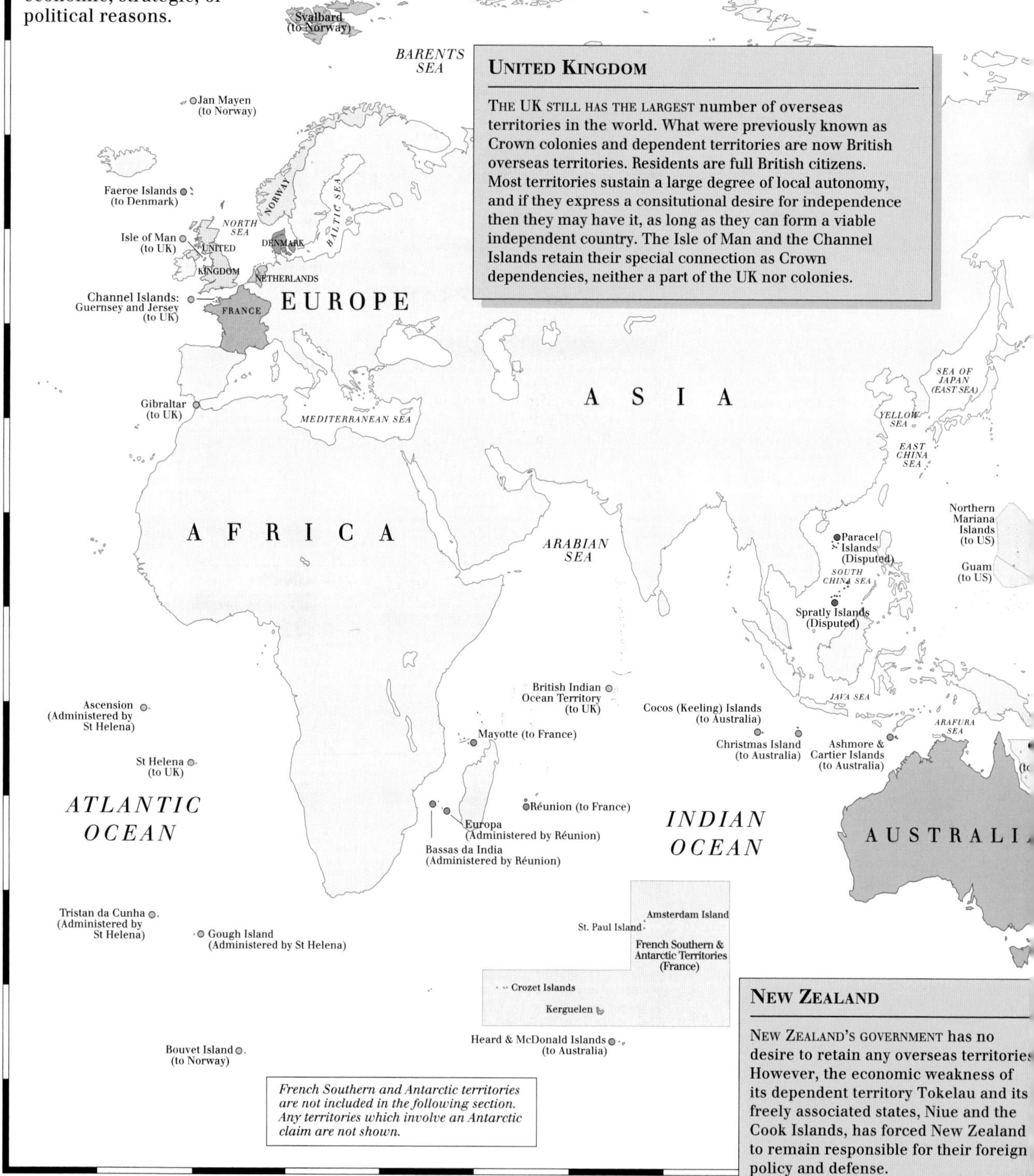
Svalbard (to Norway)
BARENTS SEA
Jan Mayen (to Norway)
Faeroe Islands (to Denmark)
NORWAY
BALTIC SEA
NORTH SEA
Isle of Man (to UK)
UNITED KINGDOM
DENMARK
NETHERLANDS
Channel Islands: Guernsey and Jersey (to UK)
FRANCE
EUROPE
A S I A
SEA OF JAPAN (EAST SEA)
Gibraltar (to UK)
MEDITERRANEAN SEA
YELLOW SEA
EAST CHINA SEA
A F R I C A
ARABIAN SEA
Northern Mariana Islands (to US)
Paracel Islands (Disputed)
SOUTH CHINA SEA
Guam (to US)
Spratly Islands (Disputed)
British Indian Ocean Territory (to UK)
JAVA SEA
Ascension (Administered by St Helena)
Cocos (Keeling) Islands (to Australia)
ARAFURA SEA
Mayotte (to France)
Christmas Island (to Australia)
Ashmore & Cartier Islands (to Australia)
St Helena (to UK)
ATLANTIC OCEAN
Réunion (to France)
INDIAN OCEAN
Europa (Administered by Réunion)
Bassas da India (Administered by Réunion)
AUSTRALI
Amsterdam Island
St. Paul Island
Tristan da Cunha (Administered by St Helena)
Gough Island (Administered by St Helena)
French Southern & Antarctic Territories (France)
Crozet Islands
Kerguelen
Heard & McDonald Islands (to Australia)
Bouvet Island (to Norway)

French Southern and Antarctic territories are not included in the following section. Any territories which involve an Antarctic claim are not shown.

United Kingdom

THE UK STILL HAS THE LARGEST number of overseas territories in the world. What were previously known as Crown colonies and dependent territories are now British overseas territories. Residents are full British citizens. Most territories sustain a large degree of local autonomy, and if they express a consitutional desire for independence then they may have it, as long as they can form a viable independent country. The Isle of Man and the Channel Islands retain their special connection as Crown dependencies, neither a part of the UK nor colonies.

New Zealand

NEW ZEALAND'S GOVERNMENT has no desire to retain any overseas territories. However, the economic weakness of its dependent territory Tokelau and its freely associated states, Niue and the Cook Islands, has forced New Zealand to remain responsible for their foreign policy and defense.

ITED STATES OF AMERICA

OVERSEAS TERRITORIES OF THE US have been seen as tegically useful, if expensive, parts of its backyard. US has, in most cases, given the local population y in deciding its own status. Thus, full sovereignty been granted to three successor states of the ner US-administered UN Trust Territory of the ific Islands. A US commonwealth territory, such as rto Rico, has a greater level of independence than of a US unincorporated or external territory.

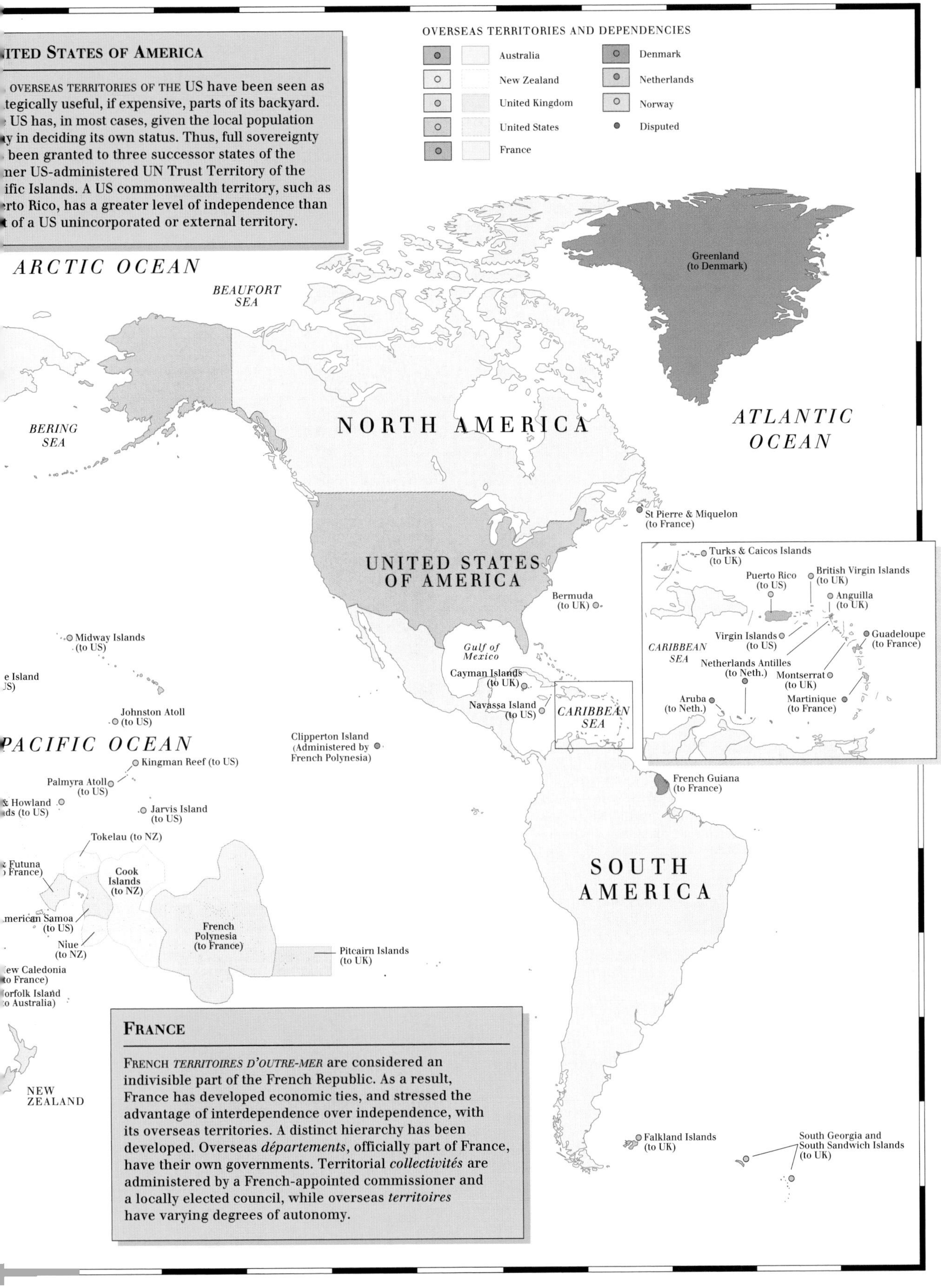
OVERSEAS TERRITORIES AND DEPENDENCIES
Australia
New Zealand
United Kingdom
United States
France
Denmark
Netherlands
Norway
Disputed
ARCTIC OCEAN
BEAUFORT SEA
BERING SEA
Greenland (to Denmark)
NORTH AMERICA
ATLANTIC OCEAN
St Pierre & Miquelon (to France)
UNITED STATES OF AMERICA
Bermuda (to UK)
Turks & Caicos Islands (to UK)
Puerto Rico (to US)
British Virgin Islands (to UK)
Anguilla (to UK)
Guadeloupe (to France)
Virgin Islands (to US)
CARIBBEAN SEA
Netherlands Antilles (to Neth.)
Montserrat (to UK)
Aruba (to Neth.)
Martinique (to France)
Midway Islands (to US)
e Island
JS)
Gulf of Mexico
Cayman Islands (to UK)
Navassa Island (to US)
CARIBBEAN SEA
Johnston Atoll (to US)
PACIFIC OCEAN
Clipperton Island (Administered by French Polynesia)
Kingman Reef (to US)
Palmyra Atoll (to US)
& Howland ds (to US)
Jarvis Island (to US)
French Guiana (to France)
Tokelau (to NZ)
Futuna France)
Cook Islands (to NZ)
SOUTH AMERICA
merican Samoa (to US)
French Polynesia (to France)
Niue (to NZ)
Pitcairn Islands (to UK)
ew Caledonia o France)
orfolk Island o Australia)
NEW ZEALAND
Falkland Islands (to UK)
South Georgia and South Sandwich Islands (to UK)

FRANCE

FRENCH *TERRITOIRES D'OUTRE-MER* are considered an indivisible part of the French Republic. As a result, France has developed economic ties, and stressed the advantage of interdependence over independence, with its overseas territories. A distinct hierarchy has been developed. Overseas *départements*, officially part of France, have their own governments. Territorial *collectivités* are administered by a French-appointed commissioner and a locally elected council, while overseas *territoires* have varying degrees of autonomy.

AMERICAN SAMOA

STATUS: Unincorporated territory of the US **CLAIMED:** 1900
CAPITAL: Pago Pago **POP.:** 70,260 **DENSITY:** 360/km² (937/mi²)

COMPRISING THE EASTERN half of the Samoan islands, American Samoa sits on the edge of Polynesia in the South Pacific Ocean. Though Christianity, introduced in the 19th century, has taken a very firm hold – Samoa is known as the "Bible Belt" of the Pacific – the traditional and conservative *fa'a Samoa* (Samoan way of life) continues to dominate the islands' culture. At its base is the extended family, the *aiga*, while traditional chiefs, or *matai*, retain their central role in government. Samoa came under the control of the US in 1900, and life there remained largely unchanged until a US-led drive for modernization in the 1960s. Along with better health care and industrial development, *fa'a Amerika* also meant unemployment, pollution, and rising petty crime fueled by alcohol. Tuna processed by Pago Pago's canneries represent 93% of American Samoa's exports. Efforts to diversify include the development of other light industries and tourism.

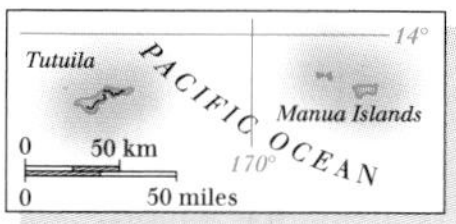
Tutuila
PACIFIC OCEAN
Manua Islands
14°
170°
0 50 km
0 50 miles

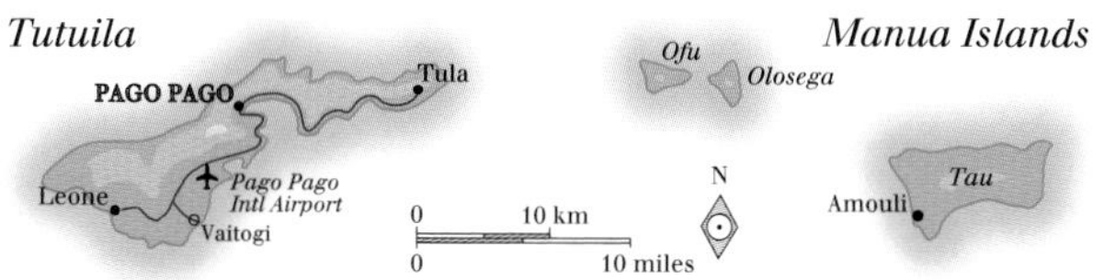
Tutuila
PAGO PAGO
Tula
Leone
Pago Pago Intl Airport
Vaitogi
Ofu
Olosega
Manua Islands
Tau
Amouli
N
0 10 km
0 10 miles

ANGUILLA

STATUS: British overseas territory **CLAIMED:** 1650
CAPITAL: The Valley **POP.:** 12,738 **DENSITY:** 133/km² (344/mi²)

LYING IN THE CENTER of the Leeward Islands, in the Caribbean, Anguilla has a subtropical climate, the heat and humidity being tempered by trade winds. Lumped by the UK into a joint colonial administration with St. Kitts and Nevis, Anguillans took up arms to protect their dependent status in 1967 when St. Kitts and Nevis was awarded internal self-government. Lacking any major industry, Anguilla relied on the economic stability that came with being an overseas territory. In the 1980s the island's government resolved to introduce a tourist industry and targeted the luxury end of the market. Tourism is now Anguilla's main source of income. Almost 50,000 tourists, around 60% from the US, visit Anguilla each year.

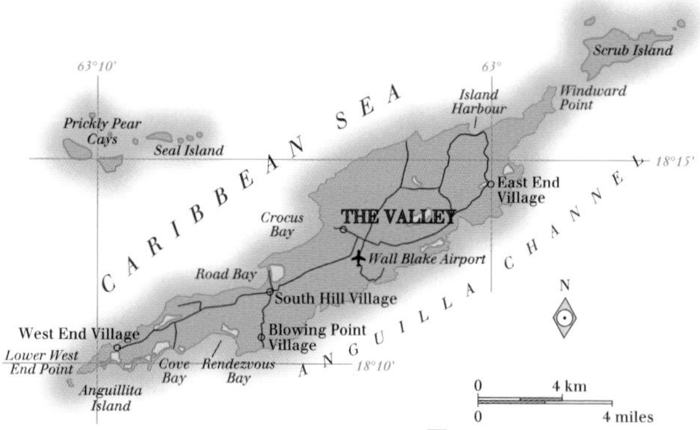
63°10'
63°
Scrub Island
Island Harbour
Windward Point
Prickly Pear Cays
Seal Island
CARIBBEAN SEA
18°15'
East End Village
THE VALLEY
Crocus Bay
Wall Blake Airport
Road Bay
South Hill Village
ANGUILLA CHANNEL
West End Village
Blowing Point Village
Lower West End Point
Cove Bay
Rendezvous Bay
18°10'
Anguillita Island
N
0 4 km
0 4 miles

ARUBA

STATUS: Autonomous part of the Netherlands **CLAIMED:** 1643
CAPITAL: Oranjestad **POP.:** 70,844 **DENSITY:** 367/km² (945/mi²)

THE MOST DEVELOPED island among the Dutch Caribbean territories, Aruba lies 25 km (15 miles) off the coast of Venezuela. Its tropical climate is moderated by constant trade winds sweeping in from the Atlantic. Formerly the richest island in the Netherlands Antilles, Aruba became a separate dependency of the Netherlands in 1986. Transition to full independence, expected in 1996, was halted in 1994 after an agreement was reached between the governments of the Netherlands, Aruba, and the Netherlands Antilles. The Netherlands voiced concern over the island's security and the danger of its becoming a base for narcotics trafficking, and the Aruban government questioned the desirability of full independence, citing high unemployment and economic instability.

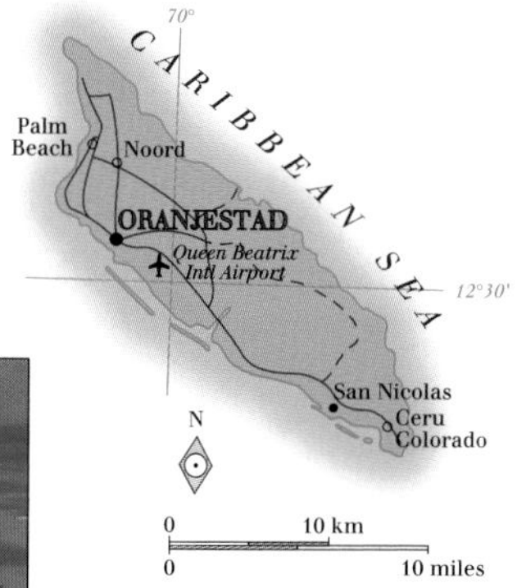
70°
CARIBBEAN SEA
Palm Beach
Noord
ORANJESTAD
Queen Beatrix Intl Airport
12°30'
San Nicolas
Ceru Colorado
N
0 10 km
0 10 miles

Since 1986, the economy of Aruba, formerly dependent on oil refining, has diversified. Tourism and offshore finance have become the most important sectors of the economy, and there are now more than 600,000 visitors annually, the majority of them from the US. The rapid expansion of tourism has, however, put considerable strain on Aruba's infrastructure, and some attempt has been made to restrict the number of visitors. At the same time facilities have been improved to encourage the growth of the data-processing industry.

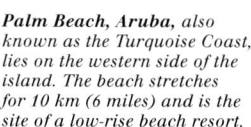

Palm Beach, Aruba, *also known as the Turquoise Coast, lies on the western side of the island. The beach stretches for 10 km (6 miles) and is the site of a low-rise beach resort.*

Oranjestad, *Aruba's capital, contains many Dutch colonial-style buildings. Though first claimed by the Spanish in 1499, Aruba was colonized by the Dutch in the 17th century.*

Aruba's cooperation with the US in the region includes support for its actions against narcotics trafficking from South America, and since the closure of the US base in Panama in 1999, US aircraft have used bases on the island to launch reconnaissance flights. Those who oppose this cooperation fear that it could drag Aruba unnecessarily into the civil conflict in Colombia.

BERMUDA

STATUS: British overseas territory **CLAIMED:** 1612
CAPITAL: Hamilton **POP.:** 64,482 **DENSITY:** 1217/km² (3224/mi²)

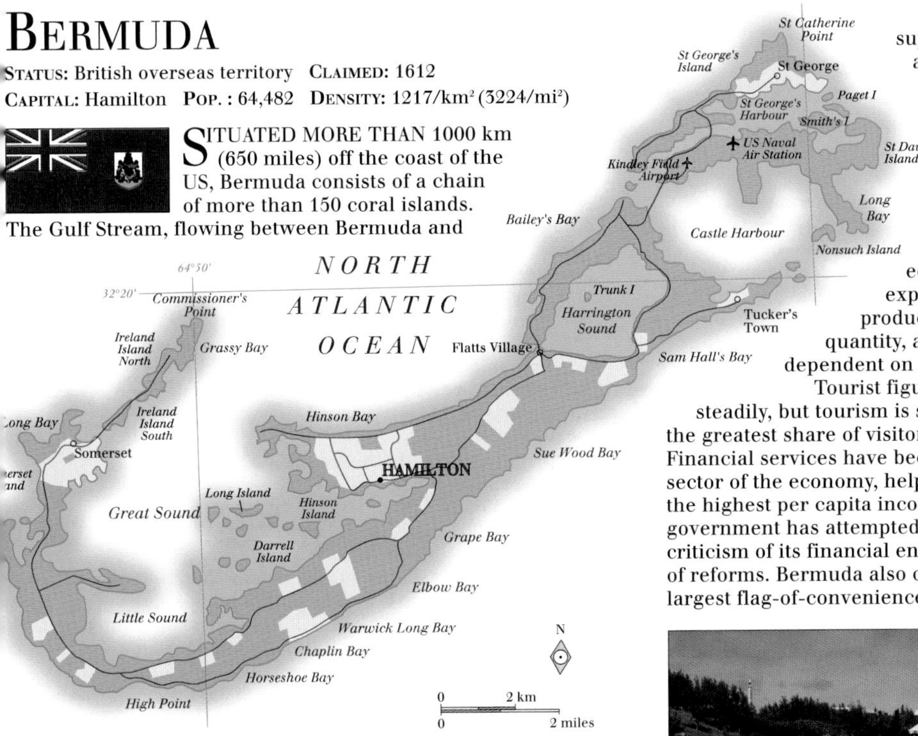

St Catherine Point
St George's Island
St George
St George's Harbour
Paget I
Smith's I
US Naval Air Station
St David's Island
Kindley Field Airport
Long Bay
Bailey's Bay
Castle Harbour
Nonsuch Island
NORTH ATLANTIC OCEAN
64°50'
32°20'
Commissioner's Point
Trunk I
Harrington Sound
Tucker's Town
Ireland Island North
Grassy Bay
Flatts Village
Sam Hall's Bay
Hinson Bay
Ireland Island South
Somerset
Sue Wood Bay
HAMILTON
Long Island
Hinson Island
Great Sound
Grape Bay
Darrell Island
Elbow Bay
Little Sound
Warwick Long Bay
Chaplin Bay
Horseshoe Bay
High Point
N
0 2 km
0 2 miles

SITUATED MORE THAN 1000 km (650 miles) off the coast of the US, Bermuda consists of a chain of more than 150 coral islands. The Gulf Stream, flowing between Bermuda and the eastern seaboard of the US, keeps the climate mild and humid. Bermuda is racially mixed; over a third of the population are of European extraction. Racial tension has lessened since the 1960s and 1970s. A more representative electoral system was established after a Royal Commission visited Bermuda in 1978.

For 30 years after the first general election, held in 1968, Bermuda was ruled by the conservative United Bermuda Party (UBP). Its veteran leader, Sir John Swan, resigned as prime minister and party leader in 1995, when a referendum decisively rejected his campaign for independence from the UK. In a general election in 1998 the UBP was heavily defeated by the Progressive Labour Party, which pledged to suppress its proindependence aspirations while in government. Major issues include the complexity of the tax structure, reform of the bloated civil service, soaring property prices, rising crime, environmental issues, and narcotics trafficking. Bermuda is overwhelmingly a service economy. Lilies are grown for export, but few other agricultural products are grown in sufficient quantity, and the islands are heavily dependent on food imports.

Tourist figures have been falling steadily, but tourism is still a significant industry, the greatest share of visitors coming from the US. Financial services have become the most important sector of the economy, helping to maintain one of the highest per capita incomes in the world. The government has attempted to head off international criticism of its financial environment through a series of reforms. Bermuda also operates one of the world's largest flag-of-convenience shipping fleets.

***Bermuda** has one of the highest densities of golf courses in the world. Nine courses have now been developed.*

BRITISH INDIAN OCEAN TERRITORY

STATUS: British overseas territory **CLAIMED:** 1814
CAPITAL: Diego Garcia **POP.:** 3000 **DENSITY:** 50/km² (130/mi²)

THE BRITISH Indian Ocean Territory, or Chagos Islands, lies in the middle of the Indian Ocean. The coral atolls are uninhabited, except for the UK–US military base on Diego Garcia, and the UK has undertaken to cede the islands to Mauritius when they are no longer required. An appeal by the Chagossians, evicted by the UK from the islands in 1968, for compensation was rejected by the UK High Court in 2003.

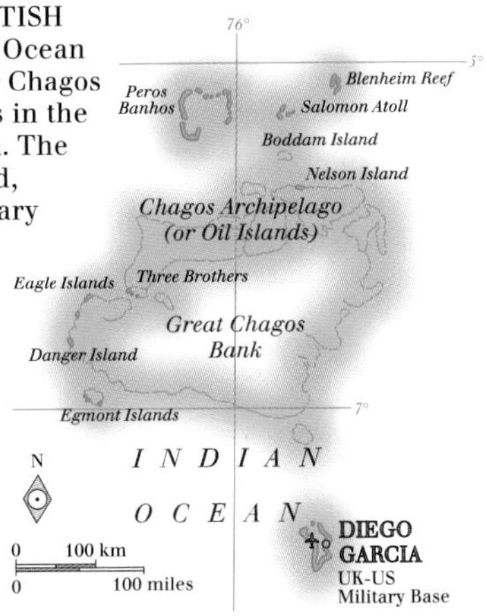

76°
5°
Blenheim Reef
Peros Banhos
Salomon Atoll
Boddam Island
Nelson Island
Chagos Archipelago (or Oil Islands)
Eagle Islands
Three Brothers
Great Chagos Bank
Danger Island
Egmont Islands
7°
N
INDIAN OCEAN
DIEGO GARCIA
UK-US Military Base
0 100 km
0 100 miles

BRITISH VIRGIN ISLANDS

STATUS: British overseas territory **CLAIMED:** 1672
CAPITAL: Road Town **POP.:** 21,730 **DENSITY:** 142/km² (368/mi²)

AN ARCHIPELAGO of 60 Caribbean islands, 15 of them inhabited, the British Virgin Islands lie at the northwestern end of the Leeward Islands chain. Tourism, now a major economic activity, is suited to the tropical climate, but there is concern about its effect on the environment. There are also fears that traditional place-names are being altered to be more tourist-friendly. The offshore finance sector is important, and has been more tightly regulated since 1990, following scandals involving foreign firms registered in the territory.

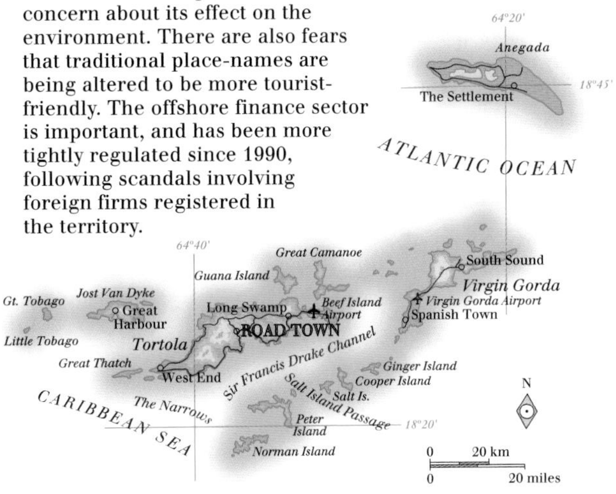

64°20'
Anegada
18°45'
The Settlement
ATLANTIC OCEAN
64°40'
Great Camanoe
South Sound
Guana Island
Virgin Gorda
Jost Van Dyke
Virgin Gorda Airport
Gt. Tobago
Great Harbour
Long Swamp
Beef Island Airport
Spanish Town
ROAD TOWN
Little Tobago
Tortola
Sir Francis Drake Channel
Great Thatch
Ginger Island
West End
Cooper Island
Salt Island Passage
Salt Is.
The Narrows
CARIBBEAN SEA
Peter Island
18°20'
Norman Island
N
0 20 km
0 20 miles

Cayman Islands

Status: British overseas territory **Claimed:** 1670
Capital: George Town **Pop.:** 41,934 **Density:** 162/km² (419/mi²)

THE LARGEST OF BRITAIN'S territories in the Caribbean, the Cayman Islands lie 225 km (140 miles) west of Jamaica and south of Cuba. The abundance of exotic wildlife, especially marine life, is a powerful draw for tourists. Grand Cayman is credited as the home of modern scuba diving, the first ever specialist shop opening there in 1957. The islanders have rejected greater autonomy, persuaded that their economic stability is linked to their status as an overseas territory. Thanks to the absence of tax and foreign-exchange controls, the islands form one of the world's largest offshore financial centers, but tourism continues to underpin the economy.

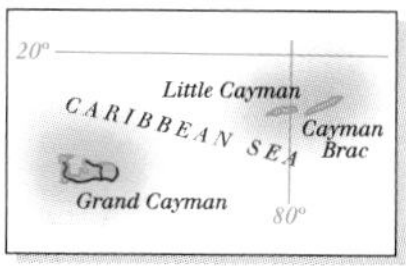
20°
Little Cayman
CARIBBEAN SEA
Cayman Brac
Grand Cayman
80°

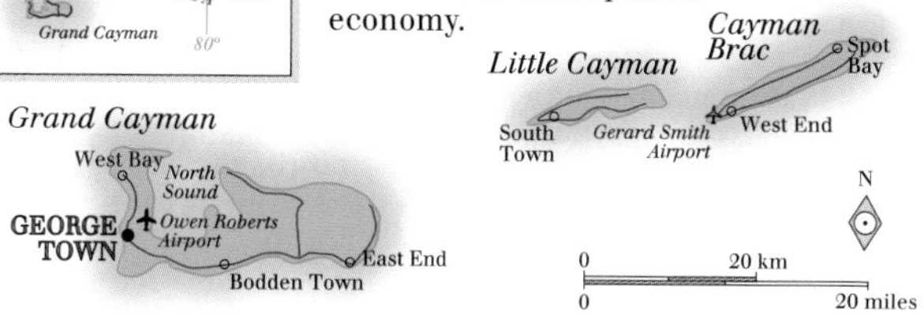
Cayman Brac
Spot Bay
Little Cayman
South Town
Gerard Smith Airport
West End
Grand Cayman
West Bay
North Sound
GEORGE TOWN
Owen Roberts Airport
East End
Bodden Town
N
0 20 km
0 20 miles

Christmas Island

Status: Australian external territory **Claimed:** 1958
Capital: Flying Fish Cove **Pop.:** 433 **Density:** 3/km² (8/mi²)

SO NAMED because it was sighted on Christmas Day in 1643, Christmas Island lies in the Indian Ocean, 380 km (240 miles) south of Java. Its population is mostly Malay and Chinese, descended from laborers imported to mine rich phosphate deposits. A national park covers some 70% of the island. In 2001 Australia agreed with Russia to begin construction of a major rocket-launching site on the island.

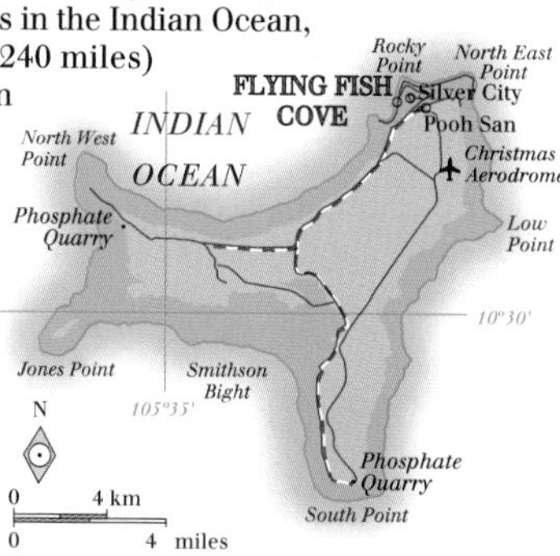
Rocky Point
North East Point
FLYING FISH COVE
Silver City
Pooh San
North West Point
INDIAN OCEAN
Christmas I Aerodrome
Phosphate Quarry
Low Point
10°30'
Jones Point
Smithson Bight
105°35'
N
Phosphate Quarry
0 4 km
0 4 miles
South Point

Cocos (Keeling) Islands

Status: Australian external territory **Claimed:** 1955
Capital: West Island **Pop.:** 630 **Density:** 45/km² (126/mi²)

IN ALL, 27 coral atolls make up the Cocos (Keeling) Islands. Situated in the Indian Ocean, roughly halfway between Australia and Sri Lanka, they have been part of the Northern Territory electoral district since 1992. The inhabited islands are the European-dominated West Island and Home Island, which has a mainly Cocos Malay community. Coconuts are the sole cash crop.

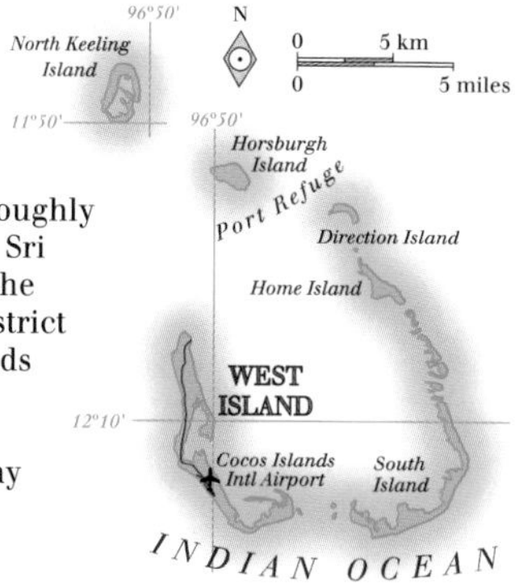
96°50'
North Keeling Island
N
0 5 km
0 5 miles
11°50'
96°50'
Horsburgh Island
Port Refuge
Direction Island
Home Island
WEST ISLAND
12°10'
Cocos Islands Intl Airport
South Island
INDIAN OCEAN

Cook Islands

Status: Territory in free association with New Zealand **Claimed:**
Capital: Avarua **Pop.:** 21,008 **Density:** 89/km² (228/mi²)

LYING IN THE MIDDLE of the South Pacific 3000 km (1900 miles) from New Zealand, the Cook Islands are a combination of 24 coral atolls and volcanic islands. Achieving self-government in 1965, they have adopted a diversified economy focusing primarily on tourism and banking, but with significant trade in giant clams and pearls.

Depopulation is of serious concern, as over 40,000 of the indigenous Maori population have migrated, seeing greater opportunities beyond the islands, and now live in New Zealand and Australia. This outflow of labor poses a major problem for the islands' future development, though remittances to relatives form an important source of income.

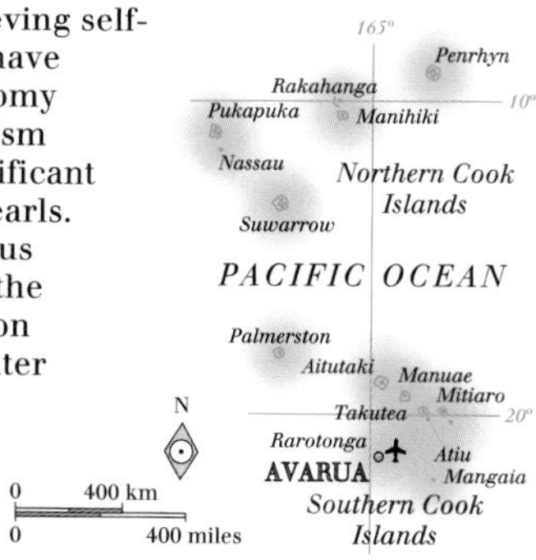
165°
Penrhyn
Rakahanga
Pukapuka
Manihiki
10°
Nassau
Northern Cook Islands
Suwarrow
PACIFIC OCEAN
Palmerston
Aitutaki
Manuae
Mitiaro
Takutea
20°
N
Rarotonga
AVARUA
Atiu
Mangaia
0 400 km
0 400 miles
Southern Cook Islands

The government of the Cook Islands, headed since 2002 by centrist prime minister Robert Woonton, is advised by a traditional council known as the House of Ariki. It is seeking a program of political reform, including devolving administration to the outer islands and cutting back an expensive bureaucracy.

Faeroe Islands

Status: Self-governing territory of Denmark **Claimed:** 1380
Capital: Tórshavn **Pop.:** 46,345 **Density:** 33/km² (86/mi²)

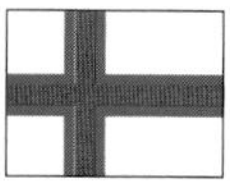

MIDWAY BETWEEN Scotland and Iceland in the north Atlantic, the Faeroe Islands have a moderate climate for their latitude – a result of the warm Gulf Stream current. Home rule since 1948 has given the Faeroese a strong sense of national identity – they voted against joining the European Communities with Denmark in 1973, but now have favorable terms of trade with most EU members. Fishing is the dominant industry, providing over 90% of exports. In the face of international criticism, the Faeroese have continued their traditional cull of pilot whales and bottle-nosed dolphins. Sheep farming is important, and there is a small textile industry which exports traditional woolens and puffin and eider-duck feathers.

Denmark's moves toward ever closer European integration have strengthened calls in the Faeroes for full independence. Negotiations to establish a "sovereign nation" under the Danish monarchy began in 1998. However, the Danish government's threat in 2001 to suspend subsidies to the islands quashed calls for a referendum.

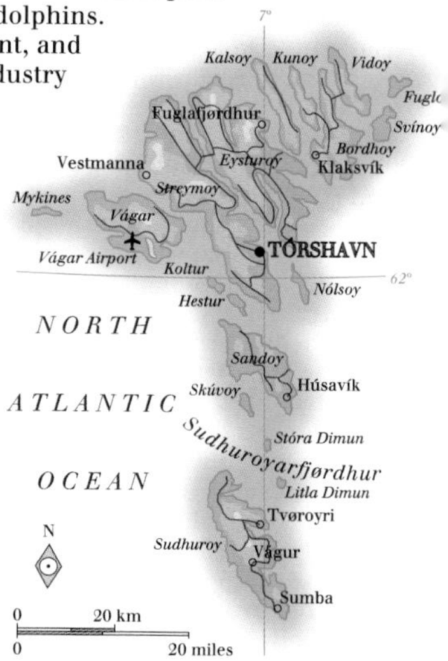
7°
Kalsoy
Kunoy
Vidoy
Fuglafjordhur
Svínoy
Bordhoy
Vestmanna
Eysturoy
Klaksvík
Mykines
Streymoy
Vágar
Vágar Airport
TÓRSHAVN
Koltur
62°
Nólsoy
Hestur
NORTH
Sandoy
Skúvoy
Húsavík
ATLANTIC
Sudhuroyarfjørdhur
Stóra Dimun
OCEAN
Litla Dimun
Tvøroyri
N
Sudhuroy
Vágur
Sumba
0 20 km
0 20 miles

LAND HEIGHT above Sea Level 200m/656ft 500m/1640ft 1000m/3281ft 1500m/4572ft above 2000m/6562ft

FALKLAND ISLANDS

STATUS: British overseas territory **CLAIMED:** 1832
CAPITAL: Port Stanley **POP.:** 2967 **DENSITY:** 0.24/km² (0.63/mi²)

SITUATED IN THE South Atlantic Ocean, over 12,000 km (7440 miles) from the UK, the Falkland Islands are influenced by the cold Antarctic current. The main islands of East and West Falkland and the hundreds of outlying islands have a cool, temperate climate with frequent strong winds.

The islands gained international attention with the Argentine invasion, and subsequent British recapture, in 1982. Since then, the UK government has invested heavily in a "Fortress Falklands" policy. A new runway and a military base to house an enlarged garrison were built at Mount Pleasant. The islanders, for their part, are determined to maintain the political status quo, but in 1999 improving relations led to the restoration of scheduled air connections with Argentina. Since the Falklands War, the economy of the islands has prospered. Falklanders invested heavily in schools, roads, and tourism in a fresh drive for a strong identity. By 1987, the Falklands had become financially solvent through the sale of fishing licenses, though sales by Argentina of cheaper, less restrictive licenses caused a fall in fishing revenues. The overexploitation of squid has seen a halt in its fishing. Depressed wool prices have caused a slump in the fortunes of the sheep-farming industry. The UK and Argentina reached agreement in 1995 on oil exploration, and it is hoped that the seabed around the islands will prove rich in reserves with great potential for the economy. Tourist numbers, including birdwatchers, photographers, and military historians, are increasing rapidly.

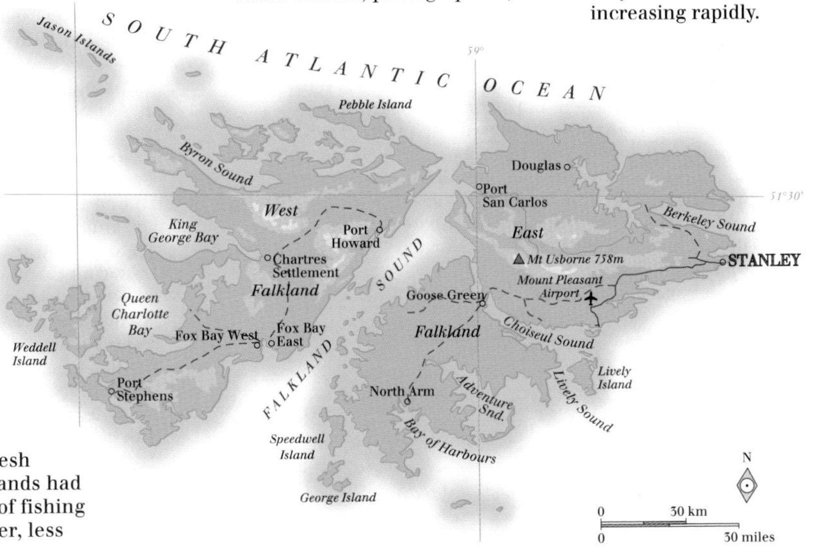

SOUTH ATLANTIC OCEAN
Jason Islands
Pebble Island
Byron Sound
Douglas
Port San Carlos
Berkeley Sound
King George Bay
West
Port Howard
East
Mt Usborne 758m
STANLEY
Chartres Settlement
Falkland
SOUND
Mount Pleasant Airport
Goose Green
Queen Charlotte Bay
Fox Bay West
Fox Bay East
Falkland
Choiseul Sound
Weddell Island
Port Stephens
FALKLAND
North Arm
Adventure Snd.
Lively Island
Lively Sound
Bay of Harbours
Speedwell Island
George Island
N
0 30 km
0 30 miles

FRENCH GUIANA

STATUS: French overseas department **CLAIMED:** 1817
CAPITAL: Cayenne **POP.:** 186,917 **DENSITY:** 2/km² (5/mi²)

SANDWICHED BETWEEN Brazil and Suriname, French Guiana is the only remaining colony in South America. A belt of coastal marsh, and an interior of equatorial jungle, combine in a location which was, for years, notorious for the offshore penal colony, Devil's Island. The rainforest, which covers 90% of the territory, is particularly rich in flora and fauna. It harbors over 400,000 species, including more different species of bird than in the whole of Europe.

Concentrated near the coast, the population is ethnically mixed. While 40% are creoles, there are around 5000 Amerindians and about 2000 Hmong refugees who fled civil war in Laos in the 1980s.

Kourou was selected for the launch of the ESA's Ariane rockets because of its equatorial site. The town has grown from 800 to 23,000 people.

A campaign for greater autonomy in the late 1970s and early 1980s led to limited devolution of power to a regional council. The grip on local power by the Guianese Socialist Party (PSG) has been undermined since 1993 by a more unified opposition, but it is still the largest party in the regional council.

During the 1990s the people became increasingly vocal in their condemnation of the French government's perceived indifference to their country's problems, and there were riots in 1996 and 1997 over the education system. The PSG has accordingly campaigned for greater autonomy. As an overseas *département* of metropolitan France, French Guiana is also a region of the EU, but it is heavily dependent on France itself for aid, food, and manufactured goods. It has a number of valuable natural resources, including gold, fishing, and forestry, and also has potential for increased tourism, but these are yet to be fully exploited because of a lack of skilled labor and investment and an underdeveloped infrastructure. The Guiana Space Center, which is situated on the coast at Kourou, has been operational since 1964. From there the Ariane rockets of the European Space Agency (ESA) are launched.

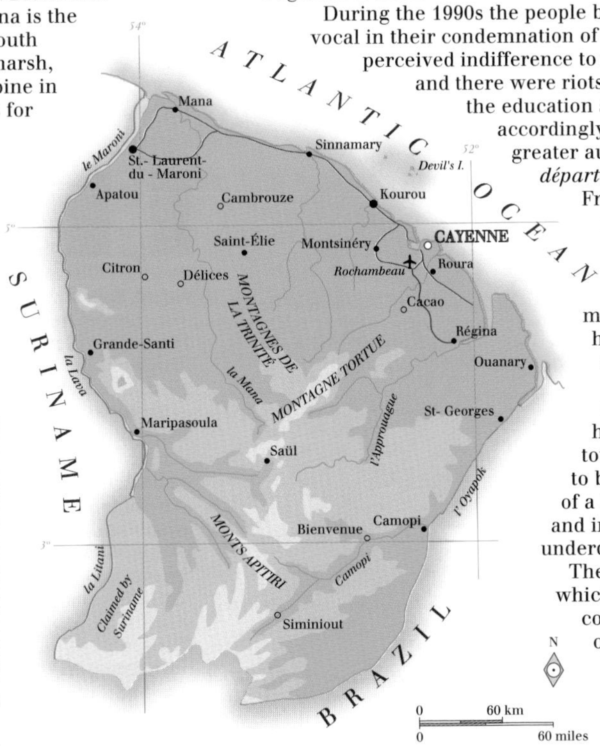

ATLANTIC OCEAN
Mana
Sinnamary
Devil's I.
le Maroni
St.-Laurent-du - Maroni
Apatou
Cambrouze
Kourou
CAYENNE
Saint-Élie
Montsinéry
Rochambeau
Roura
Citron
Délices
MONTAGNES DE LA TRINITÉ
Cacao
Régina
Grande-Santi
la Lawa
la Mana
MONTAGNE TORTUE
Ouanary
SURINAME
Maripasoula
l'Approuague
St- Georges
Saül
l'Oyapok
Bienvenue
Camopi
MONTS APITIRI
Camopi
la Litani
Claimed by Suriname
Siminiout
BRAZIL
N
0 60 km
0 60 miles

FRENCH POLYNESIA

STATUS: French overseas country **CLAIMED:** 1843
CAPITAL: Papeete **POP.:** 245,516 **DENSITY:** 70/km² (181/mi²)

A SCATTER OF 130 South Pacific islands and coral atolls over an area the size of Europe combine to form French Polynesia. The average temperature varies during the year between 20°C (68°F) and 29°C (84°F), with rainfall of over 150 cm (58 in). Nearly 75% of the population live on Tahiti, the main island. The French administration has developed the islands with little regard for local wishes, and the 70% West Polynesian (Mahoi) majority have seen their simple, self-sufficient economy transformed into one dependent on the French military and tourism. Nuclear testing on Mururoa Atoll created many jobs, but there was growing opposition, and a final series of tests, held in 1995-1996 despite widespread international protests, provoked local demonstrations and riots in Papeete.

French Polynesia became an "overseas country" in 2004. Major concerns are the growth of tourism and the rebuilding of indigenous trade. Future hopes rest largely on new tuna-fishing ventures.

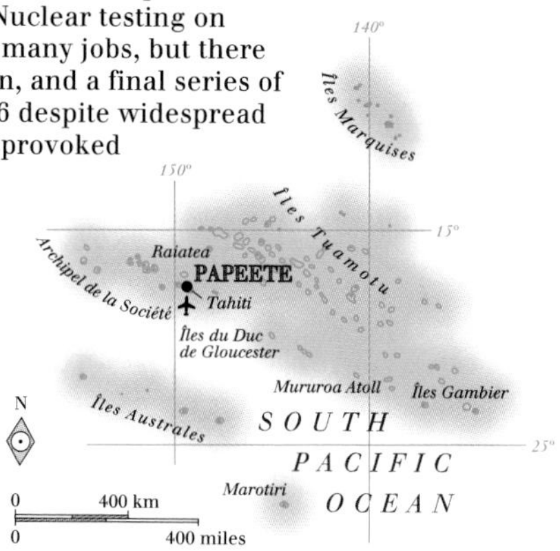

140°
Îles Marquises
150°
Îles Tuamotu
15°
Archipel de la Société
Raiatea
PAPEETE
Tahiti
Îles du Duc de Gloucester
Mururoa Atoll
Îles Gambier
Îles Australes
SOUTH PACIFIC OCEAN
Marotiri
25°
N
0 400 km
0 400 miles

GREENLAND

STATUS: Self-governing territory of Denmark **CLAIMED:** 1380
CAPITAL: Nuuk **POP.:** 56,385 **DENSITY:** 0.03/km² (0.07/mi²)

THE WORLD'S LARGEST island after Australia, Greenland is situated in the North Atlantic and surrounded by seas that are either frozen or cooled by cold Arctic currents. With an Arctic climate, much of its land is permanently ice-covered. Granted home rule in 1979, Greenlanders are of mixed Inuit and European origin. Younger islanders increasingly reject the traditional, fishing-based, subsistence lifestyle by moving to towns, placing a heavy burden on the advanced welfare system. Proposals to develop the mining of ice for drinking water could create vast revenues, even raising the possibility of economic independence.

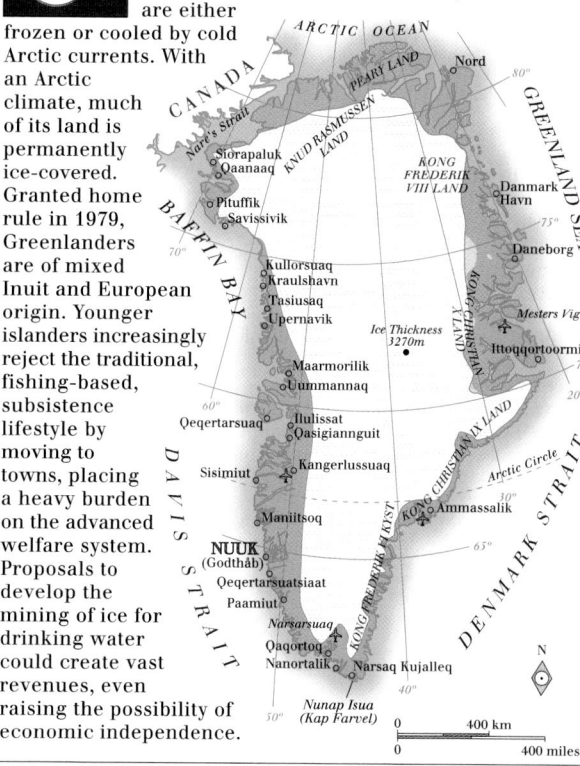

ARCTIC OCEAN
CANADA
Nare's Strait
PEARY LAND
Nord
80°
GREENLAND SEA
KNUD RASMUSSEN LAND
Siorapaluk
Qaanaaq
KONG FREDERIK VIII LAND
Danmark Havn
Pituffik
Savissivik
BAFFIN BAY
75°
70°
Daneborg
Kullorsuaq
Kraulshavn
Tasiusaq
Upernavik
KONG CHRISTIAN X LAND
Mesters Vig
Ice Thickness 3270m
Ittoqqortoormiit
Maarmorilik
Uummannaq
70°
20°
60°
Qeqertarsuaq
Ilulissat
Qasigiannguit
KONG CHRISTIAN IX LAND
Sisimiut
Kangerlussuaq
Arctic Circle
DAVIS STRAIT
KONG FREDERIK VI KYST
Ammassalik
30°
Maniitsoq
DENMARK STRAIT
NUUK (Godthåb)
65°
Qeqertarsuatsiaat
Paamiut
Narsarsuaq
Qaqortoq
Nanortalik
Narsaq Kujalleq
40°
Nunap Isua (Kap Farvel)
50°
N
0 400 km
0 400 miles

GIBRALTAR

STATUS: British overseas territory **CLAIMED:** 1713
CAPITAL: Gibraltar **POP.:** 27,776 **DENSITY:** 3968/km² (9259/mi²)

GUARDING THE western entrance to the Mediterranean, Gibraltar has survived on military and marine revenues. However, as Britain has cut defense spending, so its military presence on the Rock has declined. In response Gibraltarians have developed a vigorous offshore banking industry. Strict antismuggling legislation, in force since 1995, has curbed extensive smuggling from north Africa into Spain. Gibraltar's relationship with Britain and Spain remains contentious. The two governments' talks on the territory's status have prompted mass protests from the colony's inhabitants, who have felt sidelined in the discussions, and an unofficial referendum in 2002 rejected joint sovereignty.

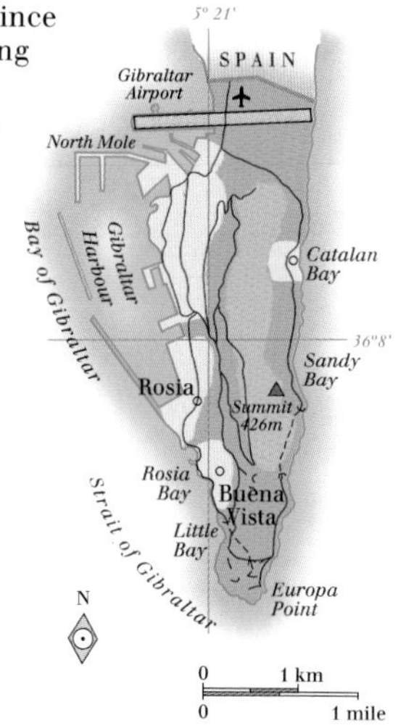

5° 21'
SPAIN
Gibraltar Airport
North Mole
Bay of Gibraltar
Gibraltar Harbour
Catalan Bay
36°8'
Sandy Bay
Rosia
Summit 426m
Rosia Bay
Buena Vista
Little Bay
Strait of Gibraltar
Europa Point
N
0 1 km
0 1 mile

The Rock of Gibraltar. The British excavated 143 caves, and built 50 km (30 miles) of roads and as many km of tunnels, for defensive purposes.

GUADELOUPE

STATUS: French overseas department **CLAIMED:** 1635
CAPITAL: Basse-Terre **POP.:** 440,000 **DENSITY:** 247/km² (640/mi²)

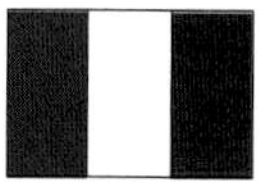

GUADELOUPE lies at the southern end of the Leeward Islands in the Caribbean and includes the north of St. Martin island and St. Barthélémy island near Anguilla. The movement for independence from France has slowly died, though the smaller islands voted in 2003 for greater autonomy. The economy is largely based on tourism and agriculture, with sugar, rum, and bananas the main exports, but the islands depend on foreign aid. The banana industry is vulnerable to hurricanes and global trade pacts prompting efforts to expand sugar production and tourism.

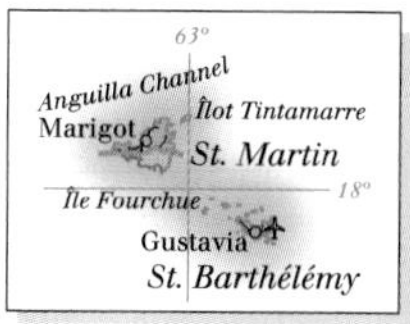

63°
Anguilla Channel
Îlot Tintamarre
Marigot
St. Martin
Île Fourchue
18°
Gustavia
St. Barthélémy

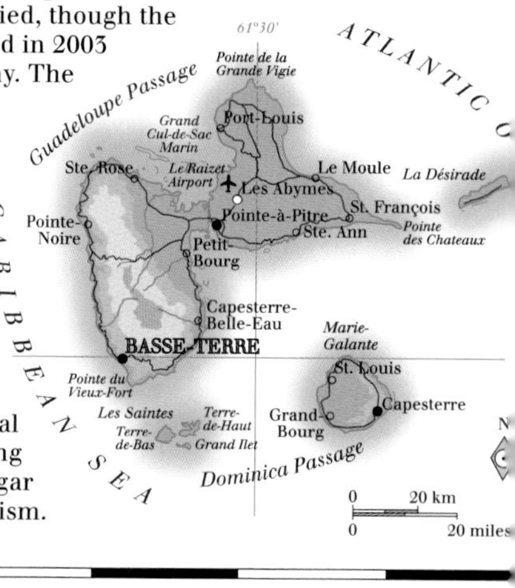

61°30'
ATLANTIC OCEAN
Pointe de la Grande Vigie
Guadeloupe Passage
Grand Cul-de-Sac Marin
Port-Louis
Ste. Rose
Le Raizet Airport
Le Moule
La Désirade
Les Abymes
St. François
Pointe des Chateaux
Pointe-Noire
Pointe-à-Pitre
Ste. Ann
Petit-Bourg
CARIBBEAN SEA
Capesterre-Belle-Eau
Marie-Galante
BASSE-TERRE
St. Louis
Pointe du Vieux-Fort
Les Saintes
Terre-de-Haut
Terre-de-Bas
Grand Ilet
Grand-Bourg
Capesterre
Dominica Passage
0 20 km
0 20 miles

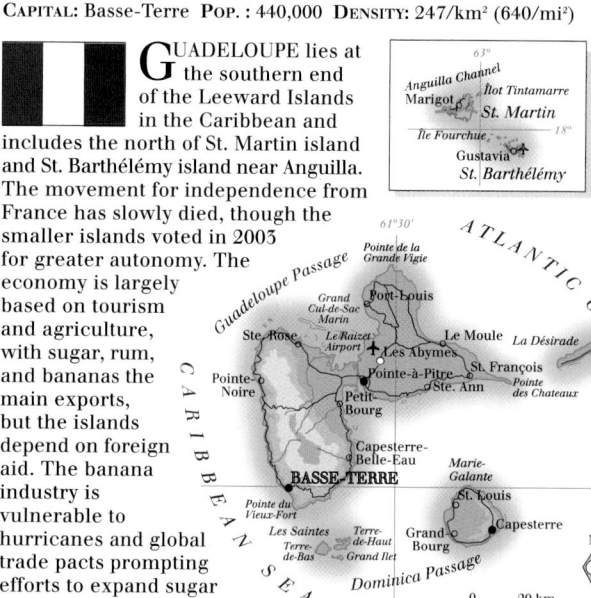

 LAND HEIGHT: above Sea Level; 200m/656ft; 500m/1640ft; 1000m/3281ft; 1500m/4572ft; above 2000m/6562ft

GUAM

STATUS: Unincorporated territory of the US **CLAIMED:** 1898
CAPITAL: Hagåtña **POP.:** 163,000 **DENSITY:** 297/km² (769/mi²)

THE VOLCANIC island of Guam lies at the southern end of the Mariana archipelago in the Pacific. Its tropical climate has encouraged tourism, though it lies in a region where typhoons are common. Guam's indigenous Chamorro people, who comprise around 40% of the population, dominate the island's political and social life. They are famous for a set of facial expressions, called "eyebrow," which virtually constitutes a language of its own. Though English is the official language, Chamorro is commonly spoken, and in 1998 the spelling of the capital was changed from Agaña to the Chamorran Hagåtña. The US military base, covering one-third of the island, has made Guam strategically important to the US. Military spending and tourism revenues have failed to benefit all islanders, and 23% live below the poverty line. The influx of US culture has also threatened to upset Guam's social stability. Greater independence has been an issue since the early 1980s, with a series of referenda since 1982. A draft Commonwealth Act was rejected by the US Congress after nearly 15 years of deliberation.

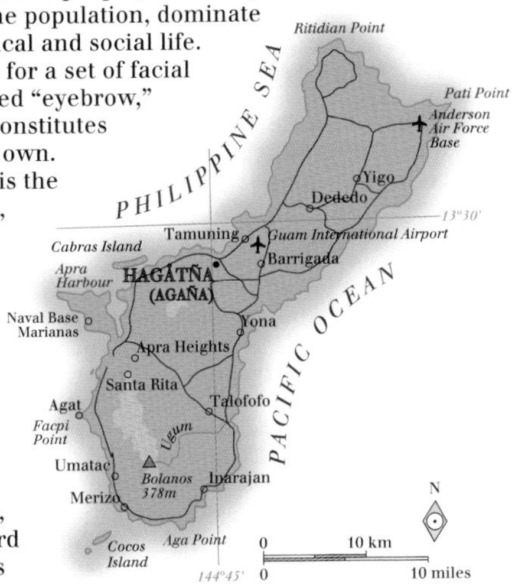

Ritidian Point
PHILIPPINE SEA
Pati Point
Anderson Air Force Base
Yigo
Dededo
13°30'
Tamuning
Guam International Airport
Cabras Island
Apra Harbour
HAGÅTÑA (AGAÑA)
Barrigada
Naval Base Marianas
Yona
PACIFIC OCEAN
Apra Heights
Santa Rita
Agat
Talofofo
Facpi Point
Ugum
Umatac
Bolanos 378m
Inarajan
Merizo
Cocos Island
Aga Point
144°45'
N
0 10 km
0 10 miles

A World War II Japanese anti-aircraft gun emplacement, *Agat Bay. Guam's history as a battle-ground during the Pacific War helps to attract tourists.*

ISLE OF MAN

STATUS: British Crown dependency **CLAIMED:** 1765
CAPITAL: Douglas **POP.:** 74,261 **DENSITY:** 130/km² (336/mi²)

LYING HALFWAY BETWEEN England and Northern Ireland in the Irish Sea, the Isle of Man has been inhabited for centuries by the Celtic Manx people. Established by the Vikings in the 9th century, the Manx parliament, the Tynwold, has autonomy from the UK in a number of matters, including taxation, and the death penalty was only officially abolished in 1993. The islanders have used this independence to establish a thriving financial and business sector, which has aided employment as the traditional industries of agriculture and fishing decline. There is still a shellfish industry, specializing in scallops. Tourism is also important: there are around 300,000 visitors each year. Publicity has been increased by the growing number of films being made on the island. Manx culture received a boost in 1993, when the local language, in danger of dying out, began to be taught in the island's schools once more. The Calf of Man, a small uninhabited island, is administered as a nature reserve.

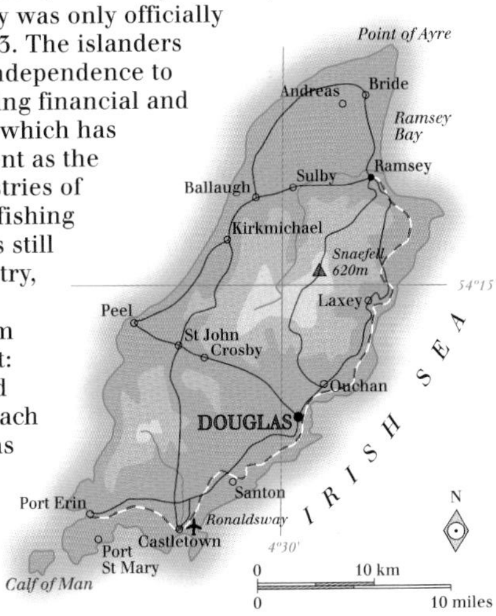

Point of Ayre
Andreas
Bride
Ramsey Bay
Sulby
Ramsey
Ballaugh
Kirkmichael
Snaefell 620m
54°15'
Peel
Laxey
St John
Crosby
IRISH SEA
Onchan
DOUGLAS
Santon
Port Erin
Ronaldsway
Port St Mary
Castletown
4°30'
Calf of Man
N
0 10 km
0 10 miles

The annual TT motorbike race *on the Isle of Man. Thousands of people come to watch the island's famous Touring Trophy race.*

GUERNSEY

STATUS: British Crown dependency **CLAIMED:** 1066
CAPITAL: St. Peter Port **POP.:** 64,818 **DENSITY:** 997/km² (2593/mi²)

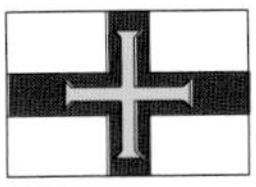

LYING 47 KM (29 miles) off the coast of France, Guernsey and its dependencies form the northwestern part of the Channel Islands, historically part of the Duchy of Normandy. English is the language most commonly used, but Norman patois is spoken in some villages, and some formal business of the legislature is conducted in French. Travel to France is easier than to the UK: Alderney is only 13 km (8 miles) from the French mainland. Residents on the smaller islands have no need for cars, and life continues in an unhurried manner that has changed little through the centuries. The islanders guard this lifestyle with strict residence laws. Guernsey's mild climate has encouraged the development of tourism and market gardening as major industries. Tomatoes and flowers are produced mainly for the UK market. The low tax system, independent of the UK, has led to a substantial and profitable financial services industry. Many international banks have Guernsey subsidiaries.

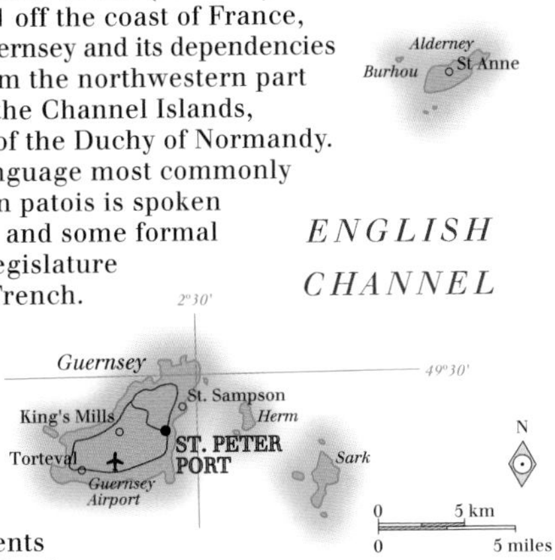

Alderney
Burhou
St Anne
ENGLISH CHANNEL
2°30'
Guernsey
49°30'
St. Sampson
Herm
King's Mills
Torteval
ST. PETER PORT
Sark
Guernsey Airport
N
0 5 km
0 5 miles

Jersey

Status: British Crown dependency **Claimed:** 1066
Capital: St. Helier **Pop.:** 90,156 **Density:** 777/km² (2003/mi²)

THE BAILIWICK OF JERSEY, the largest of the Channel Islands, lies some 22 km (14 miles) from the coast of Normandy in France. The official language (since 1960) is English, but French is still used in the courts. The island has a mild climate owing to the Gulf Stream, fine beaches, and more sunshine than anywhere else in the British Isles. Jersey has its own legislative and taxation systems which are a blend of the French and British versions. The Jersey States Assembly is one of the oldest legislative bodies in the world. Members stand as independents, rather than for political parties. It is considered a "Peculiar" of the UK monarchy, and has the right to reject "unacceptable" UK laws.

Historically, agriculture has been Jersey's most important industry, with dairy cows its most famous export, closely followed by early-harvested potatoes, tomatoes, and flowers. By the end of the 20th century, however, farming had been eclipsed by the rise of offshore finance and tourism. The growth of these sectors, and rigid controls on the rights of residence, have ensured high living standards for most of the inhabitants. Jersey is also host to a large Portuguese community which works in the island's tourist industry.

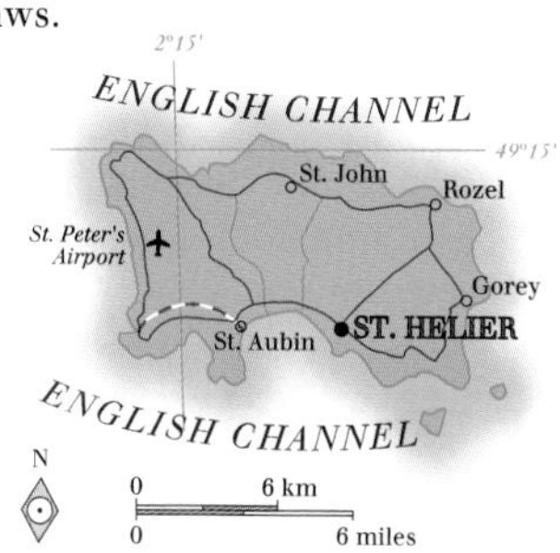
ENGLISH CHANNEL
St. John
Rozel
St. Peter's Airport
Gorey
St. Aubin
ST. HELIER
ENGLISH CHANNEL
N
0 6 km
0 6 miles

Johnston Atoll

Status: Unincorporated territory of the US **Claimed:** 1858
Capital: *Not applicable* **Pop.:** *Not applicable*

JOHNSTON ATOLL LIES 1150 km (714 miles) southwest of Hawaii. The atoll consists of a coral reef, two highly modified natural islands, Johnston and Sand, and two completely man-made islands, Akau (North) and Hikina (East). The islands, which were used by the US for nuclear weapons tests, were seriously contaminated with plutonium in 1962, when a nuclear missile exploded during testing. Regular tests began in 1971, and until 2000 the islands were also used for the storage of nuclear material and the destruction of chemical and biological weapons, including sarin nerve gas and the defoliant Agent Orange. Cleanup operations began in 2000 and since 2001 the only inhabitants left have been some US air force personnel, civilian contractors, and officials from the US Fish and Wildlife Service; the islands have been designated as a wildlife refuge: a breeding place for seabirds and green turtles.

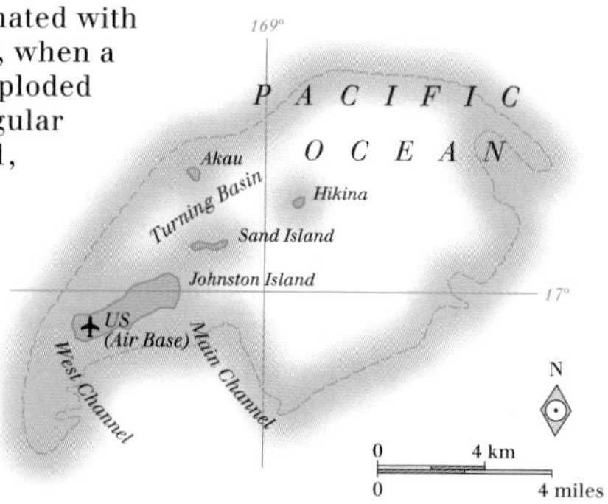
PACIFIC OCEAN
Akau
Turning Basin
Hikina
Sand Island
Johnston Island
US (Air Base)
West Channel
Main Channel
N
0 4 km
0 4 miles

Martinique

Status: French overseas department **Claimed:** 1635
Capital: Fort-de-France **Pop.:** 393,000 **Density:** 348/km² (901/m

CHRISTOPHER COLUMBUS described Martinique as "the most beautiful country in the world." It lies in the middle of the Caribbean Windward Islands but has retained remarkably close links both culturally and economically to mainland France. The island is dominated by the Montagne Pelée volcano, which violently erupted and engulfed the old capital, St. Pierre, in 1902. Situated in the Caribbean's hurricane belt, Martinique suffers an average of one natural disaster every five years.

Its long association with France and its status as an overseas *département* have left Martinique with a distinctly French feel; nonetheless nearly 90% of the population are of African or mixed ethnicity, and this influence has created a vibrant Caribbean tradition, particularly in music. Some of Martinique's more famous children include Joséphine Bonaparte (Napoléon's first wife) and Frantz Fanon, the black revolutionary who influenced anticolonial movements in the 20th century.

Economic power remains in the hands of the *Bekes* (descendants of white colonial settlers), who own most of the agricultural land. This situation has led in the past to outbreaks of violence and calls for greater autonomy. However, high living standards depend on French subsidies and a French-style social welfare system. The traditionally agricultural economy, based on the cultivation of sugarcane and bananas, has been forced to diversify as EU subsidy cuts come into effect, and high-class tourism is now the biggest source of income and the largest provider of employment. Almost 80% of the half-million annual visitors come from France. Since the late 1980s unemployment and emigration have been high, with the result that over 30% of Martiniquais nationals are resident in metropolitan France.

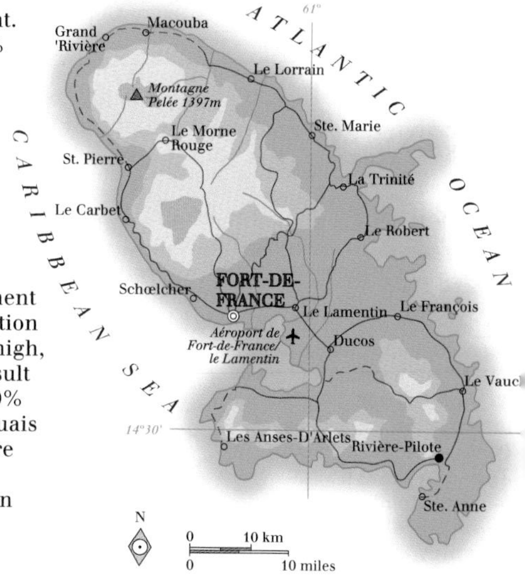
ATLANTIC OCEAN
CARIBBEAN SEA
Grand 'Rivière
Macouba
Le Lorrain
Montagne Pelée 1397m
Ste. Marie
Le Morne Rouge
St. Pierre
La Trinité
Le Carbet
Le Robert
Schœlcher
FORT-DE-FRANCE
Le Lamentin
Le François
Aéroport de Fort-de-France/ le Lamentin
Ducos
Le Vaucl
Les Anses-D'Arlets
Rivière-Pilote
Ste. Anne
N
0 10 km
0 10 miles

***Martinique.** Tourists are attracted to the island's beaches, its mountainous interior, and the historic towns of Fort-de-France and St. Pierre.*

LAND HEIGHT above Sea Level 200m/656ft 500m/1640ft 1000m/3281ft 1500m/4572ft above 2000m/6562ft

MAYOTTE

STATUS: French territorial collectivity **CLAIMED:** 1843
CAPITAL: Mamoudzou **POP.:** 178,437 **DENSITY:** 477/km² (1239/mi²)

PART OF THE COMOROS archipelago, Mayotte lies about 8000 km (5000 miles) from France, between Madagascar and the east African coast. It was the only island in the archipelago to vote against independence from France in a 1974 referendum. The other islands declared unilateral independence in 1975 and laid claim to Mayotte. Despite widespread poverty, endemic unemployment, and a cost of living twice that of France, the Mahorais voted again in 1976 to maintain the link. The main political movement has since unsuccessfully demanded that Mayotte be given the status of a French *département*, hoping that this would bring more aid to develop their largely agricultural economy. France opposes this idea because of the costs involved, but did grant the island *département*-style autonomy in 2000. The economy is still largely agricultural, producing crops both for internal consumption and for export. However, large quantities of foodstuffs are also imported. France has invested in an airport and port, but tourism has been slow to develop. Nevertheless, the relative prosperity of Mayotte has encouraged separatist movements on the two other small Comoros islands to seek closer relations with France.

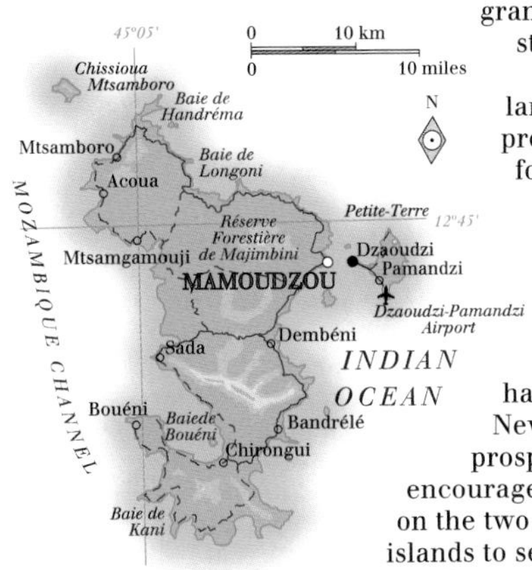
45°05'
0
10 km
0
10 miles
N
Chissioua Mtsamboro
Baie de Handréma
Mtsamboro
Baie de Longoni
Acoua
MOZAMBIQUE CHANNEL
Réserve Forestière de Majimbini
Petite-Terre
12°45'
Mtsamgamouji
Dzaoudzi
Pamandzi
MAMOUDZOU
Dzaoudzi-Pamandzi Airport
Sada
Dembéni
INDIAN OCEAN
Bouéni
Baie de Bouéni
Bandrélé
Chirongui
Baie de Kani

MIDWAY ISLANDS

STATUS: Unincorporated territory of the US **CLAIMED:** 1867
CAPITAL: *Not applicable* **POP.:** *Not applicable*

NAMED BECAUSE of its position between California and Japan, Midway is a coral atoll at the western end of the Hawaiian islands; there have been moves to make it part of Hawaii. The site of a major World War II battle, the atoll comprises two large islands, totaling over 4 sq. km (1.5 sq. miles), and several smaller ones. It functions as a naval air base and wildlife refuge. The population is limited to military personnel and civilian contractors, but some tourism is permitted, mainly connected with the wildlife.

MONTSERRAT

STATUS: British overseas territory **CLAIMED:** 1632
CAPITAL: Plymouth **POP.:** 8995 **DENSITY:** 88/km² (231/mi²)

MONTSERRAT IS ONE of the Leeward Islands chain in the eastern Caribbean. It has been devastated by volcanic eruptions which began in 1995 and culminated in massive explosions of the Soufrière Hills volcano in 1997 and 1998. As a result, the southern two-thirds of the island, where Plymouth and Blackburne airport are located, have become uninhabitable and it is illegal to enter the volcano "exclusion zone." Some two-thirds of the population left for neighboring islands or the UK in 1997. Calls for independence, based on a tourist boom in the 1980s, have been largely dropped, as the island is now dependent on UK aid. The disaster soured relations, setting off a bitter dispute over the cost of resettlement and reconstruction. A new capital, tentatively named Port Diana, is planned for the "safe" northern coast. The tourism industry is struggling to rebuild itself, but is hindered by the fact that both the airport and the seaport were closed by the eruption. Montserrat can now only be reached via neighboring Antigua.

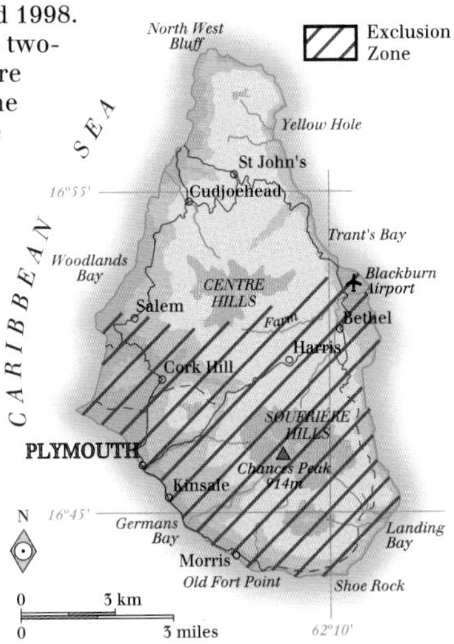
North West Bluff
Exclusion Zone
CARIBBEAN SEA
Yellow Hole
St John's
16°55'
Cudjoehead
Trant's Bay
Woodlands Bay
CENTRE HILLS
Blackburn Airport
Salem
Farm
Bethel
Harris
Cork Hill
SOUFRIÈRE HILLS
PLYMOUTH
Chances Peak 914m
Kinsale
N
16°45'
Germans Bay
Landing Bay
Morris
Old Fort Point
Shoe Rock
0
3 km
0
3 miles
62°10'

Montserrat. Known as the Caribbean's "emerald isle" because of its luxuriant flora and Irish heritage.

NETHERLANDS ANTILLES

STATUS: Autonomous part of the Netherlands **CLAIMED:** 1816
CAPITAL: Willemstad **POP.:** 221,000 **DENSITY:** 276/km² (715/mi²)

THE NETHERLANDS Antilles are composed of two Caribbean island groups. Curaçao – the richest and wealthiest island – and Bonaire lie just off the Venezuelan coast, while Saba, St. Eustatius, and Sint Maarten – whose northern half is part of Guadeloupe – lie 800 km (500 miles) to the north. Financial scandals, political instability, and the issue of the federation's future, among other things, have strained relations with the Dutch government, the major aid provider. Tourism and financial services provide the backbone of the islands' economy.

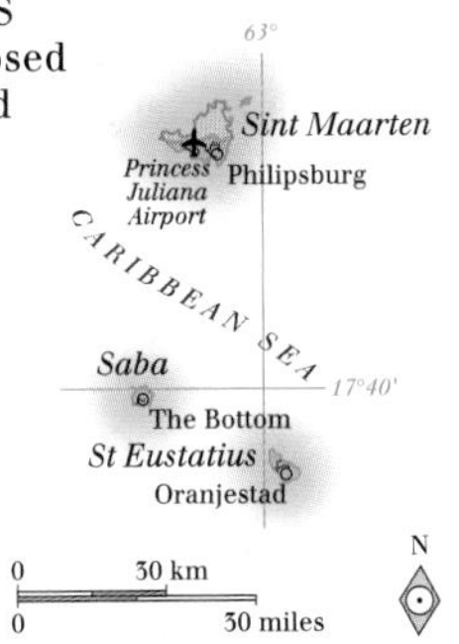
63°
Sint Maarten
Princess Juliana Airport
Philipsburg
CARIBBEAN SEA
Saba
17°40'
The Bottom
St Eustatius
Oranjestad
0
30 km
0
30 miles
N

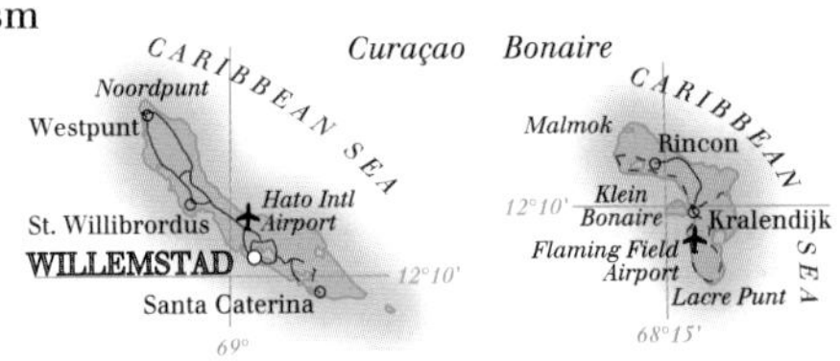
Curaçao
Bonaire
CARIBBEAN SEA
Noordpunt
Westpunt
Hato Intl Airport
St. Willibrordus
WILLEMSTAD
Santa Caterina
12°10'
69°
Malmok
Rincon
12°10'
Klein Bonaire
Kralendijk
Flaming Field Airport
Lacre Punt
68°15'
CARIBBEAN SEA

New Caledonia

Status: French overseas territory **Claimed:** 1853
Capital: Nouméa **Pop.:** 228,000 **Density:** 12/km² (31/mi²)

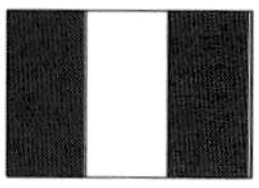

NEW CALEDONIA, or, as it is known to the indigenous Kanaks, Kanaky, is an island group 400 km (250 miles) west of Vanuatu and 1350 km (840 miles) off the coast of eastern Australia. Tension over socioeconomic inequalities and independence between the Melanesian Kanaks, who form over half of the population, and the influential expatriate *Caldoches*, resulted in a long history of political violence. Under the 1988 Matignon Accord, France imposed a year of direct rule as the prelude to a new constitutional structure which attempted to address Kanak grievances by providing greater provincial autonomy. Though some racial violence continued after 1988, it has not again reached the same level. The Nouméa accord, signed in 1998, set out a 15-year program for gradual autonomy which would end in a vote on self-determination.

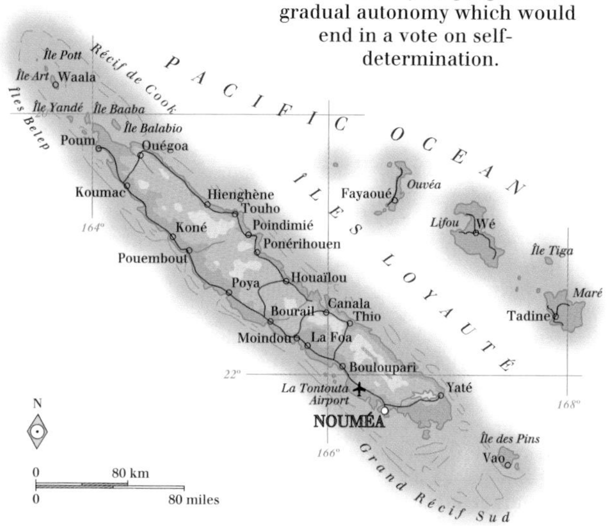
Île Pott
Île Art
Waala
Récif de Cook
Îles Belep
Île Yandé
Île Baaba
Île Balabio
Poum
Ouégoa
PACIFIC OCEAN
ÎLES LOYAUTÉ
Ouvéa
Fayaoué
Lifou
Wé
Île Tiga
Maré
Tadine
Koumac
Hienghène
Touho
Poindimié
Ponérihouen
Koné
Pouembout
Poya
Houaïlou
Canala
Thio
Bourail
Moindou
La Foa
Boulouparì
La Tontouta Airport
Yaté
NOUMÉA
Île des Pins
Vao
Grand Récif Sud
164°
166°
168°
22°
N
0 80 km
0 80 miles

Nickel mining is the territory's most valuable export industry, generating around 80% of export income. New Caledonia has about 25% of world reserves, and is the fourth-largest producer in the world, but the industry employs relatively few people, and is vulnerable to fluctuations in the world price. It was seriously affected by the Asian financial crisis of 1997–1998, but recovered on the back of high world prices in 2000. Tourism and agriculture are bigger employers, though less than 1% of total land area is cultivated. Corn, yams, sweet potatoes, and coconuts have traditionally been the main crops, and since the 1990s melons have been exported to Japan in large quantities. Fishing is important, the main catches being tuna and shrimp, most of which are also exported to Japan. A project for farming giant clams started in 1996. Unemployment nevertheless remains high among young Kanaks.

A nickel mine, *New Caledonia. The importance of the nickel industry to the territory's economy has made the control of reserves a dominant issue in politics, and in negotiations over the island's independence from France.*

Niue

Status: Territory in free association with New Zealand **Claimed:**
Capital: Alofi **Pop.:** 2145 **Density:** 8/km² (21/mi²)

THE WORLD'S LARGEST coral island, Niue lies 2400 km (1500 miles) northeast of New Zealand. Tropical fruits form part of the subsistence economy, while tourism and the sale of postage stamps provide foreign currency. Mass emigration has seen the Niuean community in New Zealand grow to over 20,000. In an effort to stem the tide, New Zealand has invested heavily in the Niuean economy, but growth remains slow and the local economy was devastated by the damage caused by Cyclone Heta in early 2004.

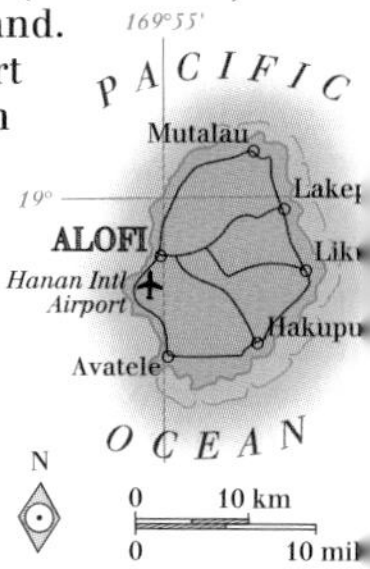
169°55'
PACIFIC
Mutalau
19°
ALOFI
Hanan Intl Airport
Avatele
OCEAN
N
0 10 km
0 10 mi

Norfolk Island

Status: Australian external territory **Claimed:** 1774
Capital: Kingston **Pop.:** 1853 **Density:** 53/km² (143/mi²)

INHABITED by Australian migrants and descendants of the mutineers of HMS *Bounty*, Norfolk Island lies 1400 km (869 miles) east of Australia. Islanders speak a hybrid language, mixing Westcountry English, Gaelic, and ancient Tahitian. They enjoy substantial autonomy, and in 1991 rejected a plan to become part of the Australian federal state. Tourists, attracted by the climate and unique flora, have brought islanders a relatively high standard of living.

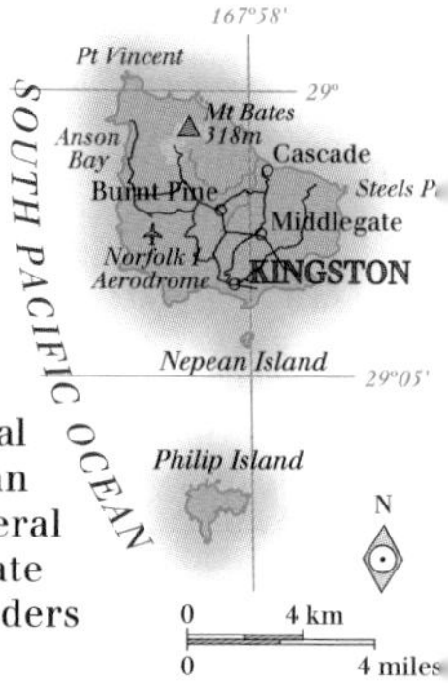
167°58'
Pt Vincent
29°
SOUTH PACIFIC OCEAN
Mt Bates 318m
Anson Bay
Cascade
Burnt Pine
Middlegate
Norfolk Aerodrome
KINGSTON
Nepean Island
29°05'
Philip Island
N
0 4 km
0 4 miles

Northern Mariana Is.

Status: Commonwealth territory of the US **Claimed:** 1947
Capital: Saipan **Pop.:** 80,006 **Density:** 175/km² (455/mi²)

A FORMER UN trust territory, the Northern Marianas preferred in 1987 to retain links with the US rather than opt for independence, though local politicians have questioned its current status. US aid fueled a boom in the 1980s, but it depended on immigrant workers who were soon more numerous than the indigenous Chamorro community, while tourism has speeded the decline of the local subsistence economy.

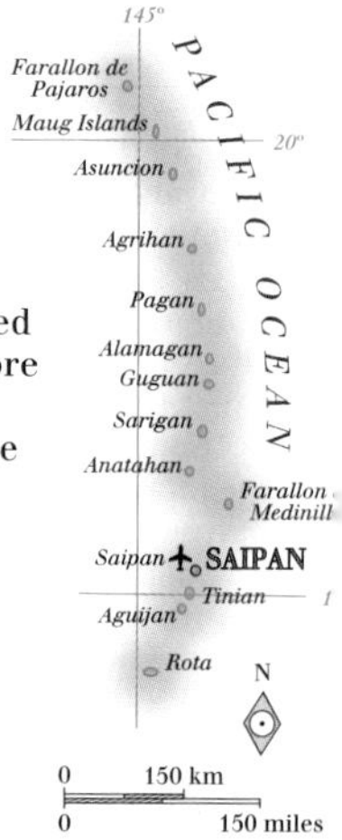
145°
Farallon de Pajaros
Maug Islands
20°
Asuncion
Agrihan
Pagan
Alamagan
Guguan
Sarigan
Anatahan
PACIFIC OCEAN
Saipan
SAIPAN
Tinian
Aguijan
Rota
N
0 150 km
0 150 miles

Rota, Northern Marianas. *The limestone outcrop of Wedding Cake Mountain overlooks the small village of Songsong.*

LAND HEIGHT: above Sea Level | 200m/656ft | 500m/1640ft | 1000m/3281ft | 1500m/4572ft | above 2000m/6562ft

PARACEL ISLANDS

STATUS: *Disputed* **CLAIMED:** *Not applicable*
CAPITAL: *Not applicable* **POPULATION:** *Unknown*

OCCUPIED BY CHINESE FORCES (who call them the Xisha Islands), but also claimed by Taiwan and Vietnam, the Paracel Islands are a small collection of coral atolls situated some 325 km (200 miles) east of Vietnam, in the South China Sea. Subject to frequent typhoons and with a tropical climate, the Paracels are at the center of a regional dispute over the vast reserves of oil and natural gas which are believed to lie beneath their territorial waters. China has built port facilities and an airstrip on Woody Island to support its claim.

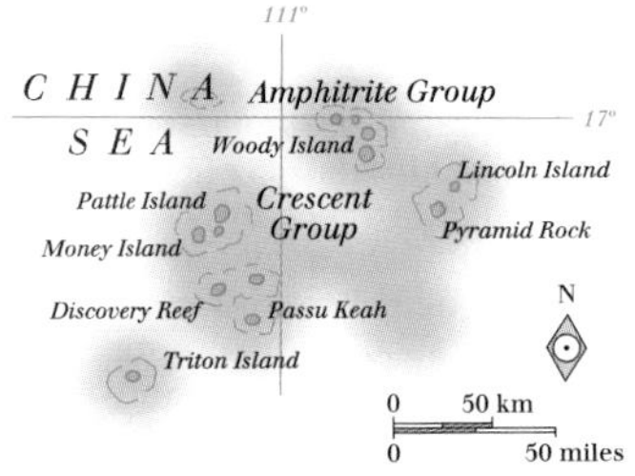

111°
CHINA SEA
Amphitrite Group
17°
Woody Island
Lincoln Island
Pattle Island
Crescent Group
Pyramid Rock
Money Island
Discovery Reef
Passu Keah
Triton Island
N
0 50 km
0 50 miles

PITCAIRN ISLANDS

STATUS: British overseas territory **CLAIMED:** 1887
CAPITAL: Adamstown **POP.:** 47 **DENSITY:** 1.3/km² (3/mi²)

A GROUP OF volcanic South Pacific islands, Pitcairn is Britain's most isolated dependency. Pitcairn Island was the last refuge for the 18th-century mutineers from HMS *Bounty*. The economy operates by barter, fishing, and subsistence farming, and is reliant on regular airdrops from New Zealand and periodic visits by supply vessels. Postage stamp sales provide foreign currency earnings. In 2003, several Pitcairn men were charged with sexual assault.

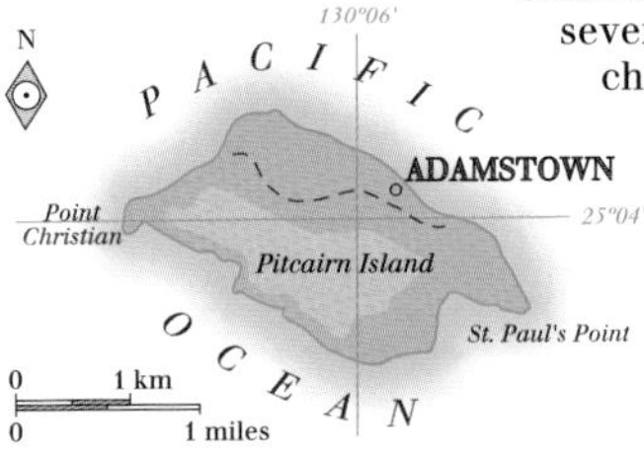

130°06'
PACIFIC
OCEAN
N
ADAMSTOWN
Point Christian
25°04'
Pitcairn Island
St. Paul's Point
0 1 km
0 1 miles

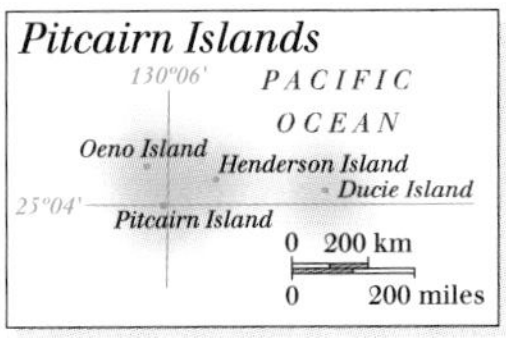

Pitcairn Islands
130°06'
PACIFIC OCEAN
Oeno Island
Henderson Island
Ducie Island
25°04'
Pitcairn Island
0 200 km
0 200 miles

PUERTO RICO

STATUS: Commonwealth territory of the US **CLAIMED:** 1898
CAPITAL: San Juan **POP.:** 3.89 million **DENSITY:** 434/km² (1123/mi²)

PUERTO RICO, a US territory since its invasion in 1898, is by far the most populous nonindependent territory. It is the easternmost of the Greater Antilles chain in the Caribbean. The population density, highest around San Juan, is comparable with the Netherlands and is higher than in any US state. The tropical climate attracts growing numbers of tourists, 85% from the US, and there have been major efforts to expand hotel and resort facilities.

Puerto Rico was granted its current commonwealth status in 1952, four years after an abortive proindependence uprising. The inhabitants have US citizenship but only limited self-government. In three plebiscites, in 1967, 1993, and 1998, the islanders endorsed continued commonwealth status rather than opting for either US statehood or independence. The most recent of these votes was extremely close, but the pro-statehood governor who called the 1993 and 1998 votes, Pedro Rossello, was replaced by the anti-statehood Sila Calderón – the first female governor of Puerto Rico – in 2001.

Though thousands of the mostly Spanish-speaking Puerto Ricans have migrated to the US mainland in search of higher wages, the islanders have one of the highest living standards in the region. Tax relief, cheap labor, and the island's role as an export-processing zone, mainly for the US market, attracted many businesses. Clothing, electronics, petrochemical, and pharmaceutical industries traditionally dominated, but the decision to phase out tax exemptions for companies reinvesting in the island caused a slump in 1996, and more emphasis is now being placed on the service sector. New industries include health care and clinical testing, biotechnology, and other knowledge-based areas.

Governor Calderón spearheaded the campaign to stop the US navy from using the populated eastern island of Vieques for bombing practice. In 2000 an invasion of the bombing range by protestors led to some high-profile arrests, including that of Robert Kennedy Jr. In response President George W. Bush agreed to hand the range back to the department of the interior and the last bombing exercise was completed in 2003.

At night, the bright lights of Puerto Rico's well-developed roads, settlements, and busy ports are in sharp contrast to the rest of the Caribbean – notably the dark outline of Haiti, just to the west.

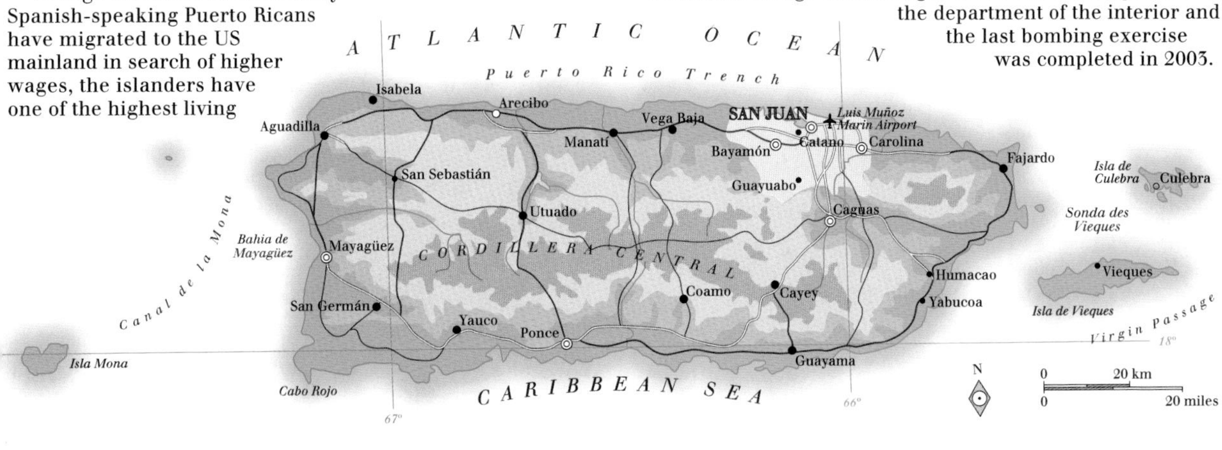

ATLANTIC OCEAN
Puerto Rico Trench
Isabela
Arecibo
Aguadilla
Vega Baja
SAN JUAN
Luis Muñoz Marín Airport
Manatí
Cataño
Carolina
Bayamón
Fajardo
Isla de Culebra
Culebra
San Sebastián
Guaynabo
Utuado
Caguas
Sonda des Vieques
Bahía de Mayagüez
Mayagüez
CORDILLERA CENTRAL
Humacao
Vieques
Canal de la Mona
Coamo
Cayey
Yabucoa
San Germán
Isla de Vieques
Yauco
Ponce
Virgin Passage
18°
Isla Mona
Guayama
Cabo Rojo
CARIBBEAN SEA
N
0 20 km
0 20 miles
67°
66°

POPULATION ○ under 5000 • under 10 000 ● over 10 000 ○ over 50 000 ◎ over 100 000 ▢ Urban areas AIRPORTS ✈ International ✈ Local

Réunion

Status: French overseas department **Claimed:** 1638
Capital: Saint-Denis **Pop.:** 756,000 **Density:** 301/km² (779/mi²)

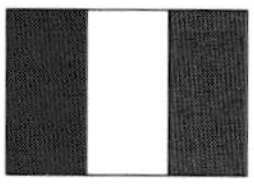

THE LARGE VOLCANIC ISLAND of Réunion, 800 km (500 miles) east of Madagascar, provides France with an important strategic presence – and a large military base – in the Indian Ocean. Its mountainous interior has forced the majority of the population to live along the coast. Tensions still exist between the very poor black community and the wealthy Indian and European groups, though the violence of 1991 has not been repeated. Despite the introduction of measures applicable to all French overseas *départements*, intended to improve social and economic standards, unemployment remains high and the cost of living very expensive. Réunion's main crop is sugarcane, though Cyclone Dina devastated production in 2002.

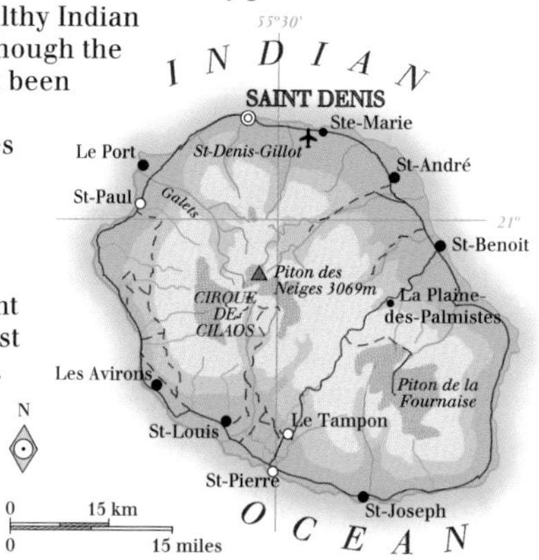

INDIAN OCEAN
SAINT DENIS
Ste-Marie
St-Denis-Gillot
Le Port
St-André
St-Paul
Galets
St-Benoit
Piton des Neiges 3069m
CIRQUE DE CILAOS
La Plaine-des-Palmistes
Les Avirons
Piton de la Fournaise
St-Louis
Le Tampon
St-Pierre
St-Joseph
55°30'
21°
N
0 15 km
0 15 miles

St. Pierre & Miquelon

Status: French territorial collectivity **Claimed:** 1604
Capital: St. Pierre **Pop.:** 6976 **Density:** 29/km² (75/mi²)

ST. PIERRE & Miquelon is a group of barren islands lying just off the south coast of Newfoundland, Canada. The islands are surrounded by some of the world's richest fishing grounds. Their inhabitants have traditionally earned a living from fishing, and from servicing foreign trawler fleets off the coast. A long-running and sometimes bitter dispute between Canada and France over fishing and mineral rights was settled in 1992. The ruling, which was generally deemed to be in Canada's favor, has led the French authorities to diversify the economy by developing port facilities and encouraging tourism.

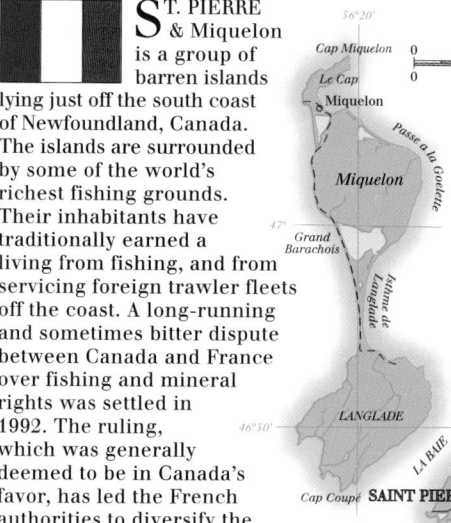

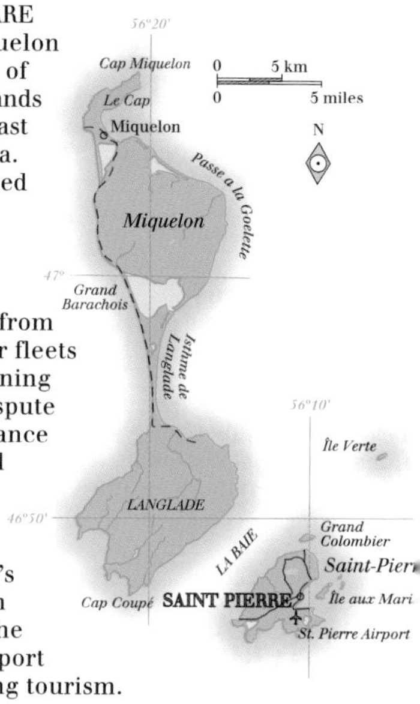

56°20'
Cap Miquelon
Le Cap
Miquelon
Passe a la Goelette
Miquelon
47°
Grand Barachois
Isthme de Langlade
56°10'
Île Verte
LANGLADE
46°50'
Grand Colombier
LA BAIE
Saint-Pierre
Cap Coupé
SAINT PIERRE
Île aux Mari
St. Pierre Airport
N
0 5 km
0 5 miles

St. Helena & Dependencies

Status: British overseas territory **Claimed:** 1673
Capital: Jamestown **Pop.:** 7367 **Density:** 60/km² (157/mi²)

TOGETHER, the islands of St. Helena, Tristan da Cunha, and Ascension form Britain's main dependency in the south Atlantic. St. Helena is famed for being the final place of exile for Napoléon. Its main economic activities – fishing, livestock farming, and the sale of handicrafts – are unable to support the population; as a result, underemployment on the island is a major problem. Many "Saints" have been forced to seek work on Ascension, which has no resident population and is operated as a military base and communications center, though civilian flights have been permitted since 1998. Tristan da Cunha, a volcanic island 2000 km (1240 miles) south of St. Helena, is inhabited by a small, closely knit farming community. It was badly hit by severe winter storms in 2001. The 2002 British Overseas Territories Act granted all overseas citizens full British citizenship, assuaging a source of local resentment.

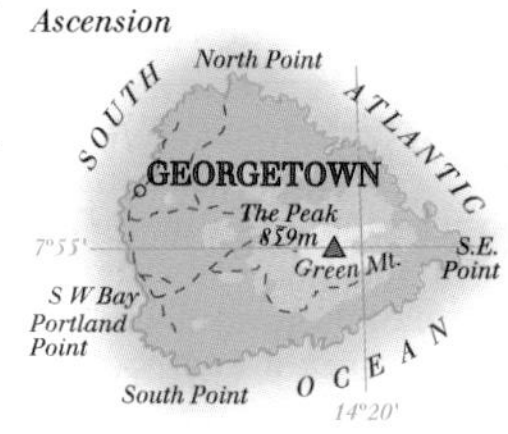

Ascension
North Point
SOUTH ATLANTIC OCEAN
GEORGETOWN
The Peak 859m
Green Mt.
S.E. Point
7°55'
S W Bay
Portland Point
South Point
14°20'

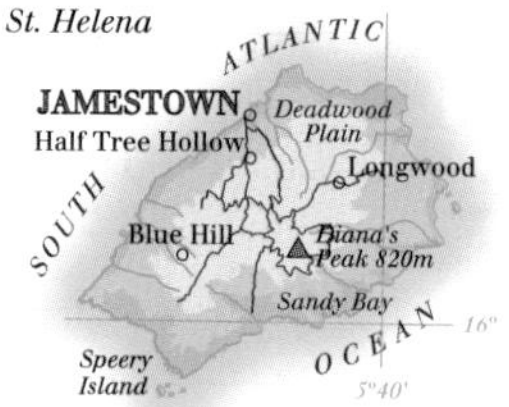

St. Helena
SOUTH ATLANTIC OCEAN
JAMESTOWN
Deadwood Plain
Half Tree Hollow
Longwood
Blue Hill
Diana's Peak 820m
Sandy Bay
Speery Island
16°
5°40'

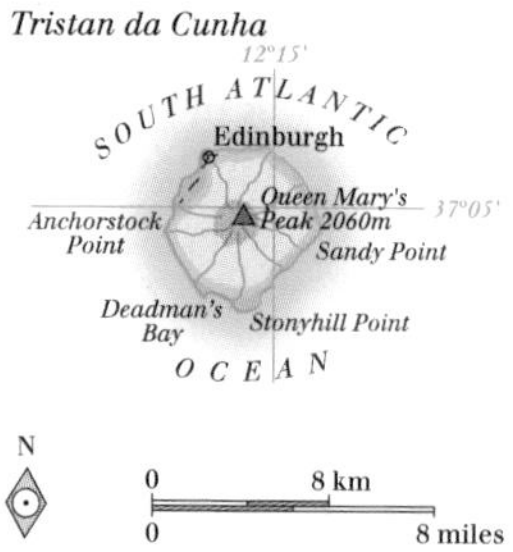

Tristan da Cunha
12°15'
SOUTH ATLANTIC OCEAN
Edinburgh
Queen Mary's Peak 2060m
37°05'
Anchorstock Point
Sandy Point
Deadman's Bay
Stonyhill Point
N
0 8 km
0 8 miles

Spratly Islands

Status: *Disputed* **Claimed:** *Not applicable*
Capital: *Not applicable* **Population:** *Unknown*

SCATTERED ACROSS a large area of the South China Sea, the reefs, islands, and atolls that make up the Spratly Islands have become one of south Asia's most serious security issues. Strategically, the islands lie in one of the world's busiest shipping areas. In addition, surveys suggest that some of the largest oil and gas reserves yet found lie in the Spratlys' territorial waters. Claimed, all or in part, by China, Taiwan, Vietnam, Brunei, Malaysia, and the Philippines, more than 40 of the larger islands now have garrisons from some of the claimant states. A code of conduct allowing freedom of navigation was agreed in 2002.

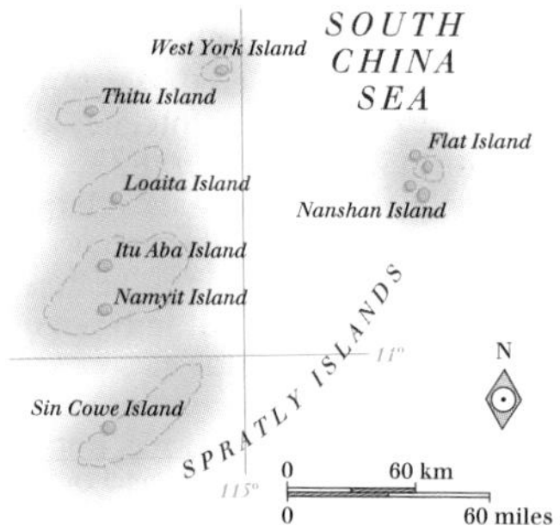

SOUTH CHINA SEA
West York Island
Thitu Island
Flat Island
Loaita Island
Nanshan Island
Itu Aba Island
Namyit Island
SPRATLY ISLANDS
11°
Sin Cowe Island
115°
N
0 60 km
0 60 miles

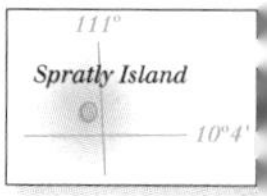

111°
Spratly Island
10°4'

The isolated Chinese occupying force on one of the Spratly Islands.

LAND HEIGHT: above Sea Level; 200m/656ft; 500m/1640ft; 1000m/3281ft; 1500m/4572ft; above 2000m/6562ft

SVALBARD

STATUS: Norwegian dependency **CLAIMED:** 1920
CAPITAL: Longyearbyen **POP.:** 2811 **DENSITY:** 0.04/km² (0.12/mi²)

MORE THAN 150 ice-covered Arctic islands 650 km (400 miles) north of Norway make up Svalbard. In accordance with the Spitsbergen Treaty of 1920, nationals of the treaty powers have equal rights to exploit the coal deposits, subject to regulation by Norway. The only companies still mining are Norwegian and Russian. There has been conflict with Iceland over fishing rights. Over half of the area of the islands is designated as environmentally protected.

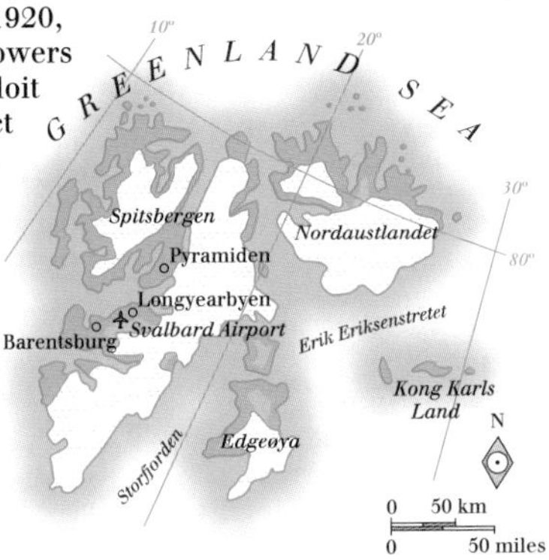
GREENLAND SEA
10°
20°
30°
80°
Spitsbergen
Nordaustlandet
Pyramiden
Longyearbyen
Svalbard Airport
Barentsburg
Erik Eriksenstretet
Kong Karls Land
Storfjorden
Edgeøya
N
0 50 km
0 50 miles

TOKELAU

STATUS: New Zealand dependent territory **CLAIMED:** 1926
CAPITAL: *Not applicable* **POP.:** 1418 **DENSITY:** 142/km² (354/mi²)

A 1989 UN REPORT states that in the 21st century these islands in the South Pacific will disappear under the sea, unless action is taken to stop global warming. The economy depends on a tuna cannery and the sale of fishing licenses, postage stamps, and coins; a catamaran link between the atolls has increased tourist potential. Tokelau's small size and economic fragility make independence unlikely, but in 1996 it gained the right to enact its own internal legislation, and since 2001 the local authorities have had full control of the islands' public services. More than 6000 Tokelauans live in New Zealand.

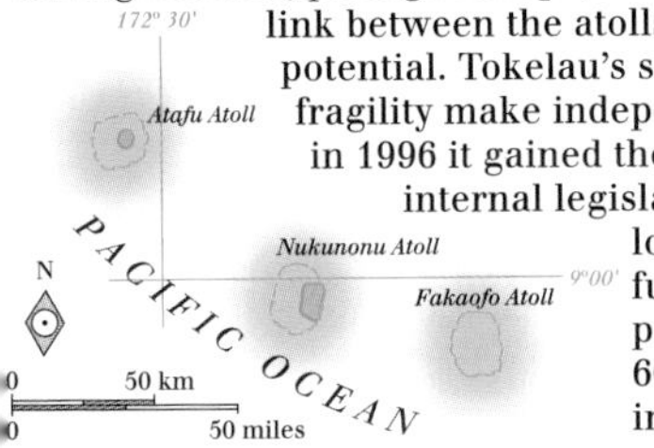
172° 30'
Atafu Atoll
Nukunonu Atoll
Fakaofo Atoll
9°00'
PACIFIC OCEAN
N
0 50 km
0 50 miles

TURKS & CAICOS ISLANDS

STATUS: British overseas territory **CLAIMED:** 1766
CAPITAL: Cockburn Town **POP.:** 19,350 **DENSITY:** 45/km² (117/mi²)

SITUATED 40 km (25 miles) south of the Bahamas, the Turks and Caicos Islands is a group of 30 low-lying islands, eight of which are inhabited. A traditional salt-based economy was exhausted in 1964, leading to two decades of stagnation. Since the 1980s, however, tourism and offshore banking have led a dramatic turnaround in the islands' fortunes.

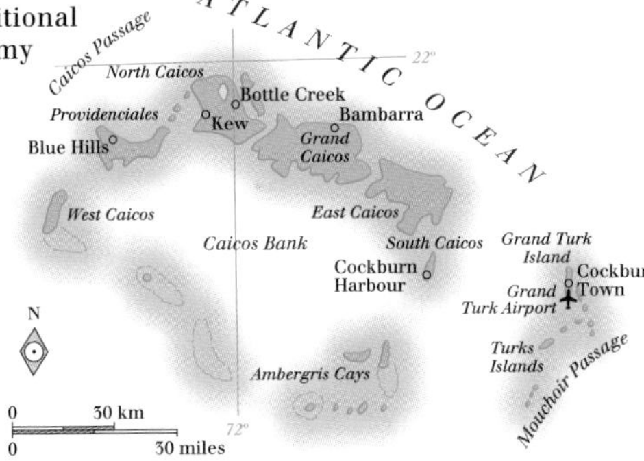
ATLANTIC OCEAN
Caicos Passage
22°
North Caicos
Bottle Creek
Bambarra
Providenciales
Kew
Grand Caicos
Blue Hills
West Caicos
East Caicos
Caicos Bank
South Caicos
Grand Turk Island
Cockburn Harbour
Cockburn Town
Grand Turk Airport
Turks Islands
Mouchoir Passage
Ambergris Cays
N
0 30 km
0 30 miles
72°

VIRGIN ISLANDS (US)

STATUS: Unincorporated territory of the US **CLAIMED:** 1917
CAPITAL: Charlotte Amalie **POP.:** 124,778 **DENS.:** 360/km² (931/mi²)

THE US VIRGIN ISLANDS are a collection of 53 volcanic islands, just to the east of Puerto Rico. Most of the population – a mix of African and European ethnic groups – live on the main islands of St. John, St. Thomas, and St. Croix. Tourism is the principal activity, though St. Croix has also used federal aid to develop industry. It has one of the world's largest oil refineries.

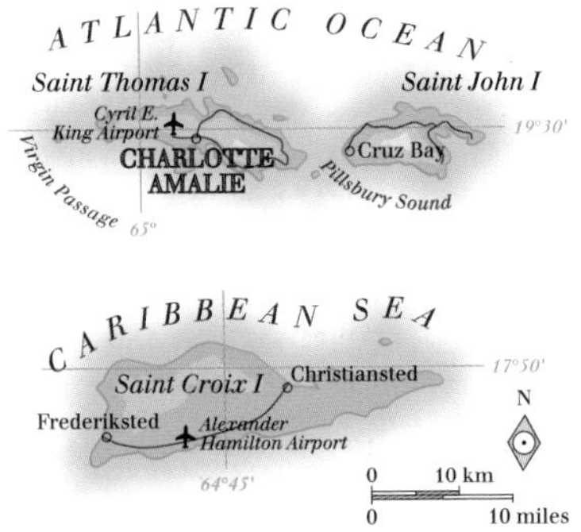
ATLANTIC OCEAN
Saint Thomas I
Saint John I
Cyril E. King Airport
CHARLOTTE AMALIE
Cruz Bay
19°30'
Virgin Passage
Pillsbury Sound
65°
CARIBBEAN SEA
Saint Croix I
Christiansted
17°50'
Frederiksted
Alexander Hamilton Airport
64°45'
N
0 10 km
0 10 miles

St. Thomas, US Virgin Islands, is a major stop-off for Caribbean cruise ships. Tourists are attracted by the island's duty-free shopping.

WAKE ISLAND

STATUS: Unincorporated territory of the US **CLAIMED:** 1898
CAPITAL: *Not applicable* **POP.:** *Not applicable*

WAKE ISLAND, in fact three islands that form the rim of an extinct volcano, has a US air base, whose airstrip can be used in emergencies by trans-Pacific flights. After widespread condemnation a 1998 proposal to store nuclear waste there was dropped. It is claimed by the Marshall Islands.

WALLIS & FUTUNA

STATUS: French overseas territory **CLAIMED:** 1842
CAPITAL: Matá'Utu **POP.:** 15,734 **DENSITY:** 57/km² (148/mi²)

UNLIKE THOSE OF France's other South Pacific overseas territories, the inhabitants of Wallis and Futuna have little desire for greater autonomy. The islands' subsistence economy produces a variety of tropical crops, while expatriate remittances and the sale of licenses to Japanese and South Korean fishing fleets provide foreign exchange. Deforestation, leading to soil erosion, is of great concern.

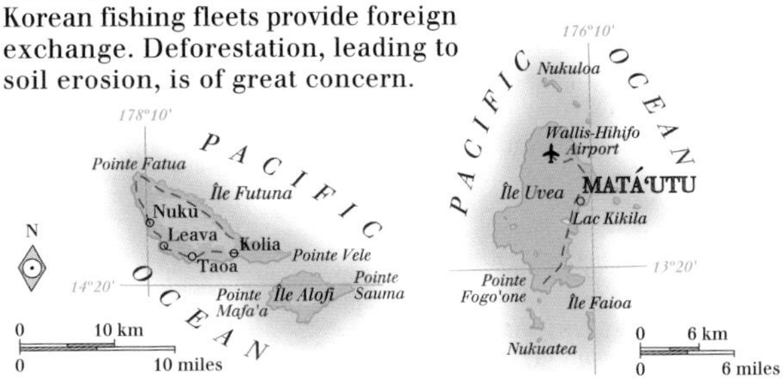
178°10'
PACIFIC OCEAN
Pointe Fatua
Île Futuna
Nuku
Leava
Kolia
Taoa
Pointe Vele
Pointe Sauma
Pointe Mafa'a
Île Alofi
14°20'
N
0 10 km
0 10 miles
176°10'
PACIFIC OCEAN
Nukuloa
Wallis-Hihifo Airport
Île Uvea
MATÁUTU
Lac Kikila
13°20'
Pointe Fogo'one
Île Faioa
Nukuatea
0 6 km
0 6 miles

Glossary of Geographical Terms

THE GLOSSARY FOLLOWING lists all geographical terms occurring on the maps and in main-entry names in the Index~Gazetteer. These terms may precede, follow, or be run together with the proper element of the name; where they precede it the term is reversed for indexing purposes – thus Poluostrov Yamal is indexed as Yamal, Poluostrov.

KEY
Geographical term *Language*, Term

A
Å *Danish, Norwegian*, River
Alpen *German*, Alps
Altiplanicie *Spanish*, Plateau
Älv(en) *Swedish*, River
Anse *French*, Bay
Archipiélago *Spanish*, Archipelago
Arcipelago *Italian*, Archipelago
Arquipélago *Portuguese*, Archipelago
Aukštuma *Lithuanian*, Upland

B
Bahía *Spanish*, Bay
Baía *Portuguese*, Bay
Baḩr *Arabic*, River
Baie *French*, Bay
Bandao *Chinese*, Peninsula
Banjaran *Malay*, Mountain range
Batang *Malay*, Stream
-berg *Afrikaans, Norwegian*, Mountain
Birket *Arabic* , Lake
Boğazı *Turkish*, Lake
Bucht *German*, Bay
Bugten *Danish*, Bay
Buḩayrat *Arabic*, Lake, reservoir
Buḩeiret *Arabic*, Lake
Bukit *Malay*, Mountain
-bukta *Norwegian*, Bay
bukten *Swedish*, Bay
Burnu *Turkish*, Cape, point
Buuraha *Somali*, Mountains

C
Cabo *Portuguese*, Cape
Cap *French*, Cape
Cascada *Portuguese*, Waterfall
Cerro *Spanish*, Mountain
Chaîne *French*, Mountain range
Chau *Cantonese*, Island
Chāy *Turkish*, River
Chhâk *Cambodian*, Bay
Chhu *Tibetan*, River
-chŏsuji *Korean*, Reservoir
Chott *Arabic*, Salt lake, depression
Ch'ün-tao *Chinese*, Island group
Chuôr Phnum *Cambodian*, Mountains
Cordillera *Spanish*, Mountain range
Costa *Spanish*, Coast
Côte *French*, Coast
Cuchilla *Spanish*, Mountains

D
Dağı *Azerbaijani, Turkish*, Mountain
Dağları *Azerbaijani, Turkish*, Mountains
-dake *Japanese*, Peak
Danau *Indonesian*, Lake
Đao *Vietnamese*, Island
Daryā *Persian*, River
Daryācheh *Persian*, Lake
Dasht *Persian*, Plain, desert
Dawḩat *Arabic*, Bay
Dere *Turkish*, Stream
Dili *Azerbaijani*, Spit
-do *Korean*, Island
Dooxo *Somali*, Valley
Düzü *Azerbaijani*, Steppe
-dwīp *Bengali*, Island

E
Embalse *Spanish*, Reservoir
Erg *Arabic*, Dunes
Estany *Catalan*, Lake
Estrecho *Spanish*, Strait
-ey *Icelandic*, Island
Ezero *Bulgarian, Macedonian*, Lake

F
Fjord *Danish*, Fjord
-fjorden *Norwegian*, Fjord
-fjørdhur *Faeroese*, Fjord
Fleuve *French*, River
Fliegu *Maltese*, Channel
-fljór *Icelandic*, River

G
-gang *Korean*, River
Ganga *Nepali, Sinhala*, River
Gaoyuan *Chinese*, Plateau
-gawa *Japanese*, River
Gebel *Arabic*, Mountain
-gebirge *German*, Mountains
Ghubbat *Arabic*, Bay
Gjiri *Albanian*, Bay
Gol *Mongolian*, River
Golfe *French*, Gulf
Golfo *Italian, Spanish*, Gulf
Gora *Russian, Serbian*, Mountain
Gory *Russian*, Mountains
Guba *Russian*, Bay
Gunung *Malay*, Mountain

H
Ḩadd *Arabic*, Spit
-haehyŏp *Korean*, Strait
Haff *German*, Lagoon
Hai *Chinese*, Sea, bay
Ḩammādat *Arabic*, Plateau
Hāmūn *Persian*, Lake
Hawr *Arabic*, Lake
Hāyk' *Amharic*, Lake
He *Chinese*, River
Helodrano *Malagasy*, Bay
-hegység *Hungarian*, Mountain range
Hka *Burmese*, River
-ho *Korean*, Lake
Hô *Korean*, Reservoir
Holot *Hebrew*, Dunes
Hora *Belarussian*, Mountain
Hrada *Belarussian*, Mountains, ridge
Hsi *Chinese*, River
Hu *Chinese*, Lake

I
Île(s) *French*, Island(s)
Ilha(s) *Portuguese*, Island(s)
Ilhéu(s) *Portuguese*, Islet(s)
Irmak *Turkish*, River
Isla(s) *Spanish*, Island(s)
Isola (Isole) *Italian*, Island(s)

J
Jabal *Arabic*, Mountain
Jāl *Arabic*, Ridge
-järvi *Finnish*, Lake
Jazīrat *Arabic*, Island
Jazīreh *Persian*, Island
Jebel *Arabic*, Mountain
Jezero *Serbo-Croat*, Lake
Jiang *Chinese*, River
-joki *Finnish*, River
-jökull *Icelandic*, Glacier
Juzur *Arabic*, Islands

K
Kaikyō *Japanese*, Strait
-kaise *Lappish*, Mountain
Kali *Nepali*, River
Kalnas *Lithuanian*, Mountain
Kalns *Latvian*, Mountain
Kang *Chinese*, Harbor
Kangri *Tibetan*, Mountain(s)
Kaôh *Cambodian*, Island
Kapp *Norwegian*, Cape
Kavīr *Persian*, Desert
K'edi *Georgian*, Mountain range
Kediet *Arabic*, Mountain
Kepulauan *Indonesian, Malay*, Island group
Khalîg, Khalīj *Arabic*, Gulf
Khawr *Arabic*, Inlet
Khola *Nepali*, River
Khrebet *Russian*, Mountain range
Ko *Thai*, Island
Kolpos *Greek*, Bay
-kopf *German*, Peak
Körfäzi *Azerbaijani*, Bay
Körfezi *Turkish*, Bay
Kõrgustik *Estonian*, Upland
Koshi *Nepali*, River
Kowtal *Persian*, Pass
Kūh(hā) *Persian*, Mountain(s)
-kundo *Korean*, Island group
-kysten *Norwegian*, Coast
Kyun *Burmese*, Island

L
Laaq *Somali*, Watercourse
Lac *French*, Lake
Lacul *Romanian*, Lake
Lago *Italian, Portuguese, Spanish*, Lake
Laguna *Spanish*, Lagoon, Lake
Laht *Estonian*, Bay
Laut *Indonesian*, Sea
Lembalemba *Malagasy*, Plateau
Lerr *Armenian*, Mountain
Lerrnashght'a *Armenian*, Mountain range
Les *Czech*, Forest
Lich *Armenian*, Lake
Liqeni *Albanian*, Lake
Lumi *Albanian*, River
Lyman *Ukrainian*, EstuaryLake

M
Mae Nam *Thai*, River
-mägi *Estonian*, Hill
Maja *Albanian*, Mountain
-man *Korean*, Bay
Marios *Lithuanian*, Lake
-meer *Dutch*, Lake
Melkosopochnik *Russian*, Plain
-meri *Estonian*, Sea
Mifraz *Hebrew*, Bay
Monkhafad *Arabic*, Depression
Mont(s) *French*, Mountain(s)
Monte *Italian, Portuguese*, Mountain
More *Russian*, Sea
Mörön *Mongolian*, River

N
Nagor'ye *Russian*, Upland
Naḩal *Hebrew*, River
Nahr *Arabic*, River
Nam *Laotian*, River
Nehri *Turkish*, River
Nevado *Spanish*, Mountain (snow-capped)
Nisoi *Greek*, Islands
Nizmennost' *Russian*, Lowland, plain
Nosy *Malagasy*, Island
Nur *Mongolian*, Lake
Nuruu *Mongolian*, Mountains
Nuur *Mongolian*, Lake
Nyzovyna *Ukrainian*, Lowland, plain

O
Ostrov(a) *Russian*, Island(s)
Oued *Arabic*, Watercourse
-oy *Faeroese*, Island
-øy(a) *Norwegian*, Island
Oya *Sinhala*, River
Ozero *Russian, Ukrainian*, Lake

P
Passo *Italian*, Pass
Pegunungan *Indonesian, Malay*, Mountain range
Pelagos *Greek*, Sea
Penisola *Italian*, Peninsula
Peski *Russian*, Sands
Phanom *Thai*, Mountain
Phou *Laotian*, Mountain
Pi *Chinese*, Point
Pic *Catalan*, Peak
Pico *Portuguese, Spanish*, Peak
Pik *Russian*, Peak
Planalto *Portuguese*, Plateau
Planina, Planini *Bulgarian, Macedonian, Serbo-Croat*, Mountain range
Ploskogor'ye *Russian*, Upland
Poluostrov *Russian*, Peninsula
Potamos *Greek*, River
Proliv *Russian*, Strait
Pulau *Indonesian, Malay*, Island
Pulu *Malay*, Island
Punta *Portuguese, Spanish*, Point

Q
Qā' *Arabic*, Depression
Qolleh *Persian*, Mountain

R
Raas *Somali*, Cape
-rags *Latvian*, Cape
Ramlat *Arabic*, Sands
Ra's *Arabic*, Cape, point, headland
Ravnina *Bulgarian, Russian*, Plain
Récif *French*, Reef
Represa (Rep.) *Spanish, Portuguese*, Reservoir
-rettō *Japanese*, Island chain
Riacho *Spanish*, Stream
Riban' *Malagasy*, Mountains
Rio *Portuguese*, River
Río *Spanish*, River
Riu *Catalan*, River
Rivier *Dutch*, River
Rivière *French*, River
Rowd *Pashtu*, River
Rūd *Persian*, River
Rudohorie *Slovak*, Mountains
Ruisseau *French*, Stream

S

Sabkhat *Arabic,* Salt marsh
Şaḩrā' *Arabic,* Desert
Samudra *Sinhala,* Reservoir
-san *Japanese, Korean,* Mountain
-sanchi *Japanese,* Mountains
-sanmaek *Korean,*
Sarīr *Arabic,* Desert
Sebkha, Sebkhet *Arabic,* Salt marsh, depression
See *German,* Lake
Selat *Indonesian,* Strait
-selkä *Finnish,* Ridge
Selseleh *Persian,* Mountain range
Serra *Portuguese,* Mountain
Serranía *Spanish,* Mountain
Sha'īb *Arabic,* Watercourse
Shamo *Chinese,* Desert
Shan *Chinese,* Mountain(s)
Shan-mo *Chinese,* Mountain range
Shaţţ *Arabic,* Distributary
-shima *Japanese,* Island
Shiqqat *Arabic,* Depression
Shui-tao *Chinese,* Channel
Sierra *Spanish,* Mountains
Sơn *Vietnamese,* Mountain
Sông *Vietnamese,* River
-spitze *German,* Peak
Štít *Slovak,* Peak
Stoeng *Cambodian,* River
Stretto *Italian,* Strait
Su Anbarı *Azerbaijani,* Reservoir
Sungai *Indonesian, Malay,* River
Suu *Turkish,* River

T

Tal *Mongolian,* Plain
Tandavan' *Malagasy,* Mountain range
Tangorombohitr' *Malagasy,* Mountain massif
Tao *Chinese,* Island
Tassili *Berber,* Plateau, mountain
Tau *Russian,* Mountain(s)
Taungdan *Burmese,* Mountain range
Teluk *Indonesian, Malay,* Bay
Terara *Amharic,* Mountain
Tog *Somali,* Valley
Tônlé *Cambodian,* Lake
Top *Dutch,* Peak
-tunturi *Finnish,* Mountain
Tur'at *Arabic,* Channel

V

Väin *Estonian,* Strait
-vatn *Icelandic,* Lake
-vesi *Finnish,* Lake
Vinh *Vietnamese,* Bay
Vodokhranilishche (Vdkhr.) *Russian,* Reservoir
Vodoskhovyshche (Vdskh.) *Ukrainian,* Reservoir
Volcán *Spanish,* Volcano
Vozvyshennost' *Russian,* Upland, plateau
Vrh *Macedonian,* Peak
Vysochyna *Ukrainian,* Upland
Vysočina *Czech,* Upland

W

Waadi *Somali,* Watercourse
Wādī *Arabic,* Watercourse
Wāḩat, Wâhat *Arabic,* Oasis
Wald *German,* Forest
Wan *Chinese,* Bay
Wyżyna *Polish,* Upland

X

Xé *Laotian,* River

Y

Yarımadası *Azerbaijani,* Peninsula
Yazovir *Bulgarian,* Reservoir
Yoma *Burmese,* Mountains
Yü *Chinese,* Island

Z

Zaliv *Bulgarian, Russian,* Bay
Zatoka *Ukrainian,* Bay
Zemlya *Russian,* Bay

GLOSSARY OF ABBREVIATIONS

THIS GLOSSARY provides a comprehensive guide to the abbreviations used.

A

abbrev. abbreviated
ABM antiballistic missile(s)
Adm. Admiral
AIDS acquired immunodeficiency syndrome
Amh. Amharic
ANC African National Congress
APC armored personnel carrier(s)
approx. approximately
ASSR Autonomous Soviet Socialist Republic

B

BBC British Broadcasting Corporation
BCE Before Common Era
b/d barrels per day
B-H Bosnia and Herzegovina
bn billion (1000 million)
Brig. Brigadier
BSE bovine spongiform encephalopathy

C

C central
c. circa
C. Cape
°C degrees (Centigrade)
cap. capita
Capt. Captain
CAR Central African Republic
CD compact disc
CE Common Era
CIA Central Intelligence Agency
cm centimeter(s)
Cmdr. Commander
CNN Cable News Network
Co. Company
Col. Colonel
Czech Rep. Czech Republic

D E

D.C. District of Columbia
Dens density
dept. department
dths deaths
dev. development
Dr. Doctor
DRC Democratic Republic of the Congo
dwt dead weight tonnage
E east
EC$ Eastern Caribbean dollar(s)
EEC/EC European Community
EEZ Exclusive Economic Zone
ECU European Currency Unit
EMS European Monetary System
est. estimated

F G

°F degrees (Fahrenheit)
Flt. Lt. Flight Lieutenant
Fr. Father
Fr. French/France
ft foot/feet
FYRM Former Yugoslav Republic of Macedonia
GATT General Agreement on Tariffs and Trade
GDP Gross Domestic Product (the total value of goods and services produced by a country excluding income from foreign countries)
Gen. General
Geplac Geplacea
GNP Gross National Product (the total value of goods and services produced by a country)
grt gross tonnage

H I

HEP hydroelectric power
HH His/Her Highness
HIPC heavily indebted poor country(ies)
hist. historical
HIV human immunodeficiency virus
H.M. His/Her Majesty
HMS His/Her Majesty's ship
H.R.H His/Her Royal Highness
H.S.H His/Her Serene Highness
I. Island
ICBM intercontinental ballistic missile(s)
in inch(es)
Intl International
IRBM intermediate-range ballistic missile(s)
Is Islands

J K L

kg kilogram(s)
km kilometer(s)
km² square kilometer (singular)
kW kilowatt(s)
kWh kilowatt hour(s)
CE Common Era
L. lower
Ltd. Limited
Lt. Lieutenant
Lux. Luxembourg

M N

m million/meter(s)
Maced. Macedonia
Maj. Major
MBA Master of Business Administration
CE Common Era
Mercsr Mercosur
mi² square mile(s)
mm millimeter(s)
Mon. Montenegro
MP Member of Parliament
MSP Member of Scottish Parliament
Mt. Mountain/Mount
Mts Mountains
MW megawatt(s)
N north
NASA National Aeronautics and Space Administration
Nepad New Partnership for Africa's Development
Neth. Netherlands
NGO Nongovernmental Organization
NIC Newly Industrialized Country
NPT Non-Proliferation Treaty
NZ New Zealand

P Q R

p.a. per annum
PLO Palestine Liberation Organization
PNG Papua New Guinea
pop. population
Rep. Republic
Res. Reservoir
Rev. Reverend
Russian Fed. Russian Federation

S

S south
S. & Mon. Serbia & Montenegro
SARS server acute respiratory syndrome
Serb. Serbia
SLBM submarine-launched ballistic missile(s)
sq. square
SSBN nuclear-fuelled ballistic-missile submarine(s)
SSR Soviet Socialist Republic
St. Saint
START Strategic Arms Reduction Treaty
Switz. Switzerland

T U

TGV *train à grande vitesse*
TV television
UAE United Arab Emirates
UK United Kingdom
UN United Nations
US/USA United States of America
USS United States ship
USSR Union of Soviet Socialist Republics
U. upper
Uzb. Uzbek

V W

VCR video cassette recorder
W west

THE MAPS

The maps in the Nations of the World section of this book have used the most up-to-date reference sources available to provide local name forms and spellings, that is to say those used within the country. In an age when international travel, on holiday or on business, is commonplace, this criterion seems the most appropriate. English conventional forms have been used for all international features and for all capital cities. English conventional forms also appear on all the maps in the World Factfile.

Acknowledgments

Dorling Kindersley would like to express their thanks to the following individuals, companies and institutions for their help in preparing this atlas:

Additional Cartography

Advanced Illustration (Congleton, UK)

Andrew Bright

Cosmographics (Watford, UK)

Malcolm Porter

Swanston Publishing (Derby, UK)

Andrew Thompson

Design

Boyd Annison, Icon Solutions (Chesham, UK) *for Macintosh consultancy and chart templates*

Bruno Maag, Dalton Maag (London, UK) *for font consultancy and production*

Research and Reference

Dr D Alkhateeb, Organization of Petroleum Exporting Countries (OPEC, Vienna, Austria)

Amnesty International (London, UK)

Caroline Blunden

CNN International (New York, USA)

Dataquest Europe SA (Paris, France)

CSL Davies

Department of Trade and Industry Export Market Information Centre (London, UK)

The Flag Institute (Chester, UK)

Foreign and Commonwealth Office (London, UK)

Alexander Fyges-Walker

Christel Heideloff, Institute of Shipping Economics and Logistics (Bremen, Germany)

International Bank for Reconstruction and Development (World Bank, Washington, DC, USA)

International Committee of the Red Cross (ICRC, Geneva, Switzerland)

International Civil Aviation Organization (ICAO, Montreal, Canada)

International Criminal Police Organization (INTERPOL, Lyon, France)

International Institute for Strategic Studies, for information from *The Military Balance* (London, UK)

International Boundaries Research Unit, University of Durham

Institute of Latin American Studies, University of London (London, UK)

Intermediate Technology Development Group (Rugby, UK)

Chris Joseph, United States Travel and Tourism Administration (USTTA, London, UK)

Latin American Bureau (London, UK)

Patrick Mahaffey, Ohio European Office (Brussels, Belgium)

Peter Mansfield

Robert Minton-Taylor

National Meteorological Library and Archive (Bracknell, UK)

Oil and Gas Journal (Houston, Texas)

Organization for Economic Cooperation and Development (OECD, Paris, France)

Penal Reform International (London, UK)

Matt Ridley

Screen Digest (London, UK)

William Smith, Chicago Sun-Times (Chicago, USA)

Tourism Concern (London, UK)

United Nations Crime Prevention and Criminal Justice Branch (UNCPC, Vienna, Austria)

United Nations Development Programme (UNDP, New York, USA)

United Nations Environment Programme (UNEP, Nairobi, Kenya)

United Nations Food and Agriculture Organization (UNFAO, Rome, Italy)

United Nations International Labour Organization (UNILO, Geneva, Switzerland)

United Nations Population Fund (UNFPA, New York, USA)

Westminster Reference Library (London, UK)

World Conservation Monitoring Centre (Cambridge, UK)

World Health Organization (WHO, Geneva, Switzerland)

World Tourism Organization (Madrid, Spain)

The many embassies, High Commissions, airports, national information and tourist offices in London and around the world.

Picture Credits

t=top, b=below, a=above, l=left, r=right, c=center

Agence France Presse: 300crb, 332tr, 445cr; Victor Drachev 123bcr; Vassil Donev 153bcr; Eric Feferberg 188br; Francois Guillot 256crb; Martyn Hayhow 256bcr; Attila Kisbenedek 293br; John MacDougall 77tr; Shah Marai 78br; Tatiana Munoz 195tcr; Keld Navntoft 219tcr; Bernd Settnik 269br; Sergei Supinsky 587tr; Weda 229tc; **Alamy: Peter Adams 327tc; Britishcolumbiaphotos.com 175bl; Bryan & Cherry Alexander 491bl;** Diomedia 512c; Jon Arnold Images 243tr; Popperfoto 245bcr; Springfield Photography 598br; Stock Connection Inc / Rob Crandall 291tc; **Ancient Art & Architecture Collection:** 44bcr; 45bl; 45cr; 47tc; G Tortoli 45tcb; **Arcaid:** P Mauss Esto 598bc; **Art Archive:** 44bl; 49bl; 49cr; 51tcl; **Aspect Picture Library:** 202tr; Brian Seed 418c; D Bayes 370bl; Fiona Nichols 304tr; **Associated Press AP:** AFP 415bcr; Aaron Favila 467crl; Humberto Pradera/Agencia Estado 149cb; Bullit Marquez 190br; **Bridgeman Art Library, London/New York:** Hermitage, St Petersburg 46bc; Lauros - Giraudon / Château de Malmaison 48bcr; National Maritime Museum, London 47br; Private Collection 48bcl; **D Donne Bryant Stock Picture Agency:** 461tc; Byron Augustin 436tr; **Dale Buckton:** 594br; **Camera Press:** A Pucciano 95cr; F Goodman 649bca; H Andrews 627bcr; S Smith 245bcl; T Charlier 607bl; **Nick Carroll:** 647tr; **The J Allan Cash Photolibrary:** 55tl; 106c; 116bc; 146br; 149tl; 168tr; 171tr; 241tr; 308tr; 320br, 339cr; 342bl; 383tc; 386c; 438bc; 440tr; 451bc; 474tr; 566bc; **CDA:** 429tcr; **Bruce Coleman Ltd:** 498bl; B&C Calhoun 174bc; Dr MP Kahl 94tr; F Prenzel 104tc; Gerald Cubitt 88tr; Gerald Cubitt 244bc; Gordon Langsbury 262bc; J Fry 511tc; J Jurka 542bc; K. Maj 470c; Kim Taylor 515tr; L Lee Rue 91tl; LC Marigo 281tc; M Berge 396tr; MPL Fogden 462ca; O Langrand 370tr; P Davey 214bc; S Prato 274bc; **Colorific:** J Polleross / M Kreiner 54cl; M Rogers 536tr; Sandro Tucci 159bl; **Comstock:** 194bc, 24tl, 535tc; Tor Eigeland 399tc; **Corbis:** AFP 233bcr, 555tcr; Ricardo Azoury 144tc; Yannis Behrakis 275tcr; Jamil Bittar 137cr; Desmond Boylan 300cbr; Dean Conger 487tr; Icone Films / Gilles Fonlupt 258bc; Bob Krist 642br; Jack Fields 648bl, 650bl; Brooks Kraft 471tr; Miki Kratsman 486br; Franz-Marc Frei 261cb; Christopher J Morris 172cbr; Bazuki Muhammad 387bcl; Reuters / Peter Andrews 471tcr; Reuters / Ceerwan Aziz 313 c; Reuters / Beawiharta 305bcl; Reuters / Michael Dalder 271bl; Reuters / Amit Gupta 303bl; Reuters / Tom Hanson 175tc; Reuters / Kamal Kishore 303tc; Reuters / William Philpott 324cbl; Reuters / Via Reuters TV / © NTV 489cl; Reuters / Darren Whiteside 337tc; Alan Schein Photography 606br; David Turnley 258tr; Nick Wheeler , 647br; Joseph Sohm 603bl; Keren Su: 189tr; **Corbis Sygma: Baldev 189br;** Vernier Jean Bernar 195tr; David Brauchli 513bcl; Patrick Durand 327bl; Shandiz Mohsen 309tcl; **James Davis Travel Photography:** 145bl; 218c; 250bc; 330bc; 379tl; 390tr; 401tc; 411tl; 428bc; 432bc; 493tc; 494bl; 496bl; 502tr; 550bc; 558tr; 586tr; 626bl; 643cr; Prisma 86cla; Prisma / Schwarz 226tr; S Begawan 151tl; S Thingeyjar 297tc; World View - Fototheek Amsterdam 177tc; **Kurt Easterwood:** 337bl; **Democratic Party of Japan: 334cbr; Mary Evans Picture Library:** 47bl, 47trb; **Chris Fairclough Colour Library:** 51cr; 375tl; 572br; **Robert Harding Picture Library:** 76tr; 180c; 225tl; 273tc; 282bl; 293tr; 312tr; 336bl; 358bc; 449tc; 466tr; 480tr; 501tc; 513tc; A Woolfitt 114bc; C Martin 266bc; C Rennie 580ca; D Hughes 259bc; Explorer 377tc; Explorer / Roy 110tr; F Dubes 148bl; Frerck / Odyssey 402tr; G Hellier 217tr; G Hellier 518tr; G Roli 444tr; Gascoine 610bl; P Craven 254tr; Photri 222ca; R Rainford 593tl; Rosehaven Management Ltd 653cr; Sassoon 134cb; Sassoon 264cl; **Paul Harris Photography:** Paul Harris Photography 484tr; **Hulton Getty:** 50bcr; 51br; 53br; **Robert Hunt Library:** 53tc; **Hutchison Library:** 136bl; 369tc; 596bc; 636tr; Andrew Hill 634bc; Bernard Gérard 261bc; Christine Pemberton 210tr; J Henderson 286ca; JG Fuller 650bcr; L Taylor 484bl; M Macintyre 568ca; Robert Francis 560tr; Trevor Page 524ca; **Image Bank:** 394bl; A Rippy 186tr; G Jung 576tr; GA Rossi 646bl; M Beebe 209cl; ME Newman 324tr; P Trummer 232tr; T Madison 187br; **Images Colour Library:** 426bl; **Image Select:** Ann Ronan 42bc; **Impact Photos:** A le Garsmeur 412ca; Ben Edwards 450tr; C Penn 584tr; G-J Norman 356tr; J Arthur 526tcr; Mark Henley 188tr; Robin Lubbock 236tr; **David King Collection:** 55tcb **Magnum:** H Cartier-Bresson 53tcb; **NATA Photo: 488bc; nPower Renewables © Dan Towers 2004 601tc; Office of Mark Latham:** 102cbr; **Office of the Prime Minister of Canada:** 172crb; **Panos Pictures:** B Tobiasson 329bc; Chris Stowers 333bl; D Hulcher 360tr; Jeremy Hartley 156bc; Marc French 289tc; Morris Carpenter 365bc; Neil Cooper 130tr; R Giling 538tr; S Sprague 160tr; Sean Sprague 136c; Michael Harvey 149cl; John Miles 189cl; 597cb; 602bl; **Pa Photos:** AFP 419cbl; EPA 146tr, 188bcr, 353bcr, 631bcr; **Popperfoto:** 51trb; 52br; 55bl; AFP / Armand 54br; David Mercado / Reuters 137crl; Reuters 271tc; Jeremy Piper / Reuters 102bcr; John Cobb / EPA 275tr; Reuters 345tr; Official U.S. Air Force Photo 55cr; **Popperfoto / Reuters:** Peter Andrews 637cr; Simon Baker 433tlb; Denis Balibouse 203cl; Russell Boyce 594cra; Bogdan Cristel 481cr; Dimitar Dilkoff 153bcl; Mohamed Hammi 573tcr; Hyungwon Kang 601bcr; Francois Lenoir 127bcr; Havakuk Levison 318bcr; David Loh 623tcl; Alexander Natruskin 487bl; Patrick de Noirmont 159bcl; Enny Nuraheni 305bcr; Pilar Olivares 463tcl; Hrvoje Polan 293bcr; Romero Ranoco 467cr; Molly Riley 268bcr; Oswaldo Rivas 555tr; Henry Romero 403bcl; Jayanta Shaw 623tl; Ruben Sprich 547cr; STR 451tr, 577car; 293bcl, 577trb, 607bcl; Sukree Sukplang 563tr; Susumu Takahashi 334cbl; Martin Thomas 182tr; Pierre Virot 476bcl; Haydn West 594tcr; Kimberly White 618tcr; Darren Whiteside 165tcr; Rick Wilking 600bcr, 600br; **Reuters:** 123bcl, tcr; 507br; **Rex Features:** 116tcbr; 172bcr; 256cb; 341bcl; 481cbr; 486bcr; 516bl; 526tr; 543tcl; 587tcr; 594tr; 594trb; 606bl; 611bc; 627bcl; Action Press 268cbr; 415bcl; 535tr; ArgenPress 95crb; Giuseppe Aresu 324cbr; Mark Brewer 320cl; Sari Gustafsson 251tcr; 487bcl; J Sutton Hibbert 597ct; Paul Browncr; David Hartley 219tr; ISOPress 251tr; 581car; ISOPress Seneport 513bcr; Keystone USA / Ku 320br; James D Morgan 105tc; F Stevens 211bcl; Farnood 309tcr; Ken McKay 531tr; Alfredo Rocha 475bcr; Ron Sachs 605bcl; 631bcl; Karl Schoendorfer 107bcl; Sipa-Press 77tcr, 83bcl, 95cbr, 127bcl, 141bc, 188bcr, 318br, 429tcl, 445c, 563tcr, 645bl; Tony Kyriacou 353bcl; Sam Tinson 601bl; Torregano 419cl; Wilhemsen 105bl; **Harry Smith Collection:** 46clb; **South American Pictures:** Jevan Berrange 206br; P Dixon 456tr; T Morrison 606tr; **Sovfoto/Eastfoto:** 652br; **Frank Spooner Pictures:** 53bl; 83bl; 324bc;345tcr; 543tr; A Denize 371tcr; Alain Morvan / Gamma 547c; Alexis Duclos 182tcr; C Poulet 647cr; Tim Crosby / Gamma - Liaison 602ct; Gamma / B Iverson 233bcl; Gamma / F Apesteguy 507bcr; Gamma / Iliona - Figaro Magazine 113tc; Gamma / K Al Arab 573tcl; Gamma / N Jallot 408tr; Gamma / Najer 387bcr; Gamma / Xinhua 188bcl; Georges Merillon 441bcl; KJ Eddy 107bcl; Liason / Peterson 441bcr; Liason / Markel 637c; N Sagansky 203cr; P Perrin 313cr; Patrick Piel 268bra; Reglain 165tr; Victoria Brynner 451tcr; **Tony Stone Images:** 179bc; 198tr; 354bl; 444br; A Cassidy 302br; Alan Kearney 182bc; Alan Smith 362c; C Waite 592bc; D Armand 172tr; D Hanson 562bl; D Schultz 50bl; Dennis Stone 344tr; G Allison 605bl; H Kurihara 270bc; J Pragen 616tr; Joe Cornish 317bc; Marcus Brooke 158tr; O Benn 93tc; 279tr; P Chesley 406ca; Penny Tweedie 384bc; R Evans 152tr; R. Everts 415tr; R Smith 102tr; R Smith 231tl; S Egan 530tr; S Egan 546tr; Steven Rothfeld 393tc; **Swiss Embassy:** 551cr; 551crr; **Sygma:** Valdev 350ca; R Reuter 502bl; **Telegraph Colour Library:** 100tr; Ford Motor Company Ltd 52clb; **Topham Picturepoint:** 133tc; 238tr; 371tr; 433cal; 478bc; 504bc; 642c; **Trip:** 506bl; G Spenceley 380tr; T Goodman 285tc; V Shuba 122c; V Sidoropolev 340tr; **Ukrainian Government:** 591tr; **World Pictures:** 83cla; 322bl; 422ca; 554tr; **Zefa Picture Library:** 80bc; 120bl; 200ca; 526bl; 570bc; 618bl; Everts 630ca; F Lanting 142tr; Streichan 268bl.